CHICANO PERIODICAL INDEX (ChPI)

CHICANO PERIODICAL INDEX (ChPI)
A Comprehensive Subject, Author, and Title Index for 1982-83

Edited by

Lillian Castillo-Speed
Francisco García-Ayvens
Richard Chabrán

Compiled by
The Chicano Periodical Indexing Project
Lillian Castillo-Speed, Director

Chicano Studies Library Publications Unit
University of California, Berkeley
1985

The Chicano Periodical Index (ChPI) was endorsed in El Paso, Texas by the National Association for Chicano Studies at its 14th Annual Conference.

ISBN 0-918520-10-X

This publication is printed on permanent/durable acid-free paper
MANUFACTURED IN THE UNITED STATES OF AMERICA

This volume is proudly dedicated to:

Lucía González Parsons
active: 1877 - 1941

&

Emma Tenayuca
active: 1931 - 1939

Two Chicana labor organizers
whose struggle for the rights of workers
continues today...

PANEL OF INDEXERS

Ivan Argüelles
Serials Department
Doe Library
University of California
Berkeley, California

Marta Stiefel Ayala
San Diego State University
Imperial Valley Campus
Calexico, California

Gilda Baeza
Mexican American Library Program
The University of Texas
Austin, Texas

Evelyn Escatiola Baca
El Monte Public Library
El Monte, California

Cesar Caballero
Library
The University of Texas
El Paso, Texas

Maria Olga Camarillo
Library Reference
California State University, Stanislaus
Turlock, California

Richard Chabrán
Chicano Studies Research Library
University of California
Los Angeles, California

Norma Corral
Reference Department
University Research Library
University of California
Los Angeles, California

Karin Duran
Oviatt Library
California State University
Northridge, California

David E. Fisher
Reference Department
Pan American University
Edinburg, Texas

Francisco García-Ayvens
Chicano Resource Center
California State University
Fullerton, California

Salvador Guereña
Colección Tloque Nahuaque
University Library
University of California
Santa Barbara, California

Antonia G. Herrera
Los Angeles Public Library
San Pedro Regional Branch
San Pedro, California

Luis Herrera
Long Beach Public Library
Long Beach, California

Pamela Howard
San Diego, California

Susan C. Luévano
Library
Santa Ana College
Santa Ana, California

Albert J. Milo
City of Commerce Public Library
Commerce, California

Mary Helen Moreno
The University Library
University of California
Davis, California

San Juanita P. Reyes
Reference Department
Library
Pan American University
Edinburg, Texas

Ronald Rodriguez
Los Angeles County Public Library
Los Angeles, California

Vivian Thomas
Green Library
Stanford University
Stanford, California

Elva K. Yanez
Pinole, California

Additional indexing by Cassandra Brush,
Christine Marín, and Robert L. McDowell.

CONTENTS

INTRODUCTION

With this third volume of the *Chicano Periodical Index (ChPI)*, the Chicano Periodical Indexing Project takes two significant steps toward providing complete author, title, and subject access to Chicano periodical literature. First, we have broadened our scope to include mainstream periodicals. Second, we are publishing *ChPI* completely in-house at the Chicano Studies Library Publications Unit of the University of California at Berkeley.

By extending our indexing coverage to non-Chicano as well as Chicano periodicals we are making *ChPI* even more inclusive than its two companion volumes published by G.K. Hall in 1981 and 1983. Now, libraries with limited collections of Chicano journals can direct users to information on Chicanos appearing in almost 500 periodical titles as varied as *Social Science Quarterly, New York Review of Books, Time Magazine*, and *American Journal of Epidemiology*. We are not limited by country of origin or by language, although the bulk of the articles are from the United States and are in English. Most of the mainstream articles were found in libraries of the University of California, California State University system, the University of Texas, and the University of Arizona. At the same time that we are broadening the scope of our literature search, we are refining the scope of the content. That is, in general we are excluding articles on South and Central America except when they deal with an aspect of Latino culture which is of interest to Chicanos, e.g., art, literature, and immigration. We have also decided to exclude less important articles appearing in periodicals we would normally index completely, e.g., articles on tourism, personal appearance, and business news not specifically about U.S. Latinos. Articles about Puerto Ricans and Cubanos were included in *ChPI* if they were identified in the general search for articles on Chicanos. However, the focus of the *Index* remains on Chicanos and the Chicano experience.

For the first time ever, the Chicano Studies Library Publications Unit will be publishing an issue of *ChPI*. It is highly appropriate that it should since the Chicano Periodical Indexing Project, the Chicano Database, the National Clearinghouse for Chicano Serials, and the Publications Unit are all headquartered at the Chicano Studies Library at UC Berkeley. These four components of the Library are committed to the goal of documenting information on Chicanos and making it as accessible as possible. The Library is now in a position to coordinate sophisticated levels of communication among professionals and to make full use of the power of the computer as a tool in the research process.

ARRANGEMENT OF THE INDEX

This issue of *ChPI* consists of three sections: the SUBJECT portion, the supplementary AUTHOR and TITLE indexes, and the current DIRECTORY of serials received by the Chicano Studies Library at UC Berkeley. A brief description of each section follows.

SUBJECT INDEX

This is the main section of *ChPI*. Here are listed over 4,000 citations arranged under appropriate descriptor (subject) terms. On average, each of the citations is indexed under three distinct descriptor terms, i.e. each of the citations is repeated in its entirety in three different locations. Each citation listing is numbered sequentially with the citation number serving as reference point for the supplementary author and title indexes.

Each of the numbered citation entries provides the unique index number, full bibliographic description, and additional descriptor terms under which that particular citation is also indexed. USE references from variant terms to the authorized form used in the *Chicano Thesaurus* are a new feature of this edition of *ChPI*.

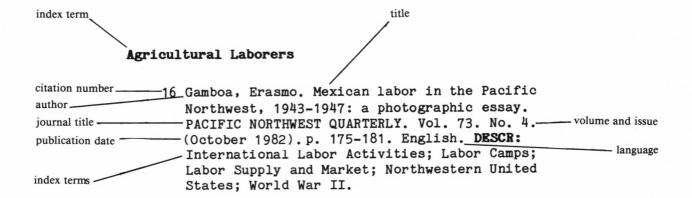

index term   title

Agricultural Laborers

citation number —— 16 Gamboa, Erasmo. Mexican labor in the Pacific
author —— Northwest, 1943-1947: a photographic essay.
journal title —— PACIFIC NORTHWEST QUARTERLY. Vol. 73. No. 4.—— volume and issue
publication date —— (October 1982). p. 175-181. English. **DESCR:**
—— International Labor Activities; Labor Camps; —— language
index terms —— Labor Supply and Market; Northwestern United
States; World War II.

AUTHOR AND TITLE INDEXES

The second major section comprises separate AUTHOR and TITLE indexes. All articles cited in this volume of *ChPI* are listed according to the author's name, when known. In the case of multiple authors, the citation is listed under each author up to a maximum of three. In the author index, entries are grouped alphabetically by author, list the full titles, and provide the citation numbers in the subject index where full citations may be located. Name USE references from variants to the authorized form used in *ChPI* are also provided here.

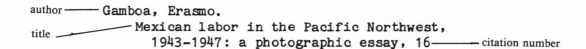

author —— Gamboa, Erasmo.
title —— Mexican labor in the Pacific Northwest,
1943-1947: a photographic essay, 16 —— citation number

Specific article titles may be located in the alphabetic title listing that follows the author index. A title entry includes the full text of an individual title and the citation number in the subject index where a full citation may be located.

title —— Mexican labor in the Pacific Northwest, 1943-1947:
a photographic essay, 16 —— citation number

DIRECTORY OF CHICANO PERIODICALS

The final section of *ChPI* is a directory of Chicano serials currently received by the Chicano Studies Library at UC Berkeley. Through this list we hope to disseminate the most current information about the publication status of a variety of important periodicals in the field of Chicano studies. As such, the list includes many more serial titles than are actually indexed in the pages of *ChPI*. The list is included as a guide to additional periodical sources and as an indicator of the vast amounts of material yet to be indexed. Moreover, the richness of the list reflects the large holdings of the Berkeley collection, recognized as the most important collection of its kind.

FUTURE DIRECTIONS FOR *ChPI*

The *Chicano Periodical Index* is the most important product to date of the Chicano Database. It is the first step toward the development of a mechanism which will eventually become the primary source of bibliographic information on Chicanos. Since the largest percentage of the most current information on Chicanos is found in periodicals, *ChPI* was the logical beginning. This volume of *ChPI* represents the next step: the broadening of our scope to include mainstream journals in our search for periodical articles.

Now we are in a position to realistically plan for the future. To reach our goal of providing complete bibliographic access to information on Chicanos, computerized on-line searching is essential. The realization of that capability is the very next step in the development of the Chicano Database. Soon after, we will be able to provide on-line modem access to the Database as well as off-line computer searches.

When the mechanism for providing up-to-date citations to Chicano materials is in place, the next step will be to expand the Database. We will then complete the next task of converting the catalogs of the Chicano Studies Library into machine-readable form. As we continue to publish Chicano bibliographic reference works, all the information used to produce those publications will become part of the Database. We intend the Chicano Database to eventually reflect the holdings of selected Chicano collections. It would then serve as a comprehensive list of Chicano Studies materials. These records could be joined to data from other projects (for example, indexing of anthologies, pamphlet files, and newspapers) to establish the Chicano Database as the major source for all kinds of information specifically on Chicanos.

As for the *Chicano Periodical Index,* we plan to keep it current. Eventually, on-line searching will be the most effective means of finding up-to-date citations, but the printed *ChPI* will continue to appear at regular and timely intervals.

ACKNOWLEDGEMENTS

So many dedicated people have helped produce our first in-house *ChPI,* and so much kind personal assistance has been lent, that it is difficult for me, as director of the indexing project, to adequately make acknowledgements here, but no one is going to keep me from trying. The third volume of *ChPI* would not have been possible without the help of the following people:

--the members of the Chicano Periodical Indexing Panel, whose dedication to the enormous task of documenting Chicano literature is the foundation of the project

--Vivian Thomas, who graciously volunteered her professional skills as a cataloger and a data editor for *Arte Chicano*

--Selimo Rael, who took the time to give his advice and actively support the publication of *ChPI*

--Ana Coronado, who cheerfully helped with data entry when we needed her

--Rosa Johnson, whose efficiency as Chicano Studies Administrative Assistant smoothed the way for the project at every step

--the backbone of the Chicano Studies Library, our student assistants: Joseph Anthony Gonzales, Martha Lucia Uribe, Dora de la Rosa, Vic Gomez, Nidia Varela, Diana Mejia, Leticia Beltran, Alonso Casas, Carl Buckhorn, Elizabeth Gonzalez, Claudia Colindrez, Carlos Escobedo, Margita Thompson, and Nancy Gomes

--Tom Holt, President of VORT Corporation, who, because of his special concern for the Chicano Database, was willing to train me to be a database manager and whose patience I strained very often

--Kyung-Hee Choi, whose special skills as data entry person and data editor I came to depend on almost as much as I depend on her friendship

--Carolyn Soto, who *is* the Publications Unit, and will someday, I hope, be adequately rewarded for her contributions as production editor and as the person whose opinions and good sense I could always trust

--Co-editor Richard Chabran, whose original dream for the development of *ChPI* has never lost its luster and who never loses sight of our goals

--Co-editor Francisco Garcia-Ayvens, my teacher, mentor, and friend, whose high standards I can only hope to emulate

and

--my husband Richard and my son Nathan, who have made everything so much easier than I had any right to expect.

KEY TO PERIODICALS INDEXED COMPLETELY
Indexing covers 1982-83 unless otherwise noted in italics.

AGENDA
Agency for International Development
Washington, DC
Vol. 11, no. 3 (1981)-(1983)

AZTLAN
Chicano Studies Center, UCLA
Los Angeles, CA

BILINGUAL JOURNAL
National Assessment and Dissemination Center
Cambridge, MA

BILINGUAL REVIEW
Eastern Michigan University
Ypsilanti, MI

BORDERLANDS JOURNAL
Texas Southmost College, Brownsville, TX

CACR REVIEW
Colorado Association for Chicano Research
Department of Sociology
Colorado State University
Fort Collins, CO

CALMECAC
Calmecac de Aztlán en Los, Inc.
Los Angeles, CA
(1980-82)

CAMINOS
Caminos Corporation
Los Angeles, CA
Vol. 2, nos. 6 & 7 (1981) - Vol. 4, no. 10 (1983)

CAMPO LIBRE
Centro de Publicaciones
Department of Chicano Studies
California State University
Los Angeles, CA
Vol. 1, no. 2 (1981)

CHICANO LAW REVIEW
Chicano Law Student Association
School of Law, UCLA
Los Angeles, CA

CHISMEARTE
Chismearte, Los Angeles, CA

COMADRE
Comadre, Santa Barbara, CA
(1977-78)

CORAZON DE AZTLAN
Los Angeles, CA
Premier Issue (1981)-Vol. 1, nos. 1 & 2 (1982)

DE COLORES
Pajarito Publications
Albuquerque, NM

HISPANIC BUSINESS
Hispanic Business, Inc.
Ridgefield, NJ

HISPANIC JOURNAL OF BEHAVIORAL SCIENCES
Spanish Speaking Mental Health Research Center
Los Angeles, CA

INTERNATIONAL MIGRATION REVIEW
Center for Migration Studies of New York, Inc.
Staten Island, NY

JOURNAL OF ETHNIC STUDIES
Ethnic Studies Program
Western Washington University
Bellingham, WA

LATINA!
Los Angeles, CA

LATINO
Denver, CO

MAIZE
Centro Cultural de la Raza Publications
San Diego, CA
(1977-1983)

MELUS: MULTI-ETHNIC LITERATURE OF THE UNITED STATES
Society for the Study of the Multi-Ethnic
Literature of the United States
Commerce, TX
Vol. 6 no. 2 (1979)-Vol. 10 (1983)

MIGRATION TODAY
Center for Migration Studies of New York, Inc.
Staten Island, NY

MINORITY VOICES
Pennsylvania State University
University Park, PN
Vol. 1, no. 2 (1977)-Vol. 5 (1981)

NATIONAL HISPANIC JOURNAL
Austin, TX

NEW SCHOLAR
University of California
Santa Barbara, CA

NUESTRO
Nuestro Publications
New York, NY
Vol. 5, no. 8 (1981)-Vol. 7 (1983)

LA PALABRA
Valle del Sol, Inc.
Tucson, AZ

LA RAZA LAW JOURNAL
Boalt Hall School of Law
University of California
Berkeley, CA

REVISTA CHICANO-RIQUENA
University of Houston
Houston, TX

SOUTHWEST ECONOMY AND SOCIETY
Albuquerque, NM
Vol.1,no.1(1976);Vol.2(1977)-Vol.6,no.2(1983)

THIRD WOMAN
Chicano-Riqueña Studies
Indiana University
Bloomington, IN

KEY TO PERIODICALS INDEXED SELECTIVELY
Indexing covers 1982-83

ABA BANKING JOURNAL
ABA Banking Journal, Bristol, CT
ACROSS THE BOARD
New York, the Conference Board
ADFL BULLETIN
Modern Language Association of America
New York, NY
ADOLESCENCE
Libra Publishers, Roslyn Height, NY
ADVERTISING AGE MAGAZINE
Crain Communications, Inc., Chicago, IL
Washington, DC
ALBERTA JOURNAL OF EDUCATIONAL RESEARCH
University of Alberta, Alberta, Canada
AMERICA
America Press, New York, NY
AMERICAN BAR ASSOCIATION JOURNAL
American Bar Association, Chicago, IL
AMERICAN BOOK REVIEW
American Book Review, Cooper Station,
New York, NY
AMERICAN CRIMINAL LAW REVIEW
American Bar Association, Chicago IL
AMERICAN DEMOGRAPHICS
American Demographics, Syracuse, NY
AMERICAN EDUCATIONAL RESEARCH JOURNAL
American Educational Research Association,
Washington, DC
AMERICAN EDUCATION
US Government Printing Office, Washington, DC
AMERICAN EDUCATOR
American Federation of Teachers, AFL-CIO,
Washington, DC
AMERICAN ETHNOLOGIST
American Ethnological Society, Washington, DC
AMERICAN FILM
American Film, Farmingdale, NY
AMERICAN HISTORICAL REVIEW
American Historical Association, Washington, DC
AMERICAN JOURNAL OF AGRICULTURAL ECONOMICS
American Farm Economic Association
Lancaster, PA
AMERICAN JOURNAL OF ARCHAEOLOGY
Archaeological Institute of America, Concord, NM
AMERICAN JOURNAL OF CLINICAL NUTRITION
American Society for Clinical Nutrition
New York, NY
AMERICAN JOURNAL OF COMMUNITY PSYCHOLOGY
Plenum Press, New York, NY
AMERICAN JOURNAL OF DISEASES OF CHILDREN
American Medical Association, Chicago, IL
AMERICAN JOURNAL OF DRUG AND ALCOHOL ABUSE
Marcel Dekker Journals, New York, NY
AMERICAN JOURNAL OF EPIDEMIOLOGY
Johns Hopkins University, Baltimore, MD
AMERICAN JOURNAL OF FAMILY THERAPY
National Alliance for Family Life
New Brunswick, NJ

AMERICAN JOURNAL OF HUMAN GENETICS
University of Chicago Press, Chicago, IL
AMERICAN JOURNAL OF INTERNATIONAL LAW
American Journal of International Law
Washington, DC
AMERICAN JOURNAL OF NURSING
American Nurses' Association, New York, NY
AMERICAN JOURNAL OF PHYSICAL ANTHROPOLOGY
Alan R. Liss, Inc., New York, NY
AMERICAN JOURNAL OF PSYCHIATRY
American Psychiatric Association, Washington, DC
AMERICAN JOURNAL OF PUBLIC HEALTH
American Public Health Association, Washington, DC
AMERICAN JOURNAL OF SOCIAL PSYCHIATRY
Brunner-Mazel, Inc., New York, NY
AMERICAN JOURNAL OF SOCIOLOGY
University of Chicago Press, Chicago, IL
AMERICAN MUSIC
Sonneck Society and the University of Illinois Press,
Champaign, IL
AMERICAN REVIEW OF RESPIRATORY DISEASE
American Lung Association, New York, NY
AMERICAN SOCIOLOGICAL REVIEW
American Sociological Association, Washington, DC
AMERICAN SCHOLAR
Phi Beta Kappa, Washington, DC
AMERICAN SOCIOLOGIST
American Sociological Association, Washington, DC
AMERICAS
Americas, Farmingdale, NY
**ANNALS OF THE AMERICAN ACADEMY OF POLITICAL
AND SOCIAL SCIENCE**
Sage Publications, Inc., Beverly Hills, CA
ANNALS OF THE ASSOCIATION OF AMERICAN GEOGRAPHERS
Association of American Geographers,
Washington, DC
ANNALS OF WYOMING
State Archives and Historical Department,
Cheyenne, Wyoming
ANS: ADVANCES IN NURSING AND SCIENCE
Aspen Systems Corporation, Germantown, MD
APPLIED RESEARCH IN MENTAL RETARDATION
Pergamon Press, Elmsford, NY
APUNTES
Centro de Investigación, Universidad del
Pacífico, Lima, Peru
ARCHIVES OF GENERAL PSYCHIATRY
American Medical Association, Chicago, IL
ARIZONA AND THE WEST
University Arizona Press, Tucson, AZ
ARIZONA BUSINESS
Arizona State University, Tempe, AZ
ART IN AMERICA
Art in America, Marion, OH
ATLANTIC
Atlantic, Greenwich, CN

BAPTIST HISTORY AND HERITAGE
Southern Baptist Convention,
Historical Commission, Nashville, TN

BAR EXAMINER
National Conference of Bar Examiners,
Chicago, IL

BAYLOR LAW REVIEW
Baylor University, Waco, TX

BILLBOARD
Billboard Publications, Los Angeles, CA

BOOKBIRD
Hermann Schaffstein Verlag, W. Germany

BOOKLIST
American Library Association, Chicago, IL

BRAIN AND LANGUAGE
Academic Press, Inc., New York, NY

BROADCASTING
Broadcasting Publications, Inc.,
Washington, DC

BULLETIN OF HISPANIC STUDIES
Liverpool University Press, Liverpool

BULLETIN OF THE HISTORY OF MEDICINE
Johns Hopkins University Press,
Baltimore, MD

BUSINESS HORIZONS
Indiana University, Bloomington, IN

BUSINESS WEEK
Business Week, Hightstown, NJ

CAHIERS DU CINEMA
Edition de L'Etoile, Paris, France

CALIFORNIA AGRICULTURE
University of California, Berkeley, CA

CALIFORNIA HISTORY
California Historical Society,
San Francisco, CA

CALIFORNIA LAWYER
State Bar of California,
San Francisco, CA

CALIFORNIA MANAGEMENT REVIEW
University of California, Berkeley, CA

CASE CURRENTS
Council for Advancement and Support of
Education, Washington, DC

CATHOLIC LIBRARY WORLD
Catholic Library Association,
Haverford, PA

CHANGE
Heldref Publications, Washington, DC

CHEST
American College of Chest Physicians,
Park Ridge, IL

CHILD WELFARE
Transaction Inc., New Brunswick, NJ

CHILDHOOD EDUCATION
Association for Childhood Education
International, Wheaton, MD

CHILDREN AND YOUTH SERVICES REVIEW
Pergamon Press, New York, NY

CHILDREN TODAY
US Government Printing Office,
Washington, DC

CHILDREN'S LEGAL RIGHTS JOURNAL
Children's Legal Rights Information and
Training Program, Washington, DC

CHOICE
Choice, Middletown, CN

CHRISTIAN CENTURY
Christian Century Foundation, Chicago, IL

CHRISTIANITY TODAY
Christianity Today, Dover, NJ

CHRONICLE OF HIGHER EDUCATION
Chronicle of Higher Education, Washington, DC

CHURCH AND SOCIETY
United Presbyterian Church in the U.S.A.,
Crawfordsville, IN

CINEASTE
Cineaste, New York, NY

THE CLEARING HOUSE
Heldref Publications, Washington, DC

CLEARINGHOUSE REVIEW
National Institute for Education in Law and
Poverty, Washington, DC

CLINICAL NEUROPSYCHOLOGY
Transaction Periodicals Consortium,
New Brunswick, NJ

COLLEGE STUDENT JOURNAL
Project Innovation, Santa Cruz Court,
Chula Vista, CA

COLUMBIA JOURNAL OF LAW AND SOCIAL PROBLEMS
Columbia University School of Law, New York, NY

COMMONWEAL
Commonweal Publications Co., Inc.,
New York, NY

COMPARATIVE STUDIES IN SOCIETY AND HISTORY
Cambridge University Press, London

CONGRESSIONAL QUARTERLY WEEKLY REPORT
Congressional Quarterly, Inc.,
Washington, DC

CONJUNTO
Ediciones Cubanas, Sub-Dirección de Exportación
La Habana, Cuba

CONTEMPORARY EDUCATION
Indiana State University, Terre Haute, IN

CONTEMPORARY EDUCATIONAL PSYCHOLOGY
Academic Press, Inc., New York, NY

CONTEMPORARY MARXISM
Synthesis Publications, San Francisco, CA

CONTEMPORARY SOCIOLOGY: A JOURNAL OF REVIEWS
American Sociological Association,
Washington, DC

CORRECTIONS TODAY
American Correction Association,
College Park, MD

COUNSELOR EDUCATION AND SUPERVISION
American Association for Counseling and
Development, Alexandria, VA

CRIME AND SOCIAL JUSTICE
Synthesis Publications, San Francisco, CA

CRIMINAL LAW REPORTER
Bureau of National Affairs, Inc.,
Washington, DC

CUADERNOS HISPANOAMERICANOS
Instituto de Cooperación Iberoamericana
Madrid, Spain

CUADERNOS POLITICOS
Ediciones Era, México

CUBAN STUDIES
University of Pittsburg, Pittsburg, PN

CULTURE, MEDICINE & PSYCHIATRY
D. Reidel Publishing Co.,
Hingham, MA
CURRENTS IN THEOLOGY AND MISSION
Evangelical Lutherans in Mission, Inc.,
St. Louis, MO
DEMOGRAFIA Y ECONOMIA
Colegio de México, México, D.F., México
DEMOGRAPHY
Population Association of America,
Washington, DC
DIABETOLOGIA
Organ of the European Association for the
Study of Diabetes, New York, NY
DIALOGOS
Colegio de México, México, D.F., México
DOLLARS AND SENSE
Economic Affairs Bureau, Inc.,
Somerville, MA
DREW GATEWAY
Drew Theological Seminary, Madison, NJ
DRUG AND ALCOHOL DEPENDENCE
Elsevier Scientific Publishers
Ireland Ltd, Limerick, Ireland
DUN'S BUSINESS MONTH
Dun & Bradstreet, New York, NY
EARLY CHILD DEVELOPMENT AND CARE
Gordon and Breach Science Publishers, Inc.,
New York, NY
ECONOMIC DEVELOPMENT AND CULTURAL CHANGE
Economic Development and Cultural Change,
Chicago, IL
ECONOMIC GEOGRAPHY
Clark University, Worcester, MA
ECONOMIC INQUIRY
Western Economic Association International,
Huntington Beach, CA
ECONOMIST
Economist Newsletter, Ltd., London, England
EDITORIAL RESEARCH REPORTS
Congressional Quarterly, Inc., Washington, DC
EDUCATIONAL AND PSYCHOLOGICAL
    MEASUREMENT
Educational and Psychological Measurement
Durham, NC
EDUCATIONAL EVALUATION AND POLICY ANALYSIS
American Educational Research Association
Washington, DC
EDUCATIONAL FORUM
Kappa Delta Pi, West Lafayette, IN
EDUCATIONAL LEADERSHIP
Association for Supervision and Curriculum
Development, Alexandria, VA
EDUCATIONAL RESEARCH QUARTERLY
University of Southern California
Los Angeles, CA
EDUCATIONAL STUDIES
University of Florida, Gainesville, FL
EMPLOYEE RELATIONS LAW JOURNAL
Executive Enterprises Publications Co.,
New York, NY
ENGLISH JOURNAL
National Council of Teachers of English
Urbana, IL
ESQUIRE
Esquire, Boulder, CO

ETHNIC AND RACIAL STUDIES
Routledge Journals, Boston, MA
ETHNOLOGY
Department of Anthropology, University of
Pittsburgh, Pittsburgh, PA
ETHNOMUSICOLOGY
Society for Ethnomusicology, Inc.,
Ann Arbor, MI
EXCEPTIONAL CHILDREN
Council for Exceptional Children,
Reston, VA
EXPERIMENTAL AGING RESEARCH
Beech Hill Enterprises, Inc.,
Southwest Harbor, ME
EXPLORATIONS IN ETHNIC STUDIES
National Association of Interdisciplinary
Ethnic Studies, University of Wisconsin,
La Crosse, WI
FAMILY PLANNING PERSPECTIVES
Alan Guttmacher Institute, New York, NY
FILM COMMENT
Film Society of Lincoln Center, New York, NY
FORBES
Forbes, New York, NY
FORDHAM INTERNATIONAL LAW FORUM
Fordham University School of Law
New York, NY
FOREIGN AFFAIRS
Foreign Affairs Reader Services, New York, NY
FOREIGN LANGUAGE ANNALS
American Council on the Teaching of Foreign
Languages, Hastings-on-Hudson, NY
THE FUTURIST
World Future Society Headquarters,
Bethesda, MD
GOLDEN GATE UNIVERSITY LAW REVIEW
School of Law, Golden Gate University,
San Francisco, CA
GREAT PLAINS QUARTERLY
Center for Great Plains Studies,
University of Nebraska, Lincoln, NK
EL GRITO DEL SOL
Tonatiuh Quinto Sol International, Inc.,
Berkeley, CA
HARVARD EDUCATIONAL REVIEW
Harvard Educational Review, Cambridge, MA
HARVARD LAW REVIEW
Harvard Law Review Association,
Cambridge, MA
HEALTH EDUCATION QUARTERLY
John Wiley & Sons, Inc., New York, NY
HETEROFONIA
Conservatorio Nacional de Música, México
HISPAMERICA: REVISTA DE LITERATURA
Saul Sosnowski, Gaithersburg, MD
HISPANIA
University of Mississippi, University, MS
HISPANIC AMERICAN HISTORICAL REVIEW
Duke University Press, Durham, NC
HISPANIC JOURNAL
Indiana University of Pennsylvania,
Indiana, PN
HISTORIA MEXICANA
Colegio de México, A.C., México, D.F.
México

HISTORIAN
Phi Alpha Theta International Honor Society
in History, Allentown, PA
HISTORY - REVIEWS OF NEW BOOKS
Reid Foundation, Washington, DC
HISTORY TEACHER
California State University, Long Beach, CA
HISTORY: JOURNAL OF THE HISTORICAL ASSOCIATION
Historical Association, London
HORN BOOK MAGAZINE
Horn Book, Inc., Boston, MA
HOSPITAL AND COMMUNITY PSYCHIATRY
American Psychiatric Association,
Washington, DC
HOSPITALS
American Hospital Publishing, Inc.,
Chicago, IL
HOUSTON JOURNAL OF INTERNATIONAL LAW
University of Houston, Houston, TX
HUMAN BIOLOGY
Wayne State University Press, Detroit, MI
HUMAN ORGANIZATION
Society for Applied Anthropology,
Oklahoma City, OK
HUMAN RELATIONS
Plenum Publishing Co., New York, NY
HUMAN SERVICES IN THE RURAL ENVIRONMENT
Center for Social Services
University of Wisconsin
ILLINOIS LIBRARIES
State Library, Springfield, IL
ILLINOIS SCHOOL RESEARCH AND DEVELOPMENT
Illinois Association for Supervision &
Curriculum Development, Illinois State
University, Normal, IL
IMMIGRATION HISTORY NEWSLETTER
Immigration History Society,
St. Paul, MN
IMPRINT
National Student Nurses' Association,
New York, NY
INDUSTRIAL AND LABOR RELATIONS REVIEW
Cornell University, Ithaca, NY
INDUSTRY WEEK
Penton-IPC, Cleveland, OH
INFORME: RELACIONES MEXICO-ESTADOS UNIDOS
Centro de Estudios Económicos y Sociales
del Tercer Mundo, México, D.F., México
INTEGRATEDUCATION
University of Massachusetts, Amherst, MA
INTER-AMERICAN ECONOMIC AFFAIRS
Inter-American Economic Affairs, Washington, DC
INTERNATIONAL JOURNAL OF GROUP
PSYCHOTHERAPY
International Universities Press, New York, NY
INTERNATIONAL JOURNAL OF SOCIAL PSYCHIATRY
Avenue Publishing Co., London, England
INTERNATIONAL JOURNAL OF THE ADDICTIONS
Marcel Dekker Journals, New York, NY
INTERNATIONAL LABOR AND WORKING CLASS HISTORY
History Department, Yale University
New Haven, CT
INTERNATIONAL LAWYER
American Bar Association, Chicago, IL
INTERNATIONAL SOCIAL SCIENCE REVIEW
Toledo University, Toledo, OH

INTERNATIONAL STUDIES NOTES
International Studies Association
University of Pittsburgh Pittsburgh, PA
INTERRACIAL BOOKS FOR CHILDREN
Council on Interracial Books for Children,
New York, NY
IRAL: INTERNATIONAL REVIEW OF APPLIED
LINGUISTICS IN LANGUAGE TEACHING
Julius Groos Verlag, Heidelberg, W. Germany
JOGN NURSING
Harper & Row, Hagerstown, MD
JOURNAL FOR RESEARCH IN MATHEMATICS EDUCATION
National Council of Teachers of Mathematics,
Reston, VA
JOURNAL OF ACADEMIC LIBRARIANSHIP
Mountainside Publishing, Ann Arbor, MI
JOURNAL OF ADOLESCENT HEALTH CARE
Society for Adolescent Medicine, New York, NY
JOURNAL OF AMERICAN CULTURE
Popular Culture Association
Bowling Green State University
Bowling Green, OH
JOURNAL OF AMERICAN ETHNIC HISTORY
Transaction Periodicals Consortium
New Brunswick, NJ
JOURNAL OF AMERICAN FOLKLORE
American Folklore Society, Washington, DC
JOURNAL OF AMERICAN HISTORY
Organization of American Historians
Bloomington, IN
JOURNAL OF AMERICAN INDIAN EDUCATION
Arizona State University, Tempe, AZ
JOURNAL OF APPLIED PSYCHOLOGY
American Psychological Association
Arlington, VA
JOURNAL OF APPLIED SOCIAL PSYCHOLOGY
V.H. Winston and Sons, Inc.
Silver Spring, MD
JOURNAL OF BEHAVIOR THERAPY AND
EXPERIMENTAL PSYCHIATRY
Pergamon Press, Elmsford, NY
JOURNAL OF BUSINESS EDUCATION
Heldref Publications, Washington, DC
JOURNAL OF CLINICAL ENDOCRINOLOGY
AND METABOLISM
Endocrine Society, Baltimore, MD
JOURNAL OF CLINICAL PSYCHOLOGY
Clinical Psychology Publishing Co., Inc.
Brandon, VT
JOURNAL OF COLLEGE STUDENT PERSONNEL
American Association for Counseling and
Development, Alexandria, VA
JOURNAL OF COMMUNITY PSYCHOLOGY
Clinical Psychology Publishing Co., Inc.
Brandon, VT
JOURNAL OF CONSULTING AND CLINICAL PSYCHOLOGY
American Psychological Association
Arlington, VA
JOURNAL OF CONSUMER AFFAIRS
University of Missouri, Columbia, MO
JOURNAL OF CONTEMPORARY HISTORY
Sage Publications, Beverly Hills, CA
JOURNAL OF COUNSELING PSYCHOLOGY
American Psychological Association, Inc.
Arlington, VA

JOURNAL OF CROSS-CULTURAL PSYCHOLOGY
Center for Cross-Cultural Research
Department of Psychology
Western Washington State College
Bellingham, WA

JOURNAL OF EARLY ADOLESCENCE
H.E.L.P. Books, Tucson, AZ

JOURNAL OF ECONOMIC HISTORY
Graduate School of Business Administration
New York University, New York, NY

JOURNAL OF EDUCATION
Boston University, Boston, MA

JOURNAL OF EDUCATIONAL EQUITY AND LEADERSHIP
University Council for Educational Administration
Columbia, OH

JOURNAL OF EDUCATIONAL PSYCHOLOGY
American Psychological Association
Arlington, VA

JOURNAL OF EDUCATIONAL TECHNOLOGY SYSTEMS
Baywood Publishing Co., Inc., Farmingdale, NY

JOURNAL OF ETHNIC STUDIES
Ethnic Studies Program, Western Washington
University, Bellingham, WA

JOURNAL OF EXPERIMENTAL EDUCATION
Heldref Publications, Washington, DC

JOURNAL OF FAMILY LAW
School of Law, University of Louisville
Louisville, KY

JOURNAL OF GENERAL PSYCHOLOGY
Provincetown, MA

JOURNAL OF GENETIC PSYCHOLOGY
Journal Press, Provincetown, MA

JOURNAL OF GERIATRIC PSYCHIATRY
Society for Gerontological Psychiatry
Boston, MA

JOURNAL OF GERONTOLOGICAL SOCIAL WORK
Haworth Press, New York, NY

JOURNAL OF GERONTOLOGY
Gerontological Society, Washington DC

JOURNAL OF HUMAN STRESS
Opinion Publications, Framingham, MA

JOURNAL OF INTERAMERICAN STUDIES AND
WORLD AFFAIRS
Sage Publications, Beverly Hills, CA

JOURNAL OF LATIN COMMUNITY HEALTH
Boston, MA

JOURNAL OF LAW AND EDUCATION
Jefferson Law Book Co., Cincinnati, OH

JOURNAL OF LEISURE RESEARCH
National Recreation & Park Association
Alexandria, VA

JOURNAL OF MARITAL AND FAMILY THERAPY
American Association of Marriage and
Family Counseling, Claremont, CA

JOURNAL OF MARRIAGE AND THE FAMILY
National Council on Family Relations
Minneapolis, MN

JOURNAL OF MEDICAL EDUCATION
Association of American Medical Colleges
Washington, DC

JOURNAL OF NERVOUS AND MENTAL DISEASE
Williams & Wilkins, Baltimore, MD

JOURNAL OF NON-WHITE CONCERNS IN PERSONNEL
AND GUIDANCE
American Association for Counseling and
Development, Alexandria, VA

JOURNAL OF OPERATIONAL PSYCHIATRY
Department of Psychiatry, University of
Missouri, Columbia, MO

JOURNAL OF PEDIATRICS
C.V. Mosby Co., St. Louis, MO

JOURNAL OF PERSONALITY AND SOCIAL PSYCHOLOGY
American Psychological Association
Arlington, VA

JOURNAL OF PERSONALITY ASSESSMENT
Society for Personality Assessment
Burbank, CA

JOURNAL OF POLITICS
University of Florida, Gainesville, FL

JOURNAL OF PSYCHOACTIVE DRUGS
Haight-Ashbury Publications, San Francisco, CA

JOURNAL OF PSYCHOSOCIAL NURSING AND
MENTAL HEALTH SERVICES
Charles B. Slack, Inc., Thorofare, NJ

JOURNAL OF REHABILITATION
National Rehabilitation Association
Alexandria, VA

JOURNAL OF RESEARCH AND DEVELOPMENT
IN EDUCATION
University of Georgia, Athens, GA

JOURNAL OF RESEARCH IN SCIENCE TEACHING
John Wiley & Sons, Inc., New York, NY

JOURNAL OF SAN DIEGO HISTORY
San Diego Historical Society, San Diego, CA

JOURNAL OF SCHOOL HEALTH
American School Health Association, Kent, OH

JOURNAL OF SCHOOL PSYCHOLOGY
Pergamon Press, Inc., Elmsford, NY

JOURNAL OF SOCIAL ISSUES
Plenum Publishing Corporation, New York, NY

JOURNAL OF SOCIAL PSYCHOLOGY
Princetown, MA

JOURNAL OF SOUTHERN HISTORY
Southern Historical Association, History Department
Tulane University, New Orleans, LA

JOURNAL OF SPORT HISTORY
North American Society for Sport History
Pennsylvania State University
University Park, PA

JOURNAL OF TEACHER EDUCATION
Journal of Teacher Education, AACTE
Washington, DC

JOURNAL OF THE AMERICAN ACADEMY OF
PSYCHOANALYSIS
John Wiley & Sons, Inc., New York, NY

JOURNAL OF THE ASSOCIATION FOR THE STUDY
OF PERCEPTION
DeKalb, IL

JOURNAL OF THE INSTITUTE FOR
SOCIOECONOMIC STUDIES
Institute for Socioeconomic Studies
White Plains, NY

JOURNAL OF THE NATIONAL ASSOCIATION OF
    COLLEGE ADMISSIONS COUNSELORS
  Stokie, IL
JOURNAL OF THE WEST
  Manhattan, KS
JOURNAL OF URBAN HISTORY
  Sage Publications, Beverly Hills, CA
JOURNAL OF VOCATIONAL BEHAVIOR
  Academic Press, Inc., New York, NY
LABOR HISTORY
  Tamiment Institute, New York University,
  New York, NY
LABOR LAW JOURNAL
  Commerce Clearing House, Chicago, IL
LATIN AMERICAN MUSIC REVIEW
  University of Texas Press, Austin, TX
LATIN AMERICAN THEATRE REVIEW
  University of Kansas, Lawrence, KS
LAW AND CONTEMPORARY PROBLEMS
  Duke University School of Law, Durham, NC
LIBRARY AND INFORMATION SCIENCE RESEARCH
  Ablex Publishing Corporation,
  Norwood, NJ
LIBRARY JOURNAL
  R.R. Bowker Co., Riverton, NJ
LOS ANGELES
  Los Angeles, Los Angeles, CA
MACLEANS
  MacLean-Hunter, Ltd., Toronto
MADISON AVENUE
  Madison Avenue Publishing Corporation
  New York, NY
MARKETING AND MEDIA DECISIONS
  Decisions Publications, New York, NY
MARRIAGE & FAMILY REVIEW
  Haworth Press, New York, NY
MEDICAL CARE
  J.B. Lippincott Co., Philadelphia, PA
MENTAL DISABILITY LAW REPORTER
  American Bar Association, Washington, DC
MESTER
  University of California, Los Angeles, CA
METAS
  New York Aspira of America, New York, NY
MICHIGAN LAW REVIEW
  Michigan Law Review Association, Ann Arbor, MI
MID-AMERICAN REVIEW OF SOCIOLOGY
  Department of Sociology, University of
  Kansas, Lawrence, KS
MIDWEST QUARTERLY
  Pittsburg State University, Pittsburg, KS
MODERN FICTION STUDIES
  Purdue University, West Lafayette, IN
MODERN LANGUAGE JOURNAL
  University of Wisconsin Press,
  Madison, WI
MOMENTUM
  National Catholic Education Association,
  Washington, DC
MONTHLY LABOR REVIEW
  US Government Printing Office,
  Washington, DC

MS. MAGAZINE
  Ms Magazine, Marion, OH
NABE JOURNAL
  NABE Central Office, Washington, DC
NATION
  Nation, Marion, OH
NATIONAL ASSOCIATION OF SECONDARY SCHOOL
PRINCIPALS: BULLETIN
  National Association of Secondary School
  Principals, Reston, VA
NATIONAL CATHOLIC REPORTER
  National Catholic Reporter Publishing Co.,
  Kansas City, MO
NATIONAL JOURNAL
  National Journal, Inc., Washington, DC
NATIONAL LAW JOURNAL
  New York Law Publishing Co., New York, NY
NATIONAL MEDICAL ASSOCIATION JOURNAL
  Appleton-Century-Crofts, Norwalk, CT
NATIONAL REVIEW
  National Review, New York, NY
NATIONAL UNDERWRITER LIFE AND HEALTH
    INSURANCE EDITION
  National Underwriter Life and Health
  Insurance Edition, Cincinnati, OH
NEW AMERICA: A REVIEW
  University of New Mexico,
  Albuquerque, NM
NEW DIRECTIONS FOR PROGRAM EVALUATION
  Jossey-Bass, Inc., Publishers,
  San Francisco, CA
NEW DIRECTIONS FOR CONTINUING EDUCATION
  Jossey-Bass, Inc., Publishers,
  San Francisco, CA
NEW JERSEY LAW JOURNAL
  Skinder-Strauss Corporation,
  Newark, NJ
NEW MEXICO HISTORICAL REVIEW
  University of New Mexico,
  Albuquerque, NM
NEW MEXICO MAGAZINE
  State of New Mexico, Santa Fe, NM
NEW REPUBLIC
  New Republic, Farmingdale, NY
NEWSWEEK
  Newsweek, Livingston, NJ
NEW YORKER
  New Yorker Magazine, New York, NY
NEW YORK LAW JOURNAL
  New York Law Publishing Co.,
  New York, NY
NEW YORK TIMES MAGAZINE
  New York Times, New York, NY
NEW YORK TIMES BOOK REVIEW
  New York Times Co., New York, NY
NOTES AND QUERIES
  Oxford University Press, London
NURSE PRACTITIONER
  Health Sciences Media and Research
  Services, Seattle, WA

NURSING RESEARCH
American Journal of Nursing Co.,
New York, NY

OHIO STATE BAR ASSOCIATION REPORT
Law Abstract Publishing Co.,
Columbus, OH

THE OTHER SIDE
Jubilee, Inc., Philadelphia, PA

PACIFIC HISTORICAL REVIEW
University of California Press,
Berkeley, CA

PACIFIC NORTHWEST QUARTERLY
University of Washington,
Seattle, WA

PACIFIC SOCIOLOGICAL REVIEW
Sage Publications, Beverly Hills, CA

PALABRA Y EL HOMBRE
Editorial de la Universidad Veracruzana,
Veracruz, México

PEABODY JOURNAL OF EDUCATION
Peabody College of Vanderbilt
University, Nashville, TN

PEDIATRICS
American Academy of Pediatrics,
Evanston, IL

PEPPERDINE LAW REVIEW
Pepperdine University Law School,
Malibu, CA

PERCEPTUAL AND MOTOR SKILLS
Perceptual and Motor Skills,
Missoula, MT

PERSPECTIVES IN PSYCHIATRIC CARE
Nursing Publications, Inc.,
Park Ridge, NJ

PHI DELTA KAPPAN
Phi Delta Kappan, Inc., Bloomington, IN

POLICE CHIEF
International Association of
Chiefs of Police
Gaithersburg, MD

POLICY REVIEW
Heritage Foundation, Inc.,
Washington, DC

POLICY STUDIES JOURNAL
University of Illinois, Urbana, IL

POLITICAL PSYCHOLOGY
Plenum Publishing Corporation,
New York, NY

PONTE RIVISTA: MENSILE DI POLITICA
E LITTERATURA
Firenze, Italy

PRINCIPAL
National Association of Elementary School
Principals, Reston, VA

PROFESSIONAL GEOGRAPHER
Association of American Geographers,
Washington, DC

THE PROGRESSIVE
The Progressive, Madison, WI

PSYCHIATRIC QUARTERLY
Human Services Press
New York, NY

PSYCHOLOGICAL REPORTS
Psychological Reports, Missoula, MT

PSYCHOLOGY IN THE SCHOOLS
Psychology in the Schools,
Brandon, VT

PSYCHOLOGY TODAY
Psychology Today, Boulder, CO

PUBLIC HEALTH REPORTS
US Government Printing Office,
Washington, DC

PUBLIC PAPERS OF THE PRESIDENT
US Government Printing Office,
Washington, DC

PUBLISHER'S WEEKLY
R.R. Bowker Co., New York, NY

R & D MEXICO
Circuito Cultural Universitario,
Ciudad Universitaria, México, D.F., México

READING TEACHER
International Reading Association,
Newark, DE

READING WORLD
College Reading Association,
Springfield, MO

REFERENCE SERVICES REVIEW
Pierian Press, Ann Arbor, MI

RELIGIOUS EDUCATION
Religious Education Association,
New Haven, CT

REVIEWS IN ANTHROPOLOGY
Redgrave Publishing Co., Salem, NY

REVISTA INTERAMERICANA DE BIBLIOGRAFIA
Organization of American States,
Washington, DC

REVUE DU CINEMA-IMAGE ET SON-ECRAN
Ligue Francaise de L'Enseignement et de
L'Education Permanente, Paris, France

REVUE FRANCAISE D'ETUDES AMERICAINES
Paris, France

ROCKY MOUNTAIN REVIEW OF LANGUAGE
AND LITERATURE
Rocky Mountain Modern Language Association,
Tempe, AZ

RQ-REFERENCE AND ADULT SERVICES DIVISION
American Library Association, Chicago, IL

S & MM [SALES & MARKETING MANAGEMENT]
Bill Communications, New York, NY

SAN DIEGO LAW REVIEW
School of Law, University of San Diego,
San Diego, CA

SAN FRANCISCO REVIEW OF BOOKS
San Francisco Publishing Co.,
San Francisco, CA

SCHOLAR AND EDUCATOR
Society of Educators and Scholars,
Danville, IL

SCHOOL COUNSELOR
American Association for Counseling
and Development, Alexandria, VA

SCHOOL LIBRARY JOURNAL
R.R. Bowker Co., Riverton, NJ

SCHOOL PSYCHOLOGY REVIEW
National Association of School
Psychologists, Kent, OH

SCHOOL PSYCHOLOGY INTERNATIONAL
School Psychology Publishing Co.,
London
SCIENCE EDUCATION
John Wiley & Sons, New York, NY
SIGNS: JOURNAL OF WOMEN IN CULTURE & SOCIETY
University of Chicago Press, Chicago, IL
SOCIAL BEHAVIOR AND PERSONALITY
Society for Personality Research
Wellington, New Zealand
SOCIAL CASEWORK
Family Service Association of America,
New York, NY
SOCIAL FORCES
University of North Carolina Press,
Chapel Hill, NC
SOCIAL PROBLEMS
Social Problems, Buffalo, NY
SOCIAL SCIENCE AND MEDICINE
Pergamon Press, Inc.,
Elmsford, NY
SOCIAL SCIENCE JOURNAL
Colorado State University,
Fort Collins, CO
SOCIAL SCIENCE QUARTERLY
University of Texas Press,
Austin, TX
SOCIAL WORK
Social Work, Silver Spring, MD
SOCIAL WORK IN HEALTH CARE
Haworth Press, New York, NY
SOCIETY
Society, New Brunswick, NJ
SOCIOLOGICAL INQUIRY
National Sociology Honor Society,
University of Illinois, Urbana-Champaign, IL
SOCIOLOGY & SOCIAL RESEARCH
University of Southern California Press,
Los Angeles, CA
SOUTH ATLANTIC QUARTERLY
Duke University Press,
Durham, NC
SOUTHERN CALIFORNIA LAW REVIEW
School of Law, University of Southern
California, Los Angeles, CA
SOUTHERN CALIFORNIA QUARTERLY
Historical Society of Southern
California, Los Angeles, CA
SOUTHERN ECONOMIC JOURNAL
Southern Economic Journal,
Chapel Hill, NC
SOUTHERN EXPOSURE
Institute for Southern Studies,
Durham, NC
SOUTHWESTERN HISTORICAL QUARTERLY
Texas State Historical Association,
Austin, TX
SOUTHERN STUDIES
University of Southwestern Louisiana,
Lafayette, LO
SOUTHWESTERN REVIEW OF MANAGEMENT
& ECONOMICS
Bureau of Business and Economic Research,
University of New Mexico, Albuquerque, NM

SUFFOLK TRANSNATIONAL LAW JOURNAL
Suffolk University Law School, Boston, MA
TEACHERS COLLEGE RECORD
Teachers College, Columbia University,
New York, NY
TELEVISION/RADIO AGE
Television Editorial Corporation,
Baltimore, MD
TESOL QUARTERLY
TESOL, Georgetown University,
Washington, DC
TEXAS BAR JOURNAL
State Bar of Texas, Austin, TX
TEXAS BUSINESS REVIEW
University of Texas, Austin, TX
TEXAS INTERNATIONAL LAW JOURNAL
School of Law, University of Texas,
Austin, TX
TEXAS MONTHLY
Texas Monthly, Austin, TX
TEXAS OBSERVOR
Texas Observor, Austin, TX
TEXAS TECH JOURNAL OF EDUCATION
Texas Tech Press, Lubbock, TX
TEXAS TECH LAW REVIEW
School of Law, Texas Tech University,
Lubbock, TX
THRUST
Association of California School
Administrators, Burlingame, CA
TIME
Time, Chicago, IL
TIMES [EDUCATIONAL SUPPLEMENT]
Times Newspapers, London
UNIVERSITY OF CALIFORNIA DAVIS LAW REVIEW
School of Law, University of California,
Davis, CA
URBAN AFFAIRS QUARTERLY
Sage Publications, Inc.,
Beverly Hills, CA
URBAN INTEREST
Department of Political Science,
University of Kansas, Lawrence, KS
URBAN LIFE
Sage Publications, Inc.,
Beverly Hills, CA
U.S. NEWS & WORLD REPORT
US News & World Report, Washington, DC
VARIETY
Variety Publishing Co., New York, NY
VILLANOVA LAW REVIEW
Villanova University Law School,
Villanova, PA
VOCATIONAL GUIDANCE QUARTERLY
American Association for Counseling
and Development, Alexandria, VA
VOGUE
Vogue, New York, NY
WALL STREET JOURNAL
Dow Jones & Company, Inc.,
Chicopee, MA
WASHINGTON UNIVERSITY LAW QUARTERLY
School of Law, Washington University,
St. Louis, MO

SUBJECT INDEX

A JULIA Y A MI

1 Umpierre, Luz Maria. La ansiedad de la influencia en Sandra Maria Esteves y Marjorie Agosin. REVISTA CHICANO-RIQUENA, Vol. 11, no. 3-4 (Fall 1983), p. 139-147. Spanish. **DESCR:** *Agosin, Magi; De Burgos, Julia; EL PAIS DIVIDIDO; *Esteves, Sandra Maria; *Literary Criticism; Neruda, Pablo; Parra, Nicanor; Poetry.

ABC-TV

2 Mexico en crisis: la incomprendida prensa norteamericana. INFORME: RELACIONES MEXICO-ESTADOS UNIDOS, Vol. 1, no. 3 (July, December, 1982), p. 256-266. Spanish. **DESCR:** *Journalism; Mass Media; NEW YORK TIMES.

Abortion

3 Lopez, Phyllis. Untitled No.1. COMADRE, no. 2 (Spring 1978), p. 10. English. **DESCR:** *Poetry.

4 Rosenhouse-Persson, Sandra and Sabagh, Georges. Attitudes toward abortion among Catholic Mexican-American women: the effects of religiosity and education. DEMOGRAPHY, Vol. 20, no. 1 (February 1983), p. 87-98. English. **DESCR:** Attitude (Psychological); *Catholic Church; Education; Religion.

5 [Summary of: Simpson, abortion, poverty, and equal protection of the law, 13 Ga. L. rev. 505 (1979)]. CHICANO LAW REVIEW, Vol. 5, (1982), p. 82-83. English. **DESCR:** *Administration of Justice; Maher v. Roe; Roe v. Wade.

Abramson, Anal J.

6 Book review of: THE FEDERAL BUDGET AND THE NON-PROFIT SECTOR. CAMINOS, Vol. 4, no. 4 (April 1983), p. 59. English. **DESCR:** Book Reviews; Federal Aid; *FEDERAL BUDGET AND THE NON-PROFIT SECTOR; Non-profit Groups; Salamon, Lester M.

Abrilz, Santos T. (Sandy)

7 Gupta, Udayan. Netting success: Apoca's approach. HISPANIC BUSINESS, Vol. 5, no. 7 (July 1983), p. 20-21+. English. **DESCR:** Business Enterprises; Businesspeople; Success; *Telecommunications.

A.C. Nielsen Company

8 Wittenauer, Cheryl. Rating Hispanic media. HISPANIC BUSINESS, Vol. 5, no. 3 (March 1983), p. 14-15. English. **DESCR:** Advertising; Arbitron; *Broadcast Media; Television.

Academic Achievement

9 Buriel, Raymond, et al. Mexican- and Anglo-American children's locus of control and achievement in relation to teachers attitudes. JOURNAL OF GENETIC PSYCHOLOGY, Vol. 140, no. 1 (March 1982), p. 131-143. English. **DESCR:** Anglo Americans; Children; Comparative Education; *Teacher Attitudes.

10 Buriel, Raymond, et al. Teacher-student interactions and their relationship to student achievement: a comparison of Mexican-American and Anglo-American children. JOURNAL OF EDUCATIONAL PSYCHOLOGY, Vol. 75, no. 6 (December 1983), p. 889-897. English. **DESCR:** Brophy-Good Dyadic Interaction System; *Primary School Education; Teacher-pupil Interaction.

11 Burke, Leslie K. Book review of: LIFE'S CAREER-AGING: CULTURAL VARIATIONS ON GROWING OLD. HISPANIC JOURNAL OF BEHAVIORAL SCIENCES, Vol. 4, no. 1 (March 1982), p. 103-107. English. **DESCR:** *LIFE'S CAREER--AGING: CULTURAL VARIATIONS ON GROWING OLD; Myerhoff, Barbara G.; Simic, Andrei.

12 Burns, Maureen. Current status of Hispanic technical professionals: how can we improve recruitment and retention. INTEGRATED EDUCATION, Vol. 20, (January, April, 1982), p. 49-55. English. **DESCR:** Academic Motivation; Counseling Services (Educational); Socioeconomic Factors; *Technical Education.

13 Calkins, E. Virginia; Willoughby, T. Lee; and Arnold, Louise M. Predictors of performance of minority students in the first two years of a BA/MD program. NATIONAL MEDICAL ASSOCIATION JOURNAL, Vol. 74, no. 7 (July 1982), p. 625-632. English. **DESCR:** Academic Motivation; Affirmative Action Programs; *Medical Education; University of Missouri-Kansas City School of Medicine.

14 de los Santos, Alfredo G. Jr.; Montemayor, Joaquin; and Solis, Enrique, Jr. Chicano students in institutions of higher education: access, attrition, and achievement. AZTLAN, Vol. 14, no. 1 (Spring 1983), p. 79-110. English. **DESCR:** Educational Statistics; Enrollment; *Higher Education; Students.

15 Dreisbach, Melanie and Keogh, Barbara K. Testwiseness as a factor in readiness test performance of young Mexican-American children. JOURNAL OF EDUCATIONAL PSYCHOLOGY, Vol. 74, no. 2 (April 1982), p. 224-229. English. **DESCR:** Bilingualism; Early Childhood Education; Educational Tests and Measurements.

16 Frazier, Donald J. and De Blassie, Richard R. Comparison of self-concept in Mexican American and non-Mexican American late adolescents. ADOLESCENCE, Vol. 17, no. 66 (Summer 1982), p. 327-334. English. **DESCR:** *Identity; Socioeconomic Factors; Students; Youth.

17 Gandara, Patricia. Passing through the eye of the needle: high-achieving Chicanas. HISPANIC JOURNAL OF BEHAVIORAL SCIENCES, Vol. 4, no. 2 (June 1982), p. 167-179. English. **DESCR:** *Chicanas; Higher Education.

18 Hispanic student study undertaken. NUESTRO, Vol. 7, no. 10 (December 1983), p. 11-12. English. **DESCR:** Dropouts; Educational Statistics; Enrollment; Hispanic Policy Development Project; *National Commission on Secondary Schooling for Hispanics; *Secondary School Education.

19 Knight, George P., et al. Cooperative-competitive social orientation and school achievement among Anglo-American and Mexican-American children. CONTEMPORARY EDUCATIONAL PSYCHOLOGY, Vol. 7, no. 2 (April 1982), p. 97-106. English. **DESCR:** Anglo Americans; Cultural Characteristics; Socialization; Students.

Academic Achievement (cont.)

20 Kugle, Cherry L.; Clements, Richard O.; and Powell, Philip M. Level and stability of self-esteem in relation to academic behavior of second graders. JOURNAL OF PERSONALITY AND SOCIAL PSYCHOLOGY, Vol. 44, no. 1 (January 1983), p. 201-207. English. **DESCR:** *Identity; PIERS-HARRIS CHILDREN'S SELF CONCEPT SCALE; Primary School Education.

21 Laosa, Luis M. School occupation, culture, and family: the impact of parental schooling on the parent-child relationship. JOURNAL OF EDUCATIONAL PSYCHOLOGY, Vol. 74, no. 6 (December 1982), p. 791-827. English. **DESCR:** Education; *Parent and Child Relationships.

22 Low, Benson P. and Clement, Paul W. Relationships of race and socioeconomic status to classroom behavior, academic achievement, and referral for special education. JOURNAL OF SCHOOL PSYCHOLOGY, Vol. 20, no. 2 (Summer 1982), p. 103-112. English. **DESCR:** Anglo Americans; Blacks; Identity; Socioeconomic Factors.

23 Maestas, Leo C. Academic performance across cultures: an examination of the effect of value similarity. EDUCATIONAL RESEARCH QUARTERLY, Vol. 7, no. 4 (Winter 1983), p. 24-34. English. **DESCR:** Cultural Customs; Ethnic Groups; Socialization; Teacher-pupil Interaction.

24 McCurdy, Jack. Chicanos mark their gains in colleges, call for more. CHRONICLE OF HIGHER EDUCATION, Vol. 25, no. 10 (November 3, 1982), p. 12. English. **DESCR:** *Higher Education; Madrid, Arturo; National Chicano Council on Higher Education (NCCHE).

25 McGroarty, Mary. English language test, school language use, and achievement in Spanish-speaking high school students. TESOL QUARTERLY, Vol. 17, no. 2 (June 1983), p. 310-311. English. **DESCR:** *English as a Second Language; High School Students; Language Assessment.

26 Mendez, Gloria I. Bilingual children's adaptation after a transitional bilingual education. METAS, Vol. 3, no. 1 (Summer 1982), p. 1-112. English. **DESCR:** Acculturation; *Bilingual Bicultural Education; Bilingualism; English as a Second Language; Identity.

27 Mishra, Shitala P. Validity of WISC-R IQs and factor scores in predicting achievement for Mexican American children. PSYCHOLOGY IN THE SCHOOLS, Vol. 20, no. 4 (October 1983), p. 442-444. English. **DESCR:** Intelligence Tests; Primary School Students; Wechsler Intelligence Scale for Children-Revised (WISC-R).

28 Moore, Helen A. Hispanic women: schooling for conformity in public education. HISPANIC JOURNAL OF BEHAVIORAL SCIENCES, Vol. 5, no. 1 (March 1983), p. 45-63. English. **DESCR:** *Chicanas; Education.

29 Nevarez, Miguel A. The Hispanic educational dilemma: a strategy for change. HISPANIC BUSINESS, Vol. 5, no. 11 (November 1983), p. 12. English. **DESCR:** Dropouts; *Education; Higher Education.

30 Oakland, Thomas. Concurrent and predictive validity estimates for the WISC-R IQ's and ELP's by racial-ethnic and SES groups. SCHOOL PSYCHOLOGY REVIEW, Vol. 12, no. 1 (Winter 1983), p. 57-61. English. **DESCR:** Estimated Learning Potential (ELP); *Intelligence Tests; Primary School Education; Wechsler Intelligence Scale for Children-Revised (WISC-R).

31 Oakland, Thomas. Joint use of adaptive behavior and IQ to predict achievement. JOURNAL OF CONSULTING AND CLINICAL PSYCHOLOGY, Vol. 51, no. 2 (April 1983), p. 298-301. English. **DESCR:** Education; Intelligence Tests; Mathematics; Reading.

32 Obrzut, John E.; Hansen, Robert L.; and Heath, Charles P. The effectiveness of visual information processing training with Hispanic children. JOURNAL OF GENERAL PSYCHOLOGY, Vol. 10, no. 2 (October 1982), p. 165-174. English. **DESCR:** Bender Gestalt Test; Colorado; Intelligence Tests; Primary School Education.

33 Powers, Stephen and Sanchez, Virginia V. Correlates of self-esteem of Mexican American adolescents. PSYCHOLOGICAL REPORTS, Vol. 51, no. 3 (December 1982), p. 771-774. English. **DESCR:** Arizona; Employment; *Identity; Junior High School Students; Nogales, AZ.

34 Saracho, Olivia N. Planning computer assisted instruction for Spanish speaking migrant students. JOURNAL OF EDUCATIONAL TECHNOLOGY SYSTEMS, Vol. 10, no. 3 (1981, 1982), p. 257-260. English. **DESCR:** Computers; Migrant Children; *Migrant Education; *Programmed Instruction.

35 Surace, Samuel J. Achievement, discrimination, and Mexican-Americans. COMPARATIVE STUDIES IN SOCIETY AND HISTORY, Vol. 24, no. 2 (1982), p. 315-339. English. **DESCR:** *Racism; Stereotypes.

36 Tienda, Marta. Sex, ethnicity and Chicano status attainment. INTERNATIONAL MIGRATION REVIEW, Vol. 16, no. 2 (Summer 1982), p. 435-473. English. **DESCR:** Chicanas; Discrimination in Education; Discrimination in Employment; Identity; Income; Language Proficiency; Sexism; *Social Classes; Social Mobility.

37 Troike, Rudolph C. Bilingual-si! PRINCIPAL, Vol. 62, no. 3 (January 1983), p. 8. English. **DESCR:** *Bilingual Bicultural Education; Bilingualism; English as a Second Language.

38 Valencia, Richard R. Predicting academic achievement of Mexican American children: preliminary analysis of the McCarthy Scales. EDUCATIONAL AND PSYCHOLOGICAL MEASUREMENT, Vol. 42, (Winter 1982), p. 1269-1278. English. **DESCR:** Children; Educational Tests and Measurements; Identity; McCarthy Scales for Children's Abilities (MSCA).

39 Vigil, James Diego. Chicano high schoolers: educational performance and acculturation. EDUCATIONAL FORUM, Vol. 47, no. 1 (Fall 1982), p. 58-73. English. **DESCR:** *Acculturation; Identity; Secondary School Education; Socioeconomic Factors.

40 Willig, Ann C. Sociocultural and educational correlates of success-failure attributions and evaluation anxiety in the school setting for Black, Hispanic, and Anglo children. AMERICAN EDUCATIONAL RESEARCH JOURNAL, Vol. 20, no. 3 (Fall 1983), p. 385-410. English. **DESCR:** *Academic Motivation; Anglo Americans; Blacks; Cultural Characteristics.

Academic Libraries

41 Perry, Charles E. Book review of: DEVELOPING
LIBRARY AND INFORMATION SERVICES FOR
AMERICANS OF HISPANIC ORIGIN. JOURNAL OF
ACADEMIC LIBRARIANSHIP, Vol. 8, no. 1 (March
1982), p. 38. English. DESCR: Book Reviews;
*DEVELOPING LIBRARY AND INFORMATION SERVICES
FOR AMERICANS OF HISPANIC ORIGIN; Haro,
Robert P.; Library Services.

Academic Motivation

42 Burns, Maureen. Current status of Hispanic
technical professionals: how can we improve
recruitment and retention. INTEGRATED
EDUCATION, Vol. 20, (January, April, 1982),
p. 49-55. English. DESCR: Academic
Achievement; Counseling Services
(Educational); Socioeconomic Factors;
*Technical Education.

43 Calkins, E. Virginia; Willoughby, T. Lee;
and Arnold, Louise M. Predictors of
performance of minority students in the
first two years of a BA/MD program. NATIONAL
MEDICAL ASSOCIATION JOURNAL, Vol. 74, no. 7
(July 1982), p. 625-632. English. DESCR:
Academic Achievement; Affirmative Action
Programs; *Medical Education; University of
Missouri-Kansas City School of Medicine.

44 Saracho, Olivia N. Effects of a
computer-assisted instruction program on
basic skills achievement and attitudes
toward instruction of Spanish-speaking
migrant children. AMERICAN EDUCATIONAL
RESEARCH JOURNAL, Vol. 19, no. 2 (Summer
1982), p. 201-219. English. DESCR:
Audiovisual Instruction; Computers; *Migrant
Children; *Migrant Education; Programmed
Instruction.

45 Vasquez, Melba J. T. Confronting barriers to
the participation of Mexican American women
in higher education. HISPANIC JOURNAL OF
BEHAVIORAL SCIENCES, Vol. 4, no. 2 (June
1982), p. 147-165. English. DESCR:
*Chicanas; Higher Education; Sex Roles;
Socioeconomic Factors.

46 Willig, Ann C. Sociocultural and educational
correlates of success-failure attributions
and evaluation anxiety in the school setting
for Black, Hispanic, and Anglo children.
AMERICAN EDUCATIONAL RESEARCH JOURNAL, Vol.
20, no. 3 (Fall 1983), p. 385-410. English.
DESCR: Academic Achievement; Anglo
Americans; Blacks; Cultural Characteristics.

Academic Performance

USE: Academic Achievement

Academy Awards

47 An Hispanic view of the 1983 Academy Awards.
CAMINOS, Vol. 4, no. 6 (June 1983), p. 59.
English. DESCR: Awards; Films.

Academy for Educational Development (AED)

48 A new direction for bilingual education in
the 1980's (originally published in FOCUS
1982). ADFL BULLETIN, Vol. 14, no. 2
(November 1982), p. 5-8. English. DESCR:
*Bilingual Bicultural Education.

Accentedness

49 Kramer, Virginia Reyes and Schell, Leo M.
English auditory discrimination skills of
Spanish-speaking children. ALBERTA JOURNAL
OF EDUCATIONAL RESEARCH, Vol. 28, no. 1
(March 1982), p. 1-8. English. DESCR:
Bilingualism; English Language; *Language
Development; Spanish Language.

50 Lipski, John M. Spanish-English language
switching in speech and literature: theories
and models. BILINGUAL REVIEW, Vol. 9, no. 3
(September, December, 1982), p. 191-212.
English. DESCR: Bilingualism; Language
Patterns.

51 Woods, Richard D. Book review of: SPANISH
AND ENGLISH OF UNITED STATES HISPANOS: A
CRITICAL, ANNOTATED, LINGUISTIC
BIBLIOGRAPHY. JOURNAL OF ETHNIC STUDIES,
Vol. 4, no. 3 (Fall 1976), p. 116. English.
DESCR: Bibliography; Bills, Garland D.; Book
Reviews; Craddock, Jerry R.; Language
Patterns; *SPANISH AND ENGLISH OF U.S.
HISPANOS: A CRITICAL, ANNOTATED, LINGUISTIC
BIBLIOGRAPHY; Spanish Language; Teschner,
Richard V.

ACCESS TO POWER: POLITICS AND THE URBAN POOR IN DEVELOPING NATIONS

52 Logan, Kathleen. The urban poor in
developing nations. JOURNAL OF URBAN
HISTORY, Vol. 9, no. 1 (November 1982), p.
108-116. English. DESCR: *Book Reviews;
BORDER BOOM TOWN: CIUDAD JUAREZ SINCE 1848;
Collier, David; Cornelius, Wayne A.;
Eckstein, Susan; Lloyd, Peter; Martinez,
Oscar J.; Nelson, Joan M.; Perlman, Janice
E.; POLITICS AND MIGRANT POOR IN MEXICO
CITY; SLUMS OF HOPE? SHANTY TOWNS OF THE
THIRD WORLD; SQUATTERS AND OLIGARCHS:
AUTHORITARIAN RULE AND POLICY CHANGE IN
PERU; THE MYTH OF MARGINALITY: URBAN POVERTY
AND POLITICS IN RIO DE JANEIRO; THE POVERTY
OF REVOLUTION: THE STATE AND THE URBAN POOR
IN MEXICO; Urban Economics.

Accion 80s

53 Gonzales, Patrisia. The two cities of
Tucson. NUESTRO, Vol. 7, no. 4 (May 1983),
p. 20-23. English. DESCR: Cultural
Organizations; *Discrimination in Education;
*Discrimination in Employment; Garcia,
Gerald; Lopez-Grant, Lillian; *Tucson, AZ;
Valdez, Joel.

Accountants

54 Lanier, Alfredo S. Making it seem easy, from
intern to account executive. HISPANIC
BUSINESS, Vol. 4, no. 8 (August 1983), p.
16-17+. English. DESCR: Careers; Chicanas;
Employment Training; *Fernandez, Margarita;
INROADS; Standard Oil Corp.

55 Sargeant, Georgia. A woman's place is in the
bank. HISPANIC BUSINESS, Vol. 5, no. 10
(October 1983), p. 20-21+. English. DESCR:
*Banking Industry; Careers; Chicanas;
*Olson, Ethel Ortega; Otero Savings and
Loan, Alamogordo, TX.

56 Vara, Richard. Cracking the Big 8. HISPANIC
BUSINESS, Vol. 4, no. 8 (August 1983), p.
18-19+. English. DESCR: Careers.

Accounting

57 Gomez, Dalia. Needed: Latino CPA's. NUESTRO,
Vol. 6, no. 1 (January, February, 1982), p.
25-28. English. DESCR: Careers; Frank,
Eleanor Marie; Karpel, Miguel; Quezada,
Felipe L.; Rodriguez, Julio H.; Umpierre,
Raphael; Zuzueta, Joseph.

Acculturation

58 Bray, Howard. The new wave of Puerto Rican immigrants. NEW YORK TIMES MAGAZINE, (July 3, 1983), p. 22. English. **DESCR:** Immigration; *Puerto Ricans.

59 Chesney, Alan P., et al. Barriers to medical care of Mexican-Americans: the role of social class, acculturation, and social isolation. MEDICAL CARE, Vol. 20, no. 9 (1982), p. 883-891. English. **DESCR:** *Medical Care; Social Classes; Surveys.

60 Craig, Richard B. and Sell, Deborah K. Values of Anglo-American, Chicano, and Mexican students at a Mexican university. BORDERLANDS JOURNAL, Vol. 6, no. 2 (Spring 1983), p. 153-169. English. **DESCR:** Cultural Characteristics.

61 Craver, Rebecca McDowell. The impact of intimacy: Mexican-Anglo intermarriage in New Mexico 1821-1846. SOUTHWESTERN STUDIES, no. 66 (1982), p. 1-79. English. **DESCR:** Assimilation; Chicanas; *Intermarriage; New Mexico; Rio Arriba Valley, New Mexico.

62 Salgado de Snyder, Nelly and Padilla, Amado M. Cultural and ethnic maintenance of interethnically married Mexican-Americans. HUMAN ORGANIZATION, Vol. 41, no. 4 (Winter 1982), p. 359-362. English. **DESCR:** *Intermarriage.

63 Delgado, Melvin. Hispanics and psychotherapeutic groups. INTERNATIONAL JOURNAL OF GROUP PSYCHOTHERAPY, Vol. 33, no. 4 (October 1983), p. 507-520. English. **DESCR:** *Psychotherapy.

64 Dolgin, Daniel L., et al. Quality of life and psychological well-being in a bicultural Latino community. HISPANIC JOURNAL OF BEHAVIORAL SCIENCES, Vol. 4, no. 4 (December 1982), p. 433-450. English. **DESCR:** *Attitude (Psychological); Depression Scale; *Global Acculturation Scale; Index of Psychological Adjustment; Psychology; Quality of Life Scale.

65 Escobar, J.I. Post-traumatic stress disorder in Hispanic Vietnam veterans. JOURNAL OF NERVOUS AND MENTAL DISEASE, Vol. 17, no. 10 (October 1983), p. 585-596. English. **DESCR:** Mental Illness; Psychiatry; Stress; *Veterans.

66 Franco, Juan N. An acculturation scale for Mexican-American children. JOURNAL OF GENERAL PSYCHOLOGY, Vol. 108, (April 1983), p. 175-181. English. **DESCR:** Children; *Children's Acculturation Scale (CAS); Psychological Testing.

67 Franco, Juan N. A developmental analysis of self concept in Mexican American and Anglo school children. HISPANIC JOURNAL OF BEHAVIORAL SCIENCES, Vol. 5, no. 2 (June 1983), p. 207-218. English. **DESCR:** Children; *Identity.

68 Garcia, Mario T. Americanization and the Mexican immigrant, 1880-1930. JOURNAL OF ETHNIC STUDIES, Vol. 6, no. 2 (Summer 1978), p. 19-34. English. **DESCR:** Cultural Characteristics; Culture; Education; Immigrant Labor; Immigration.

69 Griffith, James. Relationship between acculturation and psychological impairment in adult Mexican Americans. HISPANIC JOURNAL OF BEHAVIORAL SCIENCES, Vol. 5, no. 4 (December 1983), p. 431-459. English.

DESCR: Psychology.

70 Hernandez, Leodoro. The socialization of a Chicano family. DE COLORES, Vol. 6, no. 1-2 (1982), p. 75-84. English. **DESCR:** Family; *Socialization.

71 Herrera-Sobek, Maria. The acculturation process of the Chicana in the corrido. DE COLORES, Vol. 6, no. 1-2 (1982), p. 7-16. English. **DESCR:** *Chicanas; Corrido; Sex Roles.

72 Hough, Richard. The Los Angeles Epidemiologic Catchment Area research program and the epidemiology of psychiatric disorders among Mexican Americans. JOURNAL OF OPERATIONAL PSYCHIATRY, Vol. 14, no. 1 (1983), p. 42-51. English. **DESCR:** Diagnostic Interview Schedule (DIS); El Centro Community Health Care Center; Los Angeles, CA; *Los Angeles Epidemiologic Catchment Area Research Program (LAECA); *Mental Health.

73 Keefe, Susan Emily. Help-seeking behavior among foreign-born and native-born Mexican-Americans. SOCIAL SCIENCE AND MEDICINE, Vol. 16, no. 16 (1982), p. 1467-1472. English. **DESCR:** Immigrants; *Mental Health Programs; Santa Barbara, CA.

74 Kranau, Edgar J.; Green, Vicki; and Valencia-Weber, Gloria. Acculturation and the Hispanic woman: attitudes toward women, sex-role attribution, sex-role behavior, and demographics. HISPANIC JOURNAL OF BEHAVIORAL SCIENCES, Vol. 4, no. 1 (March 1982), p. 21-40. English. **DESCR:** *Chicanas; Demography; Sex Roles.

75 Lamare, James W. Political integration of Mexican American children: a generational analysis. INTERNATIONAL MIGRATION REVIEW, Vol. 16, no. 1 (Spring 1982), p. 169-188. English. **DESCR:** Age Groups; Assimilation; *Children; Immigration; Political Ideology; *Political Socialization.

76 Mendez, Gloria I. Bilingual children's adaptation after a transitional bilingual education. METAS, Vol. 3, no. 1 (Summer 1982), p. 1-112. English. **DESCR:** Academic Achievement; *Bilingual Bicultural Education; Bilingualism; English as a Second Language; Identity.

77 Morgan, Thomas B. The Latinization of America. ESQUIRE, Vol. 99, no. 5 (May 1983), p. 47-56. English. **DESCR:** Assimilation; Biculturalism; Bilingualism; *Population Trends.

78 Murguia, Edward and Cazares, Ralph B. Intermarriage of Mexican Americans. MARRIAGE & FAMILY REVIEW, Vol. 5, no. 1 (Spring 1982), p. 91-100. English. **DESCR:** Anglo Americans; *Intermarriage; Social Mobility.

79 Padilla, Eligio R.; Olmedo, Esteban L.; and Loya, Fred. Acculturation and the MMPI performance of Chicano and Anglo college students. HISPANIC JOURNAL OF BEHAVIORAL SCIENCES, Vol. 4, no. 4 (December 1982), p. 451-466. English. **DESCR:** *Minnesota Multiphasic Personality Inventory (MMPI); Students.

Acculturation (cont.)

80 Saragoza, Alex M. Mexican children in the U.S.: the Central San Joaquin Valley. DE COLORES, Vol. 6, no. 1-2 (1982), p. 64-74. English. DESCR: *Children; Family; Identity; Parent and Child Relationships; San Joaquin Valley.

81 Vigil, James Diego. Chicano high schoolers: educational performance and acculturation. EDUCATIONAL FORUM, Vol. 47, no. 1 (Fall 1982), p. 58-73. English. DESCR: *Academic Achievement; Identity; Secondary School Education; Socioeconomic Factors.

82 Vigil, James Diego. Towards a new perspective on understanding the Chicano people: the six C's model of sociocultural change. CAMPO LIBRE, Vol. 1, no. 2 (Summer 1981), p. 141-167. English. DESCR: Assimilation; Cultural Characteristics; History; Mexican Nationalism Period; Mexico; Nationalism; Organizations; Precolumbian Society; *Six C's Model (Theoretical Model); Social History and Conditions; Spanish Colonial Period.

83 Wurzman, Ilyana. Cultural values of Puerto Rican opiate addicts: an exploratory study. AMERICAN JOURNAL OF DRUG AND ALCOHOL ABUSE, Vol. 9, no. 2 (1982, 1983), p. 141-153. English. DESCR: Anglo Americans; Blacks; *Drug Abuse; Drug Addicts; Family; Loevinger's Sentence Completion Test; Machismo; New York, NY; Opium; Puerto Ricans; Values.

ACCULTURATION RATING SCALE FOR MEXICAN AMERICANS (ARSMA)

84 Cuellar, Israel, et al. Clinical psychiatric case presentation; culturally responsive diagnostic formulation and treatment in an Hispanic female. HISPANIC JOURNAL OF BEHAVIORAL SCIENCES, Vol. 5, no. 1 (March 1983), p. 93-103. English. DESCR: Case Study; Chicanas; Medical Care; *Psychotherapy.

ACERCA DE LITERATURA

85 Gonzalez, Maria R. Book review of: ACERCA DE LITERATURA (Dialogo con tres autores chicanos). LA PALABRA, Vol. 4, no. 1-2 (Spring, Fall, 1982, 1983), p. 170-171. Spanish. DESCR: Book Reviews; Literature; Vazquez-Castro, Javier.

Achor, Shirley

86 Cortes, Carlos E. Book review of: MEXICAN AMERICANS IN A DALLAS BARRIO. NEW SCHOLAR, Vol. 8, no. 1-2 (Spring, Fall, 1982), p. 488-489. English. DESCR: Book Reviews; *MEXICAN AMERICANS IN A DALLAS BARRIO.

87 Goldberg, Victor. Ethnic groups in the United States. REVIEWS IN ANTHROPOLOGY, Vol. 9, no. 4 (Fall 1982), p. 375-382. English. DESCR: Book Reviews; ETHNIC AMERICA, A HISTORY; MEXICAN AMERICANS IN A DALLAS BARRIO; Sowell, Thomas; *THE CHICANOS; Trejo, Arnulfo D.

88 Mata, Alberto G. Book review of: MEXICAN AMERICANS IN A DALLAS BARRIO. AZTLAN, Vol. 14, no. 1 (Spring 1983), p. 196-198. English. DESCR: Barrios; Book Reviews; Dallas, TX; *MEXICAN AMERICANS IN A DALLAS BARRIO; Urban Communities.

Acosta, Hipolito

89 Padilla, Steve. Alien smuggling and the refugee question: undercover agent for the border patrol. NUESTRO, Vol. 7, no. 5 (June, July, 1983), p. 15-17. English. DESCR: *Border Patrol; *Immigration Regulation and Control; *Undocumented Workers.

Acosta, Juan

90 Firm honors Latino workers. NUESTRO, Vol. 6, no. 5 (June, July, 1982), p. 11-12. English. DESCR: Honeywell, Inc.; Minneapolis, MN; Mural Art.

Acosta, Oscar Zeta

91 Alurista. El caso, la novela y la historia en la obra de Acosta: THE REVOLT OF THE COCKROACH PEOPLE. MAIZE, Vol. 2, no. 3 (Spring 1979), p. 6-13. Spanish. DESCR: Literary Criticism; *THE REVOLT OF THE COCKROACH PEOPLE.

92 Bruce Novoa, Juan. Fear and loathing on the buffalo trail. MELUS: MULTI-ETHNIC LITERATURE OF THE UNITED STATES, Vol. 6, no. 4 (Winter 1979), p. 39-50. English. DESCR: *Literature.

ACROSS THE BORDER: RURAL DEVELOPMENT IN MEXICO AND RECENT MIGRATION

93 Cardoso, Lawrence Anthony. Book review of: ACROSS THE BORDER: RURAL DEVELOPMENT IN MEXICO AND RECENT MIGRATION TO THE UNITED STATES. AMERICAN HISTORICAL REVIEW, Vol. 88, no. 1 (February 1983), p. 226-227. English. DESCR: Book Reviews; Cross, Harry E.; Sandos, James.

94 Cardoso, Lawrence Anthony. Book review of: ACROSS THE BORDER: RURAL DEVELOPMENT IN MEXICO AND RECENT MIGRATION TO THE UNITED STATES. AMERICAN HISTORICAL REVIEW, Vol. 88, (February 1983), p. 226. English. DESCR: Book Reviews; Cross, Harry E.; Immigration; Sandos, James.

95 Mabry, Donald J. Book review of: ACROSS THE BORDER: RURAL DEVELOPMENT IN MEXICO AND RECENT MIGRATION TO THE UNITED STATES. INTERNATIONAL MIGRATION REVIEW, Vol. 17, no. 2 (Summer 1983), p. 351. English. DESCR: Book Reviews; Cross, Harry E.; Migration; Migration Patterns; Rural Economics; Sandos, James.

Actors
USE: Artists

Actos

96 Alurista. Mal vino el tango. MAIZE, Vol. 6, no. 3-4 (Spring, Summer, 1983), p. 101-102. Spanish.

97 Alurista. Mal vino el tango. LA PALABRA, Vol. 4, no. 1-2 (Spring, Fall, 1982, 1983), p. 148-149. Spanish.

98 Lyles, Charlise L. I want to be the daisy. MAIZE, Vol. 6, no. 3-4 (Spring, Summer, 1983), p. 82-85. English.

Actresses
USE: Artists

Acuna, Rudolfo

99 Maiz, Magdalena. Book review of: OCCUPIED AMERICA. PALABRA Y EL HOMBRE, Vol. 1982, no. 42 (April, June, 1982), p. 77-79. Spanish. **DESCR:** Book Reviews; *OCCUPIED AMERICA.

Adams, Bob

100 Entertainment reviews. CAMINOS, Vol. 3, no. 8 (September 1982), p. 21. English. **DESCR:** Alpert, Herb; Books; Calvert, Robert; Jimenez, Santiago; Lopez, Lisa; Music; Myles, Carol; Paredes, Americo; Pettus, Theodore T.; *Recreation; Television.

Adaptive Behavior Inventory for Children (ABIC)

101 Scott, Leigh S., et al. Adaptive behavior inventory for children: the need for local norms. JOURNAL OF SCHOOL PSYCHOLOGY, Vol. 20, no. 1 (Spring 1982), p. 39-44. English. **DESCR:** Anglo Americans; Blacks; Corpus Christi Independent School District; Corpus Christi, TX; Placement; System of Multicultural Pluralistic Assessment (SOMPA).

Adelante Mujer Hispana Conference

102 Community watching. CAMINOS, Vol. 3, no. 5 (May 1982), p. 56-57. Bilingual. **DESCR:** Agricultural Laborers; Beilson, Anthony C.; Boycotts; Chacon, Peter R.; Chicanas; *Cultural Organizations; Farm Labor Organizing Commmittee (FLOC); Financial Aid; Hollenbeck Junior High School, Los Angeles, CA; Junior High School Students; National League of Cities; Optimist Club of Greater East Los Angeles; Organizations; Project WELL (We Enjoy Learning & Leadership); Torres, Art.

Administration of Justice

103 Brasch, Walter M. Hanigan case: hung up on racism? SOUTH ATLANTIC QUARTERLY, Vol. 81, no. 4 (Fall 1982), p. 429-435. English. **DESCR:** Arizona; Criminal Justice System; Garcia-Loya, Manuel; *Hanigan, Patrick; Hanigan, Tom; Herrera-Mata, Bernabe; *Laws; Racism; Ruelas-Zavala, Eleazar; Undocumented Workers.

104 Martinez, Elizabeth. The "Kiko" Martinez case: a sign of our times. CRIME AND SOCIAL JUSTICE, Vol. 17, (Summer 1982), p. 92-95. English. **DESCR:** Martinez Defense Committee; Martinez, Francisco; Miller, Robert; *Racism.

105 McCarthy, Martha. Legal forum. The right to an education: illegal aliens. JOURNAL OF EDUCATIONAL EQUITY AND LEADERSHIP, Vol. 2, no. 4 (Summer 1982), p. 282-287. English. **DESCR:** Doe v. Plyer [Tyler Independent School District, Texas]; Education; *Educational Law and Legislation; Migrant Children; *Migrant Education; Texas; Undocumented Workers.

106 McFadden, Bernard J. Bilingual education and the law. JOURNAL OF LAW AND EDUCATION, Vol. 12, no. 1 (January 1983), p. 1-27. English. **DESCR:** *Bilingual Bicultural Education; Discrimination in Education; Educational Law and Legislation; History.

107 [Summary of: Freeman, Legitimizing racial discrimination through anti-discrimination law: a critical review of Supreme Court doctrine, 62 Minn. L. Rev. 1049 (1978)]. CHICANO LAW REVIEW, Vol. 5, (1982), p. 78-79. English. **DESCR:** *Racism.

108 [Summary of: race as an employment qualification to meet police department operational needs, 54 N.Y.U.L. rev. 413 (1979)]. CHICANO LAW REVIEW, Vol. 5, (1982), p. 81-82. English. **DESCR:** Employment Tests; *Police.

109 [Summary of: Simpson, abortion, poverty, and equal protection of the law, 13 Ga. L. rev. 505 (1979)]. CHICANO LAW REVIEW, Vol. 5, (1982), p. 82-83. English. **DESCR:** Abortion; Maher v. Roe; Roe v. Wade.

110 Valenzuela-Crocker, Elvira. Confrontation over the Civil Rights Commission. NUESTRO, Vol. 7, no. 10 (December 1983), p. 21-27. English. **DESCR:** Affirmative Action; *Civil Rights; Education Equalization; Employment; *U.S. Commission on Civil Rights; Voting Rights.

Administrators

111 Median administrative salaries in 1981-82 for men and women and minority-group members. CHRONICLE OF HIGHER EDUCATION, Vol. 24, no. 2 (March 10, 1982), p. 10. English. **DESCR:** Chicanas; Ethnic Groups; *Income; Males.

Adolescents
USE: Youth

Adoption

112 Government review. NUESTRO, Vol. 7, no. 2 (March 1983), p. 42. English. **DESCR:** A WORKING WOMAN'S GUIDE TO HER JOB RIGHTS; Business Enterprises; Census; Chicanas; Discrimination in Employment; *Government Services; GUIDE TO FEDERAL MINORITY ENTERPRISE AND RELATED ASSISTANCE PROGRAMS; Population Trends; Study Abroad; U.S. Information Agency (USIA).

113 "Todo se puede hacer con amor..."; Hispanic adoptions recruitment program. CAMINOS, Vol. 4, no. 11 (December 1983), p. 36-37. English. **DESCR:** *Hispanic Adoption Recruitment Program (HARP).

114 Valiente-Barksdale, Clara. Recruiting Hispanic families. CHILDREN TODAY, Vol. 12, no. 2 (March, April, 1983), p. 26-28. English. **DESCR:** New York Council on Adoptable Children (COAC); New York, NY; RAICES (New York, NY).

Adult Education

115 Heaney, Thomas W. "Hanging on" or "gaining ground": educating marginal adults. NEW DIRECTIONS FOR CONTINUING EDUCATION, no. 20 (December 1983), p. 53-63. English. **DESCR:** Chicago, IL; City Colleges, Chicago, IL; General Education Diploma (GED); Gomez, Robert; Instituto del Progreso Latino; Mission District, San Francisco, CA; Project Literacy, San Francisco, CA; St. Mary's Community Educational Center; *Universidad Popular, Chicago, IL.

116 Rugsaken, Kris T. Qualifications for the bilingual vocational teacher. BILINGUAL JOURNAL, Vol. 6, no. 4 (Summer 1982), p. 22-25. English. **DESCR:** *Bilingual Bicultural Education; Teacher Training; *Vocational Education; Vocational Education Act of 1963.

Advertising

117 25 leading national Hispanic market advertisers. HISPANIC BUSINESS, Vol. 4, no. 12 (December 1982), p. 18. English. DESCR: Consumers; *Marketing.

118 Adkins, Lynn. New strategies to sell Hispanics. DUNS'S BUSINESS MONTH, Vol. 12, no. 1 (July 1983), p. 64-69. English. DESCR: Consumers; Mass Media.

119 Aguirre, Richard R. Print media at a crossroads. HISPANIC BUSINESS, Vol. 4, no. 5 (May 1982), p. 20-21+. English. DESCR: Magazines; Newspapers; *Print Media.

120 An axiom to grind: the Hispanic market - more than just a phone call away. MADISON AVENUE, Vol. 25, no. 7 (1983), p. 44-49. English. DESCR: *Marketing.

121 Balkan, D. Carlos. The crisis in Hispanic marketing. HISPANIC BUSINESS, Vol. 4, no. 12 (December 1982), p. 24-25+. English. DESCR: Consumers; *Marketing.

122 Balkan, D. Carlos. The Hispanic market: leading indicators. HISPANIC BUSINESS, Vol. 5, no. 12 (December 1983), p. 14-15. English. DESCR: Business Enterprises; *Marketing.

123 Balkan, D. Carlos. Mr. Caballero's Spanish radio network. HISPANIC BUSINESS, Vol. 4, no. 5 (May 1982), p. 18-19,26. English. DESCR: Broadcast Media; *Caballero Spanish Media, Inc. (CSM); Radio.

124 Business update: phone company issues Spanish yellow pages. NUESTRO, Vol. 7, no. 4 (May 1983), p. 42. English. DESCR: *Community Services; New York Telephone Co.

125 Cardenas, Leo. Editor's view: invisible in advertising world. LATINO, Vol. 53, no. 3 (May 1982), p. 4. English.

126 Chavarria, Jesus. The changing Hispanic market. HISPANIC BUSINESS, Vol. 5, no. 12 (December 1983), p. 6. English. DESCR: Income; *Marketing.

127 Chavarria, Jesus. The media scene. HISPANIC BUSINESS, Vol. 4, no. 5 (May 1982), p. 6. English. DESCR: Broadcast Media; Caballero Spanish Media, Inc. (CSM); *Mass Media; MIAMI MENSUAL; Print Media; Radio; Television.

128 Chavez, Lydia. The fourth network's chief executive. HISPANIC BUSINESS, Vol. 4, no. 1 (January 1982), p. 16-18. English. DESCR: Anselmo, Rene; *Biography; Cable Television; Marketing; Spanish International Network (SIN).

129 Communications/marketing. HISPANIC BUSINESS, Vol. 4, no. 12 (December 1982), p. 11. English. DESCR: Advertising Agencies; Diaz-Albertini, Luis; *Marketing; UniWorld Hispanic.

130 Communications/marketing. HISPANIC BUSINESS, Vol. 5, no. 3 (March 1983), p. 21. English. DESCR: Awards; Consumers; El Cervantes Media Awards; Marketing; Spanish Advertising and Marketing Services (S.A.M.S.)

131 Communications/marketing. HISPANIC BUSINESS, Vol. 5, no. 10 (October 1983), p. 26. English. DESCR: Arens & Gutierrez; Employment; Henry Molina, Inc.; Journals; Lionetti and Meyers Research Center, Inc.;

Marketing; *Mass Media; Midwest Hispanics in Telecommunications Symposium, Chicago, IL; NEW MANAGEMENT.

132 Gage, Theodore J. Beer still tops wine, spirits. ADVERTISING AGE MAGAZINE, Vol. 53, (February 15, 1982), p. II, M10. English. DESCR: *Alcoholic Beverages; Consumers; Market Research.

133 Gage, Theodore J. The next assignment: second-tier marketing to English-speaking Hispanics. HISPANIC BUSINESS, Vol. 5, no. 12 (December 1983), p. 22-26. English. DESCR: Bilingualism; *Marketing.

134 Galginaitis, Carol. Luring the Hispanic dollar: retailers boost ethnic image. ADVERTISING AGE MAGAZINE, Vol. 53, (February 15, 1982), p. II, M10. English. DESCR: Consumers; Market Research.

135 Guernica, Antonio. Consumer Hispanic: a dual identity. MADISON AVENUE, Vol. 25, (July 1983), p. 35-44. English. DESCR: *Marketing.

136 Gupta, Udayan. New York's WNJU Channel 47: Spanish TV's hottest item. HISPANIC BUSINESS, Vol. 5, no. 3 (March 1983), p. 16-17+. English. DESCR: Broadcast Media; Consumers; Marketing; Television; WNJU-TV, Newark, NJ [television station].

137 Heublein's Miss Black Velvet II. HISPANIC BUSINESS, Vol. 4, no. 2 (February 1982), p. 12. English. DESCR: Beauty Contests; Consumers; Heublein, Inc.; *Marketing; *Miss Black Velvet Latina.

138 Hispanics in Communications, Inc. HISPANIC BUSINESS, Vol. 4, no. 5 (May 1982), p. 12. English. DESCR: DaCosta, Jacqueline; Hispanics in Communications (HIC); *Mass Media.

139 Honomichl, Jack. Never lose sight of Hispanic pride. ADVERTISING AGE MAGAZINE, Vol. 53, (February 15, 1982), p. II, M38-39. English. DESCR: *Market Research.

140 KMEX-TV dominates the Hispanic market. HISPANIC BUSINESS, Vol. 5, no. 12 (December 1983), p. 16-17. English. DESCR: *KMEX, Los Angeles, CA [television station]; Los Angeles, CA; Marketing; *Television.

141 Mercado, Anthony. Do Hispanics use coupons? HISPANIC BUSINESS, Vol. 5, no. 12 (December 1983), p. 10. English. DESCR: Carol Wright Hispanic Program; Donnelley Marketing; *Marketing.

142 Miller Brewing is airing bilingual commercial. NUESTRO, Vol. 7, no. 9 (November 1983), p. 36. English. DESCR: Bilingualism; *Miller Brewing Company; Television.

143 Pendleton, Jennifer. Battle for the buck is the tale of two cities: marketers in San Diego and Tijuana square off. ADVERTISING AGE MAGAZINE, Vol. 53, (February 15, 1982), p. II, M42-43. English. DESCR: Border Region; Business; *Market Research; San Diego, CA; Tijuana, Mexico.

144 Segal, Madhav N. and Sosa, Lionel. Marketing to the Hispanic community. CALIFORNIA MANAGEMENT REVIEW, Vol. 26, no. 1 (Fall 1983), p. 120-134. English. DESCR: *Consumers; Mass Media; Population.

Advertising (cont.)

145 Skriloff, Lisa. Music, news dominate Spanish-language radio programming. HISPANIC BUSINESS, Vol. 5, no. 12 (December 1983), p. 34. English. **DESCR:** Los Angeles, CA; Marketing; Miami, FL; *Radio; San Antonio, TX.

146 Spanish lesson. TELEVISION/RADIO AGE, Vol. 30, no. 22 (June 6, 1983), p. 18. English. **DESCR:** Differential Survey Treatment; *Radio.

147 Think Spanish! MARKETING AND MEDIA DECISIONS, Vol. 17, (October 1982), p. 66-69. English. **DESCR:** Biography; Conill Advertising Associates, New York, NY; Conill, Alicia; Conill, Rafael; *Marketing; Scott Paper Company; Spanish Language.

148 Tips for making the right moves in today's job markets. HISPANIC BUSINESS, Vol. 5, no. 5 (May 1983), p. 30. English. **DESCR:** *Careers; Employment; Hispanic Access to Services (HAS), Denver, CO; *Working Women.

149 Volsky, George. Miami's radio S-U-A-A-A-V-E. HISPANIC BUSINESS, Vol. 4, no. 12 (December 1982), p. 22,35. English. **DESCR:** Broadcast Media; Language Usage; Marketing; Miami, FL; *Radio; Radio Station SUAVE, Miami, FL; *Radio Stations; Spanish Language.

150 Wittenauer, Cheryl. Rating Hispanic media. HISPANIC BUSINESS, Vol. 5, no. 3 (March 1983), p. 14-15. English. **DESCR:** A.C. Nielsen Company; Arbitron; *Broadcast Media; Television.

Advertising Agencies

151 Balkan, D. Carlos. The advent of Uniworld/Hispanic: an interview. HISPANIC BUSINESS, Vol. 5, no. 3 (March 1983), p. 10-11+. English. **DESCR:** Blacks; Consumers; Diaz-Albertini, Luis; Lewis, Byron; *Marketing; Spanish Advertising and Marketing Services (S.A.M.S.); Uniworld Group, Inc.; UniWorld Hispanic.

152 Communications/marketing. HISPANIC BUSINESS, Vol. 4, no. 4 (April 1982), p. 15. English. **DESCR:** Consumers; Juarez and Associates, Inc.; Las Americas, Inc.; *Marketing; Norman, Craig & Kummel Organization; Publicidad Siboney; Siboney Advertising, Inc.

153 Communications/marketing. HISPANIC BUSINESS, Vol. 4, no. 12 (December 1982), p. 11. English. **DESCR:** Advertising; Diaz-Albertini, Luis; *Marketing; UniWorld Hispanic.

154 Communications/marketing. HISPANIC BUSINESS, Vol. 5, no. 6 (June 1983), p. 16. English. **DESCR:** *Broadcast Media; Castillo & Castillo Public Relations and Advertising; Castillo, Cid; Castillo, Patricia; Latino Consortium, Los Angeles, CA; Montemayor, Carlos R.; Montemayor y Asociados, Inc.; Zubi Inc., Miami, FL.

155 Communications/marketing. HISPANIC BUSINESS, Vol. 5, no. 8 (August 1983), p. 26. English. **DESCR:** Bermudez & Associates; *Broadcast Media; Carranza Associates; Directories; Marketing.

156 Goodman, Gerson. "ES PARA USTED": CSI aims for satisfaction. HISPANIC BUSINESS, Vol. 4, no. 12 (December 1982), p. 16-17,34. English. **DESCR:** Aguirre, Jack; Business Enterprises; Consumers; CSI International,

Inc.; Fernandez, Castor A.; *Marketing.

157 People. HISPANIC BUSINESS, Vol. 4, no. 9 (September 1982), p. 7. English. **DESCR:** Appointed Officials; Awards; *Biographical Notes; Diaz-Albertini, Luis; Dimartino, Rita; Garza, Jesus; Hispanic Women in Higher Education (HWHE); League of United Latin American Citizens (LULAC); Ortega, Ray; Ortiz, George; Romero, Carlos J.; Sepulveda, Luis.

Affirmative Action

158 Affirmative action: a summary. CAMINOS, Vol. 4, no. 9 (October 1983), p. 9-10,50. Bilingual.

159 Arizona conference. HISPANIC BUSINESS, Vol. 4, no. 3 (March 1982), p. 22. English. **DESCR:** Arizona; Arizona Affirmative Action Association.

160 Atkinson, Donald R. Ethnic minority representation in counselor education. COUNSELOR EDUCATION AND SUPERVISION, Vol. 23, no. 1 (September 1983), p. 7-19. English. **DESCR:** Counseling Services (Educational); *Counselors; Recruitment.

161 Bell, Michael Davitt. Fitting into a tradition of autobiography. CHANGE, Vol. 14, no. 7 (October 1982), p. 36-39. English. **DESCR:** Assimilation; Bilingual Bicultural Education; Biography; Book Reviews; *HUNGER OF MEMORY: THE EDUCATION OF RICHARD RODRIGUEZ; Rodriguez, Richard.

162 Boycott threat leads to negociation table. NUESTRO, Vol. 6, no. 8 (October 1982), p. 48. English. **DESCR:** *Boycotts; Miller Brewing Company.

163 Executives expect little affirmative action change. HISPANIC BUSINESS, Vol. 4, no. 2 (February 1982), p. 23. English. **DESCR:** Equal Employment Opportunity Commission (EEOC).

164 Fernandez, John P. Facing the hard realities of corporate advancement. HISPANIC BUSINESS, Vol. 4, no. 4 (April 1982), p. 18-19,25. English. **DESCR:** Businesspeople; *Discrimination in Employment; Mentors; Self-Help Groups.

165 Flaherty, Francis J. The struggle continues: protecting the rights of Hispanics in the U.S. NATIONAL LAW JOURNAL, Vol. 5, (March 14, 1983), p. 1. English. **DESCR:** *Avila, Joaquin Guadalupe; Civil Rights; Hispanic Amendments; *Legal Representation; Mexican American Legal Defense and Educational Fund (MALDEF); Racism; Voting Rights.

166 Fuentes, Diana. Chicana perpectives: Ester Reyes Aguilar. COMADRE, no. 1 (Summer 1977), p. 45-48. English. **DESCR:** *Aguilar, Ester Reyes; Ballet Folkorico; *Biography; Teaching Profession.

167 Gallegos, Tony E. Why doesn't the E.E.O.C. help Hispanics? CAMINOS, Vol. 4, no. 9 (October 1983), p. 20-21,52. Bilingual. **DESCR:** Affirmative Action Programs; *Equal Employment Opportunity Commission (EEOC).

Affirmative Action (cont.)

168 Hann, Donna; Ferree, W. P.; and Flores,
    Larry. Affirmative action means progress: 2
    corporations and one federal agency look at
    affirmative action. CAMINOS, Vol. 3, no. 8
    (September 1982), p. 39-42. English. DESCR:
    General Telephone Company; Imperial Savings;
    Veteran's Administration.

169 Hiring N.J. fire fighters. NUESTRO, Vol. 6,
    no. 3 (April 1982), p. 13. English. DESCR:
    *Ethnic Groups.

170 Hispanics in federal agencies. HISPANIC
    BUSINESS, Vol. 4, no. 9 (September 1982), p.
    29. English. DESCR: *Government Employees;
    MEXICAN AMERICAN LEGAL DEFENSE AND
    EDUCATIONAL FUND NEWSLETTER.

171 Lourenzo, Susan V. Early outreach: career
    awareness for health professions. JOURNAL OF
    MEDICAL EDUCATION, Vol. 58, no. 1 (January
    1983), p. 39-44. English. DESCR: Careers;
    College Preparation; *Medical Education;
    *Recruitment.

172 Newton, Frank Cota-Robles. Perils of the
    Latino slot. NUESTRO, Vol. 6, no. 3 (April
    1982), p. 32. English. DESCR: Ethnic Groups.

173 Quevedo. The Reagan administration and
    affirmative action. CAMINOS, Vol. 4, no. 9
    (October 1983), p. 24-26. English. DESCR:
    *Reagan, Ronald.

174 Research/development: Hispanics and job
    progress. HISPANIC BUSINESS, Vol. 4, no. 4
    (April 1982), p. 29. English. DESCR:
    *Government Employees.

175 Rick Icaza on career opportunities in
    unions. CAMINOS, Vol. 3, no. 8 (September
    1982), p. 44-45. Bilingual. DESCR: Chicano
    Youth Leadership Conference; Labor Unions;
    United Food and Commercial Workers.

176 Rodriguez, Richard. A minority scholar
    speaks out. AMERICAN EDUCATION, Vol. 18, no.
    9 (November 1982), p. 2-5. English. DESCR:
    Authors; Bilingual Bicultural Education;
    *Biography; HUNGER OF MEMORY: THE EDUCATION
    OF RICHARD RODRIGUEZ; Rodriguez, Richard.

177 Rodriguez, Richard, et al. Education of
    Richard Rodriguez [excerpts from "HUNGER OF
    MEMORY", including discussion]. CHANGE, Vol.
    14, no. 7 (October 1982), p. 32-42+.
    English. DESCR: Assimilation; Bilingual
    Bicultural Education; Biography; *HUNGER OF
    MEMORY: THE EDUCATION OF RICHARD RODRIGUEZ;
    *Rodriguez, Richard.

178 Thomas, William. Affirmative action under
    fire. CAMINOS, Vol. 3, no. 8 (September
    1982), p. 47. English. DESCR: *Los Angeles
    Basin Equal Opportunity League.

179 Tovar, Irene. Affirmative action in
    California. CAMINOS, Vol. 3, no. 8
    (September 1982), p. 30-32,50+. Bilingual.
    DESCR: *California State Personnel Board;
    *Civil Service.

180 Valenzuela-Crocker, Elvira. Confrontation
    over the Civil Rights Commission. NUESTRO,
    Vol. 7, no. 10 (December 1983), p. 21-27.
    English. DESCR: Administration of Justice;
    *Civil Rights; Education Equalization;
    Employment; *U.S. Commission on Civil
    Rights; Voting Rights.

181 Villalvazo Briggs, June. Is affirmative
    action working? CAMINOS, Vol. 4, no. 9
    (October 1983), p. 12-14,50+. Bilingual.

182 Whisler, Kirk. IMAGE and affirmative action.
    CAMINOS, Vol. 3, no. 8 (September 1982), p.
    34-36. Bilingual. DESCR: *Montoya, David;
    *National Image, Inc.

183 Willie, Charles V. First learning
    unchallenged and untested. CHANGE, Vol. 14,
    no. 7 (October 1982), p. 37-41. English.
    DESCR: Bilingual Bicultural Education;
    Biography; Book Reviews; Education; *HUNGER
    OF MEMORY: THE EDUCATION OF RICHARD
    RODRIGUEZ; Rodriguez, Richard.

Affirmative Action Programs

184 Affirmative action. NUESTRO, Vol. 5, no. 8
    (November 1981), p. 11-12. English. DESCR:
    National Image, Inc.

185 Calkins, E. Virginia; Willoughby, T. Lee;
    and Arnold, Louise M. Predictors of
    performance of minority students in the
    first two years of a BA/MD program. NATIONAL
    MEDICAL ASSOCIATION JOURNAL, Vol. 74, no. 7
    (July 1982), p. 625-632. English. DESCR:
    Academic Achievement; Academic Motivation;
    *Medical Education; University of
    Missouri-Kansas City School of Medicine.

186 Career intelligencer. HISPANIC BUSINESS,
    Vol. 5, no. 10 (October 1983), p. 30.
    English. DESCR: *Careers.

187 Gallegos, Tony E. Why doesn't the E.E.O.C.
    help Hispanics? CAMINOS, Vol. 4, no. 9
    (October 1983), p. 20-21,52. Bilingual.
    DESCR: Affirmative Action; *Equal Employment
    Opportunity Commission (EEOC).

188 Levin, Betsy. An analysis of the federal
    attempt to regulate bilingual education:
    protecting civil rights or controlling
    curriculum? JOURNAL OF LAW AND EDUCATION,
    Vol. 12, no. 1 (January 1983), p. 29-60.
    English. DESCR: *Bilingual Bicultural
    Education; Civil Rights; Cultural Pluralism;
    Educational Law and Legislation; Federal
    Government.

Afro-Americans
    USE: Blacks

Agar, Michael

189 Hunsaker, Alan. Book review of: ANGEL DUST:
    AN ETHNOGRAPHIC STUDY OF PCP USERS; HEROIN
    USE IN THE BARRIO; DRUG AND ALCOHOL ABUSE: A
    CLINICAL GUIDE TO DIAGNOSIS AND TREATMENT.
    HISPANIC JOURNAL OF BEHAVIORAL SCIENCES,
    Vol. 4, no. 1 (March 1982), p. 118-121.
    English. DESCR: *ANGEL DUST: AN ETHNOGRAPHIC
    STUDY OF PCP USERS; Bescher, George; Book
    Reviews; Bullington, Bruce; *DRUG AND
    ALCOHOL ABUSE: A CLINICAL GUIDE TO DIAGNOSIS
    AND TREATMENT; Feldman, Harvey W.; *HEROIN
    USE IN THE BARRIO; Schuckit, Marc A.

Age Groups

190 Adams, Russell L.; Boake, Corwin; and Crain,
    Charles. Bias in a neuropsychological test
    classification related to education, age and
    ethnicity. JOURNAL OF CONSULTING AND
    CLINICAL PSYCHOLOGY, Vol. 50, no. 1
    (February 1982), p. 143-145. English.
    DESCR: Educational Levels; Ethnic Groups;
    Mentally Handicapped; *Psychological
    Testing.

Age Groups (cont.)

191 Lamare, James W. Political integration of
Mexican American children: a generational
analysis. INTERNATIONAL MIGRATION REVIEW,
Vol. 16, no. 1 (Spring 1982), p. 169-188.
English. DESCR: Acculturation; Assimilation;
*Children; Immigration; Political Ideology;
*Political Socialization.

192 Reisberg, Barry and Vasquez, Richard.
Stereotypes of Mexican descent persons:
attitudes of three generations of Mexican
American and Anglo-American adolescents.
JOURNAL OF CROSS-CULTURAL PSYCHOLOGY, Vol.
13, no. 1 (March 1982), p. 59-70. English.
DESCR: Anglo Americans; *Stereotypes.

193 Snipp, C. Matthew and Tienda, Marta. New
perspectives of Chicano intergenerational
occupational mobility. SOCIAL SCIENCE
JOURNAL, Vol. 19, no. 2 (April 1982), p.
37-49. English. DESCR: Careers; *Employment;
Social Mobility.

194 Zavaleta, Anthony N. and Malina, Robert M.
Growth and body composition of
Mexican-American boys 9 through 14 years of
age. AMERICAN JOURNAL OF PHYSICAL
ANTHROPOLOGY, Vol. 57, no. 3 (March 1982),
p. 261-271. English. DESCR: Anglo Americans;
*Anthropometry; Children; Socioeconomic
Factors.

Aged

USE: Ancianos

Agency for International Development (AID)

195 Foreign trade. HISPANIC BUSINESS, Vol. 5,
no. 10 (October 1983), p. 29. English.
DESCR: Caribbean Region; Economic History
and Conditions; *Foreign Trade; HOW TO
EXPORT: A MARKETING MANUAL; Mexico; Puerto
Rico; U.S. Trade Center (Mexico City).

AGING AND SOCIAL POLICY: LEADERSHIP PLANNING

196 Burke, Leslie K. Book review of: AGING AND
SOCIAL POLICY: LEADERSHIP PLANNING. HISPANIC
JOURNAL OF BEHAVIORAL SCIENCES, Vol. 4, no.
1 (March 1982), p. 115-116. English. DESCR:
Ancianos; Book Reviews; Kasschau, Patricia
L.

**AGING AND SOCIETY: CURRENT RESEARCH AND POLICY
PERSPECTIVES**

197 Burke, Leslie K. Book review of: AGING AND
SOCIETY: CURRENT RESEARCH AND POLICY
PERSPECTIVES. HISPANIC JOURNAL OF BEHAVIORAL
SCIENCES, Vol. 4, no. 1 (March 1982), p.
114-115. English. DESCR: Ancianos; Book
Reviews; Borgatta, Edgar F.; McCluskey, Neil
G.

Agosin, Magi

198 Umpierre, Luz Maria. La ansiedad de la
influencia en Sandra Maria Esteves y
Marjorie Agosin. REVISTA CHICANO-RIQUENA,
Vol. 11, no. 3-4 (Fall 1983), p. 139-147.
Spanish. DESCR: A JULIA Y A MI; De Burgos,
Julia; EL PAIS DIVIDIDO; *Esteves, Sandra
Maria; *Literary Criticism; Neruda, Pablo;
Parra, Nicanor; Poetry.

Agribusiness

199 Arnold, Frank. A history of struggle:
organizing cannery workers in the Santa
Clara Valley. SOUTHWEST ECONOMY AND SOCIETY,
Vol. 2, no. 1 (October, November, 1976), p.
26-38. English. DESCR: American Labor Union

(Santa Clara County, CA); Cannery and
Agricultural Worker's Industrial Union;
*Cannery Workers; Comite de Trabajadores de
Canerias, San Jose, CA; History; Labor
Unions; *Santa Clara Valley, CA; United
Cannery Agricultural Packing and Allied
Workers of America (UCAPAWA).

200 Barry, Tom. On strike! Undocumented workers
in Arizona. SOUTHWEST ECONOMY AND SOCIETY,
Vol. 3, no. 3 (Spring 1978), p. 52-60.
English. DESCR: Agricultural Laborers;
Arizona; *Goldmar Citrus Ranch, Phoenix, AZ;
Labor Organizing; *Maricopa County
Organizing Project (MCOP); Phoenix, AZ;
*Strikes and Lockouts; Undocumented Workers.

201 Kivisto, Peter. Book review of: FARM
WORKERS, AGRIBUSINESS, AND THE STATE.
INTERNATIONAL MIGRATION REVIEW, Vol. 17, no.
4 (Winter 1983), p. 724-726. English.
DESCR: Agricultural Laborers; Book Reviews;
*FARMWORKERS, AGRIBUSINESS, AND THE STATE;
Majka, Linda C.; Majka, Theo J.; United
Farmworkers of America (UFW).

202 Produce firm to close doors. NUESTRO, Vol.
7, no. 6 (August 1983), p. 12. English.
DESCR: Agricultural Labor Unions; Business
Enterprises; *Sun Harvest, Inc.; United
Farmworkers of America (UFW).

203 Sutton, Susan Buck and Brunner, Tracy. Life
on the road: Midwestern migrant farmworker
survival skills. MIGRATION TODAY, Vol. 11,
no. 1 (1983), p. 24-31. English. DESCR:
Agricultural Laborers; Economic History and
Conditions; Indiana; Migrant Children;
Migrant Education; *Migrant Labor;
Stereotypes.

Agricultural Cooperatives

204 Wells, Miriam J. Political mediation and
agricultural cooperation: strawberry farms
in California. ECONOMIC DEVELOPMENT AND
CULTURAL CHANGE, Vol. 30, no. 2 (January
1982), p. 413-432. English. DESCR:
Agricultural Laborers; California;
Cooperativa Campesina; Cooperativa Central;
Political Parties and Organizations; Rural
Economics.

Agricultural Labor Relations Board (ALRB)

205 California farmworkers: back to the
barricades? BUSINESS WEEK, no. 28 (September
26, 1983), p. 86+. English. DESCR:
Agricultural Labor Unions; *Agricultural
Laborers; California; United Farmworkers of
America (UFW).

206 Rodriguez, Vicente and Costello, Guy.
United farm workers. SOUTHERN EXPOSURE, Vol.
10, no. 4 (July, August, 1982), p. 14-15.
English. DESCR: Agricultural Laborers;
*United Farmworkers of America (UFW).

Agricultural Labor Unions

207 California farmworkers: back to the
barricades? BUSINESS WEEK, no. 28 (September
26, 1983), p. 86+. English. DESCR:
*Agricultural Labor Relations Board (ALRB);
*Agricultural Laborers; California; United
Farmworkers of America (UFW).

208 Chavez pinpoints Texas for bargaining
efforts. NUESTRO, Vol. 6, no. 8 (October
1982), p. 47-48. English. DESCR:
Agricultural Laborers; Collective
Bargaining; *United Farmworkers of America
(UFW).

Agricultural Labor Unions (cont.)

209 Howell, Frances Baseden. Split labor market: Mexican farm workers in the Southwest. SOCIOLOGICAL INQUIRY, Vol. 52, no. 2 (Spring 1982), p. 132-140. English. DESCR: Arizona Farm Workers (AFW); *Labor Supply and Market; Southwest United States; Undocumented Workers; United Farmworkers of America (UFW).

210 Produce firm to close doors. NUESTRO, Vol. 7, no. 6 (August 1983), p. 12. English. DESCR: *Agribusiness; Business Enterprises; *Sun Harvest, Inc.; United Farmworkers of America (UFW).

Agricultural Laborers

211 Abrams, Herbert K. Occupational and environmental health problems along the U.S.-Mexico Border. SOUTHWEST ECONOMY AND SOCIETY, Vol. 4, no. 3 (Spring, Summer, 1979), p. 3-20. English. DESCR: *Border Region; Housing; Mexican Border Industrialization Program; Nutrition; *Pollution; *Public Health; Social History and Conditions.

212 Barry, Tom. On strike! Undocumented workers in Arizona. SOUTHWEST ECONOMY AND SOCIETY, Vol. 3, no. 3 (Spring 1978), p. 52-60. English. DESCR: Agribusiness; Arizona; *Goldmar Citrus Ranch, Phoenix, AZ; Labor Organizing; *Maricopa County Organizing Project (MCOP); Phoenix, AZ; *Strikes and Lockouts; Undocumented Workers.

213 Black, Bill. Housing for farm laborers: a California solution. NUESTRO, Vol. 7, no. 6 (August 1983), p. 36-37. English. DESCR: California; *Housing.

214 California farmworkers: back to the barricades? BUSINESS WEEK, no. 28 (September 26, 1983), p. 86+. English. DESCR: *Agricultural Labor Relations Board (ALRB); Agricultural Labor Unions; California; United Farmworkers of America (UFW).

215 Chavez, Cesar E. Relentless struggle for farm workers' rights. NUESTRO, Vol. 7, no. 9 (November 1983), p. 55. English. DESCR: California; Immigrant Labor; Simpson-Mazzoli Bill.

216 Chavez pinpoints Texas for bargaining efforts. NUESTRO, Vol. 6, no. 8 (October 1982), p. 47-48. English. DESCR: Agricultural Labor Unions; Collective Bargaining; *United Farmworkers of America (UFW).

217 Chavez' union decentralizes. NUESTRO, Vol. 6, no. 7 (September 1982), p. 11-12. English. DESCR: Chavez, Cesar E.; Farmer Organizations; *United Farmworkers of America (UFW).

218 Community watching. CAMINOS, Vol. 3, no. 5 (May 1982), p. 56-57. Bilingual. DESCR: Adelante Mujer Hispana Conference; Beilson, Anthony C.; Boycotts; Chacon, Peter R.; Chicanas; *Cultural Organizations; Farm Labor Organizing Commmittee (FLOC); Financial Aid; Hollenbeck Junior High School, Los Angeles, CA; Junior High School Students; National League of Cities; Optimist Club of Greater East Los Angeles; Organizations; Project WELL (We Enjoy Learning & Leadership); Torres, Art.

219 de Armas, Isabel. Chicano, un vocablo colonizador. CUADERNOS HISPANOAMERICANOS, Vol. 394, (April 1983), p. 193-201. Spanish. DESCR: Book Reviews; Calvo Buezas, Tomas; *CHICANOS: ANTOLOGIA HISTORICA Y LITERARIA; Identity; *LOS MAS POBRES EN EL PAIS MAS RICO; Villanueva, Tino.

220 De Leon, David. Book review of: BITTER HARVEST: A HISTORY OF CALIFORNIA FARMWORKERS 1870-1941. ANNALS OF THE AMERICAN ACADEMY OF POLITICAL AND SOCIAL SCIENCE, Vol. 462, (July 1982), p. 198-199. English. DESCR: *BITTER HARVEST: A HISTORY OF CALIFORNIA FARMWORKERS, 1870-1941; Book Reviews; California; Daniel, Cletus E.

221 Farmworkers win Arkansas contract. SOUTHERN EXPOSURE, Vol. 10, no. 5 (September, October, 1982), p. 4. English. DESCR: Arkansas; *Arkansas Farmworker Civil Rights Organizing Project (AFCROP); Labor Disputes; Undocumented Workers.

222 Foster, Douglas. The desperate migrants of Devil's Canyon. THE PROGRESSIVE, Vol. 46, no. 11 (November 1982), p. 44-49. English. DESCR: California; *Devil's Canyon, Deer Canyon, CA; Growers; Labor Camps; San Diego, CA; Undocumented Workers.

223 Gamboa, Erasmo. Mexican labor in the Pacific Northwest, 1943-1947: a photographic essay. PACIFIC NORTHWEST QUARTERLY, Vol. 73, no. 4 (October 1982), p. 175-181. English. DESCR: International Labor Activities; Labor Camps; Labor Supply and Market; Northwestern United States; World War II.

224 Garcia, Ruperto. No help yet for farmworkers in Panhandle. TEXAS OBSERVOR, Vol. 74, no. 16 (September 3, 1982), p. 6-7. English. DESCR: Crops; Disasters; Economic History and Conditions; Texas Panhandle.

225 Hewitt, William L. Mexican workers in Wyoming during World War II: necessity, discrimination and protest. ANNALS OF WYOMING, Vol. 54, no. 2 (1982), p. 20-33. English. DESCR: Braceros; Migrant Labor; World War II; Wyoming.

226 Holley, Joe. Farmworker wins the right to sue. TEXAS OBSERVOR, Vol. 74, no. 13 (July 9, 1982), p. 15. English. DESCR: Donna Fruit Company; Laws; Legal Representation; Occupational Hazards; *Torrez, Juan.

227 Kivisto, Peter. Book review of: FARM WORKERS, AGRIBUSINESS, AND THE STATE. INTERNATIONAL MIGRATION REVIEW, Vol. 17, no. 4 (Winter 1983), p. 724-726. English. DESCR: Agribusiness; Book Reviews; *FARMWORKERS, AGRIBUSINESS, AND THE STATE; Majka, Linda C.; Majka, Theo J.; United Farmworkers of America (UFW).

228 Lopez, Phyllis. La campesina. COMADRE, no. 2 (Spring 1978), p. 14. English. DESCR: *Poetry.

229 Mamer, John W. and Martin, Philip. Hired workers on California farms. CALIFORNIA AGRICULTURE, Vol. 36, no. 9-10 (September, October, 1982), p. 21-23. English. DESCR: *California; *Labor Supply and Market; Statistics; Undocumented Workers.

230 Martin, Philip and Mines, Richard. Foreign workers in selected California crops. CALIFORNIA AGRICULTURE, Vol. 37, no. 3-4 (March, April, 1983), p. 6-8. English. DESCR: California; *Undocumented Workers.

Agricultural Laborers (cont.)

231 McNeil, W. K. Record Review: LAS VOCES DE
LOS CAMPESINOS. JOURNAL OF AMERICAN
FOLKLORE, Vol. 96, (1983), p. 370. English.
DESCR: Corrido; *LAS VOCES DE LOS
CAMPESINOS; Music Review; Musical Lyrics.

232 Migratory worker law increases protections.
NUESTRO, Vol. 7, no. 1 (January, February,
1983), p. 47. English. DESCR: *Migrant and
Seasonal Agricultural Worker Protection Act
(MSPA); Migrant Labor.

233 Miller, Michael V. Book review of: CHICANOS
AND RURAL POVERTY. JOURNAL OF ETHNIC
STUDIES, Vol. 5, no. 3 (Fall 1977), p.
116-117. English. DESCR: Book Reviews;
Briggs, Vernon M.; *CHICANOS AND RURAL
POVERTY; Immigration Law; Social History and
Conditions; Southwest United States.

234 Morton, Carlos and Valdez, Luis. An
interview with Luis Valdez. LATIN AMERICAN
THEATRE REVIEW, Vol. 15, no. 2 (Spring
1982), p. 73-76. English. DESCR: *Teatro;
*Valdez, Luis.

235 Murray, Douglas L. Abolition of el cortito,
the short-handled hoe: a case study in
social conflict and state policy in
California agriculture. SOCIAL PROBLEMS,
Vol. 30, no. 1 (October 1982), p. 26-39.
English. DESCR: *Occupational Hazards.

236 O'Brien, Mary Elizabeth. Reaching the
migrant worker. AMERICAN JOURNAL OF NURSING,
Vol. 83, no. 6 (June 1983), p. 895-897.
English. DESCR: Folk Medicine; Medical Care;
*Migrant Health Services.

237 Oliver, Gordon. Worker abuses claimed.
NATIONAL CATHOLIC REPORTER, Vol. 19,
(October 29, 1982), p. 7. English. DESCR:
Border Patrol; *Citizens United for
Farmworkers, Yakima WA; Immigration and
Naturalization Service (INS); *Immigration
Regulation and Control; Yakima, WA.

238 Olson, James S. Book review of: OPERATION
WETBACK: THE MASS DEPORTATION OF MEXICAN
UNDOCUMENTED WORKERS IN 1954. JOURNAL OF THE
WEST, Vol. 22, no. 1 (1983), p. 80-81.
English. DESCR: Book Reviews; Braceros;
Garcia, Juan Ramon; *OPERATION WETBACK: THE
MASS DEPORTATION OF MEXICAN UNDOCUMENTED
WORKERS IN 1954; Undocumented Workers.

239 "Racist and demeaning". NUESTRO, Vol. 7, no.
2 (March 1983), p. 7. English. DESCR: Book
Reviews; Granada, Pilar; Hagopian, Tom;
Racism; *SPANISH FOR THE CALIFORNIA FARMERS.

240 Rodriguez, Raquel. Children of the earth.
COMADRE, no. 2 (Spring 1978), p. 20.
English. DESCR: *Poetry.

241 Rodriguez, Vicente and Costello, Guy.
United farm workers. SOUTHERN EXPOSURE, Vol.
10, no. 4 (July, August, 1982), p. 14-15.
English. DESCR: Agricultural Labor Relations
Board (ALRB); *United Farmworkers of America
(UFW).

242 Sutton, Susan Buck and Brunner, Tracy. Life
on the road: Midwestern migrant farmworker
survival skills. MIGRATION TODAY, Vol. 11,
no. 1 (1983), p. 24-31. English. DESCR:
Agribusiness; Economic History and
Conditions; Indiana; Migrant Children;
Migrant Education; *Migrant Labor;
Stereotypes.

243 Walia, Adorna. Book review of: THE PLUM PLUM

PICKERS. BILINGUAL JOURNAL, Vol. 6, no. 1
(Fall 1982), p. 30-31. English. DESCR:
Barrio, Raymond; Book Reviews; California;
*Migrant Labor; Santa Clara County, CA; *THE
PLUM PLUM PICKERS.

244 Wells, Miriam J. Political mediation and
agricultural cooperation: strawberry farms
in California. ECONOMIC DEVELOPMENT AND
CULTURAL CHANGE, Vol. 30, no. 2 (January
1982), p. 413-432. English. DESCR:
*Agricultural Cooperatives; California;
Cooperativa Campesina; Cooperativa Central;
Political Parties and Organizations; Rural
Economics.

Agricultural Workers

USE: Agricultural Laborers

Agriculture

245 Martinez, Douglas R. Down on the farm with
the Cisco Kid. NUESTRO, Vol. 7, no. 2 (March
1983), p. 49. English. DESCR: Agriculture
Day USDA; Cisco Kid; Spanish Influence.

Agriculture Day USDA

246 Martinez, Douglas R. Down on the farm with
the Cisco Kid. NUESTRO, Vol. 7, no. 2 (March
1983), p. 49. English. DESCR: *Agriculture;
Cisco Kid; Spanish Influence.

Aguilar, Ester Reyes

247 Fuentes, Diana. Chicana perpectives: Ester
Reyes Aguilar. COMADRE, no. 1 (Summer 1977),
p. 45-48. English. DESCR: Affirmative
Action; Ballet Folkorico; *Biography;
Teaching Profession.

Aguilar, Gloria

248 People. HISPANIC BUSINESS, Vol. 4, no. 10
(October 1982), p. 7. English. DESCR:
Biographical Notes; *Businesspeople;
Caldera, Manuel R.; Lopez, Victor M.;
Ramirez, Steve.

Aguilar, Humberto

249 Lewis, William. Tres Plumas and his pantheon
of archetypal deities. NUESTRO, Vol. 7, no.
2 (March 1983), p. 38-40. English. DESCR:
Artists; Sculpture; Tres Plumas.

Aguilar, Richard

250 People. HISPANIC BUSINESS, Vol. 4, no. 7
(July 1982), p. 7. English. DESCR:
*Biographical Notes; Businesspeople;
Coronado, Julius; Enriquez, Rene; Garza,
Jose S.; Guerra-Martinez, Celina; Medrano,
Adan; Mota, Manny; Valenti, Frank S.

251 People. HISPANIC BUSINESS, Vol. 4, no. 8
(August 1983), p. 7. English. DESCR:
*Businesspeople; Cordero-Badillo, Atilano;
del Olmo, Frank; Infante, E. Anthony;
Levitan, Aida T.; Nunez, Luis; Quintanilla,
Guadalupe; Rivera, Victor M.

Aguirre, Horacio

252 Communications/marketing. HISPANIC BUSINESS,
Vol. 5, no. 9 (September 1983), p. 26.
English. DESCR: Business Enterprises;
Consumers; DIARIO DE LAS AMERICAS; La
Ventana; *Marketing; Miller Brewing Company;
SURVEY OF PROMOTIONAL PRACTICES.

Aguirre, Jack

253 Goodman, Gerson. "ES PARA USTED": CSI aims for satisfaction. HISPANIC BUSINESS, Vol. 4, no. 12 (December 1982), p. 16-17,34. English. **DESCR**: Advertising Agencies; Business Enterprises; Consumers; CSI International, Inc.; Fernandez, Castor A.; *Marketing.

Aguirre, Lionel

254 Cantu, Hector. Border business report: the Rio Grande Valley's economy and Mexico's lingering peso devaluation effects. NATIONAL HISPANIC JOURNAL, Vol. 2, no. 1 (Summer 1983), p. 10-13. English. **DESCR**: Border Region; Cano, Eddie; Coors Distributing Company, McAllen, TX; Cruz, Conrado; Cuevas, Betty; *Currency; Economic Development; Laredo, TX, Chamber of Commerce; Mexican American Chamber of Commerce, Austin, TX; United States-Mexico Relations.

Aguirre, Pedro

255 People. HISPANIC BUSINESS, Vol. 4, no. 6 (June 1982), p. 8. English. **DESCR**: Arellano, Richard; *Biographical Notes; Businesspeople; Cortez, Pete; De la Colina, Rafael; Hernandez, Sam; Nogales, Luis; Rodriguez, Leslie J.; Roybal, Edward R.

AIDS Hotline

256 Government review. NUESTRO, Vol. 7, no. 7 (September 1983), p. 55. English. **DESCR**: California; Education; Employment; Food for Survival, New York, NY; Funding Sources; *Government Services; Hewlett Foundation; Laborers; Mathematics, Engineering and Science Achievement (MESA); Population Trends; Public Health; Stanford University, Stanford, CA.

Aiken and Preger Revised Math Attitude Scale

257 Creswell, John L. Sex-related differences in the problem-solving abilities of rural Black, Anglo, and Chicano adolescents. TEXAS TECH JOURNAL OF EDUCATION, Vol. 10, no. 1 (Winter 1983), p. 29-33. English. **DESCR**: Anglo Americans; Blacks; California Achievement Test; Chicanas; Gender; Mathematics; National Assessment of Educational Progress; *National Council of Teachers of Mathematics (NCTM); Youth.

Air Pollution

258 Hansen, Niles. Trans boundary environmental issues in the United States-Mexico borderlands. SOUTHWESTERN REVIEW OF MANAGEMENT AND ECONOMICS, Vol. 2, no. 1 (Winter 1982), p. 61-78. English. **DESCR**: Border Region; *Pollution; Water Pollution.

Akbarian v. INS

259 Immigration and nationality symposium. SAN DIEGO LAW REVIEW, Vol. 20, no. 1 (December 1982, 1983), p. 1-231. English. **DESCR**: Deportation; Employment; Immigration and Nationality Act (INA); *Immigration Regulation and Control; Miranda v. INS; Simpson-Mazzoli Bill; Undocumented Workers.

ALAMBRISTA

260 Barrios, Gregg. Alambrista! a modern odyssey. BILINGUAL REVIEW, Vol. 10, no. 2-3 (May, December, 1983), p. 165-167. English. **DESCR**: Film Reviews.

Alambristas

USE: Undocumented Workers

Alameda County, CA

261 Medina, Antonio S. Adolescent health in Alameda county. JOURNAL OF ADOLESCENT HEALTH CARE, Vol. 2, no. 3 (March 1982), p. 175-182. English. **DESCR**: *Dentistry; Drug Abuse; Medical Care; Psychology; Youth.

Alameda Theater, San Antonio, TX

262 Southwest may lose theater. NUESTRO, Vol. 6, no. 7 (September 1982), p. 11. English. **DESCR**: Films; San Antonio, TX; Spanish Language.

Alatis, James E.

263 Amastae, Jon. The issue of language proficiency. BILINGUAL REVIEW, Vol. 10, no. 1 (January, April, 1983), p. 73-80. English. **DESCR**: Bilingual Bicultural Education; Book Reviews; *GURT 1980: CURRENT ISSUES IN BILINGUAL EDUCATION.

Alba '80 Society

264 Quinlivan, Robert and Castaneda, Jaime. Black & white ball. CAMINOS, Vol. 4, no. 1-2 (January, February, 1983), p. 68-69. Bilingual. **DESCR**: Organizations; San Diego, CA.

Albert, Margo

265 How to stuff a wild chile part II. CAMINOS, Vol. 3, no. 1 (January 1982), p. 31-32. English. **DESCR**: Chacon, Peter R.; *Icaya, Rick; Lacayo, Frank L. "Hank"; *Recipes; *Rodriguez, Edmundo; Rodriguez, Edmundo M.; *Vasquez, Victor.

Albert, Martin L.

266 Ruskin, Ellen Maria. Book review of: THE BILINGUAL BRAIN: NEURO-PSYCHOLOGICAL AND NEUROLINGUISTIC ASPECTS OF BILINGUALISM. HISPANIC JOURNAL OF BEHAVIORAL SCIENCES, Vol. 5, no. 4 (December 1983), p. 487-491. English. **DESCR**: Bilingualism; Book Reviews; Obler, Loraine K.; *THE BILINGUAL BRAIN.

Albertini, Luis Diaz

267 Media/marketing. HISPANIC BUSINESS, Vol. 5, no. 12 (December 1983), p. 38. English. **DESCR**: Computers; League of United Latin American Citizens (LULAC); Lotus-Albertini Hispanic Reps; Marketing; *Mass Media; Nuestras Noticias; Radio; Reading; Television; Tortosa, Cristobal.

Albuquerque Arts Board

268 Sculpture results in controversy. NUESTRO, Vol. 7, no. 2 (March 1983), p. 9. English. **DESCR**: *Jimenez, Luis; *Sculpture.

Alcala, Al

269 Weber, Robert. Turbo-charged MST, Inc. HISPANIC BUSINESS, Vol. 4, no. 11 (November 1982), p. 10-11,24. English. **DESCR**: Computers; *High Technology Industries; Irvine, CA; *Media Systems Technology, Inc.(MST,Inc.)

---   ---

Alcoholic Beverages

270 Davis, Susan M. A sparkling alternative to
    the cocktail party. NUESTRO, Vol. 5, no. 8
    (November 1981), p. 55-56. English.

271 Gage, Theodore J. Beer still tops wine,
    spirits. ADVERTISING AGE MAGAZINE, Vol. 53,
    (February 15, 1982), p. II, M10. English.
    DESCR: Advertising; Consumers; Market
    Research.

Alcoholism

272 Alcoholism: severe health problem for
    Latinos. NUESTRO, Vol. 6, no. 2 (March
    1982), p. 35-37. English.

273 Caetano, Raul. Drinking patterns and alcohol
    problems among Hispanics in the U.S.: a
    review. DRUG AND ALCOHOL DEPENDENCE, Vol.
    12, no. 1 (August 1983), p. 37-59. English.

274 Cayer, Shirley. Chicago's new Hispanic
    health alliance. NUESTRO, Vol. 7, no. 5
    (June, July, 1983), p. 44-48. English.
    DESCR: Chicago Hispanic Health Alliance;
    Family Planning; *Health Education; Latin
    Americans; *Medical Care.

275 Estrada, Antonio; Rabou, Jerome; and Watts,
    Ronald K. Alcohol use among Hispanic
    adolescents; a preliminary report. HISPANIC
    JOURNAL OF BEHAVIORAL SCIENCES, Vol. 4, no.
    3 (September 1982), p. 339-351. English.
    DESCR: Religion; Youth.

276 Government review. NUESTRO, Vol. 7, no. 8
    (October 1983), p. 54. English. DESCR:
    Employment; *Government Services; National
    Endowment for the Arts; Plaza de La Raza,
    Los Angeles, CA; Veterans; Working Women;
    Youth.

277 Panitz, Daniel R., et al. The role of
    machismo and the Hispanic family in the
    etiology and treatment of alcoholism in the
    Hispanic American males. AMERICAN JOURNAL OF
    FAMILY THERAPY, Vol. 11, no. 1 (Spring
    1983), p. 31-44. English. DESCR: Children;
    Family; *Machismo; Puerto Rico;
    Socioeconomic Factors.

278 Que pasa? NUESTRO, Vol. 7, no. 7 (September
    1983), p. 9. English. DESCR: Anti-Defamation
    League of B'nai B'rith; *Drug Abuse; Drug
    Programs; Employment; Kiwanis International;
    Miller Brewing Company; Racism; Sports.

279 Trotter, Robert T. Ethnic and sexual
    patterns of alcohol use: Anglo and Mexican
    American college students. ADOLESCENCE, Vol.
    17, no. 66 (Summer 1982), p. 305-325.
    English. DESCR: Anglo Americans; Chicanas;
    Cultural Characteristics; Ethnic Groups; Sex
    Roles; Youth.

Aldridge v. U.S.

280 Fram, Steven J. Restricting inquiry into
    racial attitudes during the Voir Dire.
    AMERICAN CRIMINAL REVIEW, Vol. 19, no. 4
    (Spring 1982), p. 719-750. English. DESCR:
    Ham v. South Carolina; Juries; *Racism;
    Ristaino v. Ross; Rosales v. U.S.;
    Rosales-Lopez, Humberto.

Aleman, Miguel

281 Gente: Miguel Aleman, former president,
    Mexico, dies. NUESTRO, Vol. 7, no. 5 (June,
    July, 1983), p. 49. English. DESCR: *Elected
    Officials; *Mexico.

Alfaro-Garcia, Rafael Antonio

282 Nuestra gente. LATINO, Vol. 53, no. 6
    (October 1982), p. 22. English. DESCR:
    *Biographical Notes; Quintanilla, Guadalupe;
    Salazar, Veronica.

Alice Patterson Foundation

283 Patterson fellowship to de Uriarte. LATINA,
    Vol. 1, no. 2 (February, March, 1983), p.
    20. English. DESCR: *De Uriarte, Mercedes
    Lynn; *Financial Aid.

Alicia, Ana

284 Ana Alicia. LATINO, Vol. 54, no. 7 (November
    1983), p. 6-7+. English. DESCR: Artists.

Alkali Flat Project Area Committee, Sacramento, CA

285 Did you know. LATINA, Vol. 1, no. 3 (1983),
    p. 60-63. English. DESCR: Bilingual
    Foundation of the Arts; CAFE de California,
    Inc., Sacramento, CA; *Organizations.

Allen, Kenneth

286 Allen, Kenneth. Q & A with Kenneth Allen of
    the President's Task Force on Private Sector
    initiatives (interview). CAMINOS, Vol. 4,
    no. 4 (April 1983), p. 49-50,67. Bilingual.
    DESCR: Private Funding Sources.

Allende, Fernando

287 Fernando Allende. LATINA, Vol. 1, no. 1
    (1982), p. 28+. English. DESCR: *Biography.

288 Gonzalez, Magdalena. Recognizing Hispanic
    achievements in entertainment - U.S. and
    Mexico. CAMINOS, Vol. 3, no. 7 (July,
    August, 1982), p. 18-24. Bilingual. DESCR:
    Artists; Awards; Bonilla Giannini, Roxanna;
    Eynoso, David; Felix, Maria; Films; Gallego,
    Gina; *Golden Eagle Awards; Hoyos, Rodolfo;
    Lamas, Lorenzo; Lopez, Conchita; Lopez,
    Lisa; Montalban, Ricardo; Nosotros [film
    production company]; Quintero, Jose; Rowe,
    Arthur; Television; Torres, Liz.

ALMA ABIERTA: PINTO POETRY

289 Hunsaker, Alan. Book review of: ALMA
    ABIERTA: PINTO POETRY, MAYO DE CRC. HISPANIC
    JOURNAL OF BEHAVIORAL SCIENCES, Vol. 5, no.
    1 (March 1983), p. 132-134. English. DESCR:
    Book Reviews; Mirande, Alfredo.

Alonso, Epifanio

290 Sifuentes, Roberto. Aproximaciones al
    "Corrido de los Hermanos Hernandez
    ejecutados en la camara de gas de la
    penitenciaria de Florence, Arizona el dia 6
    de julio de 1934". AZTLAN, Vol. 13, no. 1-2
    (Spring, Fall, 1982), p. 95-109. Spanish.
    DESCR: *Corrido; *CORRIDO DE LOS HERMANOS
    HERNANDEZ [song lyrics]; Folk Songs;
    Hernandez, Federico; Hernandez, Manuel;
    Music; Musical Lyrics.

Alonso, Luis Ricardo

291 Irizarry, Estelle. La abuelita in
    literature. NUESTRO, Vol. 7, no. 7
    (September 1983), p. 50. English. DESCR:
    *Ancianos; Chicanas; Cotto-Thorner,
    Guillermo; Family; Ulibarri, Sabine R.;
    Valero, Robert.

Alpert, Herb

292 Entertaiment reviews. CAMINOS, Vol. 3, no. 8
(September 1982), p. 21. English. **DESCR:**
Adams, Bob; Books; Calvert, Robert; Jimenez,
Santiago; Lopez, Lisa; Music; Myles, Carol;
Paredes, Americo; Pettus, Theodore T.;
*Recreation; Television.

AltaVision, Inc. (Denver, CO)

293 Communications/marketing. HISPANIC BUSINESS,
Vol. 5, no. 7 (July 1983), p. 24. English.
DESCR: Boycotts; Cable Television;
Marketing; Operation PUSH; Spanish Satellite
Network (SSN); *Television.

Alternative Education

294 Jensen, Joan M. Women teachers, class and
ethnicity: New Mexico 1900-1950. SOUTHWEST
ECONOMY AND SOCIETY, Vol. 4, no. 2 (Winter
1978, 1979), p. 3-13. English. **DESCR:**
*Chicanas; Cultural Pluralism; History; *New
Mexico; Spanish Language; Teaching
Profession.

Alum, Rolando

295 El profesor Alum publica capitulo en libro.
LATINO, Vol. 53, no. 1 (January, February,
1982), p. 15. Spanish. **DESCR:** Authors.

Alurista

296 Alurista and Monleon, Jose. Mesa redonda.
MAIZE, Vol. 4, no. 3-4 (Spring, Summer,
1981), p. 6-23. English. **DESCR:** Anaya,
Rudolfo A.; Herrera Sobek, Maria; Identity;
Literature; Morales, Alejandro; *Mythology;
Viramontes, Helen.

Alvarado, Angel S.

297 People on the move. CAMINOS, Vol. 2, no. 6
(October 1981), p. 7. English. **DESCR:**
Arreola, Rafael; *Biographical Notes; Diaz,
Elisa; Diaz, Elvira A.; Garcia, Jose Joel;
Garza, Florentino; Icaza, Ricardo F.;
Lacayo, Henry; Martinez, Lydia R.; Munoz,
Victor M.; Salinas, Vicente; Sanchez,
Manuel; Zuniga, Henry.

Alvarado, Anthony J.

298 People. HISPANIC BUSINESS, Vol. 5, no. 7
(July 1983), p. 8. English. **DESCR:** Appointed
Officials; *Biographical Notes;
Businesspeople; Candela, Hilario; Garcia,
Marlene; Gonzalez, Julio; Martinez, Tony;
Pla, George; Valdez, Abelardo L.

Alvarado, Bob

299 Foster, Richard. Two Alvarados make one
sucessful construction firm. HISPANIC
BUSINESS, Vol. 4, no. 10 (October 1982), p.
10-11,26. English. **DESCR:** Alvarado, Linda
M.; *Business Enterprises; Construction
Industry; Small Business Administration 8(a)
Program; U.S. Small Business Administration.

Alvarado, Linda M.

300 Foster, Richard. Two Alvarados make one
sucessful construction firm. HISPANIC
BUSINESS, Vol. 4, no. 10 (October 1982), p.
10-11,26. English. **DESCR:** Alvarado, Bob;
*Business Enterprises; Construction
Industry; Small Business Administration 8(a)
Program; U.S. Small Business Administration.

301 People. HISPANIC BUSINESS, Vol. 5, no. 4

(April 1983), p. 9. English. **DESCR:**
*Biographical Notes; Businesspeople;
Castillo, Irenemaree; Castillo, Sylvia; Del
Junco, Tirso; Gutierrez, Jose Roberto;
Juarez, Joe; Mata, Bill; Miyares, Marcelino;
Montanez Davis, Grace; Montoya, Velma;
Pineda, Pat; Siberio, Julio; Thompson, Edith
Lopez.

Alvarado, Raul, Jr.

302 Padilla, Steve. Choosing a career. NUESTRO,
Vol. 7, no. 1 (January, February, 1983), p.
13-19+. English. **DESCR:** *Careers; Computers;
Diaz, William; Engineering as a Profession;
Esparza, Alma; Flores, Francisco; Garcia,
Linda; Medical Care; Soto, John; Yanez,
Ricardo.

Alvarez, Everett, Jr.

303 Garcia, Ignacio M. America says, welcome
home. NUESTRO, Vol. 6, no. 9 (November
1982), p. 15-19+. English. **DESCR:** Political
Prisoners; *Veterans; Vietnam; Vietnam War.

304 People. HISPANIC BUSINESS, Vol. 5, no. 2
(February 1983), p. 7. English. **DESCR:**
Appointed Officials; *Biographical Notes;
Businesspeople; Guzman-Randle, Irene;
Roubin, Angel; Vasquez, Victor; Villareal,
Luis Maria.

Alvarez, Julio E.

305 Sargeant, Georgia. Young turks set new
standards. HISPANIC BUSINESS, Vol. 5, no. 11
(November 1983), p. 8-9. English. **DESCR:**
*Architecture; Business Enterprises;
Management; Marketing; Miami, FL; Taracido,
Manuel E.; Wolfberg, David A.;
*Wolfberg/Alvarez/Taracido (WAT).

Alvarez, Rodolfo

306 Furphy, Alice. Book review of:
DISCRIMINATION IN ORGANIZATIONS. HISPANIC
JOURNAL OF BEHAVIORAL SCIENCES, Vol. 5, no.
1 (March 1983), p. 115-120. English. **DESCR:**
Book Reviews; *DISCRIMINATION IN
ORGANIZATIONS; Heller, Kenneth.

Amaya-Espinoza, Isidro

307 Gente. NUESTRO, Vol. 7, no. 1 (January,
February, 1983), p. 63. English. **DESCR:**
Camargo, Mateo G.; *Latin Americans;
Musicians; Prieto, Carlos; Radio; Sports;
Trevino, Lee.

Ambassadors
USE: Appointed Officials

American Civil Liberties Union

308 Keep, Paul M. Overhauling the immigration
code: this year, Congress may finally act.
NATIONAL JOURNAL, Vol. 15, no. 12 (March 19,
1983), p. 616-619. English. **DESCR:**
Federation for American Immigration Reform
(FAIR); Immigration; *Immigration Law;
Mexican American Legal Defense and
Educational Fund (MALDEF); *Simpson-Mazzoli
Bill.

American Club of Miami

309 Volsky, George. The American club. HISPANIC
BUSINESS, Vol. 4, no. 3 (March 1982), p.
16-17+. English. **DESCR:** *Businesspeople;
Cubanos; *Cultural Organizations; Miami, FL.

American Defense Education Act (ADEA)

310 Hart, Gary. America needs to invest in the
right kind of education. LATINO, Vol. 54,
no. 2 (March 1983), p. 19-20. English.
DESCR: *Cultural Pluralism.

American Friends Service Committee

311 Klan resurgence. NUESTRO, Vol. 5, no. 8
(November 1981), p. 11. English. DESCR: Ku
Klux Klan; Racism.

American G.I. Forum

312 The California GI Forum 1982 convention.
CAMINOS, Vol. 3, no. 8 (September 1982), p.
24-25. English. DESCR: Organizations.

313 San Miguel, Guadalupe. Mexican American
organizations and the changing politics of
school desegration in Texas, 1945 to 1980.
SOCIAL SCIENCE QUARTERLY, Vol. 63,
(December 1982), p. 701-715. English.
DESCR: League of United Latin American
Citizens (LULAC); Mexican American Legal
Defense and Educational Fund (MALDEF);
Organizations; *Segregation and
Desegregation; Texas.

314 Tips for making the right moves in today's
job markets. HISPANIC BUSINESS, Vol. 4, no.
8 (August 1983), p. 11+. English. DESCR:
*Careers; Employment; Management; Military
Service.

American Indians
USE: Native Americans

American Labor Union (Santa Clara County, CA)

315 Arnold, Frank. A history of struggle:
organizing cannery workers in the Santa
Clara Valley. SOUTHWEST ECONOMY AND SOCIETY,
Vol. 2, no. 1 (October, November, 1976), p.
26-38. English. DESCR: Agribusiness; Cannery
and Agricultural Worker's Industrial Union;
*Cannery Workers; Comite de Trabajadores de
Canerias, San Jose, CA; History; Labor
Unions; *Santa Clara Valley, CA; United
Cannery Agricultural Packing and Allied
Workers of America (UCAPAWA).

American Spelling Bee

316 Martinez, Douglas R. American spelling bee:
enchilada, llano, amigo, maraca. NUESTRO,
Vol. 7, no. 5 (June, July, 1983), p. 50-51.
English. DESCR: Language Arts; *Language
Usage; *Linguistics.

Americanization
USE: Assimilation

Americas Award

317 Gente. NUESTRO, Vol. 7, no. 7 (September
1983), p. 61. English. DESCR: Chavez, Raul;
*Chicanas; Diaz-Cobo, Christine; Mexico;
Ortega, Katherine D.; Performing Arts;
Planas, Vilma; Ravard, Rafael Alonzo;
Venezuela.

Las Americas, Inc.

318 Communications/marketing. HISPANIC BUSINESS,
Vol. 4, no. 4 (April 1982), p. 15. English.
DESCR: Advertising Agencies; Consumers;
Juarez and Associates, Inc.; *Marketing;
Norman, Craig & Kummel Organization;
Publicidad Siboney; Siboney Advertising,
Inc.

AMEX Systems, Inc.

319 Balkan, D. Carlos. AMEX Systems Inc. at
transition point. HISPANIC BUSINESS, Vol. 4,
no. 6 (June 1982), p. 18-19,24. English.
DESCR: Business Enterprises; Caldera, Manuel
R.; *Corporations; High Technology
Industries; Small Business Administration
8(a) Program; U.S. Small Business
Administration.

320 Chavarria, Jesus. The largest Hispanic
firms. HISPANIC BUSINESS, Vol. 4, no. 6
(June 1982), p. 6. English. DESCR: *Business
Enterprises; Jimenez Food Products, Inc.

Amigos de las Americas

321 Amigos. LATINO, Vol. 53, no. 7 (November
1982), p. 9-10. English. DESCR: Cultural
Organizations; Public Health.

AML Instrument

322 Flores de Apodaca, Roberto. Quick
socio-emotional screening of
Mexican-American and other ethnic head start
children. HISPANIC JOURNAL OF BEHAVIORAL
SCIENCES, Vol. 5, no. 1 (March 1983), p.
81-92. English. DESCR: Children; Headstart
Program; *Mental Health.

Amnesty

323 Hing, Bill Ong. Racial disparity: the
unaddressed issues of the Simpson-Mazzoli
Bill. LA RAZA LAW JOURNAL, Vol. 1, no. 1
(June 1983), p. 21-52. English. DESCR: Asian
Americans; Ethnic Attitudes; Family;
Immigration; Immigration and Naturalization
Service (INS); Latin Americans; Mazzoli,
Romano L.; Mexican American Legal Defense
and Educational Fund (MALDEF); Simpson, Alan
K.; *Simpson-Mazzoli Bill; Temporary Worker
Program; U.S. Congresssional Subcommittee on
Immigration, Refugees and International Law.

324 Liebowitz, Arnold. Immigration challenge and
the congressional response. LA RAZA LAW
JOURNAL, Vol. 1, no. 1 (June 1983), p. 1-20.
English. DESCR: Immigration; Immigration and
Nationality Act (INA); Mazzoli, Romano L.;
*Simpson, Alan K.; *Simpson-Mazzoli Bill;
Temporary Worker Program; Undocumented
Workers; U.S. Congresssional Subcommittee on
Immigration, Refugees and International Law.

325 Schey, Peter A. Supply side immigration
theory: analysis of the Simpson-Mazzoli
Bill. LA RAZA LAW JOURNAL, Vol. 1, no. 1
(June 1983), p. 53-71. English. DESCR:
Immigration; Mazzoli, Romano L.; Migration
Patterns; Refugees; Simpson, Alan K.;
*Simpson-Mazzoli Bill; Temporary Worker
Program.

Anacani

326 Bunnell, Robert. Bravisimo! NUESTRO, Vol. 7,
no. 9 (November 1983), p. 21-25. English.
DESCR: Coca-Cola Company; Miller Brewing
Company; Palomino, Carlos; Pena, Samm;
Performing Arts; *Television.

Anaya, Rudolfo A.

327 Alurista and Monleon, Jose. Mesa redonda.
MAIZE, Vol. 4, no. 3-4 (Spring, Summer,
1981), p. 6-23. English. DESCR: Alurista;
Herrera Sobek, Maria; Identity; Literature;
Morales, Alejandro; *Mythology; Viramontes,
Helen.

Anaya, Rudolfo A. (cont.)

328 Anaya, Rudolfo A. An author's reflections:
THE SILENCE OF THE LLANO. NUESTRO, Vol. 7,
no. 3 (April 1983), p. 14-17+. English.
DESCR: Authors; *Fiction; Literary
Influence.

329 Anaya, Rudolfo A. A celebration of
grandfathers. NEW MEXICO MAGAZINE, Vol. 61,
no. 3 (March 1983), p. 35-40. English.
DESCR: *Ancianos; Biography.

330 Calderon, Hector. To read Chicano narrative:
commentary and metacommentary. MESTER, Vol.
11, no. 2 (1982), p. 3-14. English. **DESCR:**
BLESS ME, ULTIMA; Fiction; Literary
Characteristics; *Literary Criticism;
Literature; *Prose.

331 Candelaria, Cordelia. Book review of: THE
SILENCE OF THE LLANO. MELUS: MULTI-ETHNIC
LITERATURE OF THE UNITED STATES, Vol. 10,
no. 2 (Summer 1983), p. 79-82. English.
DESCR: *Literature; THE SILENCE OF THE
LLANO.

332 Candelaria, Cordelia. Book review of:
TORTUGA. LA PALABRA, Vol. 4, no. 1-2
(Spring, Fall, 1982, 1983), p. 167-169.
Spanish. **DESCR:** Book Reviews; Literature;
*TORTUGA.

333 Candelaria, Cordelia. Problems and promise
in Anaya's llano: THE SILENCE OF THE LLANO,
Rudolfo A. Anaya. AMERICAN BOOK REVIEW, Vol.
5, no. 6 (September, October, 1983), p.
18-19. English. **DESCR:** Book Reviews; *THE
SILENCE OF THE LLANO.

334 Carrasco, David. A perspective for a study
of religious dimensions in Chicano
experience: BLESS ME, ULTIMA as a religious
text. AZTLAN, Vol. 13, no. 1-2 (Spring,
Fall, 1982), p. 195-221. English. **DESCR:**
*BLESS ME, ULTIMA; Literary Criticism;
Literature; Religion.

335 Clements, William M. Way to individuation in
Anaya's BLESS ME, ULTIMA. MIDWEST QUARTERLY,
Vol. 23, no. 2 (Winter 1982), p. 131-143.
English. **DESCR:** *BLESS ME, ULTIMA; Literary
Criticism; Psychological Theory.

336 Elias, Edward. TORTUGA: a novel of
archetypal structure. BILINGUAL REVIEW, Vol.
9, no. 1 (January, April, 1982), p. 82-87.
English. **DESCR:** Book Reviews; *TORTUGA.

337 Garcia, Reyes. Politics of flesh: ethnicity
and political viability. CACR REVIEW, Vol.
1, no. 1 (September 1982), p. 102-130.
English. **DESCR:** Aristotle; Culture; Ethnic
Groups; Identity; Locke, John; Nuclear
Armament; Philosophy; *Political Repression;
Urban Communities.

338 Martinez, Douglas R. Book review of: THE
SILENCE OF THE LLANO. NUESTRO, Vol. 7, no. 1
(January, February, 1983), p. 55. English.
DESCR: Book Reviews; *THE SILENCE OF THE
LLANO.

339 Martinez, Douglas R. Sharing the silence.
LATINO, Vol. 54, no. 4 (May, June, 1983), p.
28. English. **DESCR:** Book Reviews; *THE
SILENCE OF THE LLANO.

340 A time for reflection. NUESTRO, Vol. 7, no.
9 (November 1983), p. 42-44. English.
DESCR: Arias, Beatriz; Bilingual Bicultural
Education; Computers; Financial Aid;
Folklore; Organizations; Prewitt Diaz,
Joseph (Jose); Villarreal, Sylvia; *W.K.

Kellogg Foundation National Fellowship
Program.

341 Urioste, Donaldo W. Book review of: CUENTOS
CHICANOS. LA PALABRA, Vol. 4, no. 1-2
(Spring, Fall, 1982, 1983), p. 175-177.
Spanish. **DESCR:** Book Reviews; *CUENTOS
CHICANOS; Literature.

342 Vallejos, Thomas. Ritual process and the
family in the Chicano novel. MELUS:
MULTI-ETHNIC LITERATURE OF THE UNITED
STATES, Vol. 10, no. 4 (Winter 1983, 1984),
p. 5-16. English. **DESCR:** BLESS ME, ULTIMA;
Family; *Literary Criticism; Novel; Parent
and Child Relationships; POCHO; Rivera,
Tomas; Villarreal, Jose Antonio; Y NO SE LO
TRAGO LA TIERRA/AND THE EARTH DID NOT PART.

Anaya, Toney

343 New Mexico's gubernatorial race. HISPANIC
BUSINESS, Vol. 4, no. 11 (November 1982), p.
27,30. English. **DESCR:** *Biography;
Elections; New Mexico; Political Parties and
Organizations.

344 People. HISPANIC BUSINESS, Vol. 5, no. 3
(March 1983), p. 9. English. **DESCR:**
Anguiano, Lupe; Appointed Officials; Avila,
Joaquin Guadalupe; Awards; *Biographical
Notes; de la Fuente, Emilio; del Olmo,
Frank; Godoy, Gustavo; Long, Dennis P.;
Martinez, Elias (Lee); Rivera, Joseph, Jr.

345 People. HISPANIC BUSINESS, Vol. 5, no. 10
(October 1983), p. 10. English. **DESCR:**
Arriola, Elvia Rosales; Babbitt, Bruce;
Burgos, Tony; Bush, George; *Businesspeople;
Cisneros, Henry, Mayor of San Antonio, TX;
Cruz, Jose; Kennedy, Edward M.; Montano,
Gilbert; Reagan, Ronald; White, Mark.

Ancianos

346 Aging research planned. NUESTRO, Vol. 7, no.
8 (October 1983), p. 9. English. **DESCR:**
*Public Health; Stanford University Medical
Center.

347 Anaya, Rudolfo A. A celebration of
grandfathers. NEW MEXICO MAGAZINE, Vol. 61,
no. 3 (March 1983), p. 35-40. English.
DESCR: Anaya, Rudolfo A.; Biography.

348 Burke, Leslie K. Book review of: AGING AND
SOCIETY: CURRENT RESEARCH AND POLICY
PERSPECTIVES. HISPANIC JOURNAL OF BEHAVIORAL
SCIENCES, Vol. 4, no. 1 (March 1982), p.
114-115. English. **DESCR:** *AGING AND SOCIETY:
CURRENT RESEARCH AND POLICY PERSPECTIVES;
Book Reviews; Borgatta, Edgar F.; McCluskey,
Neil G.

349 Burke, Leslie K. Book review of: AGING AND
SOCIAL POLICY: LEADERSHIP PLANNING. HISPANIC
JOURNAL OF BEHAVIORAL SCIENCES, Vol. 4, no.
1 (March 1982), p. 115-116. English. **DESCR:**
*AGING AND SOCIAL POLICY: LEADERSHIP
PLANNING; Book Reviews; Kasschau, Patricia
L.

350 Delgado, Melvin. Ethnic and cultural
variations in the care of the aged. Hispanic
elderly and natural support systems: a
special focus on Puerto Ricans. JOURNAL OF
GERIATRIC PSYCHIATRY, Vol. 15, no. 2 (1982),
p. 239-251. English. **DESCR:** Cultural
Organizations; Curanderas; Family; Natural
Support Systems; Puerto Ricans; Religion;
Santeros.

Ancianos (cont.)

351 Exum, Herbert A. The most invisible minority: the culturally diverse elderly. SCHOOL COUNSELOR, Vol. 30, no. 1 (September 1982), p. 15-24. English. **DESCR**: Asian Americans; Blacks; Counseling (Psychological); Cultural Customs; Ethnic Groups; Family; Native Americans; Stereotypes.

352 Forum to address concerns of elderly. LATINO, Vol. 54, no. 6 (October 1983), p. 5. English.

353 Franklin, Gerald S. and Kaufman, Karen S. Group psychotherapy for elderly female Hispanic outpatients. HOSPITAL AND COMMUNITY PSYCHIATRY, Vol. 33, no. 5 (May 1982), p. 385-387. English. **DESCR**: *Chicanas; Psychotherapy.

354 Greenberg, Julie L. Dating and the elderly. NUESTRO, Vol. 6, no. 5 (June, July, 1982), p. 43. English. **DESCR**: Sex Roles.

355 HHR proposes safety plan for care homes. NUESTRO, Vol. 6, no. 4 (May 1982), p. 57-58. English. **DESCR**: Public Health.

356 Irizarry, Estelle. La abuelita in literature. NUESTRO, Vol. 7, no. 7 (September 1983), p. 50. English. **DESCR**: Alonso, Luis Ricardo; Chicanas; Cotto-Thorner, Guillermo; Family; Ulibarri, Sabine R.; Valero, Robert.

357 Korte, Alvin O. Social interaction and morale of Spanish-speaking rural and urban elderly. JOURNAL OF GERONTOLOGICAL SOCIAL WORK, Vol. 4, no. 3- (Spring, Summer, 1982), p. 57-66. English. **DESCR**: New Mexico; Social Psychology.

358 Luevano, Richard L. Attitudes of elderly Mexican Americans towards nursing homes in Stanislaus county. CAMPO LIBRE, Vol. 1, no. 2 (Summer 1981), p. 213-228. English. **DESCR**: Attitude (Psychological); Cultural Characteristics; Medical Care; *Nursing Homes; Stanislaus County, CA; Surveys.

359 Markides, Kyraikos S. Aging, religiosity, and adjustment: a longitudinal analysis. JOURNAL OF GERONTOLOGY, Vol. 38, no. 5 (September 1983), p. 621-625. English. **DESCR**: *Mental Health; Psychology; Religion.

360 Markides, Kyraikos S.; Dickson, Harold; and Pappas, Christine. Characteristics of dropouts in longitudinal research on aging - a study of Mexican-Americans and Anglos. EXPERIMENTAL AGING RESEARCH, Vol. 8, no. 3-4 (1982), p. 163-167. English. **DESCR**: Comparative Psychology; *Mental Health; Psychology.

361 New nutritional research center to study aging. NUESTRO, Vol. 6, no. 4 (May 1982), p. 57. English. **DESCR**: Health Education; Public Health.

362 Ortiz, Carlos V. Growing old alone. NUESTRO, Vol. 7, no. 4 (May 1983), p. 36-38. English. **DESCR**: Drinane, Suleika Cabrera; Instituto Puertorriqueno/Hispano Para Personas Mayores; Padilla de Armas, Encarnacion; *Puerto Ricans.

363 Quinlivan, Robert. The need for Hispanic senior housing. CAMINOS, Vol. 3, no. 7 (July, August, 1982), p. 42-43. Bilingual. **DESCR**: Colonial Barrio Seniors; *Housing; San Diego, CA; Villa Merced Housing Project.

364 Regional report, health: student cited for aging work. NUESTRO, Vol. 7, no. 4 (May 1983), p. 13. English. **DESCR**: *Lopez, Isabel.

365 Rizzuto, Anna-Maria. Ethnic and cultural variations in the care of the aged. Discussion: Hispanic elderly and natural support systems: a special focus on Puerto Ricans. JOURNAL OF GERIATRIC PSYCHIATRY, Vol. 15, no. 2 (1982), p. 253-255. English. **DESCR**: Natural Support Systems; Puerto Ricans.

366 Schmidt, Lorenza. Grandparental-grandchild interaction in a Mexican American group. HISPANIC JOURNAL OF BEHAVIORAL SCIENCES, Vol. 5, no. 2 (June 1983), p. 181-198. English. **DESCR**: Children; *Grandparent and Child Relationships.

367 Szapocznik, Jose, et al. Ethnic and cultural variations in the care of the aged. New directions in the treatment of represion in the elderly: a life enhancement counseling approach. JOURNAL OF GERIATRIC PSYCHIATRY, Vol. 15, no. 2 (1982), p. 257-281. English. **DESCR**: Counseling (Psychological); Cubanos.

368 Szapocznik, Jose, et al. Life enhancement counseling and the treatment of the depressed Cuban American elders. HISPANIC JOURNAL OF BEHAVIORAL SCIENCES, Vol. 4, no. 4 (December 1982), p. 487-502. English. **DESCR**: *Counseling (Psychological); Cubanos.

369 Trilla, Francisco. The plight of the elderly Puerto Rican. JOURNAL OF LATIN COMMUNITY HEALTH, Vol. 1, no. 1 (Fall 1982), p. 89-91. English. **DESCR**: Puerto Ricans.

370 Watts, Thomas D. Social policy and the aged: transcultural perspectives. HUMAN SERVICES IN THE RURAL ENVIRONMENT, Vol. 7, no. 1 (Winter 1982), p. 32-34. English. **DESCR**: Social Services.

AND THE EARTH DID NOT PART
USE: Y NO SE LO TRAGO LA TIERRA/AND THE EARTH DID NOT PART

Anderson, John

371 Presidential election 1984. NUESTRO, Vol. 7, no. 7 (September 1983), p. 14-19. English. **DESCR**: Askew, Reubin; Cranston, Alan; Elected Officials; *Elections; Fernandez, Ben; Glenn, John; Hart, Gary; Hispanic Force '84; Hollings, Ernest "Fritz"; Mondale, Walter; Political Parties and Organizations; Reagan, Ronald.

Andrew W. Mellon Foundation

372 Math-based careers. HISPANIC BUSINESS, Vol. 5, no. 9 (September 1983), p. 28. English. **DESCR**: *Careers; Employment; Engineering as a Profession; Financial Aid; Garcia, Mary; Higher Education; National Council for Minorities in Engineering (NACME); National Medical Fellowships (NMF); Rivera, Lourdes.

Andujar, Joaquin

373 Ortiz, Carlos V. NUESTRO'S sixth annual all-star baseball team. NUESTRO, Vol. 7, no. 2 (March 1983), p. 33-37. English. **DESCR**: Barojas, Salome; *Baseball; Castillo, Manny; Concepcion, Dave; Cruz, Jose; Garcia, Damaso; Guerrero, Pedro; Hernandez, Keith; Lezcano, Sixto; Martinez, Tippy; Pena, Tony; Piniella, Lou; Sports; Valenzuela, Fernando.

ANGEL AND BIG JOE

374 Aldridge, Henry B. Angel and big Joe.
BILINGUAL REVIEW, Vol. 10, no. 2-3 (May,
December, 1983), p. 168-170. English.
DESCR: Film Reviews.

ANGEL DUST: AN ETHNOGRAPHIC STUDY OF PCP USERS

375 Hunsaker, Alan. Book review of: ANGEL DUST:
AN ETHNOGRAPHIC STUDY OF PCP USERS; HEROIN
USE IN THE BARRIO; DRUG AND ALCOHOL ABUSE: A
CLINICAL GUIDE TO DIAGNOSIS AND TREATMENT.
HISPANIC JOURNAL OF BEHAVIORAL SCIENCES,
Vol. 4, no. 1 (March 1982), p. 118-121.
English. DESCR: Agar, Michael; Bescher,
George; Book Reviews; Bullington, Bruce;
*DRUG AND ALCOHOL ABUSE: A CLINICAL GUIDE TO
DIAGNOSIS AND TREATMENT; Feldman, Harvey W.;
*HEROIN USE IN THE BARRIO; Schuckit, Marc
A.

Anglo Americans

376 Anderson, John W. The effects of culture and
social class on client preference for
counseling methods. JOURNAL OF NON-WHITE
CONCERNS IN PERSONNEL AND GUIDANCE, Vol. 11,
no. 3 (April 1983), p. 84-88. English.
DESCR: Blacks; Counseling Effectiveness
Scale; *Counseling (Psychological);
*Educational Opportunity Program (EOP);
Locus of Control; University of Illinois at
Urbana.

377 Argulewicz, Ed N.; Elliott, Stephen N.; and
Hall, Robert. Comparison of behavioral
ratings of Anglo-American and
Mexican-American gifted children. PSYCHOLOGY
IN THE SCHOOLS, Vol. 19, no. 4 (October
1982), p. 469-472. English. DESCR: Child
Study; Cultural Characteristics;
*Intelligence Tests.

378 Argulewicz, Ed N. and Sanchez, David T.
Special education evaluation process as a
moderator of false positives. EXCEPTIONAL
CHILDREN, Vol. 49, no. 5 (1983), p. 452-454.
English. DESCR: Blacks; *Special Education.

379 Ayers-Nackamkin, Beverly, et al. Sex and
ethnic differences in the use of power.
JOURNAL OF APPLIED PSYCHOLOGY, Vol. 67, no.
4 (August 1982), p. 464-471. English.
DESCR: Ethnic Groups; Management; *Personnel
Management; Sex Roles; Social Psychology.

380 Borrego, Richard L.; Chavez, Ernest L.; and
Titley, Robert W. Effect of counselor
technique on Mexican-American and
Anglo-American self-disclosure and counselor
perception. JOURNAL OF COUNSELING
PSYCHOLOGY, Vol. 29, no. 5 (September 1982),
p. 538-541. English. DESCR: *Counseling
(Psychological); Cultural Characteristics;
Identity; Personality; Sex Roles.

381 Buriel, Raymond, et al. Mexican- and
Anglo-American children's locus of control
and achievement in relation to teachers
attitudes. JOURNAL OF GENETIC PSYCHOLOGY,
Vol. 140, no. 1 (March 1982), p. 131-143.
English. DESCR: *Academic Achievement;
Children; Comparative Education; *Teacher
Attitudes.

382 Clarizio, Harvey F. Intellectual assessment
of Hispanic children. PSYCHOLOGY IN THE
SCHOOLS, Vol. 19, no. 1 (January 1982), p.
61-71. English. DESCR: Child Study; Cultural
Pluralism; *Intelligence Tests.

383 Cockerham, William C. and Alster, Joan M. A
comparison of marijuana use among

Mexican-American and Anglo rural youth
utilizing a matched-set analysis.
INTERNATIONAL JOURNAL OF THE ADDICTIONS,
Vol. 18, no. 6 (August 1983), p. 759-767.
English. DESCR: Drug Abuse; *Marijuana;
Rural Population; Youth.

384 Cortese, Anthony J., ed. A comparative
analysis of ethnicity and moral judgment.
CACR REVIEW, Vol. 1, no. 1 (September 1982),
p. 72-101. English. DESCR: Blacks; Cultural
Characteristics; Identity; *Values.

385 Creswell, John L. Sex-related differences in
the problem-solving abilities of rural
Black, Anglo, and Chicano adolescents. TEXAS
TECH JOURNAL OF EDUCATION, Vol. 10, no. 1
(Winter 1983), p. 29-33. English. DESCR:
Aiken and Preger Revised Math Attitude
Scale; Blacks; California Achievement Test;
Chicanas; Gender; Mathematics; National
Assessment of Educational Progress;
*National Council of Teachers of Mathematics
(NCTM); Youth.

386 Dean, Raymond S. Intelligence-achievement
discrepancies in diagnosing pediatric
learning disabilities. CLINICAL
NEUROPSYCHOLOGY, Vol. 4, no. 2 (1982), p.
58-62. English. DESCR: *Handicapped;
Intelligence Tests; Peabody Individual
Achievement Test (PIAT); Youth; ZOOT SUIT
[film].

387 Dodge, Russell. A comparison of the
respiratory health of Mexican-American and
non-Mexican American white children. CHEST,
Vol. 84, no. 5 (November 1983), p. 587-592.
English. DESCR: Children; *Public Health.

388 Dowdall, George W. and Flood, Lawrence G.
Correlates and consequences of socioeconomic
differences among Chicanos, Blacks and
Anglos in the Southwest: a study of
metropolitan structure. SOCIAL SCIENCE
JOURNAL, Vol. 19, no. 2 (April 1982), p.
25-36. English. DESCR: Blacks; *Ethnic
Groups; *Research Methodology; Residential
Segregation; Socioeconomic Factors;
Southwest United States.

389 Garcia, Philip. An evaluation of employment
and unemployment differences between Mexican
Americans and whites: the seventies. SOCIAL
SCIENCE JOURNAL, Vol. 20, no. 1 (January
1983), p. 51-62. English. DESCR:
*Employment; Ethnic Groups; Labor Supply and
Market.

390 Gonzalez, Alex. Sex role of the traditional
Mexican family: a comparison of Chicano and
Anglo students' attitudes. JOURNAL OF
CROSS-CULTURAL PSYCHOLOGY, Vol. 13, no. 3
(September 1982), p. 330-339. English.
DESCR: *Family; Hembrismo; Machismo; Sex
Roles.

391 Hazuda, Helen P. Ethnic differences in
health knowledge and behaviors related to
the prevention and treatment of coronary
heart disease. The San Antonio heart study.
AMERICAN JOURNAL OF EPIDEMIOLOGY, Vol. 11,
no. 6 (June 1983), p. 717-728. English.
DESCR: *Coronary Heart Disease; Health
Education; Preventative Medicine; San
Antonio, TX; Socioeconomic Factors.

Anglo Americans (cont.)

392 Henderson, Ronald W. and Brody, Gene H. Effects of ethnicity and child's age on maternal judgments of children's transgressions against persons and property. JOURNAL OF GENETIC PSYCHOLOGY, Vol. 140, no. 2 (June 1982), p. 253-263. English. **DESCR:** Arizona; Behavior Modification; *Child Rearing; Cultural Characteristics; Native Americans; *Socialization; Tucson, AZ.

393 Holck, Susan E. Lung cancer mortality and smoking habits: Mexican-American women. AMERICAN JOURNAL OF PUBLIC HEALTH, Vol. 72, no. 1 (January 1982), p. 38-42. English. **DESCR:** *Cancer; Chicanas; *Public Health.

394 Holck, Susan E., et al. Need for family planning services among Anglo and Hispanic women in the United States counties bordering Mexico. FAMILY PLANNING PERSPECTIVES, Vol. 14, no. 3 (May, June, 1982), p. 155-159. English. **DESCR:** *Family Planning.

395 Hsi, Bartholomew P.; Hsu, Katherine H.; and Jenkins, Daniel E. Ventilatory functions of normal children and young adults: Mexican-American, white and black. III. Sitting height as a predictor. JOURNAL OF PEDIATRICS, Vol. 102, no. 6 (June 1983), p. 860-865. English. **DESCR:** Blacks; Child Study; *Children; Pediatrics.

396 Kagan, Spencer and Zahn, G. Lawrence. Cultural differences in individualism? Just artifact. HISPANIC JOURNAL OF BEHAVIORAL SCIENCES, Vol. 5, no. 2 (June 1983), p. 219-232. English. **DESCR:** Blacks; Children; Competition; *Culture; Social Orientation.

397 Kagan, Spencer; Knight, George P.; and Martinez-Romero, Sergio. Culture and the development of conflict resolution style. JOURNAL OF CROSS-CULTURAL PSYCHOLOGY, Vol. 13, no. 1 (March 1982), p. 43-58. English. **DESCR:** *Conflict Resolution; Mexico.

398 Kagan, Spencer and Knudsen, Kathryn H.M. Relationship of empathy and affective role-taking in young children. JOURNAL OF GENETIC PSYCHOLOGY, Vol. 141, (September 1982), p. 149-150. English. **DESCR:** *Attitude (Psychological); Child Study; Psychological Testing; Socialization.

399 Kerr, G. R. Supermarket sales high-sugar products in predominantly Black, Hispanic and white census tracts of Houston, Texas. AMERICAN JOURNAL OF CLINICAL NUTRITION, Vol. 37, no. 4 (April 1983), p. 622-631. English. **DESCR:** Blacks; Food Practices; *Nutrition; Surveys.

400 Klein, Carol A. Children's concepts of the earth and the sun: a cross cultural study. SCIENCE EDUCATION, Vol. 66, no. 1 (January 1982), p. 95-107. English. **DESCR:** Children; Cultural Pluralism; Education; *Science.

401 Knight, George P.; Kagan, Spencer; and Buriel, Raymond. Perceived parental practices and prosocial development. JOURNAL OF GENETIC PSYCHOLOGY, Vol. 141, (September 1982), p. 57-65. English. **DESCR:** Cultural Characteristics; *Parent and Child Relationships; *Socialization; Socioeconomic Factors.

402 Knight, George P. and Kagan, Spencer. Sibling, birth order, and cooperative-competitive social behavior: a comparison of Anglo-American and Mexican-American children. JOURNAL OF CROSS-CULTURAL PSYCHOLOGY, Vol. 13, no. 2 (June 1982), p. 239-249. English. **DESCR:** Children; *Competition; Social Behavior Scale; Socialization.

403 Knight, George P., et al. Cooperative-competitive social orientation and school achievement among Anglo-American and Mexican-American children. CONTEMPORARY EDUCATIONAL PSYCHOLOGY, Vol. 7, no. 2 (April 1982), p. 97-106. English. **DESCR:** *Academic Achievement; Cultural Characteristics; Socialization; Students.

404 Knudsen, Kathryn H.M. and Kagan, Spencer. Differential development of empathy and pro-social behavior. JOURNAL OF GENETIC PSYCHOLOGY, Vol. 140, no. 2 (June 1982), p. 249-251. English. **DESCR:** *Attitude (Psychological); Child Study; Psychological Testing; Socialization.

405 Lawson, Harry H.; Kahn, Marrin W.; and Heiman, Elliott M. Psycho-pathology, treatment outcome and attitude toward mental illness in Mexican-American and European patients. INTERNATIONAL JOURNAL OF SOCIAL PSYCHIATRY, Vol. 28, no. 1 (Spring 1982), p. 20-26. English. **DESCR:** *Mental Illness; Psychotherapy.

406 Low, Benson P. and Clement, Paul W. Relationships of race and socioeconomic status to classroom behavior, academic achievement, and referral for special education. JOURNAL OF SCHOOL PSYCHOLOGY, Vol. 20, no. 2 (Summer 1982), p. 103-112. English. **DESCR:** *Academic Achievement; Blacks; Identity; Socioeconomic Factors.

407 Murguia, Edward and Cazares, Ralph B. Intermarriage of Mexican Americans. MARRIAGE & FAMILY REVIEW, Vol. 5, no. 1 (Spring 1982), p. 91-100. English. **DESCR:** Acculturation; *Intermarriage; Social Mobility.

408 Murray, James L.; Bruhn, John G.; and Bunce, Harvey. Assessment of type A behavior in preschoolers. JOURNAL OF HUMAN STRESS, Vol. 9, no. 3 (September 1983), p. 32-39. English. **DESCR:** Blacks; *Children; Early Childhood Education; Psychology.

409 Myres, Sandra Lynn. Mexican Americans and westering Anglos: a feminine perspective. NEW MEXICO HISTORICAL REVIEW, Vol. 57, no. 4 (October 1982), p. 317-333. English. **DESCR:** Chicanas; *Ethnic Attitudes; Social History and Conditions; Southwest United States; Stereotypes.

410 O'Donnell, James P., et al. Dimensions of behavior problems in Anglo-American and Mexican-American preschool children: a comparative study. JOURNAL OF CONSULTING AND CLINICAL PSYCHOLOGY, Vol. 50, no. 5 (October 1982), p. 643-651. English. **DESCR:** Children; *Comparative Psychology; Cultural Characteristics; Mental Health; Psychological Testing; Socioeconomic Factors.

411 Parra, Fernando and So, Alvin Yiu-cheong. Changing perceptions of mental illness in a Mexican-American community. JOURNAL OF SOCIAL PSYCHOLOGY, Vol. 29, (Summer 1983), p. 95-100. English. **DESCR:** Assimilation; *Los Angeles, CA; *Mental Health; Random Digit Dialling (RDD).

Anglo Americans (cont.)

412 Piersel, Wayne C., et al. Bias in content
validity on the Boehm test of basic concepts
for white and Mexican-American children.
CONTEMPORARY EDUCATIONAL PSYCHOLOGY, Vol. 7,
no. 2 (April 1982), p. 181-189. English.
DESCR: *Boehm Test of Basic Concepts;
Children; *Educational Tests and
Measurements; Language Arts.

413 Plake, Barbara S., et al. Relationship of
ethnic group membership to the measurement
and meaning of attitudes towards reading:
implications for validity of test score
interpretations. EDUCATIONAL AND
PSYCHOLOGICAL MEASUREMENT, Vol. 42, no. 4
(Winter 1982), p. 1259-1267. English.
DESCR: Attitude (Psychological); Educational
Tests and Measurements; Estes Reading
Attitude Scale; Ethnic Groups; *Reading;
Students.

414 Reisberg, Barry and Vasquez, Richard.
Stereotypes of Mexican descent persons:
attitudes of three generations of Mexican
American and Anglo-American adolescents.
JOURNAL OF CROSS-CULTURAL PSYCHOLOGY, Vol.
13, no. 1 (March 1982), p. 59-70. English.
DESCR: Age Groups; *Stereotypes.

415 Relethfold, John H., et al. Social class,
admixture, and skin color variation in
Mexican-Americans and Anglo-Americans living
in San Antonio, Texas. AMERICAN JOURNAL OF
PHYSICAL ANTHROPOLOGY, Vol. 61, no. 1 (May
1983), p. 97-102. English. **DESCR:**
Population; San Antonio, TX; *Skin Color.

416 Rueda, Robert. Interpersonal tactics and
communicative strategies of Anglo-American
and Mexican American mildly mentally
retarded and nonretarded students. APPLIED
RESEARCH IN MENTAL RETARDATION, Vol. 4, no.
2 (1983), p. 153-161. English. **DESCR:**
Children; Intelligence Tests; *Mentally
Handicapped; Test of Social Problem Solving.

417 Sattler, Jerome M. and Gwynne, John.
Ethnicity and Bender Visual Motor Gestalt
Test performance. JOURNAL OF SCHOOL
PSYCHOLOGY, Vol. 20, no. 1 (Spring 1982), p.
69-71. English. **DESCR:** *Bender Visual Motor
Gestalt Test; Psychological Testing; System
of Multicultural Pluralistic Assessment
(SOMPA).

418 Schon, Isabel. Effects of special curricular
study of Mexican culture on Anglo and
Mexican-American students perceptions of
Mexican-Americans. JOURNAL OF EXPERIMENTAL
EDUCATION, Vol. 50, no. 4 (Summer 1982), p.
215-218. English. **DESCR:** Perceptions of
Mexican Americans Scale (PMAS); Primary
School Education; *Stereotypes.

419 Scott, Leigh S., et al. Adaptive behavior
inventory for children: the need for local
norms. JOURNAL OF SCHOOL PSYCHOLOGY, Vol.
20, no. 1 (Spring 1982), p. 39-44. English.
DESCR: *Adaptive Behavior Inventory for
Children (ABIC); Blacks; Corpus Christi
Independent School District; Corpus Christi,
TX; Placement; System of Multicultural
Pluralistic Assessment (SOMPA).

420 Smith, Jack C. Trends in the incidence of
breastfeeding for Hispanics of Mexican
origin and Anglos on the US-Mexican border.
AMERICAN JOURNAL OF PUBLIC HEALTH, Vol. 72,
no. 1 (January 1982), p. 59-61. English.
DESCR: Breastfeeding; Chicanas; *Maternal
and Child Welfare.

421 Stern, Michael P. Knowledge, attitudes, and
behavior related to obesity and dieting in
Mexican-Americans and Anglos: the San
Antonio heart study. AMERICAN JOURNAL OF
EPIDEMIOLOGY, Vol. 115, no. 6 (June 1982),
p. 917-928. English. **DESCR:** Attitude
(Psychological); *Food Practices; Obesity;
San Antonio, TX; Weight Control.

422 Tienda, Marta and Angel, Ronald. Headship
and household composition among blacks,
Hispanics and other whites. SOCIAL FORCES,
Vol. 61, no. 2 (December 1982), p. 508-531.
English. **DESCR:** Blacks; Cultural
Characteristics; Extended Family; *Family;
Puerto Ricans; Single Parents.

423 Triandis, H.C., et al. Stereotyping among
Hispanics and Anglos: the uniformity,
intensity, direction and quality of auto-
and heterosterotypes. JOURNAL OF
CROSS-CULTURAL PSYCHOLOGY, Vol. 13, no. 4
(December 1982), p. 409-426. English.
DESCR: Blacks; *Stereotypes.

424 Trotter, Robert T. Ethnic and sexual
patterns of alcohol use: Anglo and Mexican
American college students. ADOLESCENCE, Vol.
17, no. 66 (Summer 1982), p. 305-325.
English. **DESCR:** *Alcoholism; Chicanas;
Cultural Characteristics; Ethnic Groups; Sex
Roles; Youth.

425 Vernon, Sally W. and Roberts, Robert E.
Prevalence of treated and untreated
psychiatric disorders in three ethnic
groups. SOCIAL SCIENCE AND MEDICINE, Vol.
16, no. 17 (1982), p. 1575-1582. English.
DESCR: Blacks; Comparative Psychology;
Mental Illness; *Psychiatry.

426 Warren, Charles W.; Smith, Jack C.; and
Rochat, Roger W. Differentials in the
planning status of the most recent live
birth to Mexican Americans and Anglos.
PUBLIC HEALTH REPORTS, Vol. 98, no. 2
(March, April, 1983), p. 152-160. English.
DESCR: *Family Planning.

427 Wheaton, Blair. A comparison of the
moderating effects of personal coping
resources in the impact of exposure to
stress in two groups. JOURNAL OF COMMUNITY
PSYCHOLOGY, Vol. 10, no. 4 (October 1982),
p. 293-311. English. **DESCR:** Comparative
Psychology; Cultural Characteristics; Mental
Health; Social Psychology; *Stress.

428 Willig, Ann C. Sociocultural and educational
correlates of success-failure attributions
and evaluation anxiety in the school setting
for Black, Hispanic, and Anglo children.
AMERICAN EDUCATIONAL RESEARCH JOURNAL, Vol.
20, no. 3 (Fall 1983), p. 385-410. English.
DESCR: Academic Achievement; *Academic
Motivation; Blacks; Cultural
Characteristics.

429 Wurzman, Ilyana. Cultural values of Puerto
Rican opiate addicts: an exploratory study.
AMERICAN JOURNAL OF DRUG AND ALCOHOL ABUSE,
Vol. 9, no. 2 (1982, 1983), p. 141-153.
English. **DESCR:** Acculturation; Blacks; *Drug
Abuse; Drug Addicts; Family; Loevinger's
Sentence Completion Test; Machismo; New
York, NY; Opium; Puerto Ricans; Values.

Anglo Americans (cont.)

430 Zavaleta, Anthony N. and Malina, Robert M. Growth and body composition of Mexican-American boys 9 through 14 years of age. AMERICAN JOURNAL OF PHYSICAL ANTHROPOLOGY, Vol. 57, no. 3 (March 1982), p. 261-271. English. **DESCR:** Age Groups; *Anthropometry; Children; Socioeconomic Factors.

431 Zeff, Shirley B. A cross-cultural study of Mexican American, Black American and white American women of a large urban university. HISPANIC JOURNAL OF BEHAVIORAL SCIENCES, Vol. 4, no. 2 (June 1982), p. 245-261. English. **DESCR:** Blacks; *Chicanas; Higher Education; Sex Roles.

Anguiano, Lupe

432 People. HISPANIC BUSINESS, Vol. 5, no. 3 (March 1983), p. 9. English. **DESCR:** Anaya, Toney; Appointed Officials; Avila, Joaquin Guadalupe; Awards; *Biographical Notes; de la Fuente, Emilio; del Olmo, Frank; Godoy, Gustavo; Long, Dennis P.; Martinez, Elias (Lee); Rivera, Joseph, Jr.

Anheuser-Busch, Inc.

433 Business notes. HISPANIC BUSINESS, Vol. 5, no. 12 (December 1983), p. 35. English. **DESCR:** *Business Enterprises; Denny's Inc.; Des Moines, IA; El Pollo Loco; Food Industry; Local Government; Martinez, Vilma Socorro; National Association of Latino Elected Officials (NALEO); Ochoa, Juan Pancho.

434 Chavarria, Jesus. Varieties of marketing strategies: the PUSH/Anheuser-Bush scrap. HISPANIC BUSINESS, Vol. 4, no. 12 (December 1982), p. 6,35. English. **DESCR:** Corporations; *Marketing; Operation PUSH; People United to Serve Humanity (PUSH).

435 Communications/marketing. HISPANIC BUSINESS, Vol. 4, no. 5 (May 1982), p. 15. English. **DESCR:** Farres, Osvaldo; Girl Scouts of the United States of America; *Marketing; Organizations; Television; Vocational Education; Voter Turnout.

436 Communications/marketing. HISPANIC BUSINESS, Vol. 5, no. 5 (May 1983), p. 24. English. **DESCR:** Arbitron; Awards; California Chicano News Media Association (CCNMA); Coca-Cola Company; Elizalde, Hector; *Marketing; Television.

437 Elizalde, Hector. How Anheuser-Busch promotions benefit the Hispanic community. CAMINOS, Vol. 4, no. 4 (April 1983), p. 51-53. Bilingual. **DESCR:** Private Funding Sources.

438 U.S. firm seeks entry to Mexican beer market. NUESTRO, Vol. 7, no. 1 (January, February, 1983), p. 36. English. **DESCR:** *Marketing; Mexico.

ANO NUEVO [film]

439 Entertainment = diversion. CAMINOS, Vol. 3, no. 1 (January 1982), p. 41-42. Bilingual. **DESCR:** Broadcast Media; *CERVANTES [film]; *Films; *SEGUIN [movie]; *Times Mirror Company.

440 Rogg, Eleanor Meyer. Film review of: ANO NUEVO. MIGRATION TODAY, Vol. 10, no. 5 (1982), p. 36. English. **DESCR:** Darling, Todd; Film Reviews; Films; Undocumented Workers.

Anselmo, Rene

441 Bagamery, Anne. SIN, the original. FORBES, Vol. 13, no. 11 (November 22, 1982), p. 96-97. English. **DESCR:** Broadcast Media; *Spanish International Network (SIN); Spanish Language; Television.

442 Chavarria, Jesus. How long will it last? HISPANIC BUSINESS, Vol. 4, no. 1 (January 1982), p. 6. English. **DESCR:** Businesspeople; Lasa, Luis; *Marketing; Spanish International Network (SIN).

443 Chavez, Lydia. The fourth network's chief executive. HISPANIC BUSINESS, Vol. 4, no. 1 (January 1982), p. 16-18. English. **DESCR:** Advertising; *Biography; Cable Television; Marketing; Spanish International Network (SIN).

Anthony, TX

444 Aptekar, Lewis. Mexican-American high school students' perception of school. ADOLESCENCE, Vol. 18, no. 70 (Summer 1983), p. 345-357. English. **DESCR:** *Attitude (Psychological); Canutillo, TX; High School Students; Texas.

Anthropology

445 Costello, J. G. Ethnoarchaeology at an Hispanic brick and tile kiln. AMERICAN JOURNAL OF ARCHAEOLOGY, Vol. 86, no. 2 (April 1982), p. 260. English. **DESCR:** *Brickmaking.

446 Ezell, P. Research on Spanish colonial sites in San Diego. AMERICAN JOURNAL OF ARCHAEOLOGY, Vol. 86, no. 2 (April 1982), p. 263. English. **DESCR:** Fort Guijanos; San Diego, CA; San Diego Mission.

447 New York's exhibition of Aztec treasures. NUESTRO, Vol. 6, no. 5 (June, July, 1982), p. 63-64. English. **DESCR:** *Aztecs; Exhibits; New York, NY.

448 Paull, Gene J. and Zavaleta, Anthony N. Archaeology and ethnohistory of the Boscaje de Palmas. BORDERLANDS JOURNAL, Vol. 6, no. 2 (Spring 1983), p. 111-150. English. **DESCR:** Texas.

449 U.S. returns stolen artifacts. NUESTRO, Vol. 6, no. 7 (September 1982), p. 10. English. **DESCR:** *Peru.

Anthropometry

450 Meredith, Howard V. Compilation and comparison of averages for standing height at late childhood ages on United States boys of several ethnic groups studied between 1875 and 1980. AMERICAN JOURNAL OF PHYSICAL ANTHROPOLOGY, Vol. 61, no. 1 (May 1983), p. 111-124. English. **DESCR:** Ethnic Groups; Socioeconomic Factors.

451 Zavaleta, Anthony N. and Malina, Robert M. Growth and body composition of Mexican-American boys 9 through 14 years of age. AMERICAN JOURNAL OF PHYSICAL ANTHROPOLOGY, Vol. 57, no. 3 (March 1982), p. 261-271. English. **DESCR:** Age Groups; Anglo Americans; Children; Socioeconomic Factors.

CHICANO PERIODICAL INDEX - SUBJECTS

Anti-Defamation League of B'nai B'rith

452 Que pasa? NUESTRO, Vol. 7, no. 7 (September 1983), p. 9. English. **DESCR:** Alcoholism; *Drug Abuse; Drug Programs; Employment; Kiwanis International; Miller Brewing Company; Racism; Sports.

ANTONIO AND THE MAYOR

453 Armas, Jose. ANTONIO AND THE MAYOR: a cultural review of the film. JOURNAL OF ETHNIC STUDIES, Vol. 3, no. 3 (Fall 1975), p. 98-101. English. **DESCR:** Broadcast Media; Columbia Broadcasting Studios (CBS); Cultural Characteristics; Film Reviews; Films; Mass Media; *Stereotypes.

Apopka, FL

454 King, Karen. Hope comes to Apopka: on working alongside the poor. THE OTHER SIDE, Vol. 18, (May 1982), p. 23-25. English. **DESCR:** Clergy; Migrant Health Services; *Migrant Labor; Office of Migrant Ministry (OMM).

Appointed Officials

455 Hispanics receive appointments. LATINO, Vol. 53, no. 1 (January, February, 1982), p. 20. English. **DESCR:** *Herrera, Maria Elena; *Naranjo, Antonio.

456 Katherine Davalos Ortega. LATINO, Vol. 54, no. 7 (November 1983), p. 8-9. English. **DESCR:** *Ortega, Katherine D.

457 Langley, Roger. Roger Langley's Hispanic beat. HISPANIC BUSINESS, Vol. 4, no. 3 (March 1982), p. 22. English. **DESCR:** Bell, William M.; Equal Employment Opportunity Commission (EEOC).

458 League protests appointment to Arizona post. LATINO, Vol. 54, no. 6 (October 1983), p. 21. English. **DESCR:** League of United Latin American Citizens (LULAC); Politics.

459 Museum official plans outreach to Latinos. NUESTRO, Vol. 6, no. 4 (May 1982), p. 27-28. English. **DESCR:** Bilingual Bicultural Education; *Metropolitan Museum of Art.

460 News at SBA: Cardenas removed as SBA chief. HISPANIC BUSINESS, Vol. 4, no. 4 (April 1982), p. 11. English. **DESCR:** *Cardenas, Michael; U.S. Small Business Administration.

461 Newsfront. HISPANIC BUSINESS, Vol. 4, no. 3 (March 1982), p. 9. English. **DESCR:** *Biographical Notes; Businesspeople; Chicano Film Exhibition and Festival, Detroit, Michigan, April 5-9, 1982; Garcia, Gloria; League of United Latin American Citizens (LULAC); Martinez, Vilma Socorro; National Association for Bilingual Education; Seaga, Edward; Suarez, Carlos R.

462 People. HISPANIC BUSINESS, Vol. 4, no. 5 (May 1982), p. 8. English. **DESCR:** Asociacion Internacional de Exportadores e Importadores (EXIMA); *Biographical Notes; Businesspeople; California Chicano News Media Association (CCNMA); de la Ossa, Ernest G.; Foreign Trade; Obledo, Mario; Rodriguez, Elias C.; Rodriguez, Samuel F.; United Way; U.S. Hispanic Chamber of Commerce.

463 People. HISPANIC BUSINESS, Vol. 4, no. 9 (September 1982), p. 7. English. **DESCR:** Advertising Agencies; Awards; *Biographical Notes; Diaz-Albertini, Luis; Dimartino,

Rita; Garza, Jesus; Hispanic Women in Higher Education (HWHE); League of United Latin American Citizens (LULAC); Ortega, Ray; Ortiz, George; Romero, Carlos J.; Sepulveda, Luis.

464 People. HISPANIC BUSINESS, Vol. 5, no. 1 (January 1983), p. 7. English. **DESCR:** *Biographical Notes; *Businesspeople; Elizalde, Hector; Mackey y Salazar, C.; Madrid, Carlos; Montoya, Velma; Nunez, Carlos; Perea, Stanley; Rodriguez, Rita; Valdes, Martha.

465 People. HISPANIC BUSINESS, Vol. 5, no. 2 (February 1983), p. 7. English. **DESCR:** Alvarez, Everett, Jr.; *Biographical Notes; Businesspeople; Guzman-Randle, Irene; Roubin, Angel; Vasquez, Victor; Villareal, Luis Maria.

466 People. HISPANIC BUSINESS, Vol. 5, no. 3 (March 1983), p. 9. English. **DESCR:** Anaya, Toney; Anguiano, Lupe; Avila, Joaquin Guadalupe; Awards; *Biographical Notes; de la Fuente, Emilio; del Olmo, Frank; Godoy, Gustavo; Long, Dennis P.; Martinez, Elias (Lee); Rivera, Joseph, Jr.

467 People. HISPANIC BUSINESS, Vol. 5, no. 6 (June 1983), p. 8. English. **DESCR:** *Biographical Notes; Businesspeople; Goizueta, Roberto C.; Guerra, Stella; Huapaya, Sixto Guillermo; Kitano, Pat; Manriquez, Suzanna; Oppenheimer-Nicolau, Siabhan; Ortiz, Solomon; Pachon, Harry P.; Richardson, Bill Lopez; Torres, Esteban E.; Torres, Johnny.

468 People. HISPANIC BUSINESS, Vol. 5, no. 7 (July 1983), p. 8. English. **DESCR:** Alvarado, Anthony J.; *Biographical Notes; Businesspeople; Candela, Hilario; Garcia, Marlene; Gonzalez, Julio; Martinez, Tony; Pla, George; Valdez, Abelardo L.

469 President Reagan's appointments. CAMINOS, Vol. 3, no. 3 (March 1982), p. 48-50. Bilingual. **DESCR:** *Federal Government; Flores Buckhart, Elizabeth; Garcia, Ernest E.; Gonzalez, Luis A.; Lozano, Diana; Pompa, Gilbert G.; Reagan, Ronald; Sanchez, Nestor D.; Zuniga, Henry.

470 Reagan, Ronald. Remarks at a White House briefing for Hispanic appointees and members of the Hispanic community (July 20, 1982). PUBLIC PAPERS OF THE PRESIDENT, Vol. 1, no. 2 (1982), p. 945-947. English.

471 Reagan's new appointee to Civil Rights Commission. NUESTRO, Vol. 6, no. 5 (June, July, 1982), p. 29-30. English. **DESCR:** *Quintanilla, Guadalupe; U.S. Commission on Civil Rights.

472 Second Latino assumes new duties at EEOC. NUESTRO, Vol. 6, no. 4 (May 1982), p. 27. English. **DESCR:** Equal Employment Opportunity Commission (EEOC); *Gallegos, Tony E.

473 Two important California appointments. HISPANIC BUSINESS, Vol. 4, no. 4 (April 1982), p. 23. English. **DESCR:** Becerra, Gloria V.; *Patino, Douglas X.

474 Virginian to head U.S.D.A. minority affairs office. NUESTRO, Vol. 6, no. 6 (August 1982), p. 34. English. **DESCR:** *Rodriguez, Isidoro.

25

Appointed Officials (cont.)

475 Woman chosen by Brown to head tax agency.
NUESTRO, Vol. 6, no. 4 (May 1982), p. 27.
English. **DESCR:** *Becerra, Gloria V.;
Taxation.

Apportionment
USE: Reapportionment

Apprenticeship
USE: Employment Training

THE AQUARIAN CONSPIRACY

476 Ferrarone, Aida. The aquarium conspiracy:
personal and social transformation in the
80's: a review. LATINA, Vol. 1, no. 2
(February, March, 1983), p. 23. English.
DESCR: Book Reviews; Ferguson, Marilyn.

Aragon, Fermin

477 People. HISPANIC BUSINESS, Vol. 5, no. 11
(November 1983), p. 10. English. **DESCR:**
*Businesspeople; De Los Reyes, Victor; Di
Martino, Rita; Garcia, Ruben; Juarez, Chris;
Lopez, Leonard; Nogales, Luis G.; Ozuna,
Bob; Rico, Jose Hipolito; Tamayo, Roberto;
Tapia, Raul R.

Aragon, Floyd

478 Caldera, Carmela. Floyd Aragon: filling
voids with his entrepreneurship. CAMINOS,
Vol. 4, no. 4 (April 1983), p. 28-30, 66.
Bilingual. **DESCR:** Business Enterprises; L.A.
Button Company; Olympics.

Arbitron

479 Communications/marketing. HISPANIC BUSINESS,
Vol. 5, no. 5 (May 1983), p. 24. English.
DESCR: Anheuser-Busch, Inc.; Awards;
California Chicano News Media Association
(CCNMA); Coca-Cola Company; Elizalde,
Hector; *Marketing; Television.

480 Wittenauer, Cheryl. Rating Hispanic media.
HISPANIC BUSINESS, Vol. 5, no. 3 (March
1983), p. 14-15. English. **DESCR:** A.C.
Nielsen Company; Advertising; *Broadcast
Media; Television.

Arce, Manuel

481 Fernandez, Enrique. Cannes and CROSSOVER
DREAMS, '83. FILM COMMENT, Vol. 19, no. 4-7
(August 1983), p. 2-7. English. **DESCR:**
Blades, Ruben; Cannes Film Festival;
*CROSSOVER DREAMS; Film Reviews; Films;
Salsa.

Archaeology
USE: Anthropology

Architecture

482 Fletcher and Valenti: Tampa's growing
arquitectural firm. HISPANIC BUSINESS, Vol.
4, no. 10 (October 1982), p. 15,26. English.
DESCR: Business Enterprises; Fletcher &
Valenti Architects/Planners, Inc.; Tampa,
FL; Valenti, Frank S.

483 Sargeant, Georgia. Young turks set new
standards. HISPANIC BUSINESS, Vol. 5, no. 11
(November 1983), p. 8-9. English. **DESCR:**
Alvarez, Julio E.; Business Enterprises;
Management; Marketing; Miami, FL; Taracido,
Manuel E.; Wolfberg, David A.;
*Wolfberg/Alvarez/Taracido (WAT).

484 Snethcamp, P. E. Reflections of the past -

public restoration and interpretation of
Hispanic sites. AMERICAN JOURNAL OF
ARCHAEOLOGY, Vol. 86, no. 2 (April 1982), p.
286. English. **DESCR:** *Public Restoration.

485 Volsky, George. Hilario Candela: designing
for Florida's future. HISPANIC BUSINESS,
Vol. 5, no. 11 (November 1983), p. 20-22.
English. **DESCR:** *Candela, Hilario; Miami,
FL; Spillis Candela & Partners; Urban
Development.

Archives

486 Richmond, Douglas W. Researching the Mexican
revolution: sources and suggestions.
BORDERLANDS JOURNAL, Vol. 6, no. 1 (Fall
1982), p. 85-91. English. **DESCR:** *Mexican
Revolution - 1910-1920.

Arco Iris [musical group]

487 Arco iris. CAMINOS, Vol. 3, no. 8 (September
1982), p. 19. English. **DESCR:** Musicians.

Arellano, Richard

488 People. HISPANIC BUSINESS, Vol. 4, no. 6
(June 1982), p. 8. English. **DESCR:** Aguirre,
Pedro; *Biographical Notes; Businesspeople;
Cortez, Pete; De la Colina, Rafael;
Hernandez, Sam; Nogales, Luis; Rodriguez,
Leslie J.; Roybal, Edward R.

Arenas, Reynaldo

489 Greenfield, Charles. Life imitating art: a
profile of Reynaldo Arenas. NUESTRO, Vol. 7,
no. 5 (June, July, 1983), p. 40-42. English.
DESCR: *Authors; *Cuba; *Cubanos; El Morro
Prison, Cuba; Political Prisoners.

Arens & Gutierrez

490 Communications/marketing. HISPANIC BUSINESS,
Vol. 5, no. 10 (October 1983), p. 26.
English. **DESCR:** Advertising; Employment;
Henry Molina, Inc.; Journals; Lionetti and
Meyers Research Center, Inc.; Marketing;
*Mass Media; Midwest Hispanics in
Telecommunications Symposium, Chicago, IL;
NEW MANAGEMENT.

Arens, W.

491 Belton, Robert T. Book review of: CANNIBALS
AND KINGS: THE ORIGINS OF CULTURE and THE
MAN-EATING MYTH: ANTHROPOLOGY AND
ANTHROPOPHAGY. HISPANIC JOURNAL OF
BEHAVIORAL SCIENCES, Vol. 4, no. 1 (March
1982), p. 129-134. English. **DESCR:** Book
Reviews; *CANNIBALS AND KINGS: THE ORIGINS
OF CULTURE; Harris, Marvin; *THE MAN-EATING
MYTH: ANTHROPOLOGY AND ANTHROPOPHAGY.

Argentina

492 Business/negocios. CAMINOS, Vol. 3, no. 2
(February 1982), p. 22-23. Bilingual.
DESCR: Brazil; *Business; Chile; Colombia;
Federation of Minority Business
Associations; FRANCHISE OPPORTUNITIES
HANDBOOK; Latin America.

493 Obejas, Achy. Argentina: back to Europe
where it belongs. NUESTRO, Vol. 6, no. 8
(October 1982), p. 51. English. **DESCR:**
Geography; Short Story.

Argentina (cont.)

494 Schon, Isabel. Recent outstanding books for young readers from Spanish speaking countries. READING TEACHER, Vol. 36, no. 2 (November 1982), p. 206-209. English. **DESCR:** *Children's Literature; Literature Reviews; Spain; Spanish Language; Venezuela.

495 Schon, Isabel. Spanish books for children. BOOKLIST, Vol. 78, no. 20 (June 15, 1982), p. 1373-1374. English. **DESCR:** *Bibliography; *Children's Literature; Mexico; Spain; Spanish Language; Venezuela.

Arias, Beatriz

496 Academic furlough for the working professional. HISPANIC BUSINESS, Vol. 4, no. 8 (August 1983), p. 15. English. **DESCR:** Financial Aid; Funding Sources; Kellogg, W.K.; *W.K. Kellogg Foundation.

497 A time for reflection. NUESTRO, Vol. 7, no. 9 (November 1983), p. 42-44. English. **DESCR:** Anaya, Rudolfo A.; Bilingual Bicultural Education; Computers; Financial Aid; Folklore; Organizations; Prewitt Diaz, Joseph (Jose); Villarreal, Sylvia; *W.K. Kellogg Foundation National Fellowship Program.

Arias, Ron

498 Arias, Ron. The rooster that called me home. NATION, Vol. 236, no. 24 (June 18, 1983), p. 758-761. English. **DESCR:** Essays; *Undocumented Workers.

499 Bruce Novoa, Juan and Arias, Ron. Interview with Ron Arias. JOURNAL OF ETHNIC STUDIES, Vol. 3, no. 4 (Winter 1976), p. 70-73. English. **DESCR:** Authors; Literary Influence; *Literature.

500 Lattin, Vernon E. La meta critica Chicana. REVISTA CHICANO-RIQUENA, Vol. 10, no. 3 (Summer 1982), p. 53-62. English. **DESCR:** Death (Concept); Literary Criticism; *THE ROAD TO TAMAZUNCHALE.

Arias v. Rogers

501 Ashman, Allan. What's new in the law: immigration ... detained aliens. AMERICAN BAR ASSOCIATION JOURNAL, Vol. 68, (June 1982), p. 745. English. **DESCR:** Deportation; Immigration Law; *Undocumented Workers.

Aristotle

502 Garcia, Reyes. Politics of flesh: ethnicity and political viability. CACR REVIEW, Vol. 1, no. 1 (September 1982), p. 102-130. English. **DESCR:** Anaya, Rudolfo A.; Culture; Ethnic Groups; Identity; Locke, John; Nuclear Armament; Philosophy; *Political Repression; Urban Communities.

Arizona

503 Arizona conference. HISPANIC BUSINESS, Vol. 4, no. 3 (March 1982), p. 22. English. **DESCR:** *Affirmative Action; Arizona Affirmative Action Association.

504 Barry, Tom. On strike! Undocumented workers in Arizona. SOUTHWEST ECONOMY AND SOCIETY, Vol. 3, no. 3 (Spring 1978), p. 52-60. English. **DESCR:** Agribusiness; Agricultural Laborers; *Goldmar Citrus Ranch, Phoenix, AZ; Labor Organizing; *Maricopa County Organizing Project (MCOP); Phoenix, AZ; *Strikes and Lockouts; Undocumented Workers.

505 Brasch, Walter M. Hanigan case: hung up on racism? SOUTH ATLANTIC QUARTERLY, Vol. 81, no. 4 (Fall 1982), p. 429-435. English. **DESCR:** Administration of Justice; Criminal Justice System; Garcia-Loya, Manuel; *Hanigan, Patrick; Hanigan, Tom; Herrera-Mata, Bernabe; *Laws; Racism; Ruelas-Zavala, Eleazar; Undocumented Workers.

506 Byrkit, James W. Walter Douglas and labor struggles in early 20th century Arizona. SOUTHWEST ECONOMY AND SOCIETY, Vol. 1, no. 1 (Spring 1976), p. 14-27. English. **DESCR:** *Biography; Bisbee, AZ; Clifton Morenci Strike, June 1903; Copper Queen Mining Co., Bisbee, AZ; *Douglas, Walter; International Workers of the World (IWW); Labor Unions; Mining Industry; Strikes and Lockouts.

507 Casillas, Mike. The Cananea strike of 1906. SOUTHWEST ECONOMY AND SOCIETY, Vol. 3, no. 2 (Winter 1977, 1978), p. 18-32. English. **DESCR:** *Cananea Mining Strike of 1906; Cananea, Sonora, Mexico; History; Mining Industry; Partido Liberal Mexicano (PLM); *Strikes and Lockouts.

508 Fernandez, Celestino and Holscher, Louis M. Chicano-Anglo intermarriage in Arizona, 1960-1980: an exploratory study of eight counties. HISPANIC JOURNAL OF BEHAVIORAL SCIENCES, Vol. 5, no. 3 (September 1983), p. 291-304. English. **DESCR:** *Intermarriage.

509 Henderson, Ronald W. and Brody, Gene H. Effects of ethnicity and child's age on maternal judgments of children's transgressions against persons and property. JOURNAL OF GENETIC PSYCHOLOGY, Vol. 140, no. 2 (June 1982), p. 253-263. English. **DESCR:** Anglo Americans; Behavior Modification; *Child Rearing; Cultural Characteristics; Native Americans; *Socialization; Tucson, AZ.

510 Jensen, Gary F.; White, C. S.; and Galliher, James M. Ethnic status and adolescent self-evaluations: an extension of research on minority self-esteem. SOCIAL PROBLEMS, Vol. 30, no. 2 (December 1982), p. 226-239. English. **DESCR:** *Identity.

511 Mendez, Jose A. and Esquer, Cecilia D. The impact of undocumented aliens on health and public health care in Arizona. ARIZONA BUSINESS, Vol. 30, no. 3 (1983), p. 3-7. English. **DESCR:** *Arizona Health Care Cost Containment System (AHCCCS); Government Funding Sources; *Public Health; Public Policy; Undocumented Workers.

512 Powers, Stephen and Sanchez, Virginia V. Correlates of self-esteem of Mexican American adolescents. PSYCHOLOGICAL REPORTS, Vol. 51, no. 3 (December 1982), p. 771-774. English. **DESCR:** Academic Achievement; Employment; *Identity; Junior High School Students; Nogales, AZ.

513 Sun Belt dominates in top housing markets. NUESTRO, Vol. 7, no. 1 (January, February, 1983), p. 36. English. **DESCR:** *Housing; Texas.

Arizona Affirmative Action Association

514 Arizona conference. HISPANIC BUSINESS, Vol. 4, no. 3 (March 1982), p. 22. English. **DESCR:** *Affirmative Action; Arizona.

Arizona Farm Workers (AFW)

515 Howell, Frances Baseden. Split labor market:
Mexican farm workers in the Southwest.
SOCIOLOGICAL INQUIRY, Vol. 52, no. 2 (Spring
1982), p. 132-140. English. DESCR:
Agricultural Labor Unions; *Labor Supply and
Market; Southwest United States;
Undocumented Workers; United Farmworkers of
America (UFW).

Arizona Health Care Cost Containment System (AHCCCS)

516 Mendez, Jose A. and Esquer, Cecilia D. The
impact of undocumented aliens on health and
public health care in Arizona. ARIZONA
BUSINESS, Vol. 30, no. 3 (1983), p. 3-7.
English. DESCR: Arizona; Government Funding
Sources; *Public Health; Public Policy;
Undocumented Workers.

Arkansas

517 Farmworkers win Arkansas contract. SOUTHERN
EXPOSURE, Vol. 10, no. 5 (September,
October, 1982), p. 4. English. DESCR:
Agricultural Laborers; *Arkansas Farmworker
Civil Rights Organizing Project (AFCROP);
Labor Disputes; Undocumented Workers.

Arkansas Farmworker Civil Rights Organizing Project (AFCROP)

518 Farmworkers win Arkansas contract. SOUTHERN
EXPOSURE, Vol. 10, no. 5 (September,
October, 1982), p. 4. English. DESCR:
Agricultural Laborers; Arkansas; Labor
Disputes; Undocumented Workers.

Arras, Raymundo

519 Padilla, Steve. Three-day siege. NUESTRO,
Vol. 6, no. 8 (October 1982), p. 19-21.
English. DESCR: Criminal Acts; Federal
Bureau of Investigation (FBI).

520 Padilla, Steve. Working for the F.B.I.
NUESTRO, Vol. 6, no. 8 (October 1982), p.
15-17. English. DESCR: *Federal Bureau of
Investigation (FBI); Latin Americans;
Marquez, Manuel; Perez, Matthew.

Arredondo, Price

521 Communications/marketing. HISPANIC BUSINESS,
Vol. 4, no. 8 (August 1983), p. 22+.
English. DESCR: Baseball; De la O, Val;
Films; Marketing; *Mass Media; Radio; San
Antonio CineFestival, TX; Television; Val De
La O Show; Valenzuela, Fernando; Wright &
Arredondo Associates; Wright, Oscar.

Arreola, Rafael

522 People on the move. CAMINOS, Vol. 2, no. 6
(October 1981), p. 7. English. DESCR:
Alvarado, Angel S.; *Biographical Notes;
Diaz, Elisa; Diaz, Elvira A.; Garcia, Jose
Joel; Garza, Florentino; Icaza, Ricardo F.;
Lacayo, Henry; Martinez, Lydia R.; Munoz,
Victor M.; Salinas, Vicente; Sanchez,
Manuel; Zuniga, Henry.

Arriola, Elvia Rosales

523 People. HISPANIC BUSINESS, Vol. 5, no. 10
(October 1983), p. 10. English. DESCR:
Anaya, Toney; Babbitt, Bruce; Burgos, Tony;
Bush, George; *Businesspeople; Cisneros,
Henry, Mayor of San Antonio, TX; Cruz, Jose;
Kennedy, Edward M.; Montano, Gilbert;
Reagan, Ronald; White, Mark.

Arrivi, Francisco

524 Griffin, Julia Ortiz. Two artists in search
of a country: Rafael Rios Rey and Francisco
Arrivi. MINORITY VOICES, Vol. 5, no. 1-2
(Spring, Fall, 1981), p. 53-58. English.
DESCR: Artists; Puerto Rican Literature;
Puerto Ricans; *Rios Rey, Rafael; Teatro.

Arrondo, Ondina

525 Naismith, Rachael. Outreach services to
Hispanics. ILLINOIS LIBRARIES, Vol. 64, no.
7 (September 1982), p. 962-966. English.
DESCR: Cubanos; La Raza Hispanica, Miami,
FL; Latin American Library/Biblioteca
Latinoamericana, Oakland, CA; *Library
Services; Lopez, Lillian; Puerto Ricans;
Ruiz, Deborah; South Bronx Project, New York
Public Library; Verges, Bruni.

Arroyos, Alex

526 Chavarria, Jesus. The entrepreneurial
reflex. HISPANIC BUSINESS, Vol. 5, no. 1
(January 1983), p. 6. English. DESCR:
*Business Enterprises; Digitron Tool
Company, Inc.; Dynamic Ocean Service, Inc.;
Fernandez, Nestor.

527 Vara, Richard. Business savvy and Capricorn
spirit: How do you spell entrepreneurship?
HISPANIC BUSINESS, Vol. 5, no. 1 (January
1983), p. 18-19+. English. DESCR:
*Biography; Business Enterprises; Export
Trade; Houston, TX.

Art

528 Aguilar, George. Raul Rodriguez, parade
artist extraordinaire. NUESTRO, Vol. 6, no.
10 (December 1982), p. 11-14. English.
DESCR: *Artists; *Rodriguez, Raul.

529 Another graphic award for Francisco
Masseria. NUESTRO, Vol. 6, no. 7 (September
1982), p. 35. English. DESCR: Artists;
Masseria, Francisco.

530 Aparicio, Frances R. Figure in dream. THIRD
WOMAN, Vol. 1, no. 2 (1982), p. 83-86.
English. DESCR: *Rivera, Diana.

531 Bruce Novoa, Juan. Artistic perceptions of
Mexico City. NUESTRO, Vol. 6, no. 4 (May
1982), p. 53-54. English. DESCR: *Mexico
City.

532 Cine-festival. CAMINOS, Vol. 4, no. 9
(October 1983), p. 58. English. DESCR:
*Fiestas; *Films; San Antonio, TX.

533 City officials decide mural must be removed.
NUESTRO, Vol. 6, no. 7 (September 1982), p.
51. English. DESCR: *Hidalgo y Costilla,
Miguel; *Mural Art; San Antonio, TX.

534 Flores, Bettina and Flores, Alfredo. Benny
Barrios, Sacramento's living landmark.
NUESTRO, Vol. 6, no. 9 (November 1982), p.
57-58. English. DESCR: Artists; Barrios,
Benny; *Sacramento, CA.

535 Goldman, Shifra. Mexican muralism: its
social-educative roles in Latin America and
the United States. AZTLAN, Vol. 13, no. 1-2
(Spring, Fall, 1982), p. 111-133. Spanish.
DESCR: Latin America; *Mexico; *Mural Art;
Social History and Conditions.

Art (cont.)

536 Gonzalez, Alicia Maria. Murals: fine, popular, or folk art? AZTLAN, Vol. 13, no. 1-2 (Spring, Fall, 1982), p. 149-163. English. **DESCR:** Art History; Folk Art; *Mural Art.

537 El Greco of Toledo: his life and his art. NUESTRO, Vol. 6, no. 6 (August 1982), p. 24-27. English. **DESCR:** Art History; Artists; Biography; *El Greco.

538 Herrera, Hayden. The elephant and the dove. NUESTRO, Vol. 7, no. 8 (October 1983), p. 40-43. English. **DESCR:** Artists; Biography; *Kahlo, Frida; Paintings; Rivera, Diego.

539 Holscher, Louis M. Tiene arte valor afuera del barrio: the murals of East Los Angeles and Boyle Heights. JOURNAL OF ETHNIC STUDIES, Vol. 4, no. 3 (Fall 1976), p. 42-52. English. **DESCR:** Boyle Heights; Culture; *East Los Angeles, CA; *Mural Art.

540 Karam, Bruce G. The murals of Tucson. NUESTRO, Vol. 5, no. 8 (November 1981), p. 58-61. English. **DESCR:** Mural Art; *Tucson, AZ.

541 Morris, Gay. The Mexican Museum has a colorful new home. CAMINOS, Vol. 3, no. 7 (July, August, 1982), p. 30-33. Bilingual. **DESCR:** *Mexican Museum, San Francisco, CA; Museums; Rodriguez, Peter; San Francisco, CA.

542 A new dimension to an ancient craft. NUESTRO, Vol. 6, no. 3 (April 1982), p. 63-64. English. **DESCR:** *Parodi, Paquita.

543 New Salazar building. NUESTRO, Vol. 6, no. 7 (September 1982), p. 9. English. **DESCR:** Culture; Education; Latin Americans; Los Angeles, CA; *Plaza de La Raza, Los Angeles, CA; Salazar, Ruben.

544 Pre-Columbian art of Costa Rica. NUESTRO, Vol. 6, no. 8 (October 1982), p. 54-55. English. **DESCR:** *Art History; Costa Rica; Exhibits.

545 Promoting the world of Hispanic art. NUESTRO, Vol. 6, no. 6 (August 1982), p. 44-46. English. **DESCR:** Moreno Vega, Marta; *Museo del Barrio, New York, NY.

546 Rose, Barbara. Frida Kahlo: the Chicana as art heroine. VOGUE, Vol. 173, (April 1983), p. 152-154. English. **DESCR:** Artists; Biography; *Kahlo, Frida; Mexico; Rivera, Diego.

547 A salute to the arts. NUESTRO, Vol. 6, no. 7 (September 1982), p. 44-45. English. **DESCR:** Artists; Congressional Hispanic Caucus; National Hispanic Heritage Week; Villa, Eduardo.

548 Shiell, Pancho. Sebastian Castro Vallejo: artist on stage and on canvas. NUESTRO, Vol. 6, no. 7 (September 1982), p. 63-64. English. **DESCR:** Artists; *Castro Vallejo, Sebastian.

549 Soto, Rose Marie. Consuelo Santos-Killins: a leader in the arts. CAMINOS, Vol. 4, no. 6 (June 1983), p. 56-57,67. Bilingual. **DESCR:** California Arts Council (C.A.C.); Cultural Organizations; *Santos-Killins, Consuelo.

550 Villa, Esteban. [Untitled art work]. CALMECAC, Vol. 2, (Spring 1981), p. 6. Bilingual.

551 Ysla, Elizabeth. King of jelly bean art. NUESTRO, Vol. 6, no. 4 (May 1982), p. 50-52. English. **DESCR:** Art History; *Rocha, Peter.

Art Galleries

552 Mexican centers advance U.S. ties. NUESTRO, Vol. 7, no. 1 (January, February, 1983), p. 10-11. English. **DESCR:** *El Centro Mexicano del Libro; Los Angeles, CA; Mexico; Museums; New York, NY; Publishing Industry.

553 Mixografia workshop gallery director Elena Cielak on collecting art. CAMINOS, Vol. 3, no. 9 (October 1982), p. 10-11. Bilingual. **DESCR:** *Cielak, Elena.

Art History

554 Gonzalez, Alicia Maria. Murals: fine, popular, or folk art? AZTLAN, Vol. 13, no. 1-2 (Spring, Fall, 1982), p. 149-163. English. **DESCR:** Art; Folk Art; *Mural Art.

555 El Greco of Toledo: his life and his art. NUESTRO, Vol. 6, no. 6 (August 1982), p. 24-27. English. **DESCR:** Art; Artists; Biography; *El Greco.

556 Lenti, Paul. Accent: the Mexican retablo - a highly collectable folk art. NUESTRO, Vol. 7, no. 4 (May 1983), p. 63-64. English. **DESCR:** *Folk Art; *Mexico; *Religious Art.

557 Pre-Columbian art of Costa Rica. NUESTRO, Vol. 6, no. 8 (October 1982), p. 54-55. English. **DESCR:** Art; Costa Rica; Exhibits.

558 Ysla, Elizabeth. King of jelly bean art. NUESTRO, Vol. 6, no. 4 (May 1982), p. 50-52. English. **DESCR:** Art; *Rocha, Peter.

Artes Antigua Society

559 Benson, Nancy C. The art of colcha-stitch embroidery: an Hispanic heritage. NEW AMERICA: A REVIEW, Vol. 4, no. 3 (1982), p. 78-81. English. **DESCR:** *Embroidery; Lujan, Maria Theofila.

Artists

560 Aguilar, George. Raul Rodriguez, parade artist extraordinaire. NUESTRO, Vol. 6, no. 10 (December 1982), p. 11-14. English. **DESCR:** *Art; *Rodriguez, Raul.

561 Ana Alicia. LATINO, Vol. 54, no. 7 (November 1983), p. 6-7+. English. **DESCR:** *Alicia, Ana.

562 Another graphic award for Francisco Masseria. NUESTRO, Vol. 6, no. 7 (September 1982), p. 35. English. **DESCR:** *Art; Masseria, Francisco.

563 Asco 83. CAMINOS, Vol. 4, no. 9 (October 1983), p. 36. English. **DESCR:** *Teatro.

564 Book review of: FRIDA: A BIOGRAPHY OF FRIDA KAHLO. BOOKLIST, Vol. 79, no. 11 (February 1, 1983), p. 708. English. **DESCR:** Biography; Book Reviews; *FRIDA: A BIOGRAPHY OF FRIDA KAHLO; Herrera, Hayden; Kahlo, Frida.

565 Breiter, Toni. Eddie Olmos and THE BALLAD OF GREGORIO CORTEZ. NUESTRO, Vol. 7, no. 4 (May 1983), p. 14-19. English. **DESCR:** *BALLAD OF GREGORIO CORTEZ [film]; Corrido; Film Reviews; *Olmos, Edward James; Prejudice (Social).

Artists (cont.)

566 Caldera, Carmela and Martinez, Alma. Alma Martinez: "I'm keeping my fingers crossed" (interview). CAMINOS, Vol. 4, no. 11 (December 1983), p. 32-35. English. **DESCR:** Films; *Martinez, Alma; Teatro.

567 Caldera, Carmela. Luis Avalos - he has it all - talent, wit, and a TV show of his own (interview). CAMINOS, Vol. 4, no. 5 (May 1983), p. 36-38. English. **DESCR:** *Avalos, Luis; Television.

568 Caldera, Carmela and De Soto, Rosana. Rosana de Soto: breaking the mold (interview). CAMINOS, Vol. 4, no. 8 (September 1983), p. 36-39. English. **DESCR:** *De Soto, Rosana; Films.

569 Campbell, Stephanie. The artist in bourgeois society, as seen in Carpentier's LA CONSAGRACION DE LA PRIMAVERA. MAIZE, Vol. 3, no. 3-4 (Spring, Summer, 1980), p. 6-16. English. **DESCR:** Carpentier, Alejo; *LA CONSAGRACION DE LA PRIMAVERA; Literary Criticism.

570 Carmen Zapata and the B.F.A. CAMINOS, Vol. 3, no. 4 (April 1982), p. 38-40. Bilingual. **DESCR:** Bilingual Foundation of the Arts; Teatro; *Zapata, Carmen.

571 Chaplik, Dorothy. Art currents from Mexico. CAMINOS, Vol. 4, no. 5 (May 1983), p. 21-25,52. English. **DESCR:** *Mexico.

572 Commercial art as a career. CAMINOS, Vol. 4, no. 9 (October 1983), p. 32-35. English. **DESCR:** *Careers; Chavez Lichwardt, Leticia; Gomez, Dario; Guerrero, Ernest R.; Melendez, Bill; Reyes, Gil; Santistevan, August.

573 Costa Rica hosts craftsmen of the Americas. NUESTRO, Vol. 6, no. 6 (August 1982), p. 63-64. English. **DESCR:** Arts and Crafts; Conventions; *Costa Rica; *Cultural Characteristics; Cultural Customs.

574 Diaz, Barbara M. The great Valentino. CAMINOS, Vol. 3, no. 9 (October 1982), p. 22-23,44. Bilingual. **DESCR:** *Valentino.

575 Diaz, Katherine A. Francisco Zuniga; el pueblo Mexicano su inspiracion. CAMINOS, Vol. 4, no. 1-2 (January, February, 1983), p. 34-38. Bilingual. **DESCR:** Mexico; *Zuniga, Francisco.

576 Diaz, Katherine A. Jose Feliciano. CAMINOS, Vol. 3, no. 8 (September 1982), p. 14-16. Bilingual. **DESCR:** *Feliciano, Jose; Musicians; Singers.

577 Diaz, Katherine A. and Gonzalez, Magdalena. Jose Guadalupe Posada: documenting his people and his times=informandonos de su gente y su epoca. CAMINOS, Vol. 2, no. 6 (October 1981), p. 18-20. Bilingual. **DESCR:** Biography; Mexico; *Posada, Jose Guadalupe.

578 Diaz, Katherine A. Mike Gomez; pursuing his dream. CAMINOS, Vol. 4, no. 9 (October 1983), p. 28-30. English. **DESCR:** Films; *Gomez, Mike.

579 Diaz, Katherine A. The model of reflection: Rita Moreno. CAMINOS, Vol. 4, no. 3 (March 1983), p. 18-21. Bilingual. **DESCR:** *Moreno, Rita; Television.

580 Entertainment = diversion. CAMINOS, Vol. 3, no. 5 (May 1982), p. 54. Bilingual. **DESCR:** Buena Vista Cablevision, Inc.; Cinco de Mayo; *Holidays; Knott's Berry Farm, Buena Park, CA; Tamayo, Rufino; Television.

581 Esperanza's Mexico; an artist speaks through her work. CAMINOS, Vol. 4, no. 5 (May 1983), p. 18-20. English. **DESCR:** *Martinez, Esperanza.

582 Fernandez, Enrique. Notas: these ladies are not waiting. BILLBOARD, Vol. 94, (November 13, 1982), p. 62. English. **DESCR:** *Chicanas; Performing Arts; Salsa; Singers.

583 Flores, Bettina and Flores, Alfredo. Benny Barrios, Sacramento's living landmark. NUESTRO, Vol. 6, no. 9 (November 1982), p. 57-58. English. **DESCR:** *Art; Barrios, Benny; *Sacramento, CA.

584 Gente. NUESTRO, Vol. 7, no. 2 (March 1983), p. 51. English. **DESCR:** Betancourt, Jose L.; *Chicanas; Crime Victims Fund; Federal Government; Juarez, Joe; Military Service; Saldana, Teresa; Vargas, Alberto; Victims for Victims.

585 Gomez, Imelda. Tamayo interview. CAMINOS, Vol. 3, no. 9 (October 1982), p. 7,44. Bilingual. **DESCR:** *Tamayo, Rufino.

586 Gonzalez, Cesar A. LA FAMILIA de Joaquin Chinas. DE COLORES, Vol. 6, no. 1-2 (1982), p. 146-149. English. **DESCR:** Chicano Movement; Chinas, Joaquin; *LA FAMILIA [poster]; Symbolism.

587 Gonzalez, Johnny. Flora and Airto; making music happen. CAMINOS, Vol. 3, no. 8 (September 1982), p. 10-13,50. Bilingual. **DESCR:** Moreira, Airto; *Musicians; Purim, Flora.

588 Gonzalez, Magdalena. Luis Mayorga. CAMINOS, Vol. 3, no. 9 (October 1982), p. 18. English. **DESCR:** *Mayorga, Luis.

589 Gonzalez, Magdalena. Ole II; BFA honors the 40's. CAMINOS, Vol. 3, no. 7 (July, August, 1982), p. 28-29. Bilingual. **DESCR:** Awards; *Bilingual Foundation of the Arts; Montalban, Ricardo; Romero, Cesar.

590 Gonzalez, Magdalena. Recognizing Hispanic achievements in entertainment - U.S. and Mexico. CAMINOS, Vol. 3, no. 7 (July, August, 1982), p. 18-24. Bilingual. **DESCR:** Allende, Fernando; Awards; Bonilla Giannini, Roxanna; Eynoso, David; Felix, Maria; Films; Gallego, Gina; *Golden Eagle Awards; Hoyos, Rodolfo; Lamas, Lorenzo; Lopez, Conchita; Lopez, Lisa; Montalban, Ricardo; Nosotros [film production company]; Quintero, Jose; Rowe, Arthur; Television; Torres, Liz.

591 El Greco of Toledo: his life and his art. NUESTRO, Vol. 6, no. 6 (August 1982), p. 24-27. English. **DESCR:** Art; Art History; Biography; *El Greco.

592 Griffin, Julia Ortiz. Two artists in search of a country: Rafael Rios Rey and Francisco Arrivi. MINORITY VOICES, Vol. 5, no. 1-2 (Spring, Fall, 1981), p. 53-58. English. **DESCR:** *Arrivi, Francisco; Puerto Rican Literature; Puerto Ricans; *Rios Rey, Rafael; Teatro.

593 Herrera, Hayden. The elephant and the dove. NUESTRO, Vol. 7, no. 8 (October 1983), p. 40-43. English. **DESCR:** Art; Biography; *Kahlo, Frida; Paintings; Rivera, Diego.

Artists (cont.)

594 A Hispanic turned Greek. LATINO, Vol. 54, no. 4 (May, June, 1983), p. 14. English. **DESCR:** *Quinn, Anthony.

595 Jan D'Esopo: a talented artist. LATINO, Vol. 54, no. 7 (November 1983), p. 23. English. **DESCR:** *D'Esopo, Jan.

596 The Julio-ization of America. LATINO, Vol. 54, no. 4 (May, June, 1983), p. 24-25. English. **DESCR:** *Iglesias, Julio; Singers.

597 Lenti, Paul. Frida Kahlo. NUESTRO, Vol. 7, no. 8 (October 1983), p. 38-39. English. **DESCR:** *Biography; *Kahlo, Frida.

598 Lenti, Paul. Special honor goes to Montalban. NUESTRO, Vol. 7, no. 2 (March 1983), p. 10-11. English. **DESCR:** Maria Teresa Montoya Award; *Montalban, Ricardo; Performing Arts.

599 Levario, Raquel. Asner tells it like it is. LATINA, Vol. 1, no. 2 (February, March, 1983), p. 14. English. **DESCR:** *Screen Actors Guild.

600 Lewis, William. Tres Plumas and his pantheon of archetypal deities. NUESTRO, Vol. 7, no. 2 (March 1983), p. 38-40. English. **DESCR:** *Aguilar, Humberto; Sculpture; Tres Plumas.

601 Lopez, Rafael and Miller, Robert. Daniel Valley and the American Zoot Band (band review). CAMINOS, Vol. 4, no. 5 (May 1983), p. 42-43,52. English. **DESCR:** Films; *Valdez, Daniel; ZOOT SUIT [film].

602 Lorenzo Lamas. LATINO, Vol. 54, no. 6 (October 1983), p. 7+. English. **DESCR:** *Lamas, Lorenzo.

603 Madre tierra press. CAMINOS, Vol. 4, no. 9 (October 1983), p. 48-49. English. **DESCR:** *Chicanas.

604 Madrid, Joe. The multi-faceted Pepe Serna (interview). CAMINOS, Vol. 4, no. 4 (April 1983), p. 32-35,66. Bilingual. **DESCR:** Films; *Serna, Pepe.

605 Madrid, Joe. Q & A with Joan Baez. CAMINOS, Vol. 3, no. 11 (December 1982), p. 44-45. English. **DESCR:** Baez, Joan; Human Rights; *Singers.

606 Madrid, Joe. Warrior of the sun. CAMINOS, Vol. 3, no. 11 (December 1982), p. 42-43. English. **DESCR:** *Baez, Joan; Singers.

607 Manuel Jaramillo Rodriguez; master portrait artist. CAMINOS, Vol. 3, no. 9 (October 1982), p. 16-17. English. **DESCR:** *Rodriguez, Manuel Jaramillo.

608 McManis, Linda. First impressions. LATINO, Vol. 54, no. 8 (December 1983), p. 24-25. English.

609 Mejias-Rentas, Antonio. Cantinflas give D.C. tribute. NUESTRO, Vol. 7, no. 5 (June, July, 1983), p. 11-12. English. **DESCR:** Films; *Moreno, Mario "Cantinflas".

610 Menudo: dishing it up in Los Angeles. CAMINOS, Vol. 4, no. 8 (September 1983), p. 46. Bilingual. **DESCR:** *Menudo [musical group]; Music; Musicians; Puerto Rican Music.

611 Moreno, Mario "Cantinflas". Ne dejen de reir. LATINO, Vol. 54, no. 4 (May, June, 1983), p. 21. English. **DESCR:** Humor; *Moreno, Mario "Cantinflas".

612 Newman, Michael. The ribbon around the bomb. ART IN AMERICA, Vol. 71, (April 1983), p. 160-169. English. **DESCR:** Kahlo, Frida; Modotti, Tina; Paintings.

613 Nontraditional street group. NUESTRO, Vol. 6, no. 6 (August 1982), p. 12. English. **DESCR:** *New Mexico; *Teatro; *Teatro Claridad, South Valley, NM.

614 Ogaz, Armando. South of the other border. CAMINOS, Vol. 3, no. 6 (June 1982), p. 26-28,36+. Bilingual. **DESCR:** Del Rio, Yolanda; Emmanuel; Nunez, Estella; Singers.

615 Padilla, Steve. The comedian. NUESTRO, Vol. 7, no. 2 (March 1983), p. 25-27. English. **DESCR:** Humor; Performing Arts; *Rodriguez, Paul.

616 Una pintora: Graciela Rolo Boulanger. NUESTRO, Vol. 7, no. 6 (August 1983), p. 30-35. English. **DESCR:** Biography; *Boulanger, Graciela Rolo; Paintings.

617 Quinlivan, Robert. Tony Orlando in concert. CAMINOS, Vol. 3, no. 9 (October 1982), p. 25. English. **DESCR:** *Orlando, Tony; Singers.

618 A real man's place in history. LATINO, Vol. 54, no. 5 (August, September, 1983), p. 23+. English. **DESCR:** *BALLAD OF GREGORIO CORTEZ [film]; Bandidos.

619 Reyes, Luis. East L.A.'s very own Anthony Quinn. CAMINOS, Vol. 4, no. 7 (July, August, 1983), p. 24-27. Bilingual. **DESCR:** Films; *Quinn, Anthony.

620 Reyes, Luis. Henry Darrow: the man behind the actor. CAMINOS, Vol. 4, no. 6 (June 1983), p. 23-25,66. Bilingual. **DESCR:** *Darrow, Henry; Films; Television.

621 Robert Beltran. LATINA, Vol. 1, no. 2 (February, March, 1983), p. 46-49. English. **DESCR:** *Beltran, Robert; Biography.

622 Rodriguez, Antonio. Tamayo: artist of great synthesis. CAMINOS, Vol. 3, no. 9 (October 1982), p. 6,8-9,44. English. **DESCR:** *Tamayo, Rufino.

623 Romero, Pedro Sababu. Pete Escovedo: a study in versatility. NUESTRO, Vol. 6, no. 10 (December 1982), p. 63-64. English. **DESCR:** Escovedo, Pete; *Musicians.

624 Rose, Barbara. Frida Kahlo: the Chicana as art heroine. VOGUE, Vol. 173, (April 1983), p. 152-154. English. **DESCR:** Art; Biography; *Kahlo, Frida; Mexico; Rivera, Diego.

625 A salute to the arts. NUESTRO, Vol. 6, no. 7 (September 1982), p. 44-45. English. **DESCR:** *Art; Congressional Hispanic Caucus; National Hispanic Heritage Week; Villa, Eduardo.

626 San Antonio: an all American city. CAMINOS, Vol. 4, no. 8 (September 1983), p. 35. English. **DESCR:** Cerda, Daniel; Congressional Arts Caucus; Gonzalez, Henry B.; *San Antonio, TX.

Artists (cont.)

627 Scott, Patricia. Book review of: FRIDA: A BIOGRAPHY OF FRIDA KAHLO. LIBRARY JOURNAL, Vol. 108, no. 2 (January 15, 1983), p. 125. English. **DESCR:** Biography; Book Reviews; *FRIDA: A BIOGRAPHY OF FRIDA KAHLO; Herrera, Hayden.

628 Shiell, Pancho. Sebastian Castro Vallejo: artist on stage and on canvas. NUESTRO, Vol. 6, no. 7 (September 1982), p. 63-64. English. **DESCR:** Art; *Castro Vallejo, Sebastian.

629 Solis, Arnaldo. El oro del barrio: maestro Montoya. CALMECAC, Vol. 3, (Spring 1982), p. 25+. Bilingual. **DESCR:** *Biography; *Montoya, Jose E.

630 Storr, Robert. Book review of: FRIDA: A BIOGRAPHY OF FRIDA KAHLO. ART IN AMERICA, Vol. 71, (April 1983), p. 19. English. **DESCR:** Book Reviews; *FRIDA: A BIOGRAPHY OF FRIDA KAHLO; Herrera, Hayden; Kahlo, Frida.

631 Tribute to 'the Love Goddess'. LATINO, Vol. 54, no. 5 (August, September, 1983), p. 16-17+. English. **DESCR:** *Hayworth, Rita.

632 Vidal, Jose. Cantinflas: Mario Moreno. CAMINOS, Vol. 3, no. 7 (July, August, 1982), p. 7-9. Bilingual. **DESCR:** Mexico; *Moreno, Mario "Cantinflas".

633 Vidal, Jose. Mexican film - a short history. CAMINOS, Vol. 3, no. 7 (July, August, 1982), p. 10-13. Bilingual. **DESCR:** *Films; Mexico.

634 Whisler, Kirk. Jose Luis Ruiz on sound festival. CAMINOS, Vol. 3, no. 8 (September 1982), p. 6-8. Bilingual. **DESCR:** Films; *Ruiz, Jose Luis; Television.

635 Whisler, Kirk. Nosotros on film in Hollywood and Latin America. CAMINOS, Vol. 3, no. 7 (July, August, 1982), p. 15-17. Bilingual. **DESCR:** Cardinale, Marcela; Espinoza, Jimmy; Films; Gomez, Mike; *Nosotros [film production company]; Ortiz, Yolanda; Television; Velasco, Jerry.

636 Whisler, Kirk. Rose Portillo: a woman on the rise. CAMINOS, Vol. 4, no. 4 (April 1983), p. 36-39. Bilingual. **DESCR:** Films; *Portillo, Rose.

637 Whisler, Kirk. A truly international artist. CAMINOS, Vol. 3, no. 9 (October 1982), p. 12-15. Bilingual. **DESCR:** *Pena, Amado Maurilio, Jr.

Arts and Crafts

638 Costa Rica hosts craftsmen of the Americas. NUESTRO, Vol. 6, no. 6 (August 1982), p. 63-64. English. **DESCR:** Artists; Conventions; *Costa Rica; *Cultural Characteristics; Cultural Customs.

639 Plaza de la Raza to host project. NUESTRO, Vol. 7, no. 10 (December 1983), p. 11. English. **DESCR:** *Folk Art; Folklife Festival (Los Angeles, CA); Olympic Arts Festival, Los Angeles, CA; *Plaza de La Raza, Los Angeles, CA.

Asian Americans

640 Exum, Herbert A. The most invisible minority: the culturally diverse elderly. SCHOOL COUNSELOR, Vol. 30, no. 1 (September 1982), p. 15-24. English. **DESCR:** *Ancianos; Blacks; Counseling (Psychological); Cultural Customs; Ethnic Groups; Family; Native Americans; Stereotypes.

641 Flaskerud, Jacquelyn H. Community mental health nursing: its unique role in the delivery of services to ethnic minorities. PERSPECTIVES IN PSYCHIATRIC CARE, Vol. 20, no. 1 (January, March, 1982), p. 37-43. English. **DESCR:** Blacks; *Community Mental Health; Cultural Characteristics; Native Americans.

642 Hing, Bill Ong. Racial disparity: the unaddressed issues of the Simpson-Mazzoli Bill. LA RAZA LAW JOURNAL, Vol. 1, no. 1 (June 1983), p. 21-52. English. **DESCR:** Amnesty; Ethnic Attitudes; Family; Immigration; Immigration and Naturalization Service (INS); Latin Americans; Mazzoli, Romano L.; Mexican American Legal Defense and Educational Fund (MALDEF); Simpson, Alan K.; *Simpson-Mazzoli Bill; Temporary Worker Program; U.S. Congresssional Subcommittee on Immigration, Refugees and International Law.

643 Yamamoto, Joe and Acosta, Frank X. Treatments of Asian Americans and Hispanic Americans: similarities and differences. JOURNAL OF THE AMERICAN ACADEMY OF PSYCHOANALYSIS, Vol. 10, no. 4 (October 1982), p. 585-607. English. **DESCR:** Comparative Psychology; Los Angeles, CA; *Mental Health; Psychotherapy; Socioeconomic Factors.

Asip, Patricia V.

644 Newsfront. HISPANIC BUSINESS, Vol. 4, no. 2 (February 1982), p. 7. English. **DESCR:** Banuelos, Ramona Acosta; *Biographical Notes; Businesspeople; Gonzalez, Henry B.; Gutierrez, Alberto; IMAGE, Washington, DC.

645 Nuestra gente. LATINO, Vol. 53, no. 2 (March, April, 1982), p. 30. English. **DESCR:** *Biographical Notes; Ceballos, Sonia Ceban; Gonzales, Modesto; Septien, Rafael.

Askew, Reubin

646 Presidential election 1984. NUESTRO, Vol. 7, no. 7 (September 1983), p. 14-19. English. **DESCR:** Anderson, John; Cranston, Alan; Elected Officials; *Elections; Fernandez, Ben; Glenn, John; Hart, Gary; Hispanic Force '84; Hollings, Ernest "Fritz"; Mondale, Walter; Political Parties and Organizations; Reagan, Ronald.

Asociacion Internacional de Exportadores e Importadores (EXIMA)

647 People. HISPANIC BUSINESS, Vol. 4, no. 5 (May 1982), p. 8. English. **DESCR:** Appointed Officials; *Biographical Notes; Businesspeople; California Chicano News Media Association (CCNMA); de la Ossa, Ernest G.; Foreign Trade; Obledo, Mario; Rodriguez, Elias C.; Rodriguez, Samuel F.; United Way; U.S. Hispanic Chamber of Commerce.

Asociacion Nacional De Grupos Folkloricos

648 Gomez, Placido. Committed to keep the culture alive. CAMINOS, Vol. 3, no. 10 (November 1982), p. 28-29,52. English. **DESCR:** *Ballet Folkorico; Organizations.

Assassination

649 Ericksen, Charles. Holdenreid and Salazar: unanswered questions. NUESTRO, Vol. 7, no. 4 (May 1983), p. 40-41. English. DESCR: Criminal Acts; Guatemala; *Holdenreid, Frank X.; *Salazar, Ruben; *Violence.

Assertiveness (Psychology)

650 Taking charge at work. HISPANIC BUSINESS, Vol. 4, no. 3 (March 1982), p. 23. English. DESCR: Nonverbal Communication (Psychology).

Assimilation

651 Baca, Reynaldo and Bryan, Dexter Edward. The "Assimilation" of unauthorized Mexican workers: another social science fiction? HISPANIC JOURNAL OF BEHAVIORAL SCIENCES, Vol. 5, no. 1 (March 1983), p. 1-20. English. DESCR: *Binationalism; Immigrants; *Undocumented Workers.

652 Bell, Michael Davitt. Fitting into a tradition of autobiography. CHANGE, Vol. 14, no. 7 (October 1982), p. 36-39. English. DESCR: Affirmative Action; Bilingual Bicultural Education; Biography; Book Reviews; *HUNGER OF MEMORY: THE EDUCATION OF RICHARD RODRIGUEZ; Rodriguez, Richard.

653 Borjas, George J. The labor supply of male Hispanic immigrants in the United States. INTERNATIONAL MIGRATION REVIEW, Vol. 17, no. 4 (Winter 1983), p. 653-671. English. DESCR: Immigration; Labor Supply and Market; *Native Americans; Puerto Ricans.

654 Chall, Jeanne. Rich and sharp memories of reading. CHANGE, Vol. 14, no. 7 (October 1982), p. 36-40. English. DESCR: Book Reviews; *HUNGER OF MEMORY: THE EDUCATION OF RICHARD RODRIGUEZ; Language Arts; Reading; Rodriguez, Richard; Socioeconomic Factors.

655 Chase, Marilyn. Mired minority: Latins rise in numbers in U.S. but don't win influence or affluence. WALL STREET JOURNAL, Vol. 19, no. 43 (June 9, 1982), p. 1+. English. DESCR: Education; Employment; *Social History and Conditions.

656 Craver, Rebecca McDowell. The impact of intimacy: Mexican-Anglo intermarriage in New Mexico 1821-1846. SOUTHWESTERN STUDIES, no. 66 (1982), p. 1-79. English. DESCR: Acculturation; Chicanas; *Intermarriage; New Mexico; Rio Arriba Valley, New Mexico.

657 DeOrtega, Manuel R. In the stomach of the shark: echoes of a culture in captivity. SOUTHWEST ECONOMY AND SOCIETY, Vol. 6, no. 1 (Fall 1982), p. 35-48. Bilingual. DESCR: Culture; Poetry; Spanish Language.

658 Fradd, Sandra. Cubans to Cuban Americans: assimilation in the United States. MIGRATION TODAY, Vol. 11, no. 4-5 (1983), p. 35-42. English. DESCR: Bilingualism; *Cubanos; Immigration.

659 Haner, Lisa G. The new wave: strangers in our land. BUSINESS HORIZONS, Vol. 26, no. 3 (May, June, 1983), p. 2-6. English. DESCR: Immigration.

660 Hispanics keep the faith, but better parish work is needed. MIGRATION TODAY, Vol. 10, no. 5 (1982), p. 35. English. DESCR: Catholic Church; Cultural Customs; *Religion.

661 Lamare, James W. Political integration of Mexican American children: a generational analysis. INTERNATIONAL MIGRATION REVIEW, Vol. 16, no. 1 (Spring 1982), p. 169-188. English. DESCR: Acculturation; Age Groups; *Children; Immigration; Political Ideology; *Political Socialization.

662 Lindsey, Alfred J. Ethnic pluralism: a misguided approach to schooling. SCHOLAR AND EDUCATOR, Vol. 6, (Spring 1982), p. 42-46. English. DESCR: Cultural Pluralism; Educational Theory and Practice.

663 Madrid, Arturo and Rodriguez, Richard. The mis-education of rich-heard road-ree-guess. MAIZE, Vol. 5, no. 3-4 (Spring, Summer, 1982), p. 88-92. English. DESCR: *Book Reviews; Education; English Language.

664 Mainstream Hispanic. AMERICAN DEMOGRAPHICS, Vol. 4, no. 1 (January 1982), p. 9-10. English.

665 Meyer Rogg, Eleanor and Holmberg, Joan J. The assimilation of Cubans in the United States. MIGRATION TODAY, Vol. 11, no. 4-5 (1983), p. 8-11. English. DESCR: *Cubanos.

666 Miller, Darlis A. Cross-cultural marriages in the Southwest: the New Mexico experience, 1846-1900. NEW MEXICO HISTORICAL REVIEW, Vol. 57, no. 4 (October 1982), p. 335-359. English. DESCR: Chicanas; Ethnic Attitudes; *Intermarriage; New Mexico; Social History and Conditions.

667 Miller, Lawrence W. A note on cultural assimilation in south Texas. BORDERLANDS JOURNAL, Vol. 6, no. 1 (Fall 1982), p. 93-98. English. DESCR: Texas.

668 Morgan, Thomas B. The Latinization of America. ESQUIRE, Vol. 99, no. 5 (May 1983), p. 47-56. English. DESCR: Acculturation; Biculturalism; Bilingualism; *Population Trends.

669 Morrissey, Marietta. Ethnic stratification and the study of Chicanos. JOURNAL OF ETHNIC STUDIES, Vol. 10, no. 4 (Winter 1983), p. 71-99. English. DESCR: *Ethnic Stratification; Internal Colonial Model (Theoretical); Marxism; Paradigm (Theoretical); Social Theory.

670 Parra, Fernando and So, Alvin Yiu-cheong. Changing perceptions of mental illness in a Mexican-American community. JOURNAL OF SOCIAL PSYCHOLOGY, Vol. 29, (Summer 1983), p. 95-100. English. DESCR: Anglo Americans; *Los Angeles, CA; *Mental Health; Random Digit Dialling (RDD).

671 Rodriguez, Richard, et al. Education of Richard Rodriguez [excerpts from "HUNGER OF MEMORY", including discussion]. CHANGE, Vol. 14, no. 7 (October 1982), p. 32-42+. English. DESCR: Affirmative Action; Bilingual Bicultural Education; Biography; *HUNGER OF MEMORY: THE EDUCATION OF RICHARD RODRIGUEZ; *Rodriguez, Richard.

672 Schoen, Robert and Cohen, Lawrence E. Theory and method in the study of ethnic endogamy among Mexican-American grooms - reply. AMERICAN JOURNAL OF SOCIOLOGY, Vol. 87, no. 4 (January 1982), p. 939-942. English. DESCR: ETHNIC ENDOGAMY: THE CASE OF THE MEXICAN-AMERICANS; Intermarriage; Mittelback, Frank G.; Moore, Joan W.; *Research Methodology.

Assimilation (cont.)

673 Vigil, James Diego. Towards a new perspective on understanding the Chicano people: the six C's model of sociocultural change. CAMPO LIBRE, Vol. 1, no. 2 (Summer 1981), p. 141-167. English. **DESCR:** Acculturation; Cultural Characteristics; History; Mexican Nationalism Period; Mexico; Nationalism; Organizations; Precolumbian Society; *Six C's Model (Theoretical Model); Social History and Conditions; Spanish Colonial Period.

674 Ward, Carmen Carole. Book review of: THE ASSIMILATION OF CUBAN EXILES: THE ROLE OF COMMUNITY AND CLASS. JOURNAL OF ETHNIC STUDIES, Vol. 3, no. 2 (Summer 1975), p. 116-119. English. **DESCR:** Book Reviews; *Cubanos; Miami, FL; *Rogg, Eleanor Meyer; Social Classes; Social History and Conditions; THE ASSIMILATION OF CUBAN EXILES: THE ROLE OF COMMUNITY AND CLASS; West New York, NJ.

675 Yovovich, B.G. Cultural pride galvanizes heritages. ADVERTISING AGE MAGAZINE, Vol. 53, (February 15, 1982), p. II, M9+. English. **DESCR:** *Market Research.

ASSIMILATION, COLONIALISM AND THE MEXICAN AMERICAN PEOPLE

676 Sierra, Christine Marie. Book review of: ASSIMILATION, COLONIALISM, AND THE MEXICAN AMERICAN PEOPLE. NEW SCHOLAR, Vol. 8, no. 1-2 (Spring, Fall, 1982), p. 490-492. English. **DESCR:** Book Reviews; Murguia, Edward.

THE ASSIMILATION OF CUBAN EXILES: THE ROLE OF COMMUNITY AND CLASS

677 Ward, Carmen Carole. Book review of: THE ASSIMILATION OF CUBAN EXILES: THE ROLE OF COMMUNITY AND CLASS. JOURNAL OF ETHNIC STUDIES, Vol. 3, no. 2 (Summer 1975), p. 116-119. English. **DESCR:** Assimilation; Book Reviews; *Cubanos; Miami, FL; *Rogg, Eleanor Meyer; Social Classes; Social History and Conditions; West New York, NJ.

Association of Mexican American Educators, Inc. (AMAE)

678 Mena, Kristena. Tomorrow's leaders (photoessays). CAMINOS, Vol. 3, no. 8 (September 1982), p. 48. English. **DESCR:** Chicano Youth Leadership Conference; *Youth.

Asthma

679 Rios, Lydia E. Determinants of asthma among Puerto Ricans. JOURNAL OF LATIN COMMUNITY HEALTH, Vol. 1, no. 1 (Fall 1982), p. 25-40. English. **DESCR:** *Puerto Ricans.

Astronauts

680 Valenzuela-Crocker, Elvira. Chang-Diaz has space shuttle role. NUESTRO, Vol. 7, no. 9 (November 1983), p. 11-12. English. **DESCR:** *Chang-Diaz, Franklin; National Aeronautics and Space Administration (NASA); Space Shuttle.

681 Vara, Richard. Reaching for the stars: Franklin Chang-Diaz, astronaut and future scientist in space. HISPANIC BUSINESS, Vol. 5, no. 11 (November 1983), p. 18-19+. English. **DESCR:** *Chang-Diaz, Franklin; National Aeronautics and Space Administration (NASA); Science as a Profession.

Ateneo de la Juventud

682 Leal, Luis. Gabino Barreda y la literatura: de la preparatoria al Ateneo. AZTLAN, Vol. 14, no. 2 (Fall 1983), p. 253-265. Spanish. **DESCR:** *Barreda, Gabino; Escuela Nacional Preparatoria; History; *Mexican Literature; Philosophy; Positivism.

Athletes

683 Salazar wins New York race. NUESTRO, Vol. 6, no. 8 (October 1982), p. 13. English. **DESCR:** New York City Marathon; *Salazar, Alberto; Sports.

Atlantic Richfield Company

684 The shaping of a career. HISPANIC BUSINESS, Vol. 4, no. 4 (April 1982), p. 14. English. **DESCR:** Biography; Businesspeople; Chicanas; *Oaxaca, Virginia.

Attitude (Psychological)

685 Adams, Phylliss J. and Anderson, Peggy L. Comparison of teachers' and Mexican-American children's perceptions of the children's competence. READING TEACHER, Vol. 36, no. 1 (October 1982), p. 8-13. English. **DESCR:** Children; Colorado; Cultural Characteristics; Learning and Cognition; Sex Roles; *Teacher Attitudes.

686 Aptekar, Lewis. Mexican-American high school students' perception of school. ADOLESCENCE, Vol. 18, no. 70 (Summer 1983), p. 345-357. English. **DESCR:** Anthony, TX; Canutillo, TX; High School Students; Texas.

687 Arce, A.A. Application of cognitive behavioral techniques in the treatment of Hispanic patients. PSYCHIATRIC QUARTERLY Vol. 54, no. 4 (March 1982), p. 230-236. English. **DESCR:** *Psychiatry.

688 Arnold, Bill R. Attitudinal research and Hispanic handicapped: a review of selected needs. JOURNAL OF REHABILITATION, Vol. 49, no. 4 (October, December, 1983), p. 36-38. English. **DESCR:** *Handicapped; Literature Reviews.

689 Book review of: HUNGER OF MEMORY: THE EDUCATION OF RICHARD RODRIGUEZ. SAN FRANCISCO REVIEW OF BOOKS, Vol. 7, (Summer 1982), p. 11. English. **DESCR:** Bilingual Bicultural Education; Book Reviews; *HUNGER OF MEMORY: THE EDUCATION OF RICHARD RODRIGUEZ; Identity; Rodriguez, Richard.

690 Bustamante, Jorge A. The Mexicans are coming: from ideology to labor relations. INTERNATIONAL MIGRATION REVIEW, Vol. 17, no. 2 (Summer 1983), p. 323-341. English. **DESCR:** *Immigration; Immigration Law; Labor Laws and Legislation; Labor Supply and Market; Migration; Policy; Political Ideology; *Simpson-Mazzoli Bill; Undocumented Workers.

691 Chavez, Ruth and Ramirez, Albert. Employment aspirations, expectations, and attitudes among employed and unemployed Chicanos. JOURNAL OF SOCIAL PSYCHOLOGY, Vol. 11, no. 1 (February 1983), p. 143-144. English. **DESCR:** *Employment; Vocational Education.

Attitude (Psychological) (cont.)

692 Cortese, Anthony. Moral development in
Chicano and Anglo children. HISPANIC JOURNAL
OF BEHAVIORAL SCIENCES, Vol. 4, no. 3
(September 1982), p. 353-366. English.
DESCR: *Ethics; *Psychology; Socialization.

693 Dolgin, Daniel L., et al. Quality of life
and psychological well-being in a bicultural
Latino community. HISPANIC JOURNAL OF
BEHAVIORAL SCIENCES, Vol. 4, no. 4 (December
1982), p. 433-450. English. DESCR:
Acculturation; Depression Scale; *Global
Acculturation Scale; Index of Psychological
Adjustment; Psychology; Quality of Life
Scale.

694 Garza, Raymond T., et al. Biculturalism,
locus of control and leader behavior in
ethnically mixed small groups. JOURNAL OF
APPLIED SOCIAL PSYCHOLOGY, Vol. 12, no. 3
(May, June, 1982), p. 237-253. English.
DESCR: *Biculturalism; Culture;
Interpersonal Relations; Leadership; *Locus
of Control; Social Psychology.

695 Jaramillo, Patricio T.; Zapata, Jesse T.;
and McPherson, Robert. Concerns of college
bound Mexican-American students. SCHOOL
COUNSELOR, Vol. 29, no. 5 (May 1982), p.
375-380. English. DESCR: College
Preparation; Counseling Services
(Educational); Identity; Stereotypes;
Students.

696 Kagan, Spencer and Knudsen, Kathryn H.M.
Relationship of empathy and affective
role-taking in young children. JOURNAL OF
GENETIC PSYCHOLOGY, Vol. 141, (September
1982), p. 149-150. English. DESCR: Anglo
Americans; Child Study; Psychological
Testing; Socialization.

697 Knudsen, Kathryn H.M. and Kagan, Spencer.
Differential development of empathy and
pro-social behavior. JOURNAL OF GENETIC
PSYCHOLOGY, Vol. 140, no. 2 (June 1982), p.
249-251. English. DESCR: Anglo Americans;
Child Study; Psychological Testing;
Socialization.

698 Luevano, Richard L. Attitudes of elderly
Mexican Americans towards nursing homes in
Stanislaus county. CAMPO LIBRE, Vol. 1, no.
2 (Summer 1981), p. 213-228. English.
DESCR: *Ancianos; Cultural Characteristics;
Medical Care; *Nursing Homes; Stanislaus
County, CA; Surveys.

699 Perales, Alonso M. Effects of
teacher-oriented and student-oriented
strategies on self-concept, English language
development, and social studies achievement
of 5th grade Mexican-American students
[research notes]. TESOL QUARTERLY, Vol. 16,
no. 1 (March 1982), p. 99-100. English.
DESCR: Identity; San Antonio, TX; *Teacher
Attitudes; Teacher-pupil Interaction.

700 Perez, Robert; Padilla, Amado M.; and
Ramirez, Alex. Expectations toward school
busing by Mexican American youth. AMERICAN
JOURNAL OF COMMUNITY PSYCHOLOGY, Vol. 10,
no. 2 (April 1982), p. 133-148. English.
DESCR: *Busing; East Los Angeles, CA;
Identity; Segregation and Desegregation;
Students; Youth.

701 Plake, Barbara S., et al. Relationship of
ethnic group membership to the measurement
and meaning of attitudes towards reading:
implications for validity of test score
interpretations. EDUCATIONAL AND
PSYCHOLOGICAL MEASUREMENT, Vol. 42, no. 4
(Winter 1982), p. 1259-1267. English.
DESCR: Anglo Americans; Educational Tests
and Measurements; Estes Reading Attitude
Scale; Ethnic Groups; *Reading; Students.

702 Rosenhouse-Persson, Sandra and Sabagh,
Georges. Attitudes toward abortion among
Catholic Mexican-American women: the effects
of religiosity and education. DEMOGRAPHY,
Vol. 20, no. 1 (February 1983), p. 87-98.
English. DESCR: Abortion; *Catholic Church;
Education; Religion.

703 Shankman, Arnold. The image of Mexico and
the Mexican-American in the Black press,
1890-1935. JOURNAL OF ETHNIC STUDIES, Vol.
3, no. 2 (Summer 1975), p. 43-56. English.
DESCR: Blacks; *Intergroup Relations;
Journalism; *Mexico.

704 Stern, Michael P. Knowledge, attitudes, and
behavior related to obesity and dieting in
Mexican-Americans and Anglos: the San
Antonio heart study. AMERICAN JOURNAL OF
EPIDEMIOLOGY, Vol. 115, no. 6 (June 1982),
p. 917-928. English. DESCR: Anglo Americans;
*Food Practices; Obesity; San Antonio, TX;
Weight Control.

Au, Kathryn Hu-Pei

705 Walia, Adorna. Book review of: CULTURE AND
THE BILINGUAL CLASSROOM: STUDIES IN
CLASSROOM ETHNOGRAPHY. BILINGUAL JOURNAL,
Vol. 6, no. 4 (Summer 1982), p. 30-31.
English. DESCR: Biculturalism; *Bilingual
Bicultural Education; Book Reviews; Cultural
Pluralism; *CULTURE AND THE BILINGUAL
CLASSROOM: STUDIES IN CLASSROOM ETHNOLOGY;
Guthrie, Grace Pung; Trueba, Henry T.

Audiovisual Instruction

706 Saracho, Olivia N. Effects of a
computer-assisted instruction program on
basic skills achievement and attitudes
toward instruction of Spanish-speaking
migrant children. AMERICAN EDUCATIONAL
RESEARCH JOURNAL, Vol. 19, no. 2 (Summer
1982), p. 201-219. English. DESCR: Academic
Motivation; Computers; *Migrant Children;
*Migrant Education; Programmed Instruction.

AURA

707 Nieto, Eva Margarita. El problema de la
juventud eterna en tres hechiceras en THE
SECOND RING OF POWER, LA MULATA DE CORDOBA y
AURA. LA PALABRA, Vol. 4, no. 1-2 (Spring,
Fall, 1982, 1983), p. 81-91. Spanish.
DESCR: Castaneda, Carlos; Fuentes, Carlos;
Gonzalez Obregon, Luis; LA MULATA DE
CORDOBA; *Literary Criticism; Literature;
Literature Reviews; THE SECOND RING OF
POWER.

AUSTIN LIGHT (TX)

708 Cantu, Hector. Aqui en Tejas: Hispanic
newspapers: city, community papers taking a
business approach to the news. NATIONAL
HISPANIC JOURNAL, Vol. 2, no. 1 (Summer
1983), p. 9. English. DESCR: EL EDITOR
(Lubbock, TX); EL SOL DE HOUSTON (TX);
Journalism; *Newspapers; THE TEXICAN
(Dallas, TX).

Austin, Robert F.

709 Jones, Richard C. Reply to Robert Austin's "Comment on 'Undocumented migration from Mexico: some geographical questions'." ANNALS OF THE ASSOCIATION OF AMERICAN GEOGRAPHERS, Vol. 72, no. 4 (December 1982), p. 561-562. English. **DESCR:** Migration Patterns; *"Undocumented migration from Mexico: some geographical questions".

Austin, TX

710 Barreto, Julio. Gathering of the Ojedas. NUESTRO, Vol. 6, no. 5 (June, July, 1982), p. 22-25. English. **DESCR:** Extended Family; Family; *Ojeda, Cecilio Colunga.

711 Cantu, Hector. Hispanic numbers rising. NATIONAL HISPANIC JOURNAL, Vol. 1, no. 3 (Summer, Fall, 1982), p. 7. English. **DESCR:** Census; Demography; Population; *Population Trends.

Authors

712 100 years of solitude. LATINO, Vol. 53, no. 4 (June 1982), p. 27. English. **DESCR:** *CIEN ANOS DE SOLEDAD; *Garcia Marquez, Gabriel.

713 Alurista and Villarreal, Jose Antonio. Jose Antonio Villarreal: entrevista. MAIZE, Vol. 5, no. 3-4 (Spring, Summer, 1982), p. 7-16. English. **DESCR:** Novel.

714 Anaya, Rudolfo A. An author's reflections: THE SILENCE OF THE LLANO. NUESTRO, Vol. 7, no. 3 (April 1983), p. 14-17+. English. **DESCR:** *Anaya, Rudolfo A.; *Fiction; Literary Influence.

715 Arias, Ron. El senor del chivo. JOURNAL OF ETHNIC STUDIES, Vol. 3, no. 4 (Winter 1976), p. 58-60. English. **DESCR:** *Fiction; *THE ROAD TO TAMAZUNCHALE.

716 Barradas, Efrain. "Todo lo que digo es cierto...": en memoria de Victor Fernandez Fragoso (1944-1982). REVISTA CHICANO-RIQUENA, Vol. 10, no. 3 (Summer 1982), p. 43-46. Spanish. **DESCR:** *Biography; Essays; *Fernandez Fragoso, Victor; New York, NY; Puerto Rican Literature.

717 Bruce Novoa, Juan. La critica chicana de Luis Leal. LA PALABRA, Vol. 4, no. 1-2 (Spring, Fall, 1982, 1983), p. 25-40. Spanish. **DESCR:** *Leal, Luis; *Literary Criticism; Literature.

718 Bruce Novoa, Juan and Arias, Ron. Interview with Ron Arias. JOURNAL OF ETHNIC STUDIES, Vol. 3, no. 4 (Winter 1976), p. 70-73. English. **DESCR:** *Arias, Ron; Literary Influence; *Literature.

719 Cantu, Roberto. El relato como articulacion infinitiva: MACARIO y el arte de Juan Rulfo. LA PALABRA, Vol. 4, no. 1-2 (Spring, Fall, 1982, 1983), p. 107-126. Spanish. **DESCR:** Literary Characteristics; Literary Criticism; *MACARIO; Mexican Literature; *Rulfo, Juan.

720 de Ortego y Gasca, Felipe. "Are there U.S. Hispanic writers?". NUESTRO, Vol. 7, no. 3 (April 1983), p. 20-21+. English. **DESCR:** Ethnic Groups; *Literary Criticism; Literature.

721 Forster, Merlin H. Luis Leal. LA PALABRA, Vol. 4, no. 1-2 (Spring, Fall, 1982, 1983), p. 19-20. Spanish. **DESCR:** *Biography; Higher Education; Latin American Literature; *Leal, Luis; Teaching Profession.

722 Garcia Marquez, Gabriel. The solitude of Latin America. NUESTRO, Vol. 6, no. 10 (December 1982), p. 46-47+. English. **DESCR:** Literature; *ONE HUNDRED YEARS OF SOLITUDE.

723 Greenfield, Charles. Cuba's matriarch of letters: Lydia Cabrera. NUESTRO, Vol. 6, no. 7 (September 1982), p. 13-15. English. **DESCR:** *Cabrera, Lydia; Cubanos.

724 Greenfield, Charles. Life imitating art: a profile of Reynaldo Arenas. NUESTRO, Vol. 7, no. 5 (June, July, 1983), p. 40-42. English. **DESCR:** Arenas, Reynaldo; *Cuba; *Cubanos; El Morro Prison, Cuba; Political Prisoners.

725 Greenfield, Charles. Q & A with Lydia Cabrera. NUESTRO, Vol. 6, no. 7 (September 1982), p. 16-17+. English. **DESCR:** *Cabrera, Lydia; Cubanos.

726 Greenfield, Charles. Writing in exile. NUESTRO, Vol. 6, no. 8 (October 1982), p. 22-24. English. **DESCR:** Cubanos; *Infante, Guillermo Cabrera.

727 Herrera-Sobek, Maria. La unidad, el hombre y el cosmos: reafirmacion del proceso vital en Estrella Portillo Trambley. LA PALABRA, Vol. 4, no. 1-2 (Spring, Fall, 1982, 1983), p. 127-141. Spanish. **DESCR:** *Literary Criticism; Literature; *Portillo Trambley, Estela.

728 Hinojosa-Smith, Rolando R. Luis (el amigo) Leal. LA PALABRA, Vol. 4, no. 1-2 (Spring, Fall, 1982, 1983), p. 17-18. Spanish. **DESCR:** *Biography; Latin American Literature; *Leal, Luis; Literature.

729 Hispanics win Nobel Prizes. LATINO, Vol. 53, no. 8 (December 1982), p. 20-21. English. **DESCR:** Garcia Marquez, Gabriel; *Nobel Prize.

730 Historia de exitos. LATINO, Vol. 53, no. 3 (May 1982), p. 9. English. **DESCR:** *Salazar, Veronica.

731 Lamento por la jubilacion de un insigne hispanista y viejo amigo (una carta anonima). LA PALABRA, Vol. 4, no. 1-2 (Spring, Fall, 1982, 1983), p. 21-24. Spanish. **DESCR:** *Biography; Higher Education; Latin American Literature; *Leal, Luis; Teaching Profession.

732 Lomeli, Francisco A. Don Luis. LA PALABRA, Vol. 4, no. 1-2 (Spring, Fall, 1982, 1983), p. IX-XI. Spanish. **DESCR:** *Biography; Latin American Literature; *Leal, Luis; Literature.

733 Lomeli, Francisco A. Entrevista con Luis Leal. LA PALABRA, Vol. 4, no. 1-2 (Spring, Fall, 1982, 1983), p. 3-15. Spanish. **DESCR:** *Biography; Latin American Literature; *Leal, Luis; Literature; Oral History.

734 Medina, Ruben and Hinojosa-Smith, Rolando R. Rolando Hinojosa: entrevista. MAIZE, Vol. 5, no. 1-2 (Fall, Winter, 1981, 1982), p. 16-31. Spanish. **DESCR:** *Hinojosa-Smith, Rolando R.; Literature.

735 Ponce, Mary Helen. Juan Gomez-Quinones: escolar y poeta. CAMINOS, Vol. 4, no. 6 (June 1983), p. 54-55,67. Bilingual. **DESCR:** *Gomez-Quinones, Juan.

Authors (cont.)

736 Prida, Dolores. Latin American women writers meet in New England. NUESTRO, Vol. 6, no. 10 (December 1982), p. 26-27. English. DESCR: *Chicanas; *Massachusetts.

737 Prida, Dolores. Playwrights Laboratory: in search of a creative formula. NUESTRO, Vol. 7, no. 10 (December 1983), p. 43. English. DESCR: Education; *Hispanic Playwrights-in-Residence Laboratory; INTAR; *Teatro.

738 El profesor Alum publica capitulo en libro. LATINO, Vol. 53, no. 1 (January, February, 1982), p. 15. Spanish. DESCR: *Alum, Rolando.

739 Rodriguez del Pino, Salvador. La intimidad poetica de Luis Leal. LA PALABRA, Vol. 4, no. 1-2 (Spring, Fall, 1982, 1983), p. 41-52. Spanish. DESCR: *Leal, Luis; Literature; *Poetry.

740 Rodriguez, Richard. A minority scholar speaks out. AMERICAN EDUCATION, Vol. 18, no. 9 (November 1982), p. 2-5. English. DESCR: Affirmative Action; Bilingual Bicultural Education; *Biography; HUNGER OF MEMORY: THE EDUCATION OF RICHARD RODRIGUEZ; Rodriguez, Richard.

741 Sanchez, Ricardo. Canto towards Ateneo. NATIONAL HISPANIC JOURNAL, Vol. 1, no. 3 (Summer, Fall, 1982), p. 19. English. DESCR: *Poetry.

742 See, Lisa. Chicano writers: looking for a breakout. PUBLISHER'S WEEKLY, Vol. 224, (September 30, 1983), p. 94. English. DESCR: Literature; Publishing Industry.

743 Soto, Gary. Luis Omar Salinas: Chicano poet. MELUS: MULTI-ETHNIC LITERATURE OF THE UNITED STATES, Vol. 9, no. 2 (Summer 1982), p. 47-82. English. DESCR: Poetry; *Salinas, Luis Omar.

744 Tatum, Charles. Book review of: CHICANO AUTHORS: INQUIRY BY INTERVIEW. HISPANIA, Vol. 65, no. 4 (December 1982), p. 668. English. DESCR: Book Reviews; Bruce Novoa, Juan; *CHICANO AUTHORS: INQUIRY BY INTERVIEW.

745 Trejo, Ernesto and Soto, Gary. An interview with Gary Soto. REVISTA CHICANO-RIQUENA, Vol. 11, no. 2 (Summer 1983), p. 25-33. English. DESCR: *Soto, Gary.

746 Vigil, Evangelina, ed. Woman of her word: Hispanic women write. REVISTA CHICANO-RIQUENA, Vol. 11, no. 3-4 (Fall 1983), p. 1-180. Bilingual. DESCR: *Chicanas.

747 Whisler, Kirk. Octavio Paz - "There will be no revolution in Mexico" (interview). CAMINOS, Vol. 4, no. 5 (May 1983), p. 10-12,48. Bilingual. DESCR: Mexico; *Paz, Octavio.

Autobiography

748 Martinez, Elisa A. Sharing her tiny pieces of the past. NUESTRO, Vol. 7, no. 7 (September 1983), p. 51-52. English. DESCR: Chicanas; *Extended Family; Reminiscences.

749 Ponce, Mary Helen. El jabon de Dona Chonita. NUESTRO, Vol. 7, no. 10 (December 1983), p. 44-45. English. DESCR: *Ponce, Mary Helen; Prose; *Reminiscences.

750 Sabat-Rivers, Georgina. Book review of: A WOMAN OF GENIUS: THE INTELLECTUAL AUTOBIOGRAPHY OF SOR JUANA INES DE LA CRUZ. NUESTRO, Vol. 7, no. 6 (August 1983), p. 62-64. English. DESCR: *A WOMAN OF GENIUS: THE INTELLECTUAL AUTOBIOGRAPHY OF SOR JUANA INES DE LA CRUZ; Book Reviews; Juana Ines de la Cruz, Sor; Peden, Margaret Sayers.

THE AUTOBIOGRAPHY OF A BROWN BUFFALO

751 Lattin, Vernon E. Ethnicity and identity in the contemporary Chicano novel. MINORITY VOICES, Vol. 2, no. 2 (Fall 1978), p. 37-44. English. DESCR: BLESS ME, ULTIMA; Identity; Literary Criticism; Literature; MEMORIES OF THE ALHAMBRA; *Novel; POCHO; Y NO SE LO TRAGO LA TIERRA/AND THE EARTH DID NOT PART.

Automobile Industry

752 Crane, Larry. Corporate personality. HISPANIC BUSINESS, Vol. 5, no. 9 (September 1983), p. 25. English. DESCR: Corporations; DeDeurwaerder, Jose.

753 Ford, Charles A. and Violante Morlock, Alejandro A. Policy concerns over the impact of trade-related performance requirements and investment incentives on the international economy: Mexican automotive policy and U.S.-Mexican relations. INTER-AMERICAN ECONOMIC AFFAIRS, Vol. 36, no. 2 (Fall 1982), p. 3-42. English. DESCR: Economic History and Conditions; *Mexico; *United States-Mexico Relations.

754 Morales, Rebecca. Transitional labor: undocumented workers in the Los Angeles automobile industry. INTERNATIONAL MIGRATION REVIEW, Vol. 17, no. 4 (Winter 1983), p. 570-596. English. DESCR: Los Angeles, CA; Transitional Labor; *Undocumented Workers.

Automobile Racing

755 Gonzalez, Magdalena. Joselo Garza: a champion for the 80's and beyond. CAMINOS, Vol. 4, no. 3 (March 1983), p. 33-35. Bilingual. DESCR: *Garza, Josele.

Automobiles

756 Solis, Arnaldo. The birth of the Ranfla. CALMECAC, Vol. 2, (Spring 1981), p. 43. Bilingual.

Avalos, Luis

757 Caldera, Carmela. Luis Avalos - he has it all - talent, wit, and a TV show of his own (interview). CAMINOS, Vol. 4, no. 5 (May 1983), p. 36-38. English. DESCR: Artists; Television.

758 Garcia, Ignacio M. Regional report, television: "Condo" canceled. NUESTRO, Vol. 7, no. 5 (June, July, 1983), p. 13. English. DESCR: Carmen, Julie; CONDO [televison series]; Latin Americans; Stereotypes; *Television.

759 Martinez, Marie. Luis Avalos: what a man, and what a talent. LATINA, Vol. 1, no. 3 (1983), p. 38-42. English. DESCR: Biography.

AVANCES EN PSICOLOGIA CONTEMPORANEA

760 Brink, T. L. Book review of: AVANCES EN
PSICOLOGIA CONTEMPORANEA. HISPANIC JOURNAL
OF BEHAVIORAL SCIENCES, Vol. 5, no. 4
(December 1983), p. 494-496. English.
DESCR: Book Reviews; Finley, Gordon E.;
Marin, Gerardo; Psychology.

Avila, Joaquin Guadalupe

761 Flaherty, Francis J. The struggle continues:
protecting the rights of Hispanics in the
U.S. NATIONAL LAW JOURNAL, Vol. 5, (March
14, 1983), p. 1. English. **DESCR:** Affirmative
Action; Civil Rights; Hispanic Amendments;
*Legal Representation; Mexican American
Legal Defense and Educational Fund (MALDEF);
Racism; Voting Rights.

762 New general counsel at MALDEF. HISPANIC
BUSINESS, Vol. 4, no. 7 (July 1982), p. 24.
English. **DESCR:** *Biography; Legal
Profession; Mexican American Legal Defense
and Educational Fund (MALDEF).

763 Nuestra gente. LATINO, Vol. 53, no. 3 (May
1982), p. 26. English. **DESCR:** *Biographical
Notes; Pompa, Gilbert G.

764 People. HISPANIC BUSINESS, Vol. 5, no. 3
(March 1983), p. 9. English. **DESCR:** Anaya,
Toney; Anguiano, Lupe; Appointed Officials;
Awards; *Biographical Notes; de la Fuente,
Emilio; del Olmo, Frank; Godoy, Gustavo;
Long, Dennis P.; Martinez, Elias (Lee);
Rivera, Joseph, Jr.

"Avocado Lake"

765 de la Fuente, Patricia. Ambiguity in the
poetry of Gary Soto. REVISTA
CHICANO-RIQUENA, Vol. 11, no. 2 (Summer
1983), p. 34-39. English. **DESCR:** "Blanco";
"Braley Street"; "Field"; *Literary
Criticism; Poetry; "Song for the pockets";
*Soto, Gary; TALE OF SUNLIGHT; "Telephoning
God"; THE ELEMENTS OF SAN JOAQUIN; "Wind".

Awards

766 1981 awards. NUESTRO, Vol. 6, no. 1
(January, February, 1982), p. 39-42.
English.

767 Agudelo, Carlos. What about Latin music?
BILLBOARD, Vol. 94, (November 20, 1982), p.
10. English. **DESCR:** *Grammy Awards; Music;
National Academy of Recording Arts and
Sciences; Performing Arts; Recording
Industry.

768 Baciu, Joyce A. The winners - Los ganadores.
CAMINOS, Vol. 3, no. 2 (February 1982), p.
14-20,45. Bilingual. **DESCR:** Caldera, Manuel;
Gomez, Ignacio; Huerta, Dolores; Lizarraga,
David C.; Obledo, Mario; Olmos, Edward
James; Rivera, Geraldo; Rivera, Tomas.

769 Business update: Ibero-American chamber has
gala, makes awards. NUESTRO, Vol. 7, no. 5
(June, July, 1983), p. 52. English. **DESCR:**
*Business Enterprises; Greater Washington
Ibero-American Chamber of Commerce.

770 CAMINO'S 1981 Chicano of the year: Fernando
Valenzuela. CAMINOS, Vol. 3, no. 2 (February
1982), p. 10-13. Bilingual. **DESCR:** *CAMINOS'
Chicano of the Year Award; *Valenzuela,
Fernando.

771 CAMINO'S fourth annual Hispanic of the year
awards: the nominees. CAMINOS, Vol. 4, no. 9
(October 1983), p. 27. English.

772 CAMINO'S fourth annual Hispanic of the year
awards: the nominees. CAMINOS, Vol. 4, no.
10 (November 1983), p. 45. English. **DESCR:**
*Hispanic of the Year Award.

773 CAMINO'S fourth annual Hispanic of the year
awards: the nominees. CAMINOS, Vol. 4, no.
11 (December 1983), p. 27. English. **DESCR:**
*Hispanic of the Year Award.

774 CAMINOS' Second Annual Chicano/a of the Year
Awards=Chicano/a del Ano. CAMINOS, Vol. 2,
no. 6 (October 1981), p. 29-33. Bilingual.
DESCR: *CAMINOS' Chicano of the Year Award.

775 CAMINO'S third annual awards finalist.
CAMINOS, Vol. 3, no. 9 (October 1982), p.
40-43. English.

776 CAMINO'S third annual awards finalist.
CAMINOS, Vol. 3, no. 10 (November 1982), p.
48-50. English.

777 Communications/marketing. HISPANIC BUSINESS,
Vol. 4, no. 7 (July 1982), p. 16. English.
DESCR: *Biographical Notes; Buena Vista
Cablevision, Inc.; Demy, Caroline;
*Marketing; Sosa de Garcia, Manuel.

778 Communications/marketing. HISPANIC BUSINESS,
Vol. 4, no. 9 (September 1982), p. 22.
English. **DESCR:** Coca-Cola Company; Domecq
Importers, Inc.; *Marketing; Western Union
Corporation.

779 Communications/marketing. HISPANIC BUSINESS,
Vol. 4, no. 10 (October 1982), p. 22.
English. **DESCR:** ENFOQUE NACIONAL [radio
program]; League of United Latin American
Citizens (LULAC); LULAC National Education
Service Centers (LNESC); Marketing; *Mass
Media.

780 Communications/marketing. HISPANIC BUSINESS,
Vol. 5, no. 3 (March 1983), p. 21. English.
DESCR: *Advertising; Consumers; El Cervantes
Media Awards; Marketing; Spanish Advertising
and Marketing Services (S.A.M.S.)

781 Communications/marketing. HISPANIC BUSINESS,
Vol. 5, no. 5 (May 1983), p. 24. English.
DESCR: Anheuser-Busch, Inc.; Arbitron;
California Chicano News Media Association
(CCNMA); Coca-Cola Company; Elizalde,
Hector; *Marketing; Television.

782 Diaz, Barbara M. Continuing the success: the
Hispanic Women's Council. CAMINOS, Vol. 4,
no. 6 (June 1983), p. 62. English. **DESCR:**
Chicanas; *Hispanic Women's Council;
Organizations; Women for Success Awards.

783 Diaz, Katherine A. "And this year's winners
are...". CAMINOS, Vol. 4, no. 1-2 (January,
February, 1983), p. 39-54,74+. English.
DESCR: Castro, Tony; Elizalde, Hector;
Flores, Tom; Martinez, Esperanza;
Mendizabal, Maritza; Molina, Gloria; Moya,
Connie; Placentia, Joe; Quesada, Leticia;
Rios, David N.; Ybarra, Lea; Zapata, Carmen.

784 Entertainment = diversion. CAMINOS, Vol. 3,
no. 2 (February 1982), p. 40-41. English.
DESCR: CHECKING IT OUT; Club Hogar Latino;
Dance; Films; Flamenco; Marley, Bob;
Montalban, Ricardo; ON GOLDEN POND;
*Recreation; Television.

Awards (cont.)

785 Fernandez, Enrique. NARAS takes a welcome step. BILLBOARD, Vol. 95, (June 18, 1983), p. 59. English. **DESCR**: Entertainers; Grammy Awards; Music; *National Academy of Recording Arts and Sciences; Performing Arts; Recording Industry.

786 Golden Eagle Awards 1983. CAMINOS, Vol. 4, no. 8 (September 1983), p. 42-43. English. **DESCR**: Nosotros [film production company]; Recreation; Sesma, Chico.

787 Gonzalez, Magdalena. Ole II; BFA honors the 40's. CAMINOS, Vol. 3, no. 7 (July, August, 1982), p. 28-29. Bilingual. **DESCR**: Artists; *Bilingual Foundation of the Arts; Montalban, Ricardo; Romero, Cesar.

788 Gonzalez, Magdalena. Recognizing Hispanic achievements in entertainment - U.S. and Mexico. CAMINOS, Vol. 3, no. 7 (July, August, 1982), p. 18-24. Bilingual. **DESCR**: Allende, Fernando; Artists; Bonilla Giannini, Roxanna; Eynoso, David; Felix, Maria; Films; Gallego, Gina; *Golden Eagle Awards; Hoyos, Rodolfo; Lamas, Lorenzo; Lopez, Conchita; Lopez, Lisa; Montalban, Ricardo; Nosotros [film production company]; Quintero, Jose; Rowe, Arthur; Television; Torres, Liz.

789 An Hispanic view of the 1983 Academy Awards. CAMINOS, Vol. 4, no. 6 (June 1983), p. 59. English. **DESCR**: *Academy Awards; Films.

790 MAGA annual scholarship awards banquet. CAMINOS, Vol. 4, no. 1-2 (January, February, 1983), p. 32. English. **DESCR**: Financial Aid; *Mexican American Grocers Association (MAGA).

791 Nobel prize recipient Marquez. LATINA, Vol. 1, no. 2 (February, March, 1983), p. 20. English. **DESCR**: Garcia Marquez, Gabriel; *Nobel Prize.

792 Our 1982 Latino awards. NUESTRO, Vol. 7, no. 1 (January, February, 1983), p. 44-46. English. **DESCR**: Escalante, Jaime; Gallegos, Gina; Grace, J. Peter; Immigration and Naturalization Service (INS); Knight, Bobby; Lamas, Fernando; *Latino Awards; Luce, Claire Boothe; Moreno, Rita; National Press Foundation; Rodriguez Hernandez, Andres; Simpson-Mazzoli Bill; Smith, Raymond; Valeri, Michele; Voting Rights Act.

793 People. HISPANIC BUSINESS, Vol. 4, no. 9 (September 1982), p. 7. English. **DESCR**: Advertising Agencies; Appointed Officials; *Biographical Notes; Diaz-Albertini, Luis; Dimartino, Rita; Garza, Jesus; Hispanic Women in Higher Education (HWHE); League of United Latin American Citizens (LULAC); Ortega, Ray; Ortiz, George; Romero, Carlos J.; Sepulveda, Luis.

794 People. HISPANIC BUSINESS, Vol. 5, no. 3 (March 1983), p. 9. English. **DESCR**: Anaya, Toney; Anguiano, Lupe; Appointed Officials; Avila, Joaquin Guadalupe; *Biographical Notes; de la Fuente, Emilio; del Olmo, Frank; Godoy, Gustavo; Long, Dennis P.; Martinez, Elias (Lee); Rivera, Joseph, Jr.

795 Quesada-Weiner, Rosemary. CAMINOS second annual Chicano of the year awards. CAMINOS, Vol. 3, no. 3 (March 1982), p. 34-36. Bilingual. **DESCR**: *CAMINOS' Chicano of the Year Award.

796 Quesada-Weiner, Rosemary. The third annual Hispanic of the Year Awards: it was an event not to be missed (photoessay). CAMINOS, Vol. 4, no. 3 (March 1983), p. 28-31. English.

797 Top talent at Tejano awards. BILLBOARD, Vol. 95, (January 29, 1983), p. 65. English. **DESCR**: Entertainers; Music; Performing Arts; *Tejano Music Awards; Texas.

Ayala, Ernesto

798 Ayala, Ernesto. My machine. NUESTRO, Vol. 6, no. 7 (September 1982), p. 31. English. **DESCR**: *Poetry; UN VERANO.

Ayudantes de los Pobres

799 Holdenreid, Frank X. Guatemala shantytown. NUESTRO, Vol. 7, no. 4 (May 1983), p. 39-41. English. **DESCR**: *Guatemala; Holdenreid, Frank X.; *Poverty; Refugees.

"The Aztecs"

800 Ruiz, Rene A. [Article review of: "The Aztecs"; "Tenochtitlan's glory"; "The Great Temple"]. HISPANIC JOURNAL OF BEHAVIORAL SCIENCES, Vol. 4, no. 3 (September 1982), p. 394-395. English. **DESCR**: Book Reviews; NATIONAL GEOGRAPHIC [magazine]; *"Tenochtitlan's glory"; *"The Great Temple".

Aztecs

801 Anderson, Arthur J.O. Aztec hymns of life and love. NEW SCHOLAR, Vol. 8, no. 1-2 (Spring, Fall, 1982), p. 1-72. English. **DESCR**: Religion.

802 Huehuetlatoli. CALMECAC, Vol. 1, (Summer 1980), p. 58-59. English.

803 New York's exhibition of Aztec treasures. NUESTRO, Vol. 6, no. 5 (June, July, 1982), p. 63-64. English. **DESCR**: Anthropology; Exhibits; New York, NY.

804 Nicholson, H. B. Treasures of Tenochtitlan. NUESTRO, Vol. 7, no. 10 (December 1983), p. 28-32. English. **DESCR**: *Mexico City; *Precolumbian Art.

805 Solis, Arnaldo. Chicano mental health. CALMECAC, Vol. 1, (Summer 1980), p. 49-56. Bilingual. **DESCR**: *Mental Health; *Values.

806 Solis, Arnaldo. Raices of the Chicano spirit. CALMECAC, Vol. 1, (Summer 1980), p. 19-27. English. **DESCR**: *Mental Health.

Aztlan

807 Chavez, John A. Aztlan, Cibola, and frontier New Spain. CAMPO LIBRE, Vol. 1, no. 2 (Summer 1981), p. 193-211. English. **DESCR**: *Explorations; Folklore; History; Mestizaje; Mexico; Missions; Native Americans; Southwest United States.

808 Farias, Eddie Jaime. Aztlan begins with the heart and the mind. CORAZON DE AZTLAN, Vol. 1, no. 3 (August, September, 1982), p. 29-30. English. **DESCR**: Chicanismo.

AZTLAN [journal]

809 Entertainment = diversion. CAMINOS, Vol. 3, no. 4 (April 1982), p. 41. Bilingual. DESCR: Committee in Solidarity with the People of El Salvador (CISPES); Cultural Organizations; Directories; DIRECTORY OF MINORITY ARTS ORGANIZATIONS; El Salvador; *National Endowment for the Arts; NOTICIERO; Organizations; Periodicals; *Recreation; Television.

Aztlan Writing Contest

810 Entertainment = diversion. CAMINOS, Vol. 3, no. 3 (March 1982), p. 55-56. Bilingual. DESCR: CORAZON DE AZTLAN; Films; Literary Contests; MISSING [film]; *Recreation; THE BORDER [film]; Young, Robert.

Azuela, Mariano

811 Beverley, John. The revolution betrayed: a note on Mariano Azuela's estridentista trilogy. MAIZE, Vol. 4, no. 1-2 (Fall, Winter, 1980, 1981), p. 27-39. English. DESCR: EL DESQUITE; LA LUCIERNAGA; LA MALHORA; Literary Criticism.

Babbitt, Bruce

812 Hamner, Richard. Hispanic update: border governors tackle U.S.-Mexico relations: much ado: but nothing on immigration. NATIONAL HISPANIC JOURNAL, Vol. 1, no. 2 (Winter 1982), p. 4-5. English. DESCR: Border Region; Brown, Edmund G., Jr., Governor of California; *Clements, Bill; Immigration; Immigration Regulation and Control; Moreno, Paul; *United States-Mexico Relations.

813 People. HISPANIC BUSINESS, Vol. 5, no. 10 (October 1983), p. 10. English. DESCR: Anaya, Toney; Arriola, Elvia Rosales; Burgos, Tony; Bush, George; *Businesspeople; Cisneros, Henry, Mayor of San Antonio, TX; Cruz, Jose; Kennedy, Edward M.; Montano, Gilbert; Reagan, Ronald; White, Mark.

Babcock, R.

814 Orlandi, Lisanio R. Book review of: WORKBOOK ON PROGRAM EVALUATION. BILINGUAL JOURNAL, Vol. 7, no. 2 (Winter 1983), p. 35-36. English. DESCR: Bilingual Bicultural Education; Book Reviews; Evaluation (Educational); Plakos, J.; Plakos, M.; *WORKBOOK ON PROGRAM EVALUATION.

Baca Barragan, Polly

815 Baca Barragan, Polly; Hamner, Richard; and Guerrero, Lena. [Untitled interview with State Senators (Colorado) Polly Baca-Barragan and Lena Guerrero. NATIONAL HISPANIC JOURNAL, Vol. 1, no. 2 (Winter 1982), p. 8-11. English. DESCR: *Carter, Jimmy (President); Chicanas; Democratic Party; Elected Officials; Guerrero, Lena; *Political Parties and Organizations.

816 N.A.L.E.O.'s "Fiesta '83". CAMINOS, Vol. 4, no. 10 (November 1983), p. 28-29. English. DESCR: Bilingual Bicultural Education; Central America; Fiesta '83; Garcia, Robert; Immigration; International Relations; Mendez, Olga; *National Association of Latino Elected Officials (NALEO); Simpson-Mazzoli Bill; United States-Mexico Relations.

Baca, Herman

817 Quinlivan, Robert. CRC's Herman Baca on the

issue. CAMINOS, Vol. 3, no. 1 (January 1982), p. 18-20. Bilingual. DESCR: *Committee on Chicano Rights; *Immigration Regulation and Control; Reagan, Ronald.

Baca Zinn, Maxine

818 Mirande, Alfredo. Sociology of Chicanos or Chicano sociology: a critical assessment of emergent paradigms. PACIFIC SOCIOLOGICAL REVIEW, Vol. 25, no. 4 (October 1982), p. 495-508. English. DESCR: Internal Colonial Model (Theoretical); *Paradigm (Theoretical); SOCIOLOGICAL THEORY IN EMERGENT CHICANO PERSPECTIVES; *Sociology.

Bacardi Imports, Inc.

819 Whitefield, Mimi. Mr. Lasa's 400,000 cases of rum. HISPANIC BUSINESS, Vol. 4, no. 1 (January 1982), p. 14-15+. English. DESCR: *Biography; Lasa, Luis; Marketing.

Back of the Yards, Chicago, IL

820 Ano Nuevo de Kerr, Louise. Chicano settlements in Chicago: a brief history. JOURNAL OF ETHNIC STUDIES, Vol. 2, no. 4 (Winter 1975), p. 22-32. English. DESCR: *Chicago, IL; Near West Side, Chicago, IL; Pilsen, IL; Social History and Conditions; South Chicago, Chicago, IL; *Urban Communities.

BAD BOYS

821 De la Rosa, Carlos. Esai Morales: a new and exciting Latino talent on the rise. LATINA, Vol. 1, no. 3 (1983), p. 19. English. DESCR: Biography; Film Reviews; Morales, Esai.

Baez, Joan

822 Barrios, Gregg. Our Lady of the Angels has no papers. LATINA, Vol. 1, no. 1 (1982), p. 36-37. English. DESCR: *Poetry.

823 Madrid, Joe. Q & A with Joan Baez. CAMINOS, Vol. 3, no. 11 (December 1982), p. 44-45. English. DESCR: *Artists; Human Rights; *Singers.

824 Madrid, Joe. Warrior of the sun. CAMINOS, Vol. 3, no. 11 (December 1982), p. 42-43. English. DESCR: *Artists; Singers.

Bahia Oral Language Test (BOLT)

825 Politzer, Robert L.; Shohamy, Elana; and McGroarty, Mary. Validation of linguistic and communicative oral language tests for Spanish-English bilingual programs. BILINGUAL REVIEW, Vol. 10, no. 1 (January, April, 1983), p. 3-20. English. DESCR: Bay Area, CA; *Bilingual Bicultural Education; Bilingual Programs; *Language Assessment; Linguistics; Sociolinguistics.

Baja California, Mexico

826 Emigrantes centroamericanos en Baja California Norte. INFORME: RELACIONES MEXICO-ESTADOS UNIDOS, Vol. 1, no. 3 (July, December, 1982), p. 227-241. Spanish. DESCR: Central America; *Immigration.

827 Historic Baja captured on film. CAMINOS, Vol. 3, no. 11 (December 1982), p. 21. English. DESCR: *Centro Cultural Fondo Nacional para Actividades Sociales (FONOPAS); Photography; *Tijuana, Mexico; *Tourism.

Baja California, Mexico (cont.)

828 Miller, Shirley and Miller, Tom. Cabo San Lucas - revisited; border updates. CAMINOS, Vol. 3, no. 1 (January 1982), p. 8-9. Bilingual. **DESCR**: Border Region; *Tourism.

829 "Tourism was benefited by the devaluation." Q and A with Hugo Torres Chabert. CAMINOS, Vol. 3, no. 11 (December 1982), p. 32-33,52+. Bilingual. **DESCR**: *Currency; *Torres Chabert, Hugo; *Tourism.

830 Whisler, Kirk. Q & A with Guillermo Schmirdhuber de la Mora, Centro Cultural FONOPAS director: "We try to balance education and culture with entertainment". CAMINOS, Vol. 3, no. 11 (December 1982), p. 19,23. Bilingual. **DESCR**: *Centro Cultural Fondo Nacional para Actividades Sociales (FONOPAS); *Schmidhuber de la Mora, Guillermo; *Tourism.

Bakke v. Regents of University of California

831 Flores, Rogelio. The struggle for minority admissions: the UCLA experience. CHICANO LAW REVIEW, Vol. 5, (1982), p. 1-12. English. **DESCR**: *Law Schools; Legal Education; Legal Profession; Student Organizations; Students; UCLA Law School.

Balderrama, Francisco E.

832 Book review of: IN DEFENSE OF LA RAZA: THE LOS ANGELES MEXICAN CONSULATE AND THE MEXICAN COMMUNITY. CHOICE, Vol. 20, no. 7 (March 1983), p. 1050. English. **DESCR**: Book Reviews; *IN DEFENSE OF LA RAZA: THE LOS ANGELES MEXICAN CONSULATE AND THE MEXICAN COMMUNITY.

833 Cuello, J. Book review of: IN DEFENSE OF LA RAZA: THE LOS ANGELES MEXICAN CONSULATE AND THE MEXICAN COMMUNITY. CALIFORNIA HISTORY, Vol. 62, no. 1 (1983), p. 70. English. **DESCR**: Book Reviews; California; History; *IN DEFENSE OF LA RAZA: THE LOS ANGELES MEXICAN CONSULATE AND THE MEXICAN COMMUNITY.

834 De Leon, Arnoldo. Book review of: IN DEFENSE OF LA RAZA: THE LOS ANGELES MEXICAN CONSULATE AND THE MEXICAN COMMUNITY. NEW MEXICO HISTORICAL REVIEW, Vol. 58, no. 3 (July 1983), p. 296-297. English. **DESCR**: Book Reviews; *IN DEFENSE OF LA RAZA: THE LOS ANGELES MEXICAN CONSULATE AND THE MEXICAN COMMUNITY.

Balestra, Victor C.

835 Volsky, George. Four careers in Miami. HISPANIC BUSINESS, Vol. 5, no. 4 (April 1983), p. 10-11+. English. **DESCR**: *Banking Industry; Biographical Notes; *Businesspeople; Harvard Business School's Latino Association; Huston, Maria Padilla; Masvidal, Sergio J.; Miami, FL; Valdes-Fauli, Gonzalo.

Ballad
USE: Corrido

BALLAD OF AN UNSUNG HERO

836 Keller, Gary. Ballad of an unsung hero. BILINGUAL REVIEW, Vol. 10, no. 2-3 (May, December, 1983), p. 171-172. English. **DESCR**: Film Reviews; Gonzalez, Pedro J.

BALLAD OF GREGORIO CORTEZ [film]

837 THE BALLAD OF GREGORIO CORTEZ (review). CAMINOS, Vol. 3, no. 8 (September 1982), p.

27. English. **DESCR**: Film Reviews.

838 THE BALLAD OF GREGORIO CORTEZ. NUESTRO, Vol. 6, no. 4 (May 1982), p. 63. English. **DESCR**: Cortez, Gregorio; Public Television; Television.

839 Breiter, Toni. Eddie Olmos and THE BALLAD OF GREGORIO CORTEZ. NUESTRO, Vol. 7, no. 4 (May 1983), p. 14-19. English. **DESCR**: Artists; Corrido; Film Reviews; *Olmos, Edward James; Prejudice (Social).

840 Bubriski, Kevin. THE BALLAD OF GREGORIO CORTEZ (photoessay). CAMINOS, Vol. 3, no. 8 (September 1982), p. 28-29. English. **DESCR**: Films.

841 Dominguez, Pia and Martinez, Marie. CORRIDO run clipped by national film distributors. LATINA, Vol. 1, no. 2 (February, March, 1983), p. 24. English. **DESCR**: Film Reviews.

842 Morales, Sylvia. Chicano-produced celluloid mujeres. BILINGUAL REVIEW, Vol. 10, no. 2-3 (May, December, 1983), p. 89-93. English. **DESCR**: *Chicanas; Film Reviews; *Films; RAICES DE SANGRE [film]; SEGUIN [movie]; *Stereotypes; ZOOT SUIT [film].

843 Olmos, Edward James. Edward James Olmos and Robert Young with 21 reasons why you should see THE BALLAD OF GREGORIO CORTEZ. CAMINOS, Vol. 3, no. 8 (September 1982), p. 26-27, 50. Bilingual. **DESCR**: Film Reviews; Olmos, Edward James; Young, Robert.

844 A real man's place in history. LATINO, Vol. 54, no. 5 (August, September, 1983), p. 23+. English. **DESCR**: Artists; Bandidos.

845 Sorell, Victor A. Ethnomusicology, folklore, and history in the filmmaker's art: THE BALLAD OF GREGORIO CORTEZ. BILINGUAL REVIEW, Vol. 10, no. 2-3 (1983), p. 153-158. English. **DESCR**: Film Reviews; Paredes, Americo; WITH HIS PISTOL IN HIS HAND.

846 Treviso, Ruben. EL CORRIDO DE GREGORIO CORTEZ. LATINO, Vol. 53, no. 5 (September 1982), p. 16-17. Spanish. **DESCR**: Film Reviews.

847 Varnez, Ginger. Film review of: THE BALLAD OF GREGORIO CORTEZ. CAMINOS, Vol. 4, no. 8 (September 1983), p. 40-41. English. **DESCR**: Film Reviews.

Ballet de Puerto Rico

848 Government review. NUESTRO, Vol. 7, no. 6 (August 1983), p. 56. English. **DESCR**: Dance; Education; Employment; *Government Funding Sources; Government Services; Housing; Income; National Fair Housing Law; Population Distribution; Urban Development Action Grant (UDAG); Veterans.

Ballet Folkorico

849 Fuentes, Diana. Chicana perpectives: Ester Reyes Aguilar. COMADRE, no. 1 (Summer 1977), p. 45-48. English. **DESCR**: Affirmative Action; *Aguilar, Ester Reyes; *Biography; Teaching Profession.

850 Gomez, Placido. Committed to keep the culture alive. CAMINOS, Vol. 3, no. 10 (November 1982), p. 28-29,52. English. **DESCR**: *Asociacion Nacional De Grupos Folkloricos; Organizations.

Banas, L.K.

851 Solis, Arnaldo. Theory of biculturality. CALMECAC, Vol. 2, (Spring 1981), p. 36-41. English. DESCR: *Biculturalism.

Bandidos

852 Mena, Jesus. Violence in the Rio Grande Valley. NUESTRO, Vol. 7, no. 1 (January, February, 1983), p. 41-42. English. DESCR: Border Region; History; *Rio Grande Valley, TX; Social History and Conditions.

853 A real man's place in history. LATINO, Vol. 54, no. 5 (August, September, 1983), p. 23+. English. DESCR: Artists; *BALLAD OF GREGORIO CORTEZ [film].

854 Ruiz, Ramon Eduardo. Book review of: DISORDER AND PROGRESS: BANDITS, POLICE, AND MEXICAN DEVELOPMENT. ARIZONA AND THE WEST, Vol. 24, no. 1 (Spring 1982), p. 75-76. English. DESCR: Book Reviews; Diaz, Porfirio; *DISORDER AND PROGRESS: BANDITS, POLICE AND MEXICAN DEVELOPMENT; Vanderwood, Paul J.

855 Schmidt, Dorothy. Book review of: MEXICANO RESISTANCE IN THE SOUTHWEST: "THE SACRED RIGHT OF SELF-PRESERVATION". WESTERN AMERICAN LITERATURE, Vol. 17, no. 1 (Spring 1982), p. 75-76. English. DESCR: Book Reviews; Insurrections; *MEXICANO RESISTANCE IN THE SOUTHWEST: "THE SACRED RIGHT OF SELF-PRESERVATION"; Rosenbaum, Robert J.

Banking Industry

856 Banking on Hispanics. HISPANIC BUSINESS, Vol. 4, no. 3 (March 1982), p. 14+. English. DESCR: California.

857 Communications/marketing. HISPANIC BUSINESS, Vol. 5, no. 1 (January 1983), p. 23. English. DESCR: Broadcast Media; Caballero Spanish Media, Inc. (CSM); Fleishman-Hillard, Inc.; *Marketing; Miami, FL; Nogales, Luis G.; Public Relations.

858 Deibel, Richard and Balkan, D. Carlos. The nation's largest little bank: Laredo's International Bank of Commerce. HISPANIC BUSINESS, Vol. 4, no. 9 (September 1982), p. 10-11,24. English. DESCR: Business Enterprises; *International Bank of Commerce (IBOC); Laredo, TX.

859 Dominguez, Richard M. Capital formulation for small businesses. HISPANIC BUSINESS, Vol. 4, no. 9 (September 1982), p. 8. English. DESCR: California; *Finance; Small Business.

860 Foreign trade. HISPANIC BUSINESS, Vol. 5, no. 4 (April 1983), p. 22. English. DESCR: Brazil; *Electronics Industry; Export Trade; *Foreign Trade; Ibero-American Chamber of Commerce; Miami, FL; Minority Bank Development Program (MBDP); Minority Export Development Consultants Program (MEDC); Peace Corps; Puerto Rico.

861 Gold coins of Mexico. NUESTRO, Vol. 6, no. 1 (January, February, 1982), p. 53-54. English. DESCR: Mexico.

862 Government review. NUESTRO, Vol. 7, no. 10 (December 1983), p. 48. English. DESCR: Child Care Centers; Chile; Clinics (Medical); Credit Unions; Employment; Employment Training; *Government Services; Medical Care; National Credit Union Administration; National Oceanic and Atmospheric Administration; SER; U.S. Department of Health and Human Services; U.S. Department of Labor.

863 Hispanic owned banks. HISPANIC BUSINESS, Vol. 5, no. 9 (September 1983), p. 13. English. DESCR: Finance; International Bank of Commerce (IBOC); Minority Bank Deposit Program (MBDP).

864 Hispanic-owned bank far exceeds expectations. ABA BANKING JOURNAL, Vol. 75, (February 1983), p. 32-34. English. DESCR: *Capital National Bank; Cordova, Carlos; New York, NY.

865 The Inter-American Development Bank at work (photoessay). CAMINOS, Vol. 4, no. 8 (September 1983), p. 22-25. English. DESCR: Economic Development; *Inter-American Development Bank; Latin America.

866 The leading US Hispanic-owned minority banks according to assets. HISPANIC BUSINESS, Vol. 4, no. 9 (September 1982), p. 14. English. DESCR: Business Enterprises; Minority Bank Deposit Program (MBDP).

867 Salvatierra, Richard. Debtors' row expands in Latin America. NUESTRO, Vol. 6, no. 9 (November 1982), p. 34-35. English. DESCR: Debt; Economics; *Latin America.

868 Sanchez, Teresa S. Banking: a diversified industry. CAMINOS, Vol. 3, no. 3 (March 1982), p. 21-22. Bilingual.

869 Sargeant, Georgia. A woman's place is in the bank. HISPANIC BUSINESS, Vol. 5, no. 10 (October 1983), p. 20-21+. English. DESCR: Accountants; Careers; Chicanas; *Olson, Ethel Ortega; Otero Savings and Loan, Alamogordo, TX.

870 Southern California's HBA. HISPANIC BUSINESS, Vol. 4, no. 9 (September 1982), p. 19. English. DESCR: California; *Hispanic Bankers Association (HBA); Organizations.

871 Volsky, George. Four careers in Miami. HISPANIC BUSINESS, Vol. 5, no. 4 (April 1983), p. 10-11+. English. DESCR: Balestra, Victor C.; Biographical Notes; *Businesspeople; Harvard Business School's Latino Association; Huston, Maria Padilla; Masvidal, Sergio J.; Miami, FL; Valdes-Fauli, Gonzalo.

872 Volsky, George and Masvidal, Raul. An interview with Raul Masvidal. HISPANIC BUSINESS, Vol. 4, no. 9 (September 1982), p. 16-17,24+. English. DESCR: Biography; Business Enterprises; Businesspeople; Cubanos; *Masvidal, Raul; Miami, FL.

Banks, James A.

873 Eaton, Joli. Book review of: EDUCATION IN THE 80's: MULTICULTURAL EDUCATION. HISPANIC JOURNAL OF BEHAVIORAL SCIENCES, Vol. 5, no. 2 (June 1983), p. 238-240. English. DESCR: Book Reviews; *EDUCATION IN THE 80'S: MULTICULTURAL EDUCATION.

Banuelos, Ramona Acosta

874 Newsfront. HISPANIC BUSINESS, Vol. 4, no. 2 (February 1982), p. 7. English. DESCR: Asip, Patricia V.; *Biographical Notes; Businesspeople; Gonzalez, Henry B.; Gutierrez, Alberto; IMAGE, Washington, DC.

Baptists

875 Grijalva, Joshua. The story of Hispanic
Southern Baptists. BAPTIST HISTORY AND
HERITAGE, Vol. 18, no. 3 (July 1983), p.
40-47. English. DESCR: History; Puerto
Ricans; Religion; *Southern Baptists.

Barcelo, Carlos Romero

876 Resign, Peter Grace. NUESTRO, Vol. 6, no. 5
(June, July, 1982), p. 9. English. DESCR:
*Grace, J. Peter; Puerto Ricans.

Barojas, Salome

877 Ortiz, Carlos V. NUESTRO'S sixth annual
all-star baseball team. NUESTRO, Vol. 7, no.
2 (March 1983), p. 33-37. English. DESCR:
Andujar, Joaquin; *Baseball; Castillo,
Manny; Concepcion, Dave; Cruz, Jose; Garcia,
Damaso; Guerrero, Pedro; Hernandez, Keith;
Lezcano, Sixto; Martinez, Tippy; Pena, Tony;
Piniella, Lou; Sports; Valenzuela, Fernando.

Baron, Augustine Jr.

878 Gonzalez, Roberto. Book review of:
EXPLORATIONS IN CHICANO PSYCHOLOGY. HISPANIC
JOURNAL OF BEHAVIORAL SCIENCES, Vol. 4, no.
4 (December 1982), p. 511-522. English.
DESCR: Book Reviews; *EXPLORATIONS IN
CHICANO PSYCHOLOGY.

Barradas, Efrain

879 Daydi-Tolson, Santiago. The right to belong:
a critic's view of Puerto Rican poetry in
the United States. BILINGUAL REVIEW, Vol.
10, no. 1 (January, April, 1983), p. 81-86.
English. DESCR: Book Reviews; *HEREJES Y
MITIFICADORES: MUESTRA DE POESIA
PUERTORRIQUENA EN LOS ESTADOS UNIDOS; Puerto
Rican Literature.

880 Mullen, E.J. Book review of: HEREJES Y
MITIFICADORES: MUESTRA DE POESIA
PUERTORRIQUENA EN LOS ESTADOS UNIDOS.
REVISTA CHICANO-RIQUENA, Vol. 10, no. 3
(Summer 1982), p. 68-70. English. DESCR:
Book Reviews; *HEREJES Y MITIFICADORES:
MUESTRA DE POESIA PUERTORRIQUENA EN LOS
ESTADOS UNIDOS; Marin, Carmen Lilianne;
Rodriguez, Rafael.

881 Rivero, Eliana S. Book review of: HEREJES Y
MITIFICADORES: MUESTRA DE POESIA
PUERTORRIQUENA EN LOS ESTADOS UNIDOS. THIRD
WOMAN, Vol. 1, no. 2 (1982), p. 91-93.
Spanish. DESCR: Book Reviews; *HEREJES Y
MITIFICADORES: MUESTRA DE POESIA
PUERTORRIQUENA EN LOS ESTADOS UNIDOS; Puerto
Rican Literature; Rodriguez, Rafael.

Barraza Sanchez, Irene

882 Reading to whet your appetite [book
reviews]. CAMINOS, Vol. 4, no. 6 (June
1983), p. 19,66. English. DESCR: Book
Reviews; *COMIDA SABROSA; Recipes; Sanchez
Yund, Gloria.

Barraza, Santa

883 Executives challenge first impressions.
HISPANIC BUSINESS, Vol. 4, no. 1 (January
1982), p. 22. English. DESCR: Job
Satisfaction.

Barreda, Gabino

884 Klor de Alva, Jorge. Gabino Barrera and
Chicano thought. AZTLAN, Vol. 14, no. 2

(Fall 1983), p. 343-358. English. DESCR:
Economic History and Conditions; History;
Mexico; Philosophy; *Positivism.

885 Leal, Luis. Gabino Barreda y la literatura:
de la preparatoria al Ateneo. AZTLAN, Vol.
14, no. 2 (Fall 1983), p. 253-265. Spanish.
DESCR: Ateneo de la Juventud; Escuela
Nacional Preparatoria; History; *Mexican
Literature; Philosophy; Positivism.

886 Marti, Oscar R. Barrera and moral
philosophy. AZTLAN, Vol. 14, no. 2 (Fall
1983), p. 373-403. English. DESCR: *Ethics;
History; Mexico; Philosophy; Positivism.

887 Marti, Oscar R. Introduction. AZTLAN, Vol.
14, no. 2 (Fall 1983), p. 209-220. English.
DESCR: *Biography; History; Mexico;
Philosophy; Positivism.

888 Marti, Oscar R., comp. Bibliography. AZTLAN,
Vol. 14, no. 2 (Fall 1983), p. 405-417.
English. DESCR: *Bibliography; History;
Mexico; Philosophy; Positivism.

889 Raat, W. Dirk. Augusto Comte, Gabino
Barreda, and positivism in Mexico. AZTLAN,
Vol. 14, no. 2 (Fall 1983), p. 235-251.
English. DESCR: *Comte, Auguste; Education;
Educational Theory and Practice; History;
Mexico; Philosophy; *Positivism.

890 Skirius, John. Barreda, Vasconcelos, and the
Mexican educational reforms. AZTLAN, Vol.
14, no. 2 (Fall 1983), p. 307-341. English.
DESCR: Education; *Educational Theory and
Practice; History; Mexico; Positivism;
*Vasconcelos, Jose.

891 Zea, Leopoldo. El sentido de la historia en
Gabino Barreda. AZTLAN, Vol. 14, no. 2 (Fall
1983), p. 221-233. Spanish. DESCR: *History;
Mexico; Philosophy; Positivism.

BARRIO BOY

892 Orozco, Febe Portillo. A bibliography of
Hispanic literature. ENGLISH JOURNAL, Vol.
71, no. 7 (November 1982), p. 58-62.
English. DESCR: *Bibliography; BLESS ME,
ULTIMA; CHICANO; EL SOL Y LOS DE ABAJO;
GRITO DEL SOL; HEART OF AZTLAN; *Literature;
POCHO; WE ARE CHICANOS.

Barrio, Raymond

893 Walia, Adorna. Book review of: THE PLUM PLUM
PICKERS. BILINGUAL JOURNAL, Vol. 6, no. 1
(Fall 1982), p. 30-31. English. DESCR:
Agricultural Laborers; Book Reviews;
California; *Migrant Labor; Santa Clara
County, CA; *THE PLUM PLUM PICKERS.

BARRIO WARRIORS: HOMEBOYS OF PEACE

894 Rodriguez, Roberto. Book review of: BARRIO
WARRIORS HOMEBOYS OF PEACE. CORAZON DE
AZTLAN, Vol. 1, no. 3 (August, September,
1982), p. 43. English. DESCR: Book Reviews;
Frias, Gustavo.

Barrios

895 Garcia, Mario T. Book review of: LOS ANGELES
BARRIO 1850-1890: A SOCIAL HISTORY. PACIFIC
HISTORICAL REVIEW, Vol. 51, no. 1 (February
1982), p. 90-91. English. DESCR: Book
Reviews; Griswold del Castillo, Ricardo; Los
Angeles, CA; *THE LOS ANGELES BARRIO
1850-1890: A SOCIAL HISTORY.

--   --

Barrios (cont.)

896 Hines, Thomas S. Housing, baseball, and
creeping socialism: the battle of Chavez
Ravine, Los Angeles, 1949-1959. JOURNAL OF
URBAN HISTORY, Vol. 8, no. 2 (1982), p.
123-143. English. **DESCR:** *Chavez Ravine, Los
Angeles, CA; Los Angeles, CA; Urban
Communities; Urban Renewal.

897 Massey, Douglas S. Research note on
residential succession: the Hispanic case.
SOCIAL FORCES, Vol. 61, (March 1983), p.
825-833. English. **DESCR:** Population Trends;
*Residential Segregation; Urban Communities.

898 Mata, Alberto G. Book review of: MEXICAN
AMERICANS IN A DALLAS BARRIO. AZTLAN, Vol.
14, no. 1 (Spring 1983), p. 196-198.
English. **DESCR:** Achor, Shirley; Book
Reviews; Dallas, TX; *MEXICAN AMERICANS IN A
DALLAS BARRIO; Urban Communities.

899 Straight, Susan. The homeboys. NUESTRO, Vol.
6, no. 6 (August 1982), p. 17-19. English.
DESCR: Frias, Gustavo; Racism; *Short Story.

900 Tenants redo neighborhood. NUESTRO, Vol. 6,
no. 2 (March 1982), p. 14. English. **DESCR:**
Police.

Barrios, Benny

901 Flores, Bettina and Flores, Alfredo. Benny
Barrios, Sacramento's living landmark.
NUESTRO, Vol. 6, no. 9 (November 1982), p.
57-58. English. **DESCR:** *Art; Artists;
*Sacramento, CA.

Barrios for Christ Program

902 Vigil, James Diego. Human revitalization:
the six tasks of victory outreach. DREW
GATEWAY, Vol. 52, no. 3 (Spring 1982), p.
49-59. English. **DESCR:** Drug Addicts; Drug
Programs; Gangs; Identity; Pentecostal
Church; Protestant Church; Religion;
*Victory Outreach; Youth.

Barrios, Gregg

903 Garcia, Ignacio M. Book review of: PURO
ROLLO. NUESTRO, Vol. 6, no. 10 (December
1982), p. 60. English. **DESCR:** Book Reviews;
*PURO ROLLO.

Baseball

904 Communications/marketing. HISPANIC BUSINESS,
Vol. 4, no. 8 (August 1983), p. 22+.
English. **DESCR:** Arredondo, Price; De la O,
Val; Films; Marketing; *Mass Media; Radio;
San Antonio CineFestival, TX; Television;
Val De La O Show; Valenzuela, Fernando;
Wright & Arredondo Associates; Wright,
Oscar.

905 Deportes. CAMINOS, Vol. 3, no. 7 (July,
August, 1982), p. 46. Spanish. **DESCR:**
Guerrero, Pedro; Los Angeles Dodgers; Romo,
Vicente.

906 Heuer, Robert J. Baseball expansion: why not
Latin America? NUESTRO, Vol. 7, no. 10
(December 1983), p. 41. English. **DESCR:**
*Latin America; Sports.

907 Ortiz, Carlos V. The Hall at last. NUESTRO,
Vol. 7, no. 1 (January, February, 1983), p.
33-35. English. **DESCR:** Baseball Hall of
Fame; *Marichal, Juan; Sports.

908 Ortiz, Carlos V. NUESTRO'S sixth annual
all-star baseball team. NUESTRO, Vol. 7, no.

2 (March 1983), p. 33-37. English. **DESCR:**
Andujar, Joaquin; Barojas, Salome; Castillo,
Manny; Concepcion, Dave; Cruz, Jose; Garcia,
Damaso; Guerrero, Pedro; Hernandez, Keith;
Lezcano, Sixto; Martinez, Tippy; Pena, Tony;
Piniella, Lou; Sports; Valenzuela, Fernando.

909 Sports updates. CAMINOS, Vol. 3, no. 4
(April 1982), p. 42. English. **DESCR:**
Maldonado, Candy; Orta, Jorge; Pena,
Alejandro; Valenzuela, Fernando.

Baseball Hall of Fame

910 Ortiz, Carlos V. The Hall at last. NUESTRO,
Vol. 7, no. 1 (January, February, 1983), p.
33-35. English. **DESCR:** *Baseball; *Marichal,
Juan; Sports.

BASIC PROBLEMS OF ETHNOPSYCHIATRY

911 Delgado, Melvin. Book review of: BASIC
PROBLEMS OF ETHNOPSYCHIATRY. HISPANIC
JOURNAL OF BEHAVIORAL SCIENCES, Vol. 4, no.
3 (September 1982), p. 380. English. **DESCR:**
Book Reviews; Devereux, George.

Bataille, Gretchen M.

912 Cripps, Thomas. Mexicans, Indians and
movies: the need for a history. WIDE ANGLE:
A FILM QUARTERLY OF THEORY, CRITICISM, AND
PRACTICE, Vol. 5, no. 1 (1982), p. 68-70.
English. **DESCR:** *Book Reviews; Films; IMAGES
OF THE MEXICAN AMERICAN IN FICTION AND FILM;
Native Americans; O'Connor, John E.; Pettit,
Arthur G.; Silet, Charles L.P.;
*Stereotypes; THE HOLLYWOOD INDIAN:
STEREOTYPES OF NATIVE AMERICANS IN FILMS;
THE PRETEND INDIANS: IMAGES OF NATIVE
AMERICANS IN THE MOVIES.

Batine, Rafael

913 Nuestra gente. LATINO, Vol. 53, no. 4 (June
1982), p. 30. English. **DESCR:** *Biographical
Notes; Gimeno, Emil; Tafoya, Tony.

Batista, Fulgencio

914 An anniversary is observed. NUESTRO, Vol. 7,
no. 8 (October 1983), p. 13. English.
DESCR: Cuba; Cubanos; Ferre, Maurice; Local
Government; Miami, FL.

Bay Area, CA

915 Politzer, Robert L.; Shohamy, Elana; and
McGroarty, Mary. Validation of linguistic
and communicative oral language tests for
Spanish-English bilingual programs.
BILINGUAL REVIEW, Vol. 10, no. 1 (January,
April, 1983), p. 3-20. English. **DESCR:** Bahia
Oral Language Test (BOLT); *Bilingual
Bicultural Education; Bilingual Programs;
*Language Assessment; Linguistics;
Sociolinguistics.

Bay Area Global Education Program (BAGEP)

916 A new global approach. NUESTRO, Vol. 7, no.
10 (December 1983), p. 9. English. **DESCR:**
Curriculum; Education; Educational
Innovations; Stanford University, Stanford,
CA.

Beauty Contests

917 Communications/marketing. HISPANIC BUSINESS, Vol. 4, no. 1 (January 1982), p. 13. English. DESCR: *Biographical Notes; Consumers; Hispanic Caucus; *Marketing; Miss Black Velvet Latina; Montemayor, Carlos R.; Philip Morris, Inc.

918 Heublein's Miss Black Velvet II. HISPANIC BUSINESS, Vol. 4, no. 2 (February 1982), p. 12. English. DESCR: Advertising; Consumers; Heublein, Inc.; *Marketing; *Miss Black Velvet Latina.

919 Rhonda Ramirez is Miss Black Velvet Latina. HISPANIC BUSINESS, Vol. 5, no. 3 (March 1983), p. 12-13. English. DESCR: *Celaya, Mona; Marketing; Miss Black Velvet Latina.

Becerra, Gloria V.

920 Two important California appointments. HISPANIC BUSINESS, Vol. 4, no. 4 (April 1982), p. 23. English. DESCR: Appointed Officials; *Patino, Douglas X.

921 Woman chosen by Brown to head tax agency. NUESTRO, Vol. 6, no. 4 (May 1982), p. 27. English. DESCR: Appointed Officials; Taxation.

BEGINNING ENGLISH THROUGH ACTION (BETA)

922 Walia, Adorna. Book review of: BEGINNING ENGLISH THROUGH ACTION. BILINGUAL JOURNAL, Vol. 7, no. 3 (Spring 1983), p. 31-32. English. DESCR: Book Reviews; English as a Second Language; Jackson, P.; Language Arts; Programmed Instruction.

Behavior Modification

923 Henderson, Ronald W. and Brody, Gene H. Effects of ethnicity and child's age on maternal judgments of children's transgressions against persons and property. JOURNAL OF GENETIC PSYCHOLOGY, Vol. 140, no. 2 (June 1982), p. 253-263. English. DESCR: Anglo Americans; Arizona; *Child Rearing; Cultural Characteristics; Native Americans; *Socialization; Tucson, AZ.

924 Hunsaker, Alan. A prompt/reward technique to elicit socially acceptable behavior with Chicano gang delinquents. HISPANIC JOURNAL OF BEHAVIORAL SCIENCES, Vol. 5, no. 1 (March 1983), p. 105-113. English. DESCR: *Gangs; Juvenile Delinquency; Socialization.

925 Stumphauzer, J.S. Training Mexican American mental health personnel in behavior therapy. JOURNAL OF BEHAVIOR THERAPY AND EXPERIMENTAL PSYCHIATRY, Vol. 14, no. 3 (September 1983), p. 215-217. English. DESCR: Mental Health; *Mental Health Personnel.

Beilson, Anthony C.

926 Community watching. CAMINOS, Vol. 3, no. 5 (May 1982), p. 56-57. Bilingual. DESCR: Adelante Mujer Hispana Conference; Agricultural Laborers; Boycotts; Chacon, Peter R.; Chicanas; *Cultural Organizations; Farm Labor Organizing Commmittee (FLOC); Financial Aid; Hollenbeck Junior High School, Los Angeles, CA; Junior High School Students; National League of Cities; Optimist Club of Greater East Los Angeles; Organizations; Project WELL (We Enjoy Learning & Leadership); Torres, Art.

Bell, Terrell H.

927 Baca, Judith F. Secretary of Education Terrell Bell speaks out. LATINO, Vol. 54, no. 2 (March 1983), p. 24+. English. DESCR: *Education.

Bell, William M.

928 Langley, Roger. Roger Langley's Hispanic beat. HISPANIC BUSINESS, Vol. 4, no. 3 (March 1982), p. 22. English. DESCR: *Appointed Officials; Equal Employment Opportunity Commission (EEOC).

Belli, Gioconda

929 Aldaraca, Bridget. The poetry of Gioconda Belli. MAIZE, Vol. 5, no. 3-4 (Spring, Summer, 1982), p. 18-21. English. DESCR: Literary Criticism; *Nicaragua; *Poetry; Revolutions.

930 Banberger, Ellen. Poesia nicaraguense. MAIZE, Vol. 5, no. 3-4 (Spring, Summer, 1982), p. 64-77. Spanish. DESCR: Cardenal, Ernesto; Carrillo, Ernesto; Coronel Urtecho, Jose; Gadea, Gerardo; Gomez, Manuel; Murillo, Rosario; *Nicaragua; Ojeda, Mirna; *Poetry; Revolutions; Rugama, Leonel.

Beltran, Robert

931 Robert Beltran. LATINA, Vol. 1, no. 2 (February, March, 1983), p. 46-49. English. DESCR: Artists; Biography.

Belvedere Childcare Center

932 A sheriff's X-mas. CAMINOS, Vol. 3, no. 1 (January 1982), p. 40. Bilingual. DESCR: *Block, Sherman; *Christmas; Holidays.

Benavidez, Roy

933 Mimiaga, Hector. Back in the step with America's Drummers: I feel good again. NUESTRO, Vol. 6, no. 9 (November 1982), p. 20. English. DESCR: Political Prisoners; Veterans; Vietnam War.

Benavidez, Virginia

934 Ramirez, Belinda. In solidarity with El Salvador. CAMINOS, Vol. 3, no. 5 (May 1982), p. 9. English. DESCR: *Committee in Solidarity with the People of El Salvador (CISPES); Organizations; San Francisco, CA.

Bender Gestalt Test

935 Obrzut, John E.; Hansen, Robert L.; and Heath, Charles P. The effectiveness of visual information processing training with Hispanic children. JOURNAL OF GENERAL PSYCHOLOGY, Vol. 10, no. 2 (October 1982), p. 165-174. English. DESCR: *Academic Achievement; Colorado; Intelligence Tests; Primary School Education.

Bender Visual Motor Gestalt Test

936 Sattler, Jerome M. and Gwynne, John. Ethnicity and Bender Visual Motor Gestalt Test performance. JOURNAL OF SCHOOL PSYCHOLOGY, Vol. 20, no. 1 (Spring 1982), p. 69-71. English. DESCR: Anglo Americans; Psychological Testing; System of Multicultural Pluralistic Assessment (SOMPA).

BENJY LOPEZ: A PICARESQUE TALE OF EMIGRATION AND RETURN

937 Hoffer, Bates L. Sociology by value systems: explication and some implications of two studies on the folklore of Hispanics in the United States. BILINGUAL REVIEW, Vol. 9, no. 2 (May, August, 1982), p. 172-177. Bilingual. **DESCR:** Braceros; *Chicanos in American Literature; Comparative Literature; Folklore; Herrera Sobek, Maria; Levine, Barry B.; THE BRACERO EXPERIENCE: ELITELORE VERSUS FOLKLORE.

Benson Latin American Collection

938 LULAC: 53 years of continued achievement (photoessay). CAMINOS, Vol. 4, no. 5 (May 1983), p. 40-41. English. **DESCR:** *League of United Latin American Citizens (LULAC); Organizations; University of Texas at Austin.

Berdeguez, Sonia Estela

939 Velez, Larry A. Sonia Berdequez; police detective. NUESTRO, Vol. 6, no. 1 (January, February, 1982), p. 20-21. English. **DESCR:** Fashion; Latin Americans; Police.

Berio, Yvonne C.

940 Reporter beaten for story pursuit. NUESTRO, Vol. 7, no. 1 (January, February, 1983), p. 11-12. English. **DESCR:** Journalists; Police; San Juan, Puerto Rico.

Berlanga, Hugo

941 Hamner, Richard. Hispanics and redistricting: what you see is not always what you get. NATIONAL HISPANIC JOURNAL, Vol. 1, no. 2 (Winter 1982), p. 25-30. English. **DESCR:** Elections; Hispanic Reapportionment District; National Association of Latino Elected Officials (NALEO); Political Representation; Politics; *Reapportionment; *Roybal, Edward R.; Santillan, Richard.

Berlin Wall

942 Buckley, William F. Doing the impossible. NATIONAL REVIEW, Vol. 35, no. 17 (September 2, 1983), p. 1097. English. **DESCR:** *Immigration; Immigration Law.

Bermudez & Associates

943 Communications/marketing. HISPANIC BUSINESS, Vol. 5, no. 8 (August 1983), p. 26. English. **DESCR:** Advertising Agencies; *Broadcast Media; Carranza Associates; Directories; Marketing.

Bermudez, Maria Teresa

944 Family favorites. NUESTRO, Vol. 7, no. 10 (December 1983), p. 36-38. English. **DESCR:** Book Reviews; *MEXICAN FAMILY FAVORITES COOKBOOK; Recipes.

Bernal, Ignacio

945 Heizer, Robert. Book review of: THE OLMEC WORLD. JOURNAL OF ETHNIC STUDIES, Vol. 15, no. 3 (Fall 1977), p. 124-125. English. **DESCR:** Book Reviews; Olmecs; *Precolumbian Society; *THE OLMEC WORLD.

Bernal, Joseph

946 Achor, Shirley. Book review of: GUNPOWDER JUSTICE: A REASSESSMENT OF THE TEXAS RANGERS. INTERNATIONAL MIGRATION REVIEW, Vol. 16, no. 2 (Summer 1982), p. 491-492. English. **DESCR:** Book Reviews; *GUNPOWDER JUSTICE: A REASSESSMENT OF THE TEXAS RANGERS; Pena, Alberto; Samora, Julian; Texas Rangers.

947 Achor, Shirley. Book review of: GUNPOWDER JUSTICE: A REASSESSMENT OF THE TEXAS RANGERS. INTERNATIONAL MIGRATION REVIEW, Vol. 16, no. 2 (Summer 1982), p. 491-492. English. **DESCR:** Book Reviews; *GUNPOWDER JUSTICE: A REASSESSMENT OF THE TEXAS RANGERS; History; Pena, Alberto; Samora, Julian; Texas Rangers.

Bernal, Louis Carlos

948 Rodriguez, Luis Javier. Profile of Luis Carlos Bernal. CORAZON DE AZTLAN, Vol. 1, no. 3 (August, September, 1982), p. 22-23. English. **DESCR:** Biography; Photography.

Bernalillo County, NM

949 Samet, Jonathan M., et al. Respiratory disease in a New Mexico population sample of Hispanic and non-Hispanic whites. AMERICAN REVIEW OF RESPIRATORY DISEASE, Vol. 125, no. 2 (February 1982), p. 152-157. English. **DESCR:** *Medical Research; Medicine; Public Health.

Bescher, George

950 Hunsaker, Alan. Book review of: ANGEL DUST: AN ETHNOGRAPHIC STUDY OF PCP USERS; HEROIN USE IN THE BARRIO; DRUG AND ALCOHOL ABUSE: A CLINICAL GUIDE TO DIAGNOSIS AND TREATMENT. HISPANIC JOURNAL OF BEHAVIORAL SCIENCES, Vol. 4, no. 1 (March 1982), p. 118-121. English. **DESCR:** Agar, Michael; *ANGEL DUST: AN ETHNOGRAPHIC STUDY OF PCP USERS; Book Reviews; Bullington, Bruce; *DRUG AND ALCOHOL ABUSE: A CLINICAL GUIDE TO DIAGNOSIS AND TREATMENT; Feldman, Harvey W.; *HEROIN USE IN THE BARRIO; Schuckit, Marc A..

Betancourt, Jose L.

951 Gente. NUESTRO, Vol. 7, no. 2 (March 1983), p. 51. English. **DESCR:** Artists; *Chicanas; Crime Victims Fund; Federal Government; Juarez, Joe; Military Service; Saldana, Teresa; Vargas, Alberto; Victims for Victims.

Bexar County, TX

952 Valdez, Avelardo. Recent increases in intermarriage by Mexican American males: Bexar County, Texas from 1971 to 1980. SOCIAL SCIENCE QUARTERLY, Vol. 64, (March 1983), p. 136-144. English. **DESCR:** *Intermarriage.

BEYOND THE NUCLEAR FAMILY MODEL

953 Vierra, Andrea. Book review of: BEYOND THE NUCLEAR FAMILY MODEL: CROSS CULTURAL PERSPECTIVES. HISPANIC JOURNAL OF BEHAVIORAL SCIENCES, Vol. 5, no. 3 (September 1983), p. 349-352. English. **DESCR:** Book Reviews; Family; Lenero-Otero, Luis.

Bibliography

954 Arora, Shirley L. A critical bibliography of Mexican American proverbs. AZTLAN, Vol. 13, no. 1-2 (Spring, Fall, 1982), p. 71-80. English. **DESCR:** Dichos; Folklore.

Bibliography (cont.)

955 Bedard, Evelyn M. Book review of: HISPANIC MENTAL HEALTH RESEARCH: A REFERENCE GUIDE. RQ - REFERENCE AND ADULT SERVICES DIVISION, Vol. 22, no. 1 (Fall 1982), p. 93. English. **DESCR:** Book Reviews; *HISPANIC MENTAL HEALTH RESEARCH: A REFERENCE GUIDE; Mental Health; Newton, Frank; Olmedo, Esteban L.; Padilla, Amado M.

956 Chavaria, Elvira. Book review of: THE MEXICAN AMERICAN: A CRITICAL GUIDE TO RESEARCH AIDS. AZTLAN, Vol. 14, no. 1 (Spring 1983), p. 192-195. English. **DESCR:** Book Reviews; Reference Works; Robinson, Barbara J.; Robinson, J. Cordell; *THE MEXICAN AMERICAN: A CRITICAL GUIDE TO RESEARCH AIDS.

957 de Cuenca, Pilar and Alvarez, Rudolph, Ines. Library holdings of the Office of Bilingual Education, city of New York: a selected bibliography. BILINGUAL REVIEW, Vol. 9, no. 2 (May, August, 1982), p. 127-152. English. **DESCR:** *Bilingual Bicultural Education; *Office of Bilingual Education Library, New York, NY; Reference Works.

958 Garza, Hector. Directory of Chicano/Latino films and their distributors. BILINGUAL REVIEW, Vol. 10, no. 2-3 (May, December, 1983), p. 191-202. English. **DESCR:** *Films.

959 Garza-Livingston, M'Liss. Annotated bibliography of selected materials on la mujer y la chicana. COMADRE, no. 1 (Summer 1977), p. 49-54. English. **DESCR:** *Chicanas.

960 Garza-Livingston, M'Liss. Annotated bibliography of selected materials on la mujer y la chicana. COMADRE, no. 2 (Spring 1978), p. 51-56. English. **DESCR:** *Chicanas.

961 Learn more about Mexico. CAMINOS, Vol. 3, no. 6 (June 1982), p. 34-35. English. **DESCR:** *Mexico.

962 Marquez, Maria Teresa. Book review of: A SELECTED AND ANNOTATED BIBLIOGRAPHY OF CHICANO STUDIES. AZTLAN, Vol. 14, no. 1 (Spring 1983), p. 191-192. English. **DESCR:** *A SELECTED AND ANNOTATED BIBLIOGRAPHY OF CHICANO STUDIES; Book Reviews; Reference Works; Tatum, Charles.

963 Marti, Oscar R., comp. Bibliography. AZTLAN, Vol. 14, no. 2 (Fall 1983), p. 405-417. English. **DESCR:** *Barreda, Gabino; History; Mexico; Philosophy; Positivism.

964 Martinez, Julio A. Book review of: A BIBLIOGRAPHY OF CRITICISM OF CONTEMPORARY CHICANO LITERATURE. RQ - REFERENCE AND ADULT SERVICES DIVISION, Vol. 22, no. 1 (Fall 1982), p. 90. English. **DESCR:** *A BIBLIOGRAPHY OF CRITICISM OF CONTEMPORARY CHICANO LITERATURE; Book Reviews; Eger, Ernestina N.; Literary Criticism; Literature.

965 Martinez, Julio A. Book review of: A DECADE OF CHICANO LITERATURE (1970-1979)-CRITICAL ESSAYS AND BIBLIOGRAPHY. RQ - REFERENCE AND ADULT SERVICES DIVISION, Vol. 22, no. 1 (Fall 1982), p. 90. English. **DESCR:** *A DECADE OF CHICANO LITERATURE (1970-1979): CRITICAL ESSAYS AND BIBLIOGRAPHY; Book Reviews; Gonzalez, Raquel Quiroz; Literary Criticism; Literatura Chicanesca; Literature; Trujillo, Robert.

966 Oczon, Annabelle M. Land grants in New Mexico: a selective bibliography. NEW MEXICO HISTORICAL REVIEW, Vol. 57, no. 1 (January 1982), p. 81-87. English. **DESCR:** *Land Grants; New Mexico.

967 Orozco, Febe Portillo. A bibliography of Hispanic literature. ENGLISH JOURNAL, Vol. 71, no. 7 (November 1982), p. 58-62. English. **DESCR:** BARRIO BOY; BLESS ME, ULTIMA; CHICANO; EL SOL Y LOS DE ABAJO; GRITO DEL SOL; HEART OF AZTLAN; *Literature; POCHO; WE ARE CHICANOS.

968 Robinson, Barbara J. Book review of: THE MEXICAN-AMERICAN WAR: AN ANNOTATED BIBLIOGRAPHY. REVISTA INTERAMERICANA DE BIBLIOGRAFIA, Vol. 32, no. 2 (1982), p. 222-223. English. **DESCR:** Book Reviews; *THE MEXICAN-AMERICAN WAR: AN ANNOTATED BIBLIOGRAPHY; Tutorow, Norman E.; War.

969 Schon, Isabel. Spanish books for children. BOOKLIST, Vol. 78, no. 20 (June 15, 1982), p. 1373-1374. English. **DESCR:** Argentina; *Children's Literature; Mexico; Spain; Spanish Language; Venezuela.

970 Schon, Isabel. Spanish books for children. BOOKLIST, Vol. 79, (February 15, 1983), p. 783-784. English. **DESCR:** *Children's Literature; Mexico; Spain; Spanish Language; Venezuela.

971 Suggested reading. CAMINOS, Vol. 3, no. 9 (October 1982), p. 19,44. English.

972 Weinberg, Meyer. Bibliography of desegration: Los Angeles. INTEGRATED EDUCATION, Vol. 20, no. 1- (January, April, 1982), p. 32-33. English. **DESCR:** Los Angeles, CA; *Segregation and Desegregation.

973 Weinberg, Meyer. Special higher education bibliography. INTEGRATED EDUCATION, Vol. 20, no. 3-5 (May 1982), p. 45-49. English. **DESCR:** *Higher Education.

974 Woods, Richard D. Book review of: SPANISH AND ENGLISH OF UNITED STATES HISPANOS: A CRITICAL, ANNOTATED, LINGUISTIC BIBLIOGRAPHY. JOURNAL OF ETHNIC STUDIES, Vol. 4, no. 3 (Fall 1976), p. 116. English. **DESCR:** Accentedness; Bills, Garland D.; Book Reviews; Craddock, Jerry R.; Language Patterns; *SPANISH AND ENGLISH OF U.S. HISPANOS: A CRITICAL, ANNOTATED, LINGUISTIC BIBLIOGRAPHY; Spanish Language; Teschner, Richard V.

975 Zimmerman, Enid. An annotated bibliography of Chicano literature: novels, short fiction, poetry, and drama, 1970-1980. BILINGUAL REVIEW, Vol. 9, no. 3 (September, December, 1982), p. 227-251. English. **DESCR:** Literature; Poetry; Teatro.

A BIBLIOGRAPHY OF CRITICISM OF CONTEMPORARY CHICANO LITERATURE

976 Martinez, Julio A. Book review of: A BIBLIOGRAPHY OF CRITICISM OF CONTEMPORARY CHICANO LITERATURE. RQ - REFERENCE AND ADULT SERVICES DIVISION, Vol. 22, no. 1 (Fall 1982), p. 90. English. **DESCR:** Bibliography; Book Reviews; Eger, Ernestina N.; Literary Criticism; Literature.

977 Woodbridge, Hensley C. Outstanding new bibliography about Chicano literature. BILINGUAL REVIEW, Vol. 10, no. 1 (January, April, 1983), p. 69-72. English. **DESCR:** Book Reviews; Eger, Ernestina N.

Bicultural Education
    USE: Bilingual Bicultural Education

Biculturalism

978 Acosta, Frank X. and Cristo, Martha H.
    Bilingual-Bicultural interpreters as
    psychotherapeutic bridges: a program note.
    JOURNAL OF COMMUNITY PSYCHOLOGY, Vol. 10,
    no. 1 (January 1982), p. 54-56. English.
    DESCR: Bilingualism; Community Mental
    Health; Doctor Patient Relations; East Los
    Angeles, CA; *Mental Health Personnel;
    Mental Health Programs; Translations.

979 Anderson, Alfred. Training teachers for the
    bicultural part of bilingual-bicultural
    education. INTEGRATED EDUCATION, Vol. 20,
    no. 1-2 (January, April, 1982), p. 73-75.
    English. **DESCR:** *Bilingual Bicultural
    Education; Teacher Attitudes; *Teacher
    Training.

980 Armengol, Armando; Manley, Joan H.; and
    Teschner, Richard V. The international
    bilingual city: how a university meets the
    challenge. FOREIGN LANGUAGE ANNALS, Vol. 15,
    no. 4 (September 1982), p. 289-295. English.
    DESCR: Bilingualism; Border Region; Ciudad
    Juarez, Chihuahua, Mexico; El Paso, TX;
    *Language Development; Spanish Language;
    University of Texas at El Paso.

981 Burns, Allan F. Politics, pedagogy, and
    culture in bilingual classrooms: a case
    study. NABE JOURNAL, Vol. 6, no. 2-3
    (Winter, Spring, 1981, 1982), p. 35-51.
    English. **DESCR:** *Bilingual Bicultural
    Education; Bilingualism; Cultural
    Characteristics; Teacher-pupil Interaction.

982 Garza, Raymond T., et al. Biculturalism,
    locus of control and leader behavior in
    ethnically mixed small groups. JOURNAL OF
    APPLIED SOCIAL PSYCHOLOGY, Vol. 12, no. 3
    (May, June, 1982), p. 237-253. English.
    DESCR: Attitude (Psychological); Culture;
    Interpersonal Relations; Leadership; *Locus
    of Control; Social Psychology.

983 Gurwitt, Rob. Widespread political efforts
    open new era for Hispanics. CONGRESSIONAL
    QUARTERLY WEEKLY REPORT, Vol. 40, (October
    23, 1982), p. 2707-2709. English. **DESCR:**
    Elected Officials; *Politics.

984 Kanellos, Nicolas. Devorados pero no
    digeridos. Paper presented at the "Dialogo
    de las Americas" conference. Mexico, D.F.
    September 9-13, 1982. REVISTA
    CHICANO-RIQUENA, Vol. 10, no. 4 (Fall 1982),
    p. 5-6. Spanish. **DESCR:** Ethnic Groups;
    Stereotypes.

985 Morgan, Thomas B. The Latinization of
    America. ESQUIRE, Vol. 99, no. 5 (May 1983),
    p. 47-56. English. **DESCR:** Acculturation;
    Assimilation; Bilingualism; *Population
    Trends.

986 Morton, Carlos. La vida: growing up in two
    cultures. NATIONAL HISPANIC JOURNAL, Vol. 1,
    no. 4 (Spring 1983), p. 23. English. **DESCR:**
    Education; *EDUCATION ACROSS CULTURES;
    Morton, Carlos.

987 Solis, Arnaldo. Theory of biculturality.
    CALMECAC, Vol. 1, no. 1 (Spring 1980), p.
    7-12. English.

988 Solis, Arnaldo. Theory of biculturality.
    CALMECAC, Vol. 2, (Spring 1981), p. 36-41.
    English. **DESCR:** *Banas, L.K.

989 Walia, Adorna. Book review of: CULTURE AND
    THE BILINGUAL CLASSROOM: STUDIES IN
    CLASSROOM ETHNOGRAPHY. BILINGUAL JOURNAL,
    Vol. 6, no. 4 (Summer 1982), p. 30-31.
    English. **DESCR:** Au, Kathryn Hu-Pei;
    *Bilingual Bicultural Education; Book
    Reviews; Cultural Pluralism; *CULTURE AND
    THE BILINGUAL CLASSROOM: STUDIES IN
    CLASSROOM ETHNOLOGY; Guthrie, Grace Pung;
    Trueba, Henry T.

Bilingual Ballots

990 Hispanic voting trends. HISPANIC BUSINESS,
    Vol. 4, no. 8 (August 1983), p. 28-29.
    English. **DESCR:** Bilingualism; California;
    *Elections; Mexican American Legal Defense
    and Educational Fund (MALDEF); Southwest
    Voter Registration Education Project (SVRP);
    Texas; Voter Turnout.

Bilingual Bicultural Education

991 Amastae, Jon. The issue of language
    proficiency. BILINGUAL REVIEW, Vol. 10, no.
    1 (January, April, 1983), p. 73-80. English.
    DESCR: Alatis, James E.; Book Reviews; *GURT
    1980: CURRENT ISSUES IN BILINGUAL EDUCATION.

992 Anderson, Alfred. Training teachers for the
    bicultural part of bilingual-bicultural
    education. INTEGRATED EDUCATION, Vol. 20,
    no. 1-2 (January, April, 1982), p. 73-75.
    English. **DESCR:** Biculturalism; Teacher
    Attitudes; *Teacher Training.

993 Aparicio, Frances R. Teaching Spanish to the
    native speaker at the college level.
    HISPANIA, Vol. 66, (May 1983), p. 232-239.
    English. **DESCR:** Spanish Language.

994 Appeals court overturns Texas bilingual
    order. PHI DELTA KAPPAN, Vol. 64, no. 1
    (September 1982), p. 75. English. **DESCR:**
    *Educational Law and Legislation; Texas.

995 Baker, Catherine A. Bilingual education: que
    pasa? CONTEMPORARY EDUCATION, Vol. 54, no. 2
    (Winter 1983), p. 105-108. English. **DESCR:**
    Educational Law and Legislation.

996 Balasubramonian, Krishna. Not on test scores
    alone: the qualitative side to program
    evaluation. BILINGUAL JOURNAL, Vol. 7, no. 2
    (Winter 1983), p. 17-21,40. English. **DESCR:**
    *Curriculum; Educational Tests and
    Measurements; ELEMENTARY AND SECONDARY
    EDUCATION ACT; Evaluation (Educational);
    Proposals.

997 Baldonado, Lisa. A university program to
    meet Chicago's bilingual needs. BILINGUAL
    JOURNAL, Vol. 7, no. 4 (Summer 1983), p.
    15-17,28. English. **DESCR:** Chicago, IL;
    Curriculum; *Teacher Training; Urban
    Education.

998 Barry, Joseph E. Politics, bilingual
    education, and the curriculum. EDUCATIONAL
    LEADERSHIP, Vol. 40, no. 8 (May 1983), p.
    56-60. English. **DESCR:** Educational Law and
    Legislation; Educational Theory and
    Practice.

999 Bell, Michael Davitt. Fitting into a
    tradition of autobiography. CHANGE, Vol. 14,
    no. 7 (October 1982), p. 36-39. English.
    DESCR: Affirmative Action; Assimilation;
    Biography; Book Reviews; *HUNGER OF MEMORY:
    THE EDUCATION OF RICHARD RODRIGUEZ;
    Rodriguez, Richard.

Bilingual Bicultural Education (cont.)

1000 Beveridge, John. Bi-lingual programs: some
     doubts and comments. THE CLEARING HOUSE,
     Vol. 55, no. 5 (January 1982), p. 214-217.
     English. **DESCR:** Bilingualism; Curriculum.

1001 Bilingual effort offers few jobs. NUESTRO,
     Vol. 7, no. 6 (August 1983), p. 13. English.
     DESCR: California; Education; Teaching
     Profession.

1002 Bilingual fund cut. NUESTRO, Vol. 6, no. 2
     (March 1914), p. 14. English.

1003 Blomstedt, Robert; Thomas, Jackie; and
     Teyna, Tadeo. Applying existential thought
     to bilingual education. BILINGUAL JOURNAL,
     Vol. 7, no. 4 (Summer 1983), p. 26,28.
     English. **DESCR:** Educational Innovations;
     *Philosophy.

1004 Book review of: HUNGER OF MEMORY: THE
     EDUCATION OF RICHARD RODRIGUEZ. SAN
     FRANCISCO REVIEW OF BOOKS, Vol. 7, (Summer
     1982), p. 11. English. **DESCR:** Attitude
     (Psychological); Book Reviews; *HUNGER OF
     MEMORY: THE EDUCATION OF RICHARD RODRIGUEZ;
     Identity; Rodriguez, Richard.

1005 Burke, P.E. Immigrant Mexican children
     hurdle the English barrier. TIMES (London)
     [EDUCATIONAL SUPPLEMENT], Vol. 3447, (July
     23, 1982), p. 15. English. **DESCR:** Children;
     English Language; Immigrants.

1006 Burns, Allan F. Politics, pedagogy, and
     culture in bilingual classrooms: a case
     study. NABE JOURNAL, Vol. 6, no. 2-3
     (Winter, Spring, 1981, 1982), p. 35-51.
     English. **DESCR:** Biculturalism; Bilingualism;
     Cultural Characteristics; Teacher-pupil
     Interaction.

1007 Burns, Melinda. Myths of bilingual
     education=Mitos de la educacion bilingue.
     CAMINOS, Vol. 2, no. 7 (December 1981), p.
     19. Bilingual.

1008 Burns, Robert C. The miracle teachers:
     portraits of women who challenged themselves
     and at the same time challenged a system
     which had relegated them to
     nonprofessional... NUESTRO, Vol. 6, no. 6
     (August 1982), p. 13-16. English. **DESCR:**
     Short Story; *Teaching Profession.

1009 Calvillo-Craig, Lorenza. Bilingual education
     and business. CAMINOS, Vol. 3, no. 10
     (November 1982), p. 41. Bilingual. **DESCR:**
     *Business.

1010 Campbell, Jack K. Senator Yarborough and the
     Texan RWY brand on bilingual education and
     federal aid. EDUCATIONAL STUDIES, Vol. 12,
     no. 4 (Winter 1981, 1982), p. 403-415.
     English. **DESCR:** Educational Law and
     Legislation; History; Social History and
     Conditions; Texas; Yarborough, Ralph
     Webster.

1011 Carrillo, Federico M. How should Spanish
     speakers be taught Spanish in the schools?
     BILINGUAL JOURNAL, Vol. 7, no. 4 (Summer
     1983), p. 18-22. English. **DESCR:** *Language
     Arts; Sociolinguistics; Spanish Language.

1012 Carrison, Muriel Paskin. Bilingual-no!
     PRINCIPAL, Vol. 62, no. 3 (January 1983), p.
     9. English. **DESCR:** Cultural Characteristics;
     Education Equalization; Socioeconomic
     Factors.

1013 Cepeda, Rita M. Healthy prospects for

bilingual education=Prospectos fructiferos
para la educacion bilingue. CAMINOS, Vol. 2,
no. 7 (December 1981), p. 24-27. Bilingual.

1014 Cervantes, Robert. Bilingual education
     questions & answers=Educacion bilingue:
     preguntas y respuestas. CAMINOS, Vol. 2, no.
     7 (December 1981), p. 18-19. Bilingual.

1015 Chacon, Peter (Assemblyman). The politics of
     bilingual education=La politica de la
     legislacion bilingue. CAMINOS, Vol. 2, no. 7
     (December 1981), p. 14-17. Bilingual.
     DESCR: Educational Law and Legislation.

1016 Chavarria, Jesus. End the bilingual
     monopoly. HISPANIC BUSINESS, Vol. 5, no. 7
     (July 1983), p. 6. English.

1017 Chesterfield, Kathleen Barrows and
     Chesterfield, Ray A. Peer interaction
     language proficiency and language preference
     in bilingual pre-school classrooms. HISPANIC
     JOURNAL OF BEHAVIORAL SCIENCES, Vol. 4, no.
     4 (December 1982), p. 467-486. English.
     DESCR: Children; Language Proficiency.

1018 Chesterfield, Ray, et al. The influence of
     teachers and peers on second language
     acquisition in bilingual preschool programs.
     TESOL QUARTERLY, Vol. 17, no. 3 (September
     1983), p. 401-419. English. **DESCR:** Early
     Childhood Education; *English as a Second
     Language; Language Development;
     Teacher-pupil Interaction.

1019 Chesterfield, Ray P.; Moll, Luis C.; and
     Perez, Ray. A naturalistic approach for
     evaluation. BILINGUAL JOURNAL, Vol. 6, no. 1
     (Fall 1982), p. 23-26. English. **DESCR:**
     Curriculum; Early Childhood Education;
     *Evaluation (Educational).

1020 Cohen, Andrew D. Researching the linguistic
     outcomes of bilingual programs. BILINGUAL
     REVIEW, Vol. 9, no. 2 (May, August, 1982),
     p. 97-108. English. **DESCR:** Linguistic
     Theory; *Linguistics.

1021 Cohen, Bernard H. It's called mainstreaming.
     LATINO, Vol. 54, no. 3 (April 1983), p.
     20-21. English.

1022 Cohen, Bernard H. Parent involvement in
     program evaluation. BILINGUAL JOURNAL, Vol.
     7, no. 2 (Winter 1983), p. 29-34. English.
     DESCR: Community School Relationships;
     Curriculum; *Evaluation (Educational);
     Project PIE (Parents Involvement in
     Evaluation).

1023 Cohen, Bernard H. Two bridges. LATINO, Vol.
     54, no. 2 (March 1983), p. 16-18. English.
     DESCR: *Cultural Pluralism.

1024 Consalvo, Robert W. Book review of: PROGRAM
     IMPACT EVALUATIONS: AN INTRODUCTION FOR
     MANAGERS OF TITLE VII PROJECTS - A DRAFT
     GUIDEBOOK. BILINGUAL JOURNAL, Vol. 7, no. 2
     (Winter 1983), p. 36-37. English. **DESCR:**
     Bissell, Joan; Book Reviews; Educational
     Administration; ELEMENTARY AND SECONDARY
     EDUCATION ACT; Evaluation (Educational);
     *PROGRAM IMPACT EVALUATIONS: AN INTRODUCTION
     FOR MANAGERS OF TITLE VII PROJECTS - A DRAFT
     GUIDEBOOK ESEA TITLE VII.

1025 Consalvo, Robert W. and Orlandi, Lisanio R.
     Principles and practices of data collection
     and management. BILINGUAL JOURNAL, Vol. 7,
     no. 2 (Winter 1983), p. 13-16. English.
     DESCR: Educational Statistics; *Evaluation
     (Educational); Research Methodology.

Bilingual Bicultural Education (cont.)

1026 Cordasco, Francesco. Bilingual education:
overview and inventory. EDUCATIONAL FORUM,
Vol. 47, (Spring 1983), p. 321-334.
English. DESCR: Educational Law and
Legislation; Educational Theory and
Practice; English as a Second Language;
History; Literature Reviews.

1027 Cordasco, Francesco. Bilingual education in
American schools: a bibliographical essay.
IMMIGRATION HISTORY NEWSLETTER, Vol. 14, no.
1 (May 1982), p. 1-8. English. DESCR:
Literature Reviews.

1028 Cunningham, John W. Library services for the
Spanish speaking. CATHOLIC LIBRARY WORLD,
Vol. 53, no. 8 (March 1982), p. 347-348.
English. DESCR: Library Education; *Library
Services.

1029 de Cuenca, Pilar and Alvarez, Rudolph, Ines.
Library holdings of the Office of Bilingual
Education, city of New York: a selected
bibliography. BILINGUAL REVIEW, Vol. 9, no.
2 (May, August, 1982), p. 127-152. English.
DESCR: Bibliography; *Office of Bilingual
Education Library, New York, NY; Reference
Works.

1030 De George, George P. The guest editor
speaks. BILINGUAL JOURNAL, Vol. 7, no. 2
(Winter 1983), p. 6. English. DESCR:
Educational Administration; *Evaluation
(Educational).

1031 De George, George P. Selecting tests for
bilingual program evaluation. BILINGUAL
JOURNAL, Vol. 7, no. 2 (Winter 1983), p.
22-28,40. English. DESCR: Curriculum;
Educational Tests and Measurements;
*Evaluation (Educational).

1032 DeMauro, Gerald E. Models and assumptions
for bilingual education evaluation.
BILINGUAL JOURNAL, Vol. 7, no. 2 (Winter
1983), p. 8-12,40. English. DESCR:
Curriculum; Educational Tests and
Measurements; *Evaluation (Educational);
Language Assessment Battery.

1033 Dickens, E. Larry. Book review of: THE
POLITICS OF BILINGUAL EDUCATION: A STUDY OF
FOUR SOUTHWEST TEXAS COMMUNITIES. SOUTHWEST
ECONOMY AND SOCIETY, Vol. 1, no. 1 (Spring
1976), p. 47-48. English. DESCR: Book
Reviews; Hardgrave, Robert L.; Hinojosa,
Santiago; *THE POLITICS OF BILINGUAL
EDUCATION: A STUDY OF FOUR SOUTHWEST TEXAS
COMMUNITIES.

1034 Dominguez, Simon. A private bilingual summer
school in San Jose" an alternative to public
education. CAMINOS, Vol. 3, no. 10 (November
1982), p. 44-45. English. DESCR: *Private
Schools.

1035 Dubois, Betty Lou. Bilingual bicultural
education: the view from across the campus.
BILINGUAL REVIEW, Vol. 9, no. 3 (September,
December, 1982), p. 272-275. English.
DESCR: ETHNOPERSPECTIVES IN BILINGUAL
EDUCATION RESEARCH: BILINGUAL EDUCATION AND
PUBLIC POLICY IN THE UNITED STATES (Vol. I);
Padilla, Raymond.

1036 Dyer, Esther and Robertson-Kozan, Concha.
Hispanics in the U.S.: implications for
library service. SCHOOL LIBRARY JOURNAL,
Vol. 29, no. 8 (April 1983), p. 27-29.
English. DESCR: *Library Services.

1037 Elford, George. Catholic schools and
bilingual education. MOMENTUM, Vol. 14, no.
1 (February 1983), p. 35-37. English.
DESCR: Catholic Church; Religious Education.

1038 Farmer, Mary. Bilingual integration in San
Diego. HISPANIA, Vol. 65, no. 3 (September
1982), p. 427-429. English. DESCR: San
Diego, CA.

1039 Fillmore, Lili Wong. Language minority
students and school participation: what kind
of English is needed? JOURNAL OF EDUCATION,
Vol. 164, no. 2 (Spring 1982), p. 143-156.
English. DESCR: Early Childhood Education;
English as a Second Language; Language
Proficiency.

1040 Fishman, Joshua A. Sociolinguistic
foundations of bilingual education.
BILINGUAL REVIEW, Vol. 9, no. 1 (January,
April, 1982), p. 1-35. English. DESCR:
Sociolinguistics.

1041 Foster, Charles R. Defusing the issues in
bilingualism and bilingual education. PHI
DELTA KAPPAN, Vol. 63, no. 5 (January 1982),
p. 342-344. English.

1042 Gallegos, Anne; Gallegos, Roberto; and
Rodriguez, Roy. Los inocentes: considering
the special need of the Mexican American
child. CONTEMPORARY EDUCATION, Vol. 54, no.
2 (Winter 1983), p. 109-112. Other. DESCR:
*Handicapped.

1043 Garcia, Herman S. Bilingualism,
biculturalism, and the educational system.
JOURNAL OF NON-WHITE CONCERNS IN PERSONNEL
AND GUIDANCE, Vol. 11, no. 2 (January 1983),
p. 67-74. English. DESCR: *Bilingualism.

1044 Garcia, Paco. Voices: Hispanic voices needed
in the education debate. NUESTRO, Vol. 7,
no. 5 (June, July, 1983), p. 53-54. English.
DESCR: *Discrimination in Education;
*Discrimination in Employment; *Education;
Federal Government; *Latin Americans;
President's Commission on Excellence in
Education; Reagan, Ronald; U.S. Department
of Health, Education and Welfare (HEW).

1045 Garza, Ana. ESL in the bilingual classroom.
BILINGUAL JOURNAL, Vol. 6, no. 4 (Summer
1982), p. 26-29,32. English. DESCR:
Bilingual Inventory of Natural Languages;
*English as a Second Language; Language
Assessment; Language Assessment Battery;
Language Assessment Scales.

1046 Gonzalez, Gustavo. Expressing time through
verb tenses and temporal expressions in
Spanish: age 2.0-4.6. NABE JOURNAL, Vol. 7,
no. 2 (Winter 1983), p. 69-82. English.
DESCR: *Language Development; *Language
Usage; Spanish Language.

1047 Haft, Jonathan D. Assuring equal educational
opportunity for language-minority students:
bilingual education and the Equal
Educational Opportunity Act of 1974.
COLUMBIA JOURNAL OF LAW AND SOCIAL PROBLEMS,
Vol. 18, no. 2 (1983), p. 209-293. English.
DESCR: Civil Rights; Educational Law and
Legislation; English as a Second Language;
*Equal Educational Opportunity Act of 1974
(EEOA); Laws; Students.

1048 Hudelson, Sarah. An introductory examination
of children's invented spelling in Spanish.
NABE JOURNAL, Vol. 6, no. 2-3 (Winter,
Spring, 1981, 1982), p. 53-67. English.
DESCR: Children; *Language Arts; Learning
and Cognition; Spanish Language.

Bilingual Bicultural Education (cont.)

1049 Improving the schools. NUESTRO, Vol. 6, no. 3 (April 1982), p. 9. English. **DESCR:** Education; Puerto Rican Education; Puerto Ricans.

1050 Kincaid, Jill. You can help 3.6 million children. LATINO, Vol. 53, no. 8 (December 1982), p. 19. English.

1051 Krashen, Stephen D. Bilingual education and the case of Richard Rodriguez. CAMINOS, Vol. 3, no. 10 (November 1982), p. 38-40,54. Bilingual. **DESCR:** *Rodriguez, Richard.

1052 Lado, Robert. Aula/the classroom: developmental reading in two languages. NABE JOURNAL, Vol. 6, no. 2-3 (Winter, Spring, 1981, 1982), p. 99-110. English. **DESCR:** Bilingualism; Language Arts; Language Development; Learning and Cognition; *Reading; Spanish Education Development (SED) Center Bilingual Reading Project; Spanish Language.

1053 Lalas, Joselito W. The influence of prior experience in ESL reading. BILINGUAL JOURNAL, Vol. 6, no. 1 (Fall 1982), p. 10-12. English. **DESCR:** English as a Second Language; Learning and Cognition; *Reading.

1054 Levin, Betsy. An analysis of the federal attempt to regulate bilingual education: protecting civil rights or controlling curriculum? JOURNAL OF LAW AND EDUCATION, Vol. 12, no. 1 (January 1983), p. 29-60. English. **DESCR:** Affirmative Action Programs; Civil Rights; Cultural Pluralism; Educational Law and Legislation; Federal Government.

1055 Liberty, Paul G. Director's notebook. BILINGUAL JOURNAL, Vol. 7, no. 4 (Summer 1983), p. 1. English.

1056 Liberty, Paul G. Director's notebook. BILINGUAL JOURNAL, Vol. 7, no. 2 (Winter 1983), p. 1,40. English. **DESCR:** *Evaluation (Educational).

1057 Liberty, Paul G. Director's notebook. BILINGUAL JOURNAL, Vol. 6, no. 2 (Winter 1982), p. 1. English.

1058 Liberty, Paul G. Director's notebook. BILINGUAL JOURNAL, Vol. 6, no. 4 (Summer 1982), p. 1,6. English. **DESCR:** BILINGUAL EDUCATION EVALUATION AND REPORTING SYSTEM; *Curriculum; Evaluation (Educational).

1059 Liberty, Paul G., et al. [Evaluation in bilingual education]. BILINGUAL JOURNAL, Vol. 7, no. 2 (Winter 1983), p. 1-40. English. **DESCR:** Curriculum; Educational Administration; ELEMENTARY AND SECONDARY EDUCATION ACT; *Evaluation (Educational).

1060 Martinez, Olivia. Bilingual education today. CAMINOS, Vol. 3, no. 10 (November 1982), p. 32-35,52+. Bilingual.

1061 Martinez, Paul E. Serna v. Portales: the plight of bilingual education four years later. JOURNAL OF ETHNIC STUDIES, Vol. 7, no. 2 (Summer 1979), p. 109-114. English. **DESCR:** Chicano Youth Organization; Civil Rights; Portales Municipal Schools; *Portales, NM; Serna v. Portales Municipal Schools.

1062 McConnell, Beverly B. Evaluating bilingual education using a time series design. NEW DIRECTIONS FOR PROGRAM EVALUATION, no. 16-12 (1982), p. 19-32. English. **DESCR:** *Evaluation (Educational).

1063 McFadden, Bernard J. Bilingual education and the law. JOURNAL OF LAW AND EDUCATION, Vol. 12, no. 1 (January 1983), p. 1-27. English. **DESCR:** Administration of Justice; Discrimination in Education; Educational Law and Legislation; History.

1064 Melendez, Melinda. Bilingual education interest groups: their past and their future=Grupos interesados en educacion bilingue: su pasado y su futuro [sic]. CAMINOS, Vol. 2, no. 7 (December 1981), p. 20-22. Bilingual. **DESCR:** Organizations.

1065 Mendez, Gloria I. Bilingual children's adaptation after a transitional bilingual education. METAS, Vol. 3, no. 1 (Summer 1982), p. 1-112. English. **DESCR:** Academic Achievement; Acculturation; Bilingualism; English as a Second Language; Identity.

1066 Michel, Jose R. For the new breed of bilingual teachers: what the future holds. CAMINOS, Vol. 2, no. 7 (December 1981), p. [29]. English. **DESCR:** *Teaching Profession.

1067 Miller, Robert. The Mexican approach to developing bilingual materials and teaching literacy to bilingual students. READING TEACHER, Vol. 35, no. 7 (April 1982), p. 800-804. English. **DESCR:** Curriculum Materials; Freire, Paulo; Mexico.

1068 Murray, Melissa and Flores, Jose. Bilingual success: a second language program that is making everyone happy (and smarter). NATIONAL HISPANIC JOURNAL, Vol. 2, no. 1 (Summer 1983), p. 14-19. English. **DESCR:** Education; Educational Innovations; *Flores, Jose; Metz Elementary School, Austin TX.

1069 Museum official plans outreach to Latinos. NUESTRO, Vol. 6, no. 4 (May 1982), p. 27-28. English. **DESCR:** *Appointed Officials; *Metropolitan Museum of Art.

1070 N.A.L.E.O.'s "Fiesta '83". CAMINOS, Vol. 4, no. 10 (November 1983), p. 28-29. English. **DESCR:** Baca Barragan, Polly; Central America; Fiesta '83; Garcia, Robert; Immigration; International Relations; Mendez, Olga; *National Association of Latino Elected Officials (NALEO); Simpson-Mazzoli Bill; United States-Mexico Relations.

1071 National Clearinghouse for Bilingual Education. Support for bilingual education. CAMINOS, Vol. 4, no. 10 (November 1983), p. 32-33,54. Bilingual.

1072 Neuman, Susan B. and Pits, Elaine F. A review of current North American television programs for bilingual children. READING TEACHER, Vol. 37, no. 3 (December 1983), p. 254-260. English. **DESCR:** Mass Media; SESAME STREET; Spanish Language; THE ELECTRIC COMPANY; VILLA ALEGRE.

1073 A new direction for bilingual education in the 1980's (originally published in FOCUS 1982). ADFL BULLETIN, Vol. 14, no. 2 (November 1982), p. 5-8. English. **DESCR:** Academy for Educational Development (AED).

1074 Nickel, Kenneth N. Bilingual education in the eighties. PHI DELTA KAPPAN, Vol. 63, (May 1982), p. 638. English. **DESCR:** Statistics.

--   --

Bilingual Bicultural Education (cont.)

1075 Olson, James S. Book review of: HUNGER OF
     MEMORY: THE EDUCATION OF RICHARD RODRIGUEZ.
     JOURNAL OF THE WEST, Vol. 22, no. 1 (1983),
     p. 80-81. English. **DESCR**: Book Reviews;
     *HUNGER OF MEMORY: THE EDUCATION OF RICHARD
     RODRIGUEZ; Identity; Rodriguez, Richard.

1076 Orlandi, Lisanio R. Book review of: WORKBOOK
     ON PROGRAM EVALUATION. BILINGUAL JOURNAL,
     Vol. 7, no. 2 (Winter 1983), p. 35-36.
     English. **DESCR**: Babcock, R.; Book Reviews;
     Evaluation (Educational); Plakos, J.;
     Plakos, M.; *WORKBOOK ON PROGRAM EVALUATION.

1077 Ortiz, Tomasita. The Spanish-speaking
     migrant child. BILINGUAL JOURNAL, Vol. 6,
     no. 4 (Summer 1982), p. 8-15,32. English.
     DESCR: English as a Second Language;
     *Migrant Children; Migrant Education;
     *MIGRANT STUDENT RECORD TRANSFER SYSTEM.

1078 Otheguy, Ricardo. Thinking about bilingual
     education: a critical appraisal. HARVARD
     EDUCATIONAL REVIEW, Vol. 52, no. 3 (August
     1982), p. 301-314. English. **DESCR**:
     Educational Law and Legislation;
     Immigration.

1079 Penichet, Carlos. Carlos Penichet on the
     market for bilingual materials. CAMINOS,
     Vol. 3, no. 10 (November 1982), p. 42-43.
     English. **DESCR**: *Bilingual Textbooks.

1080 Plata, Maximino and Jones, Priscilla.
     Bilingual vocational education for
     handicapped students. EXCEPTIONAL CHILDREN,
     Vol. 48, no. 4 (April 1982), p. 538-540.
     English. **DESCR**: *Handicapped; Limited- or
     Non-English Speaking Handicapped Students
     (LONESHS); Teaching Profession; Vocational
     Education.

1081 Politzer, Robert L.; Shohamy, Elana; and
     McGroarty, Mary. Validation of linguistic
     and communicative oral language tests for
     Spanish-English bilingual programs.
     BILINGUAL REVIEW, Vol. 10, no. 1 (January,
     April, 1983), p. 3-20. English. **DESCR**: Bahia
     Oral Language Test (BOLT); Bay Area, CA;
     Bilingual Programs; *Language Assessment;
     Linguistics; Sociolinguistics.

1082 Reusswig, Jim. Whence the National Hispanic
     Center and University? Mater artium
     necessitas. THRUST, Vol. 11, no. 3 (January,
     February, 1982), p. 32-35. English. **DESCR**:
     Education; *National Hispanic Center;
     *National Hispanic University, Oakland CA.

1083 Reyes, Ramiro. The status of bilingual
     education in California. CAMINOS, Vol. 3,
     no. 10 (November 1982), p. 36-37,54.
     English. **DESCR**: *California.

1084 Rodriguez, Richard. A minority scholar
     speaks out. AMERICAN EDUCATION, Vol. 18, no.
     9 (November 1982), p. 2-5. English. **DESCR**:
     Affirmative Action; Authors; *Biography;
     HUNGER OF MEMORY: THE EDUCATION OF RICHARD
     RODRIGUEZ; Rodriguez, Richard.

1085 Rodriguez, Richard, et al. Education of
     Richard Rodriguez [excerpts from "HUNGER OF
     MEMORY", including discussion]. CHANGE, Vol.
     14, no. 7 (October 1982), p. 32-42+.
     English. **DESCR**: Affirmative Action;
     Assimilation; Biography; *HUNGER OF MEMORY:
     THE EDUCATION OF RICHARD RODRIGUEZ;
     *Rodriguez, Richard.

1086 Rossier, Robert E. Bilingual education:
     training for the ghetto. POLICY REVIEW, Vol.

25, (Summer 1983), p. 36-45. English.
     DESCR: Bilingualism; Immigrants; Lau v.
     Nichols.

1087 Rotberg, Iris C. Some legal and research
     considerations in establishing federal
     policy in bilingual education. HARVARD
     EDUCATIONAL REVIEW, Vol. 52, no. 2 (May
     1982), p. 149-168. English. **DESCR**:
     Educational Law and Legislation; History;
     Policy Formation; Research Methodology.

1088 Rugsaken, Kris T. Qualifications for the
     bilingual vocational teacher. BILINGUAL
     JOURNAL, Vol. 6, no. 4 (Summer 1982), p.
     22-25. English. **DESCR**: Adult Education;
     Teacher Training; *Vocational Education;
     Vocational Education Act of 1963.

1089 Rugsaken, Kris T. Toward a true bilingual
     education: when federal funding ends.
     BILINGUAL JOURNAL, Vol. 7, no. 4 (Summer
     1983), p. 9-14. English. **DESCR**: Bilingual
     Education Act of 1968; *Educational Law and
     Legislation; ELEMENTARY AND SECONDARY
     EDUCATION ACT; Funding Sources.

1090 San Miguel, Guadalupe. In the background:
     conflict and controversy in the evolution of
     bilingual legislation in Texas, 1965-73.
     NABE JOURNAL, Vol. 7, no. 3 (Spring 1983),
     p. 23-40. English. **DESCR**: *Educational Law
     and Legislation; Educational Theory and
     Practice; Texas.

1091 Sandoval-Martinez, Steven. Findings from the
     Head Start bilingual curriculum development
     and evaluation effort. NABE JOURNAL, Vol. 7,
     no. 1 (Fall 1982), p. 1-12. English. **DESCR**:
     Compensatory Education; *Early Childhood
     Education; Evaluation (Educational);
     Headstart Program.

1092 Saracho, Olivia N. Essential requirements
     for teachers in early childhood
     bilingual/bicultural programs. CHILDHOOD
     EDUCATION, Vol. 60, no. 2 (November,
     December, 1983), p. 96-101. English. **DESCR**:
     *Teacher Training.

1093 Schlossman, Steven. Self-evident remedy?
     George I. Sanchez, segregation, and enduring
     dilemmas in bilingual education. TEACHERS
     COLLEGE RECORD, Vol. 84, no. 4 (Summer
     1983), p. 871-907. English. **DESCR**:
     Biography; Delgado v. Bastrop Independent
     School District of Bastrop Co., TX (1948);
     FORGOTTEN PEOPLE; History; *Sanchez, George
     I.

1094 Schon, Isabel; Hopkins, Kenneth D.; and
     Davis, W. Alan. Effects of books in Spanish
     and free reading time on Hispanic students'
     reading abilities and attitudes. NABE
     JOURNAL, Vol. 7, no. 1 (Fall 1982), p.
     13-20. English. **DESCR**: *Language Arts;
     Language Proficiency; *Reading; Spanish
     Language.

1095 School principal recognized for leadership
     efforts. NUESTRO, Vol. 6, no. 5 (June, July,
     1982), p. 30. English. **DESCR**: Leadership;
     Michigan; *Ruiz, Pablo.

1096 Spiridakis, John N. Three diagnostics tools
     for use with the bilingual child. BILINGUAL
     JOURNAL, Vol. 7, no. 4 (Summer 1983), p.
     23-25. English. **DESCR**: Educational Cognitive
     Style (ECS); Educational Psychology;
     *Educational Tests and Measurements;
     Field-Sensitive/Field-Independent Behavior
     Observation Instruments; Learning and
     Cognition; Learning Style Inventory (LSI).

Bilingual Bicultural Education (cont.)

1097 State considers English bill. NUESTRO, Vol. 6, no. 3 (April 1982), p. 12-13. English. **DESCR:** *Languages.

1098 Summary of selected bilingual legislation. CAMINOS, Vol. 2, no. 7 (December 1981), p. 28. English. **DESCR:** Educational Law and Legislation.

1099 Tikunoff, William J. and Vazquez-Faria, Jose A. Successful instruction for bilingual schooling. PEABODY JOURNAL OF EDUCATION, Vol. 59, no. 4 (July 1982), p. 234-271. English. **DESCR:** Curriculum; Educational Theory and Practice; Teacher Attitudes.

1100 A time for reflection. NUESTRO, Vol. 7, no. 9 (November 1983), p. 42-44. English. **DESCR:** Anaya, Rudolfo A.; Arias, Beatriz; Computers; Financial Aid; Folklore; Organizations; Prewitt Diaz, Joseph (Jose); Villarreal, Sylvia; *W.K. Kellogg Foundation National Fellowship Program.

1101 Tips for making the right moves in today's job markets. HISPANIC BUSINESS, Vol. 5, no. 6 (June 1983), p. 38. English. **DESCR:** *Careers.

1102 Troike, Rudolph C. Bilingual-si! PRINCIPAL, Vol. 62, no. 3 (January 1983), p. 8. English. **DESCR:** Academic Achievement; Bilingualism; English as a Second Language.

1103 Walia, Adorna. Book review of: BILINGUAL EDUCATION TEACHER HANDBOOK: LANGUAGE ISSUES IN MULTICULTURAL SETTINGS. vol. II. BILINGUAL JOURNAL, Vol. 6, no. 1 (Fall 1982), p. 29-30. English. **DESCR:** *BILINGUAL EDUCATION TEACHER HANDBOOK: LANGUAGE ISSUES IN MULTICULTURAL SETTINGS, VOL II; Book Reviews; Cultural Pluralism; Language Assessment; Montero, Martha.

1104 Walia, Adorna. Book review of: CONVERSATIONS OF MIGUEL AND MARIA: HOW CHILDREN LEARN ENGLISH AS A SECOND LANGUAGE; IMPLICATIONS FOR CLASSROOM TEACHING. BILINGUAL JOURNAL, Vol. 6, no. 1 (Fall 1982), p. 28-29. English. **DESCR:** Book Reviews; *CONVERSATIONS OF MIGUEL AND MARIA: HOW CHILDREN LEARN ENGLISH AS A SECOND LANGUAGE; IMPLICATIONS FOR CLASSROOM TEACHING; English as a Second Language; Ventriglia, Linda.

1105 Walia, Adorna. Book review of: COUNSELING THE BILINGUAL STUDENT. BILINGUAL JOURNAL, Vol. 7, no. 4 (Summer 1983), p. 27-28. English. **DESCR:** Book Reviews; Counseling Services (Educational); *COUNSELING THE BILINGUAL STUDENT; Sanchez, Antonia; Searchlight Series.

1106 Walia, Adorna. Book review of: CULTURE AND THE BILINGUAL CLASSROOM: STUDIES IN CLASSROOM ETHNOGRAPHY. BILINGUAL JOURNAL, Vol. 6, no. 4 (Summer 1982), p. 30-31. English. **DESCR:** Au, Kathryn Hu-Pei; Biculturalism; Book Reviews; Cultural Pluralism; *CULTURE AND THE BILINGUAL CLASSROOM: STUDIES IN CLASSROOM ETHNOLOGY; Guthrie, Grace Pung; Trueba, Henry T.

1107 Walia, Adorna. Book review of: DATA FORMS FOR EVALUATING BILINGUAL EDUCATION PROGRAM. BILINGUAL JOURNAL, Vol. 7, no. 2 (Winter 1983), p. 38. English. **DESCR:** Book Reviews; Cohen, Bernard H.; *DATA FORMS FOR EVALUATING BILINGUAL EDUCATION PROGRAMS; Educational Administration; Evaluation (Educational).

1108 Walia, Adorna. Book review of: DO'S AND DONT'S OF BILINGUAL PROGRAM EVALUATION. BILINGUAL JOURNAL, Vol. 7, no. 2 (Winter 1983), p. 38. English. **DESCR:** Book Reviews; Curriculum; *DO'S AND DONT'S OF BILINGUAL PROGRAM EVALUATION; Evaluation (Educational); Rodriguez-Brown, Flora V.

1109 Walia, Adorna. Book review of: THE BILINGUAL PLAY: PINOCCHIO. BILINGUAL JOURNAL, Vol. 7, no. 3 (Spring 1983), p. 31. English. **DESCR:** Book Reviews; Pastore Passaro, Maria C.; Teatro; *THE BILINGUAL PLAY: PINOCCHIO.

1110 Weber, David J. Book review of: THE NEW BILINGUALISM: AN AMERICAN DILEMMA. WESTERN HISTORICAL QUARTERLY, Vol. 14, no. 1 (1983), p. 77-79. English. **DESCR:** Bilingualism; Book Reviews; Ridge, Martin; *THE NEW BILINGUALISM: AN AMERICAN DILEMMA.

1111 Weiner, Richard E. Teaching the immigrant's child: a model plan for court-ordered bilingual education. JOURNAL OF LAW AND EDUCATION, Vol. 12, no. 1 (January 1983), p. 61-76. English. **DESCR:** Courts (Legal); Curriculum; Educational Law and Legislation; Educational Theory and Practice.

1112 What bilingual education means to the nation. NUESTRO, Vol. 7, no. 2 (March 1983), p. 52-53. English. **DESCR:** Education; Millan, Aida; Nguyen, Anh Tuan; Rodriguez, Axel.

1113 Willie, Charles V. First learning unchallenged and untested. CHANGE, Vol. 14, no. 7 (October 1982), p. 37-41. English. **DESCR:** Affirmative Action; Biography; Book Reviews; Education; *HUNGER OF MEMORY: THE EDUCATION OF RICHARD RODRIGUEZ; Rodriguez, Richard.

1114 Willig, Ann C. The effectiveness of bilingual education: review of a report. NABE JOURNAL, Vol. 6, no. 2-3 (Winter, Spring, 1981, 1982), p. 1-19. English. **DESCR:** Educational Statistics; *Research Methodology.

1115 Yvon, Bernard R. Effects of the language of a diagnostic test on math scores. BILINGUAL JOURNAL, Vol. 6, no. 1 (Fall 1982), p. 13-16. English. **DESCR:** *Educational Tests and Measurements; Key-Math Diagnostic Test; Language Proficiency; Mathematics.

1116 Zamora, Gloria L.; Mazzone, Ernest; and Calvet, Peter. Newsmakers forum (interviews with Gloria Zamora and Ernest Mazzone). BILINGUAL JOURNAL, Vol. 6, no. 2 (Winter 1982), p. 6-11,26,28. English. **DESCR:** Bilingualism; National Association for Bilingual Education.

1117 Zamora, Gloria L. Zamora speaks on bilingual education. BILINGUAL JOURNAL, Vol. 7, no. 4 (Summer 1983), p. 5-8. English. **DESCR:** Bilingual Education Act of 1968; Educational Law and Legislation; ELEMENTARY AND SECONDARY EDUCATION ACT.

THE BILINGUAL BRAIN

1118 Andrews, Ilse. Bilinguals out of focus: a critical discussion. IRAL: INT'L REVIEW OF APPLIED LINGUISTICS IN LANGUAGE TEACHING, Vol. 20, no. 4 (November 1982), p. 297-305. English. **DESCR:** *Bilingualism; Book Reviews; Literature Reviews; Martin, Albert; Obler, Loraine K.

THE BILINGUAL BRAIN (cont.)

1119 Ruskin, Ellen Maria. Book review of: THE BILINGUAL BRAIN: NEURO-PSYCHOLOGICAL AND NEUROLINGUISTIC ASPECTS OF BILINGUALISM. HISPANIC JOURNAL OF BEHAVIORAL SCIENCES, Vol. 5, no. 4 (December 1983), p. 487-491. English. **DESCR:** Albert, Martin L.; Bilingualism; Book Reviews; Obler, Loraine K.

BILINGUAL EDUCATION EVALUATION AND REPORTING SYSTEM

1120 Liberty, Paul G. Director's notebook. BILINGUAL JOURNAL, Vol. 6, no. 4 (Summer 1982), p. 1,6. English. **DESCR:** *Bilingual Bicultural Education; *Curriculum; Evaluation (Educational).

Bilingual Education Act of 1968

1121 Rugsaken, Kris T. Toward a true bilingual education: when federal funding ends. BILINGUAL JOURNAL, Vol. 7, no. 4 (Summer 1983), p. 9-14. English. **DESCR:** *Bilingual Bicultural Education; *Educational Law and Legislation; ELEMENTARY AND SECONDARY EDUCATION ACT; Funding Sources.

1122 Zamora, Gloria L. Zamora speaks on bilingual education. BILINGUAL JOURNAL, Vol. 7, no. 4 (Summer 1983), p. 5-8. English. **DESCR:** *Bilingual Bicultural Education; Educational Law and Legislation; ELEMENTARY AND SECONDARY EDUCATION ACT.

Bilingual Education

1123 Community watching: para la comunidad. CAMINOS, Vol. 2, no. 7 (December 1981), p. 42-43. Bilingual. **DESCR:** Mexican American Correctional Association (MACE); *Organizations; Student Advocates for Bilingual Education (SABE).

BILINGUAL EDUCATION TEACHER HANDBOOK: LANGUAGE ISSUES IN MULTICULTURAL SETTINGS, VOL II

1124 Walia, Adorna. Book review of: BILINGUAL EDUCATION TEACHER HANDBOOK: LANGUAGE ISSUES IN MULTICULTURAL SETTINGS. vol. II. BILINGUAL JOURNAL, Vol. 6, no. 1 (Fall 1982), p. 29-30. English. **DESCR:** Bilingual Bicultural Education; Book Reviews; Cultural Pluralism; Language Assessment; Montero, Martha.

Bilingual Foundation of the Arts

1125 Carmen Zapata and the B.F.A. CAMINOS, Vol. 3, no. 4 (April 1982), p. 38-40. Bilingual. **DESCR:** Artists; Teatro; *Zapata, Carmen.

1126 Did you know. LATINA, Vol. 1, no. 3 (1983), p. 60-63. English. **DESCR:** Alkali Flat Project Area Committee, Sacramento, CA; CAFE de California, Inc., Sacramento, CA; *Organizations.

1127 Gonzalez, Magdalena. Ole II; BFA honors the 40's. CAMINOS, Vol. 3, no. 7 (July, August, 1982), p. 28-29. Bilingual. **DESCR:** Artists; Awards; Montalban, Ricardo; Romero, Cesar.

1128 Ole carnival! CAMINOS, Vol. 4, no. 7 (July, August, 1983), p. 32-33. English. **DESCR:** *Television.

THE BILINGUAL HEART

1129 Barrio, Raymond. The bilingual heart and other adventures. BILINGUAL JOURNAL, Vol. 6, no. 2 (Winter 1982), p. 12-15. Bilingual.

DESCR: *Early Childhood Education; Ethnic Attitudes; Racism; REVERSING ROLES; THE PRINCE.

Bilingual Inventory of Natural Languages

1130 Garza, Ana. ESL in the bilingual classroom. BILINGUAL JOURNAL, Vol. 6, no. 4 (Summer 1982), p. 26-29,32. English. **DESCR:** *Bilingual Bicultural Education; *English as a Second Language; Language Assessment; Language Assessment Battery; Language Assessment Scales.

THE BILINGUAL PLAY: PINOCCHIO

1131 Walia, Adorna. Book review of: THE BILINGUAL PLAY: PINOCCHIO. BILINGUAL JOURNAL, Vol. 7, no. 3 (Spring 1983), p. 31. English. **DESCR:** Bilingual Bicultural Education; Book Reviews; Pastore Passaro, Maria C.; Teatro.

Bilingual Programs

1132 Politzer, Robert L.; Shohamy, Elana; and McGroarty, Mary. Validation of linguistic and communicative oral language tests for Spanish-English bilingual programs. BILINGUAL REVIEW, Vol. 10, no. 1 (January, April, 1983), p. 3-20. English. **DESCR:** Bahia Oral Language Test (BOLT); Bay Area, CA; *Bilingual Bicultural Education; *Language Assessment; Linguistics; Sociolinguistics.

Bilingual Textbooks

1133 Penichet, Carlos. Carlos Penichet on the market for bilingual materials. CAMINOS, Vol. 3, no. 10 (November 1982), p. 42-43. English. **DESCR:** *Bilingual Bicultural Education.

Bilingualism

1134 Acosta, Frank X. and Cristo, Martha H. Bilingual-Bicultural interpreters as psychotherapeutic bridges: a program note. JOURNAL OF COMMUNITY PSYCHOLOGY, Vol. 10, no. 1 (January 1982), p. 54-56. English. **DESCR:** Biculturalism; Community Mental Health; Doctor Patient Relations; East Los Angeles, CA; *Mental Health Personnel; Mental Health Programs; Translations.

1135 Airport charge causes conflict. NUESTRO, Vol. 7, no. 7 (September 1983), p. 12. English. **DESCR:** Language Proficiency; *Tucson International Airport.

1136 Alatorre, Alva Sylvia. Book review of: LIFE WITH TWO LANGUAGES: AN INTRODUCTION TO BILINGUALISM. HISPANIC JOURNAL OF BEHAVIORAL SCIENCES, Vol. 5, no. 4 (December 1983), p. 482-486. English. **DESCR:** Book Reviews; Grosjean, Francois; *LIFE WITH TWO LANGUAGES: AN INTRODUCTION TO BILINGUALISM.

1137 Andrews, Ilse. Bilinguals out of focus: a critical discussion. IRAL: INT'L REVIEW OF APPLIED LINGUISTICS IN LANGUAGE TEACHING, Vol. 20, no. 4 (November 1982), p. 297-305. English. **DESCR:** Book Reviews; Literature Reviews; Martin, Albert; Obler, Loraine K.; *THE BILINGUAL BRAIN.

1138 Arce, Carlos H. Language shift among Chicanos: strategies for measuring and assessing direction and rate. SOCIAL SCIENCE JOURNAL, Vol. 19, no. 2 (April 1982), p. 121-132. English. **DESCR:** Language Development; Research Methodology; *Spanish Language.

Bilingualism (cont.)

1139 Argulewicz, Ed N. and Sanchez, David T. Considerations in the assessment of reading difficulties in bilingual children. SCHOOL PSYCHOLOGY REVIEW, Vol. 11, no. 3 (Summer 1982), p. 281-289. English. DESCR: Children; *Language Assessment; Reading; Sociolinguistics.

1140 Armengol, Armando; Manley, Joan H.; and Teschner, Richard V. The international bilingual city: how a university meets the challenge. FOREIGN LANGUAGE ANNALS, Vol. 15, no. 4 (September 1982), p. 289-295. English. DESCR: Biculturalism; Border Region; Ciudad Juarez, Chihuahua, Mexico; El Paso, TX; *Language Development; Spanish Language; University of Texas at El Paso.

1141 Beveridge, John. Bi-lingual programs: some doubts and comments. THE CLEARING HOUSE, Vol. 55, no. 5 (January 1982), p. 214-217. English. DESCR: *Bilingual Bicultural Education; Curriculum.

1142 Burns, Allan F. Politics, pedagogy, and culture in bilingual classrooms: a case study. NABE JOURNAL, Vol. 6, no. 2-3 (Winter, Spring, 1981, 1982), p. 35-51. English. DESCR: Biculturalism; *Bilingual Bicultural Education; Cultural Characteristics; Teacher-pupil Interaction.

1143 Castro, Agenor L. The case for the bilingual prison. CORRECTIONS TODAY, Vol. 44, no. 4 (August 1982), p. 72-78. English. DESCR: *Prisons; Social Psychology; Socialization.

1144 Chavez, Ernest L. Analysis of a Spanish translation of the Peabody Picture Vocabulary Test. PERCEPTUAL AND MOTOR SKILLS, Vol. 54, no. 3 (June 1982), p. 1335-1338. English. DESCR: Educational Tests and Measurements; *Peabody Picture Vocabulary Test (PPVT); Spanish Language.

1145 Davila, Luis. Meditaciones. REVISTA CHICANO-RIQUENA, Vol. 10, no. 1-2 (Winter, Spring, 1982), p. 275-278. Spanish. DESCR: Cultural Customs; *Essays; Folklore; Self-Referents.

1146 Diaz, Elisa G. Bilingualism - a reality in these United States. CAMINOS, Vol. 4, no. 10 (November 1983), p. 37,54. English.

1147 Dreisbach, Melanie and Keogh, Barbara K. Testwiseness as a factor in readiness test performance of young Mexican-American children. JOURNAL OF EDUCATIONAL PSYCHOLOGY, Vol. 74, no. 2 (April 1982), p. 224-229. English. DESCR: *Academic Achievement; Early Childhood Education; Educational Tests and Measurements.

1148 Ferullo, R. J. Objectivity in the assessment of pre-school hearing impaired bilingual-Hispanic children. JOURNAL OF SCHOOL HEALTH, Vol. 53, (Fall 1983), p. 131-135. English. DESCR: Child Study; *Deaf.

1149 Fradd, Sandra. Cubans to Cuban Americans: assimilation in the United States. MIGRATION TODAY, Vol. 11, no. 4-5 (1983), p. 35-42. English. DESCR: Assimilation; *Cubanos; Immigration.

1150 France, Pauline. Working with young bilingual children. EARLY CHILD DEVELOPMENT AND CARE, Vol. 10, no. 4 (February 1983), p. 283-292. English. DESCR: *Curriculum; *Early Childhood Education.

1151 Gage, Theodore J. The next assignment: second-tier marketing to English-speaking Hispanics. HISPANIC BUSINESS, Vol. 5, no. 12 (December 1983), p. 22-26. English. DESCR: Advertising; *Marketing.

1152 Galloway, Linda M. Bilingualism: neuropsychological considerations. JOURNAL OF RESEARCH AND DEVELOPMENT IN EDUCATION, Vol. 15, no. 3 (Spring 1982), p. 12-28. English. DESCR: Language Proficiency; Psychological Theory.

1153 Galloway, Linda M. and Scarcella, Robin. Cerebral organization in adult second language acquisition: is the right hemisphere more involved. BRAIN AND LANGUAGE, Vol. 16, no. 1 (May 1982), p. 56-60. English. DESCR: English as a Second Language; Learning and Cognition.

1154 Garcia, Herman S. Bilingualism, biculturalism, and the educational system. JOURNAL OF NON-WHITE CONCERNS IN PERSONNEL AND GUIDANCE, Vol. 11, no. 2 (January 1983), p. 67-74. English. DESCR: Bilingual Bicultural Education.

1155 Goldin, Mark G. Book review of: TEACHING SPANISH TO THE HISPANIC BILINGUAL: ISSUES, AIMS AND METHODS. NABE JOURNAL, Vol. 7, no. 1 (Fall 1982), p. 53-56. English. DESCR: Book Reviews; Garcia-Moya, Rodolfo; Language Proficiency; Language Usage; Lozano, Anthony G.; Spanish Language; *TEACHING SPANISH TO THE HISPANIC BILINGUAL: ISSUES, AIMS AND METHODS; Valdez, Guadalupe.

1156 Gomez, Efrain A.; Ruiz, Pedro; and Laval, Ramon. Psychotherapy and bilingualism: is acculturation important? JOURNAL OF OPERATIONAL PSYCHIATRY, Vol. 13, no. 1 (1982), p. 13-16. English. DESCR: *Psychotherapy.

1157 Gorrell, J. Jeffrey, et al. Comparison of spatial role-taking in monolingual and bilingual children. JOURNAL OF GENETIC PSYCHOLOGY, Vol. 140, no. 1 (March 1982), p. 3-10. English. DESCR: Child Study; Cognition; *Linguistic Theory; *Perception.

1158 Gutierrez, John R. Book review of: TEACHING SPANISH TO THE HISPANIC BILINGUAL: ISSUES, AIMS AND METHODS. MODERN LANGUAGE JOURNAL, Vol. 66, no. 2 (Summer 1982), p. 234. English. DESCR: Book Reviews; Garcia-Moya, Rodolfo; Lozano, Anthony G.; Spanish Language; *TEACHING SPANISH TO THE HISPANIC BILINGUAL: ISSUES, AIMS AND METHODS; Valdez, Guadalupe.

1159 Henry, William A. Against a confusion of tongues. TIME, Vol. 121, no. 24 (June 13, 1983), p. 30-31. English.

1160 Hispanic voting trends. HISPANIC BUSINESS, Vol. 4, no. 8 (August 1983), p. 28-29. English. DESCR: Bilingual Ballots; California; *Elections; Mexican American Legal Defense and Educational Fund (MALDEF); Southwest Voter Registration Education Project (SVRP); Texas; Voter Turnout.

1161 Josel, Nathan A. Public library material selection in a bilingual community. CATHOLIC LIBRARY WORLD, Vol. 54, no. 3 (October 1982), p. 113-115. English. DESCR: El Paso, TX; Library Collections; *Public Libraries; Spanish Language.

Bilingualism (cont.)

1162 Kjolseth, Rolf. Cultural politics of bilingualism. SOCIETY, Vol. 20, no. 4 (May, June, 1983), p. 40-48. English. DESCR: Cultural Pluralism; Public Policy.

1163 Kramer, Virginia Reyes and Schell, Leo M. English auditory discrimination skills of Spanish-speaking children. ALBERTA JOURNAL OF EDUCATIONAL RESEARCH, Vol. 28, no. 1 (March 1982), p. 1-8. English. DESCR: Accentedness; English Language; *Language Development; Spanish Language.

1164 Lado, Robert. Aula/the classroom: developmental reading in two languages. NABE JOURNAL, Vol. 6, no. 2-3 (Winter, Spring, 1981, 1982), p. 99-110. English. DESCR: Bilingual Bicultural Education; Language Arts; Language Development; Learning and Cognition; *Reading; Spanish Education Development (SED) Center Bilingual Reading Project; Spanish Language.

1165 Lipski, John M. Spanish-English language switching in speech and literature: theories and models. BILINGUAL REVIEW, Vol. 9, no. 3 (September, December, 1982), p. 191-212. English. DESCR: *Accentedness; Language Patterns.

1166 Macias, Reynaldo Flores. Book review of: POLITICS AND LANGUAGE: SPANISH AND ENGLISH IN THE UNITED STATES. NABE JOURNAL, Vol. 7, no. 1 (Fall 1982), p. 61-66. English. DESCR: Book Reviews; Bruckner, D.J.R.; Cultural Pluralism; *POLITICS AND LANGUAGE: SPANISH AND ENGLISH IN THE UNITED STATES; Spanish Language.

1167 Maestas, R. W. Bilingualism in business education. JOURNAL OF BUSINESS EDUCATION, Vol. 57, (May 1982), p. 313-315. English. DESCR: *Business Education.

1168 McDowell, John H. Sociolinguistic contours in the verbal art of Chicano children. AZTLAN, Vol. 13, no. 1-2 (Spring, Fall, 1982), p. 166-193. English. DESCR: Children; Linguistics; *Sociolinguistics.

1169 Mendez, Gloria I. Bilingual children's adaptation after a transitional bilingual education. METAS, Vol. 3, no. 1 (Summer 1982), p. 1-112. English. DESCR: Academic Achievement; Acculturation; *Bilingual Bicultural Education; English as a Second Language; Identity.

1170 Miller Brewing is airing bilingual commercial. NUESTRO, Vol. 7, no. 9 (November 1983), p. 36. English. DESCR: Advertising; *Miller Brewing Company; Television.

1171 Morgan, Thomas B. The Latinization of America. ESQUIRE, Vol. 99, no. 5 (May 1983), p. 47-56. English. DESCR: Acculturation; Assimilation; Biculturalism; *Population Trends.

1172 New bilingual effort. NUESTRO, Vol. 6, no. 1 (January, February, 1982), p. 10. English. DESCR: Voting Rights.

1173 Que pasa?: future of bilingualism. NUESTRO, Vol. 7, no. 4 (May 1983), p. 9. English. DESCR: Canada; Cubanos; *Miami, FL.

1174 Ramirez, Arnulfo G.; Milk, Robert H.; and Sapiens, Alexander. Intragroup differences and attitudes toward varieties of Spanish among bilingual pupils from California and Texas. HISPANIC JOURNAL OF BEHAVIORAL SCIENCES, Vol. 5, no. 4 (December 1983), p. 417-429. English. DESCR: Spanish Language.

1175 Rodriguez, Imelda and Bethel, Lowell J. Inquiry approach to science and language teaching. JOURNAL OF RESEARCH IN SCIENCE TEACHING, Vol. 20, no. 4 (April 1983), p. 291-296. English. DESCR: Education; *Educational Tests and Measurements; Language Arts; Learning and Cognition; Primary School Education; Science.

1176 Rossier, Robert E. Bilingual education: training for the ghetto. POLICY REVIEW, Vol. 25, (Summer 1983), p. 36-45. English. DESCR: *Bilingual Bicultural Education; Immigrants; Lau v. Nichols.

1177 Ruskin, Ellen Maria. Book review of: THE BILINGUAL BRAIN: NEURO-PSYCHOLOGICAL AND NEUROLINGUISTIC ASPECTS OF BILINGUALISM. HISPANIC JOURNAL OF BEHAVIORAL SCIENCES, Vol. 5, no. 4 (December 1983), p. 487-491. English. DESCR: Albert, Martin L.; Book Reviews; Obler, Loraine K.; *THE BILINGUAL BRAIN.

1178 Staczek, John J. Code-switching in Miami Spanish: the domain of health care services. BILINGUAL REVIEW, Vol. 10, no. 1 (January, April, 1983), p. 41-46. English. DESCR: *Language Interference; Medical Care; Miami, FL; Spanish Language.

1179 Timm, Lenora A. Does code switching take time?: a comparison of results in experimental and natural setting, with some implications for bilingual language processing. HISPANIC JOURNAL OF BEHAVIORAL SCIENCES, Vol. 5, no. 4 (December 1983), p. 401-416. English. DESCR: *Language Development.

1180 Troike, Rudolph C. Bilingual-si! PRINCIPAL, Vol. 62, no. 3 (January 1983), p. 8. English. DESCR: Academic Achievement; *Bilingual Bicultural Education; English as a Second Language.

1181 Vazquez, Carol A. Research on the psychiatric evaluation of the bilingual patient: a methodological critique. HISPANIC JOURNAL OF BEHAVIORAL SCIENCES, Vol. 4, no. 1 (March 1982), p. 75-80. English. DESCR: Mental Health; *Psychiatry; Research Methodology.

1182 Wagatsuma, Yuria. Book review of: EARLY CHILDHOOD BILINGUALISM: WITH SPECIAL REFERENCE TO THE MEXICAN-AMERICAN CHILD. HISPANIC JOURNAL OF BEHAVIORAL SCIENCES, Vol. 5, no. 4 (December 1983), p. 477-481. English. DESCR: Book Reviews; *EARLY CHILDHOOD BILINGUALISM: WITH SPECIAL REFERENCE TO THE MEXICAN-AMERICAN CHILD; Garcia, Eugene E.

1183 Walsh, Catherine E. The phenomenon of educated/educado: an example for a tripartite system of semantic memory. BILINGUAL REVIEW, Vol. 10, no. 1 (January, April, 1983), p. 33-40. English. DESCR: Language Development; Semantics.

1184 Weber, David J. Book review of: THE NEW BILINGUALISM: AN AMERICAN DILEMMA. WESTERN HISTORICAL QUARTERLY, Vol. 14, no. 1 (1983), p. 77-79. English. DESCR: Bilingual Bicultural Education; Book Reviews; Ridge, Martin; *THE NEW BILINGUALISM: AN AMERICAN DILEMMA.

Bilingualism (cont.)

1185 Zamora, Gloria L.; Mazzone, Ernest; and Calvet, Peter. Newsmakers forum (interviews with Gloria Zamora and Ernest Mazzone). BILINGUAL JOURNAL, Vol. 6, no. 2 (Winter 1982), p. 6-11,26,28. English. **DESCR:** *Bilingual Bicultural Education; National Association for Bilingual Education.

BILINGUALISM IN THE SOUTHWEST

1186 Enright, Scott. Book review of: BILINGUALISM IN THE SOUTHWEST. EDUCATIONAL STUDIES, Vol. 13, no. 3-4 (Fall, Winter, 1982), p. 494-498. English. **DESCR:** Book Reviews; Turner, Paul R.

Bills, Garland D.

1187 Woods, Richard D. Book review of: SPANISH AND ENGLISH OF UNITED STATES HISPANOS: A CRITICAL, ANNOTATED, LINGUISTIC BIBLIOGRAPHY. JOURNAL OF ETHNIC STUDIES, Vol. 4, no. 3 (Fall 1976), p. 116. English. **DESCR:** Accentedness; Bibliography; Book Reviews; Craddock, Jerry R.; Language Patterns; *SPANISH AND ENGLISH OF U.S. HISPANOS: A CRITICAL, ANNOTATED, LINGUISTIC BIBLIOGRAPHY; Spanish Language; Teschner, Richard V.

Binationalism

1188 Baca, Reynaldo and Bryan, Dexter Edward. The "Assimilation" of unauthorized Mexican workers: another social science fiction? HISPANIC JOURNAL OF BEHAVIORAL SCIENCES, Vol. 5, no. 1 (March 1983), p. 1-20. English. **DESCR:** Assimilation; Immigrants; *Undocumented Workers.

Biofeedback

1189 Freeman, Frank E.; Gonzalez, Diana; and Montgomery, Gary T. Experimenter effects in biofeedback training. JOURNAL OF SOCIAL PSYCHOLOGY, Vol. 11, no. 1 (February 1983), p. 119-123. English. **DESCR:** Psychology; *Stress.

Biographical Notes USE FOR: Short biographical sketches. SEE ALSO: Biography

1190 Communications/marketing. HISPANIC BUSINESS, Vol. 4, no. 1 (January 1982), p. 13. English. **DESCR:** Beauty Contests; Consumers; Hispanic Caucus; *Marketing; Miss Black Velvet Latina; Montemayor, Carlos R.; Philip Morris, Inc.

1191 Communications/marketing. HISPANIC BUSINESS, Vol. 4, no. 7 (July 1982), p. 16. English. **DESCR:** Awards; Buena Vista Cablevision, Inc.; Demy, Caroline; *Marketing; Sosa de Garcia, Manuel.

1192 News at the SBA. HISPANIC BUSINESS, Vol. 4, no. 2 (February 1982), p. 22. English. **DESCR:** Cardenas, Michael; Castillo, Irenemaree; Lopez, Reynaldo H.; U.S. Small Business Administration.

1193 Newsfront. HISPANIC BUSINESS, Vol. 4, no. 2 (February 1982), p. 7. English. **DESCR:** Asip, Patricia V.; Banuelos, Ramona Acosta; Businesspeople; Gonzalez, Henry B.; Gutierrez, Alberto; IMAGE, Washington, DC.

1194 Newsfront. HISPANIC BUSINESS, Vol. 4, no. 1 (January 1982), p. 7. English. **DESCR:** Businesspeople; Community Development; Jimenez, Richard D.; Macias, Miguel (Mike); Oaxaca, Jaime; The East Los Angeles Community Union (TELACU); Viramontes,

Carlos.

1195 Newsfront. HISPANIC BUSINESS, Vol. 4, no. 3 (March 1982), p. 9. English. **DESCR:** Appointed Officials; Businesspeople; Chicano Film Exhibition and Festival, Detroit, Michigan, April 5-9, 1982; Garcia, Gloria; League of United Latin American Citizens (LULAC); Martinez, Vilma Socorro; National Association for Bilingual Education; Seaga, Edward; Suarez, Carlos R.

1196 Newsfront. HISPANIC BUSINESS, Vol. 4, no. 4 (April 1982), p. 8, 24. English. **DESCR:** Burgos, Elizabeth; *Businesspeople; Flores, Arturo; Garcia, Carlos E.; Garcia, Edward T.; Guzman, Ralph C.; Hernandez, Richard; National Coalition of Hispanic Mental Health and Human Services Organizations (COSSMHO); Parra, Oscar C.; Willie, Herm M.

1197 Nuestra gente. LATINO, Vol. 53, no. 3 (May 1982), p. 26. English. **DESCR:** Avila, Joaquin Guadalupe; Pompa, Gilbert G..

1198 Nuestra gente. LATINO, Vol. 53, no. 4 (June 1982), p. 30. English. **DESCR:** Batine, Rafael; Gimeno, Emil; Tafoya, Tony.

1199 Nuestra gente. LATINO, Vol. 53, no. 6 (October 1982), p. 22. English. **DESCR:** Alfaro-Garcia, Rafael Antonio; Quintanilla, Guadalupe; Salazar, Veronica.

1200 Nuestra gente. LATINO, Vol. 54, no. 8 (December 1983), p. 30. English. **DESCR:** Businesspeople; Carter, Lynda Cordoba; Duran, Sandra; Patino, Lorenzo E.; Politics; Rembis, Deborah; Vega, Christopher.

1201 Nuestra gente. LATINO, Vol. 53, no. 2 (March, April, 1982), p. 30. English. **DESCR:** Asip, Patricia V.; Ceballos, Sonia Ceban; Gonzales, Modesto; Septien, Rafael.

1202 People. HISPANIC BUSINESS, Vol. 4, no. 5 (May 1982), p. 8. English. **DESCR:** Appointed Officials; Asociacion Internacional de Exportadores e Importadores (EXIMA); Businesspeople; California Chicano News Media Association (CCNMA); de la Ossa, Ernest G.; Foreign Trade; Obledo, Mario; Rodriguez, Elias C.; Rodriguez, Samuel F.; United Way; U.S. Hispanic Chamber of Commerce.

1203 People. HISPANIC BUSINESS, Vol. 4, no. 6 (June 1982), p. 8. English. **DESCR:** Aguirre, Pedro; Arellano, Richard; Businesspeople; Cortez, Pete; De la Colina, Rafael; Hernandez, Sam; Nogales, Luis; Rodriguez, Leslie J.; Roybal, Edward R.

1204 People. HISPANIC BUSINESS, Vol. 4, no. 7 (July 1982), p. 7. English. **DESCR:** Aguilar, Richard; Businesspeople; Coronado, Julius; Enriquez, Rene; Garza, Jose S.; Guerra-Martinez, Celina; Medrano, Adan; Mota, Manny; Valenti, Frank S.

1205 People. HISPANIC BUSINESS, Vol. 4, no. 9 (September 1982), p. 7. English. **DESCR:** Advertising Agencies; Appointed Officials; Awards; Diaz-Albertini, Luis; Dimartino, Rita; Garza, Jesus; Hispanic Women in Higher Education (HWHE); League of United Latin American Citizens (LULAC); Ortega, Ray; Ortiz, George; Romero, Carlos J.; Sepulveda, Luis.

Biographical Notes (cont.)

1206 People. HISPANIC BUSINESS, Vol. 4, no. 10 (October 1982), p. 7. English. **DESCR:** Aguilar, Gloria; *Businesspeople; Caldera, Manuel R.; Lopez, Victor M.; Ramirez, Steve.

1207 People. HISPANIC BUSINESS, Vol. 4, no. 11 (November 1982), p. 7. English. **DESCR:** *Businesspeople; Diaz, Jose; Garcia-Pedrosa, Jose R.; Garza, Jose; Herrera, Heriberto; Mercado, Anthony; Rios, John F.; Solano, Faustina V.; Solis, Frank.

1208 People. HISPANIC BUSINESS, Vol. 4, no. 12 (December 1982), p. 10. English. **DESCR:** *Businesspeople; Garcia, Frances; Gort, Wilfredo; Ojeda, Armando; Olind, Rebecca Nieto; Philip Morris, Inc.; Roybal, Edward R.

1209 People. HISPANIC BUSINESS, Vol. 5, no. 1 (January 1983), p. 7. English. **DESCR:** Appointed Officials; *Businesspeople; Elizalde, Hector; Mackey y Salazar, C.; Madrid, Carlos; Montoya, Velma; Nunez, Carlos; Perea, Stanley; Rodriguez, Rita; Valdes, Martha.

1210 People. HISPANIC BUSINESS, Vol. 5, no. 2 (February 1983), p. 7. English. **DESCR:** Alvarez, Everett, Jr.; Appointed Officials; Businesspeople; Guzman-Randle, Irene; Roubin, Angel; Vasquez, Victor; Villareal, Luis Maria.

1211 People. HISPANIC BUSINESS, Vol. 5, no. 3 (March 1983), p. 9. English. **DESCR:** Anaya, Toney; Anguiano, Lupe; Appointed Officials; Avila, Joaquin Guadalupe; Awards; de la Fuente, Emilio; del Olmo, Frank; Godoy, Gustavo; Long, Dennis P.; Martinez, Elias (Lee); Rivera, Joseph, Jr.

1212 People. HISPANIC BUSINESS, Vol. 5, no. 4 (April 1983), p. 9. English. **DESCR:** Alvarado, Linda M.; Businesspeople; Castillo, Irenemaree; Castillo, Sylvia; Del Junco, Tirso; Gutierrez, Jose Roberto; Juarez, Joe; Mata, Bill; Miyares, Marcelino; Montanez Davis, Grace; Montoya, Velma; Pineda, Pat; Siberio, Julio; Thompson, Edith Lopez.

1213 People. HISPANIC BUSINESS, Vol. 5, no. 6 (June 1983), p. 8. English. **DESCR:** Appointed Officials; Businesspeople; Goizueta, Roberto C.; Guerra, Stella; Huapaya, Sixto Guillermo; Kitano, Pat; Manriquez, Suzanna; Oppenheimer-Nicolau, Siabhan; Ortiz, Solomon; Pachon, Harry P.; Richardson, Bill Lopez; Torres, Esteban E.; Torres, Johnny.

1214 People. HISPANIC BUSINESS, Vol. 5, no. 5 (May 1983), p. 8. English. **DESCR:** *Businesspeople; Duron, Armando; Espinoza, Peter; Flores, Juan; Martinez, Vilma Socorro; Molina, Gloria; Moreno, Samuel; Pantin, Leslie, Sr.; Quezada, Sylvia; Quinones, Sergio.

1215 People. HISPANIC BUSINESS, Vol. 5, no. 7 (July 1983), p. 8. English. **DESCR:** Alvarado, Anthony J.; Appointed Officials; Businesspeople; Candela, Hilario; Garcia, Marlene; Gonzalez, Julio; Martinez, Tony; Pla, George; Valdez, Abelardo L.

1216 People. HISPANIC BUSINESS, Vol. 5, no. 8 (August 1983), p. 10. English. **DESCR:** Businesspeople; Calderon, Charles M.; Esteverena, Rolando C.; General Coffee Corporation; Hispanic Bankers Association (HBA); Martinez, Olivia T.; Pallares, Mariano; Ruiz, Frederick R.; Ruiz, Louis F.; Sanchez, Joseph J.

1217 People on the move. CAMINOS, Vol. 2, no. 6 (October 1981), p. 7. English. **DESCR:** Alvarado, Angel S.; Arreola, Rafael; Diaz, Elisa; Diaz, Elvira A.; Garcia, Jose Joel; Garza, Florentino; Icaza, Ricardo F.; Lacayo, Henry; Martinez, Lydia R.; Munoz, Victor M.; Salinas, Vicente; Sanchez, Manuel; Zuniga, Henry.

1218 Research/development: books. HISPANIC BUSINESS, Vol. 5, no. 4 (April 1983), p. 28. English. **DESCR:** *Book Reviews; *"DO IT MY WAY OR YOU'RE FIRED!": EMPLOYEE RIGHTS AND THE CHANGING ROLE OF MANAGEMENT PREROGATIVES; Ewing, David W.; Garcia, Carlos; Garcia, Edward; Industrial Relations; Science; *SCIENCE OF THE SPANISH SPEAKING PEOPLE.

1219 Volsky, George. Four careers in Miami. HISPANIC BUSINESS, Vol. 5, no. 4 (April 1983), p. 10-11+. English. **DESCR:** Balestra, Victor C.; *Banking Industry; *Businesspeople; Harvard Business School's Latino Association; Huston, Maria Padilla; Masvidal, Sergio J.; Miami, FL; Valdes-Fauli, Gonzalo.

Biography SEE ALSO: Biographical Notes

1220 Alvarez, Amando. Jose Maria Morelos. LATINO, Vol. 54, no. 5 (August, September, 1983), p. 24-25. Spanish. **DESCR:** *Morelos, Jose Maria.

1221 Alvarez, Amando. Juana de Arco. LATINO, Vol. 54, no. 7 (November 1983), p. 21-22. English. **DESCR:** *De Arco, Juana; Religion.

1222 Anaya, Rudolfo A. A celebration of grandfathers. NEW MEXICO MAGAZINE, Vol. 61, no. 3 (March 1983), p. 35-40. English. **DESCR:** Anaya, Rudolfo A.; *Ancianos.

1223 Avila, Joaquin G. Remembering Matt Garcia. LATINO, Vol. 54, no. 8 (December 1983), p. 29. English. **DESCR:** *Garcia, Matt.

1224 Bachelor of the month. LATINA, Vol. 1, no. 1 (1982), p. 13. English. **DESCR:** *Varela, Gilbert.

1225 Balkan, D. Carlos. The nuclear powered Mr. Carlos Pimentel. HISPANIC BUSINESS, Vol. 4, no. 2 (February 1982), p. 16-17+. English. **DESCR:** Business Enterprises; Businesspeople; *Cataract Engineering and Construction, Inc.; Energy Industries; *Pimentel, Carlos.

1226 Ballard, Lee. Tom Marquez and the EDS mode. HISPANIC BUSINESS, Vol. 5, no. 2 (February 1983), p. 10-11+. English. **DESCR:** Businesspeople; Electronic Data Systems (EDS); Marquez, Tom; Perot, Ross; War on Drugs.

1227 Barradas, Efrain. "Todo lo que digo es cierto...": en memoria de Victor Fernandez Fragoso (1944-1982). REVISTA CHICANO-RIQUENA, Vol. 10, no. 3 (Summer 1982), p. 43-46. Spanish. **DESCR:** Authors; Essays; *Fernandez Fragoso, Victor; New York, NY; Puerto Rican Literature.

1228 Bell, Michael Davitt. Fitting into a tradition of autobiography. CHANGE, Vol. 14, no. 7 (October 1982), p. 36-39. English. **DESCR:** Affirmative Action; Assimilation; Bilingual Bicultural Education; Book Reviews; *HUNGER OF MEMORY: THE EDUCATION OF RICHARD RODRIGUEZ; Rodriguez, Richard.

Biography (cont.)

1229 Book review of: FRIDA: A BIOGRAPHY OF FRIDA KAHLO. BOOKLIST, Vol. 79, no. 11 (February 1, 1983), p. 708. English. DESCR: Artists; Book Reviews; *FRIDA: A BIOGRAPHY OF FRIDA KAHLO; Herrera, Hayden; Kahlo, Frida.

1230 Breiter, Toni. First to fall: "God just chose him to be a Marine". NUESTRO, Vol. 7, no. 9 (November 1983), p. 14-17. English. DESCR: Military Service; *Ortega, Alex.

1231 Breiter, Toni. El Libertador: a profile. NUESTRO, Vol. 7, no. 7 (September 1983), p. 32-35. English. DESCR: *Bolivar, Simon; Political History and Conditions; Revolutions; South America.

1232 Byrkit, James W. Walter Douglas and labor struggles in early 20th century Arizona. SOUTHWEST ECONOMY AND SOCIETY, Vol. 1, no. 1 (Spring 1976), p. 14-27. English. DESCR: Arizona; Bisbee, AZ; Clifton Morenci Strike, June 1903; Copper Queen Mining Co., Bisbee, AZ; *Douglas, Walter; International Workers of the World (IWW); Labor Unions; Mining Industry; Strikes and Lockouts.

1233 Cameron, Dan. Book review of: FRIDA: A BIOGRAPHY OF FRIDA KAHLO. NUESTRO, Vol. 7, no. 8 (October 1983), p. 44-45. English. DESCR: Book Reviews; *FRIDA: A BIOGRAPHY OF FRIDA KAHLO; Herrera, Hayden; Kahlo, Frida.

1234 Cardenas, Leo. The Bonilla years come to an end. LATINO, Vol. 54, no. 4 (May, June, 1983), p. 8-9+. English. DESCR: *Bonilla, Tony; Political Representation.

1235 Chavez, Lydia. The fourth network's chief executive. HISPANIC BUSINESS, Vol. 4, no. 1 (January 1982), p. 16-18. English. DESCR: Advertising; Anselmo, Rene; Cable Television; Marketing; Spanish International Network (SIN).

1236 De la Rosa, Carlos. Esai Morales: a new and exciting Latino talent on the rise. LATINA, Vol. 1, no. 3 (1983), p. 19. English. DESCR: *BAD BOYS; Film Reviews; Morales, Esai.

1237 Diaz, Katherine A. and Gonzalez, Magdalena. Jose Guadalupe Posada: documenting his people and his times=informandonos de su gente y su epoca. CAMINOS, Vol. 2, no. 6 (October 1981), p. 18-20. Bilingual. DESCR: Artists; Mexico; *Posada, Jose Guadalupe.

1238 Diaz, Katherine A. The many faceted talents of Danny Valdez=Los muchos y variados talentos de Danny Valdez. CAMINOS, Vol. 2, no. 6 (October 1981), p. [34]-36. Bilingual. DESCR: Entertainers; *Valdez, Daniel.

1239 Fernando Allende. LATINA, Vol. 1, no. 1 (1982), p. 28+. English. DESCR: *Allende, Fernando.

1240 Ferrarone, Aida. Olympic skeet-shooter. LATINA, Vol. 1, no. 3 (1983), p. 15. English. DESCR: Olympics; *Ortiz-Sherman, Nuria; Skeet-shooting; Sports.

1241 Forster, Merlin H. Luis Leal. LA PALABRA, Vol. 4, no. 1-2 (Spring, Fall, 1982, 1983), p. 19-20. Spanish. DESCR: Authors; Higher Education; Latin American Literature; *Leal, Luis; Teaching Profession.

1242 Fred Maes builds a multi-level system. HISPANIC BUSINESS, Vol. 4, no. 2 (February 1982), p. 13. English. DESCR: Consumers; Maes, Fred; *Marketing.

1243 Fuentes, Diana. Chicana perpectives: Irene Portillo. COMADRE, no. 1 (Summer 1977), p. 42-44. English. DESCR: Identity; *Portillo, Irene E.; Women's Rights.

1244 Fuentes, Diana. Chicana perpectives: Ester Reyes Aguilar. COMADRE, no. 1 (Summer 1977), p. 45-48. English. DESCR: Affirmative Action; *Aguilar, Ester Reyes; Ballet Folkorico; Teaching Profession.

1245 Fuentes, Diana. Chicana perspectives: Grace Montanez Davis. COMADRE, no. 1 (Summer 1977), p. 39-41. English. DESCR: *Montanez Davis, Grace.

1246 Gannett's Gerald Garcia goes to Tucson. HISPANIC BUSINESS, Vol. 4, no. 5 (May 1982), p. 13. English. DESCR: Gannett Co., Inc.; Garcia, Gerald; Newspapers; Tucson, AZ.

1247 Garcia, Annie. Herlinda Maxima Gonzales. COMADRE, no. 1 (Summer 1977), p. 33-38. English. DESCR: *Gonzales, Herlinda Maxima.

1248 Garcia, Art R. Star Adair Insulation Inc. spurts to new growth. HISPANIC BUSINESS, Vol. 4, no. 2 (February 1982), p. 18-19+. English. DESCR: Business Enterprises; Businesspeople; *Cisneros, Ignacio; Minority Enterprise Small Business Investment Corporation (MESBIC); *Star-Adair Insulation, Inc.

1249 Garcia, Ed. Quien es Rolando Hinojosa? TEXAS OBSERVOR, Vol. 75, no. 5 (March 11,), p. 26-29. English. DESCR: Book Reviews; *Hinojosa-Smith, Rolando R.; *RITES AND WITNESSES; THE VALLEY.

1250 Gloria Valencia: woman on the move. LATINA, Vol. 1, no. 3 (1983), p. 50-51. English. DESCR: *Valencia, Gloria; Valencia, Tony.

1251 Gozando de la vida. LATINO, Vol. 53, no. 4 (June 1982), p. 16-17. Spanish. DESCR: *Lopez, Lisa.

1252 Gradante, William. El hijo del pueblo: Jose Alfredo Jimenez and the Mexican cancion ranchera. LATIN AMERICAN MUSIC REVIEW, Vol. 3, no. 1 (Spring, Summer, 1982), p. 36-59. English. DESCR: Ethnomusicology; History; *Jimenez, Jose Alfredo.

1253 El Greco of Toledo: his life and his art. NUESTRO, Vol. 6, no. 6 (August 1982), p. 24-27. English. DESCR: Art; Art History; Artists; *El Greco.

1254 Gutierrez, Silvio. Fernando Favela: street wise and sexy. LATINA, Vol. 1, no. 3 (1983), p. 20-21. English. DESCR: *Favela, Fernando.

1255 Herrera, Hayden. The elephant and the dove. NUESTRO, Vol. 7, no. 8 (October 1983), p. 40-43. English. DESCR: Art; Artists; *Kahlo, Frida; Paintings; Rivera, Diego.

1256 Herrera, Hayden. Making an art of pain. PSYCHOLOGY TODAY, Vol. 17, no. 3 (March 1983), p. 86. English. DESCR: HENRY FORD HOSPITAL; *Kahlo, Frida; Paintings; SELF-PORTRAIT WITH PORTRAIT OF DR. FARILL; THE BROKEN COLUMN; THE LITTLE DEER; TREE OF HOPE; WITHOUT HOPE.

Biography (cont.)

1257 High energy community relations: Con
Edison's Carlota M. Maduro. HISPANIC
BUSINESS, Vol. 4, no. 2 (February 1982), p.
14. English. **DESCR:** Community Services;
Consolidated Edison Company of New York,
Inc.; *Maduro, Carlota M.; Public Relations.

1258 Hinojosa-Smith, Rolando R. Luis (el amigo)
Leal. LA PALABRA, Vol. 4, no. 1-2 (Spring,
Fall, 1982, 1983), p. 17-18. Spanish.
DESCR: Authors; Latin American Literature;
*Leal, Luis; Literature.

1259 [In memorium: Rene A. Ruiz 1929-1982].
HISPANIC JOURNAL OF BEHAVIORAL SCIENCES,
Vol. 5, no. 2 (June 1983), p. 137-140.
English. **DESCR:** *Ruiz, Rene A.

1260 Isela Sotelo. LATINA, Vol. 1, no. 1 (1982),
p. 15. English. **DESCR:** *Sotelo, Isela.

1261 Jim Blancarte, "an ace in the deck". LATINA,
Vol. 1, no. 3 (1983), p. 52-53. English.
DESCR: *Bracante, Jim; Legal Profession.

1262 Lamento por la jubilacion de un insigne
hispanista y viejo amigo (una carta
anonima). LA PALABRA, Vol. 4, no. 1-2
(Spring, Fall, 1982, 1983), p. 21-24.
Spanish. **DESCR:** Authors; Higher Education;
Latin American Literature; *Leal, Luis;
Teaching Profession.

1263 Lanier, Alfredo S. Continental's Fidel Lopez
takes an encompassing view. HISPANIC
BUSINESS, Vol. 4, no. 4 (April 1982), p.
16-17,24. English. **DESCR:** Chicago, IL;
*Lopez, Fidel; Urban Communities; Urban
Development.

1264 Lenti, Paul. Frida Kahlo. NUESTRO, Vol. 7,
no. 8 (October 1983), p. 38-39. English.
DESCR: Artists; *Kahlo, Frida.

1265 Loehr, William. Hispanic phenomenon is not
new. LATINO, Vol. 53, no. 4 (June 1982), p.
22+. English. **DESCR:** *Ferre, Maurice;
Population.

1266 Lomeli, Francisco A. Don Luis. LA PALABRA,
Vol. 4, no. 1-2 (Spring, Fall, 1982, 1983),
p. IX-XI. Spanish. **DESCR:** Authors; Latin
American Literature; *Leal, Luis;
Literature.

1267 Lomeli, Francisco A. Entrevista con Luis
Leal. LA PALABRA, Vol. 4, no. 1-2 (Spring,
Fall, 1982, 1983), p. 3-15. Spanish. **DESCR:**
Authors; Latin American Literature; *Leal,
Luis; Literature; Oral History.

1268 Lopez, Trini. Dando una mano. LATINO, Vol.
53, no. 7 (November 1982), p. 11. Spanish.
DESCR: *Lopez, Trini; Musicians.

1269 La lucha por la independencia. LATINO, Vol.
54, no. 6 (October 1983), p. 16-17. Spanish.
DESCR: *History; *Morelos, Jose Maria.

1270 LA LUZ MAGAZINE founder victim of cancer.
LATINO, Vol. 53, no. 4 (June 1982), p. 8.
English. **DESCR:** *Valdes y Tapia, Daniel T.

1271 Marti, Oscar R. Introduction. AZTLAN, Vol.
14, no. 2 (Fall 1983), p. 209-220. English.
DESCR: *Barreda, Gabino; History; Mexico;
Philosophy; Positivism.

1272 Martinez, Marie. Luis Avalos: what a man,
and what a talent. LATINA, Vol. 1, no. 3
(1983), p. 38-42. English. **DESCR:** *Avalos,
Luis.

1273 Martinez, Marie. Lynda Cordoba Carter.
LATINA, Vol. 1, no. 3 (1983), p. 16-17.
English. **DESCR:** *Carter, Lynda Cordoba.

1274 Mimiaga, Hector. Greatest ambition. LATINO,
Vol. 53, no. 4 (June 1982), p. 25. English.
DESCR: *Gonzalez, Ruben; Musicians.

1275 New general counsel at MALDEF. HISPANIC
BUSINESS, Vol. 4, no. 7 (July 1982), p. 24.
English. **DESCR:** *Avila, Joaquin Guadalupe;
Legal Profession; Mexican American Legal
Defense and Educational Fund (MALDEF).

1276 New Mexico's gubernatorial race. HISPANIC
BUSINESS, Vol. 4, no. 11 (November 1982), p.
27,30. English. **DESCR:** Anaya, Toney;
Elections; New Mexico; Political Parties and
Organizations.

1277 Olivas, Michael A. Painful to write, painful
to read. CHANGE, Vol. 14, no. 7 (October
1982), p. 37-42. English. **DESCR:** Book
Reviews; *HUNGER OF MEMORY: THE EDUCATION OF
RICHARD RODRIGUEZ; Rodriguez, Richard.

1278 Paul Rodriguez. LATINA, Vol. 1, no. 2
(February, March, 1983), p. 44-45. English.
DESCR: *Rodriguez, Paul.

1279 Pena takes Denver. HISPANIC BUSINESS, Vol.
5, no. 8 (August 1983), p. 13+. English.
DESCR: Denver, CO; Elected Officials; Pena,
Federico.

1280 Perales, Leon. Rockwell International's
highest ranking Hispanic. LATINA, Vol. 1,
no. 3 (1983), p. 46. English. **DESCR:**
*Martinez, Anita V.

1281 Una pintora: Graciela Rolo Boulanger.
NUESTRO, Vol. 7, no. 6 (August 1983), p.
30-35. English. **DESCR:** Artists; *Boulanger,
Graciela Rolo; Paintings.

1282 Reavis, Dick J. Growing up gringo. TEXAS
MONTHLY, Vol. 10, no. 8 (August 1982), p.
110-112+. English. **DESCR:** Dumas, TX;
*Rodriguez, Adan; Zinc Mining.

1283 Robert Beltran. LATINA, Vol. 1, no. 2
(February, March, 1983), p. 46-49. English.
DESCR: Artists; *Beltran, Robert.

1284 Rodriguez, Luis Javier. Profile of Luis
Carlos Bernal. CORAZON DE AZTLAN, Vol. 1,
no. 3 (August, September, 1982), p. 22-23.
English. **DESCR:** *Bernal, Louis Carlos;
Photography.

1285 Rodriguez, Richard. A minority scholar
speaks out. AMERICAN EDUCATION, Vol. 18, no.
9 (November 1982), p. 2-5. English. **DESCR:**
Affirmative Action; Authors; Bilingual
Bicultural Education; HUNGER OF MEMORY: THE
EDUCATION OF RICHARD RODRIGUEZ; Rodriguez,
Richard.

1286 Rodriguez, Richard, et al. Education of
Richard Rodriguez [excerpts from "HUNGER OF
MEMORY", including discussion]. CHANGE, Vol.
14, no. 7 (October 1982), p. 32-42+.
English. **DESCR:** Affirmative Action;
Assimilation; Bilingual Bicultural
Education; *HUNGER OF MEMORY: THE EDUCATION
OF RICHARD RODRIGUEZ; *Rodriguez, Richard.

1287 Rose, Barbara. Frida Kahlo: the Chicana as
art heroine. VOGUE, Vol. 173, (April 1983),
p. 152-154. English. **DESCR:** Art; Artists;
*Kahlo, Frida; Mexico; Rivera, Diego.

Biography (cont.)

1288 Sagel, Jaime. Patriarch of San Juan Pueblo.
NUESTRO, Vol. 6, no. 8 (October 1982), p.
52-53. English. DESCR: Montoya, Liberato;
San Juan Pueblo, NM.

1289 Schlossman, Steven. Self-evident remedy?
George I. Sanchez, segregation, and enduring
dilemmas in bilingual education. TEACHERS
COLLEGE RECORD, Vol. 84, no. 4 (Summer
1983), p. 871-907. English. DESCR:
*Bilingual Bicultural Education; Delgado v.
Bastrop Independent School District of
Bastrop Co., TX (1948); FORGOTTEN PEOPLE;
History; *Sanchez, George I.

1290 Scott, Patricia. Book review of: FRIDA: A
BIOGRAPHY OF FRIDA KAHLO. LIBRARY JOURNAL,
Vol. 108, no. 2 (January 15, 1983), p. 125.
English. DESCR: Artists; Book Reviews;
*FRIDA: A BIOGRAPHY OF FRIDA KAHLO; Herrera,
Hayden.

1291 The shaping of a career. HISPANIC BUSINESS,
Vol. 4, no. 4 (April 1982), p. 14. English.
DESCR: Atlantic Richfield Company;
Businesspeople; Chicanas; *Oaxaca, Virginia.

1292 Slade, Santiago. From Michoacan to Southern
California: the story of an undocumented
Mexican. SOUTHWEST ECONOMY AND SOCIETY, Vol.
3, no. 1 (Fall 1977), p. 5-18. English.
DESCR: *Oral History; *Puruaran, Michoacan,
Mexico; *Undocumented Workers.

1293 Solis, Arnaldo. El oro del barrio: maestro
Montoya. CALMECAC, Vol. 3, (Spring 1982),
p. 25+. Bilingual. DESCR: Artists; *Montoya,
Jose E.

1294 Think Spanish! MARKETING AND MEDIA
DECISIONS, Vol. 17, (October 1982), p.
66-69. English. DESCR: Advertising; Conill
Advertising Associates, New York, NY;
Conill, Alicia; Conill, Rafael; *Marketing;
Scott Paper Company; Spanish Language.

1295 Vara, Richard. Business savvy and Capricorn
spirit: How do you spell entrepreneurship?
HISPANIC BUSINESS, Vol. 5, no. 1 (January
1983), p. 18-19+. English. DESCR: Arroyos,
Alex; Business Enterprises; Export Trade;
Houston, TX.

1296 Villa, Esteban. Chicano wisdom. CALMECAC,
Vol. 2, (Spring 1981), p. 16-17. English.
DESCR: *Villa, Esteban.

1297 Villarreal, Maria; Tirado, Miguel David; and
Lopez, Ronald W. Abelardo Villarreal: a
teacher's teacher. CAMINOS, no. 12 (1981),
p. 30, 46. Bilingual. DESCR: Teaching
Profession; *Villarreal, Abelardo.

1298 Volsky, George and Masvidal, Raul. An
interview with Raul Masvidal. HISPANIC
BUSINESS, Vol. 4, no. 9 (September 1982), p.
16-17,24+. English. DESCR: Banking Industry;
Business Enterprises; Businesspeople;
Cubanos; *Masvidal, Raul; Miami, FL.

1299 Whitefield, Mimi. Mr. Lasa's 400,000 cases
of rum. HISPANIC BUSINESS, Vol. 4, no. 1
(January 1982), p. 14-15+. English. DESCR:
*Bacardi Imports, Inc.; Lasa, Luis;
Marketing.

1300 Willie, Charles V. First learning
unchallenged and untested. CHANGE, Vol. 14,
no. 7 (October 1982), p. 37-41. English.
DESCR: Affirmative Action; Bilingual
Bicultural Education; Book Reviews;
Education; *HUNGER OF MEMORY: THE EDUCATION
OF RICHARD RODRIGUEZ; Rodriguez, Richard.

1301 Ybarra-Frausto, Tomas. La Chata Noloesca:
figura del donaire. REVISTA CHICANO-RIQUENA,
Vol. 11, no. 1 (Spring 1983), p. 41-51.
English. DESCR: *La Chata Noloesca; Teatro.

Birth Control

1302 Davis, Sally M. and Harris, Mary B. Sexual
knowledge, sexual interests, and sources of
sexual information of rural and urban
adolescents from three cultures.
ADOLESCENCE, Vol. 17, no. 66 (Summer 1982),
p. 471-492. English. DESCR: Cultural
Characteristics; Identity; Rural Population;
*Sex Education; Sex Roles; *Sexual Behavior;
Urban Communities; Youth.

Bisbee, AZ

1303 Byrkit, James W. Walter Douglas and labor
struggles in early 20th century Arizona.
SOUTHWEST ECONOMY AND SOCIETY, Vol. 1, no. 1
(Spring 1976), p. 14-27. English. DESCR:
Arizona; *Biography; Clifton Morenci Strike,
June 1903; Copper Queen Mining Co., Bisbee,
AZ; *Douglas, Walter; International Workers
of the World (IWW); Labor Unions; Mining
Industry; Strikes and Lockouts.

Bissell, Joan

1304 Consalvo, Robert W. Book review of: PROGRAM
IMPACT EVALUATIONS: AN INTRODUCTION FOR
MANAGERS OF TITLE VII PROJECTS - A DRAFT
GUIDEBOOK. BILINGUAL JOURNAL, Vol. 7, no. 2
(Winter 1983), p. 36-37. English. DESCR:
Bilingual Bicultural Education; Book
Reviews; Educational Administration;
ELEMENTARY AND SECONDARY EDUCATION ACT;
Evaluation (Educational); *PROGRAM IMPACT
EVALUATIONS: AN INTRODUCTION FOR MANAGERS OF
TITLE VII PROJECTS - A DRAFT GUIDEBOOK ESEA
TITLE VII.

BITTER HARVEST: A HISTORY OF CALIFORNIA FARMWORKERS, 1870-1941

1305 De Leon, David. Book review of: BITTER
HARVEST: A HISTORY OF CALIFORNIA FARMWORKERS
1870-1941. ANNALS OF THE AMERICAN ACADEMY OF
POLITICAL AND SOCIAL SCIENCE, Vol. 462,
(July 1982), p. 198-199. English. DESCR:
Agricultural Laborers; Book Reviews;
California; Daniel, Cletus E.

Blackie's House of Beef v. Castillo

1306 Aragon, Ellen Weis. The factory raid: an
unconstitutional act. SOUTHERN CALIFORNIA
LAW REVIEW, Vol. 56, no. 2 (January 1983),
p. 605-645. English. DESCR: Deportation;
Immigration and Naturalization Service
(INS); International Ladies Garment Workers
Union (ILGWU) v. Sureck; Racism; Search and
Seizure; *Undocumented Workers.

Blacks

1307 Anderson, John W. The effects of culture and
social class on client preference for
counseling methods. JOURNAL OF NON-WHITE
CONCERNS IN PERSONNEL AND GUIDANCE, Vol. 11,
no. 3 (April 1983), p. 84-88. English.
DESCR: Anglo Americans; Counseling
Effectiveness Scale; *Counseling
(Psychological); *Educational Opportunity
Program (EOP); Locus of Control; University
of Illinois at Urbana.

Blacks (cont.)

1308 Applebome, Peter. The unkindest cut. TEXAS MONTHLY, Vol. 11, no. 1 (January 1983), p. 74-80. English. **DESCR**: Corpus Christi, TX; Political Representation; Voter Turnout.

1309 Argulewicz, Ed N. and Sanchez, David T. Special education evaluation process as a moderator of false positives. EXCEPTIONAL CHILDREN, Vol. 49, no. 5 (1983), p. 452-454. English. **DESCR**: Anglo Americans; *Special Education.

1310 Bailey, Lynn B., et al. Folacin and iron status and hematological finding in Blacks and Spanish-American adolescents from urban low-income households. AMERICAN JOURNAL OF CLINICAL NUTRITION, Vol. 35, no. 5 (May 1982), p. 1023-1032. English. **DESCR**: Low Income; Public Health; Surveys; *Youth.

1311 Balkan, D. Carlos. The advent of Uniworld/Hispanic: an interview. HISPANIC BUSINESS, Vol. 5, no. 3 (March 1983), p. 10-11+. English. **DESCR**: *Advertising Agencies; Consumers; Diaz-Albertini, Luis; Lewis, Byron; *Marketing; Spanish Advertising and Marketing Services (S.A.M.S.); Uniworld Group, Inc.; UniWorld Hispanic.

1312 Black-Hispanic coalition. LATINO, Vol. 53, no. 2 (March, April, 1982), p. 25. English. **DESCR**: King, Coretta Scott; Politics.

1313 Cortese, Anthony J., ed. A comparative analysis of ethnicity and moral judgment. CACR REVIEW, Vol. 1, no. 1 (September 1982), p. 72-101. English. **DESCR**: Anglo Americans; Cultural Characteristics; Identity; *Values.

1314 Creswell, John L. and Exezidis, Roxane H. Research brief: sex and ethnic differences in mathematics achievement of Black and Mexican-American adolescents. TEXAS TECH JOURNAL OF EDUCATION, Vol. 9, no. 3 (Fall 1982), p. 219-222. English. **DESCR**: Chicanas; Gender; *Mathematics; Youth.

1315 Creswell, John L. Sex-related differences in the problem-solving abilities of rural Black, Anglo, and Chicano adolescents. TEXAS TECH JOURNAL OF EDUCATION, Vol. 10, no. 1 (Winter 1983), p. 29-33. English. **DESCR**: Aiken and Preger Revised Math Attitude Scale; Anglo Americans; California Achievement Test; Chicanas; Gender; Mathematics; National Assessment of Educational Progress; *National Council of Teachers of Mathematics (NCTM); Youth.

1316 Dolan, Michael. Personality differences among Black, white, and Hispanic-American male heroin addicts on MMPI content scales. JOURNAL OF CLINICAL PSYCHOLOGY, Vol. 39, no. 5 (September 1983), p. 807-813. English. **DESCR**: Drug Addicts; *Heroin Addicts; Minnesota Multiphasic Personality Inventory (MMPI); Personality.

1317 Dowdall, George W. and Flood, Lawrence G. Correlates and consequences of socioeconomic differences among Chicanos, Blacks and Anglos in the Southwest: a study of metropolitan structure. SOCIAL SCIENCE JOURNAL, Vol. 19, no. 2 (April 1982), p. 25-36. English. **DESCR**: Anglo Americans; *Ethnic Groups; *Research Methodology; Residential Segregation; Socioeconomic Factors; Southwest United States.

1318 Exum, Herbert A. The most invisible minority: the culturally diverse elderly.
SCHOOL COUNSELOR, Vol. 30, no. 1 (September 1982), p. 15-24. English. **DESCR**: *Ancianos; Asian Americans; Counseling (Psychological); Cultural Customs; Ethnic Groups; Family; Native Americans; Stereotypes.

1319 Flaskerud, Jacquelyn H. Community mental health nursing: its unique role in the delivery of services to ethnic minorities. PERSPECTIVES IN PSYCHIATRIC CARE, Vol. 20, no. 1 (January, March, 1982), p. 37-43. English. **DESCR**: *Asian Americans; *Community Mental Health; Cultural Characteristics; Native Americans.

1320 Gober, Patricia and Behr, Michelle. Central cities and suburbs as distinct place types: myth or fact? ECONOMIC GEOGRAPHY, Vol. 58, no. 4 (October 1982), p. 371-385. English. **DESCR**: Census; Population Distribution; Suburban Communities; *Urban Communities.

1321 Hines, Bea L. and Fabricio, Roberto. Voices. NUESTRO, Vol. 7, no. 10 (December 1983), p. 57-58. English. **DESCR**: Cubanos; *Elections; Ferre, Maurice; *Miami, FL; Suarez, Xavier.

1322 Hsi, Bartholomew P.; Hsu, Katherine H.; and Jenkins, Daniel E. Ventilatory functions of normal children and young adults: Mexican-American, white and black. III. Sitting height as a predictor. JOURNAL OF PEDIATRICS, Vol. 102, no. 6 (June 1983), p. 860-865. English. **DESCR**: Anglo Americans; Child Study; *Children; Pediatrics.

1323 Kagan, Spencer and Zahn, G. Lawrence. Cultural differences in individualism? Just artifact. HISPANIC JOURNAL OF BEHAVIORAL SCIENCES, Vol. 5, no. 2 (June 1983), p. 219-232. English. **DESCR**: Anglo Americans; Children; Competition; *Culture; Social Orientation.

1324 Kerr, G. R. Supermarket sales high-sugar products in predominantly Black, Hispanic and white census tracts of Houston, Texas. AMERICAN JOURNAL OF CLINICAL NUTRITION, Vol. 37, no. 4 (April 1983), p. 622-631. English. **DESCR**: Anglo Americans; Food Practices; *Nutrition; Surveys.

1325 Low, Benson P. and Clement, Paul W. Relationships of race and socioeconomic status to classroom behavior, academic achievement, and referral for special education. JOURNAL OF SCHOOL PSYCHOLOGY, Vol. 20, no. 2 (Summer 1982), p. 103-112. English. **DESCR**: *Academic Achievement; Anglo Americans; Identity; Socioeconomic Factors.

1326 MacManus, Susan A. and Cassel, Carol A. Mexican-Americans in city-politics: participation, representation, and policy preferences. URBAN INTEREST, Vol. 4, no. 1 (Spring 1982), p. 57-69. English. **DESCR**: Houston, TX; Local Government; *Political Representation; Public Opinion; Public Policy.

1327 Murray, James L.; Bruhn, John G.; and Bunce, Harvey. Assessment of type A behavior in preschoolers. JOURNAL OF HUMAN STRESS, Vol. 9, no. 3 (September 1983), p. 32-39. English. **DESCR**: Anglo Americans; *Children; Early Childhood Education; Psychology.

Blacks (cont.)

1328 Scott, Leigh S., et al. Adaptive behavior inventory for children: the need for local norms. JOURNAL OF SCHOOL PSYCHOLOGY, Vol. 20, no. 1 (Spring 1982), p. 39-44. English. **DESCR:** *Adaptive Behavior Inventory for Children (ABIC); Anglo Americans; Corpus Christi Independent School District; Corpus Christi, TX; Placement; System of Multicultural Pluralistic Assessment (SOMPA).

1329 Shankman, Arnold. The image of Mexico and the Mexican-American in the Black press, 1890-1935. JOURNAL OF ETHNIC STUDIES, Vol. 3, no. 2 (Summer 1975), p. 43-56. English. **DESCR:** Attitude (Psychological); *Intergroup Relations; Journalism; *Mexico.

1330 Tienda, Marta and Angel, Ronald. Headship and household composition among blacks, Hispanics and other whites. SOCIAL FORCES, Vol. 61, no. 2 (December 1982), p. 508-531. English. **DESCR:** Anglo Americans; Cultural Characteristics; Extended Family; *Family; Puerto Ricans; Single Parents.

1331 Triandis, H.C., et al. Stereotyping among Hispanics and Anglos: the uniformity, intensity, direction and quality of auto- and heterosterotypes. JOURNAL OF CROSS-CULTURAL PSYCHOLOGY, Vol. 13, no. 4 (December 1982), p. 409-426. English. **DESCR:** Anglo Americans; *Stereotypes.

1332 Vernon, Sally W. and Roberts, Robert E. Prevalence of treated and untreated psychiatric disorders in three ethnic groups. SOCIAL SCIENCE AND MEDICINE, Vol. 16, no. 17 (1982), p. 1575-1582. English. **DESCR:** Anglo Americans; Comparative Psychology; Mental Illness; *Psychiatry.

1333 Willig, Ann C. Sociocultural and educational correlates of success-failure attributions and evaluation anxiety in the school setting for Black, Hispanic, and Anglo children. AMERICAN EDUCATIONAL RESEARCH JOURNAL, Vol. 20, no. 3 (Fall 1983), p. 385-410. English. **DESCR:** Academic Achievement; *Academic Motivation; Anglo Americans; Cultural Characteristics.

1334 Wurzman, Ilyana. Cultural values of Puerto Rican opiate addicts: an exploratory study. AMERICAN JOURNAL OF DRUG AND ALCOHOL ABUSE, Vol. 9, no. 2 (1982, 1983), p. 141-153. English. **DESCR:** Acculturation; Anglo Americans; *Drug Abuse; Drug Addicts; Family; Loevinger's Sentence Completion Test; Machismo; New York, NY; Opium; Puerto Ricans; Values.

1335 Zeff, Shirley B. A cross-cultural study of Mexican American, Black American and white American women of a large urban university. HISPANIC JOURNAL OF BEHAVIORAL SCIENCES, Vol. 4, no. 2 (June 1982), p. 245-261. English. **DESCR:** Anglo Americans; *Chicanas; Higher Education; Sex Roles.

Blades, Ruben

1336 Fernandez, Enrique. Cannes and CROSSOVER DREAMS, '83. FILM COMMENT, Vol. 19, no. 4-7 (August 1983), p. 2-7. English. **DESCR:** Arce, Manuel; Cannes Film Festival; *CROSSOVER DREAMS; Film Reviews; Films; Salsa.

"Blanco"

1337 de la Fuente, Patricia. Ambiguity in the poetry of Gary Soto. REVISTA

CHICANO-RIQUENA, Vol. 11, no. 2 (Summer 1983), p. 34-39. English. **DESCR:** "Avocado Lake"; "Braley Street"; "Field"; *Literary Criticism; Poetry; "Song for the pockets"; *Soto, Gary; TALE OF SUNLIGHT; "Telephoning God"; THE ELEMENTS OF SAN JOAQUIN; "Wind".

Blanco, Salvador Jorge

1338 Blanco seeks votes in U.S. NUESTRO, Vol. 6, no. 3 (April 1982), p. 11. English. **DESCR:** Politics.

Blank, Les

1339 Beaver, Frank E. CHULAS FRONTERAS. BILINGUAL REVIEW, Vol. 10, no. 2-3 (May, December, 1983), p. 176. English. **DESCR:** *CHULAS FRONTERAS [film]; Film Reviews; Music.

1340 Herrera-Sobek, Maria. Film review of: DEL MERO CORAZON (STRAIGHT FROM THE HEART). JOURNAL OF AMERICAN FOLKLORE, Vol. 95, (March 1982), p. 123. English. **DESCR:** *DEL MERO CORAZON; Film Reviews; Gosling, Maureen; Hernandez, Guillermo; Norteno; Strachwitz, Chris.

BLESS ME, ULTIMA

1341 Calderon, Hector. To read Chicano narrative: commentary and metacommentary. MESTER, Vol. 11, no. 2 (1982), p. 3-14. English. **DESCR:** Anaya, Rudolfo A.; Fiction; Literary Characteristics; *Literary Criticism; Literature; *Prose.

1342 Carrasco, David. A perspective for a study of religious dimensions in Chicano experience: BLESS ME, ULTIMA as a religious text. AZTLAN, Vol. 13, no. 1-2 (Spring, Fall, 1982), p. 195-221. English. **DESCR:** Anaya, Rudolfo A.; Literary Criticism; Literature; Religion.

1343 Clements, William M. Way to individuation in Anaya's BLESS ME, ULTIMA. MIDWEST QUARTERLY, Vol. 23, no. 2 (Winter 1982), p. 131-143. English. **DESCR:** Anaya, Rudolfo A.; Literary Criticism; Psychological Theory.

1344 Lattin, Vernon E. Ethnicity and identity in the contemporary Chicano novel. MINORITY VOICES, Vol. 2, no. 2 (Fall 1978), p. 37-44. English. **DESCR:** Identity; Literary Criticism; Literature; MEMORIES OF THE ALHAMBRA; *Novel; POCHO; THE AUTOBIOGRAPHY OF A BROWN BUFFALO; Y NO SE LO TRAGO LA TIERRA/AND THE EARTH DID NOT PART.

1345 Orozco, Febe Portillo. A bibliography of Hispanic literature. ENGLISH JOURNAL, Vol. 71, no. 7 (November 1982), p. 58-62. English. **DESCR:** BARRIO BOY; *Bibliography; CHICANO; EL SOL Y LOS DE ABAJO; GRITO DEL SOL; HEART OF AZTLAN; *Literature; POCHO; WE ARE CHICANOS.

1346 Vallejos, Thomas. Ritual process and the family in the Chicano novel. MELUS: MULTI-ETHNIC LITERATURE OF THE UNITED STATES, Vol. 10, no. 4 (Winter 1983, 1984), p. 5-16. English. **DESCR:** Anaya, Rudolfo A.; Family; *Literary Criticism; Novel; Parent and Child Relationships; POCHO; Rivera, Tomas; Villarreal, Jose Antonio; Y NO SE LO TRAGO LA TIERRA/AND THE EARTH DID NOT PART.

Block, Sherman

1347 A sheriff's X-mas. CAMINOS, Vol. 3, no. 1 (January 1982), p. 40. Bilingual. DESCR: *Belvedere Childcare Center; *Christmas; Holidays.

Blood Examination

1348 Sussman, Leon N. Paternity blood tests. NEW YORK LAW JOURNAL, Vol. 188, (October 6, 1982), p. 2. English. DESCR: Blood Groups; Genetics; *Paternity.

Blood Groups

1349 Sussman, Leon N. Paternity blood tests. NEW YORK LAW JOURNAL, Vol. 188, (October 6, 1982), p. 2. English. DESCR: Blood Examination; Genetics; *Paternity.

Blue Cross of Southern California

1350 Manuel Sanchez: the joy of big business. CAMINOS, Vol. 3, no. 2 (February 1982), p. 34-36. Bilingual. DESCR: Businesspeople; *Sanchez, Manuel.

Board of Education of Hudson Central School District v. Rowley Individualized Educational Program (IEP)

1351 Opportunity knocks ... but it needn't be equal. CHILDREN'S LEGAL RIGHTS JOURNAL, Vol. 4, no. 1 (August 1982), p. 14-17. English. DESCR: Doe v. Plyer [Tyler Independent School District, Texas]; Handicapped; *Undocumented Workers.

Board of Immigration Appeals (BIA)

1352 Roma, Thomas E., Jr. Not my father's son: obtaining preferred immigration status through paternal affiliation. JOURNAL OF FAMILY LAW, Vol. 20, no. 2 (January 1982), p. 323-335. English. DESCR: Immigration; Immigration and Nationality Act (INA); *Visa.

Body Measurements
USE: Anthropometry

Boehm Test of Basic Concepts

1353 Piersel, Wayne C., et al. Bias in content validity on the Boehm test of basic concepts for white and Mexican-American children. CONTEMPORARY EDUCATIONAL PSYCHOLOGY, Vol. 7, no. 2 (April 1982), p. 181-189. English. DESCR: Anglo Americans; Children; *Educational Tests and Measurements; Language Arts.

Bolivar, Simon

1354 Alvarez, Amando. Simon Bolivar. LATINO, Vol. 54, no. 8 (December 1983), p. 26-28. Spanish. DESCR: History.

1355 Breiter, Toni. El Libertador: a profile. NUESTRO, Vol. 7, no. 7 (September 1983), p. 32-35. English. DESCR: Biography; Political History and Conditions; Revolutions; South America.

1356 de Olmedo, Jose Joaquin. The victory at Junin: song to Bolivar. NUESTRO, Vol. 7, no. 7 (September 1983), p. 41. English. DESCR: Poetry.

1357 Palacios, Gonzalo. Bolivar and contemporary Latin America. NUESTRO, Vol. 7, no. 7 (September 1983), p. 36-37. English. DESCR: Latin America; Political History and Conditions; Political Ideology; South America.

1358 Valdez, Abelardo L. From Simon Bolivar to the Malvinas and beyond. NUESTRO, Vol. 7, no. 7 (September 1983), p. 38-41. English. DESCR: Latin America; Political Economy; *Political History and Conditions; South America.

Bonilla Giannini, Roxanna

1359 Gonzalez, Magdalena. Recognizing Hispanic achievements in entertainment - U.S. and Mexico. CAMINOS, Vol. 3, no. 7 (July, August, 1982), p. 18-24. Bilingual. DESCR: Allende, Fernando; Artists; Awards; Eynoso, David; Felix, Maria; Films; Gallego, Gina; *Golden Eagle Awards; Hoyos, Rodolfo; Lamas, Lorenzo; Lopez, Conchita; Lopez, Lisa; Montalban, Ricardo; Nosotros [film production company]; Quintero, Jose; Rowe, Arthur; Television; Torres, Liz.

Bonilla, Ruben

1360 Hamner, Richard. Hispanic update: changing of the LULAC guard--almost. NATIONAL HISPANIC JOURNAL, Vol. 1, no. 2 (Winter 1982), p. 6. English. DESCR: Bonilla, Tony; *League of United Latin American Citizens (LULAC).

1361 Two Hispanics on top ten list. LATINO, Vol. 53, no. 2 (March, April, 1982), p. 14. English. DESCR: *Cisneros, Henry, Mayor of San Antonio, TX; Politics; U.S. Junior Chamber of Commerce.

Bonilla, Tony

1362 Bonilla, Tony. 'We gave it our best shot'. LATINO, Vol. 54, no. 4 (May, June, 1983), p. 6. English. DESCR: Cultural Organizations.

1363 Brocksbank, Bonilla are winners of LNESC award. LATINO, Vol. 53, no. 8 (December 1982), p. 26. English. DESCR: Brocksbank, Robert W.; *Education; *League of United Latin American Citizens (LULAC); LULAC National Education Service Centers (LNESC).

1364 Cardenas, Leo. The Bonilla years come to an end. LATINO, Vol. 54, no. 4 (May, June, 1983), p. 8-9+. English. DESCR: Biography; Political Representation.

1365 Hamner, Richard. Hispanic update: changing of the LULAC guard--almost. NATIONAL HISPANIC JOURNAL, Vol. 1, no. 2 (Winter 1982), p. 6. English. DESCR: Bonilla, Ruben; *League of United Latin American Citizens (LULAC).

1366 Latinos evident in 1983 march. NUESTRO, Vol. 7, no. 7 (September 1983), p. 11-12. English. DESCR: Cuban-American Coordinating Committee; *Demonstrations; IMAGE, Washington, DC; Jackson, Jesse; League of United Latin American Citizens (LULAC); National Congress for Puerto Rican Rights (NCPRR); National Council of La Raza (NCLR); Velasquez, Baldemar; Zamora, Reuben.

1367 LULAC files complaint against TV networks. NUESTRO, Vol. 6, no. 8 (October 1982), p. 48. English. DESCR: Employment; Equal Employment Opportunity Commission (EEOC); *League of United Latin American Citizens (LULAC); Racism; Television.

Bonilla, Tony (cont.)

1368 The LULAC/PUSH dialog. HISPANIC BUSINESS, Vol. 5, no. 4 (April 1983), p. 15. English. **DESCR:** *Economic Development; Jackson, Jesse; League of United Latin American Citizens (LULAC); Operation PUSH.

1369 Rainbow coalition. LATINO, Vol. 54, no. 6 (October 1983), p. 10. Spanish. **DESCR:** *Jackson, Jesse; Political Representation.

1370 Zuniga, Jo Ann and Bonilla, Tony. Talking Texas: turning the tables with LULAC. HISPANIC BUSINESS, Vol. 5, no. 9 (September 1983), p. 18-19+. English. **DESCR:** Business Enterprises; Consumers; Economic History and Conditions; League of United Latin American Citizens (LULAC); Marketing; Texas.

Book Industry
    USE: Publishing Industry

Book Reviews

1371 Abu Bakr, Virginia. Book review of: MENTAL-HEALTH RESEARCH: A REFERENCE GUIDE. SOCIAL CASEWORK: JOURNAL OF CONTEMPORARY SOCIAL WORK, Vol. 63, no. 7 (September 1982), p. 443-444. English. **DESCR:** Cota-Robles Newton, Frank; *HISPANIC MENTAL HEALTH RESEARCH: A REFERENCE GUIDE; Mental Health; Reference Works.

1372 Achor, Shirley. Book review of: GUNPOWDER JUSTICE: A REASSESSMENT OF THE TEXAS RANGERS. INTERNATIONAL MIGRATION REVIEW, Vol. 16, no. 2 (Summer 1982), p. 491-492. English. **DESCR:** Bernal, Joseph; *GUNPOWDER JUSTICE: A REASSESSMENT OF THE TEXAS RANGERS; Pena, Alberto; Samora, Julian; Texas Rangers.

1373 Achor, Shirley. Book review of: GUNPOWDER JUSTICE: A REASSESSMENT OF THE TEXAS RANGERS. INTERNATIONAL MIGRATION REVIEW, Vol. 16, no. 2 (Summer 1982), p. 491-492. English. **DESCR:** Bernal, Joseph; *GUNPOWDER JUSTICE: A REASSESSMENT OF THE TEXAS RANGERS; History; Pena, Alberto; Samora, Julian; Texas Rangers.

1374 Acuna, Rodolfo. Book review of: THE MEXICAN FRONTIER 1821-1846: THE AMERICAN SOUTHWEST UNDER MEXICO. AMERICAN HISTORICAL REVIEW, Vol. 88, no. 2 (April 1983), p. 504-505. English. **DESCR:** *THE MEXICAN FRONTIER, 1821-1846: THE AMERICAN SOUTHWEST UNDER MEXICO; Weber, David J.

1375 Acuna, Rodolfo. Book review of: THE TEJANO COMMUNITY 1836-1900. WESTERN HISTORICAL QUARTERLY, Vol. 14, no. 2, p. 207-208. English. **DESCR:** De Leon, Arnoldo; Texas; *THE TEJANO COMMUNITY, 1836-1900.

1376 Adams, Alice. To see you again. NUESTRO, Vol. 6, no. 6 (August 1982), p. 55. English.

1377 Agosin, Marjorie. Book review of: ENTRE LA VIGILIA Y EL SUENO. THIRD WOMAN, Vol. 1, no. 2 (1982), p. 94-95. Spanish. **DESCR:** *ENTRE LA VIGILIA Y EL SUENO; Matte Alessandri, Ester.

1378 Alarcon, Justo S. Resena de EL DIABLO EN TEXAS. MAIZE, Vol. 3, no. 1-2 (Fall, Winter, 1979, 1980), p. 6-8. Spanish. **DESCR:** Brito, Aristeo; *EL DIABLO EN TEXAS.

1379 Alatorre, Alva Sylvia. Book review of: LIFE WITH TWO LANGUAGES: AN INTRODUCTION TO BILINGUALISM. HISPANIC JOURNAL OF BEHAVIORAL SCIENCES, Vol. 5, no. 4 (December 1983), p.

482-486. English. **DESCR:** Bilingualism; Grosjean, Francois; *LIFE WITH TWO LANGUAGES: AN INTRODUCTION TO BILINGUALISM.

1380 Allen, Virginia. Book review of: A CHICANO CHRISTMAS STORY. MODERN LANGUAGE JOURNAL, Vol. 66, no. 3 (Fall 1982), p. 353-354. English. **DESCR:** *A CHICANO CHRISTMAS STORY; Children's Literature; Cruz, Manuel; Cruz, Ruth.

1381 Almaraz, Felix D., Jr. Book review of: MEXICAN EMIGRATION TO THE UNITED STATES, 1897-1931: SOCIO-ECONOMIC PATTERNS. GREAT PLAINS QUARTERLY, Vol. 3, no. 2 (Spring 1983), p. 123-124. English. **DESCR:** Cardoso, Lawrence A.; *MEXICAN EMIGRATION TO THE UNITED STATES 1897-1931: SOCIO-ECONOMIC PATTERNS.

1382 Alvarez, Amando. A clash of cultures. LATINO, Vol. 54, no. 8 (December 1983), p. 18+. English. **DESCR:** De Leon, Arnoldo; *THEY CALLED THEM GREASERS: ANGLO ATTITUDES TOWARD MEXICANS IN TEXAS, 1821-1900.

1383 Alves Pereira, Teresinka. Book review of: CHICANOS: ANTOLOGIA HISTORICA Y LITERARIA. ROCKY MOUNTAIN REVIEW OF LANGUAGE AND LITERATURE, Vol. 36, no. 4 (1982), p. 301-302. Spanish. **DESCR:** *CHICANOS: ANTOLOGIA HISTORICA Y LITERARIA; Villanueva, Tino.

1384 Amastae, Jon. The issue of language proficiency. BILINGUAL REVIEW, Vol. 10, no. 1 (January, April, 1983), p. 73-80. English. **DESCR:** Alatis, James E.; Bilingual Bicultural Education; *GURT 1980: CURRENT ISSUES IN BILINGUAL EDUCATION.

1385 Andrews, Ilse. Bilinguals out of focus: a critical discussion. IRAL: INT'L REVIEW OF APPLIED LINGUISTICS IN LANGUAGE TEACHING, Vol. 20, no. 4 (November 1982), p. 297-305. English. **DESCR:** *Bilingualism; Literature Reviews; Martin, Albert; Obler, Loraine K.; *THE BILINGUAL BRAIN.

1386 Ano Nuevo de Kerr, Louise. Book review of: HUNGER OF MEMORY: THE EDUCATION OF RICHARD RODRIGUEZ. COMMONWEAL, Vol. 110, no. 1 (January 14, 1983), p. 26-28. English. **DESCR:** *HUNGER OF MEMORY: THE EDUCATION OF RICHARD RODRIGUEZ; Rodriguez, Richard.

1387 Arias, Ron. Book review of: CONTEMPORARY CHICANO THEATRE. JOURNAL OF ETHNIC STUDIES, Vol. 5, no. 1 (Spring 1977), p. 122-123. English. **DESCR:** *CONTEMPORARY CHICANO THEATRE; Garza, Roberto; Teatro.

1388 Avendano, Fausto. Book review of: HAY PLESHA LICHANS TO DI FLAC. LA PALABRA, Vol. 4, no. 1-2 (Spring, Fall, 1982, 1983), p. 165-167. Spanish. **DESCR:** *HAY PLESHA LICHANS TU DI FLAC; Literature; Sanchez, Saul.

1389 Baca Zinn, Maxine. Book review of: LA CHICANA: THE MEXICAN AMERICAN WOMAN. SIGNS: JOURNAL OF WOMEN IN CULTURE AND SOCIETY, Vol. 8, no. 2 (Winter 1982), p. 259-272. English. **DESCR:** Chicanas; Enriquez, Evangelina; *LA CHICANA: THE MEXICAN AMERICAN WOMAN; Literature Reviews; Mirande, Alfredo; Social Science.

Book Reviews (cont.)

1390 Baca Zinn, Maxine. Book review of: MEXICAN
WOMEN IN THE UNITED STATES: STRUGGLES PAST
AND PRESENT. SIGNS: JOURNAL OF WOMEN IN
CULTURE AND SOCIETY, Vol. 8, no. 2 (Winter
1982), p. 259-272. English. **DESCR:** Chicanas;
Del Castillo, Adelaida R.; Literature
Reviews; *MEXICAN WOMEN IN THE UNITED
STATES: STRUGGLES PAST AND PRESENT; Mora,
Magdalena; Social Science.

1391 Baca Zinn, Maxine. Book review of: TWICE A
MINORITY; MEXICAN-AMERICAN WOMEN. SIGNS:
JOURNAL OF WOMEN IN CULTURE AND SOCIETY,
Vol. 8, no. 2 (Winter 1982), p. 259-272.
English. **DESCR:** Chicanas; Literature
Reviews; Melville, Margarita B.; Social
Science; *TWICE A MINORITY: MEXICAN-AMERICAN
WOMEN.

1392 Balakian, Anna. Book review of: THE
PERPETUAL PRESENT: THE POETRY AND PROSE OF
OCTAVIO PAZ. JOURNAL OF ETHNIC STUDIES, Vol.
2, no. 3 (Fall 1974), p. 84-88. English.
DESCR: Mexican Literature; Paz, Octavio;
*THE PERPETUAL PRESENT: THE POETRY AND PROSE
OF OCTAVIO PAZ.

1393 Barber, Gary. Book review of: DICTIONARY OF
MEXICAN-AMERICAN HISTORY. REFERENCE SERVICES
REVIEW, Vol. 10, no. 3 (October 1982), p.
41. English. **DESCR:** Dictionaries;
*DICTIONARY OF MEXICAN AMERICAN HISTORY;
Meier, Matt S.; Rivera, Feliciano.

1394 Barradas, Efrain. Book review of: EN EL PAIS
DE LAS MARAVILLAS (KEMPIS PUERTORRIQUENO).
REVISTA CHICANO-RIQUENA, Vol. 10, no. 4
(Fall 1982), p. 67-68. Spanish. **DESCR:** *EN
EL PAIS DE LAS MARAVILLAS (KEMPIS
PUERTORRIQUENO); Umpierre, Maria.

1395 Barradas, Efrain. NOO JORK. REVISTA
CHICANO-RIQUENA, Vol. 10, no. 3 (Summer
1982), p. 65-67. Spanish. **DESCR:** Fernandez
Fragoso, Victor; Figueroa, Jose Angel; *NOO
JORK.

1396 Bauer, Karl Jack. Book review of: THE
MEXICAN-AMERICAN WAR: AN ANNOTATED
BIBLIOGRAPHY. JOURNAL OF THE WEST, Vol. 21,
no. 3 (April 1982), p. 73. English. **DESCR:**
Mexican American War; *THE MEXICAN-AMERICAN
WAR: AN ANNOTATED BIBLIOGRAPHY; Tutorow,
Norman E.; United States-Mexico Relations.

1397 Bean, Frank D. Book review of: MEXICAN
EMIGRATION TO THE UNITED STATES, 1897-1931:
SOCIO-ECONOMIC PATTERNS. INTERNATIONAL
MIGRATION REVIEW, Vol. 16, no. 2 (Summer
1982), p. 493-494. English. **DESCR:** Cardoso,
Lawrence A.; *MEXICAN EMIGRATION TO THE
UNITED STATES 1897-1931: SOCIO-ECONOMIC
PATTERNS.

1398 Beaupre, Shirley. Book review of: CROSS
CULTURAL PSYCHOLOGY: HUMAN BEHAVIOR IN
GLOBAL PERSPECTIVE. HISPANIC JOURNAL OF
BEHAVIORAL SCIENCES, Vol. 4, no. 1 (March
1982), p. 134-137. English. **DESCR:** *CROSS
CULTURAL PSYCHOLOGY: HUMAN BEHAVIOR IN
GLOBAL PERSPECTIVE; Segall, Marshall H.

1399 Bedard, Evelyn M. Book review of: HISPANIC
MENTAL HEALTH RESEARCH: A REFERENCE GUIDE.
RQ - REFERENCE AND ADULT SERVICES DIVISION,
Vol. 22, no. 1 (Fall 1982), p. 93. English.
DESCR: Bibliography; *HISPANIC MENTAL HEALTH
RESEARCH: A REFERENCE GUIDE; Mental Health;
Newton, Frank; Olmedo, Esteban L.; Padilla,
Amado M.

1400 Bell, Michael Davitt. Fitting into a

tradition of autobiography. CHANGE, Vol. 14,
no. 7 (October 1982), p. 36-39. English.
DESCR: Affirmative Action; Assimilation;
Bilingual Bicultural Education; Biography;
*HUNGER OF MEMORY: THE EDUCATION OF RICHARD
RODRIGUEZ; Rodriguez, Richard.

1401 Bell-Villada, G. H. Book review of: CHICANO
AUTHORS, INQUIRY BY INTERVIEW v. 228. NOTES
AND QUERIES, Vol. 30, no. 2 (1983), p.
186-188. English. **DESCR:** Bruce Novoa, Juan;
*CHICANO POETRY: A RESPONSE TO CHAOS;
Literary Criticism.

1402 Belton, Robert T. Book review of: CANNIBALS
AND KINGS: THE ORIGINS OF CULTURE and THE
MAN-EATING MYTH: ANTHROPOLOGY AND
ANTHROPOPHAGY. HISPANIC JOURNAL OF
BEHAVIORAL SCIENCES, Vol. 4, no. 1 (March
1982), p. 129-134. English. **DESCR:** Arens,
W.; *CANNIBALS AND KINGS: THE ORIGINS OF
CULTURE; Harris, Marvin, *THE MAN-EATING
MYTH: ANTHROPOLOGY AND ANTHROPOPHAGY.

1403 Berg, Charles. Book review of: CHRONIQUE OF
A DEATH FORETOLD. NUESTRO, Vol. 7, no. 4
(May 1983), p. 62. English. **DESCR:** CHRONICLE
OF A DEATH FORETOLD; *Criminal Acts; *Death
(Concept); Garcia Marquez, Gabriel.

1404 Blea, Irene I. Book review of: BUT TIME AND
CHANCE. CACR REVIEW, Vol. 1, no. 1
(September 1982), p. 132-133. English.
DESCR: *BUT TIME AND CHANCE; Catholic
Church; Chavez, Fray Angelico; Lamy, J.B.;
Machelbeuf, Joseph P., Vicar; Martinez,
Antonio, Fray; New Mexico.

1405 Bloodworth, William A., Jr. Book review of:
IMAGES OF THE MEXICAN-AMERICAN IN FICTION
AND FILM. WESTERN AMERICAN LITERATURE, Vol.
16, no. 4 (Winter 1982), p. 323-325.
English. **DESCR:** Chicanos in American
Literature; Films; *IMAGES OF THE MEXICAN
AMERICAN IN FICTION AND FILM; Pettit, Arthur
G.; Showalter, Dennis E.; Stereotypes.

1406 Bodayla, Stephen D. Book review of: ORIGINS
OF THE MEXICAN WAR: A DOCUMENTARY SOURCE
BOOK. HISTORY - REVIEWS OF NEW BOOKS, Vol.
11, no. 7 (May, June, 1983), p. 149-150.
English. **DESCR:** McAfee, Ward; *ORIGINS OF
THE MEXICAN WAR: A DOCUMENTARY SOURCE BOOK;
Robinson, J. Cordell.

1407 Book review of: BORDER BOOMTOWN, CIUDAD
JUAREZ SINCE 1848. NUESTRO, Vol. 5, no. 8
(November 1981), p. 51. English.

1408 Book review of: BORDERLANDS SOURCEBOOK.
LIBRARY JOURNAL, Vol. 108, no. 4 (February
15, 1983), p. 385. English. **DESCR:**
*BORDERLANDS SOURCEBOOK; Stoddard, Ellwyn
R.

1409 Book review of: CHICANO THEATER: THEMES AND
FORMS. CHOICE, Vol. 20, no. 2 (October
1982), p. 280. English. **DESCR:** *CHICANO
THEATER: THEMES AND FORMS; History; Huerta,
Jorge A.; Teatro.

1410 Book review of: CHICANO POETRY: A RESPONSE
TO CHAOS. CHOICE, Vol. 20, no. 6 (February
1983), p. 827. English. **DESCR:** Bruce Novoa,
Juan; *CHICANO POETRY: A RESPONSE TO CHAOS.

1411 Book review of: DICTIONARY OF
MEXICAN-AMERICAN HISTORY. LIBRARY JOURNAL,
Vol. 108, no. 10 (May 15, 1983), p. 965.
English. **DESCR:** *DICTIONARY OF MEXICAN
AMERICAN HISTORY; Meier, Matt S.; Rivera,
Feliciano.

Book Reviews (cont.)

1412 Book review of: EAST LOS ANGELES. LIBRARY
     JOURNAL, Vol. 107, no. 22 (December 15,
     1982), p. 2349. English. **DESCR:** *EAST LOS
     ANGELES: HISTORY OF A BARRIO; Romo, Ricardo.

1413 Book review of: FAMOUS ALL OVER TOWN. NEW
     YORKER, Vol. 59, no. 11 (May 2, 1983), p.
     126. English. **DESCR:** *FAMOUS ALL OVER TOWN;
     James, Dan.

1414 Book review of: FAMOUS ALL OVER TOWN.
     BOOKLIST, Vol. 79, no. 15 (April 1, 1983),
     p. 1016. English. **DESCR:** *FAMOUS ALL OVER
     TOWN; James, Dan.

1415 Book review of: FRIDA: A BIOGRAPHY OF FRIDA
     KAHLO. BOOKLIST, Vol. 79, no. 11 (February
     1, 1983), p. 708. English. **DESCR:** Artists;
     Biography; *FRIDA: A BIOGRAPHY OF FRIDA
     KAHLO; Herrera, Hayden; Kahlo, Frida.

1416 Book review of: HUNGER OF MEMORY: THE
     EDUCATION OF RICHARD RODRIGUEZ. SAN
     FRANCISCO REVIEW OF BOOKS, Vol. 7, (Summer
     1982), p. 11. English. **DESCR:** Attitude
     (Psychological); Bilingual Bicultural
     Education; *HUNGER OF MEMORY: THE EDUCATION
     OF RICHARD RODRIGUEZ; Identity; Rodriguez,
     Richard.

1417 Book review of: IMAGES OF THE
     MEXICAN-AMERICAN IN FICTION AND FILM. MODERN
     FICTION STUDIES, Vol. 28, (Summer 1982), p.
     367-369. English. **DESCR:** Fiction; Films;
     *IMAGES OF THE MEXICAN AMERICAN IN FICTION
     AND FILM; Mass Media; Pettit, Arthur G.

1418 Book review of: IN DEFENSE OF LA RAZA: THE
     LOS ANGELES MEXICAN CONSULATE AND THE
     MEXICAN COMMUNITY. CHOICE, Vol. 20, no. 7
     (March 1983), p. 1050. English. **DESCR:**
     Balderrama, Francisco E.; *IN DEFENSE OF LA
     RAZA: THE LOS ANGELES MEXICAN CONSULATE AND
     THE MEXICAN COMMUNITY.

1419 Book review of: MEGATRENDS. NUESTRO, Vol. 7,
     no. 9 (November 1983), p. 61-62. English.
     DESCR: *MEGATRENDS; Naisbitt, John.

1420 Book review of: MEXICAN CINEMA: REFLECTIONS
     OF A SOCIETY. CHOICE, Vol. 20, no. 2
     (October 1982), p. 276. English. **DESCR:**
     *MEXICAN CINEMA: REFLECTIONS OF A SOCIETY;
     Mora, Carl J.

1421 Book review of: OVER THE CHIHUAHUA AND SANTA
     FE TRAILS, 1847-1848: GEORGE RUTLEDGE
     GIBSON'S JOURNAL. HISPANIC BUSINESS, Vol. 4,
     no. 8 (August 1983), p. 27. English. **DESCR:**
     Frazer, Robert W.; Gibson, George Rutledge;
     *OVER THE CHIHUAHUA AND SANTA FE
     TRAILS, 1847-1848.

1422 Book review of: THE FEDERAL BUDGET AND THE
     NON-PROFIT SECTOR. CAMINOS, Vol. 4, no. 4
     (April 1983), p. 59. English. **DESCR:**
     Abramson, Anal J.; Federal Aid; *FEDERAL
     BUDGET AND THE NON-PROFIT SECTOR; Non-profit
     Groups; Salamon, Lester M.

1423 Book review of: THE MEXICAN FRONTIER,
     1821-1846: THE AMERICAN SOUTHWEST UNDER
     MEXICO. CHOICE, Vol. 20, no. 3 (November
     1982), p. 494. English. **DESCR:** *THE MEXICAN
     FRONTIER, 1821-1846: THE AMERICAN SOUTHWEST
     UNDER MEXICO; Weber, David J.

1424 Borland, James J. Book review of: COUNSELING
     THE CULTURALLY DIFFERENT. INTERNATIONAL
     MIGRATION REVIEW, Vol. 16, no. 4 (Winter
     1982), p. 910-911. English. **DESCR:**
     Counseling (Psychological); *COUNSELING THE

CULTURALLY DIFFERENT; Sue, Derald Wing.

1425 Brack, Gene M. Book review of: THE MEXICAN
     FRONTIER, 1821-1846: THE AMERICAN SOUTHWEST
     UNDER MEXICO. HISPANIC AMERICAN HISTORICAL
     REVIEW, Vol. 63, no. 2 (1983), p. 396-397.
     English. **DESCR:** *THE MEXICAN FRONTIER,
     1821-1846: THE AMERICAN SOUTHWEST UNDER
     MEXICO; Weber, David J.

1426 Brink, T. L. Book review of: AVANCES EN
     PSICOLOGIA CONTEMPORANEA. HISPANIC JOURNAL
     OF BEHAVIORAL SCIENCES, Vol. 5, no. 4
     (December 1983), p. 494-496. English.
     DESCR: *AVANCES EN PSICOLOGIA CONTEMPORANEA;
     Finley, Gordon E.; Marin, Gerardo;
     Psychology.

1427 Brink, T. L. Book review of: PSYCHOLOGY
     MISDIRECTED. HISPANIC JOURNAL OF BEHAVIORAL
     SCIENCES, Vol. 5, no. 3 (September 1983), p.
     363. English. **DESCR:** Psychiatry; *PSYCHOLOGY
     MISDIRECTED; Sarason, Seymour B.

1428 Brink, T. L. Book review of: WORKING-CLASS
     EMIGRES FROM CUBA. HISPANIC JOURNAL OF
     BEHAVIORAL SCIENCES, Vol. 5, no. 3
     (September 1983), p. 363-365. English.
     DESCR: Cubanos; Fox, Geoffrey E.; Laborers;
     *WORKING CLASS EMIGRES FROM CUBA.

1429 Britt, Anita. Book review of: THE LOS
     ANGELES BARRIO 1850-1890: A SOCIAL HISTORY.
     HISPANIC JOURNAL OF BEHAVIORAL SCIENCES,
     Vol. 4, no. 3 (September 1982), p. 388-391.
     English. **DESCR:** Griswold del Castillo,
     Ricardo; *THE LOS ANGELES BARRIO 1850-1890:
     A SOCIAL HISTORY.

1430 Brue de Lorenzo, Kathryn. Book review of:
     ETHNIC LEADERSHIP IN A NEW ENGLAND
     COMMUNITY: THREE PUERTO RICAN FAMILIES.
     HISPANIC JOURNAL OF BEHAVIORAL SCIENCES,
     Vol. 5, no. 2 (June 1983), p. 245-247.
     English. **DESCR:** *ETHNIC LEADERSHIP IN A NEW
     ENGLAND COMMUNITY: THREE PUERTO RICAN
     FAMILIES; Westfried, Alex Huxley.

1431 Bunker, Stephen G. Book review of: THE
     CHANGING DEMOGRAPHY OF SPANISH-AMERICANS.
     CONTEMPORARY SOCIOLOGY: A JOURNAL OF
     REVIEWS, Vol. 11, no. 3 (May 1982), p.
     270-273. English. **DESCR:** Jaffee, A.J.; *THE
     CHANGING DEMOGRAPHY OF SPANISH-AMERICANS.

1432 Burke, Leslie K. Book review of: AGING AND
     SOCIETY: CURRENT RESEARCH AND POLICY
     PERSPECTIVES. HISPANIC JOURNAL OF BEHAVIORAL
     SCIENCES, Vol. 4, no. 1 (March 1982), p.
     114-115. English. **DESCR:** *AGING AND SOCIETY:
     CURRENT RESEARCH AND POLICY PERSPECTIVES;
     Ancianos; Borgatta, Edgar F.; McCluskey,
     Neil G.

1433 Burke, Leslie K. Book review of: AGING AND
     SOCIAL POLICY: LEADERSHIP PLANNING. HISPANIC
     JOURNAL OF BEHAVIORAL SCIENCES, Vol. 4, no.
     1 (March 1982), p. 115-116. English. **DESCR:**
     *AGING AND SOCIAL POLICY: LEADERSHIP
     PLANNING; Ancianos; Kasschau, Patricia L.

1434 Burke, Leslie K. Book review of: ETHNICITY
     AND AGING: THEORY, RESEARCH AND POLICY.
     HISPANIC JOURNAL OF BEHAVIORAL SCIENCES,
     Vol. 4, no. 1 (March 1982), p. 107-112.
     English. **DESCR:** *ETHNICITY AND AGING:
     THEORY, RESEARCH, AND POLICY; Gelfland,
     Donald E.; Kutzik, Alfred J.

Book Reviews (cont.)

1435 Burke, Leslie K. Book review of: THE LATER YEARS: SOCIAL APPLICATIONS OF GERONTOLOGY. HISPANIC JOURNAL OF BEHAVIORAL SCIENCES, Vol. 4, no. 1 (March 1982), p. 116-117. English. DESCR: Kalish, Richard A.; *THE LATER YEARS: SOCIAL APPLICATIONS OF GERONTOLOGY.

1436 Burke, Leslie K. Book review of: WORK AND RETIREMENT: POLICY ISSUES. HISPANIC JOURNAL OF BEHAVIORAL SCIENCES, Vol. 4, no. 1 (March 1982), p. 112-114. English. DESCR: Ragan, Pauline K.; *WORK AND RETIREMENT: POLICY ISSUES.

1437 Camarillo, Alberto M. Book review of: DICTIONARY OF MEXICAN-AMERICAN HISTORY. JOURNAL OF AMERICAN HISTORY, Vol. 69, no. 4 (March 1983), p. 953-954. English. DESCR: *DICTIONARY OF MEXICAN AMERICAN HISTORY; Meier, Matt S.; Rivera, Feliciano.

1438 Camarillo, Alberto M. Book review of: MEXICANO RESISTANCE IN THE SOUTHWEST: "THE SACRED RIGHT OF SELF-PRESERVATION". WESTERN HISTORICAL QUARTERLY, Vol. 14, no. 1 (1983), p. 79-80. English. DESCR: History; *MEXICANO RESISTANCE IN THE SOUTHWEST: "THE SACRED RIGHT OF SELF-PRESERVATION"; New Mexico; Rosenbaum, Robert J.

1439 Cameron, Dan. Book review of: FRIDA: A BIOGRAPHY OF FRIDA KAHLO. NUESTRO, Vol. 7, no. 8 (October 1983), p. 44-45. English. DESCR: Biography; *FRIDA: A BIOGRAPHY OF FRIDA KAHLO; Herrera, Hayden; Kahlo, Frida.

1440 Candelaria, Cordelia. Book review of: TORTUGA. LA PALABRA, Vol. 4, no. 1-2 (Spring, Fall, 1982, 1983), p. 167-169. Spanish. DESCR: Anaya, Rudolfo A.; Literature; *TORTUGA.

1441 Candelaria, Cordelia. Problems and promise in Anaya's llano: THE SILENCE OF THE LLANO, Rudolfo A. Anaya. AMERICAN BOOK REVIEW, Vol. 5, no. 6 (September, October, 1983), p. 18-19. English. DESCR: Anaya, Rudolfo A.; *THE SILENCE OF THE LLANO.

1442 Cardenas, Lupe and Alarcon, Justo S. Book review of: CHULIFEAS FRONTERAS. MAIZE, Vol. 6, no. 3-4 (Spring, Summer, 1983), p. 60-61. Spanish. DESCR: Border Region.

1443 Cardoso, Lawrence Anthony. Book review of: ACROSS THE BORDER: RURAL DEVELOPMENT IN MEXICO AND RECENT MIGRATION TO THE UNITED STATES. AMERICAN HISTORICAL REVIEW, Vol. 88, no. 1 (February 1983), p. 226-227. English. DESCR: *ACROSS THE BORDER: RURAL DEVELOPMENT IN MEXICO AND RECENT MIGRATION; Cross, Harry E.; Sandos, James.

1444 Cardoso, Lawrence Anthony. Book review of: ACROSS THE BORDER: RURAL DEVELOPMENT IN MEXICO AND RECENT MIGRATION TO THE UNITED STATES. AMERICAN HISTORICAL REVIEW, Vol. 88, (February 1983), p. 226. English. DESCR: *ACROSS THE BORDER: RURAL DEVELOPMENT IN MEXICO AND RECENT MIGRATION; Cross, Harry E.; Immigration; Sandos, James.

1445 Cardoso, Lawrence Anthony. Book review of: DESERT IMMIGRANTS: THE MEXICANS OF EL PASO 1880-1920. WESTERN HISTORICAL QUARTERLY, Vol. 13, (April 1982), p. 197. English. DESCR: *DESERT IMMIGRANTS: THE MEXICANS OF EL PASO 1880-1920; Garcia, Mario T.

1446 Cardoso, Lawrence Anthony. Book review of: LOS MEXICANOS QUE DEVOLVIO LA CRISIS, 1929-1932. JOURNAL OF ETHNIC STUDIES, Vol. 5, no. 1 (Spring 1977), p. 120-122. Spanish. DESCR: Carreras de Velasco, Mercedes; Deportation; Immigrant Labor; Immigration; Immigration Regulation and Control; *LOS MEXICANOS QUE DEVOLVIO LA CRISIS 1929-1932; Mexico; Social History and Conditions.

1447 Cardoso, Lawrence Anthony. Book review of: REVOLTOSOS: MEXICO'S REBELS IN THE UNITED STATES 1903-1923. JOURNAL OF THE WEST, Vol. 22, no. 1 (1983), p. 90. English. DESCR: History; Immigration; Mexico; Raat, W. Dirk; *REVOLTOSOS: MEXICO'S REBELS IN THE UNITED STATES, 1903-1923.

1448 Cardoso, Lawrence Anthony. Book review of: UNWANTED MEXICAN AMERICANS IN THE GREAT DEPRESSION: REPATRIATION PRESSURES, 1929-1939. JOURNAL OF ETHNIC STUDIES, Vol. 5, no. 1 (Spring 1977), p. 120-122. English. DESCR: Deportation; Hoffman, Abraham; Immigrant Labor; Immigration; Immigration Regulation and Control; Mexico; Social History and Conditions; *UNWANTED MEXICAN AMERICANS IN THE GREAT DEPRESSION.

1449 Cardoso, Lawrence Anthony. "Wetbacks" and "slaves": recent additions to the literature. JOURNAL OF AMERICAN ETHNIC HISTORY, Vol. 1, no. 2 (Spring 1982), p. 68-71. English. DESCR: Garcia, Juan Ramon; Lewis, Sasha G.; *OPERATION WETBACK: THE MASS DEPORTATION OF MEXICAN UNDOCUMENTED WORKERS IN 1954; *SLAVE TRADE TODAY: AMERICAN EXPLOITATION OF ILLEGAL ALIENS; Undocumented Workers.

1450 Carlson, Alvar W. Book review of: CANONES: VALUES, CRISIS, AND SURVIVAL IN A NORTHERN NEW MEXICO VILLAGE. NEW MEXICO HISTORICAL REVIEW, Vol. 58, no. 3 (July 1983), p. 294. English. DESCR: *CANONES: VALUES, CRISIS AND SURVIVAL IN A NORTHERN NEW MEXICO VILLAGE; Kutsche, Paul; Van Ness, John R.

1451 Cazemajou, Jean. Book review of: LES FILS DU SOLEIL: LA MINORITE MEXICAINE A TRAVERS LA LITTERATURE DES ETATS-UNIS. REVUE FRANCAISE D'ETUDES AMERICAINES. Vol. 83, no. 16 (February 1983), p. 153-155. Other. DESCR: *LES FILS DU SOLEIL: LA MINORITE MEXICAINE A TRAVERS LA LITTERATURE DES ETATS-UNIS; Rocard, Marcienne.

1452 Cervantes, Lorna Dee. Book review of: EMPLUMADA. NUESTRO, Vol. 6, no. 5 (June, July, 1982), p. 56. English. DESCR: Cervantes, Lorna Dee; *EMPLUMADA.

1453 Chall, Jeanne. Rich and sharp memories of reading. CHANGE, Vol. 14, no. 7 (October 1982), p. 36-40. English. DESCR: Assimilation; *HUNGER OF MEMORY: THE EDUCATION OF RICHARD RODRIGUEZ; Language Arts; Reading; Rodriguez, Richard; Socioeconomic Factors.

1454 Chavaria, Elvira. Book review of: THE MEXICAN AMERICAN: A CRITICAL GUIDE TO RESEARCH AIDS. AZTLAN, Vol. 14, no. 1 (Spring 1983), p. 192-195. English. DESCR: Bibliography; Reference Works; Robinson, Barbara J.; Robinson, J. Cordell; *THE MEXICAN AMERICAN: A CRITICAL GUIDE TO RESEARCH AIDS.

1455 Chavez, Linda. HUNGER OF MEMORY: the metamorphosis of a disadvantaged child. AMERICAN EDUCATOR, Vol. 6, no. 3 (Fall 1982), p. 14-16. English. DESCR: *HUNGER OF MEMORY: THE EDUCATION OF RICHARD RODRIGUEZ; Rodriguez, Richard.

Book Reviews (cont.)

1456 Chavez, Mauro. Book review of: ESSAYS ON LA
MUJER. JOURNAL OF ETHNIC STUDIES, Vol. 8,
no. 2 (Summer 1980), p. 117-120. English.
DESCR: *Chicanas; Cruz, Rosa Martinez;
Economic History and Conditions; *ESSAYS ON
LA MUJER; Sanchez, Rosaura; Social History
and Conditions; Socioeconomic Factors;
Women's Rights.

1457 Chavez, Mauro. Carranza's CHICANISMO:
PHILOSOPHICAL FRAGMENTS. JOURNAL OF ETHNIC
STUDIES, Vol. 7, no. 3 (Fall 1979), p.
95-100. English. **DESCR:** Carranza, Elihu;
*Chicanismo; *CHICANISMO: PHILOSOPHICAL
FRAGMENTS; Philosophy; Research Methodology.

1458 Churchhill, Ward. Implications of publishing
ROOTS OF RESISTANCE. JOURNAL OF ETHNIC
STUDIES, Vol. 9, no. 3 (Fall 1981), p.
83-89. English. **DESCR:** Colonialism; Dunbar
Ortiz, Roxanne; Land Tenure; Native
Americans; New Mexico; Publishing Industry;
*ROOTS OF RESISTANCE: LAND TENURE IN NEW
MEXICO, 1680-1980; Social History and
Conditions.

1459 Clifford, Terry. Book review of: PARENTING
IN A MULTI-CULTURAL SOCIETY. HISPANIC
JOURNAL OF BEHAVIORAL SCIENCES, Vol. 4, no.
3 (September 1982), p. 385-387. English.
DESCR: Cardenas, Rene; Fantini, Mario;
*PARENTING IN A MULTI-CULTURAL SOCIETY.

1460 Consalvo, Robert W. Book review of: PROGRAM
IMPACT EVALUATIONS: AN INTRODUCTION FOR
MANAGERS OF TITLE VII PROJECTS - A DRAFT
GUIDEBOOK. BILINGUAL JOURNAL, Vol. 7, no. 2
(Winter 1983), p. 36-37. English. **DESCR:**
Bilingual Bicultural Education; Bissell,
Joan; Educational Administration; ELEMENTARY
AND SECONDARY EDUCATION ACT; Evaluation
(Educational); *PROGRAM IMPACT EVALUATIONS:
AN INTRODUCTION FOR MANAGERS OF TITLE VII
PROJECTS - A DRAFT GUIDEBOOK ESEA TITLE VII.

1461 Coolson, Freda L. Book review of: THE
QUESTION OF SEX DIFFERENCES: BIOLOGICAL,
CULTURAL AND PSYCHOLOGICAL ISSUES. HISPANIC
JOURNAL OF BEHAVIORAL SCIENCES, Vol. 4, no.
3 (September 1982), p. 391-393. English.
DESCR: Hoyenga, Katherine Blick; Hoyenga,
Kermit T.; *THE QUESTION OF SEX DIFFERENCES:
BIOLOGICAL, CULTURAL, AND PSYCHOLOGICAL
ISSUES.

1462 Cortes, Carlos E. Book review of: DESERT
IMMIGRANTS: THE MEXICANS OF EL PASO
1880-1920. PACIFIC HISTORICAL REVIEW, Vol.
52, no. 1 (February 1983), p. 119-120.
English. **DESCR:** *DESERT IMMIGRANTS: THE
MEXICANS OF EL PASO 1880-1920; Garcia, Mario
T.

1463 Cortes, Carlos E. Book review of: MEXICAN
AMERICANS IN A DALLAS BARRIO. NEW SCHOLAR,
Vol. 8, no. 1-2 (Spring, Fall, 1982), p.
488-489. English. **DESCR:** Achor, Shirley;
*MEXICAN AMERICANS IN A DALLAS BARRIO.

1464 Corwin, Arthur F. Book review of: DESERT
IMMIGRANTS: THE MEXICANS OF EL PASO
1880-1920. HISTORIAN, Vol. 45, no. 2
(February 1983), p. 279-280. English.
DESCR: *DESERT IMMIGRANTS: THE MEXICANS OF
EL PASO 1880-1920; Garcia, Mario T.

1465 Cotera, Martha P. Rich-heard rod-ree-guess.
LATINA, Vol. 1, no. 1 (1982), p. 27+.
English. **DESCR:** *HUNGER OF MEMORY: THE
EDUCATION OF RICHARD RODRIGUEZ; Rodriguez,
Richard.

1466 Craver, Rebecca McDowell. Book review of:
CHICANO INTERMARRIAGE: A THEORETICAL AND
EMPIRICAL STUDY. NEW MEXICO HISTORICAL
REVIEW, Vol. 58, no. 3 (July 1983), p.
295-296. English. **DESCR:** *CHICANO
INTERMARRIAGE: A THEORETICAL AND EMPIRICAL
STUDY; Murguia, Edward.

1467 Cripps, Thomas. Mexicans, Indians and
movies: the need for a history. WIDE ANGLE:
A FILM QUARTERLY OF THEORY, CRITICISM, AND
PRACTICE, Vol. 5, no. 1 (1982), p. 68-70.
English. **DESCR:** Bataille, Gretchen M.;
Films; IMAGES OF THE MEXICAN AMERICAN IN
FICTION AND FILM; Native Americans;
O'Connor, John E.; Pettit, Arthur G.; Silet,
Charles L.P.; *Stereotypes; THE HOLLYWOOD
INDIAN: STEREOTYPES OF NATIVE AMERICANS IN
FILMS; THE PRETEND INDIANS: IMAGES OF NATIVE
AMERICANS IN THE MOVIES.

1468 Crisp, James E. Book review of: MEXICANO
RESISTANCE IN THE SOUTHWEST: "THE SACRED
RIGHT OF SELF-PRESERVATION". JOURNAL OF
SOUTHERN HISTORY, Vol. 48, no. 1 (1982), p.
138-139. English. **DESCR:** *MEXICANO
RESISTANCE IN THE SOUTHWEST: "THE SACRED
RIGHT OF SELF-PRESERVATION"; Political
History and Conditions; Rosenbaum, Robert
J.; United States-Mexico Relations.

1469 Crisp, James E. Book review of: THE TEJANO
COMMUNITY 1836-1900. JOURNAL OF ECONOMIC
HISTORY, Vol. 42, no. 4 (December 1982), p.
951-953. English. **DESCR:** De Leon, Arnoldo;
Texas; *THE TEJANO COMMUNITY, 1836-1900.

1470 Cuello, J. Book review of: IN DEFENSE OF LA
RAZA: THE LOS ANGELES MEXICAN CONSULATE AND
THE MEXICAN COMMUNITY. CALIFORNIA HISTORY,
Vol. 62, no. 1 (1983), p. 70. English.
DESCR: Balderrama, Francisco E.; California;
History; *IN DEFENSE OF LA RAZA: THE LOS
ANGELES MEXICAN CONSULATE AND THE MEXICAN
COMMUNITY.

1471 Cummins, Light Townsend. Book review of: THE
MEXICAN FRONTIER 1821-1846: THE AMERICAN
SOUTHWEST UNDER MEXICO. JOURNAL OF SOUTHERN
HISTORY, Vol. 49, no. 3 (August 1983), p.
453-455. English. **DESCR:** *THE MEXICAN
FRONTIER, 1821-1846: THE AMERICAN SOUTHWEST
UNDER MEXICO; Weber, David J.

1472 Daydi-Tolson, Santiago. The right to belong:
a critic's view of Puerto Rican poetry in
the United States. BILINGUAL REVIEW, Vol.
10, no. 1 (January, April, 1983), p. 81-86.
English. **DESCR:** Barradas, Efrain; *HEREJES Y
MITIFICADORES: MUESTRA DE POESIA
PUERTORRIQUENA EN LOS ESTADOS UNIDOS; Puerto
Rican Literature.

1473 de Armas, Isabel. Chicano, un vocablo
colonizador. CUADERNOS HISPANOAMERICANOS,
Vol. 394, (April 1983), p. 193-201.
Spanish. **DESCR:** Agricultural Laborers; Calvo
Buezas, Tomas; *CHICANOS: ANTOLOGIA
HISTORICA Y LITERARIA; Identity; *LOS MAS
POBRES EN EL PAIS MAS RICO; Villanueva,
Tino.

1474 De Leon, Arnoldo. Book review of: DICTIONARY
OF MEXICAN-AMERICAN HISTORY. NEW MEXICO
HISTORICAL REVIEW, Vol. 58, no. 1 (January
1983), p. 101-102. English. **DESCR:**
*DICTIONARY OF MEXICAN AMERICAN HISTORY;
Meier, Matt S.; Rivera, Feliciano.

Book Reviews (cont.)

1475 De Leon, Arnoldo. Book review of: IN DEFENSE OF LA RAZA: THE LOS ANGELES MEXICAN CONSULATE AND THE MEXICAN COMMUNITY. NEW MEXICO HISTORICAL REVIEW, Vol. 58, no. 3 (July 1983), p. 296-297. English. **DESCR:** Balderrama, Francisco E.; *IN DEFENSE OF LA RAZA: THE LOS ANGELES MEXICAN CONSULATE AND THE MEXICAN COMMUNITY.

1476 De Leon, Arnoldo. Book review of: ON THE BORDER: PORTRAITS OF AMERICA'S SOUTHWESTERN FRONTIER. SOUTHWESTERN HISTORICAL QUARTERLY, Vol. 86, no. 2 (1982), p. 367-368. English. **DESCR:** History; Mexico; Miller, Tom; *ON THE BORDER: PORTRAITS OF AMERICA'S SOUTHWESTERN FRONTIER; Texas.

1477 De Leon, David. Book review of: BITTER HARVEST: A HISTORY OF CALIFORNIA FARMWORKERS 1870-1941. ANNALS OF THE AMERICAN ACADEMY OF POLITICAL AND SOCIAL SCIENCE, Vol. 462, (July 1982), p. 198-199. English. **DESCR:** Agricultural Laborers; *BITTER HARVEST: A HISTORY OF CALIFORNIA FARMWORKERS, 1870-1941; California; Daniel, Cletus E.

1478 Delgado, Melvin. Book review of: BASIC PROBLEMS OF ETHNOPSYCHIATRY. HISPANIC JOURNAL OF BEHAVIORAL SCIENCES, Vol. 4, no. 3 (September 1982), p. 380. English. **DESCR:** *BASIC PROBLEMS OF ETHNOPSYCHIATRY; Devereux, George.

1479 Dickens, E. Larry. Book review of: THE POLITICS OF BILINGUAL EDUCATION: A STUDY OF FOUR SOUTHWEST TEXAS COMMUNITIES. SOUTHWEST ECONOMY AND SOCIETY, Vol. 1, no. 1 (Spring 1976), p. 47-48. English. **DESCR:** Bilingual Bicultural Education; Hardgrave, Robert L.; Hinojosa, Santiago; *THE POLITICS OF BILINGUAL EDUCATION: A STUDY OF FOUR SOUTHWEST TEXAS COMMUNITIES.

1480 Dyer, Nancy Joe. Book review of: TEACHING SPANISH TO THE HISPANIC BILINGUAL: ISSUES, AIMS AND METHODS. HISPANIA, Vol. 65, no. 3 (September 1982), p. 474-475. English. **DESCR:** Garcia-Moya, Rodolfo; Lozano, Anthony G.; Spanish Language; *TEACHING SPANISH TO THE HISPANIC BILINGUAL: ISSUES, AIMS AND METHODS; Valdez, Guadalupe.

1481 Eaton, Joli. Book review of: EDUCATION IN THE 80's: MULTICULTURAL EDUCATION. HISPANIC JOURNAL OF BEHAVIORAL SCIENCES, Vol. 5, no. 2 (June 1983), p. 238-240. English. **DESCR:** Banks, James A.; *EDUCATION IN THE 80'S: MULTICULTURAL EDUCATION.

1482 Elias, Edward. TORTUGA: a novel of archetypal structure. BILINGUAL REVIEW, Vol. 9, no. 1 (January, April, 1982), p. 82-87. English. **DESCR:** Anaya, Rudolfo A.; *TORTUGA.

1483 Elizondo, Sergio D. Book review of: LITERATURA CHICANA: TEXTO Y CONTEXTO. JOURNAL OF ETHNIC STUDIES, Vol. 1, no. 1 (Spring 1973), p. 68-70. Bilingual. **DESCR:** Castaneda Shular, Antonia; Literary Criticism; Literary History; Literary Influence; *LITERATURA CHICANA: TEXTO Y CONTEXTO; Literature; Sommers, Joseph; Teatro; Ybarra-Frausto, Tomas.

1484 Elsenberg, Ann R. Book review of: LATINO LANGUAGE AND COMMUNICATIVE BEHAVIOR. HISPANIC JOURNAL OF BEHAVIORAL SCIENCES, Vol. 5, no. 3 (September 1983), p. 347-349. English. **DESCR:** Duran, Richard P.; Languages; *LATINO LANGUAGE AND COMMUNICATIVE BEHAVIOR; Sociolinguistics.

1485 Enright, Scott. Book review of: BILINGUALISM IN THE SOUTHWEST. EDUCATIONAL STUDIES, Vol. 13, no. 3-4 (Fall, Winter, 1982), p. 494-498. English. **DESCR:** *BILINGUALISM IN THE SOUTHWEST; Turner, Paul R.

1486 Escobedo, Theresa Herrera. Book review of: CHICANAS IN THE NATIONAL LANDSCAPE. JOURNAL OF AMERICAN ETHNIC HISTORY, Vol. 1, no. 2 (Spring 1982), p. 101-103. English. **DESCR:** Candelaria, Cordelia; Chicanas; *CHICANAS EN EL AMBIENTE NACIONAL/CHICANAS IN THE NATIONAL LANDSCAPE.

1487 Escobedo, Theresa Herrera. Book review of: CHICANAS IN THE NATIONAL LANDSCAPE. HISPANIC JOURNAL OF BEHAVIORAL SCIENCES, Vol. 4, no. 2 (June 1982), p. 263-267. English. **DESCR:** *CHICANAS EN EL AMBIENTE NACIONAL/CHICANAS IN THE NATIONAL LANDSCAPE; FRONTIERS: A JOURNAL OF WOMEN STUDIES, Vol. 5, no. 2(Summer 1980).

1488 Esman, Milton J. Book review of: THE ETHNIC REVIVAL IN THE MODERN WORLD. ETHNIC AND RACIAL STUDIES, Vol. 5, no. 3 (1982), p. 378-379. English. **DESCR:** Ethnic Groups; *ETHNIC REVIVAL IN THE MODERN WORLD; Smith, Anthony D.

1489 Fabre, Michel. Book review of: LES FILS DU SOLEIL: LA MINORITE MEXICAINE A TRAVERS LA LITTERATURE DES ETATS-UNIS. MELUS: MULTI-ETHNIC LITERATURE OF THE UNITED STATES, Vol. 8, no. 1 (Spring 1981), p. 65-68. English. **DESCR:** *LES FILS DU SOLEIL: LA MINORITE MEXICAINE A TRAVERS LA LITTERATURE DES ETATS-UNIS; Literature; Rocard, Marcienne.

1490 Fainberg, Louise Vasvari. HUNGER OF MEMORY: review of a review. NABE JOURNAL, Vol. 6, no. 2-3 (Winter, Spring, 1981, 1982), p. 115-116. English. **DESCR:** *HUNGER OF MEMORY: THE EDUCATION OF RICHARD RODRIGUEZ; Rodriguez, Richard; Zweig, Paul.

1491 Family favorites. NUESTRO, Vol. 7, no. 10 (December 1983), p. 36-38. English. **DESCR:** Bermudez, Maria Teresa; *MEXICAN FAMILY FAVORITES COOKBOOK; Recipes.

1492 Feliciano-Foster, Wilma. A comparison of three current first-year college-level Spanish-for-native-speakers textbooks. BILINGUAL REVIEW, Vol. 9, no. 1 (January, April, 1982), p. 72-81. English. **DESCR:** ESPANOL ESCRITO; Garza-Swan, Gloria; *Language Development; Mejias, Hugo A.; MEJORA TU ESPANOL; NUESTRO ESPANOL: CURSO PARA ESTUDIANTES BILINGUES; Portilla, Marta de la; Spanish Language Textbooks; Teschner, Richard V.; Valdes Fallis, Guadalupe; Varela, Beatriz.

1493 Fernandez, Celestino. The neglected dimension: ethnicity in American life. AZTLAN, Vol. 14, no. 1 (Spring 1983), p. 199-201. English. **DESCR:** Ethnic Groups; Identity; Rosen, Philip; *THE NEGLECTED DIMENSION: ETHNICITY IN AMERICAN LIFE.

1494 Fernandez, Jose B. Book review of: HISPANICS IN THE UNITED STATES: AN ANTHOLOGY OF CREATIVE LITERATURE. ROCKY MOUNTAIN REVIEW OF LANGUAGE AND LITERATURE, Vol. 36, no. 1 (1982), p. 65-66. English. **DESCR:** *HISPANICS IN THE UNITED STATES: AN ANTHOLOGY OF CREATIVE WRITING; Jimenez, Francisco; Keller, Gary D.

Book Reviews (cont.)

1495 Fernandez, Jose B. Book review of: LA
LLEGADA. REVISTA CHICANO-RIQUENA, Vol. 10,
no. 3 (Summer 1982), p. 67-68. Spanish.
DESCR: Gonzalez, Jose Luis; *LA LLEGADA.

1496 Fernandez, Maria Patricia. Book review of:
TWICE A MINORITY; MEXICAN-AMERICAN WOMEN.
CONTEMPORARY SOCIOLOGY: A JOURNAL OF
REVIEWS, Vol. 11, no. 3 (May 1982), p.
342-343. English. **DESCR:** Melville, Margarita
B.; *TWICE A MINORITY: MEXICAN-AMERICAN
WOMEN.

1497 Ferrarone, Aida. The aquarium conspiracy:
personal and social transformation in the
80's: a review. LATINA, Vol. 1, no. 2
(February, March, 1983), p. 23. English.
DESCR: Ferguson, Marilyn; *THE AQUARIAN
CONSPIRACY.

1498 Flemming, Donald N. Book review of:
EXPLORACIONES CHICANO-RIQUENAS. MODERN
LANGUAGE JOURNAL, Vol. 66, no. 2 (Summer
1982), p. 233-234. English. **DESCR:**
Burgos-Sasscer. Ruth; *EXPLORACIONES
CHICANO-RIQUENAS; Textbooks; Williams,
Shirley.

1499 Franco, Juan N. Book review of: COUNSELING
ACROSS CULTURES. HISPANIC JOURNAL OF
BEHAVIORAL SCIENCES, Vol. 5, no. 2 (June),
p. 233-237. English. **DESCR:** *COUNSELING
ACROSS CULTURES; Draguns, Juris G.; Lonner,
Walter J.; Pedersen, Paul P.; Trimble,
Joseph E.

1500 Furphy, Alice. Book review of:
DISCRIMINATION IN ORGANIZATIONS. HISPANIC
JOURNAL OF BEHAVIORAL SCIENCES, Vol. 5, no.
1 (March 1983), p. 115-120. English. **DESCR:**
Alvarez, Rodolfo; *DISCRIMINATION IN
ORGANIZATIONS; Heller, Kenneth.

1501 Garcia, Ed. Book review of: HUNGER OF
MEMORY: THE EDUCATION OF RICHARD RODRIGUEZ.
TEXAS OBSERVOR, Vol. 74, no. 12 (June 18,
1982), p. 23-24. English. **DESCR:** *HUNGER OF
MEMORY: THE EDUCATION OF RICHARD RODRIGUEZ;
Rodriguez, Richard.

1502 Garcia, Ed. Quien es Rolando Hinojosa? TEXAS
OBSERVOR, Vol. 75, no. 5 (March 11,), p.
26-29. English. **DESCR:** Biography;
*Hinojosa-Smith, Rolando R.; *RITES AND
WITNESSES; THE VALLEY.

1503 Garcia, Ignacio M. Book review of: PURO
ROLLO. NUESTRO, Vol. 6, no. 10 (December
1982), p. 60. English. **DESCR:** Barrios,
Gregg; *PURO ROLLO.

1504 Garcia, Juan R. Book review of: MEXICANO
RESISTANCE IN THE SOUTHWEST: "THE SACRED
RIGHT OF SELF-PRESERVATION". ARIZONA AND THE
WEST, Vol. 24, no. 1 (Spring 1982), p.
81-82. English. **DESCR:** *MEXICANO RESISTANCE
IN THE SOUTHWEST: "THE SACRED RIGHT OF
SELF-PRESERVATION"; New Mexico; Rosenbaum,
Robert J.; Social History and Conditions.

1505 Garcia, Mario T. Book review of: LA CLASE
OBRERA EN LA HISTORIA DE MEXICO: AL NORTE
DEL RIO BRAVO (PASADO INMEDIATO, 1930-1981).
HISPANIC AMERICAN HISTORICAL REVIEW, Vol.
62, no. 4 (November 1982), p. 694-696.
English. **DESCR:** History; *LA CLASE OBRERA EN
LA HISTORIA DE MEXICO: AL NORTE DEL RIO
BRAVO (PASADO INMEDIATO, 1930-1981); Labor
Disputes; Laboring Classes; Maciel, David
R.

1506 Garcia, Mario T. Book review of: LOS ANGELES

BARRIO 1850-1890: A SOCIAL HISTORY. PACIFIC
HISTORICAL REVIEW, Vol. 51, no. 1 (February
1982), p. 90-91. English. **DESCR:** Barrios;
Griswold del Castillo, Ricardo; Los Angeles,
CA; *THE LOS ANGELES BARRIO 1850-1890: A
SOCIAL HISTORY.

1507 Garcia, Mario T. Book review of: LOS
MOJADOS: THE WETBACK STORY. JOURNAL OF
ETHNIC STUDIES, Vol. 1, no. 1 (Spring 1973),
p. 66-68. English. **DESCR:** Immigrant Labor;
*LOS MOJADOS: THE WETBACK STORY; Mexico;
Samora, Julian; Southwest United States;
Undocumented Workers; United States.

1508 Garcia, Mario T. Book review of: MEXICANO
RESISTANCE IN THE SOUTHWEST: "THE SACRED
RIGHT OF SELF-PRESERVATION". PACIFIC
HISTORICAL REVIEW, Vol. 51, no. 3 (August
1982), p. 331-332. English. **DESCR:** *MEXICANO
RESISTANCE IN THE SOUTHWEST: "THE SACRED
RIGHT OF SELF-PRESERVATION"; Rosenbaum,
Robert J.

1509 Garcia, Mario T. History, culture, and
society of the borderlands. NEW SCHOLAR,
Vol. 8, no. 1-2 (Spring, Fall, 1982), p.
467-472. English. **DESCR:** Border Studies;
*VIEWS ACROSS THE BORDER: THE UNITED STATES
AND MEXICO.

1510 Garcia, Mario T. On Mexican immigration, the
United States, and Chicano history. JOURNAL
OF ETHNIC STUDIES, Vol. 7, no. 1 (Spring
1979), p. 80-88. English. **DESCR:** *BY THE
SWEAT OF THEIR BROW: MEXICAN IMMIGRANT LABOR
IN THE UNITED STATES, 1900-1940; History;
Immigrant Labor; Immigration; Immigration
Law; Mexico; Reisler, Mark; Research
Methodology; Southwest United States.

1511 Garcia, Wilfred F. Book review of: NUESTRO
ESPANOL: CURSO PARA ESTUDIANTES BILINGUES,
BILINGUAL NATIVE SPANISH SPEAKERS FROM THE
SOUTHWESTERN UNITED STATES. HISPANIA, Vol.
65, no. 2 (May 1982), p. 320-321. English.
DESCR: Garza-Swan, Gloria; Mejias, Hugo A.;
*NUESTRO ESPANOL: CURSO PARA ESTUDIANTES
BILINGUES; Southwest United States; Spanish
Language; Textbooks.

1512 Gates, Paul W. Book review of: ROOTS OF
RESISTANCE: LAND TENURE IN NEW MEXICO,
1680-1980. WESTERN HISTORICAL QUARTERLY,
Vol. 13, no. 1 (January 1982), p. 76-77.
English. **DESCR:** Ortiz, Roxanne Dunbar;
*ROOTS OF RESISTANCE: LAND TENURE IN NEW
MEXICO, 1680-1980.

1513 Gifford, Douglas. Book review of: HISPANIC
FOLK MUSIC OF NEW MEXICO AND THE SOUTHWEST:
A SELF-PORTRAIT OF A PEOPLE. BULLETIN OF
HISPANIC STUDIES, Vol. 59, no. 2 (April
1982), p. 162-163. English. **DESCR:** Folk
Songs; *HISPANIC FOLK MUSIC OF NEW MEXICO
AND THE SOUTHWEST: A SELF-PORTRAIT OF A
PEOPLE; New Mexico; Robb, John Donald.

1514 Gil, Carlos B. Miguel Antonio Otero, first
Chicano governor. JOURNAL OF ETHNIC STUDIES,
Vol. 4, no. 3 (Fall 1976), p. 95-102.
English. **DESCR:** *Elected Officials; *New
Mexico; OTERO: AN AUTOBIOGRAPHICAL TRILOGY;
Otero, Miguel A.; Social History and
Conditions; United States History.

1515 Goldberg, Victor. Ethnic groups in the
United States. REVIEWS IN ANTHROPOLOGY, Vol.
9, no. 4 (Fall 1982), p. 375-382. English.
DESCR: Achor, Shirley; ETHNIC AMERICA, A
HISTORY; MEXICAN AMERICANS IN A DALLAS
BARRIO; Sowell, Thomas; *THE CHICANOS;
Trejo, Arnulfo D.

Book Reviews (cont.)

1516 Goldin, Mark G. Book review of: TEACHING SPANISH TO THE HISPANIC BILINGUAL: ISSUES, AIMS AND METHODS. NABE JOURNAL, Vol. 7, no. 1 (Fall 1982), p. 53-56. English. **DESCR:** Bilingualism; Garcia-Moya, Rodolfo; Language Proficiency; Language Usage; Lozano, Anthony G.; Spanish Language; *TEACHING SPANISH TO THE HISPANIC BILINGUAL: ISSUES, AIMS AND METHODS; Valdez, Guadalupe.

1517 Gonzalez, LaVerne. Book review of: BY LINGUAL WHOLES. REVISTA CHICANO-RIQUENA, Vol. 11, no. 2 (Summer 1983), p. 75-77. English. **DESCR:** *BY LINGUAL WHOLES; Hernandez Cruz, Victor.

1518 Gonzalez, Maria R. Book review of: ACERCA DE LITERATURA (Dialogo con tres autores chicanos). LA PALABRA, Vol. 4, no. 1-2 (Spring, Fall, 1982, 1983), p. 170-171. Spanish. **DESCR:** *ACERCA DE LITERATURA; Literature; Vazquez-Castro, Javier.

1519 Gonzalez, Roberto. Book review of: EXPLORATIONS IN CHICANO PSYCHOLOGY. HISPANIC JOURNAL OF BEHAVIORAL SCIENCES, Vol. 4, no. 4 (December 1982), p. 511-522. English. **DESCR:** Baron, Augustine Jr.; *EXPLORATIONS IN CHICANO PSYCHOLOGY.

1520 Graebner, Norman A. Book review of: ORIGINS OF THE MEXICAN WAR: A DOCUMENTARY SOURCE BOOK. NEW MEXICO HISTORICAL REVIEW, Vol. 58, no. 3 (July 1983), p. 291-292. English. **DESCR:** McAfee, Ward; *ORIGINS OF THE MEXICAN WAR: A DOCUMENTARY SOURCE BOOK; Robinson, J. Cordell.

1521 Griswold del Castillo, Richard. Book review of: DICTIONARY OF MEXICAN-AMERICAN HISTORY. SOUTHWESTERN HISTORICAL QUARTERLY, Vol. 86, no. 4 (April 1983), p. 579-580. English. **DESCR:** *DICTIONARY OF MEXICAN AMERICAN HISTORY; Meier, Matt S.; Rivera, Feliciano.

1522 Griswold del Castillo, Richard. Book review of: IMAGES OF THE MEXICAN-AMERICAN IN FICTION AND FILM. JOURNAL OF THE WEST, Vol. 22, no. 2 (April 1983), p. 94. English. **DESCR:** *IMAGES OF THE MEXICAN AMERICAN IN FICTION AND FILM; Pettit, Arthur G.

1523 Griswold del Castillo, Richard. Book review of: REVOLTOSOS: MEXICO'S REBELS IN THE UNITED STATES 1903-1923. JOURNAL OF SAN DIEGO HISTORY, Vol. 28, no. 2 (Spring 1982), p. 143-144. English. **DESCR:** Raat, W. Dirk; *REVOLTOSOS: MEXICO'S REBELS IN THE UNITED STATES, 1903-1923.

1524 Griswold del Castillo, Richard. Book review of: THE CHICANOS OF EL PASO: AN ASSESSMENT OF PROGRESS. PACIFIC HISTORICAL REVIEW, Vol. 51, no. 3 (August 1982), p. 337-338. English. **DESCR:** El Paso, TX; Martinez, Oscar J.; *THE CHICANOS OF EL PASO: AN ASSESSMENT OF PROGRESS.

1525 Gutierrez, John R. Book review of: TEACHING SPANISH TO THE HISPANIC BILINGUAL: ISSUES, AIMS AND METHODS. MODERN LANGUAGE JOURNAL, Vol. 66, no. 2 (Summer 1982), p. 234. English. **DESCR:** Bilingualism; Garcia-Moya, Rodolfo; Lozano, Anthony G.; Spanish Language; *TEACHING SPANISH TO THE HISPANIC BILINGUAL: ISSUES, AIMS AND METHODS; Valdez, Guadalupe.

1526 Hartman, Harriet. Book review of: MEXICAN WOMEN IN THE UNITED STATES: STRUGGLES PAST AND PRESENT. INTERNATIONAL MIGRATION REVIEW, Vol. 16, no. 1 (Spring 1982), p. 228-229.

English. **DESCR:** Chicanas; Del Castillo, Adelaida R.; *MEXICAN WOMEN IN THE UNITED STATES: STRUGGLES PAST AND PRESENT; Mora, Magdalena; Sexism.

1527 Hartzler, Kaye. Book review of: YUCATAN BEFORE AND AFTER THE CONQUEST. HISPANIC JOURNAL OF BEHAVIORAL SCIENCES, Vol. 4, no. 3 (September 1982), p. 381-383. English. **DESCR:** De Landa, Friar Diego; Gates, William; *YUCATAN BEFORE AND AFTER THE CONQUEST.

1528 Heizer, Robert. Book review of: THE OLMEC WORLD. JOURNAL OF ETHNIC STUDIES, Vol. 15, no. 3 (Fall 1977), p. 124-125. English. **DESCR:** Bernal, Ignacio; Olmecs; *Precolumbian Society; *THE OLMEC WORLD.

1529 Henson, Margaret S. Book review of: THE MEXICAN FRONTIER 1821-1846: THE AMERICAN SOUTHWEST UNDER MEXICO. SOUTHWESTERN HISTORICAL QUARTERLY, Vol. 86, no. 3 (1983), p. 441-443. English. **DESCR:** *THE MEXICAN FRONTIER, 1821-1846: THE AMERICAN SOUTHWEST UNDER MEXICO; Weber, David J.

1530 Herman, Janice. Book review of: THE INTELLIGENCE CONTROVERSY. HISPANIC JOURNAL OF BEHAVIORAL SCIENCES, Vol. 4, no. 3 (September 1982), p. 384-385. English. **DESCR:** Eysenck, H.J.; Kamin, Leon; *THE INTELLIGENCE CONTROVERSY.

1531 Hill, Patricia Liggins. Book review of: THE THIRD WOMAN: MINORITY WRITERS OF THE UNITED STATES. MELUS: MULTI-ETHNIC LITERATURE OF THE UNITED STATES, Vol. 7, no. 3 (Fall 1980), p. 87-89. English. **DESCR:** *Fisher, Dexter; THIRD WOMAN: MINORITY WOMEN WRITERS OF THE UNITED STATES; *Third World Literature (U.S.)

1532 Hoffman, Abraham. Book review of: MEXICANO RESISTANCE IN THE SOUTHWEST: "THE SACRED RIGHT OF SELF-PRESERVATION". JOURNAL OF AMERICAN HISTORY, Vol. 68, no. 4 (March 1982), p. 911. English. **DESCR:** *MEXICANO RESISTANCE IN THE SOUTHWEST: "THE SACRED RIGHT OF SELF-PRESERVATION"; Rosenbaum, Robert J.

1533 Hoffman, Abraham. Book review of: MEXICANO RESISTANCE IN THE SOUTHWEST: "THE SACRED RIGHT OF SELF-PRESERVATION". PACIFIC HISTORICAL REVIEW, Vol. 51, no. 2 (May 1982), p. 230-231. English. **DESCR:** Cardoso, Lawrence A.; *MEXICAN EMIGRATION TO THE UNITED STATES 1897-1931: SOCIO-ECONOMIC PATTERNS; Migration.

1534 Holmberg, Joan J. Book review of: THE CHANGING DEMOGRAPHY OF SPANISH-AMERICANS. INTERNATIONAL MIGRATION REVIEW, Vol. 17, no. 3 (Fall 1983), p. 506-507. English. **DESCR:** Jaffee, A.J.; *THE CHANGING DEMOGRAPHY OF SPANISH-AMERICANS.

1535 Hornbeck, David. Book review of: STUDIES IN SPANISH-AMERICAN POPULATION HISTORY. PROFESSIONAL GEOGRAPHER, Vol. 34, no. 4 (1982), p. 480. English. **DESCR:** Demography; Latin America; Robinson, David J.; *STUDIES IN SPANISH-AMERICAN POPULATION HISTORY.

1536 Huerta, Jorge A. Book review of: CHICANO THEATER: THEMES AND FORMS. NUESTRO, Vol. 6, no. 8 (October 1982), p. 45. English. **DESCR:** Teatro.

Book Reviews (cont.)

1537 HUNGER OF MEMORY: THE EDUCATION OF RICHARD RODRIGUEZ. NUESTRO, Vol. 6, no. 3 (April 1982), p. 52-53. English. **DESCR:** *HUNGER OF MEMORY: THE EDUCATION OF RICHARD RODRIGUEZ; Rodriguez, Richard.

1538 Hunsaker, Alan. Book review of: ALMA ABIERTA: PINTO POETRY, MAYO DE CRC. HISPANIC JOURNAL OF BEHAVIORAL SCIENCES, Vol. 5, no. 1 (March 1983), p. 132-134. English. **DESCR:** *ALMA ABIERTA: PINTO POETRY; Mirande, Alfredo.

1539 Hunsaker, Alan. Book review of: ANGEL DUST: AN ETHNOGRAPHIC STUDY OF PCP USERS; HEROIN USE IN THE BARRIO; DRUG AND ALCOHOL ABUSE: A CLINICAL GUIDE TO DIAGNOSIS AND TREATMENT. HISPANIC JOURNAL OF BEHAVIORAL SCIENCES, Vol. 4, no. 1 (March 1982), p. 118-121. English. **DESCR:** Agar, Michael; *ANGEL DUST: AN ETHNOGRAPHIC STUDY OF PCP USERS; Bescher, George; Bullington, Bruce; *DRUG AND ALCOHOL ABUSE: A CLINICAL GUIDE TO DIAGNOSIS AND TREATMENT; Feldman, Harvey W.; *HEROIN USE IN THE BARRIO; Schuckit, Marc A.

1540 Hunsaker, Alan. Book review of: PSYCHOLOGY AND COMMUNITY CHANGE; SOCIAL AND PSYCHOLOGICAL RESEARCH IN COMMUNITY SETTING; COMMUNITY PSYCHOLOGY: THEORETICAL AND EMPIRICAL APPROACHES. HISPANIC JOURNAL OF BEHAVIORAL SCIENCES, Vol. 5, no. 1 (March 1983), p. 121-124. English. **DESCR:** *COMMUNITY PSYCHOLOGY: THEORETICAL AND EMPIRICAL APPROACHES; Gibbs, Margaret S.; Heller, Kenneth; Kelly, James G.; Lachenmeyer, Juliana Rasic; Monahan, John; Munoz, Ricardo F.; *PSYCHOLOGY AND COMMUNITY CHANGE; Sigal, Janet; Snowden, Lonnie R.; *SOCIAL AND PSYCHOLOGICAL RESEARCH IN COMMUNITY SETTINGS.

1541 Hunsaker, Alan. Book review of: STRESSFUL LIFE EVENTS: THEIR NATURE AND EFFECTS. HISPANIC JOURNAL OF BEHAVIORAL SCIENCES, Vol. 5, no. 1 (March 1983), p. 130-132. English. **DESCR:** Dohrenwend, Barbara Snell; Dohrenwend, Bruce P.; *STRESSFUL LIFE EVENTS: THEIR NATURE AND EFFECTS.

1542 Jamail, Milton H. Book review of: MEXICO IN TRANSITION. SOUTHWEST ECONOMY AND SOCIETY, Vol. 4, no. 2 (Winter 1978, 1979), p. 47-49. English. **DESCR:** History; Mexico; *MEXICO IN TRANSITION; Russell, Philip.

1543 Cruz, Amaury. Book review of: AZTEC. NUESTRO, Vol. 6, no. 7 (September 1982), p. 53-54. English. **DESCR:** *Cortes, Hernan.

1544 John, Elizabeth A.H. Book review of: THE MEXICAN FRONTIER, 1821-1846: THE AMERICAN SOUTHWEST UNDER MEXICO. NEW MEXICO HISTORICAL REVIEW, Vol. 57, no. 3 (July 1982), p. 289-293. English. **DESCR:** Border Region; Southwest United States; *THE MEXICAN FRONTIER, 1821-1846: THE AMERICAN SOUTHWEST UNDER MEXICO; Weber, David J.

1545 Jones, Errol D. Book review of: DICTIONARY OF MEXICAN-AMERICAN HISTORY. WESTERN HISTORICAL QUARTERLY, Vol. 14, no. 3 (1983), p. 339-340. English. **DESCR:** *DICTIONARY OF MEXICAN AMERICAN HISTORY; History; Meier, Matt S.; Reference Works; Rivera, Feliciano.

1546 Jones, Oakah L. Book review of: THE MEXICAN FRONTIER, 1821-1846: THE AMERICAN SOUTHWEST UNDER MEXICO. ARIZONA AND THE WEST, Vol. 25, no. 2 (1983), p. 168-169. English. **DESCR:** History; Mexico; Southwest United States; *THE MEXICAN FRONTIER, 1821-1846: THE AMERICAN SOUTHWEST UNDER MEXICO; Weber, David J.

1547 Kelly, Philip. Book review of: OPERATION WETBACK: THE MASS DEPORTATION OF MEXICAN UNDOCUMENTED WORKERS IN 1954. SOCIAL SCIENCE JOURNAL, Vol. 19, no. 2 (April 1982), p. 133-134. English. **DESCR:** Garcia, Juan Ramon; *OPERATION WETBACK: THE MASS DEPORTATION OF MEXICAN UNDOCUMENTED WORKERS IN 1954; Undocumented Workers.

1548 Kivisto, Peter. Book review of: FARM WORKERS, AGRIBUSINESS, AND THE STATE. INTERNATIONAL MIGRATION REVIEW, Vol. 17, no. 4 (Winter 1983), p. 724-726. English. **DESCR:** Agribusiness; Agricultural Laborers; *FARMWORKERS, AGRIBUSINESS, AND THE STATE; Majka, Linda C.; Majka, Theo J.; United Farmworkers of America (UFW).

1549 Klor de Alva, Jorge. Book review of: PELON DROPS OUT. LA PALABRA, Vol. 4, no. 1-2 (Spring, Fall, 1982, 1983), p. 172-174. Spanish. **DESCR:** De Casas, Celso A.; Literature; *PELON DROPS OUT.

1550 Knight, Alan. Book review of: THE GREAT REBELLION: MEXICO 1905-1924 and DESERT IMMIGRANTS: THE MEXICANS OF EL PASO 1880-1920. HISTORY: THE JOURNAL OF THE HISTORICAL ASSOCIATION [London], Vol. 67, (October 1982), p. 450-451. English. **DESCR:** *DESERT IMMIGRANTS: THE MEXICANS OF EL PASO 1880-1920; Garcia, Mario T.; Ruiz, Ramon Eduardo; *THE GREAT REBELLION: MEXICO 1905-1924.

1551 Laguardia, Gari. The canon and the air-conditioner: modern Puerto Rican poetry. BILINGUAL REVIEW, Vol. 9, no. 2 (May, August, 1982), p. 178-181. English. **DESCR:** *INVENTING A WORD, AN ANTHOLOGY OF TWENTIETH CENTURY PUERTO RICAN POETRY; Marzan, Julio; Poetry; Puerto Rican Literature.

1552 Laska, Vera. Book review of: DICTIONARY OF MEXICAN-AMERICAN HISTORY. INTERNATIONAL SOCIAL SCIENCE, Vol. 57, no. 3 (Summer 1982), p. 184. English. **DESCR:** Dictionaries; *DICTIONARY OF MEXICAN AMERICAN HISTORY; History; Meier, Matt S.; Rivera, Feliciano.

1553 Lattin, Vernon E. Book review of: THE DOCILE PUERTO RICAN. MINORITY VOICES, Vol. 2, no. 1 (Spring 1978), p. 62-63. English. **DESCR:** Marques, Rene; Puerto Ricans; *THE DOCILE PUERTO RICAN.

1554 Lewis, Marvin A. Book review of: THE IDENTIFICATION AND ANALYSIS OF CHICANO LITERATURE. MELUS: MULTI-ETHNIC LITERATURE OF THE UNITED STATES, Vol. 7, no. 1 (Spring 1980), p. 82-85. English. **DESCR:** IDENTIFICATION AND ANALYSIS OF CHICANO LITERATURE; *Jimenez, Francisco; *Literature.

1555 Lippard, Lucy R. Book review of: FRIDA: A BIOGRAPHY OF FRIDA KAHLO. NEW YORK TIMES BOOK REVIEW, Vol. 88, (April 24, 1983), p. 10+. English. **DESCR:** *FRIDA: A BIOGRAPHY OF FRIDA KAHLO; Herrera, Hayden; Kahlo, Frida.

Book Reviews (cont.)

1556 Logan, Kathleen. The urban poor in developing nations. JOURNAL OF URBAN HISTORY, Vol. 9, no. 1 (November 1982), p. 108-116. English. **DESCR:** ACCESS TO POWER: POLITICS AND THE URBAN POOR IN DEVELOPING NATIONS; BORDER BOOM TOWN: CIUDAD JUAREZ SINCE 1848; Collier, David; Cornelius, Wayne A.; Eckstein, Susan; Lloyd, Peter; Martinez, Oscar J.; Nelson, Joan M.; Perlman, Janice E.; POLITICS AND MIGRANT POOR IN MEXICO CITY; SLUMS OF HOPE? SHANTY TOWNS OF THE THIRD WORLD; SQUATTERS AND OLIGARCHS: AUTHORITARIAN RULE AND POLICY CHANGE IN PERU; THE MYTH OF MARGINALITY: URBAN POVERTY AND POLITICS IN RIO DE JANEIRO; THE POVERTY OF REVOLUTION: THE STATE AND THE URBAN POOR IN MEXICO; Urban Economics.

1557 Lomeli, Francisco A. Book review of: MY PENITENTE LAND: REFLECTIONS ON SPANISH NEW MEXICO. NEW SCHOLAR, Vol. 8, no. 1-2 (Spring, Fall, 1982), p. 495-498. English. **DESCR:** Chavez, Fray Angelico; *MY PENITENTE LAND: REFLECTIONS ON SPANISH NEW MEXICO.

1558 Lomeli, Francisco A. Book review of: MY PENITENTE LAND: REFLECTIONS ON SPANISH NEW MEXICO. NEW SCHOLAR, Vol. 8, no. 1-2 (Spring, Fall, 1982), p. 495-498. English. **DESCR:** Chavez, Fray Angelico; *MY PENITENTE LAND: REFLECTIONS ON SPANISH NEW MEXICO.

1559 Mabry, Donald J. Book review of: ACROSS THE BORDER: RURAL DEVELOPMENT IN MEXICO AND RECENT MIGRATION TO THE UNITED STATES. INTERNATIONAL MIGRATION REVIEW, Vol. 17, no. 2 (Summer 1983), p. 351. English. **DESCR:** *ACROSS THE BORDER: RURAL DEVELOPMENT IN MEXICO AND RECENT MIGRATION; Cross, Harry E.; Migration; Migration Patterns; Rural Economics; Sandos, James.

1560 Macias, Reynaldo Flores. Book review of: POLITICS AND LANGUAGE: SPANISH AND ENGLISH IN THE UNITED STATES. NABE JOURNAL, Vol. 7, no. 1 (Fall 1982), p. 61-66. English. **DESCR:** Bilingualism; Bruckner, D.J.R.; Cultural Pluralism; *POLITICS AND LANGUAGE: SPANISH AND ENGLISH IN THE UNITED STATES; Spanish Language.

1561 Maciel, David R. and Bergaila, Christine. Book review of: CHICANOS: THE STORY OF THE MEXICAN AMERICANS. JOURNAL OF ETHNIC STUDIES, Vol. 2, no. 3 (Fall 1974), p. 94-95. English. **DESCR:** *CHICANOS: THE STORY OF MEXICAN AMERICANS; de Garza, Patricia; History.

1562 Maciel, David R. Book review of: THE KENNEDY CORRIDOS: A STUDY OF THE BALLADS OF A MEXICAN AMERICAN HERO. AZTLAN, Vol. 13, no. 1-2 (Spring, Fall, 1982), p. 335-337. English. **DESCR:** Corrido; Dickey, Dan William; Folk Songs; *Kennedy, John Fitzgerald; Music.

1563 Madrid, Arturo. Book review of: HUNGER OF MEMORY: THE EDUCATION OF RICHARD RODRIGUEZ. TEXAS OBSERVOR, Vol. 74, no. 13 (July 9, 1982), p. 14+. English. **DESCR:** *HUNGER OF MEMORY: THE EDUCATION OF RICHARD RODRIGUEZ; Rodriguez, Richard.

1564 Madrid, Arturo and Rodriguez, Richard. The mis-education of rich-heard road-ree-guess. MAIZE, Vol. 5, no. 3-4 (Spring, Summer, 1982), p. 88-92. English. **DESCR:** Assimilation; Education; English Language.

1565 Maiz, Magdalena. Book review of: OCCUPIED AMERICA. PALABRA Y EL HOMBRE, Vol. 1982, no. 42 (April, June, 1982), p. 77-79. Spanish. **DESCR:** Acuna, Rudolfo; *OCCUPIED AMERICA.

1566 Manning, Roberta. Book review of: CHICANO INTERMARRIAGE: A THEORETICAL AND EMPIRICAL STUDY. HISPANIC JOURNAL OF BEHAVIORAL SCIENCES, Vol. 5, no. 3 (September 1983), p. 353-356. English. **DESCR:** *CHICANO INTERMARRIAGE: A THEORETICAL AND EMPIRICAL STUDY; Intermarriage; Murguia, Edward.

1567 Markiewicz, Dana. Book review of: MEXICAN CINEMA: REFLECTIONS OF SOCIETY, 1896-1980. HISPANIC JOURNAL OF BEHAVIORAL SCIENCES, Vol. 5, no. 4 (December 1983), p. 491-494. English. **DESCR:** Films; *MEXICAN CINEMA: REFLECTIONS OF A SOCIETY; Mora, Carl J.

1568 Marquez, Maria Teresa. Book review of: A SELECTED AND ANNOTATED BIBLIOGRAPHY OF CHICANO STUDIES. AZTLAN, Vol. 14, no. 1 (Spring 1983), p. 191-192. English. **DESCR:** *A SELECTED AND ANNOTATED BIBLIOGRAPHY OF CHICANO STUDIES; Bibliography; Reference Works; Tatum, Charles.

1569 Martinez, Douglas R. Book review of: THE SILENCE OF THE LLANO. NUESTRO, Vol. 7, no. 1 (January, February, 1983), p. 55. English. **DESCR:** Anaya, Rudolfo A.; *THE SILENCE OF THE LLANO.

1570 Martinez, Douglas R. Sharing the silence. LATINO, Vol. 54, no. 4 (May, June, 1983), p. 28. English. **DESCR:** Anaya, Rudolfo A.; *THE SILENCE OF THE LLANO.

1571 Martinez, Julio A. Book review of: A BIBLIOGRAPHY OF CRITICISM OF CONTEMPORARY CHICANO LITERATURE. RQ - REFERENCE AND ADULT SERVICES DIVISION, Vol. 22, no. 1 (Fall 1982), p. 90. English. **DESCR:** *A BIBLIOGRAPHY OF CRITICISM OF CONTEMPORARY CHICANO LITERATURE; Bibliography; Eger, Ernestina N.; Literary Criticism; Literature.

1572 Martinez, Julio A. Book review of: A DECADE OF CHICANO LITERATURE (1970-1979)-CRITICAL ESSAYS AND BIBLIOGRAPHY. RQ - REFERENCE AND ADULT SERVICES DIVISION, Vol. 22, no. 1 (Fall 1982), p. 90. English. **DESCR:** *A DECADE OF CHICANO LITERATURE (1970-1979): CRITICAL ESSAYS AND BIBLIOGRAPHY; Bibliography; Gonzalez, Raquel Quiroz; Literary Criticism; Literatura Chicanesca; Literature; Trujillo, Robert.

1573 Martinez, Julio A. Book review of: DICTIONARY OF MEXICAN-AMERICAN HISTORY. RQ - REFERENCE AND ADULT SERVICES DIVISION, Vol. 21, no. 3 (Spring 1982), p. 297-298. English. **DESCR:** Dictionaries; *DICTIONARY OF MEXICAN AMERICAN HISTORY; History; Meier, Matt S.; Rivera, Feliciano.

1574 Martinez, Oscar J. Book review of: DESERT IMMIGRANTS: THE MEXICANS OF EL PASO 1880-1920. HISPANIC AMERICAN HISTORICAL REVIEW, Vol. 62, no. 2 (May 1982), p. 289-291. English. **DESCR:** *DESERT IMMIGRANTS: THE MEXICANS OF EL PASO 1880-1920; El Paso, TX; Garcia, Mario T.; Immigration.

1575 Martinez, Oscar J. Book review of: OPERATION WETBACK: THE MASS DEPORTATION OF MEXICAN UNDOCUMENTED WORKERS IN 1954. NEW MEXICO HISTORICAL REVIEW, Vol. 57, no. 2 (April 1982), p. 201-202. English. **DESCR:** Garcia, Juan Ramon; *OPERATION WETBACK: THE MASS DEPORTATION OF MEXICAN UNDOCUMENTED WORKERS IN 1954; Undocumented Workers.

Book Reviews (cont.)

1576 Martinez, Oscar J. Book review of: REVOLTOSOS: MEXICO'S REBELS IN THE UNITED STATES 1903-1923. ARIZONA AND THE WEST, Vol. 24, no. 1 (Spring 1982), p. 69-70. English. **DESCR:** Mexico; Raat, W. Dirk; *REVOLTOSOS: MEXICO'S REBELS IN THE UNITED STATES, 1903-1923; United States History.

1577 Mata, Alberto G. Book review of: MEXICAN AMERICANS IN A DALLAS BARRIO. AZTLAN, Vol. 14, no. 1 (Spring 1983), p. 196-198. English. **DESCR:** Achor, Shirley; Barrios; Dallas, TX; *MEXICAN AMERICANS IN A DALLAS BARRIO; Urban Communities.

1578 Mathes, W. Michael. Book review of: JOAQUIN MURRIETA AND HIS HORSE GANGS. CALIFORNIA HISTORY, Vol. 61, no. 4 (1983), p. 306-308. English. **DESCR:** California; History; Latta, Frank F.; *Murieta, Joaquin.

1579 Mathes, W. Michael. Book review of: THE MEXICAN-AMERICAN WAR: AN ANNOTATED BIBLIOGRAPHY. CALIFORNIA HISTORY, Vol. 60, no. 4 (Winter 1981, 1982), p. 379-380. English. **DESCR:** *THE MEXICAN-AMERICAN WAR: AN ANNOTATED BIBLIOGRAPHY; Tutorow, Norman E.; United States-Mexico War.

1580 McCracken, Ellen. Book review of: IDENTIFICATION AND ANALYSIS OF CHICANO LITERATURE. NEW SCHOLAR, Vol. 8, no. 1-2 (Spring, Fall, 1982), p. 493-495. English. **DESCR:** *IDENTIFICATION AND ANALYSIS OF CHICANO LITERATURE; Jimenez, Francisco.

1581 McCracken, Ellen. Book review of: SALT OF THE EARTH. JOURNAL OF ETHNIC STUDIES, Vol. 8, no. 1 (Spring 1980), p. 116-120. English. **DESCR:** Chicanas; Films; Hanover, NM; International Union of Mine, Mill and Smelter Workers; *SALT OF THE EARTH; Silverton Rosenfelt, Deborah; Strikes and Lockouts; Women Men Relations; Women's Rights.

1582 McKinney, J.E. Book review of: MOSAICO DE LA VIDA: CHICANO, CUBAN AND PUERTO RICAN PROSE. HISPANIA, Vol. 65, no. 2 (May 1982), p. 321. English. **DESCR:** Jimenez, Francisco; *MOSAICO DE LA VIDA: CHICANO, CUBAN AND PUERTO RICAN PROSE; Prose; Spanish Language; Textbooks.

1583 Meier, Matt S. Book review of: MEXICAN IMMIGRANT WORKERS IN THE UNITED STATES and OPERATION WETBACK: THE MASS DEPORTATION OF MEXICAN UNDOCUMENTED WORKERS IN 1954. PACIFIC HISTORICAL REVIEW, Vol. 52, no. 1 (February 1983), p. 126-128. English. **DESCR:** Garcia, Juan Ramon; *MEXICAN IMMIGRANT WORKERS IN THE U.S.; *Operation Wetback; Rios-Bustamante, Antonio.

1584 Meyer, Michael C. Book review of: THE MEXICAN FRONTIER, 1821-1846: THE AMERICAN SOUTHWEST UNDER MEXICO. WESTERN HISTORICAL QUARTERLY, Vol. 14, no. 3 (1983), p. 337-338. English. **DESCR:** History; Mexico; Southwest United States; *THE MEXICAN FRONTIER, 1821-1846: THE AMERICAN SOUTHWEST UNDER MEXICO; Weber, David J.

1585 Miller, Darlis A. Book review of: THE IMPACT OF INTIMACY: MEXICAN-ANGLO INTERMARRIAGE IN NEW MEXICO, 1821-1846. NEW MEXICO HISTORICAL REVIEW, Vol. 57, no. 4 (October 1982), p. 407-408. English. **DESCR:** Craver, Rebecca McDowell; Intermarriage; *THE IMPACT OF INTIMACY: MEXICAN-ANGLO INTERMARRIAGE IN NEW MEXICO, 1821-1846.

1586 Miller, John C. Book review of: NUEVOS PASOS: CHICANO AND PUERTO RICAN DRAMA. MELUS: MULTI-ETHNIC LITERATURE OF THE UNITED STATES, Vol. 6, no. 3 (Fall 1979), p. 99-100. English. **DESCR:** Huerta, Jorge A.; *Kanellos, Nicolas; NUEVOS PASOS: CHICANO AND PUERTO RICAN DRAMA (thematic issue of REVISTA CHICANO-RIQUENA); *Teatro.

1587 Miller, Michael V. Book review of: CHICANOS AND RURAL POVERTY. JOURNAL OF ETHNIC STUDIES, Vol. 5, no. 3 (Fall 1977), p. 116-117. English. **DESCR:** Agricultural Laborers; Briggs, Vernon M.; *CHICANOS AND RURAL POVERTY; Immigration Law; Social History and Conditions; Southwest United States.

1588 Miller, Robert. Bilingual education in Mexico. EDUCATIONAL LEADERSHIP, Vol. 40, no. 8 (May 1983), p. 59. English. **DESCR:** Mexico.

1589 Monjaras-Ruiz, Jesus. Book review of: DOLLARS OVER DOMINION: THE TRIUMPH OF LIBERALISM IN MEXICAN-UNITED STATES RELATIONS, 1861-1867. HISTORIA MEXICANA, Vol. 31, no. 4 (April, June, 1982), p. 642-646. Spanish. **DESCR:** *DOLLARS OVER DOMINION: THE TRIUMPH OF LIBERALISM IN MEXICAN-UNITED STATES RELATIONS, 1861-1867; Schoonover, Thomas David.

1590 Moore, Richard J. Book review of: "TEMPORARY" ALIEN WORKERS IN THE UNITED STATES: DESIGNING POLICY FROM FACT AND OPINION. INTERNATIONAL MIGRATION REVIEW, Vol. 16, no. 4 (Winter 1982), p. 909-910. English. **DESCR:** Braceros; Ross, Stanley R.; *"TEMPORARY" ALIEN WORKERS IN THE UNITED STATES: DESIGNING POLICY FROM FACT AND OPINION; Undocumented Workers; Weintraub, Sidney.

1591 Moore, Richard J. Book review of: "TEMPORARY" ALIEN WORKERS IN THE UNITED STATES: DESIGNING POLICY FROM FACT AND OPINION. INTERNATIONAL MIGRATION REVIEW, Vol. 16, no. 4 (Winter 1982), p. 909-910. English. **DESCR:** Immigration Law; Literature Reviews; Ross, Stanley R.; *"TEMPORARY" ALIEN WORKERS IN THE UNITED STATES: DESIGNING POLICY FROM FACT AND OPINION; Undocumented Workers; Weintraub, Sidney.

1592 Mosier, Pat. Book review of: PRIMEROS ENCUENTROS/FIRST ENCOUNTERS. REVISTA CHICANO-RIQUENA, Vol. 10, no. 4 (Fall 1982), p. 69-70. English. **DESCR:** *PRIMEROS ENCUENTROS/FIRST ENCOUNTERS; Ulibarri, Sabine R.

1593 Mullen, E.J. Book review of: HEREJES Y MITIFICADORES: MUESTRA DE POESIA PUERTORRIQUENA EN LOS ESTADOS UNIDOS. REVISTA CHICANO-RIQUENA, Vol. 10, no. 3 (Summer 1982), p. 68-70. English. **DESCR:** Barradas, Efrain; *HEREJES Y MITIFICADORES: MUESTRA DE POESIA PUERTORRIQUENA EN LOS ESTADOS UNIDOS; Marin, Carmen Lilianne; Rodriguez, Rafael.

1594 Murphy, Lawrence R. Book review of: ROOTS OF RESISTANCE: LAND TENURE IN NEW MEXICO, 1680-1980. NEW MEXICO HISTORICAL REVIEW, Vol. 57, no. 1 (January 1982), p. 89-90. English. **DESCR:** New Mexico; Ortiz, Roxanne Dunbar; *ROOTS OF RESISTANCE: LAND TENURE IN NEW MEXICO, 1680-1980.

Book Reviews (cont.)

1595 Nalven, Joseph. Resolving the undocumented worker problem. NEW SCHOLAR, Vol. 8, no. 1-2 (Spring, Fall, 1982), p. 473-481. English. **DESCR:** *MEXICAN WORKERS IN THE UNITED STATES; *MIGRANT WORKERS IN WESTERN EUROPE AND THE UNITED STATES; Undocumented Workers.

1596 Nasatir, A. P. Book review of: THE MEXICAN-AMERICAN WAR: AN ANNOTATED BIBLIOGRAPHY. JOURNAL OF SAN DIEGO HISTORY, Vol. 28, no. 3 (Summer 1982) p. 210-211. English. **DESCR:** Mexican American War; *THE MEXICAN-AMERICAN WAR: AN ANNOTATED BIBLIOGRAPHY; Tutorow, Norman E.; United States-Mexico Relations.

1597 Nelson, Ann. Book review of: THE SELF-CONCEPT (Rev. ed.). Volume 2: THEORY AND RESEARCH ON SELECTED TOPICS. HISPANIC JOURNAL OF BEHAVIORAL SCIENCES, Vol. 4, no. 3 (September 1982), p. 396-397. English. **DESCR:** *THE SELF-CONCEPT (REV. ED) VOLUME 2: THEORY AND RESEARCH ON SELECTED TOPICS; Wylie, Ruth C.

1598 North, David S. Book review of: ILLEGAL ALIENS IN THE WESTERN HEMISPHERE: POLITICAL AND ECONOMIC FACTORS. INTERNATIONAL MIGRATION REVIEW, Vol. 16, no. 3 (Fall 1982), p. 682-683. English. **DESCR:** *ILLEGAL ALIENS IN THE WESTERN HEMISPHERE: POLITICAL AND ECONOMIC FACTORS; Johnson, Kenneth F.; Undocumented Workers; Williams, Miles W.

1599 Olivas, Michael A. Painful to write, painful to read. CHANGE, Vol. 14, no. 7 (October 1982), p. 37-42. English. **DESCR:** Biography; *HUNGER OF MEMORY: THE EDUCATION OF RICHARD RODRIGUEZ; Rodriguez, Richard.

1600 Olson, James S. Book review of: HUNGER OF MEMORY: THE EDUCATION OF RICHARD RODRIGUEZ. JOURNAL OF THE WEST, Vol. 22, no. 1 (1983), p. 80-81. English. **DESCR:** Bilingual Bicultural Education; *HUNGER OF MEMORY: THE EDUCATION OF RICHARD RODRIGUEZ; Identity; Rodriguez, Richard.

1601 Olson, James S. Book review of: OPERATION WETBACK: THE MASS DEPORTATION OF MEXICAN UNDOCUMENTED WORKERS IN 1954. JOURNAL OF THE WEST, Vol. 22, no. 1 (1983), p. 80-81. English. **DESCR:** Agricultural Laborers; Braceros; Garcia, Juan Ramon; *OPERATION WETBACK: THE MASS DEPORTATION OF MEXICAN UNDOCUMENTED WORKERS IN 1954; Undocumented Workers.

1602 Olszewski, Lawrence. Book review of: CHICANO LITERATURE: A CRITICAL HISTORY. LIBRARY JOURNAL, Vol. 108, no. 2 (January 15, 1983), p. 132. English. **DESCR:** *CHICANO LITERATURE: A CRITICAL HISTORY; History; Poetry; *Tatum, Charles.

1603 Orlandi, Lisanio R. Book review of: WORKBOOK ON PROGRAM EVALUATION. BILINGUAL JOURNAL, Vol. 7, no. 2 (Winter 1983), p. 35-36. English. **DESCR:** Babcock, R.; Bilingual Bicultural Education; Evaluation (Educational); Plakos, J.; Plakos, M.; *WORKBOOK ON PROGRAM EVALUATION.

1604 Over a million barrio. LATINO, Vol. 54, no. 4 (May, June, 1983), p. 28. English. **DESCR:** *EAST LOS ANGELES: HISTORY OF A BARRIO; Romo, Ricardo.

1605 Padilla, Amado M. Book review of: ETHNIC CHANGE. HISPANIC JOURNAL OF BEHAVIORAL SCIENCES, Vol. 4, no. 3 (September 1982), p. 393-394. English. **DESCR:** *ETHNIC CHANGE;

Keyes, Charles F.

1606 Palacios, Maria. Book review of: LA CHICANA: THE MEXICAN AMERICAN WOMAN. HISPANIC JOURNAL OF BEHAVIORAL SCIENCES, Vol. 4, no. 2 (June 1982), p. 272-275. English. **DESCR:** Enriquez, Evangelina; *LA CHICANA: THE MEXICAN AMERICAN WOMAN; Mirande, Alfredo.

1607 Paredes, Raymund A. Book review of: THE ELEMENTS OF SAN JOAQUIN. MINORITY VOICES, Vol. 1, no. 2 (Fall 1977), p. 106-108. English. **DESCR:** Poetry; Soto, Gary; *THE ELEMENTS OF SAN JOAQUIN.

1608 Paredes, Raymund A. Book review of: THE TALE OF SUNLIGHT. MINORITY VOICES, Vol. 2, no. 2 (Fall 1978), p. 67-68. English. **DESCR:** Poetry; Soto, Gary; *TALE OF SUNLIGHT.

1609 Pena, Manuel H. Book review of: FOLK MUSIC OF NEW MEXICO AND THE SOUTHWEST: A SELF-PORTRAIT OF A PEOPLE. AMERICAN MUSIC, Vol. 1, no. 2 (Summer 1983), p. 102-105. English. **DESCR:** *HISPANIC FOLK MUSIC OF NEW MEXICO AND THE SOUTHWEST: A SELF-PORTRAIT OF A PEOPLE; Music; Robb, John Donald.

1610 Perry, Charles E. Book review of: DEVELOPING LIBRARY AND INFORMATION SERVICES FOR AMERICANS OF HISPANIC ORIGIN. JOURNAL OF ACADEMIC LIBRARIANSHIP, Vol. 8, no. 1 (March 1982), p. 38. English. **DESCR:** Academic Libraries; *DEVELOPING LIBRARY AND INFORMATION SERVICES FOR AMERICANS OF HISPANIC ORIGIN; Haro, Robert P.; Library Services.

1611 Portales, Marco A. Anglo villains and Chicano writers. JOURNAL OF ETHNIC STUDIES, Vol. 9, no. 3 (Fall 1981), p. 78-82. English. **DESCR:** *HAY PLESHA LICHANS TU DI FLAC; Literature; Sanchez, Saul; Stereotypes.

1612 Porter, Horace A. Book review of: HUNGER OF MEMORY: THE EDUCATION OF RICHARD RODRIGUEZ. AMERICAN SCHOLAR, Vol. 52, no. 2 (Spring 1983), p. 278-285. English. **DESCR:** *HUNGER OF MEMORY: THE EDUCATION OF RICHARD RODRIGUEZ; Rodriguez, Richard.

1613 Powell, T. G. Book review of: DISORDER AND PROGRESS: BANDITS, POLICE, AND MEXICAN DEVELOPMENT. AMERICAS, Vol. 38, no. 4 (1982), p. 540-541. English. **DESCR:** *DISORDER AND PROGRESS: BANDITS, POLICE AND MEXICAN DEVELOPMENT; Vanderwood, Paul J.

1614 Prichard, Sue. Book review of: HISTORY AS NEUROSIS: PATERNALISM AND MACHISMO IN SPANISH AMERICA. HISPANIC JOURNAL OF BEHAVIORAL SCIENCES, Vol. 5, no. 3 (September 1983), p. 356-360. English. **DESCR:** Goldwert, Marvin; *HISTORY AS NEUROSIS: PATERNALISM AND MACHISMO IN SPANISH AMERICA; Machismo.

1615 Quammen, David. Book review of: FAMOUS ALL OVER TOWN. NEW YORK TIMES BOOK REVIEW, Vol. 88, (April 24, 1983), p. 12+. English. **DESCR:** *FAMOUS ALL OVER TOWN; James, Dan.

1616 Quirarte, Jacinto. Book review of: OLMEC: AN EARLY ART STYLE OF PRECOLUMBIAN MEXICO. JOURNAL OF ETHNIC STUDIES, Vol. 1, no. 3 (Fall 1973), p. 92-95. English. **DESCR:** La Venta, Mexico; *OLMEC: AN EARLY ART STYLE OF PRECOLUMBIAN MEXICO; Precolumbian Art; Precolumbian Society; San Lorenzo, Mexico; Tres Zapotes, Mexico; Wicke, Charles R.

Book Reviews (cont.)

1617 "Racist and demeaning". NUESTRO, Vol. 7, no. 2 (March 1983), p. 7. English. **DESCR:** Agricultural Laborers; Granada, Pilar; Hagopian, Tom; Racism; *SPANISH FOR THE CALIFORNIA FARMERS.

1618 Ramirez, Arthur. Book review of: OLD FACES AND NEW WINE. REVISTA CHICANO-RIQUENA, Vol. 10, no. 4 (Fall 1982), p. 65-67. English. **DESCR:** CARAS VIEJAS Y VINO NUEVO; Morales, Alejandro; *OLD FACES AND NEW WINE.

1619 Ramirez, Nora E. Book review of: OPERATION WETBACK: THE MASS DEPORTATION OF MEXICAN UNDOCUMENTED WORKERS IN 1954. WESTERN HISTORICAL QUARTERLY, Vol. 13, no. 2 (April 1982), p. 198. English. **DESCR:** Garcia, Juan Ramon; *OPERATION WETBACK: THE MASS DEPORTATION OF MEXICAN UNDOCUMENTED WORKERS IN 1954.

1620 Rangel-Guerrero, Daniel. Book review of: CHICANO AUTHORS: INQUIRY BY INTERVIEW. JOURNAL OF ETHNIC STUDIES, Vol. 10, no. 2 (Summer 1982), p. 117-119. English. **DESCR:** Bruce Novoa, Juan; *CHICANO AUTHORS: INQUIRY BY INTERVIEW; Comparative Literature; Literary Criticism; Literary History; Literary Influence; Literature.

1621 Reading to whet your appetite [book reviews]. CAMINOS, Vol. 4, no. 6 (June 1983), p. 19,66. English. **DESCR:** Barraza Sanchez, Irene; *COMIDA SABROSA; Recipes; Sanchez Yund, Gloria.

1622 Reimers, David M. Book review of: TODAY'S IMMIGRANTS, THEIR STORIES. INTERNATIONAL MIGRATION REVIEW, Vol. 16, no. 4 (Winter 1982), p. 900. English. **DESCR:** Caroli, Betty; Immigrants; Kessner, Thomas; Oral History; *TODAY'S IMMIGRANTS, THEIR STORIES.

1623 Reisler, Mark. Book review of: CHICANOS IN A CHANGING SOCIETY: FROM MEXICAN PUEBLOS TO AMERICAN BARRIOS IN SANTA BARBARA AND SOUTHERN CALIFORNIA, 1848-1930. NEW MEXICO HISTORICAL REVIEW, Vol. 57, no. 2 (April 1982), p. 200-201. English. **DESCR:** Camarillo, Alberto; *CHICANOS IN A CHANGING SOCIETY; Social History and Conditions.

1624 Reisler, Mark. Book review of: DESERT IMMIGRANTS: THE MEXICANS OF EL PASO 1880-1920. AMERICAN HISTORICAL REVIEW, Vol. 87, no. 1 (February 1982), p. 271-272. English. **DESCR:** *DESERT IMMIGRANTS: THE MEXICANS OF EL PASO 1880-1920; El Paso, TX; Garcia, Mario T.; History; Immigration.

1625 Renzi, Mario. A review of the ethnic groups in American life series. MID-AMERICAN REVIEW OF SOCIOLOGY, Vol. 7, no. 1 (Spring 1982), p. 109-123. English. **DESCR:** *MEXICAN AMERICANS, 2nd. ed.

1626 Research/development: books. HISPANIC BUSINESS, Vol. 4, no. 2 (February 1982), p. 28. English. **DESCR:** Business; Business Enterprises; *FINANCING YOUR BUSINESS; *Loffel, Egon W.; *National Hispanic Center for Advanced Studies and Policy Analysis (NHCAS); Public Policy; *THE STATE OF HISPANIC AMERICA.

1627 Research/development: books. HISPANIC BUSINESS, Vol. 4, no. 1 (January 1982), p. 27. English. **DESCR:** *Discrimination in Employment; *Fernandez, John P.; Racism; *RACISM AND SEXISM IN CORPORATE LIFE; Sexism.

1628 Research/development: books. HISPANIC BUSINESS, Vol. 4, no. 4 (April 1982), p. 28. English. **DESCR:** Engineering; Financial Aid; FINANCIAL AID FOR MINORITIES IN ENGINEERING; Kennedy, David W.; PERFECTLY LEGAL - 275 FOOLPROOF METHODS FOR PAYING LESS TAXES; Steiner, Barry R.; Swann, Ruth N.; Taxation.

1629 Research/development: books. HISPANIC BUSINESS, Vol. 4, no. 7 (July 1982), p. 27. English. **DESCR:** De Leon, Arnoldo; Finance; History; Spiro, Herbert T.; Texas; THE TEJANO COMMUNITY, 1836-1900.

1630 Research/development: books. HISPANIC BUSINESS, Vol. 4, no. 11 (November 1982), p. 28. English. **DESCR:** Border Industries; Border Region; *ESTUDIOS FRONTERIZOS: PONENCIAS Y COMENTARIOS; Jamail, Milton H.; *THE UNITED STATES-MEXICO BORDER: A GUIDE TO INSTITUTIONS, ORGANIZATIONS AND SCHOLARS; United States-Mexico Relations.

1631 Research/development: books. HISPANIC BUSINESS, Vol. 4, no. 12 (December 1982), p. 36. English. **DESCR:** Consumers; Guernica, A.; Kasperuk, I.; Marketing; *REACHING THE HISPANIC MARKET EFFECTIVELY.

1632 Research/development: books. HISPANIC BUSINESS, Vol. 5, no. 4 (April 1983), p. 28. English. **DESCR:** Biographical Notes; *"DO IT MY WAY OR YOU'RE FIRED!": EMPLOYEE RIGHTS AND THE CHANGING ROLE OF MANAGEMENT PREROGATIVES; Ewing, David W.; Garcia, Carlos; Garcia, Edward; Industrial Relations; Science; *SCIENCE OF THE SPANISH SPEAKING PEOPLE.

1633 Riley, Michael N. Book review of: HUNGER OF MEMORY: THE EDUCATION OF RICHARD RODRIGUEZ. NATIONAL ASSOCIATION OF SECONDARY SCHOOL PRINCIPALS: BULLETIN, Vol. 66, no. 45 (December 1982), p. 112-113. English. **DESCR:** HUNGER OF MEMORY: THE EDUCATION OF RICHARD RODRIGUEZ; Rodriguez, Richard.

1634 Rivera, Julius. Book review of: VARIETIES OF AMERICA. NEW SCHOLAR, Vol. 8, no. 1-2 (Spring, Fall, 1982), p. 523-527. English. **DESCR:** Ethnology; *HISPANIC AMERICA AND ITS CIVILIZATIONS, SPANISH AMERICANS, AND ANGLO-AMERICANS.

1635 Rivera, Mario A. Book review of: CUBAN AMERICANS: MASTERS OF SURVIVAL. MIGRATION TODAY, Vol. 11, no. 4-5 (1983), p. 53. English. **DESCR:** *CUBAN AMERICANS: MASTERS OF SURVIVAL; Cubanos; *Llanes, Jose.

1636 Rivero, Eliana S. Book review of: HEREJES Y MITIFICADORES: MUESTRA DE POESIA PUERTORRIQUENA EN LOS ESTADOS UNIDOS. THIRD WOMAN, Vol. 1, no. 2 (1982), p. 91-93. Spanish. **DESCR:** Barradas, Efrain; *HEREJES Y MITIFICADORES: MUESTRA DE POESIA PUERTORRIQUENA EN LOS ESTADOS UNIDOS; Puerto Rican Literature; Rodriguez, Rafael.

1637 Robinson, Barbara J. Book review of: THE MEXICAN-AMERICAN WAR: AN ANNOTATED BIBLIOGRAPHY. REVISTA INTERAMERICANA DE BIBLIOGRAFIA, Vol. 32, no. 2 (1982), p. 222-223. English. **DESCR:** Bibliography; *THE MEXICAN-AMERICAN WAR: AN ANNOTATED BIBLIOGRAPHY; Tutorow, Norman E.; War.

1638 Rochester, R. C. Book review of: IMPACT OF RACISM ON WHITE AMERICANS. HISPANIC JOURNAL OF BEHAVIORAL SCIENCES, Vol. 5, no. 1 (March 1983), p. 125-129. English. **DESCR:** Bowser, Benjamin P.; Hunt, Raymond G.; *IMPACT OF RACISM ON WHITE AMERICANS.

Book Reviews (cont.)

1639 Rodriguez, Roberto. Book review of: BARRIO WARRIORS HOMEBOYS OF PEACE. CORAZON DE AZTLAN, Vol. 1, no. 3 (August, September, 1982), p. 43. English. **DESCR:** *BARRIO WARRIORS: HOMEBOYS OF PEACE; Frias, Gustavo.

1640 Romo, Ricardo. Book review of: MEXICAN EMIGRATION TO THE UNITED STATES, 1897-1931: SOCIO-ECONOMIC PATTERNS. SOUTHWESTERN HISTORICAL QUARTERLY, Vol. 86, no. 4 (April 1983), p. 576-577. English. **DESCR:** Cardoso, Lawrence A.; *MEXICAN EMIGRATION TO THE UNITED STATES 1897-1931: SOCIO-ECONOMIC PATTERNS.

1641 Rosales, Francisco Arturo. Book review of: DESERT IMMIGRANTS: THE MEXICANS OF EL PASO 1880-1920. ARIZONA AND THE WEST, Vol. 24, no. 1 (Spring 1982), p. 79-80. English. **DESCR:** *DESERT IMMIGRANTS: THE MEXICANS OF EL PASO 1880-1920; Garcia, Mario T.; Immigrants; Texas.

1642 Ruiz, Ramon Eduardo. Book review of: DISORDER AND PROGRESS: BANDITS, POLICE, AND MEXICAN DEVELOPMENT. ARIZONA AND THE WEST, Vol. 24, no. 1 (Spring 1982), p. 75-76. English. **DESCR:** Bandidos; Diaz, Porfirio; *DISORDER AND PROGRESS: BANDITS, POLICE AND MEXICAN DEVELOPMENT; Vanderwood, Paul J.

1643 Ruiz, Rene A. [Article review of: "The Aztecs"; "Tenochtitlan's glory"; "The Great Temple"]. HISPANIC JOURNAL OF BEHAVIORAL SCIENCES, Vol. 4, no. 3 (September 1982), p. 394-395. English. **DESCR:** NATIONAL GEOGRAPHIC [magazine]; *"Tenochtitlan's glory"; *"The Aztecs"; *"The Great Temple".

1644 Ruiz, Rene A. and LeVine, Elaine S. Book review of: PSYCHOLOGY OF THE MEXICAN CULTURE AND PERSONALITY. JOURNAL OF ETHNIC STUDIES, Vol. 4, no. 2 (Summer 1976), p. 104-107. English. **DESCR:** *Cultural Characteristics; Culture; *Diaz-Guerrero, Rogelio; Personality; Psychology; PSYCHOLOGY OF THE MEXICAN CULTURE AND PERSONALITY.

1645 Ruskin, Ellen Maria. Book review of: THE BILINGUAL BRAIN: NEURO-PSYCHOLOGICAL AND NEUROLINGUISTIC ASPECTS OF BILINGUALISM. HISPANIC JOURNAL OF BEHAVIORAL SCIENCES, Vol. 5, no. 4 (December 1983), p. 487-491. English. **DESCR:** Albert, Martin L.; Bilingualism; Obler, Loraine K.; *THE BILINGUAL BRAIN.

1646 Sabat-Rivers, Georgina. Book review of: A WOMAN OF GENIUS: THE INTELLECTUAL AUTOBIOGRAPHY OF SOR JUANA INES DE LA CRUZ. NUESTRO, Vol. 7, no. 6 (August 1983), p. 62-64. English. **DESCR:** *A WOMAN OF GENIUS: THE INTELLECTUAL AUTOBIOGRAPHY OF SOR JUANA INES DE LA CRUZ; Autobiography; Juana Ines de la Cruz, Sor; Peden, Margaret Sayers.

1647 Sagarin, Edward. Book review of: LIFE WITH TWO LANGUAGES: AN INTRODUCTION TO BILINGUALISM. INTERNATIONAL MIGRATION REVIEW, Vol. 17, no. 3 (Fall 1983), p. 505-506. English. **DESCR:** Grosjean, Francois; *LIFE WITH TWO LANGUAGES: AN INTRODUCTION TO BILINGUALISM.

1648 Saldivar, Jose David. Book review of: CHICANO POETRY: A RESPONSE TO CHAOS. MELUS: MULTI-ETHNIC LITERATURE OF THE UNITED STATES, Vol. 10, no. 2 (Summer 1983), p. 83-85. English. **DESCR:** Bruce Novoa, Juan; *CHICANO POETRY: A RESPONSE TO CHAOS; Poetry.

1649 Saldivar, Jose David. Book review of: WHISPERING TO FOOL THE WIND. REVISTA CHICANO-RIQUENA, Vol. 11, no. 2 (Summer 1983), p. 72-74. English. **DESCR:** Rios, Alberto; *WHISPERING TO FOOL THE WIND.

1650 Salgado de Snyder, Nelly. Book review of: LA CHICANA: THE MEXICAN AMERICAN WOMAN. HISPANIC JOURNAL OF BEHAVIORAL SCIENCES, Vol. 4, no. 2 (June 1982), p. 268-272. English. **DESCR:** Enriquez, Evangelina; *LA CHICANA: THE MEXICAN AMERICAN WOMAN; Mirande, Alfredo.

1651 Salmon, Roberto Mario. Book review of: SPANISH AND MEXICAN LAND GRANTS IN NEW MEXICO AND COLORADO. JOURNAL OF ETHNIC STUDIES, Vol. 9, no. 3 (Fall 1981), p. 120-121. English. **DESCR:** Colorado; *Land Grants; New Mexico; *SPANISH AND MEXICAN LAND GRANTS IN NEW MEXICO AND COLORADO; Van Ness, Christine M.; Van Ness, John R.

1652 Saragoza, Alex M. The florescence of Chicano historical scholarship. NEW SCHOLAR, Vol. 8, no. 1-2 (Spring, Fall, 1982), p. 483-487. English. **DESCR:** Camarillo, Alberto; *CHICANOS IN A CHANGING SOCIETY; History.

1653 Schmidt, Dorothy. Book review of: MEXICANO RESISTANCE IN THE SOUTHWEST: "THE SACRED RIGHT OF SELF-PRESERVATION". WESTERN AMERICAN LITERATURE, Vol. 17, no. 1 (Spring 1982), p. 75-76. English. **DESCR:** Bandidos; Insurrections; *MEXICANO RESISTANCE IN THE SOUTHWEST: "THE SACRED RIGHT OF SELF-PRESERVATION"; Rosenbaum, Robert J.

1654 Schmidt, Dorothy. Book review of: ON THE BORDER: PORTRAITS OF AMERICA'S SOUTHWESTERN FRONTIER. WESTERN AMERICAN LITERATURE, Vol. 17, no. 1 (Spring 1982), p. 74. English. **DESCR:** Miller, Tom; *ON THE BORDER: PORTRAITS OF AMERICA'S SOUTHWESTERN FRONTIER; Photography.

1655 Schmitt, Karl M. Book review of: HISPANIC FOLK MUSIC OF NEW MEXICO AND THE SOUTHWEST: A SELF-PORTRAIT OF A PEOPLE. HISPANIC AMERICAN HISTORICAL REVIEW, Vol. 63, no. 1 (1983), p. 209-210. English. **DESCR:** Mabry, Donald; *NEIGHBORS, MEXICO AND THE UNITED STATES: WETBACKS AND OIL; Shafer, Robert Jones; United States-Mexico Relations.

1656 Scott, Patricia. Book review of: FRIDA: A BIOGRAPHY OF FRIDA KAHLO. LIBRARY JOURNAL, Vol. 108, no. 2 (January 15, 1983), p. 125. English. **DESCR:** Artists; Biography; *FRIDA: A BIOGRAPHY OF FRIDA KAHLO; Herrera, Hayden.

1657 Shepperson, Wilbur S. Book review of: THE MEXICANS IN OKLAHOMA. NEW MEXICO HISTORICAL REVIEW, Vol. 57, no. 3 (July 1982), p. 304-305. English. **DESCR:** Immigration; Oklahoma; Smith, Michael M.; *THE MEXICANS IN OKLAHOMA.

1658 Shirley, Paula. Book review of: MEMORIES OF THE ALHAMBRA. MELUS: MULTI-ETHNIC LITERATURE OF THE UNITED STATES, Vol. 6, no. 2 (Summer 1979), p. 100-103. English. **DESCR:** Candelaria, Nash; Literature; *MEMORIES OF THE ALHAMBRA.

1659 Sierra, Christine Marie. Book review of: ASSIMILATION, COLONIALISM, AND THE MEXICAN AMERICAN PEOPLE. NEW SCHOLAR, Vol. 8, no. 1-2 (Spring, Fall, 1982), p. 490-492. English. **DESCR:** *ASSIMILATION, COLONIALISM AND THE MEXICAN AMERICAN PEOPLE; Murguia, Edward.

Book Reviews (cont.)

1660 Silber, Joan. Book review of: FRIDA: A BIOGRAPHY OF FRIDA KAHLO. MS. MAGAZINE, Vol. 11, no. 12 (June 1983), p. 40. English. **DESCR:** *FRIDA: A BIOGRAPHY OF FRIDA KAHLO; Herrera, Hayden.

1661 Smith, Bruce M. Book review of: HUNGER OF MEMORY: THE EDUCATION OF RICHARD RODRIGUEZ. PHI DELTA KAPPAN, Vol. 64, no. 4 (December 1982), p. 289-290. English. **DESCR:** *HUNGER OF MEMORY: THE EDUCATION OF RICHARD RODRIGUEZ; Rodriguez, Richard.

1662 Smith, Sherman W. Book review of: FAMOUS ALL OVER TOWN. WEST COAST REVIEW OF BOOKS, Vol. 9, no. 2 (1983), p. 40. English. **DESCR:** *FAMOUS ALL OVER TOWN; James, Dan.

1663 Soens. Adolph L. Book review of: CHICANOS: ANTOLOGIA HISTORICA Y LITERARIA. MINORITY VOICES, Vol. 5, no. 1-2 (Spring, Fall, 1981), p. 69-71. English. **DESCR:** *CHICANOS: ANTOLOGIA HISTORICA Y LITERARIA; Literature; Villanueva, Tino.

1664 Somoza, Oscar U. Book review of: CHICANO AUTHORS: INQUIRY BY INTERVIEW. HISPAMERICA: REVISTA DE LITERATURA, Vol. 11, no. 31 (1982), p. 101-102. Spanish. **DESCR:** Bruce Novoa, Juan; *CHICANO AUTHORS: INQUIRY BY INTERVIEW.

1665 Somoza, Oscar U. Book review of: EXPLORACIONES CHICANO-RIQUENAS. HISPANIA, Vol. 65, no. 4 (December 1982), p. 668-669. Spanish. **DESCR:** Burgos-Sasscer. Ruth; *EXPLORACIONES CHICANO-RIQUENAS; Textbooks; Williams, Shirley.

1666 Stephens, Doris T. Book review of: IMAGES OF THE MEXICAN-AMERICAN IN FICTION AND FILM. JOURNAL OF AMERICAN CULTURE, Vol. 5, no. 4 (Winter 1982), p. 112-113. English. **DESCR:** *IMAGES OF THE MEXICAN AMERICAN IN FICTION AND FILM; Pettit, Arthur G.

1667 Stoller, Marianne L. Book review of: LA CHICANA: THE MEXICAN AMERICAN WOMAN. SOCIAL SCIENCE JOURNAL, Vol. 19, no. 2 (April 1982), p. 134-136. English. **DESCR:** Chicanas; Enriquez, Evangelina; *LA CHICANA: THE MEXICAN AMERICAN WOMAN; Mirande, Alfredo.

1668 Storr, Robert. Book review of: FRIDA: A BIOGRAPHY OF FRIDA KAHLO. ART IN AMERICA, Vol. 71, (April 1983), p. 19. English. **DESCR:** Artists; *FRIDA: A BIOGRAPHY OF FRIDA KAHLO; Herrera, Hayden; Kahlo, Frida.

1669 Sunseri, Alvin R. Book review of: DESERT IMMIGRANTS: THE MEXICANS OF EL PASO 1880-1920. JOURNAL OF THE WEST, Vol. 21, no. 2 (April 1982), p. 111. English. **DESCR:** *DESERT IMMIGRANTS: THE MEXICANS OF EL PASO 1880-1920; Garcia, Mario T.; Immigration.

1670 Swink, Sue. Book review of: LA CHICANA: THE MEXICAN AMERICAN WOMAN. HISPANIC JOURNAL OF BEHAVIORAL SCIENCES, Vol. 4, no. 2 (June 1982), p. 275-277. English. **DESCR:** Enriquez, Evangelina; *LA CHICANA: THE MEXICAN AMERICAN WOMAN; Mirande, Alfredo.

1671 Tabet, Nita. Book review of: RX: DISCOVERY AND NURTURANCE OF GIFTEDNESS IN THE CULTURALLY DIFFERENT. HISPANIC JOURNAL OF BEHAVIORAL SCIENCES, Vol. 4, no. 4 (December 1982), p. 526-527. English. **DESCR:** *RX: DISCOVERY AND NURTURANCE OF GIFTEDNESS IN THE CULTURALLY DIFFERENT; Torrance, E. Paul.

1672 Tammaro, Thom. Book review of: CHICANO POETRY: A RESPONSE TO CHAOS. LIBRARY JOURNAL, Vol. 107, no. 16 (September 15, 1982), p. 1755-1756. English. **DESCR:** Bruce Novoa, Juan; *CHICANO POETRY: A RESPONSE TO CHAOS.

1673 Tatum, Charles. Book review of: CHICANO AUTHORS: INQUIRY BY INTERVIEW. HISPANIA, Vol. 65, no. 4 (December 1982), p. 668. English. **DESCR:** Authors; Bruce Novoa, Juan; *CHICANO AUTHORS: INQUIRY BY INTERVIEW.

1674 Taylor, William B. Book review of: LABOR AND LABORERS THROUGH MEXICAN HISTORY. NEW MEXICO HISTORICAL REVIEW, Vol. 57, no. 1 (January 1982), p. 91-92. English. **DESCR:** *EL TRABAJO Y LOS TRABAJADORES EN LA HISTORIA DE MEXICO = LABOR AND LABORERS THROUGH MEXICAN HISTORY; Frost, Elsa Cecilia; Laborers; Mexico.

1675 Tiano, Susan B. El programa mexicano de maquiladoras: una respuesta a las necesidades de la industria norteamericana. AZTLAN, Vol. 14, no. 1 (Spring 1983), p. 201-208. English. **DESCR:** *EL PROGRAMA MEXICANO DE MAQUILADORAS: UNA RESPUESTA A LAS NECESIDADES DE LA INDUSTRIA NORTEAMERICANA; Industrial Workers; Industries; International Labor Activities; Maquiladoras; Woog, Mario Arriola.

1676 Tomayo, Maria. Book review of: CUNDE AMORES. NUESTRO, Vol. 7, no. 2 (March 1983), p. 57-59. Bilingual. **DESCR:** *CUNDE AMORES; Morales-Deeny, Carmen A.

1677 Torbert, Eugene C. Book review of: NUEVOS HORIZONTES: CHICANO, PUERTO-RICAN AND CUBAN SHORT STORIES. HISPANIA, Vol. 66, no. 1 (1983), p. 151. English. **DESCR:** *Multinational Literature; *NUEVOS-HORIZONTES: CHICANO, PUERTO-RICAN, AND CUBAN SHORT STORIES.

1678 Torres, Sylvia. Book review of: ROSIE: THE INVESTIGATION OF A WRONGFUL DEATH. HISPANIC JOURNAL OF BEHAVIORAL SCIENCES, Vol. 4, no. 2 (June 1982), p. 279-280. English. **DESCR:** Frankfort, Ellen; Kissling, Frances; *ROSIE: THE INVESTIGATION OF A WRONGFUL DEATH.

1679 Trujillo, Larry. Book review of: GUNPOWDER JUSTICE: A REASSESSMENT OF THE TEXAS RANGERS [reprinted from CRIME AND SOCIAL JUSTICE, 61 (Summer 1980)]. CHICANO LAW REVIEW, Vol. 6, (1983), p. 148-155. English. **DESCR:** *GUNPOWDER JUSTICE: A REASSESSMENT OF THE TEXAS RANGERS; Samora, Julian; *Texas Rangers.

1680 Tucker, Sally. Book review of: THE TESTING TRAP. HISPANIC JOURNAL OF BEHAVIORAL SCIENCES, Vol. 5, no. 2 (June 1983), p. 241-244. English. **DESCR:** Strenio, Andrew J., Jr.; *THE TESTING TRAP.

1681 Tyler, Joseph. Basque Ball in Bridgeport. HISPANIA, Vol. 66, no. 1 (1983), p. 144. English. **DESCR:** *Chicanos in American Literature; *LES FILS DU SOLEIL: LA MINORITE MEXICAINE A TRAVERS LA LITTERATURE DES ETATS-UNIS.

1682 Umpierre, Luz Maria. Book review of: KILIAGONIA. THIRD WOMAN, Vol. 1, no. 2 (1982), p. 87-90. Spanish. **DESCR:** *KILIAGONIA; Zavala, Iris M.

Book Reviews (cont.)

1683 Umpierre, Luz Maria. Un manifiesto
literario: PAPELES DE PANDERA DE ROSARIO
FERRE. BILINGUAL REVIEW, Vol. 9, no. 2 (May,
August, 1982), p. 120126. Spanish. **DESCR:**
Ferre, Rosario; *PAPELES DE PANDORA; Poetry;
Puerto Rican Literature.

1684 Urioste, Donaldo W. Book review of: CUENTOS
CHICANOS. LA PALABRA, Vol. 4, no. 1-2
(Spring, Fall, 1982, 1983), p. 175-177.
Spanish. **DESCR:** Anaya, Rudolfo A.; *CUENTOS
CHICANOS; Literature.

1685 Van den Berghe, Pierre L. Book review of:
ETHNIC AMERICA, A HISTORY. INTERNATIONAL
MIGRATION REVIEW, Vol. 16, no. 4 (Winter
1982), p. 900-902. English. **DESCR:** *ETHNIC
AMERICA, A HISTORY; Ethnic Groups; History;
Migration; Sowell, Thomas.

1686 Vega, Ed. Book review of: OUR HOUSE IN THE
LAST WORLD. NUESTRO, Vol. 7, no. 10
(December 1983), p. 54-55. English. **DESCR:**
Hijuelos, Oscar; *OUR HOUSE IN THE LAST
WORLD.

1687 Venier, M.E. Literatura chicana. DIALOGOS,
Vol. 18, (May, June, 1982), p. 62-63.
Spanish. **DESCR:** *IDENTIFICATION AND ANALYSIS
OF CHICANO LITERATURE; Jimenez, Francisco.

1688 Vierra, Andrea. Book review of: BEYOND THE
NUCLEAR FAMILY MODEL: CROSS CULTURAL
PERSPECTIVES. HISPANIC JOURNAL OF BEHAVIORAL
SCIENCES, Vol. 5, no. 3 (September 1983), p.
349-352. English. **DESCR:** *BEYOND THE NUCLEAR
FAMILY; Family; Lenero-Otero, Luis.

1689 Vigil, Ralph H. Book review of: DESERT
IMMIGRANTS: THE MEXICANS OF EL PASO
1880-1920. INTERNATIONAL MIGRATION REVIEW,
Vol. 16, no. 1 (Spring 1982), p. 223-224.
English. **DESCR:** *DESERT IMMIGRANTS: THE
MEXICANS OF EL PASO 1880-1920; El Paso, TX;
Garcia, Mario T.; History; Immigrants.

1690 Vigil, Ralph H. Book review of: MEXICANO
RESISTANCE IN THE SOUTHWEST: "THE SACRED
RIGHT OF SELF-PRESERVATION". NEW MEXICO
HISTORICAL REVIEW, Vol. 58, no. 1 (January
1983), p. 104-105. English. **DESCR:** *MEXICANO
RESISTANCE IN THE SOUTHWEST: "THE SACRED
RIGHT OF SELF-PRESERVATION"; Rosenbaum,
Robert J.

1691 Villarreal, Diana Judith. For Spanish
children. HORN BOOK MAGAZINE, Vol. 58,
(June 1982), p. 312-313. English. **DESCR:**
Griego, Margo C.; *PARA LOS NINOS, vols.
1&2; Pena, Graciela; *TORTILLITAS PARA MAMA.

1692 Vincent, J. Book review of: HISPANIC FOLK
MUSIC OF NEW MEXICO AND THE SOUTHWEST: A
SELF-PORTRAIT OF A PEOPLE. ETHNOMUSICOLOGY,
Vol. 26, no. 2 (May 1982), p. 326-327.
English. **DESCR:** Ethnomusicology; Folk Songs;
*HISPANIC FOLK MUSIC OF NEW MEXICO AND THE
SOUTHWEST: A SELF-PORTRAIT OF A PEOPLE; New
Mexico; Robb, John Donald; *THE SOUTHWEST: A
SELF-PORTRAIT.

1693 Vivo, Paquita. Book review of: PUERTO RICO:
A POLITICAL AND CULTURAL HISTORY. NUESTRO,
Vol. 7, no. 5 (June, July, 1983), p. 63.
English. **DESCR:** Carrion, Arturo Morales;
History; Puerto Rican Studies; Puerto Rico;
*PUERTO RICO: A POLITICAL AND CULTURAL
HISTORY; United States History.

1694 Wagatsuma, Yuria. Book review of: EARLY
CHILDHOOD BILINGUALISM: WITH SPECIAL
REFERENCE TO THE MEXICAN-AMERICAN CHILD.
HISPANIC JOURNAL OF BEHAVIORAL SCIENCES,
Vol. 5, no. 4 (December 1983), p. 477-481.
English. **DESCR:** Bilingualism; *EARLY
CHILDHOOD BILINGUALISM: WITH SPECIAL
REFERENCE TO THE MEXICAN-AMERICAN CHILD;
Garcia, Eugene E.

1695 Walia, Adorna. Book review of: BEGINNING
ENGLISH THROUGH ACTION. BILINGUAL JOURNAL,
Vol. 7, no. 3 (Spring 1983), p. 31-32.
English. **DESCR:** *BEGINNING ENGLISH THROUGH
ACTION (BETA); English as a Second Language;
Jackson, P.; Language Arts; Programmed
Instruction.

1696 Walia, Adorna. Book review of: BILINGUAL
EDUCATION TEACHER HANDBOOK: LANGUAGE ISSUES
IN MULTICULTURAL SETTINGS. vol. II.
BILINGUAL JOURNAL, Vol. 6, no. 1 (Fall
1982), p. 29-30. English. **DESCR:** Bilingual
Bicultural Education; *BILINGUAL EDUCATION
TEACHER HANDBOOK: LANGUAGE ISSUES IN
MULTICULTURAL SETTINGS, VOL II; Cultural
Pluralism; Language Assessment; Montero,
Martha.

1697 Walia, Adorna. Book review of: CONVERSATIONS
OF MIGUEL AND MARIA: HOW CHILDREN LEARN
ENGLISH AS A SECOND LANGUAGE; IMPLICATIONS
FOR CLASSROOM TEACHING. BILINGUAL JOURNAL,
Vol. 6, no. 1 (Fall 1982), p. 28-29.
English. **DESCR:** Bilingual Bicultural
Education; *CONVERSATIONS OF MIGUEL AND
MARIA: HOW CHILDREN LEARN ENGLISH AS A
SECOND LANGUAGE; IMPLICATIONS FOR CLASSROOM
TEACHING; English as a Second Language;
Ventriglia, Linda.

1698 Walia, Adorna. Book review of: COUNSELING
THE BILINGUAL STUDENT. BILINGUAL JOURNAL,
Vol. 7, no. 4 (Summer 1983), p. 27-28.
English. **DESCR:** Bilingual Bicultural
Education; Counseling Services
(Educational); *COUNSELING THE BILINGUAL
STUDENT; Sanchez, Antonia; Searchlight
Series.

1699 Walia, Adorna. Book review of: CULTURE AND
THE BILINGUAL CLASSROOM: STUDIES IN
CLASSROOM ETHNOGRAPHY. BILINGUAL JOURNAL,
Vol. 6, no. 4 (Summer 1982), p. 30-31.
English. **DESCR:** Au, Kathryn Hu-Pei;
Biculturalism; *Bilingual Bicultural
Education; Cultural Pluralism; *CULTURE AND
THE BILINGUAL CLASSROOM: STUDIES IN
CLASSROOM ETHNOLOGY; Guthrie, Grace Pung;
Trueba, Henry T.

1700 Walia, Adorna. Book review of: DATA FORMS
FOR EVALUATING BILINGUAL EDUCATION PROGRAM.
BILINGUAL JOURNAL, Vol. 7, no. 2 (Winter
1983), p. 38. English. **DESCR:** Bilingual
Bicultural Education; Cohen, Bernard H.;
*DATA FORMS FOR EVALUATING BILINGUAL
EDUCATION PROGRAMS; Educational
Administration; Evaluation (Educational).

1701 Walia, Adorna. Book review of: DO'S AND
DONT'S OF BILINGUAL PROGRAM EVALUATION.
BILINGUAL JOURNAL, Vol. 7, no. 2 (Winter
1983), p. 38. English. **DESCR:** Bilingual
Bicultural Education; Curriculum; *DO'S AND
DONT'S OF BILINGUAL PROGRAM EVALUATION;
Evaluation (Educational); Rodriguez-Brown,
Flora V.

Book Reviews (cont.)

1702 Walia, Adorna. Book review of: EL GOBIERNO Y LOS PRESIDENTES DE LOS ESTADOS UNIDOS DE AMERICA. BILINGUAL JOURNAL, Vol. 6, no. 3 (Spring 1982), p. 22. English. **DESCR:** Constitution of the United States; *EL GOBIERNO Y LOS PRESIDENTES DE LOS ESTADOS UNIDOS DE AMERICA; *Government; Roy, Joaquin; United States; *United States History.

1703 Walia, Adorna. Book review of: THE BILINGUAL PLAY: PINOCCHIO. BILINGUAL JOURNAL, Vol. 7, no. 3 (Spring 1983), p. 31. English. **DESCR:** Bilingual Bicultural Education; Pastore Passaro, Maria C.; Teatro; *THE BILINGUAL PLAY: PINOCCHIO.

1704 Walia, Adorna. Book review of: THE PLUM PLUM PICKERS. BILINGUAL JOURNAL, Vol. 6, no. 1 (Fall 1982), p. 30-31. English. **DESCR:** Agricultural Laborers; Barrio, Raymond; California; *Migrant Labor; Santa Clara County, CA; *THE PLUM PLUM PICKERS.

1705 Walia, Adorna. Book review of: WOMEN AND MEN SPEAKING: FRAMEWORK FOR ANALYSIS. BILINGUAL JOURNAL, Vol. 6, no. 3 (Spring 1982), p. 20-22. English. **DESCR:** Kramarae, Cheris; Language Usage; Sex Stereotypes; Sexism; Sociolinguistics; *WOMEN AND MEN SPEAKING: FRAMEWORK FOR ANALYSIS.

1706 Ward, Carmen Carole. Book review of: THE ASSIMILATION OF CUBAN EXILES: THE ROLE OF COMMUNITY AND CLASS. JOURNAL OF ETHNIC STUDIES, Vol. 3, no. 2 (Summer 1975), p. 116-119. English. **DESCR:** Assimilation; *Cubanos; Miami, FL; *Rogg, Eleanor Meyer; Social Classes; Social History and Conditions; THE ASSIMILATION OF CUBAN EXILES: THE ROLE OF COMMUNITY AND CLASS; West New York, NJ.

1707 Weber, David J. Book review of: MEXICANO RESISTANCE IN THE SOUTHWEST: "THE SACRED RIGHT OF SELF-PRESERVATION". AMERICAN HISTORICAL REVIEW, Vol. 87, no. 1 (February 1982), p. 272-273. English. **DESCR:** Insurrections; *MEXICANO RESISTANCE IN THE SOUTHWEST: "THE SACRED RIGHT OF SELF-PRESERVATION"; Rosenbaum, Robert J.; Southwest United States.

1708 Weber, David J. Book review of: THE NEW BILINGUALISM: AN AMERICAN DILEMMA. WESTERN HISTORICAL QUARTERLY, Vol. 14, no. 1 (1983), p. 77-79. English. **DESCR:** Bilingual Bicultural Education; Bilingualism; Ridge, Martin; *THE NEW BILINGUALISM: AN AMERICAN DILEMMA.

1709 Weber, Kenneth R. Book review of: CANONES: VALUES, CRISIS, AND SURVIVAL IN A NORTHERN NEW MEXICO VILLAGE. JOURNAL OF ETHNIC STUDIES, Vol. 11, no. 2 (Summer 1983), p. 119-123. English. **DESCR:** Canones, NM; *CANONES: VALUES, CRISIS AND SURVIVAL IN A NORTHERN NEW MEXICO VILLAGE; Ethnology; History; Kutsche, Paul; New Mexico; Northern New Mexico; Van Ness, John R.

1710 Weber, Kenneth R. Book review of: HISPANIC VILLAGES OF NORTHERN NEW MEXICO. SOUTHWEST ECONOMY AND SOCIETY, Vol. 1, no. 1 (Spring 1976), p. 48. English. **DESCR:** Economic History and Conditions; Great Depression, 1929-1933; *HISPANIC VILLAGES OF NORTHERN NEW MEXICO; New Mexico; Tewa Basin, NM; Weigle, Marta.

1711 Weber, Kenneth R. Book review of: MY PENITENTE LAND: REFLECTIONS ON SPANISH NEW MEXICO. JOURNAL OF ETHNIC STUDIES, Vol. 3, no. 2 (Summer 1975), p. 119-121. English. **DESCR:** Chavez, Fray Angelico; *Hermanos Penitentes; MY PENITENTE LAND: REFLECTIONS ON SPANISH NEW MEXICO; *New Mexico; Religion.

1712 Weigle, Marta. Book review of: HISPANIC LEGENDS FROM NEW MEXICO: NARRATIVES FROM THE R.D. JAMESON COLLECTION. JOURNAL OF AMERICAN FOLKLORE, Vol. 96, , p. 238-239. English. **DESCR:** Cuentos; *HISPANIC LEGENDS FROM NEW MEXICO: NARRATIVES FROM THE R.D. JAMESON COLLECTION; Robe, Stanley L.

1713 Weiss, Richard. Book review of: LEGISLATIVE HISTORY OF AMERICAN IMMIGRATION POLICY, 1798-1965. INTERNATIONAL MIGRATION REVIEW, Vol. 16, no. 3 (Fall 1982), p. 683. English. **DESCR:** Hutchinson, E.P.; Immigration Law; *LEGISLATIVE HISTORY OF AMERICAN IMMIGRATION POLICY, 1798-1965.

1714 West, Dennis. Book review of: IMAGES OF THE MEXICAN-AMERICAN IN FICTION AND FILM. CINEASTE, Vol. 12, no. 1 (1982), p. 41. English. **DESCR:** Chicanos in American Literature; Films; *IMAGES OF THE MEXICAN AMERICAN IN FICTION AND FILM; Pettit, Arthur G.; Stereotypes.

1715 West, John O. Book review of: HISPANIC FOLK MUSIC OF NEW MEXICO AND THE SOUTHWEST: A SELF-PORTRAIT OF A PEOPLE. JOURNAL OF AMERICAN FOLKLORE, Vol. 96, (April, May, 1983), p. 239. English. **DESCR:** Folk Songs; *HISPANIC FOLK MUSIC OF NEW MEXICO AND THE SOUTHWEST: A SELF-PORTRAIT OF A PEOPLE; Robb, John Donald.

1716 Westphall, Victor. Book review of: ROOTS OF RESISTANCE: LAND TENURE IN NEW MEXICO, 1680-1980. ARIZONA AND THE WEST, Vol. 24, no. 2 (Summer 1982), p. 192-193. English. **DESCR:** Land Tenure; Ortiz, Roxanne Dunbar; *ROOTS OF RESISTANCE: LAND TENURE IN NEW MEXICO, 1680-1980.

1717 White, Tim. Book review of: INTELLIGENCE AND RACE. THE ORIGINS AND DIMENSIONS OF THE IQ CONTROVERSY. HISPANIC JOURNAL OF BEHAVIORAL SCIENCES, Vol. 4, no. 4 (December 1982), p. 522-525. English. **DESCR:** Eckberg, Douglas Lee; *INTELLIGENCE AND RACE: THE ORIGINS AND DIMENSIONS OF THE IQ CONTROVERSY.

1718 Willie, Charles V. First learning unchallenged and untested. CHANGE, Vol. 14, no. 7 (October 1982), p. 37-41. English. **DESCR:** Affirmative Action; Bilingual Bicultural Education; Biography; Education; *HUNGER OF MEMORY: THE EDUCATION OF RICHARD RODRIGUEZ; Rodriguez, Richard.

1719 Wimsatt, Margaret. Book review of: FAMOUS ALL OVER TOWN. COMMONWEAL, Vol. 110, no. 10 (May 20, 1983), p. 309-312. English. **DESCR:** *FAMOUS ALL OVER TOWN; James, Dan.

1720 Woodbridge, Hensley C. Outstanding new bibliography about Chicano literature. BILINGUAL REVIEW, Vol. 10, no. 1 (January, April, 1983), p. 69-72. English. **DESCR:** *A BIBLIOGRAPHY OF CRITICISM OF CONTEMPORARY CHICANO LITERATURE; Eger, Ernestina N.

Book Reviews (cont.)

1721 Woods, Richard D. Book review of: SPANISH AND ENGLISH OF UNITED STATES HISPANOS: A CRITICAL, ANNOTATED, LINGUISTIC BIBLIOGRAPHY. JOURNAL OF ETHNIC STUDIES, Vol. 4, no. 3 (Fall 1976), p. 116. English. DESCR: Accentedness; Bibliography; Bills, Garland D.; Craddock, Jerry R.; Language Patterns; *SPANISH AND ENGLISH OF U.S. HISPANOS: A CRITICAL, ANNOTATED, LINGUISTIC BIBLIOGRAPHY; Spanish Language; Teschner, Richard V.

1722 Ybarra, Lea. Book review of: LAS MUJERES: CONVERSATIONS FROM A HISPANIC COMMUNITY [reprinted from LA RED/THE NET 5 (Sept. 1982)]. CHICANO LAW REVIEW, Vol. 6, (1983), p. 146-147. English. DESCR: Chicanas; Elsasser, Nan; *LAS MUJERES: CONVERSATIONS FROM A HISPANIC COMMUNITY; MacKenzie, Kyle; Oral History; Tixier y Vigil, Yvonne.

1723 Zaks, Vivian Calderon. Book review of: ETHNIC FAMILIES IN AMERICA: PATTERNS AND VARIATIONS. HISPANIC JOURNAL OF BEHAVIORAL SCIENCES, Vol. 4, no. 1 (March 1982), p. 122-128. English. DESCR: *ETHNIC FAMILIES IN AMERICA: PATTERNS AND VARIATIONS; Habenstein, Robert W.; Mindel, Charles H.

1724 Zalazar, Daniel E. Book review of: HISPANIC FOLK MUSIC OF NEW MEXICO AND THE SOUTHWEST: A SELF-PORTRAIT OF A PEOPLE. HISPANIC JOURNAL, Vol. 3, no. 2 (Spring 1982), p. 139-140. Spanish. DESCR: *HISPANIC FOLK MUSIC OF NEW MEXICO AND THE SOUTHWEST: A SELF-PORTRAIT OF A PEOPLE; Robb, John Donald.

1725 Zamora, Carlos. Book review of: MOSAICO DE LA VIDA: CHICANO, CUBAN AND PUERTO RICAN PROSE. MINORITY VOICES, Vol. 5, no. 1-2 (Spring, Fall, 1981), p. 71-72. English. DESCR: Jimenez, Francisco; Literature; *MOSAICO DE LA VIDA: CHICANO, CUBAN AND PUERTO RICAN PROSE.

Book Sellers and Distributors
USE: Publishing Industry

Bookkeeping
USE: Accounting

Books and Reading for Children
USE: Children's Literature

BOQUITAS PINTADAS

1727 Alurista. BOQUITAS PINTADAS, produccion folletinesca bajo el militarismo. MAIZE, Vol. 4, no. 1-2 (Fall, Winter, 1980, 1981), p. 21-26. Spanish. DESCR: Literary Criticism; Puig, Manuel.

BORDER BOOM TOWN: CIUDAD JUAREZ SINCE 1848

1728 Logan, Kathleen. The urban poor in developing nations. JOURNAL OF URBAN HISTORY, Vol. 9, no. 1 (November 1982), p. 108-116. English. DESCR: ACCESS TO POWER: POLITICS AND THE URBAN POOR IN DEVELOPING NATIONS; *Book Reviews; Collier, David; Cornelius, Wayne A.; Eckstein, Susan; Lloyd, Peter; Martinez, Oscar J.; Nelson, Joan M.; Perlman, Janice E.; POLITICS AND MIGRANT POOR IN MEXICO CITY; SLUMS OF HOPE? SHANTY TOWNS OF THE THIRD WORLD; SQUATTERS AND OLIGARCHS: AUTHORITARIAN RULE AND POLICY CHANGE IN PERU; THE MYTH OF MARGINALITY: URBAN POVERTY AND POLITICS IN RIO DE JANEIRO; THE POVERTY OF REVOLUTION: THE STATE AND THE URBAN POOR IN MEXICO; Urban Economics.

THE BORDER [film]

1729 Entertainment = diversion. CAMINOS, Vol. 3, no. 3 (March 1982), p. 55-56. Bilingual. DESCR: Aztlan Writing Contest; CORAZON DE AZTLAN; Films; Literary Contests; MISSING [film]; *Recreation; Young, Robert.

Border Industrialization Program
USE: Mexican Border Industrialization Program

Border Industries

1730 Deibel, Richard and Sanchez, Tony, Jr. Business on the border: attracting venture capital. HISPANIC BUSINESS, Vol. 5, no. 9 (September 1983), p. 20-21+. English. DESCR: Border Region; Finance; *Sanchez, Tony, Jr.; Texas.

1731 Research/development: books. HISPANIC BUSINESS, Vol. 4, no. 11 (November 1982), p. 28. English. DESCR: Book Reviews; Border Region; *ESTUDIOS FRONTERIZOS: PONENCIAS Y COMENTARIOS; Jamail, Milton H.; *THE UNITED STATES-MEXICO BORDER: A GUIDE TO INSTITUTIONS, ORGANIZATIONS AND SCHOLARS; United States-Mexico Relations.

Border Patrol

1732 Brooks, Douglas Montgomery. Aliens - civil rights - illegal aliens are inhabitants within meaning of U.S.C 242. SUFFOLK TRANSNATIONAL LAW JOURNAL, Vol. 6, no. 1 (Spring 1982), p. 117-131. English. DESCR: Constitutional Amendments - Fourteenth; Immigration Regulation and Control; *Undocumented Workers; U.S. v. Otherson.

1733 Castro, Mike. Alien smuggling and the refugee question: caught between the border patrol and the river. NUESTRO, Vol. 7, no. 5 (June, July, 1983), p. 18. English. DESCR: California Rural Legal Assistance (CRLA); *Immigration Regulation and Control; *Sacramento, CA; *Undocumented Workers.

1734 Castro, Mike. OAS investigates California deaths. NUESTRO, Vol. 7, no. 9 (November 1983), p. 12-13. English. DESCR: California Rural Legal Assistance (CRLA); Immigration Regulation and Control; *Organization of American States.

1735 Chavira, Ricardo. Refugees from poverty: a San Diego perspective. NUESTRO, Vol. 7, no. 4 (May 1983), p. 24-25. English. DESCR: *Immigration Regulation and Control; *San Diego, CA; *Undocumented Workers.

1736 Day, Mark R. 'Traffic darn heavy' to U.S. NATIONAL CATHOLIC REPORTER, Vol. 19, (October 29, 1982), p. 3. English. DESCR: Immigration Regulation and Control; *Undocumented Workers.

Border Patrol (cont.)

1737 Dowd, Maureen. Losing control of the borders. TIME, Vol. 121, no. 24 (June 13, 1983), p. 26-27. English. DESCR: *Immigration; Immigration and Naturalization Service (INS); Immigration Regulation and Control.

1738 Long, William J. and Pohl, Christopher M. Joint foot patrols succeed in El Paso. POLICE CHIEF, Vol. 50, no. 4 (April 1983), p. 49-51. English. DESCR: Ciudad Juarez, Chihuahua, Mexico; Criminal Acts; *El Paso, TX; Immigration Regulation and Control; *Police; Undocumented Workers; Youth.

1739 Mena, Jesus. Refugees from poverty: a Brownsville perspective. NUESTRO, Vol. 7, no. 4 (May 1983), p. 26. English. DESCR: Brownsville, TX; *Immigration Regulation and Control; *Undocumented Workers.

1740 Mexican woman seriously injured. NUESTRO, Vol. 6, no. 10 (December 1982), p. 9. English. DESCR: *Immigrants; Immigration Regulation and Control.

1741 Oliver, Gordon. Worker abuses claimed. NATIONAL CATHOLIC REPORTER, Vol. 19, (October 29, 1982), p. 7. English. DESCR: Agricultural Laborers; *Citizens United for Farmworkers, Yakima WA; Immigration and Naturalization Service (INS); *Immigration Regulation and Control; Yakima, WA.

1742 Padilla, Steve. Alien smuggling and the refugee question: undercover agent for the border patrol. NUESTRO, Vol. 7, no. 5 (June, July, 1983), p. 15-17. English. DESCR: Acosta, Hipolito; *Immigration Regulation and Control; *Undocumented Workers.

1743 Police and immigration. NUESTRO, Vol. 7, no. 2 (March 1983), p. 7. English. DESCR: El Paso, TX; Federal Government; *Immigration Law; Immigration Regulation and Control; Police.

1744 Que pasa? NUESTRO, Vol. 7, no. 3 (April 1983), p. 9. English. DESCR: *Cisneros, Henry, Mayor of San Antonio, TX; Elections; Immigration Regulation and Control; Rocky Mountain Spotted Fever; Servas; Tourism.

1745 Rivera, Julius and Goodman, Paul Wershub. Clandestine labor circulation: a case on the U.S.-Mexico border. MIGRATION TODAY, Vol. 10, no. 1 (1982), p. 21-26. English. DESCR: Border Region; Ciudad Juarez, Chihuahua, Mexico; El Paso, TX; Immigration Regulation and Control; Migration Patterns; Social Classes; Social Mobility; Socioeconomic Factors; *Undocumented Workers.

1746 Salgado, J. F. Alien smugglers: an escalating war. NUESTRO, Vol. 7, no. 1 (January, February, 1983), p. 39. English. DESCR: Immigration and Naturalization Service (INS); Immigration Regulation and Control; *Undocumented Workers.

1747 Turansick, Michael F. A critique of proposed amendments to the immigration and nationality act. FORDHAM INTERNATIONAL LAW FORUM, Vol. 5, no. 1 (Winter 1981, 1982), p. 213-238. English. DESCR: Braceros; *Immigration and Nationality Act (INA); Immigration Regulation and Control; Public Law 78; Undocumented Workers.

Border Region

1748 Abrams, Herbert K. Occupational and environmental health problems along the U.S.-Mexico Border. SOUTHWEST ECONOMY AND SOCIETY, Vol. 4, no. 3 (Spring, Summer, 1979), p. 3-20. English. DESCR: Agricultural Laborers; Housing; Mexican Border Industrialization Program; Nutrition; *Pollution; *Public Health; Social History and Conditions.

1749 Armengol, Armando; Manley, Joan H.; and Teschner, Richard V. The international bilingual city: how a university meets the challenge. FOREIGN LANGUAGE ANNALS, Vol. 15, no. 4 (September 1982), p. 289-295. English. DESCR: Biculturalism; Bilingualism; Ciudad Juarez, Chihuahua, Mexico; El Paso, TX; *Language Development; Spanish Language; University of Texas at El Paso.

1750 Babbitt, Bruce. Reagan approach to aliens simply wishful thinking. NATIONAL HISPANIC JOURNAL, Vol. 1, no. 2 (Winter 1982), p. 6-7. English. DESCR: Braceros; Immigration Regulation and Control; *Reagan, Ronald; Select Commission on Immigration and Refugee Policy; *Undocumented Workers; United States-Mexico Relations.

1751 Bath, C. Richard. Health and environmental problems: the role of the border in El Paso-Ciudad Juarez coordination. JOURNAL OF INTERAMERICAN STUDIES AND WORLD AFFAIRS, Vol. 24, no. 3 (August 1982), p. 375-392. English. DESCR: Ciudad Juarez, Chihuahua, Mexico; *El Paso, TX; International Boundary and Water Commission; Nationalism; Pollution; *Public Health; United States-Mexico Relations; U.S Border Public Health Association (AFMES).

1752 Bell, Samuel E. and Smallwood, James M. Zona libre: trade and diplomacy on the Mexican border, 1858-1905. ARIZONA AND THE WEST, Vol. 24, no. 2 (Summer 1982), p. 119-152. English. DESCR: *Foreign Trade; International Relations; Mexico; United States History.

1753 Cantu, Hector. Border business report: the Rio Grande Valley's economy and Mexico's lingering peso devaluation effects. NATIONAL HISPANIC JOURNAL, Vol. 2, no. 1 (Summer 1983), p. 10-13. English. DESCR: Aguirre, Lionel; Cano, Eddie; Coors Distributing Company, McAllen, TX; Cruz, Conrado; Cuevas, Betty; *Currency; Economic Development; Laredo, TX, Chamber of Commerce; Mexican American Chamber of Commerce, Austin, TX; United States-Mexico Relations.

1754 Cardenas, Lupe and Alarcon, Justo S. Book review of: CHULIFEAS FRONTERAS. MAIZE, Vol. 6, no. 3-4 (Spring, Summer, 1983), p. 60-61. Spanish. DESCR: *Book Reviews.

1755 Chaze, William L. Invasion from Mexico: it just keeps growing. U.S. NEWS & WORLD REPORT, Vol. 94, no. 9 (March 7, 1983), p. 37-41. English. DESCR: *Immigration Regulation and Control; Smuggling; *Undocumented Workers.

1756 Day, Mark R. Border group feeds, clothes dispossessed. NATIONAL CATHOLIC REPORTER, Vol. 19, (October 22, 1982), p. 5. English. DESCR: Catholic Church; Colonia Reforma, Tijuana, Baja California, Mexico; *Mexican American Neighborhood Organization (MANO).

1757 Day, Mark R. Hopes of jobs lure Mexicans. NATIONAL CATHOLIC REPORTER, Vol. 19, (October 29, 1982), p. 3. English. DESCR: *Undocumented Workers; U.S. Border Patrol.

Border Region (cont.)

1758 Deibel, Richard. Business along la frontera. HISPANIC BUSINESS, Vol. 5, no. 1 (January 1983), p. 14-15. English. **DESCR:** *Currency; Laredo, TX; Mexico.

1759 Deibel, Richard and Sanchez, Tony, Jr. Business on the border: attracting venture capital. HISPANIC BUSINESS, Vol. 5, no. 9 (September 1983), p. 20-21+. English. **DESCR:** Border Industries; Finance; *Sanchez, Tony, Jr.; Texas.

1760 Deukmejian, George. Welcoming the Commission of the Californias. CAMINOS, Vol. 4, no. 11 (December 1983), p. 19. English. **DESCR:** California; *Commission of the Californias; United States-Mexico Relations.

1761 Duncan, Cameron. The runaway shop and the Mexican border industrialization program. SOUTHWEST ECONOMY AND SOCIETY, Vol. 2, no. 1 (October, November, 1976), p. 4-25. English. **DESCR:** Labor Supply and Market; *Maquiladoras; *Mexican Border Industrialization Program; Multinational Corporations.

1762 Edmunds, Stahrl W. California-Mexico trade relations. CAMINOS, Vol. 4, no. 11 (December 1983), p. 20-21,38. Bilingual. **DESCR:** Business; *California; *United States-Mexico Relations.

1763 Hamner, Richard. Hispanic update: border governors tackle U.S.-Mexico relations: much ado: but nothing on immigration. NATIONAL HISPANIC JOURNAL, Vol. 1, no. 2 (Winter 1982), p. 4-5. English. **DESCR:** Babbitt, Bruce; Brown, Edmund G., Jr., Governor of California; *Clements, Bill; Immigration; Immigration Regulation and Control; Moreno, Paul; *United States-Mexico Relations.

1764 Hansen, Niles. Trans boundary environmental issues in the United States-Mexico borderlands. SOUTHWESTERN REVIEW OF MANAGEMENT AND ECONOMICS, Vol. 2, no. 1 (Winter 1982), p. 61-78. English. **DESCR:** Air Pollution; *Pollution; Water Pollution.

1765 Illegal aliens vital to economy, mayor says. NUESTRO, Vol. 7, no. 2 (March 1983), p. 54. English. **DESCR:** Cisneros, Henry, Mayor of San Antonio, TX; Economics; *Undocumented Workers.

1766 John, Elizabeth A.H. Book review of: THE MEXICAN FRONTIER, 1821-1846: THE AMERICAN SOUTHWEST UNDER MEXICO. NEW MEXICO HISTORICAL REVIEW, Vol. 57, no. 3 (July 1982), p. 289-293. English. **DESCR:** Book Reviews; Southwest United States; *THE MEXICAN FRONTIER, 1821-1846: THE AMERICAN SOUTHWEST UNDER MEXICO; Weber, David J.

1767 Juarez, Richard. Third international conference of the U.S.- Mexico border governors. CAMINOS, Vol. 3, no. 11 (December 1982), p. 35-36. English. **DESCR:** United States-Mexico Governors' Conference; *United States-Mexico Relations.

1768 Mena, Jesus. Violence in the Rio Grande Valley. NUESTRO, Vol. 7, no. 1 (January, February, 1983), p. 41-42. English. **DESCR:** *Bandidos; History; *Rio Grande Valley, TX; Social History and Conditions.

1769 Mexican border crossing survey. CAMINOS, Vol. 3, no. 11 (December 1982), p. 40-41. English. **DESCR:** *United States-Mexico Relations.

1770 Mexican border sounds travel the folk circuit. BILLBOARD, Vol. 95, (February 26, 1983), p. 46. English. **DESCR:** Music; *Norteno.

1771 Miller, Shirley and Miller, Tom. Cabo San Lucas - revisited; border updates. CAMINOS, Vol. 3, no. 1 (January 1982), p. 8-9. Bilingual. **DESCR:** *Baja California, Mexico; *Tourism.

1772 Moody, George F. Mexicans and Americans should be the best of friends. CAMINOS, Vol. 3, no. 11 (December 1982), p. 37. Bilingual. **DESCR:** *United States-Mexico Relations.

1773 Morrison, Thomas K. The relationship of U.S. aid, trade and investment to migration pressures in major sending countries. INTERNATIONAL MIGRATION REVIEW, Vol. 16, no. 1 (Spring 1982), p. 4-26. English. **DESCR:** International Economic Relations; Investments; Mexican Border Industrialization Program; *Migration Patterns; PIDER Project; Rural Economics; Rural Urban Migration; Undocumented Workers; United States-Mexico Relations.

1774 Mumme, Stephen P. and Jamail, Milton H. The International Boundary and Water Commission as a conflict management agency in the U.S.-Mexico borderlands. SOCIAL SCIENCE JOURNAL, Vol. 19, no. 1 (January 1982), p. 46-62. English. **DESCR:** Conflict Resolution; *International Boundary and Water Commission; Rio Grande; United States-Mexico Relations; *Water.

1775 Pendleton, Jennifer. Battle for the buck is the tale of two cities: marketers in San Diego and Tijuana square off. ADVERTISING AGE MAGAZINE, Vol. 53, (February 15, 1982), p. II, M42-43. English. **DESCR:** Advertising; Business; *Market Research; San Diego, CA; Tijuana, Mexico.

1776 Que pasa?: Mexican border caucus. NUESTRO, Vol. 7, no. 5 (June, July, 1983), p. 9. English. **DESCR:** Congressional Border Caucus; *United States-Mexico Relations.

1777 Research/development: books. HISPANIC BUSINESS, Vol. 4, no. 11 (November 1982), p. 28. English. **DESCR:** Book Reviews; Border Industries; *ESTUDIOS FRONTERIZOS: PONENCIAS Y COMENTARIOS; Jamail, Milton H.; *THE UNITED STATES-MEXICO BORDER: A GUIDE TO INSTITUTIONS, ORGANIZATIONS AND SCHOLARS; United States-Mexico Relations.

1778 Richmond, Douglas W. Mexican immigration and border strategy during the revolution, 1910-1920. NEW MEXICO HISTORICAL REVIEW, Vol. 57, no. 3 (July 1982), p. 269-288. English. **DESCR:** Carranza, Venustiano; History; Immigration; Mexican Revolution - 1910-1920; Mexico; Social History and Conditions; United States-Mexico Relations.

1779 Rivera, Julius and Goodman, Paul Wershub. Clandestine labor circulation: a case on the U.S.-Mexico border. MIGRATION TODAY, Vol. 10, no. 1 (1982), p. 21-26. English. **DESCR:** Border Patrol; Ciudad Juarez, Chihuahua, Mexico; El Paso, TX; Immigration Regulation and Control; Migration Patterns; Social Classes; Social Mobility; Socioeconomic Factors; *Undocumented Workers.

Border Region (cont.)

1780 Sanchez, Ricardo. El lencho y los chenchos.
NATIONAL HISPANIC JOURNAL, Vol. 1, no. 3
(Summer, Fall, 1982), p. 20. Calo. **DESCR:**
*Ciudad Juarez, Chihuahua, Mexico; El Paso,
TX; *Short Story.

1781 Starr, Mark; McGuire, Stryker; and
Contreras, Joe. The border: a world apart.
NEWSWEEK, Vol. 10, (April 11, 1983), p.
36-40. English. **DESCR:** Immigration; United
States-Mexico Relations.

1782 Timmons, Wilbert H. American El Paso: the
formative years, 1848-1854. SOUTHWESTERN
HISTORICAL QUARTERLY, Vol. 87, no. 1 (July
1983), p. 1-36. English. **DESCR:** *El Paso,
TX; Guadalupe Hidalgo, Treaty of 1848;
History; Social History and Conditions.

1783 UC MEXUS consortium established. CAMINOS,
Vol. 3, no. 6 (June 1982), p. 38. English.
DESCR: United States-Mexico Relations;
University of California; *University of
California Consortium on Mexico and the
United States (UC MEXUS).

1784 U.S. Mexico border region economic report.
CAMINOS, Vol. 3, no. 11 (December 1982), p.
38-39. English. **DESCR:** *Economic
Development; *United States-Mexico
Relations.

1785 Utton, Albert E. The present status of water
issues in the United States-Mexico border
region. SOUTHWESTERN REVIEW OF MANAGEMENT
AND ECONOMICS, Vol. 2, no. 1 (Winter 1982),
p. 79-81. English. **DESCR:** *Water.

1786 Whisler, Kirk. There are no easy solutions.
CAMINOS, Vol. 3, no. 11 (December 1982), p.
34. English. **DESCR:** *Juarez, Richard.

Border Studies

1787 Garcia, Mario T. History, culture, and
society of the borderlands. NEW SCHOLAR,
Vol. 8, no. 1-2 (Spring, Fall, 1982), p.
467-472. English. **DESCR:** Book Reviews;
*VIEWS ACROSS THE BORDER: THE UNITED STATES
AND MEXICO.

1788 Stoddard, Ellwyn R. Multidisciplinary
research funding: a "Catch 22" enigma.
AMERICAN SOCIOLOGIST, Vol. 17, no. 4
(November 1982), p. 210-216. English.
DESCR: Funding Sources.

BORDERLANDS [film]

1789 Ruiz, Reynaldo. BORDERLANDS. BILINGUAL
REVIEW, Vol. 10, no. 2-3 (May, December,
1983), p. 173-175. English. **DESCR:** Film
Reviews.

BORDERLANDS SOURCEBOOK

1790 Book review of: BORDERLANDS SOURCEBOOK.
LIBRARY JOURNAL, Vol. 108, no. 4 (February
15, 1983), p. 385. English. **DESCR:** Book
Reviews; Stoddard, Ellwyn R.

Borgatta, Edgar F.

1791 Burke, Leslie K. Book review of: AGING AND
SOCIETY: CURRENT RESEARCH AND POLICY
PERSPECTIVES. HISPANIC JOURNAL OF BEHAVIORAL
SCIENCES, Vol. 4, no. 1 (March 1982), p.
114-115. English. **DESCR:** *AGING AND SOCIETY:
CURRENT RESEARCH AND POLICY PERSPECTIVES;
Ancianos; Book Reviews; McCluskey, Neil G.

Boston Archdiocese Justice and Peace Commission

1792 Askin, Steve. Boston church encourages labor
talks. NATIONAL CATHOLIC REPORTER, Vol. 18,
(July 30, 1982), p. 6. English. **DESCR:**
Boycotts; Campbell Soup Co.; Catholic
Church; *Farm Labor Organizing Commmittee
(FLOC); Labor Unions.

Boston, MA

1793 Perez, Ana M. Issues in Hispanic foster
care: the Boston experience. JOURNAL OF
LATIN COMMUNITY HEALTH, Vol. 1, no. 1 (Fall
1982), p. 81-88. English. **DESCR:** *Foster
Care.

Boulanger, Graciela Rolo

1794 Una pintora: Graciela Rolo Boulanger.
NUESTRO, Vol. 7, no. 6 (August 1983), p.
30-35. English. **DESCR:** Artists; Biography;
Paintings.

Bowser, Benjamin P.

1795 Rochester, R. C. Book review of: IMPACT OF
RACISM ON WHITE AMERICANS. HISPANIC JOURNAL
OF BEHAVIORAL SCIENCES, Vol. 5, no. 1 (March
1983), p. 125-129. English. **DESCR:** Book
Reviews; Hunt, Raymond G.; *IMPACT OF RACISM
ON WHITE AMERICANS.

Boy Scouts of America

1796 Que pasa? NUESTRO, Vol. 7, no. 6 (August
1983), p. 9. English. **DESCR:** *Court System;
Criminal Justice System; Diabetes;
Education; Judicial Review; Petersilia,
Joan; PREPARED FOR TODAY; RACIAL DISPARITIES
IN THE CRIMINAL JUSTICE SYSTEM; Reagan,
Ronald.

1797 Sacramento youth wins leadership
scholarship. NUESTRO, Vol. 6, no. 8 (October
1982), p. 43. English. **DESCR:** Sacramento,
CA.

Boycotts

1798 Askin, Steve. Boston church encourages labor
talks. NATIONAL CATHOLIC REPORTER, Vol. 18,
(July 30, 1982), p. 6. English. **DESCR:**
Boston Archdiocese Justice and Peace
Commission; Campbell Soup Co.; Catholic
Church; *Farm Labor Organizing Commmittee
(FLOC); Labor Unions.

1799 Boycott threat leads to negociation table.
NUESTRO, Vol. 6, no. 8 (October 1982), p.
48. English. **DESCR:** *Affirmative Action;
Miller Brewing Company.

1800 Communications/marketing. HISPANIC BUSINESS,
Vol. 5, no. 7 (July 1983), p. 24. English.
DESCR: AltaVision, Inc. (Denver, CO); Cable
Television; Marketing; Operation PUSH;
Spanish Satellite Network (SSN);
*Television.

1801 Community watching. CAMINOS, Vol. 3, no. 5
(May 1982), p. 56-57. Bilingual. **DESCR:**
Adelante Mujer Hispana Conference;
Agricultural Laborers; Beilson, Anthony C.;
Chacon, Peter R.; Chicanas; *Cultural
Organizations; Farm Labor Organizing
Commmittee (FLOC); Financial Aid; Hollenbeck
Junior High School, Los Angeles, CA; Junior
High School Students; National League of
Cities; Optimist Club of Greater East Los
Angeles; Organizations; Project WELL (We
Enjoy Learning & Leadership); Torres, Art.

Boycotts (cont.)

1802 FLOC, Campbell labels. NUESTRO, Vol. 6, no.
1 (January, February, 1982), p. 10. English.
DESCR: *Farm Labor Organizing Commmittee
(FLOC); Migrant Labor.

Boyle Heights

1803 Holscher, Louis M. Tiene arte valor afuera
del barrio: the murals of East Los Angeles
and Boyle Heights. JOURNAL OF ETHNIC
STUDIES, Vol. 4, no. 3 (Fall 1976), p.
42-52. English. **DESCR:** Art; Culture; *East
Los Angeles, CA; *Mural Art.

Bracante, Jim

1804 Jim Blancarte, "an ace in the deck". LATINA,
Vol. 1, no. 3 (1983), p. 52-53. English.
DESCR: Biography; Legal Profession.

THE BRACERO EXPERIENCE: ELITELORE VERSUS FOLKLORE

1805 Hoffer, Bates L. Sociology by value systems:
explication and some implications of two
studies on the folklore of Hispanics in the
United States. BILINGUAL REVIEW, Vol. 9, no.
2 (May, August, 1982), p. 172-177.
Bilingual. **DESCR:** BENJY LOPEZ: A PICARESQUE
TALE OF EMIGRATION AND RETURN; Braceros;
*Chicanos in American Literature;
Comparative Literature; Folklore; Herrera
Sobek, Maria; Levine, Barry B.

Bracero Program

1806 Rodriguez, Roberto. "Guest worker program".
CORAZON DE AZTLAN, Vol. 1, no. 2 (March,
April, 1982), p. 36-39. Bilingual. **DESCR:**
Immigration.

Braceros

1807 Babbitt, Bruce. Reagan approach to aliens
simply wishful thinking. NATIONAL HISPANIC
JOURNAL, Vol. 1, no. 2 (Winter 1982), p.
6-7. English. **DESCR:** Border Region;
Immigration Regulation and Control; *Reagan,
Ronald; Select Commission on Immigration and
Refugee Policy; *Undocumented Workers;
United States-Mexico Relations.

1808 Hewitt, William L. Mexican workers in
Wyoming during World War II: necessity,
discrimination and protest. ANNALS OF
WYOMING, Vol. 54, no. 2 (1982), p. 20-33.
English. **DESCR:** *Agricultural Laborers;
Migrant Labor; World War II; Wyoming.

1809 Hoffer, Bates L. Sociology by value systems:
explication and some implications of two
studies on the folklore of Hispanics in the
United States. BILINGUAL REVIEW, Vol. 9, no.
2 (May, August, 1982), p. 172-177.
Bilingual. **DESCR:** BENJY LOPEZ: A PICARESQUE
TALE OF EMIGRATION AND RETURN; *Chicanos in
American Literature; Comparative Literature;
Folklore; Herrera Sobek, Maria; Levine,
Barry B.; THE BRACERO EXPERIENCE: ELITELORE
VERSUS FOLKLORE.

1810 Moore, Richard J. Book review of:
"TEMPORARY" ALIEN WORKERS IN THE UNITED
STATES: DESIGNING POLICY FROM FACT AND
OPINION. INTERNATIONAL MIGRATION REVIEW,
Vol. 16, no. 4 (Winter 1982), p. 909-910.
English. **DESCR:** Book Reviews; Ross, Stanley
R.; *"TEMPORARY" ALIEN WORKERS IN THE UNITED
STATES: DESIGNING POLICY FROM FACT AND
OPINION; Undocumented Workers; Weintraub,
Sidney.

1811 Olson, James S. Book review of: OPERATION

WETBACK: THE MASS DEPORTATION OF MEXICAN
UNDOCUMENTED WORKERS IN 1954. JOURNAL OF THE
WEST, Vol. 22, no. 1 (1983), p. 80-81.
English. **DESCR:** Agricultural Laborers; Book
Reviews; Garcia, Juan Ramon; *OPERATION
WETBACK: THE MASS DEPORTATION OF MEXICAN
UNDOCUMENTED WORKERS IN 1954; Undocumented
Workers.

1812 Sandos, James A. and Cross, Harry E.
National development and international
labour migration: Mexico 1940-1965. JOURNAL
OF CONTEMPORARY HISTORY, Vol. 18, no. 1
(January 1983), p. 43-60. English. **DESCR:**
Immigrant Labor; Mexico.

1813 Turansick, Michael F. A critique of proposed
amendments to the immigration and
nationality act. FORDHAM INTERNATIONAL LAW
FORUM, Vol. 5, no. 1 (Winter 1981, 1982), p.
213-238. English. **DESCR:** Border Patrol;
*Immigration and Nationality Act (INA);
Immigration Regulation and Control; Public
Law 78; Undocumented Workers.

1814 Weintraub, Sidney and Ross, Stanley R. Poor
United States, so close to Mexico. ACROSS
THE BOARD, Vol. 19, no. 3 (March 1982), p.
54-61. English. **DESCR:** Immigrants;
*Immigration; Undocumented Workers.

Bradley, Tom

1815 Tom Bradley. CAMINOS, Vol. 3, no. 4 (April
1982), p. 21-23. Bilingual. **DESCR:** Obledo,
Mario; State Government.

"Braley Street"

1816 de la Fuente, Patricia. Ambiguity in the
poetry of Gary Soto. REVISTA
CHICANO-RIQUENA, Vol. 11, no. 2 (Summer
1983), p. 34-39. English. **DESCR:** "Avocado
Lake"; "Blanco"; "Field"; *Literary
Criticism; Poetry; "Song for the pockets";
*Soto, Gary; TALE OF SUNLIGHT; "Telephoning
God"; THE ELEMENTS OF SAN JOAQUIN; "Wind".

Brand, Othal

1817 Rivas, Mike. Keeping peace in paradise.
NATIONAL HISPANIC JOURNAL, Vol. 1, no. 2
(Winter 1982), p. 13-20. English. **DESCR:**
Casso, Ramiro; Elections; Police; Police
Brutality; *Political Repression; Rio Grande
Valley, TX; THE MEXICAN AMERICAN: QUEST FOR
EQUALITY; Voter Turnout.

The Brat [musical group]

1818 Madrid, Joe. The brat; looking for the best.
CAMINOS, Vol. 3, no. 8 (September 1982), p.
20. English. **DESCR:** Musicians.

BRAVISIMO

1819 Caldera, Carmela. Coca-Cola president Bryan
Dyson on BRAVISIMO. CAMINOS, Vol. 4, no. 4
(April 1983), p. 44-45,48. Bilingual.
DESCR: Coca-Cola Company; Dyson, Bryan;
Private Funding Sources; Television.

1820 Ogaz, Antonio and Caldera, Carmela. What do
you think of Coca-Cola's sponsorship of
Bravisimo? CAMINOS, Vol. 4, no. 4 (April
1983), p. 46-47. English. **DESCR:** Coca-Cola
Company; Private Funding Sources;
Television.

BRAVISIMO (cont.)

1821 Sutherland, Sam. TV series eyes crossover: BRAVISIMO sets its sights on mainstream audience. BILLBOARD, Vol. 95, (July 30, 1983), p. 50. English. **DESCR:** Broadcast Media; Mass Media; Television.

Brazil

1822 Business/negocios. CAMINOS, Vol. 3, no. 2 (February 1982), p. 22-23. Bilingual. **DESCR:** Argentina; *Business; Chile; Colombia; Federation of Minority Business Associations; FRANCHISE OPPORTUNITIES HANDBOOK; Latin America.

1823 Foreign trade. HISPANIC BUSINESS, Vol. 5, no. 4 (April 1983), p. 22. English. **DESCR:** Banking Industry; *Electronics Industry; Export Trade; *Foreign Trade; Ibero-American Chamber of Commerce; Miami, FL; Minority Bank Development Program (MBDP); Minority Export Development Consultants Program (MEDC); Peace Corps; Puerto Rico.

Breastfeeding

1824 Smith, Jack C. Trends in the incidence of breastfeeding for Hispanics of Mexican origin and Anglos on the US-Mexican border. AMERICAN JOURNAL OF PUBLIC HEALTH, Vol. 72, no. 1 (January 1982), p. 59-61. English. **DESCR:** Anglo Americans; Chicanas; *Maternal and Child Welfare.

Brickmaking

1825 Costello, J. G. Ethnoarchaeology at an Hispanic brick and tile kiln. AMERICAN JOURNAL OF ARCHAEOLOGY, Vol. 86, no. 2 (April 1982), p. 260. English. **DESCR:** Anthropology.

Brigands and Robbers
USE: Bandidos

Briggs, Vernon M.

1826 Miller, Michael V. Book review of: CHICANOS AND RURAL POVERTY. JOURNAL OF ETHNIC STUDIES, Vol. 5, no. 3 (Fall 1977), p. 116-117. English. **DESCR:** Agricultural Laborers; Book Reviews; *CHICANOS AND RURAL POVERTY; Immigration Law; Social History and Conditions; Southwest United States.

Brigham Young University

1827 Math-based careers. HISPANIC BUSINESS, Vol. 4, no. 8 (August 1983), p. 20. English. **DESCR:** Business Administration; *Careers; Coalition of Spanish-Speaking Mental Health Organization (COSSMHO), Annual Regional Conference, Los Angeles, March 14-15, 1975; Cooperative Extension Programs; Education; Employment Training; Financial Aid; Medical Personnel.

Brito, Aristeo

1828 Alarcon, Justo S. Resena de EL DIABLO EN TEXAS. MAIZE, Vol. 3, no. 1-2 (Fall, Winter, 1979, 1980), p. 6-8. Spanish. **DESCR:** Book Reviews; *EL DIABLO EN TEXAS.

Broadcast Media

1829 Armas, Jose. ANTONIO AND THE MAYOR: a cultural review of the film. JOURNAL OF ETHNIC STUDIES, Vol. 3, no. 3 (Fall 1975), p. 98-101. English. **DESCR:** *ANTONIO AND THE MAYOR; Columbia Broadcasting Studios (CBS); Cultural Characteristics; Film Reviews; Films; Mass Media; *Stereotypes.

1830 Bagamery, Anne. SIN, the original. FORBES, Vol. 13, no. 11 (November 22, 1982), p. 96-97. English. **DESCR:** Anselmo, Rene; *Spanish International Network (SIN); Spanish Language; Television.

1831 Balkan, D. Carlos. Mr. Caballero's Spanish radio network. HISPANIC BUSINESS, Vol. 4, no. 5 (May 1982), p. 18-19,26. English. **DESCR:** Advertising; *Caballero Spanish Media, Inc. (CSM); Radio.

1832 Chavarria, Jesus. The media scene. HISPANIC BUSINESS, Vol. 4, no. 5 (May 1982), p. 6. English. **DESCR:** Advertising; Caballero Spanish Media, Inc. (CSM); *Mass Media; MIAMI MENSUAL; Print Media; Radio; Television.

1833 Communications/marketing. HISPANIC BUSINESS, Vol. 5, no. 1 (January 1983), p. 23. English. **DESCR:** Banking Industry; Caballero Spanish Media, Inc. (CSM); Fleishman-Hillard, Inc.; *Marketing; Miami, FL; Nogales, Luis G.; Public Relations.

1834 Communications/marketing. HISPANIC BUSINESS, Vol. 5, no. 2 (February 1983), p. 23. English. **DESCR:** Coopers and Lybrand; Domecq Importers, Inc.; Latin American Feature Syndicate (ALA); *Mass Media; Phoenix, AZ.

1835 Communications/marketing. HISPANIC BUSINESS, Vol. 5, no. 6 (June 1983), p. 16. English. **DESCR:** *Advertising Agencies; Castillo & Castillo Public Relations and Advertising; Castillo, Cid; Castillo, Patricia; Latino Consortium, Los Angeles, CA; Montemayor, Carlos R.; Montemayor y Asociados, Inc.; Zubi Inc., Miami, FL.

1836 Communications/marketing. HISPANIC BUSINESS, Vol. 5, no. 8 (August 1983), p. 26. English. **DESCR:** Advertising Agencies; Bermudez & Associates; Carranza Associates; Directories; Marketing.

1837 Desde Anchorage hasta San Juan. LATINO, Vol. 53, no. 4 (June 1982), p. 14-15. Spanish.

1838 Entertainment = diversion. CAMINOS, Vol. 3, no. 1 (January 1982), p. 41-42. Bilingual. **DESCR:** ANO NUEVO [film]; *CERVANTES [film]; *Films; *SEGUIN [movie]; *Times Mirror Company.

1839 Excerpts from FCC Commissioner Henry M. Rivera. HISPANIC BUSINESS, Vol. 4, no. 5 (May 1982), p. 23. English. **DESCR:** Federal Communications Commission (FCC).

1840 Fantin, Joyce. Some Hispanic stations trying bilingual approach. BILLBOARD, Vol. 94, (November 13, 1982), p. 164. English. **DESCR:** Mass Media; *Radio.

1841 Greenberg, Bradley S. and Heeter, Carrie. Mass media orientations among Hispanic youth. HISPANIC JOURNAL OF BEHAVIORAL SCIENCES, Vol. 5, no. 3 (September 1983), p. 305-323. English. **DESCR:** *Mass Media; Television.

1842 Gupta, Udayan. New York's WNJU Channel 47: Spanish TV's hottest item. HISPANIC BUSINESS, Vol. 5, no. 3 (March 1983), p. 16-17+. English. **DESCR:** *Advertising; Consumers; Marketing; Television; WNJU-TV, Newark, NJ [television station].

Broadcast Media (cont.)

1843 Hispanic owned stations. HISPANIC BUSINESS,
Vol. 4, no. 5 (May 1982), p. 28. English.
DESCR: Radio; Radio Stations; Television;
Television Stations.

1844 Hulin-Salkin, Belinda. Films need mass
appeal. ADVERTISING AGE MAGAZINE, Vol. 53,
(February 15, 1982), p. II, M10. English.
DESCR: Films; *Market Research; Television.

1845 The invisible American. LATINO, Vol. 53, no.
8 (December 1982), p. 8-9. English.

1846 Langley, Roger. Roger Langley's Hispanic
beat. HISPANIC BUSINESS, Vol. 4, no. 5 (May
1982), p. 24. English. **DESCR:** *Television.

1847 McGuire, Jack. Hispanic TV network thrives:
this SIN is legit. ADVERTISING AGE MAGAZINE,
Vol. 53, (February 15, 1982), p. II,
M34-35. English. **DESCR:** *Spanish
International Network (SIN); Spanish
Language; Television.

1848 Navarrete, Diana. Broadcasting role model.
NUESTRO, Vol. 6, no. 1 (January, February,
1982), p. 22-23. English. **DESCR:** Fashion;
Latin Americans; *Navarrete, Diana.

1849 Obledo, Mario. Where are the Latinos?
LATINO, Vol. 54, no. 7 (November 1983), p.
4. English. **DESCR:** Television.

1850 Prime time brown out. LATINO, Vol. 54, no. 8
(December 1983), p. 16-17. English. **DESCR:**
*Television.

1851 Sutherland, Sam. TV series eyes crossover:
BRAVISIMO sets its sights on mainstream
audience. BILLBOARD, Vol. 95, (July 30,
1983), p. 50. English. **DESCR:** *BRAVISIMO;
Mass Media; Television.

1852 Volsky, George. Miami's radio S-U-A-A-V-E.
HISPANIC BUSINESS, Vol. 4, no. 12 (December
1982), p. 22,35. English. **DESCR:**
Advertising; Language Usage; Marketing;
Miami, FL; *Radio; Radio Station SUAVE,
Miami, FL; *Radio Stations; Spanish
Language.

1853 Wittenauer, Cheryl. Dallas Hispanic media.
HISPANIC BUSINESS, Vol. 5, no. 2 (February
1983), p. 12-13+. English. **DESCR:**
*Consumers; Dallas, TX; English Language;
Marketing; Mass Media; Newspapers; Spanish
Language.

1854 Wittenauer, Cheryl. Rating Hispanic media.
HISPANIC BUSINESS, Vol. 5, no. 3 (March
1983), p. 14-15. English. **DESCR:** A.C.
Nielsen Company; Advertising; Arbitron;
Television.

Brocksbank, Robert W.

1855 Brocksbank, Bonilla are winners of LNESC
award. LATINO, Vol. 53, no. 8 (December
1982), p. 26. English. **DESCR:** Bonilla, Tony;
*Education; *League of United Latin American
Citizens (LULAC); LULAC National Education
Service Centers (LNESC).

THE BROKEN COLUMN

1856 Herrera, Hayden. Making an art of pain.
PSYCHOLOGY TODAY, Vol. 17, no. 3 (March
1983), p. 86. English. **DESCR:** Biography;
HENRY FORD HOSPITAL; *Kahlo, Frida;
Paintings; SELF-PORTRAIT WITH PORTRAIT OF
DR. FARILL; THE LITTLE DEER; TREE OF HOPE;
WITHOUT HOPE.

Bronx, NY

1857 Jones, B.E. Manic-depressive illness among
poor urban Hispanics. AMERICAN JOURNAL OF
PSYCHIATRY, Vol. 14, no. 9 (September 1983),
p. 1208-1210. English. **DESCR:** *Mental
Health; Puerto Ricans.

Brooklyn, NY

1858 Fox, Martin. Grand Jury selection upheld
against test by Hispanics. NEW YORK LAW
JOURNAL, Vol. 188, (October 1, 1982), p. 1.
English. **DESCR:** *Juries; People v. Guzman.

Brophy-Good Dyadic Interaction System

1859 Buriel, Raymond, et al. Teacher-student
interactions and their relationship to
student achievement: a comparison of
Mexican-American and Anglo-American
children. JOURNAL OF EDUCATIONAL PSYCHOLOGY,
Vol. 75, no. 6 (December 1983), p. 889-897.
English. **DESCR:** Academic Achievement;
*Primary School Education; Teacher-pupil
Interaction.

Brothers of Light
USE: Hermanos Penitentes

Brown, Edmund G., Jr., Governor of California

1860 Hamner, Richard. Hispanic update: border
governors tackle U.S.-Mexico relations: much
ado: but nothing on immigration. NATIONAL
HISPANIC JOURNAL, Vol. 1, no. 2 (Winter
1982), p. 4-5. English. **DESCR:** Babbitt,
Bruce; Border Region; *Clements, Bill;
Immigration; Immigration Regulation and
Control; Moreno, Paul; *United States-Mexico
Relations.

Brown, Susan E.

1861 Minority access to legal profession is still
limited. CALIFORNIA LAWYER, Vol. 3, no. 4
(April 1983), p. 72. English. **DESCR:** Ethnic
Groups; *Legal Education; Mexican American
Legal Defense and Educational Fund (MALDEF).

1862 Study details minority access to legal
education. NEW JERSEY LAW JOURNAL, Vol. 112,
no. 1 (July 7, 1983), p. 28. English.
DESCR: *Ethnic Groups; *Legal Education;
Mexican American Legal Defense and
Educational Fund (MALDEF); PLURALISM IN THE
LEGAL PROFESSION: MODELS FOR MINORITY
ACCESS; Vasquez, Hector G.

Brownsville, TX

1863 Mena, Jesus. Refugees from poverty: a
Brownsville perspective. NUESTRO, Vol. 7,
no. 4 (May 1983), p. 26. English. **DESCR:**
Border Patrol; *Immigration Regulation and
Control; *Undocumented Workers.

1864 Richardson, Chad and Yanez, Linda. "Equal
justice" and Jose Reyna. NUESTRO, Vol. 6,
no. 5 (June, July, 1982), p. 17. English.
DESCR: *Children; Education; Education
Equalization; Immigration Law; *Legislation;
Reyna, Jose; Undocumented Workers.

Bruce Novoa, Juan

1865 Bell-Villada, G. H. Book review of: CHICANO
AUTHORS, INQUIRY BY INTERVIEW v. 228. NOTES
AND QUERIES, Vol. 30, no. 2 (1983), p.
186-188. English. **DESCR:** Book Reviews;
*CHICANO POETRY: A RESPONSE TO CHAOS;
Literary Criticism.

Bruce Novoa, Juan (cont.)

1866 Book review of: CHICANO POETRY: A RESPONSE TO CHAOS. CHOICE, Vol. 20, no. 6 (February 1983), p. 827. English. **DESCR:** Book Reviews; *CHICANO POETRY: A RESPONSE TO CHAOS.

1867 Bruce Novoa, Juan. Round table on Chicano literature. JOURNAL OF ETHNIC STUDIES, Vol. 3, no. 1 (Spring 1975), p. 99-103. English. **DESCR:** *Literature; Montejano, David; Morton, Carlos; Ortego y Gasca, Felipe de; Teatro.

1868 Lizarraga, Sylvia S. Observaciones acerca de la critica literaria Chicana. REVISTA CHICANO-RIQUENA, Vol. 10, no. 4 (Fall 1982), p. 55-64. Spanish. **DESCR:** CITY OF NIGHT; El Teatro Campesino; *Literary Criticism; Literature; POCHO; THE SPACE OF CHICANO LITERATURE.

1869 Rangel-Guerrero, Daniel. Book review of: CHICANO AUTHORS: INQUIRY BY INTERVIEW. JOURNAL OF ETHNIC STUDIES, Vol. 10, no. 2 (Summer 1982), p. 117-119. English. **DESCR:** Book Reviews; *CHICANO AUTHORS: INQUIRY BY INTERVIEW; Comparative Literature; Literary Criticism; Literary History; Literary Influence; Literature.

1870 Saldivar, Jose David. Book review of: CHICANO POETRY: A RESPONSE TO CHAOS. MELUS: MULTI-ETHNIC LITERATURE OF THE UNITED STATES, Vol. 10, no. 2 (Summer 1983), p. 83-85. English. **DESCR:** Book Reviews; *CHICANO POETRY: A RESPONSE TO CHAOS; Poetry.

1871 Somoza, Oscar U. Book review of: CHICANO AUTHORS: INQUIRY BY INTERVIEW. HISPAMERICA: REVISTA DE LITERATURA, Vol. 11, no. 31 (1982), p. 101-102. Spanish. **DESCR:** Book Reviews; *CHICANO AUTHORS: INQUIRY BY INTERVIEW.

1872 Tammaro, Thom. Book review of: CHICANO POETRY: A RESPONSE TO CHAOS. LIBRARY JOURNAL, Vol. 107, no. 16 (September 15, 1982), p. 1755-1756. English. **DESCR:** Book Reviews; *CHICANO POETRY: A RESPONSE TO CHAOS.

1873 Tatum, Charles. Book review of: CHICANO AUTHORS: INQUIRY BY INTERVIEW. HISPANIA, Vol. 65, no. 4 (December 1982), p. 668. English. **DESCR:** Authors; Book Reviews; *CHICANO AUTHORS: INQUIRY BY INTERVIEW.

Bruckner, D.J.R.

1874 Macias, Reynaldo Flores. Book review of: POLITICS AND LANGUAGE: SPANISH AND ENGLISH IN THE UNITED STATES. NABE JOURNAL, Vol. 7, no. 1 (Fall 1982), p. 61-66. English. **DESCR:** Bilingualism; Book Reviews; Cultural Pluralism; *POLITICS AND LANGUAGE: SPANISH AND ENGLISH IN THE UNITED STATES; Spanish Language.

Brujo

1875 Richardson, Lynette. Caring through understanding, part II: folk medicine in the Hispanic population. IMPRINT, Vol. 29, no. 2 (April 1982), p. 21, 72-77. English. **DESCR:** Caida de Mollera; Curanderas; Empacho; *Folk Medicine; Mal de Ojo; Mal Puesto; Susto.

Buena Vista Cablevision, Inc.

1876 Communications/marketing. HISPANIC BUSINESS, Vol. 4, no. 7 (July 1982), p. 16. English. **DESCR:** Awards; *Biographical Notes; Demy, Caroline; *Marketing; Sosa de Garcia, Manuel.

1877 Entertainment = diversion. CAMINOS, Vol. 3, no. 5 (May 1982), p. 54. Bilingual. **DESCR:** Artists; Cinco de Mayo; *Holidays; Knott's Berry Farm, Buena Park, CA; Tamayo, Rufino; Television.

Building
USE: Architecture

Bullington, Bruce

1878 Hunsaker, Alan. Book review of: ANGEL DUST: AN ETHNOGRAPHIC STUDY OF PCP USERS; HEROIN USE IN THE BARRIO; DRUG AND ALCOHOL ABUSE: A CLINICAL GUIDE TO DIAGNOSIS AND TREATMENT. HISPANIC JOURNAL OF BEHAVIORAL SCIENCES, Vol. 4, no. 1 (March 1982), p. 118-121. English. **DESCR:** Agar, Michael; *ANGEL DUST: AN ETHNOGRAPHIC STUDY OF PCP USERS; Bescher, George; Book Reviews; *DRUG AND ALCOHOL ABUSE: A CLINICAL GUIDE TO DIAGNOSIS AND TREATMENT; Feldman, Harvey W.; *HEROIN USE IN THE BARRIO; Schuckit, Marc A.

Bumpers, Dale

1879 Midwest senator addresses NALEO. NUESTRO, Vol. 6, no. 9 (November 1982), p. 13. English. **DESCR:** Funding Sources; *National Association of Latino Elected Officials (NALEO).

Bunuel, Luis

1880 Monsivais, Carlos. No te muevas, paisaje (sobre el cincuentenario del cine sonoro en Mexico). AZTLAN, Vol. 14, no. 1 (Spring 1983), p. 1-19. Spanish. **DESCR:** Felix, Maria; Fernandez, Emilio; *Films; Mass Media; *Mexico.

Burgillo, Luis

1881 Politicians you didn't vote for. NUESTRO, Vol. 5, no. 8 (November 1981), p. 18-20. English. **DESCR:** *Congressional Aides; Latin Americans; Political Parties and Organizations; *Politics.

Burgos, Elizabeth

1882 Newsfront. HISPANIC BUSINESS, Vol. 4, no. 4 (April 1982), p. 8, 24. English. **DESCR:** *Biographical Notes; *Businesspeople; Flores, Arturo; Garcia, Carlos E.; Garcia, Edward T.; Guzman, Ralph C.; Hernandez, Richard; National Coalition of Hispanic Mental Health and Human Services Organizations (COSSMHO); Parra, Oscar C.; Willie, Herm M.

Burgos, Tony

1883 People. HISPANIC BUSINESS, Vol. 5, no. 10 (October 1983), p. 10. English. **DESCR:** Anaya, Toney; Arriola, Elvia Rosales; Babbitt, Bruce; Bush, George; *Businesspeople; Cisneros, Henry, Mayor of San Antonio, TX; Cruz, Jose; Kennedy, Edward M.; Montano, Gilbert; Reagan, Ronald; White, Mark.

Burgos-Sasscer. Ruth

1884 Flemming, Donald N. Book review of: EXPLORACIONES CHICANO-RIQUENAS. MODERN LANGUAGE JOURNAL, Vol. 66, no. 2 (Summer 1982), p. 233-234. English. **DESCR:** Book Reviews; *EXPLORACIONES CHICANO-RIQUENAS; Textbooks; Williams, Shirley.

Burgos-Sasscer. Ruth (cont.)

1885 Somoza, Oscar U. Book review of:
EXPLORACIONES CHICANO-RIQUENAS. HISPANIA,
Vol. 65, no. 4 (December 1982), p. 668-669.
Spanish. **DESCR:** Book Reviews; *EXPLORACIONES
CHICANO-RIQUENAS; Textbooks; Williams,
Shirley.

Bush, George

1886 People. HISPANIC BUSINESS, Vol. 5, no. 10
(October 1983), p. 10. English. **DESCR:**
Anaya, Toney; Arriola, Elvia Rosales;
Babbitt, Bruce; Burgos, Tony;
*Businesspeople; Cisneros, Henry, Mayor of
San Antonio, TX; Cruz, Jose; Kennedy, Edward
M.; Montano, Gilbert; Reagan, Ronald; White,
Mark.

Business

1887 7-Eleven does it right. LATINO, Vol. 54, no.
5 (August, September, 1983), p. 18-19.
English.

1888 Acosta, Maria D. Hispanic business in the
80's/el negocio Hispanico en los ochentas.
CAMINOS, Vol. 3, no. 2 (February 1982), p.
24-26. Bilingual. **DESCR:** *U.S. Small
Business Administration.

1889 Alvarado, Linda. A new day for Hispanic
business. LATINO, Vol. 53, no. 1 (January,
February, 1982), p. 8-9. English.

1890 Barreto, Julio. Where the jobs are: tips
from Latinos in key occupations. NUESTRO,
Vol. 6, no. 7 (September 1982), p. 18-23.
English. **DESCR:** Businesspeople; Curriculum;
*Employment.

1891 Booming Latino business. LATINO, Vol. 54,
no. 5 (August, September, 1983), p. 28.
English.

1892 Boost for Hispanic business. LATINO, Vol.
53, no. 6 (October 1982), p. 5. English.

1893 Business/negocios. CAMINOS, Vol. 3, no. 2
(February 1982), p. 22-23. Bilingual.
DESCR: Argentina; Brazil; Chile; Colombia;
Federation of Minority Business
Associations; FRANCHISE OPPORTUNITIES
HANDBOOK; Latin America.

1894 Calero, Jose. Opportunity or obstacle (it's
your choice) [editorial]. CAMINOS, Vol. 3,
no. 2 (February 1982), p. 21. English.

1895 Calvillo-Craig, Lorenza. Bilingual education
and business. CAMINOS, Vol. 3, no. 10
(November 1982), p. 41. Bilingual. **DESCR:**
*Bilingual Bicultural Education.

1896 Castor wins Michelob account. LATINO, Vol.
54, no. 5 (August, September, 1983), p. 28.
English.

1897 Chamber, construction group given SBA aid.
NUESTRO, Vol. 6, no. 7 (September 1982), p.
51. English. **DESCR:** *Businesspeople; *U.S.
Small Business Administration.

1898 Chamber, Peace Corps join in training
effort. NUESTRO, Vol. 7, no. 1 (January,
February, 1983), p. 36. English. **DESCR:**
Caribbean Basin Initiative (CBI);
*Ibero-American Chamber of Commerce; Latin
America; Peace Corps.

1899 Chavarria, Jesus. The world according to
Miami. HISPANIC BUSINESS, Vol. 4, no. 3
(March 1982), p. 6. English. **DESCR:** Carnaval

Miami 82; Cubanos; Miami, FL; *Urban
Communities.

1900 Coca-Cola USA Today outlines Latino agenda.
NUESTRO, Vol. 7, no. 9 (November 1983), p.
36. English. **DESCR:** Coca-Cola Company;
*Coca-Cola National Hispanic Education Fund;
Education; *Financial Aid; Funding Sources.

1901 Corporate-education team. LATINO, Vol. 53,
no. 2 (March, April, 1982), p. 11+. English.
DESCR: *League of United Latin American
Citizens (LULAC).

1902 Davis, Lisa. Workers or owners. LATINO, Vol.
53, no. 1 (January, February, 1982), p. 16.
English.

1903 Edmunds, Stahrl W. California-Mexico trade
relations. CAMINOS, Vol. 4, no. 11 (December
1983), p. 20-21,38. Bilingual. **DESCR:** Border
Region; *California; *United States-Mexico
Relations.

1904 Ferre, Maurice A. Marketplace of the
Americas. HISPANIC BUSINESS, Vol. 4, no. 3
(March 1982), p. 8. English. **DESCR:** Miami,
FL; *Urban Communities.

1905 From the SBA. CAMINOS, Vol. 3, no. 2
(February 1982), p. 42. English. **DESCR:**
*Statistics; *U.S. Small Business
Administration.

1906 The future beckons, USC's LBSA responds.
HISPANIC BUSINESS, Vol. 4, no. 4 (April
1982), p. 12, 25. English. **DESCR:** Business
Education; Business Schools and Colleges;
Educational Opportunities; *Latino Business
Students Association (LBSA); University of
Southern California.

1907 Guernica, Antonio. El mercado hispano.
LATINO, Vol. 53, no. 6 (October 1982), p.
12. Spanish.

1908 The Hispanic market: a reality of the 1980s.
LATINO, Vol. 53, no. 2 (March, April, 1982),
p. 29. English.

1909 Houstonite builds successful business:
home-started business exceeds millions in
foreign trade sales. NATIONAL HISPANIC
JOURNAL, Vol. 1, no. 4 (Spring 1983), p. 7.
English. **DESCR:** *Business Enterprises;
Businesspeople; Cavazos, Roy; Minority
Business Development Agency (MBDA);
*National Economic Development Association
(NEDA); U.S. Small Business Administration.

1910 Latino business study launched by chamber.
NUESTRO, Vol. 6, no. 3 (April 1982), p. 45.
English. **DESCR:** Latin Americans.

1911 Mexican business update. HISPANIC BUSINESS,
Vol. 4, no. 1 (January 1982), p. 24.
English. **DESCR:** Export Trade; *Foreign
Trade; Mexico; *U.S.-Mexico Joint Commission
on Commerce and Trade.

1912 Minority business week observed. LATINO,
Vol. 54, no. 6 (October 1983), p. 5.
English.

1913 Molina, Raymond. Como mantener la tecnologia
moderna? LATINO, Vol. 53, no. 4 (June 1982),
p. 13. Spanish.

Business (cont.)

1914 Movement of illegal alien laborers into United States is Hobbs act "Commerce". CRIMINAL LAW REPORTER, Vol. 31, no. 19 (August 18, 1982), p. 2394. English. **DESCR**: Hobbs Act; *Undocumented Workers; U.S. v. Hanigan.

1915 NEDA is out of business. LATINO, Vol. 53, no. 1 (January, February, 1982), p. 17. English.

1916 News at the SBA. HISPANIC BUSINESS, Vol. 4, no. 3 (March 1982), p. 14. English. **DESCR**: Business Enterprises; Cardenas, Maria Elena; Small Business Administration 8(a) Program; U.S. Small Business Administration.

1917 Obledo, Mario. End the dairy subsidy. LATINO, Vol. 54, no. 8 (December 1983), p. 6. English. **DESCR**: *Government Contracts.

1918 Pacific direct mail services. CAMINOS, Vol. 3, no. 2 (February 1982), p. 30-32. Bilingual. **DESCR**: Businesspeople; *Pacific Direct Mail Service, Inc., Los Angeles, CA; *Rivera, Julio.

1919 Pendleton, Jennifer. Battle for the buck is the tale of two cities: marketers in San Diego and Tijuana square off. ADVERTISING AGE MAGAZINE, Vol. 53, (February 15, 1982), p. II, M42-43. English. **DESCR**: Advertising; Border Region; *Market Research; San Diego, CA; Tijuana, Mexico.

1920 Quesada-Weiner, Rosemary. Latin Business Association (photoessay). CAMINOS, Vol. 3, no. 2 (February 1982), p. 33. Bilingual. **DESCR**: *Professional Organizations.

1921 Quijada. What the corporate world wants and expects. CAMINOS, Vol. 4, no. 1-2 (January, February, 1983), p. 13-14,16+. Bilingual. **DESCR**: *Careers.

1922 Research/development: books. HISPANIC BUSINESS, Vol. 4, no. 2 (February 1982), p. 28. English. **DESCR**: Book Reviews; Business Enterprises; *FINANCING YOUR BUSINESS; *Loffel, Egon W.; *National Hispanic Center for Advanced Studies and Policy Analysis (NHCAS); Public Policy; *THE STATE OF HISPANIC AMERICA.

1923 Rinco, Marcos. U.S. Hispanic Chamber's national convention. CAMINOS, Vol. 3, no. 10 (November 1982), p. 30-31. English. **DESCR**: *U.S. Hispanic Chamber of Commerce.

1924 Rivera, Victor M. Goal for the 1980s for minority-owned businesses is expansion. LATINO, Vol. 53, no. 1 (January, February, 1982), p. 10-11+. English.

1925 Riverside's Hispanic Chamber of Commerce. CAMINOS, Vol. 3, no. 8 (September 1982), p. 46. English. **DESCR**: *Organizations; Riverside, CA.

1926 Roberto Varela and TLC. CAMINOS, Vol. 3, no. 2 (February 1982), p. 27-29. Bilingual. **DESCR**: *Businesspeople; Tape & Label Converters (TLC); *Varela, Robert.

1927 Southwest regional conference of Hispanic Chamber of Commerce. CAMINOS, Vol. 4, no. 9 (October 1983), p. 60. English. **DESCR**: Clergy; *U.S. Hispanic Chamber of Commerce.

1928 Students view career option. NUESTRO, Vol. 6, no. 6 (August 1982), p. 12. English. **DESCR**: Careers; Phoenix, AZ; Students.

1929 Superlearning for business. LATINO, Vol. 53, no. 4 (June 1982), p. 24. English.

1930 Trujillo, Leo G. Don't forget corporate business as a career. CAMINOS, Vol. 4, no. 1-2 (January, February, 1983), p. 7-8,71. Bilingual. **DESCR**: *Careers.

1931 Whitefield, Mimi. Miami, Caribbean megalopolis. HISPANIC BUSINESS, Vol. 4, no. 3 (March 1982), p. 18-19+. English. **DESCR**: Dade County, FL; Foreign Trade; Miami, FL; *Urban Communities.

Business Administration

1932 Business notes. HISPANIC BUSINESS, Vol. 5, no. 10 (October 1983), p. 13. English. **DESCR**: Business Enterprises; Claudio, Irma; Investments; Los Angeles Board of Public Works; Oakland, CA; Taxation; Tri-Oakland Development Corporation; Wisconsin Minority Business Forum '83.

1933 Math-based careers. HISPANIC BUSINESS, Vol. 4, no. 8 (August 1983), p. 20. English. **DESCR**: Brigham Young University; *Careers; Coalition of Spanish-Speaking Mental Health Organization (COSSMHO), Annual Regional Conference, Los Angeles, March 14-15, 1975; Cooperative Extension Programs; Education; Employment Training; Financial Aid; Medical Personnel.

1934 Mestre, Mercedes. Paving the path. HISPANIC BUSINESS, Vol. 5, no. 10 (October 1983), p. 9. English. **DESCR**: Education; *Employment; Employment Training; *Korn/Ferry International.

Business Education

1935 The future beckons, USC's LBSA responds. HISPANIC BUSINESS, Vol. 4, no. 4 (April 1982), p. 12, 25. English. **DESCR**: Business; Business Schools and Colleges; Educational Opportunities; *Latino Business Students Association (LBSA); University of Southern California.

1936 Maestas, R. W. Bilingualism in business education. JOURNAL OF BUSINESS EDUCATION, Vol. 57, (May 1982), p. 313-315. English. **DESCR**: *Bilingualism.

Business Enterprises

1937 Administration unveils minority business enterprise initiative. HISPANIC BUSINESS, Vol. 4, no. 10 (October 1982), p. 18. English. **DESCR**: Minority Business Development Agency (MBDA).

1938 AM-COR Architects & Engineers, Inc. aligns growth. HISPANIC BUSINESS, Vol. 4, no. 7 (July 1982), p. 12-13. English. **DESCR**: *Engineering; Engineering as a Profession; Pueblo, CO.

1939 Balkan, D. Carlos. AMEX Systems Inc. at transition point. HISPANIC BUSINESS, Vol. 4, no. 6 (June 1982), p. 18-19,24. English. **DESCR**: AMEX Systems, Inc.; Caldera, Manuel R.; *Corporations; High Technology Industries; Small Business Administration 8(a) Program; U.S. Small Business Administration.

1940 Balkan, D. Carlos. The Hispanic business top 400 in sales. HISPANIC BUSINESS, Vol. 5, no. 6 (June 1983), p. 18-20+. English. **DESCR**: *Directories.

Business Enterprises (cont.)

1941 Balkan, D. Carlos. The Hispanic market: leading indicators. HISPANIC BUSINESS, Vol. 5, no. 12 (December 1983), p. 14-15. English. **DESCR:** Advertising; *Marketing.

1942 Balkan, D. Carlos. The nuclear powered Mr. Carlos Pimentel. HISPANIC BUSINESS, Vol. 4, no. 2 (February 1982), p. 16-17+. English. **DESCR:** Biography; Businesspeople; *Cataract Engineering and Construction, Inc.; Energy Industries; *Pimentel, Carlos.

1943 Balkan, D. Carlos and Cruz, Franklin D. Space-Craft's strategy for re-industrialization. HISPANIC BUSINESS, Vol. 4, no. 11 (November 1982), p. 16-17,26. English. **DESCR:** Connecticut; *High Technology Industries; Soto, John; Space-Craft Manufacturing, Inc.

1944 Business notes. HISPANIC BUSINESS, Vol. 5, no. 10 (October 1983), p. 13. English. **DESCR:** *Business Administration; Claudio, Irma; Investments; Los Angeles Board of Public Works; Oakland, CA; Taxation; Tri-Oakland Development Corporation; Wisconsin Minority Business Forum '83.

1945 Business notes. HISPANIC BUSINESS, Vol. 5, no. 11 (November 1983), p. 27. English. **DESCR:** Garment Industry; High Tech '84; Personnel Management; Puerto Rico; Taxation; U.S. Department of Housing and Urban Development (HUD).

1946 Business notes. HISPANIC BUSINESS, Vol. 5, no. 12 (December 1983), p. 35. English. **DESCR:** Anheuser-Busch, Inc.; Denny's Inc.; Des Moines, IA; El Pollo Loco; Food Industry; Local Government; Martinez, Vilma Socorro; National Association of Latino Elected Officials (NALEO); Ochoa, Juan Pancho.

1947 Business update: Ibero-American chamber has gala, makes awards. NUESTRO, Vol. 7, no. 5 (June, July, 1983), p. 52. English. **DESCR:** Awards; Greater Washington Ibero-American Chamber of Commerce.

1948 Business update: West Coast food firm given special honors. NUESTRO, Vol. 7, no. 4 (May 1983), p. 42. English. **DESCR:** Food Industry; *Ruiz Food Products, Inc., Tulare, CA.

1949 Caldera, Carmela. The consummate salesman: Rudy Cervantes. CAMINOS, Vol. 4, no. 4 (April 1983), p. 25-27. Bilingual. **DESCR:** *Cervantes, Rudy; Olympics.

1950 Caldera, Carmela. Floyd Aragon: filling voids with his entrepreneurship. CAMINOS, Vol. 4, no. 4 (April 1983), p. 28-30, 66. Bilingual. **DESCR:** *Aragon, Floyd; L.A. Button Company; Olympics.

1951 Cantu, Hector. Aqui en Texas: ex-boxer finds success in restaurant: Matt's of Austin one of Texas's most successful restaurants. NATIONAL HISPANIC JOURNAL, Vol. 2, no. 1 (Summer 1983), p. 6. English. **DESCR:** Martinez, Matt.

1952 Cantu, Hector. The island. NATIONAL HISPANIC JOURNAL, Vol. 1, no. 3 (Summer, Fall, 1982), p. 6. English. **DESCR:** *Castanon, Rudy; *Curanderismo.

1953 Chavarria, Jesus. The entrepreneurial reflex. HISPANIC BUSINESS, Vol. 5, no. 1 (January 1983), p. 6. English. **DESCR:** Arroyos, Alex; Digitron Tool Company, Inc.; Dynamic Ocean Service, Inc.; Fernandez, Nestor.

1954 Chavarria, Jesus. The largest Hispanic firms. HISPANIC BUSINESS, Vol. 4, no. 6 (June 1982), p. 6. English. **DESCR:** AMEX Systems, Inc.; Jimenez Food Products, Inc.

1955 Chavarria, Jesus. Researching the 400. HISPANIC BUSINESS, Vol. 5, no. 6 (June 1983), p. 6. English. **DESCR:** *Directories; Hispanic Business 400.

1956 Chavarria, Jesus. Varieties of energy. HISPANIC BUSINESS, Vol. 4, no. 2 (February 1982), p. 6. English. **DESCR:** *Cataract Engineering and Construction, Inc.; Energy Industries; *Star-Adair Insulation, Inc.

1957 Communications/marketing. HISPANIC BUSINESS, Vol. 5, no. 9 (September 1983), p. 26. English. **DESCR:** Aguirre, Horacio; Consumers; DIARIO DE LAS AMERICAS; La Ventana; *Marketing; Miller Brewing Company; SURVEY OF PROMOTIONAL PRACTICES.

1958 Deibel, Richard and Balkan, D. Carlos. The nation's largest little bank: Laredo's International Bank of Commerce. HISPANIC BUSINESS, Vol. 4, no. 9 (September 1982), p. 10-11,24. English. **DESCR:** Banking Industry; *International Bank of Commerce (IBOC); Laredo, TX.

1959 Entrepreneurial incentives. HISPANIC BUSINESS, Vol. 5, no. 6 (June 1983), p. 42. English. **DESCR:** Businesspeople.

1960 Fletcher and Valenti: Tampa's growing arquitectural firm. HISPANIC BUSINESS, Vol. 4, no. 10 (October 1982), p. 15,26. English. **DESCR:** *Architecture; Fletcher & Valenti Architects/Planners, Inc.; Tampa, FL; Valenti, Frank S.

1961 Foster, Richard. Two Alvarados make one sucessful construction firm. HISPANIC BUSINESS, Vol. 4, no. 10 (October 1982), p. 10-11,26. English. **DESCR:** Alvarado, Bob; Alvarado, Linda M.; Construction Industry; Small Business Administration 8(a) Program; U.S. Small Business Administration.

1962 Garcia, Art R. Star Adair Insulation Inc. spurts to new growth. HISPANIC BUSINESS, Vol. 4, no. 2 (February 1982), p. 18-19+. English. **DESCR:** Biography; Businesspeople; *Cisneros, Ignacio; Minority Enterprise Small Business Investment Corporation (MESBIC); *Star-Adair Insulation, Inc.

1963 Goodman, Gerson. "ES PARA USTED": CSI aims for satisfaction. HISPANIC BUSINESS, Vol. 4, no. 12 (December 1982), p. 16-17,34. English. **DESCR:** Advertising Agencies; Aguirre, Jack; Consumers; CSI International, Inc.; Fernandez, Castor A.; *Marketing.

1964 Goodman, Gerson. LRF takes on Battery Park City. HISPANIC BUSINESS, Vol. 4, no. 10 (October 1982), p. 16-17,24. English. **DESCR:** Construction Industry; *LRF Developers, Inc.; NEW YORK; *Real Estate.

1965 Government review. NUESTRO, Vol. 7, no. 2 (March 1983), p. 42. English. **DESCR:** A WORKING WOMAN'S GUIDE TO HER JOB RIGHTS; Adoption; Census; Chicanas; Discrimination in Employment; *Government Services; GUIDE TO FEDERAL MINORITY ENTERPRISE AND RELATED ASSISTANCE PROGRAMS; Population Trends; Study Abroad; U.S. Information Agency (USIA).

Business Enterprises (cont.)

1966 Gupta, Udayan. Netting success: Apoca's approach. HISPANIC BUSINESS, Vol. 5, no. 7 (July 1983), p. 20-21+. English. **DESCR:** Abrilz, Santos T. (Sandy); Businesspeople; Success; *Telecommunications.

1967 The Hispanic business directory of the 400 largest corporations. HISPANIC BUSINESS, Vol. 4, no. 6 (June 1982), p. 11-16. English. **DESCR:** *Corporations; *Television.

1968 Houstonite builds successful business: home-started business exceeds millions in foreign trade sales. NATIONAL HISPANIC JOURNAL, Vol. 1, no. 4 (Spring 1983), p. 7. English. **DESCR:** Business; Businesspeople; Cavazos, Roy; Minority Business Development Agency (MBDA); *National Economic Development Association (NEDA); U.S. Small Business Administration.

1969 The leading US Hispanic-owned minority banks according to assets. HISPANIC BUSINESS, Vol. 4, no. 9 (September 1982), p. 14. English. **DESCR:** *Banking Industry; Minority Bank Deposit Program (MBDP).

1970 NALEO audits the Feds. HISPANIC BUSINESS, Vol. 5, no. 10 (October 1983), p. 16. English. **DESCR:** Federal Government; *Government Contracts; Minority Business Development Agency (MBDA); *National Association of Latino Elected Officials (NALEO); U.S. Department of Defense (DOD); U.S. Department of Health and Human Services.

1971 New York's tele-signal corporation. HISPANIC BUSINESS, Vol. 4, no. 11 (November 1982), p. 20. English. **DESCR:** *High Technology Industries; NEW YORK; *Tele-Signal Corporation; Toracida, Esteben.

1972 News at the SBA. HISPANIC BUSINESS, Vol. 4, no. 3 (March 1982), p. 14. English. **DESCR:** *Business; Cardenas, Maria Elena; Small Business Administration 8(a) Program; U.S. Small Business Administration.

1973 Padilla, Steve. You've come a long way, baby. Or have you? NUESTRO, Vol. 7, no. 6 (August 1983), p. 38-41. English. **DESCR:** Chicanas; Minority Business Development Agency (MBDA); National Alliance of Homebased Businesswomen.

1974 Produce firm to close doors. NUESTRO, Vol. 7, no. 6 (August 1983), p. 12. English. **DESCR:** *Agribusiness; Agricultural Labor Unions; *Sun Harvest, Inc.; United Farmworkers of America (UFW).

1975 Research/development: books. HISPANIC BUSINESS, Vol. 4, no. 2 (February 1982), p. 28. English. **DESCR:** Book Reviews; Business; *FINANCING YOUR BUSINESS; *Loffel, Egon W.; *National Hispanic Center for Advanced Studies and Policy Analysis (NHCAS); Public Policy; *THE STATE OF HISPANIC AMERICA.

1976 Rivera, Victor M. Trends in minority business enterprise. HISPANIC BUSINESS, Vol. 5, no. 6 (June 1983), p. 12. English.

1977 Salazar, Pamela Eoff. Selling $25 million of Jimenez Food Products. HISPANIC BUSINESS, Vol. 4, no. 6 (June 1982), p. 20-21,24. English. **DESCR:** Food Industry; *Jimenez Food Products, Inc.; Recipes.

1978 Sargeant, Georgia. Young turks set new standards. HISPANIC BUSINESS, Vol. 5, no. 11 (November 1983), p. 8-9. English. **DESCR:** Alvarez, Julio E.; *Architecture; Management; Marketing; Miami, FL; Taracido, Manuel E.; Wolfberg, David A.; *Wolfberg/Alvarez/Taracido (WAT).

1979 Triana, Armando R. and Balkan, D. Carlos. Four little-known facts about Hispanic business firms. HISPANIC BUSINESS, Vol. 5, no. 6 (June 1983), p. 10-11. English. **DESCR:** Small Business.

1980 Vara, Richard. Business savvy and Capricorn spirit: How do you spell entrepreneurship? HISPANIC BUSINESS, Vol. 5, no. 1 (January 1983), p. 18-19+. English. **DESCR:** Arroyos, Alex; *Biography; Export Trade; Houston, TX.

1981 Volsky, George and Masvidal, Raul. An interview with Raul Masvidal. HISPANIC BUSINESS, Vol. 4, no. 9 (September 1982), p. 16-17,24+. English. **DESCR:** Banking Industry; Biography; Businesspeople; Cubanos; *Masvidal, Raul; Miami, FL.

1982 Weber, Robert. Rising star: Satelco. HISPANIC BUSINESS, Vol. 5, no. 9 (September 1983), p. 14. English. **DESCR:** Lagueruela, Andy; *Satelco, Inc.; Telecommunications; Veve, Rafael.

1983 Weber, Robert. The special talent of digitron's Nestor Fernandez. HISPANIC BUSINESS, Vol. 5, no. 1 (January 1983), p. 10-11+. English. **DESCR:** Dayton, Ohio; Digitron Tool Company, Inc.; Fernandez, Nestor; Financial Planning.

1984 Weber, Robert. Summa's Tumortec/hCG. HISPANIC BUSINESS, Vol. 5, no. 7 (July 1983), p. 18-19+. English. **DESCR:** Businesspeople; *Medical Research; Summa Medical Corporation.

1985 White House honors three minority firms. NUESTRO, Vol. 7, no. 8 (October 1983), p. 51. English. **DESCR:** Businesspeople; Carson, Norris L.; H & H Meat Products, Mercedes, TX; Hinojosa, Liborio; J.T. Construction Co., El Paso, TX; National Minority Enterprise Development Week; N.L. Carson Construction, Inc., Carthage, MS; Torres, Jaime.

1986 Women entrepreneurs offered SBA assistance. NUESTRO, Vol. 7, no. 1 (January, February, 1983), p. 47. English. **DESCR:** Businesspeople; *Chicanas; U.S. Small Business Administration.

1987 Zuniga, Jo Ann and Bonilla, Tony. Talking Texas: turning the tables with LULAC. HISPANIC BUSINESS, Vol. 5, no. 9 (September 1983), p. 18-19+. English. **DESCR:** *Bonilla, Tony; Consumers; Economic History and Conditions; League of United Latin American Citizens (LULAC); Marketing; Texas.

Business Schools and Colleges

1988 The future beckons, USC's LBSA responds. HISPANIC BUSINESS, Vol. 4, no. 4 (April 1982), p. 12, 25. English. **DESCR:** Business; Business Education; Educational Opportunities; *Latino Business Students Association (LBSA); University of Southern California.

Business Schools and Colleges (cont.)

1989 Wittenauer, Cheryl. Harvard's Latino Association. HISPANIC BUSINESS, Vol. 5, no. 4 (April 1983), p. 12-13+. English. DESCR: *Harvard Business School's Latino Association; Harvard University; Student Organizations.

Businesspeople

1990 Balkan, D. Carlos. The nuclear powered Mr. Carlos Pimentel. HISPANIC BUSINESS, Vol. 4, no. 2 (February 1982), p. 16-17+. English. DESCR: Biography; Business Enterprises; *Cataract Engineering and Construction, Inc.; Energy Industries; *Pimentel, Carlos.

1991 Ballard, Lee. Tom Marquez and the EDS mode. HISPANIC BUSINESS, Vol. 5, no. 2 (February 1983), p. 10-11+. English. DESCR: *Biography; Electronic Data Systems (EDS); Marquez, Tom; Perot, Ross; War on Drugs.

1992 Barreto, Julio. Where the jobs are: tips from Latinos in key occupations. NUESTRO, Vol. 6, no. 7 (September 1982), p. 18-23. English. DESCR: Business; Curriculum; *Employment.

1993 Barry, Patrick. Saturdays are wedding cakes. NUESTRO, Vol. 6, no. 9 (November 1982), p. 31-33. English. DESCR: Chicago, IL; Fasco, Luis; Weddings.

1994 Chamber, construction group given SBA aid. NUESTRO, Vol. 6, no. 7 (September 1982), p. 51. English. DESCR: *Business; *U.S. Small Business Administration.

1995 Chavarria, Jesus. Chambers meet, Minnesota shines. HISPANIC BUSINESS, Vol. 4, no. 10 (October 1982), p. 6. English. DESCR: *Chamber of Commerce; U.S. Hispanic Chamber of Commerce.

1996 Chavarria, Jesus. How long will it last? HISPANIC BUSINESS, Vol. 4, no. 1 (January 1982), p. 6. English. DESCR: Anselmo, Rene; Lasa, Luis; *Marketing; Spanish International Network (SIN).

1997 Entrepreneurial incentives. HISPANIC BUSINESS, Vol. 5, no. 6 (June 1983), p. 42. English. DESCR: *Business Enterprises.

1998 Fernandez, John P. Facing the hard realities of corporate advancement. HISPANIC BUSINESS, Vol. 4, no. 4 (April 1982), p. 18-19,25. English. DESCR: *Affirmative Action; *Discrimination in Employment; Mentors; Self-Help Groups.

1999 Garcia, Art R. Star Adair Insulation Inc. spurts to new growth. HISPANIC BUSINESS, Vol. 4, no. 2 (February 1982), p. 18-19+. English. DESCR: Biography; Business Enterprises; *Cisneros, Ignacio; Minority Enterprise Small Business Investment Corporation (MESBIC); *Star-Adair Insulation, Inc.

2000 Gupta, Udayan. Netting success: Apoca's approach. HISPANIC BUSINESS, Vol. 5, no. 7 (July 1983), p. 20-21+. English. DESCR: Abrilz, Santos T. (Sandy); Business Enterprises; Success; *Telecommunications.

2001 Houstonite builds successful business: home-started business exceeds millions in foreign trade sales. NATIONAL HISPANIC JOURNAL, Vol. 1, no. 4 (Spring 1983), p. 7. English. DESCR: Business; *Business Enterprises; Cavazos, Roy; Minority Business

Development Agency (MBDA); *National Economic Development Association (NEDA); U.S. Small Business Administration.

2002 Manuel Sanchez: the joy of big business. CAMINOS, Vol. 3, no. 2 (February 1982), p. 34-36. Bilingual. DESCR: Blue Cross of Southern California; *Sanchez, Manuel.

2003 Miami's thriving Camacol. HISPANIC BUSINESS, Vol. 4, no. 3 (March 1982), p. 12-13. English. DESCR: Camara de Comercio Latina de Los Estados Unidos (CAMACOL); *Chamber of Commerce; Miami, FL.

2004 Newsfront. HISPANIC BUSINESS, Vol. 4, no. 2 (February 1982), p. 7. English. DESCR: Asip, Patricia V.; Banuelos, Ramona Acosta; *Biographical Notes; Gonzalez, Henry B.; Gutierrez, Alberto; IMAGE, Washington, DC.

2005 Newsfront. HISPANIC BUSINESS, Vol. 4, no. 1 (January 1982), p. 7. English. DESCR: *Biographical Notes; Community Development; Jimenez, Richard D.; Macias, Miguel (Mike); Oaxaca, Jaime; The East Los Angeles Community Union (TELACU); Viramontes, Carlos.

2006 Newsfront. HISPANIC BUSINESS, Vol. 4, no. 3 (March 1982), p. 9. English. DESCR: Appointed Officials; *Biographical Notes; Chicano Film Exhibition and Festival, Detroit, Michigan, April 5-9, 1982; Garcia, Gloria; League of United Latin American Citizens (LULAC); Martinez, Vilma Socorro; National Association for Bilingual Education; Seaga, Edward; Suarez, Carlos R.

2007 Newsfront. HISPANIC BUSINESS, Vol. 4, no. 4 (April 1982), p. 8, 24. English. DESCR: *Biographical Notes; Burgos, Elizabeth; Flores, Arturo; Garcia, Carlos E.; Garcia, Edward T.; Guzman, Ralph C.; Hernandez, Richard; National Coalition of Hispanic Mental Health and Human Services Organizations (COSSMHO); Parra, Oscar C.; Willie, Herm M.

2008 Nuestra gente. LATINO, Vol. 54, no. 4 (May, June, 1983), p. 30. English.

2009 Nuestra gente. LATINO, Vol. 54, no. 6 (October 1983), p. 22. English.

2010 Nuestra gente. LATINO, Vol. 54, no. 8 (December 1983), p. 30. English. DESCR: *Biographical Notes; Carter, Lynda Cordoba; Duran, Sandra; Patino, Lorenzo E.; Politics; Rembis, Deborah; Vega, Christopher.

2011 Pacific direct mail services. CAMINOS, Vol. 3, no. 2 (February 1982), p. 30-32. Bilingual. DESCR: *Business; *Pacific Direct Mail Service, Inc., Los Angeles, CA; *Rivera, Julio.

2012 Padilla, Steve. Adelina Pena Callahan: restaurateur. NUESTRO, Vol. 7, no. 4 (May 1983), p. 26-29. English. DESCR: *Callahan, Adelina Pena; *Careers; Food Industry; La Fonda Restaurant; Working Women.

2013 People. HISPANIC BUSINESS, Vol. 4, no. 5 (May 1982), p. 8. English. DESCR: Appointed Officials; Asociacion Internacional de Exportadores e Importadores (EXIMA); *Biographical Notes; California Chicano News Media Association (CCNMA); de la Ossa, Ernest G.; Foreign Trade; Obledo, Mario; Rodriguez, Elias C.; Rodriguez, Samuel F.; United Way; U.S. Hispanic Chamber of Commerce.

Businesspeople (cont.)

2014 People. HISPANIC BUSINESS, Vol. 4, no. 6 (June 1982), p. 8. English. **DESCR:** Aguirre, Pedro; Arellano, Richard; *Biographical Notes; Cortez, Pete; De la Colina, Rafael; Hernandez, Sam; Nogales, Luis; Rodriguez, Leslie J.; Roybal, Edward R.

2015 People. HISPANIC BUSINESS, Vol. 4, no. 7 (July 1982), p. 7. English. **DESCR:** Aguilar, Richard; *Biographical Notes; Coronado, Julius; Enriquez, Rene; Garza, Jose S.; Guerra-Martinez, Celina; Medrano, Adan; Mota, Manny; Valenti, Frank S.

2016 People. HISPANIC BUSINESS, Vol. 4, no. 10 (October 1982), p. 7. English. **DESCR:** Aguilar, Gloria; Biographical Notes; Caldera, Manuel R.; Lopez, Victor M.; Ramirez, Steve.

2017 People. HISPANIC BUSINESS, Vol. 4, no. 11 (November 1982), p. 7. English. **DESCR:** Biographical Notes; Diaz, Jose; Garcia-Pedrosa, Jose R.; Garza, Jose; Herrera, Heriberto; Mercado, Anthony; Rios, John F.; Solano, Faustina V.; Solis, Frank.

2018 People. HISPANIC BUSINESS, Vol. 4, no. 12 (December 1982), p. 10. English. **DESCR:** *Biographical Notes; Garcia, Frances; Gort, Wilfredo; Ojeda, Armando; Olind, Rebecca Nieto; Philip Morris, Inc.; Roybal, Edward R.

2019 People. HISPANIC BUSINESS, Vol. 5, no. 1 (January 1983), p. 7. English. **DESCR:** Appointed Officials; *Biographical Notes; Elizalde, Hector; Mackey y Salazar, C.; Madrid, Carlos; Montoya, Velma; Nunez, Carlos; Perea, Stanley; Rodriguez, Rita; Valdes, Martha.

2020 People. HISPANIC BUSINESS, Vol. 5, no. 2 (February 1983), p. 7. English. **DESCR:** Alvarez, Everett, Jr.; Appointed Officials; *Biographical Notes; Guzman-Randle, Irene; Roubin, Angel; Vasquez, Victor; Villareal, Luis Maria.

2021 People. HISPANIC BUSINESS, Vol. 5, no. 4 (April 1983), p. 9. English. **DESCR:** Alvarado, Linda M.; *Biographical Notes; Castillo, Irenemaree; Castillo, Sylvia; Del Junco, Tirso; Gutierrez, Jose Roberto; Juarez, Joe; Mata, Bill; Miyares, Marcelino; Montanez Davis, Grace; Montoya, Velma; Pineda, Pat; Siberio, Julio; Thompson, Edith Lopez.

2022 People. HISPANIC BUSINESS, Vol. 5, no. 6 (June 1983), p. 8. English. **DESCR:** Appointed Officials; *Biographical Notes; Goizueta, Roberto C.; Guerra, Stella; Huapaya, Sixto Guillermo; Kitano, Pat; Manriquez, Suzanna; Oppenheimer-Nicolau, Siabhan; Ortiz, Solomon; Pachon, Harry P.; Richardson, Bill Lopez; Torres, Esteban E.; Torres, Johnny.

2023 People. HISPANIC BUSINESS, Vol. 5, no. 5 (May 1983), p. 8. English. **DESCR:** Biographical Notes; Duron, Armando; Espinoza, Peter; Flores, Juan; Martinez, Vilma Socorro; Molina, Gloria; Moreno, Samuel; Pantin, Leslie, Sr.; Quezada, Sylvia; Quinones, Sergio.

2024 People. HISPANIC BUSINESS, Vol. 5, no. 7 (July 1983), p. 8. English. **DESCR:** Alvarado, Anthony J.; Appointed Officials; *Biographical Notes; Candela, Hilario; Garcia, Marlene; Gonzalez, Julio; Martinez, Tony; Pla, George; Valdez, Abelardo L.

2025 People. HISPANIC BUSINESS, Vol. 5, no. 8 (August 1983), p. 10. English. **DESCR:** *Biographical Notes; Calderon, Charles M.; Esteverena, Rolando C.; General Coffee Corporation; Hispanic Bankers Association (HBA); Martinez, Olivia T.; Pallares, Mariano; Ruiz, Frederick R.; Ruiz, Louis F.; Sanchez, Joseph J.

2026 People. HISPANIC BUSINESS, Vol. 5, no. 9 (September 1983), p. 10. English. **DESCR:** Chavez, Chris; Diez de Onate, Jorge; Franco Garcia, Freddie; Garcia, Hector P.; Lozano, Leticia Eugenia; Ravard, Rafael Alonzo; Rodriguez, Alberto Duque; Sanchez, Philip V.; Villalpando, Catalina.

2027 People. HISPANIC BUSINESS, Vol. 5, no. 10 (October 1983), p. 10. English. **DESCR:** Anaya, Toney; Arriola, Elvia Rosales; Babbitt, Bruce; Burgos, Tony; Bush, George; Cisneros, Henry, Mayor of San Antonio, TX; Cruz, Jose; Kennedy, Edward M.; Montano, Gilbert; Reagan, Ronald; White, Mark.

2028 People. HISPANIC BUSINESS, Vol. 5, no. 11 (November 1983), p. 10. English. **DESCR:** Aragon, Fermin; De Los Reyes, Victor; Di Martino, Rita; Garcia, Ruben; Juarez, Chris; Lopez, Leonard; Nogales, Luis G.; Ozuna, Bob; Rico, Jose Hipolito; Tamayo, Roberto; Tapia, Raul R.

2029 People. HISPANIC BUSINESS, Vol. 5, no. 12 (December 1983), p. 9. English. **DESCR:** Cantu, Norma V.; Cruz, Jose; Masvidal, Sergio J.; Ortega, Katherine D.; Planas, Maria Bordas; Rodriguez, Ismael D.; Romero, Estella E.

2030 People. HISPANIC BUSINESS, Vol. 4, no. 8 (August 1983), p. 7. English. **DESCR:** Aguilar, Richard; Cordero-Badillo, Atilano; del Olmo, Frank; Infante, E. Anthony; Levitan, Aida T.; Nunez, Luis; Quintanilla, Guadalupe; Rivera, Victor M.

2031 Roberto Varela and TLC. CAMINOS, Vol. 3, no. 2 (February 1982), p. 27-29. Bilingual. **DESCR:** Business; Tape & Label Converters (TLC); *Varela, Robert.

2032 SBA reports on help to minority businesses. NUESTRO, Vol. 6, no. 4 (May 1982), p. 48. English. **DESCR:** Ethnic Groups; *U.S. Small Business Administration.

2033 The shaping of a career. HISPANIC BUSINESS, Vol. 4, no. 4 (April 1982), p. 14. English. **DESCR:** Atlantic Richfield Company; Biography; Chicanas; *Oaxaca, Virginia.

2034 Volsky, George. The American club. HISPANIC BUSINESS, Vol. 4, no. 3 (March 1982), p. 16-17+. English. **DESCR:** American Club of Miami; Cubanos; *Cultural Organizations; Miami, FL.

2035 Volsky, George. Four careers in Miami. HISPANIC BUSINESS, Vol. 5, no. 4 (April 1983), p. 10-11+. English. **DESCR:** Balestra, Victor C.; *Banking Industry; Biographical Notes; Harvard Business School's Latino Association; Huston, Maria Padilla; Masvidal, Sergio J.; Miami, FL; Valdes-Fauli, Gonzalo.

Businesspeople (cont.)

2036 Volsky, George and Masvidal, Raul. An interview with Raul Masvidal. HISPANIC BUSINESS, Vol. 4, no. 9 (September 1982), p. 16-17,24+. English. **DESCR:** Banking Industry; Biography; Business Enterprises; Cubanos; *Masvidal, Raul; Miami, FL.

2037 Weber, Robert. Summa's Tumortec/hCG. HISPANIC BUSINESS, Vol. 5, no. 7 (July 1983), p. 18-19+. English. **DESCR:** *Business Enterprises; *Medical Research; Summa Medical Corporation.

2038 White House honors three minority firms. NUESTRO, Vol. 7, no. 8 (October 1983), p. 51. English. **DESCR:** *Business Enterprises; Carson, Norris L.; H & H Meat Products, Mercedes, TX; Hinojosa, Liborio; J.T. Construction Co., El Paso, TX; National Minority Enterprise Development Week; N.L. Carson Construction, Inc., Carthage, MS; Torres, Jaime.

2039 Women entrepreneurs offered SBA assistance. NUESTRO, Vol. 7, no. 1 (January, February, 1983), p. 47. English. **DESCR:** *Business Enterprises; *Chicanas; U.S. Small Business Administration.

Busing

2040 Perez, Robert; Padilla, Amado M.; and Ramirez, Alex. Expectations toward school busing by Mexican American youth. AMERICAN JOURNAL OF COMMUNITY PSYCHOLOGY, Vol. 10, no. 2 (April 1982), p. 133-148. English. **DESCR:** Attitude (Psychological); East Los Angeles, CA; Identity; Segregation and Desegregation; Students; Youth.

Bustamante, Jorge A.

2041 Bustamante, Jorge A. Relief from illegals? Perhaps in 50 years. U.S. NEWS & WORLD REPORT, Vol. 94, no. 9 (March 7, 1983), p. 44. English. **DESCR:** *Migration; *Undocumented Workers.

2042 Corwin, Arthur F. The numbers game: estimates of illegal aliens in the United States, 1970-1981. LAW AND CONTEMPORARY PROBLEMS, Vol. 45, no. 2 (Spring 1982), p. 223-297. English. **DESCR:** Centro Nacional de Informacion y Estadistica del Trabajo (CENINET); Demography; Federation for American Immigration Reform (FAIR); Mexican American Legal Defense and Educational Fund (MALDEF); *Select Commission on Immigration and Refugee Policy; Simpson-Mazzoli Bill; *Statistics; *Undocumented Workers.

Bustelo, Manuel A.

2043 Manuel Bustelo heads youth effort. NUESTRO, Vol. 5, no. 8 (November 1981), p. 42-43. English. **DESCR:** National Youth Employment Coalition; *Organizations.

2044 Uehling, Mark D. Rivalry in New York: a profile of two newspapers. NUESTRO, Vol. 7, no. 7 (September 1983), p. 20-21. English. **DESCR:** DIARIO LA PRENSA [newspaper], New York, NY; Espinal, Antonio; Gannett Co., Inc.; Journalism; New York, NY; *Newspapers; NOTICIAS DEL MUNDO; Patino, Luis; Unification Church.

BUT TIME AND CHANCE

2045 Blea, Irene I. Book review of: BUT TIME AND CHANCE. CACR REVIEW, Vol. 1, no. 1 (September 1982), p. 132-133. English.

DESCR: Book Reviews; Catholic Church; Chavez, Fray Angelico; Lamy, J.B.; Machelbeuf, Joseph P., Vicar; Martinez, Antonio, Fray; New Mexico.

BY LINGUAL WHOLES

2046 Gonzalez, LaVerne. Book review of: BY LINGUAL WHOLES. REVISTA CHICANO-RIQUENA, Vol. 11, no. 2 (Summer 1983), p. 75-77. English. **DESCR:** Book Reviews; Hernandez Cruz, Victor.

BY THE SWEAT OF THEIR BROW: MEXICAN IMMIGRANT LABOR IN THE UNITED STATES, 1900-1940

2047 Garcia, Mario T. On Mexican immigration, the United States, and Chicano history. JOURNAL OF ETHNIC STUDIES, Vol. 7, no. 1 (Spring 1979), p. 80-88. English. **DESCR:** Book Reviews; History; Immigrant Labor; Immigration; Immigration Law; Mexico; Reisler, Mark; Research Methodology; Southwest United States.

Caballero Spanish Media, Inc. (CSM)

2048 Balkan, D. Carlos. Mr. Caballero's Spanish radio network. HISPANIC BUSINESS, Vol. 4, no. 5 (May 1982), p. 18-19,26. English. **DESCR:** Advertising; Broadcast Media; Radio.

2049 Chavarria, Jesus. The media scene. HISPANIC BUSINESS, Vol. 4, no. 5 (May 1982), p. 6. English. **DESCR:** Advertising; Broadcast Media; *Mass Media; MIAMI MENSUAL; Print Media; Radio; Television.

2050 Communications/marketing. HISPANIC BUSINESS, Vol. 5, no. 1 (January 1983), p. 23. English. **DESCR:** Banking Industry; Broadcast Media; Fleishman-Hillard, Inc.; *Marketing; Miami, FL; Nogales, Luis G.; Public Relations.

2051 Media/marketing. HISPANIC BUSINESS, Vol. 5, no. 11 (November 1983), p. 30. English. **DESCR:** California Chicano News Media Association (CCNMA); Employment Training; Federal Communications Commission (FCC); HISPANEX (Oakland, CA); *Mass Media; Michell, Pat; Radio; Radio Station KALI, Los Angeles, CA.

Caballero-Perez, Diana

2052 Barreto, Julio. A new force in the barrio. NUESTRO, Vol. 7, no. 4 (May 1983), p. 43-45. English. **DESCR:** *Community Development; *Cultural Organizations; National Congress for Puerto Rican Rights (NCPRR); *Puerto Ricans.

Cabell v. Chavez-Salido

2053 Richard, John E. Public employment rights of aliens. BAYLOR LAW REVIEW, Vol. 34, no. 3 (Summer 1982), p. 371-385. English. **DESCR:** Employment; *Naturalization; Sugarman v. Dougall.

Cabinet Committee on Opportunity for Spanish-Speaking People (CCOSSP)

2054 Bustelo, Manuel A. Ending an era of Hispanic isolation. NUESTRO, Vol. 6, no. 7 (September 1982), p. 60. English. **DESCR:** *Culture; *Family; *Identity.

Cable Television

2055 Chavez, Lydia. The fourth network's chief executive. HISPANIC BUSINESS, Vol. 4, no. 1 (January 1982), p. 16-18. English. DESCR: Advertising; Anselmo, Rene; *Biography; Marketing; Spanish International Network (SIN).

2056 Communications/marketing. HISPANIC BUSINESS, Vol. 4, no. 2 (February 1982), p. 15. English. DESCR: Congressional Hispanic Caucus; El Teatro Campesino; GalaVision; Labor Unions; *Marketing; Philip Morris, Inc.; Publishing Industry; Spanish International Network (SIN).

2057 Communications/marketing. HISPANIC BUSINESS, Vol. 5, no. 7 (July 1983), p. 24. English. DESCR: AltaVision, Inc. (Denver, CO); Boycotts; Marketing; Operation PUSH; Spanish Satellite Network (SSN); *Television.

2058 Figueroa, John. Pueden los Hispanos costearse la television por cable? LATINO, Vol. 53, no. 7 (November 1982), p. 15. Spanish. DESCR: *Television.

2059 Siccardi, Maria C. Cable T.V.: new opportunities for Hispanic communities. AGENDA, Vol. 11, no. 3 (May, June, 1981), p. 20-22. English. DESCR: Television.

Cabrera, Lydia

2060 Greenfield, Charles. Cuba's matriarch of letters: Lydia Cabrera. NUESTRO, Vol. 6, no. 7 (September 1982), p. 13-15. English. DESCR: Authors; Cubanos.

2061 Greenfield, Charles. Q & A with Lydia Cabrera. NUESTRO, Vol. 6, no. 7 (September 1982), p. 16-17+. English. DESCR: Authors; Cubanos.

Cache Restaurant

2062 It's not all rice & beans, part III (restaurant reviews). CAMINOS, Vol. 4, no. 6 (June 1983), p. 15-18. Bilingual. DESCR: El Cochinito Yucateco Restaurant; El Tepeyac Restaurant; La Parrilla Restaurant; *Restaurants.

CAFE de California, Inc., Sacramento, CA

2063 Did you know. LATINA, Vol. 1, no. 3 (1983), p. 60-63. English. DESCR: Alkali Flat Project Area Committee, Sacramento, CA; Bilingual Foundation of the Arts; *Organizations.

Caida de Mollera

2064 Richardson, Lynette. Caring through understanding, part II: folk medicine in the Hispanic population. IMPRINT, Vol. 29, no. 2 (April 1982), p. 21, 72-77. English. DESCR: Brujo; Curanderas; Empacho; *Folk Medicine; Mal de Ojo; Mal Puesto; Susto.

Cal International

2065 Burritos to Lebanon. LATINA, Vol. 1, no. 2 (February, March, 1983), p. 19. English. DESCR: Maria's Burritos; *Recipes.

Caldera, Manuel

2066 Baciu, Joyce A. The winners - Los ganadores. CAMINOS, Vol. 3, no. 2 (February 1982), p. 14-20,45. Bilingual. DESCR: *Awards; Gomez, Ignacio; Huerta, Dolores; Lizarraga, David C.; Obledo, Mario; Olmos, Edward James;

Rivera, Geraldo; Rivera, Tomas.

Caldera, Manuel R.

2067 Balkan, D. Carlos. AMEX Systems Inc. at transition point. HISPANIC BUSINESS, Vol. 4, no. 6 (June 1982), p. 18-19,24. English. DESCR: AMEX Systems, Inc.; Business Enterprises; *Corporations; High Technology Industries; Small Business Administration 8(a) Program; U.S. Small Business Administration.

2068 People. HISPANIC BUSINESS, Vol. 4, no. 10 (October 1982), p. 7. English. DESCR: Aguilar, Gloria; Biographical Notes; *Businesspeople; Lopez, Victor M.; Ramirez, Steve.

Calderon, Charles M.

2069 People. HISPANIC BUSINESS, Vol. 5, no. 8 (August 1983), p. 10. English. DESCR: *Biographical Notes; Businesspeople; Esteverena, Rolando C.; General Coffee Corporation; Hispanic Bankers Association (HBA); Martinez, Olivia T.; Pallares, Mariano; Ruiz, Frederick R.; Ruiz, Louis F.; Sanchez, Joseph J.

Calderon, Tony

2070 Gus Garcia Foundation. LATINO, Vol. 54, no. 4 (May, June, 1983), p. 29. English. DESCR: *Films; Financial Aid; Garcia, Gus.

California

2071 Balkan, D. Carlos. Being a start-up manager at San Onofre II & III. HISPANIC BUSINESS, Vol. 4, no. 7 (July 1982), p. 18-19,26. English. DESCR: Chavez, Gabriel A.; Engineering as a Profession; *Management; Nuclear Energy.

2072 Banking on Hispanics. HISPANIC BUSINESS, Vol. 4, no. 3 (March 1982), p. 14+. English. DESCR: *Banking Industry.

2073 Barber, Bob. UFW and the class struggle. SOUTHWEST ECONOMY AND SOCIETY, Vol. 1, no. 1 (Spring 1976), p. 28-35. English. DESCR: *Labor Unions; Undocumented Workers; *United Farmworkers of America (UFW).

2074 Bilingual effort offers few jobs. NUESTRO, Vol. 7, no. 6 (August 1983), p. 13. English. DESCR: *Bilingual Bicultural Education; Education; Teaching Profession.

2075 Black, Bill. Housing for farm laborers: a California solution. NUESTRO, Vol. 7, no. 6 (August 1983), p. 36-37. English. DESCR: Agricultural Laborers; *Housing.

2076 California farmworkers: back to the barricades? BUSINESS WEEK, no. 28 (September 26, 1983), p. 86+. English. DESCR: *Agricultural Labor Relations Board (ALRB); Agricultural Labor Unions; *Agricultural Laborers; United Farmworkers of America (UFW).

2077 Chavez, Cesar E. Relentless struggle for farm workers' rights. NUESTRO, Vol. 7, no. 9 (November 1983), p. 55. English. DESCR: *Agricultural Laborers; Immigrant Labor; Simpson-Mazzoli Bill.

California (cont.)

2078 Chavez, Leo R. Undocumented immigrants and access to health services: a game of pass the buck. MIGRATION TODAY, Vol. 11, no. 1 (1983), p. 14-19. English. **DESCR:** *Immigrants; Medical Care; Migrant Health Services; Public Health Legislation; Simpson-Mazzoli Bill; Social Services; Undocumented Workers.

2079 Communications/marketing. HISPANIC BUSINESS, Vol. 4, no. 3 (March 1982), p. 15. English. **DESCR:** Herrera, Maria Elena; *Marketing; Philip Morris, Inc.; Publicidad Siboney; Siboney Advertising, Inc.; SRI International.

2080 Cuello, J. Book review of: IN DEFENSE OF LA RAZA: THE LOS ANGELES MEXICAN CONSULATE AND THE MEXICAN COMMUNITY. CALIFORNIA HISTORY, Vol. 62, no. 1 (1983), p. 70. English. **DESCR:** Balderrama, Francisco E.; Book Reviews; History; *IN DEFENSE OF LA RAZA: THE LOS ANGELES MEXICAN CONSULATE AND THE MEXICAN COMMUNITY.

2081 De Leon, David. Book review of: BITTER HARVEST: A HISTORY OF CALIFORNIA FARMWORKERS 1870-1941. ANNALS OF THE AMERICAN ACADEMY OF POLITICAL AND SOCIAL SCIENCE, Vol. 462, (July 1982), p. 198-199. English. **DESCR:** Agricultural Laborers; *BITTER HARVEST: A HISTORY OF CALIFORNIA FARMWORKERS, 1870-1941; Book Reviews; Daniel, Cletus E.

2082 Deukmejian, George. Welcoming the Commission of the Californias. CAMINOS, Vol. 4, no. 11 (December 1983), p. 19. English. **DESCR:** Border Region; *Commission of the Californias; United States-Mexico Relations.

2083 Dominguez, Richard M. Capital formulation for small businesses. HISPANIC BUSINESS, Vol. 4, no. 9 (September 1982), p. 8. English. **DESCR:** Banking Industry; *Finance; Small Business.

2084 Edmunds, Stahrl W. California-Mexico trade relations. CAMINOS, Vol. 4, no. 11 (December 1983), p. 20-21,38. Bilingual. **DESCR:** Border Region; Business; *United States-Mexico Relations.

2085 Foreign trade. HISPANIC BUSINESS, Vol. 5, no. 11 (November 1983), p. 31. English. **DESCR:** *Foreign Trade; HOW TO EXPORT: A MARKETING MANUAL; Marketing; Miami, FL; Miami Free Zone; Puerto Rico.

2086 Foster, Douglas. The desperate migrants of Devil's Canyon. THE PROGRESSIVE, Vol. 46, no. 11 (November 1982), p. 44-49. English. **DESCR:** *Agricultural Laborers; *Devil's Canyon, Deer Canyon, CA; Growers; Labor Camps; San Diego, CA; Undocumented Workers.

2087 Government review. NUESTRO, Vol. 7, no. 7 (September 1983), p. 55. English. **DESCR:** AIDS Hotline; Education; Employment; Food for Survival, New York, NY; Funding Sources; *Government Services; Hewlett Foundation; Laborers; Mathematics, Engineering and Science Achievement (MESA); Population Trends; Public Health; Stanford University, Stanford, CA.

2088 Haro, Carlos Manuel. Chicanos and higher education: a review of selected literature. AZTLAN, Vol. 14, no. 1 (Spring 1983), p. 35-77. English. **DESCR:** Education; *Higher Education; Literature Reviews; Students.

2089 Hernandez, Leodoro and Luevano, Richard L. A program for the recruitment of Chicanos into higher education. COLLEGE STUDENT JOURNAL, Vol. 17, no. 2 (Summer 1983), p. 166-171. English. **DESCR:** California State University, Stanislaus; *Enrollment; Higher Education; *Student Ambassador Recruitment Program, California State University, Stanislaus.

2090 Hispanic victories; seats gained. CAMINOS, Vol. 3, no. 7 (July, August, 1982), p. 34-35. English. **DESCR:** *Elections.

2091 Hispanic voting trends. HISPANIC BUSINESS, Vol. 4, no. 8 (August 1983), p. 28-29. English. **DESCR:** Bilingual Ballots; Bilingualism; *Elections; Mexican American Legal Defense and Educational Fund (MALDEF); Southwest Voter Registration Education Project (SVRP); Texas; Voter Turnout.

2092 Kanellos, Nicolas. Two centuries of Hispanic theatre in the Southwest. REVISTA CHICANO-RIQUENA, Vol. 11, no. 1 (Spring 1983), p. 17-39. English. **DESCR:** History; Los Angeles, CA; Photography; San Antonio, TX; Southwest United States; *Teatro; Texas.

2093 Langum, D.J. From condemnation to praise: shifting perspectives on Hispanic California. CALIFORNIA HISTORY, Vol. 61, no. 4 (1983), p. 282-291. English. **DESCR:** *Cultural Characteristics; Ethnic Attitudes; Stereotypes.

2094 Mamer, John W. and Martin, Philip. Hired workers on California farms. CALIFORNIA AGRICULTURE, Vol. 36, no. 9-10 (September, October, 1982), p. 21-23. English. **DESCR:** *Agricultural Laborers; *Labor Supply and Market; Statistics; Undocumented Workers.

2095 Martin, Philip and Mines, Richard. Foreign workers in selected California crops. CALIFORNIA AGRICULTURE, Vol. 37, no. 3-4 (March, April, 1983), p. 6-8. English. **DESCR:** Agricultural Laborers; *Undocumented Workers.

2096 Mathes, W. Michael. Book review of: JOAQUIN MURRIETA AND HIS HORSE GANGS. CALIFORNIA HISTORY, Vol. 61, no. 4 (1983), p. 306-308. English. **DESCR:** Book Reviews; History; Latta, Frank F.; *Murieta, Joaquin.

2097 Mathes, W. Michael. Sources in Mexico for the history of Spanish California. CALIFORNIA HISTORY, Vol. 61, no. 3 (1982), p. 223-226. English. **DESCR:** *Historiography; Mexico; Spanish Influence.

2098 Munoz, Carlos, Jr. and Barrera, Mario. La Raza Unida Party and the Chicano student movement in California. SOCIAL SCIENCE JOURNAL, Vol. 19, no. 2 (April 1982), p. 101-119. English. **DESCR:** *Chicano Movement; *La Raza Unida Party; Political History and Conditions; Political Ideology; Political Parties and Organizations; Student Movements.

2099 Occupational distribution of Hispanics in California. HISPANIC BUSINESS, Vol. 5, no. 9 (September 1983), p. 33-34. English. **DESCR:** Employment; *Population Distribution; Population Trends.

2100 Professional network. HISPANIC BUSINESS, Vol. 4, no. 9 (September 1982), p. 18,26+. English. **DESCR:** Castillo, Sylvia; Higher Education; Hispanic Women in Higher Education (HWHE); Mentors; *Self-Help Groups.

California (cont.)

2101 Reapportionment [panel discussion at the LATINOS IN THE LAW symposium, UCLA, 1982]. CHICANO LAW REVIEW, Vol. 6, (1983), p. 34-62. English. DESCR: Californios for Fair Representation; Common Cause; *Reapportionment.

2102 Reyes, Ramiro. The status of bilingual education in California. CAMINOS, Vol. 3, no. 10 (November 1982), p. 36-37,54. English. DESCR: *Bilingual Bicultural Education.

2103 Southern California's HBA. HISPANIC BUSINESS, Vol. 4, no. 9 (September 1982), p. 19. English. DESCR: Banking Industry; *Hispanic Bankers Association (HBA); Organizations.

2104 A statistical profile of California public schools. CAMINOS, Vol. 3, no. 10 (November 1982), p. 46-47. English. DESCR: *Education; *Statistics.

2105 US-Mexican trade relations. HISPANIC BUSINESS, Vol. 4, no. 9 (September 1982), p. 23. English. DESCR: Export Trade; *Foreign Trade; Mexico; United States-Mexico Relations.

2106 Walia, Adorna. Book review of: THE PLUM PLUM PICKERS. BILINGUAL JOURNAL, Vol. 6, no. 1 (Fall 1982), p. 30-31. English. DESCR: Agricultural Laborers; Barrio, Raymond; Book Reviews; *Migrant Labor; Santa Clara County, CA; *THE PLUM PLUM PICKERS.

2107 Wells, Miriam J. Political mediation and agricultural cooperation: strawberry farms in California. ECONOMIC DEVELOPMENT AND CULTURAL CHANGE, Vol. 30, no. 2 (January 1982), p. 413-432. English. DESCR: *Agricultural Cooperatives; Agricultural Laborers; Cooperativa Campesina; Cooperativa Central; Political Parties and Organizations; Rural Economics.

2108 Whisler, Kirk. Hispanic representation in California's cities: progress??? CAMINOS, Vol. 4, no. 3 (March 1983), p. 42-43,49. English. DESCR: *Elected Officials; *Local Government.

California Achievement Test

2109 Creswell, John L. Sex-related differences in the problem-solving abilities of rural Black, Anglo, and Chicano adolescents. TEXAS TECH JOURNAL OF EDUCATION, Vol. 10, no. 1 (Winter 1983), p. 29-33. English. DESCR: Aiken and Preger Revised Math Attitude Scale; Anglo Americans; Blacks; Chicanas; Gender; Mathematics; National Assessment of Educational Progress; *National Council of Teachers of Mathematics (NCTM); Youth.

California Arts Council (C.A.C.)

2110 Soto, Rose Marie. Consuelo Santos-Killins: a leader in the arts. CAMINOS, Vol. 4, no. 6 (June 1983), p. 56-57,67. Bilingual. DESCR: Art; Cultural Organizations; *Santos-Killins, Consuelo.

California Chicano News Media Association (CCNMA)

2111 Career intelligencer. HISPANIC BUSINESS, Vol. 5, no. 9 (September 1983), p. 30. English. DESCR: *Careers; Journalism; National Consortium for Graduate Degrees for Minorities in Engineering.

2112 Communications/marketing. HISPANIC BUSINESS, Vol. 4, no. 11 (November 1982), p. 18. English. DESCR: Diaz-Albertini, Luis; Domecq Importers, Inc.; *Marketing; National Hispanic Media Conference, San Diego, CA, December 2-5, 1982; Pacific Telephone; Television.

2113 Communications/marketing. HISPANIC BUSINESS, Vol. 5, no. 5 (May 1983), p. 24. English. DESCR: Anheuser-Busch, Inc.; Arbitron; Awards; Coca-Cola Company; Elizalde, Hector; *Marketing; Television.

2114 Ericksen, Charles and Treviso, Ruben. Latino journalists make their move. NUESTRO, Vol. 6, no. 5 (June, July, 1982), p. 45-47. English. DESCR: *Journalists; Latin American Studies.

2115 Media/marketing. HISPANIC BUSINESS, Vol. 5, no. 11 (November 1983), p. 30. English. DESCR: Caballero Spanish Media, Inc. (CSM); Employment Training; Federal Communications Commission (FCC); HISPANEX (Oakland, CA); *Mass Media; Michell, Pat; Radio; Radio Station KALI, Los Angeles, CA.

2116 People. HISPANIC BUSINESS, Vol. 4, no. 5 (May 1982), p. 8. English. DESCR: Appointed Officials; Asociacion Internacional de Exportadores e Importadores (EXIMA); *Biographical Notes; Businesspeople; de la Ossa, Ernest G.; Foreign Trade; Obledo, Mario; Rodriguez, Elias C.; Rodriguez, Samuel F.; United Way; U.S. Hispanic Chamber of Commerce.

2117 Tips for making the right moves in today's job markets. HISPANIC BUSINESS, Vol. 4, no. 5 (May 1982), p. 16. English. DESCR: *Careers; Mass Media.

2118 Tips for making the right moves in today's job markets. HISPANIC BUSINESS, Vol. 4, no. 7 (July 1982), p. 14. English. DESCR: *Careers; Employment.

California Farm Bureau Federation

2119 King, John S. California Farm Bureau Federation: addressing the issue/conduciendo el topico. CAMINOS, Vol. 3, no. 1 (January 1982), p. 16-17. Bilingual. DESCR: *Immigration Regulation and Control; Reagan, Ronald.

California National Guard

2120 Paredes, Michael J. The California National Guard. CAMINOS, Vol. 3, no. 3 (March 1982), p. 26-27. Bilingual. DESCR: Military Service.

California Republican Hispanic Council

2121 Whisler, Kirk. The California Republican Hispanic Council: a new force/un nuevo poder. CAMINOS, Vol. 3, no. 3 (March 1982), p. 44-46. Bilingual. DESCR: Politics; Republican Party.

California Rural Legal Assistance (CRLA)

2122 Castro, Mike. Alien smuggling and the refugee question: caught between the border patrol and the river. NUESTRO, Vol. 7, no. 5 (June, July, 1983), p. 18. English. DESCR: *Border Patrol; *Immigration Regulation and Control; *Sacramento, CA; *Undocumented Workers.

California Rural Legal Assistance (CRLA) (cont.)

2123 Castro, Mike. OAS investigates California deaths. NUESTRO, Vol. 7, no. 9 (November 1983), p. 12-13. English. **DESCR:** *Border Patrol; Immigration Regulation and Control; *Organization of American States.

California Spanish Language Data Base (CSLDB)
USE: HISPANEX (Oakland, CA)

California State Personnel Board

2124 Tovar, Irene. Affirmative action in California. CAMINOS, Vol. 3, no. 8 (September 1982), p. 30-32,50+. Bilingual. **DESCR:** *Affirmative Action; *Civil Service.

California State University, Los Angeles

2125 McCurdy, Jack. L.A. violence linked to Chicano-studies dispute. CHRONICLE OF HIGHER EDUCATION, Vol. 24, no. 14 (June 2, 1982), p. 8. English. **DESCR:** *Chicano Studies; Corona, Bert; Faculty; Violence.

California State University, Stanislaus

2126 Hernandez, Leodoro and Luevano, Richard L. A program for the recruitment of Chicanos into higher education. COLLEGE STUDENT JOURNAL, Vol. 17, no. 2 (Summer 1983), p. 166-171. English. **DESCR:** California; *Enrollment; Higher Education; *Student Ambassador Recruitment Program, California State University, Stanislaus.

California v. Prysock

2127 Miranda warnings were adequate despite deviations from strict form. CRIMINAL LAW REPORTER, Vol. 30, no. 22 (October 3, 1982), p. 2427-2428. English. **DESCR:** Drug Traffic; *Legal Aid; U.S. v. Contreras.

Californios for Fair Representation

2128 Reapportionment [panel discussion at the LATINOS IN THE LAW symposium, UCLA, 1982]. CHICANO LAW REVIEW, Vol. 6, (1983), p. 34-62. English. **DESCR:** California; Common Cause; *Reapportionment.

2129 Santillan, Richard. [Translating population numbers into political power]. CHICANO LAW REVIEW, Vol. 6, (1983), p. 16-21. English. **DESCR:** Carrillo v. Whittier Union High School; LATINOS IN THE LAW [symposium], UCLA, 1982; MEXICAN AMERICAN LEGAL DEFENSE AND EDUCATIONAL FUND NEWSLETTER; Political Representation; Reapportionment; *Voter Turnout.

Callahan, Adelina Pena

2130 Padilla, Steve. Adelina Pena Callahan: restaurateur. NUESTRO, Vol. 7, no. 4 (May 1983), p. 26-29. English. **DESCR:** Businesspeople; *Careers; Food Industry; La Fonda Restaurant; Working Women.

Calvert, Robert

2131 Entertaiment reviews. CAMINOS, Vol. 3, no. 8 (September 1982), p. 21. English. **DESCR:** Adams, Bob; Alpert, Herb; Books; Jimenez, Santiago; Lopez, Lisa; Music; Myles, Carol; Paredes, Americo; Pettus, Theodore T.; *Recreation; Television.

Calvo Buezas, Tomas

2132 de Armas, Isabel. Chicano, un vocablo colonizador. CUADERNOS HISPANOAMERICANOS, Vol. 394, (April 1983), p. 193-201. Spanish. **DESCR:** Agricultural Laborers; Book Reviews; *CHICANOS: ANTOLOGIA HISTORICA Y LITERARIA; Identity; *LOS MAS POBRES EN EL PAIS MAS RICO; Villanueva, Tino.

Camara de Comercio Latina de Los Estados Unidos (CAMACOL)

2133 Miami's thriving Camacol. HISPANIC BUSINESS, Vol. 4, no. 3 (March 1982), p. 12-13. English. **DESCR:** Businesspeople; *Chamber of Commerce; Miami, FL.

Camargo, Mateo G.

2134 Gente. NUESTRO, Vol. 7, no. 1 (January, February, 1983), p. 63. English. **DESCR:** Amaya-Espinoza, Isidro; *Latin Americans; Musicians; Prieto, Carlos; Radio; Sports; Trevino, Lee.

Camarillo, Alberto

2135 Lotchin, Roger W. New Chicano history: an urban history perspective. HISTORY TEACHER, Vol. 16, no. 2 (February 1983), p. 229-247. English. **DESCR:** CHICANOS IN A CHANGING SOCIETY; DESERT IMMIGRANTS: THE MEXICANS OF EL PASO 1880-1920; Garcia, Mario T.; Griswold del Castillo, Ricardo; *Historiography; History; Social History and Conditions; THE LOS ANGELES BARRIO 1850-1890: A SOCIAL HISTORY; Urban Communities.

2136 Reisler, Mark. Book review of: CHICANOS IN A CHANGING SOCIETY: FROM MEXICAN PUEBLOS TO AMERICAN BARRIOS IN SANTA BARBARA AND SOUTHERN CALIFORNIA, 1848-1930. NEW MEXICO HISTORICAL REVIEW, Vol. 57, no. 2 (April 1982), p. 200-201. English. **DESCR:** Book Reviews; *CHICANOS IN A CHANGING SOCIETY; Social History and Conditions.

2137 Saragoza, Alex M. The florescence of Chicano historical scholarship. NEW SCHOLAR, Vol. 8, no. 1-2 (Spring, Fall, 1982), p. 483-487. English. **DESCR:** Book Reviews; *CHICANOS IN A CHANGING SOCIETY; History.

2138 Weber, David J. and Lotchin, Roger W. The new Chicano history: two perspectives. HISTORY TEACHER, Vol. 16, no. 2 (February 1983), p. 219-247. English. **DESCR:** *CHICANOS IN A CHANGING SOCIETY; DESERT IMMIGRANTS: THE MEXICANS OF EL PASO 1880-1920; Garcia, Mario T.; Griswold del Castillo, Ricardo; *Historiography; History; Social History and Conditions; *THE LOS ANGELES BARRIO 1850-1890: A SOCIAL HISTORY; *Urban Communities.

2139 Weber, David J. The new Chicano urban history. HISTORY TEACHER, Vol. 16, no. 2 (February 1983), p. 223-229. English. **DESCR:** *CHICANOS IN A CHANGING SOCIETY; DESERT IMMIGRANTS: THE MEXICANS OF EL PASO 1880-1920; Garcia, Mario T.; Griswold del Castillo, Ricardo; *Historiography; History; Social History and Conditions; *THE LOS ANGELES BARRIO 1850-1890: A SOCIAL HISTORY; Urban Communities.

CAMINOS' Chicano of the Year Award

2140 CAMINO'S 1981 Chicano of the year: Fernando Valenzuela. CAMINOS, Vol. 3, no. 2 (February 1982), p. 10-13. Bilingual. **DESCR:** Awards; *Valenzuela, Fernando.

CAMINOS' Chicano of the Year Award (cont.)

2141 CAMINOS' Second Annual Chicano/a of the Year Awards=Chicano/a del Ano. CAMINOS, Vol. 2, no. 6 (October 1981), p. 29-33. Bilingual. **DESCR:** Awards.

2142 Quesada-Weiner, Rosemary. CAMINOS second annual Chicano of the year awards. CAMINOS, Vol. 3, no. 3 (March 1982), p. 34-36. Bilingual. **DESCR:** Awards.

Campbell Soup Co.

2143 Askin, Steve. Boston church encourages labor talks. NATIONAL CATHOLIC REPORTER, Vol. 18, (July 30, 1982), p. 6. English. **DESCR:** Boston Archdiocese Justice and Peace Commission; Boycotts; Catholic Church; *Farm Labor Organizing Commmittee (FLOC); Labor Unions.

Campesinos
USE: Agricultural Laborers

Campos, Olga

2144 Cantu, Hector. Aqui en Austin: this is Olga Campos reporting. NATIONAL HISPANIC JOURNAL, Vol. 1, no. 3 (Summer, Fall, 1982), p. 7. English. **DESCR:** Careers; *KTBC-TV, Austin, TX [television station]; Mass Media; Television.

Canada

2145 Que pasa?: future of bilingualism. NUESTRO, Vol. 7, no. 4 (May 1983), p. 9. English. **DESCR:** *Bilingualism; Cubanos; *Miami, FL.

Cananea Mining Strike of 1906

2146 Casillas, Mike. The Cananea strike of 1906. SOUTHWEST ECONOMY AND SOCIETY, Vol. 3, no. 2 (Winter 1977, 1978), p. 18-32. English. **DESCR:** Arizona; Cananea, Sonora, Mexico; History; Mining Industry; Partido Liberal Mexicano (PLM); *Strikes and Lockouts.

Cananea, Sonora, Mexico

2147 Casillas, Mike. The Cananea strike of 1906. SOUTHWEST ECONOMY AND SOCIETY, Vol. 3, no. 2 (Winter 1977, 1978), p. 18-32. English. **DESCR:** Arizona; *Cananea Mining Strike of 1906; History; Mining Industry; Partido Liberal Mexicano (PLM); *Strikes and Lockouts.

Cancer

2148 Breast examination. LATINA, Vol. 1, no. 1 (1982), p. 56+. Bilingual.

2149 Cancer protection project. LATINO, Vol. 54, no. 5 (August, September, 1983), p. 14. English. **DESCR:** *Public Health.

2150 Effective ways to fight cancer in new publication. LATINO, Vol. 54, no. 8 (December 1983), p. 24. English. **DESCR:** *Preventative Medicine; Public Health.

2151 Holck, Susan E. Lung cancer mortality and smoking habits: Mexican-American women. AMERICAN JOURNAL OF PUBLIC HEALTH, Vol. 72, no. 1 (January 1982), p. 38-42. English. **DESCR:** Anglo Americans; Chicanas; *Public Health.

2152 Ponce-Adame, Merrihelen. Latinas and breast cancer. NUESTRO, Vol. 6, no. 8 (October 1982), p. 30-31. English. **DESCR:** Chicanas; *Public Health.

2153 Ponce-Adame, Merrihelen. Women and cancer. CORAZON DE AZTLAN, Vol. 1, no. 2 (March, April, 1982), p. 32. English. **DESCR:** Chicanas; Medical Care; Preventative Medicine.

Candela, Hilario

2154 People. HISPANIC BUSINESS, Vol. 5, no. 7 (July 1983), p. 8. English. **DESCR:** Alvarado, Anthony J.; Appointed Officials; *Biographical Notes; Businesspeople; Garcia, Marlene; Gonzalez, Julio; Martinez, Tony; Pla, George; Valdez, Abelardo L.

2155 Volsky, George. Hilario Candela: designing for Florida's future. HISPANIC BUSINESS, Vol. 5, no. 11 (November 1983), p. 20-22. English. **DESCR:** Architecture; Miami, FL; Spillis Candela & Partners; Urban Development.

Candelaria, Cordelia

2156 Escobedo, Theresa Herrera. Book review of: CHICANAS IN THE NATIONAL LANDSCAPE. JOURNAL OF AMERICAN ETHNIC HISTORY, Vol. 1, no. 2 (Spring 1982), p. 101-103. English. **DESCR:** Book Reviews; Chicanas; *CHICANAS EN EL AMBIENTE NACIONAL/CHICANAS IN THE NATIONAL LANDSCAPE.

Candelaria, Nash

2157 Shirley, Paula. Book review of: MEMORIES OF THE ALHAMBRA. MELUS: MULTI-ETHNIC LITERATURE OF THE UNITED STATES, Vol. 6, no. 2 (Summer 1979), p. 100-103. English. **DESCR:** Book Reviews; Literature; *MEMORIES OF THE ALHAMBRA.

Cannery and Agricultural Worker's Industrial Union

2158 Arnold, Frank. A history of struggle: organizing cannery workers in the Santa Clara Valley. SOUTHWEST ECONOMY AND SOCIETY, Vol. 2, no. 1 (October, November, 1976), p. 26-38. English. **DESCR:** Agribusiness; American Labor Union (Santa Clara County, CA); *Cannery Workers; Comite de Trabajadores de Canerias, San Jose, CA; History; Labor Unions; *Santa Clara Valley, CA; United Cannery Agricultural Packing and Allied Workers of America (UCAPAWA).

2159 Monroy, Douglas. Anarquismo y comunismo: Mexican radicalism and the Communist Party in Los Angeles during the 1930's. LABOR HISTORY, Vol. 24, no. 1 (Winter 1983), p. 34-59. English. **DESCR:** *Communist Party; Confederacion de Uniones de Obreros Mexicanos (CUOM); History; International Ladies Garment Workers Union (ILGWU); Labor; Labor Organizing; *Los Angeles, CA; Tenayuca, Emma; Worker's Alliance (WA), Los Angeles, CA.

Cannery Workers

2160 Arnold, Frank. A history of struggle: organizing cannery workers in the Santa Clara Valley. SOUTHWEST ECONOMY AND SOCIETY, Vol. 2, no. 1 (October, November, 1976), p. 26-38. English. **DESCR:** Agribusiness; American Labor Union (Santa Clara County, CA); Cannery and Agricultural Worker's Industrial Union; Comite de Trabajadores de Canerias, San Jose, CA; History; Labor Unions; *Santa Clara Valley, CA; United Cannery Agricultural Packing and Allied Workers of America (UCAPAWA).

Cannery Workers (cont.)

2161 Jensen, Joan M. Canning comes to New Mexico: women and the agricultural extension service, 1914-1919. NEW MEXICO HISTORICAL REVIEW, Vol. 57, no. 4 (October 1982), p. 361-386. English. DESCR: Chicanas; Food Industry; New Mexico; New Mexico Agricultural Extension Service.

Cannes Film Festival

2162 Fernandez, Enrique. Cannes and CROSSOVER DREAMS, '83. FILM COMMENT, Vol. 19, no. 4-7 (August 1983), p. 2-7. English. DESCR: Arce, Manuel; Blades, Ruben; *CROSSOVER DREAMS; Film Reviews; Films; Salsa.

CANNIBALS AND KINGS: THE ORIGINS OF CULTURE

2163 Belton, Robert T. Book review of: CANNIBALS AND KINGS: THE ORIGINS OF CULTURE and THE MAN-EATING MYTH: ANTHROPOLOGY AND ANTHROPOPHAGY. HISPANIC JOURNAL OF BEHAVIORAL SCIENCES, Vol. 4, no. 1 (March 1982), p. 129-134. English. DESCR: Arens, W.; Book Reviews; Harris, Marvin; *THE MAN-EATING MYTH: ANTHROPOLOGY AND ANTHROPOPHAGY.

Cano, Eddie

2164 Cantu, Hector. Border business report: the Rio Grande Valley's economy and Mexico's lingering peso devaluation effects. NATIONAL HISPANIC JOURNAL, Vol. 2, no. 1 (Summer 1983), p. 10-13. English. DESCR: Aguirre, Lionel; Border Region; Coors Distributing Company, McAllen, TX; Cruz, Conrado; Cuevas, Betty; *Currency; Economic Development; Laredo, TX, Chamber of Commerce; Mexican American Chamber of Commerce, Austin, TX; United States-Mexico Relations.

Canones, NM

2165 Weber, Kenneth R. Book review of: CANONES: VALUES, CRISIS, AND SURVIVAL IN A NORTHERN NEW MEXICO VILLAGE. JOURNAL OF ETHNIC STUDIES, Vol. 11, no. 2 (Summer 1983), p. 119-123. English. DESCR: Book Reviews; *CANONES: VALUES, CRISIS AND SURVIVAL IN A NORTHERN NEW MEXICO VILLAGE; Ethnology; History; Kutsche, Paul; New Mexico; Northern New Mexico; Van Ness, John R.

CANONES: VALUES, CRISIS AND SURVIVAL IN A NORTHERN NEW MEXICO VILLAGE

2166 Carlson, Alvar W. Book review of: CANONES: VALUES, CRISIS, AND SURVIVAL IN A NORTHERN NEW MEXICO VILLAGE. NEW MEXICO HISTORICAL REVIEW, Vol. 58, no. 3 (July 1983), p. 294. English. DESCR: Book Reviews; Kutsche, Paul; Van Ness, John R.

2167 Weber, Kenneth R. Book review of: CANONES: VALUES, CRISIS, AND SURVIVAL IN A NORTHERN NEW MEXICO VILLAGE. JOURNAL OF ETHNIC STUDIES, Vol. 11, no. 2 (Summer 1983), p. 119-123. English. DESCR: Book Reviews; Canones, NM; Ethnology; History; Kutsche, Paul; New Mexico; Northern New Mexico; Van Ness, John R.

Cantu, Norma V.

2168 People. HISPANIC BUSINESS, Vol. 5, no. 12 (December 1983), p. 9. English. DESCR: *Businesspeople; Cruz, Jose; Masvidal, Sergio J.; Ortega, Katherine D.; Planas, Maria Bordas; Rodriguez, Ismael D.; Romero, Estella E.

Canutillo, TX

2169 Aptekar, Lewis. Mexican-American high school students' perception of school. ADOLESCENCE, Vol. 18, no. 70 (Summer 1983), p. 345-357. English. DESCR: Anthony, TX; *Attitude (Psychological); High School Students; Texas.

Capital National Bank

2170 Hispanic-owned bank far exceeds expectations. ABA BANKING JOURNAL, Vol. 75, (February 1983), p. 32-34. English. DESCR: Banking Industry; Cordova, Carlos; New York, NY.

Capitalism

2171 Law of productivity. LATINO, Vol. 53, no. 1 (January, February, 1982), p. 18. English.

2172 Maldonado-Denis, Manuel. El problema de las nacionalidades: la experiencia caribena. Paper presented at the "Dialogo de las Americas" conference. Mexico, D.F. September 9-14, 1982. REVISTA CHICANO-RIQUENA, Vol. 10, no. 4 (Fall 1982), p. 39-45. Spanish. DESCR: Carpentier, Alejo; Cuba; El Salvador; Grenada; Guatemala; Imperialism; Marti, Jose; Nicaragua; *Political History and Conditions; Puerto Rico; United States.

2173 Manta, Ben. Toward economic development of the Chicano barrio: alternative strategies and their implications [reprint of DE COLORES article]. SOUTHWEST ECONOMY AND SOCIETY, Vol. 1, no. 1 (Spring 1976), p. 35-41. English. DESCR: *Economic History and Conditions; Internal Colonial Model (Theoretical).

2174 Weiss, Lawrence D. Industrial reserve armies of the southwest: Navajo and Mexican. SOUTHWEST ECONOMY AND SOCIETY, Vol. 3, no. 1 (Fall 1977), p. 19-29. English. DESCR: History; *Labor Supply and Market; Native Americans; Navaho Indians; Railroads; *Southwest United States.

CAPITULOS DE HISTORIA MEDICA MEXICANA

2175 Risse, Gunter B. Book review of: CAPITULOS DE HISTORIA MEDICA MEXICANA. BULLETIN OF THE HISTORY OF MEDICINE, Vol. 56, no. 4 (1982), p. 591-592. English. DESCR: Folk Medicine; Medicine; Mexico; Precolumbian Medicine; Somolinos D'Ardois, German.

Car Clubs

2176 Mendoza, Ruben G. The lowrider happening: hydraulics and the hopping competition. CAMINOS, Vol. 4, no. 7 (July, August, 1983), p. 34,44. English. DESCR: *Low Riders.

2177 Whisler, Kirk. It can work. CAMINOS, Vol. 3, no. 6 (June 1982), p. 46. Bilingual. DESCR: Low Riders; San Bernardino, CA.

CARAS VIEJAS Y VINO NUEVO

2178 Monleon, Jose. Dos novelas de Alejandro Morales. MAIZE, Vol. 4, no. 1-2 (Fall, Winter, 1980, 1981), p. 6-8. Spanish. DESCR: *LA VERDAD SIN VOZ; Literary Criticism; Morales, Alejandro.

CARAS VIEJAS Y VINO NUEVO (cont.)

2179 Ramirez, Arthur. Book review of: OLD FACES
AND NEW WINE. REVISTA CHICANO-RIQUENA, Vol.
10, no. 4 (Fall 1982), p. 65-67. English.
DESCR: Book Reviews; Morales, Alejandro;
*OLD FACES AND NEW WINE.

Cardenal, Ernesto

2180 Banberger, Ellen. Poesia nicaraguense.
MAIZE, Vol. 5, no. 3-4 (Spring, Summer,
1982), p. 64-77. Spanish. **DESCR:** Belli,
Gioconda; Carrillo, Ernesto; Coronel
Urtecho, Jose; Gadea, Gerardo; Gomez,
Manuel; Murillo, Rosario; *Nicaragua; Ojeda,
Mirna; *Poetry; Revolutions; Rugama, Leonel.

Cardenas, Maria Elena

2181 News at the SBA. HISPANIC BUSINESS, Vol. 4,
no. 3 (March 1982), p. 14. English. **DESCR:**
*Business; Business Enterprises; Small
Business Administration 8(a) Program; U.S.
Small Business Administration.

Cardenas, Michael

2182 News at SBA: Cardenas removed as SBA chief.
HISPANIC BUSINESS, Vol. 4, no. 4 (April
1982), p. 11. English. **DESCR:** Appointed
Officials; U.S. Small Business
Administration.

2183 News at the SBA. HISPANIC BUSINESS, Vol. 4,
no. 2 (February 1982), p. 22. English.
DESCR: *Biographical Notes; Castillo,
Irenemaree; Lopez, Reynaldo H.; U.S. Small
Business Administration.

2184 Top ranking Latino resigns from SBA.
NUESTRO, Vol. 6, no. 2 (March 1982), p. 45.
English. **DESCR:** Government; U.S. Small
Business Administration.

Cardenas, Rene

2185 Clifford, Terry. Book review of: PARENTING
IN A MULTI-CULTURAL SOCIETY. HISPANIC
JOURNAL OF BEHAVIORAL SCIENCES, Vol. 4, no.
3 (September 1982), p. 385-387. English.
DESCR: Book Reviews; Fantini, Mario;
*PARENTING IN A MULTI-CULTURAL SOCIETY.

Cardinale, Marcela

2186 Whisler, Kirk. Nosotros on film in Hollywood
and Latin America. CAMINOS, Vol. 3, no. 7
(July, August, 1982), p. 15-17. Bilingual.
DESCR: Artists; Espinoza, Jimmy; Films;
Gomez, Mike; *Nosotros [film production
company]; Ortiz, Yolanda; Television;
Velasco, Jerry.

Cardoso, Lawrence A.

2187 Almaraz, Felix D., Jr. Book review of:
MEXICAN EMIGRATION TO THE UNITED STATES,
1897-1931: SOCIO-ECONOMIC PATTERNS. GREAT
PLAINS QUARTERLY, Vol. 3, no. 2 (Spring
1983), p. 123-124. English. **DESCR:** Book
Reviews; *MEXICAN EMIGRATION TO THE UNITED
STATES 1897-1931: SOCIO-ECONOMIC PATTERNS.

2188 Bean, Frank D. Book review of: MEXICAN
EMIGRATION TO THE UNITED STATES, 1897-1931:
SOCIO-ECONOMIC PATTERNS. INTERNATIONAL
MIGRATION REVIEW, Vol. 16, no. 2 (Summer
1982), p. 493-494. English. **DESCR:** Book
Reviews; *MEXICAN EMIGRATION TO THE UNITED
STATES 1897-1931: SOCIO-ECONOMIC PATTERNS.

2189 Hoffman, Abraham. Book review of: MEXICANO

RESISTANCE IN THE SOUTHWEST: "THE SACRED
RIGHT OF SELF-PRESERVATION". PACIFIC
HISTORICAL REVIEW, Vol. 51, no. 2 (May
1982), p. 230-231. English. **DESCR:** Book
Reviews; *MEXICAN EMIGRATION TO THE UNITED
STATES 1897-1931: SOCIO-ECONOMIC PATTERNS;
Migration.

2190 Romo, Ricardo. Book review of: MEXICAN
EMIGRATION TO THE UNITED STATES, 1897-1931:
SOCIO-ECONOMIC PATTERNS. SOUTHWESTERN
HISTORICAL QUARTERLY, Vol. 86, no. 4 (April
1983), p. 576-577. English. **DESCR:** Book
Reviews; *MEXICAN EMIGRATION TO THE UNITED
STATES 1897-1931: SOCIO-ECONOMIC PATTERNS.

Cardova, Mark

2191 Clarence and angel. NUESTRO, Vol. 6, no. 1
(January, February, 1982), p. 61. English.
DESCR: Films.

Careers

2192 Aqui en Tejas: staying on that long road to
success: mentors, how to find a helping hand
to assist you achieve educational goals.
NATIONAL HISPANIC JOURNAL, Vol. 2, no. 1
(Summer 1983), p. 8. English. **DESCR:**
Education; Fashion; *Mentors.

2193 Borman, Adele T. "Who do you think you are,
anyway? CAMINOS, Vol. 4, no. 1-2 (January,
February, 1983), p. 24-25,71. English.
DESCR: *Identity.

2194 Bunuel, Janie. The need for goal setting.
CAMINOS, Vol. 4, no. 1-2 (January, February,
1983), p. 20. English.

2195 Cantu, Hector. Aqui en Austin: this is Olga
Campos reporting. NATIONAL HISPANIC JOURNAL,
Vol. 1, no. 3 (Summer, Fall, 1982), p. 7.
English. **DESCR:** Campos, Olga; *KTBC-TV,
Austin, TX [television station]; Mass Media;
Television.

2196 Captor, Rich. College and the Navy. CAMINOS,
Vol. 4, no. 1-2 (January, February, 1983),
p. 26-27. Bilingual. **DESCR:** *Military;
Reserve Officer Training Corps (ROTC); U.S.
Navy.

2197 Career intelligencer. HISPANIC BUSINESS,
Vol. 5, no. 9 (September 1983), p. 30.
English. **DESCR:** California Chicano News
Media Association (CCNMA); Journalism;
National Consortium for Graduate Degrees for
Minorities in Engineering.

2198 Career intelligencer. HISPANIC BUSINESS,
Vol. 5, no. 10 (October 1983), p. 30.
English. **DESCR:** Affirmative Action Programs.

2199 Careers: formula for jobs '82. LATINO, Vol.
53, no. 2 (March, April, 1982), p. 9+.
English.

2200 Careers: recipe for success. LATINO, Vol.
53, no. 2 (March, April, 1982), p. 22-24.
English. **DESCR:** *Cisneros, Henry, Mayor of
San Antonio, TX; *Colleges and Universities.

2201 Chavarria, Jesus. The systems way. HISPANIC
BUSINESS, Vol. 4, no. 4 (April 1982), p. 6.
English. **DESCR:** College Graduates;
Employment; *Higher Education.

Careers (cont.)

2202 Chavez, Rigo. Job counseling, role models mean a lot. HISPANIC BUSINESS, Vol. 4, no. 8 (August 1983), p. 12. English. **DESCR:** *Counseling Services (Educational); Cuevas, Hector; Escobedo, Ed; Professional Opportunities Program (POP); *Stanford University, Stanford, CA.

2203 Commercial art as a career. CAMINOS, Vol. 4, no. 9 (October 1983), p. 32-35. English. **DESCR:** Artists; Chavez Lichwardt, Leticia; Gomez, Dario; Guerrero, Ernest R.; Melendez, Bill; Reyes, Gil; Santistevan, August.

2204 de la Isla, Jose. Math-based careers. HISPANIC BUSINESS, Vol. 5, no. 4 (April 1983), p. 20. English. **DESCR:** Engineering; Mathematics, Engineering and Science Achievement (MESA); Medical Personnel.

2205 Garcia, Ray J. The technological challenge: Hispanics as participants or observers. HISPANIC BUSINESS, Vol. 4, no. 7 (July 1982), p. 20-21,26. English. **DESCR:** Education; *Engineering as a Profession; Technology.

2206 Gente; FBI head, two agents praised by Texas house. NUESTRO, Vol. 7, no. 4 (May 1983), p. 52. English. **DESCR:** *Federal Bureau of Investigation (FBI); Salinas, Raul; *Texas.

2207 Gomez, Dalia. Needed: Latino CPA's. NUESTRO, Vol. 6, no. 1 (January, February, 1982), p. 25-28. English. **DESCR:** *Accounting; Frank, Eleanor Marie; Karpel, Miguel; Quezada, Felipe L.; Rodriguez, Julio H.; Umpierre, Raphael; Zuzueta, Joseph.

2208 Gould, Sam. Correlates of career progression among Mexican-American college graduates. JOURNAL OF VOCATIONAL BEHAVIOR, Vol. 20, no. 1 (February 1982), p. 93-110. English. **DESCR:** *College Graduates; Colleges and Universities; Cultural Characteristics; Social Mobility.

2209 Hawley, Peggy and Even, Brenda. Work and sex-role attitudes in relation to education and other characteristics. VOCATIONAL GUIDANCE QUARTERLY, Vol. 31, no. 2 (December 1982), p. 101-108. English. **DESCR:** Chicanas; Ethnic Groups; Psychological Testing; *Sex Roles; Working Women.

2210 Hispanic caucus offers Washington, fellowships. NUESTRO, Vol. 6, no. 3 (April 1982), p. 62. English. **DESCR:** *Congressional Hispanic Caucus; Political Science.

2211 Hughes invests in the future. HISPANIC BUSINESS, Vol. 4, no. 11 (November 1982), p. 8-9,26. English. **DESCR:** *Educational Opportunities; *Engineering as a Profession; Minority Introduction to Engineering (MITE); University of California, Los Angeles (UCLA).

2212 Job hunting & bolts. CAMINOS, Vol. 4, no. 1-2 (January, February, 1983), p. 19. English. **DESCR:** Discrimination in Employment.

2213 Lanier, Alfredo S. Making it seem easy, from intern to account executive. HISPANIC BUSINESS, Vol. 4, no. 8 (August 1983), p. 16-17+. English. **DESCR:** *Accountants; Chicanas; Employment Training; *Fernandez, Margarita; INROADS; Standard Oil Corp.

2214 Lourenzo, Susan V. Early outreach: career awareness for health professions. JOURNAL OF MEDICAL EDUCATION, Vol. 58, no. 1 (January 1983), p. 39-44. English. **DESCR:** Affirmative Action; College Preparation; *Medical Education; *Recruitment.

2215 Math-based careers. HISPANIC BUSINESS, Vol. 4, no. 1 (January 1982), p. 20. English. **DESCR:** *College Graduates; *Cox, George; Employment; Engineering as a Profession; *Hispanic Society of Engineers and Scientists (HSES); *Leadership, Education and Development Program in Business (LEAD).

2216 Math-based careers. HISPANIC BUSINESS, Vol. 4, no. 3 (March 1982), p. 20. English. **DESCR:** Congressional Hispanic Caucus; Consortium for Graduate Study in Management; *Educational Opportunities; *Financial Aid.

2217 Math-based careers. HISPANIC BUSINESS, Vol. 4, no. 4 (April 1982), p. 20,24. English. **DESCR:** Chicanas; *Engineering as a Profession; Government Employees; National Action Council for Minorities in Engineering (NACME); National Hispanic Field Service Program.

2218 Math-based careers. HISPANIC BUSINESS, Vol. 4, no. 5 (May 1982), p. 22. English. **DESCR:** Education; Engineering as a Profession; *Financial Aid; National Action Council for Minorities in Engineering (NACME); Society for Hispanic Professional Engineers (SHPE).

2219 Math-based careers. HISPANIC BUSINESS, Vol. 4, no. 7 (July 1982), p. 22. English. **DESCR:** Engineering as a Profession; LULAC National Education Service Centers (LNESC); National Action Council for Minorities in Engineering (NACME).

2220 Math-based careers. HISPANIC BUSINESS, Vol. 4, no. 10 (October 1982), p. 20. English. **DESCR:** Educational Opportunities; Engineering as a Profession; Financial Aid; Minority Business Development Agency (MBDA); National Action Council for Minorities in Engineering (NACME); National Association of Independent Schools (NAIS).

2221 Math-based careers. HISPANIC BUSINESS, Vol. 5, no. 2 (February 1983), p. 22. English. **DESCR:** Engineering; Financial Aid; Mathematics; Mathematics, Engineering and Science Achievement (MESA); National Action Council for Minorities in Engineering (NACME).

2222 Math-based careers. HISPANIC BUSINESS, Vol. 5, no. 5 (May 1983), p. 26. English. **DESCR:** Engineering as a Profession; Financial Aid; Income; Labor Supply and Market; Mexican American Engineering Society (MAES) National Symposium (5th), Fullerton, CA, April 13-15, 1980; University of California, Santa Barbara.

2223 Math-based careers. HISPANIC BUSINESS, Vol. 5, no. 7 (July 1983), p. 22. English. **DESCR:** Education; Mathematics; National Council for Minorities in Engineering (NACME); Nursing.

2224 Math-based careers. HISPANIC BUSINESS, Vol. 5, no. 9 (September 1983), p. 28. English. **DESCR:** Andrew W. Mellon Foundation; Employment; Engineering as a Profession; Financial Aid; Garcia, Mary; Higher Education; National Council for Minorities in Engineering (NACME); National Medical Fellowships (NMF); Rivera, Lourdes.

Careers (cont.)

2225 Math-based careers. HISPANIC BUSINESS, Vol. 5, no. 10 (October 1983), p. 28. English. **DESCR:** Carnation Company; Chicanas; Education; Engineering as a Profession; Hispanic Policy Development Project; Minority Engineering Education Center, University of California, Los Angeles; Science as a Profession; University of California, Los Angeles (UCLA).

2226 Math-based careers. HISPANIC BUSINESS, Vol. 5, no. 11 (November 1983), p. 32. English. **DESCR:** Education; Employment Training; INROADS; Mathematics, Engineering and Science Achievement (MESA); Mexican American Legal Defense and Educational Fund (MALDEF); Soriano, Esteban.

2227 Math-based careers. HISPANIC BUSINESS, Vol. 5, no. 12 (December 1983), p. 40. English. **DESCR:** Council on Legal Education Opportunities (CLEO); Education; Employment Training; Graduate Schools; High Technology High School, San Antonio, TX; Legal Education; Mexican American Legal Defense and Educational Fund (MALDEF); San Antonio, TX; Science as a Profession.

2228 Math-based careers. HISPANIC BUSINESS, Vol. 4, no. 8 (August 1983), p. 20. English. **DESCR:** Brigham Young University; Business Administration; Coalition of Spanish-Speaking Mental Health Organization (COSSMHO), Annual Regional Conference, Los Angeles, March 14-15, 1975; Cooperative Extension Programs; Education; Employment Training; Financial Aid; Medical Personnel.

2229 Mendoza, Samuel M. Careers for Chicanos: computers, engineering, science/computadoras, ingenieria, ciencia. CAMINOS, Vol. 3, no. 3 (March 1982), p. 14-16. Bilingual. **DESCR:** Computers; Engineering as a Profession; Science as a Profession.

2230 Padilla, Steve. Adelina Pena Callahan: restaurateur. NUESTRO, Vol. 7, no. 4 (May 1983), p. 26-29. English. **DESCR:** Businesspeople; *Callahan, Adelina Pena; Food Industry; La Fonda Restaurant; Working Women.

2231 Padilla, Steve. Choosing a career. NUESTRO, Vol. 7, no. 1 (January, February, 1983), p. 13-19+. English. **DESCR:** Alvarado, Raul, Jr.; Computers; Diaz, William; Engineering as a Profession; Esparza, Alma; Flores, Francisco; Garcia, Linda; Medical Care; Soto, John; Yanez, Ricardo.

2232 Phillips, Susan D., et al. Career development of special populations: a framework for research. JOURNAL OF VOCATIONAL BEHAVIOR, Vol. 22, no. 1 (February 1983), p. 12-29. English. **DESCR:** College Graduates; *Research Methodology; Vocational Education.

2233 Q & A with Fernando Niebla: "You have to present yourself as a person that knows what he wants". CAMINOS, Vol. 4, no. 1-2 (January, February, 1983), p. 22-23,71. English. **DESCR:** Computers; Electronics Industry; *Niebla, Fernando.

2234 Quijada. What the corporate world wants and expects. CAMINOS, Vol. 4, no. 1-2 (January, February, 1983), p. 13-14,16+. Bilingual. **DESCR:** Business.

2235 Sargeant, Georgia. A woman's place is in the

bank. HISPANIC BUSINESS, Vol. 5, no. 10 (October 1983), p. 20-21+. English. **DESCR:** Accountants; *Banking Industry; Chicanas; *Olson, Ethel Ortega; Otero Savings and Loan, Alamogordo, TX.

2236 Snipp, C. Matthew and Tienda, Marta. New perspectives of Chicano intergenerational occupational mobility. SOCIAL SCIENCE JOURNAL, Vol. 19, no. 2 (April 1982), p. 37-49. English. **DESCR:** Age Groups; *Employment; Social Mobility.

2237 Students view career option. NUESTRO, Vol. 6, no. 6 (August 1982), p. 12. English. **DESCR:** *Business; Phoenix, AZ; Students.

2238 Tips for making the right moves in today's job markets. HISPANIC BUSINESS, Vol. 4, no. 4 (April 1982), p. 10. English.

2239 Tips for making the right moves in today's job markets. HISPANIC BUSINESS, Vol. 4, no. 5 (May 1982), p. 16. English. **DESCR:** California Chicano News Media Association (CCNMA); Mass Media.

2240 Tips for making the right moves in today's job markets. HISPANIC BUSINESS, Vol. 4, no. 7 (July 1982), p. 14. English. **DESCR:** California Chicano News Media Association (CCNMA); Employment.

2241 Tips for making the right moves in today's job markets. HISPANIC BUSINESS, Vol. 4, no. 12 (December 1982), p. 28. English. **DESCR:** Marketing.

2242 Tips for making the right moves in today's job markets. HISPANIC BUSINESS, Vol. 5, no. 5 (May 1983), p. 30. English. **DESCR:** Advertising; Employment; Hispanic Access to Services (HAS), Denver, CO; *Working Women.

2243 Tips for making the right moves in today's job markets. HISPANIC BUSINESS, Vol. 5, no. 6 (June 1983), p. 38. English. **DESCR:** Bilingual Bicultural Education.

2244 Tips for making the right moves in today's job markets. HISPANIC BUSINESS, Vol. 4, no. 8 (August 1983), p. 11+. English. **DESCR:** American G.I. Forum; Employment; Management; Military Service.

2245 Tom Velez: a man in control of his future. CAMINOS, Vol. 4, no. 1-2 (January, February, 1983), p. 9-10+. English. **DESCR:** Computer Technology Associates (CTA); Computers; *Velez, Tom.

2246 Trujillo, Leo G. Don't forget corporate business as a career. CAMINOS, Vol. 4, no. 1-2 (January, February, 1983), p. 7-8,71. Bilingual. **DESCR:** Business.

2247 Vara, Richard. Cracking the Big 8. HISPANIC BUSINESS, Vol. 4, no. 8 (August 1983), p. 18-19+. English. **DESCR:** *Accountants.

2248 Whisler, Kirk. Martha Cornejo Rottenberg: on opportunities & advancement. CAMINOS, Vol. 4, no. 1-2 (January, February, 1983), p. 17-18,71+. English. **DESCR:** *Cornejo Rottenberg, Martha; Electronics Industry; Mining Industry; TRW Defense Systems Group.

Caribbean Basin Initiative (CBI)

2249 Chamber, Peace Corps join in training effort. NUESTRO, Vol. 7, no. 1 (January, February, 1983), p. 36. English. DESCR: Business; *Ibero-American Chamber of Commerce; Latin America; Peace Corps.

2250 Foreign trade: outlook for the Caribbean Basin Initiative. HISPANIC BUSINESS, Vol. 4, no. 8 (August 1983), p. 23+. English. DESCR: *Foreign Trade; International Economic Relations; Latin America.

Caribbean Region

2251 Bunnell, Robert. A conversation with Commodore Diego Hernandez. NUESTRO, Vol. 7, no. 8 (October 1983), p. 15-17. English. DESCR: *Hernandez, Diego; Military Service; U.S. Navy.

2252 Foreign trade. HISPANIC BUSINESS, Vol. 5, no. 3 (March 1983), p. 23. English. DESCR: Export Trade; *Foreign Trade; Minority Business Development Agency (MBDA).

2253 Foreign trade. HISPANIC BUSINESS, Vol. 5, no. 5 (May 1983), p. 32. English. DESCR: Export Trade; *Foreign Trade; Latin America; Minority Business Development Agency (MBDA); Panama.

2254 Foreign trade. HISPANIC BUSINESS, Vol. 5, no. 10 (October 1983), p. 29. English. DESCR: Agency for International Development (AID); Economic History and Conditions; *Foreign Trade; HOW TO EXPORT: A MARKETING MANUAL; Mexico; Puerto Rico; U.S. Trade Center (Mexico City).

Caribbean Relief Program

2255 Estevez, Guillermo. Resettling the Cuban refugees in New Jersey. MIGRATION TODAY, Vol. 11, no. 4-5 (1983), p. 28-33. English. DESCR: *Cubanos; Immigration; International Rescue Committee; *New Jersey; Refugees.

Caricature

2256 Al dia. LATINA, Vol. 1, no. 1 (1982), p. 64. English.

2257 Efren. [Untitled]. MAIZE, Vol. 3, no. 1-2 (Fall, Winter, 1979, 1980), p. 67. Spanish. DESCR: *Graphics.

2258 Naranjo. Excerpts from la escena politica 1975. MAIZE, Vol. 2, no. 1 (Fall 1978), p. 6,61. English.

2259 Naranjo. El mundo. MAIZE, Vol. 1, no. 4 (Summer 1978), p. 46,60. English.

2260 La Nopalera. Hace un chingo de anos ... [drawing]. MAIZE, Vol. 1, no. 2 (Winter 1978), p. 18. Spanish.

2261 Ortego y Gasca, Felipe de. Fables of identity: stereotype and caricature of Chicanos in Steinbeck's TORTILLA FLAT. JOURNAL OF ETHNIC STUDIES, Vol. 1, no. 1 (Spring 1973), p. 39-43. English. DESCR: Chicanos in American Literature; Literature; Steinbeck, John; *Stereotypes; TORTILLA FLAT.

2262 Romano, Branko E. Chicken toons. EL GRITO DEL SOL, Vol. 6, no. 1-2 (1981), p. 1-93. English.

Carlos, Juan, King of Spain

2263 Mimiaga, Hector. El rey saluda a America. LATINO, Vol. 53, no. 2 (March, April, 1982), p. 13. English. DESCR: Politics.

Carmen, Julie

2264 Garcia, Ignacio M. Regional report, television: "Condo" canceled. NUESTRO, Vol. 7, no. 5 (June, July, 1983), p. 13. English. DESCR: Avalos, Luis; CONDO [televison series]; Latin Americans; Stereotypes; *Television.

Carnation Company

2265 Math-based careers. HISPANIC BUSINESS, Vol. 5, no. 10 (October 1983), p. 28. English. DESCR: *Careers; Chicanas; Education; Engineering as a Profession; Hispanic Policy Development Project; Minority Engineering Education Center, University of California, Los Angeles; Science as a Profession; University of California, Los Angeles (UCLA).

Carnaval Miami 82

2266 Chavarria, Jesus. The world according to Miami. HISPANIC BUSINESS, Vol. 4, no. 3 (March 1982), p. 6. English. DESCR: *Business; Cubanos; Miami, FL; *Urban Communities.

2267 The Little Havana development authority. HISPANIC BUSINESS, Vol. 4, no. 3 (March 1982), p. 10+. English. DESCR: *Community Development; Cubanos; Little Havana; Miami, FL.

Carol Wright Hispanic Program

2268 Mercado, Anthony. Do Hispanics use coupons? HISPANIC BUSINESS, Vol. 5, no. 12 (December 1983), p. 10. English. DESCR: Advertising; Donnelley Marketing; *Marketing.

Caroli, Betty

2269 Reimers, David M. Book review of: TODAY'S IMMIGRANTS, THEIR STORIES. INTERNATIONAL MIGRATION REVIEW, Vol. 16, no. 4 (Winter 1982), p. 900. English. DESCR: Book Reviews; Immigrants; Kessner, Thomas; Oral History; *TODAY'S IMMIGRANTS, THEIR STORIES.

Carpentier, Alejo

2270 Campbell, Stephanie. The artist in bourgeois society, as seen in Carpentier's LA CONSAGRACION DE LA PRIMAVERA. MAIZE, Vol. 3, no. 3-4 (Spring, Summer, 1980), p. 6-16. English. DESCR: Artists; *LA CONSAGRACION DE LA PRIMAVERA; Literary Criticism.

2271 Espinoza, Roberto. Sintesis vs. analysis: un problema de historicidad en las novelas de las dictaduras. MAIZE, Vol. 6, no. 1-2 (Fall, Winter, 1982, 1983), p. 7-27. Spanish. DESCR: Dictatorships; Garcia Marquez, Gabriel; Latin American Literature; *Literary Criticism; Novel; Roa Bastos, Augustos; Valle Inclan, Ramon; White, Lucas Edward.

Carpentier, Alejo (cont.)

2272 Maldonado-Denis, Manuel. El problema de las nacionalidades: la experiencia caribena. Paper presented at the "Dialogo de las Americas" conference. Mexico, D.F. September 9-14, 1982. REVISTA CHICANO-RIQUENA, Vol. 10, no. 4 (Fall 1982), p. 39-45. Spanish. DESCR: Capitalism; Cuba; El Salvador; Grenada; Guatemala; Imperialism; Marti, Jose; Nicaragua; *Political History and Conditions; Puerto Rico; United States.

Carr, Vikki

2273 Phillips, Melody. The Chicana: her attitudes towards the woman's liberation movement. COMADRE, no. 2 (Spring 1978), p. 42-50. English. DESCR: *Chicanas; FAMOUS MEXICAN-AMERICANS; Newton, Clark; Social History and Conditions; Women's Rights.

2274 Rosales, John. Holy Cross High: a Texas success story. NUESTRO, Vol. 6, no. 9 (November 1982), p. 41-42. English. DESCR: *Education; Holy Cross High School, San Antonio, TX; *San Antonio, TX.

Carranza Associates

2275 Communications/marketing. HISPANIC BUSINESS, Vol. 5, no. 8 (August 1983), p. 26. English. DESCR: Advertising Agencies; Bermudez & Associates; *Broadcast Media; Directories; Marketing.

Carranza, Elihu

2276 Chavez, Mauro. Carranza's CHICANISMO: PHILOSOPHICAL FRAGMENTS. JOURNAL OF ETHNIC STUDIES, Vol. 7, no. 3 (Fall 1979), p. 95-100. English. DESCR: Book Reviews; *Chicanismo; *CHICANISMO: PHILOSOPHICAL FRAGMENTS; Philosophy; Research Methodology.

Carranza, Venustiano

2277 Richmond, Douglas W. Mexican immigration and border strategy during the revolution, 1910-1920. NEW MEXICO HISTORICAL REVIEW, Vol. 57, no. 3 (July 1982), p. 269-288. English. DESCR: *Border Region; History; Immigration; Mexican Revolution - 1910-1920; Mexico; Social History and Conditions; United States-Mexico Relations.

Carrasco, Barbara

2278 The history of Los Angeles: a Mexican perspective. CHISMEARTE, no. 9 (September 1983), p. 20-21. English. DESCR: Los Angeles, CA; *Mural Art.

Carreras de Velasco, Mercedes

2279 Cardoso, Lawrence Anthony. Book review of: LOS MEXICANOS QUE DEVOLVIO LA CRISIS, 1929-1932. JOURNAL OF ETHNIC STUDIES, Vol. 5, no. 1 (Spring 1977), p. 120-122. Spanish. DESCR: Book Reviews; Deportation; Immigrant Labor; Immigration; Immigration Regulation and Control; *LOS MEXICANOS QUE DEVOLVIO LA CRISIS 1929-1932; Mexico; Social History and Conditions.

LA CARRETA MADE A U-TURN

2280 Clarke, Gerard R. Book review of: LA CARRETA MADE A U-TURN. MELUS: MULTI-ETHNIC LITERATURE OF THE UNITED STATES, Vol. 8, no. 1 (Spring 1981), p. 81-83. English. DESCR: *Laviera, Tato.

Carrillo, Ernesto

2281 Banberger, Ellen. Poesia nicaraguense. MAIZE, Vol. 5, no. 3-4 (Spring, Summer, 1982), p. 64-77. Spanish. DESCR: Belli, Gioconda; Cardenal, Ernesto; Coronel Urtecho, Jose; Gadea, Gerardo; Gomez, Manuel; Murillo, Rosario; *Nicaragua; Ojeda, Mirna; *Poetry; Revolutions; Rugama, Leonel.

Carrillo v. Whittier Union High School

2282 Santillan, Richard. [Translating population numbers into political power]. CHICANO LAW REVIEW, Vol. 6, (1983), p. 16-21. English. DESCR: Californios for Fair Representation; LATINOS IN THE LAW [symposium], UCLA, 1982; MEXICAN AMERICAN LEGAL DEFENSE AND EDUCATIONAL FUND NEWSLETTER; Political Representation; Reapportionment; *Voter Turnout.

Carrion, Arturo Morales

2283 Vivo, Paquita. Book review of: PUERTO RICO: A POLITICAL AND CULTURAL HISTORY. NUESTRO, Vol. 7, no. 5 (June, July, 1983), p. 63. English. DESCR: Book Reviews; History; Puerto Rican Studies; Puerto Rico; *PUERTO RICO: A POLITICAL AND CULTURAL HISTORY; United States History.

Carson, Norris L.

2284 White House honors three minority firms. NUESTRO, Vol. 7, no. 8 (October 1983), p. 51. English. DESCR: *Business Enterprises; Businesspeople; H & H Meat Products, Mercedes, TX; Hinojosa, Liborio; J.T. Construction Co., El Paso, TX; National Minority Enterprise Development Week; N.L. Carson Construction, Inc., Carthage, MS; Torres, Jaime.

Carter, Jimmy (President)

2285 Baca Barragan, Polly; Hamner, Richard; and Guerrero, Lena. [Untitled interview with State Senators (Colorado) Polly Baca-Barragan and Lena Guerrero. NATIONAL HISPANIC JOURNAL, Vol. 1, no. 2 (Winter 1982), p. 8-11. English. DESCR: Baca Barragan, Polly; Chicanas; Democratic Party; Elected Officials; Guerrero, Lena; *Political Parties and Organizations.

Carter, Lynda Cordoba

2286 Martinez, Marie. Lynda Cordoba Carter. LATINA, Vol. 1, no. 3 (1983), p. 16-17. English. DESCR: Biography.

2287 Nuestra gente. LATINO, Vol. 54, no. 8 (December 1983), p. 30. English. DESCR: *Biographical Notes; Businesspeople; Duran, Sandra; Patino, Lorenzo E.; Politics; Rembis, Deborah; Vega, Christopher.

Casa Aztlan

2288 Venerable, W. R. Student and parent attitudes toward college at five Hispanic learning centers in Illinois. JOURNAL OF THE NATIONAL ASSOC. OF COLLEGE ADMISSIONS COUNSELORS, Vol. 26, (April 1982), p. 19-23. English. DESCR: Chicago, IL; *Higher Education; Illinois Migrant Council; Lakeview Learning Center, Chicago, IL; *Secondary School Education.

Casa Blanca Youth Project

2289 Community watching: para la comunidad.
CAMINOS, Vol. 3, no. 2 (February 1982), p.
43-44. Bilingual. **DESCR:** Colegio Cesar
Chavez, Mt. Angel, OR; Colleges and
Universities; *Cultural Organizations;
Financial Aid; LULAC National Education
Service Centers (LNESC); Tonatiuh-Quinto Sol
Award for Literature, 1977-78; University of
California, Riverside.

Casado, Frank

2290 Diaz, Katherine A. El Adobe Cafe: a recipe
for success. CAMINOS, Vol. 3, no. 1 (January
1982), p. 33-34. Bilingual. **DESCR:**
*Restaurants.

Casado, Lucy

2291 Q & A: in the Hispanic community who are the
winners and losers of Reaganomics? CAMINOS,
Vol. 3, no. 3 (March 1982), p. 47.
Bilingual. **DESCR:** Echeveste, John; *Federal
Government; Flores, Bob; Leon, Virginia;
Mendoza, John; *Reagan, Ronald;
Sanchez-Alvarez, Gloria; Vidal de Neri,
Julieta.

Casas, Myrna

2292 Umpierre, Luz Maria. Introduccion al teatro
de Myrna Casas. THIRD WOMAN, Vol. 1, no. 2
(1982), p. 52-58. Spanish. **DESCR:** *Teatro.

Casasola, Agustin V.

2293 Quinlivan, Robert. The photographs of
Agustin V. Casasola; un epilogo de la
revolucion Mexicana de 1910. CAMINOS, Vol.
3, no. 1 (January 1982), p. 38-40.
Bilingual. **DESCR:** *Mexican Revolution -
1910-1920; *Photography.

Case Study

2294 Cuellar, Israel, et al. Clinical psychiatric
case presentation; culturally responsive
diagnostic formulation and treatment in an
Hispanic female. HISPANIC JOURNAL OF
BEHAVIORAL SCIENCES, Vol. 5, no. 1 (March
1983), p. 93-103. English. **DESCR:**
*ACCULTURATION RATING SCALE FOR MEXICAN
AMERICANS (ARSMA); Chicanas; Medical Care;
*Psychotherapy.

Casso, Ramiro

2295 Rivas, Mike. Keeping peace in paradise.
NATIONAL HISPANIC JOURNAL, Vol. 1, no. 2
(Winter 1982), p. 13-20. English. **DESCR:**
*Brand, Othal; Elections; Police; Police
Brutality; *Political Repression; Rio Grande
Valley, TX; THE MEXICAN AMERICAN: QUEST FOR
EQUALITY; Voter Turnout.

Castaneda, Carlos

2296 Nieto, Eva Margarita. El problema de la
juventud eterna en tres hechiceras en THE
SECOND RING OF POWER, LA MULATA DE CORDOBA y
AURA. LA PALABRA, Vol. 4, no. 1-2 (Spring,
Fall, 1982, 1983), p. 81-91. Spanish.
DESCR: AURA; Fuentes, Carlos; Gonzalez
Obregon, Luis; LA MULATA DE CORDOBA;
*Literary Criticism; Literature; Literature
Reviews; THE SECOND RING OF POWER.

Castaneda, Jaime

2297 Quinlivan, Robert. The Mexican and American
Foundation. CAMINOS, Vol. 3, no. 4 (April
1982), p. 24-25. Bilingual. **DESCR:**
*Organizations; San Diego, CA; United
States-Mexico Relations.

Castaneda Shular, Antonia

2298 Elizondo, Sergio D. Book review of:
LITERATURA CHICANA: TEXTO Y CONTEXTO.
JOURNAL OF ETHNIC STUDIES, Vol. 1, no. 1
(Spring 1973), p. 68-70. Bilingual. **DESCR:**
Book Reviews; Literary Criticism; Literary
History; Literary Influence; *LITERATURA
CHICANA: TEXTO Y CONTEXTO; Literature;
Sommers, Joseph; Teatro; Ybarra-Frausto,
Tomas.

Castanon, Rudy

2299 Cantu, Hector. The island. NATIONAL HISPANIC
JOURNAL, Vol. 1, no. 3 (Summer, Fall, 1982),
p. 6. English. **DESCR:** Business Enterprises;
*Curanderismo.

Castillo & Castillo Public Relations and Advertising

2300 Communications/marketing. HISPANIC BUSINESS,
Vol. 5, no. 6 (June 1983), p. 16. English.
DESCR: *Advertising Agencies; *Broadcast
Media; Castillo, Cid; Castillo, Patricia;
Latino Consortium, Los Angeles, CA;
Montemayor, Carlos R.; Montemayor y
Asociados, Inc.; Zubi Inc., Miami, FL.

Castillo, Cid

2301 Communications/marketing. HISPANIC BUSINESS,
Vol. 5, no. 6 (June 1983), p. 16. English.
DESCR: *Advertising Agencies; *Broadcast
Media; Castillo & Castillo Public Relations
and Advertising; Castillo, Patricia; Latino
Consortium, Los Angeles, CA; Montemayor,
Carlos R.; Montemayor y Asociados, Inc.;
Zubi Inc., Miami, FL.

Castillo, Irenemaree

2302 News at the SBA. HISPANIC BUSINESS, Vol. 4,
no. 2 (February 1982), p. 22. English.
DESCR: *Biographical Notes; Cardenas,
Michael; Lopez, Reynaldo H.; U.S. Small
Business Administration.

2303 People. HISPANIC BUSINESS, Vol. 5, no. 4
(April 1983), p. 9. English. **DESCR:**
Alvarado, Linda M.; *Biographical Notes;
Businesspeople; Castillo, Sylvia; Del Junco,
Tirso; Gutierrez, Jose Roberto; Juarez, Joe;
Mata, Bill; Miyares, Marcelino; Montanez
Davis, Grace; Montoya, Velma; Pineda, Pat;
Siberio, Julio; Thompson, Edith Lopez.

2304 Stockton woman named regional head of SBA.
NUESTRO, Vol. 6, no. 1 (January, February,
1982), p. 47. English. **DESCR:** U.S. Small
Business Administration.

Castillo, Manny

2305 Ortiz, Carlos V. NUESTRO'S sixth annual
all-star baseball team. NUESTRO, Vol. 7, no.
2 (March 1983), p. 33-37. English. **DESCR:**
Andujar, Joaquin; Barojas, Salome;
*Baseball; Concepcion, Dave; Cruz, Jose;
Garcia, Damaso; Guerrero, Pedro; Hernandez,
Keith; Lezcano, Sixto; Martinez, Tippy;
Pena, Tony; Piniella, Lou; Sports;
Valenzuela, Fernando.

Castillo, Patricia

2306 Communications/marketing. HISPANIC BUSINESS, Vol. 5, no. 6 (June 1983), p. 16. English. **DESCR:** *Advertising Agencies; *Broadcast Media; Castillo & Castillo Public Relations and Advertising; Castillo, Cid; Latino Consortium, Los Angeles, CA; Montemayor, Carlos R.; Montemayor y Asociados, Inc.; Zubi Inc., Miami, FL.

Castillo, Sylvia

2307 People. HISPANIC BUSINESS, Vol. 5, no. 4 (April 1983), p. 9. English. **DESCR:** Alvarado, Linda M.; *Biographical Notes; Businesspeople; Castillo, Irenemaree; Del Junco, Tirso; Gutierrez, Jose Roberto; Juarez, Joe; Mata, Bill; Miyares, Marcelino; Montanez Davis, Grace; Montoya, Velma; Pineda, Pat; Siberio, Julio; Thompson, Edith Lopez.

2308 Professional network. HISPANIC BUSINESS, Vol. 4, no. 9 (September 1982), p. 18,26+. English. **DESCR:** California; Higher Education; Hispanic Women in Higher Education (HWHE); Mentors; *Self-Help Groups.

Castro, Fidel

2309 Castro's sister takes U.S. citizenship oath. NUESTRO, Vol. 6, no. 3 (April 1982), p. 38. English. **DESCR:** *Castro, Juanita; Cubanos.

2310 Garcia, Margarita. The last days in Cuba: personal accounts of the circumstances of the exit. MIGRATION TODAY, Vol. 11, no. 4-5 (1983), p. 13-26. English. **DESCR:** Cuba; *Cuban Boatlift; *Cubanos; Hudson County, NJ; Immigration; Peruvian Embassy (Cuba).

Castro, Juanita

2311 Castro's sister takes U.S. citizenship oath. NUESTRO, Vol. 6, no. 3 (April 1982), p. 38. English. **DESCR:** Castro, Fidel; Cubanos.

Castro, Thomas

2312 Diaz, Katherine A. Commercial radio and Hispanic community. CAMINOS, Vol. 3, no. 5 (May 1982), p. 40-41. Bilingual. **DESCR:** *Radio.

Castro, Tony

2313 Diaz, Katherine A. "And this year's winners are...". CAMINOS, Vol. 4, no. 1-2 (January, February, 1983), p. 39-54,74+. English. **DESCR:** *Awards; Elizalde, Hector; Flores, Tom; Martinez, Esperanza; Mendizabal, Maritza; Molina, Gloria; Moya, Connie; Placentia, Joe; Quesada, Leticia; Rios, David N.; Ybarra, Lea; Zapata, Carmen.

Castro Vallejo, Sebastian

2314 Shiell, Pancho. Sebastian Castro Vallejo: artist on stage and on canvas. NUESTRO, Vol. 6, no. 7 (September 1982), p. 63-64. English. **DESCR:** Art; Artists.

Catalogues

2315 Cabello-Argandona, Roberto; Crary, Eleanor R.; and Pisano, Vivian M. Subject access for Hispanic library users. LIBRARY JOURNAL, Vol. 107, no. 14 (August 1982), p. 1383-1385. English. **DESCR:** *HISPANEX (Oakland, CA); Library Services; Public Libraries.

Cataract Engineering and Construction, Inc.

2316 Balkan, D. Carlos. The nuclear powered Mr. Carlos Pimentel. HISPANIC BUSINESS, Vol. 4, no. 2 (February 1982), p. 16-17+. English. **DESCR:** Biography; Business Enterprises; Businesspeople; Energy Industries; *Pimentel, Carlos.

2317 Chavarria, Jesus. Varieties of energy. HISPANIC BUSINESS, Vol. 4, no. 2 (February 1982), p. 6. English. **DESCR:** Business Enterprises; Energy Industries; *Star-Adair Insulation, Inc.

Catholic Church

2318 Askin, Steve. Boston church encourages labor talks. NATIONAL CATHOLIC REPORTER, Vol. 18, (July 30, 1982), p. 6. English. **DESCR:** Boston Archdiocese Justice and Peace Commission; Boycotts; Campbell Soup Co.; *Farm Labor Organizing Commmittee (FLOC); Labor Unions.

2319 Blea, Irene I. Book review of: BUT TIME AND CHANCE. CACR REVIEW, Vol. 1, no. 1 (September 1982), p. 132-133. English. **DESCR:** Book Reviews; *BUT TIME AND CHANCE; Chavez, Fray Angelico; Lamy, J.B.; Machelbeuf, Joseph P., Vicar; Martinez, Antonio, Fray; New Mexico.

2320 Carlos, Jess. The Filipinos: our forgotten cultural cousins. NUESTRO, Vol. 7, no. 8 (October 1983), p. 19-21. English. **DESCR:** Cultural Characteristics; *Philippines; Social History and Conditions.

2321 Day, Mark R. and Ramirez, Ricardo (Bishop of Las Cruces, NM),. Bishop: why have we had to wait so long for Hispanic leaders. NATIONAL CATHOLIC REPORTER, Vol. 19, (December 24, 1982), p. 6-7. English. **DESCR:** *Clergy; Leadership; *Ramirez, Ricardo (Bishop of Las Cruces, NM).

2322 Day, Mark R. Border group feeds, clothes dispossessed. NATIONAL CATHOLIC REPORTER, Vol. 19, (October 22, 1982), p. 5. English. **DESCR:** Border Region; Colonia Reforma, Tijuana, Baja California, Mexico; *Mexican American Neighborhood Organization (MANO).

2323 Day, Mark R. Hispanics 'want more bishops, input in church'. NATIONAL CATHOLIC REPORTER, Vol. 18, (March 12, 1982), p. 1. English. **DESCR:** Clergy; Cursillo Movement; Monterey, CA; Religion.

2324 Day, Mark R. Immigrants ... and Mexican citizens. NATIONAL CATHOLIC REPORTER, Vol. 18, (February 5, 1982), p. 3. English. **DESCR:** *Immigrants; Immigration and Naturalization Service (INS); Undocumented Workers.

2325 Deck, Allan Figueroa and Nunez, J. A. Religious enthusiasm and Hispanic youths. AMERICA [America Press, New York, NY], Vol. 147, (October 23, 1982), p. 232-234. English. **DESCR:** Religious Education.

2326 Doyle, Janet. Escoja educacion catolica! MOMENTUM, Vol. 14, no. 1 (February 1983), p. 37-38. English. **DESCR:** *Enrollment; *Religious Education; Toledo, OH.

Catholic Church (cont.)

2327 Elford, George. Catholic schools and bilingual education. MOMENTUM, Vol. 14, no. 1 (February 1983), p. 35-37. English. DESCR: *Bilingual Bicultural Education; Religious Education.

2328 Gibeau, Dawn. Mexican-American Center forges new vision. NATIONAL CATHOLIC REPORTER, Vol. 18, (July 30, 1982), p. 5+. English. DESCR: Elizondo, Virgilio; *Mexican American Cultural Center, San Antonio, TX; Religion.

2329 Gil, Carlos B. Withstanding time: the miracle of the Virgin of Guadalupe. NUESTRO, Vol. 7, no. 10 (December 1983), p. 46-47. English. DESCR: *Guadalupanismo; Mexico City; Religion; *Virgin of Guadalupe.

2330 Gonzalez, Juan. Caribbean voodoo: a Catholic response, a private encounter. NUESTRO, Vol. 7, no. 1 (January, February, 1983), p. 37. English. DESCR: Gods and Dieties; *Religion.

2331 Gumperz, John J. Hispanic Catholics. SOCIETY, Vol. 20, no. 3 (March, April, 1983), p. 2-3. English. DESCR: New York, NY.

2332 Hispanics keep the faith, but better parish work is needed. MIGRATION TODAY, Vol. 10, no. 5 (1982), p. 35. English. DESCR: Assimilation; Cultural Customs; *Religion.

2333 Morales, Cecilio J. The bishops' pastoral on Hispanic ministry. AMERICA [America Press, New York, NY], Vol. 149, (June, July, 1983), p. 7-9. English. DESCR: Clergy; Religion.

2334 Morales, Cecilio J. Challenges in Catholicism. NUESTRO, Vol. 6, no. 3 (April 1982), p. 26-27+. English. DESCR: *Religion.

2335 Morales, Cecilio J. Hispanics are moving toward the front pew. NATIONAL CATHOLIC REPORTER, Vol. 19, (December 31, 1982), p. 11. English. DESCR: *Clergy; Identity.

2336 Ramirez named bishop of Las Cruces diocese. NUESTRO, Vol. 6, no. 8 (October 1982), p. 43. English. DESCR: *Ramirez, Ricardo (Bishop of Las Cruces, NM); *Religion.

2337 Ramirez, Ricardo. Reflections on the Hispanicization of the liturgy. WORSHIP, Vol. 57, no. 1 (January 1983), p. 26-34. English. DESCR: Clergy; *Liturgy; Religion; Third General Conference of the Latin American Episcopate.

2338 Rosenhouse-Persson, Sandra and Sabagh, Georges. Attitudes toward abortion among Catholic Mexican-American women: the effects of religiosity and education. DEMOGRAPHY, Vol. 20, no. 1 (February 1983), p. 87-98. English. DESCR: Abortion; Attitude (Psychological); Education; Religion.

2339 Salvatierra, Richard. Christmas mass at the Vatican: a burning memory. NUESTRO, Vol. 6, no. 10 (December 1982), p. 38-40. English. DESCR: *Short Story.

Catholic University, Washington, D.C.

2340 School focuses on Latino needs. NUESTRO, Vol. 7, no. 1 (January, February, 1983), p. 12. English. DESCR: Colleges and Universities; Education; *Hispanidad '83.

Cavazos, Richard E.

2341 Cavazos is nominated army four-star-general.

NUESTRO, Vol. 6, no. 1 (January, February, 1982), p. 47. English. DESCR: *Military Service.

Cavazos, Roy

2342 Houstonite builds successful business: home-started business exceeds millions in foreign trade sales. NATIONAL HISPANIC JOURNAL, Vol. 1, no. 4 (Spring 1983), p. 7. English. DESCR: Business; *Business Enterprises; Businesspeople; Minority Business Development Agency (MBDA); *National Economic Development Association (NEDA); U.S. Small Business Administration.

Ceballos, Sonia Ceban

2343 Nuestra gente. LATINO, Vol. 53, no. 2 (March, April, 1982), p. 30. English. DESCR: Asip, Patricia V.; *Biographical Notes; Gonzales, Modesto; Septien, Rafael.

Celaya, Mona

2344 Rhonda Ramirez is Miss Black Velvet Latina. HISPANIC BUSINESS, Vol. 5, no. 3 (March 1983), p. 12-13. English. DESCR: *Beauty Contests; Marketing; Miss Black Velvet Latina.

La Cena Fine Foods, Ltd.

2345 Gupta, Udayan. Hispanic foods in New York: the race for number two. HISPANIC BUSINESS, Vol. 5, no. 8 (August 1983), p. 18-19+. English. DESCR: Condal Distributor, Inc.; Consumers; *Food Industry; Goya Foods; Iberia Foods Corp.; Recipes.

Census

2346 1980 census data on Hispanics. CAMINOS, Vol. 3, no. 9 (October 1982), p. 35-39. English.

2347 1983 U.S. population reaches 232.6 million. NUESTRO, Vol. 7, no. 1 (January, February, 1983), p. 47. English. DESCR: *Population; Population Trends.

2348 Bean, Frank D.; King, Allan G.; and Passel, Jeffrey S. The number of illegal migrants of Mexican origin in the United States: sex ratio-based estimates for 1980. DEMOGRAPHY, Vol. 20, no. 1 (February 1983), p. 99-109. English. DESCR: Migration; *Population; Statistics; Undocumented Workers.

2349 Bletzer, Keith V. A follow-up note on census techniques for enumerating the Hispanic population. HUMAN ORGANIZATION, Vol. 41, no. 3 (Fall 1982), p. 281-282. English.

2350 Cantu, Hector. Hispanic numbers rising. NATIONAL HISPANIC JOURNAL, Vol. 1, no. 3 (Summer, Fall, 1982), p. 7. English. DESCR: Austin, TX; Demography; Population; *Population Trends.

2351 Census information: 1980 U.S. census report on nation's racial group. NUESTRO, Vol. 5, no. 8 (November 1981), p. 34-37. English. DESCR: *Ethnic Groups.

2352 Commerce department releases census data. NUESTRO, Vol. 6, no. 4 (May 1982), p. 58. English.

2353 Data sources for information on Hispanics. CAMINOS, Vol. 3, no. 9 (October 1982), p. 34. Bilingual.

Census (cont.)

2354 Estrada, Leobardo F. Significance of the 1980 census to Latinos. CAMINOS, Vol. 3, no. 9 (October 1982), p. 29-31. Bilingual.

2355 Garcia, Philip and Maldonado, Lionel A. America's Mexicans: a plea for specificity. SOCIAL SCIENCE JOURNAL, Vol. 19, no. 2 (April 1982), p. 9-24. English. DESCR: *Demography; Ethnic Groups; Statistics.

2356 Gay, Eva. How to understand the 1980 census data. CAMINOS, Vol. 3, no. 9 (October 1982), p. 33-34. Bilingual.

2357 Gay, Eva. What the 1980 census means to Hispanics. CAMINOS, Vol. 3, no. 9 (October 1982), p. 26-28. Bilingual.

2358 Giachello, Aida L., et al. Uses of the 1980 census for Hispanic health services research. AMERICAN JOURNAL OF PUBLIC HEALTH, Vol. 73, no. 3 (March 1983), p. 266-274. English. DESCR: Public Health; Research Methodology; *Surveys.

2359 Gober, Patricia and Behr, Michelle. Central cities and suburbs as distinct place types: myth or fact? ECONOMIC GEOGRAPHY, Vol. 58, no. 4 (October 1982), p. 371-385. English. DESCR: Blacks; Population Distribution; Suburban Communities; *Urban Communities.

2360 Government review. NUESTRO, Vol. 7, no. 2 (March 1983), p. 42. English. DESCR: A WORKING WOMAN'S GUIDE TO HER JOB RIGHTS; Adoption; Business Enterprises; Chicanas; Discrimination in Employment; *Government Services; GUIDE TO FEDERAL MINORITY ENTERPRISE AND RELATED ASSISTANCE PROGRAMS; Population Trends; Study Abroad; U.S. Information Agency (USIA).

2361 Hispanics and the census. NUESTRO, Vol. 6, no. 7 (September 1982), p. 46-47. English. DESCR: *Congressional Hispanic Caucus.

2362 Huerta, John. The future of Latino political power. CAMINOS, Vol. 4, no. 3 (March 1983), p. 44-46,49. English. DESCR: *Politics; *Voter Turnout.

2363 Russell, Cheryl. The news about Hispanics. AMERICAN DEMOGRAPHICS, Vol. 5, no. 3 (March 1983), p. 14-25. English. DESCR: Cubanos; *Population; Puerto Ricans.

2364 A territorial approach to representation for illegal aliens. MICHIGAN LAW REVIEW, Vol. 80, no. 6 (May 1982), p. 1342-1371. English. DESCR: Federation for American Immigration Reform (FAIR); Population; Reapportionment; Reynolds, Steve; *Undocumented Workers; Voting Rights.

2365 Vidal, Jose and Galarza, Carlos V. CAMINO'S census effectiveness poll. CAMINOS, Vol. 3, no. 9 (October 1982), p. 32. English.

Central America

2366 Caldera, Carmela. Two views on Central America (interview). CAMINOS, Vol. 4, no. 8 (September 1983), p. 12-16,50. Bilingual. DESCR: *International Relations; Sanchez, Philip V.; Torres, Esteban E.

2367 Chacon, Jose Mividal. Resena historica del periodismo en Centroamerica. CAMINOS, Vol. 4, no. 8 (September 1983), p. 20-21,50+. Spanish. DESCR: History; *Journalism.

2368 Diaz, Katherine A. Henry G. Cisneros on

Central American commission (interview). CAMINOS, Vol. 4, no. 8 (September 1983), p. 10,48. English. DESCR: *Cisneros, Henry, Mayor of San Antonio, TX; International Relations; National Bipartisan Commission on Central America; United States.

2369 Emigrantes centroamericanos en Baja California Norte. INFORME: RELACIONES MEXICO-ESTADOS UNIDOS, Vol. 1, no. 3 (July, December, 1982), p. 227-241. Spanish. DESCR: *Baja California, Mexico; *Immigration.

2370 N.A.L.E.O.'s "Fiesta '83". CAMINOS, Vol. 4, no. 10 (November 1983), p. 28-29. English. DESCR: Baca Barragan, Polly; Bilingual Bicultural Education; Fiesta '83; Garcia, Robert; Immigration; International Relations; Mendez, Olga; *National Association of Latino Elected Officials (NALEO); Simpson-Mazzoli Bill; United States-Mexico Relations.

2371 Reagan, Ronald. "There is a war in Central America" (speech). CAMINOS, Vol. 4, no. 8 (September 1983), p. 9. English. DESCR: *International Relations; United States.

2372 Regional report, Latin America: marchers oppose Reagan policies. NUESTRO, Vol. 7, no. 4 (May 1983), p. 11. English. DESCR: Demonstrations; International Relations; *Latin America; *Reagan, Ronald; Stanford University, Stanford, CA.

El Centro Community Health Care Center

2373 Hough, Richard. The Los Angeles Epidemiologic Catchment Area research program and the epidemiology of psychiatric disorders among Mexican Americans. JOURNAL OF OPERATIONAL PSYCHIATRY, Vol. 14, no. 1 (1983), p. 42-51. English. DESCR: Acculturation; Diagnostic Interview Schedule (DIS); Los Angeles, CA; *Los Angeles Epidemiologic Catchment Area Research Program (LAECA); *Mental Health.

Centro Cultural Fondo Nacional para Actividades Sociales (FONOPAS)

2374 Esparza, Antonio. The new spectacular Tijuana cultural center. CAMINOS, Vol. 3, no. 11 (December 1982), p. 18,20,22. English. DESCR: Tijuana, Mexico; *Tourism.

2375 Historic Baja captured on film. CAMINOS, Vol. 3, no. 11 (December 1982), p. 21. English. DESCR: *Baja California, Mexico; Photography; *Tijuana, Mexico; *Tourism.

2376 Whisler, Kirk. Q & A with Guillermo Schmirdhuber de la Mora, Centro Cultural FONOPAS director: "We try to balance education and culture with entertainment". CAMINOS, Vol. 3, no. 11 (December 1982), p. 19,23. Bilingual. DESCR: *Baja California, Mexico; *Schmidhuber de la Mora, Guillermo; *Tourism.

Centro de Ninos

2377 For children - Centros de Ninos. CAMINOS, Vol. 4, no. 8 (September 1983), p. 44. English. DESCR: *Child Care Centers.

El Centro Mexicano del Libro

2378 Mexican centers advance U.S. ties. NUESTRO, Vol. 7, no. 1 (January, February, 1983), p. 10-11. English. DESCR: Art Galleries; Los Angeles, CA; Mexico; Museums; New York, NY; Publishing Industry.

Centro Nacional de Informacion y Estadistica del Trabajo (CENINET)

2379 Corwin, Arthur F. The numbers game: estimates of illegal aliens in the United States, 1970-1981. LAW AND CONTEMPORARY PROBLEMS, Vol. 45, no. 2 (Spring 1982), p. 223-297. English. DESCR: Bustamante, Jorge A.; Demography; Federation for American Immigration Reform (FAIR); Mexican American Legal Defense and Educational Fund (MALDEF); *Select Commission on Immigration and Refugee Policy; Simpson-Mazzoli Bill; *Statistics; *Undocumented Workers.

CERAMIC TOMB SCULPTURE FROM ANCIENT WEST MEXICO

2380 A potpourri of pre-Columbian art. NUESTRO, Vol. 7, no. 6 (August 1983), p. 59-60. English. DESCR: Ceramics; Exhibits; Frederick S. Wright Art Gallery, University of California, Los Angeles; Museum of Cultural History, University of California, Los Angeles; *Precolumbian Art; Sculpture.

Ceramics

2381 A potpourri of pre-Columbian art. NUESTRO, Vol. 7, no. 6 (August 1983), p. 59-60. English. DESCR: CERAMIC TOMB SCULPTURE FROM ANCIENT WEST MEXICO; Exhibits; Frederick S. Wright Art Gallery, University of California, Los Angeles; Museum of Cultural History, University of California, Los Angeles; *Precolumbian Art; Sculpture.

Cerda, Daniel

2382 San Antonio: an all American city. CAMINOS, Vol. 4, no. 8 (September 1983), p. 35. English. DESCR: *Artists; Congressional Arts Caucus; Gonzalez, Henry B.; *San Antonio, TX.

CERVANTES [film]

2383 Entertainment = diversion. CAMINOS, Vol. 3, no. 1 (January 1982), p. 41-42. Bilingual. DESCR: ANO NUEVO [film]; Broadcast Media; *Films; *SEGUIN [movie]; *Times Mirror Company.

Cervantes, Lorna Dee

2384 Cervantes, Lorna Dee. Book review of: EMPLUMADA. NUESTRO, Vol. 6, no. 5 (June, July, 1982), p. 56. English. DESCR: Book Reviews; *EMPLUMADA.

El Cervantes Media Awards

2385 Communications/marketing. HISPANIC BUSINESS, Vol. 5, no. 3 (March 1983), p. 21. English. DESCR: *Advertising; Awards; Consumers; Marketing; Spanish Advertising and Marketing Services (S.A.M.S.).

Cervantes, Rudy

2386 Caldera, Carmela. The consummate salesman: Rudy Cervantes. CAMINOS, Vol. 4, no. 4 (April 1983), p. 25-27. Bilingual. DESCR: Business Enterprises; Olympics.

Chacon, Peter R.

2387 Community watching. CAMINOS, Vol. 3, no. 5 (May 1982), p. 56-57. Bilingual. DESCR: Adelante Mujer Hispana Conference; Agricultural Laborers; Beilson, Anthony C.; Boycotts; Chicanas; *Cultural Organizations; Farm Labor Organizing Commmittee (FLOC); Financial Aid; Hollenbeck Junior High School, Los Angeles, CA; Junior High School Students; National League of Cities; Optimist Club of Greater East Los Angeles; Organizations; Project WELL (We Enjoy Learning & Leadership); Torres, Art.

2388 How to stuff a wild chile part II. CAMINOS, Vol. 3, no. 1 (January 1982), p. 31-32. English. DESCR: Albert, Margo; *Icaya, Rick; Lacayo, Frank L. "Hank"; *Recipes; *Rodriguez, Edmundo; Rodriguez, Edmundo M.; *Vasquez, Victor.

Chamber of Commerce

2389 Chavarria, Jesus. Chambers meet, Minnesota shines. HISPANIC BUSINESS, Vol. 4, no. 10 (October 1982), p. 6. English. DESCR: Businesspeople; U.S. Hispanic Chamber of Commerce.

2390 Miami's thriving Camacol. HISPANIC BUSINESS, Vol. 4, no. 3 (March 1982), p. 12-13. English. DESCR: Businesspeople; Camara de Comercio Latina de Los Estados Unidos (CAMACOL); Miami, FL.

Chang-Diaz, Franklin

2391 Valenzuela-Crocker, Elvira. Chang-Diaz has space shuttle role. NUESTRO, Vol. 7, no. 9 (November 1983), p. 11-12. English. DESCR: *Astronauts; National Aeronautics and Space Administration (NASA); Space Shuttle.

2392 Vara, Richard. Reaching for the stars: Franklin Chang-Diaz, astronaut and future scientist in space. HISPANIC BUSINESS, Vol. 5, no. 11 (November 1983), p. 18-19+. English. DESCR: Astronauts; National Aeronautics and Space Administration (NASA); Science as a Profession.

THE CHANGING DEMOGRAPHY OF SPANISH-AMERICANS

2393 Bunker, Stephen G. Book review of: THE CHANGING DEMOGRAPHY OF SPANISH-AMERICANS. CONTEMPORARY SOCIOLOGY: A JOURNAL OF REVIEWS, Vol. 11, no. 3 (May 1982), p. 270-273. English. DESCR: Book Reviews; Jaffee, A.J..

2394 Holmberg, Joan J. Book review of: THE CHANGING DEMOGRAPHY OF SPANISH-AMERICANS. INTERNATIONAL MIGRATION REVIEW, Vol. 17, no. 3 (Fall 1983), p. 506-507. English. DESCR: Book Reviews; Jaffee, A.J..

Charreada

2396 LeCompte, Mary Lou. The first American rodeo never happened. JOURNAL OF SPORT HISTORY, Vol. 9, no. 2 (Summer 1982), p. 89-96. English. DESCR: History.

La Chata Noloesca

2397 Ybarra-Frausto, Tomas. La Chata Noloesca: figura del donaire. REVISTA CHICANO-RIQUENA, Vol. 11, no. 1 (Spring 1983), p. 41-51. English. DESCR: Biography; Teatro.

Chavez, Carlos

2398 Mead, R. H. Latin American accents in new music. LATIN AMERICAN MUSIC REVIEW, Vol. 3, no. 2 (Fall, Winter, 1982), p. 207-228. English. DESCR: Cowell, Henry; *Music; *New Music.

2399 Stevenson, Robert. Carlos Chavez's United States press coverage. AZTLAN, Vol. 14, no. 1 (Spring 1983), p. 21-33. English. DESCR: Ethnomusicology; *Journalism; Musicians; Print Media.

2400 Stevenson, Robert. Relaciones de Carlos Chavez en Los Angeles. HETEROFONIA, Vol. 15, no. 1 (January, March, 1982), p. 3-19. Spanish. DESCR: Music.

Chavez, Cesar E.

2401 Brigham, Jack. Tribute to Cesar Chavez. CAMINOS, Vol. 4, no. 7 (July, August, 1983), p. 36. English.

2402 Chavez' union decentralizes. NUESTRO, Vol. 6, no. 7 (September 1982), p. 11-12. English. DESCR: Agricultural Laborers; Farmer Organizations; *United Farmworkers of America (UFW).

Chavez, Chris

2403 People. HISPANIC BUSINESS, Vol. 5, no. 9 (September 1983), p. 10. English. DESCR: *Businesspeople; Diez de Onate, Jorge; Franco Garcia, Freddie; Garcia, Hector P.; Lozano, Leticia Eugenia; Ravard, Rafael Alonzo; Rodriguez, Alberto Duque; Sanchez, Philip V.; Villalpando, Catalina.

Chavez, Fray Angelico

2404 Blea, Irene I. Book review of: BUT TIME AND CHANCE. CACR REVIEW, Vol. 1, no. 1 (September 1982), p. 132-133. English. DESCR: Book Reviews; *BUT TIME AND CHANCE; Catholic Church; Lamy, J.B.; Machelbeuf, Joseph P., Vicar; Martinez, Antonio, Fray; New Mexico.

2405 Lomeli, Francisco A. Book review of: MY PENITENTE LAND: REFLECTIONS ON SPANISH NEW MEXICO. NEW SCHOLAR, Vol. 8, no. 1-2 (Spring, Fall, 1982), p. 495-498. English. DESCR: Book Reviews; *MY PENITENTE LAND: REFLECTIONS ON SPANISH NEW MEXICO.

2406 Lomeli, Francisco A. Book review of: MY PENITENTE LAND: REFLECTIONS ON SPANISH NEW MEXICO. NEW SCHOLAR, Vol. 8, no. 1-2 (Spring, Fall, 1982), p. 495-498. English. DESCR: Book Reviews; *MY PENITENTE LAND: REFLECTIONS ON SPANISH NEW MEXICO.

2407 Weber, Kenneth R. Book review of: MY PENITENTE LAND: REFLECTIONS ON SPANISH NEW MEXICO. JOURNAL OF ETHNIC STUDIES, Vol. 3, no. 2 (Summer 1975), p. 119-121. English. DESCR: Book Reviews; *Hermanos Penitentes;

MY PENITENTE LAND: REFLECTIONS ON SPANISH NEW MEXICO; *New Mexico; Religion.

Chavez, Gabriel A.

2408 Balkan, D. Carlos. Being a start-up manager at San Onofre II & III. HISPANIC BUSINESS, Vol. 4, no. 7 (July 1982), p. 18-19,26. English. DESCR: California; Engineering as a Profession; *Management; Nuclear Energy.

Chavez Lichwardt, Leticia

2409 Commercial art as a career. CAMINOS, Vol. 4, no. 9 (October 1983), p. 32-35. English. DESCR: Artists; *Careers; Gomez, Dario; Guerrero, Ernest R.; Melendez, Bill; Reyes, Gil; Santistevan, August.

Chavez, Raul

2410 Gente. NUESTRO, Vol. 7, no. 7 (September 1983), p. 61. English. DESCR: Americas Award; *Chicanas; Diaz-Cobo, Christine; Mexico; Ortega, Katherine D.; Performing Arts; Planas, Vilma; Ravard, Rafael Alonzo; Venezuela.

Chavez Ravine, Los Angeles, CA

2411 The battle of Chavez Ravine, 1949-1959. CAMINOS, Vol. 4, no. 7 (July, August, 1983), p. 11-14,38. Bilingual. DESCR: History; Los Angeles, CA.

2412 Hines, Thomas S. Housing, baseball, and creeping socialism: the battle of Chavez Ravine, Los Angeles, 1949-1959. JOURNAL OF URBAN HISTORY, Vol. 8, no. 2 (1982), p. 123-143. English. DESCR: Barrios; Los Angeles, CA; Urban Communities; Urban Renewal.

CHECKING IT OUT

2413 Entertainment = diversion. CAMINOS, Vol. 3, no. 2 (February 1982), p. 40-41. English. DESCR: Awards; Club Hogar Latino; Dance; Films; Flamenco; Marley, Bob; Montalban, Ricardo; ON GOLDEN POND; *Recreation; Television.

Chicago Hispanic Health Alliance

2414 Cayer, Shirley. Chicago's new Hispanic health alliance. NUESTRO, Vol. 7, no. 5 (June, July, 1983), p. 44-48. English. DESCR: Alcoholism; Family Planning; *Health Education; Latin Americans; *Medical Care.

Chicago, IL

2415 Ano Nuevo de Kerr, Louise. Chicano settlements in Chicago: a brief history. JOURNAL OF ETHNIC STUDIES, Vol. 2, no. 4 (Winter 1975), p. 22-32. English. DESCR: Back of the Yards, Chicago, IL; Near West Side, Chicago, IL; Pilsen, IL; Social History and Conditions; South Chicago, Chicago, IL; *Urban Communities.

2416 Baldonado, Lisa. A university program to meet Chicago's bilingual needs. BILINGUAL JOURNAL, Vol. 7, no. 4 (Summer 1983), p. 15-17,28. English. DESCR: *Bilingual Bicultural Education; Curriculum; *Teacher Training; Urban Education.

Chicago, IL (cont.)

2417 Barry, Patrick and Zavala, Antonio. Election '83: Chicago's Latinos awake, but not united. NUESTRO, Vol. 7, no. 1 (January, February, 1983), p. 20-23. English. **DESCR:** *Elections; Political Representation; Voter Turnout.

2418 Barry, Patrick. Progress at La Paz: a chance for the retarded. NUESTRO, Vol. 6, no. 6 (August 1982), p. 20-23. English. **DESCR:** *Child Care Centers; *Child Study.

2419 Barry, Patrick. Saturdays are wedding cakes. NUESTRO, Vol. 6, no. 9 (November 1982), p. 31-33. English. **DESCR:** *Businesspeople; Fasco, Luis; Weddings.

2420 Barry, Patrick. Trouble in the bush: neighborhood house fights back. NUESTRO, Vol. 6, no. 3 (April 1982), p. 21-24. English. **DESCR:** *Economic History and Conditions.

2421 Chicago: a case study of minority participation in city government and industry. HISPANIC BUSINESS, Vol. 5, no. 1 (January 1983), p. 28-29. English. **DESCR:** *Employment; *Ethnic Groups; Government.

2422 Chicago's mayoralty race. HISPANIC BUSINESS, Vol. 5, no. 7 (July 1983), p. 27-28. English. **DESCR:** Elections; Local Government; *Voter Turnout.

2423 Endicott, Craig. Chicago Hispanics to get new channel. ADVERTISING AGE MAGAZINE, Vol. 53, (February 15, 1982), p. II, M36-37. English. **DESCR:** *HATCO/60 [television station], Chicago IL; Television.

2424 Gaviria, Moises; Stern, Gwen; and Schensul, Stephen L. Sociocultural factors and perinatal health in a Mexican-American community. NATIONAL MEDICAL ASSOCIATION JOURNAL, Vol. 74, no. 10 (October 1982), p. 983-989. English. **DESCR:** Migration Patterns; *Prenatal Care; Public Health; Socioeconomic Factors.

2425 Glick, R. Dealing, demoralization and addiction: heroin in the Chicago Puerto Rican community. JOURNAL OF PSYCHOACTIVE DRUGS, Vol. 15, no. 4 (October, December, 1983), p. 281-292. English. **DESCR:** Culture; *Drug Abuse; Puerto Ricans.

2426 Heaney, Thomas W. "Hanging on" or "gaining ground": educating marginal adults. NEW DIRECTIONS FOR CONTINUING EDUCATION, no. 20 (December 1983), p. 53-63. English. **DESCR:** *Adult Education; City Colleges, Chicago, IL; General Education Diploma (GED); Gomez, Robert; Instituto del Progreso Latino; Mission District, San Francisco, CA; Project Literacy, San Francisco, CA; St. Mary's Community Educational Center; *Universidad Popular, Chicago, IL.

2427 Lanier, Alfredo S. Continental's Fidel Lopez takes an encompassing view. HISPANIC BUSINESS, Vol. 4, no. 4 (April 1982), p. 16-17,24. English. **DESCR:** Biography; *Lopez, Fidel; Urban Communities; Urban Development.

2428 Triana, Armando R. Changing demographics, consumer patterns in the Chicago marketplace. HISPANIC BUSINESS, Vol. 5, no. 12 (December 1983), p. 20-21+. English. **DESCR:** Income; *Marketing; Population Trends.

2429 Venerable, W. R. Student and parent

attitudes toward college at five Hispanic learning centers in Illinois. JOURNAL OF THE NATIONAL ASSOC. OF COLLEGE ADMISSIONS COUNSELORS, Vol. 26, (April 1982), p. 19-23. English. **DESCR:** Casa Aztlan; *Higher Education; Illinois Migrant Council; Lakeview Learning Center, Chicago, IL; *Secondary School Education.

2430 Zavala, Antonio. The end of another summer. NUESTRO, Vol. 7, no. 8 (October 1983), p. 64. English. **DESCR:** Urban Communities.

Chicago Park District

2431 Park inequity pursued. NUESTRO, Vol. 7, no. 1 (January, February, 1983), p. 9. English. **DESCR:** Local Government; Racism.

THE CHICANA FEMINIST

2432 Garza-Livingston, M'Liss, ed. and Mercado, Olivia, ed. New book on the Chicana. COMADRE, no. 3 (Fall 1978), p. 38. English. **DESCR:** Cotera, Marta.

Chicana Rights Project

2434 Mexican American Legal Defense and Education Fund (MALDEF). Chicana rights: a major MALDEF issue (reprinted from MALDEF Newsletter, Fall 1977). COMADRE, no. 2 (Spring 1978), p. 31-33. English. **DESCR:** Chicanas; *Mexican American Legal Defense and Educational Fund (MALDEF); Statistics; Vasquez, Patricia; *Women's Rights.

2435 Mexican American Legal Defense and Education Fund (MALDEF). Chicana rights: a major MALDEF issue (reprinted from MALDEF Newsletter, Fall 1977). COMADRE, no. 3 (Fall 1978), p. 31-35. English. **DESCR:** Chicanas; *Mexican American Legal Defense and Educational Fund (MALDEF); Statistics; Vasquez, Patricia; *Women's Rights.

Chicana Service Action Center, Los Angeles, CA

2436 Quesada-Weiner, Rosemary. Chicana Service Action Center. CAMINOS, Vol. 2, no. 6 (October 1981), p. 39. Bilingual. **DESCR:** Chicanas; Cultural Organizations.

LA CHICANA: THE MEXICAN AMERICAN WOMAN

2437 Baca Zinn, Maxine. Book review of: LA CHICANA: THE MEXICAN AMERICAN WOMAN. SIGNS: JOURNAL OF WOMEN IN CULTURE AND SOCIETY, Vol. 8, no. 2 (Winter 1982), p. 259-272. English. **DESCR:** Book Reviews; Chicanas; Enriquez, Evangelina; Literature Reviews; Mirande, Alfredo; Social Science.

2438 Palacios, Maria. Book review of: LA CHICANA: THE MEXICAN AMERICAN WOMAN. HISPANIC JOURNAL OF BEHAVIORAL SCIENCES, Vol. 4, no. 2 (June 1982), p. 272-275. English. **DESCR:** Book Reviews; Enriquez, Evangelina; Mirande, Alfredo.

2439 Salgado de Snyder, Nelly. Book review of: LA CHICANA: THE MEXICAN AMERICAN WOMAN. HISPANIC JOURNAL OF BEHAVIORAL SCIENCES, Vol. 4, no. 2 (June 1982), p. 268-272. English. **DESCR:** Book Reviews; Enriquez, Evangelina; Mirande, Alfredo.

LA CHICANA: THE MEXICAN AMERICAN WOMAN (cont.)

2440 Stoller, Marianne L. Book review of: LA
CHICANA: THE MEXICAN AMERICAN WOMAN. SOCIAL
SCIENCE JOURNAL, Vol. 19, no. 2 (April
1982), p. 134-136. English. **DESCR**: Book
Reviews; Chicanas; Enriquez, Evangelina;
Mirande, Alfredo.

2441 Swink, Sue. Book review of: LA CHICANA: THE
MEXICAN AMERICAN WOMAN. HISPANIC JOURNAL OF
BEHAVIORAL SCIENCES, Vol. 4, no. 2 (June
1982), p. 275-277. English. **DESCR**: Book
Reviews; Enriquez, Evangelina; Mirande,
Alfredo.

Chicana Welfare Rights Organization

2442 Young, Rowland L. Exclusion hearing enough
for illegal alien smuggler. AMERICAN BAR
ASSOCIATION JOURNAL, Vol. 69, (March 1983),
p. 352. English. **DESCR**: Landon v. Plasencia;
Laws; *Undocumented Workers.

Chicanas
   SEE ALSO: Women
2443 Adelante, mujer hispana. LATINO, Vol. 53,
no. 2 (March, April, 1982), p. 26. English.

2444 Agosin, Marjorie. Elucubraciones y
antielucubraciones: critica feminista desde
perspectivas poeticas. THIRD WOMAN, Vol. 1,
no. 2 (1982), p. 65-69. Spanish. **DESCR**:
Essays; Literature.

2445 Alvarez, Amando. La mujer enigmatica.
LATINO, Vol. 53, no. 3 (May 1982), p. 10.
Spanish.

2446 Andrade, Sally J. Social science stereotypes
of the Mexican American woman: policy
implications for research. HISPANIC JOURNAL
OF BEHAVIORAL SCIENCES, Vol. 4, no. 2 (June
1982), p. 223-244. English. **DESCR**: Sex
Roles; Stereotypes.

2447 Baca Barragan, Polly; Hamner, Richard; and
Guerrero, Lena. [Untitled interview with
State Senators (Colorado) Polly
Baca-Barragan and Lena Guerrero. NATIONAL
HISPANIC JOURNAL, Vol. 1, no. 2 (Winter
1982), p. 8-11. English. **DESCR**: Baca
Barragan, Polly; *Carter, Jimmy (President);
Democratic Party; Elected Officials;
Guerrero, Lena; *Political Parties and
Organizations.

2448 Baca Zinn, Maxine. Book review of: LA
CHICANA: THE MEXICAN AMERICAN WOMAN. SIGNS:
JOURNAL OF WOMEN IN CULTURE AND SOCIETY,
Vol. 8, no. 2 (Winter 1982), p. 259-272.
English. **DESCR**: Book Reviews; Enriquez,
Evangelina; *LA CHICANA: THE MEXICAN
AMERICAN WOMAN; Literature Reviews; Mirande,
Alfredo; Social Science.

2449 Baca Zinn, Maxine. Book review of: MEXICAN
WOMEN IN THE UNITED STATES: STRUGGLES PAST
AND PRESENT. SIGNS: JOURNAL OF WOMEN IN
CULTURE AND SOCIETY, Vol. 8, no. 2 (Winter
1982), p. 259-272. English. **DESCR**: Book
Reviews; Del Castillo, Adelaida R.;
Literature Reviews; *MEXICAN WOMEN IN THE
UNITED STATES: STRUGGLES PAST AND PRESENT;
Mora, Magdalena; Social Science.

2450 Baca Zinn, Maxine. Book review of: TWICE A
MINORITY; MEXICAN-AMERICAN WOMEN. SIGNS:
JOURNAL OF WOMEN IN CULTURE AND SOCIETY,
Vol. 8, no. 2 (Winter 1982), p. 259-272.
English. **DESCR**: Book Reviews; Literature
Reviews; Melville, Margarita B.; Social
Science; *TWICE A MINORITY: MEXICAN-AMERICAN
WOMEN.

2451 Baca Zinn, Maxine. Mexican American women in
the social sciences. SIGNS: JOURNAL OF WOMEN
IN CULTURE AND SOCIETY, Vol. 8, no. 2
(Winter 1982), p. 259-272. English. **DESCR**:
*Literature Reviews; Social Science.

2452 Barreto, Julio. Seven women honored. LATINO,
Vol. 53, no. 5 (September 1982), p. 22.
English.

2453 Bean, Frank D. and Swicegood, Gray.
Generation, female education and Mexican
American fertility. SOCIAL SCIENCE
QUARTERLY, Vol. 63, (March 1982), p.
131-144. English. **DESCR**: Family Planning;
*Fertility.

2454 Benardo, Margot L. and Anthony, Darius.
Hispanic women and their men. LATINA, Vol.
1, no. 3 (1983), p. 24-29. English. **DESCR**:
Photography; *Women Men Relations.

2455 Benton, Patricia Moran. Mother's Day
reflections: keepers of the faith. NUESTRO,
Vol. 7, no. 4 (May 1983), p. 49. English.
DESCR: Family; *Parent and Child
Relationships.

2456 Candelaria, Cordelia. Social equity in film
criticism. BILINGUAL REVIEW, Vol. 10, no.
2-3 (May, December, 1983), p. 64-70.
English. **DESCR**: *Film Criticism;
Stereotypes.

2457 Castro, Rafaela. Mexican women's sexual
jokes. AZTLAN, Vol. 13, no. 1-2 (Spring,
Fall, 1982), p. 275-293. English. **DESCR**:
*Chistes; Humor.

2458 Chavez, Mauro. Book review of: ESSAYS ON LA
MUJER. JOURNAL OF ETHNIC STUDIES, Vol. 8,
no. 2 (Summer 1980), p. 117-120. English.
DESCR: Book Reviews; Cruz, Rosa Martinez;
Economic History and Conditions; *ESSAYS ON
LA MUJER; Sanchez, Rosaura; Social History
and Conditions; Socioeconomic Factors;
Women's Rights.

2459 Community watching. CAMINOS, Vol. 3, no. 5
(May 1982), p. 56-57. Bilingual. **DESCR**:
Adelante Mujer Hispana Conference;
Agricultural Laborers; Beilson, Anthony C.;
Boycotts; Chacon, Peter R.; *Cultural
Organizations; Farm Labor Organizing
Commmittee (FLOC); Financial Aid; Hollenbeck
Junior High School, Los Angeles, CA; Junior
High School Students; National League of
Cities; Optimist Club of Greater East Los
Angeles; Organizations; Project WELL (We
Enjoy Learning & Leadership); Torres, Art.

2460 Cooney, Rosemary Santana and Ortiz, Vilma.
Nativity, national origin, and Hispanic
female participation in the labor force.
SOCIAL SCIENCE QUARTERLY, Vol. 64,
(September 1983), p. 510-523. English.
DESCR: Working Women.

2461 Corbit, Gladys Benavides. Sharing with a
spiritual sister. NUESTRO, Vol. 7, no. 6
(August 1983), p. 50. English. **DESCR**:
Family; Parent and Child Relationships.

2462 Cordelia, Candelaria. Film portrayals of La
Mujer Hispana. AGENDA, Vol. 11, no. 3 (May,
June, 1981), p. 32-36. English. **DESCR**:
*Films.

Chicanas (cont.)

2463 Cortes, Carlos E. Chicanas in film: history of an image. BILINGUAL REVIEW, Vol. 10, no. 2-3 (May, December, 1983), p. 94-108. English. **DESCR:** Film Criticism; *Films; *Stereotypes.

2464 Craver, Rebecca McDowell. The impact of intimacy: Mexican-Anglo intermarriage in New Mexico 1821-1846. SOUTHWESTERN STUDIES, no. 66 (1982), p. 1-79. English. **DESCR:** Acculturation; Assimilation; *Intermarriage; New Mexico; Rio Arriba Valley, New Mexico.

2465 Creswell, John L. and Exezidis, Roxane H. Research brief: sex and ethnic differences in mathematics achievement of Black and Mexican-American adolescents. TEXAS TECH JOURNAL OF EDUCATION, Vol. 9, no. 3 (Fall 1982), p. 219-222. English. **DESCR:** Blacks; Gender; *Mathematics; Youth.

2466 Creswell, John L. Sex-related differences in the problem-solving abilities of rural Black, Anglo, and Chicano adolescents. TEXAS TECH JOURNAL OF EDUCATION, Vol. 10, no. 1 (Winter 1983), p. 29-33. English. **DESCR:** Aiken and Preger Revised Math Attitude Scale; Anglo Americans; Blacks; California Achievement Test; Gender; Mathematics; National Assessment of Educational Progress; *National Council of Teachers of Mathematics (NCTM); Youth.

2467 Cuellar, Israel, et al. Clinical psychiatric case presentation; culturally responsive diagnostic formulation and treatment in an Hispanic female. HISPANIC JOURNAL OF BEHAVIORAL SCIENCES, Vol. 5, no. 1 (March 1983), p. 93-103. English. **DESCR:** *ACCULTURATION RATING SCALE FOR MEXICAN AMERICANS (ARSMA); Case Study; Medical Care; *Psychotherapy.

2468 Davis, Lisa. La mujer hispana. LATINO, Vol. 53, no. 3 (May 1982), p. 5-6. English.

2469 De Anda, Diane. A study of the interaction of Hispanic junior high school students and their teachers. HISPANIC JOURNAL OF BEHAVIORAL SCIENCES, Vol. 4, no. 1 (March 1982), p. 57-74. English. **DESCR:** Dropouts; Teacher-pupil Interaction.

2470 De Blassie, Richard R. and Franco, Juan N. The differences between personality inventory scores and self-rating in a sample of Hispanic subjects. JOURNAL OF NON-WHITE CONCERNS IN PERSONNEL AND GUIDANCE, Vol. 11, no. 2 (January 1983), p. 43-46. English. **DESCR:** Hispanic Education [program]; New Mexico State University; *Personality; *Sixteen Personality Factor Questionnaire.

2471 Delgado, Abelardo "Lalo". An open letter to Carolina... or relations between men and women. REVISTA CHICANO-RIQUENA, Vol. 10, no. 1-2 (Winter, Spring, 1982), p. 279-284. English. **DESCR:** *Essays; Machismo; Sex Roles; Sex Stereotypes.

2472 Diaz, Barbara M. Continuing the success: the Hispanic Women's Council. CAMINOS, Vol. 4, no. 6 (June 1983), p. 62. English. **DESCR:** Awards; *Hispanic Women's Council; Organizations; Women for Success Awards.

2473 Escobedo, Theresa Herrera. Book review of: CHICANAS IN THE NATIONAL LANDSCAPE. JOURNAL OF AMERICAN ETHNIC HISTORY, Vol. 1, no. 2 (Spring 1982), p. 101-103. English. **DESCR:** Book Reviews; Candelaria, Cordelia; *CHICANAS EN EL AMBIENTE NACIONAL/CHICANAS

IN THE NATIONAL LANDSCAPE.

2474 Escobedo, Theresa Herrera, ed. Thematic issue: Chicana issues. HISPANIC JOURNAL OF BEHAVIORAL SCIENCES, Vol. 4, no. 2 (June 1982), p. 145-286. English.

2475 Espinoza, Ana Luisa. La Chicana cosmica. CALMECAC, Vol. 3, (Spring 1982), p. 42-46. English.

2476 Fernandez, Enrique. Notas: these ladies are not waiting. BILLBOARD, Vol. 94, (November 13, 1982), p. 62. English. **DESCR:** Artists; Performing Arts; Salsa; Singers.

2477 Fleming, Marilyn B. Problems experienced by Anglo, Hispanic and Navajo Indian women college students. JOURNAL OF AMERICAN INDIAN EDUCATION, Vol. 22, no. 1 (October 1982), p. 7-17. English. **DESCR:** Community Colleges; Ethnic Groups; Identity; Medical Education; Native Americans.

2478 Flores, Henry. Some different thoughts concerning "machismo". COMADRE, no. 3 (Fall 1978), p. 7-9. English. **DESCR:** *Machismo; Mythology; Sex Roles.

2479 Fostering the advancement of Latinas. NUESTRO, Vol. 6, no. 10 (December 1982), p. 48-49. English. **DESCR:** *Mexican American Women's National Association (MANA); Women Men Relations.

2480 Franklin, Gerald S. and Kaufman, Karen S. Group psychotherapy for elderly female Hispanic outpatients. HOSPITAL AND COMMUNITY PSYCHIATRY, Vol. 33, no. 5 (May 1982), p. 385-387. English. **DESCR:** Ancianos; Psychotherapy.

2481 Fu, Victoria R.; Hinkle, Dennis E.; and Korslund, Mary K. A development study of ethnic self-concept among pre-adolescent girls. JOURNAL OF GENETIC PSYCHOLOGY, Vol. 14, (March 1983), p. 67-73. English. **DESCR:** Comparative Psychology; *Identity; Junior High School Students; Self-Concept Self Report Scale.

2482 Gallego, Grace Griego. Survival. LATINO, Vol. 53, no. 6 (October 1982), p. 10+. English.

2483 Gandara, Patricia. Passing through the eye of the needle: high-achieving Chicanas. HISPANIC JOURNAL OF BEHAVIORAL SCIENCES, Vol. 4, no. 2 (June 1982), p. 167-179. English. **DESCR:** Academic Achievement; Higher Education.

2484 Garza, M'Liss, ed. and Mercado, Olivia, ed. Chicana journals. COMADRE, no. 3 (Fall 1978), p. 38. Bilingual. **DESCR:** *Journals.

2485 Garza-Livingston, M'Liss. Annotated bibliography of selected materials on la mujer y la chicana. COMADRE, no. 1 (Summer 1977), p. 49-54. English. **DESCR:** *Bibliography.

2486 Garza-Livingston, M'Liss. Annotated bibliography of selected materials on la mujer y la chicana. COMADRE, no. 2 (Spring 1978), p. 51-56. English. **DESCR:** *Bibliography.

Chicanas (cont.)

2487 Gente. NUESTRO, Vol. 7, no. 7 (September 1983), p. 61. English. **DESCR:** Americas Award; Chavez, Raul; Diaz-Cobo, Christine; Mexico; Ortega, Katherine D.; Performing Arts; Planas, Vilma; Ravard, Rafael Alonzo; Venezuela.

2488 Gente. NUESTRO, Vol. 7, no. 2 (March 1983), p. 51. English. **DESCR:** Artists; Betancourt, Jose L.; Crime Victims Fund; Federal Government; Juarez, Joe; Military Service; Saldana, Teresa; Vargas, Alberto; Victims for Victims.

2489 Gibbs, Jewelle Taylor. Personality patterns of delinquent females: ethnic and sociocultural variations. JOURNAL OF CLINICAL PSYCHOLOGY, Vol. 38, no. 1 (January 1982), p. 198-206. English. **DESCR:** Ethnic Groups; Identity; *Juvenile Delinquency; Personality; Psychological Testing; Socioeconomic Factors.

2490 Girls explore new job fields. NUESTRO, Vol. 7, no. 8 (October 1983), p. 13. English. **DESCR:** *Discrimination in Employment; Mi Carrera Program; Mi Casa Women's Resource Center, Denver, CO.

2491 Gloria Molina spells winner. LATINA, Vol. 1, no. 1 (1982), p. 4-5. English. **DESCR:** Elected Officials.

2492 Gonzalez, Alicia. Women for success. CAMINOS, Vol. 3, no. 6 (June 1982), p. 42-43. Bilingual. **DESCR:** *Hispanic Women's Council; Moreno, Rita; Organizations; Saavedra, Denise; Terrazas, Carmen.

2493 Government review. NUESTRO, Vol. 7, no. 2 (March 1983), p. 42. English. **DESCR:** A WORKING WOMAN'S GUIDE TO HER JOB RIGHTS; Adoption; Business Enterprises; Census; Discrimination in Employment; *Government Services; GUIDE TO FEDERAL MINORITY ENTERPRISE AND RELATED ASSISTANCE PROGRAMS; Population Trends; Study Abroad; U.S. Information Agency (USIA).

2494 Hartman, Harriet. Book review of: MEXICAN WOMEN IN THE UNITED STATES: STRUGGLES PAST AND PRESENT. INTERNATIONAL MIGRATION REVIEW, Vol. 16, no. 1 (Spring 1982), p. 228-229. English. **DESCR:** Book Reviews; Del Castillo, Adelaida R.; *MEXICAN WOMEN IN THE UNITED STATES: STRUGGLES PAST AND PRESENT; Mora, Magdalena; Sexism.

2495 Hawley, Peggy and Even, Brenda. Work and sex-role attitudes in relation to education and other characteristics. VOCATIONAL GUIDANCE QUARTERLY, Vol. 31, no. 2 (December 1982), p. 101-108. English. **DESCR:** Careers; Ethnic Groups; Psychological Testing; *Sex Roles; Working Women.

2496 Herrera-Sobek, Maria. The acculturation process of the Chicana in the corrido. DE COLORES, Vol. 6, no. 1-2 (1982), p. 7-16. English. **DESCR:** Acculturation; Corrido; Sex Roles.

2497 Herrera-Sobek, Maria. The treacherous woman archetype: a structuring agent in the corrido. AZTLAN, Vol. 13, no. 1-2 (Spring, Fall, 1982), p. 135-148. English. **DESCR:** *Corrido; Folk Songs; Music.

2498 Hispanic wages and employment slow to rise. HISPANIC BUSINESS, Vol. 5, no. 11 (November 1983), p. 36-37. English. **DESCR:** Congressional Hispanic Caucus; *Employment;

Income.

2499 Holck, Susan E. Lung cancer mortality and smoking habits: Mexican-American women. AMERICAN JOURNAL OF PUBLIC HEALTH, Vol. 72, no. 1 (January 1982), p. 38-42. English. **DESCR:** Anglo Americans; *Cancer; *Public Health.

2500 Huerta, Grace C. Mother's day reflections: a woman of means. NUESTRO, Vol. 7, no. 4 (May 1983), p. 48-49. English. **DESCR:** Family; *Parent and Child Relationships.

2501 Hunt, Isabelle F., et al. Zinc supplementation during pregnancy: zinc concentration of serum and hair from low-income women of Mexican descent. AMERICAN JOURNAL OF CLINICAL NUTRITION, Vol. 37, no. 4 (April 1983), p. 572-582. English. **DESCR:** Low Income; Nutrition; *Prenatal Care; Surveys.

2502 Introduction. REVISTA CHICANO-RIQUENA, Vol. 11, no. 3-4 (Fall 1983), p. 7-17. English. **DESCR:** Literature.

2503 Irizarry, Estelle. La abuelita in literature. NUESTRO, Vol. 7, no. 7 (September 1983), p. 50. English. **DESCR:** Alonso, Luis Ricardo; *Ancianos; Cotto-Thorner, Guillermo; Family; Ulibarri, Sabine R.; Valero, Robert.

2504 Jenoveva and Solis, Arnaldo. La Chicana: principle of life, survival and endurance. CALMECAC, Vol. 1, (Summer 1980), p. 7-10. English.

2505 Jensen, Joan M. Canning comes to New Mexico: women and the agricultural extension service, 1914-1919. NEW MEXICO HISTORICAL REVIEW, Vol. 57, no. 4 (October 1982), p. 361-386. English. **DESCR:** *Cannery Workers; Food Industry; New Mexico; New Mexico Agricultural Extension Service.

2506 Jensen, Joan M. Women teachers, class and ethnicity: New Mexico 1900-1950. SOUTHWEST ECONOMY AND SOCIETY, Vol. 4, no. 2 (Winter 1978, 1979), p. 3-13. English. **DESCR:** Alternative Education; Cultural Pluralism; History; *New Mexico; Spanish Language; Teaching Profession.

2507 Kranau, Edgar J.; Green, Vicki; and Valencia-Weber, Gloria. Acculturation and the Hispanic woman: attitudes toward women, sex-role attribution, sex-role behavior, and demographics. HISPANIC JOURNAL OF BEHAVIORAL SCIENCES, Vol. 4, no. 1 (March 1982), p. 21-40. English. **DESCR:** Acculturation; Demography; Sex Roles.

2508 Lampe, Philip E. Female Mexican Americans: minority within a minority. BORDERLANDS JOURNAL, Vol. 6, no. 2 (Spring 1983), p. 99-109. English.

2509 Lanier, Alfredo S. Making it seem easy, from intern to account executive. HISPANIC BUSINESS, Vol. 4, no. 8 (August 1983), p. 16-17+. English. **DESCR:** *Accountants; Careers; Employment Training; *Fernandez, Margarita; INROADS; Standard Oil Corp.

2510 Levario, Raquel. Our children are watching. LATINA, Vol. 1, no. 1 (1982), p. 30. English. **DESCR:** Stereotypes; Television.

2511 Madre tierra press. CAMINOS, Vol. 4, no. 9 (October 1983), p. 48-49. English. **DESCR:** *Artists.

Chicanas (cont.)

2512 Martinez, Elisa A. Sharing her tiny pieces of the past. NUESTRO, Vol. 7, no. 7 (September 1983), p. 51-52. English. **DESCR:** Autobiography; *Extended Family; Reminiscences.

2513 Math-based careers. HISPANIC BUSINESS, Vol. 4, no. 4 (April 1982), p. 20,24. English. **DESCR:** *Careers; *Engineering as a Profession; Government Employees; National Action Council for Minorities in Engineering (NACME); National Hispanic Field Service Program.

2514 Math-based careers. HISPANIC BUSINESS, Vol. 5, no. 10 (October 1983), p. 28. English. **DESCR:** *Careers; Carnation Company; Education; Engineering as a Profession; Hispanic Policy Development Project; Minority Engineering Education Center, University of California, Los Angeles; Science as a Profession; University of California, Los Angeles (UCLA).

2515 Matute-Bianchi, Maria Eugenia. A Chicana in academe. WOMEN'S STUDIES QUARTERLY, Vol. 10, no. 1 (Spring 1982), p. 14-17. English. **DESCR:** *Higher Education; Matute-Bianchi, Maria Eugenia; Racism; Sex Roles; Sexism.

2516 McCracken, Ellen. Book review of: SALT OF THE EARTH. JOURNAL OF ETHNIC STUDIES, Vol. 8, no. 1 (Spring 1980), p. 116-120. English. **DESCR:** Book Reviews; Films; Hanover, NM; International Union of Mine, Mill and Smelter Workers; *SALT OF THE EARTH; Silverton Rosenfelt, Deborah; Strikes and Lockouts; Women Men Relations; Women's Rights.

2517 Median administrative salaries in 1981-82 for men and women and minority-group members. CHRONICLE OF HIGHER EDUCATION, Vol. 24, no. 2 (March 10, 1982), p. 10. English. **DESCR:** *Administrators; Ethnic Groups; *Income; Males.

2518 Mendez Gonzalez, Rosalinda. Mexican women and families: rural-to-urban and international migration. SOUTHWEST ECONOMY AND SOCIETY, Vol. 4, no. 2 (Winter 1978, 1979), p. 14-27. English. **DESCR:** Employment; *Family; Garment Industry; Immigration; International Ladies Garment Workers Union (ILGWU); Labor Organizing; Los Angeles, CA; Undocumented Workers.

2519 Mercado, Olivia. Chicanas: myths and roles. COMADRE, no. 1 (Summer 1977), p. 26-32. English. **DESCR:** Gallo, Juana; Huerta, Dolores; *Identity; Leadership; Sex Roles; Women's Rights.

2520 Mercado, Olivia; Corrales, Ramona; and Segovia, Sara. Las hermanas. COMADRE, no. 2 (Spring 1978), p. 34-41. English. **DESCR:** *Clergy; Religion.

2521 Mexican American Legal Defense and Education Fund (MALDEF). Chicana rights: a major MALDEF issue (reprinted from MALDEF Newsletter, Fall 1977). COMADRE, no. 2 (Spring 1978), p. 31-33. English. **DESCR:** Chicana Rights Project; *Mexican American Legal Defense and Educational Fund (MALDEF); Statistics; Vasquez, Patricia; *Women's Rights.

2522 Mexican American Legal Defense and Education Fund (MALDEF). Chicana rights: a major MALDEF issue (reprinted from MALDEF Newsletter, Fall 1977). COMADRE, no. 3 (Fall 1978), p. 31-35. English. **DESCR:** Chicana Rights Project; *Mexican American Legal Defense and Educational Fund (MALDEF); Statistics; Vasquez, Patricia; *Women's Rights.

2523 Miller, Darlis A. Cross-cultural marriages in the Southwest: the New Mexico experience, 1846-1900. NEW MEXICO HISTORICAL REVIEW, Vol. 57, no. 4 (October 1982), p. 335-359. English. **DESCR:** Assimilation; Ethnic Attitudes; *Intermarriage; New Mexico; Social History and Conditions.

2524 Montenegro, Marilyn. Latinas in the work force. LATINA, Vol. 1, no. 1 (1982), p. 16. English. **DESCR:** *Working Women.

2525 Moore, Helen A. Hispanic women: schooling for conformity in public education. HISPANIC JOURNAL OF BEHAVIORAL SCIENCES, Vol. 5, no. 1 (March 1983), p. 45-63. English. **DESCR:** Academic Achievement; Education.

2526 Morales, Sylvia. Chicano-produced celluloid mujeres. BILINGUAL REVIEW, Vol. 10, no. 2-3 (May, December, 1983), p. 89-93. English. **DESCR:** BALLAD OF GREGORIO CORTEZ [film]; Film Reviews; *Films; RAICES DE SANGRE [film]; SEGUIN [movie]; *Stereotypes; ZOOT SUIT [film].

2527 Myres, Sandra Lynn. Mexican Americans and westering Anglos: a feminine perspective. NEW MEXICO HISTORICAL REVIEW, Vol. 57, no. 4 (October 1982), p. 317-333. English. **DESCR:** Anglo Americans; *Ethnic Attitudes; Social History and Conditions; Southwest United States; Stereotypes.

2528 NATIONAL HISPANIC WOMEN'S NETWORK DIRECTORY: LULAC mujeres en accion. LATINO, Vol. 53, no. 3 (May 1982), p. 13-18. English. **DESCR:** Directories; *League of United Latin American Citizens (LULAC).

2529 NATIONAL HISPANIC WOMEN'S NETWORK DIRECTORY, June 1983. LATINO, Vol. 54, no. 7 (January 1983), p. 13-20. English. **DESCR:** *Directories; *NATIONAL HISPANIC WOMEN'S NETWORK DIRECTORY.

2530 Ortiz, Flora Ida. The distribution of Mexican American women in school organizations. HISPANIC JOURNAL OF BEHAVIORAL SCIENCES, Vol. 4, no. 2 (June 1982), p. 181-198. English. **DESCR:** Educational Administration; Educational Organizations; Teaching Profession.

2531 Padilla, Steve. A Latino voice on the Parole Commission. NUESTRO, Vol. 7, no. 7 (September 1983), p. 42-43. English. **DESCR:** Discrimination in Employment; *Kaslow, Audrey; Racism; U.S. Parole Commission.

2532 Padilla, Steve. You've come a long way, baby. Or have you? NUESTRO, Vol. 7, no. 6 (August 1983), p. 38-41. English. **DESCR:** *Business Enterprises; Minority Business Development Agency (MBDA); National Alliance of Homebased Businesswomen.

2533 People behind the shield: profiles. LATINO, Vol. 54, no. 7 (November 1983), p. 24+. English.

2534 Perez, Robert. Effects of stress, social support and coping style on adjustment to pregnancy among Hispanic women. HISPANIC JOURNAL OF BEHAVIORAL SCIENCES, Vol. 5, no. 2 (June 1983), p. 141-161. English. **DESCR:** *Pregnancy; Stress.

Chicanas (cont.)

2535 Phillips, Melody. The Chicana: her attitudes towards the woman's liberation movement. COMADRE, no. 2 (Spring 1978), p. 42-50. English. **DESCR:** Carr, Vikki; FAMOUS MEXICAN-AMERICANS; Newton, Clark; Social History and Conditions; Women's Rights.

2536 Ponce-Adame, Merrihelen. Latinas and breast cancer. NUESTRO, Vol. 6, no. 8 (October 1982), p. 30-31. English. **DESCR:** Cancer; *Public Health.

2537 Ponce-Adame, Merrihelen. Women and cancer. CORAZON DE AZTLAN, Vol. 1, no. 2 (March, April, 1982), p. 32. English. **DESCR:** *Cancer; Medical Care; Preventative Medicine.

2538 Popp, Gary E. and Muhs, William F. Fears of success and women employees. HUMAN RELATIONS, Vol. 35, no. 7 (July 1982), p. 511-519. English. **DESCR:** Employment.

2539 Prida, Dolores. Latin American women writers meet in New England. NUESTRO, Vol. 6, no. 10 (December 1982), p. 26-27. English. **DESCR:** Authors; *Massachusetts.

2540 Quesada-Weiner, Rosemary. Chicana Service Action Center. CAMINOS, Vol. 2, no. 6 (October 1981), p. 39. Bilingual. **DESCR:** *Chicana Service Action Center, Los Angeles, CA; Cultural Organizations.

2541 Quesada-Weiner, Rosemary. Soy Chicana. CAMINOS, Vol. 3, no. 3 (March 1982), p. 52-53. English.

2542 Rebolledo, Tey Diana. Abuelitas: mythology and integration in Chicana literature. REVISTA CHICANO-RIQUENA, Vol. 11, no. 3-4 (Fall 1983), p. 148-158. English. **DESCR:** *Literary Criticism; Poetry.

2543 Rebolledo, Tey Diana. Game theory in Chicana poetry. REVISTA CHICANO-RIQUENA, Vol. 11, no. 3-4 (Fall 1983), p. 159-168. English. **DESCR:** *Literary Criticism; Poetry.

2544 Rita Moreno: Hispanic woman of the year. LATINO, Vol. 53, no. 3 (May 1982), p. 9. English. **DESCR:** *Moreno, Rita.

2545 Roberts, Robert E. and Roberts, Catharine Ramsay. Marriage, work and depressive symptoms among Mexican Americans. HISPANIC JOURNAL OF BEHAVIORAL SCIENCES, Vol. 4, no. 2 (June 1982), p. 199-221. English. **DESCR:** Employment; Marriage; *Mental Health.

2546 Sargeant, Georgia. A woman's place is in the bank. HISPANIC BUSINESS, Vol. 5, no. 10 (October 1983), p. 20-21+. English. **DESCR:** Accountants; *Banking Industry; Careers; *Olson, Ethel Ortega; Otero Savings and Loan, Alamogordo, TX.

2547 The shaping of a career. HISPANIC BUSINESS, Vol. 4, no. 4 (April 1982), p. 14. English. **DESCR:** Atlantic Richfield Company; Biography; Businesspeople; *Oaxaca, Virginia.

2548 Smith, Jack C. Trends in the incidence of breastfeeding for Hispanics of Mexican origin and Anglos on the US-Mexican border. AMERICAN JOURNAL OF PUBLIC HEALTH, Vol. 72, no. 1 (January 1982), p. 59-61. English. **DESCR:** Anglo Americans; Breastfeeding; *Maternal and Child Welfare.

2549 Soto, Grace. Editorial. LATINA, Vol. 1, no. 3 (1983), p. 4. English. **DESCR:** Editorials; *LATINA [magazine].

2550 Soto, Shirlene Ann. The emerging Chicana: a review of the journals. SOUTHWEST ECONOMY AND SOCIETY, Vol. 2, no. 1 (October, November, 1976), p. 39-45. English. **DESCR:** Directories; *Literature Reviews; Periodicals.

2551 A special dress for a special person. LATINO, Vol. 53, no. 5 (September 1982), p. 23. English.

2552 Stoller, Marianne L. Book review of: LA CHICANA: THE MEXICAN AMERICAN WOMAN. SOCIAL SCIENCE JOURNAL, Vol. 19, no. 2 (April 1982), p. 134-136. English. **DESCR:** Book Reviews; Enriquez, Evangelina; *LA CHICANA: THE MEXICAN AMERICAN WOMAN; Mirande, Alfredo.

2553 Tienda, Marta. Sex, ethnicity and Chicano status attainment. INTERNATIONAL MIGRATION REVIEW, Vol. 16, no. 2 (Summer 1982), p. 435-473. English. **DESCR:** Academic Achievement; Discrimination in Education; Discrimination in Employment; Identity; Income; Language Proficiency; Sexism; *Social Classes; Social Mobility.

2554 Trotter, Robert T. Ethnic and sexual patterns of alcohol use: Anglo and Mexican American college students. ADOLESCENCE, Vol. 17, no. 66 (Summer 1982), p. 305-325. English. **DESCR:** *Alcoholism; Anglo Americans; Cultural Characteristics; Ethnic Groups; Sex Roles; Youth.

2555 Valadez, Esther. [The role of the Latina]. CHICANO LAW REVIEW, Vol. 6, (1983), p. 21-24. English. **DESCR:** LATINOS IN THE LAW [symposium], UCLA, 1982; Voter Turnout.

2556 Vasquez, Melba J. T. Confronting barriers to the participation of Mexican American women in higher education. HISPANIC JOURNAL OF BEHAVIORAL SCIENCES, Vol. 4, no. 2 (June 1982), p. 147-165. English. **DESCR:** Academic Motivation; Higher Education; Sex Roles; Socioeconomic Factors.

2557 Vigil, Evangelina, ed. Woman of her word: Hispanic women write. REVISTA CHICANO-RIQUENA, Vol. 11, no. 3-4 (Fall 1983), p. 1-180. Bilingual. **DESCR:** Authors.

2558 Villa Romo, Velma. Rape in the barrio. COMADRE, no. 3 (Fall 1978), p. 19-29. English. **DESCR:** Identity; Rape; Santa Barbara Rape Crisis Center; Social History and Conditions.

2559 Villanueva Collado, Alfredo. Fili-Mele: simbolo y mujer en la poesia de Luis Pales Matos e Ivan Silen. REVISTA CHICANO-RIQUENA, Vol. 10, no. 4 (Fall 1982), p. 47-54. Spanish. **DESCR:** Literary Criticism; LOS POEMAS DE FILI-MELE; *Pales Matos, Luis; Ribes Tovar, Federico; *Silen, Ivan; Symbolism; TUNTUN DE PASA Y GRIFERIA.

2560 Whiteford, Linda. Migrants no longer: changing family structure of Mexican Americans in South Texas. DE COLORES, Vol. 6, no. 1-2 (1982), p. 99-108. English. **DESCR:** *Family; Sex Roles; *South Texas.

2561 Women entrepreneurs offered SBA assistance. NUESTRO, Vol. 7, no. 1 (January, February, 1983), p. 47. English. **DESCR:** *Business Enterprises; Businesspeople; U.S. Small Business Administration.

Chicanas (cont.)

2562 Women's role in politics to receive new boost. LATINO, Vol. 53, no. 1 (January, February, 1982), p. 17. English.

2563 Yarbro-Bejarano, Yvonne. Teatropoesia by Chicanas in the Bay Area: tongues of fire. REVISTA CHICANO-RIQUENA, Vol. 11, no. 1 (Spring 1983), p. 78-94. English. **DESCR:** El Teatro Nacional de Aztlan (TENAZ); Poetry; Teatro; *TONGUES OF FIRE.

2564 Ybarra, Lea. Book review of: LAS MUJERES: CONVERSATIONS FROM A HISPANIC COMMUNITY [reprinted from LA RED/THE NET 5 (Sept. 1982)]. CHICANO LAW REVIEW, Vol. 6, (1983), p. 146-147. English. **DESCR:** Book Reviews; Elsasser, Nan; *LAS MUJERES: CONVERSATIONS FROM A HISPANIC COMMUNITY; MacKenzie, Kyle; Oral History; Tixier y Vigil, Yvonne.

2565 Zavala, Iris M. Ideologias y autobiografias: perspectivas femeninas. THIRD WOMAN, Vol. 1, no. 2 (1982), p. 35-39. Spanish. **DESCR:** *Essays.

2566 Zeff, Shirley B. A cross-cultural study of Mexican American, Black American and white American women of a large urban university. HISPANIC JOURNAL OF BEHAVIORAL SCIENCES, Vol. 4, no. 2 (June 1982), p. 245-261. English. **DESCR:** Anglo Americans; Blacks; Higher Education; Sex Roles.

CHICANAS EN EL AMBIENTE NACIONAL/CHICANAS IN THE NATIONAL LANDSCAPE

2567 Escobedo, Theresa Herrera. Book review of: CHICANAS IN THE NATIONAL LANDSCAPE. JOURNAL OF AMERICAN ETHNIC HISTORY, Vol. 1, no. 2 (Spring 1982), p. 101-103. English. **DESCR:** Book Reviews; Candelaria, Cordelia; Chicanas.

2568 Escobedo, Theresa Herrera. Book review of: CHICANAS IN THE NATIONAL LANDSCAPE. HISPANIC JOURNAL OF BEHAVIORAL SCIENCES, Vol. 4, no. 2 (June 1982), p. 263-267. English. **DESCR:** Book Reviews; FRONTIERS: A JOURNAL OF WOMEN STUDIES, Vol. 5, no. 2(Summer 1980).

Chicanismo

2569 Barrera, Jose J. Jesus "Chuy" Negrete: the Chicano vote. NUESTRO, Vol. 5, no. 8 (November 1981), p. 40-41. English. **DESCR:** *Negrete, Jesus "Chuy"; *Recreation.

2570 Chavez, Mauro. Carranza's CHICANISMO: PHILOSOPHICAL FRAGMENTS. JOURNAL OF ETHNIC STUDIES, Vol. 7, no. 3 (Fall 1979), p. 95-100. English. **DESCR:** Book Reviews; Carranza, Elihu; *CHICANISMO: PHILOSOPHICAL FRAGMENTS; Philosophy; Research Methodology.

2571 Farias, Eddie Jaime. Aztlan begins with the heart and the mind. CORAZON DE AZTLAN, Vol. 1, no. 3 (August, September, 1982), p. 29-30. English. **DESCR:** *Aztlan.

2572 Solis, A. A Chicano Tloque Nahuaque in the 20th century. CORAZON DE AZTLAN, Vol. 1, no. 1 (January, February, 1982), p. 33. English.

CHICANISMO DEFINED

2573 Banas, L. K. Donde estas? Conflicts in the Chicano movement (reprinted CARACOL June 1977). CALMECAC, Vol. 2, (Spring 1981), p. 28-33. English. **DESCR:** *Philosophy; Political Ideology.

CHICANISMO: PHILOSOPHICAL FRAGMENTS

2574 Chavez, Mauro. Carranza's CHICANISMO: PHILOSOPHICAL FRAGMENTS. JOURNAL OF ETHNIC STUDIES, Vol. 7, no. 3 (Fall 1979), p. 95-100. English. **DESCR:** Book Reviews; Carranza, Elihu; *Chicanismo; Philosophy; Research Methodology.

CHICANO

2575 Orozco, Febe Portillo. A bibliography of Hispanic literature. ENGLISH JOURNAL, Vol. 71, no. 7 (November 1982), p. 58-62. English. **DESCR:** BARRIO BOY; *Bibliography; BLESS ME, ULTIMA; EL SOL Y LOS DE ABAJO; GRITO DEL SOL; HEART OF AZTLAN; *Literature; POCHO; WE ARE CHICANOS.

CHICANO AUTHORS: INQUIRY BY INTERVIEW

2576 Rangel-Guerrero, Daniel. Book review of: CHICANO AUTHORS: INQUIRY BY INTERVIEW. JOURNAL OF ETHNIC STUDIES, Vol. 10, no. 2 (Summer 1982), p. 117-119. English. **DESCR:** Book Reviews; Bruce Novoa, Juan; Comparative Literature; Literary Criticism; Literary History; Literary Influence; Literature.

2577 Somoza, Oscar U. Book review of: CHICANO AUTHORS: INQUIRY BY INTERVIEW. HISPAMERICA: REVISTA DE LITERATURA, Vol. 11, no. 31 (1982), p. 101-102. Spanish. **DESCR:** Book Reviews; Bruce Novoa, Juan.

2578 Tatum, Charles. Book review of: CHICANO AUTHORS: INQUIRY BY INTERVIEW. HISPANIA, Vol. 65, no. 4 (December 1982), p. 668. English. **DESCR:** Authors; Book Reviews; Bruce Novoa, Juan.

A CHICANO CHRISTMAS STORY

2579 Allen, Virginia. Book review of: A CHICANO CHRISTMAS STORY. MODERN LANGUAGE JOURNAL, Vol. 66, no. 3 (Fall 1982), p. 353-354. English. **DESCR:** Book Reviews; Children's Literature; Cruz, Manuel; Cruz, Ruth.

Chicano Federation of San Diego Co., Inc

2580 Quinlivan, Robert. Another milestone for the Chicano federation. CAMINOS, Vol. 3, no. 6 (June 1982), p. 41. English. **DESCR:** Cultural Organizations.

Chicano Film Exhibition and Festival, Detroit, Michigan, April 5-9, 1982

2581 Broyles, Yolanda Julia. Chicano film festivals: an examination. BILINGUAL REVIEW, Vol. 10, no. 2-3 (May, December, 1983), p. 116-120. English. **DESCR:** *Film Festivals; San Antonio CineFestival, TX.

2582 Newsfront. HISPANIC BUSINESS, Vol. 4, no. 3 (March 1982), p. 9. English. **DESCR:** Appointed Officials; *Biographical Notes; Businesspeople; Garcia, Gloria; League of United Latin American Citizens (LULAC); Martinez, Vilma Socorro; National Association for Bilingual Education; Seaga, Edward; Suarez, Carlos R.

CHICANO INTERMARRIAGE: A THEORETICAL AND EMPIRICAL STUDY

2583 Craver, Rebecca McDowell. Book review of: CHICANO INTERMARRIAGE: A THEORETICAL AND EMPIRICAL STUDY. NEW MEXICO HISTORICAL REVIEW, Vol. 58, no. 3 (July 1983), p. 295-296. English. **DESCR**: Book Reviews; Murguia, Edward.

2584 Manning, Roberta. Book review of: CHICANO INTERMARRIAGE: A THEORETICAL AND EMPIRICAL STUDY. HISPANIC JOURNAL OF BEHAVIORAL SCIENCES, Vol. 5, no. 3 (September 1983), p. 353-356. English. **DESCR**: Book Reviews; Intermarriage; Murguia, Edward.

CHICANO LITERATURE: A CRITICAL HISTORY

2585 Olszewski, Lawrence. Book review of: CHICANO LITERATURE: A CRITICAL HISTORY. LIBRARY JOURNAL, Vol. 108, no. 2 (January 15, 1983), p. 132. English. **DESCR**: Book Reviews; History; Poetry; *Tatum, Charles.

Chicano, Meaning Of
USE: Self-Referents

Chicano Moratorium

2586 Herrera, Juan Felipe. Photo-poem of the Chicano Moratorium 1980/L.A. REVISTA CHICANO-RIQUENA, Vol. 10, no. 3 (Summer 1982), p. 5-9. English. **DESCR**: Photography; *Poetry.

Chicano Movement

2587 Acuna, Rodolfo. La generacion de '68: unfulfilled dreams. CORAZON DE AZTLAN, Vol. 1, no. 1 (January, February, 1982), p. 6-7. English.

2588 Fernandez, Peter. The incredible F.P. hopper of varrio nuevo. CHISMEARTE, (1982), p. 11-12. English. **DESCR**: Short Story.

2589 Fraser Rothenberg, Irene. Mexican-American views of U.S. relations with Latin America. JOURNAL OF ETHNIC STUDIES, Vol. 6, no. 1 (Spring 1978), p. 62-78. English. **DESCR**: Culture; Identity; International Relations; Latin America; Lobbying; Mexico; *Nationalism; Political History and Conditions; Politics.

2590 Garcia, Richard A. Chicano intellectual history: myth and realities. REVISTA CHICANO-RIQUENA, Vol. 10, no. 1-2 (Winter, Spring, 1982), p. 285-289. English. **DESCR**: *Essays; History; Self-Referents; Stereotypes.

2591 Gonzalez, Cesar A. LA FAMILIA de Joaquin Chinas. DE COLORES, Vol. 6, no. 1-2 (1982), p. 146-149. English. **DESCR**: Artists; Chinas, Joaquin; *LA FAMILIA [poster]; Symbolism.

2592 Jensen, Richard J. and Hammerback, John C. "No revolutions without poets": the rhetoric of Rodolfo "Corky" Gonzales. WESTERN JOURNAL OF SPEECH COMMUNICATION, Vol. 46, no. 1 (Winter 1982), p. 72-91. English. **DESCR**: *Gonzales, Rodolfo (Corky); Literary Criticism; Poetry; Rhetoric.

2593 Lopez, Enrique Hank. Overkill at the silver dollar. CHISMEARTE, (1982), p. 6-8. English. **DESCR**: Riots.

2594 Lopez, Phyllis. Recollections. COMADRE, no. 2 (Spring 1978), p. 15. English. **DESCR**: *Poetry.

2595 Miller, Michael V. Chicano community control in South Texas: problems and prospects. JOURNAL OF ETHNIC STUDIES, Vol. 3, no. 3 (Fall 1975), p. 70-89. English. **DESCR**: Crystal City, TX; Gutierrez, Jose Angel; History; La Raza Unida Party; Patron System; *Political Parties and Organizations; Social Classes; Social History and Conditions; *South Texas.

2596 Molina-Pick, Gracia. The emergence of Chicano leadership: 1930-1950. CAMINOS, Vol. 4, no. 7 (July, August, 1983), p. 7-10. English. **DESCR**: History; Leadership.

2597 Munoz, Carlos, Jr. and Barrera, Mario. La Raza Unida Party and the Chicano student movement in California. SOCIAL SCIENCE JOURNAL, Vol. 19, no. 2 (April 1982), p. 101-119. English. **DESCR**: California; *La Raza Unida Party; Political History and Conditions; Political Ideology; Political Parties and Organizations; Student Movements.

2598 Regional report, education: NMSU schedules Chicano week. NUESTRO, Vol. 7, no. 4 (May 1983), p. 11-12. English. **DESCR**: New Mexico State University.

2599 Rodriguez, Luis. La veintinueve. CHISMEARTE, (1982), p. 9-10. English. **DESCR**: Riots.

2600 Rodriguez, Roberto. Who declared war on the word Chicano? CORAZON DE AZTLAN, Vol. 1, no. 2 (March, April, 1982), p. 17-20. English. **DESCR**: *Self-Referents.

CHICANO POETRY: A RESPONSE TO CHAOS

2601 Bell-Villada, G. H. Book review of: CHICANO AUTHORS, INQUIRY BY INTERVIEW v. 228. NOTES AND QUERIES, Vol. 30, no. 2 (1983), p. 186-188. English. **DESCR**: Book Reviews; Bruce Novoa, Juan; Literary Criticism.

2602 Book review of: CHICANO POETRY: A RESPONSE TO CHAOS. CHOICE, Vol. 20, no. 6 (February 1983), p. 827. English. **DESCR**: Book Reviews; Bruce Novoa, Juan.

2603 Saldivar, Jose David. Book review of: CHICANO POETRY: A RESPONSE TO CHAOS. MELUS: MULTI-ETHNIC LITERATURE OF THE UNITED STATES, Vol. 10, no. 2 (Summer 1983), p. 83-85. English. **DESCR**: Book Reviews; Bruce Novoa, Juan; Poetry.

2604 Tammaro, Thom. Book review of: CHICANO POETRY: A RESPONSE TO CHAOS. LIBRARY JOURNAL, Vol. 107, no. 16 (September 15, 1982), p. 1755-1756. English. **DESCR**: Book Reviews; Bruce Novoa, Juan.

Chicano Studies

2605 Cortese, Anthony J., ed. Contemporary trends in Chicano studies. CACR REVIEW, Vol. 1, no. 1 (September 1982), p. 1-133. English. **DESCR**: Colorado Association of Chicano Research (CACR); Journals.

2606 McCurdy, Jack. L.A. violence linked to Chicano-studies dispute. CHRONICLE OF HIGHER EDUCATION, Vol. 24, no. 14 (June 2, 1982), p. 8. English. **DESCR**: California State University, Los Angeles; Corona, Bert; Faculty; Violence.

2607 Romo, Ricardo. Unfinished story: Chicanos in the West. WESTERN HISTORICAL QUARTERLY, Vol. 13, no. 3 (July 1982), p. 299-302. English. **DESCR**: *Historiography; History.

CHICANO THEATER: THEMES AND FORMS

2608 Book review of: CHICANO THEATER: THEMES AND FORMS. CHOICE, Vol. 20, no. 2 (October 1982), p. 280. English. DESCR: Book Reviews; History; Huerta, Jorge A.; Teatro.

Chicano Youth Leadership Conference

2609 Mena, Kristena. Tomorrow's leaders (photoessays). CAMINOS, Vol. 3, no. 8 (September 1982), p. 48. English. DESCR: *Association of Mexican American Educators, Inc. (AMAE); *Youth.

2610 Rick Icaza on career opportunities in unions. CAMINOS, Vol. 3, no. 8 (September 1982), p. 44-45. Bilingual. DESCR: *Affirmative Action; Labor Unions; United Food and Commercial Workers.

Chicano Youth Organization

2611 Martinez, Paul E. Serna v. Portales: the plight of bilingual education four years later. JOURNAL OF ETHNIC STUDIES, Vol. 7, no. 2 (Summer 1979), p. 109-114. English. DESCR: *Bilingual Bicultural Education; Civil Rights; Portales Municipal Schools; *Portales, NM; Serna v. Portales Municipal Schools.

THE CHICANOS

2612 Goldberg, Victor. Ethnic groups in the United States. REVIEWS IN ANTHROPOLOGY, Vol. 9, no. 4 (Fall 1982), p. 375-382. English. DESCR: Achor, Shirley; Book Reviews; ETHNIC AMERICA, A HISTORY; MEXICAN AMERICANS IN A DALLAS BARRIO; Sowell, Thomas; Trejo, Arnulfo D.

CHICANOS AND RURAL POVERTY

2613 Miller, Michael V. Book review of: CHICANOS AND RURAL POVERTY. JOURNAL OF ETHNIC STUDIES, Vol. 5, no. 3 (Fall 1977), p. 116-117. English. DESCR: Agricultural Laborers; Book Reviews; Briggs, Vernon M.; Immigration Law; Social History and Conditions; Southwest United States.

CHICANOS: ANTOLOGIA HISTORICA Y LITERARIA

2614 Alves Pereira, Teresinka. Book review of: CHICANOS: ANTOLOGIA HISTORICA Y LITERARIA. ROCKY MOUNTAIN REVIEW OF LANGUAGE AND LITERATURE, Vol. 36, no. 4 (1982), p. 301-302. Spanish. DESCR: Book Reviews; Villanueva, Tino.

2615 de Armas, Isabel. Chicano, un vocablo colonizador. CUADERNOS HISPANOAMERICANOS, Vol. 394, (April 1983), p. 193-201. Spanish. DESCR: Agricultural Laborers; Book Reviews; Calvo Buezas, Tomas; Identity; *LOS MAS POBRES EN EL PAIS MAS RICO; Villanueva, Tino.

2616 Soens. Adolph L. Book review of: CHICANOS: ANTOLOGIA HISTORICA Y LITERARIA. MINORITY VOICES, Vol. 5, no. 1-2 (Spring, Fall, 1981), p. 69-71. English. DESCR: Book Reviews; Literature; Villanueva, Tino.

Chicanos for Fair Representation (CFR), Los Angeles, CA

2617 Santillan, Richard. The Chicano community and the redistricting of the Los Angeles city council, 1971-1973. CHICANO LAW REVIEW, Vol. 6, (1983), p. 122-145. English. DESCR: Los Angeles City Council; Mexican American Legal Defense and Educational Fund (MALDEF); *Political Representation; Snyder, Art, Councilman.

CHICANOS IN A CHANGING SOCIETY

2618 Lotchin, Roger W. New Chicano history: an urban history perspective. HISTORY TEACHER, Vol. 16, no. 2 (February 1983), p. 229-247. English. DESCR: Camarillo, Alberto; DESERT IMMIGRANTS: THE MEXICANS OF EL PASO 1880-1920; Garcia, Mario T.; Griswold del Castillo, Ricardo; *Historiography; History; Social History and Conditions; THE LOS ANGELES BARRIO 1850-1890: A SOCIAL HISTORY; Urban Communities.

2619 Reisler, Mark. Book review of: CHICANOS IN A CHANGING SOCIETY: FROM MEXICAN PUEBLOS TO AMERICAN BARRIOS IN SANTA BARBARA AND SOUTHERN CALIFORNIA, 1848-1930. NEW MEXICO HISTORICAL REVIEW, Vol. 57, no. 2 (April 1982), p. 200-201. English. DESCR: Book Reviews; Camarillo, Alberto; Social History and Conditions.

2620 Saragoza, Alex M. The florescence of Chicano historical scholarship. NEW SCHOLAR, Vol. 8, no. 1-2 (Spring, Fall, 1982), p. 483-487. English. DESCR: Book Reviews; Camarillo, Alberto; History.

2621 Weber, David J. and Lotchin, Roger W. The new Chicano history: two perspectives. HISTORY TEACHER, Vol. 16, no. 2 (February 1983), p. 219-247. English. DESCR: Camarillo, Alberto; DESERT IMMIGRANTS: THE MEXICANS OF EL PASO 1880-1920; Garcia, Mario T.; Griswold del Castillo, Ricardo; *Historiography; History; Social History and Conditions; *THE LOS ANGELES BARRIO 1850-1890: A SOCIAL HISTORY; *Urban Communities.

2622 Weber, David J. The new Chicano urban history. HISTORY TEACHER, Vol. 16, no. 2 (February 1983), p. 223-229. English. DESCR: Camarillo, Alberto; DESERT IMMIGRANTS: THE MEXICANS OF EL PASO 1880-1920; Garcia, Mario T.; Griswold del Castillo, Ricardo; *Historiography; History; Social History and Conditions; *THE LOS ANGELES BARRIO 1850-1890: A SOCIAL HISTORY; Urban Communities.

Chicanos in American Literature

2623 Bloodworth, William A., Jr. Book review of: IMAGES OF THE MEXICAN-AMERICAN IN FICTION AND FILM. WESTERN AMERICAN LITERATURE, Vol. 16, no. 4 (Winter 1982), p. 323-325. English. DESCR: Book Reviews; Films; *IMAGES OF THE MEXICAN AMERICAN IN FICTION AND FILM; Pettit, Arthur G.; Showalter, Dennis E.; Stereotypes.

2624 Hoffer, Bates L. Sociology by value systems: explication and some implications of two studies on the folklore of Hispanics in the United States. BILINGUAL REVIEW, Vol. 9, no. 2 (May, August, 1982), p. 172-177. Bilingual. DESCR: BENJY LOPEZ: A PICARESQUE TALE OF EMIGRATION AND RETURN; Braceros; Comparative Literature; Folklore; Herrera Sobek, Maria; Levine, Barry B.; THE BRACERO EXPERIENCE: ELITELORE VERSUS FOLKLORE.

2625 Ortego y Gasca, Felipe de. Fables of identity: stereotype and caricature of Chicanos in Steinbeck's TORTILLA FLAT. JOURNAL OF ETHNIC STUDIES, Vol. 1, no. 1 (Spring 1973), p. 39-43. English. DESCR: Caricature; Literature; Steinbeck, John; *Stereotypes; TORTILLA FLAT.

Chicanos in American Literature (cont.)

2626 Tyler, Joseph. Basque Ball in Bridgeport. HISPANIA, Vol. 66, no. 1 (1983), p. 144. English. **DESCR:** Book Reviews; *LES FILS DU SOLEIL: LA MINORITE MEXICAINE A TRAVERS LA LITTERATURE DES ETATS-UNIS.

2627 West, Dennis. Book review of: IMAGES OF THE MEXICAN-AMERICAN IN FICTION AND FILM. CINEASTE, Vol. 12, no. 1 (1982), p. 41. English. **DESCR:** Book Reviews; Films; *IMAGES OF THE MEXICAN AMERICAN IN FICTION AND FILM; Pettit, Arthur G.; Stereotypes.

THE CHICANOS OF EL PASO: AN ASSESSMENT OF PROGRESS

2628 Griswold del Castillo, Richard. Book review of: THE CHICANOS OF EL PASO: AN ASSESSMENT OF PROGRESS. PACIFIC HISTORICAL REVIEW, Vol. 51, no. 3 (August 1982), p. 337-338. English. **DESCR:** Book Reviews; El Paso, TX; Martinez, Oscar J.

CHICANOS: THE STORY OF MEXICAN AMERICANS

2629 Maciel, David R. and Bergaila, Christine. Book review of: CHICANOS: THE STORY OF THE MEXICAN AMERICANS. JOURNAL OF ETHNIC STUDIES, Vol. 2, no. 3 (Fall 1974), p. 94-95. English. **DESCR:** Book Reviews; de Garza, Patricia; History.

Child Care Centers

2630 Barry, Patrick. Progress at La Paz: a chance for the retarded. NUESTRO, Vol. 6, no. 6 (August 1982), p. 20-23. English. **DESCR:** *Chicago, IL; *Child Study.

2631 For children - Centros de Ninos. CAMINOS, Vol. 4, no. 8 (September 1983), p. 44. English. **DESCR:** *Centro de Ninos.

2632 Government review. NUESTRO, Vol. 7, no. 10 (December 1983), p. 48. English. **DESCR:** Banking Industry; Chile; Clinics (Medical); Credit Unions; Employment; Employment Training; *Government Services; Medical Care; National Credit Union Administration; National Oceanic and Atmospheric Administration; SER; U.S. Department of Health and Human Services; U.S. Department of Labor.

Child Development Associate (CDA) Program

2633 Riley, Mary Tom and Taylor, Vincent. Threading the needle: IEP's for teachers? EDUCATIONAL RESEARCH QUARTERLY, Vol. 7, no. 1 (Spring 1982), p. 2-6. English. **DESCR:** Ethnic Groups; *Teacher Training.

Child Rearing

2634 Escovar, Peggy L. and Lazarus, Philip J. Cross-cultural child-rearing practices: implications for school psychologists. SCHOOL PSYCHOLOGY INTERNATIONAL, Vol. 3, no. 3 (July, September, 1982), p. 143-148. English. **DESCR:** Children; Counseling (Psychological); Cultural Characteristics.

2635 Henderson, Ronald W. and Brody, Gene H. Effects of ethnicity and child's age on maternal judgments of children's transgressions against persons and property. JOURNAL OF GENETIC PSYCHOLOGY, Vol. 140, no. 2 (June 1982), p. 253-263. English. **DESCR:** Anglo Americans; Arizona; Behavior Modification; Cultural Characteristics; Native Americans; *Socialization; Tucson, AZ.

2636 Johnson, Dale L. and Breckenridge, James N. The Houston Parent-Child Development Center and the primary prevention of behavior problems in young children. AMERICAN JOURNAL OF COMMUNITY PSYCHOLOGY, Vol. 10, no. 3 (June 1982), p. 305-316. English. **DESCR:** Children; Early Childhood Education; *Houston Parent-Child Development Center(PCDC); Parent and Child Relationships; Social Classes.

2637 Rivera-Cano, Andrea. Parenting: four families' stories. LATINA, Vol. 1, no. 2 (February, March, 1983), p. 66-73+. English. **DESCR:** Children; Elias, Bob; Hernandez, Jesus; Hernandez, Virginia; Lopez, Genevieve; Ojalvo, Juana.

2638 Zepeda, Marlene. Selected maternal-infant care practices of Spanish-speaking women. JOGN NURSING, Vol. 11, no. 6 (November, December, 1982), p. 371-374. English. **DESCR:** *Maternal and Child Welfare.

Child Study

2639 Argulewicz, Ed N.; Elliott, Stephen N.; and Hall, Robert. Comparison of behavioral ratings of Anglo-American and Mexican-American gifted children. PSYCHOLOGY IN THE SCHOOLS, Vol. 19, no. 4 (October 1982), p. 469-472. English. **DESCR:** Anglo Americans; Cultural Characteristics; *Intelligence Tests.

2640 Barry, Patrick. Progress at La Paz: a chance for the retarded. NUESTRO, Vol. 6, no. 6 (August 1982), p. 20-23. English. **DESCR:** *Chicago, IL; *Child Care Centers.

2641 Clarizio, Harvey F. Intellectual assessment of Hispanic children. PSYCHOLOGY IN THE SCHOOLS, Vol. 19, no. 1 (January 1982), p. 61-71. English. **DESCR:** Anglo Americans; Cultural Pluralism; *Intelligence Tests.

2642 Ferullo, R. J. Objectivity in the assessment of pre-school hearing impaired bilingual-Hispanic children. JOURNAL OF SCHOOL HEALTH, Vol. 53, (Fall 1983), p. 131-135. English. **DESCR:** Bilingualism; *Deaf.

2643 Gorrell, J. Jeffrey, et al. Comparison of spatial role-taking in monolingual and bilingual children. JOURNAL OF GENETIC PSYCHOLOGY, Vol. 140, no. 1 (March 1982), p. 3-10. English. **DESCR:** Bilingualism; Cognition; *Linguistic Theory; *Perception.

2644 Hsi, Bartholomew P.; Hsu, Katherine H.; and Jenkins, Daniel E. Ventilatory functions of normal children and young adults: Mexican-American, white and black. III. Sitting height as a predictor. JOURNAL OF PEDIATRICS, Vol. 102, no. 6 (June 1983), p. 860-865. English. **DESCR:** Anglo Americans; Blacks; *Children; Pediatrics.

2645 Kagan, Spencer and Knudsen, Kathryn H.M. Relationship of empathy and affective role-taking in young children. JOURNAL OF GENETIC PSYCHOLOGY, Vol. 141, (September 1982), p. 149-150. English. **DESCR:** Anglo Americans; *Attitude (Psychological); Psychological Testing; Socialization.

Child Study (cont.)

2646 Knudsen, Kathryn H.M. and Kagan, Spencer. Differential development of empathy and pro-social behavior. JOURNAL OF GENETIC PSYCHOLOGY, Vol. 140, no. 2 (June 1982), p. 249-251. English. **DESCR:** Anglo Americans; *Attitude (Psychological); Psychological Testing; Socialization.

2647 Montalvo, Frank F.; Lasater, Tonia Tash; and Valdez, Nancy Garza. Training child welfare workers for cultural awareness: the culture simulator technique. CHILD WELFARE, Vol. 61, no. 6 (June 1982), p. 341-352. English. **DESCR:** Cultural Pluralism; Social Work.

2648 Peterson, Marilyn L. Mexican-American children: what do they prefer to read? READING WORLD, Vol. 22, no. 2 (December 1982), p. 129-131. English. **DESCR:** *Reading.

2649 Valencia, Richard R. Stability of the McCarthy scales of children's abilities over a one-year period for Mexican-American children. PSYCHOLOGY IN THE SCHOOLS, Vol. 20, no. 1 (January 1983), p. 29-34. English. **DESCR:** Cultural Characteristics; *Intelligence Tests; McCarthy Scales for Children's Abilities (MSCA); Socioeconomic Factors.

Children

2650 Adams, Phylliss J. and Anderson, Peggy L. Comparison of teachers' and Mexican-American children's perceptions of the children's competence. READING TEACHER, Vol. 36, no. 1 (October 1982), p. 8-13. English. **DESCR:** Attitude (Psychological); Colorado; Cultural Characteristics; Learning and Cognition; Sex Roles; *Teacher Attitudes.

2651 Argulewicz, Ed N. and Sanchez, David T. Considerations in the assessment of reading difficulties in bilingual children. SCHOOL PSYCHOLOGY REVIEW, Vol. 11, no. 3 (Summer 1982), p. 281-289. English. **DESCR:** Bilingualism; *Language Assessment; Reading; Sociolinguistics.

2652 Blake, Robert. Mood selection among Spanish-speaking children, ages 4 to 12. BILINGUAL REVIEW, Vol. 10, no. 1 (January, April, 1983), p. 21-32. English. **DESCR:** Grammar; *Language Development; Language Usage; Spanish Language.

2653 Bonilla, Tony. A decade of success. LATINO, Vol. 54, no. 2 (March 1983), p. 4. English. **DESCR:** *Education.

2654 Bose, Aruna; Vashistha, Krishan; and O'Loughlin, Bernard J. Azarcon por empacho - another cause of lead toxicity. PEDIATRICS, Vol. 72, no. 1 (July 1983), p. 106-108. English. **DESCR:** Folk Medicine; *Lead Poisoning; Public Health.

2655 Buriel, Raymond, et al. Mexican- and Anglo-American children's locus of control and achievement in relation to teachers attitudes. JOURNAL OF GENETIC PSYCHOLOGY, Vol. 140, no. 1 (March 1982), p. 131-143. English. **DESCR:** *Academic Achievement; Anglo Americans; Comparative Education; *Teacher Attitudes.

2656 Burke, P.E. Immigrant Mexican children hurdle the English barrier. TIMES (London) [EDUCATIONAL SUPPLEMENT], Vol. 3447, (July 23, 1982), p. 15. English. **DESCR:** *Bilingual Bicultural Education; English Language; Immigrants.

2657 Canales, Judy. Preparing your child for a higher education: staying on that long road to sucess. NATIONAL HISPANIC JOURNAL, Vol. 1, no. 4 (Spring 1983), p. 6. English. **DESCR:** Education; Educational Psychology; *Higher Education.

2658 Chesterfield, Kathleen Barrows and Chesterfield, Ray A. Peer interaction language proficiency and language preference in bilingual pre-school classrooms. HISPANIC JOURNAL OF BEHAVIORAL SCIENCES, Vol. 4, no. 4 (December 1982), p. 467-486. English. **DESCR:** *Bilingual Bicultural Education; Language Proficiency.

2659 Constantino, Guiseppe and Malgady, Robert G. Verbal fluency of Hispanic, Black and white children on TAT and TEMAS, a new thematic apperception test. HISPANIC JOURNAL OF BEHAVIORAL SCIENCES, Vol. 5, no. 2 (June 1983), p. 199-206. English. **DESCR:** Ethnic Groups; *Language Proficiency; TAT; TEMAS.

2660 De Barbosa, Liliam Coya. "Mastering learning" como metodo psicoeducativo para ninos con problemas especificos de aprendizaje. HISPANIC JOURNAL OF BEHAVIORAL SCIENCES, Vol. 4, no. 4 (December 1982), p. 503-510. Spanish. **DESCR:** Learning and Cognition; *Mastery Learning; Puerto Ricans; *Reading.

2661 Dodge, Russell. A comparison of the respiratory health of Mexican-American and non-Mexican American white children. CHEST, Vol. 84, no. 5 (November 1983), p. 587-592. English. **DESCR:** Anglo Americans; *Public Health.

2662 Dressing up the children. LATINA, Vol. 1, no. 2 (February, March, 1983), p. 39-41. English. **DESCR:** *Fashion.

2663 Equal protection: right of illegal alien children to state provided education. HARVARD LAW REVIEW, Vol. 96, no. 1 (November 1982), p. 130-140. English. **DESCR:** Civil Rights; Discrimination in Education; Doe v. Plyer [Tyler Independent School District, Texas]; *Education; *Undocumented Workers.

2664 Escovar, Peggy L. and Lazarus, Philip J. Cross-cultural child-rearing practices: implications for school psychologists. SCHOOL PSYCHOLOGY INTERNATIONAL, Vol. 3, no. 3 (July, September, 1982), p. 143-148. English. **DESCR:** *Child Rearing; Counseling (Psychological); Cultural Characteristics.

2665 Espinoza, Ana Luisa. Los ninos: la cosecha del futuro. CALMECAC, Vol. 2, (Spring 1981), p. 20-25. English. **DESCR:** *Short Story.

2666 Flores de Apodaca, Roberto. Quick socio-emotional screening of Mexican-American and other ethnic head start children. HISPANIC JOURNAL OF BEHAVIORAL SCIENCES, Vol. 5, no. 1 (March 1983), p. 81-92. English. **DESCR:** *AML Instrument; Headstart Program; *Mental Health.

2667 Franco, Juan N. An acculturation scale for Mexican-American children. JOURNAL OF GENERAL PSYCHOLOGY, Vol. 108, (April 1983), p. 175-181. English. **DESCR:** *Acculturation; *Children's Acculturation Scale (CAS); Psychological Testing.

Children (cont.)

2668 Franco, Juan N. A developmental analysis of self concept in Mexican American and Anglo school children. HISPANIC JOURNAL OF BEHAVIORAL SCIENCES, Vol. 5, no. 2 (June 1983), p. 207-218. English. **DESCR:** Acculturation; *Identity.

2669 Gallo, Adrien. Children of Guatemala: a pictoral essay. NUESTRO, Vol. 7, no. 2 (March 1983), p. 43-45. English. **DESCR:** *Guatemala; Photography.

2670 Guendelman, Sylvia. Developing responsiveness to health needs of Hispanic children and families. SOCIAL WORK IN HEALTH CARE, Vol. 8, no. 4 (Summer 1983), p. 1-15. English. **DESCR:** Family; Public Health; *Social Psychology.

2671 Heberton Craig N. To educate and not to educate: the plight of undocumented alien children in Texas. WASHINGTON UNIVERSITY LAW QUARTERLY, Vol. 60, no. 1 (Spring 1982), p. 119-159. English. **DESCR:** Doe v. Plyer [Tyler Independent School District, Texas]; Education; San Antonio School District v. Rodriguez; *Undocumented Workers.

2672 Hsi, Bartholomew P.; Hsu, Katherine H.; and Jenkins, Daniel E. Ventilatory functions of normal children and young adults: Mexican-American, white and black. III. Sitting height as a predictor. JOURNAL OF PEDIATRICS, Vol. 102, no. 6 (June 1983), p. 860-865. English. **DESCR:** Anglo Americans; Blacks; Child Study; Pediatrics.

2673 Hudelson, Sarah. An introductory examination of children's invented spelling in Spanish. NABE JOURNAL, Vol. 6, no. 2-3 (Winter, Spring, 1981, 1982), p. 53-67. English. **DESCR:** Bilingual Bicultural Education; *Language Arts; Learning and Cognition; Spanish Language.

2674 Johnson, Dale L. and Breckenridge, James N. The Houston Parent-Child Development Center and the primary prevention of behavior problems in young children. AMERICAN JOURNAL OF COMMUNITY PSYCHOLOGY, Vol. 10, no. 3 (June 1982), p. 305-316. English. **DESCR:** *Child Rearing; Early Childhood Education; *Houston Parent-Child Development Center(PCDC); Parent and Child Relationships; Social Classes.

2675 Kagan, Spencer and Zahn, G. Lawrence. Cultural differences in individualism? Just artifact. HISPANIC JOURNAL OF BEHAVIORAL SCIENCES, Vol. 5, no. 2 (June 1983), p. 219-232. English. **DESCR:** Anglo Americans; Blacks; Competition; *Culture; Social Orientation.

2676 Klein, Carol A. Children's concepts of the earth and the sun: a cross cultural study. SCIENCE EDUCATION, Vol. 66, no. 1 (January 1982), p. 95-107. English. **DESCR:** Anglo Americans; Cultural Pluralism; Education; *Science.

2677 Knight, George P. and Kagan, Spencer. Sibling, birth order, and cooperative-competitive social behavior: a comparison of Anglo-American and Mexican-American children. JOURNAL OF CROSS-CULTURAL PSYCHOLOGY, Vol. 13, no. 2 (June 1982), p. 239-249. English. **DESCR:** Anglo Americans; *Competition; Social Behavior Scale; Socialization.

2678 Lamare, James W. Political integration of Mexican American children: a generational analysis. INTERNATIONAL MIGRATION REVIEW, Vol. 16, no. 1 (Spring 1982), p. 169-188. English. **DESCR:** Acculturation; Age Groups; Assimilation; Immigration; Political Ideology; *Political Socialization.

2679 Leigh, Monroe. United States Constitution - equal protection deprivation of education in illegal alien school-children not justified by substantial state goal. AMERICAN JOURNAL OF INTERNATIONAL LAW, Vol. 77, no. 1 (January 1983), p. 151-153. English. **DESCR:** Discrimination in Education; Doe v. Plyer [Tyler Independent School District, Texas]; *Education; Texas; *Undocumented Workers.

2680 Lopez-Moreno, Amelia. For the Apache infants in the mountains of Arizona. COMADRE, no. 1 (Summer 1977), p. 6. English. **DESCR:** *Poetry.

2681 McDowell, John H. Sociolinguistic contours in the verbal art of Chicano children. AZTLAN, Vol. 13, no. 1-2 (Spring, Fall, 1982), p. 166-193. English. **DESCR:** Bilingualism; Linguistics; *Sociolinguistics.

2682 Morrison, J. A. and Michael, W.B. Development and validation of an auditory perception test in Spanish for Hispanic children receiving reading instruction in Spanish. EDUCATIONAL AND PSYCHOLOGICAL MEASUREMENT, Vol. 42, (Summer 1982), p. 657-669. English. **DESCR:** Educational Tests and Measurements; *Language Arts; Prueba de Analisis Auditivo (PAA); Reading; Spanish Language.

2683 Murray, James L.; Bruhn, John G.; and Bunce, Harvey. Assessment of type A behavior in preschoolers. JOURNAL OF HUMAN STRESS, Vol. 9, no. 3 (September 1983), p. 32-39. English. **DESCR:** Anglo Americans; Blacks; Early Childhood Education; Psychology.

2684 New program on parenting. NUESTRO, Vol. 6, no. 3 (April 1982), p. 11-12. English. **DESCR:** Parent and Child Relationships.

2685 O'Donnell, James P., et al. Dimensions of behavior problems in Anglo-American and Mexican-American preschool children: a comparative study. JOURNAL OF CONSULTING AND CLINICAL PSYCHOLOGY, Vol. 50, no. 5 (October 1982), p. 643-651. English. **DESCR:** Anglo Americans; *Comparative Psychology; Cultural Characteristics; Mental Health; Psychological Testing; Socioeconomic Factors.

2686 Panitz, Daniel R., et al. The role of machismo and the Hispanic family in the etiology and treatment of alcoholism in the Hispanic American males. AMERICAN JOURNAL OF FAMILY THERAPY, Vol. 11, no. 1 (Spring 1983), p. 31-44. English. **DESCR:** *Alcoholism; Family; *Machismo; Puerto Rico; Socioeconomic Factors.

2687 Parents' corner: kids/discipline and you. LATINA, Vol. 1, no. 1 (1982), p. 43+. English.

2688 Piersel, Wayne C., et al. Bias in content validity on the Boehm test of basic concepts for white and Mexican-American children. CONTEMPORARY EDUCATIONAL PSYCHOLOGY, Vol. 7, no. 2 (April 1982), p. 181-189. English. **DESCR:** Anglo Americans; *Boehm Test of Basic Concepts; *Educational Tests and Measurements; Language Arts.

Children (cont.)

2689 Quinn, Michael Sean. Educating alien kids. TEXAS OBSERVOR, Vol. 74, no. 18 (September 17, 1982), p. 5-6. English. **DESCR:** *Doe v. Plyer [Tyler Independent School District, Texas]; Education; Undocumented Workers.

2690 Reaves, Gayle. Supreme Court rules for alien children. NUESTRO, Vol. 6, no. 5 (June, July, 1982), p. 14-16. English. **DESCR:** Education; Education Equalization; Immigration Law; *Legislation; Undocumented Workers; U.S. Supreme Court.

2691 Richardson, Chad and Yanez, Linda. "Equal justice" and Jose Reyna. NUESTRO, Vol. 6, no. 5 (June, July, 1982), p. 17. English. **DESCR:** Brownsville, TX; Education; Education Equalization; Immigration Law; *Legislation; Reyna, Jose; Undocumented Workers.

2692 Rising star in the music world. NUESTRO, Vol. 6, no. 1 (January, February, 1982), p. 64. English. **DESCR:** Music; *Romero, Gustavo.

2693 Rivera-Cano, Andrea. Parenting: four families' stories. LATINA, Vol. 1, no. 2 (February, March, 1983), p. 66-73+. English. **DESCR:** *Child Rearing; Elias, Bob; Hernandez, Jesus; Hernandez, Virginia; Lopez, Genevieve; Ojalvo, Juana.

2694 Rodriguez, Andres and De Blassie, Richard R. Ethnic designation, identification, and preference as they relate to Chicano children. JOURNAL OF NON-WHITE CONCERNS IN PERSONNEL AND GUIDANCE, Vol. 11, no. 3 (April 1983), p. 99-106. English. **DESCR:** *Identity.

2695 Rueda, Robert. Interpersonal tactics and communicative strategies of Anglo-American and Mexican American mildly mentally retarded and nonretarded students. APPLIED RESEARCH IN MENTAL RETARDATION, Vol. 4, no. 2 (1983), p. 153-161. English. **DESCR:** Anglo Americans; Intelligence Tests; *Mentally Handicapped; Test of Social Problem Solving.

2696 Saragoza, Alex M. Mexican children in the U.S.: the Central San Joaquin Valley. DE COLORES, Vol. 6, no. 1-2 (1982), p. 64-74. English. **DESCR:** Acculturation; Family; Identity; Parent and Child Relationships; San Joaquin Valley.

2697 Schmidt, Lorenza. Grandparental-grandchild interaction in a Mexican American group. HISPANIC JOURNAL OF BEHAVIORAL SCIENCES, Vol. 5, no. 2 (June 1983), p. 181-198. English. **DESCR:** Ancianos; *Grandparent and Child Relationships.

2698 Student at New Jersey school saves classmate. NUESTRO, Vol. 6, no. 4 (May 1982), p. 28. English. **DESCR:** *New Jersey.

2699 Tejani, Amir et al. Lupus nephritis in Black and Hispanic children. AMERICAN JOURNAL OF DISEASES OF CHILDREN, Vol. 137, no. 5 (May 1983), p. 481-483. English. **DESCR:** Medical Care; *Medical Research; Public Health.

2700 Torres, Arnold. Looking out for America's children. LATINO, Vol. 53, no. 8 (December 1982), p. 23. English.

2701 U.S. workers tutor students. NUESTRO, Vol. 6, no. 4 (May 1982), p. 13. English. **DESCR:** *Education; Rios, Al.

2702 Valencia, Richard R. Predicting academic achievement of Mexican American children: preliminary analysis of the McCarthy Scales. EDUCATIONAL AND PSYCHOLOGICAL MEASUREMENT, Vol. 42, (Winter 1982), p. 1269-1278. English. **DESCR:** *Academic Achievement; Educational Tests and Measurements; Identity; McCarthy Scales for Children's Abilities (MSCA).

2703 Zavaleta, Anthony N. and Malina, Robert M. Growth and body composition of Mexican-American boys 9 through 14 years of age. AMERICAN JOURNAL OF PHYSICAL ANTHROPOLOGY, Vol. 57, no. 3 (March 1982), p. 261-271. English. **DESCR:** Age Groups; Anglo Americans; *Anthropometry; Socioeconomic Factors.

Children of the Undocumented
   USE: Undocumented Children

Children's Acculturation Scale (CAS)

2704 Franco, Juan N. An acculturation scale for Mexican-American children. JOURNAL OF GENERAL PSYCHOLOGY, Vol. 108, (April 1983), p. 175-181. English. **DESCR:** *Acculturation; Children; Psychological Testing.

Children's Literature

2705 Allen, Virginia. Book review of: A CHICANO CHRISTMAS STORY. MODERN LANGUAGE JOURNAL, Vol. 66, no. 3 (Fall 1982), p. 353-354. English. **DESCR:** *A CHICANO CHRISTMAS STORY; Book Reviews; Cruz, Manuel; Cruz, Ruth.

2706 Dujoune, Marta. The image of Latin America in children's literature of developed countries. BOOKBIRD, Vol. 20, no. 1-2 (1982), p. 5-10. English. **DESCR:** Stereotypes.

2707 Ferrarone, Aida. Chasqui: a children's story. LATINA, Vol. 1, no. 2 (February, March, 1983), p. 42-43. English.

2708 Nieto, Sonia. Children's literature on Puerto Rican themes -- the messages of fiction; non-fiction. INTERRACIAL BOOKS FOR CHILDREN, Vol. 14, no. 1-2 (1983), p. 6-12. English. **DESCR:** Puerto Rican Literature; Puerto Ricans.

2709 Schon, Isabel. Books in Spanish and bilingual books for young readers: some good, some bad. SCHOOL LIBRARY JOURNAL, Vol. 29, (March 1983), p. 87-91. English. **DESCR:** Publishing Industry.

2710 Schon, Isabel. Recent outstanding books for young readers from Spanish speaking countries. READING TEACHER, Vol. 36, no. 2 (November 1982), p. 206-209. English. **DESCR:** Argentina; Literature Reviews; Spain; Spanish Language; Venezuela.

2711 Schon, Isabel. Spanish books for children. BOOKLIST, Vol. 78, no. 20 (June 15, 1982), p. 1373-1374. English. **DESCR:** Argentina; *Bibliography; Mexico; Spain; Spanish Language; Venezuela.

2712 Schon, Isabel. Spanish books for children. BOOKLIST, Vol. 79, (February 15, 1983), p. 783-784. English. **DESCR:** *Bibliography; Mexico; Spain; Spanish Language; Venezuela.

2713 Wagoner, Shirley A. Mexican-Americans in children's literature since 1970. READING TEACHER, Vol. 36, no. 3 (December 1982), p. 274-279. English. **DESCR:** Literature Reviews; Stereotypes.

Chile

2714 Business/negocios. CAMINOS, Vol. 3, no. 2 (February 1982), p. 22-23. Bilingual. **DESCR:** Argentina; Brazil; *Business; Colombia; Federation of Minority Business Associations; FRANCHISE OPPORTUNITIES HANDBOOK; Latin America.

2715 Concha, Jaime. Exilio, conciencia: coda sobre la poesia de Millan. MAIZE, Vol. 5, no. 1-2 (Fall, Winter, 1981, 1982), p. 7-15. Spanish. **DESCR:** Jesuits; Literary Criticism; Literary History; *Millan, Gonzalo; Poetry; Political Refugees.

2716 Government review. NUESTRO, Vol. 7, no. 10 (December 1983), p. 48. English. **DESCR:** Banking Industry; Child Care Centers; Clinics (Medical); Credit Unions; Employment; Employment Training; *Government Services; Medical Care; National Credit Union Administration; National Oceanic and Atmospheric Administration; SER; U.S. Department of Health and Human Services; U.S. Department of Labor.

2717 Perez, Juan. Chile, poema en cuatro augustias y un iris aura. MAIZE, Vol. 3, no. 3-4 (Spring, Summer, 1980), p. 70-73. Spanish. **DESCR:** *Poetry.

Chile (Food)

2718 Kopp, April. Chile, spice of the southwest. NUESTRO, Vol. 6, no. 10 (December 1982), p. 22-25+. English. **DESCR:** *Recipes.

Chinas, Joaquin

2719 Gonzalez, Cesar A. LA FAMILIA de Joaquin Chinas. DE COLORES, Vol. 6, no. 1-2 (1982), p. 146-149. English. **DESCR:** Artists; Chicano Movement; *LA FAMILIA [poster]; Symbolism.

Chisholm, Shirley

2720 Migrant farm workers. NUESTRO, Vol. 5, no. 8 (November 1981), p. 10-11. English. **DESCR:** *Migrant Labor; U.S. Commission on Farmworkers.

Chistes

2721 Castro, Rafaela. Mexican women's sexual jokes. AZTLAN, Vol. 13, no. 1-2 (Spring, Fall, 1982), p. 275-293. English. **DESCR:** Chicanas; Humor.

2722 Limon, Jose. History, Chicano joking, and the varieties of higher-education: tradition and performance as critical symbolic action. JOURNAL OF THE FOLKLORE INSTITUTE, Vol. 19, no. 2-3 (1982), p. 146-166. English. **DESCR:** Folklore; Higher Education; Humor; Interpersonal Relations; Texas; University of Texas at Austin.

Chiswick, Barry R.

2723 Bronfenbrenner, Martin. Hyphenated Americans-economic aspects. LAW AND CONTEMPORARY PROBLEMS, Vol. 45, no. 2 (Spring 1982), p. 9-27. English. **DESCR:** *Economics; *Immigrants; Racism; Smith, James P.; Welch, Finis R.

Cholos, Images of
USE: Pachuco Images

Christianity
USE: Religion

Christmas

2724 Burciaga, Jose Antonio. Hannukkah, navidad and christmas. NUESTRO, Vol. 5, no. 8 (November 1981), p. 22-23. English. **DESCR:** *Holidays.

2725 Lenti, Paul. Mexico's posadas a unique experience. NUESTRO, Vol. 6, no. 10 (December 1982), p. 52-55. English. **DESCR:** Las Posadas; Mexico; Tourism.

2726 Melendez, Carmelo. Chasing a Puerto Rican Christmas. NUESTRO, Vol. 5, no. 8 (November 1981), p. 33. English. **DESCR:** *Family; Puerto Rico.

2727 Padilla, Steve. Granny's bunuelos and other secrets. NUESTRO, Vol. 6, no. 10 (December 1982), p. 45. English. **DESCR:** *Short Story.

2728 A sheriff's X-mas. CAMINOS, Vol. 3, no. 1 (January 1982), p. 40. Bilingual. **DESCR:** *Belvedere Childcare Center; *Block, Sherman; Holidays.

2729 Vigil, Maurilio E. Recollections of New Mexico Christmas. NUESTRO, Vol. 6, no. 10 (December 1982), p. 41-44. English. **DESCR:** New Mexico; *Short Story.

CHRONICLE OF A DEATH FORETOLD

2730 Berg, Charles. Book review of: CHRONIQUE OF A DEATH FORETOLD. NUESTRO, Vol. 7, no. 4 (May 1983), p. 62. English. **DESCR:** *Book Reviews; *Criminal Acts; *Death (Concept); Garcia Marquez, Gabriel.

CHULAS FRONTERAS [film]

2731 Beaver, Frank E. CHULAS FRONTERAS. BILINGUAL REVIEW, Vol. 10, no. 2-3 (May, December, 1983), p. 176. English. **DESCR:** Blank, Les; Film Reviews; Music.

Church of Jesus Christ of Latter-Day Saints (Mormons)

2732 Garcia, Ignacio M. Latino-ization of the Mormon church. NUESTRO, Vol. 7, no. 2 (March 1983), p. 20-24+. English. **DESCR:** Molina, Alberto; Religion.

Cielak, Elena

2733 Mixografia workshop gallery director Elena Cielak on collecting art. CAMINOS, Vol. 3, no. 9 (October 1982), p. 10-11. Bilingual. **DESCR:** *Art Galleries.

CIEN ANOS DE SOLEDAD

2734 100 years of solitude. LATINO, Vol. 53, no. 4 (June 1982), p. 27. English. **DESCR:** Authors; *Garcia Marquez, Gabriel.

2735 Monleon, Jose. Historia de una contradiccion. MAIZE, Vol. 3, no. 3-4 (Spring, Summer, 1980), p. 17-22. Spanish. **DESCR:** Garcia Marquez, Gabriel; Literary Criticism.

Cinco de Mayo

2736 Entertainment = diversion. CAMINOS, Vol. 3, no. 5 (May 1982), p. 54. Bilingual. **DESCR:** Artists; Buena Vista Cablevision, Inc.; *Holidays; Knott's Berry Farm, Buena Park, CA; Tamayo, Rufino; Television.

CINCO VIDAS

2737 Ruiz, Reynaldo. CINCO VIDAS. BILINGUAL REVIEW, Vol. 10, no. 2-3 (May, December, 1983), p. 177-178. English. **DESCR:** Film Reviews.

Circus

2738 McManis, Linda. Flying Hispanics: a constant gamble with death. LATINO, Vol. 54, no. 6 (October 1983), p. 12-13. English. **DESCR:** Recreation.

Cisco Kid

2739 Martinez, Douglas R. Down on the farm with the Cisco Kid. NUESTRO, Vol. 7, no. 2 (March 1983), p. 49. English. **DESCR:** *Agriculture; Agriculture Day USDA; Spanish Influence.

Cisneros, Henry, Mayor of San Antonio, TX

2740 Careers: recipe for success. LATINO, Vol. 53, no. 2 (March, April, 1982), p. 22-24. English. **DESCR:** Careers; *Colleges and Universities.

2741 Diaz, Katherine A. Henry Cisneros: our hope for today & tomorrow. CAMINOS, Vol. 4, no. 3 (March 1983), p. 38-41,49+. Bilingual. **DESCR:** Elected Officials.

2742 Diaz, Katherine A. Henry G. Cisneros on Central American commission (interview). CAMINOS, Vol. 4, no. 8 (September 1983), p. 10,48. English. **DESCR:** Central America; International Relations; National Bipartisan Commission on Central America; United States.

2743 Illegal aliens vital to economy, mayor says. NUESTRO, Vol. 7, no. 2 (March 1983), p. 54. English. **DESCR:** Border Region; Economics; *Undocumented Workers.

2744 Morton, Carlos. People: back on top with Bernardo Eureste. NATIONAL HISPANIC JOURNAL, Vol. 2, no. 1 (Summer 1983), p. 20-21. English. **DESCR:** Elected Officials; Elections; *Eureste, Bernardo; San Antonio Police Department; San Antonio, TX; Valdez, Jesse.

2745 Old and new in San Antonio. ECONOMIST (London), Vol. 288, (August 13, 1983), p. 26. English. **DESCR:** San Antonio, TX; Voter Turnout.

2746 People. HISPANIC BUSINESS, Vol. 5, no. 10 (October 1983), p. 10. English. **DESCR:** Anaya, Toney; Arriola, Elvia Rosales; Babbitt, Bruce; Burgos, Tony; Bush, George; *Businesspeople; Cruz, Jose; Kennedy, Edward M.; Montano, Gilbert; Reagan, Ronald; White, Mark.

2747 Que pasa? NUESTRO, Vol. 7, no. 3 (April 1983), p. 9. English. **DESCR:** Border Patrol; Elections; Immigration Regulation and Control; Rocky Mountain Spotted Fever; Servas; Tourism.

2748 Two Hispanics on top ten list. LATINO, Vol. 53, no. 2 (March, April, 1982), p. 14. English. **DESCR:** *Bonilla, Ruben; Politics; U.S. Junior Chamber of Commerce.

2749 Wittenauer, Cheryl. The mayor markets San Antonio. HISPANIC BUSINESS, Vol. 5, no. 7 (July 1983), p. 12-13+. English. **DESCR:** *Economic Development; *Marketing; San Antonio, TX.

Cisneros, Ignacio

2750 Garcia, Art R. Star Adair Insulation Inc. spurts to new growth. HISPANIC BUSINESS, Vol. 4, no. 2 (February 1982), p. 18-19+. English. **DESCR:** Biography; Business Enterprises; Businesspeople; Minority Enterprise Small Business Investment Corporation (MESBIC); *Star-Adair Insulation, Inc.

Cities
USE: Urban Communities

Citizens United for Farmworkers, Yakima WA

2751 Oliver, Gordon. Worker abuses claimed. NATIONAL CATHOLIC REPORTER, Vol. 19, (October 29, 1982), p. 7. English. **DESCR:** Agricultural Laborers; Border Patrol; Immigration and Naturalization Service (INS); *Immigration Regulation and Control; Yakima, WA.

Citizenship
USE: Naturalization

City Colleges, Chicago, IL

2752 Heaney, Thomas W. "Hanging on" or "gaining ground": educating marginal adults. NEW DIRECTIONS FOR CONTINUING EDUCATION, no. 20 (December 1983), p. 53-63. English. **DESCR:** *Adult Education; Chicago, IL; General Education Diploma (GED); Gomez, Robert; Instituto del Progreso Latino; Mission District, San Francisco, CA; Project Literacy, San Francisco, CA; St. Mary's Community Educational Center; *Universidad Popular, Chicago, IL.

CITY OF NIGHT

2753 Lizarraga, Sylvia S. Observaciones acerca de la critica literaria Chicana. REVISTA CHICANO-RIQUENA, Vol. 10, no. 4 (Fall 1982), p. 55-64. Spanish. **DESCR:** *Bruce Novoa, Juan; El Teatro Campesino; *Literary Criticism; Literature; POCHO; THE SPACE OF CHICANO LITERATURE.

2754 Tatum, Charles. The sexual underworld of John Rechy. MINORITY VOICES, Vol. 3, no. 1 (Fall 1979), p. 47-52. English. **DESCR:** Literature; *Rechy, John.

2755 Zamora, Carlos. Odysseus in John Rechy's CITY OF NIGHT: the epistemological journey. MINORITY VOICES, Vol. 3, no. 1 (Fall 1979), p. 53-62. English. **DESCR:** Literature; *Rechy, John.

Ciudad Juarez, Chihuahua, Mexico

2756 Armengol, Armando; Manley, Joan H.; and Teschner, Richard V. The international bilingual city: how a university meets the challenge. FOREIGN LANGUAGE ANNALS, Vol. 15, no. 4 (September 1982), p. 289-295. English. **DESCR:** Biculturalism; Bilingualism; Border Region; El Paso, TX; *Language Development; Spanish Language; University of Texas at El Paso.

Ciudad Juarez, Chihuahua, Mexico (cont.)

2757 Bath, C. Richard. Health and environmental problems: the role of the border in El Paso-Ciudad Juarez coordination. JOURNAL OF INTERAMERICAN STUDIES AND WORLD AFFAIRS, Vol. 24, no. 3 (August 1982), p. 375-392. English. **DESCR:** Border Region; *El Paso, TX; International Boundary and Water Commission; Nationalism; Pollution; *Public Health; United States-Mexico Relations; U.S Border Public Health Association (AFMES).

2758 Long, William J. and Pohl, Christopher M. Joint foot patrols succeed in El Paso. POLICE CHIEF, Vol. 50, no. 4 (April 1983), p. 49-51. English. **DESCR:** Border Patrol; Criminal Acts; *El Paso, TX; Immigration Regulation and Control; *Police; Undocumented Workers; Youth.

2759 Mirowsky, John and Ross, Catherine E. Paranoia and the structure of powerlessness. AMERICAN SOCIOLOGICAL REVIEW, Vol. 48, no. 2 (April 1983), p. 228-239. English. **DESCR:** *El Paso, TX; *Social Psychology.

2760 Rivera, Julius and Goodman, Paul Wershub. Clandestine labor circulation: a case on the U.S.-Mexico border. MIGRATION TODAY, Vol. 10, no. 1 (1982), p. 21-26. English. **DESCR:** Border Patrol; Border Region; El Paso, TX; Immigration Regulation and Control; Migration Patterns; Social Classes; Social Mobility; Socioeconomic Factors; *Undocumented Workers.

2761 Sanchez, Ricardo. El lencho y los chenchos. NATIONAL HISPANIC JOURNAL, Vol. 1, no. 3 (Summer, Fall, 1982), p. 20. Calo. **DESCR:** Border Region; El Paso, TX; *Short Story.

Civil Rights

2762 Civil Rights Commission. LATINO, Vol. 54, no. 8 (December 1983), p. 21. English. **DESCR:** *U.S. Commission on Civil Rights.

2763 Equal protection: right of illegal alien children to state provided education. HARVARD LAW REVIEW, Vol. 96, no. 1 (November 1982), p. 130-140. English. **DESCR:** *Children; Discrimination in Education; Doe v. Plyer [Tyler Independent School District, Texas]; *Education; *Undocumented Workers.

2764 Flaherty, Francis J. The struggle continues: protecting the rights of Hispanics in the U.S. NATIONAL LAW JOURNAL, Vol. 5, (March 14, 1983), p. 1. English. **DESCR:** Affirmative Action; *Avila, Joaquin Guadalupe; Hispanic Amendments; *Legal Representation; Mexican American Legal Defense and Educational Fund (MALDEF); Racism; Voting Rights.

2765 Haft, Jonathan D. Assuring equal educational opportunity for language-minority students: bilingual education and the Equal Educational Opportunity Act of 1974. COLUMBIA JOURNAL OF LAW AND SOCIAL PROBLEMS, Vol. 18, no. 2 (1983), p. 209-293. English. **DESCR:** *Bilingual Bicultural Education; Educational Law and Legislation; English as a Second Language; *Equal Educational Opportunity Act of 1974 (EEOA); Laws; Students.

2766 Hopson, Susan B. Immigration: indefinite detention of excluded aliens held illegal. TEXAS INTERNATIONAL LAW JOURNAL, Vol. 17, (Winter 1982), p. 101-110. English. **DESCR:** Deportation; *Detention of Persons; Immigration; International Law; Rodriguez-Fernandez v. Wilkinson;

Shaughnessy v. Mezei; *Undocumented Workers.

2767 Is the answer right at home? LATINO, Vol. 53, no. 5 (September 1982), p. 25. English.

2768 Levin, Betsy. An analysis of the federal attempt to regulate bilingual education: protecting civil rights or controlling curriculum? JOURNAL OF LAW AND EDUCATION, Vol. 12, no. 1 (January 1983), p. 29-60. English. **DESCR:** Affirmative Action Programs; *Bilingual Bicultural Education; Cultural Pluralism; Educational Law and Legislation; Federal Government.

2769 Lopez, Victor Manuel. Equal protection for undocumented aliens. CHICANO LAW REVIEW, Vol. 5, (1982), p. 29-54. English. **DESCR:** Discrimination in Education; Legal Reform; Medical Care Laws and Legislation; *Undocumented Workers.

2770 Martinez, Paul E. Serna v. Portales: the plight of bilingual education four years later. JOURNAL OF ETHNIC STUDIES, Vol. 7, no. 2 (Summer 1979), p. 109-114. English. **DESCR:** *Bilingual Bicultural Education; Chicano Youth Organization; Portales Municipal Schools; *Portales, NM; Serna v. Portales Municipal Schools.

2771 Osifchok, Diane I. The utilization of immediate scrutiny in establishing the right to education for undocumented alien children. PEPPERDINE LAW REVIEW, Vol. 10, no. 1 (December 1982), p. 139-165. English. **DESCR:** Doe v. Plyer [Tyler Independent School District, Texas]; Education; *Undocumented Workers.

2772 Parr, Julie A. Immigration law and the excluded alien: potential for human rights violations. UNIVERSITY OF CALIFORNIA DAVIS LAW REVIEW, Vol. 15, no. 3 (Spring 1982), p. 723-740. English. **DESCR:** Deportation; *Detention of Persons; Internal Security Act of 1950; Rodriguez-Fernandez v. Wilkinson; *Undocumented Workers.

2773 Reagan's report card: F. LATINO, Vol. 53, no. 3 (May 1982), p. 24-25. English. **DESCR:** *Politics; *Reagan Administration.

2774 Valenzuela-Crocker, Elvira. Confrontation over the Civil Rights Commission. NUESTRO, Vol. 7, no. 10 (December 1983), p. 21-27. English. **DESCR:** Administration of Justice; Affirmative Action; Education Equalization; Employment; *U.S. Commission on Civil Rights; Voting Rights.

Civil Service

2775 Tovar, Irene. Affirmative action in California. CAMINOS, Vol. 3, no. 8 (September 1982), p. 30-32,50+. Bilingual. **DESCR:** *Affirmative Action; *California State Personnel Board.

LA CLASE OBRERA EN LA HISTORIA DE MEXICO: AL NORTE DEL RIO BRAVO (PASADO INMEDIATO, 1930-1981)

2776 Garcia, Mario T. Book review of: LA CLASE OBRERA EN LA HISTORIA DE MEXICO: AL NORTE DEL RIO BRAVO (PASADO INMEDIATO, 1930-1981). HISPANIC AMERICAN HISTORICAL REVIEW, Vol. 62, no. 4 (November 1982), p. 694-696. English. **DESCR:** Book Reviews; History; Labor Disputes; Laboring Classes; Maciel, David R.

Class Distinction
  USE: Social Classes

Classical Music

2777 Laguna, Jaime. Enrique Serin: Mexico's
violin ambassador. CAMINOS, Vol. 4, no. 10
(November 1983), p. 17-19. Bilingual.
DESCR: Music; *Serin, Enrique.

Claudio, Irma

2778 Business notes. HISPANIC BUSINESS, Vol. 5,
no. 10 (October 1983), p. 13. English.
DESCR: *Business Administration; Business
Enterprises; Investments; Los Angeles Board
of Public Works; Oakland, CA; Taxation;
Tri-Oakland Development Corporation;
Wisconsin Minority Business Forum '83.

Clements, Bill

2779 Hamner, Richard. Hispanic update: border
governors tackle U.S.-Mexico relations: much
ado: but   nothing on immigration. NATIONAL
HISPANIC JOURNAL, Vol. 1, no. 2 (Winter
1982), p. 4-5. English. **DESCR:** Babbitt,
Bruce; Border Region; Brown, Edmund G., Jr.,
Governor of California; Immigration;
Immigration Regulation and Control; Moreno,
Paul; *United States-Mexico Relations.

2780 Hispanic leader reaction to Governor White:
Republicans fail to overcome Democratic
one-two punch. NATIONAL HISPANIC JOURNAL,
Vol. 1, no. 4 (Spring 1983), p. 8. English.
DESCR: Mexican American Republicans of
Texas; Political Parties and Organizations;
*Voter Turnout; White, Mark.

2781 Murray, Melissa and De Leon, Hector. Texas
politics: a frank talk about leadership,
Austin, state government and attorney Hector
de Leon. NATIONAL HISPANIC JOURNAL, Vol. 1,
no. 4 (Spring 1983), p. 10-13. English.
DESCR: De Leon, Hector; *Politics; Texas;
White, Mark.

2782 O'Leary, Tim. David Ruiz brings justice to
Texas prisons. NATIONAL HISPANIC JOURNAL,
Vol. 1, no. 2 (Winter 1982), p. 21-24.
English. **DESCR:** Legal Reform; Prisoners;
Prisons; *Ruiz, David; Texas Department of
Corrections.

Clergy

2783 Day, Mark R. and Ramirez, Ricardo (Bishop of
Las Cruces, NM),. Bishop: why have we had to
wait so long for Hispanic leaders. NATIONAL
CATHOLIC REPORTER, Vol. 19, (December 24,
1982), p. 6-7. English. **DESCR:** Catholic
Church; Leadership; *Ramirez, Ricardo
(Bishop of Las Cruces, NM).

2784 Day, Mark R. Hispanics 'want more bishops,
input in church'. NATIONAL CATHOLIC
REPORTER, Vol. 18, (March 12, 1982), p. 1.
English. **DESCR:** *Catholic Church; Cursillo
Movement; Monterey, CA; Religion.

2785 Gomez, Roberto L. Pastoral care and
counseling in a Mexican American setting.
APUNTES, Vol. 2, no. 2 (Summer 1982), p.
31-39. English. **DESCR:** *Counseling
(Religious); Cultural Characteristics;
Religion.

2786 King, Karen. Hope comes to Apopka: on
working alongside the poor. THE OTHER SIDE,
Vol. 18, (May 1982), p. 23-25. English.
DESCR: Apopka, FL; Migrant Health Services;
*Migrant Labor; Office of Migrant Ministry
(OMM).

2787 Mercado, Olivia; Corrales, Ramona; and
Segovia, Sara. Las hermanas. COMADRE, no. 2
(Spring 1978), p. 34-41. English. **DESCR:**
Chicanas; Religion.

2788 Morales, Cecilio J. The bishops' pastoral on
Hispanic ministry. AMERICA [America Press,
New York, NY], Vol. 149, (June, July,
1983), p. 7-9. English. **DESCR:** *Catholic
Church; Religion.

2789 Morales, Cecilio J. Hispanics are moving
toward the front pew. NATIONAL CATHOLIC
REPORTER, Vol. 19, (December 31, 1982), p.
11. English. **DESCR:** *Catholic Church;
Identity.

2790 Ramirez, Ricardo. Reflections on the
Hispanicization of the liturgy. WORSHIP,
Vol. 57, no. 1 (January 1983), p. 26-34.
English. **DESCR:** Catholic Church; *Liturgy;
Religion; Third General Conference of the
Latin American Episcopate.

2791 Southwest regional conference of Hispanic
Chamber of Commerce. CAMINOS, Vol. 4, no. 9
(October 1983), p. 60. English. **DESCR:**
Business; *U.S. Hispanic Chamber of
Commerce.

Clifton Morenci Strike, June 1903

2792 Byrkit, James W. Walter Douglas and labor
struggles in early 20th century Arizona.
SOUTHWEST ECONOMY AND SOCIETY, Vol. 1, no. 1
(Spring 1976), p. 14-27. English. **DESCR:**
Arizona; *Biography; Bisbee, AZ; Copper
Queen Mining Co., Bisbee, AZ; *Douglas,
Walter; International Workers of the World
(IWW); Labor Unions; Mining Industry;
Strikes and Lockouts.

Clinical Psychiatry

2793 Good, Byron J. Reflexivity and
countertransference in a psychiatric
cultural consultation clinic. CULTURE,
MEDICINE & PSYCHIATRY, Vol. 6, no. 3
(September 1982), p. 281-303. English.
DESCR: *Cultural Consultation Clinic;
Psychiatry.

Clinics (Medical)

2794 Cohen, Leslie G. Neighborhood health
centers: the promise, the rhetoric, and the
reality. JOURNAL OF LATIN COMMUNITY HEALTH,
Vol. 1, no. 1 (Fall 1982), p. 92-100.
English.

2795 Government review. NUESTRO, Vol. 7, no. 10
(December 1983), p. 48. English. **DESCR:**
Banking Industry; Child Care Centers; Chile;
Credit Unions; Employment; Employment
Training; *Government Services; Medical
Care; National Credit Union Administration;
National Oceanic and Atmospheric
Administration; SER; U.S. Department of
Health and Human Services; U.S. Department
of Labor.

Clothing Trade
USE: Garment Industry

Club Hogar Latino

2796 Entertainment = diversion. CAMINOS, Vol. 3,
no. 2 (February 1982), p. 40-41. English.
DESCR: Awards; CHECKING IT OUT; Dance;
Films; Flamenco; Marley, Bob; Montalban,
Ricardo; ON GOLDEN POND; *Recreation;
Television.

Coalition of Spanish-Speaking Mental Health Organization (COSSMHO), Annual Regional Conference, Los Angeles, March 14-15, 1975

2797 Math-based careers. HISPANIC BUSINESS, Vol. 4, no. 8 (August 1983), p. 20. English. DESCR: Brigham Young University; Business Administration; *Careers; Cooperative Extension Programs; Education; Employment Training; Financial Aid; Medical Personnel.

Coca-Cola Company

2798 Bunnell, Robert. Bravisimo! NUESTRO, Vol. 7, no. 9 (November 1983), p. 21-25. English. DESCR: Anacani; Miller Brewing Company; Palomino, Carlos; Pena, Samm; Performing Arts; *Television.

2799 Caldera, Carmela. Coca-Cola president Bryan Dyson on BRAVISIMO. CAMINOS, Vol. 4, no. 4 (April 1983), p. 44-45,48. Bilingual. DESCR: *BRAVISIMO; Dyson, Bryan; Private Funding Sources; Television.

2800 Coca-Cola USA Today outlines Latino agenda. NUESTRO, Vol. 7, no. 9 (November 1983), p. 36. English. DESCR: Business; *Coca-Cola National Hispanic Education Fund; Education; *Financial Aid; Funding Sources.

2801 Communications/marketing. HISPANIC BUSINESS, Vol. 4, no. 9 (September 1982), p. 22. English. DESCR: Awards; Domecq Importers, Inc.; *Marketing; Western Union Corporation.

2802 Communications/marketing. HISPANIC BUSINESS, Vol. 5, no. 5 (May 1983), p. 24. English. DESCR: Anheuser-Busch, Inc.; Arbitron; Awards; California Chicano News Media Association (CCNMA); Elizalde, Hector; *Marketing; Television.

2803 Ogaz, Antonio and Caldera, Carmela. What do you think of Coca-Cola's sponsorship of Bravisimo? CAMINOS, Vol. 4, no. 4 (April 1983), p. 46-47. English. DESCR: *BRAVISIMO; Private Funding Sources; Television.

Coca-Cola National Hispanic Education Fund

2804 Coca-Cola USA Today outlines Latino agenda. NUESTRO, Vol. 7, no. 9 (November 1983), p. 36. English. DESCR: Business; Coca-Cola Company; Education; *Financial Aid; Funding Sources.

El Cochinito Yucateco Restaurant

2805 It's not all rice & beans, part III (restaurant reviews). CAMINOS, Vol. 4, no. 6 (June 1983), p. 15-18. Bilingual. DESCR: Cache Restaurant; El Tepeyac Restaurant; La Parrilla Restaurant; *Restaurants.

Cockroft, James

2806 Alvarez, Alejandro. Economic crisis and migration: comments on James Cockcroft's article. CONTEMPORARY MARXISM, Vol. 5, (Summer 1982), p. 62-66. English. DESCR: International Economic Relations; Laboring Classes; Legislation; MEXICAN MIGRATION, CRISIS, AND THE INTERNATIONALIZATION OF LABOR STRUGGLES; *Undocumented Workers.

Codices

2807 Brotherston, Gordon. Year 13 reed equals 31113 BC: a clue to Mesoamerican chronology. NEW SCHOLAR, Vol. 8, no. 1-2 (Spring, Fall, 1982), p. 75-84. English. DESCR: *Precolumbian Society.

Cognition

2808 Gorrell, J. Jeffrey, et al. Comparison of spatial role-taking in monolingual and bilingual children. JOURNAL OF GENETIC PSYCHOLOGY, Vol. 140, no. 1 (March 1982), p. 3-10. English. DESCR: Bilingualism; Child Study; *Linguistic Theory; *Perception.

2809 Saracho, Olivia N. Cultural differences in the cognitive style of Mexican American students. JOURNAL OF THE ASSOCIATION FOR THE STUDY OF PERCEPTION, Vol. 18, no. 1 (Spring 1983), p. 3-10. English.

Cohen, Bernard H.

2810 Walia, Adorna. Book review of: DATA FORMS FOR EVALUATING BILINGUAL EDUCATION PROGRAM. BILINGUAL JOURNAL, Vol. 7, no. 2 (Winter 1983), p. 38. English. DESCR: Bilingual Bicultural Education; Book Reviews; *DATA FORMS FOR EVALUATING BILINGUAL EDUCATION PROGRAMS; Educational Administration; Evaluation (Educational).

Cohen, Lawrence E.

2811 Alba, Richard D. A comment on Schoen and Cohen. AMERICAN JOURNAL OF SOCIOLOGY, Vol. 87, no. 4 (January 1982), p. 935-939. English. DESCR: ETHNIC ENDOGAMY AMONG MEXICAN AMERICAN GROOMS; Intermarriage; *Research Methodology; Schoen, Robert.

Colegio Cesar Chavez, Mt. Angel, OR

2812 Community watching: para la comunidad. CAMINOS, Vol. 3, no. 2 (February 1982), p. 43-44. Bilingual. DESCR: Casa Blanca Youth Project; Colleges and Universities; *Cultural Organizations; Financial Aid; LULAC National Education Service Centers (LNESC); Tonatiuh-Quinto Sol Award for Literature, 1977-78; University of California, Riverside.

Collective Bargaining

2813 Chavez pinpoints Texas for bargaining efforts. NUESTRO, Vol. 6, no. 8 (October 1982), p. 47-48. English. DESCR: Agricultural Labor Unions; Agricultural Laborers; *United Farmworkers of America (UFW).

Collective Farms
USE: Agricultural Cooperatives

College and University Students

2814 Mestre, Jose P. and Robinson, Holly. Academic, socio-economic, and motivational characteristics of Hispanic college students enrolled in technical programs. VOCATIONAL GUIDANCE QUARTERLY, Vol. 31, no. 3 (March 1983), p. 187-194. English. DESCR: Counseling Services (Educational); Enrollment; Vocational Guidance.

College Graduates

2815 Chavarria, Jesus. The systems way. HISPANIC BUSINESS, Vol. 4, no. 4 (April 1982), p. 6. English. DESCR: *Careers; Employment; *Higher Education.

College Graduates (cont.)

2816 Gould, Sam. Correlates of career progression among Mexican-American college graduates. JOURNAL OF VOCATIONAL BEHAVIOR, Vol. 20, no. 1 (February 1982), p. 93-110. English. **DESCR:** *Careers; Colleges and Universities; Cultural Characteristics; Social Mobility.

2817 Math-based careers. HISPANIC BUSINESS, Vol. 4, no. 1 (January 1982), p. 20. English. **DESCR:** Careers; *Cox, George; Employment; Engineering as a Profession; *Hispanic Society of Engineers and Scientists (HSES); *Leadership, Education and Development Program in Business (LEAD).

2818 Phillips, Susan D., et al. Career development of special populations: a framework for research. JOURNAL OF VOCATIONAL BEHAVIOR, Vol. 22, no. 1 (February 1983), p. 12-29. English. **DESCR:** Careers; *Research Methodology; Vocational Education.

2819 Raymond, Richard and Sesnowitz, Michael. Labor market discrimination against Mexican American college graduates. SOUTHERN ECONOMIC JOURNAL, Vol. 49, no. 4 (April 1983), p. 1122-1136. English. **DESCR:** *Employment; Income; Racism.

2820 Taylor, Karla and Vargas, Raul. Entrevista/interview: Q: How to raise money for your Hispanic students? A: Involve your alumni and their corporate contacts. CASE CURRENTS, Vol. 9, no. 4 (April 1983), p. 18-21. English. **DESCR:** Funding Sources; Higher Education; *Office for Mexican American Programs, University of Southern California; Vargas, Raul.

College Preparation

2821 Jaramillo, Patricio T.; Zapata, Jesse T.; and McPherson, Robert. Concerns of college bound Mexican-American students. SCHOOL COUNSELOR, Vol. 29, no. 5 (May 1982), p. 375-380. English. **DESCR:** *Attitude (Psychological); Counseling Services (Educational); Identity; Stereotypes; Students.

2822 Lourenzo, Susan V. Early outreach: career awareness for health professions. JOURNAL OF MEDICAL EDUCATION, Vol. 58, no. 1 (January 1983), p. 39-44. English. **DESCR:** Affirmative Action; Careers; *Medical Education; *Recruitment.

Colleges and Universities

2823 Baltodano, J. C. Success. CAMINOS, Vol. 4, no. 6 (June 1983), p. 32,34+. English. **DESCR:** Gallegos, Genevie; Gutierrez, Jorge; Sotelo, Priscilla Elvira; *Students; Torres, Juan; University of California, Berkeley.

2824 Careers: recipe for success. LATINO, Vol. 53, no. 2 (March, April, 1982), p. 22-24. English. **DESCR:** Careers; *Cisneros, Henry, Mayor of San Antonio, TX.

2825 Community watching: para la comunidad. CAMINOS, Vol. 3, no. 2 (February 1982), p. 43-44. Bilingual. **DESCR:** Casa Blanca Youth Project; Colegio Cesar Chavez, Mt. Angel, OR; *Cultural Organizations; Financial Aid; LULAC National Education Service Centers (LNESC); Tonatiuh-Quinto Sol Award for Literature, 1977-78; University of California, Riverside.

2826 Gould, Sam. Correlates of career progression among Mexican-American college graduates. JOURNAL OF VOCATIONAL BEHAVIOR, Vol. 20, no. 1 (February 1982), p. 93-110. English. **DESCR:** *Careers; *College Graduates; Cultural Characteristics; Social Mobility.

2827 Justiz, Manuel J. Six community colleges share resources to meet the needs of Mexican-American students linking together to solve a common need. BORDERLANDS JOURNAL, Vol. 6, no. 1 (Fall 1982), p. 41-48. English.

2828 Lujan, Sylvia and Zapata, Jesse T. Personality differences among Mexican-American college freshmen. JOURNAL OF COLLEGE STUDENT PERSONNEL, Vol. 24, no. 2 (March 1983), p. 105-111. English. **DESCR:** *Personality; Socioeconomic Factors; *Students.

2829 Navarro, Susana. Access to higher education: a state of crisis. CAMINOS, Vol. 4, no. 6 (June 1983), p. 29-30,66+. Bilingual. **DESCR:** *Higher Education.

2830 Olivas, Michael A. Indian, Chicano and Puerto Rican colleges: status and issues. BILINGUAL REVIEW, Vol. 9, no. 1 (January, March, 1982), p. 36-58. English. **DESCR:** Education; Native Americans; Puerto Rican Education; Treaties.

2831 Rivera, Roberto. Selected topics on Latino access to Illinois colleges and universities. INTEGRATED EDUCATION, Vol. 20, no. 3-5 (May, October, 1982), p. 101-105. English. **DESCR:** Discrimination in Education; *Higher Education; Illinois; Racism.

2832 Rivera, Tomas. The importance of college. CAMINOS, Vol. 4, no. 6 (June 1983), p. 26-27. Bilingual. **DESCR:** Higher Education.

2833 School focuses on Latino needs. NUESTRO, Vol. 7, no. 1 (January, February, 1983), p. 12. English. **DESCR:** Catholic University, Washington, D.C.; Education; *Hispanidad '83.

2834 Valverde, Leonard. Hispanic academics organized for the greater good. CAMINOS, Vol. 4, no. 6 (June 1983), p. 50-51. Bilingual. **DESCR:** Higher Education; Organizations; *Texas Association of Chicanos in Higher Education (TACHE).

2835 Zamudio, Anthony; Padilla, Amado M.; and Comrey, Andrew L. Personality structure of Mexican Americans using the Comrey Personality Scales. JOURNAL OF PERSONALITY ASSESSMENT, Vol. 47, no. 1 (February 1983), p. 100-106. English. **DESCR:** Comrey Personality Scales (CPS); Minnesota Multiphasic Personality Inventory (MMPI); *Personality; Psychological Testing; Students.

Collier, David

2836 Logan, Kathleen. The urban poor in
developing nations. JOURNAL OF URBAN
HISTORY, Vol. 9, no. 1 (November 1982), p.
108-116. English. **DESCR:** ACCESS TO POWER:
POLITICS AND THE URBAN POOR IN DEVELOPING
NATIONS; *Book Reviews; BORDER BOOM TOWN:
CIUDAD JUAREZ SINCE 1848; Cornelius, Wayne
A.; Eckstein, Susan; Lloyd, Peter; Martinez,
Oscar J.; Nelson, Joan M.; Perlman, Janice
E.; POLITICS AND MIGRANT POOR IN MEXICO
CITY; SLUMS OF HOPE? SHANTY TOWNS OF THE
THIRD WORLD; SQUATTERS AND OLIGARCHS:
AUTHORITARIAN RULE AND POLICY CHANGE IN
PERU; THE MYTH OF MARGINALITY: URBAN POVERTY
AND POLITICS IN RIO DE JANEIRO; THE POVERTY
OF REVOLUTION: THE STATE AND THE URBAN POOR
IN MEXICO; Urban Economics.

Colombia

2837 Business/negocios. CAMINOS, Vol. 3, no. 2
(February 1982), p. 22-23. Bilingual.
DESCR: Argentina; Brazil; *Business; Chile;
Federation of Minority Business
Associations; FRANCHISE OPPORTUNITIES
HANDBOOK; Latin America.

2838 Carreras, Peter Nares. Strong concern over
searches. NUESTRO, Vol. 7, no. 10 (December
1983), p. 12-13. English. **DESCR:** *Drug Laws;
Drug Traffic; *U.S. Customs.

Colonia
USE: Barrios

Colonia Reforma, Tijuana, Baja California, Mexico

2839 Day, Mark R. Border group feeds, clothes
dispossessed. NATIONAL CATHOLIC REPORTER,
Vol. 19, (October 22, 1982), p. 5. English.
DESCR: Border Region; Catholic Church;
*Mexican American Neighborhood Organization
(MANO).

Colonial Barrio Seniors

2840 Quinlivan, Robert. The need for Hispanic
senior housing. CAMINOS, Vol. 3, no. 7
(July, August, 1982), p. 42-43. Bilingual.
DESCR: *Ancianos; *Housing; San Diego, CA;
Villa Merced Housing Project.

Colonialism

2841 Barrios-Martinez, Ruben. Should Puerto Rico
become a state?: against statehood. NUESTRO,
Vol. 7, no. 5 (June, July, 1983), p. 37-39.
English. **DESCR:** *International Relations;
Puerto Rican Independence Party; *Puerto
Rico; Racism; United States.

2842 Churchhill, Ward. Implications of publishing
ROOTS OF RESISTANCE. JOURNAL OF ETHNIC
STUDIES, Vol. 9, no. 3 (Fall 1981), p.
83-89. English. **DESCR:** Book Reviews; Dunbar
Ortiz, Roxanne; Land Tenure; Native
Americans; New Mexico; Publishing Industry;
*ROOTS OF RESISTANCE: LAND TENURE IN NEW
MEXICO, 1680-1980; Social History and
Conditions.

2843 Romero-Barcelo, Carlos. Should Puerto Rico
become a state?: for statehood. NUESTRO,
Vol. 7, no. 5 (June, July, 1983), p. 34-37.
English. **DESCR:** *International Relations;
Munoz Marin, Luis; *Puerto Rico; United
States.

2844 Sandoval, David A. What do I call them: the
Chicano experience. CACR REVIEW, Vol. 1, no.
1 (September 1982), p. 3-25. English.
DESCR: Identity; Intergroup Relations;

*Self-Referents.

Colonies
USE: Colonialism

Colorado

2845 Adams, Phylliss J. and Anderson, Peggy L.
Comparison of teachers' and Mexican-American
children's perceptions of the children's
competence. READING TEACHER, Vol. 36, no. 1
(October 1982), p. 8-13. English. **DESCR:**
Attitude (Psychological); Children; Cultural
Characteristics; Learning and Cognition; Sex
Roles; *Teacher Attitudes.

2846 Colorado confrontation. NUESTRO, Vol. 6, no.
6 (August 1982), p. 9. English. **DESCR:**
Riots; *Violence.

2847 Obrzut, John E.; Hansen, Robert L.; and
Heath, Charles P. The effectiveness of
visual information processing training with
Hispanic children. JOURNAL OF GENERAL
PSYCHOLOGY, Vol. 10, no. 2 (October 1982),
p. 165-174. English. **DESCR:** *Academic
Achievement; Bender Gestalt Test;
Intelligence Tests; Primary School
Education.

2848 Salmon, Roberto Mario. Book review of:
SPANISH AND MEXICAN LAND GRANTS IN NEW
MEXICO AND COLORADO. JOURNAL OF ETHNIC
STUDIES, Vol. 9, no. 3 (Fall 1981), p.
120-121. English. **DESCR:** Book Reviews; *Land
Grants; New Mexico; *SPANISH AND MEXICAN
LAND GRANTS IN NEW MEXICO AND COLORADO; Van
Ness, Christine M.; Van Ness, John R.

Colorado Association of Chicano Research (CACR)

2849 Cortese, Anthony J., ed. Contemporary trends
in Chicano studies. CACR REVIEW, Vol. 1, no.
1 (September 1982), p. 1-133. English.
DESCR: *Chicano Studies; Journals.

Columbia Broadcasting Studios (CBS)

2850 Armas, Jose. ANTONIO AND THE MAYOR: a
cultural review of the film. JOURNAL OF
ETHNIC STUDIES, Vol. 3, no. 3 (Fall 1975),
p. 98-101. English. **DESCR:** *ANTONIO AND THE
MAYOR; Broadcast Media; Cultural
Characteristics; Film Reviews; Films; Mass
Media; *Stereotypes.

COMIDA SABROSA

2851 Reading to whet your appetite [book
reviews]. CAMINOS, Vol. 4, no. 6 (June
1983), p. 19,66. English. **DESCR:** Barraza
Sanchez, Irene; Book Reviews; Recipes;
Sanchez Yund, Gloria.

Comite de Trabajadores de Canerias, San Jose, CA

2852 Arnold, Frank. A history of struggle:
organizing cannery workers in the Santa
Clara Valley. SOUTHWEST ECONOMY AND SOCIETY,
Vol. 2, no. 1 (October, November, 1976), p.
26-38. English. **DESCR:** Agribusiness;
American Labor Union (Santa Clara County,
CA); Cannery and Agricultural Worker's
Industrial Union; *Cannery Workers; History;
Labor Unions; *Santa Clara Valley, CA;
United Cannery Agricultural Packing and
Allied Workers of America (UCAPAWA).

Commerce
USE: Business

Commission of the Californias

2853 Deukmejian, George. Welcoming the Commission of the Californias. CAMINOS, Vol. 4, no. 11 (December 1983), p. 19. English. DESCR: Border Region; California; United States-Mexico Relations.

Committee in Solidarity with the People of El Salvador (CISPES)

2854 Entertainment = diversion. CAMINOS, Vol. 3, no. 4 (April 1982), p. 41. Bilingual. DESCR: AZTLAN [journal]; Cultural Organizations; Directories; DIRECTORY OF MINORITY ARTS ORGANIZATIONS; El Salvador; *National Endowment for the Arts; NOTICIERO; Organizations; Periodicals; *Recreation; Television.

2855 Ramirez, Belinda. In solidarity with El Salvador. CAMINOS, Vol. 3, no. 5 (May 1982), p. 9. English. DESCR: Benavidez, Virginia; Organizations; San Francisco, CA.

Committee on Chicano Rights

2856 Quinlivan, Robert. CRC's Herman Baca on the issue. CAMINOS, Vol. 3, no. 1 (January 1982), p. 18-20. Bilingual. DESCR: *Baca, Herman; *Immigration Regulation and Control; Reagan, Ronald.

Common Cause

2857 Reapportionment [panel discussion at the LATINOS IN THE LAW symposium, UCLA, 1982]. CHICANO LAW REVIEW, Vol. 6, (1983), p. 34-62. English. DESCR: California; Californios for Fair Representation; *Reapportionment.

Communications and Spanish Speaking Americans (CASA)

2858 Avila, Carmen. Assessing the casa study. AGENDA, Vol. 11, no. 3 (May, June, 1981), p. 45-47,60. English. DESCR: Mass Media.

Communist Party

2859 Monroy, Douglas. Anarquismo y comunismo: Mexican radicalism and the Communist Party in Los Angeles during the 1930's. LABOR HISTORY, Vol. 24, no. 1 (Winter 1983), p. 34-59. English. DESCR: Cannery and Agricultural Worker's Industrial Union; Confederacion de Uniones de Obreros Mexicanos (CUOM); History; International Ladies Garment Workers Union (ILGWU); Labor; Labor Organizing; *Los Angeles, CA; Tenayuca, Emma; Worker's Alliance (WA), Los Angeles, CA.

Communities Organized for Public Service (COPS)

2860 COPS. LATINO, Vol. 53, no. 4 (June 1982), p. 7. English. DESCR: Cultural Organizations.

2861 Holley, Joe. Page two. TEXAS OBSERVER, Vol. 75, no. 1 (January 14, 1983), p. 2-3. English. DESCR: Cultural Organizations; Educational Law and Legislation; Political Parties and Organizations.

2862 Rips, Geoffrey. COPS educates. TEXAS OBSERVER, Vol. 75, no. 4 (February 25, 1983), p. 1-2. English. DESCR: Cultural Organizations; Educational Law and Legislation; Political Parties and Organizations.

2863 Rips, Geoffrey. New politics in Texas: COPS comes to Austin. TEXAS OBSERVER, Vol. 75,

no. 1 (January 14, 1983), p. 1+. English. DESCR: Cultural Organizations; Educational Law and Legislation; Political Parties and Organizations.

Community Colleges

2864 Fleming, Marilyn B. Problems experienced by Anglo, Hispanic and Navajo Indian women college students. JOURNAL OF AMERICAN INDIAN EDUCATION, Vol. 22, no. 1 (October 1982), p. 7-17. English. DESCR: *Chicanas; Ethnic Groups; Identity; Medical Education; Native Americans.

Community Development

2865 Barreto, Julio. A new force in the barrio. NUESTRO, Vol. 7, no. 4 (May 1983), p. 43-45. English. DESCR: Caballero-Perez, Diana; *Cultural Organizations; National Congress for Puerto Rican Rights (NCPRR); *Puerto Ricans.

2866 Community development. LATINO, Vol. 54, no. 4 (May, June, 1983), p. 27+. English.

2867 The Little Havana development authority. HISPANIC BUSINESS, Vol. 4, no. 3 (March 1982), p. 10+. English. DESCR: Carnaval Miami 82; Cubanos; Little Havana; Miami, FL.

2868 Newsfront. HISPANIC BUSINESS, Vol. 4, no. 1 (January 1982), p. 7. English. DESCR: *Biographical Notes; Businesspeople; Jimenez, Richard D.; Macias, Miguel (Mike); Oaxaca, Jaime; The East Los Angeles Community Union (TELACU); Viramontes, Carlos.

Community Mental Health

2869 Acosta, Frank X. and Cristo, Martha H. Bilingual-Bicultural interpreters as psychotherapeutic bridges: a program note. JOURNAL OF COMMUNITY PSYCHOLOGY, Vol. 10, no. 1 (January 1982), p. 54-56. English. DESCR: Biculturalism; Bilingualism; Doctor Patient Relations; East Los Angeles, CA; *Mental Health Personnel; Mental Health Programs; Translations.

2870 Flaskerud, Jacquelyn H. Community mental health nursing: its unique role in the delivery of services to ethnic minorities. PERSPECTIVES IN PSYCHIATRIC CARE, Vol. 20, no. 1 (January, March, 1982), p. 37-43. English. DESCR: *Asian Americans; Blacks; Cultural Characteristics; Native Americans.

2871 Roberts, Robert E.; Attkisson, C. Clifford; and Stegner, Bruce L. A client satisfaction scale suitable for use with Hispanics? HISPANIC JOURNAL OF BEHAVIORAL SCIENCES, Vol. 5, no. 4 (December 1983), p. 461-476. English. DESCR: Public Health.

Community Organizations
USE: Cultural Organizations

Community Outreach Project

2872 Training, fellowships. NUESTRO, Vol. 7, no. 1 (January, February, 1983), p. 9. English. DESCR: Employment Training; Financial Aid; Medical Personnel; Stanford University Medical Center.

COMMUNITY PSYCHOLOGY: THEORETICAL AND EMPIRICAL APPROACHES

2873 Hunsaker, Alan. Book review of: PSYCHOLOGY AND COMMUNITY CHANGE; SOCIAL AND PSYCHOLOGICAL RESEARCH IN COMMUNITY SETTING; COMMUNITY PSYCHOLOGY: THEORETICAL AND EMPIRICAL APPROACHES. HISPANIC JOURNAL OF BEHAVIORAL SCIENCES, Vol. 5, no. 1 (March 1983), p. 121-124. English. DESCR: Book Reviews; Gibbs, Margaret S.; Heller, Kenneth; Kelly, James G.; Lachenmeyer, Juliana Rasic; Monahan, John; Munoz, Ricardo F.; *PSYCHOLOGY AND COMMUNITY CHANGE; Sigal, Janet; Snowden, Lonnie R.; *SOCIAL AND PSYCHOLOGICAL RESEARCH IN COMMUNITY SETTINGS.

Community School Relationships

2874 Cohen, Bernard H. Parent involvement in program evaluation. BILINGUAL JOURNAL, Vol. 7, no. 2 (Winter 1983), p. 29-34. English. DESCR: *Bilingual Bicultural Education; Curriculum; *Evaluation (Educational); Project PIE (Parents Involvement in Evaluation).

2875 Flori, Monica. The Hispanic community as a resource for a practical Spanish program. FOREIGN LANGUAGE ANNALS, Vol. 15, no. 3 (May 1982), p. 213-215. English. DESCR: Curriculum; Educational Innovations; Language Development; Lewis and Clark College, Portland, OR; *Spanish Language.

2876 Pride in school. LATINO, Vol. 54, no. 5 (August, September, 1983), p. 4. English. DESCR: Education.

Community Services

2877 Business update: phone company issues Spanish yellow pages. NUESTRO, Vol. 7, no. 4 (May 1983), p. 42. English. DESCR: Advertising; New York Telephone Co..

2878 Contributions to the Hispanic community. LATINO, Vol. 54, no. 7 (November 1983), p. 29. English.

2879 High energy community relations: Con Edison's Carlota M. Maduro. HISPANIC BUSINESS, Vol. 4, no. 2 (February 1982), p. 14. English. DESCR: Biography; Consolidated Edison Company of New York, Inc.; *Maduro, Carlota M.; Public Relations.

Compadrazgo

2880 Baca Zinn, Maxine. Urban kinship and Midwest Chicano families: evidence in support of revision. DE COLORES, Vol. 6, no. 1-2 (1982), p. 85-98. English. DESCR: *Extended Family; Family; *Midwestern States; Urban Communities.

Comparative Education

2881 Buriel, Raymond, et al. Mexican- and Anglo-American children's locus of control and achievement in relation to teachers attitudes. JOURNAL OF GENETIC PSYCHOLOGY, Vol. 140, no. 1 (March 1982), p. 131-143. English. DESCR: *Academic Achievement; Anglo Americans; Children; *Teacher Attitudes.

2882 Heathcote, Olivia D. Sex stereotyping in Mexican reading primers. READING TEACHER, Vol. 36, no. 2 (November 1982), p. 158-165. English. DESCR: Curriculum Materials; Mexico; Primary School Education; *Sex Stereotypes.

2883 Iadicola, Peter and Moore, Helen A. The desegregated school and status relations among Anglo and Hispanic students: the dilemma of school desegregation. AZTLAN, Vol. 14, no. 1 (Spring 1983), p. 147-173. English. DESCR: Educational Theory and Practice; *Segregation and Desegregation; Students.

2884 Mahan, James M. and Miller, Shawn M. Concerns of Anglo secondary student teachers in Hispanic communities: a pilot study. ILLINOIS SCHOOL RESEARCH AND DEVELOPMENT, Vol. 19, no. 2 (Winter 1983), p. 28-34. English. DESCR: *Frequent Concerns of Student Teachers Survey; Teacher Training.

Comparative Literature

2885 Hoffer, Bates L. Sociology by value systems: explication and some implications of two studies on the folklore of Hispanics in the United States. BILINGUAL REVIEW, Vol. 9, no. 2 (May, August, 1982), p. 172-177. Bilingual. DESCR: BENJY LOPEZ: A PICARESQUE TALE OF EMIGRATION AND RETURN; Braceros; *Chicanos in American Literature; Folklore; Herrera Sobek, Maria; Levine, Barry B.; THE BRACERO EXPERIENCE: ELITELORE VERSUS FOLKLORE.

2886 Rangel-Guerrero, Daniel. Book review of: CHICANO AUTHORS: INQUIRY BY INTERVIEW. JOURNAL OF ETHNIC STUDIES, Vol. 10, no. 2 (Summer 1982), p. 117-119. English. DESCR: Book Reviews; Bruce Novoa, Juan; *CHICANO AUTHORS: INQUIRY BY INTERVIEW; Literary Criticism; Literary History; Literary Influence; Literature.

Comparative Psychology

2887 Aneshensel, Carol S.; Clark, Virginia A.; and Frerichs, Ralph R. Race, ethnicity, and depression: a confirmatory analysis. JOURNAL OF PERSONALITY AND SOCIAL PSYCHOLOGY, Vol. 44, no. 2 (February 1983), p. 385-398. English. DESCR: Los Angeles County, CA.

2888 Davis, James Alston. Does authority generalize? Locus of control perceptions in Anglo-American and Mexican-American adolescents. POLITICAL PSYCHOLOGY, Vol. 4, no. 1 (March 1983), p. 101-120. English. DESCR: Family; High School Students; Internal-External Reinforcement Scale; *Locus of Control; Political Ideology.

2889 Fu, Victoria R.; Hinkle, Dennis E.; and Korslund, Mary K. A development study of ethnic self-concept among pre-adolescent girls. JOURNAL OF GENETIC PSYCHOLOGY, Vol. 14, (March 1983), p. 67-73. English. DESCR: Chicanas; *Identity; Junior High School Students; Self-Concept Self Report Scale.

2890 Gonzales, Eloy. A cross-cultural comparison of the developmental items of five ethnic groups in the Southwest. JOURNAL OF PERSONALITY ASSESSMENT, Vol. 46, no. 1 (February 1982), p. 26-31. English. DESCR: Draw-A-Person (DAP) [psychological test]; Ethnic Groups; Psychological Testing; Southwest United States.

2891 Hui, C. Harry. Analysis of the modernity scale: an item response theory approach. JOURNAL OF CROSS-CULTURAL PSYCHOLOGY, Vol. 14, no. 3 (September 1983), p. 259-278. English. DESCR: *Military Personnel; Overall Modernity Scale (OM).

Comparative Psychology (cont.)

2892 Hui, C. Harry. Multistrategy approach to cross-cultural research: the case of locus of control. JOURNAL OF CROSS-CULTURAL PSYCHOLOGY, Vol. 14, no. 1 (March 1983), p. 65-83. English. DESCR: *Locus of Control; *Military Personnel; Psychological Testing.

2893 Markides, Kyraikos S.; Dickson, Harold; and Pappas, Christine. Characteristics of dropouts in longitudinal research on aging - a study of Mexican-Americans and Anglos. EXPERIMENTAL AGING RESEARCH, Vol. 8, no. 3-4 (1982), p. 163-167. English. DESCR: *Ancianos; *Mental Health; Psychology.

2894 O'Donnell, James P., et al. Dimensions of behavior problems in Anglo-American and Mexican-American preschool children: a comparative study. JOURNAL OF CONSULTING AND CLINICAL PSYCHOLOGY, Vol. 50, no. 5 (October 1982), p. 643-651. English. DESCR: Anglo Americans; Children; Cultural Characteristics; Mental Health; Psychological Testing; Socioeconomic Factors.

2895 Ross-Reynolds, Jane and Reschly, Daniel J. An investigation of item bias on the WISC-R with four sociocultural groups. JOURNAL OF CONSULTING AND CLINICAL PSYCHOLOGY, Vol. 51, no. 1 (February 1983), p. 144-146. English. DESCR: Ethnic Groups; Psychological Testing; *Wechsler Intelligence Scale for Children-Revised (WISC-R).

2896 Vernon, Sally W. and Roberts, Robert E. Prevalence of treated and untreated psychiatric disorders in three ethnic groups. SOCIAL SCIENCE AND MEDICINE, Vol. 16, no. 17 (1982), p. 1575-1582. English. DESCR: Anglo Americans; Blacks; Mental Illness; *Psychiatry.

2897 Warheit, George. Interpersonal coping networks and mental health problems among four race-ethnic groups. JOURNAL OF COMMUNITY PSYCHOLOGY, Vol. 10, no. 4 (October 1982), p. 312-324. English. DESCR: Family; Mental Health; Stress; *Support Groups.

2898 Wheaton, Blair. A comparison of the moderating effects of personal coping resources in the impact of exposure to stress in two groups. JOURNAL OF COMMUNITY PSYCHOLOGY, Vol. 10, no. 4 (October 1982), p. 293-311. English. DESCR: Anglo Americans; Cultural Characteristics; Mental Health; Social Psychology; *Stress.

2899 Yamamoto, Joe and Acosta, Frank X. Treatments of Asian Americans and Hispanic Americans: similarities and differences. JOURNAL OF THE AMERICAN ACADEMY OF PSYCHOANALYSIS, Vol. 10, no. 4 (October 1982), p. 585-607. English. DESCR: Asian Americans; Los Angeles, CA; *Mental Health; Psychotherapy; Socioeconomic Factors.

Compensatory Education

2900 Sandoval-Martinez, Steven. Findings from the Head Start bilingual curriculum development and evaluation effort. NABE JOURNAL, Vol. 7, no. 1 (Fall 1982), p. 1-12. English. DESCR: *Bilingual Bicultural Education; *Early Childhood Education; Evaluation (Educational); Headstart Program.

Competition

2901 Kagan, Spencer and Zahn, G. Lawrence.

Cultural differences in individualism? Just artifact. HISPANIC JOURNAL OF BEHAVIORAL SCIENCES, Vol. 5, no. 2 (June 1983), p. 219-232. English. DESCR: Anglo Americans; Blacks; Children; *Culture; Social Orientation.

2902 Knight, George P. and Kagan, Spencer. Sibling, birth order, and cooperative-competitive social behavior: a comparison of Anglo-American and Mexican-American children. JOURNAL OF CROSS-CULTURAL PSYCHOLOGY, Vol. 13, no. 2 (June 1982), p. 239-249. English. DESCR: Anglo Americans; Children; Social Behavior Scale; Socialization.

Comprehensive Test of Basic Skills (CTBS)

2903 Llabre, Maria M. and Cuevas, Gilberto. Effects of test language and mathematical skills assessed on the scores of bilingual Hispanic students. JOURNAL FOR RESEARCH IN MATHEMATICS EDUCATION, Vol. 14, no. 4 (November 1983), p. 318-324. English. DESCR: Dade County, FL; *Educational Tests and Measurements; Mathematics; Stanford Achievement Test.

Computer Technology Associates (CTA)

2904 Tom Velez: a man in control of his future. CAMINOS, Vol. 4, no. 1-2 (January, February, 1983), p. 9-10+. English. DESCR: Careers; Computers; *Velez, Tom.

Computers

2905 Avila, Joaquin G. The computer revolution: only for the few? NUESTRO, Vol. 7, no. 6 (August 1983), p. 29. English. DESCR: Education; Mexican American Legal Defense and Educational Fund (MALDEF).

2906 Media/marketing. HISPANIC BUSINESS, Vol. 5, no. 12 (December 1983), p. 38. English. DESCR: Albertini, Luis Diaz; League of United Latin American Citizens (LULAC); Lotus-Albertini Hispanic Reps; Marketing; *Mass Media; Nuestras Noticias; Radio; Reading; Television; Tortosa, Cristobal.

2907 Mendoza, Samuel M. Careers for Chicanos: computers, engineering, science/computadoras, ingenieria, ciencia. CAMINOS, Vol. 3, no. 3 (March 1982), p. 14-16. Bilingual. DESCR: *Careers; Engineering as a Profession; Science as a Profession.

2908 Padilla, Steve. Choosing a career. NUESTRO, Vol. 7, no. 1 (January, February, 1983), p. 13-19+. English. DESCR: Alvarado, Raul, Jr.; *Careers; Diaz, William; Engineering as a Profession; Esparza, Alma; Flores, Francisco; Garcia, Linda; Medical Care; Soto, John; Yanez, Ricardo.

2909 Q & A with Fernando Niebla: "You have to present yourself as a person that knows what he wants". CAMINOS, Vol. 4, no. 1-2 (January, February, 1983), p. 22-23,71. English. DESCR: Careers; Electronics Industry; *Niebla, Fernando.

2910 Rodriguez, Eddie. Computer sciences: a special challenge. CAMINOS, Vol. 3, no. 3 (March 1982), p. 18-20. Bilingual. DESCR: Parra, Raymond A.

Computers (cont.)

2911 Saracho, Olivia N. Effects of a computer-assisted instruction program on basic skills achievement and attitudes toward instruction of Spanish-speaking migrant children. AMERICAN EDUCATIONAL RESEARCH JOURNAL, Vol. 19, no. 2 (Summer 1982), p. 201-219. English. DESCR: Academic Motivation; Audiovisual Instruction; *Migrant Children; *Migrant Education; Programmed Instruction.

2912 Saracho, Olivia N. Planning computer assisted instruction for Spanish speaking migrant students. JOURNAL OF EDUCATIONAL TECHNOLOGY SYSTEMS, Vol. 10, no. 3 (1981, 1982), p. 257-260. English. DESCR: Academic Achievement; Migrant Children; *Migrant Education; *Programmed Instruction.

2913 A time for reflection. NUESTRO, Vol. 7, no. 9 (November 1983), p. 42-44. English. DESCR: Anaya, Rudolfo A.; Arias, Beatriz; Bilingual Bicultural Education; Financial Aid; Folklore; Organizations; Prewitt Diaz, Joseph (Jose); Villarreal, Sylvia; *W.K. Kellogg Foundation National Fellowship Program.

2914 Tom Velez: a man in control of his future. CAMINOS, Vol. 4, no. 1-2 (January, February, 1983), p. 9-10+. English. DESCR: Careers; Computer Technology Associates (CTA); *Velez, Tom.

2915 Weber, Robert. Turbo-charged MST, Inc. HISPANIC BUSINESS, Vol. 4, no. 11 (November 1982), p. 10-11,24. English. DESCR: Alcala, Al; *High Technology Industries; Irvine, CA; *Media Systems Technology, Inc.(MST,Inc.)

Comrey Personality Scales (CPS)

2916 Zamudio, Anthony; Padilla, Amado M.; and Comrey, Andrew L. Personality structure of Mexican Americans using the Comrey Personality Scales. JOURNAL OF PERSONALITY ASSESSMENT, Vol. 47, no. 1 (February 1983), p. 100-106. English. DESCR: Colleges and Universities; Minnesota Multiphasic Personality Inventory (MMPI); *Personality; Psychological Testing; Students.

Comte, Auguste

2917 Raat, W. Dirk. Augusto Comte, Gabino Barreda, and positivism in Mexico. AZTLAN, Vol. 14, no. 2 (Fall 1983), p. 235-251. English. DESCR: *Barreda, Gabino; Education; Educational Theory and Practice; History; Mexico; Philosophy; *Positivism.

Concepcion, Dave

2918 Ortiz, Carlos V. NUESTRO'S sixth annual all-star baseball team. NUESTRO, Vol. 7, no. 2 (March 1983), p. 33-37. English. DESCR: Andujar, Joaquin; Barojas, Salome; *Baseball; Castillo, Manny; Cruz, Jose; Garcia, Damaso; Guerrero, Pedro; Hernandez, Keith; Lezcano, Sixto; Martinez, Tippy; Pena, Tony; Piniella, Lou; Sports; Valenzuela, Fernando.

Condal Distributor, Inc.

2919 Gupta, Udayan. Hispanic foods in New York: the race for number two. HISPANIC BUSINESS, Vol. 5, no. 8 (August 1983), p. 18-19+. English. DESCR: Consumers; *Food Industry; Goya Foods; Iberia Foods Corp.; La Cena Fine Foods, Ltd.; Recipes.

CONDO [televison series]

2920 Garcia, Ignacio M. Regional report, television: "Condo" canceled. NUESTRO, Vol. 7, no. 5 (June, July, 1983), p. 13. English. DESCR: Avalos, Luis; Carmen, Julie; Latin Americans; Stereotypes; *Television.

Condominiums

2921 Mexican condo buyer in Texas-sized trouble. SOUTHERN EXPOSURE, Vol. 11, no. 1 (January 1983), p. 8-9. English. DESCR: Mexico; Peso Devaluation; *Real Estate.

Confederacion de Uniones de Obreros Mexicanos (CUOM)

2922 Monroy, Douglas. Anarquismo y comunismo: Mexican radicalism and the Communist Party in Los Angeles during the 1930's. LABOR HISTORY, Vol. 24, no. 1 (Winter 1983), p. 34-59. English. DESCR: Cannery and Agricultural Worker's Industrial Union; *Communist Party; History; International Ladies Garment Workers Union (ILGWU); Labor; Labor Organizing; *Los Angeles, CA; Tenayuca, Emma; Worker's Alliance (WA), Los Angeles, CA.

CONFEMAR

2923 Mexico y Estados Unidos ante la tercera Confemar: resultados e implicaciones. INFORME: RELACIONES MEXICO-ESTADOS UNIDOS, Vol. 1, no. 3 (July, December, 1982), p. 215-226. Spanish. DESCR: *Maritime Law; Multinational Corporations; Reagan Administration; United States-Mexico Relations.

Conflict Resolution

2924 Kagan, Spencer; Knight, George P.; and Martinez-Romero, Sergio. Culture and the development of conflict resolution style. JOURNAL OF CROSS-CULTURAL PSYCHOLOGY, Vol. 13, no. 1 (March 1982), p. 43-58. English. DESCR: Anglo Americans; Mexico.

2925 Mumme, Stephen P. and Jamail, Milton H. The International Boundary and Water Commission as a conflict management agency in the U.S.-Mexico borderlands. SOCIAL SCIENCE JOURNAL, Vol. 19, no. 1 (January 1982), p. 46-62. English. DESCR: Border Region; *International Boundary and Water Commission; Rio Grande; United States-Mexico Relations; *Water.

Congreso Nacional Para Pueblos Unidos (CPU)

2926 Community watching: para la comunidad. CAMINOS, Vol. 3, no. 1 (January 1982), p. 43-44. Bilingual. DESCR: *Financial Aid; *Food Programs; *Journalists; National Association for Chicano Studies (NACS); *Radio; Summer Program for Minority Journalists; Zozaya, Julia S.

2927 Navarro, Armando. Operation corporate responsibility: a movement for Latino economic empowerment. CAMINOS, Vol. 4, no. 7 (July, August, 1983), p. 28-31,43. Bilingual. DESCR: Economic Development; *Operation Corporate Responsibility (OCR).

Congress for United Communities (CPU)

2928 Garcia, Miguel. Are you registered to vote? CAMINOS, Vol. 3, no. 4 (April 1982), p. 33-34. English. **DESCR:** Mexican American Latino Voter Registration Alliance (MALVRA); *Voter Turnout.

Congressional Aides

2929 Politicians you didn't vote for. NUESTRO, Vol. 5, no. 8 (November 1981), p. 18-20. English. **DESCR:** Burgillo, Luis; Latin Americans; Political Parties and Organizations; *Politics.

Congressional Arts Caucus

2930 San Antonio: an all American city. CAMINOS, Vol. 4, no. 8 (September 1983), p. 35. English. **DESCR:** *Artists; Cerda, Daniel; Gonzalez, Henry B.; *San Antonio, TX.

Congressional Border Caucus

2931 Que pasa?: Mexican border caucus. NUESTRO, Vol. 7, no. 5 (June, July, 1983), p. 9. English. **DESCR:** Border Region; *United States-Mexico Relations.

Congressional Hispanic Caucus

2932 Caucus highlights. NUESTRO, Vol. 6, no. 7 (September 1982), p. 43. English. **DESCR:** Elected Officials; Garcia, Robert.

2933 Communications/marketing. HISPANIC BUSINESS, Vol. 4, no. 2 (February 1982), p. 15. English. **DESCR:** Cable Television; El Teatro Campesino; GalaVision; Labor Unions; *Marketing; Philip Morris, Inc.; Publishing Industry; Spanish International Network (SIN).

2934 Hispanic caucus announces plans. NUESTRO, Vol. 7, no. 6 (August 1983), p. 12-13. English. **DESCR:** National Hispanic Heritage Week; Political Parties and Organizations.

2935 Hispanic caucus offers Washington, fellowships. NUESTRO, Vol. 6, no. 3 (April 1982), p. 62. English. **DESCR:** *Careers; Political Science.

2936 Hispanic wages and employment slow to rise. HISPANIC BUSINESS, Vol. 5, no. 11 (November 1983), p. 36-37. English. **DESCR:** Chicanas; *Employment; Income.

2937 Hispanics and the census. NUESTRO, Vol. 6, no. 7 (September 1982), p. 46-47. English. **DESCR:** *Census.

2938 Hispanics wooed by Reagan, Demos. NUESTRO, Vol. 7, no. 8 (October 1983), p. 11-12. English. **DESCR:** *National Hispanic Heritage Week; *Political Parties and Organizations; Reagan, Ronald.

2939 Math-based careers. HISPANIC BUSINESS, Vol. 4, no. 3 (March 1982), p. 20. English. **DESCR:** Careers; Consortium for Graduate Study in Management; *Educational Opportunities; *Financial Aid.

2940 Members of the caucus. NUESTRO, Vol. 6, no. 7 (September 1982), p. 42. English. **DESCR:** De la Garza, Kika; Elected Officials.

2941 A salute to the arts. NUESTRO, Vol. 6, no. 7 (September 1982), p. 44-45. English. **DESCR:** *Art; Artists; National Hispanic Heritage Week; Villa, Eduardo.

2942 Su voto es su voz. NUESTRO, Vol. 6, no. 7 (September 1982), p. 41. English. **DESCR:** Political Representation; Political System; Politics; *Voter Turnout; *Voting Rights; *Voting Rights Act.

2943 Whisler, Kirk. Robert Garcia: the mover in the Congressional Hispanic Caucus. CAMINOS, Vol. 3, no. 7 (July, August, 1982), p. 36-37,44. Bilingual. **DESCR:** Elected Officials; Federal Government; *Garcia, Robert.

Conill Advertising Associates, New York, NY

2944 Think Spanish! MARKETING AND MEDIA DECISIONS, Vol. 17, (October 1982), p. 66-69. English. **DESCR:** Advertising; Biography; Conill, Alicia; Conill, Rafael; *Marketing; Scott Paper Company; Spanish Language.

Conill, Alicia

2945 Think Spanish! MARKETING AND MEDIA DECISIONS, Vol. 17, (October 1982), p. 66-69. English. **DESCR:** Advertising; Biography; Conill Advertising Associates, New York, NY; Conill, Rafael; *Marketing; Scott Paper Company; Spanish Language.

Conill, Rafael

2946 Think Spanish! MARKETING AND MEDIA DECISIONS, Vol. 17, (October 1982), p. 66-69. English. **DESCR:** Advertising; Biography; Conill Advertising Associates, New York, NY; Conill, Alicia; *Marketing; Scott Paper Company; Spanish Language.

Conjunto

2947 Reyna, Jose R. Notes on Tejano music. AZTLAN, Vol. 13, no. 1-2 (Spring, Fall, 1982), p. 81-94. English. **DESCR:** Ethnomusicology; *Music; Texas.

Connecticut

2948 Balkan, D. Carlos and Cruz, Franklin D. Space-Craft's strategy for re-industrialization. HISPANIC BUSINESS, Vol. 4, no. 11 (November 1982), p. 16-17,26. English. **DESCR:** Business Enterprises; *High Technology Industries; Soto, John; Space-Craft Manufacturing, Inc.

Connolly, Patrick J.

2949 Garza, Hector. El grito de las madres dolorosas. BILINGUAL REVIEW, Vol. 10, no. 2-3 (May, December, 1983), p. 184-186. English. **DESCR:** *EL GRITO DE LAS MADRES DOLOROSAS; Film Reviews.

LA CONSAGRACION DE LA PRIMAVERA

2950 Campbell, Stephanie. The artist in bourgeois society, as seen in Carpentier's LA CONSAGRACION DE LA PRIMAVERA. MAIZE, Vol. 3, no. 3-4 (Spring, Summer, 1980), p. 6-16. English. **DESCR:** Artists; Carpentier, Alejo; Literary Criticism.

Consolidated Edison Company of New York, Inc.

2951 High energy community relations: Con Edison's Carlota M. Maduro. HISPANIC BUSINESS, Vol. 4, no. 2 (February 1982), p. 14. English. **DESCR:** Biography; Community Services; *Maduro, Carlota M.; Public Relations.

Consortium for Graduate Study in Management

2952 Math-based careers. HISPANIC BUSINESS, Vol. 4, no. 3 (March 1982), p. 20. English. **DESCR:** Careers; Congressional Hispanic Caucus; *Educational Opportunities; *Financial Aid.

Constitution of the United States

2953 Walia, Adorna. Book review of: EL GOBIERNO Y LOS PRESIDENTES DE LOS ESTADOS UNIDOS DE AMERICA. BILINGUAL JOURNAL, Vol. 6, no. 3 (Spring 1982), p. 22. English. **DESCR:** Book Reviews; *EL GOBIERNO Y LOS PRESIDENTES DE LOS ESTADOS UNIDOS DE AMERICA; *Government; Roy, Joaquin; United States; *United States History.

Constitutional Amendments - Fourteenth

2954 Brooks, Douglas Montgomery. Aliens - civil rights - illegal aliens are inhabitants within meaning of U.S.C 242. SUFFOLK TRANSNATIONAL LAW JOURNAL, Vol. 6, no. 1 (Spring 1982), p. 117-131. English. **DESCR:** Border Patrol; Immigration Regulation and Control; *Undocumented Workers; U.S. v. Otherson.

2955 Gallagher, Michael P. Constitutional law - equal protection: a Texas statute which withholds state funds for the education of illegal alien children ... VILLANOVA LAW REVIEW, Vol. 28, no. 1 (November 1982), p. 198-224. English. **DESCR:** Doe v. Plyer [Tyler Independent School District, Texas]; Education; Tyler Independent School District, Texas; *Undocumented Workers.

2956 Packard, Mark. Equal protection clause requires a free public education for illegal alien children. TEXAS TECH LAW REVIEW, Vol. 14, (May 1983), p. 531-547. English. **DESCR:** Doe v. Plyer [Tyler Independent School District, Texas]; Education; *Undocumented Workers.

2957 Schey, Peter A. Unnamed witness number 1: now attending the Texas public schools. MIGRATION TODAY, Vol. 10, no. 5 (1982), p. 22-27. English. **DESCR:** Education; Education Equalization; Educational Law and Legislation; Equal Protection Clause; Migrant Children; Texas Public Schools; *Undocumented Children; U.S. Supreme Court Case.

2958 School house door must be open to children of illegal aliens. CHILDREN'S LEGAL RIGHTS JOURNAL, Vol. 3, (June 1982), p. 19-21. English. **DESCR:** Doe v. Plyer [Tyler Independent School District, Texas]; *Education; Texas; Undocumented Workers.

2959 Vasquez, Ivan. Analysis of June 15, 1982 opinion issued by the U.S. Supreme Court in the case of Texas undocumented children. MIGRATION TODAY, Vol. 10, no. 3-4 (1982), p. 49-51. English. **DESCR:** Education; *Education Equalization; Educational Law and Legislation; Equal Protection Clause; Migrant Children; *Undocumented Children; U.S. Supreme Court Case.

2960 Young, Rowland L. Schools ... illegal aliens ... AMERICAN BAR ASSOCIATION JOURNAL, Vol. 68, (September 1982), p. 1156-1157. English. **DESCR:** *Education; Undocumented Workers.

Constitutional Amendments - Fourth

2961 Appleson, Gail. Court to review INS stop-and-quiz policy. AMERICAN BAR ASSOCIATION JOURNAL, Vol. 68, (July 1982), p. 791-792. English. **DESCR:** Immigration and Naturalization Service (INS); Immigration Regulation and Control; Search and Seizure; *Undocumented Workers.

2962 INS sweep searches of work areas must meet fourth amendment standards. CRIMINAL LAW REPORTER, Vol. 31, no. 18 (August 11, 1982), p. 2366-2367. English. **DESCR:** Immigration and Naturalization Service (INS); Immigration Regulation and Control; International Ladies Garment Workers Union (ILGWU); *Search and Seizure; Undocumented Workers.

Construction Industry

2963 Foster, Richard. Two Alvarados make one sucessful construction firm. HISPANIC BUSINESS, Vol. 4, no. 10 (October 1982), p. 10-11,26. English. **DESCR:** Alvarado, Bob; Alvarado, Linda M.; *Business Enterprises; Small Business Administration 8(a) Program; U.S. Small Business Administration.

2964 Goodman, Gerson. LRF takes on Battery Park City. HISPANIC BUSINESS, Vol. 4, no. 10 (October 1982), p. 16-17,24. English. **DESCR:** Business Enterprises; *LRF Developers, Inc.; NEW YORK; *Real Estate.

2965 NHACE is born. LATINO, Vol. 53, no. 1 (January, February, 1982), p. 19. English. **DESCR:** Hispanic American Construction Industry Association (HACIA); *National Hispanic Association of Construction Enterprises (NHACE).

2966 Organizing Hispanics in construction. HISPANIC BUSINESS, Vol. 4, no. 10 (October 1982), p. 14,26. English. **DESCR:** National Hispanic Association of Construction Enterprises (NHACE).

CONSUELO: QUIENES SOMOS?

2967 McCloud, George E. Film review of: CONSUELO: QUIENES SOMOS? BILINGUAL REVIEW, Vol. 10, no. 2-3 (May, December, 1983), p. 181-182. English. **DESCR:** Film Reviews.

Consultants

2968 Garcia, Art R. Art Garcia's capital gains: the consultant's consultant. HISPANIC BUSINESS, Vol. 4, no. 12 (December 1982), p. 12. English.

2969 Garcia, Art R. Art Garcia's capital gains: staying on top of the public relations games. HISPANIC BUSINESS, Vol. 5, no. 5 (May 1983), p. 12. English. **DESCR:** *Public Relations.

Consumers

2970 25 leading national Hispanic market advertisers. HISPANIC BUSINESS, Vol. 4, no. 12 (December 1982), p. 18. English. **DESCR:** Advertising; *Marketing.

2971 The activist Dallas Hispanic chamber of commerce. HISPANIC BUSINESS, Vol. 5, no. 2 (February 1983), p. 16-17. English. **DESCR:** Dallas Hispanic Chamber of Commerce; Dallas, TX.

2972 Adkins, Lynn. New strategies to sell Hispanics. DUNS'S BUSINESS MONTH, Vol. 12, no. 1 (July 1983), p. 64-69. English. **DESCR:** *Advertising; Mass Media.

Consumers (cont.)

2973 Andreasen, Alan R. Disadvantaged Hispanic consumers: a research perspective and agenda. JOURNAL OF CONSUMER AFFAIRS, Vol. 16, no. 1 (Summer 1982), p. 46-61. English. **DESCR**: Marketing; Socioeconomic Factors.

2974 Balkan, D. Carlos. The advent of Uniworld/Hispanic: an interview. HISPANIC BUSINESS, Vol. 5, no. 3 (March 1983), p. 10-11+. English. **DESCR**: *Advertising Agencies; Blacks; Diaz-Albertini, Luis; Lewis, Byron; *Marketing; Spanish Advertising and Marketing Services (S.A.M.S.); Uniworld Group, Inc.; UniWorld Hispanic.

2975 Balkan, D. Carlos. The crisis in Hispanic marketing. HISPANIC BUSINESS, Vol. 4, no. 12 (December 1982), p. 24-25+. English. **DESCR**: Advertising; *Marketing.

2976 Bellenger, Danny N. and Valencia, Humberto. Understanding the Hispanic market. BUSINESS HORIZONS, Vol. 25, no. 3 (May, June, 1982), p. 47-50. English. **DESCR**: *Market Research.

2977 Brusco, Bernadette A. Hispanic marketing: new applications for old methodologies. AGENDA, Vol. 11, no. 3 (May, June, 1981), p. 8-9. English. **DESCR**: *Marketing.

2978 Chavarria, Jesus. Dallas. HISPANIC BUSINESS, Vol. 5, no. 2 (February 1983), p. 6. English. **DESCR**: Dallas, TX.

2979 Communications/marketing. HISPANIC BUSINESS, Vol. 4, no. 1 (January 1982), p. 13. English. **DESCR**: Beauty Contests; *Biographical Notes; Hispanic Caucus; *Marketing; Miss Black Velvet Latina; Montemayor, Carlos R.; Philip Morris, Inc.

2980 Communications/marketing. HISPANIC BUSINESS, Vol. 4, no. 4 (April 1982), p. 15. English. **DESCR**: Advertising Agencies; Juarez and Associates, Inc.; Las Americas, Inc.; *Marketing; Norman, Craig & Kummel Organization; Publicidad Siboney; Siboney Advertising, Inc.

2981 Communications/marketing. HISPANIC BUSINESS, Vol. 5, no. 3 (March 1983), p. 21. English. **DESCR**: *Advertising; Awards; El Cervantes Media Awards; Marketing; Spanish Advertising and Marketing Services (S.A.M.S.).

2982 Communications/marketing. HISPANIC BUSINESS, Vol. 5, no. 9 (September 1983), p. 26. English. **DESCR**: Aguirre, Horacio; Business Enterprises; DIARIO DE LAS AMERICAS; La Ventana; *Marketing; Miller Brewing Company; SURVEY OF PROMOTIONAL PRACTICES.

2983 The compleat Hispanic marketing guide. HISPANIC BUSINESS, Vol. 4, no. 1 (January 1982), p. 10. English. **DESCR**: *Marketing; Rios, Conrad R.

2984 The Dallas bilingual yellow pages. HISPANIC BUSINESS, Vol. 4, no. 1 (January 1982), p. 11. English. **DESCR**: Dallas, TX; Gonzalez, John David; Gonzalez, Michael; *Marketing.

2985 Demographic profile of Hispanics in the Dallas/Fort Worth SMSA. HISPANIC BUSINESS, Vol. 5, no. 2 (February 1983), p. 29-30. English. **DESCR**: Dallas, TX; Dallas/Ft. Worth SMSA; *Demography; Fort Worth, Texas; Marketing.

2986 Fred Maes builds a multi-level system. HISPANIC BUSINESS, Vol. 4, no. 2 (February

1982), p. 13. English. **DESCR**: *Biography; Maes, Fred; *Marketing.

2987 Gage, Theodore J. Beer still tops wine, spirits. ADVERTISING AGE MAGAZINE, Vol. 53, (February 15, 1982), p. II, M10. English. **DESCR**: Advertising; *Alcoholic Beverages; Market Research.

2988 Galginaitis, Carol. Luring the Hispanic dollar: retailers boost ethnic image. ADVERTISING AGE MAGAZINE, Vol. 53, (February 15, 1982), p. II, M10. English. **DESCR**: *Advertising; Market Research.

2989 Goodman, Gerson. "ES PARA USTED": CSI aims for satisfaction. HISPANIC BUSINESS, Vol. 4, no. 12 (December 1982), p. 16-17,34. English. **DESCR**: Advertising Agencies; Aguirre, Jack; Business Enterprises; CSI International, Inc.; Fernandez, Castor A.; *Marketing.

2990 Guernica, Antonio. The Hispanic market: a profile. AGENDA, Vol. 11, no. 3 (May, June, 1981), p. 4-7. English. **DESCR**: Marketing; Mass Media; *Population; Population Distribution; Population Trends.

2991 Gupta, Udayan. Hispanic foods in New York: the race for number two. HISPANIC BUSINESS, Vol. 5, no. 8 (August 1983), p. 18-19+. English. **DESCR**: Condal Distributor, Inc.; *Food Industry; Goya Foods; Iberia Foods Corp.; La Cena Fine Foods, Ltd.; Recipes.

2992 Gupta, Udayan. New York's WNJU Channel 47: Spanish TV's hottest item. HISPANIC BUSINESS, Vol. 5, no. 3 (March 1983), p. 16-17+. English. **DESCR**: *Advertising; Broadcast Media; Marketing; Television; WNJU-TV, Newark, NJ [television station].

2993 Hartenstein, Roslyn and Balkan, D. Carlos. Packaging the Dallas Hispanic consumer. HISPANIC BUSINESS, Vol. 5, no. 2 (February 1983), p. 18-19+. English. **DESCR**: Dallas, TX; Fort Worth, Texas; *Marketing.

2994 Heublein's Miss Black Velvet II. HISPANIC BUSINESS, Vol. 4, no. 2 (February 1982), p. 12. English. **DESCR**: Advertising; Beauty Contests; Heublein, Inc.; *Marketing; *Miss Black Velvet Latina.

2995 Metro market ranking: Spanish-origin population. S & MM [SALES & MARKETING MANAGEMENT], Vol. 13, (July 25, 1983), p. B17. English. **DESCR**: Population; Statistics.

2996 Research/development: books. HISPANIC BUSINESS, Vol. 4, no. 12 (December 1982), p. 36. English. **DESCR**: Book Reviews; Guernica, A.; Kasperuk, I.; Marketing; *REACHING THE HISPANIC MARKET EFFECTIVELY.

2997 Segal, Madhav N. and Sosa, Lionel. Marketing to the Hispanic community. CALIFORNIA MANAGEMENT REVIEW, Vol. 26, no. 1 (Fall 1983), p. 120-134. English. **DESCR**: Advertising; Mass Media; Population.

2998 Stroud, Ruth. New products target Hispanics, men. ADVERTISING AGE MAGAZINE, Vol. 54, (September 19, 1983), p. 37. English. **DESCR**: Cosmetology; *Mas Distributors.

2999 Triana, Armando R. The trendy Hispanic market. HISPANIC BUSINESS, Vol. 4, no. 12 (December 1982), p. 8. English. **DESCR**: Marketing.

Consumers (cont.)

3000 Unanue, Joseph F. The two Hispanic markets.
HISPANIC BUSINESS, Vol. 5, no. 8 (August
1983), p. 8. English. **DESCR:** *Food Industry.

3001 Upscale Hispanic consumer demographics in
the top 15 SMSAS. HISPANIC BUSINESS, Vol. 4,
no. 12 (December 1982), p. 37-38. English.
DESCR: *Demography; Income; Population.

3002 Wittenauer, Cheryl. Dallas Hispanic media.
HISPANIC BUSINESS, Vol. 5, no. 2 (February
1983), p. 12-13+. English. **DESCR:** Broadcast
Media; Dallas, TX; English Language;
Marketing; Mass Media; Newspapers; Spanish
Language.

3003 Wittenauer, Cheryl. The Maga Saga. HISPANIC
BUSINESS, Vol. 5, no. 8 (August 1983), p.
14+. English. **DESCR:** *Food Industry; Mexican
American Grocers Association (MAGA).

3004 Zuniga, Jo Ann and Bonilla, Tony. Talking
Texas: turning the tables with LULAC.
HISPANIC BUSINESS, Vol. 5, no. 9 (September
1983), p. 18-19+. English. **DESCR:** *Bonilla,
Tony; Business Enterprises; Economic History
and Conditions; League of United Latin
American Citizens (LULAC); Marketing; Texas.

CONTEMPORARY CHICANO THEATRE

3005 Arias, Ron. Book review of: CONTEMPORARY
CHICANO THEATRE. JOURNAL OF ETHNIC STUDIES,
Vol. 5, no. 1 (Spring 1977), p. 122-123.
English. **DESCR:** Book Reviews; Garza,
Roberto; Teatro.

Contraception
USE: Birth Control

CONTRASTES [exhibit]

3006 Puerto Rico: images from the past. NUESTRO,
Vol. 7, no. 9 (November 1983), p. 48-53.
English. **DESCR:** *Delano, Jack; Hostos
Community College, New York, NY;
*Photography; Puerto Rico.

Conventions

3007 Costa Rica hosts craftsmen of the Americas.
NUESTRO, Vol. 6, no. 6 (August 1982), p.
63-64. English. **DESCR:** Artists; Arts and
Crafts; *Costa Rica; *Cultural
Characteristics; Cultural Customs.

3008 Latinos from 21 states attend chamber
confab. NUESTRO, Vol. 6, no. 6 (August
1982), p. 51. English. **DESCR:** Latin
Americans; *U.S. Chamber of Commerce.

CONVERSATIONS OF MIGUEL AND MARIA: HOW CHILDREN LEARN ENGLISH AS A SECOND LANGUAGE; IMPLICATIONS FOR CLASSROOM TEACHING

3009 Walia, Adorna. Book review of: CONVERSATIONS
OF MIGUEL AND MARIA: HOW CHILDREN LEARN
ENGLISH AS A SECOND LANGUAGE; IMPLICATIONS
FOR CLASSROOM TEACHING. BILINGUAL JOURNAL,
Vol. 6, no. 1 (Fall 1982), p. 28-29.
English. **DESCR:** Bilingual Bicultural
Education; Book Reviews; English as a Second
Language; Ventriglia, Linda.

Cookery
USE: Recipes

Cooperativa Campesina

3010 Wells, Miriam J. Political mediation and
agricultural cooperation: strawberry farms
in California. ECONOMIC DEVELOPMENT AND
CULTURAL CHANGE, Vol. 30, no. 2 (January
1982), p. 413-432. English. **DESCR:**
*Agricultural Cooperatives; Agricultural
Laborers; California; Cooperativa Central;
Political Parties and Organizations; Rural
Economics.

Cooperativa Central

3011 Wells, Miriam J. Political mediation and
agricultural cooperation: strawberry farms
in California. ECONOMIC DEVELOPMENT AND
CULTURAL CHANGE, Vol. 30, no. 2 (January
1982), p. 413-432. English. **DESCR:**
*Agricultural Cooperatives; Agricultural
Laborers; California; Cooperativa Campesina;
Political Parties and Organizations; Rural
Economics.

Cooperative Education

3012 Gonzalez, Alex. Classroom cooperation and
ethnic balance: Chicanos and equal status.
CACR REVIEW, Vol. 1, no. 1 (September 1982),
p. 42-71. English. **DESCR:** Curriculum;
Intergroup Relations; *Prejudice (Social);
Segregation and Desegregation.

Cooperative Extension Programs

3013 Math-based careers. HISPANIC BUSINESS, Vol.
4, no. 8 (August 1983), p. 20. English.
DESCR: Brigham Young University; Business
Administration; *Careers; Coalition of
Spanish-Speaking Mental Health Organization
(COSSMHO), Annual Regional Conference, Los
Angeles, March 14-15, 1975; Education;
Employment Training; Financial Aid; Medical
Personnel.

Coopers and Lybrand

3014 Communications/marketing. HISPANIC BUSINESS,
Vol. 5, no. 2 (February 1983), p. 23.
English. **DESCR:** *Broadcast Media; Domecq
Importers, Inc.; Latin American Feature
Syndicate (ALA); *Mass Media; Phoenix, AZ.

Coors, Adolf

3015 Ogaz, Armando. National menudo cook-off.
CAMINOS, Vol. 4, no. 4 (April 1983), p. 60.
English. **DESCR:** *Private Funding Sources.

Coors Distributing Company, McAllen, TX

3016 Cantu, Hector. Border business report: the
Rio Grande Valley's economy and Mexico's
lingering peso devaluation effects. NATIONAL
HISPANIC JOURNAL, Vol. 2, no. 1 (Summer
1983), p. 10-13. English. **DESCR:** Aguirre,
Lionel; Border Region; Cano, Eddie; Cruz,
Conrado; Cuevas, Betty; *Currency; Economic
Development; Laredo, TX, Chamber of
Commerce; Mexican American Chamber of
Commerce, Austin, TX; United States-Mexico
Relations.

3017 Office manager hired under Coors grant.
LATINO, Vol. 53, no. 1 (January, February,
1982), p. 6. English. **DESCR:** *Management.

Copper Queen Mining Co., Bisbee, AZ

3018 Byrkit, James W. Walter Douglas and labor
     struggles in early 20th century Arizona.
     SOUTHWEST ECONOMY AND SOCIETY, Vol. 1, no. 1
     (Spring 1976), p. 14-27. English. DESCR:
     Arizona; *Biography; Bisbee, AZ; Clifton
     Morenci Strike, June 1903; *Douglas, Walter;
     International Workers of the World (IWW);
     Labor Unions; Mining Industry; Strikes and
     Lockouts.

Copyright
     USE: Publishing Industry

CORAZON DE AZTLAN

3019 Entertainment = diversion. CAMINOS, Vol. 3,
     no. 3 (March 1982), p. 55-56. Bilingual.
     DESCR: Aztlan Writing Contest; Films;
     Literary Contests; MISSING [film];
     *Recreation; THE BORDER [film]; Young,
     Robert.

Cordero-Badillo, Atilano

3020 People. HISPANIC BUSINESS, Vol. 4, no. 8
     (August 1983), p. 7. English. DESCR:
     Aguilar, Richard; *Businesspeople; del Olmo,
     Frank; Infante, E. Anthony; Levitan, Aida
     T.; Nunez, Luis; Quintanilla, Guadalupe;
     Rivera, Victor M.

Cordova, Carlos

3021 Hispanic-owned bank far exceeds
     expectations. ABA BANKING JOURNAL, Vol. 75,
     (February 1983), p. 32-34. English. DESCR:
     Banking Industry; *Capital National Bank;
     New York, NY.

Cornejo Rottenberg, Martha

3022 Whisler, Kirk. Martha Cornejo Rottenberg: on
     opportunities & advancement. CAMINOS, Vol.
     4, no. 1-2 (January, February, 1983), p.
     17-18,71+. English. DESCR: Careers;
     Electronics Industry; Mining Industry; TRW
     Defense Systems Group.

Cornelius, Wayne A.

3023 Logan, Kathleen. The urban poor in
     developing nations. JOURNAL OF URBAN
     HISTORY, Vol. 9, no. 1 (November 1982), p.
     108-116. English. DESCR: ACCESS TO POWER:
     POLITICS AND THE URBAN POOR IN DEVELOPING
     NATIONS; *Book Reviews; BORDER BOOM TOWN:
     CIUDAD JUAREZ SINCE 1848; Collier, David;
     Eckstein, Susan; Lloyd, Peter; Martinez,
     Oscar J.; Nelson, Joan M.; Perlman, Janice
     E.; POLITICS AND MIGRANT POOR IN MEXICO
     CITY; SLUMS OF HOPE? SHANTY TOWNS OF THE
     THIRD WORLD; SQUATTERS AND OLIGARCHS:
     AUTHORITARIAN RULE AND POLICY CHANGE IN
     PERU; THE MYTH OF MARGINALITY: URBAN POVERTY
     AND POLITICS IN RIO DE JANEIRO; THE POVERTY
     OF REVOLUTION: THE STATE AND THE URBAN POOR
     IN MEXICO; Urban Economics.

Corona, Bert

3024 McCurdy, Jack. L.A. violence linked to
     Chicano-studies dispute. CHRONICLE OF HIGHER
     EDUCATION, Vol. 24, no. 14 (June 2, 1982),
     p. 8. English. DESCR: California State
     University, Los Angeles; *Chicano Studies;
     Faculty; Violence.

3025 Mena, Jesus. Testimonio de Bert Corona:
     struggle is the ultimate teacher.
     CHISMEARTE, (1982), p. 27-36. English.
     DESCR: *Labor.

Coronado, Julius

3026 People. HISPANIC BUSINESS, Vol. 4, no. 7
     (July 1982), p. 7. English. DESCR: Aguilar,
     Richard; *Biographical Notes;
     Businesspeople; Enriquez, Rene; Garza, Jose
     S.; Guerra-Martinez, Celina; Medrano, Adan;
     Mota, Manny; Valenti, Frank S.

Coronary Heart Disease

3027 Hazuda, Helen P. Ethnic differences in
     health knowledge and behaviors related to
     the prevention and treatment of coronary
     heart disease. The San Antonio heart study.
     AMERICAN JOURNAL OF EPIDEMIOLOGY, Vol. 11,
     no. 6 (June 1983), p. 717-728. English.
     DESCR: Anglo Americans; Health Education;
     Preventative Medicine; San Antonio, TX;
     Socioeconomic Factors.

Coronel Urtecho, Jose

3028 Banberger, Ellen. Poesia nicaraguense.
     MAIZE, Vol. 5, no. 3-4 (Spring, Summer,
     1982), p. 64-77. Spanish. DESCR: Belli,
     Gioconda; Cardenal, Ernesto; Carrillo,
     Ernesto; Gadea, Gerardo; Gomez, Manuel;
     Murillo, Rosario; *Nicaragua; Ojeda, Mirna;
     *Poetry; Revolutions; Rugama, Leonel.

Corporations

3029 Balkan, D. Carlos. AMEX Systems Inc. at
     transition point. HISPANIC BUSINESS, Vol. 4,
     no. 6 (June 1982), p. 18-19,24. English.
     DESCR: AMEX Systems, Inc.; Business
     Enterprises; Caldera, Manuel R.; High
     Technology Industries; Small Business
     Administration 8(a) Program; U.S. Small
     Business Administration.

3030 Balkan, D. Carlos. The subtleties of
     corporate boardsmanship. HISPANIC BUSINESS,
     Vol. 5, no. 5 (May 1983), p. 10-11+.
     English. DESCR: Executives.

3031 Chavarria, Jesus. Varieties of marketing
     strategies: the PUSH/Anheuser-Bush scrap.
     HISPANIC BUSINESS, Vol. 4, no. 12 (December
     1982), p. 6,35. English. DESCR:
     Anheuser-Busch, Inc.; *Marketing; Operation
     PUSH; People United to Serve Humanity
     (PUSH).

3032 Crane, Larry. Corporate personality.
     HISPANIC BUSINESS, Vol. 5, no. 9 (September
     1983), p. 25. English. DESCR: *Automobile
     Industry; DeDeurwaerder, Jose.

3033 The Hispanic business directory of the 400
     largest corporations. HISPANIC BUSINESS,
     Vol. 4, no. 6 (June 1982), p. 11-16.
     English. DESCR: Business Enterprises;
     *Television.

3034 Philanthropy: Hispanic-corporate
     partnership. LATINO, Vol. 53, no. 5
     (September 1982), p. 19. English. DESCR:
     *Foundations; Funding Sources.

Corpus Christi Independent School District

3035 Scott, Leigh S., et al. Adaptive behavior
     inventory for children: the need for local
     norms. JOURNAL OF SCHOOL PSYCHOLOGY, Vol.
     20, no. 1 (Spring 1982), p. 39-44. English.
     DESCR: *Adaptive Behavior Inventory for
     Children (ABIC); Anglo Americans; Blacks;
     Corpus Christi, TX; Placement; System of
     Multicultural Pluralistic Assessment
     (SOMPA).

Corpus Christi, TX

3036 Applebome, Peter. The unkindest cut. TEXAS MONTHLY, Vol. 11, no. 1 (January 1983), p. 74-80. English. **DESCR:** *Blacks; Political Representation; Voter Turnout.

3037 Election change sought by Garcia. NUESTRO, Vol. 6, no. 10 (December 1982), p. 9-10. English. **DESCR:** Garcia, Hector; Government; *Urban Communities.

3038 Food stamp recovery. NUESTRO, Vol. 6, no. 10 (December 1982), p. 8. English. **DESCR:** *Food Stamps; *Naturalization.

3039 LULAC is building $2.6 million housing project in Corpus Christi. LATINO, Vol. 53, no. 8 (December 1982), p. 18. English. **DESCR:** *Housing; *League of United Latin American Citizens (LULAC).

3040 Scott, Leigh S., et al. Adaptive behavior inventory for children: the need for local norms. JOURNAL OF SCHOOL PSYCHOLOGY, Vol. 20, no. 1 (Spring 1982), p. 39-44. English. **DESCR:** *Adaptive Behavior Inventory for Children (ABIC); Anglo Americans; Blacks; Corpus Christi Independent School District; Placement; System of Multicultural Pluralistic Assessment (SOMPA).

Corrido

3041 Breiter, Toni. Eddie Olmos and THE BALLAD OF GREGORIO CORTEZ. NUESTRO, Vol. 7, no. 4 (May 1983), p. 14-19. English. **DESCR:** Artists; *BALLAD OF GREGORIO CORTEZ [film]; Film Reviews; *Olmos, Edward James; Prejudice (Social).

3042 Burciaga, Jose Antonio. Theatre: CORRIDOS - sad and happy masks. NUESTRO, Vol. 7, no. 4 (May 1983), p. 53. English. **DESCR:** *CORRIDOS [play]; El Teatro Campesino; Valdez, Luis.

3043 Calderon, Roberto R. Corridos of Ynocencio Ramos Jimenez. CAMINOS, Vol. 4, no. 10 (November 1983), p. 26-27,48+. Bilingual. **DESCR:** *Ramos Jimenez, Ynocencio.

3044 Herrera-Sobek, Maria. The acculturation process of the Chicana in the corrido. DE COLORES, Vol. 6, no. 1-2 (1982), p. 7-16. English. **DESCR:** Acculturation; *Chicanas; Sex Roles.

3045 Herrera-Sobek, Maria. The treacherous woman archetype: a structuring agent in the corrido. AZTLAN, Vol. 13, no. 1-2 (Spring, Fall, 1982), p. 135-148. English. **DESCR:** Chicanas; Folk Songs; Music.

3046 Maciel, David R. Book review of: THE KENNEDY CORRIDOS: A STUDY OF THE BALLADS OF A MEXICAN AMERICAN HERO. AZTLAN, Vol. 13, no. 1-2 (Spring, Fall, 1982), p. 335-337. English. **DESCR:** Book Reviews; Dickey, Dan William; Folk Songs; *Kennedy, John Fitzgerald; Music.

3047 Mascarenas, Etta Delgado. Corrido de las comadres: (sung to the music of a traditional Mexican corrido). COMADRE, no. 3 (Fall 1978), p. 37. Spanish. **DESCR:** *Poetry.

3048 McNeil, W. K. Record Review: LAS VOCES DE LOS CAMPESINOS. JOURNAL OF AMERICAN FOLKLORE, Vol. 96, (1983), p. 370. English. **DESCR:** Agricultural Laborers; *LAS VOCES DE LOS CAMPESINOS; Music Review; Musical Lyrics.

3049 Paredes, Americo. Texas-Mexican cancionero: folk song of the lower (excerpts). SOUTHERN EXPOSURE, Vol. 10, no. 4 (July, August, 1982), p. 50-57. Bilingual. **DESCR:** *Folk Songs; Music.

3050 Pena, Manuel H. Folksong and social change: two corridos as interpretive sources. AZTLAN, Vol. 13, no. 1-2 (Spring, Fall, 1982), p. 12-42. English. **DESCR:** Cortez, Gregorio; *DISCRIMINACION A UN MARTIR [corrido]; *EL CORRIDO DE GREGORIO CORTE [corrido]; *Folk Songs; Longoria, Felix; Music.

3051 Prof pushes for recognition of Chicano's music. VARIETY, Vol. 306, (March 10, 1982), p. 184. English. **DESCR:** *Folk Songs; Reidel, Johannes.

3052 Sifuentes, Roberto. Aproximaciones al "Corrido de los Hermanos Hernandez ejecutados en la camara de gas de la penitenciaria de Florence, Arizona el dia 6 de julio de 1934". AZTLAN, Vol. 13, no. 1-2 (Spring, Fall, 1982), p. 95-109. Spanish. **DESCR:** Alonso, Epifanio; *CORRIDO DE LOS HERMANOS HERNANDEZ [song lyrics]; Folk Songs; Hernandez, Federico; Hernandez, Manuel; Music; Musical Lyrics.

EL CORRIDO DE GREGORIO CORTE [corrido]

3053 Pena, Manuel H. Folksong and social change: two corridos as interpretive sources. AZTLAN, Vol. 13, no. 1-2 (Spring, Fall, 1982), p. 12-42. English. **DESCR:** Corrido; Cortez, Gregorio; *DISCRIMINACION A UN MARTIR [corrido]; *Folk Songs; Longoria, Felix; Music.

CORRIDO DE LOS HERMANOS HERNANDEZ [song lyrics]

3054 Sifuentes, Roberto. Aproximaciones al "Corrido de los Hermanos Hernandez ejecutados en la camara de gas de la penitenciaria de Florence, Arizona el dia 6 de julio de 1934". AZTLAN, Vol. 13, no. 1-2 (Spring, Fall, 1982), p. 95-109. Spanish. **DESCR:** Alonso, Epifanio; *Corrido; Folk Songs; Hernandez, Federico; Hernandez, Manuel; Music; Musical Lyrics.

CORRIDOS [play]

3055 Burciaga, Jose Antonio. Theatre: CORRIDOS - sad and happy masks. NUESTRO, Vol. 7, no. 4 (May 1983), p. 53. English. **DESCR:** Corrido; El Teatro Campesino; Valdez, Luis.

Cortazar, Julio

3056 Araya, Juan Gabriel. La autocontemplacion literaria en LIBRO DE MANUEL. MAIZE, Vol. 6, no. 3-4 (Spring, Summer, 1983), p. 7-16. Spanish. **DESCR:** *Latin American Literature; Literary Characteristics; Literary Criticism; Novel.

Cortes, Hernan

3057 Jennings, Gary. Book review of: AZTEC. NUESTRO, Vol. 6, no. 7 (September 1982), p. 53-54. English. **DESCR:** *Book Reviews.

Cortez, Gregorio

3058 THE BALLAD OF GREGORIO CORTEZ. NUESTRO, Vol. 6, no. 4 (May 1982), p. 63. English. **DESCR:** *BALLAD OF GREGORIO CORTEZ [film]; Public Television; Television.

Cortez, Gregorio (cont.)

3059 Pena, Manuel H. Folksong and social change: two corridos as interpretive sources. AZTLAN, Vol. 13, no. 1-2 (Spring, Fall, 1982). English. DESCR: Corrido; *DISCRIMINACION A UN MARTIR [corrido]; *EL CORRIDO DE GREGORIO CORTE [corrido]; *Folk Songs; Longoria, Felix; Music.

Cortez, Pete

3060 People. HISPANIC BUSINESS, Vol. 4, no. 6 (June 1982), p. 8. English. DESCR: Aguirre, Pedro; Arellano, Richard; *Biographical Notes; Businesspeople; De la Colina, Rafael; Hernandez, Sam; Nogales, Luis; Rodriguez, Leslie J.; Roybal, Edward R.

Cosmetology

3061 Gonzalez, Kenneth. Eye don't, eye do's. LATINA, Vol. 1, no. 2 (February, March, 1983), p. 80-81. English.

3062 It's in the cut. LATINA, Vol. 1, no. 2 (February, March, 1983), p. 50-54. English.

3063 Martinez, Marie. A morenita and a rubia visit Rodeo Drive for a sleek make-over. LATINA, Vol. 1, no. 2 (February, March, 1983), p. 30-32+. English. DESCR: *Fashion.

3064 Stroud, Ruth. New products target Hispanics, men. ADVERTISING AGE MAGAZINE, Vol. 54, (September 19, 1983), p. 37. English. DESCR: *Consumers; *Mas Distributors.

Costa Rica

3065 Arias, Ron. Los que emigran desde Costa Rica hacia el norte. LATINO, Vol. 53, no. 1 (January, February, 1982), p. 15. Spanish. DESCR: Immigrants.

3066 Costa Rica hosts craftsmen of the Americas. NUESTRO, Vol. 6, no. 6 (August 1982), p. 63-64. English. DESCR: Artists; Arts and Crafts; Conventions; *Cultural Characteristics; Cultural Customs.

3067 Pre-Columbian art of Costa Rica. NUESTRO, Vol. 6, no. 8 (October 1982), p. 54-55. English. DESCR: Art; *Art History; Exhibits.

Cota-Robles Newton, Frank

3068 Abu Bakr, Virginia. Book review of: MENTAL-HEALTH RESEARCH: A REFERENCE GUIDE. SOCIAL CASEWORK: JOURNAL OF CONTEMPORARY SOCIAL WORK, Vol. 63, no. 7 (September 1982), p. 443-444. English. DESCR: Book Reviews; *HISPANIC MENTAL HEALTH RESEARCH: A REFERENCE GUIDE; Mental Health; Reference Works.

3069 Hispanic journalists assemble in California. NUESTRO, Vol. 6, no. 10 (December 1982), p. 28-30. English. DESCR: Journalism; *Journalists; *Martinez, Vilma Socorro.

Cotera, Marta

3070 Garza-Livingston, M'Liss, ed. and Mercado, Olivia, ed. New book on the Chicana. COMADRE, no. 3 (Fall 1978), p. 38. English. DESCR: *THE CHICANA FEMINIST.

Cotto-Thorner, Guillermo

3071 Irizarry, Estelle. La abuelita in literature. NUESTRO, Vol. 7, no. 7 (September 1983), p. 50. English. DESCR:

Alonso, Luis Ricardo; *Ancianos; Chicanas; Family; Ulibarri, Sabine R.; Valero, Robert.

Council on Legal Education Opportunities (CLEO)

3072 Math-based careers. HISPANIC BUSINESS, Vol. 5, no. 12 (December 1983), p. 40. English. DESCR: *Careers; Education; Employment Training; Graduate Schools; High Technology High School, San Antonio, TX; Legal Education; Mexican American Legal Defense and Educational Fund (MALDEF); San Antonio, TX; Science as a Profession.

COUNSELING ACROSS CULTURES

3073 Franco, Juan N. Book review of: COUNSELING ACROSS CULTURES. HISPANIC JOURNAL OF BEHAVIORAL SCIENCES, Vol. 5, no. 2 (June), p. 233-237. English. DESCR: Book Reviews; Draguns, Juris G.; Lonner, Walter J.; Pedersen, Paul P.; Trimble, Joseph E.

Counseling Effectiveness Scale

3074 Anderson, John W. The effects of culture and social class on client preference for counseling methods. JOURNAL OF NON-WHITE CONCERNS IN PERSONNEL AND GUIDANCE, Vol. 11, no. 3 (April 1983), p. 84-88. English. DESCR: Anglo Americans; Blacks; *Counseling (Psychological); *Educational Opportunity Program (EOP); Locus of Control; University of Illinois at Urbana.

Counseling (Psychological)

3075 Anderson, John W. The effects of culture and social class on client preference for counseling methods. JOURNAL OF NON-WHITE CONCERNS IN PERSONNEL AND GUIDANCE, Vol. 11, no. 3 (April 1983), p. 84-88. English. DESCR: Anglo Americans; Blacks; Counseling Effectiveness Scale; *Educational Opportunity Program (EOP); Locus of Control; University of Illinois at Urbana.

3077 Borland, James J. Book review of: COUNSELING THE CULTURALLY DIFFERENT. INTERNATIONAL MIGRATION REVIEW, Vol. 16, no. 4 (Winter 1982), p. 910-911. English. DESCR: Book Reviews; *COUNSELING THE CULTURALLY DIFFERENT; Sue, Derald Wing.

3078 Borrego, Richard L.; Chavez, Ernest L.; and Titley, Robert W. Effect of counselor technique on Mexican-American and Anglo-American self-disclosure and counselor perception. JOURNAL OF COUNSELING PSYCHOLOGY, Vol. 29, no. 5 (September 1982), p. 538-541. English. DESCR: Anglo Americans; Cultural Characteristics; Identity; Personality; Sex Roles.

3079 Escovar, Peggy L. and Lazarus, Philip J. Cross-cultural child-rearing practices: implications for school psychologists. SCHOOL PSYCHOLOGY INTERNATIONAL, Vol. 3, no. 3 (July, September, 1982), p. 143-148. English. DESCR: *Child Rearing; Children; Cultural Characteristics.

3080 Exum, Herbert A. The most invisible minority: the culturally diverse elderly. SCHOOL COUNSELOR, Vol. 30, no. 1 (September 1982), p. 15-24. English. DESCR: *Ancianos; Asian Americans; Blacks; Cultural Customs; Ethnic Groups; Family; Native Americans; Stereotypes.

Counseling (Psychological) (cont.)

3081 Pilar. Ask pilar. LATINA, Vol. 1, no. 3 (1983), p. 22-23. English.

3082 Sanchez, Arthur R. and Atkinson, Donald R. Mexican-American cultural commitment, preference for counselor ethnicity, and willingness to use counseling. JOURNAL OF COUNSELING PSYCHOLOGY, Vol. 30, no. 2 (April 1983), p. 215-220. English. DESCR: Cultural Characteristics; Identity; Mental Health; *Mental Health Personnel.

3083 Szapocznik, Jose, et al. Ethnic and cultural variations in the care of the aged. New directions in the treatment of represion in the elderly: a life enhancement counseling approach. JOURNAL OF GERIATRIC PSYCHIATRY, Vol. 15, no. 2 (1982), p. 257-281. English. DESCR: *Ancianos; Cubanos.

3084 Szapocznik, Jose, et al. Life enhancement counseling and the treatment of the depressed Cuban American elders. HISPANIC JOURNAL OF BEHAVIORAL SCIENCES, Vol. 4, no. 4 (December 1982), p. 487-502. English. DESCR: Ancianos; Cubanos.

Counseling (Religious)

3085 Gomez, Roberto L. Pastoral care and counseling in a Mexican American setting. APUNTES, Vol. 2, no. 2 (Summer 1982), p. 31-39. English. DESCR: *Clergy; Cultural Characteristics; Religion.

Counseling Services (Educational)

3086 Atkinson, Donald R. Ethnic minority representation in counselor education. COUNSELOR EDUCATION AND SUPERVISION, Vol. 23, no. 1 (September 1983), p. 7-19. English. DESCR: Affirmative Action; *Counselors; Recruitment.

3087 Burns, Maureen. Current status of Hispanic technical professionals: how can we improve recruitment and retention. INTEGRATED EDUCATION, Vol. 20, (January, April, 1982), p. 49-55. English. DESCR: Academic Achievement; Academic Motivation; Socioeconomic Factors; *Technical Education.

3088 Chavez, Rigo. Job counseling, role models mean a lot. HISPANIC BUSINESS, Vol. 4, no. 8 (August 1983), p. 12. English. DESCR: Careers; Cuevas, Hector; Escobedo, Ed; Professional Opportunities Program (POP); *Stanford University, Stanford, CA.

3089 Gonzalez, Gilbert G. Educational reform and the Mexican community in Los Angeles. SOUTHWEST ECONOMY AND SOCIETY, Vol. 3, no. 3 (Spring 1978), p. 24-51. English. DESCR: Curriculum; *Education; Enrollment; *History; Intelligence Tests; Los Angeles, CA; *Los Angeles City School District; Tracking (Educational); Vocational Education.

3090 Jaramillo, Patricio T.; Zapata, Jesse T.; and McPherson, Robert. Concerns of college bound Mexican-American students. SCHOOL COUNSELOR, Vol. 29, no. 5 (May 1982), p. 375-380. English. DESCR: *Attitude (Psychological); College Preparation; Identity; Stereotypes; Students.

3091 LeVine, Elaine S. and Franco, Juan N. Effects of therapist's gender, ethnicity, and verbal style on client's willingness to seek therapy. JOURNAL OF SOCIAL PSYCHOLOGY, Vol. 12, no. 1 (October 1983), p. 51-57. English. DESCR: Jourard's (3) Self-Disclosure Questionnaire; Mental Health; Psychotherapy; Social Services.

3092 Mestre, Jose P. and Robinson, Holly. Academic, socio-economic, and motivational characteristics of Hispanic college students enrolled in technical programs. VOCATIONAL GUIDANCE QUARTERLY, Vol. 31, no. 3 (March 1983), p. 187-194. English. DESCR: *College and University Students; Enrollment; Vocational Guidance.

3093 Walia, Adorna. Book review of: COUNSELING THE BILINGUAL STUDENT. BILINGUAL JOURNAL, Vol. 7, no. 4 (Summer 1983), p. 27-28. English. DESCR: Bilingual Bicultural Education; Book Reviews; *COUNSELING THE BILINGUAL STUDENT; Sanchez, Antonia; Searchlight Series.

3094 Watkins, Ted R. and Gonzalez, Richard. Outreach to Mexican-Americans. SOCIAL WORK, Vol. 27, no. 1 (January 1982), p. 68-73. English. DESCR: Cultural Organizations; Social Services.

COUNSELING THE BILINGUAL STUDENT

3095 Walia, Adorna. Book review of: COUNSELING THE BILINGUAL STUDENT. BILINGUAL JOURNAL, Vol. 7, no. 4 (Summer 1983), p. 27-28. English. DESCR: Bilingual Bicultural Education; Book Reviews; Counseling Services (Educational); Sanchez, Antonia; Searchlight Series.

COUNSELING THE CULTURALLY DIFFERENT

3096 Borland, James J. Book review of: COUNSELING THE CULTURALLY DIFFERENT. INTERNATIONAL MIGRATION REVIEW, Vol. 16, no. 4 (Winter 1982), p. 910-911. English. DESCR: Book Reviews; Counseling (Psychological); Sue, Derald Wing.

Counselors

3097 Atkinson, Donald R. Ethnic minority representation in counselor education. COUNSELOR EDUCATION AND SUPERVISION, Vol. 23, no. 1 (September 1983), p. 7-19. English. DESCR: Affirmative Action; Counseling Services (Educational); Recruitment.

Court Decisions
USE: Administration of Justice

Court System

3098 Lipton, Jack P. Racism in the jury box: the Hispanic defendant. HISPANIC JOURNAL OF BEHAVIORAL SCIENCES, Vol. 5, no. 3 (September 1983), p. 275-290. English. DESCR: *Juries.

3099 Obledo, Mario. What kind of justice? LATINO, Vol. 54, no. 6 (October 1983), p. 4. English.

3100 Que pasa? NUESTRO, Vol. 7, no. 6 (August 1983), p. 9. English. DESCR: Boy Scouts of America; Criminal Justice System; Diabetes; Education; Judicial Review; Petersilia, Joan; PREPARED FOR TODAY; RACIAL DISPARITIES IN THE CRIMINAL JUSTICE SYSTEM; Reagan, Ronald.

Courts (Legal)

3101 Weiner, Richard E. Teaching the immigrant's
      child: a model plan for court-ordered
      bilingual education. JOURNAL OF LAW AND
      EDUCATION, Vol. 12, no. 1 (January 1983), p.
      61-76. English. DESCR: *Bilingual Bicultural
      Education; Curriculum; Educational Law and
      Legislation; Educational Theory and
      Practice.

Cowell, Henry

3102 Mead, R. H. Latin American accents in new
      music. LATIN AMERICAN MUSIC REVIEW, Vol. 3,
      no. 2 (Fall, Winter, 1982), p. 207-228.
      English. DESCR: Chavez, Carlos; *Music; *New
      Music.

Cox, George

3103 Math-based careers. HISPANIC BUSINESS, Vol.
      4, no. 1 (January 1982), p. 20. English.
      DESCR: Careers; *College Graduates;
      Employment; Engineering as a Profession;
      *Hispanic Society of Engineers and
      Scientists (HSES); *Leadership, Education
      and Development Program in Business (LEAD).

Coyote [folkloric symbol]

3104 Melendez, Theresa. Coyote: towards a
      definition of a concept. AZTLAN, Vol. 13,
      no. 1-2 (Spring, Fall, 1982), p. 295-307.
      English. DESCR: Folklore; Leyendas; Mitos.

Craddock, Jerry R.

3105 Woods, Richard D. Book review of: SPANISH
      AND ENGLISH OF UNITED STATES HISPANOS: A
      CRITICAL, ANNOTATED, LINGUISTIC
      BIBLIOGRAPHY. JOURNAL OF ETHNIC STUDIES,
      Vol. 4, no. 3 (Fall 1976), p. 116. English.
      DESCR: Accentedness; Bibliography; Bills,
      Garland D.; Book Reviews; Language Patterns;
      *SPANISH AND ENGLISH OF U.S. HISPANOS: A
      CRITICAL, ANNOTATED, LINGUISTIC
      BIBLIOGRAPHY; Spanish Language; Teschner,
      Richard V.

Cranston, Alan

3106 Presidential election 1984. NUESTRO, Vol. 7,
      no. 7 (September 1983), p. 14-19. English.
      DESCR: Anderson, John; Askew, Reubin;
      Elected Officials; *Elections; Fernandez,
      Ben; Glenn, John; Hart, Gary; Hispanic Force
      '84; Hollings, Ernest "Fritz"; Mondale,
      Walter; Political Parties and Organizations;
      Reagan, Ronald.

Craver, Rebecca McDowell

3107 Miller, Darlis A. Book review of: THE IMPACT
      OF INTIMACY: MEXICAN-ANGLO INTERMARRIAGE IN
      NEW MEXICO, 1821-1846. NEW MEXICO HISTORICAL
      REVIEW, Vol. 57, no. 4 (October 1982), p.
      407-408. English. DESCR: Book Reviews;
      Intermarriage; *THE IMPACT OF INTIMACY:
      MEXICAN-ANGLO INTERMARRIAGE IN NEW MEXICO,
      1821-1846.

Credit

3108 Velez-I., Carlos G. Social diversity,
      commercialization, and organizational
      complexity of urban Mexican Chicano rotating
      credit associations- theorical and empirical
      issues of adaptation. HUMAN ORGANIZATION,
      Vol. 41, no. 2 (Summer 1982), p. 107-120.
      English.

Credit Unions

3109 Government review. NUESTRO, Vol. 7, no. 10
      (December 1983), p. 48. English. DESCR:
      Banking Industry; Child Care Centers; Chile;
      Clinics (Medical); Employment; Employment
      Training; *Government Services; Medical
      Care; National Credit Union Administration;
      National Oceanic and Atmospheric
      Administration; SER; U.S. Department of
      Health and Human Services; U.S. Department
      of Labor.

Crime Victims Fund

3110 Gente. NUESTRO, Vol. 7, no. 2 (March 1983),
      p. 51. English. DESCR: Artists; Betancourt,
      Jose L.; *Chicanas; Federal Government;
      Juarez, Joe; Military Service; Saldana,
      Teresa; Vargas, Alberto; Victims for
      Victims.

Criminal Acts

3111 Berg, Charles. Book review of: CHRONIQUE OF
      A DEATH FORETOLD. NUESTRO, Vol. 7, no. 4
      (May 1983), p. 62. English. DESCR: *Book
      Reviews; CHRONICLE OF A DEATH FORETOLD;
      *Death (Concept); Garcia Marquez, Gabriel.

3112 Ericksen, Charles. Holdenreid and Salazar:
      unanswered questions. NUESTRO, Vol. 7, no. 4
      (May 1983), p. 40-41. English. DESCR:
      Assassination; Guatemala; *Holdenreid, Frank
      X.; *Salazar, Ruben; *Violence.

3113 Gonzalez, Juan. Arson wave threatens Puerto
      Ricans in inner cities. NUESTRO, Vol. 6, no.
      7 (September 1982), p. 27-28. English.
      DESCR: Firefighters; Hoboken, NJ; *Puerto
      Ricans.

3114 Long, William J. and Pohl, Christopher M.
      Joint foot patrols succeed in El Paso.
      POLICE CHIEF, Vol. 50, no. 4 (April 1983),
      p. 49-51. English. DESCR: Border Patrol;
      Ciudad Juarez, Chihuahua, Mexico; *El Paso,
      TX; Immigration Regulation and Control;
      *Police; Undocumented Workers; Youth.

3115 Lopez, Marcos. Legal affair. LATINA, Vol. 1,
      no. 2 (February, March, 1983), p. 85.
      English. DESCR: Employment; Housing; *Legal
      Aid.

3116 Padilla, Steve. Three-day siege. NUESTRO,
      Vol. 6, no. 8 (October 1982), p. 19-21.
      English. DESCR: *Arras, Raymundo; Federal
      Bureau of Investigation (FBI).

3117 Regional report, antiquities: stolen
      treasure begins U.S. tour. NUESTRO, Vol. 7,
      no. 4 (May 1983), p. 12-13. English. DESCR:
      *Peru; Precolumbian Art.

3118 [Summary of: Hollander, defending the
      criminal alien in New Mexico: tactics and
      strategy to avoid deportation, 9 N.M.L. rev.
      45 (1979)]. CHICANO LAW REVIEW, Vol. 5,
      (1982), p. 79-80. English. DESCR:
      Deportation; *Legal Representation;
      Undocumented Workers.

Criminal Justice System

3119 Brasch, Walter M. Hanigan case: hung up on racism? SOUTH ATLANTIC QUARTERLY, Vol. 81, no. 4 (Fall 1982), p. 429-435. English. DESCR: Administration of Justice; Arizona; Garcia-Loya, Manuel; *Hanigan, Patrick; Hanigan, Tom; Herrera-Mata, Bernabe; *Laws; Racism; Ruelas-Zavala, Eleazar; Undocumented Workers.

3120 Hail to the chief. HISPANIC BUSINESS, Vol. 4, no. 8 (August 1983), p. 10+. English. DESCR: *Ortega, Ruben; Phoenix, AZ; Police.

3121 Latinos in the law: meeting the challenge [a symposium]. CHICANO LAW REVIEW, Vol. 6, (1983), p. 1-121. English. DESCR: Demography; Legal Profession; Los Angeles Police Department; Love, Eulia; Police Brutality; Political Representation; Reapportionment; Settles, Ron.

3122 Nuestra gente. LATINO, Vol. 54, no. 5 (August, September, 1983), p. 29. English. DESCR: *Law; Paintings.

3123 Que pasa? NUESTRO, Vol. 7, no. 6 (August 1983), p. 9. English. DESCR: Boy Scouts of America; *Court System; Diabetes; Education; Judicial Review; Petersilia, Joan; PREPARED FOR TODAY; RACIAL DISPARITIES IN THE CRIMINAL JUSTICE SYSTEM; Reagan, Ronald.

Cronkite, Walter

3124 Holston, Mark. The Walter Cronkite of Mexico. NUESTRO, Vol. 7, no. 5 (June, July, 1983), p. 58-59. English. DESCR: Journalists; *Television; *Zabludovsky, Jacobo.

Crops

3125 Garcia, Ruperto. No help yet for farmworkers in Panhandle. TEXAS OBSERVER, Vol. 74, no. 16 (September 3, 1982), p. 6-7. English. DESCR: *Agricultural Laborers; Disasters; Economic History and Conditions; Texas Panhandle.

CROSS CULTURAL PSYCHOLOGY: HUMAN BEHAVIOR IN GLOBAL PERSPECTIVE

3126 Beaupre, Shirley. Book review of: CROSS CULTURAL PSYCHOLOGY: HUMAN BEHAVIOR IN GLOBAL PERSPECTIVE. HISPANIC JOURNAL OF BEHAVIORAL SCIENCES, Vol. 4, no. 1 (March 1982), p. 134-137. English. DESCR: Book Reviews; Segall, Marshall H.

Cross, Harry E.

3127 Cardoso, Lawrence Anthony. Book review of: ACROSS THE BORDER: RURAL DEVELOPMENT IN MEXICO AND RECENT MIGRATION TO THE UNITED STATES. AMERICAN HISTORICAL REVIEW, Vol. 88, no. 1 (February 1983), p. 226-227. English. DESCR: *ACROSS THE BORDER: RURAL DEVELOPMENT IN MEXICO AND RECENT MIGRATION; Book Reviews; Sandos, James.

3128 Cardoso, Lawrence Anthony. Book review of: ACROSS THE BORDER: RURAL DEVELOPMENT IN MEXICO AND RECENT MIGRATION TO THE UNITED STATES. AMERICAN HISTORICAL REVIEW, Vol. 88, (February 1983), p. 226. English. DESCR: *ACROSS THE BORDER: RURAL DEVELOPMENT IN MEXICO AND RECENT MIGRATION; Book Reviews; Immigration; Sandos, James.

3129 Mabry, Donald J. Book review of: ACROSS THE BORDER: RURAL DEVELOPMENT IN MEXICO AND RECENT MIGRATION TO THE UNITED STATES. INTERNATIONAL MIGRATION REVIEW, Vol. 17, no. 2 (Summer 1983), p. 351. English. DESCR: *ACROSS THE BORDER: RURAL DEVELOPMENT IN MEXICO AND RECENT MIGRATION; Book Reviews; Migration; Migration Patterns; Rural Economics; Sandos, James.

CROSSOVER DREAMS

3130 Fernandez, Enrique. Cannes and CROSSOVER DREAMS, '83. FILM COMMENT, Vol. 19, no. 4-7 (August 1983), p. 2-7. English. DESCR: Arce, Manuel; Blades, Ruben; Cannes Film Festival; Film Reviews; Films; Salsa.

Cruz, Conrado

3131 Cantu, Hector. Border business report: the Rio Grande Valley's economy and Mexico's lingering peso devaluation effects. NATIONAL HISPANIC JOURNAL, Vol. 2, no. 1 (Summer 1983), p. 10-13. English. DESCR: Aguirre, Lionel; Border Region; Cano, Eddie; Coors Distributing Company, McAllen, TX; Cuevas, Betty; *Currency; Economic Development; Laredo, TX, Chamber of Commerce; Mexican American Chamber of Commerce, Austin, TX; United States-Mexico Relations.

Cruz, Dan

3132 Caldera, Carmela. Dan Cruz: making the Olympics happen for the community. CAMINOS, Vol. 4, no. 4 (April 1983), p. 10-13,64. Bilingual. DESCR: *Los Angeles Olympic Organizing Committee; Olympics; Sports.

Cruz, Jose

3133 Ortiz, Carlos V. NUESTRO'S sixth annual all-star baseball team. NUESTRO, Vol. 7, no. 2 (March 1983), p. 33-37. English. DESCR: Andujar, Joaquin; Barojas, Salome; *Baseball; Castillo, Manny; Concepcion, Dave; Garcia, Damaso; Guerrero, Pedro; Hernandez, Keith; Lezcano, Sixto; Martinez, Tippy; Pena, Tony; Piniella, Lou; Sports; Valenzuela, Fernando.

3134 People. HISPANIC BUSINESS, Vol. 5, no. 10 (October 1983), p. 10. English. DESCR: Anaya, Toney; Arriola, Elvia Rosales; Babbitt, Bruce; Burgos, Tony; Bush, George; *Businesspeople; Cisneros, Henry, Mayor of San Antonio, TX; Kennedy, Edward M.; Montano, Gilbert; Reagan, Ronald; White, Mark.

3135 People. HISPANIC BUSINESS, Vol. 5, no. 12 (December 1983), p. 9. English. DESCR: *Businesspeople; Cantu, Norma V.; Masvidal, Sergio J.; Ortega, Katherine D.; Planas, Maria Bordas; Rodriguez, Ismael D.; Romero, Estella E.

Cruz, Manuel

3136 Allen, Virginia. Book review of: A CHICANO CHRISTMAS STORY. MODERN LANGUAGE JOURNAL, Vol. 66, no. 3 (Fall 1982), p. 353-354. English. DESCR: *A CHICANO CHRISTMAS STORY; Book Reviews; Children's Literature; Cruz, Ruth.

Cruz, Rosa Martinez

3137 Chavez, Mauro. Book review of: ESSAYS ON LA MUJER. JOURNAL OF ETHNIC STUDIES, Vol. 8, no. 2 (Summer 1980), p. 117-120. English. DESCR: Book Reviews; *Chicanas; Economic History and Conditions; *ESSAYS ON LA MUJER; Sanchez, Rosaura; Social History and Conditions; Socioeconomic Factors; Women's Rights.

Cruz, Ruth

3138 Allen, Virginia. Book review of: A CHICANO CHRISTMAS STORY. MODERN LANGUAGE JOURNAL, Vol. 66, no. 3 (Fall 1982), p. 353-354. English. DESCR: *A CHICANO CHRISTMAS STORY; Book Reviews; Children's Literature; Cruz, Manuel.

Crystal City, TX

3139 Laws, Bart. Raza unida de Cristal. SOUTHERN EXPOSURE, Vol. 10, no. 2 (March, April, 1982), p. 67-72. English. DESCR: Gurule, Dorothy; History; La Raza Unida Party; Mexican American Youth Organization (MAYO); *Political Parties and Organizations; Reyes, Carlos.

3140 Miller, Michael V. Chicano community control in South Texas: problems and prospects. JOURNAL OF ETHNIC STUDIES, Vol. 3, no. 3 (Fall 1975), p. 70-89. English. DESCR: Chicano Movement; Gutierrez, Jose Angel; History; La Raza Unida Party; Patron System; *Political Parties and Organizations; Social Classes; Social History and Conditions; *South Texas.

CSI International, Inc.

3141 Goodman, Gerson. "ES PARA USTED": CSI aims for satisfaction. HISPANIC BUSINESS, Vol. 4, no. 12 (December 1982), p. 16-17,34. English. DESCR: Advertising Agencies; Aguirre, Jack; Business Enterprises; Consumers; Fernandez, Castor A.; *Marketing.

Cuba

3142 An anniversary is observed. NUESTRO, Vol. 7, no. 8 (October 1983), p. 13. English. DESCR: *Batista, Fulgencio; Cubanos; Ferre, Maurice; Local Government; Miami, FL.

3143 Anti-Castro effort. NUESTRO, Vol. 6, no. 7 (September 1982), p. 9. English. DESCR: *Radio; Radio Marti.

3144 Burciaga, Jose Antonio. 20 nuclear years later: still holding my breath. NUESTRO, Vol. 6, no. 8 (October 1982), p. 35. English. DESCR: *Cuban Missile Crisis, October 1962; Nuclear Armament; *War.

3145 Carrion, Arturo Morales. Puerto Rico: the coming of the Americans. NUESTRO, Vol. 7, no. 5 (June, July, 1983), p. 25-30. English. DESCR: *International Relations; *Puerto Rico; Spain; *United States History; *War.

3146 Garcia, Margarita. The last days in Cuba: personal accounts of the circumstances of the exit. MIGRATION TODAY, Vol. 11, no. 4-5 (1983), p. 13-26. English. DESCR: Castro, Fidel; *Cuban Boatlift; *Cubanos; Hudson County, NJ; Immigration; Peruvian Embassy (Cuba).

3147 Gonzalez Cruz, Luis F. Quest and discovery in Oscar Hurtado's THE DEAD CITY OF KORAD: a unique experiment in science fiction poetry.

MAIZE, Vol. 5, no. 1-2 (Fall, Winter, 1981, 1982), p. 74-85. English. DESCR: *Hurtado, Oscar; Latin American Literature; *Literary Criticism; Poetry.

3148 Greenfield, Charles. Armando Valladares: twenty-two years of solitude. NUESTRO, Vol. 7, no. 10 (December 1983), p. 14-18+. English. DESCR: *Political Prisoners; Political Repression; *Valladares, Armando.

3149 Greenfield, Charles. Life imitating art: a profile of Reynaldo Arenas. NUESTRO, Vol. 7, no. 5 (June, July, 1983), p. 40-42. English. DESCR: Arenas, Reynaldo; *Authors; *Cubanos; El Morro Prison, Cuba; Political Prisoners.

3150 Maldonado-Denis, Manuel. El problema de las nacionalidades: la experiencia caribena. Paper presented at the "Dialogo de las Americas" conference. Mexico, D.F. September 9-14, 1982. REVISTA CHICANO-RIQUENA, Vol. 10, no. 4 (Fall 1982), p. 39-45. Spanish. DESCR: Capitalism; Carpentier, Alejo; El Salvador; Grenada; Guatemala; Imperialism; Marti, Jose; Nicaragua; *Political History and Conditions; Puerto Rico; United States.

Cuban Americans
USE: Cubanos

CUBAN AMERICANS: MASTERS OF SURVIVAL

3151 Rivera, Mario A. Book review of: CUBAN AMERICANS: MASTERS OF SURVIVAL. MIGRATION TODAY, Vol. 11, no. 4-5 (1983), p. 53. English. DESCR: Book Reviews; Cubanos; *Llanes, Jose.

Cuban Boatlift

3152 Garcia, Margarita. The last days in Cuba: personal accounts of the circumstances of the exit. MIGRATION TODAY, Vol. 11, no. 4-5 (1983), p. 13-26. English. DESCR: Castro, Fidel; Cuba; *Cubanos; Hudson County, NJ; Immigration; Peruvian Embassy (Cuba).

Cuban Haitian Task Force

3153 Gil, Rosa Maria. Issues in the delivery of mental health services to Cuban entrants. MIGRATION TODAY, Vol. 11, no. 4-5 (1983), p. 44-48. English. DESCR: Cubanos; Immigration; *Mental Health Programs; National Institute of Mental Health.

Cuban Missile Crisis, October 1962

3154 Burciaga, Jose Antonio. 20 nuclear years later: still holding my breath. NUESTRO, Vol. 6, no. 8 (October 1982), p. 35. English. DESCR: Cuba; Nuclear Armament; *War.

Cuban-American Coordinating Committee

3155 Latinos evident in 1983 march. NUESTRO, Vol. 7, no. 7 (September 1983), p. 11-12. English. DESCR: Bonilla, Tony; *Demonstrations; IMAGE, Washington, DC; Jackson, Jesse; League of United Latin American Citizens (LULAC); National Congress for Puerto Rican Rights (NCPRR); National Council of La Raza (NCLR); Velasquez, Baldemar; Zamora, Reuben.

Cubanos

3156 An anniversary is observed. NUESTRO, Vol. 7, no. 8 (October 1983), p. 13. English. DESCR: *Batista, Fulgencio; Cuba; Ferre, Maurice; Local Government; Miami, FL.

3157 Borjas, George J. Earnings of male Hispanic immigrants in the United States. INDUSTRIAL AND LABOR RELATIONS REVIEW, Vol. 35, no. 3 (April 1982), p. 343-353. English. DESCR: Ethnic Groups; *Immigrants; *Income; Puerto Ricans; Social Mobility.

3158 Brink, T. L. Book review of: WORKING-CLASS EMIGRES FROM CUBA. HISPANIC JOURNAL OF BEHAVIORAL SCIENCES, Vol. 5, no. 3 (September 1983), p. 363-365. English. DESCR: Book Reviews; Fox, Geoffrey E.; Laborers; *WORKING CLASS EMIGRES FROM CUBA.

3159 Castro's sister takes U.S. citizenship oath. NUESTRO, Vol. 6, no. 3 (April 1982), p. 38. English. DESCR: Castro, Fidel; *Castro, Juanita.

3160 Chavarria, Jesus. The world according to Miami. HISPANIC BUSINESS, Vol. 4, no. 3 (March 1982), p. 6. English. DESCR: *Business; Carnaval Miami 82; Miami, FL; *Urban Communities.

3161 Cuban exile chosen teacher of the year. NUESTRO, Vol. 6, no. 3 (April 1982), p. 37. English. DESCR: *Teaching Profession.

3162 Cuban-exile community protests deportation of recent escapee. NUESTRO, Vol. 6, no. 2 (March 1982), p. 32-34. English. DESCR: Immigration and Naturalization Service (INS); Political Asylum; *Rodriguez Hernandez, Andres.

3163 Cubans enjoy New Jersey town. NUESTRO, Vol. 7, no. 3 (April 1983), p. 10-11. English. DESCR: New Jersey; *Union City, NJ.

3164 Engle, Margarita Mondrus. Mother's Day reflections: a "traditional" Latina. NUESTRO, Vol. 7, no. 4 (May 1983), p. 46. Portuguese. DESCR: *Family; *Women's Rights.

3165 Estevez, Guillermo. Resettling the Cuban refugees in New Jersey. MIGRATION TODAY, Vol. 11, no. 4-5 (1983), p. 28-33. English. DESCR: Caribbean Relief Program; Immigration; International Rescue Committee; *New Jersey; Refugees.

3166 Ferre, Maurice A. Decade of the Hispanic. ADVERTISING AGE MAGAZINE, Vol. 53, (February 15, 1982), p. II, M14+. English. DESCR: *Population Trends; Puerto Ricans.

3167 First Cuban since 1890 in Florida legislature. NUESTRO, Vol. 6, no. 3 (April 1982), p. 37-38. English.

3168 Fradd, Sandra. Cubans to Cuban Americans: assimilation in the United States. MIGRATION TODAY, Vol. 11, no. 4-5 (1983), p. 35-42. English. DESCR: Assimilation; Bilingualism; Immigration.

3169 Garcia, Margarita. The last days in Cuba: personal accounts of the circumstances of the exit. MIGRATION TODAY, Vol. 11, no. 4-5 (1983), p. 13-26. English. DESCR: Castro, Fidel; Cuba; *Cuban Boatlift; Hudson County, NJ; Immigration; Peruvian Embassy (Cuba).

3170 Gil, Rosa Maria. Issues in the delivery of mental health services to Cuban entrants. MIGRATION TODAY, Vol. 11, no. 4-5 (1983), p.

44-48. English. DESCR: Cuban Haitian Task Force; Immigration; *Mental Health Programs; National Institute of Mental Health.

3171 Greenfield, Charles. Cuban theater in exile: Miami's little Broadway. NUESTRO, Vol. 6, no. 9 (November 1982), p. 36-38. English. DESCR: Little Havana; *Miami, FL; *Teatro.

3172 Greenfield, Charles. Cuba's matriarch of letters: Lydia Cabrera. NUESTRO, Vol. 6, no. 7 (September 1982), p. 13-15. English. DESCR: Authors; *Cabrera, Lydia.

3173 Greenfield, Charles. Life imitating art: a profile of Reynaldo Arenas. NUESTRO, Vol. 7, no. 5 (June, July, 1983), p. 40-42. English. DESCR: Arenas, Reynaldo; *Authors; *Cuba; El Morro Prison, Cuba; Political Prisoners.

3174 Greenfield, Charles. Q & A with Lydia Cabrera. NUESTRO, Vol. 6, no. 7 (September 1982), p. 16-17+. English. DESCR: Authors; *Cabrera, Lydia.

3175 Greenfield, Charles. Writing in exile. NUESTRO, Vol. 6, no. 8 (October 1982), p. 22-24. English. DESCR: Authors; *Infante, Guillermo Cabrera.

3176 Haggerty, Alfred G. Occidental goes after Hispanic market. NATIONAL UNDERWRITER LIFE AND HEALTH INSURANCE EDITION, Vol. 86, no. 1 (January 2, 1982), p. 22. English. DESCR: *Insurance; Market Research; Transamerica Occidental Life.

3177 Hines, Bea L. and Fabricio, Roberto. Voices. NUESTRO, Vol. 7, no. 10 (December 1983), p. 57-58. English. DESCR: Blacks; *Elections; Ferre, Maurice; *Miami, FL; Suarez, Xavier.

3178 House panel limits Radio Marti effort. NUESTRO, Vol. 6, no. 4 (May 1982), p. 57. English. DESCR: Radio; *Radio Marti.

3179 The Little Havana development authority. HISPANIC BUSINESS, Vol. 4, no. 3 (March 1982), p. 10+. English. DESCR: Carnaval Miami 82; *Community Development; Little Havana; Miami, FL.

3180 Meyer Rogg, Eleanor and Holmberg, Joan J. The assimilation of Cubans in the United States. MIGRATION TODAY, Vol. 11, no. 4-5 (1983), p. 8-11. English. DESCR: Assimilation.

3181 Naismith, Rachael. Outreach services to Hispanics. ILLINOIS LIBRARIES, Vol. 64, no. 7 (September 1982), p. 962-966. English. DESCR: Arrondo, Ondina; La Raza Hispanica, Miami, FL; Latin American Library/Biblioteca Latinoamericana, Oakland, CA; *Library Services; Lopez, Lillian; Puerto Ricans; Ruiz, Deborah; South Bronx Project, New York Public Library; Verges, Bruni.

3182 A new understanding of Cuban Americans. LATINO, Vol. 54, no. 8 (December 1983), p. 20. English.

3183 Pedraza Bailey, Silvia. Cubans and Mexicans in the United States: the functions of political and economic migration. CUBAN STUDIES, Vol. 11, no. 2-1 (1981, 1982), p. 70-103. English. DESCR: Immigrants; *Migration; Political Economy; Political Refugees.

Cubanos (cont.)

3184 Perez, Lisandro. Comment: Cubans and Mexicans in the United States. CUBAN STUDIES, Vol. 11, no. 2-1 (1981, 1982), p. 99-103. English. **DESCR:** *Migration; Social Research.

3185 Que pasa?: future of bilingualism. NUESTRO, Vol. 7, no. 4 (May 1983), p. 9. English. **DESCR:** *Bilingualism; Canada; *Miami, FL.

3186 Rivera, Mario A. Book review of: CUBAN AMERICANS: MASTERS OF SURVIVAL. MIGRATION TODAY, Vol. 11, no. 4-5 (1983), p. 53. English. **DESCR:** Book Reviews; *CUBAN AMERICANS: MASTERS OF SURVIVAL; *Llanes, Jose.

3187 Russell, Cheryl. The news about Hispanics. AMERICAN DEMOGRAPHICS, Vol. 5, no. 3 (March 1983), p. 14-25. English. **DESCR:** Census; *Population; Puerto Ricans.

3188 Sierra, Jerry A. Faces [photographs]. CAMINOS, Vol. 4, no. 8 (September 1983), p. 28-30. English. **DESCR:** Los Marielitos; *Photography.

3189 Szapocznik, Jose, et al. Ethnic and cultural variations in the care of the aged. New directions in the treatment of represion in the elderly: a life enhancement counseling approach. JOURNAL OF GERIATRIC PSYCHIATRY, Vol. 15, no. 2 (1982), p. 257-281. English. **DESCR:** *Ancianos; Counseling (Psychological).

3190 Szapocznik, Jose, et al. Life enhancement counseling and the treatment of the depressed Cuban American elders. HISPANIC JOURNAL OF BEHAVIORAL SCIENCES, Vol. 4, no. 4 (December 1982), p. 487-502. English. **DESCR:** Ancianos; *Counseling (Psychological).

3191 Tattered borders. NEW REPUBLIC, Vol. 189, no. 2 (July 11, 1983), p. 9-11. English. **DESCR:** *Immigration; *Simpson-Mazzoli Bill; Undocumented Workers.

3192 Volsky, George. The American club. HISPANIC BUSINESS, Vol. 4, no. 3 (March 1982), p. 16-17+. English. **DESCR:** American Club of Miami; *Businesspeople; *Cultural Organizations; Miami, FL.

3193 Volsky, George and Masvidal, Raul. An interview with Raul Masvidal. HISPANIC BUSINESS, Vol. 4, no. 9 (September 1982), p. 16-17,24+. English. **DESCR:** Banking Industry; Biography; Business Enterprises; Businesspeople; *Masvidal, Raul; Miami, FL.

3194 Ward, Carmen Carole. Book review of: THE ASSIMILATION OF CUBAN EXILES: THE ROLE OF COMMUNITY AND CLASS. JOURNAL OF ETHNIC STUDIES, Vol. 3, no. 2 (Summer 1975), p. 116-119. English. **DESCR:** Assimilation; Book Reviews; Miami, FL; *Rogg, Eleanor Meyer; Social Classes; Social History and Conditions; THE ASSIMILATION OF CUBAN EXILES: THE ROLE OF COMMUNITY AND CLASS; West New York, NJ.

3195 West, Dennis. Film review of: EL SUPER. MINORITY VOICES, Vol. 4, no. 2 (Fall 1980), p. 85-87. English. **DESCR:** *EL SUPER; Film Reviews; Ichaso, Leon; Jimenez-Leal, Orlando.

Cuellar, Israel

3196 Vazquez, Carol A. Reply to Cuellar and

Price. HISPANIC JOURNAL OF BEHAVIORAL SCIENCES, Vol. 4, no. 1 (March 1982), p. 85-88. English. **DESCR:** Price, Criselda S.; *Psychological Theory.

Cuentos

For written short stories USE Short Stories

3197 Weigle, Marta. Book review of: HISPANIC LEGENDS FROM NEW MEXICO: NARRATIVES FROM THE R.D. JAMESON COLLECTION. JOURNAL OF AMERICAN FOLKLORE, Vol. 96, , p. 238-239. English. **DESCR:** Book Reviews; *HISPANIC LEGENDS FROM NEW MEXICO: NARRATIVES FROM THE R.D. JAMESON COLLECTION; Robe, Stanley L.

CUENTOS CHICANOS

3198 Urioste, Donaldo W. Book review of: CUENTOS CHICANOS. LA PALABRA, Vol. 4, no. 1-2 (Spring, Fall, 1982, 1983), p. 175-177. Spanish. **DESCR:** Anaya, Rudolfo A.; Book Reviews; Literature.

Cuevas, Betty

3199 Cantu, Hector. Border business report: the Rio Grande Valley's economy and Mexico's lingering peso devaluation effects. NATIONAL HISPANIC JOURNAL, Vol. 2, no. 1 (Summer 1983), p. 10-13. English. **DESCR:** Aguirre, Lionel; Border Region; Cano, Eddie; Coors Distributing Company, McAllen, TX; Cruz, Conrado; *Currency; Economic Development; Laredo, TX, Chamber of Commerce; Mexican American Chamber of Commerce, Austin, TX; United States-Mexico Relations.

Cuevas, Hector

3200 Chavez, Rigo. Job counseling, role models mean a lot. HISPANIC BUSINESS, Vol. 4, no. 8 (August 1983), p. 12. English. **DESCR:** Careers; *Counseling Services (Educational); Escobedo, Ed; Professional Opportunities Program (POP); *Stanford University, Stanford, CA.

Culinary Institute of America, Hyde Park, NY

3201 Shiell, Pancho. The food world's CIA. NUESTRO, Vol. 7, no. 2 (March 1983), p. 28-32. English. **DESCR:** Employment Training; Figueroa, Roberto; Recipes.

Cultural Characteristics

3202 Adams, Phylliss J. and Anderson, Peggy L. Comparison of teachers' and Mexican-American children's perceptions of the children's competence. READING TEACHER, Vol. 36, no. 1 (October 1982), p. 8-13. English. **DESCR:** Attitude (Psychological); Children; Colorado; Learning and Cognition; Sex Roles; *Teacher Attitudes.

3203 Ambert, Alba N. The identification of LEP children with special needs. BILINGUAL JOURNAL, Vol. 6, no. 1 (Fall 1982), p. 17-22. English. **DESCR:** Handicapped; Language Interference; Limited-English Proficient (LEP); *Special Education.

3204 Argulewicz, Ed N.; Elliott, Stephen N.; and Hall, Robert. Comparison of behavioral ratings of Anglo-American and Mexican-American gifted children. PSYCHOLOGY IN THE SCHOOLS, Vol. 19, no. 4 (October 1982), p. 469-472. English. **DESCR:** Anglo Americans; Child Study; *Intelligence Tests.

Cultural Characteristics (cont.)

3205 Armas, Jose. ANTONIO AND THE MAYOR: a cultural review of the film. JOURNAL OF ETHNIC STUDIES, Vol. 3, no. 3 (Fall 1975), p. 98-101. English. DESCR: *ANTONIO AND THE MAYOR; Broadcast Media; Columbia Broadcasting Studios (CBS); Film Reviews; Films; Mass Media; *Stereotypes.

3206 Baca Zinn, Maxine. Chicano family research: conceptual distortions and alternative directions. JOURNAL OF ETHNIC STUDIES, Vol. 7, no. 3 (Fall 1979), p. 59-71. English. DESCR: Culture; *Family; Research Methodology; Social Research; Stereotypes.

3207 Baca Zinn, Maxine. Chicano men and masculinity. JOURNAL OF ETHNIC STUDIES, Vol. 10, no. 2 (Summer 1982), p. 29-44. English. DESCR: Ethnic Stratification; *Machismo; Sex Roles; Sex Stereotypes; Socioeconomic Factors; Women Men Relations.

3208 Borrego, Richard L.; Chavez, Ernest L.; and Titley, Robert W. Effect of counselor technique on Mexican-American and Anglo-American self-disclosure and counselor perception. JOURNAL OF COUNSELING PSYCHOLOGY, Vol. 29, no. 5 (September 1982), p. 538-541. English. DESCR: Anglo Americans; *Counseling (Psychological); Identity; Personality; Sex Roles.

3209 Burns, Allan F. Politics, pedagogy, and culture in bilingual classrooms: a case study. NABE JOURNAL, Vol. 6, no. 2-3 (Winter, Spring, 1981, 1982), p. 35-51. English. DESCR: Biculturalism; *Bilingual Bicultural Education; Bilingualism; Teacher-pupil Interaction.

3210 Cantu, Roberto. Nota preliminar: de Samuel Ramos a Emilio Uranga. CAMPO LIBRE, Vol. 1, no. 2 (Summer 1981), p. 239-272. Spanish. DESCR: Identity; Mexico; Philosophy; *Ramos, Samuel; *Uranga, Emilio.

3211 Carlos, Jess. The Filipinos: our forgotten cultural cousins. NUESTRO, Vol. 7, no. 8 (October 1983), p. 19-21. English. DESCR: Catholic Church; *Philippines; Social History and Conditions.

3212 Carrison, Muriel Paskin. Bilingual-no! PRINCIPAL, Vol. 62, no. 3 (January 1983), p. 9. English. DESCR: *Bilingual Bicultural Education; Education Equalization; Socioeconomic Factors.

3213 Cortese, Anthony J., ed. A comparative analysis of ethnicity and moral judgment. CACR REVIEW, Vol. 1, no. 1 (September 1982), p. 72-101. English. DESCR: Anglo Americans; Blacks; Identity; *Values.

3214 Costa Rica hosts craftsmen of the Americas. NUESTRO, Vol. 6, no. 6 (August 1982), p. 63-64. English. DESCR: Artists; Arts and Crafts; Conventions; *Costa Rica; Cultural Customs.

3215 Craig, Richard B. and Sell, Deborah K. Values of Anglo-American, Chicano, and Mexican students at a Mexican university. BORDERLANDS JOURNAL, Vol. 6, no. 2 (Spring 1983), p. 153-169. English. DESCR: *Acculturation.

3216 Davis, Sally M. and Harris, Mary B. Sexual knowledge, sexual interests, and sources of sexual information of rural and urban adolescents from three cultures. ADOLESCENCE, Vol. 17, no. 66 (Summer 1982), p. 471-492. English. DESCR: Birth Control; Identity; Rural Population; *Sex Education; Sex Roles; *Sexual Behavior; Urban Communities; Youth.

3217 Delgado, Melvin and Humm-Delgado, Denise. Natural support systems: source of strength in Hispanic communities. SOCIAL WORK, Vol. 27, no. 1 (January 1982), p. 83-89. English. DESCR: Cultural Organizations; *Social Work.

3218 Escovar, Peggy L. and Lazarus, Philip J. Cross-cultural child-rearing practices: implications for school psychologists. SCHOOL PSYCHOLOGY INTERNATIONAL, Vol. 3, no. 3 (July, September, 1982), p. 143-148. English. DESCR: *Child Rearing; Children; Counseling (Psychological).

3219 Flaskerud, Jacquelyn H. Community mental health nursing: its unique role in the delivery of services to ethnic minorities. PERSPECTIVES IN PSYCHIATRIC CARE, Vol. 20, no. 1 (January, March, 1982), p. 37-43. English. DESCR: *Asian Americans; Blacks; *Community Mental Health; Native Americans.

3220 Garcia, Mario T. Americanization and the Mexican immigrant, 1880-1930. JOURNAL OF ETHNIC STUDIES, Vol. 6, no. 2 (Summer 1978), p. 19-34. English. DESCR: *Acculturation; Culture; Education; Immigrant Labor; Immigration.

3221 Gomez, Roberto L. Pastoral care and counseling in a Mexican American setting. APUNTES, Vol. 2, no. 2 (Summer 1982), p. 31-39. English. DESCR: *Clergy; *Counseling (Religious); Religion.

3222 Gonzalez, Roseann Duenas. Teaching Mexican American students to write: capitalizing on the culture. ENGLISH JOURNAL, Vol. 71, no. 7 (November 1982), p. 20-24. English. DESCR: Education; Educational Innovations; *Language Arts; Style and Composition.

3223 Gould, Sam. Correlates of career progression among Mexican-American college graduates. JOURNAL OF VOCATIONAL BEHAVIOR, Vol. 20, no. 1 (February 1982), p. 93-110. English. DESCR: *Careers; *College Graduates; Colleges and Universities; Social Mobility.

3224 Henderson, Ronald W. and Brody, Gene H. Effects of ethnicity and child's age on maternal judgments of children's transgressions against persons and property. JOURNAL OF GENETIC PSYCHOLOGY, Vol. 140, no. 2 (June 1982), p. 253-263. English. DESCR: Anglo Americans; Arizona; Behavior Modification; *Child Rearing; Native Americans; *Socialization; Tucson, AZ.

3225 Jimenez, Ricardo. Understanding the culture and learning styles of Hispanic students. MOMENTUM, Vol. 14, no. 1 (February 1983), p. 15-18. English. DESCR: Learning and Cognition; Socioeconomic Factors.

3226 Knight, George P.; Kagan, Spencer; and Buriel, Raymond. Perceived parental practices and prosocial development. JOURNAL OF GENETIC PSYCHOLOGY, Vol. 141, (September 1982), p. 57-65. English. DESCR: Anglo Americans; *Parent and Child Relationships; *Socialization; Socioeconomic Factors.

Cultural Characteristics (cont.)

Mental Health; *Mental Health Personnel.

3227 Knight, George P., et al. Cooperative-competitive social orientation and school achievement among Anglo-American and Mexican-American children. CONTEMPORARY EDUCATIONAL PSYCHOLOGY, Vol. 7, no. 2 (April 1982), p. 97-106. English. DESCR: Academic Achievement; Anglo Americans; Socialization; Students.

3228 Langum, D.J. From condemnation to praise: shifting perspectives on Hispanic California. CALIFORNIA HISTORY, Vol. 61, no. 4 (1983), p. 282-291. English. DESCR: *California; Ethnic Attitudes; Stereotypes.

3229 Lasater, Tonia Tash and Montalvo, Frank F. Understanding Mexican American culture: a training program. CHILDREN TODAY, Vol. 11, no. 3 (May, June, 1982), p. 23-25+. English. DESCR: *Cultural Customs; Employment Training; Mexican American Culture Simulator; Social Services.

3230 Luevano, Richard L. Attitudes of elderly Mexican Americans towards nursing homes in Stanislaus county. CAMPO LIBRE, Vol. 1, no. 2 (Summer 1981), p. 213-228. English. DESCR: *Ancianos; Attitude (Psychological); Medical Care; *Nursing Homes; Stanislaus County, CA; Surveys.

3231 McMillen, Jay B. The social organization of leisure among Mexican-Americans. JOURNAL OF LEISURE RESEARCH, Vol. 15, no. 2 (1983), p. 164-173. English. DESCR: Leisure; *Socialization.

3232 O'Donnell, James P., et al. Dimensions of behavior problems in Anglo-American and Mexican-American preschool children: a comparative study. JOURNAL OF CONSULTING AND CLINICAL PSYCHOLOGY, Vol. 50, no. 5 (October 1982), p. 643-651. English. DESCR: Anglo Americans; Children; *Comparative Psychology; Mental Health; Psychological Testing; Socioeconomic Factors.

3233 Perry, Ronald W. Crisis communications: ethnic differentials in interpreting and acting on disaster warnings. SOCIAL BEHAVIOR AND PERSONALITY, Vol. 10, no. 1 (1982), p. 97-104. English. DESCR: *Disasters; *Social Psychology.

3234 Poma, Pedro A. Hispanic cultural influences on medical practices. NATIONAL MEDICAL ASSOCIATION JOURNAL, Vol. 75, no. 10 (October 1983), p. 941-946. English. DESCR: Hospitals and the Community; *Medical Care.

3235 Ramos, Manuel. En torno a las ideas sobre EL MEXICANO. CAMPO LIBRE, Vol. 1, no. 2 (Summer 1981), p. 273-282. Spanish. DESCR: *EL MEXICANO; Identity; Mexico; Philosophy; *Uranga, Emilio.

3236 Ruiz, Rene A. and LeVine, Elaine S. Book review of: PSYCHOLOGY OF THE MEXICAN CULTURE AND PERSONALITY. JOURNAL OF ETHNIC STUDIES, Vol. 4, no. 2 (Summer 1976), p. 104-107. English. DESCR: Book Reviews; Culture; *Diaz-Guerrero, Rogelio; Personality; Psychology; PSYCHOLOGY OF THE MEXICAN CULTURE AND PERSONALITY.

3237 Sanchez, Arthur R. and Atkinson, Donald R. Mexican-American cultural commitment, preference for counselor ethnicity, and willingness to use counseling. JOURNAL OF COUNSELING PSYCHOLOGY, Vol. 30, no. 2 (April 1983), p. 215-220. English. DESCR: *Counseling (Psychological); Identity;

3238 Seilhamer, E. Stella and Prewitt-Diaz, Joseph O. The return and circulatory migrant student: a perception of teachers, schools and self. MIGRATION TODAY, Vol. 11, no. 1 (1983), p. 21-23. English. DESCR: Identity; Migration Patterns; *Puerto Rican Education; Puerto Ricans.

3239 Tienda, Marta and Angel, Ronald. Headship and household composition among blacks, Hispanics and other whites. SOCIAL FORCES, Vol. 61, no. 2 (December 1982), p. 508-531. English. DESCR: Anglo Americans; Blacks; Extended Family; *Family; Puerto Ricans; Single Parents.

3240 Tomasi, Lydio F. Of diversity and strength [editorial]. MIGRATION TODAY, Vol. 11, no. 4-5 (1983), p. 7. English. DESCR: *Los Angeles, CA.

3241 Trotter, Robert T. Contrasting models of the healer's role: south Texas case examples. HISPANIC JOURNAL OF BEHAVIORAL SCIENCES, Vol. 4, no. 3 (September 1982), p. 315-327. English. DESCR: *Curanderismo; Medical Care; Public Health.

3242 Trotter, Robert T. Ethnic and sexual patterns of alcohol use: Anglo and Mexican American college students. ADOLESCENCE, Vol. 17, no. 66 (Summer 1982), p. 305-325. English. DESCR: *Alcoholism; Anglo Americans; Chicanas; Ethnic Groups; Sex Roles; Youth.

3243 Uranga, Emilio. Notas para un estudio del mexicano. CAMPO LIBRE, Vol. 1, no. 2 (Summer 1981), p. 283-295. Spanish. DESCR: Gaos, Jose; Identity; Mexico; Philosophy; *Ramos, Samuel.

3244 Valencia, Richard R. Stability of the McCarthy scales of children's abilities over a one-year period for Mexican-American children. PSYCHOLOGY IN THE SCHOOLS, Vol. 20, no. 1 (January 1983), p. 29-34. English. DESCR: Child Study; *Intelligence Tests; McCarthy Scales for Children's Abilities (MSCA); Socioeconomic Factors.

3245 Vigil, James Diego. Towards a new perspective on understanding the Chicano people: the six C's model of sociocultural change. CAMPO LIBRE, Vol. 1, no. 2 (Summer 1981), p. 141-167. English. DESCR: Acculturation; Assimilation; History; Mexican Nationalism Period; Mexico; Nationalism; Organizations; Precolumbian Society; *Six C's Model (Theoretical Model); Social History and Conditions; Spanish Colonial Period.

3246 Wheaton, Blair. A comparison of the moderating effects of personal coping resources in the impact of exposure to stress in two groups. JOURNAL OF COMMUNITY PSYCHOLOGY, Vol. 10, no. 4 (October 1982), p. 293-311. English. DESCR: Anglo Americans; Comparative Psychology; Mental Health; Social Psychology; *Stress.

3247 Willig, Ann C. Sociocultural and educational correlates of success-failure attributions and evaluation anxiety in the school setting for Black, Hispanic, and Anglo children. AMERICAN EDUCATIONAL RESEARCH JOURNAL, Vol. 20, no. 3 (Fall 1983), p. 385-410. English. DESCR: Academic Achievement; *Academic Motivation; Anglo Americans; Blacks.

Cultural Consultation Clinic

3248 Good, Byron J. Reflexivity and countertransference in a psychiatric cultural consultation clinic. CULTURE, MEDICINE & PSYCHIATRY, Vol. 6, no. 3 (September 1982), p. 281-303. English. **DESCR:** Clinical Psychiatry; Psychiatry.

Cultural Customs

3249 Costa Rica hosts craftsmen of the Americas. NUESTRO, Vol. 6, no. 6 (August 1982), p. 63-64. English. **DESCR:** Artists; Arts and Crafts; Conventions; *Costa Rica; *Cultural Characteristics.

3250 Davila, Luis. Meditaciones. REVISTA CHICANO-RIQUENA, Vol. 10, no. 1-2 (Winter, Spring, 1982), p. 275-278. Spanish. **DESCR:** Bilingualism; *Essays; Folklore; Self-Referents.

3251 Exum, Herbert A. The most invisible minority: the culturally diverse elderly. SCHOOL COUNSELOR, Vol. 30, no. 1 (September 1982), p. 15-24. English. **DESCR:** *Ancianos; Asian Americans; Blacks; Counseling (Psychological); Ethnic Groups; Family; Native Americans; Stereotypes.

3252 Hispanic heritage month celebrated by Newark public. LIBRARY JOURNAL, Vol. 107, no. 17 (October 1, 1982), p. 1801. English. **DESCR:** National Hispanic Heritage Week.

3253 Hispanics keep the faith, but better parish work is needed. MIGRATION TODAY, Vol. 10, no. 5 (1982), p. 35. English. **DESCR:** Assimilation; Catholic Church; *Religion.

3254 Lasater, Tonia Tash and Montalvo, Frank F. Understanding Mexican American culture: a training program. CHILDREN TODAY, Vol. 11, no. 3 (May, June, 1982), p. 23-25+. English. **DESCR:** Cultural Characteristics; Employment Training; Mexican American Culture Simulator; Social Services.

3255 Living traditions of the days of the dead. NUESTRO, Vol. 6, no. 6 (August 1982), p. 41-43. English. **DESCR:** Death (Concept); *Dia de los Muertos; Mexico.

3256 Maestas, Leo C. Academic performance across cultures: an examination of the effect of value similarity. EDUCATIONAL RESEARCH QUARTERLY, Vol. 7, no. 4 (Winter 1983), p. 24-34. English. **DESCR:** *Academic Achievement; Ethnic Groups; Socialization; Teacher-pupil Interaction.

3257 Miccaihuitl. CALMECAC, Vol. 1, (Summer 1980), p. 34-37. Bilingual. **DESCR:** *Dia de los Muertos; Self-Help Graphics, Los Angeles, CA.

Cultural Organizations

3258 1983 SER theme: a new reality. LATINO, Vol. 54, no. 3 (April 1983), p. 8. English. **DESCR:** *SER.

3259 Alvarez, Carlos. 1983 LULAC convention. LATINO, Vol. 54, no. 6 (October 1983), p. 8. English. **DESCR:** *League of United Latin American Citizens (LULAC).

3260 Amigos. LATINO, Vol. 53, no. 7 (November 1982), p. 9-10. English. **DESCR:** *Amigos de las Americas; Public Health.

3261 Barreto, Julio. A new force in the barrio. NUESTRO, Vol. 7, no. 4 (May 1983), p. 43-45. English. **DESCR:** Caballero-Perez, Diana; *Community Development; National Congress for Puerto Rican Rights (NCPRR); *Puerto Ricans.

3262 Bonilla, Tony. 'We gave it our best shot'. LATINO, Vol. 54, no. 4 (May, June, 1983), p. 6. English. **DESCR:** *Bonilla, Tony.

3263 Community watching. CAMINOS, Vol. 3, no. 5 (May 1982), p. 56-57. Bilingual. **DESCR:** Adelante Mujer Hispana Conference; Agricultural Laborers; Beilson, Anthony C.; Boycotts; Chacon, Peter R.; Chicanas; Farm Labor Organizing Commmittee (FLOC); Financial Aid; Hollenbeck Junior High School, Los Angeles, CA; Junior High School Students; National League of Cities; Optimist Club of Greater East Los Angeles; Organizations; Project WELL (We Enjoy Learning & Leadership); Torres, Art.

3264 Community watching: para la comunidad. CAMINOS, Vol. 3, no. 2 (February 1982), p. 43-44. Bilingual. **DESCR:** Casa Blanca Youth Project; Colegio Cesar Chavez, Mt. Angel, OR; Colleges and Universities; Financial Aid; LULAC National Education Service Centers (LNESC); Tonatiuh-Quinto Sol Award for Literature, 1977-78; University of California, Riverside.

3265 Community watching: para la comunidad. CAMINOS, Vol. 3, no. 3 (March 1982), p. 58-59. Bilingual. **DESCR:** *Engineering as a Profession; Financial Aid; Harvard University; Latino Business Students Association (LBSA); Rodolfo H. Castro Fellowship; Society for Hispanic Professional Engineers (SHPE); Student Organizations; University of Southern California.

3266 Community watching: para la comunidad. CAMINOS, Vol. 2, no. 6 (October 1981), p. 40-41+. English. **DESCR:** Hispanic Women in Higher Education (HWHE); La Plaza Senior Citizens, Los Angeles, CA; Mexican American Political Association (MAPA); Reapportionment.

3267 COPS. LATINO, Vol. 53, no. 4 (June 1982), p. 7. English. **DESCR:** *Communities Organized for Public Service (COPS).

3268 Delgado, Melvin. Ethnic and cultural variations in the care of the aged. Hispanic elderly and natural support systems: a special focus on Puerto Ricans. JOURNAL OF GERIATRIC PSYCHIATRY, Vol. 15, no. 2 (1982), p. 239-251. English. **DESCR:** *Ancianos; Curanderas; Family; Natural Support Systems; Puerto Ricans; Religion; Santeros.

3269 Delgado, Melvin and Humm-Delgado, Denise. Natural support systems: source of strength in Hispanic communities. SOCIAL WORK, Vol. 27, no. 1 (January 1982), p. 83-89. English. **DESCR:** Cultural Characteristics; *Social Work.

3270 Dreams come true ... a celebration (photoessay). CAMINOS, Vol. 3, no. 11 (December 1982), p. 46-47. English. **DESCR:** *Plaza de La Raza, Los Angeles, CA.

Cultural Organizations (cont.)

3271 Entertainment = diversion. CAMINOS, Vol. 3, no. 4 (April 1982), p. 41. Bilingual. **DESCR:** AZTLAN [journal]; Committee in Solidarity with the People of El Salvador (CISPES); Directories; DIRECTORY OF MINORITY ARTS ORGANIZATIONS; El Salvador; *National Endowment for the Arts; NOTICIERO; Organizations; Periodicals; *Recreation; Television.

3272 Gonzales, Patrisia. The two cities of Tucson. NUESTRO, Vol. 7, no. 4 (May 1983), p. 20-23. English. **DESCR:** Accion 80s; *Discrimination in Education; *Discrimination in Employment; Garcia, Gerald; Lopez-Grant, Lillian; *Tucson, AZ; Valdez, Joel.

3273 Holley, Joe. Page two. TEXAS OBSERVOR, Vol. 75, no. 1 (January 14, 1983), p. 2-3. English. **DESCR:** *Communities Organized for Public Service (COPS); Educational Law and Legislation; Political Parties and Organizations.

3274 LNESC tenth anniversary banquet set for March 24. LATINO, Vol. 54, no. 2 (March 1983), p. 7. English. **DESCR:** *LULAC National Education Service Centers (LNESC).

3275 The Mexican and American Foundation. LATINA, Vol. 1, no. 3 (1983), p. 51. English. **DESCR:** *Mexican and American Foundation.

3276 "Our success is to see someone get a job with MGM"; Q and A with Edmundo M. Rodriguez. CAMINOS, Vol. 3, no. 11 (December 1982), p. 48-49,54. English. **DESCR:** *Plaza de La Raza, Los Angeles, CA; Rodriguez, Edmundo M.

3277 Quesada-Weiner, Rosemary. Chicana Service Action Center. CAMINOS, Vol. 2, no. 6 (October 1981), p. 39. Bilingual. **DESCR:** *Chicana Service Action Center, Los Angeles, CA; Chicanas.

3278 Quinlivan, Robert. Another milestone for the Chicano federation. CAMINOS, Vol. 3, no. 6 (June 1982), p. 41. English. **DESCR:** *Chicano Federation of San Diego Co., Inc.

3279 Rips, Geoffrey. COPS educates. TEXAS OBSERVOR, Vol. 75, no. 4 (February 25, 1983), p. 1-2. English. **DESCR:** *Communities Organized for Public Service (COPS); Educational Law and Legislation; Political Parties and Organizations.

3280 Rips, Geoffrey. New politics in Texas: COPS comes to Austin. TEXAS OBSERVOR, Vol. 75, no. 1 (January 14, 1983), p. 1+. English. **DESCR:** *Communities Organized for Public Service (COPS); Educational Law and Legislation; Political Parties and Organizations.

3281 Soto, Rose Marie. Consuelo Santos-Killins: a leader in the arts. CAMINOS, Vol. 4, no. 6 (June 1983), p. 56-57,67. Bilingual. **DESCR:** Art; California Arts Council (C.A.C.); *Santos-Killins, Consuelo.

3282 Volsky, George. The American club. HISPANIC BUSINESS, Vol. 4, no. 3 (March 1982), p. 16-17+. English. **DESCR:** American Club of Miami; *Businesspeople; Cubanos; Miami, FL.

3283 Watkins, Ted R. and Gonzalez, Richard. Outreach to Mexican-Americans. SOCIAL WORK, Vol. 27, no. 1 (January 1982), p. 68-73. English. **DESCR:** *Counseling Services (Educational); Social Services.

3284 Whisler, Kirk. Menudo cook-off and much more (photoessay). CAMINOS, Vol. 3, no. 8 (September 1982), p. 49. English. **DESCR:** Riverside, CA.

3285 Whole lot of love. LATINO, Vol. 53, no. 5 (September 1982), p. 12. English.

3286 Wittenauer, Cheryl. The economics of culture: L.A.'s most successful Plaza de la Raza. HISPANIC BUSINESS, Vol. 5, no. 1 (January 1983), p. 12-13+. English. **DESCR:** Funding Sources; Plaza de La Raza, Los Angeles, CA; Ruben Salazar Bicentennial Building.

Cultural Pluralism

3287 Bradley, Curtis H. and Friedenberg, Joan E. Tips for the English speaking multicultural vocational teacher. BILINGUAL JOURNAL, Vol. 6, no. 1 (Fall 1982), p. 6-9. English. **DESCR:** Educational Innovations; Limited-English Proficient (LEP); Teacher-pupil Interaction; *Vocational Education.

3288 Brooks, C.K. Verbal giftedness in the minority student: a NEWT questions a SOT. ENGLISH JOURNAL, Vol. 72, (January 1983), p. 18-21. English. **DESCR:** Curriculum; *Language Arts; Language Development.

3289 Clarizio, Harvey F. Intellectual assessment of Hispanic children. PSYCHOLOGY IN THE SCHOOLS, Vol. 19, no. 1 (January 1982), p. 61-71. English. **DESCR:** Anglo Americans; Child Study; *Intelligence Tests.

3290 Cohen, Bernard H. Two bridges. LATINO, Vol. 54, no. 2 (March 1983), p. 16-18. English. **DESCR:** Bilingual Bicultural Education.

3291 Costas, Orlando E. The Hispanics next door. CHRISTIAN CENTURY, Vol. 99, no. 26 (August 18, 1982), p. 851-856. English. **DESCR:** Latin Americans; *Liberation Theology; Religion.

3292 Guckert, John C. Multiculturalism: a democratic approach to education. SCHOLAR AND EDUCATOR, Vol. 6, (Spring 1982), p. 37-41. English. **DESCR:** *Educational Theory and Practice; Identity.

3293 Hart, Gary. America needs to invest in the right kind of education. LATINO, Vol. 54, no. 2 (March 1983), p. 19-20. English. **DESCR:** *American Defense Education Act (ADEA).

3294 Jensen, Joan M. Women teachers, class and ethnicity: New Mexico 1900-1950. SOUTHWEST ECONOMY AND SOCIETY, Vol. 4, no. 2 (Winter 1978, 1979), p. 3-13. English. **DESCR:** Alternative Education; *Chicanas; History; *New Mexico; Spanish Language; Teaching Profession.

3295 Kjolseth, Rolf. Cultural politics of bilingualism. SOCIETY, Vol. 20, no. 4 (May, June, 1983), p. 40-48. English. **DESCR:** *Bilingualism; Public Policy.

3296 Klein, Carol A. Children's concepts of the earth and the sun: a cross cultural study. SCIENCE EDUCATION, Vol. 66, no. 1 (January 1982), p. 95-107. English. **DESCR:** Anglo Americans; Children; Education; *Science.

Cultural Pluralism (cont.)

3297 Levin, Betsy. An analysis of the federal attempt to regulate bilingual education: protecting civil rights or controlling curriculum? JOURNAL OF LAW AND EDUCATION, Vol. 12, no. 1 (January 1983), p. 29-60. English. DESCR: Affirmative Action Programs; *Bilingual Bicultural Education; Civil Rights; Educational Law and Legislation; Federal Government.

3298 Lindsey, Alfred J. Ethnic pluralism: a misguided approach to schooling. SCHOLAR AND EDUCATOR, Vol. 6, (Spring 1982), p. 42-46. English. DESCR: *Assimilation; Educational Theory and Practice.

3299 Macias, Reynaldo Flores. Book review of: POLITICS AND LANGUAGE: SPANISH AND ENGLISH IN THE UNITED STATES. NABE JOURNAL, Vol. 7, no. 1 (Fall 1982), p. 61-66. English. DESCR: Bilingualism; Book Reviews; Bruckner, D.J.R.; *POLITICS AND LANGUAGE: SPANISH AND ENGLISH IN THE UNITED STATES; Spanish Language.

3300 Montalvo, Frank F.; Lasater, Tonia Tash; and Valdez, Nancy Garza. Training child welfare workers for cultural awareness: the culture simulator technique. CHILD WELFARE, Vol. 61, no. 6 (June 1982), p. 341-352. English. DESCR: *Child Study; Social Work.

3301 Walia, Adorna. Book review of: BILINGUAL EDUCATION TEACHER HANDBOOK: LANGUAGE ISSUES IN MULTICULTURAL SETTINGS. vol. II. BILINGUAL JOURNAL, Vol. 6, no. 1 (Fall 1982), p. 29-30. English. DESCR: Bilingual Bicultural Education; *BILINGUAL EDUCATION TEACHER HANDBOOK: LANGUAGE ISSUES IN MULTICULTURAL SETTINGS, VOL II; Book Reviews; Language Assessment; Montero, Martha.

3302 Walia, Adorna. Book review of: CULTURE AND THE BILINGUAL CLASSROOM: STUDIES IN CLASSROOM ETHNOGRAPHY. BILINGUAL JOURNAL, Vol. 6, no. 4 (Summer 1982), p. 30-31. English. DESCR: Au, Kathryn Hu-Pei; Biculturalism; *Bilingual Bicultural Education; Book Reviews; *CULTURE AND THE BILINGUAL CLASSROOM: STUDIES IN CLASSROOM ETHNOLOGY; Guthrie, Grace Pung; Trueba, Henry T.

Culture

3303 Baca Zinn, Maxine. Chicano family research: conceptual distortions and alternative directions. JOURNAL OF ETHNIC STUDIES, Vol. 7, no. 3 (Fall 1979), p. 59-71. English. DESCR: Cultural Characteristics; *Family; Research Methodology; Social Research; Stereotypes.

3304 Bejar, Rebecca. Mejor en grupo. CALMECAC, Vol. 1, no. 1 (Spring 1980), p. 25-26. English. DESCR: *Mental Health Programs.

3305 Buriel, Raymond; Calzada, Silverio; and Vasquez, Richard. The relationship of traditional Mexican American culture to adjustment and delinquency among three generations of Mexican American male adolescents. HISPANIC JOURNAL OF BEHAVIORAL SCIENCES, Vol. 4, no. 1 (March 1982), p. 41-55. English. DESCR: Juvenile Delinquency.

3306 Bustelo, Manuel A. Ending an era of Hispanic isolation. NUESTRO, Vol. 6, no. 7 (September 1982), p. 60. English. DESCR: *Cabinet Committee on Opportunity for Spanish-Speaking People (CCOSSP); *Family;

*Identity.

3307 De la Carcela, Victor and Martinez, Iris Zavala. An analysis of culturalism in Latino mental health: folk medicine as a case in point. HISPANIC JOURNAL OF BEHAVIORAL SCIENCES, Vol. 5, no. 3 (September 1983), p. 251-274. English. DESCR: *Folk Medicine.

3308 DeOrtega, Manuel R. In the stomach of the shark: echoes of a culture in captivity. SOUTHWEST ECONOMY AND SOCIETY, Vol. 6, no. 1 (Fall 1982), p. 35-48. Bilingual. DESCR: *Assimilation; Poetry; Spanish Language.

3309 Fraser Rothenberg, Irene. Mexican-American views of U.S. relations with Latin America. JOURNAL OF ETHNIC STUDIES, Vol. 6, no. 1 (Spring 1978), p. 62-78. English. DESCR: Chicano Movement; Identity; International Relations; Latin America; Lobbying; Mexico; *Nationalism; Political History and Conditions; Politics.

3310 Garcia, Mario T. Americanization and the Mexican immigrant, 1880-1930. JOURNAL OF ETHNIC STUDIES, Vol. 6, no. 2 (Summer 1978), p. 19-34. English. DESCR: *Acculturation; Cultural Characteristics; Education; Immigrant Labor; Immigration.

3311 Garcia, Reyes. Politics of flesh: ethnicity and political viability. CACR REVIEW, Vol. 1, no. 1 (September 1982), p. 102-130. English. DESCR: Anaya, Rudolfo A.; Aristotle; Ethnic Groups; Identity; Locke, John; Nuclear Armament; Philosophy; *Political Repression; Urban Communities.

3312 Garza, Raymond T. and Lipton, Jack P. Theoretical perspectives on Chicano personality development. HISPANIC JOURNAL OF BEHAVIORAL SCIENCES, Vol. 4, no. 4 (December 1982), p. 407-432. English. DESCR: *Personality.

3313 Garza, Raymond T., et al. Biculturalism, locus of control and leader behavior in ethnically mixed small groups. JOURNAL OF APPLIED SOCIAL PSYCHOLOGY, Vol. 12, no. 3 (May, June, 1982), p. 237-253. English. DESCR: Attitude (Psychological); *Biculturalism; Interpersonal Relations; Leadership; *Locus of Control; Social Psychology.

3314 Glick, R. Dealing, demoralization and addiction: heroin in the Chicago Puerto Rican community. JOURNAL OF PSYCHOACTIVE DRUGS, Vol. 15, no. 4 (October, December, 1983), p. 281-292. English. DESCR: Chicago, IL; *Drug Abuse; Puerto Ricans.

3315 Gomez-Quinones, Juan. On culture. REVISTA CHICANO-RIQUENA, Vol. 10, no. 1-2 (Winter, Spring, 1982), p. 290-308. English. DESCR: *Essays; Identity.

3316 Holscher, Louis M. Tiene arte valor afuera del barrio: the murals of East Los Angeles and Boyle Heights. JOURNAL OF ETHNIC STUDIES, Vol. 4, no. 3 (Fall 1976), p. 42-52. English. DESCR: Art; Boyle Heights; *East Los Angeles, CA; *Mural Art.

3317 Kagan, Spencer and Zahn, G. Lawrence. Cultural differences in individualism? Just artifact. HISPANIC JOURNAL OF BEHAVIORAL SCIENCES, Vol. 5, no. 2 (June 1983), p. 219-232. English. DESCR: Anglo Americans; Blacks; Children; Competition; Social Orientation.

Culture (cont.)

3318 Karno, M. Development of the
Spanish-language version of the National
Institute of Mental Health Diagnostic
Interview Schedule. ARCHIVES OF GENERAL
PSYCHIATRY, Vol. 40, no. 11 (November 1983),
p. 1183-1188. English. DESCR: Languages;
Mental Health; *National Institute of Mental
Health Diagnostic Interview Schedule;
Spanish Language.

3319 Maduro, Renaldo J. Working with Latinos and
the use of dream analysis. JOURNAL OF THE
AMERICAN ACADEMY OF PSYCHOANALYSIS, Vol. 10,
no. 4 (October 1982), p. 609-628. English.
DESCR: Dream Analysis; *Mental Health;
Psychiatry.

3320 Murray, Anne M. and Mishra, Shitala P.
Judgments of item bias in the McCarthy
scales of children's abilities. HISPANIC
JOURNAL OF BEHAVIORAL SCIENCES, Vol. 5, no.
3 (September 1983), p. 325-336. English.
DESCR: *McCarthy Scales for Children's
Abilities (MSCA); *Psychological Testing.

3321 New Salazar building. NUESTRO, Vol. 6, no. 7
(September 1982), p. 9. English. DESCR:
*Art; Education; Latin Americans; Los
Angeles, CA; *Plaza de La Raza, Los Angeles,
CA; Salazar, Ruben.

3322 Ross, Catherine E.; Mirowsky, John; and
Cockerham, William C. Social class, Mexican
culture, and fatalism: their effects on
psychological distress. AMERICAN JOURNAL OF
COMMUNITY PSYCHOLOGY, Vol. 11, no. 4 (August
1983), p. 383-399. English. DESCR:
*Fatalism; Mental Health.

3323 Ruiz, Rene A. and LeVine, Elaine S. Book
review of: PSYCHOLOGY OF THE MEXICAN CULTURE
AND PERSONALITY. JOURNAL OF ETHNIC STUDIES,
Vol. 4, no. 2 (Summer 1976), p. 104-107.
English. DESCR: Book Reviews; *Cultural
Characteristics; *Diaz-Guerrero, Rogelio;
Personality; Psychology; PSYCHOLOGY OF THE
MEXICAN CULTURE AND PERSONALITY.

CULTURE AND THE BILINGUAL CLASSROOM: STUDIES IN CLASSROOM ETHNOLOGY

3324 Walia, Adorna. Book review of: CULTURE AND
THE BILINGUAL CLASSROOM: STUDIES IN
CLASSROOM ETHNOGRAPHY. BILINGUAL JOURNAL,
Vol. 6, no. 4 (Summer 1982), p. 30-31.
English. DESCR: Au, Kathryn Hu-Pei;
Biculturalism; *Bilingual Bicultural
Education; Book Reviews; Cultural Pluralism;
Guthrie, Grace Pung; Trueba, Henry T.

Cumberland County Library, NJ

3325 Naismith, Rachael. Field work: outreach to
migrants. RQ - REFERENCE AND ADULT SERVICES
DIVISION, Vol. 22, no. 1 (Fall 1982), p.
33-35. English. DESCR: Fresno County Public
Library, CA; *Library Services; *Migrant
Labor; Public Libraries.

CUNDE AMORES

3326 Tomayo, Maria. Book review of: CUNDE AMORES.
NUESTRO, Vol. 7, no. 2 (March 1983), p.
57-59. Bilingual. DESCR: Book Reviews;
Morales-Deeny, Carmen A.

Curanderas

3327 Delgado, Melvin. Ethnic and cultural
variations in the care of the aged. Hispanic
elderly and natural support systems: a
special focus on Puerto Ricans. JOURNAL OF
GERIATRIC PSYCHIATRY, Vol. 15, no. 2 (1982),
p. 239-251. English. DESCR: *Ancianos;
Cultural Organizations; Family; Natural
Support Systems; Puerto Ricans; Religion;
Santeros.

3328 Delgado, Melvin. Hispanic natural support
systems: implications for mental health
services. JOURNAL OF PSYCHOSOCIAL NURSING
AND MENTAL HEALTH SERVICES, Vol. 21, no. 4
(April 1983), p. 19-24. English. DESCR:
Family; *Mental Health; Religion; Support
Groups.

3329 Richardson, Lynette. Caring through
understanding, part II: folk medicine in the
Hispanic population. IMPRINT, Vol. 29, no. 2
(April 1982), p. 21, 72-77. English. DESCR:
Brujo; Caida de Mollera; Empacho; *Folk
Medicine; Mal de Ojo; Mal Puesto; Susto.

Curanderismo

3330 Cantu, Hector. The island. NATIONAL HISPANIC
JOURNAL, Vol. 1, no. 3 (Summer, Fall, 1982),
p. 6. English. DESCR: Business Enterprises;
*Castanon, Rudy.

3331 Gonzalez-Swafford, Maria J. and Gutierrez,
Mary Grace. Ethno-medical beliefs and
practices of Mexican-Americans. NURSE
PRACTITIONER, Vol. 8, no. 10 (November,
December, 1983), p. 29-30. English. DESCR:
Ethnic Attitudes; *Folk Medicine.

3332 O'Brien, Mary Elizabeth. Pragmatic
survivalism: behavior patterns affecting
low-level wellness among minority group
members. ANS: ADVANCES IN NURSING SCIENCE,
Vol. 4, no. 3 (April 1982), p. 13-26.
English. DESCR: Ethnic Attitudes;
Immigrants; *Medical Care; *Nursing; Public
Health.

3333 Rodriguez, Josie. Mexican-Americans: factors
influencing health practices. JOURNAL OF
SCHOOL HEALTH, Vol. 53, no. 2 (Fall 1983),
p. 136-139. English. DESCR: Medical Care;
*Public Health.

3334 Trotter, Robert T. Contrasting models of the
healer's role: south Texas case examples.
HISPANIC JOURNAL OF BEHAVIORAL SCIENCES,
Vol. 4, no. 3 (September 1982), p. 315-327.
English. DESCR: Cultural Characteristics;
Medical Care; Public Health.

3335 Zabaleta, Antonio N. The medieval
antecedents of border pseudo-religious folk
beliefs. BORDERLANDS JOURNAL, Vol. 5, no. 2
(Spring 1982), p. 185-200. English. DESCR:
*Religion.

Curb, Mike

3336 Whisler, Kirk. Lt. Governor Mike Curb.
CAMINOS, Vol. 3, no. 5 (May 1982), p. 11-13.
Bilingual. DESCR: *Elected Officials.

Currency

3337 Cantu, Hector. Border business report: the
Rio Grande Valley's economy and Mexico's
lingering peso devaluation effects. NATIONAL
HISPANIC JOURNAL, Vol. 2, no. 1 (Summer
1983), p. 10-13. English. DESCR: Aguirre,
Lionel; Border Region; Cano, Eddie; Coors
Distributing Company, McAllen, TX; Cruz,
Conrado; Cuevas, Betty; Economic
Development; Laredo, TX, Chamber of
Commerce; Mexican American Chamber of
Commerce, Austin, TX; United States-Mexico
Relations.

Currency (cont.)

3338 Deibel, Richard. Business along la frontera. HISPANIC BUSINESS, Vol. 5, no. 1 (January 1983), p. 14-15. English. DESCR: Border Region; Laredo, TX; Mexico.

3339 Foreign trade. HISPANIC BUSINESS, Vol. 5, no. 2 (February 1983), p. 25. English. DESCR: Mexico; Small Business; U.S. Small Business Administration; U.S. Trade Center (Mexico City).

3340 Ogaz, Armando. "It has been very confusing" Q and A with Hector Santillan. CAMINOS, Vol. 3, no. 11 (December 1982), p. 30-31. Bilingual. DESCR: *Santillan Munoz, Hector; *Tijuana, Mexico; *Tourism.

3341 Peso devaluation hurts Rio Grande economy. NUESTRO, Vol. 6, no. 3 (April 1982), p. 46. English. DESCR: Rio Grande Valley, TX.

3342 Some useful advise [sic] on currency regulations in Mexico. CAMINOS, Vol. 3, no. 11 (December 1982), p. 28. English. DESCR: *Mexico; *Tourism.

3343 "Tourism was benefited by the devaluation." Q and A with Hugo Torres Chabert. CAMINOS, Vol. 3, no. 11 (December 1982), p. 32-33,52+. Bilingual. DESCR: *Baja California, Mexico; *Torres Chabert, Hugo; *Tourism.

Curriculum

3344 Balasubramonian, Krishna. Not on test scores alone: the qualitative side to program evaluation. BILINGUAL JOURNAL, Vol. 7, no. 2 (Winter 1983), p. 17-21,40. English. DESCR: *Bilingual Bicultural Education; Educational Tests and Measurements; ELEMENTARY AND SECONDARY EDUCATION ACT; Evaluation (Educational); Proposals.

3345 Baldonado, Lisa. A university program to meet Chicago's bilingual needs. BILINGUAL JOURNAL, Vol. 7, no. 4 (Summer 1983), p. 15-17,28. English. DESCR: *Bilingual Bicultural Education; Chicago, IL; *Teacher Training; Urban Education.

3346 Barreto, Julio. Where the jobs are: tips from Latinos in key occupations. NUESTRO, Vol. 6, no. 7 (September 1982), p. 18-23. English. DESCR: Business; Businesspeople; *Employment.

3347 Beveridge, John. Bi-lingual programs: some doubts and comments. THE CLEARING HOUSE, Vol. 55, no. 5 (January 1982), p. 214-217. English. DESCR: *Bilingual Bicultural Education; Bilingualism.

3348 Brooks, C.K. Verbal giftedness in the minority student: a NEWT questions a SOT. ENGLISH JOURNAL, Vol. 72, (January 1983), p. 18-21. English. DESCR: Cultural Pluralism; *Language Arts; Language Development.

3349 Chesterfield, Ray P.; Moll, Luis C.; and Perez, Ray. A naturalistic approach for evaluation. BILINGUAL JOURNAL, Vol. 6, no. 1 (Fall 1982), p. 23-26. English. DESCR: Bilingual Bicultural Education; Early Childhood Education; *Evaluation (Educational).

3350 Cohen, Bernard H. Parent involvement in program evaluation. BILINGUAL JOURNAL, Vol. 7, no. 2 (Winter 1983), p. 29-34. English. DESCR: *Bilingual Bicultural Education;

Community School Relationships; *Evaluation (Educational); Project PIE (Parents Involvement in Evaluation).

3351 De George, George P. Selecting tests for bilingual program evaluation. BILINGUAL JOURNAL, Vol. 7, no. 2 (Winter 1983), p. 22-28,40. English. DESCR: *Bilingual Bicultural Education; Educational Tests and Measurements; *Evaluation (Educational).

3352 DeMauro, Gerald E. Models and assumptions for bilingual education evaluation. BILINGUAL JOURNAL, Vol. 7, no. 2 (Winter 1983), p. 8-12,40. English. DESCR: *Bilingual Bicultural Education; Educational Tests and Measurements; *Evaluation (Educational); Language Assessment Battery.

3353 Englebrecht, Guillermina. And now Domingo... in school in the United States. CHILDHOOD EDUCATION, Vol. 60, no. 2 (November, December, 1983), p. 90-95. English. DESCR: Education; Mexico; Textbooks; *Undocumented Children.

3354 Flori, Monica. The Hispanic community as a resource for a practical Spanish program. FOREIGN LANGUAGE ANNALS, Vol. 15, no. 3 (May 1982), p. 213-215. English. DESCR: Community School Relationships; Educational Innovations; Language Development; Lewis and Clark College, Portland, OR; *Spanish Language.

3355 France, Pauline. Working with young bilingual children. EARLY CHILD DEVELOPMENT AND CARE, Vol. 10, no. 4 (February 1983), p. 283-292. English. DESCR: Bilingualism; *Early Childhood Education.

3356 Gonzalez, Alex. Classroom cooperation and ethnic balance: Chicanos and equal status. CACR REVIEW, Vol. 1, no. 1 (September 1982), p. 42-71. English. DESCR: Cooperative Education; Intergroup Relations; *Prejudice (Social); Segregation and Desegregation.

3357 Gonzalez, Gilbert G. Educational reform and the Mexican community in Los Angeles. SOUTHWEST ECONOMY AND SOCIETY, Vol. 3, no. 3 (Spring 1978), p. 24-51. English. DESCR: Counseling Services (Educational); *Education; Enrollment; *History; Intelligence Tests; Los Angeles, CA; *Los Angeles City School District; Tracking (Educational); Vocational Education.

3358 Liberty, Paul G. Director's notebook. BILINGUAL JOURNAL, Vol. 6, no. 4 (Summer 1982), p. 1,6. English. DESCR: *Bilingual Bicultural Education; BILINGUAL EDUCATION EVALUATION AND REPORTING SYSTEM; Evaluation (Educational).

3359 Liberty, Paul G., et al. [Evaluation in bilingual education]. BILINGUAL JOURNAL, Vol. 7, no. 2 (Winter 1983), p. 1-40. English. DESCR: *Bilingual Bicultural Education; Educational Administration; ELEMENTARY AND SECONDARY EDUCATION ACT; *Evaluation (Educational).

3360 Miller, Robert. Reading instruction and primary school education - Mexican teachers' viewpoints. READING TEACHER, Vol. 35, no. 8 (May 1982), p. 890-894. English. DESCR: Early Childhood Education; Educational Theory and Practice; Mexico; Teacher Attitudes.

Curriculum (cont.)

3361 A new global approach. NUESTRO, Vol. 7, no. 10 (December 1983), p. 9. English. DESCR: *Bay Area Global Education Program (BAGEP); Education; Educational Innovations; Stanford University, Stanford, CA.

3362 Tikunoff, William J. and Vazquez-Faria, Jose A. Successful instruction for bilingual schooling. PEABODY JOURNAL OF EDUCATION, Vol. 59, no. 4 (July 1982), p. 234-271. English. DESCR: *Bilingual Bicultural Education; Educational Theory and Practice; Teacher Attitudes.

3363 Walia, Adorna. Book review of: DO'S AND DONT'S OF BILINGUAL PROGRAM EVALUATION. BILINGUAL JOURNAL, Vol. 7, no. 2 (Winter 1983), p. 38. English. DESCR: Bilingual Bicultural Education; Book Reviews; *DO'S AND DONT'S OF BILINGUAL PROGRAM EVALUATION; Evaluation (Educational); Rodriguez-Brown, Flora V.

3364 Weiner, Richard E. Teaching the immigrant's child: a model plan for court-ordered bilingual education. JOURNAL OF LAW AND EDUCATION, Vol. 12, no. 1 (January 1983), p. 61-76. English. DESCR: *Bilingual Bicultural Education; Courts (Legal); Educational Law and Legislation; Educational Theory and Practice.

Curriculum Materials

3365 Heathcote, Olivia D. Sex stereotyping in Mexican reading primers. READING TEACHER, Vol. 36, no. 2 (November 1982), p. 158-165. English. DESCR: Comparative Education; Mexico; Primary School Education; *Sex Stereotypes.

3366 Miller, Robert. The Mexican approach to developing bilingual materials and teaching literacy to bilingual students. READING TEACHER, Vol. 35, no. 7 (April 1982), p. 800-804. English. DESCR: *Bilingual Bicultural Education; Freire, Paulo; Mexico.

Cursillo Movement

3367 Day, Mark R. Hispanics 'want more bishops, input in church'. NATIONAL CATHOLIC REPORTER, Vol. 18, (March 12, 1982), p. 1. English. DESCR: *Catholic Church; Clergy; Monterey, CA; Religion.

DaCosta, Jacqueline

3368 Hispanics in Communications, Inc. HISPANIC BUSINESS, Vol. 4, no. 5 (May 1982), p. 12. English. DESCR: Advertising; Hispanics in Communications (HIC); *Mass Media.

Dade County, FL

3369 Llabre, Maria M. and Cuevas, Gilberto. Effects of test language and mathematical skills assessed on the scores of bilingual Hispanic students. JOURNAL FOR RESEARCH IN MATHEMATICS EDUCATION, Vol. 14, no. 4 (November 1983), p. 318-324. English. DESCR: Comprehensive Test of Basic Skills (CTBS); *Educational Tests and Measurements; Mathematics; Stanford Achievement Test.

3370 Whitefield, Mimi. Miami, Caribbean megalopolis. HISPANIC BUSINESS, Vol. 4, no. 3 (March 1982), p. 18-19+. English. DESCR: Business; Foreign Trade; Miami, FL; *Urban Communities.

Dallas Hispanic Chamber of Commerce

3371 The activist Dallas Hispanic chamber of commerce. HISPANIC BUSINESS, Vol. 5, no. 2 (February 1983), p. 16-17. English. DESCR: *Consumers; Dallas, TX.

Dallas, TX

3372 The activist Dallas Hispanic chamber of commerce. HISPANIC BUSINESS, Vol. 5, no. 2 (February 1983), p. 16-17. English. DESCR: *Consumers; Dallas Hispanic Chamber of Commerce.

3373 Chavarria, Jesus. Dallas. HISPANIC BUSINESS, Vol. 5, no. 2 (February 1983), p. 6. English. DESCR: *Consumers.

3374 The Dallas bilingual yellow pages. HISPANIC BUSINESS, Vol. 4, no. 1 (January 1982), p. 11. English. DESCR: *Consumers; Gonzalez, John David; Gonzalez, Michael; *Marketing.

3375 Demographic profile of Hispanics in the Dallas/Fort Worth SMSA. HISPANIC BUSINESS, Vol. 5, no. 2 (February 1983), p. 29-30. English. DESCR: *Consumers; Dallas/Ft. Worth SMSA; *Demography; Fort Worth, Texas; Marketing.

3376 Hartenstein, Roslyn and Balkan, D. Carlos. Packaging the Dallas Hispanic consumer. HISPANIC BUSINESS, Vol. 5, no. 2 (February 1983), p. 18-19+. English. DESCR: *Consumers; Fort Worth, Texas; *Marketing.

3377 Mata, Alberto G. Book review of: MEXICAN AMERICANS IN A DALLAS BARRIO. AZTLAN, Vol. 14, no. 1 (Spring 1983), p. 196-198. English. DESCR: Achor, Shirley; Barrios; Book Reviews; *MEXICAN AMERICANS IN A DALLAS BARRIO; Urban Communities.

3378 Wittenauer, Cheryl. Dallas Hispanic media. HISPANIC BUSINESS, Vol. 5, no. 2 (February 1983), p. 12-13+. English. DESCR: Broadcast Media; *Consumers; English Language; Marketing; Mass Media; Newspapers; Spanish Language.

Dallas/Ft. Worth SMSA

3379 Demographic profile of Hispanics in the Dallas/Fort Worth SMSA. HISPANIC BUSINESS, Vol. 5, no. 2 (February 1983), p. 29-30. English. DESCR: *Consumers; Dallas, TX; *Demography; Fort Worth, Texas; Marketing.

Dance

3380 Alvarez, Amando. There is no way to go but up. LATINO, Vol. 53, no. 6 (October 1982), p. 17+. English.

3381 The culture is alive at the schools of East Los Angeles. CAMINOS, Vol. 3, no. 6 (June 1982), p. 30-31. Bilingual. DESCR: East Los Angeles, CA.

3382 Entertainment = diversion. CAMINOS, Vol. 3, no. 2 (February 1982), p. 40-41. English. DESCR: Awards; CHECKING IT OUT; Club Hogar Latino; Films; Flamenco; Marley, Bob; Montalban, Ricardo; ON GOLDEN POND; *Recreation; Television.

Dance (cont.)

3383 Government review. NUESTRO, Vol. 7, no. 6 (August 1983), p. 56. English. DESCR: Ballet de Puerto Rico; Education; Employment; *Government Funding Sources; Government Services; Housing; Income; National Fair Housing Law; Population Distribution; Urban Development Action Grant (UDAG); Veterans.

3384 Kappel, Mark. A new career direction for Hilda Morales. NUESTRO, Vol. 7, no. 1 (January, February, 1983), p. 24-27. English. DESCR: *Morales, Hilda; Performing Arts.

3385 Leal, Luis. Los voladores: from ritual to game. NEW SCHOLAR, Vol. 8, no. 1-2 (Spring, Fall, 1982), p. 129-142. English. DESCR: Folklore.

3386 Loza, Steven J. Origins, form, and development of the Son Jarocho: Veracruz, Mexico. AZTLAN, Vol. 13, no. 1-2 (Spring, Fall, 1982), p. 257-274. English. DESCR: Folk Songs; Music; *Son Jarocho; Veracruz, Mexico.

3387 Loza, Steven J. The Son Jarocho: the history, style and repertory of a changing Mexican musical tradition. AZTLAN, Vol. 13, no. 1-2 (Spring, Fall, 1982), p. 327-334. English. DESCR: Folk Songs; Music; Sheehy, Daniel E.; *Son Jarocho; Veracruz, Mexico.

3388 Pilar Rioja and the magic of duende. NUESTRO, Vol. 7, no. 6 (August 1983), p. 47-48. English. DESCR: Performing Arts; *Rioja, Pilar.

3389 Quesada-Weiner, Rosemary. Relampago del Cielo. CAMINOS, Vol. 3, no. 6 (June 1982), p. 23-25. English.

3390 Shay, Anthony. Fandangos and bailes: dancing and dance events in early California. SOUTHERN CALIFORNIA QUARTERLY, Vol. 64, no. 2 (Summer 1982), p. 99-113. English. DESCR: Fandango.

Daniel, Cletus E.

3391 De Leon, David. Book review of: BITTER HARVEST: A HISTORY OF CALIFORNIA FARMWORKERS 1870-1941. ANNALS OF THE AMERICAN ACADEMY OF POLITICAL AND SOCIAL SCIENCE, Vol. 462, (July 1982), p. 198-199. English. DESCR: Agricultural Laborers; *BITTER HARVEST: A HISTORY OF CALIFORNIA FARMWORKERS, 1870-1941; Book Reviews; California.

Darling, Todd

3392 Rogg, Eleanor Meyer. Film review of: ANO NUEVO. MIGRATION TODAY, Vol. 10, no. 5 (1982), p. 36. English. DESCR: *ANO NUEVO [film]; Film Reviews; Films; Undocumented Workers.

Darrow, Henry

3393 Reyes, Luis. Henry Darrow: the man behind the actor. CAMINOS, Vol. 4, no. 6 (June 1983), p. 23-25,66. Bilingual. DESCR: Artists; Films; Television.

DATA FORMS FOR EVALUATING BILINGUAL EDUCATION PROGRAMS

3394 Walia, Adorna. Book review of: DATA FORMS FOR EVALUATING BILINGUAL EDUCATION PROGRAM. BILINGUAL JOURNAL, Vol. 7, no. 2 (Winter 1983), p. 38. English. DESCR: Bilingual Bicultural Education; Book Reviews; Cohen, Bernard H.; Educational Administration; Evaluation (Educational).

Davila, Leonard

3395 Chicano music: from country and rock to soul and Mexican rancheras. NATIONAL HISPANIC JOURNAL, Vol. 1, no. 4 (Spring 1983), p. 9. English. DESCR: *Music.

Day Care Centers
USE: Child Care Centers

Day of the Dead
USE: Dia de los Muertos

Days, Drew

3396 Mexican American Legal Defense and Education Fund (MALDEF). MALDEF on the Reagan plan. CAMINOS, Vol. 3, no. 1 (January 1982), p. 23-25. English. DESCR: *Immigration Regulation and Control; Mexican American Legal Defense and Educational Fund (MALDEF).

Dayton, Ohio

3397 Weber, Robert. The special talent of digitron's Nestor Fernandez. HISPANIC BUSINESS, Vol. 5, no. 1 (January 1983), p. 10-11+. English. DESCR: *Business Enterprises; Digitron Tool Company, Inc.; Fernandez, Nestor; Financial Planning.

De Arco, Juana

3398 Alvarez, Amando. Juana de Arco. LATINO, Vol. 54, no. 7 (November 1983), p. 21-22. English. DESCR: Biography; Religion.

De Baca, Fernando E.C.

3399 Hispanic coalition formed on economy. NUESTRO, Vol. 5, no. 8 (November 1981), p. 38. English. DESCR: *Economic Policy; Hispanic Coalition for Economic Recovery.

De Burgos, Julia

3400 Umpierre, Luz Maria. La ansiedad de la influencia en Sandra Maria Esteves y Marjorie Agosin. REVISTA CHICANO-RIQUENA, Vol. 11, no. 3-4 (Fall 1983), p. 139-147. Spanish. DESCR: A JULIA Y A MI; *Agosin, Magi; EL PAIS DIVIDIDO; *Esteves, Sandra Maria; *Literary Criticism; Neruda, Pablo; Parra, Nicanor; Poetry.

De Casas, Celso A.

3401 Klor de Alva, Jorge. Book review of: PELON DROPS OUT. LA PALABRA, Vol. 4, no. 1-2 (Spring, Fall, 1982, 1983), p. 172-174. Spanish. DESCR: Book Reviews; Literature; *PELON DROPS OUT.

De Galvez, Bernardo

3402 New calendar salutes Latino military men. NUESTRO, Vol. 6, no. 4 (May 1982), p. 47. English. DESCR: *Farragut, David G.; *Publishing Industry.

de Garza, Patricia

3403 Maciel, David R. and Bergaila, Christine. Book review of: CHICANOS: THE STORY OF THE MEXICAN AMERICANS. JOURNAL OF ETHNIC STUDIES, Vol. 2, no. 3 (Fall 1974), p. 94-95. English. DESCR: Book Reviews; *CHICANOS: THE STORY OF MEXICAN AMERICANS; History.

DE -DE

De la Colina, Rafael

3404 People. HISPANIC BUSINESS, Vol. 4, no. 6 (June 1982), p. 8. English. DESCR: Aguirre, Pedro; Arellano, Richard; *Biographical Notes; Businesspeople; Cortez, Pete; Hernandez, Sam; Nogales, Luis; Rodriguez, Leslie J.; Roybal, Edward R.

de la Fuente, Emilio

3405 People. HISPANIC BUSINESS, Vol. 5, no. 3 (March 1983), p. 9. English. DESCR: Anaya, Toney; Anguiano, Lupe; Appointed Officials; Avila, Joaquin Guadalupe; Awards; *Biographical Notes; del Olmo, Frank; Godoy, Gustavo; Long, Dennis P.; Martinez, Elias (Lee); Rivera, Joseph, Jr.

De la Garza, Kika

3406 Members of the caucus. NUESTRO, Vol. 6, no. 7 (September 1982), p. 42. English. DESCR: *Congressional Hispanic Caucus; Elected Officials.

3407 Padilla, Steve. Latinos wield political clout in midterm election. NUESTRO, Vol. 6, no. 9 (November 1982), p. 28-30. English. DESCR: *Elected Officials; Garcia, Robert; Gonzales, Henry B.; Lujan, Manuel, Jr.; Martinez, Matthew G. "Marty", Assemblyman; Ortiz, Solomon; *Politics; Richardson, William; Roybal, Edward R.; *Torres, Esteban E.

3408 Texans name highway for Kiko de la Garza. NUESTRO, Vol. 6, no. 1 (January, February, 1982), p. 47. English.

De la Madrid, Miguel

3409 Eliminating corruption. NUESTRO, Vol. 6, no. 10 (December 1982), p. 8. English. DESCR: Government; *Mexico.

3410 Martinez, Vilma. Working with de la Madrid. CAMINOS, Vol. 3, no. 6 (June 1982), p. 10-11,36. Bilingual. DESCR: Elected Officials; Mexico.

3411 Miguel de la Madrid en la prensa norteamericana. INFORME: RELACIONES MEXICO-ESTADOS UNIDOS, Vol. 1, no. 2 (July, December, 1982), p. 176-183. Spanish. DESCR: *Journalism; Lopez Portillo, Jose; LOS ANGELES TIMES; NEW YORK TIMES; Newspapers; WALL STREET JOURNAL; WASHINGTON POST.

3412 Salvatierra, Richard. Tiempos dificiles. LATINO, Vol. 53, no. 5 (September 1982), p. 13,26. Spanish. DESCR: Mexico.

3413 Vidal. The next president of Mexico: Miguel de la Madrid. CAMINOS, Vol. 3, no. 6 (June 1982), p. 9. Bilingual. DESCR: Elected Officials; Mexico.

De la O, Val

3414 Communications/marketing. HISPANIC BUSINESS, Vol. 4, no. 8 (August 1983), p. 22+. English. DESCR: Arredondo, Price; Baseball; Films; Marketing; *Mass Media; Radio; San Antonio CineFestival, TX; Television; Val De La O Show; Valenzuela, Fernando; Wright & Arredondo Associates; Wright, Oscar.

de la Ossa, Ernest G.

3415 People. HISPANIC BUSINESS, Vol. 4, no. 5 (May 1982), p. 8. English. DESCR: Appointed Officials; Asociacion Internacional de Exportadores e Importadores (EXIMA); *Biographical Notes; Businesspeople; California Chicano News Media Association (CCNMA); Foreign Trade; Obledo, Mario; Rodriguez, Elias C.; Rodriguez, Samuel F.; United Way; U.S. Hispanic Chamber of Commerce.

De Landa, Friar Diego

3416 Hartzler, Kaye. Book review of: YUCATAN BEFORE AND AFTER THE CONQUEST. HISPANIC JOURNAL OF BEHAVIORAL SCIENCES, Vol. 4, no. 3 (September 1982), p. 381-383. English. DESCR: Book Reviews; Gates, William; *YUCATAN BEFORE AND AFTER THE CONQUEST.

De Leon, Arnoldo

3417 Acuna, Rodolfo. Book review of: THE TEJANO COMMUNITY 1836-1900. WESTERN HISTORICAL QUARTERLY, Vol. 14, no. 2, p. 207-208. English. DESCR: Book Reviews; Texas; *THE TEJANO COMMUNITY, 1836-1900.

3418 Alvarez, Amando. A clash of cultures. LATINO, Vol. 54, no. 8 (December 1983), p. 18+. English. DESCR: Book Reviews; *THEY CALLED THEM GREASERS: ANGLO ATTITUDES TOWARD MEXICANS IN TEXAS, 1821-1900.

3419 Crisp, James E. Book review of: THE TEJANO COMMUNITY 1836-1900. JOURNAL OF ECONOMIC HISTORY, Vol. 42, no. 4 (December 1982), p. 951-953. English. DESCR: Book Reviews; Texas; *THE TEJANO COMMUNITY, 1836-1900.

3420 Research/development: books. HISPANIC BUSINESS, Vol. 4, no. 7 (July 1982), p. 27. English. DESCR: *Book Reviews; Finance; History; Spiro, Herbert T.; Texas; THE TEJANO COMMUNITY, 1836-1900.

De Leon, Hector

3421 Murray, Melissa and De Leon, Hector. Texas politics: a frank talk about leadership, Austin, state government and attorney Hector de Leon. NATIONAL HISPANIC JOURNAL, Vol. 1, no. 4 (Spring 1983), p. 10-13. English. DESCR: Clements, Bill; *Politics; Texas; White, Mark.

De Los Reyes, Victor

3422 People. HISPANIC BUSINESS, Vol. 5, no. 11 (November 1983), p. 10. English. DESCR: Aragon, Fermin; *Businesspeople; Di Martino, Rita; Garcia, Ruben; Juarez, Chris; Lopez, Leonard; Nogales, Luis G.; Ozuna, Bob; Rico, Jose Hipolito; Tamayo, Roberto; Tapia, Raul R.

De Soto, Rosana

3423 Caldera, Carmela and De Soto, Rosana. Rosana de Soto: breaking the mold (interview). CAMINOS, Vol. 4, no. 8 (September 1983), p. 36-39. English. DESCR: Artists; Films.

De Uriarte, Mercedes Lynn

3424 Patterson fellowship to de Uriarte. LATINA, Vol. 1, no. 2 (February, March, 1983), p. 20. English. DESCR: Alice Patterson Foundation; *Financial Aid.

De Valle-Inclan, Ramon

3425 Espinoza, Herbert O. Lope de Aguirre y santos banderas, la manipulacion del mito. MAIZE, Vol. 4, no. 3-4 (Spring, Summer, 1981), p. 32-43. Spanish. **DESCR:** Literary Criticism; Mythology; *TIRANO BANDERAS.

Deaf

3426 Ferullo, R. J. Objectivity in the assessment of pre-school hearing impaired bilingual-Hispanic children. JOURNAL OF SCHOOL HEALTH, Vol. 53, (Fall 1983), p. 131-135. English. **DESCR:** Bilingualism; Child Study.

Death (Concept)

3427 Berg, Charles. Book review of: CHRONIQUE OF A DEATH FORETOLD. NUESTRO, Vol. 7, no. 4 (May 1983), p. 62. English. **DESCR:** *Book Reviews; CHRONICLE OF A DEATH FORETOLD; *Criminal Acts; Garcia Marquez, Gabriel.

3428 Lattin, Vernon E. La meta critica Chicana. REVISTA CHICANO-RIQUENA, Vol. 10, no. 3 (Summer 1982), p. 53-62. English. **DESCR:** *Arias, Ron; Literary Criticism; *THE ROAD TO TAMAZUNCHALE.

3429 Living traditions of the days of the dead. NUESTRO, Vol. 6, no. 6 (August 1982), p. 41-43. English. **DESCR:** Cultural Customs; *Dia de los Muertos; Mexico.

3430 Salvadorans left in truck to die. NUESTRO, Vol. 6, no. 8 (October 1982), p. 12. English. **DESCR:** Deportation; *Edinburg, TX; Undocumented Workers.

Debt

3431 Salvatierra, Richard. Debtors' row expands in Latin America. NUESTRO, Vol. 6, no. 9 (November 1982), p. 34-35. English. **DESCR:** Banking Industry; Economics; *Latin America.

A DECADE OF CHICANO LITERATURE (1970-1979): CRITICAL ESSAYS AND BIBLIOGRAPHY

3432 Martinez, Julio A. Book review of: A DECADE OF CHICANO LITERATURE (1970-1979)-CRITICAL ESSAYS AND BIBLIOGRAPHY. RQ - REFERENCE AND ADULT SERVICES DIVISION, Vol. 22, no. 1 (Fall 1982), p. 90. English. **DESCR:** Bibliography; Book Reviews; Gonzalez, Raquel Quiroz; Literary Criticism; Literatura Chicanesca; Literature; Trujillo, Robert.

Decorative Arts
USE: Arts and Crafts

DeDeurwaerder, Jose

3433 Crane, Larry. Corporate personality. HISPANIC BUSINESS, Vol. 5, no. 9 (September 1983), p. 25. English. **DESCR:** *Automobile Industry; Corporations.

Del Castillo, Adelaida R.

3434 Baca Zinn, Maxine. Book review of: MEXICAN WOMEN IN THE UNITED STATES: STRUGGLES PAST AND PRESENT. SIGNS: JOURNAL OF WOMEN IN CULTURE AND SOCIETY, Vol. 8, no. 2 (Winter 1982), p. 259-272. English. **DESCR:** Book Reviews; Chicanas; Literature Reviews; *MEXICAN WOMEN IN THE UNITED STATES: STRUGGLES PAST AND PRESENT; Mora, Magdalena; Social Science.

3435 Hartman, Harriet. Book review of: MEXICAN

WOMEN IN THE UNITED STATES: STRUGGLES PAST AND PRESENT. INTERNATIONAL MIGRATION REVIEW, Vol. 16, no. 1 (Spring 1982), p. 228-229. English. **DESCR:** Book Reviews; Chicanas; *MEXICAN WOMEN IN THE UNITED STATES: STRUGGLES PAST AND PRESENT; Mora, Magdalena; Sexism.

Del Junco, Tirso

3436 People. HISPANIC BUSINESS, Vol. 5, no. 4 (April 1983), p. 9. English. **DESCR:** Alvarado, Linda M.; *Biographical Notes; Businesspeople; Castillo, Irenemaree; Castillo, Sylvia; Gutierrez, Jose Roberto; Juarez, Joe; Mata, Bill; Miyares, Marcelino; Montanez Davis, Grace; Montoya, Velma; Pineda, Pat; Siberio, Julio; Thompson, Edith Lopez.

DEL MERO CORAZON

3437 Beaver, Frank E. DEL MERO CORAZON. BILINGUAL REVIEW, Vol. 10, no. 2-3 (May, December, 1983), p. 183. English. **DESCR:** Film Reviews.

3438 Herrera-Sobek, Maria. Film review of: DEL MERO CORAZON (STRAIGHT FROM THE HEART). JOURNAL OF AMERICAN FOLKLORE, Vol. 95, (March 1982), p. 123. English. **DESCR:** Blank, Les; Film Reviews; Gosling, Maureen; Hernandez, Guillermo; Norteno; Strachwitz, Chris.

del Olmo, Frank

3439 People. HISPANIC BUSINESS, Vol. 5, no. 3 (March 1983), p. 9. English. **DESCR:** Anaya, Toney; Anguiano, Lupe; Appointed Officials; Avila, Joaquin Guadalupe; Awards; *Biographical Notes; de la Fuente, Emilio; Godoy, Gustavo; Long, Dennis P.; Martinez, Elias (Lee); Rivera, Joseph, Jr.

3440 People. HISPANIC BUSINESS, Vol. 4, no. 8 (August 1983), p. 7. English. **DESCR:** Aguilar, Richard; *Businesspeople; Cordero-Badillo, Atilano; Infante, E. Anthony; Levitan, Aida T.; Nunez, Luis; Quintanilla, Guadalupe; Rivera, Victor M.

Del Rio, Yolanda

3441 Ogaz, Armando. South of the other border. CAMINOS, Vol. 3, no. 6 (June 1982), p. 26-28,36+. Bilingual. **DESCR:** *Artists; Emmanuel; Nunez, Estella; Singers.

Del Valle, Pedro A.

3442 Weinberger, Caspar W. A heritage of valor - Hispanics in America's defense: remarks... at the recent unveiling of paintings of Hispanic heroes at the Pentagon. NUESTRO, Vol. 7, no. 9 (November 1983), p. 18. English. **DESCR:** Gabaldon, Guy; Lopez, Jose; *Military Service; Paintings; Rivero, Horacio.

Delano, Jack

3443 Puerto Rico: images from the past. NUESTRO, Vol. 7, no. 9 (November 1983), p. 48-53. English. **DESCR:** CONTRASTES [exhibit]; Hostos Community College, New York, NY; *Photography; Puerto Rico.

Delgado v. Bastrop Independent School District of Bastrop Co., TX (1948)

3444 Schlossman, Steven. Self-evident remedy? George I. Sanchez, segregation, and enduring dilemmas in bilingual education. TEACHERS COLLEGE RECORD, Vol. 84, no. 4 (Summer 1983), p. 871-907. English. DESCR: *Bilingual Bicultural Education; Biography; FORGOTTEN PEOPLE; History; *Sanchez, George I.

Democratic Party

3445 Baca Barragan, Polly; Hamner, Richard; and Guerrero, Lena. [Untitled interview with State Senators (Colorado) Polly Baca-Barragan and Lena Guerrero. NATIONAL HISPANIC JOURNAL, Vol. 1, no. 2 (Winter 1982), p. 8-11. English. DESCR: Baca Barragan, Polly; *Carter, Jimmy (President); Chicanas; Elected Officials; Guerrero, Lena; *Political Parties and Organizations.

3446 Conservative Hispanic groups gaining strength attracting suitors. HISPANIC BUSINESS, Vol. 4, no. 2 (February 1982), p. 29. English. DESCR: *Political Parties and Organizations; Politics; Republican Party.

3447 Kirschten, Dick. The Hispanic vote: parties can't gamble that the sleeping giant won't awaken. NATIONAL JOURNAL, Vol. 15, no. 47 (November 19, 1983), p. 2410-2411. English. DESCR: *Hispanic Caucus; Republican Party; Southwest Voter Registration Education Project (SVRP); *Voter Turnout.

3448 Lacayo, Carmela G. A response to conservatism: a Democrat's opinion. CAMINOS, Vol. 3, no. 3 (March 1982), p. 42-43,62. Bilingual. DESCR: *Politics.

3449 Rips, Geoffrey. Mexican Americans jalaron la palanca, Democrats say ole. TEXAS OBSERVOR, Vol. 75, (January 1983), p. 6-7. English. DESCR: Political Representation; Texas; *Voter Turnout.

3450 Whisler, Kirk. Hispanic Democrats. CAMINOS, Vol. 3, no. 4 (April 1982), p. 37. English. DESCR: Politics.

Demography

3451 Alba, Francisco. La fecundidad entre los Mexicano-Norteamericanos en relacion a los cambiantes patrones reproductivos en Mexico y los Estados Unidos. DEMOGRAFIA Y ECONOMIA, Vol. 16, no. 2 (1982), p. 236-249. Spanish. DESCR: *Fertility; *Mexico; Population Trends; Social Research.

3452 American as apple pie and tortillas. AMERICAN DEMOGRAPHICS, Vol. 4, (October 1982), p. 9. English. DESCR: Population.

3453 Andersen, Kurt. The new Ellis Island. TIME, Vol. 121, no. 24 (June 13, 1983), p. 18-25. English. DESCR: *Ethnic Groups; Los Angeles, CA.

3454 Cantu, Hector. Hispanic numbers rising. NATIONAL HISPANIC JOURNAL, Vol. 1, no. 3 (Summer, Fall, 1982), p. 7. English. DESCR: Austin, TX; Census; Population; *Population Trends.

3455 Corwin, Arthur F. The numbers game: estimates of illegal aliens in the United States, 1970-1981. LAW AND CONTEMPORARY PROBLEMS, Vol. 45, no. 2 (Spring 1982), p. 223-297. English. DESCR: Bustamante, Jorge A.; Centro Nacional de Informacion y Estadistica del Trabajo (CENINET); Federation for American Immigration Reform (FAIR); Mexican American Legal Defense and Educational Fund (MALDEF); *Select Commission on Immigration and Refugee Policy; Simpson-Mazzoli Bill; *Statistics; *Undocumented Workers.

3456 Demographic profile of Hispanics in the Dallas/Fort Worth SMSA. HISPANIC BUSINESS, Vol. 5, no. 2 (February 1983), p. 29-30. English. DESCR: *Consumers; Dallas, TX; Dallas/Ft. Worth SMSA; Fort Worth, Texas; Marketing.

3457 Estrada, Leobardo F. [Demographic characteristics of Latinos]. CHICANO LAW REVIEW, Vol. 6, (1983), p. 9-16. English. DESCR: Internal Migration; LATINOS IN THE LAW [symposium], UCLA, 1982; Los Angeles County, CA; Migration; Migration Patterns; Spanish Language.

3458 Garcia, Philip and Maldonado, Lionel A. America's Mexicans: a plea for specificity. SOCIAL SCIENCE JOURNAL, Vol. 19, no. 2 (April 1982), p. 9-24. English. DESCR: Census; Ethnic Groups; Statistics.

3459 Gottlieb, Karen. Genetic demography of Denver, Colorado: Spanish surname as a market of Mexican ancestry. HUMAN BIOLOGY, Vol. 55, no. 2 (May 1983), p. 227-234. English. DESCR: Denver, CO; Personal Names; *Population Genetics; Research Methodology; Sociology.

3460 Gottlieb, Karen. Spanish surname as a market of Mexican heritage in Denver, Colorado. AMERICAN JOURNAL OF PHYSICAL ANTHROPOLOGY, Vol. 57, no. 2 (February 1982), p. 194. English. DESCR: Population; *Spanish Surname.

3461 Grimond, John. The reconquista begins. LOS ANGELES, Vol. 27, (May 1982), p. 190-195. English. DESCR: *Los Angeles, CA; United Neighborhoods Organization (UNO).

3462 Hedderson, John and Daudistel, Howard C. Infant mortality of the Spanish surname population. SOCIAL SCIENCE JOURNAL, Vol. 19, no. 4 (October 1982), p. 67-78. English. DESCR: El Paso County, TX; *Infant Mortality; Medical Care; Statistics; Vital Statistics.

3463 Hornbeck, David. Book review of: STUDIES IN SPANISH-AMERICAN POPULATION HISTORY. PROFESSIONAL GEOGRAPHER, Vol. 34, no. 4 (1982), p. 480. English. DESCR: Book Reviews; Latin America; Robinson, David J.; *STUDIES IN SPANISH-AMERICAN POPULATION HISTORY.

3464 Kranau, Edgar J.; Green, Vicki; and Valencia-Weber, Gloria. Acculturation and the Hispanic woman: attitudes toward women, sex-role attribution, sex-role behavior, and demographics. HISPANIC JOURNAL OF BEHAVIORAL SCIENCES, Vol. 4, no. 1 (March 1982), p. 21-40. English. DESCR: Acculturation; *Chicanas; Sex Roles.

3465 Latinos in the law: meeting the challenge [a symposium]. CHICANO LAW REVIEW, Vol. 6, (1983), p. 1-121. English. DESCR: *Criminal Justice System; Legal Profession; Los Angeles Police Department; Love, Eulia; Police Brutality; Political Representation; Reapportionment; Settles, Ron.

Demography (cont.)

3466 Total persons and Spanish origin persons by type of Spanish origin. AMERICAN DEMOGRAPHICS, Vol. 4, (September 1982), p. 3. English.

3467 Upscale Hispanic consumer demographics in the top 15 SMSAS. HISPANIC BUSINESS, Vol. 4, no. 12 (December 1982), p. 37-38. English. DESCR: *Consumers; Income; Population.

Demonstrations

3468 Latinos evident in 1983 march. NUESTRO, Vol. 7, no. 7 (September 1983), p. 11-12. English. DESCR: Bonilla, Tony; Cuban-American Coordinating Committee; IMAGE, Washington, DC; Jackson, Jesse; League of United Latin American Citizens (LULAC); National Congress for Puerto Rican Rights (NCPRR); National Council of La Raza (NCLR); Velasquez, Baldemar; Zamora, Reuben.

3469 Regional report, Latin America: marchers oppose Reagan policies. NUESTRO, Vol. 7, no. 4 (May 1983), p. 11. English. DESCR: Central America; International Relations; *Latin America; *Reagan, Ronald; Stanford University, Stanford, CA.

Demy, Caroline

3470 Communications/marketing. HISPANIC BUSINESS, Vol. 4, no. 7 (July 1982), p. 16. English. DESCR: Awards; *Biographical Notes; Buena Vista Cablevision, Inc.; *Marketing; Sosa de Garcia, Manuel.

Denny's Inc.

3471 Business notes. HISPANIC BUSINESS, Vol. 5, no. 12 (December 1983), p. 35. English. DESCR: Anheuser-Busch, Inc.; *Business Enterprises; Des Moines, IA; El Pollo Loco; Food Industry; Local Government; Martinez, Vilma Socorro; National Association of Latino Elected Officials (NALEO); Ochoa, Juan Pancho.

Dentistry

3472 Gum disease: a problem of epidemic proportions. NUESTRO, Vol. 7, no. 9 (November 1983), p. 39-41. English. DESCR: Medical Care.

3473 Medina, Antonio S. Adolescent health in Alameda county. JOURNAL OF ADOLESCENT HEALTH CARE, Vol. 2, no. 3 (March 1982), p. 175-182. English. DESCR: Alameda County, CA; Drug Abuse; Medical Care; Psychology; Youth.

Denver, CO

3474 Gottlieb, Karen. Genetic demography of Denver, Colorado: Spanish surname as a market of Mexican ancestry. HUMAN BIOLOGY, Vol. 55, no. 2 (May 1983), p. 227-234. English. DESCR: Demography; Personal Names; *Population Genetics; Research Methodology; Sociology.

3475 Hispanic power arrives at the ballot box. BUSINESS WEEK, no. 27 (July 4, 1983), p. 32. English. DESCR: *Pena, Federico; *Voter Turnout.

3476 Martinez, Chip. Federico Pena: Denver's first Hispanic mayor. NUESTRO, Vol. 7, no. 6 (August 1983), p. 14-20. English. DESCR: Elections; Local Government; *Pena, Federico; Voter Turnout.

3477 Pena takes Denver. HISPANIC BUSINESS, Vol. 5, no. 8 (August 1983), p. 13+. English. DESCR: *Biography; Elected Officials; Pena, Federico.

3478 Racial problems at Denver school. NUESTRO, Vol. 6, no. 9 (November 1982), p. 11-12. English. DESCR: *Racism.

3479 Young Latino goes to prison. NUESTRO, Vol. 6, no. 8 (October 1982), p. 11. English. DESCR: *Juvenile Delinquency; *Mental Health; Prisoners; Prisons.

Deportation

3480 Aragon, Ellen Weis. The factory raid: an unconstitutional act. SOUTHERN CALIFORNIA LAW REVIEW, Vol. 56, no. 2 (January 1983), p. 605-645. English. DESCR: Blackie's House of Beef v. Castillo; Immigration and Naturalization Service (INS); International Ladies Garment Workers Union (ILGWU) v. Sureck; Racism; Search and Seizure; *Undocumented Workers.

3481 Ashman, Allan. What's new in the law: immigration ... detained aliens. AMERICAN BAR ASSOCIATION JOURNAL, Vol. 68, (June 1982), p. 745. English. DESCR: Arias v. Rogers; Immigration Law; *Undocumented Workers.

3482 Cardoso, Lawrence Anthony. Book review of: LOS MEXICANOS QUE DEVOLVIO LA CRISIS, 1929-1932. JOURNAL OF ETHNIC STUDIES, Vol. 5, no. 1 (Spring 1977), p. 120-122. Spanish. DESCR: Book Reviews; Carreras de Velasco, Mercedes; Immigrant Labor; Immigration; Immigration Regulation and Control; *LOS MEXICANOS QUE DEVOLVIO LA CRISIS 1929-1932; Mexico; Social History and Conditions.

3483 Cardoso, Lawrence Anthony. Book review of: UNWANTED MEXICAN AMERICANS IN THE GREAT DEPRESSION: REPATRIATION PRESSURES, 1929-1939. JOURNAL OF ETHNIC STUDIES, Vol. 5, no. 1 (Spring 1977), p. 120-122. English. DESCR: Book Reviews; Hoffman, Abraham; Immigrant Labor; Immigration; Immigration Regulation and Control; Mexico; Social History and Conditions; *UNWANTED MEXICAN AMERICANS IN THE GREAT DEPRESSION.

3484 Fernandez, Enrique and Valle, Eunice. Latin drop: retail sales decrease attributed to sweeps by Dept. of Immigration raids. BILLBOARD, Vol. 94, no. 25 (June 26, 1982), p. 3. English. DESCR: Immigration Regulation and Control; Marketing; *Music.

3485 Helbush, Terry. INS violations of its own regulations: relief for the aliens. GOLDEN GATE UNIVERSITY LAW REVIEW, Vol. 12, (Spring 1982), p. 217-225. English. DESCR: *Immigration Law; Tejeda-Mata v. INS; Undocumented Workers; U.S. v. Calderon-Medina.

3486 Hopson, Susan B. Immigration: indefinite detention of excluded aliens held illegal. TEXAS INTERNATIONAL LAW JOURNAL, Vol. 17, (Winter 1982), p. 101-110. English. DESCR: Civil Rights; *Detention of Persons; Immigration; International Law; Rodriguez-Fernandez v. Wilkinson; Shaughnessy v. Mezei; *Undocumented Workers.

Deportation (cont.)

3487 Immigration and nationality symposium. SAN DIEGO LAW REVIEW, Vol. 20, no. 1 (December 1982, 1983), p. 1-231. English. **DESCR:** Akbarian v. INS; Employment; Immigration and Nationality Act (INA); *Immigration Regulation and Control; Miranda v. INS; Simpson-Mazzoli Bill; Undocumented Workers.

3488 Joe, Harry J. Judicial recommendation against deportation. TEXAS BAR JOURNAL, Vol. 45, no. 6 (June 1982), p. 712-716. English. **DESCR:** Legal Aid; Undocumented Workers.

3489 Parr, Julie A. Immigration law and the excluded alien: potential for human rights violations. UNIVERSITY OF CALIFORNIA DAVIS LAW REVIEW, Vol. 15, no. 3 (Spring 1982), p. 723-740. English. **DESCR:** *Civil Rights; *Detention of Persons; Internal Security Act of 1950; Rodriguez-Fernandez v. Wilkinson; *Undocumented Workers.

3490 Salvadorans left in truck to die. NUESTRO, Vol. 6, no. 8 (October 1982), p. 12. English. **DESCR:** Death (Concept); *Edinburg, TX; Undocumented Workers.

3491 Simon, Daniel T. Mexican repatriation in East Chicago, Indiana. JOURNAL OF ETHNIC STUDIES, Vol. 2, no. 2 (Summer 1974), p. 11-23. English. **DESCR:** *East Chicago, IN; History; Immigrant Labor; Immigration; Immigration Regulation and Control; Inland Steel Company; Mexico; Social History and Conditions.

3492 [Summary of: Hollander, defending the criminal alien in New Mexico: tactics and strategy to avoid deportation, 9 N.M.L. rev. 45 (1979)]. CHICANO LAW REVIEW, Vol. 5, (1982), p. 79-80. English. **DESCR:** Criminal Acts; *Legal Representation; Undocumented Workers.

3493 Young, Rowland L. Witnesses ... deportation. AMERICAN BAR ASSOCIATION JOURNAL, Vol. 68, (November 1982), p. 1493. English. **DESCR:** Jury Trials; Undocumented Workers; U.S. v. Valenzuela-Bernal.

Depression Scale

3494 Dolgin, Daniel L., et al. Quality of life and psychological well-being in a bicultural Latino community. HISPANIC JOURNAL OF BEHAVIORAL SCIENCES, Vol. 4, no. 4 (December 1982), p. 433-450. English. **DESCR:** Acculturation; *Attitude (Psychological); *Global Acculturation Scale; Index of Psychological Adjustment; Psychology; Quality of Life Scale.

Des Moines, IA

3495 Business notes. HISPANIC BUSINESS, Vol. 5, no. 12 (December 1983), p. 35. English. **DESCR:** Anheuser-Busch, Inc.; *Business Enterprises; Denny's Inc.; El Pollo Loco; Food Industry; Local Government; Martinez, Vilma Socorro; National Association of Latino Elected Officials (NALEO); Ochoa, Juan Pancho.

Desegregation
USE: Segregation and Desegregation

DESERT IMMIGRANTS: THE MEXICANS OF EL PASO 1880-1920

3496 Cardoso, Lawrence Anthony. Book review of: DESERT IMMIGRANTS: THE MEXICANS OF EL PASO 1880-1920. WESTERN HISTORICAL QUARTERLY, Vol. 13, (April 1982), p. 197. English. **DESCR:** Book Reviews; Garcia, Mario T.

3497 Cortes, Carlos E. Book review of: DESERT IMMIGRANTS: THE MEXICANS OF EL PASO 1880-1920. PACIFIC HISTORICAL REVIEW, Vol. 52, no. 1 (February 1983), p. 119-120. English. **DESCR:** Book Reviews; Garcia, Mario T.

3498 Corwin, Arthur F. Book review of: DESERT IMMIGRANTS: THE MEXICANS OF EL PASO 1880-1920. HISTORIAN, Vol. 45, no. 2 (February 1983), p. 279-280. English. **DESCR:** Book Reviews; Garcia, Mario T.

3499 Knight, Alan. Book review of: THE GREAT REBELLION: MEXICO 1905-1924 and DESERT IMMIGRANTS: THE MEXICANS OF EL PASO 1880-1920. HISTORY: THE JOURNAL OF THE HISTORICAL ASSOCIATION [London], Vol. 67, (October 1982), p. 450-451. English. **DESCR:** Book Reviews; Garcia, Mario T.; Ruiz, Ramon Eduardo; *THE GREAT REBELLION: MEXICO 1905-1924.

3500 Lotchin, Roger W. New Chicano history: an urban history perspective. HISTORY TEACHER, Vol. 16, no. 2 (February 1983), p. 229-247. English. **DESCR:** Camarillo, Alberto; CHICANOS IN A CHANGING SOCIETY; Garcia, Mario T.; Griswold del Castillo, Ricardo; *Historiography; History; Social History and Conditions; THE LOS ANGELES BARRIO 1850-1890: A SOCIAL HISTORY; Urban Communities.

3501 Martinez, Oscar J. Book review of: DESERT IMMIGRANTS: THE MEXICANS OF EL PASO 1880-1920. HISPANIC AMERICAN HISTORICAL REVIEW, Vol. 62, no. 2 (May 1982), p. 289-291. English. **DESCR:** Book Reviews; El Paso, TX; Garcia, Mario T.; Immigration.

3502 Reisler, Mark. Book review of: DESERT IMMIGRANTS: THE MEXICANS OF EL PASO 1880-1920. AMERICAN HISTORICAL REVIEW, Vol. 87, no. 1 (February 1982), p. 271-272. English. **DESCR:** Book Reviews; El Paso, TX; Garcia, Mario T.; History; Immigration.

3503 Rosales, Francisco Arturo. Book review of: DESERT IMMIGRANTS: THE MEXICANS OF EL PASO 1880-1920. ARIZONA AND THE WEST, Vol. 24, no. 1 (Spring 1982), p. 79-80. English. **DESCR:** Book Reviews; Garcia, Mario T.; Immigrants; Texas.

3504 Sunseri, Alvin R. Book review of: DESERT IMMIGRANTS: THE MEXICANS OF EL PASO 1880-1920. JOURNAL OF THE WEST, Vol. 21, no. 2 (April 1982), p. 111. English. **DESCR:** Book Reviews; Garcia, Mario T.; Immigration.

3505 Vigil, Ralph H. Book review of: DESERT IMMIGRANTS: THE MEXICANS OF EL PASO 1880-1920. INTERNATIONAL MIGRATION REVIEW, Vol. 16, no. 1 (Spring 1982), p. 223-224. English. **DESCR:** Book Reviews; El Paso, TX; Garcia, Mario T.; History; Immigrants.

3506 Weber, David J. and Lotchin, Roger W. The new Chicano history: two perspectives. HISTORY TEACHER, Vol. 16, no. 2 (February 1983), p. 219-247. English. **DESCR:** Camarillo, Alberto; *CHICANOS IN A CHANGING SOCIETY; Garcia, Mario T.; Griswold del Castillo, Ricardo; *Historiography; History; Social History and Conditions; *THE LOS ANGELES BARRIO 1850-1890: A SOCIAL HISTORY; *Urban Communities.

DESERT IMMIGRANTS: THE MEXICANS OF EL PASO 1880-1920 (cont.)

3507 Weber, David J. The new Chicano urban history. HISTORY TEACHER, Vol. 16, no. 2 (February 1983), p. 223-229. English. **DESCR:** Camarillo, Alberto; *CHICANOS IN A CHANGING SOCIETY; Garcia, Mario T.; Griswold del Castillo, Ricardo; *Historiography; History; Social History and Conditions; *THE LOS ANGELES BARRIO 1850-1890: A SOCIAL HISTORY; Urban Communities.

Design

3508 LULAC national scholarship fund. LATINO, Vol. 54, no. 2 (March 1983), p. 22. English. **DESCR:** *League of United Latin American Citizens (LULAC).

D'Esopo, Jan

3509 Jan D'Esopo: a talented artist. LATINO, Vol. 54, no. 7 (November 1983), p. 23. English. **DESCR:** Artists.

EL DESQUITE

3510 Beverley, John. The revolution betrayed: a note on Mariano Azuela's estridentista trilogy. MAIZE, Vol. 4, no. 1-2 (Fall, Winter, 1980, 1981), p. 27-39. English. **DESCR:** *Azuela, Mariano; LA LUCIERNAGA; LA MALHORA; Literary Criticism.

Detention of Persons

3511 Hopson, Susan B. Immigration: indefinite detention of excluded aliens held illegal. TEXAS INTERNATIONAL LAW JOURNAL, Vol. 17, (Winter 1982), p. 101-110. English. **DESCR:** Civil Rights; Deportation; Immigration; International Law; Rodriguez-Fernandez v. Wilkinson; Shaughnessy v. Mezei; *Undocumented Workers.

3512 Parr, Julie A. Immigration law and the excluded alien: potential for human rights violations. UNIVERSITY OF CALIFORNIA DAVIS LAW REVIEW, Vol. 15, no. 3 (Spring 1982), p. 723-740. English. **DESCR:** *Civil Rights; Deportation; Internal Security Act of 1950; Rodriguez-Fernandez v. Wilkinson; *Undocumented Workers.

Detroit, MI

3513 Sepulveda, Ciro. Detroit's great mural battle. CAMINOS, Vol. 4, no. 9 (October 1983), p. 38-41. Bilingual. **DESCR:** *Mural Art.

Deukmejian, George

3514 Whisler, Kirk. Attorney General George Deukmejian. CAMINOS, Vol. 3, no. 5 (May 1982), p. 14-16. Bilingual. **DESCR:** *Elected Officials.

DEVELOPING LIBRARY AND INFORMATION SERVICES FOR AMERICANS OF HISPANIC ORIGIN

3515 Perry, Charles E. Book review of: DEVELOPING LIBRARY AND INFORMATION SERVICES FOR AMERICANS OF HISPANIC ORIGIN. JOURNAL OF ACADEMIC LIBRARIANSHIP, Vol. 8, no. 1 (March 1982), p. 38. English. **DESCR:** Academic Libraries; Book Reviews; Haro, Robert P.; Library Services.

Devereux Elementary School Behavior Rating Scale (DESBRS)

3516 Elliott, Stephen N. and Argulewicz, Ed N.

The influence of student ethnicity on teachers' behavior ratings of normal and learning disabled children. HISPANIC JOURNAL OF BEHAVIORAL SCIENCES, Vol. 5, no. 3 (September 1983), p. 337-345. English. **DESCR:** *Ethnic Attitudes; Teacher Attitudes.

Devereux, George

3517 Delgado, Melvin. Book review of: BASIC PROBLEMS OF ETHNOPSYCHIATRY. HISPANIC JOURNAL OF BEHAVIORAL SCIENCES, Vol. 4, no. 3 (September 1982), p. 380. English. **DESCR:** *BASIC PROBLEMS OF ETHNOPSYCHIATRY; Book Reviews.

Devil's Canyon, Deer Canyon, CA

3518 Foster, Douglas. The desperate migrants of Devil's Canyon. THE PROGRESSIVE, Vol. 46, no. 11 (November 1982), p. 44-49. English. **DESCR:** *Agricultural Laborers; California; Growers; Labor Camps; San Diego, CA; Undocumented Workers.

Di Martino, Rita

3519 People. HISPANIC BUSINESS, Vol. 5, no. 11 (November 1983), p. 10. English. **DESCR:** Aragon, Fermin; *Businesspeople; De Los Reyes, Victor; Garcia, Ruben; Juarez, Chris; Lopez, Leonard; Nogales, Luis G.; Ozuna, Bob; Rico, Jose Hipolito; Tamayo, Roberto; Tapia, Raul R.

Dia de los Muertos

3520 Living traditions of the days of the dead. NUESTRO, Vol. 6, no. 6 (August 1982), p. 41-43. English. **DESCR:** Cultural Customs; Death (Concept); Mexico.

3521 Miccaihuitl. CALMECAC, Vol. 1, (Summer 1980), p. 34-37. Bilingual. **DESCR:** *Cultural Customs; Self-Help Graphics, Los Angeles, CA.

Diabetes

3522 Hanis, Craig L., et al. Diabetes among Mexican Americans in Starr County, Texas. AMERICAN JOURNAL OF EPIDEMIOLOGY, Vol. 118, no. 5 (November 1983), p. 659-672. English. **DESCR:** Starr County, TX.

3523 Que pasa? NUESTRO, Vol. 7, no. 6 (August 1983), p. 9. English. **DESCR:** Boy Scouts of America; *Court System; Criminal Justice System; Education; Judicial Review; Petersilia, Joan; PREPARED FOR TODAY; RACIAL DISPARITIES IN THE CRIMINAL JUSTICE SYSTEM; Reagan, Ronald.

3524 Stern, Michael P., et al. Does obesity explain excess prevalence of diabetes among Mexican Americans? Results of the San Antonio Heart Study. DIABETOLOGIA, Vol. 24, no. 4 (April 1983), p. 272-277. English. **DESCR:** Medical Research; Medicine; Obesity; Public Health; *San Antonio Heart Study.

3525 Zeidler, Adina S. Histocompatibility antigens and immunoglobulin G insulin antibodies in Mexican-American insulin-dependent diabetic patients. JOURNAL OF CLINICAL ENDOCRINOLOGY AND METABOLISM, Vol. 54, no. 3 (March 1982), p. 569-573. English. **DESCR:** Medical Research; Medicine.

Diabetes (cont.)

3526 Zeidler, Adina S. Pancreatic islet cell and
     thyroid antibodies, and islet cell function
     in diabetic patients of Mexico-American
     origin. JOURNAL OF CLINICAL ENDOCRINOLOGY
     AND METABOLISM, Vol. 54, no. 5 (May 1982),
     p. 949-954. English. **DESCR:** Medical
     Research; Medicine.

EL DIABLO EN TEXAS

3527 Alarcon, Justo S. Resena de EL DIABLO EN
     TEXAS. MAIZE, Vol. 3, no. 1-2 (Fall, Winter,
     1979, 1980), p. 6-8. Spanish. **DESCR:** Book
     Reviews; Brito, Aristeo.

Diagnostic Interview Schedule (DIS)

3528 Hough, Richard. The Los Angeles
     Epidemiologic Catchment Area research
     program and the epidemiology of psychiatric
     disorders among Mexican Americans. JOURNAL
     OF OPERATIONAL PSYCHIATRY, Vol. 14, no. 1
     (1983), p. 42-51. English. **DESCR:**
     Acculturation; El Centro Community Health
     Care Center; Los Angeles, CA; *Los Angeles
     Epidemiologic Catchment Area Research
     Program (LAECA); *Mental Health.

DIARIO DE LAS AMERICAS

3529 Communications/marketing. HISPANIC BUSINESS,
     Vol. 5, no. 9 (September 1983), p. 26.
     English. **DESCR:** Aguirre, Horacio; Business
     Enterprises; Consumers; La Ventana;
     *Marketing; Miller Brewing Company; SURVEY
     OF PROMOTIONAL PRACTICES.

DIARIO LA PRENSA [newspaper], New York, NY

3530 Uehling, Mark D. Rivalry in New York: a
     profile of two newspapers. NUESTRO, Vol. 7,
     no. 7 (September 1983), p. 20-21. English.
     DESCR: Bustelo, Manuel A.; Espinal, Antonio;
     Gannett Co., Inc.; Journalism; New York, NY;
     *Newspapers; NOTICIAS DEL MUNDO; Patino,
     Luis; Unification Church.

Dietetics
     USE: Nutrition

Diaz, Elisa

3531 People on the move. CAMINOS, Vol. 2, no. 6
     (October 1981), p. 7. English. **DESCR:**
     Alvarado, Angel S.; Arreola, Rafael;
     *Biographical Notes; Diaz, Elvira A.;
     Garcia, Jose Joel; Garza, Florentino; Icaza,
     Ricardo F.; Lacayo, Henry; Martinez, Lydia
     R.; Munoz, Victor M.; Salinas, Vicente;
     Sanchez, Manuel; Zuniga, Henry.

Diaz, Elvira A.

3532 People on the move. CAMINOS, Vol. 2, no. 6
     (October 1981), p. 7. English. **DESCR:**
     Alvarado, Angel S.; Arreola, Rafael;
     *Biographical Notes; Diaz, Elisa; Garcia,
     Jose Joel; Garza, Florentino; Icaza, Ricardo
     F.; Lacayo, Henry; Martinez, Lydia R.;
     Munoz, Victor M.; Salinas, Vicente; Sanchez,
     Manuel; Zuniga, Henry.

Diaz, Jose

3533 People. HISPANIC BUSINESS, Vol. 4, no. 11
     (November 1982), p. 7. English. **DESCR:**
     Biographical Notes; *Businesspeople;
     Garcia-Pedrosa, Jose R.; Garza, Jose;
     Herrera, Heriberto; Mercado, Anthony; Rios,
     John F.; Solano, Faustina V.; Solis, Frank.

Diaz, Porfirio

3534 Ruiz, Ramon Eduardo. Book review of:
     DISORDER AND PROGRESS: BANDITS, POLICE, AND
     MEXICAN DEVELOPMENT. ARIZONA AND THE WEST,
     Vol. 24, no. 1 (Spring 1982), p. 75-76.
     English. **DESCR:** Bandidos; Book Reviews;
     *DISORDER AND PROGRESS: BANDITS, POLICE AND
     MEXICAN DEVELOPMENT; Vanderwood, Paul J.

Diaz, William

3535 Padilla, Steve. Choosing a career. NUESTRO,
     Vol. 7, no. 1 (January, February, 1983), p.
     13-19+. English. **DESCR:** Alvarado, Raul, Jr.;
     *Careers; Computers; Engineering as a
     Profession; Esparza, Alma; Flores,
     Francisco; Garcia, Linda; Medical Care;
     Soto, John; Yanez, Ricardo.

Diaz-Albertini, Luis

3536 Balkan, D. Carlos. The advent of
     Uniworld/Hispanic: an interview. HISPANIC
     BUSINESS, Vol. 5, no. 3 (March 1983), p.
     10-11+. English. **DESCR:** *Advertising
     Agencies; Blacks; Consumers; Lewis, Byron;
     *Marketing; Spanish Advertising and
     Marketing Services (S.A.M.S.); Uniworld
     Group, Inc.; UniWorld Hispanic.

3537 Communications/marketing. HISPANIC BUSINESS,
     Vol. 4, no. 11 (November 1982), p. 18.
     English. **DESCR:** California Chicano News
     Media Association (CCNMA); Domecq Importers,
     Inc.; *Marketing; National Hispanic Media
     Conference, San Diego, CA, December 2-5,
     1982; Pacific Telephone; Television.

3538 Communications/marketing. HISPANIC BUSINESS,
     Vol. 4, no. 12 (December 1982), p. 11.
     English. **DESCR:** Advertising; Advertising
     Agencies; *Marketing; UniWorld Hispanic.

3539 People. HISPANIC BUSINESS, Vol. 4, no. 9
     (September 1982), p. 7. English. **DESCR:**
     Advertising Agencies; Appointed Officials;
     Awards; *Biographical Notes; Dimartino,
     Rita; Garza, Jesus; Hispanic Women in Higher
     Education (HWHE); League of United Latin
     American Citizens (LULAC); Ortega, Ray;
     Ortiz, George; Romero, Carlos J.; Sepulveda,
     Luis.

Diaz-Cobo, Christine

3540 Gente. NUESTRO, Vol. 7, no. 7 (September
     1983), p. 61. English. **DESCR:** Americas
     Award; Chavez, Raul; *Chicanas; Mexico;
     Ortega, Katherine D.; Performing Arts;
     Planas, Vilma; Ravard, Rafael Alonzo;
     Venezuela.

Diaz-Guerrero, Rogelio

3541 Ruiz, Rene A. and LeVine, Elaine S. Book
     review of: PSYCHOLOGY OF THE MEXICAN CULTURE
     AND PERSONALITY. JOURNAL OF ETHNIC STUDIES,
     Vol. 4, no. 2 (Summer 1976), p. 104-107.
     English. **DESCR:** Book Reviews; *Cultural
     Characteristics; Culture; Personality;
     Psychology; PSYCHOLOGY OF THE MEXICAN
     CULTURE AND PERSONALITY.

Dichos

3542 Arora, Shirley L. A critical bibliography of
     Mexican American proverbs. AZTLAN, Vol. 13,
     no. 1-2 (Spring, Fall, 1982), p. 71-80.
     English. **DESCR:** *Bibliography; Folklore.

Dichos (cont.)

3543 Arora, Shirley L. Proverbs in Mexican American tradition. AZTLAN, Vol. 13, no. 1-2 (Spring, Fall, 1982), p. 43-69. English. **DESCR**: Identity; Spanish Language; Surveys.

3544 Paredes, Americo. Folklore, lo mexicano, and proverbs. AZTLAN, Vol. 13, no. 1-2 (Spring, Fall, 1982), p. 1-11. English. **DESCR**: *Folklore; Identity.

Dickey, Dan William

3545 Maciel, David R. Book review of: THE KENNEDY CORRIDOS: A STUDY OF THE BALLADS OF A MEXICAN AMERICAN HERO. AZTLAN, Vol. 13, no. 1-2 (Spring, Fall, 1982), p. 335-337. English. **DESCR**: Book Reviews; Corrido; Folk Songs; *Kennedy, John Fitzgerald; Music.

Dictatorships

3546 Espinoza, Roberto. Sintesis vs. analysis: un problema de historicidad en las novelas de las dictaduras. MAIZE, Vol. 6, no. 1-2 (Fall, Winter, 1982, 1983), p. 7-27. Spanish. **DESCR**: Carpentier, Alejo; Garcia Marquez, Gabriel; Latin American Literature; *Literary Criticism; Novel; Roa Bastos, Augustos; Valle Inclan, Ramon; White, Lucas Edward.

Dictionaries

3547 Barber, Gary. Book review of: DICTIONARY OF MEXICAN-AMERICAN HISTORY. REFERENCE SERVICES REVIEW, Vol. 10, no. 3 (October 1982), p. 41. English. **DESCR**: Book Reviews; *DICTIONARY OF MEXICAN AMERICAN HISTORY; Meier, Matt S.; Rivera, Feliciano.

3548 Laska, Vera. Book review of: DICTIONARY OF MEXICAN-AMERICAN HISTORY. INTERNATIONAL SOCIAL SCIENCE, Vol. 57, no. 3 (Summer 1982), p. 184. English. **DESCR**: Book Reviews; *DICTIONARY OF MEXICAN AMERICAN HISTORY; History; Meier, Matt S.; Rivera, Feliciano.

3549 Martinez, Julio A. Book review of: DICTIONARY OF MEXICAN-AMERICAN HISTORY. RQ - REFERENCE AND ADULT SERVICES DIVISION, Vol. 21, no. 3 (Spring 1982), p. 297-298. English. **DESCR**: Book Reviews; *DICTIONARY OF MEXICAN AMERICAN HISTORY; History; Meier, Matt S.; Rivera, Feliciano.

DICTIONARY OF MEXICAN AMERICAN HISTORY

3550 Barber, Gary. Book review of: DICTIONARY OF MEXICAN-AMERICAN HISTORY. REFERENCE SERVICES REVIEW, Vol. 10, no. 3 (October 1982), p. 41. English. **DESCR**: Book Reviews; Dictionaries; Meier, Matt S.; Rivera, Feliciano.

3551 Book review of: DICTIONARY OF MEXICAN-AMERICAN HISTORY. LIBRARY JOURNAL, Vol. 108, no. 10 (May 15, 1983), p. 965. English. **DESCR**: Book Reviews; Meier, Matt S.; Rivera, Feliciano.

3552 Camarillo, Alberto M. Book review of: DICTIONARY OF MEXICAN-AMERICAN HISTORY. JOURNAL OF AMERICAN HISTORY, Vol. 69, no. 4 (March 1983), p. 953-954. English. **DESCR**: Book Reviews; Meier, Matt S.; Rivera, Feliciano.

3553 De Leon, Arnoldo. Book review of: DICTIONARY OF MEXICAN-AMERICAN HISTORY. NEW MEXICO HISTORICAL REVIEW, Vol. 58, no. 1 (January 1983), p. 101-102. English. **DESCR**: Book Reviews; Meier, Matt S.; Rivera, Feliciano.

3554 Griswold del Castillo, Richard. Book review of: DICTIONARY OF MEXICAN-AMERICAN HISTORY. SOUTHWESTERN HISTORICAL QUARTERLY, Vol. 86, no. 4 (April 1983), p. 579-580. English. **DESCR**: Book Reviews; Meier, Matt S.; Rivera, Feliciano.

3555 Jones, Errol D. Book review of: DICTIONARY OF MEXICAN-AMERICAN HISTORY. WESTERN HISTORICAL QUARTERLY, Vol. 14, no. 3 (1983), p. 339-340. English. **DESCR**: Book Reviews; History; Meier, Matt S.; Reference Works; Rivera, Feliciano.

3556 Laska, Vera. Book review of: DICTIONARY OF MEXICAN-AMERICAN HISTORY. INTERNATIONAL SOCIAL SCIENCE, Vol. 57, no. 3 (Summer 1982), p. 184. English. **DESCR**: Book Reviews; Dictionaries; History; Meier, Matt S.; Rivera, Feliciano.

3557 Martinez, Julio A. Book review of: DICTIONARY OF MEXICAN-AMERICAN HISTORY. RQ - REFERENCE AND ADULT SERVICES DIVISION, Vol. 21, no. 3 (Spring 1982), p. 297-298. English. **DESCR**: Book Reviews; Dictionaries; History; Meier, Matt S.; Rivera, Feliciano.

Dieciseis de Septiembre

3558 Moreno, Mario "Cantinflas". Observations on Mexico today. CAMINOS, Vol. 3, no. 10 (November 1982), p. 20,45. Bilingual. **DESCR**: *Holidays; Mexico; *Moreno, Mario "Cantinflas".

3559 Whisler, Kirk. Everyone in town was there (photoessay). CAMINOS, Vol. 3, no. 10 (November 1982), p. 26-27. English. **DESCR**: East Los Angeles, CA; *Mexican Independence Parade; Parades.

Diez de Onate, Jorge

3560 People. HISPANIC BUSINESS, Vol. 5, no. 9 (September 1983), p. 10. English. **DESCR**: *Businesspeople; Chavez, Chris; Franco Garcia, Freddie; Garcia, Hector P.; Lozano, Leticia Eugenia; Ravard, Rafael Alonzo; Rodriguez, Alberto Duque; Sanchez, Philip V.; Villalpando, Catalina.

Differential Survey Treatment

3561 Spanish lesson. TELEVISION/RADIO AGE, Vol. 30, no. 22 (June 6, 1983), p. 18. English. **DESCR**: Advertising; *Radio.

Digitron Tool Company, Inc.

3562 Chavarria, Jesus. The entrepreneurial reflex. HISPANIC BUSINESS, Vol. 5, no. 1 (January 1983), p. 6. English. **DESCR**: Arroyos, Alex; *Business Enterprises; Dynamic Ocean Service, Inc.; Fernandez, Nestor.

3563 Weber, Robert. The special talent of digitron's Nestor Fernandez. HISPANIC BUSINESS, Vol. 5, no. 1 (January 1983), p. 10-11+. English. **DESCR**: *Business Enterprises; Dayton, Ohio; Fernandez, Nestor; Financial Planning.

Dimartino, Rita

3564 People. HISPANIC BUSINESS, Vol. 4, no. 9 (September 1982), p. 7. English. **DESCR:** Advertising Agencies; Appointed Officials; Awards; *Biographical Notes; Diaz-Albertini, Luis; Garza, Jesus; Hispanic Women in Higher Education (HWHE); League of United Latin American Citizens (LULAC); Ortega, Ray; Ortiz, George; Romero, Carlos J.; Sepulveda, Luis.

Directories

3565 Balkan, D. Carlos. The Hispanic business top 400 in sales. HISPANIC BUSINESS, Vol. 5, no. 6 (June 1983), p. 18-20+. English. **DESCR:** *Business Enterprises.

3566 Chavarria, Jesus. Researching the 400. HISPANIC BUSINESS, Vol. 5, no. 6 (June 1983), p. 6. English. **DESCR:** Business Enterprises; Hispanic Business 400.

3567 Communications/marketing. HISPANIC BUSINESS, Vol. 5, no. 8 (August 1983), p. 26. English. **DESCR:** Advertising Agencies; Bermudez & Associates; *Broadcast Media; Carranza Associates; Marketing.

3568 Entertainment = diversion. CAMINOS, Vol. 3, no. 4 (April 1982), p. 41. Bilingual. **DESCR:** AZTLAN [journal]; Committee in Solidarity with the People of El Salvador (CISPES); Cultural Organizations; DIRECTORY OF MINORITY ARTS ORGANIZATIONS; El Salvador; *National Endowment for the Arts; NOTICIERO; Organizations; Periodicals; *Recreation; Television.

3569 NATIONAL HISPANIC WOMEN'S NETWORK DIRECTORY: LULAC mujeres en accion. LATINO, Vol. 53, no. 3 (May 1982), p. 13-18. English. **DESCR:** *Chicanas; *League of United Latin American Citizens (LULAC).

3570 NATIONAL HISPANIC WOMEN'S NETWORK DIRECTORY, June 1983. LATINO, Vol. 54, no. 7 (January 1983), p. 13-20. English. **DESCR:** *Chicanas; *NATIONAL HISPANIC WOMEN'S NETWORK DIRECTORY.

3571 Philip Morris publishes guide. LATINO, Vol. 54, no. 5 (August, September, 1983), p. 28. English. **DESCR:** *Philip Morris, Inc.

3572 Soto, Shirlene Ann. The emerging Chicana: a review of the journals. SOUTHWEST ECONOMY AND SOCIETY, Vol. 2, no. 1 (October, November, 1976), p. 39-45. English. **DESCR:** *Chicanas; *Literature Reviews; Periodicals.

DIRECTORY OF MINORITY ARTS ORGANIZATIONS

3573 Entertainment = diversion. CAMINOS, Vol. 3, no. 4 (April 1982), p. 41. Bilingual. **DESCR:** AZTLAN [journal]; Committee in Solidarity with the People of El Salvador (CISPES); Cultural Organizations; Directories; El Salvador; *National Endowment for the Arts; NOTICIERO; Organizations; Periodicals; *Recreation; Television.

Disasters

3574 Garcia, Ruperto. No help yet for farmworkers in Panhandle. TEXAS OBSERVER, Vol. 74, no. 16 (September 3, 1982), p. 6-7. English. **DESCR:** *Agricultural Laborers; Crops; Economic History and Conditions; Texas Panhandle.

3575 Perry, Ronald W. Crisis communications: ethnic differentials in interpreting and acting on disaster warnings. SOCIAL BEHAVIOR AND PERSONALITY, Vol. 10, no. 1 (1982), p. 97-104. English. **DESCR:** Cultural Characteristics; *Social Psychology.

DISCRIMINACION A UN MARTIR [corrido]

3576 Pena, Manuel H. Folksong and social change: two corridos as interpretive sources. AZTLAN, Vol. 13, no. 1-2 (Spring, Fall, 1982), p. 12-42. English. **DESCR:** Corrido; Cortez, Gregorio; *EL CORRIDO DE GREGORIO CORTE [corrido]; *Folk Songs; Longoria, Felix; Music.

Discrimination
USE: Racism

Discrimination in Education

3577 Equal protection: right of illegal alien children to state provided education. HARVARD LAW REVIEW, Vol. 96, no. 1 (November 1982), p. 130-140. English. **DESCR:** *Children; Civil Rights; Doe v. Plyer [Tyler Independent School District, Texas]; *Education; *Undocumented Workers.

3578 Garcia, Paco. Voices: Hispanic voices needed in the education debate. NUESTRO, Vol. 7, no. 5 (June, July, 1983), p. 53-54. English. **DESCR:** Bilingual Bicultural Education; *Discrimination in Employment; *Education; Federal Government; *Latin Americans; President's Commission on Excellence in Education; Reagan, Ronald; U.S. Department of Health, Education and Welfare (HEW).

3579 Gonzales, Patrisia. The two cities of Tucson. NUESTRO, Vol. 7, no. 4 (May 1983), p. 20-23. English. **DESCR:** Accion 80s; Cultural Organizations; *Discrimination in Employment; Garcia, Gerald; Lopez-Grant, Lillian; *Tucson, AZ; Valdez, Joel.

3580 Leigh, Monroe. United States Constitution - equal protection deprivation of education in illegal alien school-children not justified by substantial state goal. AMERICAN JOURNAL OF INTERNATIONAL LAW, Vol. 77, no. 1 (January 1983), p. 151-153. English. **DESCR:** *Children; Doe v. Plyer [Tyler Independent School District, Texas]; *Education; Texas; *Undocumented Workers.

3581 Lopez, Victor Manuel. Equal protection for undocumented aliens. CHICANO LAW REVIEW, Vol. 5, (1982), p. 29-54. English. **DESCR:** Civil Rights; Legal Reform; Medical Care Laws and Legislation; *Undocumented Workers.

3582 McFadden, Bernard J. Bilingual education and the law. JOURNAL OF LAW AND EDUCATION, Vol. 12, no. 1 (January 1983), p. 1-27. English. **DESCR:** Administration of Justice; *Bilingual Bicultural Education; Educational Law and Legislation; History.

3583 Olivas, Michael A. Federal higher education policy: the case of Hispanics. EDUCATIONAL EVALUATION AND POLICY ANALYSIS, Vol. 4, no. 3 (Fall 1982), p. 301-310. English. **DESCR:** Education Equalization; Educational Law and Legislation; Federal Government; *Higher Education; Policy Formation.

Discrimination in Education (cont.)

3584 Rivera, Roberto. Selected topics on Latino access to Illinois colleges and universities. INTEGRATED EDUCATION, Vol. 20, no. 3-5 (May, October, 1982), p. 101-105. English. DESCR: Colleges and Universities; *Higher Education; Illinois; Racism.

3585 Tienda, Marta. Sex, ethnicity and Chicano status attainment. INTERNATIONAL MIGRATION REVIEW, Vol. 16, no. 2 (Summer 1982), p. 435-473. English. DESCR: Academic Achievement; Chicanas; Discrimination in Employment; Identity; Income; Language Proficiency; Sexism; *Social Classes; Social Mobility.

Discrimination in Employment

3586 Fernandez, John P. Facing the hard realities of corporate advancement. HISPANIC BUSINESS, Vol. 4, no. 4 (April 1982), p. 18-19,25. English. DESCR: *Affirmative Action; Businesspeople; Mentors; Self-Help Groups.

3587 Garcia, Paco. Voices: Hispanic voices needed in the education debate. NUESTRO, Vol. 7, no. 5 (June, July, 1983), p. 53-54. English. DESCR: Bilingual Bicultural Education; *Discrimination in Education; *Education; Federal Government; *Latin Americans; President's Commission on Excellence in Education; Reagan, Ronald; U.S. Department of Health, Education and Welfare (HEW).

3588 Girls explore new job fields. NUESTRO, Vol. 7, no. 8 (October 1983), p. 13. English. DESCR: *Chicanas; Mi Carrera Program; Mi Casa Women's Resource Center, Denver, CO.

3589 Gonzales, Patrisia. The two cities of Tucson. NUESTRO, Vol. 7, no. 4 (May 1983), p. 20-23. English. DESCR: Accion 80s; Cultural Organizations; *Discrimination in Education; Garcia, Gerald; Lopez-Grant, Lillian; *Tucson, AZ; Valdez, Joel.

3590 Government review. NUESTRO, Vol. 7, no. 2 (March 1983), p. 42. English. DESCR: A WORKING WOMAN'S GUIDE TO HER JOB RIGHTS; Adoption; Business Enterprises; Census; Chicanas; *Government Services; GUIDE TO FEDERAL MINORITY ENTERPRISE AND RELATED ASSISTANCE PROGRAMS; Population Trends; Study Abroad; U.S. Information Agency (USIA).

3591 Job hunting & bolts. CAMINOS, Vol. 4, no. 1-2 (January, February, 1983), p. 19. English. DESCR: *Careers.

3592 Padilla, Steve. A Latino voice on the Parole Commission. NUESTRO, Vol. 7, no. 7 (September 1983), p. 42-43. English. DESCR: *Chicanas; *Kaslow, Audrey; Racism; U.S. Parole Commission.

3593 Research/development: books. HISPANIC BUSINESS, Vol. 4, no. 1 (January 1982), p. 27. English. DESCR: *Book Reviews; *Fernandez, John P.; Racism; *RACISM AND SEXISM IN CORPORATE LIFE; Sexism.

3594 Tienda, Marta. Sex, ethnicity and Chicano status attainment. INTERNATIONAL MIGRATION REVIEW, Vol. 16, no. 2 (Summer 1982), p. 435-473. English. DESCR: Academic Achievement; Chicanas; Discrimination in Education; Identity; Income; Language Proficiency; Sexism; *Social Classes; Social Mobility.

Discrimination in Housing
USE: Residential Segregation

DISCRIMINATION IN ORGANIZATIONS

3595 Furphy, Alice. Book review of: DISCRIMINATION IN ORGANIZATIONS. HISPANIC JOURNAL OF BEHAVIORAL SCIENCES, Vol. 5, no. 1 (March 1983), p. 115-120. English. DESCR: Alvarez, Rodolfo; Book Reviews; Heller, Kenneth.

Discriminatory Hiring Practices
USE: Discrimination in Employment

Disease Prevention and Control
USE: Preventative Medicine

DISORDER AND PROGRESS: BANDITS, POLICE AND MEXICAN DEVELOPMENT

3596 Powell, T. G. Book review of: DISORDER AND PROGRESS: BANDITS, POLICE, AND MEXICAN DEVELOPMENT. AMERICAS, Vol. 38, no. 4 (1982), p. 540-541. English. DESCR: Book Reviews; Vanderwood, Paul J..

3597 Ruiz, Ramon Eduardo. Book review of: DISORDER AND PROGRESS: BANDITS, POLICE, AND MEXICAN DEVELOPMENT. ARIZONA AND THE WEST, Vol. 24, no. 1 (Spring 1982), p. 75-76. English. DESCR: Bandidos; Book Reviews; Diaz, Porfirio; Vanderwood, Paul J.

Divorce

3598 Nieto, Daniel S. Hispanic fathers: the growing phenomenon of single fathers keeping their children. NATIONAL HISPANIC JOURNAL, Vol. 1, no. 4 (Spring 1983), p. 15-19. English. DESCR: Family; Parent and Child Relationships; *Single Parents.

"DO IT MY WAY OR YOU'RE FIRED!": EMPLOYEE RIGHTS AND THE CHANGING ROLE OF MANAGEMENT PREROGATIVES

3599 Research/development: books. HISPANIC BUSINESS, Vol. 5, no. 4 (April 1983), p. 28. English. DESCR: Biographical Notes; *Book Reviews; Ewing, David W.; Garcia, Carlos; Garcia, Edward; Industrial Relations; Science; *SCIENCE OF THE SPANISH SPEAKING PEOPLE.

THE DOCILE PUERTO RICAN

3600 Lattin, Vernon E. Book review of: THE DOCILE PUERTO RICAN. MINORITY VOICES, Vol. 2, no. 1 (Spring 1978), p. 62-63. English. DESCR: Book Reviews; Marques, Rene; Puerto Ricans.

Doctor Patient Relations

3601 Acosta, Frank X. and Cristo, Martha H. Bilingual-Bicultural interpreters as psychotherapeutic bridges: a program note. JOURNAL OF COMMUNITY PSYCHOLOGY, Vol. 10, no. 1 (January 1982), p. 54-56. English. DESCR: Biculturalism; Bilingualism; Community Mental Health; East Los Angeles, CA; *Mental Health Personnel; Mental Health Programs; Translations.

3602 Gombeski, William R., Jr., et al. Communicating health information to urban Mexican-Americans: sources of health information. HEALTH EDUCATION QUARTERLY, Vol. 9, no. 4 (Winter 1982), p. 293-309. English. DESCR: Health Education; Mass Media; *Public Health; Surveys.

Dodge County Library System, WI

3603 Naismith, Rachael. Moveable library: serving migrant farm workers. WILSON LIBRARY BULLETIN, Vol. 57, no. 7 (March 1983), p. 571-575. English. **DESCR:** #Fresno County Public Library, CA; Library Services; Migrant Labor; Public Libraries.

Doe v. Plyer [Tyler Independent School District, Texas]

3604 Equal protection: right of illegal alien children to state provided education. HARVARD LAW REVIEW, Vol. 96, no. 1 (November 1982), p. 130-140. English. **DESCR:** #Children; Civil Rights; Discrimination in Education; #Education; #Undocumented Workers.

3605 Gallagher, Michael P. Constitutional law - equal protection: a Texas statute which withholds state funds for the education of illegal alien children ... VILLANOVA LAW REVIEW, Vol. 28, no. 1 (November 1982), p. 198-224. English. **DESCR:** Constitutional Amendments - Fourteenth; Education; Tyler Independent School District, Texas; #Undocumented Workers.

3606 Heberton Craig N. To educate and not to educate: the plight of undocumented alien children in Texas. WASHINGTON UNIVERSITY LAW QUARTERLY, Vol. 60, no. 1 (Spring 1982), p. 119-159. English. **DESCR:** #Children; Education; San Antonio School District v. Rodriguez; #Undocumented Workers.

3607 Leigh, Monroe. United States Constitution - equal protection deprivation of education in illegal alien school-children not justified by substantial state goal. AMERICAN JOURNAL OF INTERNATIONAL LAW, Vol. 77, no. 1 (January 1983), p. 151-153. English. **DESCR:** #Children; Discrimination in Education; #Education; Texas; #Undocumented Workers.

3608 McCarthy, Martha. Legal forum. The right to an education: illegal aliens. JOURNAL OF EDUCATIONAL EQUITY AND LEADERSHIP, Vol. 2, no. 4 (Summer 1982), p. 282-287. English. **DESCR:** Administration of Justice; Education; #Educational Law and Legislation; Migrant Children; #Migrant Education; Texas; Undocumented Workers.

3609 Opportunity knocks ... but it needn't be equal. CHILDREN'S LEGAL RIGHTS JOURNAL, Vol. 4, no. 1 (August 1982), p. 14-17. English. **DESCR:** Board of Education of Hudson Central School District v. Rowley Individualized Educational Program (IEP); Handicapped; #Undocumented Workers.

3610 Osifchok, Diane I. The utilization of immediate scrutiny in establishing the right to education for undocumented alien children. PEPPERDINE LAW REVIEW, Vol. 10, no. 1 (December 1982), p. 139-165. English. **DESCR:** Civil Rights; Education; #Undocumented Workers.

3611 Packard, Mark. Equal protection clause requires a free public education for illegal alien children. TEXAS TECH LAW REVIEW, Vol. 14, (May 1983), p. 531-547. English. **DESCR:** Constitutional Amendments - Fourteenth; Education; #Undocumented Workers.

3612 Quinn, Michael Sean. Educating alien kids. TEXAS OBSERVOR, Vol. 74, no. 18 (September 17, 1982), p. 5-6. English. **DESCR:** Children; Education; Undocumented Workers.

3613 School house door must be open to children of illegal aliens. CHILDREN'S LEGAL RIGHTS JOURNAL, Vol. 3, (June 1982), p. 19-21. English. **DESCR:** Constitutional Amendments - Fourteenth; #Education; Texas; Undocumented Workers.

3614 Supreme Court recognizes special importance of education. MENTAL DISABILITY LAW REPORTER, Vol. 6, (July, August, 1982), p. 227-229. English. **DESCR:** #Education; San Antonio School District v. Rodriguez; THE PLUM PLUM PICKERS; Undocumented Workers.

3615 Witt, Elder. Court rules illegal aliens entitled to public schooling. CONGRESSIONAL QUARTERLY WEEKLY REPORT, Vol. 40, (June 19, 1982), p. 1479-1480. English. **DESCR:** Education; Immigration; Texas v. Certain Undocumented Alien Children; Undocumented Children; #Undocumented Workers.

Dohrenwend, Barbara Snell

3616 Hunsaker, Alan. Book review of: STRESSFUL LIFE EVENTS: THEIR NATURE AND EFFECTS. HISPANIC JOURNAL OF BEHAVIORAL SCIENCES, Vol. 5, no. 1 (March 1983), p. 130-132. English. **DESCR:** Book Reviews; Dohrenwend, Bruce P.; #STRESSFUL LIFE EVENTS: THEIR NATURE AND EFFECTS.

Dohrenwend, Bruce P.

3617 Hunsaker, Alan. Book review of: STRESSFUL LIFE EVENTS: THEIR NATURE AND EFFECTS. HISPANIC JOURNAL OF BEHAVIORAL SCIENCES, Vol. 5, no. 1 (March 1983), p. 130-132. English. **DESCR:** Book Reviews; Dohrenwend, Barbara Snell; #STRESSFUL LIFE EVENTS: THEIR NATURE AND EFFECTS.

DOLLARS OVER DOMINION: THE TRIUMPH OF LIBERALISM IN MEXICAN-UNITED STATES RELATIONS, 1861-1867

3618 Monjaras-Ruiz, Jesus. Book review of: DOLLARS OVER DOMINION: THE TRIUMPH OF LIBERALISM IN MEXICAN-UNITED STATES RELATIONS, 1861-1867. HISTORIA MEXICANA, Vol. 31, no. 4 (April, June, 1982), p. 642-646. Spanish. **DESCR:** Book Reviews; Schoonover, Thomas David.

Domecq Importers, Inc.

3619 Communications/marketing. HISPANIC BUSINESS, Vol. 4, no. 9 (September 1982), p. 22. English. **DESCR:** Awards; Coca-Cola Company; #Marketing; Western Union Corporation.

3620 Communications/marketing. HISPANIC BUSINESS, Vol. 4, no. 11 (November 1982), p. 18. English. **DESCR:** California Chicano News Media Association (CCNMA); Diaz-Albertini, Luis; #Marketing; National Hispanic Media Conference, San Diego, CA, December 2-5, 1982; Pacific Telephone; Television.

3621 Communications/marketing. HISPANIC BUSINESS, Vol. 5, no. 2 (February 1983), p. 23. English. **DESCR:** #Broadcast Media; Coopers and Lybrand; Latin American Feature Syndicate (ALA); #Mass Media; Phoenix, AZ.

Donna Fruit Company

3622 Holley, Joe. Farmworker wins the right to sue. TEXAS OBSERVOR, Vol. 74, no. 13 (July 9, 1982), p. 15. English. **DESCR:** *Agricultural Laborers; Laws; Legal Representation; Occupational Hazards; *Torrez, Juan.

Donnelley Marketing

3623 Mercado, Anthony. Do Hispanics use coupons? HISPANIC BUSINESS, Vol. 5, no. 12 (December 1983), p. 10. English. **DESCR:** Advertising; Carol Wright Hispanic Program; *Marketing.

DO'S AND DONT'S OF BILINGUAL PROGRAM EVALUATION

3624 Walia, Adorna. Book review of: DO'S AND DONT'S OF BILINGUAL PROGRAM EVALUATION. BILINGUAL JOURNAL, Vol. 7, no. 2 (Winter 1983), p. 38. English. **DESCR:** Bilingual Bicultural Education; Book Reviews; Curriculum; Evaluation (Educational); Rodriguez-Brown, Flora V.

Douglas, Walter

3625 Byrkit, James W. Walter Douglas and labor struggles in early 20th century Arizona. SOUTHWEST ECONOMY AND SOCIETY, Vol. 1, no. 1 (Spring 1976), p. 14-27. English. **DESCR:** Arizona; *Biography; Bisbee, AZ; Clifton Morenci Strike, June 1903; Copper Queen Mining Co., Bisbee, AZ; International Workers of the World (IWW); Labor Unions; Mining Industry; Strikes and Lockouts.

DOWN THESE MEAN STREETS

3626 Binder, Wolfgang and Thomas, Piri. An interview with Piri Thomas. MINORITY VOICES, Vol. 4, no. 1 (Spring 1980), p. 63-78. English. **DESCR:** Puerto Rican Literature; *Thomas, Piri.

Draft
USE: Military Service

Draguns, Juris G.

3627 Franco, Juan N. Book review of: COUNSELING ACROSS CULTURES. HISPANIC JOURNAL OF BEHAVIORAL SCIENCES, Vol. 5, no. 2 (June), p. 233-237. English. **DESCR:** Book Reviews; *COUNSELING ACROSS CULTURES; Lonner, Walter J.; Pedersen, Paul P.; Trimble, Joseph E.

Draw-A-Person (DAP) [psychological test]

3628 Gonzales, Eloy. A cross-cultural comparison of the developmental items of five ethnic groups in the Southwest. JOURNAL OF PERSONALITY ASSESSMENT, Vol. 46, no. 1 (February 1982), p. 26-31. English. **DESCR:** *Comparative Psychology; Ethnic Groups; Psychological Testing; Southwest United States.

Drawings

3629 Acevedo, Guillermo. Portfolio-arte. MAIZE, Vol. 1, no. 1 (Fall 1977), p. 25-30. English.

3630 Acevedo, Mario (Torero). [La race (drawing)]. MAIZE, Vol. 1, no. 2 (Winter 1978), p. 12. English.

3631 Callejo, Carlos. [Untitled drawing]. CORAZON DE AZTLAN, Vol. 1, no. 1 (January, February, 1982), p. 19. English.

3632 Chinas, Joaquin. Panchito [drawing]. MAIZE,

Vol. 2, no. 2 (Winter 1979), p. 27. English.

3633 Chinas, Joaquin. [Untitled drawing]. MAIZE, Vol. 1, no. 1 (Fall 1977), p. 49-50. English.

3634 Chinas, Joaquin. Yalateca [drawing]. MAIZE, Vol. 2, no. 2 (Winter 1979), p. 26. English.

3635 Garcia Perez, Linda Mary. Mejico [drawing]. MAIZE, Vol. 2, no. 3 (Spring 1979), p. 32-33. English.

3636 Garcia-Camarillo, Mia. [Untitled drawing]. MAIZE, Vol. 1, no. 1 (Fall 1977), p. Bk cover. Spanish.

3637 Martinez, D. G. [Untitled drawing]. CORAZON DE AZTLAN, Vol. 1, no. 1 (January, February, 1982), p. 45. English.

3638 Mascarenas, Stella. [Untitled drawings]. CALMECAC, Vol. 3, (Spring 1982), p. 47. Bilingual.

3639 Montoya, Jose E. Chuco series [drawings]. MAIZE, Vol. 2, no. 1 (Fall 1978), p. Bk cover. English. **DESCR:** Pachuco Images.

3640 Montoya, Jose E. [Untitled drawing]. CALMECAC, Vol. 3, (Spring 1982), p. 52. Bilingual.

3641 Montoya, Jose E. [Untitled drawings]. CALMECAC, Vol. 3, (Spring 1982), p. 5+. Bilingual.

3642 Montoya, Jose E. [Untitled drawings]. CALMECAC, Vol. 3, (Spring 1982), p. 24-29. Bilingual.

3643 Montoya, Jose E. [Untitled drawings]. CALMECAC, Vol. 3, (Spring 1982), p. 35+. Bilingual.

3644 Montoya, Jose E. [Untitled drawings from the CHUCO SERIES]. MAIZE, Vol. 2, no. 1 (Fall 1978), p. 32-35. English. **DESCR:** Pachuco Images.

3645 Morales, Maria A. Moliendo cafe. THIRD WOMAN, Vol. 1, no. 2 (1982), p. 30. Spanish.

3646 Morales, Maria A. Vida criolla. THIRD WOMAN, Vol. 1, no. 2 (1982), p. 29. Spanish.

3647 Moreno, Juan M. [Untitled drawings]. MAIZE, Vol. 2, no. 1 (Fall 1978), p. 18-19. English.

3648 Norte. [Untitled drawing]. CORAZON DE AZTLAN, Vol. 1, no. 1 (January, February, 1982), p. 34. English.

3649 Nuestra libertad. CORAZON DE AZTLAN, Vol. 1, no. 2 (March, April, 1982), p. 24-25. Spanish.

3650 Ochoa, Victor Orozco. Centerfold-arte [drawing]. MAIZE, Vol. 1, no. 1 (Fall 1977), p. 32-33. English.

3651 Ochoa, Victor Orozco. [La tierra mia, all the way to the Bay (drawing)]. MAIZE, Vol. 2, no. 2 (Winter 1979), p. 6. English.

3652 Rivera, Diana. Woman with black kerchief. THIRD WOMAN, Vol. 1, no. 2 (1982), p. 85. English.

3653 Sanchez, Rita. [Untitled drawing]. MAIZE, Vol. 1, no. 4 (Summer 1978), p. 32-33. English.

Drawings (cont.)

3654 Singing of life en el Valle de Califas.
CALMECAC, Vol. 1, (Summer 1980), p. 57.
English.

3655 Tello, Jerry. [Untitled drawing]. CALMECAC,
Vol. 2, (Spring 1981), p. 6. Bilingual.

3656 Tizoc. Arte. MAIZE, Vol. 1, no. 1 (Fall
1977), p. 45.

3657 Tizoc. Breaking the needle [drawing]. MAIZE,
Vol. 1, no. 2 (Winter 1978), p. 37. English.

3658 Tizoc. [Levantate campesino! (drawing)].
MAIZE, Vol. 1, no. 1 (Fall 1977), p. 48.
English.

3659 Ulloa, Domingo. [Untitled drawing]. MAIZE,
Vol. 1, no. 1 (Fall 1977), p. 40. English.

3660 Unzueta, Manuel. La chiclera [drawing].
MAIZE, Vol. 1, no. 3 (Spring 1978), p. 37.
English.

3661 Valdes, Rosalia Hayakawa. [Untitled
drawing]. MAIZE, Vol. 2, no. 2 (Winter
1979), p. 49. English.

3662 Villa, Esteban. Coacihuatl - serpent woman.
CALMECAC, Vol. 2, (Spring 1981), p. 44.
English.

3663 Villa, Esteban. La Colonia. CALMECAC, Vol.
2, (Spring 1981), p. 34. Spanish.

3664 Villa, Esteban. La jennie de sacra.
CALMECAC, Vol. 2, (Spring 1981), p. 42.
Spanish.

3665 Villa, Esteban. RCAF c/s. CALMECAC, Vol. 2,
(Spring 1981), p. 48. English.

3666 Villa, Esteban. Reflection = action c/s.
CALMECAC, Vol. 2, (Spring 1981), p. 52.
English.

3667 Villa, Esteban. [Untitled drawings].
CALMECAC, Vol. 2, (Spring 1981), p. 17.
Bilingual.

3668 Villa, Esteban. [Untitled drawings].
CALMECAC, Vol. 2, (Spring 1981), p. 25-26+.
Bilingual.

3669 Villa, Esteban. [Untitled drawings].
CALMECAC, Vol. 2, (Spring 1981), p. 38-39.
Bilingual.

3670 Villa, Esteban. [Untitled drawings].
CALMECAC, Vol. 2, (Spring 1981), p. 55.
Bilingual.

Dream Analysis

3671 Maduro, Renaldo J. Working with Latinos and
the use of dream analysis. JOURNAL OF THE
AMERICAN ACADEMY OF PSYCHOANALYSIS, Vol. 10,
no. 4 (October 1982), p. 609-628. English.
DESCR: Culture; *Mental Health; Psychiatry.

Drinane, Suleika Cabrera

3672 Ortiz, Carlos V. Growing old alone. NUESTRO,
Vol. 7, no. 4 (May 1983), p. 36-38. English.
DESCR: *Ancianos; Instituto
Puertorriqueno/Hispano Para Personas
Mayores; Padilla de Armas, Encarnacion;
*Puerto Ricans.

Dropouts

3673 Barry, Patrick. Alternative high school

provides dropouts a second chance. NUESTRO,
Vol. 6, no. 7 (September 1982), p. 29-30.
English. DESCR: *Pilsen, IL.

3674 Burciaga, Cecilia Preciado. Cap and gown vs.
cap and apron. NUESTRO, Vol. 6, no. 4 (May
1982), p. 43. English. DESCR: *Education.

3675 Burciaga, Cecilia Preciado. High school
dropouts: remedies. CAMINOS, Vol. 4, no. 10
(November 1983), p. 38-40,54. Bilingual.
DESCR: Secondary School Education.

3676 De Anda, Diane. A study of the interaction
of Hispanic junior high school students and
their teachers. HISPANIC JOURNAL OF
BEHAVIORAL SCIENCES, Vol. 4, no. 1 (March
1982), p. 57-74. English. DESCR: *Chicanas;
Teacher-pupil Interaction.

3677 Hispanic student study undertaken. NUESTRO,
Vol. 7, no. 10 (December 1983), p. 11-12.
English. DESCR: Academic Achievement;
Educational Statistics; Enrollment; Hispanic
Policy Development Project; *National
Commission on Secondary Schooling for
Hispanics; *Secondary School Education.

3678 Nevarez, Miguel A. The Hispanic educational
dilemma: a strategy for change. HISPANIC
BUSINESS, Vol. 5, no. 11 (November 1983), p.
12. English. DESCR: Academic Achievement;
*Education; Higher Education.

3679 Webster, David S. Chicano students in
American higher education: a review of the
literature. CAMPO LIBRE, Vol. 1, no. 2
(Summer 1981), p. 169-192. English. DESCR:
Educational Statistics; Enrollment; Graduate
Schools; *Higher Education; Literature
Reviews; Professional Schools.

Drug Abuse

3680 Cockerham, William C. and Alster, Joan M. A
comparison of marijuana use among
Mexican-American and Anglo rural youth
utilizing a matched-set analysis.
INTERNATIONAL JOURNAL OF THE ADDICTIONS,
Vol. 18, no. 6 (August 1983), p. 759-767.
English. DESCR: Anglo Americans; *Marijuana;
Rural Population; Youth.

3681 Glick, R. Dealing, demoralization and
addiction: heroin in the Chicago Puerto
Rican community. JOURNAL OF PSYCHOACTIVE
DRUGS, Vol. 15, no. 4 (October, December,
1983), p. 281-292. English. DESCR: Chicago,
IL; Culture; Puerto Ricans.

3682 Medina, Antonio S. Adolescent health in
Alameda county. JOURNAL OF ADOLESCENT HEALTH
CARE, Vol. 2, no. 3 (March 1982), p.
175-182. English. DESCR: Alameda County, CA;
*Dentistry; Medical Care; Psychology; Youth.

3683 Moreno, Rita. No, not my kid. LATINO, Vol.
54, no. 7 (November 1983), p. 26+. English.

3684 Que pasa? NUESTRO, Vol. 7, no. 7 (September
1983), p. 9. English. DESCR: Alcoholism;
Anti-Defamation League of B'nai B'rith; Drug
Programs; Employment; Kiwanis International;
Miller Brewing Company; Racism; Sports.

Drug Abuse (cont.)

3685 Wurzman, Ilyana. Cultural values of Puerto Rican opiate addicts: an exploratory study. AMERICAN JOURNAL OF DRUG AND ALCOHOL ABUSE, Vol. 9, no. 2 (1982, 1983), p. 141-153. English. DESCR: Acculturation; Anglo Americans; Blacks; Drug Addicts; Family; Loevinger's Sentence Completion Test; Machismo; New York, NY; Opium; Puerto Ricans; Values.

Drug Addicts

3686 Dolan, Michael. Personality differences among Black, white, and Hispanic-American male heroin addicts on MMPI content scales. JOURNAL OF CLINICAL PSYCHOLOGY, Vol. 39, no. 5 (September 1983), p. 807-813. English. DESCR: Blacks; *Heroin Addicts; Minnesota Multiphasic Personality Inventory (MMPI); Personality.

3687 Vigil, James Diego. Human revitalization: the six tasks of victory outreach. DREW GATEWAY, Vol. 52, no. 3 (Spring 1982), p. 49-59. English. DESCR: Barrios for Christ Program; Drug Programs; Gangs; Identity; Pentecostal Church; Protestant Church; Religion; *Victory Outreach; Youth.

3688 Wurzman, Ilyana. Cultural values of Puerto Rican opiate addicts: an exploratory study. AMERICAN JOURNAL OF DRUG AND ALCOHOL ABUSE, Vol. 9, no. 2 (1982, 1983), p. 141-153. English. DESCR: Acculturation; Anglo Americans; Blacks; *Drug Abuse; Family; Loevinger's Sentence Completion Test; Machismo; New York, NY; Opium; Puerto Ricans; Values.

DRUG AND ALCOHOL ABUSE: A CLINICAL GUIDE TO DIAGNOSIS AND TREATMENT

3689 Hunsaker, Alan. Book review of: ANGEL DUST: AN ETHNOGRAPHIC STUDY OF PCP USERS; HEROIN USE IN THE BARRIO; DRUG AND ALCOHOL ABUSE: A CLINICAL GUIDE TO DIAGNOSIS AND TREATMENT. HISPANIC JOURNAL OF BEHAVIORAL SCIENCES, Vol. 4, no. 1 (March 1982), p. 118-121. English. DESCR: Agar, Michael; *ANGEL DUST: AN ETHNOGRAPHIC STUDY OF PCP USERS; Bescher, George; Book Reviews; Bullington, Bruce; Feldman, Harvey W.; *HEROIN USE IN THE BARRIO; Schuckit, Marc A.

Drug Laws

3690 Carreras, Peter Nares. Strong concern over searches. NUESTRO, Vol. 7, no. 10 (December 1983), p. 12-13. English. DESCR: Colombia; Drug Traffic; *U.S. Customs.

Drug Programs

3691 Que pasa? NUESTRO, Vol. 7, no. 7 (September 1983), p. 9. English. DESCR: Alcoholism; Anti-Defamation League of B'nai B'rith; *Drug Abuse; Employment; Kiwanis International; Miller Brewing Company; Racism; Sports.

3692 Vigil, James Diego. Human revitalization: the six tasks of victory outreach. DREW GATEWAY, Vol. 52, no. 3 (Spring 1982), p. 49-59. English. DESCR: Barrios for Christ Program; Drug Addicts; Gangs; Identity; Pentecostal Church; Protestant Church; Religion; *Victory Outreach; Youth.

Drug Traffic

3693 Carreras, Peter Nares. Strong concern over searches. NUESTRO, Vol. 7, no. 10 (December 1983), p. 12-13. English. DESCR: Colombia; *Drug Laws; *U.S. Customs.

3694 Miranda warnings were adequate despite deviations from strict form. CRIMINAL LAW REPORTER, Vol. 30, no. 22 (October 3, 1982), p. 2427-2428. English. DESCR: California v. Prysock; *Legal Aid; U.S. v. Contreras.

Duarte, Rodrigo

3695 Guerra, Victor and Duarte, Rodrigo. An interview with Rodrigo Duarte of Teatro de la Esperanza, August 13, 1982/New York City. REVISTA CHICANO-RIQUENA, Vol. 11, no. 1 (Spring 1983), p. 112-120. English. DESCR: *El Teatro de la Esperanza; Teatro.

Dumas, TX

3696 Reavis, Dick J. Growing up gringo. TEXAS MONTHLY, Vol. 10, no. 8 (August 1982), p. 110-112+. English. DESCR: Biography; *Rodriguez, Adan; Zinc Mining.

Dunbar Ortiz, Roxanne

3697 Churchhill, Ward. Implications of publishing ROOTS OF RESISTANCE. JOURNAL OF ETHNIC STUDIES, Vol. 9, no. 3 (Fall 1981), p. 83-89. English. DESCR: Book Reviews; Colonialism; Land Tenure; Native Americans; New Mexico; Publishing Industry; *ROOTS OF RESISTANCE: LAND TENURE IN NEW MEXICO, 1680-1980; Social History and Conditions.

Duran, Richard P.

3698 Elsenberg, Ann R. Book review of: LATINO LANGUAGE AND COMMUNICATIVE BEHAVIOR. HISPANIC JOURNAL OF BEHAVIORAL SCIENCES, Vol. 5, no. 3 (September 1983), p. 347-349. English. DESCR: Book Reviews; Languages; *LATINO LANGUAGE AND COMMUNICATIVE BEHAVIOR; Sociolinguistics.

Duran, Sandra

3699 Nuestra gente. LATINO, Vol. 54, no. 8 (December 1983), p. 30. English. DESCR: *Biographical Notes; Businesspeople; Carter, Lynda Cordoba; Patino, Lorenzo E.; Politics; Rembis, Deborah; Vega, Christopher.

Durfee Award

3700 Perales, Velasco win special Durfee award. NUESTRO, Vol. 6, no. 8 (October 1982), p. 43. English. DESCR: *Perales, Cesar A.; *Velasco, Eugenio.

Duron, Armando

3701 People. HISPANIC BUSINESS, Vol. 5, no. 5 (May 1983), p. 8. English. DESCR: Biographical Notes; *Businesspeople; Espinoza, Peter; Flores, Juan; Martinez, Vilma Socorro; Molina, Gloria; Moreno, Samuel; Pantin, Leslie, Sr.; Quezada, Sylvia; Quinones, Sergio.

Dynamic Ocean Service, Inc.

3702 Chavarria, Jesus. The entrepreneurial reflex. HISPANIC BUSINESS, Vol. 5, no. 1 (January 1983), p. 6. English. DESCR: Arroyos, Alex; *Business Enterprises; Digitron Tool Company, Inc.; Fernandez, Nestor.

Dyson, Bryan

3703 Caldera, Carmela. Coca-Cola president Bryan Dyson on BRAVISIMO. CAMINOS, Vol. 4, no. 4 (April 1983), p. 44-45,48. Bilingual. **DESCR:** *BRAVISIMO; Coca-Cola Company; Private Funding Sources; Television.

EARLY CHILDHOOD BILINGUALISM: WITH SPECIAL REFERENCE TO THE MEXICAN-AMERICAN CHILD

3704 Wagatsuma, Yuria. Book review of: EARLY CHILDHOOD BILINGUALISM: WITH SPECIAL REFERENCE TO THE MEXICAN-AMERICAN CHILD. HISPANIC JOURNAL OF BEHAVIORAL SCIENCES, Vol. 5, no. 4 (December 1983), p. 477-481. English. **DESCR:** Bilingualism; Book Reviews; Garcia, Eugene E.

Early Childhood Education

3705 Barrio, Raymond. The bilingual heart and other adventures. BILINGUAL JOURNAL, Vol. 6, no. 2 (Winter 1982), p. 12-15. Bilingual. **DESCR:** Ethnic Attitudes; Racism; REVERSING ROLES; THE BILINGUAL HEART; THE PRINCE.

3706 Chesterfield, Ray, et al. The influence of teachers and peers on second language acquisition in bilingual preschool programs. TESOL QUARTERLY, Vol. 17, no. 3 (September 1983), p. 401-419. English. **DESCR:** Bilingual Bicultural Education; *English as a Second Language; Language Development; Teacher-pupil Interaction.

3707 Chesterfield, Ray P.; Moll, Luis C.; and Perez, Ray. A naturalistic approach for evaluation. BILINGUAL JOURNAL, Vol. 6, no. 1 (Fall 1982), p. 23-26. English. **DESCR:** Bilingual Bicultural Education; Curriculum; *Evaluation (Educational).

3708 Dreisbach, Melanie and Keogh, Barbara K. Testwiseness as a factor in readiness test performance of young Mexican-American children. JOURNAL OF EDUCATIONAL PSYCHOLOGY, Vol. 74, no. 2 (April 1982), p. 224-229. English. **DESCR:** *Academic Achievement; Bilingualism; Educational Tests and Measurements.

3709 Fillmore, Lili Wong. Language minority students and school participation: what kind of English is needed? JOURNAL OF EDUCATION, Vol. 164, no. 2 (Spring 1982), p. 143-156. English. **DESCR:** *Bilingual Bicultural Education; English as a Second Language; Language Proficiency.

3710 France, Pauline. Working with young bilingual children. EARLY CHILD DEVELOPMENT AND CARE, Vol. 10, no. 4 (February 1983), p. 283-292. English. **DESCR:** Bilingualism; *Curriculum.

3711 Johnson, Dale L. and Breckenridge, James N. The Houston Parent-Child Development Center and the primary prevention of behavior problems in young children. AMERICAN JOURNAL OF COMMUNITY PSYCHOLOGY, Vol. 10, no. 3 (June 1982), p. 305-316. English. **DESCR:** *Child Rearing; Children; *Houston Parent-Child Development Center(PCDC); Parent and Child Relationships; Social Classes.

3712 Miller, Robert. Reading instruction and primary school education - Mexican teachers' viewpoints. READING TEACHER, Vol. 35, no. 8 (May 1982), p. 890-894. English. **DESCR:** *Curriculum; Educational Theory and Practice; Mexico; Teacher Attitudes.

3713 Murray, James L.; Bruhn, John G.; and Bunce, Harvey. Assessment of type A behavior in preschoolers. JOURNAL OF HUMAN STRESS, Vol. 9, no. 3 (September 1983), p. 32-39. English. **DESCR:** Anglo Americans; Blacks; *Children; Psychology.

3714 Sandoval-Martinez, Steven. Findings from the Head Start bilingual curriculum development and evaluation effort. NABE JOURNAL, Vol. 7, no. 1 (Fall 1982), p. 1-12. English. **DESCR:** *Bilingual Bicultural Education; Compensatory Education; Evaluation (Educational); Headstart Program.

3715 YMCA. LATINA, Vol. 1, no. 3 (1983), p. 44-45+. English. **DESCR:** *YMCA.

East Chicago, IN

3716 Simon, Daniel T. Mexican repatriation in East Chicago, Indiana. JOURNAL OF ETHNIC STUDIES, Vol. 2, no. 2 (Summer 1974), p. 11-23. English. **DESCR:** *Deportation; History; Immigrant Labor; Immigration; Immigration Regulation and Control; Inland Steel Company; Mexico; Social History and Conditions.

East Los Angeles, CA

3717 Acosta, Frank X. and Cristo, Martha H. Bilingual-Bicultural interpreters as psychotherapeutic bridges: a program note. JOURNAL OF COMMUNITY PSYCHOLOGY, Vol. 10, no. 1 (January 1982), p. 54-56. English. **DESCR:** Biculturalism; Bilingualism; Community Mental Health; Doctor Patient Relations; *Mental Health Personnel; Mental Health Programs; Translations.

3718 The battle of the bands in East Los Angeles. CAMINOS, Vol. 4, no. 10 (November 1983), p. 9-11,47. Bilingual. **DESCR:** *Musicians.

3719 The culture is alive at the schools of East Los Angeles. CAMINOS, Vol. 3, no. 6 (June 1982), p. 30-31. Bilingual. **DESCR:** *Dance.

3720 Education center named Alfonso B. Perez. NUESTRO, Vol. 6, no. 5 (June, July, 1982), p. 30. English. **DESCR:** Education; Educational Services; *Perez, Alfonso B.

3721 Holscher, Louis M. Tiene arte valor afuera del barrio: the murals of East Los Angeles and Boyle Heights. JOURNAL OF ETHNIC STUDIES, Vol. 4, no. 3 (Fall 1976), p. 42-52. English. **DESCR:** Art; Boyle Heights; Culture; *Mural Art.

3722 Life in a Mexican-American barrio: gangs alongside middle-class striving. WALL STREET JOURNAL, Vol. 199, no. 43 (June 9, 1982), p. 26. English. **DESCR:** Frias, Gustavo; *Gangs; Social History and Conditions.

3723 Pearlman, Steven Ray. Mariachi music in Los Angeles. CAMINOS, Vol. 4, no. 10 (November 1983), p. 12,47. English. **DESCR:** *Mariachis.

3724 Perez, Robert; Padilla, Amado M.; and Ramirez, Alex. Expectations toward school busing by Mexican American youth. AMERICAN JOURNAL OF COMMUNITY PSYCHOLOGY, Vol. 10, no. 2 (April 1982), p. 133-148. English. **DESCR:** Attitude (Psychological); *Busing; Identity; Segregation and Desegregation; Students; Youth.

East Los Angeles, CA (cont.)

3725 Quesada-Weiner, Rosemary. EL ARCA. CAMINOS, Vol. 3, no. 1 (January 1982), p. 45. Bilingual. **DESCR:** East Los Angeles Retarded Citizen's Association (EL ARCA); *Mentally Handicapped.

3726 Salcido, Ramon M. The undocumented alien family. DE COLORES, Vol. 6, no. 1-2 (1982), p. 109-119. English. **DESCR:** Family; Green Carders; Social Services; *Undocumented Workers.

3727 Whisler, Kirk. Everyone in town was there (photoessay). CAMINOS, Vol. 3, no. 10 (November 1982), p. 26-27. English. **DESCR:** *Dieciseis de Septiembre; *Mexican Independence Parade; Parades.

EAST LOS ANGELES: HISTORY OF A BARRIO

3728 Book review of: EAST LOS ANGELES. LIBRARY JOURNAL, Vol. 107, no. 22 (December 15, 1982), p. 2349. English. **DESCR:** Book Reviews; Romo, Ricardo.

3729 Over a million barrio. LATINO, Vol. 54, no. 4 (May, June, 1983), p. 28. English. **DESCR:** Book Reviews; Romo, Ricardo.

East Los Angeles Retarded Citizen's Association (EL ARCA)

3730 Quesada-Weiner, Rosemary. EL ARCA. CAMINOS, Vol. 3, no. 1 (January 1982), p. 45. Bilingual. **DESCR:** *East Los Angeles, CA; *Mentally Handicapped.

Echeveste, John

3731 Q & A: in the Hispanic community who are the winners and losers of Reaganomics? CAMINOS, Vol. 3, no. 3 (March 1982), p. 47. Bilingual. **DESCR:** Casado, Lucy; *Federal Government; Flores, Bob; Leon, Virginia; Mendoza, John; *Reagan, Ronald; Sanchez-Alvarez, Gloria; Vidal de Neri, Julieta.

Eckberg, Douglas Lee

3732 White, Tim. Book review of: INTELLIGENCE AND RACE. THE ORIGINS AND DIMENSIONS OF THE IQ CONTROVERSY. HISPANIC JOURNAL OF BEHAVIORAL SCIENCES, Vol. 4, no. 4 (December 1982), p. 522-525. English. **DESCR:** Book Reviews; *INTELLIGENCE AND RACE: THE ORIGINS AND DIMENSIONS OF THE IQ CONTROVERSY.

Eckstein, Susan

3733 Logan, Kathleen. The urban poor in developing nations. JOURNAL OF URBAN HISTORY, Vol. 9, no. 1 (November 1982), p. 108-116. English. **DESCR:** ACCESS TO POWER: POLITICS AND THE URBAN POOR IN DEVELOPING NATIONS; *Book Reviews; BORDER BOOM TOWN: CIUDAD JUAREZ SINCE 1848; Collier, David; Cornelius, Wayne A.; Lloyd, Peter; Martinez, Oscar J.; Nelson, Joan M.; Perlman, Janice E.; POLITICS AND MIGRANT POOR IN MEXICO CITY; SLUMS OF HOPE? SHANTY TOWNS OF THE THIRD WORLD; SQUATTERS AND OLIGARCHS: AUTHORITARIAN RULE AND POLICY CHANGE IN PERU; THE MYTH OF MARGINALITY: URBAN POVERTY AND POLITICS IN RIO DE JANEIRO; THE POVERTY OF REVOLUTION: THE STATE AND THE URBAN POOR IN MEXICO; Urban Economics.

Economic Development

3734 Cantu, Hector. Border business report: the Rio Grande Valley's economy and Mexico's lingering peso devaluation effects. NATIONAL HISPANIC JOURNAL, Vol. 2, no. 1 (Summer 1983), p. 10-13. English. **DESCR:** Aguirre, Lionel; Border Region; Cano, Eddie; Coors Distributing Company, McAllen, TX; Cruz, Conrado; Cuevas, Betty; *Currency; Laredo, TX, Chamber of Commerce; Mexican American Chamber of Commerce, Austin, TX; United States-Mexico Relations.

3735 The Inter-American Development Bank at work (photoessay). CAMINOS, Vol. 4, no. 8 (September 1983), p. 22-25. English. **DESCR:** Banking Industry; *Inter-American Development Bank; Latin America.

3736 The LULAC/PUSH dialog. HISPANIC BUSINESS, Vol. 5, no. 4 (April 1983), p. 15. English. **DESCR:** Bonilla, Tony; Jackson, Jesse; League of United Latin American Citizens (LULAC); Operation PUSH.

3737 Mexico's export production map. CAMINOS, Vol. 3, no. 6 (June 1982), p. 20-21. Bilingual. **DESCR:** *Export Trade; Mexico.

3738 Navarro, Armando. Operation corporate responsibility: a movement for Latino economic empowerment. CAMINOS, Vol. 4, no. 7 (July, August, 1983), p. 28-31,43. Bilingual. **DESCR:** Congreso Nacional Para Pueblos Unidos (CPU); *Operation Corporate Responsibility (OCR).

3739 Nieto, Jesus G. Mexico & its economy - some keen insights. CAMINOS, Vol. 4, no. 5 (May 1983), p. 6-9,48. Bilingual. **DESCR:** *Mexico.

3740 U.S. Mexico border region economic report. CAMINOS, Vol. 3, no. 11 (December 1982), p. 38-39. English. **DESCR:** *Border Region; *United States-Mexico Relations.

3741 Vidal, Jose. Oil pluses - economic woes. CAMINOS, Vol. 3, no. 6 (June 1982), p. 18-19. Bilingual. **DESCR:** Mexico; Petroleum Industry; *United States-Mexico Relations.

3742 Wittenauer, Cheryl. The mayor markets San Antonio. HISPANIC BUSINESS, Vol. 5, no. 7 (July 1983), p. 12-13+. English. **DESCR:** Cisneros, Henry, Mayor of San Antonio, TX; *Marketing; San Antonio, TX.

Economic History and Conditions

3743 Barry, Patrick. Trouble in the bush: neighborhood house fights back. NUESTRO, Vol. 6, no. 3 (April 1982), p. 21-24. English. **DESCR:** *Chicago, IL.

3744 Burciaga, Jose Antonio. Death of el senor Peso. NUESTRO, Vol. 6, no. 7 (September 1982), p. 52. English. **DESCR:** *Economics; Mexico.

3745 Castillo, Pedro. Letter to the editor. SOUTHWEST ECONOMY AND SOCIETY, Vol. 3, no. 1 (Fall 1977), p. 55-56. English. **DESCR:** Internal Colonial Model (Theoretical); *Manta, Ben; TOWARD ECONOMIC DEVELOPMENT OF THE CHICANO BARRIO.

3746 Chavarria, Jesus. The two faces of progress. HISPANIC BUSINESS, Vol. 5, no. 9 (September 1983), p. 6. English. **DESCR:** League of United Latin American Citizens (LULAC).

Economic History and Conditions (cont.)

3747 Chavez, Mauro. Book review of: ESSAYS ON LA MUJER. JOURNAL OF ETHNIC STUDIES, Vol. 8, no. 2 (Summer 1980), p. 117-120. English. **DESCR:** Book Reviews; *Chicanas; Cruz, Rosa Martinez; *ESSAYS ON LA MUJER; Sanchez, Rosaura; Social History and Conditions; Socioeconomic Factors; Women's Rights.

3748 Ford, Charles A. and Violante Morlock, Alejandro A. Policy concerns over the impact of trade-related performance requirements and investment incentives on the international economy: Mexican automotive policy and U.S.-Mexican relations. INTER-AMERICAN ECONOMIC AFFAIRS, Vol. 36, no. 2 (Fall 1982), p. 3-42. English. **DESCR:** Automobile Industry; *Mexico; *United States-Mexico Relations.

3749 Foreign trade. HISPANIC BUSINESS, Vol. 5, no. 10 (October 1983), p. 29. English. **DESCR:** Agency for International Development (AID); Caribbean Region; *Foreign Trade; HOW TO EXPORT: A MARKETING MANUAL; Mexico; Puerto Rico; U.S. Trade Center (Mexico City).

3750 Gallegos, Herman. Making a dent in the corporate hierarchy. NUESTRO, Vol. 6, no. 9 (November 1982), p. 49-51. English. **DESCR:** *Economics; Latin Americans.

3751 Garcia, Ruperto. No help yet for farmworkers in Panhandle. TEXAS OBSERVOR, Vol. 74, no. 16 (September 3, 1982), p. 6-7. English. **DESCR:** *Agricultural Laborers; Crops; Disasters; Texas Panhandle.

3752 Hansen, Niles. Location preference and opportunity cost: a South Texas perspective. SOCIAL SCIENCE QUARTERLY, Vol. 63, (September 1982), p. 506-516. English. **DESCR:** Employment; Texas.

3753 The impact of undocumented migration on the U.S. labor market. HOUSTON JOURNAL OF INTERNATIONAL LAW, Vol. 5, no. 2 (Spring 1983), p. 287-321. English. **DESCR:** Employment; Immigrant Labor; Immigration and Nationality Act (INA); Immigration Law; Labor Supply and Market; Research Methodology; Simpson-Mazzoli Bill; *Undocumented Workers.

3754 Klor de Alva, Jorge. Gabino Barrera and Chicano thought. AZTLAN, Vol. 14, no. 2 (Fall 1983), p. 343-358. English. **DESCR:** *Barreda, Gabino; History; Mexico; Philosophy; *Positivism.

3755 Manta, Ben. Toward economic development of the Chicano barrio: alternative strategies and their implications [reprint of DE COLORES article]. SOUTHWEST ECONOMY AND SOCIETY, Vol. 1, no. 1 (Spring 1976), p. 35-41. English. **DESCR:** Capitalism; Internal Colonial Model (Theoretical).

3756 Mexican migration to the United States: challenge to Christian witness and national policy. CHURCH AND SOCIETY, Vol. 72, no. 5 (May, June, 1982), p. 29-46. English. **DESCR:** Immigration Regulation and Control; Religion; *Undocumented Workers; United States-Mexico Relations.

3757 Meyer, Lorenzo. Mexico frente a los Estados Unidos, 1971-1980. DIALOGOS, Vol. 18, (January, February, 1982), p. 3-12. Spanish. **DESCR:** *Mexico; *United States-Mexico Relations.

3758 Migdail, Carl J. Mexico's poverty: driving force for border jumpers. U.S. NEWS & WORLD REPORT, Vol. 94, no. 9 (March 7, 1983), p. 42-44. English. **DESCR:** Mexico; Migration; *Poverty.

3759 Morales, Cesareo. El impacto norteamericano en la politica economica de Mexico (1970-1983). CUADERNOS POLITICOS, Vol. 38, (October, December, 1983), p. 81-101. Spanish. **DESCR:** Mexico; Political History and Conditions; *United States-Mexico Relations.

3760 Newman, Allen R. The impacts of emigration on the Mexican economy. MIGRATION TODAY, Vol. 10, no. 2 (1982), p. 17-21. English. **DESCR:** Employment; *Mexican Economy; *Migration; Socioeconomic Factors; Undocumented Workers.

3761 Peso pack announced for border businesses. NUESTRO, Vol. 6, no. 7 (September 1982), p. 52. English. **DESCR:** *Economic Policy; *Economics; *U.S. Small Business Administration.

3762 Stacy, Gerald F. From stranger to neighbor. CHURCH AND SOCIETY, Vol. 72, no. 5 (May, June, 1982), p. 1-71. English. **DESCR:** *Migration; Religion; Undocumented Workers.

3763 Sutton, Susan Buck and Brunner, Tracy. Life on the road: Midwestern migrant farmworker survival skills. MIGRATION TODAY, Vol. 11, no. 1 (1983), p. 24-31. English. **DESCR:** Agribusiness; Agricultural Laborers; Indiana; Migrant Children; Migrant Education; *Migrant Labor; Stereotypes.

3764 Weber, Kenneth R. Book review of: HISPANIC VILLAGES OF NORTHERN NEW MEXICO. SOUTHWEST ECONOMY AND SOCIETY, Vol. 1, no. 1 (Spring 1976), p. 48. English. **DESCR:** Book Reviews; Great Depression, 1929-1933; *HISPANIC VILLAGES OF NORTHERN NEW MEXICO; New Mexico; Tewa Basin, NM; Weigle, Marta.

3765 Zuniga, Jo Ann and Bonilla, Tony. Talking Texas: turning the tables with LULAC. HISPANIC BUSINESS, Vol. 5, no. 9 (September 1983), p. 18-19+. English. **DESCR:** *Bonilla, Tony; Business Enterprises; Consumers; League of United Latin American Citizens (LULAC); Marketing; Texas.

Economic Policy

3766 Hispanic coalition formed on economy. NUESTRO, Vol. 5, no. 8 (November 1981), p. 38. English. **DESCR:** *De Baca, Fernando E.C.; Hispanic Coalition for Economic Recovery.

3767 Peso pack announced for border businesses. NUESTRO, Vol. 6, no. 7 (September 1982), p. 52. English. **DESCR:** *Economic History and Conditions; *Economics; *U.S. Small Business Administration.

Economic Refugees

3768 Haitian boat people. NUESTRO, Vol. 5, no. 8 (November 1981), p. 10. English. **DESCR:** *Haiti; Political Refugees; World Bank.

Economically Disadvantaged
    USE: Poverty

Economics

3769 Bonilla, Tony. New doors of opportunity. LATINO, Vol. 53, no. 3 (May 1982), p. 7. English.

Economics (cont.)

3770 Bronfenbrenner, Martin. Hyphenated Americans-economic aspects. LAW AND CONTEMPORARY PROBLEMS, Vol. 45, no. 2 (Spring 1982), p. 9-27. English. DESCR: *Chiswick, Barry R.; *Immigrants; Racism; Smith, James P.; Welch, Finis R.

3771 Burciaga, Jose Antonio. Death of el senor Peso. NUESTRO, Vol. 6, no. 7 (September 1982), p. 52. English. DESCR: *Economic History and Conditions; Mexico.

3772 Chavarria, Jesus. How are we doing? HISPANIC BUSINESS, Vol. 4, no. 8 (August 1983), p. 6. English. DESCR: Elected Officials; *Finance; Voter Turnout.

3773 De la Garza, Rodolfo O. Chicano-Mexican relations: a framework for research. SOCIAL SCIENCE QUARTERLY, Vol. 63, (March 1982), p. 115-130. English. DESCR: *International Economic Relations.

3774 Economic conference to be held in Phoenix. LATINO, Vol. 54, no. 3 (April 1983), p. 8. English.

3775 Estado, cerco financiero y proyecto nacional. INFORME: RELACIONES MEXICO-ESTADOS UNIDOS, Vol. 1, no. 3 (July, December, 1982), p. 160-197. Spanish. DESCR: *Mexico; *Nationalization.

3776 Gallegos, Herman. Making a dent in the corporate hierarchy. NUESTRO, Vol. 6, no. 9 (November 1982), p. 49-51. English. DESCR: *Economic History and Conditions; Latin Americans.

3777 Growth of U.S. Hispanic income: 1950-1982. HISPANIC BUSINESS, Vol. 5, no. 12 (December 1983), p. 46. English. DESCR: *Income; Research Methodology.

3778 Illegal aliens vital to economy, mayor says. NUESTRO, Vol. 7, no. 2 (March 1983), p. 54. English. DESCR: Border Region; Cisneros, Henry, Mayor of San Antonio, TX; *Undocumented Workers.

3779 Latin America booming. HISPANIC BUSINESS, Vol. 4, no. 1 (January 1982), p. 25. English. DESCR: Latin America.

3780 Navarro, Armando. Project 1983. LATINO, Vol. 54, no. 1 (January, February, 1983), p. 20-21. English.

3781 Peso pack announced for border businesses. NUESTRO, Vol. 6, no. 7 (September 1982), p. 52. English. DESCR: *Economic History and Conditions; *Economic Policy; *U.S. Small Business Administration.

3782 Petroleo, negociaciones fiancieras y nueva estrategia economica de Mexico. INFORME: RELACIONES MEXICO-ESTADOS UNIDOS, Vol. 1, no. 3 (July, December, 1982), p. 198-208. Spanish. DESCR: Mexico; *Petroleum Industry.

3783 Reaganomics. LATINO, Vol. 53, no. 7 (November 1982), p. 18-20. English. DESCR: *Reagan Administration.

3784 Salvatierra, Richard. Debtors' row expands in Latin America. NUESTRO, Vol. 6, no. 9 (November 1982), p. 34-35. English. DESCR: Banking Industry; Debt; *Latin America.

3785 Tracking the recovery. HISPANIC BUSINESS, Vol. 5, no. 7 (July 1983), p. 14. English. DESCR: *Employment.

3786 Turnure, Juan C. Hemisphere bulletin. AGENDA, Vol. 11, no. 3 (May, June, 1981), p. 56-57. English. DESCR: Latin American Studies; Latin Americans; Politics.

Ecuador

3787 Ecuadorian president Osvaldo Hurtado Larrea on the future of Ecuador. CAMINOS, Vol. 4, no. 1-2 (January, February, 1983), p. 56-57,61. Bilingual. DESCR: Hurtado Larrea, Osvaldo; International Relations.

Edible Plants

USE: Herbal Medicine

Edinburg, TX

3788 Salvadorans left in truck to die. NUESTRO, Vol. 6, no. 8 (October 1982), p. 12. English. DESCR: Death (Concept); Deportation; Undocumented Workers.

EL EDITOR (Lubbock, TX)

3789 Cantu, Hector. Aqui en Tejas: Hispanic newspapers: city, community papers taking a business approach to the news. NATIONAL HISPANIC JOURNAL, Vol. 2, no. 1 (Summer 1983), p. 9. English. DESCR: AUSTIN LIGHT (TX); EL SOL DE HOUSTON (TX); Journalism; *Newspapers; THE TEXICAN (Dallas, TX).

Editorials

3790 Soto, Grace. Editorial. LATINA, Vol. 1, no. 3 (1983), p. 4. English. DESCR: Chicanas; *LATINA [magazine].

3791 Stone, Marvin. The illegals: one more try. U.S. NEWS & WORLD REPORT, Vol. 94, no. 15 (April 18, 1983), p. 94. English. DESCR: Immigration Law; *Immigration Regulation and Control; Simpson-Mazzoli Bill.

Education

3792 Amador, Richard S. Raising our expectations of Hispanic students. CAMINOS, Vol. 4, no. 10 (November 1983), p. 30. English. DESCR: Students.

3793 America's most important investment. LATINO, Vol. 54, no. 2 (March 1983), p. 13+. English.

3794 Aqui en Tejas: staying on that long road to success: mentors, how to find a helping hand to assist you achieve educational goals. NATIONAL HISPANIC JOURNAL, Vol. 2, no. 1 (Summer 1983), p. 8. English. DESCR: Careers; Fashion; *Mentors.

3795 Avila, Joaquin G. The computer revolution: only for the few? NUESTRO, Vol. 7, no. 6 (August 1983), p. 29. English. DESCR: *Computers; Mexican American Legal Defense and Educational Fund (MALDEF).

3796 Baca, Judith F. Secretary of Education Terrell Bell speaks out. LATINO, Vol. 54, no. 2 (March 1983), p. 24+. English. DESCR: *Bell, Terrell H.

3797 Barclay, Lisa K. Using Spanish as the language of instruction with Mexican-American Head Start children: a re-evaluation using meta-analysis. PERCEPTUAL AND MOTOR SKILLS, Vol. 56, no. 2-4 (1983), p. 359-366. English. DESCR: Languages; Psychological Testing; *Spanish Language.

Education (cont.)

3798 Bilingual effort offers few jobs. NUESTRO, Vol. 7, no. 6 (August 1983), p. 13. English. **DESCR:** *Bilingual Bicultural Education; California; Teaching Profession.

3799 Bonilla, Tony. A decade of success. LATINO, Vol. 54, no. 2 (March 1983), p. 4. English. **DESCR:** Children.

3800 Bonilla, Tony. There is trouble in our schools. LATINO, Vol. 53, no. 4 (June 1982), p. 6. English.

3801 Brocksbank, Bonilla are winners of LNESC award. LATINO, Vol. 53, no. 8 (December 1982), p. 26. English. **DESCR:** Bonilla, Tony; Brocksbank, Robert W.; *League of United Latin American Citizens (LULAC); LULAC National Education Service Centers (LNESC).

3802 Burciaga, Cecilia Preciado. Cap and gown vs. cap and apron. NUESTRO, Vol. 6, no. 4 (May 1982), p. 43. English. **DESCR:** *Dropouts.

3803 Canales, Judy. Preparing your child for a higher education: staying on that long road to sucess. NATIONAL HISPANIC JOURNAL, Vol. 1, no. 4 (Spring 1983), p. 6. English. **DESCR:** Children; Educational Psychology; *Higher Education.

3804 Canchola, E. M. School daze: reflections on what school days were like for some Latinos in the 1940's. NUESTRO, Vol. 6, no. 4 (May 1982), p. 30-33. English. **DESCR:** *Short Story.

3805 Chase, Marilyn. Mired minority: Latins rise in numbers in U.S. but don't win influence or affluence. WALL STREET JOURNAL, Vol. 19, no. 43 (June 9, 1982), p. 1+. English. **DESCR:** Assimilation; Employment; *Social History and Conditions.

3806 Coca-Cola USA Today outlines Latino agenda. NUESTRO, Vol. 7, no. 9 (November 1983), p. 36. English. **DESCR:** Business; Coca-Cola Company; *Coca-Cola National Hispanic Education Fund; *Financial Aid; Funding Sources.

3807 Conoley, Martin. The hidden threat of underemployment. HISPANIC BUSINESS, Vol. 5, no. 10 (October 1983), p. 14+. English. **DESCR:** *Employment; Employment Training; Labor Supply and Market; Personnel Management.

3808 Education center named Alfonso B. Perez. NUESTRO, Vol. 6, no. 5 (June, July, 1982), p. 30. English. **DESCR:** East Los Angeles, CA; Educational Services; *Perez, Alfonso B.

3809 Education: is it only for the elitist? LATINO, Vol. 53, no. 2 (March, April, 1982), p. 27-28. English. **DESCR:** Politics.

3810 Englebrecht, Guillermina. And now Domingo... in school in the United States. CHILDHOOD EDUCATION, Vol. 60, no. 2 (November, December, 1983), p. 90-95. English. **DESCR:** Curriculum; Mexico; Textbooks; *Undocumented Children.

3811 Equal protection: right of illegal alien children to state provided education. HARVARD LAW REVIEW, Vol. 96, no. 1 (November 1982), p. 130-140. English. **DESCR:** *Children; Civil Rights; Discrimination in Education; Doe v. Plyer [Tyler Independent School District, Texas]; *Undocumented Workers.

3812 Gallagher, Michael P. Constitutional law - equal protection: a Texas statute which withholds state funds for the education of illegal alien children ... VILLANOVA LAW REVIEW, Vol. 28, no. 1 (November 1982), p. 198-224. English. **DESCR:** Constitutional Amendments - Fourteenth; Doe v. Plyer [Tyler Independent School District, Texas]; Tyler Independent School District, Texas; *Undocumented Workers.

3813 Garcia, Mario T. Americanization and the Mexican immigrant, 1880-1930. JOURNAL OF ETHNIC STUDIES, Vol. 6, no. 2 (Summer 1978), p. 19-34. English. **DESCR:** *Acculturation; Cultural Characteristics; Culture; Immigrant Labor; Immigration.

3814 Garcia, Paco. Voices: Hispanic voices needed in the education debate. NUESTRO, Vol. 7, no. 5 (June, July, 1983), p. 53-54. English. **DESCR:** Bilingual Bicultural Education; *Discrimination in Education; *Discrimination in Employment; Federal Government; *Latin Americans; President's Commission on Excellence in Education; Reagan, Ronald; U.S. Department of Health, Education and Welfare (HEW).

3815 Garcia, Ray J. The technological challenge: Hispanics as participants or observers. HISPANIC BUSINESS, Vol. 4, no. 7 (July 1982), p. 20-21,26. English. **DESCR:** *Careers; *Engineering as a Profession; Technology.

3816 Giamatti, A. Bartlett. Government has a role to promote access to education. LATINO, Vol. 54, no. 2 (March 1983), p. 21+. English. **DESCR:** Government.

3817 Gonzalez, Gilbert G. Educational reform and the Mexican community in Los Angeles. SOUTHWEST ECONOMY AND SOCIETY, Vol. 3, no. 3 (Spring 1978), p. 24-51. English. **DESCR:** Counseling Services (Educational); Curriculum; Enrollment; *History; Intelligence Tests; Los Angeles, CA; *Los Angeles City School District; Tracking (Educational); Vocational Education.

3818 Gonzalez, Larry. Serving our students: Larry Gonzalez (interview). CAMINOS, Vol. 4, no. 10 (November 1983), p. 34-36. English. **DESCR:** *Gonzalez, Larry; Los Angeles Unified School District; *Primary School Education.

3819 Gonzalez, Roseann Duenas. Teaching Mexican American students to write: capitalizing on the culture. ENGLISH JOURNAL, Vol. 71, no. 7 (November 1982), p. 20-24. English. **DESCR:** Cultural Characteristics; Educational Innovations; *Language Arts; Style and Composition.

3820 Government review. NUESTRO, Vol. 7, no. 7 (September 1983), p. 55. English. **DESCR:** AIDS Hotline; California; Employment; Food for Survival, New York, NY; Funding Sources; *Government Services; Hewlett Foundation; Laborers; Mathematics, Engineering and Science Achievement (MESA); Population Trends; Public Health; Stanford University, Stanford, CA.

3821 Government review. NUESTRO, Vol. 7, no. 6 (August 1983), p. 56. English. **DESCR:** Ballet de Puerto Rico; Dance; Employment; *Government Funding Sources; Government Services; Housing; Income; National Fair Housing Law; Population Distribution; Urban Development Action Grant (UDAG); Veterans.

Education (cont.)

3822 Griego, Richard J. Crisis in science
education: from Sputnik to Pac-man. CAMINOS,
Vol. 4, no. 6 (June 1983), p. 47-49,67.
English. **DESCR:** *Science.

3823 Haro, Carlos Manuel. Chicanos and higher
education: a review of selected literature.
AZTLAN, Vol. 14, no. 1 (Spring 1983), p.
35-77. English. **DESCR:** California; *Higher
Education; Literature Reviews; Students.

3824 Heberton Craig N. To educate and not to
educate: the plight of undocumented alien
children in Texas. WASHINGTON UNIVERSITY LAW
QUARTERLY, Vol. 60, no. 1 (Spring 1982), p.
119-159. English. **DESCR:** *Children; Doe v.
Plyer [Tyler Independent School District,
Texas]; San Antonio School District v.
Rodriguez; *Undocumented Workers.

3825 Improving the schools. NUESTRO, Vol. 6, no.
3 (April 1982), p. 9. English. **DESCR:**
*Bilingual Bicultural Education; Puerto
Rican Education; Puerto Ricans.

3826 Jimenez, Carlos M. Crisis in Chicano
schools. CORAZON DE AZTLAN, Vol. 1, no. 2
(March, April, 1982), p. 12-15. English.

3827 Klein, Carol A. Children's concepts of the
earth and the sun: a cross cultural study.
SCIENCE EDUCATION, Vol. 66, no. 1 (January
1982), p. 95-107. English. **DESCR:** Anglo
Americans; Children; Cultural Pluralism;
*Science.

3828 Laosa, Luis M. School occupation, culture,
and family: the impact of parental schooling
on the parent-child relationship. JOURNAL OF
EDUCATIONAL PSYCHOLOGY, Vol. 74, no. 6
(December 1982), p. 791-827. English.
DESCR: Academic Achievement; *Parent and
Child Relationships.

3829 Latinos and higher education. NUESTRO, Vol.
6, no. 10 (December 1982), p. 18-19.
English. **DESCR:** *Higher Education; Hispanic
Higher Education Coalition (HHEC).

3830 Leigh, Monroe. United States Constitution -
equal protection deprivation of education in
illegal alien school-children not justified
by substantial state goal. AMERICAN JOURNAL
OF INTERNATIONAL LAW, Vol. 77, no. 1
(January 1983), p. 151-153. English. **DESCR:**
*Children; Discrimination in Education; Doe
v. Plyer [Tyler Independent School District,
Texas]; Texas; *Undocumented Workers.

3831 Let pac man do it. LATINO, Vol. 54, no. 3
(April 1983), p. 5. English.

3832 Madrid, Arturo and Rodriguez, Richard. The
mis-education of rich-heard road-ree-guess.
MAIZE, Vol. 5, no. 3-4 (Spring, Summer,
1982), p. 88-92. English. **DESCR:**
Assimilation; *Book Reviews; English
Language.

3833 MALDEF's goal: a fair opportunity for
Hispanics to compete. NUESTRO, Vol. 7, no. 6
(August 1983), p. 26-28+. English. **DESCR:**
Employment; *Legal Reform; *Mexican American
Legal Defense and Educational Fund (MALDEF).

3834 Math-based careers. HISPANIC BUSINESS, Vol.
4, no. 5 (May 1982), p. 22. English. **DESCR:**
Careers; Engineering as a Profession;
*Financial Aid; National Action Council for
Minorities in Engineering (NACME); Society
for Hispanic Professional Engineers (SHPE).

3835 Math-based careers. HISPANIC BUSINESS, Vol.
5, no. 7 (July 1983), p. 22. English.
DESCR: *Careers; Mathematics; National
Council for Minorities in Engineering
(NACME); Nursing.

3836 Math-based careers. HISPANIC BUSINESS, Vol.
5, no. 10 (October 1983), p. 28. English.
DESCR: *Careers; Carnation Company;
Chicanas; Engineering as a Profession;
Hispanic Policy Development Project;
Minority Engineering Education Center,
University of California, Los Angeles;
Science as a Profession; University of
California, Los Angeles (UCLA).

3837 Math-based careers. HISPANIC BUSINESS, Vol.
5, no. 11 (November 1983), p. 32. English.
DESCR: *Careers; Employment Training;
INROADS; Mathematics, Engineering and
Science Achievement (MESA); Mexican American
Legal Defense and Educational Fund (MALDEF);
Soriano, Esteban.

3838 Math-based careers. HISPANIC BUSINESS, Vol.
5, no. 12 (December 1983), p. 40. English.
DESCR: *Careers; Council on Legal Education
Opportunities (CLEO); Employment Training;
Graduate Schools; High Technology High
School, San Antonio, TX; Legal Education;
Mexican American Legal Defense and
Educational Fund (MALDEF); San Antonio, TX;
Science as a Profession.

3839 Math-based careers. HISPANIC BUSINESS, Vol.
4, no. 8 (August 1983), p. 20. English.
DESCR: Brigham Young University; Business
Administration; *Careers; Coalition of
Spanish-Speaking Mental Health Organization
(COSSMHO), Annual Regional Conference Los
Angeles, March 14-15, 1975; Cooperative
Extension Programs; Employment Training;
Financial Aid; Medical Personnel.

3840 Mayers, Raymond Sanchez. The school and
labor-force status of Hispanic youth:
implications for social policy. CHILDREN AND
YOUTH SERVICES REVIEW, Vol. 4, no. 1-
(1982), p. 175-192. English. **DESCR:**
Laborers; *Youth.

3841 McCarthy, Martha. Legal forum. The right to
an education: illegal aliens. JOURNAL OF
EDUCATIONAL EQUITY AND LEADERSHIP, Vol. 2,
no. 4 (Summer 1982), p. 282-287. English.
DESCR: Administration of Justice; Doe v.
Plyer [Tyler Independent School District,
Texas]; *Educational Law and Legislation;
Migrant Children; *Migrant Education; Texas;
Undocumented Workers.

3842 McKone, Jerry. Texas Spanish: not standard:
but not bad. NATIONAL HISPANIC JOURNAL, Vol.
1, no. 4 (Spring 1983), p. 20-21. English.
DESCR: Folk Medicine; Mejias, Hugo A.;
*Spanish Language.

3843 Mestre, Mercedes. Paving the path. HISPANIC
BUSINESS, Vol. 5, no. 10 (October 1983), p.
9. English. **DESCR:** Business Administration;
*Employment; Employment Training;
*Korn/Ferry International.

3844 Minority students given assistance. NUESTRO,
Vol. 7, no. 2 (March 1983), p. 10. English.
DESCR: Engineering as a Profession;
*Minority Engineering Education Center,
University of California, Los Angeles;
University of California, Los Angeles
(UCLA).

Education (cont.)

3845 Moore, Helen A. Hispanic women: schooling for conformity in public education. HISPANIC JOURNAL OF BEHAVIORAL SCIENCES, Vol. 5, no. 1 (March 1983), p. 45-63. English. DESCR: Academic Achievement; *Chicanas.

3846 Morton, Carlos. La vida: growing up in two cultures. NATIONAL HISPANIC JOURNAL, Vol. 1, no. 4 (Spring 1983), p. 23. English. DESCR: *Biculturalism; *EDUCATION ACROSS CULTURES; Morton, Carlos.

3847 Murray, Melissa. Aqui en Tejas: de Zabala youth session set for August: students from throughout state to attend. NATIONAL HISPANIC JOURNAL, Vol. 2, no. 1 (Summer 1983), p. 7. English. DESCR: National Hispanic Institute; Politics; Students; *Youth.

3848 Murray, Melissa and Flores, Jose. Bilingual success: a second language program that is making everyone happy (and smarter). NATIONAL HISPANIC JOURNAL, Vol. 2, no. 1 (Summer 1983), p. 14-19. English. DESCR: *Bilingual Bicultural Education; Educational Innovations; *Flores, Jose; Metz Elementary School, Austin TX.

3849 Nevarez, Miguel A. The Hispanic educational dilemma: a strategy for change. HISPANIC BUSINESS, Vol. 5, no. 11 (November 1983), p. 12. English. DESCR: Academic Achievement; Dropouts; Higher Education.

3850 A new global approach. NUESTRO, Vol. 7, no. 10 (December 1983), p. 9. English. DESCR: *Bay Area Global Education Program (BAGEP); Curriculum; Educational Innovations; Stanford University, Stanford, CA.

3851 New Salazar building. NUESTRO, Vol. 6, no. 7 (September 1982), p. 9. English. DESCR: *Art; Culture; Latin Americans; Los Angeles, CA; *Plaza de La Raza, Los Angeles, CA; Salazar, Ruben.

3852 Oakland, Thomas. Joint use of adaptive behavior and IQ to predict achievement. JOURNAL OF CONSULTING AND CLINICAL PSYCHOLOGY, Vol. 51, no. 2 (April 1983), p. 298-301. English. DESCR: *Academic Achievement; Intelligence Tests; Mathematics; Reading.

3853 Olivas, Michael. The worsening condition of Hispanic education. CAMINOS, Vol. 4, no. 6 (June 1983), p. 42-44,67. Bilingual.

3854 Olivas, Michael A. Indian, Chicano and Puerto Rican colleges: status and issues. BILINGUAL REVIEW, Vol. 9, no. 1 (January, March, 1982), p. 36-58. English. DESCR: *Colleges and Universities; Native Americans; Puerto Rican Education; Treaties.

3855 Osifchok, Diane I. The utilization of immediate scrutiny in establishing the right to education for undocumented alien children. PEPPERDINE LAW REVIEW, Vol. 10, no. 1 (December 1982), p. 139-165. English. DESCR: Civil Rights; Doe v. Plyer [Tyler Independent School District, Texas]; *Undocumented Workers.

3856 Packard, Mark. Equal protection clause requires a free public education for illegal alien children. TEXAS TECH LAW REVIEW, Vol. 14, (May 1983), p. 531-547. English. DESCR: Constitutional Amendments - Fourteenth; Doe v. Plyer [Tyler Independent School District, Texas]; *Undocumented Workers.

3857 Prida, Dolores. Playwrights Laboratory: in search of a creative formula. NUESTRO, Vol. 7, no. 10 (December 1983), p. 43. English. DESCR: Authors; *Hispanic Playwrights-in-Residence Laboratory; INTAR; *Teatro.

3858 Pride in school. LATINO, Vol. 54, no. 5 (August, September, 1983), p. 4. English. DESCR: *Community School Relationships.

3859 Que pasa? NUESTRO, Vol. 7, no. 6 (August 1983), p. 9. English. DESCR: Boy Scouts of America; *Court System; Criminal Justice System; Diabetes; Judicial Review; Petersilia, Joan; PREPARED FOR TODAY; RACIAL DISPARITIES IN THE CRIMINAL JUSTICE SYSTEM; Reagan, Ronald.

3860 Quinn, Michael Sean. Educating alien kids. TEXAS OBSERVOR, Vol. 74, no. 18 (September 17, 1982), p. 5-6. English. DESCR: Children; *Doe v. Plyer [Tyler Independent School District, Texas]; Undocumented Workers.

3861 Raat, W. Dirk. Augusto Comte, Gabino Barreda, and positivism in Mexico. AZTLAN, Vol. 14, no. 2 (Fall 1983), p. 235-251. English. DESCR: *Barreda, Gabino; *Comte, Auguste; Educational Theory and Practice; History; Mexico; Philosophy; *Positivism.

3862 Reaves, Gayle. Supreme Court rules for alien children. NUESTRO, Vol. 6, no. 5 (June, July, 1982), p. 14-16. English. DESCR: *Children; Education Equalization; Immigration Law; *Legislation; Undocumented Workers; U.S. Supreme Court.

3863 Reinstate the American dream for our children. LATINO, Vol. 54, no. 4 (May, June, 1983), p. 23+. English.

3864 Reusswig, Jim. Whence the National Hispanic Center and University? Mater artium necessitas. THRUST, Vol. 11, no. 3 (January, February, 1982), p. 32-35. English. DESCR: Bilingual Bicultural Education; *National Hispanic Center; *National Hispanic University, Oakland CA.

3865 Richardson, Chad and Yanez, Linda. "Equal justice" and Jose Reyna. NUESTRO, Vol. 6, no. 5 (June, July, 1982), p. 17. English. DESCR: Brownsville, TX; *Children; Education Equalization; Immigration Law; *Legislation; Reyna, Jose; Undocumented Workers.

3866 Rodriguez, Imelda and Bethel, Lowell J. Inquiry approach to science and language teaching. JOURNAL OF RESEARCH IN SCIENCE TEACHING, Vol. 20, no. 4 (April 1983), p. 291-296. English. DESCR: Bilingualism; *Educational Tests and Measurements; Language Arts; Learning and Cognition; Primary School Education; Science.

3867 Rosales, John. Holy Cross High: a Texas success story. NUESTRO, Vol. 6, no. 9 (November 1982), p. 41-42. English. DESCR: Carr, Vikki; Holy Cross High School, San Antonio, TX; *San Antonio, TX.

3868 Rosenhouse-Persson, Sandra and Sabagh, Georges. Attitudes toward abortion among Catholic Mexican-American women: the effects of religiosity and education. DEMOGRAPHY, Vol. 20, no. 1 (February 1983), p. 87-98. English. DESCR: Abortion; Attitude (Psychological); *Catholic Church; Religion.

Education (cont.)

3869 Schey, Peter A. Unnamed witness number 1: now attending the Texas public schools. MIGRATION TODAY, Vol. 10, no. 5 (1982), p. 22-27. English. **DESCR:** Constitutional Amendments - Fourteenth; Education Equalization; Educational Law and Legislation; Equal Protection Clause; Migrant Children; Texas Public Schools; *Undocumented Children; U.S. Supreme Court Case.

3870 School focuses on Latino needs. NUESTRO, Vol. 7, no. 1 (January, February, 1983), p. 12. English. **DESCR:** Catholic University, Washington, D.C.; Colleges and Universities; *Hispanidad '83.

3871 School house door must be open to children of illegal aliens. CHILDREN'S LEGAL RIGHTS JOURNAL, Vol. 3, (June 1982), p. 19-21. English. **DESCR:** Constitutional Amendments - Fourteenth; Doe v. Plyer [Tyler Independent School District, Texas]; Texas; Undocumented Workers.

3872 Skirius, John. Barreda, Vasconcelos, and the Mexican educational reforms. AZTLAN, Vol. 14, no. 2 (Fall 1983), p. 307-341. English. **DESCR:** *Barreda, Gabino; *Educational Theory and Practice; History; Mexico; Positivism; *Vasconcelos, Jose.

3873 A statistical profile of California public schools. CAMINOS, Vol. 3, no. 10 (November 1982), p. 46-47. English. **DESCR:** *California; *Statistics.

3874 Supreme Court recognizes special importance of education. MENTAL DISABILITY LAW REPORTER, Vol. 6, (July, August, 1982), p. 227-229. English. **DESCR:** Doe v. Plyer [Tyler Independent School District, Texas]; San Antonio School District v. Rodriguez; THE PLUM PLUM PICKERS; Undocumented Workers.

3875 Tio Pepe habla espanol. CAMINOS, Vol. 4, no. 10 (November 1983), p. 31. English. **DESCR:** *Spanish Language; *Suarez Weiss, Patricia.

3876 U.S. workers tutor students. NUESTRO, Vol. 6, no. 4 (May 1982), p. 13. English. **DESCR:** Children; Rios, Al.

3877 Vasquez, Ivan. Analysis of June 15, 1982 opinion issued by the U.S. Supreme Court in the case of Texas undocumented children. MIGRATION TODAY, Vol. 10, no. 3-4 (1982), p. 49-51. English. **DESCR:** Constitutional Amendments - Fourteenth; *Education Equalization; Educational Law and Legislation; Equal Protection Clause; Migrant Children; *Undocumented Children; U.S. Supreme Court Case.

3878 What bilingual education means to the nation. NUESTRO, Vol. 7, no. 2 (March 1983), p. 52-53. English. **DESCR:** *Bilingual Bicultural Education; Millan, Aida; Nguyen, Anh Tuan; Rodriguez, Axel.

3879 Willie, Charles V. First learning unchallenged and untested. CHANGE, Vol. 14, no. 7 (October 1982), p. 37-41. English. **DESCR:** Affirmative Action; Bilingual Bicultural Education; Biography; Book Reviews; *HUNGER OF MEMORY: THE EDUCATION OF RICHARD RODRIGUEZ; Rodriguez, Richard.

3880 Witt, Elder. Court rules illegal aliens entitled to public schooling. CONGRESSIONAL QUARTERLY WEEKLY REPORT, Vol. 40, (June 19, 1982), p. 1479-1480. English. **DESCR:** Doe v. Plyer [Tyler Independent School District, Texas]; Immigration; Texas v. Certain Undocumented Alien Children; Undocumented Children; *Undocumented Workers.

3881 Young, Rowland L. Schools ... illegal aliens ... AMERICAN BAR ASSOCIATION JOURNAL, Vol. 68, (September 1982), p. 1156-1157. English. **DESCR:** Constitutional Amendments - Fourteenth; Undocumented Workers.

EDUCATION ACROSS CULTURES

3882 Morton, Carlos. La vida: growing up in two cultures. NATIONAL HISPANIC JOURNAL, Vol. 1, no. 4 (Spring 1983), p. 23. English. **DESCR:** *Biculturalism; Education; Morton, Carlos.

Education Equalization

3883 Carrison, Muriel Paskin. Bilingual-no! PRINCIPAL, Vol. 62, no. 3 (January 1983), p. 9. English. **DESCR:** *Bilingual Bicultural Education; Cultural Characteristics; Socioeconomic Factors.

3884 Olivas, Michael A. Federal higher education policy: the case of Hispanics. EDUCATIONAL EVALUATION AND POLICY ANALYSIS, Vol. 4, no. 3 (Fall 1982), p. 301-310. English. **DESCR:** Discrimination in Education; Educational Law and Legislation; Federal Government; *Higher Education; Policy Formation.

3885 Reaves, Gayle. Supreme Court rules for alien children. NUESTRO, Vol. 6, no. 5 (June, July, 1982), p. 14-16. English. **DESCR:** *Children; Education; Immigration Law; *Legislation; Undocumented Workers; U.S. Supreme Court.

3886 Richardson, Chad and Yanez, Linda. "Equal justice" and Jose Reyna. NUESTRO, Vol. 6, no. 5 (June, July, 1982), p. 17. English. **DESCR:** Brownsville, TX; *Children; Education; Immigration Law; *Legislation; Reyna, Jose; Undocumented Workers.

3887 Schey, Peter A. Unnamed witness number 1: now attending the Texas public schools. MIGRATION TODAY, Vol. 10, no. 5 (1982), p. 22-27. English. **DESCR:** Constitutional Amendments - Fourteenth; Education; Educational Law and Legislation; Equal Protection Clause; Migrant Children; Texas Public Schools; *Undocumented Children; U.S. Supreme Court Case.

3888 Valenzuela-Crocker, Elvira. Confrontation over the Civil Rights Commission. NUESTRO, Vol. 7, no. 10 (December 1983), p. 21-27. English. **DESCR:** Administration of Justice; Affirmative Action; *Civil Rights; Employment; *U.S. Commission on Civil Rights; Voting Rights.

3889 Vasquez, Ivan. Analysis of June 15, 1982 opinion issued by the U.S. Supreme Court in the case of Texas undocumented children. MIGRATION TODAY, Vol. 10, no. 3-4 (1982), p. 49-51. English. **DESCR:** Constitutional Amendments - Fourteenth; Education; Educational Law and Legislation; Equal Protection Clause; Migrant Children; *Undocumented Children; U.S. Supreme Court Case.

EDUCATION IN THE 80'S: MULTICULTURAL EDUCATION

3890 Eaton, Joli. Book review of: EDUCATION IN THE 80's: MULTICULTURAL EDUCATION. HISPANIC JOURNAL OF BEHAVIORAL SCIENCES, Vol. 5, no. 2 (June 1983), p. 238-240. English. **DESCR:** Banks, James A.; Book Reviews.

Educational Administration

3891 Consalvo, Robert W. Book review of: PROGRAM IMPACT EVALUATIONS: AN INTRODUCTION FOR MANAGERS OF TITLE VII PROJECTS - A DRAFT GUIDEBOOK. BILINGUAL JOURNAL, Vol. 7, no. 2 (Winter 1983), p. 36-37. English. **DESCR:** Bilingual Bicultural Education; Bissell, Joan; Book Reviews; ELEMENTARY AND SECONDARY EDUCATION ACT; Evaluation (Educational); *PROGRAM IMPACT EVALUATIONS: AN INTRODUCTION FOR MANAGERS OF TITLE VII PROJECTS - A DRAFT GUIDEBOOK ESEA TITLE VII.

3892 De George, George P. The guest editor speaks. BILINGUAL JOURNAL, Vol. 7, no. 2 (Winter 1983), p. 6. English. **DESCR:** *Bilingual Bicultural Education; *Evaluation (Educational).

3893 Liberty, Paul G., et al. [Evaluation in bilingual education]. BILINGUAL JOURNAL, Vol. 7, no. 2 (Winter 1983), p. 1-40. English. **DESCR:** *Bilingual Bicultural Education; Curriculum; ELEMENTARY AND SECONDARY EDUCATION ACT; *Evaluation (Educational).

3894 Murphy, John W. and Redden, Richard. The use of management by objectives in medical education enrichment programs. JOURNAL OF MEDICAL EDUCATION, Vol. 57, no. 12 (December 1982), p. 911-917. English. **DESCR:** Educational Innovations; Evaluation (Educational); Management by Objectives (MBO); *Medical Education.

3895 Olivas, Michael A. Research and theory on Hispanic education: students, finance, and governance. AZTLAN, Vol. 14, no. 1 (Spring 1983), p. 111-146. English. **DESCR:** *Educational Theory and Practice; School Finance; Students.

3896 Ortiz, Flora Ida. The distribution of Mexican American women in school organizations. HISPANIC JOURNAL OF BEHAVIORAL SCIENCES, Vol. 4, no. 2 (June 1982), p. 181-198. English. **DESCR:** *Chicanas; Educational Organizations; Teaching Profession.

3897 Walia, Adorna. Book review of: DATA FORMS FOR EVALUATING BILINGUAL EDUCATION PROGRAM. BILINGUAL JOURNAL, Vol. 7, no. 2 (Winter 1983), p. 38. English. **DESCR:** Bilingual Bicultural Education; Book Reviews; Cohen, Bernard H.; *DATA FORMS FOR EVALUATING BILINGUAL EDUCATION PROGRAMS; Evaluation (Educational).

Educational Cognitive Style (ECS)

3898 Spiridakis, John N. Three diagnostics tools for use with the bilingual child. BILINGUAL JOURNAL, Vol. 7, no. 4 (Summer 1983), p. 23-25. English. **DESCR:** *Bilingual Bicultural Education; Educational Psychology; *Educational Tests and Measurements; Field-Sensitive/Field-Independent Behavior Observation Instruments; Learning and Cognition; Learning Style Inventory (LSI).

Educational Desegregation
USE: Busing

Educational Innovations

3899 Beyer, Sandra S. and Kluck, Frederick J. French via Spanish: a positive approach to language learning for minority students. FOREIGN LANGUAGE ANNALS, Vol. 15, no. 2 (April 1982), p. 123-126. English. **DESCR:** *French Language; Language Development; Spanish Language; University of Texas at El Paso.

3900 Blomstedt, Robert; Thomas, Jackie; and Teyna, Tadeo. Applying existential thought to bilingual education. BILINGUAL JOURNAL, Vol. 7, no. 4 (Summer 1983), p. 26,28. English. **DESCR:** *Bilingual Bicultural Education; *Philosophy.

3901 Bradley, Curtis H. and Friedenberg, Joan E. Tips for the English speaking multicultural vocational teacher. BILINGUAL JOURNAL, Vol. 6, no. 1 (Fall 1982), p. 6-9. English. **DESCR:** *Cultural Pluralism; Limited-English Proficient (LEP); Teacher-pupil Interaction; *Vocational Education.

3902 Flori, Monica. The Hispanic community as a resource for a practical Spanish program. FOREIGN LANGUAGE ANNALS, Vol. 15, no. 3 (May 1982), p. 213-215. English. **DESCR:** Community School Relationships; Curriculum; Language Development; Lewis and Clark College, Portland, OR; *Spanish Language.

3903 Gonzalez, Roseann Duenas. Teaching Mexican American students to write: capitalizing on the culture. ENGLISH JOURNAL, Vol. 71, no. 7 (November 1982), p. 20-24. English. **DESCR:** Cultural Characteristics; Education; *Language Arts; Style and Composition.

3904 Murphy, John W. and Redden, Richard. The use of management by objectives in medical education enrichment programs. JOURNAL OF MEDICAL EDUCATION, Vol. 57, no. 12 (December 1982), p. 911-917. English. **DESCR:** *Educational Administration; Evaluation (Educational); Management by Objectives (MBO); *Medical Education.

3905 Murray, Melissa and Flores, Jose. Bilingual success: a second language program that is making everyone happy (and smarter). NATIONAL HISPANIC JOURNAL, Vol. 2, no. 1 (Summer 1983), p. 14-19. English. **DESCR:** *Bilingual Bicultural Education; Education; *Flores, Jose; Metz Elementary School, Austin TX.

3906 A new global approach. NUESTRO, Vol. 7, no. 10 (December 1983), p. 9. English. **DESCR:** *Bay Area Global Education Program (BAGEP); Curriculum; Education; Stanford University, Stanford, CA.

3907 Taylor, Karla. Accion/action: a coast-to-coast sampling of innovative Hispanic programs. CASE CURRENTS, Vol. 9, no. 4 (April 1983), p. 11-13. English. **DESCR:** *Enrollment; Higher Education.

Educational Law and Legislation

3908 Appeals court overturns Texas bilingual order. PHI DELTA KAPPAN, Vol. 64, no. 1 (September 1982), p. 75. English. **DESCR:** Bilingual Bicultural Education; Texas.

3909 Baker, Catherine A. Bilingual education: que pasa? CONTEMPORARY EDUCATION, Vol. 54, no. 2 (Winter 1983), p. 105-108. English. **DESCR:** *Bilingual Bicultural Education.

Educational Law and Legislation (cont.)

3910 Barry, Joseph E. Politics, bilingual education, and the curriculum. EDUCATIONAL LEADERSHIP, Vol. 40, no. 8 (May 1983), p. 56-60. English. **DESCR:** *Bilingual Bicultural Education; Educational Theory and Practice.

3911 Campbell, Jack K. Senator Yarborough and the Texan RWY brand on bilingual education and federal aid. EDUCATIONAL STUDIES, Vol. 12, no. 4 (Winter 1981, 1982), p. 403-415. English. **DESCR:** *Bilingual Bicultural Education; History; Social History and Conditions; Texas; Yarborough, Ralph Webster.

3912 Chacon, Peter (Assemblyman). The politics of bilingual education=La politica de la legislacion bilingue. CAMINOS, Vol. 2, no. 7 (December 1981), p. 14-17. Bilingual. **DESCR:** *Bilingual Bicultural Education.

3913 Cordasco, Francesco. Bilingual education: overview and inventory. EDUCATIONAL FORUM, Vol. 47, (Spring 1983), p. 321-334. English. **DESCR:** *Bilingual Bicultural Education; Educational Theory and Practice; English as a Second Language; History; Literature Reviews.

3914 Haft, Jonathan D. Assuring equal educational opportunity for language-minority students: bilingual education and the Equal Educational Opportunity Act of 1974. COLUMBIA JOURNAL OF LAW AND SOCIAL PROBLEMS, Vol. 18, no. 2 (1983), p. 209-293. English. **DESCR:** *Bilingual Bicultural Education; Civil Rights; English as a Second Language; *Equal Educational Opportunity Act of 1974 (EEOA); Laws; Students.

3915 Holley, Joe. Page two. TEXAS OBSERVOR, Vol. 75, no. 1 (January 14, 1983), p. 2-3. English. **DESCR:** *Communities Organized for Public Service (COPS); Cultural Organizations; Political Parties and Organizations.

3916 Levin, Betsy. An analysis of the federal attempt to regulate bilingual education: protecting civil rights or controlling curriculum? JOURNAL OF LAW AND EDUCATION, Vol. 12, no. 1 (January 1983), p. 29-60. English. **DESCR:** Affirmative Action Programs; *Bilingual Bicultural Education; Civil Rights; Cultural Pluralism; Federal Government.

3917 McCarthy, Martha. Legal forum. The right to an education: illegal aliens. JOURNAL OF EDUCATIONAL EQUITY AND LEADERSHIP, Vol. 2, no. 4 (Summer 1982), p. 282-287. English. **DESCR:** Administration of Justice; Doe v. Plyer [Tyler Independent School District, Texas]; Education; Migrant Children; *Migrant Education; Texas; Undocumented Workers.

3918 McFadden, Bernard J. Bilingual education and the law. JOURNAL OF LAW AND EDUCATION, Vol. 12, no. 1 (January 1983), p. 1-27. English. **DESCR:** Administration of Justice; *Bilingual Bicultural Education; Discrimination in Education; History.

3919 Olivas, Michael A. Federal higher education policy: the case of Hispanics. EDUCATIONAL EVALUATION AND POLICY ANALYSIS, Vol. 4, no. 3 (Fall 1982), p. 301-310. English. **DESCR:** Discrimination in Education; Education Equalization; Federal Government; *Higher Education; Policy Formation.

3920 Otheguy, Ricardo. Thinking about bilingual education: a critical appraisal. HARVARD EDUCATIONAL REVIEW, Vol. 52, no. 3 (August 1982), p. 301-314. English. **DESCR:** *Bilingual Bicultural Education; Immigration.

3921 Rips, Geoffrey. COPS educates. TEXAS OBSERVOR, Vol. 75, no. 4 (February 25, 1983), p. 1-2. English. **DESCR:** *Communities Organized for Public Service (COPS); Cultural Organizations; Political Parties and Organizations.

3922 Rips, Geoffrey. New politics in Texas: COPS comes to Austin. TEXAS OBSERVOR, Vol. 75, no. 1 (January 14, 1983), p. 1+. English. **DESCR:** *Communities Organized for Public Service (COPS); Cultural Organizations; Political Parties and Organizations.

3923 Rotberg, Iris C. Some legal and research considerations in establishing federal policy in bilingual education. HARVARD EDUCATIONAL REVIEW, Vol. 52, no. 2 (May 1982), p. 149-168. English. **DESCR:** *Bilingual Bicultural Education; History; Policy Formation; Research Methodology.

3924 Rugsaken, Kris T. Toward a true bilingual education: when federal funding ends. BILINGUAL JOURNAL, Vol. 7, no. 4 (Summer 1983), p. 9-14. English. **DESCR:** *Bilingual Bicultural Education; Bilingual Education Act of 1968; ELEMENTARY AND SECONDARY EDUCATION ACT; Funding Sources.

3925 San Miguel, Guadalupe. In the background: conflict and controversy in the evolution of bilingual legislation in Texas, 1965-73. NABE JOURNAL, Vol. 7, no. 3 (Spring 1983), p. 23-40. English. **DESCR:** *Bilingual Bicultural Education; Educational Theory and Practice; Texas.

3926 Schey, Peter A. Unnamed witness number 1: now attending the Texas public schools. MIGRATION TODAY, Vol. 10, no. 5 (1982), p. 22-27. English. **DESCR:** Constitutional Amendments - Fourteenth; Education; Education Equalization; Equal Protection Clause; Migrant Children; Texas Public Schools; *Undocumented Children; U.S. Supreme Court Case.

3927 Speight, Tamara D. Current legislation of significance to the English as a second language and bilingual education communities. FOREIGN LANGUAGE ANNALS, Vol. 15, no. 4 (September 1982), p. 245-247. English. **DESCR:** Immigration Law.

3928 Summary of selected bilingual legislation. CAMINOS, Vol. 2, no. 7 (December 1981), p. 28. English. **DESCR:** *Bilingual Bicultural Education.

3929 Vasquez, Ivan. Analysis of June 15, 1982 opinion issued by the U.S. Supreme Court in the case of Texas undocumented children. MIGRATION TODAY, Vol. 10, no. 3-4 (1982), p. 49-51. English. **DESCR:** Constitutional Amendments - Fourteenth; Education; *Education Equalization; Equal Protection Clause; Migrant Children; *Undocumented Children; U.S. Supreme Court Case.

Educational Law and Legislation (cont.)

3930 Weiner, Richard E. Teaching the immigrant's child: a model plan for court-ordered bilingual education. JOURNAL OF LAW AND EDUCATION, Vol. 12, no. 1 (January 1983), p. 61-76. English. DESCR: *Bilingual Bicultural Education; Courts (Legal); Curriculum; Educational Theory and Practice.

3931 Zamora, Gloria L. Zamora speaks on bilingual education. BILINGUAL JOURNAL, Vol. 7, no. 4 (Summer 1983), p. 5-8. English. DESCR: *Bilingual Bicultural Education; Bilingual Education Act of 1968; ELEMENTARY AND SECONDARY EDUCATION ACT.

Educational Levels

3932 Adams, Russell L.; Boake, Corwin; and Crain, Charles. Bias in a neuropsychological test classification related to education, age and ethnicity. JOURNAL OF CONSULTING AND CLINICAL PSYCHOLOGY, Vol. 50, no. 1 (February 1982), p. 143-145. English. DESCR: Age Groups; Ethnic Groups; Mentally Handicapped; *Psychological Testing.

Educational Materials
USE: Curriculum Materials

Educational Opportunities

3933 The future beckons, USC's LBSA responds. HISPANIC BUSINESS, Vol. 4, no. 4 (April 1982), p. 12, 25. English. DESCR: Business; Business Education; Business Schools and Colleges; *Latino Business Students Association (LBSA); University of Southern California.

3934 Hughes invests in the future. HISPANIC BUSINESS, Vol. 4, no. 11 (November 1982), p. 8-9,26. English. DESCR: Careers; *Engineering as a Profession; Minority Introduction to Engineering (MITE); University of California, Los Angeles (UCLA).

3935 Math-based careers. HISPANIC BUSINESS, Vol. 4, no. 3 (March 1982), p. 20. English. DESCR: Careers; Congressional Hispanic Caucus; Consortium for Graduate Study in Management; *Financial Aid.

3936 Math-based careers. HISPANIC BUSINESS, Vol. 4, no. 10 (October 1982), p. 20. English. DESCR: *Careers; Engineering as a Profession; Financial Aid; Minority Business Development Agency (MBDA); National Action Council for Minorities in Engineering (NACME); National Association of Independent Schools (NAIS).

Educational Opportunity Program (EOP)

3937 Anderson, John W. The effects of culture and social class on client preference for counseling methods. JOURNAL OF NON-WHITE CONCERNS IN PERSONNEL AND GUIDANCE, Vol. 11, no. 3 (April 1983), p. 84-88. English. DESCR: Anglo Americans; Blacks; Counseling Effectiveness Scale; *Counseling (Psychological); Locus of Control; University of Illinois at Urbana.

Educational Organizations

3938 Ortiz, Flora Ida. The distribution of Mexican American women in school organizations. HISPANIC JOURNAL OF BEHAVIORAL SCIENCES, Vol. 4, no. 2 (June 1982), p. 181-198. English. DESCR: *Chicanas; Educational Administration; Teaching Profession.

Educational Psychology

3939 Canales, Judy. Preparing your child for a higher education: staying on that long road to sucess. NATIONAL HISPANIC JOURNAL, Vol. 1, no. 4 (Spring 1983), p. 6. English. DESCR: Children; Education; *Higher Education.

3940 Spiridakis, John N. Three diagnostics tools for use with the bilingual child. BILINGUAL JOURNAL, Vol. 7, no. 4 (Summer 1983), p. 23-25. English. DESCR: *Bilingual Bicultural Education; Educational Cognitive Style (ECS); *Educational Tests and Measurements; Field-Sensitive/Field-Independent Behavior Observation Instruments; Learning and Cognition; Learning Style Inventory (LSI).

Educational Services

3941 Education center named Alfonso B. Perez. NUESTRO, Vol. 6, no. 5 (June, July, 1982), p. 30. English. DESCR: East Los Angeles, CA; Education; *Perez, Alfonso B.

3942 Twelfth educational center opens. LATINO, Vol. 53, no. 8 (December 1982), p. 24-25. English.

Educational Statistics

3943 Consalvo, Robert W. and Orlandi, Lisanio R. Principles and practices of data collection and management. BILINGUAL JOURNAL, Vol. 7, no. 2 (Winter 1983), p. 13-16. English. DESCR: *Bilingual Bicultural Education; *Evaluation (Educational); Research Methodology.

3944 de los Santos, Alfredo G. Jr.; Montemayor, Joaquin; and Solis, Enrique, Jr. Chicano students in institutions of higher education: access, attrition, and achievement. AZTLAN, Vol. 14, no. 1 (Spring 1983), p. 79-110. English. DESCR: Academic Achievement; Enrollment; *Higher Education; Students.

3945 Hispanic student study undertaken. NUESTRO, Vol. 7, no. 10 (December 1983), p. 11-12. English. DESCR: Academic Achievement; Dropouts; Enrollment; Hispanic Policy Development Project; *National Commission on Secondary Schooling for Hispanics; *Secondary School Education.

3946 Sherman, Susan N., comp. Applicants to U.S. medical schools, 1977-78 to 1981-82. JOURNAL OF MEDICAL EDUCATION, Vol. 57, no. 11 (November 1982), p. 882-884. English. DESCR: Ethnic Groups; *Medical Education; Medical Students.

3947 Webster, David S. Chicano students in American higher education: a review of the literature. CAMPO LIBRE, Vol. 1, no. 2 (Summer 1981), p. 169-192. English. DESCR: Dropouts; Enrollment; Graduate Schools; *Higher Education; Literature Reviews; Professional Schools.

3948 Willig, Ann C. The effectiveness of bilingual education: review of a report. NABE JOURNAL, Vol. 6, no. 2-3 (Winter, Spring, 1981, 1982), p. 1-19. English. DESCR: *Bilingual Bicultural Education; *Research Methodology.

Educational Tests and Measurements

3949 Balasubramonian, Krishna. Not on test scores alone: the qualitative side to program evaluation. BILINGUAL JOURNAL, Vol. 7, no. 2 (Winter 1983), p. 17-21,40. English. **DESCR:** *Bilingual Bicultural Education; *Curriculum; ELEMENTARY AND SECONDARY EDUCATION ACT; Evaluation (Educational); Proposals.

3950 Chavez, Ernest L. Analysis of a Spanish translation of the Peabody Picture Vocabulary Test. PERCEPTUAL AND MOTOR SKILLS, Vol. 54, no. 3 (June 1982), p. 1335-1338. English. **DESCR:** Bilingualism; *Peabody Picture Vocabulary Test (PPVT); Spanish Language.

3951 De George, George P. Selecting tests for bilingual program evaluation. BILINGUAL JOURNAL, Vol. 7, no. 2 (Winter 1983), p. 22-28,40. English. **DESCR:** *Bilingual Bicultural Education; Curriculum; *Evaluation (Educational).

3952 Dejnozka, Edward L. and Smiley, Lydia R. Selective admissions criteria in graduate teacher education programs. JOURNAL OF TEACHER EDUCATION, Vol. 34, no. 1 (January, February, 1983), p. 24-27. English. **DESCR:** Graduate Schools; Teaching Profession.

3953 DeMauro, Gerald E. Models and assumptions for bilingual education evaluation. BILINGUAL JOURNAL, Vol. 7, no. 2 (Winter 1983), p. 8-12,40. English. **DESCR:** *Bilingual Bicultural Education; Curriculum; *Evaluation (Educational); Language Assessment Battery.

3954 Dreisbach, Melanie and Keogh, Barbara K. Testwiseness as a factor in readiness test performance of young Mexican-American children. JOURNAL OF EDUCATIONAL PSYCHOLOGY, Vol. 74, no. 2 (April 1982), p. 224-229. English. **DESCR:** *Academic Achievement; Bilingualism; Early Childhood Education.

3955 Friedman, Mary Lusky. Notes on the grading of advanced placement Spanish language examination. HISPANIA, Vol. 66, (May 1983), p. 239-241. English. **DESCR:** *Spanish Language.

3956 Llabre, Maria M. and Cuevas, Gilberto. Effects of test language and mathematical skills assessed on the scores of bilingual Hispanic students. JOURNAL FOR RESEARCH IN MATHEMATICS EDUCATION, Vol. 14, no. 4 (November 1983), p. 318-324. English. **DESCR:** Comprehensive Test of Basic Skills (CTBS); Dade County, FL; Mathematics; Stanford Achievement Test.

3957 Morrison, J. A. and Michael, W.B. Development and validation of an auditory perception test in Spanish for Hispanic children receiving reading instruction in Spanish. EDUCATIONAL AND PSYCHOLOGICAL MEASUREMENT, Vol. 42, (Summer 1982), p. 657-669. English. **DESCR:** Children; *Language Arts; Prueba de Analisis Auditivo (PAA); Reading; Spanish Language.

3958 Piersel, Wayne C., et al. Bias in content validity on the Boehm test of basic concepts for white and Mexican-American children. CONTEMPORARY EDUCATIONAL PSYCHOLOGY, Vol. 7, no. 2 (April 1982), p. 181-189. English. **DESCR:** Anglo Americans; *Boehm Test of Basic Concepts; Children; Language Arts.

3959 Plake, Barbara S., et al. Relationship of ethnic group membership to the measurement and meaning of attitudes towards reading: implications for validity of test score interpretations. EDUCATIONAL AND PSYCHOLOGICAL MEASUREMENT, Vol. 42, no. 4 (Winter 1982), p. 1259-1267. English. **DESCR:** Anglo Americans; Attitude (Psychological); Estes Reading Attitude Scale; Ethnic Groups; *Reading; Students.

3960 Ramirez, Albert and Soriano, Fernando. Social power in educational systems: its effect on Chicanos' attitudes toward the school experience. JOURNAL OF SOCIAL PSYCHOLOGY, Vol. 118, no. 1 (October 1982), p. 113-119. English. **DESCR:** Identity; Secondary School Education; *Social Psychology.

3961 Rodriguez, Imelda and Bethel, Lowell J. Inquiry approach to science and language teaching. JOURNAL OF RESEARCH IN SCIENCE TEACHING, Vol. 20, no. 4 (April 1983), p. 291-296. English. **DESCR:** Bilingualism; Education; Language Arts; Learning and Cognition; Primary School Education; Science.

3962 Sandoval, Jonathan; Zimmerman, Irla L.; and Woo-Sam, James M. Cultural difference on WISC-R verbal items. JOURNAL OF SCHOOL PSYCHOLOGY, Vol. 21, no. 1 (Spring 1983), p. 49-55. English. **DESCR:** *Intelligence Tests; Wechsler Intelligence Scale for Children-Revised (WISC-R).

3963 Sandoval, Joseph. WISC-R factoral validity for minority groups and Spearman's hypothesis. JOURNAL OF SCHOOL PSYCHOLOGY, Vol. 20, (Fall 1982), p. 198-204. English. **DESCR:** *Intelligence Tests; Wechsler Intelligence Scale for Children-Revised (WISC-R).

3964 Spiridakis, John N. Three diagnostics tools for use with the bilingual child. BILINGUAL JOURNAL, Vol. 7, no. 4 (Summer 1983), p. 23-25. English. **DESCR:** *Bilingual Bicultural Education; Educational Cognitive Style (ECS); Educational Psychology; Field-Sensitive/Field-Independent Behavior Observation Instruments; Learning and Cognition; Learning Style Inventory (LSI).

3965 Valencia, Richard R. and Rankin, Richard J. Concurrent validity and reliability of the Kaufman version of the McCarthy scales short form for a sample of Mexican-American children. EDUCATIONAL AND PSYCHOLOGICAL MEASUREMENT, Vol. 43, no. 3 (Fall 1983), p. 915-925. English. **DESCR:** Learning and Cognition; *McCarthy Scales for Children's Abilities (MSCA).

3966 Valencia, Richard R. Predicting academic achievement of Mexican American children: preliminary analysis of the McCarthy Scales. EDUCATIONAL AND PSYCHOLOGICAL MEASUREMENT, Vol. 42, (Winter 1982), p. 1269-1278. English. **DESCR:** *Academic Achievement; Children; Identity; McCarthy Scales for Children's Abilities (MSCA).

3967 Yvon, Bernard R. Effects of the language of a diagnostic test on math scores. BILINGUAL JOURNAL, Vol. 6, no. 1 (Fall 1982), p. 13-16. English. **DESCR:** Bilingual Bicultural Education; Key-Math Diagnostic Test; Language Proficiency; Mathematics.

Educational Theory and Practice

3968 Barry, Joseph E. Politics, bilingual education, and the curriculum. EDUCATIONAL LEADERSHIP, Vol. 40, no. 8 (May 1983), p. 56-60. English. DESCR: *Bilingual Bicultural Education; Educational Law and Legislation.

3969 Cordasco, Francesco. Bilingual education: overview and inventory. EDUCATIONAL FORUM, Vol. 47, (Spring 1983), p. 321-334. English. DESCR: *Bilingual Bicultural Education; Educational Law and Legislation; English as a Second Language; History; Literature Reviews.

3970 Guckert, John C. Multiculturalism: a democratic approach to education. SCHOLAR AND EDUCATOR, Vol. 6, (Spring 1982), p. 37-41. English. DESCR: *Cultural Pluralism; Identity.

3971 Iadicola, Peter and Moore, Helen A. The desegregated school and status relations among Anglo and Hispanic students: the dilemma of school desegregation. AZTLAN, Vol. 14, no. 1 (Spring 1983), p. 147-173. English. DESCR: Comparative Education; *Segregation and Desegregation; Students.

3972 Lindsey, Alfred J. Ethnic pluralism: a misguided approach to schooling. SCHOLAR AND EDUCATOR, Vol. 6, (Spring 1982), p. 42-46. English. DESCR: *Assimilation; Cultural Pluralism.

3973 Miller, Robert. Reading instruction and primary school education - Mexican teachers' viewpoints. READING TEACHER, Vol. 35, no. 8 (May 1982), p. 890-894. English. DESCR: *Curriculum; Early Childhood Education; Mexico; Teacher Attitudes.

3974 Olivas, Michael A. Research and theory on Hispanic education: students, finance, and governance. AZTLAN, Vol. 14, no. 1 (Spring 1983), p. 111-146. English. DESCR: Educational Administration; School Finance; Students.

3975 Raat, W. Dirk. Augusto Comte, Gabino Barreda, and positivism in Mexico. AZTLAN, Vol. 14, no. 2 (Fall 1983), p. 235-251. English. DESCR: *Barreda, Gabino; *Comte, Auguste; Education; History; Mexico; Philosophy; *Positivism.

3976 San Miguel, Guadalupe. In the background: conflict and controversy in the evolution of bilingual legislation in Texas, 1965-73. NABE JOURNAL, Vol. 7, no. 3 (Spring 1983), p. 23-40. English. DESCR: *Bilingual Bicultural Education; *Educational Law and Legislation; Texas.

3977 Skirius, John. Barreda, Vasconcelos, and the Mexican educational reforms. AZTLAN, Vol. 14, no. 2 (Fall 1983), p. 307-341. English. DESCR: *Barreda, Gabino; Education; History; Mexico; Positivism; *Vasconcelos, Jose.

3978 Tikunoff, William J. and Vazquez-Faria, Jose A. Successful instruction for bilingual schooling. PEABODY JOURNAL OF EDUCATION, Vol. 59, no. 4 (July 1982), p. 234-271. English. DESCR: *Bilingual Bicultural Education; Curriculum; Teacher Attitudes.

3979 Weiner, Richard E. Teaching the immigrant's child: a model plan for court-ordered bilingual education. JOURNAL OF LAW AND EDUCATION, Vol. 12, no. 1 (January 1983), p. 61-76. English. DESCR: *Bilingual Bicultural Education; Courts (Legal); Curriculum; Educational Law and Legislation.

Educational Travel
USE: Study Abroad

Eger, Ernestina N.

3980 Martinez, Julio A. Book review of: A BIBLIOGRAPHY OF CRITICISM OF CONTEMPORARY CHICANO LITERATURE. RQ - REFERENCE AND ADULT SERVICES DIVISION, Vol. 22, no. 1 (Fall 1982), p. 90. English. DESCR: *A BIBLIOGRAPHY OF CRITICISM OF CONTEMPORARY CHICANO LITERATURE; Bibliography; Book Reviews; Literary Criticism; Literature.

3981 Woodbridge, Hensley C. Outstanding new bibliography about Chicano literature. BILINGUAL REVIEW, Vol. 10, no. 1 (January, April, 1983), p. 69-72. English. DESCR: *A BIBLIOGRAPHY OF CRITICISM OF CONTEMPORARY CHICANO LITERATURE; Book Reviews.

El Paso County, TX

3982 Hedderson, John and Daudistel, Howard C. Infant mortality of the Spanish surname population. SOCIAL SCIENCE JOURNAL, Vol. 19, no. 4 (October 1982), p. 67-78. English. DESCR: Demography; *Infant Mortality; Medical Care; Statistics; Vital Statistics.

El Paso Electric Company

3983 Positioning growth at El Paso Electric Co. HISPANIC BUSINESS, Vol. 4, no. 2 (February 1982), p. 10+. English. DESCR: El Paso, TX; Employment; *Energy Industries; *Labor Supply and Market; Wall, Evern R.

El Paso Jesters

3984 Cantu, Hector. Softball Texas style. NATIONAL HISPANIC JOURNAL, Vol. 1, no. 3 (Summer, Fall, 1982), p. 9-11. English. DESCR: Mexico City All Stars; Pan American Softball League; Recreation; *Softball; Sports.

El Paso, TX

3985 Armengol, Armando; Manley, Joan H.; and Teschner, Richard V. The international bilingual city: how a university meets the challenge. FOREIGN LANGUAGE ANNALS, Vol. 15, no. 4 (September 1982), p. 289-295. English. DESCR: Biculturalism; Bilingualism; Border Region; Ciudad Juarez, Chihuahua, Mexico; *Language Development; Spanish Language; University of Texas at El Paso.

3986 Bath, C. Richard. Health and environmental problems: the role of the border in El Paso-Ciudad Juarez coordination. JOURNAL OF INTERAMERICAN STUDIES AND WORLD AFFAIRS, Vol. 24, no. 3 (August 1982), p. 375-392. English. DESCR: Border Region; Ciudad Juarez, Chihuahua, Mexico; International Boundary and Water Commission; Nationalism; Pollution; *Public Health; United States-Mexico Relations; U.S Border Public Health Association (AFMES).

3987 Griswold del Castillo, Richard. Book review of: THE CHICANOS OF EL PASO: AN ASSESSMENT OF PROGRESS. PACIFIC HISTORICAL REVIEW, Vol. 51, no. 3 (August 1982), p. 337-338. English. DESCR: Book Reviews; Martinez, Oscar J.; *THE CHICANOS OF EL PASO: AN ASSESSMENT OF PROGRESS.

Educational Law and Legislation.

El Paso, TX (cont.)

3988 Josel, Nathan A. Public library material selection in a bilingual community. CATHOLIC LIBRARY WORLD, Vol. 54, no. 3 (October 1982), p. 113-115. English. **DESCR:** Bilingualism; Library Collections; *Public Libraries; Spanish Language.

3989 Long, William J. and Pohl, Christopher M. Joint foot patrols succeed in El Paso. POLICE CHIEF, Vol. 50, no. 4 (April 1983), p. 49-51. English. **DESCR:** Border Patrol; Ciudad Juarez, Chihuahua, Mexico; Criminal Acts; Immigration Regulation and Control; *Police; Undocumented Workers; Youth.

3990 Martinez, Oscar J. Book review of: DESERT IMMIGRANTS: THE MEXICANS OF EL PASO 1880-1920. HISPANIC AMERICAN HISTORICAL REVIEW, Vol. 62, no. 2 (May 1982), p. 289-291. English. **DESCR:** Book Reviews; *DESERT IMMIGRANTS: THE MEXICANS OF EL PASO 1880-1920; Garcia, Mario T.; Immigration.

3991 Mirowsky, John and Ross, Catherine E. Paranoia and the structure of powerlessness. AMERICAN SOCIOLOGICAL REVIEW, Vol. 48, no. 2 (April 1983), p. 228-239. English. **DESCR:** Ciudad Juarez, Chihuahua, Mexico; *Social Psychology.

3992 Police and immigration. NUESTRO, Vol. 7, no. 2 (March 1983), p. 7. English. **DESCR:** *Border Patrol; Federal Government; *Immigration Law; Immigration Regulation and Control; Police.

3993 Positioning growth at El Paso Electric Co. HISPANIC BUSINESS, Vol. 4, no. 2 (February 1982), p. 10+. English. **DESCR:** El Paso Electric Company; Employment; *Energy Industries; *Labor Supply and Market; Wall, Evern R.

3994 Reisler, Mark. Book review of: DESERT IMMIGRANTS: THE MEXICANS OF EL PASO 1880-1920. AMERICAN HISTORICAL REVIEW, Vol. 87, no. 1 (February 1982), p. 271-272. English. **DESCR:** Book Reviews; *DESERT IMMIGRANTS: THE MEXICANS OF EL PASO 1880-1920; Garcia, Mario T.; History; Immigration.

3995 Rivera, Julius and Goodman, Paul Wershub. Clandestine labor circulation: a case on the U.S.-Mexico border. MIGRATION TODAY, Vol. 10, no. 1 (1982), p. 21-26. English. **DESCR:** Border Patrol; Border Region; Ciudad Juarez, Chihuahua, Mexico; Immigration Regulation and Control; Migration Patterns; Social Classes; Social Mobility; Socioeconomic Factors; *Undocumented Workers.

3996 Sanchez, Ricardo. El lencho y los chenchos. NATIONAL HISPANIC JOURNAL, Vol. 1, no. 3 (Summer, Fall, 1982), p. 20. Calo. **DESCR:** Border Region; *Ciudad Juarez, Chihuahua, Mexico; *Short Story.

3997 Timmons, Wilbert H. American El Paso: the formative years, 1848-1854. SOUTHWESTERN HISTORICAL QUARTERLY, Vol. 87, no. 1 (July 1983), p. 1-36. English. **DESCR:** Border Region; Guadalupe Hidalgo, Treaty of 1848; History; Social History and Conditions.

3998 Vigil, Ralph H. Book review of: DESERT IMMIGRANTS: THE MEXICANS OF EL PASO 1880-1920. INTERNATIONAL MIGRATION REVIEW, Vol. 16, no. 1 (Spring 1982), p. 223-224. English. **DESCR:** Book Reviews; *DESERT IMMIGRANTS: THE MEXICANS OF EL PASO 1880-1920; Garcia, Mario T.; History; Immigrants.

El Salvador

3999 Altman, Barbara. El Salvador. LATINO, Vol. 54, no. 4 (May, June, 1983), p. 10-11. English. **DESCR:** Latin Americans; War.

4000 Baker, Edward, trans. and Dalton, Roque. The poetry of Roque Dalton: We all, Typist, Latinoamerica, Love poem, O.A.S. MAIZE, Vol. 5, no. 3-4 (Spring, Summer, 1982), p. 37-46. English. **DESCR:** *Poetry; Revolutions.

4001 Barrio, Raymond. Resurrection 1999. NUESTRO, Vol. 7, no. 4 (May 1983), p. 50-51. English. **DESCR:** *Fiction; Nuclear Armament.

4002 Cruz, Amaury. El Salvador: realities of a country at war. NUESTRO, Vol. 6, no. 3 (April 1982), p. 14-17+. English. **DESCR:** Political History and Conditions; Poverty; Short Story; Tourism.

4003 Dalton, Roque. Poema de amor. NUESTRO, Vol. 7, no. 8 (October 1983), p. 37. Spanish. **DESCR:** *Poetry.

4004 Entertainment = diversion. CAMINOS, Vol. 3, no. 4 (April 1982), p. 41. Bilingual. **DESCR:** AZTLAN [journal]; Committee in Solidarity with the People of El Salvador (CISPES); Cultural Organizations; Directories; DIRECTORY OF MINORITY ARTS ORGANIZATIONS; *National Endowment for the Arts; NOTICIERO; Organizations; Periodicals; *Recreation; Television.

4005 Garcia, Ignacio M. El Salvador: profile of a nation at war. NUESTRO, Vol. 7, no. 8 (October 1983), p. 26-36. English. **DESCR:** Guerrillas; Military; Political History and Conditions; War.

4006 Maldonado-Denis, Manuel. El problema de las nacionalidades: la experiencia caribena. Paper presented at the "Dialogo de las Americas" conference. Mexico, D.F. September 9-14, 1982. REVISTA CHICANO-RIQUENA, Vol. 10, no. 4 (Fall 1982), p. 39-45. Spanish. **DESCR:** Capitalism; Carpentier, Alejo; Cuba; Grenada; Guatemala; Imperialism; Marti, Jose; Nicaragua; *Political History and Conditions; Puerto Rico; United States.

4007 Uriarte, Ivan. Introduccion a la poesia revolucionaria de El Salvador. MAIZE, Vol. 6, no. 1-2 (Fall, Winter, 1982, 1983), p. 34-40. Spanish. **DESCR:** Latin American Literature; *Poetry; Revolutions.

El Teatro Nacional de Aztlan (TENAZ)

4008 Yarbro-Bejarano, Yvonne. Teatropoesia by Chicanas in the Bay Area: tongues of fire. REVISTA CHICANO-RIQUENA, Vol. 11, no. 1 (Spring 1983), p. 78-94. English. **DESCR:** Chicanas; Poetry; Teatro; *TONGUES OF FIRE.

Elected Officials

4009 Baca Barragan, Polly; Hamner, Richard; and Guerrero, Lena. [Untitled interview with State Senators (Colorado) Polly Baca-Barragan and Lena Guerrero. NATIONAL HISPANIC JOURNAL, Vol. 1, no. 2 (Winter 1982), p. 8-11. English. **DESCR:** Baca Barragan, Polly; *Carter, Jimmy (President); Chicanas; Democratic Party; Guerrero, Lena; *Political Parties and Organizations.

Elected Officials (cont.)

4010 Burciaga, Jose Antonio. Mosca en la leche. LATINO, Vol. 54, no. 5 (August, September, 1983), p. 15. Spanish. **DESCR:** *Terrazas, Francisco Barrio.

4011 Candidates for congressional seats. CAMINOS, Vol. 3, no. 5 (May 1982), p. 26-34. English. **DESCR:** U.S. Congress.

4012 Caucus highlights. NUESTRO, Vol. 6, no. 7 (September 1982), p. 43. English. **DESCR:** *Congressional Hispanic Caucus; Garcia, Robert.

4013 Chavarria, Jesus. How are we doing? HISPANIC BUSINESS, Vol. 4, no. 8 (August 1983), p. 6. English. **DESCR:** Economics; *Finance; Voter Turnout.

4014 A close look at Mario Obledo. LATINO, Vol. 54, no. 5 (August, September, 1983), p. 10. English. **DESCR:** *Obledo, Mario; Politics.

4015 Diaz, Katherine A. Henry Cisneros: our hope for today & tomorrow. CAMINOS, Vol. 4, no. 3 (March 1983), p. 38-41,49+. Bilingual. **DESCR:** *Cisneros, Henry, Mayor of San Antonio, TX.

4016 Gente: Miguel Aleman, former president, Mexico, dies. NUESTRO, Vol. 7, no. 5 (June, July, 1983), p. 49. English. **DESCR:** Aleman, Miguel; *Mexico.

4017 Gil, Carlos B. Miguel Antonio Otero, first Chicano governor. JOURNAL OF ETHNIC STUDIES, Vol. 4, no. 3 (Fall 1976), p. 95-102. English. **DESCR:** Book Reviews; *New Mexico; OTERO: AN AUTOBIOGRAPHICAL TRILOGY; Otero, Miguel A.; Social History and Conditions; United States History.

4018 Gloria Molina spells winner. LATINA, Vol. 1, no. 1 (1982), p. 4-5. English. **DESCR:** *Chicanas.

4019 Gurwitt, Rob. Widespread political efforts open new era for Hispanics. CONGRESSIONAL QUARTERLY WEEKLY REPORT, Vol. 40, (October 23, 1982), p. 2707-2709. English. **DESCR:** Biculturalism; *Politics.

4020 Martinez, Vilma. Working with de la Madrid. CAMINOS, Vol. 3, no. 6 (June 1982), p. 10-11,36. Bilingual. **DESCR:** *De la Madrid, Miguel; Mexico.

4021 Members of the caucus. NUESTRO, Vol. 6, no. 7 (September 1982), p. 42. English. **DESCR:** *Congressional Hispanic Caucus; De la Garza, Kika.

4022 Mile high Pena fever. LATINO, Vol. 54, no. 4 (May, June, 1983), p. 4. English. **DESCR:** *Pena, Federico; Voter Turnout.

4023 Morton, Carlos. People: back on top with Bernardo Eureste. NATIONAL HISPANIC JOURNAL, Vol. 2, no. 1 (Summer 1983), p. 20-21. English. **DESCR:** Cisneros, Henry, Mayor of San Antonio, TX; Elections; *Eureste, Bernardo; San Antonio Police Department; San Antonio, TX; Valdez, Jesse.

4024 Padilla, Steve. Latinos wield political clout in midterm election. NUESTRO, Vol. 6, no. 9 (November 1982), p. 28-30. English. **DESCR:** De la Garza, Kika; Garcia, Robert; Gonzales, Henry B.; Lujan, Manuel, Jr.; Martinez, Matthew G. "Marty", Assemblyman; Ortiz, Solomon; *Politics; Richardson, William; Roybal, Edward R.; *Torres, Esteban E.

4025 Pena takes Denver. HISPANIC BUSINESS, Vol. 5, no. 8 (August 1983), p. 13+. English. **DESCR:** *Biography; Denver, CO; Pena, Federico.

4026 Presidential election 1984. NUESTRO, Vol. 7, no. 7 (September 1983), p. 14-19. English. **DESCR:** Anderson, John; Askew, Reubin; Cranston, Alan; *Elections; Fernandez, Ben; Glenn, John; Hart, Gary; Hispanic Force '84; Hollings, Ernest "Fritz"; Mondale, Walter; Political Parties and Organizations; Reagan, Ronald.

4027 Profile of a public man. NUESTRO, Vol. 7, no. 2 (March 1983), p. 13-19+. English. **DESCR:** *Gonzalez, Henry B.; Politics; Texas.

4028 Rodriguez, Roberto. Cal Worthington politics and 1982. CORAZON DE AZTLAN, Vol. 1, no. 1 (January, February, 1982), p. 40. English. **DESCR:** Elections.

4029 Vidal. The next president of Mexico: Miguel de la Madrid. CAMINOS, Vol. 3, no. 6 (June 1982), p. 9. Bilingual. **DESCR:** *De la Madrid, Miguel; Mexico.

4030 Vidal, Jose. Lopez Portillo's accomplishments. CAMINOS, Vol. 3, no. 6 (June 1982), p. 22. Bilingual. **DESCR:** *Lopez Portillo, Jose.

4031 Whisler, Kirk. Attorney General George Deukmejian. CAMINOS, Vol. 3, no. 5 (May 1982), p. 14-16. Bilingual. **DESCR:** *Deukmejian, George.

4032 Whisler, Kirk. Hispanic representation in California's cities: progress??? CAMINOS, Vol. 4, no. 3 (March 1983), p. 42-43,49. English. **DESCR:** California; *Local Government.

4033 Whisler, Kirk. Lt. Governor Mike Curb. CAMINOS, Vol. 3, no. 5 (May 1982), p. 11-13. Bilingual. **DESCR:** *Curb, Mike.

4034 Whisler, Kirk. Robert Garcia: the mover in the Congressional Hispanic Caucus. CAMINOS, Vol. 3, no. 7 (July, August, 1982), p. 36-37,44. Bilingual. **DESCR:** Congressional Hispanic Caucus; Federal Government; *Garcia, Robert.

4035 Whisler, Kirk. State Senator John Garamendi. CAMINOS, Vol. 3, no. 5 (May 1982), p. 17-19. Bilingual. **DESCR:** *Garamendi, John.

Elections

4036 Barry, Patrick and Zavala, Antonio. Election '83: Chicago's Latinos awake, but not united. NUESTRO, Vol. 7, no. 1 (January, February, 1983), p. 20-23. English. **DESCR:** *Chicago, IL; Political Representation; Voter Turnout.

4037 Chicago's mayoralty race. HISPANIC BUSINESS, Vol. 5, no. 7 (July 1983), p. 27-28. English. **DESCR:** Chicago, IL; Local Government; *Voter Turnout.

4038 Councilman wins despite problems. NUESTRO, Vol. 7, no. 3 (April 1983), p. 12. English. **DESCR:** *Eureste, Bernardo; Local Government.

4039 Election '82: the Hispanic vote. CAMINOS, Vol. 4, no. 1-2 (January, February, 1983), p. 65,75. English. **DESCR:** *Voter Turnout.

Elections (cont.)

4040 Hamner, Richard. Hispanics and redistricting: what you see is not always what you get. NATIONAL HISPANIC JOURNAL, Vol. 1, no. 2 (Winter 1982), p. 25-30. English. **DESCR**: Berlanga, Hugo; Hispanic Reapportionment District; National Association of Latino Elected Officials (NALEO); Political Representation; Politics; *Reapportionment; *Roybal, Edward R.; Santillan, Richard.

4041 Hines, Bea L. and Fabricio, Roberto. Voices. NUESTRO, Vol. 7, no. 10 (December 1983), p. 57-58. English. **DESCR**: Blacks; Cubanos; Ferre, Maurice; *Miami, FL; Suarez, Xavier.

4042 Hispanic victories; seats gained. CAMINOS, Vol. 3, no. 7 (July, August, 1982), p. 34-35. English. **DESCR**: *California.

4043 Hispanic voting trends. HISPANIC BUSINESS, Vol. 4, no. 8 (August 1983), p. 28-29. English. **DESCR**: Bilingual Ballots; Bilingualism; California; Mexican American Legal Defense and Educational Fund (MALDEF); Southwest Voter Registration Education Project (SVRP); Texas; Voter Turnout.

4044 The invisible Puerto Rican vote. HISPANIC BUSINESS, Vol. 5, no. 10 (October 1983), p. 34-36. English. **DESCR**: Political Parties and Organizations; Puerto Ricans; *Voter Turnout.

4045 Lowther, William. Reagan hunts for the Hispanic vote. MACLEANS, Vol. 96, no. 34 (August 22, 1983), p. 21-22. English. **DESCR**: League of United Latin American Citizens (LULAC); Reagan, Ronald; *Voter Turnout.

4046 Martinez, Chip. Federico Pena: Denver's first Hispanic mayor. NUESTRO, Vol. 7, no. 6 (August 1983), p. 14-20. English. **DESCR**: Denver, CO; Local Government; *Pena, Federico; Voter Turnout.

4047 Morton, Carlos. People: back on top with Bernardo Eureste. NATIONAL HISPANIC JOURNAL, Vol. 2, no. 1 (Summer 1983), p. 20-21. English. **DESCR**: Cisneros, Henry, Mayor of San Antonio, TX; Elected Officials; *Eureste, Bernardo; San Antonio Police Department; San Antonio, TX; Valdez, Jesse.

4048 New Mexico's gubernatorial race. HISPANIC BUSINESS, Vol. 4, no. 11 (November 1982), p. 27,30. English. **DESCR**: Anaya, Toney; *Biography; New Mexico; Political Parties and Organizations.

4049 Nieto, Ernesto. Politics: powers that struggled in the Texas Valley. NATIONAL HISPANIC JOURNAL, Vol. 2, no. 1 (Summer 1983), p. 22-23. English. **DESCR**: McAllen, TX; *Politics; *Rio Grande Valley, TX; Voter Turnout.

4050 Padilla, Steve. In search of Hispanic voters. NUESTRO, Vol. 7, no. 6 (August 1983), p. 20. English. **DESCR**: National Hispanic Voter Registration Campaign; *Voter Turnout.

4051 Presidential election 1984. NUESTRO, Vol. 7, no. 7 (September 1983), p. 14-19. English. **DESCR**: Anderson, John; Askew, Reubin; Cranston, Alan; Elected Officials; Fernandez, Ben; Glenn, John; Hart, Gary; Hispanic Force '84; Hollings, Ernest "Fritz"; Mondale, Walter; Political Parties and Organizations; Reagan, Ronald.

4052 Que pasa? NUESTRO, Vol. 7, no. 3 (April 1983), p. 9. English. **DESCR**: Border Patrol; *Cisneros, Henry, Mayor of San Antonio, TX; Immigration Regulation and Control; Rocky Mountain Spotted Fever; Servas; Tourism.

4053 Rivas, Mike. Keeping peace in paradise. NATIONAL HISPANIC JOURNAL, Vol. 1, no. 2 (Winter 1982), p. 13-20. English. **DESCR**: *Brand, Othal; Casso, Ramiro; Police; Police Brutality; *Political Repression; Rio Grande Valley, TX; THE MEXICAN AMERICAN: QUEST FOR EQUALITY; Voter Turnout.

4054 Rivera, Elaine. Fernandez envies Jackson effort. NUESTRO, Vol. 7, no. 9 (November 1983), p. 13. English. **DESCR**: *Fernandez, Ben; Jackson, Jesse; Politics.

4055 Rodriguez, Roberto. Cal Worthington politics and 1982. CORAZON DE AZTLAN, Vol. 1, no. 1 (January, February, 1982), p. 40. English. **DESCR**: *Elected Officials.

4056 Whisler, Kirk. Hispanic candidates: getting serious. CAMINOS, Vol. 3, no. 5 (May 1982), p. 24-25. Bilingual. **DESCR**: *Political Representation.

THE ELECTRIC COMPANY

4057 Neuman, Susan B. and Pits, Elaine F. A review of current North American television programs for bilingual children. READING TEACHER, Vol. 37, no. 3 (December 1983), p. 254-260. English. **DESCR**: *Bilingual Bicultural Education; Mass Media; SESAME STREET; Spanish Language; VILLA ALEGRE.

Electronic Data Systems (EDS)

4058 Ballard, Lee. Tom Marquez and the EDS mode. HISPANIC BUSINESS, Vol. 5, no. 2 (February 1983), p. 10-11+. English. **DESCR**: *Biography; Businesspeople; Marquez, Tom; Perot, Ross; War on Drugs.

Electronics Industry

4059 Foreign trade. HISPANIC BUSINESS, Vol. 5, no. 4 (April 1983), p. 22. English. **DESCR**: Banking Industry; Brazil; Export Trade; *Foreign Trade; Ibero-American Chamber of Commerce; Miami, FL; Minority Bank Development Program (MBDP); Minority Export Development Consultants Program (MEDC); Peace Corps; Puerto Rico.

4060 Q & A with Fernando Niebla: "You have to present yourself as a person that knows what he wants". CAMINOS, Vol. 4, no. 1-2 (January, February, 1983), p. 22-23,71. English. **DESCR**: Careers; Computers; *Niebla, Fernando.

4061 Whisler, Kirk. Martha Cornejo Rottenberg: on opportunities & advancement. CAMINOS, Vol. 4, no. 1-2 (January, February, 1983), p. 17-18,71+. English. **DESCR**: Careers; *Cornejo Rottenberg, Martha; Mining Industry; TRW Defense Systems Group.

ELEMENTARY AND SECONDARY EDUCATION ACT

4062 Balasubramonian, Krishna. Not on test scores alone: the qualitative side to program evaluation. BILINGUAL JOURNAL, Vol. 7, no. 2 (Winter 1983), p. 17-21,40. English. **DESCR**: *Bilingual Bicultural Education; *Curriculum; Educational Tests and Measurements; Evaluation (Educational); Proposals.

ELEMENTARY AND SECONDARY EDUCATION ACT (cont.)

4063 Consalvo, Robert W. Book review of: PROGRAM IMPACT EVALUATIONS: AN INTRODUCTION FOR MANAGERS OF TITLE VII PROJECTS - A DRAFT GUIDEBOOK. BILINGUAL JOURNAL, Vol. 7, no. 2 (Winter 1983), p. 36-37. English. DESCR: Bilingual Bicultural Education; Bissell, Joan; Book Reviews; Educational Administration; Evaluation (Educational); *PROGRAM IMPACT EVALUATIONS: AN INTRODUCTION FOR MANAGERS OF TITLE VII PROJECTS - A DRAFT GUIDEBOOK ESEA TITLE VII.

4064 Liberty, Paul G., et al. [Evaluation in bilingual education]. BILINGUAL JOURNAL, Vol. 7, no. 2 (Winter 1983), p. 1-40. English. DESCR: *Bilingual Bicultural Education; Curriculum; Educational Administration; *Evaluation (Educational).

4065 Rugsaken, Kris T. Toward a true bilingual education: when federal funding ends. BILINGUAL JOURNAL, Vol. 7, no. 4 (Summer 1983), p. 9-14. English. DESCR: *Bilingual Bicultural Education; Bilingual Education Act of 1968; *Educational Law and Legislation; Funding Sources.

4066 Zamora, Gloria L. Zamora speaks on bilingual education. BILINGUAL JOURNAL, Vol. 7, no. 4 (Summer 1983), p. 5-8. English. DESCR: *Bilingual Bicultural Education; Bilingual Education Act of 1968; Educational Law and Legislation.

THE ELEMENTS OF SAN JOAQUIN

4067 de la Fuente, Patricia. Ambiguity in the poetry of Gary Soto. REVISTA CHICANO-RIQUENA, Vol. 11, no. 2 (Summer 1983), p. 34-39. English. DESCR: "Avocado Lake"; "Blanco"; "Braley Street"; "Field"; *Literary Criticism; Poetry; "Song for the pockets"; *Soto, Gary; TALE OF SUNLIGHT; "Telephoning God"; "Wind".

4068 Paredes, Raymund A. Book review of: THE ELEMENTS OF SAN JOAQUIN. MINORITY VOICES, Vol. 1, no. 2 (Fall 1977), p. 106-108. English. DESCR: Book Reviews; Poetry; Soto, Gary.

Eleventh International Chicano Latino Teatro Festival, Mission Cultural Center, San Francisco, CA

4069 Lira, Pedro Antonio. El Onceno Festival Chicano-Latino de Teatro. CONJUNTO, no. 51 (January, March, 1982), p. 113-117. Spanish. DESCR: Teatro.

4070 Padilla-Sanchez, Beverly. T.E.N.A.Z.: Teatro Chicano/Teatro Latino. CAMINOS, Vol. 2, no. 7 (December 1981), p. 34-35. Bilingual. DESCR: Huerta, Jorge A.; Teatro.

Elias, Bob

4071 Rivera-Cano, Andrea. Parenting: four families' stories. LATINA, Vol. 1, no. 2 (February, March, 1983), p. 66-73+. English. DESCR: *Child Rearing; Children; Hernandez, Jesus; Hernandez, Virginia; Lopez, Genevieve; Ojalvo, Juana.

Elizalde, Hector

4072 Communications/marketing. HISPANIC BUSINESS, Vol. 5, no. 5 (May 1983), p. 24. English. DESCR: Anheuser-Busch, Inc.; Arbitron; Awards; California Chicano News Media Association (CCNMA); Coca-Cola Company; *Marketing; Television.

4073 Diaz, Katherine A. "And this year's winners are...". CAMINOS, Vol. 4, no. 1-2 (January, February, 1983), p. 39-54,74+. English. DESCR: *Awards; Castro, Tony; Flores, Tom; Martinez, Esperanza; Mendizabal, Maritza; Molina, Gloria; Moya, Connie; Placentia, Joe; Quesada, Leticia; Rios, David N.; Ybarra, Lea; Zapata, Carmen.

4074 People. HISPANIC BUSINESS, Vol. 5, no. 1 (January 1983), p. 7. English. DESCR: Appointed Officials; *Biographical Notes; *Businesspeople; Mackey y Salazar, C.; Madrid, Carlos; Montoya, Velma; Nunez, Carlos; Perea, Stanley; Rodriguez, Rita; Valdes, Martha.

Elizondo, Virgilio

4075 Gibeau, Dawn. Mexican-American Center forges new vision. NATIONAL CATHOLIC REPORTER, Vol. 18, (July 30, 1982), p. 5+. English. DESCR: Catholic Church; *Mexican American Cultural Center, San Antonio, TX; Religion.

Elsasser, Nan

4076 Ybarra, Lea. Book review of: LAS MUJERES: CONVERSATIONS FROM A HISPANIC COMMUNITY [reprinted from LA RED/THE NET 5 (Sept. 1982)]. CHICANO LAW REVIEW, Vol. 6, (1983), p. 146-147. English. DESCR: Book Reviews; Chicanas; *LAS MUJERES: CONVERSATIONS FROM A HISPANIC COMMUNITY; MacKenzie, Kyle; Oral History; Tixier y Vigil, Yvonne.

Embassy Communications

4077 Nevarez, Armando. We're with you, Norman Lear, but watching you closely. NUESTRO, Vol. 7, no. 8 (October 1983), p. 47. English. DESCR: *Lear, Norman; Stereotypes; *Television.

Embroidery

4078 Benson, Nancy C. The art of colcha-stitch embroidery: an Hispanic heritage. NEW AMERICA: A REVIEW, Vol. 4, no. 3 (1982), p. 78-81. English. DESCR: Artes Antigua Society; Lujan, Maria Theofila.

Emigration
USE: Migration

Emmanuel

4079 Ogaz, Armando. South of the other border. CAMINOS, Vol. 3, no. 6 (June 1982), p. 26-28,36+. Bilingual. DESCR: *Artists; Del Rio, Yolanda; Nunez, Estella; Singers.

Empacho

4080 Richardson, Lynette. Caring through understanding, part II: folk medicine in the Hispanic population. IMPRINT, Vol. 29, no. 2 (April 1982), p. 21, 72-77. English. DESCR: Brujo; Caida de Mollera; Curanderas; *Folk Medicine; Mal de Ojo; Mal Puesto; Susto.

Employee Management Relations
USE: Industrial Relations

Employment

4081 Are you a good job hunter? Test yourself. LATINA, Vol. 1, no. 1 (1982), p. 57. English.

Employment (cont.)

4082 Baciu, Joyce A. How to prepare a resume/como redactar un resumen. CAMINOS, Vol. 4, no. 1-2 (January, February, 1983), p. 28. Bilingual. **DESCR:** *Resumes.

4083 Barreto, Julio. Where the jobs are: tips from Latinos in key occupations. NUESTRO, Vol. 6, no. 7 (September 1982), p. 18-23. English. **DESCR:** Business; Businesspeople; Curriculum.

4084 Boiston, Bernard G. The Simpson-Mazzoli bill: the first major immigration bill in thirty years. OHIO STATE BAR ASSOCIATION REPORT, Vol. 55, no. 39 (October 11, 1982), p. 1738-1743. English. **DESCR:** Immigration; *Undocumented Workers; Visa.

4085 Bonham, G.W. Moral imperative. CHANGE, Vol. 15, (January, February, 1983), p. 14-15. English. **DESCR:** *Higher Education; National Chicano Council on Higher Education (NCCHE).

4086 Buffenstein, Darryl F. The proposed immigration reform and control act of 1982: a new epoch in immigration law and a new headache for employers. EMPLOYEE RELATIONS LAW JOURNAL, Vol. 8, no. 3 (Winter 1983), p. 450-462. English. **DESCR:** Immigration Law; *Immigration Regulation and Control; Labor Certification; Undocumented Workers.

4087 Chase, Marilyn. Mired minority: Latins rise in numbers in U.S. but don't win influence or affluence. WALL STREET JOURNAL, Vol. 19, no. 43 (June 9, 1982), p. 1+. English. **DESCR:** Assimilation; Education; *Social History and Conditions.

4088 Chavarria, Jesus. The systems way. HISPANIC BUSINESS, Vol. 4, no. 4 (April 1982), p. 6. English. **DESCR:** *Careers; College Graduates; *Higher Education.

4089 Chavez, Ruth and Ramirez, Albert. Employment aspirations, expectations, and attitudes among employed and unemployed Chicanos. JOURNAL OF SOCIAL PSYCHOLOGY, Vol. 11, no. 1 (February 1983), p. 143-144. English. **DESCR:** Attitude (Psychological); Vocational Education.

4090 Chicago: a case study of minority participation in city government and industry. HISPANIC BUSINESS, Vol. 5, no. 1 (January 1983), p. 28-29. English. **DESCR:** Chicago, IL; *Ethnic Groups; Government.

4091 Communications/marketing. HISPANIC BUSINESS, Vol. 5, no. 10 (October 1983), p. 26. English. **DESCR:** Advertising; Arens & Gutierrez; Henry Molina, Inc.; Journals; Lionetti and Meyers Research Center, Inc.; Marketing; *Mass Media; Midwest Hispanics in Telecommunications Symposium, Chicago, IL; NEW MANAGEMENT.

4092 Conoley, Martin. The hidden threat of underemployment. HISPANIC BUSINESS, Vol. 5, no. 10 (October 1983), p. 14+. English. **DESCR:** Education; Employment Training; Labor Supply and Market; Personnel Management.

4093 Expected but shocking. NUESTRO, Vol. 6, no. 8 (October 1982), p. 9. English. **DESCR:** Federal Aid.

4094 Full employment is theme of SER annual conference. LATINO, Vol. 53, no. 2 (March, April, 1982), p. 20. English. **DESCR:** SER.

4095 Furin, Gary C. Immigration law: alien employment certification. INTERNATIONAL LAWYER, Vol. 16, no. 1 (Winter 1982), p. 111-119. English. **DESCR:** Immigration and Nationality Act (INA); *Labor Certification; Undocumented Workers.

4096 Garcia, Art R. The executive market. HISPANIC BUSINESS, Vol. 5, no. 10 (October 1983), p. 12. English. **DESCR:** *Management.

4097 Garcia, Philip. An evaluation of employment and unemployment differences between Mexican Americans and whites: the seventies. SOCIAL SCIENCE JOURNAL, Vol. 20, no. 1 (January 1983), p. 51-62. English. **DESCR:** Anglo Americans; Ethnic Groups; Labor Supply and Market.

4098 Government review. NUESTRO, Vol. 7, no. 10 (December 1983), p. 48. English. **DESCR:** Banking Industry; Child Care Centers; Chile; Clinics (Medical); Credit Unions; Employment Training; *Government Services; Medical Care; National Credit Union Administration; National Oceanic and Atmospheric Administration; SER; U.S. Department of Health and Human Services; U.S. Department of Labor.

4099 Government review. NUESTRO, Vol. 7, no. 8 (October 1983), p. 54. English. **DESCR:** Alcoholism; *Government Services; National Endowment for the Arts; Plaza de La Raza, Los Angeles, CA; Veterans; Working Women; Youth.

4100 Government review. NUESTRO, Vol. 7, no. 7 (September 1983), p. 55. English. **DESCR:** AIDS Hotline; California; Education; Food for Survival, New York, NY; Funding Sources; *Government Services; Hewlett Foundation; Laborers; Mathematics, Engineering and Science Achievement (MESA); Population Trends; Public Health; Stanford University, Stanford, CA.

4101 Government review. NUESTRO, Vol. 7, no. 6 (August 1983), p. 56. English. **DESCR:** Ballet de Puerto Rico; Dance; Education; *Government Funding Sources; Government Services; Housing; Income; National Fair Housing Law; Population Distribution; Urban Development Action Grant (UDAG); Veterans.

4102 Gutierrez, Felix. Breaking through the media employment wall. AGENDA, Vol. 11, no. 3 (May, June, 1981), p. 13-19. English. **DESCR:** Journalism; Mass Media; Torres, Luis.

4103 Hansen, Niles. Location preference and opportunity cost: a South Texas perspective. SOCIAL SCIENCE QUARTERLY, Vol. 63, (September 1982), p. 506-516. English. **DESCR:** *Economic History and Conditions; Texas.

4104 Hispanic employment reviews. HISPANIC BUSINESS, Vol. 4, no. 6 (June 1982), p. 28-29. English. **DESCR:** Labor Supply and Market; Laborers.

4105 Hispanic income still lower. HISPANIC BUSINESS, Vol. 4, no. 1 (January 1982), p. 29. English. **DESCR:** *Income.

4106 Hispanic wages and employment slow to rise. HISPANIC BUSINESS, Vol. 5, no. 11 (November 1983), p. 36-37. English. **DESCR:** Chicanas; Congressional Hispanic Caucus; Income.

4107 How to keep your job. LATINO, Vol. 54, no. 3 (April 1983), p. 12-13. English.

Employment (cont.)

4108 Immigration and nationality symposium. SAN DIEGO LAW REVIEW, Vol. 20, no. 1 (December 1982, 1983), p. 1-231. English. **DESCR:** Akbarian v. INS; Deportation; Immigration and Nationality Act (INA); *Immigration Regulation and Control; Miranda v. INS; Simpson-Mazzoli Bill; Undocumented Workers.

4109 The impact of undocumented migration on the U.S. labor market. HOUSTON JOURNAL OF INTERNATIONAL LAW, Vol. 5, no. 2 (Spring 1983), p. 287-321. English. **DESCR:** Economic History and Conditions; Immigrant Labor; Immigration and Nationality Act (INA); Immigration Law; Labor Supply and Market; Research Methodology; Simpson-Mazzoli Bill; *Undocumented Workers.

4110 Jobs for peace initiative. CAMINOS, Vol. 4, no. 11 (December 1983), p. 26. English. **DESCR:** Federal Government.

4111 Lopez, Marcos. Legal affair. LATINA, Vol. 1, no. 2 (February, March, 1983), p. 85. English. **DESCR:** Criminal Acts; Housing; *Legal Aid.

4112 LULAC files complaint against TV networks. NUESTRO, Vol. 6, no. 8 (October 1982), p. 48. English. **DESCR:** Bonilla, Tony; Equal Employment Opportunity Commission (EEOC); *League of United Latin American Citizens (LULAC); Racism; Television.

4113 MALDEF's goal: a fair opportunity for Hispanics to compete. NUESTRO, Vol. 7, no. 6 (August 1983), p. 26-28+. English. **DESCR:** Education; *Legal Reform; *Mexican American Legal Defense and Educational Fund (MALDEF).

4114 Martinez, Arthur D. Mexican-Americans: Qua the assistant-Americans. SOUTHWEST ECONOMY AND SOCIETY, Vol. 2, no. 2 (Winter 1977), p. 34-36. English. **DESCR:** Management; Racism; *Self-Determination.

4115 Math-based careers. HISPANIC BUSINESS, Vol. 4, no. 1 (January 1982), p. 20. English. **DESCR:** Careers; *College Graduates; *Cox, George; Engineering as a Profession; *Hispanic Society of Engineers and Scientists (HSES); *Leadership, Education and Development Program in Business (LEAD).

4116 Math-based careers. HISPANIC BUSINESS, Vol. 5, no. 9 (September 1983), p. 28. English. **DESCR:** Andrew W. Mellon Foundation; *Careers; Engineering as a Profession; Financial Aid; Garcia, Mary; Higher Education; National Council for Minorities in Engineering (NACME); National Medical Fellowships (NMF); Rivera, Lourdes.

4117 Mendez Gonzalez, Rosalinda. Mexican women and families: rural-to-urban and international migration. SOUTHWEST ECONOMY AND SOCIETY, Vol. 4, no. 2 (Winter 1978, 1979), p. 14-27. English. **DESCR:** Chicanas; *Family; Garment Industry; Immigration; International Ladies Garment Workers Union (ILGWU); Labor Organizing; Los Angeles, CA; Undocumented Workers.

4118 Mestre, Mercedes. Paving the path. HISPANIC BUSINESS, Vol. 5, no. 10 (October 1983), p. 9. English. **DESCR:** Business Administration; Education; Employment Training; *Korn/Ferry International.

4119 Morales, Rebecca. Unions and undocumented workers. SOUTHWEST ECONOMY AND SOCIETY, Vol. 6, no. 1 (Fall 1982), p. 3-11. English.

DESCR: Immigration and Naturalization Service (INS); Labor Unions; *Operation Jobs; *Undocumented Workers.

4120 New thrust in public jobs. LATINO, Vol. 53, no. 4 (June 1982), p. 29. English.

4121 Newman, Allen R. The impacts of emigration on the Mexican economy. MIGRATION TODAY, Vol. 10, no. 2 (1982), p. 17-21. English. **DESCR:** Economic History and Conditions; *Mexican Economy; *Migration; Socioeconomic Factors; Undocumented Workers.

4122 Occupational distribution of Hispanics in California. HISPANIC BUSINESS, Vol. 5, no. 9 (September 1983), p. 33-34. English. **DESCR:** California; *Population Distribution; Population Trends.

4123 Operation Jobs is a failure. LATINO, Vol. 53, no. 4 (June 1982), p. 21. English. **DESCR:** *Operation Jobs.

4124 Opportunities in the military. NUESTRO, Vol. 6, no. 1 (January, February, 1982), p. 29. English. **DESCR:** *Military Service.

4125 Paul, Jan S. The changing work week. HISPANIC BUSINESS, Vol. 5, no. 9 (September 1983), p. 16. English. **DESCR:** Labor Laws and Legislation; *Labor Supply and Market; Personnel Management.

4126 Popp, Gary E. and Muhs, William F. Fears of success and women employees. HUMAN RELATIONS, Vol. 35, no. 7 (July 1982), p. 511-519. English. **DESCR:** *Chicanas.

4127 Positioning growth at El Paso Electric Co. HISPANIC BUSINESS, Vol. 4, no. 2 (February 1982), p. 10+. English. **DESCR:** El Paso Electric Company; El Paso, TX; *Energy Industries; *Labor Supply and Market; Wall, Evern R.

4128 Powers, Stephen and Sanchez, Virginia V. Correlates of self-esteem of Mexican American adolescents. PSYCHOLOGICAL REPORTS, Vol. 51, no. 3 (December 1982), p. 771-774. English. **DESCR:** Academic Achievement; Arizona; *Identity; Junior High School Students; Nogales, AZ.

4129 Que pasa? NUESTRO, Vol. 7, no. 7 (September 1983), p. 9. English. **DESCR:** Alcoholism; Anti-Defamation League of B'nai B'rith; *Drug Abuse; Drug Programs; Kiwanis International; Miller Brewing Company; Racism; Sports.

4130 Raymond, Richard and Sesnowitz, Michael. Labor market discrimination against Mexican American college graduates. SOUTHERN ECONOMIC JOURNAL, Vol. 49, no. 4 (April 1983), p. 1122-1136. English. **DESCR:** College Graduates; Income; Racism.

4131 Research/development: employment update. HISPANIC BUSINESS, Vol. 4, no. 11 (November 1982), p. 29-30. English.

4132 Richard, John E. Public employment rights of aliens. BAYLOR LAW REVIEW, Vol. 34, no. 3 (Summer 1982), p. 371-385. English. **DESCR:** Cabell v. Chavez-Salido; *Naturalization; Sugarman v. Dougall.

Employment (cont.)

4133 Roberts, Robert E. and Roberts, Catharine
Ramsay. Marriage, work and depressive
symptoms among Mexican Americans. HISPANIC
JOURNAL OF BEHAVIORAL SCIENCES, Vol. 4, no.
2 (June 1982), p. 199-221. English. **DESCR:**
Chicanas; Marriage; *Mental Health.

4134 Santos, Richard. Earning among
Spanish-origin males in the Midwest. SOCIAL
SCIENCE JOURNAL, Vol. 19, no. 2 (April
1982), p. 51-59. English. **DESCR:** *Income;
Labor; Midwestern States.

4135 Snipp, C. Matthew and Tienda, Marta. New
perspectives of Chicano intergenerational
occupational mobility. SOCIAL SCIENCE
JOURNAL, Vol. 19, no. 2 (April 1982), p.
37-49. English. **DESCR:** Age Groups; Careers;
Social Mobility.

4136 Tips for making the right moves in today's
job markets. HISPANIC BUSINESS, Vol. 4, no.
6 (June 1982), p. 26. English. **DESCR:**
Recruitment.

4137 Tips for making the right moves in today's
job markets. HISPANIC BUSINESS, Vol. 4, no.
7 (July 1982), p. 14. English. **DESCR:**
California Chicano News Media Association
(CCNMA); *Careers.

4138 Tips for making the right moves in today's
job markets. HISPANIC BUSINESS, Vol. 5, no.
3 (March 1983), p. 24. English. **DESCR:**
National Image, Inc.

4139 Tips for making the right moves in today's
job markets. HISPANIC BUSINESS, Vol. 5, no.
5 (May 1983), p. 30. English. **DESCR:**
Advertising; *Careers; Hispanic Access to
Services (HAS), Denver, CO; *Working Women.

4140 Tips for making the right moves in today's
job markets. HISPANIC BUSINESS, Vol. 4, no.
8 (August 1983), p. 11+. English. **DESCR:**
American G.I. Forum; *Careers; Management;
Military Service.

4141 Tracking the recovery. HISPANIC BUSINESS,
Vol. 5, no. 7 (July 1983), p. 14. English.
DESCR: *Economics.

4142 Valenzuela-Crocker, Elvira. Confrontation
over the Civil Rights Commission. NUESTRO,
Vol. 7, no. 10 (December 1983), p. 21-27.
English. **DESCR:** Administration of Justice;
Affirmative Action; *Civil Rights; Education
Equalization; *U.S. Commission on Civil
Rights; Voting Rights.

4143 Watson, Roy J., Jr. The Simpson-Mazzoli
bill: an analysis of selected policies. SAN
DIEGO LAW REVIEW, Vol. 20, no. 1 (December
1982), p. 97-116. English. **DESCR:**
Immigration Regulation and Control; Labor
Certification; Mazzoli, Romano L.; Simpson,
Alan K.; *Simpson-Mazzoli Bill;
*Undocumented Workers.

Employment Tests

4144 [Summary of: race as an employment
qualification to meet police department
operational needs, 54 N.Y.U.L. rev. 413
(1979)]. CHICANO LAW REVIEW, Vol. 5,
(1982), p. 81-82. English. **DESCR:**
Administration of Justice; *Police.

Employment Training

4145 Buckholtz, Marjorie Weidenfeld. Technical
training in two languages helps Houston stay

cool. AMERICAN EDUCATION, Vol. 18, no. 3
(April 1982), p. 11-14. English. **DESCR:**
Houston Community College; Language Arts;
Language Proficiency; Vocational Education.

4146 Conoley, Martin. The hidden threat of
underemployment. HISPANIC BUSINESS, Vol. 5,
no. 10 (October 1983), p. 14+. English.
DESCR: Education; *Employment; Labor Supply
and Market; Personnel Management.

4147 Five-part series on youth jobs. NUESTRO,
Vol. 7, no. 7 (September 1983), p. 13.
English. **DESCR:** KCET-TV, Los Angeles, CA
[television station]; Television; *Y.E.S.
INC.; Youth.

4148 Government review. NUESTRO, Vol. 7, no. 10
(December 1983), p. 48. English. **DESCR:**
Banking Industry; Child Care Centers; Chile;
Clinics (Medical); Credit Unions;
Employment; *Government Services; Medical
Care; National Credit Union Administration;
National Oceanic and Atmospheric
Administration; SER; U.S. Department of
Health and Human Services; U.S. Department
of Labor.

4149 Lanier, Alfredo S. Making it seem easy, from
intern to account executive. HISPANIC
BUSINESS, Vol. 4, no. 8 (August 1983), p.
16-17+. English. **DESCR:** *Accountants;
Careers; Chicanas; *Fernandez, Margarita;
INROADS; Standard Oil Corp.

4150 Lasater, Tonia Tash and Montalvo, Frank F.
Understanding Mexican American culture: a
training program. CHILDREN TODAY, Vol. 11,
no. 3 (May, June, 1982), p. 23-25+. English.
DESCR: Cultural Characteristics; *Cultural
Customs; Mexican American Culture Simulator;
Social Services.

4151 Math-based careers. HISPANIC BUSINESS, Vol.
5, no. 11 (November 1983), p. 32. English.
DESCR: *Careers; Education; INROADS;
Mathematics, Engineering and Science
Achievement (MESA); Mexican American Legal
Defense and Educational Fund (MALDEF);
Soriano, Esteban.

4152 Math-based careers. HISPANIC BUSINESS, Vol.
5, no. 12 (December 1983), p. 40. English.
DESCR: *Careers; Council on Legal Education
Opportunities (CLEO); Education; Graduate
Schools; High Technology High School, San
Antonio, TX; Legal Education; Mexican
American Legal Defense and Educational Fund
(MALDEF); San Antonio, TX; Science as a
Profession.

4153 Math-based careers. HISPANIC BUSINESS, Vol.
4, no. 8 (August 1983), p. 20. English.
DESCR: Brigham Young University; Business
Administration; *Careers; Coalition of
Spanish-Speaking Mental Health Organization
(COSSMHO), Annual Regional Conference, Los
Angeles, March 14-15, 1975; Cooperative
Extension Programs; Education; Financial
Aid; Medical Personnel.

4154 Media/marketing. HISPANIC BUSINESS, Vol. 5,
no. 11 (November 1983), p. 30. English.
DESCR: Caballero Spanish Media, Inc. (CSM);
California Chicano News Media Association
(CCNMA); Federal Communications Commission
(FCC); HISPANEX (Oakland, CA); *Mass Media;
Michell, Pat; Radio; Radio Station KALI, Los
Angeles, CA.

Employment Training (cont.)

4155 Mestre, Mercedes. Paving the path. HISPANIC BUSINESS, Vol. 5, no. 10 (October 1983), p. 9. English. DESCR: Business Administration; Education; *Employment; *Korn/Ferry International.

4156 Shiell, Pancho. The food world's CIA. NUESTRO, Vol. 7, no. 2 (March 1983), p. 28-32. English. DESCR: *Culinary Institute of America, Hyde Park, NY; Figueroa, Roberto; Recipes.

4157 Training, fellowships. NUESTRO, Vol. 7, no. 1 (January, February, 1983), p. 9. English. DESCR: *Community Outreach Project; Financial Aid; Medical Personnel; Stanford University Medical Center.

EMPLUMADA

4158 Cervantes, Lorna Dee. Book review of: EMPLUMADA. NUESTRO, Vol. 6, no. 5 (June, July, 1982), p. 56. English. DESCR: Book Reviews; Cervantes, Lorna Dee.

EN EL PAIS DE LAS MARAVILLAS (KEMPIS PUERTORRIQUENO)

4159 Barradas, Efrain. Book review of: EN EL PAIS DE LAS MARAVILLAS (KEMPIS PUERTORRIQUENO). REVISTA CHICANO-RIQUENA, Vol. 10, no. 4 (Fall 1982), p. 67-68. Spanish. DESCR: *Book Reviews; Umpierre, Maria.

Energy Industries

4160 Balkan, D. Carlos. The nuclear powered Mr. Carlos Pimentel. HISPANIC BUSINESS, Vol. 4, no. 2 (February 1982), p. 16-17+. English. DESCR: Biography; Business Enterprises; Businesspeople; *Cataract Engineering and Construction, Inc.; *Pimentel, Carlos.

4161 Chavarria, Jesus. Varieties of energy. HISPANIC BUSINESS, Vol. 4, no. 2 (February 1982), p. 6. English. DESCR: Business Enterprises; *Cataract Engineering and Construction, Inc.; *Star-Adair Insulation, Inc.

4162 Positioning growth at El Paso Electric Co. HISPANIC BUSINESS, Vol. 4, no. 2 (February 1982), p. 10+. English. DESCR: El Paso Electric Company; El Paso, TX; Employment; *Labor Supply and Market; Wall, Evern R.

ENFOQUE NACIONAL [radio program]

4163 Communications/marketing. HISPANIC BUSINESS, Vol. 4, no. 10 (October 1982), p. 22. English. DESCR: Awards; League of United Latin American Citizens (LULAC); LULAC National Education Service Centers (LNESC); Marketing; *Mass Media.

4164 Villegas, Jim. Enfoque nacional: created from a need for information. CAMINOS, Vol. 3, no. 5 (May 1982), p. 42-43. Bilingual. DESCR: Radio.

Engineering

4165 AM-COR Architects & Engineers, Inc. aligns growth. HISPANIC BUSINESS, Vol. 4, no. 7 (July 1982), p. 12-13. English. DESCR: Business Enterprises; Engineering as a Profession; Pueblo, CO.

4166 Chavarria, Jesus. Hispanic engineers. HISPANIC BUSINESS, Vol. 4, no. 7 (July 1982), p. 6. English. DESCR: *Engineering as a Profession; National Action Council for

Minorities in Engineering (NACME).

4167 de la Isla, Jose. Math-based careers. HISPANIC BUSINESS, Vol. 5, no. 4 (April 1983), p. 20. English. DESCR: *Careers; Mathematics, Engineering and Science Achievement (MESA); Medical Personnel.

4168 Hernandez, Carlos A. State of the art. HISPANIC BUSINESS, Vol. 4, no. 7 (July 1982), p. 8. English. DESCR: *Engineering as a Profession.

4169 Math-based careers. HISPANIC BUSINESS, Vol. 5, no. 2 (February 1983), p. 22. English. DESCR: *Careers; Financial Aid; Mathematics; Mathematics, Engineering and Science Achievement (MESA); National Action Council for Minorities in Engineering (NACME).

4170 Research/development: books. HISPANIC BUSINESS, Vol. 4, no. 4 (April 1982), p. 28. English. DESCR: *Book Reviews; Financial Aid; FINANCIAL AID FOR MINORITIES IN ENGINEERING; Kennedy, David W.; PERFECTLY LEGAL - 275 FOOLPROOF METHODS FOR PAYING LESS TAXES; Steiner, Barry R.; Swann, Ruth N.; Taxation.

Engineering as a Profession

4171 AM-COR Architects & Engineers, Inc. aligns growth. HISPANIC BUSINESS, Vol. 4, no. 7 (July 1982), p. 12-13. English. DESCR: Business Enterprises; *Engineering; Pueblo, CO.

4172 Balkan, D. Carlos. Being a start-up manager at San Onofre II & III. HISPANIC BUSINESS, Vol. 4, no. 7 (July 1982), p. 18-19,26. English. DESCR: California; Chavez, Gabriel A.; *Management; Nuclear Energy.

4173 Chavarria, Jesus. Hispanic engineers. HISPANIC BUSINESS, Vol. 4, no. 7 (July 1982), p. 6. English. DESCR: Engineering; National Action Council for Minorities in Engineering (NACME).

4174 Community watching: para la comunidad. CAMINOS, Vol. 3, no. 3 (March 1982), p. 58-59. Bilingual. DESCR: Cultural Organizations; Financial Aid; Harvard University; Latino Business Students Association (LBSA); Rodolfo H. Castro Fellowship; Society for Hispanic Professional Engineers (SHPE); Student Organizations; University of Southern California.

4175 The future of minority engineering. HISPANIC BUSINESS, Vol. 4, no. 7 (July 1982), p. 28. English.

4176 Garcia, Ray J. The technological challenge: Hispanics as participants or observers. HISPANIC BUSINESS, Vol. 4, no. 7 (July 1982), p. 20-21,26. English. DESCR: *Careers; Education; Technology.

4177 Hernandez, Carlos A. State of the art. HISPANIC BUSINESS, Vol. 4, no. 7 (July 1982), p. 8. English. DESCR: Engineering.

4178 Hughes invests in the future. HISPANIC BUSINESS, Vol. 4, no. 11 (November 1982), p. 8-9,26. English. DESCR: Careers; *Educational Opportunities; Minority Introduction to Engineering (MITE); University of California, Los Angeles (UCLA).

Engineering as a Profession (cont.)

4179 Math-based careers. HISPANIC BUSINESS, Vol. 4, no. 1 (January 1982), p. 20. English. DESCR: Careers; *College Graduates; *Cox, George; Employment; *Hispanic Society of Engineers and Scientists (HSES); *Leadership, Education and Development Program in Business (LEAD).

4180 Math-based careers. HISPANIC BUSINESS, Vol. 4, no. 4 (April 1982), p. 20,24. English. DESCR: *Careers; Chicanas; Government Employees; National Action Council for Minorities in Engineering (NACME); National Hispanic Field Service Program.

4181 Math-based careers. HISPANIC BUSINESS, Vol. 4, no. 5 (May 1982), p. 22. English. DESCR: Careers; Education; *Financial Aid; National Action Council for Minorities in Engineering (NACME); Society for Hispanic Professional Engineers (SHPE).

4182 Math-based careers. HISPANIC BUSINESS, Vol. 4, no. 7 (July 1982), p. 22. English. DESCR: *Careers; LULAC National Education Service Centers (LNESC); National Action Council for Minorities in Engineering (NACME).

4183 Math-based careers. HISPANIC BUSINESS, Vol. 4, no. 10 (October 1982), p. 20. English. DESCR: *Careers; Educational Opportunities; Financial Aid; Minority Business Development Agency (MBDA); National Action Council for Minorities in Engineering (NACME); National Association of Independent Schools (NAIS).

4184 Math-based careers. HISPANIC BUSINESS, Vol. 5, no. 5 (May 1983), p. 26. English. DESCR: *Careers; Financial Aid; Income; Labor Supply and Market; Mexican American Engineering Society (MAES) National Symposium (5th), Fullerton, CA, April 13-15, 1980; University of California, Santa Barbara.

4185 Math-based careers. HISPANIC BUSINESS, Vol. 5, no. 9 (September 1983), p. 28. English. DESCR: Andrew W. Mellon Foundation; *Careers; Employment; Financial Aid; Garcia, Mary; Higher Education; National Council for Minorities in Engineering (NACME); National Medical Fellowships (NMF); Rivera, Lourdes.

4186 Math-based careers. HISPANIC BUSINESS, Vol. 5, no. 10 (October 1983), p. 28. English. DESCR: *Careers; Carnation Company; Chicanas; Education; Hispanic Policy Development Project; Minority Engineering Education Center, University of California, Los Angeles; Science as a Profession; University of California, Los Angeles (UCLA).

4187 Mendoza, Samuel M. Careers for Chicanos: computers, engineering, science/computadoras, ingenieria, ciencia. CAMINOS, Vol. 3, no. 3 (March 1982), p. 14-16. Bilingual. DESCR: *Careers; Computers; Science as a Profession.

4188 Minority students given assistance. NUESTRO, Vol. 7, no. 2 (March 1983), p. 10. English. DESCR: Education; *Minority Engineering Education Center, University of California, Los Angeles; University of California, Los Angeles (UCLA).

4189 Padilla, Steve. Choosing a career. NUESTRO, Vol. 7, no. 1 (January, February, 1983), p. 13-19+. English. DESCR: Alvarado, Raul, Jr.; *Careers; Computers; Diaz, William; Esparza, Alma; Flores, Francisco; Garcia, Linda; Medical Care; Soto, John; Yanez, Ricardo.

4190 Thomas Fuentes: community builder. HISPANIC BUSINESS, Vol. 5, no. 11 (November 1983), p. 16-17. English. DESCR: *Fuentes, Thomas; Local Government; Orange County, CA; Urban Development.

English as a Second Language

4191 Chesterfield, Ray, et al. The influence of teachers and peers on second language acquisition in bilingual preschool programs. TESOL QUARTERLY, Vol. 17, no. 3 (September 1983), p. 401-419. English. DESCR: Bilingual Bicultural Education; Early Childhood Education; Language Development; Teacher-pupil Interaction.

4192 Cordasco, Francesco. Bilingual education: overview and inventory. EDUCATIONAL FORUM, Vol. 47, (Spring 1983), p. 321-334. English. DESCR: *Bilingual Bicultural Education; Educational Law and Legislation; Educational Theory and Practice; History; Literature Reviews.

4193 Fillmore, Lili Wong. Language minority students and school participation: what kind of English is needed? JOURNAL OF EDUCATION, Vol. 164, no. 2 (Spring 1982), p. 143-156. English. DESCR: *Bilingual Bicultural Education; Early Childhood Education; Language Proficiency.

4194 Galloway, Linda M. and Scarcella, Robin. Cerebral organization in adult second language acquisition: is the right hemisphere more involved. BRAIN AND LANGUAGE, Vol. 16, no. 1 (May 1982), p. 56-60. English. DESCR: *Bilingualism; Learning and Cognition.

4195 Garza, Ana. ESL in the bilingual classroom. BILINGUAL JOURNAL, Vol. 6, no. 4 (Summer 1982), p. 26-29,32. English. DESCR: *Bilingual Bicultural Education; Bilingual Inventory of Natural Languages; Language Assessment; Language Assessment Battery; Language Assessment Scales.

4196 Haft, Jonathan D. Assuring equal educational opportunity for language-minority students: bilingual education and the Equal Educational Opportunity Act of 1974. COLUMBIA JOURNAL OF LAW AND SOCIAL PROBLEMS, Vol. 18, no. 2 (1983), p. 209-293. English. DESCR: *Bilingual Bicultural Education; Civil Rights; Educational Law and Legislation; *Equal Educational Opportunity Act of 1974 (EEOA); Laws; Students.

4197 Johnson, Donna M. Natural language learning by design: a classroom experiment in social interaction and second language acquisition. TESOL QUARTERLY, Vol. 17, no. 1 (March 1983), p. 55-68. English. DESCR: Inter-Ethnolinguistic Peer Tutoring (IEPT); Language Development; Primary School Education.

4198 Lalas, Joselito W. The influence of prior experience in ESL reading. BILINGUAL JOURNAL, Vol. 6, no. 1 (Fall 1982), p. 10-12. English. DESCR: Bilingual Bicultural Education; Learning and Cognition; *Reading.

English as a Second Language (cont.)

4199 McGroarty, Mary. English language test, school language use, and achievement in Spanish-speaking high school students. TESOL QUARTERLY, Vol. 17, no. 2 (June 1983), p. 310-311. English. **DESCR:** Academic Achievement; High School Students; Language Assessment.

4200 Mendez, Gloria I. Bilingual children's adaptation after a transitional bilingual education. METAS, Vol. 3, no. 1 (Summer 1982), p. 1-112. English. **DESCR:** Academic Achievement; Acculturation; *Bilingual Bicultural Education; Bilingualism; Identity.

4201 Ortiz, Tomasita. The Spanish-speaking migrant child. BILINGUAL JOURNAL, Vol. 6, no. 4 (Summer 1982), p. 8-15,32. English. **DESCR:** Bilingual Bicultural Education; *Migrant Children; Migrant Education; *MIGRANT STUDENT RECORD TRANSFER SYSTEM.

4202 Schorr, Burt. Language lab: grade-school project helps Hispanic pupils learn English quickly; but Texas test's avoidance of bilingual approach is source of controversy. WALL STREET JOURNAL, Vol. 202, (November 30, 1983), p. 1. English. **DESCR:** Primary School Education; *Texas.

4203 Troike, Rudolph C. Bilingual-si! PRINCIPAL, Vol. 62, no. 3 (January 1983), p. 8. English. **DESCR:** Academic Achievement; *Bilingual Bicultural Education; Bilingualism.

4204 Walia, Adorna. Book review of: BEGINNING ENGLISH THROUGH ACTION. BILINGUAL JOURNAL, Vol. 7, no. 3 (Spring 1983), p. 31-32. English. **DESCR:** *BEGINNING ENGLISH THROUGH ACTION (BETA); Book Reviews; Jackson, P.; Language Arts; Programmed Instruction.

4205 Walia, Adorna. Book review of: CONVERSATIONS OF MIGUEL AND MARIA: HOW CHILDREN LEARN ENGLISH AS A SECOND LANGUAGE; IMPLICATIONS FOR CLASSROOM TEACHING. BILINGUAL JOURNAL, Vol. 6, no. 1 (Fall 1982), p. 28-29. English. **DESCR:** Bilingual Bicultural Education; Book Reviews; *CONVERSATIONS OF MIGUEL AND MARIA: HOW CHILDREN LEARN ENGLISH AS A SECOND LANGUAGE; IMPLICATIONS FOR CLASSROOM TEACHING; Ventriglia, Linda.

4206 Walker de Felix, Judith. The language arts approach: planned eclecticism in ESL teaching in the elementary school. BILINGUAL REVIEW, Vol. 10, no. 1 (January, April, 1983), p. 87-89. English. **DESCR:** *Language Arts Approach (LAA); Primary School Education.

English Language

4207 Burke, P.E. Immigrant Mexican children hurdle the English barrier. TIMES (London) [EDUCATIONAL SUPPLEMENT], Vol. 3447, (July 23, 1982), p. 15. English. **DESCR:** *Bilingual Bicultural Education; Children; Immigrants.

4208 Hernandez, Rudy. English, yes! Spanish, si! Spanglish, no! NUESTRO, Vol. 7, no. 8 (October 1983), p. 53. English. **DESCR:** Language Proficiency; *Language Usage; Spanish Language.

4209 Kramer, Virginia Reyes and Schell, Leo M. English auditory discrimination skills of Spanish-speaking children. ALBERTA JOURNAL OF EDUCATIONAL RESEARCH, Vol. 28, no. 1 (March 1982), p. 1-8. English. **DESCR:**

Accentedness; Bilingualism; *Language Development; Spanish Language.

4210 Madrid, Arturo and Rodriguez, Richard. The mis-education of rich-heard road-ree-guess. MAIZE, Vol. 5, no. 3-4 (Spring, Summer, 1982), p. 88-92. English. **DESCR:** Assimilation; *Book Reviews; Education.

4211 Savage, David G. Is the market going English? HISPANIC BUSINESS, Vol. 4, no. 12 (December 1982), p. 20-21. English. **DESCR:** Language Proficiency; *Language Usage; *Spanish Language.

4212 Wittenauer, Cheryl. Dallas Hispanic media. HISPANIC BUSINESS, Vol. 5, no. 2 (February 1983), p. 12-13+. English. **DESCR:** Broadcast Media; *Consumers; Dallas, TX; Marketing; Mass Media; Newspapers; Spanish Language.

Enriquez, Evangelina

4213 Baca Zinn, Maxine. Book review of: LA CHICANA: THE MEXICAN AMERICAN WOMAN. SIGNS: JOURNAL OF WOMEN IN CULTURE AND SOCIETY, Vol. 8, no. 2 (Winter 1982), p. 259-272. English. **DESCR:** Book Reviews; Chicanas; *LA CHICANA: THE MEXICAN AMERICAN WOMAN; Literature Reviews; Mirande, Alfredo; Social Science.

4214 Palacios, Maria. Book review of: LA CHICANA: THE MEXICAN AMERICAN WOMAN. HISPANIC JOURNAL OF BEHAVIORAL SCIENCES, Vol. 4, no. 2 (June 1982), p. 272-275. English. **DESCR:** Book Reviews; *LA CHICANA: THE MEXICAN AMERICAN WOMAN; Mirande, Alfredo.

4215 Salgado de Snyder, Nelly. Book review of: LA CHICANA: THE MEXICAN AMERICAN WOMAN. HISPANIC JOURNAL OF BEHAVIORAL SCIENCES, Vol. 4, no. 2 (June 1982), p. 268-272. English. **DESCR:** Book Reviews; *LA CHICANA: THE MEXICAN AMERICAN WOMAN; Mirande, Alfredo.

4216 Stoller, Marianne L. Book review of: LA CHICANA: THE MEXICAN AMERICAN WOMAN. SOCIAL SCIENCE JOURNAL, Vol. 19, no. 2 (April 1982), p. 134-136. English. **DESCR:** Book Reviews; Chicanas; *LA CHICANA: THE MEXICAN AMERICAN WOMAN; Mirande, Alfredo.

4217 Swink, Sue. Book review of: LA CHICANA: THE MEXICAN AMERICAN WOMAN. HISPANIC JOURNAL OF BEHAVIORAL SCIENCES, Vol. 4, no. 2 (June 1982), p. 275-277. English. **DESCR:** Book Reviews; *LA CHICANA: THE MEXICAN AMERICAN WOMAN; Mirande, Alfredo.

Enriquez, Rene

4218 People. HISPANIC BUSINESS, Vol. 4, no. 7 (July 1982), p. 7. English. **DESCR:** Aguilar, Richard; *Biographical Notes; Businesspeople; Coronado, Julius; Garza, Jose S.; Guerra-Martinez, Celina; Medrano, Adan; Mota, Manny; Valenti, Frank S.

Enrollment

4219 Cantu, Hector. Hispanic students wanted. NATIONAL HISPANIC JOURNAL, Vol. 1, no. 3 (Summer, Fall, 1982), p. 8. English. **DESCR:** Higher Education; Recruitment; Students; *University of Texas at Austin.

Enrollment (cont.)

4220 de los Santos, Alfredo G. Jr.; Montemayor, Joaquin; and Solis, Enrique, Jr. Chicano students in institutions of higher education: access, attrition, and achievement. AZTLAN, Vol. 14, no. 1 (Spring 1983), p. 79-110. English. DESCR: Academic Achievement; Educational Statistics; *Higher Education; Students.

4221 Doyle, Janet. Escoja educacion catolica! MOMENTUM, Vol. 14, no. 1 (February 1983), p. 37-38. English. DESCR: Catholic Church; *Religious Education; Toledo, OH.

4222 Gonzalez, Gilbert G. Educational reform and the Mexican community in Los Angeles. SOUTHWEST ECONOMY AND SOCIETY, Vol. 3, no. 3 (Spring 1978), p. 24-51. English. DESCR: Counseling Services (Educational); Curriculum; *Education; *History; Intelligence Tests; Los Angeles, CA; *Los Angeles City School District; Tracking (Educational); Vocational Education.

4223 Hernandez, Leodoro and Luevano, Richard L. A program for the recruitment of Chicanos into higher education. COLLEGE STUDENT JOURNAL, Vol. 17, no. 2 (Summer 1983), p. 166-171. English. DESCR: California; California State University, Stanislaus; Higher Education; *Student Ambassador Recruitment Program, California State University, Stanislaus.

4224 Hispanic student study undertaken. NUESTRO, Vol. 7, no. 10 (December 1983), p. 11-12. English. DESCR: Academic Achievement; Dropouts; Educational Statistics; Hispanic Policy Development Project; *National Commission on Secondary Schooling for Hispanics; *Secondary School Education.

4225 Mestre, Jose P. and Robinson, Holly. Academic, socio-economic, and motivational characteristics of Hispanic college students enrolled in technical programs. VOCATIONAL GUIDANCE QUARTERLY, Vol. 31, no. 3 (March 1983), p. 187-194. English. DESCR: *College and University Students; Counseling Services (Educational); Vocational Guidance.

4226 Schlef, Aileen. Estudio/survey: what higher education does (and doesn't do) for Hispanics. CASE CURRENTS, Vol. 9, no. 4 (April 1983), p. 14-17. English. DESCR: *Higher Education.

4227 Taylor, Karla. Accion/action: a coast-to-coast sampling of innovative Hispanic programs. CASE CURRENTS, Vol. 9, no. 4 (April 1983), p. 11-13. English. DESCR: Educational Innovations; Higher Education.

4228 Webster, David S. Chicano students in American higher education: a review of the literature. CAMPO LIBRE, Vol. 1, no. 2 (Summer 1981), p. 169-192. English. DESCR: Dropouts; Educational Statistics; Graduate Schools; *Higher Education; Literature Reviews; Professional Schools.

Entertainers

4229 Diaz, Katherine A. The many faceted talents of Danny Valdez=Los muchos y variados talentos de Danny Valdez. CAMINOS, Vol. 2, no. 6 (October 1981), p. [34]-36. Bilingual. DESCR: Biography; *Valdez, Daniel.

4230 Fernandez, Enrique. NARAS takes a welcome step. BILLBOARD, Vol. 95, (June 18, 1983), p. 59. English. DESCR: Awards; Grammy Awards; Music; *National Academy of Recording Arts and Sciences; Performing Arts; Recording Industry.

4231 Fernandez, Enrique. Youth acts dominating markets: labels woo kids with Spanish-language rock product. BILLBOARD, Vol. 95, (March 12, 1983), p. 58. English. DESCR: Music; Recording Industry; Youth.

4232 Greenfield, Charles. Spanish prince of song. NUESTRO, Vol. 6, no. 5 (June, July, 1982), p. 18-21. English. DESCR: *Iglesias, Julio; Recreation.

4233 Top talent at Tejano awards. BILLBOARD, Vol. 95, (January 29, 1983), p. 65. English. DESCR: Awards; Music; Performing Arts; *Tejano Music Awards; Texas.

Entertainment
USE: Recreation

ENTRE LA VIGILIA Y EL SUENO

4234 Agosin, Marjorie. Book review of: ENTRE LA VIGILIA Y EL SUENO. THIRD WOMAN, Vol. 1, no. 2 (1982), p. 94-95. Spanish. DESCR: Book Reviews; Matte Alessandri, Ester.

Environmental Pollution
USE: Pollution

Equal Educational Opportunity Act of 1974 (EEOA)

4235 Haft, Jonathan D. Assuring equal educational opportunity for language-minority students: bilingual education and the Equal Educational Opportunity Act of 1974. COLUMBIA JOURNAL OF LAW AND SOCIAL PROBLEMS, Vol. 18, no. 2 (1983), p. 209-293. English. DESCR: *Bilingual Bicultural Education; Civil Rights; Educational Law and Legislation; English as a Second Language; Laws; Students.

Equal Employment Opportunity Commission (EEOC)

4236 Executives expect little affirmative action change. HISPANIC BUSINESS, Vol. 4, no. 2 (February 1982), p. 23. English. DESCR: *Affirmative Action.

4237 Gallegos, Tony E. Why doesn't the E.E.O.C. help Hispanics? CAMINOS, Vol. 4, no. 9 (October 1983), p. 20-21,52. Bilingual. DESCR: Affirmative Action; Affirmative Action Programs.

4238 Langley, Roger. Roger Langley's Hispanic beat. HISPANIC BUSINESS, Vol. 4, no. 3 (March 1982), p. 22. English. DESCR: *Appointed Officials; Bell, William M.

4239 Levario, Raquel. LULAC takes a stand against mainstream media. LATINA, Vol. 1, no. 3 (1983), p. 49. English. DESCR: *League of United Latin American Citizens (LULAC); *Mass Media.

4240 LULAC files complaint against TV networks. NUESTRO, Vol. 6, no. 8 (October 1982), p. 48. English. DESCR: Bonilla, Tony; Employment; *League of United Latin American Citizens (LULAC); Racism; Television.

Equal Employment Opportunity Commission (EEOC)
(cont.)

4241 Rivera, Henry M. Hispanics need to effectively translate potential into political and economic clout. TELEVISION/RADIO AGE, Vol. 31, no. 4 (September 12, 1983), p. 117-118. English. **DESCR:** Federal Communications Commission (FCC); *Minority Telecommunications Ownership Act of 1983 (HR 2331); *Radio.

4242 Second Latino assumes new duties at EEOC. NUESTRO, Vol. 6, no. 4 (May 1982), p. 27. English. **DESCR:** Appointed Officials; *Gallegos, Tony E.

Equal Opportunity
USE: Affirmative Action

Equal Opportunity Programs
USE: Affirmative Action Programs

Equal Protection Clause

4243 Schey, Peter A. Unnamed witness number 1: now attending the Texas public schools. MIGRATION TODAY, Vol. 10, no. 5 (1982), p. 22-27. English. **DESCR:** Constitutional Amendments - Fourteenth; Education; Education Equalization; Educational Law and Legislation; Migrant Children; Texas Public Schools; *Undocumented Children; U.S. Supreme Court Case.

4244 Vasquez, Ivan. Analysis of June 15, 1982 opinion issued by the U.S. Supreme Court in the case of Texas undocumented children. MIGRATION TODAY, Vol. 10, no. 3-4 (1982), p. 49-51. English. **DESCR:** Constitutional Amendments - Fourteenth; Education; *Education Equalization; Educational Law and Legislation; Migrant Children; *Undocumented Children; U.S. Supreme Court Case.

Equal Rights Amendment (ERA)

4245 Cotera, Martha P. ERA: the Latina challenge. NUESTRO, Vol. 5, no. 8 (November 1981), p. 47-48. English. **DESCR:** *Women Men Relations; Women's Rights.

Equality Before the Law
USE: Civil Rights

Equality in Education
USE: Discrimination in Education

Escalante, Jaime

4246 Our 1982 Latino awards. NUESTRO, Vol. 7, no. 1 (January, February, 1983), p. 44-46. English. **DESCR:** Awards; Gallegos, Gina; Grace, J. Peter; Immigration and Naturalization Service (INS); Knight, Bobby; Lamas, Fernando; *Latino Awards; Luce, Claire Boothe; Moreno, Rita; National Press Foundation; Rodriguez Hernandez, Andres; Simpson-Mazzoli Bill; Smith, Raymond; Valeri, Michele; Voting Rights Act.

Escobedo, Ed

4247 Chavez, Rigo. Job counseling, role models mean a lot. HISPANIC BUSINESS, Vol. 4, no. 8 (August 1983), p. 12. English. **DESCR:** Careers; *Counseling Services (Educational); Cuevas, Hector; Professional Opportunities Program (POP); *Stanford University, Stanford, CA.

Escovedo, Pete

4248 Romero, Pedro Sababu. Pete Escovedo: a study

in versatility. NUESTRO, Vol. 6, no. 10 (December 1982), p. 63-64. English. **DESCR:** *Artists; *Musicians.

Escuela Nacional Preparatoria

4249 Leal, Luis. Gabino Barreda y la literatura: de la preparatoria al Ateneo. AZTLAN, Vol. 14, no. 2 (Fall 1983), p. 253-265. Spanish. **DESCR:** Ateneo de la Juventud; *Barreda, Gabino; History; *Mexican Literature; Philosophy; Positivism.

ESEA Title VII
USE: ELEMENTARY AND SECONDARY EDUCATION ACT

ESENCIA [magazine]

4250 New tabloid magazines developed in Bay Area. NUESTRO, Vol. 6, no. 2 (March 1982), p. 48. English. **DESCR:** *Magazines; UNO [magazine], Fremont, CA.

ESL
USE: English as a Second Language

Espada, Frank

4251 The Puerto Rican diaspora: the dispersal of a people. NUESTRO, Vol. 6, no. 5 (June, July, 1982), p. 32-41. English. **DESCR:** Ethnic Groups; Ethnic Stratification; Population Distribution; *Puerto Ricans.

ESPANOL ESCRITO

4252 Feliciano-Foster, Wilma. A comparison of three current first-year college-level Spanish-for-native-speakers textbooks. BILINGUAL REVIEW, Vol. 9, no. 1 (January, April, 1982), p. 72-81. English. **DESCR:** *Book Reviews; Garza-Swan, Gloria; *Language Development; Mejias, Hugo A.; MEJORA TU ESPANOL; NUESTRO ESPANOL: CURSO PARA ESTUDIANTES BILINGUES; Portilla, Marta de la; Spanish Language Textbooks; Teschner, Richard V.; Valdes Fallis, Guadalupe; Varela, Beatriz.

Esparza, Alma

4253 Padilla, Steve. Choosing a career. NUESTRO, Vol. 7, no. 1 (January, February, 1983), p. 13-19+. English. **DESCR:** Alvarado, Raul, Jr.; *Careers; Computers; Diaz, William; Engineering as a Profession; Flores, Francisco; Garcia, Linda; Medical Care; Soto, John; Yanez, Ricardo.

Esparza, Moctezuma

4254 Breiter, Toni. La raza. AGENDA, Vol. 11, no. 3 (May, June, 1981), p. 28-29. English. **DESCR:** Mass Media.

Espinal, Antonio

4255 Uehling, Mark D. Rivalry in New York: a profile of two newspapers. NUESTRO, Vol. 7, no. 7 (September 1983), p. 20-21. English. **DESCR:** Bustelo, Manuel A.; DIARIO LA PRENSA [newspaper], New York, NY; Gannett Co., Inc.; Journalism; New York, NY; *Newspapers; NOTICIAS DEL MUNDO; Patino, Luis; Unification Church.

Espinosa, Victoria

4256 Lopez, Yvette. Victoria Espinoza and the development of theater in Puerto Rico. THIRD WOMAN, Vol. 1, no. 2 (1982), p. 56-64. English. **DESCR:** Teatro.

Espinoza, Jimmy

4257 Whisler, Kirk. Nosotros on film in Hollywood and Latin America. CAMINOS, Vol. 3, no. 7 (July, August, 1982), p. 15-17. Bilingual. DESCR: Artists; Cardinale, Marcela; Films; Gomez, Mike; *Nosotros [film production company]; Ortiz, Yolanda; Television; Velasco, Jerry.

Espinoza, Peter

4258 People. HISPANIC BUSINESS, Vol. 5, no. 5 (May 1983), p. 8. English. DESCR: Biographical Notes; *Businesspeople; Duron, Armando; Flores, Juan; Martinez, Vilma Socorro; Molina, Gloria; Moreno, Samuel; Pantin, Leslie, Sr.; Quezada, Sylvia; Quinones, Sergio.

Essays

4259 Agosin, Marjorie. Elucubraciones y antielucubraciones: critica feminista desde perspectivas poeticas. THIRD WOMAN, Vol. 1, no. 2 (1982), p. 65-69. Spanish. DESCR: *Chicanas; Literature.

4260 Alarcon, Justo S. La meta critica Chicana. REVISTA CHICANO-RIQUENA, Vol. 10, no. 3 (Summer 1982), p. 47-52. Spanish. DESCR: *Humor; Literary Criticism.

4261 Arias, Ron. The rooster that called me home. NATION, Vol. 236, no. 24 (June 18, 1983), p. 758-761. English. DESCR: Arias, Ron; *Undocumented Workers.

4262 Barradas, Efrain. "Todo lo que digo es cierto...": en memoria de Victor Fernandez Fragoso (1944-1982). REVISTA CHICANO-RIQUENA, Vol. 10, no. 3 (Summer 1982), p. 43-46. Spanish. DESCR: Authors; *Biography; *Fernandez Fragoso, Victor; New York, NY; Puerto Rican Literature.

4263 Davila, Luis. Meditaciones. REVISTA CHICANO-RIQUENA, Vol. 10, no. 1-2 (Winter, Spring, 1982), p. 275-278. Spanish. DESCR: Bilingualism; Cultural Customs; Folklore; Self-Referents.

4264 A decade of Hispanic literature: an anniversary anthology. REVISTA CHICANO-RIQUENA, Vol. 10, no. 1-2 (Winter, Spring, 1982), p. 1-310. Bilingual. DESCR: *Literature; Poetry; Prose.

4265 Delgado, Abelardo "Lalo". An open letter to Carolina... or relations between men and women. REVISTA CHICANO-RIQUENA, Vol. 10, no. 1-2 (Winter, Spring, 1982), p. 279-284. English. DESCR: Chicanas; Machismo; Sex Roles; Sex Stereotypes.

4266 Fernandez Olmos, Margarite. From the metropolis: Puerto Rican women poets and the immigration experience. THIRD WOMAN, Vol. 1, no. 2 (1982), p. 40-51. English. DESCR: *Puerto Rican Literature; *Women.

4267 Garcia, Jorge. Somewhere. CORAZON DE AZTLAN, Vol. 1, no. 3 (August, September, 1982), p. 11. English.

4268 Garcia, Richard A. Chicano intellectual history: myth and realities. REVISTA CHICANO-RIQUENA, Vol. 10, no. 1-2 (Winter, Spring, 1982), p. 285-289. English. DESCR: Chicano Movement; History; Self-Referents; Stereotypes.

4269 Gomez-Quinones, Juan. On culture. REVISTA CHICANO-RIQUENA, Vol. 10, no. 1-2 (Winter, Spring, 1982), p. 290-308. English. DESCR: Culture; Identity.

4270 Zavala, Iris M. Ideologias y autobiografias: perspectivas femeninas. THIRD WOMAN, Vol. 1, no. 2 (1982), p. 35-39. Spanish. DESCR: *Chicanas.

ESSAYS ON LA MUJER

4271 Chavez, Mauro. Book review of: ESSAYS ON LA MUJER. JOURNAL OF ETHNIC STUDIES, Vol. 8, no. 2 (Summer 1980), p. 117-120. English. DESCR: Book Reviews; *Chicanas; Cruz, Rosa Martinez; Economic History and Conditions; Sanchez, Rosaura; Social History and Conditions; Socioeconomic Factors; Women's Rights.

Estassi, Pilar

4272 PA trained for Venezuela. NUESTRO, Vol. 6, no. 6 (August 1982), p. 10. English. DESCR: Medical Care; Venezuela.

Estes Reading Attitude Scale

4273 Plake, Barbara S., et al. Relationship of ethnic group membership to the measurement and meaning of attitudes towards reading: implications for validity of test score interpretations. EDUCATIONAL AND PSYCHOLOGICAL MEASUREMENT, Vol. 42, no. 4 (Winter 1982), p. 1259-1267. English. DESCR: Anglo Americans; Attitude (Psychological); Educational Tests and Measurements; Ethnic Groups; *Reading; Students.

Esteverena, Rolando C.

4274 People. HISPANIC BUSINESS, Vol. 5, no. 8 (August 1983), p. 10. English. DESCR: *Biographical Notes; Businesspeople; Calderon, Charles M.; General Coffee Corporation; Hispanic Bankers Association (HBA); Martinez, Olivia T.; Pallares, Mariano; Ruiz, Frederick R.; Ruiz, Louis F.; Sanchez, Joseph J.

Esteves, Sandra Maria

4275 Barradas, Efrain. Conciencia femenina, conciencia social: la voz poetica de Sandra Maria Esteves. THIRD WOMAN, Vol. 1, no. 2 (1982), p. 31-34. Spanish. DESCR: *Literature Reviews.

4276 Umpierre, Luz Maria. La ansiedad de la influencia en Sandra Maria Esteves y Marjorie Agosin. REVISTA CHICANO-RIQUENA, Vol. 11, no. 3-4 (Fall 1983), p. 139-147. Spanish. DESCR: A JULIA Y A MI; *Agosin, Magi; De Burgos, Julia; EL PAIS DIVIDIDO; *Literary Criticism; Neruda, Pablo; Parra, Nicanor; Poetry.

Estimated Learning Potential (ELP)

4277 Oakland, Thomas. Concurrent and predictive validity estimates for the WISC-R IQ's and ELP's by racial-ethnic and SES groups. SCHOOL PSYCHOLOGY REVIEW, Vol. 12, no. 1 (Winter 1983), p. 57-61. English. DESCR: Academic Achievement; *Intelligence Tests; Primary School Education; Wechsler Intelligence Scale for Children-Revised (WISC-R).

ESTUDIOS FRONTERIZOS: PONENCIAS Y COMENTARIOS

4278 Research/development: books. HISPANIC
BUSINESS, Vol. 4, no. 11 (November 1982), p.
28. English. DESCR: Book Reviews; Border
Industries; Border Region; Jamail, Milton
H.; *THE UNITED STATES-MEXICO BORDER: A
GUIDE TO INSTITUTIONS, ORGANIZATIONS AND
SCHOLARS; United States-Mexico Relations.

Ethics

4279 Cortese, Anthony. Moral development in
Chicano and Anglo children. HISPANIC JOURNAL
OF BEHAVIORAL SCIENCES, Vol. 4, no. 3
(September 1982), p. 353-366. English.
DESCR: Attitude (Psychological);
*Psychology; Socialization.

4280 Marti, Oscar R. Barrera and moral
philosophy. AZTLAN, Vol. 14, no. 2 (Fall
1983), p. 373-403. English. DESCR: *Barreda,
Gabino; History; Mexico; Philosophy;
Positivism.

ETHNIC AMERICA, A HISTORY

4281 Goldberg, Victor. Ethnic groups in the
United States. REVIEWS IN ANTHROPOLOGY, Vol.
9, no. 4 (Fall 1982), p. 375-382. English.
DESCR: Achor, Shirley; Book Reviews; MEXICAN
AMERICANS IN A DALLAS BARRIO; Sowell,
Thomas; *THE CHICANOS; Trejo, Arnulfo D.

4282 Van den Berghe, Pierre L. Book review of:
ETHNIC AMERICA, A HISTORY. INTERNATIONAL
MIGRATION REVIEW, Vol. 16, no. 4 (Winter
1982), p. 900-902. English. DESCR: Book
Reviews; Ethnic Groups; History; Migration;
Sowell, Thomas.

Ethnic Attitudes

4283 Barrio, Raymond. The bilingual heart and
other adventures. BILINGUAL JOURNAL, Vol. 6,
no. 2 (Winter 1982), p. 12-15. Bilingual.
DESCR: *Early Childhood Education; Racism;
REVERSING ROLES; THE BILINGUAL HEART; THE
PRINCE.

4284 Diaz, Tom. "Wetbacks" and other fellow
Americans. NUESTRO, Vol. 7, no. 8 (October
1983), p. 63. English. DESCR: *Hollings,
Ernest "Fritz"; *Racism.

4285 Elliott, Stephen N. and Argulewicz, Ed N.
The influence of student ethnicity on
teachers' behavior ratings of normal and
learning disabled children. HISPANIC JOURNAL
OF BEHAVIORAL SCIENCES, Vol. 5, no. 3
(September 1983), p. 337-345. English.
DESCR: *Devereux Elementary School Behavior
Rating Scale (DESBRS); Teacher Attitudes.

4286 Gonzalez-Swafford, Maria J. and Gutierrez,
Mary Grace. Ethno-medical beliefs and
practices of Mexican-Americans. NURSE
PRACTITIONER, Vol. 8, no. 10 (November,
December, 1983), p. 29-30. English. DESCR:
Curanderismo; *Folk Medicine.

4287 Hing, Bill Ong. Racial disparity: the
unaddressed issues of the Simpson-Mazzoli
Bill. LA RAZA LAW JOURNAL, Vol. 1, no. 1
(June 1983), p. 21-52. English. DESCR:
Amnesty; Asian Americans; Family;
Immigration; Immigration and Naturalization
Service (INS); Latin Americans; Mazzoli,
Romano L.; Mexican American Legal Defense
and Educational Fund (MALDEF); Simpson, Alan
K.; *Simpson-Mazzoli Bill; Temporary Worker
Program; U.S. Congresssional Subcommittee on
Immigration, Refugees and International Law.

4288 Langum, D.J. From condemnation to praise:
shifting perspectives on Hispanic
California. CALIFORNIA HISTORY, Vol. 61, no.
4 (1983), p. 282-291. English. DESCR:
*California; *Cultural Characteristics;
Stereotypes.

4289 Mejias-Rentas, Antonio. "I love Latinos
because they love to smile". NUESTRO, Vol.
7, no. 7 (September 1983), p. 53. English.
DESCR: *Identity.

4290 Miller, Darlis A. Cross-cultural marriages
in the Southwest: the New Mexico experience,
1846-1900. NEW MEXICO HISTORICAL REVIEW,
Vol. 57, no. 4 (October 1982), p. 335-359.
English. DESCR: Assimilation; Chicanas;
*Intermarriage; New Mexico; Social History
and Conditions.

4291 Myres, Sandra Lynn. Mexican Americans and
westering Anglos: a feminine perspective.
NEW MEXICO HISTORICAL REVIEW, Vol. 57, no. 4
(October 1982), p. 317-333. English. DESCR:
Anglo Americans; Chicanas; Social History
and Conditions; Southwest United States;
Stereotypes.

4292 O'Brien, Mary Elizabeth. Pragmatic
survivalism: behavior patterns affecting
low-level wellness among minority group
members. ANS: ADVANCES IN NURSING SCIENCE,
Vol. 4, no. 3 (April 1982), p. 13-26.
English. DESCR: Curanderismo; Immigrants;
*Medical Care; *Nursing; Public Health.

4293 Steigelfest, Annette. Ethnicity and sex role
socialization. BILINGUAL JOURNAL, Vol. 6,
no. 3 (Spring 1982), p. 11-15,24. English.
DESCR: Halacha Institute; *Identity;
Orthodox Jews; *Sex Roles; Sex Stereotypes;
Socialization.

ETHNIC CHANGE

4294 Padilla, Amado M. Book review of: ETHNIC
CHANGE. HISPANIC JOURNAL OF BEHAVIORAL
SCIENCES, Vol. 4, no. 3 (September 1982), p.
393-394. English. DESCR: Book Reviews;
Keyes, Charles F.

ETHNIC ENDOGAMY AMONG MEXICAN AMERICAN GROOMS

4295 Alba, Richard D. A comment on Schoen and
Cohen. AMERICAN JOURNAL OF SOCIOLOGY, Vol.
87, no. 4 (January 1982), p. 935-939.
English. DESCR: Cohen, Lawrence E.;
Intermarriage; *Research Methodology;
Schoen, Robert.

ETHNIC ENDOGAMY: THE CASE OF THE MEXICAN-AMERICANS

4296 Schoen, Robert and Cohen, Lawrence E. Theory
and method in the study of ethnic endogamy
among Mexican-American grooms - reply.
AMERICAN JOURNAL OF SOCIOLOGY, Vol. 87, no.
4 (January 1982), p. 939-942. English.
DESCR: Assimilation; Intermarriage;
Mittelback, Frank G.; Moore, Joan W.;
*Research Methodology.

ETHNIC FAMILIES IN AMERICA: PATTERNS AND VARIATIONS

4297 Zaks, Vivian Calderon. Book review of:
ETHNIC FAMILIES IN AMERICA: PATTERNS AND
VARIATIONS. HISPANIC JOURNAL OF BEHAVIORAL
SCIENCES, Vol. 4, no. 1 (March 1982), p.
122-128. English. DESCR: Book Reviews;
Habenstein, Robert W.; Mindel, Charles H.

Ethnic Groups

4298 Adams, Russell L.; Boake, Corwin; and Crain,
Charles. Bias in a neuropsychological test
classification related to education, age and
ethnicity. JOURNAL OF CONSULTING AND
CLINICAL PSYCHOLOGY, Vol. 50, no. 1
(February 1982), p. 143-145. English.
DESCR: Age Groups; Educational Levels;
Mentally Handicapped; *Psychological
Testing.

4299 Andersen, Kurt. The new Ellis Island. TIME,
Vol. 121, no. 24 (June 13, 1983), p. 18-25.
English. **DESCR:** Demography; Los Angeles, CA.

4300 Ayers-Nackamkin, Beverly, et al. Sex and
ethnic differences in the use of power.
JOURNAL OF APPLIED PSYCHOLOGY, Vol. 67, no.
4 (August 1982), p. 464-471. English.
DESCR: Anglo Americans; Management;
*Personnel Management; Sex Roles; Social
Psychology.

4301 Borjas, George J. Earnings of male Hispanic
immigrants in the United States. INDUSTRIAL
AND LABOR RELATIONS REVIEW, Vol. 35, no. 3
(April 1982), p. 343-353. English. **DESCR:**
Cubanos; *Immigrants; *Income; Puerto
Ricans; Social Mobility.

4302 Census information: 1980 U.S. census report
on nation's racial group. NUESTRO, Vol. 5,
no. 8 (November 1981), p. 34-37. English.
DESCR: *Census.

4303 Chicago: a case study of minority
participation in city government and
industry. HISPANIC BUSINESS, Vol. 5, no. 1
(January 1983), p. 28-29. English. **DESCR:**
Chicago, IL; *Employment; Government.

4304 Constantino, Guiseppe and Malgady, Robert G.
Verbal fluency of Hispanic, Black and white
children on TAT and TEMAS, a new thematic
apperception test. HISPANIC JOURNAL OF
BEHAVIORAL SCIENCES, Vol. 5, no. 2 (June
1983), p. 199-206. English. **DESCR:** Children;
*Language Proficiency; TAT; TEMAS.

4305 de Ortego y Gasca, Felipe. "Are there U.S.
Hispanic writers?". NUESTRO, Vol. 7, no. 3
(April 1983), p. 20-21+. English. **DESCR:**
Authors; *Literary Criticism; Literature.

4306 Dowdall, George W. and Flood, Lawrence G.
Correlates and consequences of socioeconomic
differences among Chicanos, Blacks and
Anglos in the Southwest: a study of
metropolitan structure. SOCIAL SCIENCE
JOURNAL, Vol. 19, no. 2 (April 1982), p.
25-36. English. **DESCR:** Anglo Americans;
Blacks; *Research Methodology; Residential
Segregation; Socioeconomic Factors;
Southwest United States.

4307 Esman, Milton J. Book review of: THE ETHNIC
REVIVAL IN THE MODERN WORLD. ETHNIC AND
RACIAL STUDIES, Vol. 5, no. 3 (1982), p.
378-379. English. **DESCR:** Book Reviews;
*ETHNIC REVIVAL IN THE MODERN WORLD; Smith,
Anthony D.

4308 Espada, Frank. Who am I?: Puerto Rican
Hawaiians ask. NUESTRO, Vol. 6, no. 8
(October 1982), p. 32-33. English. **DESCR:**
Identity; *Puerto Rican Hawaiians; *Puerto
Ricans.

4309 Exum, Herbert A. The most invisible
minority: the culturally diverse elderly.
SCHOOL COUNSELOR, Vol. 30, no. 1 (September
1982), p. 15-24. English. **DESCR:** *Ancianos;
Asian Americans; Blacks; Counseling
(Psychological); Cultural Customs; Family;
Native Americans; Stereotypes.

4310 Fernandez, Celestino. The neglected
dimension: ethnicity in American life.
AZTLAN, Vol. 14, no. 1 (Spring 1983), p.
199-201. English. **DESCR:** Book Reviews;
Identity; Rosen, Philip; *THE NEGLECTED
DIMENSION: ETHNICITY IN AMERICAN LIFE.

4311 Fleming, Marilyn B. Problems experienced by
Anglo, Hispanic and Navajo Indian women
college students. JOURNAL OF AMERICAN INDIAN
EDUCATION, Vol. 22, no. 1 (October 1982), p.
7-17. English. **DESCR:** *Chicanas; Community
Colleges; Identity; Medical Education;
Native Americans.

4312 Forbes, Jack D. Hispanic-Mexican pioneers of
the San Francisco Bay region: an analysis of
racial origins. AZTLAN, Vol. 14, no. 1
(Spring 1983), p. 175-189. English. **DESCR:**
Identity; *Pioneers; *San Francisco Bay.

4313 Foster, Charles R. Political culture and
regional ethnic minorities. JOURNAL OF
POLITICS, Vol. 44, no. 2 (May 1982), p.
560-568. English. **DESCR:** Politics.

4314 Garcia, Philip and Maldonado, Lionel A.
America's Mexicans: a plea for specificity.
SOCIAL SCIENCE JOURNAL, Vol. 19, no. 2
(April 1982), p. 9-24. English. **DESCR:**
Census; *Demography; Statistics.

4315 Garcia, Philip. An evaluation of employment
and unemployment differences between Mexican
Americans and whites: the seventies. SOCIAL
SCIENCE JOURNAL, Vol. 20, no. 1 (January
1983), p. 51-62. English. **DESCR:** Anglo
Americans; *Employment; Labor Supply and
Market.

4316 Garcia, Reyes. Politics of flesh: ethnicity
and political viability. CACR REVIEW, Vol.
1, no. 1 (September 1982), p. 102-130.
English. **DESCR:** Anaya, Rudolfo A.;
Aristotle; Culture; Identity; Locke, John;
Nuclear Armament; Philosophy; *Political
Repression; Urban Communities.

4317 Gibbs, Jewelle Taylor. Personality patterns
of delinquent females: ethnic and
sociocultural variations. JOURNAL OF
CLINICAL PSYCHOLOGY, Vol. 38, no. 1 (January
1982), p. 198-206. English. **DESCR:** Chicanas;
Identity; *Juvenile Delinquency;
Personality; Psychological Testing;
Socioeconomic Factors.

4318 Gonzales, Eloy. A cross-cultural comparison
of the developmental items of five ethnic
groups in the Southwest. JOURNAL OF
PERSONALITY ASSESSMENT, Vol. 46, no. 1
(February 1982), p. 26-31. English. **DESCR:**
*Comparative Psychology; Draw-A-Person (DAP)
[psychological test]; Psychological Testing;
Southwest United States.

4319 Gonzalez, Josue M. The pentagon and genetic
inferiority. NUESTRO, Vol. 6, no. 3 (April
1982), p. 44. English. **DESCR:** *Government;
*Racism.

4320 Hawley, Peggy and Even, Brenda. Work and
sex-role attitudes in relation to education
and other characteristics. VOCATIONAL
GUIDANCE QUARTERLY, Vol. 31, no. 2 (December
1982), p. 101-108. English. **DESCR:** Careers;
Chicanas; Psychological Testing; *Sex Roles;
Working Women.

Ethnic Groups (cont.)

4321 Hiring N.J. fire fighters. NUESTRO, Vol. 6, no. 3 (April 1982), p. 13. English. **DESCR:** Affirmative Action.

4322 Kanellos, Nicolas. Devorados pero no digeridos. Paper presented at the "Dialogo de las Americas" conference. Mexico, D.F. September 9-13, 1982. REVISTA CHICANO-RIQUENA, Vol. 10, no. 4 (Fall 1982), p. 5-6. Spanish. **DESCR:** *Biculturalism; Stereotypes.

4323 Lum, Doman. Toward a framework for social work practice with minorities. SOCIAL WORK, Vol. 27, no. 3 (May 1982), p. 244-249. English. **DESCR:** *Social Work.

4324 Maestas, Leo C. Academic performance across cultures: an examination of the effect of value similarity. EDUCATIONAL RESEARCH QUARTERLY, Vol. 7, no. 4 (Winter 1983), p. 24-34. English. **DESCR:** *Academic Achievement; Cultural Customs; Socialization; Teacher-pupil Interaction.

4325 Median administrative salaries in 1981-82 for men and women and minority-group members. CHRONICLE OF HIGHER EDUCATION, Vol. 24, no. 2 (March 10, 1982), p. 10. English. **DESCR:** *Administrators; Chicanas; *Income; Males.

4326 Meredith, Howard V. Compilation and comparison of averages for standing height at late childhood ages on United States boys of several ethnic groups studied between 1875 and 1980. AMERICAN JOURNAL OF PHYSICAL ANTHROPOLOGY, Vol. 61, no. 1 (May 1983), p. 111-124. English. **DESCR:** *Anthropometry; Socioeconomic Factors.

4327 Minority access to legal profession is still limited. CALIFORNIA LAWYER, Vol. 3, no. 4 (April 1983), p. 72. English. **DESCR:** *Brown, Susan E.; *Legal Education; Mexican American Legal Defense and Educational Fund (MALDEF).

4328 Newton, Frank Cota-Robles. Perils of the Latino slot. NUESTRO, Vol. 6, no. 3 (April 1982), p. 32. English. **DESCR:** *Affirmative Action.

4329 Plake, Barbara S., et al. Relationship of ethnic group membership to the measurement and meaning of attitudes towards reading: implications for validity of test score interpretations. EDUCATIONAL AND PSYCHOLOGICAL MEASUREMENT, Vol. 42, no. 4 (Winter 1982), p. 1259-1267. English. **DESCR:** Anglo Americans; Attitude (Psychological); Educational Tests and Measurements; Estes Reading Attitude Scale; *Reading; Students.

4330 The Puerto Rican diaspora: the dispersal of a people. NUESTRO, Vol. 6, no. 5 (June, July, 1982), p. 32-41. English. **DESCR:** Espada, Frank; Ethnic Stratification; Population Distribution; *Puerto Ricans.

4331 Ramos, Alfonso Pena. Voices: Gandhi: the Mahatma's message to Hispanics. NUESTRO, Vol. 7, no. 4 (May 1983), p. 59-60. English. **DESCR:** Gandhi, Mahatma; *Identity; *Philosophy; Welfare.

4332 Riley, Mary Tom and Taylor, Vincent. Threading the needle: IEP's for teachers? EDUCATIONAL RESEARCH QUARTERLY, Vol. 7, no. 1 (Spring 1982), p. 2-6. English. **DESCR:** Child Development Associate (CDA) Program; *Teacher Training.

4333 Ross-Reynolds, Jane and Reschly, Daniel J. An investigation of item bias on the WISC-R with four sociocultural groups. JOURNAL OF CONSULTING AND CLINICAL PSYCHOLOGY, Vol. 51, no. 1 (February 1983), p. 144-146. English. **DESCR:** Comparative Psychology; Psychological Testing; *Wechsler Intelligence Scale for Children-Revised (WISC-R).

4334 SBA reports on help to minority businesses. NUESTRO, Vol. 6, no. 4 (May 1982), p. 48. English. **DESCR:** *Businesspeople; *U.S. Small Business Administration.

4335 Sherman, Susan N., comp. Applicants to U.S. medical schools, 1977-78 to 1981-82. JOURNAL OF MEDICAL EDUCATION, Vol. 57, no. 11 (November 1982), p. 882-884. English. **DESCR:** Educational Statistics; *Medical Education; Medical Students.

4336 Stehno, S. M. Differential treatment of minority children in service systems. SOCIAL WORK, Vol. 27, (January 1982), p. 39-45. English. **DESCR:** Racism; Social Services; Youth.

4337 Study details minority access to legal education. NEW JERSEY LAW JOURNAL, Vol. 112, no. 1 (July 7, 1983), p. 28. English. **DESCR:** Brown, Susan E.; *Legal Education; Mexican American Legal Defense and Educational Fund (MALDEF); PLURALISM IN THE LEGAL PROFESSION: MODELS FOR MINORITY ACCESS; Vasquez, Hector G.

4338 Trotter, Robert T. Ethnic and sexual patterns of alcohol use: Anglo and Mexican American college students. ADOLESCENCE, Vol. 17, no. 66 (Summer 1982), p. 305-325. English. **DESCR:** *Alcoholism; Anglo Americans; Chicanas; Cultural Characteristics; Sex Roles; Youth.

4339 Van den Berghe, Pierre L. Book review of: ETHNIC AMERICA, A HISTORY. INTERNATIONAL MIGRATION REVIEW, Vol. 16, no. 4 (Winter 1982), p. 900-902. English. **DESCR:** Book Reviews; *ETHNIC AMERICA, A HISTORY; History; Migration; Sowell, Thomas.

4340 Vernon, Sally W. and Roberts, Robert E. Use of the SADS-RDC in a tri-ethnic community survey. ARCHIVES OF GENERAL PSYCHIATRY, Vol. 39, no. 1 (January 1982), p. 47-52. English. **DESCR:** Mental Health; Psychiatry; Psychotherapy; *Schedule for Affective Disorders and Schizophrenia-Research Diagnostic Criteria (SADS-RDC).

Ethnic Identity
USE: Identity

ETHNIC LEADERSHIP IN A NEW ENGLAND COMMUNITY: THREE PUERTO RICAN FAMILIES

4341 Brue de Lorenzo, Kathryn. Book review of: ETHNIC LEADERSHIP IN A NEW ENGLAND COMMUNITY: THREE PUERTO RICAN FAMILIES. HISPANIC JOURNAL OF BEHAVIORAL SCIENCES, Vol. 5, no. 2 (June 1983), p. 245-247. English. **DESCR:** Book Reviews; Westfried, Alex Huxley.

ETHNIC REVIVAL IN THE MODERN WORLD

4342 Esman, Milton J. Book review of: THE ETHNIC REVIVAL IN THE MODERN WORLD. ETHNIC AND RACIAL STUDIES, Vol. 5, no. 3 (1982), p. 378-379. English. **DESCR:** Book Reviews; Ethnic Groups; Smith, Anthony D.

Ethnic Stratification

4343 Baca Zinn, Maxine. Chicano men and masculinity. JOURNAL OF ETHNIC STUDIES, Vol. 10, no. 2 (Summer 1982), p. 29-44. English. **DESCR:** Cultural Characteristics; *Machismo; Sex Roles; Sex Stereotypes; Socioeconomic Factors; Women Men Relations.

4344 Morrissey, Marietta. Ethnic stratification and the study of Chicanos. JOURNAL OF ETHNIC STUDIES, Vol. 10, no. 4 (Winter 1983), p. 71-99. English. **DESCR:** Assimilation; Internal Colonial Model (Theoretical); Marxism; Paradigm (Theoretical); Social Theory.

4345 The Puerto Rican diaspora: the dispersal of a people. NUESTRO, Vol. 6, no. 5 (June, July, 1982), p. 32-41. English. **DESCR:** Espada, Frank; Ethnic Groups; Population Distribution; *Puerto Ricans.

Ethnicity

USE: Identity

ETHNICITY AND AGING: THEORY, RESEARCH, AND POLICY

4346 Burke, Leslie K. Book review of: ETHNICITY AND AGING: THEORY, RESEARCH AND POLICY. HISPANIC JOURNAL OF BEHAVIORAL SCIENCES, Vol. 4, no. 1 (March 1982), p. 107-112. English. **DESCR:** Book Reviews; Gelfland, Donald E.; Kutzik, Alfred J.

Ethnobotany

USE: Herbal Medicine

Ethnology

4347 Rivera, Julius. Book review of: VARIETIES OF AMERICA. NEW SCHOLAR, Vol. 8, no. 1-2 (Spring, Fall, 1982), p. 523-527. English. **DESCR:** Book Reviews; *HISPANIC AMERICA AND ITS CIVILIZATIONS, SPANISH AMERICANS, AND ANGLO-AMERICANS.

4348 Weber, Kenneth R. Book review of: CANONES: VALUES, CRISIS, AND SURVIVAL IN A NORTHERN NEW MEXICO VILLAGE. JOURNAL OF ETHNIC STUDIES, Vol. 11, no. 2 (Summer 1983), p. 119-123. English. **DESCR:** Book Reviews; Canones, NM; *CANONES: VALUES, CRISIS AND SURVIVAL IN A NORTHERN NEW MEXICO VILLAGE; History; Kutsche, Paul; New Mexico; Northern New Mexico; Van Ness, John R.

Ethnomethodology

4349 Ramos, Reyes. Discovering the production of Mexican American family structure. DE COLORES, Vol. 6, no. 1-2 (1982), p. 120-134. English. **DESCR:** *Family; Research Methodology.

Ethnomusicology

4350 Gradante, William. El hijo del pueblo: Jose Alfredo Jimenez and the Mexican cancion ranchera. LATIN AMERICAN MUSIC REVIEW, Vol. 3, no. 1 (Spring, Summer, 1982), p. 36-59. English. **DESCR:** Biography; History; *Jimenez, Jose Alfredo.

4351 Reyna, Jose R. Notes on Tejano music. AZTLAN, Vol. 13, no. 1-2 (Spring, Fall, 1982), p. 81-94. English. **DESCR:** Conjunto; *Music; Texas.

4352 Stevenson, Robert. Carlos Chavez's United States press coverage. AZTLAN, Vol. 14, no. 1 (Spring 1983), p. 21-33. English. **DESCR:** *Chavez, Carlos; *Journalism; Musicians; Print Media.

4353 Vincent, J. Book review of: HISPANIC FOLK MUSIC OF NEW MEXICO AND THE SOUTHWEST: A SELF-PORTRAIT OF A PEOPLE. ETHNOMUSICOLOGY, Vol. 26, no. 2 (May 1982), p. 326-327. English. **DESCR:** Book Reviews; Folk Songs; *HISPANIC FOLK MUSIC OF NEW MEXICO AND THE SOUTHWEST: A SELF-PORTRAIT OF A PEOPLE; New Mexico; Robb, John Donald; *THE SOUTHWEST: A SELF-PORTRAIT.

ETHNOPERSPECTIVES IN BILINGUAL EDUCATION RESEARCH: BILINGUAL EDUCATION AND PUBLIC POLICY IN THE UNITED STATES (Vol. I)

4354 Dubois, Betty Lou. Bilingual bicultural education: the view from across the campus. BILINGUAL REVIEW, Vol. 9, no. 3 (September, December, 1982), p. 272-275. English. **DESCR:** *Bilingual Bicultural Education; Padilla, Raymond.

Ethnopsychology

USE: Social Psychology

Eureste, Bernardo

4355 Councilman wins despite problems. NUESTRO, Vol. 7, no. 3 (April 1983), p. 12. English. **DESCR:** Elections; Local Government.

4356 Morton, Carlos. People: back on top with Bernardo Eureste. NATIONAL HISPANIC JOURNAL, Vol. 2, no. 1 (Summer 1983), p. 20-21. English. **DESCR:** Cisneros, Henry, Mayor of San Antonio, TX; Elected Officials; Elections; San Antonio Police Department; San Antonio, TX; Valdez, Jesse.

Evaluation (Educational)

4357 Balasubramonian, Krishna. Not on test scores alone: the qualitative side to program evaluation. BILINGUAL JOURNAL, Vol. 7, no. 2 (Winter 1983), p. 17-21,40. English. **DESCR:** *Bilingual Bicultural Education; *Curriculum; Educational Tests and Measurements; ELEMENTARY AND SECONDARY EDUCATION ACT; Proposals.

4358 Chesterfield, Ray P.; Moll, Luis C.; and Perez, Ray. A naturalistic approach for evaluation. BILINGUAL JOURNAL, Vol. 6, no. 1 (Fall 1982), p. 23-26. English. **DESCR:** Bilingual Bicultural Education; Curriculum; Early Childhood Education.

4359 Cohen, Bernard H. Parent involvement in program evaluation. BILINGUAL JOURNAL, Vol. 7, no. 2 (Winter 1983), p. 29-34. English. **DESCR:** *Bilingual Bicultural Education; Community School Relationships; Curriculum; Project PIE (Parents Involvement in Evaluation).

4360 Consalvo, Robert W. Book review of: PROGRAM IMPACT EVALUATIONS: AN INTRODUCTION FOR MANAGERS OF TITLE VII PROJECTS - A DRAFT GUIDEBOOK. BILINGUAL JOURNAL, Vol. 7, no. 2 (Winter 1983), p. 36-37. English. **DESCR:** Bilingual Bicultural Education; Bissell, Joan; Book Reviews; Educational Administration; ELEMENTARY AND SECONDARY EDUCATION ACT; *PROGRAM IMPACT EVALUATIONS: AN INTRODUCTION FOR MANAGERS OF TITLE VII PROJECTS - A DRAFT GUIDEBOOK ESEA TITLE VII.

Evaluation (Educational) (cont.)

4361 Consalvo, Robert W. and Orlandi, Lisanio R.
Principles and practices of data collection
and management. BILINGUAL JOURNAL, Vol. 7,
no. 2 (Winter 1983), p. 13-16. English.
DESCR: *Bilingual Bicultural Education;
Educational Statistics; Research
Methodology.

4362 De George, George P. The guest editor
speaks. BILINGUAL JOURNAL, Vol. 7, no. 2
(Winter 1983), p. 6. English. **DESCR:**
*Bilingual Bicultural Education; Educational
Administration.

4363 De George, George P. Selecting tests for
bilingual program evaluation. BILINGUAL
JOURNAL, Vol. 7, no. 2 (Winter 1983), p.
22-28,40. English. **DESCR:** *Bilingual
Bicultural Education; Curriculum;
Educational Tests and Measurements.

4364 DeMauro, Gerald E. Models and assumptions
for bilingual education evaluation.
BILINGUAL JOURNAL, Vol. 7, no. 2 (Winter
1983), p. 8-12,40. English. **DESCR:**
*Bilingual Bicultural Education; Curriculum;
Educational Tests and Measurements; Language
Assessment Battery.

4365 Liberty, Paul G. Director's notebook.
BILINGUAL JOURNAL, Vol. 7, no. 2 (Winter
1983), p. 1,40. English. **DESCR:** *Bilingual
Bicultural Education.

4366 Liberty, Paul G. Director's notebook.
BILINGUAL JOURNAL, Vol. 6, no. 4 (Summer
1982), p. 1,6. English. **DESCR:** *Bilingual
Bicultural Education; BILINGUAL EDUCATION
EVALUATION AND REPORTING SYSTEM;
*Curriculum.

4367 Liberty, Paul G., et al. [Evaluation in
bilingual education]. BILINGUAL JOURNAL,
Vol. 7, no. 2 (Winter 1983), p. 1-40.
English. **DESCR:** *Bilingual Bicultural
Education; Curriculum; Educational
Administration; ELEMENTARY AND SECONDARY
EDUCATION ACT.

4368 McConnell, Beverly B. Evaluating bilingual
education using a time series design. NEW
DIRECTIONS FOR PROGRAM EVALUATION, no. 16-12
(1982), p. 19-32. English. **DESCR:** Bilingual
Bicultural Education.

4369 Murphy, John W. and Redden, Richard. The use
of management by objectives in medical
education enrichment programs. JOURNAL OF
MEDICAL EDUCATION, Vol. 57, no. 12 (December
1982), p. 911-917. English. **DESCR:**
*Educational Administration; Educational
Innovations; Management by Objectives (MBO);
*Medical Education.

4370 Orlandi, Lisanio R. Book review of: WORKBOOK
ON PROGRAM EVALUATION. BILINGUAL JOURNAL,
Vol. 7, no. 2 (Winter 1983), p. 35-36.
English. **DESCR:** Babcock, R.; Bilingual
Bicultural Education; Book Reviews; Plakos,
J.; Plakos, M.; *WORKBOOK ON PROGRAM
EVALUATION.

4371 Sandoval-Martinez, Steven. Findings from the
Head Start bilingual curriculum development
and evaluation effort. NABE JOURNAL, Vol. 7,
no. 1 (Fall 1982), p. 1-12. English. **DESCR:**
*Bilingual Bicultural Education;
Compensatory Education; *Early Childhood
Education; Headstart Program.

4372 Walia, Adorna. Book review of: DATA FORMS
FOR EVALUATING BILINGUAL EDUCATION PROGRAM.
BILINGUAL JOURNAL, Vol. 7, no. 2 (Winter
1983), p. 38. English. **DESCR:** Bilingual
Bicultural Education; Book Reviews; Cohen,
Bernard H.; *DATA FORMS FOR EVALUATING
BILINGUAL EDUCATION PROGRAMS; Educational
Administration.

4373 Walia, Adorna. Book review of: DO'S AND
DONT'S OF BILINGUAL PROGRAM EVALUATION.
BILINGUAL JOURNAL, Vol. 7, no. 2 (Winter
1983), p. 38. English. **DESCR:** Bilingual
Bicultural Education; Book Reviews;
Curriculum; *DO'S AND DONT'S OF BILINGUAL
PROGRAM EVALUATION; Rodriguez-Brown, Flora
V.

Ewing, David W.

4374 Research/development: books. HISPANIC
BUSINESS, Vol. 5, no. 4 (April 1983), p. 28.
English. **DESCR:** Biographical Notes; *Book
Reviews; *"DO IT MY WAY OR YOU'RE FIRED!":
EMPLOYEE RIGHTS AND THE CHANGING ROLE OF
MANAGEMENT PREROGATIVES; Garcia, Carlos;
Garcia, Edward; Industrial Relations;
Science; *SCIENCE OF THE SPANISH SPEAKING
PEOPLE.

Excavations
USE: Anthropology

Executives

4375 Balkan, D. Carlos. The subtleties of
corporate boardsmanship. HISPANIC BUSINESS,
Vol. 5, no. 5 (May 1983), p. 10-11+.
English. **DESCR:** *Corporations.

Exhibits

4376 New York's exhibition of Aztec treasures.
NUESTRO, Vol. 6, no. 5 (June, July, 1982),
p. 63-64. English. **DESCR:** Anthropology;
*Aztecs; New York, NY.

4377 A potpourri of pre-Columbian art. NUESTRO,
Vol. 7, no. 6 (August 1983), p. 59-60.
English. **DESCR:** CERAMIC TOMB SCULPTURE FROM
ANCIENT WEST MEXICO; Ceramics; Frederick S.
Wright Art Gallery, University of
California, Los Angeles; Museum of Cultural
History, University of California, Los
Angeles; *Precolumbian Art; Sculpture.

4378 Pre-Columbian art of Costa Rica. NUESTRO,
Vol. 6, no. 8 (October 1982), p. 54-55.
English. **DESCR:** Art; *Art History; Costa
Rica.

EXITO

4379 Whisler, Kirk. Exito - an East coast play
for the whole nation. CAMINOS, Vol. 4, no. 6
(June 1983), p. 58,67. Bilingual. **DESCR:**
Gala Hispanic Theatre; Teatro.

Expansionism
USE: Imperialism

EXPLORACIONES CHICANO-RIQUENAS

4380 Flemming, Donald N. Book review of:
EXPLORACIONES CHICANO-RIQUENAS. MODERN
LANGUAGE JOURNAL, Vol. 66, no. 2 (Summer
1982), p. 233-234. English. **DESCR:** Book
Reviews; Burgos-Sasscer. Ruth; Textbooks;
Williams, Shirley.

EXPLORACIONES CHICANO-RIQUENAS (cont.)

4381 Somoza, Oscar U. Book review of: EXPLORACIONES CHICANO-RIQUENAS. HISPANIA, Vol. 65, no. 4 (December 1982), p. 668-669. Spanish. **DESCR**: Book Reviews; Burgos-Sasscer. Ruth; Textbooks; Williams, Shirley.

Explorations

4382 Alvarez, Amando. Aguas milagrosas. LATINO, Vol. 54, no. 5 (August, September, 1983), p. 21-22. English. **DESCR**: History.

4383 Barrio, Raymond. Dando gracias al Rey Ocho Ciervos. LATINO, Vol. 53, no. 7 (November 1982), p. 16. Spanish.

4384 Chavez, John A. Aztlan, Cibola, and frontier New Spain. CAMPO LIBRE, Vol. 1, no. 2 (Summer 1981), p. 193-211. English. **DESCR**: *Aztlan; Folklore; History; Mestizaje; Mexico; Missions; Native Americans; Southwest United States.

EXPLORATIONS IN CHICANO PSYCHOLOGY

4385 Gonzalez, Roberto. Book review of: EXPLORATIONS IN CHICANO PSYCHOLOGY. HISPANIC JOURNAL OF BEHAVIORAL SCIENCES, Vol. 4, no. 4 (December 1982), p. 511-522. English. **DESCR**: Baron, Augustine Jr.; Book Reviews.

Export Trade

4386 Foreign trade. HISPANIC BUSINESS, Vol. 5, no. 3 (March 1983), p. 23. English. **DESCR**: Caribbean Region; *Foreign Trade; Minority Business Development Agency (MBDA).

4387 Foreign trade. HISPANIC BUSINESS, Vol. 5, no. 4 (April 1983), p. 22. English. **DESCR**: Banking Industry; Brazil; *Electronics Industry; *Foreign Trade; Ibero-American Chamber of Commerce; Miami, FL; Minority Bank Development Program (MBDP); Minority Export Development Consultants Program (MEDC); Peace Corps; Puerto Rico.

4388 Foreign trade. HISPANIC BUSINESS, Vol. 5, no. 5 (May 1983), p. 32. English. **DESCR**: Caribbean Region; *Foreign Trade; Latin America; Minority Business Development Agency (MBDA); Panama.

4389 Mexican business update. HISPANIC BUSINESS, Vol. 4, no. 1 (January 1982), p. 24. English. **DESCR**: Business; *Foreign Trade; Mexico; *U.S.-Mexico Joint Commission on Commerce and Trade.

4390 Mexico's export production map. CAMINOS, Vol. 3, no. 6 (June 1982), p. 20-21. Bilingual. **DESCR**: Economic Development; Mexico.

4391 US-Mexican trade relations. HISPANIC BUSINESS, Vol. 4, no. 9 (September 1982), p. 23. English. **DESCR**: California; *Foreign Trade; Mexico; United States-Mexico Relations.

4392 Vara, Richard. Business savvy and Capricorn spirit: How do you spell entrepreneurship? HISPANIC BUSINESS, Vol. 5, no. 1 (January 1983), p. 18-19+. English. **DESCR**: Arroyos, Alex; *Biography; Business Enterprises; Houston, TX.

Extended Family

4393 Angel, Ronald and Tienda, Marta. Determinants of extended household

structure: cultural pattern or economical need? AMERICAN JOURNAL OF SOCIOLOGY, Vol. 87, no. 6 (May 1982), p. 1360-1383. English. **DESCR**: Income.

4394 Baca Zinn, Maxine. Urban kinship and Midwest Chicano families: evidence in support of revision. DE COLORES, Vol. 6, no. 1-2 (1982), p. 85-98. English. **DESCR**: Compadrazgo; Family; *Midwestern States; Urban Communities.

4395 Barreto, Julio. Gathering of the Ojedas. NUESTRO, Vol. 6, no. 5 (June, July, 1982), p. 22-25. English. **DESCR**: Austin, TX; Family; *Ojeda, Cecilio Colunga.

4396 Griffith, James. Re-examination of Mexican American service utilization and mental health need. HISPANIC JOURNAL OF BEHAVIORAL SCIENCES, Vol. 5, no. 2 (June 1983), p. 163-180. English. **DESCR**: *Mental Health.

4397 Martinez, Elisa A. Sharing her tiny pieces of the past. NUESTRO, Vol. 7, no. 7 (September 1983), p. 51-52. English. **DESCR**: Autobiography; Chicanas; Reminiscences.

4398 Tienda, Marta and Angel, Ronald. Headship and household composition among blacks, Hispanics and other whites. SOCIAL FORCES, Vol. 61, no. 2 (December 1982), p. 508-531. English. **DESCR**: Anglo Americans; Blacks; Cultural Characteristics; *Family; Puerto Ricans; Single Parents.

Eynoso, David

4399 Gonzalez, Magdalena. Recognizing Hispanic achievements in entertainment - U.S. and Mexico. CAMINOS, Vol. 3, no. 7 (July, August, 1982), p. 18-24. Bilingual. **DESCR**: Allende, Fernando; Artists; Awards; Bonilla Giannini, Roxanna; Felix, Maria; Films; Gallego, Gina; *Golden Eagle Awards; Hoyos, Rodolfo; Lamas, Lorenzo; Lopez, Conchita; Lopez, Lisa; Montalban, Ricardo; Nosotros [film production company]; Quintero, Jose; Rowe, Arthur; Television; Torres, Liz.

Eysenck, H.J.

4400 Herman, Janice. Book review of: THE INTELLIGENCE CONTROVERSY. HISPANIC JOURNAL OF BEHAVIORAL SCIENCES, Vol. 4, no. 3 (September 1982), p. 384-385. English. **DESCR**: Book Reviews; Kamin, Leon; *THE INTELLIGENCE CONTROVERSY.

Fables

USE: Cuentos

Faculty

4401 McCurdy, Jack. L.A. violence linked to Chicano-studies dispute. CHRONICLE OF HIGHER EDUCATION, Vol. 24, no. 14 (June 2, 1982), p. 8. English. **DESCR**: California State University, Los Angeles; *Chicano Studies; Corona, Bert; Violence.

Fair Labor Standards Act (FLSA)

4402 Developments in migrant workers programs: 1981. CLEARINGHOUSE REVIEW, Vol. 15, (January 1982), p. 797-805. English. **DESCR**: Farm Labor Contractor Registration Act (FLCRA); Migrant Education; Migrant Housing; *Migrant Labor; Migrant Legal Action Program (MLAP); Occupational Safety and Health Administration; Pesticides; Undocumented Workers; Wagner-Peyser Act.

Fairytales
    USE: Cuentos

Familia
    USE: Family

LA FAMILIA [poster]

4403 Gonzalez, Cesar A. LA FAMILIA de Joaquin
     Chinas. DE COLORES, Vol. 6, no. 1-2 (1982),
     p. 146-149. English. **DESCR:** Artists; Chicano
     Movement; Chinas, Joaquin; Symbolism.

Familias Unidas Latinas

4404 Espinoza, Ana Luisa. Approaching our
     familias con corazon. CALMECAC, Vol. 1, no.
     1 (Spring 1980), p. 15-17. English. **DESCR:**
     Family; *Mental Health.

Family

4405 Baca Zinn, Maxine. Chicano family research:
     conceptual distortions and alternative
     directions. JOURNAL OF ETHNIC STUDIES, Vol.
     7, no. 3 (Fall 1979), p. 59-71. English.
     DESCR: Cultural Characteristics; Culture;
     Research Methodology; Social Research;
     Stereotypes.

4406 Baca Zinn, Maxine. Urban kinship and Midwest
     Chicano families: evidence in support of
     revision. DE COLORES, Vol. 6, no. 1-2
     (1982), p. 85-98. English. **DESCR:**
     Compadrazgo; *Extended Family; *Midwestern
     States; Urban Communities.

4407 Barreto, Julio. Cecilio's dream. LATINO,
     Vol. 53, no. 7 (November 1982), p. 12-14+.
     English. **DESCR:** *Ojeda, Cecilio Colunga.

4408 Barreto, Julio. Gathering of the Ojedas.
     NUESTRO, Vol. 6, no. 5 (June, July, 1982),
     p. 22-25. English. **DESCR:** Austin, TX;
     Extended Family; *Ojeda, Cecilio Colunga.

4409 Benton, Patricia Moran. Mother's Day
     reflections: keepers of the faith. NUESTRO,
     Vol. 7, no. 4 (May 1983), p. 49. English.
     DESCR: *Chicanas; *Parent and Child
     Relationships.

4410 Bernal, Guillermo and Flores-Ortiz, Yvette.
     Latino families in therapy: engagement and
     evaluation. JOURNAL OF MARITAL AND FAMILY
     THERAPY, Vol. 8, no. 3 (July 1982), p.
     357-365. English. **DESCR:** Mental Health;
     Social Psychology.

4411 Bustelo, Manuel A. Ending an era of Hispanic
     isolation. NUESTRO, Vol. 6, no. 7 (September
     1982), p. 60. English. **DESCR:** *Cabinet
     Committee on Opportunity for
     Spanish-Speaking People (CCOSSP); *Culture;
     *Identity.

4412 Carlos, Manuel L. Chicano households, the
     structure of parental information networks,
     and family use of child-related social
     services. BORDERLANDS JOURNAL, Vol. 6, no. 1
     (Fall 1982), p. 49-68. English. **DESCR:**
     *Social Services.

4413 Corbit, Gladys Benavides. Sharing with a
     spiritual sister. NUESTRO, Vol. 7, no. 6
     (August 1983), p. 50. English. **DESCR:**
     *Chicanas; Parent and Child Relationships.

4414 Davis, James Alston. Does authority
     generalize? Locus of control perceptions in
     Anglo-American and Mexican-American
     adolescents. POLITICAL PSYCHOLOGY, Vol. 4,
     no. 1 (March 1983), p. 101-120. English.
     DESCR: Comparative Psychology; High School

Students; Internal-External Reinforcement
Scale; *Locus of Control; Political
Ideology.

4415 Delgado, Melvin. Ethnic and cultural
     variations in the care of the aged. Hispanic
     elderly and natural support systems: a
     special focus on Puerto Ricans. JOURNAL OF
     GERIATRIC PSYCHIATRY, Vol. 15, no. 2 (1982),
     p. 239-251. English. **DESCR:** *Ancianos;
     Cultural Organizations; Curanderas; Natural
     Support Systems; Puerto Ricans; Religion;
     Santeros.

4416 Delgado, Melvin. Hispanic natural support
     systems: implications for mental health
     services. JOURNAL OF PSYCHOSOCIAL NURSING
     AND MENTAL HEALTH SERVICES, Vol. 21, no. 4
     (April 1983), p. 19-24. English. **DESCR:**
     Curanderas; *Mental Health; Religion;
     Support Groups.

4417 Engle, Margarita Mondrus. Mother's Day
     reflections: a "traditional" Latina.
     NUESTRO, Vol. 7, no. 4 (May 1983), p. 46.
     Portuguese. **DESCR:** *Cubanos; *Women's
     Rights.

4418 Espinoza, Ana Luisa. Approaching our
     familias con corazon. CALMECAC, Vol. 1, no.
     1 (Spring 1980), p. 15-17. English. **DESCR:**
     *Familias Unidas Latinas; *Mental Health.

4419 Espinoza, Ana Luisa. Los tatas. CALMECAC,
     Vol. 1, (Summer 1980), p. 29-33. Bilingual.
     DESCR: Interpersonal Relations.

4420 Exum, Herbert A. The most invisible
     minority: the culturally diverse elderly.
     SCHOOL COUNSELOR, Vol. 30, no. 1 (September
     1982), p. 15-24. English. **DESCR:** *Ancianos;
     Asian Americans; Blacks; Counseling
     (Psychological); Cultural Customs; Ethnic
     Groups; Native Americans; Stereotypes.

4421 La familia [special issue of DE COLORES]. DE
     COLORES, Vol. 6, no. 1-2 (1982), p. 1-149.
     Bilingual.

4422 Father, son attend UCLA school of law.
     NUESTRO, Vol. 5, no. 8 (November 1981), p.
     42. English. **DESCR:** Students; UCLA Law
     School.

4423 Gonzalez, Alex. Sex role of the traditional
     Mexican family: a comparison of Chicano and
     Anglo students' attitudes. JOURNAL OF
     CROSS-CULTURAL PSYCHOLOGY, Vol. 13, no. 3
     (September 1982), p. 330-339. English.
     DESCR: Anglo Americans; Hembrismo; Machismo;
     Sex Roles.

4424 Griswold del Castillo, Richard. La familia
     Chicana: social change in the Chicano family
     of Los Angeles, 1850-1880. JOURNAL OF ETHNIC
     STUDIES, Vol. 3, no. 1 (Spring 1975), p.
     41-58. English. **DESCR:** Industrialization;
     *Los Angeles, CA; Social History and
     Conditions.

4425 Guendelman, Sylvia. Developing
     responsiveness to health needs of Hispanic
     children and families. SOCIAL WORK IN HEALTH
     CARE, Vol. 8, no. 4 (Summer 1983), p. 1-15.
     English. **DESCR:** Children; Public Health;
     *Social Psychology.

4426 Hernandez, Leodoro. The socialization of a
     Chicano family. DE COLORES, Vol. 6, no. 1-2
     (1982), p. 75-84. English. **DESCR:**
     Acculturation; *Socialization.

Family (cont.)

4427 Hing, Bill Ong. Racial disparity: the unaddressed issues of the Simpson-Mazzoli Bill. LA RAZA LAW JOURNAL, Vol. 1, no. 1 (June 1983), p. 21-52. English. **DESCR:** Amnesty; Asian Americans; Ethnic Attitudes; Immigration; Immigration and Naturalization Service (INS); Latin Americans; Mazzoli, Romano L.; Mexican American Legal Defense and Educational Fund (MALDEF); Simpson, Alan K.; *Simpson-Mazzoli Bill; Temporary Worker Program; U.S. Congresssional Subcommittee on Immigration, Refugees and International Law.

4428 Hinojosa-Smith, Rolando R. Reflections on fathers: out of many lives: one. NUESTRO, Vol. 7, no. 5 (June, July, 1983), p. 62. English. **DESCR:** Hinojosa, Manuel G.; *Parent and Child Relationships.

4429 Huerta, Grace C. Mother's day reflections: a woman of means. NUESTRO, Vol. 7, no. 4 (May 1983), p. 48-49. English. **DESCR:** *Chicanas; *Parent and Child Relationships.

4430 Irizarry, Estelle. La abuelita in literature. NUESTRO, Vol. 7, no. 7 (September 1983), p. 50. English. **DESCR:** Alonso, Luis Ricardo; *Ancianos; Chicanas; Cotto-Thorner, Guillermo; Ulibarri, Sabine R.; Valero, Robert.

4431 Martinez, Danny. Mother's Day reflections: master gardener. NUESTRO, Vol. 7, no. 4 (May 1983), p. 48. English. **DESCR:** *Parent and Child Relationships; *Salvadorans.

4432 Martinez, Elisa A. Sharing her tiny pieces of the past. LATINO, Vol. 54, no. 7 (November 1983), p. 10-11+. English.

4433 Mejias-Rentas, Antonio. Reflections on fathers: my three fathers. NUESTRO, Vol. 7, no. 5 (June, July, 1983), p. 61-62. English. **DESCR:** Marin, Luis Munoz; Partido Popular Democratico (PPD); *Puerto Ricans; *Puerto Rico.

4434 Melendez, Carmelo. Chasing a Puerto Rican Christmas. NUESTRO, Vol. 5, no. 8 (November 1981), p. 33. English. **DESCR:** *Christmas; Puerto Rico.

4435 Melendez, Carmelo. Mother's Day reflections: "I will get to him". NUESTRO, Vol. 7, no. 4 (May 1983), p. 47. English. **DESCR:** *Parent and Child Relationships; *Puerto Ricans.

4436 Mendez Gonzalez, Rosalinda. Mexican women and families: rural-to-urban and international migration. SOUTHWEST ECONOMY AND SOCIETY, Vol. 4, no. 2 (Winter 1978, 1979), p. 14-27. English. **DESCR:** Chicanas; Employment; Garment Industry; Immigration; International Ladies Garment Workers Union (ILGWU); Labor Organizing; Los Angeles, CA; Undocumented Workers.

4437 Mirande, Alfredo. The Chicano family and sex roles: an overview and introduction. DE COLORES, Vol. 6, no. 1-2 (1982), p. 1-6. English. **DESCR:** Sex Roles.

4438 Nieto, Daniel S. Hispanic fathers: the growing phenomenon of single fathers keeping their children. NATIONAL HISPANIC JOURNAL, Vol. 1, no. 4 (Spring 1983), p. 15-19. English. **DESCR:** Divorce; Parent and Child Relationships; *Single Parents.

4439 Panitz, Daniel R., et al. The role of machismo and the Hispanic family in the etiology and treatment of alcoholism in the Hispanic American males. AMERICAN JOURNAL OF FAMILY THERAPY, Vol. 11, no. 1 (Spring 1983), p. 31-44. English. **DESCR:** *Alcoholism; Children; *Machismo; Puerto Rico; Socioeconomic Factors.

4440 Ramos, Reyes. Discovering the production of Mexican American family structure. DE COLORES, Vol. 6, no. 1-2 (1982), p. 120-134. English. **DESCR:** *Ethnomethodology; Research Methodology.

4441 Salcido, Ramon M. The undocumented alien family. DE COLORES, Vol. 6, no. 1-2 (1982), p. 109-119. English. **DESCR:** East Los Angeles, CA; Green Carders; Social Services; *Undocumented Workers.

4442 Santiago, Esmerelda. Madre de madre. NUESTRO, Vol. 6, no. 1 (January, February, 1982), p. 59. English. **DESCR:** *Short Story.

4443 Saragoza, Alex M. Mexican children in the U.S.: the Central San Joaquin Valley. DE COLORES, Vol. 6, no. 1-2 (1982), p. 64-74. English. **DESCR:** Acculturation; *Children; Identity; Parent and Child Relationships; San Joaquin Valley.

4444 Tello, Jerry. Platicando (relationships III). CALMECAC, Vol. 2, (Spring 1981), p. 6-15. English. **DESCR:** Interpersonal Relations.

4445 Tello, Jerry. Relationship entre nuestra gente. CALMECAC, Vol. 1, no. 1 (Spring 1980), p. 20-22. English. **DESCR:** Interpersonal Relations.

4446 Tienda, Marta and Angel, Ronald. Headship and household composition among blacks, Hispanics and other whites. SOCIAL FORCES, Vol. 61, no. 2 (December 1982), p. 508-531. English. **DESCR:** Anglo Americans; Blacks; Cultural Characteristics; Extended Family; Puerto Ricans; Single Parents.

4447 Valdez, Diana. Mexican American family research: a critical review and conceptual framework. DE COLORES, Vol. 6, no. 1-2 (1982), p. 48-63. English. **DESCR:** Research Methodology.

4448 Vallejos, Thomas. Ritual process and the family in the Chicano novel. MELUS: MULTI-ETHNIC LITERATURE OF THE UNITED STATES, Vol. 10, no. 4 (Winter 1983, 1984), p. 5-16. English. **DESCR:** Anaya, Rudolfo A.; BLESS ME, ULTIMA; *Literary Criticism; Novel; Parent and Child Relationships; POCHO; Rivera, Tomas; Villarreal, Jose Antonio; Y NO SE LO TRAGO LA TIERRA/AND THE EARTH DID NOT PART.

4449 Vierra, Andrea. Book review of: BEYOND THE NUCLEAR FAMILY MODEL: CROSS CULTURAL PERSPECTIVES. HISPANIC JOURNAL OF BEHAVIORAL SCIENCES, Vol. 5, no. 3 (September 1983), p. 349-352. English. **DESCR:** *BEYOND THE NUCLEAR FAMILY; Book Reviews; Lenero-Otero, Luis.

4450 Warheit, George. Interpersonal coping networks and mental health problems among four race-ethnic groups. JOURNAL OF COMMUNITY PSYCHOLOGY, Vol. 10, no. 4 (October 1982), p. 312-324. English. **DESCR:** Comparative Psychology; Mental Health; Stress; *Support Groups.

Family (cont.)

4451 Whiteford, Linda. Migrants no longer: changing family structure of Mexican Americans in South Texas. DE COLORES, Vol. 6, no. 1-2 (1982), p. 99-108. English. **DESCR:** Chicanas; Sex Roles; *South Texas.

4452 Wurzman, Ilyana. Cultural values of Puerto Rican opiate addicts: an exploratory study. AMERICAN JOURNAL OF DRUG AND ALCOHOL ABUSE, Vol. 9, no. 2 (1982, 1983), p. 141-153. English. **DESCR:** Acculturation; Anglo Americans; Blacks; *Drug Abuse; Drug Addicts; Loevinger's Sentence Completion Test; Machismo; New York, NY; Opium; Puerto Ricans; Values.

4453 Ybarra, Lea. Marital decision-making and the role of machismo in the Chicano family. DE COLORES, Vol. 6, no. 1-2 (1982), p. 32-47. English. **DESCR:** *Machismo; Marriage; Sex Roles.

4454 Ybarra, Lea. When wives work: the impact on the Chicano family. JOURNAL OF MARRIAGE AND THE FAMILY, Vol. 44, (February 1982), p. 169-178. English. **DESCR:** *Working Women.

Family Planning

4455 Bean, Frank D. and Swicegood, Gray. Generation, female education and Mexican American fertility. SOCIAL SCIENCE QUARTERLY, Vol. 63, (March 1982), p. 131-144. English. **DESCR:** Chicanas; *Fertility.

4456 Cayer, Shirley. Chicago's new Hispanic health alliance. NUESTRO, Vol. 7, no. 5 (June, July, 1983), p. 44-48. English. **DESCR:** Alcoholism; Chicago Hispanic Health Alliance; *Health Education; Latin Americans; *Medical Care.

4457 Holck, Susan E., et al. Need for family planning services among Anglo and Hispanic women in the United States counties bordering Mexico. FAMILY PLANNING PERSPECTIVES, Vol. 14, no. 3 (May, June, 1982), p. 155-159. English. **DESCR:** Anglo Americans.

4458 Warren, Charles W.; Smith, Jack C.; and Rochat, Roger W. Differentials in the planning status of the most recent live birth to Mexican Americans and Anglos. PUBLIC HEALTH REPORTS, Vol. 98, no. 2 (March, April, 1983), p. 152-160. English. **DESCR:** Anglo Americans.

Family Therapy

4459 Inclan, Jaime. Structural family therapy training in family medicine. JOURNAL OF LATIN COMMUNITY HEALTH, Vol. 1, no. 1 (Fall 1982), p. 55-69. English.

FAMOUS ALL OVER TOWN

4460 Book review of: FAMOUS ALL OVER TOWN. NEW YORKER, Vol. 59, no. 11 (May 2, 1983), p. 126. English. **DESCR:** Book Reviews; James, Dan.

4461 Book review of: FAMOUS ALL OVER TOWN. BOOKLIST, Vol. 79, no. 15 (April 1, 1983), p. 1016. English. **DESCR:** Book Reviews; James, Dan.

4462 Quammen, David. Book review of: FAMOUS ALL OVER TOWN. NEW YORK TIMES BOOK REVIEW, Vol. 88, (April 24, 1983), p. 12+. English. **DESCR:** Book Reviews; James, Dan.

4463 Smith, Sherman W. Book review of: FAMOUS ALL OVER TOWN. WEST COAST REVIEW OF BOOKS, Vol. 9, no. 2 (1983), p. 40. English. **DESCR:** Book Reviews; James, Dan.

4464 Wimsatt, Margaret. Book review of: FAMOUS ALL OVER TOWN. COMMONWEAL, Vol. 110, no. 10 (May 20, 1983), p. 309-312. English. **DESCR:** Book Reviews; James, Dan.

FAMOUS MEXICAN-AMERICANS

4465 Phillips, Melody. The Chicana: her attitudes towards the woman's liberation movement. COMADRE, no. 2 (Spring 1978), p. 42-50. English. **DESCR:** Carr, Vikki; *Chicanas; Newton, Clark; Social History and Conditions; Women's Rights.

Fandango

4466 Shay, Anthony. Fandangos and bailes: dancing and dance events in early California. SOUTHERN CALIFORNIA QUARTERLY, Vol. 64, no. 2 (Summer 1982), p. 99-113. English. **DESCR:** *Dance.

Fantini, Mario

4467 Clifford, Terry. Book review of: PARENTING IN A MULTI-CULTURAL SOCIETY. HISPANIC JOURNAL OF BEHAVIORAL SCIENCES, Vol. 4, no. 3 (September 1982), p. 385-387. English. **DESCR:** Book Reviews; Cardenas, Rene; *PARENTING IN A MULTI-CULTURAL SOCIETY.

Farm Labor Contractor Registration Act (FLCRA)

4468 Developments in migrant workers programs: 1981. CLEARINGHOUSE REVIEW, Vol. 15, (January 1982), p. 797-805. English. **DESCR:** Fair Labor Standards Act (FLSA); Migrant Education; Migrant Housing; *Migrant Labor; Migrant Legal Action Program (MLAP); Occupational Safety and Health Administration; Pesticides; Undocumented Workers; Wagner-Peyser Act.

Farm Labor Organizing Commmittee (FLOC)

4469 Askin, Steve. Boston church encourages labor talks. NATIONAL CATHOLIC REPORTER, Vol. 18, (July 30, 1982), p. 6. English. **DESCR:** Boston Archdiocese Justice and Peace Commission; Boycotts; Campbell Soup Co.; Catholic Church; Labor Unions.

4470 Community watching. CAMINOS, Vol. 3, no. 5 (May 1982), p. 56-57. Bilingual. **DESCR:** Adelante Mujer Hispana Conference; Agricultural Laborers; Beilson, Anthony C.; Boycotts; Chacon, Peter R.; Chicanas; *Cultural Organizations; Financial Aid; Hollenbeck Junior High School, Los Angeles, CA; Junior High School Students; National League of Cities; Optimist Club of Greater East Los Angeles; Organizations; Project WELL (We Enjoy Learning & Leadership); Torres, Art.

4471 FLOC, Campbell labels. NUESTRO, Vol. 6, no. 1 (January, February, 1982), p. 10. English. **DESCR:** Boycotts; Migrant Labor.

Farm Women
USE: Working Women

Farm Workers
USE: Agricultural Laborers

Farmer Organizations

4472 Chavez' union decentralizes. NUESTRO, Vol. 6, no. 7 (September 1982), p. 11-12. English. **DESCR:** Agricultural Laborers; Chavez, Cesar E.; *United Farmworkers of America (UFW).

FARMWORKERS, AGRIBUSINESS, AND THE STATE

4473 Kivisto, Peter. Book review of: FARM WORKERS, AGRIBUSINESS, AND THE STATE. INTERNATIONAL MIGRATION REVIEW, Vol. 17, no. 4 (Winter 1983), p. 724-726. English. **DESCR:** Agribusiness; Agricultural Laborers; Book Reviews; Majka, Linda C.; Majka, Theo J.; United Farmworkers of America (UFW).

Farragut, David G.

4474 New calendar salutes Latino military men. NUESTRO, Vol. 6, no. 4 (May 1982), p. 47. English. **DESCR:** De Galvez, Bernardo; *Publishing Industry.

Farres, Osvaldo

4475 Communications/marketing. HISPANIC BUSINESS, Vol. 4, no. 5 (May 1982), p. 15. English. **DESCR:** Anheuser-Busch, Inc.; Girl Scouts of the United States of America; *Marketing; Organizations; Television; Vocational Education; Voter Turnout.

Fasco, Luis

4476 Barry, Patrick. Saturdays are wedding cakes. NUESTRO, Vol. 6, no. 9 (November 1982), p. 31-33. English. **DESCR:** *Businesspeople; Chicago, IL; Weddings.

Fashion

4477 All dressed up... LATINA, Vol. 1, no. 2 (February, March, 1983), p. 15-16. English.

4478 Aqui en Tejas: staying on that long road to success: mentors, how to find a helping hand to assist you achieve educational goals. NATIONAL HISPANIC JOURNAL, Vol. 2, no. 1 (Summer 1983), p. 8. English. **DESCR:** Careers; Education; *Mentors.

4479 Dressing up the children. LATINA, Vol. 1, no. 2 (February, March, 1983), p. 39-41. English. **DESCR:** Children.

4480 Flores, Fernando. Flores on fashion. LATINA, Vol. 1, no. 1 (1982), p. 39-41+. English. **DESCR:** *Flores Fashions.

4481 Hawkins, Timothy. Confessions of a bargain hunter. LATINA, Vol. 1, no. 1 (1982), p. 38. English.

4482 Martinez, Marie. A morenita and a rubia visit Rodeo Drive for a sleek make-over. LATINA, Vol. 1, no. 2 (February, March, 1983), p. 30-32+. English. **DESCR:** Cosmetology.

4483 McManis, Linda. Fashion is international. LATINO, Vol. 54, no. 3 (April 1983), p. 18-19. English.

4484 Navarrete, Diana. Broadcasting role model. NUESTRO, Vol. 6, no. 1 (January, February, 1982), p. 22-23. English. **DESCR:** Broadcast Media; Latin Americans; *Navarrete, Diana.

4485 Romero, Karen. A sense of inner beauty. LATINO, Vol. 54, no. 7 (November 1983), p. 25+. English.

4486 Velez, Larry A. Sonia Berdequez; police detective. NUESTRO, Vol. 6, no. 1 (January, February, 1982), p. 20-21. English. **DESCR:** *Berdeguez, Sonia Estela; Latin Americans; Police.

4487 You're cordially invited. LATINA, Vol. 1, no. 2 (February, March, 1983), p. 55-58. English.

Fatalism

4488 Medinnus, Gene R.; Ford, Martin Z.; and Tack-Robinson, Susan. Locus of control: a cross-cultural comparison. PSYCHOLOGICAL REPORTS, Vol. 53, no. 1 (August 1983), p. 131-134. English. **DESCR:** Junior High School Students; *Locus of Control; Personality.

4489 Ross, Catherine E.; Mirowsky, John; and Cockerham, William C. Social class, Mexican culture, and fatalism: their effects on psychological distress. AMERICAN JOURNAL OF COMMUNITY PSYCHOLOGY, Vol. 11, no. 4 (August 1983), p. 383-399. English. **DESCR:** Culture; Mental Health.

Faultless Starch/Bon Ami Company

4490 Communications/marketing. HISPANIC BUSINESS, Vol. 5, no. 4 (April 1983), p. 23. English. **DESCR:** Garcia, Marti; *Marketing; Mejias, Hugo A.; Pan American University, Edinburg, TX; Spanish Language.

Favela, Fernando

4491 Gutierrez, Silvio. Fernando Favela: street wise and sexy. LATINA, Vol. 1, no. 3 (1983), p. 20-21. English. **DESCR:** Biography.

Federal Aid

4492 Book review of: THE FEDERAL BUDGET AND THE NON-PROFIT SECTOR. CAMINOS, Vol. 4, no. 4 (April 1983), p. 59. English. **DESCR:** Abramson, Anal J.; Book Reviews; *FEDERAL BUDGET AND THE NON-PROFIT SECTOR; Non-profit Groups; Salamon, Lester M.

4493 Expected but shocking. NUESTRO, Vol. 6, no. 8 (October 1982), p. 9. English. **DESCR:** *Employment.

4494 The new federalism. NUESTRO, Vol. 6, no. 2 (March 1982), p. 10. English. **DESCR:** *Government; *Government Services; *Social Services.

FEDERAL BUDGET AND THE NON-PROFIT SECTOR

4495 Book review of: THE FEDERAL BUDGET AND THE NON-PROFIT SECTOR. CAMINOS, Vol. 4, no. 4 (April 1983), p. 59. English. **DESCR:** Abramson, Anal J.; Book Reviews; Federal Aid; Non-profit Groups; Salamon, Lester M.

Federal Bureau of Investigation (FBI)

4496 Gente; FBI head, two agents praised by Texas house. NUESTRO, Vol. 7, no. 4 (May 1983), p. 52. English. **DESCR:** Careers; Salinas, Raul; *Texas.

4497 Padilla, Steve. Three-day siege. NUESTRO, Vol. 6, no. 8 (October 1982), p. 19-21. English. **DESCR:** *Arras, Raymundo; Criminal Acts.

Federal Bureau of Investigation (FBI) (cont.)

4498 Padilla, Steve. Working for the F.B.I.
NUESTRO, Vol. 6, no. 8 (October 1982), p.
15-17. English. DESCR: Arras, Raymundo;
Latin Americans; Marquez, Manuel; Perez,
Matthew.

Federal Communications Commission (FCC)

4499 Excerpts from FCC Commissioner Henry M.
Rivera. HISPANIC BUSINESS, Vol. 4, no. 5
(May 1982), p. 23. English. DESCR:
*Broadcast Media.

4500 Gutierrez, Felix. Henry Rivera: our Hispanic
on the FCC. CAMINOS, Vol. 4, no. 3 (March
1983), p. 22-24,50. Bilingual. DESCR: Mass
Media; *Rivera, Henry; Television.

4501 Media/marketing. HISPANIC BUSINESS, Vol. 5,
no. 11 (November 1983), p. 30. English.
DESCR: Caballero Spanish Media, Inc. (CSM);
California Chicano News Media Association
(CCNMA); Employment Training; HISPANEX
(Oakland, CA); *Mass Media; Michell, Pat;
Radio; Radio Station KALI, Los Angeles, CA.

4502 Research and ownership among Hispanic
concerns. BROADCASTING, Vol. 102, no. 15
(April 12, 1982), p. 66. English. DESCR:
*Radio; Rivera, Henry.

4503 Rivera, Henry M. Hispanics need to
effectively translate potential into
political and economic clout.
TELEVISION/RADIO AGE, Vol. 31, no. 4
(September 12, 1983), p. 117-118. English.
DESCR: Equal Employment Opportunity
Commission (EEOC); *Minority
Telecommunications Ownership Act of 1983 (HR
2331); *Radio.

Federal Drug Administration (FDA)

4504 Folk remedy dangerous. NUESTRO, Vol. 7, no.
2 (March 1983), p. 7. English. DESCR: *Folk
Medicine; Medicine; Trotter, Robert.

Federal Government

4505 Garcia, Paco. Voices: Hispanic voices needed
in the education debate. NUESTRO, Vol. 7,
no. 5 (June, July, 1983), p. 53-54. English.
DESCR: Bilingual Bicultural Education;
*Discrimination in Education;
*Discrimination in Employment; *Education;
*Latin Americans; President's Commission on
Excellence in Education; Reagan, Ronald;
U.S. Department of Health, Education and
Welfare (HEW).

4506 Gente. NUESTRO, Vol. 7, no. 2 (March 1983),
p. 51. English. DESCR: Artists; Betancourt,
Jose L.; *Chicanas; Crime Victims Fund;
Juarez, Joe; Military Service; Saldana,
Teresa; Vargas, Alberto; Victims for
Victims.

4507 Jobs for peace initiative. CAMINOS, Vol. 4,
no. 11 (December 1983), p. 26. English.
DESCR: *Employment.

4508 Levin, Betsy. An analysis of the federal
attempt to regulate bilingual education:
protecting civil rights or controlling
curriculum? JOURNAL OF LAW AND EDUCATION,
Vol. 12, no. 1 (January 1983), p. 29-60.
English. DESCR: Affirmative Action Programs;
*Bilingual Bicultural Education; Civil
Rights; Cultural Pluralism; Educational Law
and Legislation.

4509 NALEO audits the Feds. HISPANIC BUSINESS,

Vol. 5, no. 10 (October 1983), p. 16.
English. DESCR: Business Enterprises;
*Government Contracts; Minority Business
Development Agency (MBDA); *National
Association of Latino Elected Officials
(NALEO); U.S. Department of Defense (DOD);
U.S. Department of Health and Human
Services.

4510 Olivas, Michael A. Federal higher education
policy: the case of Hispanics. EDUCATIONAL
EVALUATION AND POLICY ANALYSIS, Vol. 4, no.
3 (Fall 1982), p. 301-310. English. DESCR:
Discrimination in Education; Education
Equalization; Educational Law and
Legislation; *Higher Education; Policy
Formation.

4511 Police and immigration. NUESTRO, Vol. 7, no.
2 (March 1983), p. 7. English. DESCR:
*Border Patrol; El Paso, TX; *Immigration
Law; Immigration Regulation and Control;
Police.

4512 President Reagan's appointments. CAMINOS,
Vol. 3, no. 3 (March 1982), p. 48-50.
Bilingual. DESCR: Appointed Officials;
Flores Buckhart, Elizabeth; Garcia, Ernest
E.; Gonzalez, Luis A.; Lozano, Diana; Pompa,
Gilbert G.; Reagan, Ronald; Sanchez, Nestor
D.; Zuniga, Henry.

4513 Q & A: in the Hispanic community who are the
winners and losers of Reaganomics? CAMINOS,
Vol. 3, no. 3 (March 1982), p. 47.
Bilingual. DESCR: Casado, Lucy; Echeveste,
John; Flores, Bob; Leon, Virginia; Mendoza,
John; *Reagan, Ronald; Sanchez-Alvarez,
Gloria; Vidal de Neri, Julieta.

4514 Whisler, Kirk. Robert Garcia: the mover in
the Congressional Hispanic Caucus. CAMINOS,
Vol. 3, no. 7 (July, August, 1982), p.
36-37,44. Bilingual. DESCR: Congressional
Hispanic Caucus; Elected Officials; *Garcia,
Robert.

4515 Zapanta, Albert C. President Reagan and the
Hispanic community/El presidente Reagan y la
comunidad Hispanica. CAMINOS, Vol. 3, no. 3
(March 1982), p. 38-39. Bilingual. DESCR:
*Reagan, Ronald.

Federal Reserve Board

4516 Congressman questions federal reserve role.
NUESTRO, Vol. 5, no. 8 (November 1981), p.
38. English. DESCR: *Gonzales, Henry B.;
*Legislation.

Federation for American Immigration Reform (FAIR)

4517 Corwin, Arthur F. The numbers game:
estimates of illegal aliens in the United
States, 1970-1981. LAW AND CONTEMPORARY
PROBLEMS, Vol. 45, no. 2 (Spring 1982), p.
223-297. English. DESCR: Bustamante, Jorge
A.; Centro Nacional de Informacion y
Estadistica del Trabajo (CENINET);
Demography; Mexican American Legal Defense
and Educational Fund (MALDEF); *Select
Commission on Immigration and Refugee
Policy; Simpson-Mazzoli Bill; *Statistics;
*Undocumented Workers.

4518 Keep, Paul M. Overhauling the immigration
code: this year, Congress may finally act.
NATIONAL JOURNAL, Vol. 15, no. 12 (March 19,
1983), p. 616-619. English. DESCR: American
Civil Liberties Union; Immigration;
*Immigration Law; Mexican American Legal
Defense and Educational Fund (MALDEF);
*Simpson-Mazzoli Bill.

Federation for American Immigration Reform (FAIR) (cont.)

4519 MALDEF critical of FAIR study. NUESTRO, Vol. 7, no. 7 (September 1983), p. 12-13. English. **DESCR:** *Immigration Regulation and Control; *Mexican American Legal Defense and Educational Fund (MALDEF); Simpson-Mazzoli Bill.

4520 Salvatierra, Richard. Alien smuggling and the refugee question: U.S. must set a limit on refugees. NUESTRO, Vol. 7, no. 5 (June, July, 1983), p. 19. English. **DESCR:** *Immigration Regulation and Control; *Political Refugees; Refugees; *Undocumented Workers.

4521 A territorial approach to representation for illegal aliens. MICHIGAN LAW REVIEW, Vol. 80, no. 6 (May 1982), p. 1342-1371. English. **DESCR:** Census; Population; Reapportionment; Reynolds, Steve; *Undocumented Workers; Voting Rights.

Federation of Minority Business Associations

4522 Business/negocios. CAMINOS, Vol. 3, no. 2 (February 1982), p. 22-23. Bilingual. **DESCR:** Argentina; Brazil; *Business; Chile; Colombia; FRANCHISE OPPORTUNITIES HANDBOOK; Latin America.

Feldman, Harvey W.

4523 Hunsaker, Alan. Book review of: ANGEL DUST: AN ETHNOGRAPHIC STUDY OF PCP USERS; HEROIN USE IN THE BARRIO; DRUG AND ALCOHOL ABUSE: A CLINICAL GUIDE TO DIAGNOSIS AND TREATMENT. HISPANIC JOURNAL OF BEHAVIORAL SCIENCES, Vol. 4, no. 1 (March 1982), p. 118-121. English. **DESCR:** Agar, Michael; *ANGEL DUST: AN ETHNOGRAPHIC STUDY OF PCP USERS; Bescher, George; Book Reviews; Bullington, Bruce; *DRUG AND ALCOHOL ABUSE: A CLINICAL GUIDE TO DIAGNOSIS AND TREATMENT; *HEROIN USE IN THE BARRIO; Schuckit, Marc A.

Feliciano, Jose

4524 Diaz, Katherine A. Jose Feliciano. CAMINOS, Vol. 3, no. 8 (September 1982), p. 14-16. Bilingual. **DESCR:** Artists; Musicians; Singers.

Felix, Maria

4525 Gonzalez, Magdalena. Recognizing Hispanic achievements in entertainment - U.S. and Mexico. CAMINOS, Vol. 3, no. 7 (July, August, 1982), p. 18-24. Bilingual. **DESCR:** Allende, Fernando; Artists; Awards; Bonilla Giannini, Roxanna; Eynoso, David; Films; Gallego, Gina; *Golden Eagle Awards; Hoyos, Rodolfo; Lamas, Lorenzo; Lopez, Conchita; Lopez, Lisa; Montalban, Ricardo; Nosotros [film production company]; Quintero, Jose; Rowe, Arthur; Television; Torres, Liz.

4526 Monsivais, Carlos. No te muevas, paisaje (sobre el cincuentenario del cine sonoro en Mexico). AZTLAN, Vol. 14, no. 1 (Spring 1983), p. 1-19. Spanish. **DESCR:** Bunuel, Luis; Fernandez, Emilio; *Films; Mass Media; *Mexico.

Fellowship

USE: Financial Aid

Females

USE: Chicanas

Feminism

USE: Women's Rights

Ferguson, Marilyn

4527 Ferrarone, Aida. The aquarium conspiracy: personal and social transformation in the 80's: a review. LATINA, Vol. 1, no. 2 (February, March, 1983), p. 23. English. **DESCR:** Book Reviews; *THE AQUARIAN CONSPIRACY.

Fernandez, Ben

4528 California economist considering candidacy. NUESTRO, Vol. 6, no. 5 (June, July, 1982), p. 29. English. **DESCR:** *Politics.

4529 Presidential election 1984. NUESTRO, Vol. 7, no. 7 (September 1983), p. 14-19. English. **DESCR:** Anderson, John; Askew, Reubin; Cranston, Alan; Elected Officials; *Elections; Glenn, John; Hart, Gary; Hispanic Force '84; Hollings, Ernest "Fritz"; Mondale, Walter; Political Parties and Organizations; Reagan, Ronald.

4530 Rivera, Elaine. Fernandez envies Jackson effort. NUESTRO, Vol. 7, no. 9 (November 1983), p. 13. English. **DESCR:** Elections; Jackson, Jesse; Politics.

Fernandez, Castor A.

4531 Goodman, Gerson. "ES PARA USTED": CSI aims for satisfaction. HISPANIC BUSINESS, Vol. 4, no. 12 (December 1982), p. 16-17,34. English. **DESCR:** Advertising Agencies; Aguirre, Jack; Business Enterprises; Consumers; CSI International, Inc.; *Marketing.

Fernandez, Emilio

4532 Monsivais, Carlos. No te muevas, paisaje (sobre el cincuentenario del cine sonoro en Mexico). AZTLAN, Vol. 14, no. 1 (Spring 1983), p. 1-19. Spanish. **DESCR:** Bunuel, Luis; Felix, Maria; *Films; Mass Media; *Mexico.

Fernandez Fragoso, Victor

4533 Barradas, Efrain. NOO JORK. REVISTA CHICANO-RIQUENA, Vol. 10, no. 3 (Summer 1982), p. 65-67. Spanish. **DESCR:** Book Reviews; Figueroa, Jose Angel; *NOO JORK.

4534 Barradas, Efrain. "Todo lo que digo es cierto...": en memoria de Victor Fernandez Fragoso (1944-1982). REVISTA CHICANO-RIQUENA, Vol. 10, no. 3 (Summer 1982), p. 43-46. Spanish. **DESCR:** Authors; *Biography; Essays; New York, NY; Puerto Rican Literature.

Fernandez, John P.

4535 Research/development: books. HISPANIC BUSINESS, Vol. 4, no. 1 (January 1982), p. 27. English. **DESCR:** *Book Reviews; *Discrimination in Employment; Racism; *RACISM AND SEXISM IN CORPORATE LIFE; Sexism.

Fernandez, Margarita

4536 Lanier, Alfredo S. Making it seem easy, from intern to account executive. HISPANIC BUSINESS, Vol. 4, no. 8 (August 1983), p. 16-17+. English. **DESCR**: *Accountants; Careers; Chicanas; Employment Training; INROADS; Standard Oil Corp.

Fernandez, Nestor

4537 Chavarria, Jesus. The entrepreneurial reflex. HISPANIC BUSINESS, Vol. 5, no. 1 (January 1983), p. 6. English. **DESCR**: Arroyos, Alex; *Business Enterprises; Digitron Tool Company, Inc.; Dynamic Ocean Service, Inc.

4538 Weber, Robert. The special talent of digitron's Nestor Fernandez. HISPANIC BUSINESS, Vol. 5, no. 1 (January 1983), p. 10-11+. English. **DESCR**: *Business Enterprises; Dayton, Ohio; Digitron Tool Company, Inc.; Financial Planning.

Ferre, Don Luis A.

4539 Ferre honored at concert. NUESTRO, Vol. 6, no. 4 (May 1982), p. 12-13. English. **DESCR**: Puerto Ricans.

Ferre, Maurice

4540 An anniversary is observed. NUESTRO, Vol. 7, no. 8 (October 1983), p. 13. English. **DESCR**: *Batista, Fulgencio; Cuba; Cubanos; Local Government; Miami, FL.

4541 Hines, Bea L. and Fabricio, Roberto. Voices. NUESTRO, Vol. 7, no. 10 (December 1983), p. 57-58. English. **DESCR**: Blacks; Cubanos; *Elections; *Miami, FL; Suarez, Xavier.

4542 Loehr, William. Hispanic phenomenon is not new. LATINO, Vol. 53, no. 4 (June 1982), p. 22+. English. **DESCR**: Biography; Population.

Ferre, Rosario

4543 Umpierre, Luz Maria. Un manifiesto literario: PAPELES DE PANDERA DE ROSARIO FERRE. BILINGUAL REVIEW, Vol. 9, no. 2 (May, August, 1982), p. 120126. Spanish. **DESCR**: Book Reviews; *PAPELES DE PANDORA; Poetry; Puerto Rican Literature.

Fertility

4544 Alba, Francisco. La fecundidad entre los Mexicano-Norteamericanos en relacion a los cambiantes patrones reproductivos en Mexico y los Estados Unidos. DEMOGRAFIA Y ECONOMIA, Vol. 16, no. 2 (1982), p. 236-249. Spanish. **DESCR**: Demography; *Mexico; Population Trends; Social Research.

4545 Bean, Frank D. and Swicegood, Gray. Generation, female education and Mexican American fertility. SOCIAL SCIENCE QUARTERLY, Vol. 63, (March 1982), p. 131-144. English. **DESCR**: Chicanas; Family Planning.

4546 Lindemann, Constance and Scott, Wilbur. The fertility related behavior of Mexican American adolescents. JOURNAL OF EARLY ADOLESCENCE, Vol. 2, no. 1 (Spring 1982), p. 31-38. English. **DESCR**: Migration Patterns; Youth.

Festival Internacional Cervantino

4547 Festival international Cervantino. NUESTRO, Vol. 6, no. 5 (June, July, 1982), p. 60-61.

English. **DESCR**: Fiestas.

Festivals
USE: Fiestas

Fiction

4548 Anaya, Rudolfo A. An author's reflections: THE SILENCE OF THE LLANO. NUESTRO, Vol. 7, no. 3 (April 1983), p. 14-17+. English. **DESCR**: *Anaya, Rudolfo A.; Authors; Literary Influence.

4549 Arias, Ron. El senor del chivo. JOURNAL OF ETHNIC STUDIES, Vol. 3, no. 4 (Winter 1976), p. 58-60. English. **DESCR**: Authors; *THE ROAD TO TAMAZUNCHALE.

4550 Barrio, Raymond. Resurrection 1999. NUESTRO, Vol. 7, no. 4 (May 1983), p. 50-51. English. **DESCR**: El Salvador; Nuclear Armament.

4551 Book review of: IMAGES OF THE MEXICAN-AMERICAN IN FICTION AND FILM. MODERN FICTION STUDIES, Vol. 28, (Summer 1982), p. 367-369. English. **DESCR**: Book Reviews; Films; *IMAGES OF THE MEXICAN AMERICAN IN FICTION AND FILM; Mass Media; Pettit, Arthur G.

4552 Calderon, Hector. To read Chicano narrative: commentary and metacommentary. MESTER, Vol. 11, no. 2 (1982), p. 3-14. English. **DESCR**: Anaya, Rudolfo A.; BLESS ME, ULTIMA; Literary Characteristics; *Literary Criticism; Literature; *Prose.

4553 Lopez, Felice. Word woman. NUESTRO, Vol. 7, no. 9 (November 1983), p. 56-59. English. **DESCR**: *Short Story.

4554 A showcase of fiction: NUESTRO's sixth anniversary edition. NUESTRO, Vol. 7, no. 3 (April 1983), p. 13. English. **DESCR**: Literature.

Fiction and Juvenile Literature
USE: Children's Literature

"Field"

4555 de la Fuente, Patricia. Ambiguity in the poetry of Gary Soto. REVISTA CHICANO-RIQUENA, Vol. 11, no. 2 (Summer 1983), p. 34-39. English. **DESCR**: "Avocado Lake"; "Blanco"; "Braley Street"; *Literary Criticism; Poetry; "Song for the pockets"; *Soto, Gary; TALE OF SUNLIGHT; "Telephoning God"; THE ELEMENTS OF SAN JOAQUIN; "Wind".

Field Crops
USE: Crops

Field-Sensitive/Field-Independent Behavior Observation Instruments

4556 Spiridakis, John N. Three diagnostics tools for use with the bilingual child. BILINGUAL JOURNAL, Vol. 7, no. 4 (Summer 1983), p. 23-25. English. **DESCR**: *Bilingual Bicultural Education; Educational Cognitive Style (ECS); Educational Psychology; *Educational Tests and Measurements; Learning and Cognition; Learning Style Inventory (LSI).

Fiesta '83

4557 N.A.L.E.O.'s "Fiesta '83". CAMINOS, Vol. 4,
no. 10 (November 1983), p. 28-29. English.
DESCR: Baca Barragan, Polly; Bilingual
Bicultural Education; Central America;
Garcia, Robert; Immigration; International
Relations; Mendez, Olga; *National
Association of Latino Elected Officials
(NALEO); Simpson-Mazzoli Bill; United
States-Mexico Relations.

Fiesta de Santiago Apostol

4558 100.000 people attend little Spain's fiesta.
NUESTRO, Vol. 6, no. 6 (August 1982), p. 52.
English. **DESCR:** Fiestas.

Fiesta en Washington

4559 70.000 enjoy cultural confab. NUESTRO, Vol.
6, no. 7 (September 1982), p. 12. English.
DESCR: Fiestas; Washington, DC.

Fiestas

4560 100.000 people attend little Spain's fiesta.
NUESTRO, Vol. 6, no. 6 (August 1982), p. 52.
English. **DESCR:** *Fiesta de Santiago Apostol.

4561 70.000 enjoy cultural confab. NUESTRO, Vol.
6, no. 7 (September 1982), p. 12. English.
DESCR: *Fiesta en Washington; Washington,
DC.

4562 Cine-festival. CAMINOS, Vol. 4, no. 9
(October 1983), p. 58. English. **DESCR:** Art;
*Films; San Antonio, TX.

4563 Festival international Cervantino. NUESTRO,
Vol. 6, no. 5 (June, July, 1982), p. 60-61.
English. **DESCR:** *Festival Internacional
Cervantino.

4564 Hispanidad parades: New York and world.
NUESTRO, Vol. 5, no. 8 (November 1981), p.
25-27. English.

Figueroa, Jose Angel

4565 Barradas, Efrain. NOO JORK. REVISTA
CHICANO-RIQUENA, Vol. 10, no. 3 (Summer
1982), p. 65-67. Spanish. **DESCR:** Book
Reviews; Fernandez Fragoso, Victor; *NOO
JORK.

Figueroa, Roberto

4566 Shiell, Pancho. The food world's CIA.
NUESTRO, Vol. 7, no. 2 (March 1983), p.
28-32. English. **DESCR:** *Culinary Institute
of America, Hyde Park, NY; Employment
Training; Recipes.

Film Criticism

4567 Candelaria, Cordelia. Social equity in film
criticism. BILINGUAL REVIEW, Vol. 10, no.
2-3 (May, December, 1983), p. 64-70.
English. **DESCR:** Chicanas; Stereotypes.

4568 Cortes, Carlos E. Chicanas in film: history
of an image. BILINGUAL REVIEW, Vol. 10, no.
2-3 (May, December, 1983), p. 94-108.
English. **DESCR:** *Chicanas; *Films;
*Stereotypes.

Film Festivals

4569 Broyles, Yolanda Julia. Chicano film
festivals: an examination. BILINGUAL REVIEW,
Vol. 10, no. 2-3 (May, December, 1983), p.
116-120. English. **DESCR:** Chicano Film
Exhibition and Festival, Detroit, Michigan,
April 5-9, 1982; San Antonio CineFestival,
TX.

Film Reviews

4570 Aldridge, Henry B. Angel and big Joe.
BILINGUAL REVIEW, Vol. 10, no. 2-3 (May,
December, 1983), p. 168-170. English.
DESCR: *ANGEL AND BIG JOE.

4571 Armas, Jose. ANTONIO AND THE MAYOR: a
cultural review of the film. JOURNAL OF
ETHNIC STUDIES, Vol. 3, no. 3 (Fall 1975),
p. 98-101. English. **DESCR:** *ANTONIO AND THE
MAYOR; Broadcast Media; Columbia
Broadcasting Studios (CBS); Cultural
Characteristics; Films; Mass Media;
*Stereotypes.

4572 THE BALLAD OF GREGORIO CORTEZ (review).
CAMINOS, Vol. 3, no. 8 (September 1982), p.
27. English. **DESCR:** *BALLAD OF GREGORIO
CORTEZ [film].

4573 Barrios, Gregg. Alambrista! a modern
odyssey. BILINGUAL REVIEW, Vol. 10, no. 2-3
(May, December, 1983), p. 165-167. English.
DESCR: *ALAMBRISTA.

4574 Barrios, Gregg. A cinema of failure, a
cinema of hunger: the films of Efrain
Gutierrez. BILINGUAL REVIEW, Vol. 10, no.
2-3 (May, December, 1983), p. 179-180.
English. **DESCR:** *Gutierrez, Efrain.

4575 Barrios, Gregg. Zoot Suit: the man, the
myth, still lives. BILINGUAL REVIEW, Vol.
10, no. 2-3 (May, December, 1983), p.
159-164. English. **DESCR:** Valdez, Luis; *ZOOT
SUIT [film].

4576 Beaver, Frank E. CHULAS FRONTERAS. BILINGUAL
REVIEW, Vol. 10, no. 2-3 (May, December,
1983), p. 176. English. **DESCR:** Blank, Les;
*CHULAS FRONTERAS [film]; Music.

4577 Beaver, Frank E. DEL MERO CORAZON. BILINGUAL
REVIEW, Vol. 10, no. 2-3 (May, December,
1983), p. 183. English. **DESCR:** *DEL MERO
CORAZON.

4578 BLOOD WEDDING. NUESTRO, Vol. 5, no. 8
(November 1981), p. 50. English. **DESCR:**
Gades, Antonio; Lorca, Federico Garcia;
*Saura, Carlos.

4579 Breiter, Toni. Eddie Olmos and THE BALLAD OF
GREGORIO CORTEZ. NUESTRO, Vol. 7, no. 4 (May
1983), p. 14-19. English. **DESCR:** Artists;
*BALLAD OF GREGORIO CORTEZ [film]; Corrido;
*Olmos, Edward James; Prejudice (Social).

4580 De la Rosa, Carlos. Esai Morales: a new and
exciting Latino talent on the rise. LATINA,
Vol. 1, no. 3 (1983), p. 19. English.
DESCR: *BAD BOYS; Biography; Morales, Esai.

4581 Dominguez, Pia and Martinez, Marie. CORRIDO
run clipped by national film distributors.
LATINA, Vol. 1, no. 2 (February, March,
1983), p. 24. English. **DESCR:** *BALLAD OF
GREGORIO CORTEZ [film].

4582 Fernandez, Enrique. Cannes and CROSSOVER
DREAMS, '83. FILM COMMENT, Vol. 19, no. 4-7
(August 1983), p. 2-7. English. **DESCR:** Arce,
Manuel; Blades, Ruben; Cannes Film Festival;
*CROSSOVER DREAMS; Films; Salsa.

Film Reviews (cont.)

4583 Fregoso, Linda. Sequin: the same side of the Alamo. BILINGUAL REVIEW, Vol. 10, no. 2-3 (May, December, 1983), p. 146-152. English. **DESCR:** *SEGUIN [movie]; Trevino, Jesus Salvador.

4584 Garza, Hector. El grito de las madres dolorosas. BILINGUAL REVIEW, Vol. 10, no. 2-3 (May, December, 1983), p. 184-186. English. **DESCR:** Connolly, Patrick J.; *EL GRITO DE LAS MADRES DOLOROSAS.

4585 Grelier, Robert. Film review of: CHICANOS STORY. REVUE DU CINEMA - IMAGE ET SON - ECRAN, (May 1983), p. 30. Other. **DESCR:** *Valdez, Luis; ZOOT SUIT [film].

4586 Gutierrez, Chela. Flicks in review. LATINA, Vol. 1, no. 1 (1982), p. 46+. English. **DESCR:** *AN OFFICER AND A GENTLEMAN; *THINGS ARE TOUGH ALL OVER.

4587 Gutierrez, Silvio. Cinema. LATINA, Vol. 1, no. 3 (1983), p. 18-19+. English. **DESCR:** *LIANNA; *VOLVER A EMPEZAR.

4588 Herrera-Sobek, Maria. Film review of: DEL MERO CORAZON (STRAIGHT FROM THE HEART). JOURNAL OF AMERICAN FOLKLORE, Vol. 95, (March 1982), p. 123. English. **DESCR:** Blank, Les; *DEL MERO CORAZON; Gosling, Maureen; Hernandez, Guillermo; Norteno; Strachwitz, Chris.

4589 Hinojosa-Smith, Rolando R. I AM JOAQUIN: relationships between the text and the film. BILINGUAL REVIEW, Vol. 10, no. 2-3 (May, December, 1983), p. 142-145. English. **DESCR:** Gonzales, Rodolfo (Corky); I AM JOAQUIN [book]; *I AM JOAQUIN [film]; Valdez, Luis.

4590 Keller, Gary. Ballad of an unsung hero. BILINGUAL REVIEW, Vol. 10, no. 2-3 (May, December, 1983), p. 171-172. English. **DESCR:** *BALLAD OF AN UNSUNG HERO; Gonzalez, Pedro J.

4591 Keller, Gary. The image of the Chicano in Mexican, Chicano, and Chicano cinema: an overview. BILINGUAL REVIEW, Vol. 10, no. 2-3 (May, December, 1983), p. 13-58. English. **DESCR:** *Films; *Stereotypes.

4592 Levine, Paul G. Remember the Alamo? AMERICAN FILM, Vol. 7, no. 4 (January, February, 1982), p. 47-49. English. **DESCR:** Films; LA HISTORIA [film series]; *SEGUIN [movie]; Trevino, Jesus Salvador.

4593 Maciel, David R. Visions of the other Mexico: Chicanos and undocumented workers in Mexican cinema, 1954-1982. BILINGUAL REVIEW, Vol. 10, no. 2-3 (May, December, 1983), p. 71-88. English. **DESCR:** *Films; Mexican Cinema; *Mexico; *Undocumented Workers.

4594 McCloud, George E. Film review of: CONSUELO: QUIENES SOMOS? BILINGUAL REVIEW, Vol. 10, no. 2-3 (May, December, 1983), p. 181-182. English. **DESCR:** *CONSUELO: QUIENES SOMOS?.

4595 Morales, Alejandro. Expanding the meaning of Chicano cinema: YO SOY CHICANO, RAICES DE SANGRE, SEGUIN. BILINGUAL REVIEW, Vol. 10, no. 2-3 (May, December, 1983), p. 121-137. English. **DESCR:** *Films; RAICES DE SANGRE [film]; SEGUIN [movie]; YO SOY CHICANO [film].

4596 Morales, Sylvia. Chicano-produced celluloid mujeres. BILINGUAL REVIEW, Vol. 10, no. 2-3 (May, December, 1983), p. 89-93. English. **DESCR:** BALLAD OF GREGORIO CORTEZ [film]; *Chicanas; *Films; RAICES DE SANGRE [film]; SEGUIN [movie]; *Stereotypes; ZOOT SUIT [film].

4597 Munoz, Carlos, Jr. The unwanted. BILINGUAL REVIEW, Vol. 10, no. 2-3 (May, December, 1983), p. 187-188. English. **DESCR:** *THE UNWANTED.

4598 Ochoa Thompson, Guadalupe. RAICES DE SANGRE: roots of lineage, sources of life. BILINGUAL REVIEW, Vol. 10, no. 2-3 (May, December, 1983), p. 138-141. English. **DESCR:** *RAICES DE SANGRE [film]; Trevino, Jesus Salvador.

4599 Olmos, Edward James. Edward James Olmos and Robert Young with 21 reasons why you should see THE BALLAD OF GREGORIO CORTEZ. CAMINOS, Vol. 3, no. 8 (September 1982), p. 26-27, 50. Bilingual. **DESCR:** *BALLAD OF GREGORIO CORTEZ [film]; Olmos, Edward James; Young, Robert.

4600 Ostria, Vincent. Film review of: CHICANOS STORY. CAHIERS DU CINEMA, Vol. 36, (June, July, 1983), p. 90. Other. **DESCR:** Valdez, Luis; *ZOOT SUIT [film].

4601 Quesada-Weiner, Rosemary and Diaz, Katherine A. ZOOT SUIT. CAMINOS, Vol. 2, no. 7 (December 1981), p. 38-39. English. **DESCR:** *ZOOT SUIT [film].

4602 Ramirez Berg, Charles. ZOOT SUIT. BILINGUAL REVIEW, Vol. 10, no. 2-3 (May, December, 1983), p. 189-190. English. **DESCR:** *ZOOT SUIT [film].

4603 Rogg, Eleanor Meyer. Film review of: ANO NUEVO. MIGRATION TODAY, Vol. 10, no. 5 (1982), p. 36. English. **DESCR:** *ANO NUEVO [film]; Darling, Todd; Films; Undocumented Workers.

4604 Ruiz, Reynaldo. BORDERLANDS. BILINGUAL REVIEW, Vol. 10, no. 2-3 (May, December, 1983), p. 173-175. English. **DESCR:** *BORDERLANDS [film].

4605 Ruiz, Reynaldo. CINCO VIDAS. BILINGUAL REVIEW, Vol. 10, no. 2-3 (May, December, 1983), p. 177-178. English. **DESCR:** *CINCO VIDAS.

4606 Sorell, Victor A. Ethnomusicology, folklore, and history in the filmmaker's art: THE BALLAD OF GREGORIO CORTEZ. BILINGUAL REVIEW, Vol. 10, no. 2-3 (1983), p. 153-158. English. **DESCR:** *BALLAD OF GREGORIO CORTEZ [film]; Paredes, Americo; WITH HIS PISTOL IN HIS HAND.

4607 Treviso, Ruben. EL CORRIDO DE GREGORIO CORTEZ. LATINO, Vol. 53, no. 5 (September 1982), p. 16-17. Spanish. **DESCR:** *BALLAD OF GREGORIO CORTEZ [film].

4608 Varnez, Ginger. Film review of: THE BALLAD OF GREGORIO CORTEZ. CAMINOS, Vol. 4, no. 8 (September 1983), p. 40-41. English. **DESCR:** *BALLAD OF GREGORIO CORTEZ [film].

4609 West, Dennis. Film review of: EL SUPER. MINORITY VOICES, Vol. 4, no. 2 (Fall 1980), p. 85-87. English. **DESCR:** Cubanos; *EL SUPER; Ichaso, Leon; Jimenez-Leal, Orlando.

Films

4610 Los Alvarez. CAMINOS, Vol. 4, no. 4 (April 1983), p. 40-41, 66. English. **DESCR:** *Reyes, Luis.

Films (cont.)

4611 Alvarez, Amando. Daniel Valdez: su vida y su carrera. LATINO, Vol. 53, no. 2 (March, April, 1982), p. 16-17. Spanish. **DESCR:** *Valdez, Daniel; ZOOT SUIT [film].

4612 Armas, Jose. ANTONIO AND THE MAYOR: a cultural review of the film. JOURNAL OF ETHNIC STUDIES, Vol. 3, no. 3 (Fall 1975), p. 98-101. English. **DESCR:** *ANTONIO AND THE MAYOR; Broadcast Media; Columbia Broadcasting Studios (CBS); Cultural Characteristics; Film Reviews; Mass Media; *Stereotypes.

4613 Barrios, Gregg. The Latino genre in American film 1980-81. LATINA, Vol. 1, no. 1 (1982), p. 54-55. English.

4614 Bloodworth, William A., Jr. Book review of: IMAGES OF THE MEXICAN-AMERICAN IN FICTION AND FILM. WESTERN AMERICAN LITERATURE, Vol. 16, no. 4 (Winter 1982), p. 323-325. English. **DESCR:** Book Reviews; Chicanos in American Literature; *IMAGES OF THE MEXICAN AMERICAN IN FICTION AND FILM; Pettit, Arthur G.; Showalter, Dennis E.; Stereotypes.

4615 Bonilla, Ruben. Soliciten aqui dentro el presidente continua su busqueda. LATINO, Vol. 53, no. 2 (March, April, 1982), p. 18+. Spanish.

4616 Book review of: IMAGES OF THE MEXICAN-AMERICAN IN FICTION AND FILM. MODERN FICTION STUDIES, Vol. 28, (Summer 1982), p. 367-369. English. **DESCR:** Book Reviews; Fiction; *IMAGES OF THE MEXICAN AMERICAN IN FICTION AND FILM; Mass Media; Pettit, Arthur G.

4617 Bubriski, Kevin. THE BALLAD OF GREGORIO CORTEZ (photoessay). CAMINOS, Vol. 3, no. 8 (September 1982), p. 28-29. English. **DESCR:** *BALLAD OF GREGORIO CORTEZ [film].

4618 Caldera, Carmela and Martinez, Alma. Alma Martinez: "I'm keeping my fingers crossed" (interview). CAMINOS, Vol. 4, no. 11 (December 1983), p. 32-35. English. **DESCR:** Artists; *Martinez, Alma; Teatro.

4619 Caldera, Carmela and De Soto, Rosana. Rosana de Soto: breaking the mold (interview). CAMINOS, Vol. 4, no. 8 (September 1983), p. 36-39. English. **DESCR:** Artists; *De Soto, Rosana.

4620 Cine-festival. CAMINOS, Vol. 4, no. 9 (October 1983), p. 58. English. **DESCR:** Art; *Fiestas; San Antonio, TX.

4621 Clarence and angel. NUESTRO, Vol. 6, no. 1 (January, February, 1982), p. 61. English. **DESCR:** *Cardova, Mark.

4622 Communications/marketing. HISPANIC BUSINESS, Vol. 4, no. 8 (August 1983), p. 22+. English. **DESCR:** Arredondo, Price; Baseball; De la O, Val; Marketing; *Mass Media; Radio; San Antonio CineFestival, TX; Television; Val De La O Show; Valenzuela, Fernando; Wright & Arredondo Associates; Wright, Oscar.

4623 Cordelia, Candelaria. Film portrayals of La Mujer Hispana. AGENDA, Vol. 11, no. 3 (May, June, 1981), p. 32-36. English. **DESCR:** *Chicanas.

4624 Cortes, Carlos E. Chicanas in film: history of an image. BILINGUAL REVIEW, Vol. 10, no. 2-3 (May, December, 1983), p. 94-108.

English. **DESCR:** *Chicanas; Film Criticism; *Stereotypes.

4625 Cripps, Thomas. Mexicans, Indians and movies: the need for a history. WIDE ANGLE: A FILM QUARTERLY OF THEORY, CRITICISM, AND PRACTICE, Vol. 5, no. 1 (1982), p. 68-70. English. **DESCR:** Bataille, Gretchen M.; *Book Reviews; IMAGES OF THE MEXICAN AMERICAN IN FICTION AND FILM; Native Americans; O'Connor, John E.; Pettit, Arthur G.; Silet, Charles L.P.; *Stereotypes; THE HOLLYWOOD INDIAN: STEREOTYPES OF NATIVE AMERICANS IN FILMS; THE PRETEND INDIANS: IMAGES OF NATIVE AMERICANS IN THE MOVIES.

4626 Diaz, Katherine A. Mike Gomez; pursuing his dream. CAMINOS, Vol. 4, no. 9 (October 1983), p. 28-30. English. **DESCR:** Artists; *Gomez, Mike.

4627 Diaz, Katherine A. The people who make films happen. CAMINOS, Vol. 3, no. 10 (November 1982), p. 16-17,45. English.

4628 Entertainment = diversion. CAMINOS, Vol. 3, no. 1 (January 1982), p. 41-42. Bilingual. **DESCR:** ANO NUEVO [film]; Broadcast Media; *CERVANTES [film]; *SEGUIN [movie]; *Times Mirror Company.

4629 Entertainment = diversion. CAMINOS, Vol. 3, no. 2 (February 1982), p. 40-41. English. **DESCR:** Awards; CHECKING IT OUT; Club Hogar Latino; Dance; Flamenco; Marley, Bob; Montalban, Ricardo; ON GOLDEN POND; *Recreation; Television.

4630 Entertainment = diversion. CAMINOS, Vol. 3, no. 3 (March 1982), p. 55-56. Bilingual. **DESCR:** Aztlan Writing Contest; CORAZON DE AZTLAN; Literary Contests; MISSING [film]; *Recreation; THE BORDER [film]; Young, Robert.

4631 Fernandez, Enrique. Cannes and CROSSOVER DREAMS, '83. FILM COMMENT, Vol. 19, no. 4-7 (August 1983), p. 2-7. English. **DESCR:** Arce, Manuel; Blades, Ruben; Cannes Film Festival; *CROSSOVER DREAMS; Film Reviews; Salsa.

4632 Film distributors. CAMINOS, Vol. 3, no. 10 (November 1982), p. 15. English.

4633 Gamboa, Harry, Jr. Chicano cinema update. CAMINOS, Vol. 3, no. 10 (November 1982), p. 18-19. Bilingual.

4634 Garza, Hector. Directory of Chicano/Latino films and their distributors. BILINGUAL REVIEW, Vol. 10, no. 2-3 (May, December, 1983), p. 191-202. English. **DESCR:** *Bibliography.

4635 Gonzalez, Magdalena. Recognizing Hispanic achievements in entertainment - U.S. and Mexico. CAMINOS, Vol. 3, no. 7 (July, August, 1982), p. 18-24. Bilingual. **DESCR:** Allende, Fernando; Artists; Awards; Bonilla Giannini, Roxanna; Eynoso, David; Felix, Maria; Gallego, Gina; *Golden Eagle Awards; Hoyos, Rodolfo; Lamas, Lorenzo; Lopez, Conchita; Lopez, Lisa; Montalban, Ricardo; Nosotros [film production company]; Quintero, Jose; Rowe, Arthur; Television; Torres, Liz.

4636 Gus Garcia Foundation. LATINO, Vol. 54, no. 4 (May, June, 1983), p. 29. English. **DESCR:** Calderon, Tony; Financial Aid; Garcia, Gus.

Films (cont.)

4637 An Hispanic view of the 1983 Academy Awards. CAMINOS, Vol. 4, no. 6 (June 1983), p. 59. English. **DESCR:** *Academy Awards; Awards.

4638 Hulin-Salkin, Belinda. Films need mass appeal. ADVERTISING AGE MAGAZINE, Vol. 53, (February 15, 1982), p. II, M10. English. **DESCR:** Broadcast Media; *Market Research; Television.

4639 Keller, Gary. The image of the Chicano in Mexican, Chicano, and Chicano cinema: an overview. BILINGUAL REVIEW, Vol. 10, no. 2-3 (May, December, 1983), p. 13-58. English. **DESCR:** Film Reviews; *Stereotypes.

4640 Keller, Gary D., ed. Chicano cinema research, reviews, and resources. BILINGUAL REVIEW, Vol. 10, no. 2-3 (May, December, 1983), p. 1-209. English.

4641 Latino filmmaking is artistic renaissance. LATINO, Vol. 53, no. 5 (September 1982), p. 8. English.

4642 Levine, Paul G. Remember the Alamo? AMERICAN FILM, Vol. 7, no. 4 (January, February, 1982), p. 47-49. English. **DESCR:** Film Reviews; LA HISTORIA [film series]; *SEGUIN [movie]; Trevino, Jesus Salvador.

4643 Lopez, Rafael and Miller, Robert. Daniel Valley and the American Zoot Band (band review). CAMINOS, Vol. 4, no. 5 (May 1983), p. 42-43,52. English. **DESCR:** Artists; *Valdez, Daniel; ZOOT SUIT [film].

4644 Maciel, David R. Visions of the other Mexico: Chicanos and undocumented workers in Mexican cinema, 1954-1982. BILINGUAL REVIEW, Vol. 10, no. 2-3 (May, December, 1983), p. 71-88. English. **DESCR:** Film Reviews; Mexican Cinema; *Mexico; *Undocumented Workers.

4645 Madrid, Joe. The multi-faceted Pepe Serna (interview). CAMINOS, Vol. 4, no. 4 (April 1983), p. 32-35,66. Bilingual. **DESCR:** Artists; *Serna, Pepe.

4646 Markiewicz, Dana. Book review of: MEXICAN CINEMA: REFLECTIONS OF SOCIETY, 1896-1980. HISPANIC JOURNAL OF BEHAVIORAL SCIENCES, Vol. 5, no. 4 (December 1983), p. 491-494. English. **DESCR:** Book Reviews; *MEXICAN CINEMA: REFLECTIONS OF A SOCIETY; Mora, Carl J.

4647 McCracken, Ellen. Book review of: SALT OF THE EARTH. JOURNAL OF ETHNIC STUDIES, Vol. 8, no. 1 (Spring 1980), p. 116-120. English. **DESCR:** Book Reviews; Chicanas; Hanover, NM; International Union of Mine, Mill and Smelter Workers; *SALT OF THE EARTH; Silverton Rosenfelt, Deborah; Strikes and Lockouts; Women Men Relations; Women's Rights.

4648 Mejias-Rentas, Antonio. Cantinflas give D.C. tribute. NUESTRO, Vol. 7, no. 5 (June, July, 1983), p. 11-12. English. **DESCR:** Artists; *Moreno, Mario "Cantinflas".

4649 Monsivais, Carlos. No te muevas, paisaje (sobre el cincuentenario del cine sonoro en Mexico). AZTLAN, Vol. 14, no. 1 (Spring 1983), p. 1-19. Spanish. **DESCR:** Bunuel, Luis; Felix, Maria; Fernandez, Emilio; Mass Media; *Mexico.

4650 Morales, Alejandro. Expanding the meaning of Chicano cinema: YO SOY CHICANO, RAICES DE SANGRE, SEGUIN. BILINGUAL REVIEW, Vol. 10, no. 2-3 (May, December, 1983), p. 121-137. English. **DESCR:** Film Reviews; RAICES DE SANGRE [film]; SEGUIN [movie]; YO SOY CHICANO [film].

4651 Morales, Sylvia. Chicano-produced celluloid mujeres. BILINGUAL REVIEW, Vol. 10, no. 2-3 (May, December, 1983), p. 89-93. English. **DESCR:** BALLAD OF GREGORIO CORTEZ [film]; *Chicanas; Film Reviews; RAICES DE SANGRE [film]; SEGUIN [movie]; *Stereotypes; ZOOT SUIT [film].

4652 Reyes, Luis. East L.A.'s very own Anthony Quinn. CAMINOS, Vol. 4, no. 7 (July, August, 1983), p. 24-27. Bilingual. **DESCR:** Artists; *Quinn, Anthony.

4653 Reyes, Luis. Henry Darrow: the man behind the actor. CAMINOS, Vol. 4, no. 6 (June 1983), p. 23-25,66. Bilingual. **DESCR:** Artists; *Darrow, Henry; Television.

4654 Reyes, Luis. The Hispanic movie market. CAMINOS, Vol. 3, no. 10 (November 1982), p. 12-14. English.

4655 Rogg, Eleanor Meyer. Film review of: ANO NUEVO. MIGRATION TODAY, Vol. 10, no. 5 (1982), p. 36. English. **DESCR:** *ANO NUEVO [film]; Darling, Todd; Film Reviews; Undocumented Workers.

4656 Southwest may lose theater. NUESTRO, Vol. 6, no. 7 (September 1982), p. 11. English. **DESCR:** *Alameda Theater, San Antonio, TX; San Antonio, TX; Spanish Language.

4657 Torres, Luis. The Chicano image in film. CAMINOS, Vol. 3, no. 10 (November 1982), p. 8-11,51. Bilingual. **DESCR:** Stereotypes.

4658 Torres, Luis. Distortions in celluloid: Hispanics and film. AGENDA, Vol. 11, no. 3 (May, June, 1981), p. 37-40. English. **DESCR:** Hispano.

4659 Trevino, Jesus Salvador. Chicano cinema. NEW SCHOLAR, Vol. 8, no. 1-2 (Spring, Fall, 1982), p. 167-180. English.

4660 Trevino, Jesus Salvador. Chicano films and beyond. CAMINOS, Vol. 3, no. 10 (November 1982), p. 6-7,51. Bilingual.

4661 Trevino, Jesus Salvador. Form and technique in Chicano cinema. BILINGUAL REVIEW, Vol. 10, no. 2-3 (May, December, 1983), p. 109-115. English. **DESCR:** Political Ideology.

4662 A very special gift. LATINO, Vol. 53, no. 5 (September 1982), p. 7-8+. English. **DESCR:** *Martinez, A.; SEGUIN [movie].

4663 Vidal, Jose. Mexican film - a short history. CAMINOS, Vol. 3, no. 7 (July, August, 1982), p. 10-13. Bilingual. **DESCR:** Artists; Mexico.

4664 West, Dennis. Book review of: IMAGES OF THE MEXICAN-AMERICAN IN FICTION AND FILM. CINEASTE, Vol. 12, no. 1 (1982), p. 41. English. **DESCR:** Book Reviews; Chicanos in American Literature; *IMAGES OF THE MEXICAN AMERICAN IN FICTION AND FILM; Pettit, Arthur G.; Stereotypes.

4665 Whisler, Kirk. Jose Luis Ruiz on sound festival. CAMINOS, Vol. 3, no. 8 (September 1982), p. 6-8. Bilingual. **DESCR:** Artists; *Ruiz, Jose Luis; Television.

Films (cont.)

4666 Whisler, Kirk. Nosotros on film in Hollywood and Latin America. CAMINOS, Vol. 3, no. 7 (July, August, 1982), p. 15-17. Bilingual. DESCR: Artists; Cardinale, Marcela; Espinoza, Jimmy; Gomez, Mike; *Nosotros [film production company]; Ortiz, Yolanda; Television; Velasco, Jerry.

4667 Whisler, Kirk. Rose Portillo: a woman on the rise. CAMINOS, Vol. 4, no. 4 (April 1983), p. 36-39. Bilingual. DESCR: Artists; *Portillo, Rose.

4668 Williams, Linda. Type and stereotype: Chicano images in film. BILINGUAL REVIEW, Vol. 10, no. 2-3 (May, December, 1983), p. 59-63. English. DESCR: *Stereotypes.

4669 ZOOT SUIT. NUESTRO, Vol. 6, no. 2 (March 1982), p. 46-47. English. DESCR: *ZOOT SUIT [film].

LES FILS DU SOLEIL: LA MINORITE MEXICAINE A TRAVERS LA LITTERATURE DES ETATS-UNIS

4670 Cazemajou, Jean. Book review of: LES FILS DU SOLEIL: LA MINORITE MEXICAINE A TRAVERS LA LITTERATURE DES ETATS-UNIS. REVUE FRANCAISE D'ETUDES AMERICAINES. Vol. 83, no. 16 (February 1983), p. 153-155. Other. DESCR: *LES FILS DU SOLEIL; Book Reviews; Rocard, Marcienne.

4671 Fabre, Michel. Book review of: LES FILS DU SOLEIL: LA MINORITE MEXICAINE A TRAVERS LA LITTERATURE DES ETATS-UNIS. MELUS: MULTI-ETHNIC LITERATURE OF THE UNITED STATES, Vol. 8, no. 1 (Spring 1981), p. 65-68. English. DESCR: Book Reviews; Literature; Rocard, Marcienne.

4672 Tyler, Joseph. Basque Ball in Bridgeport. HISPANIA, Vol. 66, no. 1 (1983), p. 144. English. DESCR: Book Reviews; *Chicanos in American Literature.

Finance

4673 Chavarria, Jesus. How are we doing? HISPANIC BUSINESS, Vol. 4, no. 8 (August 1983), p. 6. English. DESCR: Economics; Elected Officials; Voter Turnout.

4674 Deibel, Richard and Sanchez, Tony, Jr. Business on the border: attracting venture capital. HISPANIC BUSINESS, Vol. 5, no. 9 (September 1983), p. 20-21+. English. DESCR: Border Industries; Border Region; *Sanchez, Tony, Jr.; Texas.

4675 Dominguez, Richard M. Capital formulation for small businesses. HISPANIC BUSINESS, Vol. 4, no. 9 (September 1982), p. 8. English. DESCR: Banking Industry; California; Small Business.

4676 Hispanic owned banks. HISPANIC BUSINESS, Vol. 5, no. 9 (September 1983), p. 13. English. DESCR: *Banking Industry; International Bank of Commerce (IBOC); Minority Bank Deposit Program (MBDP).

4677 Research/development: books. HISPANIC BUSINESS, Vol. 4, no. 7 (July 1982), p. 27. English. DESCR: *Book Reviews; De Leon, Arnoldo; History; Spiro, Herbert T.; Texas; THE TEJANO COMMUNITY, 1836-1900.

Financial Aid

4678 1982 scholarship fund past half-way mark. LATINO, Vol. 53, no. 2 (March, April, 1982), p. 28. English.

4679 30 Urban Fellowships to be awarded. LATINO, Vol. 53, no. 1 (January, February, 1982), p. 21. English. DESCR: *National Urban Fellows, Inc..

4680 Academic furlough for the working professional. HISPANIC BUSINESS, Vol. 4, no. 8 (August 1983), p. 15. English. DESCR: Arias, Beatriz; Funding Sources; Kellogg, W.K.; *W.K. Kellogg Foundation.

4681 Baca, Judith F. Class II: young and energetic leaders. LATINO, Vol. 54, no. 2 (March 1983), p. 29-30. English. DESCR: Students.

4682 Chavira, Ricardo. Gutierrez, first Latino recipient. NUESTRO, Vol. 7, no. 3 (April 1983), p. 11-12. English. DESCR: *Gutierrez, Ramon; History; MacArthur Foundation; New Mexico.

4683 Coca-Cola USA Today outlines Latino agenda. NUESTRO, Vol. 7, no. 9 (November 1983), p. 36. English. DESCR: Business; Coca-Cola Company; *Coca-Cola National Hispanic Education Fund; Education; Funding Sources.

4684 Community watching. CAMINOS, Vol. 3, no. 5 (May 1982), p. 56-57. Bilingual. DESCR: Adelante Mujer Hispana Conference; Agricultural Laborers; Beilson, Anthony C.; Boycotts; Chacon, Peter R.; Chicanas; *Cultural Organizations; Farm Labor Organizing Commmittee (FLOC); Hollenbeck Junior High School, Los Angeles, CA; Junior High School Students; National League of Cities; Optimist Club of Greater East Los Angeles; Organizations; Project WELL (We Enjoy Learning & Leadership); Torres, Art.

4685 Community watching: para la comunidad. CAMINOS, Vol. 3, no. 1 (January 1982), p. 43-44. Bilingual. DESCR: Congreso Nacional Para Pueblos Unidos (CPU); *Food Programs; *Journalists; National Association for Chicano Studies (NACS); *Radio; Summer Program for Minority Journalists; Zozaya, Julia S.

4686 Community watching: para la comunidad. CAMINOS, Vol. 3, no. 2 (February 1982), p. 43-44. Bilingual. DESCR: Casa Blanca Youth Project; Colegio Cesar Chavez, Mt. Angel, OR; Colleges and Universities; *Cultural Organizations; LULAC National Education Service Centers (LNESC); Tonatiuh-Quinto Sol Award for Literature, 1977-78; University of California, Riverside.

4687 Community watching: para la comunidad. CAMINOS, Vol. 3, no. 3 (March 1982), p. 58-59. Bilingual. DESCR: Cultural Organizations; *Engineering as a Profession; Harvard University; Latino Business Students Association (LBSA); Rodolfo H. Castro Fellowship; Society for Hispanic Professional Engineers (SHPE); Student Organizations; University of Southern California.

4688 Gus Garcia Foundation. LATINO, Vol. 54, no. 4 (May, June, 1983), p. 29. English. DESCR: Calderon, Tony; *Films; Garcia, Gus.

4689 MAGA annual scholarship awards banquet. CAMINOS, Vol. 4, no. 1-2 (January, February, 1983), p. 32. English. DESCR: Awards; *Mexican American Grocers Association (MAGA).

Financial Aid (cont.)

4690 Math-based careers. HISPANIC BUSINESS, Vol. 4, no. 3 (March 1982), p. 20. English. **DESCR:** Careers; Congressional Hispanic Caucus; Consortium for Graduate Study in Management; *Educational Opportunities.

4691 Math-based careers. HISPANIC BUSINESS, Vol. 4, no. 5 (May 1982), p. 22. English. **DESCR:** Careers; Education; Engineering as a Profession; National Action Council for Minorities in Engineering (NACME); Society for Hispanic Professional Engineers (SHPE).

4692 Math-based careers. HISPANIC BUSINESS, Vol. 4, no. 10 (October 1982), p. 20. English. **DESCR:** *Careers; Educational Opportunities; Engineering as a Profession; Minority Business Development Agency (MBDA); National Action Council for Minorities in Engineering (NACME); National Association of Independent Schools (NAIS).

4693 Math-based careers. HISPANIC BUSINESS, Vol. 5, no. 2 (February 1983), p. 22. English. **DESCR:** *Careers; Engineering; Mathematics; Mathematics, Engineering and Science Achievement (MESA); National Action Council for Minorities in Engineering (NACME).

4694 Math-based careers. HISPANIC BUSINESS, Vol. 5, no. 5 (May 1983), p. 26. English. **DESCR:** *Careers; Engineering as a Profession; Income; Labor Supply and Market; Mexican American Engineering Society (MAES) National Symposium (5th), Fullerton, CA, April 13-15, 1980; University of California, Santa Barbara.

4695 Math-based careers. HISPANIC BUSINESS, Vol. 5, no. 9 (September 1983), p. 28. English. **DESCR:** Andrew W. Mellon Foundation; *Careers; Employment; Engineering as a Profession; Garcia, Mary; Higher Education; National Council for Minorities in Engineering (NACME); National Medical Fellowships (NMF); Rivera, Lourdes.

4696 Math-based careers. HISPANIC BUSINESS, Vol. 4, no. 8 (August 1983), p. 20. English. **DESCR:** Brigham Young University; Business Administration; *Careers; Coalition of Spanish-Speaking Mental Health Organization (COSSMHO), Annual Regional Conference, Los Angeles, March 14-15, 1975; Cooperative Extension Programs; Education; Employment Training; Medical Personnel.

4697 Omaha awards $8,000 in scholarships to 12. LATINO, Vol. 54, no. 6 (October 1983), p. 5. English.

4698 The path to college. LATINO, Vol. 54, no. 2 (March 1983), p. 8-11+. English. **DESCR:** Higher Education; *Students.

4699 Patterson fellowship to de Uriarte. LATINA, Vol. 1, no. 2 (February, March, 1983), p. 20. English. **DESCR:** Alice Patterson Foundation; *De Uriarte, Mercedes Lynn.

4700 Reagan, Ronald. Remarks at a White House reception for the National Coalition of Hispanic Mental Health and Human Services Organization (September 23, 1982). PUBLIC PAPERS OF THE PRESIDENT, Vol. 1, no. 2 (1982), p. 1209-1211. English. **DESCR:** *National Coalition of Hispanic Mental Health and Human Services Organizations (COSSMHO).

4701 Redmond, Deborah L. Young achievers recognized. LATINO, Vol. 53, no. 5 (September 1982), p. 27. English.

4702 Research/development: books. HISPANIC BUSINESS, Vol. 4, no. 4 (April 1982), p. 28. English. **DESCR:** *Book Reviews; Engineering; FINANCIAL AID FOR MINORITIES IN ENGINEERING; Kennedy, David W.; PERFECTLY LEGAL - 275 FOOLPROOF METHODS FOR PAYING LESS TAXES; Steiner, Barry R.; Swann, Ruth N.; Taxation.

4703 RJR supports four year scholarships. LATINO, Vol. 54, no. 5 (August, September, 1983), p. 14. English.

4704 The scholarship challenge. LATINO, Vol. 54, no. 4 (May, June, 1983), p. 23. English.

4705 Texas teenager wins scholarship. NUESTRO, Vol. 7, no. 10 (December 1983), p. 13. English. **DESCR:** Girl Scouts of the United States of America; Leadership; *Turincio, Giovanne.

4706 Thirty fellowships to be awarded in 1983. LATINO, Vol. 54, no. 4 (May, June, 1983), p. 27. English.

4707 A time for reflection. NUESTRO, Vol. 7, no. 9 (November 1983), p. 42-44. English. **DESCR:** Anaya, Rudolfo A.; Arias, Beatriz; Bilingual Bicultural Education; Computers; Folklore; Organizations; Prewitt Diaz, Joseph (Jose); Villarreal, Sylvia; *W.K. Kellogg Foundation National Fellowship Program.

4708 Training, fellowships. NUESTRO, Vol. 7, no. 1 (January, February, 1983), p. 9. English. **DESCR:** *Community Outreach Project; Employment Training; Medical Personnel; Stanford University Medical Center.

FINANCIAL AID FOR MINORITIES IN ENGINEERING

4709 Research/development: books. HISPANIC BUSINESS, Vol. 4, no. 4 (April 1982), p. 28. English. **DESCR:** *Book Reviews; Engineering; Financial Aid; Kennedy, David W.; PERFECTLY LEGAL - 275 FOOLPROOF METHODS FOR PAYING LESS TAXES; Steiner, Barry R.; Swann, Ruth N.; Taxation.

Financial Planning

4710 Weber, Robert. The special talent of digitron's Nestor Fernandez. HISPANIC BUSINESS, Vol. 5, no. 1 (January 1983), p. 10-11+. English. **DESCR:** *Business Enterprises; Dayton, Ohio; Digitron Tool Company, Inc.; Fernandez, Nestor.

FINANCING YOUR BUSINESS

4711 Research/development: books. HISPANIC BUSINESS, Vol. 4, no. 2 (February 1982), p. 28. English. **DESCR:** Book Reviews; Business; Business Enterprises; *Loffel, Egon W.; *National Hispanic Center for Advanced Studies and Policy Analysis (NHCAS); Public Policy; *THE STATE OF HISPANIC AMERICA.

Finley, Gordon E.

4712 Brink, T. L. Book review of: AVANCES EN PSICOLOGIA CONTEMPORANEA. HISPANIC JOURNAL OF BEHAVIORAL SCIENCES, Vol. 5, no. 4 (December 1983), p. 494-496. English. **DESCR:** *AVANCES EN PSICOLOGIA CONTEMPORANEA; Book Reviews; Marin, Gerardo; Psychology.

Firefighters

4713 Gonzalez, Juan. Arson wave threatens Puerto Ricans in inner cities. NUESTRO, Vol. 6, no. 7 (September 1982), p. 27-28. English. DESCR: *Criminal Acts; Hoboken, NJ; *Puerto Ricans.

Fisher, Dexter

4714 Hill, Patricia Liggins. Book review of: THE THIRD WOMAN: MINORITY WRITERS OF THE UNITED STATES. MELUS: MULTI-ETHNIC LITERATURE OF THE UNITED STATES, Vol. 7, no. 3 (Fall 1980), p. 87-89. English. DESCR: Book Reviews; THIRD WOMAN: MINORITY WOMEN WRITERS OF THE UNITED STATES; *Third World Literature (U.S.)

Flagellants and Flagellation
USE: Hermanos Penitentes

Flamenco

4715 Entertainment = diversion. CAMINOS, Vol. 3, no. 2 (February 1982), p. 40-41. English. DESCR: Awards; CHECKING IT OUT; Club Hogar Latino; Dance; Films; Marley, Bob; Montalban, Ricardo; ON GOLDEN POND; *Recreation; Television.

Fleishman-Hillard, Inc.

4716 Communications/marketing. HISPANIC BUSINESS, Vol. 5, no. 1 (January 1983), p. 23. English. DESCR: Banking Industry; Broadcast Media; Caballero Spanish Media, Inc. (CSM); *Marketing; Miami, FL; Nogales, Luis G.; Public Relations.

Fletcher & Valenti Architects/Planners, Inc.

4717 Fletcher and Valenti: Tampa's growing arquitectural firm. HISPANIC BUSINESS, Vol. 4, no. 10 (October 1982), p. 15,26. English. DESCR: *Architecture; Business Enterprises; Tampa, FL; Valenti, Frank S.

Flores, Arturo

4718 Newsfront. HISPANIC BUSINESS, Vol. 4, no. 4 (April 1982), p. 8, 24. English. DESCR: *Biographical Notes; Burgos, Elizabeth; *Businesspeople; Garcia, Carlos E.; Garcia, Edward T.; Guzman, Ralph C.; Hernandez, Richard; National Coalition of Hispanic Mental Health and Human Services Organizations (COSSMHO); Parra, Oscar C.; Willie, Herm M.

Flores, Bob

4719 Q & A: in the Hispanic community who are the winners and losers of Reaganomics? CAMINOS, Vol. 3, no. 3 (March 1982), p. 47. Bilingual. DESCR: Casado, Lucy; Echeveste, John; *Federal Government; Leon, Virginia; Mendoza, John; *Reagan, Ronald; Sanchez-Alvarez, Gloria; Vidal de Neri, Julieta.

Flores Buckhart, Elizabeth

4720 President Reagan's appointments. CAMINOS, Vol. 3, no. 3 (March 1982), p. 48-50. Bilingual. DESCR: Appointed Officials; *Federal Government; Garcia, Ernest E.; Gonzalez, Luis A.; Lozano, Diana; Pompa, Gilbert G.; Reagan, Ronald; Sanchez, Nestor D.; Zuniga, Henry.

Flores Fashions

4721 Flores, Fernando. Flores on fashion. LATINA, Vol. 1, no. 1 (1982), p. 39-41+. English. DESCR: *Fashion.

Flores, Francisco

4722 Padilla, Steve. Choosing a career. NUESTRO, Vol. 7, no. 1 (January, February, 1983), p. 13-19+. English. DESCR: Alvarado, Raul, Jr.; *Careers; Computers; Diaz, William; Engineering as a Profession; Esparza, Alma; Garcia, Linda; Medical Care; Soto, John; Yanez, Ricardo.

Flores, Jose

4723 Murray, Melissa and Flores, Jose. Bilingual success: a second language program that is making everyone happy (and smarter). NATIONAL HISPANIC JOURNAL, Vol. 2, no. 1 (Summer 1983), p. 14-19. English. DESCR: *Bilingual Bicultural Education; Education; Educational Innovations; Metz Elementary School, Austin TX.

Flores, Juan

4724 People. HISPANIC BUSINESS, Vol. 5, no. 5 (May 1983), p. 8. English. DESCR: Biographical Notes; *Businesspeople; Duron, Armando; Espinoza, Peter; Martinez, Vilma Socorro; Molina, Gloria; Moreno, Samuel; Pantin, Leslie, Sr.; Quezada, Sylvia; Quinones, Sergio.

Flores Magon, Ricardo

4725 Devis, Rey. Prisons can't contain freedom. CAMINOS, Vol. 4, no. 11 (December 1983), p. 22-23. English. DESCR: Prisoners; Prisons; Yuma Penitentiary.

Flores, Tom

4726 Alvarez, Amando. Tall and mighty proud. LATINO, Vol. 53, no. 6 (October 1982), p. 18+. English. DESCR: *Sports.

4727 Diaz, Katherine A. "And this year's winners are...". CAMINOS, Vol. 4, no. 1-2 (January, February, 1983), p. 39-54,74+. English. DESCR: *Awards; Castro, Tony; Elizalde, Hector; Martinez, Esperanza; Mendizabal, Maritza; Molina, Gloria; Moya, Connie; Placentia, Joe; Quesada, Leticia; Rios, David N.; Ybarra, Lea; Zapata, Carmen.

Folk Art

4728 Gonzalez, Alicia Maria. Murals: fine, popular, or folk art? AZTLAN, Vol. 13, no. 1-2 (Spring, Fall, 1982), p. 149-163. English. DESCR: Art; Art History; *Mural Art.

4729 Lenti, Paul. Accent: the Mexican retablo - a highly collectable folk art. NUESTRO, Vol. 7, no. 4 (May 1983), p. 63-64. English. DESCR: *Art History; *Mexico; *Religious Art.

4730 Plaza de la Raza to host project. NUESTRO, Vol. 7, no. 10 (December 1983), p. 11. English. DESCR: Arts and Crafts; Folklife Festival (Los Angeles, CA); Olympic Arts Festival, Los Angeles, CA; *Plaza de La Raza, Los Angeles, CA.

Folk Dancing
USE: Dance

Folk Drama

4731 Kanellos, Nicolas. The flourishing of Hispanic theater in the Southwest, 1920-30s. LATIN AMERICAN THEATRE REVIEW, Vol. 16, no. 1 (1982), p. 29-40. English. **DESCR:** History; Social History and Conditions; *Teatro.

Folk Healing
USE: Curanderismo

Folk Medicine

4732 Bose, Aruna; Vashistha, Krishan; and O'Loughlin, Bernard J. Azarcon por empacho - another cause of lead toxicity. PEDIATRICS, Vol. 72, no. 1 (July 1983), p. 106-108. English. **DESCR:** Children; *Lead Poisoning; Public Health.

4733 De la Carcela, Victor and Martinez, Iris Zavala. An analysis of culturalism in Latino mental health: folk medicine as a case in point. HISPANIC JOURNAL OF BEHAVIORAL SCIENCES, Vol. 5, no. 3 (September 1983), p. 251-274. English. **DESCR:** Culture.

4734 Folk remedy dangerous. NUESTRO, Vol. 7, no. 2 (March 1983), p. 7. English. **DESCR:** Federal Drug Administration (FDA); Medicine; Trotter, Robert.

4735 Gonzalez-Swafford, Maria J. and Gutierrez, Mary Grace. Ethno-medical beliefs and practices of Mexican-Americans. NURSE PRACTITIONER, Vol. 8, no. 10 (November, December, 1983), p. 29-30. English. **DESCR:** Curanderismo; Ethnic Attitudes.

4736 McKone, Jerry. Texas Spanish: not standard: but not bad. NATIONAL HISPANIC JOURNAL, Vol. 1, no. 4 (Spring 1983), p. 20-21. English. **DESCR:** Education; Mejias, Hugo A.; *Spanish Language.

4737 O'Brien, Mary Elizabeth. Reaching the migrant worker. AMERICAN JOURNAL OF NURSING, Vol. 83, no. 6 (June 1983), p. 895-897. English. **DESCR:** Agricultural Laborers; Medical Care; *Migrant Health Services.

4738 Richardson, Lynette. Caring through understanding, part II: folk medicine in the Hispanic population. IMPRINT, Vol. 29, no. 2 (April 1982), p. 21, 72-77. English. **DESCR:** Brujo; Caida de Mollera; Curanderas; Empacho; Mal de Ojo; Mal Puesto; Susto.

4739 Risse, Gunter B. Book review of: CAPITULOS DE HISTORIA MEDICA MEXICANA. BULLETIN OF THE HISTORY OF MEDICINE, Vol. 56, no. 4 (1982), p. 591-592. English. **DESCR:** *CAPITULOS DE HISTORIA MEDICA MEXICANA; Medicine; Mexico; Precolumbian Medicine; Somolinos D'Ardois, German.

4740 Roeder, Beatrice A. Health care beliefs and practices among the Mexican Americans. AZTLAN, Vol. 13, no. 1-2 (Spring, Fall, 1982), p. 223-256. English. **DESCR:** *Literature Reviews; Medical Care; Public Health.

4741 Trotter, Robert T. Susto: the context of community morbidity patterns. ETHNOLOGY, Vol. 21, no. 3 (July 1982), p. 215-226. English. **DESCR:** Medical Anthropology; *Susto.

4742 Vigil, Maria. Regional report, health: Tucson students study herbal arts. NUESTRO, Vol. 7, no. 5 (June, July, 1983), p. 12-13. English. **DESCR:** Herbal Medicine; *Tucson, AZ.

Folk Songs

4743 Gifford, Douglas. Book review of: HISPANIC FOLK MUSIC OF NEW MEXICO AND THE SOUTHWEST: A SELF-PORTRAIT OF A PEOPLE. BULLETIN OF HISPANIC STUDIES, Vol. 59, no. 2 (April 1982), p. 162-163. English. **DESCR:** Book Reviews; *HISPANIC FOLK MUSIC OF NEW MEXICO AND THE SOUTHWEST: A SELF-PORTRAIT OF A PEOPLE; New Mexico; Robb, John Donald.

4744 Herrera-Sobek, Maria. The treacherous woman archetype: a structuring agent in the corrido. AZTLAN, Vol. 13, no. 1-2 (Spring, Fall, 1982), p. 135-148. English. **DESCR:** Chicanas; *Corrido; Music.

4745 Loza, Steven J. Origins, form, and development of the Son Jarocho: Veracruz, Mexico. AZTLAN, Vol. 13, no. 1-2 (Spring, Fall, 1982), p. 257-274. English. **DESCR:** Dance; Music; *Son Jarocho; Veracruz, Mexico.

4746 Loza, Steven J. The Son Jarocho: the history, style and repertory of a changing Mexican musical tradition. AZTLAN, Vol. 13, no. 1-2 (Spring, Fall, 1982), p. 327-334. English. **DESCR:** Dance; Music; Sheehy, Daniel E.; *Son Jarocho; Veracruz, Mexico.

4747 Maciel, David R. Book review of: THE KENNEDY CORRIDOS: A STUDY OF THE BALLADS OF A MEXICAN AMERICAN HERO. AZTLAN, Vol. 13, no. 1-2 (Spring, Fall, 1982), p. 335-337. English. **DESCR:** Book Reviews; Corrido; Dickey, Dan William; *Kennedy, John Fitzgerald; Music.

4748 Paredes, Americo. Texas-Mexican cancionero: folk song of the lower (excerpts). SOUTHERN EXPOSURE, Vol. 10, no. 4 (July, August, 1982), p. 50-57. Bilingual. **DESCR:** *Corrido; Music.

4749 Pena, Manuel H. Folksong and social change: two corridos as interpretive sources. AZTLAN, Vol. 13, no. 1-2 (Spring, Fall, 1982), p. 12-42. English. **DESCR:** Corrido; Cortez, Gregorio; *DISCRIMINACION A UN MARTIR [corrido]; *EL CORRIDO DE GREGORIO CORTE [corrido]; Longoria, Felix; Music.

4750 Prof pushes for recognition of Chicano's music. VARIETY, Vol. 306, (March 10, 1982), p. 184. English. **DESCR:** Corrido; Reidel, Johannes.

4751 Sifuentes, Roberto. Aproximaciones al "Corrido de los Hermanos Hernandez ejecutados en la camara de gas de la penitenciaria de Florence, Arizona el dia 6 de julio de 1934". AZTLAN, Vol. 13, no. 1-2 (Spring, Fall, 1982), p. 95-109. Spanish. **DESCR:** Alonso, Epifanio; *Corrido; *CORRIDO DE LOS HERMANOS HERNANDEZ [song lyrics]; Hernandez, Federico; Hernandez, Manuel; Music; Musical Lyrics.

4752 Vincent, J. Book review of: HISPANIC FOLK MUSIC OF NEW MEXICO AND THE SOUTHWEST: A SELF-PORTRAIT OF A PEOPLE. ETHNOMUSICOLOGY, Vol. 26, no. 2 (May 1982), p. 326-327. English. **DESCR:** Book Reviews; Ethnomusicology; *HISPANIC FOLK MUSIC OF NEW MEXICO AND THE SOUTHWEST: A SELF-PORTRAIT OF A PEOPLE; New Mexico; Robb, John Donald; *THE SOUTHWEST: A SELF-PORTRAIT.

Folk Songs (cont.)

4753 West, John O. Book review of: HISPANIC FOLK
     MUSIC OF NEW MEXICO AND THE SOUTHWEST: A
     SELF-PORTRAIT OF A PEOPLE. JOURNAL OF
     AMERICAN FOLKLORE, Vol. 96, (April, May,
     1983), p. 239. English. **DESCR**: Book Reviews;
     *HISPANIC FOLK MUSIC OF NEW MEXICO AND THE
     SOUTHWEST: A SELF-PORTRAIT OF A PEOPLE;
     Robb, John Donald.

Folklife
     USE: Cultural Customs

Folklife Festival (Los Angeles, CA)

4754 Plaza de la Raza to host project. NUESTRO,
     Vol. 7, no. 10 (December 1983), p. 11.
     English. **DESCR**: Arts and Crafts; *Folk Art;
     Olympic Arts Festival, Los Angeles, CA;
     *Plaza de La Raza, Los Angeles, CA.

Folklore

4755 Arora, Shirley L. A critical bibliography of
     Mexican American proverbs. AZTLAN, Vol. 13,
     no. 1-2 (Spring, Fall, 1982), p. 71-80.
     English. **DESCR**: *Bibliography; Dichos.

4756 Chavez, John A. Aztlan, Cibola, and frontier
     New Spain. CAMPO LIBRE, Vol. 1, no. 2
     (Summer 1981), p. 193-211. English. **DESCR**:
     *Aztlan; *Explorations; History; Mestizaje;
     Mexico; Missions; Native Americans;
     Southwest United States.

4757 Davila, Luis. Meditaciones. REVISTA
     CHICANO-RIQUENA, Vol. 10, no. 1-2 (Winter,
     Spring, 1982), p. 275-278. Spanish. **DESCR**:
     Bilingualism; Cultural Customs; *Essays;
     Self-Referents.

4758 Hoffer, Bates L. Sociology by value systems:
     explication and some implications of two
     studies on the folklore of Hispanics in the
     United States. BILINGUAL REVIEW, Vol. 9, no.
     2 (May, August, 1982), p. 172-177.
     Bilingual. **DESCR**: BENJY LOPEZ: A PICARESQUE
     TALE OF EMIGRATION AND RETURN; Braceros;
     *Chicanos in American Literature;
     Comparative Literature; Herrera Sobek,
     Maria; Levine, Barry B.; THE BRACERO
     EXPERIENCE: ELITELORE VERSUS FOLKLORE.

4759 Leal, Luis. Los voladores: from ritual to
     game. NEW SCHOLAR, Vol. 8, no. 1-2 (Spring,
     Fall, 1982), p. 129-142. English. **DESCR**:
     *Dance.

4760 Limon, Jose. History, Chicano joking, and
     the varieties of higher-education: tradition
     and performance as critical symbolic action.
     JOURNAL OF THE FOLKLORE INSTITUTE, Vol. 19,
     no. 2-3 (1982), p. 146-166. English. **DESCR**:
     *Chistes; Higher Education; Humor;
     Interpersonal Relations; Texas; University
     of Texas at Austin.

4761 Melendez, Theresa. Coyote: towards a
     definition of a concept. AZTLAN, Vol. 13,
     no. 1-2 (Spring, Fall, 1982), p. 295-307.
     English. **DESCR**: *Coyote [folkloric symbol];
     Leyendas; Mitos.

4762 Paredes, Americo. Folklore, lo mexicano, and
     proverbs. AZTLAN, Vol. 13, no. 1-2 (Spring,
     Fall, 1982), p. 1-11. English. **DESCR**:
     Dichos; Identity.

4763 A time for reflection. NUESTRO, Vol. 7, no.
     9 (November 1983), p. 42-44. English.
     DESCR: Anaya, Rudolfo A.; Arias, Beatriz;
     Bilingual Bicultural Education; Computers;
     Financial Aid; Organizations; Prewitt Diaz,

Joseph (Jose); Villarreal, Sylvia; *W.K.
Kellogg Foundation National Fellowship
Program.

Folktales
     USE: Cuentos

Food
     USE: Recipes

Food for Survival, New York, NY

4764 Government review. NUESTRO, Vol. 7, no. 7
     (September 1983), p. 55. English. **DESCR**:
     AIDS Hotline; California; Education;
     Employment; Funding Sources; *Government
     Services; Hewlett Foundation; Laborers;
     Mathematics, Engineering and Science
     Achievement (MESA); Population Trends;
     Public Health; Stanford University,
     Stanford, CA.

Food Industry

4765 Business notes. HISPANIC BUSINESS, Vol. 5,
     no. 12 (December 1983), p. 35. English.
     DESCR: Anheuser-Busch, Inc.; *Business
     Enterprises; Denny's Inc.; Des Moines, IA;
     El Pollo Loco; Local Government; Martinez,
     Vilma Socorro; National Association of
     Latino Elected Officials (NALEO); Ochoa,
     Juan Pancho.

4766 Business update: West Coast food firm given
     special honors. NUESTRO, Vol. 7, no. 4 (May
     1983), p. 42. English. **DESCR**: Business
     Enterprises; *Ruiz Food Products, Inc.,
     Tulare, CA.

4767 Casey, G.M. Marketing to Mexican-Americans:
     just a bit of insight. ADVERTISING AGE
     MAGAZINE, Vol. 53, no. 11 (March 15, 1982),
     p. II, M34-35. English. **DESCR**: *Market
     Research; Southern California.

4768 Chavarria, Jesus. Hispanic food producers:
     the top ten. HISPANIC BUSINESS, Vol. 5, no.
     8 (August 1983), p. 6. English. **DESCR**:
     Jimenez Food Products, Inc.

4769 Grocery chains fight for San Antonio market.
     NUESTRO, Vol. 7, no. 2 (March 1983), p. 54.
     English. **DESCR**: Marketing; San Antonio, TX.

4770 Gupta, Udayan. Hispanic foods in New York:
     the race for number two. HISPANIC BUSINESS,
     Vol. 5, no. 8 (August 1983), p. 18-19+.
     English. **DESCR**: Condal Distributor, Inc.;
     Consumers; Goya Foods; Iberia Foods Corp.;
     La Cena Fine Foods, Ltd.; Recipes.

4771 Jensen, Joan M. Canning comes to New Mexico:
     women and the agricultural extension
     service, 1914-1919. NEW MEXICO HISTORICAL
     REVIEW, Vol. 57, no. 4 (October 1982), p.
     361-386. English. **DESCR**: *Cannery Workers;
     Chicanas; New Mexico; New Mexico
     Agricultural Extension Service.

4772 Langley, Roger. Roger Langley's Hispanic
     beat. HISPANIC BUSINESS, Vol. 4, no. 1
     (January 1982), p. 22. English. **DESCR**:
     Restaurants.

4773 Molina, Robert A. The Mexican food industry.
     CAMINOS, Vol. 4, no. 6 (June 1983), p.
     7-9,66. Bilingual.

4774 Ogaz, Armando. The chicken wars. CAMINOS,
     Vol. 4, no. 6 (June 1983), p. 10-11.
     Bilingual. **DESCR**: El Pollo Loco; Pioneer
     Chicken; *Restaurants.

Food Industry (cont.)

4775 Padilla, Steve. Adelina Pena Callahan: restaurateur. NUESTRO, Vol. 7, no. 4 (May 1983), p. 26-29. English. **DESCR:** Businesspeople; *Callahan, Adelina Pena; *Careers; La Fonda Restaurant; Working Women.

4776 Salazar, Pamela Eoff. Selling $25 million of Jimenez Food Products. HISPANIC BUSINESS, Vol. 4, no. 6 (June 1982), p. 20-21,24. English. **DESCR:** Business Enterprises; *Jimenez Food Products, Inc.; Recipes.

4777 Sullivan, Jim. The Puerto Rican powerhouse: Goya. CAMINOS, Vol. 4, no. 6 (June 1983), p. 12-13,66. Bilingual. **DESCR:** *Goya Foods.

4778 Unanue, Joseph F. The two Hispanic markets. HISPANIC BUSINESS, Vol. 5, no. 8 (August 1983), p. 8. English. **DESCR:** Consumers.

4779 Weber, Robert and Balkan, D. Carlos. Hispanic foods in Southern California: anatomy of a market in flux. HISPANIC BUSINESS, Vol. 5, no. 8 (August 1983), p. 24-25+. English. **DESCR:** Recipes.

4780 Wittenauer, Cheryl. The Maga Saga. HISPANIC BUSINESS, Vol. 5, no. 8 (August 1983), p. 14+. English. **DESCR:** Consumers; Mexican American Grocers Association (MAGA).

Food Practices

4781 Irizarry, Estelle. Frijoles boiling musically. LATINO, Vol. 54, no. 7 (November 1983), p. 27. English.

4782 Kerr, G. R. Supermarket sales high-sugar products in predominantly Black, Hispanic and white census tracts of Houston, Texas. AMERICAN JOURNAL OF CLINICAL NUTRITION, Vol. 37, no. 4 (April 1983), p. 622-631. English. **DESCR:** Anglo Americans; Blacks; *Nutrition; Surveys.

4783 Stern, Michael P. Knowledge, attitudes, and behavior related to obesity and dieting in Mexican-Americans and Anglos: the San Antonio heart study. AMERICAN JOURNAL OF EPIDEMIOLOGY, Vol. 115, no. 6 (June 1982), p. 917-928. English. **DESCR:** Anglo Americans; Attitude (Psychological); Obesity; San Antonio, TX; Weight Control.

Food Programs

4784 Community watching: para la comunidad. CAMINOS, Vol. 3, no. 1 (January 1982), p. 43-44. Bilingual. **DESCR:** Congreso Nacional Para Pueblos Unidos (CPU); *Financial Aid; *Journalists; National Association for Chicano Studies (NACS); *Radio; Summer Program for Minority Journalists; Zozaya, Julia S.

Food Stamps

4785 Food stamp cheaters. NUESTRO, Vol. 5, no. 8 (November 1981), p. 10. English. **DESCR:** Human Resources Administration; *Richmond, Frederick W.; *Welfare.

4786 Food stamp recovery. NUESTRO, Vol. 6, no. 10 (December 1982), p. 8. English. **DESCR:** Corpus Christi, TX; *Naturalization.

Foreign Policy
USE: International Relations

Foreign Trade

4787 Bell, Samuel E. and Smallwood, James M. Zona libre: trade and diplomacy on the Mexican border, 1858-1905. ARIZONA AND THE WEST, Vol. 24, no. 2 (Summer 1982), p. 119-152. English. **DESCR:** Border Region; International Relations; Mexico; United States History.

4788 Foreign trade. HISPANIC BUSINESS, Vol. 5, no. 3 (March 1983), p. 23. English. **DESCR:** Caribbean Region; Export Trade; Minority Business Development Agency (MBDA).

4789 Foreign trade. HISPANIC BUSINESS, Vol. 5, no. 4 (April 1983), p. 22. English. **DESCR:** Banking Industry; Brazil; *Electronics Industry; Export Trade; Ibero-American Chamber of Commerce; Miami, FL; Minority Bank Development Program (MBDP); Minority Export Development Consultants Program (MEDC); Peace Corps; Puerto Rico.

4790 Foreign trade. HISPANIC BUSINESS, Vol. 5, no. 5 (May 1983), p. 32. English. **DESCR:** Caribbean Region; Export Trade; Latin America; Minority Business Development Agency (MBDA); Panama.

4791 Foreign trade. HISPANIC BUSINESS, Vol. 5, no. 10 (October 1983), p. 29. English. **DESCR:** Agency for International Development (AID); Caribbean Region; Economic History and Conditions; HOW TO EXPORT: A MARKETING MANUAL; Mexico; Puerto Rico; U.S. Trade Center (Mexico City).

4792 Foreign trade. HISPANIC BUSINESS, Vol. 5, no. 11 (November 1983), p. 31. English. **DESCR:** California; HOW TO EXPORT: A MARKETING MANUAL; Marketing; Miami, FL; Miami Free Zone; Puerto Rico.

4793 Foreign trade: outlook for the Caribbean Basin Initiative. HISPANIC BUSINESS, Vol. 4, no. 8 (August 1983), p. 23+. English. **DESCR:** *Caribbean Basin Initiative (CBI); International Economic Relations; Latin America.

4794 Mexican business update. HISPANIC BUSINESS, Vol. 4, no. 1 (January 1982), p. 24. English. **DESCR:** Business; Export Trade; Mexico; *U.S.-Mexico Joint Commission on Commerce and Trade.

4795 Mexican market hints. HISPANIC BUSINESS, Vol. 4, no. 6 (June 1982), p. 25. English. **DESCR:** *Marketing; Mexico.

4796 People. HISPANIC BUSINESS, Vol. 4, no. 5 (May 1982), p. 8. English. **DESCR:** Appointed Officials; Asociacion Internacional de Exportadores e Importadores (EXIMA); *Biographical Notes; Businesspeople; California Chicano News Media Association (CCNMA); de la Ossa, Ernest G.; Obledo, Mario; Rodriguez, Elias C.; Rodriguez, Samuel F.; United Way; U.S. Hispanic Chamber of Commerce.

4797 Sanchez-Devanny, Jorge. Inseparable United States Mexico business relations. CAMINOS, Vol. 3, no. 6 (June 1982), p. 12-14. English. **DESCR:** Mexico; *United States-Mexico Relations.

4798 US-Mexican trade relations. HISPANIC BUSINESS, Vol. 4, no. 9 (September 1982), p. 23. English. **DESCR:** California; Export Trade; Mexico; United States-Mexico Relations.

Foreign Trade (cont.)

4799 Whitefield, Mimi. Miami, Caribbean megalopolis. HISPANIC BUSINESS, Vol. 4, no. 3 (March 1982), p. 18-19+. English. DESCR: Business; Dade County, FL; Miami, FL; *Urban Communities.

FORGOTTEN PEOPLE

4800 Schlossman, Steven. Self-evident remedy? George I. Sanchez, segregation, and enduring dilemmas in bilingual education. TEACHERS COLLEGE RECORD, Vol. 84, no. 4 (Summer 1983), p. 871-907. English. DESCR: *Bilingual Bicultural Education; Biography; Delgado v. Bastrop Independent School District of Bastrop Co., TX (1948); History; *Sanchez, George I.

Foro Nacional Puertorriqueno

4801 Bustelo, Manuel A. Una epoca del Foro Nacional Puertorriqueno. LATINO, Vol. 53, no. 2 (March, April, 1982), p. 15. Spanish. DESCR: Newspapers; Print Media.

Fort Guijanos

4802 Ezell, P. Research on Spanish colonial sites in San Diego. AMERICAN JOURNAL OF ARCHAEOLOGY, Vol. 86, no. 2 (April 1982), p. 263. English. DESCR: *Anthropology; San Diego, CA; San Diego Mission.

Fort Worth, Texas

4803 Demographic profile of Hispanics in the Dallas/Fort Worth SMSA. HISPANIC BUSINESS, Vol. 5, no. 2 (February 1983), p. 29-30. English. DESCR: *Consumers; Dallas, TX; Dallas/Ft. Worth SMSA; *Demography; Marketing.

4804 Hartenstein, Roslyn and Balkan, D. Carlos. Packaging the Dallas Hispanic consumer. HISPANIC BUSINESS, Vol. 5, no. 2 (February 1983), p. 18-19+. English. DESCR: *Consumers; Dallas, TX; *Marketing.

Forum of National Hispanic Organizations

4805 Latinas on the march, NUESTRO survey reveals: organizations assess achievements during 1981. NUESTRO, Vol. 6, no. 2 (March 1982), p. 16-28+. English. DESCR: Hispanic Health Council; Latin Americans; League of United Latin American Citizens (LULAC); National Coalition of Hispanic Mental Health and Human Services Organizations (COSSMHO); National Council of La Raza (NCLR); National Hispanic Bar Association; *National Image, Inc.; National Puerto Rican Forum, Inc.; *Organizations; Yzaguirre, Raul.

Foster Care

4806 Behind the scenes. LATINA, Vol. 1, no. 2 (February, March, 1983), p. 38. English.

4807 Gale, Kenneth. A home at last. LATINA, Vol. 1, no. 2 (February, March, 1983), p. 34-38. English.

4808 Perez, Ana M. Issues in Hispanic foster care: the Boston experience. JOURNAL OF LATIN COMMUNITY HEALTH, Vol. 1, no. 1 (Fall 1982), p. 81-88. English. DESCR: *Boston, MA.

Foundations

4809 Fundraising resources. CAMINOS, Vol. 4, no. 4 (April 1983), p. 58. English. DESCR: *Private Funding Sources.

4810 Philanthropy: Hispanic-corporate partnership. LATINO, Vol. 53, no. 5 (September 1982), p. 19. English. DESCR: Corporations; Funding Sources.

Fourteenth Amendment

USE: Constitutional Amendments - Fourteenth

Fourth Amendment

USE: Constitutional Amendments - Fourth

Fox, Geoffrey E.

4811 Brink, T. L. Book review of: WORKING-CLASS EMIGRES FROM CUBA. HISPANIC JOURNAL OF BEHAVIORAL SCIENCES, Vol. 5, no. 3 (September 1983), p. 363-365. English. DESCR: Book Reviews; Cubanos; Laborers; *WORKING CLASS EMIGRES FROM CUBA.

FRANCHISE OPPORTUNITIES HANDBOOK

4812 Business/negocios. CAMINOS, Vol. 3, no. 2 (February 1982), p. 22-23. Bilingual. DESCR: Argentina; Brazil; *Business; Chile; Colombia; Federation of Minority Business Associations; Latin America.

Franco Garcia, Freddie

4813 People. HISPANIC BUSINESS, Vol. 5, no. 9 (September 1983), p. 10. English. DESCR: *Businesspeople; Chavez, Chris; Diez de Onate, Jorge; Garcia, Hector P.; Lozano, Leticia Eugenia; Ravard, Rafael Alonzo; Rodriguez, Alberto Duque; Sanchez, Philip V.; Villalpando, Catalina.

Frank, Eleanor Marie

4814 Gomez, Dalia. Needed: Latino CPA's. NUESTRO, Vol. 6, no. 1 (January, February, 1982), p. 25-28. English. DESCR: *Accounting; Careers; Karpel, Miguel; Quezada, Felipe L.; Rodriguez, Julio H.; Umpierre, Raphael; Zuzueta, Joseph.

Frankfort, Ellen

4815 Torres, Sylvia. Book review of: ROSIE: THE INVESTIGATION OF A WRONGFUL DEATH. HISPANIC JOURNAL OF BEHAVIORAL SCIENCES, Vol. 4, no. 2 (June 1982), p. 279-280. English. DESCR: Book Reviews; Kissling, Frances; *ROSIE: THE INVESTIGATION OF A WRONGFUL DEATH.

Frazer, Robert W.

4816 Book review of: OVER THE CHIHUAHUA AND SANTA FE TRAILS, 1847-1848: GEORGE RUTLEDGE GIBSON'S JOURNAL. HISPANIC BUSINESS, Vol. 4, no. 8 (August 1983), p. 27. English. DESCR: Book Reviews; Gibson, George Rutledge; *OVER THE CHIHUAHUA AND SANTA FE TRAILS, 1847-1848.

Frederick S. Wright Art Gallery, University of California, Los Angeles

4817 A potpourri of pre-Columbian art. NUESTRO, Vol. 7, no. 6 (August 1983), p. 59-60. English. DESCR: CERAMIC TOMB SCULPTURE FROM ANCIENT WEST MEXICO; Ceramics; Exhibits; Museum of Cultural History, University of California, Los Angeles; *Precolumbian Art; Sculpture.

Freire, Paulo

4818 Miller, Robert. The Mexican approach to developing bilingual materials and teaching literacy to bilingual students. READING TEACHER, Vol. 35, no. 7 (April 1982), p. 800-804. English. **DESCR:** *Bilingual Bicultural Education; Curriculum Materials; Mexico.

French Language

4819 Beyer, Sandra S. and Kluck, Frederick J. French via Spanish: a positive approach to language learning for minority students. FOREIGN LANGUAGE ANNALS, Vol. 15, no. 2 (April 1982), p. 123-126. English. **DESCR:** Educational Innovations; Language Development; Spanish Language; University of Texas at El Paso.

Frequent Concerns of Student Teachers Survey

4820 Mahan, James M. and Miller, Shawn M. Concerns of Anglo secondary student teachers in Hispanic communities: a pilot study. ILLINOIS SCHOOL RESEARCH AND DEVELOPMENT, Vol. 19, no. 2 (Winter 1983), p. 28-34. English. **DESCR:** Comparative Education; Teacher Training.

Fresno, CA

4821 Silva, Vicente. Community supported radio bilingue: FM 91. CAMINOS, Vol. 3, no. 5 (May 1982), p. 46-48. Bilingual. **DESCR:** *KSJV, Fresno, CA [radio station]; Radio.

Fresno County Public Library, CA

4822 Naismith, Rachael. Field work: outreach to migrants. RQ - REFERENCE AND ADULT SERVICES DIVISION, Vol. 22, no. 1 (Fall 1982), p. 33-35. English. **DESCR:** Cumberland County Library, NJ; *Library Services; *Migrant Labor; Public Libraries.

4823 Naismith, Rachael. Moveable library: serving migrant farm workers. WILSON LIBRARY BULLETIN, Vol. 57, no. 7 (March 1983), p. 571-575. English. **DESCR:** *Dodge County Library System, WI; Library Services; Migrant Labor; Public Libraries.

Freud, Sigmund

4824 Satow, Robert. A severe case of penis envy: the convergence of cultural and individual intra-psychic factors. JOURNAL OF THE AMERICAN ACADEMY OF PSYCHOANALYSIS, Vol. 11, no. 4 (October 1983), p. 547-556. English. **DESCR:** *Psychotherapy; Puerto Ricans; Women.

Frias, Gustavo

4825 Life in a Mexican-American barrio: gangs alongside middle-class striving. WALL STREET JOURNAL, Vol. 199, no. 43 (June 9, 1982), p. 26. English. **DESCR:** East Los Angeles, CA; *Gangs; Social History and Conditions.

4826 Rodriguez, Roberto. Book review of: BARRIO WARRIORS HOMEBOYS OF PEACE. CORAZON DE AZTLAN, Vol. 1, no. 3 (August, September, 1982), p. 43. English. **DESCR:** *BARRIO WARRIORS: HOMEBOYS OF PEACE; Book Reviews.

4827 Straight, Susan. The homeboys. NUESTRO, Vol. 6, no. 6 (August 1982), p. 17-19. English. **DESCR:** Barrios; Racism; *Short Story.

FRIDA: A BIOGRAPHY OF FRIDA KAHLO

4828 Book review of: FRIDA: A BIOGRAPHY OF FRIDA KAHLO. BOOKLIST, Vol. 79, no. 11 (February 1, 1983), p. 708. English. **DESCR:** Artists; Biography; Book Reviews; Herrera, Hayden; Kahlo, Frida.

4829 Cameron, Dan. Book review of: FRIDA: A BIOGRAPHY OF FRIDA KAHLO. NUESTRO, Vol. 7, no. 8 (October 1983), p. 44-45. English. **DESCR:** Biography; Book Reviews; Herrera, Hayden; Kahlo, Frida.

4830 Lippard, Lucy R. Book review of: FRIDA: A BIOGRAPHY OF FRIDA KAHLO. NEW YORK TIMES BOOK REVIEW, Vol. 88, (April 24, 1983), p. 10+. English. **DESCR:** Book Reviews; Herrera, Hayden; Kahlo, Frida.

4831 Scott, Patricia. Book review of: FRIDA: A BIOGRAPHY OF FRIDA KAHLO. LIBRARY JOURNAL, Vol. 108, no. 2 (January 15, 1983), p. 125. English. **DESCR:** Artists; Biography; Book Reviews; Herrera, Hayden.

4832 Silber, Joan. Book review of: FRIDA: A BIOGRAPHY OF FRIDA KAHLO. MS. MAGAZINE, Vol. 11, no. 12 (June 1983), p. 40. English. **DESCR:** Book Reviews; Herrera, Hayden.

4833 Storr, Robert. Book review of: FRIDA: A BIOGRAPHY OF FRIDA KAHLO. ART IN AMERICA, Vol. 71, (April 1983), p. 19. English. **DESCR:** Artists; Book Reviews; Herrera, Hayden; Kahlo, Frida.

FRONTIERS: A JOURNAL OF WOMEN STUDIES, Vol. 5, no. 2(Summer 1980)

4834 Escobedo, Theresa Herrera. Book review of: CHICANAS IN THE NATIONAL LANDSCAPE. HISPANIC JOURNAL OF BEHAVIORAL SCIENCES, Vol. 4, no. 2 (June 1982), p. 263-267. English. **DESCR:** Book Reviews; *CHICANAS EN EL AMBIENTE NACIONAL/CHICANAS IN THE NATIONAL LANDSCAPE.

Frost, Elsa Cecilia

4835 Taylor, William B. Book review of: LABOR AND LABORERS THROUGH MEXICAN HISTORY. NEW MEXICO HISTORICAL REVIEW, Vol. 57, no. 1 (January 1982), p. 91-92. English. **DESCR:** Book Reviews; *EL TRABAJO Y LOS TRABAJADORES EN LA HISTORIA DE MEXICO = LABOR AND LABORERS THROUGH MEXICAN HISTORY; Laborers; Mexico.

Fuentes, Carlos

4836 Nieto, Eva Margarita. El problema de la juventud eterna en tres hechiceras en THE SECOND RING OF POWER, LA MULATA DE CORDOBA y AURA. LA PALABRA, Vol. 4, no. 1-2 (Spring, Fall, 1982, 1983), p. 81-91. Spanish. **DESCR:** AURA; Castaneda, Carlos; Gonzalez Obregon, Luis; LA MULATA DE CORDOBA; *Literary Criticism; Literature; Literature Reviews; THE SECOND RING OF POWER.

Fuentes, Thomas

4837 Thomas Fuentes: community builder. HISPANIC BUSINESS, Vol. 5, no. 11 (November 1983), p. 16-17. English. **DESCR:** Engineering as a Profession; Local Government; Orange County, CA; Urban Development.

Funding Sources

4838 Academic furlough for the working professional. HISPANIC BUSINESS, Vol. 4, no. 8 (August 1983), p. 15. English. **DESCR:** Arias, Beatriz; Financial Aid; Kellogg, W.K.; *W.K. Kellogg Foundation.

4839 Camayd-Freixas, Yohel. Hispanic mental health and the Omnibus Budget Reconciliation Act of 1981 (editorial board special report). JOURNAL OF LATIN COMMUNITY HEALTH, Vol. 1, no. 1 (Fall 1982), p. 5-24. English. **DESCR:** *Mental Health; *Omnibus Budget Reconciliation Act of 1981.

4840 Coca-Cola USA Today outlines Latino agenda. NUESTRO, Vol. 7, no. 9 (November 1983), p. 36. English. **DESCR:** Business; Coca-Cola Company; *Coca-Cola National Hispanic Education Fund; Education; *Financial Aid.

4841 Council donates $500 to national office. LATINO, Vol. 54, no. 8 (December 1983), p. 21. English.

4842 First race for scouts occurs in East L.A. NUESTRO, Vol. 6, no. 1 (January, February, 1982), p. 47. English. **DESCR:** *Godoy, Carlos Piloy; Los Angeles, CA; Palomino, Carlos.

4843 Government review. NUESTRO, Vol. 7, no. 7 (September 1983), p. 55. English. **DESCR:** AIDS Hotline; California; Education; Employment; Food for Survival, New York, NY; *Government Services; Hewlett Foundation; Laborers; Mathematics, Engineering and Science Achievement (MESA); Population Trends; Public Health; Stanford University, Stanford, CA.

4844 How have Hispanic organizations fared with the cutbacks: a survey. CAMINOS, Vol. 4, no. 4 (April 1983), p. 54-55. English. **DESCR:** Organizations.

4845 Midwest senator addresses NALEO. NUESTRO, Vol. 6, no. 9 (November 1982), p. 13. English. **DESCR:** Bumpers, Dale; *National Association of Latino Elected Officials (NALEO).

4846 Philanthropy: Hispanic-corporate partnership. LATINO, Vol. 53, no. 5 (September 1982), p. 19. English. **DESCR:** Corporations; *Foundations.

4847 Quinlivan, Robert. An evening with the stars '82. CAMINOS, Vol. 3, no. 9 (October 1982), p. 24-25. English. **DESCR:** Mexican and American Foundation; Organizations.

4848 Rugsaken, Kris T. Toward a true bilingual education: when federal funding ends. BILINGUAL JOURNAL, Vol. 7, no. 4 (Summer 1983), p. 9-14. English. **DESCR:** *Bilingual Bicultural Education; Bilingual Education Act of 1968; *Educational Law and Legislation; ELEMENTARY AND SECONDARY EDUCATION ACT.

4849 Saucedo, Concha. Chingaderas in mental health funding. CALMECAC, Vol. 1, (Summer 1980), p. 45-47. Bilingual. **DESCR:** *Mental Health.

4850 Stoddard, Ellwyn R. Multidisciplinary research funding: a "Catch 22" enigma. AMERICAN SOCIOLOGIST, Vol. 17, no. 4 (November 1982), p. 210-216. English. **DESCR:** *Border Studies.

4851 Taylor, Karla and Vargas, Raul. Entrevista/interview: Q: How to raise money for your Hispanic students? A: Involve your alumni and their corporate contacts. CASE CURRENTS, Vol. 9, no. 4 (April 1983), p. 18-21. English. **DESCR:** College Graduates; Higher Education; *Office for Mexican American Programs, University of Southern California; Vargas, Raul.

4852 Wittenauer, Cheryl. The economics of culture: L.A.'s most successful Plaza de la Raza. HISPANIC BUSINESS, Vol. 5, no. 1 (January 1983), p. 12-13+. English. **DESCR:** *Cultural Organizations; Plaza de La Raza, Los Angeles, CA; Ruben Salazar Bicentennial Building.

4853 Women aid global partners. LATINA, Vol. 1, no. 2 (February, March, 1983), p. 18. English. **DESCR:** *Overseas Education Fund.

Gabacho
USE: Anglo Americans

Gabaldon, Guy

4854 Weinberger, Caspar W. A heritage of valor - Hispanics in America's defense: remarks... at the recent unveiling of paintings of Hispanic heroes at the Pentagon. NUESTRO, Vol. 7, no. 9 (November 1983), p. 18. English. **DESCR:** Del Valle, Pedro A.; Lopez, Jose; *Military Service; Paintings; Rivero, Horacio.

Gadea, Gerardo

4855 Banberger, Ellen. Poesia nicaraguense. MAIZE, Vol. 5, no. 3-4 (Spring, Summer, 1982), p. 64-77. Spanish. **DESCR:** Belli, Gioconda; Cardenal, Ernesto; Carrillo, Ernesto; Coronel Urtecho, Jose; Gomez, Manuel; Murillo, Rosario; *Nicaragua; Ojeda, Mirna; *Poetry; Revolutions; Rugama, Leonel.

Gades, Antonio

4856 BLOOD WEDDING. NUESTRO, Vol. 5, no. 8 (November 1981), p. 50. English. **DESCR:** *Film Reviews; Lorca, Federico Garcia; *Saura, Carlos.

Gala Hispanic Theatre

4857 Whisler, Kirk. Exito - an East coast play for the whole nation. CAMINOS, Vol. 4, no. 6 (June 1983), p. 58,67. Bilingual. **DESCR:** *EXITO; Teatro.

Galarza, Ernesto

4858 Morris, Gabrielle and Beard, Timothy. Ernesto Galarza: early organizing efforts and the community. CAMINOS, Vol. 4, no. 7 (July, August, 1983), p. 18-21. Bilingual. **DESCR:** History.

GalaVision

4859 Communications/marketing. HISPANIC BUSINESS, Vol. 4, no. 2 (February 1982), p. 15. English. **DESCR:** Cable Television; Congressional Hispanic Caucus; El Teatro Campesino; Labor Unions; *Marketing; Philip Morris, Inc.; Publishing Industry; Spanish International Network (SIN).

Galindo, P. (Pseud. for Rolando Hinojosa-Smith)
USE: Hinojosa-Smith, Rolando R.

Gallego, Gina

4860 Gonzalez, Magdalena. Recognizing Hispanic
     achievements in entertainment - U.S. and
     Mexico. CAMINOS, Vol. 3, no. 7 (July,
     August, 1982), p. 18-24. Bilingual. **DESCR:**
     Allende, Fernando; Artists; Awards; Bonilla
     Giannini, Roxanna; Eynoso, David; Felix,
     Maria; Films; *Golden Eagle Awards; Hoyos,
     Rodolfo; Lamas, Lorenzo; Lopez, Conchita;
     Lopez, Lisa; Montalban, Ricardo; Nosotros
     [film production company]; Quintero, Jose;
     Rowe, Arthur; Television; Torres, Liz.

Gallegos, Amanda M.

4861 A career line. HISPANIC BUSINESS, Vol. 4,
     no. 11 (November 1982), p. 14-15. English.
     DESCR: Small Business; U.S. Small Business
     Administration.

Gallegos, Genevie

4862 Baltodano, J. C. Success. CAMINOS, Vol. 4,
     no. 6 (June 1983), p. 32,34+. English.
     DESCR: Colleges and Universities; Gutierrez,
     Jorge; Sotelo, Priscilla Elvira; *Students;
     Torres, Juan; University of California,
     Berkeley.

Gallegos, Gina

4863 Our 1982 Latino awards. NUESTRO, Vol. 7, no.
     1 (January, February, 1983), p. 44-46.
     English. **DESCR:** Awards; Escalante, Jaime;
     Grace, J. Peter; Immigration and
     Naturalization Service (INS); Knight, Bobby;
     Lamas, Fernando; *Latino Awards; Luce,
     Claire Boothe; Moreno, Rita; National Press
     Foundation; Rodriguez Hernandez, Andres;
     Simpson-Mazzoli Bill; Smith, Raymond;
     Valeri, Michele; Voting Rights Act.

Gallegos, Tony E.

4864 Second Latino assumes new duties at EEOC.
     NUESTRO, Vol. 6, no. 4 (May 1982), p. 27.
     English. **DESCR:** Appointed Officials; Equal
     Employment Opportunity Commission (EEOC).

Galleries, Chicano

4865 La Nueva Raza Bookstore y Galeria. CAMINOS,
     Vol. 2, no. 6 (October 1981), p. 23.
     English. **DESCR:** *La Nueva Raza Bookstore y
     Galeria, Sacramento, CA.

Gallo, Juana

4866 Mercado, Olivia. Chicanas: myths and roles.
     COMADRE, no. 1 (Summer 1977), p. 26-32.
     English. **DESCR:** *Chicanas; Huerta, Dolores;
     *Identity; Leadership; Sex Roles; Women's
     Rights.

Gallup Coal Strike of 1933

4867 Rubenstein, Harry R. The great Gallup Coal
     strike of 1933. SOUTHWEST ECONOMY AND
     SOCIETY, Vol. 3, no. 2 (Winter 1977, 1978),
     p. 34-53. English. **DESCR:** Labor Unions;
     Mining Industry; National Miner's Union
     (NMU); New Mexico; *Strikes and Lockouts;
     United Mineworkers of America (UMWA).

Games

4868 Games helps study effort. NUESTRO, Vol. 6,
     no. 4 (May 1982), p. 11-12. English. **DESCR:**
     Language Development; Language Proficiency.

Gandhi, Mahatma

4869 Ramos, Alfonso Pena. Voices: Gandhi: the
     Mahatma's message to Hispanics. NUESTRO,
     Vol. 7, no. 4 (May 1983), p. 59-60. English.
     DESCR: *Ethnic Groups; *Identity;
     *Philosophy; Welfare.

Gangs

4870 Harowitz, Ruth. Adult delinquent gangs in a
     Chicano community: masked intimacy and
     marginality. URBAN LIFE, Vol. 11, no. 1
     (April 1982), p. 3-26. English. **DESCR:**
     Identity; Lions, 32nd Street.

4871 Hunsaker, Alan. A prompt/reward technique to
     elicit socially acceptable behavior with
     Chicano gang delinquents. HISPANIC JOURNAL
     OF BEHAVIORAL SCIENCES, Vol. 5, no. 1 (March
     1983), p. 105-113. English. **DESCR:** Behavior
     Modification; Juvenile Delinquency;
     Socialization.

4872 Life in a Mexican-American barrio: gangs
     alongside middle-class striving. WALL STREET
     JOURNAL, Vol. 199, no. 43 (June 9, 1982), p.
     26. English. **DESCR:** East Los Angeles, CA;
     Frias, Gustavo; Social History and
     Conditions.

4873 Vigil, James Diego. Human revitalization:
     the six tasks of victory outreach. DREW
     GATEWAY, Vol. 52, no. 3 (Spring 1982), p.
     49-59. English. **DESCR:** Barrios for Christ
     Program; Drug Addicts; Drug Programs;
     Identity; Pentecostal Church; Protestant
     Church; Religion; *Victory Outreach; Youth.

Gannett Co., Inc.

4874 Gannett's Gerald Garcia goes to Tucson.
     HISPANIC BUSINESS, Vol. 4, no. 5 (May 1982),
     p. 13. English. **DESCR:** *Biography; Garcia,
     Gerald; Newspapers; Tucson, AZ.

4875 Uehling, Mark D. Rivalry in New York: a
     profile of two newspapers. NUESTRO, Vol. 7,
     no. 7 (September 1983), p. 20-21. English.
     DESCR: Bustelo, Manuel A.; DIARIO LA PRENSA
     [newspaper], New York, NY; Espinal, Antonio;
     Journalism; New York, NY; *Newspapers;
     NOTICIAS DEL MUNDO; Patino, Luis;
     Unification Church.

Gaos, Jose

4876 Uranga, Emilio. Notas para un estudio del
     mexicano. CAMPO LIBRE, Vol. 1, no. 2 (Summer
     1981), p. 283-295. Spanish. **DESCR:** Cultural
     Characteristics; Identity; Mexico;
     Philosophy; *Ramos, Samuel.

Garamendi, John

4877 Whisler, Kirk. State Senator John Garamendi.
     CAMINOS, Vol. 3, no. 5 (May 1982), p. 17-19.
     Bilingual. **DESCR:** Elected Officials.

Garcia, Carlos

4878 Research/development: books. HISPANIC
     BUSINESS, Vol. 5, no. 4 (April 1983), p. 28.
     English. **DESCR:** Biographical Notes; *Book
     Reviews; *"DO IT MY WAY OR YOU'RE FIRED!":
     EMPLOYEE RIGHTS AND THE CHANGING ROLE OF
     MANAGEMENT PREROGATIVES; Ewing, David W.;
     Garcia, Edward; Industrial Relations;
     Science; *SCIENCE OF THE SPANISH SPEAKING
     PEOPLE.

Garcia, Carlos E.

4879 Newsfront. HISPANIC BUSINESS, Vol. 4, no. 4 (April 1982), p. 8, 24. English. DESCR: *Biographical Notes; Burgos, Elizabeth; *Businesspeople; Flores, Arturo; Garcia, Edward T.; Guzman, Ralph C.; Hernandez, Richard; National Coalition of Hispanic Mental Health and Human Services Organizations (COSSMHO); Parra, Oscar C.; Willie, Herm M.

Garcia, Damaso

4880 Ortiz, Carlos V. NUESTRO'S sixth annual all-star baseball team. NUESTRO, Vol. 7, no. 2 (March 1983), p. 33-37. English. DESCR: Andujar, Joaquin; Barojas, Salome; *Baseball; Castillo, Manny; Concepcion, Dave; Cruz, Jose; Guerrero, Pedro; Hernandez, Keith; Lezcano, Sixto; Martinez, Tippy; Pena, Tony; Piniella, Lou; Sports; Valenzuela, Fernando.

Garcia, Edward

4881 Research/development: books. HISPANIC BUSINESS, Vol. 5, no. 4 (April 1983), p. 28. English. DESCR: Biographical Notes; *Book Reviews; *"DO IT MY WAY OR YOU'RE FIRED!": EMPLOYEE RIGHTS AND THE CHANGING ROLE OF MANAGEMENT PREROGATIVES; Ewing, David W.; Garcia, Carlos; Industrial Relations; Science; *SCIENCE OF THE SPANISH SPEAKING PEOPLE.

Garcia, Edward T.

4882 Newsfront. HISPANIC BUSINESS, Vol. 4, no. 4 (April 1982), p. 8, 24. English. DESCR: *Biographical Notes; Burgos, Elizabeth; *Businesspeople; Flores, Arturo; Garcia, Carlos E.; Guzman, Ralph C.; Hernandez, Richard; National Coalition of Hispanic Mental Health and Human Services Organizations (COSSMHO); Parra, Oscar C.; Willie, Herm M.

Garcia, Ernest E.

4883 President Reagan's appointments. CAMINOS, Vol. 3, no. 3 (March 1982), p. 48-50. Bilingual. DESCR: Appointed Officials; *Federal Government; Flores Buckhart, Elizabeth; Gonzalez, Luis A.; Lozano, Diana; Pompa, Gilbert G.; Reagan, Ronald; Sanchez, Nestor D.; Zuniga, Henry.

Garcia, Eugene E.

4884 Wagatsuma, Yuria. Book review of: EARLY CHILDHOOD BILINGUALISM: WITH SPECIAL REFERENCE TO THE MEXICAN-AMERICAN CHILD. HISPANIC JOURNAL OF BEHAVIORAL SCIENCES, Vol. 5, no. 4 (December 1983), p. 477-481. English. DESCR: Bilingualism; Book Reviews; *EARLY CHILDHOOD BILINGUALISM: WITH SPECIAL REFERENCE TO THE MEXICAN-AMERICAN CHILD.

Garcia, Frances

4885 People. HISPANIC BUSINESS, Vol. 4, no. 12 (December 1982), p. 10. English. DESCR: *Biographical Notes; *Businesspeople; Gort, Wilfredo; Ojeda, Armando; Olind, Rebecca Nieto; Philip Morris, Inc.; Roybal, Edward R.

Garcia, Gerald

4886 Gannett's Gerald Garcia goes to Tucson. HISPANIC BUSINESS, Vol. 4, no. 5 (May 1982), p. 13. English. DESCR: *Biography; Gannett Co., Inc.; Newspapers; Tucson, AZ.

4887 Gonzales, Patrisia. The two cities of Tucson. NUESTRO, Vol. 7, no. 4 (May 1983), p. 20-23. English. DESCR: Accion 80s; Cultural Organizations; *Discrimination in Education; *Discrimination in Employment; Lopez-Grant, Lillian; *Tucson, AZ; Valdez, Joel.

Garcia, Gloria

4888 Newsfront. HISPANIC BUSINESS, Vol. 4, no. 3 (March 1982), p. 9. English. DESCR: Appointed Officials; *Biographical Notes; Businesspeople; Chicano Film Exhibition and Festival, Detroit, Michigan, April 5-9, 1982; League of United Latin American Citizens (LULAC); Martinez, Vilma Socorro; National Association for Bilingual Education; Seaga, Edward; Suarez, Carlos R.

Garcia, Gus

4889 Gus Garcia Foundation. LATINO, Vol. 54, no. 4 (May, June, 1983), p. 29. English. DESCR: Calderon, Tony; *Films; Financial Aid.

Garcia, Hector

4890 Election change sought by Garcia. NUESTRO, Vol. 6, no. 10 (December 1982), p. 9-10. English. DESCR: *Corpus Christi, TX; Government; *Urban Communities.

Garcia, Hector P.

4891 People. HISPANIC BUSINESS, Vol. 5, no. 9 (September 1983), p. 10. English. DESCR: *Businesspeople; Chavez, Chris; Diez de Onate, Jorge; Franco Garcia, Freddie; Lozano, Leticia Eugenia; Ravard, Rafael Alonzo; Rodriguez, Alberto Duque; Sanchez, Philip V.; Villalpando, Catalina.

Garcia, Jose Joel

4892 People on the move. CAMINOS, Vol. 2, no. 6 (October 1981), p. 7. English. DESCR: Alvarado, Angel S.; Arreola, Rafael; *Biographical Notes; Diaz, Elisa; Diaz, Elvira A.; Garza, Florentino; Icaza, Ricardo F.; Lacayo, Henry; Martinez, Lydia R.; Munoz, Victor M.; Salinas, Vicente; Sanchez, Manuel; Zuniga, Henry.

Garcia, Juan Ramon

4893 Cardoso, Lawrence Anthony. "Wetbacks" and "slaves": recent additions to the literature. JOURNAL OF AMERICAN ETHNIC HISTORY, Vol. 1, no. 2 (Spring 1982), p. 68-71. English. DESCR: Book Reviews; Lewis, Sasha G.; *OPERATION WETBACK: THE MASS DEPORTATION OF MEXICAN UNDOCUMENTED WORKERS IN 1954; *SLAVE TRADE TODAY: AMERICAN EXPLOITATION OF ILLEGAL ALIENS; Undocumented Workers.

4894 Kelly, Philip. Book review of: OPERATION WETBACK: THE MASS DEPORTATION OF MEXICAN UNDOCUMENTED WORKERS IN 1954. SOCIAL SCIENCE JOURNAL, Vol. 19, no. 2 (April 1982), p. 133-134. English. DESCR: Book Reviews; *OPERATION WETBACK: THE MASS DEPORTATION OF MEXICAN UNDOCUMENTED WORKERS IN 1954; Undocumented Workers.

Garcia, Juan Ramon (cont.)

4895 Martinez, Oscar J. Book review of: OPERATION WETBACK: THE MASS DEPORTATION OF MEXICAN UNDOCUMENTED WORKERS IN 1954. NEW MEXICO HISTORICAL REVIEW, Vol. 57, no. 2 (April 1982), p. 201-202. English. **DESCR:** Book Reviews; *OPERATION WETBACK: THE MASS DEPORTATION OF MEXICAN UNDOCUMENTED WORKERS IN 1954; Undocumented Workers.

4896 Meier, Matt S. Book review of: MEXICAN IMMIGRANT WORKERS IN THE UNITED STATES and OPERATION WETBACK: THE MASS DEPORTATION OF MEXICAN UNDOCUMENTED WORKERS IN 1954. PACIFIC HISTORICAL REVIEW, Vol. 52, no. 1 (February 1983), p. 126-128. English. **DESCR:** Book Reviews; *MEXICAN IMMIGRANT WORKERS IN THE U.S.; *Operation Wetback; Rios-Bustamante, Antonio.

4897 Olson, James S. Book review of: OPERATION WETBACK: THE MASS DEPORTATION OF MEXICAN UNDOCUMENTED WORKERS IN 1954. JOURNAL OF THE WEST, Vol. 22, no. 1 (1983), p. 80-81. English. **DESCR:** Agricultural Laborers; Book Reviews; Braceros; *OPERATION WETBACK: THE MASS DEPORTATION OF MEXICAN UNDOCUMENTED WORKERS IN 1954; Undocumented Workers.

4898 Ramirez, Nora E. Book review of: OPERATION WETBACK: THE MASS DEPORTATION OF MEXICAN UNDOCUMENTED WORKERS IN 1954. WESTERN HISTORICAL QUARTERLY, Vol. 13, no. 2 (April 1982), p. 198. English. **DESCR:** Book Reviews; *OPERATION WETBACK: THE MASS DEPORTATION OF MEXICAN UNDOCUMENTED WORKERS IN 1954.

Garcia, Linda

4899 Padilla, Steve. Choosing a career. NUESTRO, Vol. 7, no. 1 (January, February, 1983), p. 13-19+. English. **DESCR:** Alvarado, Raul, Jr.; *Careers; Computers; Diaz, William; Engineering as a Profession; Esparza, Alma; Flores, Francisco; Medical Care; Soto, John; Yanez, Ricardo.

Garcia, Mario T.

4900 Cardoso, Lawrence Anthony. Book review of: DESERT IMMIGRANTS: THE MEXICANS OF EL PASO 1880-1920. WESTERN HISTORICAL QUARTERLY, Vol. 13, (April 1982), p. 197. English. **DESCR:** Book Reviews; *DESERT IMMIGRANTS: THE MEXICANS OF EL PASO 1880-1920.

4901 Cortes, Carlos E. Book review of: DESERT IMMIGRANTS: THE MEXICANS OF EL PASO 1880-1920. PACIFIC HISTORICAL REVIEW, Vol. 52, no. 1 (February 1983), p. 119-120. English. **DESCR:** Book Reviews; *DESERT IMMIGRANTS: THE MEXICANS OF EL PASO 1880-1920.

4902 Corwin, Arthur F. Book review of: DESERT IMMIGRANTS: THE MEXICANS OF EL PASO 1880-1920. HISTORIAN, Vol. 45, no. 2 (February 1983), p. 279-280. English. **DESCR:** Book Reviews; *DESERT IMMIGRANTS: THE MEXICANS OF EL PASO 1880-1920.

4903 Knight, Alan. Book review of: THE GREAT REBELLION: MEXICO 1905-1924 and DESERT IMMIGRANTS: THE MEXICANS OF EL PASO 1880-1920. HISTORY: THE JOURNAL OF THE HISTORICAL ASSOCIATION [London], Vol. 67, (October 1982), p. 450-451. English. **DESCR:** Book Reviews; *DESERT IMMIGRANTS: THE MEXICANS OF EL PASO 1880-1920; Ruiz, Ramon Eduardo; *THE GREAT REBELLION: MEXICO 1905-1924.

4904 Lotchin, Roger W. New Chicano history: an

urban history perspective. HISTORY TEACHER, Vol. 16, no. 2 (February 1983), p. 229-247. English. **DESCR:** Camarillo, Alberto; CHICANOS IN A CHANGING SOCIETY; DESERT IMMIGRANTS: THE MEXICANS OF EL PASO 1880-1920; Griswold del Castillo, Ricardo; *Historiography; History; Social History and Conditions; THE LOS ANGELES BARRIO 1850-1890: A SOCIAL HISTORY; Urban Communities.

4905 Martinez, Oscar J. Book review of: DESERT IMMIGRANTS: THE MEXICANS OF EL PASO 1880-1920. HISPANIC AMERICAN HISTORICAL REVIEW, Vol. 62, no. 2 (May 1982), p. 289-291. English. **DESCR:** Book Reviews; *DESERT IMMIGRANTS: THE MEXICANS OF EL PASO 1880-1920; El Paso, TX; Immigration.

4906 Reisler, Mark. Book review of: DESERT IMMIGRANTS: THE MEXICANS OF EL PASO 1880-1920. AMERICAN HISTORICAL REVIEW, Vol. 87, no. 1 (February 1982), p. 271-272. English. **DESCR:** Book Reviews; *DESERT IMMIGRANTS: THE MEXICANS OF EL PASO 1880-1920; El Paso, TX; History; Immigration.

4907 Rosales, Francisco Arturo. Book review of: DESERT IMMIGRANTS: THE MEXICANS OF EL PASO 1880-1920. ARIZONA AND THE WEST, Vol. 24, no. 1 (Spring 1982), p. 79-80. English. **DESCR:** Book Reviews; *DESERT IMMIGRANTS: THE MEXICANS OF EL PASO 1880-1920; Immigrants; Texas.

4908 Sunseri, Alvin R. Book review of: DESERT IMMIGRANTS: THE MEXICANS OF EL PASO 1880-1920. JOURNAL OF THE WEST, Vol. 21, no. 2 (April 1982), p. 111. English. **DESCR:** Book Reviews; *DESERT IMMIGRANTS: THE MEXICANS OF EL PASO 1880-1920; Immigration.

4909 Vigil, Ralph H. Book review of: DESERT IMMIGRANTS: THE MEXICANS OF EL PASO 1880-1920. INTERNATIONAL MIGRATION REVIEW, Vol. 16, no. 1 (Spring 1982), p. 223-224. English. **DESCR:** Book Reviews; *DESERT IMMIGRANTS: THE MEXICANS OF EL PASO 1880-1920; El Paso, TX; History; Immigrants.

4910 Weber, David J. and Lotchin, Roger W. The new Chicano history: two perspectives. HISTORY TEACHER, Vol. 16, no. 2 (February 1983), p. 219-247. English. **DESCR:** Camarillo, Alberto; *CHICANOS IN A CHANGING SOCIETY; DESERT IMMIGRANTS: THE MEXICANS OF EL PASO 1880-1920; Griswold del Castillo, Ricardo; *Historiography; History; Social History and Conditions; *THE LOS ANGELES BARRIO 1850-1890: A SOCIAL HISTORY; *Urban Communities.

4911 Weber, David J. The new Chicano urban history. HISTORY TEACHER, Vol. 16, no. 2 (February 1983), p. 223-229. English. **DESCR:** Camarillo, Alberto; *CHICANOS IN A CHANGING SOCIETY; DESERT IMMIGRANTS: THE MEXICANS OF EL PASO 1880-1920; Griswold del Castillo, Ricardo; *Historiography; History; Social History and Conditions; *THE LOS ANGELES BARRIO 1850-1890: A SOCIAL HISTORY; Urban Communities.

Garcia, Marlene

4912 People. HISPANIC BUSINESS, Vol. 5, no. 7 (July 1983), p. 8. English. **DESCR:** Alvarado, Anthony J.; Appointed Officials; *Biographical Notes; Businesspeople; Candela, Hilario; Gonzalez, Julio; Martinez, Tony; Pla, George; Valdez, Abelardo L.

Garcia Marquez, Gabriel

4913 100 years of solitude. LATINO, Vol. 53, no. 4 (June 1982), p. 27. English. DESCR: Authors; *CIEN ANOS DE SOLEDAD.

4914 Berg, Charles. Book review of: CHRONIQUE OF A DEATH FORETOLD. NUESTRO, Vol. 7, no. 4 (May 1983), p. 62. English. DESCR: *Book Reviews; CHRONICLE OF A DEATH FORETOLD; *Criminal Acts; *Death (Concept).

4915 Espinoza, Roberto. Sintesis vs. analysis: un problema de historicidad en las novelas de las dictaduras. MAIZE, Vol. 6, no. 1-2 (Fall, Winter, 1982, 1983), p. 7-27. Spanish. DESCR: Carpentier, Alejo; Dictatorships; Latin American Literature; *Literary Criticism; Novel; Roa Bastos, Augustos; Valle Inclan, Ramon; White, Lucas Edward.

4916 Hispanics win Nobel Prizes. LATINO, Vol. 53, no. 8 (December 1982), p. 20-21. English. DESCR: Authors; *Nobel Prize.

4917 Monleon, Jose. Historia de una contradiccion. MAIZE, Vol. 3, no. 3-4 (Spring, Summer, 1980), p. 17-22. Spanish. DESCR: *CIEN ANOS DE SOLEDAD; Literary Criticism.

4918 Nobel prize recipient Marquez. LATINA, Vol. 1, no. 2 (February, March, 1983), p. 20. English. DESCR: *Awards; *Nobel Prize.

Garcia, Marti

4919 Communications/marketing. HISPANIC BUSINESS, Vol. 5, no. 4 (April 1983), p. 23. English. DESCR: Faultless Starch/Bon Ami Company; *Marketing; Mejias, Hugo A.; Pan American University, Edinburg, TX; Spanish Language.

Garcia, Mary

4920 Math-based careers. HISPANIC BUSINESS, Vol. 5, no. 9 (September 1983), p. 28. English. DESCR: Andrew W. Mellon Foundation; *Careers; Employment; Engineering as a Profession; Financial Aid; Higher Education; National Council for Minorities in Engineering (NACME); National Medical Fellowships (NMF); Rivera, Lourdes.

Garcia, Matt

4921 Avila, Joaquin G. Remembering Matt Garcia. LATINO, Vol. 54, no. 8 (December 1983), p. 29. English. DESCR: Biography.

Garcia, Robert

4922 Caucus highlights. NUESTRO, Vol. 6, no. 7 (September 1982), p. 43. English. DESCR: *Congressional Hispanic Caucus; Elected Officials.

4923 N.A.L.E.O.'s "Fiesta '83". CAMINOS, Vol. 4, no. 10 (November 1983), p. 28-29. English. DESCR: Baca Barragan, Polly; Bilingual Bicultural Education; Central America; Fiesta '83; Immigration; International Relations; Mendez, Olga; *National Association of Latino Elected Officials (NALEO); Simpson-Mazzoli Bill; United States-Mexico Relations.

4924 Padilla, Steve. Latinos wield political clout in midterm election. NUESTRO, Vol. 6, no. 9 (November 1982), p. 28-30. English. DESCR: De la Garza, Kika; *Elected Officials; Gonzales, Henry B.; Lujan, Manuel, Jr.; Martinez, Matthew G. "Marty",

Assemblyman; Ortiz, Solomon; *Politics; Richardson, William; Roybal, Edward R.; *Torres, Esteban E.

4925 Solon opposes military support for Guatemala. NUESTRO, Vol. 6, no. 5 (June, July, 1982), p. 53. English. DESCR: Government; *Guatemala; *Military.

4926 Whisler, Kirk. Robert Garcia: the mover in the Congressional Hispanic Caucus. CAMINOS, Vol. 3, no. 7 (July, August, 1982), p. 36-37,44. Bilingual. DESCR: Congressional Hispanic Caucus; Elected Officials; Federal Government.

Garcia, Ruben

4927 People. HISPANIC BUSINESS, Vol. 5, no. 11 (November 1983), p. 10. English. DESCR: Aragon, Fermin; *Businesspeople; De Los Reyes, Victor; Di Martino, Rita; Juarez, Chris; Lopez, Leonard; Nogales, Luis G.; Ozuna, Bob; Rico, Jose Hipolito; Tamayo, Roberto; Tapia, Raul R.

Garcia-Loya, Manuel

4928 Brasch, Walter M. Hanigan case: hung up on racism? SOUTH ATLANTIC QUARTERLY, Vol. 81, no. 4 (Fall 1982), p. 429-435. English. DESCR: Administration of Justice; Arizona; Criminal Justice System; *Hanigan, Patrick; Hanigan, Tom; Herrera-Mata, Bernabe; *Laws; Racism; Ruelas-Zavala, Eleazar; Undocumented Workers.

Garcia-Moya, Rodolfo

4929 Dyer, Nancy Joe. Book review of: TEACHING SPANISH TO THE HISPANIC BILINGUAL: ISSUES, AIMS AND METHODS. HISPANIA, Vol. 65, no. 3 (September 1982), p. 474-475. English. DESCR: Book Reviews; Lozano, Anthony G.; Spanish Language; *TEACHING SPANISH TO THE HISPANIC BILINGUAL: ISSUES, AIMS AND METHODS; Valdez, Guadalupe.

4930 Goldin, Mark G. Book review of: TEACHING SPANISH TO THE HISPANIC BILINGUAL: ISSUES, AIMS AND METHODS. NABE JOURNAL, Vol. 7, no. 1 (Fall 1982), p. 53-56. English. DESCR: Bilingualism; Book Reviews; Language Proficiency; Language Usage; Lozano, Anthony G.; Spanish Language; *TEACHING SPANISH TO THE HISPANIC BILINGUAL: ISSUES, AIMS AND METHODS; Valdez, Guadalupe.

4931 Gutierrez, John R. Book review of: TEACHING SPANISH TO THE HISPANIC BILINGUAL: ISSUES, AIMS AND METHODS. MODERN LANGUAGE JOURNAL, Vol. 66, no. 2 (Summer 1982), p. 234. English. DESCR: Bilingualism; Book Reviews; Lozano, Anthony G.; Spanish Language; *TEACHING SPANISH TO THE HISPANIC BILINGUAL: ISSUES, AIMS AND METHODS; Valdez, Guadalupe.

Garcia-Pedrosa, Jose R.

4932 People. HISPANIC BUSINESS, Vol. 4, no. 11 (November 1982), p. 7. English. DESCR: Biographical Notes; *Businesspeople; Diaz, Jose; Garza, Jose; Herrera, Heriberto; Mercado, Anthony; Rios, John F.; Solano, Faustina V.; Solis, Frank.

Garment Industry

4933 Business notes. HISPANIC BUSINESS, Vol. 5, no. 11 (November 1983), p. 27. English. DESCR: *Business Enterprises; High Tech '84; Personnel Management; Puerto Rico; Taxation; U.S. Department of Housing and Urban Development (HUD).

4934 Jaech, Richard E. Latin American undocumented women in the United States. CURRENTS IN THEOLOGY AND MISSION, Vol. 9, no. 4 (August 1982), p. 196-211. English. DESCR: Latin Americans; Protestant Church; Socioeconomic Factors; *Undocumented Workers; *Women.

4935 Mendez Gonzalez, Rosalinda. Mexican women and families: rural-to-urban and international migration. SOUTHWEST ECONOMY AND SOCIETY, Vol. 4, no. 2 (Winter 1978, 1979), p. 14-27. English. DESCR: Chicanas; Employment; *Family; Immigration; International Ladies Garment Workers Union (ILGWU); Labor Organizing; Los Angeles, CA; Undocumented Workers.

Garment Workers
USE: Industrial Workers

Garreau, Joel

4936 Castagnera-Cain, Jim. Garreau's nine nations offer immigation insights. TEXAS OBSERVOR, Vol. 74, (October 15, 1982), p. 12+. English. DESCR: Immigration Law; Immigration Regulation and Control; *THE NINE NATIONS OF NORTH AMERICA; Undocumented Workers.

Garza, Florentino

4937 People on the move. CAMINOS, Vol. 2, no. 6 (October 1981), p. 7. English. DESCR: Alvarado, Angel S.; Arreola, Rafael; *Biographical Notes; Diaz, Elisa; Diaz, Elvira A.; Garcia, Jose Joel; Icaza, Ricardo F.; Lacayo, Henry; Martinez, Lydia R.; Munoz, Victor M.; Salinas, Vicente; Sanchez, Manuel; Zuniga, Henry.

Garza, Jesus

4938 People. HISPANIC BUSINESS, Vol. 4, no. 9 (September 1982), p. 7. English. DESCR: Advertising Agencies; Appointed Officials; Awards; *Biographical Notes; Diaz-Albertini, Luis; Dimartino, Rita; Hispanic Women in Higher Education (HWHE); League of United Latin American Citizens (LULAC); Ortega, Ray; Ortiz, George; Romero, Carlos J.; Sepulveda, Luis.

Garza, Jose

4939 People. HISPANIC BUSINESS, Vol. 4, no. 11 (November 1982), p. 7. English. DESCR: Biographical Notes; *Businesspeople; Diaz, Jose; Garcia-Pedrosa, Jose R.; Herrera, Heriberto; Mercado, Anthony; Rios, John F.; Solano, Faustina V.; Solis, Frank.

Garza, Jose S.

4940 People. HISPANIC BUSINESS, Vol. 4, no. 7 (July 1982), p. 7. English. DESCR: Aguilar, Richard; *Biographical Notes; Businesspeople; Coronado, Julius; Enriquez, Rene; Guerra-Martinez, Celina; Medrano, Adan; Mota, Manny; Valenti, Frank S.

Garza, Josele

4941 Gonzalez, Magdalena. Joselo Garza: a champion for the 80's and beyond. CAMINOS,

Vol. 4, no. 3 (March 1983), p. 33-35. Bilingual. DESCR: Automobile Racing.

Garza, Roberto

4942 Arias, Ron. Book review of: CONTEMPORARY CHICANO THEATRE. JOURNAL OF ETHNIC STUDIES, Vol. 5, no. 1 (Spring 1977), p. 122-123. English. DESCR: Book Reviews; *CONTEMPORARY CHICANO THEATRE; Teatro.

Garza Travel Bureau, San Antonio, TX

4943 Applebome, Peter. The Laredo express. TEXAS MONTHLY, Vol. 10, no. 4 (April 1982), p. 100-106. English. DESCR: *Transportation.

Garza-Swan, Gloria

4944 Feliciano-Foster, Wilma. A comparison of three current first-year college-level Spanish-for-native-speakers textbooks. BILINGUAL REVIEW, Vol. 9, no. 1 (January, April, 1982), p. 72-81. English. DESCR: *Book Reviews; ESPANOL ESCRITO; *Language Development; Mejias, Hugo A.; MEJORA TU ESPANOL; NUESTRO ESPANOL: CURSO PARA ESTUDIANTES BILINGUES; Portilla, Marta de la; Spanish Language Textbooks; Teschner, Richard V.; Valdes Fallis, Guadalupe; Varela, Beatriz.

4945 Garcia, Wilfred F. Book review of: NUESTRO ESPANOL: CURSO PARA ESTUDIANTES BILINGUES, BILINGUAL NATIVE SPANISH SPEAKERS FROM THE SOUTHWESTERN UNITED STATES. HISPANIA, Vol. 65, no. 2 (May 1982), p. 320-321. English. DESCR: Book Reviews; Mejias, Hugo A.; *NUESTRO ESPANOL: CURSO PARA ESTUDIANTES BILINGUES; Southwest United States; Spanish Language; Textbooks.

Gates, William

4946 Hartzler, Kaye. Book review of: YUCATAN BEFORE AND AFTER THE CONQUEST. HISPANIC JOURNAL OF BEHAVIORAL SCIENCES, Vol. 4, no. 3 (September 1982), p. 381-383. English. DESCR: Book Reviews; De Landa, Friar Diego; *YUCATAN BEFORE AND AFTER THE CONQUEST.

Gelfland, Donald E.

4947 Burke, Leslie K. Book review of: ETHNICITY AND AGING: THEORY, RESEARCH AND POLICY. HISPANIC JOURNAL OF BEHAVIORAL SCIENCES, Vol. 4, no. 1 (March 1982), p. 107-112. English. DESCR: Book Reviews; *ETHNICITY AND AGING: THEORY, RESEARCH, AND POLICY; Kutzik, Alfred J.

Gender

4948 Creswell, John L. and Exezidis, Roxane H. Research brief: sex and ethnic differences in mathematics achievement of Black and Mexican-American adolescents. TEXAS TECH JOURNAL OF EDUCATION, Vol. 9, no. 3 (Fall 1982), p. 219-222. English. DESCR: Blacks; Chicanas; *Mathematics; Youth.

4949 Creswell, John L. Sex-related differences in the problem-solving abilities of rural Black, Anglo, and Chicano adolescents. TEXAS TECH JOURNAL OF EDUCATION, Vol. 10, no. 1 (Winter 1983), p. 29-33. English. DESCR: Aiken and Preger Revised Math Attitude Scale; Anglo Americans; Blacks; California Achievement Test; Chicanas; Mathematics; National Assessment of Educational Progress; *National Council of Teachers of Mathematics (NCTM); Youth.

General Coffee Corporation

4950 People. HISPANIC BUSINESS, Vol. 5, no. 8 (August 1983), p. 10. English. **DESCR:** *Biographical Notes; Businesspeople; Calderon, Charles M.; Esteverena, Rolando C.; Hispanic Bankers Association (HBA); Martinez, Olivia T.; Pallares, Mariano; Ruiz, Frederick R.; Ruiz, Louis F.; Sanchez, Joseph J.

General Education Diploma (GED)

4951 Heaney, Thomas W. "Hanging on" or "gaining ground": educating marginal adults. NEW DIRECTIONS FOR CONTINUING EDUCATION, no. 20 (December 1983), p. 53-63. English. **DESCR:** *Adult Education; Chicago, IL; City Colleges, Chicago, IL; Gomez, Robert; Instituto del Progreso Latino; Mission District, San Francisco, CA; Project Literacy, San Francisco, CA; St. Mary's Community Educational Center; *Universidad Popular, Chicago, IL.

General Telephone Company

4952 Hann, Donna; Ferree, W. P.; and Flores, Larry. Affirmative action means progress: 2 corporations and one federal agency look at affirmative action. CAMINOS, Vol. 3, no. 8 (September 1982), p. 39-42. English. **DESCR:** *Affirmative Action; Imperial Savings; Veteran's Administration.

Generally Useful Ethnic Search System (GUESS)

4953 Camayd-Freixas, Yohel. A critical assessment of a computer program designed to identify Hispanic surnames in archival data. JOURNAL OF LATIN COMMUNITY HEALTH, Vol. 1, no. 1 (Fall 1982), p. 41-54. English. **DESCR:** *Survey Research.

Generations
USE: Age Groups

Genetics

4954 Garber, Ronald A. PGM1 and Ge subtype gene frequencies in a California Hispanic population. AMERICAN JOURNAL OF HUMAN GENETICS, Vol. 35, no. 4 (July 1983), p. 773-776. English. **DESCR:** Paternity; *Population Genetics.

4955 Sussman, Leon N. Paternity blood tests. NEW YORK LAW JOURNAL, Vol. 188, (October 6, 1982), p. 2. English. **DESCR:** Blood Examination; Blood Groups; *Paternity.

Geography

4956 Engle, Margarita Mondrus. Quien mato a la geografia? LATINO, Vol. 54, no. 8 (December 1983), p. 14. English. **DESCR:** *Language Usage.

4957 Jones, Richard C. Undocumented migration from Mexico: some geographical questions. ANNALS OF THE ASSOCIATION OF AMERICAN GEOGRAPHERS, Vol. 72, no. 1 (March 1982), p. 77-87. English. **DESCR:** Immigration; Mexico; *Migration Patterns; Undocumented Workers.

4958 Obejas, Achy. Argentina: back to Europe where it belongs. NUESTRO, Vol. 6, no. 8 (October 1982), p. 51. English. **DESCR:** *Argentina; Short Story.

Gerrymandering
USE: Reapportionment

Ghetto
USE: Barrios

Gibbs, Margaret S.

4959 Hunsaker, Alan. Book review of: PSYCHOLOGY AND COMMUNITY CHANGE; SOCIAL AND PSYCHOLOGICAL RESEARCH IN COMMUNITY SETTING; COMMUNITY PSYCHOLOGY: THEORETICAL AND EMPIRICAL APPROACHES. HISPANIC JOURNAL OF BEHAVIORAL SCIENCES, Vol. 5, no. 1 (March 1983), p. 121-124. English. **DESCR:** Book Reviews; *COMMUNITY PSYCHOLOGY: THEORETICAL AND EMPIRICAL APPROACHES; Heller, Kenneth; Kelly, James G.; Lachenmeyer, Juliana Rasic; Monahan, John; Munoz, Ricardo F.; *PSYCHOLOGY AND COMMUNITY CHANGE; Sigal, Janet; Snowden, Lonnie R.; *SOCIAL AND PSYCHOLOGICAL RESEARCH IN COMMUNITY SETTINGS.

Gibson, George Rutledge

4960 Book review of: OVER THE CHIHUAHUA AND SANTA FE TRAILS, 1847-1848: GEORGE RUTLEDGE GIBSON'S JOURNAL. HISPANIC BUSINESS, Vol. 4, no. 8 (August 1983), p. 27. English. **DESCR:** Book Reviews; Frazer, Robert W.; *OVER THE CHIHUAHUA AND SANTA FE TRAILS, 1847-1848.

Gimeno, Emil

4961 Nuestra gente. LATINO, Vol. 53, no. 4 (June 1982), p. 30. English. **DESCR:** Batine, Rafael; *Biographical Notes; Tafoya, Tony.

Girl Scouts of the United States of America

4962 Communications/marketing. HISPANIC BUSINESS, Vol. 4, no. 5 (May 1982), p. 15. English. **DESCR:** Anheuser-Busch, Inc.; Farres, Osvaldo; *Marketing; Organizations; Television; Vocational Education; Voter Turnout.

4963 Texas teenager wins scholarship. NUESTRO, Vol. 7, no. 10 (December 1983), p. 13. English. **DESCR:** *Financial Aid; Leadership; *Turincio, Giovanne.

Glenn, John

4964 Presidential election 1984. NUESTRO, Vol. 7, no. 7 (September 1983), p. 14-19. English. **DESCR:** Anderson, John; Askew, Reubin; Cranston, Alan; Elected Officials; *Elections; Fernandez, Ben; Hart, Gary; Hispanic Force '84; Hollings, Ernest "Fritz"; Mondale, Walter; Political Parties and Organizations; Reagan, Ronald.

Global Acculturation Scale

4965 Dolgin, Daniel L., et al. Quality of life and psychological well-being in a bicultural Latino community. HISPANIC JOURNAL OF BEHAVIORAL SCIENCES, Vol. 4, no. 4 (December 1982), p. 433-450. English. **DESCR:** Acculturation; *Attitude (Psychological); Depression Scale; Index of Psychological Adjustment; Psychology; Quality of Life Scale.

EL GOBIERNO Y LOS PRESIDENTES DE LOS ESTADOS UNIDOS DE AMERICA

4966 Walia, Adorna. Book review of: EL GOBIERNO Y LOS PRESIDENTES DE LOS ESTADOS UNIDOS DE AMERICA. BILINGUAL JOURNAL, Vol. 6, no. 3 (Spring 1982), p. 22. English. DESCR: Book Reviews; Constitution of the United States; *Government; Roy, Joaquin; United States; *United States History.

Godoy, Carlos Piloy

4967 First race for scouts occurs in East L.A. NUESTRO, Vol. 6, no. 1 (January, February, 1982), p. 47. English. DESCR: Funding Sources; Los Angeles, CA; Palomino, Carlos.

Godoy, Gustavo

4968 People. HISPANIC BUSINESS, Vol. 5, no. 3 (March 1983), p. 9. English. DESCR: Anaya, Toney; Anguiano, Lupe; Appointed Officials; Avila, Joaquin Guadalupe; Awards; *Biographical Notes; de la Fuente, Emilio; del Olmo, Frank; Long, Dennis P.; Martinez, Elias (Lee); Rivera, Joseph, Jr.

Godparents
USE: Compadrazgo

Gods and Dieties

4969 Gonzalez, Juan. Caribbean voodoo: a Catholic response, a private encounter. NUESTRO, Vol. 7, no. 1 (January, February, 1983), p. 37. English. DESCR: Catholic Church; *Religion.

Goizueta, Roberto C.

4970 People. HISPANIC BUSINESS, Vol. 5, no. 6 (June 1983), p. 8. English. DESCR: Appointed Officials; *Biographical Notes; Businesspeople; Guerra, Stella; Huapaya, Sixto Guillermo; Kitano, Pat; Manriquez, Suzanna; Oppenheimer-Nicolau, Siabhan; Ortiz, Solomon; Pachon, Harry P.; Richardson, Bill Lopez; Torres, Esteban E.; Torres, Johnny.

Golden Eagle Awards

4971 Gonzalez, Magdalena. Recognizing Hispanic achievements in entertainment - U.S. and Mexico. CAMINOS, Vol. 3, no. 7 (July, August, 1982), p. 18-24. Bilingual. DESCR: Allende, Fernando; Artists; Awards; Bonilla Giannini, Roxanna; Eynoso, David; Felix, Maria; Films; Gallego, Gina; Hoyos, Rodolfo; Lamas, Lorenzo; Lopez, Conchita; Lopez, Lisa; Montalban, Ricardo; Nosotros [film production company]; Quintero, Jose; Rowe, Arthur; Television; Torres, Liz.

Goldmar Citrus Ranch, Phoenix, AZ

4972 Barry, Tom. On strike! Undocumented workers in Arizona. SOUTHWEST ECONOMY AND SOCIETY, Vol. 3, no. 3 (Spring 1978), p. 52-60. English. DESCR: Agribusiness; Agricultural Laborers; Arizona; Labor Organizing; *Maricopa County Organizing Project (MCOP); Phoenix, AZ; *Strikes and Lockouts; Undocumented Workers.

Goldwert, Marvin

4973 Prichard, Sue. Book review of: HISTORY AS NEUROSIS: PATERNALISM AND MACHISMO IN SPANISH AMERICA. HISPANIC JOURNAL OF BEHAVIORAL SCIENCES, Vol. 5, no. 3 (September 1983), p. 356-360. English. DESCR: Book Reviews; *HISTORY AS NEUROSIS: PATERNALISM AND MACHISMO IN SPANISH AMERICA; Machismo.

Gomez, Dario

4974 Commercial art as a career. CAMINOS, Vol. 4, no. 9 (October 1983), p. 32-35. English. DESCR: Artists; *Careers; Chavez Lichwardt, Leticia; Guerrero, Ernest R.; Melendez, Bill; Reyes, Gil; Santistevan, August.

Gomez, Ignacio

4975 Baciu, Joyce A. The winners - Los ganadores. CAMINOS, Vol. 3, no. 2 (February 1982), p. 14-20,45. Bilingual. DESCR: *Awards; Caldera, Manuel; Huerta, Dolores; Lizarraga, David C.; Obledo, Mario; Olmos, Edward James; Rivera, Geraldo; Rivera, Tomas.

Gomez, Manuel

4976 Banberger, Ellen. Poesia nicaraguense. MAIZE, Vol. 5, no. 3-4 (Spring, Summer, 1982), p. 64-77. Spanish. DESCR: Belli, Gioconda; Cardenal, Ernesto; Carrillo, Ernesto; Coronel Urtecho, Jose; Gadea, Gerardo; Murillo, Rosario; *Nicaragua; Ojeda, Mirna; *Poetry; Revolutions; Rugama, Leonel.

Gomez, Mike

4977 Diaz, Katherine A. Mike Gomez; pursuing his dream. CAMINOS, Vol. 4, no. 9 (October 1983), p. 28-30. English. DESCR: Artists; Films.

4978 Whisler, Kirk. Nosotros on film in Hollywood and Latin America. CAMINOS, Vol. 3, no. 7 (July, August, 1982), p. 15-17. Bilingual. DESCR: Artists; Cardinale, Marcela; Espinoza, Jimmy; Films; *Nosotros [film production company]; Ortiz, Yolanda; Television; Velasco, Jerry.

Gomez, Robert

4979 Heaney, Thomas W. "Hanging on" or "gaining ground": educating marginal adults. NEW DIRECTIONS FOR CONTINUING EDUCATION, no. 20 (December 1983), p. 53-63. English. DESCR: *Adult Education; Chicago, IL; City Colleges, Chicago, IL; General Education Diploma (GED); Instituto del Progreso Latino; Mission District, San Francisco, CA; Project Literacy, San Francisco, CA; St. Mary's Community Educational Center; *Universidad Popular, Chicago, IL.

Gomez-Quinones, Juan

4980 Ponce, Mary Helen. Juan Gomez-Quinones: escolar y poeta. CAMINOS, Vol. 4, no. 6 (June 1983), p. 54-55,67. Bilingual. DESCR: Authors.

Gonzales, Ciriaco Q.

4981 Role model for aspiring researchers. NUESTRO, Vol. 6, no. 4 (May 1982), p. 34-36. English. DESCR: *Research Methodology; *Short Story.

Gonzales, Henry B.

4982 Congressman questions federal reserve role. NUESTRO, Vol. 5, no. 8 (November 1981), p. 38. English. DESCR: Federal Reserve Board; *Legislation.

Gonzales, Henry B. (cont.)

4983 Padilla, Steve. Latinos wield political
     clout in midterm election. NUESTRO, Vol. 6,
     no. 9 (November 1982), p. 28-30. English.
     DESCR: De la Garza, Kika; *Elected
     Officials; Garcia, Robert; Lujan, Manuel,
     Jr.; Martinez, Matthew G. "Marty",
     Assemblyman; Ortiz, Solomon; *Politics;
     Richardson, William; Roybal, Edward R.;
     *Torres, Esteban E.

Gonzales, Herlinda Maxima

4984 Garcia, Annie. Herlinda Maxima Gonzales.
     COMADRE, no. 1 (Summer 1977), p. 33-38.
     English. **DESCR:** *Biography.

Gonzales, Modesto

4985 Nuestra gente. LATINO, Vol. 53, no. 2
     (March, April, 1982), p. 30. English.
     DESCR: Asip, Patricia V.; *Biographical
     Notes; Ceballos, Sonia Ceban; Septien,
     Rafael.

Gonzales, Rodolfo (Corky)

4986 Hinojosa-Smith, Rolando R. I AM JOAQUIN:
     relationships between the text and the film.
     BILINGUAL REVIEW, Vol. 10, no. 2-3 (May,
     December, 1983), p. 142-145. English.
     DESCR: Film Reviews; I AM JOAQUIN [book]; *I
     AM JOAQUIN [film]; Valdez, Luis.

4987 Jensen, Richard J. and Hammerback, John C.
     "No revolutions without poets": the rhetoric
     of Rodolfo "Corky" Gonzales. WESTERN JOURNAL
     OF SPEECH COMMUNICATION, Vol. 46, no. 1
     (Winter 1982), p. 72-91. English. **DESCR:**
     Chicano Movement; Literary Criticism;
     Poetry; Rhetoric.

Gonzalez, Arthur

4988 Garcia, Ignacio M. Miracles at Kino
     Hospital. NUESTRO, Vol. 7, no. 6 (August
     1983), p. 11-12. English. **DESCR:** Hospitals
     and the Community; *Kino Community Hospital,
     Tucson, AZ; Medical Care; Public Health.

Gonzalez, Gilbert G.

4989 Cortese, Anthony J., ed.; Santillan,
     Richard; and Mercado, Olivia. Chicano
     psychological assessment: a critique of
     "Racial intelligence and the Mexican people"
     [sic]. EXPLORATIONS IN ETHNIC STUDIES, Vol.
     5, no. 2 (July 1982), p. 50-51. English.
     DESCR: *Intelligence Tests; "Racial
     intelligence testing and the Mexican
     people".

4990 Santillan, Richard. Critique. EXPLORATIONS
     IN ETHNIC STUDIES, Vol. 5, no. 2 (July
     1982), p. 54-55. English. **DESCR:**
     *Intelligence Tests; "Racial intelligence
     testing and the Mexican people".

Gonzalez, Henry B.

4991 Newsfront. HISPANIC BUSINESS, Vol. 4, no. 2
     (February 1982), p. 7. English. **DESCR:** Asip,
     Patricia V.; Banuelos, Ramona Acosta;
     *Biographical Notes; Businesspeople;
     Gutierrez, Alberto; IMAGE, Washington, DC.

4992 Profile of a public man. NUESTRO, Vol. 7,
     no. 2 (March 1983), p. 13-19+. English.
     DESCR: Elected Officials; Politics; Texas.

4993 San Antonio: an all American city. CAMINOS,
     Vol. 4, no. 8 (September 1983), p. 35.
     English. **DESCR:** *Artists; Cerda, Daniel;

Congressional Arts Caucus; *San Antonio, TX.

Gonzalez, John David

4994 The Dallas bilingual yellow pages. HISPANIC
     BUSINESS, Vol. 4, no. 1 (January 1982), p.
     11. English. **DESCR:** *Consumers; Dallas, TX;
     Gonzalez, Michael; *Marketing.

Gonzalez, Jose Luis

4995 Fernandez, Jose B. Book review of: LA
     LLEGADA. REVISTA CHICANO-RIQUENA, Vol. 10,
     no. 3 (Summer 1982), p. 67-68. Spanish.
     DESCR: Book Reviews; *LA LLEGADA.

Gonzalez, Julio

4996 People. HISPANIC BUSINESS, Vol. 5, no. 7
     (July 1983), p. 8. English. **DESCR:** Alvarado,
     Anthony J.; Appointed Officials;
     *Biographical Notes; Businesspeople;
     Candela, Hilario; Garcia, Marlene; Martinez,
     Tony; Pla, George; Valdez, Abelardo L.

Gonzalez, Larry

4997 Gonzalez, Larry. Serving our students: Larry
     Gonzalez (interview). CAMINOS, Vol. 4, no.
     10 (November 1983), p. 34-36. English.
     DESCR: Education; Los Angeles Unified School
     District; *Primary School Education.

Gonzalez, Luis A.

4998 President Reagan's appointments. CAMINOS,
     Vol. 3, no. 3 (March 1982), p. 48-50.
     Bilingual. **DESCR:** Appointed Officials;
     *Federal Government; Flores Buckhart,
     Elizabeth; Garcia, Ernest E.; Lozano, Diana;
     Pompa, Gilbert G.; Reagan, Ronald; Sanchez,
     Nestor D.; Zuniga, Henry.

Gonzalez, Michael

4999 The Dallas bilingual yellow pages. HISPANIC
     BUSINESS, Vol. 4, no. 1 (January 1982), p.
     11. English. **DESCR:** *Consumers; Dallas, TX;
     Gonzalez, John David; *Marketing.

Gonzalez Obregon, Luis

5000 Nieto, Eva Margarita. El problema de la
     juventud eterna en tres hechiceras en THE
     SECOND RING OF POWER, LA MULATA DE CORDOBA y
     AURA. LA PALABRA, Vol. 4, no. 1-2 (Spring,
     Fall, 1983), p. 81-91. Spanish.
     DESCR: AURA; Castaneda, Carlos; Fuentes,
     Carlos; LA MULATA DE CORDOBA; *Literary
     Criticism; Literature; Literature Reviews;
     THE SECOND RING OF POWER.

Gonzalez, Pedro J.

5001 Keller, Gary. Ballad of an unsung hero.
     BILINGUAL REVIEW, Vol. 10, no. 2-3 (May,
     December, 1983), p. 171-172. English.
     DESCR: *BALLAD OF AN UNSUNG HERO; Film
     Reviews.

Gonzalez, Raquel Quiroz

5002 Martinez, Julio A. Book review of: A DECADE
     OF CHICANO LITERATURE (1970-1979)-CRITICAL
     ESSAYS AND BIBLIOGRAPHY. RQ - REFERENCE AND
     ADULT SERVICES DIVISION, Vol. 22, no. 1
     (Fall 1982), p. 90. English. **DESCR:** *A
     DECADE OF CHICANO LITERATURE (1970-1979):
     CRITICAL ESSAYS AND BIBLIOGRAPHY;
     Bibliography; Book Reviews; Literary
     Criticism; Literatura Chicanesca;
     Literature; Trujillo, Robert.

Gonzalez, Ruben

5003 Mimiaga, Hector. Greatest ambition. LATINO, Vol. 53, no. 4 (June 1982), p. 25. English. DESCR: Biography; Musicians.

Gort, Wilfredo

5004 People. HISPANIC BUSINESS, Vol. 4, no. 12 (December 1982), p. 10. English. DESCR: *Biographical Notes; *Businesspeople; Garcia, Frances; Ojeda, Armando; Olind, Rebecca Nieto; Philip Morris, Inc.; Roybal, Edward R.

Gosling, Maureen

5005 Herrera-Sobek, Maria. Film review of: DEL MERO CORAZON (STRAIGHT FROM THE HEART). JOURNAL OF AMERICAN FOLKLORE, Vol. 95, (March 1982), p. 123. English. DESCR: Blank, Les; *DEL MERO CORAZON; Film Reviews; Hernandez, Guillermo; Norteno; Strachwitz, Chris.

Government

5006 Chicago: a case study of minority participation in city government and industry. HISPANIC BUSINESS, Vol. 5, no. 1 (January 1983), p. 28-29. English. DESCR: Chicago, IL; *Employment; *Ethnic Groups.

5007 Election change sought by Garcia. NUESTRO, Vol. 6, no. 10 (December 1982), p. 9-10. English. DESCR: *Corpus Christi, TX; Garcia, Hector; *Urban Communities.

5008 Eliminating corruption. NUESTRO, Vol. 6, no. 10 (December 1982), p. 8. English. DESCR: De la Madrid, Miguel; *Mexico.

5009 Giamatti, A. Bartlett. Government has a role to promote access to education. LATINO, Vol. 54, no. 2 (March 1983), p. 21+. English. DESCR: *Education.

5010 Gonzalez, Josue M. The pentagon and genetic inferiority. NUESTRO, Vol. 6, no. 3 (April 1982), p. 44. English. DESCR: *Ethnic Groups; *Racism.

5011 Government maze. NUESTRO, Vol. 6, no. 4 (May 1982), p. 9. English. DESCR: Government Services.

5012 The new federalism. NUESTRO, Vol. 6, no. 2 (March 1982), p. 10. English. DESCR: *Federal Aid; *Government Services; *Social Services.

5013 Solon opposes military support for Guatemala. NUESTRO, Vol. 6, no. 5 (June, July, 1982), p. 53. English. DESCR: Garcia, Robert; *Guatemala; *Military.

5014 Top ranking Latino resigns from SBA. NUESTRO, Vol. 6, no. 2 (March 1982), p. 45. English. DESCR: *Cardenas, Michael; U.S. Small Business Administration.

5015 Walia, Adorna. Book review of: EL GOBIERNO Y LOS PRESIDENTES DE LOS ESTADOS UNIDOS DE AMERICA. BILINGUAL JOURNAL, Vol. 6, no. 3 (Spring 1982), p. 22. English. DESCR: Book Reviews; Constitution of the United States; *EL GOBIERNO Y LOS PRESIDENTES DE LOS ESTADOS UNIDOS DE AMERICA; Roy, Joaquin; United States; *United States History.

Government Contracts

5016 NALEO audits the Feds. HISPANIC BUSINESS, Vol. 5, no. 10 (October 1983), p. 16. English. DESCR: Business Enterprises; Federal Government; Minority Business Development Agency (MBDA); *National Association of Latino Elected Officials (NALEO); U.S. Department of Defense (DOD); U.S. Department of Health and Human Services.

5017 Obledo, Mario. End the dairy subsidy. LATINO, Vol. 54, no. 8 (December 1983), p. 6. English. DESCR: Business.

Government Employees

5018 Hispanics in federal agencies. HISPANIC BUSINESS, Vol. 4, no. 9 (September 1982), p. 29. English. DESCR: Affirmative Action; MEXICAN AMERICAN LEGAL DEFENSE AND EDUCATIONAL FUND NEWSLETTER.

5019 Langley, Roger. Roger Langley's Hispanic beat. HISPANIC BUSINESS, Vol. 4, no. 4 (April 1982), p. 23. English.

5020 Math-based careers. HISPANIC BUSINESS, Vol. 4, no. 4 (April 1982), p. 20,24. English. DESCR: *Careers; Chicanas; *Engineering as a Profession; National Action Council for Minorities in Engineering (NACME); National Hispanic Field Service Program.

5021 Research/development: Hispanics and job progress. HISPANIC BUSINESS, Vol. 4, no. 4 (April 1982), p. 29. English. DESCR: *Affirmative Action.

Government Funding Sources

5022 Government review. NUESTRO, Vol. 7, no. 6 (August 1983), p. 56. English. DESCR: Ballet de Puerto Rico; Dance; Education; Employment; Government Services; Housing; Income; National Fair Housing Law; Population Distribution; Urban Development Action Grant (UDAG); Veterans.

5023 Mendez, Jose A. and Esquer, Cecilia D. The impact of undocumented aliens on health and public health care in Arizona. ARIZONA BUSINESS, Vol. 30, no. 3 (1983), p. 3-7. English. DESCR: Arizona; *Arizona Health Care Cost Containment System (AHCCCS); *Public Health; Public Policy; Undocumented Workers.

Government Services

5024 Baca-Ramirez, Reynaldo and Bryan, Dexter Edward. The undocumented Mexican worker: a social problem? JOURNAL OF ETHNIC STUDIES, Vol. 8, no. 1 (Spring 1980), p. 55-69. English. DESCR: Immigrant Labor; Immigration; Immigration Regulation and Control; Mexico; Social History and Conditions; Social Services; *Undocumented Workers.

5025 Ericksen, Charles. Si no fuera por la gente: podriamos servir el publico. LATINO, Vol. 54, no. 3 (April 1983), p. 9+. Spanish.

5026 Government maze. NUESTRO, Vol. 6, no. 4 (May 1982), p. 9. English. DESCR: *Government.

Government Services (cont.)

5027 Government review. NUESTRO, Vol. 7, no. 10 (December 1983), p. 48. English. **DESCR:** Banking Industry; Child Care Centers; Chile; Clinics (Medical); Credit Unions; Employment; Employment Training; Medical Care; National Credit Union Administration; National Oceanic and Atmospheric Administration; SER; U.S. Department of Health and Human Services; U.S. Department of Labor.

5028 Government review. NUESTRO, Vol. 7, no. 8 (October 1983), p. 54. English. **DESCR:** Alcoholism; Employment; National Endowment for the Arts; Plaza de La Raza, Los Angeles, CA; Veterans; Working Women; Youth.

5029 Government review. NUESTRO, Vol. 7, no. 7 (September 1983), p. 55. English. **DESCR:** AIDS Hotline; California; Education; Employment; Food for Survival, New York, NY; Funding Sources; Hewlett Foundation; Laborers; Mathematics, Engineering and Science Achievement (MESA); Population Trends; Public Health; Stanford University, Stanford, CA.

5030 Government review. NUESTRO, Vol. 7, no. 6 (August 1983), p. 56. English. **DESCR:** Ballet de Puerto Rico; Dance; Education; Employment; *Government Funding Sources; Housing; Income; National Fair Housing Law; Population Distribution; Urban Development Action Grant (UDAG); Veterans.

5031 Government review. NUESTRO, Vol. 7, no. 2 (March 1983), p. 42. English. **DESCR:** A WORKING WOMAN'S GUIDE TO HER JOB RIGHTS; Adoption; Business Enterprises; Census; Chicanas; Discrimination in Employment; GUIDE TO FEDERAL MINORITY ENTERPRISE AND RELATED ASSISTANCE PROGRAMS; Population Trends; Study Abroad; U.S. Information Agency (USIA).

5032 The new federalism. NUESTRO, Vol. 6, no. 2 (March 1982), p. 10. English. **DESCR:** *Federal Aid; *Government; *Social Services.

Goya Foods

5033 Gupta, Udayan. Hispanic foods in New York: the race for number two. HISPANIC BUSINESS, Vol. 5, no. 8 (August 1983), p. 18-19+. English. **DESCR:** Condal Distributor, Inc.; Consumers; *Food Industry; Iberia Foods Corp.; La Cena Fine Foods, Ltd.; Recipes.

5034 Sullivan, Jim. The Puerto Rican powerhouse: Goya. CAMINOS, Vol. 4, no. 6 (June 1983), p. 12-13,66. Bilingual. **DESCR:** Food Industry.

Grace, J. Peter

5035 Our 1982 Latino awards. NUESTRO, Vol. 7, no. 1 (January, February, 1983), p. 44-46. English. **DESCR:** Awards; Escalante, Jaime; Gallegos, Gina; Immigration and Naturalization Service (INS); Knight, Bobby; Lamas, Fernando; *Latino Awards; Luce, Claire Boothe; Moreno, Rita; National Press Foundation; Rodriguez Hernandez, Andres; Simpson-Mazzoli Bill; Smith, Raymond; Valeri, Michele; Voting Rights Act.

5036 Resign, Peter Grace. NUESTRO, Vol. 6, no. 5 (June, July, 1982), p. 9. English. **DESCR:** Barcelo, Carlos Romero; Puerto Ricans.

Graduate Schools

5037 Dejnozka, Edward L. and Smiley, Lydia R. Selective admissions criteria in graduate teacher education programs. JOURNAL OF TEACHER EDUCATION, Vol. 34, no. 1 (January, February, 1983), p. 24-27. English. **DESCR:** *Educational Tests and Measurements; Teaching Profession.

5038 Math-based careers. HISPANIC BUSINESS, Vol. 5, no. 12 (December 1983), p. 40. English. **DESCR:** *Careers; Council on Legal Education Opportunities (CLEO); Education; Employment Training; High Technology High School, San Antonio, TX; Legal Education; Mexican American Legal Defense and Educational Fund (MALDEF); San Antonio, TX; Science as a Profession.

5039 Webster, David S. Chicano students in American higher education: a review of the literature. CAMPO LIBRE, Vol. 1, no. 2 (Summer 1981), p. 169-192. English. **DESCR:** Dropouts; Educational Statistics; Enrollment; *Higher Education; Literature Reviews; Professional Schools.

Graffiti

5040 Adrien Gallo's les tap - tap of Haiti. NUESTRO, Vol. 6, no. 1 (January, February, 1982), p. 56-58. English. **DESCR:** *Haiti.

Grammar

5041 Blake, Robert. Mood selection among Spanish-speaking children, ages 4 to 12. BILINGUAL REVIEW, Vol. 10, no. 1 (January, April, 1983), p. 21-32. English. **DESCR:** Children; *Language Development; Language Usage; Spanish Language.

5042 Kirschner, Carl. Spanish and English inchoatives and the Spanish-English bilingual: got anything to se? BILINGUAL REVIEW, Vol. 9, no. 3 (September, December, 1982), p. 213-219. English. **DESCR:** *Semantics; Slang; Syntax.

Grammy Awards

5043 Agudelo, Carlos. What about Latin music? BILLBOARD, Vol. 94, (November 20, 1982), p. 10. English. **DESCR:** *Awards; Music; National Academy of Recording Arts and Sciences; Performing Arts; Recording Industry.

5044 Fernandez, Enrique. NARAS takes a welcome step. BILLBOARD, Vol. 95, (June 18, 1983), p. 59. English. **DESCR:** Awards; Entertainers; Music; *National Academy of Recording Arts and Sciences; Performing Arts; Recording Industry.

Granada, Pilar

5045 "Racist and demeaning". NUESTRO, Vol. 7, no. 2 (March 1983), p. 7. English. **DESCR:** Agricultural Laborers; Book Reviews; Hagopian, Tom; Racism; *SPANISH FOR THE CALIFORNIA FARMERS.

Grandparent and Child Relationships

5046 Schmidt, Lorenza. Grandparental-grandchild interaction in a Mexican American group. HISPANIC JOURNAL OF BEHAVIORAL SCIENCES, Vol. 5, no. 2 (June 1983), p. 181-198. English. **DESCR:** Ancianos; Children.

Grape Boycott
   USE: Boycotts

Graphics

5047 Carreon, Ernesto. [Untitled drawing]. MAIZE,
   Vol. 2, no. 2 (Winter 1979), p. 39. English.

5048 Cedrins, Inara. [Untitled wood engraving].
   MAIZE, Vol. 3, no. 3-4 (Spring, Summer,
   1980), p. 42. Bilingual.

5049 Cedrins, Inara. [Untitled wood engraving].
   MAIZE, Vol. 3, no. 3-4 (Spring, Summer,
   1980), p. 56. Bilingual.

5050 Efren. [Untitled]. MAIZE, Vol. 3, no. 1-2
   (Fall, Winter, 1979, 1980), p. 67. Spanish.
   DESCR: Caricature.

5051 Garcia Perez, Linda Mary. Cactus prisoner.
   MAIZE, Vol. 2, no. 3 (Spring 1979), p. 35.
   English.

5052 Garcia-Camarillo, Cecilio. Medianoche
   [graphic]. MAIZE, Vol. 1, no. 4 (Summer
   1978), p. 42. Spanish.

5053 Lujan, Otono Amarillo. An indian. MAIZE,
   Vol. 2, no. 4 (Summer 1979), p. 29. English.

5054 Lujan, Otono Amarillo. [Untitled pencil line
   drawings]. MAIZE, Vol. 2, no. 1 (Fall 1978),
   p. 48-49. English.

5055 Marta. [Untitled graphic]. MAIZE, Vol. 1,
   no. 2 (Winter 1978), p. 32-33. English.

5056 Ochoa, Victor Orozco. Posadas [graphic].
   MAIZE, Vol. 1, no. 2 (Winter 1978), p. Ft
   cover. English.

5057 Palma Castroman, Janis. Infantes. MAIZE,
   Vol. 1, no. 3 (Spring 1978), p. 23-25.
   English.

5058 Pazos, Antonio. [Untitled graphics]. MAIZE,
   Vol. 2, no. 1 (Fall 1978), p. 59-60,[65].
   English.

5059 Pena, Gerardo. Sidro. MAIZE, Vol. 3, no. 1-2
   (Fall, Winter, 1979, 1980), p. Ft cover.
   English.

5060 Polkinhorn, Harry. [Untitled]. MAIZE, Vol.
   4, no. 3-4 (Spring, Summer, 1981), p. Ft
   cover. Bilingual.

5061 Polkinhorn, Harry. [Untitled graphics].
   MAIZE, Vol. 4, no. 3-4 (Spring, Summer,
   1981), p. 9+. Spanish.

5062 Tizoc. [Untitled graphics]. MAIZE, Vol. 1,
   no. 4 (Summer 1978), p. 50-51. English.

5063 Tizocurista. [Untitled pen line drawings].
   MAIZE, Vol. 2, no. 1 (Fall 1978), p. 50-51.
   English.

5064 Tizocurista. [Untitled pen line drawings].
   MAIZE, Vol. 2, no. 4 (Summer 1979), p. 50.
   English.

5065 Tremblay, Gail. Remembering the way ... old
   woman's fire. MAIZE, Vol. 2, no. 3 (Spring
   1979), p. 25,39. English.

5066 Tremblay, Gail. Young man's fire. MAIZE,
   Vol. 2, no. 3 (Spring 1979), p. 41. English.

5067 Urista, Tizoc. [Untitled]. MAIZE, Vol. 3,
   no. 1-2 (Fall, Winter, 1979, 1980), p. 35.
   English.

Great Depression, 1929-1933

5068 Weber, Kenneth R. Book review of: HISPANIC
   VILLAGES OF NORTHERN NEW MEXICO. SOUTHWEST
   ECONOMY AND SOCIETY, Vol. 1, no. 1 (Spring
   1976), p. 48. English. **DESCR:** Book Reviews;
   Economic History and Conditions; *HISPANIC
   VILLAGES OF NORTHERN NEW MEXICO; New Mexico;
   Tewa Basin, NM; Weigle, Marta.

THE GREAT REBELLION: MEXICO 1905-1924

5069 Knight, Alan. Book review of: THE GREAT
   REBELLION: MEXICO 1905-1924 and DESERT
   IMMIGRANTS: THE MEXICANS OF EL PASO
   1880-1920. HISTORY: THE JOURNAL OF THE
   HISTORICAL ASSOCIATION [London], Vol. 67,
   (October 1982), p. 450-451. English. **DESCR:**
   Book Reviews; *DESERT IMMIGRANTS: THE
   MEXICANS OF EL PASO 1880-1920; Garcia, Mario
   T.; Ruiz, Ramon Eduardo.

**Greater Washington Ibero-American Chamber of
   Commerce**

5070 Business update: Ibero-American chamber has
   gala, makes awards. NUESTRO, Vol. 7, no. 5
   (June, July, 1983), p. 52. English. **DESCR:**
   Awards; *Business Enterprises.

El Greco

5071 El Greco of Toledo: his life and his art.
   NUESTRO, Vol. 6, no. 6 (August 1982), p.
   24-27. English. **DESCR:** Art; Art History;
   Artists; Biography.

Green Carders

5072 Salcido, Ramon M. The undocumented alien
   family. DE COLORES, Vol. 6, no. 1-2 (1982),
   p. 109-119. English. **DESCR:** East Los
   Angeles, CA; Family; Social Services;
   *Undocumented Workers.

Grenada

5073 Maldonado-Denis, Manuel. El problema de las
   nacionalidades: la experiencia caribena.
   Paper presented at the "Dialogo de las
   Americas" conference. Mexico, D.F.
   September 9-14, 1982. REVISTA
   CHICANO-RIQUENA, Vol. 10, no. 4 (Fall 1982),
   p. 39-45. Spanish. **DESCR:** Capitalism;
   Carpentier, Alejo; Cuba; El Salvador;
   Guatemala; Imperialism; Marti, Jose;
   Nicaragua; *Political History and
   Conditions; Puerto Rico; United States.

Griego, Margo C.

5074 Villarreal, Diana Judith. For Spanish
   children. HORN BOOK MAGAZINE, Vol. 58,
   (June 1982), p. 312-313. English. **DESCR:**
   Book Reviews; *PARA LOS NINOS, vols. 1&2;
   Pena, Graciela; *TORTILLITAS PARA MAMA.

Gringo
   USE: Anglo Americans

Griswold del Castillo, Ricardo

5075 Britt, Anita. Book review of: THE LOS
   ANGELES BARRIO 1850-1890: A SOCIAL HISTORY.
   HISPANIC JOURNAL OF BEHAVIORAL SCIENCES,
   Vol. 4, no. 3 (September 1982), p. 388-391.
   English. **DESCR:** Book Reviews; *THE LOS
   ANGELES BARRIO 1850-1890: A SOCIAL HISTORY.

Griswold del Castillo, Ricardo (cont.)

5076 Garcia, Mario T. Book review of: LOS ANGELES BARRIO 1850-1890: A SOCIAL HISTORY. PACIFIC HISTORICAL REVIEW, Vol. 51, no. 1 (February 1982), p. 90-91. English. **DESCR:** Barrios; Book Reviews; Los Angeles, CA; *THE LOS ANGELES BARRIO 1850-1890: A SOCIAL HISTORY.

5077 Lotchin, Roger W. New Chicano history: an urban history perspective. HISTORY TEACHER, Vol. 16, no. 2 (February 1983), p. 229-247. English. **DESCR:** Camarillo, Alberto; CHICANOS IN A CHANGING SOCIETY; DESERT IMMIGRANTS: THE MEXICANS OF EL PASO 1880-1920; Garcia, Mario T.; *Historiography; History; Social History and Conditions; THE LOS ANGELES BARRIO 1850-1890: A SOCIAL HISTORY; Urban Communities.

5078 Weber, David J. and Lotchin, Roger W. The new Chicano history: two perspectives. HISTORY TEACHER, Vol. 16, no. 2 (February 1983), p. 219-247. English. **DESCR:** Camarillo, Alberto; *CHICANOS IN A CHANGING SOCIETY; DESERT IMMIGRANTS: THE MEXICANS OF EL PASO 1880-1920; Garcia, Mario T.; *Historiography; History; Social History and Conditions; *THE LOS ANGELES BARRIO 1850-1890: A SOCIAL HISTORY; *Urban Communities.

5079 Weber, David J. The new Chicano urban history. HISTORY TEACHER, Vol. 16, no. 2 (February 1983), p. 223-229. English. **DESCR:** Camarillo, Alberto; *CHICANOS IN A CHANGING SOCIETY; DESERT IMMIGRANTS: THE MEXICANS OF EL PASO 1880-1920; Garcia, Mario T.; *Historiography; History; Social History and Conditions; *THE LOS ANGELES BARRIO 1850-1890: A SOCIAL HISTORY; Urban Communities.

EL GRITO DE LAS MADRES DOLOROSAS

5080 Garza, Hector. El grito de las madres dolorosas. BILINGUAL REVIEW, Vol. 10, no. 2-3 (May, December, 1983), p. 184-186. English. **DESCR:** Connolly, Patrick J.; Film Reviews.

GRITO DEL SOL

5081 Orozco, Febe Portillo. A bibliography of Hispanic literature. ENGLISH JOURNAL, Vol. 71, no. 7 (November 1982), p. 58-62. English. **DESCR:** BARRIO BOY; *Bibliography; BLESS ME, ULTIMA; CHICANO; EL SOL Y LOS DE ABAJO; HEART OF AZTLAN; *Literature; POCHO; WE ARE CHICANOS.

Grocery Trade

5082 Shiell, Pancho. East Harlem's La Marqueta offers fascinating potpourri of produce and dry goods. NUESTRO, Vol. 6, no. 7 (September 1982), p. 24-26. English.

Grosjean, Francois

5083 Alatorre, Alva Sylvia. Book review of: LIFE WITH TWO LANGUAGES: AN INTRODUCTION TO BILINGUALISM. HISPANIC JOURNAL OF BEHAVIORAL SCIENCES, Vol. 5, no. 4 (December 1983), p. 482-486. English. **DESCR:** Bilingualism; Book Reviews; *LIFE WITH TWO LANGUAGES: AN INTRODUCTION TO BILINGUALISM.

5084 Sagarin, Edward. Book review of: LIFE WITH TWO LANGUAGES: AN INTRODUCTION TO BILINGUALISM. INTERNATIONAL MIGRATION REVIEW, Vol. 17, no. 3 (Fall 1983), p. 505-506. English. **DESCR:** Book Reviews; *LIFE WITH TWO LANGUAGES: AN INTRODUCTION TO BILINGUALISM.

Growers

5085 Foster, Douglas. The desperate migrants of Devil's Canyon. THE PROGRESSIVE, Vol. 46, no. 11 (November 1982), p. 44-49. English. **DESCR:** *Agricultural Laborers; California; *Devil's Canyon, Deer Canyon, CA; Labor Camps; San Diego, CA; Undocumented Workers.

Guadalupanismo

5086 Gil, Carlos B. Withstanding time: the miracle of the Virgin of Guadalupe. NUESTRO, Vol. 7, no. 10 (December 1983), p. 46-47. English. **DESCR:** Catholic Church; Mexico City; Religion; *Virgin of Guadalupe.

Guadalupe Hidalgo, Treaty of 1848

5087 Hernandez, Philip A. The Treaty of Guadalupe Hidalgo: a matter of precision. CACR REVIEW, Vol. 1, no. 1 (September 1982), p. 26-41. English. **DESCR:** Treaties; United States History.

5088 Timmons, Wilbert H. American El Paso: the formative years, 1848-1854. SOUTHWESTERN HISTORICAL QUARTERLY, Vol. 87, no. 1 (July 1983), p. 1-36. English. **DESCR:** Border Region; *El Paso, TX; History; Social History and Conditions.

Guatemala

5089 Camacho de Schmidt, Aurora. Alien smuggling and the refugee question: the INS and sojourners from Yalaj. NUESTRO, Vol. 7, no. 5 (June, July, 1983), p. 20. English. **DESCR:** *Immigration Regulation and Control; *Political Refugees; Refugees; *Undocumented Workers.

5090 Ericksen, Charles. Holdenreid and Salazar: unanswered questions. NUESTRO, Vol. 7, no. 4 (May 1983), p. 40-41. English. **DESCR:** Assassination; Criminal Acts; *Holdenreid, Frank X.; *Salazar, Ruben; *Violence.

5091 Gallo, Adrien. Children of Guatemala: a pictoral essay. NUESTRO, Vol. 7, no. 2 (March 1983), p. 43-45. English. **DESCR:** *Children; Photography.

5092 Holdenreid, Frank X. Guatemala shantytown. NUESTRO, Vol. 7, no. 4 (May 1983), p. 39-41. English. **DESCR:** Ayudantes de los Pobres; Holdenreid, Frank X.; *Poverty; Refugees.

5093 Maldonado-Denis, Manuel. El problema de las nacionalidades: la experiencia caribena. Paper presented at the "Dialogo de las Americas" conference. Mexico, D.F. September 9-14, 1982. REVISTA CHICANO-RIQUENA, Vol. 10, no. 4 (Fall 1982), p. 39-45. Spanish. **DESCR:** Capitalism; Carpentier, Alejo; Cuba; El Salvador; Grenada; Imperialism; Marti, Jose; Nicaragua; *Political History and Conditions; Puerto Rico; United States.

5094 Simon, Jean-Marie. Five days in Nebaj: one perspective. NUESTRO, Vol. 7, no. 1 (January, February, 1983), p. 28-32. English. **DESCR:** Nebaj, Guatemala; *Political History and Conditions.

5095 Solon opposes military support for Guatemala. NUESTRO, Vol. 6, no. 5 (June, July, 1982), p. 53. English. **DESCR:** Garcia, Robert; Government; *Military.

Guatemala (cont.)

5096 Trevino, Jesus and Ruiz, Jose Luis.
Guatemalan refugees - the tip of the
iceberg. CAMINOS, Vol. 4, no. 5 (May 1983),
p. 13-15,48. English. **DESCR:** International
Relations; Mexico; MEXICO: THE FUTURE;
*Refugees.

5097 Wise, Robert P. The persistence of poor
health in Guatemala: a preventive medical
perspective. JOURNAL OF LATIN COMMUNITY
HEALTH, Vol. 1, no. 1 (Fall 1982), p. 71-79.
English. **DESCR:** *Public Health.

Guernica, A.

5098 Research/development: books. HISPANIC
BUSINESS, Vol. 4, no. 12 (December 1982), p.
36. English. **DESCR:** Book Reviews; Consumers;
Kasperuk, I.; Marketing; *REACHING THE
HISPANIC MARKET EFFECTIVELY.

Guernica, Antonio

5099 Breiter, Toni. An interview with some
experts. AGENDA, Vol. 11, no. 3 (May, June,
1981), p. 48-52. English. **DESCR:** Gutierrez,
Felix; *Mass Media; Morales, Rosa; Schement,
Jorge Reina; Valenzuela, Nicholas.

Guerra, Stella

5100 People. HISPANIC BUSINESS, Vol. 5, no. 6
(June 1983), p. 8. English. **DESCR:** Appointed
Officials; *Biographical Notes;
Businesspeople; Goizueta, Roberto C.;
Huapaya, Sixto Guillermo; Kitano, Pat;
Manriquez, Suzanna; Oppenheimer-Nicolau,
Siabhan; Ortiz, Solomon; Pachon, Harry P.;
Richardson, Bill Lopez; Torres, Esteban E.;
Torres, Johnny.

Guerra-Martinez, Celina

5101 People. HISPANIC BUSINESS, Vol. 4, no. 7
(July 1982), p. 7. English. **DESCR:** Aguilar,
Richard; *Biographical Notes;
Businesspeople; Coronado, Julius; Enriquez,
Rene; Garza, Jose S.; Medrano, Adan; Mota,
Manny; Valenti, Frank S.

Guerrero, Ernest R.

5102 Commercial art as a career. CAMINOS, Vol. 4,
no. 9 (October 1983), p. 32-35. English.
DESCR: Artists; *Careers; Chavez Lichwardt,
Leticia; Gomez, Dario; Melendez, Bill;
Reyes, Gil; Santistevan, August.

Guerrero, Lena

5103 Baca Barragan, Polly; Hamner, Richard; and
Guerrero, Lena. [Untitled interview with
State Senators (Colorado) Polly
Baca-Barragan and Lena Guerrero. NATIONAL
HISPANIC JOURNAL, Vol. 1, no. 2 (Winter
1982), p. 8-11. English. **DESCR:** Baca
Barragan, Polly; *Carter, Jimmy (President);
Chicanas; Democratic Party; Elected
Officials; *Political Parties and
Organizations.

Guerrero, Pedro

5104 Deportes. CAMINOS, Vol. 3, no. 7 (July,
August, 1982), p. 46. Spanish. **DESCR:**
*Baseball; Los Angeles Dodgers; Romo,
Vicente.

5105 Ortiz, Carlos V. NUESTRO'S sixth annual
all-star baseball team. NUESTRO, Vol. 7, no.
2 (March 1983), p. 33-37. English. **DESCR:**
Andujar, Joaquin; Barojas, Salome;

*Baseball; Castillo, Manny; Concepcion,
Dave; Cruz, Jose; Garcia, Damaso; Hernandez,
Keith; Lezcano, Sixto; Martinez, Tippy;
Pena, Tony; Piniella, Lou; Sports;
Valenzuela, Fernando.

Guerrillas

5106 Garcia, Ignacio M. El Salvador: profile of a
nation at war. NUESTRO, Vol. 7, no. 8
(October 1983), p. 26-36. English. **DESCR:**
*El Salvador; Military; Political History
and Conditions; War.

Guevara, Che

5107 Acevedo, Mario (Torero). Big brother speaks
from the dead [poster]. MAIZE, Vol. 1, no. 2
(Winter 1978), p. 13. English. **DESCR:**
*Posters.

**GUIDE TO FEDERAL MINORITY ENTERPRISE AND RELATED
ASSISTANCE PROGRAMS**

5108 Government review. NUESTRO, Vol. 7, no. 2
(March 1983), p. 42. English. **DESCR:** A
WORKING WOMAN'S GUIDE TO HER JOB RIGHTS;
Adoption; Business Enterprises; Census;
Chicanas; Discrimination in Employment;
*Government Services; Population Trends;
Study Abroad; U.S. Information Agency
(USIA).

Guitar Music

5109 Santana's guitar work still sharp and crisp.
NUESTRO, Vol. 6, no. 9 (November 1982), p.
60. English. **DESCR:** Guitarists; Music;
*Santana, Carlos.

Guitarists

5110 Santana's guitar work still sharp and crisp.
NUESTRO, Vol. 6, no. 9 (November 1982), p.
60. English. **DESCR:** Guitar Music; Music;
*Santana, Carlos.

**GUNPOWDER JUSTICE: A REASSESSMENT OF THE TEXAS
RANGERS**

5111 Achor, Shirley. Book review of: GUNPOWDER
JUSTICE: A REASSESSMENT OF THE TEXAS
RANGERS. INTERNATIONAL MIGRATION REVIEW,
Vol. 16, no. 2 (Summer 1982), p. 491-492.
English. **DESCR:** Bernal, Joseph; Book
Reviews; Pena, Alberto; Samora, Julian;
Texas Rangers.

5112 Achor, Shirley. Book review of: GUNPOWDER
JUSTICE: A REASSESSMENT OF THE TEXAS
RANGERS. INTERNATIONAL MIGRATION REVIEW,
Vol. 16, no. 2 (Summer 1982), p. 491-492.
English. **DESCR:** Bernal, Joseph; Book
Reviews; History; Pena, Alberto; Samora,
Julian; Texas Rangers.

5113 Trujillo, Larry. Book review of: GUNPOWDER
JUSTICE: A REASSESSMENT OF THE TEXAS RANGERS
[reprinted from CRIME AND SOCIAL JUSTICE, 61
(Summer 1980)]. CHICANO LAW REVIEW, Vol. 6,
(1983), p. 148-155. English. **DESCR:** Book
Reviews; Samora, Julian; *Texas Rangers.

GURT 1980: CURRENT ISSUES IN BILINGUAL EDUCATION

5114 Amastae, Jon. The issue of language
proficiency. BILINGUAL REVIEW, Vol. 10, no.
1 (January, April, 1983), p. 73-80. English.
DESCR: Alatis, James E.; Bilingual
Bicultural Education; Book Reviews.

Gurule, Dorothy

5115 Laws, Bart. Raza unida de Cristal. SOUTHERN
EXPOSURE, Vol. 10, no. 2 (March, April,
1982), p. 67-72. English. DESCR: Crystal
City, TX; History; La Raza Unida Party;
Mexican American Youth Organization (MAYO);
*Political Parties and Organizations; Reyes,
Carlos.

Guthrie, Grace Pung

5116 Walia, Adorna. Book review of: CULTURE AND
THE BILINGUAL CLASSROOM: STUDIES IN
CLASSROOM ETHNOGRAPHY. BILINGUAL JOURNAL,
Vol. 6, no. 4 (Summer 1982), p. 30-31.
English. DESCR: Au, Kathryn Hu-Pei;
Biculturalism; *Bilingual Bicultural
Education; Book Reviews; Cultural Pluralism;
*CULTURE AND THE BILINGUAL CLASSROOM:
STUDIES IN CLASSROOM ETHNOLOGY; Trueba,
Henry T.

Gutierrez, Alberto

5117 Newsfront. HISPANIC BUSINESS, Vol. 4, no. 2
(February 1982), p. 7. English. DESCR: Asip,
Patricia V.; Banuelos, Ramona Acosta;
*Biographical Notes; Businesspeople;
Gonzalez, Henry B.; IMAGE, Washington, DC.

Gutierrez, Efrain

5118 Barrios, Gregg. A cinema of failure, a
cinema of hunger: the films of Efrain
Gutierrez. BILINGUAL REVIEW, Vol. 10, no.
2-3 (May, December, 1983), p. 179-180.
English. DESCR: Film Reviews.

Gutierrez, Felix

5119 Breiter, Toni. An interview with some
experts. AGENDA, Vol. 11, no. 3 (May, June,
1981), p. 48-52. English. DESCR: Guernica,
Antonio; *Mass Media; Morales, Rosa;
Schement, Jorge Reina; Valenzuela, Nicholas.

Gutierrez, Jorge

5120 Baltodano, J. C. Success. CAMINOS, Vol. 4,
no. 6 (June 1983), p. 32,34+. English.
DESCR: Colleges and Universities; Gallegos,
Genevie; Sotelo, Priscilla Elvira;
*Students; Torres, Juan; University of
California, Berkeley.

Gutierrez, Jose Angel

5121 Miller, Michael V. Chicano community control
in South Texas: problems and prospects.
JOURNAL OF ETHNIC STUDIES, Vol. 3, no. 3
(Fall 1975), p. 70-89. English. DESCR:
Chicano Movement; Crystal City, TX; History;
La Raza Unida Party; Patron System;
*Political Parties and Organizations; Social
Classes; Social History and Conditions;
*South Texas.

Gutierrez, Jose Roberto

5122 People. HISPANIC BUSINESS, Vol. 5, no. 4
(April 1983), p. 9. English. DESCR:
Alvarado, Linda M.; *Biographical Notes;
Businesspeople; Castillo, Irenemaree;
Castillo, Sylvia; Del Junco, Tirso; Juarez,
Joe; Mata, Bill; Miyares, Marcelino;
Montanez Davis, Grace; Montoya, Velma;
Pineda, Pat; Siberio, Julio; Thompson, Edith
Lopez.

Gutierrez, Ramon

5123 Chavira, Ricardo. Gutierrez, first Latino

recipient. NUESTRO, Vol. 7, no. 3 (April
1983), p. 11-12. English. DESCR: Financial
Aid; History; MacArthur Foundation; New
Mexico.

Guzman, Ralph C.

5124 Newsfront. HISPANIC BUSINESS, Vol. 4, no. 4
(April 1982), p. 8, 24. English. DESCR:
*Biographical Notes; Burgos, Elizabeth;
*Businesspeople; Flores, Arturo; Garcia,
Carlos E.; Garcia, Edward T.; Hernandez,
Richard; National Coalition of Hispanic
Mental Health and Human Services
Organizations (COSSMHO); Parra, Oscar C.;
Willie, Herm M.

Guzman-Randle, Irene

5125 People. HISPANIC BUSINESS, Vol. 5, no. 2
(February 1983), p. 7. English. DESCR:
Alvarez, Everett, Jr.; Appointed Officials;
*Biographical Notes; Businesspeople; Roubin,
Angel; Vasquez, Victor; Villareal, Luis
Maria.

H & H Meat Products, Mercedes, TX

5126 White House honors three minority firms.
NUESTRO, Vol. 7, no. 8 (October 1983), p.
51. English. DESCR: *Business Enterprises;
Businesspeople; Carson, Norris L.; Hinojosa,
Liborio; J.T. Construction Co., El Paso, TX;
National Minority Enterprise Development
Week; N.L. Carson Construction, Inc.,
Carthage, MS; Torres, Jaime.

HABANA! ANTOLOGIA MUSICAL

5127 Whitney, James. Habana! comes to Manhattan.
NUESTRO, Vol. 7, no. 2 (March 1983), p.
55-56. English. DESCR: HAVANA SINGS;
Musicals; Performing Arts.

Habenstein, Robert W.

5128 Zaks, Vivian Calderon. Book review of:
ETHNIC FAMILIES IN AMERICA: PATTERNS AND
VARIATIONS. HISPANIC JOURNAL OF BEHAVIORAL
SCIENCES, Vol. 4, no. 1 (March 1982), p.
122-128. English. DESCR: Book Reviews;
*ETHNIC FAMILIES IN AMERICA: PATTERNS AND
VARIATIONS; Mindel, Charles H.

Hagopian, Tom

5129 "Racist and demeaning". NUESTRO, Vol. 7, no.
2 (March 1983), p. 7. English. DESCR:
Agricultural Laborers; Book Reviews;
Granada, Pilar; Racism; *SPANISH FOR THE
CALIFORNIA FARMERS.

Haiti

5130 Adrien Gallo's les tap - tap of Haiti.
NUESTRO, Vol. 6, no. 1 (January, February,
1982), p. 56-58. English. DESCR: *Graffiti.

5131 Equity for camp victims. NUESTRO, Vol. 6,
no. 1 (January, February, 1982), p. 10-11.
English. DESCR: Immigration and
Naturalization Service (INS); *Immigration
Law; Refugees.

5132 Haitian boat people. NUESTRO, Vol. 5, no. 8
(November 1981), p. 10. English. DESCR:
*Economic Refugees; Political Refugees;
World Bank.

Halacha Institute

5133 Steigelfest, Annette. Ethnicity and sex role socialization. BILINGUAL JOURNAL, Vol. 6, no. 3 (Spring 1982), p. 11-15,24. English. **DESCR:** Ethnic Attitudes; *Identity; Orthodox Jews; *Sex Roles; Sex Stereotypes; Socialization.

Ham v. South Carolina

5134 Fram, Steven J. Restricting inquiry into racial attitudes during the Voir Dire. AMERICAN CRIMINAL REVIEW, Vol. 19, no. 4 (Spring 1982), p. 719-750. English. **DESCR:** Aldridge v. U.S.; Juries; *Racism; Ristaino v. Ross; Rosales v. U.S.; Rosales-Lopez, Humberto.

Handicapped

5135 Achievements of social security worker noted. NUESTRO, Vol. 6, no. 10 (December 1982), p. 31. English. **DESCR:** *Social Security Administration.

5136 Ambert, Alba N. The identification of LEP children with special needs. BILINGUAL JOURNAL, Vol. 6, no. 1 (Fall 1982), p. 17-22. English. **DESCR:** Cultural Characteristics; Language Interference; Limited-English Proficient (LEP); *Special Education.

5137 Arnold, Bill R. Attitudinal research and Hispanic handicapped: a review of selected needs. JOURNAL OF REHABILITATION, Vol. 49, no. 4 (October, December, 1983), p. 36-38. English. **DESCR:** Attitude (Psychological); Literature Reviews.

5138 Dean, Raymond S. Intelligence-achievement discrepancies in diagnosing pediatric learning disabilities. CLINICAL NEUROPSYCHOLOGY, Vol. 4, no. 2 (1982), p. 58-62. English. **DESCR:** Anglo Americans; Intelligence Tests; Peabody Individual Achievement Test (PIAT); Youth; ZOOT SUIT [film].

5139 Gallegos, Anne; Gallegos, Roberto; and Rodriguez, Roy. Los inocentes: considering the special need of the Mexican American child. CONTEMPORARY EDUCATION, Vol. 54, no. 2 (Winter 1983), p. 109-112. Other. **DESCR:** Bilingual Bicultural Education.

5140 Gonzales, Juan. Puerto Rico to Philadelphia: a cure connection. NUESTRO, Vol. 7, no. 5 (June, July, 1983), p. 21-24. English. **DESCR:** Hospitals and the Community; Medical Care; Puerto Ricans; Shriner's Hospital for Crippled Children, Philadelphia, PA.

5141 Opportunity knocks ... but it needn't be equal. CHILDREN'S LEGAL RIGHTS JOURNAL, Vol. 4, no. 1 (August 1982), p. 14-17. English. **DESCR:** Board of Education of Hudson Central School District v. Rowley Individualized Educational Program (IEP); Doe v. Plyer [Tyler Independent School District, Texas]; *Undocumented Workers.

5142 Plata, Maximino and Jones, Priscilla. Bilingual vocational education for handicapped students. EXCEPTIONAL CHILDREN, Vol. 48, no. 4 (April 1982), p. 538-540. English. **DESCR:** *Bilingual Bicultural Education; Limited- or Non-English Speaking Handicapped Students (LONESHS); Teaching Profession; Vocational Education.

Handicrafts
    USE: Arts and Crafts

Hanigan, Patrick

5143 Brasch, Walter M. Hanigan case: hung up on racism? SOUTH ATLANTIC QUARTERLY, Vol. 81, no. 4 (Fall 1982), p. 429-435. English. **DESCR:** Administration of Justice; Arizona; Criminal Justice System; Garcia-Loya, Manuel; Herrera-Mata, Bernabe; Hanigan, Tom; *Laws; Racism; Ruelas-Zavala, Eleazar; Undocumented Workers.

Hanigan, Tom

5144 Brasch, Walter M. Hanigan case: hung up on racism? SOUTH ATLANTIC QUARTERLY, Vol. 81, no. 4 (Fall 1982), p. 429-435. English. **DESCR:** Administration of Justice; Arizona; Criminal Justice System; Garcia-Loya, Manuel; *Hanigan, Patrick; Herrera-Mata, Bernabe; *Laws; Racism; Ruelas-Zavala, Eleazar; Undocumented Workers.

Hanover, NM

5145 McCracken, Ellen. Book review of: SALT OF THE EARTH. JOURNAL OF ETHNIC STUDIES, Vol. 8, no. 1 (Spring 1980), p. 116-120. English. **DESCR:** Book Reviews; Chicanas; Films; International Union of Mine, Mill and Smelter Workers; *SALT OF THE EARTH; Silverton Rosenfelt, Deborah; Strikes and Lockouts; Women Men Relations; Women's Rights.

Hardgrave, Robert L.

5146 Dickens, E. Larry. Book review of: THE POLITICS OF BILINGUAL EDUCATION: A STUDY OF FOUR SOUTHWEST TEXAS COMMUNITIES. SOUTHWEST ECONOMY AND SOCIETY, Vol. 1, no. 1 (Spring 1976), p. 47-48. English. **DESCR:** Bilingual Bicultural Education; Book Reviews; Hinojosa, Santiago; *THE POLITICS OF BILINGUAL EDUCATION: A STUDY OF FOUR SOUTHWEST TEXAS COMMUNITIES.

Haro, Robert P.

5147 Perry, Charles E. Book review of: DEVELOPING LIBRARY AND INFORMATION SERVICES FOR AMERICANS OF HISPANIC ORIGIN. JOURNAL OF ACADEMIC LIBRARIANSHIP, Vol. 8, no. 1 (March 1982), p. 38. English. **DESCR:** Academic Libraries; Book Reviews; *DEVELOPING LIBRARY AND INFORMATION SERVICES FOR AMERICANS OF HISPANIC ORIGIN; Library Services.

Harris, Marvin

5148 Belton, Robert T. Book review of: CANNIBALS AND KINGS: THE ORIGINS OF CULTURE and THE MAN-EATING MYTH: ANTHROPOLOGY AND ANTHROPOPHAGY. HISPANIC JOURNAL OF BEHAVIORAL SCIENCES, Vol. 4, no. 1 (March 1982), p. 129-134. English. **DESCR:** Arens, W.; Book Reviews; *CANNIBALS AND KINGS: THE ORIGINS OF CULTURE; *THE MAN-EATING MYTH: ANTHROPOLOGY AND ANTHROPOPHAGY.

Hart, Gary

5149 Presidential election 1984. NUESTRO, Vol. 7, no. 7 (September 1983), p. 14-19. English. **DESCR:** Anderson, John; Askew, Reubin; Cranston, Alan; Elected Officials; *Elections; Fernandez, Ben; Glenn, John; Hispanic Force '84; Hollings, Ernest "Fritz"; Mondale, Walter; Political Parties and Organizations; Reagan, Ronald.

Harvard Business School's Latino Association

5150 Volsky, George. Four careers in Miami. HISPANIC BUSINESS, Vol. 5, no. 4 (April 1983), p. 10-11+. English. DESCR: Balestra, Victor C.; *Banking Industry; Biographical Notes; *Businesspeople; Huston, Maria Padilla; Masvidal, Sergio J.; Miami, FL; Valdes-Fauli, Gonzalo.

5151 Wittenauer, Cheryl. Harvard's Latino Association. HISPANIC BUSINESS, Vol. 5, no. 4 (April 1983), p. 12-13+. English. DESCR: Business Schools and Colleges; Harvard University; Student Organizations.

Harvard University

5152 Community watching: para la comunidad. CAMINOS, Vol. 3, no. 3 (March 1982), p. 58-59. Bilingual. DESCR: Cultural Organizations; *Engineering as a Profession; Financial Aid; Latino Business Students Association (LBSA); Rodolfo H. Castro Fellowship; Society for Hispanic Professional Engineers (SHPE); Student Organizations; University of Southern California.

5153 Wittenauer, Cheryl. Harvard's Latino Association. HISPANIC BUSINESS, Vol. 5, no. 4 (April 1983), p. 12-13+. English. DESCR: Business Schools and Colleges; *Harvard Business School's Latino Association; Student Organizations.

HATCO/60 [television station], Chicago IL

5154 Endicott, Craig. Chicago Hispanics to get new channel. ADVERTISING AGE MAGAZINE, Vol. 53, (February 15, 1982), p. II, M36-37. English. DESCR: Chicago, IL; Television.

HAVANA SINGS

5155 Whitney, James. Habana! comes to Manhattan. NUESTRO, Vol. 7, no. 2 (March 1983), p. 55-56. English. DESCR: *HABANA! ANTOLOGIA MUSICAL; Musicals; Performing Arts.

HAY PLESHA LICHANS TU DI FLAC

5156 Avendano, Fausto. Book review of: HAY PLESHA LICHANS TO DI FLAC. LA PALABRA, Vol. 4, no. 1-2 (Spring, Fall, 1982, 1983), p. 165-167. Spanish. DESCR: Book Reviews; Literature; Sanchez, Saul.

5157 Portales, Marco A. Anglo villains and Chicano writers. JOURNAL OF ETHNIC STUDIES, Vol. 9, no. 3 (Fall 1981), p. 78-82. English. DESCR: Book Reviews; Literature; Sanchez, Saul; Stereotypes.

Hayworth, Rita

5158 Tribute to 'the Love Goddess'. LATINO, Vol. 54, no. 5 (August, September, 1983), p. 16-17+. English. DESCR: Artists.

Headstart Program

5159 Flores de Apodaca, Roberto. Quick socio-emotional screening of Mexican-American and other ethnic head start children. HISPANIC JOURNAL OF BEHAVIORAL SCIENCES, Vol. 5, no. 1 (March 1983), p. 81-92. English. DESCR: *AML Instrument; Children; *Mental Health.

5160 Sandoval-Martinez, Steven. Findings from the Head Start bilingual curriculum development and evaluation effort. NABE JOURNAL, Vol. 7, no. 1 (Fall 1982), p. 1-12. English. DESCR:

*Bilingual Bicultural Education; Compensatory Education; *Early Childhood Education; Evaluation (Educational).

Health
USE: Public Health

Health Care
USE: Medical Care

Health Education

5161 Cayer, Shirley. Chicago's new Hispanic health alliance. NUESTRO, Vol. 7, no. 5 (June, July, 1983), p. 44-48. English. DESCR: Alcoholism; Chicago Hispanic Health Alliance; Family Planning; Latin Americans; *Medical Care.

5162 Dienhart, Paul. Minnesota support groups help Latinos through medical school. NUESTRO, Vol. 6, no. 6 (August 1982), p. 39-40. English. DESCR: Latin Americans; Medical Education; Medical Students; Minnesota; Public Health; *University of Minnesota.

5163 Gombeski, William R., Jr., et al. Communicating health information to urban Mexican-Americans: sources of health information. HEALTH EDUCATION QUARTERLY, Vol. 9, no. 4 (Winter 1982), p. 293-309. English. DESCR: Doctor Patient Relations; Mass Media; *Public Health; Surveys.

5164 Hazuda, Helen P. Ethnic differences in health knowledge and behaviors related to the prevention and treatment of coronary heart disease. The San Antonio heart study. AMERICAN JOURNAL OF EPIDEMIOLOGY, Vol. 11, no. 6 (June 1983), p. 717-728. English. DESCR: Anglo Americans; *Coronary Heart Disease; Preventative Medicine; San Antonio, TX; Socioeconomic Factors.

5165 New nutritional research center to study aging. NUESTRO, Vol. 6, no. 4 (May 1982), p. 57. English. DESCR: *Ancianos; Public Health.

Health Status
USE: Public Health

Health Survey
USE: Public Health

Hearing Impaired
USE: Deaf

HEART OF AZTLAN

5166 Orozco, Febe Portillo. A bibliography of Hispanic literature. ENGLISH JOURNAL, Vol. 71, no. 7 (November 1982), p. 58-62. English. DESCR: BARRIO BOY; *Bibliography; BLESS ME, ULTIMA; CHICANO; EL SOL Y LOS DE ABAJO; GRITO DEL SOL; *Literature; POCHO; WE ARE CHICANOS.

HECHIZOSPELLS

5167 Ortego y Gasca, Felipe de. An appreciation of "Hechizospells" by Ricardo Sanchez. MELUS: MULTI-ETHNIC LITERATURE OF THE UNITED STATES, Vol. 7, no. 2 (Summer 1980), p. 73-77. English. DESCR: *Literature; *Sanchez, Ricardo.

Heller, Kenneth

5168 Furphy, Alice. Book review of:
DISCRIMINATION IN ORGANIZATIONS. HISPANIC
JOURNAL OF BEHAVIORAL SCIENCES, Vol. 5, no.
1 (March 1983), p. 115-120. English. DESCR:
Alvarez, Rodolfo; Book Reviews;
*DISCRIMINATION IN ORGANIZATIONS.

5169 Hunsaker, Alan. Book review of: PSYCHOLOGY
AND COMMUNITY CHANGE; SOCIAL AND
PSYCHOLOGICAL RESEARCH IN COMMUNITY SETTING;
COMMUNITY PSYCHOLOGY: THEORETICAL AND
EMPIRICAL APPROACHES. HISPANIC JOURNAL OF
BEHAVIORAL SCIENCES, Vol. 5, no. 1 (March
1983), p. 121-124. English. DESCR: Book
Reviews; *COMMUNITY PSYCHOLOGY: THEORETICAL
AND EMPIRICAL APPROACHES; Gibbs, Margaret
S.; Kelly, James G.; Lachenmeyer, Juliana
Rasic; Monahan, John; Munoz, Ricardo F.;
*PSYCHOLOGY AND COMMUNITY CHANGE; Sigal,
Janet; Snowden, Lonnie R.; *SOCIAL AND
PSYCHOLOGICAL RESEARCH IN COMMUNITY
SETTINGS.

Hembrismo

5170 Gonzalez, Alex. Sex role of the traditional
Mexican family: a comparison of Chicano and
Anglo students' attitudes. JOURNAL OF
CROSS-CULTURAL PSYCHOLOGY, Vol. 13, no. 3
(September 1982), p. 330-339. English.
DESCR: Anglo Americans; *Family; Machismo;
Sex Roles.

HENRY FORD HOSPITAL

5171 Herrera, Hayden. Making an art of pain.
PSYCHOLOGY TODAY, Vol. 17, no. 3 (March
1983), p. 86. English. DESCR: Biography;
*Kahlo, Frida; Paintings; SELF-PORTRAIT WITH
PORTRAIT OF DR. FARILL; THE BROKEN COLUMN;
THE LITTLE DEER; TREE OF HOPE; WITHOUT HOPE.

Henry Molina, Inc.

5172 Communications/marketing. HISPANIC BUSINESS,
Vol. 5, no. 10 (October 1983), p. 26.
English. DESCR: Advertising; Arens &
Gutierrez; Employment; Journals; Lionetti
and Meyers Research Center, Inc.; Marketing;
*Mass Media; Midwest Hispanics in
Telecommunications Symposium, Chicago, IL;
NEW MANAGEMENT.

Herbal Medicine

5173 Vigil, Maria. Regional report, health:
Tucson students study herbal arts. NUESTRO,
Vol. 7, no. 5 (June, July, 1983), p. 12-13.
English. DESCR: *Folk Medicine; *Tucson, AZ.

HEREJES Y MITIFICADORES: MUESTRA DE POESIA PUERTORRIQUENA EN LOS ESTADOS UNIDOS

5174 Daydi-Tolson, Santiago. The right to belong:
a critic's view of Puerto Rican poetry in
the United States. BILINGUAL REVIEW, Vol.
10, no. 1 (January, April, 1983), p. 81-86.
English. DESCR: Barradas, Efrain; Book
Reviews; Puerto Rican Literature.

5175 Mullen, E.J. Book review of: HEREJES Y
MITIFICADORES: MUESTRA DE POESIA
PUERTORRIQUENA EN LOS ESTADOS UNIDOS.
REVISTA CHICANO-RIQUENA, Vol. 10, no. 3
(Summer 1982), p. 68-70. English. DESCR:
Barradas, Efrain; Book Reviews; Marin,
Carmen Lilianne; Rodriguez, Rafael.

5176 Rivero, Eliana S. Book review of: HEREJES Y
MITIFICADORES: MUESTRA DE POESIA

PUERTORRIQUENA EN LOS ESTADOS UNIDOS. THIRD
WOMAN, Vol. 1, no. 2 (1982), p. 91-93.
Spanish. DESCR: Barradas, Efrain; Book
Reviews; Puerto Rican Literature; Rodriguez,
Rafael.

Hermanos de Luz
USE: Hermanos Penitentes

Hermanos de Sangre de Cristo
USE: Hermanos Penitentes

Hermanos Penitentes

5177 Weber, Kenneth R. Book review of: MY
PENITENTE LAND: REFLECTIONS ON SPANISH NEW
MEXICO. JOURNAL OF ETHNIC STUDIES, Vol. 3,
no. 2 (Summer 1975), p. 119-121. English.
DESCR: Book Reviews; Chavez, Fray Angelico;
MY PENITENTE LAND: REFLECTIONS ON SPANISH
NEW MEXICO; *New Mexico; Religion.

Hernandez Cruz, Victor

5178 Gonzalez, LaVerne. Book review of: BY
LINGUAL WHOLES. REVISTA CHICANO-RIQUENA,
Vol. 11, no. 2 (Summer 1983), p. 75-77.
English. DESCR: Book Reviews; *BY LINGUAL
WHOLES.

Hernandez, Diego

5179 Bunnell, Robert. A conversation with
Commodore Diego Hernandez. NUESTRO, Vol. 7,
no. 8 (October 1983), p. 15-17. English.
DESCR: Caribbean Region; Military Service;
U.S. Navy.

Hernandez, Federico

5180 Sifuentes, Roberto. Aproximaciones al
"Corrido de los Hermanos Hernandez
ejecutados en la camara de gas de la
penitenciaria de Florence, Arizona el dia 6
de julio de 1934". AZTLAN, Vol. 13, no. 1-2
(Spring, Fall, 1982), p. 95-109. Spanish.
DESCR: Alonso, Epifanio; *Corrido; *CORRIDO
DE LOS HERMANOS HERNANDEZ [song lyrics];
Folk Songs; Hernandez, Manuel; Music;
Musical Lyrics.

Hernandez, Gilbert L.

5181 Gilbert L. Hernandez. LATINO, Vol. 53, no. 8
(December 1982), p. 26. English. DESCR:
*Marketing.

Hernandez, Guillermo

5182 Herrera-Sobek, Maria. Film review of: DEL
MERO CORAZON (STRAIGHT FROM THE HEART).
JOURNAL OF AMERICAN FOLKLORE, Vol. 95,
(March 1982), p. 123. English. DESCR: Blank,
Les; *DEL MERO CORAZON; Film Reviews;
Gosling, Maureen; Norteno; Strachwitz,
Chris.

Hernandez, Jesus

5183 Rivera-Cano, Andrea. Parenting: four
families' stories. LATINA, Vol. 1, no. 2
(February, March, 1983), p. 66-73+. English.
DESCR: *Child Rearing; Children; Elias, Bob;
Hernandez, Virginia; Lopez, Genevieve;
Ojalvo, Juana.

Hernandez, Joe

5184 Hernandez, Al Carlos. "Redneck Meskin" world
tour of Texas starring Joe, Johnny, y la
familia. NUESTRO, Vol. 6, no. 2 (March
1982), p. 40-42. English. DESCR: *Music.

Hernandez, Keith

5185 Ortiz, Carlos V. NUESTRO'S sixth annual
all-star baseball team. NUESTRO, Vol. 7, no.
2 (March 1983), p. 33-37. English. DESCR:
Andujar, Joaquin; Barojas, Salome;
*Baseball; Castillo, Manny; Concepcion,
Dave; Cruz, Jose; Garcia, Damaso; Guerrero,
Pedro; Lezcano, Sixto; Martinez, Tippy;
Pena, Tony; Piniella, Lou; Sports;
Valenzuela, Fernando.

Hernandez, Manuel

5186 Sifuentes, Roberto. Aproximaciones al
"Corrido de los Hermanos Hernandez
ejecutados en la camara de gas de la
penitenciaria de Florence, Arizona el dia 6
de julio de 1934". AZTLAN, Vol. 13, no. 1-2
(Spring, Fall, 1982), p. 95-109. Spanish.
DESCR: Alonso, Epifanio; *Corrido; *CORRIDO
DE LOS HERMANOS HERNANDEZ [song lyrics];
Folk Songs; Hernandez, Federico; Music;
Musical Lyrics.

Hernandez, Richard

5187 Newsfront. HISPANIC BUSINESS, Vol. 4, no. 4
(April 1982), p. 8, 24. English. DESCR:
*Biographical Notes; Burgos, Elizabeth;
*Businesspeople; Flores, Arturo; Garcia,
Carlos E.; Garcia, Edward T.; Guzman, Ralph
C.; National Coalition of Hispanic Mental
Health and Human Services Organizations
(COSSMHO); Parra, Oscar C.; Willie, Herm M.

Hernandez, Sam

5188 People. HISPANIC BUSINESS, Vol. 4, no. 6
(June 1982), p. 8. English. DESCR: Aguirre,
Pedro; Arellano, Richard; *Biographical
Notes; Businesspeople; Cortez, Pete; De la
Colina, Rafael; Nogales, Luis; Rodriguez,
Leslie J.; Roybal, Edward R.

Hernandez, Virginia

5189 Rivera-Cano, Andrea. Parenting: four
families' stories. LATINA, Vol. 1, no. 2
(February, March, 1983), p. 66-73+. English.
DESCR: *Child Rearing; Children; Elias, Bob;
Hernandez, Jesus; Lopez, Genevieve; Ojalvo,
Juana.

Heroin Addicts

5190 Dolan, Michael. Personality differences
among Black, white, and Hispanic-American
male heroin addicts on MMPI content scales.
JOURNAL OF CLINICAL PSYCHOLOGY, Vol. 39, no.
5 (September 1983), p. 807-813. English.
DESCR: Blacks; Drug Addicts; Minnesota
Multiphasic Personality Inventory (MMPI);
Personality.

HEROIN USE IN THE BARRIO

5191 Hunsaker, Alan. Book review of: ANGEL DUST:
AN ETHNOGRAPHIC STUDY OF PCP USERS; HEROIN
USE IN THE BARRIO; DRUG AND ALCOHOL ABUSE: A
CLINICAL GUIDE TO DIAGNOSIS AND TREATMENT.
HISPANIC JOURNAL OF BEHAVIORAL SCIENCES,
Vol. 4, no. 1 (March 1982), p. 118-121.
English. DESCR: Agar, Michael; *ANGEL DUST:
AN ETHNOGRAPHIC STUDY OF PCP USERS; Bescher,
George; Book Reviews; Bullington, Bruce;
*DRUG AND ALCOHOL ABUSE: A CLINICAL GUIDE TO
DIAGNOSIS AND TREATMENT; Feldman, Harvey W.;
Schuckit, Marc A.

Herrera, Hayden

5192 Book review of: FRIDA: A BIOGRAPHY OF FRIDA
KAHLO. BOOKLIST, Vol. 79, no. 11 (February
1, 1983), p. 708. English. DESCR: Artists;
Biography; Book Reviews; *FRIDA: A BIOGRAPHY
OF FRIDA KAHLO; Kahlo, Frida.

5193 Cameron, Dan. Book review of: FRIDA: A
BIOGRAPHY OF FRIDA KAHLO. NUESTRO, Vol. 7,
no. 8 (October 1983), p. 44-45. English.
DESCR: Biography; Book Reviews; *FRIDA: A
BIOGRAPHY OF FRIDA KAHLO; Kahlo, Frida.

5194 Lippard, Lucy R. Book review of: FRIDA: A
BIOGRAPHY OF FRIDA KAHLO. NEW YORK TIMES
BOOK REVIEW, Vol. 88, (April 24, 1983), p.
10+. English. DESCR: Book Reviews; *FRIDA: A
BIOGRAPHY OF FRIDA KAHLO; Kahlo, Frida.

5195 Scott, Patricia. Book review of: FRIDA: A
BIOGRAPHY OF FRIDA KAHLO. LIBRARY JOURNAL,
Vol. 108, no. 2 (January 15, 1983), p. 125.
English. DESCR: Artists; Biography; Book
Reviews; *FRIDA: A BIOGRAPHY OF FRIDA KAHLO.

5196 Silber, Joan. Book review of: FRIDA: A
BIOGRAPHY OF FRIDA KAHLO. MS. MAGAZINE, Vol.
11, no. 12 (June 1983), p. 40. English.
DESCR: Book Reviews; *FRIDA: A BIOGRAPHY OF
FRIDA KAHLO.

5197 Storr, Robert. Book review of: FRIDA: A
BIOGRAPHY OF FRIDA KAHLO. ART IN AMERICA,
Vol. 71, (April 1983), p. 19. English.
DESCR: Artists; Book Reviews; *FRIDA: A
BIOGRAPHY OF FRIDA KAHLO; Kahlo, Frida.

Herrera, Heriberto

5198 People. HISPANIC BUSINESS, Vol. 4, no. 11
(November 1982), p. 7. English. DESCR:
Biographical Notes; *Businesspeople; Diaz,
Jose; Garcia-Pedrosa, Jose R.; Garza, Jose;
Mercado, Anthony; Rios, John F.; Solano,
Faustina V.; Solis, Frank.

Herrera, Juan Felipe

5199 La muerte y el deseo: notas sobre la poesia
de Juan Felipe Herrera. LA PALABRA, Vol. 4,
no. 1-2 (Spring, Fall, 1982, 1983), p.
97-106. Spanish. DESCR: Literary Criticism;
Literature; *Poetry.

Herrera, Maria Elena

5200 Communications/marketing. HISPANIC BUSINESS,
Vol. 4, no. 3 (March 1982), p. 15. English.
DESCR: California; *Marketing; Philip
Morris, Inc.; Publicidad Siboney; Siboney
Advertising, Inc.; SRI International.

5201 Hispanics receive appointments. LATINO, Vol.
53, no. 1 (January, February, 1982), p. 20.
English. DESCR: Appointed Officials;
*Naranjo, Antonio.

Herrera Sobek, Maria

5202 Alurista and Monleon, Jose. Mesa redonda.
MAIZE, Vol. 4, no. 3-4 (Spring, Summer,
1981), p. 6-23. English. DESCR: Alurista;
Anaya, Rudolfo A.; Identity; Literature;
Morales, Alejandro; *Mythology; Viramontes,
Helen.

Herrera Sobek, Maria (cont.)

5203 Hoffer, Bates L. Sociology by value systems: explication and some implications of two studies on the folklore of Hispanics in the United States. BILINGUAL REVIEW, Vol. 9, no. 2 (May, August, 1982), p. 172-177. Bilingual. DESCR: BENJY LOPEZ: A PICARESQUE TALE OF EMIGRATION AND RETURN; Braceros; *Chicanos in American Literature; Comparative Literature; Folklore; Levine, Barry B.; THE BRACERO EXPERIENCE: ELITELORE VERSUS FOLKLORE.

Herrera-Mata, Bernabe

5204 Brasch, Walter M. Hanigan case: hung up on racism? SOUTH ATLANTIC QUARTERLY, Vol. 81, no. 4 (Fall 1982), p. 429-435. English. DESCR: Administration of Justice; Arizona; Criminal Justice System; Garcia-Loya, Manuel; *Hanigan, Patrick; Hanigan, Tom; *Laws; Racism; Ruelas-Zavala, Eleazar; Undocumented Workers.

Heublein, Inc.

5205 Heublein's Miss Black Velvet II. HISPANIC BUSINESS, Vol. 4, no. 2 (February 1982), p. 12. English. DESCR: Advertising; Beauty Contests; Consumers; *Marketing; *Miss Black Velvet Latina.

Hewlett Foundation

5206 Government review. NUESTRO, Vol. 7, no. 7 (September 1983), p. 55. English. DESCR: AIDS Hotline; California; Education; Employment; Food for Survival, New York, NY; Funding Sources; *Government Services; Laborers; Mathematics, Engineering and Science Achievement (MESA); Population Trends; Public Health; Stanford University, Stanford, CA.

Hidalgo y Costilla, Miguel

5207 City officials decide mural must be removed. NUESTRO, Vol. 6, no. 7 (September 1982), p. 51. English. DESCR: *Art; *Mural Art; San Antonio, TX.

High School Education
USE: Secondary School Education

High School Students

5208 Aptekar, Lewis. Mexican-American high school students' perception of school. ADOLESCENCE, Vol. 18, no. 70 (Summer 1983), p. 345-357. English. DESCR: Anthony, TX; *Attitude (Psychological); Canutillo, TX; Texas.

5209 Davis, James Alston. Does authority generalize? Locus of control perceptions in Anglo-American and Mexican-American adolescents. POLITICAL PSYCHOLOGY, Vol. 4, no. 1 (March 1983), p. 101-120. English. DESCR: Comparative Psychology; Family; Internal-External Reinforcement Scale; *Locus of Control; Political Ideology.

5210 McGroarty, Mary. English language test, school language use, and achievement in Spanish-speaking high school students. TESOL QUARTERLY, Vol. 17, no. 2 (June 1983), p. 310-311. English. DESCR: Academic Achievement; *English as a Second Language; Language Assessment.

High Tech '84

5211 Business notes. HISPANIC BUSINESS, Vol. 5, no. 11 (November 1983), p. 27. English.

DESCR: *Business Enterprises; Garment Industry; Personnel Management; Puerto Rico; Taxation; U.S. Department of Housing and Urban Development (HUD).

High Technology High School, San Antonio, TX

5212 Math-based careers. HISPANIC BUSINESS, Vol. 5, no. 12 (December 1983), p. 40. English. DESCR: *Careers; Council on Legal Education Opportunities (CLEO); Education; Employment Training; Graduate Schools; Legal Education; Mexican American Legal Defense and Educational Fund (MALDEF); San Antonio, TX; Science as a Profession.

High Technology Industries

5213 Balkan, D. Carlos. AMEX Systems Inc. at transition point. HISPANIC BUSINESS, Vol. 4, no. 6 (June 1982), p. 18-19,24. English. DESCR: AMEX Systems, Inc.; Business Enterprises; Caldera, Manuel R.; *Corporations; Small Business Administration 8(a) Program; U.S. Small Business Administration.

5214 Balkan, D. Carlos and Cruz, Franklin D. Space-Craft's strategy for re-industrialization. HISPANIC BUSINESS, Vol. 4, no. 11 (November 1982), p. 16-17,26. English. DESCR: Business Enterprises; Connecticut; Soto, John; Space-Craft Manufacturing, Inc.

5215 Chavarria, Jesus. Forging technologies. HISPANIC BUSINESS, Vol. 4, no. 11 (November 1982), p. 6. English.

5216 New York's tele-signal corporation. HISPANIC BUSINESS, Vol. 4, no. 11 (November 1982), p. 20. English. DESCR: Business Enterprises; NEW YORK; *Tele-Signal Corporation; Toracida, Esteben.

5217 SBA update. HISPANIC BUSINESS, Vol. 5, no. 3 (March 1983), p. 18. English. DESCR: Minority Business Development Agency (MBDA); *Small Business; Small Business Innovation Research Act; Technology.

5218 Weber, Robert. Turbo-charged MST, Inc. HISPANIC BUSINESS, Vol. 4, no. 11 (November 1982), p. 10-11,24. English. DESCR: Alcala, Al; Computers; Irvine, CA; *Media Systems Technology, Inc.(MST,Inc.)

Higher Education

5219 Bonham, G.W. Moral imperative. CHANGE, Vol. 15, (January, February, 1983), p. 14-15. English. DESCR: Employment; National Chicano Council on Higher Education (NCCHE).

5220 Canales, Judy. Preparing your child for a higher education: staying on that long road to sucess. NATIONAL HISPANIC JOURNAL, Vol. 1, no. 4 (Spring 1983), p. 6. English. DESCR: Children; Education; Educational Psychology.

5221 Cantu, Hector. Hispanic students wanted. NATIONAL HISPANIC JOURNAL, Vol. 1, no. 3 (Summer, Fall, 1982), p. 8. English. DESCR: *Enrollment; Recruitment; Students; *University of Texas at Austin.

5222 Chavarria, Jesus. The systems way. HISPANIC BUSINESS, Vol. 4, no. 4 (April 1982), p. 6. English. DESCR: *Careers; College Graduates; Employment.

Higher Education (cont.)

5223 de los Santos, Alfredo G. Jr.; Montemayor, Joaquin; and Solis, Enrique, Jr. Chicano students in institutions of higher education: access, attrition, and achievement. AZTLAN, Vol. 14, no. 1 (Spring 1983), p. 79-110. English. **DESCR**: Academic Achievement; Educational Statistics; Enrollment; Students.

5224 de Ortego y Gasca, Felipe. Puntos para los alumnos hispanos. LATINO, Vol. 54, no. 2 (March 1983), p. 12. Spanish.

5225 Diaz, Katherine A. Chancellor Tomas Rivera on today's graduates. CAMINOS, Vol. 3, no. 3 (March 1982), p. 11-13. English. **DESCR**: Rivera, Tomas.

5226 The entrepreneurial profile. HISPANIC BUSINESS, Vol. 5, no. 1 (January 1983), p. 16+. English.

5227 Forster, Merlin H. Luis Leal. LA PALABRA, Vol. 4, no. 1-2 (Spring, Fall, 1982, 1983), p. 19-20. Spanish. **DESCR**: Authors; *Biography; Latin American Literature; *Leal, Luis; Teaching Profession.

5228 Gandara, Patricia. Passing through the eye of the needle: high-achieving Chicanas. HISPANIC JOURNAL OF BEHAVIORAL SCIENCES, Vol. 4, no. 2 (June 1982), p. 167-179. English. **DESCR**: Academic Achievement; *Chicanas.

5229 Haro, Carlos Manuel. Chicanos and higher education: a review of selected literature. AZTLAN, Vol. 14, no. 1 (Spring 1983), p. 35-77. English. **DESCR**: California; Education; Literature Reviews; Students.

5230 Hernandez, Leodoro and Luevano, Richard L. A program for the recruitment of Chicanos into higher education. COLLEGE STUDENT JOURNAL, Vol. 17, no. 2 (Summer 1983), p. 166-171. English. **DESCR**: California; California State University, Stanislaus; *Enrollment; *Student Ambassador Recruitment Program, California State University, Stanislaus.

5231 Increasingly educated work force. HISPANIC BUSINESS, Vol. 4, no. 1 (January 1982), p. 29. English. **DESCR**: *Labor Supply and Market.

5232 Lamento por la jubilacion de un insigne hispanista y viejo amigo (una carta anonima). LA PALABRA, Vol. 4, no. 1-2 (Spring, Fall, 1982, 1983), p. 21-24. Spanish. **DESCR**: Authors; *Biography; Latin American Literature; *Leal, Luis; Teaching Profession.

5233 Latinos and higher education. NUESTRO, Vol. 6, no. 10 (December 1982), p. 18-19. English. **DESCR**: Education; Hispanic Higher Education Coalition (HHEC).

5234 Limon, Jose. History, Chicano joking, and the varieties of higher-education: tradition and performance as critical symbolic action. JOURNAL OF THE FOLKLORE INSTITUTE, Vol. 19, no. 2-3 (1982), p. 146-166. English. **DESCR**: *Chistes; Folklore; Humor; Interpersonal Relations; Texas; University of Texas at Austin.

5235 Longoria, Jose L. Future scenarios for Hispanics in higher education. LATINO, Vol. 54, no. 2 (March 1983), p. 6. English.

5236 Magallan, Rafael J. Resume/overview: insights into the needs of a new source of students. CASE CURRENTS, Vol. 9, no. 4 (April 1983), p. 8-10. English. **DESCR**: Students.

5237 Math-based careers. HISPANIC BUSINESS, Vol. 5, no. 9 (September 1983), p. 28. English. **DESCR**: Andrew W. Mellon Foundation; *Careers; Employment; Engineering as a Profession; Financial Aid; Garcia, Mary; National Council for Minorities in Engineering (NACME); National Medical Fellowships (NMF); Rivera, Lourdes.

5238 Matute-Bianchi, Maria Eugenia. A Chicana in academe. WOMEN'S STUDIES QUARTERLY, Vol. 10, no. 1 (Spring 1982), p. 14-17. English. **DESCR**: *Chicanas; Matute-Bianchi, Maria Eugenia; Racism; Sex Roles; Sexism.

5239 McCurdy, Jack. Chicanos mark their gains in colleges, call for more. CHRONICLE OF HIGHER EDUCATION, Vol. 25, no. 10 (November 3, 1982), p. 12. English. **DESCR**: Academic Achievement; Madrid, Arturo; National Chicano Council on Higher Education (NCCHE).

5240 Navarro, Susana. Access to higher education: a state of crisis. CAMINOS, Vol. 4, no. 6 (June 1983), p. 29-30,66+. Bilingual. **DESCR**: Colleges and Universities.

5241 Nevarez, Miguel A. The Hispanic educational dilemma: a strategy for change. HISPANIC BUSINESS, Vol. 5, no. 11 (November 1983), p. 12. English. **DESCR**: Academic Achievement; Dropouts; *Education.

5242 Olivas, Michael A. Federal higher education policy: the case of Hispanics. EDUCATIONAL EVALUATION AND POLICY ANALYSIS, Vol. 4, no. 3 (Fall 1982), p. 301-310. English. **DESCR**: Discrimination in Education; Education Equalization; Educational Law and Legislation; Federal Government; Policy Formation.

5243 The path to college. LATINO, Vol. 54, no. 2 (March 1983), p. 8-11+. English. **DESCR**: Financial Aid; *Students.

5244 Professional network. HISPANIC BUSINESS, Vol. 4, no. 9 (September 1982), p. 18,26+. English. **DESCR**: California; Castillo, Sylvia; Hispanic Women in Higher Education (HWHE); Mentors; *Self-Help Groups.

5245 Rivera, Roberto. Selected topics on Latino access to Illinois colleges and universities. INTEGRATED EDUCATION, Vol. 20, no. 3-5 (May, October, 1982), p. 101-105. English. **DESCR**: Colleges and Universities; Discrimination in Education; Illinois; Racism.

5246 Rivera, Tomas. The importance of college. CAMINOS, Vol. 4, no. 6 (June 1983), p. 26-27. Bilingual. **DESCR**: *Colleges and Universities.

5247 Schlef, Aileen. Estudio/survey: what higher education does (and doesn't do) for Hispanics. CASE CURRENTS, Vol. 9, no. 4 (April 1983), p. 14-17. English. **DESCR**: Enrollment.

5248 Taylor, Karla. Accion/action: a coast-to-coast sampling of innovative Hispanic programs. CASE CURRENTS, Vol. 9, no. 4 (April 1983), p. 11-13. English. **DESCR**: Educational Innovations; *Enrollment.

Higher Education (cont.)

5249 Taylor, Karla and Vargas, Raul. Entrevista/interview: Q: How to raise money for your Hispanic students? A: Involve your alumni and their corporate contacts. CASE CURRENTS, Vol. 9, no. 4 (April 1983), p. 18-21. English. DESCR: College Graduates; Funding Sources; *Office for Mexican American Programs, University of Southern California; Vargas, Raul.

5250 Valverde, Leonard. Hispanic academics organized for the greater good. CAMINOS, Vol. 4, no. 6 (June 1983), p. 50-51. Bilingual. DESCR: Colleges and Universities; Organizations; *Texas Association of Chicanos in Higher Education (TACHE).

5251 Vasquez, Melba J. T. Confronting barriers to the participation of Mexican American women in higher education. HISPANIC JOURNAL OF BEHAVIORAL SCIENCES, Vol. 4, no. 2 (June 1982), p. 147-165. English. DESCR: Academic Motivation; *Chicanas; Sex Roles; Socioeconomic Factors.

5252 Venerable, W. R. Student and parent attitudes toward college at five Hispanic learning centers in Illinois. JOURNAL OF THE NATIONAL ASSOC. OF COLLEGE ADMISSIONS COUNSELORS, Vol. 26, (April 1982), p. 19-23. English. DESCR: Casa Aztlan; Chicago, IL; Illinois Migrant Council; Lakeview Learning Center, Chicago, IL; *Secondary School Education.

5253 Webster, David S. Chicano students in American higher education: a review of the literature. CAMPO LIBRE, Vol. 1, no. 2 (Summer 1981), p. 169-192. English. DESCR: Dropouts; Educational Statistics; Enrollment; Graduate Schools; Literature Reviews; Professional Schools.

5254 Weinberg, Meyer. Special higher education bibliography. INTEGRATED EDUCATION, Vol. 20, no. 3-5 (May 1982), p. 45-49. English. DESCR: Bibliography.

5255 Zeff, Shirley B. A cross-cultural study of Mexican American, Black American and white American women of a large urban university. HISPANIC JOURNAL OF BEHAVIORAL SCIENCES, Vol. 4, no. 2 (June 1982), p. 245-261. English. DESCR: Anglo Americans; Blacks; *Chicanas; Sex Roles.

Hijuelos, Oscar

5256 Vega, Ed. Book review of: OUR HOUSE IN THE LAST WORLD. NUESTRO, Vol. 7, no. 10 (December 1983), p. 54-55. English. DESCR: Book Reviews; *OUR HOUSE IN THE LAST WORLD.

Hinojosa, Liborio

5257 White House honors three minority firms. NUESTRO, Vol. 7, no. 8 (October 1983), p. 51. English. DESCR: *Business Enterprises; Businesspeople; Carson, Norris L.; H & H Meat Products, Mercedes, TX; J.T. Construction Co., El Paso, TX; National Minority Enterprise Development Week; N.L. Carson Construction, Inc., Carthage, MS; Torres, Jaime.

Hinojosa, Manuel G.

5258 Hinojosa-Smith, Rolando R. Reflections on fathers: out of many lives: one. NUESTRO, Vol. 7, no. 5 (June, July, 1983), p. 62. English. DESCR: *Family; *Parent and Child Relationships.

Hinojosa, Santiago

5259 Dickens, E. Larry. Book review of: THE POLITICS OF BILINGUAL EDUCATION: A STUDY OF FOUR SOUTHWEST TEXAS COMMUNITIES. SOUTHWEST ECONOMY AND SOCIETY, Vol. 1, no. 1 (Spring 1976), p. 47-48. English. DESCR: Bilingual Bicultural Education; Book Reviews; Hardgrave, Robert L.; *THE POLITICS OF BILINGUAL EDUCATION: A STUDY OF FOUR SOUTHWEST TEXAS COMMUNITIES.

Hinojosa-Smith, Rolando R.

5260 Garcia, Ed. Quien es Rolando Hinojosa? TEXAS OBSERVOR, Vol. 75, no. 5 (March 11,), p. 26-29. English. DESCR: Biography; Book Reviews; *RITES AND WITNESSES; THE VALLEY.

5261 Medina, Ruben and Hinojosa-Smith, Rolando R. Rolando Hinojosa: entrevista. MAIZE, Vol. 5, no. 1-2 (Fall, Winter, 1981, 1982), p. 16-31. Spanish. DESCR: Authors; Literature.

HISPANEX (Oakland, CA)

5262 Cabello-Argandona, Roberto; Crary, Eleanor R.; and Pisano, Vivian M. Subject access for Hispanic library users. LIBRARY JOURNAL, Vol. 107, no. 14 (August 1982), p. 1383-1385. English. DESCR: Catalogues; Library Services; Public Libraries.

5263 Media/marketing. HISPANIC BUSINESS, Vol. 5, no. 11 (November 1983), p. 30. English. DESCR: Caballero Spanish Media, Inc. (CSM); California Chicano News Media Association (CCNMA); Employment Training; Federal Communications Commission (FCC); *Mass Media; Michell, Pat; Radio; Radio Station KALI, Los Angeles, CA.

Hispanic Access to Services (HAS), Denver, CO

5264 Tips for making the right moves in today's job markets. HISPANIC BUSINESS, Vol. 5, no. 5 (May 1983), p. 30. English. DESCR: Advertising; *Careers; Employment; *Working Women.

Hispanic Adoption Recruitment Program (HARP)

5265 "Todo se puede hacer con amor..."; Hispanic adoptions recruitment program. CAMINOS, Vol. 4, no. 11 (December 1983), p. 36-37. English. DESCR: Adoption.

Hispanic Amendments

5266 Flaherty, Francis J. The struggle continues: protecting the rights of Hispanics in the U.S. NATIONAL LAW JOURNAL, Vol. 5, (March 14, 1983), p. 1. English. DESCR: Affirmative Action; *Avila, Joaquin Guadalupe; Civil Rights; *Legal Representation; Mexican American Legal Defense and Educational Fund (MALDEF); Racism; Voting Rights.

HISPANIC AMERICA AND ITS CIVILIZATIONS, SPANISH AMERICANS, AND ANGLO-AMERICANS

5267 Rivera, Julius. Book review of: VARIETIES OF AMERICA. NEW SCHOLAR, Vol. 8, no. 1-2 (Spring, Fall, 1982), p. 523-527. English. DESCR: Book Reviews; Ethnology.

Hispanic American Construction Industry Association (HACIA)

5268 NHACE is born. LATINO, Vol. 53, no. 1 (January, February, 1982), p. 19. English. **DESCR:** Construction Industry; *National Hispanic Association of Construction Enterprises (NHACE).

Hispanic Association for Professional Advancement (HAPA)

5269 Fostering Hispanic professionalism. HISPANIC BUSINESS, Vol. 5, no. 4 (April 1983), p. 18. English. **DESCR:** *Organizations; *Professional Organizations.

Hispanic Bankers Association (HBA)

5270 People. HISPANIC BUSINESS, Vol. 5, no. 8 (August 1983), p. 10. English. **DESCR:** *Biographical Notes; Businesspeople; Calderon, Charles M.; Esteverena, Rolando C.; General Coffee Corporation; Martinez, Olivia T.; Pallares, Mariano; Ruiz, Frederick R.; Ruiz, Louis F.; Sanchez, Joseph J.

5271 Southern California's HBA. HISPANIC BUSINESS, Vol. 4, no. 9 (September 1982), p. 19. English. **DESCR:** Banking Industry; California; Organizations.

Hispanic Business 400

5272 Chavarria, Jesus. Researching the 400. HISPANIC BUSINESS, Vol. 5, no. 6 (June 1983), p. 6. English. **DESCR:** Business Enterprises; *Directories.

Hispanic Caucus

5273 Communications/marketing. HISPANIC BUSINESS, Vol. 4, no. 1 (January 1982), p. 13. English. **DESCR:** Beauty Contests; *Biographical Notes; Consumers; *Marketing; Miss Black Velvet Latina; Montemayor, Carlos R.; Philip Morris, Inc.

5274 Kirschten, Dick. The Hispanic vote: parties can't gamble that the sleeping giant won't awaken. NATIONAL JOURNAL, Vol. 15, no. 47 (November 19, 1983), p. 2410-2411. English. **DESCR:** Democratic Party; Republican Party; Southwest Voter Registration Education Project (SVRP); *Voter Turnout.

Hispanic Coalition for Economic Recovery

5275 Hispanic coalition formed on economy. NUESTRO, Vol. 5, no. 8 (November 1981), p. 38. English. **DESCR:** *De Baca, Fernando E.C.; *Economic Policy.

Hispanic Education [program]

5276 De Blassie, Richard R. and Franco, Juan N. The differences between personality inventory scores and self-rating in a sample of Hispanic subjects. JOURNAL OF NON-WHITE CONCERNS IN PERSONNEL AND GUIDANCE, Vol. 11, no. 2 (January 1983), p. 43-46. English. **DESCR:** Chicanas; New Mexico State University; *Personality; *Sixteen Personality Factor Questionnaire.

Hispanic Employment Program (HEP)

5277 NATIVE ALIENS (videotape). CAMINOS, Vol. 3, no. 8 (September 1982), p. 43. English. **DESCR:** *Manpower Programs; Veteran's Administration.

HISPANIC FOLK MUSIC OF NEW MEXICO AND THE SOUTHWEST: A SELF-PORTRAIT OF A PEOPLE

5278 Gifford, Douglas. Book review of: HISPANIC FOLK MUSIC OF NEW MEXICO AND THE SOUTHWEST: A SELF-PORTRAIT OF A PEOPLE. BULLETIN OF HISPANIC STUDIES, Vol. 59, no. 2 (April 1982), p. 162-163. English. **DESCR:** Book Reviews; Folk Songs; New Mexico; Robb, John Donald.

5279 Pena, Manuel H. Book review of: FOLK MUSIC OF NEW MEXICO AND THE SOUTHWEST: A SELF-PORTRAIT OF A PEOPLE. AMERICAN MUSIC, Vol. 1, no. 2 (Summer 1983), p. 102-105. English. **DESCR:** Book Reviews; Music; Robb, John Donald.

5280 Vincent, J. Book review of: HISPANIC FOLK MUSIC OF NEW MEXICO AND THE SOUTHWEST: A SELF-PORTRAIT OF A PEOPLE. ETHNOMUSICOLOGY, Vol. 26, no. 2 (May 1982), p. 326-327. English. **DESCR:** Book Reviews; Ethnomusicology; Folk Songs; New Mexico; Robb, John Donald; *THE SOUTHWEST: A SELF-PORTRAIT.

5281 West, John O. Book review of: HISPANIC FOLK MUSIC OF NEW MEXICO AND THE SOUTHWEST: A SELF-PORTRAIT OF A PEOPLE. JOURNAL OF AMERICAN FOLKLORE, Vol. 96, (April, May, 1983), p. 239. English. **DESCR:** Book Reviews; Folk Songs; Robb, John Donald.

5282 Zalazar, Daniel E. Book review of: HISPANIC FOLK MUSIC OF NEW MEXICO AND THE SOUTHWEST: A SELF-PORTRAIT OF A PEOPLE. HISPANIC JOURNAL, Vol. 3, no. 2 (Spring 1982), p. 139-140. Spanish. **DESCR:** Book Reviews; Robb, John Donald.

Hispanic Force '84

5283 Presidential election 1984. NUESTRO, Vol. 7, no. 7 (September 1983), p. 14-19. English. **DESCR:** Anderson, John; Askew, Reubin; Cranston, Alan; Elected Officials; *Elections; Fernandez, Ben; Glenn, John; Hart, Gary; Hollings, Ernest "Fritz"; Mondale, Walter; Political Parties and Organizations; Reagan, Ronald.

Hispanic Health and Nutrition Examination Survey (HHANES)

5284 Hispanics responding well to health survey. NUESTRO, Vol. 7, no. 1 (January, February, 1983), p. 47. English. **DESCR:** National Center for Health Statistics; Public Health.

5285 Major health survey of Latinos undertaken. NUESTRO, Vol. 6, no. 7 (September 1982), p. 56. English. **DESCR:** Public Health.

Hispanic Health Council

5286 Latinas on the march, NUESTRO survey reveals: organizations assess achievements during 1981. NUESTRO, Vol. 6, no. 2 (March 1982), p. 16-28+. English. **DESCR:** Forum of National Hispanic Organizations; Latin Americans; League of United Latin American Citizens (LULAC); National Coalition of Hispanic Mental Health and Human Services Organizations (COSSMHO); National Council of La Raza (NCLR); National Hispanic Bar Association; *National Image, Inc.; National Puerto Rican Forum, Inc.; *Organizations; Yzaguirre, Raul.

Hispanic Higher Education Coalition (HHEC)

5287 Latinos and higher education. NUESTRO, Vol. 6, no. 10 (December 1982), p. 18-19. English. DESCR: Education; *Higher Education.

HISPANIC LEGENDS FROM NEW MEXICO: NARRATIVES FROM THE R.D. JAMESON COLLECTION

5288 Weigle, Marta. Book review of: HISPANIC LEGENDS FROM NEW MEXICO: NARRATIVES FROM THE R.D. JAMESON COLLECTION. JOURNAL OF AMERICAN FOLKLORE, Vol. 96, , p. 238-239. English. DESCR: Book Reviews; Cuentos; Robe, Stanley L.

HISPANIC MENTAL HEALTH RESEARCH: A REFERENCE GUIDE

5289 Abu Bakr, Virginia. Book review of: MENTAL-HEALTH RESEARCH: A REFERENCE GUIDE. SOCIAL CASEWORK: JOURNAL OF CONTEMPORARY SOCIAL WORK, Vol. 63, no. 7 (September 1982), p. 443-444. English. DESCR: Book Reviews; Cota-Robles Newton, Frank; Mental Health; Reference Works.

5290 Bedard, Evelyn M. Book review of: HISPANIC MENTAL HEALTH RESEARCH: A REFERENCE GUIDE. RQ - REFERENCE AND ADULT SERVICES DIVISION, Vol. 22, no. 1 (Fall 1982), p. 93. English. DESCR: Bibliography; Book Reviews; Mental Health; Newton, Frank; Olmedo, Esteban L.; Padilla, Amado M.

Hispanic of the Year Award

5291 CAMINO'S fourth annual Hispanic of the year awards: the nominees. CAMINOS, Vol. 4, no. 10 (November 1983), p. 45. English. DESCR: Awards.

5292 CAMINO'S fourth annual Hispanic of the year awards: the nominees. CAMINOS, Vol. 4, no. 11 (December 1983), p. 27. English. DESCR: Awards.

Hispanic Playwrights-in-Residence Laboratory

5293 Prida, Dolores. Playwrights Laboratory: in search of a creative formula. NUESTRO, Vol. 7, no. 10 (December 1983), p. 43. English. DESCR: Authors; Education; INTAR; *Teatro.

Hispanic Policy Development Project

5294 Breiter, Toni. Hispanic policy development project. CAMINOS, Vol. 4, no. 10 (November 1983), p. 42-43,54. Bilingual. DESCR: *National Commission on Secondary Schooling for Hispanics; Secondary School Education.

5295 Hispanic student study undertaken. NUESTRO, Vol. 7, no. 10 (December 1983), p. 11-12. English. DESCR: Academic Achievement; Dropouts; Educational Statistics; Enrollment; *National Commission on Secondary Schooling for Hispanics; *Secondary School Education.

5296 Math-based careers. HISPANIC BUSINESS, Vol. 5, no. 10 (October 1983), p. 28. English. DESCR: *Careers; Carnation Company; Chicanas; Education; Engineering as a Profession; Minority Engineering Education Center, University of California, Los Angeles; Science as a Profession; University of California, Los Angeles (UCLA).

Hispanic Reading Room, Library of Congress

5297 Dorn, Georgette Magassy. Hispanic collections of the Library of Congress. NUESTRO, Vol. 6, no. 6 (August 1982), p.

35-38. English. DESCR: Libraries; Library Collections; Library of Congress; Washington, DC.

Hispanic Reapportionment District

5298 Hamner, Richard. Hispanics and redistricting: what you see is not always what you get. NATIONAL HISPANIC JOURNAL, Vol. 1, no. 2 (Winter 1982), p. 25-30. English. DESCR: Berlanga, Hugo; Elections; National Association of Latino Elected Officials (NALEO); Political Representation; Politics; *Reapportionment; *Roybal, Edward R.; Santillan, Richard.

Hispanic Society of Engineers and Scientists (HSES)

5299 Math-based careers. HISPANIC BUSINESS, Vol. 4, no. 1 (January 1982), p. 20. English. DESCR: Careers; *College Graduates; *Cox, George; Employment; Engineering as a Profession; *Leadership, Education and Development Program in Business (LEAD).

HISPANIC VILLAGES OF NORTHERN NEW MEXICO

5300 Weber, Kenneth R. Book review of: HISPANIC VILLAGES OF NORTHERN NEW MEXICO. SOUTHWEST ECONOMY AND SOCIETY, Vol. 1, no. 1 (Spring 1976), p. 48. English. DESCR: Book Reviews; Economic History and Conditions; Great Depression, 1929-1933; New Mexico; Tewa Basin, NM; Weigle, Marta.

Hispanic Women in Higher Education (HWHE)

5301 Community watching: para la comunidad. CAMINOS, Vol. 2, no. 6 (October 1981), p. 40-41+. English. DESCR: *Cultural Organizations; La Plaza Senior Citizens, Los Angeles, CA; Mexican American Political Association (MAPA); Reapportionment.

5302 People. HISPANIC BUSINESS, Vol. 4, no. 9 (September 1982), p. 7. English. DESCR: Advertising Agencies; Appointed Officials; Awards; *Biographical Notes; Diaz-Albertini, Luis; Dimartino, Rita; Garza, Jesus; League of United Latin American Citizens (LULAC); Ortega, Ray; Ortiz, George; Romero, Carlos J.; Sepulveda, Luis.

5303 Professional network. HISPANIC BUSINESS, Vol. 4, no. 9 (September 1982), p. 18,26+. English. DESCR: California; Castillo, Sylvia; Higher Education; Mentors; *Self-Help Groups.

Hispanic Women's Council

5304 Diaz, Barbara M. Continuing the success: the Hispanic Women's Council. CAMINOS, Vol. 4, no. 6 (June 1983), p. 62. English. DESCR: Awards; Chicanas; Organizations; Women for Success Awards.

5305 Gonzalez, Alicia. Women for success. CAMINOS, Vol. 3, no. 6 (June 1982), p. 42-43. Bilingual. DESCR: *Chicanas; Moreno, Rita; Organizations; Saavedra, Denise; Terrazas, Carmen.

Hispanics in Communications (HIC)

5306 Hispanics in Communications, Inc. HISPANIC BUSINESS, Vol. 4, no. 5 (May 1982), p. 12. English. DESCR: Advertising; DaCosta, Jacqueline; *Mass Media.

HISPANICS IN THE UNITED STATES: AN ANTHOLOGY OF CREATIVE WRITING

5307 Fernandez, Jose B. Book review of: HISPANICS IN THE UNITED STATES: AN ANTHOLOGY OF CREATIVE LITERATURE. ROCKY MOUNTAIN REVIEW OF LANGUAGE AND LITERATURE, Vol. 36, no. 1 (1982), p. 65-66. English. **DESCR:** Book Reviews; Jimenez, Francisco; Keller, Gary D.

Hispanidad '83

5308 School focuses on Latino needs. NUESTRO, Vol. 7, no. 1 (January, February, 1983), p. 12. English. **DESCR:** Catholic University, Washington, D.C.; Colleges and Universities; Education.

Hispano

5309 Torres, Luis. Distortions in celluloid: Hispanics and film. AGENDA, Vol. 11, no. 3 (May, June, 1981), p. 37-40. English. **DESCR:** *Films.

LA HISTORIA [film series]

5310 Levine, Paul G. Remember the Alamo? AMERICAN FILM, Vol. 7, no. 4 (January, February, 1982), p. 47-49. English. **DESCR:** Film Reviews; Films; *SEGUIN [movie]; Trevino, Jesus Salvador.

Historiography

5311 Lotchin, Roger W. New Chicano history: an urban history perspective. HISTORY TEACHER, Vol. 16, no. 2 (February 1983), p. 229-247. English. **DESCR:** Camarillo, Alberto; CHICANOS IN A CHANGING SOCIETY; DESERT IMMIGRANTS: THE MEXICANS OF EL PASO 1880-1920; Garcia, Mario T.; Griswold del Castillo, Ricardo; History; Social History and Conditions; THE LOS ANGELES BARRIO 1850-1890: A SOCIAL HISTORY; Urban Communities.

5312 Mathes, W. Michael. Sources in Mexico for the history of Spanish California. CALIFORNIA HISTORY, Vol. 61, no. 3 (1982), p. 223-226. English. **DESCR:** *California; Mexico; Spanish Influence.

5313 Romo, Ricardo. Unfinished story: Chicanos in the West. WESTERN HISTORICAL QUARTERLY, Vol. 13, no. 3 (July 1982), p. 299-302. English. **DESCR:** Chicano Studies; History.

5314 Weber, David J. and Lotchin, Roger W. The new Chicano history: two perspectives. HISTORY TEACHER, Vol. 16, no. 2 (February 1983), p. 219-247. English. **DESCR:** Camarillo, Alberto; *CHICANOS IN A CHANGING SOCIETY; DESERT IMMIGRANTS: THE MEXICANS OF EL PASO 1880-1920; Garcia, Mario T.; Griswold del Castillo, Ricardo; History; Social History and Conditions; *THE LOS ANGELES BARRIO 1850-1890: A SOCIAL HISTORY; *Urban Communities.

5315 Weber, David J. The new Chicano urban history. HISTORY TEACHER, Vol. 16, no. 2 (February 1983), p. 223-229. English. **DESCR:** Camarillo, Alberto; *CHICANOS IN A CHANGING SOCIETY; DESERT IMMIGRANTS: THE MEXICANS OF EL PASO 1880-1920; Garcia, Mario T.; Griswold del Castillo, Ricardo; History; Social History and Conditions; *THE LOS ANGELES BARRIO 1850-1890: A SOCIAL HISTORY; Urban Communities.

History

5316 Achor, Shirley. Book review of: GUNPOWDER JUSTICE: A REASSESSMENT OF THE TEXAS RANGERS. INTERNATIONAL MIGRATION REVIEW, Vol. 16, no. 2 (Summer 1982), p. 491-492. English. **DESCR:** Bernal, Joseph; Book Reviews; *GUNPOWDER JUSTICE: A REASSESSMENT OF THE TEXAS RANGERS; Pena, Alberto; Samora, Julian; Texas Rangers.

5317 Alvarez, Amando. Aguas milagrosas. LATINO, Vol. 54, no. 5 (August, September, 1983), p. 21-22. English. **DESCR:** *Explorations.

5318 Alvarez, Amando. Benito Juarez. LATINO, Vol. 54, no. 4 (May, June, 1983), p. 12-13. Spanish. **DESCR:** *Juarez, Benito; Mexico.

5319 Alvarez, Amando. Simon Bolivar. LATINO, Vol. 54, no. 8 (December 1983), p. 26-28. Spanish. **DESCR:** *Bolivar, Simon.

5320 Arnold, Frank. A history of struggle: organizing cannery workers in the Santa Clara Valley. SOUTHWEST ECONOMY AND SOCIETY, Vol. 2, no. 1 (October, November, 1976), p. 26-38. English. **DESCR:** Agribusiness; American Labor Union (Santa Clara County, CA); Cannery and Agricultural Worker's Industrial Union; *Cannery Workers; Comite de Trabajadores de Canerias, San Jose, CA; Labor Unions; *Santa Clara Valley, CA; United Cannery Agricultural Packing and Allied Workers of America (UCAPAWA).

5321 Barberis, Mary. Hispanic America. EDITORIAL RESEARCH REPORTS, no. 7 (30, 1982), p. 551-568. English. **DESCR:** Immigration; Marketing; *Population Trends.

5322 The battle of Chavez Ravine, 1949-1959. CAMINOS, Vol. 4, no. 7 (July, August, 1983), p. 11-14,38. Bilingual. **DESCR:** *Chavez Ravine, Los Angeles, CA; Los Angeles, CA.

5323 Bonilla, Tony. Toward a land of opportunity. LATINO, Vol. 54, no. 1 (January, February, 1983), p. 5+. English.

5324 Book review of: CHICANO THEATER: THEMES AND FORMS. CHOICE, Vol. 20, no. 2 (October 1982), p. 280. English. **DESCR:** Book Reviews; *CHICANO THEATER: THEMES AND FORMS; Huerta, Jorge A.; Teatro.

5325 Camarillo, Alberto M. Book review of: MEXICANO RESISTANCE IN THE SOUTHWEST: "THE SACRED RIGHT OF SELF-PRESERVATION". WESTERN HISTORICAL QUARTERLY, Vol. 14, no. 1 (1983), p. 79-80. English. **DESCR:** Book Reviews; *MEXICANO RESISTANCE IN THE SOUTHWEST: "THE SACRED RIGHT OF SELF-PRESERVATION"; New Mexico; Rosenbaum, Robert J.

5326 Campbell, Jack K. Senator Yarborough and the Texan RWY brand on bilingual education and federal aid. EDUCATIONAL STUDIES, Vol. 12, no. 4 (Winter 1981, 1982), p. 403-415. English. **DESCR:** *Bilingual Bicultural Education; Educational Law and Legislation; Social History and Conditions; Texas; Yarborough, Ralph Webster.

5327 Cardoso, Lawrence Anthony. Book review of: REVOLTOSOS: MEXICO'S REBELS IN THE UNITED STATES 1903-1923. JOURNAL OF THE WEST, Vol. 22, no. 1 (1983). p. 90. English. **DESCR:** Book Reviews; Immigration; Mexico; Raat, W. Dirk; *REVOLTOSOS: MEXICO'S REBELS IN THE UNITED STATES, 1903-1923.

History (cont.)

5328 Casillas, Mike. The Cananea strike of 1906.
SOUTHWEST ECONOMY AND SOCIETY, Vol. 3, no. 2
(Winter 1977, 1978), p. 18-32. English.
DESCR: Arizona; *Cananea Mining Strike of
1906; Cananea, Sonora, Mexico; Mining
Industry; Partido Liberal Mexicano (PLM);
*Strikes and Lockouts.

5329 Chacon, Jose Mividal. Resena historica del
periodismo en Centroamerica. CAMINOS, Vol.
4, no. 8 (September 1983), p. 20-21,50+.
Spanish. **DESCR:** Central America;
*Journalism.

5330 Chavez, John A. Aztlan, Cibola, and frontier
New Spain. CAMPO LIBRE, Vol. 1, no. 2
(Summer 1981), p. 193-211. English. **DESCR:**
*Aztlan; *Explorations; Folklore; Mestizaje;
Mexico; Missions; Native Americans;
Southwest United States.

5331 Chavira, Ricardo. Gutierrez, first Latino
recipient. NUESTRO, Vol. 7, no. 3 (April
1983), p. 11-12. English. **DESCR:** Financial
Aid; *Gutierrez, Ramon; MacArthur
Foundation; New Mexico.

5332 Conflict occurs over city statue. NUESTRO,
Vol. 6, no. 9 (November 1982), p. 11.
English. **DESCR:** Mexico; *Tucson, AZ; *Villa,
Pancho.

5333 Cordasco, Francesco. Bilingual education:
overview and inventory. EDUCATIONAL FORUM,
Vol. 47, (Spring 1983), p. 321-334.
English. **DESCR:** *Bilingual Bicultural
Education; Educational Law and Legislation;
Educational Theory and Practice; English as
a Second Language; Literature Reviews.

5334 Cuello, J. Book review of: IN DEFENSE OF LA
RAZA: THE LOS ANGELES MEXICAN CONSULATE AND
THE MEXICAN COMMUNITY. CALIFORNIA HISTORY,
Vol. 62, no. 1 (1983), p. 70. English.
DESCR: Balderrama, Francisco E.; Book
Reviews; California; *IN DEFENSE OF LA RAZA:
THE LOS ANGELES MEXICAN CONSULATE AND THE
MEXICAN COMMUNITY.

5335 De Leon, Arnoldo. Book review of: ON THE
BORDER: PORTRAITS OF AMERICA'S SOUTHWESTERN
FRONTIER. SOUTHWESTERN HISTORICAL QUARTERLY,
Vol. 86, no. 2 (1982), p. 367-368. English.
DESCR: Book Reviews; Mexico; Miller, Tom;
*ON THE BORDER: PORTRAITS OF AMERICA'S
SOUTHWESTERN FRONTIER; Texas.

5336 De Leon, Arnoldo and Stewart, Kenneth L.
Lost dream and found fortunes: Mexican and
Anglo immigrants in South Texas,1850 -1900.
WESTERN HISTORICAL QUARTERLY, Vol. 14, no. 3
(1983), p. 291-310. English. **DESCR:** Migrant
Labor; *Migration; Texas.

5337 Diaz, Katherine A. Congressman Edward
Roybal: Los Angeles before the 1960's
(interview). CAMINOS, Vol. 4, no. 7 (July,
August, 1983), p. 15-17,38. Bilingual.
DESCR: Los Angeles, CA; *Roybal, Edward R.

5338 Garcia, Mario T. Book review of: LA CLASE
OBRERA EN LA HISTORIA DE MEXICO: AL NORTE
DEL RIO BRAVO (PASADO INMEDIATO, 1930-1981).
HISPANIC AMERICAN HISTORICAL REVIEW, Vol.
62, no. 4 (November 1982), p. 694-696.
English. **DESCR:** Book Reviews; *LA CLASE
OBRERA EN LA HISTORIA DE MEXICO: AL NORTE
DEL RIO BRAVO (PASADO INMEDIATO, 1930-1981);
Labor Disputes; Laboring Classes; Maciel,
David R.

5339 Garcia, Mario T. On Mexican immigration, the

United States, and Chicano history. JOURNAL
OF ETHNIC STUDIES, Vol. 7, no. 1 (Spring
1979), p. 80-88. English. **DESCR:** Book
Reviews; *BY THE SWEAT OF THEIR BROW:
MEXICAN IMMIGRANT LABOR IN THE UNITED
STATES, 1900-1940; Immigrant Labor;
Immigration; Immigration Law; Mexico;
Reisler, Mark; Research Methodology;
Southwest United States.

5340 Garcia, Richard A. Chicano intellectual
history: myth and realities. REVISTA
CHICANO-RIQUENA, Vol. 10, no. 1-2 (Winter,
Spring, 1982), p. 285-289. English. **DESCR:**
Chicano Movement; *Essays; Self-Referents;
Stereotypes.

5341 Gonzalez, Gilbert G. Educational reform and
the Mexican community in Los Angeles.
SOUTHWEST ECONOMY AND SOCIETY, Vol. 3, no. 3
(Spring 1978), p. 24-51. English. **DESCR:**
Counseling Services (Educational);
Curriculum; *Education; Enrollment;
Intelligence Tests; Los Angeles, CA; *Los
Angeles City School District; Tracking
(Educational); Vocational Education.

5342 Gradante, William. El hijo del pueblo: Jose
Alfredo Jimenez and the Mexican cancion
ranchera. LATIN AMERICAN MUSIC REVIEW, Vol.
3, no. 1 (Spring, Summer, 1982), p. 36-59.
English. **DESCR:** Biography; Ethnomusicology;
*Jimenez, Jose Alfredo.

5343 Grijalva, Joshua. The story of Hispanic
Southern Baptists. BAPTIST HISTORY AND
HERITAGE, Vol. 18, no. 3 (July 1983), p.
40-47. English. **DESCR:** *Baptists; Puerto
Ricans; Religion; *Southern Baptists.

5344 Hernandez, Guillermo. A history of la musica
mexicana in the U.S. CAMINOS, Vol. 4, no. 10
(November 1983), p. 24,47-48. Bilingual.
DESCR: *Music.

5345 Hoffman, Abraham. Chicano history: problems
and potentialities. JOURNAL OF ETHNIC
STUDIES, Vol. 1, no. 1 (Spring 1973), p.
6-12. English. **DESCR:** Research Methodology.

5346 Jamail, Milton H. Book review of: MEXICO IN
TRANSITION. SOUTHWEST ECONOMY AND SOCIETY,
Vol. 4, no. 2 (Winter 1978, 1979), p. 47-49.
English. **DESCR:** Book Reviews; Mexico;
*MEXICO IN TRANSITION; Russell, Philip.

5347 Jensen, Joan M. Women teachers, class and
ethnicity: New Mexico 1900-1950. SOUTHWEST
ECONOMY AND SOCIETY, Vol. 4, no. 2 (Winter
1978, 1979), p. 3-13. English. **DESCR:**
Alternative Education; *Chicanas; Cultural
Pluralism; *New Mexico; Spanish Language;
Teaching Profession.

5348 Jones, Errol D. Book review of: DICTIONARY
OF MEXICAN-AMERICAN HISTORY. WESTERN
HISTORICAL QUARTERLY, Vol. 14, no. 3 (1983),
p. 339-340. English. **DESCR:** Book Reviews;
*DICTIONARY OF MEXICAN AMERICAN HISTORY;
Meier, Matt S.; Reference Works; Rivera,
Feliciano.

5349 Jones, Oakah L. Book review of: THE MEXICAN
FRONTIER, 1821-1846: THE AMERICAN SOUTHWEST
UNDER MEXICO. ARIZONA AND THE WEST, Vol. 25,
no. 2 (1983), p. 168-169. English. **DESCR:**
Book Reviews; Mexico; Southwest United
States; *THE MEXICAN FRONTIER, 1821-1846:
THE AMERICAN SOUTHWEST UNDER MEXICO; Weber,
David J.

History (cont.)

5350 Kanellos, Nicolas. The flourishing of Hispanic theater in the Southwest, 1920-30s. LATIN AMERICAN THEATRE REVIEW, Vol. 16, no. 1 (1982), p. 29-40. English. **DESCR:** Folk Drama; Social History and Conditions; *Teatro.

5351 Kanellos, Nicolas. Two centuries of Hispanic theatre in the Southwest. REVISTA CHICANO-RIQUENA, Vol. 11, no. 1 (Spring 1983), p. 17-39. English. **DESCR:** California; Los Angeles, CA; Photography; San Antonio, TX; Southwest United States; *Teatro; Texas.

5352 Klor de Alva, Jorge. Gabino Barrera and Chicano thought. AZTLAN, Vol. 14, no. 2 (Fall 1983), p. 343-358. English. **DESCR:** *Barreda, Gabino; Economic History and Conditions; Mexico; Philosophy; *Positivism.

5353 Laska, Vera. Book review of: DICTIONARY OF MEXICAN-AMERICAN HISTORY. INTERNATIONAL SOCIAL SCIENCE, Vol. 57, no. 3 (Summer 1982), p. 184. English. **DESCR:** Book Reviews; Dictionaries; *DICTIONARY OF MEXICAN AMERICAN HISTORY; Meier, Matt S.; Rivera, Feliciano.

5354 Laws, Bart. Raza unida de Cristal. SOUTHERN EXPOSURE, Vol. 10, no. 2 (March, April, 1982), p. 67-72. English. **DESCR:** Crystal City, TX; Gurule, Dorothy; La Raza Unida Party; Mexican American Youth Organization (MAYO); *Political Parties and Organizations; Reyes, Carlos.

5355 Leal, Luis. Gabino Barreda y la literatura: de la preparatoria al Ateneo. AZTLAN, Vol. 14, no. 2 (Fall 1983), p. 253-265. Spanish. **DESCR:** Ateneo de la Juventud; *Barreda, Gabino; Escuela Nacional Preparatoria; *Mexican Literature; Philosophy; Positivism.

5356 Learning more about Mexico. CAMINOS, Vol. 4, no. 5 (May 1983), p. 16-17. English. **DESCR:** *Mexico.

5357 LeCompte, Mary Lou. The first American rodeo never happened. JOURNAL OF SPORT HISTORY, Vol. 9, no. 2 (Summer 1982), p. 89-96. English. **DESCR:** *Charreada.

5358 Lotchin, Roger W. New Chicano history: an urban history perspective. HISTORY TEACHER, Vol. 16, no. 2 (February 1983), p. 229-247. English. **DESCR:** Camarillo, Alberto; CHICANOS IN A CHANGING SOCIETY; DESERT IMMIGRANTS: THE MEXICANS OF EL PASO 1880-1920; Garcia, Mario T.; Griswold del Castillo, Ricardo; *Historiography; Social History and Conditions; THE LOS ANGELES BARRIO 1850-1890: A SOCIAL HISTORY; Urban Communities.

5359 La lucha por la independencia. LATINO, Vol. 54, no. 6 (October 1983), p. 16-17. Spanish. **DESCR:** Biography; *Morelos, Jose Maria.

5360 Maciel, David R. and Bergaila, Christine. Book review of: CHICANOS: THE STORY OF THE MEXICAN AMERICANS. JOURNAL OF ETHNIC STUDIES, Vol. 2, no. 3 (Fall 1974), p. 94-95. English. **DESCR:** Book Reviews; *CHICANOS: THE STORY OF MEXICAN AMERICANS; de Garza, Patricia.

5361 Maciel, David R. Nacionalismo cultural y politica liberal en la Republica Restaurada, 1867-1876. AZTLAN, Vol. 14, no. 2 (Fall 1983), p. 267-287. Spanish. **DESCR:** *Mexico; *Physical Education; Political History and Conditions; Political Ideology.

5362 Marti, Oscar R. Barrera and moral philosophy. AZTLAN, Vol. 14, no. 2 (Fall 1983), p. 373-403. English. **DESCR:** *Barreda, Gabino; *Ethics; Mexico; Philosophy; Positivism.

5363 Marti, Oscar R. Introduction. AZTLAN, Vol. 14, no. 2 (Fall 1983), p. 209-220. English. **DESCR:** *Barreda, Gabino; *Biography; Mexico; Philosophy; Positivism.

5364 Marti, Oscar R., comp. Bibliography. AZTLAN, Vol. 14, no. 2 (Fall 1983), p. 405-417. English. **DESCR:** *Barreda, Gabino; *Bibliography; Mexico; Philosophy; Positivism.

5365 Martinez, Julio A. Book review of: DICTIONARY OF MEXICAN-AMERICAN HISTORY. RQ - REFERENCE AND ADULT SERVICES DIVISION, Vol. 21, no. 3 (Spring 1982), p. 297-298. English. **DESCR:** Book Reviews; Dictionaries; *DICTIONARY OF MEXICAN AMERICAN HISTORY; Meier, Matt S.; Rivera, Feliciano.

5366 Mathes, W. Michael. Book review of: JOAQUIN MURRIETA AND HIS HORSE GANGS. CALIFORNIA HISTORY, Vol. 61, no. 4 (1983), p. 306-308. English. **DESCR:** Book Reviews; California; Latta, Frank F.; *Murieta, Joaquin.

5367 McFadden, Bernard J. Bilingual education and the law. JOURNAL OF LAW AND EDUCATION, Vol. 12, no. 1 (January 1983), p. 1-27. English. **DESCR:** Administration of Justice; *Bilingual Bicultural Education; Discrimination in Education; Educational Law and Legislation.

5368 Mena, Jesus. Violence in the Rio Grande Valley. NUESTRO, Vol. 7, no. 1 (January, February, 1983), p. 41-42. English. **DESCR:** *Bandidos; Border Region; *Rio Grande Valley, TX; Social History and Conditions.

5369 Meyer, Michael C. Book review of: THE MEXICAN FRONTIER, 1821-1846: THE AMERICAN SOUTHWEST UNDER MEXICO. WESTERN HISTORICAL QUARTERLY, Vol. 14, no. 3 (1983), p. 337-338. English. **DESCR:** Book Reviews; Mexico; Southwest United States; *THE MEXICAN FRONTIER, 1821-1846: THE AMERICAN SOUTHWEST UNDER MEXICO; Weber, David J.

5370 Miller, Michael V. Chicano community control in South Texas: problems and prospects. JOURNAL OF ETHNIC STUDIES, Vol. 3, no. 3 (Fall 1975), p. 70-89. English. **DESCR:** Chicano Movement; Crystal City, TX; Gutierrez, Jose Angel; La Raza Unida Party; Patron System; *Political Parties and Organizations; Social Classes; Social History and Conditions; *South Texas.

5371 Molina-Pick, Gracia. The emergence of Chicano leadership: 1930-1950. CAMINOS, Vol. 4, no. 7 (July, August, 1983), p. 7-10. English. **DESCR:** *Chicano Movement; Leadership.

5372 Monroy, Douglas. Anarquismo y comunismo: Mexican radicalism and the Communist Party in Los Angeles during the 1930's. LABOR HISTORY, Vol. 24, no. 1 (Winter 1983), p. 34-59. English. **DESCR:** Cannery and Agricultural Worker's Industrial Union; *Communist Party; Confederacion de Uniones de Obreros Mexicanos (CUOM); International Ladies Garment Workers Union (ILGWU); Labor; Labor Organizing; *Los Angeles, CA; Tenayuca, Emma; Worker's Alliance (WA), Los Angeles, CA.

History (cont.)

5373 Morris, Gabrielle and Beard, Timothy.
Ernesto Galarza: early organizing efforts
and the community. CAMINOS, Vol. 4, no. 7
(July, August, 1983), p. 18-21. Bilingual.
DESCR: *Galarza, Ernesto.

5374 Olszewski, Lawrence. Book review of: CHICANO
LITERATURE: A CRITICAL HISTORY. LIBRARY
JOURNAL, Vol. 108, no. 2 (January 15, 1983),
p. 132. English. **DESCR:** Book Reviews;
*CHICANO LITERATURE: A CRITICAL HISTORY;
Poetry; *Tatum, Charles.

5375 Raat, W. Dirk. Augusto Comte, Gabino
Barreda, and positivism in Mexico. AZTLAN,
Vol. 14, no. 2 (Fall 1983), p. 235-251.
English. **DESCR:** *Barreda, Gabino; *Comte,
Auguste; Education; Educational Theory and
Practice; Mexico; Philosophy; *Positivism.

5376 Reisler, Mark. Book review of: DESERT
IMMIGRANTS: THE MEXICANS OF EL PASO
1880-1920. AMERICAN HISTORICAL REVIEW, Vol.
87, no. 1 (February 1982), p. 271-272.
English. **DESCR:** Book Reviews; *DESERT
IMMIGRANTS: THE MEXICANS OF EL PASO
1880-1920; El Paso, TX; Garcia, Mario T.;
Immigration.

5377 Research/development: books. HISPANIC
BUSINESS, Vol. 4, no. 7 (July 1982), p. 27.
English. **DESCR:** *Book Reviews; De Leon,
Arnoldo; Finance; Spiro, Herbert T.; Texas;
THE TEJANO COMMUNITY, 1836-1900.

5378 Rice, Jacqueline. Beyond the cientificos:
the educational background of the Porfirian
Elite. AZTLAN, Vol. 14, no. 2 (Fall 1983),
p. 289-306. English. **DESCR:** La Union
Liberal; Leadership; *Mexico; Political
History and Conditions; Political Parties
and Organizations; *Social Classes.

5379 Richmond, Douglas W. Mexican immigration and
border strategy during the revolution,
1910-1920. NEW MEXICO HISTORICAL REVIEW,
Vol. 57, no. 3 (July 1982), p. 269-288.
English. **DESCR:** *Border Region; Carranza,
Venustiano; Immigration; Mexican Revolution
- 1910-1920; Mexico; Social History and
Conditions; United States-Mexico Relations.

5380 Rios-Bustamante, Antonio. The Pan American
games 1951-1983. CAMINOS, Vol. 4, no. 8
(September 1983), p. 31-33,51+. Bilingual.
DESCR: Latin America; *Pan American Games;
*Sports.

5381 Rocco, Raymond. Positivism and Mexican
identity: then and now. AZTLAN, Vol. 14, no.
2 (Fall 1983), p. 359-371. English. **DESCR:**
Identity; Mexico; Philosophy; *Positivism.

5382 Romo, Ricardo. Unfinished story: Chicanos in
the West. WESTERN HISTORICAL QUARTERLY, Vol.
13, no. 3 (July 1982), p. 299-302. English.
DESCR: Chicano Studies; *Historiography.

5383 Rotberg, Iris C. Some legal and research
considerations in establishing federal
policy in bilingual education. HARVARD
EDUCATIONAL REVIEW, Vol. 52, no. 2 (May
1982), p. 149-168. English. **DESCR:**
*Bilingual Bicultural Education; Educational
Law and Legislation; Policy Formation;
Research Methodology.

5384 Saragoza, Alex M. The florescence of Chicano
historical scholarship. NEW SCHOLAR, Vol. 8,
no. 1-2 (Spring, Fall, 1982), p. 483-487.
English. **DESCR:** Book Reviews; Camarillo,
Alberto; *CHICANOS IN A CHANGING SOCIETY.

5385 Schlossman, Steven. Self-evident remedy?
George I. Sanchez, segregation, and enduring
dilemmas in bilingual education. TEACHERS
COLLEGE RECORD, Vol. 84, no. 4 (Summer
1983), p. 871-907. English. **DESCR:**
*Bilingual Bicultural Education; Biography;
Delgado v. Bastrop Independent School
District of Bastrop Co., TX (1948);
FORGOTTEN PEOPLE; *Sanchez, George I.

5386 Serafino, Nina M. U.S.-Latinoamerican
relations: 1960 to the present. CAMINOS,
Vol. 4, no. 8 (September 1983), p. 6-8,48.
Bilingual. **DESCR:** *International Relations;
Latin America; United States; United
States-Mexico Relations.

5387 Simon, Daniel T. Mexican repatriation in
East Chicago, Indiana. JOURNAL OF ETHNIC
STUDIES, Vol. 2, no. 2 (Summer 1974), p.
11-23. English. **DESCR:** *Deportation; *East
Chicago, IN; Immigrant Labor; Immigration;
Immigration Regulation and Control; Inland
Steel Company; Mexico; Social History and
Conditions.

5388 Skirius, John. Barreda, Vasconcelos, and the
Mexican educational reforms. AZTLAN, Vol.
14, no. 2 (Fall 1983), p. 307-341. English.
DESCR: *Barreda, Gabino; Education;
*Educational Theory and Practice; Mexico;
Positivism; *Vasconcelos, Jose.

5389 Through the revolution door: undocumented
workers and the U.S. economy. DOLLARS AND
SENSE, Vol. 83, (January 1983), p. 8-9+.
English. **DESCR:** *Immigration Law;
Simpson-Mazzoli Bill.

5390 Timmons, Wilbert H. American El Paso: the
formative years, 1848-1854. SOUTHWESTERN
HISTORICAL QUARTERLY, Vol. 87, no. 1 (July
1983), p. 1-36. English. **DESCR:** Border
Region; *El Paso, TX; Guadalupe Hidalgo,
Treaty of 1848; Social History and
Conditions.

5391 Van den Berghe, Pierre L. Book review of:
ETHNIC AMERICA, A HISTORY. INTERNATIONAL
MIGRATION REVIEW, Vol. 16, no. 4 (Winter
1982), p. 900-902. English. **DESCR:** Book
Reviews; *ETHNIC AMERICA, A HISTORY; Ethnic
Groups; Migration; Sowell, Thomas.

5392 Vigil, James Diego. Towards a new
perspective on understanding the Chicano
people: the six C's model of sociocultural
change. CAMPO LIBRE, Vol. 1, no. 2 (Summer
1981), p. 141-167. English. **DESCR:**
Acculturation; Assimilation; Cultural
Characteristics; Mexican Nationalism Period;
Mexico; Nationalism; Organizations;
Precolumbian Society; *Six C's Model
(Theoretical Model); Social History and
Conditions; Spanish Colonial Period.

5393 Vigil, Ralph H. Book review of: DESERT
IMMIGRANTS: THE MEXICANS OF EL PASO
1880-1920. INTERNATIONAL MIGRATION REVIEW,
Vol. 16, no. 1 (Spring 1982), p. 223-224.
English. **DESCR:** Book Reviews; *DESERT
IMMIGRANTS: THE MEXICANS OF EL PASO
1880-1920; El Paso, TX; Garcia, Mario T.;
Immigrants.

5394 Vivo, Paquita. Book review of: PUERTO RICO:
A POLITICAL AND CULTURAL HISTORY. NUESTRO,
Vol. 7, no. 5 (June, July, 1983), p. 63.
English. **DESCR:** Book Reviews; Carrion,
Arturo Morales; Puerto Rican Studies; Puerto
Rico; *PUERTO RICO: A POLITICAL AND CULTURAL
HISTORY; United States History.

History (cont.)

5395 Weber, David J. and Lotchin, Roger W. The new Chicano history: two perspectives. HISTORY TEACHER, Vol. 16, no. 2 (February 1983), p. 219-247. English. **DESCR:** Camarillo, Alberto; *CHICANOS IN A CHANGING SOCIETY; DESERT IMMIGRANTS: THE MEXICANS OF EL PASO 1880-1920; Garcia, Mario T.; Griswold del Castillo, Ricardo; *Historiography; Social History and Conditions; *THE LOS ANGELES BARRIO 1850-1890: A SOCIAL HISTORY; *Urban Communities.

5396 Weber, David J. The new Chicano urban history. HISTORY TEACHER, Vol. 16, no. 2 (February 1983), p. 223-229. English. **DESCR:** Camarillo, Alberto; *CHICANOS IN A CHANGING SOCIETY; DESERT IMMIGRANTS: THE MEXICANS OF EL PASO 1880-1920; Garcia, Mario T.; Griswold del Castillo, Ricardo; *Historiography; Social History and Conditions; *THE LOS ANGELES BARRIO 1850-1890: A SOCIAL HISTORY; Urban Communities.

5397 Weber, Kenneth R. Book review of: CANONES: VALUES, CRISIS, AND SURVIVAL IN A NORTHERN NEW MEXICO VILLAGE. JOURNAL OF ETHNIC STUDIES, Vol. 11, no. 2 (Summer 1983), p. 119-123. English. **DESCR:** Book Reviews; Canones, NM; *CANONES: VALUES, CRISIS AND SURVIVAL IN A NORTHERN NEW MEXICO VILLAGE; Ethnology; Kutsche, Paul; New Mexico; Northern New Mexico; Van Ness, John R.

5398 Weiss, Lawrence D. Industrial reserve armies of the southwest: Navajo and Mexican. SOUTHWEST ECONOMY AND SOCIETY, Vol. 3, no. 1 (Fall 1977), p. 19-29. English. **DESCR:** Capitalism; *Labor Supply and Market; Native Americans; Navaho Indians; Railroads; *Southwest United States.

5399 Zea, Leopoldo. El sentido de la historia en Gabino Barreda. AZTLAN, Vol. 14, no. 2 (Fall 1983), p. 221-233. Spanish. **DESCR:** *Barreda, Gabino; Mexico; Philosophy; Positivism.

HISTORY AS NEUROSIS: PATERNALISM AND MACHISMO IN SPANISH AMERICA

5400 Prichard, Sue. Book review of: HISTORY AS NEUROSIS: PATERNALISM AND MACHISMO IN SPANISH AMERICA. HISPANIC JOURNAL OF BEHAVIORAL SCIENCES, Vol. 5, no. 3 (September 1983), p. 356-360. English. **DESCR:** Book Reviews; Goldwert, Marvin; Machismo.

Hobbs Act

5401 Movement of illegal alien laborers into United States is Hobbs act "Commerce". CRIMINAL LAW REPORTER, Vol. 31, no. 19 (August 18, 1982), p. 2394. English. **DESCR:** Business; *Undocumented Workers; U.S. v. Hanigan.

Hoboken, NJ

5402 Gonzalez, Juan. Arson wave threatens Puerto Ricans in inner cities. NUESTRO, Vol. 6, no. 7 (September 1982), p. 27-28. English. **DESCR:** *Criminal Acts; Firefighters; *Puerto Ricans.

Hoffman, Abraham

5403 Cardoso, Lawrence Anthony. Book review of: UNWANTED MEXICAN AMERICANS IN THE GREAT DEPRESSION: REPATRIATION PRESSURES, 1929-1939. JOURNAL OF ETHNIC STUDIES, Vol.

5, no. 1 (Spring 1977), p. 120-122. English. **DESCR:** Book Reviews; Deportation; Immigrant Labor; Immigration; Immigration Regulation and Control; Mexico; Social History and Conditions; *UNWANTED MEXICAN AMERICANS IN THE GREAT DEPRESSION.

Holdenreid, Frank X.

5404 Ericksen, Charles. Holdenreid and Salazar: unanswered questions. NUESTRO, Vol. 7, no. 4 (May 1983), p. 40-41. English. **DESCR:** Assassination; Criminal Acts; Guatemala; *Salazar, Ruben; *Violence.

5405 Holdenreid, Frank X. Guatemala shantytown. NUESTRO, Vol. 7, no. 4 (May 1983), p. 39-41. English. **DESCR:** Ayudantes de los Pobres; *Guatemala; *Poverty; Refugees.

Holidays

5406 Alvarez, Amando. El Cinco de Mayo. LATINO, Vol. 53, no. 3 (May 1982), p. 19-25. Spanish.

5407 Alvarez, Amando. El Grito de Dolores. LATINO, Vol. 53, no. 5 (September 1982), p. 29-30. Spanish.

5408 Burciaga, Jose Antonio. Hannukkah, navidad and christmas. NUESTRO, Vol. 5, no. 8 (November 1981), p. 22-23. English. **DESCR:** *Christmas.

5409 Deep in the heart of Texas. LATINO, Vol. 53, no. 4 (June 1982), p. 8. English. **DESCR:** *Texas.

5410 El dia de los enamorados. LATINO, Vol. 54, no. 1 (January, February, 1983), p. 11. Spanish.

5411 Entertainment = diversion. CAMINOS, Vol. 3, no. 5 (May 1982), p. 54. Bilingual. **DESCR:** Artists; Buena Vista Cablevision, Inc.; Cinco de Mayo; Knott's Berry Farm, Buena Park, CA; Tamayo, Rufino; Television.

5412 Mimiaga, Hector. Una semana de lujo. LATINO, Vol. 54, no. 8 (December 1983), p. 22+. English.

5413 Moreno, Mario "Cantinflas". Observations on Mexico today. CAMINOS, Vol. 3, no. 10 (November 1982), p. 20,45. Bilingual. **DESCR:** Dieciseis de Septiembre; Mexico; *Moreno, Mario "Cantinflas".

5414 A sheriff's X-mas. CAMINOS, Vol. 3, no. 1 (January 1982), p. 40. Bilingual. **DESCR:** *Belvedere Childcare Center; *Block, Sherman; *Christmas.

5415 Tlaquepaque. LATINO, Vol. 53, no. 8 (December 1982), p. 13. Spanish.

Hollenbeck Junior High School, Los Angeles, CA

5416 Community watching. CAMINOS, Vol. 3, no. 5 (May 1982), p. 56-57. Bilingual. **DESCR:** Adelante Mujer Hispana Conference; Agricultural Laborers; Beilson, Anthony C.; Boycotts; Chacon, Peter R.; Chicanas; *Cultural Organizations; Farm Labor Organizing Commmittee (FLOC); Financial Aid; Junior High School Students; National League of Cities; Optimist Club of Greater East Los Angeles; Organizations; Project WELL (We Enjoy Learning & Leadership); Torres, Art.

Hollings, Ernest "Fritz"

5417 Diaz, Tom. "Wetbacks" and other fellow Americans. NUESTRO, Vol. 7, no. 8 (October 1983), p. 63. English. DESCR: Ethnic Attitudes; *Racism.

5418 Presidential election 1984. NUESTRO, Vol. 7, no. 7 (September 1983), p. 14-19. English. DESCR: Anderson, John; Askew, Reubin; Cranston, Alan; Elected Officials; *Elections; Fernandez, Ben; Glenn, John; Hart, Gary; Hispanic Force '84; Mondale, Walter; Political Parties and Organizations; Reagan, Ronald.

THE HOLLYWOOD INDIAN: STEREOTYPES OF NATIVE AMERICANS IN FILMS

5419 Cripps, Thomas. Mexicans, Indians and movies: the need for a history. WIDE ANGLE: A FILM QUARTERLY OF THEORY, CRITICISM, AND PRACTICE, Vol. 5, no. 1 (1982), p. 68-70. English. DESCR: Bataille, Gretchen M.; *Book Reviews; Films; IMAGES OF THE MEXICAN AMERICAN IN FICTION AND FILM; Native Americans; O'Connor, John E.; Pettit, Arthur G.; Silet, Charles L.P.; *Stereotypes; THE PRETEND INDIANS: IMAGES OF NATIVE AMERICANS IN THE MOVIES.

Holy Cross High School, San Antonio, TX

5420 Rosales, John. Holy Cross High: a Texas success story. NUESTRO, Vol. 6, no. 9 (November 1982), p. 41-42. English. DESCR: Carr, Vikki; *Education; *San Antonio, TX.

Home Altars

5421 Turner, Kay F. Mexican American home altars: towards their interpretation. AZTLAN, Vol. 13, no. 1-2 (Spring, Fall, 1982), p. 309-326. English. DESCR: Icons; Religion.

Homeless Persons

5422 Gonzales, Juan. Town without fear. NUESTRO, Vol. 6, no. 10 (December 1982), p. 15-17. English. DESCR: *Housing; *Puerto Rico.

Honeywell, Inc.

5423 Firm honors Latino workers. NUESTRO, Vol. 6, no. 5 (June, July, 1982), p. 11-12. English. DESCR: *Acosta, Juan; Minneapolis, MN; Mural Art.

Hospitals and the Community

5425 Fischman, Gladys, et al. Day treatment programs for the Spanish speaking: a response to underutilization. INTERNATIONAL JOURNAL OF SOCIAL PSYCHIATRY, Vol. 29, no. 3 (Fall 1983), p. 215-219. English. DESCR: *Mental Health Clinics.

5426 Garcia, Ignacio M. Miracles at Kino Hospital. NUESTRO, Vol. 7, no. 6 (August 1983), p. 11-12. English. DESCR: *Gonzalez, Arthur; *Kino Community Hospital, Tucson, AZ; Medical Care; Public Health.

5427 Gonzales, Juan. Puerto Rico to Philadelphia: a cure connection. NUESTRO, Vol. 7, no. 5 (June, July, 1983), p. 21-24. English. DESCR: *Handicapped; Medical Care; Puerto Ricans; Shriner's Hospital for Crippled Children, Philadelphia, PA.

5428 Hospital produces television series for Spanish-speaking viewers. HOSPITALS, Vol. 56, no. 8 (April 16, 1982), p. 36. English. DESCR: *Television.

5429 Poma, Pedro A. Hispanic cultural influences on medical practices. NATIONAL MEDICAL ASSOCIATION JOURNAL, Vol. 75, no. 10 (October 1983), p. 941-946. English. DESCR: Cultural Characteristics; *Medical Care.

Hostos Community College, New York, NY

5430 Puerto Rico: images from the past. NUESTRO, Vol. 7, no. 9 (November 1983), p. 48-53. English. DESCR: CONTRASTES [exhibit]; *Delano, Jack; *Photography; Puerto Rico.

HOT LAND, COLD SEASON

5431 Seda-Bonilla, Eduardo. On the vicissitudes of being "Puerto Rican": an exploration of Pedro Juan Soto's "Hot land, cold season". MELUS: MULTI-ETHNIC LITERATURE OF THE UNITED STATES, Vol. 6, no. 3 (Fall 1979), p. 27-40. English. DESCR: Puerto Ricans; Soto, Pedro Juan.

Housing

5432 Abrams, Herbert K. Occupational and environmental health problems along the U.S.-Mexico Border. SOUTHWEST ECONOMY AND SOCIETY, Vol. 4, no. 3 (Spring, Summer, 1979), p. 3-20. English. DESCR: Agricultural Laborers; *Border Region; Mexican Border Industrialization Program; Nutrition; *Pollution; *Public Health; Social History and Conditions.

5433 Arroyo, Sara G. and Tucker, M. Belinda. Black residential mobility: trends and characteristics. JOURNAL OF SOCIAL ISSUES, Vol. 38, no. 3 (1982), p. 51-74. English. DESCR: Los Angeles, CA; Undocumented Children; Watts, CA.

5434 Black, Bill. Housing for farm laborers: a California solution. NUESTRO, Vol. 7, no. 6 (August 1983), p. 36-37. English. DESCR: Agricultural Laborers; California.

5435 Garza, Jose S. Housing: Hispanic America's unfulfilled dream. HISPANIC BUSINESS, Vol. 4, no. 10 (October 1982), p. 8. English.

5436 Gonzales, Juan. Town without fear. NUESTRO, Vol. 6, no. 10 (December 1982), p. 15-17. English. DESCR: Homeless Persons; *Puerto Rico.

5437 Government review. NUESTRO, Vol. 7, no. 6 (August 1983), p. 56. English. DESCR: Ballet de Puerto Rico; Dance; Education; Employment; *Government Funding Sources; Government Services; Income; National Fair Housing Law; Population Distribution; Urban Development Action Grant (UDAG); Veterans.

5438 Hwang, Sean-Shong and Murdock, Steve H. Residential segregation in Texas in 1980. SOCIAL SCIENCE QUARTERLY, Vol. 63, (December 1982), p. 737-748. English. DESCR: *Segregation and Desegregation; Texas.

5439 Krivo, Lauren J. Housing price inequalities: a comparison of Anglos, Blacks, and Spanish-origin populations. URBAN AFFAIRS QUARTERLY, Vol. 17, no. 4 (1982), p. 445-462. English. DESCR: Residential Segregation; *Urban Housing.

Housing (cont.)

5440 Lopez, Marcos. Legal affair. LATINA, Vol. 1,
no. 2 (February, March, 1983), p. 85.
English. DESCR: Criminal Acts; Employment;
*Legal Aid.

5441 LULAC is building $2.6 million housing
project in Corpus Christi. LATINO, Vol. 53,
no. 8 (December 1982), p. 18. English.
DESCR: Corpus Christi, TX; *League of United
Latin American Citizens (LULAC).

5442 Public housing vital. NUESTRO, Vol. 6, no. 9
(November 1982), p. 9. English. DESCR:
Poverty.

5443 Quinlivan, Robert. The need for Hispanic
senior housing. CAMINOS, Vol. 3, no. 7
(July, August, 1982), p. 42-43. Bilingual.
DESCR: *Ancianos; Colonial Barrio Seniors;
San Diego, CA; Villa Merced Housing Project.

5444 Rosales, John. Life at the "Chicano Hilton".
NUESTRO, Vol. 6, no. 4 (May 1982), p. 23-26.
English. DESCR: Washington, DC.

5445 Sun Belt dominates in top housing markets.
NUESTRO, Vol. 7, no. 1 (January, February,
1983), p. 36. English. DESCR: Arizona;
Texas.

5446 Washington carousel. HISPANIC BUSINESS, Vol.
4, no. 10 (October 1982), p. 23. English.
DESCR: *Legislation.

Houston Community College

5447 Buckholtz, Marjorie Weidenfeld. Technical
training in two languages helps Houston stay
cool. AMERICAN EDUCATION, Vol. 18, no. 3
(April 1982), p. 11-14. English. DESCR:
*Employment Training; Language Arts;
Language Proficiency; Vocational Education.

Houston Parent-Child Development Center(PCDC)

5448 Johnson, Dale L. and Breckenridge, James N.
The Houston Parent-Child Development Center
and the primary prevention of behavior
problems in young children. AMERICAN JOURNAL
OF COMMUNITY PSYCHOLOGY, Vol. 10, no. 3
(June 1982), p. 305-316. English. DESCR:
*Child Rearing; Children; Early Childhood
Education; Parent and Child Relationships;
Social Classes.

Houston, TX

5449 MacManus, Susan A. and Cassel, Carol A.
Mexican-Americans in city-politics:
participation, representation, and policy
preferences. URBAN INTEREST, Vol. 4, no. 1
(Spring 1982), p. 57-69. English. DESCR:
Blacks; Local Government; *Political
Representation; Public Opinion; Public
Policy.

5450 Vara, Richard. Business savvy and Capricorn
spirit: How do you spell entrepreneurship?
HISPANIC BUSINESS, Vol. 5, no. 1 (January
1983), p. 18-19+. English. DESCR: Arroyos,
Alex; *Biography; Business Enterprises;
Export Trade.

HOW TO EXPORT: A MARKETING MANUAL

5451 Foreign trade. HISPANIC BUSINESS, Vol. 5,
no. 10 (October 1983), p. 29. English.
DESCR: Agency for International Development
(AID); Caribbean Region; Economic History
and Conditions; *Foreign Trade; Mexico;
Puerto Rico; U.S. Trade Center (Mexico
City).

5452 Foreign trade. HISPANIC BUSINESS, Vol. 5,
no. 11 (November 1983), p. 31. English.
DESCR: California; *Foreign Trade;
Marketing; Miami, FL; Miami Free Zone;
Puerto Rico.

Hoyenga, Katherine Blick

5453 Coolson, Freda L. Book review of: THE
QUESTION OF SEX DIFFERENCES: BIOLOGICAL,
CULTURAL AND PSYCHOLOGICAL ISSUES. HISPANIC
JOURNAL OF BEHAVIORAL SCIENCES, Vol. 4, no.
3 (September 1982), p. 391-393. English.
DESCR: Book Reviews; Hoyenga, Kermit T.;
*THE QUESTION OF SEX DIFFERENCES:
BIOLOGICAL, CULTURAL, AND PSYCHOLOGICAL
ISSUES.

Hoyenga, Kermit T.

5454 Coolson, Freda L. Book review of: THE
QUESTION OF SEX DIFFERENCES: BIOLOGICAL,
CULTURAL AND PSYCHOLOGICAL ISSUES. HISPANIC
JOURNAL OF BEHAVIORAL SCIENCES, Vol. 4, no.
3 (September 1982), p. 391-393. English.
DESCR: Book Reviews; Hoyenga, Katherine
Blick; *THE QUESTION OF SEX DIFFERENCES:
BIOLOGICAL, CULTURAL, AND PSYCHOLOGICAL
ISSUES.

Hoyos, Rodolfo

5455 Gonzalez, Magdalena. Recognizing Hispanic
achievements in entertainment - U.S. and
Mexico. CAMINOS, Vol. 3, no. 7 (July,
August, 1982), p. 18-24. Bilingual. DESCR:
Allende, Fernando; Artists; Awards; Bonilla
Giannini, Roxanna; Eynoso, David; Felix,
Maria; Films; Gallego, Gina; *Golden Eagle
Awards; Lamas, Lorenzo; Lopez, Conchita;
Lopez, Lisa; Montalban, Ricardo; Nosotros
[film production company]; Quintero, Jose;
Rowe, Arthur; Television; Torres, Liz.

Huapaya, Sixto Guillermo

5456 People. HISPANIC BUSINESS, Vol. 5, no. 6
(June 1983), p. 8. English. DESCR: Appointed
Officials; *Biographical Notes;
Businesspeople; Goizueta, Roberto C.;
Guerra, Stella; Kitano, Pat; Manriquez,
Suzanna; Oppenheimer-Nicolau, Siabhan;
Ortiz, Solomon; Pachon, Harry P.;
Richardson, Bill Lopez; Torres, Esteban E.;
Torres, Johnny.

Hudson County, NJ

5457 Garcia, Margarita. The last days in Cuba:
personal accounts of the circumstances of
the exit. MIGRATION TODAY, Vol. 11, no. 4-5
(1983), p. 13-26. English. DESCR: Castro,
Fidel; Cuba; *Cuban Boatlift; *Cubanos;
Immigration; Peruvian Embassy (Cuba).

La Huelga
USE: Boycotts

Huerta, Dolores

5458 Baciu, Joyce A. The winners - Los ganadores.
CAMINOS, Vol. 3, no. 2 (February 1982), p.
14-20,45. Bilingual. DESCR: *Awards;
Caldera, Manuel; Gomez, Ignacio; Lizarraga,
David C.; Obledo, Mario; Olmos, Edward
James; Rivera, Geraldo; Rivera, Tomas.

5459 Mercado, Olivia. Chicanas: myths and roles.
COMADRE, no. 1 (Summer 1977), p. 26-32.
English. DESCR: *Chicanas; Gallo, Juana;
*Identity; Leadership; Sex Roles; Women's
Rights.

Huerta, Jorge A.

5460 Book review of: CHICANO THEATER: THEMES AND
FORMS. CHOICE, Vol. 20, no. 2 (October
1982), p. 280. English. DESCR: Book Reviews;
*CHICANO THEATER: THEMES AND FORMS; History;
Teatro.

5461 Miller, John C. Book review of: NUEVOS
PASOS: CHICANO AND PUERTO RICAN DRAMA.
MELUS: MULTI-ETHNIC LITERATURE OF THE UNITED
STATES, Vol. 6, no. 3 (Fall 1979), p.
99-100. English. DESCR: Book Reviews;
*Kanellos, Nicolas; NUEVOS PASOS: CHICANO
AND PUERTO RICAN DRAMA (thematic issue of
REVISTA CHICANO-RIQUENA); *Teatro.

5462 Padilla-Sanchez, Beverly. T.E.N.A.Z.: Teatro
Chicano/Teatro Latino. CAMINOS, Vol. 2, no.
7 (December 1981), p. 34-35. Bilingual.
DESCR: *Eleventh International Chicano
Latino Teatro Festival, Mission Cultural
Center, San Francisco, CA; Teatro.

Human Relations Commission, Los Angeles, CA

5463 Olguin, Hank S. Images: minorities in the
media. LATINA, Vol. 1, no. 2 (February,
March, 1983), p. 21. English. DESCR: *Mass
Media; Media Artists Against Discrimination
(MAAD); Stereotypes.

Human Resources Administration

5464 Food stamp cheaters. NUESTRO, Vol. 5, no. 8
(November 1981), p. 10. English. DESCR: Food
Stamps; *Richmond, Frederick W.; *Welfare.

Human Rights

5465 Madrid, Joe. Q & A with Joan Baez. CAMINOS,
Vol. 3, no. 11 (December 1982), p. 44-45.
English. DESCR: *Artists; Baez, Joan;
*Singers.

Human Services
USE: Community Services

Humor

5466 Alarcon, Justo S. La meta critica Chicana.
REVISTA CHICANO-RIQUENA, Vol. 10, no. 3
(Summer 1982), p. 47-52. Spanish. DESCR:
Essays; Literary Criticism.

5467 Cardenas, Leo. The day E.T. met T.B. and
A.T. LATINO, Vol. 53, no. 8 (December 1982),
p. 5. English.

5468 Castro, Rafaela. Mexican women's sexual
jokes. AZTLAN, Vol. 13, no. 1-2 (Spring,
Fall, 1982), p. 275-293. English. DESCR:
Chicanas; *Chistes.

5469 Limon, Jose. History, Chicano joking, and
the varieties of higher-education: tradition
and performance as critical symbolic action.
JOURNAL OF THE FOLKLORE INSTITUTE, Vol. 19,
no. 2-3 (1982), p. 146-166. English. DESCR:
*Chistes; Folklore; Higher Education;
Interpersonal Relations; Texas; University
of Texas at Austin.

5470 McGhee, Paul E. and Duffy, Nelda S.
Children's appreciation of humor victimizing
different racial-ethnic groups: racial
ethnic differences. JOURNAL OF
CROSS-CULTURAL PSYCHOLOGY, Vol. 14, no. 1
(March 1983), p. 29-40. English. DESCR:
Primary School Students; Racism.

5471 Montez, Philip. How to spot a Chicano from
New Texicaloradizona. NUESTRO, Vol. 7, no. 7
(September 1983), p. 54. English. DESCR:

*Identity.

5472 Moreno, Mario "Cantinflas". Ne dejen de
reir. LATINO, Vol. 54, no. 4 (May, June,
1983), p. 21. English. DESCR: Artists;
*Moreno, Mario "Cantinflas".

5473 New mecca for comedians. NUESTRO, Vol. 6,
no. 5 (June, July, 1982), p. 12. English.
DESCR: *San Francisco, CA; Simon, Jose.

5474 Padilla, Steve. The comedian. NUESTRO, Vol.
7, no. 2 (March 1983), p. 25-27. English.
DESCR: Artists; Performing Arts; *Rodriguez,
Paul.

5475 Valdez, Cynthia. Toro-cicletas y agua
potable de Mexico. LATINO, Vol. 53, no. 1
(January, February, 1982), p. 12. Spanish.

HUNGER OF MEMORY: THE EDUCATION OF RICHARD RODRIGUEZ

5476 Ano Nuevo de Kerr, Louise. Book review of:
HUNGER OF MEMORY: THE EDUCATION OF RICHARD
RODRIGUEZ. COMMONWEAL, Vol. 110, no. 1
(January 14, 1983), p. 26-28. English.
DESCR: Book Reviews; Rodriguez, Richard.

5477 Bell, Michael Davitt. Fitting into a
tradition of autobiography. CHANGE, Vol. 14,
no. 7 (October 1982), p. 36-39. English.
DESCR: Affirmative Action; Assimilation;
Bilingual Bicultural Education; Biography;
Book Reviews; Rodriguez, Richard.

5478 Book review of: HUNGER OF MEMORY: THE
EDUCATION OF RICHARD RODRIGUEZ. SAN
FRANCISCO REVIEW OF BOOKS, Vol. 7, (Summer
1982), p. 11. English. DESCR: Attitude
(Psychological); Bilingual Bicultural
Education; Book Reviews; Identity;
Rodriguez, Richard.

5479 Chall, Jeanne. Rich and sharp memories of
reading. CHANGE, Vol. 14, no. 7 (October
1982), p. 36-40. English. DESCR:
Assimilation; Book Reviews; Language Arts;
Reading; Rodriguez, Richard; Socioeconomic
Factors.

5480 Chavez, Linda. HUNGER OF MEMORY: the
metamorphosis of a disadvantaged child.
AMERICAN EDUCATOR, Vol. 6, no. 3 (Fall
1982), p. 14-16. English. DESCR: Book
Reviews; Rodriguez, Richard.

5481 Cotera, Martha P. Rich-heard rod-ree-guess.
LATINA, Vol. 1, no. 1 (1982), p. 27+.
English. DESCR: Book Reviews; Rodriguez,
Richard.

5482 Fainberg, Louise Vasvari. HUNGER OF MEMORY:
review of a review. NABE JOURNAL, Vol. 6,
no. 2-3 (Winter, Spring, 1981, 1982), p.
115-116. English. DESCR: Book Reviews;
Rodriguez, Richard; Zweig, Paul.

5483 Garcia, Ed. Book review of: HUNGER OF
MEMORY: THE EDUCATION OF RICHARD RODRIGUEZ.
TEXAS OBSERVOR, Vol. 74, no. 12 (June 18,
1982), p. 23-24. English. DESCR: Book
Reviews; Rodriguez, Richard.

5484 HUNGER OF MEMORY: THE EDUCATION OF RICHARD
RODRIGUEZ. NUESTRO, Vol. 6, no. 3 (April
1982), p. 52-53. English. DESCR: Book
Reviews; Rodriguez, Richard.

HUNGER OF MEMORY: THE EDUCATION OF RICHARD RODRIGUEZ (cont.)

5485 Madrid, Arturo. Book review of: HUNGER OF MEMORY: THE EDUCATION OF RICHARD RODRIGUEZ. TEXAS OBSERVOR, Vol. 74, no. 13 (July 9, 1982), p. 14+. English. DESCR: Book Reviews; Rodriguez, Richard.

5486 Olivas, Michael A. Painful to write, painful to read. CHANGE, Vol. 14, no. 7 (October 1982), p. 37-42. English. DESCR: Biography; Book Reviews; Rodriguez, Richard.

5487 Olson, James S. Book review of: HUNGER OF MEMORY: THE EDUCATION OF RICHARD RODRIGUEZ. JOURNAL OF THE WEST, Vol. 22, no. 1 (1983), p. 80-81. English. DESCR: Bilingual Bicultural Education; Book Reviews; Identity; Rodriguez, Richard.

5488 Porter, Horace A. Book review of: HUNGER OF MEMORY: THE EDUCATION OF RICHARD RODRIGUEZ. AMERICAN SCHOLAR, Vol. 52, no. 2 (Spring 1983), p. 278-285. English. DESCR: Book Reviews; Rodriguez, Richard.

5489 Riley, Michael N. Book review of: HUNGER OF MEMORY: THE EDUCATION OF RICHARD RODRIGUEZ. NATIONAL ASSOCIATION OF SECONDARY SCHOOL PRINCIPALS: BULLETIN, Vol. 66, no. 45 (December 1982), p. 112-113. English. DESCR: *Book Reviews; Rodriguez, Richard.

5490 Rodriguez, Richard. A minority scholar speaks out. AMERICAN EDUCATION, Vol. 18, no. 9 (November 1982), p. 2-5. English. DESCR: Affirmative Action; Authors; Bilingual Bicultural Education; *Biography; Rodriguez, Richard.

5491 Rodriguez, Richard, et al. Education of Richard Rodriguez [excerpts from "HUNGER OF MEMORY", including discussion]. CHANGE, Vol. 14, no. 7 (October 1982), p. 32-42+. English. DESCR: Affirmative Action; Assimilation; Bilingual Bicultural Education; Biography; *Rodriguez, Richard.

5492 Smith, Bruce M. Book review of: HUNGER OF MEMORY: THE EDUCATION OF RICHARD RODRIGUEZ. PHI DELTA KAPPAN, Vol. 64, no. 4 (December 1982), p. 289-290. English. DESCR: Book Reviews; Rodriguez, Richard.

5493 Willie, Charles V. First learning unchallenged and untested. CHANGE, Vol. 14, no. 7 (October 1982), p. 37-41. English. DESCR: Affirmative Action; Bilingual Bicultural Education; Biography; Book Reviews; Education; Rodriguez, Richard.

Hunt, Raymond G.

5494 Rochester, R. C. Book review of: IMPACT OF RACISM ON WHITE AMERICANS. HISPANIC JOURNAL OF BEHAVIORAL SCIENCES, Vol. 5, no. 1 (March 1983), p. 125-129. English. DESCR: Book Reviews; Bowser, Benjamin P.; *IMPACT OF RACISM ON WHITE AMERICANS.

Hurtado Larrea, Osvaldo

5495 Ecuadorian president Osvaldo Hurtado Larrea on the future of Ecuador. CAMINOS, Vol. 4, no. 1-2 (January, February, 1983), p. 56-57,61. Bilingual. DESCR: *Ecuador; International Relations.

Hurtado, Oscar

5496 Gonzalez Cruz, Luis F. Quest and discovery in Oscar Hurtado's THE DEAD CITY OF KORAD: a unique experiment in science fiction poetry.

MAIZE, Vol. 5, no. 1-2 (Fall, Winter, 1981, 1982), p. 74-85. English. DESCR: Cuba; Latin American Literature; *Literary Criticism; Poetry.

Huston, Maria Padilla

5497 Volsky, George. Four careers in Miami. HISPANIC BUSINESS, Vol. 5, no. 4 (April 1983), p. 10-11+. English. DESCR: Balestra, Victor C.; *Banking Industry; Biographical Notes; *Businesspeople; Harvard Business School's Latino Association; Masvidal, Sergio J.; Miami, FL; Valdes-Fauli, Gonzalo.

Hutchinson, E.P.

5498 Weiss, Richard. Book review of: LEGISLATIVE HISTORY OF AMERICAN IMMIGRATION POLICY, 1798-1965. INTERNATIONAL MIGRATION REVIEW, Vol. 16, no. 3 (Fall 1982), p. 683. English. DESCR: Book Reviews; Immigration Law; *LEGISLATIVE HISTORY OF AMERICAN IMMIGRATION POLICY, 1798-1965.

Hypertension

5499 Ailinger, Rita L. Hypertension knowledge in a Hispanic community. NURSING RESEARCH, Vol. 31, no. 4 (July, August, 1982), p. 207-210. English. DESCR: Medical Care; Surveys.

I AM JOAQUIN [book]

5500 Hinojosa-Smith, Rolando R. I AM JOAQUIN: relationships between the text and the film. BILINGUAL REVIEW, Vol. 10, no. 2-3 (May, December, 1983), p. 142-145. English. DESCR: Film Reviews; Gonzales, Rodolfo (Corky); *I AM JOAQUIN [film]; Valdez, Luis.

I AM JOAQUIN [film]

5501 Hinojosa-Smith, Rolando R. I AM JOAQUIN: relationships between the text and the film. BILINGUAL REVIEW, Vol. 10, no. 2-3 (May, December, 1983), p. 142-145. English. DESCR: Film Reviews; Gonzales, Rodolfo (Corky); I AM JOAQUIN [book]; Valdez, Luis.

Iberia Foods Corp.

5502 Gupta, Udayan. Hispanic foods in New York: the race for number two. HISPANIC BUSINESS, Vol. 5, no. 8 (August 1983), p. 18-19+. English. DESCR: Condal Distributor, Inc.; Consumers; *Food Industry; Goya Foods; La Cena Fine Foods, Ltd.; Recipes.

Ibero-American Chamber of Commerce

5503 Chamber, Peace Corps join in training effort. NUESTRO, Vol. 7, no. 1 (January, February, 1983), p. 36. English. DESCR: Business; Caribbean Basin Initiative (CBI); Latin America; Peace Corps.

5504 Foreign trade. HISPANIC BUSINESS, Vol. 5, no. 4 (April 1983), p. 22. English. DESCR: Banking Industry; Brazil; *Electronics Industry; Export Trade; *Foreign Trade; Miami, FL; Minority Bank Development Program (MBDP); Minority Export Development Consultants Program (MEDC); Peace Corps; Puerto Rico.

Icaya, Rick

5505 How to stuff a wild chile part II. CAMINOS, Vol. 3, no. 1 (January 1982), p. 31-32. English. DESCR: Albert, Margo; Chacon, Peter R.; Lacayo, Frank L. "Hank"; *Recipes; *Rodriguez, Edmundo; Rodriguez, Edmundo M.; *Vasquez, Victor.

Icaza, Ricardo F.

5506 People on the move. CAMINOS, Vol. 2, no. 6 (October 1981), p. 7. English. DESCR: Alvarado, Angel S.; Arreola, Rafael; *Biographical Notes; Diaz, Elisa; Diaz, Elvira A.; Garcia, Jose Joel; Garza, Florentino; Lacayo, Henry; Martinez, Lydia R.; Munoz, Victor M.; Salinas, Vicente; Sanchez, Manuel; Zuniga, Henry.

Ichaso, Leon

5507 West, Dennis. Film review of: EL SUPER. MINORITY VOICES, Vol. 4, no. 2 (Fall 1980), p. 85-87. English. DESCR: Cubanos; *EL SUPER; Film Reviews; Jimenez-Leal, Orlando.

Icons

5508 Turner, Kay F. Mexican American home altars: towards their interpretation. AZTLAN, Vol. 13, no. 1-2 (Spring, Fall, 1982), p. 309-326. English. DESCR: *Home Altars; Religion.

IDENTIFICATION AND ANALYSIS OF CHICANO LITERATURE

5509 Lewis, Marvin A. Book review of: THE IDENTIFICATION AND ANALYSIS OF CHICANO LITERATURE. MELUS: MULTI-ETHNIC LITERATURE OF THE UNITED STATES, Vol. 7, no. 1 (Spring 1980), p. 82-85. English. DESCR: Book Reviews; *Jimenez, Francisco; *Literature.

5510 McCracken, Ellen. Book review of: IDENTIFICATION AND ANALYSIS OF CHICANO LITERATURE. NEW SCHOLAR, Vol. 8, no. 1-2 (Spring, Fall, 1982), p. 493-495. English. DESCR: Book Reviews; Jimenez, Francisco.

5511 Venier, M.E. Literatura chicana. DIALOGOS, Vol. 18, (May, June, 1982), p. 62-63. Spanish. DESCR: Book Reviews; Jimenez, Francisco.

Identity

5512 Alurista and Monleon, Jose. Mesa redonda. MAIZE, Vol. 4, no. 3-4 (Spring, Summer, 1981), p. 6-23. English. DESCR: Alurista; Anaya, Rudolfo A.; Herrera Sobek, Maria; Literature; Morales, Alejandro; *Mythology; Viramontes, Helen.

5513 Arora, Shirley L. Proverbs in Mexican American tradition. AZTLAN, Vol. 13, no. 1-2 (Spring, Fall, 1982), p. 43-69. English. DESCR: *Dichos; Spanish Language; Surveys.

5514 Book review of: HUNGER OF MEMORY: THE EDUCATION OF RICHARD RODRIGUEZ. SAN FRANCISCO REVIEW OF BOOKS, Vol. 7, (Summer 1982), p. 11. English. DESCR: Attitude (Psychological); Bilingual Bicultural Education; Book Reviews; *HUNGER OF MEMORY: THE EDUCATION OF RICHARD RODRIGUEZ; Rodriguez, Richard.

5515 Borman, Adele T. "Who do you think you are, anyway? CAMINOS, Vol. 4, no. 1-2 (January, February, 1983), p. 24-25,71. English. DESCR: *Careers.

5516 Borrego, Richard L.; Chavez, Ernest L.; and

Titley, Robert W. Effect of counselor technique on Mexican-American and Anglo-American self-disclosure and counselor perception. JOURNAL OF COUNSELING PSYCHOLOGY, Vol. 29, no. 5 (September 1982), p. 538-541. English. DESCR: Anglo Americans; *Counseling (Psychological); Cultural Characteristics; Personality; Sex Roles.

5517 Burciaga, Jose Antonio. Me, E.T. and other alien beings. NUESTRO, Vol. 7, no. 2 (March 1983), p. 41. English. DESCR: Racism.

5518 Bustelo, Manuel A. Ending an era of Hispanic isolation. NUESTRO, Vol. 6, no. 7 (September 1982), p. 60. English. DESCR: *Cabinet Committee on Opportunity for Spanish-Speaking People (CCOSSP); *Culture; *Family.

5519 Cantu, Roberto. Nota preliminar: de Samuel Ramos a Emilio Uranga. CAMPO LIBRE, Vol. 1, no. 2 (Summer 1981), p. 239-272. Spanish. DESCR: Cultural Characteristics; Mexico; Philosophy; *Ramos, Samuel; *Uranga, Emilio.

5520 La Chrisx. La loca de la raza cosmica. COMADRE, no. 2 (Spring 1978), p. 5-9. Bilingual. DESCR: *Poetry.

5521 Cohen, Gaynor. Alliance and conflict among Mexican-Americans. ETHNIC AND RACIAL STUDIES, Vol. 5, no. 2 (April 1982), p. 175-195. English. DESCR: *Political History and Conditions; Segregation and Desegregation.

5522 Cortese, Anthony J., ed. A comparative analysis of ethnicity and moral judgment. CACR REVIEW, Vol. 1, no. 1 (September 1982), p. 72-101. English. DESCR: Anglo Americans; Blacks; Cultural Characteristics; *Values.

5523 Davis, Sally M. and Harris, Mary B. Sexual knowledge, sexual interests, and sources of sexual information of rural and urban adolescents from three cultures. ADOLESCENCE, Vol. 17, no. 66 (Summer 1982), p. 471-492. English. DESCR: Birth Control; Cultural Characteristics; Rural Population; *Sex Education; Sex Roles; *Sexual Behavior; Urban Communities; Youth.

5524 de Armas, Isabel. Chicano, un vocablo colonizador. CUADERNOS HISPANOAMERICANOS, Vol. 394, (April 1983), p. 193-201. Spanish. DESCR: Agricultural Laborers; Book Reviews; Calvo Buezas, Tomas; *CHICANOS: ANTOLOGIA HISTORICA Y LITERARIA; *LOS MAS POBRES EN EL PAIS MAS RICO; Villanueva, Tino.

5525 Eberstein, Isaac W. and Pol, Louis G. Mexican-American ethnicity, socioeconomic status, and infant mortality: a county level analysis. SOCIAL SCIENCE JOURNAL, Vol. 19, no. 2 (April 1982), p. 61-71. English. DESCR: *Infant Mortality; Socioeconomic Factors; Southwest United States.

5526 Erdman, Daniel. Liberation and identity: Indo-Hispano youth. RELIGIOUS EDUCATION, Vol. 78, no. 1 (Winter 1983), p. 76-89. English. DESCR: *Liberation Theology; *Religion.

5527 Espada, Frank. Who am I?: Puerto Rican Hawaiians ask. NUESTRO, Vol. 6, no. 8 (October 1982), p. 32-33. English. DESCR: Ethnic Groups; *Puerto Rican Hawaiians; *Puerto Ricans.

Identity (cont.)

5528 Fernandez, Celestino. The neglected dimension: ethnicity in American life. AZTLAN, Vol. 14, no. 1 (Spring 1983), p. 199-201. English. **DESCR**: Book Reviews; Ethnic Groups; Rosen, Philip; *THE NEGLECTED DIMENSION: ETHNICITY IN AMERICAN LIFE.

5529 Fleming, Marilyn B. Problems experienced by Anglo, Hispanic and Navajo Indian women college students. JOURNAL OF AMERICAN INDIAN EDUCATION, Vol. 22, no. 1 (October 1982), p. 7-17. English. **DESCR**: *Chicanas; Community Colleges; Ethnic Groups; Medical Education; Native Americans.

5530 Forbes, Jack D. Hispanic-Mexican pioneers of the San Francisco Bay region: an analysis of racial origins. AZTLAN, Vol. 14, no. 1 (Spring 1983), p. 175-189. English. **DESCR**: Ethnic Groups; *Pioneers; *San Francisco Bay.

5531 Franco, Juan N. A developmental analysis of self concept in Mexican American and Anglo school children. HISPANIC JOURNAL OF BEHAVIORAL SCIENCES, Vol. 5, no. 2 (June 1983), p. 207-218. English. **DESCR**: Acculturation; Children.

5532 Fraser Rothenberg, Irene. Mexican-American views of U.S. relations with Latin America. JOURNAL OF ETHNIC STUDIES, Vol. 6, no. 1 (Spring 1978), p. 62-78. English. **DESCR**: Chicano Movement; Culture; International Relations; Latin America; Lobbying; Mexico; *Nationalism; Political History and Conditions; Politics.

5533 Frazier, Donald J. and De Blassie, Richard R. Comparison of self-concept in Mexican American and non-Mexican American late adolescents. ADOLESCENCE, Vol. 17, no. 66 (Summer 1982), p. 327-334. English. **DESCR**: Academic Achievement; Socioeconomic Factors; Students; Youth.

5534 Fu, Victoria R.; Hinkle, Dennis E.; and Korslund, Mary K. A development study of ethnic self-concept among pre-adolescent girls. JOURNAL OF GENETIC PSYCHOLOGY, Vol. 14, (March 1983), p. 67-73. English. **DESCR**: Chicanas; Comparative Psychology; Junior High School Students; Self-Concept Self Report Scale.

5535 Fuentes, Diana. Chicana perpectives: Irene Portillo. COMADRE, no. 1 (Summer 1977), p. 42-44. English. **DESCR**: *Biography; *Portillo, Irene E.; Women's Rights.

5536 Garcia, John A. Ethnicity and Chicanos: measurement of ethnic identification, identity and consciousness. HISPANIC JOURNAL OF BEHAVIORAL SCIENCES, Vol. 4, no. 3 (September 1982), p. 295-314. English. **DESCR**: *National Chicano Survey of Mexicans; Politics.

5537 Garcia, Juan R. Midwest Mexicanos in the 1920's: issues, questions, and directions. SOCIAL SCIENCE JOURNAL, Vol. 19, no. 2 (April 1982), p. 89-99. English. **DESCR**: Midwestern States; *Social History and Conditions; Social Research.

5538 Garcia Nunez, Fernando. La poesia chicana en espanol. CUADERNOS HISPANOAMERICANOS, Vol. 397, (July 1983), p. 117-123. Spanish. **DESCR**: Literary Criticism; *Poetry.

5539 Garcia, Reyes. Politics of flesh: ethnicity and political viability. CACR REVIEW, Vol.

1, no. 1 (September 1982), p. 102-130. English. **DESCR**: Anaya, Rudolfo A.; Aristotle; Culture; Ethnic Groups; Locke, John; Nuclear Armament; Philosophy; *Political Repression; Urban Communities.

5540 Gibbs, Jewelle Taylor. Personality patterns of delinquent females: ethnic and sociocultural variations. JOURNAL OF CLINICAL PSYCHOLOGY, Vol. 38, no. 1 (January 1982), p. 198-206. English. **DESCR**: Chicanas; Ethnic Groups; *Juvenile Delinquency; Personality; Psychological Testing; Socioeconomic Factors.

5541 Gomez-Quinones, Juan. On culture. REVISTA CHICANO-RIQUENA, Vol. 10, no. 1-2 (Winter, Spring, 1982), p. 290-308. English. **DESCR**: Culture; *Essays.

5542 Grant, Carmencita. From the daughter of the deceased. COMADRE, no. 2 (Spring 1978), p. 24. English. **DESCR**: *Poetry.

5543 Guckert, John C. Multiculturalism: a democratic approach to education. SCHOLAR AND EDUCATOR, Vol. 6, (Spring 1982), p. 37-41. English. **DESCR**: *Cultural Pluralism; *Educational Theory and Practice.

5544 Harowitz, Ruth. Adult delinquent gangs in a Chicano community: masked intimacy and marginality. URBAN LIFE, Vol. 11, no. 1 (April 1982), p. 3-26. English. **DESCR**: *Gangs; Lions, 32nd Street.

5545 Iadicola, Peter. Schooling and symbolic violence: the effect of power differences and curriculum factors on Hispanic students' attitudes toward their own ethnicity. HISPANIC JOURNAL OF BEHAVIORAL SCIENCES, Vol. 5, no. 1 (March 1983), p. 21-43. English. **DESCR**: Parent and Child Relationships.

5546 Jaramillo, Patricio T.; Zapata, Jesse T.; and McPherson, Robert. Concerns of college bound Mexican-American students. SCHOOL COUNSELOR, Vol. 29, no. 5 (May 1982), p. 375-380. English. **DESCR**: *Attitude (Psychological); College Preparation; Counseling Services (Educational); Stereotypes; Students.

5547 Jensen, Gary F.; White, C. S.; and Galliher, James M. Ethnic status and adolescent self-evaluations: an extension of research on minority self-esteem. SOCIAL PROBLEMS, Vol. 30, no. 2 (December 1982), p. 226-239. English. **DESCR**: Arizona.

5548 Kugle, Cherry L.; Clements, Richard O.; and Powell, Philip M. Level and stability of self-esteem in relation to academic behavior of second graders. JOURNAL OF PERSONALITY AND SOCIAL PSYCHOLOGY, Vol. 44, no. 1 (January 1983), p. 201-207. English. **DESCR**: Academic Achievement; PIERS-HARRIS CHILDREN'S SELF CONCEPT SCALE; Primary School Education.

5549 Lattin, Vernon E. Ethnicity and identity in the contemporary Chicano novel. MINORITY VOICES, Vol. 2, no. 2 (Fall 1978), p. 37-44. English. **DESCR**: BLESS ME, ULTIMA; Literary Criticism; Literature; MEMORIES OF THE ALHAMBRA; *Novel; POCHO; THE AUTOBIOGRAPHY OF A BROWN BUFFALO; Y NO SE LO TRAGO LA TIERRA/AND THE EARTH DID NOT PART.

5550 Lopez, Phyllis. La Chicana. COMADRE, no. 2 (Spring 1978), p. 12. English. **DESCR**: *Poetry.

Identity (cont.)

East Los Angeles, CA; Segregation and
Desegregation; Students; Youth.

5551 Lopez, Phyllis. Sentimientos sin nombre.
COMADRE, no. 1 (Summer 1977), p. 10-12.
Bilingual. **DESCR:** *Poetry.

5552 Low, Benson P. and Clement, Paul W.
Relationships of race and socioeconomic
status to classroom behavior, academic
achievement, and referral for special
education. JOURNAL OF SCHOOL PSYCHOLOGY,
Vol. 20, no. 2 (Summer 1982), p. 103-112.
English. **DESCR:** *Academic Achievement; Anglo
Americans; Blacks; Socioeconomic Factors.

5553 Mejias-Rentas, Antonio. "I love Latinos
because they love to smile". NUESTRO, Vol.
7, no. 7 (September 1983), p. 53. English.
DESCR: Ethnic Attitudes.

5554 Mendez, Gloria I. Bilingual children's
adaptation after a transitional bilingual
education. METAS, Vol. 3, no. 1 (Summer
1982), p. 1-112. English. **DESCR:** Academic
Achievement; Acculturation; *Bilingual
Bicultural Education; Bilingualism; English
as a Second Language.

5555 Mercado, Olivia. Chicanas: myths and roles.
COMADRE, no. 1 (Summer 1977), p. 26-32.
English. **DESCR:** *Chicanas; Gallo, Juana;
Huerta, Dolores; Leadership; Sex Roles;
Women's Rights.

5556 Montez, Philip. How to spot a Chicano from
New Texicaloradizona. NUESTRO, Vol. 7, no. 7
(September 1983), p. 54. English. **DESCR:**
Humor.

5557 Morales, Cecilio J. Hispanics are moving
toward the front pew. NATIONAL CATHOLIC
REPORTER, Vol. 19, (December 31, 1982), p.
11. English. **DESCR:** *Catholic Church;
*Clergy.

5558 Morton, Carlos. A racial and cultural
menudo. NUESTRO, Vol. 7, no. 6 (August
1983), p. 49. English. **DESCR:** Mestizaje.

5559 Olson, James S. Book review of: HUNGER OF
MEMORY: THE EDUCATION OF RICHARD RODRIGUEZ.
JOURNAL OF THE WEST, Vol. 22, no. 1 (1983),
p. 80-81. English. **DESCR:** Bilingual
Bicultural Education; Book Reviews; *HUNGER
OF MEMORY: THE EDUCATION OF RICHARD
RODRIGUEZ; Rodriguez, Richard.

5560 Ortega Acevedo, Zoila. Ethnic, racial
identification: a problem. NUESTRO, Vol. 6,
no. 1 (January, February, 1982), p. 31-32.
English.

5561 Paredes, Americo. Folklore, lo mexicano, and
proverbs. AZTLAN, Vol. 13, no. 1-2 (Spring,
Fall, 1982), p. 1-11. English. **DESCR:**
Dichos; *Folklore.

5562 Perales, Alonso M. Effects of
teacher-oriented and student-oriented
strategies on self-concept, English language
development, and social studies achievement
of 5th grade Mexican-American students
[research notes]. TESOL QUARTERLY, Vol. 16,
no. 1 (March 1982), p. 99-100. English.
DESCR: Attitude (Psychological); San
Antonio, TX; *Teacher Attitudes;
Teacher-pupil Interaction.

5563 Perez, Robert; Padilla, Amado M.; and
Ramirez, Alex. Expectations toward school
busing by Mexican American youth. AMERICAN
JOURNAL OF COMMUNITY PSYCHOLOGY, Vol. 10,
no. 2 (April 1982), p. 133-148. English.
DESCR: Attitude (Psychological); *Busing;

5564 Powers, Stephen and Sanchez, Virginia V.
Correlates of self-esteem of Mexican
American adolescents. PSYCHOLOGICAL REPORTS,
Vol. 51, no. 3 (December 1982), p. 771-774.
English. **DESCR:** Academic Achievement;
Arizona; Employment; Junior High School
Students; Nogales, AZ.

5565 Ramirez, Albert and Soriano, Fernando.
Social power in educational systems: its
effect on Chicanos' attitudes toward the
school experience. JOURNAL OF SOCIAL
PSYCHOLOGY, Vol. 118, no. 1 (October 1982),
p. 113-119. English. **DESCR:** Educational
Tests and Measurements; Secondary School
Education; *Social Psychology.

5566 Ramos, Alfonso Pena. Voices: Gandhi: the
Mahatma's message to Hispanics. NUESTRO,
Vol. 7, no. 4 (May 1983), p. 59-60. English.
DESCR: *Ethnic Groups; Gandhi, Mahatma;
*Philosophy; Welfare.

5567 Ramos, Manuel. En torno a las ideas sobre EL
MEXICANO. CAMPO LIBRE, Vol. 1, no. 2 (Summer
1981), p. 273-282. Spanish. **DESCR:** Cultural
Characteristics; *EL MEXICANO; Mexico;
Philosophy; *Uranga, Emilio.

5568 Rivas, Yolanda E. Confrontacion y
reconciliacion. APUNTES, Vol. 2, no. 2
(Summer 1982), p. 40-47. Spanish. **DESCR:**
*Religion.

5569 Rocco, Raymond. Positivism and Mexican
identity: then and now. AZTLAN, Vol. 14, no.
2 (Fall 1983), p. 359-371. English. **DESCR:**
History; Mexico; Philosophy; *Positivism.

5570 Rodriguez, Andres and De Blassie, Richard R.
Ethnic designation, identification, and
preference as they relate to Chicano
children. JOURNAL OF NON-WHITE CONCERNS IN
PERSONNEL AND GUIDANCE, Vol. 11, no. 3
(April 1983), p. 99-106. English. **DESCR:**
Children.

5571 Rodriguez, Joe. Chicano poetry: mestizaje
and the use of irony. CAMPO LIBRE, Vol. 1,
no. 2 (Summer 1981), p. 229-235. English.
DESCR: Literary Characteristics; *Literary
Criticism; *Mestizaje; Poetry.

5572 Salmon, Roberto Mario. Comment: is this our
decade in the sun? NATIONAL HISPANIC
JOURNAL, Vol. 2, no. 1 (Summer 1983), p.
24-25. English. **DESCR:** Machismo; *Mass
Media; National Council of La Raza (NCLR).

5573 Sanchez, Arthur R. and Atkinson, Donald R.
Mexican-American cultural commitment,
preference for counselor ethnicity, and
willingness to use counseling. JOURNAL OF
COUNSELING PSYCHOLOGY, Vol. 30, no. 2 (April
1983), p. 215-220. English. **DESCR:**
*Counseling (Psychological); Cultural
Characteristics; Mental Health; *Mental
Health Personnel.

5574 Sanchez, Saul. La incipiente narrativa
chicana: un espejo de telaranas. CUADERNOS
HISPANOAMERICANOS, Vol. 390, (December
1982), p. 641-645. Spanish. **DESCR:**
*Literature.

5575 Sandoval, David A. What do I call them: the
Chicano experience. CACR REVIEW, Vol. 1, no.
1 (September 1982), p. 3-25. English.
DESCR: Colonialism; Intergroup Relations;
*Self-Referents.

Identity (cont.)

5576 Saragoza, Alex M. Mexican children in the
U.S.: the Central San Joaquin Valley. DE
COLORES, Vol. 6, no. 1-2 (1982), p. 64-74.
English. DESCR: Acculturation; *Children;
Family; Parent and Child Relationships; San
Joaquin Valley.

5577 Saucedo, Concha. No me llames Hispanic.
CALMECAC, Vol. 2, (Spring 1981), p. 35.
Bilingual. DESCR: *Poetry.

5578 Seilhamer, E. Stella and Prewitt-Diaz,
Joseph O. The return and circulatory migrant
student: a perception of teachers, schools
and self. MIGRATION TODAY, Vol. 11, no. 1
(1983), p. 21-23. English. DESCR: Cultural
Characteristics; Migration Patterns; *Puerto
Rican Education; Puerto Ricans.

5579 Sifuentes, Frank. Notes from a 9 to 5
Hispanic. CORAZON DE AZTLAN, Vol. 1, no. 2
(March, April, 1982), p. 31. English.

5580 Sifuentes, Frank. Tio tacos are people too.
CHISMEARTE, (1982), p. 14. English. DESCR:
*Short Story.

5581 Steigelfest, Annette. Ethnicity and sex role
socialization. BILINGUAL JOURNAL, Vol. 6,
no. 3 (Spring 1982), p. 11-15,24. English.
DESCR: Ethnic Attitudes; Halacha Institute;
Orthodox Jews; *Sex Roles; Sex Stereotypes;
Socialization.

5582 Tienda, Marta. Sex, ethnicity and Chicano
status attainment. INTERNATIONAL MIGRATION
REVIEW, Vol. 16, no. 2 (Summer 1982), p.
435-473. English. DESCR: Academic
Achievement; Chicanas; Discrimination in
Education; Discrimination in Employment;
Income; Language Proficiency; Sexism;
*Social Classes; Social Mobility.

5583 Uranga, Emilio. Notas para un estudio del
mexicano. CAMPO LIBRE, Vol. 1, no. 2 (Summer
1981), p. 283-295. Spanish. DESCR: Cultural
Characteristics; Gaos, Jose; Mexico;
Philosophy; *Ramos, Samuel.

5584 Valencia, Richard R. Predicting academic
achievement of Mexican American children:
preliminary analysis of the McCarthy Scales.
EDUCATIONAL AND PSYCHOLOGICAL MEASUREMENT,
Vol. 42, (Winter 1982), p. 1269-1278.
English. DESCR: *Academic Achievement;
Children; Educational Tests and
Measurements; McCarthy Scales for Children's
Abilities (MSCA).

5585 Vigil, James Diego. Chicano high schoolers:
educational performance and acculturation.
EDUCATIONAL FORUM, Vol. 47, no. 1 (Fall
1982), p. 58-73. English. DESCR: *Academic
Achievement; *Acculturation; Secondary
School Education; Socioeconomic Factors.

5586 Vigil, James Diego. Human revitalization:
the six tasks of victory outreach. DREW
GATEWAY, Vol. 52, no. 3 (Spring 1982), p.
49-59. English. DESCR: Barrios for Christ
Program; Drug Addicts; Drug Programs; Gangs;
Pentecostal Church; Protestant Church;
Religion; *Victory Outreach; Youth.

5587 Villa Romo, Velma. Rape in the barrio.
COMADRE, no. 3 (Fall 1978), p. 19-29.
English. DESCR: *Chicanas; Rape; Santa
Barbara Rape Crisis Center; Social History
and Conditions.

Ideology
USE: Political Ideology

Iglesias, Julio

5588 Greenfield, Charles. Spanish prince of song.
NUESTRO, Vol. 6, no. 5 (June, July, 1982),
p. 18-21. English. DESCR: Entertainers;
Recreation.

5589 The Julio-ization of America. LATINO, Vol.
54, no. 4 (May, June, 1983), p. 24-25.
English. DESCR: Artists; Singers.

5590 Obejas, Achy. My mother, the groupie.
NUESTRO, Vol. 7, no. 9 (November 1983), p.
47. English. DESCR: Performing Arts.

Illegal Aliens
USE: Undocumented Workers

ILLEGAL ALIENS IN THE WESTERN HEMISPHERE: POLITICAL AND ECONOMIC FACTORS

5591 North, David S. Book review of: ILLEGAL
ALIENS IN THE WESTERN HEMISPHERE: POLITICAL
AND ECONOMIC FACTORS. INTERNATIONAL
MIGRATION REVIEW, Vol. 16, no. 3 (Fall
1982), p. 682-683. English. DESCR: Book
Reviews; Johnson, Kenneth F.; Undocumented
Workers; Williams, Miles W.

Los Illegals [musical group]

5592 Madrid, Joe. Los Illegals. CAMINOS, Vol. 3,
no. 8 (September 1982), p. 18-19. English.
DESCR: Musicians.

Illinois

5593 Rivera, Roberto. Selected topics on Latino
access to Illinois colleges and
universities. INTEGRATED EDUCATION, Vol. 20,
no. 3-5 (May, October, 1982), p. 101-105.
English. DESCR: Colleges and Universities;
Discrimination in Education; *Higher
Education; Racism.

Illinois Migrant Council

5594 Venerable, W. R. Student and parent
attitudes toward college at five Hispanic
learning centers in Illinois. JOURNAL OF THE
NATIONAL ASSOC. OF COLLEGE ADMISSIONS
COUNSELORS, Vol. 26, (April 1982), p.
19-23. English. DESCR: Casa Aztlan; Chicago,
IL; *Higher Education; Lakeview Learning
Center, Chicago, IL; *Secondary School
Education.

IMAGE, Washington, DC

5595 Latinos evident in 1983 march. NUESTRO, Vol.
7, no. 7 (September 1983), p. 11-12.
English. DESCR: Bonilla, Tony;
Cuban-American Coordinating Committee;
*Demonstrations; Jackson, Jesse; League of
United Latin American Citizens (LULAC);
National Congress for Puerto Rican Rights
(NCPRR); National Council of La Raza (NCLR);
Velasquez, Baldemar; Zamora, Reuben.

5596 Newsfront. HISPANIC BUSINESS, Vol. 4, no. 2
(February 1982), p. 7. English. DESCR: Asip,
Patricia V.; Banuelos, Ramona Acosta;
*Biographical Notes; Businesspeople;
Gonzalez, Henry B.; Gutierrez, Alberto.

IMAGES OF THE MEXICAN AMERICAN IN FICTION AND FILM

5597 Bloodworth, William A., Jr. Book review of: IMAGES OF THE MEXICAN-AMERICAN IN FICTION AND FILM. WESTERN AMERICAN LITERATURE, Vol. 16, no. 4 (Winter 1982), p. 323-325. English. DESCR: Book Reviews; Chicanos in American Literature; Films; Pettit, Arthur G.; Showalter, Dennis E.; Stereotypes.

5598 Book review of: IMAGES OF THE MEXICAN-AMERICAN IN FICTION AND FILM. MODERN FICTION STUDIES, Vol. 28, (Summer 1982), p. 367-369. English. DESCR: Book Reviews; Fiction; Films; Mass Media; Pettit, Arthur G.

5599 Cripps, Thomas. Mexicans, Indians and movies: the need for a history. WIDE ANGLE: A FILM QUARTERLY OF THEORY, CRITICISM, AND PRACTICE, Vol. 5, no. 1 (1982), p. 68-70. English. DESCR: Bataille, Gretchen M.; *Book Reviews; Films; Native Americans; O'Connor, John E.; Pettit, Arthur G.; Silet, Charles L.P.; *Stereotypes; THE HOLLYWOOD INDIAN: STEREOTYPES OF NATIVE AMERICANS IN FILMS; THE PRETEND INDIANS: IMAGES OF NATIVE AMERICANS IN THE MOVIES.

5600 Griswold del Castillo, Richard. Book review of: IMAGES OF THE MEXICAN-AMERICAN IN FICTION AND FILM. JOURNAL OF THE WEST, Vol. 22, no. 2 (April 1983), p. 94. English. DESCR: Book Reviews; Pettit, Arthur G.

5601 Stephens, Doris T. Book review of: IMAGES OF THE MEXICAN-AMERICAN IN FICTION AND FILM. JOURNAL OF AMERICAN CULTURE, Vol. 5, no. 4 (Winter 1982), p. 112-113. English. DESCR: Book Reviews; Pettit, Arthur G.

5602 West, Dennis. Book review of: IMAGES OF THE MEXICAN-AMERICAN IN FICTION AND FILM. CINEASTE, Vol. 12, no. 1 (1982), p. 41. English. DESCR: Book Reviews; Chicanos in American Literature; Films; Pettit, Arthur G.; Stereotypes.

Immigrant Labor

5603 Baca-Ramirez, Reynaldo and Bryan, Dexter Edward. The undocumented Mexican worker: a social problem? JOURNAL OF ETHNIC STUDIES, Vol. 8, no. 1 (Spring 1980), p. 55-69. English. DESCR: Government Services; Immigration; Immigration Regulation and Control; Mexico; Social History and Conditions; Social Services; *Undocumented Workers.

5604 Cardoso, Lawrence Anthony. Book review of: LOS MEXICANOS QUE DEVOLVIO LA CRISIS, 1929-1932. JOURNAL OF ETHNIC STUDIES, Vol. 5, no. 1 (Spring 1977), p. 120-122. Spanish. DESCR: Book Reviews; Carreras de Velasco, Mercedes; Deportation; Immigration; Immigration Regulation and Control; *LOS MEXICANOS QUE DEVOLVIO LA CRISIS 1929-1932; Mexico; Social History and Conditions.

5605 Cardoso, Lawrence Anthony. Book review of: UNWANTED MEXICAN AMERICANS IN THE GREAT DEPRESSION: REPATRIATION PRESSURES, 1929-1939. JOURNAL OF ETHNIC STUDIES, Vol. 5, no. 1 (Spring 1977), p. 120-122. English. DESCR: Book Reviews; Deportation; Hoffman, Abraham; Immigration; Immigration Regulation and Control; Mexico; Social History and Conditions; *UNWANTED MEXICAN AMERICANS IN THE GREAT DEPRESSION.

5606 Chavez, Cesar E. Relentless struggle for farm workers' rights. NUESTRO, Vol. 7, no. 9 (November 1983), p. 55. English. DESCR:

*Agricultural Laborers; California; Simpson-Mazzoli Bill.

5607 Cornelius, Wayne A. Interviewing undocumented immigrants: methodological reflections based on fieldwork in Mexico and the U.S. INTERNATIONAL MIGRATION REVIEW, Vol. 16, no. 2 (Summer 1982), p. 378-411. English. DESCR: Immigrants; Migrant Labor; Research Methodology; *Undocumented Workers.

5608 Garcia, Mario T. Americanization and the Mexican immigrant, 1880-1930. JOURNAL OF ETHNIC STUDIES, Vol. 6, no. 2 (Summer 1978), p. 19-34. English. DESCR: *Acculturation; Cultural Characteristics; Culture; Education; Immigration.

5609 Garcia, Mario T. Book review of: LOS MOJADOS: THE WETBACK STORY. JOURNAL OF ETHNIC STUDIES, Vol. 1, no. 1 (Spring 1973), p. 66-68. English. DESCR: Book Reviews; *LOS MOJADOS: THE WETBACK STORY; Mexico; Samora, Julian; Southwest United States; Undocumented Workers; United States.

5610 Garcia, Mario T. On Mexican immigration, the United States, and Chicano history. JOURNAL OF ETHNIC STUDIES, Vol. 7, no. 1 (Spring 1979), p. 80-88. English. DESCR: Book Reviews; *BY THE SWEAT OF THEIR BROW: MEXICAN IMMIGRANT LABOR IN THE UNITED STATES, 1900-1940; History; Immigration; Immigration Law; Mexico; Reisler, Mark; Research Methodology; Southwest United States.

5611 Garcia, Philip. Trends in the relative income position of Mexican-origin workers in the United States: the early seventies. SOCIOLOGY & SOCIAL RESEARCH, Vol. 66, no. 4 (June 1982), p. 467-483. English. DESCR: *Income.

5612 Hewlett, Sylvia Ann. Coping with illegal immigrants. FOREIGN AFFAIRS, Vol. 60, no. 2 (Winter 1981, 1982), p. 358-378. English. DESCR: Immigration; Immigration Law; *Immigration Regulation and Control; Policy Formation; Undocumented Workers.

5613 Immigration questions. NUESTRO, Vol. 6, no. 2 (March 1982), p. 10-11. English. DESCR: Immigration Law; Silva, Refugio.

5614 The impact of undocumented migration on the U.S. labor market. HOUSTON JOURNAL OF INTERNATIONAL LAW, Vol. 5, no. 2 (Spring 1983), p. 287-321. English. DESCR: Economic History and Conditions; Employment; Immigration and Nationality Act (INA); Immigration Law; Labor Supply and Market; Research Methodology; Simpson-Mazzoli Bill; *Undocumented Workers.

5615 Sandos, James A. and Cross, Harry E. National development and international labour migration: Mexico 1940-1965. JOURNAL OF CONTEMPORARY HISTORY, Vol. 18, no. 1 (January 1983), p. 43-60. English. DESCR: *Braceros; Mexico.

5616 Simon, Daniel T. Mexican repatriation in East Chicago, Indiana. JOURNAL OF ETHNIC STUDIES, Vol. 2, no. 2 (Summer 1974), p. 11-23. English. DESCR: *Deportation; *East Chicago, IN; History; Immigration; Immigration Regulation and Control; Inland Steel Company; Mexico; Social History and Conditions.

Immigrant Labor (cont.)

5617 Wolin, Merle Linda. Dirty work: Americans turn down many jobs vacated by ouster of aliens. WALL STREET JOURNAL, Vol. 200, (December 6, 1982), p. 1. English. **DESCR:** Labor; *Undocumented Workers.

Immigrants

5618 Arias, Ron. Los que emigran desde Costa Rica hacia el norte. LATINO, Vol. 53, no. 1 (January, February, 1982), p. 15. Spanish. **DESCR:** *Costa Rica.

5619 Baca, Reynaldo and Bryan, Dexter Edward. The "Assimilation" of unauthorized Mexican workers: another social science fiction? HISPANIC JOURNAL OF BEHAVIORAL SCIENCES, Vol. 5, no. 1 (March 1983), p. 1-20. English. **DESCR:** Assimilation; *Binationalism; *Undocumented Workers.

5620 Borjas, George J. Earnings of male Hispanic immigrants in the United States. INDUSTRIAL AND LABOR RELATIONS REVIEW, Vol. 35, no. 3 (April 1982), p. 343-353. English. **DESCR:** Cubanos; Ethnic Groups; *Income; Puerto Ricans; Social Mobility.

5621 Bronfenbrenner, Martin. Hyphenated Americans-economic aspects. LAW AND CONTEMPORARY PROBLEMS, Vol. 45, no. 2 (Spring 1982), p. 9-27. English. **DESCR:** *Chiswick, Barry R.; *Economics; Racism; Smith, James P.; Welch, Finis R.

5622 Burke, P.E. Immigrant Mexican children hurdle the English barrier. TIMES (London) [EDUCATIONAL SUPPLEMENT], Vol. 3447, (July 23, 1982), p. 15. English. **DESCR:** *Bilingual Bicultural Education; Children; English Language.

5623 Chavez, Leo R. Undocumented immigrants and access to health services: a game of pass the buck. MIGRATION TODAY, Vol. 11, no. 1 (1983), p. 14-19. English. **DESCR:** California; Medical Care; Migrant Health Services; Public Health Legislation; Simpson-Mazzoli Bill; Social Services; Undocumented Workers.

5624 Cornelius, Wayne A. Interviewing undocumented immigrants: methodological reflections based on fieldwork in Mexico and the U.S. INTERNATIONAL MIGRATION REVIEW, Vol. 16, no. 2 (Summer 1982), p. 378-411. English. **DESCR:** Immigrant Labor; Migrant Labor; Research Methodology; *Undocumented Workers.

5625 Day, Mark R. Immigrants ... and Mexican citizens. NATIONAL CATHOLIC REPORTER, Vol. 18, (February 5, 1982), p. 3. English. **DESCR:** Catholic Church; Immigration and Naturalization Service (INS); Undocumented Workers.

5626 Espada, Frank. Regreso a la patria. LATINO, Vol. 53, no. 4 (June 1982), p. 20+. Spanish.

5627 Keefe, Susan Emily. Help-seeking behavior among foreign-born and native-born Mexican-Americans. SOCIAL SCIENCE AND MEDICINE, Vol. 16, no. 16 (1982), p. 1467-1472. English. **DESCR:** Acculturation; *Mental Health Programs; Santa Barbara, CA.

5628 Lopez, Hugo L. Toward a theology of migration. APUNTES, Vol. 2, no. 3 (Fall 1982), p. 68-71. English. **DESCR:** *Liberation Theology; Religion.

5629 Massey, Douglas S. and Schnabel, Kathleen M. Background and characteristics of undocumented Hispanic migrants to the United States: a review of recent research. MIGRATION TODAY, Vol. 11, no. 1 (1983), p. 6-13. English. **DESCR:** Migration; Migration Patterns; Socioeconomic Factors; *Undocumented Workers.

5630 Mexican woman seriously injured. NUESTRO, Vol. 6, no. 10 (December 1982), p. 9. English. **DESCR:** Border Patrol; Immigration Regulation and Control.

5631 Nalven, Joseph. Health research on undocumented Mexicans. SOCIAL SCIENCE JOURNAL, Vol. 19, no. 2 (April 1982), p. 73-88. English. **DESCR:** Immigration Law; Medical Care; *Public Health; *Undocumented Workers.

5632 O'Brien, Mary Elizabeth. Pragmatic survivalism: behavior patterns affecting low-level wellness among minority group members. ANS: ADVANCES IN NURSING SCIENCE, Vol. 4, no. 3 (April 1982), p. 13-26. English. **DESCR:** Curanderismo; Ethnic Attitudes; *Medical Care; *Nursing; Public Health.

5633 Pedraza Bailey, Silvia. Cubans and Mexicans in the United States: the functions of political and economic migration. CUBAN STUDIES, Vol. 11, no. 2-1 (1981, 1982), p. 70-103. English. **DESCR:** Cubanos; *Migration; Political Economy; Political Refugees.

5634 Reimers, David M. Book review of: TODAY'S IMMIGRANTS, THEIR STORIES. INTERNATIONAL MIGRATION REVIEW, Vol. 16, no. 4 (Winter 1982), p. 900. English. **DESCR:** Book Reviews; Caroli, Betty; Kessner, Thomas; Oral History; *TODAY'S IMMIGRANTS, THEIR STORIES.

5635 Rosales, Francisco Arturo. Book review of: DESERT IMMIGRANTS: THE MEXICANS OF EL PASO 1880-1920. ARIZONA AND THE WEST, Vol. 24, no. 1 (Spring 1982), p. 79-80. English. **DESCR:** Book Reviews; *DESERT IMMIGRANTS: THE MEXICANS OF EL PASO 1880-1920; Garcia, Mario T.; Texas.

5636 Rossier, Robert E. Bilingual education: training for the ghetto. POLICY REVIEW, Vol. 25, (Summer 1983), p. 36-45. English. **DESCR:** *Bilingual Bicultural Education; Bilingualism; Lau v. Nichols.

5637 Vigil, Ralph H. Book review of: DESERT IMMIGRANTS: THE MEXICANS OF EL PASO 1880-1920. INTERNATIONAL MIGRATION REVIEW, Vol. 16, no. 1 (Spring 1982), p. 223-224. English. **DESCR:** Book Reviews; *DESERT IMMIGRANTS: THE MEXICANS OF EL PASO 1880-1920; El Paso, TX; Garcia, Mario T.; History.

5638 Weintraub, Sidney and Ross, Stanley R. Poor United States, so close to Mexico. ACROSS THE BOARD, Vol. 19, no. 3 (March 1982), p. 54-61. English. **DESCR:** Braceros; *Immigration; Undocumented Workers.

--   --

Immigration

5639 Baca-Ramirez, Reynaldo and Bryan, Dexter
Edward. The undocumented Mexican worker: a
social problem? JOURNAL OF ETHNIC STUDIES,
Vol. 8, no. 1 (Spring 1980), p. 55-69.
English. **DESCR:** Government Services;
Immigrant Labor; Immigration Regulation and
Control; Mexico; Social History and
Conditions; Social Services; *Undocumented
Workers.

5640 Barberis, Mary. Hispanic America. EDITORIAL
RESEARCH REPORTS, no. 7 (30, 1982), p.
551-568. English. **DESCR:** History; Marketing;
*Population Trends.

5641 Baruch, Jeremiah (pseud.). Half-open door.
COMMONWEAL, Vol. 110, no. 13 (July 15,
1983), p. 389-390. English. **DESCR:**
*Immigration Law; *Simpson-Mazzoli Bill.

5642 Bethell, Tom. Immigration and the economy.
NATIONAL REVIEW, Vol. 35, no. 13 (July 8,
1983), p. 802. English. **DESCR:** Immigration
Law; *Simpson-Mazzoli Bill.

5643 Boiston, Bernard G. The Simpson-Mazzoli
bill: the first major immigration bill in
thirty years. OHIO STATE BAR ASSOCIATION
REPORT, Vol. 55, no. 39 (October 11, 1982),
p. 1738-1743. English. **DESCR:** Employment;
*Undocumented Workers; Visa.

5644 Borjas, George J. The labor supply of male
Hispanic immigrants in the United States.
INTERNATIONAL MIGRATION REVIEW, Vol. 17, no.
4 (Winter 1983), p. 653-671. English.
DESCR: Assimilation; Labor Supply and
Market; *Native Americans; Puerto Ricans.

5645 Bradshaw, Benjamin S. and Frisbie, W.
Parker. Potential labor force supply and
replacement in Mexico and the states of the
Mexican cession and Texas: 1980-2000.
INTERNATIONAL MIGRATION REVIEW, Vol. 17, no.
3 (Fall 1983), p. 394-409. English. **DESCR:**
*Labor Supply and Market; *Mexico; Texas.

5646 Bray, Howard. The new wave of Puerto Rican
immigrants. NEW YORK TIMES MAGAZINE, (July
3, 1983), p. 22. English. **DESCR:**
Acculturation; *Puerto Ricans.

5647 Buckley, William F. Doing the impossible.
NATIONAL REVIEW, Vol. 35, no. 17 (September
2, 1983), p. 1097. English. **DESCR:** Berlin
Wall; Immigration Law.

5648 Bustamante, Jorge A. The Mexicans are
coming: from ideology to labor relations.
INTERNATIONAL MIGRATION REVIEW, Vol. 17, no.
2 (Summer 1983), p. 323-341. English.
DESCR: Attitude (Psychological); Immigration
Law; Labor Laws and Legislation; Labor
Supply and Market; Migration; Policy;
Political Ideology; *Simpson-Mazzoli Bill;
Undocumented Workers.

5649 Can America get control of its border?
ECONOMIST (London), Vol. 286, (February 26,
1983), p. 43-44. English. **DESCR:** Immigration
Regulation and Control; Simpson-Mazzoli
Bill; Undocumented Workers.

5650 Cardoso, Lawrence Anthony. Book review of:
ACROSS THE BORDER: RURAL DEVELOPMENT IN
MEXICO AND RECENT MIGRATION TO THE UNITED
STATES. AMERICAN HISTORICAL REVIEW, Vol. 88,
(February 1983), p. 226. English. **DESCR:**
*ACROSS THE BORDER: RURAL DEVELOPMENT IN
MEXICO AND RECENT MIGRATION; Book Reviews;
Cross, Harry E.; Sandos, James.

5651 Cardoso, Lawrence Anthony. Book review of:
LOS MEXICANOS QUE DEVOLVIO LA CRISIS,
1929-1932. JOURNAL OF ETHNIC STUDIES, Vol.
5, no. 1 (Spring 1977), p. 120-122. Spanish.
DESCR: Book Reviews; Carreras de Velasco,
Mercedes; Deportation; Immigrant Labor;
Immigration Regulation and Control; *LOS
MEXICANOS QUE DEVOLVIO LA CRISIS 1929-1932;
Mexico; Social History and Conditions.

5652 Cardoso, Lawrence Anthony. Book review of:
REVOLTOSOS: MEXICO'S REBELS IN THE UNITED
STATES 1903-1923. JOURNAL OF THE WEST, Vol.
22, no. 1 (1983), p. 90. English. **DESCR:**
Book Reviews; History; Mexico; Raat, W.
Dirk; *REVOLTOSOS: MEXICO'S REBELS IN THE
UNITED STATES, 1903-1923.

5653 Cardoso, Lawrence Anthony. Book review of:
UNWANTED MEXICAN AMERICANS IN THE GREAT
DEPRESSION: REPATRIATION PRESSURES,
1929-1939. JOURNAL OF ETHNIC STUDIES, Vol.
5, no. 1 (Spring 1977), p. 120-122. English.
DESCR: Book Reviews; Deportation; Hoffman,
Abraham; Immigrant Labor; Immigration
Regulation and Control; Mexico; Social
History and Conditions; *UNWANTED MEXICAN
AMERICANS IN THE GREAT DEPRESSION.

5654 Congressional hearings proceed on
immigration. NUESTRO, Vol. 6, no. 3 (April
1982), p. 62. English. **DESCR:**
*Simpson-Mazzoli Bill.

5655 Corona, Bert. Unidad no deportaciones.
CORAZON DE AZTLAN, Vol. 1, no. 2 (March,
April, 1982), p. 6. English. **DESCR:**
*Immigration and Naturalization Service
(INS).

5656 Diez-Canedo, Juan. Undocumented migration to
the United States: a new perspective.
SOUTHWESTERN REVIEW OF MANAGEMENT AND
ECONOMICS, Vol. 2, no. 1 (Winter 1982), p.
1-59. English. **DESCR:** *Undocumented Workers.

5657 Dowd, Maureen. Losing control of the
borders. TIME, Vol. 121, no. 24 (June 13,
1983), p. 26-27. English. **DESCR:** Border
Patrol; Immigration and Naturalization
Service (INS); Immigration Regulation and
Control.

5658 Emigrantes centroamericanos en Baja
California Norte. INFORME: RELACIONES
MEXICO-ESTADOS UNIDOS, Vol. 1, no. 3 (July,
December, 1982), p. 227-241. Spanish.
DESCR: *Baja California, Mexico; Central
America.

5659 Estevez, Guillermo. Resettling the Cuban
refugees in New Jersey. MIGRATION TODAY,
Vol. 11, no. 4-5 (1983), p. 28-33. English.
DESCR: Caribbean Relief Program; *Cubanos;
International Rescue Committee; *New Jersey;
Refugees.

5660 Fradd, Sandra. Cubans to Cuban Americans:
assimilation in the United States. MIGRATION
TODAY, Vol. 11, no. 4-5 (1983), p. 35-42.
English. **DESCR:** Assimilation; Bilingualism;
*Cubanos.

5661 Garcia, Margarita. The last days in Cuba:
personal accounts of the circumstances of
the exit. MIGRATION TODAY, Vol. 11, no. 4-5
(1983), p. 13-26. English. **DESCR:** Castro,
Fidel; Cuba; *Cuban Boatlift; *Cubanos;
Hudson County, NJ; Peruvian Embassy (Cuba).

Immigration (cont.)

5662 Garcia, Mario T. Americanization and the
Mexican immigrant, 1880-1930. JOURNAL OF
ETHNIC STUDIES, Vol. 6, no. 2 (Summer 1978),
p. 19-34. English. **DESCR:** *Acculturation;
Cultural Characteristics; Culture;
Education; Immigrant Labor.

5663 Garcia, Mario T. On Mexican immigration, the
United States, and Chicano history. JOURNAL
OF ETHNIC STUDIES, Vol. 7, no. 1 (Spring
1979), p. 80-88. English. **DESCR:** Book
Reviews; *BY THE SWEAT OF THEIR BROW:
MEXICAN IMMIGRANT LABOR IN THE UNITED
STATES, 1900-1940; History; Immigrant Labor;
Immigration Law; Mexico; Reisler, Mark;
Research Methodology; Southwest United
States.

5664 Gil, Rosa Maria. Issues in the delivery of
mental health services to Cuban entrants.
MIGRATION TODAY, Vol. 11, no. 4-5 (1983), p.
44-48. English. **DESCR:** Cuban Haitian Task
Force; Cubanos; *Mental Health Programs;
National Institute of Mental Health.

5665 Hamner, Richard. Hispanic update: border
governors tackle U.S.-Mexico relations: much
ado: but   nothing on immigration. NATIONAL
HISPANIC JOURNAL, Vol. 1, no. 2 (Winter
1982), p. 4-5. English. **DESCR:** Babbitt,
Bruce; Border Region; Brown, Edmund G., Jr.,
Governor of California; *Clements, Bill;
Immigration Regulation and Control; Moreno,
Paul; *United States-Mexico Relations.

5666 Haner, Lisa G. The new wave: strangers in
our land. BUSINESS HORIZONS, Vol. 26, no. 3
(May, June, 1983), p. 2-6. English. **DESCR:**
*Assimilation.

5667 Hewlett, Sylvia Ann. Coping with illegal
immigrants. FOREIGN AFFAIRS, Vol. 60, no. 2
(Winter 1981, 1982), p. 358-378. English.
DESCR: Immigrant Labor; Immigration Law;
*Immigration Regulation and Control; Policy
Formation; Undocumented Workers.

5668 Hing, Bill Ong. Racial disparity: the
unaddressed issues of the Simpson-Mazzoli
Bill. LA RAZA LAW JOURNAL, Vol. 1, no. 1
(June 1983), p. 21-52. English. **DESCR:**
Amnesty; Asian Americans; Ethnic Attitudes;
Family; Immigration and Naturalization
Service (INS); Latin Americans; Mazzoli,
Romano L.; Mexican American Legal Defense
and Educational Fund (MALDEF); Simpson, Alan
K.; *Simpson-Mazzoli Bill; Temporary Worker
Program; U.S. Congresssional Subcommittee on
Immigration, Refugees and International Law.

5669 Hopson, Susan B. Immigration: indefinite
detention of excluded aliens held illegal.
TEXAS INTERNATIONAL LAW JOURNAL, Vol. 17,
(Winter 1982), p. 101-110. English. **DESCR:**
Civil Rights; Deportation; *Detention of
Persons; International Law;
Rodriguez-Fernandez v. Wilkinson;
Shaughnessy v. Mezei; *Undocumented Workers.

5670 Howard, David. For "illegals" migration goes
both ways. R & D MEXICO, Vol. 2, no. 3-4
(December, January, 1981, 1982), p. 14-17.
English. **DESCR:** Migration; Migration
Patterns; NATIONAL SURVEY ON EMIGRATION TO
THE NORTHERN BORDER AND THE UNITED STATES;
Surveys; *Undocumented Workers.

5671 Immigration, jobs. NUESTRO, Vol. 6, no. 4
(May 1982), p. 8. English. **DESCR:**
*Immigration and Naturalization Service
(INS); Immigration Law; Undocumented
Workers.

5672 Immigration reform again. AMERICA [America
Press, New York, NY], Vol. 149, (December
22, 1983), p. 221-222. English. **DESCR:**
Immigration Law; *Immigration Regulation and
Control.

5673 Immigration reform is alive. LATINO, Vol.
54, no. 8 (December 1983), p. 21. English.

5674 Jones, Richard C. Undocumented migration
from Mexico: some geographical questions.
ANNALS OF THE ASSOCIATION OF AMERICAN
GEOGRAPHERS, Vol. 72, no. 1 (March 1982), p.
77-87. English. **DESCR:** Geography; Mexico;
*Migration Patterns; Undocumented Workers.

5675 Jones, Robert C. Channelization of
undocumented Mexican migrants to the U.S.
ECONOMIC GEOGRAPHY, Vol. 58, (April 1982),
p. 156-176. English. **DESCR:** *Undocumented
Workers.

5676 Keep, Paul M. Overhauling the immigration
code: this year, Congress may finally act.
NATIONAL JOURNAL, Vol. 15, no. 12 (March 19,
1983), p. 616-619. English. **DESCR:** American
Civil Liberties Union; Federation for
American Immigration Reform (FAIR);
*Immigration Law; Mexican American Legal
Defense and Educational Fund (MALDEF);
*Simpson-Mazzoli Bill.

5677 Lamare, James W. Political integration of
Mexican American children: a generational
analysis. INTERNATIONAL MIGRATION REVIEW,
Vol. 16, no. 1 (Spring 1982), p. 169-188.
English. **DESCR:** Acculturation; Age Groups;
Assimilation; *Children; Political Ideology;
*Political Socialization.

5678 Lamm, Richard D. Why the U.S. closed its
borders. FUTURIST, Vol. 16, no. 6 (December
1982), p. 4-8. English. **DESCR:** United
Nations.

5679 Latinos and Mrs. Luce. NUESTRO, Vol. 6, no.
8 (October 1982), p. 9. English. **DESCR:**
*Luce, Claire Boothe; Prejudice (Social).

5680 Liebowitz, Arnold. Immigration challenge and
the congressional response. LA RAZA LAW
JOURNAL, Vol. 1, no. 1 (June 1983), p. 1-20.
English. **DESCR:** Amnesty; Immigration and
Nationality Act (INA); Mazzoli, Romano L.;
*Simpson, Alan K.; *Simpson-Mazzoli Bill;
Temporary Worker Program; Undocumented
Workers; U.S. Congresssional Subcommittee on
Immigration, Refugees and International Law.

5681 Martin, Philip L. Select Commission suggests
changes in immigration policy: a review
essay. MONTHLY LABOR REVIEW, Vol. 105, no. 2
(February 1982), p. 31-37. English. **DESCR:**
*Immigration Regulation and Control; Select
Commission on Immigration and Refugee
Policy; Undocumented Workers.

5682 Martinez, Oscar J. Book review of: DESERT
IMMIGRANTS: THE MEXICANS OF EL PASO
1880-1920. HISPANIC AMERICAN HISTORICAL
REVIEW, Vol. 62, no. 2 (May 1982), p.
289-291. English. **DESCR:** Book Reviews;
*DESERT IMMIGRANTS: THE MEXICANS OF EL PASO
1880-1920; El Paso, TX; Garcia, Mario T.

5683 Massey, Douglas S. and Schnabel, Kathleen M.
Recent trends in Hispanic immigration to the
United States. INTERNATIONAL MIGRATION
REVIEW, Vol. 17, no. 2 (Summer 1983), p.
212-244. English. **DESCR:** Migration Patterns;
Population Trends; Rural Urban Migration;
Socioeconomic Factors.

Immigration (cont.)

5684 Mendez Gonzalez, Rosalinda. Mexican women and families: rural-to-urban and international migration. SOUTHWEST ECONOMY AND SOCIETY, Vol. 4, no. 2 (Winter 1978, 1979), p. 14-27. English. **DESCR:** Chicanas; Employment; *Family; Garment Industry; International Ladies Garment Workers Union (ILGWU); Labor Organizing; Los Angeles, CA; Undocumented Workers.

5685 N.A.L.E.O.'s "Fiesta '83". CAMINOS, Vol. 4, no. 10 (November 1983), p. 28-29. English. **DESCR:** Baca Barragan, Polly; Bilingual Bicultural Education; Central America; Fiesta '83; Garcia, Robert; International Relations; Mendez, Olga; *National Association of Latino Elected Officials (NALEO); Simpson-Mazzoli Bill; United States-Mexico Relations.

5686 Otheguy, Ricardo. Thinking about bilingual education: a critical appraisal. HARVARD EDUCATIONAL REVIEW, Vol. 52, no. 3 (August 1982), p. 301-314. English. **DESCR:** *Bilingual Bicultural Education; Educational Law and Legislation.

5687 Plaza, Eva. Interest group politics and U.S. immigration policy towards Mexico. LA RAZA LAW JOURNAL, Vol. 1, no. 1 (June 1983), p. 76-100. English. **DESCR:** Immigration Law; Immigration Regulation and Control; *Interest Groups; Mexico; *Simpson-Mazzoli Bill; United States-Mexico Relations.

5688 Reisler, Mark. Book review of: DESERT IMMIGRANTS: THE MEXICANS OF EL PASO 1880-1920. AMERICAN HISTORICAL REVIEW, Vol. 87, no. 1 (February 1982), p. 271-272. English. **DESCR:** Book Reviews; *DESERT IMMIGRANTS: THE MEXICANS OF EL PASO 1880-1920; El Paso, TX; Garcia, Mario T.; History.

5689 Richmond, Douglas W. Mexican immigration and border strategy during the revolution, 1910-1920. NEW MEXICO HISTORICAL REVIEW, Vol. 57, no. 3 (July 1982), p. 269-288. English. **DESCR:** *Border Region; Carranza, Venustiano; History; Mexican Revolution - 1910-1920; Mexico; Social History and Conditions; United States-Mexico Relations.

5690 Rodriguez, Roberto. "Guest worker program". CORAZON DE AZTLAN, Vol. 1, no. 2 (March, April, 1982), p. 36-39. Bilingual. **DESCR:** *Bracero Program.

5691 Roma, Thomas E., Jr. Not my father's son: obtaining preferred immigration status through paternal affiliation. JOURNAL OF FAMILY LAW, Vol. 20, no. 2 (January 1982), p. 323-335. English. **DESCR:** Board of Immigration Appeals (BIA); Immigration and Nationality Act (INA); *Visa.

5692 Schey, Peter A. Supply side immigration theory: analysis of the Simpson-Mazzoli Bill. LA RAZA LAW JOURNAL, Vol. 1, no. 1 (June 1983), p. 53-71. English. **DESCR:** Amnesty; Mazzoli, Romano L.; Migration Patterns; Refugees; Simpson, Alan K.; *Simpson-Mazzoli Bill; Temporary Worker Program.

5693 Schmeltzer, Mike. Mexicans asked to report. MIGRATION TODAY, Vol. 10, no. 1 (1982), p. 29. English. **DESCR:** *Immigration Regulation and Control; Silva Letters; Silva, Refugio; Visa.

5694 Senate passes immigration reform bill.

CONGRESSIONAL QUARTERLY WEEKLY REPORT, Vol. 41, (May 21, 1983), p. 1006-1007. English. **DESCR:** Immigration Law; *Simpson-Mazzoli Bill.

5695 Shapiro, Walter, et al. Immigration: failure of will. NEWSWEEK, Vol. 102, no. 16 (October 17, 1983), p. 32. English. **DESCR:** *Immigration Law; Simpson-Mazzoli Bill.

5696 Shepperson, Wilbur S. Book review of: THE MEXICANS IN OKLAHOMA. NEW MEXICO HISTORICAL REVIEW, Vol. 57, no. 3 (July 1982), p. 304-305. English. **DESCR:** Book Reviews; Oklahoma; Smith, Michael M.; *THE MEXICANS IN OKLAHOMA.

5697 Simon, Daniel T. Mexican repatriation in East Chicago, Indiana. JOURNAL OF ETHNIC STUDIES, Vol. 2, no. 2 (Summer 1974), p. 11-23. English. **DESCR:** *Deportation; *East Chicago, IN; History; Immigrant Labor; Immigration Regulation and Control; Inland Steel Company; Mexico; Social History and Conditions.

5698 Starr, Mark; McGuire, Stryker; and Contreras, Joe. The border: a world apart. NEWSWEEK, Vol. 10, (April 11, 1983), p. 36-40. English. **DESCR:** *Border Region; United States-Mexico Relations.

5699 Sunseri, Alvin R. Book review of: DESERT IMMIGRANTS: THE MEXICANS OF EL PASO 1880-1920. JOURNAL OF THE WEST, Vol. 21, no. 2 (April 1982), p. 111. English. **DESCR:** Book Reviews; *DESERT IMMIGRANTS: THE MEXICANS OF EL PASO 1880-1920; Garcia, Mario T.

5700 Tattered borders. NEW REPUBLIC, Vol. 189, no. 2 (July 11, 1983), p. 9-11. English. **DESCR:** Cubanos; *Simpson-Mazzoli Bill; Undocumented Workers.

5701 Weintraub, Sidney and Ross, Stanley R. Poor United States, so close to Mexico. ACROSS THE BOARD, Vol. 19, no. 3 (March 1982), p. 54-61. English. **DESCR:** Braceros; Immigrants; Undocumented Workers.

5702 Witt, Elder. Court rules illegal aliens entitled to public schooling. CONGRESSIONAL QUARTERLY WEEKLY REPORT, Vol. 40, (June 19, 1982), p. 1479-1480. English. **DESCR:** Doe v. Plyer [Tyler Independent School District, Texas]; Education; Texas v. Certain Undocumented Alien Children; Undocumented Children; *Undocumented Workers.

Immigration and Nationality Act (INA)

5703 Furin, Gary C. Immigration law: alien employment certification. INTERNATIONAL LAWYER, Vol. 16, no. 1 (Winter 1982), p. 111-119. English. **DESCR:** Employment; *Labor Certification; Undocumented Workers.

5704 Immigration and nationality symposium. SAN DIEGO LAW REVIEW, Vol. 20, no. 1 (December 1982, 1983), p. 1-231. English. **DESCR:** Akbarian v. INS; Deportation; Employment; *Immigration Regulation and Control; Miranda v. INS; Simpson-Mazzoli Bill; Undocumented Workers.

5705 The impact of undocumented migration on the U.S. labor market. HOUSTON JOURNAL OF INTERNATIONAL LAW, Vol. 5, no. 2 (Spring 1983), p. 287-321. English. **DESCR:** Economic History and Conditions; Employment; Immigrant Labor; Immigration Law; Labor Supply and Market; Research Methodology; Simpson-Mazzoli Bill; *Undocumented Workers.

Immigration and Nationality Act (INA) (cont.)

5706 Liebowitz, Arnold. Immigration challenge and the congressional response. LA RAZA LAW JOURNAL, Vol. 1, no. 1 (June 1983), p. 1-20. English. **DESCR:** Amnesty; Immigration; Mazzoli, Romano L.; *Simpson, Alan K.; *Simpson-Mazzoli Bill; Temporary Worker Program; Undocumented Workers; U.S. Congresssional Subcommittee on Immigration, Refugees and International Law.

5707 Roma, Thomas E., Jr. Not my father's son: obtaining preferred immigration status through paternal affiliation. JOURNAL OF FAMILY LAW, Vol. 20, no. 2 (January 1982), p. 323-335. English. **DESCR:** Board of Immigration Appeals (BIA); Immigration; *Visa.

5708 Turansick, Michael F. A critique of proposed amendments to the immigration and nationality act. FORDHAM INTERNATIONAL LAW FORUM, Vol. 5, no. 1 (Winter 1981, 1982), p. 213-238. English. **DESCR:** Border Patrol; Braceros; Immigration Regulation and Control; Public Law 78; Undocumented Workers.

Immigration and Naturalization Service (INS)

5709 Appleson, Gail. Court to review INS stop-and-quiz policy. AMERICAN BAR ASSOCIATION JOURNAL, Vol. 68, (July 1982), p. 791-792. English. **DESCR:** Constitutional Amendments - Fourth; Immigration Regulation and Control; Search and Seizure; *Undocumented Workers.

5710 Aragon, Ellen Weis. The factory raid: an unconstitutional act. SOUTHERN CALIFORNIA LAW REVIEW, Vol. 56, no. 2 (January 1983), p. 605-645. English. **DESCR:** Blackie's House of Beef v. Castillo; Deportation; International Ladies Garment Workers Union (ILGWU) v. Sureck; Racism; Search and Seizure; *Undocumented Workers.

5711 Corona, Bert. Unidad no deportaciones. CORAZON DE AZTLAN, Vol. 1, no. 2 (March, April, 1982), p. 6. English. **DESCR:** Immigration.

5712 Cuban-exile community protests deportation of recent escapee. NUESTRO, Vol. 6, no. 2 (March 1982), p. 32-34. English. **DESCR:** Cubanos; Political Asylum; *Rodriguez Hernandez, Andres.

5713 Day, Mark R. Immigrants ... and Mexican citizens. NATIONAL CATHOLIC REPORTER, Vol. 18, (February 5, 1982), p. 3. English. **DESCR:** Catholic Church; *Immigrants; Undocumented Workers.

5714 Dowd, Maureen. Losing control of the borders. TIME, Vol. 121, no. 24 (June 13, 1983), p. 26-27. English. **DESCR:** Border Patrol; *Immigration; Immigration Regulation and Control.

5715 Equity for camp victims. NUESTRO, Vol. 6, no. 1 (January, February, 1982), p. 10-11. English. **DESCR:** Haiti; *Immigration Law; Refugees.

5716 Hing, Bill Ong. Racial disparity: the unaddressed issues of the Simpson-Mazzoli Bill. LA RAZA LAW JOURNAL, Vol. 1, no. 1 (June 1983), p. 21-52. English. **DESCR:** Amnesty; Asian Americans; Ethnic Attitudes; Family; Immigration; Latin Americans; Mazzoli, Romano L.; Mexican American Legal Defense and Educational Fund (MALDEF); Simpson, Alan K.; *Simpson-Mazzoli Bill; Temporary Worker Program; U.S. Congresssional Subcommittee on Immigration, Refugees and International Law.

5717 Immigration, jobs. NUESTRO, Vol. 6, no. 4 (May 1982), p. 8. English. **DESCR:** *Immigration; Immigration Law; Undocumented Workers.

5718 INS raids challenged. NUESTRO, Vol. 6, no. 6 (August 1982), p. 9. English. **DESCR:** Immigration Regulation and Control; *Undocumented Workers.

5719 INS sweep searches of work areas must meet fourth amendment standards. CRIMINAL LAW REPORTER, Vol. 31, no. 18 (August 11, 1982), p. 2366-2367. English. **DESCR:** Constitutional Amendments - Fourth; Immigration Regulation and Control; International Ladies Garment Workers Union (ILGWU); *Search and Seizure; Undocumented Workers.

5720 Morales, Rebecca. Unions and undocumented workers. SOUTHWEST ECONOMY AND SOCIETY, Vol. 6, no. 1 (Fall 1982), p. 3-11. English. **DESCR:** Employment; Labor Unions; *Operation Jobs; *Undocumented Workers.

5721 Oliver, Gordon. Worker abuses claimed. NATIONAL CATHOLIC REPORTER, Vol. 19, (October 29, 1982), p. 7. English. **DESCR:** Agricultural Laborers; Border Patrol; *Citizens United for Farmworkers, Yakima WA; *Immigration Regulation and Control; Yakima, WA.

5722 Our 1982 Latino awards. NUESTRO, Vol. 7, no. 1 (January, February, 1983), p. 44-46. English. **DESCR:** Awards; Escalante, Jaime; Gallegos, Gina; Grace, J. Peter; Knight, Bobby; Lamas, Fernando; *Latino Awards; Luce, Claire Boothe; Moreno, Rita; National Press Foundation; Rodriguez Hernandez, Andres; Simpson-Mazzoli Bill; Smith, Raymond; Valeri, Michele; Voting Rights Act.

5723 Richardson, Chad and Feagin, Joe. After crossing Rio Bravo. TEXAS OBSERVOR, Vol. 74, no. 12 (June 18, 1982), p. 1, 4-7. English. **DESCR:** *Immigration Regulation and Control; Undocumented Workers.

5724 Rout, Lawrence. For most Mexicans, legal entry to U.S. is impossible dream. WALL STREET JOURNAL, Vol. 19, no. 43 (March 4, 1982), p. 1+. English. **DESCR:** *Immigration Regulation and Control.

5725 Salgado, J. F. Alien smugglers: an escalating war. NUESTRO, Vol. 7, no. 1 (January, February, 1983), p. 39. English. **DESCR:** Border Patrol; Immigration Regulation and Control; *Undocumented Workers.

5726 Wong, Linda. Simpson-Mazzoli Bill in the Ninety-eighth Congress. LA RAZA LAW JOURNAL, Vol. 1, no. 1 (June 1983), p. 72-75. English. **DESCR:** Immigration Law; Mazzoli, Romano L.; Simpson, Alan K.; *Simpson-Mazzoli Bill.

Immigration Law

5727 Ashman, Allan. What's new in the law: immigration ... detained aliens. AMERICAN BAR ASSOCIATION JOURNAL, Vol. 68, (June 1982), p. 745. English. **DESCR:** Arias v. Rogers; Deportation; *Undocumented Workers.

Immigration Law (cont.)

5728 Baruch, Jeremiah (pseud.). Half-open door. COMMONWEAL, Vol. 110, no. 13 (July 15, 1983), p. 389-390. English. **DESCR:** Immigration; *Simpson-Mazzoli Bill.

5729 Bethell, Tom. Immigration and the economy. NATIONAL REVIEW, Vol. 35, no. 13 (July 8, 1983), p. 802. English. **DESCR:** *Immigration; *Simpson-Mazzoli Bill.

5730 Bracamonte, Jose A. The national labor relations act and undaunted workers: the alienation of American labor. SAN DIEGO LAW REVIEW, Vol. 21, no. 1 (December 1983), p. 29-86. English. **DESCR:** Labor Unions; National Labor Relations Act (NLRA); Sure-Tan; *Undocumented Workers.

5731 Bridling at a U.S. immigration bill. BUSINESS WEEK, (February 28, 1983), p. 43-44. English. **DESCR:** Immigration Regulation and Control; *Simpson-Mazzoli Bill; Undocumented Workers.

5732 Buckley, William F. Doing the impossible. NATIONAL REVIEW, Vol. 35, no. 17 (September 2, 1983), p. 1097. English. **DESCR:** Berlin Wall; *Immigration.

5733 Buffenstein, Darryl F. The proposed immigration reform and control act of 1982: a new epoch in immigration law and a new headache for employers. EMPLOYEE RELATIONS LAW JOURNAL, Vol. 8, no. 3 (Winter 1983), p. 450-462. English. **DESCR:** Employment; *Immigration Regulation and Control; Labor Certification; Undocumented Workers.

5734 Bustamante, Jorge A. The Mexicans are coming: from ideology to labor relations. INTERNATIONAL MIGRATION REVIEW, Vol. 17, no. 2 (Summer 1983), p. 323-341. English. **DESCR:** Attitude (Psychological); *Immigration; Labor Laws and Legislation; Labor Supply and Market; Migration; Policy; Political Ideology; *Simpson-Mazzoli Bill; Undocumented Workers.

5735 Castagnera-Cain, Jim. Garreau's nine nations offer immigation insights. TEXAS OBSERVER, Vol. 74, (October 15, 1982), p. 12+. English. **DESCR:** Garreau, Joel; Immigration Regulation and Control; *THE NINE NATIONS OF NORTH AMERICA; Undocumented Workers.

5736 Chaikin, Sol C. and Comstock, Phil. Toward a rational immigration policy. JOURNAL OF THE INSTITUTE FOR SOCIOECONOMIC STUDIES, Vol. 7, no. 1 (Spring 1982), p. 48-61. English. **DESCR:** Immigration Regulation and Control; Socioeconomic Factors; *Undocumented Workers.

5737 Chavez, Leo R. Hispanics and immigration reform. NUESTRO, Vol. 7, no. 8 (October 1983), p. 23-24. English. **DESCR:** *Immigration Regulation and Control; *Simpson-Mazzoli Bill; Undocumented Workers.

5738 Cohodas, Nadine. Senate passes legislation to curb illegal immigration. CONGRESSIONAL QUARTERLY WEEKLY REPORT, Vol. 40, (August 21, 1982), p. 2053-2055. English. **DESCR:** Simpson-Mazzoli Bill; *Undocumented Workers.

5739 Countdown for the immigration bill. AMERICA [America Press, New York, NY], Vol. 147, (December 25, 1982), p. 403. English. **DESCR:** Immigration Regulation and Control.

5740 Employers may pay if they hire illegals. BUSINESS WEEK, (June 21, 1982), p. 38. English. **DESCR:** Immigration Regulation and Control; *Simpson-Mazzoli Bill; Undocumented Workers.

5741 Equity for camp victims. NUESTRO, Vol. 6, no. 1 (January, February, 1982), p. 10-11. English. **DESCR:** Haiti; Immigration and Naturalization Service (INS); Refugees.

5742 Evolucion del proyecto Simpson-Mazzoli. INFORME: RELACIONES MEXICO-ESTADOS UNIDOS, Vol. 1, no. 3 (July, December, 1982), p. 209-214. Spanish. **DESCR:** *Simpson-Mazzoli Bill.

5743 Garcia, Mario T. On Mexican immigration, the United States, and Chicano history. JOURNAL OF ETHNIC STUDIES, Vol. 7, no. 1 (Spring 1979), p. 80-88. English. **DESCR:** Book Reviews; *BY THE SWEAT OF THEIR BROW: MEXICAN IMMIGRANT LABOR IN THE UNITED STATES, 1900-1940; History; Immigrant Labor; Immigration; Mexico; Reisler, Mark; Research Methodology; Southwest United States.

5744 Harwood, Edwin. Congress's bad immigration bill. WALL STREET JOURNAL, Vol. 200, (September 17, 1982), p. 28. English. **DESCR:** Immigration Regulation and Control.

5745 Helbush, Terry. INS violations of its own regulations: relief for the aliens. GOLDEN GATE UNIVERSITY LAW REVIEW, Vol. 12, (Spring 1982), p. 217-225. English. **DESCR:** Deportation; Tejeda-Mata v. INS; Undocumented Workers; U.S. v. Calderon-Medina.

5746 Hewlett, Sylvia Ann. Coping with illegal immigrants. FOREIGN AFFAIRS, Vol. 60, no. 2 (Winter 1981, 1982), p. 358-378. English. **DESCR:** Immigrant Labor; Immigration; *Immigration Regulation and Control; Policy Formation; Undocumented Workers.

5747 Immigration, jobs. NUESTRO, Vol. 6, no. 4 (May 1982), p. 8. English. **DESCR:** *Immigration; *Immigration and Naturalization Service (INS); Undocumented Workers.

5748 Immigration pols. NATION, Vol. 237, no. 10 (October 15, 1983), p. 324. English. **DESCR:** *Simpson-Mazzoli Bill.

5749 Immigration questions. NUESTRO, Vol. 6, no. 2 (March 1982), p. 10-11. English. **DESCR:** *Immigrant Labor; Silva, Refugio.

5750 Immigration reform. NUESTRO, Vol. 5, no. 8 (November 1981), p. 11. English. **DESCR:** *Rodino, Peter W.

5751 Immigration reform again. AMERICA [America Press, New York, NY], Vol. 149, (December 22, 1983), p. 221-222. English. **DESCR:** Immigration; *Immigration Regulation and Control.

5752 Immigration reform overdue. AMERICA [America Press, New York, NY], Vol. 148, (June 4, 1983), p. 430. English. **DESCR:** Immigration Regulation and Control.

5753 The impact of undocumented migration on the U.S. labor market. HOUSTON JOURNAL OF INTERNATIONAL LAW, Vol. 5, no. 2 (Spring 1983), p. 287-321. English. **DESCR:** Economic History and Conditions; Employment; Immigrant Labor; Immigration and Nationality Act (INA); Labor Supply and Market; Research Methodology; Simpson-Mazzoli Bill; *Undocumented Workers.

Immigration Law (cont.)

5754 Keep, Paul M. Overhauling the immigration code: this year, Congress may finally act. NATIONAL JOURNAL, Vol. 15, no. 12 (March 19, 1983), p. 616-619. English. **DESCR:** American Civil Liberties Union; Federation for American Immigration Reform (FAIR); Immigration; Mexican American Legal Defense and Educational Fund (MALDEF); *Simpson-Mazzoli Bill.

5755 Miller, Michael V. Book review of: CHICANOS AND RURAL POVERTY. JOURNAL OF ETHNIC STUDIES, Vol. 5, no. 3 (Fall 1977), p. 116-117. English. **DESCR:** Agricultural Laborers; Book Reviews; Briggs, Vernon M.; *CHICANOS AND RURAL POVERTY; Social History and Conditions; Southwest United States.

5756 Moore, Richard J. Book review of: "TEMPORARY" ALIEN WORKERS IN THE UNITED STATES: DESIGNING POLICY FROM FACT AND OPINION. INTERNATIONAL MIGRATION REVIEW, Vol. 16, no. 4 (Winter 1982), p. 909-910. English. **DESCR:** Book Reviews; Literature Reviews; Ross, Stanley R.; *"TEMPORARY" ALIEN WORKERS IN THE UNITED STATES: DESIGNING POLICY FROM FACT AND OPINION; Undocumented Workers; Weintraub, Sidney.

5757 Morganthau, Tom and Camper, Diane. An amnesty for illegal aliens? NEWSWEEK, Vol. 101, no. 22 (May 30, 1983), p. 41. English. **DESCR:** *Simpson-Mazzoli Bill.

5758 Nalven, Joseph. Health research on undocumented Mexicans. SOCIAL SCIENCE JOURNAL, Vol. 19, no. 2 (April 1982), p. 73-88. English. **DESCR:** Immigrants; Medical Care; *Public Health; *Undocumented Workers.

5759 O'Neill shifts his course on immigration (NEW YORK TIMES 12-4-83). MIGRATION TODAY, Vol. 11, no. 4-5 (1983), p. 52. English. **DESCR:** *O'Neill, Thomas P.; Simpson-Mazzoli Bill.

5760 Plaza, Eva. Interest group politics and U.S. immigration policy towards Mexico. LA RAZA LAW JOURNAL, Vol. 1, no. 1 (June 1983), p. 76-100. English. **DESCR:** Immigration; Immigration Regulation and Control; *Interest Groups; Mexico; *Simpson-Mazzoli Bill; United States-Mexico Relations.

5761 Police and immigration. NUESTRO, Vol. 7, no. 2 (March 1983), p. 7. English. **DESCR:** *Border Patrol; El Paso, TX; Federal Government; Immigration Regulation and Control; Police.

5762 Praise for the speaker. NUESTRO, Vol. 7, no. 8 (October 1983), p. 9. English. **DESCR:** Mexican American Legal Defense and Educational Fund (MALDEF); *Simpson-Mazzoli Bill.

5763 El proyecto Simpson-Mazzoli para el control de la inmigracion de los trabajadores mexicanos a Estados Unidos. INFORME: RELACIONES MEXICO-ESTADOS UNIDOS, Vol. 1, no. 2 (July, December, 1982), p. 75-87. Spanish. **DESCR:** *Simpson-Mazzoli Bill.

5764 Reaves, Gayle. Supreme Court rules for alien children. NUESTRO, Vol. 6, no. 5 (June, July, 1982), p. 14-16. English. **DESCR:** *Children; Education; Education Equalization; *Legislation; Undocumented Workers; U.S. Supreme Court.

5765 Reza, H. G. Immigration: restriction or reform? CALIFORNIA LAWYER, Vol. 2, no. 11

(December 1982), p. 32-35. English. **DESCR:** Immigration Regulation and Control; Simpson-Mazzoli Bill; Undocumented Workers.

5766 Richardson, Chad and Yanez, Linda. "Equal justice" and Jose Reyna. NUESTRO, Vol. 6, no. 5 (June, July, 1982), p. 17. English. **DESCR:** Brownsville, TX; *Children; Education; Education Equalization; *Legislation; Reyna, Jose; Undocumented Workers.

5767 Rips, Geoffrey. Supply-side immigration reform. NATION, Vol. 237, no. 10 (October 8, 1983), p. 289,303+. English. **DESCR:** Simpson-Mazzoli Bill; Undocumented Workers.

5768 Romero, Tina. The undocumented worker: how will the United States deal with him? NATIONAL HISPANIC JOURNAL, Vol. 1, no. 3 (Summer, Fall, 1982), p. 13-15. English. **DESCR:** Immigration Regulation and Control; Reagan, Ronald; *Undocumented Workers.

5769 Schey, Peter A. The Reagan and Simpson/Mazzoli immigration proposals: supply side immigration policy. MIGRATION TODAY, Vol. 11, no. 2-3 (1983), p. 35-38. English. **DESCR:** *Simpson-Mazzoli Bill.

5770 Senate passes immigration reform bill. CONGRESSIONAL QUARTERLY WEEKLY REPORT, Vol. 41, (May 21, 1983), p. 1006-1007. English. **DESCR:** Immigration; *Simpson-Mazzoli Bill.

5771 Shapiro, Walter, et al. Immigration: failure of will. NEWSWEEK, Vol. 102, no. 16 (October 17, 1983), p. 32. English. **DESCR:** Immigration; Simpson-Mazzoli Bill.

5772 Side-by-side comparison of House and Senate bills. MIGRATION TODAY, Vol. 11, no. 2-3 (1983), p. 7. English. **DESCR:** *Simpson-Mazzoli Bill.

5773 Simpson, Alan K. Immigration reform and control. LABOR LAW JOURNAL, Vol. 34, no. 4 (April 1983), p. 195-200. English. **DESCR:** *Simpson-Mazzoli Bill.

5774 Smith, William French. A look at the immigration laws. TEXAS BAR JOURNAL, Vol. 45, no. 2 (February 1982), p. 224-225. English. **DESCR:** Undocumented Workers.

5775 Speight, Tamara D. Current legislation of significance to the English as a second language and bilingual education communities. FOREIGN LANGUAGE ANNALS, Vol. 15, no. 4 (September 1982), p. 245-247. English. **DESCR:** *Educational Law and Legislation.

5776 Stone, Marvin. The illegals: one more try. U.S. NEWS & WORLD REPORT, Vol. 94, no. 15 (April 18, 1983), p. 94. English. **DESCR:** Editorials; *Immigration Regulation and Control; Simpson-Mazzoli Bill.

5777 Taylor, Robert E. New fight on illegal aliens planned amid signs opposition is softening. WALL STREET JOURNAL, Vol. 19, no. 43 (March 10, 1982), p. 33. English. **DESCR:** *Simpson-Mazzoli Bill.

5778 Thomas, Evan. Playing politics with immigration. TIME, Vol. 122, no. 17 (October 17, 1983), p. 19. English. **DESCR:** *Immigration Regulation and Control; Simpson-Mazzoli Bill.

---   ---

Immigration Law (cont.)

5779 Through the revolution door: undocumented
     workers and the U.S. economy. DOLLARS AND
     SENSE, Vol. 83, (January 1983), p. 8-9+.
     English. **DESCR:** History; Simpson-Mazzoli
     Bill.

5780 Torres, Arnold. Immigration bill defeated.
     LATINO, Vol. 53, no. 6 (October 1982), p. 7.
     English.

5781 Torres, Arnold. Special report on the
     Simpson-Mazzoli Bill. LATINO, Vol. 53, no. 8
     (December 1982), p. 16-18. English. **DESCR:**
     *Simpson-Mazzoli Bill.

5782 Weiss, Richard. Book review of: LEGISLATIVE
     HISTORY OF AMERICAN IMMIGRATION POLICY,
     1798-1965. INTERNATIONAL MIGRATION REVIEW,
     Vol. 16, no. 3 (Fall 1982), p. 683. English.
     DESCR: Book Reviews; Hutchinson, E.P.;
     *LEGISLATIVE HISTORY OF AMERICAN IMMIGRATION
     POLICY, 1798-1965.

5783 Wong, Linda. Simpson-Mazzoli Bill in the
     Ninety-eighth Congress. LA RAZA LAW JOURNAL,
     Vol. 1, no. 1 (June 1983), p. 72-75.
     English. **DESCR:** Immigration and
     Naturalization Service (INS); Mazzoli,
     Romano L.; Simpson, Alan K.;
     *Simpson-Mazzoli Bill.

Immigration Raids
     USE: Immigration Regulation and Control

Immigration Reform and Control Act of 1982
     USE: Simpson-Mazzoli Bill

Immigration Regulation and Control

5784 Appleson, Gail. Court to review INS
     stop-and-quiz policy. AMERICAN BAR
     ASSOCIATION JOURNAL, Vol. 68, (July 1982),
     p. 791-792. English. **DESCR:** Constitutional
     Amendments - Fourth; Immigration and
     Naturalization Service (INS); Search and
     Seizure; *Undocumented Workers.

5785 Babbitt, Bruce. Reagan approach to aliens
     simply wishful thinking. NATIONAL HISPANIC
     JOURNAL, Vol. 1, no. 2 (Winter 1982), p.
     6-7. English. **DESCR:** Border Region;
     Braceros; *Reagan, Ronald; Select Commission
     on Immigration and Refugee Policy;
     *Undocumented Workers; United States-Mexico
     Relations.

5786 Baca-Ramirez, Reynaldo and Bryan, Dexter
     Edward. The undocumented Mexican worker: a
     social problem? JOURNAL OF ETHNIC STUDIES,
     Vol. 8, no. 1 (Spring 1980), p. 55-69.
     English. **DESCR:** Government Services;
     Immigrant Labor; Immigration; Mexico; Social
     History and Conditions; Social Services;
     *Undocumented Workers.

5787 Bridling at a U.S. immigration bill.
     BUSINESS WEEK, (February 28, 1983), p.
     43-44. English. **DESCR:** *Immigration Law;
     *Simpson-Mazzoli Bill; Undocumented Workers.

5788 Brooks, Douglas Montgomery. Aliens - civil
     rights - illegal aliens are inhabitants
     within meaning of U.S.C 242. SUFFOLK
     TRANSNATIONAL LAW JOURNAL, Vol. 6, no. 1
     (Spring 1982), p. 117-131. English. **DESCR:**
     Border Patrol; Constitutional Amendments -
     Fourteenth; *Undocumented Workers; U.S. v.
     Otherson.

5789 Buffenstein, Darryl F. The proposed
     immigration reform and control act of 1982:
     a new epoch in immigration law and a new

     headache for employers. EMPLOYEE RELATIONS
     LAW JOURNAL, Vol. 8, no. 3 (Winter 1983), p.
     450-462. English. **DESCR:** Employment;
     Immigration Law; Labor Certification;
     Undocumented Workers.

5790 Camacho de Schmidt, Aurora. Alien smuggling
     and the refugee question: the INS and
     sojourners from Yalaj. NUESTRO, Vol. 7, no.
     5 (June, July, 1983), p. 20. English.
     DESCR: *Guatemala; *Political Refugees;
     Refugees; *Undocumented Workers.

5791 Can America get control of its border?
     ECONOMIST (London), Vol. 286, (February 26,
     1983), p. 43-44. English. **DESCR:**
     *Immigration; Simpson-Mazzoli Bill;
     Undocumented Workers.

5792 Cardoso, Lawrence Anthony. Book review of:
     LOS MEXICANOS QUE DEVOLVIO LA CRISIS,
     1929-1932. JOURNAL OF ETHNIC STUDIES, Vol.
     5, no. 1 (Spring 1977), p. 120-122. Spanish.
     DESCR: Book Reviews; Carreras de Velasco,
     Mercedes; Deportation; Immigrant Labor;
     Immigration; *LOS MEXICANOS QUE DEVOLVIO LA
     CRISIS 1929-1932; Mexico; Social History and
     Conditions.

5793 Cardoso, Lawrence Anthony. Book review of:
     UNWANTED MEXICAN AMERICANS IN THE GREAT
     DEPRESSION: REPATRIATION PRESSURES,
     1929-1939. JOURNAL OF ETHNIC STUDIES, Vol.
     5, no. 1 (Spring 1977), p. 120-122. English.
     DESCR: Book Reviews; Deportation; Hoffman,
     Abraham; Immigrant Labor; Immigration;
     Mexico; Social History and Conditions;
     *UNWANTED MEXICAN AMERICANS IN THE GREAT
     DEPRESSION.

5794 Castagnera-Cain, Jim. Garreau's nine nations
     offer immigation insights. TEXAS OBSERVOR,
     Vol. 74, (October 15, 1982), p. 12+.
     English. **DESCR:** Garreau, Joel; Immigration
     Law; *THE NINE NATIONS OF NORTH AMERICA;
     Undocumented Workers.

5795 Castillo, Leonel J. A response to the Reagan
     plan: respuesta al plan Reagan. CAMINOS,
     Vol. 3, no. 1 (January 1982), p. 13-15.
     Bilingual. **DESCR:** *Reagan, Ronald.

5796 Castro, Mike. Alien smuggling and the
     refugee question: caught between the border
     patrol and the river. NUESTRO, Vol. 7, no. 5
     (June, July, 1983), p. 18. English. **DESCR:**
     *Border Patrol; California Rural Legal
     Assistance (CRLA); *Sacramento, CA;
     *Undocumented Workers.

5797 Castro, Mike. OAS investigates California
     deaths. NUESTRO, Vol. 7, no. 9 (November
     1983), p. 12-13. English. **DESCR:** *Border
     Patrol; California Rural Legal Assistance
     (CRLA); *Organization of American States.

5798 Chaikin, Sol C. and Comstock, Phil. Toward a
     rational immigration policy. JOURNAL OF THE
     INSTITUTE FOR SOCIOECONOMIC STUDIES, Vol. 7,
     no. 1 (Spring 1982), p. 48-61. English.
     DESCR: Immigration Law; Socioeconomic
     Factors; *Undocumented Workers.

5799 Chavez, Leo R. Hispanics and immigration
     reform. NUESTRO, Vol. 7, no. 8 (October
     1983), p. 23-24. English. **DESCR:** Immigration
     Law; *Simpson-Mazzoli Bill; Undocumented
     Workers.

Immigration Regulation and Control (cont.)

5800 Chavira, Ricardo. Refugees from poverty: a San Diego perspective. NUESTRO, Vol. 7, no. 4 (May 1983), p. 24-25. English. **DESCR**: Border Patrol; *San Diego, CA; *Undocumented Workers.

5801 Chaze, William L. Invasion from Mexico: it just keeps growing. U.S. NEWS & WORLD REPORT, Vol. 94, no. 9 (March 7, 1983), p. 37-41. English. **DESCR**: Border Region; Smuggling; *Undocumented Workers.

5802 Cortez, Hector. The undocumented alien and the law. CHRISTIAN CENTURY, Vol. 100, (July 6, 1983), p. 650-652. English. **DESCR**: Religion; *Undocumented Workers.

5803 Countdown for the immigration bill. AMERICA [America Press, New York, NY], Vol. 147, (December 25, 1982), p. 403. English. **DESCR**: *Immigration Law.

5804 Day, Mark R. 'Traffic darn heavy' to U.S. NATIONAL CATHOLIC REPORTER, Vol. 19, (October 29, 1982), p. 3. English. **DESCR**: Border Patrol; *Undocumented Workers.

5805 Dowd, Maureen. Losing control of the borders. TIME, Vol. 121, no. 24 (June 13, 1983), p. 26-27. English. **DESCR**: Border Patrol; *Immigration; Immigration and Naturalization Service (INS).

5806 Employers may pay if they hire illegals. BUSINESS WEEK, (June 21, 1982), p. 38. English. **DESCR**: *Immigration Law; *Simpson-Mazzoli Bill; Undocumented Workers.

5807 Fernandez, Enrique and Valle, Eunice. Latin drop: retail sales decrease attributed to sweeps by Dept. of Immigration raids. BILLBOARD, Vol. 94, no. 25 (June 26, 1982), p. 3. English. **DESCR**: Deportation; Marketing; *Music.

5808 Hamner, Richard. Hispanic update: border governors tackle U.S.-Mexico relations: much ado: but nothing on immigration. NATIONAL HISPANIC JOURNAL, Vol. 1, no. 2 (Winter 1982), p. 4-5. English. **DESCR**: Babbitt, Bruce; Border Region; Brown, Edmund G., Jr., Governor of California; *Clements, Bill; Immigration; Moreno, Paul; *United States-Mexico Relations.

5809 Harwood, Edwin. Congress's bad immigration bill. WALL STREET JOURNAL, Vol. 200, (September 17, 1982), p. 28. English. **DESCR**: *Immigration Law.

5810 Hewlett, Sylvia Ann. Coping with illegal immigrants. FOREIGN AFFAIRS, Vol. 60, no. 2 (Winter 1981, 1982), p. 358-378. English. **DESCR**: Immigrant Labor; Immigration; Immigration Law; Policy Formation; Undocumented Workers.

5811 Immigration and nationality symposium. SAN DIEGO LAW REVIEW, Vol. 20, no. 1 (December 1982, 1983), p. 1-231. English. **DESCR**: Akbarian v. INS; Deportation; Employment; Immigration and Nationality Act (INA); Miranda v. INS; Simpson-Mazzoli Bill; Undocumented Workers.

5812 Immigration reform again. AMERICA [America Press, New York, NY], Vol. 149, (December 22, 1983), p. 221-222. English. **DESCR**: Immigration; Immigration Law.

5813 Immigration reform overdue. AMERICA [America Press, New York, NY], Vol. 148, (June 4,

1983), p. 430. English. **DESCR**: *Immigration Law.

5814 INS raids challenged. NUESTRO, Vol. 6, no. 6 (August 1982), p. 9. English. **DESCR**: *Immigration and Naturalization Service (INS); *Undocumented Workers.

5815 INS sweep searches of work areas must meet fourth amendment standards. CRIMINAL LAW REPORTER, Vol. 31, no. 18 (August 11, 1982), p. 2366-2367. English. **DESCR**: Constitutional Amendments - Fourth; Immigration and Naturalization Service (INS); International Ladies Garment Workers Union (ILGWU); *Search and Seizure; Undocumented Workers.

5816 King, John S. California Farm Bureau Federation: addressing the issue/conduciendo el topico. CAMINOS, Vol. 3, no. 1 (January 1982), p. 16-17. Bilingual. **DESCR**: *California Farm Bureau Federation; Reagan, Ronald.

5817 Long, William J. and Pohl, Christopher M. Joint foot patrols succeed in El Paso. POLICE CHIEF, Vol. 50, no. 4 (April 1983), p. 49-51. English. **DESCR**: Border Patrol; Ciudad Juarez, Chihuahua, Mexico; Criminal Acts; *El Paso, TX; *Police; Undocumented Workers; Youth.

5818 MALDEF critical of FAIR study. NUESTRO, Vol. 7, no. 7 (September 1983), p. 12-13. English. **DESCR**: Federation for American Immigration Reform (FAIR); *Mexican American Legal Defense and Educational Fund (MALDEF); Simpson-Mazzoli Bill.

5819 Martin, Philip L. Select Commission suggests changes in immigration policy: a review essay. MONTHLY LABOR REVIEW, Vol. 105, no. 2 (February 1982), p. 31-37. English. **DESCR**: Immigration; Select Commission on Immigration and Refugee Policy; Undocumented Workers.

5820 Mena, Jesus. Refugees from poverty: a Brownsville perspective. NUESTRO, Vol. 7, no. 4 (May 1983), p. 26. English. **DESCR**: Border Patrol; Brownsville, TX; *Undocumented Workers.

5821 Mexican American Legal Defense and Education Fund (MALDEF). MALDEF on the Reagan plan. CAMINOS, Vol. 3, no. 1 (January 1982), p. 23-25. English. **DESCR**: *Days, Drew; Mexican American Legal Defense and Educational Fund (MALDEF).

5822 Mexican migration to the United States: challenge to Christian witness and national policy. CHURCH AND SOCIETY, Vol. 72, no. 5 (May, June, 1982), p. 29-46. English. **DESCR**: Economic History and Conditions; Religion; *Undocumented Workers; United States-Mexico Relations.

5823 Mexican woman seriously injured. NUESTRO, Vol. 6, no. 10 (December 1982), p. 9. English. **DESCR**: Border Patrol; *Immigrants.

5824 Oliver, Gordon. Worker abuses claimed. NATIONAL CATHOLIC REPORTER, Vol. 19, (October 29, 1982), p. 7. English. **DESCR**: Agricultural Laborers; Border Patrol; *Citizens United for Farmworkers, Yakima WA; Immigration and Naturalization Service (INS); Yakima, WA.

Immigration Regulation and Control (cont.)

5825 Padilla, Steve. Alien smuggling and the
     refugee question: undercover agent for the
     border patrol. NUESTRO, Vol. 7, no. 5 (June,
     July, 1983), p. 15-17. English. DESCR:
     Acosta, Hipolito; *Border Patrol;
     *Undocumented Workers.

5826 Plaza, Eva. Interest group politics and U.S.
     immigration policy towards Mexico. LA RAZA
     LAW JOURNAL, Vol. 1, no. 1 (June 1983), p.
     76-100. English. DESCR: Immigration;
     Immigration Law; *Interest Groups; Mexico;
     *Simpson-Mazzoli Bill; United States-Mexico
     Relations.

5827 Police and immigration. NUESTRO, Vol. 7, no.
     2 (March 1983), p. 7. English. DESCR:
     *Border Patrol; El Paso, TX; Federal
     Government; *Immigration Law; Police.

5828 Que pasa? NUESTRO, Vol. 7, no. 3 (April
     1983), p. 9. English. DESCR: Border Patrol;
     *Cisneros, Henry, Mayor of San Antonio, TX;
     Elections; Rocky Mountain Spotted Fever;
     Servas; Tourism.

5829 Quinlivan, Robert. CRC's Herman Baca on the
     issue. CAMINOS, Vol. 3, no. 1 (January
     1982), p. 18-20. Bilingual. DESCR: *Baca,
     Herman; *Committee on Chicano Rights;
     Reagan, Ronald.

5830 Reza, H. G. Immigration: restriction or
     reform? CALIFORNIA LAWYER, Vol. 2, no. 11
     (December 1982), p. 32-35. English. DESCR:
     *Immigration Law; Simpson-Mazzoli Bill;
     Undocumented Workers.

5831 Richardson, Chad and Feagin, Joe. After
     crossing Rio Bravo. TEXAS OBSERVOR, Vol. 74,
     no. 12 (June 18, 1982), p. 1, 4-7. English.
     DESCR: Immigration and Naturalization
     Service (INS); Undocumented Workers.

5832 Rios, Madeline. Operation Jobs: one year
     later. CAMINOS, Vol. 4, no. 11 (December
     1983), p. 28-30. Bilingual. DESCR:
     *Operation Jobs; Undocumented Workers.

5833 Rivera, Julius and Goodman, Paul Wershub.
     Clandestine labor circulation: a case on the
     U.S.-Mexico border. MIGRATION TODAY, Vol.
     10, no. 1 (1982), p. 21-26. English. DESCR:
     Border Patrol; Border Region; Ciudad Juarez,
     Chihuahua, Mexico; El Paso, TX; Migration
     Patterns; Social Classes; Social Mobility;
     Socioeconomic Factors; *Undocumented
     Workers.

5834 Romero, Tina. The undocumented worker: how
     will the United States deal with him?
     NATIONAL HISPANIC JOURNAL, Vol. 1, no. 3
     (Summer, Fall, 1982), p. 13-15. English.
     DESCR: Immigration Law; Reagan, Ronald;
     *Undocumented Workers.

5835 Rout, Lawrence. For most Mexicans, legal
     entry to U.S. is impossible dream. WALL
     STREET JOURNAL, Vol. 19, no. 43 (March 4,
     1982), p. 1+. English. DESCR: Immigration
     and Naturalization Service (INS).

5836 Salgado, J. F. Alien smugglers: an
     escalating war. NUESTRO, Vol. 7, no. 1
     (January, February, 1983), p. 39. English.
     DESCR: Border Patrol; Immigration and
     Naturalization Service (INS); *Undocumented
     Workers.

5837 Salvatierra, Richard. Alien smuggling and
     the refugee question: U.S. must set a limit
     on refugees. NUESTRO, Vol. 7, no. 5 (June,

July, 1983), p. 19. English. DESCR:
Federation for American Immigration Reform
(FAIR); *Political Refugees; Refugees;
*Undocumented Workers.

5838 Schmeltzer, Mike. Mexicans asked to report.
     MIGRATION TODAY, Vol. 10, no. 1 (1982), p.
     29. English. DESCR: Immigration; Silva
     Letters; Silva, Refugio; Visa.

5839 Simon, Daniel T. Mexican repatriation in
     East Chicago, Indiana. JOURNAL OF ETHNIC
     STUDIES, Vol. 2, no. 2 (Summer 1974), p.
     11-23. English. DESCR: *Deportation; *East
     Chicago, IN; History; Immigrant Labor;
     Immigration; Inland Steel Company; Mexico;
     Social History and Conditions.

5840 Stone, Marvin. The illegals: one more try.
     U.S. NEWS & WORLD REPORT, Vol. 94, no. 15
     (April 18, 1983), p. 94. English. DESCR:
     Editorials; Immigration Law; Simpson-Mazzoli
     Bill.

5841 A summary of the Reagan administration's
     proposed immigration policies/compendio de
     la propuesta politica de inmigracion de la
     administracion Reagan. CAMINOS, Vol. 3, no.
     1 (January 1982), p. 11-12. Bilingual.
     DESCR: *Reagan, Ronald.

5842 Thomas, Evan. Playing politics with
     immigration. TIME, Vol. 122, no. 17 (October
     17, 1983), p. 19. English. DESCR:
     Immigration Law; Simpson-Mazzoli Bill.

5843 Turansick, Michael F. A critique of proposed
     amendments to the immigration and
     nationality act. FORDHAM INTERNATIONAL LAW
     FORUM, Vol. 5, no. 1 (Winter 1981, 1982), p.
     213-238. English. DESCR: Border Patrol;
     Braceros; *Immigration and Nationality Act
     (INA); Public Law 78; Undocumented Workers.

5844 Watson, Roy J., Jr. The Simpson-Mazzoli
     bill: an analysis of selected policies. SAN
     DIEGO LAW REVIEW, Vol. 20, no. 1 (December
     1982), p. 97-116. English. DESCR:
     Employment; Labor Certification; Mazzoli,
     Romano L.; Simpson, Alan K.;
     *Simpson-Mazzoli Bill; *Undocumented
     Workers.

Immunization
     USE: Preventative Medicine

**THE IMPACT OF INTIMACY: MEXICAN-ANGLO
INTERMARRIAGE IN NEW MEXICO, 1821-1846**

5845 Miller, Darlis A. Book review of: THE IMPACT
     OF INTIMACY: MEXICAN-ANGLO INTERMARRIAGE IN
     NEW MEXICO, 1821-1846. NEW MEXICO HISTORICAL
     REVIEW, Vol. 57, no. 4 (October 1982), p.
     407-408. English. DESCR: Book Reviews;
     Craver, Rebecca McDowell; Intermarriage.

IMPACT OF RACISM ON WHITE AMERICANS

5846 Rochester, R. C. Book review of: IMPACT OF
     RACISM ON WHITE AMERICANS. HISPANIC JOURNAL
     OF BEHAVIORAL SCIENCES, Vol. 5, no. 1 (March
     1983), p. 125-129. English. DESCR: Book
     Reviews; Bowser, Benjamin P.; Hunt, Raymond
     G.

Imperial Savings

5847 Hann, Donna; Ferree, W. P.; and Flores, Larry. Affirmative action means progress: 2 corporations and one federal agency look at affirmative action. CAMINOS, Vol. 3, no. 8 (September 1982), p. 39-42. English. DESCR: *Affirmative Action; General Telephone Company; Veteran's Administration.

Imperialism

5848 Maldonado-Denis, Manuel. El problema de las nacionalidades: la experiencia caribena. Paper presented at the "Dialogo de las Americas" conference. Mexico, D.F. September 9-14, 1982. REVISTA CHICANO-RIQUENA, Vol. 10, no. 4 (Fall 1982), p. 39-45. Spanish. DESCR: Capitalism; Carpentier, Alejo; Cuba; El Salvador; Grenada; Guatemala; Marti, Jose; Nicaragua; *Political History and Conditions; Puerto Rico; United States.

IN DEFENSE OF LA RAZA: THE LOS ANGELES MEXICAN CONSULATE AND THE MEXICAN COMMUNITY

5849 Book review of: IN DEFENSE OF LA RAZA: THE LOS ANGELES MEXICAN CONSULATE AND THE MEXICAN COMMUNITY. CHOICE, Vol. 20, no. 7 (March 1983), p. 1050. English. DESCR: Balderrama, Francisco E.; Book Reviews.

5850 Cuello, J. Book review of: IN DEFENSE OF LA RAZA: THE LOS ANGELES MEXICAN CONSULATE AND THE MEXICAN COMMUNITY. CALIFORNIA HISTORY, Vol. 62, no. 1 (1983), p. 70. English. DESCR: Balderrama, Francisco E.; Book Reviews; California; History.

5851 De Leon, Arnoldo. Book review of: IN DEFENSE OF LA RAZA: THE LOS ANGELES MEXICAN CONSULATE AND THE MEXICAN COMMUNITY. NEW MEXICO HISTORICAL REVIEW, Vol. 58, no. 3 (July 1983), p. 296-297. English. DESCR: Balderrama, Francisco E.; Book Reviews.

Income

5852 Angel, Ronald and Tienda, Marta. Determinants of extended household structure: cultural pattern or economical need? AMERICAN JOURNAL OF SOCIOLOGY, Vol. 87, no. 6 (May 1982), p. 1360-1383. English. DESCR: *Extended Family.

5853 Borjas, George J. Earnings of male Hispanic immigrants in the United States. INDUSTRIAL AND LABOR RELATIONS REVIEW, Vol. 35, no. 3 (April 1982), p. 343-353. English. DESCR: Cubanos; Ethnic Groups; *Immigrants; Puerto Ricans; Social Mobility.

5854 Borjas, George J. The substitutability of Black, Hispanic and white labor. ECONOMIC INQUIRY, Vol. 21, no. 1 (January 1983), p. 93-106. English. DESCR: *Labor Supply and Market.

5855 Chavarria, Jesus. The changing Hispanic market. HISPANIC BUSINESS, Vol. 5, no. 12 (December 1983), p. 6. English. DESCR: Advertising; *Marketing.

5856 Garcia, Philip. Trends in the relative income position of Mexican-origin workers in the United States: the early seventies. SOCIOLOGY & SOCIAL RESEARCH, Vol. 66, no. 4 (June 1982), p. 467-483. English. DESCR: Immigrant Labor.

5857 Government review. NUESTRO, Vol. 7, no. 6 (August 1983), p. 56. English. DESCR: Ballet de Puerto Rico; Dance; Education; Employment; *Government Funding Sources; Government Services; Housing; National Fair Housing Law; Population Distribution; Urban Development Action Grant (UDAG); Veterans.

5858 Growth of U.S. Hispanic income: 1950-1982. HISPANIC BUSINESS, Vol. 5, no. 12 (December 1983), p. 46. English. DESCR: Economics; Research Methodology.

5859 Hispanic income still lower. HISPANIC BUSINESS, Vol. 4, no. 1 (January 1982), p. 29. English. DESCR: Employment.

5860 Hispanic wages and employment slow to rise. HISPANIC BUSINESS, Vol. 5, no. 11 (November 1983), p. 36-37. English. DESCR: Chicanas; Congressional Hispanic Caucus; *Employment.

5861 Hispanics: don't they know there's a recession on? S & MM [SALES & MARKETING MANAGEMENT], Vol. 12, no. 2 (July 26, 1982), p. A41. English. DESCR: *Labor Supply and Market.

5862 Kincaid, Jill. LULAC opposes youth subminimum wage proposal. LATINO, Vol. 54, no. 4 (May, June, 1983), p. 27. English. DESCR: *League of United Latin American Citizens (LULAC); Youth.

5863 Math-based careers. HISPANIC BUSINESS, Vol. 5, no. 5 (May 1983), p. 26. English. DESCR: *Careers; Engineering as a Profession; Financial Aid; Labor Supply and Market; Mexican American Engineering Society (MAES) National Symposium (5th), Fullerton, CA, April 13-15, 1980; University of California, Santa Barbara.

5864 Median administrative salaries in 1981-82 for men and women and minority-group members. CHRONICLE OF HIGHER EDUCATION, Vol. 24, no. 2 (March 10, 1982), p. 10. English. DESCR: *Administrators; Chicanas; Ethnic Groups; Males.

5865 Raymond, Richard and Sesnowitz, Michael. Labor market discrimination against Mexican American college graduates. SOUTHERN ECONOMIC JOURNAL, Vol. 49, no. 4 (April 1983), p. 1122-1136. English. DESCR: College Graduates; *Employment; Racism.

5866 Santos, Richard. Earning among Spanish-origin males in the Midwest. SOCIAL SCIENCE JOURNAL, Vol. 19, no. 2 (April 1982), p. 51-59. English. DESCR: Employment; Labor; Midwestern States.

5867 Tienda, Marta. Market characteristics and Hispanic earnings: a comparison of natives and immigrants. SOCIAL PROBLEMS, Vol. 31, no. 1 (October 1983), p. 59-72. English. DESCR: Labor Supply and Market.

5868 Tienda, Marta. Sex, ethnicity and Chicano status attainment. INTERNATIONAL MIGRATION REVIEW, Vol. 16, no. 2 (Summer 1982), p. 435-473. English. DESCR: Academic Achievement; Chicanas; Discrimination in Education; Discrimination in Employment; Identity; Language Proficiency; Sexism; *Social Classes; Social Mobility.

5869 Triana, Armando R. Changing demographics, consumer patterns in the Chicago marketplace. HISPANIC BUSINESS, Vol. 5, no. 12 (December 1983), p. 20-21+. English. DESCR: *Chicago, IL; *Marketing; Population Trends.

Income (cont.)

5870 Upscale Hispanic consumer demographics in
     the top 15 SMSAS. HISPANIC BUSINESS, Vol. 4,
     no. 12 (December 1982), p. 37-38. English.
     DESCR: *Consumers; *Demography; Population.

Index of Psychological Adjustment

5871 Dolgin, Daniel L., et al. Quality of life
     and psychological well-being in a bicultural
     Latino community. HISPANIC JOURNAL OF
     BEHAVIORAL SCIENCES, Vol. 4, no. 4 (December
     1982), p. 433-450. English. **DESCR:**
     Acculturation; *Attitude (Psychological);
     Depression Scale; *Global Acculturation
     Scale; Psychology; Quality of Life Scale.

Indiana

5872 Sutton, Susan Buck and Brunner, Tracy. Life
     on the road: Midwestern migrant farmworker
     survival skills. MIGRATION TODAY, Vol. 11,
     no. 1 (1983), p. 24-31. English. **DESCR:**
     Agribusiness; Agricultural Laborers;
     Economic History and Conditions; Migrant
     Children; Migrant Education; *Migrant Labor;
     Stereotypes.

Industrial Productivity

5873 Productivity measurement: balancing input &
     output. HISPANIC BUSINESS, Vol. 4, no. 2
     (February 1982), p. 23. English.

Industrial Relations

5874 Research/development: books. HISPANIC
     BUSINESS, Vol. 5, no. 4 (April 1983), p. 28.
     English. **DESCR:** Biographical Notes; *Book
     Reviews; *"DO IT MY WAY OR YOU'RE FIRED!":
     EMPLOYEE RIGHTS AND THE CHANGING ROLE OF
     MANAGEMENT PREROGATIVES; Ewing, David W.;
     Garcia, Carlos; Garcia, Edward; Science;
     *SCIENCE OF THE SPANISH SPEAKING PEOPLE.

Industrial Workers

5875 Tiano, Susan B. El programa mexicano de
     maquiladoras: una respuesta a las
     necesidades de la industria norteamericana.
     AZTLAN, Vol. 14, no. 1 (Spring 1983), p.
     201-208. English. **DESCR:** Book Reviews; *EL
     PROGRAMA MEXICANO DE MAQUILADORAS: UNA
     RESPUESTA A LAS NECESIDADES DE LA INDUSTRIA
     NORTEAMERICANA; Industries; International
     Labor Activities; Maquiladoras; Woog, Mario
     Arriola.

Industrialization

5876 Griswold del Castillo, Richard. La familia
     Chicana: social change in the Chicano family
     of Los Angeles, 1850-1880. JOURNAL OF ETHNIC
     STUDIES, Vol. 3, no. 1 (Spring 1975), p.
     41-58. English. **DESCR:** *Family; *Los
     Angeles, CA; Social History and Conditions.

Industries

5877 Johnson, Greg. Administracion en un medio
     ambiente hispanico. INDUSTRY WEEK, Vol. 212,
     no. 2 (January 25, 1982), p. 30-34. English.
     DESCR: *Labor Supply and Market; Spanish
     Language; Undocumented Workers.

5878 Tiano, Susan B. El programa mexicano de
     maquiladoras: una respuesta a las
     necesidades de la industria norteamericana.
     AZTLAN, Vol. 14, no. 1 (Spring 1983), p.
     201-208. English. **DESCR:** Book Reviews; *EL
     PROGRAMA MEXICANO DE MAQUILADORAS: UNA
     RESPUESTA A LAS NECESIDADES DE LA INDUSTRIA
     NORTEAMERICANA; Industrial Workers;

International Labor Activities;
Maquiladoras; Woog, Mario Arriola.

Infant Mortality

5879 Eberstein, Isaac W. and Pol, Louis G.
     Mexican-American ethnicity, socioeconomic
     status, and infant mortality: a county level
     analysis. SOCIAL SCIENCE JOURNAL, Vol. 19,
     no. 2 (April 1982), p. 61-71. English.
     DESCR: Identity; Socioeconomic Factors;
     Southwest United States.

5880 Hedderson, John and Daudistel, Howard C.
     Infant mortality of the Spanish surname
     population. SOCIAL SCIENCE JOURNAL, Vol. 19,
     no. 4 (October 1982), p. 67-78. English.
     DESCR: Demography; El Paso County, TX;
     Medical Care; Statistics; Vital Statistics.

5881 Powell-Griner, Eve and Streck, Dan. A closer
     examination of neonatal mortality rates
     among the Texas Spanish surname population.
     AMERICAN JOURNAL OF PUBLIC HEALTH, Vol. 72,
     no. 9 (September 1982), p. 993-999. English.
     DESCR: Texas.

Infante, E. Anthony

5882 People. HISPANIC BUSINESS, Vol. 4, no. 8
     (August 1983), p. 7. English. **DESCR:**
     Aguilar, Richard; *Businesspeople;
     Cordero-Badillo, Atilano; del Olmo, Frank;
     Levitan, Aida T.; Nunez, Luis; Quintanilla,
     Guadalupe; Rivera, Victor M.

Infante, Guillermo Cabrera

5883 Greenfield, Charles. Writing in exile.
     NUESTRO, Vol. 6, no. 8 (October 1982), p.
     22-24. English. **DESCR:** Authors; Cubanos.

Iniciativa Para la Cuenca del Caribe (ICC)

5884 El futuro de la cuenca del Caribe segun la
     administracion Reagan. INFORME: RELACIONES
     MEXICO-ESTADOS UNIDOS, Vol. 1, no. 2 (July,
     December, 1982), p. 10-56. Spanish. **DESCR:**
     Reagan, Ronald; *United States-Latin
     American Relations.

Inland Steel Company

5885 Simon, Daniel T. Mexican repatriation in
     East Chicago, Indiana. JOURNAL OF ETHNIC
     STUDIES, Vol. 2, no. 2 (Summer 1974), p.
     11-23. English. **DESCR:** *Deportation; *East
     Chicago, IN; History; Immigrant Labor;
     Immigration; Immigration Regulation and
     Control; Mexico; Social History and
     Conditions.

Inner City
     USE: Urban Communities

INROADS

5886 Lanier, Alfredo S. Making it seem easy, from
     intern to account executive. HISPANIC
     BUSINESS, Vol. 4, no. 8 (August 1983), p.
     16-17+. English. **DESCR:** *Accountants;
     Careers; Chicanas; Employment Training;
     *Fernandez, Margarita; Standard Oil Corp..

5887 Math-based careers. HISPANIC BUSINESS, Vol.
     5, no. 11 (November 1983), p. 32. English.
     DESCR: *Careers; Education; Employment
     Training; Mathematics; Engineering and
     Science Achievement (MESA); Mexican American
     Legal Defense and Educational Fund (MALDEF);
     Soriano, Esteban.

Insecticides
USE: Pesticides

Institute for Hispanic Media and Culture

5888 Cuenca, Ramon Araluce. USC forms institute for Hispanic media & culture. CAMINOS, Vol. 4, no. 3 (March 1983), p. 32. English. **DESCR:** Mass Media; University of Southern California.

Instituto del Progreso Latino

5889 Heaney, Thomas W. "Hanging on" or "gaining ground": educating marginal adults. NEW DIRECTIONS FOR CONTINUING EDUCATION, no. 20 (December 1983), p. 53-63. English. **DESCR:** *Adult Education; Chicago, IL; City Colleges, Chicago, IL; General Education Diploma (GED); Gomez, Robert; Mission District, San Francisco, CA; Project Literacy, San Francisco, CA; St. Mary's Community Educational Center; *Universidad Popular, Chicago, IL.

Instituto Puertorriqueno/Hispano Para Personas Mayores

5890 Ortiz, Carlos V. Growing old alone. NUESTRO, Vol. 7, no. 4 (May 1983), p. 36-38. English. **DESCR:** *Ancianos; Drinane, Suleika Cabrera; Padilla de Armas, Encarnacion; *Puerto Ricans.

Insurance

5891 Haggerty, Alfred G. Occidental goes after Hispanic market. NATIONAL UNDERWRITER LIFE AND HEALTH INSURANCE EDITION, Vol. 86, no. 1 (January 2, 1982), p. 22. English. **DESCR:** Cubanos; Market Research; Transamerica Occidental Life.

Insurrections

5892 Schmidt, Dorothy. Book review of: MEXICANO RESISTANCE IN THE SOUTHWEST: "THE SACRED RIGHT OF SELF-PRESERVATION". WESTERN AMERICAN LITERATURE, Vol. 17, no. 1 (Spring 1982), p. 75-76. English. **DESCR:** Bandidos; Book Reviews; *MEXICANO RESISTANCE IN THE SOUTHWEST: "THE SACRED RIGHT OF SELF-PRESERVATION"; Rosenbaum, Robert J.

5893 Weber, David J. Book review of: MEXICANO RESISTANCE IN THE SOUTHWEST: "THE SACRED RIGHT OF SELF-PRESERVATION". AMERICAN HISTORICAL REVIEW, Vol. 87, no. 1 (February 1982), p. 272-273. English. **DESCR:** Book Reviews; *MEXICANO RESISTANCE IN THE SOUTHWEST: "THE SACRED RIGHT OF SELF-PRESERVATION"; Rosenbaum, Robert J.; Southwest United States.

INTAR

5894 Prida, Dolores. Playwrights Laboratory: in search of a creative formula. NUESTRO, Vol. 7, no. 10 (December 1983), p. 43. English. **DESCR:** Authors; Education; *Hispanic Playwrights-in-Residence Laboratory; *Teatro.

Integration
USE: Segregation and Desegregation

INTELLIGENCE AND RACE: THE ORIGINS AND DIMENSIONS OF THE IQ CONTROVERSY

5895 White, Tim. Book review of: INTELLIGENCE AND RACE. THE ORIGINS AND DIMENSIONS OF THE IQ CONTROVERSY. HISPANIC JOURNAL OF BEHAVIORAL SCIENCES, Vol. 4, no. 4 (December 1982), p. 522-525. English. **DESCR:** Book Reviews; Eckberg, Douglas Lee.

THE INTELLIGENCE CONTROVERSY

5896 Herman, Janice. Book review of: THE INTELLIGENCE CONTROVERSY. HISPANIC JOURNAL OF BEHAVIORAL SCIENCES, Vol. 4, no. 3 (September 1982), p. 384-385. English. **DESCR:** Book Reviews; Eysenck, H.J.; Kamin, Leon.

Intelligence Levels
USE: Intelligence Tests

Intelligence Tests

5897 Argulewicz, Ed N.; Elliott, Stephen N.; and Hall, Robert. Comparison of behavioral ratings of Anglo-American and Mexican-American gifted children. PSYCHOLOGY IN THE SCHOOLS, Vol. 19, no. 4 (October 1982), p. 469-472. English. **DESCR:** Anglo Americans; Child Study; Cultural Characteristics.

5898 Clarizio, Harvey F. Intellectual assessment of Hispanic children. PSYCHOLOGY IN THE SCHOOLS, Vol. 19, no. 1 (January 1982), p. 61-71. English. **DESCR:** Anglo Americans; Child Study; Cultural Pluralism.

5899 Cortese, Anthony J., ed.; Santillan, Richard; and Mercado, Olivia. Chicano psychological assessment: a critique of "Racial intelligence and the Mexican people" [sic]. EXPLORATIONS IN ETHNIC STUDIES, Vol. 5, no. 2 (July 1982), p. 50-51. English. **DESCR:** *Gonzalez, Gilbert G.; "Racial intelligence testing and the Mexican people".

5900 Dean, Raymond S. Intelligence-achievement discrepancies in diagnosing pediatric learning disabilities. CLINICAL NEUROPSYCHOLOGY, Vol. 4, no. 2 (1982), p. 58-62. English. **DESCR:** Anglo Americans; *Handicapped; Peabody Individual Achievement Test (PIAT); Youth; ZOOT SUIT [film].

5901 Gonzalez, Gilbert G. Educational reform and the Mexican community in Los Angeles. SOUTHWEST ECONOMY AND SOCIETY, Vol. 3, no. 3 (Spring 1978), p. 24-51. English. **DESCR:** Counseling Services (Educational); Curriculum; *Education; Enrollment; *History; Los Angeles, CA; *Los Angeles City School District; Tracking (Educational); Vocational Education.

5902 Gonzalez, Gilbert G. Racial intelligence testing and the Mexican people. EXPLORATIONS IN ETHNIC STUDIES, Vol. 5, no. 2 (July 1982), p. 36-49. English.

5903 Mishra, Shitala P. Validity of WISC-R IQs and factor scores in predicting achievement for Mexican American children. PSYCHOLOGY IN THE SCHOOLS, Vol. 20, no. 4 (October 1983), p. 442-444. English. **DESCR:** *Academic Achievement; Primary School Students; Wechsler Intelligence Scale for Children-Revised (WISC-R).

5904 Oakland, Thomas. Concurrent and predictive validity estimates for the WISC-R IQ's and ELP's by racial-ethnic and SES groups. SCHOOL PSYCHOLOGY REVIEW, Vol. 12, no. 1 (Winter 1983), p. 57-61. English. **DESCR:** Academic Achievement; Estimated Learning Potential (ELP); Primary School Education; Wechsler Intelligence Scale for Children-Revised (WISC-R).

Intelligence Tests (cont.)

5905 Oakland, Thomas. Joint use of adaptive behavior and IQ to predict achievement. JOURNAL OF CONSULTING AND CLINICAL PSYCHOLOGY, Vol. 51, no. 2 (April 1983), p. 298-301. English. DESCR: *Academic Achievement; Education; Mathematics; Reading.

5906 Obrzut, John E.; Hansen, Robert L.; and Heath, Charles P. The effectiveness of visual information processing training with Hispanic children. JOURNAL OF GENERAL PSYCHOLOGY, Vol. 10, no. 2 (October 1982), p. 165-174. English. DESCR: *Academic Achievement; Bender Gestalt Test; Colorado; Primary School Education.

5907 Rueda, Robert. Interpersonal tactics and communicative strategies of Anglo-American and Mexican American mildly mentally retarded and nonretarded students. APPLIED RESEARCH IN MENTAL RETARDATION, Vol. 4, no. 2 (1983), p. 153-161. English. DESCR: Anglo Americans; Children; *Mentally Handicapped; Test of Social Problem Solving.

5908 Sandoval, Jonathan; Zimmerman, Irla L.; and Woo-Sam, James M. Cultural difference on WISC-R verbal items. JOURNAL OF SCHOOL PSYCHOLOGY, Vol. 21, no. 1 (Spring 1983), p. 49-55. English. DESCR: Educational Tests and Measurements; Wechsler Intelligence Scale for Children-Revised (WISC-R).

5909 Sandoval, Joseph. WISC-R factoral validity for minority groups and Spearman's hypothesis. JOURNAL OF SCHOOL PSYCHOLOGY, Vol. 20, (Fall 1982), p. 198-204. English. DESCR: Educational Tests and Measurements; Wechsler Intelligence Scale for Children-Revised (WISC-R).

5910 Santillan, Richard. Critique. EXPLORATIONS IN ETHNIC STUDIES, Vol. 5, no. 2 (July 1982), p. 54-55. English. DESCR: *Gonzalez, Gilbert G.; "Racial intelligence testing and the Mexican people".

5911 Scruggs, Thomas E.; Mastropieri, Margo A.; and Argulewicz, Ed N. Stability of performance on the PPVT-R for three ethnic groups attending a bilingual kindergarten. PSYCHOLOGY IN THE SCHOOLS, Vol. 20, (October 1983), p. 433-435. English. DESCR: Peabody Picture Vocabulary Test-Revised (PPVT-R); Primary School Students.

5912 Shellenberger, Sylvia. Assessment of Puerto Rican children: a cross-culture study with the Spanish McCarthy scales of children's abilities. BILINGUAL REVIEW, Vol. 9, no. 2 (May, August, 1982), p. 109-119. English. DESCR: Sociology; Spanish Language.

5913 Valencia, Richard R. Stability of the McCarthy scales of children's abilities over a one-year period for Mexican-American children. PSYCHOLOGY IN THE SCHOOLS, Vol. 20, no. 1 (January 1983), p. 29-34. English. DESCR: Child Study; Cultural Characteristics; McCarthy Scales for Children's Abilities (MSCA); Socioeconomic Factors.

Inter-American Development Bank

5914 The Inter-American Development Bank at work (photoessay). CAMINOS, Vol. 4, no. 8 (September 1983), p. 22-25. English. DESCR: Banking Industry; Economic Development; Latin America.

Intercultural Education
USE: Cultural Pluralism

Interest Groups

5915 Plaza, Eva. Interest group politics and U.S. immigration policy towards Mexico. LA RAZA LAW JOURNAL, Vol. 1, no. 1 (June 1983), p. 76-100. English. DESCR: Immigration; Immigration Law; Immigration Regulation and Control; Mexico; *Simpson-Mazzoli Bill; United States-Mexico Relations.

Interethnic Relationships
USE: Intergroup Relations

Inter-Ethnolinguistic Peer Tutoring (IEPT)

5916 Johnson, Donna M. Natural language learning by design: a classroom experiment in social interaction and second language acquisition. TESOL QUARTERLY, Vol. 17, no. 1 (March 1983), p. 55-68. English. DESCR: *English as a Second Language; Language Development; Primary School Education.

Intergroup Relations

5917 Gonzalez, Alex. Classroom cooperation and ethnic balance: Chicanos and equal status. CACR REVIEW, Vol. 1, no. 1 (September 1982), p. 42-71. English. DESCR: Cooperative Education; Curriculum; *Prejudice (Social); Segregation and Desegregation.

5918 Sandoval, David A. What do I call them: the Chicano experience. CACR REVIEW, Vol. 1, no. 1 (September 1982), p. 3-25. English. DESCR: Colonialism; Identity; *Self-Referents.

5919 Shankman, Arnold. The image of Mexico and the Mexican-American in the Black press, 1890-1935. JOURNAL OF ETHNIC STUDIES, Vol. 3, no. 2 (Summer 1975), p. 43-56. English. DESCR: Attitude (Psychological); Blacks; Journalism; *Mexico.

5920 UCLA effort aids students. NUESTRO, Vol. 6, no. 5 (June, July, 1982), p. 11. English. DESCR: Students; *University of California, Los Angeles (UCLA).

Intermarriage

5921 Alba, Richard D. A comment on Schoen and Cohen. AMERICAN JOURNAL OF SOCIOLOGY, Vol. 87, no. 4 (January 1982), p. 935-939. English. DESCR: Cohen, Lawrence E.; ETHNIC ENDOGAMY AMONG MEXICAN AMERICAN GROOMS; *Research Methodology; Schoen, Robert.

5922 Craver, Rebecca McDowell. The impact of intimacy: Mexican-Anglo intermarriage in New Mexico 1821-1846. SOUTHWESTERN STUDIES, no. 66 (1982), p. 1-79. English. DESCR: Acculturation; Assimilation; Chicanas; New Mexico; Rio Arriba Valley, New Mexico.

5923 Salgado de Snyder, Nelly and Padilla, Amado M. Cultural and ethnic maintenance of interethnically married Mexican-Americans. HUMAN ORGANIZATION, Vol. 41, no. 4 (Winter 1982), p. 359-362. English. DESCR: Acculturation.

5924 Fernandez, Celestino and Holscher, Louis M. Chicano-Anglo intermarriage in Arizona, 1960-1980: an exploratory study of eight counties. HISPANIC JOURNAL OF BEHAVIORAL SCIENCES, Vol. 5, no. 3 (September 1983), p. 291-304. English. DESCR: Arizona.

Intermarriage (cont.)

5925 Gurak, Douglas T. and Fitzpatrick, Joseph P. Intermarriage among Hispanic ethnic groups in New York City. AMERICAN JOURNAL OF SOCIOLOGY, Vol. 87, no. 4 (January 1982), p. 921-934. English. **DESCR:** New York, NY; Puerto Ricans.

5926 Manning, Roberta. Book review of: CHICANO INTERMARRIAGE: A THEORETICAL AND EMPIRICAL STUDY. HISPANIC JOURNAL OF BEHAVIORAL SCIENCES, Vol. 5, no. 3 (September 1983), p. 353-356. English. **DESCR:** Book Reviews; *CHICANO INTERMARRIAGE: A THEORETICAL AND EMPIRICAL STUDY; Murguia, Edward.

5927 Miller, Darlis A. Book review of: THE IMPACT OF INTIMACY: MEXICAN-ANGLO INTERMARRIAGE IN NEW MEXICO, 1821-1846. NEW MEXICO HISTORICAL REVIEW, Vol. 57, no. 4 (October 1982), p. 407-408. English. **DESCR:** Book Reviews; Craver, Rebecca McDowell; *THE IMPACT OF INTIMACY: MEXICAN-ANGLO INTERMARRIAGE IN NEW MEXICO, 1821-1846.

5928 Miller, Darlis A. Cross-cultural marriages in the Southwest: the New Mexico experience, 1846-1900. NEW MEXICO HISTORICAL REVIEW, Vol. 57, no. 4 (October 1982), p. 335-359. English. **DESCR:** Assimilation; Chicanas; Ethnic Attitudes; New Mexico; Social History and Conditions.

5929 Murguia, Edward and Cazares, Ralph B. Intermarriage of Mexican Americans. MARRIAGE & FAMILY REVIEW, Vol. 5, no. 1 (Spring 1982), p. 91-100. English. **DESCR:** Acculturation; Anglo Americans; Social Mobility.

5930 Schoen, Robert and Cohen, Lawrence E. Theory and method in the study of ethnic endogamy among Mexican-American grooms - reply. AMERICAN JOURNAL OF SOCIOLOGY, Vol. 87, no. 4 (January 1982), p. 939-942. English. **DESCR:** Assimilation; ETHNIC ENDOGAMY: THE CASE OF THE MEXICAN-AMERICANS; Mittelback, Frank G.; Moore, Joan W.; *Research Methodology.

5931 Valdez, Avelardo. Recent increases in intermarriage by Mexican American males: Bexar County, Texas from 1971 to 1980. SOCIAL SCIENCE QUARTERLY, Vol. 64, (March 1983), p. 136-144. English. **DESCR:** Bexar County, TX.

Internal Colonial Model (Theoretical)

5932 Castillo, Pedro. Letter to the editor. SOUTHWEST ECONOMY AND SOCIETY, Vol. 3, no. 1 (Fall 1977), p. 55-56. English. **DESCR:** Economic History and Conditions; *Manta, Ben; TOWARD ECONOMIC DEVELOPMENT OF THE CHICANO BARRIO.

5933 Manta, Ben. Toward economic development of the Chicano barrio: alternative strategies and their implications [reprint of DE COLORES article]. SOUTHWEST ECONOMY AND SOCIETY, Vol. 1, no. 1 (Spring 1976), p. 35-41. English. **DESCR:** Capitalism; *Economic History and Conditions.

5934 Mirande, Alfredo. Sociology of Chicanos or Chicano sociology: a critical assessment of emergent paradigms. PACIFIC SOCIOLOGICAL REVIEW, Vol. 25, no. 4 (October 1982), p. 495-508. English. **DESCR:** Baca Zinn, Maxine; *Paradigm (Theoretical); SOCIOLOGICAL THEORY IN EMERGENT CHICANO PERSPECTIVES; *Sociology.

5935 Morrissey, Marietta. Ethnic stratification and the study of Chicanos. JOURNAL OF ETHNIC STUDIES, Vol. 10, no. 4 (Winter 1983), p. 71-99. English. **DESCR:** Assimilation; *Ethnic Stratification; Marxism; Paradigm (Theoretical); Social Theory.

Internal Migration

5936 Estrada, Leobardo F. [Demographic characteristics of Latinos]. CHICANO LAW REVIEW, Vol. 6, (1983), p. 9-16. English. **DESCR:** *Demography; LATINOS IN THE LAW [symposium], UCLA, 1982; Los Angeles County, CA; Migration; Migration Patterns; Spanish Language.

Internal Security Act of 1950

5937 Parr, Julie A. Immigration law and the excluded alien: potential for human rights violations. UNIVERSITY OF CALIFORNIA DAVIS LAW REVIEW, Vol. 15, no. 3 (Spring 1982), p. 723-740. English. **DESCR:** *Civil Rights; Deportation; *Detention of Persons; Rodriguez-Fernandez v. Wilkinson; *Undocumented Workers.

Internal-External Reinforcement Scale

5938 Davis, James Alston. Does authority generalize? Locus of control perceptions in Anglo-American and Mexican-American adolescents. POLITICAL PSYCHOLOGY, Vol. 4, no. 1 (March 1983), p. 101-120. English. **DESCR:** Comparative Psychology; Family; High School Students; *Locus of Control; Political Ideology.

International Bank of Commerce (IBOC)

5939 Deibel, Richard and Balkan, D. Carlos. The nation's largest little bank: Laredo's International Bank of Commerce. HISPANIC BUSINESS, Vol. 4, no. 9 (September 1982), p. 10-11,24. English. **DESCR:** Banking Industry; Business Enterprises; Laredo, TX.

5940 Hispanic owned banks. HISPANIC BUSINESS, Vol. 5, no. 9 (September 1983), p. 13. English. **DESCR:** *Banking Industry; Finance; Minority Bank Deposit Program (MBDP).

International Boundary and Water Commission

5941 Bath, C. Richard. Health and environmental problems: the role of the border in El Paso-Ciudad Juarez coordination. JOURNAL OF INTERAMERICAN STUDIES AND WORLD AFFAIRS, Vol. 24, no. 3 (August 1982), p. 375-392. English. **DESCR:** Border Region; Ciudad Juarez, Chihuahua, Mexico; *El Paso, TX; Nationalism; Pollution; *Public Health; United States-Mexico Relations; U.S Border Public Health Association (AFMES).

5942 Mumme, Stephen P. and Jamail, Milton H. The International Boundary and Water Commission as a conflict management agency in the U.S.-Mexico borderlands. SOCIAL SCIENCE JOURNAL, Vol. 19, no. 1 (January 1982), p. 46-62. English. **DESCR:** Border Region; Conflict Resolution; Rio Grande; United States-Mexico Relations; *Water.

International Economic Relations

5943 Alvarez, Alejandro. Economic crisis and migration: comments on James Cockcroft's article. CONTEMPORARY MARXISM, Vol. 5, (Summer 1982), p. 62-66. English. DESCR: Cockroft, James; Laboring Classes; Legislation; MEXICAN MIGRATION, CRISIS, AND THE INTERNATIONALIZATION OF LABOR STRUGGLES; *Undocumented Workers.

5944 Cockcroft, James D. Mexican migration, crisis, and the internationalization of labor struggle. CONTEMPORARY MARXISM, Vol. 5, (Summer 1982), p. 48-61. English. DESCR: International Labor Activities; Labor Unions; Legislation; Racism; *Undocumented Workers.

5945 De la Garza, Rodolfo O. Chicano-Mexican relations: a framework for research. SOCIAL SCIENCE QUARTERLY, Vol. 63, (March 1982), p. 115-130. English. DESCR: Economics.

5946 Foreign trade: outlook for the Caribbean Basin Initiative. HISPANIC BUSINESS, Vol. 4, no. 8 (August 1983), p. 23+. English. DESCR: *Caribbean Basin Initiative (CBI); *Foreign Trade; Latin America.

5947 Morrison, Thomas K. The relationship of U.S. aid, trade and investment to migration pressures in major sending countries. INTERNATIONAL MIGRATION REVIEW, Vol. 16, no. 1 (Spring 1982), p. 4-26. English. DESCR: Border Region; Investments; Mexican Border Industrialization Program; *Migration Patterns; PIDER Project; Rural Economics; Rural Urban Migration; Undocumented Workers; United States-Mexico Relations.

5948 Las tendencias de la relacion economica Mexico-Estados Unidos. INFORME: RELACIONES MEXICO-ESTADOS UNIDOS, Vol. 1, no. 2 (July, December, 1982), p. 88-108. Spanish. DESCR: United States-Mexico Relations.

International Labor Activities

5949 Cockcroft, James D. Mexican migration, crisis, and the internationalization of labor struggle. CONTEMPORARY MARXISM, Vol. 5, (Summer 1982), p. 48-61. English. DESCR: International Economic Relations; Labor Unions; Legislation; Racism; *Undocumented Workers.

5950 Gamboa, Erasmo. Mexican labor in the Pacific Northwest, 1943-1947: a photographic essay. PACIFIC NORTHWEST QUARTERLY, Vol. 73, no. 4 (October 1982), p. 175-181. English. DESCR: *Agricultural Laborers; Labor Camps; Labor Supply and Market; Northwestern United States; World War II.

5951 Tiano, Susan B. El programa mexicano de maquiladoras: una respuesta a las necesidades de la industria norteamericana. AZTLAN, Vol. 14, no. 1 (Spring 1983), p. 201-208. English. DESCR: Book Reviews; *EL PROGRAMA MEXICANO DE MAQUILADORAS: UNA RESPUESTA A LAS NECESIDADES DE LA INDUSTRIA NORTEAMERICANA; Industrial Workers; Industries; Maquiladoras; Woog, Mario Arriola.

International Ladies Garment Workers Union (ILGWU) v. Sureck

5952 Aragon, Ellen Weis. The factory raid: an unconstitutional act. SOUTHERN CALIFORNIA LAW REVIEW, Vol. 56, no. 2 (January 1983), p. 605-645. English. DESCR: Blackie's House of Beef v. Castillo; Deportation; Immigration and Naturalization Service (INS); Racism; Search and Seizure; *Undocumented Workers.

International Ladies Garment Workers Union (ILGWU)

5953 INS sweep searches of work areas must meet fourth amendment standards. CRIMINAL LAW REPORTER, Vol. 31, no. 18 (August 11, 1982), p. 2366-2367. English. DESCR: Constitutional Amendments - Fourth; Immigration and Naturalization Service (INS); Immigration Regulation and Control; *Search and Seizure; Undocumented Workers.

5954 Mendez Gonzalez, Rosalinda. Mexican women and families: rural-to-urban and international migration. SOUTHWEST ECONOMY AND SOCIETY, Vol. 4, no. 2 (Winter 1978, 1979), p. 14-27. English. DESCR: Chicanas; Employment; *Family; Garment Industry; Immigration; Labor Organizing; Los Angeles, CA; Undocumented Workers.

5955 Monroy, Douglas. Anarquismo y comunismo: Mexican radicalism and the Communist Party in Los Angeles during the 1930's. LABOR HISTORY, Vol. 24, no. 1 (Winter 1983), p. 34-59. English. DESCR: Cannery and Agricultural Worker's Industrial Union; *Communist Party; Confederacion de Uniones de Obreros Mexicanos (CUOM); History; Labor; Labor Organizing; *Los Angeles, CA; Tenayuca, Emma; Worker's Alliance (WA), Los Angeles, CA.

International Law

5956 Hopson, Susan B. Immigration: indefinite detention of excluded aliens held illegal. TEXAS INTERNATIONAL LAW JOURNAL, Vol. 17, (Winter 1982), p. 101-110. English. DESCR: Civil Rights; Deportation; *Detention of Persons; Immigration; Rodriguez-Fernandez v. Wilkinson; Shaughnessy v. Mezei; *Undocumented Workers.

International Relations

5957 Barrios-Martinez, Ruben. Should Puerto Rico become a state?: against statehood. NUESTRO, Vol. 7, no. 5 (June, July, 1983), p. 37-39. English. DESCR: *Colonialism; Puerto Rican Independence Party; *Puerto Rico; Racism; United States.

5958 Bell, Samuel E. and Smallwood, James M. Zona libre: trade and diplomacy on the Mexican border, 1858-1905. ARIZONA AND THE WEST, Vol. 24, no. 2 (Summer 1982), p. 119-152. English. DESCR: Border Region; *Foreign Trade; Mexico; United States History.

5959 Caldera, Carmela. Two views on Central America (interview). CAMINOS, Vol. 4, no. 8 (September 1983), p. 12-16,50. Bilingual. DESCR: *Central America; Sanchez, Philip V.; Torres, Esteban E.

5960 Carrion, Arturo Morales. Puerto Rico: the coming of the Americans. NUESTRO, Vol. 7, no. 5 (June, July, 1983), p. 25-30. English. DESCR: Cuba; *Puerto Rico; Spain; *United States History; *War.

5961 Diaz, Katherine A. Henry G. Cisneros on Central American commission (interview). CAMINOS, Vol. 4, no. 8 (September 1983), p. 10,48. English. DESCR: Central America; *Cisneros, Henry, Mayor of San Antonio, TX; National Bipartisan Commission on Central America; United States.

International Relations (cont.)

5962 Ecuadorian president Osvaldo Hurtado Larrea on the future of Ecuador. CAMINOS, Vol. 4, no. 1-2 (January, February, 1983), p. 56-57,61. Bilingual. DESCR: *Ecuador; Hurtado Larrea, Osvaldo.

5963 Fraser Rothenberg, Irene. Chicanos, the Panama Canal issues and the Reagan campaign: reflections from 1976 and projections for 1980. JOURNAL OF ETHNIC STUDIES, Vol. 7, no. 4 (Winter 1980), p. 37-49. English. DESCR: Lobbying; Nationalism; Newspapers; Panama; *Panama Canal; Politics; Reagan, Ronald.

5964 Fraser Rothenberg, Irene. Mexican-American views of U.S. relations with Latin America. JOURNAL OF ETHNIC STUDIES, Vol. 6, no. 1 (Spring 1978), p. 62-78. English. DESCR: Chicano Movement; Culture; Identity; Latin America; Lobbying; Mexico; *Nationalism; Political History and Conditions; Politics.

5965 Gonzalez, Raymond J. U.S. support of military in Latin America. CAMINOS, Vol. 4, no. 8 (September 1983), p. 18-19,50. Bilingual. DESCR: *Latin America; United States.

5966 N.A.L.E.O.'s "Fiesta '83". CAMINOS, Vol. 4, no. 10 (November 1983), p. 28-29. English. DESCR: Baca Barragan, Polly; Bilingual Bicultural Education; Central America; Fiesta '83; Garcia, Robert; Immigration; Mendez, Olga; *National Association of Latino Elected Officials (NALEO); Simpson-Mazzoli Bill; United States-Mexico Relations.

5967 Reagan, Ronald. "There is a war in Central America" (speech). CAMINOS, Vol. 4, no. 8 (September 1983), p. 9. English. DESCR: Central America; United States.

5968 Regional report, Latin America: marchers oppose Reagan policies. NUESTRO, Vol. 7, no. 4 (May 1983), p. 11. English. DESCR: Central America; Demonstrations; *Latin America; *Reagan, Ronald; Stanford University, Stanford, CA.

5969 Romero-Barcelo, Carlos. Should Puerto Rico become a state?: for statehood. NUESTRO, Vol. 7, no. 5 (June, July, 1983), p. 34-37. English. DESCR: *Colonialism; Munoz Marin, Luis; *Puerto Rico; United States.

5970 Serafino, Nina M. U.S.-Latinoamerican relations: 1960 to the present. CAMINOS, Vol. 4, no. 8 (September 1983), p. 6-8,48. Bilingual. DESCR: History; Latin America; United States; United States-Mexico Relations.

5971 Trevino, Jesus and Ruiz, Jose Luis. Guatemalan refugees - the tip of the iceberg. CAMINOS, Vol. 4, no. 5 (May 1983), p. 13-15,48. English. DESCR: Guatemala; Mexico; MEXICO: THE FUTURE; *Refugees.

5972 Villarreal, Roberto E. and Kelly, Philip. Mexican Americans as participants in United States-Mexico relations. INTERNATIONAL STUDIES NOTES, Vol. 9, no. 4 (Winter 1982), p. 1-6. English. DESCR: Mexico; Political Representation; *United States-Mexico Relations.

International Rescue Committee

5973 Estevez, Guillermo. Resettling the Cuban refugees in New Jersey. MIGRATION TODAY, Vol. 11, no. 4-5 (1983), p. 28-33. English. DESCR: Caribbean Relief Program; *Cubanos; Immigration; *New Jersey; Refugees.

International Union of Mine, Mill and Smelter Workers

5974 McCracken, Ellen. Book review of: SALT OF THE EARTH. JOURNAL OF ETHNIC STUDIES, Vol. 8, no. 1 (Spring 1980), p. 116-120. English. DESCR: Book Reviews; Chicanas; Films; Hanover, NM; *SALT OF THE EARTH; Silverton Rosenfelt, Deborah; Strikes and Lockouts; Women Men Relations; Women's Rights.

International Workers of the World (IWW)

5975 Byrkit, James W. Walter Douglas and labor struggles in early 20th century Arizona. SOUTHWEST ECONOMY AND SOCIETY, Vol. 1, no. 1 (Spring 1976), p. 14-27. English. DESCR: Arizona; *Biography; Bisbee, AZ; Clifton Morenci Strike, June 1903; Copper Queen Mining Co., Bisbee, AZ; *Douglas, Walter; Labor Unions; Mining Industry; Strikes and Lockouts.

Interpersonal Relations

5976 Espinoza, Ana Luisa. Los tatas. CALMECAC, Vol. 1, (Summer 1980), p. 29-33. Bilingual. DESCR: *Family.

5977 Garza, Raymond T., et al. Biculturalism, locus of control and leader behavior in ethnically mixed small groups. JOURNAL OF APPLIED SOCIAL PSYCHOLOGY, Vol. 12, no. 3 (May, June, 1982), p. 237-253. English. DESCR: Attitude (Psychological); *Biculturalism; Culture; Leadership; *Locus of Control; Social Psychology.

5978 Limon, Jose. History, Chicano joking, and the varieties of higher-education: tradition and performance as critical symbolic action. JOURNAL OF THE FOLKLORE INSTITUTE, Vol. 19, no. 2-3 (1982), p. 146-166. English. DESCR: *Chistes; Folklore; Higher Education; Humor; Texas; University of Texas at Austin.

5979 Tello, Jerry. Platicando (relationships III). CALMECAC, Vol. 2, (Spring 1981), p. 6-15. English. DESCR: *Family.

5980 Tello, Jerry. Relationship entre nuestra gente. CALMECAC, Vol. 1, no. 1 (Spring 1980), p. 20-22. English. DESCR: *Family.

5981 Tello, Jerry. Relationship entre nuestra gente II. CALMECAC, Vol. 1, (Summer 1980), p. 12-15. Bilingual. DESCR: Values.

INVENTING A WORD, AN ANTHOLOGY OF TWENTIETH CENTURY PUERTO RICAN POETRY

5982 Binder, Wolfgang. Book review of: INVENTING A WORD: AN ANTHOLOGY OF TWENTIETH CENTURY PUERTO RICAN POETRY. MELUS: MULTI-ETHNIC LITERATURE OF THE UNITED STATES, Vol. 8, no. 1 (Spring 1981), p. 77-79. English. DESCR: *Marzan, Julio; *Puerto Rican Literature.

5983 Laguardia, Gari. The canon and the air-conditioner: modern Puerto Rican poetry. BILINGUAL REVIEW, Vol. 9, no. 2 (May, August, 1982), p. 178-181. English. DESCR: Book Reviews; Marzan, Julio; Poetry; Puerto Rican Literature.

Investments

5984 Business notes. HISPANIC BUSINESS, Vol. 5, no. 10 (October 1983), p. 13. English. DESCR: *Business Administration; Business Enterprises; Claudio, Irma; Los Angeles Board of Public Works; Oakland, CA; Taxation; Tri-Oakland Development Corporation; Wisconsin Minority Business Forum '83.

5985 Morrison, Thomas K. The relationship of U.S. aid, trade and investment to migration pressures in major sending countries. INTERNATIONAL MIGRATION REVIEW, Vol. 16, no. 1 (Spring 1982), p. 4-26. English. DESCR: Border Region; International Economic Relations; Mexican Border Industrialization Program; *Migration Patterns; PIDER Project; Rural Economics; Rural Urban Migration; Undocumented Workers; United States-Mexico Relations.

I.Q. Test
USE: Intelligence Tests

I.Q. Testing
USE: Intelligence Tests

Irvine, CA

5986 Weber, Robert. Turbo-charged MST, Inc. HISPANIC BUSINESS, Vol. 4, no. 11 (November 1982), p. 10-11,24. English. DESCR: Alcala, Al; Computers; *High Technology Industries; *Media Systems Technology, Inc.(MST,Inc.)

Jackson, Jesse

5987 An Indian treaty. NUESTRO, Vol. 6, no. 5 (June, July, 1982), p. 9. English. DESCR: *Voting Rights; *Voting Rights Act.

5988 Latinos evident in 1983 march. NUESTRO, Vol. 7, no. 7 (September 1983), p. 11-12. English. DESCR: Bonilla, Tony; Cuban-American Coordinating Committee; *Demonstrations; IMAGE, Washington, DC; League of United Latin American Citizens (LULAC); National Congress for Puerto Rican Rights (NCPRR); National Council of La Raza (NCLR); Velasquez, Baldemar; Zamora, Reuben.

5989 The LULAC/PUSH dialog. HISPANIC BUSINESS, Vol. 5, no. 4 (April 1983), p. 15. English. DESCR: Bonilla, Tony; *Economic Development; League of United Latin American Citizens (LULAC); Operation PUSH.

5990 Rainbow coalition. LATINO, Vol. 54, no. 6 (October 1983), p. 10. Spanish. DESCR: Bonilla, Tony; Political Representation.

5991 Rivera, Elaine. Fernandez envies Jackson effort. NUESTRO, Vol. 7, no. 9 (November 1983), p. 13. English. DESCR: Elections; *Fernandez, Ben; Politics.

Jackson, P.

5992 Walia, Adorna. Book review of: BEGINNING ENGLISH THROUGH ACTION. BILINGUAL JOURNAL, Vol. 7, no. 3 (Spring 1983), p. 31-32. English. DESCR: *BEGINNING ENGLISH THROUGH ACTION (BETA); Book Reviews; English as a Second Language; Language Arts; Programmed Instruction.

Jaffee, A.J.

5993 Bunker, Stephen G. Book review of: THE CHANGING DEMOGRAPHY OF SPANISH-AMERICANS. CONTEMPORARY SOCIOLOGY: A JOURNAL OF REVIEWS, Vol. 11, no. 3 (May 1982), p.

270-273. English. DESCR: Book Reviews; *THE CHANGING DEMOGRAPHY OF SPANISH-AMERICANS.

5994 Holmberg, Joan J. Book review of: THE CHANGING DEMOGRAPHY OF SPANISH-AMERICANS. INTERNATIONAL MIGRATION REVIEW, Vol. 17, no. 3 (Fall 1983), p. 506-507. English. DESCR: Book Reviews; *THE CHANGING DEMOGRAPHY OF SPANISH-AMERICANS.

Jails
USE: Prisons

Jamail, Milton H.

5995 Research/development: books. HISPANIC BUSINESS, Vol. 4, no. 11 (November 1982), p. 28. English. DESCR: Book Reviews; Border Industries; Border Region; *ESTUDIOS FRONTERIZOS: PONENCIAS Y COMENTARIOS; *THE UNITED STATES-MEXICO BORDER: A GUIDE TO INSTITUTIONS, ORGANIZATIONS AND SCHOLARS; United States-Mexico Relations.

James, Dan

5996 Book review of: FAMOUS ALL OVER TOWN. NEW YORKER, Vol. 59, no. 11 (May 2, 1983), p. 126. English. DESCR: Book Reviews; *FAMOUS ALL OVER TOWN.

5997 Book review of: FAMOUS ALL OVER TOWN. BOOKLIST, Vol. 79, no. 15 (April 1, 1983), p. 1016. English. DESCR: Book Reviews; *FAMOUS ALL OVER TOWN.

5998 Quammen, David. Book review of: FAMOUS ALL OVER TOWN. NEW YORK TIMES BOOK REVIEW, Vol. 88, (April 24, 1983), p. 12+. English. DESCR: Book Reviews; *FAMOUS ALL OVER TOWN.

5999 Smith, Sherman W. Book review of: FAMOUS ALL OVER TOWN. WEST COAST REVIEW OF BOOKS, Vol. 9, no. 2 (1983), p. 40. English. DESCR: Book Reviews; *FAMOUS ALL OVER TOWN.

6000 Wimsatt, Margaret. Book review of: FAMOUS ALL OVER TOWN. COMMONWEAL, Vol. 110, no. 10 (May 20, 1983), p. 309-312. English. DESCR: Book Reviews; *FAMOUS ALL OVER TOWN.

Jaramillo, Cleofas M.

6001 Jensen, Carol. Cleofas M. Jaramillo on marriage in territorial Northern New Mexico. NEW MEXICO HISTORICAL REVIEW, Vol. 58, no. 2 (April 1983), p. 153-171. English. DESCR: *Marriage; *New Mexico.

Jarrin, Jaime

6002 Diaz, Katherine A. The Dodger's Spanish voice: Jaime Jarrin. CAMINOS, Vol. 3, no. 5 (May 1982), p. 50-51. English. DESCR: Radio; Sports.

Jazz

6003 Diaz, Katherine A. El rey del timbal Tito Puente (interview). CAMINOS, Vol. 4, no. 10 (November 1983), p. 14-16. English. DESCR: *Puente, Tito.

Jesuits

6004 Concha, Jaime. Exilio, conciencia: coda sobre la poesia de Millan. MAIZE, Vol. 5, no. 1-2 (Fall, Winter, 1981, 1982), p. 7-15. Spanish. DESCR: Chile; Literary Criticism; Literary History; *Millan, Gonzalo; Poetry; Political Refugees.

Jews

6005 Walden, Daniel. Parallels between Chicano and Jewish-American writing. MELUS: MULTI-ETHNIC LITERATURE OF THE UNITED STATES, Vol. 8, no. 2 (Summer 1981), p. 57-60. English. **DESCR:** *Literature.

Jimenez, Flaco

6006 Dickey, Dan W. and Van Osdol, Scott. La musica nortena: a photographic essay. SOUTHERN EXPOSURE, Vol. 11, no. 1 (1983), p. 38-41. English. **DESCR:** *Music; Norteno.

Jimenez Food Products, Inc.

6007 Chavarria, Jesus. Hispanic food producers: the top ten. HISPANIC BUSINESS, Vol. 5, no. 8 (August 1983), p. 6. English. **DESCR:** *Food Industry.

6008 Chavarria, Jesus. The largest Hispanic firms. HISPANIC BUSINESS, Vol. 4, no. 6 (June 1982), p. 6. English. **DESCR:** AMEX Systems, Inc.; *Business Enterprises.

6009 Salazar, Pamela Eoff. Selling $25 million of Jimenez Food Products. HISPANIC BUSINESS, Vol. 4, no. 6 (June 1982), p. 20-21,24. English. **DESCR:** Business Enterprises; Food Industry; Recipes.

Jimenez, Francisco

6010 Fernandez, Jose B. Book review of: HISPANICS IN THE UNITED STATES: AN ANTHOLOGY OF CREATIVE LITERATURE. ROCKY MOUNTAIN REVIEW OF LANGUAGE AND LITERATURE, Vol. 36, no. 1 (1982), p. 65-66. English. **DESCR:** Book Reviews; *HISPANICS IN THE UNITED STATES: AN ANTHOLOGY OF CREATIVE WRITING; Keller, Gary D.

6011 Lewis, Marvin A. Book review of: THE IDENTIFICATION AND ANALYSIS OF CHICANO LITERATURE. MELUS: MULTI-ETHNIC LITERATURE OF THE UNITED STATES, Vol. 7, no. 1 (Spring 1980), p. 82-85. English. **DESCR:** Book Reviews; IDENTIFICATION AND ANALYSIS OF CHICANO LITERATURE; *Literature.

6012 McCracken, Ellen. Book review of: IDENTIFICATION AND ANALYSIS OF CHICANO LITERATURE. NEW SCHOLAR, Vol. 8, no. 1-2 (Spring, Fall, 1982), p. 493-495. English. **DESCR:** Book Reviews; *IDENTIFICATION AND ANALYSIS OF CHICANO LITERATURE.

6013 McKinney, J.E. Book review of: MOSAICO DE LA VIDA: CHICANO, CUBAN AND PUERTO RICAN PROSE. HISPANIA, Vol. 65, no. 2 (May 1982), p. 321. English. **DESCR:** Book Reviews; *MOSAICO DE LA VIDA: CHICANO, CUBAN AND PUERTO RICAN PROSE; Prose; Spanish Language; Textbooks.

6014 Venier, M.E. Literatura chicana. DIALOGOS, Vol. 18, (May, June, 1982), p. 62-63. Spanish. **DESCR:** Book Reviews; *IDENTIFICATION AND ANALYSIS OF CHICANO LITERATURE.

6015 Zamora, Carlos. Book review of: MOSAICO DE LA VIDA: CHICANO, CUBAN AND PUERTO RICAN PROSE. MINORITY VOICES, Vol. 5, no. 1-2 (Spring, Fall, 1981), p. 71-72. English. **DESCR:** Book Reviews; Literature; *MOSAICO DE LA VIDA: CHICANO, CUBAN AND PUERTO RICAN PROSE.

Jimenez, Jose Alfredo

6016 Gradante, William. El hijo del pueblo: Jose Alfredo Jimenez and the Mexican cancion ranchera. LATIN AMERICAN MUSIC REVIEW, Vol. 3, no. 1 (Spring, Summer, 1982), p. 36-59. English. **DESCR:** Biography; Ethnomusicology; History.

Jimenez, Julian

6017 Friedman, Florence. Living and working in a lighthouse. CAMINOS, Vol. 4, no. 9 (October 1983), p. 16-18. Bilingual. **DESCR:** *Parks.

Jimenez, Luis

6018 Sculpture results in controversy. NUESTRO, Vol. 7, no. 2 (March 1983), p. 9. English. **DESCR:** Albuquerque Arts Board; *Sculpture.

Jimenez, Richard D.

6019 Newsfront. HISPANIC BUSINESS, Vol. 4, no. 1 (January 1982), p. 7. English. **DESCR:** *Biographical Notes; Businesspeople; Community Development; Macias, Miguel (Mike); Oaxaca, Jaime; The East Los Angeles Community Union (TELACU); Viramontes, Carlos.

Jimenez, Santiago

6020 Entertaiment reviews. CAMINOS, Vol. 3, no. 8 (September 1982), p. 21. English. **DESCR:** Adams, Bob; Alpert, Herb; Books; Calvert, Robert; Lopez, Lisa; Music; Myles, Carol; Paredes, Americo; Pettus, Theodore T.; *Recreation; Television.

Jimenez-Leal, Orlando

6021 West, Dennis. Film review of: EL SUPER. MINORITY VOICES, Vol. 4, no. 2 (Fall 1980), p. 85-87. English. **DESCR:** Cubanos; *EL SUPER; Film Reviews; Ichaso, Leon.

Job Discrimination
USE: Discrimination in Employment

Job Interviews

6022 Baciu, Joyce A. How to handle a job interview. CAMINOS, Vol. 3, no. 3 (March 1982), p. 32. English.

6023 Baciu, Joyce A. How to handle a job interview/como prepararse para una entrevista. CAMINOS, Vol. 4, no. 1-2 (January, February, 1983), p. 30-31. Bilingual.

Job Opportunities
USE: Discrimination in Employment

Job Satisfaction

6024 Executives challenge first impressions. HISPANIC BUSINESS, Vol. 4, no. 1 (January 1982), p. 22. English. **DESCR:** *Barraza, Santa.

Johnson, Kenneth F.

6025 North, David S. Book review of: ILLEGAL ALIENS IN THE WESTERN HEMISPHERE: POLITICAL AND ECONOMIC FACTORS. INTERNATIONAL MIGRATION REVIEW, Vol. 16, no. 3 (Fall 1982), p. 682-683. English. **DESCR:** Book Reviews; *ILLEGAL ALIENS IN THE WESTERN HEMISPHERE: POLITICAL AND ECONOMIC FACTORS; Undocumented Workers; Williams, Miles W.

Jokes
USE: Chistes

Jones, Richard C.

6026 Austin, Robert F. Comment on "Undocumented migration from Mexico: some geographical questions". ANNALS OF THE ASSOCIATION OF AMERICAN GEOGRAPHERS, Vol. 72, no. 4 (December 1982), p. 559-560. English. **DESCR:** Migration Patterns; *"Undocumented migration from Mexico: some geographical questions".

Jourard's (3) Self-Disclosure Questionnaire

6027 LeVine, Elaine S. and Franco, Juan N. Effects of therapist's gender, ethnicity, and verbal style on client's willingness to seek therapy. JOURNAL OF SOCIAL PSYCHOLOGY, Vol. 12, no. 1 (October 1983), p. 51-57. English. **DESCR:** *Counseling Services (Educational); Mental Health; Psychotherapy; Social Services.

JOURNAL OF LATIN COMMUNITY HEALTH

6028 Camarillo, J. Emilio. THE JOURNAL OF LATIN COMMUNITY HEALTH. JOURNAL OF LATIN COMMUNITY HEALTH, Vol. 1, no. 1 (Fall 1982), p. 1-3. English.

Journalism

6029 Cantu, Hector. Aqui en Tejas: Hispanic newspapers: city, community papers taking a business approach to the news. NATIONAL HISPANIC JOURNAL, Vol. 2, no. 1 (Summer 1983), p. 9. English. **DESCR:** AUSTIN LIGHT (TX); EL EDITOR (Lubbock, TX); EL SOL DE HOUSTON (TX); *Newspapers; THE TEXICAN (Dallas, TX).

6030 Career intelligencer. HISPANIC BUSINESS, Vol. 5, no. 9 (September 1983), p. 30. English. **DESCR:** California Chicano News Media Association (CCNMA); *Careers; National Consortium for Graduate Degrees for Minorities in Engineering.

6031 Chacon, Jose Mividal. Resena historica del periodismo en Centroamerica. CAMINOS, Vol. 4, no. 8 (September 1983), p. 20-21,50+. Spanish. **DESCR:** Central America; History.

6032 Gutierrez, Felix. Breaking through the media employment wall. AGENDA, Vol. 11, no. 3 (May, June, 1981), p. 13-19. English. **DESCR:** *Employment; Mass Media; Torres, Luis.

6033 Hispanic journalists assemble in California. NUESTRO, Vol. 6, no. 10 (December 1982), p. 28-30. English. **DESCR:** Cota-Robles Newton, Frank; *Journalists; *Martinez, Vilma Socorro.

6034 Lanier, Alfredo S. The quicksilver world of television news: Phil Ponce's Chicago beat. HISPANIC BUSINESS, Vol. 5, no. 10 (October 1983), p. 18-19+. English. **DESCR:** *Ponce, Phil; *Television; WBBM-TV, Chicago, IL [television station].

6035 Mexico en crisis: la incomprendida prensa norteamericana. INFORME: RELACIONES MEXICO-ESTADOS UNIDOS, Vol. 1, no. 3 (July, December, 1982), p. 256-266. Spanish. **DESCR:** *ABC-TV; Mass Media; NEW YORK TIMES.

6036 Miguel de la Madrid en la prensa norteamericana. INFORME: RELACIONES MEXICO-ESTADOS UNIDOS, Vol. 1, no. 2 (July, December, 1982), p. 176-183. Spanish. **DESCR:** *De la Madrid, Miguel; Lopez Portillo, Jose; LOS ANGELES TIMES; NEW YORK TIMES; Newspapers; WALL STREET JOURNAL;

WASHINGTON POST.

6037 Shankman, Arnold. The image of Mexico and the Mexican-American in the Black press, 1890-1935. JOURNAL OF ETHNIC STUDIES, Vol. 3, no. 2 (Summer 1975), p. 43-56. English. **DESCR:** Attitude (Psychological); Blacks; *Intergroup Relations; *Mexico.

6038 Stevenson, Robert. Carlos Chavez's United States press coverage. AZTLAN, Vol. 14, no. 1 (Spring 1983), p. 21-33. English. **DESCR:** *Chavez, Carlos; Ethnomusicology; Musicians; Print Media.

6039 Uehling, Mark D. Rivalry in New York: a profile of two newspapers. NUESTRO, Vol. 7, no. 7 (September 1983), p. 20-21. English. **DESCR:** Bustelo, Manuel A.; DIARIO LA PRENSA [newspaper], New York, NY; Espinal, Antonio; Gannett Co., Inc.; New York, NY; *Newspapers; NOTICIAS DEL MUNDO; Patino, Luis; Unification Church.

Journalists

6040 Community watching: para la comunidad. CAMINOS, Vol. 3, no. 1 (January 1982), p. 43-44. Bilingual. **DESCR:** Congreso Nacional Para Pueblos Unidos (CPU); *Financial Aid; *Food Programs; National Association for Chicano Studies (NACS); *Radio; Summer Program for Minority Journalists; Zozaya, Julia S.

6041 Ericksen, Charles and Treviso, Ruben. Latino journalists make their move. NUESTRO, Vol. 6, no. 5 (June, July, 1982), p. 45-47. English. **DESCR:** California Chicano News Media Association (CCNMA); Latin American Studies.

6042 Esther Manzano. CAMINOS, Vol. 3, no. 3 (March 1982), p. 30. Bilingual. **DESCR:** EL MEXICALO; *Manzano, Esther; Newspapers.

6043 Hispanic journalists assemble in California. NUESTRO, Vol. 6, no. 10 (December 1982), p. 28-30. English. **DESCR:** Cota-Robles Newton, Frank; Journalism; *Martinez, Vilma Socorro.

6044 Holston, Mark. The Walter Cronkite of Mexico. NUESTRO, Vol. 7, no. 5 (June, July, 1983), p. 58-59. English. **DESCR:** Cronkite, Walter; *Television; *Zabludovsky, Jacobo.

6045 Reporter beaten for story pursuit. NUESTRO, Vol. 7, no. 1 (January, February, 1983), p. 11-12. English. **DESCR:** *Berio, Yvonne C.; Police; San Juan, Puerto Rico.

Journals

6046 Communications/marketing. HISPANIC BUSINESS, Vol. 5, no. 10 (October 1983), p. 26. English. **DESCR:** Advertising; Arens & Gutierrez; Employment; Henry Molina, Inc.; Lionetti and Meyers Research Center, Inc.; Marketing; *Mass Media; Midwest Hispanics in Telecommunications Symposium, Chicago, IL; NEW MANAGEMENT.

6047 Cortese, Anthony J., ed. Contemporary trends in Chicano studies. CACR REVIEW, Vol. 1, no. 1 (September 1982), p. 1-133. English. **DESCR:** *Chicano Studies; Colorado Association of Chicano Research (CACR).

6048 Garza, M'Liss, ed. and Mercado, Olivia, ed. Chicana journals. COMADRE, no. 3 (Fall 1978), p. 38. Bilingual. **DESCR:** Chicanas.

Journals (cont.)

6049 Kanellos, Nicolas. REVISTA
CHICANO-RIQUENA/Arte Publico Press. CAMINOS,
Vol. 4, no. 6 (June 1983), p. 52-53,67.
English. DESCR: Periodicals; *REVISTA
CHICANO-RIQUENA.

J.T. Construction Co., El Paso, TX

6050 White House honors three minority firms.
NUESTRO, Vol. 7, no. 8 (October 1983), p.
51. English. DESCR: *Business Enterprises;
Businesspeople; Carson, Norris L.; H & H
Meat Products, Mercedes, TX; Hinojosa,
Liborio; National Minority Enterprise
Development Week; N.L. Carson Construction,
Inc., Carthage, MS; Torres, Jaime.

Juana Ines de la Cruz, Sor

6051 Sabat-Rivers, Georgina. Book review of: A
WOMAN OF GENIUS: THE INTELLECTUAL
AUTOBIOGRAPHY OF SOR JUANA INES DE LA CRUZ.
NUESTRO, Vol. 7, no. 6 (August 1983), p.
62-64. English. DESCR: *A WOMAN OF GENIUS:
THE INTELLECTUAL AUTOBIOGRAPHY OF SOR JUANA
INES DE LA CRUZ; Autobiography; Book
Reviews; Peden, Margaret Sayers.

Juarez and Associates, Inc.

6052 Communications/marketing. HISPANIC BUSINESS,
Vol. 4, no. 4 (April 1982), p. 15. English.
DESCR: Advertising Agencies; Consumers; Las
Americas, Inc.; *Marketing; Norman, Craig &
Kummel Organization; Publicidad Siboney;
Siboney Advertising, Inc.

Juarez, Benito

6053 Alvarez, Amando. Benito Juarez. LATINO, Vol.
54, no. 4 (May, June, 1983), p. 12-13.
Spanish. DESCR: History; Mexico.

Juarez, Chris

6054 People. HISPANIC BUSINESS, Vol. 5, no. 11
(November 1983), p. 10. English. DESCR:
Aragon, Fermin; *Businesspeople; De Los
Reyes, Victor; Di Martino, Rita; Garcia,
Ruben; Lopez, Leonard; Nogales, Luis G.;
Ozuna, Bob; Rico, Jose Hipolito; Tamayo,
Roberto; Tapia, Raul R.

Juarez, Joe

6055 Gente. NUESTRO, Vol. 7, no. 2 (March 1983),
p. 51. English. DESCR: Artists; Betancourt,
Jose L.; *Chicanas; Crime Victims Fund;
Federal Government; Military Service;
Saldana, Teresa; Vargas, Alberto; Victims
for Victims.

6056 People. HISPANIC BUSINESS, Vol. 5, no. 4
(April 1983), p. 9. English. DESCR:
Alvarado, Linda M.; *Biographical Notes;
Businesspeople; Castillo, Irenemaree;
Castillo, Sylvia; Del Junco, Tirso;
Gutierrez, Jose Roberto; Mata, Bill;
Miyares, Marcelino; Montanez Davis, Grace;
Montoya, Velma; Pineda, Pat; Siberio, Julio;
Thompson, Edith Lopez.

Juarez, Richard

6057 Whisler, Kirk. There are no easy solutions.
CAMINOS, Vol. 3, no. 11 (December 1982), p.
34. English. DESCR: *Border Region.

Judges

6058 Hernandez, Dennis. Group works to ensure
Reynoso election. CAMINOS, Vol. 3, no. 9
(October 1982), p. 46. English. DESCR:
*Reynoso, Cruz.

Judicial Review

6059 Que pasa? NUESTRO, Vol. 7, no. 6 (August
1983), p. 9. English. DESCR: Boy Scouts of
America; *Court System; Criminal Justice
System; Diabetes; Education; Petersilia,
Joan; PREPARED FOR TODAY; RACIAL DISPARITIES
IN THE CRIMINAL JUSTICE SYSTEM; Reagan,
Ronald.

Junior Colleges
USE: Community Colleges

Junior High School Students

6060 Community watching. CAMINOS, Vol. 3, no. 5
(May 1982), p. 56-57. Bilingual. DESCR:
Adelante Mujer Hispana Conference;
Agricultural Laborers; Beilson, Anthony C.;
Boycotts; Chacon, Peter R.; Chicanas;
*Cultural Organizations; Farm Labor
Organizing Commmittee (FLOC); Financial Aid;
Hollenbeck Junior High School, Los Angeles,
CA; National League of Cities; Optimist Club
of Greater East Los Angeles; Organizations;
Project WELL (We Enjoy Learning &
Leadership); Torres, Art.

6061 Fu, Victoria R.; Hinkle, Dennis E.; and
Korslund, Mary K. A development study of
ethnic self-concept among pre-adolescent
girls. JOURNAL OF GENETIC PSYCHOLOGY, Vol.
14, (March 1983), p. 67-73. English.
DESCR: Chicanas; Comparative Psychology;
*Identity; Self-Concept Self Report Scale.

6062 Medinnus, Gene R.; Ford, Martin Z.; and
Tack-Robinson, Susan. Locus of control: a
cross-cultural comparison. PSYCHOLOGICAL
REPORTS, Vol. 53, no. 1 (August 1983), p.
131-134. English. DESCR: *Fatalism; *Locus
of Control; Personality.

6063 Powers, Stephen and Sanchez, Virginia V.
Correlates of self-esteem of Mexican
American adolescents. PSYCHOLOGICAL REPORTS,
Vol. 51, no. 3 (December 1982), p. 771-774.
English. DESCR: Academic Achievement;
Arizona; Employment; *Identity; Nogales, AZ.

Juries

6064 Fox, Martin. Grand Jury selection upheld
against test by Hispanics. NEW YORK LAW
JOURNAL, Vol. 188, (October 1, 1982), p. 1.
English. DESCR: Brooklyn, NY; People v.
Guzman.

6065 Fram, Steven J. Restricting inquiry into
racial attitudes during the Voir Dire.
AMERICAN CRIMINAL REVIEW, Vol. 19, no. 4
(Spring 1982), p. 719-750. English. DESCR:
Aldridge v. U.S.; Ham v. South Carolina;
*Racism; Ristaino v. Ross; Rosales v. U.S.;
Rosales-Lopez, Humberto.

6066 Lipton, Jack P. Racism in the jury box: the
Hispanic defendant. HISPANIC JOURNAL OF
BEHAVIORAL SCIENCES, Vol. 5, no. 3
(September 1983), p. 275-290. English.
DESCR: Court System.

Jury Trials

6067 Young, Rowland L. Witnesses ... deportation.
AMERICAN BAR ASSOCIATION JOURNAL, Vol. 68,
(November 1982), p. 1493. English. DESCR:
*Deportation; Undocumented Workers; U.S. v.
Valenzuela-Bernal.

Juvenile Delinquency

6068 Buriel, Raymond; Calzada, Silverio; and Vasquez, Richard. The relationship of traditional Mexican American culture to adjustment and delinquency among three generations of Mexican American male adolescents. HISPANIC JOURNAL OF BEHAVIORAL SCIENCES, Vol. 4, no. 1 (March 1982), p. 41-55. English. DESCR: *Culture.

6069 Gibbs, Jewelle Taylor. Personality patterns of delinquent females: ethnic and sociocultural variations. JOURNAL OF CLINICAL PSYCHOLOGY, Vol. 38, no. 1 (January 1982), p. 198-206. English. DESCR: Chicanas; Ethnic Groups; Identity; Personality; Psychological Testing; Socioeconomic Factors.

6070 Hunsaker, Alan. A prompt/reward technique to elicit socially acceptable behavior with Chicano gang delinquents. HISPANIC JOURNAL OF BEHAVIORAL SCIENCES, Vol. 5, no. 1 (March 1983), p. 105-113. English. DESCR: Behavior Modification; *Gangs; Socialization.

6071 Young Latino goes to prison. NUESTRO, Vol. 6, no. 8 (October 1982), p. 11. English. DESCR: Denver, CO; *Mental Health; Prisoners; Prisons.

Kahlo, Frida

6072 Book review of: FRIDA: A BIOGRAPHY OF FRIDA KAHLO. BOOKLIST, Vol. 79, no. 11 (February 1, 1983), p. 708. English. DESCR: Artists; Biography; Book Reviews; *FRIDA: A BIOGRAPHY OF FRIDA KAHLO; Herrera, Hayden.

6073 Cameron, Dan. Book review of: FRIDA: A BIOGRAPHY OF FRIDA KAHLO. NUESTRO, Vol. 7, no. 8 (October 1983), p. 44-45. English. DESCR: Biography; Book Reviews; *FRIDA: A BIOGRAPHY OF FRIDA KAHLO; Herrera, Hayden.

6074 Herrera, Hayden. The elephant and the dove. NUESTRO, Vol. 7, no. 8 (October 1983), p. 40-43. English. DESCR: Art; Artists; Biography; Paintings; Rivera, Diego.

6075 Herrera, Hayden. Making an art of pain. PSYCHOLOGY TODAY, Vol. 17, no. 3 (March 1983), p. 86. English. DESCR: Biography; HENRY FORD HOSPITAL; Paintings; SELF-PORTRAIT WITH PORTRAIT OF DR. FARILL; THE BROKEN COLUMN; THE LITTLE DEER; TREE OF HOPE; WITHOUT HOPE.

6076 Lenti, Paul. Frida Kahlo. NUESTRO, Vol. 7, no. 8 (October 1983), p. 38-39. English. DESCR: Artists; *Biography.

6077 Lippard, Lucy R. Book review of: FRIDA: A BIOGRAPHY OF FRIDA KAHLO. NEW YORK TIMES BOOK REVIEW, Vol. 88, (April 24, 1983), p. 10+. English. DESCR: Book Reviews; *FRIDA: A BIOGRAPHY OF FRIDA KAHLO; Herrera, Hayden.

6078 Newman, Michael. The ribbon around the bomb. ART IN AMERICA, Vol. 71, (April 1983), p. 160-169. English. DESCR: *Artists; Modotti, Tina; Paintings.

6079 Rose, Barbara. Frida Kahlo: the Chicana as art heroine. VOGUE, Vol. 173, (April 1983), p. 152-154. English. DESCR: Art; Artists; Biography; Mexico; Rivera, Diego.

6080 Storr, Robert. Book review of: FRIDA: A BIOGRAPHY OF FRIDA KAHLO. ART IN AMERICA, Vol. 71, (April 1983), p. 19. English. DESCR: Artists; Book Reviews; *FRIDA: A BIOGRAPHY OF FRIDA KAHLO; Herrera, Hayden.

Kalish, Richard A.

6081 Burke, Leslie K. Book review of: THE LATER YEARS: SOCIAL APPLICATIONS OF GERONTOLOGY. HISPANIC JOURNAL OF BEHAVIORAL SCIENCES, Vol. 4, no. 1 (March 1982), p. 116-117. English. DESCR: Book Reviews; *THE LATER YEARS: SOCIAL APPLICATIONS OF GERONTOLOGY.

Kamin, Leon

6082 Herman, Janice. Book review of: THE INTELLIGENCE CONTROVERSY. HISPANIC JOURNAL OF BEHAVIORAL SCIENCES, Vol. 4, no. 3 (September 1982), p. 384-385. English. DESCR: Book Reviews; Eysenck, H.J.; *THE INTELLIGENCE CONTROVERSY.

Kanellos, Nicolas

6083 Miller, John C. Book review of: NUEVOS PASOS: CHICANO AND PUERTO RICAN DRAMA. MELUS: MULTI-ETHNIC LITERATURE OF THE UNITED STATES, Vol. 6, no. 3 (Fall 1979), p. 99-100. English. DESCR: Book Reviews; Huerta, Jorge A.; NUEVOS PASOS: CHICANO AND PUERTO RICAN DRAMA (thematic issue of REVISTA CHICANO-RIQUENA); *Teatro.

Karpel, Miguel

6084 Gomez, Dalia. Needed: Latino CPA's. NUESTRO, Vol. 6, no. 1 (January, February, 1982), p. 25-28. English. DESCR: *Accounting; Careers; Frank, Eleanor Marie; Quezada, Felipe L.; Rodriguez, Julio H.; Umpierre, Raphael; Zuzueta, Joseph.

Kaslow, Audrey

6085 Padilla, Steve. A Latino voice on the Parole Commission. NUESTRO, Vol. 7, no. 7 (September 1983), p. 42-43. English. DESCR: *Chicanas; Discrimination in Employment; Racism; U.S. Parole Commission.

Kasperuk, I.

6086 Research/development: books. HISPANIC BUSINESS, Vol. 4, no. 12 (December 1982), p. 36. English. DESCR: Book Reviews; Consumers; Guernica, A.; Marketing; *REACHING THE HISPANIC MARKET EFFECTIVELY.

Kasschau, Patricia L.

6087 Burke, Leslie K. Book review of: AGING AND SOCIAL POLICY: LEADERSHIP PLANNING. HISPANIC JOURNAL OF BEHAVIORAL SCIENCES, Vol. 4, no. 1 (March 1982), p. 115-116. English. DESCR: *AGING AND SOCIAL POLICY: LEADERSHIP PLANNING; Ancianos; Book Reviews.

KCET-TV, Los Angeles, CA [television station]

6088 Five-part series on youth jobs. NUESTRO, Vol. 7, no. 7 (September 1983), p. 13. English. DESCR: *Employment Training; Television; *Y.E.S. INC.; Youth.

Keller, Gary D.

6089 Fernandez, Jose B. Book review of: HISPANICS IN THE UNITED STATES: AN ANTHOLOGY OF CREATIVE LITERATURE. ROCKY MOUNTAIN REVIEW OF LANGUAGE AND LITERATURE, Vol. 36, no. 1 (1982), p. 65-66. English. DESCR: Book Reviews; *HISPANICS IN THE UNITED STATES: AN ANTHOLOGY OF CREATIVE WRITING; Jimenez, Francisco.

Kellogg, W.K.

6090 Academic furlough for the working professional. HISPANIC BUSINESS, Vol. 4, no. 8 (August 1983), p. 15. English. DESCR: Arias, Beatriz; Financial Aid; Funding Sources; *W.K. Kellogg Foundation.

Kelly, James G.

6091 Hunsaker, Alan. Book review of: PSYCHOLOGY AND COMMUNITY CHANGE; SOCIAL AND PSYCHOLOGICAL RESEARCH IN COMMUNITY SETTING; COMMUNITY PSYCHOLOGY: THEORETICAL AND EMPIRICAL APPROACHES. HISPANIC JOURNAL OF BEHAVIORAL SCIENCES, Vol. 5, no. 1 (March 1983), p. 121-124. English. DESCR: Book Reviews; *COMMUNITY PSYCHOLOGY: THEORETICAL AND EMPIRICAL APPROACHES; Gibbs, Margaret S.; Heller, Kenneth; Lachenmeyer, Juliana Rasic; Monahan, John; Munoz, Ricardo F.; *PSYCHOLOGY AND COMMUNITY CHANGE; Sigal, Janet; Snowden, Lonnie R.; *SOCIAL AND PSYCHOLOGICAL RESEARCH IN COMMUNITY SETTINGS.

Kennedy, David W.

6092 Research/development: books. HISPANIC BUSINESS, Vol. 4, no. 4 (April 1982), p. 28. English. DESCR: *Book Reviews; Engineering; Financial Aid; FINANCIAL AID FOR MINORITIES IN ENGINEERING; PERFECTLY LEGAL - 275 FOOLPROOF METHODS FOR PAYING LESS TAXES; Steiner, Barry R.; Swann, Ruth N.; Taxation.

Kennedy, Edward M.

6093 People. HISPANIC BUSINESS, Vol. 5, no. 10 (October 1983), p. 10. English. DESCR: Anaya, Toney; Arriola, Elvia Rosales; Babbitt, Bruce; Burgos, Tony; Bush, George; *Businesspeople; Cisneros, Henry, Mayor of San Antonio, TX; Cruz, Jose; Montano, Gilbert; Reagan, Ronald; White, Mark.

Kennedy, John Fitzgerald

6094 Kennedy, Edward M. Twentieth anniversary tribute to President John F. Kennedy. NUESTRO, Vol. 7, no. 9 (November 1983), p. 9. English. DESCR: Statesmanship.

6095 Maciel, David R. Book review of: THE KENNEDY CORRIDOS: A STUDY OF THE BALLADS OF A MEXICAN AMERICAN HERO. AZTLAN, Vol. 13, no. 1-2 (Spring, Fall, 1982), p. 335-337. English. DESCR: Book Reviews; Corrido; Dickey, Dan William; Folk Songs; Music.

Kessner, Thomas

6096 Reimers, David M. Book review of: TODAY'S IMMIGRANTS, THEIR STORIES. INTERNATIONAL MIGRATION REVIEW, Vol. 16, no. 4 (Winter 1982), p. 900. English. DESCR: Book Reviews; Caroli, Betty; Immigrants; Oral History; *TODAY'S IMMIGRANTS, THEIR STORIES.

Keyes, Charles F.

6097 Padilla, Amado M. Book review of: ETHNIC CHANGE. HISPANIC JOURNAL OF BEHAVIORAL SCIENCES, Vol. 4, no. 3 (September 1982), p. 393-394. English. DESCR: Book Reviews; *ETHNIC CHANGE.

Key-Math Diagnostic Test

6098 Yvon, Bernard R. Effects of the language of a diagnostic test on math scores. BILINGUAL JOURNAL, Vol. 6, no. 1 (Fall 1982), p. 13-16. English. DESCR: Bilingual Bicultural Education; *Educational Tests and Measurements; Language Proficiency; Mathematics.

KILIAGONIA

6099 Umpierre, Luz Maria. Book review of: KILIAGONIA. THIRD WOMAN, Vol. 1, no. 2 (1982), p. 87-90. Spanish. DESCR: Book Reviews; Zavala, Iris M.

King, Coretta Scott

6100 Black-Hispanic coalition. LATINO, Vol. 53, no. 2 (March, April, 1982), p. 25. English. DESCR: *Blacks; Politics.

Kino Community Hospital, Tucson, AZ

6101 Garcia, Ignacio M. Miracles at Kino Hospital. NUESTRO, Vol. 7, no. 6 (August 1983), p. 11-12. English. DESCR: *Gonzalez, Arthur; Hospitals and the Community; Medical Care; Public Health.

Kissling, Frances

6102 Torres, Sylvia. Book review of: ROSIE: THE INVESTIGATION OF A WRONGFUL DEATH. HISPANIC JOURNAL OF BEHAVIORAL SCIENCES, Vol. 4, no. 2 (June 1982), p. 279-280. English. DESCR: Book Reviews; Frankfort, Ellen; *ROSIE: THE INVESTIGATION OF A WRONGFUL DEATH.

Kitano, Pat

6103 People. HISPANIC BUSINESS, Vol. 5, no. 6 (June 1983), p. 8. English. DESCR: Appointed Officials; *Biographical Notes; Businesspeople; Goizueta, Roberto C.; Guerra, Stella; Huapaya, Sixto Guillermo; Manriquez, Suzanna; Oppenheimer-Nicolau, Siabhan; Ortiz, Solomon; Pachon, Harry P.; Richardson, Bill Lopez; Torres, Esteban E.; Torres, Johnny.

Kiwanis International

6104 Que pasa? NUESTRO, Vol. 7, no. 7 (September 1983), p. 9. English. DESCR: Alcoholism; Anti-Defamation League of B'nai B'rith; *Drug Abuse; Drug Programs; Employment; Miller Brewing Company; Racism; Sports.

Klein, Stephen P.

6105 Brown, Susan E. and Levoy, Claire. Melendez v. Burciaga: revealing the state of the art in bar examinations. BAR EXAMINER, Vol. 51, (May 1982), p. 4-15. English. DESCR: *Legal Profession; Melendez v. Burciaga; Mexican American Legal Defense and Educational Fund (MALDEF); Multistate Bar Examination (MBE).

KMEX, Los Angeles, CA [television station]

6106 KMEX-TV dominates the Hispanic market. HISPANIC BUSINESS, Vol. 5, no. 12 (December 1983), p. 16-17. English. DESCR: Advertising; Los Angeles, CA; Marketing; *Television.

Knight, Bobby

6107 Bobby Knight must go. NUESTRO, Vol. 7, no. 1 (January, February, 1983), p. 9. English. DESCR: Olympic Committee (U.S.); Racism; Sports.

Knight, Bobby (cont.)

6108 Our 1982 Latino awards. NUESTRO, Vol. 7, no.
1 (January, February, 1983), p. 44-46.
English. DESCR: Awards; Escalante, Jaime;
Gallegos, Gina; Grace, J. Peter; Immigration
and Naturalization Service (INS); Lamas,
Fernando; *Latino Awards; Luce, Claire
Boothe; Moreno, Rita; National Press
Foundation; Rodriguez Hernandez, Andres;
Simpson-Mazzoli Bill; Smith, Raymond;
Valeri, Michele; Voting Rights Act.

Knott's Berry Farm, Buena Park, CA

6109 Entertainment = diversion. CAMINOS, Vol. 3,
no. 5 (May 1982), p. 54. Bilingual. DESCR:
Artists; Buena Vista Cablevision, Inc.;
Cinco de Mayo; *Holidays; Tamayo, Rufino;
Television.

Korn/Ferry International

6110 Mestre, Mercedes. Paving the path. HISPANIC
BUSINESS, Vol. 5, no. 10 (October 1983), p.
9. English. DESCR: Business Administration;
Education; *Employment; Employment Training.

Kramarae, Cheris

6111 Walia, Adorna. Book review of: WOMEN AND MEN
SPEAKING: FRAMEWORK FOR ANALYSIS. BILINGUAL
JOURNAL, Vol. 6, no. 3 (Spring 1982), p.
20-22. English. DESCR: Book Reviews;
Language Usage; Sex Stereotypes; Sexism;
Sociolinguistics; *WOMEN AND MEN SPEAKING:
FRAMEWORK FOR ANALYSIS.

KSJV, Fresno, CA [radio station]

6112 Silva, Vicente. Community supported radio
bilingue: FM 91. CAMINOS, Vol. 3, no. 5 (May
1982), p. 46-48. Bilingual. DESCR: Fresno,
CA; Radio.

KTBC-TV, Austin, TX [television station]

6113 Cantu, Hector. Aqui en Austin: this is Olga
Campos reporting. NATIONAL HISPANIC JOURNAL,
Vol. 1, no. 3 (Summer, Fall, 1982), p. 7.
English. DESCR: Campos, Olga; Careers; Mass
Media; Television.

Ku Klux Klan

6114 Klan resurgence. NUESTRO, Vol. 5, no. 8
(November 1981), p. 11. English. DESCR:
*American Friends Service Committee; Racism.

KUBO, Salinas, CA [radio station]

6115 Baciu, Joyce A. KUBO-FM 90.9; the nation's
fourth bilingual radio station. CAMINOS,
Vol. 3, no. 5 (May 1982), p. 44-45,59.
Bilingual. DESCR: Radio; Salinas, CA.

Kutsche, Paul

6116 Carlson, Alvar W. Book review of: CANONES:
VALUES, CRISIS, AND SURVIVAL IN A NORTHERN
NEW MEXICO VILLAGE. NEW MEXICO HISTORICAL
REVIEW, Vol. 58, no. 3 (July 1983), p. 294.
English. DESCR: Book Reviews; *CANONES:
VALUES, CRISIS AND SURVIVAL IN A NORTHERN
NEW MEXICO VILLAGE; Van Ness, John R.

6117 Weber, Kenneth R. Book review of: CANONES:
VALUES, CRISIS, AND SURVIVAL IN A NORTHERN
NEW MEXICO VILLAGE. JOURNAL OF ETHNIC
STUDIES, Vol. 11, no. 2 (Summer 1983), p.
119-123. English. DESCR: Book Reviews;
Canones, NM; *CANONES: VALUES, CRISIS AND

SURVIVAL IN A NORTHERN NEW MEXICO VILLAGE;
Ethnology; History; New Mexico; Northern New
Mexico; Van Ness, John R.

Kutzik, Alfred J.

6118 Burke, Leslie K. Book review of: ETHNICITY
AND AGING: THEORY, RESEARCH AND POLICY.
HISPANIC JOURNAL OF BEHAVIORAL SCIENCES,
Vol. 4, no. 1 (March 1982), p. 107-112.
English. DESCR: Book Reviews; *ETHNICITY AND
AGING: THEORY, RESEARCH, AND POLICY;
Gelfland, Donald E.

L.A. Button Company

6119 Caldera, Carmela. Floyd Aragon: filling
voids with his entrepreneurship. CAMINOS,
Vol. 4, no. 4 (April 1983), p. 28-30, 66.
Bilingual. DESCR: *Aragon, Floyd; Business
Enterprises; Olympics.

La Fonda Restaurant

6120 Padilla, Steve. Adelina Pena Callahan:
restaurateur. NUESTRO, Vol. 7, no. 4 (May
1983), p. 26-29. English. DESCR:
Businesspeople; *Callahan, Adelina Pena;
*Careers; Food Industry; Working Women.

La Parrilla Restaurant

6121 It's not all rice & beans, part III
(restaurant reviews). CAMINOS, Vol. 4, no. 6
(June 1983), p. 15-18. Bilingual. DESCR:
Cache Restaurant; El Cochinito Yucateco
Restaurant; El Tepeyac Restaurant;
*Restaurants.

La Venta, Mexico

6122 Quirarte, Jacinto. Book review of: OLMEC: AN
EARLY ART STYLE OF PRECOLUMBIAN MEXICO.
JOURNAL OF ETHNIC STUDIES, Vol. 1, no. 3
(Fall 1973), p. 92-95. English. DESCR: Book
Reviews; *OLMEC: AN EARLY ART STYLE OF
PRECOLUMBIAN MEXICO; Precolumbian Art;
Precolumbian Society; San Lorenzo, Mexico;
Tres Zapotes, Mexico; Wicke, Charles R.

Labels
USE: Self-Referents

Labor

6123 Garcia, Ignacio M. Linda Ramirez: labor
leader. NUESTRO, Vol. 6, no. 5 (June, July,
1982), p. 26-28. English. DESCR: Labor
Unions; Latin Americans; Leadership;
Ramirez, Linda; San Antonio, TX.

6124 Hispanic solidarity. CAMINOS, Vol. 3, no. 7
(July, August, 1982), p. 38-39. Bilingual.
DESCR: *Labor Council for Latin American
Advancement; Organizations.

6125 Mena, Jesus. Testimonio de Bert Corona:
struggle is the ultimate teacher.
CHISMEARTE, (1982), p. 27-36. English.
DESCR: *Corona, Bert.

6126 Monroy, Douglas. Anarquismo y comunismo:
Mexican radicalism and the Communist Party
in Los Angeles during the 1930's. LABOR
HISTORY, Vol. 24, no. 1 (Winter 1983), p.
34-59. English. DESCR: Cannery and
Agricultural Worker's Industrial Union;
*Communist Party; Confederacion de Uniones
de Obreros Mexicanos (CUOM); History;
International Ladies Garment Workers Union
(ILGWU); Labor Organizing; *Los Angeles, CA;
Tenayuca, Emma; Worker's Alliance (WA), Los
Angeles, CA.

Labor (cont.)

6127 Santos, Richard. Earning among Spanish-origin males in the Midwest. SOCIAL SCIENCE JOURNAL, Vol. 19, no. 2 (April 1982), p. 51-59. English. **DESCR:** Employment; *Income; Midwestern States.

6128 Whisler, Kirk. There are 1 1/2 million Hispanics in labor unions. CAMINOS, Vol. 3, no. 7 (July, August, 1982), p. 40. English. **DESCR:** *Labor Council for Latin American Advancement; *Labor Unions; Montoya, Al.

6129 Wolin, Merle Linda. Dirty work: Americans turn down many jobs vacated by ouster of aliens. WALL STREET JOURNAL, Vol. 200, (December 6, 1982), p. 1. English. **DESCR:** Immigrant Labor; *Undocumented Workers.

Labor Camps

6130 Foster, Douglas. The desperate migrants of Devil's Canyon. THE PROGRESSIVE, Vol. 46, no. 11 (November 1982), p. 44-49. English. **DESCR:** *Agricultural Laborers; California; *Devil's Canyon, Deer Canyon, CA; Growers; San Diego, CA; Undocumented Workers.

6131 Gamboa, Erasmo. Mexican labor in the Pacific Northwest, 1943-1947: a photographic essay. PACIFIC NORTHWEST QUARTERLY, Vol. 73, no. 4 (October 1982), p. 175-181. English. **DESCR:** *Agricultural Laborers; International Labor Activities; Labor Supply and Market; Northwestern United States; World War II.

Labor Certification

6132 Buffenstein, Darryl F. The proposed immigration reform and control act of 1982: a new epoch in immigration law and a new headache for employers. EMPLOYEE RELATIONS LAW JOURNAL, Vol. 8, no. 3 (Winter 1983), p. 450-462. English. **DESCR:** Employment; Immigration Law; *Immigration Regulation and Control; Undocumented Workers.

6133 Furin, Gary C. Immigration law: alien employment certification. INTERNATIONAL LAWYER, Vol. 16, no. 1 (Winter 1982), p. 111-119. English. **DESCR:** Employment; Immigration and Nationality Act (INA); Undocumented Workers.

6134 Watson, Roy J., Jr. The Simpson-Mazzoli bill: an analysis of selected policies. SAN DIEGO LAW REVIEW, Vol. 20, no. 1 (December 1982), p. 97-116. English. **DESCR:** Employment; Immigration Regulation and Control; Mazzoli, Romano L.; Simpson, Alan K.; *Simpson-Mazzoli Bill; *Undocumented Workers.

Labor Classes
USE: Laboring Classes

Labor Council for Latin American Advancement

6135 Hispanic solidarity. CAMINOS, Vol. 3, no. 7 (July, August, 1982), p. 38-39. Bilingual. **DESCR:** Labor; Organizations.

6136 Whisler, Kirk. There are 1 1/2 million Hispanics in labor unions. CAMINOS, Vol. 3, no. 7 (July, August, 1982), p. 40. English. **DESCR:** Labor; *Labor Unions; Montoya, Al.

6137 Whisler, Kirk. Winners from the LCLAA. CAMINOS, Vol. 3, no. 1 (January 1982), p. 36. Bilingual. **DESCR:** *Labor Unions.

Labor Disputes

6138 Farmworkers win Arkansas contract. SOUTHERN EXPOSURE, Vol. 10, no. 5 (September, October, 1982), p. 4. English. **DESCR:** Agricultural Laborers; Arkansas; *Arkansas Farmworker Civil Rights Organizing Project (AFCROP); Undocumented Workers.

6139 Garcia, Mario T. Book review of: LA CLASE OBRERA EN LA HISTORIA DE MEXICO: AL NORTE DEL RIO BRAVO (PASADO INMEDIATO, 1930-1981). HISPANIC AMERICAN HISTORICAL REVIEW, Vol. 62, no. 4 (November 1982), p. 694-696. English. **DESCR:** Book Reviews; History; *LA CLASE OBRERA EN LA HISTORIA DE MEXICO: AL NORTE DEL RIO BRAVO (PASADO INMEDIATO, 1930-1981); Laboring Classes; Maciel, David R.

Labor Laws and Legislation

6140 Bustamante, Jorge A. The Mexicans are coming: from ideology to labor relations. INTERNATIONAL MIGRATION REVIEW, Vol. 17, no. 2 (Summer 1983), p. 323-341. English. **DESCR:** Attitude (Psychological); *Immigration; Immigration Law; Labor Supply and Market; Migration; Policy; Political Ideology; *Simpson-Mazzoli Bill; Undocumented Workers.

6141 Paul, Jan S. The changing work week. HISPANIC BUSINESS, Vol. 5, no. 9 (September 1983), p. 16. English. **DESCR:** Employment; *Labor Supply and Market; Personnel Management.

Labor Organizing

6142 Barry, Tom. On strike! Undocumented workers in Arizona. SOUTHWEST ECONOMY AND SOCIETY, Vol. 3, no. 3 (Spring 1978), p. 52-60. English. **DESCR:** Agribusiness; Agricultural Laborers; Arizona; *Goldmar Citrus Ranch, Phoenix, AZ; *Maricopa County Organizing Project (MCOP); Phoenix, AZ; *Strikes and Lockouts; Undocumented Workers.

6143 Mendez Gonzalez, Rosalinda. Mexican women and families: rural-to-urban and international migration. SOUTHWEST ECONOMY AND SOCIETY, Vol. 4, no. 2 (Winter 1978, 1979), p. 14-27. English. **DESCR:** Chicanas; Employment; *Family; Garment Industry; Immigration; International Ladies Garment Workers Union (ILGWU); Los Angeles, CA; Undocumented Workers.

6144 Monroy, Douglas. Anarquismo y comunismo: Mexican radicalism and the Communist Party in Los Angeles during the 1930's. LABOR HISTORY, Vol. 24, no. 1 (Winter 1983), p. 34-59. English. **DESCR:** Cannery and Agricultural Worker's Industrial Union; *Communist Party; Confederacion de Uniones de Obreros Mexicanos (CUOM); History; International Ladies Garment Workers Union (ILGWU); Labor; *Los Angeles, CA; Tenayuca, Emma; Worker's Alliance (WA), Los Angeles, CA.

Labor Supply and Market

6145 Borjas, George J. The labor supply of male Hispanic immigrants in the United States. INTERNATIONAL MIGRATION REVIEW, Vol. 17, no. 4 (Winter 1983), p. 653-671. English. **DESCR:** Assimilation; Immigration; *Native Americans; Puerto Ricans.

Labor Supply and Market (cont.)

6146 Borjas, George J. The substitutability of
Black, Hispanic and white labor. ECONOMIC
INQUIRY, Vol. 21, no. 1 (January 1983), p.
93-106. English. **DESCR:** Income.

6147 Bradshaw, Benjamin S. and Frisbie, W.
Parker. Potential labor force supply and
replacement in Mexico and the states of the
Mexican cession and Texas: 1980-2000.
INTERNATIONAL MIGRATION REVIEW, Vol. 17, no.
3 (Fall 1983), p. 394-409. English. **DESCR:**
Immigration; *Mexico; Texas.

6148 Bustamante, Jorge A. The Mexicans are
coming: from ideology to labor relations.
INTERNATIONAL MIGRATION REVIEW, Vol. 17, no.
2 (Summer 1983), p. 323-341. English.
DESCR: Attitude (Psychological);
*Immigration; Immigration Law; Labor Laws
and Legislation; Migration; Policy;
Political Ideology; *Simpson-Mazzoli Bill;
Undocumented Workers.

6149 Conoley, Martin. The hidden threat of
underemployment. HISPANIC BUSINESS, Vol. 5,
no. 10 (October 1983), p. 14+. English.
DESCR: Education; *Employment; Employment
Training; Personnel Management.

6150 Duncan, Cameron. The runaway shop and the
Mexican border industrialization program.
SOUTHWEST ECONOMY AND SOCIETY, Vol. 2, no. 1
(October, November, 1976), p. 4-25. English.
DESCR: Border Region; *Maquiladoras;
*Mexican Border Industrialization Program;
Multinational Corporations.

6151 Gamboa, Erasmo. Mexican labor in the Pacific
Northwest, 1943-1947: a photographic essay.
PACIFIC NORTHWEST QUARTERLY, Vol. 73, no. 4
(October 1982), p. 175-181. English. **DESCR:**
*Agricultural Laborers; International Labor
Activities; Labor Camps; Northwestern United
States; World War II.

6152 Garcia, Philip. An evaluation of employment
and unemployment differences between Mexican
Americans and whites: the seventies. SOCIAL
SCIENCE JOURNAL, Vol. 20, no. 1 (January
1983), p. 51-62. English. **DESCR:** Anglo
Americans; *Employment; Ethnic Groups.

6153 Hispanic employment reviews. HISPANIC
BUSINESS, Vol. 4, no. 6 (June 1982), p.
28-29. English. **DESCR:** *Employment;
Laborers.

6154 Hispanics: don't they know there's a
recession on? S & MM [SALES & MARKETING
MANAGEMENT], Vol. 12, no. 2 (July 26, 1982),
p. A41. English. **DESCR:** Income.

6155 Howell, Frances Baseden. Split labor market:
Mexican farm workers in the Southwest.
SOCIOLOGICAL INQUIRY, Vol. 52, no. 2 (Spring
1982), p. 132-140. English. **DESCR:**
Agricultural Labor Unions; Arizona Farm
Workers (AFW); Southwest United States;
Undocumented Workers; United Farmworkers of
America (UFW).

6156 The impact of undocumented migration on the
U.S. labor market. HOUSTON JOURNAL OF
INTERNATIONAL LAW, Vol. 5, no. 2 (Spring
1983), p. 287-321. English. **DESCR:** Economic
History and Conditions; Employment;
Immigrant Labor; Immigration and Nationality
Act (INA); Immigration Law; Research
Methodology; Simpson-Mazzoli Bill;
*Undocumented Workers.

6157 Increasingly educated work force. HISPANIC

BUSINESS, Vol. 4, no. 1 (January 1982), p.
29. English. **DESCR:** Higher Education.

6158 Johnson, Greg. Administracion en un medio
ambiente hispanico. INDUSTRY WEEK, Vol. 212,
no. 2 (January 25, 1982), p. 30-34. English.
DESCR: Industries; Spanish Language;
Undocumented Workers.

6159 Mamer, John W. and Martin, Philip. Hired
workers on California farms. CALIFORNIA
AGRICULTURE, Vol. 36, no. 9-10 (September,
October, 1982), p. 21-23. English. **DESCR:**
*Agricultural Laborers; *California;
Statistics; Undocumented Workers.

6160 Manpower Inc. Hispanics in the labor force:
data. CAMINOS, Vol. 3, no. 3 (March 1982),
p. 23-25. English. **DESCR:** *Statistics.

6161 Math-based careers. HISPANIC BUSINESS, Vol.
5, no. 5 (May 1983), p. 26. English. **DESCR:**
*Careers; Engineering as a Profession;
Financial Aid; Income; Mexican American
Engineering Society (MAES) National
Symposium (5th), Fullerton, CA, April 13-15,
1980; University of California, Santa
Barbara.

6162 Paul, Jan S. The changing work week.
HISPANIC BUSINESS, Vol. 5, no. 9 (September
1983), p. 16. English. **DESCR:** Employment;
Labor Laws and Legislation; Personnel
Management.

6163 Positioning growth at El Paso Electric Co.
HISPANIC BUSINESS, Vol. 4, no. 2 (February
1982), p. 10+. English. **DESCR:** El Paso
Electric Company; El Paso, TX; Employment;
*Energy Industries; Wall, Evern R.

6164 Tienda, Marta. Market characteristics and
Hispanic earnings: a comparison of natives
and immigrants. SOCIAL PROBLEMS, Vol. 31,
no. 1 (October 1983), p. 59-72. English.
DESCR: *Income.

6165 Weiss, Lawrence D. Industrial reserve armies
of the southwest: Navajo and Mexican.
SOUTHWEST ECONOMY AND SOCIETY, Vol. 3, no. 1
(Fall 1977), p. 19-29. English. **DESCR:**
Capitalism; History; Native Americans;
Navaho Indians; Railroads; *Southwest United
States.

Labor Unions

6166 Arnold, Frank. A history of struggle:
organizing cannery workers in the Santa
Clara Valley. SOUTHWEST ECONOMY AND SOCIETY,
Vol. 2, no. 1 (October, November, 1976), p.
26-38. English. **DESCR:** Agribusiness;
American Labor Union (Santa Clara County,
CA); Cannery and Agricultural Worker's
Industrial Union; *Cannery Workers; Comite
de Trabajadores de Canerias, San Jose, CA;
History; *Santa Clara Valley, CA; United
Cannery Agricultural Packing and Allied
Workers of America (UCAPAWA).

6167 Askin, Steve. Boston church encourages labor
talks. NATIONAL CATHOLIC REPORTER, Vol. 18,
(July 30, 1982), p. 6. English. **DESCR:**
Boston Archdiocese Justice and Peace
Commission; Boycotts; Campbell Soup Co.;
Catholic Church; *Farm Labor Organizing
Commmittee (FLOC).

6168 Barber, Bob. UFW and the class struggle.
SOUTHWEST ECONOMY AND SOCIETY, Vol. 1, no. 1
(Spring 1976), p. 28-35. English. **DESCR:**
California; Undocumented Workers; *United
Farmworkers of America (UFW).

Labor Unions (cont.)

6169 Bracamonte, Jose A. The national labor relations act and undaunted workers: the alienation of American labor. SAN DIEGO LAW REVIEW, Vol. 21, no. 1 (December 1983), p. 29-86. English. **DESCR:** Immigration Law; National Labor Relations Act (NLRA); Sure-Tan; *Undocumented Workers.

6170 Byrkit, James W. Walter Douglas and labor struggles in early 20th century Arizona. SOUTHWEST ECONOMY AND SOCIETY, Vol. 1, no. 1 (Spring 1976), p. 14-27. English. **DESCR:** Arizona; *Biography; Bisbee, AZ; Clifton Morenci Strike, June 1903; Copper Queen Mining Co., Bisbee, AZ; *Douglas, Walter; International Workers of the World (IWW); Mining Industry; Strikes and Lockouts.

6171 Cockcroft, James D. Mexican migration, crisis, and the internationalization of labor struggle. CONTEMPORARY MARXISM, Vol. 5, (Summer 1982), p. 48-61. English. **DESCR:** International Economic Relations; International Labor Activities; Legislation; Racism; *Undocumented Workers.

6172 Communications/marketing. HISPANIC BUSINESS, Vol. 4, no. 2 (February 1982), p. 15. English. **DESCR:** Cable Television; Congressional Hispanic Caucus; El Teatro Campesino; GalaVision; *Marketing; Philip Morris, Inc.; Publishing Industry; Spanish International Network (SIN).

6173 Garcia, Ignacio M. Linda Ramirez: labor leader. NUESTRO, Vol. 6, no. 5 (June, July, 1982), p. 26-28. English. **DESCR:** *Labor; Latin Americans; Leadership; Ramirez, Linda; San Antonio, TX.

6174 Morales, Rebecca. Unions and undocumented workers. SOUTHWEST ECONOMY AND SOCIETY, Vol. 6, no. 1 (Fall 1982), p. 3-11. English. **DESCR:** Employment; Immigration and Naturalization Service (INS); *Operation Jobs; *Undocumented Workers.

6175 Negrete, Louis R. Labor unions and undocumented workers. BORDERLANDS JOURNAL, Vol. 6, no. 1 (Fall 1982), p. 1-10. English. **DESCR:** *Undocumented Workers.

6176 Rick Icaza on career opportunities in unions. CAMINOS, Vol. 3, no. 8 (September 1982), p. 44-45. Bilingual. **DESCR:** *Affirmative Action; Chicano Youth Leadership Conference; United Food and Commercial Workers.

6177 Rubenstein, Harry R. The great Gallup Coal strike of 1933. SOUTHWEST ECONOMY AND SOCIETY, Vol. 3, no. 2 (Winter 1977, 1978), p. 34-53. English. **DESCR:** *Gallup Coal Strike of 1933; Mining Industry; National Miner's Union (NMU); New Mexico; *Strikes and Lockouts; United Mineworkers of America (UMWA).

6178 Torres, Lorenzo. Short history of Chicano workers. SOUTHWEST ECONOMY AND SOCIETY, Vol. 3, no. 2 (Winter 1977, 1978), p. 4-17. English. **DESCR:** Marxism; *Mine, Mill and Smelter Workers Union; Mining Industry; Racism.

6179 Whisler, Kirk. There are 1 1/2 million Hispanics in labor unions. CAMINOS, Vol. 3, no. 7 (July, August, 1982), p. 40. English. **DESCR:** Labor; *Labor Council for Latin American Advancement; Montoya, Al.

6180 Whisler, Kirk. Winners from the LCLAA. CAMINOS, Vol. 3, no. 1 (January 1982), p. 36. Bilingual. **DESCR:** *Labor Council for Latin American Advancement.

Laborers

6181 Brink, T. L. Book review of: WORKING-CLASS EMIGRES FROM CUBA. HISPANIC JOURNAL OF BEHAVIORAL SCIENCES, Vol. 5, no. 3 (September 1983), p. 363-365. English. **DESCR:** Book Reviews; Cubanos; Fox, Geoffrey E.; *WORKING CLASS EMIGRES FROM CUBA.

6182 Government review. NUESTRO, Vol. 7, no. 7 (September 1983), p. 55. English. **DESCR:** AIDS Hotline; California; Education; Employment; Food for Survival, New York, NY; Funding Sources; *Government Services; Hewlett Foundation; Mathematics, Engineering and Science Achievement (MESA); Population Trends; Public Health; Stanford University, Stanford, CA.

6183 Hispanic employment reviews. HISPANIC BUSINESS, Vol. 4, no. 6 (June 1982), p. 28-29. English. **DESCR:** *Employment; Labor Supply and Market.

6184 Mayers, Raymond Sanchez. The school and labor-force status of Hispanic youth: implications for social policy. CHILDREN AND YOUTH SERVICES REVIEW, Vol. 4, no. 1- (1982), p. 175-192. English. **DESCR:** Education; *Youth.

6185 Taylor, William B. Book review of: LABOR AND LABORERS THROUGH MEXICAN HISTORY. NEW MEXICO HISTORICAL REVIEW, Vol. 57, no. 1 (January 1982), p. 91-92. English. **DESCR:** Book Reviews; *EL TRABAJO Y LOS TRABAJADORES EN LA HISTORIA DE MEXICO = LABOR AND LABORERS THROUGH MEXICAN HISTORY; Frost, Elsa Cecilia; Mexico.

Laboring Classes

6186 Alvarez, Alejandro. Economic crisis and migration: comments on James Cockcroft's article. CONTEMPORARY MARXISM, Vol. 5, (Summer 1982), p. 62-66. English. **DESCR:** Cockroft, James; International Economic Relations; Legislation; MEXICAN MIGRATION, CRISIS, AND THE INTERNATIONALIZATION OF LABOR STRUGGLES; *Undocumented Workers.

6187 Garcia, Mario T. Book review of: LA CLASE OBRERA EN LA HISTORIA DE MEXICO: AL NORTE DEL RIO BRAVO (PASADO INMEDIATO, 1930-1981). HISPANIC AMERICAN HISTORICAL REVIEW, Vol. 62, no. 4 (November 1982), p. 694-696. English. **DESCR:** Book Reviews; History; *LA CLASE OBRERA EN LA HISTORIA DE MEXICO: AL NORTE DEL RIO BRAVO (PASADO INMEDIATO, 1930-1981); Labor Disputes; Maciel, David R.

Lacayo, Frank L. "Hank"

6188 How to stuff a wild chile part II. CAMINOS, Vol. 3, no. 1 (January 1982), p. 31-32. English. **DESCR:** Albert, Margo; Chacon, Peter R.; *Icaya, Rick; *Recipes; *Rodriguez, Edmundo; Rodriguez, Edmundo M.; *Vasquez, Victor.

Lacayo, Henry

6189 People on the move. CAMINOS, Vol. 2, no. 6
(October 1981), p. 7. English. DESCR:
Alvarado, Angel S.; Arreola, Rafael;
*Biographical Notes; Diaz, Elisa; Diaz,
Elvira A.; Garcia, Jose Joel; Garza,
Florentino; Icaza, Ricardo F.; Martinez,
Lydia R.; Munoz, Victor M.; Salinas,
Vicente; Sanchez, Manuel; Zuniga, Henry.

Lachenmeyer, Juliana Rasic

6190 Hunsaker, Alan. Book review of: PSYCHOLOGY
AND COMMUNITY CHANGE; SOCIAL AND
PSYCHOLOGICAL RESEARCH IN COMMUNITY SETTING;
COMMUNITY PSYCHOLOGY: THEORETICAL AND
EMPIRICAL APPROACHES. HISPANIC JOURNAL OF
BEHAVIORAL SCIENCES, Vol. 5, no. 1 (March
1983), p. 121-124. English. DESCR: Book
Reviews; *COMMUNITY PSYCHOLOGY: THEORETICAL
AND EMPIRICAL APPROACHES; Gibbs, Margaret
S.; Heller, Kenneth; Kelly, James G.;
Monahan, John; Munoz, Ricardo F.;
*PSYCHOLOGY AND COMMUNITY CHANGE; Sigal,
Janet; Snowden, Lonnie R.; *SOCIAL AND
PSYCHOLOGICAL RESEARCH IN COMMUNITY
SETTINGS.

Lagueruela, Andy

6191 Weber, Robert. Rising star: Satelco.
HISPANIC BUSINESS, Vol. 5, no. 9 (September
1983), p. 14. English. DESCR: Business
Enterprises; *Satelco, Inc.;
Telecommunications; Veve, Rafael.

Lakeview Learning Center, Chicago, IL

6192 Venerable, W. R. Student and parent
attitudes toward college at five Hispanic
learning centers in Illinois. JOURNAL OF THE
NATIONAL ASSOC. OF COLLEGE ADMISSIONS
COUNSELORS, Vol. 26, (April 1982), p.
19-23. English. DESCR: Casa Aztlan; Chicago,
IL; *Higher Education; Illinois Migrant
Council; *Secondary School Education.

Lamas, Fernando

6193 Our 1982 Latino awards. NUESTRO, Vol. 7, no.
1 (January, February, 1983), p. 44-46.
English. DESCR: Awards; Escalante, Jaime;
Gallegos, Gina; Grace, J. Peter; Immigration
and Naturalization Service (INS); Knight,
Bobby; *Latino Awards; Luce, Claire Boothe;
Moreno, Rita; National Press Foundation;
Rodriguez Hernandez, Andres; Simpson-Mazzoli
Bill; Smith, Raymond; Valeri, Michele;
Voting Rights Act.

Lamas, Lorenzo

6194 Gonzalez, Magdalena. Recognizing Hispanic
achievements in entertainment - U.S. and
Mexico. CAMINOS, Vol. 3, no. 7 (July,
August, 1982), p. 18-24. Bilingual. DESCR:
Allende, Fernando; Artists; Awards; Bonilla
Giannini, Roxanna; Eynoso, David; Felix,
Maria; Films; Gallego, Gina; *Golden Eagle
Awards; Hoyos, Rodolfo; Lopez, Conchita;
Lopez, Lisa; Montalban, Ricardo; Nosotros
[film production company]; Quintero, Jose;
Rowe, Arthur; Television; Torres, Liz.

6195 Lorenzo Lamas. LATINO, Vol. 54, no. 6
(October 1983), p. 7+. English. DESCR:
Artists.

Lamy, J.B.

6196 Blea, Irene I. Book review of: BUT TIME AND
CHANCE. CACR REVIEW, Vol. 1, no. 1
(September 1982), p. 132-133. English.

DESCR: Book Reviews; *BUT TIME AND CHANCE;
Catholic Church; Chavez, Fray Angelico;
Machelbeuf, Joseph P., Vicar; Martinez,
Antonio, Fray; New Mexico.

Land Grants

6197 Oczon, Annabelle M. Land grants in New
Mexico: a selective bibliography. NEW MEXICO
HISTORICAL REVIEW, Vol. 57, no. 1 (January
1982), p. 81-87. English. DESCR:
Bibliography; New Mexico.

6198 Salmon, Roberto Mario. Book review of:
SPANISH AND MEXICAN LAND GRANTS IN NEW
MEXICO AND COLORADO. JOURNAL OF ETHNIC
STUDIES, Vol. 9, no. 3 (Fall 1981), p.
120-121. English. DESCR: Book Reviews;
Colorado; New Mexico; *SPANISH AND MEXICAN
LAND GRANTS IN NEW MEXICO AND COLORADO; Van
Ness, Christine M.; Van Ness, John R.

Land Tenure

6199 Churchhill, Ward. Implications of publishing
ROOTS OF RESISTANCE. JOURNAL OF ETHNIC
STUDIES, Vol. 9, no. 3 (Fall 1981), p.
83-89. English. DESCR: Book Reviews;
Colonialism; Dunbar Ortiz, Roxanne; Native
Americans; New Mexico; Publishing Industry;
*ROOTS OF RESISTANCE: LAND TENURE IN NEW
MEXICO, 1680-1980; Social History and
Conditions.

6200 Dunbar Ortiz, Roxanne. The roots of
resistance: Pueblo land tenure and Spanish
colonization. JOURNAL OF ETHNIC STUDIES,
Vol. 5, no. 4 (Winter 1977), p. 33-53.
English. DESCR: Native Americans; New
Mexico; Pueblo Indians; Social History and
Conditions.

6201 Westphall, Victor. Book review of: ROOTS OF
RESISTANCE: LAND TENURE IN NEW MEXICO,
1680-1980. ARIZONA AND THE WEST, Vol. 24,
no. 2 (Summer 1982), p. 192-193. English.
DESCR: Book Reviews; Ortiz, Roxanne Dunbar;
*ROOTS OF RESISTANCE: LAND TENURE IN NEW
MEXICO, 1680-1980.

Land Titles

USE: Land Grants

Landon v. Plasencia

6202 Young, Rowland L. Exclusion hearing enough
for illegal alien smuggler. AMERICAN BAR
ASSOCIATION JOURNAL, Vol. 69, (March 1983),
p. 352. English. DESCR: Chicana Welfare
Rights Organization; Laws; *Undocumented
Workers.

Language Arts

6203 Brooks, C.K. Verbal giftedness in the
minority student: a NEWT questions a SOT.
ENGLISH JOURNAL, Vol. 72, (January 1983),
p. 18-21. English. DESCR: Cultural
Pluralism; Curriculum; Language Development.

6204 Buckholtz, Marjorie Weidenfeld. Technical
training in two languages helps Houston stay
cool. AMERICAN EDUCATION, Vol. 18, no. 3
(April 1982), p. 11-14. English. DESCR:
*Employment Training; Houston Community
College; Language Proficiency; Vocational
Education.

Language Arts (cont.)

6205 Carrillo, Federico M. How should Spanish speakers be taught Spanish in the schools? BILINGUAL JOURNAL, Vol. 7, no. 4 (Summer 1983), p. 18-22. English. **DESCR:** *Bilingual Bicultural Education; Sociolinguistics; Spanish Language.

6206 Chall, Jeanne. Rich and sharp memories of reading. CHANGE, Vol. 14, no. 7 (October 1982), p. 36-40. English. **DESCR:** Assimilation; Book Reviews; *HUNGER OF MEMORY: THE EDUCATION OF RICHARD RODRIGUEZ; Reading; Rodriguez, Richard; Socioeconomic Factors.

6207 Gonzalez, Roseann Duenas. Teaching Mexican American students to write: capitalizing on the culture. ENGLISH JOURNAL, Vol. 71, no. 7 (November 1982), p. 20-24. English. **DESCR:** Cultural Characteristics; Education; Educational Innovations; Style and Composition.

6208 Hudelson, Sarah. An introductory examination of children's invented spelling in Spanish. NABE JOURNAL, Vol. 6, no. 2-3 (Winter, Spring, 1981, 1982), p. 53-67. English. **DESCR:** Bilingual Bicultural Education; Children; Learning and Cognition; Spanish Language.

6209 Lado, Robert. Aula/the classroom: developmental reading in two languages. NABE JOURNAL, Vol. 6, no. 2-3 (Winter, Spring, 1981, 1982), p. 99-110. English. **DESCR:** Bilingual Bicultural Education; Bilingualism; Language Development; Learning and Cognition; *Reading; Spanish Education Development (SED) Center Bilingual Reading Project; Spanish Language.

6210 Martinez, Douglas R. American spelling bee: enchilada, llano, amigo, maraca. NUESTRO, Vol. 7, no. 5 (June, July, 1983), p. 50-51. English. **DESCR:** American Spelling Bee; *Language Usage; *Linguistics.

6211 Morrison, J. A. and Michael, W.B. Development and validation of an auditory perception test in Spanish for Hispanic children receiving reading instruction in Spanish. EDUCATIONAL AND PSYCHOLOGICAL MEASUREMENT, Vol. 42, (Summer 1982), p. 657-669. English. **DESCR:** Children; Educational Tests and Measurements; Prueba de Analisis Auditivo (PAA); Reading; Spanish Language.

6212 Piersel, Wayne C., et al. Bias in content validity on the Boehm test of basic concepts for white and Mexican-American children. CONTEMPORARY EDUCATIONAL PSYCHOLOGY, Vol. 7, no. 2 (April 1982), p. 181-189. English. **DESCR:** Anglo Americans; *Boehm Test of Basic Concepts; Children; *Educational Tests and Measurements.

6213 Rodriguez, Imelda and Bethel, Lowell J. Inquiry approach to science and language teaching. JOURNAL OF RESEARCH IN SCIENCE TEACHING, Vol. 20, no. 4 (April 1983), p. 291-296. English. **DESCR:** Bilingualism; Education; *Educational Tests and Measurements; Learning and Cognition; Primary School Education; Science.

6214 Schon, Isabel; Hopkins, Kenneth D.; and Davis, W. Alan. Effects of books in Spanish and free reading time on Hispanic students' reading abilities and attitudes. NABE JOURNAL, Vol. 7, no. 1 (Fall 1982), p. 13-20. English. **DESCR:** Bilingual Bicultural Education; Language Proficiency; *Reading; Spanish Language.

6215 Walia, Adorna. Book review of: BEGINNING ENGLISH THROUGH ACTION. BILINGUAL JOURNAL, Vol. 7, no. 3 (Spring 1983), p. 31-32. English. **DESCR:** *BEGINNING ENGLISH THROUGH ACTION (BETA); Book Reviews; English as a Second Language; Jackson, P.; Programmed Instruction.

Language Arts Approach (LAA)

6216 Walker de Felix, Judith. The language arts approach: planned eclecticism in ESL teaching in the elementary school. BILINGUAL REVIEW, Vol. 10, no. 1 (January, April, 1983), p. 87-89. English. **DESCR:** *English as a Second Language; Primary School Education.

Language Assessment

6217 Argulewicz, Ed N. and Sanchez, David T. Considerations in the assessment of reading difficulties in bilingual children. SCHOOL PSYCHOLOGY REVIEW, Vol. 11, no. 3 (Summer 1982), p. 281-289. English. **DESCR:** Bilingualism; Children; Reading; Sociolinguistics.

6218 Garza, Ana. ESL in the bilingual classroom. BILINGUAL JOURNAL, Vol. 6, no. 4 (Summer 1982), p. 26-29,32. English. **DESCR:** *Bilingual Bicultural Education; Bilingual Inventory of Natural Languages; *English as a Second Language; Language Assessment Battery; Language Assessment Scales.

6219 McGroarty, Mary. English language test, school language use, and achievement in Spanish-speaking high school students. TESOL QUARTERLY, Vol. 17, no. 2 (June 1983), p. 310-311. English. **DESCR:** Academic Achievement; *English as a Second Language; High School Students.

6220 Politzer, Robert L.; Shohamy, Elana; and McGroarty, Mary. Validation of linguistic and communicative oral language tests for Spanish-English bilingual programs. BILINGUAL REVIEW, Vol. 10, no. 1 (January, April, 1983), p. 3-20. English. **DESCR:** Bahia Oral Language Test (BOLT); Bay Area, CA; *Bilingual Bicultural Education; Bilingual Programs; Linguistics; Sociolinguistics.

6221 Walia, Adorna. Book review of: BILINGUAL EDUCATION TEACHER HANDBOOK: LANGUAGE ISSUES IN MULTICULTURAL SETTINGS. vol. II. BILINGUAL JOURNAL, Vol. 6, no. 1 (Fall 1982), p. 29-30. English. **DESCR:** Bilingual Bicultural Education; *BILINGUAL EDUCATION TEACHER HANDBOOK: LANGUAGE ISSUES IN MULTICULTURAL SETTINGS, VOL II; Book Reviews; Cultural Pluralism; Montero, Martha.

Language Assessment Scales

6222 Garza, Ana. ESL in the bilingual classroom. BILINGUAL JOURNAL, Vol. 6, no. 4 (Summer 1982), p. 26-29,32. English. **DESCR:** *Bilingual Bicultural Education; Bilingual Inventory of Natural Languages; *English as a Second Language; Language Assessment; Language Assessment Battery.

Language Assessment Battery

6223 DeMauro, Gerald E. Models and assumptions for bilingual education evaluation. BILINGUAL JOURNAL, Vol. 7, no. 2 (Winter 1983), p. 8-12,40. English. DESCR: *Bilingual Bicultural Education; Curriculum; Educational Tests and Measurements; *Evaluation (Educational).

6224 Garza, Ana. ESL in the bilingual classroom. BILINGUAL JOURNAL, Vol. 6, no. 4 (Summer 1982), p. 26-29,32. English. DESCR: *Bilingual Bicultural Education; Bilingual Inventory of Natural Languages; *English as a Second Language; Language Assessment; Language Assessment Scales.

Language Development

6225 Arce, Carlos H. Language shift among Chicanos: strategies for measuring and assessing direction and rate. SOCIAL SCIENCE JOURNAL, Vol. 19, no. 2 (April 1982), p. 121-132. English. DESCR: Bilingualism; Research Methodology; *Spanish Language.

6226 Armengol, Armando; Manley, Joan H.; and Teschner, Richard V. The international bilingual city: how a university meets the challenge. FOREIGN LANGUAGE ANNALS, Vol. 15, no. 4 (September 1982), p. 289-295. English. DESCR: Biculturalism; Bilingualism; Border Region; Ciudad Juarez, Chihuahua, Mexico; El Paso, TX; Spanish Language; University of Texas at El Paso.

6227 Beyer, Sandra S. and Kluck, Frederick J. French via Spanish: a positive approach to language learning for minority students. FOREIGN LANGUAGE ANNALS, Vol. 15, no. 2 (April 1982), p. 123-126. English. DESCR: Educational Innovations; *French Language; Spanish Language; University of Texas at El Paso.

6228 Blake, Robert. Mood selection among Spanish-speaking children, ages 4 to 12. BILINGUAL REVIEW, Vol. 10, no. 1 (January, April, 1983), p. 21-32. English. DESCR: Children; Grammar; Language Usage; Spanish Language.

6229 Brooks, C.K. Verbal giftedness in the minority student: a NEWT questions a SOT. ENGLISH JOURNAL, Vol. 72, (January 1983), p. 18-21. English. DESCR: Cultural Pluralism; Curriculum; *Language Arts.

6230 Chesterfield, Ray, et al. The influence of teachers and peers on second language acquisition in bilingual preschool programs. TESOL QUARTERLY, Vol. 17, no. 3 (September 1983), p. 401-419. English. DESCR: Bilingual Bicultural Education; Early Childhood Education; *English as a Second Language; Teacher-pupil Interaction.

6231 Fallows, James. Language. ATLANTIC, Vol. 252, (November 1983), p. 62+. English. DESCR: *Languages; Spanish Language.

6232 Feliciano-Foster, Wilma. A comparison of three current first-year college-level Spanish-for-native-speakers textbooks. BILINGUAL REVIEW, Vol. 9, no. 1 (January, April, 1982), p. 72-81. English. DESCR: *Book Reviews; ESPANOL ESCRITO; Garza-Swan, Gloria; Mejias, Hugo A.; MEJORA TU ESPANOL; NUESTRO ESPANOL: CURSO PARA ESTUDIANTES BILINGUES; Portilla, Marta de la; Spanish Language Textbooks; Teschner, Richard V.; Valdes Fallis, Guadalupe; Varela, Beatriz.

6233 Flori, Monica. The Hispanic community as a resource for a practical Spanish program. FOREIGN LANGUAGE ANNALS, Vol. 15, no. 3 (May 1982), p. 213-215. English. DESCR: Community School Relationships; Curriculum; Educational Innovations; Lewis and Clark College, Portland, OR; *Spanish Language.

6234 Games helps study effort. NUESTRO, Vol. 6, no. 4 (May 1982), p. 11-12. English. DESCR: *Games; Language Proficiency.

6235 Gonzalez, Gustavo. Expressing time through verb tenses and temporal expressions in Spanish: age 2.0-4.6. NABE JOURNAL, Vol. 7, no. 2 (Winter 1983), p. 69-82. English. DESCR: *Bilingual Bicultural Education; *Language Usage; Spanish Language.

6236 Johnson, Donna M. Natural language learning by design: a classroom experiment in social interaction and second language acquisition. TESOL QUARTERLY, Vol. 17, no. 1 (March 1983), p. 55-68. English. DESCR: *English as a Second Language; Inter-Ethnolinguistic Peer Tutoring (IEPT); Primary School Education.

6237 Kramer, Virginia Reyes and Schell, Leo M. English auditory discrimination skills of Spanish-speaking children. ALBERTA JOURNAL OF EDUCATIONAL RESEARCH, Vol. 28, no. 1 (March 1982), p. 1-8. English. DESCR: Accentedness; Bilingualism; English Language; Spanish Language.

6238 Lado, Robert. Aula/the classroom: developmental reading in two languages. NABE JOURNAL, Vol. 6, no. 2-3 (Winter, Spring, 1981, 1982), p. 99-110. English. DESCR: Bilingual Bicultural Education; Bilingualism; Language Arts; Learning and Cognition; *Reading; Spanish Education Development (SED) Center Bilingual Reading Project; Spanish Language.

6239 Merino, Barbara J. Language development in normal and language handicapped Spanish-speaking children. HISPANIC JOURNAL OF BEHAVIORAL SCIENCES, Vol. 5, no. 4 (December 1983), p. 379-400. English. DESCR: Language Usage.

6240 Robey, Bryant. Speaking of Hispanics. AMERICAN DEMOGRAPHICS, Vol. 5, (June 1983), p. 2. English. DESCR: *Language Proficiency.

6241 Strong, Michael. Social styles and the second language acquisition of Spanish-speaking kindergartners. TESOL QUARTERLY, Vol. 17, no. 2 (June 1983), p. 241-258. English. DESCR: Personality; Primary School Education.

6242 Timm, Lenora A. Does code switching take time?: a comparison of results in experimental and natural setting, with some implications for bilingual language processing. HISPANIC JOURNAL OF BEHAVIORAL SCIENCES, Vol. 5, no. 4 (December 1983), p. 401-416. English. DESCR: Bilingualism.

6243 Walsh, Catherine E. The phenomenon of educated/educado: an example for a tripartite system of semantic memory. BILINGUAL REVIEW, Vol. 10, no. 1 (January, April, 1983), p. 33-40. English. DESCR: *Bilingualism; Semantics.

6244 Wiedmer, Jack. Through the language gates. NUESTRO, Vol. 6, no. 6 (August 1982), p. 29-30. English. DESCR: *Language Patterns; *Language Usage.

Language Fluency
    USE: Language Proficiency

Language Interference

6245 Ambert, Alba N. The identification of LEP
    children with special needs. BILINGUAL
    JOURNAL, Vol. 6, no. 1 (Fall 1982), p.
    17-22. English. DESCR: Cultural
    Characteristics; Handicapped;
    Limited-English Proficient (LEP); *Special
    Education.

6246 Staczek, John J. Code-switching in Miami
    Spanish: the domain of health care services.
    BILINGUAL REVIEW, Vol. 10, no. 1 (January,
    April, 1983), p. 41-46. English. DESCR:
    *Bilingualism; Medical Care; Miami, FL;
    Spanish Language.

Language Patterns

6247 Common Spanish book provided by Romagosa.
    NUESTRO, Vol. 6, no. 5 (June, July, 1982),
    p. 30. English. DESCR: Language Usage;
    Languages; *Romagosa, Guillermo.

6248 Freeman, Marion. La onda and other youthful
    Mexican expressions. HISPANIA, Vol. 66,
    (May 1983), p. 260-261. English. DESCR:
    *Slang.

6249 Lipski, John M. Spanish-English language
    switching in speech and literature: theories
    and models. BILINGUAL REVIEW, Vol. 9, no. 3
    (September, December, 1982), p. 191-212.
    English. DESCR: *Accentedness; Bilingualism.

6250 Wiedmer, Jack. Through the language gates.
    NUESTRO, Vol. 6, no. 6 (August 1982), p.
    29-30. English. DESCR: *Language
    Development; *Language Usage.

6251 Woods, Richard D. Book review of: SPANISH
    AND ENGLISH OF UNITED STATES HISPANOS: A
    CRITICAL, ANNOTATED, LINGUISTIC
    BIBLIOGRAPHY. JOURNAL OF ETHNIC STUDIES,
    Vol. 4, no. 3 (Fall 1976), p. 116. English.
    DESCR: Accentedness; Bibliography; Bills,
    Garland D.; Book Reviews; Craddock, Jerry
    R.; *SPANISH AND ENGLISH OF U.S. HISPANOS: A
    CRITICAL, ANNOTATED, LINGUISTIC
    BIBLIOGRAPHY; Spanish Language; Teschner,
    Richard V.

Language Proficiency

6252 Airport charge causes conflict. NUESTRO,
    Vol. 7, no. 7 (September 1983), p. 12.
    English. DESCR: Bilingualism; *Tucson
    International Airport.

6253 Buckholtz, Marjorie Weidenfeld. Technical
    training in two languages helps Houston stay
    cool. AMERICAN EDUCATION, Vol. 18, no. 3
    (April 1982), p. 11-14. English. DESCR:
    *Employment Training; Houston Community
    College; Language Arts; Vocational
    Education.

6254 Chesterfield, Kathleen Barrows and
    Chesterfield, Ray A. Peer interaction
    language proficiency and language preference
    in bilingual pre-school classrooms. HISPANIC
    JOURNAL OF BEHAVIORAL SCIENCES, Vol. 4, no.
    4 (December 1982), p. 467-486. English.
    DESCR: *Bilingual Bicultural Education;
    Children.

6255 Constantino, Guiseppe and Malgady, Robert G.
    Verbal fluency of Hispanic, Black and white
    children on TAT and TEMAS, a new thematic
    apperception test. HISPANIC JOURNAL OF
    BEHAVIORAL SCIENCES, Vol. 5, no. 2 (June

1983), p. 199-206. English. DESCR: Children;
Ethnic Groups; TAT; TEMAS.

6256 Fillmore, Lili Wong. Language minority
    students and school participation: what kind
    of English is needed? JOURNAL OF EDUCATION,
    Vol. 164, no. 2 (Spring 1982), p. 143-156.
    English. DESCR: *Bilingual Bicultural
    Education; Early Childhood Education;
    English as a Second Language.

6257 Galloway, Linda M. Bilingualism:
    neuropsychological considerations. JOURNAL
    OF RESEARCH AND DEVELOPMENT IN EDUCATION,
    Vol. 15, no. 3 (Spring 1982), p. 12-28.
    English. DESCR: *Bilingualism; Psychological
    Theory.

6258 Games helps study effort. NUESTRO, Vol. 6,
    no. 4 (May 1982), p. 11-12. English. DESCR:
    *Games; Language Development.

6259 Goldin, Mark G. Book review of: TEACHING
    SPANISH TO THE HISPANIC BILINGUAL: ISSUES,
    AIMS AND METHODS. NABE JOURNAL, Vol. 7, no.
    1 (Fall 1982), p. 53-56. English. DESCR:
    Bilingualism; Book Reviews; Garcia-Moya,
    Rodolfo; Language Usage; Lozano, Anthony G.;
    Spanish Language; *TEACHING SPANISH TO THE
    HISPANIC BILINGUAL: ISSUES, AIMS AND
    METHODS; Valdez, Guadalupe.

6260 Hernandez, Rudy. English, yes! Spanish, si!
    Spanglish, no! NUESTRO, Vol. 7, no. 8
    (October 1983), p. 53. English. DESCR:
    English Language; *Language Usage; Spanish
    Language.

6261 Robey, Bryant. Speaking of Hispanics.
    AMERICAN DEMOGRAPHICS, Vol. 5, (June 1983),
    p. 2. English. DESCR: Language Development.

6262 Savage, David G. Is the market going
    English? HISPANIC BUSINESS, Vol. 4, no. 12
    (December 1982), p. 20-21. English. DESCR:
    English Language; *Language Usage; *Spanish
    Language.

6263 Schon, Isabel; Hopkins, Kenneth D.; and
    Davis, W. Alan. Effects of books in Spanish
    and free reading time on Hispanic students'
    reading abilities and attitudes. NABE
    JOURNAL, Vol. 7, no. 1 (Fall 1982), p.
    13-20. English. DESCR: Bilingual Bicultural
    Education; *Language Arts; *Reading; Spanish
    Language.

6264 Tienda, Marta. Sex, ethnicity and Chicano
    status attainment. INTERNATIONAL MIGRATION
    REVIEW, Vol. 16, no. 2 (Summer 1982), p.
    435-473. English. DESCR: Academic
    Achievement; Chicanas; Discrimination in
    Education; Discrimination in Employment;
    Identity; Income; Sexism; *Social Classes;
    Social Mobility.

6265 Yvon, Bernard R. Effects of the language of
    a diagnostic test on math scores. BILINGUAL
    JOURNAL, Vol. 6, no. 1 (Fall 1982), p.
    13-16. English. DESCR: Bilingual Bicultural
    Education; *Educational Tests and
    Measurements; Key-Math Diagnostic Test;
    Mathematics.

Language Usage

6266 Blake, Robert. Mood selection among
    Spanish-speaking children, ages 4 to 12.
    BILINGUAL REVIEW, Vol. 10, no. 1 (January,
    April, 1983), p. 21-32. English. DESCR:
    Children; Grammar; *Language Development;
    Spanish Language.

Language Usage (cont.)

6267 Common Spanish book provided by Romagosa. NUESTRO, Vol. 6, no. 5 (June, July, 1982), p. 30. English. **DESCR**: Language Patterns; Languages; *Romagosa, Guillermo.

6268 Engle, Margarita Mondrus. Quien mato a la geografia? LATINO, Vol. 54, no. 8 (December 1983), p. 14. English. **DESCR**: *Geography.

6269 Goldin, Mark G. Book review of: TEACHING SPANISH TO THE HISPANIC BILINGUAL: ISSUES, AIMS AND METHODS. NABE JOURNAL, Vol. 7, no. 1 (Fall 1982), p. 53-56. English. **DESCR**: Bilingualism; Book Reviews; Garcia-Moya, Rodolfo; Language Proficiency; Lozano, Anthony G.; Spanish Language; *TEACHING SPANISH TO THE HISPANIC BILINGUAL: ISSUES, AIMS AND METHODS; Valdez, Guadalupe.

6270 Gonzalez, Gustavo. Expressing time through verb tenses and temporal expressions in Spanish: age 2.0-4.6. NABE JOURNAL, Vol. 7, no. 2 (Winter 1983), p. 69-82. English. **DESCR**: *Bilingual Bicultural Education; *Language Development; Spanish Language.

6271 Gumperz, John J. Interethnic discourse. SOCIETY, Vol. 20, no. 4 (May, June, 1983), p. 64-69. English. **DESCR**: *Sociolinguistics.

6272 Hernandez, Rudy. English, yes! Spanish, si! Spanglish, no! NUESTRO, Vol. 7, no. 8 (October 1983), p. 53. English. **DESCR**: English Language; Language Proficiency; Spanish Language.

6273 Martinez, Douglas R. American spelling bee: enchilada, llano, amigo, maraca. NUESTRO, Vol. 7, no. 5 (June, July, 1983), p. 50-51. English. **DESCR**: American Spelling Bee; Language Arts; *Linguistics.

6274 Merino, Barbara J. Language development in normal and language handicapped Spanish-speaking children. HISPANIC JOURNAL OF BEHAVIORAL SCIENCES, Vol. 5, no. 4 (December 1983), p. 379-400. English. **DESCR**: *Language Development.

6275 Savage, David G. Is the market going English? HISPANIC BUSINESS, Vol. 4, no. 12 (December 1982), p. 20-21. English. **DESCR**: English Language; Language Proficiency; *Spanish Language.

6276 Volsky, George. Miami's radio S-U-A-A-V-E. HISPANIC BUSINESS, Vol. 4, no. 12 (December 1982), p. 22,35. English. **DESCR**: Advertising; Broadcast Media; Marketing; Miami, FL; *Radio; Radio Station SUAVE, Miami, FL; *Radio Stations; Spanish Language.

6277 Walia, Adorna. Book review of: WOMEN AND MEN SPEAKING: FRAMEWORK FOR ANALYSIS. BILINGUAL JOURNAL, Vol. 6, no. 3 (Spring 1982), p. 20-22. English. **DESCR**: Book Reviews; Kramarae, Cheris; Sex Stereotypes; Sexism; Sociolinguistics; *WOMEN AND MEN SPEAKING: FRAMEWORK FOR ANALYSIS.

6278 Wiedmer, Jack. Through the language gates. NUESTRO, Vol. 6, no. 6 (August 1982), p. 29-30. English. **DESCR**: *Language Development; *Language Patterns.

Languages

6279 Barclay, Lisa K. Using Spanish as the language of instruction with Mexican-American Head Start children: a re-evaluation using meta-analysis.

PERCEPTUAL AND MOTOR SKILLS, Vol. 56, no. 2-4 (1983), p. 359-366. English. **DESCR**: Education; Psychological Testing; *Spanish Language.

6280 Common Spanish book provided by Romagosa. NUESTRO, Vol. 6, no. 5 (June, July, 1982), p. 30. English. **DESCR**: Language Patterns; Language Usage; *Romagosa, Guillermo.

6281 Elsenberg, Ann R. Book review of: LATINO LANGUAGE AND COMMUNICATIVE BEHAVIOR. HISPANIC JOURNAL OF BEHAVIORAL SCIENCES, Vol. 5, no. 3 (September 1983), p. 347-349. English. **DESCR**: Book Reviews; Duran, Richard P.; *LATINO LANGUAGE AND COMMUNICATIVE BEHAVIOR; Sociolinguistics.

6282 Fallows, James. Language. ATLANTIC, Vol. 252, (November 1983), p. 62+. English. **DESCR**: Language Development; Spanish Language.

6283 Karno, M. Development of the Spanish-language version of the National Institute of Mental Health Diagnostic Interview Schedule. ARCHIVES OF GENERAL PSYCHIATRY, Vol. 40, no. 11 (November 1983), p. 1183-1188. English. **DESCR**: Culture; Mental Health; *National Institute of Mental Health Diagnostic Interview Schedule; Spanish Language.

6284 State considers English bill. NUESTRO, Vol. 6, no. 3 (April 1982), p. 12-13. English. **DESCR**: Bilingual Bicultural Education.

Laredo, TX

6285 Deibel, Richard. Business along la frontera. HISPANIC BUSINESS, Vol. 5, no. 1 (January 1983), p. 14-15. English. **DESCR**: Border Region; *Currency; Mexico.

6286 Deibel, Richard and Balkan, D. Carlos. The nation's largest little bank: Laredo's International Bank of Commerce. HISPANIC BUSINESS, Vol. 4, no. 9 (September 1982), p. 10-11,24. English. **DESCR**: Banking Industry; Business Enterprises; *International Bank of Commerce (IBOC).

Laredo, TX, Chamber of Commerce

6287 Cantu, Hector. Border business report: the Rio Grande Valley's economy and Mexico's lingering peso devaluation effects. NATIONAL HISPANIC JOURNAL, Vol. 2, no. 1 (Summer 1983), p. 10-13. English. **DESCR**: Aguirre, Lionel; Border Region; Cano, Eddie; Coors Distributing Company, McAllen, TX; Cruz, Conrado; Cuevas, Betty; *Currency; Economic Development; Mexican American Chamber of Commerce, Austin, TX; United States-Mexico Relations.

Lasa, Luis

6288 Chavarria, Jesus. How long will it last? HISPANIC BUSINESS, Vol. 4, no. 1 (January 1982), p. 6. English. **DESCR**: Anselmo, Rene; Businesspeople; *Marketing; Spanish International Network (SIN).

6289 Whitefield, Mimi. Mr. Lasa's 400,000 cases of rum. HISPANIC BUSINESS, Vol. 4, no. 1 (January 1982), p. 14-15+. English. **DESCR**: *Bacardi Imports, Inc.; *Biography; Marketing.

**THE LATER YEARS: SOCIAL APPLICATIONS OF
GERONTOLOGY**

6290 Burke, Leslie K. Book review of: THE LATER
YEARS: SOCIAL APPLICATIONS OF GERONTOLOGY.
HISPANIC JOURNAL OF BEHAVIORAL SCIENCES,
Vol. 4, no. 1 (March 1982), p. 116-117.
English. DESCR: Book Reviews; Kalish,
Richard A.

Latin America

6291 Business/negocios. CAMINOS, Vol. 3, no. 2
(February 1982), p. 22-23. Bilingual.
DESCR: Argentina; Brazil; *Business; Chile;
Colombia; Federation of Minority Business
Associations; FRANCHISE OPPORTUNITIES
HANDBOOK.

6292 Chamber, Peace Corps join in training
effort. NUESTRO, Vol. 7, no. 1 (January,
February, 1983), p. 36. English. DESCR:
Business; Caribbean Basin Initiative (CBI);
*Ibero-American Chamber of Commerce; Peace
Corps.

6293 Foreign trade. HISPANIC BUSINESS, Vol. 5,
no. 5 (May 1983), p. 32. English. DESCR:
Caribbean Region; Export Trade; *Foreign
Trade; Minority Business Development Agency
(MBDA); Panama.

6294 Foreign trade: outlook for the Caribbean
Basin Initiative. HISPANIC BUSINESS, Vol. 4,
no. 8 (August 1983), p. 23+. English.
DESCR: *Caribbean Basin Initiative (CBI);
*Foreign Trade; International Economic
Relations.

6295 Fraser Rothenberg, Irene. Mexican-American
views of U.S. relations with Latin America.
JOURNAL OF ETHNIC STUDIES, Vol. 6, no. 1
(Spring 1978), p. 62-78. English. DESCR:
Chicano Movement; Culture; Identity;
International Relations; Lobbying; Mexico;
*Nationalism; Political History and
Conditions; Politics.

6296 Garcia Marquez, Gabriel. La soledad de la
America Latina. LATINO, Vol. 54, no. 1
(January, February, 1983), p. 9. Spanish.
DESCR: *Latin Americans.

6297 Goldman, Shifra. Mexican muralism: its
social-educative roles in Latin America and
the United States. AZTLAN, Vol. 13, no. 1-2
(Spring, Fall, 1982), p. 111-133. Spanish.
DESCR: Art; *Mexico; *Mural Art; Social
History and Conditions.

6298 Gonzalez, Raymond J. U.S. support of
military in Latin America. CAMINOS, Vol. 4,
no. 8 (September 1983), p. 18-19,50.
Bilingual. DESCR: *International Relations;
United States.

6299 Heuer, Robert J. Baseball expansion: why not
Latin America? NUESTRO, Vol. 7, no. 10
(December 1983), p. 41. English. DESCR:
*Baseball; Sports.

6300 Hornbeck, David. Book review of: STUDIES IN
SPANISH-AMERICAN POPULATION HISTORY.
PROFESSIONAL GEOGRAPHER, Vol. 34, no. 4
(1982), p. 480. English. DESCR: Book
Reviews; Demography; Robinson, David J.;
*STUDIES IN SPANISH-AMERICAN POPULATION
HISTORY.

6301 Huerta, Jorge A. The influences of Latin
American theatre on teatro Chicano. REVISTA
CHICANO-RIQUENA, Vol. 11, no. 1 (Spring
1983), p. 68-77. English. DESCR: *El Teatro
Campesino; Teatro; Valdez, Luis.

6302 The Inter-American Development Bank at work
(photoessay). CAMINOS, Vol. 4, no. 8
(September 1983), p. 22-25. English. DESCR:
Banking Industry; Economic Development;
*Inter-American Development Bank.

6303 Latin America booming. HISPANIC BUSINESS,
Vol. 4, no. 1 (January 1982), p. 25.
English. DESCR: *Economics.

6304 Palacios, Gonzalo. Bolivar and contemporary
Latin America. NUESTRO, Vol. 7, no. 7
(September 1983), p. 36-37. English. DESCR:
*Bolivar, Simon; Political History and
Conditions; Political Ideology; South
America.

6305 Pena-Ramos, Alfonso. The Latin American
disease: an essay. NUESTRO, Vol. 7, no. 6
(August 1983), p. 42-43. English. DESCR:
*Political History and Conditions;
Revolutions; Social History and Conditions.

6306 Regional report, Latin America: marchers
oppose Reagan policies. NUESTRO, Vol. 7, no.
4 (May 1983), p. 11. English. DESCR: Central
America; Demonstrations; International
Relations; *Reagan, Ronald; Stanford
University, Stanford, CA.

6307 Rios-Bustamante, Antonio. The Pan American
games 1951-1983. CAMINOS, Vol. 4, no. 8
(September 1983), p. 31-33,51+. Bilingual.
DESCR: History; *Pan American Games;
*Sports.

6308 Salvatierra, Richard. Debtors' row expands
in Latin America. NUESTRO, Vol. 6, no. 9
(November 1982), p. 34-35. English. DESCR:
Banking Industry; Debt; Economics.

6309 Serafino, Nina M. U.S.-Latinoamerican
relations: 1960 to the present. CAMINOS,
Vol. 4, no. 8 (September 1983), p. 6-8,48.
Bilingual. DESCR: History; *International
Relations; United States; United
States-Mexico Relations.

6310 Valdez, Abelardo L. From Simon Bolivar to
the Malvinas and beyond. NUESTRO, Vol. 7,
no. 7 (September 1983), p. 38-41. English.
DESCR: *Bolivar, Simon; Political Economy;
*Political History and Conditions; South
America.

Latin American Feature Syndicate (ALA)

6311 Communications/marketing. HISPANIC BUSINESS,
Vol. 5, no. 2 (February 1983), p. 23.
English. DESCR: *Broadcast Media; Coopers
and Lybrand; Domecq Importers, Inc.; *Mass
Media; Phoenix, AZ.

**Latin American Library/Biblioteca Latinoamericana,
Oakland, CA**

6312 Naismith, Rachael. Outreach services to
Hispanics. ILLINOIS LIBRARIES, Vol. 64, no.
7 (September 1982), p. 962-966. English.
DESCR: Arrondo, Ondina; Cubanos; La Raza
Hispanica, Miami, FL; *Library Services;
Lopez, Lillian; Puerto Ricans; Ruiz,
Deborah; South Bronx Project, New York
Public Library; Verges, Bruni.

Latin American Literature

6313 Araya, Juan Gabriel. La autocontemplacion
literaria en LIBRO DE MANUEL. MAIZE, Vol. 6,
no. 3-4 (Spring, Summer, 1983), p. 7-16.
Spanish. DESCR: *Cortazar, Julio; Literary
Characteristics; Literary Criticism; Novel.

Latin American Literature (cont.)

6314 Espinoza, Roberto. Sintesis vs. analysis: un problema de historicidad en las novelas de las dictaduras. MAIZE, Vol. 6, no. 1-2 (Fall, Winter, 1982, 1983), p. 7-27. Spanish. DESCR: Carpentier, Alejo; Dictatorships; Garcia Marquez, Gabriel; *Literary Criticism; Novel; Roa Bastos, Augustos; Valle Inclan, Ramon; White, Lucas Edward.

6315 Forster, Merlin H. Luis Leal. LA PALABRA, Vol. 4, no. 1-2 (Spring, Fall, 1982, 1983), p. 19-20. Spanish. DESCR: Authors; *Biography; Higher Education; *Leal, Luis; Teaching Profession.

6316 Gonzalez Cruz, Luis F. Quest and discovery in Oscar Hurtado's THE DEAD CITY OF KORAD: a unique experiment in science fiction poetry. MAIZE, Vol. 5, no. 1-2 (Fall, Winter, 1981, 1982), p. 74-85. English. DESCR: Cuba; *Hurtado, Oscar; *Literary Criticism; Poetry.

6317 Hinojosa-Smith, Rolando R. Luis (el amigo) Leal. LA PALABRA, Vol. 4, no. 1-2 (Spring, Fall, 1982, 1983), p. 17-18. Spanish. DESCR: Authors; *Biography; *Leal, Luis; Literature.

6318 Lamento por la jubilacion de un insigne hispanista y viejo amigo (una carta anonima). LA PALABRA, Vol. 4, no. 1-2 (Spring, Fall, 1982, 1983), p. 21-24. Spanish. DESCR: Authors; *Biography; Higher Education; *Leal, Luis; Teaching Profession.

6319 Lomeli, Francisco A. Don Luis. LA PALABRA, Vol. 4, no. 1-2 (Spring, Fall, 1982, 1983), p. IX-XI. Spanish. DESCR: Authors; *Biography; *Leal, Luis; Literature.

6320 Lomeli, Francisco A. Entrevista con Luis Leal. LA PALABRA, Vol. 4, no. 1-2 (Spring, Fall, 1982, 1983), p. 3-15. Spanish. DESCR: Authors; *Biography; *Leal, Luis; Literature; Oral History.

6321 Sohn, Jeanne and Davidson, Russ. Out of the morass: acquiring Spanish language materials from Latin America. LIBRARY JOURNAL, Vol. 10, no. 13 (July 1982), p. 1290-1293. English. DESCR: *Library Collections; Library Services; Spanish Language.

6322 Uriarte, Ivan. Introduccion a la poesia revolucionaria de El Salvador. MAIZE, Vol. 6, no. 1-2 (Fall, Winter, 1982, 1983), p. 34-40. Spanish. DESCR: *El Salvador; *Poetry; Revolutions.

Latin American Studies

6323 Ericksen, Charles and Treviso, Ruben. Latino journalists make their move. NUESTRO, Vol. 6, no. 5 (June, July, 1982), p. 45-47. English. DESCR: California Chicano News Media Association (CCNMA); *Journalists.

6324 Turnure, Juan C. Hemisphere bulletin. AGENDA, Vol. 11, no. 3 (May, June, 1981), p. 56-57. English. DESCR: *Economics; Latin Americans; Politics.

Latin Americans

6325 1982 business persons announced by chamber. NUESTRO, Vol. 6, no. 5 (June, July, 1982), p. 44. English. DESCR: *Roubin, Angel; *Vasquez, Victor.

6326 Altman, Barbara. El Salvador. LATINO, Vol.

54, no. 4 (May, June, 1983), p. 10-11. English. DESCR: *El Salvador; War.

6327 Cayer, Shirley. Chicago's new Hispanic health alliance. NUESTRO, Vol. 7, no. 5 (June, July, 1983), p. 44-48. English. DESCR: Alcoholism; Chicago Hispanic Health Alliance; Family Planning; *Health Education; *Medical Care.

6328 Costas, Orlando E. The Hispanics next door. CHRISTIAN CENTURY, Vol. 99, no. 26 (August 18, 1982), p. 851-856. English. DESCR: Cultural Pluralism; *Liberation Theology; Religion.

6329 Dienhart, Paul. Minnesota support groups help Latinos through medical school. NUESTRO, Vol. 6, no. 6 (August 1982), p. 39-40. English. DESCR: Health Education; Medical Education; Medical Students; Minnesota; Public Health; *University of Minnesota.

6330 Gallegos, Herman. Making a dent in the corporate hierarchy. NUESTRO, Vol. 6, no. 9 (November 1982), p. 49-51. English. DESCR: *Economic History and Conditions; *Economics.

6331 Garcia, Ignacio M. Linda Ramirez: labor leader. NUESTRO, Vol. 6, no. 5 (June, July, 1982), p. 26-28. English. DESCR: *Labor; Labor Unions; Leadership; Ramirez, Linda; San Antonio, TX.

6332 Garcia, Ignacio M. Regional report, television: "Condo" canceled. NUESTRO, Vol. 7, no. 5 (June, July, 1983), p. 13. English. DESCR: Avalos, Luis; Carmen, Julie; CONDO [televison series]; Stereotypes; *Television.

6333 Garcia Marquez, Gabriel. La soledad de la America Latina. LATINO, Vol. 54, no. 1 (January, February, 1983), p. 9. Spanish. DESCR: *Latin America.

6334 Garcia, Paco. Voices: Hispanic voices needed in the education debate. NUESTRO, Vol. 7, no. 5 (June, July, 1983), p. 53-54. English. DESCR: Bilingual Bicultural Education; *Discrimination in Education; *Discrimination in Employment; *Education; Federal Government; President's Commission on Excellence in Education; Reagan, Ronald; U.S. Department of Health, Education and Welfare (HEW).

6335 Gaviria, Moises and Wintrob, Ronald. Latin American medical graduates: I. determinants of the decision to remain in the United States. HISPANIC JOURNAL OF BEHAVIORAL SCIENCES, Vol. 4, no. 1 (March 1982), p. 89-101. English. DESCR: Medical Education; Medical Personnel; *Medical Students.

6336 Gente. NUESTRO, Vol. 7, no. 1 (January, February, 1983), p. 63. English. DESCR: Amaya-Espinoza, Isidro; Camargo, Mateo G.; Musicians; Prieto, Carlos; Radio; Sports; Trevino, Lee.

Latin Americans (cont.)

6337 Hing, Bill Ong. Racial disparity: the unaddressed issues of the Simpson-Mazzoli Bill. LA RAZA LAW JOURNAL, Vol. 1, no. 1 (June 1983), p. 21-52. English. DESCR: Amnesty; Asian Americans; Ethnic Attitudes; Family; Immigration; Immigration and Naturalization Service (INS); Mazzoli, Romano L.; Mexican American Legal Defense and Educational Fund (MALDEF); Simpson, Alan K.; *Simpson-Mazzoli Bill; Temporary Worker Program; U.S. Congresssional Subcommittee on Immigration, Refugees and International Law.

6338 Jaech, Richard E. Latin American undocumented women in the United States. CURRENTS IN THEOLOGY AND MISSION, Vol. 9, no. 4 (August 1982), p. 196-211. English. DESCR: Garment Industry; Protestant Church; Socioeconomic Factors; *Undocumented Workers; *Women.

6339 Latinas on the march, NUESTRO survey reveals: organizations assess achievements during 1981. NUESTRO, Vol. 6, no. 2 (March 1982), p. 16-28+. English. DESCR: Forum of National Hispanic Organizations; Hispanic Health Council; League of United Latin American Citizens (LULAC); National Coalition of Hispanic Mental Health and Human Services Organizations (COSSMHO); National Council of La Raza (NCLR); National Hispanic Bar Association; *National Image, Inc.; National Puerto Rican Forum, Inc.; *Organizations; Yzaguirre, Raul.

6340 Latino business study launched by chamber. NUESTRO, Vol. 6, no. 3 (April 1982), p. 45. English. DESCR: *Business.

6341 Latino vs. Latino. LATINO, Vol. 54, no. 8 (December 1983), p. 21+. English.

6342 Latinos from 21 states attend chamber confab. NUESTRO, Vol. 6, no. 6 (August 1982), p. 51. English. DESCR: Conventions; *U.S. Chamber of Commerce.

6343 Navarrete, Diana. Broadcasting role model. NUESTRO, Vol. 6, no. 1 (January, February, 1982), p. 22-23. English. DESCR: Broadcast Media; Fashion; *Navarrete, Diana.

6344 New Salazar building. NUESTRO, Vol. 6, no. 7 (September 1982), p. 9. English. DESCR: *Art; Culture; Education; Los Angeles, CA; *Plaza de La Raza, Los Angeles, CA; Salazar, Ruben.

6345 Padilla, Steve. Working for the F.B.I. NUESTRO, Vol. 6, no. 8 (October 1982), p. 15-17. English. DESCR: Arras, Raymundo; *Federal Bureau of Investigation (FBI); Marquez, Manuel; Perez, Matthew.

6346 Politicians you didn't vote for. NUESTRO, Vol. 5, no. 8 (November 1981), p. 18-20. English. DESCR: Burgillo, Luis; *Congressional Aides; Political Parties and Organizations; *Politics.

6347 Three Latinos in training. NUESTRO, Vol. 6, no. 5 (June, July, 1982), p. 10-11. English. DESCR: *Sports.

6348 Turnure, Juan C. Hemisphere bulletin. AGENDA, Vol. 11, no. 3 (May, June, 1981), p. 56-57. English. DESCR: *Economics; Latin American Studies; Politics.

6349 Velez, Larry A. Sonia Berdequez; police detective. NUESTRO, Vol. 6, no. 1 (January, February, 1982), p. 20-21. English. DESCR: *Berdeguez, Sonia Estela; Fashion; Police.

LATINA [magazine]

6350 Dear reader. LATINA, Vol. 1, no. 2 (February, March, 1983), p. 92-94. English. DESCR: Market Research.

6351 Soto, Grace. Editorial. LATINA, Vol. 1, no. 3 (1983), p. 4. English. DESCR: Chicanas; Editorials.

Latino Awards

6352 Our 1982 Latino awards. NUESTRO, Vol. 7, no. 1 (January, February, 1983), p. 44-46. English. DESCR: Awards; Escalante, Jaime; Gallegos, Gina; Grace, J. Peter; Immigration and Naturalization Service (INS); Knight, Bobby; Lamas, Fernando; Luce, Claire Boothe; Moreno, Rita; National Press Foundation; Rodriguez Hernandez, Andres; Simpson-Mazzoli Bill; Smith, Raymond; Valeri, Michele; Voting Rights Act.

Latino Business Students Association (LBSA)

6353 Community watching: para la comunidad. CAMINOS, Vol. 3, no. 3 (March 1982), p. 58-59. Bilingual. DESCR: Cultural Organizations; *Engineering as a Profession; Financial Aid; Harvard University; Rodolfo H. Castro Fellowship; Society for Hispanic Professional Engineers (SHPE); Student Organizations; University of Southern California.

6354 The future beckons, USC's LBSA responds. HISPANIC BUSINESS, Vol. 4, no. 4 (April 1982), p. 12, 25. English. DESCR: Business; Business Education; Business Schools and Colleges; Educational Opportunities; University of Southern California.

Latino Consortium, Los Angeles, CA

6355 Communications/marketing. HISPANIC BUSINESS, Vol. 5, no. 6 (June 1983), p. 16. English. DESCR: *Advertising Agencies; *Broadcast Media; Castillo & Castillo Public Relations and Advertising; Castillo, Cid; Castillo, Patricia; Montemayor, Carlos R.; Montemayor y Asociados, Inc.; Zubi Inc., Miami, FL.

LATINO LANGUAGE AND COMMUNICATIVE BEHAVIOR

6356 Elsenberg, Ann R. Book review of: LATINO LANGUAGE AND COMMUNICATIVE BEHAVIOR. HISPANIC JOURNAL OF BEHAVIORAL SCIENCES, Vol. 5, no. 3 (September 1983), p. 347-349. English. DESCR: Book Reviews; Duran, Richard P.; Languages; Sociolinguistics.

LATINO [magazine]

6357 Support LATINO MAGAZINE. LATINO, Vol. 53, no. 2 (March, April, 1982), p. 21. English. DESCR: Magazines.

Latino Olympians Project

6358 Rios-Bustamante, Antonio. The Latino Olympians project and what it means to you. CAMINOS, Vol. 4, no. 4 (April 1983), p. 19. Bilingual. DESCR: Mass Media; Olympics; Sports.

LATINOS IN THE LAW [symposium], UCLA, 1982

6359 de Avila, Edward A. [Combining political strategies for effective representation]. CHICANO LAW REVIEW, Vol. 6, (1983), p. 24-29. English. DESCR: *Voter Turnout.

LATINOS IN THE LAW [symposium], UCLA, 1982 (cont.)

6360 Estrada, Leobardo F. [Demographic
characteristics of Latinos]. CHICANO LAW
REVIEW, Vol. 6, (1983), p. 9-16. English.
DESCR: *Demography; Internal Migration; Los
Angeles County, CA; Migration; Migration
Patterns; Spanish Language.

6361 Santillan, Richard. [Translating population
numbers into political power]. CHICANO LAW
REVIEW, Vol. 6, (1983), p. 16-21. English.
DESCR: Californios for Fair Representation;
Carrillo v. Whittier Union High School;
MEXICAN AMERICAN LEGAL DEFENSE AND
EDUCATIONAL FUND NEWSLETTER; Political
Representation; Reapportionment; *Voter
Turnout.

6362 Valadez, Esther. [The role of the Latina].
CHICANO LAW REVIEW, Vol. 6, (1983), p.
21-24. English. **DESCR:** *Chicanas; Voter
Turnout.

Latta, Frank F.

6363 Mathes, W. Michael. Book review of: JOAQUIN
MURRIETA AND HIS HORSE GANGS. CALIFORNIA
HISTORY, Vol. 61, no. 4 (1983), p. 306-308.
English. **DESCR:** Book Reviews; California;
History; *Murieta, Joaquin.

Lau v. Nichols

6364 Rossier, Robert E. Bilingual education:
training for the ghetto. POLICY REVIEW, Vol.
25, (Summer 1983), p. 36-45. English.
DESCR: *Bilingual Bicultural Education;
Bilingualism; Immigrants.

Laviera, Tato

6365 Clarke, Gerard R. Book review of: LA CARRETA
MADE A U-TURN. MELUS: MULTI-ETHNIC
LITERATURE OF THE UNITED STATES, Vol. 8, no.
1 (Spring 1981), p. 81-83. English. **DESCR:**
LA CARRETA MADE A U-TURN.

Law

6366 Nuestra gente. LATINO, Vol. 54, no. 5
(August, September, 1983), p. 29. English.
DESCR: Criminal Justice System; Paintings.

Law School Admission Test (LSAT)

6367 Minority access to legal education. HISPANIC
BUSINESS, Vol. 5, no. 4 (April 1983), p.
29-30. English. **DESCR:** *Legal Education;
Melendez v. Burciaga.

Law Schools

6368 Flores, Rogelio. The struggle for minority
admissions: the UCLA experience. CHICANO LAW
REVIEW, Vol. 5, (1982), p. 1-12. English.
DESCR: Bakke v. Regents of University of
California; Legal Education; Legal
Profession; Student Organizations; Students;
UCLA Law School.

6369 Moss, Bernard H. Political values and career
aspirations of UCLA law students: the 70's
generation. CHICANO LAW REVIEW, Vol. 5,
(1982), p. 13-28. English. **DESCR:** Legal
Education; Legal Profession; Political
Ideology; Student Movements; Students.

Laws

6370 Brasch, Walter M. Hanigan case: hung up on
racism? SOUTH ATLANTIC QUARTERLY, Vol. 81,
no. 4 (Fall 1982), p. 429-435. English.
DESCR: Administration of Justice; Arizona;
Criminal Justice System; Garcia-Loya,
Manuel; *Hanigan, Patrick; Hanigan, Tom;
Herrera-Mata, Bernabe; Racism;
Ruelas-Zavala, Eleazar; Undocumented
Workers.

6371 Haft, Jonathan D. Assuring equal educational
opportunity for language-minority students:
bilingual education and the Equal
Educational Opportunity Act of 1974.
COLUMBIA JOURNAL OF LAW AND SOCIAL PROBLEMS,
Vol. 18, no. 2 (1983), p. 209-293. English.
DESCR: *Bilingual Bicultural Education;
Civil Rights; Educational Law and
Legislation; English as a Second Language;
*Equal Educational Opportunity Act of 1974
(EEOA); Students.

6372 Holley, Joe. Farmworker wins the right to
sue. TEXAS OBSERVOR, Vol. 74, no. 13 (July
9, 1982), p. 15. English. **DESCR:**
*Agricultural Laborers; Donna Fruit Company;
Legal Representation; Occupational Hazards;
*Torrez, Juan.

6373 SIN seeks FCC review of Hughes performance.
NUESTRO, Vol. 6, no. 1 (January, February,
1982), p. 50. English. **DESCR:** *Spanish
International Network (SIN); Television.

6374 Young, Rowland L. Exclusion hearing enough
for illegal alien smuggler. AMERICAN BAR
ASSOCIATION JOURNAL, Vol. 69, (March 1983),
p. 352. English. **DESCR:** Chicana Welfare
Rights Organization; Landon v. Plasencia;
*Undocumented Workers.

Lawyers
USE: Legal Profession

Lead Poisoning

6375 Bose, Aruna; Vashistha, Krishan; and
O'Loughlin, Bernard J. Azarcon por empacho -
another cause of lead toxicity. PEDIATRICS,
Vol. 72, no. 1 (July 1983), p. 106-108.
English. **DESCR:** Children; Folk Medicine;
Public Health.

Leadership

6376 100 influentials survey findings. HISPANIC
BUSINESS, Vol. 5, no. 5 (May 1983), p. 36+.
English. **DESCR:** *Surveys.

6377 Balkan, D. Carlos. 100 influentials and
their critical issues for the eighties.
HISPANIC BUSINESS, Vol. 5, no. 5 (May 1983),
p. 14-22. English. **DESCR:** *Surveys.

6378 Chavarria, Jesus. Assembling 100
influentials. HISPANIC BUSINESS, Vol. 5, no.
5 (May 1983), p. 6. English.

6379 Day, Mark R. and Ramirez, Ricardo (Bishop of
Las Cruces, NM),. Bishop: why have we had to
wait so long for Hispanic leaders. NATIONAL
CATHOLIC REPORTER, Vol. 19, (December 24,
1982), p. 6-7. English. **DESCR:** Catholic
Church; *Clergy; *Ramirez, Ricardo (Bishop
of Las Cruces, NM).

6380 Garcia, Ignacio M. Linda Ramirez: labor
leader. NUESTRO, Vol. 6, no. 5 (June, July,
1982), p. 26-28. English. **DESCR:** *Labor;
Labor Unions; Latin Americans; Ramirez,
Linda; San Antonio, TX.

Leadership (cont.)

6381 Garza, Raymond T., et al. Biculturalism, locus of control and leader behavior in ethnically mixed small groups. JOURNAL OF APPLIED SOCIAL PSYCHOLOGY, Vol. 12, no. 3 (May, June, 1982), p. 237-253. English. **DESCR:** Attitude (Psychological); *Biculturalism; Culture; Interpersonal Relations; *Locus of Control; Social Psychology.

6382 Mercado, Olivia. Chicanas: myths and roles. COMADRE, no. 1 (Summer 1977), p. 26-32. English. **DESCR:** *Chicanas; Gallo, Juana; Huerta, Dolores; *Identity; Sex Roles; Women's Rights.

6383 Molina-Pick, Gracia. The emergence of Chicano leadership: 1930-1950. CAMINOS, Vol. 4, no. 7 (July, August, 1983), p. 7-10. English. **DESCR:** *Chicano Movement; History.

6384 Nuestra gente. LATINO, Vol. 54, no. 3 (April 1983), p. 22. English.

6385 Rice, Jacqueline. Beyond the cientificos: the educational background of the Porfirian Elite. AZTLAN, Vol. 14, no. 2 (Fall 1983), p. 289-306. English. **DESCR:** History; La Union Liberal; *Mexico; Political History and Conditions; Political Parties and Organizations; *Social Classes.

6386 Salute to Hispanic leaders. LATINO, Vol. 54, no. 3 (April 1983), p. 15. English.

6387 School principal recognized for leadership efforts. NUESTRO, Vol. 6, no. 5 (June, July, 1982), p. 30. English. **DESCR:** Bilingual Bicultural Education; Michigan; *Ruiz, Pablo.

6388 Texas teenager wins scholarship. NUESTRO, Vol. 7, no. 10 (December 1983), p. 13. English. **DESCR:** *Financial Aid; Girl Scouts of the United States of America; *Turincio, Giovanne.

6389 Wittenauer, Cheryl. MALDEF's strategies for leadership. HISPANIC BUSINESS, Vol. 5, no. 5 (May 1983), p. 28-29. English. **DESCR:** MEXICAN AMERICAN LEGAL DEFENSE AND EDUCATIONAL FUND NEWSLETTER.

6390 Wittenauer, Cheryl. Stanford students set it straight. HISPANIC BUSINESS, Vol. 5, no. 7 (July 1983), p. 15. English. **DESCR:** Success.

6391 Youth leadership conference set. LATINO, Vol. 53, no. 8 (December 1982), p. 24. English.

Leadership, Education and Development Program in Business (LEAD)

6392 Math-based careers. HISPANIC BUSINESS, Vol. 4, no. 1 (January 1982), p. 20. English. **DESCR:** Careers; *College Graduates; *Cox, George; Employment; Engineering as a Profession; *Hispanic Society of Engineers and Scientists (HSES).

League of United Latin American Citizens (LULAC)

6393 1983 LULAC convention election excitement. LATINO, Vol. 54, no. 5 (August, September, 1983), p. 11. English. **DESCR:** Organizations.

6394 54th annual LULAC convention. LATINO, Vol. 54, no. 4 (May, June, 1983), p. 16-17. English. **DESCR:** Organizations.

6395 Alvarez, Carlos. 1983 LULAC convention.

LATINO, Vol. 54, no. 6 (October 1983), p. 8. English. **DESCR:** Cultural Organizations.

6396 Brocksbank, Bonilla are winners of LNESC award. LATINO, Vol. 53, no. 8 (December 1982), p. 26. English. **DESCR:** Bonilla, Tony; Brocksbank, Robert W.; *Education; LULAC National Education Service Centers (LNESC).

6397 Chavarria, Jesus. The two faces of progress. HISPANIC BUSINESS, Vol. 5, no. 9 (September 1983), p. 6. English. **DESCR:** *Economic History and Conditions.

6398 Communications/marketing. HISPANIC BUSINESS, Vol. 4, no. 10 (October 1982), p. 22. English. **DESCR:** Awards; ENFOQUE NACIONAL [radio program]; LULAC National Education Service Centers (LNESC); Marketing; *Mass Media.

6399 Corporate-education team. LATINO, Vol. 53, no. 2 (March, April, 1982), p. 11+. English. **DESCR:** *Business.

6400 Hamner, Richard. Hispanic update: changing of the LULAC guard--almost. NATIONAL HISPANIC JOURNAL, Vol. 1, no. 2 (Winter 1982), p. 6. English. **DESCR:** Bonilla, Ruben; Bonilla, Tony.

6401 Kincaid, Jill. LULAC opposes youth subminimum wage proposal. LATINO, Vol. 54, no. 4 (May, June, 1983), p. 27. English. **DESCR:** *Income; Youth.

6402 Latinas on the march, NUESTRO survey reveals: organizations assess achievements during 1981. NUESTRO, Vol. 6, no. 2 (March 1982), p. 16-28+. English. **DESCR:** Forum of National Hispanic Organizations; Hispanic Health Council; Latin Americans; National Coalition of Hispanic Mental Health and Human Services Organizations (COSSMHO); National Council of La Raza (NCLR); National Hispanic Bar Association; *National Image, Inc.; National Puerto Rican Forum, Inc.; *Organizations; Yzaguirre, Raul.

6403 Latinos evident in 1983 march. NUESTRO, Vol. 7, no. 7 (September 1983), p. 11-12. English. **DESCR:** Bonilla, Tony; Cuban-American Coordinating Committee; *Demonstrations; IMAGE, Washington, DC; Jackson, Jesse; National Congress for Puerto Rican Rights (NCPRR); National Council of La Raza (NCLR); Velasquez, Baldemar; Zamora, Reuben.

6404 League protests appointment to Arizona post. LATINO, Vol. 54, no. 6 (October 1983), p. 21. English. **DESCR:** *Appointed Officials; Politics.

6405 Levario, Raquel. LULAC takes a stand against mainstream media. LATINA, Vol. 1, no. 3 (1983), p. 49. English. **DESCR:** Equal Employment Opportunity Commission (EEOC); *Mass Media.

6406 Lowther, William. Reagan hunts for the Hispanic vote. MACLEANS, Vol. 96, no. 34 (August 22, 1983), p. 21-22. English. **DESCR:** Elections; Reagan, Ronald; *Voter Turnout.

6407 LULAC 1983 national convention to be in Detroit. LATINO, Vol. 53, no. 8 (December 1982), p. 25. English. **DESCR:** *Politics.

League of United Latin American Citizens (LULAC)
(cont.)

6408 LULAC: 53 years of continued achievement (photoessay). CAMINOS, Vol. 4, no. 5 (May 1983), p. 40-41. English. DESCR: Benson Latin American Collection; Organizations; University of Texas at Austin.

6409 LULAC '83: 54th annual LULAC national convention agenda. LATINO, Vol. 54, no. 4 (May, June, 1983), p. 18-19. English. DESCR: Organizations.

6410 LULAC board appointments. LATINO, Vol. 54, no. 8 (December 1983), p. 20. English. DESCR: Politics.

6411 LULAC board's Washington meeting set October 6-8. LATINO, Vol. 54, no. 5 (August, September, 1983), p. 27. English. DESCR: Organizations.

6412 LULAC files complaint against TV networks. NUESTRO, Vol. 6, no. 8 (October 1982), p. 48. English. DESCR: Bonilla, Tony; Employment; Equal Employment Opportunity Commission (EEOC); Racism; Television.

6413 LULAC foundation moves to Washington D.C. LATINO, Vol. 54, no. 5 (August, September, 1983), p. 14. English. DESCR: Organizations.

6414 LULAC is building $2.6 million housing project in Corpus Christi. LATINO, Vol. 53, no. 8 (December 1982), p. 18. English. DESCR: Corpus Christi, TX; *Housing.

6415 LULAC national scholarship fund. LATINO, Vol. 54, no. 2 (March 1983), p. 22. English. DESCR: *Design.

6416 LULAC reports new stance. NUESTRO, Vol. 6, no. 3 (April 1982), p. 13. English. DESCR: *Voter Turnout.

6417 LULAC survey approved. LATINO, Vol. 53, no. 8 (December 1982), p. 26. English. DESCR: *Surveys.

6418 LULAC train is rolling. LATINO, Vol. 53, no. 5 (September 1982), p. 9-11. English. DESCR: Politics.

6419 The LULAC/PUSH dialog. HISPANIC BUSINESS, Vol. 5, no. 4 (April 1983), p. 15. English. DESCR: Bonilla, Tony; *Economic Development; Jackson, Jesse; Operation PUSH.

6420 LULAC-Red Cross agreement. LATINO, Vol. 53, no. 8 (December 1982), p. 25. English. DESCR: *Public Health.

6421 Media/marketing. HISPANIC BUSINESS, Vol. 5, no. 12 (December 1983), p. 38. English. DESCR: Albertini, Luis Diaz; Computers; Lotus-Albertini Hispanic Reps; Marketing; *Mass Media; Nuestras Noticias; Radio; Reading; Television; Tortosa, Cristobal.

6422 Members to LULAC boards named. LATINO, Vol. 53, no. 8 (December 1982), p. 26. English. DESCR: *Politics.

6423 NATIONAL HISPANIC WOMEN'S NETWORK DIRECTORY: LULAC mujeres en accion. LATINO, Vol. 53, no. 3 (May 1982), p. 13-18. English. DESCR: *Chicanas; Directories.

6424 Newsfront. HISPANIC BUSINESS, Vol. 4, no. 3 (March 1982), p. 9. English. DESCR: Appointed Officials; *Biographical Notes; Businesspeople; Chicano Film Exhibition and Festival, Detroit, Michigan, April 5-9, 1982; Garcia, Gloria; Martinez, Vilma Socorro; National Association for Bilingual Education; Seaga, Edward; Suarez, Carlos R.

6425 Only two remain. LATINO, Vol. 54, no. 1 (January, February, 1983), p. 4. English. DESCR: *Wilmot, Luis G.

6426 People. HISPANIC BUSINESS, Vol. 4, no. 9 (September 1982), p. 7. English. DESCR: Advertising Agencies; Appointed Officials; Awards; *Biographical Notes; Diaz-Albertini, Luis; Dimartino, Rita; Garza, Jesus; Hispanic Women in Higher Education (HWHE); Ortega, Ray; Ortiz, George; Romero, Carlos J.; Sepulveda, Luis.

6427 San Miguel, Guadalupe. Mexican American organizations and the changing politics of school desegregation in Texas, 1945 to 1980. SOCIAL SCIENCE QUARTERLY, Vol. 63, (December 1982), p. 701-715. English. DESCR: American G.I. Forum; Mexican American Legal Defense and Educational Fund (MALDEF); Organizations; *Segregation and Desegregation; Texas.

6428 Sandoval, Moises. Why LULAC was founded. LATINO, Vol. 54, no. 1 (January, February, 1983), p. 12-19. English. DESCR: Organizations.

6429 Zuniga, Jo Ann and Bonilla, Tony. Talking Texas: turning the tables with LULAC. HISPANIC BUSINESS, Vol. 5, no. 9 (September 1983), p. 18-19+. English. DESCR: *Bonilla, Tony; Business Enterprises; Consumers; Economic History and Conditions; Marketing; Texas.

Leal, Luis

6430 Bruce Novoa, Juan. La critica chicana de Luis Leal. LA PALABRA, Vol. 4, no. 1-2 (Spring, Fall, 1982, 1983), p. 25-40. Spanish. DESCR: Authors; *Literary Criticism; Literature.

6431 Forster, Merlin H. Luis Leal. LA PALABRA, Vol. 4, no. 1-2 (Spring, Fall, 1982, 1983), p. 19-20. Spanish. DESCR: Authors; *Biography; Higher Education; Latin American Literature; Teaching Profession.

6432 Hinojosa-Smith, Rolando R. Luis (el amigo) Leal. LA PALABRA, Vol. 4, no. 1-2 (Spring, Fall, 1982, 1983), p. 17-18. Spanish. DESCR: Authors; *Biography; Latin American Literature; Literature.

6433 Lamento por la jubilacion de un insigne hispanista y viejo amigo (una carta anonima). LA PALABRA, Vol. 4, no. 1-2 (Spring, Fall, 1982, 1983), p. 21-24. Spanish. DESCR: Authors; *Biography; Higher Education; Latin American Literature; Teaching Profession.

6434 Lomeli, Francisco A. Don Luis. LA PALABRA, Vol. 4, no. 1-2 (Spring, Fall, 1982, 1983), p. IX-XI. Spanish. DESCR: Authors; *Biography; Latin American Literature; Literature.

6435 Lomeli, Francisco A. Entrevista con Luis Leal. LA PALABRA, Vol. 4, no. 1-2 (Spring, Fall, 1982, 1983), p. 3-15. Spanish. DESCR: Authors; *Biography; Latin American Literature; Literature; Oral History.

Leal, Luis (cont.)

6436 Rodriguez del Pino, Salvador. La intimidad poetica de Luis Leal. LA PALABRA, Vol. 4, no. 1-2 (Spring, Fall, 1982, 1983), p. 41-52. Spanish. DESCR: Authors; Literature; *Poetry.

Lear, Norman

6437 Nevarez, Armando. We're with you, Norman Lear, but watching you closely. NUESTRO, Vol. 7, no. 8 (October 1983), p. 47. English. DESCR: Embassy Communications; Stereotypes; *Television.

Learning and Cognition

6438 Adams, Phyliss J. and Anderson, Peggy L. Comparison of teachers' and Mexican-American children's perceptions of the children's competence. READING TEACHER, Vol. 36, no. 1 (October 1982), p. 8-13. English. DESCR: Attitude (Psychological); Children; Colorado; Cultural Characteristics; Sex Roles; *Teacher Attitudes.

6439 De Barbosa, Liliam Coya. "Mastering learning" como metodo psicoeducativo para ninos con problemas especificos de aprendizaje. HISPANIC JOURNAL OF BEHAVIORAL SCIENCES, Vol. 4, no. 4 (December 1982), p. 503-510. Spanish. DESCR: Children; *Mastery Learning; Puerto Ricans; *Reading.

6440 Galloway, Linda M. and Scarcella, Robin. Cerebral organization in adult second language acquisition: is the right hemisphere more involved. BRAIN AND LANGUAGE, Vol. 16, no. 1 (May 1982), p. 56-60. English. DESCR: *Bilingualism; English as a Second Language.

6441 Hudelson, Sarah. An introductory examination of children's invented spelling in Spanish. NABE JOURNAL, Vol. 6, no. 2-3 (Winter, Spring, 1981, 1982), p. 53-67. English. DESCR: Bilingual Bicultural Education; Children; *Language Arts; Spanish Language.

6442 Jimenez, Ricardo. Understanding the culture and learning styles of Hispanic students. MOMENTUM, Vol. 14, no. 1 (February 1983), p. 15-18. English. DESCR: *Cultural Characteristics; Socioeconomic Factors.

6443 Lado, Robert. Aula/the classroom: developmental reading in two languages. NABE JOURNAL, Vol. 6, no. 2-3 (Winter, Spring, 1981, 1982), p. 99-110. English. DESCR: Bilingual Bicultural Education; Bilingualism; Language Arts; Language Development; *Reading; Spanish Education Development (SED) Center Bilingual Reading Project; Spanish Language.

6444 Lalas, Joselito W. The influence of prior experience in ESL reading. BILINGUAL JOURNAL, Vol. 6, no. 1 (Fall 1982), p. 10-12. English. DESCR: Bilingual Bicultural Education; English as a Second Language; *Reading.

6445 Rodriguez, Imelda and Bethel, Lowell J. Inquiry approach to science and language teaching. JOURNAL OF RESEARCH IN SCIENCE TEACHING, Vol. 20, no. 4 (April 1983), p. 291-296. English. DESCR: Bilingualism; Education; *Educational Tests and Measurements; Language Arts; Primary School Education; Science.

6446 Spiridakis, John N. Three diagnostics tools for use with the bilingual child. BILINGUAL JOURNAL, Vol. 7, no. 4 (Summer 1983), p. 23-25. English. DESCR: *Bilingual Bicultural Education; Educational Cognitive Style (ECS); Educational Psychology; *Educational Tests and Measurements; Field-Sensitive/Field-Independent Behavior Observation Instruments; Learning Style Inventory (LSI).

6447 Valencia, Richard R. and Rankin, Richard J. Concurrent validity and reliability of the Kaufman version of the McCarthy scales short form for a sample of Mexican-American children. EDUCATIONAL AND PSYCHOLOGICAL MEASUREMENT, Vol. 43, no. 3 (Fall 1983), p. 915-925. English. DESCR: Educational Tests and Measurements; *McCarthy Scales for Children's Abilities (MSCA).

Learning Style Inventory (LSI)

6448 Spiridakis, John N. Three diagnostics tools for use with the bilingual child. BILINGUAL JOURNAL, Vol. 7, no. 4 (Summer 1983), p. 23-25. English. DESCR: *Bilingual Bicultural Education; Educational Cognitive Style (ECS); Educational Psychology; *Educational Tests and Measurements; Field-Sensitive/Field-Independent Behavior Observation Instruments; Learning and Cognition.

Legal Aid

6449 Bonilla, Tony. Law services for the poor. LATINO, Vol. 53, no. 2 (March, April, 1982), p. 6. English. DESCR: Legal Profession.

6450 Cardenas, Leo. Ruben Sandoval's quiet work. LATINO, Vol. 53, no. 4 (June 1982), p. 4. English. DESCR: *Sandoval, Ruben.

6451 Joe, Harry J. Judicial recommendation against deportation. TEXAS BAR JOURNAL, Vol. 45, no. 6 (June 1982), p. 712-716. English. DESCR: *Deportation; Undocumented Workers.

6452 Lopez, Marcos. Legal affair. LATINA, Vol. 1, no. 2 (February, March, 1983), p. 85. English. DESCR: Criminal Acts; Employment; Housing.

6453 Miranda warnings were adequate despite deviations from strict form. CRIMINAL LAW REPORTER, Vol. 30, no. 22 (October 3, 1982), p. 2427-2428. English. DESCR: California v. Prysock; Drug Traffic; U.S. v. Contreras.

Legal Assistance
USE: Legal Aid

Legal Brief and Records

6454 Gomez, Fernando. Past and precedent. AGENDA, Vol. 11, no. 3 (May, June, 1981), p. 54-55. English.

Legal Cases
USE: Laws

Legal Defense
USE: Legal Representation

Legal Education

6455 Flores, Rogelio. The struggle for minority admissions: the UCLA experience. CHICANO LAW REVIEW, Vol. 5, (1982), p. 1-12. English. DESCR: Bakke v. Regents of University of California; *Law Schools; Legal Profession; Student Organizations; Students; UCLA Law School.

Legal Education (cont.)

6456 Math-based careers. HISPANIC BUSINESS, Vol. 5, no. 12 (December 1983), p. 40. English. **DESCR:** *Careers; Council on Legal Education Opportunities (CLEO); Education; Employment Training; Graduate Schools; High Technology High School, San Antonio, TX; Mexican American Legal Defense and Educational Fund (MALDEF); San Antonio, TX; Science as a Profession.

6457 Minority access to legal profession is still limited. CALIFORNIA LAWYER, Vol. 3, no. 4 (April 1983), p. 72. English. **DESCR:** *Brown, Susan E.; Ethnic Groups; Mexican American Legal Defense and Educational Fund (MALDEF).

6458 Minority access to legal education. HISPANIC BUSINESS, Vol. 5, no. 4 (April 1983), p. 29-30. English. **DESCR:** Law School Admission Test (LSAT); Melendez v. Burciaga.

6459 Moss, Bernard H. Political values and career aspirations of UCLA law students: the 70's generation. CHICANO LAW REVIEW, Vol. 5, (1982), p. 13-28. English. **DESCR:** *Law Schools; Legal Profession; Political Ideology; Student Movements; Students.

6460 Study details minority access to legal education. NEW JERSEY LAW JOURNAL, Vol. 112, no. 1 (July 7, 1983), p. 28. English. **DESCR:** Brown, Susan E.; *Ethnic Groups; Mexican American Legal Defense and Educational Fund (MALDEF); PLURALISM IN THE LEGAL PROFESSION: MODELS FOR MINORITY ACCESS; Vasquez, Hector G.

Legal Profession

6461 Bonilla, Tony. Law services for the poor. LATINO, Vol. 53, no. 2 (March, April, 1982), p. 6. English. **DESCR:** *Legal Aid.

6462 Brown, Susan E. and Levoy, Claire. Melendez v. Burciaga: revealing the state of the art in bar examinations. BAR EXAMINER, Vol. 51, (May 1982), p. 4-15. English. **DESCR:** Klein, Stephen P.; Melendez v. Burciaga; Mexican American Legal Defense and Educational Fund (MALDEF); Multistate Bar Examination (MBE).

6463 Cazares, Allen E. Adventures in careers: los desafios del periodismo y la profesion legal. CAMINOS, Vol. 3, no. 3 (March 1982), p. 29. Bilingual.

6464 Flores, Rogelio. The struggle for minority admissions: the UCLA experience. CHICANO LAW REVIEW, Vol. 5, (1982), p. 1-12. English. **DESCR:** Bakke v. Regents of University of California; *Law Schools; Legal Education; Student Organizations; Students; UCLA Law School.

6465 Garcia, Daniel P. Where are the Hispanic partners? Only two out of 530 partners in eight large California firms are Hispanic. CALIFORNIA LAWYER, Vol. 3, no. 3 (March 1983), p. 11-12. English.

6466 Jim Blancarte, "an ace in the deck". LATINA, Vol. 1, no. 3 (1983), p. 52-53. English. **DESCR:** Biography; *Bracante, Jim.

6467 Latinos in the law: meeting the challenge [a symposium]. CHICANO LAW REVIEW, Vol. 6, (1983), p. 1-121. English. **DESCR:** *Criminal Justice System; Demography; Los Angeles Police Department; Love, Eulia; Police Brutality; Political Representation; Reapportionment; Settles, Ron.

6468 Moss, Bernard H. Political values and career aspirations of UCLA law students: the 70's generation. CHICANO LAW REVIEW, Vol. 5, (1982), p. 13-28. English. **DESCR:** *Law Schools; Legal Education; Political Ideology; Student Movements; Students.

6469 New general counsel at MALDEF. HISPANIC BUSINESS, Vol. 4, no. 7 (July 1982), p. 24. English. **DESCR:** *Avila, Joaquin Guadalupe; *Biography; Mexican American Legal Defense and Educational Fund (MALDEF).

6470 Whisler, Kirk. M.A.B.A. CAMINOS, Vol. 3, no. 5 (May 1982), p. 36-37. English. **DESCR:** *Mexican American Bar Association (MABA); Professional Organizations.

Legal Reform

6471 Lopez, Victor Manuel. Equal protection for undocumented aliens. CHICANO LAW REVIEW, Vol. 5, (1982), p. 29-54. English. **DESCR:** Civil Rights; Discrimination in Education; Medical Care Laws and Legislation; *Undocumented Workers.

6472 MALDEF's goal: a fair opportunity for Hispanics to compete. NUESTRO, Vol. 7, no. 6 (August 1983), p. 26-28+. English. **DESCR:** Education; Employment; *Mexican American Legal Defense and Educational Fund (MALDEF).

6473 O`Leary, Tim. David Ruiz brings justice to Texas prisons. NATIONAL HISPANIC JOURNAL, Vol. 1, no. 2 (Winter 1982), p. 21-24. English. **DESCR:** Clements, Bill; Prisoners; Prisons; *Ruiz, David; Texas Department of Corrections.

Legal Representation

6474 Beyette, Beverly. A time of transition for MALDEF. CALIFORNIA LAWYER, Vol. 2, no. 5 (May 1982), p. 28-32. English. **DESCR:** Martinez, Vilma Socorro; Mexican American Legal Defense and Educational Fund (MALDEF); Tijerina, Pete.

6475 Flaherty, Francis J. The struggle continues: protecting the rights of Hispanics in the U.S. NATIONAL LAW JOURNAL, Vol. 5, (March 14, 1983), p. 1. English. **DESCR:** Affirmative Action; *Avila, Joaquin Guadalupe; Civil Rights; Hispanic Amendments; Mexican American Legal Defense and Educational Fund (MALDEF); Racism; Voting Rights.

6476 Garcia, Art R. Art Garcia's capital gains: keeping down legal fees. HISPANIC BUSINESS, Vol. 4, no. 10 (October 1982), p. 12. English.

6477 Holley, Joe. Farmworker wins the right to sue. TEXAS OBSERVOR, Vol. 74, no. 13 (July 9, 1982), p. 15. English. **DESCR:** *Agricultural Laborers; Donna Fruit Company; Laws; Occupational Hazards; *Torrez, Juan.

6478 [Summary of: Hollander, defending the criminal alien in New Mexico: tactics and strategy to avoid deportation, 9 N.M.L. rev. 45 (1979)]. CHICANO LAW REVIEW, Vol. 5, (1982), p. 79-80. English. **DESCR:** Criminal Acts; Deportation; Undocumented Workers.

Legal Services
USE: Legal Aid

Legends
USE: Leyendas

Legislation

6479 Alvarez, Alejandro. Economic crisis and migration: comments on James Cockcroft's article. CONTEMPORARY MARXISM, Vol. 5, (Summer 1982), p. 62-66. English. DESCR: Cockcroft, James; International Economic Relations; Laboring Classes; MEXICAN MIGRATION, CRISIS, AND THE INTERNATIONALIZATION OF LABOR STRUGGLES; *Undocumented Workers.

6480 Cockcroft, James D. Mexican migration, crisis, and the internationalization of labor struggle. CONTEMPORARY MARXISM, Vol. 5, (Summer 1982), p. 48-61. English. DESCR: International Economic Relations; International Labor Activities; Labor Unions; Racism; *Undocumented Workers.

6481 Congressman questions federal reserve role. NUESTRO, Vol. 5, no. 8 (November 1981), p. 38. English. DESCR: Federal Reserve Board; *Gonzales, Henry B.

6482 Reaves, Gayle. Supreme Court rules for alien children. NUESTRO, Vol. 6, no. 5 (June, July, 1982), p. 14-16. English. DESCR: *Children; Education; Education Equalization; Immigration Law; Undocumented Workers; U.S. Supreme Court.

6483 Richardson, Chad and Yanez, Linda. "Equal justice" and Jose Reyna. NUESTRO, Vol. 6, no. 5 (June, July, 1982), p. 17. English. DESCR: Brownsville, TX; *Children; Education; Education Equalization; Immigration Law; Reyna, Jose; Undocumented Workers.

6484 Washington carousel. HISPANIC BUSINESS, Vol. 4, no. 7 (July 1982), p. 24. English. DESCR: Small Business.

6485 Washington carousel. HISPANIC BUSINESS, Vol. 4, no. 10 (October 1982), p. 23. English. DESCR: Housing.

LEGISLATIVE HISTORY OF AMERICAN IMMIGRATION POLICY, 1798-1965

6486 Weiss, Richard. Book review of: LEGISLATIVE HISTORY OF AMERICAN IMMIGRATION POLICY, 1798-1965. INTERNATIONAL MIGRATION REVIEW, Vol. 16, no. 3 (Fall 1982), p. 683. English. DESCR: Book Reviews; Hutchinson, E.P.; Immigration Law.

Leisure

6487 McMillen, Jay B. The social organization of leisure among Mexican-Americans. JOURNAL OF LEISURE RESEARCH, Vol. 15, no. 2 (1983), p. 164-173. English. DESCR: Cultural Characteristics; *Socialization.

Lenero-Otero, Luis

6488 Vierra, Andrea. Book review of: BEYOND THE NUCLEAR FAMILY MODEL: CROSS CULTURAL PERSPECTIVES. HISPANIC JOURNAL OF BEHAVIORAL SCIENCES, Vol. 5, no. 3 (September 1983), p. 349-352. English. DESCR: *BEYOND THE NUCLEAR FAMILY; Book Reviews; Family.

Leon, Virginia

6489 Q & A: in the Hispanic community who are the winners and losers of Reaganomics? CAMINOS, Vol. 3, no. 3 (March 1982), p. 47. Bilingual. DESCR: Casado, Lucy; Echeveste, John; *Federal Government; Flores, Bob; Mendoza, John; *Reagan, Ronald; Sanchez-Alvarez, Gloria; Vidal de Neri, Julieta

Lerma, Everardo Carlos

6490 Flores, David. 30's gridder recalls pain of prejudice. NUESTRO, Vol. 6, no. 8 (October 1982), p. 25-26. English. DESCR: Rio Grande Valley, TX; Sports; Texas.

6491 Garcia, Ignacio M. Realizing the dream. NUESTRO, Vol. 6, no. 8 (October 1982), p. 27-29. English. DESCR: Sports.

Lettuce Boycotts
USE: Boycotts

Levine, Barry B.

6492 Hoffer, Bates L. Sociology by value systems: explication and some implications of two studies on the folklore of Hispanics in the United States. BILINGUAL REVIEW, Vol. 9, no. 2 (May, August, 1982), p. 172-177. Bilingual. DESCR: BENJY LOPEZ: A PICARESQUE TALE OF EMIGRATION AND RETURN; Braceros; *Chicanos in American Literature; Comparative Literature; Folklore; Herrera Sobek, Maria; THE BRACERO EXPERIENCE: ELITELORE VERSUS FOLKLORE.

Levitan, Aida T.

6493 People. HISPANIC BUSINESS, Vol. 4, no. 8 (August 1983), p. 7. English. DESCR: Aguilar, Richard; *Businesspeople; Cordero-Badillo, Atilano; del Olmo, Frank; Infante, E. Anthony; Nunez, Luis; Quintanilla, Guadalupe; Rivera, Victor M.

Lew, Salvador

6494 Fifth member leaves panel. NUESTRO, Vol. 6, no. 4 (May 1982), p. 11. English. DESCR: Little Havana; Miami, FL; Police; Violence.

Lewis and Clark College, Portland, OR

6495 Flori, Monica. The Hispanic community as a resource for a practical Spanish program. FOREIGN LANGUAGE ANNALS, Vol. 15, no. 3 (May 1982), p. 213-215. English. DESCR: Community School Relationships; Curriculum; Educational Innovations; Language Development; *Spanish Language.

Lewis, Byron

6496 Balkan, D. Carlos. The advent of Uniworld/Hispanic: an interview. HISPANIC BUSINESS, Vol. 5, no. 3 (March 1983), p. 10-11+. English. DESCR: *Advertising Agencies; Blacks; Consumers; Diaz-Albertini, Luis; *Marketing; Spanish Advertising and Marketing Services (S.A.M.S.); Uniworld Group, Inc.; UniWorld Hispanic.

Lewis, Sasha G.

6497 Cardoso, Lawrence Anthony. "Wetbacks" and "slaves": recent additions to the literature. JOURNAL OF AMERICAN ETHNIC HISTORY, Vol. 1, no. 2 (Spring 1982), p. 68-71. English. DESCR: Book Reviews; Garcia, Juan Ramon; *OPERATION WETBACK: THE MASS DEPORTATION OF MEXICAN UNDOCUMENTED WORKERS IN 1954; *SLAVE TRADE TODAY: AMERICAN EXPLOITATION OF ILLEGAL ALIENS; Undocumented Workers.

Leyendas

6498 Melendez, Theresa. Coyote: towards a definition of a concept. AZTLAN, Vol. 13, no. 1-2 (Spring, Fall, 1982), p. 295-307. English. DESCR: *Coyote [folkloric symbol]; Folklore; Mitos.

Lezcano, Sixto

6499 Ortiz, Carlos V. NUESTRO'S sixth annual all-star baseball team. NUESTRO, Vol. 7, no. 2 (March 1983), p. 33-37. English. DESCR: Andujar, Joaquin; Barojas, Salome; *Baseball; Castillo, Manny; Concepcion, Dave; Cruz, Jose; Garcia, Damaso; Guerrero, Pedro; Hernandez, Keith; Martinez, Tippy; Pena, Tony; Piniella, Lou; Sports; Valenzuela, Fernando.

LIANNA

6500 Gutierrez, Silvio. Cinema. LATINA, Vol. 1, no. 3 (1983), p. 18-19+. English. DESCR: Film Reviews; *VOLVER A EMPEZAR.

Liberation Theology

6501 Costas, Orlando E. The Hispanics next door. CHRISTIAN CENTURY, Vol. 99, no. 26 (August 18, 1982), p. 851-856. English. DESCR: Cultural Pluralism; Latin Americans; Religion.

6502 Erdman, Daniel. Liberation and identity: Indo-Hispano youth. RELIGIOUS EDUCATION, Vol. 78, no. 1 (Winter 1983), p. 76-89. English. DESCR: Identity; *Religion.

6503 Lopez, Hugo L. Toward a theology of migration. APUNTES, Vol. 2, no. 3 (Fall 1982), p. 68-71. English. DESCR: *Immigrants; Religion.

Librarians

6504 Fisher, Edith Maureen. Minority librarianship research: a state-of-the-art review. LIBRARY AND INFORMATION SCIENCE RESEARCH, Vol. 5, no. 1 (Spring 1983), p. 5-65. English. DESCR: Library and Information Studies; *Recruitment.

Libraries

6505 Dorn, Georgette Magassy. Hispanic collections of the Library of Congress. NUESTRO, Vol. 6, no. 6 (August 1982), p. 35-38. English. DESCR: *Hispanic Reading Room, Library of Congress; Library Collections; Library of Congress; Washington, DC.

Library and Information Studies

6506 Fisher, Edith Maureen. Minority librarianship research: a state-of-the-art review. LIBRARY AND INFORMATION SCIENCE RESEARCH, Vol. 5, no. 1 (Spring 1983), p. 5-65. English. DESCR: *Librarians; *Recruitment.

Library Collections

6507 Dorn, Georgette Magassy. Hispanic collections of the Library of Congress. NUESTRO, Vol. 6, no. 6 (August 1982), p. 35-38. English. DESCR: *Hispanic Reading Room, Library of Congress; Libraries; Library of Congress; Washington, DC.

6508 Josel, Nathan A. Public library material selection in a bilingual community. CATHOLIC LIBRARY WORLD, Vol. 54, no. 3 (October 1982), p. 113-115. English. DESCR: Bilingualism; El Paso, TX; *Public Libraries; Spanish Language.

6509 Sohn, Jeanne and Davidson, Russ. Out of the morass: acquiring Spanish language materials from Latin America. LIBRARY JOURNAL, Vol. 10, no. 13 (July 1982), p. 1290-1293. English. DESCR: Latin American Literature; Library Services; Spanish Language.

Library Education

6510 Cunningham, John W. Library services for the Spanish speaking. CATHOLIC LIBRARY WORLD, Vol. 53, no. 8 (March 1982), p. 347-348. English. DESCR: Bilingual Bicultural Education; *Library Services.

Library of Congress

6511 Dorn, Georgette Magassy. Hispanic collections of the Library of Congress. NUESTRO, Vol. 6, no. 6 (August 1982), p. 35-38. English. DESCR: *Hispanic Reading Room, Library of Congress; Libraries; Library Collections; Washington, DC.

Library Services

6512 Cabello-Argandona, Roberto; Crary, Eleanor R.; and Pisano, Vivian M. Subject access for Hispanic library users. LIBRARY JOURNAL, Vol. 107, no. 14 (August 1982), p. 1383-1385. English. DESCR: Catalogues; *HISPANEX (Oakland, CA); Public Libraries.

6513 Cunningham, John W. Library services for the Spanish speaking. CATHOLIC LIBRARY WORLD, Vol. 53, no. 8 (March 1982), p. 347-348. English. DESCR: Bilingual Bicultural Education; Library Education.

6514 Dyer, Esther and Robertson-Kozan, Concha. Hispanics in the U.S.: implications for library service. SCHOOL LIBRARY JOURNAL, Vol. 29, no. 8 (April 1983), p. 27-29. English. DESCR: Bilingual Bicultural Education.

6515 Naismith, Rachael. Field work: outreach to migrants. RQ - REFERENCE AND ADULT SERVICES DIVISION, Vol. 22, no. 1 (Fall 1982), p. 33-35. English. DESCR: Cumberland County Library, NJ; Fresno County Public Library, CA; *Migrant Labor; Public Libraries.

6516 Naismith, Rachael. Moveable library: serving migrant farm workers. WILSON LIBRARY BULLETIN, Vol. 57, no. 7 (March 1983), p. 571-575. English. DESCR: *Dodge County Library System, WI; *Fresno County Public Library, CA; Migrant Labor; Public Libraries.

6517 Naismith, Rachael. Outreach services to Hispanics. ILLINOIS LIBRARIES, Vol. 64, no. 7 (September 1982), p. 962-966. English. DESCR: Arrondo, Ondina; Cubanos; La Raza Hispanica, Miami, FL; Latin American Library/Biblioteca Latinoamericana, Oakland, CA; Lopez, Lillian; Puerto Ricans; Ruiz, Deborah; South Bronx Project, New York Public Library; Verges, Bruni.

6518 Perry, Charles E. Book review of: DEVELOPING LIBRARY AND INFORMATION SERVICES FOR AMERICANS OF HISPANIC ORIGIN. JOURNAL OF ACADEMIC LIBRARIANSHIP, Vol. 8, no. 1 (March 1982), p. 38. English. DESCR: Academic Libraries; Book Reviews; *DEVELOPING LIBRARY AND INFORMATION SERVICES FOR AMERICANS OF HISPANIC ORIGIN; Haro, Robert P.

Library Services (cont.)

6519 Sohn, Jeanne and Davidson, Russ. Out of the morass: acquiring Spanish language materials from Latin America. LIBRARY JOURNAL, Vol. 10, no. 13 (July 1982), p. 1290-1293. English. DESCR: Latin American Literature; *Library Collections; Spanish Language.

LIFE WITH TWO LANGUAGES: AN INTRODUCTION TO BILINGUALISM

6520 Alatorre, Alva Sylvia. Book review of: LIFE WITH TWO LANGUAGES: AN INTRODUCTION TO BILINGUALISM. HISPANIC JOURNAL OF BEHAVIORAL SCIENCES, Vol. 5, no. 4 (December 1983), p. 482-486. English. DESCR: Bilingualism; Book Reviews; Grosjean, Francois.

6521 Sagarin, Edward. Book review of: LIFE WITH TWO LANGUAGES: AN INTRODUCTION TO BILINGUALISM. INTERNATIONAL MIGRATION REVIEW, Vol. 17, no. 3 (Fall 1983), p. 505-506. English. DESCR: Book Reviews; Grosjean, Francois.

LIFE'S CAREER--AGING: CULTURAL VARIATIONS ON GROWING OLD

6522 Burke, Leslie K. Book review of: LIFE'S CAREER-AGING: CULTURAL VARIATIONS ON GROWING OLD. HISPANIC JOURNAL OF BEHAVIORAL SCIENCES, Vol. 4, no. 1 (March 1982), p. 103-107. English. DESCR: Academic Achievement; Myerhoff, Barbara G.; Simic, Andrei.

Limited- or Non-English Speaking Handicapped Students (LONESHS)

6523 Plata, Maximino and Jones, Priscilla. Bilingual vocational education for handicapped students. EXCEPTIONAL CHILDREN, Vol. 48, no. 4 (April 1982), p. 538-540. English. DESCR: *Bilingual Bicultural Education; *Handicapped; Teaching Profession; Vocational Education.

Limited-English Proficient (LEP)

6524 Ambert, Alba N. The identification of LEP children with special needs. BILINGUAL JOURNAL, Vol. 6, no. 1 (Fall 1982), p. 17-22. English. DESCR: Cultural Characteristics; Handicapped; Language Interference; *Special Education.

6525 Bradley, Curtis H. and Friedenberg, Joan E. Tips for the English speaking multicultural vocational teacher. BILINGUAL JOURNAL, Vol. 6, no. 1 (Fall 1982), p. 6-9. English. DESCR: *Cultural Pluralism; Educational Innovations; Teacher-pupil Interaction; *Vocational Education.

Linguistic Theory

6526 Cohen, Andrew D. Researching the linguistic outcomes of bilingual programs. BILINGUAL REVIEW, Vol. 9, no. 2 (May, August, 1982), p. 97-108. English. DESCR: *Bilingual Bicultural Education; *Linguistics.

6527 Gorrell, J. Jeffrey, et al. Comparison of spatial role-taking in monolingual and bilingual children. JOURNAL OF GENETIC PSYCHOLOGY, Vol. 140, no. 1 (March 1982), p. 3-10. English. DESCR: Bilingualism; Child Study; Cognition; *Perception.

Linguistics

6528 Cohen, Andrew D. Researching the linguistic outcomes of bilingual programs. BILINGUAL

REVIEW, Vol. 9, no. 2 (May, August, 1982), p. 97-108. English. DESCR: *Bilingual Bicultural Education; Linguistic Theory.

6529 Martinez, Douglas R. American spelling bee: enchilada, llano, amigo, maraca. NUESTRO, Vol. 7, no. 5 (June, July, 1983), p. 50-51. English. DESCR: American Spelling Bee; Language Arts; *Language Usage.

6530 McDowell, John H. Sociolinguistic contours in the verbal art of Chicano children. AZTLAN, Vol. 13, no. 1-2 (Spring, Fall, 1982), p. 166-193. English. DESCR: Bilingualism; Children; *Sociolinguistics.

6531 Politzer, Robert L.; Shohamy, Elana; and McGroarty, Mary. Validation of linguistic and communicative oral language tests for Spanish-English bilingual programs. BILINGUAL REVIEW, Vol. 10, no. 1 (January, April, 1983), p. 3-20. English. DESCR: Bahia Oral Language Test (BOLT); Bay Area, CA; *Bilingual Bicultural Education; Bilingual Programs; *Language Assessment; Sociolinguistics.

Lionetti and Meyers Research Center, Inc.

6532 Communications/marketing. HISPANIC BUSINESS, Vol. 5, no. 10 (October 1983), p. 26. English. DESCR: Advertising; Arens & Gutierrez; Employment; Henry Molina, Inc.; Journals; Marketing; *Mass Media; Midwest Hispanics in Telecommunications Symposium, Chicago, IL; NEW MANAGEMENT.

Lions, 32nd Street

6533 Harowitz, Ruth. Adult delinquent gangs in a Chicano community: masked intimacy and marginality. URBAN LIFE, Vol. 11, no. 1 (April 1982), p. 3-26. English. DESCR: *Gangs; Identity.

Literary Characteristics

6534 Araya, Juan Gabriel. La autocontemplacion literaria en LIBRO DE MANUEL. MAIZE, Vol. 6, no. 3-4 (Spring, Summer, 1983), p. 7-16. Spanish. DESCR: *Cortazar, Julio; *Latin American Literature; Literary Criticism; Novel.

6535 Calderon, Hector. To read Chicano narrative: commentary and metacommentary. MESTER, Vol. 11, no. 2 (1982), p. 3-14. English. DESCR: Anaya, Rudolfo A.; BLESS ME, ULTIMA; Fiction; *Literary Criticism; Literature; *Prose.

6536 Cantu, Roberto. El relato como articulacion infinitiva: MACARIO y el arte de Juan Rulfo. LA PALABRA, Vol. 4, no. 1-2 (Spring, Fall, 1982, 1983), p. 107-126. Spanish. DESCR: Authors; Literary Criticism; *MACARIO; Mexican Literature; *Rulfo, Juan.

6537 Rodriguez, Joe. Chicano poetry: mestizaje and the use of irony. CAMPO LIBRE, Vol. 1, no. 2 (Summer 1981), p. 229-235. English. DESCR: Identity; *Literary Criticism; *Mestizaje; Poetry.

Literary Contests

6538 Entertainment = diversion. CAMINOS, Vol. 3, no. 3 (March 1982), p. 55-56. Bilingual. DESCR: Aztlan Writing Contest; CORAZON DE AZTLAN; Films; MISSING [film]; *Recreation; THE BORDER [film]; Young, Robert.

Literary Criticism

6539 Alarcon, Justo S. La meta critica Chicana. REVISTA CHICANO-RIQUENA, Vol. 10, no. 3 (Summer 1982), p. 47-52. Spanish. DESCR: Essays; *Humor.

6540 Aldaraca, Bridget. The poetry of Gioconda Belli. MAIZE, Vol. 5, no. 3-4 (Spring, Summer, 1982), p. 18-21. English. DESCR: Belli, Gioconda; *Nicaragua; *Poetry; Revolutions.

6541 Alurista. BOQUITAS PINTADAS, produccion folletinesca bajo el militarismo. MAIZE, Vol. 4, no. 1-2 (Fall, Winter, 1980, 1981), p. 21-26. Spanish. DESCR: *BOQUITAS PINTADAS; Puig, Manuel.

6542 Alurista. El caso, la novela y la historia en la obra de Acosta: THE REVOLT OF THE COCKROACH PEOPLE. MAIZE, Vol. 2, no. 3 (Spring 1979), p. 6-13. Spanish. DESCR: Acosta, Oscar Zeta; *THE REVOLT OF THE COCKROACH PEOPLE.

6543 Araya, Juan Gabriel. La autocontemplacion literaria en LIBRO DE MANUEL. MAIZE, Vol. 6, no. 3-4 (Spring, Summer, 1983), p. 7-16. Spanish. DESCR: *Cortazar, Julio; *Latin American Literature; Literary Characteristics; Novel.

6544 Bell-Villada, G. H. Book review of: CHICANO AUTHORS, INQUIRY BY INTERVIEW v. 228. NOTES AND QUERIES, Vol. 30, no. 2 (1983), p. 186-188. English. DESCR: Book Reviews; Bruce Novoa, Juan; *CHICANO POETRY: A RESPONSE TO CHAOS.

6545 Beverley, John. The revolution betrayed: a note on Mariano Azuela's estridentista trilogy. MAIZE, Vol. 4, no. 1-2 (Fall, Winter, 1980, 1981), p. 27-39. English. DESCR: *Azuela, Mariano; EL DESQUITE; LA LUCIERNAGA; LA MALHORA.

6546 Bruce Novoa, Juan. La critica chicana de Luis Leal. LA PALABRA, Vol. 4, no. 1-2 (Spring, Fall, 1982, 1983), p. 25-40. Spanish. DESCR: Authors; *Leal, Luis; Literature.

6547 Calderon, Hector. To read Chicano narrative: commentary and metacommentary. MESTER, Vol. 11, no. 2 (1982), p. 3-14. English. DESCR: Anaya, Rudolfo A.; BLESS ME, ULTIMA; Fiction; Literary Characteristics; Literature; *Prose.

6548 Campbell, Stephanie. The artist in bourgeois society, as seen in Carpentier's LA CONSAGRACION DE LA PRIMAVERA. MAIZE, Vol. 3, no. 3-4 (Spring, Summer, 1980), p. 6-16. English. DESCR: Artists; Carpentier, Alejo; *LA CONSAGRACION DE LA PRIMAVERA.

6549 Cantu, Roberto. El relato como articulacion infinitiva: MACARIO y el arte de Juan Rulfo. LA PALABRA, Vol. 4, no. 1-2 (Spring, Fall, 1982, 1983), p. 107-126. Spanish. DESCR: Authors; Literary Characteristics; *MACARIO; Mexican Literature; *Rulfo, Juan.

6550 Carrasco, David. A perspective for a study of religious dimensions in Chicano experience: BLESS ME, ULTIMA as a religious text. AZTLAN, Vol. 13, no. 1-2 (Spring, Fall, 1982), p. 195-221. English. DESCR: Anaya, Rudolfo A.; *BLESS ME, ULTIMA; Literature; Religion.

6551 Clements, William M. Way to individuation in Anaya's BLESS ME, ULTIMA. MIDWEST QUARTERLY, Vol. 23, no. 2 (Winter 1982), p. 131-143. English. DESCR: Anaya, Rudolfo A.; *BLESS ME, ULTIMA; Psychological Theory.

6552 Concha, Jaime. Exilio, conciencia: coda sobre la poesia de Millan. MAIZE, Vol. 5, no. 1-2 (Fall, Winter, 1981, 1982), p. 7-15. Spanish. DESCR: Chile; Jesuits; Literary History; *Millan, Gonzalo; Poetry; Political Refugees.

6553 de la Fuente, Patricia. Ambiguity in the poetry of Gary Soto. REVISTA CHICANO-RIQUENA, Vol. 11, no. 2 (Summer 1983), p. 34-39. English. DESCR: "Avocado Lake"; "Blanco"; "Braley Street"; "Field"; Poetry; "Song for the pockets"; *Soto, Gary; TALE OF SUNLIGHT; "Telephoning God"; THE ELEMENTS OF SAN JOAQUIN; "Wind".

6554 de Ortego y Gasca, Felipe. "Are there U.S. Hispanic writers?". NUESTRO, Vol. 7, no. 3 (April 1983), p. 20-21+. English. DESCR: Authors; Ethnic Groups; Literature.

6555 Elizondo, Sergio D. Book review of: LITERATURA CHICANA: TEXTO Y CONTEXTO. JOURNAL OF ETHNIC STUDIES, Vol. 1, no. 1 (Spring 1973), p. 68-70. Bilingual. DESCR: Book Reviews; Castaneda Shular, Antonia; Literary History; Literary Influence; *LITERATURA CHICANA: TEXTO Y CONTEXTO; Literature; Sommers, Joseph; Teatro; Ybarra-Frausto, Tomas.

6556 Espinoza, Herbert O. Lope de Aguirre y santos banderas, la manipulacion del mito. MAIZE, Vol. 4, no. 3-4 (Spring, Summer, 1981), p. 32-43. Spanish. DESCR: De Valle-Inclan, Ramon; Mythology; *TIRANO BANDERAS.

6557 Espinoza, Roberto. Sintesis vs. analysis: un problema de historicidad en las novelas de las dictaduras. MAIZE, Vol. 6, no. 1-2 (Fall, Winter, 1982, 1983), p. 7-27. Spanish. DESCR: Carpentier, Alejo; Dictatorships; Garcia Marquez, Gabriel; Latin American Literature; Novel; Roa Bastos, Augustos; Valle Inclan, Ramon; White, Lucas Edward.

6558 Garcia Nunez, Fernando. La poesia chicana en espanol. CUADERNOS HISPANOAMERICANOS, Vol. 397, (July 1983), p. 117-123. Spanish. DESCR: Identity; *Poetry.

6559 Gonzalez Cruz, Luis F. Quest and discovery in Oscar Hurtado's THE DEAD CITY OF KORAD: a unique experiment in science fiction poetry. MAIZE, Vol. 5, no. 1-2 (Fall, Winter, 1981, 1982), p. 74-85. English. DESCR: Cuba; *Hurtado, Oscar; Latin American Literature; Poetry.

6560 Guerrero, Yolanda E. La funcion del mito: NAMBE-YEAR ONE. MAIZE, Vol. 4, no. 3-4 (Spring, Summer, 1981), p. 51-59. Spanish. DESCR: Mythology; *NAMBE: YEAR ONE; Romero, Orlando.

6561 Herrera-Sobek, Maria. La unidad, el hombre y el cosmos: reafirmacion del proceso vital en Estrella Portillo Trambley. LA PALABRA, Vol. 4, no. 1-2 (Spring, Fall, 1982, 1983), p. 127-141. Spanish. DESCR: Authors; Literature; *Portillo Trambley, Estela.

Literary Criticism (cont.)

6562 Jensen, Richard J. and Hammerback, John C.
"No revolutions without poets": the rhetoric
of Rodolfo "Corky" Gonzales. WESTERN JOURNAL
OF SPEECH COMMUNICATION, Vol. 46, no. 1
(Winter 1982), p. 72-91. English. DESCR:
Chicano Movement; *Gonzales, Rodolfo
(Corky); Poetry; Rhetoric.

6563 Lattin, Vernon E. Ethnicity and identity in
the contemporary Chicano novel. MINORITY
VOICES, Vol. 2, no. 2 (Fall 1978), p. 37-44.
English. DESCR: BLESS ME, ULTIMA; Identity;
Literature; MEMORIES OF THE ALHAMBRA;
*Novel; POCHO; THE AUTOBIOGRAPHY OF A BROWN
BUFFALO; Y NO SE LO TRAGO LA TIERRA/AND THE
EARTH DID NOT PART.

6564 Lattin, Vernon E. La meta critica Chicana.
REVISTA CHICANO-RIQUENA, Vol. 10, no. 3
(Summer 1982), p. 53-62. English. DESCR:
*Arias, Ron; Death (Concept); *THE ROAD TO
TAMAZUNCHALE.

6565 Lizarraga, Sylvia S. Observaciones acerca de
la critica literaria Chicana. REVISTA
CHICANO-RIQUENA, Vol. 10, no. 4 (Fall 1982),
p. 55-64. Spanish. DESCR: *Bruce Novoa,
Juan; CITY OF NIGHT; El Teatro Campesino;
Literature; POCHO; THE SPACE OF CHICANO
LITERATURE.

6566 Madrid, A. The problematics of the Chicano
experience and its literature. PONTE
RIVISTA: MENSILE DI POLITICA E LITTERATURA,
Vol. 38, no. 6 (1982), p. 627-634. English.

6567 Marquez, Antonio. The American dream in the
Chicano novel. ROCKY MOUNTAIN REVIEW OF
LANGUAGE AND LITERATURE, Vol. 37, no. 1-2
(1983), p. 4-19. English. DESCR: *Novel.

6568 Martinez, Julio A. Book review of: A
BIBLIOGRAPHY OF CRITICISM OF CONTEMPORARY
CHICANO LITERATURE. RQ - REFERENCE AND ADULT
SERVICES DIVISION, Vol. 22, no. 1 (Fall
1982), p. 90. English. DESCR: *A
BIBLIOGRAPHY OF CRITICISM OF CONTEMPORARY
CHICANO LITERATURE; Bibliography; Book
Reviews; Eger, Ernestina N.; Literature.

6569 Martinez, Julio A. Book review of: A DECADE
OF CHICANO LITERATURE (1970-1979)-CRITICAL
ESSAYS AND BIBLIOGRAPHY. RQ - REFERENCE AND
ADULT SERVICES DIVISION, Vol. 22, no. 1
(Fall 1982), p. 90. English. DESCR: *A
DECADE OF CHICANO LITERATURE (1970-1979):
CRITICAL ESSAYS AND BIBLIOGRAPHY;
Bibliography; Book Reviews; Gonzalez, Raquel
Quiroz; Literatura Chicanesca; Literature;
Trujillo, Robert.

6570 Menton, Seymour. EL LLANO EN LLAMAS:
anti-epopeya de la revolucion. LA PALABRA,
Vol. 4, no. 1-2 (Spring, Fall, 1982, 1983),
p. 93-96. Spanish. DESCR: *EL LLANO EN
LLAMAS; Literature; *Rulfo, Juan.

6571 Monleon, Jose. Dos novelas de Alejandro
Morales. MAIZE, Vol. 4, no. 1-2 (Fall,
Winter, 1980, 1981), p. 6-8. Spanish.
DESCR: *CARAS VIEJAS Y VINO NUEVO; *LA
VERDAD SIN VOZ; Morales, Alejandro.

6572 Monleon, Jose. Historia de una
contradiccion. MAIZE, Vol. 3, no. 3-4
(Spring, Summer, 1980), p. 17-22. Spanish.
DESCR: *CIEN ANOS DE SOLEDAD; Garcia
Marquez, Gabriel.

6573 La muerte y el deseo: notas sobre la poesia
de Juan Felipe Herrera. LA PALABRA, Vol. 4,
no. 1-2 (Spring, Fall, 1982, 1983), p.

97-106. Spanish. DESCR: *Herrera, Juan
Felipe; Literature; *Poetry.

6574 The new literature: a look at current
trends. NUESTRO, Vol. 7, no. 3 (April 1983),
p. 22. English. DESCR: Literary Influence;
*Literature.

6575 Nieto, Eva Margarita. El problema de la
juventud eterna en tres hechiceras en THE
SECOND RING OF POWER, LA MULATA DE CORDOBA y
AURA. LA PALABRA, Vol. 4, no. 1-2 (Spring,
Fall, 1982, 1983), p. 81-91. Spanish.
DESCR: AURA; Castaneda, Carlos; Fuentes,
Carlos; Gonzalez Obregon, Luis; LA MULATA DE
CORDOBA; Literature; Literature Reviews; THE
SECOND RING OF POWER.

6576 Ortiz Griffin, Julia. The Puerto Rican woman
in Rene Marques' drama. REVISTA
CHICANO-RIQUENA, Vol. 11, no. 3-4 (Fall
1983), p. 169-176. English. DESCR: *Marques,
Rene; Teatro; Women.

6577 Rangel-Guerrero, Daniel. Book review of:
CHICANO AUTHORS: INQUIRY BY INTERVIEW.
JOURNAL OF ETHNIC STUDIES, Vol. 10, no. 2
(Summer 1982), p. 117-119. English. DESCR:
Book Reviews; Bruce Novoa, Juan; *CHICANO
AUTHORS: INQUIRY BY INTERVIEW; Comparative
Literature; Literary History; Literary
Influence; Literature.

6578 Rebolledo, Tey Diana. Abuelitas: mythology
and integration in Chicana literature.
REVISTA CHICANO-RIQUENA, Vol. 11, no. 3-4
(Fall 1983), p. 148-158. English. DESCR:
Chicanas; Poetry.

6579 Rebolledo, Tey Diana. Game theory in Chicana
poetry. REVISTA CHICANO-RIQUENA, Vol. 11,
no. 3-4 (Fall 1983), p. 159-168. English.
DESCR: Chicanas; Poetry.

6580 Rodriguez, Joe. Chicano poetry: mestizaje
and the use of irony. CAMPO LIBRE, Vol. 1,
no. 2 (Summer 1981), p. 229-235. English.
DESCR: Identity; Literary Characteristics;
*Mestizaje; Poetry.

6581 Soto, Gary; Trejo, Ernesto; and de la
Fuente, Patricia. Special focus on Gary
Soto. REVISTA CHICANO-RIQUENA, Vol. 11, no.
2 (Summer 1983), p. 7-39. English. DESCR:
*Poetry; Prose; *Soto, Gary.

6582 Umpierre, Luz Maria. La ansiedad de la
influencia en Sandra Maria Esteves y
Marjorie Agosin. REVISTA CHICANO-RIQUENA,
Vol. 11, no. 3-4 (Fall 1983), p. 139-147.
Spanish. DESCR: A JULIA Y A MI; *Agosin,
Magi; De Burgos, Julia; EL PAIS DIVIDIDO;
*Esteves, Sandra Maria; Neruda, Pablo;
Parra, Nicanor; Poetry.

6583 Vallejos, Thomas. Ritual process and the
family in the Chicano novel. MELUS:
MULTI-ETHNIC LITERATURE OF THE UNITED
STATES, Vol. 10, no. 4 (Winter 1983, 1984),
p. 5-16. English. DESCR: Anaya, Rudolfo A.;
BLESS ME, ULTIMA; Family; Novel; Parent and
Child Relationships; POCHO; Rivera, Tomas;
Villarreal, Jose Antonio; Y NO SE LO TRAGO
LA TIERRA/AND THE EARTH DID NOT PART.

6584 Villanueva Collado, Alfredo. Fili-Mele:
simbolo y mujer en la poesia de Luis Pales
Matos e Ivan Silen. REVISTA CHICANO-RIQUENA,
Vol. 10, no. 4 (Fall 1982), p. 47-54.
Spanish. DESCR: Chicanas; LOS POEMAS DE
FILI-MELE; *Pales Matos, Luis; Ribes Tovar,
Federico; *Silen, Ivan; Symbolism; TUNTUN DE
PASA Y GRIFERIA.

Literary History

6585 Alurista. El capital y su genero: la
novela/... material, instrumento y dinero,
producto y mercado. MAIZE, Vol. 3, no. 3-4
(Spring, Summer, 1980), p. 23-41. Spanish.
DESCR: *Novel.

6586 Concha, Jaime. Exilio, conciencia: coda
sobre la poesia de Millan. MAIZE, Vol. 5,
no. 1-2 (Fall, Winter, 1981, 1982), p. 7-15.
Spanish. **DESCR:** Chile; Jesuits; Literary
Criticism; *Millan, Gonzalo; Poetry;
Political Refugees.

6587 Elizondo, Sergio D. Book review of:
LITERATURA CHICANA: TEXTO Y CONTEXTO.
JOURNAL OF ETHNIC STUDIES, Vol. 1, no. 1
(Spring 1973), p. 68-70. Bilingual. **DESCR:**
Book Reviews; Castaneda Shular, Antonia;
Literary Criticism; Literary Influence;
*LITERATURA CHICANA: TEXTO Y CONTEXTO;
Literature; Sommers, Joseph; Teatro;
Ybarra-Frausto, Tomas.

6588 Rangel-Guerrero, Daniel. Book review of:
CHICANO AUTHORS: INQUIRY BY INTERVIEW.
JOURNAL OF ETHNIC STUDIES, Vol. 10, no. 2
(Summer 1982), p. 117-119. English. **DESCR:**
Book Reviews; Bruce Novoa, Juan; *CHICANO
AUTHORS: INQUIRY BY INTERVIEW; Comparative
Literature; Literary Criticism; Literary
Influence; Literature.

Literary Influence

6589 Anaya, Rudolfo A. An author's reflections:
THE SILENCE OF THE LLANO. NUESTRO, Vol. 7,
no. 3 (April 1983), p. 14-17+. English.
DESCR: *Anaya, Rudolfo A.; Authors;
*Fiction.

6590 Bruce Novoa, Juan and Arias, Ron. Interview
with Ron Arias. JOURNAL OF ETHNIC STUDIES,
Vol. 3, no. 4 (Winter 1976), p. 70-73.
English. **DESCR:** *Arias, Ron; Authors;
*Literature.

6591 Elizondo, Sergio D. Book review of:
LITERATURA CHICANA: TEXTO Y CONTEXTO.
JOURNAL OF ETHNIC STUDIES, Vol. 1, no. 1
(Spring 1973), p. 68-70. Bilingual. **DESCR:**
Book Reviews; Castaneda Shular, Antonia;
Literary Criticism; Literary History;
*LITERATURA CHICANA: TEXTO Y CONTEXTO;
Literature; Sommers, Joseph; Teatro;
Ybarra-Frausto, Tomas.

6592 The new literature: a look at current
trends. NUESTRO, Vol. 7, no. 3 (April 1983),
p. 22. English. **DESCR:** Literary Criticism;
*Literature.

6593 Rangel-Guerrero, Daniel. Book review of:
CHICANO AUTHORS: INQUIRY BY INTERVIEW.
JOURNAL OF ETHNIC STUDIES, Vol. 10, no. 2
(Summer 1982), p. 117-119. English. **DESCR:**
Book Reviews; Bruce Novoa, Juan; *CHICANO
AUTHORS: INQUIRY BY INTERVIEW; Comparative
Literature; Literary Criticism; Literary
History; Literature.

LITERATURA CHICANA: TEXTO Y CONTEXTO

6594 Elizondo, Sergio D. Book review of:
LITERATURA CHICANA: TEXTO Y CONTEXTO.
JOURNAL OF ETHNIC STUDIES, Vol. 1, no. 1
(Spring 1973), p. 68-70. Bilingual. **DESCR:**
Book Reviews; Castaneda Shular, Antonia;
Literary Criticism; Literary History;
Literary Influence; Literature; Sommers,
Joseph; Teatro; Ybarra-Frausto, Tomas.

Literatura Chicanesca

6595 Martinez, Julio A. Book review of: A DECADE
OF CHICANO LITERATURE (1970-1979)-CRITICAL
ESSAYS AND BIBLIOGRAPHY. RQ - REFERENCE AND
ADULT SERVICES DIVISION, Vol. 22, no. 1
(Fall 1982), p. 90. English. **DESCR:** *A
DECADE OF CHICANO LITERATURE (1970-1979):
CRITICAL ESSAYS AND BIBLIOGRAPHY;
Bibliography; Book Reviews; Gonzalez, Raquel
Quiroz; Literary Criticism; Literature;
Trujillo, Robert.

Literature

6596 Agosin, Marjorie. Elucubraciones y
antielucubraciones: critica feminista desde
perspectivas poeticas. THIRD WOMAN, Vol. 1,
no. 2 (1982), p. 65-69. Spanish. **DESCR:**
*Chicanas; Essays.

6597 Aguilar, Ricardo D. Chicano poetry and new
places. JOURNAL OF ETHNIC STUDIES, Vol. 5,
no. 1 (Spring 1977), p. 59-61. English.
DESCR: Poetry; Seattle, WA.

6598 Alarcon, Justo S. Hacia la nada ... o la
religion en POCHO. MINORITY VOICES, Vol. 1,
no. 2 (Fall 1977), p. 17-26. English.
DESCR: *POCHO; Religion; Villarreal, Jose
Antonio.

6599 Alurista. Cultural nationalism and Xicano
literature during the decade of 1965-1975.
MELUS: MULTI-ETHNIC LITERATURE OF THE UNITED
STATES, Vol. 8, no. 2 (Summer 1981), p.
22-34. English. **DESCR:** Nationalism.

6600 Alurista and Monleon, Jose. Mesa redonda.
MAIZE, Vol. 4, no. 3-4 (Spring, Summer,
1981), p. 6-23. English. **DESCR:** Alurista;
Anaya, Rudolfo A.; Herrera Sobek, Maria;
Identity; Morales, Alejandro; *Mythology;
Viramontes, Helen.

6601 Avendano, Fausto. Book review of: HAY PLESHA
LICHANS TO DI FLAC. LA PALABRA, Vol. 4, no.
1-2 (Spring, Fall, 1982, 1983), p. 165-167.
Spanish. **DESCR:** Book Reviews; *HAY PLESHA
LICHANS TU DI FLAC; Sanchez, Saul.

6602 Bruce Novoa, Juan. La critica chicana de
Luis Leal. LA PALABRA, Vol. 4, no. 1-2
(Spring, Fall, 1982, 1983), p. 25-40.
Spanish. **DESCR:** Authors; *Leal, Luis;
*Literary Criticism.

6603 Bruce Novoa, Juan. Fear and loathing on the
buffalo trail. MELUS: MULTI-ETHNIC
LITERATURE OF THE UNITED STATES, Vol. 6, no.
4 (Winter 1979), p. 39-50. English. **DESCR:**
*Acosta, Oscar Zeta.

6604 Bruce Novoa, Juan. In search of the honest
outlaw: John Rechy. MINORITY VOICES, Vol. 3,
no. 1 (Fall 1979), p. 37-45. English.
DESCR: *Rechy, John.

6605 Bruce Novoa, Juan and Arias, Ron. Interview
with Ron Arias. JOURNAL OF ETHNIC STUDIES,
Vol. 3, no. 4 (Winter 1976), p. 70-73.
English. **DESCR:** *Arias, Ron; Authors;
Literary Influence.

6606 Bruce Novoa, Juan. Round table on Chicano
literature. JOURNAL OF ETHNIC STUDIES, Vol.
3, no. 1 (Spring 1975), p. 99-103. English.
DESCR: *Bruce Novoa, Juan; Montejano, David;
Morton, Carlos; Ortego y Gasca, Felipe de;
Teatro.

Literature (cont.)

6607 Calderon, Hector. To read Chicano narrative: commentary and metacommentary. MESTER, Vol. 11, no. 2 (1982), p. 3-14. English. **DESCR:** Anaya, Rudolfo A.; BLESS ME, ULTIMA; Fiction; Literary Characteristics; *Literary Criticism; *Prose.

6608 Candelaria, Cordelia. Another reading of three poems by Zamora. MELUS: MULTI-ETHNIC LITERATURE OF THE UNITED STATES, Vol. 7, no. 4 (Winter 1980), p. 102-104. English. **DESCR:** *Zamora, Bernice.

6609 Candelaria, Cordelia. Book review of: THE SILENCE OF THE LLANO. MELUS: MULTI-ETHNIC LITERATURE OF THE UNITED STATES, Vol. 10, no. 2 (Summer 1983), p. 79-82. English. **DESCR:** *Anaya, Rudolfo A.; THE SILENCE OF THE LLANO.

6610 Candelaria, Cordelia. Book review of: TORTUGA. LA PALABRA, Vol. 4, no. 1-2 (Spring, Fall, 1982, 1983), p. 167-169. Spanish. **DESCR:** Anaya, Rudolfo A.; Book Reviews; *TORTUGA.

6611 Cardenas de Dwyer, Carlota. Cultural nationalism and Chicano literature in the eighties. MELUS: MULTI-ETHNIC LITERATURE OF THE UNITED STATES, Vol. 8, no. 2 (Summer 1981), p. 40-47. English. **DESCR:** Nationalism.

6612 Carrasco, David. A perspective for a study of religious dimensions in Chicano experience: BLESS ME, ULTIMA as a religious text. AZTLAN, Vol. 13, no. 1-2 (Spring, Fall, 1982), p. 195-221. English. **DESCR:** Anaya, Rudolfo A.; *BLESS ME, ULTIMA; Literary Criticism; Religion.

6613 de Ortego y Gasca, Felipe. "Are there U.S. Hispanic writers?". NUESTRO, Vol. 7, no. 3 (April 1983), p. 20-21+. English. **DESCR:** Authors; Ethnic Groups; *Literary Criticism.

6614 De Vallbona, Rima. El nagual de mi amiga Irene. LA PALABRA, Vol. 4, no. 1-2 (Spring, Fall, 1982, 1983), p. 151-157. Spanish. **DESCR:** Prose; *Short Story.

6615 A decade of Hispanic literature: an anniversary anthology. REVISTA CHICANO-RIQUENA, Vol. 10, no. 1-2 (Winter, Spring, 1982), p. 1-310. Bilingual. **DESCR:** Essays; Poetry; Prose.

6616 Elizondo, Sergio D. Book review of: LITERATURA CHICANA: TEXTO Y CONTEXTO. JOURNAL OF ETHNIC STUDIES, Vol. 1, no. 1 (Spring 1973), p. 68-70. Bilingual. **DESCR:** Book Reviews; Castaneda Shular, Antonia; Literary Criticism; Literary History; Literary Influence; *LITERATURA CHICANA: TEXTO Y CONTEXTO; Sommers, Joseph; Teatro; Ybarra-Frausto, Tomas.

6617 Fabre, Michel. Book review of: LES FILS DU SOLEIL: LA MINORITE MEXICAINE A TRAVERS LA LITTERATURE DES ETATS-UNIS. MELUS: MULTI-ETHNIC LITERATURE OF THE UNITED STATES, Vol. 8, no. 1 (Spring 1981), p. 65-68. English. **DESCR:** Book Reviews; *LES FILS DU SOLEIL: LA MINORITE MEXICAINE A TRAVERS LA LITTERATURE DES ETATS-UNIS; Rocard, Marcienne.

6618 Garcia Marquez, Gabriel. The solitude of Latin America. NUESTRO, Vol. 6, no. 10 (December 1982), p. 46-47+. English. **DESCR:** *Authors; *ONE HUNDRED YEARS OF SOLITUDE.

6619 Gonzalez, Maria R. Book review of: ACERCA DE LITERATURA (Dialogo con tres autores chicanos). LA PALABRA, Vol. 4, no. 1-2 (Spring, Fall, 1982, 1983), p. 170-171. Spanish. **DESCR:** *ACERCA DE LITERATURA; Book Reviews; Vazquez-Castro, Javier.

6620 Herrera-Sobek, Maria. La unidad, el hombre y el cosmos: reafirmacion del proceso vital en Estrella Portillo Trambley. LA PALABRA, Vol. 4, no. 1-2 (Spring, Fall, 1982, 1983), p. 127-141. Spanish. **DESCR:** Authors; *Literary Criticism; *Portillo Trambley, Estela.

6621 Hinojosa-Smith, Rolando R. Luis (el amigo) Leal. LA PALABRA, Vol. 4, no. 1-2 (Spring, Fall, 1982, 1983), p. 17-18. Spanish. **DESCR:** Authors; *Biography; Latin American Literature; *Leal, Luis.

6622 Introduction. REVISTA CHICANO-RIQUENA, Vol. 11, no. 3-4 (Fall 1983), p. 7-17. English. **DESCR:** *Chicanas.

6623 Klor de Alva, Jorge. Book review of: PELON DROPS OUT. LA PALABRA, Vol. 4, no. 1-2 (Spring, Fall, 1982, 1983), p. 172-174. Spanish. **DESCR:** Book Reviews; De Casas, Celso A.; *PELON DROPS OUT.

6624 Lattin, Vernon E. Ethnicity and identity in the contemporary Chicano novel. MINORITY VOICES, Vol. 2, no. 2 (Fall 1978), p. 37-44. English. **DESCR:** BLESS ME, ULTIMA; Identity; Literary Criticism; MEMORIES OF THE ALHAMBRA; *Novel; POCHO; THE AUTOBIOGRAPHY OF A BROWN BUFFALO; Y NO SE LO TRAGO LA TIERRA/AND THE EARTH DID NOT PART.

6625 Lattin, Vernon E. Novelistic structure and myth in ...Y NO SE LO TRAGO LA TIERRA. BILINGUAL REVIEW, Vol. 9, no. 3 (September, December, 1982), p. 220-226. English. **DESCR:** Novel; Rivera, Tomas; United Mexican Americans, South Bend, IN; *Y NO SE LO TRAGO LA TIERRA/AND THE EARTH DID NOT PART.

6626 Leudtke, Luther S. POCHO and the American dream. MINORITY VOICES, Vol. 1, no. 2 (Fall 1977), p. 1-16. English. **DESCR:** *POCHO; Villarreal, Jose Antonio.

6627 Lewis, Marvin A. Book review of: THE IDENTIFICATION AND ANALYSIS OF CHICANO LITERATURE. MELUS: MULTI-ETHNIC LITERATURE OF THE UNITED STATES, Vol. 7, no. 1 (Spring 1980), p. 82-85. English. **DESCR:** Book Reviews; IDENTIFICATION AND ANALYSIS OF CHICANO LITERATURE; *Jimenez, Francisco.

6628 Lizarraga, Sylvia S. Observaciones acerca de la critica literaria Chicana. REVISTA CHICANO-RIQUENA, Vol. 10, no. 4 (Fall 1982), p. 55-64. Spanish. **DESCR:** *Bruce Novoa, Juan; CITY OF NIGHT; El Teatro Campesino; *Literary Criticism; POCHO; THE SPACE OF CHICANO LITERATURE.

6629 Lomeli, Francisco A. Don Luis. LA PALABRA, Vol. 4, no. 1-2 (Spring, Fall, 1982, 1983), p. IX-XI. Spanish. **DESCR:** Authors; *Biography; Latin American Literature; *Leal, Luis.

6630 Lomeli, Francisco A. Entrevista con Luis Leal. LA PALABRA, Vol. 4, no. 1-2 (Spring, Fall, 1982, 1983), p. 3-15. Spanish. **DESCR:** Authors; *Biography; Latin American Literature; *Leal, Luis; Oral History.

Literature (cont.)

6631 Lomeli, Francisco A. Isabella Rios and the Chicano psychic novel. MINORITY VOICES, Vol. 4, no. 1 (Spring 1980), p. 49-61. English. **DESCR:** Lopez, Diana; Novel; *Rios, Isabella; VICTUUM.

6632 Lopez, Tom. Pilsen. NUESTRO, Vol. 6, no. 7 (September 1982), p. 31. English. **DESCR:** *Pilsen, IL.

6633 Marquez, Antonio. A discordant image: the Mexican in American literature. MINORITY VOICES, Vol. 5, no. 1-2 (Spring, Fall, 1981), p. 41-51. English. **DESCR:** Stereotypes.

6634 Martinez, Julio A. Book review of: A BIBLIOGRAPHY OF CRITICISM OF CONTEMPORARY CHICANO LITERATURE. RQ - REFERENCE AND ADULT SERVICES DIVISION, Vol. 22, no. 1 (Fall 1982), p. 90. English. **DESCR:** *A BIBLIOGRAPHY OF CRITICISM OF CONTEMPORARY CHICANO LITERATURE; Bibliography; Book Reviews; Eger, Ernestina N.; Literary Criticism.

6635 Martinez, Julio A. Book review of: A DECADE OF CHICANO LITERATURE (1970-1979)-CRITICAL ESSAYS AND BIBLIOGRAPHY. RQ - REFERENCE AND ADULT SERVICES DIVISION, Vol. 22, no. 1 (Fall 1982), p. 90. English. **DESCR:** *A DECADE OF CHICANO LITERATURE (1970-1979): CRITICAL ESSAYS AND BIBLIOGRAPHY; Bibliography; Book Reviews; Gonzalez, Raquel Quiroz; Literary Criticism; Literatura Chicanesca; Trujillo, Robert.

6636 Medina, Ruben and Hinojosa-Smith, Rolando R. Rolando Hinojosa: entrevista. MAIZE, Vol. 5, no. 1-2 (Fall, Winter, 1981, 1982), p. 16-31. Spanish. **DESCR:** Authors; *Hinojosa-Smith, Rolando R.

6637 Menton, Seymour. EL LLANO EN LLAMAS: anti-epopeya de la revolucion. LA PALABRA, Vol. 4, no. 1-2 (Spring, Fall, 1982, 1983), p. 93-96. Spanish. **DESCR:** *EL LLANO EN LLAMAS; Literary Criticism; *Rulfo, Juan.

6638 Monleon, Jose and Morales, Alejandro. Entrevista con Alejandro Morales. MAIZE, Vol. 4, no. 1-2 (Fall, Winter, 1980, 1981), p. 9-20. Spanish. **DESCR:** Morales, Alejandro.

6639 La muerte y el deseo: notas sobre la poesia de Juan Felipe Herrera. LA PALABRA, Vol. 4, no. 1-2 (Spring, Fall, 1982, 1983), p. 97-106. Spanish. **DESCR:** *Herrera, Juan Felipe; Literary Criticism; *Poetry.

6640 The new literature: a look at current trends. NUESTRO, Vol. 7, no. 3 (April 1983), p. 22. English. **DESCR:** Literary Criticism; Literary Influence.

6641 Nieto, Eva Margarita. El problema de la juventud eterna en tres hechiceras en THE SECOND RING OF POWER, LA MULATA DE CORDOBA y AURA. LA PALABRA, Vol. 4, no. 1-2 (Spring, Fall, 1982, 1983), p. 81-91. Spanish. **DESCR:** AURA; Castaneda, Carlos; Fuentes, Carlos; Gonzalez Obregon, Luis; LA MULATA DE CORDOBA; *Literary Criticism; Literature Reviews; THE SECOND RING OF POWER.

6642 Orozco, Febe Portillo. A bibliography of Hispanic literature. ENGLISH JOURNAL, Vol. 71, no. 7 (November 1982), p. 58-62. English. **DESCR:** BARRIO BOY; *Bibliography; BLESS ME, ULTIMA; CHICANO; EL SOL Y LOS DE ABAJO; GRITO DEL SOL; HEART OF AZTLAN; POCHO; WE ARE CHICANOS.

6643 Ortego y Gasca, Felipe de. An appreciation of "Hechizospells" by Ricardo Sanchez. MELUS: MULTI-ETHNIC LITERATURE OF THE UNITED STATES, Vol. 7, no. 2 (Summer 1980), p. 73-77. English. **DESCR:** HECHIZOSPELLS; *Sanchez, Ricardo.

6644 Ortego y Gasca, Felipe de. Fables of identity: stereotype and caricature of Chicanos in Steinbeck's TORTILLA FLAT. JOURNAL OF ETHNIC STUDIES, Vol. 1, no. 1 (Spring 1973), p. 39-43. English. **DESCR:** Caricature; Chicanos in American Literature; Steinbeck, John; *Stereotypes; TORTILLA FLAT.

6645 Paredes, Raymund A. Mexican American authors and the American dream. MELUS: MULTI-ETHNIC LITERATURE OF THE UNITED STATES, Vol. 8, no. 4 (Winter 1981), p. 71-80. English.

6646 Parr, Carmen Salazar. Surrealism in the work of Estela Portillo. MELUS: MULTI-ETHNIC LITERATURE OF THE UNITED STATES, Vol. 7, no. 4 (Winter 1980), p. 85-92. English. **DESCR:** *Portillo Trambley, Estela; Surrealism.

6647 Portales, Marco A. Anglo villains and Chicano writers. JOURNAL OF ETHNIC STUDIES, Vol. 9, no. 3 (Fall 1981), p. 78-82. English. **DESCR:** Book Reviews; *HAY PLESHA LICHANS TU DI FLAC; Sanchez, Saul; Stereotypes.

6648 Rangel-Guerrero, Daniel. Book review of: CHICANO AUTHORS: INQUIRY BY INTERVIEW. JOURNAL OF ETHNIC STUDIES, Vol. 10, no. 2 (Summer 1982), p. 117-119. English. **DESCR:** Book Reviews; Bruce Novoa, Juan; *CHICANO AUTHORS: INQUIRY BY INTERVIEW; Comparative Literature; Literary Criticism; Literary History; Literary Influence.

6649 Riesco, Laura. Laura Riesco y el truco de los ojos: entrevista. THIRD WOMAN, Vol. 1, no. 2 (1982), p. 76-82. Spanish. **DESCR:** Literature Reviews; *Riesco, Laura.

6650 Rodriguez del Pino, Salvador. La intimidad poetica de Luis Leal. LA PALABRA, Vol. 4, no. 1-2 (Spring, Fall, 1982, 1983), p. 41-52. Spanish. **DESCR:** Authors; *Leal, Luis; *Poetry.

6651 Saldivar, Ramon. Chicano literature and ideology: prospectus for the 80's: part II: the present. MELUS: MULTI-ETHNIC LITERATURE OF THE UNITED STATES, Vol. 8, no. 2 (Summer 1981), p. 35-39. English.

6652 Saldivar, Ramon. A dialectic of difference: towards a theory of the Chicano novel. MELUS: MULTI-ETHNIC LITERATURE OF THE UNITED STATES, Vol. 6, no. 3 (Fall 1979), p. 73-92. English. **DESCR:** Novel.

6653 Sanchez, Marta. Inter-sexual and intertextual codes in the poetry of Bernice Zamora. MELUS: MULTI-ETHNIC LITERATURE OF THE UNITED STATES, Vol. 7, no. 3 (Fall 1980), p. 55-68. English. **DESCR:** RESTLESS SERPENTS; *Zamora, Bernice.

6654 Sanchez, Saul. La incipiente narrativa chicana: un espejo de telaranas. CUADERNOS HISPANOAMERICANOS, Vol. 390, (December 1982), p. 641-645. Spanish. **DESCR:** Identity.

6655 See, Lisa. Chicano writers: looking for a breakout. PUBLISHER'S WEEKLY, Vol. 224, (September 30, 1983), p. 94. English. **DESCR:** *Authors; Publishing Industry.

Literature (cont.)

6656 Shirley, Paula. Book review of: MEMORIES OF
THE ALHAMBRA. MELUS: MULTI-ETHNIC LITERATURE
OF THE UNITED STATES, Vol. 6, no. 2 (Summer
1979), p. 100-103. English. **DESCR:** Book
Reviews; Candelaria, Nash; *MEMORIES OF THE
ALHAMBRA.

6657 A showcase of fiction: NUESTRO's sixth
anniversary edition. NUESTRO, Vol. 7, no. 3
(April 1983), p. 13. English. **DESCR:**
*Fiction.

6658 Soens. Adolph L. Book review of: CHICANOS:
ANTOLOGIA HISTORICA Y LITERARIA. MINORITY
VOICES, Vol. 5, no. 1-2 (Spring, Fall,
1981), p. 69-71. English. **DESCR:** Book
Reviews; *CHICANOS: ANTOLOGIA HISTORICA Y
LITERARIA; Villanueva, Tino.

6659 Tatum, Charles. The sexual underworld of
John Rechy. MINORITY VOICES, Vol. 3, no. 1
(Fall 1979), p. 47-52. English. **DESCR:** CITY
OF NIGHT; *Rechy, John.

6660 Urioste, Donaldo W. Book review of: CUENTOS
CHICANOS. LA PALABRA, Vol. 4, no. 1-2
(Spring, Fall, 1982, 1983), p. 175-177.
Spanish. **DESCR:** Anaya, Rudolfo A.; Book
Reviews; *CUENTOS CHICANOS.

6661 Valencia, Juan O. Salud Pacheco. LA PALABRA,
Vol. 4, no. 1-2 (Spring, Fall, 1982, 1983),
p. 159-162. Spanish. **DESCR:** Prose; *Short
Story.

6662 Vowell, Faye Nell and Portillo Trambley,
Estela. A MELUS interview: Estela
Portillo-Trambley. MELUS: MULTI-ETHNIC
LITERATURE OF THE UNITED STATES, Vol. 9, no.
4 (Winter 1982), p. 59-66. English. **DESCR:**
*Portillo Trambley, Estela.

6663 Walden, Daniel. Parallels between Chicano
and Jewish-American writing. MELUS:
MULTI-ETHNIC LITERATURE OF THE UNITED
STATES, Vol. 8, no. 2 (Summer 1981), p.
57-60. English. **DESCR:** Jews.

6664 Zamora, Carlos. Book review of: MOSAICO DE
LA VIDA: CHICANO, CUBAN AND PUERTO RICAN
PROSE. MINORITY VOICES, Vol. 5, no. 1-2
(Spring, Fall, 1981), p. 71-72. English.
DESCR: Book Reviews; Jimenez, Francisco;
*MOSAICO DE LA VIDA: CHICANO, CUBAN AND
PUERTO RICAN PROSE.

6665 Zamora, Carlos. Odysseus in John Rechy's
CITY OF NIGHT: the epistemological journey.
MINORITY VOICES, Vol. 3, no. 1 (Fall 1979),
p. 53-62. English. **DESCR:** *CITY OF NIGHT;
*Rechy, John.

6666 Zimmerman, Enid. An annotated bibliography
of Chicano literature: novels, short
fiction, poetry, and drama, 1970-1980.
BILINGUAL REVIEW, Vol. 9, no. 3 (September,
December, 1982), p. 227-251. English.
DESCR: *Bibliography; Poetry; Teatro.

Literature Reviews

6667 Andrews, Ilse. Bilinguals out of focus: a
critical discussion. IRAL: INT'L REVIEW OF
APPLIED LINGUISTICS IN LANGUAGE TEACHING,
Vol. 20, no. 4 (November 1982), p. 297-305.
English. **DESCR:** *Bilingualism; Book Reviews;
Martin, Albert; Obler, Loraine K.; *THE
BILINGUAL BRAIN.

6668 Arnold, Bill R. Attitudinal research and
Hispanic handicapped: a review of selected
needs. JOURNAL OF REHABILITATION, Vol. 49,

no. 4 (October, December, 1983), p. 36-38.
English. **DESCR:** Attitude (Psychological);
*Handicapped.

6669 Baca Zinn, Maxine. Book review of: LA
CHICANA: THE MEXICAN AMERICAN WOMAN. SIGNS:
JOURNAL OF WOMEN IN CULTURE AND SOCIETY,
Vol. 8, no. 2 (Winter 1982), p. 259-272.
English. **DESCR:** Book Reviews; Chicanas;
Enriquez, Evangelina; *LA CHICANA: THE
MEXICAN AMERICAN WOMAN; Mirande, Alfredo;
Social Science.

6670 Baca Zinn, Maxine. Book review of: MEXICAN
WOMEN IN THE UNITED STATES: STRUGGLES PAST
AND PRESENT. SIGNS: JOURNAL OF WOMEN IN
CULTURE AND SOCIETY, Vol. 8, no. 2 (Winter
1982), p. 259-272. English. **DESCR:** Book
Reviews; Chicanas; Del Castillo, Adelaida
R.; *MEXICAN WOMEN IN THE UNITED STATES:
STRUGGLES PAST AND PRESENT; Mora, Magdalena;
Social Science.

6671 Baca Zinn, Maxine. Book review of: TWICE A
MINORITY; MEXICAN-AMERICAN WOMEN. SIGNS:
JOURNAL OF WOMEN IN CULTURE AND SOCIETY,
Vol. 8, no. 2 (Winter 1982), p. 259-272.
English. **DESCR:** Book Reviews; Chicanas;
Melville, Margarita B.; Social Science;
*TWICE A MINORITY: MEXICAN-AMERICAN WOMEN.

6672 Baca Zinn, Maxine. Mexican American women in
the social sciences. SIGNS: JOURNAL OF WOMEN
IN CULTURE AND SOCIETY, Vol. 8, no. 2
(Winter 1982), p. 259-272. English. **DESCR:**
*Chicanas; Social Science.

6673 Barradas, Efrain. Conciencia femenina,
conciencia social: la voz poetica de Sandra
Maria Esteves. THIRD WOMAN, Vol. 1, no. 2
(1982), p. 31-34. Spanish. **DESCR:** *Esteves,
Sandra Maria.

6674 Cordasco, Francesco. Bilingual education:
overview and inventory. EDUCATIONAL FORUM,
Vol. 47, (Spring 1983), p. 321-334.
English. **DESCR:** *Bilingual Bicultural
Education; Educational Law and Legislation;
Educational Theory and Practice; English as
a Second Language; History.

6675 Cordasco, Francesco. Bilingual education in
American schools: a bibliographical essay.
IMMIGRATION HISTORY NEWSLETTER, Vol. 14, no.
1 (May 1982), p. 1-8. English. **DESCR:**
*Bilingual Bicultural Education.

6676 Duncan, Erika. Myriam Diaz - Diocaretz:
letting the sun look into our eyes. THIRD
WOMAN, Vol. 1, no. 2 (1982), p. 70-75.
English. **DESCR:** *Poetry.

6677 Greenblatt, Milton and Norman, Margie.
Hispanic mental health and use of mental
health services: a critical review of the
literature. AMERICAN JOURNAL OF SOCIAL
PSYCHIATRY, Vol. 2, no. 3 (Summer 1982), p.
25-31. English. **DESCR:** *Mental Health.

6678 Haro, Carlos Manuel. Chicanos and higher
education: a review of selected literature.
AZTLAN, Vol. 14, no. 1 (Spring 1983), p.
35-77. English. **DESCR:** California;
Education; *Higher Education; Students.

Literature Reviews (cont.)

6679 Moore, Richard J. Book review of: "TEMPORARY" ALIEN WORKERS IN THE UNITED STATES: DESIGNING POLICY FROM FACT AND OPINION. INTERNATIONAL MIGRATION REVIEW, Vol. 16, no. 4 (Winter 1982), p. 909-910. English. DESCR: Book Reviews; Immigration Law; Ross, Stanley R.; *"TEMPORARY" ALIEN WORKERS IN THE UNITED STATES: DESIGNING POLICY FROM FACT AND OPINION; Undocumented Workers; Weintraub, Sidney.

6680 Nieto, Eva Margarita. El problema de la juventud eterna en tres hechiceras en THE SECOND RING OF POWER, LA MULATA DE CORDOBA y AURA. LA PALABRA, Vol. 4, no. 1-2 (Spring, Fall, 1982, 1983), p. 81-91. Spanish. DESCR: AURA; Castaneda, Carlos; Fuentes, Carlos; Gonzalez Obregon, Luis; LA MULATA DE CORDOBA; *Literary Criticism; Literature; THE SECOND RING OF POWER.

6681 Riesco, Laura. Laura Riesco y el truco de los ojos: entrevista. THIRD WOMAN, Vol. 1, no. 2 (1982), p. 76-82. Spanish. DESCR: Literature; *Riesco, Laura.

6682 Roeder, Beatrice A. Health care beliefs and practices among the Mexican Americans. AZTLAN, Vol. 13, no. 1-2 (Spring, Fall, 1982), p. 223-256. English. DESCR: Folk Medicine; Medical Care; Public Health.

6683 Schon, Isabel. Recent outstanding books for young readers from Spanish speaking countries. READING TEACHER, Vol. 36, no. 2 (November 1982), p. 206-209. English. DESCR: Argentina; *Children's Literature; Spain; Spanish Language; Venezuela.

6684 Soto, Shirlene Ann. The emerging Chicana: a review of the journals. SOUTHWEST ECONOMY AND SOCIETY, Vol. 2, no. 1 (October, November, 1976), p. 39-45. English. DESCR: *Chicanas; Directories; Periodicals.

6685 Wagoner, Shirley A. Mexican-Americans in children's literature since 1970. READING TEACHER, Vol. 36, no. 3 (December 1982), p. 274-279. English. DESCR: *Children's Literature; Stereotypes.

6686 Webster, David S. Chicano students in American higher education: a review of the literature. CAMPO LIBRE, Vol. 1, no. 2 (Summer 1981), p. 169-192. English. DESCR: Dropouts; Educational Statistics; Enrollment; Graduate Schools; *Higher Education; Professional Schools.

Lithographs

6687 Lopez, Oscar. Untitled lithograph. MAIZE, Vol. 5, no. 1-2 (Fall, Winter, 1981, 1982), p. 32.

6688 Lopez, Oscar. Untitled lithograph. MAIZE, Vol. 5, no. 1-2 (Fall, Winter, 1981, 1982), p. 47.

THE LITTLE DEER

6689 Herrera, Hayden. Making an art of pain. PSYCHOLOGY TODAY, Vol. 17, no. 3 (March 1983), p. 86. English. DESCR: Biography; HENRY FORD HOSPITAL; *Kahlo, Frida; Paintings; SELF-PORTRAIT WITH PORTRAIT OF DR. FARILL; THE BROKEN COLUMN; TREE OF HOPE; WITHOUT HOPE.

Little Havana

6690 Fifth member leaves panel. NUESTRO, Vol. 6, no. 4 (May 1982), p. 11. English. DESCR: *Lew, Salvador; Miami, FL; Police; Violence.

6691 Greenfield, Charles. Cuban theater in exile: Miami's little Broadway. NUESTRO, Vol. 6, no. 9 (November 1982), p. 36-38. English. DESCR: Cubanos; *Miami, FL; *Teatro.

6692 The Little Havana development authority. HISPANIC BUSINESS, Vol. 4, no. 3 (March 1982), p. 10+. English. DESCR: Carnaval Miami 82; *Community Development; Cubanos; Miami, FL.

Little People of America

6693 Family displays special courage. NUESTRO, Vol. 7, no. 1 (January, February, 1983), p. 10. English. DESCR: *Luna, Brian; Medicine.

Liturgy

6694 Ramirez, Ricardo. Reflections on the Hispanicization of the liturgy. WORSHIP, Vol. 57, no. 1 (January 1983), p. 26-34. English. DESCR: Catholic Church; Clergy; Religion; Third General Conference of the Latin American Episcopate.

Lizarraga, David C.

6695 Baciu, Joyce A. The winners - Los ganadores. CAMINOS, Vol. 3, no. 2 (February 1982), p. 14-20,45. Bilingual. DESCR: *Awards; Caldera, Manuel; Gomez, Ignacio; Huerta, Dolores; Obledo, Mario; Olmos, Edward James; Rivera, Geraldo; Rivera, Tomas.

Llanes, Jose

6696 Rivera, Mario A. Book review of: CUBAN AMERICANS: MASTERS OF SURVIVAL. MIGRATION TODAY, Vol. 11, no. 4-5 (1983), p. 53. English. DESCR: Book Reviews; *CUBAN AMERICANS: MASTERS OF SURVIVAL; Cubanos.

EL LLANO EN LLAMAS

6697 Menton, Seymour. EL LLANO EN LLAMAS: anti-epopeya de la revolucion. LA PALABRA, Vol. 4, no. 1-2 (Spring, Fall, 1982, 1983), p. 93-96. Spanish. DESCR: Literary Criticism; Literature; *Rulfo, Juan.

LA LLEGADA

6698 Fernandez, Jose B. Book review of: LA LLEGADA. REVISTA CHICANO-RIQUENA, Vol. 10, no. 3 (Summer 1982), p. 67-68. Spanish. DESCR: Book Reviews; Gonzalez, Jose Luis.

Lloyd, Peter

6699 Logan, Kathleen. The urban poor in developing nations. JOURNAL OF URBAN HISTORY, Vol. 9, no. 1 (November 1982), p. 108-116. English. DESCR: ACCESS TO POWER: POLITICS AND THE URBAN POOR IN DEVELOPING NATIONS; *Book Reviews; BORDER BOOM TOWN: CIUDAD JUAREZ SINCE 1848; Collier, David; Cornelius, Wayne A.; Eckstein, Susan; Martinez, Oscar J.; Nelson, Joan M.; Perlman, Janice E.; POLITICS AND MIGRANT POOR IN MEXICO CITY; SLUMS OF HOPE? SHANTY TOWNS OF THE THIRD WORLD; SQUATTERS AND OLIGARCHS: AUTHORITARIAN RULE AND POLICY CHANGE IN PERU; THE MYTH OF MARGINALITY: URBAN POVERTY AND POLITICS IN RIO DE JANEIRO; THE POVERTY OF REVOLUTION: THE STATE AND THE URBAN POOR IN MEXICO; Urban Economics.

Loans (Student)
USE: Financial Aid

Lobbying

6700 Fraser Rothenberg, Irene. Chicanos, the
Panama Canal issues and the Reagan campaign:
reflections from 1976 and projections for
1980. JOURNAL OF ETHNIC STUDIES, Vol. 7, no.
4 (Winter 1980), p. 37-49. English. DESCR:
*International Relations; Nationalism;
Newspapers; Panama; *Panama Canal; Politics;
Reagan, Ronald.

6701 Fraser Rothenberg, Irene. Mexican-American
views of U.S. relations with Latin America.
JOURNAL OF ETHNIC STUDIES, Vol. 6, no. 1
(Spring 1978), p. 62-78. English. DESCR:
Chicano Movement; Culture; Identity;
International Relations; Latin America;
Mexico; *Nationalism; Political History and
Conditions; Politics.

Local Government

6702 An anniversary is observed. NUESTRO, Vol. 7,
no. 8 (October 1983), p. 13. English.
DESCR: *Batista, Fulgencio; Cuba; Cubanos;
Ferre, Maurice; Miami, FL.

6703 Bonilla, Tony. Local government is no
answer. LATINO, Vol. 53, no. 7 (November
1982), p. 5. English.

6704 Business notes. HISPANIC BUSINESS, Vol. 5,
no. 12 (December 1983), p. 35. English.
DESCR: Anheuser-Busch, Inc.; *Business
Enterprises; Denny's Inc.; Des Moines, IA;
El Pollo Loco; Food Industry; Martinez,
Vilma Socorro; National Association of
Latino Elected Officials (NALEO); Ochoa,
Juan Pancho.

6705 Chicago's mayoralty race. HISPANIC BUSINESS,
Vol. 5, no. 7 (July 1983), p. 27-28.
English. DESCR: Chicago, IL; Elections;
*Voter Turnout.

6706 Councilman wins despite problems. NUESTRO,
Vol. 7, no. 3 (April 1983), p. 12. English.
DESCR: Elections; *Eureste, Bernardo.

6707 MacManus, Susan A. and Cassel, Carol A.
Mexican-Americans in city-politics:
participation, representation, and policy
preferences. URBAN INTEREST, Vol. 4, no. 1
(Spring 1982), p. 57-69. English. DESCR:
Blacks; Houston, TX; *Political
Representation; Public Opinion; Public
Policy.

6708 Martinez, Chip. Federico Pena: Denver's
first Hispanic mayor. NUESTRO, Vol. 7, no. 6
(August 1983), p. 14-20. English. DESCR:
Denver, CO; Elections; *Pena, Federico;
Voter Turnout.

6709 Park inequity pursued. NUESTRO, Vol. 7, no.
1 (January, February, 1983), p. 9. English.
DESCR: *Chicago Park District; Racism.

6710 Thomas Fuentes: community builder. HISPANIC
BUSINESS, Vol. 5, no. 11 (November 1983), p.
16-17. English. DESCR: Engineering as a
Profession; *Fuentes, Thomas; Orange County,
CA; Urban Development.

6711 Whisler, Kirk. Hispanic representation in
California's cities: progress??? CAMINOS,
Vol. 4, no. 3 (March 1983), p. 42-43,49.
English. DESCR: California; *Elected
Officials.

Locke, John

6712 Garcia, Reyes. Politics of flesh: ethnicity
and political viability. CACR REVIEW, Vol.
1, no. 1 (September 1982), p. 102-130.
English. DESCR: Anaya, Rudolfo A.;
Aristotle; Culture; Ethnic Groups; Identity;
Nuclear Armament; Philosophy; *Political
Repression; Urban Communities.

Locus of Control

6713 Anderson, John W. The effects of culture and
social class on client preference for
counseling methods. JOURNAL OF NON-WHITE
CONCERNS IN PERSONNEL AND GUIDANCE, Vol. 11,
no. 3 (April 1983), p. 84-88. English.
DESCR: Anglo Americans; Blacks; Counseling
Effectiveness Scale; *Counseling
(Psychological); *Educational Opportunity
Program (EOP); University of Illinois at
Urbana.

6714 Davis, James Alston. Does authority
generalize? Locus of control perceptions in
Anglo-American and Mexican-American
adolescents. POLITICAL PSYCHOLOGY, Vol. 4,
no. 1 (March 1983), p. 101-120. English.
DESCR: Comparative Psychology; Family; High
School Students; Internal-External
Reinforcement Scale; Political Ideology.

6715 Garza, Raymond T., et al. Biculturalism,
locus of control and leader behavior in
ethnically mixed small groups. JOURNAL OF
APPLIED SOCIAL PSYCHOLOGY, Vol. 12, no. 3
(May, June, 1982), p. 237-253. English.
DESCR: Attitude (Psychological);
*Biculturalism; Culture; Interpersonal
Relations; Leadership; Social Psychology.

6716 Hui, C. Harry. Multistrategy approach to
cross-cultural research: the case of locus
of control. JOURNAL OF CROSS-CULTURAL
PSYCHOLOGY, Vol. 14, no. 1 (March 1983), p.
65-83. English. DESCR: Comparative
Psychology; *Military Personnel;
Psychological Testing.

6717 Medinnus, Gene R.; Ford, Martin Z.; and
Tack-Robinson, Susan. Locus of control: a
cross-cultural comparison. PSYCHOLOGICAL
REPORTS, Vol. 53, no. 1 (August 1983), p.
131-134. English. DESCR: *Fatalism; Junior
High School Students; Personality.

Loevinger's Sentence Completion Test

6718 Wurzman, Ilyana. Cultural values of Puerto
Rican opiate addicts: an exploratory study.
AMERICAN JOURNAL OF DRUG AND ALCOHOL ABUSE,
Vol. 9, no. 2 (1982, 1983), p. 141-153.
English. DESCR: Acculturation; Anglo
Americans; Blacks; *Drug Abuse; Drug
Addicts; Family; Machismo; New York, NY;
Opium; Puerto Ricans; Values.

Loffel, Egon W.

6719 Research/development: books. HISPANIC
BUSINESS, Vol. 4, no. 2 (February 1982), p.
28. English. DESCR: Book Reviews; Business;
Business Enterprises; *FINANCING YOUR
BUSINESS; *National Hispanic Center for
Advanced Studies and Policy Analysis
(NHCAS); Public Policy; *THE STATE OF
HISPANIC AMERICA.

Logos or Symbols
USE: Symbolism

Long, Dennis P.

6720 People. HISPANIC BUSINESS, Vol. 5, no. 3 (March 1983), p. 9. English. **DESCR**: Anaya, Toney; Anguiano, Lupe; Appointed Officials; Avila, Joaquin Guadalupe; Awards; *Biographical Notes; de la Fuente, Emilio; del Olmo, Frank; Godoy, Gustavo; Martinez, Elias (Lee); Rivera, Joseph, Jr.

Longoria, Felix

6721 Pena, Manuel H. Folksong and social change: two corridos as interpretive sources. AZTLAN, Vol. 13, no. 1-2 (Spring, Fall, 1982), p. 12-42. English. **DESCR**: Corrido; Cortez, Gregorio; *DISCRIMINACION A UN MARTIR [corrido]; *EL CORRIDO DE GREGORIO CORTE [corrido]; *Folk Songs; Music.

Lonner, Walter J.

6722 Franco, Juan N. Book review of: COUNSELING ACROSS CULTURES. HISPANIC JOURNAL OF BEHAVIORAL SCIENCES, Vol. 5, no. 2 (June), p. 233-237. English. **DESCR**: Book Reviews; *COUNSELING ACROSS CULTURES; Draguns, Juris G.; Pedersen, Paul P.; Trimble, Joseph E.

Lopez, Antonio

6723 Ramirez, Sylvia E. Bilingual radio: reaching new horizons. CAMINOS, Vol. 3, no. 5 (May 1982), p. 38-39. Bilingual. **DESCR**: *Radio; Ramos, Juan; WCBR (Western Community Bilingual Radio) [radio station].

Lopez, Aurelia

6724 Ortiz, Carlos V. NUESTRO's 1981 all-star baseball team. NUESTRO, Vol. 6, no. 2 (March 1982), p. 55-58. English. **DESCR**: Martinez, Felix; *Sports.

Lopez, Conchita

6725 Gonzalez, Magdalena. Recognizing Hispanic achievements in entertainment - U.S. and Mexico. CAMINOS, Vol. 3, no. 7 (July, August, 1982), p. 18-24. Bilingual. **DESCR**: Allende, Fernando; Artists; Awards; Bonilla Giannini, Roxanna; Eynoso, David; Felix, Maria; Films; Gallego, Gina; *Golden Eagle Awards; Hoyos, Rodolfo; Lamas, Lorenzo; Lopez, Lisa; Montalban, Ricardo; Nosotros [film production company]; Quintero, Jose; Rowe, Arthur; Television; Torres, Liz.

Lopez, Diana

6726 Lomeli, Francisco A. Isabella Rios and the Chicano psychic novel. MINORITY VOICES, Vol. 4, no. 1 (Spring 1980), p. 49-61. English. **DESCR**: Literature; Novel; *Rios, Isabella; VICTUUM.

Lopez, Fidel

6727 Lanier, Alfredo S. Continental's Fidel Lopez takes an encompassing view. HISPANIC BUSINESS, Vol. 4, no. 4 (April 1982), p. 16-17,24. English. **DESCR**: Biography; Chicago, IL; Urban Communities; Urban Development.

Lopez, Genevieve

6728 Rivera-Cano, Andrea. Parenting: four families' stories. LATINA, Vol. 1, no. 2 (February, March, 1983), p. 66-73+. English. **DESCR**: *Child Rearing; Children; Elias, Bob; Hernandez, Jesus; Hernandez, Virginia; Ojalvo, Juana.

Lopez, Isabel

6729 Regional report, health: student cited for aging work. NUESTRO, Vol. 7, no. 4 (May 1983), p. 13. English. **DESCR**: Ancianos.

Lopez, Jose

6730 Weinberger, Caspar W. A heritage of valor - Hispanics in America's defense: remarks... at the recent unveiling of paintings of Hispanic heroes at the Pentagon. NUESTRO, Vol. 7, no. 9 (November 1983), p. 18. English. **DESCR**: Del Valle, Pedro A.; Gabaldon, Guy; *Military Service; Paintings; Rivero, Horacio.

Lopez, Leonard

6731 People. HISPANIC BUSINESS, Vol. 5, no. 11 (November 1983), p. 10. English. **DESCR**: Aragon, Fermin; *Businesspeople; De Los Reyes, Victor; Di Martino, Rita; Garcia, Ruben; Juarez, Chris; Nogales, Luis G.; Ozuna, Bob; Rico, Jose Hipolito; Tamayo, Roberto; Tapia, Raul R.

Lopez, Lillian

6732 Naismith, Rachael. Outreach services to Hispanics. ILLINOIS LIBRARIES, Vol. 64, no. 7 (September 1982), p. 962-966. English. **DESCR**: Arrondo, Ondina; Cubanos; La Raza Hispanica, Miami, FL; Latin American Library/Biblioteca Latinoamericana, Oakland, CA; *Library Services; Puerto Ricans; Ruiz, Deborah; South Bronx Project, New York Public Library; Verges, Bruni.

Lopez, Lisa

6733 Entertaiment reviews. CAMINOS, Vol. 3, no. 8 (September 1982), p. 21. English. **DESCR**: Adams, Bob; Alpert, Herb; Books; Calvert, Robert; Jimenez, Santiago; Music; Myles, Carol; Paredes, Americo; Pettus, Theodore T.; *Recreation; Television.

6734 Gonzalez, Magdalena. Recognizing Hispanic achievements in entertainment - U.S. and Mexico. CAMINOS, Vol. 3, no. 7 (July, August, 1982), p. 18-24. Bilingual. **DESCR**: Allende, Fernando; Artists; Awards; Bonilla Giannini, Roxanna; Eynoso, David; Felix, Maria; Films; Gallego, Gina; *Golden Eagle Awards; Hoyos, Rodolfo; Lamas, Lorenzo; Lopez, Conchita; Montalban, Ricardo; Nosotros [film production company]; Quintero, Jose; Rowe, Arthur; Television; Torres, Liz.

6735 Gozando de la vida. LATINO, Vol. 53, no. 4 (June 1982), p. 16-17. Spanish. **DESCR**: Biography.

Lopez, Nancy

6736 Cardenas, Leo. Family unit. LATINO, Vol. 53, no. 6 (October 1982), p. 14-15. English. **DESCR**: Sports.

Lopez Portillo, Jose

6737 Miguel de la Madrid en la prensa norteamericana. INFORME: RELACIONES MEXICO-ESTADOS UNIDOS, Vol. 1, no. 2 (July, December, 1982), p. 176-183. Spanish. **DESCR**: *De la Madrid, Miguel; *Journalism; LOS ANGELES TIMES; NEW YORK TIMES; Newspapers; WALL STREET JOURNAL; WASHINGTON POST.

Lopez Portillo, Jose (cont.)

6738 Vidal, Jose. Lopez Portillo's
     accomplishments. CAMINOS, Vol. 3, no. 6
     (June 1982), p. 22. Bilingual. DESCR:
     Elected Officials.

Lopez, Reynaldo H.

6739 News at the SBA. HISPANIC BUSINESS, Vol. 4,
     no. 2 (February 1982), p. 22. English.
     DESCR: *Biographical Notes; Cardenas,
     Michael; Castillo, Irenemaree; U.S. Small
     Business Administration.

Lopez, Trini

6740 Lopez, Trini. Dando una mano. LATINO, Vol.
     53, no. 7 (November 1982), p. 11. Spanish.
     DESCR: Biography; Musicians.

Lopez, Victor M.

6741 People. HISPANIC BUSINESS, Vol. 4, no. 10
     (October 1982), p. 7. English. DESCR:
     Aguilar, Gloria; Biographical Notes;
     *Businesspeople; Caldera, Manuel R.;
     Ramirez, Steve.

Lopez-Grant, Lillian

6742 Gonzales, Patrisia. The two cities of
     Tucson. NUESTRO, Vol. 7, no. 4 (May 1983),
     p. 20-23. English. DESCR: Accion 80s;
     Cultural Organizations; *Discrimination in
     Education; *Discrimination in Employment;
     Garcia, Gerald; *Tucson, AZ; Valdez, Joel.

Lorca, Federico Garcia

6743 BLOOD WEDDING. NUESTRO, Vol. 5, no. 8
     (November 1981), p. 50. English. DESCR:
     *Film Reviews; Gades, Antonio; *Saura,
     Carlos.

Lorenzo de Zavala Mock Legislative Session

6744 Marquez, Roberto. Experiencing state
     government. NATIONAL HISPANIC JOURNAL, Vol.
     1, no. 3 (Summer, Fall, 1982), p. 16-18.
     English. DESCR: *National Hispanic
     Institute; *State Government.

THE LOS ANGELES BARRIO 1850-1890: A SOCIAL HISTORY

6745 Britt, Anita. Book review of: THE LOS
     ANGELES BARRIO 1850-1890: A SOCIAL HISTORY.
     HISPANIC JOURNAL OF BEHAVIORAL SCIENCES,
     Vol. 4, no. 3 (September 1982), p. 388-391.
     English. DESCR: Book Reviews; Griswold del
     Castillo, Ricardo.

6746 Garcia, Mario T. Book review of: LOS ANGELES
     BARRIO 1850-1890: A SOCIAL HISTORY. PACIFIC
     HISTORICAL REVIEW, Vol. 51, no. 1 (February
     1982), p. 90-91. English. DESCR: Barrios;
     Book Reviews; Griswold del Castillo,
     Ricardo; Los Angeles, CA.

6747 Lotchin, Roger W. New Chicano history: an
     urban history perspective. HISTORY TEACHER,
     Vol. 16, no. 2 (February 1983), p. 229-247.
     English. DESCR: Camarillo, Alberto; CHICANOS
     IN A CHANGING SOCIETY; DESERT IMMIGRANTS:
     THE MEXICANS OF EL PASO 1880-1920; Garcia,
     Mario T.; Griswold del Castillo, Ricardo;
     *Historiography; History; Social History and
     Conditions; Urban Communities.

6748 Weber, David J. and Lotchin, Roger W. The
     new Chicano history: two perspectives.
     HISTORY TEACHER, Vol. 16, no. 2 (February
     1983), p. 219-247. English. DESCR:
     Camarillo, Alberto; *CHICANOS IN A CHANGING
     SOCIETY; DESERT IMMIGRANTS: THE MEXICANS OF
     EL PASO 1880-1920; Garcia, Mario T.;
     Griswold del Castillo, Ricardo;
     *Historiography; History; Social History and
     Conditions; *Urban Communities.

6749 Weber, David J. The new Chicano urban
     history. HISTORY TEACHER, Vol. 16, no. 2
     (February 1983), p. 223-229. English.
     DESCR: Camarillo, Alberto; *CHICANOS IN A
     CHANGING SOCIETY; DESERT IMMIGRANTS: THE
     MEXICANS OF EL PASO 1880-1920; Garcia, Mario
     T.; Griswold del Castillo, Ricardo;
     *Historiography; History; Social History and
     Conditions; Urban Communities.

Los Angeles Basin Equal Opportunity League

6750 Thomas, William. Affirmative action under
     fire. CAMINOS, Vol. 3, no. 8 (September
     1982), p. 47. English. DESCR: *Affirmative
     Action.

Los Angeles Bicentennial

6751 201 [special issue of CHISMEARTE].
     CHISMEARTE, (1982), p. 6-66. Bilingual.
     DESCR: *Los Angeles, CA; U.S.A.
     Bicentennial.

6752 Quesada-Weiner, Rosemary. Blowing out the
     candles on 200 years=Apagando las velas de
     los 200 anos de L.A. CAMINOS, Vol. 2, no. 6
     (October 1981), p. 26-27. Bilingual. DESCR:
     Los Angeles, CA.

Los Angeles Board of Public Works

6753 Business notes. HISPANIC BUSINESS, Vol. 5,
     no. 10 (October 1983), p. 13. English.
     DESCR: *Business Administration; Business
     Enterprises; Claudio, Irma; Investments;
     Oakland, CA; Taxation; Tri-Oakland
     Development Corporation; Wisconsin Minority
     Business Forum '83.

6754 Olympic$. Who's going to profit? LATINA,
     Vol. 1, no. 2 (February, March, 1983), p.
     76. English. DESCR: *Olympics.

Los Angeles, CA

6755 201 [special issue of CHISMEARTE].
     CHISMEARTE, (1982), p. 6-66. Bilingual.
     DESCR: *Los Angeles Bicentennial; U.S.A.
     Bicentennial.

6756 Andersen, Kurt. The new Ellis Island. TIME,
     Vol. 121, no. 24 (June 13, 1983), p. 18-25.
     English. DESCR: Demography; *Ethnic Groups.

6757 Arroyo, Sara G. and Tucker, M. Belinda.
     Black residential mobility: trends and
     characteristics. JOURNAL OF SOCIAL ISSUES,
     Vol. 38, no. 3 (1982), p. 51-74. English.
     DESCR: *Housing; Undocumented Children;
     Watts, CA.

6758 The battle of Chavez Ravine, 1949-1959.
     CAMINOS, Vol. 4, no. 7 (July, August, 1983),
     p. 11-14,38. Bilingual. DESCR: *Chavez
     Ravine, Los Angeles, CA; History.

6759 Changing Hispanic political loyalties.
     HISPANIC BUSINESS, Vol. 4, no. 6 (June
     1982), p. 23. English. DESCR: *Political
     Parties and Organizations; Politics; Public
     Policy; San Antonio, TX; *Surveys.

Los Angeles, CA (cont.)

6760 Del Olmo, Frank. Latinos: they were a people living between two worlds (reprinted LOS ANGELES TIMES August 14, 1983). MIGRATION TODAY, Vol. 11, no. 4-5 (1983), p. 5-6+. English.

6761 Diaz, Katherine A. Congressman Edward Roybal: Los Angeles before the 1960's (interview). CAMINOS, Vol. 4, no. 7 (July, August, 1983), p. 15-17,38. Bilingual. **DESCR**: History; *Roybal, Edward R.

6762 First race for scouts occurs in East L.A. NUESTRO, Vol. 6, no. 1 (January, February, 1982), p. 47. English. **DESCR**: Funding Sources; *Godoy, Carlos Piloy; Palomino, Carlos.

6763 Garcia, Mario T. Book review of: LOS ANGELES BARRIO 1850-1890: A SOCIAL HISTORY. PACIFIC HISTORICAL REVIEW, Vol. 51, no. 1 (February 1982), p. 90-91. English. **DESCR**: Barrios; Book Reviews; Griswold del Castillo, Ricardo; *THE LOS ANGELES BARRIO 1850-1890: A SOCIAL HISTORY.

6764 Gonzalez, Gilbert G. Educational reform and the Mexican community in Los Angeles. SOUTHWEST ECONOMY AND SOCIETY, Vol. 3, no. 3 (Spring 1978), p. 24-51. English. **DESCR**: Counseling Services (Educational); Curriculum; *Education; Enrollment; *History; Intelligence Tests; *Los Angeles City School District; Tracking (Educational); Vocational Education.

6765 The great wall of Los Angeles. CAMINOS, Vol. 4, no. 9 (October 1983), p. 46-47. English. **DESCR**: *Mural Art.

6766 Grimond, John. The reconquista begins. LOS ANGELES, Vol. 27, (May 1982), p. 190-195. English. **DESCR**: Demography; United Neighborhoods Organization (UNO).

6767 Griswold del Castillo, Richard. La familia Chicana: social change in the Chicano family of Los Angeles, 1850-1880. JOURNAL OF ETHNIC STUDIES, Vol. 3, no. 1 (Spring 1975), p. 41-58. English. **DESCR**: *Family; Industrialization; Social History and Conditions.

6768 Hines, Thomas S. Housing, baseball, and creeping socialism: the battle of Chavez Ravine, Los Angeles, 1949-1959. JOURNAL OF URBAN HISTORY, Vol. 8, no. 2 (1982), p. 123-143. English. **DESCR**: Barrios; *Chavez Ravine, Los Angeles, CA; Urban Communities; Urban Renewal.

6769 The history of Los Angeles: a Mexican perspective. CHISMEARTE, no. 9 (September 1983), p. 20-21. English. **DESCR**: Carrasco, Barbara; *Mural Art.

6770 Hough, Richard. The Los Angeles Epidemiologic Catchment Area research program and the epidemiology of psychiatric disorders among Mexican Americans. JOURNAL OF OPERATIONAL PSYCHIATRY, Vol. 14, no. 1 (1983), p. 42-51. English. **DESCR**: Acculturation; Diagnostic Interview Schedule (DIS); El Centro Community Health Care Center; *Los Angeles Epidemiologic Catchment Area Research Program (LAECA); *Mental Health.

6771 Kanellos, Nicolas. Two centuries of Hispanic theatre in the Southwest. REVISTA CHICANO-RIQUENA, Vol. 11, no. 1 (Spring 1983), p. 17-39. English. **DESCR**: California; History; Photography; San Antonio, TX; Southwest United States; *Teatro; Texas.

6772 KMEX-TV dominates the Hispanic market. HISPANIC BUSINESS, Vol. 5, no. 12 (December 1983), p. 16-17. English. **DESCR**: Advertising; *KMEX, Los Angeles, CA [television station]; Marketing; *Television.

6773 Latino students rapidly increase. NUESTRO, Vol. 6, no. 10 (December 1982), p. 10. English. **DESCR**: *Population; *Population Distribution; *Population Trends.

6774 Mendez Gonzalez, Rosalinda. Mexican women and families: rural-to-urban and international migration. SOUTHWEST ECONOMY AND SOCIETY, Vol. 4, no. 2 (Winter 1978, 1979), p. 14-27. English. **DESCR**: Chicanas; Employment; *Family; Garment Industry; Immigration; International Ladies Garment Workers Union (ILGWU); Labor Organizing; Undocumented Workers.

6775 Mexican centers advance U.S. ties. NUESTRO, Vol. 7, no. 1 (January, February, 1983), p. 10-11. English. **DESCR**: Art Galleries; *El Centro Mexicano del Libro; Mexico; Museums; New York, NY; Publishing Industry.

6776 Monroy, Douglas. Anarquismo y comunismo: Mexican radicalism and the Communist Party in Los Angeles during the 1930's. LABOR HISTORY, Vol. 24, no. 1 (Winter 1983), p. 34-59. English. **DESCR**: Cannery and Agricultural Worker's Industrial Union; *Communist Party; Confederacion de Uniones de Obreros Mexicanos (CUOM); History; International Ladies Garment Workers Union (ILGWU); Labor; Labor Organizing; Tenayuca, Emma; Worker's Alliance (WA), Los Angeles, CA.

6777 Morales, Rebecca. Transitional labor: undocumented workers in the Los Angeles automobile industry. INTERNATIONAL MIGRATION REVIEW, Vol. 17, no. 4 (Winter 1983), p. 570-596. English. **DESCR**: Automobile Industry; Transitional Labor; *Undocumented Workers.

6778 New Salazar building. NUESTRO, Vol. 6, no. 7 (September 1982), p. 9. English. **DESCR**: *Art; Culture; Education; Latin Americans; *Plaza de La Raza, Los Angeles, CA; Salazar, Ruben.

6779 Olvera Street - a Mexican mercado in the heart of Los Angeles. CAMINOS, Vol. 4, no. 5 (May 1983), p. 26-35,51+. Bilingual. **DESCR**: *Olvera Street, Los Angeles, CA; Tourism.

6780 Parra, Fernando and So, Alvin Yiu-cheong. Changing perceptions of mental illness in a Mexican-American community. JOURNAL OF SOCIAL PSYCHOLOGY, Vol. 29, (Summer 1983), p. 95-100. English. **DESCR**: Anglo Americans; Assimilation; *Mental Health; Random Digit Dialling (RDD).

6781 Quesada-Weiner, Rosemary. Blowing out the candles on 200 years=Apagando las velas de los 200 anos de L.A. CAMINOS, Vol. 2, no. 6 (October 1981), p. 26-27. Bilingual. **DESCR**: *Los Angeles Bicentennial.

6782 Skriloff, Lisa. Music, news dominate Spanish-language radio programming. HISPANIC BUSINESS, Vol. 5, no. 12 (December 1983), p. 34. English. **DESCR**: Advertising; Marketing; Miami, FL; *Radio; San Antonio, TX.

Los Angeles, CA (cont.)

6783 Tomasi, Lydio F. Of diversity and strength [editorial]. MIGRATION TODAY, Vol. 11, no. 4-5 (1983), p. 7. English. **DESCR:** Cultural Characteristics.

6784 Weinberg, Meyer. Bibliography of desegration: Los Angeles. INTEGRATED EDUCATION, Vol. 20, no. 1- (January, April, 1982), p. 32-33. English. **DESCR:** Bibliography; *Segregation and Desegregation.

6785 Yamamoto, Joe and Acosta, Frank X. Treatments of Asian Americans and Hispanic Americans: similarities and differences. JOURNAL OF THE AMERICAN ACADEMY OF PSYCHOANALYSIS, Vol. 10, no. 4 (October 1982), p. 585-607. English. **DESCR:** Asian Americans; Comparative Psychology; *Mental Health; Psychotherapy; Socioeconomic Factors.

Los Angeles City Council

6786 Santillan, Richard. The Chicano community and the redistricting of the Los Angeles city council, 1971-1973. CHICANO LAW REVIEW, Vol. 6, (1983), p. 122-145. English. **DESCR:** Chicanos for Fair Representation (CFR), Los Angeles, CA; Mexican American Legal Defense and Educational Fund (MALDEF); *Political Representation; Snyder, Art, Councilman.

Los Angeles City School District

6787 Gonzalez, Gilbert G. Educational reform and the Mexican community in Los Angeles. SOUTHWEST ECONOMY AND SOCIETY, Vol. 3, no. 3 (Spring 1978), p. 24-51. English. **DESCR:** Counseling Services (Educational); Curriculum; *Education; Enrollment; *History; Intelligence Tests; Los Angeles, CA; Tracking (Educational); Vocational Education.

Los Angeles County, CA

6788 Aneshensel, Carol S.; Clark, Virginia A.; and Frerichs, Ralph R. Race, ethnicity, and depression: a confirmatory analysis. JOURNAL OF PERSONALITY AND SOCIAL PSYCHOLOGY, Vol. 44, no. 2 (February 1983), p. 385-398. English. **DESCR:** *Comparative Psychology.

6789 Estrada, Leobardo F. [Demographic characteristics of Latinos]. CHICANO LAW REVIEW, Vol. 6, (1983), p. 9-16. English. **DESCR:** *Demography; Internal Migration; LATINOS IN THE LAW [symposium], UCLA, 1982; Migration; Migration Patterns; Spanish Language.

Los Angeles Dodgers

6790 Deportes. CAMINOS, Vol. 3, no. 7 (July, August, 1982), p. 46. Spanish. **DESCR:** *Baseball; Guerrero, Pedro; Romo, Vicente.

Los Angeles Epidemiologic Catchment Area Research Program (LAECA)

6791 Hough, Richard. The Los Angeles Epidemiologic Catchment Area research program and the epidemiology of psychiatric disorders among Mexican Americans. JOURNAL OF OPERATIONAL PSYCHIATRY, Vol. 14, no. 1 (1983), p. 42-51. English. **DESCR:** Acculturation; Diagnostic Interview Schedule (DIS); El Centro Community Health Care Center; Los Angeles, CA; *Mental Health.

Los Angeles Olympic Organizing Committee

6792 Caldera, Carmela. Dan Cruz: making the Olympics happen for the community. CAMINOS, Vol. 4, no. 4 (April 1983), p. 10-13,64. Bilingual. **DESCR:** *Cruz, Dan; Olympics; Sports.

Los Angeles Police Department

6793 Latinos in the law: meeting the challenge [a symposium]. CHICANO LAW REVIEW, Vol. 6, (1983), p. 1-121. English. **DESCR:** *Criminal Justice System; Demography; Legal Profession; Love, Eulia; Police Brutality; Political Representation; Reapportionment; Settles, Ron.

6794 Police misconduct [panel discussion at the LATINOS IN THE LAW symposium, UCLA, 1982]. CHICANO LAW REVIEW, Vol. 6, (1983), p. 63-121. English. **DESCR:** Love, Eulia; Nettles, Ron; Police; *Police Brutality.

LOS ANGELES TIMES

6795 Miguel de la Madrid en la prensa norteamericana. INFORME: RELACIONES MEXICO-ESTADOS UNIDOS, Vol. 1, no. 2 (July, December, 1982), p. 176-183. Spanish. **DESCR:** *De la Madrid, Miguel; *Journalism; Lopez Portillo, Jose; NEW YORK TIMES; Newspapers; WALL STREET JOURNAL; WASHINGTON POST.

Los Angeles Unified School District

6796 Gonzalez, Larry. Serving our students: Larry Gonzalez (interview). CAMINOS, Vol. 4, no. 10 (November 1983), p. 34-36. English. **DESCR:** Education; *Gonzalez, Larry; *Primary School Education.

Lotus-Albertini Hispanic Reps

6797 Media/marketing. HISPANIC BUSINESS, Vol. 5, no. 12 (December 1983), p. 38. English. **DESCR:** Albertini, Luis Diaz; Computers; League of United Latin American Citizens (LULAC); Marketing; *Mass Media; Nuestras Noticias; Radio; Reading; Television; Tortosa, Cristobal.

Love, Eulia

6798 Latinos in the law: meeting the challenge [a symposium]. CHICANO LAW REVIEW, Vol. 6, (1983), p. 1-121. English. **DESCR:** *Criminal Justice System; Demography; Legal Profession; Los Angeles Police Department; Police Brutality; Political Representation; Reapportionment; Settles, Ron.

6799 Police misconduct [panel discussion at the LATINOS IN THE LAW symposium, UCLA, 1982]. CHICANO LAW REVIEW, Vol. 6, (1983), p. 63-121. English. **DESCR:** Los Angeles Police Department; Nettles, Ron; Police; *Police Brutality.

Low Income

6800 Bailey, Lynn B., et al. Folacin and iron status and hematological finding in Blacks and Spanish-American adolescents from urban low-income households. AMERICAN JOURNAL OF CLINICAL NUTRITION, Vol. 35, no. 5 (May 1982), p. 1023-1032. English. **DESCR:** Blacks; Public Health; Surveys; *Youth.

Low Income (cont.)

6801 Hunt, Isabelle F., et al. Zinc
supplementation during pregnancy: zinc
concentration of serum and hair from
low-income women of Mexican descent.
AMERICAN JOURNAL OF CLINICAL NUTRITION, Vol.
37, no. 4 (April 1983), p. 572-582. English.
DESCR: Chicanas; Nutrition; *Prenatal Care;
Surveys.

Low Riders

6802 Bustamante, Anna Luisa. Low riding to
positive mental health. CALMECAC, Vol. 1,
no. 1 (Spring 1980), p. 29-33. English.
DESCR: Mental Health.

6803 Mendoza, Ruben G. The lowrider happening:
hydraulics and the hopping competition.
CAMINOS, Vol. 4, no. 7 (July, August, 1983),
p. 34,44. English. **DESCR:** Car Clubs.

6804 Whisler, Kirk. It can work. CAMINOS, Vol. 3,
no. 6 (June 1982), p. 46. Bilingual. **DESCR:**
*Car Clubs; San Bernardino, CA.

Lower Class
USE: Social Classes

Lozano, Anthony G.

6805 Dyer, Nancy Joe. Book review of: TEACHING
SPANISH TO THE HISPANIC BILINGUAL: ISSUES,
AIMS AND METHODS. HISPANIA, Vol. 65, no. 3
(September 1982), p. 474-475. English.
DESCR: Book Reviews; Garcia-Moya, Rodolfo;
Spanish Language; *TEACHING SPANISH TO THE
HISPANIC BILINGUAL: ISSUES, AIMS AND
METHODS; Valdez, Guadalupe.

6806 Goldin, Mark G. Book review of: TEACHING
SPANISH TO THE HISPANIC BILINGUAL: ISSUES,
AIMS AND METHODS. NABE JOURNAL, Vol. 7, no.
1 (Fall 1982), p. 53-56. English. **DESCR:**
Bilingualism; Book Reviews; Garcia-Moya,
Rodolfo; Language Proficiency; Language
Usage; Spanish Language; *TEACHING SPANISH
TO THE HISPANIC BILINGUAL: ISSUES, AIMS AND
METHODS; Valdez, Guadalupe.

6807 Gutierrez, John R. Book review of: TEACHING
SPANISH TO THE HISPANIC BILINGUAL: ISSUES,
AIMS AND METHODS. MODERN LANGUAGE JOURNAL,
Vol. 66, no. 2 (Summer 1982), p. 234.
English. **DESCR:** Bilingualism; Book Reviews;
Garcia-Moya, Rodolfo; Spanish Language;
*TEACHING SPANISH TO THE HISPANIC BILINGUAL:
ISSUES, AIMS AND METHODS; Valdez, Guadalupe.

Lozano, Diana

6808 President Reagan's appointments. CAMINOS,
Vol. 3, no. 3 (March 1982), p. 48-50.
Bilingual. **DESCR:** Appointed Officials;
*Federal Government; Flores Buckhart,
Elizabeth; Garcia, Ernest E.; Gonzalez, Luis
A.; Pompa, Gilbert G.; Reagan, Ronald;
Sanchez, Nestor D.; Zuniga, Henry.

Lozano, Leticia Eugenia

6809 People. HISPANIC BUSINESS, Vol. 5, no. 9
(September 1983), p. 10. English. **DESCR:**
*Businesspeople; Chavez, Chris; Diez de
Onate, Jorge; Franco Garcia, Freddie;
Garcia, Hector P.; Ravard, Rafael Alonzo;
Rodriguez, Alberto Duque; Sanchez, Philip
V.; Villalpando, Catalina.

LRF Developers, Inc.

6810 Goodman, Gerson. LRF takes on Battery Park

City. HISPANIC BUSINESS, Vol. 4, no. 10
(October 1982), p. 16-17,24. English.
DESCR: Business Enterprises; Construction
Industry; NEW YORK; *Real Estate.

Luce, Claire Boothe

6811 Latinos and Mrs. Luce. NUESTRO, Vol. 6, no.
8 (October 1982), p. 9. English. **DESCR:**
Immigration; Prejudice (Social).

6812 Our 1982 Latino awards. NUESTRO, Vol. 7, no.
1 (January, February, 1983), p. 44-46.
English. **DESCR:** Awards; Escalante, Jaime;
Gallegos, Gina; Grace, J. Peter; Immigration
and Naturalization Service (INS); Knight,
Bobby; Lamas, Fernando; *Latino Awards;
Moreno, Rita; National Press Foundation;
Rodriguez Hernandez, Andres; Simpson-Mazzoli
Bill; Smith, Raymond; Valeri, Michele;
Voting Rights Act.

LA LUCIERNAGA

6813 Beverley, John. The revolution betrayed: a
note on Mariano Azuela's estridentista
trilogy. MAIZE, Vol. 4, no. 1-2 (Fall,
Winter, 1980, 1981), p. 27-39. English.
DESCR: *Azuela, Mariano; EL DESQUITE; LA
MALHORA; Literary Criticism.

Lujan, Manuel, Jr.

6814 Padilla, Steve. Latinos wield political
clout in midterm election. NUESTRO, Vol. 6,
no. 9 (November 1982), p. 28-30. English.
DESCR: De la Garza, Kika; *Elected
Officials; Garcia, Robert; Gonzales, Henry
B.; Martinez, Matthew G. "Marty",
Assemblyman; Ortiz, Solomon; *Politics;
Richardson, William; Roybal, Edward R.;
*Torres, Esteban E.

Lujan, Maria Theofila

6815 Benson, Nancy C. The art of colcha-stitch
embroidery: an Hispanic heritage. NEW
AMERICA: A REVIEW, Vol. 4, no. 3 (1982), p.
78-81. English. **DESCR:** Artes Antigua
Society; *Embroidery.

LULAC National Education Service Centers (LNESC)

6816 Brocksbank, Bonilla are winners of LNESC
award. LATINO, Vol. 53, no. 8 (December
1982), p. 26. English. **DESCR:** Bonilla, Tony;
Brocksbank, Robert W.; *Education; *League
of United Latin American Citizens (LULAC).

6817 Communications/marketing. HISPANIC BUSINESS,
Vol. 4, no. 10 (October 1982), p. 22.
English. **DESCR:** Awards; ENFOQUE NACIONAL
[radio program]; League of United Latin
American Citizens (LULAC); Marketing; *Mass
Media.

6818 Community watching: para la comunidad.
CAMINOS, Vol. 3, no. 2 (February 1982), p.
43-44. Bilingual. **DESCR:** Casa Blanca Youth
Project; Colegio Cesar Chavez, Mt. Angel,
OR; Colleges and Universities; *Cultural
Organizations; Financial Aid;
Tonatiuh-Quinto Sol Award for Literature,
1977-78; University of California,
Riverside.

6819 LNESC tenth anniversary banquet set for
March 24. LATINO, Vol. 54, no. 2 (March
1983), p. 7. English. **DESCR:** Cultural
Organizations.

LULAC National Education Service Centers (LNESC) (cont.)

6820 Math-based careers. HISPANIC BUSINESS, Vol. 4, no. 7 (July 1982). p. 22. English. **DESCR:** *Careers; Engineering as a Profession; National Action Council for Minorities in Engineering (NACME).

6821 Redmond, Debbie. Most elegant event. LATINO, Vol. 54, no. 4 (May, June, 1983), p. 22. English. **DESCR:** *Organizations.

Luna, Brian

6822 Family displays special courage. NUESTRO, Vol. 7, no. 1 (January, February, 1983), p. 10. English. **DESCR:** Little People of America; Medicine.

Mabry, Donald

6823 Schmitt, Karl M. Book review of: HISPANIC FOLK MUSIC OF NEW MEXICO AND THE SOUTHWEST: A SELF-PORTRAIT OF A PEOPLE. HISPANIC AMERICAN HISTORICAL REVIEW, Vol. 63, no. 1 (1983), p. 209-210. English. **DESCR:** Book Reviews; *NEIGHBORS, MEXICO AND THE UNITED STATES: WETBACKS AND OIL; Shafer, Robert Jones; United States-Mexico Relations.

MACARIO

6824 Cantu, Roberto. El relato como articulacion infinitiva: MACARIO y el arte de Juan Rulfo. LA PALABRA, Vol. 4, no. 1-2 (Spring, Fall, 1982, 1983), p. 107-126. Spanish. **DESCR:** Authors; Literary Characteristics; Literary Criticism; Mexican Literature; *Rulfo, Juan.

MacArthur Foundation

6825 Chavira, Ricardo. Gutierrez, first Latino recipient. NUESTRO, Vol. 7, no. 3 (April 1983), p. 11-12. English. **DESCR:** Financial Aid; *Gutierrez, Ramon; History; New Mexico.

Machelbeuf, Joseph P., Vicar

6826 Blea, Irene I. Book review of: BUT TIME AND CHANCE. CACR REVIEW, Vol. 1, no. 1 (September 1982), p. 132-133. English. **DESCR:** Book Reviews; *BUT TIME AND CHANCE; Catholic Church; Chavez, Fray Angelico; Lamy, J.B.; Martinez, Antonio, Fray; New Mexico.

Machismo

6827 Baca Zinn, Maxine. Chicano men and masculinity. JOURNAL OF ETHNIC STUDIES, Vol. 10, no. 2 (Summer 1982), p. 29-44. English. **DESCR:** Cultural Characteristics; Ethnic Stratification; Sex Roles; Sex Stereotypes; Socioeconomic Factors; Women Men Relations.

6828 Delgado, Abelardo "Lalo". An open letter to Carolina... or relations between men and women. REVISTA CHICANO-RIQUENA, Vol. 10, no. 1-2 (Winter, Spring, 1982), p. 279-284. English. **DESCR:** Chicanas; *Essays; Sex Roles; Sex Stereotypes.

6829 Flores, Henry. Some different thoughts concerning "machismo". COMADRE, no. 3 (Fall 1978), p. 7-9. English. **DESCR:** Chicanas; Mythology; Sex Roles.

6830 Gonzalez, Alex. Sex role of the traditional Mexican family: a comparison of Chicano and Anglo students' attitudes. JOURNAL OF CROSS-CULTURAL PSYCHOLOGY, Vol. 13, no. 3 (September 1982), p. 330-339. English. **DESCR:** Anglo Americans; *Family; Hembrismo; Sex Roles.

6831 Lewis, William. Machismo and the will to win. NUESTRO, Vol. 7, no. 9 (November 1983), p. 32-34. English. **DESCR:** Psychology; *Sports.

6832 Mirande, Alfredo. Machismo: rucas, chingasos, y chingaderas. DE COLORES, Vol. 6, no. 1-2 (1982), p. 17-31. English. **DESCR:** Sex Roles.

6833 Panitz, Daniel R., et al. The role of machismo and the Hispanic family in the etiology and treatment of alcoholism in the Hispanic American males. AMERICAN JOURNAL OF FAMILY THERAPY, Vol. 11, no. 1 (Spring 1983), p. 31-44. English. **DESCR:** *Alcoholism; Children; Family; Puerto Rico; Socioeconomic Factors.

6834 Prichard, Sue. Book review of: HISTORY AS NEUROSIS: PATERNALISM AND MACHISMO IN SPANISH AMERICA. HISPANIC JOURNAL OF BEHAVIORAL SCIENCES, Vol. 5, no. 3 (September 1983), p. 356-360. English. **DESCR:** Book Reviews; Goldwert, Marvin; *HISTORY AS NEUROSIS: PATERNALISM AND MACHISMO IN SPANISH AMERICA.

6835 Salmon, Roberto Mario. Comment: is this our decade in the sun? NATIONAL HISPANIC JOURNAL, Vol. 2, no. 1 (Summer 1983), p. 24-25. English. **DESCR:** Identity; *Mass Media; National Council of La Raza (NCLR).

6836 Wurzman, Ilyana. Cultural values of Puerto Rican opiate addicts: an exploratory study. AMERICAN JOURNAL OF DRUG AND ALCOHOL ABUSE, Vol. 9, no. 2 (1982, 1983), p. 141-153. English. **DESCR:** Acculturation; Anglo Americans; Blacks; *Drug Abuse; Drug Addicts; Family; Loevinger's Sentence Completion Test; New York, NY; Opium; Puerto Ricans; Values.

6837 Ybarra, Lea. Marital decision-making and the role of machismo in the Chicano family. DE COLORES, Vol. 6, no. 1-2 (1982), p. 32-47. English. **DESCR:** Family; Marriage; Sex Roles.

Macias, Miguel (Mike)

6838 Newsfront. HISPANIC BUSINESS, Vol. 4, no. 1 (January 1982), p. 7. English. **DESCR:** *Biographical Notes; Businesspeople; Community Development; Jimenez, Richard D.; Oaxaca, Jaime; The East Los Angeles Community Union (TELACU); Viramontes, Carlos.

Maciel, David R.

6839 Garcia, Mario T. Book review of: LA CLASE OBRERA EN LA HISTORIA DE MEXICO: AL NORTE DEL RIO BRAVO (PASADO INMEDIATO, 1930-1981). HISPANIC AMERICAN HISTORICAL REVIEW, Vol. 62, no. 4 (November 1982), p. 694-696. English. **DESCR:** Book Reviews; History; *LA CLASE OBRERA EN LA HISTORIA DE MEXICO: AL NORTE DEL RIO BRAVO (PASADO INMEDIATO, 1930-1981); Labor Disputes; Laboring Classes.

MacKenzie, Kyle

6840 Ybarra, Lea. Book review of: LAS MUJERES: CONVERSATIONS FROM A HISPANIC COMMUNITY [reprinted from LA RED/THE NET 5 (Sept. 1982)]. CHICANO LAW REVIEW, Vol. 6, (1983), p. 146-147. English. DESCR: Book Reviews; Chicanas; Elsasser, Nan; *LAS MUJERES: CONVERSATIONS FROM A HISPANIC COMMUNITY; Oral History; Tixier y Vigil, Yvonne.

Mackey y Salazar, C.

6841 People. HISPANIC BUSINESS, Vol. 5, no. 1 (January 1983), p. 7. English. DESCR: Appointed Officials; *Biographical Notes; *Businesspeople; Elizalde, Hector; Madrid, Carlos; Montoya, Velma; Nunez, Carlos; Perea, Stanley; Rodriguez, Rita; Valdes, Martha.

Madrid, Arturo

6842 McCurdy, Jack. Chicanos mark their gains in colleges, call for more. CHRONICLE OF HIGHER EDUCATION, Vol. 25, no. 10 (November 3, 1982), p. 12. English. DESCR: Academic Achievement; *Higher Education; National Chicano Council on Higher Education (NCCHE).

Madrid, Carlos

6843 People. HISPANIC BUSINESS, Vol. 5, no. 1 (January 1983), p. 7. English. DESCR: Appointed Officials; *Biographical Notes; *Businesspeople; Elizalde, Hector; Mackey y Salazar, C.; Montoya, Velma; Nunez, Carlos; Perea, Stanley; Rodriguez, Rita; Valdes, Martha.

Maduro, Carlota M.

6844 High energy community relations: Con Edison's Carlota M. Maduro. HISPANIC BUSINESS, Vol. 4, no. 2 (February 1982), p. 14. English. DESCR: Biography; Community Services; Consolidated Edison Company of New York, Inc.; Public Relations.

Maes, Fred

6845 Fred Maes builds a multi-level system. HISPANIC BUSINESS, Vol. 4, no. 2 (February 1982), p. 13. English. DESCR: *Biography; Consumers; *Marketing.

Magazines

6846 Aguirre, Richard R. Print media at a crossroads. HISPANIC BUSINESS, Vol. 4, no. 5 (May 1982), p. 20-21+. English. DESCR: *Advertising; Newspapers; *Print Media.

6847 Lopez, Daniel M. The founding of NUESTRO. NUESTRO, Vol. 6, no. 3 (April 1982), p. 41-43. English. DESCR: *Short Story.

6848 More news for Latinos. LATINO, Vol. 54, no. 6 (October 1983), p. 14. English. DESCR: *Print Media.

6849 New tabloid magazines developed in Bay Area. NUESTRO, Vol. 6, no. 2 (March 1982), p. 48. English. DESCR: ESENCIA [magazine]; UNO [magazine], Fremont, CA.

6850 Support LATINO MAGAZINE. LATINO, Vol. 53, no. 2 (March, April, 1982), p. 21. English. DESCR: *LATINO [magazine].

Maher v. Roe

6851 [Summary of: Simpson, abortion, poverty, and equal protection of the law, 13 Ga. L. rev. 505 (1979)]. CHICANO LAW REVIEW, Vol. 5, (1982), p. 82-83. English. DESCR: Abortion; *Administration of Justice; Roe v. Wade.

Majka, Linda C.

6852 Kivisto, Peter. Book review of: FARM WORKERS, AGRIBUSINESS, AND THE STATE. INTERNATIONAL MIGRATION REVIEW, Vol. 17, no. 4 (Winter 1983), p. 724-726. English. DESCR: Agribusiness; Agricultural Laborers; Book Reviews; *FARMWORKERS, AGRIBUSINESS, AND THE STATE; Majka, Theo J.; United Farmworkers of America (UFW).

Majka, Theo J.

6853 Kivisto, Peter. Book review of: FARM WORKERS, AGRIBUSINESS, AND THE STATE. INTERNATIONAL MIGRATION REVIEW, Vol. 17, no. 4 (Winter 1983), p. 724-726. English. DESCR: Agribusiness; Agricultural Laborers; Book Reviews; *FARMWORKERS, AGRIBUSINESS, AND THE STATE; Majka, Linda C.; United Farmworkers of America (UFW).

Make up
USE: Fashion

Mal de Ojo

6854 Richardson, Lynette. Caring through understanding, part II: folk medicine in the Hispanic population. IMPRINT, Vol. 29, no. 2 (April 1982), p. 21, 72-77. English. DESCR: Brujo; Caida de Mollera; Curanderas; Empacho; *Folk Medicine; Mal Puesto; Susto.

Mal Puesto

6855 Richardson, Lynette. Caring through understanding, part II: folk medicine in the Hispanic population. IMPRINT, Vol. 29, no. 2 (April 1982), p. 21, 72-77. English. DESCR: Brujo; Caida de Mollera; Curanderas; Empacho; *Folk Medicine; Mal de Ojo; Susto.

Maldonado, Candy

6856 Sports updates. CAMINOS, Vol. 3, no. 4 (April 1982), p. 42. English. DESCR: *Baseball; Orta, Jorge; Pena, Alejandro; Valenzuela, Fernando.

Male and Female Roles
USE: Sex Roles

Males

6857 Median administrative salaries in 1981-82 for men and women and minority-group members. CHRONICLE OF HIGHER EDUCATION, Vol. 24, no. 2 (March 10, 1982), p. 10. English. DESCR: *Administrators; Chicanas; Ethnic Groups; *Income.

LA MALHORA

6858 Beverley, John. The revolution betrayed: a note on Mariano Azuela's estridentista trilogy. MAIZE, Vol. 4, no. 1-2 (Fall, Winter, 1980, 1981), p. 27-39. English. DESCR: *Azuela, Mariano; EL DESQUITE; LA LUCIERNAGA; Literary Criticism.

Management

6859 Ayers-Nackamkin, Beverly, et al. Sex and ethnic differences in the use of power. JOURNAL OF APPLIED PSYCHOLOGY, Vol. 67, no. 4 (August 1982), p. 464-471. English. DESCR: Anglo Americans; Ethnic Groups; *Personnel Management; Sex Roles; Social Psychology.

6860 Balkan, D. Carlos. Being a start-up manager at San Onofre II & III. HISPANIC BUSINESS, Vol. 4, no. 7 (July 1982), p. 18-19,26. English. DESCR: California; Chavez, Gabriel A.; Engineering as a Profession; Nuclear Energy.

6861 Garcia, Art R. The executive market. HISPANIC BUSINESS, Vol. 5, no. 10 (October 1983), p. 12. English. DESCR: Employment.

6862 Martinez, Arthur D. Mexican-Americans: Qua the assistant-Americans. SOUTHWEST ECONOMY AND SOCIETY, Vol. 2, no. 2 (Winter 1977), p. 34-36. English. DESCR: *Employment; Racism; *Self-Determination.

6863 Office manager hired under Coors grant. LATINO, Vol. 53, no. 1 (January, February, 1982), p. 6. English. DESCR: *Coors Distributing Company, McAllen, TX.

6864 Sargeant, Georgia. Young turks set new standards. HISPANIC BUSINESS, Vol. 5, no. 11 (November 1983), p. 8-9. English. DESCR: Alvarez, Julio E.; *Architecture; Business Enterprises; Marketing; Miami, FL; Taracido, Manuel E.; Wolfberg, David A.; *Wolfberg/Alvarez/Taracido (WAT).

6865 Tips for making the right moves in today's job markets. HISPANIC BUSINESS, Vol. 4, no. 8 (August 1983), p. 11+. English. DESCR: American G.I. Forum; *Careers; Employment; Military Service.

Management by Objectives (MBO)

6866 Murphy, John W. and Redden, Richard. The use of management by objectives in medical education enrichment programs. JOURNAL OF MEDICAL EDUCATION, Vol. 57, no. 12 (December 1982), p. 911-917. English. DESCR: *Educational Administration; Educational Innovations; Evaluation (Educational); *Medical Education.

THE MAN-EATING MYTH: ANTHROPOLOGY AND ANTHROPOPHAGY

6867 Belton, Robert T. Book review of: CANNIBALS AND KINGS: THE ORIGINS OF CULTURE and THE MAN-EATING MYTH: ANTHROPOLOGY AND ANTHROPOPHAGY. HISPANIC JOURNAL OF BEHAVIORAL SCIENCES, Vol. 4, no. 1 (March 1982), p. 129-134. English. DESCR: Arens, W.; Book Reviews; *CANNIBALS AND KINGS: THE ORIGINS OF CULTURE; Harris, Marvin.

Manpower Programs

6868 NATIVE ALIENS (videotape). CAMINOS, Vol. 3, no. 8 (September 1982), p. 43. English. DESCR: Hispanic Employment Program (HEP); Veteran's Administration.

Manriquez, Suzanna

6869 People. HISPANIC BUSINESS, Vol. 5, no. 6 (June 1983), p. 8. English. DESCR: Appointed Officials; *Biographical Notes; Businesspeople; Goizueta, Roberto C.; Guerra, Stella; Huapaya, Sixto Guillermo; Kitano, Pat; Oppenheimer-Nicolau, Siabhan; Ortiz, Solomon; Pachon, Harry P.; Richardson, Bill Lopez; Torres, Esteban E.; Torres, Johnny.

Manta, Ben

6870 Castillo, Pedro. Letter to the editor. SOUTHWEST ECONOMY AND SOCIETY, Vol. 3, no. 1 (Fall 1977), p. 55-56. English. DESCR: Economic History and Conditions; Internal Colonial Model (Theoretical); TOWARD ECONOMIC DEVELOPMENT OF THE CHICANO BARRIO.

Manzano, Esther

6871 Esther Manzano. CAMINOS, Vol. 3, no. 3 (March 1982), p. 30. Bilingual. DESCR: EL MEXICALO; Journalists; Newspapers.

Maquiladoras

6872 Duncan, Cameron. The runaway shop and the Mexican border industrialization program. SOUTHWEST ECONOMY AND SOCIETY, Vol. 2, no. 1 (October, November, 1976), p. 4-25. English. DESCR: Border Region; Labor Supply and Market; *Mexican Border Industrialization Program; Multinational Corporations.

6873 Tiano, Susan B. El programa mexicano de maquiladoras: una respuesta a las necesidades de la industria norteamericana. AZTLAN, Vol. 14, no. 1 (Spring 1983), p. 201-208. English. DESCR: Book Reviews; *EL PROGRAMA MEXICANO DE MAQUILADORAS: UNA RESPUESTA A LAS NECESIDADES DE LA INDUSTRIA NORTEAMERICANA; Industrial Workers; Industries; International Labor Activities; Woog, Mario Arriola.

Maria Teresa Montoya Award

6874 Lenti, Paul. Special honor goes to Montalban. NUESTRO, Vol. 7, no. 2 (March 1983), p. 10-11. English. DESCR: Artists; *Montalban, Ricardo; Performing Arts.

Mariachis

6875 Pearlman, Steven Ray. Mariachi music in Los Angeles. CAMINOS, Vol. 4, no. 10 (November 1983), p. 12,47. English. DESCR: East Los Angeles, CA.

Maria's Burritos

6876 Burritos to Lebanon. LATINA, Vol. 1, no. 2 (February, March, 1983), p. 19. English. DESCR: *Cal International; *Recipes.

Marichal, Juan

6877 Ortiz, Carlos V. The Hall at last. NUESTRO, Vol. 7, no. 1 (January, February, 1983), p. 33-35. English. DESCR: *Baseball; Baseball Hall of Fame; Sports.

Maricopa County Organizing Project (MCOP)

6878 Barry, Tom. On strike! Undocumented workers in Arizona. SOUTHWEST ECONOMY AND SOCIETY, Vol. 3, no. 3 (Spring 1978), p. 52-60. English. DESCR: Agribusiness; Agricultural Laborers; Arizona; *Goldmar Citrus Ranch, Phoenix, AZ; Labor Organizing; Phoenix, AZ; *Strikes and Lockouts; Undocumented Workers.

Los Marielitos

6879 Sierra, Jerry A. Faces [photographs].
CAMINOS, Vol. 4, no. 8 (September 1983), p.
28-30. English. DESCR: *Cubanos;
*Photography.

Marijuana

6880 Cockerham, William C. and Alster, Joan M. A
comparison of marijuana use among
Mexican-American and Anglo rural youth
utilizing a matched-set analysis.
INTERNATIONAL JOURNAL OF THE ADDICTIONS,
Vol. 18, no. 6 (August 1983), p. 759-767.
English. DESCR: Anglo Americans; Drug Abuse;
Rural Population; Youth.

Marin, Carmen Lilianne

6881 Mullen, E.J. Book review of: HEREJES Y
MITIFICADORES: MUESTRA DE POESIA
PUERTORRIQUENA EN LOS ESTADOS UNIDOS.
REVISTA CHICANO-RIQUENA, Vol. 10, no. 3
(Summer 1982), p. 68-70. English. DESCR:
Barradas, Efrain; Book Reviews; *HEREJES Y
MITIFICADORES: MUESTRA DE POESIA
PUERTORRIQUENA EN LOS ESTADOS UNIDOS;
Rodriguez, Rafael.

Marin, Gerardo

6882 Brink, T. L. Book review of: AVANCES EN
PSICOLOGIA CONTEMPORANEA. HISPANIC JOURNAL
OF BEHAVIORAL SCIENCES, Vol. 5, no. 4
(December 1983), p. 494-496. English.
DESCR: *AVANCES EN PSICOLOGIA CONTEMPORANEA;
Book Reviews; Finley, Gordon E.; Psychology.

Marin, Luis Munoz

6883 Mejias-Rentas, Antonio. Reflections on
fathers: my three fathers. NUESTRO, Vol. 7,
no. 5 (June, July, 1983), p. 61-62. English.
DESCR: *Family; Partido Popular Democratico
(PPD); *Puerto Ricans; *Puerto Rico.

Maritime Law

6884 Mexico y Estados Unidos ante la tercera
Confemar: resultados e implicaciones.
INFORME: RELACIONES MEXICO-ESTADOS UNIDOS,
Vol. 1, no. 3 (July, December, 1982), p.
215-226. Spanish. DESCR: CONFEMAR;
Multinational Corporations; Reagan
Administration; United States-Mexico
Relations.

Market Research

6885 Bellenger, Danny N. and Valencia, Humberto.
Understanding the Hispanic market. BUSINESS
HORIZONS, Vol. 25, no. 3 (May, June, 1982),
p. 47-50. English. DESCR: Consumers.

6886 Casey, G.M. Marketing to Mexican-Americans:
just a bit of insight. ADVERTISING AGE
MAGAZINE, Vol. 53, no. 11 (March 15, 1982),
p. II, M34-35. English. DESCR: Food
Industry; Southern California.

6887 Dear reader. LATINA, Vol. 1, no. 2
(February, March, 1983), p. 92-94. English.
DESCR: *LATINA [magazine].

6888 Gage, Theodore J. Beer still tops wine,
spirits. ADVERTISING AGE MAGAZINE, Vol. 53,
(February 15, 1982), p. II, M10. English.
DESCR: Advertising; *Alcoholic Beverages;
Consumers.

6889 Galginaitis, Carol. Luring the Hispanic
dollar: retailers boost ethnic image.
ADVERTISING AGE MAGAZINE, Vol. 53,
(February 15, 1982), p. II, M10. English.
DESCR: *Advertising; Consumers.

6890 Haggerty, Alfred G. Occidental goes after
Hispanic market. NATIONAL UNDERWRITER LIFE
AND HEALTH INSURANCE EDITION, Vol. 86, no. 1
(January 2, 1982), p. 22. English. DESCR:
Cubanos; *Insurance; Transamerica Occidental
Life.

6891 Honomichl, Jack. How to research U.S.
Hispanic market. ADVERTISING AGE MAGAZINE,
Vol. 53, (January 18, 1982), p. 22-24.
English. DESCR: *Marketing.

6892 Honomichl, Jack. Never lose sight of
Hispanic pride. ADVERTISING AGE MAGAZINE,
Vol. 53, (February 15, 1982), p. II,
M38-39. English. DESCR: Advertising.

6893 Hulin-Salkin, Belinda. Films need mass
appeal. ADVERTISING AGE MAGAZINE, Vol. 53,
(February 15, 1982), p. II, M10. English.
DESCR: Broadcast Media; Films; Television.

6894 Pendleton, Jennifer. Battle for the buck is
the tale of two cities: marketers in San
Diego and Tijuana square off. ADVERTISING
AGE MAGAZINE, Vol. 53, (February 15, 1982),
p. II, M42-43. English. DESCR: Advertising;
Border Region; Business; San Diego, CA;
Tijuana, Mexico.

6895 Yovovich, B.G. Cultural pride galvanizes
heritages. ADVERTISING AGE MAGAZINE, Vol.
53, (February 15, 1982), p. II, M9+.
English. DESCR: Assimilation.

6896 Zotti, Ed. An idea whose time has not quite
arrived: Spanish sections in newspapers
still struggling. ADVERTISING AGE MAGAZINE,
Vol. 53, (February 15, 1982), p. II, M29+.
English. DESCR: *Newspapers; Spanish
Language.

Marketing

6897 25 leading national Hispanic market
advertisers. HISPANIC BUSINESS, Vol. 4, no.
12 (December 1982), p. 18. English. DESCR:
Advertising; Consumers.

6898 Andreasen, Alan R. Disadvantaged Hispanic
consumers: a research perspective and
agenda. JOURNAL OF CONSUMER AFFAIRS, Vol.
16, no. 1 (Summer 1982), p. 46-61. English.
DESCR: *Consumers; Socioeconomic Factors.

6899 An axiom to grind: the Hispanic market -
more than just a phone call away. MADISON
AVENUE, Vol. 25, no. 7 (1983), p. 44-49.
English. DESCR: Advertising.

6900 Balkan, D. Carlos. The advent of
Uniworld/Hispanic: an interview. HISPANIC
BUSINESS, Vol. 5, no. 3 (March 1983), p.
10-11+. English. DESCR: *Advertising
Agencies; Blacks; Consumers; Diaz-Albertini,
Luis; Lewis, Byron; Spanish Advertising and
Marketing Services (S.A.M.S.); Uniworld
Group, Inc.; UniWorld Hispanic.

6901 Balkan, D. Carlos. The crisis in Hispanic
marketing. HISPANIC BUSINESS, Vol. 4, no. 12
(December 1982), p. 24-25+. English. DESCR:
Advertising; Consumers.

6902 Balkan, D. Carlos. The Hispanic market:
leading indicators. HISPANIC BUSINESS, Vol.
5, no. 12 (December 1983), p. 14-15.
English. DESCR: Advertising; Business
Enterprises.

Marketing (cont.)

6903 Barberis, Mary. Hispanic America. EDITORIAL RESEARCH REPORTS, no. 7 (30, 1982), p. 551-568. English. DESCR: History; Immigration; *Population Trends.

6904 Brusco, Bernadette A. Hispanic marketing: new applications for old methodologies. AGENDA, Vol. 11, no. 3 (May, June, 1981), p. 8-9. English. DESCR: *Consumers.

6905 Chavarria, Jesus. The changing Hispanic market. HISPANIC BUSINESS, Vol. 5, no. 12 (December 1983), p. 6. English. DESCR: Advertising; Income.

6906 Chavarria, Jesus. How long will it last? HISPANIC BUSINESS, Vol. 4, no. 1 (January 1982), p. 6. English. DESCR: Anselmo, Rene; Businesspeople; Lasa, Luis; Spanish International Network (SIN).

6907 Chavarria, Jesus. Varieties of marketing strategies: the PUSH/Anheuser-Bush scrap. HISPANIC BUSINESS, Vol. 4, no. 12 (December 1982), p. 6,35. English. DESCR: Anheuser-Busch, Inc.; Corporations; Operation PUSH; People United to Serve Humanity (PUSH).

6908 Chavez, Lydia. The fourth network's chief executive. HISPANIC BUSINESS, Vol. 4, no. 1 (January 1982), p. 16-18. English. DESCR: Advertising; Anselmo, Rene; *Biography; Cable Television; Spanish International Network (SIN).

6909 Communications/marketing. HISPANIC BUSINESS, Vol. 4, no. 2 (February 1982), p. 15. English. DESCR: Cable Television; Congressional Hispanic Caucus; El Teatro Campesino; GalaVision; Labor Unions; Philip Morris, Inc.; Publishing Industry; Spanish International Network (SIN).

6910 Communications/marketing. HISPANIC BUSINESS, Vol. 4, no. 1 (January 1982), p. 13. English. DESCR: Beauty Contests; *Biographical Notes; Consumers; Hispanic Caucus; Miss Black Velvet Latina; Montemayor, Carlos R.; Philip Morris, Inc.

6911 Communications/marketing. HISPANIC BUSINESS, Vol. 4, no. 3 (March 1982), p. 15. English. DESCR: California; Herrera, Maria Elena; Philip Morris, Inc.; Publicidad Siboney; Siboney Advertising, Inc.; SRI International.

6912 Communications/marketing. HISPANIC BUSINESS, Vol. 4, no. 4 (April 1982), p. 15. English. DESCR: Advertising Agencies; Consumers; Juarez and Associates, Inc.; Las Americas, Inc.; Norman, Craig & Kummel Organization; Publicidad Siboney; Siboney Advertising, Inc.

6913 Communications/marketing. HISPANIC BUSINESS, Vol. 4, no. 5 (May 1982), p. 15. English. DESCR: Anheuser-Busch, Inc.; Farres, Osvaldo; Girl Scouts of the United States of America; Organizations; Television; Vocational Education; Voter Turnout.

6914 Communications/marketing. HISPANIC BUSINESS, Vol. 4, no. 7 (July 1982), p. 16. English. DESCR: Awards; *Biographical Notes; Buena Vista Cablevision, Inc.; Demy, Caroline; Sosa de Garcia, Manuel.

6915 Communications/marketing. HISPANIC BUSINESS, Vol. 4, no. 9 (September 1982), p. 22. English. DESCR: Awards; Coca-Cola Company;

Domecq Importers, Inc.; Western Union Corporation.

6916 Communications/marketing. HISPANIC BUSINESS, Vol. 4, no. 10 (October 1982), p. 22. English. DESCR: Awards; ENFOQUE NACIONAL [radio program]; League of United Latin American Citizens (LULAC); LULAC National Education Service Centers (LNESC); *Mass Media.

6917 Communications/marketing. HISPANIC BUSINESS, Vol. 4, no. 11 (November 1982), p. 18. English. DESCR: California Chicano News Media Association (CCNMA); Diaz-Albertini, Luis; Domecq Importers, Inc.; National Hispanic Media Conference, San Diego, CA, December 2-5, 1982; Pacific Telephone; Television.

6918 Communications/marketing. HISPANIC BUSINESS, Vol. 4, no. 12 (December 1982), p. 11. English. DESCR: Advertising; Advertising Agencies; Diaz-Albertini, Luis; UniWorld Hispanic.

6919 Communications/marketing. HISPANIC BUSINESS, Vol. 5, no. 1 (January 1983), p. 23. English. DESCR: Banking Industry; Broadcast Media; Caballero Spanish Media, Inc. (CSM); Fleishman-Hillard, Inc.; Miami, FL; Nogales, Luis G.; Public Relations.

6920 Communications/marketing. HISPANIC BUSINESS, Vol. 5, no. 3 (March 1983), p. 21. English. DESCR: *Advertising; Awards; Consumers; El Cervantes Media Awards; Spanish Advertising and Marketing Services (S.A.M.S.)

6921 Communications/marketing. HISPANIC BUSINESS, Vol. 5, no. 4 (April 1983), p. 23. English. DESCR: Faultless Starch/Bon Ami Company; Garcia, Marti; Mejias, Hugo A.; Pan American University, Edinburg, TX; Spanish Language.

6922 Communications/marketing. HISPANIC BUSINESS, Vol. 5, no. 5 (May 1983), p. 24. English. DESCR: Anheuser-Busch, Inc.; Arbitron; Awards; California Chicano News Media Association (CCNMA); Coca-Cola Company; Elizalde, Hector; Television.

6923 Communications/marketing. HISPANIC BUSINESS, Vol. 5, no. 7 (July 1983), p. 24. English. DESCR: AltaVision, Inc. (Denver, CO); Boycotts; Cable Television; Operation PUSH; Spanish Satellite Network (SSN); *Television.

6924 Communications/marketing. HISPANIC BUSINESS, Vol. 5, no. 8 (August 1983), p. 26. English. DESCR: Advertising Agencies; Bermudez & Associates; *Broadcast Media; Carranza Associates; Directories.

6925 Communications/marketing. HISPANIC BUSINESS, Vol. 5, no. 9 (September 1983), p. 26. English. DESCR: Aguirre, Horacio; Business Enterprises; Consumers; DIARIO DE LAS AMERICAS; La Ventana; Miller Brewing Company; SURVEY OF PROMOTIONAL PRACTICES.

6926 Communications/marketing. HISPANIC BUSINESS, Vol. 5, no. 10 (October 1983), p. 26. English. DESCR: Advertising; Arens & Gutierrez; Employment; Henry Molina, Inc.; Journals; Lionetti and Meyers Research Center, Inc.; *Mass Media; Midwest Hispanics in Telecommunications Symposium, Chicago, IL; NEW MANAGEMENT.

Marketing (cont.)

6927 Communications/marketing. HISPANIC BUSINESS, Vol. 4, no. 8 (August 1983), p. 22+. English. DESCR: Arredondo, Price; Baseball; De la O, Val; Films; *Mass Media; Radio; San Antonio CineFestival, TX; Television; Val De La O Show; Valenzuela, Fernando; Wright & Arredondo Associates; Wright, Oscar.

6928 The compleat Hispanic marketing guide. HISPANIC BUSINESS, Vol. 4, no. 1 (January 1982), p. 10. English. DESCR: *Consumers; Rios, Conrad R.

6929 The Dallas bilingual yellow pages. HISPANIC BUSINESS, Vol. 4, no. 1 (January 1982), p. 11. English. DESCR: *Consumers; Dallas, TX; Gonzalez, John David; Gonzalez, Michael.

6930 Dear reader. LATINA, Vol. 1, no. 3 (1983), p. 76-78. English. DESCR: Surveys.

6931 Demographic profile of Hispanics in the Dallas/Fort Worth SMSA. HISPANIC BUSINESS, Vol. 5, no. 2 (February 1983), p. 29-30. English. DESCR: *Consumers; Dallas, TX; Dallas/Ft. Worth SMSA; *Demography; Fort Worth, Texas.

6932 Fernandez, Enrique and Valle, Eunice. Latin drop: retail sales decrease attributed to sweeps by Dept. of Immigration raids. BILLBOARD, Vol. 94, no. 25 (June 26, 1982), p. 3. English. DESCR: Deportation; Immigration Regulation and Control; *Music.

6933 Foreign trade. HISPANIC BUSINESS, Vol. 5, no. 11 (November 1983), p. 31. English. DESCR: California; *Foreign Trade; HOW TO EXPORT: A MARKETING MANUAL; Miami, FL; Miami Free Zone; Puerto Rico.

6934 Fred Maes builds a multi-level system. HISPANIC BUSINESS, Vol. 4, no. 2 (February 1982), p. 13. English. DESCR: *Biography; Consumers; Maes, Fred.

6935 Gage, Theodore J. The next assignment: second-tier marketing to English-speaking Hispanics. HISPANIC BUSINESS, Vol. 5, no. 12 (December 1983), p. 22-26. English. DESCR: Advertising; Bilingualism.

6936 Gilbert L. Hernandez. LATINO, Vol. 53, no. 8 (December 1982), p. 26. English. DESCR: *Hernandez, Gilbert L.

6937 Goodman, Gerson. "ES PARA USTED": CSI aims for satisfaction. HISPANIC BUSINESS, Vol. 4, no. 12 (December 1982), p. 16-17,34. English. DESCR: Advertising Agencies; Aguirre, Jack; Business Enterprises; Consumers; CSI International, Inc.; Fernandez, Castor A.

6938 Grocery chains fight for San Antonio market. NUESTRO, Vol. 7, no. 2 (March 1983), p. 54. English. DESCR: *Food Industry; San Antonio, TX.

6939 Guernica, Antonio. Consumer Hispanic: a dual identity. MADISON AVENUE, Vol. 25, (July 1983), p. 35-44. English. DESCR: Advertising.

6940 Guernica, Antonio. The Hispanic market: a profile. AGENDA, Vol. 11, no. 3 (May, June, 1981), p. 4-7. English. DESCR: *Consumers; Mass Media; *Population; Population Distribution; Population Trends.

6941 Gupta, Udayan. New York's WNJU Channel 47: Spanish TV's hottest item. HISPANIC BUSINESS, Vol. 5, no. 3 (March 1983), p. 16-17+. English. DESCR: *Advertising; Broadcast Media; Consumers; Television; WNJU-TV, Newark, NJ [television station].

6942 Hartenstein, Roslyn and Balkan, D. Carlos. Packaging the Dallas Hispanic consumer. HISPANIC BUSINESS, Vol. 5, no. 2 (February 1983), p. 18-19+. English. DESCR: *Consumers; Dallas, TX; Fort Worth, Texas.

6943 Heublein's Miss Black Velvet II. HISPANIC BUSINESS, Vol. 4, no. 2 (February 1982), p. 12. English. DESCR: Advertising; Beauty Contests; Consumers; Heublein, Inc.; *Miss Black Velvet Latina.

6944 Hispanic television. AMERICAN DEMOGRAPHICS, Vol. 4, no. 6 (June 1982), p. 11. English. DESCR: *Television.

6945 Honomichl, Jack. How to research U.S. Hispanic market. ADVERTISING AGE MAGAZINE, Vol. 53, (January 18, 1982), p. 22-24. English. DESCR: Market Research.

6946 KMEX-TV dominates the Hispanic market. HISPANIC BUSINESS, Vol. 5, no. 12 (December 1983), p. 16-17. English. DESCR: Advertising; *KMEX, Los Angeles, CA [television station]; Los Angeles, CA; *Television.

6947 Media/marketing. HISPANIC BUSINESS, Vol. 5, no. 12 (December 1983), p. 38. English. DESCR: Albertini, Luis Diaz; Computers; League of United Latin American Citizens (LULAC); Lotus-Albertini Hispanic Reps; *Mass Media; Nuestras Noticias; Radio; Reading; Television; Tortosa, Cristobal.

6948 Mercado, Anthony. Do Hispanics use coupons? HISPANIC BUSINESS, Vol. 5, no. 12 (December 1983), p. 10. English. DESCR: Advertising; Carol Wright Hispanic Program; Donnelley Marketing.

6949 Mexican market hints. HISPANIC BUSINESS, Vol. 4, no. 6 (June 1982), p. 25. English. DESCR: *Foreign Trade; Mexico.

6950 Record marketing effort aimed at Latino buyer. NUESTRO, Vol. 6, no. 2 (March 1982), p. 48. English. DESCR: Music; Recording Industry.

6951 Research/development: books. HISPANIC BUSINESS, Vol. 4, no. 12 (December 1982), p. 36. English. DESCR: Book Reviews; Consumers; Guernica, A.; Kasperuk, I.; *REACHING THE HISPANIC MARKET EFFECTIVELY.

6952 Rhonda Ramirez is Miss Black Velvet Latina. HISPANIC BUSINESS, Vol. 5, no. 3 (March 1983), p. 12-13. English. DESCR: *Beauty Contests; *Celaya, Mona; Miss Black Velvet Latina.

6953 Sargeant, Georgia. Young turks set new standards. HISPANIC BUSINESS, Vol. 5, no. 11 (November 1983), p. 8-9. English. DESCR: Alvarez, Julio E.; *Architecture; Business Enterprises; Management; Miami, FL; Taracido, Manuel E.; Wolfberg, David A.; *Wolfberg/Alvarez/Taracido (WAT).

Marketing (cont.)

6954 Skriloff, Lisa. Music, news dominate Spanish-language radio programming. HISPANIC BUSINESS, Vol. 5, no. 12 (December 1983), p. 34. English. **DESCR:** Advertising; Los Angeles, CA; Miami, FL; *Radio; San Antonio, TX.

6955 Tabla raza. AMERICAN DEMOGRAPHICS, Vol. 4, no. 7 (August 1982), p. 46-47. English.

6956 Think Spanish! MARKETING AND MEDIA DECISIONS, Vol. 17, (October 1982), p. 66-69. English. **DESCR:** Advertising; Biography; Conill Advertising Associates, New York, NY; Conill, Alicia; Conill, Rafael; Scott Paper Company; Spanish Language.

6957 Tips for making the right moves in today's job markets. HISPANIC BUSINESS, Vol. 4, no. 12 (December 1982), p. 28. English. **DESCR:** *Careers.

6958 Triana, Armando R. Changing demographics, consumer patterns in the Chicago marketplace. HISPANIC BUSINESS, Vol. 5, no. 12 (December 1983), p. 20-21+. English. **DESCR:** *Chicago, IL; Income; Population Trends.

6959 Triana, Armando R. The trendy Hispanic market. HISPANIC BUSINESS, Vol. 4, no. 12 (December 1982), p. 8. English. **DESCR:** *Consumers.

6960 U.S. firm seeks entry to Mexican beer market. NUESTRO, Vol. 7, no. 1 (January, February, 1983), p. 36. English. **DESCR:** *Anheuser-Busch, Inc.; Mexico.

6961 Volsky, George. Miami's radio S-U-A-A-A-V-E. HISPANIC BUSINESS, Vol. 4, no. 12 (December 1982), p. 22,35. English. **DESCR:** Advertising; Broadcast Media; Language Usage; Miami, FL; *Radio; Radio Station SUAVE, Miami, FL; *Radio Stations; Spanish Language.

6962 Whitefield, Mimi. Mr. Lasa's 400,000 cases of rum. HISPANIC BUSINESS, Vol. 4, no. 1 (January 1982), p. 14-15+. English. **DESCR:** *Bacardi Imports, Inc.; *Biography; Lasa, Luis.

6963 Wittenauer, Cheryl. Dallas Hispanic media. HISPANIC BUSINESS, Vol. 5, no. 2 (February 1983), p. 12-13+. English. **DESCR:** Broadcast Media; *Consumers; Dallas, TX; English Language; Mass Media; Newspapers; Spanish Language.

6964 Wittenauer, Cheryl. The mayor markets San Antonio. HISPANIC BUSINESS, Vol. 5, no. 7 (July 1983), p. 12-13+. English. **DESCR:** Cisneros, Henry, Mayor of San Antonio, TX; *Economic Development; San Antonio, TX.

6965 Zuniga, Jo Ann and Bonilla, Tony. Talking Texas: turning the tables with LULAC. HISPANIC BUSINESS, Vol. 5, no. 9 (September 1983), p. 18-19+. English. **DESCR:** *Bonilla, Tony; Business Enterprises; Consumers; Economic History and Conditions; League of United Latin American Citizens (LULAC); Texas.

Marley, Bob

6966 Entertainment = diversion. CAMINOS, Vol. 3, no. 2 (February 1982), p. 40-41. English. **DESCR:** Awards; CHECKING IT OUT; Club Hogar Latino; Dance; Films; Flamenco; Montalban, Ricardo; ON GOLDEN POND; *Recreation; Television.

Marques, Rene

6967 Lattin, Vernon E. Book review of: THE DOCILE PUERTO RICAN. MINORITY VOICES, Vol. 2, no. 1 (Spring 1978), p. 62-63. English. **DESCR:** Book Reviews; Puerto Ricans; *THE DOCILE PUERTO RICAN.

6968 Ortiz Griffin, Julia. The Puerto Rican woman in Rene Marques' drama. REVISTA CHICANO-RIQUENA, Vol. 11, no. 3-4 (Fall 1983), p. 169-176. English. **DESCR:** Literary Criticism; Teatro; Women.

Marquez, Manuel

6969 Padilla, Steve. Working for the F.B.I. NUESTRO, Vol. 6, no. 8 (October 1982), p. 15-17. English. **DESCR:** Arras, Raymundo; *Federal Bureau of Investigation (FBI); Latin Americans; Perez, Matthew.

Marquez, Tom

6970 Ballard, Lee. Tom Marquez and the EDS mode. HISPANIC BUSINESS, Vol. 5, no. 2 (February 1983), p. 10-11+. English. **DESCR:** *Biography; Businesspeople; Electronic Data Systems (EDS); Perot, Ross; War on Drugs.

Marriage

6971 Jensen, Carol. Cleofas M. Jaramillo on marriage in territorial Northern New Mexico. NEW MEXICO HISTORICAL REVIEW, Vol. 58, no. 2 (April 1983), p. 153-171. English. **DESCR:** Jaramillo, Cleofas M.; *New Mexico.

6972 Roberts, Robert E. and Roberts, Catharine Ramsay. Marriage, work and depressive symptoms among Mexican Americans. HISPANIC JOURNAL OF BEHAVIORAL SCIENCES, Vol. 4, no. 2 (June 1982), p. 199-221. English. **DESCR:** Chicanas; Employment; *Mental Health.

6973 Ybarra, Lea. Marital decision-making and the role of machismo in the Chicano family. DE COLORES, Vol. 6, no. 1-2 (1982), p. 32-47. English. **DESCR:** Family; *Machismo; Sex Roles.

Marti, Jose

6974 Maldonado-Denis, Manuel. El problema de las nacionalidades: la experiencia caribena. Paper presented at the "Dialogo de las Americas" conference. Mexico, D.F. September 9-14, 1982. REVISTA CHICANO-RIQUENA, Vol. 10, no. 4 (Fall 1982), p. 39-45. Spanish. **DESCR:** Capitalism; Carpentier, Alejo; Cuba; El Salvador; Grenada; Guatemala; Imperialism; Nicaragua; *Political History and Conditions; Puerto Rico; United States.

6975 New city park for Miamians. NUESTRO, Vol. 6, no. 9 (November 1982), p. 13. English. **DESCR:** *Miami, FL; *Recreation.

Martin, Albert

6976 Andrews, Ilse. Bilinguals out of focus: a critical discussion. IRAL: INT'L REVIEW OF APPLIED LINGUISTICS IN LANGUAGE TEACHING, Vol. 20, no. 4 (November 1982), p. 297-305. English. **DESCR:** *Bilingualism; Book Reviews; Literature Reviews; Obler, Loraine K.; *THE BILINGUAL BRAIN.

Martinez, A.

6977 A very special gift. LATINO, Vol. 53, no. 5 (September 1982), p. 7-8+. English. **DESCR:** Films; SEGUIN [movie].

Martinez, Alma

6978 Caldera, Carmela and Martinez, Alma. Alma Martinez: "I'm keeping my fingers crossed" (interview). CAMINOS, Vol. 4, no. 11 (December 1983), p. 32-35. English. **DESCR:** Artists; Films; Teatro.

Martinez, Anita V.

6979 Perales, Leon. Rockwell International's highest ranking Hispanic. LATINA, Vol. 1, no. 3 (1983), p. 46. English. **DESCR:** Biography.

Martinez, Antonio, Fray

6980 Blea, Irene I. Book review of: BUT TIME AND CHANCE. CACR REVIEW, Vol. 1, no. 1 (September 1982), p. 132-133. English. **DESCR:** Book Reviews; *BUT TIME AND CHANCE; Catholic Church; Chavez, Fray Angelico; Lamy, J.B.; Machelbeuf, Joseph P., Vicar; New Mexico.

Martinez Defense Committee

6981 Martinez, Elizabeth. The "Kiko" Martinez case: a sign of our times. CRIME AND SOCIAL JUSTICE, Vol. 17, (Summer 1982), p. 92-95. English. **DESCR:** Administration of Justice; Martinez, Francisco; Miller, Robert; *Racism.

Martinez, Elias (Lee)

6982 People. HISPANIC BUSINESS, Vol. 5, no. 3 (March 1983), p. 9. English. **DESCR:** Anaya, Toney; Anguiano, Lupe; Appointed Officials; Avila, Joaquin Guadalupe; Awards; *Biographical Notes; de la Fuente, Emilio; del Olmo, Frank; Godoy, Gustavo; Long, Dennis P.; Rivera, Joseph, Jr.

Martinez, Enrique

6983 Diaz, Katherine A. Enrique Martinez: why I became a U.S. citizen. CAMINOS, Vol. 3, no. 4 (April 1982), p. 35-36. Bilingual. **DESCR:** Naturalization.

Martinez, Esperanza

6984 Diaz, Katherine A. "And this year's winners are...". CAMINOS, Vol. 4, no. 1-2 (January, February, 1983), p. 39-54,74+. English. **DESCR:** *Awards; Castro, Tony; Elizalde, Hector; Flores, Tom; Mendizabal, Maritza; Molina, Gloria; Moya, Connie; Placentia, Joe; Quesada, Leticia; Rios, David N.; Ybarra, Lea; Zapata, Carmen.

6985 Esperanza's Mexico; an artist speaks through her work. CAMINOS, Vol. 4, no. 5 (May 1983), p. 18-20. English. **DESCR:** Artists.

Martinez, Felix

6986 Ortiz, Carlos V. NUESTRO's 1981 all-star baseball team. NUESTRO, Vol. 6, no. 2 (March 1982), p. 55-58. English. **DESCR:** Lopez, Aurelia; *Sports.

Martinez, Francisco

6987 Martinez, Elizabeth. The "Kiko" Martinez case: a sign of our times. CRIME AND SOCIAL JUSTICE, Vol. 17, (Summer 1982), p. 92-95.

English. **DESCR:** Administration of Justice; Martinez Defense Committee; Miller, Robert; *Racism.

Martinez, Lydia R.

6988 People on the move. CAMINOS, Vol. 2, no. 6 (October 1981), p. 7. English. **DESCR:** Alvarado, Angel S.; Arreola, Rafael; *Biographical Notes; Diaz, Elisa; Diaz, Elvira A.; Garcia, Jose Joel; Garza, Florentino; Icaza, Ricardo F.; Lacayo, Henry; Munoz, Victor M.; Salinas, Vicente; Sanchez, Manuel; Zuniga, Henry.

Martinez, Matt

6989 Cantu, Hector. Aqui en Texas: ex-boxer finds success in restaurant: Matt's of Austin one of Texas's most successful restaurants. NATIONAL HISPANIC JOURNAL, Vol. 2, no. 1 (Summer 1983), p. 6. English. **DESCR:** *Business Enterprises.

Martinez, Matthew G. "Marty", Assemblyman

6990 Padilla, Steve. Latinos wield political clout in midterm election. NUESTRO, Vol. 6, no. 9 (November 1982), p. 28-30. English. **DESCR:** De la Garza, Kika; *Elected Officials; Garcia, Robert; Gonzales, Henry B.; Lujan, Manuel, Jr.; Ortiz, Solomon; *Politics; Richardson, William; Roybal, Edward R.; *Torres, Esteban E.

Martinez, Olivia T.

6991 People. HISPANIC BUSINESS, Vol. 5, no. 8 (August 1983), p. 10. English. **DESCR:** *Biographical Notes; Businesspeople; Calderon, Charles M.; Esteverena, Rolando C.; General Coffee Corporation; Hispanic Bankers Association (HBA); Pallares, Mariano; Ruiz, Frederick R.; Ruiz, Louis F.; Sanchez, Joseph J.

Martinez, Oscar J.

6992 Griswold del Castillo, Richard. Book review of: THE CHICANOS OF EL PASO: AN ASSESSMENT OF PROGRESS. PACIFIC HISTORICAL REVIEW, Vol. 51, no. 3 (August 1982), p. 337-338. English. **DESCR:** Book Reviews; El Paso, TX; *THE CHICANOS OF EL PASO: AN ASSESSMENT OF PROGRESS.

6993 Logan, Kathleen. The urban poor in developing nations. JOURNAL OF URBAN HISTORY, Vol. 9, no. 1 (November 1982), p. 108-116. English. **DESCR:** ACCESS TO POWER: POLITICS AND THE URBAN POOR IN DEVELOPING NATIONS; *Book Reviews; BORDER BOOM TOWN: CIUDAD JUAREZ SINCE 1848; Collier, David; Cornelius, Wayne A.; Eckstein, Susan; Lloyd, Peter; Nelson, Joan M.; Perlman, Janice E.; POLITICS AND MIGRANT POOR IN MEXICO CITY; SLUMS OF HOPE? SHANTY TOWNS OF THE THIRD WORLD; SQUATTERS AND OLIGARCHS: AUTHORITARIAN RULE AND POLICY CHANGE IN PERU; THE MYTH OF MARGINALITY: URBAN POVERTY AND POLITICS IN RIO DE JANEIRO; THE POVERTY OF REVOLUTION: THE STATE AND THE URBAN POOR IN MEXICO; Urban Economics.

Martinez, Tippy

6994 Ortiz, Carlos V. NUESTRO'S sixth annual
all-star baseball team. NUESTRO, Vol. 7, no.
2 (March 1983), p. 33-37. English. DESCR:
Andujar, Joaquin; Barojas, Salome;
*Baseball; Castillo, Manny; Concepcion,
Dave; Cruz, Jose; Garcia, Damaso; Guerrero,
Pedro; Hernandez, Keith; Lezcano, Sixto;
Pena, Tony; Piniella, Lou; Sports;
Valenzuela, Fernando.

Martinez, Tony

6995 People. HISPANIC BUSINESS, Vol. 5, no. 7
(July 1983), p. 8. English. DESCR: Alvarado,
Anthony J.; Appointed Officials;
*Biographical Notes; Businesspeople;
Candela, Hilario; Garcia, Marlene; Gonzalez,
Julio; Pla, George; Valdez, Abelardo L.

Martinez, Vilma Socorro

6996 Beyette, Beverly. A time of transition for
MALDEF. CALIFORNIA LAWYER, Vol. 2, no. 5
(May 1982), p. 28-32. English. DESCR: *Legal
Representation; Mexican American Legal
Defense and Educational Fund (MALDEF);
Tijerina, Pete.

6997 Business notes. HISPANIC BUSINESS, Vol. 5,
no. 12 (December 1983), p. 35. English.
DESCR: Anheuser-Busch, Inc.; *Business
Enterprises; Denny's Inc.; Des Moines, IA;
El Pollo Loco; Food Industry; Local
Government; National Association of Latino
Elected Officials (NALEO); Ochoa, Juan
Pancho.

6998 Hispanic journalists assemble in California.
NUESTRO, Vol. 6, no. 10 (December 1982), p.
28-30. English. DESCR: Cota-Robles Newton,
Frank; Journalism; *Journalists.

6999 Newsfront. HISPANIC BUSINESS, Vol. 4, no. 3
(March 1982), p. 9. English. DESCR:
Appointed Officials; *Biographical Notes;
Businesspeople; Chicano Film Exhibition and
Festival, Detroit, Michigan, April 5-9,
1982; Garcia, Gloria; League of United Latin
American Citizens (LULAC); National
Association for Bilingual Education; Seaga,
Edward; Suarez, Carlos R.

7000 People. HISPANIC BUSINESS, Vol. 5, no. 5
(May 1983), p. 8. English. DESCR:
Biographical Notes; *Businesspeople; Duron,
Armando; Espinoza, Peter; Flores, Juan;
Molina, Gloria; Moreno, Samuel; Pantin,
Leslie, Sr.; Quezada, Sylvia; Quinones,
Sergio.

Marxism

7001 Morrissey, Marietta. Ethnic stratification
and the study of Chicanos. JOURNAL OF ETHNIC
STUDIES, Vol. 10, no. 4 (Winter 1983), p.
71-99. English. DESCR: Assimilation; *Ethnic
Stratification; Internal Colonial Model
(Theoretical); Paradigm (Theoretical);
Social Theory.

7002 Torres, Lorenzo. Short history of Chicano
workers. SOUTHWEST ECONOMY AND SOCIETY, Vol.
3, no. 2 (Winter 1977, 1978), p. 4-17.
English. DESCR: *Labor Unions; *Mine, Mill
and Smelter Workers Union; Mining Industry;
Racism.

Marzan, Julio

7003 Binder, Wolfgang. Book review of: INVENTING
A WORD: AN ANTHOLOGY OF TWENTIETH CENTURY
PUERTO RICAN POETRY. MELUS: MULTI-ETHNIC
LITERATURE OF THE UNITED STATES, Vol. 8, no.
1 (Spring 1981), p. 77-79. English. DESCR:
INVENTING A WORD, AN ANTHOLOGY OF TWENTIETH
CENTURY PUERTO RICAN POETRY; *Puerto Rican
Literature.

7004 Laguardia, Gari. The canon and the
air-conditioner: modern Puerto Rican poetry.
BILINGUAL REVIEW, Vol. 9, no. 2 (May,
August, 1982), p. 178-181. English. DESCR:
Book Reviews; *INVENTING A WORD, AN
ANTHOLOGY OF TWENTIETH CENTURY PUERTO RICAN
POETRY; Poetry; Puerto Rican Literature.

Mas Distributors

7005 Stroud, Ruth. New products target Hispanics,
men. ADVERTISING AGE MAGAZINE, Vol. 54,
(September 19, 1983), p. 37. English.
DESCR: *Consumers; Cosmetology.

LOS MAS POBRES EN EL PAIS MAS RICO

7006 de Armas, Isabel. Chicano, un vocablo
colonizador. CUADERNOS HISPANOAMERICANOS,
Vol. 394, (April 1983), p. 193-201.
Spanish. DESCR: Agricultural Laborers; Book
Reviews; Calvo Buezas, Tomas; *CHICANOS:
ANTOLOGIA HISTORICA Y LITERARIA; Identity;
Villanueva, Tino.

Mass Media

7007 Adkins, Lynn. New strategies to sell
Hispanics. DUNS'S BUSINESS MONTH, Vol. 12,
no. 1 (July 1983), p. 64-69. English.
DESCR: *Advertising; Consumers.

7008 Armas, Jose. ANTONIO AND THE MAYOR: a
cultural review of the film. JOURNAL OF
ETHNIC STUDIES, Vol. 3, no. 3 (Fall 1975),
p. 98-101. English. DESCR: *ANTONIO AND THE
MAYOR; Broadcast Media; Columbia
Broadcasting Studios (CBS); Cultural
Characteristics; Film Reviews; Films;
*Stereotypes.

7009 Avila, Carmen. Assessing the casa study.
AGENDA, Vol. 11, no. 3 (May, June, 1981), p.
45-47,60. English. DESCR: *Communications
and Spanish Speaking Americans (CASA).

7010 Bonilla, Tony. Hispanics in the media.
LATINO, Vol. 53, no. 1 (January, February,
1982), p. 7. English.

7011 Bonilla, Tony. It's time for us to watch the
media. LATINO, Vol. 53, no. 6 (October
1982), p. 4. English.

7012 Bonilla, Tony. Life in these United States.
LATINO, Vol. 53, no. 5 (September 1982), p.
6. English.

7013 Book review of: IMAGES OF THE
MEXICAN-AMERICAN IN FICTION AND FILM. MODERN
FICTION STUDIES, Vol. 28, (Summer 1982), p.
367-369. English. DESCR: Book Reviews;
Fiction; Films; *IMAGES OF THE MEXICAN
AMERICAN IN FICTION AND FILM; Pettit, Arthur
G.

7014 Breiter, Toni. An interview with some
experts. AGENDA, Vol. 11, no. 3 (May, June,
1981), p. 48-52. English. DESCR: Guernica,
Antonio; Gutierrez, Felix; Morales, Rosa;
Schement, Jorge Reina; Valenzuela, Nicholas.

7015 Breiter, Toni. La raza. AGENDA, Vol. 11, no.
3 (May, June, 1981), p. 28-29. English.
DESCR: *Esparza, Moctezuma.

Mass Media (cont.)

7016 Cantu, Hector. Aqui en Austin: this is Olga Campos reporting. NATIONAL HISPANIC JOURNAL, Vol. 1, no. 3 (Summer, Fall, 1982), p. 7. English. **DESCR:** Campos, Olga; Careers; *KTBC-TV, Austin, TX [television station]; Television.

7017 Cardenas, Leo. How Hispanics are really influencing the networks. LATINO, Vol. 54, no. 3 (April 1983), p. 16-17. English.

7018 Chavarria, Jesus. The media scene. HISPANIC BUSINESS, Vol. 4, no. 5 (May 1982), p. 6. English. **DESCR:** Advertising; Broadcast Media; Caballero Spanish Media, Inc. (CSM); MIAMI MENSUAL; Print Media; Radio; Television.

7019 Communications/marketing. HISPANIC BUSINESS, Vol. 4, no. 10 (October 1982), p. 22. English. **DESCR:** Awards; ENFOQUE NACIONAL [radio program]; League of United Latin American Citizens (LULAC); LULAC National Education Service Centers (LNESC); Marketing.

7020 Communications/marketing. HISPANIC BUSINESS, Vol. 5, no. 2 (February 1983), p. 23. English. **DESCR:** *Broadcast Media; Coopers and Lybrand; Domecq Importers, Inc.; Latin American Feature Syndicate (ALA); Phoenix, AZ.

7021 Communications/marketing. HISPANIC BUSINESS, Vol. 5, no. 10 (October 1983), p. 26. English. **DESCR:** Advertising; Arens & Gutierrez; Employment; Henry Molina, Inc.; Journals; Lionetti and Meyers Research Center, Inc.; Marketing; Midwest Hispanics in Telecommunications Symposium, Chicago, IL; NEW MANAGEMENT.

7022 Communications/marketing. HISPANIC BUSINESS, Vol. 4, no. 8 (August 1983), p. 22+. English. **DESCR:** Arredondo, Price; Baseball; De la O, Val; Films; Marketing; Radio; San Antonio CineFestival, TX; Television; Val De La O Show; Valenzuela, Fernando; Wright & Arredondo Associates; Wright, Oscar.

7023 Cuenca, Ramon Araluce. USC forms institute for Hispanic media & culture. CAMINOS, Vol. 4, no. 3 (March 1983), p. 32. English. **DESCR:** *Institute for Hispanic Media and Culture; University of Southern California.

7024 Dear Santa, we want to see more Hispanics on television, movies, radio, magazines, and newspapers, Teresa and Carlos. LATINO, Vol. 53, no. 8 (December 1982), p. 7. English.

7025 Ericksen, Charles. Hispanics still ignored. LATINO, Vol. 53, no. 6 (October 1982), p. 20-21. English.

7026 Fantin, Joyce. Some Hispanic stations trying bilingual approach. BILLBOARD, Vol. 94, (November 13, 1982), p. 164. English. **DESCR:** Broadcast Media; *Radio.

7027 Gombeski, William R., Jr., et al. Communicating health information to urban Mexican-Americans: sources of health information. HEALTH EDUCATION QUARTERLY, Vol. 9, no. 4 (Winter 1982), p. 293-309. English. **DESCR:** Doctor Patient Relations; Health Education; *Public Health; Surveys.

7028 Greenberg, Bradley S. and Heeter, Carrie. Mass media orientations among Hispanic youth. HISPANIC JOURNAL OF BEHAVIORAL SCIENCES, Vol. 5, no. 3 (September 1983), p. 305-323. English. **DESCR:** Broadcast Media; Television.

7029 Guernica, Antonio. The Hispanic market: a profile. AGENDA, Vol. 11, no. 3 (May, June, 1981), p. 4-7. English. **DESCR:** *Consumers; Marketing; *Population; Population Distribution; Population Trends.

7030 Gutierrez, Felix. Breaking through the media employment wall. AGENDA, Vol. 11, no. 3 (May, June, 1981), p. 13-19. English. **DESCR:** *Employment; Journalism; Torres, Luis.

7031 Gutierrez, Felix. Henry Rivera: our Hispanic on the FCC. CAMINOS, Vol. 4, no. 3 (March 1983), p. 22-24,50. Bilingual. **DESCR:** Federal Communications Commission (FCC); *Rivera, Henry; Television.

7032 Hispanics in Communications, Inc. HISPANIC BUSINESS, Vol. 4, no. 5 (May 1982), p. 12. English. **DESCR:** Advertising; DaCosta, Jacqueline; Hispanics in Communications (HIC).

7033 Levario, Raquel. LULAC takes a stand against mainstream media. LATINA, Vol. 1, no. 3 (1983), p. 49. English. **DESCR:** Equal Employment Opportunity Commission (EEOC); *League of United Latin American Citizens (LULAC).

7034 Lewels, Francisco J. Un mensaje. LATINO, Vol. 53, no. 7 (November 1982), p. 17. Spanish. **DESCR:** *Rivera, Henry.

7035 McDougall, George. The press and Puerto Rico. NUESTRO, Vol. 7, no. 6 (August 1983), p. 21-25. English. **DESCR:** Political History and Conditions; *Puerto Rico.

7036 Media/marketing. HISPANIC BUSINESS, Vol. 5, no. 11 (November 1983), p. 30. English. **DESCR:** Caballero Spanish Media, Inc. (CSM); California Chicano News Media Association (CCNMA); Employment Training; Federal Communications Commission (FCC); HISPANEX (Oakland, CA); Michell, Pat; Radio; Radio Station KALI, Los Angeles, CA.

7037 Media/marketing. HISPANIC BUSINESS, Vol. 5, no. 12 (December 1983), p. 38. English. **DESCR:** Albertini, Luis Diaz; Computers; League of United Latin American Citizens (LULAC); Lotus-Albertini Hispanic Reps; Marketing; Nuestras Noticias; Radio; Reading; Television; Tortosa, Cristobal.

7038 The Mexican-American electorate. HISPANIC BUSINESS, Vol. 5, no. 8 (August 1983), p. 34-36. English. **DESCR:** Surveys.

7039 Mexico en crisis: la incomprendida prensa norteamericana. INFORME: RELACIONES MEXICO-ESTADOS UNIDOS, Vol. 1, no. 3 (July, December, 1982), p. 256-266. Spanish. **DESCR:** *ABC-TV; *Journalism; NEW YORK TIMES.

7040 Monsivais, Carlos. No te muevas, paisaje (sobre el cincuentenario del cine sonoro en Mexico). AZTLAN, Vol. 14, no. 1 (Spring 1983), p. 1-19. Spanish. **DESCR:** Bunuel, Luis; Felix, Maria; Fernandez, Emilio; *Films; *Mexico.

Mass Media (cont.)

7041 Neuman, Susan B. and Pits, Elaine F. A review of current North American television programs for bilingual children. READING TEACHER, Vol. 37, no. 3 (December 1983), p. 254-260. English. **DESCR**: *Bilingual Bicultural Education; SESAME STREET; Spanish Language; THE ELECTRIC COMPANY; VILLA ALEGRE.

7042 Olguin, Hank S. Images: minorities in the media. LATINA, Vol. 1, no. 2 (February, March, 1983), p. 21. English. **DESCR**: *Human Relations Commission, Los Angeles, CA; Media Artists Against Discrimination (MAAD); Stereotypes.

7043 Rangel, Jesus. Hispanic print media: alive and growing. AGENDA, Vol. 11, no. 3 (May, June, 1981), p. 10-12. English.

7044 Rios-Bustamante, Antonio. The Latino Olympians project and what it means to you. CAMINOS, Vol. 4, no. 4 (April 1983), p. 19. Bilingual. **DESCR**: *Latino Olympians Project; Olympics; Sports.

7045 Rosales, John. El perro favorito. LATINO, Vol. 53, no. 1 (January, February, 1982), p. 14. Spanish.

7046 Salmon, Roberto Mario. Comment: is this our decade in the sun? NATIONAL HISPANIC JOURNAL, Vol. 2, no. 1 (Summer 1983), p. 24-25. English. **DESCR**: Identity; Machismo; National Council of La Raza (NCLR).

7047 Sandoval, Alicia. Images and the media. LATINA, Vol. 1, no. 3 (1983), p. 37. English.

7048 Segal, Madhav N. and Sosa, Lionel. Marketing to the Hispanic community. CALIFORNIA MANAGEMENT REVIEW, Vol. 26, no. 1 (Fall 1983), p. 120-134. English. **DESCR**: Advertising; *Consumers; Population.

7049 Superbowl losers. LATINO, Vol. 53, no. 1 (January, February, 1982), p. 4. English.

7050 Sutherland, Sam. TV series eyes crossover: BRAVISIMO sets its sights on mainstream audience. BILLBOARD, Vol. 95, (July 30, 1983), p. 50. English. **DESCR**: *BRAVISIMO; Broadcast Media; Television.

7051 Tips for making the right moves in today's job markets. HISPANIC BUSINESS, Vol. 4, no. 5 (May 1982), p. 16. English. **DESCR**: California Chicano News Media Association (CCNMA); *Careers.

7052 A torch of diversity. LATINO, Vol. 54, no. 8 (December 1983), p. 15. English. **DESCR**: Television.

7053 Valenzuela, Nicholas. Ensuring future Hispanic participation in telecommunications. AGENDA, Vol. 11, no. 3 (May, June, 1981), p. 24-27. English. **DESCR**: *Telecommunications; Television.

7054 Viamonte, Norberto. Media and politics. LATINO, Vol. 53, no. 1 (January, February, 1982), p. 6. English.

7055 Wittenauer, Cheryl. Dallas Hispanic media. HISPANIC BUSINESS, Vol. 5, no. 2 (February 1983), p. 12-13+. English. **DESCR**: Broadcast Media; *Consumers; Dallas, TX; English Language; Marketing; Newspapers; Spanish Language.

Massachusetts

7056 Prida, Dolores. Latin American women writers meet in New England. NUESTRO, Vol. 6, no. 10 (December 1982), p. 26-27. English. **DESCR**: Authors; *Chicanas.

Masseria, Francisco

7057 Another graphic award for Francisco Masseria. NUESTRO, Vol. 6, no. 7 (September 1982), p. 35. English. **DESCR**: *Art; Artists.

Mastery Learning

7058 De Barbosa, Liliam Coya. "Mastering learning" como metodo psicoeducativo para ninos con problemas especificos de aprendizaje. HISPANIC JOURNAL OF BEHAVIORAL SCIENCES, Vol. 4, no. 4 (December 1982), p. 503-510. Spanish. **DESCR**: Children; Learning and Cognition; Puerto Ricans; *Reading.

Masvidal, Raul

7059 Volsky, George and Masvidal, Raul. An interview with Raul Masvidal. HISPANIC BUSINESS, Vol. 4, no. 9 (September 1982), p. 16-17,24+. English. **DESCR**: Banking Industry; Biography; Business Enterprises; Businesspeople; Cubanos; Miami, FL.

Masvidal, Sergio J.

7060 People. HISPANIC BUSINESS, Vol. 5, no. 12 (December 1983), p. 9. English. **DESCR**: *Businesspeople; Cantu, Norma V.; Cruz, Jose; Ortega, Katherine D.; Planas, Maria Bordas; Rodriguez, Ismael D.; Romero, Estella E.

7061 Volsky, George. Four careers in Miami. HISPANIC BUSINESS, Vol. 5, no. 4 (April 1983), p. 10-11+. English. **DESCR**: Balestra, Victor C.; *Banking Industry; Biographical Notes; *Businesspeople; Harvard Business School's Latino Association; Huston, Maria Padilla; Miami, FL; Valdes-Fauli, Gonzalo.

Mata, Bill

7062 People. HISPANIC BUSINESS, Vol. 5, no. 4 (April 1983), p. 9. English. **DESCR**: Alvarado, Linda M.; *Biographical Notes; Businesspeople; Castillo, Irenemaree; Castillo, Sylvia; Del Junco, Tirso; Gutierrez, Jose Roberto; Juarez, Joe; Miyares, Marcelino; Montanez Davis, Grace; Montoya, Velma; Pineda, Pat; Siberio, Julio; Thompson, Edith Lopez.

Maternal and Child Welfare

7063 Smith, Jack C. Trends in the incidence of breastfeeding for Hispanics of Mexican origin and Anglos on the US-Mexican border. AMERICAN JOURNAL OF PUBLIC HEALTH, Vol. 72, no. 1 (January 1982), p. 59-61. English. **DESCR**: Anglo Americans; Breastfeeding; Chicanas.

7064 Zepeda, Marlene. Selected maternal-infant care practices of Spanish-speaking women. JOGN NURSING, Vol. 11, no. 6 (November, December, 1982), p. 371-374. English. **DESCR**: Child Rearing.

Mathematics

7065 Creswell, John L. and Exezidis, Roxane H.
Research brief: sex and ethnic differences
in mathematics achievement of Black and
Mexican-American adolescents. TEXAS TECH
JOURNAL OF EDUCATION, Vol. 9, no. 3 (Fall
1982), p. 219-222. English. DESCR: Blacks;
Chicanas; Gender; Youth.

7066 Creswell, John L. Sex-related differences in
the problem-solving abilities of rural
Black, Anglo, and Chicano adolescents. TEXAS
TECH JOURNAL OF EDUCATION, Vol. 10, no. 1
(Winter 1983), p. 29-33. English. DESCR:
Aiken and Preger Revised Math Attitude
Scale; Anglo Americans; Blacks; California
Achievement Test; Chicanas; Gender; National
Assessment of Educational Progress;
*National Council of Teachers of Mathematics
(NCTM); Youth.

7067 Llabre, Maria M. and Cuevas, Gilberto.
Effects of test language and mathematical
skills assessed on the scores of bilingual
Hispanic students. JOURNAL FOR RESEARCH IN
MATHEMATICS EDUCATION, Vol. 14, no. 4
(November 1983), p. 318-324. English.
DESCR: Comprehensive Test of Basic Skills
(CTBS); Dade County, FL; *Educational Tests
and Measurements; Stanford Achievement Test.

7068 Math-based careers. HISPANIC BUSINESS, Vol.
5, no. 2 (February 1983), p. 22. English.
DESCR: *Careers; Engineering; Financial Aid;
Mathematics, Engineering and Science
Achievement (MESA); National Action Council
for Minorities in Engineering (NACME).

7069 Math-based careers. HISPANIC BUSINESS, Vol.
5, no. 7 (July 1983), p. 22. English.
DESCR: *Careers; Education; National Council
for Minorities in Engineering (NACME);
Nursing.

7070 Oakland, Thomas. Joint use of adaptive
behavior and IQ to predict achievement.
JOURNAL OF CONSULTING AND CLINICAL
PSYCHOLOGY, Vol. 51, no. 2 (April 1983), p.
298-301. English. DESCR: *Academic
Achievement; Education; Intelligence Tests;
Reading.

7071 Yvon, Bernard R. Effects of the language of
a diagnostic test on math scores. BILINGUAL
JOURNAL, Vol. 6, no. 1 (Fall 1982), p.
13-16. English. DESCR: Bilingual Bicultural
Education; *Educational Tests and
Measurements; Key-Math Diagnostic Test;
Language Proficiency.

Mathematics, Engineering and Science Achievement (MESA)

7072 de la Isla, Jose. Math-based careers.
HISPANIC BUSINESS, Vol. 5, no. 4 (April
1983), p. 20. English. DESCR: *Careers;
Engineering; Medical Personnel.

7073 Government review. NUESTRO, Vol. 7, no. 7
(September 1983), p. 55. English. DESCR:
AIDS Hotline; California; Education;
Employment; Food for Survival, New York, NY;
Funding Sources; *Government Services;
Hewlett Foundation; Laborers; Population
Trends; Public Health; Stanford University,
Stanford, CA.

7074 Math-based careers. HISPANIC BUSINESS, Vol.
5, no. 2 (February 1983), p. 22. English.
DESCR: *Careers; Engineering; Financial Aid;
Mathematics; National Action Council for
Minorities in Engineering (NACME).

7075 Math-based careers. HISPANIC BUSINESS, Vol.
5, no. 11 (November 1983), p. 32. English.
DESCR: *Careers; Education; Employment
Training; INROADS; Mexican American Legal
Defense and Educational Fund (MALDEF);
Soriano, Esteban.

Matte Alessandri, Ester

7076 Agosin, Marjorie. Book review of: ENTRE LA
VIGILIA Y EL SUENO. THIRD WOMAN, Vol. 1, no.
2 (1982), p. 94-95. Spanish. DESCR: Book
Reviews; *ENTRE LA VIGILIA Y EL SUENO.

Matute-Bianchi, Maria Eugenia

7077 Matute-Bianchi, Maria Eugenia. A Chicana in
academe. WOMEN'S STUDIES QUARTERLY, Vol. 10,
no. 1 (Spring 1982), p. 14-17. English.
DESCR: *Chicanas; *Higher Education; Racism;
Sex Roles; Sexism.

Maxims

USE: Dichos

Mayas

7078 Rodriguez, Roberto. The Maya: from
oppression to resistence. CORAZON DE AZTLAN,
Vol. 1, no. 1 (January, February, 1982), p.
11-14. English.

Mayorga, Luis

7079 Gonzalez, Magdalena. Luis Mayorga. CAMINOS,
Vol. 3, no. 9 (October 1982), p. 18.
English. DESCR: *Artists.

Mazzoli, Romano L.

7080 Hing, Bill Ong. Racial disparity: the
unaddressed issues of the Simpson-Mazzoli
Bill. LA RAZA LAW JOURNAL, Vol. 1, no. 1
(June 1983), p. 21-52. English. DESCR:
Amnesty; Asian Americans; Ethnic Attitudes;
Family; Immigration; Immigration and
Naturalization Service (INS); Latin
Americans; Mexican American Legal Defense
and Educational Fund (MALDEF); Simpson, Alan
K.; *Simpson-Mazzoli Bill; Temporary Worker
Program; U.S. Congresssional Subcommittee on
Immigration, Refugees and International Law.

7081 Liebowitz, Arnold. Immigration challenge and
the congressional response. LA RAZA LAW
JOURNAL, Vol. 1, no. 1 (June 1983), p. 1-20.
English. DESCR: Amnesty; Immigration;
Immigration and Nationality Act (INA);
*Simpson, Alan K.; *Simpson-Mazzoli Bill;
Temporary Worker Program; Undocumented
Workers; U.S. Congresssional Subcommittee on
Immigration, Refugees and International Law.

7082 Schey, Peter A. Supply side immigration
theory: analysis of the Simpson-Mazzoli
Bill. LA RAZA LAW JOURNAL, Vol. 1, no. 1
(June 1983), p. 53-71. English. DESCR:
Amnesty; Immigration; Migration Patterns;
Refugees; Simpson, Alan K.; *Simpson-Mazzoli
Bill; Temporary Worker Program.

7083 Watson, Roy J., Jr. The Simpson-Mazzoli
bill: an analysis of selected policies. SAN
DIEGO LAW REVIEW, Vol. 20, no. 1 (December
1982), p. 97-116. English. DESCR:
Employment; Immigration Regulation and
Control; Labor Certification; Simpson, Alan
K.; *Simpson-Mazzoli Bill; *Undocumented
Workers.

Mazzoli, Romano L. (cont.)

7084 Wong, Linda. Simpson-Mazzoli Bill in the
     Ninety-eighth Congress. LA RAZA LAW JOURNAL,
     Vol. 1, no. 1 (June 1983), p. 72-75.
     English. DESCR: Immigration and
     Naturalization Service (INS); Immigration
     Law; Simpson, Alan K.; *Simpson-Mazzoli
     Bill.

McAfee, Ward

7085 Bodayla, Stephen D. Book review of: ORIGINS
     OF THE MEXICAN WAR: A DOCUMENTARY SOURCE
     BOOK. HISTORY - REVIEWS OF NEW BOOKS, Vol.
     11, no. 7 (May, June, 1983), p. 149-150.
     English. DESCR: Book Reviews; *ORIGINS OF
     THE MEXICAN WAR: A DOCUMENTARY SOURCE BOOK;
     Robinson, J. Cordell.

7086 Graebner, Norman A. Book review of: ORIGINS
     OF THE MEXICAN WAR: A DOCUMENTARY SOURCE
     BOOK. NEW MEXICO HISTORICAL REVIEW, Vol. 58,
     no. 3 (July 1983), p. 291-292. English.
     DESCR: Book Reviews; *ORIGINS OF THE MEXICAN
     WAR: A DOCUMENTARY SOURCE BOOK; Robinson, J.
     Cordell.

McAllen, TX

7087 Nieto, Ernesto. Politics: powers that
     struggled in the Texas Valley. NATIONAL
     HISPANIC JOURNAL, Vol. 2, no. 1 (Summer
     1983), p. 22-23. English. DESCR: Elections;
     *Politics; *Rio Grande Valley, TX; Voter
     Turnout.

McCarthy Scales for Children's Abilities (MSCA)

7088 Murray, Anne M. and Mishra, Shitala P.
     Judgments of item bias in the McCarthy
     scales of children's abilities. HISPANIC
     JOURNAL OF BEHAVIORAL SCIENCES, Vol. 5, no.
     3 (September 1983), p. 325-336. English.
     DESCR: Culture; *Psychological Testing.

7089 Valencia, Richard R. and Rankin, Richard J.
     Concurrent validity and reliability of the
     Kaufman version of the McCarthy scales short
     form for a sample of Mexican-American
     children. EDUCATIONAL AND PSYCHOLOGICAL
     MEASUREMENT, Vol. 43, no. 3 (Fall 1983), p.
     915-925. English. DESCR: Educational Tests
     and Measurements; Learning and Cognition.

7090 Valencia, Richard R. Predicting academic
     achievement of Mexican American children:
     preliminary analysis of the McCarthy Scales.
     EDUCATIONAL AND PSYCHOLOGICAL MEASUREMENT,
     Vol. 42, (Winter 1982), p. 1269-1278.
     English. DESCR: *Academic Achievement;
     Children; Educational Tests and
     Measurements; Identity.

7091 Valencia, Richard R. Stability of the
     McCarthy scales of children's abilities over
     a one-year period for Mexican-American
     children. PSYCHOLOGY IN THE SCHOOLS, Vol.
     20, no. 1 (January 1983), p. 29-34. English.
     DESCR: Child Study; Cultural
     Characteristics; *Intelligence Tests;
     Socioeconomic Factors.

McCluskey, Neil G.

7092 Burke, Leslie K. Book review of: AGING AND
     SOCIETY: CURRENT RESEARCH AND POLICY
     PERSPECTIVES. HISPANIC JOURNAL OF BEHAVIORAL
     SCIENCES, Vol. 4, no. 1 (March 1982), p.
     114-115. English. DESCR: *AGING AND SOCIETY:
     CURRENT RESEARCH AND POLICY PERSPECTIVES;
     Ancianos; Book Reviews; Borgatta, Edgar F.

Medal of Honor

7093 Madrid, Joe and Gonzalez, Magdalena. NALEO -
     honoring the Hispanic Medal of Honor
     winners. CAMINOS, Vol. 3, no. 10 (November
     1982), p. 22-25. English. DESCR: *Military
     Service; *National Association of Latino
     Elected Officials (NALEO).

7094 Ponce, Mary Helen. Recuerdo: the funeral of
     Daniel Torres, winner of the Medal of Honor.
     CHISMEARTE, no. 9 (September 1983), p.
     35-37. English. DESCR: Military Service;
     *Torres, Daniel.

Media

USE: Mass Media

Media Artists Against Discrimination (MAAD)

7095 Olguin, Hank S. Images: minorities in the
     media. LATINA, Vol. 1, no. 2 (February,
     March, 1983), p. 21. English. DESCR: *Human
     Relations Commission, Los Angeles, CA; *Mass
     Media; Stereotypes.

Media Systems Technology, Inc.(MST,Inc.)

7096 Weber, Robert. Turbo-charged MST, Inc.
     HISPANIC BUSINESS, Vol. 4, no. 11 (November
     1982), p. 10-11,24. English. DESCR: Alcala,
     Al; Computers; *High Technology Industries;
     Irvine, CA.

Medical Anthropology

7097 Trotter, Robert T. Susto: the context of
     community morbidity patterns. ETHNOLOGY,
     Vol. 21, no. 3 (July 1982), p. 215-226.
     English. DESCR: Folk Medicine; *Susto.

Medical Botany

USE: Herbal Medicine

Medical Care

7098 Ailinger, Rita L. Hypertension knowledge in
     a Hispanic community. NURSING RESEARCH, Vol.
     31, no. 4 (July, August, 1982), p. 207-210.
     English. DESCR: *Hypertension; Surveys.

7099 Cayer, Shirley. Chicago's new Hispanic
     health alliance. NUESTRO, Vol. 7, no. 5
     (June, July, 1983), p. 44-48. English.
     DESCR: Alcoholism; Chicago Hispanic Health
     Alliance; Family Planning; *Health
     Education; Latin Americans.

7100 Chavez, Leo R. Undocumented immigrants and
     access to health services: a game of pass
     the buck. MIGRATION TODAY, Vol. 11, no. 1
     (1983), p. 14-19. English. DESCR:
     California; *Immigrants; Migrant Health
     Services; Public Health Legislation;
     Simpson-Mazzoli Bill; Social Services;
     Undocumented Workers.

7101 Chesney, Alan P., et al. Barriers to medical
     care of Mexican-Americans: the role of
     social class, acculturation, and social
     isolation. MEDICAL CARE, Vol. 20, no. 9
     (1982), p. 883-891. English. DESCR:
     Acculturation; Social Classes; Surveys.

Medical Care (cont.)

7102 Cuellar, Israel, et al. Clinical psychiatric case presentation; culturally responsive diagnostic formulation and treatment in an Hispanic female. HISPANIC JOURNAL OF BEHAVIORAL SCIENCES, Vol. 5, no. 1 (March 1983), p. 93-103. English. **DESCR**: *ACCULTURATION RATING SCALE FOR MEXICAN AMERICANS (ARSMA); Case Study; Chicanas; *Psychotherapy.

7103 Garcia, Ignacio M. Miracles at Kino Hospital. NUESTRO, Vol. 7, no. 6 (August 1983), p. 11-12. English. **DESCR**: *Gonzalez, Arthur; Hospitals and the Community; *Kino Community Hospital, Tucson, AZ; Public Health.

7104 Gonzales, Juan. Puerto Rico to Philadelphia: a cure connection. NUESTRO, Vol. 7, no. 5 (June, July, 1983), p. 21-24. English. **DESCR**: *Handicapped; Hospitals and the Community; Puerto Ricans; Shriner's Hospital for Crippled Children, Philadelphia, PA.

7105 Government review. NUESTRO, Vol. 7, no. 10 (December 1983), p. 48. English. **DESCR**: Banking Industry; Child Care Centers; Chile; Clinics (Medical); Credit Unions; Employment; Employment Training; *Government Services; National Credit Union Administration; National Oceanic and Atmospheric Administration; SER; U.S. Department of Health and Human Services; U.S. Department of Labor.

7106 Gum disease: a problem of epidemic proportions. NUESTRO, Vol. 7, no. 9 (November 1983), p. 39-41. English. **DESCR**: *Dentistry.

7107 Hedderson, John and Daudistel, Howard C. Infant mortality of the Spanish surname population. SOCIAL SCIENCE JOURNAL, Vol. 19, no. 4 (October 1982), p. 67-78. English. **DESCR**: Demography; El Paso County, TX; *Infant Mortality; Statistics; Vital Statistics.

7108 Luevano, Richard L. Attitudes of elderly Mexican Americans towards nursing homes in Stanislaus county. CAMPO LIBRE, Vol. 1, no. 2 (Summer 1981), p. 213-228. English. **DESCR**: *Ancianos; Attitude (Psychological); Cultural Characteristics; *Nursing Homes; Stanislaus County, CA; Surveys.

7109 Marin, Barbara Van Oss, et al. Utilization of traditional and non-traditional sources of health care among Hispanics. HISPANIC JOURNAL OF BEHAVIORAL SCIENCES, Vol. 5, no. 1 (March 1983), p. 65-80. English. **DESCR**: Public Health.

7110 Medina, Antonio S. Adolescent health in Alameda county. JOURNAL OF ADOLESCENT HEALTH CARE, Vol. 2, no. 3 (March 1982), p. 175-182. English. **DESCR**: Alameda County, CA; *Dentistry; Drug Abuse; Psychology; Youth.

7111 Nalven, Joseph. Health research on undocumented Mexicans. SOCIAL SCIENCE JOURNAL, Vol. 19, no. 2 (April 1982), p. 73-88. English. **DESCR**: Immigrants; Immigration Law; *Public Health; *Undocumented Workers.

7112 O'Brien, Mary Elizabeth. Pragmatic survivalism: behavior patterns affecting low-level wellness among minority group members. ANS: ADVANCES IN NURSING SCIENCE, Vol. 4, no. 3 (April 1982), p. 13-26. English. **DESCR**: Curanderismo; Ethnic Attitudes; Immigrants; *Nursing; Public Health.

7113 O'Brien, Mary Elizabeth. Reaching the migrant worker. AMERICAN JOURNAL OF NURSING, Vol. 83, no. 6 (June 1983), p. 895-897. English. **DESCR**: Agricultural Laborers; Folk Medicine; *Migrant Health Services.

7114 PA trained for Venezuela. NUESTRO, Vol. 6, no. 6 (August 1982), p. 10. English. **DESCR**: *Estassi, Pilar; Venezuela.

7115 Padilla, Steve. Choosing a career. NUESTRO, Vol. 7, no. 1 (January, February, 1983), p. 13-19+. English. **DESCR**: Alvarado, Raul, Jr.; *Careers; Computers; Diaz, William; Engineering as a Profession; Esparza, Alma; Flores, Francisco; Garcia, Linda; Soto, John; Yanez, Ricardo.

7116 Poma, Pedro A. Hispanic cultural influences on medical practices. NATIONAL MEDICAL ASSOCIATION JOURNAL, Vol. 75, no. 10 (October 1983), p. 941-946. English. **DESCR**: Cultural Characteristics; Hospitals and the Community.

7117 Ponce-Adame, Merrihelen. Women and cancer. CORAZON DE AZTLAN, Vol. 1, no. 2 (March, April, 1982), p. 32. English. **DESCR**: *Cancer; Chicanas; Preventative Medicine.

7118 Reid, Richard A.; Bartlett, Edward E.; and Kozoll, Richard. Checkerboard area health system: delivering comprehensive care in a remote region of New Mexico. HUMAN ORGANIZATION, Vol. 41, no. 2 (Summer 1982), p. 147-155. English. **DESCR**: New Mexico; Rural Population.

7119 Rodriguez, Josie. Mexican-Americans: factors influencing health practices. JOURNAL OF SCHOOL HEALTH, Vol. 53, no. 2 (Fall 1983), p. 136-139. English. **DESCR**: Curanderismo; *Public Health.

7120 Roeder, Beatrice A. Health care beliefs and practices among the Mexican Americans. AZTLAN, Vol. 13, no. 1-2 (Spring, Fall, 1982), p. 223-256. English. **DESCR**: Folk Medicine; *Literature Reviews; Public Health.

7121 Staczek, John J. Code-switching in Miami Spanish: the domain of health care services. BILINGUAL REVIEW, Vol. 10, no. 1 (January, April, 1983), p. 41-46. English. **DESCR**: *Bilingualism; *Language Interference; Miami, FL; Spanish Language.

7122 [Summary of: Note, medical benefits awarded to an alien: Perez v. health and social services, 9 N.M.L. rev. 89 (1979)]. CHICANO LAW REVIEW, Vol. 5, (1982), p. 80-81. English. **DESCR**: *Medical Care Laws and Legislation; Perez v. Health and Social Services; Undocumented Workers.

7123 Tejani, Amir et al. Lupus nephritis in Black and Hispanic children. AMERICAN JOURNAL OF DISEASES OF CHILDREN, Vol. 137, no. 5 (May 1983), p. 481-483. English. **DESCR**: *Children; *Medical Research; Public Health.

7124 Trotter, Robert T. Contrasting models of the healer's role: south Texas case examples. HISPANIC JOURNAL OF BEHAVIORAL SCIENCES, Vol. 4, no. 3 (September 1982), p. 315-327. English. **DESCR**: Cultural Characteristics; *Curanderismo; Public Health.

Medical Care Laws and Legislation

7125 Lopez, Victor Manuel. Equal protection for undocumented aliens. CHICANO LAW REVIEW, Vol. 5, (1982), p. 29-54. English. DESCR: Civil Rights; Discrimination in Education; Legal Reform; *Undocumented Workers.

7126 [Summary of: Note, medical benefits awarded to an alien: Perez v. health and social services, 9 N.M.L. rev. 89 (1979)]. CHICANO LAW REVIEW, Vol. 5, (1982), p. 80-81. English. DESCR: Medical Care; Perez v. Health and Social Services; Undocumented Workers.

Medical Education

7127 Calkins, E. Virginia; Willoughby, T. Lee; and Arnold, Louise M. Predictors of performance of minority students in the first two years of a BA/MD program. NATIONAL MEDICAL ASSOCIATION JOURNAL, Vol. 74, no. 7 (July 1982), p. 625-632. English. DESCR: Academic Achievement; Academic Motivation; Affirmative Action Programs; University of Missouri-Kansas City School of Medicine.

7128 Dienhart, Paul. Minnesota support groups help Latinos through medical school. NUESTRO, Vol. 6, no. 6 (August 1982), p. 39-40. English. DESCR: Health Education; Latin Americans; Medical Students; Minnesota; Public Health; *University of Minnesota.

7129 Fleming, Marilyn B. Problems experienced by Anglo, Hispanic and Navajo Indian women college students. JOURNAL OF AMERICAN INDIAN EDUCATION, Vol. 22, no. 1 (October 1982), p. 7-17. English. DESCR: *Chicanas; Community Colleges; Ethnic Groups; Identity; Native Americans.

7130 Gaviria, Moises and Wintrob, Ronald. Latin American medical graduates: I. determinants of the decision to remain in the United States. HISPANIC JOURNAL OF BEHAVIORAL SCIENCES, Vol. 4, no. 1 (March 1982), p. 89-101. English. DESCR: Latin Americans; Medical Personnel; *Medical Students.

7131 Gaviria, Moises and Wintrob, Ronald. Latin American medical graduates: II the readaptation process for those who return home. HISPANIC JOURNAL OF BEHAVIORAL SCIENCES, Vol. 4, no. 3 (September 1982), p. 367-379. English. DESCR: *Medical Students.

7132 Lourenzo, Susan V. Early outreach: career awareness for health professions. JOURNAL OF MEDICAL EDUCATION, Vol. 58, no. 1 (January 1983), p. 39-44. English. DESCR: Affirmative Action; Careers; College Preparation; *Recruitment.

7133 Murphy, John W. and Redden, Richard. The use of management by objectives in medical education enrichment programs. JOURNAL OF MEDICAL EDUCATION, Vol. 57, no. 12 (December 1982), p. 911-917. English. DESCR: *Educational Administration; Educational Innovations; Evaluation (Educational); Management by Objectives (MBO).

7134 Sherman, Susan N., comp. Applicants to U.S. medical schools, 1977-78 to 1981-82. JOURNAL OF MEDICAL EDUCATION, Vol. 57, no. 11 (November 1982), p. 882-884. English. DESCR: Educational Statistics; Ethnic Groups; Medical Students.

Medical Personnel

7135 de la Isla, Jose. Math-based careers. HISPANIC BUSINESS, Vol. 5, no. 4 (April 1983), p. 20. English. DESCR: *Careers; Engineering; Mathematics, Engineering and Science Achievement (MESA).

7136 Gaviria, Moises and Wintrob, Ronald. Latin American medical graduates: I. determinants of the decision to remain in the United States. HISPANIC JOURNAL OF BEHAVIORAL SCIENCES, Vol. 4, no. 1 (March 1982), p. 89-101. English. DESCR: Latin Americans; Medical Education; *Medical Students.

7137 Math-based careers. HISPANIC BUSINESS, Vol. 4, no. 8 (August 1983), p. 20. English. DESCR: Brigham Young University; Business Administration; *Careers; Coalition of Spanish-Speaking Mental Health Organization (COSSMHO), Annual Regional Conference, Los Angeles, March 14-15, 1975; Cooperative Extension Programs; Education; Employment Training; Financial Aid.

7138 Training, fellowships. NUESTRO, Vol. 7, no. 1 (January, February, 1983), p. 9. English. DESCR: *Community Outreach Project; Employment Training; Financial Aid; Stanford University Medical Center.

Medical Research

7139 Cox, Rebecca A., et al. HLA phenotypes in Mexican-Americans with tuberculosis. AMERICAN REVIEW OF RESPIRATORY DISEASE, Vol. 126, no. 4 (October 1982), p. 653-655. English. DESCR: Medicine; Public Health; *Tuberculosis.

7140 Samet, Jonathan M., et al. Respiratory disease in a New Mexico population sample of Hispanic and non-Hispanic whites. AMERICAN REVIEW OF RESPIRATORY DISEASE, Vol. 125, no. 2 (February 1982), p. 152-157. English. DESCR: Bernalillo County, NM; Medicine; Public Health.

7141 Stern, Michael P., et al. Does obesity explain excess prevalence of diabetes among Mexican Americans? Results of the San Antonio Heart Study. DIABETOLOGIA, Vol. 24, no. 4 (April 1983), p. 272-277. English. DESCR: *Diabetes; Medicine; Obesity; Public Health; *San Antonio Heart Study.

7142 Tejani, Amir et al. Lupus nephritis in Black and Hispanic children. AMERICAN JOURNAL OF DISEASES OF CHILDREN, Vol. 137, no. 5 (May 1983), p. 481-483. English. DESCR: *Children; Medical Care; Public Health.

7143 Weber, Robert. Summa's Tumortec/hCG. HISPANIC BUSINESS, Vol. 5, no. 7 (July 1983), p. 18-19+. English. DESCR: *Business Enterprises; Businesspeople; Summa Medical Corporation.

7144 Zeidler, Adina S. Histocompatibility antigens and immunoglobulin G insulin antibodies in Mexican-American insulin-dependent diabetic patients. JOURNAL OF CLINICAL ENDOCRINOLOGY AND METABOLISM, Vol. 54, no. 3 (March 1982), p. 569-573. English. DESCR: *Diabetes; Medicine.

Medical Research (cont.)

7145 Zeidler, Adina S. Pancreatic islet cell and thyroid antibodies, and islet cell function in diabetic patients of Mexico-American origin. JOURNAL OF CLINICAL ENDOCRINOLOGY AND METABOLISM, Vol. 54, no. 5 (May 1982), p. 949-954. English. DESCR: *Diabetes; Medicine.

Medical Services
USE: Medical Care

Medical Students

7146 Dienhart, Paul. Minnesota support groups help Latinos through medical school. NUESTRO, Vol. 6, no. 6 (August 1982), p. 39-40. English. DESCR: Health Education; Latin Americans; Medical Education; Minnesota; Public Health; *University of Minnesota.

7147 Gaviria, Moises and Wintrob, Ronald. Latin American medical graduates: I. determinants of the decision to remain in the United States. HISPANIC JOURNAL OF BEHAVIORAL SCIENCES, Vol. 4, no. 1 (March 1982), p. 89-101. English. DESCR: Latin Americans; Medical Education; Medical Personnel.

7148 Gaviria, Moises and Wintrob, Ronald. Latin American medical graduates: II the readaptation process for those who return home. HISPANIC JOURNAL OF BEHAVIORAL SCIENCES, Vol. 4, no. 3 (September 1982), p. 367-379. English. DESCR: Medical Education.

7149 Martinez, Rick. Migrant worker to M.D. NUESTRO, Vol. 6, no. 1 (January, February, 1982), p. 16-17. English. DESCR: *Sandoval, Jose.

7150 Sherman, Susan N., comp. Applicants to U.S. medical schools, 1977-78 to 1981-82. JOURNAL OF MEDICAL EDUCATION, Vol. 57, no. 11 (November 1982), p. 882-884. English. DESCR: Educational Statistics; Ethnic Groups; *Medical Education.

Medicine

7151 Cox, Rebecca A., et al. HLA phenotypes in Mexican-Americans with tuberculosis. AMERICAN REVIEW OF RESPIRATORY DISEASE, Vol. 126, no. 4 (October 1982), p. 653-655. English. DESCR: *Medical Research; Public Health; *Tuberculosis.

7152 Family displays special courage. NUESTRO, Vol. 7, no. 1 (January, February, 1983), p. 10. English. DESCR: Little People of America; *Luna, Brian.

7153 Folk remedy dangerous. NUESTRO, Vol. 7, no. 2 (March 1983), p. 7. English. DESCR: Federal Drug Administration (FDA); *Folk Medicine; Trotter, Robert.

7154 Risse, Gunter B. Book review of: CAPITULOS DE HISTORIA MEDICA MEXICANA. BULLETIN OF THE HISTORY OF MEDICINE, Vol. 56, no. 4 (1982), p. 591-592. English. DESCR: *CAPITULOS DE HISTORIA MEDICA MEXICANA; Folk Medicine; Mexico; Precolumbian Medicine; Somolinos D'Ardois, German.

7155 Samet, Jonathan M., et al. Respiratory disease in a New Mexico population sample of Hispanic and non-Hispanic whites. AMERICAN REVIEW OF RESPIRATORY DISEASE, Vol. 125, no. 2 (February 1982), p. 152-157. English. DESCR: Bernalillo County, NM; *Medical Research; Public Health.

7156 Stern, Michael P., et al. Does obesity explain excess prevalence of diabetes among Mexican Americans? Results of the San Antonio Heart Study. DIABETOLOGIA, Vol. 24, no. 4 (April 1983), p. 272-277. English. DESCR: *Diabetes; Medical Research; Obesity; Public Health; *San Antonio Heart Study.

7157 Zeidler, Adina S. Histocompatibility antigens and immunoglobulin G insulin antibodies in Mexican-American insulin-dependent diabetic patients. JOURNAL OF CLINICAL ENDOCRINOLOGY AND METABOLISM, Vol. 54, no. 3 (March 1982), p. 569-573. English. DESCR: *Diabetes; Medical Research.

7158 Zeidler, Adina S. Pancreatic islet cell and thyroid antibodies, and islet cell function in diabetic patients of Mexico-American origin. JOURNAL OF CLINICAL ENDOCRINOLOGY AND METABOLISM, Vol. 54, no. 5 (May 1982), p. 949-954. English. DESCR: *Diabetes; Medical Research.

Medrano, Adan

7159 People. HISPANIC BUSINESS, Vol. 4, no. 7 (July 1982), p. 7. English. DESCR: Aguilar, Richard; *Biographical Notes; Businesspeople; Coronado, Julius; Enriquez, Rene; Garza, Jose S.; Guerra-Martinez, Celina; Mota, Manny; Valenti, Frank S.

MEGATRENDS

7160 Book review of: MEGATRENDS. NUESTRO, Vol. 7, no. 9 (November 1983), p. 61-62. English. DESCR: Book Reviews; Naisbitt, John.

Meier, Matt S.

7161 Barber, Gary. Book review of: DICTIONARY OF MEXICAN-AMERICAN HISTORY. REFERENCE SERVICES REVIEW, Vol. 10, no. 3 (October 1982), p. 41. English. DESCR: Book Reviews; Dictionaries; *DICTIONARY OF MEXICAN AMERICAN HISTORY; Rivera, Feliciano.

7162 Book review of: DICTIONARY OF MEXICAN-AMERICAN HISTORY. LIBRARY JOURNAL, Vol. 108, no. 10 (May 15, 1983), p. 965. English. DESCR: Book Reviews; *DICTIONARY OF MEXICAN AMERICAN HISTORY; Rivera, Feliciano.

7163 Camarillo, Alberto M. Book review of: DICTIONARY OF MEXICAN-AMERICAN HISTORY. JOURNAL OF AMERICAN HISTORY, Vol. 69, no. 4 (March 1983), p. 953-954. English. DESCR: Book Reviews; *DICTIONARY OF MEXICAN AMERICAN HISTORY; Rivera, Feliciano.

7164 De Leon, Arnoldo. Book review of: DICTIONARY OF MEXICAN-AMERICAN HISTORY. NEW MEXICO HISTORICAL REVIEW, Vol. 58, no. 1 (January 1983), p. 101-102. English. DESCR: Book Reviews; *DICTIONARY OF MEXICAN AMERICAN HISTORY; Rivera, Feliciano.

7165 Griswold del Castillo, Richard. Book review of: DICTIONARY OF MEXICAN-AMERICAN HISTORY. SOUTHWESTERN HISTORICAL QUARTERLY, Vol. 86, no. 4 (April 1983), p. 579-580. English. DESCR: Book Reviews; *DICTIONARY OF MEXICAN AMERICAN HISTORY; Rivera, Feliciano.

7166 Jones, Errol D. Book review of: DICTIONARY OF MEXICAN-AMERICAN HISTORY. WESTERN HISTORICAL QUARTERLY, Vol. 14, no. 3 (1983), p. 339-340. English. DESCR: Book Reviews; *DICTIONARY OF MEXICAN AMERICAN HISTORY; History; Reference Works; Rivera, Feliciano.

Meier, Matt S. (cont.)

7167 Laska, Vera. Book review of: DICTIONARY OF MEXICAN-AMERICAN HISTORY. INTERNATIONAL SOCIAL SCIENCE, Vol. 57, no. 3 (Summer 1982), p. 184. English. **DESCR:** Book Reviews; Dictionaries; *DICTIONARY OF MEXICAN AMERICAN HISTORY; History; Rivera, Feliciano.

7168 Martinez, Julio A. Book review of: DICTIONARY OF MEXICAN-AMERICAN HISTORY. RQ - REFERENCE AND ADULT SERVICES DIVISION, Vol. 21, no. 3 (Spring 1982), p. 297-298. English. **DESCR:** Book Reviews; Dictionaries; *DICTIONARY OF MEXICAN AMERICAN HISTORY; History; Rivera, Feliciano.

Mejias, Hugo A.

7169 Communications/marketing. HISPANIC BUSINESS, Vol. 5, no. 4 (April 1983), p. 23. English. **DESCR:** Faultless Starch/Bon Ami Company; Garcia, Marti; *Marketing; Pan American University, Edinburg, TX; Spanish Language.

7170 Feliciano-Foster, Wilma. A comparison of three current first-year college-level Spanish-for-native-speakers textbooks. BILINGUAL REVIEW, Vol. 9, no. 1 (January, April, 1982), p. 72-81. English. **DESCR:** *Book Reviews; ESPANOL ESCRITO; Garza-Swan, Gloria; *Language Development; MEJORA TU ESPANOL; NUESTRO ESPANOL: CURSO PARA ESTUDIANTES BILINGUES; Portilla, Marta de la; Spanish Language Textbooks; Teschner, Richard V.; Valdes Fallis, Guadalupe; Varela, Beatriz.

7171 Garcia, Wilfred F. Book review of: NUESTRO ESPANOL: CURSO PARA ESTUDIANTES BILINGUES, BILINGUAL NATIVE SPANISH SPEAKERS FROM THE SOUTHWESTERN UNITED STATES. HISPANIA, Vol. 65, no. 2 (May 1982), p. 320-321. English. **DESCR:** Book Reviews; Garza-Swan, Gloria; *NUESTRO ESPANOL: CURSO PARA ESTUDIANTES BILINGUES; Southwest United States; Spanish Language; Textbooks.

7172 McKone, Jerry. Texas Spanish: not standard: but not bad. NATIONAL HISPANIC JOURNAL, Vol. 1, no. 4 (Spring 1983), p. 20-21. English. **DESCR:** Education; Folk Medicine; *Spanish Language.

MEJORA TU ESPANOL

7173 Feliciano-Foster, Wilma. A comparison of three current first-year college-level Spanish-for-native-speakers textbooks. BILINGUAL REVIEW, Vol. 9, no. 1 (January, April, 1982), p. 72-81. English. **DESCR:** *Book Reviews; ESPANOL ESCRITO; Garza-Swan, Gloria; *Language Development; Mejias, Hugo A.; NUESTRO ESPANOL: CURSO PARA ESTUDIANTES BILINGUES; Portilla, Marta de la; Spanish Language Textbooks; Teschner, Richard V.; Valdes Fallis, Guadalupe; Varela, Beatriz.

Melendez, Bill

7174 Commercial art as a career. CAMINOS, Vol. 4, no. 9 (October 1983), p. 32-35. English. **DESCR:** Artists; *Careers; Chavez Lichwardt, Leticia; Gomez, Dario; Guerrero, Ernest R.; Reyes, Gil; Santistevan, August.

Melendez v. Burciaga

7175 Brown, Susan E. and Levoy, Claire. Melendez v. Burciaga: revealing the state of the art in bar examinations. BAR EXAMINER, Vol. 51, (May 1982), p. 4-15. English. **DESCR:** Klein, Stephen P.; *Legal Profession; Mexican American Legal Defense and Educational Fund (MALDEF); Multistate Bar Examination (MBE).

7176 Minority access to legal education. HISPANIC BUSINESS, Vol. 5, no. 4 (April 1983), p. 29-30. English. **DESCR:** Law School Admission Test (LSAT); *Legal Education.

Melville, Margarita B.

7177 Baca Zinn, Maxine. Book review of: TWICE A MINORITY; MEXICAN-AMERICAN WOMEN. SIGNS: JOURNAL OF WOMEN IN CULTURE AND SOCIETY, Vol. 8, no. 2 (Winter 1982), p. 259-272. English. **DESCR:** Book Reviews; Chicanas; Literature Reviews; Social Science; *TWICE A MINORITY: MEXICAN-AMERICAN WOMEN.

7178 Fernandez, Maria Patricia. Book review of: TWICE A MINORITY; MEXICAN-AMERICAN WOMEN. CONTEMPORARY SOCIOLOGY: A JOURNAL OF REVIEWS, Vol. 11, no. 3 (May 1982), p. 342-343. English. **DESCR:** Book Reviews; *TWICE A MINORITY: MEXICAN-AMERICAN WOMEN.

MEMORIES OF THE ALHAMBRA

7179 Lattin, Vernon E. Ethnicity and identity in the contemporary Chicano novel. MINORITY VOICES, Vol. 2, no. 2 (Fall 1978), p. 37-44. English. **DESCR:** BLESS ME, ULTIMA; Identity; Literary Criticism; Literature; *Novel; POCHO; THE AUTOBIOGRAPHY OF A BROWN BUFFALO; Y NO SE LO TRAGO LA TIERRA/AND THE EARTH DID NOT PART.

7180 Shirley, Paula. Book review of: MEMORIES OF THE ALHAMBRA. MELUS: MULTI-ETHNIC LITERATURE OF THE UNITED STATES, Vol. 6, no. 2 (Summer 1979), p. 100-103. English. **DESCR:** Book Reviews; Candelaria, Nash; Literature.

Mendez M., Miguel

7181 Katra, William H. 'Taller de imagenes': a poetic cosmovision. MINORITY VOICES, Vol. 4, no. 2 (Fall 1980), p. 75-84. English. **DESCR:** Poetry; *TALLER DE IMAGENES.

Mendez, Olga

7182 N.A.L.E.O.'s "Fiesta '83". CAMINOS, Vol. 4, no. 10 (November 1983), p. 28-29. English. **DESCR:** Baca Barragan, Polly; Bilingual Bicultural Education; Central America; Fiesta '83; Garcia, Robert; Immigration; International Relations; *National Association of Latino Elected Officials (NALEO); Simpson-Mazzoli Bill; United States-Mexico Relations.

Mendizabal, Maritza

7183 Diaz, Katherine A. "And this year's winners are...". CAMINOS, Vol. 4, no. 1-2 (January, February, 1983), p. 39-54,74+. English. **DESCR:** *Awards; Castro, Tony; Elizalde, Hector; Flores, Tom; Martinez, Esperanza; Molina, Gloria; Moya, Connie; Placentia, Joe; Quesada, Leticia; Rios, David N.; Ybarra, Lea; Zapata, Carmen.

Mendoza, John

7184 Q & A: in the Hispanic community who are the winners and losers of Reaganomics? CAMINOS, Vol. 3, no. 3 (March 1982), p. 47. Bilingual. **DESCR:** Casado, Lucy; Echeveste, John; *Federal Government; Flores, Bob; Leon, Virginia; *Reagan, Ronald; Sanchez-Alvarez, Gloria; Vidal de Neri, Julieta.

Mental Health

7185 Abu Bakr, Virginia. Book review of: MENTAL-HEALTH RESEARCH: A REFERENCE GUIDE. SOCIAL CASEWORK: JOURNAL OF CONTEMPORARY SOCIAL WORK, Vol. 63, no. 7 (September 1982), p. 443-444. English. **DESCR:** Book Reviews; Cota-Robles Newton, Frank; *HISPANIC MENTAL HEALTH RESEARCH: A REFERENCE GUIDE; Reference Works.

7186 Aguilar, Nacho. Cultural awareness and sensitivity in mental health with Chicanos. CALMECAC, Vol. 1, (Summer 1980), p. 39-42. English.

7187 Bedard, Evelyn M. Book review of: HISPANIC MENTAL HEALTH RESEARCH: A REFERENCE GUIDE. RQ - REFERENCE AND ADULT SERVICES DIVISION, Vol. 22, no. 1 (Fall 1982), p. 93. English. **DESCR:** Bibliography; Book Reviews; *HISPANIC MENTAL HEALTH RESEARCH: A REFERENCE GUIDE; Newton, Frank; Olmedo, Esteban L.; Padilla, Amado M.

7188 Bernal, Guillermo and Flores-Ortiz, Yvette. Latino families in therapy: engagement and evaluation. JOURNAL OF MARITAL AND FAMILY THERAPY, Vol. 8, no. 3 (July 1982), p. 357-365. English. **DESCR:** *Family; Social Psychology.

7189 Bustamante, Anna Luisa. Low riding to positive mental health. CALMECAC, Vol. 1, no. 1 (Spring 1980), p. 29-33. English. **DESCR:** *Low Riders.

7190 Camayd-Freixas, Yohel. Hispanic mental health and the Omnibus Budget Reconciliation Act of 1981 (editorial board special report). JOURNAL OF LATIN COMMUNITY HEALTH, Vol. 1, no. 1 (Fall 1982), p. 5-24. English. **DESCR:** Funding Sources; *Omnibus Budget Reconciliation Act of 1981.

7191 Delgado, Melvin. Hispanic natural support systems: implications for mental health services. JOURNAL OF PSYCHOSOCIAL NURSING AND MENTAL HEALTH SERVICES, Vol. 21, no. 4 (April 1983), p. 19-24. English. **DESCR:** Curanderas; Family; Religion; Support Groups.

7192 Espinoza, Ana Luisa. Approaching our familias con corazon. CALMECAC, Vol. 1, no. 1 (Spring 1980), p. 15-17. English. **DESCR:** *Familias Unidas Latinas; Family.

7193 Flores de Apodaca, Roberto. Quick socio-emotional screening of Mexican-American and other ethnic head start children. HISPANIC JOURNAL OF BEHAVIORAL SCIENCES, Vol. 5, no. 1 (March 1983), p. 81-92. English. **DESCR:** *AML Instrument; Children; Headstart Program.

7194 Greenblatt, Milton and Norman, Margie. Hispanic mental health and use of mental health services: a critical review of the literature. AMERICAN JOURNAL OF SOCIAL PSYCHIATRY, Vol. 2, no. 3 (Summer 1982), p. 25-31. English. **DESCR:** *Literature Reviews.

7195 Griffith, James. Re-examination of Mexican American service utilization and mental health need. HISPANIC JOURNAL OF BEHAVIORAL SCIENCES, Vol. 5, no. 2 (June 1983), p. 163-180. English. **DESCR:** Extended Family.

7196 Hough, Richard. The Los Angeles Epidemiologic Catchment Area research program and the epidemiology of psychiatric disorders among Mexican Americans. JOURNAL OF OPERATIONAL PSYCHIATRY, Vol. 14, no. 1 (1983), p. 42-51. English. **DESCR:** Acculturation; Diagnostic Interview Schedule (DIS); El Centro Community Health Care Center; Los Angeles, CA; *Los Angeles Epidemiologic Catchment Area Research Program (LAECA).

7197 Jones, B.E. Manic-depressive illness among poor urban Hispanics. AMERICAN JOURNAL OF PSYCHIATRY, Vol. 14, no. 9 (September 1983), p. 1208-1210. English. **DESCR:** Bronx, NY; Puerto Ricans.

7198 Karno, M. Development of the Spanish-language version of the National Institute of Mental Health Diagnostic Interview Schedule. ARCHIVES OF GENERAL PSYCHIATRY, Vol. 40, no. 11 (November 1983), p. 1183-1188. English. **DESCR:** Culture; Languages; *National Institute of Mental Health Diagnostic Interview Schedule; Spanish Language.

7199 LeVine, Elaine S. and Franco, Juan N. Effects of therapist's gender, ethnicity, and verbal style on client's willingness to seek therapy. JOURNAL OF SOCIAL PSYCHOLOGY, Vol. 12, no. 1 (October 1983), p. 51-57. English. **DESCR:** *Counseling Services (Educational); Jourard's (3) Self-Disclosure Questionnaire; Psychotherapy; Social Services.

7200 Maduro, Renaldo J. Working with Latinos and the use of dream analysis. JOURNAL OF THE AMERICAN ACADEMY OF PSYCHOANALYSIS, Vol. 10, no. 4 (October 1982), p. 609-628. English. **DESCR:** Culture; Dream Analysis; Psychiatry.

7201 Markides, Kyraikos S. Aging, religiosity, and adjustment: a longitudinal analysis. JOURNAL OF GERONTOLOGY, Vol. 38, no. 5 (September 1983), p. 621-625. English. **DESCR:** *Ancianos; Psychology; Religion.

7202 Markides, Kyraikos S.; Dickson, Harold; and Pappas, Christine. Characteristics of dropouts in longitudinal research on aging - a study of Mexican-Americans and Anglos. EXPERIMENTAL AGING RESEARCH, Vol. 8, no. 3-4 (1982), p. 163-167. English. **DESCR:** *Ancianos; Comparative Psychology; Psychology.

7203 Mukherjee, Sukdeb. Misdiagnosis of schizophrenia in bipolar patients: a multiethnic comparison. AMERICAN JOURNAL OF PSYCHIATRY, Vol. 14, no. 12 (December 1983), p. 1571-1574. English. **DESCR:** NEW YORK; Puerto Ricans.

7204 O'Donnell, James P., et al. Dimensions of behavior problems in Anglo-American and Mexican-American preschool children: a comparative study. JOURNAL OF CONSULTING AND CLINICAL PSYCHOLOGY, Vol. 50, no. 5 (October 1982), p. 643-651. English. **DESCR:** Anglo Americans; Children; *Comparative Psychology; Cultural Characteristics; Psychological Testing; Socioeconomic Factors.

7205 Parra, Fernando and So, Alvin Yiu-cheong. Changing perceptions of mental illness in a Mexican-American community. JOURNAL OF SOCIAL PSYCHOLOGY, Vol. 29, (Summer 1983), p. 95-100. English. **DESCR:** Anglo Americans; Assimilation; *Los Angeles, CA; Random Digit Dialling (RDD).

Mental Health (cont.)

7206 Roberts, Robert E. and Roberts, Catharine Ramsay. Marriage, work and depressive symptoms among Mexican Americans. HISPANIC JOURNAL OF BEHAVIORAL SCIENCES, Vol. 4, no. 2 (June 1982), p. 199-221. English. **DESCR:** Chicanas; Employment; Marriage.

7207 Ross, Catherine E.; Mirowsky, John; and Cockerham, William C. Social class, Mexican culture, and fatalism: their effects on psychological distress. AMERICAN JOURNAL OF COMMUNITY PSYCHOLOGY, Vol. 11, no. 4 (August 1983), p. 383-399. English. **DESCR:** Culture; *Fatalism.

7208 Sanchez, Arthur R. and Atkinson, Donald R. Mexican-American cultural commitment, preference for counselor ethnicity, and willingness to use counseling. JOURNAL OF COUNSELING PSYCHOLOGY, Vol. 30, no. 2 (April 1983), p. 215-220. English. **DESCR:** *Counseling (Psychological); Cultural Characteristics; Identity; *Mental Health Personnel.

7209 Saucedo, Concha. Chingaderas in mental health funding. CALMECAC, Vol. 1, (Summer 1980), p. 45-47. Bilingual. **DESCR:** Funding Sources.

7210 Solis, Arnaldo. Chicano mental health. CALMECAC, Vol. 1, (Summer 1980), p. 49-56. Bilingual. **DESCR:** Aztecs; *Values.

7211 Solis, Arnaldo. Prevention in Chicano mental health. CALMECAC, Vol. 1, no. 1 (Spring 1980), p. 35. English.

7212 Solis, Arnaldo. Raices of the Chicano spirit. CALMECAC, Vol. 1, (Summer 1980), p. 19-27. English. **DESCR:** Aztecs.

7213 Stumphauzer, J.S. Training Mexican American mental health personnel in behavior therapy. JOURNAL OF BEHAVIOR THERAPY AND EXPERIMENTAL PSYCHIATRY, Vol. 14, no. 3 (September 1983), p. 215-217. English. **DESCR:** Behavior Modification; *Mental Health Personnel.

7214 Vazquez, Carol A. Research on the psychiatric evaluation of the bilingual patient: a methodological critique. HISPANIC JOURNAL OF BEHAVIORAL SCIENCES, Vol. 4, no. 1 (March 1982), p. 75-80. English. **DESCR:** Bilingualism; *Psychiatry; Research Methodology.

7215 Vernon, Sally W. and Roberts, Robert E. Use of the SADS-RDC in a tri-ethnic community survey. ARCHIVES OF GENERAL PSYCHIATRY, Vol. 39, no. 1 (January 1982), p. 47-52. English. **DESCR:** Ethnic Groups; Psychiatry; Psychotherapy; *Schedule for Affective Disorders and Schizophrenia-Research Diagnostic Criteria (SADS-RDC).

7216 Warheit, George. Interpersonal coping networks and mental health problems among four race-ethnic groups. JOURNAL OF COMMUNITY PSYCHOLOGY, Vol. 10, no. 4 (October 1982), p. 312-324. English. **DESCR:** Comparative Psychology; Family; Stress; *Support Groups.

7217 Wheaton, Blair. A comparison of the moderating effects of personal coping resources in the impact of exposure to stress in two groups. JOURNAL OF COMMUNITY PSYCHOLOGY, Vol. 10, no. 4 (October 1982), p. 293-311. English. **DESCR:** Anglo Americans; Comparative Psychology; Cultural Characteristics; Social Psychology; *Stress.

7218 Yamamoto, Joe and Acosta, Frank X. Treatments of Asian Americans and Hispanic Americans: similarities and differences. JOURNAL OF THE AMERICAN ACADEMY OF PSYCHOANALYSIS, Vol. 10, no. 4 (October 1982), p. 585-607. English. **DESCR:** Asian Americans; Comparative Psychology; Los Angeles, CA; Psychotherapy; Socioeconomic Factors.

7219 Young Latino goes to prison. NUESTRO, Vol. 6, no. 8 (October 1982), p. 11. English. **DESCR:** Denver, CO; *Juvenile Delinquency; Prisoners; Prisons.

Mental Health Clinics

7220 Fischman, Gladys, et al. Day treatment programs for the Spanish speaking: a response to underutilization. INTERNATIONAL JOURNAL OF SOCIAL PSYCHIATRY, Vol. 29, no. 3 (Fall 1983), p. 215-219. English. **DESCR:** Hospitals and the Community.

Mental Health Personnel

7221 Acosta, Frank X. and Cristo, Martha H. Bilingual-Bicultural interpreters as psychotherapeutic bridges: a program note. JOURNAL OF COMMUNITY PSYCHOLOGY, Vol. 10, no. 1 (January 1982), p. 54-56. English. **DESCR:** Biculturalism; Bilingualism; Community Mental Health; Doctor Patient Relations; East Los Angeles, CA; Mental Health Programs; Translations.

7222 Sanchez, Arthur R. and Atkinson, Donald R. Mexican-American cultural commitment, preference for counselor ethnicity, and willingness to use counseling. JOURNAL OF COUNSELING PSYCHOLOGY, Vol. 30, no. 2 (April 1983), p. 215-220. English. **DESCR:** *Counseling (Psychological); Cultural Characteristics; Identity; Mental Health.

7223 Stumphauzer, J.S. Training Mexican American mental health personnel in behavior therapy. JOURNAL OF BEHAVIOR THERAPY AND EXPERIMENTAL PSYCHIATRY, Vol. 14, no. 3 (September 1983), p. 215-217. English. **DESCR:** Behavior Modification; Mental Health.

Mental Health Programs

7224 Acosta, Frank X. and Cristo, Martha H. Bilingual-Bicultural interpreters as psychotherapeutic bridges: a program note. JOURNAL OF COMMUNITY PSYCHOLOGY, Vol. 10, no. 1 (January 1982), p. 54-56. English. **DESCR:** Biculturalism; Bilingualism; Community Mental Health; Doctor Patient Relations; East Los Angeles, CA; *Mental Health Personnel; Translations.

7225 Bejar, Rebecca. Mejor en grupo. CALMECAC, Vol. 1, no. 1 (Spring 1980), p. 25-26. English. **DESCR:** Culture.

7226 Gil, Rosa Maria. Issues in the delivery of mental health services to Cuban entrants. MIGRATION TODAY, Vol. 11, no. 4-5 (1983), p. 44-48. English. **DESCR:** Cuban Haitian Task Force; Cubanos; Immigration; National Institute of Mental Health.

7227 Keefe, Susan Emily. Help-seeking behavior among foreign-born and native-born Mexican-Americans. SOCIAL SCIENCE AND MEDICINE, Vol. 16, no. 16 (1982), p. 1467-1472. English. **DESCR:** Acculturation; Immigrants; Santa Barbara, CA.

Mental Hygiene
USE: Mental Health

Mental Illness

7228 Dolgin, Daniel L., et al. Discriminant analysis of behavioral symptomatology in hospitalized Hispanic and Anglo patients. HISPANIC JOURNAL OF BEHAVIORAL SCIENCES, Vol. 4, no. 3 (September 1982), p. 329-351. English. **DESCR:** *Patients.

7229 Escobar, J.I. Post-traumatic stress disorder in Hispanic Vietnam veterans. JOURNAL OF NERVOUS AND MENTAL DISEASE, Vol. 17, no. 10 (October 1983), p. 585-596. English. **DESCR:** Acculturation; Psychiatry; Stress; *Veterans.

7230 Lawson, Harry H.; Kahn, Marrin W.; and Heiman, Elliott M. Psycho-pathology, treatment outcome and attitude toward mental illness in Mexican-American and European patients. INTERNATIONAL JOURNAL OF SOCIAL PSYCHIATRY, Vol. 28, no. 1 (Spring 1982), p. 20-26. English. **DESCR:** Anglo Americans; Psychotherapy.

7231 Vernon, Sally W. and Roberts, Robert E. Prevalence of treated and untreated psychiatric disorders in three ethnic groups. SOCIAL SCIENCE AND MEDICINE, Vol. 16, no. 17 (1982), p. 1575-1582. English. **DESCR:** Anglo Americans; Blacks; Comparative Psychology; *Psychiatry.

Mentally Handicapped

7232 Adams, Russell L.; Boake, Corwin; and Crain, Charles. Bias in a neuropsychological test classification related to education, age and ethnicity. JOURNAL OF CONSULTING AND CLINICAL PSYCHOLOGY, Vol. 50, no. 1 (February 1982), p. 143-145. English. **DESCR:** Age Groups; Educational Levels; Ethnic Groups; *Psychological Testing.

7233 Quesada-Weiner, Rosemary. EL ARCA. CAMINOS, Vol. 3, no. 1 (January 1982), p. 45. Bilingual. **DESCR:** *East Los Angeles, CA; East Los Angeles Retarded Citizen's Association (EL ARCA).

7234 Rueda, Robert. Interpersonal tactics and communicative strategies of Anglo-American and Mexican American mildly mentally retarded and nonretarded students. APPLIED RESEARCH IN MENTAL RETARDATION, Vol. 4, no. 2 (1983), p. 153-161. English. **DESCR:** Anglo Americans; Children; Intelligence Tests; Test of Social Problem Solving.

Mentors

7235 Aqui en Tejas: staying on that long road to success: mentors, how to find a helping hand to assist you achieve educational goals. NATIONAL HISPANIC JOURNAL, Vol. 2, no. 1 (Summer 1983), p. 8. English. **DESCR:** Careers; Education; Fashion.

7236 Fernandez, John P. Facing the hard realities of corporate advancement. HISPANIC BUSINESS, Vol. 4, no. 4 (April 1982), p. 18-19,25. English. **DESCR:** *Affirmative Action; Businesspeople; *Discrimination in Employment; Self-Help Groups.

7237 Professional network. HISPANIC BUSINESS, Vol. 4, no. 9 (September 1982), p. 18,26+. English. **DESCR:** California; Castillo, Sylvia; Higher Education; Hispanic Women in Higher Education (HWHE); *Self-Help Groups.

Menudo [musical group]

7238 Andersen, Kurt. A Puerto Rican pop music machine. TIME, Vol. 121, no. 26 (June 27, 1983), p. 46. English. **DESCR:** Musicians; Puerto Rican Music.

7239 Latino of the Year 1983: Menudo. LATINO, Vol. 54, no. 8 (December 1983), p. 8-11. English. **DESCR:** *Musicians; Puerto Rican Music.

7240 Mejias-Rentas, Antonio. Una dosis puertorriquena de Menudo. LATINO, Vol. 54, no. 8 (December 1983), p. 12. Spanish. **DESCR:** *Musicians; Puerto Rican Music.

7241 Mejias-Rentas, Antonio. A Puerto Rican dose of Menudo. NUESTRO, Vol. 7, no. 7 (September 1983), p. 49. English. **DESCR:** Musicians; Puerto Rican Music.

7242 Menudo: dishing it up in Los Angeles. CAMINOS, Vol. 4, no. 8 (September 1983), p. 46. Bilingual. **DESCR:** Artists; Music; Musicians; Puerto Rican Music.

Mercado, Anthony

7243 People. HISPANIC BUSINESS, Vol. 4, no. 11 (November 1982), p. 7. English. **DESCR:** Biographical Notes; *Businesspeople; Diaz, Jose; Garcia-Pedrosa, Jose R.; Garza, Jose; Herrera, Heriberto; Rios, John F.; Solano, Faustina V.; Solis, Frank.

Mestizaje

7244 Chavez, John A. Aztlan, Cibola, and frontier New Spain. CAMPO LIBRE, Vol. 1, no. 2 (Summer 1981), p. 193-211. English. **DESCR:** *Aztlan; *Explorations; Folklore; History; Mexico; Missions; Native Americans; Southwest United States.

7245 Morton, Carlos. A racial and cultural menudo. NUESTRO, Vol. 7, no. 6 (August 1983), p. 49. English. **DESCR:** *Identity.

7246 Rodriguez, Joe. Chicano poetry: mestizaje and the use of irony. CAMPO LIBRE, Vol. 1, no. 2 (Summer 1981), p. 229-235. English. **DESCR:** Identity; Literary Characteristics; *Literary Criticism; Poetry.

Methadone
USE: Drug Programs

Methodology
USE: Research Methodology

Metropolitan Museum of Art

7247 Museum official plans outreach to Latinos. NUESTRO, Vol. 6, no. 4 (May 1982), p. 27-28. English. **DESCR:** *Appointed Officials; Bilingual Bicultural Education.

Metz Elementary School, Austin TX

7248 Murray, Melissa and Flores, Jose. Bilingual success: a second language program that is making everyone happy (and smarter). NATIONAL HISPANIC JOURNAL, Vol. 2, no. 1 (Summer 1983), p. 14-19. English. **DESCR:** *Bilingual Bicultural Education; Education; Educational Innovations; *Flores, Jose.

EL MEXICALO

7249 Esther Manzano. CAMINOS, Vol. 3, no. 3 (March 1982), p. 30. Bilingual. **DESCR:** Journalists; *Manzano, Esther; Newspapers.

THE MEXICAN AMERICAN: A CRITICAL GUIDE TO RESEARCH AIDS

7250 Chavaria, Elvira. Book review of: THE MEXICAN AMERICAN: A CRITICAL GUIDE TO RESEARCH AIDS. AZTLAN, Vol. 14, no. 1 (Spring 1983), p. 192-195. English. **DESCR:** Bibliography; Book Reviews; Reference Works; Robinson, Barbara J.; Robinson, J. Cordell.

Mexican American Bar Association (MABA)

7251 Whisler, Kirk. M.A.B.A. CAMINOS, Vol. 3, no. 5 (May 1982), p. 36-37. English. **DESCR:** Legal Profession; Professional Organizations.

Mexican American Chamber of Commerce, Austin, TX

7252 Cantu, Hector. Border business report: the Rio Grande Valley's economy and Mexico's lingering peso devaluation effects. NATIONAL HISPANIC JOURNAL, Vol. 2, no. 1 (Summer 1983), p. 10-13. English. **DESCR:** Aguirre, Lionel; Border Region; Cano, Eddie; Coors Distributing Company, McAllen, TX; Cruz, Conrado; Cuevas, Betty; *Currency; Economic Development; Laredo, TX, Chamber of Commerce; United States-Mexico Relations.

Mexican American Correctional Association (MACE)

7253 Community watching: para la comunidad. CAMINOS, Vol. 2, no. 7 (December 1981), p. 42-43. Bilingual. **DESCR:** Bilingual Education; *Organizations; Student Advocates for Bilingual Education (SABE).

Mexican American Cultural Center, San Antonio, TX

7254 Gibeau, Dawn. Mexican-American Center forges new vision. NATIONAL CATHOLIC REPORTER, Vol. 18, (July 30, 1982), p. 5+. English. **DESCR:** Catholic Church; Elizondo, Virgilio; Religion.

Mexican American Culture Simulator

7255 Lasater, Tonia Tash and Montalvo, Frank F. Understanding Mexican American culture: a training program. CHILDREN TODAY, Vol. 11, no. 3 (May, June, 1982), p. 23-25+. English. **DESCR:** Cultural Characteristics; *Cultural Customs; Employment Training; Social Services.

Mexican American Engineering Society (MAES) National Symposium (5th), Fullerton, CA, April 13-15, 1980

7256 Math-based careers. HISPANIC BUSINESS, Vol. 5, no. 5 (May 1983), p. 26. English. **DESCR:** *Careers; Engineering as a Profession; Financial Aid; Income; Labor Supply and Market; University of California, Santa Barbara.

Mexican American Grocers Association (MAGA)

7257 MAGA annual scholarship awards banquet. CAMINOS, Vol. 4, no. 1-2 (January, February, 1983), p. 32. English. **DESCR:** Awards; Financial Aid.

7258 Wittenauer, Cheryl. The Maga Saga. HISPANIC BUSINESS, Vol. 5, no. 8 (August 1983), p. 14+. English. **DESCR:** Consumers; *Food Industry.

Mexican American Latino Voter Registration Alliance (MALVRA)

7259 Garcia, Miguel. Are you registered to vote? CAMINOS, Vol. 3, no. 4 (April 1982), p. 33-34. English. **DESCR:** Congress for United Communities (CPU); *Voter Turnout.

Mexican American Legal Defense and Educational Fund (MALDEF)

7260 Avila, Joaquin G. The computer revolution: only for the few? NUESTRO, Vol. 7, no. 6 (August 1983), p. 29. English. **DESCR:** *Computers; Education.

7261 Beyette, Beverly. A time of transition for MALDEF. CALIFORNIA LAWYER, Vol. 2, no. 5 (May 1982), p. 28-32. English. **DESCR:** *Legal Representation; Martinez, Vilma Socorro; Tijerina, Pete.

7262 Brown, Susan E. and Levoy, Claire. Melendez v. Burciaga: revealing the state of the art in bar examinations. BAR EXAMINER, Vol. 51, (May 1982), p. 4-15. English. **DESCR:** Klein, Stephen P.; *Legal Profession; Melendez v. Burciaga; Multistate Bar Examination (MBE).

7263 Corwin, Arthur F. The numbers game: estimates of illegal aliens in the United States, 1970-1981. LAW AND CONTEMPORARY PROBLEMS, Vol. 45, no. 2 (Spring 1982), p. 223-297. English. **DESCR:** Bustamante, Jorge A.; Centro Nacional de Informacion y Estadistica del Trabajo (CENINET); Demography; Federation for American Immigration Reform (FAIR); *Select Commission on Immigration and Refugee Policy; Simpson-Mazzoli Bill; *Statistics; *Undocumented Workers.

7264 Flaherty, Francis J. The struggle continues: protecting the rights of Hispanics in the U.S. NATIONAL LAW JOURNAL, Vol. 5, (March 14, 1983), p. 1. English. **DESCR:** Affirmative Action; *Avila, Joaquin Guadalupe; Civil Rights; Hispanic Amendments; *Legal Representation; Racism; Voting Rights.

7265 Hing, Bill Ong. Racial disparity: the unaddressed issues of the Simpson-Mazzoli Bill. LA RAZA LAW JOURNAL, Vol. 1, no. 1 (June 1983), p. 21-52. English. **DESCR:** Amnesty; Asian Americans; Ethnic Attitudes; Family; Immigration; Immigration and Naturalization Service (INS); Latin Americans; Mazzoli, Romano L.; Simpson, Alan K.; *Simpson-Mazzoli Bill; Temporary Worker Program; U.S. Congresssional Subcommittee on Immigration, Refugees and International Law.

7266 Hispanic voting trends. HISPANIC BUSINESS, Vol. 4, no. 8 (August 1983), p. 28-29. English. **DESCR:** Bilingual Ballots; Bilingualism; California; *Elections; Southwest Voter Registration Education Project (SVRP); Texas; Voter Turnout.

7267 Keep, Paul M. Overhauling the immigration code: this year, Congress may finally act. NATIONAL JOURNAL, Vol. 15, no. 12 (March 19, 1983), p. 616-619. English. **DESCR:** American Civil Liberties Union; Federation for American Immigration Reform (FAIR); Immigration; *Immigration Law; *Simpson-Mazzoli Bill.

Mexican American Legal Defense and Educational Fund (MALDEF) (cont.)

7268 MALDEF critical of FAIR study. NUESTRO, Vol. 7, no. 7 (September 1983), p. 12-13. English. DESCR: Federation for American Immigration Reform (FAIR); *Immigration Regulation and Control; Simpson-Mazzoli Bill.

7269 MALDEF's goal: a fair opportunity for Hispanics to compete. NUESTRO, Vol. 7, no. 6 (August 1983), p. 26-28+. English. DESCR: Education; Employment; *Legal Reform.

7270 Math-based careers. HISPANIC BUSINESS, Vol. 5, no. 11 (November 1983), p. 32. English. DESCR: *Careers; Education; Employment Training; INROADS; Mathematics, Engineering and Science Achievement (MESA); Soriano, Esteban.

7271 Math-based careers. HISPANIC BUSINESS, Vol. 5, no. 12 (December 1983), p. 40. English. DESCR: *Careers; Council on Legal Education Opportunities (CLEO); Education; Employment Training; Graduate Schools; High Technology High School, San Antonio, TX; Legal Education; San Antonio, TX; Science as a Profession.

7272 Mexican American Legal Defense and Education Fund (MALDEF). Chicana rights: a major MALDEF issue (reprinted from MALDEF Newsletter, Fall 1977). COMADRE, no. 2 (Spring 1978), p. 31-33. English. DESCR: Chicana Rights Project; Chicanas; Statistics; Vasquez, Patricia; *Women's Rights.

7273 Mexican American Legal Defense and Education Fund (MALDEF). Chicana rights: a major MALDEF issue (reprinted from MALDEF Newsletter, Fall 1977). COMADRE, no. 3 (Fall 1978), p. 31-35. English. DESCR: Chicana Rights Project; Chicanas; Statistics; Vasquez, Patricia; *Women's Rights.

7274 Mexican American Legal Defense and Education Fund (MALDEF). MALDEF on the Reagan plan. CAMINOS, Vol. 3, no. 1 (January 1982), p. 23-25. English. DESCR: *Days, Drew; *Immigration Regulation and Control.

7275 Minority access to legal profession is still limited. CALIFORNIA LAWYER, Vol. 3, no. 4 (April 1983), p. 72. English. DESCR: *Brown, Susan E.; Ethnic Groups; *Legal Education.

7276 New general counsel at MALDEF. HISPANIC BUSINESS, Vol. 4, no. 7 (July 1982), p. 24. English. DESCR: *Avila, Joaquin Guadalupe; *Biography; Legal Profession.

7277 Praise for the speaker. NUESTRO, Vol. 7, no. 8 (October 1983), p. 9. English. DESCR: Immigration Law; *Simpson-Mazzoli Bill.

7278 Promoting U.S. citizenship. CAMINOS, Vol. 3, no. 7 (July, August, 1982), p. 27. English. DESCR: *Naturalization.

7279 Quesada-Weiner, Rosemary. MALDEF (photoessay). CAMINOS, Vol. 3, no. 2 (February 1982), p. 38-39. English. DESCR: Organizations.

7280 San Miguel, Guadalupe. Mexican American organizations and the changing politics of school desegration in Texas, 1945 to 1980. SOCIAL SCIENCE QUARTERLY, Vol. 63, (December 1982), p. 701-715. English. DESCR: American G.I. Forum; League of United Latin American Citizens (LULAC); Organizations; *Segregation and Desegregation; Texas.

7281 Santillan, Richard. The Chicano community and the redistricting of the Los Angeles city council, 1971-1973. CHICANO LAW REVIEW, Vol. 6, (1983), p. 122-145. English. DESCR: Chicanos for Fair Representation (CFR), Los Angeles, CA; Los Angeles City Council; *Political Representation; Snyder, Art, Councilman.

7282 Study details minority access to legal education. NEW JERSEY LAW JOURNAL, Vol. 112, no. 1 (July 7, 1983), p. 28. English. DESCR: Brown, Susan E.; *Ethnic Groups; *Legal Education; PLURALISM IN THE LEGAL PROFESSION: MODELS FOR MINORITY ACCESS; Vasquez, Hector G.

MEXICAN AMERICAN LEGAL DEFENSE AND EDUCATIONAL FUND NEWSLETTER

7283 Hispanics in federal agencies. HISPANIC BUSINESS, Vol. 4, no. 9 (September 1982), p. 29. English. DESCR: Affirmative Action; *Government Employees.

7284 Santillan, Richard. [Translating population numbers into political power]. CHICANO LAW REVIEW, Vol. 6, (1983), p. 16-21. English. DESCR: Californios for Fair Representation; Carrillo v. Whittier Union High School; LATINOS IN THE LAW [symposium], UCLA, 1982; Political Representation; Reapportionment; *Voter Turnout.

7285 Wittenauer, Cheryl. MALDEF's strategies for leadership. HISPANIC BUSINESS, Vol. 5, no. 5 (May 1983), p. 28-29. English. DESCR: *Leadership.

Mexican American Neighborhood Organization (MANO)

7286 Day, Mark R. Border group feeds, clothes dispossessed. NATIONAL CATHOLIC REPORTER, Vol. 19, (October 22, 1982), p. 5. English. DESCR: Border Region; Catholic Church; Colonia Reforma, Tijuana, Baja California, Mexico.

Mexican American Political Association (MAPA)

7287 Community watching: para la comunidad. CAMINOS, Vol. 2, no. 6 (October 1981), p. 40-41+. English. DESCR: *Cultural Organizations; Hispanic Women in Higher Education (HWHE); La Plaza Senior Citizens, Los Angeles, CA; Reapportionment.

7288 The rebirth of MAPA??? CAMINOS, Vol. 3, no. 9 (October 1982), p. 21. English. DESCR: Organizations; *Politics.

THE MEXICAN AMERICAN: QUEST FOR EQUALITY

7289 Rivas, Mike. Keeping peace in paradise. NATIONAL HISPANIC JOURNAL, Vol. 1, no. 2 (Winter 1982), p. 13-20. English. DESCR: *Brand, Othal; Casso, Ramiro; Elections; Police; Police Brutality; *Political Repression; Rio Grande Valley, TX; Voter Turnout.

Mexican American Republicans of Texas

7290 Hispanic leader reaction to Governor White: Republicans fail to overcome Democratic one-two punch. NATIONAL HISPANIC JOURNAL, Vol. 1, no. 4 (Spring 1983), p. 8. English. DESCR: Clements, Bill; Political Parties and Organizations; *Voter Turnout; White, Mark.

Mexican American War

7291 Bauer, Karl Jack. Book review of: THE
MEXICAN-AMERICAN WAR: AN ANNOTATED
BIBLIOGRAPHY. JOURNAL OF THE WEST, Vol. 21,
no. 3 (April 1982), p. 73. English. DESCR:
Book Reviews; *THE MEXICAN-AMERICAN WAR: AN
ANNOTATED BIBLIOGRAPHY; Tutorow, Norman E.;
United States-Mexico Relations.

7292 Nasatir, A. P. Book review of: THE
MEXICAN-AMERICAN WAR: AN ANNOTATED
BIBLIOGRAPHY. JOURNAL OF SAN DIEGO HISTORY,
Vol. 28, no. 3 (Summer 1982), p. 210-211.
English. DESCR: Book Reviews; *THE
MEXICAN-AMERICAN WAR: AN ANNOTATED
BIBLIOGRAPHY; Tutorow, Norman E.; United
States-Mexico Relations.

Mexican American Women's National Association (MANA)

7293 Fostering the advancement of Latinas.
NUESTRO, Vol. 6, no. 10 (December 1982), p.
48-49. English. DESCR: *Chicanas; Women Men
Relations.

Mexican American Youth Organization (MAYO)

7294 Laws, Bart. Raza unida de Cristal. SOUTHERN
EXPOSURE, Vol. 10, no. 2 (March, April,
1982), p. 67-72. English. DESCR: Crystal
City, TX; Gurule, Dorothy; History; La Raza
Unida Party; *Political Parties and
Organizations; Reyes, Carlos.

MEXICAN AMERICANS, 2nd. ed.

7295 Renzi, Mario. A review of the ethnic groups
in American life series. MID-AMERICAN REVIEW
OF SOCIOLOGY, Vol. 7, no. 1 (Spring 1982),
p. 109-123. English. DESCR: Book Reviews.

MEXICAN AMERICANS IN A DALLAS BARRIO

7296 Cortes, Carlos E. Book review of: MEXICAN
AMERICANS IN A DALLAS BARRIO. NEW SCHOLAR,
Vol. 8, no. 1-2 (Spring, Fall, 1982), p.
488-489. English. DESCR: Achor, Shirley;
Book Reviews.

7297 Goldberg, Victor. Ethnic groups in the
United States. REVIEWS IN ANTHROPOLOGY, Vol.
9, no. 4 (Fall 1982), p. 375-382. English.
DESCR: Achor, Shirley; Book Reviews; ETHNIC
AMERICA, A HISTORY; Sowell, Thomas; *THE
CHICANOS; Trejo, Arnulfo D.

7298 Mata, Alberto G. Book review of: MEXICAN
AMERICANS IN A DALLAS BARRIO. AZTLAN, Vol.
14, no. 1 (Spring 1983), p. 196-198.
English. DESCR: Achor, Shirley; Barrios;
Book Reviews; Dallas, TX; Urban Communities.

Mexican and American Foundation

7299 The Mexican and American Foundation. LATINA,
Vol. 1, no. 3 (1983), p. 51. English.
DESCR: Cultural Organizations.

7300 Quinlivan, Robert. An evening with the stars
'82. CAMINOS, Vol. 3, no. 9 (October 1982),
p. 24-25. English. DESCR: *Funding Sources;
Organizations.

Mexican Border Industrialization Program

7301 Abrams, Herbert K. Occupational and
environmental health problems along the
U.S.-Mexico Border. SOUTHWEST ECONOMY AND
SOCIETY, Vol. 4, no. 3 (Spring, Summer,
1979), p. 3-20. English. DESCR: Agricultural
Laborers; *Border Region; Housing;
Nutrition; *Pollution; *Public Health;
Social History and Conditions.

7302 Duncan, Cameron. The runaway shop and the
Mexican border industrialization program.
SOUTHWEST ECONOMY AND SOCIETY, Vol. 2, no. 1
(October, November, 1976), p. 4-25. English.
DESCR: Border Region; Labor Supply and
Market; *Maquiladoras; Multinational
Corporations.

7303 Morrison, Thomas K. The relationship of U.S.
aid, trade and investment to migration
pressures in major sending countries.
INTERNATIONAL MIGRATION REVIEW, Vol. 16, no.
1 (Spring 1982), p. 4-26. English. DESCR:
Border Region; International Economic
Relations; Investments; *Migration Patterns;
PIDER Project; Rural Economics; Rural Urban
Migration; Undocumented Workers; United
States-Mexico Relations.

Mexican Cinema

7304 Maciel, David R. Visions of the other
Mexico: Chicanos and undocumented workers in
Mexican cinema, 1954-1982. BILINGUAL REVIEW,
Vol. 10, no. 2-3 (May, December, 1983), p.
71-88. English. DESCR: Film Reviews; *Films;
*Mexico; *Undocumented Workers.

MEXICAN CINEMA: REFLECTIONS OF A SOCIETY

7305 Book review of: MEXICAN CINEMA: REFLECTIONS
OF A SOCIETY. CHOICE, Vol. 20, no. 2
(October 1982), p. 276. English. DESCR: Book
Reviews; Mora, Carl J.

7306 Markiewicz, Dana. Book review of: MEXICAN
CINEMA: REFLECTIONS OF SOCIETY, 1896-1980.
HISPANIC JOURNAL OF BEHAVIORAL SCIENCES,
Vol. 5, no. 4 (December 1983), p. 491-494.
English. DESCR: Book Reviews; Films; Mora,
Carl J.

Mexican Economy

7307 Newman, Allen R. The impacts of emigration
on the Mexican economy. MIGRATION TODAY,
Vol. 10, no. 2 (1982), p. 17-21. English.
DESCR: Economic History and Conditions;
Employment; *Migration; Socioeconomic
Factors; Undocumented Workers.

MEXICAN EMIGRATION TO THE UNITED STATES 1897-1931: SOCIO-ECONOMIC PATTERNS

7308 Almaraz, Felix D., Jr. Book review of:
MEXICAN EMIGRATION TO THE UNITED STATES,
1897-1931: SOCIO-ECONOMIC PATTERNS. GREAT
PLAINS QUARTERLY, Vol. 3, no. 2 (Spring
1983), p. 123-124. English. DESCR: Book
Reviews; Cardoso, Lawrence A.

7309 Bean, Frank D. Book review of: MEXICAN
EMIGRATION TO THE UNITED STATES, 1897-1931:
SOCIO-ECONOMIC PATTERNS. INTERNATIONAL
MIGRATION REVIEW, Vol. 16, no. 2 (Summer
1982), p. 493-494. English. DESCR: Book
Reviews; Cardoso, Lawrence A.

7310 Hoffman, Abraham. Book review of: MEXICANO
RESISTANCE IN THE SOUTHWEST: "THE SACRED
RIGHT OF SELF-PRESERVATION". PACIFIC
HISTORICAL REVIEW, Vol. 51, no. 2 (May
1982), p. 230-231. English. DESCR: Book
Reviews; Cardoso, Lawrence A.; Migration.

MEXICAN EMIGRATION TO THE UNITED STATES 1897-1931: SOCIO-ECONOMIC PATTERNS (cont.)

7311 Romo, Ricardo. Book review of: MEXICAN EMIGRATION TO THE UNITED STATES, 1897-1931: SOCIO-ECONOMIC PATTERNS. SOUTHWESTERN HISTORICAL QUARTERLY, Vol. 86, no. 4 (April 1983), p. 576-577. English. DESCR: Book Reviews; Cardoso, Lawrence A.

MEXICAN FAMILY FAVORITES COOKBOOK

7312 Family favorites. NUESTRO, Vol. 7, no. 10 (December 1983), p. 36-38. English. DESCR: Bermudez, Maria Teresa; Book Reviews; Recipes.

THE MEXICAN FRONTIER, 1821-1846: THE AMERICAN SOUTHWEST UNDER MEXICO

7313 Acuna, Rodolfo. Book review of: THE MEXICAN FRONTIER 1821-1846: THE AMERICAN SOUTHWEST UNDER MEXICO. AMERICAN HISTORICAL REVIEW, Vol. 88, no. 2 (April 1983), p. 504-505. English. DESCR: Book Reviews; Weber, David J.

7314 Book review of: THE MEXICAN FRONTIER, 1821-1846: THE AMERICAN SOUTHWEST UNDER MEXICO. CHOICE, Vol. 20, no. 3 (November 1982), p. 494. English. DESCR: Book Reviews; Weber, David J.

7315 Brack, Gene M. Book review of: THE MEXICAN FRONTIER, 1821-1846: THE AMERICAN SOUTHWEST UNDER MEXICO. HISPANIC AMERICAN HISTORICAL REVIEW, Vol. 63, no. 2 (1983), p. 396-397. English. DESCR: Book Reviews; Weber, David J.

7316 Cummins, Light Townsend. Book review of: THE MEXICAN FRONTIER 1821-1846: THE AMERICAN SOUTHWEST UNDER MEXICO. JOURNAL OF SOUTHERN HISTORY, Vol. 49, no. 3 (August 1983), p. 453-455. English. DESCR: Book Reviews; Weber, David J.

7317 Henson, Margaret S. Book review of: THE MEXICAN FRONTIER 1821-1846: THE AMERICAN SOUTHWEST UNDER MEXICO. SOUTHWESTERN HISTORICAL QUARTERLY, Vol. 86, no. 3 (1983), p. 441-443. English. DESCR: Book Reviews; Weber, David J.

7318 John, Elizabeth A.H. Book review of: THE MEXICAN FRONTIER 1821-1846: THE AMERICAN SOUTHWEST UNDER MEXICO. NEW MEXICO HISTORICAL REVIEW, Vol. 57, no. 3 (July 1982), p. 289-293. English. DESCR: Book Reviews; Border Region; Southwest United States; Weber, David J.

7319 Jones, Oakah L. Book review of: THE MEXICAN FRONTIER, 1821-1846: THE AMERICAN SOUTHWEST UNDER MEXICO. ARIZONA AND THE WEST, Vol. 25, no. 2 (1983), p. 168-169. English. DESCR: Book Reviews; History; Mexico; Southwest United States; Weber, David J.

7320 Meyer, Michael C. Book review of: THE MEXICAN FRONTIER, 1821-1846: THE AMERICAN SOUTHWEST UNDER MEXICO. WESTERN HISTORICAL QUARTERLY, Vol. 14, no. 3 (1983), p. 337-338. English. DESCR: Book Reviews; History; Mexico; Southwest United States; Weber, David J.

MEXICAN IMMIGRANT WORKERS IN THE U.S.

7321 Meier, Matt S. Book review of: MEXICAN IMMIGRANT WORKERS IN THE UNITED STATES and OPERATION WETBACK: THE MASS DEPORTATION OF MEXICAN UNDOCUMENTED WORKERS IN 1954. PACIFIC HISTORICAL REVIEW, Vol. 52, no. 1 (February 1983), p. 126-128. English. DESCR: Book Reviews; Garcia, Juan Ramon; *Operation Wetback; Rios-Bustamante, Antonio.

Mexican Independence Parade

7322 Whisler, Kirk. Everyone in town was there (photoessay). CAMINOS, Vol. 3, no. 10 (November 1982), p. 26-27. English. DESCR: *Dieciseis de Septiembre; East Los Angeles, CA; Parades.

Mexican Literature

7323 Balakian, Anna. Book review of: THE PERPETUAL PRESENT: THE POETRY AND PROSE OF OCTAVIO PAZ. JOURNAL OF ETHNIC STUDIES, Vol. 2, no. 3 (Fall 1974), p. 84-88. English. DESCR: Book Reviews; Paz, Octavio; *THE PERPETUAL PRESENT: THE POETRY AND PROSE OF OCTAVIO PAZ.

7324 Cantu, Roberto. El relato como articulacion infinitiva: MACARIO y el arte de Juan Rulfo. LA PALABRA, Vol. 4, no. 1-2 (Spring, Fall, 1982, 1983), p. 107-126. Spanish. DESCR: Authors; Literary Characteristics; Literary Criticism; *MACARIO; *Rulfo, Juan.

7325 Leal, Luis. Gabino Barreda y la literatura: de la preparatoria al Ateneo. AZTLAN, Vol. 14, no. 2 (Fall 1983), p. 253-265. Spanish. DESCR: Ateneo de la Juventud; *Barreda, Gabino; Escuela Nacional Preparatoria; History; Philosophy; Positivism.

MEXICAN MIGRATION, CRISIS, AND THE INTERNATIONALIZATION OF LABOR STRUGGLES

7326 Alvarez, Alejandro. Economic crisis and migration: comments on James Cockcroft's article. CONTEMPORARY MARXISM, Vol. 5, (Summer 1982), p. 62-66. English. DESCR: Cockroft, James; International Economic Relations; Laboring Classes; Legislation; *Undocumented Workers.

Mexican Museum, San Francisco, CA

7327 Morris, Gay. The Mexican Museum has a colorful new home. CAMINOS, Vol. 3, no. 7 (July, August, 1982), p. 30-33. Bilingual. DESCR: Art; Museums; Rodriguez, Peter; San Francisco, CA.

Mexican Nationalism Period

7328 Vigil, James Diego. Towards a new perspective on understanding the Chicano people: the six C's model of sociocultural change. CAMPO LIBRE, Vol. 1, no. 2 (Summer 1981), p. 141-167. English. DESCR: Acculturation; Assimilation; Cultural Characteristics; History; Mexico; Nationalism; Organizations; Precolumbian Society; *Six C's Model (Theoretical Model); Social History and Conditions; Spanish Colonial Period.

Mexican Revolution - 1910-1920

7329 Quinlivan, Robert. The photographs of Agustin V. Casasola; un epilogo de la revolucion Mexicana de 1910. CAMINOS, Vol. 3, no. 1 (January 1982), p. 38-40. Bilingual. DESCR: *Casasola, Agustin V.; *Photography.

Mexican Revolution - 1910-1920 (cont.)

7330 Richmond, Douglas W. Mexican immigration and
border strategy during the revolution,
1910-1920. NEW MEXICO HISTORICAL REVIEW,
Vol. 57, no. 3 (July 1982), p. 269-288.
English. **DESCR:** *Border Region; Carranza,
Venustiano; History; Immigration; Mexico;
Social History and Conditions; United
States-Mexico Relations.

7331 Richmond, Douglas W. Researching the Mexican
revolution: sources and suggestions.
BORDERLANDS JOURNAL, Vol. 6, no. 1 (Fall
1982), p. 85-91. English. **DESCR:** Archives.

**MEXICAN WOMEN IN THE UNITED STATES: STRUGGLES PAST
AND PRESENT**

7332 Baca Zinn, Maxine. Book review of: MEXICAN
WOMEN IN THE UNITED STATES: STRUGGLES PAST
AND PRESENT. SIGNS: JOURNAL OF WOMEN IN
CULTURE AND SOCIETY, Vol. 8, no. 2 (Winter
1982). English. **DESCR:** Book
Reviews; Chicanas; Del Castillo, Adelaida
R.; Literature Reviews; Mora, Magdalena;
Social Science.

7333 Hartman, Harriet. Book review of: MEXICAN
WOMEN IN THE UNITED STATES: STRUGGLES PAST
AND PRESENT. INTERNATIONAL MIGRATION REVIEW,
Vol. 16, no. 1 (Spring 1982), p. 228-229.
English. **DESCR:** Book Reviews; Chicanas; Del
Castillo, Adelaida R.; Mora, Magdalena;
Sexism.

MEXICAN WORKERS IN THE UNITED STATES

7334 Nalven, Joseph. Resolving the undocumented
worker problem. NEW SCHOLAR, Vol. 8, no. 1-2
(Spring, Fall, 1982), p. 473-481. English.
DESCR: Book Reviews; *MIGRANT WORKERS IN
WESTERN EUROPE AND THE UNITED STATES;
Undocumented Workers.

**THE MEXICAN-AMERICAN WAR: AN ANNOTATED
BIBLIOGRAPHY**

7335 Bauer, Karl Jack. Book review of: THE
MEXICAN-AMERICAN WAR: AN ANNOTATED
BIBLIOGRAPHY. JOURNAL OF THE WEST, Vol. 21,
no. 3 (April 1982), p. 73. English. **DESCR:**
Book Reviews; Mexican American War; Tutorow,
Norman E.; United States-Mexico Relations.

7336 Mathes, W. Michael. Book review of: THE
MEXICAN-AMERICAN WAR: AN ANNOTATED
BIBLIOGRAPHY. CALIFORNIA HISTORY, Vol. 60,
no. 4 (Winter 1981, 1982), p. 379-380.
English. **DESCR:** Book Reviews; Tutorow,
Norman E.; United States-Mexico War.

7337 Nasatir, A. P. Book review of: THE
MEXICAN-AMERICAN WAR: AN ANNOTATED
BIBLIOGRAPHY. JOURNAL OF SAN DIEGO HISTORY,
Vol. 28, no. 3 (Summer 1982), p. 210-211.
English. **DESCR:** Book Reviews; Mexican
American War; Tutorow, Norman E.; United
States-Mexico Relations.

7338 Robinson, Barbara J. Book review of: THE
MEXICAN-AMERICAN WAR: AN ANNOTATED
BIBLIOGRAPHY. REVISTA INTERAMERICANA DE
BIBLIOGRAFIA, Vol. 32, no. 2 (1982), p.
222-223. English. **DESCR:** Bibliography; Book
Reviews; Tutorow, Norman E.; War.

Mexicanism
USE: Nationalism

EL MEXICANO

7339 Ramos, Manuel. En torno a las ideas sobre EL
MEXICANO. CAMPO LIBRE, Vol. 1, no. 2 (Summer

1981), p. 273-282. Spanish. **DESCR:** Cultural
Characteristics; Identity; Mexico;
Philosophy; *Uranga, Emilio.

**MEXICANO RESISTANCE IN THE SOUTHWEST: "THE SACRED
RIGHT OF SELF-PRESERVATION"**

7340 Camarillo, Alberto M. Book review of:
MEXICANO RESISTANCE IN THE SOUTHWEST: "THE
SACRED RIGHT OF SELF-PRESERVATION". WESTERN
HISTORICAL QUARTERLY, Vol. 14, no. 1 (1983),
p. 79-80. English. **DESCR:** Book Reviews;
History; New Mexico; Rosenbaum, Robert J.

7341 Crisp, James E. Book review of: MEXICANO
RESISTANCE IN THE SOUTHWEST: "THE SACRED
RIGHT OF SELF-PRESERVATION". JOURNAL OF
SOUTHERN HISTORY, Vol. 48, no. 1 (1982), p.
138-139. English. **DESCR:** Book Reviews;
Political History and Conditions; Rosenbaum,
Robert J.; United States-Mexico Relations.

7342 Garcia, Juan R. Book review of: MEXICANO
RESISTANCE IN THE SOUTHWEST: "THE SACRED
RIGHT OF SELF-PRESERVATION". ARIZONA AND THE
WEST, Vol. 24, no. 1 (Spring 1982), p.
81-82. English. **DESCR:** Book Reviews; New
Mexico; Rosenbaum, Robert J.; Social History
and Conditions.

7343 Garcia, Mario T. Book review of: MEXICANO
RESISTANCE IN THE SOUTHWEST: "THE SACRED
RIGHT OF SELF-PRESERVATION". PACIFIC
HISTORICAL REVIEW, Vol. 51, no. 3 (August
1982), p. 331-332. English. **DESCR:** Book
Reviews; Rosenbaum, Robert J.

7344 Hoffman, Abraham. Book review of: MEXICANO
RESISTANCE IN THE SOUTHWEST: "THE SACRED
RIGHT OF SELF-PRESERVATION". JOURNAL OF
AMERICAN HISTORY, Vol. 68, no. 4 (March
1982), p. 911. English. **DESCR:** Book Reviews;
Rosenbaum, Robert J.

7345 Schmidt, Dorothy. Book review of: MEXICANO
RESISTANCE IN THE SOUTHWEST: "THE SACRED
RIGHT OF SELF-PRESERVATION". WESTERN
AMERICAN LITERATURE, Vol. 17, no. 1 (Spring
1982), p. 75-76. English. **DESCR:** Bandidos;
Book Reviews; Insurrections; Rosenbaum,
Robert J.

7346 Vigil, Ralph H. Book review of: MEXICANO
RESISTANCE IN THE SOUTHWEST: "THE SACRED
RIGHT OF SELF-PRESERVATION". NEW MEXICO
HISTORICAL REVIEW, Vol. 58, no. 1 (January
1983), p. 104-105. English. **DESCR:** Book
Reviews; Rosenbaum, Robert J.

7347 Weber, David J. Book review of: MEXICANO
RESISTANCE IN THE SOUTHWEST: "THE SACRED
RIGHT OF SELF-PRESERVATION". AMERICAN
HISTORICAL REVIEW, Vol. 87, no. 1 (February
1982), p. 272-273. English. **DESCR:** Book
Reviews; Insurrections; Rosenbaum, Robert
J.; Southwest United States.

LOS MEXICANOS QUE DEVOLVIO LA CRISIS 1929-1932

7348 Cardoso, Lawrence Anthony. Book review of:
LOS MEXICANOS QUE DEVOLVIO LA CRISIS,
1929-1932. JOURNAL OF ETHNIC STUDIES, Vol.
5, no. 1 (Spring 1977), p. 120-122. Spanish.
DESCR: Book Reviews; Carreras de Velasco,
Mercedes; Deportation; Immigrant Labor;
Immigration; Immigration Regulation and
Control; Mexico; Social History and
Conditions.

THE MEXICANS IN OKLAHOMA

7349 Shepperson, Wilbur S. Book review of: THE
MEXICANS IN OKLAHOMA. NEW MEXICO HISTORICAL
REVIEW, Vol. 57, no. 3 (July 1982), p.
304-305. English. **DESCR:** Book Reviews;
Immigration; Oklahoma; Smith, Michael M.

Mexico

7350 Alba, Francisco. La fecundidad entre los
Mexicano-Norteamericanos en relacion a los
cambiantes patrones reproductivos en Mexico
y los Estados Unidos. DEMOGRAFIA Y ECONOMIA,
Vol. 16, no. 2 (1982), p. 236-249. Spanish.
DESCR: Demography; *Fertility; Population
Trends; Social Research.

7351 Alvarez, Amando. Benito Juarez. LATINO, Vol.
54, no. 4 (May, June, 1983), p. 12-13.
Spanish. **DESCR:** History; *Juarez, Benito.

7352 Baca-Ramirez, Reynaldo and Bryan, Dexter
Edward. The undocumented Mexican worker: a
social problem? JOURNAL OF ETHNIC STUDIES,
Vol. 8, no. 1 (Spring 1980), p. 55-69.
English. **DESCR:** Government Services;
Immigrant Labor; Immigration; Immigration
Regulation and Control; Social History and
Conditions; Social Services; *Undocumented
Workers.

7353 Bell, Samuel E. and Smallwood, James M. Zona
libre: trade and diplomacy on the Mexican
border, 1858-1905. ARIZONA AND THE WEST,
Vol. 24, no. 2 (Summer 1982), p. 119-152.
English. **DESCR:** Border Region; *Foreign
Trade; International Relations; United
States History.

7354 Bradshaw, Benjamin S. and Frisbie, W.
Parker. Potential labor force supply and
replacement in Mexico and the states of the
Mexican cession and Texas: 1980-2000.
INTERNATIONAL MIGRATION REVIEW, Vol. 17, no.
3 (Fall 1983), p. 394-409. English. **DESCR:**
Immigration; *Labor Supply and Market;
Texas.

7355 Burciaga, Jose Antonio. Death of el senor
Peso. NUESTRO, Vol. 6, no. 7 (September
1982), p. 52. English. **DESCR:** *Economic
History and Conditions; *Economics.

7356 Burciaga, Jose Antonio. The Mexican
archipelago. NUESTRO, Vol. 6, no. 6 (August
1982), p. 47. English. **DESCR:** *Treaties.

7357 Cantu, Roberto. Nota preliminar: de Samuel
Ramos a Emilio Uranga. CAMPO LIBRE, Vol. 1,
no. 2 (Summer 1981), p. 239-272. Spanish.
DESCR: Cultural Characteristics; Identity;
Philosophy; *Ramos, Samuel; *Uranga, Emilio.

7358 Cardoso, Lawrence Anthony. Book review of:
LOS MEXICANOS QUE DEVOLVIO LA CRISIS,
1929-1932. JOURNAL OF ETHNIC STUDIES, Vol.
5, no. 1 (Spring 1977), p. 120-122. Spanish.
DESCR: Book Reviews; Carreras de Velasco,
Mercedes; Deportation; Immigrant Labor;
Immigration; Immigration Regulation and
Control; *LOS MEXICANOS QUE DEVOLVIO LA
CRISIS 1929-1932; Social History and
Conditions.

7359 Cardoso, Lawrence Anthony. Book review of:
REVOLTOSOS: MEXICO'S REBELS IN THE UNITED
STATES 1903-1923. JOURNAL OF THE WEST, Vol.
22, no. 1 (1983), p. 90. English. **DESCR:**
Book Reviews; History; Immigration; Raat, W.
Dirk; *REVOLTOSOS: MEXICO'S REBELS IN THE
UNITED STATES, 1903-1923.

7360 Cardoso, Lawrence Anthony. Book review of:

UNWANTED MEXICAN AMERICANS IN THE GREAT
DEPRESSION: REPATRIATION PRESSURES,
1929-1939. JOURNAL OF ETHNIC STUDIES, Vol.
5, no. 1 (Spring 1977), p. 120-122. English.
DESCR: Book Reviews; Deportation; Hoffman,
Abraham; Immigrant Labor; Immigration;
Immigration Regulation and Control; Social
History and Conditions; *UNWANTED MEXICAN
AMERICANS IN THE GREAT DEPRESSION.

7361 Casanova, Steve. Oaxaca and the ancient
ruins of Monte Alban and Mitla. NUESTRO,
Vol. 6, no. 9 (November 1982), p. 62-64.
English. **DESCR:** *Oaxaca, Mexico; Tourism.

7362 Chaplik, Dorothy. Art currents from Mexico.
CAMINOS, Vol. 4, no. 5 (May 1983), p.
21-25,52. English. **DESCR:** *Artists.

7363 Chavez, John A. Aztlan, Cibola, and frontier
New Spain. CAMPO LIBRE, Vol. 1, no. 2
(Summer 1981), p. 193-211. English. **DESCR:**
*Aztlan; *Explorations; Folklore; History;
Mestizaje; Missions; Native Americans;
Southwest United States.

7364 Conflict occurs over city statue. NUESTRO,
Vol. 6, no. 9 (November 1982), p. 11.
English. **DESCR:** History; *Tucson, AZ;
*Villa, Pancho.

7365 De Leon, Arnoldo. Book review of: ON THE
BORDER: PORTRAITS OF AMERICA'S SOUTHWESTERN
FRONTIER. SOUTHWESTERN HISTORICAL QUARTERLY,
Vol. 86, no. 2 (1982), p. 367-368. English.
DESCR: Book Reviews; History; Miller, Tom;
*ON THE BORDER: PORTRAITS OF AMERICA'S
SOUTHWESTERN FRONTIER; Texas.

7366 Deibel, Richard. Business along la frontera.
HISPANIC BUSINESS, Vol. 5, no. 1 (January
1983), p. 14-15. English. **DESCR:** Border
Region; *Currency; Laredo, TX.

7367 Diaz, Katherine A. Francisco Zuniga; el
pueblo Mexicano su inspiracion. CAMINOS,
Vol. 4, no. 1-2 (January, February, 1983),
p. 34-38. Bilingual. **DESCR:** Artists;
*Zuniga, Francisco.

7368 Diaz, Katherine A. and Gonzalez, Magdalena.
Jose Guadalupe Posada: documenting his
people and his times=informandonos de su
gente y su epoca. CAMINOS, Vol. 2, no. 6
(October 1981), p. 18-20. Bilingual. **DESCR:**
Artists; Biography; *Posada, Jose Guadalupe.

7369 Dr. Julian Nava on Mexico. CAMINOS, Vol. 3,
no. 6 (June 1982), p. 7-8. Bilingual.
DESCR: Nava, Julian; *United States-Mexico
Relations.

7370 Eliminating corruption. NUESTRO, Vol. 6, no.
10 (December 1982), p. 8. English. **DESCR:** De
la Madrid, Miguel; Government.

7371 Englebrecht, Guillermina. And now Domingo...
in school in the United States. CHILDHOOD
EDUCATION, Vol. 60, no. 2 (November,
December, 1983), p. 90-95. English. **DESCR:**
Curriculum; Education; Textbooks;
*Undocumented Children.

7372 Estado, cerco financiero y proyecto
nacional. INFORME: RELACIONES MEXICO-ESTADOS
UNIDOS, Vol. 1, no. 3 (July, December,
1982), p. 160-197. Spanish. **DESCR:**
Economics; *Nationalization.

Mexico (cont.)

7373 Ford, Charles A. and Violante Morlock, Alejandro A. Policy concerns over the impact of trade-related performance requirements and investment incentives on the international economy: Mexican automotive policy and U.S.-Mexican relations. INTER-AMERICAN ECONOMIC AFFAIRS, Vol. 36, no. 2 (Fall 1982), p. 3-42. English. **DESCR:** Automobile Industry; Economic History and Conditions; *United States-Mexico Relations.

7374 Foreign trade. HISPANIC BUSINESS, Vol. 5, no. 2 (February 1983), p. 25. English. **DESCR:** *Currency; Small Business; U.S. Small Business Administration; U.S. Trade Center (Mexico City).

7375 Foreign trade. HISPANIC BUSINESS, Vol. 5, no. 10 (October 1983), p. 29. English. **DESCR:** Agency for International Development (AID); Caribbean Region; Economic History and Conditions; *Foreign Trade; HOW TO EXPORT: A MARKETING MANUAL; Puerto Rico; U.S. Trade Center (Mexico City).

7376 Fraser Rothenberg, Irene. Mexican-American views of U.S. relations with Latin America. JOURNAL OF ETHNIC STUDIES, Vol. 6, no. 1 (Spring 1978), p. 62-78. English. **DESCR:** Chicano Movement; Culture; Identity; International Relations; Latin America; Lobbying; *Nationalism; Political History and Conditions; Politics.

7377 Galarza, Carlos V. Deportes en Mexico. CAMINOS, Vol. 3, no. 6 (June 1982), p. 29,40. Bilingual. **DESCR:** Soccer; *Sports.

7378 Garcia, Mario T. Book review of: LOS MOJADOS: THE WETBACK STORY. JOURNAL OF ETHNIC STUDIES, Vol. 1, no. 1 (Spring 1973), p. 66-68. English. **DESCR:** Book Reviews; Immigrant Labor; *LOS MOJADOS: THE WETBACK STORY; Samora, Julian; Southwest United States; Undocumented Workers; United States.

7379 Garcia, Mario T. On Mexican immigration, the United States, and Chicano history. JOURNAL OF ETHNIC STUDIES, Vol. 7, no. 1 (Spring 1979), p. 80-88. English. **DESCR:** Book Reviews; *BY THE SWEAT OF THEIR BROW: MEXICAN IMMIGRANT LABOR IN THE UNITED STATES, 1900-1940; History; Immigrant Labor; Immigration; Immigration Law; Reisler, Mark; Research Methodology; Southwest United States.

7380 Gavin, John. A productive year. CAMINOS, Vol. 3, no. 6 (June 1982), p. 6-17,36. English. **DESCR:** *United States-Mexico Relations.

7381 Geary, Richard. The faces of San Miguel: a photo essay. NUESTRO, Vol. 7, no. 4 (May 1983), p. 31-34. English. **DESCR:** *Photography; *San Miguel de Allende, Mexico.

7382 Gente. NUESTRO, Vol. 7, no. 7 (September 1983), p. 61. English. **DESCR:** Americas Award; Chavez, Raul; *Chicanas; Diaz-Cobo, Christine; Ortega, Katherine D.; Performing Arts; Planas, Vilma; Ravard, Rafael Alonzo; Venezuela.

7383 Gente: Miguel Aleman, former president, Mexico, dies. NUESTRO, Vol. 7, no. 5 (June, July, 1983), p. 49. English. **DESCR:** Aleman, Miguel; *Elected Officials.

7384 Gold coins of Mexico. NUESTRO, Vol. 6, no. 1 (January, February, 1982), p. 53-54.

English. **DESCR:** *Banking Industry.

7385 Goldman, Shifra. Mexican muralism: its social-educative roles in Latin America and the United States. AZTLAN, Vol. 13, no. 1-2 (Spring, Fall, 1982), p. 111-133. Spanish. **DESCR:** Art; Latin America; *Mural Art; Social History and Conditions.

7386 Gonzales, Patrisia. Nogales: view from a cardboard box. NUESTRO, Vol. 6, no. 9 (November 1982), p. 21-27. English. **DESCR:** Nogales, Mexico; *Poverty.

7387 Heathcote, Olivia D. Sex stereotyping in Mexican reading primers. READING TEACHER, Vol. 36, no. 2 (November 1982), p. 158-165. English. **DESCR:** Comparative Education; Curriculum Materials; Primary School Education; *Sex Stereotypes.

7388 Jamail, Milton H. Book review of: MEXICO IN TRANSITION. SOUTHWEST ECONOMY AND SOCIETY, Vol. 4, no. 2 (Winter 1978, 1979), p. 47-49. English. **DESCR:** Book Reviews; History; *MEXICO IN TRANSITION; Russell, Philip.

7389 Jones, Oakah L. Book review of: THE MEXICAN FRONTIER, 1821-1846: THE AMERICAN SOUTHWEST UNDER MEXICO. ARIZONA AND THE WEST, Vol. 25, no. 2 (1983), p. 168-169. English. **DESCR:** Book Reviews; History; Southwest United States; *THE MEXICAN FRONTIER, 1821-1846: THE AMERICAN SOUTHWEST UNDER MEXICO; Weber, David J.

7390 Jones, Richard C. Undocumented migration from Mexico: some geographical questions. ANNALS OF THE ASSOCIATION OF AMERICAN GEOGRAPHERS, Vol. 72, no. 1 (March 1982), p. 77-87. English. **DESCR:** Geography; Immigration; *Migration Patterns; Undocumented Workers.

7391 Kagan, Spencer; Knight, George P.; and Martinez-Romero, Sergio. Culture and the development of conflict resolution style. JOURNAL OF CROSS-CULTURAL PSYCHOLOGY, Vol. 13, no. 1 (March 1982), p. 43-58. English. **DESCR:** Anglo Americans; *Conflict Resolution.

7392 Klor de Alva, Jorge. Gabino Barrera and Chicano thought. AZTLAN, Vol. 14, no. 2 (Fall 1983), p. 343-358. English. **DESCR:** *Barreda, Gabino; Economic History and Conditions; History; Philosophy; *Positivism.

7393 Langley, Roger. Roger Langley's Hispanic beat. HISPANIC BUSINESS, Vol. 4, no. 7 (July 1982), p. 29. English. **DESCR:** *Nuclear Energy.

7394 Learn more about Mexico. CAMINOS, Vol. 3, no. 6 (June 1982), p. 34-35. English. **DESCR:** *Bibliography.

7395 Learning more about Mexico. CAMINOS, Vol. 4, no. 5 (May 1983), p. 16-17. English. **DESCR:** History.

7396 Lenti, Paul. Accent: the Mexican retablo - a highly collectable folk art. NUESTRO, Vol. 7, no. 4 (May 1983), p. 63-64. English. **DESCR:** *Art History; *Folk Art; *Religious Art.

7397 Lenti, Paul. Mexico's posadas a unique experience. NUESTRO, Vol. 6, no. 10 (December 1982), p. 52-55. English. **DESCR:** *Christmas; Las Posadas; Tourism.

Mexico (cont.)

7398 Living traditions of the days of the dead. NUESTRO, Vol. 6, no. 6 (August 1982), p. 41-43. English. **DESCR:** Cultural Customs; Death (Concept); *Dia de los Muertos.

7399 Loza, Steven J. The great Mexican legends in music. CAMINOS, Vol. 4, no. 10 (November 1983), p. 20-23,47. Bilingual. **DESCR:** *Music.

7400 Maciel, David R. Nacionalismo cultural y politica liberal en la Republica Restaurada, 1867-1876. AZTLAN, Vol. 14, no. 2 (Fall 1983), p. 267-287. Spanish. **DESCR:** History; *Physical Education; Political History and Conditions; Political Ideology.

7401 Maciel, David R. Visions of the other Mexico: Chicanos and undocumented workers in Mexican cinema, 1954-1982. BILINGUAL REVIEW, Vol. 10, no. 2-3 (May, December, 1983), p. 71-88. English. **DESCR:** Film Reviews; *Films; Mexican Cinema; *Undocumented Workers.

7402 Marti, Oscar R. Barrera and moral philosophy. AZTLAN, Vol. 14, no. 2 (Fall 1983), p. 373-403. English. **DESCR:** *Barreda, Gabino; *Ethics; History; Philosophy; Positivism.

7403 Marti, Oscar R. Introduction. AZTLAN, Vol. 14, no. 2 (Fall 1983), p. 209-220. English. **DESCR:** *Barreda, Gabino; *Biography; History; Philosophy; Positivism.

7404 Marti, Oscar R., comp. Bibliography. AZTLAN, Vol. 14, no. 2 (Fall 1983), p. 405-417. English. **DESCR:** *Barreda, Gabino; *Bibliography; History; Philosophy; Positivism.

7405 Martinez, Ollin. Visitas e imagenes mexicanas; reflections of a photographer (photoessay). CAMINOS, Vol. 4, no. 11 (December 1983), p. 16-18. English. **DESCR:** *Photography.

7406 Martinez, Oscar J. Book review of: REVOLTOSOS: MEXICO'S REBELS IN THE UNITED STATES 1903-1923. ARIZONA AND THE WEST, Vol. 24, no. 1 (Spring 1982), p. 69-70. English. **DESCR:** Book Reviews; Raat, W. Dirk; *REVOLTOSOS: MEXICO'S REBELS IN THE UNITED STATES, 1903-1923; United States History.

7407 Martinez, Vilma. Working with de la Madrid. CAMINOS, Vol. 3, no. 6 (June 1982), p. 10-11,36. Bilingual. **DESCR:** *De la Madrid, Miguel; Elected Officials.

7408 Mathes, W. Michael. Sources in Mexico for the history of Spanish California. CALIFORNIA HISTORY, Vol. 61, no. 3 (1982), p. 223-226. English. **DESCR:** *California; *Historiography; Spanish Influence.

7409 Mecht, Richard L. U.S. real estate owners in Mexico face huge losses. CAMINOS, Vol. 3, no. 11 (December 1982), p. 27,52. Bilingual. **DESCR:** *Real Estate.

7410 Mexican business update. HISPANIC BUSINESS, Vol. 4, no. 1 (January 1982), p. 24. English. **DESCR:** Business; Export Trade; *Foreign Trade; *U.S.-Mexico Joint Commission on Commerce and Trade.

7411 Mexican centers advance U.S. ties. NUESTRO, Vol. 7, no. 1 (January, February, 1983), p. 10-11. English. **DESCR:** Art Galleries; *El Centro Mexicano del Libro; Los Angeles, CA; Museums; New York, NY; Publishing Industry.

7412 Mexican condo buyer in Texas-sized trouble. SOUTHERN EXPOSURE, Vol. 11, no. 1 (January 1983), p. 8-9. English. **DESCR:** Condominiums; Peso Devaluation; *Real Estate.

7413 Mexican market hints. HISPANIC BUSINESS, Vol. 4, no. 6 (June 1982), p. 25. English. **DESCR:** *Foreign Trade; *Marketing.

7414 Mexico's export production map. CAMINOS, Vol. 3, no. 6 (June 1982), p. 20-21. Bilingual. **DESCR:** Economic Development; *Export Trade.

7415 Meyer, Lorenzo. Mexico frente a los Estados Unidos, 1971-1980. DIALOGOS, Vol. 18, (January, February, 1982), p. 3-12. Spanish. **DESCR:** Economic History and Conditions; *United States-Mexico Relations.

7416 Meyer, Michael C. Book review of: THE MEXICAN FRONTIER, 1821-1846: THE AMERICAN SOUTHWEST UNDER MEXICO. WESTERN HISTORICAL QUARTERLY, Vol. 14, no. 3 (1983), p. 337-338. English. **DESCR:** Book Reviews; History; Southwest United States; *THE MEXICAN FRONTIER, 1821-1846: THE AMERICAN SOUTHWEST UNDER MEXICO; Weber, David J.

7417 Migdail, Carl J. Mexico's poverty: driving force for border jumpers. U.S. NEWS & WORLD REPORT, Vol. 94, no. 9 (March 7, 1983), p. 42-44. English. **DESCR:** Economic History and Conditions; Migration; *Poverty.

7418 Miller, Robert. Bilingual education in Mexico. EDUCATIONAL LEADERSHIP, Vol. 40, no. 8 (May 1983), p. 59. English. **DESCR:** *Book Reviews.

7419 Miller, Robert. The Mexican approach to developing bilingual materials and teaching literacy to bilingual students. READING TEACHER, Vol. 35, no. 7 (April 1982), p. 800-804. English. **DESCR:** *Bilingual Bicultural Education; Curriculum Materials; Freire, Paulo.

7420 Miller, Robert. Reading instruction and primary school education - Mexican teachers' viewpoints. READING TEACHER, Vol. 35, no. 8 (May 1982), p. 890-894. English. **DESCR:** *Curriculum; Early Childhood Education; Educational Theory and Practice; Teacher Attitudes.

7421 Monsivais, Carlos. No te muevas, paisaje (sobre el cincuentenario del cine sonoro en Mexico). AZTLAN, Vol. 14, no. 1 (Spring 1983), p. 1-19. Spanish. **DESCR:** Bunuel, Luis; Felix, Maria; Fernandez, Emilio; *Films; Mass Media.

7422 Morales, Cesareo. El impacto norteamericano en la politica economica de Mexico (1970-1983). CUADERNOS POLITICOS, Vol. 38, (October, December, 1983), p. 81-101. Spanish. **DESCR:** Economic History and Conditions; Political History and Conditions; *United States-Mexico Relations.

7423 Moreno, Mario "Cantinflas". Observations on Mexico today. CAMINOS, Vol. 3, no. 10 (November 1982), p. 20,45. Bilingual. **DESCR:** Dieciseis de Septiembre; *Holidays; *Moreno, Mario "Cantinflas".

7424 Nieto, Jesus G. Mexico & its economy - some keen insights. CAMINOS, Vol. 4, no. 5 (May 1983), p. 6-9,48. Bilingual. **DESCR:** *Economic Development.

Mexico (cont.)

7425 Petroleo, negociaciones fiancieras y nueva estrategia economica de Mexico. INFORME: RELACIONES MEXICO-ESTADOS UNIDOS, Vol. 1, no. 3 (July, December, 1982), p. 198-208. Spanish. **DESCR:** Economics; *Petroleum Industry.

7426 Plaza, Eva. Interest group politics and U.S. immigration policy towards Mexico. LA RAZA LAW JOURNAL, Vol. 1, no. 1 (June 1983), p. 76-100. English. **DESCR:** Immigration; Immigration Law; Immigration Regulation and Control; *Interest Groups; *Simpson-Mazzoli Bill; United States-Mexico Relations.

7427 Raat, W. Dirk. Augusto Comte, Gabino Barreda, and positivism in Mexico. AZTLAN, Vol. 14, no. 2 (Fall 1983), p. 235-251. English. **DESCR:** *Barreda, Gabino; *Comte, Auguste; Education; Educational Theory and Practice; History; Philosophy; *Positivism.

7428 Ramos, Manuel. En torno a las ideas sobre EL MEXICANO. CAMPO LIBRE, Vol. 1, no. 2 (Summer 1981), p. 273-282. Spanish. **DESCR:** Cultural Characteristics; *EL MEXICANO; Identity; Philosophy; *Uranga, Emilio.

7429 Reichert, Joshua. Town divided: economic stratification and social relations in a Mexican migrant community. SOCIAL PROBLEMS, Vol. 29, no. 4 (April 1982), p. 411-423. English. **DESCR:** *Migration; Social Classes.

7430 Rice, Jacqueline. Beyond the cientificos: the educational background of the Porfirian Elite. AZTLAN, Vol. 14, no. 2 (Fall 1983), p. 289-306. English. **DESCR:** History; La Union Liberal; Leadership; Political History and Conditions; Political Parties and Organizations; *Social Classes.

7431 Richmond, Douglas W. Mexican immigration and border strategy during the revolution, 1910-1920. NEW MEXICO HISTORICAL REVIEW, Vol. 57, no. 3 (July 1982), p. 269-288. English. **DESCR:** *Border Region; Carranza, Venustiano; History; Immigration; Mexican Revolution - 1910-1920; Social History and Conditions; United States-Mexico Relations.

7432 Risse, Gunter B. Book review of: CAPITULOS DE HISTORIA MEDICA MEXICANA. BULLETIN OF THE HISTORY OF MEDICINE, Vol. 56, no. 4 (1982), p. 591-592. English. **DESCR:** *CAPITULOS DE HISTORIA MEDICA MEXICANA; Folk Medicine; Medicine; Precolumbian Medicine; Somolinos D'Ardois, German.

7433 Rocco, Raymond. Positivism and Mexican identity: then and now. AZTLAN, Vol. 14, no. 2 (Fall 1983), p. 359-371. English. **DESCR:** History; Identity; Philosophy; *Positivism.

7434 Rose, Barbara. Frida Kahlo: the Chicana as art heroine. VOGUE, Vol. 173, (April 1983), p. 152-154. English. **DESCR:** Art; Artists; Biography; *Kahlo, Frida; Rivera, Diego.

7435 Salvatierra, Richard. Tiempos dificiles. LATINO, Vol. 53, no. 5 (September 1982), p. 13,26. Spanish. **DESCR:** *De la Madrid, Miguel.

7436 Sanchez-Devanny, Jorge. Inseparable United States Mexico business relations. CAMINOS, Vol. 3, no. 6 (June 1982), p. 12-14. English. **DESCR:** Foreign Trade; *United States-Mexico Relations.

7437 Sandos, James A. and Cross, Harry E. National development and international

labour migration: Mexico 1940-1965. JOURNAL OF CONTEMPORARY HISTORY, Vol. 18, no. 1 (January 1983), p. 43-60. English. **DESCR:** *Braceros; Immigrant Labor.

7438 Schon, Isabel. Spanish books for children. BOOKLIST, Vol. 78, no. 20 (June 15, 1982), p. 1373-1374. English. **DESCR:** Argentina; *Bibliography; *Children's Literature; Spain; Spanish Language; Venezuela.

7439 Schon, Isabel. Spanish books for children. BOOKLIST, Vol. 79, (February 15, 1983), p. 783-784. English. **DESCR:** *Bibliography; *Children's Literature; Spain; Spanish Language; Venezuela.

7440 Shankman, Arnold. The image of Mexico and the Mexican-American in the Black press, 1890-1935. JOURNAL OF ETHNIC STUDIES, Vol. 3, no. 2 (Summer 1975), p. 43-56. English. **DESCR:** Attitude (Psychological); Blacks; *Intergroup Relations; Journalism.

7441 Simon, Daniel T. Mexican repatriation in East Chicago, Indiana. JOURNAL OF ETHNIC STUDIES, Vol. 2, no. 2 (Summer 1974), p. 11-23. English. **DESCR:** *Deportation; *East Chicago, IN; History; Immigrant Labor; Immigration; Immigration Regulation and Control; Inland Steel Company; Social History and Conditions.

7442 Skirius, John. Barreda, Vasconcelos, and the Mexican educational reforms. AZTLAN, Vol. 14, no. 2 (Fall 1983), p. 307-341. English. **DESCR:** *Barreda, Gabino; Education; *Educational Theory and Practice; History; Positivism; *Vasconcelos, Jose.

7443 Some useful advise [sic] on currency regulations in Mexico. CAMINOS, Vol. 3, no. 11 (December 1982), p. 28. English. **DESCR:** *Currency; *Tourism.

7444 Taylor, William B. Book review of: LABOR AND LABORERS THROUGH MEXICAN HISTORY. NEW MEXICO HISTORICAL REVIEW, Vol. 57, no. 1 (January 1982), p. 91-92. English. **DESCR:** Book Reviews; *EL TRABAJO Y LOS TRABAJADORES EN LA HISTORIA DE MEXICO = LABOR AND LABORERS THROUGH MEXICAN HISTORY; Frost, Elsa Cecilia; Laborers.

7445 Trevino, Jesus and Ruiz, Jose Luis. Guatemalan refugees - the tip of the iceberg. CAMINOS, Vol. 4, no. 5 (May 1983), p. 13-15,48. English. **DESCR:** Guatemala; International Relations; MEXICO: THE FUTURE; *Refugees.

7446 Uranga, Emilio. Notas para un estudio del mexicano. CAMPO LIBRE, Vol. 1, no. 2 (Summer 1981), p. 283-295. Spanish. **DESCR:** Cultural Characteristics; Gaos, Jose; Identity; Philosophy; *Ramos, Samuel.

7447 U.S. firm seeks entry to Mexican beer market. NUESTRO, Vol. 7, no. 1 (January, February, 1983), p. 36. English. **DESCR:** *Anheuser-Busch, Inc.; *Marketing.

7448 US-Mexican trade relations. HISPANIC BUSINESS, Vol. 4, no. 9 (September 1982), p. 23. English. **DESCR:** California; Export Trade; *Foreign Trade; United States-Mexico Relations.

7449 Vidal. The next president of Mexico: Miguel de la Madrid. CAMINOS, Vol. 3, no. 6 (June 1982), p. 9. Bilingual. **DESCR:** *De la Madrid, Miguel; Elected Officials.

Mexico (cont.)

7450 Vidal, Jose. Cantinflas: Mario Moreno.
CAMINOS, Vol. 3, no. 7 (July, August, 1982),
p. 7-9. Bilingual. **DESCR:** Artists; *Moreno,
Mario "Cantinflas".

7451 Vidal, Jose. Mexican film - a short history.
CAMINOS, Vol. 3, no. 7 (July, August, 1982),
p. 10-13. Bilingual. **DESCR:** Artists; *Films.

7452 Vidal, Jose. Oil pluses - economic woes.
CAMINOS, Vol. 3, no. 6 (June 1982), p.
18-19. Bilingual. **DESCR:** Economic
Development; Petroleum Industry; *United
States-Mexico Relations.

7453 Vigil, James Diego. Towards a new
perspective on understanding the Chicano
people: the six C's model of sociocultural
change. CAMPO LIBRE, Vol. 1, no. 2 (Summer
1981), p. 141-167. English. **DESCR:**
Acculturation; Assimilation; Cultural
Characteristics; History; Mexican
Nationalism Period; Nationalism;
Organizations; Precolumbian Society; *Six
C's Model (Theoretical Model); Social
History and Conditions; Spanish Colonial
Period.

7454 Villarreal, Roberto E. and Kelly, Philip.
Mexican Americans as participants in United
States-Mexico relations. INTERNATIONAL
STUDIES NOTES, Vol. 9, no. 4 (Winter 1982),
p. 1-6. English. **DESCR:** International
Relations; Political Representation; *United
States-Mexico Relations.

7455 Whisler, Kirk. Octavio Paz - "There will be
no revolution in Mexico" (interview).
CAMINOS, Vol. 4, no. 5 (May 1983), p.
10-12,48. Bilingual. **DESCR:** Authors; *Paz,
Octavio.

7456 Zea, Leopoldo. El sentido de la historia en
Gabino Barreda. AZTLAN, Vol. 14, no. 2 (Fall
1983), p. 221-233. Spanish. **DESCR:** *Barreda,
Gabino; *History; Philosophy; Positivism.

Mexico City

7457 Bruce Novoa, Juan. Artistic perceptions of
Mexico City. NUESTRO, Vol. 6, no. 4 (May
1982), p. 53-54. English. **DESCR:** *Art.

7458 Gil, Carlos B. Withstanding time: the
miracle of the Virgin of Guadalupe. NUESTRO,
Vol. 7, no. 10 (December 1983), p. 46-47.
English. **DESCR:** Catholic Church;
*Guadalupanismo; Religion; *Virgin of
Guadalupe.

7459 Nicholson, H. B. Treasures of Tenochtitlan.
NUESTRO, Vol. 7, no. 10 (December 1983), p.
28-32. English. **DESCR:** Aztecs; *Precolumbian
Art.

Mexico City All Stars

7460 Cantu, Hector. Softball Texas style.
NATIONAL HISPANIC JOURNAL, Vol. 1, no. 3
(Summer, Fall, 1982), p. 9-11. English.
DESCR: El Paso Jesters; Pan American
Softball League; Recreation; *Softball;
Sports.

MEXICO IN TRANSITION

7461 Jamail, Milton H. Book review of: MEXICO IN
TRANSITION. SOUTHWEST ECONOMY AND SOCIETY,
Vol. 4, no. 2 (Winter 1978, 1979), p. 47-49.
English. **DESCR:** Book Reviews; History;
Mexico; Russell, Philip.

MEXICO: THE FUTURE

7462 Trevino, Jesus and Ruiz, Jose Luis.
Guatemalan refugees - the tip of the
iceberg. CAMINOS, Vol. 4, no. 5 (May 1983),
p. 13-15,48. English. **DESCR:** Guatemala;
International Relations; Mexico; *Refugees.

Mi Carrera Program

7463 Girls explore new job fields. NUESTRO, Vol.
7, no. 8 (October 1983), p. 13. English.
DESCR: *Chicanas; *Discrimination in
Employment; Mi Casa Women's Resource Center,
Denver, CO.

Mi Casa Women's Resource Center, Denver, CO

7464 Girls explore new job fields. NUESTRO, Vol.
7, no. 8 (October 1983), p. 13. English.
DESCR: *Chicanas; *Discrimination in
Employment; Mi Carrera Program.

MIAMI EN SUS MANOS

7465 Southern Bell faces directory competition.
NUESTRO, Vol. 6, no. 8 (October 1982), p.
47. English. **DESCR:** Publishing Industry;
SPANISH YELLOW PAGES.

Miami, FL

7466 An anniversary is observed. NUESTRO, Vol. 7,
no. 8 (October 1983), p. 13. English.
DESCR: *Batista, Fulgencio; Cuba; Cubanos;
Ferre, Maurice; Local Government.

7467 Chavarria, Jesus. The world according to
Miami. HISPANIC BUSINESS, Vol. 4, no. 3
(March 1982), p. 6. English. **DESCR:**
*Business; Carnaval Miami 82; Cubanos;
*Urban Communities.

7468 Communications/marketing. HISPANIC BUSINESS,
Vol. 5, no. 1 (January 1983), p. 23.
English. **DESCR:** Banking Industry; Broadcast
Media; Caballero Spanish Media, Inc. (CSM);
Fleishman-Hillard, Inc.; *Marketing;
Nogales, Luis G.; Public Relations.

7469 EFE announces opening of Miami News Bureau.
NUESTRO, Vol. 6, no. 6 (August 1982), p. 52.
English. **DESCR:** *News Agencies; Spain;
Spanish Language.

7470 Ferre, Maurice A. Marketplace of the
Americas. HISPANIC BUSINESS, Vol. 4, no. 3
(March 1982), p. 8. English. **DESCR:**
Business; *Urban Communities.

7471 Fifth member leaves panel. NUESTRO, Vol. 6,
no. 4 (May 1982), p. 11. English. **DESCR:**
*Lew, Salvador; Little Havana; Police;
Violence.

7472 Foreign trade. HISPANIC BUSINESS, Vol. 5,
no. 4 (April 1983), p. 22. English. **DESCR:**
Banking Industry; Brazil; *Electronics
Industry; Export Trade; *Foreign Trade;
Ibero-American Chamber of Commerce; Minority
Bank Development Program (MBDP); Minority
Export Development Consultants Program
(MEDC); Peace Corps; Puerto Rico.

7473 Foreign trade. HISPANIC BUSINESS, Vol. 5,
no. 11 (November 1983), p. 31. English.
DESCR: California; *Foreign Trade; HOW TO
EXPORT: A MARKETING MANUAL; Marketing; Miami
Free Zone; Puerto Rico.

Miami, FL (cont.)

7474 Greenfield, Charles. Cuban theater in exile: Miami's little Broadway. NUESTRO, Vol. 6, no. 9 (November 1982), p. 36-38. English. **DESCR:** Cubanos; Little Havana; *Teatro.

7475 Hines, Bea L. and Fabricio, Roberto. Voices. NUESTRO, Vol. 7, no. 10 (December 1983), p. 57-58. English. **DESCR:** Blacks; Cubanos; *Elections; Ferre, Maurice; Suarez, Xavier.

7476 The Little Havana development authority. HISPANIC BUSINESS, Vol. 4, no. 3 (March 1982), p. 10+. English. **DESCR:** Carnaval Miami 82; *Community Development; Cubanos; Little Havana.

7477 Miami's thriving Camacol. HISPANIC BUSINESS, Vol. 4, no. 3 (March 1982), p. 12-13. English. **DESCR:** Businesspeople; Camara de Comercio Latina de Los Estados Unidos (CAMACOL); *Chamber of Commerce.

7478 New city park for Miamians. NUESTRO, Vol. 6, no. 9 (November 1982), p. 13. English. **DESCR:** Marti, Jose; *Recreation.

7479 Que pasa?: future of bilingualism. NUESTRO, Vol. 7, no. 4 (May 1983), p. 9. English. **DESCR:** *Bilingualism; Canada; Cubanos.

7480 Sargeant, Georgia. Young turks set new standards. HISPANIC BUSINESS, Vol. 5, no. 11 (November 1983), p. 8-9. English. **DESCR:** Alvarez, Julio E.; *Architecture; Business Enterprises; Management; Marketing; Taracido, Manuel E.; Wolfberg, David A.; *Wolfberg/Alvarez/Taracido (WAT).

7481 Skriloff, Lisa. Music, news dominate Spanish-language radio programming. HISPANIC BUSINESS, Vol. 5, no. 12 (December 1983), p. 34. English. **DESCR:** Advertising; Los Angeles, CA; Marketing; *Radio; San Antonio, TX.

7482 Staczek, John J. Code-switching in Miami Spanish: the domain of health care services. BILINGUAL REVIEW, Vol. 10, no. 1 (January, April, 1983), p. 41-46. English. **DESCR:** *Bilingualism; *Language Interference; Medical Care; Spanish Language.

7483 Volsky, George. The American club. HISPANIC BUSINESS, Vol. 4, no. 3 (March 1982), p. 16-17+. English. **DESCR:** American Club of Miami; *Businesspeople; Cubanos; *Cultural Organizations.

7484 Volsky, George. Four careers in Miami. HISPANIC BUSINESS, Vol. 5, no. 4 (April 1983), p. 10-11+. English. **DESCR:** Balestra, Victor C.; *Banking Industry; Biographical Notes; *Businesspeople; Harvard Business School's Latino Association; Huston, Maria Padilla; Masvidal, Sergio J.; Valdes-Fauli, Gonzalo.

7485 Volsky, George. Hilario Candela: designing for Florida's future. HISPANIC BUSINESS, Vol. 5, no. 11 (November 1983), p. 20-22. English. **DESCR:** Architecture; *Candela, Hilario; Spillis Candela & Partners; Urban Development.

7486 Volsky, George and Masvidal, Raul. An interview with Raul Masvidal. HISPANIC BUSINESS, Vol. 4, no. 9 (September 1982), p. 16-17,24+. English. **DESCR:** Banking Industry; Biography; Business Enterprises; Businesspeople; Cubanos; *Masvidal, Raul.

7487 Volsky, George. Miami's radio S-U-A-A-V-E.

HISPANIC BUSINESS, Vol. 4, no. 12 (December 1982), p. 22,35. English. **DESCR:** Advertising; Broadcast Media; Language Usage; Marketing; *Radio; Radio Station SUAVE, Miami, FL; *Radio Stations; Spanish Language.

7488 Ward, Carmen Carole. Book review of: THE ASSIMILATION OF CUBAN EXILES: THE ROLE OF COMMUNITY AND CLASS. JOURNAL OF ETHNIC STUDIES, Vol. 3, no. 2 (Summer 1975), p. 116-119. English. **DESCR:** Assimilation; Book Reviews; *Cubanos; *Rogg, Eleanor Meyer; Social Classes; Social History and Conditions; THE ASSIMILATION OF CUBAN EXILES: THE ROLE OF COMMUNITY AND CLASS; West New York, NJ.

7489 Whitefield, Mimi. Miami, Caribbean megalopolis. HISPANIC BUSINESS, Vol. 4, no. 3 (March 1982), p. 18-19+. English. **DESCR:** Business; Dade County, FL; Foreign Trade; *Urban Communities.

Miami Free Zone

7490 Foreign trade. HISPANIC BUSINESS, Vol. 5, no. 11 (November 1983), p. 31. English. **DESCR:** California; *Foreign Trade; HOW TO EXPORT: A MARKETING MANUAL; Marketing; Miami, FL; Puerto Rico.

MIAMI MENSUAL

7491 Chavarria, Jesus. The media scene. HISPANIC BUSINESS, Vol. 4, no. 5 (May 1982), p. 6. English. **DESCR:** Advertising; Broadcast Media; Caballero Spanish Media, Inc. (CSM); *Mass Media; Print Media; Radio; Television.

Michell, Pat

7492 Media/marketing. HISPANIC BUSINESS, Vol. 5, no. 11 (November 1983), p. 30. English. **DESCR:** Caballero Spanish Media, Inc. (CSM); California Chicano News Media Association (CCNMA); Employment Training; Federal Communications Commission (FCC); HISPANEX (Oakland, CA); *Mass Media; Radio; Radio Station KALI, Los Angeles, CA.

Michigan

7493 School principal recognized for leadership efforts. NUESTRO, Vol. 6, no. 5 (June, July, 1982), p. 30. English. **DESCR:** Bilingual Bicultural Education; Leadership; *Ruiz, Pablo.

Middle Class
    USE: Social Classes

Midwest Hispanics in Telecommunications Symposium, Chicago, IL

7494 Communications/marketing. HISPANIC BUSINESS, Vol. 5, no. 10 (October 1983), p. 26. English. **DESCR:** Advertising; Arens & Gutierrez; Employment; Henry Molina, Inc.; Journals; Lionetti and Meyers Research Center, Inc.; Marketing; *Mass Media; NEW MANAGEMENT.

Midwestern States

7495 Baca Zinn, Maxine. Urban kinship and Midwest Chicano families: evidence in support of revision. DE COLORES, Vol. 6, no. 1-2 (1982), p. 85-98. English. **DESCR:** Compadrazgo; *Extended Family; Family; Urban Communities.

Midwestern States (cont.)

7496 Garcia, Juan R. Midwest Mexicanos in the
     1920's: issues, questions, and directions.
     SOCIAL SCIENCE JOURNAL, Vol. 19, no. 2
     (April 1982), p. 89-99. English. **DESCR:**
     Identity; *Social History and Conditions;
     Social Research.

7497 Santos, Richard. Earning among
     Spanish-origin males in the Midwest. SOCIAL
     SCIENCE JOURNAL, Vol. 19, no. 2 (April
     1982), p. 51-59. English. **DESCR:** Employment;
     *Income; Labor.

La Migra
     USE: Immigration Regulation and Control

**Migrant and Seasonal Agricultural Worker
Protection Act (MSPA)**

7498 Migratory worker law increases protections.
     NUESTRO, Vol. 7, no. 1 (January, February,
     1983), p. 47. English. **DESCR:** Agricultural
     Laborers; Migrant Labor.

Migrant Children

7499 Alvarez, Amando. From Texas to Idaho.
     LATINO, Vol. 53, no. 4 (June 1982), p. 26.
     English. **DESCR:** *Undocumented Workers.

7500 McCarthy, Martha. Legal forum. The right to
     an education: illegal aliens. JOURNAL OF
     EDUCATIONAL EQUITY AND LEADERSHIP, Vol. 2,
     no. 4 (Summer 1982), p. 282-287. English.
     DESCR: Administration of Justice; Doe v.
     Plyer [Tyler Independent School District,
     Texas]; Education; *Educational Law and
     Legislation; *Migrant Education; Texas;
     Undocumented Workers.

7501 Ortiz, Tomasita. The Spanish-speaking
     migrant child. BILINGUAL JOURNAL, Vol. 6,
     no. 4 (Summer 1982), p. 8-15,32. English.
     DESCR: Bilingual Bicultural Education;
     English as a Second Language; Migrant
     Education; *MIGRANT STUDENT RECORD TRANSFER
     SYSTEM.

7502 Saracho, Olivia N. Effects of a
     computer-assisted instruction program on
     basic skills achievement and attitudes
     toward instruction of Spanish-speaking
     migrant children. AMERICAN EDUCATIONAL
     RESEARCH JOURNAL, Vol. 19, no. 2 (Summer
     1982), p. 201-219. English. **DESCR:** Academic
     Motivation; Audiovisual Instruction;
     Computers; *Migrant Education; Programmed
     Instruction.

7503 Saracho, Olivia N. Planning computer
     assisted instruction for Spanish speaking
     migrant students. JOURNAL OF EDUCATIONAL
     TECHNOLOGY SYSTEMS, Vol. 10, no. 3 (1981,
     1982), p. 257-260. English. **DESCR:** Academic
     Achievement; Computers; *Migrant Education;
     *Programmed Instruction.

7504 Schey, Peter A. Unnamed witness number 1:
     now attending the Texas public schools.
     MIGRATION TODAY, Vol. 10, no. 5 (1982), p.
     22-27. English. **DESCR:** Constitutional
     Amendments - Fourteenth; Education;
     Education Equalization; Educational Law and
     Legislation; Equal Protection Clause; Texas
     Public Schools; *Undocumented Children; U.S.
     Supreme Court Case.

7505 Sutton, Susan Buck and Brunner, Tracy. Life
     on the road: Midwestern migrant farmworker
     survival skills. MIGRATION TODAY, Vol. 11,
     no. 1 (1983), p. 24-31. English. **DESCR:**
     Agribusiness; Agricultural Laborers;

Economic History and Conditions; Indiana;
Migrant Education; *Migrant Labor;
Stereotypes.

7506 Vasquez, Ivan. Analysis of June 15, 1982
     opinion issued by the U.S. Supreme Court in
     the case of Texas undocumented children.
     MIGRATION TODAY, Vol. 10, no. 3-4 (1982), p.
     49-51. English. **DESCR:** Constitutional
     Amendments - Fourteenth; Education;
     *Education Equalization; Educational Law and
     Legislation; Equal Protection Clause;
     *Undocumented Children; U.S. Supreme Court
     Case.

Migrant Education

7507 Developments in migrant workers programs:
     1981. CLEARINGHOUSE REVIEW, Vol. 15,
     (January 1982), p. 797-805. English. **DESCR:**
     Fair Labor Standards Act (FLSA); Farm Labor
     Contractor Registration Act (FLCRA); Migrant
     Housing; *Migrant Labor; Migrant Legal
     Action Program (MLAP); Occupational Safety
     and Health Administration; Pesticides;
     Undocumented Workers; Wagner-Peyser Act.

7508 McCarthy, Martha. Legal forum. The right to
     an education: illegal aliens. JOURNAL OF
     EDUCATIONAL EQUITY AND LEADERSHIP, Vol. 2,
     no. 4 (Summer 1982), p. 282-287. English.
     DESCR: Administration of Justice; Doe v.
     Plyer [Tyler Independent School District,
     Texas]; Education; *Educational Law and
     Legislation; Migrant Children; Texas;
     Undocumented Workers.

7509 Ortiz, Tomasita. The Spanish-speaking
     migrant child. BILINGUAL JOURNAL, Vol. 6,
     no. 4 (Summer 1982), p. 8-15,32. English.
     DESCR: Bilingual Bicultural Education;
     English as a Second Language; *Migrant
     Children; *MIGRANT STUDENT RECORD TRANSFER
     SYSTEM.

7510 Saracho, Olivia N. Effects of a
     computer-assisted instruction program on
     basic skills achievement and attitudes
     toward instruction of Spanish-speaking
     migrant children. AMERICAN EDUCATIONAL
     RESEARCH JOURNAL, Vol. 19, no. 2 (Summer
     1982), p. 201-219. English. **DESCR:** Academic
     Motivation; Audiovisual Instruction;
     Computers; *Migrant Children; Programmed
     Instruction.

7511 Saracho, Olivia N. Planning computer
     assisted instruction for Spanish speaking
     migrant students. JOURNAL OF EDUCATIONAL
     TECHNOLOGY SYSTEMS, Vol. 10, no. 3 (1981,
     1982), p. 257-260. English. **DESCR:** Academic
     Achievement; Computers; Migrant Children;
     *Programmed Instruction.

7512 Sutton, Susan Buck and Brunner, Tracy. Life
     on the road: Midwestern migrant farmworker
     survival skills. MIGRATION TODAY, Vol. 11,
     no. 1 (1983), p. 24-31. English. **DESCR:**
     Agribusiness; Agricultural Laborers;
     Economic History and Conditions; Indiana;
     Migrant Children; *Migrant Labor;
     Stereotypes.

Migrant Health Services

7513 Chavez, Leo R. Undocumented immigrants and
     access to health services: a game of pass
     the buck. MIGRATION TODAY, Vol. 11, no. 1
     (1983), p. 14-19. English. **DESCR:**
     California; *Immigrants; Medical Care;
     Public Health Legislation; Simpson-Mazzoli
     Bill; Social Services; Undocumented Workers.

Migrant Health Services (cont.)

7514 King, Karen. Hope comes to Apopka: on working alongside the poor. THE OTHER SIDE, Vol. 18, (May 1982), p. 23-25. English. **DESCR:** Apopka, FL; Clergy; *Migrant Labor; Office of Migrant Ministry (OMM).

7515 O'Brien, Mary Elizabeth. Reaching the migrant worker. AMERICAN JOURNAL OF NURSING, Vol. 83, no. 6 (June 1983), p. 895-897. English. **DESCR:** Agricultural Laborers; Folk Medicine; Medical Care.

Migrant Housing

7516 Developments in migrant workers programs: 1981. CLEARINGHOUSE REVIEW, Vol. 15, (January 1982), p. 797-805. English. **DESCR:** Fair Labor Standards Act (FLSA); Farm Labor Contractor Registration Act (FLCRA); Migrant Education; *Migrant Labor; Migrant Legal Action Program (MLAP); Occupational Safety and Health Administration; Pesticides; Undocumented Workers; Wagner-Peyser Act.

Migrant Labor

7517 Cornelius, Wayne A. Interviewing undocumented immigrants: methodological reflections based on fieldwork in Mexico and the U.S. INTERNATIONAL MIGRATION REVIEW, Vol. 16, no. 2 (Summer 1982), p. 378-411. English. **DESCR:** Immigrant Labor; Immigrants; Research Methodology; *Undocumented Workers.

7518 De Leon, Arnoldo and Stewart, Kenneth L. Lost dream and found fortunes: Mexican and Anglo immigrants in South Texas,1850 -1900. WESTERN HISTORICAL QUARTERLY, Vol. 14, no. 3 (1983), p. 291-310. English. **DESCR:** History; *Migration; Texas.

7519 Developments in migrant workers programs: 1981. CLEARINGHOUSE REVIEW, Vol. 15, (January 1982), p. 797-805. English. **DESCR:** Fair Labor Standards Act (FLSA); Farm Labor Contractor Registration Act (FLCRA); Migrant Education; Migrant Housing; Migrant Legal Action Program (MLAP); Occupational Safety and Health Administration; Pesticides; Undocumented Workers; Wagner-Peyser Act.

7520 FLOC, Campbell labels. NUESTRO, Vol. 6, no. 1 (January, February, 1982), p. 10. English. **DESCR:** Boycotts; *Farm Labor Organizing Commmittee (FLOC).

7521 Hewitt, William L. Mexican workers in Wyoming during World War II: necessity, discrimination and protest. ANNALS OF WYOMING, Vol. 54, no. 2 (1982), p. 20-33. English. **DESCR:** *Agricultural Laborers; Braceros; World War II; Wyoming.

7522 King, Karen. Hope comes to Apopka: on working alongside the poor. THE OTHER SIDE, Vol. 18, (May 1982), p. 23-25. English. **DESCR:** Apopka, FL; Clergy; Migrant Health Services; Office of Migrant Ministry (OMM).

7523 Linguistic confusion. NUESTRO, Vol. 6, no. 4 (May 1982), p. 9. English.

7524 Migrant farm workers. NUESTRO, Vol. 5, no. 8 (November 1981), p. 10-11. English. **DESCR:** *Chisholm, Shirley; U.S. Commission on Farmworkers.

7525 Migratory worker law increases protections. NUESTRO, Vol. 7, no. 1 (January, February, 1983), p. 47. English. **DESCR:** Agricultural Laborers; *Migrant and Seasonal Agricultural Worker Protection Act (MSPA).

7526 Naismith, Rachael. Field work: outreach to migrants. RQ - REFERENCE AND ADULT SERVICES DIVISION, Vol. 22, no. 1 (Fall 1982), p. 33-35. English. **DESCR:** Cumberland County Library, NJ; Fresno County Public Library, CA; *Library Services; Public Libraries.

7527 Naismith, Rachael. Moveable library: serving migrant farm workers. WILSON LIBRARY BULLETIN, Vol. 57, no. 7 (March 1983), p. 571-575. English. **DESCR:** *Dodge County Library System, WI; *Fresno County Public Library, CA; Library Services; Public Libraries.

7528 Sutton, Susan Buck and Brunner, Tracy. Life on the road: Midwestern migrant farmworker survival skills. MIGRATION TODAY, Vol. 11, no. 1 (1983), p. 24-31. English. **DESCR:** Agribusiness; Agricultural Laborers; Economic History and Conditions; Indiana; Migrant Children; Migrant Education; Stereotypes.

7529 Walia, Adorna. Book review of: THE PLUM PLUM PICKERS. BILINGUAL JOURNAL, Vol. 6, no. 1 (Fall 1982), p. 30-31. English. **DESCR:** Agricultural Laborers; Barrio, Raymond; Book Reviews; California; Santa Clara County, CA; *THE PLUM PLUM PICKERS.

Migrant Legal Action Program (MLAP)

7530 Developments in migrant workers programs: 1981. CLEARINGHOUSE REVIEW, Vol. 15, (January 1982), p. 797-805. English. **DESCR:** Fair Labor Standards Act (FLSA); Farm Labor Contractor Registration Act (FLCRA); Migrant Education; Migrant Housing; *Migrant Labor; Occupational Safety and Health Administration; Pesticides; Undocumented Workers; Wagner-Peyser Act.

MIGRANT STUDENT RECORD TRANSFER SYSTEM

7531 Ortiz, Tomasita. The Spanish-speaking migrant child. BILINGUAL JOURNAL, Vol. 6, no. 4 (Summer 1982), p. 8-15,32. English. **DESCR:** Bilingual Bicultural Education; English as a Second Language; *Migrant Children; Migrant Education.

MIGRANT WORKERS IN WESTERN EUROPE AND THE UNITED STATES

7532 Nalven, Joseph. Resolving the undocumented worker problem. NEW SCHOLAR, Vol. 8, no. 1-2 (Spring, Fall, 1982), p. 473-481. English. **DESCR:** Book Reviews; *MEXICAN WORKERS IN THE UNITED STATES; Undocumented Workers.

Migration

7533 Bean, Frank D.; King, Allan G.; and Passel, Jeffrey S. The number of illegal migrants of Mexican origin in the United States: sex ratio-based estimates for 1980. DEMOGRAPHY, Vol. 20, no. 1 (February 1983), p. 99-109. English. **DESCR:** Census; *Population; Statistics; Undocumented Workers.

7534 Bustamante, Jorge A. The Mexicans are coming: from ideology to labor relations. INTERNATIONAL MIGRATION REVIEW, Vol. 17, no. 2 (Summer 1983), p. 323-341. English. **DESCR:** Attitude (Psychological); *Immigration; Immigration Law; Labor Laws and Legislation; Labor Supply and Market; Policy; Political Ideology; *Simpson-Mazzoli Bill; Undocumented Workers.

Migration (cont.)

7535 Bustamante, Jorge A. Relief from illegals? Perhaps in 50 years. U.S. NEWS & WORLD REPORT, Vol. 94, no. 9 (March 7, 1983), p. 44. English. DESCR: Bustamante, Jorge A.; *Undocumented Workers.

7536 De Leon, Arnoldo and Stewart, Kenneth L. Lost dream and found fortunes: Mexican and Anglo immigrants in South Texas,1850 -1900. WESTERN HISTORICAL QUARTERLY, Vol. 14, no. 3 (1983), p. 291-310. English. DESCR: History; Migrant Labor; Texas.

7537 Estrada, Leobardo F. [Demographic characteristics of Latinos]. CHICANO LAW REVIEW, Vol. 6, (1983), p. 9-16. English. DESCR: *Demography; Internal Migration; LATINOS IN THE LAW [symposium], UCLA, 1982; Los Angeles County, CA; Migration Patterns; Spanish Language.

7538 Hoffman, Abraham. Book review of: MEXICANO RESISTANCE IN THE SOUTHWEST: "THE SACRED RIGHT OF SELF-PRESERVATION". PACIFIC HISTORICAL REVIEW, Vol. 51, no. 2 (May 1982), p. 230-231. English. DESCR: Book Reviews; Cardoso, Lawrence A.; *MEXICAN EMIGRATION TO THE UNITED STATES 1897-1931: SOCIO-ECONOMIC PATTERNS.

7539 Howard, David. For "illegals" migration goes both ways. R & D MEXICO, Vol. 2, no. 3-4 (December, January, 1981, 1982), p. 14-17. English. DESCR: Immigration; Migration Patterns; NATIONAL SURVEY ON EMIGRATION TO THE NORTHERN BORDER AND THE UNITED STATES; Surveys; *Undocumented Workers.

7540 Mabry, Donald J. Book review of: ACROSS THE BORDER: RURAL DEVELOPMENT IN MEXICO AND RECENT MIGRATION TO THE UNITED STATES. INTERNATIONAL MIGRATION REVIEW, Vol. 17, no. 2 (Summer 1983), p. 351. English. DESCR: *ACROSS THE BORDER: RURAL DEVELOPMENT IN MEXICO AND RECENT MIGRATION; Book Reviews; Cross, Harry E.; Migration Patterns; Rural Economics; Sandos, James.

7541 Massey, Douglas S. and Schnabel, Kathleen M. Background and characteristics of undocumented Hispanic migrants to the United States: a review of recent research. MIGRATION TODAY, Vol. 11, no. 1 (1983), p. 6-13. English. DESCR: Immigrants; Migration Patterns; Socioeconomic Factors; *Undocumented Workers.

7542 Migdail, Carl J. Mexico's poverty: driving force for border jumpers. U.S. NEWS & WORLD REPORT, Vol. 94, no. 9 (March 7, 1983), p. 42-44. English. DESCR: Economic History and Conditions; Mexico; *Poverty.

7543 Migration: a problem. NUESTRO, Vol. 6, no. 10 (December 1982), p. 8. English. DESCR: *Puerto Rico.

7544 Mines, Richard and de Janvry, Alain. Migration to the United States and Mexican rural developments: a case study. AMERICAN JOURNAL OF AGRICULTURAL ECONOMICS, Vol. 64, no. 3 (August 1982), p. 444-454. English.

7545 Newman, Allen R. The impacts of emigration on the Mexican economy. MIGRATION TODAY, Vol. 10, no. 2 (1982), p. 17-21. English. DESCR: Economic History and Conditions; Employment; *Mexican Economy; Socioeconomic Factors; Undocumented Workers.

7546 Pedraza Bailey, Silvia. Cubans and Mexicans in the United States: the functions of political and economic migration. CUBAN STUDIES, Vol. 11, no. 2-1 (1981, 1982), p. 70-103. English. DESCR: Cubanos; Immigrants; Political Economy; Political Refugees.

7547 Perez, Lisandro. Comment: Cubans and Mexicans in the United States. CUBAN STUDIES, Vol. 11, no. 2-1 (1981, 1982), p. 99-103. English. DESCR: Cubanos; Social Research.

7548 Reichert, Joshua. Town divided: economic stratification and social relations in a Mexican migrant community. SOCIAL PROBLEMS, Vol. 29, no. 4 (April 1982), p. 411-423. English. DESCR: Mexico; Social Classes.

7549 Stacy, Gerald F. From stranger to neighbor. CHURCH AND SOCIETY, Vol. 72, no. 5 (May, June, 1982), p. 1-71. English. DESCR: Economic History and Conditions; Religion; Undocumented Workers.

7550 Van den Berghe, Pierre L. Book review of: ETHNIC AMERICA, A HISTORY. INTERNATIONAL MIGRATION REVIEW, Vol. 16, no. 4 (Winter 1982), p. 900-902. English. DESCR: Book Reviews; *ETHNIC AMERICA, A HISTORY; Ethnic Groups; History; Sowell, Thomas.

Migration Patterns

7551 Arrastia, Cecilio. The Hispanics in the U.S.A.: drama and challenge. CHURCH AND SOCIETY, Vol. 72, no. 4 (March, April, 1982), p. 31-35. English. DESCR: *Presbyterian Church; Religion.

7552 Austin, Robert F. Comment on "Undocumented migration from Mexico: some geographical questions". ANNALS OF THE ASSOCIATION OF AMERICAN GEOGRAPHERS, Vol. 72, no. 4 (December 1982), p. 559-560. English. DESCR: Jones, Richard C.; *"Undocumented migration from Mexico: some geographical questions".

7553 Estrada, Leobardo F. [Demographic characteristics of Latinos]. CHICANO LAW REVIEW, Vol. 6, (1983), p. 9-16. English. DESCR: *Demography; Internal Migration; LATINOS IN THE LAW [symposium], UCLA, 1982; Los Angeles County, CA; Migration; Spanish Language.

7554 Gaviria, Moises; Stern, Gwen; and Schensul, Stephen L. Sociocultural factors and perinatal health in a Mexican-American community. NATIONAL MEDICAL ASSOCIATION JOURNAL, Vol. 74, no. 10 (October 1982), p. 983-989. English. DESCR: Chicago, IL; *Prenatal Care; Public Health; Socioeconomic Factors.

7555 Howard, David. For "illegals" migration goes both ways. R & D MEXICO, Vol. 2, no. 3-4 (December, January, 1981, 1982), p. 14-17. English. DESCR: Immigration; Migration; NATIONAL SURVEY ON EMIGRATION TO THE NORTHERN BORDER AND THE UNITED STATES; Surveys; *Undocumented Workers.

7556 Jones, Richard C. Reply to Robert Austin's "Comment on 'Undocumented migration from Mexico: some geographical questions'." ANNALS OF THE ASSOCIATION OF AMERICAN GEOGRAPHERS, Vol. 72, no. 4 (December 1982), p. 561-562. English. DESCR: Austin, Robert F.; *"Undocumented migration from Mexico: some geographical questions".

Migration Patterns (cont.)

7557 Jones, Richard C. Undocumented migration from Mexico: some geographical questions. ANNALS OF THE ASSOCIATION OF AMERICAN GEOGRAPHERS, Vol. 72, no. 1 (March 1982), p. 77-87. English. DESCR: Geography; Immigration; Mexico; Undocumented Workers.

7558 Lindemann, Constance and Scott, Wilbur. The fertility related behavior of Mexican American adolescents. JOURNAL OF EARLY ADOLESCENCE, Vol. 2, no. 1 (Spring 1982), p. 31-38. English. DESCR: *Fertility; Youth.

7559 Mabry, Donald J. Book review of: ACROSS THE BORDER: RURAL DEVELOPMENT IN MEXICO AND RECENT MIGRATION TO THE UNITED STATES. INTERNATIONAL MIGRATION REVIEW, Vol. 17, no. 2 (Summer 1983), p. 351. English. DESCR: *ACROSS THE BORDER: RURAL DEVELOPMENT IN MEXICO AND RECENT MIGRATION; Book Reviews; Cross, Harry E.; Migration; Rural Economics; Sandos, James.

7560 Massey, Douglas S. and Schnabel, Kathleen M. Background and characteristics of undocumented Hispanic migrants to the United States: a review of recent research. MIGRATION TODAY, Vol. 11, no. 1 (1983), p. 6-13. English. DESCR: Immigrants; Migration; Socioeconomic Factors; *Undocumented Workers.

7561 Massey, Douglas S. and Schnabel, Kathleen M. Recent trends in Hispanic immigration to the United States. INTERNATIONAL MIGRATION REVIEW, Vol. 17, no. 2 (Summer 1983), p. 212-244. English. DESCR: *Immigration; Population Trends; Rural Urban Migration; Socioeconomic Factors.

7562 Morrison, Thomas K. The relationship of U.S. aid, trade and investment to migration pressures in major sending countries. INTERNATIONAL MIGRATION REVIEW, Vol. 16, no. 1 (Spring 1982), p. 4-26. English. DESCR: Border Region; International Economic Relations; Investments; Mexican Border Industrialization Program; PIDER Project; Rural Economics; Rural Urban Migration; Undocumented Workers; United States-Mexico Relations.

7563 Rivera, Julius and Goodman, Paul Wershub. Clandestine labor circulation: a case on the U.S.-Mexico border. MIGRATION TODAY, Vol. 10, no. 1 (1982), p. 21-26. English. DESCR: Border Patrol; Border Region; Ciudad Juarez, Chihuahua, Mexico; El Paso, TX; Immigration Regulation and Control; Social Classes; Social Mobility; Socioeconomic Factors; *Undocumented Workers.

7564 Schey, Peter A. Supply side immigration theory: analysis of the Simpson-Mazzoli Bill. LA RAZA LAW JOURNAL, Vol. 1, no. 1 (June 1983), p. 53-71. English. DESCR: Amnesty; Immigration; Mazzoli, Romano L.; Refugees; Simpson, Alan K.; *Simpson-Mazzoli Bill; Temporary Worker Program.

7565 Seilhamer, E. Stella and Prewitt-Diaz, Joseph O. The return and circulatory migrant student: a perception of teachers, schools and self. MIGRATION TODAY, Vol. 11, no. 1 (1983), p. 21-23. English. DESCR: Cultural Characteristics; Identity; *Puerto Rican Education; Puerto Ricans.

Migratory Labor
USE: Migrant Labor

Military

7566 Captor, Rich. College and the Navy. CAMINOS, Vol. 4, no. 1-2 (January, February, 1983), p. 26-27. Bilingual. DESCR: *Careers; Reserve Officer Training Corps (ROTC); U.S. Navy.

7567 Garcia, Ignacio M. El Salvador: profile of a nation at war. NUESTRO, Vol. 7, no. 8 (October 1983), p. 26-36. English. DESCR: *El Salvador; Guerrillas; Political History and Conditions; War.

7568 Solon opposes military support for Guatemala. NUESTRO, Vol. 6, no. 5 (June, July, 1982), p. 53. English. DESCR: Garcia, Robert; Government; *Guatemala.

7569 Treviso, Ruben. Strength through dollars. LATINO, Vol. 53, no. 5 (September 1982), p. 28. English.

Military Personnel

7570 Hui, C. Harry. Analysis of the modernity scale: an item response theory approach. JOURNAL OF CROSS-CULTURAL PSYCHOLOGY, Vol. 14, no. 3 (September 1983), p. 259-278. English. DESCR: Comparative Psychology; Overall Modernity Scale (OM).

7571 Hui, C. Harry. Multistrategy approach to cross-cultural research: the case of locus of control. JOURNAL OF CROSS-CULTURAL PSYCHOLOGY, Vol. 14, no. 1 (March 1983), p. 65-83. English. DESCR: Comparative Psychology; *Locus of Control; Psychological Testing.

Military Service

7572 Breiter, Toni. First to fall: "God just chose him to be a Marine". NUESTRO, Vol. 7, no. 9 (November 1983), p. 14-17. English. DESCR: Biography; *Ortega, Alex.

7573 Bunnell, Robert. A conversation with Commodore Diego Hernandez. NUESTRO, Vol. 7, no. 8 (October 1983), p. 15-17. English. DESCR: Caribbean Region; *Hernandez, Diego; U.S. Navy.

7574 Cavazos is nominated army four-star-general. NUESTRO, Vol. 6, no. 1 (January, February, 1982), p. 47. English. DESCR: *Cavazos, Richard E.

7575 Gente. NUESTRO, Vol. 7, no. 2 (March 1983), p. 51. English. DESCR: Artists; Betancourt, Jose L.; *Chicanas; Crime Victims Fund; Federal Government; Juarez, Joe; Saldana, Teresa; Vargas, Alberto; Victims for Victims.

7576 Madrid, Joe and Gonzalez, Magdalena. NALEO - honoring the Hispanic Medal of Honor winners. CAMINOS, Vol. 3, no. 10 (November 1982), p. 22-25. English. DESCR: *Medal of Honor; *National Association of Latino Elected Officials (NALEO).

7577 Opportunities in the military. NUESTRO, Vol. 6, no. 1 (January, February, 1982), p. 29. English. DESCR: Employment.

7578 Paredes, Michael J. The California National Guard. CAMINOS, Vol. 3, no. 3 (March 1982), p. 26-27. Bilingual. DESCR: *California National Guard.

Military Service (cont.)

7579 Ponce, Mary Helen. Recuerdo: the funeral of Daniel Torres, winner of the Medal of Honor. CHISMEARTE, no. 9 (September 1983), p. 35-37. English. **DESCR:** Medal of Honor; *Torres, Daniel.

7580 Tips for making the right moves in today's job markets. HISPANIC BUSINESS, Vol. 4, no. 8 (August 1983), p. 11+. English. **DESCR:** American G.I. Forum; *Careers; Employment; Management.

7581 Weinberger, Caspar W. A heritage of valor - Hispanics in America's defense: remarks... at the recent unveiling of paintings of Hispanic heroes at the Pentagon. NUESTRO, Vol. 7, no. 9 (November 1983), p. 18. English. **DESCR:** Del Valle, Pedro A.; Gabaldon, Guy; Lopez, Jose; Paintings; Rivero, Horacio.

7582 "With pride and courage". NUESTRO, Vol. 7, no. 8 (October 1983), p. 9. English. **DESCR:** *U.S. Postal Service; *Veterans.

Millan, Aida

7583 What bilingual education means to the nation. NUESTRO, Vol. 7, no. 2 (March 1983), p. 52-53. English. **DESCR:** *Bilingual Bicultural Education; Education; Nguyen, Anh Tuan; Rodriguez, Axel.

Millan, Gonzalo

7584 Concha, Jaime. Exilio, conciencia: coda sobre la poesia de Millan. MAIZE, Vol. 5, no. 1-2 (Fall, Winter, 1981, 1982), p. 7-15. Spanish. **DESCR:** Chile; Jesuits; Literary Criticism; Literary History; Poetry; Political Refugees.

Miller Brewing Company

7585 Boycott threat leads to negociation table. NUESTRO, Vol. 6, no. 8 (October 1982), p. 48. English. **DESCR:** *Affirmative Action; *Boycotts.

7586 Bunnell, Robert. Bravisimo! NUESTRO, Vol. 7, no. 9 (November 1983), p. 21-25. English. **DESCR:** Anacani; Coca-Cola Company; Palomino, Carlos; Pena, Samm; Performing Arts; *Television.

7587 Communications/marketing. HISPANIC BUSINESS, Vol. 5, no. 9 (September 1983), p. 26. English. **DESCR:** Aguirre, Horacio; Business Enterprises; Consumers; DIARIO DE LAS AMERICAS; La Ventana; *Marketing; SURVEY OF PROMOTIONAL PRACTICES.

7588 Miller Brewing is airing bilingual commercial. NUESTRO, Vol. 7, no. 9 (November 1983), p. 36. English. **DESCR:** Advertising; Bilingualism; Television.

7589 Que pasa? NUESTRO, Vol. 7, no. 7 (September 1983), p. 9. English. **DESCR:** Alcoholism; Anti-Defamation League of B'nai B'rith; *Drug Abuse; Drug Programs; Employment; Kiwanis International; Racism; Sports.

Miller, Robert

7590 Martinez, Elizabeth. The "Kiko" Martinez case: a sign of our times. CRIME AND SOCIAL JUSTICE, Vol. 17, (Summer 1982), p. 92-95. English. **DESCR:** Administration of Justice; Martinez Defense Committee; Martinez, Francisco; *Racism.

Miller, Tom

7591 De Leon, Arnoldo. Book review of: ON THE BORDER: PORTRAITS OF AMERICA'S SOUTHWESTERN FRONTIER. SOUTHWESTERN HISTORICAL QUARTERLY, Vol. 86, no. 2 (1982), p. 367-368. English. **DESCR:** Book Reviews; History; Mexico; *ON THE BORDER: PORTRAITS OF AMERICA'S SOUTHWESTERN FRONTIER; Texas.

7592 Schmidt, Dorothy. Book review of: ON THE BORDER: PORTRAITS OF AMERICA'S SOUTHWESTERN FRONTIER. WESTERN AMERICAN LITERATURE, Vol. 17, no. 1 (Spring 1982), p. 74. English. **DESCR:** Book Reviews; *ON THE BORDER: PORTRAITS OF AMERICA'S SOUTHWESTERN FRONTIER; Photography.

Mindel, Charles H.

7593 Zaks, Vivian Calderon. Book review of: ETHNIC FAMILIES IN AMERICA: PATTERNS AND VARIATIONS. HISPANIC JOURNAL OF BEHAVIORAL SCIENCES, Vol. 4, no. 1 (March 1982), p. 122-128. English. **DESCR:** Book Reviews; *ETHNIC FAMILIES IN AMERICA: PATTERNS AND VARIATIONS; Habenstein, Robert W.

Mine, Mill and Smelter Workers Union

7594 Torres, Lorenzo. Short history of Chicano workers. SOUTHWEST ECONOMY AND SOCIETY, Vol. 3, no. 2 (Winter 1977, 1978), p. 4-17. English. **DESCR:** *Labor Unions; Marxism; Mining Industry; Racism.

Mining Industry

7595 Byrkit, James W. Walter Douglas and labor struggles in early 20th century Arizona. SOUTHWEST ECONOMY AND SOCIETY, Vol. 1, no. 1 (Spring 1976), p. 14-27. English. **DESCR:** Arizona; *Biography; Bisbee, AZ; Clifton Morenci Strike, June 1903; Copper Queen Mining Co., Bisbee, AZ; *Douglas, Walter; International Workers of the World (IWW); Labor Unions; Strikes and Lockouts.

7596 Casillas, Mike. The Cananea strike of 1906. SOUTHWEST ECONOMY AND SOCIETY, Vol. 3, no. 2 (Winter 1977, 1978), p. 18-32. English. **DESCR:** Arizona; *Cananea Mining Strike of 1906; Cananea, Sonora, Mexico; History; Partido Liberal Mexicano (PLM); *Strikes and Lockouts.

7597 Rubenstein, Harry R. The great Gallup Coal strike of 1933. SOUTHWEST ECONOMY AND SOCIETY, Vol. 3, no. 2 (Winter 1977, 1978), p. 34-53. English. **DESCR:** *Gallup Coal Strike of 1933; Labor Unions; National Miner's Union (NMU); New Mexico; *Strikes and Lockouts; United Mineworkers of America (UMWA).

7598 Torres, Lorenzo. Short history of Chicano workers. SOUTHWEST ECONOMY AND SOCIETY, Vol. 3, no. 2 (Winter 1977, 1978), p. 4-17. English. **DESCR:** *Labor Unions; Marxism; *Mine, Mill and Smelter Workers Union; Racism.

7599 Whisler, Kirk. Martha Cornejo Rottenberg: on opportunities & advancement. CAMINOS, Vol. 4, no. 1-2 (January, February, 1983), p. 17-18,71+. English. **DESCR:** Careers; *Cornejo Rottenberg, Martha; Electronics Industry; TRW Defense Systems Group.

Minneapolis, MN

7600 Firm honors Latino workers. NUESTRO, Vol. 6, no. 5 (June, July, 1982), p. 11-12. English. **DESCR:** *Acosta, Juan; Honeywell, Inc.; Mural Art.

Minnesota

7601 Dienhart, Paul. Minnesota support groups help Latinos through medical school. NUESTRO, Vol. 6, no. 6 (August 1982), p. 39-40. English. **DESCR:** Health Education; Latin Americans; Medical Education; Medical Students; Public Health; *University of Minnesota.

Minnesota Multiphasic Personality Inventory (MMPI)

7602 Dolan, Michael. Personality differences among Black, white, and Hispanic-American male heroin addicts on MMPI content scales. JOURNAL OF CLINICAL PSYCHOLOGY, Vol. 39, no. 5 (September 1983), p. 807-813. English. **DESCR:** Blacks; Drug Addicts; *Heroin Addicts; Personality.

7603 Padilla, Eligio R.; Olmedo, Esteban L.; and Loya, Fred. Acculturation and the MMPI performance of Chicano and Anglo college students. HISPANIC JOURNAL OF BEHAVIORAL SCIENCES, Vol. 4, no. 4 (December 1982), p. 451-466. English. **DESCR:** *Acculturation; Students.

7604 Zamudio, Anthony; Padilla, Amado M.; and Comrey, Andrew L. Personality structure of Mexican Americans using the Comrey Personality Scales. JOURNAL OF PERSONALITY ASSESSMENT, Vol. 47, no. 1 (February 1983), p. 100-106. English. **DESCR:** Colleges and Universities; Comrey Personality Scales (CPS); *Personality; Psychological Testing; Students.

Minorities
USE: Ethnic Groups

Minority Bank Deposit Program (MBDP)

7605 Hispanic owned banks. HISPANIC BUSINESS, Vol. 5, no. 9 (September 1983), p. 13. English. **DESCR:** *Banking Industry; Finance; International Bank of Commerce (IBOC).

7606 The leading US Hispanic-owned minority banks according to assets. HISPANIC BUSINESS, Vol. 4, no. 9 (September 1982), p. 14. English. **DESCR:** *Banking Industry; Business Enterprises.

Minority Bank Development Program (MBDP)

7607 Foreign trade. HISPANIC BUSINESS, Vol. 5, no. 4 (April 1983), p. 22. English. **DESCR:** Banking Industry; Brazil; *Electronics Industry; Export Trade; *Foreign Trade; Ibero-American Chamber of Commerce; Miami, FL; Minority Export Development Consultants Program (MEDC); Peace Corps; Puerto Rico.

Minority Business Development Agency (MBDA)

7608 Administration unveils minority business enterprise initiative. HISPANIC BUSINESS, Vol. 4, no. 10 (October 1982), p. 18. English. **DESCR:** *Business Enterprises.

7609 Foreign trade. HISPANIC BUSINESS, Vol. 5, no. 3 (March 1983), p. 23. English. **DESCR:** Caribbean Region; Export Trade; *Foreign Trade.

7610 Foreign trade. HISPANIC BUSINESS, Vol. 5,

no. 5 (May 1983), p. 32. English. **DESCR:** Caribbean Region; Export Trade; *Foreign Trade; Latin America; Panama.

7611 Houstonite builds successful business: home-started business exceeds millions in foreign trade sales. NATIONAL HISPANIC JOURNAL, Vol. 1, no. 4 (Spring 1983), p. 7. English. **DESCR:** Business; *Business Enterprises; Businesspeople; Cavazos, Roy; *National Economic Development Association (NEDA); U.S. Small Business Administration.

7612 Math-based careers. HISPANIC BUSINESS, Vol. 4, no. 10 (October 1982), p. 20. English. **DESCR:** *Careers; Educational Opportunities; Engineering as a Profession; Financial Aid; National Action Council for Minorities in Engineering (NACME); National Association of Independent Schools (NAIS).

7613 NALEO audits the Feds. HISPANIC BUSINESS, Vol. 5, no. 10 (October 1983), p. 16. English. **DESCR:** Business Enterprises; Federal Government; *Government Contracts; *National Association of Latino Elected Officials (NALEO); U.S. Department of Defense (DOD); U.S. Department of Health and Human Services.

7614 Padilla, Steve. You've come a long way, baby. Or have you? NUESTRO, Vol. 7, no. 6 (August 1983), p. 38-41. English. **DESCR:** *Business Enterprises; Chicanas; National Alliance of Homebased Businesswomen.

7615 SBA update. HISPANIC BUSINESS, Vol. 5, no. 3 (March 1983), p. 18. English. **DESCR:** High Technology Industries; *Small Business; Small Business Innovation Research Act; Technology.

Minority Engineering Education Center, University of California, Los Angeles

7616 Math-based careers. HISPANIC BUSINESS, Vol. 5, no. 10 (October 1983), p. 28. English. **DESCR:** *Careers; Carnation Company; Chicanas; Education; Engineering as a Profession; Hispanic Policy Development Project; Science as a Profession; University of California, Los Angeles (UCLA).

7617 Minority students given assistance. NUESTRO, Vol. 7, no. 2 (March 1983), p. 10. English. **DESCR:** Education; Engineering as a Profession; University of California, Los Angeles (UCLA).

Minority Enterprise Small Business Investment Corporation (MESBIC)

7618 Garcia, Art R. Star Adair Insulation Inc. spurts to new growth. HISPANIC BUSINESS, Vol. 4, no. 2 (February 1982), p. 18-19+. English. **DESCR:** Biography; Business Enterprises; Businesspeople; *Cisneros, Ignacio; *Star-Adair Insulation, Inc.

Minority Export Development Consultants Program (MEDC)

7619 Foreign trade. HISPANIC BUSINESS, Vol. 5, no. 4 (April 1983), p. 22. English. **DESCR:** Banking Industry; Brazil; *Electronics Industry; Export Trade; *Foreign Trade; Ibero-American Chamber of Commerce; Miami, FL; Minority Bank Development Program (MBDP); Peace Corps; Puerto Rico.

Minority Introduction to Engineering (MITE)

7620 Hughes invests in the future. HISPANIC BUSINESS, Vol. 4, no. 11 (November 1982), p. 8-9,26. English. DESCR: Careers; *Educational Opportunities; *Engineering as a Profession; University of California, Los Angeles (UCLA).

Minority Literature
USE: Third World Literature (U.S.)

Minority Telecommunications Ownership Act of 1983 (HR 2331)

7621 Rivera, Henry M. Hispanics need to effectively translate potential into political and economic clout. TELEVISION/RADIO AGE, Vol. 31, no. 4 (September 12, 1983), p. 117-118. English. DESCR: Equal Employment Opportunity Commission (EEOC); Federal Communications Commission (FCC); *Radio.

Miranda v. INS

7622 Immigration and nationality symposium. SAN DIEGO LAW REVIEW, Vol. 20, no. 1 (December 1982, 1983), p. 1-231. English. DESCR: Akbarian v. INS; Deportation; Employment; Immigration and Nationality Act (INA); *Immigration Regulation and Control; Simpson-Mazzoli Bill; Undocumented Workers.

Mirande, Alfredo

7623 Baca Zinn, Maxine. Book review of: LA CHICANA: THE MEXICAN AMERICAN WOMAN. SIGNS: JOURNAL OF WOMEN IN CULTURE AND SOCIETY, Vol. 8, no. 2 (Winter 1982), p. 259-272. English. DESCR: Book Reviews; Chicanas; Enriquez, Evangelina; *LA CHICANA: THE MEXICAN AMERICAN WOMAN; Literature Reviews; Social Science.

7624 Hunsaker, Alan. Book review of: ALMA ABIERTA: PINTO POETRY, MAYO DE CRC. HISPANIC JOURNAL OF BEHAVIORAL SCIENCES, Vol. 5, no. 1 (March 1983), p. 132-134. English. DESCR: *ALMA ABIERTA: PINTO POETRY; Book Reviews.

7625 Palacios, Maria. Book review of: LA CHICANA: THE MEXICAN AMERICAN WOMAN. HISPANIC JOURNAL OF BEHAVIORAL SCIENCES, Vol. 4, no. 2 (June 1982), p. 272-275. English. DESCR: Book Reviews; Enriquez, Evangelina; *LA CHICANA: THE MEXICAN AMERICAN WOMAN.

7626 Salgado de Snyder, Nelly. Book review of: LA CHICANA: THE MEXICAN AMERICAN WOMAN. HISPANIC JOURNAL OF BEHAVIORAL SCIENCES, Vol. 4, no. 2 (June 1982), p. 268-272. English. DESCR: Book Reviews; Enriquez, Evangelina; *LA CHICANA: THE MEXICAN AMERICAN WOMAN.

7627 Stoller, Marianne L. Book review of: LA CHICANA: THE MEXICAN AMERICAN WOMAN. SOCIAL SCIENCE JOURNAL, Vol. 19, no. 2 (April 1982), p. 134-136. English. DESCR: Book Reviews; Chicanas; Enriquez, Evangelina; *LA CHICANA: THE MEXICAN AMERICAN WOMAN.

7628 Swink, Sue. Book review of: LA CHICANA: THE MEXICAN AMERICAN WOMAN. HISPANIC JOURNAL OF BEHAVIORAL SCIENCES, Vol. 4, no. 2 (June 1982), p. 275-277. English. DESCR: Book Reviews; Enriquez, Evangelina; *LA CHICANA: THE MEXICAN AMERICAN WOMAN.

Miscegenation
USE: Intermarriage

Miss Black Velvet Latina

7629 Communications/marketing. HISPANIC BUSINESS, Vol. 4, no. 1 (January 1982), p. 13. English. DESCR: Beauty Contests; *Biographical Notes; Consumers; Hispanic Caucus; *Marketing; Montemayor, Carlos R.; Philip Morris, Inc.

7630 Heublein's Miss Black Velvet II. HISPANIC BUSINESS, Vol. 4, no. 2 (February 1982), p. 12. English. DESCR: Advertising; Beauty Contests; Consumers; Heublein, Inc.; *Marketing.

7631 Rhonda Ramirez is Miss Black Velvet Latina. HISPANIC BUSINESS, Vol. 5, no. 3 (March 1983), p. 12-13. English. DESCR: *Beauty Contests; *Celaya, Mona; Marketing.

MISSING [film]

7632 Entertainment = diversion. CAMINOS, Vol. 3, no. 3 (March 1982), p. 55-56. Bilingual. DESCR: Aztlan Writing Contest; CORAZON DE AZTLAN; Films; Literary Contests; *Recreation; THE BORDER [film]; Young, Robert.

Mission District, San Francisco, CA

7633 Heaney, Thomas W. "Hanging on" or "gaining ground": educating marginal adults. NEW DIRECTIONS FOR CONTINUING EDUCATION, no. 20 (December 1983), p. 53-63. English. DESCR: *Adult Education; Chicago, IL; City Colleges, Chicago, IL; General Education Diploma (GED); Gomez, Robert; Instituto del Progreso Latino; Project Literacy, San Francisco, CA; St. Mary's Community Educational Center; *Universidad Popular, Chicago, IL.

Missions

7634 Camino real. LATINO, Vol. 53, no. 6 (October 1982), p. 19. English.

7635 Chavez, John A. Aztlan, Cibola, and frontier New Spain. CAMPO LIBRE, Vol. 1, no. 2 (Summer 1981), p. 193-211. English. DESCR: *Aztlan; *Explorations; Folklore; History; Mestizaje; Mexico; Native Americans; Southwest United States.

Mitos

7636 Melendez, Theresa. Coyote: towards a definition of a concept. AZTLAN, Vol. 13, no. 1-2 (Spring, Fall, 1982), p. 295-307. English. DESCR: *Coyote [folkloric symbol]; Folklore; Leyendas.

Mittelback, Frank G.

7637 Schoen, Robert and Cohen, Lawrence E. Theory and method in the study of ethnic endogamy among Mexican-American grooms - reply. AMERICAN JOURNAL OF SOCIOLOGY, Vol. 87, no. 4 (January 1982), p. 939-942. English. DESCR: Assimilation; ETHNIC ENDOGAMY: THE CASE OF THE MEXICAN-AMERICANS; Intermarriage; Moore, Joan W.; *Research Methodology.

Miyares, Marcelino

7638 People. HISPANIC BUSINESS, Vol. 5, no. 4
(April 1983), p. 9. English. **DESCR:**
Alvarado, Linda M.; *Biographical Notes;
Businesspeople; Castillo, Irenemaree;
Castillo, Sylvia; Del Junco, Tirso;
Gutierrez, Jose Roberto; Juarez, Joe; Mata,
Bill; Montanez Davis, Grace; Montoya, Velma;
Pineda, Pat; Siberio, Julio; Thompson, Edith
Lopez.

Model Housing
USE: Urban Housing

Models
USE: Fashion

Modotti, Tina

7639 Newman, Michael. The ribbon around the bomb.
ART IN AMERICA, Vol. 71, (April 1983), p.
160-169. English. **DESCR:** *Artists; Kahlo,
Frida; Paintings.

Mohr, Eugene V.

7640 Turner, Faythe. Book review of: THE
NUYORICAN EXPERIENCE: LITERATURE OF THE
PUERTO RICAN MINORITY. MELUS: MULTI-ETHNIC
LITERATURE OF THE UNITED STATES, Vol. 10,
no. 2 (Summer 1983), p. 85-88. English.
DESCR: *Puerto Rican Literature; THE
NUYORICAN EXPERIENCE: LITERATURE OF THE
PUERTO RICAN MINORITY.

Mojados
USE: Undocumented Workers

LOS MOJADOS: THE WETBACK STORY

7641 Garcia, Mario T. Book review of: LOS
MOJADOS: THE WETBACK STORY. JOURNAL OF
ETHNIC STUDIES, Vol. 1, no. 1 (Spring 1973),
p. 66-68. English. **DESCR:** Book Reviews;
Immigrant Labor; Mexico; Samora, Julian;
Southwest United States; Undocumented
Workers; United States.

Molina, Alberto

7642 Garcia, Ignacio M. Latino-ization of the
Mormon church. NUESTRO, Vol. 7, no. 2 (March
1983), p. 20-24+. English. **DESCR:** *Church of
Jesus Christ of Latter-Day Saints (Mormons);
Religion.

Molina, Gloria

7643 Diaz, Katherine A. "And this year's winners
are...". CAMINOS, Vol. 4, no. 1-2 (January,
February, 1983), p. 39-54,74+. English.
DESCR: *Awards; Castro, Tony; Elizalde,
Hector; Flores, Tom; Martinez, Esperanza;
Mendizabal, Maritza; Moya, Connie;
Placentia, Joe; Quesada, Leticia; Rios,
David N.; Ybarra, Lea; Zapata, Carmen.

7644 People. HISPANIC BUSINESS, Vol. 5, no. 5
(May 1983), p. 8. English. **DESCR:**
Biographical Notes; *Businesspeople; Duron,
Armando; Espinoza, Peter; Flores, Juan;
Martinez, Vilma Socorro; Moreno, Samuel;
Pantin, Leslie, Sr.; Quezada, Sylvia;
Quinones, Sergio.

Monahan, John

7645 Hunsaker, Alan. Book review of: PSYCHOLOGY
AND COMMUNITY CHANGE; SOCIAL AND
PSYCHOLOGICAL RESEARCH IN COMMUNITY SETTING;
COMMUNITY PSYCHOLOGY: THEORETICAL AND
EMPIRICAL APPROACHES. HISPANIC JOURNAL OF
BEHAVIORAL SCIENCES, Vol. 5, no. 1 (March
1983), p. 121-124. English. **DESCR:** Book
Reviews; *COMMUNITY PSYCHOLOGY: THEORETICAL
AND EMPIRICAL APPROACHES; Gibbs, Margaret
S.; Heller, Kenneth; Kelly, James G.;
Lachenmeyer, Juliana Rasic; Munoz, Ricardo
F.; *PSYCHOLOGY AND COMMUNITY CHANGE; Sigal,
Janet; Snowden, Lonnie R.; *SOCIAL AND
PSYCHOLOGICAL RESEARCH IN COMMUNITY
SETTINGS.

Mondale, Walter

7646 Presidential election 1984. NUESTRO, Vol. 7,
no. 7 (September 1983), p. 14-19. English.
DESCR: Anderson, John; Askew, Reubin;
Cranston, Alan; Elected Officials;
*Elections; Fernandez, Ben; Glenn, John;
Hart, Gary; Hispanic Force '84; Hollings,
Ernest "Fritz"; Political Parties and
Organizations; Reagan, Ronald.

Montage

7647 Lopez, Yolanda M. [Untitled montage from the
SERIE GUADALUPE]. MAIZE, Vol. 1, no. 4
(Summer 1978), p. Ft cover. English. **DESCR:**
*Virgin of Guadalupe.

7648 Lopez, Yolanda M. [Untitled montage from the
SERIE GUADALUPE]. MAIZE, Vol. 1, no. 4
(Summer 1978), p. 55-59. English. **DESCR:**
Virgin of Guadalupe.

Montalban, Ricardo

7649 Entertainment = diversion. CAMINOS, Vol. 3,
no. 2 (February 1982), p. 40-41. English.
DESCR: Awards; CHECKING IT OUT; Club Hogar
Latino; Dance; Films; Flamenco; Marley, Bob;
ON GOLDEN POND; *Recreation; Television.

7650 Gonzalez, Magdalena. Ole II; BFA honors the
40's. CAMINOS, Vol. 3, no. 7 (July, August,
1982), p. 28-29. Bilingual. **DESCR:** Artists;
Awards; *Bilingual Foundation of the Arts;
Romero, Cesar.

7651 Gonzalez, Magdalena. Recognizing Hispanic
achievements in entertainment - U.S. and
Mexico. CAMINOS, Vol. 3, no. 7 (July,
August, 1982), p. 18-24. Bilingual. **DESCR:**
Allende, Fernando; Artists; Awards; Bonilla
Giannini, Roxanna; Eynoso, David; Felix,
Maria; Films; Gallego, Gina; *Golden Eagle
Awards; Hoyos, Rodolfo; Lamas, Lorenzo;
Lopez, Conchita; Lopez, Lisa; Nosotros [film
production company]; Quintero, Jose; Rowe,
Arthur; Television; Torres, Liz.

7652 Lenti, Paul. Special honor goes to
Montalban. NUESTRO, Vol. 7, no. 2 (March
1983), p. 10-11. English. **DESCR:** Artists;
Maria Teresa Montoya Award; Performing Arts.

Montanez Davis, Grace

7653 Fuentes, Diana. Chicana perspectives: Grace
Montanez Davis. COMADRE, no. 1 (Summer
1977), p. 39-41. English. **DESCR:** *Biography.

7654 People. HISPANIC BUSINESS, Vol. 5, no. 4
(April 1983), p. 9. English. **DESCR:**
Alvarado, Linda M.; *Biographical Notes;
Businesspeople; Castillo, Irenemaree;
Castillo, Sylvia; Del Junco, Tirso;
Gutierrez, Jose Roberto; Juarez, Joe; Mata,
Bill; Miyares, Marcelino; Montoya, Velma;
Pineda, Pat; Siberio, Julio; Thompson, Edith
Lopez.

Montano, Gilbert

7655 People. HISPANIC BUSINESS, Vol. 5, no. 10
(October 1983), p. 10. English. DESCR:
Anaya, Toney; Arriola, Elvia Rosales;
Babbitt, Bruce; Burgos, Tony; Bush, George;
*Businesspeople; Cisneros, Henry, Mayor of
San Antonio, TX; Cruz, Jose; Kennedy, Edward
M.; Reagan, Ronald; White, Mark.

Montejano, David

7656 Bruce Novoa, Juan. Round table on Chicano
literature. JOURNAL OF ETHNIC STUDIES, Vol.
3, no. 1 (Spring 1975), p. 99-103. English.
DESCR: *Bruce Novoa, Juan; *Literature;
Morton, Carlos; Ortego y Gasca, Felipe de;
Teatro.

Montemayor, Carlos R.

7657 Communications/marketing. HISPANIC BUSINESS,
Vol. 4, no. 1 (January 1982), p. 13.
English. DESCR: Beauty Contests;
*Biographical Notes; Consumers; Hispanic
Caucus; *Marketing; Miss Black Velvet
Latina; Philip Morris, Inc.

7658 Communications/marketing. HISPANIC BUSINESS,
Vol. 5, no. 6 (June 1983), p. 16. English.
DESCR: *Advertising Agencies; *Broadcast
Media; Castillo & Castillo Public Relations
and Advertising; Castillo, Cid; Castillo,
Patricia; Latino Consortium, Los Angeles,
CA; Montemayor y Asociados, Inc.; Zubi Inc.,
Miami, FL.

Montemayor y Asociados, Inc.

7659 Communications/marketing. HISPANIC BUSINESS,
Vol. 5, no. 6 (June 1983), p. 16. English.
DESCR: *Advertising Agencies; *Broadcast
Media; Castillo & Castillo Public Relations
and Advertising; Castillo, Cid; Castillo,
Patricia; Latino Consortium, Los Angeles,
CA; Montemayor, Carlos R.; Zubi Inc., Miami,
FL.

Monterey, CA

7660 Day, Mark R. Hispanics 'want more bishops,
input in church'. NATIONAL CATHOLIC
REPORTER, Vol. 18, (March 12, 1982), p. 1.
English. DESCR: *Catholic Church; Clergy;
Cursillo Movement; Religion.

Montero, Martha

7661 Walia, Adorna. Book review of: BILINGUAL
EDUCATION TEACHER HANDBOOK: LANGUAGE ISSUES
IN MULTICULTURAL SETTINGS. vol. II.
BILINGUAL JOURNAL, Vol. 6, no. 1 (Fall
1982), p. 29-30. English. DESCR: Bilingual
Bicultural Education; *BILINGUAL EDUCATION
TEACHER HANDBOOK: LANGUAGE ISSUES IN
MULTICULTURAL SETTINGS, VOL II; Book
Reviews; Cultural Pluralism; Language
Assessment.

Montoya, Al

7662 Whisler, Kirk. There are 1 1/2 million
Hispanics in labor unions. CAMINOS, Vol. 3,
no. 7 (July, August, 1982), p. 40. English.
DESCR: Labor; *Labor Council for Latin
American Advancement; *Labor Unions.

Montoya, David

7663 Whisler, Kirk. IMAGE and affirmative action.
CAMINOS, Vol. 3, no. 8 (September 1982), p.
34-36. Bilingual. DESCR: *Affirmative
Action; *National Image, Inc.

Montoya, Jose E.

7664 Solis, Arnaldo. El oro del barrio: maestro
Montoya. CALMECAC, Vol. 3, (Spring 1982),
p. 25+. Bilingual. DESCR: Artists;
*Biography.

Montoya, Liberato

7665 Sagel, Jaime. Patriarch of San Juan Pueblo.
NUESTRO, Vol. 6, no. 8 (October 1982), p.
52-53. English. DESCR: *Biography; San Juan
Pueblo, NM.

Montoya, Velma

7666 People. HISPANIC BUSINESS, Vol. 5, no. 1
(January 1983), p. 7. English. DESCR:
Appointed Officials; *Biographical Notes;
*Businesspeople; Elizalde, Hector; Mackey y
Salazar, C.; Madrid, Carlos; Nunez, Carlos;
Perea, Stanley; Rodriguez, Rita; Valdes,
Martha.

7667 People. HISPANIC BUSINESS, Vol. 5, no. 4
(April 1983), p. 9. English. DESCR:
Alvarado, Linda M.; *Biographical Notes;
Businesspeople; Castillo, Irenemaree;
Castillo, Sylvia; Del Junco, Tirso;
Gutierrez, Jose Roberto; Juarez, Joe; Mata,
Bill; Miyares, Marcelino; Montanez Davis,
Grace; Pineda, Pat; Siberio, Julio;
Thompson, Edith Lopez.

Moore, Joan W.

7668 Schoen, Robert and Cohen, Lawrence E. Theory
and method in the study of ethnic endogamy
among Mexican-American grooms - reply.
AMERICAN JOURNAL OF SOCIOLOGY, Vol. 87, no.
4 (January 1982), p. 939-942. English.
DESCR: Assimilation; ETHNIC ENDOGAMY: THE
CASE OF THE MEXICAN-AMERICANS;
Intermarriage; Mittelback, Frank G.;
*Research Methodology.

Mora, Carl J.

7669 Book review of: MEXICAN CINEMA: REFLECTIONS
OF A SOCIETY. CHOICE, Vol. 20, no. 2
(October 1982), p. 276. English. DESCR: Book
Reviews; *MEXICAN CINEMA: REFLECTIONS OF A
SOCIETY.

7670 Markiewicz, Dana. Book review of: MEXICAN
CINEMA: REFLECTIONS OF SOCIETY, 1896-1980.
HISPANIC JOURNAL OF BEHAVIORAL SCIENCES,
Vol. 5, no. 4 (December 1983), p. 491-494.
English. DESCR: Book Reviews; Films;
*MEXICAN CINEMA: REFLECTIONS OF A SOCIETY.

Mora, Magdalena

7671 Baca Zinn, Maxine. Book review of: MEXICAN
WOMEN IN THE UNITED STATES: STRUGGLES PAST
AND PRESENT. SIGNS: JOURNAL OF WOMEN IN
CULTURE AND SOCIETY, Vol. 8, no. 2 (Winter
1982), p. 259-272. English. DESCR: Book
Reviews; Chicanas; Del Castillo, Adelaida
R.; Literature Reviews; *MEXICAN WOMEN IN
THE UNITED STATES: STRUGGLES PAST AND
PRESENT; Social Science.

7672 Hartman, Harriet. Book review of: MEXICAN
WOMEN IN THE UNITED STATES: STRUGGLES PAST
AND PRESENT. INTERNATIONAL MIGRATION REVIEW,
Vol. 16, no. 1 (Spring 1982), p. 228-229.
English. DESCR: Book Reviews; Chicanas; Del
Castillo, Adelaida R.; *MEXICAN WOMEN IN THE
UNITED STATES: STRUGGLES PAST AND PRESENT;
Sexism.

Morales, Alejandro

7673 Alurista and Monleon, Jose. Mesa redonda. MAIZE, Vol. 4, no. 3-4 (Spring, Summer, 1981), p. 6-23. English. **DESCR:** Alurista; Anaya, Rudolfo A.; Herrera Sobek, Maria; Identity; Literature; *Mythology; Viramontes, Helen.

7674 Gonzales-Berry, Erlinda. Doctor, writer, warrior chief. BILINGUAL REVIEW, Vol. 9, no. 3 (September, December, 1982), p. 276-279. English. **DESCR:** LA VERDAD SIN VOZ.

7675 Monleon, Jose. Dos novelas de Alejandro Morales. MAIZE, Vol. 4, no. 1-2 (Fall, Winter, 1980, 1981), p. 6-8. Spanish. **DESCR:** *CARAS VIEJAS Y VINO NUEVO; *LA VERDAD SIN VOZ; Literary Criticism.

7676 Monleon, Jose and Morales, Alejandro. Entrevista con Alejandro Morales. MAIZE, Vol. 4, no. 1-2 (Fall, Winter, 1980, 1981), p. 9-20. Spanish. **DESCR:** *Literature.

7677 Ramirez, Arthur. Book review of: OLD FACES AND NEW WINE. REVISTA CHICANO-RIQUENA, Vol. 10, no. 4 (Fall 1982), p. 65-67. English. **DESCR:** Book Reviews; CARAS VIEJAS Y VINO NUEVO; *OLD FACES AND NEW WINE.

Morales, Esai

7678 De la Rosa, Carlos. Esai Morales: a new and exciting Latino talent on the rise. LATINA, Vol. 1, no. 3 (1983), p. 19. English. **DESCR:** *BAD BOYS; Biography; Film Reviews.

Morales, Hilda

7679 Kappel, Mark. A new career direction for Hilda Morales. NUESTRO, Vol. 7, no. 1 (January, February, 1983), p. 24-27. English. **DESCR:** *Dance; Performing Arts.

Morales, Rosa

7680 Breiter, Toni. An interview with some experts. AGENDA, Vol. 11, no. 3 (May, June, 1981), p. 48-52. English. **DESCR:** Guernica, Antonio; Gutierrez, Felix; *Mass Media; Schement, Jorge Reina; Valenzuela, Nicholas.

Morales-Deeny, Carmen A.

7681 Tomayo, Maria. Book review of: CUNDE AMORES. NUESTRO, Vol. 7, no. 2 (March 1983), p. 57-59. Bilingual. **DESCR:** Book Reviews; *CUNDE AMORES.

Moreira, Airto

7682 Gonzalez, Johnny. Flora and Airto; making music happen. CAMINOS, Vol. 3, no. 8 (September 1982), p. 10-13,50. Bilingual. **DESCR:** Artists; *Musicians; Purim, Flora.

Morelos, Jose Maria

7683 Alvarez, Amando. Jose Maria Morelos. LATINO, Vol. 54, no. 5 (August, September, 1983), p. 24-25. Spanish. **DESCR:** Biography.

7684 La lucha por la independencia. LATINO, Vol. 54, no. 6 (October 1983), p. 16-17. Spanish. **DESCR:** Biography; *History.

Moreno, Mario "Cantinflas"

7685 Mejias-Rentas, Antonio. Cantinflas give D.C. tribute. NUESTRO, Vol. 7, no. 5 (June, July, 1983), p. 11-12. English. **DESCR:** Artists; Films.

7686 Moreno, Mario "Cantinflas". Ne dejen de reir. LATINO, Vol. 54, no. 4 (May, June, 1983), p. 21. English. **DESCR:** Artists; Humor.

7687 Moreno, Mario "Cantinflas". Observations on Mexico today. CAMINOS, Vol. 3, no. 10 (November 1982), p. 20,45. Bilingual. **DESCR:** Dieciseis de Septiembre; *Holidays; Mexico.

7688 Vidal, Jose. Cantinflas: Mario Moreno. CAMINOS, Vol. 3, no. 7 (July, August, 1982), p. 7-9. Bilingual. **DESCR:** Artists; Mexico.

Moreno, Paul

7689 Hamner, Richard. Hispanic update: border governors tackle U.S.-Mexico relations: much ado: but nothing on immigration. NATIONAL HISPANIC JOURNAL, Vol. 1, no. 2 (Winter 1982), p. 4-5. English. **DESCR:** Babbitt, Bruce; Border Region; Brown, Edmund G., Jr., Governor of California; *Clements, Bill; Immigration; Immigration Regulation and Control; *United States-Mexico Relations.

Moreno, Rita

7690 Diaz, Katherine A. The model of reflection: Rita Moreno. CAMINOS, Vol. 4, no. 3 (March 1983), p. 18-21. Bilingual. **DESCR:** Artists; Television.

7691 Gonzalez, Alicia. Women for success. CAMINOS, Vol. 3, no. 6 (June 1982), p. 42-43. Bilingual. **DESCR:** *Chicanas; *Hispanic Women's Council; Organizations; Saavedra, Denise; Terrazas, Carmen.

7692 Our 1982 Latino awards. NUESTRO, Vol. 7, no. 1 (January, February, 1983), p. 44-46. English. **DESCR:** Awards; Escalante, Jaime; Gallegos, Gina; Grace, J. Peter; Immigration and Naturalization Service (INS); Knight, Bobby; Lamas, Fernando; *Latino Awards; Luce, Claire Boothe; National Press Foundation; Rodriguez Hernandez, Andres; Simpson-Mazzoli Bill; Smith, Raymond; Valeri, Michele; Voting Rights Act.

7693 Rita Moreno: Hispanic woman of the year. LATINO, Vol. 53, no. 3 (May 1982), p. 9. English. **DESCR:** Chicanas.

Moreno, Samuel

7694 People. HISPANIC BUSINESS, Vol. 5, no. 5 (May 1983), p. 8. English. **DESCR:** Biographical Notes; *Businesspeople; Duron, Armando; Espinoza, Peter; Flores, Juan; Martinez, Vilma Socorro; Molina, Gloria; Pantin, Leslie, Sr.; Quezada, Sylvia; Quinones, Sergio.

Moreno Vega, Marta

7695 Promoting the world of Hispanic art. NUESTRO, Vol. 6, no. 6 (August 1982), p. 44-46. English. **DESCR:** Art; *Museo del Barrio, New York, NY.

El Morro Prison, Cuba

7696 Greenfield, Charles. Life imitating art: a profile of Reynaldo Arenas. NUESTRO, Vol. 7, no. 5 (June, July, 1983), p. 40-42. English. **DESCR:** Arenas, Reynaldo; *Authors; *Cuba; *Cubanos; Political Prisoners.

Morton, Carlos

7697 Bruce Novoa, Juan. Round table on Chicano literature. JOURNAL OF ETHNIC STUDIES, Vol. 3, no. 1 (Spring 1975), p. 99-103. English. DESCR: *Bruce Novoa, Juan; *Literature; Montejano, David; Ortego y Gasca, Felipe de; Teatro.

7698 Morton, Carlos. La vida: growing up in two cultures. NATIONAL HISPANIC JOURNAL, Vol. 1, no. 4 (Spring 1983), p. 23. English. DESCR: *Biculturalism; Education; *EDUCATION ACROSS CULTURES.

MOSAICO DE LA VIDA: CHICANO, CUBAN AND PUERTO RICAN PROSE

7699 McKinney, J.E. Book review of: MOSAICO DE LA VIDA: CHICANO, CUBAN AND PUERTO RICAN PROSE. HISPANIA, Vol. 65, no. 2 (May 1982), p. 321. English. DESCR: Book Reviews; Jimenez, Francisco; Prose; Spanish Language; Textbooks.

7700 Zamora, Carlos. Book review of: MOSAICO DE LA VIDA: CHICANO, CUBAN AND PUERTO RICAN PROSE. MINORITY VOICES, Vol. 5, no. 1-2 (Spring, Fall, 1981), p. 71-72. English. DESCR: Book Reviews; Jimenez, Francisco; Literature.

Mota, Manny

7701 People. HISPANIC BUSINESS, Vol. 4, no. 7 (July 1982), p. 7. English. DESCR: Aguilar, Richard; *Biographical Notes; Businesspeople; Coronado, Julius; Enriquez, Rene; Garza, Jose S.; Guerra-Martinez, Celina; Medrano, Adan; Valenti, Frank S.

Motion Pictures
USE: Films

Moya, Connie

7702 Diaz, Katherine A. "And this year's winners are...". CAMINOS, Vol. 4, no. 1-2 (January, February, 1983), p. 39-54,74+. English. DESCR: *Awards; Castro, Tony; Elizalde, Hector; Flores, Tom; Martinez, Esperanza; Mendizabal, Maritza; Molina, Gloria; Placentia, Joe; Quesada, Leticia; Rios, David N.; Ybarra, Lea; Zapata, Carmen.

LAS MUJERES: CONVERSATIONS FROM A HISPANIC COMMUNITY

7703 Ybarra, Lea. Book review of: LAS MUJERES: CONVERSATIONS FROM A HISPANIC COMMUNITY [reprinted from LA RED/THE NET 5 (Sept. 1982)]. CHICANO LAW REVIEW, Vol. 6, (1983), p. 146-147. English. DESCR: Book Reviews; Chicanas; Elsasser, Nan; MacKenzie, Kyle; Oral History; Tixier y Vigil, Yvonne.

LA MULATA DE CORDOBA

7704 Nieto, Eva Margarita. El problema de la juventud eterna en tres hechiceras en THE SECOND RING OF POWER, LA MULATA DE CORDOBA y AURA. LA PALABRA, Vol. 4, no. 1-2 (Spring, Fall, 1982, 1983), p. 81-91. Spanish. DESCR: AURA; Castaneda, Carlos; Fuentes, Carlos; Gonzalez Obregon, Luis; *Literary Criticism; Literature; Literature Reviews; THE SECOND RING OF POWER.

Multicultural Education
USE: Cultural Pluralism

Multinational Corporations

7705 Duncan, Cameron. The runaway shop and the Mexican border industrialization program. SOUTHWEST ECONOMY AND SOCIETY, Vol. 2, no. 1 (October, November, 1976), p. 4-25. English. DESCR: Border Region; Labor Supply and Market; *Maquiladoras; *Mexican Border Industrialization Program.

7706 Mexico y Estados Unidos ante la tercera Confemar: resultados e implicaciones. INFORME: RELACIONES MEXICO-ESTADOS UNIDOS, Vol. 1, no. 3 (July, December, 1982), p. 215-226. Spanish. DESCR: CONFEMAR; *Maritime Law; Reagan Administration; United States-Mexico Relations.

Multinational Literature

7707 Torbert, Eugene C. Book review of: NUEVOS HORIZONTES: CHICANO, PUERTO-RICAN AND CUBAN SHORT STORIES. HISPANIA, Vol. 66, no. 1 (1983), p. 151. English. DESCR: Book Reviews; *NUEVOS-HORIZONTES: CHICANO, PUERTO-RICAN, AND CUBAN SHORT STORIES.

Multistate Bar Examination (MBE)

7708 Brown, Susan E. and Levoy, Claire. Melendez v. Burciaga: revealing the state of the art in bar examinations. BAR EXAMINER, Vol. 51, (May 1982), p. 4-15. English. DESCR: Klein, Stephen P.; *Legal Profession; Melendez v. Burciaga; Mexican American Legal Defense and Educational Fund (MALDEF).

Municipal Government
USE: Local Government

Munoz Marin, Luis

7709 Romero-Barcelo, Carlos. Should Puerto Rico become a state?: for statehood. NUESTRO, Vol. 7, no. 5 (June, July, 1983), p. 34-37. English. DESCR: *Colonialism; *International Relations; *Puerto Rico; United States.

Munoz, Ricardo F.

7710 Hunsaker, Alan. Book review of: PSYCHOLOGY AND COMMUNITY CHANGE; SOCIAL AND PSYCHOLOGICAL RESEARCH IN COMMUNITY SETTING; COMMUNITY PSYCHOLOGY: THEORETICAL AND EMPIRICAL APPROACHES. HISPANIC JOURNAL OF BEHAVIORAL SCIENCES, Vol. 5, no. 1 (March 1983), p. 121-124. English. DESCR: Book Reviews; *COMMUNITY PSYCHOLOGY: THEORETICAL AND EMPIRICAL APPROACHES; Gibbs, Margaret S.; Heller, Kenneth; Kelly, James G.; Lachenmeyer, Juliana Rasic; Monahan, John; *PSYCHOLOGY AND COMMUNITY CHANGE; Sigal, Janet; Snowden, Lonnie R.; *SOCIAL AND PSYCHOLOGICAL RESEARCH IN COMMUNITY SETTINGS.

Munoz, Victor M.

7711 People on the move. CAMINOS, Vol. 2, no. 6 (October 1981), p. 7. English. DESCR: Alvarado, Angel S.; Arreola, Rafael; *Biographical Notes; Diaz, Elisa; Diaz, Elvira A.; Garcia, Jose Joel; Garza, Florentino; Icaza, Ricardo F.; Lacayo, Henry; Martinez, Lydia R.; Salinas, Vicente; Sanchez, Manuel; Zuniga, Henry.

Mural Art

7712 Bejarano, William. Murals of Los Angeles. CHISMEARTE, (1982), p. 38-43. English.

7713 City officials decide mural must be removed. NUESTRO, Vol. 6, no. 7 (September 1982), p. 51. English. DESCR: *Art; *Hidalgo y Costilla, Miguel; San Antonio, TX.

Mural Art (cont.)

7714 East Los Streetscapers. Death of a homeboy. MAIZE, Vol. 6, no. 3-4 (Spring, Summer, 1983), p. 59. English.

7715 Firm honors Latino workers. NUESTRO, Vol. 6, no. 5 (June, July, 1982), p. 11-12. English. **DESCR:** *Acosta, Juan; Honeywell, Inc.; Minneapolis, MN.

7716 Fuentes, Juan and Mouton, Regina. The last supper. MAIZE, Vol. 6, no. 3-4 (Spring, Summer, 1983), p. Ft cover. English.

7717 Goldman, Shifra. Mexican muralism: its social-educative roles in Latin America and the United States. AZTLAN, Vol. 13, no. 1-2 (Spring, Fall, 1982), p. 111-133. Spanish. **DESCR:** Art; Latin America; *Mexico; Social History and Conditions.

7718 Gonzalez, Alicia Maria. Murals: fine, popular, or folk art? AZTLAN, Vol. 13, no. 1-2 (Spring, Fall, 1982), p. 149-163. English. **DESCR:** Art; Art History; Folk Art.

7719 The great wall of Los Angeles. CAMINOS, Vol. 4, no. 9 (October 1983), p. 46-47. English. **DESCR:** Los Angeles, CA.

7720 The history of Los Angeles: a Mexican perspective. CHISMEARTE, no. 9 (September 1983), p. 20-21. English. **DESCR:** Carrasco, Barbara; Los Angeles, CA.

7721 Holscher, Louis M. Tiene arte valor afuera del barrio: the murals of East Los Angeles and Boyle Heights. JOURNAL OF ETHNIC STUDIES, Vol. 4, no. 3 (Fall 1976), p. 42-52. English. **DESCR:** Art; Boyle Heights; Culture; *East Los Angeles, CA.

7722 Imagenes de mi pueblo. LATINO, Vol. 53, no. 5 (September 1982), p. 20-21. English.

7723 Karam, Bruce G. The murals of Tucson. NUESTRO, Vol. 5, no. 8 (November 1981), p. 58-61. English. **DESCR:** *Art; *Tucson, AZ.

7724 Message to Rudy Acuna...stop... the Spanish boys have returned...stop... business as usual...stop,spot. MAIZE, Vol. 6, no. 3-4 (Spring, Summer, 1983), p. 77. English.

7725 Montoya, Emmanuel. Reagan's carcajada/ Reagan's sarcastic laugh: detail... MAIZE, Vol. 6, no. 3-4 (Spring, Summer, 1983), p. Bk cover. English.

7726 No nukes for mother nature. MAIZE, Vol. 6, no. 3-4 (Spring, Summer, 1983), p. 47. English.

7727 Rodriguez, Patricia. Goddess Tlazolteotl. MAIZE, Vol. 6, no. 3-4 (Spring, Summer, 1983), p. 25. English.

7728 Royal Chicano Air Force (RCAF). Untitled. CALMECAC, Vol. 1, (Summer 1980), p. 38. English.

7729 Sepulveda, Ciro. Detroit's great mural battle. CAMINOS, Vol. 4, no. 9 (October 1983), p. 38-41. Bilingual. **DESCR:** Detroit, MI.

Murguia, Edward

7730 Craver, Rebecca McDowell. Book review of: CHICANO INTERMARRIAGE: A THEORETICAL AND EMPIRICAL STUDY. NEW MEXICO HISTORICAL REVIEW, Vol. 58, no. 3 (July 1983), p. 295-296. English. **DESCR:** Book Reviews; *CHICANO INTERMARRIAGE: A THEORETICAL AND EMPIRICAL STUDY.

7731 Manning, Roberta. Book review of: CHICANO INTERMARRIAGE: A THEORETICAL AND EMPIRICAL STUDY. HISPANIC JOURNAL OF BEHAVIORAL SCIENCES, Vol. 5, no. 3 (September 1983), p. 353-356. English. **DESCR:** Book Reviews; *CHICANO INTERMARRIAGE: A THEORETICAL AND EMPIRICAL STUDY; Intermarriage.

7732 Sierra, Christine Marie. Book review of: ASSIMILATION, COLONIALISM, AND THE MEXICAN AMERICAN PEOPLE. NEW SCHOLAR, Vol. 8, no. 1-2 (Spring, Fall, 1982), p. 490-492. English. **DESCR:** *ASSIMILATION, COLONIALISM AND THE MEXICAN AMERICAN PEOPLE; Book Reviews.

Murieta, Joaquin

7733 Mathes, W. Michael. Book review of: JOAQUIN MURRIETA AND HIS HORSE GANGS. CALIFORNIA HISTORY, Vol. 61, no. 4 (1983), p. 306-308. English. **DESCR:** Book Reviews; California; History; Latta, Frank F.

Murillo, Rosario

7734 Banberger, Ellen. Poesia nicaraguense. MAIZE, Vol. 5, no. 3-4 (Spring, Summer, 1982), p. 64-77. Spanish. **DESCR:** Belli, Gioconda; Cardenal, Ernesto; Carrillo, Ernesto; Coronel Urtecho, Jose; Gadea, Gerardo; Gomez, Manuel; *Nicaragua; Ojeda, Mirna; *Poetry; Revolutions; Rugama, Leonel.

Museo del Barrio, New York, NY

7735 Promoting the world of Hispanic art. NUESTRO, Vol. 6, no. 6 (August 1982), p. 44-46. English. **DESCR:** Art; Moreno Vega, Marta.

Museum of Cultural History, University of California, Los Angeles

7736 A potpourri of pre-Columbian art. NUESTRO, Vol. 7, no. 6 (August 1983), p. 59-60. English. **DESCR:** CERAMIC TOMB SCULPTURE FROM ANCIENT WEST MEXICO; Ceramics; Exhibits; Frederick S. Wright Art Gallery, University of California, Los Angeles; *Precolumbian Art; Sculpture.

Museums

7737 Mexican centers advance U.S. ties. NUESTRO, Vol. 7, no. 1 (January, February, 1983), p. 10-11. English. **DESCR:** Art Galleries; *El Centro Mexicano del Libro; Los Angeles, CA; Mexico; New York, NY; Publishing Industry.

7738 Morris, Gay. The Mexican Museum has a colorful new home. CAMINOS, Vol. 3, no. 7 (July, August, 1982), p. 30-33. Bilingual. **DESCR:** Art; *Mexican Museum, San Francisco, CA; Rodriguez, Peter; San Francisco, CA.

Music

7739 Agudelo, Carlos. What about Latin music? BILLBOARD, Vol. 94, (November 20, 1982), p. 10. English. **DESCR:** *Awards; *Grammy Awards; National Academy of Recording Arts and Sciences; Performing Arts; Recording Industry.

7740 Beaver, Frank E. CHULAS FRONTERAS. BILINGUAL REVIEW, Vol. 10, no. 2-3 (May, December, 1983), p. 176. English. **DESCR:** Blank, Les; *CHULAS FRONTERAS [film]; Film Reviews.

Music (cont.)

7741 Chicano music: from country and rock to soul and Mexican rancheras. NATIONAL HISPANIC JOURNAL, Vol. 1, no. 4 (Spring 1983), p. 9. English. **DESCR:** Davila, Leonard.

7742 Communications and announcements: raices y ritmos/roots and rythms: our heritage of Latin American music. LATIN AMERICAN MUSIC REVIEW, Vol. 3, no. 1 (Spring, Summer, 1982), p. 139-145. English. **DESCR:** Radio; *RAICES Y RITMOS/ROOTS AND RHYTHMS.

7743 Dickey, Dan W. and Van Osdol, Scott. La musica nortena: a photographic essay. SOUTHERN EXPOSURE, Vol. 11, no. 1 (1983), p. 38-41. English. **DESCR:** Jimenez, Flaco; Norteno.

7744 Entertaiment reviews. CAMINOS, Vol. 3, no. 8 (September 1982), p. 21. English. **DESCR:** Adams, Bob; Alpert, Herb; Books; Calvert, Robert; Jimenez, Santiago; Lopez, Lisa; Myles, Carol; Paredes, Americo; Pettus, Theodore T.; *Recreation; Television.

7745 Fantin, Joyce and Fernandez, Diana. Undocumented aliens ease concern over younger generation's cultural drift. BILLBOARD, Vol. 94, (September 11, 1982), p. T20+. English. **DESCR:** Recording Industry; Undocumented Workers.

7746 Feliciano, Jose. Escenas de amor: Jose Feliciano. NUESTRO, Vol. 6, no. 8 (October 1982), p. 46. English. **DESCR:** Musicians.

7747 Fernandez, Enrique and Valle, Eunice. Latin drop: retail sales decrease attributed to sweeps by Dept. of Immigration raids. BILLBOARD, Vol. 94, no. 25 (June 26, 1982), p. 3. English. **DESCR:** Deportation; Immigration Regulation and Control; Marketing.

7748 Fernandez, Enrique. NARAS takes a welcome step. BILLBOARD, Vol. 95, (June 18, 1983), p. 59. English. **DESCR:** Awards; Entertainers; Grammy Awards; *National Academy of Recording Arts and Sciences; Performing Arts; Recording Industry.

7749 Fernandez, Enrique. Youth acts dominating markets: labels woo kids with Spanish-language rock product. BILLBOARD, Vol. 95, (March 12, 1983), p. 58. English. **DESCR:** *Entertainers; Recording Industry; Youth.

7750 Hernandez, Al Carlos. BAD CITY BOYS: Tierra. NUESTRO, Vol. 6, no. 8 (October 1982), p. 46. English. **DESCR:** Musicians; *Tierra [musical group].

7751 Hernandez, Al Carlos. "Redneck Meskin" world tour of Texas starring Joe, Johnny, y la familia. NUESTRO, Vol. 6, no. 2 (March 1982), p. 40-42. English. **DESCR:** *Hernandez, Joe.

7752 Hernandez, Guillermo. A history of la musica mexicana in the U.S. CAMINOS, Vol. 4, no. 10 (November 1983), p. 24,47-48. Bilingual. **DESCR:** History.

7753 Herrera-Sobek, Maria. The treacherous woman archetype: a structuring agent in the corrido. AZTLAN, Vol. 13, no. 1-2 (Spring, Fall, 1982), p. 135-148. English. **DESCR:** Chicanas; *Corrido; Folk Songs.

7754 Laguna, Jaime. Enrique Serin: Mexico's violin ambassador. CAMINOS, Vol. 4, no. 10 (November 1983), p. 17-19. Bilingual. **DESCR:** Classical Music; *Serin, Enrique.

7755 Lopez, Raymond. Manuel M. Ponce visto por un profesor norteamericano de ascendencia mexicana. HETEROFONIA, Vol. 15, no. 4 (October, December, 1982), p. 30-35. Spanish. **DESCR:** *Ponce, Manuel M.

7756 Loza, Steven J. The great Mexican legends in music. CAMINOS, Vol. 4, no. 10 (November 1983), p. 20-23,47. Bilingual. **DESCR:** Mexico.

7757 Loza, Steven J. Origins, form, and development of the Son Jarocho: Veracruz, Mexico. AZTLAN, Vol. 13, no. 1-2 (Spring, Fall, 1982), p. 257-274. English. **DESCR:** Dance; Folk Songs; *Son Jarocho; Veracruz, Mexico.

7758 Loza, Steven J. The Son Jarocho: the history, style and repertory of a changing Mexican musical tradition. AZTLAN, Vol. 13, no. 1-2 (Spring, Fall, 1982), p. 327-334. English. **DESCR:** Dance; Folk Songs; Sheehy, Daniel E.; *Son Jarocho; Veracruz, Mexico.

7759 Maciel, David R. Book review of: THE KENNEDY CORRIDOS: A STUDY OF THE BALLADS OF A MEXICAN AMERICAN HERO. AZTLAN, Vol. 13, no. 1-2 (Spring, Fall, 1982), p. 335-337. English. **DESCR:** Book Reviews; Corrido; Dickey, Dan William; Folk Songs; *Kennedy, John Fitzgerald.

7760 Mead, R. H. Latin American accents in new music. LATIN AMERICAN MUSIC REVIEW, Vol. 3, no. 2 (Fall, Winter, 1982), p. 207-228. English. **DESCR:** Chavez, Carlos; Cowell, Henry; *New Music.

7761 Menudo: dishing it up in Los Angeles. CAMINOS, Vol. 4, no. 8 (September 1983), p. 46. Bilingual. **DESCR:** Artists; *Menudo [musical group]; Musicians; Puerto Rican Music.

7762 Mexican border sounds travel the folk circuit. BILLBOARD, Vol. 95, (February 26, 1983), p. 46. English. **DESCR:** Border Region; *Norteno.

7763 Mi casa es su casa. NUESTRO, Vol. 6, no. 4 (May 1982), p. 64. English. **DESCR:** Valeri, Michele.

7764 Mismanagement hampers TOGETHER AGAIN album. NUESTRO, Vol. 6, no. 3 (April 1982), p. 54. English. **DESCR:** *Tierra [musical group].

7765 Paredes, Americo. Texas-Mexican cancionero: folk song of the lower (excerpts). SOUTHERN EXPOSURE, Vol. 10, no. 4 (July, August, 1982), p. 50-57. Bilingual. **DESCR:** *Corrido; *Folk Songs.

7766 Pena, Manuel H. Book review of: FOLK MUSIC OF NEW MEXICO AND THE SOUTHWEST: A SELF-PORTRAIT OF A PEOPLE. AMERICAN MUSIC, Vol. 1, no. 2 (Summer 1983), p. 102-105. English. **DESCR:** Book Reviews; *HISPANIC FOLK MUSIC OF NEW MEXICO AND THE SOUTHWEST: A SELF-PORTRAIT OF A PEOPLE; Robb, John Donald.

Music (cont.)

7767 Pena, Manuel H. Folksong and social change:
two corridos as interpretive sources.
AZTLAN, Vol. 13, no. 1-2 (Spring, Fall,
1982), p. 12-42. English. DESCR: Corrido;
Cortez, Gregorio; *DISCRIMINACION A UN
MARTIR [corrido]; *EL CORRIDO DE GREGORIO
CORTE [corrido]; *Folk Songs; Longoria,
Felix.

7768 Record marketing effort aimed at Latino
buyer. NUESTRO, Vol. 6, no. 2 (March 1982),
p. 48. English. DESCR: *Marketing; Recording
Industry.

7769 Reyna, Jose R. Musica tejana. CAMINOS, Vol.
4, no. 10 (November 1983), p. 25,48.
English. DESCR: Texas.

7770 Reyna, Jose R. Notes on Tejano music.
AZTLAN, Vol. 13, no. 1-2 (Spring, Fall,
1982), p. 81-94. English. DESCR: Conjunto;
Ethnomusicology; Texas.

7771 Rising star in the music world. NUESTRO,
Vol. 6, no. 1 (January, February, 1982), p.
64. English. DESCR: Children; *Romero,
Gustavo.

7772 Santana's guitar work still sharp and crisp.
NUESTRO, Vol. 6, no. 9 (November 1982), p.
60. English. DESCR: Guitar Music;
Guitarists; *Santana, Carlos.

7773 Sifuentes, Roberto. Aproximaciones al
"Corrido de los Hermanos Hernandez
ejecutados en la camara de gas de la
penitenciaria de Florence, Arizona el dia 6
de julio de 1934". AZTLAN, Vol. 13, no. 1-2
(Spring, Fall, 1982), p. 95-109. Spanish.
DESCR: Alonso, Epifanio; *Corrido; *CORRIDO
DE LOS HERMANOS HERNANDEZ [song lyrics];
Folk Songs; Hernandez, Federico; Hernandez,
Manuel; Musical Lyrics.

7774 Sound impact. LATINO, Vol. 53, no. 7
(November 1982), p. 21. English.

7775 Stevenson, Robert. Relaciones de Carlos
Chavez en Los Angeles. HETEROFONIA, Vol. 15,
no. 1 (January, March, 1982), p. 3-19.
Spanish. DESCR: *Chavez, Carlos.

7776 Tierra. LATINO, Vol. 54, no. 1 (January,
February, 1983), p. 8. English. DESCR:
Musicians; *Tierra [musical group].

7777 Top talent at Tejano awards. BILLBOARD, Vol.
95, (January 29, 1983), p. 65. English.
DESCR: Awards; Entertainers; Performing
Arts; *Tejano Music Awards; Texas.

7778 Ucalatino: salsa music comes to UCLA.
NUESTRO, Vol. 6, no. 9 (November 1982), p.
59-60. English. DESCR: Salsa; UCALATINO
[musical group]; University of California,
Los Angeles (UCLA).

Music Review

7779 McNeil, W. K. Record Review: LAS VOCES DE
LOS CAMPESINOS. JOURNAL OF AMERICAN
FOLKLORE, Vol. 96, (1983), p. 370. English.
DESCR: Agricultural Laborers; Corrido; *LAS
VOCES DE LOS CAMPESINOS; Musical Lyrics.

Musical Lyrics

7780 Canto sacro mexica: 'en la tierra tan solo
es el bello cantar, la flor hermosa'.
CALMECAC, Vol. 1, no. 1 (Spring 1980), p.

19. Bilingual.

7781 McNeil, W. K. Record Review: LAS VOCES DE
LOS CAMPESINOS. JOURNAL OF AMERICAN
FOLKLORE, Vol. 96, (1983), p. 370. English.
DESCR: Agricultural Laborers; Corrido; *LAS
VOCES DE LOS CAMPESINOS; Music Review.

7782 Los pasos de la vida c/s. CALMECAC, Vol. 2,
(Spring 1981), p. 49. English. DESCR:
*Poetry.

7783 Rangel, Irma "La Cui Cui". The children are
the healing. CALMECAC, Vol. 2, (Spring
1981), p. 27. English. DESCR: *Poetry.

7784 Rangel, Irma "La Cui Cui". L.A.'s dust.
CALMECAC, Vol. 1, no. 1 (Spring 1980), p.
27. English.

7785 Rangel, Irma "La Cui Cui". Lullaby for baby.
CALMECAC, Vol. 2, (Spring 1981), p. 26.
English. DESCR: *Poetry.

7786 Sifuentes, Roberto. Aproximaciones al
"Corrido de los Hermanos Hernandez
ejecutados en la camara de gas de la
penitenciaria de Florence, Arizona el dia 6
de julio de 1934". AZTLAN, Vol. 13, no. 1-2
(Spring, Fall, 1982), p. 95-109. Spanish.
DESCR: Alonso, Epifanio; *Corrido; *CORRIDO
DE LOS HERMANOS HERNANDEZ [song lyrics];
Folk Songs; Hernandez, Federico; Hernandez,
Manuel; Music.

7787 Xochicuitcatl. CALMECAC, Vol. 3, (Spring
1982), p. 38. English. DESCR: *Poetry.

Musicals

7788 Whitney, James. Habana! comes to Manhattan.
NUESTRO, Vol. 7, no. 2 (March 1983), p.
55-56. English. DESCR: *HABANA! ANTOLOGIA
MUSICAL; HAVANA SINGS; Performing Arts.

Musicians

7789 Andersen, Kurt. A Puerto Rican pop music
machine. TIME, Vol. 121, no. 26 (June 27,
1983), p. 46. English. DESCR: *Menudo
[musical group]; Puerto Rican Music.

7790 Arco iris. CAMINOS, Vol. 3, no. 8 (September
1982), p. 19. English. DESCR: *Arco Iris
[musical group].

7791 The battle of the bands in East Los Angeles.
CAMINOS, Vol. 4, no. 10 (November 1983), p.
9-11,47. Bilingual. DESCR: East Los Angeles,
CA.

7792 Diaz, Katherine A. Jose Feliciano. CAMINOS,
Vol. 3, no. 8 (September 1982), p. 14-16.
Bilingual. DESCR: Artists; *Feliciano, Jose;
Singers.

7793 Feliciano, Jose. Escenas de amor: Jose
Feliciano. NUESTRO, Vol. 6, no. 8 (October
1982), p. 46. English. DESCR: *Music.

7794 Gente. NUESTRO, Vol. 7, no. 1 (January,
February, 1983), p. 63. English. DESCR:
Amaya-Espinoza, Isidro; Camargo, Mateo G.;
*Latin Americans; Prieto, Carlos; Radio;
Sports; Trevino, Lee.

7795 Gonzalez, Johnny. Flora and Airto; making
music happen. CAMINOS, Vol. 3, no. 8
(September 1982), p. 10-13,50. Bilingual.
DESCR: Artists; Moreira, Airto; Purim,
Flora.

Musicians (cont.)

7796 Hernandez, Al Carlos. BAD CITY BOYS: Tierra. NUESTRO, Vol. 6, no. 8 (October 1982), p. 46. English. DESCR: Music; *Tierra [musical group].

7797 Latino of the Year 1983: Menudo. LATINO, Vol. 54, no. 8 (December 1983), p. 8-11. English. DESCR: *Menudo [musical group]; Puerto Rican Music.

7798 Lopez, Trini. Dando una mano. LATINO, Vol. 53, no. 7 (November 1982), p. 11. Spanish. DESCR: Biography; *Lopez, Trini.

7799 Madrid, Joe. The brat; looking for the best. CAMINOS, Vol. 3, no. 8 (September 1982), p. 20. English. DESCR: *The Brat [musical group].

7800 Madrid, Joe. Los Illegals. CAMINOS, Vol. 3, no. 8 (September 1982), p. 18-19. English. DESCR: *Los Illegals [musical group].

7801 Mejias-Rentas, Antonio. Una dosis puertorriquena de Menudo. LATINO, Vol. 54, no. 8 (December 1983), p. 12. Spanish. DESCR: *Menudo [musical group]; Puerto Rican Music.

7802 Mejias-Rentas, Antonio. A Puerto Rican dose of Menudo. NUESTRO, Vol. 7, no. 7 (September 1983), p. 49. English. DESCR: *Menudo [musical group]; Puerto Rican Music.

7803 Menudo: dishing it up in Los Angeles. CAMINOS, Vol. 4, no. 8 (September 1983), p. 46. Bilingual. DESCR: Artists; *Menudo [musical group]; Music; Puerto Rican Music.

7804 Mimiaga, Hector. Greatest ambition. LATINO, Vol. 53, no. 4 (June 1982), p. 25. English. DESCR: Biography; *Gonzalez, Ruben.

7805 Romero, Pedro Sababu. Pete Escovedo: a study in versatility. NUESTRO, Vol. 6, no. 10 (December 1982), p. 63-64. English. DESCR: *Artists; Escovedo, Pete.

7806 Segovia: un retrato musical. LATINO, Vol. 54, no. 3 (April 1983), p. 10. Spanish. DESCR: *Segovia, Andres.

7807 Stevenson, Robert. Carlos Chavez's United States press coverage. AZTLAN, Vol. 14, no. 1 (Spring 1983), p. 21-33. English. DESCR: *Chavez, Carlos; Ethnomusicology; *Journalism; Print Media.

7808 Tierra. LATINO, Vol. 54, no. 1 (January, February, 1983), p. 8. English. DESCR: Music; *Tierra [musical group].

7809 UC Latino: salsa music comes to UCLA. CAMINOS, Vol. 4, no. 5 (May 1983), p. 46,48. English. DESCR: Salsa; *UC Latino; University of California, Los Angeles (UCLA).

MY PENITENTE LAND: REFLECTIONS ON SPANISH NEW MEXICO

7810 Lomeli, Francisco A. Book review of: MY PENITENTE LAND: REFLECTIONS ON SPANISH NEW MEXICO. NEW SCHOLAR, Vol. 8, no. 1-2 (Spring, Fall, 1982), p. 495-498. English. DESCR: Book Reviews; Chavez, Fray Angelico.

7811 Lomeli, Francisco A. Book review of: MY PENITENTE LAND: REFLECTIONS ON SPANISH NEW MEXICO. NEW SCHOLAR, Vol. 8, no. 1-2 (Spring, Fall, 1982), p. 495-498. English. DESCR: Book Reviews; Chavez, Fray Angelico.

7812 Weber, Kenneth R. Book review of: MY PENITENTE LAND: REFLECTIONS ON SPANISH NEW MEXICO. JOURNAL OF ETHNIC STUDIES, Vol. 3, no. 2 (Summer 1975), p. 119-121. English. DESCR: Book Reviews; Chavez, Fray Angelico; *Hermanos Penitentes; *New Mexico; Religion.

Myerhoff, Barbara G.

7813 Burke, Leslie K. Book review of: LIFE'S CAREER-AGING: CULTURAL VARIATIONS ON GROWING OLD. HISPANIC JOURNAL OF BEHAVIORAL SCIENCES, Vol. 4, no. 1 (March 1982), p. 103-107. English. DESCR: Academic Achievement; *LIFE'S CAREER--AGING: CULTURAL VARIATIONS ON GROWING OLD; Simic, Andrei.

Myles, Carol

7814 Entertaiment reviews. CAMINOS, Vol. 3, no. 8 (September 1982), p. 21. English. DESCR: Adams, Bob; Alpert, Herb; Books; Calvert, Robert; Jimenez, Santiago; Lopez, Lisa; Music; Paredes, Americo; Pettus, Theodore T.; *Recreation; Television.

THE MYTH OF MARGINALITY: URBAN POVERTY AND POLITICS IN RIO DE JANEIRO

7815 Logan, Kathleen. The urban poor in developing nations. JOURNAL OF URBAN HISTORY, Vol. 9, no. 1 (November 1982), p. 108-116. English. DESCR: ACCESS TO POWER: POLITICS AND THE URBAN POOR IN DEVELOPING NATIONS; *Book Reviews; BORDER BOOM TOWN: CIUDAD JUAREZ SINCE 1848; Collier, David; Cornelius, Wayne A.; Eckstein, Susan; Lloyd, Peter; Martinez, Oscar J.; Nelson, Joan M.; Perlman, Janice E.; POLITICS AND MIGRANT POOR IN MEXICO CITY; SLUMS OF HOPE? SHANTY TOWNS OF THE THIRD WORLD; SQUATTERS AND OLIGARCHS: AUTHORITARIAN RULE AND POLICY CHANGE IN PERU; THE POVERTY OF REVOLUTION: THE STATE AND THE URBAN POOR IN MEXICO; Urban Economics.

Mythology

7816 Alurista and Monleon, Jose. Mesa redonda. MAIZE, Vol. 4, no. 3-4 (Spring, Summer, 1981), p. 6-23. English. DESCR: Alurista; Anaya, Rudolfo A.; Herrera Sobek, Maria; Identity; Literature; Morales, Alejandro; Viramontes, Helen.

7817 Carr, Pat and Gingerich, Willard. The vagina dentata motif in Nahuatl and Pueblo mythic narratives: a comparative study. NEW SCHOLAR, Vol. 8, no. 1-2 (Spring, Fall, 1982), p. 85-101. English. DESCR: *Precolumbian Literature.

7818 Espinoza, Herbert O. Lope de Aguirre y santos banderas, la manipulacion del mito. MAIZE, Vol. 4, no. 3-4 (Spring, Summer, 1981), p. 32-43. Spanish. DESCR: De Valle-Inclan, Ramon; Literary Criticism; *TIRANO BANDERAS.

7819 Flores, Henry. Some different thoughts concerning "machismo". COMADRE, no. 3 (Fall 1978), p. 7-9. English. DESCR: Chicanas; *Machismo; Sex Roles.

7820 Guerrero, Yolanda E. La funcion del mito: NAMBE-YEAR ONE. MAIZE, Vol. 4, no. 3-4 (Spring, Summer, 1981), p. 51-59. Spanish. DESCR: Literary Criticism; *NAMBE: YEAR ONE; Romero, Orlando.

Nahuatl Literature
  USE: Precolumbian Literature

Naisbitt, John

  7821 Book review of: MEGATRENDS. NUESTRO, Vol. 7,
    no. 9 (November 1983), p. 61-62. English.
    DESCR: Book Reviews; *MEGATRENDS.

NAMBE: YEAR ONE

  7822 Guerrero, Yolanda E. La funcion del mito:
    NAMBE-YEAR ONE. MAIZE, Vol. 4, no. 3-4
    (Spring, Summer, 1981), p. 51-59. Spanish.
    DESCR: Literary Criticism; Mythology;
    Romero, Orlando.

Names, Spanish

  7823 Woods, Richard D. Sources of identification
    of Spanish names. JOURNAL OF ETHNIC STUDIES,
    Vol. 4, no. 2 (Summer 1976), p. 92-94.
    English. **DESCR:** *Personal Names; Spanish
    Language.

Naranjo, Antonio

  7824 Hispanics receive appointments. LATINO, Vol.
    53, no. 1 (January, February, 1982), p. 20.
    English. **DESCR:** Appointed Officials;
    *Herrera, Maria Elena.

Narcotic Addicts
  USE: Drug Addicts

Narcotic Laws
  USE: Drug Laws

Narcotic Traffic
  USE: Drug Traffic

Narcotics

  7825 Emboden, William A. The Water Lily and the
    Maya Scribe: an ethnobotanical
    interpretation. NEW SCHOLAR, Vol. 8, no. 1-2
    (Spring, Fall, 1982), p. 103-127. English.
    DESCR: *Precolumbian Society.

National Academy of Recording Arts and Sciences

  7826 Agudelo, Carlos. What about Latin music?
    BILLBOARD, Vol. 94, (November 20, 1982), p.
    10. English. **DESCR:** *Awards; *Grammy Awards;
    Music; Performing Arts; Recording Industry.

  7827 Fernandez, Enrique. NARAS takes a welcome
    step. BILLBOARD, Vol. 95, (June 18, 1983),
    p. 59. English. **DESCR:** Awards; Entertainers;
    Grammy Awards; Music; Performing Arts;
    Recording Industry.

National Action Council for Minorities in Engineering (NACME)

  7828 Chavarria, Jesus. Hispanic engineers.
    HISPANIC BUSINESS, Vol. 4, no. 7 (July
    1982), p. 6. English. **DESCR:** Engineering;
    *Engineering as a Profession.

  7829 Math-based careers. HISPANIC BUSINESS, Vol.
    4, no. 4 (April 1982), p. 20,24. English.
    DESCR: *Careers; Chicanas; *Engineering as a
    Profession; Government Employees; National
    Hispanic Field Service Program.

  7830 Math-based careers. HISPANIC BUSINESS, Vol.
    4, no. 5 (May 1982), p. 22. English. **DESCR:**
    Careers; Education; Engineering as a
    Profession; *Financial Aid; Society for
    Hispanic Professional Engineers (SHPE).

  7831 Math-based careers. HISPANIC BUSINESS, Vol.
    4, no. 7 (July 1982), p. 22. English.

    DESCR: *Careers; Engineering as a
    Profession; LULAC National Education Service
    Centers (LNESC).

  7832 Math-based careers. HISPANIC BUSINESS, Vol.
    4, no. 10 (October 1982), p. 20. English.
    DESCR: *Careers; Educational Opportunities;
    Engineering as a Profession; Financial Aid;
    Minority Business Development Agency (MBDA);
    National Association of Independent Schools
    (NAIS).

  7833 Math-based careers. HISPANIC BUSINESS, Vol.
    5, no. 2 (February 1983), p. 22. English.
    DESCR: *Careers; Engineering; Financial Aid;
    Mathematics; Mathematics, Engineering and
    Science Achievement (MESA).

National Aeronautics and Space Administration (NASA)

  7834 Valenzuela-Crocker, Elvira. Chang-Diaz has
    space shuttle role. NUESTRO, Vol. 7, no. 9
    (November 1983), p. 11-12. English. **DESCR:**
    *Astronauts; *Chang-Diaz, Franklin; Space
    Shuttle.

  7835 Vara, Richard. Reaching for the stars:
    Franklin Chang-Diaz, astronaut and future
    scientist in space. HISPANIC BUSINESS, Vol.
    5, no. 11 (November 1983), p. 18-19+.
    English. **DESCR:** Astronauts; *Chang-Diaz,
    Franklin; Science as a Profession.

National Alliance of Homebased Businesswomen

  7836 Padilla, Steve. You've come a long way,
    baby. Or have you? NUESTRO, Vol. 7, no. 6
    (August 1983), p. 38-41. English. **DESCR:**
    *Business Enterprises; Chicanas; Minority
    Business Development Agency (MBDA).

National Assessment of Educational Progress

  7837 Creswell, John L. Sex-related differences in
    the problem-solving abilities of rural
    Black, Anglo, and Chicano adolescents. TEXAS
    TECH JOURNAL OF EDUCATION, Vol. 10, no. 1
    (Winter 1983), p. 29-33. English. **DESCR:**
    Aiken and Preger Revised Math Attitude
    Scale; Anglo Americans; Blacks; California
    Achievement Test; Chicanas; Gender;
    Mathematics; *National Council of Teachers
    of Mathematics (NCTM); Youth.

National Association of Latino Elected Officials (NALEO)

  7838 Business notes. HISPANIC BUSINESS, Vol. 5,
    no. 12 (December 1983), p. 35. English.
    DESCR: Anheuser-Busch, Inc.; *Business
    Enterprises; Denny's Inc.; Des Moines, IA;
    El Pollo Loco; Food Industry; Local
    Government; Martinez, Vilma Socorro; Ochoa,
    Juan Pancho.

  7839 Hamner, Richard. Hispanics and
    redistricting: what you see is not always
    what you get. NATIONAL HISPANIC JOURNAL,
    Vol. 1, no. 2 (Winter 1982), p. 25-30.
    English. **DESCR:** Berlanga, Hugo; Elections;
    Hispanic Reapportionment District; Political
    Representation; Politics; *Reapportionment;
    *Roybal, Edward R.; Santillan, Richard.

  7840 Madrid, Joe and Gonzalez, Magdalena. NALEO -
    honoring the Hispanic Medal of Honor
    winners. CAMINOS, Vol. 3, no. 10 (November
    1982), p. 22-25. English. **DESCR:** *Medal of
    Honor; *Military Service.

National Association of Latino Elected Officials (NALEO) (cont.)

7841 Midwest senator addresses NALEO. NUESTRO, Vol. 6, no. 9 (November 1982), p. 13. English. DESCR: Bumpers, Dale; Funding Sources.

7842 NALEO audits the Feds. HISPANIC BUSINESS, Vol. 5, no. 10 (October 1983), p. 16. English. DESCR: Business Enterprises; Federal Government; *Government Contracts; Minority Business Development Agency (MBDA); U.S. Department of Defense (DOD); U.S. Department of Health and Human Services.

7843 N.A.L.E.O.'s "Fiesta '83". CAMINOS, Vol. 4, no. 10 (November 1983), p. 28-29. English. DESCR: Baca Barragan, Polly; Bilingual Bicultural Education; Central America; Fiesta '83; Garcia, Robert; Immigration; International Relations; Mendez, Olga; Simpson-Mazzoli Bill; United States-Mexico Relations.

7844 Quesada-Weiner, Rosemary. NALEO's Fiesta '81. CAMINOS, Vol. 2, no. 7 (December 1981), p. 45. English.

National Association of Independent Schools (NAIS)

7845 Math-based careers. HISPANIC BUSINESS, Vol. 4, no. 10 (October 1982), p. 20. English. DESCR: *Careers; Educational Opportunities; Engineering as a Profession; Financial Aid; Minority Business Development Agency (MBDA); National Action Council for Minorities in Engineering (NACME).

National Association for Chicano Studies (NACS)

7846 Community watching: para la comunidad. CAMINOS, Vol. 3, no. 1 (January 1982), p. 43-44. Bilingual. DESCR: Congreso Nacional Para Pueblos Unidos (CPU); *Financial Aid; *Food Programs; *Journalists; *Radio; Summer Program for Minority Journalists; Zozaya, Julia S.

National Association for Bilingual Education

7847 Newsfront. HISPANIC BUSINESS, Vol. 4, no. 3 (March 1982), p. 9. English. DESCR: Appointed Officials; *Biographical Notes; Businesspeople; Chicano Film Exhibition and Festival, Detroit, Michigan, April 5-9, 1982; Garcia, Gloria; League of United Latin American Citizens (LULAC); Martinez, Vilma Socorro; Seaga, Edward; Suarez, Carlos R.

7848 Zamora, Gloria L.; Mazzone, Ernest; and Calvet, Peter. Newsmakers forum (interviews with Gloria Zamora and Ernest Mazzone). BILINGUAL JOURNAL, Vol. 6, no. 2 (Winter 1982), p. 6-11,26,28. English. DESCR: *Bilingual Bicultural Education; Bilingualism.

National Bipartisan Commission on Central America

7849 Diaz, Katherine A. Henry G. Cisneros on Central American commission (interview). CAMINOS, Vol. 4, no. 8 (September 1983), p. 10,48. English. DESCR: Central America; *Cisneros, Henry, Mayor of San Antonio, TX; International Relations; United States.

National Center for Health Statistics

7850 Hispanics responding well to health survey. NUESTRO, Vol. 7, no. 1 (January, February, 1983), p. 47. English. DESCR: *Hispanic Health and Nutrition Examination Survey (HHANES); Public Health.

National Chicano Council on Higher Education (NCCHE)

7851 Bonham, G.W. Moral imperative. CHANGE, Vol. 15, (January, February, 1983), p. 14-15. English. DESCR: Employment; *Higher Education.

7852 McCurdy, Jack. Chicanos mark their gains in colleges, call for more. CHRONICLE OF HIGHER EDUCATION, Vol. 25, no. 10 (November 3, 1982), p. 12. English. DESCR: Academic Achievement; *Higher Education; Madrid, Arturo.

National Chicano Survey of Mexicans

7853 Garcia, John A. Ethnicity and Chicanos: measurement of ethnic identification, identity and consciousness. HISPANIC JOURNAL OF BEHAVIORAL SCIENCES, Vol. 4, no. 3 (September 1982), p. 295-314. English. DESCR: *Identity; Politics.

National Coalition of Hispanic Mental Health and Human Services Organizations (COSSMHO)

7854 Capital events honor achievers. NUESTRO, Vol. 6, no. 9 (November 1982), p. 12. English. DESCR: *Youth.

7855 Latinas on the march, NUESTRO survey reveals: organizations assess achievements during 1981. NUESTRO, Vol. 6, no. 2 (March 1982), p. 16-28+. English. DESCR: Forum of National Hispanic Organizations; Hispanic Health Council; Latin Americans; League of United Latin American Citizens (LULAC); National Council of La Raza (NCLR); National Hispanic Bar Association; *National Image, Inc.; National Puerto Rican Forum, Inc.; *Organizations; Yzaguirre, Raul.

7856 Newsfront. HISPANIC BUSINESS, Vol. 4, no. 4 (April 1982), p. 8, 24. English. DESCR: *Biographical Notes; Burgos, Elizabeth; *Businesspeople; Flores, Arturo; Garcia, Carlos E.; Garcia, Edward T.; Guzman, Ralph C.; Hernandez, Richard; Parra, Oscar C.; Willie, Herm M.

7857 Reagan, Ronald. Remarks at a White House reception for the National Coalition of Hispanic Mental Health and Human Services Organization (September 23, 1982). PUBLIC PAPERS OF THE PRESIDENT, Vol. 1, no. 2 (1982), p. 1209-1211. English. DESCR: Financial Aid.

National Coalition on Violence

7858 Too much TV and violence in cartoons. LATINA, Vol. 1, no. 2 (February, March, 1983), p. 74. English. DESCR: *Television; *Violence.

National Commission on Secondary Schooling for Hispanics

7859 Breiter, Toni. Hispanic policy development project. CAMINOS, Vol. 4, no. 10 (November 1983), p. 42-43,54. Bilingual. DESCR: *Hispanic Policy Development Project; Secondary School Education.

7860 Hispanic student study undertaken. NUESTRO, Vol. 7, no. 10 (December 1983), p. 11-12. English. DESCR: Academic Achievement; Dropouts; Educational Statistics; Enrollment; Hispanic Policy Development Project; *Secondary School Education.

National Commission on Working Women (NCWW)

7861 Women & economic progress. HISPANIC
BUSINESS, Vol. 4, no. 1 (January 1982), p.
28. English. DESCR: *Working Women.

National Congress for Puerto Rican Rights (NCPRR)

7862 Barreto, Julio. A new force in the barrio.
NUESTRO, Vol. 7, no. 4 (May 1983), p. 43-45.
English. DESCR: Caballero-Perez, Diana;
*Community Development; *Cultural
Organizations; *Puerto Ricans.

7863 Latinos evident in 1983 march. NUESTRO, Vol.
7, no. 7 (September 1983), p. 11-12.
English. DESCR: Bonilla, Tony;
Cuban-American Coordinating Committee;
*Demonstrations; IMAGE, Washington, DC;
Jackson, Jesse; League of United Latin
American Citizens (LULAC); National Council
of La Raza (NCLR); Velasquez, Baldemar;
Zamora, Reuben.

National Consortium for Graduate Degrees for Minorities in Engineering

7864 Career intelligencer. HISPANIC BUSINESS,
Vol. 5, no. 9 (September 1983), p. 30.
English. DESCR: California Chicano News
Media Association (CCNMA); *Careers;
Journalism.

National Council for Minorities in Engineering (NACME)

7865 Math-based careers. HISPANIC BUSINESS, Vol.
5, no. 7 (July 1983), p. 22. English.
DESCR: *Careers; Education; Mathematics;
Nursing.

7866 Math-based careers. HISPANIC BUSINESS, Vol.
5, no. 9 (September 1983), p. 28. English.
DESCR: Andrew W. Mellon Foundation;
*Careers; Employment; Engineering as a
Profession; Financial Aid; Garcia, Mary;
Higher Education; National Medical
Fellowships (NMF); Rivera, Lourdes.

National Council of Churches

7867 Inter faith unity. LATINA, Vol. 1, no. 2
(February, March, 1983), p. 19. English.
DESCR: *Religion.

National Council of Teachers of Mathematics (NCTM)

7868 Creswell, John L. Sex-related differences in
the problem-solving abilities of rural
Black, Anglo, and Chicano adolescents. TEXAS
TECH JOURNAL OF EDUCATION, Vol. 10, no. 1
(Winter 1983), p. 29-33. English. DESCR:
Aiken and Preger Revised Math Attitude
Scale; Anglo Americans; Blacks; California
Achievement Test; Chicanas; Gender;
Mathematics; National Assessment of
Educational Progress; Youth.

National Council of La Raza (NCLR)

7869 Latinas on the march, NUESTRO survey
reveals: organizations assess achievements
during 1981. NUESTRO, Vol. 6, no. 2 (March
1982), p. 16-28+. English. DESCR: Forum of
National Hispanic Organizations; Hispanic
Health Council; Latin Americans; League of
United Latin American Citizens (LULAC);
National Coalition of Hispanic Mental Health
and Human Services Organizations (COSSMHO);
National Hispanic Bar Association; *National
Image, Inc.; National Puerto Rican Forum,
Inc.; *Organizations; Yzaguirre, Raul.

7870 Latinos evident in 1983 march. NUESTRO, Vol.

7, no. 7 (September 1983), p. 11-12.
English. DESCR: Bonilla, Tony;
Cuban-American Coordinating Committee;
*Demonstrations; IMAGE, Washington, DC;
Jackson, Jesse; League of United Latin
American Citizens (LULAC); National Congress
for Puerto Rican Rights (NCPRR); Velasquez,
Baldemar; Zamora, Reuben.

7871 Salmon, Roberto Mario. Comment: is this our
decade in the sun? NATIONAL HISPANIC
JOURNAL, Vol. 2, no. 1 (Summer 1983), p.
24-25. English. DESCR: Identity; Machismo;
*Mass Media.

7872 Whisler, Kirk. Hispanics and the private
sector. CAMINOS, Vol. 3, no. 8 (September
1982), p. 22-23. Bilingual. DESCR:
*Organizations; Private Funding Sources.

National Credit Union Administration

7873 Government review. NUESTRO, Vol. 7, no. 10
(December 1983), p. 48. English. DESCR:
Banking Industry; Child Care Centers; Chile;
Clinics (Medical); Credit Unions;
Employment; Employment Training; *Government
Services; Medical Care; National Oceanic and
Atmospheric Administration; SER; U.S.
Department of Health and Human Services;
U.S. Department of Labor.

National Economic Development Association (NEDA)

7874 Houstonite builds successful business:
home-started business exceeds millions in
foreign trade sales. NATIONAL HISPANIC
JOURNAL, Vol. 1, no. 4 (Spring 1983), p. 7.
English. DESCR: Business; *Business
Enterprises; Businesspeople; Cavazos, Roy;
Minority Business Development Agency (MBDA);
U.S. Small Business Administration.

National Endowment for the Arts

7875 Entertainment = diversion. CAMINOS, Vol. 3,
no. 4 (April 1982), p. 41. Bilingual.
DESCR: AZTLAN [journal];
Committee in Solidarity with the People of
El Salvador (CISPES); Cultural
Organizations; Directories; DIRECTORY OF
MINORITY ARTS ORGANIZATIONS; El Salvador;
NOTICIERO; Organizations; Periodicals;
*Recreation; Television.

7876 Government review. NUESTRO, Vol. 7, no. 8
(October 1983), p. 54. English. DESCR:
Alcoholism; Employment; *Government
Services; Plaza de La Raza, Los Angeles, CA;
Veterans; Working Women; Youth.

National Fair Housing Law

7877 Government review. NUESTRO, Vol. 7, no. 6
(August 1983), p. 56. English. DESCR: Ballet
de Puerto Rico; Dance; Education;
Employment; *Government Funding Sources;
Government Services; Housing; Income;
Population Distribution; Urban Development
Action Grant (UDAG); Veterans.

NATIONAL GEOGRAPHIC [magazine]

7878 Ruiz, Rene A. [Article review of: "The
Aztecs"; "Tenochtitlan's glory"; "The Great
Temple"]. HISPANIC JOURNAL OF BEHAVIORAL
SCIENCES, Vol. 4, no. 3 (September 1982), p.
394-395. English. DESCR: Book Reviews;
*"Tenochtitlan's glory"; *"The Aztecs";
*"The Great Temple".

National Hispanic Association of Construction Enterprises (NHACE)

7879 NHACE is born. LATINO, Vol. 53, no. 1 (January, February, 1982), p. 19. English. **DESCR:** Construction Industry; Hispanic American Construction Industry Association (HACIA).

7880 Organizing Hispanics in construction. HISPANIC BUSINESS, Vol. 4, no. 10 (October 1982), p. 14,26. English. **DESCR:** *Construction Industry.

National Hispanic Bar Association

7881 Latinas on the march, NUESTRO survey reveals: organizations assess achievements during 1981. NUESTRO, Vol. 6, no. 2 (March 1982), p. 16-28+. English. **DESCR:** Forum of National Hispanic Organizations; Hispanic Health Council; Latin Americans; League of United Latin American Citizens (LULAC); National Coalition of Hispanic Mental Health and Human Services Organizations (COSSMHO); National Council of La Raza (NCLR); *National Image, Inc.; National Puerto Rican Forum, Inc.; *Organizations; Yzaguirre, Raul.

National Hispanic Center

7882 Reusswig, Jim. Whence the National Hispanic Center and University? Mater artium necessitas. THRUST, Vol. 11, no. 3 (January, February, 1982), p. 32-35. English. **DESCR:** Bilingual Bicultural Education; Education; *National Hispanic University, Oakland CA.

National Hispanic Center for Advanced Studies and Policy Analysis (NHCAS)

7883 Research/development: books. HISPANIC BUSINESS, Vol. 4, no. 2 (February 1982), p. 28. English. **DESCR:** Book Reviews; Business; Business Enterprises; *FINANCING YOUR BUSINESS; *Loffel, Egon W.; Public Policy; *THE STATE OF HISPANIC AMERICA.

National Hispanic Field Service Program

7884 Math-based careers. HISPANIC BUSINESS, Vol. 4, no. 4 (April 1982), p. 20,24. English. **DESCR:** *Careers; Chicanas; *Engineering as a Profession; Government Employees; National Action Council for Minorities in Engineering (NACME).

National Hispanic Heritage Week

7885 Hispanic caucus announces plans. NUESTRO, Vol. 7, no. 6 (August 1983), p. 12-13. English. **DESCR:** *Congressional Hispanic Caucus; Political Parties and Organizations.

7886 Hispanic heritage month celebrated by Newark public. LIBRARY JOURNAL, Vol. 107, no. 17 (October 1, 1982), p. 1801. English. **DESCR:** *Cultural Customs.

7887 Hispanics wooed by Reagan, Demos. NUESTRO, Vol. 7, no. 8 (October 1983), p. 11-12. English. **DESCR:** Congressional Hispanic Caucus; *Political Parties and Organizations; Reagan, Ronald.

7888 Nation observes Hispanic Heritage Week. NUESTRO, Vol. 6, no. 8 (October 1982), p. 36-37. English.

7889 Proclamation 4956 - National Hispanic Heritage Week, 1982 (July 30, 1982). PUBLIC PAPERS OF THE PRESIDENT, Vol. 1, no. 2 (1982), p. 995-996. English.

7890 Reagan, Ronald. Remarks at a White House ceremony celebrating Hispanic heritage week (September 15, 1982). PUBLIC PAPERS OF THE PRESIDENT, Vol. 1, no. 2 (1982), p. 1157-1159. English.

7891 A salute to the arts. NUESTRO, Vol. 6, no. 7 (September 1982), p. 44-45. English. **DESCR:** *Art; Artists; Congressional Hispanic Caucus; Villa, Eduardo.

National Hispanic Institute

7892 Marquez, Roberto. Experiencing state government. NATIONAL HISPANIC JOURNAL, Vol. 1, no. 3 (Summer, Fall, 1982), p. 16-18. English. **DESCR:** Lorenzo de Zavala Mock Legislative Session; *State Government.

7893 Murray, Melissa. Aqui en Tejas: de Zabala youth session set for August: students from throughout state to attend. NATIONAL HISPANIC JOURNAL, Vol. 2, no. 1 (Summer 1983), p. 7. English. **DESCR:** Education; Politics; Students; *Youth.

National Hispanic Media Conference, San Diego, CA, December 2-5, 1982

7894 Communications/marketing. HISPANIC BUSINESS, Vol. 4, no. 11 (November 1982), p. 18. English. **DESCR:** California Chicano News Media Association (CCNMA); Diaz-Albertini, Luis; Domecq Importers, Inc.; *Marketing; Pacific Telephone; Television.

National Hispanic University, Oakland CA

7895 Reusswig, Jim. Whence the National Hispanic Center and University? Mater artium necessitas. THRUST, Vol. 11, no. 3 (January, February, 1982), p. 32-35. English. **DESCR:** Bilingual Bicultural Education; Education; *National Hispanic Center.

National Hispanic Voter Registration Campaign

7896 Padilla, Steve. In search of Hispanic voters. NUESTRO, Vol. 7, no. 6 (August 1983), p. 20. English. **DESCR:** Elections; *Voter Turnout.

NATIONAL HISPANIC WOMEN'S NETWORK DIRECTORY

7897 NATIONAL HISPANIC WOMEN'S NETWORK DIRECTORY, June 1983. LATINO, Vol. 54, no. 7 (January 1983), p. 13-20. English. **DESCR:** *Chicanas; *Directories.

National Image, Inc.

7898 Affirmative action. NUESTRO, Vol. 5, no. 8 (November 1981), p. 11-12. English. **DESCR:** *Affirmative Action Programs.

7899 Latinas on the march, NUESTRO survey reveals: organizations assess achievements during 1981. NUESTRO, Vol. 6, no. 2 (March 1982), p. 16-28+. English. **DESCR:** Forum of National Hispanic Organizations; Hispanic Health Council; Latin Americans; League of United Latin American Citizens (LULAC); National Coalition of Hispanic Mental Health and Human Services Organizations (COSSMHO); National Council of La Raza (NCLR); National Hispanic Bar Association; National Puerto Rican Forum, Inc.; *Organizations; Yzaguirre, Raul.

National Image, Inc. (cont.)

7900 Tips for making the right moves in today's job markets. HISPANIC BUSINESS, Vol. 5, no. 3 (March 1983), p. 24. English. DESCR: *Employment.

7901 Treviso, Ruben. National IMAGE. CAMINOS, Vol. 3, no. 8 (September 1982), p. 37-38,51. Bilingual. DESCR: *Organizations.

7902 Whisler, Kirk. IMAGE and affirmative action. CAMINOS, Vol. 3, no. 8 (September 1982), p. 34-36. Bilingual. DESCR: *Affirmative Action; *Montoya, David.

National Institute of Mental Health

7903 Gil, Rosa Maria. Issues in the delivery of mental health services to Cuban entrants. MIGRATION TODAY, Vol. 11, no. 4-5 (1983), p. 44-48. English. DESCR: Cuban Haitian Task Force; Cubanos; Immigration; *Mental Health Programs.

National Institute of Mental Health Diagnostic Interview Schedule

7904 Karno, M. Development of the Spanish-language version of the National Institute of Mental Health Diagnostic Interview Schedule. ARCHIVES OF GENERAL PSYCHIATRY, Vol. 40, no. 11 (November 1983), p. 1183-1188. English. DESCR: Culture; Languages; Mental Health; Spanish Language.

National Labor Relations Act (NLRA)

7905 Bracamonte, Jose A. The national labor relations act and undaunted workers: the alienation of American labor. SAN DIEGO LAW REVIEW, Vol. 21, no. 1 (December 1983), p. 29-86. English. DESCR: Immigration Law; Labor Unions; Sure-Tan; *Undocumented Workers.

National League of Cities

7906 Community watching. CAMINOS, Vol. 3, no. 5 (May 1982), p. 56-57. Bilingual. DESCR: Adelante Mujer Hispana Conference; Agricultural Laborers; Beilson, Anthony C.; Boycotts; Chacon, Peter R.; Chicanas; *Cultural Organizations; Farm Labor Organizing Commmittee (FLOC); Financial Aid; Hollenbeck Junior High School, Los Angeles, CA; Junior High School Students; Optimist Club of Greater East Los Angeles; Organizations; Project WELL (We Enjoy Learning & Leadership); Torres, Art.

National Medical Fellowships (NMF)

7907 Math-based careers. HISPANIC BUSINESS, Vol. 5, no. 9 (September 1983), p. 28. English. DESCR: Andrew W. Mellon Foundation; *Careers; Employment; Engineering as a Profession; Financial Aid; Garcia, Mary; Higher Education; National Council for Minorities in Engineering (NACME); Rivera, Lourdes.

National Miner's Union (NMU)

7908 Rubenstein, Harry R. The great Gallup Coal strike of 1933. SOUTHWEST ECONOMY AND SOCIETY, Vol. 3, no. 2 (Winter 1977, 1978), p. 34-53. English. DESCR: *Gallup Coal Strike of 1933; Labor Unions; Mining Industry; New Mexico; *Strikes and Lockouts; United Mineworkers of America (UMWA).

National Minority Enterprise Development Week

7909 White House honors three minority firms. NUESTRO, Vol. 7, no. 8 (October 1983), p. 51. English. DESCR: *Business Enterprises; Businesspeople; Carson, Norris L.; H & H Meat Products, Mercedes, TX; Hinojosa, Liborio; J.T. Construction Co., El Paso, TX; N.L. Carson Construction, Inc., Carthage, MS; Torres, Jaime.

National Oceanic and Atmospheric Administration

7910 Government review. NUESTRO, Vol. 7, no. 10 (December 1983), p. 48. English. DESCR: Banking Industry; Child Care Centers; Chile; Clinics (Medical); Credit Unions; Employment; Employment Training; *Government Services; Medical Care; National Credit Union Administration; SER; U.S. Department of Health and Human Services; U.S. Department of Labor.

National Press Foundation

7911 Our 1982 Latino awards. NUESTRO, Vol. 7, no. 1 (January, February, 1983), p. 44-46. English. DESCR: Awards; Escalante, Jaime; Gallegos, Gina; Grace, J. Peter; Immigration and Naturalization Service (INS); Knight, Bobby; Lamas, Fernando; *Latino Awards; Luce, Claire Boothe; Moreno, Rita; Rodriguez Hernandez, Andres; Simpson-Mazzoli Bill; Smith, Raymond; Valeri, Michele; Voting Rights Act.

National Puerto Rican Coalition

7912 Diaz, Tom. Turning numbers into clout. NUESTRO, Vol. 7, no. 10 (December 1983), p. 34-35. English. DESCR: *National Puerto Rican/Hispanic Voter Participation Project; Puerto Ricans; *Voter Turnout.

National Puerto Rican Forum, Inc.

7913 Latinas on the march, NUESTRO survey reveals: organizations assess achievements during 1981. NUESTRO, Vol. 6, no. 2 (March 1982), p. 16-28+. English. DESCR: Forum of National Hispanic Organizations; Hispanic Health Council; Latin Americans; League of United Latin American Citizens (LULAC); National Coalition of Hispanic Mental Health and Human Services Organizations (COSSMHO); National Council of La Raza (NCLR); National Hispanic Bar Association; *National Image, Inc.; *Organizations; Yzaguirre, Raul.

National Puerto Rican/Hispanic Voter Participation Project

7914 Diaz, Tom. Turning numbers into clout. NUESTRO, Vol. 7, no. 10 (December 1983), p. 34-35. English. DESCR: National Puerto Rican Coalition; Puerto Ricans; *Voter Turnout.

NATIONAL SURVEY ON EMIGRATION TO THE NORTHERN BORDER AND THE UNITED STATES

7915 Howard, David. For "illegals" migration goes both ways. R & D MEXICO, Vol. 2, no. 3-4 (December, January, 1981, 1982), p. 14-17. English. DESCR: Immigration; Migration; Migration Patterns; Surveys; *Undocumented Workers.

National Urban Fellows, Inc.

7916 30 Urban Fellowships to be awarded. LATINO, Vol. 53, no. 1 (January, February, 1982), p. 21. English. DESCR: Financial Aid.

National Youth Employment Coalition

7917 Manuel Bustelo heads youth effort. NUESTRO,
Vol. 5, no. 8 (November 1981), p. 42-43.
English. DESCR: Bustelo, Manuel A.;
*Organizations.

Nationalism

7918 Alurista. Cultural nationalism and Xicano
literature during the decade of 1965-1975.
MELUS: MULTI-ETHNIC LITERATURE OF THE UNITED
STATES, Vol. 8, no. 2 (Summer 1981), p.
22-34. English. DESCR: *Literature.

7919 Bath, C. Richard. Health and environmental
problems: the role of the border in El
Paso-Ciudad Juarez coordination. JOURNAL OF
INTERAMERICAN STUDIES AND WORLD AFFAIRS,
Vol. 24, no. 3 (August 1982), p. 375-392.
English. DESCR: Border Region; Ciudad
Juarez, Chihuahua, Mexico; *El Paso, TX;
International Boundary and Water Commission;
Pollution; *Public Health; United
States-Mexico Relations; U.S Border Public
Health Association (AFMES).

7920 Cardenas de Dwyer, Carlota. Cultural
nationalism and Chicano literature in the
eighties. MELUS: MULTI-ETHNIC LITERATURE OF
THE UNITED STATES, Vol. 8, no. 2 (Summer
1981), p. 40-47. English. DESCR:
*Literature.

7921 Fraser Rothenberg, Irene. Chicanos, the
Panama Canal issues and the Reagan campaign:
reflections from 1976 and projections for
1980. JOURNAL OF ETHNIC STUDIES, Vol. 7, no.
4 (Winter 1980), p. 37-49. English. DESCR:
*International Relations; Lobbying;
Newspapers; Panama; *Panama Canal; Politics;
Reagan, Ronald.

7922 Fraser Rothenberg, Irene. Mexican-American
views of U.S. relations with Latin America.
JOURNAL OF ETHNIC STUDIES, Vol. 6, no. 1
(Spring 1978), p. 62-78. English. DESCR:
Chicano Movement; Culture; Identity;
International Relations; Latin America;
Lobbying; Mexico; Political History and
Conditions; Politics.

7923 Vigil, James Diego. Towards a new
perspective on understanding the Chicano
people: the six C's model of sociocultural
change. CAMPO LIBRE, Vol. 1, no. 2 (Summer
1981), p. 141-167. English. DESCR:
Acculturation; Assimilation; Cultural
Characteristics; History; Mexican
Nationalism Period; Mexico; Organizations;
Precolumbian Society; *Six C's Model
(Theoretical Model); Social History and
Conditions; Spanish Colonial Period.

Nationalization

7924 Estado, cerco financiero y proyecto
nacional. INFORME: RELACIONES MEXICO-ESTADOS
UNIDOS, Vol. 1, no. 3 (July, December,
1982), p. 160-197. Spanish. DESCR:
Economics; *Mexico.

Native Americans

7925 Big mountain Dine nation. CORAZON DE AZTLAN,
Vol. 1, no. 1 (January, February, 1982), p.
22. English.

7926 Borjas, George J. The labor supply of male
Hispanic immigrants in the United States.
INTERNATIONAL MIGRATION REVIEW, Vol. 17, no.
4 (Winter 1983), p. 653-671. English.
DESCR: Assimilation; Immigration; Labor
Supply and Market; Puerto Ricans.

7927 Chavez, John A. Aztlan, Cibola, and frontier
New Spain. CAMPO LIBRE, Vol. 1, no. 2
(Summer 1981), p. 193-211. English. DESCR:
*Aztlan; *Explorations; Folklore; History;
Mestizaje; Mexico; Missions; Southwest
United States.

7928 Churchhill, Ward. Implications of publishing
ROOTS OF RESISTANCE. JOURNAL OF ETHNIC
STUDIES, Vol. 9, no. 3 (Fall 1981), p.
83-89. English. DESCR: Book Reviews;
Colonialism; Dunbar Ortiz, Roxanne; Land
Tenure; New Mexico; Publishing Industry;
*ROOTS OF RESISTANCE: LAND TENURE IN NEW
MEXICO, 1680-1980; Social History and
Conditions.

7929 Cripps, Thomas. Mexicans, Indians and
movies: the need for a history. WIDE ANGLE:
A FILM QUARTERLY OF THEORY, CRITICISM, AND
PRACTICE, Vol. 5, no. 1 (1982), p. 68-70.
English. DESCR: Bataille, Gretchen M.; *Book
Reviews; Films; IMAGES OF THE MEXICAN
AMERICAN IN FICTION AND FILM; O'Connor, John
E.; Pettit, Arthur G.; Silet, Charles L.P.;
*Stereotypes; THE HOLLYWOOD INDIAN:
STEREOTYPES OF NATIVE AMERICANS IN FILMS;
THE PRETEND INDIANS: IMAGES OF NATIVE
AMERICANS IN THE MOVIES.

7930 Dunbar Ortiz, Roxanne. The roots of
resistance: Pueblo land tenure and Spanish
colonization. JOURNAL OF ETHNIC STUDIES,
Vol. 5, no. 4 (Winter 1977), p. 33-53.
English. DESCR: *Land Tenure; New Mexico;
Pueblo Indians; Social History and
Conditions.

7931 Exum, Herbert A. The most invisible
minority: the culturally diverse elderly.
SCHOOL COUNSELOR, Vol. 30, no. 1 (September
1982), p. 15-24. English. DESCR: *Ancianos;
Asian Americans; Blacks; Counseling
(Psychological); Cultural Customs; Ethnic
Groups; Family; Stereotypes.

7932 Flaskerud, Jacquelyn H. Community mental
health nursing: its unique role in the
delivery of services to ethnic minorities.
PERSPECTIVES IN PSYCHIATRIC CARE, Vol. 20,
no. 1 (January, March, 1982), p. 37-43.
English. DESCR: *Asian Americans; Blacks;
*Community Mental Health; Cultural
Characteristics.

7933 Fleming, Marilyn B. Problems experienced by
Anglo, Hispanic and Navajo Indian women
college students. JOURNAL OF AMERICAN INDIAN
EDUCATION, Vol. 22, no. 1 (October 1982), p.
7-17. English. DESCR: *Chicanas; Community
Colleges; Ethnic Groups; Identity; Medical
Education.

7934 Henderson, Ronald W. and Brody, Gene H.
Effects of ethnicity and child's age on
maternal judgments of children's
transgressions against persons and property.
JOURNAL OF GENETIC PSYCHOLOGY, Vol. 140, no.
2 (June 1982), p. 253-263. English. DESCR:
Anglo Americans; Arizona; Behavior
Modification; *Child Rearing; Cultural
Characteristics; *Socialization; Tucson, AZ.

7935 The land is not for sale. CORAZON DE AZTLAN,
Vol. 1, no. 1 (January, February, 1982), p.
21. English.

Native Americans (cont.)

7936 Olivas, Michael A. Indian, Chicano and Puerto Rican colleges: status and issues. BILINGUAL REVIEW, Vol. 9, no. 1 (January, March, 1982), p. 36-58. English. DESCR: *Colleges and Universities; Education; Puerto Rican Education; Treaties.

7937 Weiss, Lawrence D. Industrial reserve armies of the southwest: Navajo and Mexican. SOUTHWEST ECONOMY AND SOCIETY, Vol. 3, no. 1 (Fall 1977), p. 19-29. English. DESCR: Capitalism; History; *Labor Supply and Market; Navaho Indians; Railroads; *Southwest United States.

Nativism

USE: Assimilation

Natural Support Systems

7938 Delgado, Melvin. Ethnic and cultural variations in the care of the aged. Hispanic elderly and natural support systems: a special focus on Puerto Ricans. JOURNAL OF GERIATRIC PSYCHIATRY, Vol. 15, no. 2 (1982), p. 239-251. English. DESCR: *Ancianos; Cultural Organizations; Curanderas; Family; Puerto Ricans; Religion; Santeros.

7939 Rizzuto, Anna-Maria. Ethnic and cultural variations in the care of the aged. Discussion: Hispanic elderly and natural support systems: a special focus on Puerto Ricans. JOURNAL OF GERIATRIC PSYCHIATRY, Vol. 15, no. 2 (1982), p. 253-255. English. DESCR: *Ancianos; Puerto Ricans.

Naturalization

7940 Diaz, Katherine A. Enrique Martinez: why I became a U.S. citizen. CAMINOS, Vol. 3, no. 4 (April 1982), p. 35-36. Bilingual. DESCR: *Martinez, Enrique.

7941 Food stamp recovery. NUESTRO, Vol. 6, no. 10 (December 1982), p. 8. English. DESCR: Corpus Christi, TX; *Food Stamps.

7942 Promoting U.S. citizenship. CAMINOS, Vol. 3, no. 7 (July, August, 1982), p. 27. English. DESCR: *Mexican American Legal Defense and Educational Fund (MALDEF).

7943 Richard, John E. Public employment rights of aliens. BAYLOR LAW REVIEW, Vol. 34, no. 3 (Summer 1982), p. 371-385. English. DESCR: Cabell v. Chavez-Salido; Employment; Sugarman v. Dougall.

Nava, Julian

7944 Dr. Julian Nava on Mexico. CAMINOS, Vol. 3, no. 6 (June 1982), p. 7-8. Bilingual. DESCR: Mexico; *United States-Mexico Relations.

Navaho Indians

7945 Weiss, Lawrence D. Industrial reserve armies of the southwest: Navajo and Mexican. SOUTHWEST ECONOMY AND SOCIETY, Vol. 3, no. 1 (Fall 1977), p. 19-29. English. DESCR: Capitalism; History; *Labor Supply and Market; Native Americans; Railroads; *Southwest United States.

Navarrete, Diana

7946 Navarrete, Diana. Broadcasting role model. NUESTRO, Vol. 6, no. 1 (January, February, 1982), p. 22-23. English. DESCR: Broadcast Media; Fashion; Latin Americans.

NBC [television network]

7947 Television: Hispanics: unexplored territory. LATINO, Vol. 53, no. 2 (March, April, 1982), p. 21+. English. DESCR: *Television.

NCCHE

USE: National Chicano Council on Higher Education (NCCHE)

Near West Side, Chicago, IL

7948 Ano Nuevo de Kerr, Louise. Chicano settlements in Chicago: a brief history. JOURNAL OF ETHNIC STUDIES, Vol. 2, no. 4 (Winter 1975), p. 22-32. English. DESCR: Back of the Yards, Chicago, IL; *Chicago, IL; Pilsen, IL; Social History and Conditions; South Chicago, Chicago, IL; *Urban Communities.

Nebaj, Guatemala

7949 Simon, Jean-Marie. Five days in Nebaj: one perspective. NUESTRO, Vol. 7, no. 1 (January, February, 1983), p. 28-32. English. DESCR: *Guatemala; *Political History and Conditions.

THE NEGLECTED DIMENSION: ETHNICITY IN AMERICAN LIFE

7950 Fernandez, Celestino. The neglected dimension: ethnicity in American life. AZTLAN, Vol. 14, no. 1 (Spring 1983), p. 199-201. English. DESCR: Book Reviews; Ethnic Groups; Identity; Rosen, Philip.

Negrete, Jesus "Chuy"

7951 Barrera, Jose J. Jesus "Chuy" Negrete: the Chicano vote. NUESTRO, Vol. 5, no. 8 (November 1981), p. 40-41. English. DESCR: Chicanismo; *Recreation.

NEIGHBORS, MEXICO AND THE UNITED STATES: WETBACKS AND OIL

7952 Schmitt, Karl M. Book review of: HISPANIC FOLK MUSIC OF NEW MEXICO AND THE SOUTHWEST: A SELF-PORTRAIT OF A PEOPLE. HISPANIC AMERICAN HISTORICAL REVIEW, Vol. 63, no. 1 (1983), p. 209-210. English. DESCR: Book Reviews; Mabry, Donald; Shafer, Robert Jones; United States-Mexico Relations.

Nelson, Joan M.

7953 Logan, Kathleen. The urban poor in developing nations. JOURNAL OF URBAN HISTORY, Vol. 9, no. 1 (November 1982), p. 108-116. English. DESCR: ACCESS TO POWER: POLITICS AND THE URBAN POOR IN DEVELOPING NATIONS; *Book Reviews; BORDER BOOM TOWN: CIUDAD JUAREZ SINCE 1848; Collier, David; Cornelius, Wayne A.; Eckstein, Susan; Lloyd, Peter; Martinez, Oscar J.; Perlman, Janice E.; POLITICS AND MIGRANT POOR IN MEXICO CITY; SLUMS OF HOPE? SHANTY TOWNS OF THE THIRD WORLD; SQUATTERS AND OLIGARCHS: AUTHORITARIAN RULE AND POLICY CHANGE IN PERU; THE MYTH OF MARGINALITY: URBAN POVERTY AND POLITICS IN RIO DE JANEIRO; THE POVERTY OF REVOLUTION: THE STATE AND THE URBAN POOR IN MEXICO; Urban Economics.

Neruda, Pablo

7954 Umpierre, Luz Maria. La ansiedad de la influencia en Sandra Maria Esteves y Marjorie Agosin. REVISTA CHICANO-RIQUENA, Vol. 11, no. 3-4 (Fall 1983), p. 139-147. Spanish. DESCR: A JULIA Y A MI; *Agosin, Magi; De Burgos, Julia; EL PAIS DIVIDIDO; *Esteves, Sandra Maria; *Literary Criticism; Parra, Nicanor; Poetry.

Nettles, Ron

7955 Police misconduct [panel discussion at the LATINOS IN THE LAW symposium, UCLA, 1982]. CHICANO LAW REVIEW, Vol. 6, (1983), p. 63-121. English. DESCR: Los Angeles Police Department; Love, Eulia; Police; *Police Brutality.

THE NEW BILINGUALISM: AN AMERICAN DILEMMA

7956 Weber, David J. Book review of: THE NEW BILINGUALISM: AN AMERICAN DILEMMA. WESTERN HISTORICAL QUARTERLY, Vol. 14, no. 1 (1983), p. 77-79. English. DESCR: Bilingual Bicultural Education; Bilingualism; Book Reviews; Ridge, Martin.

New Jersey

7957 Cubans enjoy New Jersey town. NUESTRO, Vol. 7, no. 3 (April 1983), p. 10-11. English. DESCR: Cubanos; *Union City, NJ.

7958 Estevez, Guillermo. Resettling the Cuban refugees in New Jersey. MIGRATION TODAY, Vol. 11, no. 4-5 (1983), p. 28-33. English. DESCR: Caribbean Relief Program; *Cubanos; Immigration; International Rescue Committee; Refugees.

7959 Student at New Jersey school saves classmate. NUESTRO, Vol. 6, no. 4 (May 1982), p. 28. English. DESCR: *Children.

NEW MANAGEMENT

7960 Communications/marketing. HISPANIC BUSINESS, Vol. 5, no. 10 (October 1983), p. 26. English. DESCR: Advertising; Arens & Gutierrez; Employment; Henry Molina, Inc.; Journals; Lionetti and Meyers Research Center, Inc.; Marketing; *Mass Media; Midwest Hispanics in Telecommunications Symposium, Chicago, IL.

New Mexico

7961 Blea, Irene I. Book review of: BUT TIME AND CHANCE. CACR REVIEW, Vol. 1, no. 1 (September 1982), p. 132-133. English. DESCR: Book Reviews; *BUT TIME AND CHANCE; Catholic Church; Chavez, Fray Angelico; Lamy, J.B.; Machelbeuf, Joseph P., Vicar; Martinez, Antonio, Fray.

7962 Camarillo, Alberto M. Book review of: MEXICANO RESISTANCE IN THE SOUTHWEST: "THE SACRED RIGHT OF SELF-PRESERVATION". WESTERN HISTORICAL QUARTERLY, Vol. 14, no. 1 (1983), p. 79-80. English. DESCR: Book Reviews; History; *MEXICANO RESISTANCE IN THE SOUTHWEST: "THE SACRED RIGHT OF SELF-PRESERVATION"; Rosenbaum, Robert J.

7963 Chavira, Ricardo. Gutierrez, first Latino recipient. NUESTRO, Vol. 7, no. 3 (April 1983), p. 11-12. English. DESCR: Financial Aid; *Gutierrez, Ramon; History; MacArthur Foundation.

7964 Churchhill, Ward. Implications of publishing ROOTS OF RESISTANCE. JOURNAL OF ETHNIC STUDIES, Vol. 9, no. 3 (Fall 1981), p. 83-89. English. DESCR: Book Reviews; Colonialism; Dunbar Ortiz, Roxanne; Land Tenure; Native Americans; Publishing Industry; *ROOTS OF RESISTANCE: LAND TENURE IN NEW MEXICO, 1680-1980; Social History and Conditions.

7965 Craver, Rebecca McDowell. The impact of intimacy: Mexican-Anglo intermarriage in New Mexico 1821-1846. SOUTHWESTERN STUDIES, no. 66 (1982), p. 1-79. English. DESCR: Acculturation; Assimilation; Chicanas; *Intermarriage; Rio Arriba Valley, New Mexico.

7966 Dunbar Ortiz, Roxanne. The roots of resistance: Pueblo land tenure and Spanish colonization. JOURNAL OF ETHNIC STUDIES, Vol. 5, no. 4 (Winter 1977), p. 33-53. English. DESCR: *Land Tenure; Native Americans; Pueblo Indians; Social History and Conditions.

7967 Garcia, Juan R. Book review of: MEXICANO RESISTANCE IN THE SOUTHWEST: "THE SACRED RIGHT OF SELF-PRESERVATION". ARIZONA AND THE WEST, Vol. 24, no. 1 (Spring 1982), p. 81-82. English. DESCR: Book Reviews; *MEXICANO RESISTANCE IN THE SOUTHWEST: "THE SACRED RIGHT OF SELF-PRESERVATION"; Rosenbaum, Robert J.; Social History and Conditions.

7968 Gifford, Douglas. Book review of: HISPANIC FOLK MUSIC OF NEW MEXICO AND THE SOUTHWEST: A SELF-PORTRAIT OF A PEOPLE. BULLETIN OF HISPANIC STUDIES, Vol. 59, no. 2 (April 1982), p. 162-163. English. DESCR: Book Reviews; Folk Songs; *HISPANIC FOLK MUSIC OF NEW MEXICO AND THE SOUTHWEST: A SELF-PORTRAIT OF A PEOPLE; Robb, John Donald.

7969 Gil, Carlos B. Miguel Antonio Otero, first Chicano governor. JOURNAL OF ETHNIC STUDIES, Vol. 4, no. 3 (Fall 1976), p. 95-102. English. DESCR: Book Reviews; *Elected Officials; OTERO: AN AUTOBIOGRAPHICAL TRILOGY; Otero, Miguel A.; Social History and Conditions; United States History.

7970 Jensen, Carol. Cleofas M. Jaramillo on marriage in territorial Northern New Mexico. NEW MEXICO HISTORICAL REVIEW, Vol. 58, no. 2 (April 1983), p. 153-171. English. DESCR: Jaramillo, Cleofas M.; *Marriage.

7971 Jensen, Joan M. Canning comes to New Mexico: women and the agricultural extension service, 1914-1919. NEW MEXICO HISTORICAL REVIEW, Vol. 57, no. 4 (October 1982), p. 361-386. English. DESCR: *Cannery Workers; Chicanas; Food Industry; New Mexico Agricultural Extension Service.

7972 Jensen, Joan M. Women teachers, class and ethnicity: New Mexico 1900-1950. SOUTHWEST ECONOMY AND SOCIETY, Vol. 4, no. 2 (Winter 1978, 1979), p. 3-13. English. DESCR: Alternative Education; *Chicanas; Cultural Pluralism; History; Spanish Language; Teaching Profession.

7973 Korte, Alvin O. Social interaction and morale of Spanish-speaking rural and urban elderly. JOURNAL OF GERONTOLOGICAL SOCIAL WORK, Vol. 4, no. 3- (Spring, Summer, 1982), p. 57-66. English. DESCR: *Ancianos; Social Psychology.

New Mexico (cont.)

7974 Miller, Darlis A. Cross-cultural marriages
in the Southwest: the New Mexico experience,
1846-1900. NEW MEXICO HISTORICAL REVIEW,
Vol. 57, no. 4 (October 1982), p. 335-359.
English. DESCR: Assimilation; Chicanas;
Ethnic Attitudes; *Intermarriage; Social
History and Conditions.

7975 Murphy, Lawrence R. Book review of: ROOTS OF
RESISTANCE: LAND TENURE IN NEW MEXICO,
1680-1980. NEW MEXICO HISTORICAL REVIEW,
Vol. 57, no. 1 (January 1982), p. 89-90.
English. DESCR: Book Reviews; Ortiz, Roxanne
Dunbar; *ROOTS OF RESISTANCE: LAND TENURE IN
NEW MEXICO, 1680-1980.

7976 New Mexico's gubernatorial race. HISPANIC
BUSINESS, Vol. 4, no. 11 (November 1982), p.
27,30. English. DESCR: Anaya, Toney;
*Biography; Elections; Political Parties and
Organizations.

7977 Nontraditional street group. NUESTRO, Vol.
6, no. 6 (August 1982), p. 12. English.
DESCR: Artists; *Teatro; *Teatro Claridad,
South Valley, NM.

7978 Oczon, Annabelle M. Land grants in New
Mexico: a selective bibliography. NEW MEXICO
HISTORICAL REVIEW, Vol. 57, no. 1 (January
1982), p. 81-87. English. DESCR:
Bibliography; *Land Grants.

7979 Reid, Richard A.; Bartlett, Edward E.; and
Kozoll, Richard. Checkerboard area health
system: delivering comprehensive care in a
remote region of New Mexico. HUMAN
ORGANIZATION, Vol. 41, no. 2 (Summer 1982),
p. 147-155. English. DESCR: *Medical Care;
Rural Population.

7980 Rubenstein, Harry R. The great Gallup Coal
strike of 1933. SOUTHWEST ECONOMY AND
SOCIETY, Vol. 3, no. 2 (Winter 1977, 1978),
p. 34-53. English. DESCR: *Gallup Coal
Strike of 1933; Labor Unions; Mining
Industry; National Miner's Union (NMU);
*Strikes and Lockouts; United Mineworkers of
America (UMWA).

7981 Salmon, Roberto Mario. Book review of:
SPANISH AND MEXICAN LAND GRANTS IN NEW
MEXICO AND COLORADO. JOURNAL OF ETHNIC
STUDIES, Vol. 9, no. 3 (Fall 1981), p.
120-121. English. DESCR: Book Reviews;
Colorado; *Land Grants; *SPANISH AND MEXICAN
LAND GRANTS IN NEW MEXICO AND COLORADO; Van
Ness, Christine M.; Van Ness, John R.

7982 Vigil, Maurilio E. Recollections of New
Mexico Christmas. NUESTRO, Vol. 6, no. 10
(December 1982), p. 41-44. English. DESCR:
*Christmas; *Short Story.

7983 Vincent, J. Book review of: HISPANIC FOLK
MUSIC OF NEW MEXICO AND THE SOUTHWEST: A
SELF-PORTRAIT OF A PEOPLE. ETHNOMUSICOLOGY,
Vol. 26, no. 2 (May 1982), p. 326-327.
English. DESCR: Book Reviews;
Ethnomusicology; Folk Songs; *HISPANIC FOLK
MUSIC OF NEW MEXICO AND THE SOUTHWEST: A
SELF-PORTRAIT OF A PEOPLE; Robb, John
Donald; *THE SOUTHWEST: A SELF-PORTRAIT.

7984 Weber, Kenneth R. Book review of: CANONES:
VALUES, CRISIS, AND SURVIVAL IN A NORTHERN
NEW MEXICO VILLAGE. JOURNAL OF ETHNIC
STUDIES, Vol. 11, no. 2 (Summer 1983), p.
119-123. English. DESCR: Book Reviews;
Canones, NM; *CANONES: VALUES, CRISIS AND
SURVIVAL IN A NORTHERN NEW MEXICO VILLAGE;
Ethnology; History; Kutsche, Paul; Northern

New Mexico; Van Ness, John R.

7985 Weber, Kenneth R. Book review of: HISPANIC
VILLAGES OF NORTHERN NEW MEXICO. SOUTHWEST
ECONOMY AND SOCIETY, Vol. 1, no. 1 (Spring
1976), p. 48. English. DESCR: Book Reviews;
Economic History and Conditions; Great
Depression, 1929-1933; *HISPANIC VILLAGES OF
NORTHERN NEW MEXICO; Tewa Basin, NM; Weigle,
Marta.

7986 Weber, Kenneth R. Book review of: MY
PENITENTE LAND: REFLECTIONS ON SPANISH NEW
MEXICO. JOURNAL OF ETHNIC STUDIES, Vol. 3,
no. 2 (Summer 1975), p. 119-121. English.
DESCR: Book Reviews; Chavez, Fray Angelico;
*Hermanos Penitentes; MY PENITENTE LAND:
REFLECTIONS ON SPANISH NEW MEXICO; Religion.

New Mexico Agricultural Extension Service

7987 Jensen, Joan M. Canning comes to New Mexico:
women and the agricultural extension
service, 1914-1919. NEW MEXICO HISTORICAL
REVIEW, Vol. 57, no. 4 (October 1982), p.
361-386. English. DESCR: *Cannery Workers;
Chicanas; Food Industry; New Mexico.

New Mexico State University

7988 De Blassie, Richard R. and Franco, Juan N.
The differences between personality
inventory scores and self-rating in a sample
of Hispanic subjects. JOURNAL OF NON-WHITE
CONCERNS IN PERSONNEL AND GUIDANCE, Vol. 11,
no. 2 (January 1983), p. 43-46. English.
DESCR: Chicanas; Hispanic Education
[program]; *Personality; *Sixteen
Personality Factor Questionnaire.

7989 Regional report, education: NMSU schedules
Chicano week. NUESTRO, Vol. 7, no. 4 (May
1983), p. 11-12. English. DESCR: *Chicano
Movement.

New Music

7990 Mead, R. H. Latin American accents in new
music. LATIN AMERICAN MUSIC REVIEW, Vol. 3,
no. 2 (Fall, Winter, 1982), p. 207-228.
English. DESCR: Chavez, Carlos; Cowell,
Henry; *Music.

NEW YORK

7991 Goodman, Gerson. LRF takes on Battery Park
City. HISPANIC BUSINESS, Vol. 4, no. 10
(October 1982), p. 16-17,24. English.
DESCR: Business Enterprises; Construction
Industry; *LRF Developers, Inc.; *Real
Estate.

7992 Mukherjee, Sukdeb. Misdiagnosis of
schizophrenia in bipolar patients: a
multiethnic comparison. AMERICAN JOURNAL OF
PSYCHIATRY, Vol. 14, no. 12 (December 1983),
p. 1571-1574. English. DESCR: *Mental
Health; Puerto Ricans.

7993 New York's tele-signal corporation. HISPANIC
BUSINESS, Vol. 4, no. 11 (November 1982), p.
20. English. DESCR: Business Enterprises;
*High Technology Industries; *Tele-Signal
Corporation; Toracida, Esteben.

New York

7994 Dvorak, Trisha and Kirschner, Carl. Mary likes fishes: reverse psychological phenomena in New York Puerto Rican Spanish. BILINGUAL REVIEW, Vol. 9, no. 1 (January, April, 1982), p. 59-65. English. **DESCR:** Puerto Ricans; *Spanish Language; *Syntax.

New York City Marathon

7995 Salazar wins New York race. NUESTRO, Vol. 6, no. 8 (October 1982), p. 13. English. **DESCR:** Athletes; *Salazar, Alberto; Sports.

New York Council on Adoptable Children (COAC)

7996 Valiente-Barksdale, Clara. Recruiting Hispanic families. CHILDREN TODAY, Vol. 12, no. 2 (March, April, 1983), p. 26-28. English. **DESCR:** *Adoption; New York, NY; RAICES (New York, NY).

New York, NY

7997 Barradas, Efrain. "Todo lo que digo es cierto...": en memoria de Victor Fernandez Fragoso (1944-1982). REVISTA CHICANO-RIQUENA, Vol. 10, no. 3 (Summer 1982), p. 43-46. Spanish. **DESCR:** Authors; *Biography; Essays; *Fernandez Fragoso, Victor; Puerto Rican Literature.

7998 Gumperz, John J. Hispanic Catholics. SOCIETY, Vol. 20, no. 3 (March, April, 1983), p. 2-3. English. **DESCR:** *Catholic Church.

7999 Gurak, Douglas T. and Fitzpatrick, Joseph P. Intermarriage among Hispanic ethnic groups in New York City. AMERICAN JOURNAL OF SOCIOLOGY, Vol. 87, no. 4 (January 1982), p. 921-934. English. **DESCR:** *Intermarriage; Puerto Ricans.

8000 Hispanic-owned bank far exceeds expectations. ABA BANKING JOURNAL, Vol. 75, (February 1983), p. 32-34. English. **DESCR:** Banking Industry; *Capital National Bank; Cordova, Carlos.

8001 Mexican centers advance U.S. ties. NUESTRO, Vol. 7, no. 1 (January, February, 1983), p. 10-11. English. **DESCR:** Art Galleries; *El Centro Mexicano del Libro; Los Angeles, CA; Mexico; Museums; Publishing Industry.

8002 New York's exhibition of Aztec treasures. NUESTRO, Vol. 6, no. 5 (June, July, 1982), p. 63-64. English. **DESCR:** Anthropology; *Aztecs; Exhibits.

8003 Uehling, Mark D. Rivalry in New York: a profile of two newspapers. NUESTRO, Vol. 7, no. 7 (September 1982), p. 20-21. English. **DESCR:** Bustelo, Manuel A.; DIARIO LA PRENSA [newspaper], New York, NY; Espinal, Antonio; Gannett Co., Inc.; Journalism; *Newspapers; NOTICIAS DEL MUNDO; Patino, Luis; Unification Church.

8004 Valiente-Barksdale, Clara. Recruiting Hispanic families. CHILDREN TODAY, Vol. 12, no. 2 (March, April, 1983), p. 26-28. English. **DESCR:** *Adoption; New York Council on Adoptable Children (COAC); RAICES (New York, NY).

8005 Wurzman, Ilyana. Cultural values of Puerto Rican opiate addicts: an exploratory study. AMERICAN JOURNAL OF DRUG AND ALCOHOL ABUSE, Vol. 9, no. 2 (1982, 1983), p. 141-153. English. **DESCR:** Acculturation; Anglo Americans; Blacks; *Drug Abuse; Drug

Addicts; Family; Loevinger's Sentence Completion Test; Machismo; Opium; Puerto Ricans; Values.

New York Telephone Co.

8006 Business update: phone company issues Spanish yellow pages. NUESTRO, Vol. 7, no. 4 (May 1983), p. 42. English. **DESCR:** Advertising; *Community Services.

NEW YORK TIMES

8007 Mexico en crisis: la incomprendida prensa norteamericana. INFORME: RELACIONES MEXICO-ESTADOS UNIDOS, Vol. 1, no. 3 (July, December, 1982), p. 256-266. Spanish. **DESCR:** *ABC-TV; *Journalism; Mass Media.

8008 Miguel de la Madrid en la prensa norteamericana. INFORME: RELACIONES MEXICO-ESTADOS UNIDOS, Vol. 1, no. 2 (July, December, 1982), p. 176-183. Spanish. **DESCR:** *De la Madrid, Miguel; *Journalism; Lopez Portillo, Jose; LOS ANGELES TIMES; Newspapers; WALL STREET JOURNAL; WASHINGTON POST.

News Agencies

8009 EFE announces opening of Miami News Bureau. NUESTRO, Vol. 6, no. 6 (August 1982), p. 52. English. **DESCR:** Miami, FL; Spain; Spanish Language.

Newspapers

8010 Aguirre, Richard R. Print media at a crossroads. HISPANIC BUSINESS, Vol. 4, no. 5 (May 1982), p. 20-21+. English. **DESCR:** *Advertising; Magazines; *Print Media.

8011 Bustelo, Manuel A. Una epoca del Foro Nacional Puertorriqueno. LATINO, Vol. 53, no. 2 (March, April, 1982), p. 15. Spanish. **DESCR:** *Foro Nacional Puertorriqueno; Print Media.

8012 Cantu, Hector. Aqui en Tejas: Hispanic newspapers: city, community papers taking a business approach to the news. NATIONAL HISPANIC JOURNAL, Vol. 2, no. 1 (Summer 1983), p. 9. English. **DESCR:** AUSTIN LIGHT (TX); EL EDITOR (Lubbock, TX); EL SOL DE HOUSTON (TX); Journalism; THE TEXICAN (Dallas, TX).

8013 Esther Manzano. CAMINOS, Vol. 3, no. 3 (March 1982), p. 30. Bilingual. **DESCR:** EL MEXICALO; Journalists; *Manzano, Esther.

8014 Fraser Rothenberg, Irene. Chicanos, the Panama Canal issues and the Reagan campaign: reflections from 1976 and projections for 1980. JOURNAL OF ETHNIC STUDIES, Vol. 7, no. 4 (Winter 1980), p. 37-49. English. **DESCR:** *International Relations; Lobbying; Nationalism; Panama; *Panama Canal; Politics; Reagan, Ronald.

8015 Gannett's Gerald Garcia goes to Tucson. HISPANIC BUSINESS, Vol. 4, no. 5 (May 1982), p. 13. English. **DESCR:** *Biography; Gannett Co., Inc.; Garcia, Gerald; Tucson, AZ.

8016 Miguel de la Madrid en la prensa norteamericana. INFORME: RELACIONES MEXICO-ESTADOS UNIDOS, Vol. 1, no. 2 (July, December, 1982), p. 176-183. Spanish. **DESCR:** *De la Madrid, Miguel; *Journalism; Lopez Portillo, Jose; LOS ANGELES TIMES; NEW YORK TIMES; WALL STREET JOURNAL; WASHINGTON POST.

Newspapers (cont.)

8017 Uehling, Mark D. Rivalry in New York: a profile of two newspapers. NUESTRO, Vol. 7, no. 7 (September 1983), p. 20-21. English. DESCR: Bustelo, Manuel A.; DIARIO LA PRENSA [newspaper], New York, NY; Espinal, Antonio; Gannett Co., Inc.; Journalism; New York, NY; NOTICIAS DEL MUNDO; Patino, Luis; Unification Church.

8018 Wittenauer, Cheryl. Dallas Hispanic media. HISPANIC BUSINESS, Vol. 5, no. 2 (February 1983), p. 12-13+. English. DESCR: Broadcast Media; *Consumers; Dallas, TX; English Language; Marketing; Mass Media; Spanish Language.

8019 Zotti, Ed. An idea whose time has not quite arrived: Spanish sections in newspapers still struggling. ADVERTISING AGE MAGAZINE, Vol. 53, (February 15, 1982), p. II, M29+. English. DESCR: Market Research; Spanish Language.

Newton, Clark

8020 Phillips, Melody. The Chicana: her attitudes towards the woman's liberation movement. COMADRE, no. 2 (Spring 1978), p. 42-50. English. DESCR: Carr, Vikki; *Chicanas; FAMOUS MEXICAN-AMERICANS; Social History and Conditions; Women's Rights.

Newton, Frank

8021 Bedard, Evelyn M. Book review of: HISPANIC MENTAL HEALTH RESEARCH: A REFERENCE GUIDE. RQ - REFERENCE AND ADULT SERVICES DIVISION, Vol. 22, no. 1 (Fall 1982), p. 93. English. DESCR: Bibliography; Book Reviews; *HISPANIC MENTAL HEALTH RESEARCH: A REFERENCE GUIDE; Mental Health; Olmedo, Esteban L.; Padilla, Amado M.

Nguyen, Anh Tuan

8022 What bilingual education means to the nation. NUESTRO, Vol. 7, no. 2 (March 1983), p. 52-53. English. DESCR: *Bilingual Bicultural Education; Education; Millan, Aida; Rodriguez, Axel.

Nicaragua

8023 Aldaraca, Bridget. The poetry of Gioconda Belli. MAIZE, Vol. 5, no. 3-4 (Spring, Summer, 1982), p. 18-21. English. DESCR: Belli, Gioconda; Literary Criticism; *Poetry; Revolutions.

8024 Banberger, Ellen. Poesia nicaraguense. MAIZE, Vol. 5, no. 3-4 (Spring, Summer, 1982), p. 64-77. Spanish. DESCR: Belli, Gioconda; Cardenal, Ernesto; Carrillo, Ernesto; Coronel Urtecho, Jose; Gadea, Gerardo; Gomez, Manuel; Murillo, Rosario; Ojeda, Mirna; *Poetry; Revolutions; Rugama, Leonel.

8025 Belli, Gioconda. Dynamite dresses: vestidos de dinamita. MAIZE, Vol. 5, no. 3-4 (Spring, Summer, 1982), p. 22. Bilingual. DESCR: *Poetry.

8026 Bernal, Juan Manuel. Happy happy. MAIZE, Vol. 5, no. 3-4 (Spring, Summer, 1982), p. 23. Bilingual. DESCR: *Poetry.

8027 Bernal, Juan Manuel. Mientras. MAIZE, Vol. 5, no. 3-4 (Spring, Summer, 1982), p. 24. Spanish. DESCR: *Poetry.

8028 Maldonado-Denis, Manuel. El problema de las nacionalidades: la experiencia caribena. Paper presented at the "Dialogo de las Americas" conference. Mexico, D.F. September 9-14, 1982. REVISTA CHICANO-RIQUENA, Vol. 10, no. 4 (Fall 1982), p. 39-45. Spanish. DESCR: Capitalism; Carpentier, Alejo; Cuba; El Salvador; Grenada; Guatemala; Imperialism; Marti, Jose; *Political History and Conditions; Puerto Rico; United States.

Niebla, Fernando

8029 Q & A with Fernando Niebla: "You have to present yourself as a person that knows what he wants". CAMINOS, Vol. 4, no. 1-2 (January, February, 1983), p. 22-23,71. English. DESCR: Careers; Computers; Electronics Industry.

THE NINE NATIONS OF NORTH AMERICA

8030 Castagnera-Cain, Jim. Garreau's nine nations offer immigration insights. TEXAS OBSERVER, Vol. 74, (October 15, 1982), p. 12+. English. DESCR: Garreau, Joel; Immigration Law; Immigration Regulation and Control; Undocumented Workers.

N.L. Carson Construction, Inc., Carthage, MS

8031 White House honors three minority firms. NUESTRO, Vol. 7, no. 8 (October 1983), p. 51. English. DESCR: *Business Enterprises; Businesspeople; Carson, Norris L.; H & H Meat Products, Mercedes, TX; Hinojosa, Liborio; J.T. Construction Co., El Paso, TX; National Minority Enterprise Development Week; Torres, Jaime.

Nobel Prize

8032 Hispanics win Nobel Prizes. LATINO, Vol. 53, no. 8 (December 1982), p. 20-21. English. DESCR: Authors; Garcia Marquez, Gabriel.

8033 Nobel prize recipient Marquez. LATINA, Vol. 1, no. 2 (February, March, 1983), p. 20. English. DESCR: *Awards; Garcia Marquez, Gabriel.

Nochebuena
USE: Christmas

Nogales, AZ

8034 Powers, Stephen and Sanchez, Virginia V. Correlates of self-esteem of Mexican American adolescents. PSYCHOLOGICAL REPORTS, Vol. 51, no. 3 (December 1982), p. 771-774. English. DESCR: Academic Achievement; Arizona; Employment; *Identity; Junior High School Students.

Nogales, Luis

8035 People. HISPANIC BUSINESS, Vol. 4, no. 6 (June 1982), p. 8. English. DESCR: Aguirre, Pedro; Arellano, Richard; *Biographical Notes; Businesspeople; Cortez, Pete; De la Colina, Rafael; Hernandez, Sam; Rodriguez, Leslie J.; Roybal, Edward R.

Nogales, Luis G.

8036 Communications/marketing. HISPANIC BUSINESS, Vol. 5, no. 1 (January 1983), p. 23. English. DESCR: Banking Industry; Broadcast Media; Caballero Spanish Media, Inc. (CSM); Fleishman-Hillard, Inc.; *Marketing; Miami, FL; Public Relations.

Nogales, Luis G. (cont.)

8037 People. HISPANIC BUSINESS, Vol. 5, no. 11
(November 1983), p. 10. English. **DESCR:**
Aragon, Fermin; *Businesspeople; De Los
Reyes, Victor; Di Martino, Rita; Garcia,
Ruben; Juarez, Chris; Lopez, Leonard; Ozuna,
Bob; Rico, Jose Hipolito; Tamayo, Roberto;
Tapia, Raul R.

Nogales, Mexico

8038 Gonzales, Patrisia. Nogales: view from a
cardboard box. NUESTRO, Vol. 6, no. 9
(November 1982), p. 21-27. English. **DESCR:**
*Mexico; *Poverty.

Non-profit Groups

8039 Book review of: THE FEDERAL BUDGET AND THE
NON-PROFIT SECTOR. CAMINOS, Vol. 4, no. 4
(April 1983), p. 59. English. **DESCR:**
Abramson, Anal J.; Book Reviews; Federal
Aid; *FEDERAL BUDGET AND THE NON-PROFIT
SECTOR; Salamon, Lester M.

Nonverbal Communication (Psychology)

8040 Taking charge at work. HISPANIC BUSINESS,
Vol. 4, no. 3 (March 1982), p. 23. English.
DESCR: *Assertiveness (Psychology).

NOO JORK

8041 Barradas, Efrain. NOO JORK. REVISTA
CHICANO-RIQUENA, Vol. 10, no. 3 (Summer
1982), p. 65-67. Spanish. **DESCR:** Book
Reviews; Fernandez Fragoso, Victor;
Figueroa, Jose Angel.

Norman, Craig & Kummel Organization

8042 Communications/marketing. HISPANIC BUSINESS,
Vol. 4, no. 4 (April 1982), p. 15. English.
DESCR: Advertising Agencies; Consumers;
Juarez and Associates, Inc.; Las Americas,
Inc.; *Marketing; Publicidad Siboney;
Siboney Advertising, Inc.

Norteno

8043 Dickey, Dan W. and Van Osdol, Scott. La
musica nortena: a photographic essay.
SOUTHERN EXPOSURE, Vol. 11, no. 1 (1983), p.
38-41. English. **DESCR:** Jimenez, Flaco;
*Music.

8044 Herrera-Sobek, Maria. Film review of: DEL
MERO CORAZON (STRAIGHT FROM THE HEART).
JOURNAL OF AMERICAN FOLKLORE, Vol. 95,
(March 1982), p. 123. English. **DESCR:** Blank,
Les; *DEL MERO CORAZON; Film Reviews;
Gosling, Maureen; Hernandez, Guillermo;
Strachwitz, Chris.

8045 Mexican border sounds travel the folk
circuit. BILLBOARD, Vol. 95, (February 26,
1983), p. 46. English. **DESCR:** Border Region;
Music.

Northern New Mexico

8046 Weber, Kenneth R. Book review of: CANONES:
VALUES, CRISIS, AND SURVIVAL IN A NORTHERN
NEW MEXICO VILLAGE. JOURNAL OF ETHNIC
STUDIES, Vol. 11, no. 2 (Summer 1983), p.
119-123. English. **DESCR:** Book Reviews;
Canones, NM; *CANONES: VALUES, CRISIS AND
SURVIVAL IN A NORTHERN NEW MEXICO VILLAGE;
Ethnology; History; Kutsche, Paul; New
Mexico; Van Ness, John R.

Northwestern United States

8047 Gamboa, Erasmo. Mexican labor in the Pacific
Northwest, 1943-1947: a photographic essay.
PACIFIC NORTHWEST QUARTERLY, Vol. 73, no. 4
(October 1982), p. 175-181. English. **DESCR:**
*Agricultural Laborers; International Labor
Activities; Labor Camps; Labor Supply and
Market; World War II.

Nosotros [film production company]

8048 Golden Eagle Awards 1983. CAMINOS, Vol. 4,
no. 8 (September 1983), p. 42-43. English.
DESCR: *Awards; Recreation; Sesma, Chico.

8049 Gonzalez, Magdalena. Recognizing Hispanic
achievements in entertainment - U.S. and
Mexico. CAMINOS, Vol. 3, no. 7 (July,
August, 1982), p. 18-24. Bilingual. **DESCR:**
Allende, Fernando; Artists; Awards; Bonilla
Giannini, Roxanna; Eynoso, David; Felix,
Maria; Films; Gallego, Gina; *Golden Eagle
Awards; Hoyos, Rodolfo; Lamas, Lorenzo;
Lopez, Conchita; Lopez, Lisa; Montalban,
Ricardo; Quintero, Jose; Rowe, Arthur;
Television; Torres, Liz.

8050 Whisler, Kirk. Nosotros on film in Hollywood
and Latin America. CAMINOS, Vol. 3, no. 7
(July, August, 1982), p. 15-17. Bilingual.
DESCR: Artists; Cardinale, Marcela;
Espinoza, Jimmy; Films; Gomez, Mike; Ortiz,
Yolanda; Television; Velasco, Jerry.

NOTICIAS DEL MUNDO

8051 Uehling, Mark D. Rivalry in New York: a
profile of two newspapers. NUESTRO, Vol. 7,
no. 7 (September 1983), p. 20-21. English.
DESCR: Bustelo, Manuel A.; DIARIO LA PRENSA
[newspaper], New York, NY; Espinal, Antonio;
Gannett Co., Inc.; Journalism; New York, NY;
*Newspapers; Patino, Luis; Unification
Church.

NOTICIERO

8052 Entertainment = diversion. CAMINOS, Vol. 3,
no. 4 (April 1982), p. 41. Bilingual.
DESCR: AZTLAN [journal];
Committee in Solidarity with the People of
El Salvador (CISPES); Cultural
Organizations; Directories; DIRECTORY OF
MINORITY ARTS ORGANIZATIONS; El Salvador;
*National Endowment for the Arts;
Organizations; Periodicals; *Recreation;
Television.

Novel

8053 Alurista. El capital y su genero: la
novela/... material, instrumento y dinero,
producto y mercado. MAIZE, Vol. 3, no. 3-4
(Spring, Summer, 1980), p. 23-41. Spanish.
DESCR: Literary History.

8054 Alurista and Villarreal, Jose Antonio. Jose
Antonio Villarreal: entrevista. MAIZE, Vol.
5, no. 3-4 (Spring, Summer, 1982), p. 7-16.
English. **DESCR:** *Authors.

8055 Araya, Juan Gabriel. La autocontemplacion
literaria en LIBRO DE MANUEL. MAIZE, Vol. 6,
no. 3-4 (Spring, Summer, 1983), p. 7-16.
Spanish. **DESCR:** *Cortazar, Julio; *Latin
American Literature; Literary
Characteristics; Literary Criticism.

Novel (cont.)

8056 Arias, Ron. The road to Tamazunchale
(excerpt from novel). JOURNAL OF ETHNIC
STUDIES, Vol. 3, no. 4 (Winter 1976), p.
61-69. English.

8057 Espinoza, Roberto. Sintesis vs. analysis: un
problema de historicidad en las novelas de
las dictaduras. MAIZE, Vol. 6, no. 1-2
(Fall, Winter, 1982, 1983), p. 7-27.
Spanish. DESCR: Carpentier, Alejo;
Dictatorships; Garcia Marquez, Gabriel;
Latin American Literature; *Literary
Criticism; Roa Bastos, Augustos; Valle
Inclan, Ramon; White, Lucas Edward.

8058 Lattin, Vernon E. Ethnicity and identity in
the contemporary Chicano novel. MINORITY
VOICES, Vol. 2, no. 2 (Fall 1978), p. 37-44.
English. DESCR: BLESS ME, ULTIMA; Identity;
Literary Criticism; Literature; MEMORIES OF
THE ALHAMBRA; POCHO; THE AUTOBIOGRAPHY OF A
BROWN BUFFALO; Y NO SE LO TRAGO LA
TIERRA/AND THE EARTH DID NOT PART.

8059 Lattin, Vernon E. Novelistic structure and
myth in ...Y NO SE LO TRAGO LA TIERRA.
BILINGUAL REVIEW, Vol. 9, no. 3 (September,
December, 1982), p. 220-226. English.
DESCR: Literature; Rivera, Tomas; United
Mexican Americans, South Bend, IN; *Y NO SE
LO TRAGO LA TIERRA/AND THE EARTH DID NOT
PART.

8060 Lomeli, Francisco A. Isabella Rios and the
Chicano psychic novel. MINORITY VOICES, Vol.
4, no. 1 (Spring 1980), p. 49-61. English.
DESCR: Literature; Lopez, Diana; *Rios,
Isabella; VICTUUM.

8061 Marquez, Antonio. The American dream in the
Chicano novel. ROCKY MOUNTAIN REVIEW OF
LANGUAGE AND LITERATURE, Vol. 37, no. 1-2
(1983), p. 4-19. English. DESCR: Literary
Criticism.

8062 Saldivar, Ramon. A dialectic of difference:
towards a theory of the Chicano novel.
MELUS: MULTI-ETHNIC LITERATURE OF THE UNITED
STATES, Vol. 6, no. 3 (Fall 1979), p. 73-92.
English. DESCR: *Literature.

8063 Vallejos, Thomas. Ritual process and the
family in the Chicano novel. MELUS:
MULTI-ETHNIC LITERATURE OF THE UNITED
STATES, Vol. 10, no. 4 (Winter 1983, 1984),
p. 5-16. English. DESCR: Anaya, Rudolfo A.;
BLESS ME, ULTIMA; Family; *Literary
Criticism; Parent and Child Relationships;
POCHO; Rivera, Tomas; Villarreal, Jose
Antonio; Y NO SE LO TRAGO LA TIERRA/AND THE
EARTH DID NOT PART.

Novelists
USE: Authors

Nuclear Armament

8064 Barrio, Raymond. Resurrection 1999. NUESTRO,
Vol. 7, no. 4 (May 1983), p. 50-51. English.
DESCR: El Salvador; *Fiction.

8065 Burciaga, Jose Antonio. 20 nuclear years
later: still holding my breath. NUESTRO,
Vol. 6, no. 8 (October 1982), p. 35.
English. DESCR: Cuba; *Cuban Missile Crisis,
October 1962; *War.

8066 Garcia, Reyes. Politics of flesh: ethnicity
and political viability. CACR REVIEW, Vol.
1, no. 1 (September 1982), p. 102-130.
English. DESCR: Anaya, Rudolfo A.;
Aristotle; Culture; Ethnic Groups; Identity;

Locke, John; Philosophy; *Political
Repression; Urban Communities.

Nuclear Energy

8067 Balkan, D. Carlos. Being a start-up manager
at San Onofre II & III. HISPANIC BUSINESS,
Vol. 4, no. 7 (July 1982), p. 18-19,26.
English. DESCR: California; Chavez, Gabriel
A.; Engineering as a Profession;
*Management.

8068 Langley, Roger. Roger Langley's Hispanic
beat. HISPANIC BUSINESS, Vol. 4, no. 7 (July
1982), p. 29. English. DESCR: Mexico.

Nuestras Noticias

8069 Media/marketing. HISPANIC BUSINESS, Vol. 5,
no. 12 (December 1983), p. 38. English.
DESCR: Albertini, Luis Diaz; Computers;
League of United Latin American Citizens
(LULAC); Lotus-Albertini Hispanic Reps;
Marketing; *Mass Media; Radio; Reading;
Television; Tortosa, Cristobal.

NUESTRO ESPANOL: CURSO PARA ESTUDIANTES BILINGUES

8070 Feliciano-Foster, Wilma. A comparison of
three current first-year college-level
Spanish-for-native-speakers textbooks.
BILINGUAL REVIEW, Vol. 9, no. 1 (January,
April, 1982), p. 72-81. English. DESCR:
*Book Reviews; ESPANOL ESCRITO; Garza-Swan,
Gloria; *Language Development; Mejias, Hugo
A.; MEJORA TU ESPANOL; Portilla, Marta de
la; Spanish Language Textbooks; Teschner,
Richard V.; Valdes Fallis, Guadalupe;
Varela, Beatriz.

8071 Garcia, Wilfred F. Book review of: NUESTRO
ESPANOL: CURSO PARA ESTUDIANTES BILINGUES,
BILINGUAL NATIVE SPANISH SPEAKERS FROM THE
SOUTHWESTERN UNITED STATES. HISPANIA, Vol.
65, no. 2 (May 1982), p. 320-321. English.
DESCR: Book Reviews; Garza-Swan, Gloria;
Mejias, Hugo A.; Southwest United States;
Spanish Language; Textbooks.

La Nueva Raza Bookstore y Galeria, Sacramento, CA

8072 La Nueva Raza Bookstore y Galeria. CAMINOS,
Vol. 2, no. 6 (October 1981), p. 23.
English. DESCR: Galleries, Chicano.

**NUEVOS PASOS: CHICANO AND PUERTO RICAN DRAMA
(thematic issue of REVISTA CHICANO-RIQUENA)**

8073 Miller, John C. Book review of: NUEVOS
PASOS: CHICANO AND PUERTO RICAN DRAMA.
MELUS: MULTI-ETHNIC LITERATURE OF THE UNITED
STATES, Vol. 6, no. 3 (Fall 1979), p.
99-100. English. DESCR: Book Reviews;
Huerta, Jorge A.; *Kanellos, Nicolas;
*Teatro.

**NUEVOS-HORIZONTES: CHICANO, PUERTO-RICAN, AND
CUBAN SHORT STORIES**

8074 Torbert, Eugene C. Book review of: NUEVOS
HORIZONTES: CHICANO, PUERTO-RICAN AND CUBAN
SHORT STORIES. HISPANIA, Vol. 66, no. 1
(1983), p. 151. English. DESCR: Book
Reviews; *Multinational Literature.

Nunez, Carlos

8075 People. HISPANIC BUSINESS, Vol. 5, no. 1
(January 1983), p. 7. English. DESCR:
Appointed Officials; *Biographical Notes;
*Businesspeople; Elizalde, Hector; Mackey y
Salazar, C.; Madrid, Carlos; Montoya, Velma;
Perea, Stanley; Rodriguez, Rita; Valdes,
Martha.

Nunez, Estella

8076 Ogaz, Armando. South of the other border.
CAMINOS, Vol. 3, no. 6 (June 1982), p.
26-28,36+. Bilingual. DESCR: *Artists; Del
Rio, Yolanda; Emmanuel; Singers.

Nunez, Luis

8077 People. HISPANIC BUSINESS, Vol. 4, no. 8
(August 1983), p. 7. English. DESCR:
Aguilar, Richard; *Businesspeople;
Cordero-Badillo, Atilano; del Olmo, Frank;
Infante, E. Anthony; Levitan, Aida T.;
Quintanilla, Guadalupe; Rivera, Victor M.

Nurseries (Children)
     USE: Child Care Centers

Nursery School
     USE: Child Care Centers

Nursing

8078 Math-based careers. HISPANIC BUSINESS, Vol.
5, no. 7 (July 1983), p. 22. English.
DESCR: *Careers; Education; Mathematics;
National Council for Minorities in
Engineering (NACME).

8079 O'Brien, Mary Elizabeth. Pragmatic
survivalism: behavior patterns affecting
low-level wellness among minority group
members. ANS: ADVANCES IN NURSING SCIENCE,
Vol. 4, no. 3 (April 1982), p. 13-26.
English. DESCR: Curanderismo; Ethnic
Attitudes; Immigrants; *Medical Care; Public
Health.

Nursing Homes

8080 Luevano, Richard L. Attitudes of elderly
Mexican Americans towards nursing homes in
Stanislaus county. CAMPO LIBRE, Vol. 1, no.
2 (Summer 1981), p. 213-228. English.
DESCR: *Ancianos; Attitude (Psychological);
Cultural Characteristics; Medical Care;
Stanislaus County, CA; Surveys.

Nutrition

8081 Abrams, Herbert K. Occupational and
environmental health problems along the
U.S.-Mexico Border. SOUTHWEST ECONOMY AND
SOCIETY, Vol. 4, no. 3 (Spring, Summer,
1979), p. 3-20. English. DESCR: Agricultural
Laborers; *Border Region; Housing; Mexican
Border Industrialization Program;
*Pollution; *Public Health; Social History
and Conditions.

8082 Burciaga, Jose Antonio. La dieta del ano.
LATINO, Vol. 53, no. 4 (June 1982), p. 18.
Spanish.

8083 Hunt, Isabelle F., et al. Zinc
supplementation during pregnancy: zinc
concentration of serum and hair from
low-income women of Mexican descent.
AMERICAN JOURNAL OF CLINICAL NUTRITION, Vol.
37, no. 4 (April 1983), p. 572-582. English.
DESCR: Chicanas; Low Income; *Prenatal Care;
Surveys.

8084 Kerr, G. R. Supermarket sales high-sugar
products in predominantly Black, Hispanic
and white census tracts of Houston, Texas.
AMERICAN JOURNAL OF CLINICAL NUTRITION, Vol.
37, no. 4 (April 1983), p. 622-631. English.
DESCR: Anglo Americans; Blacks; Food
Practices; Surveys.

**THE NUYORICAN EXPERIENCE: LITERATURE OF THE PUERTO
RICAN MINORITY**

8085 Turner, Faythe. Book review of: THE
NUYORICAN EXPERIENCE: LITERATURE OF THE
PUERTO RICAN MINORITY. MELUS: MULTI-ETHNIC
LITERATURE OF THE UNITED STATES, Vol. 10,
no. 2 (Summer 1983), p. 85-88. English.
DESCR: *Mohr, Eugene V.; *Puerto Rican
Literature.

Oakland, CA

8086 Business notes. HISPANIC BUSINESS, Vol. 5,
no. 10 (October 1983), p. 13. English.
DESCR: *Business Administration; Business
Enterprises; Claudio, Irma; Investments; Los
Angeles Board of Public Works; Taxation;
Tri-Oakland Development Corporation;
Wisconsin Minority Business Forum '83.

Oaxaca, Jaime

8087 Newsfront. HISPANIC BUSINESS, Vol. 4, no. 1
(January 1982), p. 7. English. DESCR:
*Biographical Notes; Businesspeople;
Community Development; Jimenez, Richard D.;
Macias, Miguel (Mike); The East Los Angeles
Community Union (TELACU); Viramontes,
Carlos.

Oaxaca, Mexico

8088 Casanova, Steve. Oaxaca and the ancient
ruins of Monte Alban and Mitla. NUESTRO,
Vol. 6, no. 9 (November 1982), p. 62-64.
English. DESCR: Mexico; Tourism.

Oaxaca, Virginia

8089 The shaping of a career. HISPANIC BUSINESS,
Vol. 4, no. 4 (April 1982), p. 14. English.
DESCR: Atlantic Richfield Company;
Biography; Businesspeople; Chicanas.

Obesity

8090 Stern, Michael P. Knowledge, attitudes, and
behavior related to obesity and dieting in
Mexican-Americans and Anglos: the San
Antonio heart study. AMERICAN JOURNAL OF
EPIDEMIOLOGY, Vol. 115, no. 6 (June 1982),
p. 917-928. English. DESCR: Anglo Americans;
Attitude (Psychological); *Food Practices;
San Antonio, TX; Weight Control.

8091 Stern, Michael P., et al. Does obesity
explain excess prevalence of diabetes among
Mexican Americans? Results of the San
Antonio Heart Study. DIABETOLOGIA, Vol. 24,
no. 4 (April 1983), p. 272-277. English.
DESCR: *Diabetes; Medical Research;
Medicine; Public Health; *San Antonio Heart
Study.

Obledo, Mario

8092 Baciu, Joyce A. The winners - Los ganadores.
CAMINOS, Vol. 3, no. 2 (February 1982), p.
14-20,45. Bilingual. DESCR: *Awards;
Caldera, Manuel; Gomez, Ignacio; Huerta,
Dolores; Lizarraga, David C.; Olmos, Edward
James; Rivera, Geraldo; Rivera, Tomas.

Obledo, Mario (cont.)

8093 A close look at Mario Obledo. LATINO, Vol. 54, no. 5 (August, September, 1983), p. 10. English. **DESCR:** Elected Officials; Politics.

8094 Obledo to lecture at University of Madrid. LATINO, Vol. 54, no. 8 (December 1983), p. 21. English. **DESCR:** Politics.

8095 People. HISPANIC BUSINESS, Vol. 4, no. 5 (May 1982), p. 8. English. **DESCR:** Appointed Officials; Asociacion Internacional de Exportadores e Importadores (EXIMA); *Biographical Notes; Businesspeople; California Chicano News Media Association (CCNMA); de la Ossa, Ernest G.; Foreign Trade; Rodriguez, Elias C.; Rodriguez, Samuel F.; United Way; U.S. Hispanic Chamber of Commerce.

8096 Peterson, Sarah; Mashek, John W.; and Obledo, Mario. Hispanics set their sights on ballot box. U.S. NEWS & WORLD REPORT, Vol. 95, no. 8 (August 22, 1983), p. 48-49. English. **DESCR:** Political Repression; *Voter Turnout.

8097 Tom Bradley. CAMINOS, Vol. 3, no. 4 (April 1982), p. 21-23. Bilingual. **DESCR:** *Bradley, Tom; State Government.

8098 Viva Obledo. LATINO, Vol. 54, no. 5 (August, September, 1983), p. 8-9. English. **DESCR:** *Voter Turnout.

8099 Whisler, Kirk. Mario Obledo. CAMINOS, Vol. 3, no. 4 (April 1982), p. 18-20. Bilingual. **DESCR:** State Government.

Obler, Loraine K.

8100 Andrews, Ilse. Bilinguals out of focus: a critical discussion. IRAL: INT'L REVIEW OF APPLIED LINGUISTICS IN LANGUAGE TEACHING, Vol. 20, no. 4 (November 1982), p. 297-305. English. **DESCR:** *Bilingualism; Book Reviews; Literature Reviews; Martin, Albert; *THE BILINGUAL BRAIN.

8101 Ruskin, Ellen Maria. Book review of: THE BILINGUAL BRAIN: NEURO-PSYCHOLOGICAL AND NEUROLINGUISTIC ASPECTS OF BILINGUALISM. HISPANIC JOURNAL OF BEHAVIORAL SCIENCES, Vol. 5, no. 4 (December 1983), p. 487-491. English. **DESCR:** Albert, Martin L.; Bilingualism; Book Reviews; *THE BILINGUAL BRAIN.

Occupational Aspirations
    USE: Careers

Occupational Hazards

8102 Dicker, Lois and Dicker, Marvin. Occupational health hazards faced by Hispanic workers: an exploratory discussion. JOURNAL OF LATIN COMMUNITY HEALTH, Vol. 1, no. 1 (Fall 1982), p. 101-107. English.

8103 Holley, Joe. Farmworker wins the right to sue. TEXAS OBSERVOR, Vol. 74, no. 13 (July 9, 1982), p. 15. English. **DESCR:** *Agricultural Laborers; Donna Fruit Company; Laws; Legal Representation; *Torrez, Juan.

8104 Murray, Douglas L. Abolition of el cortito, the short-handled hoe: a case study in social conflict and state policy in California agriculture. SOCIAL PROBLEMS, Vol. 30, no. 1 (October 1982), p. 26-39. English. **DESCR:** Agricultural Laborers.

Occupational Safety and Health Administration

8105 Developments in migrant workers programs: 1981. CLEARINGHOUSE REVIEW, Vol. 15, (January 1982), p. 797-805. English. **DESCR:** Fair Labor Standards Act (FLSA); Farm Labor Contractor Registration Act (FLCRA); Migrant Education; Migrant Housing; *Migrant Labor; Migrant Legal Action Program (MLAP); Pesticides; Undocumented Workers; Wagner-Peyser Act.

Occupational Training
    USE: Vocational Education

OCCUPIED AMERICA

8106 Maiz, Magdalena. Book review of: OCCUPIED AMERICA. PALABRA Y EL HOMBRE, Vol. 1982, no. 42 (April, June, 1982), p. 77-79. Spanish. **DESCR:** Acuna, Rudolfo; Book Reviews.

Ochoa, Juan Pancho

8107 Business notes. HISPANIC BUSINESS, Vol. 5, no. 12 (December 1983), p. 35. English. **DESCR:** Anheuser-Busch, Inc.; *Business Enterprises; Denny's Inc.; Des Moines, IA; El Pollo Loco; Food Industry; Local Government; Martinez, Vilma Socorro; National Association of Latino Elected Officials (NALEO).

O'Connor, John E.

8108 Cripps, Thomas. Mexicans, Indians and movies: the need for a history. WIDE ANGLE: A FILM QUARTERLY OF THEORY, CRITICISM, AND PRACTICE, Vol. 5, no. 1 (1982), p. 68-70. English. **DESCR:** Bataille, Gretchen M.; *Book Reviews; Films; IMAGES OF THE MEXICAN AMERICAN IN FICTION AND FILM; Native Americans; Pettit, Arthur G.; Silet, Charles L.P.; *Stereotypes; THE HOLLYWOOD INDIAN: STEREOTYPES OF NATIVE AMERICANS IN FILMS; THE PRETEND INDIANS: IMAGES OF NATIVE AMERICANS IN THE MOVIES.

Office for Mexican American Programs, University of Southern California

8109 Taylor, Karla and Vargas, Raul. Entrevista/interview: Q: How to raise money for your Hispanic students? A: Involve your alumni and their corporate contacts. CASE CURRENTS, Vol. 9, no. 4 (April 1983), p. 18-21. English. **DESCR:** College Graduates; Funding Sources; Higher Education; Vargas, Raul.

Office of Bilingual Education Library, New York, NY

8110 de Cuenca, Pilar and Alvarez, Rudolph, Ines. Library holdings of the Office of Bilingual Education, city of New York: a selected bibliography. BILINGUAL REVIEW, Vol. 9, no. 2 (May, August, 1982), p. 127-152. English. **DESCR:** Bibliography; *Bilingual Bicultural Education; Reference Works.

Office of Migrant Ministry (OMM)

8111 King, Karen. Hope comes to Apopka: on working alongside the poor. THE OTHER SIDE, Vol. 18, (May 1982), p. 23-25. English. **DESCR:** Apopka, FL; Clergy; Migrant Health Services; *Migrant Labor.

AN OFFICER AND A GENTLEMAN

8112 Gutierrez, Chela. Flicks in review. LATINA, Vol. 1, no. 1 (1982), p. 46+. English. DESCR: Film Reviews; *THINGS ARE TOUGH ALL OVER.

Oil Industry
USE: Petroleum Industry

Ojalvo, Juana

8113 Rivera-Cano, Andrea. Parenting: four families' stories. LATINA, Vol. 1, no. 2 (February, March, 1983), p. 66-73+. English. DESCR: *Child Rearing; Children; Elias, Bob; Hernandez, Jesus; Hernandez, Virginia; Lopez, Genevieve.

Ojeda, Armando

8114 People. HISPANIC BUSINESS, Vol. 4, no. 12 (December 1982), p. 10. English. DESCR: *Biographical Notes; *Businesspeople; Garcia, Frances; Gort, Wilfredo; Olind, Rebecca Nieto; Philip Morris, Inc.; Roybal, Edward R.

Ojeda, Cecilio Colunga

8115 Barreto, Julio. Cecilio's dream. LATINO, Vol. 53, no. 7 (November 1982), p. 12-14+. English. DESCR: *Family.

8116 Barreto, Julio. Gathering of the Ojedas. NUESTRO, Vol. 6, no. 5 (June, July, 1982), p. 22-25. English. DESCR: Austin, TX; Extended Family; Family.

Ojeda, Mirna

8117 Banberger, Ellen. Poesia nicaraguense. MAIZE, Vol. 5, no. 3-4 (Spring, Summer, 1982), p. 64-77. Spanish. DESCR: Belli, Gioconda; Cardenal, Ernesto; Carrillo, Ernesto; Coronel Urtecho, Jose; Gadea, Gerardo; Gomez, Manuel; Murillo, Rosario; *Nicaragua; *Poetry; Revolutions; Rugama, Leonel.

Oklahoma

8118 Shepperson, Wilbur S. Book review of: THE MEXICANS IN OKLAHOMA. NEW MEXICO HISTORICAL REVIEW, Vol. 57, no. 3 (July 1982), p. 304-305. English. DESCR: Book Reviews; Immigration; Smith, Michael M.; *THE MEXICANS IN OKLAHOMA.

Old Age
USE: Ancianos

OLD FACES AND NEW WINE

8119 Ramirez, Arthur. Book review of: OLD FACES AND NEW WINE. REVISTA CHICANO-RIQUENA, Vol. 10, no. 4 (Fall 1982), p. 65-67. English. DESCR: Book Reviews; CARAS VIEJAS Y VINO NUEVO; Morales, Alejandro.

Olind, Rebecca Nieto

8120 People. HISPANIC BUSINESS, Vol. 4, no. 12 (December 1982), p. 10. English. DESCR: *Biographical Notes; *Businesspeople; Garcia, Frances; Gort, Wilfredo; Ojeda, Armando; Philip Morris, Inc.; Roybal, Edward R.

OLMEC: AN EARLY ART STYLE OF PRECOLUMBIAN MEXICO

8121 Quirarte, Jacinto. Book review of: OLMEC: AN EARLY ART STYLE OF PRECOLUMBIAN MEXICO. JOURNAL OF ETHNIC STUDIES, Vol. 1, no. 3 (Fall 1973), p. 92-95. English. DESCR: Book Reviews; La Venta, Mexico; Precolumbian Art; Precolumbian Society; San Lorenzo, Mexico; Tres Zapotes, Mexico; Wicke, Charles R.

THE OLMEC WORLD

8122 Heizer, Robert. Book review of: THE OLMEC WORLD. JOURNAL OF ETHNIC STUDIES, Vol. 15, no. 3 (Fall 1977), p. 124-125. English. DESCR: Bernal, Ignacio; Book Reviews; Olmecs; *Precolumbian Society.

Olmecs

8123 Heizer, Robert. Book review of: THE OLMEC WORLD. JOURNAL OF ETHNIC STUDIES, Vol. 15, no. 3 (Fall 1977), p. 124-125. English. DESCR: Bernal, Ignacio; Book Reviews; *Precolumbian Society; *THE OLMEC WORLD.

Olmedo, Esteban L.

8124 Bedard, Evelyn M. Book review of: HISPANIC MENTAL HEALTH RESEARCH: A REFERENCE GUIDE. RQ - REFERENCE AND ADULT SERVICES DIVISION, Vol. 22, no. 1 (Fall 1982), p. 93. English. DESCR: Bibliography; Book Reviews; *HISPANIC MENTAL HEALTH RESEARCH: A REFERENCE GUIDE; Mental Health; Newton, Frank; Padilla, Amado M.

Olmos, Edward James

8125 Baciu, Joyce A. The winners - Los ganadores. CAMINOS, Vol. 3, no. 2 (February 1982), p. 14-20,45. Bilingual. DESCR: *Awards; Caldera, Manuel; Gomez, Ignacio; Huerta, Dolores; Lizarraga, David C.; Obledo, Mario; Rivera, Geraldo; Rivera, Tomas.

8126 Breiter, Toni. Eddie Olmos and THE BALLAD OF GREGORIO CORTEZ. NUESTRO, Vol. 7, no. 4 (May 1983), p. 14-19. English. DESCR: Artists; *BALLAD OF GREGORIO CORTEZ [film]; Corrido; Film Reviews; Prejudice (Social).

8127 Olmos, Edward James. Edward James Olmos and Robert Yound with 21 reasons why you should see THE BALLAD OF GREGORIO CORTEZ. CAMINOS, Vol. 3, no. 8 (September 1982), p. 26-27, 50. Bilingual. DESCR: *BALLAD OF GREGORIO CORTEZ [film]; Film Reviews; Young, Robert.

Olson, Ethel Ortega

8128 Sargeant, Georgia. A woman's place is in the bank. HISPANIC BUSINESS, Vol. 5, no. 10 (October 1983), p. 20-21+. English. DESCR: Accountants; *Banking Industry; Careers; Chicanas; Otero Savings and Loan, Alamogordo, TX.

Olvera Street, Los Angeles, CA

8129 Olvera Street - a Mexican mercado in the heart of Los Angeles. CAMINOS, Vol. 4, no. 5 (May 1983), p. 26-35,51+. Bilingual. DESCR: Los Angeles, CA; Tourism.

Olympic Arts Festival, Los Angeles, CA

8130 Plaza de la Raza to host project. NUESTRO, Vol. 7, no. 10 (December 1983), p. 11. English. DESCR: Arts and Crafts; *Folk Art; Folklife Festival (Los Angeles, CA); *Plaza de La Raza, Los Angeles, CA.

Olympic Committee (U.S.)

8131 Bobby Knight must go. NUESTRO, Vol. 7, no. 1 (January, February, 1983), p. 9. English. DESCR: *Knight, Bobby; Racism; Sports.

Olympics

8132 Caldera, Carmela. The consummate salesman: Rudy Cervantes. CAMINOS, Vol. 4, no. 4 (April 1983), p. 25-27. Bilingual. **DESCR:** Business Enterprises; *Cervantes, Rudy.

8133 Caldera, Carmela. Dan Cruz: making the Olympics happen for the community. CAMINOS, Vol. 4, no. 4 (April 1983), p. 10-13,64. Bilingual. **DESCR:** *Cruz, Dan; *Los Angeles Olympic Organizing Committee; Sports.

8134 Caldera, Carmela. Floyd Aragon: filling voids with his entrepreneurship. CAMINOS, Vol. 4, no. 4 (April 1983), p. 28-30, 66. Bilingual. **DESCR:** *Aragon, Floyd; Business Enterprises; L.A. Button Company.

8135 Caldera, Carmela. You and the 1984 Olympics. CAMINOS, Vol. 4, no. 4 (April 1983), p. 7-9,64. Bilingual. **DESCR:** Sports.

8136 Ferrarone, Aida. Olympic skeet-shooter. LATINA, Vol. 1, no. 3 (1983), p. 15. English. **DESCR:** Biography; *Ortiz-Sherman, Nuria; Skeet-shooting; Sports.

8137 Olympic$. Who's going to profit? LATINA, Vol. 1, no. 2 (February, March, 1983), p. 76. English. **DESCR:** *Los Angeles Board of Public Works.

8138 Rios-Bustamante, Antonio and Estrada, William. The Latino Olympians: Latin American participation in the Olympic Games 1896-1980. CAMINOS, Vol. 4, no. 4 (April 1983), p. 14-18,20+. Bilingual. **DESCR:** Sports.

8139 Rios-Bustamante, Antonio. The Latino Olympians project and what it means to you. CAMINOS, Vol. 4, no. 4 (April 1983), p. 19. Bilingual. **DESCR:** *Latino Olympians Project; Mass Media; Sports.

8140 Rios-Bustamante, Antonio. Latino Olympians project. CAMINOS, Vol. 4, no. 7 (July, August, 1983), p. 22. English.

Omnibus Budget Reconciliation Act of 1981

8141 Camayd-Freixas, Yohel. Hispanic mental health and the Omnibus Budget Reconciliation Act of 1981 (editorial board special report). JOURNAL OF LATIN COMMUNITY HEALTH, Vol. 1, no. 1 (Fall 1982), p. 5-24. English. **DESCR:** Funding Sources; *Mental Health.

ON GOLDEN POND

8142 Entertainment = diversion. CAMINOS, Vol. 3, no. 2 (February 1982), p. 40-41. English. **DESCR:** Awards; CHECKING IT OUT; Club Hogar Latino; Dance; Films; Flamenco; Marley, Bob; Montalban, Ricardo; *Recreation; Television.

ON THE BORDER: PORTRAITS OF AMERICA'S SOUTHWESTERN FRONTIER

8143 De Leon, Arnoldo. Book review of: ON THE BORDER: PORTRAITS OF AMERICA'S SOUTHWESTERN FRONTIER. SOUTHWESTERN HISTORICAL QUARTERLY, Vol. 86, no. 2 (1982), p. 367-368. English. **DESCR:** Book Reviews; History; Mexico; Miller, Tom; Texas.

8144 Schmidt, Dorothy. Book review of: ON THE BORDER: PORTRAITS OF AMERICA'S SOUTHWESTERN FRONTIER. WESTERN AMERICAN LITERATURE, Vol. 17, no. 1 (Spring 1982), p. 74. English. **DESCR:** Book Reviews; Miller, Tom; Photography.

El Onceno Festival Chicano-Latino de Teatro, San Francisco, September 11-20, 1981
USE: Eleventh International Chicano Latino Teatro Festival, Mission Cultural Center, San Francisco, CA

ONE ACT PLAYS
USE: Actos

ONE HUNDRED YEARS OF SOLITUDE

8145 Garcia Marquez, Gabriel. The solitude of Latin America. NUESTRO, Vol. 6, no. 10 (December 1982), p. 46-47+. English. **DESCR:** *Authors; Literature.

O'Neill, Thomas P.

8146 O'Neill shifts his course on immigration (NEW YORK TIMES 12-4-83). MIGRATION TODAY, Vol. 11, no. 4-5 (1983), p. 52. English. **DESCR:** *Immigration Law; Simpson-Mazzoli Bill.

Operation Corporate Responsibility (OCR)

8147 Navarro, Armando. Operation corporate responsibility: a movement for Latino economic empowerment. CAMINOS, Vol. 4, no. 7 (July, August, 1983), p. 28-31,43. Bilingual. **DESCR:** Congreso Nacional Para Pueblos Unidos (CPU); Economic Development.

Operation Jobs

8148 Morales, Rebecca. Unions and undocumented workers. SOUTHWEST ECONOMY AND SOCIETY, Vol. 6, no. 1 (Fall 1982), p. 3-11. English. **DESCR:** Employment; Immigration and Naturalization Service (INS); Labor Unions; *Undocumented Workers.

8149 Operation Jobs is a failure. LATINO, Vol. 53, no. 4 (June 1982), p. 21. English. **DESCR:** Employment.

8150 Rios, Madeline. Operation Jobs: one year later. CAMINOS, Vol. 4, no. 11 (December 1983), p. 28-30. Bilingual. **DESCR:** Immigration Regulation and Control; Undocumented Workers.

Operation PUSH

8151 Chavarria, Jesus. Varieties of marketing strategies: the PUSH/Anheuser-Bush scrap. HISPANIC BUSINESS, Vol. 4, no. 12 (December 1982), p. 6,35. English. **DESCR:** Anheuser-Busch, Inc.; Corporations; *Marketing; People United to Serve Humanity (PUSH).

8152 Communications/marketing. HISPANIC BUSINESS, Vol. 5, no. 7 (July 1983), p. 24. English. **DESCR:** AltaVision, Inc. (Denver, CO); Boycotts; Cable Television; Marketing; Spanish Satellite Network (SSN); *Television.

8153 The LULAC/PUSH dialog. HISPANIC BUSINESS, Vol. 5, no. 4 (April 1983), p. 15. English. **DESCR:** Bonilla, Tony; *Economic Development; Jackson, Jesse; League of United Latin American Citizens (LULAC).

Operation Wetback

8154 Meier, Matt S. Book review of: MEXICAN
     IMMIGRANT WORKERS IN THE UNITED STATES and
     OPERATION WETBACK: THE MASS DEPORTATION OF
     MEXICAN UNDOCUMENTED WORKERS IN 1954.
     PACIFIC HISTORICAL REVIEW, Vol. 52, no. 1
     (February 1983), p. 126-128. English.
     DESCR: Book Reviews; Garcia, Juan Ramon;
     *MEXICAN IMMIGRANT WORKERS IN THE U.S.;
     Rios-Bustamante, Antonio.

**OPERATION WETBACK: THE MASS DEPORTATION OF MEXICAN
UNDOCUMENTED WORKERS IN 1954**

8155 Cardoso, Lawrence Anthony. "Wetbacks" and
     "slaves": recent additions to the
     literature. JOURNAL OF AMERICAN ETHNIC
     HISTORY, Vol. 1, no. 2 (Spring 1982), p.
     68-71. English. DESCR: Book Reviews; Garcia,
     Juan Ramon; Lewis, Sasha G.; *SLAVE TRADE
     TODAY: AMERICAN EXPLOITATION OF ILLEGAL
     ALIENS; Undocumented Workers.

8156 Kelly, Philip. Book review of: OPERATION
     WETBACK: THE MASS DEPORTATION OF MEXICAN
     UNDOCUMENTED WORKERS IN 1954. SOCIAL SCIENCE
     JOURNAL, Vol. 19, no. 2 (April 1982), p.
     133-134. English. DESCR: Book Reviews;
     Garcia, Juan Ramon; Undocumented Workers.

8157 Martinez, Oscar J. Book review of: OPERATION
     WETBACK: THE MASS DEPORTATION OF MEXICAN
     UNDOCUMENTED WORKERS IN 1954. NEW MEXICO
     HISTORICAL REVIEW, Vol. 57, no. 2 (April
     1982), p. 201-202. English. DESCR: Book
     Reviews; Garcia, Juan Ramon; Undocumented
     Workers.

8158 Olson, James S. Book review of: OPERATION
     WETBACK: THE MASS DEPORTATION OF MEXICAN
     UNDOCUMENTED WORKERS IN 1954. JOURNAL OF THE
     WEST, Vol. 22, no. 1 (1983), p. 80-81.
     English. DESCR: Agricultural Laborers; Book
     Reviews; Braceros; Garcia, Juan Ramon;
     Undocumented Workers.

8159 Ramirez, Nora E. Book review of: OPERATION
     WETBACK: THE MASS DEPORTATION OF MEXICAN
     UNDOCUMENTED WORKERS IN 1954. WESTERN
     HISTORICAL QUARTERLY, Vol. 13, no. 2 (April
     1982), p. 198. English. DESCR: Book Reviews;
     Garcia, Juan Ramon.

Opium

8160 Wurzman, Ilyana. Cultural values of Puerto
     Rican opiate addicts: an exploratory study.
     AMERICAN JOURNAL OF DRUG AND ALCOHOL ABUSE,
     Vol. 9, no. 2 (1982, 1983), p. 141-153.
     English. DESCR: Acculturation; Anglo
     Americans; Blacks; *Drug Abuse; Drug
     Addicts; Family; Loevinger's Sentence
     Completion Test; Machismo; New York, NY;
     Puerto Ricans; Values.

Oppenheimer-Nicolau, Siabhan

8161 People. HISPANIC BUSINESS, Vol. 5, no. 6
     (June 1983), p. 8. English. DESCR: Appointed
     Officials; *Biographical Notes;
     Businesspeople; Goizueta, Roberto C.;
     Guerra, Stella; Huapaya, Sixto Guillermo;
     Kitano, Pat; Manriquez, Suzanna; Ortiz,
     Solomon; Pachon, Harry P.; Richardson, Bill
     Lopez; Torres, Esteban E.; Torres, Johnny.

Optimist Club of Greater East Los Angeles

8162 Community watching. CAMINOS, Vol. 3, no. 5
     (May 1982), p. 56-57. Bilingual. DESCR:
     Adelante Mujer Hispana Conference;
     Agricultural Laborers; Beilson, Anthony C.;
     Boycotts; Chacon, Peter R.; Chicanas;

*Cultural Organizations; Farm Labor
Organizing Commmittee (FLOC); Financial Aid;
Hollenbeck Junior High School, Los Angeles,
CA; Junior High School Students; National
League of Cities; Organizations; Project
WELL (We Enjoy Learning & Leadership);
Torres, Art.

Oral History

8163 Lomeli, Francisco A. Entrevista con Luis
     Leal. LA PALABRA, Vol. 4, no. 1-2 (Spring,
     Fall, 1982, 1983), p. 3-15. Spanish. DESCR:
     Authors; *Biography; Latin American
     Literature; *Leal, Luis; Literature.

8164 Reimers, David M. Book review of: TODAY'S
     IMMIGRANTS, THEIR STORIES. INTERNATIONAL
     MIGRATION REVIEW, Vol. 16, no. 4 (Winter
     1982), p. 900. English. DESCR: Book Reviews;
     Caroli, Betty; Immigrants; Kessner, Thomas;
     *TODAY'S IMMIGRANTS, THEIR STORIES.

8165 Slade, Santiago. From Michoacan to Southern
     California: the story of an undocumented
     Mexican. SOUTHWEST ECONOMY AND SOCIETY, Vol.
     3, no. 1 (Fall 1977), p. 5-18. English.
     DESCR: Biography; *Puruaran, Michoacan,
     Mexico; *Undocumented Workers.

8166 Weber, Devra. Oral sources and the history
     of Mexican workers in the United States.
     INTERNATIONAL LABOR AND WORKING CLASS
     HISTORY, Vol. 23, (1983), p. 47-50.
     English.

8167 Ybarra, Lea. Book review of: LAS MUJERES:
     CONVERSATIONS FROM A HISPANIC COMMUNITY
     [reprinted from LA RED/THE NET 5 (Sept.
     1982)]. CHICANO LAW REVIEW, Vol. 6, (1983),
     p. 146-147. English. DESCR: Book Reviews;
     Chicanas; Elsasser, Nan; *LAS MUJERES:
     CONVERSATIONS FROM A HISPANIC COMMUNITY;
     MacKenzie, Kyle; Tixier y Vigil, Yvonne.

Orange County, CA

8168 Thomas Fuentes: community builder. HISPANIC
     BUSINESS, Vol. 5, no. 11 (November 1983), p.
     16-17. English. DESCR: Engineering as a
     Profession; *Fuentes, Thomas; Local
     Government; Urban Development.

Organization of American States

8169 Castro, Mike. OAS investigates California
     deaths. NUESTRO, Vol. 7, no. 9 (November
     1983), p. 12-13. English. DESCR: *Border
     Patrol; California Rural Legal Assistance
     (CRLA); Immigration Regulation and Control.

Organizations

8170 1983 LULAC convention election excitement.
     LATINO, Vol. 54, no. 5 (August, September,
     1983), p. 11. English. DESCR: *League of
     United Latin American Citizens (LULAC).

8171 54th annual LULAC convention. LATINO, Vol.
     54, no. 4 (May, June, 1983), p. 16-17.
     English. DESCR: *League of United Latin
     American Citizens (LULAC).

8172 The California GI Forum 1982 convention.
     CAMINOS, Vol. 3, no. 8 (September 1982), p.
     24-25. English. DESCR: *American G.I. Forum.

8173 Communications/marketing. HISPANIC BUSINESS,
     Vol. 4, no. 5 (May 1982), p. 15. English.
     DESCR: Anheuser-Busch, Inc.; Farres,
     Osvaldo; Girl Scouts of the United States of
     America; *Marketing; Television; Vocational
     Education; Voter Turnout.

Organizations (cont.)

8174 Community watching. CAMINOS, Vol. 3, no. 5 (May 1982), p. 56-57. Bilingual. **DESCR:** Adelante Mujer Hispana Conference; Agricultural Laborers; Beilson, Anthony C.; Boycotts; Chacon, Peter R.; Chicanas; *Cultural Organizations; Farm Labor Organizing Commmittee (FLOC); Financial Aid; Hollenbeck Junior High School, Los Angeles, CA; Junior High School Students; National League of Cities; Optimist Club of Greater East Los Angeles; Project WELL (We Enjoy Learning & Leadership); Torres, Art.

8175 Community watching: para la comunidad. CAMINOS, Vol. 2, no. 7 (December 1981), p. 42-43. Bilingual. **DESCR:** Bilingual Education; Mexican American Correctional Association (MACE); Student Advocates for Bilingual Education (SABE).

8176 Diaz, Barbara M. Continuing the success: the Hispanic Women's Council. CAMINOS, Vol. 4, no. 6 (June 1983), p. 62. English. **DESCR:** Awards; Chicanas; *Hispanic Women's Council; Women for Success Awards.

8177 Did you know. LATINA, Vol. 1, no. 3 (1983), p. 60-63. English. **DESCR:** Alkali Flat Project Area Committee, Sacramento, CA; Bilingual Foundation of the Arts; CAFE de California, Inc., Sacramento, CA.

8178 Entertainment = diversion. CAMINOS, Vol. 3, no. 4 (April 1982), p. 41. Bilingual. **DESCR:** AZTLAN [journal]; Committee in Solidarity with the People of El Salvador (CISPES); Cultural Organizations; Directories; DIRECTORY OF MINORITY ARTS ORGANIZATIONS; El Salvador; *National Endowment for the Arts; NOTICIERO; Periodicals; *Recreation; Television.

8179 Fostering Hispanic professionalism. HISPANIC BUSINESS, Vol. 5, no. 4 (April 1983), p. 18. English. **DESCR:** Hispanic Association for Professional Advancement (HAPA); *Professional Organizations.

8180 Gomez, Placido. Committed to keep the culture alive. CAMINOS, Vol. 3, no. 10 (November 1982), p. 28-29,52. English. **DESCR:** *Asociacion Nacional De Grupos Folkloricos; *Ballet Folkorico.

8181 Gonzalez, Alicia. Women for success. CAMINOS, Vol. 3, no. 6 (June 1982), p. 42-43. Bilingual. **DESCR:** *Chicanas; *Hispanic Women's Council; Moreno, Rita; Saavedra, Denise; Terrazas, Carmen.

8182 Hispanic solidarity. CAMINOS, Vol. 3, no. 7 (July, August, 1982), p. 38-39. Bilingual. **DESCR:** Labor; *Labor Council for Latin American Advancement.

8183 How have Hispanic organizations fared with the cutbacks: a survey. CAMINOS, Vol. 4, no. 4 (April 1983), p. 54-55. English. **DESCR:** *Funding Sources.

8184 Latinas on the march, NUESTRO survey reveals: organizations assess achievements during 1981. NUESTRO, Vol. 6, no. 2 (March 1982), p. 16-28+. English. **DESCR:** Forum of National Hispanic Organizations; Hispanic Health Council; Latin Americans; League of United Latin American Citizens (LULAC); National Coalition of Hispanic Mental Health and Human Services Organizations (COSSMHO); National Council of La Raza (NCLR); National Hispanic Bar Association; *National Image, Inc.; National Puerto Rican Forum, Inc.; Yzaguirre, Raul.

8185 LULAC: 53 years of continued achievement (photoessay). CAMINOS, Vol. 4, no. 5 (May 1983), p. 40-41. English. **DESCR:** Benson Latin American Collection; *League of United Latin American Citizens (LULAC); University of Texas at Austin.

8186 LULAC '83: 54th annual LULAC national convention agenda. LATINO, Vol. 54, no. 4 (May, June, 1983), p. 18-19. English. **DESCR:** *League of United Latin American Citizens (LULAC).

8187 LULAC board's Washington meeting set October 6-8. LATINO, Vol. 54, no. 5 (August, September, 1983), p. 27. English. **DESCR:** *League of United Latin American Citizens (LULAC).

8188 LULAC foundation moves to Washington D.C. LATINO, Vol. 54, no. 5 (August, September, 1983), p. 14. English. **DESCR:** *League of United Latin American Citizens (LULAC).

8189 Manuel Bustelo heads youth effort. NUESTRO, Vol. 5, no. 8 (November 1981), p. 42-43. English. **DESCR:** Bustelo, Manuel A.; National Youth Employment Coalition.

8190 Melendez, Melinda. Bilingual education interest groups: their past and their future=Grupos interesados en educacion bilingue: su pasado y su futuro [sic]. CAMINOS, Vol. 2, no. 7 (December 1981), p. 20-22. Bilingual. **DESCR:** *Bilingual Bicultural Education.

8191 New corporate structure approved for national SER. LATINO, Vol. 53, no. 6 (October 1982), p. 16. English. **DESCR:** *SER.

8192 Quesada-Weiner, Rosemary. MALDEF (photoessay). CAMINOS, Vol. 3, no. 2 (February 1982), p. 38-39. English. **DESCR:** *Mexican American Legal Defense and Educational Fund (MALDEF).

8193 Quinlivan, Robert and Castaneda, Jaime. Black & white ball. CAMINOS, Vol. 4, no. 1-2 (January, February, 1983), p. 68-69. Bilingual. **DESCR:** *Alba '80 Society; San Diego, CA.

8194 Quinlivan, Robert. An evening with the stars '82. CAMINOS, Vol. 3, no. 9 (October 1982), p. 24-25. English. **DESCR:** *Funding Sources; Mexican and American Foundation.

8195 Quinlivan, Robert. The Mexican and American Foundation. CAMINOS, Vol. 3, no. 4 (April 1982), p. 24-25. Bilingual. **DESCR:** Castaneda, Jaime; San Diego, CA; United States-Mexico Relations.

8196 Ramirez, Belinda. In solidarity with El Salvador. CAMINOS, Vol. 3, no. 5 (May 1982), p. 9. English. **DESCR:** Benavidez, Virginia; *Committee in Solidarity with the People of El Salvador (CISPES); San Francisco, CA.

8197 The rebirth of MAPA??? CAMINOS, Vol. 3, no. 9 (October 1982), p. 21. English. **DESCR:** *Mexican American Political Association (MAPA); *Politics.

8198 Redmond, Debbie. Most elegant event. LATINO, Vol. 54, no. 4 (May, June, 1983), p. 22. English. **DESCR:** LULAC National Education Service Centers (LNESC).

Organizations (cont.)

8199 Riverside's Hispanic Chamber of Commerce.
CAMINOS, Vol. 3, no. 8 (September 1982), p.
46. English. **DESCR**: *Business; Riverside,
CA.

8200 San Miguel, Guadalupe. Mexican American
organizations and the changing politics of
school desegration in Texas, 1945 to 1980.
SOCIAL SCIENCE QUARTERLY, Vol. 63,
(December 1982), p. 701-715. English.
DESCR: American G.I. Forum; League of United
Latin American Citizens (LULAC); Mexican
American Legal Defense and Educational Fund
(MALDEF); *Segregation and Desegregation;
Texas.

8201 Sandoval, Moises. Why LULAC was founded.
LATINO, Vol. 54, no. 1 (January, February,
1983), p. 12-19. English. **DESCR**: *League of
United Latin American Citizens (LULAC).

8202 Southern California's HBA. HISPANIC
BUSINESS, Vol. 4, no. 9 (September 1982), p.
19. English. **DESCR**: Banking Industry;
California; *Hispanic Bankers Association
(HBA).

8203 A time for reflection. NUESTRO, Vol. 7, no.
9 (November 1983), p. 42-44. English.
DESCR: Anaya, Rudolfo A.; Arias, Beatriz;
Bilingual Bicultural Education; Computers;
Financial Aid; Folklore; Prewitt Diaz,
Joseph (Jose); Villarreal, Sylvia; *W.K.
Kellogg Foundation National Fellowship
Program.

8204 Treviso, Ruben. National IMAGE. CAMINOS,
Vol. 3, no. 8 (September 1982), p. 37-38,51.
Bilingual. **DESCR**: *National Image, Inc.

8205 Valverde, Leonard. Hispanic academics
organized for the greater good. CAMINOS,
Vol. 4, no. 6 (June 1983), p. 50-51.
Bilingual. **DESCR**: Colleges and Universities;
Higher Education; *Texas Association of
Chicanos in Higher Education (TACHE).

8206 Vigil, James Diego. Towards a new
perspective on understanding the Chicano
people: the six C's model of sociocultural
change. CAMPO LIBRE, Vol. 1, no. 2 (Summer
1981), p. 141-167. English. **DESCR**:
Acculturation; Assimilation; Cultural
Characteristics; History; Mexican
Nationalism Period; Mexico; Nationalism;
Precolumbian Society; *Six C's Model
(Theoretical Model); Social History and
Conditions; Spanish Colonial Period.

8207 Whisler, Kirk. Hispanics and the private
sector. CAMINOS, Vol. 3, no. 8 (September
1982), p. 22-23. Bilingual. **DESCR**: *National
Council of La Raza (NCLR); Private Funding
Sources.

**ORIGINS OF THE MEXICAN WAR: A DOCUMENTARY SOURCE
    BOOK**

8208 Bodayla, Stephen D. Book review of: ORIGINS
OF THE MEXICAN WAR: A DOCUMENTARY SOURCE
BOOK. HISTORY - REVIEWS OF NEW BOOKS, Vol.
11, no. 7 (May, June, 1983), p. 149-150.
English. **DESCR**: Book Reviews; McAfee, Ward;
Robinson, J. Cordell.

8209 Graebner, Norman A. Book review of: ORIGINS
OF THE MEXICAN WAR: A DOCUMENTARY SOURCE
BOOK. NEW MEXICO HISTORICAL REVIEW, Vol. 58,
no. 3 (July 1983), p. 291-292. English.
DESCR: Book Reviews; McAfee, Ward; Robinson,
J. Cordell.

Orlando, Tony

8210 Quinlivan, Robert. Tony Orlando in concert.
CAMINOS, Vol. 3, no. 9 (October 1982), p.
25. English. **DESCR**: Artists; Singers.

Orta, Jorge

8211 Sports updates. CAMINOS, Vol. 3, no. 4
(April 1982), p. 42. English. **DESCR**:
*Baseball; Maldonado, Candy; Pena,
Alejandro; Valenzuela, Fernando.

Ortega, Alex

8212 Breiter, Toni. First to fall: "God just
chose him to be a Marine". NUESTRO, Vol. 7,
no. 9 (November 1983), p. 14-17. English.
DESCR: Biography; Military Service.

Ortega, Katherine D.

8213 Gente. NUESTRO, Vol. 7, no. 7 (September
1983), p. 61. English. **DESCR**: Americas
Award; Chavez, Raul; *Chicanas; Diaz-Cobo,
Christine; Mexico; Performing Arts; Planas,
Vilma; Ravard, Rafael Alonzo; Venezuela.

8214 Katherine Davalos Ortega. LATINO, Vol. 54,
no. 7 (November 1983), p. 8-9. English.
DESCR: Appointed Officials.

8215 People. HISPANIC BUSINESS, Vol. 5, no. 12
(December 1983), p. 9. English. **DESCR**:
*Businesspeople; Cantu, Norma V.; Cruz,
Jose; Masvidal, Sergio J.; Planas, Maria
Bordas; Rodriguez, Ismael D.; Romero,
Estella E.

Ortega, Ray

8216 People. HISPANIC BUSINESS, Vol. 4, no. 9
(September 1982), p. 7. English. **DESCR**:
Advertising Agencies; Appointed Officials;
Awards; *Biographical Notes; Diaz-Albertini,
Luis; Dimartino, Rita; Garza, Jesus;
Hispanic Women in Higher Education (HWHE);
League of United Latin American Citizens
(LULAC); Ortiz, George; Romero, Carlos J.;
Sepulveda, Luis.

Ortega, Ruben

8217 Hail to the chief. HISPANIC BUSINESS, Vol.
4, no. 8 (August 1983), p. 10+. English.
DESCR: Criminal Justice System; Phoenix, AZ;
Police.

Ortego y Gasca, Felipe de

8218 Bruce Novoa, Juan. Round table on Chicano
literature. JOURNAL OF ETHNIC STUDIES, Vol.
3, no. 1 (Spring 1975), p. 99-103. English.
DESCR: *Bruce Novoa, Juan; *Literature;
Montejano, David; Morton, Carlos; Teatro.

Ortego y Gasca, Philip D.
    USE: Ortego y Gasca, Felipe de

Orthodox Jews

8219 Steigelfest, Annette. Ethnicity and sex role
socialization. BILINGUAL JOURNAL, Vol. 6,
no. 3 (Spring 1982), p. 11-15,24. English.
DESCR: Ethnic Attitudes; Halacha Institute;
*Identity; *Sex Roles; Sex Stereotypes;
Socialization.

Ortiz, George

8220 People. HISPANIC BUSINESS, Vol. 4, no. 9 (September 1982), p. 7. English. **DESCR:** Advertising Agencies; Appointed Officials; Awards; *Biographical Notes; Diaz-Albertini, Luis; Dimartino, Rita; Garza, Jesus; Hispanic Women in Higher Education (HWHE); League of United Latin American Citizens (LULAC); Ortega, Ray; Romero, Carlos J.; Sepulveda, Luis.

Ortiz, Roxanne Dunbar

8221 Gates, Paul W. Book review of: ROOTS OF RESISTANCE: LAND TENURE IN NEW MEXICO, 1680-1980. WESTERN HISTORICAL QUARTERLY, Vol. 13, no. 1 (January 1982), p. 76-77. English. **DESCR:** Book Reviews; *ROOTS OF RESISTANCE: LAND TENURE IN NEW MEXICO, 1680-1980.

8222 Murphy, Lawrence R. Book review of: ROOTS OF RESISTANCE: LAND TENURE IN NEW MEXICO, 1680-1980. NEW MEXICO HISTORICAL REVIEW, Vol. 57, no. 1 (January 1982), p. 89-90. English. **DESCR:** Book Reviews; New Mexico; *ROOTS OF RESISTANCE: LAND TENURE IN NEW MEXICO, 1680-1980.

8223 Westphall, Victor. Book review of: ROOTS OF RESISTANCE: LAND TENURE IN NEW MEXICO, 1680-1980. ARIZONA AND THE WEST, Vol. 24, no. 2 (Summer 1982), p. 192-193. English. **DESCR:** Book Reviews; Land Tenure; *ROOTS OF RESISTANCE: LAND TENURE IN NEW MEXICO, 1680-1980.

Ortiz, Solomon

8224 Padilla, Steve. Latinos wield political clout in midterm election. NUESTRO, Vol. 6, no. 9 (November 1982), p. 28-30. English. **DESCR:** De la Garza, Kika; *Elected Officials; Garcia, Robert; Gonzales, Henry B.; Lujan, Manuel, Jr.; Martinez, Matthew G. "Marty", Assemblyman; *Politics; Richardson, William; Roybal, Edward R.; *Torres, Esteban E.

8225 People. HISPANIC BUSINESS, Vol. 5, no. 6 (June 1983), p. 8. English. **DESCR:** Appointed Officials; *Biographical Notes; Businesspeople; Goizueta, Roberto C.; Guerra, Stella; Huapaya, Sixto Guillermo; Kitano, Pat; Manriquez, Suzanna; Oppenheimer-Nicolau, Siabhan; Pachon, Harry P.; Richardson, Bill Lopez; Torres, Esteban E.; Torres, Johnny.

Ortiz, Yolanda

8226 Whisler, Kirk. Nosotros on film in Hollywood and Latin America. CAMINOS, Vol. 3, no. 7 (July, August, 1982), p. 15-17. Bilingual. **DESCR:** Artists; Cardinale, Marcela; Espinoza, Jimmy; Films; Gomez, Mike; *Nosotros [film production company]; Television; Velasco, Jerry.

Ortiz-Sherman, Nuria

8227 Ferrarone, Aida. Olympic skeet-shooter. LATINA, Vol. 1, no. 3 (1983), p. 15. English. **DESCR:** Biography; Olympics; Skeet-shooting; Sports.

Osteopathy

USE: Curanderismo

OTERO: AN AUTOBIOGRAPHICAL TRILOGY

8228 Gil, Carlos B. Miguel Antonio Otero, first Chicano governor. JOURNAL OF ETHNIC STUDIES,

Vol. 4, no. 3 (Fall 1976), p. 95-102. English. **DESCR:** Book Reviews; *Elected Officials; *New Mexico; Otero, Miguel A.; Social History and Conditions; United States History.

Otero, Miguel A.

8229 Gil, Carlos B. Miguel Antonio Otero, first Chicano governor. JOURNAL OF ETHNIC STUDIES, Vol. 4, no. 3 (Fall 1976), p. 95-102. English. **DESCR:** Book Reviews; *Elected Officials; *New Mexico; OTERO: AN AUTOBIOGRAPHICAL TRILOGY; Social History and Conditions; United States History.

Otero Savings and Loan, Alamogordo, TX

8230 Sargeant, Georgia. A woman's place is in the bank. HISPANIC BUSINESS, Vol. 5, no. 10 (October 1983), p. 20-21+. English. **DESCR:** Accountants; *Banking Industry; Careers; Chicanas; *Olson, Ethel Ortega.

OUR HOUSE IN THE LAST WORLD

8231 Vega, Ed. Book review of: OUR HOUSE IN THE LAST WORLD. NUESTRO, Vol. 7, no. 10 (December 1983), p. 54-55. English. **DESCR:** Book Reviews; Hijuelos, Oscar.

Outlaws

USE: Bandidos

OVER THE CHIHUAHUA AND SANTA FE TRAILS, 1847-1848

8232 Book review of: OVER THE CHIHUAHUA AND SANTA FE TRAILS, 1847-1848: GEORGE RUTLEDGE GIBSON'S JOURNAL. HISPANIC BUSINESS, Vol. 4, no. 8 (August 1983), p. 27. English. **DESCR:** Book Reviews; Frazer, Robert W.; Gibson, George Rutledge.

Overall Modernity Scale (OM)

8233 Hui, C. Harry. Analysis of the modernity scale: an item response theory approach. JOURNAL OF CROSS-CULTURAL PSYCHOLOGY, Vol. 14, no. 3 (September 1983), p. 259-278. English. **DESCR:** Comparative Psychology; *Military Personnel.

Overseas Education Fund

8234 Women aid global partners. LATINA, Vol. 1, no. 2 (February, March, 1983), p. 18. English. **DESCR:** *Funding Sources.

Ozuna, Bob

8235 People. HISPANIC BUSINESS, Vol. 5, no. 11 (November 1983), p. 10. English. **DESCR:** Aragon, Fermin; *Businesspeople; De Los Reyes, Victor; Di Martino, Rita; Garcia, Ruben; Juarez, Chris; Lopez, Leonard; Nogales, Luis G.; Rico, Jose Hipolito; Tamayo, Roberto; Tapia, Raul R.

Pachon, Harry P.

8236 People. HISPANIC BUSINESS, Vol. 5, no. 6 (June 1983), p. 8. English. **DESCR:** Appointed Officials; *Biographical Notes; Businesspeople; Goizueta, Roberto C.; Guerra, Stella; Huapaya, Sixto Guillermo; Kitano, Pat; Manriquez, Suzanna; Oppenheimer-Nicolau, Siabhan; Ortiz, Solomon; Richardson, Bill Lopez; Torres, Esteban E.; Torres, Johnny.

--   --

Pachuco Images

8237 Montoya, Jose E. Chuco series [drawings].
MAIZE, Vol. 2, no. 1 (Fall 1978), p. Bk
cover. English. **DESCR**: *Drawings.

8238 Montoya, Jose E. [Untitled drawings from the
CHUCO SERIES]. MAIZE, Vol. 2, no. 1 (Fall
1978), p. 32-35. English. **DESCR**: *Drawings.

Pachucos

8239 Orona-Cordova, Roberta and Valdez, Luis.
ZOOT SUIT and the Pachuco phenomenon: an
interview with Luis Valdez. REVISTA
CHICANO-RIQUENA, Vol. 11, no. 1 (Spring
1983), p. 95-111. English. **DESCR**: Teatro;
Valdez, Luis; *ZOOT SUIT [play].

Pacific Direct Mail Service, Inc., Los Angeles, CA

8240 Pacific direct mail services. CAMINOS, Vol.
3, no. 2 (February 1982), p. 30-32.
Bilingual. **DESCR**: *Business; Businesspeople;
*Rivera, Julio.

Pacific Telephone

8241 Communications/marketing. HISPANIC BUSINESS,
Vol. 4, no. 11 (November 1982), p. 18.
English. **DESCR**: California Chicano News
Media Association (CCNMA); Diaz-Albertini,
Luis; Domecq Importers, Inc.; *Marketing;
National Hispanic Media Conference, San
Diego, CA, December 2-5, 1982; Television.

Padilla, Amado M.

8242 Bedard, Evelyn M. Book review of: HISPANIC
MENTAL HEALTH RESEARCH: A REFERENCE GUIDE.
RQ - REFERENCE AND ADULT SERVICES DIVISION,
Vol. 22, no. 1 (Fall 1982), p. 93. English.
DESCR: Bibliography; Book Reviews; *HISPANIC
MENTAL HEALTH RESEARCH: A REFERENCE GUIDE;
Mental Health; Newton, Frank; Olmedo,
Esteban L.

Padilla de Armas, Encarnacion

8243 Ortiz, Carlos V. Growing old alone. NUESTRO,
Vol. 7, no. 4 (May 1983), p. 36-38. English.
DESCR: *Ancianos; Drinane, Suleika Cabrera;
Instituto Puertorriqueno/Hispano Para
Personas Mayores; *Puerto Ricans.

Padilla, Raymond

8244 Dubois, Betty Lou. Bilingual bicultural
education: the view from across the campus.
BILINGUAL REVIEW, Vol. 9, no. 3 (September,
December, 1982), p. 272-275. English.
DESCR: *Bilingual Bicultural Education;
ETHNOPERSPECTIVES IN BILINGUAL EDUCATION
RESEARCH: BILINGUAL EDUCATION AND PUBLIC
POLICY IN THE UNITED STATES (Vol. I).

Painters
USE: Artists

Paintings

8245 Acevedo, Mario (Torero). Trapezoid man
[painting]. MAIZE, Vol. 1, no. 2 (Winter
1978), p. 9. English.

8246 Acevedo, Mario (Torero) and Sanchez, Rita.
[Untitled painting]. MAIZE, Vol. 1, no. 1
(Fall 1977), p. Ft cover. English.

8247 Barajas, Salvador. A mi amor [painting].
MAIZE, Vol. 1, no. 3 (Spring 1978), p. Bk
cover. Spanish.

8248 Barajas, Salvador. Primavera [painting].

MAIZE, Vol. 1, no. 3 (Spring 1978), p.
32-33. English.

8249 East Los Streetscapers 1981. CORAZON DE
AZTLAN, Vol. 1, no. 1 (January, February,
1982), p. 24-25. English.

8250 Garcia Perez, Linda Mary. Chicano nights
[painting]. MAIZE, Vol. 2, no. 3 (Spring
1979), p. 17. English.

8251 Garcia Perez, Linda Mary. El otro mundo
[painting]. MAIZE, Vol. 2, no. 3 (Spring
1979), p. 3. English.

8252 Garcia Perez, Linda Mary. Tortilla bits
[painting]. MAIZE, Vol. 2, no. 3 (Spring
1979), p. 9. English.

8253 Garcia Perez, Linda Mary. Tortilla curtain.
MAIZE, Vol. 2, no. 3 (Spring 1979), p. Bk
cover. English.

8254 Gerardo, Rocky. Albert Einstein [painting].
MAIZE, Vol. 2, no. 3 (Spring 1979), p. In
FtCover. English.

8255 Gerardo, Rocky. Children of the sun
[painting]. MAIZE, Vol. 2, no. 3 (Spring
1979), p. 51. English.

8256 Gerardo, Rocky. El Sandinista [painting].
MAIZE, Vol. 2, no. 3 (Spring 1979), p. In
BkCover. English.

8257 Gerardo, Rocky. Twilight cat [painting].
MAIZE, Vol. 2, no. 3 (Spring 1979), p. 61.
English.

8258 Herrera, Hayden. The elephant and the dove.
NUESTRO, Vol. 7, no. 8 (October 1983), p.
40-43. English. **DESCR**: Art; Artists;
Biography; *Kahlo, Frida; Rivera, Diego.

8259 Herrera, Hayden. Making an art of pain.
PSYCHOLOGY TODAY, Vol. 17, no. 3 (March
1983), p. 86. English. **DESCR**: Biography;
HENRY FORD HOSPITAL; *Kahlo, Frida;
SELF-PORTRAIT WITH PORTRAIT OF DR. FARILL;
THE BROKEN COLUMN; THE LITTLE DEER; TREE OF
HOPE; WITHOUT HOPE.

8260 Newman, Michael. The ribbon around the bomb.
ART IN AMERICA, Vol. 71, (April 1983), p.
160-169. English. **DESCR**: *Artists; Kahlo,
Frida; Modotti, Tina.

8261 Nuestra gente. LATINO, Vol. 54, no. 5
(August, September, 1983), p. 29. English.
DESCR: Criminal Justice System; *Law.

8262 Orozco, Jose Clemente. Tres generaciones
[detail]. CALMECAC, Vol. 1, (Summer 1980),
p. 28. Spanish.

8263 Una pintora: Graciela Rolo Boulanger.
NUESTRO, Vol. 7, no. 6 (August 1983), p.
30-35. English. **DESCR**: Artists; Biography;
*Boulanger, Graciela Rolo.

8264 Terronez, Irene R. [Untitled painting].
MAIZE, Vol. 2, no. 4 (Summer 1979), p. 31.

8265 Terronez, Irene R. [Untitled paintings].
MAIZE, Vol. 2, no. 4 (Summer 1979), p. Ft
cover. English.

Paintings (cont.)

8266 Weinberger, Caspar W. A heritage of valor - Hispanics in America's defense: remarks... at the recent unveiling of paintings of Hispanic heroes at the Pentagon. NUESTRO, Vol. 7, no. 9 (November 1983), p. 18. English. DESCR: Del Valle, Pedro A.; Gabaldon, Guy; Lopez, Jose; *Military Service; Rivero, Horacio.

EL PAIS DIVIDIDO

8267 Umpierre, Luz Maria. La ansiedad de la influencia en Sandra Maria Esteves y Marjorie Agosin. REVISTA CHICANO-RIQUENA, Vol. 11, no. 3-4 (Fall 1983), p. 139-147. Spanish. DESCR: A JULIA Y A MI; *Agosin, Magi; De Burgos, Julia; *Esteves, Sandra Maria; *Literary Criticism; Neruda, Pablo; Parra, Nicanor; Poetry.

Pales Matos, Luis

8268 Villanueva Collado, Alfredo. Fili-Mele: simbolo y mujer en la poesia de Luis Pales Matos e Ivan Silen. REVISTA CHICANO-RIQUENA, Vol. 10, no. 4 (Fall 1982), p. 47-54. Spanish. DESCR: Chicanas; Literary Criticism; LOS POEMAS DE FILI-MELE; Ribes Tovar, Federico; *Silen, Ivan; Symbolism; TUNTUN DE PASA Y GRIFERIA.

Pallares, Mariano

8269 People. HISPANIC BUSINESS, Vol. 5, no. 8 (August 1983), p. 10. English. DESCR: *Biographical Notes; Businesspeople; Calderon, Charles M.; Esteverena, Rolando C.; General Coffee Corporation; Hispanic Bankers Association (HBA); Martinez, Olivia T.; Ruiz, Frederick R.; Ruiz, Louis F.; Sanchez, Joseph J.

Palomino, Carlos

8270 Bunnell, Robert. Bravisimo! NUESTRO, Vol. 7, no. 9 (November 1983), p. 21-25. English. DESCR: Anacani; Coca-Cola Company; Miller Brewing Company; Pena, Samm; Performing Arts; *Television.

8271 First race for scouts occurs in East L.A. NUESTRO, Vol. 6, no. 1 (January, February, 1982), p. 47. English. DESCR: Funding Sources; *Godoy, Carlos Piloy; Los Angeles, CA.

Pan American Games

8272 Rios-Bustamante, Antonio. The Pan American games 1951-1983. CAMINOS, Vol. 4, no. 8 (September 1983), p. 31-33,51+. Bilingual. DESCR: History; Latin America; *Sports.

Pan American Softball League

8273 Cantu, Hector. Softball Texas style. NATIONAL HISPANIC JOURNAL, Vol. 1, no. 3 (Summer, Fall, 1982), p. 9-11. English. DESCR: El Paso Jesters; Mexico City All Stars; Recreation; *Softball; Sports.

Pan American University, Edinburg, TX

8274 Communications/marketing. HISPANIC BUSINESS, Vol. 5, no. 4 (April 1983), p. 23. English. DESCR: Faultless Starch/Bon Ami Company; Garcia, Marti; *Marketing; Mejias, Hugo A.; Spanish Language.

8275 Whittaker, Michael. New career opportunity in social services agencies. NUESTRO, Vol. 6, no. 3 (April 1982), p. 28-30. English.

DESCR: *Social Services.

Panama

8276 Foreign trade. HISPANIC BUSINESS, Vol. 5, no. 5 (May 1983), p. 32. English. DESCR: Caribbean Region; Export Trade; *Foreign Trade; Latin America; Minority Business Development Agency (MBDA).

8277 Fraser Rothenberg, Irene. Chicanos, the Panama Canal issues and the Reagan campaign: reflections from 1976 and projections for 1980. JOURNAL OF ETHNIC STUDIES, Vol. 7, no. 4 (Winter 1980), p. 37-49. English. DESCR: *International Relations; Lobbying; Nationalism; Newspapers; *Panama Canal; Politics; Reagan, Ronald.

Panama Canal

8278 Fraser Rothenberg, Irene. Chicanos, the Panama Canal issues and the Reagan campaign: reflections from 1976 and projections for 1980. JOURNAL OF ETHNIC STUDIES, Vol. 7, no. 4 (Winter 1980), p. 37-49. English. DESCR: *International Relations; Lobbying; Nationalism; Newspapers; Panama; Politics; Reagan, Ronald.

Pantin, Leslie, Sr.

8279 People. HISPANIC BUSINESS, Vol. 5, no. 5 (May 1983), p. 8. English. DESCR: Biographical Notes; *Businesspeople; Duron, Armando; Espinoza, Peter; Flores, Juan; Martinez, Vilma Socorro; Molina, Gloria; Moreno, Samuel; Quezada, Sylvia; Quinones, Sergio.

PAPELES DE PANDORA

8280 Umpierre, Luz Maria. Un manifiesto literario: PAPELES DE PANDERA DE ROSARIO FERRE. BILINGUAL REVIEW, Vol. 9, no. 2 (May, August, 1982), p. 120126. Spanish. DESCR: Book Reviews; Ferre, Rosario; Poetry; Puerto Rican Literature.

PARA LOS NINOS, vols. 1&2

8281 Villarreal, Diana Judith. For Spanish children. HORN BOOK MAGAZINE, Vol. 58, (June 1982), p. 312-313. English. DESCR: Book Reviews; Griego, Margo C.; Pena, Graciela; *TORTILLITAS PARA MAMA.

Parades

8282 Whisler, Kirk. Everyone in town was there (photoessay). CAMINOS, Vol. 3, no. 10 (November 1982), p. 26-27. English. DESCR: *Dieciseis de Septiembre; East Los Angeles, CA; *Mexican Independence Parade.

Paradigm (Theoretical)

8283 Mirande, Alfredo. Sociology of Chicanos or Chicano sociology: a critical assessment of emergent paradigms. PACIFIC SOCIOLOGICAL REVIEW, Vol. 25, no. 4 (October 1982), p. 495-508. English. DESCR: Baca Zinn, Maxine; Internal Colonial Model (Theoretical); SOCIOLOGICAL THEORY IN EMERGENT CHICANO PERSPECTIVES; *Sociology.

8284 Morrissey, Marietta. Ethnic stratification and the study of Chicanos. JOURNAL OF ETHNIC STUDIES, Vol. 10, no. 4 (Winter 1983), p. 71-99. English. DESCR: Assimilation; *Ethnic Stratification; Internal Colonial Model (Theoretical); Marxism; Social Theory.

Paredes, Americo

8285 Entertaiment reviews. CAMINOS, Vol. 3, no. 8 (September 1982), p. 21. English. DESCR: Adams, Bob; Alpert, Herb; Books; Calvert, Robert; Jimenez, Santiago; Lopez, Lisa; Music; Myles, Carol; Pettus, Theodore T.; *Recreation; Television.

8286 Sorell, Victor A. Ethnomusicology, folklore, and history in the filmmaker's art: THE BALLAD OF GREGORIO CORTEZ. BILINGUAL REVIEW, Vol. 10, no. 2-3 (1983), p. 153-158. English. DESCR: *BALLAD OF GREGORIO CORTEZ [film]; Film Reviews; WITH HIS PISTOL IN HIS HAND.

Parent and Child Relationships

8287 Benton, Patricia Moran. Mother's Day reflections: keepers of the faith. NUESTRO, Vol. 7, no. 4 (May 1983), p. 49. English. DESCR: *Chicanas; Family.

8288 Corbit, Gladys Benavides. Sharing with a spiritual sister. NUESTRO, Vol. 7, no. 6 (August 1983), p. 50. English. DESCR: *Chicanas; Family.

8289 Hinojosa-Smith, Rolando R. Reflections on fathers: out of many lives: one. NUESTRO, Vol. 7, no. 5 (June, July, 1983), p. 62. English. DESCR: *Family; Hinojosa, Manuel G.

8290 Huerta, Grace C. Mother's day reflections: a woman of means. NUESTRO, Vol. 7, no. 4 (May 1983), p. 48-49. English. DESCR: *Chicanas; Family.

8291 Iadicola, Peter. Schooling and symbolic violence: the effect of power differences and curriculum factors on Hispanic students' attitudes toward their own ethnicity. HISPANIC JOURNAL OF BEHAVIORAL SCIENCES, Vol. 5, no. 1 (March 1983), p. 21-43. English. DESCR: *Identity.

8292 Johnson, Dale L. and Breckenridge, James N. The Houston Parent-Child Development Center and the primary prevention of behavior problems in young children. AMERICAN JOURNAL OF COMMUNITY PSYCHOLOGY, Vol. 10, no. 3 (June 1982), p. 305-316. English. DESCR: *Child Rearing; Children; Early Childhood Education; *Houston Parent-Child Development Center(PCDC); Social Classes.

8293 Knight, George P.; Kagan, Spencer; and Buriel, Raymond. Perceived parental practices and prosocial development. JOURNAL OF GENETIC PSYCHOLOGY, Vol. 141, (September 1982), p. 57-65. English. DESCR: Anglo Americans; Cultural Characteristics; *Socialization; Socioeconomic Factors.

8294 Laosa, Luis M. School occupation, culture, and family: the impact of parental schooling on the parent-child relationship. JOURNAL OF EDUCATIONAL PSYCHOLOGY, Vol. 74, no. 6 (December 1982), p. 791-827. English. DESCR: Academic Achievement; Education.

8295 Martinez, Danny. Mother's Day reflections: master gardener. NUESTRO, Vol. 7, no. 4 (May 1983), p. 48. English. DESCR: *Family; *Salvadorans.

8296 Melendez, Carmelo. Mother's Day reflections: "I will get to him". NUESTRO, Vol. 7, no. 4 (May 1983), p. 47. English. DESCR: *Family; *Puerto Ricans.

8297 New program on parenting. NUESTRO, Vol. 6, no. 3 (April 1982), p. 11-12. English. DESCR: *Children.

8298 Nieto, Daniel S. Hispanic fathers: the growing phenomenon of single fathers keeping their children. NATIONAL HISPANIC JOURNAL, Vol. 1, no. 4 (Spring 1983), p. 15-19. English. DESCR: Divorce; Family; *Single Parents.

8299 Saragoza, Alex M. Mexican children in the U.S.: the Central San Joaquin Valley. DE COLORES, Vol. 6, no. 1-2 (1982), p. 64-74. English. DESCR: Acculturation; *Children; Family; Identity; San Joaquin Valley.

8300 Vallejos, Thomas. Ritual process and the family in the Chicano novel. MELUS: MULTI-ETHNIC LITERATURE OF THE UNITED STATES, Vol. 10, no. 4 (Winter 1983, 1984), p. 5-16. English. DESCR: Anaya, Rudolfo A.; BLESS ME, ULTIMA; Family; *Literary Criticism; Novel; POCHO; Rivera, Tomas; Villarreal, Jose Antonio; Y NO SE LO TRAGO LA TIERRA/AND THE EARTH DID NOT PART.

PARENTING IN A MULTI-CULTURAL SOCIETY

8301 Clifford, Terry. Book review of: PARENTING IN A MULTI-CULTURAL SOCIETY. HISPANIC JOURNAL OF BEHAVIORAL SCIENCES, Vol. 4, no. 3 (September 1982), p. 385-387. English. DESCR: Book Reviews; Cardenas, Rene; Fantini, Mario.

Parks

8302 Friedman, Florence. Living and working in a lighthouse. CAMINOS, Vol. 4, no. 9 (October 1983), p. 16-18. Bilingual. DESCR: *Jimenez, Julian.

Parodi, Paquita

8303 A new dimension to an ancient craft. NUESTRO, Vol. 6, no. 3 (April 1982), p. 63-64. English. DESCR: Art.

Parra, Nicanor

8304 Umpierre, Luz Maria. La ansiedad de la influencia en Sandra Maria Esteves y Marjorie Agosin. REVISTA CHICANO-RIQUENA, Vol. 11, no. 3-4 (Fall 1983), p. 139-147. Spanish. DESCR: A JULIA Y A MI; *Agosin, Magi; De Burgos, Julia; EL PAIS DIVIDIDO; *Esteves, Sandra Maria; *Literary Criticism; Neruda, Pablo; Poetry.

Parra, Oscar C.

8305 Newsfront. HISPANIC BUSINESS, Vol. 4, no. 4 (April 1982), p. 8, 24. English. DESCR: *Biographical Notes; Burgos, Elizabeth; *Businesspeople; Flores, Arturo; Garcia, Carlos E.; Garcia, Edward T.; Guzman, Ralph C.; Hernandez, Richard; National Coalition of Hispanic Mental Health and Human Services Organizations (COSSMHO); Willie, Herm M.

Parra, Raymond A.

8306 Rodriguez, Eddie. Computer sciences: a special challenge. CAMINOS, Vol. 3, no. 3 (March 1982), p. 18-20. Bilingual. DESCR: *Computers.

Partido Liberal Mexicano (PLM)

8307 Casillas, Mike. The Cananea strike of 1906. SOUTHWEST ECONOMY AND SOCIETY, Vol. 3, no. 2 (Winter 1977, 1978), p. 18-32. English. **DESCR:** Arizona; *Cananea Mining Strike of 1906; Cananea, Sonora, Mexico; History; Mining Industry; *Strikes and Lockouts.

Partido Popular Democratico (PPD)

8308 Mejias-Rentas, Antonio. Reflections on fathers: my three fathers. NUESTRO, Vol. 7, no. 5 (June, July, 1983), p. 61-62. English. **DESCR:** *Family; Marin, Luis Munoz; *Puerto Ricans; *Puerto Rico.

Passports
USE: Visa

Pastoral Drama
USE: Folk Drama

Pastore Passaro, Maria C.

8309 Walia, Adorna. Book review of: THE BILINGUAL PLAY: PINOCCHIO. BILINGUAL JOURNAL, Vol. 7, no. 3 (Spring 1983), p. 31. English. **DESCR:** Bilingual Bicultural Education; Book Reviews; Teatro; *THE BILINGUAL PLAY: PINOCCHIO.

Paternity

8310 Garber, Ronald A. PGM1 and Ge subtype gene frequencies in a California Hispanic population. AMERICAN JOURNAL OF HUMAN GENETICS, Vol. 35, no. 4 (July 1983), p. 773-776. English. **DESCR:** Genetics; *Population Genetics.

8311 Sussman, Leon N. Paternity blood tests. NEW YORK LAW JOURNAL, Vol. 188, (October 6, 1982), p. 2. English. **DESCR:** Blood Examination; Blood Groups; Genetics.

Patients

8312 Dolgin, Daniel L., et al. Discriminant analysis of behavioral symptomatology in hospitalized Hispanic and Anglo patients. HISPANIC JOURNAL OF BEHAVIORAL SCIENCES, Vol. 4, no. 3 (September 1982), p. 329-351. English. **DESCR:** *Mental Illness.

Patino, Douglas X.

8313 Two important California appointments. HISPANIC BUSINESS, Vol. 4, no. 4 (April 1982), p. 23. English. **DESCR:** Appointed Officials; *Becerra, Gloria V.

Patino, Lorenzo E.

8314 Nuestra gente. LATINO, Vol. 54, no. 8 (December 1983), p. 30. English. **DESCR:** *Biographical Notes; Businesspeople; Carter, Lynda Cordoba; Duran, Sandra; Politics; Rembis, Deborah; Vega, Christopher.

Patino, Luis

8315 Uehling, Mark D. Rivalry in New York: a profile of two newspapers. NUESTRO, Vol. 7, no. 7 (September 1983), p. 20-21. English. **DESCR:** Bustelo, Manuel A.; DIARIO LA PRENSA [newspaper], New York, NY; Espinal, Antonio; Gannett Co., Inc.; Journalism; New York, NY; *Newspapers; NOTICIAS DEL MUNDO; Unification Church.

Patron System

8316 Miller, Michael V. Chicano community control

in South Texas: problems and prospects. JOURNAL OF ETHNIC STUDIES, Vol. 3, no. 3 (Fall 1975), p. 70-89. English. **DESCR:** Chicano Movement; Crystal City, TX; Gutierrez, Jose Angel; History; La Raza Unida Party; *Political Parties and Organizations; Social Classes; Social History and Conditions; *South Texas.

Paz, Octavio

8317 Balakian, Anna. Book review of: THE PERPETUAL PRESENT: THE POETRY AND PROSE OF OCTAVIO PAZ. JOURNAL OF ETHNIC STUDIES, Vol. 2, no. 3 (Fall 1974), p. 84-88. English. **DESCR:** Book Reviews; Mexican Literature; *THE PERPETUAL PRESENT: THE POETRY AND PROSE OF OCTAVIO PAZ.

8318 Whisler, Kirk. Octavio Paz - "There will be no revolution in Mexico" (interview). CAMINOS, Vol. 4, no. 5 (May 1983), p. 10-12,48. Bilingual. **DESCR:** Authors; Mexico.

Peabody Individual Achievement Test (PIAT)

8319 Dean, Raymond S. Intelligence-achievement discrepancies in diagnosing pediatric learning disabilities. CLINICAL NEUROPSYCHOLOGY, Vol. 4, no. 2 (1982), p. 58-62. English. **DESCR:** Anglo Americans; *Handicapped; Intelligence Tests; Youth; ZOOT SUIT [film].

Peabody Picture Vocabulary Test-Revised (PPVT-R)

8320 Scruggs, Thomas E.; Mastropieri, Margo A.; and Argulewicz, Ed N. Stability of performance on the PPVT-R for three ethnic groups attending a bilingual kindergarten. PSYCHOLOGY IN THE SCHOOLS, Vol. 20, (October 1983), p. 433-435. English. **DESCR:** *Intelligence Tests; Primary School Students.

Peabody Picture Vocabulary Test (PPVT)

8321 Chavez, Ernest L. Analysis of a Spanish translation of the Peabody Picture Vocabulary Test. PERCEPTUAL AND MOTOR SKILLS, Vol. 54, no. 3 (June 1982), p. 1335-1338. English. **DESCR:** Bilingualism; Educational Tests and Measurements; Spanish Language.

Peace Corps

8322 Chamber, Peace Corps join in training effort. NUESTRO, Vol. 7, no. 1 (January, February, 1983), p. 36. English. **DESCR:** Business; Caribbean Basin Initiative (CBI); *Ibero-American Chamber of Commerce; Latin America.

8323 Foreign trade. HISPANIC BUSINESS, Vol. 5, no. 4 (April 1983), p. 22. English. **DESCR:** Banking Industry; Brazil; *Electronics Industry; Export Trade; *Foreign Trade; Ibero-American Chamber of Commerce; Miami, FL; Minority Bank Development Program (MBDP); Minority Export Development Consultants Program (MEDC); Puerto Rico.

Peden, Margaret Sayers

8324 Sabat-Rivers, Georgina. Book review of: A WOMAN OF GENIUS: THE INTELLECTUAL AUTOBIOGRAPHY OF SOR JUANA INES DE LA CRUZ. NUESTRO, Vol. 7, no. 6 (August 1983), p. 62-64. English. **DESCR:** *A WOMAN OF GENIUS: THE INTELLECTUAL AUTOBIOGRAPHY OF SOR JUANA INES DE LA CRUZ; Autobiography; Book Reviews; Juana Ines de la Cruz, Sor.

Pedersen, Paul P.

8325 Franco, Juan N. Book review of: COUNSELING ACROSS CULTURES. HISPANIC JOURNAL OF BEHAVIORAL SCIENCES, Vol. 5, no. 2 (June), p. 233-237. English. **DESCR:** Book Reviews; *COUNSELING ACROSS CULTURES; Draguns, Juris G.; Lonner, Walter J.; Trimble, Joseph E.

Pediatrics

8326 Hsi, Bartholomew P.; Hsu, Katherine H.; and Jenkins, Daniel E. Ventilatory functions of normal children and young adults: Mexican-American, white and black. III. Sitting height as a predictor. JOURNAL OF PEDIATRICS, Vol. 102, no. 6 (June 1983), p. 860-865. English. **DESCR:** Anglo Americans; Blacks; Child Study; *Children.

PELON DROPS OUT

8327 Klor de Alva, Jorge. Book review of: PELON DROPS OUT. LA PALABRA, Vol. 4, no. 1-2 (Spring, Fall, 1982, 1983), p. 172-174. Spanish. **DESCR:** Book Reviews; De Casas, Celso A.; Literature.

Pena, Alberto

8328 Achor, Shirley. Book review of: GUNPOWDER JUSTICE: A REASSESSMENT OF THE TEXAS RANGERS. INTERNATIONAL MIGRATION REVIEW, Vol. 16, no. 2 (Summer 1982), p. 491-492. English. **DESCR:** Bernal, Joseph; Book Reviews; *GUNPOWDER JUSTICE: A REASSESSMENT OF THE TEXAS RANGERS; Samora, Julian; Texas Rangers.

8329 Achor, Shirley. Book review of: GUNPOWDER JUSTICE: A REASSESSMENT OF THE TEXAS RANGERS. INTERNATIONAL MIGRATION REVIEW, Vol. 16, no. 2 (Summer 1982), p. 491-492. English. **DESCR:** Bernal, Joseph; Book Reviews; *GUNPOWDER JUSTICE: A REASSESSMENT OF THE TEXAS RANGERS; History; Samora, Julian; Texas Rangers.

Pena, Alejandro

8330 Sports updates. CAMINOS, Vol. 3, no. 4 (April 1982), p. 42. English. **DESCR:** *Baseball; Maldonado, Candy; Orta, Jorge; Valenzuela, Fernando.

Pena, Amado Maurilio, Jr.

8331 Whisler, Kirk. A truly international artist. CAMINOS, Vol. 3, no. 9 (October 1982), p. 12-15. Bilingual. **DESCR:** *Artists.

Pena, Federico

8332 Hispanic power arrives at the ballot box. BUSINESS WEEK, no. 27 (July 4, 1983), p. 32. English. **DESCR:** Denver, CO; *Voter Turnout.

8333 Martinez, Chip. Federico Pena: Denver's first Hispanic mayor. NUESTRO, Vol. 7, no. 6 (August 1983), p. 14-20. English. **DESCR:** Denver, CO; Elections; Local Government; Voter Turnout.

8334 Mile high Pena fever. LATINO, Vol. 54, no. 4 (May, June, 1983), p. 4. English. **DESCR:** Elected Officials; Voter Turnout.

8335 Pena takes Denver. HISPANIC BUSINESS, Vol. 5, no. 8 (August 1983), p. 13+. English. **DESCR:** *Biography; Denver, CO; Elected Officials.

Pena, Graciela

8336 Villarreal, Diana Judith. For Spanish children. HORN BOOK MAGAZINE, Vol. 58, (June 1982), p. 312-313. English. **DESCR:** Book Reviews; Griego, Margo C.; *PARA LOS NINOS, vols. 1&2; *TORTILLITAS PARA MAMA.

Pena, Samm

8337 Bunnell, Robert. Bravisimo! NUESTRO, Vol. 7, no. 9 (November 1983), p. 21-25. English. **DESCR:** Anacani; Coca-Cola Company; Miller Brewing Company; Palomino, Carlos; Performing Arts; *Television.

Pena, Tony

8338 Ortiz, Carlos V. NUESTRO'S sixth annual all-star baseball team. NUESTRO, Vol. 7, no. 2 (March 1983), p. 33-37. English. **DESCR:** Andujar, Joaquin; Barojas, Salome; *Baseball; Castillo, Manny; Concepcion, Dave; Cruz, Jose; Garcia, Damaso; Guerrero, Pedro; Hernandez, Keith; Lezcano, Sixto; Martinez, Tippy; Piniella, Lou; Sports; Valenzuela, Fernando.

Penitentes
USE: Hermanos Penitentes

Pentecostal Church

8339 Vigil, James Diego. Human revitalization: the six tasks of victory outreach. DREW GATEWAY, Vol. 52, no. 3 (Spring 1982), p. 49-59. English. **DESCR:** Barrios for Christ Program; Drug Addicts; Drug Programs; Gangs; Identity; Protestant Church; Religion; *Victory Outreach; Youth.

Peonage
USE: Patron System

People United to Serve Humanity (PUSH)

8340 Chavarria, Jesus. Varieties of marketing strategies: the PUSH/Anheuser-Bush scrap. HISPANIC BUSINESS, Vol. 4, no. 12 (December 1982), p. 6,35. English. **DESCR:** Anheuser-Busch, Inc.; Corporations; *Marketing; Operation PUSH.

People v. Guzman

8341 Fox, Martin. Grand Jury selection upheld against test by Hispanics. NEW YORK LAW JOURNAL, Vol. 188, (October 1, 1982), p. 1. English. **DESCR:** Brooklyn, NY; *Juries.

Perales, Cesar A.

8342 Perales, Velasco win special Durfee award. NUESTRO, Vol. 6, no. 8 (October 1982), p. 43. English. **DESCR:** *Durfee Award; *Velasco, Eugenio.

Perception

8343 Gorrell, J. Jeffrey, et al. Comparison of spatial role-taking in monolingual and bilingual children. JOURNAL OF GENETIC PSYCHOLOGY, Vol. 140, no. 1 (March 1982), p. 3-10. English. DESCR: Bilingualism; Child Study; Cognition; *Linguistic Theory.

Perceptions of Mexican Americans Scale (PMAS)

8344 Schon, Isabel. Effects of special curricular study of Mexican culture on Anglo and Mexican-American students perceptions of Mexican-Americans. JOURNAL OF EXPERIMENTAL EDUCATION, Vol. 50, no. 4 (Summer 1982), p. 215-218. English. DESCR: Anglo Americans; Primary School Education; *Stereotypes.

Perea, Stanley

8345 People. HISPANIC BUSINESS, Vol. 5, no. 1 (January 1983), p. 7. English. DESCR: Appointed Officials; *Biographical Notes; *Businesspeople; Elizalde, Hector; Mackey y Salazar, C.; Madrid, Carlos; Montoya, Velma; Nunez, Carlos; Rodriguez, Rita; Valdes, Martha.

Perez, Alfonso B.

8346 Education center named Alfonso B. Perez. NUESTRO, Vol. 6, no. 5 (June, July, 1982), p. 30. English. DESCR: East Los Angeles, CA; Education; Educational Services.

Perez, Matthew

8347 Padilla, Steve. Working for the F.B.I. NUESTRO, Vol. 6, no. 8 (October 1982), p. 15-17. English. DESCR: Arras, Raymundo; *Federal Bureau of Investigation (FBI); Latin Americans; Marquez, Manuel.

Perez v. Health and Social Services

8348 [Summary of: Note, medical benefits awarded to an alien: Perez v. health and social services, 9 N.M.L. rev. 89 (1979)]. CHICANO LAW REVIEW, Vol. 5, (1982), p. 80-81. English. DESCR: Medical Care; *Medical Care Laws and Legislation; Undocumented Workers.

PERFECTLY LEGAL - 275 FOOLPROOF METHODS FOR PAYING LESS TAXES

8349 Research/development: books. HISPANIC BUSINESS, Vol. 4, no. 4 (April 1982), p. 28. English. DESCR: *Book Reviews; Engineering; Financial Aid; FINANCIAL AID FOR MINORITIES IN ENGINEERING; Kennedy, David W.; Steiner, Barry R.; Swann, Ruth N.; Taxation.

Performing Arts

8350 Agudelo, Carlos. What about Latin music? BILLBOARD, Vol. 94, (November 20, 1982), p. 10. English. DESCR: *Awards; *Grammy Awards; Music; National Academy of Recording Arts and Sciences; Recording Industry.

8351 Bunnell, Robert. Bravisimo! NUESTRO, Vol. 7, no. 9 (November 1983), p. 21-25. English. DESCR: Anacani; Coca-Cola Company; Miller Brewing Company; Palomino, Carlos; Pena, Samm; *Television.

8352 Fernandez, Enrique. NARAS takes a welcome step. BILLBOARD, Vol. 95, (June 18, 1983), p. 59. English. DESCR: Awards; Entertainers; Grammy Awards; Music; *National Academy of Recording Arts and Sciences; Recording Industry.

8353 Fernandez, Enrique. Notas: these ladies are not waiting. BILLBOARD, Vol. 94, (November 13, 1982), p. 62. English. DESCR: Artists; *Chicanas; Salsa; Singers.

8354 Gente. NUESTRO, Vol. 7, no. 7 (September 1983), p. 61. English. DESCR: Americas Award; Chavez, Raul; *Chicanas; Diaz-Cobo, Christine; Mexico; Ortega, Katherine D.; Planas, Vilma; Ravard, Rafael Alonzo; Venezuela.

8355 Kappel, Mark. A new career direction for Hilda Morales. NUESTRO, Vol. 7, no. 1 (January, February, 1983), p. 24-27. English. DESCR: *Dance; *Morales, Hilda.

8356 Lenti, Paul. Special honor goes to Montalban. NUESTRO, Vol. 7, no. 2 (March 1983), p. 10-11. English. DESCR: Artists; Maria Teresa Montoya Award; *Montalban, Ricardo.

8357 Obejas, Achy. My mother, the groupie. NUESTRO, Vol. 7, no. 9 (November 1983), p. 47. English. DESCR: *Iglesias, Julio.

8358 Padilla, Steve. The comedian. NUESTRO, Vol. 7, no. 2 (March 1983), p. 25-27. English. DESCR: Artists; Humor; *Rodriguez, Paul.

8359 Pilar Rioja and the magic of duende. NUESTRO, Vol. 7, no. 6 (August 1983), p. 47-48. English. DESCR: *Dance; *Rioja, Pilar.

8360 Top talent at Tejano awards. BILLBOARD, Vol. 95, (January 29, 1983), p. 65. English. DESCR: Awards; Entertainers; Music; *Tejano Music Awards; Texas.

8361 Whitney, James. Habana! comes to Manhattan. NUESTRO, Vol. 7, no. 2 (March 1983), p. 55-56. English. DESCR: *HABANA! ANTOLOGIA MUSICAL; HAVANA SINGS; Musicals.

Periodicals

8362 Entertainment = diversion. CAMINOS, Vol. 3, no. 4 (April 1982), p. 41. Bilingual. DESCR: AZTLAN [journal]; Committee in Solidarity with the People of El Salvador (CISPES); Cultural Organizations; Directories; DIRECTORY OF MINORITY ARTS ORGANIZATIONS; El Salvador; *National Endowment for the Arts; NOTICIERO; Organizations; *Recreation; Television.

8363 Kanellos, Nicolas. REVISTA CHICANO-RIQUENA/Arte Publico Press. CAMINOS, Vol. 4, no. 6 (June 1983), p. 52-53,67. English. DESCR: Journals; *REVISTA CHICANO-RIQUENA.

8364 Soto, Shirlene Ann. The emerging Chicana: a review of the journals. SOUTHWEST ECONOMY AND SOCIETY, Vol. 2, no. 1 (October, November, 1976), p. 39-45. English. DESCR: *Chicanas; Directories; *Literature Reviews.

Perlman, Janice E.

8365 Logan, Kathleen. The urban poor in developing nations. JOURNAL OF URBAN HISTORY, Vol. 9, no. 1 (November 1982), p. 108-116. English. **DESCR:** ACCESS TO POWER: POLITICS AND THE URBAN POOR IN DEVELOPING NATIONS; *Book Reviews; BORDER BOOM TOWN: CIUDAD JUAREZ SINCE 1848; Collier, David; Cornelius, Wayne A.; Eckstein, Susan; Lloyd, Peter; Martinez, Oscar J.; Nelson, Joan M.; POLITICS AND MIGRANT POOR IN MEXICO CITY; SLUMS OF HOPE? SHANTY TOWNS OF THE THIRD WORLD; SQUATTERS AND OLIGARCHS: AUTHORITARIAN RULE AND POLICY CHANGE IN PERU; THE MYTH OF MARGINALITY: URBAN POVERTY AND POLITICS IN RIO DE JANEIRO; THE POVERTY OF REVOLUTION: THE STATE AND THE URBAN POOR IN MEXICO; Urban Economics.

Perot, Ross

8366 Ballard, Lee. Tom Marquez and the EDS mode. HISPANIC BUSINESS, Vol. 5, no. 2 (February 1983), p. 10-11+. English. **DESCR:** *Biography; Businesspeople; Electronic Data Systems (EDS); Marquez, Tom; War on Drugs.

THE PERPETUAL PRESENT: THE POETRY AND PROSE OF OCTAVIO PAZ

8367 Balakian, Anna. Book review of: THE PERPETUAL PRESENT: THE POETRY AND PROSE OF OCTAVIO PAZ. JOURNAL OF ETHNIC STUDIES, Vol. 2, no. 3 (Fall 1974), p. 84-88. English. **DESCR:** Book Reviews; Mexican Literature; Paz, Octavio.

Personal Names

8368 Gottlieb, Karen. Genetic demography of Denver, Colorado: Spanish surname as a market of Mexican ancestry. HUMAN BIOLOGY, Vol. 55, no. 2 (May 1983), p. 227-234. English. **DESCR:** Demography; Denver, CO; *Population Genetics; Research Methodology; Sociology.

8369 Woods, Richard D. Sources of identification of Spanish names. JOURNAL OF ETHNIC STUDIES, Vol. 4, no. 2 (Summer 1976), p. 92-94. English. **DESCR:** Names, Spanish; Spanish Language.

Personality

8370 Borrego, Richard L.; Chavez, Ernest L.; and Titley, Robert W. Effect of counselor technique on Mexican-American and Anglo-American self-disclosure and counselor perception. JOURNAL OF COUNSELING PSYCHOLOGY, Vol. 29, no. 5 (September 1982), p. 538-541. English. **DESCR:** Anglo Americans; *Counseling (Psychological); Cultural Characteristics; Identity; Sex Roles.

8371 De Blassie, Richard R. and Franco, Juan N. The differences between personality inventory scores and self-rating in a sample of Hispanic subjects. JOURNAL OF NON-WHITE CONCERNS IN PERSONNEL AND GUIDANCE, Vol. 11, no. 2 (January 1983), p. 43-46. English. **DESCR:** Chicanas; Hispanic Education [program]; New Mexico State University; *Sixteen Personality Factor Questionnaire.

8372 Dolan, Michael. Personality differences among Black, white, and Hispanic-American male heroin addicts on MMPI content scales. JOURNAL OF CLINICAL PSYCHOLOGY, Vol. 39, no. 5 (September 1983), p. 807-813. English. **DESCR:** Blacks; Drug Addicts; *Heroin Addicts; Minnesota Multiphasic Personality Inventory (MMPI).

8373 Garza, Raymond T. and Lipton, Jack P. Theoretical perspectives on Chicano personality development. HISPANIC JOURNAL OF BEHAVIORAL SCIENCES, Vol. 4, no. 4 (December 1982), p. 407-432. English. **DESCR:** Culture.

8374 Gibbs, Jewelle Taylor. Personality patterns of delinquent females: ethnic and sociocultural variations. JOURNAL OF CLINICAL PSYCHOLOGY, Vol. 38, no. 1 (January 1982), p. 198-206. English. **DESCR:** Chicanas; Ethnic Groups; Identity; *Juvenile Delinquency; Psychological Testing; Socioeconomic Factors.

8375 Lujan, Sylvia and Zapata, Jesse T. Personality differences among Mexican-American college freshmen. JOURNAL OF COLLEGE STUDENT PERSONNEL, Vol. 24, no. 2 (March 1983), p. 105-111. English. **DESCR:** Colleges and Universities; Socioeconomic Factors; *Students.

8376 Medinnus, Gene R.; Ford, Martin Z.; and Tack-Robinson, Susan. Locus of control: a cross-cultural comparison. PSYCHOLOGICAL REPORTS, Vol. 53, no. 1 (August 1983), p. 131-134. English. **DESCR:** *Fatalism; Junior High School Students; *Locus of Control.

8377 Ruiz, Rene A. and LeVine, Elaine S. Book review of: PSYCHOLOGY OF THE MEXICAN CULTURE AND PERSONALITY. JOURNAL OF ETHNIC STUDIES, Vol. 4, no. 2 (Summer 1976), p. 104-107. English. **DESCR:** Book Reviews; *Cultural Characteristics; Culture; *Diaz-Guerrero, Rogelio; Psychology; PSYCHOLOGY OF THE MEXICAN CULTURE AND PERSONALITY.

8378 Strong, Michael. Social styles and the second language acquisition of Spanish-speaking kindergartners. TESOL QUARTERLY, Vol. 17, no. 2 (June 1983), p. 241-258. English. **DESCR:** *Language Development; Primary School Education.

8379 Zamudio, Anthony; Padilla, Amado M.; and Comrey, Andrew L. Personality structure of Mexican Americans using the Comrey Personality Scales. JOURNAL OF PERSONALITY ASSESSMENT, Vol. 47, no. 1 (February 1983), p. 100-106. English. **DESCR:** Colleges and Universities; Comrey Personality Scales (CPS); Minnesota Multiphasic Personality Inventory (MMPI); Psychological Testing; Students.

Personnel Management

8380 Ayers-Nackamkin, Beverly, et al. Sex and ethnic differences in the use of power. JOURNAL OF APPLIED PSYCHOLOGY, Vol. 67, no. 4 (August 1982), p. 464-471. English. **DESCR:** Anglo Americans; Ethnic Groups; Management; Sex Roles; Social Psychology.

8381 Business notes. HISPANIC BUSINESS, Vol. 5, no. 11 (November 1983), p. 27. English. **DESCR:** *Business Enterprises; Garment Industry; High Tech '84; Puerto Rico; Taxation; U.S. Department of Housing and Urban Development (HUD).

8382 Conoley, Martin. The hidden threat of underemployment. HISPANIC BUSINESS, Vol. 5, no. 10 (October 1983), p. 14+. English. **DESCR:** Education; *Employment; Employment Training; Labor Supply and Market.

Personnel Management (cont.)

8383 Paul, Jan S. The changing work week.
HISPANIC BUSINESS, Vol. 5, no. 9 (September
1983), p. 16. English. DESCR: Employment;
Labor Laws and Legislation; *Labor Supply
and Market.

Peru

8384 Regional report, antiquities: stolen
treasure begins U.S. tour. NUESTRO, Vol. 7,
no. 4 (May 1983), p. 12-13. English. DESCR:
*Criminal Acts; Precolumbian Art.

8385 U.S. returns stolen artifacts. NUESTRO, Vol.
6, no. 7 (September 1982), p. 10. English.
DESCR: *Anthropology.

Peruvian Embassy (Cuba)

8386 Garcia, Margarita. The last days in Cuba:
personal accounts of the circumstances of
the exit. MIGRATION TODAY, Vol. 11, no. 4-5
(1983), p. 13-26. English. DESCR: Castro,
Fidel; Cuba; *Cuban Boatlift; *Cubanos;
Hudson County, NJ; Immigration.

Peso Devaluation

8387 Mexican condo buyer in Texas-sized trouble.
SOUTHERN EXPOSURE, Vol. 11, no. 1 (January
1983), p. 8-9. English. DESCR: Condominiums;
Mexico; *Real Estate.

Pesticides

8388 Developments in migrant workers programs:
1981. CLEARINGHOUSE REVIEW, Vol. 15,
(January 1982), p. 797-805. English. DESCR:
Fair Labor Standards Act (FLSA); Farm Labor
Contractor Registration Act (FLCRA); Migrant
Education; Migrant Housing; *Migrant Labor;
Migrant Legal Action Program (MLAP);
Occupational Safety and Health
Administration; Undocumented Workers;
Wagner-Peyser Act.

Petersilia, Joan

8389 Que pasa? NUESTRO, Vol. 7, no. 6 (August
1983), p. 9. English. DESCR: Boy Scouts of
America; *Court System; Criminal Justice
System; Diabetes; Education; Judicial
Review; PREPARED FOR TODAY; RACIAL
DISPARITIES IN THE CRIMINAL JUSTICE SYSTEM;
Reagan, Ronald.

Petroleum Industry

8390 Petroleo, negociaciones fiancieras y nueva
estrategia economica de Mexico. INFORME:
RELACIONES MEXICO-ESTADOS UNIDOS, Vol. 1,
no. 3 (July, December, 1982), p. 198-208.
Spanish. DESCR: Economics; Mexico.

8391 Vidal, Jose. Oil pluses - economic woes.
CAMINOS, Vol. 3, no. 6 (June 1982), p.
18-19. Bilingual. DESCR: Economic
Development; Mexico; *United States-Mexico
Relations.

Pettit, Arthur G.

8392 Bloodworth, William A., Jr. Book review of:
IMAGES OF THE MEXICAN-AMERICAN IN FICTION
AND FILM. WESTERN AMERICAN LITERATURE, Vol.
16, no. 4 (Winter 1982), p. 323-325.
English. DESCR: Book Reviews; Chicanos in
American Literature; Films; *IMAGES OF THE
MEXICAN AMERICAN IN FICTION AND FILM;
Showalter, Dennis E.; Stereotypes.

8393 Book review of: IMAGES OF THE

MEXICAN-AMERICAN IN FICTION AND FILM. MODERN
FICTION STUDIES, Vol. 28, (Summer 1982), p.
367-369. English. DESCR: Book Reviews;
Fiction; Films; *IMAGES OF THE MEXICAN
AMERICAN IN FICTION AND FILM; Mass Media.

8394 Cripps, Thomas. Mexicans, Indians and
movies: the need for a history. WIDE ANGLE:
A FILM QUARTERLY OF THEORY, CRITICISM, AND
PRACTICE, Vol. 5, no. 1 (1982), p. 68-70.
English. DESCR: Bataille, Gretchen M.; *Book
Reviews; Films; IMAGES OF THE MEXICAN
AMERICAN IN FICTION AND FILM; Native
Americans; O'Connor, John E.; Silet, Charles
L.P.; *Stereotypes; THE HOLLYWOOD INDIAN:
STEREOTYPES OF NATIVE AMERICANS IN FILMS;
THE PRETEND INDIANS: IMAGES OF NATIVE
AMERICANS IN THE MOVIES.

8395 Griswold del Castillo, Richard. Book review
of: IMAGES OF THE MEXICAN-AMERICAN IN
FICTION AND FILM. JOURNAL OF THE WEST, Vol.
22, no. 2 (April 1983), p. 94. English.
DESCR: Book Reviews; *IMAGES OF THE MEXICAN
AMERICAN IN FICTION AND FILM.

8396 Stephens, Doris T. Book review of: IMAGES OF
THE MEXICAN-AMERICAN IN FICTION AND FILM.
JOURNAL OF AMERICAN CULTURE, Vol. 5, no. 4
(Winter 1982), p. 112-113. English. DESCR:
Book Reviews; *IMAGES OF THE MEXICAN
AMERICAN IN FICTION AND FILM.

8397 West, Dennis. Book review of: IMAGES OF THE
MEXICAN-AMERICAN IN FICTION AND FILM.
CINEASTE, Vol. 12, no. 1 (1982), p. 41.
English. DESCR: Book Reviews; Chicanos in
American Literature; Films; *IMAGES OF THE
MEXICAN AMERICAN IN FICTION AND FILM;
Stereotypes.

Pettus, Theodore T.

8398 Entertaiment reviews. CAMINOS, Vol. 3, no. 8
(September 1982), p. 21. English. DESCR:
Adams, Bob; Alpert, Herb; Books; Calvert,
Robert; Jimenez, Santiago; Lopez, Lisa;
Music; Myles, Carol; Paredes, Americo;
*Recreation; Television.

Philip Morris, Inc.

8399 Communications/marketing. HISPANIC BUSINESS,
Vol. 4, no. 2 (February 1982), p. 15.
English. DESCR: Cable Television;
Congressional Hispanic Caucus; El Teatro
Campesino; GalaVision; Labor Unions;
*Marketing; Publishing Industry; Spanish
International Network (SIN).

8400 Communications/marketing. HISPANIC BUSINESS,
Vol. 4, no. 1 (January 1982), p. 13.
English. DESCR: Beauty Contests;
*Biographical Notes; Consumers; Hispanic
Caucus; *Marketing; Miss Black Velvet
Latina; Montemayor, Carlos R.

8401 Communications/marketing. HISPANIC BUSINESS,
Vol. 4, no. 3 (March 1982), p. 15. English.
DESCR: California; Herrera, Maria Elena;
*Marketing; Publicidad Siboney; Siboney
Advertising, Inc.; SRI International.

8402 People. HISPANIC BUSINESS, Vol. 4, no. 12
(December 1982), p. 10. English. DESCR:
*Biographical Notes; *Businesspeople;
Garcia, Frances; Gort, Wilfredo; Ojeda,
Armando; Olind, Rebecca Nieto; Roybal,
Edward R.

8403 Philip Morris publishes guide. LATINO, Vol.
54, no. 5 (August, September, 1983), p. 28.
English. DESCR: Directories.

Philippines

8404 Carlos, Jess. The Filipinos: our forgotten cultural cousins. NUESTRO, Vol. 7, no. 8 (October 1983), p. 19-21. English. DESCR: Catholic Church; Cultural Characteristics; Social History and Conditions.

Philology
USE: Linguistics

Philosophy

8405 Banas, L. K. Donde estas? Conflicts in the Chicano movement (reprinted CARACOL June 1977). CALMECAC, Vol. 2, (Spring 1981), p. 28-33. English. DESCR: *CHICANISMO DEFINED; Political Ideology.

8406 Blomstedt, Robert; Thomas, Jackie; and Teyna, Tadeo. Applying existential thought to bilingual education. BILINGUAL JOURNAL, Vol. 7, no. 4 (Summer 1983), p. 26,28. English. DESCR: *Bilingual Bicultural Education; Educational Innovations.

8407 Bustamante, Anna Luisa. La ciencia en la tradicion. CALMECAC, Vol. 3, (Spring 1982), p. 11-17. English. DESCR: *Precolumbian Science.

8408 Cantu, Roberto. Nota preliminar: de Samuel Ramos a Emilio Uranga. CAMPO LIBRE, Vol. 1, no. 2 (Summer 1981), p. 239-272. Spanish. DESCR: Cultural Characteristics; Identity; Mexico; *Ramos, Samuel; *Uranga, Emilio.

8409 Chavez, Mauro. Carranza's CHICANISMO: PHILOSOPHICAL FRAGMENTS. JOURNAL OF ETHNIC STUDIES, Vol. 7, no. 3 (Fall 1979), p. 95-100. English. DESCR: Book Reviews; Carranza, Elihu; *Chicanismo; *CHICANISMO: PHILOSOPHICAL FRAGMENTS; Research Methodology.

8410 Garcia, Reyes. Politics of flesh: ethnicity and political viability. CACR REVIEW, Vol. 1, no. 1 (September 1982), p. 102-130. English. DESCR: Anaya, Rudolfo A.; Aristotle; Culture; Ethnic Groups; Identity; Locke, John; Nuclear Armament; *Political Repression; Urban Communities.

8411 Klor de Alva, Jorge. Gabino Barrera and Chicano thought. AZTLAN, Vol. 14, no. 2 (Fall 1983), p. 343-358. English. DESCR: *Barreda, Gabino; Economic History and Conditions; History; Mexico; *Positivism.

8412 Leal, Luis. Gabino Barreda y la literatura: de la preparatoria al Ateneo. AZTLAN, Vol. 14, no. 2 (Fall 1983), p. 253-265. Spanish. DESCR: Ateneo de la Juventud; *Barreda, Gabino; Escuela Nacional Preparatoria; History; *Mexican Literature; Positivism.

8413 Marti, Oscar R. Barrera and moral philosophy. AZTLAN, Vol. 14, no. 2 (Fall 1983), p. 373-403. English. DESCR: *Barreda, Gabino; *Ethics; History; Mexico; Positivism.

8414 Marti, Oscar R. Introduction. AZTLAN, Vol. 14, no. 2 (Fall 1983), p. 209-220. English. DESCR: *Barreda, Gabino; *Biography; History; Mexico; Positivism.

8415 Marti, Oscar R., comp. Bibliography. AZTLAN, Vol. 14, no. 2 (Fall 1983), p. 405-417. English. DESCR: *Barreda, Gabino; *Bibliography; History; Mexico; Positivism.

8416 Raat, W. Dirk. Augusto Comte, Gabino Barreda, and positivism in Mexico. AZTLAN, Vol. 14, no. 2 (Fall 1983), p. 235-251. English. DESCR: *Barreda, Gabino; *Comte, Auguste; Education; Educational Theory and Practice; History; Mexico; *Positivism.

8417 Ramos, Alfonso Pena. Voices: Gandhi: the Mahatma's message to Hispanics. NUESTRO, Vol. 7, no. 4 (May 1983), p. 59-60. English. DESCR: *Ethnic Groups; Gandhi, Mahatma; *Identity; Welfare.

8418 Ramos, Manuel. En torno a las ideas sobre EL MEXICANO. CAMPO LIBRE, Vol. 1, no. 2 (Summer 1981), p. 273-282. Spanish. DESCR: Cultural Characteristics; *EL MEXICANO; Identity; Mexico; *Uranga, Emilio.

8419 Rocco, Raymond. Positivism and Mexican identity: then and now. AZTLAN, Vol. 14, no. 2 (Fall 1983), p. 359-371. English. DESCR: History; Identity; Mexico; *Positivism.

8420 Solis, Arnaldo. Calmecac. CALMECAC, Vol. 3, (Spring 1982), p. 8-9. English.

8421 Uranga, Emilio. Notas para un estudio del mexicano. CAMPO LIBRE, Vol. 1, no. 2 (Summer 1981), p. 283-295. Spanish. DESCR: Cultural Characteristics; Gaos, Jose; Identity; Mexico; *Ramos, Samuel.

8422 Zea, Leopoldo. El sentido de la historia en Gabino Barreda. AZTLAN, Vol. 14, no. 2 (Fall 1983), p. 221-233. Spanish. DESCR: *Barreda, Gabino; *History; Mexico; Positivism.

Phoenix, AZ

8423 Barry, Tom. On strike! Undocumented workers in Arizona. SOUTHWEST ECONOMY AND SOCIETY, Vol. 3, no. 3 (Spring 1978), p. 52-60. English. DESCR: Agribusiness; Agricultural Laborers; Arizona; *Goldmar Citrus Ranch, Phoenix, AZ; Labor Organizing; *Maricopa County Organizing Project (MCOP); *Strikes and Lockouts; Undocumented Workers.

8424 Communications/marketing. HISPANIC BUSINESS, Vol. 5, no. 2 (February 1983), p. 23. English. DESCR: *Broadcast Media; Coopers and Lybrand; Domecq Importers, Inc.; Latin American Feature Syndicate (ALA); *Mass Media.

8425 Hail to the chief. HISPANIC BUSINESS, Vol. 4, no. 8 (August 1983), p. 10+. English. DESCR: Criminal Justice System; *Ortega, Ruben; Police.

8426 Students view career option. NUESTRO, Vol. 6, no. 6 (August 1982), p. 12. English. DESCR: *Business; Careers; Students.

Photography

8427 Benardo, Margot L. and Anthony, Darius. Hispanic women and their men. LATINA, Vol. 1, no. 3 (1983), p. 24-29. English. DESCR: Chicanas; *Women Men Relations.

8428 Buitron, Robert C. Loteria: las manos. MAIZE, Vol. 3, no. 3-4 (Spring, Summer, 1980), p. 21.

8429 Buitron, Robert C. [Untitled]. MAIZE, Vol. 3, no. 3-4 (Spring, Summer, 1980), p. 31.

8430 Gallo, Adrien. Children of Guatemala: a pictoral essay. NUESTRO, Vol. 7, no. 2 (March 1983), p. 43-45. English. DESCR: *Children; *Guatemala.

Photography (cont.)

8431 Garcia de Fernando, Armando. [Untitled photograph]. MAIZE, Vol. 2, no. 2 (Winter 1979), p. 32-33.

8432 Garcia de Fernando, Armando. [Untitled photograph]. MAIZE, Vol. 2, no. 2 (Winter 1979), p. 57.

8433 Geary, Richard. The faces of San Miguel: a photo essay. NUESTRO, Vol. 7, no. 4 (May 1983), p. 31-34. English. **DESCR:** Mexico; *San Miguel de Allende, Mexico.

8434 Herrera, Juan Felipe. Photo-poem of the Chicano Moratorium 1980/L.A. REVISTA CHICANO-RIQUENA, Vol. 10, no. 3 (Summer 1982), p. 5-9. English. **DESCR:** Chicano Moratorium; *Poetry.

8435 Historic Baja captured on film. CAMINOS, Vol. 3, no. 11 (December 1982), p. 21. English. **DESCR:** *Baja California, Mexico; *Centro Cultural Fondo Nacional para Actividades Sociales (FONOPAS); *Tijuana, Mexico; *Tourism.

8436 Kanellos, Nicolas. Two centuries of Hispanic theatre in the Southwest. REVISTA CHICANO-RIQUENA, Vol. 11, no. 1 (Spring 1983), p. 17-39. English. **DESCR:** California; History; Los Angeles, CA; San Antonio, TX; Southwest United States; *Teatro; Texas.

8437 Marshall, Peter. [Untitled photograph]. MAIZE, Vol. 1, no. 4 (Summer 1978), p. 20-23.

8438 Martinez, Ollin. Visitas e imagenes mexicanas; reflections of a photographer (photoessay). CAMINOS, Vol. 4, no. 11 (December 1983), p. 16-18. English. **DESCR:** Mexico.

8439 Montoya, Delilah Merriman. [Untitled photograph]. MAIZE, Vol. 2, no. 4 (Summer 1979), p. 24.

8440 Montoya, Delilah Merriman. [Untitled photograph]. MAIZE, Vol. 2, no. 4 (Summer 1979), p. 59.

8441 Naranjo. Los campesinos [photograph]. MAIZE, Vol. 1, no. 4 (Summer 1978), p. 13.

8442 Ochoa, Victor Orozco. [Untitled photographs]. MAIZE, Vol. 1, no. 3 (Spring 1978), p. 45-47,50+. **DESCR:** Precolumbian Art.

8443 Polkinhorn, Harry. [Untitled]. MAIZE, Vol. 3, no. 3-4 (Spring, Summer, 1980), p. Bk cover.

8444 Ponce, Miguel. [Untitled photographs]. MAIZE, Vol. 1, no. 2 (Winter 1978), p. 26-27.

8445 Puerto Rico: images from the past. NUESTRO, Vol. 7, no. 9 (November 1983), p. 48-53. English. **DESCR:** CONTRASTES [exhibit]; *Delano, Jack; Hostos Community College, New York, NY; Puerto Rico.

8446 Quinlivan, Robert. The photographs of Agustin V. Casasola; un epilogo de la revolucion Mexicana de 1910. CAMINOS, Vol. 3, no. 1 (January 1982), p. 38-40. Bilingual. **DESCR:** *Casasola, Agustin V.; *Mexican Revolution - 1910-1920.

8447 Rocha, Julie. Ano de la mujer-Tenochtitlan [photograph]. MAIZE, Vol. 1, no. 2 (Winter 1977), p. 58-60.

8448 Rodriguez, Luis Javier. Profile of Luis Carlos Bernal. CORAZON DE AZTLAN, Vol. 1, no. 3 (August, September, 1982), p. 22-23. English. **DESCR:** *Bernal, Louis Carlos; Biography.

8449 Roitman, Daniel. [Untitled]. MAIZE, Vol. 3, no. 1-2 (Fall, Winter, 1979, 1980), p. 23. English.

8450 Schmidt, Dorothy. Book review of: ON THE BORDER: PORTRAITS OF AMERICA'S SOUTHWESTERN FRONTIER. WESTERN AMERICAN LITERATURE, Vol. 17, no. 1 (Spring 1982), p. 74. English. **DESCR:** Book Reviews; Miller, Tom; *ON THE BORDER: PORTRAITS OF AMERICA'S SOUTHWESTERN FRONTIER.

8451 Sierra, Jerry A. Faces [photographs]. CAMINOS, Vol. 4, no. 8 (September 1983), p. 28-30. English. **DESCR:** *Cubanos; Los Marielitos.

8452 Smith, Dana M. [Untitled photographs]. MAIZE, Vol. 1, no. 2 (Winter 1978), p. 49-51.

Physical Education

8453 Maciel, David R. Nacionalismo cultural y politica liberal en la Republica Restaurada, 1867-1876. AZTLAN, Vol. 14, no. 2 (Fall 1983), p. 267-287. Spanish. **DESCR:** History; *Mexico; Political History and Conditions; Political Ideology.

Picardias
USE: Chistes

PIDER Project

8454 Morrison, Thomas K. The relationship of U.S. aid, trade and investment to migration pressures in major sending countries. INTERNATIONAL MIGRATION REVIEW, Vol. 16, no. 1 (Spring 1982), p. 4-26. English. **DESCR:** Border Region; International Economic Relations; Investments; Mexican Border Industrialization Program; *Migration Patterns; Rural Economics; Rural Urban Migration; Undocumented Workers; United States-Mexico Relations.

PIERS-HARRIS CHILDREN'S SELF CONCEPT SCALE

8455 Kugle, Cherry L.; Clements, Richard O.; and Powell, Philip M. Level and stability of self-esteem in relation to academic behavior of second graders. JOURNAL OF PERSONALITY AND SOCIAL PSYCHOLOGY, Vol. 44, no. 1 (January 1983), p. 201-207. English. **DESCR:** Academic Achievement; *Identity; Primary School Education.

Pilsen, IL

8456 Ano Nuevo de Kerr, Louise. Chicano settlements in Chicago: a brief history. JOURNAL OF ETHNIC STUDIES, Vol. 2, no. 4 (Winter 1975), p. 22-32. English. **DESCR:** Back of the Yards, Chicago, IL; *Chicago, IL; Near West Side, Chicago, IL; Social History and Conditions; South Chicago, Chicago, IL; *Urban Communities.

8457 Barry, Patrick. Alternative high school provides dropouts a second chance. NUESTRO, Vol. 6, no. 7 (September 1982), p. 29-30. English. **DESCR:** *Dropouts.

Pilsen, IL (cont.)

8458 Lopez, Tom. Pilsen. NUESTRO, Vol. 6, no. 7 (September 1982), p. 31. English. DESCR: *Literature.

Pimentel, Carlos

8459 Balkan, D. Carlos. The nuclear powered Mr. Carlos Pimentel. HISPANIC BUSINESS, Vol. 4, no. 2 (February 1982), p. 16-17+. English. DESCR: Biography; Business Enterprises; Businesspeople; *Cataract Engineering and Construction, Inc.; Energy Industries.

Pineda, Pat

8460 People. HISPANIC BUSINESS, Vol. 5, no. 4 (April 1983), p. 9. English. DESCR: Alvarado, Linda M.; *Biographical Notes; Businesspeople; Castillo, Irenemaree; Castillo, Sylvia; Del Junco, Tirso; Gutierrez, Jose Roberto; Juarez, Joe; Mata, Bill; Miyares, Marcelino; Montanez Davis, Grace; Montoya, Velma; Siberio, Julio; Thompson, Edith Lopez.

Piniella, Lou

8461 Ortiz, Carlos V. NUESTRO'S sixth annual all-star baseball team. NUESTRO, Vol. 7, no. 2 (March 1983), p. 33-37. English. DESCR: Andujar, Joaquin; Barojas, Salome; *Baseball; Castillo, Manny; Concepcion, Dave; Cruz, Jose; Garcia, Damaso; Guerrero, Pedro; Hernandez, Keith; Lezcano, Sixto; Martinez, Tippy; Pena, Tony; Sports; Valenzuela, Fernando.

Pintos
USE: Prisoners

Pioneer Chicken

8462 Ogaz, Armando. The chicken wars. CAMINOS, Vol. 4, no. 6 (June 1983), p. 10-11. Bilingual. DESCR: El Pollo Loco; Food Industry; *Restaurants.

Pioneers

8463 Forbes, Jack D. Hispanic-Mexican pioneers of the San Francisco Bay region: an analysis of racial origins. AZTLAN, Vol. 14, no. 1 (Spring 1983), p. 175-189. English. DESCR: Ethnic Groups; Identity; *San Francisco Bay.

Pla, George

8464 People. HISPANIC BUSINESS, Vol. 5, no. 7 (July 1983), p. 8. English. DESCR: Alvarado, Anthony J.; Appointed Officials; *Biographical Notes; Businesspeople; Candela, Hilario; Garcia, Marlene; Gonzalez, Julio; Martinez, Tony; Valdez, Abelardo L.

Placa
USE: Graffiti

Placement

8465 Scott, Leigh S., et al. Adaptive behavior inventory for children: the need for local norms. JOURNAL OF SCHOOL PSYCHOLOGY, Vol. 20, no. 1 (Spring 1982), p. 39-44. English. DESCR: *Adaptive Behavior Inventory for Children (ABIC); Anglo Americans; Blacks; Corpus Christi Independent School District; Corpus Christi, TX; System of Multicultural Pluralistic Assessment (SOMPA).

Placentia, Joe

8466 Diaz, Katherine A. "And this year's winners are...". CAMINOS, Vol. 4, no. 1-2 (January, February, 1983), p. 39-54,74+. English. DESCR: *Awards; Castro, Tony; Elizalde, Hector; Flores, Tom; Martinez, Esperanza; Mendizabal, Maritza; Molina, Gloria; Moya, Connie; Quesada, Leticia; Rios, David N.; Ybarra, Lea; Zapata, Carmen.

Plakos, J.

8467 Orlandi, Lisanio R. Book review of: WORKBOOK ON PROGRAM EVALUATION. BILINGUAL JOURNAL, Vol. 7, no. 2 (Winter 1983), p. 35-36. English. DESCR: Babcock, R.; Bilingual Bicultural Education; Book Reviews; Evaluation (Educational); Plakos, M.; *WORKBOOK ON PROGRAM EVALUATION.

Plakos, M.

8468 Orlandi, Lisanio R. Book review of: WORKBOOK ON PROGRAM EVALUATION. BILINGUAL JOURNAL, Vol. 7, no. 2 (Winter 1983), p. 35-36. English. DESCR: Babcock, R.; Bilingual Bicultural Education; Book Reviews; Evaluation (Educational); Plakos, J.; *WORKBOOK ON PROGRAM EVALUATION.

Planas, Maria Bordas

8469 People. HISPANIC BUSINESS, Vol. 5, no. 12 (December 1983), p. 9. English. DESCR: *Businesspeople; Cantu, Norma V.; Cruz, Jose; Masvidal, Sergio J.; Ortega, Katherine D.; Rodriguez, Ismael D.; Romero, Estella E.

Planas, Vilma

8470 Gente. NUESTRO, Vol. 7, no. 7 (September 1983), p. 61. English. DESCR: Americas Award; Chavez, Raul; *Chicanas; Diaz-Cobo, Christine; Mexico; Ortega, Katherine D.; Performing Arts; Ravard, Rafael Alonzo; Venezuela.

Plays
USE: Teatro

Plaza de La Raza, Los Angeles, CA

8471 Dreams come true ... a celebration (photoessay). CAMINOS, Vol. 3, no. 11 (December 1982), p. 46-47. English. DESCR: Cultural Organizations.

8472 Government review. NUESTRO, Vol. 7, no. 8 (October 1983), p. 54. English. DESCR: Alcoholism; Employment; *Government Services; National Endowment for the Arts; Veterans; Working Women; Youth.

8473 New Salazar building. NUESTRO, Vol. 6, no. 7 (September 1982), p. 9. English. DESCR: *Art; Culture; Education; Latin Americans; Los Angeles, CA; Salazar, Ruben.

8474 "Our success is to see someone get a job with MGM"; Q and A with Edmundo M. Rodriguez. CAMINOS, Vol. 3, no. 11 (December 1982), p. 48-49,54. English. DESCR: Cultural Organizations; Rodriguez, Edmundo M.

8475 Plaza de la Raza to host project. NUESTRO, Vol. 7, no. 10 (December 1983), p. 11. English. DESCR: Arts and Crafts; *Folk Art; Folklife Festival (Los Angeles, CA); Olympic Arts Festival, Los Angeles, CA.

Plaza de La Raza, Los Angeles, CA (cont.)

8476 Wittenauer, Cheryl. The economics of
culture: L.A.'s most successful Plaza de la
Raza. HISPANIC BUSINESS, Vol. 5, no. 1
(January 1983), p. 12-13+. English. DESCR:
*Cultural Organizations; Funding Sources;
Ruben Salazar Bicentennial Building.

La Plaza Senior Citizens, Los Angeles, CA

8477 Community watching: para la comunidad.
CAMINOS, Vol. 2, no. 6 (October 1981), p.
40-41+. English. DESCR: *Cultural
Organizations; Hispanic Women in Higher
Education (HWHE); Mexican American Political
Association (MAPA); Reapportionment.

THE PLUM PLUM PICKERS

8478 Supreme Court recognizes special importance
of education. MENTAL DISABILITY LAW
REPORTER, Vol. 6, (July, August, 1982), p.
227-229. English. DESCR: Doe v. Plyer [Tyler
Independent School District, Texas];
*Education; San Antonio School District v.
Rodriguez; Undocumented Workers.

8479 Walia, Adorna. Book review of: THE PLUM PLUM
PICKERS. BILINGUAL JOURNAL, Vol. 6, no. 1
(Fall 1982), p. 30-31. English. DESCR:
Agricultural Laborers; Barrio, Raymond; Book
Reviews; California; *Migrant Labor; Santa
Clara County, CA.

Pluralism
USE: Cultural Pluralism

PLURALISM IN THE LEGAL PROFESSION: MODELS FOR MINORITY ACCESS

8480 Study details minority access to legal
education. NEW JERSEY LAW JOURNAL, Vol. 112,
no. 1 (July 7, 1983), p. 28. English.
DESCR: Brown, Susan E.; *Ethnic Groups;
*Legal Education; Mexican American Legal
Defense and Educational Fund (MALDEF);
Vasquez, Hector G.

POCHO

8481 Alarcon, Justo S. Hacia la nada ... o la
religion en POCHO. MINORITY VOICES, Vol. 1,
no. 2 (Fall 1977), p. 17-26. English.
DESCR: Literature; Religion; Villarreal,
Jose Antonio.

8482 Lattin, Vernon E. Ethnicity and identity in
the contemporary Chicano novel. MINORITY
VOICES, Vol. 2, no. 2 (Fall 1978), p. 37-44.
English. DESCR: BLESS ME, ULTIMA; Identity;
Literary Criticism; Literature; MEMORIES OF
THE ALHAMBRA; *Novel; THE AUTOBIOGRAPHY OF A
BROWN BUFFALO; Y NO SE LO TRAGO LA
TIERRA/AND THE EARTH DID NOT PART.

8483 Leudtke, Luther S. POCHO and the American
dream. MINORITY VOICES, Vol. 1, no. 2 (Fall
1977), p. 1-16. English. DESCR: Literature;
Villarreal, Jose Antonio.

8484 Lizarraga, Sylvia S. Observaciones acerca de
la critica literaria Chicana. REVISTA
CHICANO-RIQUENA, Vol. 10, no. 4 (Fall 1982),
p. 55-64. Spanish. DESCR: *Bruce Novoa,
Juan; CITY OF NIGHT; El Teatro Campesino;
*Literary Criticism; Literature; THE SPACE
OF CHICANO LITERATURE.

8485 Orozco, Febe Portillo. A bibliography of
Hispanic literature. ENGLISH JOURNAL, Vol.
71, no. 7 (November 1982), p. 58-62.
English. DESCR: BARRIO BOY; *Bibliography;
BLESS ME, ULTIMA; CHICANO; EL SOL Y LOS DE
ABAJO; GRITO DEL SOL; HEART OF AZTLAN;
*Literature; WE ARE CHICANOS.

8486 Vallejos, Thomas. Ritual process and the
family in the Chicano novel. MELUS:
MULTI-ETHNIC LITERATURE OF THE UNITED
STATES, Vol. 10, no. 4 (Winter 1983, 1984),
p. 5-16. English. DESCR: Anaya, Rudolfo A.;
BLESS ME, ULTIMA; Family; *Literary
Criticism; Novel; Parent and Child
Relationships; Rivera, Tomas; Villarreal,
Jose Antonio; Y NO SE LO TRAGO LA TIERRA/AND
THE EARTH DID NOT PART.

LOS POEMAS DE FILI-MELE

8487 Villanueva Collado, Alfredo. Fili-Mele:
simbolo y mujer en la poesia de Luis Pales
Matos e Ivan Silen. REVISTA CHICANO-RIQUENA,
Vol. 10, no. 4 (Fall 1982), p. 47-54.
Spanish. DESCR: Chicanas; Literary
Criticism; *Pales Matos, Luis; Ribes Tovar,
Federico; *Silen, Ivan; Symbolism; TUNTUN DE
PASA Y GRIFERIA.

Poetry

8488 Accion de gracias. MAIZE, Vol. 5, no. 3-4
(Spring, Summer, 1982), p. 86. Spanish.

8489 Acuna, Carlos. Alcon Moco's ballet (a border
question). MAIZE, Vol. 5, no. 1-2 (Fall,
Winter, 1981, 1982), p. 33-37. Bilingual.

8490 Adnan, Etel. Pablo Neruda is a banana tree.
MAIZE, Vol. 6, no. 1-2 (Fall, Winter, 1982,
1983), p. 44-47. English.

8491 Adrienne, K. Memories of you. MAIZE, Vol. 2,
no. 4 (Summer 1979), p. 28. English.

8492 Agosin, Marjorie. Donde estan? REVISTA
CHICANO-RIQUENA, Vol. 11, no. 3-4 (Fall
1983), p. 76. Spanish.

8493 Agosin, Marjorie. Estados Unidos. REVISTA
CHICANO-RIQUENA, Vol. 11, no. 3-4 (Fall
1983), p. 73. Spanish.

8494 Agosin, Marjorie. La mesa de billar en New
Bedford, Mass. REVISTA CHICANO-RIQUENA, Vol.
11, no. 3-4 (Fall 1983), p. 72-73. Spanish.

8495 Aguila, Pancho. Before the aquarians. MAIZE,
Vol. 6, no. 1-2 (Fall, Winter, 1982, 1983),
p. 48. English.

8496 Aguila, Pancho. Existential. MAIZE, Vol. 6,
no. 1-2 (Fall, Winter, 1982, 1983), p. 49.
English.

8497 Aguila, Pancho. The ex-marine. MAIZE, Vol.
6, no. 1-2 (Fall, Winter, 1982, 1983), p.
50. English.

8498 Aguila, Pancho. Folsom. MAIZE, Vol. 6, no.
1-2 (Fall, Winter, 1982, 1983), p. 51.
English.

8499 Aguila, Pancho. Marilyn. MAIZE, Vol. 4, no.
3-4 (Spring, Summer, 1981), p. 44-45.
English.

8500 Aguila, Pancho. The nuts and bolts.
CHISMEARTE, no. 9 (September 1983), p.
30-31. English.

8501 Aguilar, Ricardo D. Aeroplanos de papel.
JOURNAL OF ETHNIC STUDIES, Vol. 5, no. 1
(Spring 1977), p. 63-64. Spanish.

Poetry (cont.)

8502 Aguilar, Ricardo D. Al regreso. JOURNAL OF ETHNIC STUDIES, Vol. 4, no. 4 (Winter 1977), p. 83. English.

8503 Aguilar, Ricardo D. Cancion de viaje. JOURNAL OF ETHNIC STUDIES, Vol. 5, no. 1 (Spring 1977), p. 65. Spanish.

8504 Aguilar, Ricardo D. Chicano poetry and new places. JOURNAL OF ETHNIC STUDIES, Vol. 5, no. 1 (Spring 1977), p. 59-61. English. **DESCR:** *Literature; Seattle, WA.

8505 Aguilar, Ricardo D. Definicion de la vida -o- agarrala que se escapa. JOURNAL OF ETHNIC STUDIES, Vol. 5, no. 1 (Spring 1977), p. 62. Spanish.

8506 Aguilar, Ricardo D. Gabi. JOURNAL OF ETHNIC STUDIES, Vol. 5, no. 1 (Spring 1977), p. 67. Spanish.

8507 Aguilar, Ricardo D. Hacia donde? JOURNAL OF ETHNIC STUDIES, Vol. 5, no. 1 (Spring 1977), p. 68-69. Bilingual.

8508 Aguilar, Ricardo D. Marinero. JOURNAL OF ETHNIC STUDIES, Vol. 5, no. 1 (Spring 1977), p. 66. Spanish.

8509 Aguilar, Ricardo D. Pica pica pica perico pica pica pica la rama. JOURNAL OF ETHNIC STUDIES, Vol. 4, no. 4 (Winter 1977), p. 84. English.

8510 Aguirre, Javier. Las lagrimas se secan. DE COLORES, Vol. 6, no. 1-2 (1982), p. 141. Spanish.

8511 Aguirre, Javier. Oda para la jefita. DE COLORES, Vol. 6, no. 1-2 (1982), p. 142-143. Spanish.

8512 Aguirre, Javier. Pa' mi asi fue. DE COLORES, Vol. 6, no. 1-2 (1982), p. 140. Bilingual.

8513 Akbar, Karim. Death. MAIZE, Vol. 2, no. 1 (Fall 1978), p. 23. English.

8514 Akbar, Karim. I am tired. MAIZE, Vol. 2, no. 1 (Fall 1978), p. 22. English.

8515 Akbar, Karim. People. MAIZE, Vol. 2, no. 1 (Fall 1978), p. 20-21. English.

8516 Alcaraz, Edward. Tecate soldiers. CORAZON DE AZTLAN, Vol. 1, no. 3 (August, September, 1982), p. 42. English.

8517 Aldaraca, Bridget. The poetry of Gioconda Belli. MAIZE, Vol. 5, no. 3-4 (Spring, Summer, 1982), p. 18-21. English. **DESCR:** Belli, Gioconda; Literary Criticism; *Nicaragua; Revolutions.

8518 Alegria, Claribel. Requiem. MAIZE, Vol. 6, no. 1-2 (Fall, Winter, 1982, 1983), p. 92-93. Spanish.

8519 Alejandro, Brenda. La paraplejica se vistio de largo. THIRD WOMAN, Vol. 1, no. 2 (1982), p. 24. Spanish.

8520 Algarin, Miguel. Albuquerque. REVISTA CHICANO-RIQUENA, Vol. 10, no. 1-2 (Winter, Spring, 1982), p. 13-14. Bilingual.

8521 Algarin, Miguel. El jibarito moderno. REVISTA CHICANO-RIQUENA, Vol. 10, no. 1-2 (Winter, Spring, 1982), p. 7. Bilingual.

8522 Algarin, Miguel. Paris. REVISTA CHICANO-RIQUENA, Vol. 10, no. 1-2 (Winter, Spring, 1982), p. 15-19. English.

8523 Algarin, Miguel. Paterson. REVISTA CHICANO-RIQUENA, Vol. 10, no. 1-2 (Winter, Spring, 1982), p. 8-9. English.

8524 Algarin, Miguel. Taos Pueblo Indians: 700 strong according to Bobby's last census. REVISTA CHICANO-RIQUENA, Vol. 10, no. 1-2 (Winter, Spring, 1982), p. 10-12. English.

8525 Almanza, Antonio. A......lone. MAIZE, Vol. 2, no. 3 (Spring 1979), p. 50. English.

8526 Almanza, Antonio. Charade. MAIZE, Vol. 2, no. 3 (Spring 1979), p. 53. English.

8527 Almanza, Antonio. The panhandle. MAIZE, Vol. 2, no. 3 (Spring 1979), p. 52. English.

8528 Altschul, Fernando. The siren rang. MAIZE, Vol. 6, no. 1-2 (Fall, Winter, 1982, 1983), p. 62. English.

8529 Alurista. A. MAIZE, Vol. 1, no. 4 (Summer 1978), p. 52. Spanish.

8530 Alurista. All over. MAIZE, Vol. 3, no. 1-2 (Fall, Winter, 1979, 1980), p. 68. English.

8531 Alurista. Aztlan, quo vadis? MAIZE, Vol. 4, no. 1-2 (Fall, Winter, 1980, 1981), p. 64. Bilingual.

8532 Alurista. Been. MAIZE, Vol. 1, no. 4 (Summer 1978), p. 53. English.

8533 Alurista. Cabezeando. MAIZE, Vol. 1, no. 4 (Summer 1978), p. 54. Spanish.

8534 Alurista. Caudillos de arena. MAIZE, Vol. 1, no. 2 (Winter 1977), p. 39. English.

8535 Alurista. Chuck. MAIZE, Vol. 2, no. 4 (Summer 1979), p. [60]. English.

8536 Alurista. [Corn stalks]. MAIZE, Vol. 1, no. 3 (Spring 1978), p. Ft Cover. English.

8537 Alurista. Cornfields thaw out. REVISTA CHICANO-RIQUENA, Vol. 10, no. 1-2 (Winter, Spring, 1982), p. 21. English.

8538 Alurista. Cornfields thaw out. MAIZE, Vol. 3, no. 1-2 (Fall, Winter, 1979, 1980), p. 66. English.

8539 Alurista. Do u remember. REVISTA CHICANO-RIQUENA, Vol. 10, no. 1-2 (Winter, Spring, 1982), p. 20. English.

8540 Alurista. En. MAIZE, Vol. 6, no. 1-2 (Fall, Winter, 1982, 1983), p. 89. Spanish.

8541 Alurista. I hate. MAIZE, Vol. 1, no. 1 (Fall 1977), p. 34. English.

8542 Alurista. Jc's mono jog at camp slingshot. MAIZE, Vol. 2, no. 2 (Winter 1979), p. 59. English.

8543 Alurista. Left just. MAIZE, Vol. 4, no. 3-4 (Spring, Summer, 1981), p. 68. English.

8544 Alurista. Ms. x. MAIZE, Vol. 3, no. 1-2 (Fall, Winter, 1979, 1980), p. 69. Spanish.

8545 Alurista. Pues. MAIZE, Vol. 2, no. 2 (Winter 1979), p. 60. Calo.

Poetry (cont.)

8546 Alurista. Scratching six, plucking one. REVISTA CHICANO-RIQUENA, Vol. 10, no. 1-2 (Winter, Spring, 1982), p. 22-23. English.

8547 Alurista. Siers robo. MAIZE, Vol. 1, no. 1 (Fall 1977), p. 31. Bilingual.

8548 Alurista. Thee gone? MAIZE, Vol. 1, no. 2 (Winter 1977), p. [65]. English.

8549 Alves Pereira, Teresinka. Espera sin odio. MAIZE, Vol. 3, no. 1-2 (Fall, Winter, 1979, 1980), p. 29. Spanish.

8550 Alves Pereira, Teresinka. Roberto. CHISMEARTE, no. 9 (September 1983), p. 18. Bilingual.

8551 Alves Pereira, Teresinka. Roberto Santoro, desaparecido. MAIZE, Vol. 5, no. 3-4 (Spring, Summer, 1982), p. 62. Spanish.

8552 Anaya, Jose Vicente. La nave de la locura (excerpt). MAIZE, Vol. 1, no. 3 (Spring 1978), p. 58-59. Spanish.

8553 Ando sangrando! (I am bleeding), a study of Mexican American - Police conflict and an analysis of the East Los Angeles 1970 riots. CORAZON DE AZTLAN, Vol. 1, no. 2 (March, April, 1982), p. 35. Bilingual.

8554 Arguelles, Ivan. The conquest of Mexico. REVISTA CHICANO-RIQUENA, Vol. 10, no. 1-2 (Winter, Spring, 1982), p. 26. English.

8555 Arguelles, Ivan. "The Cuban decision". REVISTA CHICANO-RIQUENA, Vol. 10, no. 1-2 (Winter, Spring, 1982), p. 27. English.

8556 Arguelles, Ivan. Echoes of life. MAIZE, Vol. 5, no. 1-2 (Fall, Winter, 1981, 1982), p. 92. English.

8557 Arguelles, Ivan. Maquina de coser. REVISTA CHICANO-RIQUENA, Vol. 10, no. 1-2 (Winter, Spring, 1982), p. 28. English.

8558 Arguelles, Ivan. Modern Mexico. REVISTA CHICANO-RIQUENA, Vol. 10, no. 1-2 (Winter, Spring, 1982), p. 25. English.

8559 Arguelles, Ivan. Mr. Gonzalez makes a speech. REVISTA CHICANO-RIQUENA, Vol. 10, no. 1-2 (Winter, Spring, 1982), p. 29. English.

8560 Arguelles, Ivan. El Quijote de la maquina de coser. REVISTA CHICANO-RIQUENA, Vol. 11, no. 2 (Summer 1983), p. 49. English.

8561 Arguelles, Ivan. Republica Mexicana. REVISTA CHICANO-RIQUENA, Vol. 10, no. 1-2 (Winter, Spring, 1982), p. 24. English.

8562 Arguelles, Ivan. La vida no es un sueno. REVISTA CHICANO-RIQUENA, Vol. 11, no. 2 (Summer 1983), p. 50. English.

8563 Ayala, Ernesto. My machine. NUESTRO, Vol. 6, no. 7 (September 1982), p. 31. English. DESCR: Ayala, Ernesto; UN VERANO.

8564 Aztlan, Perico. The sewer society. CORAZON DE AZTLAN, Vol. 1, no. 1 (January, February, 1982), p. 35. English.

8565 Baca, Jimmy Santiago. For a Chicano brother of mine. REVISTA CHICANO-RIQUENA, Vol. 10, no. 1-2 (Winter, Spring, 1982), p. 33-34. English.

8566 Baca, Jimmy Santiago. Sun calendar. REVISTA CHICANO-RIQUENA, Vol. 10, no. 1-2 (Winter, Spring, 1982), p. 31. English.

8567 Baca, Jimmy Santiago. They're used to putting things in the ground. REVISTA CHICANO-RIQUENA, Vol. 10, no. 1-2 (Winter, Spring, 1982), p. 34-35. English.

8568 Baca, Jimmy Santiago. We knew it. REVISTA CHICANO-RIQUENA, Vol. 10, no. 1-2 (Winter, Spring, 1982), p. 32-33. English.

8569 Baca, Jimmy Santiago. The word love. REVISTA CHICANO-RIQUENA, Vol. 10, no. 1-2 (Winter, Spring, 1982), p. 30-31. English.

8570 Baker, Edward, trans. and Dalton, Roque. The poetry of Roque Dalton: We all, Typist, Latinoamerica, Love poem, O.A.S. MAIZE, Vol. 5, no. 3-4 (Spring, Summer, 1982), p. 37-46. English. DESCR: *El Salvador; Revolutions.

8571 Baldwin, Deirdra. The empty room. MAIZE, Vol. 3, no. 1-2 (Fall, Winter, 1979, 1980), p. 71. English.

8572 Baldwin, Deirdra. Stopping by the sauna. MAIZE, Vol. 3, no. 1-2 (Fall, Winter, 1979, 1980), p. 70. English.

8573 Banberger, Ellen. Poesia nicaraguense. MAIZE, Vol. 5, no. 3-4 (Spring, Summer, 1982), p. 64-77. Spanish. DESCR: Belli, Gioconda; Cardenal, Ernesto; Carrillo, Ernesto; Coronel Urtecho, Jose; Gadea, Gerardo; Gomez, Manuel; Murillo, Rosario; *Nicaragua; Ojeda, Mirna; Revolutions; Rugama, Leonel.

8574 Barrio, Raymond. Un breviario mexicano. BILINGUAL JOURNAL, Vol. 6, no. 4 (Summer 1982), p. 16-17. Bilingual.

8575 Barrios, Gregg. Advertisement for Chicano unity. NUESTRO, Vol. 6, no. 10 (December 1982), p. 60. English.

8576 Barrios, Gregg. Del mero corazon. NUESTRO, Vol. 6, no. 10 (December 1982), p. 60. English.

8577 Barrios, Gregg. I am an American too. NUESTRO, Vol. 6, no. 10 (December 1982), p. 61. English.

8578 Barrios, Gregg. Our Lady of the Angels has no papers. LATINA, Vol. 1, no. 1 (1982), p. 36-37. English. DESCR: *Baez, Joan.

8579 Baxter, Carolyn. E. 100th st. (8th grade). MAIZE, Vol. 2, no. 4 (Summer 1979), p. 41. English.

8580 Baxter, Carolyn. Street. MAIZE, Vol. 2, no. 4 (Summer 1979), p. 42. English.

8581 Belli, Gioconda. Dynamite dresses: vestidos de dinamita. MAIZE, Vol. 5, no. 3-4 (Spring, Summer, 1982), p. 22. Bilingual. DESCR: *Nicaragua.

8582 Benavidez, Max. Los Angeles. MAIZE, Vol. 3, no. 3-4 (Spring, Summer, 1980), p. 60. English.

8583 Benavidez, Max. Los Angeles. CHISMEARTE, (1982), p. 62. English.

8584 Benavidez, Max. Nada. MAIZE, Vol. 3, no. 3-4 (Spring, Summer, 1980), p. 61. English.

Poetry (cont.)

8585 Bernal, Juan Manuel. [Cheech and Chong together]. MAIZE, Vol. 4, no. 3-4 (Spring, Summer, 1981), p. 78. Spanish.

8586 Bernal, Juan Manuel. Happy happy. MAIZE, Vol. 5, no. 3-4 (Spring, Summer, 1982), p. 23. Bilingual. **DESCR:** *Nicaragua.

8587 Bernal, Juan Manuel. [It took ten powerful trucks to haul]. MAIZE, Vol. 4, no. 3-4 (Spring, Summer, 1981), p. 80. Bilingual.

8588 Bernal, Juan Manuel. Mientras. MAIZE, Vol. 5, no. 3-4 (Spring, Summer, 1982), p. 24. Spanish. **DESCR:** *Nicaragua.

8589 Bernal, Juan Manuel. Monologo congruente. MAIZE, Vol. 4, no. 3-4 (Spring, Summer, 1981), p. 80. Spanish.

8590 Bernal, Juan Manuel. Oda a garcia lorca. MAIZE, Vol. 4, no. 3-4 (Spring, Summer, 1981), p. 79. Spanish.

8591 Bernal, Juan Manuel. [Quiero jugar bebeleche y la cebolla]. MAIZE, Vol. 4, no. 3-4 (Spring, Summer, 1981), p. 79. Spanish.

8592 Bernal, Juan Manuel. La vida fascinante de un individuo trivial. MAIZE, Vol. 4, no. 3-4 (Spring, Summer, 1981), p. 78. Spanish.

8593 Berssenbrugge, Mei Mei. The beautiful moth. MAIZE, Vol. 5, no. 1-2 (Fall, Winter, 1981, 1982), p. 55. English.

8594 Betancourt, Mary. La educacion de Jesus. MAIZE, Vol. 1, no. 2 (Winter 1977), p. 28-29. Bilingual.

8595 Beveridge, Kriss. Chubasco. MAIZE, Vol. 2, no. 2 (Winter 1979), p. 34-35. English.

8596 Beveridge, Kriss. La isla de nadie. MAIZE, Vol. 2, no. 2 (Winter 1979), p. 36. English.

8597 Bisconte, Sarah R. [Untitled poems]. MAIZE, Vol. 6, no. 3-4 (Spring, Summer, 1983), p. 62-63. Spanish.

8598 Blanche, Ella. Ghost people. MAIZE, Vol. 3, no. 1-2 (Fall, Winter, 1979, 1980), p. 28. English.

8599 Blanche, Ella. I have seen her. MAIZE, Vol. 3, no. 12 (Fall, Winter, 1979, 1980), p. 28. English.

8600 Bogrand, Ricardo. Dentro de un pozo. MAIZE, Vol. 6, no. 1-2 (Fall, Winter, 1982, 1983), p. 98. Spanish.

8601 Bolano, Roberto. Bienvenida. MAIZE, Vol. 3, no. 3-4 (Spring, Summer, 1980), p. 74-75. Spanish.

8602 Bolano, Roberto. Estos patios parecen playas. MAIZE, Vol. 2, no. 3 (Spring 1979), p. 21. Spanish.

8603 Bolano, Roberto. Rojo/burbujeante. MAIZE, Vol. 2, no. 3 (Spring 1979), p. 18-20. Spanish.

8604 Bolivar, Maria Dolores. Al hombre. MAIZE, Vol. 3, no. 1-2 (Fall, Winter, 1979, 1980), p. 52-53. Spanish.

8605 Brinson-Pineda, Barbara. Fire. REVISTA CHICANO-RIQUENA, Vol. 10, no. 1-2 (Winter, Spring, 1982), p. 36-37. English.

8606 Brinson-Pineda, Barbara. Maria la O. REVISTA CHICANO-RIQUENA, Vol. 10, no. 1-2 (Winter, Spring, 1982), p. 38-41. English.

8607 Burciaga, Jose Antonio. Ghost riders. MAIZE, Vol. 2, no. 1 (Fall 1978), p. 46-47. English.

8608 Burk, Ronnie. Cihuacoatl. MAIZE, Vol. 1, no. 4 (Summer 1978), p. 29. English.

8609 Burk, Ronnie. In the park. MAIZE, Vol. 3, no. 1-2 (Fall, Winter, 1979, 1980), p. 77. English.

8610 Burk, Ronnie. Ogre woman's song. MAIZE, Vol. 1, no. 4 (Summer 1978), p. 29. English.

8611 Bush, Roberta F. Cowboys and indians. MAIZE, Vol. 1, no. 4 (Summer 1978), p. 10. Bilingual.

8612 Bush, Roberta F. Para mi esposo. MAIZE, Vol. 1, no. 4 (Summer 1978), p. 9. Bilingual.

8613 Bustamante, Anna Luisa. In ixtli, in yollotl - rostro y corazon. CALMECAC, Vol. 1, no. 1 (Spring 1980), p. 23. English.

8614 Bustamante, Anna Luisa. Rain feather. CALMECAC, Vol. 2, (Spring 1981), p. 54. English.

8615 Bustamante, Anna Luisa. Senor Pascua. CALMECAC, Vol. 3, (Spring 1982), p. 49. Spanish.

8616 Caballero, Raul. Festival a puertas abiertas. MAIZE, Vol. 4, no. 3-4 (Spring, Summer, 1981), p. 83. Spanish.

8617 Caballero, Raul. El jazz del vagabundo. MAIZE, Vol. 4, no. 3-4 (Spring, Summer, 1981), p. 82. Spanish.

8618 Caballero, Raul. Parque de diversiones. MAIZE, Vol. 4, no. 3-4 (Spring, Summer, 1981), p. 81. Spanish.

8619 Cabanas, Suzana. A song to women. THIRD WOMAN, Vol. 1, no. 2 (1982), p. 21-22. English.

8620 Calderon, Beto. Esta noche. MAIZE, Vol. 1, no. 3 (Spring 1978), p. 30-31. Spanish.

8621 Calderon, Beto. Me imagino una lucha llena de amor. MAIZE, Vol. 3, no. 1-2 (Fall, Winter, 1979, 1980), p. 32-33. Spanish.

8622 Calderon, Beto. Poema decisivo. MAIZE, Vol. 3, no. 1-2 (Fall, Winter, 1979, 1980), p. 30-31. Spanish.

8623 Caly, Eugenia. Cadiz de lien tan. MAIZE, Vol. 6, no. 3-4 (Spring, Summer, 1983), p. 28. Spanish.

8624 Caly, Eugenia. Las eras imaginarias. MAIZE, Vol. 6, no. 3-4 (Spring, Summer, 1983), p. 29. Spanish.

8625 Caly, Eugenia. La partida. MAIZE, Vol. 6, no. 3-4 (Spring, Summer, 1983), p. 26. Spanish.

8626 Caly, Eugenia. Rio de Plata. MAIZE, Vol. 6, no. 3-4 (Spring, Summer, 1983), p. 27. Spanish.

8627 Caly, Eugenia. Ritzama. MAIZE, Vol. 6, no. 3-4 (Spring, Summer, 1983), p. 30. Spanish.

Poetry (cont.)

8628 Camarillo, Tina. Quetzals. MAIZE, Vol. 1, no. 3 (Spring 1978), p. 38. English.

8629 Candelaria, Cordelia. Fresh mint garden. REVISTA CHICANO-RIQUENA, Vol. 11, no. 3-4 (Fall 1983), p. 66. English.

8630 Candelaria, Cordelia. Sin raices hay flor? REVISTA CHICANO-RIQUENA, Vol. 11, no. 3-4 (Fall 1983), p. 65. English.

8631 Cannstatt, Christian. On sancta maria-ave euroshima. MAIZE, Vol. 5, no. 3-4 (Spring, Summer, 1982), p. 31-32. English.

8632 Cardona-Hine, Alvaro. The croupiers. BILINGUAL REVIEW, Vol. 9, no. 2 (May, August, 1982), p. 165. English.

8633 Castillo, Ana. 1975. REVISTA CHICANO-RIQUENA, Vol. 10, no. 1-2 (Winter, Spring, 1982), p. 45-46. English.

8634 Castillo, Ana. The antihero. REVISTA CHICANO-RIQUENA, Vol. 11, no. 3-4 (Fall 1983), p. 41. English.

8635 Castillo, Ana. Cartas. REVISTA CHICANO-RIQUENA, Vol. 10, no. 1-2 (Winter, Spring, 1982), p. 43. Spanish.

8636 Castillo, Ana. Encuentros #1. REVISTA CHICANO-RIQUENA, Vol. 10, no. 1-2 (Winter, Spring, 1982), p. 42. Spanish.

8637 Castillo, Ana. I don't want to know. REVISTA CHICANO-RIQUENA, Vol. 11, no. 3-4 (Fall 1983), p. 39. English.

8638 Castillo, Ana. Napa, California. REVISTA CHICANO-RIQUENA, Vol. 10, no. 1-2 (Winter, Spring, 1982), p. 44. Bilingual.

8639 Castillo, Ana. Not just because my husband said. REVISTA CHICANO-RIQUENA, Vol. 11, no. 3-4 (Fall 1983), p. 40. English.

8640 Castro, Tony. I still love you. LATINA, Vol. 1, no. 1 (1982), p. 60-61. English.

8641 Catala, Rafael. Danzon Peruano. MAIZE, Vol. 5, no. 3-4 (Spring, Summer, 1982), p. 85. Spanish.

8642 Cavazos, David S. Chile bruja. MAIZE, Vol. 1, no. 4 (Summer 1978), p. 30. Spanish.

8643 Caviness, Denise. The battered woman. MAIZE, Vol. 3, no. 1-2 (Fall, Winter, 1979, 1980), p. 13-15. English.

8644 Caviness, Denise. The battering. MAIZE, Vol. 3, no. 1-2 (Fall, Winter, 1979, 1980), p. 12. English.

8645 Cea, Jose Roberto. El potrero. MAIZE, Vol. 6, no. 1-2 (Fall, Winter, 1982, 1983), p. 96-97. Spanish.

8646 Cervantes, Lorna Dee. Heritage. REVISTA CHICANO-RIQUENA, Vol. 10, no. 1-2 (Winter, Spring, 1982), p. 47. English.

8647 Cervantes, Lorna Dee. Refugee ship. REVISTA CHICANO-RIQUENA, Vol. 10, no. 1-2 (Winter, Spring, 1982), p. 48. English.

8648 Cervantes, Lorna Dee. Shells. REVISTA CHICANO-RIQUENA, Vol. 10, no. 1-2 (Winter, Spring, 1982), p. 50-53. English.

8649 Cervantes, Lorna Dee. You are like a weed.

8650 Cervantez, Tony "Blue Crow". America linda. CALMECAC, Vol. 2, (Spring 1981), p. 18. English.

8651 Cervantez, Tony "Blue Crow". Madrugada. CALMECAC, Vol. 3, (Spring 1982), p. 6. Bilingual.

8652 Cervantez, Tony "Blue Crow". Nino. CALMECAC, Vol. 3, (Spring 1982), p. 20. English.

8653 Chavez-Trejo, Felipe. No tengas miedo. CHISMEARTE, (1982), p. 64. Spanish.

8654 La Chrisx. La loca de la raza cosmica. COMADRE, no. 2 (Spring 1978), p. 5-9. Bilingual. **DESCR**: Identity.

8655 Cipriano, Arturo and Alejandro, Marcial. Un canto. MAIZE, Vol. 1, no. 2 (Winter 1977), p. 17. Spanish.

8656 Cipriano, Arturo. Hora precisa. MAIZE, Vol. 2, no. 1 (Fall 1978), p. 40. Spanish.

8657 Cisneros, Sandra. Arturo Burro. REVISTA CHICANO-RIQUENA, Vol. 10, no. 1-2 (Winter, Spring, 1982), p. 58. English.

8658 Cisneros, Sandra. Letter to Ilona from the south of France. REVISTA CHICANO-RIQUENA, Vol. 11, no. 3-4 (Fall 1983), p. 23. English.

8659 Cisneros, Sandra. Love poem # 1. REVISTA CHICANO-RIQUENA, Vol. 11, no. 3-4 (Fall 1983), p. 22. English.

8660 Cisneros, Sandra. No mercy. REVISTA CHICANO-RIQUENA, Vol. 11, no. 3-4 (Fall 1983), p. 19. English.

8661 Cisneros, Sandra. North Avenue/1600 North. REVISTA CHICANO-RIQUENA, Vol. 10, no. 1-2 (Winter, Spring, 1982), p. 54-55. English.

8662 Cisneros, Sandra. The so-and-so's. REVISTA CHICANO-RIQUENA, Vol. 11, no. 3-4 (Fall 1983), p. 20-21. English.

8663 Cisneros, Sandra. Stone men. REVISTA CHICANO-RIQUENA, Vol. 10, no. 1-2 (Winter, Spring, 1982), p. 56-57. English.

8664 Cobian, Ricardo. Despues del sueno. MAIZE, Vol. 4, no. 3-4 (Spring, Summer, 1981), p. 66-67. Spanish.

8665 Cobian, Ricardo. En visperas de todos nosotros. MAIZE, Vol. 3, no. 3-4 (Spring, Summer, 1980), p. 50-53. Spanish.

8666 Cobian, Ricardo. Hostia del salario. MAIZE, Vol. 6, no. 1-2 (Fall, Winter, 1982, 1983), p. 90-91. Spanish.

8667 Cobian, Ricardo. Ocurre a veces, que no quepo en mi dolor. MAIZE, Vol. 4, no. 3-4 (Spring, Summer, 1981), p. 64-65. Spanish.

8668 Cobian, Ricardo. Saludo a mi vecino. MAIZE, Vol. 4, no. 3-4 (Spring, Summer, 1981), p. 65. Spanish.

8669 Concha, Jaime. Exilio, conciencia: coda sobre la poesia de Millan. MAIZE, Vol. 5, no. 1-2 (Fall, Winter, 1981, 1982), p. 7-15. Spanish. **DESCR**: Chile; Jesuits; Literary Criticism; Literary History; *Millan, Gonzalo; Political Refugees.

Poetry (cont.)

8670 Contreras, Juan. Limbo. MAIZE, Vol. 1, no. 2 (Winter 1977), p. 31. English.

8671 Contreras, Juan. Twixt. MAIZE, Vol. 2, no. 1 (Fall 1978), p. 57-58. English.

8672 Cook, Rhoby. Signs your wife is going crazy. MAIZE, Vol. 5, no. 3-4 (Spring, Summer, 1982), p. 28. English.

8673 Cook, Rhoby. Subtle as growth, the process has begun. MAIZE, Vol. 5, no. 3-4 (Spring, Summer, 1982), p. 29-30. English.

8674 Cordova, Roberto H. A la flor de nuestra herencia. DE COLORES, Vol. 6, no. 1-2 (1982), p. 144. Spanish.

8675 Cordova, Roberto H. A nuestro carinoso antecesor chicano. DE COLORES, Vol. 6, no. 1-2 (1982), p. 145. Spanish.

8676 Corpi, Lucha [pseud.]. Denuncia. REVISTA CHICANO-RIQUENA, Vol. 10, no. 1-2 (Winter, Spring, 1982), p. 59. Spanish.

8677 Corpi, Lucha [pseud.]. Lamento. REVISTA CHICANO-RIQUENA, Vol. 10, no. 1-2 (Winter, Spring, 1982), p. 60-61. Spanish.

8678 Cottam, R.V. And thus and thus. MAIZE, Vol. 6, no. 3-4 (Spring, Summer, 1983), p. 43. English.

8679 Cottam, R.V. The confessional. MAIZE, Vol. 6, no. 3-4 (Spring, Summer, 1983), p. 41-42. English.

8680 Cottam, R.V. Those were the days. MAIZE, Vol. 6, no. 3-4 (Spring, Summer, 1983), p. 44-45. English.

8681 Cuervo, Jose S. Los estragos del progreso. MAIZE, Vol. 5, no. 1-2 (Fall, Winter, 1981, 1982), p. 51. Spanish.

8682 Curiel, Marco Antonio. Black Greg. MAIZE, Vol. 1, no. 2 (Winter 1977), p. 55. English.

8683 Curiel, Marco Antonio. Carlitos. MAIZE, Vol. 1, no. 2 (Winter 1977), p. 56. Spanish.

8684 Curiel, Marco Antonio. Fears. MAIZE, Vol. 1, no. 2 (Winter 1977), p. 57. Spanish.

8685 Curiel, Marco Antonio. Para vicente. MAIZE, Vol. 2, no. 2 (Winter 1979), p. 30-31. English.

8686 Dalton, Roque. Poema de amor. NUESTRO, Vol. 7, no. 8 (October 1983), p. 37. Spanish. DESCR: *El Salvador.

8687 Davila, Martin. Cuando hay nieve. MAIZE, Vol. 1, no. 2 (Winter 1977), p. 36. Spanish.

8688 De Hoyos, Angela. The final laugh. REVISTA CHICANO-RIQUENA, Vol. 10, no. 1-2 (Winter, Spring, 1982), p. 78. English.

8689 De Hoyos, Angela. How to eat crow on a cold Sunday morning. REVISTA CHICANO-RIQUENA, Vol. 11, no. 3-4 (Fall 1983), p. 43. English.

8690 De Hoyos, Angela. Un llanto en seco. REVISTA CHICANO-RIQUENA, Vol. 10, no. 1-2 (Winter, Spring, 1982), p. 77. Spanish.

8691 De Hoyos, Angela. The missing ingredient. REVISTA CHICANO-RIQUENA, Vol. 10, no. 1-2 (Winter, Spring, 1982), p. 79. English.

8692 De Hoyos, Angela. San antonio rose era xicana. MAIZE, Vol. 1, no. 3 (Spring 1978), p. 7. English.

8693 De Hoyos, Angela. Ten dry summers ago. REVISTA CHICANO-RIQUENA, Vol. 11, no. 3-4 (Fall 1983), p. 42. English.

8694 de la Fuente, Patricia. Ambiguity in the poetry of Gary Soto. REVISTA CHICANO-RIQUENA, Vol. 11, no. 2 (Summer 1983), p. 34-39. English. DESCR: "Avocado Lake"; "Blanco"; "Braley Street"; "Field"; *Literary Criticism; "Song for the pockets"; *Soto, Gary; TALE OF SUNLIGHT; "Telephoning God"; THE ELEMENTS OF SAN JOAQUIN; "Wind".

8695 de Leon Hernandez, Victor. Recuerdos de Manolo. REVISTA CHICANO-RIQUENA, Vol. 10, no. 3 (Summer 1982), p. 18-20. Spanish.

8696 De los Angeles Ruano, Isabel. El cadaver. MAIZE, Vol. 4, no. 1-2 (Fall, Winter, 1980, 1981), p. 62. Spanish.

8697 De los Angeles Ruano, Isabel. No son muchos. MAIZE, Vol. 4, no. 1-2 (Fall, Winter, 1980, 1981), p. 63. Spanish.

8698 de Olmedo, Jose Joaquin. The victory at Junin: song to Bolivar. NUESTRO, Vol. 7, no. 7 (September 1983), p. 41. English. DESCR: *Bolivar, Simon.

8699 A decade of Hispanic literature: an anniversary anthology. REVISTA CHICANO-RIQUENA, Vol. 10, no. 1-2 (Winter, Spring, 1982), p. 1-310. Bilingual. DESCR: Essays; *Literature; Prose.

8700 Decormier-Shekerjian, Regina. Her hands. MAIZE, Vol. 6, no. 3-4 (Spring, Summer, 1983), p. 39-40. English.

8701 Decormier-Shekerjian, Regina. Pigeons limping in Venice...special to the New York Times. MAIZE, Vol. 6, no. 3-4 (Spring, Summer, 1983), p. 37-38. English.

8702 Dedicacion. CALMECAC, Vol. 1, no. 1 (Spring 1980), p. 5. English.

8703 Dedicacion. CALMECAC, Vol. 1, (Summer 1980), p. 5. Bilingual.

8704 Dedicacion. CALMECAC, Vol. 2, (Spring 1981), p. 4. Bilingual.

8705 Dedicacion. CALMECAC, Vol. 3, (Spring 1982), p. 4. English.

8706 del Castillo, Amelia. Cara al viento. THIRD WOMAN, Vol. 1, no. 2 (1982), p. 28. Spanish.

8707 del Castillo, Amelia. Mi poesia y yo. THIRD WOMAN, Vol. 1, no. 2 (1982), p. 28. Spanish.

8708 Delgado, Abelardo "Lalo". From Garden City to Hays. REVISTA CHICANO-RIQUENA, Vol. 10, no. 1-2 (Winter, Spring, 1982), p. 62-63. English.

8709 Delgado, Abelardo "Lalo". The last wow. REVISTA CHICANO-RIQUENA, Vol. 10, no. 1-2 (Winter, Spring, 1982), p. 64-66. English.

8710 Delgado, Alberto. Los mexicanos. MAIZE, Vol. 1, no. 1 (Fall 1977), p. 46. English.

Poetry (cont.)

8711 DeOrtega, Manuel R. In the stomach of the shark: echoes of a culture in captivity. SOUTHWEST ECONOMY AND SOCIETY, Vol. 6, no. 1 (Fall 1982), p. 35-48. Bilingual. **DESCR:** *Assimilation; Culture; Spanish Language.

8712 Desleal, Alvaro Menen. Oracion que ayuda a bien condenarse a un tirano. MAIZE, Vol. 6, no. 1-2 (Fall, Winter, 1982, 1983), p. 80-81. Spanish.

8713 Diaz, David. Cosmopolitan Angel Dust. CHISMEARTE, no. 9 (September 1983), p. 27-28. English.

8714 Diaz-Diocaretz, Myriam. Mujer de la tierra. THIRD WOMAN, Vol. 1, no. 2 (1982), p. 19-20. Spanish.

8715 Diaz-Diocaretz, Myriam. Musa amordazada. THIRD WOMAN, Vol. 1, no. 2 (1982), p. 18. Spanish.

8716 Dochniak, Jim. Pro-life)maybe(/el salvador. MAIZE, Vol. 6, no. 3-4 (Spring, Summer, 1983), p. 19-20. English.

8717 Dominguez, Marco. En el corazon de Aztlan. CORAZON DE AZTLAN, Vol. 1, no. 1 (January, February, 1982), p. 8-9. Spanish.

8718 Duboy, Maria E. Evita. MAIZE, Vol. 6, no. 3-4 (Spring, Summer, 1983), p. 24. English.

8719 Duncan, Erika. Myriam Diaz - Diocaretz: letting the sun look into our eyes. THIRD WOMAN, Vol. 1, no. 2 (1982), p. 70-75. English. **DESCR:** *Literature Reviews.

8720 Duran, Manuel. Valle de Mexico. LA PALABRA, Vol. 4, no. 1-2 (Spring, Fall, 1982, 1983), p. 145. Spanish.

8721 Elizondo, Raquel. Voy a vengo? MAIZE, Vol. 1, no. 3 (Spring 1977), p. 17. Spanish.

8722 Elizondo, Sergio D. Cantar de las gentiles damas. REVISTA CHICANO-RIQUENA, Vol. 10, no. 1-2 (Winter, Spring, 1982), p. 67. Spanish.

8723 Elizondo, Sergio D. Este es un cuento. REVISTA CHICANO-RIQUENA, Vol. 10, no. 1-2 (Winter, Spring, 1982), p. 68. Spanish.

8724 Elizondo, Sergio D. He sabido, Carnala. REVISTA CHICANO-RIQUENA, Vol. 10, no. 1-2 (Winter, Spring, 1982), p. 69. Spanish.

8725 Epple, Juan Armando. Tiempo Chicano. MAIZE, Vol. 6, no. 1-2 (Fall, Winter, 1982, 1983), p. 100-101. Bilingual.

8726 Escandell, Noemi. Elegia. THIRD WOMAN, Vol. 1, no. 2 (1982), p. 17. Spanish.

8727 Escandell, Noemi. Ritz-Carlton. THIRD WOMAN, Vol. 1, no. 2 (1982), p. 16. Spanish.

8728 Espada, Martin. The firing squad is singing in Chile. BILINGUAL REVIEW, Vol. 9, no. 2 (May, August, 1982), p. 156-158. English.

8729 Espada, Martin. Power. BILINGUAL REVIEW, Vol. 9, no. 2 (May, August, 1982), p. 160. English.

8730 Espada, Martin. Tato hates the New York Yankees. BILINGUAL REVIEW, Vol. 9, no. 2 (May, August, 1982), p. 158-160. English.

8731 Espinosa, Luis P. Erendira. CALMECAC, Vol. 2, (Spring 1981), p. 19. Spanish.

8732 Espinoza, Ana Luisa. Untitled Poem. CALMECAC, Vol. 1, (Summer 1980), p. 44. English.

8733 Espinoza, Danny J. Life is. MAIZE, Vol. 6, no. 1-2 (Fall, Winter, 1982, 1983), p. 52. English.

8734 Espinoza, Danny J. Video games video games. MAIZE, Vol. 6, no. 1-2 (Fall, Winter, 1982, 1983), p. 53. English.

8735 Espinoza, Herbert O. Examen final de literatura. MAIZE, Vol. 2, no. 4 (Summer 1979), p. 18-22. Spanish.

8736 Esteves, Sandra Maria. Amor negro. REVISTA CHICANO-RIQUENA, Vol. 11, no. 3-4 (Fall 1983), p. 30. English.

8737 Esteves, Sandra Maria. A celebration of home birth. REVISTA CHICANO-RIQUENA, Vol. 11, no. 3-4 (Fall 1983), p. 31-32. English.

8738 Esteves, Sandra Maria. For Noel Rico. REVISTA CHICANO-RIQUENA, Vol. 10, no. 1-2 (Winter, Spring, 1982), p. 71. English.

8739 Esteves, Sandra Maria. A Julia y a mi. THIRD WOMAN, Vol. 1, no. 2 (1982), p. 14-15. Bilingual.

8740 Esteves, Sandra Maria. Portraits for Shamsul Alam. REVISTA CHICANO-RIQUENA, Vol. 11, no. 3-4 (Fall 1983), p. 33-34. English.

8741 Esteves, Sandra Maria. Transference. REVISTA CHICANO-RIQUENA, Vol. 11, no. 3-4 (Fall 1983), p. 34-35. English.

8742 Esteves, Sandra Maria. [Untitled poem]. REVISTA CHICANO-RIQUENA, Vol. 10, no. 1-2 (Winter, Spring, 1982), p. 70. English.

8743 Esteves, Sandra Maria. [Untitled poem]. REVISTA CHICANO-RIQUENA, Vol. 10, no. 1-2 (Winter, Spring, 1982), p. 71-72. English.

8744 Fernandez, Angel Jose. Balada (en tono menor) para el culpable. MAIZE, Vol. 3, no. 3-4 (Spring, Summer, 1980), p. 66-69. Spanish.

8745 Fiesta de los colores de sacra: fiesta de colores. CALMECAC, Vol. 3, (Spring 1982), p. 37-38. English.

8746 Flores de Aztlan. CALMECAC, Vol. 2, (Spring 1981), p. 50-51. English.

8747 Flores, Jose. Las manos (para 'pa Agapito). MAIZE, Vol. 1, no. 4 (Summer 1978), p. 26-27. Spanish.

8748 Flores, Jose. Sabado. MAIZE, Vol. 1, no. 4 (Summer 1978), p. 28. Spanish.

8749 Fox-Chandonnet, Ann. Masks. MAIZE, Vol. 5, no. 1-2 (Fall, Winter, 1981, 1982), p. 38. English.

8750 Francis, Reynold S. Cost efficency. MAIZE, Vol. 6, no. 1-2 (Fall, Winter, 1982, 1983), p. 106. Spanish.

8751 Freed, Ray. Josephina. MAIZE, Vol. 1, no. 4 (Summer 1978), p. 31. English.

8752 Fussell, Edwin Sill. A suite of locals. MAIZE, Vol. 6, no. 1-2 (Fall, Winter, 1982, 1983), p. 28-29. English.

Poetry (cont.)

8753 Gallardo, Josefina "Nicte Ha". I do what needs to be done. CALMECAC, Vol. 3, (Spring 1982), p. 10. English.

8754 Gallegos, Robert. Tokay. CHISMEARTE, no. 9 (September 1983), p. 4-5. English.

8755 Gamboa, Manuel "Manazar". 1953 chicano tanke in the old county jail: the jam session. CHISMEARTE, (1982), p. 20. English.

8756 Gamboa, Manuel "Manazar". Buttonwillow. CHISMEARTE, no. 9 (September 1983), p. 22. English.

8757 Garcia Nunez, Fernando. La poesia chicana en espanol. CUADERNOS HISPANOAMERICANOS, Vol. 397, (July 1983), p. 117-123. Spanish. **DESCR:** Identity; Literary Criticism.

8758 Garcia-Camarillo, Cecilio. Alma. MAIZE, Vol. 1, no. 2 (Winter 1977), p. 14-15. Spanish.

8759 Garcia-Camarillo, Cecilio. Chivo. REVISTA CHICANO-RIQUENA, Vol. 10, no. 1-2 (Winter, Spring, 1982), p. 76. English.

8760 Garcia-Camarillo, Cecilio. Compassionate heart. REVISTA CHICANO-RIQUENA, Vol. 10, no. 1-2 (Winter, Spring, 1982), p. 75. English.

8761 Garcia-Camarillo, Cecilio. Hoeing. MAIZE, Vol. 6, no. 3-4 (Spring, Summer, 1983), p. 58. English.

8762 Garcia-Camarillo, Cecilio. Juvencio. REVISTA CHICANO-RIQUENA, Vol. 10, no. 1-2 (Winter, Spring, 1982), p. 73-74. Spanish.

8763 Garcia-Camarillo, Cecilio. Una pila de anteojos. MAIZE, Vol. 2, no. 4 (Summer 1979), p. 6. Spanish.

8764 Garcia-Camarillo, Cecilio. Rancho. REVISTA CHICANO-RIQUENA, Vol. 10, no. 1-2 (Winter, Spring, 1982), p. 74. Bilingual.

8765 Garcia-Camarillo, Cecilio. Wachando el jardin. MAIZE, Vol. 2, no. 4 (Summer 1979), p. [61]. Spanish.

8766 Gaspar de Alba, Alice. Easter: the lame bull. REVISTA CHICANO-RIQUENA, Vol. 10, no. 3 (Summer 1982), p. 13. English.

8767 Gayton, Thomas. Long journey home. MAIZE, Vol. 3, no. 3-4 (Spring, Summer, 1980), p. 48. English.

8768 Gayton, Thomas. Why Western man? II. MAIZE, Vol. 3, no. 3-4 (Spring, Summer, 1980), p. 48. English.

8769 Georgakas, Dan. Enemy. MAIZE, Vol. 1, no. 3 (Spring 1978), p. 44. English.

8770 Georgakas, Dan. Growing. MAIZE, Vol. 1, no. 3 (Spring 1978), p. 42. English.

8771 Georgakas, Dan. Junta. MAIZE, Vol. 1, no. 3 (Spring 1978), p. 43. English.

8772 Georgakas, Dan. Lamentation. MAIZE, Vol. 1, no. 3 (Spring 1978), p. 44. English.

8773 Godinez, Art. Corridos de Tony Guzman. CHISMEARTE, (1982), p. 62. Bilingual.

8774 Godinez, Art. El hoyo. CHISMEARTE, (1982), p. 18. English.

8775 Gomez, Cristina. Desempleo. MAIZE, Vol. 4,

no. 1-2 (Fall, Winter, 1980, 1981), p. 60. Spanish.

8776 Gomez, Cristina. En memoria. MAIZE, Vol. 2, no. 2 (Winter 1979), p. 23-24. Spanish.

8777 Gomez, Cristina. Exilio. MAIZE, Vol. 4, no. 1-2 (Fall, Winter, 1980, 1981), p. 59. Spanish.

8778 Gomez, Cristina. Hasta siempre companero revueltas! MAIZE, Vol. 2, no. 2 (Winter 1979), p. 25. Spanish.

8779 Gomez, Cristina. Para escribir distinto. MAIZE, Vol. 2, no. 2 (Winter 1979), p. 22. Spanish.

8780 Gomez, Cristina. Sin que nadie la vea... MAIZE, Vol. 4, no. 1-2 (Fall, Winter, 1980, 1981), p. 61. Spanish.

8781 Gomez-Quinones, Juan. Canto al trabajador: a Juan Gomez Duarte. CHISMEARTE, (1982), p. 25. Bilingual.

8782 Gonsalves, Ricardo. And. MAIZE, Vol. 1, no. 3 (Spring 1978), p. 14-15. English.

8783 Gonsalves, Ricardo. Gritos. MAIZE, Vol. 1, no. 3 (Spring 1977), p. 16. English.

8784 Gonzalez, Cesar. Balboa Park. MAIZE, Vol. 1, no. 1 (Fall 1977), p. 60. English.

8785 Gonzalez, Cesar. Jose. MAIZE, Vol. 1, no. 1 (Fall 1977), p. 57. Spanish.

8786 Gonzalez, Cesar. The women of Zuniga. MAIZE, Vol. 1, no. 1 (Fall 1977), p. 58-59. English.

8787 Gonzalez Cruz, Luis F. Quest and discovery in Oscar Hurtado's THE DEAD CITY OF KORAD: a unique experiment in science fiction poetry. MAIZE, Vol. 5, no. 1-2 (Fall, Winter, 1981, 1982), p. 74-85. English. **DESCR:** Cuba; *Hurtado, Oscar; Latin American Literature; *Literary Criticism.

8788 Gonzalez, Francisca. Recuerdo. MAIZE, Vol. 1, no. 2 (Winter 1977), p. 38. Spanish.

8789 Gonzalez, Rafael Jesus. Consejo. MAIZE, Vol. 1, no. 4 (Summer 1978), p. 44. Spanish.

8790 Gonzalez, Rafael Jesus. Estrofas a la libelula. MAIZE, Vol. 1, no. 4 (Summer 1978), p. 43. Spanish.

8791 Gonzalez, Rafael Jesus. Suenos de plomo. MAIZE, Vol. 1, no. 4 (Summer 1978), p. 45. Spanish.

8792 Goodwin, Sister. Alpenglow. MAIZE, Vol. 2, no. 1 (Fall 1978), p. 31. English.

8793 Goodwin, Sister. Quivinna. MAIZE, Vol. 2, no. 1 (Fall 1978), p. 28-30. English.

8794 Grant, Carmencita. From the daughter of the deceased. COMADRE, no. 2 (Spring 1978), p. 24. English. **DESCR:** Identity.

8795 Grant, Carmencita. Grandmother's ghetto. COMADRE, no. 2 (Spring 1978), p. 25. English.

8796 Greenleaf, Cynthia. Legacy. MAIZE, Vol. 5, no. 3-4 (Spring, Summer, 1982), p. 81-84. English.

Poetry (cont.)

8797 Guerra, Vicente. Hermandad iberoamericana.
LATINO, Vol. 53, no. 7 (November 1982), p.
22. Spanish.

8798 Guerra-Garza, Victor. Ecos del barrio.
MAIZE, Vol. 1, no. 3 (Spring 1978), p.
34-35. Bilingual.

8799 Guillen, Pablo. Que puedo darte... MAIZE,
Vol. 4, no. 1-2 (Fall, Winter, 1980, 1981),
p. 49. Spanish.

8800 Guillen, Pablo. Volver a empezar. MAIZE,
Vol. 4, no. 1-2 (Fall, Winter, 1980, 1981),
p. 52. Spanish.

8801 Guillen, Pablo. Voy a denunciar al silencio.
MAIZE, Vol. 4, no. 1-2 (Fall, Winter, 1980,
1981), p. 50-51. Spanish.

8802 Gutierrez, Adolfo. El cinco. MAIZE, Vol. 1,
no. 1 (Fall 1977), p. 47. Spanish.

8803 Gutierrez-Revuelta, Pedro. A marilyn con
unas violetas. MAIZE, Vol. 4, no. 3-4
(Spring, Summer, 1981), p. 47-50. Spanish.

8804 Gutierrez-Revuelta, Pedro and Monleon, Jose.
Democracia a blas de otero. MAIZE, Vol. 2,
no. 2 (Winter 1979), p. 9. Spanish.

8805 Gutierrez-Revuelta, Pedro. No draft, no war,
U.S. out of El Salvador. MAIZE, Vol. 5, no.
3-4 (Spring, Summer, 1982), p. 78-79.
Bilingual.

8806 Gutierrez-Revuelta, Pedro and Monleon, Jose.
Oda a san diego. MAIZE, Vol. 2, no. 2
(Winter 1979), p. 14-16. Spanish.

8807 Gutierrez-Revuelta, Pedro and Monleon, Jose.
Oda a walt disney (pacto con china). MAIZE,
Vol. 2, no. 2 (Winter 1979), p. 10-11.
Spanish.

8808 Gutierrez-Revuelta, Pedro and Monleon, Jose.
Take 5. MAIZE, Vol. 2, no. 2 (Winter 1979),
p. 17-18. Spanish.

8809 Gutierrez-Revuelta, Pedro. Una dos y tres.
MAIZE, Vol. 5, no. 3-4 (Spring, Summer,
1982), p. 80. Spanish.

8810 Gutierrez-Revuelta, Pedro and Monleon, Jose.
U.s.a. MAIZE, Vol. 2, no. 2 (Winter 1979),
p. 13. Spanish.

8811 Hasan, Rabiul. The little bighorn, montana,
1980. MAIZE, Vol. 4, no. 1-2 (Fall, Winter,
1980, 1981), p. 72. English.

8812 Hasan, Rabiul. Report from the Delta:
Central Mississippi. MAIZE, Vol. 4, no. 1-2
(Fall, Winter, 1980, 1981), p. 73. English.

8813 Hasan, Rabiul. Seven page note to a choctaw
indian girl at a claiborne county school in
mississippi. MAIZE, Vol. 3, no. 1-2 (Fall,
Winter, 1979, 1980), p. 54. English.

8814 Hashmi, Alamgir. Gautum. MAIZE, Vol. 1, no.
4 (Summer 1978), p. 14-15. English.

8815 Hernandez Cruz, Victor. Table of contents.
MAIZE, Vol. 1, no. 4 (Summer 1978), p. 7-8.
English.

8816 Herrera Isla, Nelson. Ah, viejo constructor.
MAIZE, Vol. 3, no. 3-4 (Spring, Summer,
1980), p. 79. Spanish.

8817 Herrera Isla, Nelson. Cambiar la vida.

MAIZE, Vol. 3, no. 3-4 (Spring, Summer,
1980), p. 78. Spanish.

8818 Herrera, Juan Felipe. At the moon cafe.
MAIZE, Vol. 1, no. 3 (Spring 1978), p. 53.
English.

8819 Herrera, Juan Felipe. Evaluacion. MAIZE,
Vol. 1, no. 3 (Spring 1978), p. 54. Spanish.

8820 Herrera, Juan Felipe. Febrero. MAIZE, Vol.
1, no. 3 (Spring 1978), p. 52. English.

8821 Herrera, Juan Felipe. Photo-poem of the
Chicano Moratorium 1980/L.A. REVISTA
CHICANO-RIQUENA, Vol. 10, no. 3 (Summer
1982), p. 5-9. English. DESCR: Chicano
Moratorium; Photography.

8822 Herrera-Sobek, Maria. Abuelas
revolucionarias. REVISTA CHICANO-RIQUENA,
Vol. 10, no. 1-2 (Winter, Spring, 1982), p.
128. Spanish.

8823 Herrera-Sobek, Maria. Colores de un hombre
fuerte. REVISTA CHICANO-RIQUENA, Vol. 10,
no. 1-2 (Winter, Spring, 1982), p. 129.
Spanish.

8824 Herrera-Sobek, Maria. Mantillas. REVISTA
CHICANO-RIQUENA, Vol. 10, no. 1-2 (Winter,
Spring, 1982), p. 130. Spanish.

8825 Herrera-Sobek, Maria. Native son home from
asia. MAIZE, Vol. 1, no. 3 (Spring 1978), p.
60. English.

8826 Herrera-Sobek, Maria. No supimos amarnos.
MAIZE, Vol. 4, no. 3-4 (Spring, Summer,
1981), p. 85. Spanish.

8827 Herrera-Sobek, Maria. Noches perdidas.
MAIZE, Vol. 4, no. 3-4 (Spring, Summer,
1981), p. 86. Spanish.

8828 Herrera-Sobek, Maria. Nos encontramos.
REVISTA CHICANO-RIQUENA, Vol. 10, no. 1-2
(Winter, Spring, 1982), p. 131. Spanish.

8829 Herrera-Sobek, Maria. Tomate rojo. MAIZE,
Vol. 4, no. 3-4 (Spring, Summer, 1981), p.
87. Spanish.

8830 Los hijos de Quetzalcoatl. CALMECAC, Vol. 3,
(Spring 1982), p. 39. English.

8831 Hinestrosa, Dukardo. Canto sin estrellas.
CHISMEARTE, (1982), p. 56. Bilingual.

8832 Hinojosa-Smith, Rolando R. Retaguardia en no
noviembre which means: the 219th isn't doing
well at all. MAIZE, Vol. 4, no. 3-4 (Spring,
Summer, 1981), p. 61-63. Spanish.

8833 Hitchens, Theresa. Astronomy. NUESTRO, Vol.
6, no. 7 (September 1982), p. 55. English.

8834 Hitchens, Theresa. Harvest. NUESTRO, Vol. 6,
no. 3 (April 1982), p. 47. English.

8835 Hitchens, Theresa. In black and white.
NUESTRO, Vol. 6, no. 7 (September 1982), p.
55. English.

8836 Hitchens, Theresa. Tristan. NUESTRO, Vol. 6,
no. 7 (September 1982), p. 55. English.

8837 Hitchens, Theresa. Winter feeding (to little
sis). NUESTRO, Vol. 6, no. 3 (April 1982),
p. 47. English.

Poetry (cont.)

8838 Holzman, Michael. Tar. MAIZE, Vol. 5, no. 3-4 (Spring, Summer, 1982), p. 57-61. English.

8839 HRV. Time and time again. MAIZE, Vol. 5, no. 3-4 (Spring, Summer, 1982), p. 52. English.

8840 Ibargoyen Islas, Saul. Soledad propia. MAIZE, Vol. 3, no. 1-2 (Fall, Winter, 1979, 1980), p. 61. Spanish.

8841 Islas, Maya. He dudado. MAIZE, Vol. 1, no. 3 (Spring 1978), p. 48-49. Spanish.

8842 Islas, Maya. Palabras del ave. MAIZE, Vol. 2, no. 2 (Winter 1979), p. 19-20. Spanish.

8843 Islas, Saul. Otra vez octubre. MAIZE, Vol. 3, no. 3-4 (Spring, Summer, 1980), p. 82. Spanish.

8844 Jacobs, Teresa. Ara. MAIZE, Vol. 4, no. 1-2 (Fall, Winter, 1980, 1981), p. 43. English.

8845 Jacobs, Teresa. Ceremonies. MAIZE, Vol. 4, no. 1-2 (Fall, Winter, 1980, 1981), p. 42. English.

8846 Jacobs, Teresa. Metamorfose. MAIZE, Vol. 4, no. 1-2 (Fall, Winter, 1980, 1981), p. 41. Portuguese.

8847 Jensen, Richard J. and Hammerback, John C. "No revolutions without poets": the rhetoric of Rodolfo "Corky" Gonzales. WESTERN JOURNAL OF SPEECH COMMUNICATION, Vol. 46, no. 1 (Winter 1982), p. 72-91. English. **DESCR:** Chicano Movement; *Gonzales, Rodolfo (Corky); Literary Criticism; Rhetoric.

8848 Josber. A la siega. MAIZE, Vol. 1, no. 4 (Summer 1978), p. 49. Spanish.

8849 Josber. Ansias. MAIZE, Vol. 1, no. 4 (Summer 1978), p. 47. Spanish.

8850 Karanikas, Marianthe. A boa from Brazil. NUESTRO, Vol. 6, no. 1 (January, February, 1982), p. 63. English.

8851 Karanikas, Marianthe. Tu companera Guachita. NUESTRO, Vol. 6, no. 1 (January, February, 1982), p. 63. English.

8852 Katra, William H. 'Taller de imagenes': a poetic cosmovision. MINORITY VOICES, Vol. 4, no. 2 (Fall 1980), p. 75-84. English. **DESCR:** Mendez M., Miguel; *TALLER DE IMAGENES.

8853 Kerns, Chloe Jane. Now, I just dance. MAIZE, Vol. 6, no. 3-4 (Spring, Summer, 1983), p. 17. English.

8854 Kerns, Chloe Jane. Shock treatment. MAIZE, Vol. 6, no. 3-4 (Spring, Summer, 1983), p. 18. English.

8855 Kerns, Chloe Jane. Untitled #73. MAIZE, Vol. 6, no. 3-4 (Spring, Summer, 1983), p. 18. English.

8856 La Fond, Vita. Calexico, where windows. MAIZE, Vol. 2, no. 4 (Summer 1979), p. 11. English.

8857 Laguardia, Gari. The canon and the air-conditioner: modern Puerto Rican poetry. BILINGUAL REVIEW, Vol. 9, no. 2 (May, August, 1982), p. 178-181. English. **DESCR:** Book Reviews; *INVENTING A WORD, AN ANTHOLOGY OF TWENTIETH CENTURY PUERTO RICAN POETRY; Marzan, Julio; Puerto Rican Literature.

8858 Laraque, Paul. El reino del hombre. MAIZE, Vol. 3, no. 3-4 (Spring, Summer, 1980), p. 54-55. Spanish.

8859 Larrosa, Mara. Espaldas negras. MAIZE, Vol. 2, no. 3 (Spring 1979), p. 49. Spanish.

8860 Laviera, Tato. Angelito's eulogy in anger. REVISTA CHICANO-RIQUENA, Vol. 10, no. 1-2 (Winter, Spring, 1982), p. 83-85. Bilingual.

8861 Laviera, Tato. The song of an oppressor. REVISTA CHICANO-RIQUENA, Vol. 10, no. 1-2 (Winter, Spring, 1982), p. 80-82. Bilingual.

8862 Laviera, Tato. Standards. REVISTA CHICANO-RIQUENA, Vol. 10, no. 1-2 (Winter, Spring, 1982), p. 86. English.

8863 Laviera, Tato. Tito Madera Smith. REVISTA CHICANO-RIQUENA, Vol. 10, no. 1-2 (Winter, Spring, 1982), p. 87-88. English.

8864 Leal, Luis. Aves zancudas. LA PALABRA, Vol. 4, no. 1-2 (Spring, Fall, 1982, 1983), p. 68-69. Spanish.

8865 Leal, Luis. Caracol. LA PALABRA, Vol. 4, no. 1-2 (Spring, Fall, 1982, 1983), p. 60-61. Spanish.

8866 Leal, Luis. Con Borges en el sueno. LA PALABRA, Vol. 4, no. 1-2 (Spring, Fall, 1982, 1983), p. 65. Spanish.

8867 Leal, Luis. Coyolxauhqui. LA PALABRA, Vol. 4, no. 1-2 (Spring, Fall, 1982, 1983), p. 74-75. Spanish.

8868 Leal, Luis. El Dios viejo. LA PALABRA, Vol. 4, no. 1-2 (Spring, Fall, 1982, 1983), p. 62-63. Spanish.

8869 Leal, Luis. Fabula de la luna y el astro. LA PALABRA, Vol. 4, no. 1-2 (Spring, Fall, 1982, 1983), p. 76-77. Spanish.

8870 Leal, Luis. Magueyes. LA PALABRA, Vol. 4, no. 1-2 (Spring, Fall, 1982, 1983), p. 72-73. Spanish.

8871 Leal, Luis. La noche triste. LA PALABRA, Vol. 4, no. 1-2 (Spring, Fall, 1982, 1983), p. 70-71. Spanish.

8872 Leal, Luis. La noria del tiempo. LA PALABRA, Vol. 4, no. 1-2 (Spring, Fall, 1982, 1983), p. 57. Spanish.

8873 Leal, Luis. Pavo irreal. LA PALABRA, Vol. 4, no. 1-2 (Spring, Fall, 1982, 1983), p. 56. Spanish.

8874 Leal, Luis. El retorno. LA PALABRA, Vol. 4, no. 1-2 (Spring, Fall, 1982, 1983), p. 54-55. Spanish.

8875 Leal, Luis. El sarape de la existencia. LA PALABRA, Vol. 4, no. 1-2 (Spring, Fall, 1982, 1983), p. 67. Spanish.

8876 Leal, Luis. Tlapala. LA PALABRA, Vol. 4, no. 1-2 (Spring, Fall, 1982, 1983), p. 65. Spanish.

8877 Leal, Luis. Xibalba. LA PALABRA, Vol. 4, no. 1-2 (Spring, Fall, 1982, 1983), p. 58-59. Spanish.

Poetry (cont.)

8878 Let us delight ourselves. CALMECAC, Vol. 3, (Spring 1982), p. 39. English.

8879 Leyna, Mariano. El miedo de la muerte. CALMECAC, Vol. 1, (Summer 1980), p. 37. Bilingual.

8880 Lezcano, Manuel. Read this when I die (again) please. REVISTA CHICANO-RIQUENA, Vol. 11, no. 2 (Summer 1983), p. 48. English.

8881 Limon, Margarita. Las flores. MAIZE, Vol. 1, no. 3 (Spring 1978), p. 36. Spanish.

8882 Limon, Mercedes. Esperame en la historia Che Guevara. MAIZE, Vol. 6, no. 1-2 (Fall, Winter, 1982, 1983), p. 103-104. Spanish.

8883 Limon, Mercedes. Mentira. MAIZE, Vol. 6, no. 1-2 (Fall, Winter, 1982, 1983), p. 102. Spanish.

8884 Lockett, Reginald. The killing ground. MAIZE, Vol. 2, no. 4 (Summer 1979), p. 8-9. English.

8885 Lockett, Reginald. The other side of what's happening (or takin the bunk outta the funk). MAIZE, Vol. 2, no. 4 (Summer 1979), p. 7-8. English.

8886 Lockett, Reginald. There's a pain in my upper back. MAIZE, Vol. 2, no. 4 (Summer 1979), p. 10. English.

8887 Lockwood Barletta, Naomi. En el norte. REVISTA CHICANO-RIQUENA, Vol. 11, no. 3-4 (Fall 1983), p. 71. Spanish.

8888 Lockwood Barletta, Naomi. El Salvador. REVISTA CHICANO-RIQUENA, Vol. 11, no. 3-4 (Fall 1983), p. 71. Spanish.

8889 Lopez, Emy. Los que lo saben lo ignoran los que lo ignoran...yo se los cuento. MAIZE, Vol. 6, no. 1-2 (Fall, Winter, 1982, 1983), p. 94-95. Spanish.

8890 Lopez, Phyllis. La campesina. COMADRE, no. 2 (Spring 1978), p. 14. English. **DESCR:** Agricultural Laborers.

8891 Lopez, Phyllis. La Chicana. COMADRE, no. 2 (Spring 1978), p. 12. English. **DESCR:** Identity.

8892 Lopez, Phyllis. De la vina. COMADRE, no. 3 (Fall 1978), p. 1. English.

8893 Lopez, Phyllis. En mi barrio. COMADRE, no. 2 (Spring 1978), p. 13. English.

8894 Lopez, Phyllis. Migrant life. COMADRE, no. 3 (Fall 1978), p. 4. English. **DESCR:** Undocumented Workers.

8895 Lopez, Phyllis. Para mi gente. COMADRE, no. 1 (Summer 1977), p. 9. Bilingual.

8896 Lopez, Phyllis. Recollections. COMADRE, no. 2 (Spring 1978), p. 15. English. **DESCR:** Chicano Movement.

8897 Lopez, Phyllis. Sentimientos sin nombre. COMADRE, no. 1 (Summer 1977), p. 10-12. Bilingual. **DESCR:** Identity.

8898 Lopez, Phyllis. Social workers? COMADRE, no. 3 (Fall 1978), p. 2. Bilingual.

8899 Lopez, Phyllis. Untitled No.1. COMADRE, no. 2 (Spring 1978), p. 10. English. **DESCR:** Abortion.

8900 Lopez, Phyllis. Untitled No.2. COMADRE, no. 2 (Spring 1978), p. 11. English. **DESCR:** Poverty.

8901 Lopez, Phyllis. Untitled poem: I. COMADRE, no. 1 (Summer 1977), p. 13. Spanish.

8902 Lopez, Phyllis. Untitled poem: II. COMADRE, no. 1 (Summer 1977), p. 14. English.

8903 Lopez, Phyllis. Untitled poem: III. COMADRE, no. 1 (Summer 1977), p. 15-16. English. **DESCR:** Prejudices.

8904 Lopez, Phyllis. The unwanted emigrants. COMADRE, no. 3 (Fall 1978), p. 3. Bilingual. **DESCR:** Undocumented Workers.

8905 Lopez-Moreno, Amelia. For the Apache infants in the mountains of Arizona. COMADRE, no. 1 (Summer 1977), p. 6. English. **DESCR:** Children.

8906 Lopez-Moreno, Amelia. Humanidad. COMADRE, no. 1 (Summer 1977), p. 3-5. Spanish.

8907 Lopez-Moreno, Amelia. Montanas Blancas. COMADRE, no. 1 (Summer 1977), p. 7-8. Spanish.

8908 Lopez-Moreno, Amelia. Untitled Poem. COMADRE, no. 1 (Summer 1977), p. 2. Spanish.

8909 Luzma. Homenaje a un labrador. CALMECAC, Vol. 1, (Summer 1980), p. 16-17. Spanish.

8910 Luzma. Mariposas. CALMECAC, Vol. 1, (Summer 1980), p. 48. Spanish.

8911 Luzma. Woman-mujer. CALMECAC, Vol. 1, (Summer 1980), p. 11. English.

8912 Lyles, Charlise L. Combing my hair. MAIZE, Vol. 6, no. 3-4 (Spring, Summer, 1983), p. 80-81. English.

8913 Lyles, Charlise L. Miami. MAIZE, Vol. 6, no. 3-4 (Spring, Summer, 1983), p. 88-89. English.

8914 Lyles, Charlise L. Negress on the bridge. MAIZE, Vol. 6, no. 3-4 (Spring, Summer, 1983), p. 86-87. English.

8915 Lyles, Charlise L. The savior. MAIZE, Vol. 6, no. 3-4 (Spring, Summer, 1983), p. 79. English.

8916 Macias, Enrique. A David Huerta. MAIZE, Vol. 6, no. 3-4 (Spring, Summer, 1983), p. 36. Spanish.

8917 Macias, Enrique. En el ombligo de la soledad (Babilonia New York USA). MAIZE, Vol. 6, no. 3-4 (Spring, Summer, 1983), p. 34. Spanish.

8918 Macias, Enrique. Hoy amaneci. MAIZE, Vol. 6, no. 3-4 (Spring, Summer, 1983), p. 35. Spanish.

8919 Magorian, James. Blizzard. MAIZE, Vol. 2, no. 3 (Spring 1979), p. 15. English.

8920 Magorian, James. Small town. MAIZE, Vol. 2, no. 3 (Spring 1979), p. 14. English.

8921 Mansilla, Juan. Alabanza a pinochet. MAIZE, Vol. 3, no. 1-2 (Fall, Winter, 1979, 1980), p. 62-65. Spanish.

Poetry (cont.)

8922 Mariaurelia. Explanation. NUESTRO, Vol. 6, no. 6 (August 1982), p. 53. English.

8923 Mariaurelia. Mallory Docks, Key West. NUESTRO, Vol. 6, no. 6 (August 1982), p. 53. English.

8924 Marquez, Alberto. Bomba de gasolina. HISPAMERICA: REVISTA DE LITERATURA, Vol. 11, no. 32 (1982), p. 121. Spanish.

8925 Marquez, Alberto. Madre. HISPAMERICA: REVISTA DE LITERATURA, Vol. 11, no. 32 (1982), p. 121. Spanish.

8926 Martinez, Mardell. La banda. COMADRE, no. 3 (Fall 1978), p. 13. Bilingual.

8927 Martinez, Mardell. Come again. COMADRE, no. 3 (Fall 1978), p. 11. English.

8928 Martinez, Mardell. Por mi padre. COMADRE, no. 3 (Fall 1978), p. 12. English.

8929 Martinez, Maria. The kiss of the butterfly. NUESTRO, Vol. 6, no. 8 (October 1982), p. 49. English.

8930 Martinez, Maria. Sterling silver roses. NUESTRO, Vol. 6, no. 8 (October 1982), p. 49. English.

8931 Martinez, Ramon E. The jockey. BILINGUAL REVIEW, Vol. 9, no. 2 (May, August, 1982), p. 166-167. English.

8932 Martinez, Renato. Cancion de cuna para una nina que no comio pan. MAIZE, Vol. 5, no. 3-4 (Spring, Summer, 1982), p. 35-36. Spanish.

8933 Mascarenas, Etta Delgado. Corrido de las comadres: (sung to the music of a traditional Mexican corrido). COMADRE, no. 3 (Fall 1978), p. 37. Spanish. **DESCR:** Corrido.

8934 McCaffrey, Mark. Laura Allende. MAIZE, Vol. 1, no. 1 (Fall 1977), p. 55-56. Spanish.

8935 Medina, Jose M. Angela before an earthquake. MAIZE, Vol. 1, no. 2 (Winter 1977), p. 53. English.

8936 Medina, Jose M. Holy week. MAIZE, Vol. 2, no. 2 (Winter 1979), p. 37-38. English.

8937 Medina, Jose M. Pool of bad luck. MAIZE, Vol. 1, no. 2 (Winter 1977), p. 54. English.

8938 Medina, Ruben. Acuarela. MAIZE, Vol. 3, no. 1-2 (Fall, Winter, 1979, 1980), p. 10. Spanish.

8939 Medina, Ruben. Angels of the city. MAIZE, Vol. 4, no. 1-2 (Fall, Winter, 1980, 1981), p. 58. Spanish.

8940 Medina, Ruben. Clasificados. MAIZE, Vol. 4, no. 1-2 (Fall, Winter, 1980, 1981), p. 56-57. Spanish.

8941 Medina, Ruben. Desaparecido. MAIZE, Vol. 2, no. 3 (Spring 1979), p. 37. Spanish.

8942 Medina, Ruben. Fotografias. MAIZE, Vol. 2, no. 3 (Spring 1979), p. 37-38. Spanish.

8943 Medina, Ruben. Has vuelto a casa como un silencio: rimbaud. MAIZE, Vol. 3, no. 1-2 (Fall, Winter, 1979, 1980), p. 11. Spanish.

8944 Medina, Ruben. Los muchachos de matagalpa.

MAIZE, Vol. 2, no. 3 (Spring 1979), p. 36. Spanish.

8945 Medina, Ruben. Para un album. MAIZE, Vol. 3, no. 1-2 (Fall, Winter, 1979, 1980), p. 9. Spanish.

8946 Medina, Ruben. Post card. MAIZE, Vol. 4, no. 1-2 (Fall, Winter, 1980, 1981), p. 55. Spanish.

8947 Medina-Nguyen, Suzanne. Age. COMADRE, no. 2 (Spring 1978), p. 21. English.

8948 Medina-Nguyen, Suzanne. One, two, three. COMADRE, no. 3 (Fall 1978), p. 17. English.

8949 Medina-Nguyen, Suzanne. Reality. COMADRE, no. 2 (Spring 1978), p. 22. English.

8950 Melendez, Jesus Papoleto. Antonia. MAIZE, Vol. 4, no. 1-2 (Fall, Winter, 1980, 1981), p. 67. English.

8951 Melendez, Jesus Papoleto. Story from a mountain. MAIZE, Vol. 4, no. 1-2 (Fall, Winter, 1980, 1981), p. 68-69. English.

8952 Melendez, Jesus Papoleto. Who i am/who i touch. MAIZE, Vol. 4, no. 1-2 (Fall, Winter, 1980, 1981), p. 70. English.

8953 Mendez, Cuauhtemoc. Cancion cansada. MAIZE, Vol. 2, no. 3 (Spring 1979), p. 54-55. Spanish.

8954 Mendez, Luis. La muerte que adelanto. MAIZE, Vol. 6, no. 1-2 (Fall, Winter, 1982, 1983), p. 86. Spanish.

8955 Mendoza, Amelia. Son paginas. CORAZON DE AZTLAN, Vol. 1, no. 3 (August, September, 1982), p. 35. Spanish.

8956 Mendoza, Pablo. Dreams. CORAZON DE AZTLAN, Vol. 1, no. 1 (January, February, 1982), p. 16. English.

8957 Mendoza, Rafael. Secreto profesional. MAIZE, Vol. 6, no. 1-2 (Fall, Winter, 1982, 1983), p. 88. Spanish.

8958 Millar, Pat. Ce Acatl. CHISMEARTE, no. 9 (September 1983), p. 19. English.

8959 Monleon, Jose. Este hombre. MAIZE, Vol. 3, no. 1-2 (Fall, Winter, 1979, 1980), p. 78-79. Spanish.

8960 Montane, Bruno. Cronica de los anos azules: mareas de metal n.4. MAIZE, Vol. 2, no. 3 (Spring 1979), p. 34. Spanish.

8961 Montane, Bruno. Cronica de los anos azules: mareas de metal n.2. MAIZE, Vol. 2, no. 3 (Spring 1979), p. 34. Spanish.

8962 Montane, Bruno. Exilio. MAIZE, Vol. 3, no. 3-4 (Spring, Summer, 1980), p. 76. Spanish.

8963 Montanez, Mary Ann. Old Lady -- New Woman: (a poem -- cycle). COMADRE, no. 1 (Summer 1977), p. 17-23. English.

8964 Montecino A., Sonia. Tres poemas y una impresion etnografica. MAIZE, Vol. 4, no. 3-4 (Spring, Summer, 1981), p. 70-73. Spanish.

8965 Montenegro, Raquel. Ausencia. MAIZE, Vol. 5, no. 3-4 (Spring, Summer, 1982), p. 53. Spanish.

Poetry (cont.)

8966 Montes, Ana. Adelita. COMADRE, no. 2 (Spring 1978), p. 23. English.

8967 Montes, Ana. Bus stop macho. COMADRE, no. 1 (Summer 1977), p. 24-25. English.

8968 Montoya, Deborah. Creativity. NUESTRO, Vol. 6, no. 7 (September 1982), p. 31. English. **DESCR:** UN VERANO.

8969 Montoya, Jose E. El corrido de mi jefe. CALMECAC, Vol. 1, (Summer 1980), p. 18. Bilingual.

8970 Montoya, Jose E. Eslipping and esliding. MAIZE, Vol. 2, no. 1 (Fall 1978), p. 41-43. English.

8971 Montoya, Jose E. It's my turn to kick the can. CALMECAC, Vol. 1, (Summer 1980), p. 43. Bilingual.

8972 Mora, Pat. Bailando. REVISTA CHICANO-RIQUENA, Vol. 11, no. 3-4 (Fall 1983), p. 60. English.

8973 Mora, Pat. Chuparrosa: humingbird. REVISTA CHICANO-RIQUENA, Vol. 10, no. 3 (Summer 1982), p. 11. English.

8974 Mora, Pat. Cool love. REVISTA CHICANO-RIQUENA, Vol. 10, no. 3 (Summer 1982), p. 10. English.

8975 Mora, Pat. Elena. REVISTA CHICANO-RIQUENA, Vol. 11, no. 3-4 (Fall 1983), p. 61. English.

8976 Mora, Pat. Plot. NEW AMERICA: A REVIEW, Vol. 4, no. 3 (1982), p. 41. English.

8977 Mora, Pat. Sola. REVISTA CHICANO-RIQUENA, Vol. 10, no. 3 (Summer 1982), p. 12. English.

8978 Mora, Pat. Unrefined. NEW AMERICA: A REVIEW, Vol. 4, no. 3 (1982), p. 41. English.

8979 Moraga, Cherrie. Passage. MAIZE, Vol. 6, no. 1-2 (Fall, Winter, 1982, 1983), p. 105. English.

8980 Morales, Carlos. Un borracho cargado a tu cuenta bancaria. MAIZE, Vol. 5, no. 1-2 (Fall, Winter, 1981, 1982), p. 69. Spanish.

8981 Morales, Carlos. Hoy. MAIZE, Vol. 5, no. 1-2 (Fall, Winter, 1981, 1982), p. 70-71. Spanish.

8982 Morra, Lynn. Morning after blues. MAIZE, Vol. 6, no. 1-2 (Fall, Winter, 1982, 1983), p. 43. English.

8983 Morra, Lynn. Recipe for hatred. MAIZE, Vol. 6, no. 1-2 (Fall, Winter, 1982, 1983), p. 42. English.

8984 La muerte y el deseo: notas sobre la poesia de Juan Felipe Herrera. LA PALABRA, Vol. 4, no. 1-2 (Spring, Fall, 1982, 1983), p. 97-106. Spanish. **DESCR:** *Herrera, Juan Felipe; Literary Criticism; Literature.

8985 Munoz, Amina. Muerte en Nueva York. THIRD WOMAN, Vol. 1, no. 2 (1982), p. 10-12. English.

8986 Munoz, Elias Miguel. Guernica 1980. MAIZE, Vol. 5, no. 1-2 (Fall, Winter, 1981, 1982), p. 48-50. Spanish.

8987 Norte, Marisela. Salmo para ella. CORAZON DE AZTLAN, Vol. 1, no. 2 (March, April, 1982), p. 8-9. Spanish.

8988 Nower, Joyce. No legend here. MAIZE, Vol. 2, no. 2 (Winter 1979), p. 48. English.

8989 Obejas, Achy. Kimberle. REVISTA CHICANO-RIQUENA, Vol. 11, no. 3-4 (Fall 1983), p. 47. English.

8990 Obejas, Achy. Sugarcane. REVISTA CHICANO-RIQUENA, Vol. 11, no. 3-4 (Fall 1983), p. 48-49. Bilingual.

8991 Ochart, Luz Ivonne. Su calle. THIRD WOMAN, Vol. 1, no. 2 (1982), p. 13. Spanish.

8992 Ochoa, Victor Orozco. Pa' la bestia. MAIZE, Vol. 1, no. 2 (Winter 1977), p. 32-33. Bilingual.

8993 O'Donnell, Patti. The newsboy. MAIZE, Vol. 5, no. 1-2 (Fall, Winter, 1981, 1982), p. 90-91. English.

8994 Ojeda, Patrick. Alleycats. MAIZE, Vol. 1, no. 4 (Summer 1978), p. 25. English.

8995 Ojeda, Patrick. Nana. MAIZE, Vol. 1, no. 4 (Summer 1978), p. 24. English.

8996 Olmstead, Clark. Inlak'ech. MAIZE, Vol. 2, no. 4 (Summer 1979), p. 23. English.

8997 Olszewski, Lawrence. Book review of: CHICANO LITERATURE: A CRITICAL HISTORY. LIBRARY JOURNAL, Vol. 108, no. 2 (January 15, 1983), p. 132. English. **DESCR:** Book Reviews; *CHICANO LITERATURE: A CRITICAL HISTORY; History; *Tatum, Charles.

8998 Opere, Fernando. Las madres de la Plaza de Mayo en Buenos Aires. REVISTA CHICANO-RIQUENA, Vol. 10, no. 4 (Fall 1982), p. 11. Spanish.

8999 Opere, Fernando. Por que se fue Teresa? REVISTA CHICANO-RIQUENA, Vol. 10, no. 4 (Fall 1982), p. 12. Spanish.

9000 Opere, Fernando. Por que se marcho Miguel? REVISTA CHICANO-RIQUENA, Vol. 10, no. 4 (Fall 1982), p. 13. Spanish.

9001 Ortega, Melquiade Antonio. Soneto. LA PALABRA, Vol. 4, no. 1-2 (Spring, Fall, 1982, 1983), p. 150. Spanish.

9002 Ortega-Neal, S. Mario. Ojazo. MAIZE, Vol. 2, no. 3 (Spring 1979), p. 56-57. English.

9003 Ortiz Cofer, Judith. Progress report to a dead father. REVISTA CHICANO-RIQUENA, Vol. 11, no. 3-4 (Fall 1983), p. 45. English.

9004 Ortiz Cofer, Judith. What the gypsy said to her children. REVISTA CHICANO-RIQUENA, Vol. 11, no. 3-4 (Fall 1983), p. 46. English.

9005 Pacheco, Javier. Book 1 of manifestations... Mrs. Trocayo's falacy fantancy trip book 1. CHISMEARTE, no. 9 (September 1983), p. 11-13. English.

9006 Pacheco, Javier. Creacion del mundo mudo. MAIZE, Vol. 3, no. 1-2 (Fall, Winter, 1979, 1980), p. 24. Spanish.

9007 Pacheco, Javier. Decadecima. MAIZE, Vol. 3, no. 1-2 (Fall, Winter, 1979, 1980), p. 25-27. English.

Poetry (cont.)

9008 Padilla, Gary. The blacksmith. JOURNAL OF ETHNIC STUDIES, Vol. 5, no. 1 (Spring 1977), p. 70. English.

9009 Padilla, Gary. The campesina's breakdown. JOURNAL OF ETHNIC STUDIES, Vol. 5, no. 1 (Spring 1977), p. 74-76. English.

9010 Padilla, Gary. Night visions of the blacksmith and the campesina. JOURNAL OF ETHNIC STUDIES, Vol. 5, no. 1 (Spring 1977), p. 71-73. English.

9011 Painter, Vita. Token mexican. MAIZE, Vol. 2, no. 2 (Winter 1979), p. 7. English.

9012 Painter, Vita. Woman in the field. MAIZE, Vol. 2, no. 2 (Winter 1979), p. 8. English.

9013 Paredes, Americo. A Sandino cinco anos despues de su muerte. MAIZE, Vol. 1, no. 1 (Fall 1977), p. 6. Spanish.

9014 Paredes, Americo. Coplas. MAIZE, Vol. 1, no. 1 (Fall 1977), p. 7-8. Spanish.

9015 Paredes, Americo. Mi pueblo. MAIZE, Vol. 1, no. 2 (Winter 1977), p. 23-25. Spanish.

9016 Paredes, Americo. Pa que. MAIZE, Vol. 1, no. 1 (Fall 1977), p. 9. Spanish.

9017 Paredes, Americo. El pocho. MAIZE, Vol. 1, no. 1 (Fall 1977), p. 5. Spanish.

9018 Paredes, Raymund A. Book review of: THE ELEMENTS OF SAN JOAQUIN. MINORITY VOICES, Vol. 1, no. 2 (Fall 1977), p. 106-108. English. **DESCR:** Book Reviews; Soto, Gary; *THE ELEMENTS OF SAN JOAQUIN.

9019 Paredes, Raymund A. Book review of: THE TALE OF SUNLIGHT. MINORITY VOICES, Vol. 2, no. 2 (Fall 1978), p. 67-68. English. **DESCR:** Book Reviews; Soto, Gary; *TALE OF SUNLIGHT.

9020 Los pasos de la vida c/s. CALMECAC, Vol. 2, (Spring 1981), p. 49. English. **DESCR:** *Musical Lyrics.

9021 Pau-Llosa, Ricardo. The sugar mill. BILINGUAL REVIEW, Vol. 9, no. 2 (May, August, 1982), p. 153-155. English.

9022 Pena, Devon G. Migra three points blue. MAIZE, Vol. 1, no. 3 (Spring 1978), p. 26-27. English.

9023 Pena, Devon G. Untitled. MAIZE, Vol. 1, no. 3 (Spring 1978), p. 28. English.

9024 Pena, Silvia Novo. Sonata nuevomejicana. REVISTA CHICANO-RIQUENA, Vol. 10, no. 3 (Summer 1982), p. 16-17. Spanish.

9025 The people of Quinto Sol. CALMECAC, Vol. 3, (Spring 1982), p. 40. English.

9026 Perez Firmat, Gustavo. Carolina Cuban. BILINGUAL REVIEW, Vol. 9, no. 2 (May, August, 1982), p. 170. English.

9027 Perez Firmat, Gustavo. Home. BILINGUAL REVIEW, Vol. 9, no. 2 (May, August, 1982), p. 171. English.

9028 Perez, Juan. Chile, poema en cuatro augustias y un iris aura. MAIZE, Vol. 3, no. 3-4 (Spring, Summer, 1980), p. 70-73. Spanish. **DESCR:** *Chile.

9029 Pinero, Miguel. A Lower East Side poem.

REVISTA CHICANO-RIQUENA, Vol. 10, no. 1-2 (Winter, Spring, 1982), p. 90-91. English.

9030 Pinero, Miguel. New York City hard times blues. REVISTA CHICANO-RIQUENA, Vol. 10, no. 1-2 (Winter, Spring, 1982), p. 92-97. English.

9031 Pinero, Miguel. Requiem for the men's shelter. REVISTA CHICANO-RIQUENA, Vol. 10, no. 1-2 (Winter, Spring, 1982), p. 89. English.

9032 Planting-time. NUESTRO, Vol. 6, no. 3 (April 1982), p. 47. English.

9033 Prepare me. CALMECAC, Vol. 3, (Spring 1982), p. 48. English.

9034 Pursifull, Carmen M. Going for the land of the living. REVISTA CHICANO-RIQUENA, Vol. 11, no. 2 (Summer 1983), p. 47. English.

9035 Pursifull, Carmen M. Papa. REVISTA CHICANO-RIQUENA, Vol. 11, no. 2 (Summer 1983), p. 45-46. English.

9036 Pursifull, Carmen M. The poltergeist. REVISTA CHICANO-RIQUENA, Vol. 11, no. 2 (Summer 1983), p. 44. English.

9037 Quinonez, Naomi. Central Califas. CHISMEARTE, no. 9 (September 1983), p. 17. English.

9038 Quinonez, Naomi. Educators. CHISMEARTE, (1982), p. 55. English.

9039 Quinonez, Naomi. L.A.: a face only a mother could love. MAIZE, Vol. 6, no. 1-2 (Fall, Winter, 1982, 1983), p. 32-33. English.

9040 Quinonez, Naomi. El Salvador. MAIZE, Vol. 6, no. 1-2 (Fall, Winter, 1982, 1983), p. 31. English.

9041 Quintana Pigno, Antonia. Isleta. REVISTA CHICANO-RIQUENA, Vol. 11, no. 3-4 (Fall 1983), p. 67-70. English.

9042 Quintana, Vicente. Mourn not. MAIZE, Vol. 1, no. 2 (Winter 1977), p. 30. English.

9043 Ramirez Garcia, Raul. A las botas que me dio mi apa. MAIZE, Vol. 6, no. 1-2 (Fall, Winter, 1982, 1983), p. 84. Spanish.

9044 Ramirez Garcia, Raul. Mi fella epoca. MAIZE, Vol. 6, no. 1-2 (Fall, Winter, 1982, 1983), p. 83. Spanish.

9045 Ramirez Garcia, Raul. El tiempo es un suicida que nos arrastra. MAIZE, Vol. 6, no. 1-2 (Fall, Winter, 1982, 1983), p. 82. Spanish.

9046 Rangel, Irma "La Cui Cui". The children are the healing. CALMECAC, Vol. 2, (Spring 1981), p. 27. English. **DESCR:** Musical Lyrics.

9047 Rangel, Irma "La Cui Cui". Lullaby for baby. CALMECAC, Vol. 2, (Spring 1981), p. 26. English. **DESCR:** Musical Lyrics.

9048 Rangel, Irma "La Cui Cui". A tender gift. CALMECAC, Vol. 3, (Spring 1982), p. 36. English.

Poetry (cont.)

9049 Rebolledo, Tey Diana. Abuelitas: mythology and integration in Chicana literature. REVISTA CHICANO-RIQUENA, Vol. 11, no. 3-4 (Fall 1983), p. 148-158. English. DESCR: Chicanas; *Literary Criticism.

9050 Rebolledo, Tey Diana. Game theory in Chicana poetry. REVISTA CHICANO-RIQUENA, Vol. 11, no. 3-4 (Fall 1983), p. 159-168. English. DESCR: Chicanas; *Literary Criticism.

9051 Retana, Nicolas. Decia grandpa. MAIZE, Vol. 6, no. 3-4 (Spring, Summer, 1983), p. 51. Bilingual.

9052 Retana, Nicolas. Drum sounds of peace. MAIZE, Vol. 6, no. 3-4 (Spring, Summer, 1983), p. 52-54. English.

9053 Rico, Noel. The Bronx, 1979. REVISTA CHICANO-RIQUENA, Vol. 10, no. 1-2 (Winter, Spring, 1982), p. 99. English.

9054 Rico, Noel. Excerpt from the South Bronx. REVISTA CHICANO-RIQUENA, Vol. 10, no. 1-2 (Winter, Spring, 1982), p. 101. English.

9055 Rico, Noel. Excerpt from the South Bronx II. REVISTA CHICANO-RIQUENA, Vol. 10, no. 1-2 (Winter, Spring, 1982), p. 101. English.

9056 Rico, Noel. A hot August night on the lower east side. BILINGUAL REVIEW, Vol. 9, no. 2 (May, August, 1982), p. 168-169. English.

9057 Rico, Noel. It is only the flowers. REVISTA CHICANO-RIQUENA, Vol. 10, no. 1-2 (Winter, Spring, 1982), p. 100. English.

9058 Rico, Noel. A late afternoon. REVISTA CHICANO-RIQUENA, Vol. 10, no. 1-2 (Winter, Spring, 1982), p. 103. English.

9059 Rico, Noel. The Lower East Side: after having witnessed a man beating up a woman underneath a balcony overlooking Avenue C. REVISTA CHICANO-RIQUENA, Vol. 10, no. 1-2 (Winter, Spring, 1982), p. 98. English.

9060 Rico, Noel. The first place. REVISTA CHICANO-RIQUENA, Vol. 10, no. 1-2 (Winter, Spring, 1982), p. 102. English.

9061 Riddell, Adaljiza. Assault and battery. JOURNAL OF ETHNIC STUDIES, Vol. 2, no. 2 (Summer 1974), p. 52. English.

9062 Riddell, Adaljiza. Como duele. JOURNAL OF ETHNIC STUDIES, Vol. 2, no. 2 (Summer 1974), p. 59-60. Bilingual.

9063 Riddell, Adaljiza. Looking backwards down. JOURNAL OF ETHNIC STUDIES, Vol. 2, no. 2 (Summer 1974), p. 50-51. Bilingual.

9064 Riddell, Adaljiza. Ode to Jose Montoya, un poeta Chicano. JOURNAL OF ETHNIC STUDIES, Vol. 2, no. 2 (Summer 1974), p. 56-58. Bilingual.

9065 Riddell, Adaljiza. Orfeo Azteca. JOURNAL OF ETHNIC STUDIES, Vol. 2, no. 2 (Summer 1974), p. 54-55. English.

9066 Riddell, Adaljiza. San Juan Capistrano - at the sacred fountain. JOURNAL OF ETHNIC STUDIES, Vol. 2, no. 2 (Summer 1974), p. 53. English.

9067 Rios, Denise. Survival of the female fetus. THIRD WOMAN, Vol. 1, no. 2 (1982), p. 23. English.

9068 Rivera, Diana. ChildEternal. THIRD WOMAN, Vol. 1, no. 2 (1982), p. 25-26. English.

9069 Rivera, Marina. Bees, birds, moths, chickens. REVISTA CHICANO-RIQUENA, Vol. 10, no. 1-2 (Winter, Spring, 1982), p. 107. English.

9070 Rivera, Marina. Esteban. REVISTA CHICANO-RIQUENA, Vol. 10, no. 1-2 (Winter, Spring, 1982), p. 105. English.

9071 Rivera, Marina. Pan. REVISTA CHICANO-RIQUENA, Vol. 10, no. 1-2 (Winter, Spring, 1982), p. 108. English.

9072 Rivera, Marina. Villa. REVISTA CHICANO-RIQUENA, Vol. 10, no. 1-2 (Winter, Spring, 1982), p. 104. English.

9073 Rivera, Marina. Why. REVISTA CHICANO-RIQUENA, Vol. 10, no. 1-2 (Winter, Spring, 1982), p. 106. English.

9074 Rivero, Eliana S. En el lugar que corresponde. REVISTA CHICANO-RIQUENA, Vol. 11, no. 3-4 (Fall 1983), p. 36. Spanish.

9075 Rivero, Eliana S. Gloria. REVISTA CHICANO-RIQUENA, Vol. 11, no. 3-4 (Fall 1983), p. 38. Spanish.

9076 Rivero, Eliana S. Salutacion: Ave. REVISTA CHICANO-RIQUENA, Vol. 11, no. 3-4 (Fall 1983), p. 37. Spanish.

9077 Riveros, Enrique. Carta a un poeta. MAIZE, Vol. 2, no. 3 (Spring 1979), p. 45. Spanish.

9078 Riveros, Enrique. Despues del golpe. MAIZE, Vol. 2, no. 3 (Spring 1979), p. 44-45. Spanish.

9079 Riveros, Enrique. La esperanza vuelve desde el horizonte. MAIZE, Vol. 2, no. 3 (Spring 1979), p. 48. Spanish.

9080 Riveros, Enrique. Mientras tanto. MAIZE, Vol. 2, no. 3 (Spring 1979), p. 46-47. Spanish.

9081 Riveros, Enrique. Paisaje. MAIZE, Vol. 2, no. 3 (Spring 1979), p. 46. Spanish.

9082 Rivers, J.W. Guerrillas. MAIZE, Vol. 6, no. 1-2 (Fall, Winter, 1982, 1983), p. 30. English.

9083 Rivers, J.W. MSFW: migrant seasonal farm worker. MAIZE, Vol. 6, no. 1-2 (Fall, Winter, 1982, 1983), p. 85. Spanish.

9084 Rivers, J.W. The municipal president of tequistalpa to general felix diaz. MAIZE, Vol. 3, no. 3-4 (Spring, Summer, 1980), p. 65. English.

9085 Rivers, J.W. Pascual orozco. MAIZE, Vol. 3, no. 3-4 (Spring, Summer, 1980), p. 64. English.

9086 Robertson, Sandra. Para que me mueras. MAIZE, Vol. 3, no. 1-2 (Fall, Winter, 1979, 1980), p. 76. Spanish.

9087 Robles, Mireya. Trilogia en punto final. MAIZE, Vol. 1, no. 3 (Spring 1978), p. 55-57. Spanish.

9088 Rocha, Thomas. Drink into the early dawn: on the death of an uncle. NUESTRO, Vol. 6, no. 2 (March 1982), p. 39. English.

Poetry (cont.)

9089 Rocha, Thomas. Reflejos. NUESTRO, Vol. 6, no. 2 (March 1982), p. 39. English.

9090 Rocha, Thomas. Torment. NUESTRO, Vol. 6, no. 2 (March 1982), p. 39. English.

9091 Rodriguez, Alfonso. Ideologia. LA PALABRA, Vol. 4, no. 1-2 (Spring, Fall, 1982, 1983), p. 146-147. Spanish.

9092 Rodriguez, Andres. Hunters tell at midnight. MAIZE, Vol. 4, no. 3-4 (Spring, Summer, 1981), p. 75. English.

9093 Rodriguez, Andres. Irises. MAIZE, Vol. 4, no. 3-4 (Spring, Summer, 1981), p. 75. English.

9094 Rodriguez, Andres. The island. MAIZE, Vol. 4, no. 3-4 (Spring, Summer, 1981), p. 74. English.

9095 Rodriguez del Pino, Salvador. Implorasion a mi lengua. MAIZE, Vol. 1, no. 2 (Winter 1977), p. 52. Spanish.

9096 Rodriguez del Pino, Salvador. La intimidad poetica de Luis Leal. LA PALABRA, Vol. 4, no. 1-2 (Spring, Fall, 1982, 1983), p. 41-52. Spanish. DESCR: Authors; *Leal, Luis; Literature.

9097 Rodriguez, Joe. Chicano poetry: mestizaje and the use of irony. CAMPO LIBRE, Vol. 1, no. 2 (Summer 1981), p. 229-235. English. DESCR: Identity; Literary Characteristics; *Literary Criticism; *Mestizaje.

9098 Rodriguez, Luis. Soldados. MAIZE, Vol. 3, no. 3-4 (Spring, Summer, 1980), p. 62. Spanish.

9099 Rodriguez, Luis. Vengan. MAIZE, Vol. 3, no. 3-4 (Spring, Summer, 1980), p. 62. English.

9100 Rodriguez, Raquel. Children of the earth. COMADRE, no. 2 (Spring 1978), p. 20. English. DESCR: Agricultural Laborers.

9101 Rodriguez, Raquel. Cry to the wind. COMADRE, no. 3 (Fall 1978), p. 5. English.

9102 Rodriguez, Raquel. My mother will no longer cry. COMADRE, no. 2 (Spring 1978), p. 17. English.

9103 Rodriguez, Raquel. This woman. COMADRE, no. 2 (Spring 1978), p. 19. English.

9104 Rodriguez, Raquel. Tomorrow. COMADRE, no. 2 (Spring 1978), p. 16. English.

9105 Rodriguez, Raquel. Yo soy mujer. COMADRE, no. 2 (Spring 1978), p. 18. English.

9106 Roman, James. Haiku. MAIZE, Vol. 6, no. 1-2 (Fall, Winter, 1982, 1983), p. 59. English.

9107 Romano, James V. Spanish scene. MAIZE, Vol. 6, no. 1-2 (Fall, Winter, 1982, 1983), p. 58. English.

9108 Romero, Leo. The dark side of the moon. REVISTA CHICANO-RIQUENA, Vol. 10, no. 1-2 (Winter, Spring, 1982), p. 109. English.

9109 Romero, Leo. Earth, Texas. BILINGUAL REVIEW, Vol. 9, no. 2 (May, August, 1982), p. 164. English.

9110 Romero, Leo. Fear of the moon. REVISTA CHICANO-RIQUENA, Vol. 10, no. 1-2 (Winter, Spring, 1982), p. 110-111. English.

9111 Romero, Leo. I came to earth. REVISTA CHICANO-RIQUENA, Vol. 10, no. 1-2 (Winter, Spring, 1982), p. 113. English.

9112 Romero, Leo. The moon is lost. REVISTA CHICANO-RIQUENA, Vol. 10, no. 1-2 (Winter, Spring, 1982), p. 112. English.

9113 Romero, Leo. Moonstruck. BILINGUAL REVIEW, Vol. 9, no. 2 (May, August, 1982), p. 163-164. English.

9114 Romero, Leo. The night is overwhelmed. REVISTA CHICANO-RIQUENA, Vol. 10, no. 1-2 (Winter, Spring, 1982), p. 111. English.

9115 Romero, Leo. The ocean is not red. REVISTA CHICANO-RIQUENA, Vol. 10, no. 1-2 (Winter, Spring, 1982), p. 112-113. English.

9116 Ruben Salazar: a most uncommon man. NUESTRO, Vol. 6, no. 4 (May 1982), p. 44-45. English. DESCR: *Salazar, Ruben.

9117 Sabino, Osvaldo R. La magia y el mito. MAIZE, Vol. 6, no. 3-4 (Spring, Summer, 1983), p. 98-100. Spanish.

9118 Sabino, Osvaldo R. Ronda infantil. MAIZE, Vol. 6, no. 3-4 (Spring, Summer, 1983), p. 96-97. Spanish.

9119 Sagel, Jaime. Abuela. CHISMEARTE, no. 9 (September 1983), p. 6-10. Bilingual.

9120 Sagel, Jaime. Frigid. MAIZE, Vol. 5, no. 1-2 (Fall, Winter, 1981, 1982), p. 53-54. Spanish.

9121 Sagel, Jaime. Low rider. MAIZE, Vol. 2, no. 2 (Winter 1979), p. 28-29. English.

9122 Salazar, Alejandro. Indio. MAIZE, Vol. 2, no. 1 (Fall 1978), p. 27. English.

9123 Saldivar, Jose David. Book review of: CHICANO POETRY: A RESPONSE TO CHAOS. MELUS: MULTI-ETHNIC LITERATURE OF THE UNITED STATES, Vol. 10, no. 2 (Summer 1983), p. 83-85. English. DESCR: Book Reviews; Bruce Novoa, Juan; *CHICANO POETRY: A RESPONSE TO CHAOS.

9124 Salinas Jaramillo, Miguel A. Canto al hombre nuevo. MAIZE, Vol. 5, no. 1-2 (Fall, Winter, 1981, 1982), p. 86-87. Spanish.

9125 Salinas, Omar. As I look to the literate. REVISTA CHICANO-RIQUENA, Vol. 10, no. 1-2 (Winter, Spring, 1982), p. 116. English.

9126 Salinas, Omar. I am America. REVISTA CHICANO-RIQUENA, Vol. 10, no. 1-2 (Winter, Spring, 1982), p. 114-115. English.

9127 Salinas, Omar. My father is a simple man. REVISTA CHICANO-RIQUENA, Vol. 10, no. 1-2 (Winter, Spring, 1982), p. 117. English.

9128 Salinas, Omar. When this life no longer smells of roses. REVISTA CHICANO-RIQUENA, Vol. 10, no. 1-2 (Winter, Spring, 1982), p. 118. English.

9129 Sanchez, Ricardo. Canto towards Ateneo. NATIONAL HISPANIC JOURNAL, Vol. 1, no. 3 (Summer, Fall, 1982), p. 19. English. DESCR: Authors.

Poetry (cont.)

9130 Sanchez, Ricardo. Coronado. REVISTA CHICANO-RIQUENA, Vol. 10, no. 1-2 (Winter, Spring, 1982), p. 123-124. English.

9131 Sanchez, Ricardo. Entequila. REVISTA CHICANO-RIQUENA, Vol. 10, no. 1-2 (Winter, Spring, 1982), p. 119-122. Bilingual.

9132 Sanchez, Ricardo. Letter to my ex-Texas sanity. REVISTA CHICANO-RIQUENA, Vol. 10, no. 1-2 (Winter, Spring, 1982), p. 125-127. English.

9133 Santiago Baca, Jimmy. Dark innocence. REVISTA CHICANO-RIQUENA, Vol. 11, no. 2 (Summer 1983), p. 42. English.

9134 Santiago Baca, Jimmy. Mr. Valdez. REVISTA CHICANO-RIQUENA, Vol. 11, no. 2 (Summer 1983), p. 41. English.

9135 Santiago Baca, Jimmy. On this side of the mountain. CHISMEARTE, no. 9 (September 1983), p. 32-34. English.

9136 Santiago Baca, Jimmy. Spring burning. REVISTA CHICANO-RIQUENA, Vol. 11, no. 2 (Summer 1983), p. 43. English.

9137 Santiago, Esmerelda. Paseo. NUESTRO, Vol. 5, no. 8 (November 1981), p. 45. English.

9138 Santiago, Esmerelda. Recordando un verano. NUESTRO, Vol. 5, no. 8 (November 1981), p. 45. English.

9139 Santiago, Esmerelda. Wintercool. NUESTRO, Vol. 5, no. 8 (November 1981), p. 45. English.

9140 Santiago, Mario. Imaginense. MAIZE, Vol. 2, no. 3 (Spring 1979), p. 16. Spanish.

9141 Sapia, Yvonne. Another poem about breasts. REVISTA CHICANO-RIQUENA, Vol. 10, no. 4 (Fall 1982), p. 8. English.

9142 Sapia, Yvonne. Del medio del sueno. REVISTA CHICANO-RIQUENA, Vol. 11, no. 3-4 (Fall 1983), p. 58. English.

9143 Sapia, Yvonne. The figure at the door. REVISTA CHICANO-RIQUENA, Vol. 10, no. 4 (Fall 1982), p. 7. English.

9144 Sapia, Yvonne. Inside the room of ruined light. REVISTA CHICANO-RIQUENA, Vol. 10, no. 4 (Fall 1982), p. 9. English.

9145 Sapia, Yvonne. The landlord's dream of hell. REVISTA CHICANO-RIQUENA, Vol. 11, no. 3-4 (Fall 1983), p. 57. English.

9146 Sapia, Yvonne. The posture of the dance. REVISTA CHICANO-RIQUENA, Vol. 11, no. 3-4 (Fall 1983), p. 59. English.

9147 Sapia, Yvonne. The second person. REVISTA CHICANO-RIQUENA, Vol. 10, no. 4 (Fall 1982), p. 10. English.

9148 Sapia, Yvonne. Southern boulevard. REVISTA CHICANO-RIQUENA, Vol. 11, no. 3-4 (Fall 1983), p. 56. English.

9149 Saucedo, Concha. No me llames Hispanic. CALMECAC, Vol. 2, (Spring 1981), p. 35. Bilingual. **DESCR**: Identity.

9150 Savren, Shelley. Discovering the source. MAIZE, Vol. 6, no. 3-4 (Spring, Summer, 1983), p. 78. English.

9151 Schmidt, Lorenza. Birth. JOURNAL OF ETHNIC STUDIES, Vol. 2, no. 2 (Summer 1974), p. 62-64. Bilingual.

9152 Schmidt, Lorenza. Death of mi abuelito. JOURNAL OF ETHNIC STUDIES, Vol. 2, no. 2 (Summer 1974), p. 65. Bilingual.

9153 Schmidt, Lorenza. La Llorona. JOURNAL OF ETHNIC STUDIES, Vol. 2, no. 2 (Summer 1974), p. 61. Bilingual.

9154 Segade, Gustavo V. Dog days in paradise. MAIZE, Vol. 2, no. 4 (Summer 1979), p. 39-40. English.

9155 Segade, Gustavo V. Luisa/louise (mothersong). MAIZE, Vol. 2, no. 4 (Summer 1979), p. 36-38. English.

9156 Shahnaz, Fatima. I am Sita. MAIZE, Vol. 5, no. 3-4 (Spring, Summer, 1982), p. 48-51. English.

9157 Sierra Foothills. CALMECAC, Vol. 2, (Spring 1981), p. 53. English.

9158 Silver, Chitra. At a pipe factory in Fontana. MAIZE, Vol. 5, no. 1-2 (Fall, Winter, 1981, 1982), p. 88. English.

9159 Soto, Gary. Black hair. REVISTA CHICANO-RIQUENA, Vol. 11, no. 2 (Summer 1983), p. 8. English.

9160 Soto, Gary. Brown like us. REVISTA CHICANO-RIQUENA, Vol. 10, no. 1-2 (Winter, Spring, 1982), p. 132-134. English.

9161 Soto, Gary. Eating. REVISTA CHICANO-RIQUENA, Vol. 11, no. 2 (Summer 1983), p. 10. English.

9162 Soto, Gary. A few coins. REVISTA CHICANO-RIQUENA, Vol. 10, no. 1-2 (Winter, Spring, 1982), p. 140. English.

9163 Soto, Gary. Girls among waves, 1967. REVISTA CHICANO-RIQUENA, Vol. 11, no. 2 (Summer 1983), p. 9. English.

9164 Soto, Gary. Hard times. REVISTA CHICANO-RIQUENA, Vol. 11, no. 2 (Summer 1983), p. 7. English.

9165 Soto, Gary. In the madness of love. REVISTA CHICANO-RIQUENA, Vol. 11, no. 2 (Summer 1983), p. 13. English.

9166 Soto, Gary. Joey the midget. REVISTA CHICANO-RIQUENA, Vol. 10, no. 1-2 (Winter, Spring, 1982), p. 134-135. English.

9167 Soto, Gary. Litany after a mexican prayer of the poor. MAIZE, Vol. 2, no. 1 (Fall 1978), p. 9. English.

9168 Soto, Gary. Luis Omar Salinas: Chicano poet. MELUS: MULTI-ETHNIC LITERATURE OF THE UNITED STATES, Vol. 9, no. 2 (Summer 1982), p. 47-82. English. **DESCR**: Authors; *Salinas, Luis Omar.

9169 Soto, Gary. Mexicans begin jogging. REVISTA CHICANO-RIQUENA, Vol. 10, no. 1-2 (Winter, Spring, 1982), p. 136. English.

9170 Soto, Gary. Mission tire factory, 1969. REVISTA CHICANO-RIQUENA, Vol. 10, no. 1-2 (Winter, Spring, 1982), p. 136. English.

Poetry (cont.)

9171 Soto, Gary. Nada. REVISTA CHICANO-RIQUENA, Vol. 10, no. 1-2 (Winter, Spring, 1982), p. 139. English.

9172 Soto, Gary. The ring. REVISTA CHICANO-RIQUENA, Vol. 10, no. 1-2 (Winter, Spring, 1982), p. 138-139. English.

9173 Soto, Gary. Ritual. REVISTA CHICANO-RIQUENA, Vol. 11, no. 2 (Summer 1983), p. 11. English.

9174 Soto, Gary; Trejo, Ernesto; and de la Fuente, Patricia. Special focus on Gary Soto. REVISTA CHICANO-RIQUENA, Vol. 11, no. 2 (Summer 1983), p. 7-39. English. **DESCR:** Literary Criticism; Prose; *Soto, Gary.

9175 Soto, Gary. Uncle: 1957: after being rejected by the Marines. REVISTA CHICANO-RIQUENA, Vol. 10, no. 1-2 (Winter, Spring, 1982), p. 137. English.

9176 Soto, Gary. Who are you? REVISTA CHICANO-RIQUENA, Vol. 11, no. 2 (Summer 1983), p. 12. English.

9177 Suarez, Elena. Encuentro de dos expatriados. MAIZE, Vol. 2, no. 4 (Summer 1979), p. 48. Spanish.

9178 Suarez, Elena. Marginacion. MAIZE, Vol. 2, no. 4 (Summer 1979), p. 46-47. Spanish.

9179 Suro, Xiomara. Do you remember my love. NUESTRO, Vol. 6, no. 5 (June, July, 1982), p. 55. English.

9180 Suro, Xiomara. The horizon. NUESTRO, Vol. 6, no. 5 (June, July, 1982), p. 55. English.

9181 Suro, Xiomara. Loneliness. NUESTRO, Vol. 6, no. 5 (June, July, 1982), p. 55. English.

9182 Tafolla, Carmen. Caminitos. MAIZE, Vol. 4, no. 3-4 (Spring, Summer, 1981), p. 76-77. English.

9183 Tafolla, Carmen. Casa. REVISTA CHICANO-RIQUENA, Vol. 11, no. 3-4 (Fall 1983), p. 27. Bilingual.

9184 Tafolla, Carmen. MotherMother. REVISTA CHICANO-RIQUENA, Vol. 11, no. 3-4 (Fall 1983), p. 26. English.

9185 Tafolla, Carmen. Soulpain. REVISTA CHICANO-RIQUENA, Vol. 11, no. 3-4 (Fall 1983), p. 25. English.

9186 Tafolla, Carmen. Woman-hole. REVISTA CHICANO-RIQUENA, Vol. 11, no. 3-4 (Fall 1983), p. 24. Bilingual.

9187 Tawese. Tia Ester. REVISTA CHICANO-RIQUENA, Vol. 11, no. 3-4 (Fall 1983), p. 62-64. English.

9188 Tejeda, Juan. Aztlan 1976. MAIZE, Vol. 1, no. 3 (Spring 1978), p. 29. Bilingual.

9189 Tello, Jerry. De donde eres? que te importa. LATINA, Vol. 1, no. 1 (1982), p. 14. Bilingual.

9190 Thompson, Laurie. Active verbs. MAIZE, Vol. 3, no. 3-4 (Spring, Summer, 1980), p. 49. English.

9191 Thompson, Laurie. Amen. MAIZE, Vol. 2, no. 4 (Summer 1979), p. 14-15. English.

9192 Thompson, Laurie. Far away. MAIZE, Vol. 3, no. 3-4 (Spring, Summer, 1980), p. 49. English.

9193 Thompson, Laurie. Manzanas amargas. MAIZE, Vol. 2, no. 4 (Summer 1979), p. 12-14. English.

9194 Thompson, Laurie. To the quetzal. MAIZE, Vol. 2, no. 4 (Summer 1979), p. 16-17. English.

9195 Tirado, Evie. In the damp sienna hills. MAIZE, Vol. 5, no. 1-2 (Fall, Winter, 1981, 1982), p. 66. English.

9196 Tirado, Evie. Today. MAIZE, Vol. 5, no. 1-2 (Fall, Winter, 1981, 1982), p. 67-68. English.

9197 Tizocurista. Papa sun. MAIZE, Vol. 2, no. 4 (Summer 1979), p. 49. English.

9198 Torrens, James. The American way. BILINGUAL REVIEW, Vol. 10, no. 1 (January, April, 1983), p. 68. English.

9199 Torrens, James. Shine on, la rubia. BILINGUAL REVIEW, Vol. 10, no. 1 (January, April, 1983), p. 68. English.

9200 Tremblay, Gail. Night gives old woman the word. MAIZE, Vol. 3, no. 1-2 (Fall, Winter, 1979, 1980), p. 48. English.

9201 Trevino, Gloria L. Recuerdos. MAIZE, Vol. 2, no. 1 (Fall 1978), p. 17. Spanish.

9202 Trujillo Munoz, Gabriel. Alien. MAIZE, Vol. 5, no. 3-4 (Spring, Summer, 1982), p. 54. Spanish.

9203 Trujillo Munoz, Gabriel. Anos luz. MAIZE, Vol. 5, no. 3-4 (Spring, Summer, 1982), p. 55. Spanish.

9204 Trujillo, Paul. Before and after noon. MAIZE, Vol. 3, no. 1-2 (Fall, Winter, 1979, 1980), p. 47. English.

9205 Trujillo, Paul. Damage. BILINGUAL REVIEW, Vol. 9, no. 2 (May, August, 1982), p. 161. English.

9206 Trujillo, Paul. Letters. BILINGUAL REVIEW, Vol. 9, no. 2 (May, August, 1982), p. 161. English.

9207 Trujillo, Paul. Motion. MAIZE, Vol. 3, no. 1-2 (Fall, Winter, 1979, 1980), p. 46. English.

9208 Trujillo, Paul. Prayer for evening. BILINGUAL REVIEW, Vol. 9, no. 2 (May, August, 1982), p. 162. English.

9209 Trujillo, Paul. Winter. MAIZE, Vol. 3, no. 1-2 (Fall, Winter, 1979, 1980), p. 46. English.

9210 Turner, Lance M. On a hill, sitting. MAIZE, Vol. 6, no. 1-2 (Fall, Winter, 1982, 1983), p. 61. English.

9211 Turner, Lance M. [Untitled poem]. MAIZE, Vol. 6, no. 1-2 (Fall, Winter, 1982, 1983), p. 60. English.

9212 Tyler, Joseph. Loaned lawns. MAIZE, Vol. 6, no. 3-4 (Spring, Summer, 1983), p. 46. Bilingual.

Poetry (cont.)

9213 Umpierre, Luz Maria. La ansiedad de la influencia en Sandra Maria Esteves y Marjorie Agosin. REVISTA CHICANO-RIQUENA, Vol. 11, no. 3-4 (Fall 1983), p. 139-147. Spanish. **DESCR:** A JULIA Y A MI; *Agosin, Magi; De Burgos, Julia; EL PAIS DIVIDIDO; *Esteves, Sandra Maria; *Literary Criticism; Neruda, Pablo; Parra, Nicanor.

9214 Umpierre, Luz Maria. Carta a los Hispanos. BILINGUAL REVIEW, Vol. 10, no. 1 (January, April, 1983), p. 67. Spanish.

9215 Umpierre, Luz Maria. Cuento sin hadas. THIRD WOMAN, Vol. 1, no. 2 (1982), p. 6. Spanish.

9216 Umpierre, Luz Maria. Un manifiesto literario: PAPELES DE PANDERA DE ROSARIO FERRE. BILINGUAL REVIEW, Vol. 9, no. 2 (May, August, 1982), p. 120126. Spanish. **DESCR:** Book Reviews; Ferre, Rosario; *PAPELES DE PANDORA; Puerto Rican Literature.

9217 Umpierre, Luz Maria. Miscelanea. THIRD WOMAN, Vol. 1, no. 2 (1982), p. 8-9. Spanish.

9218 Umpierre, Luz Maria. Oracion ante una imagen derrumbada. BILINGUAL REVIEW, Vol. 10, no. 1 (January, April, 1983), p. 66. Spanish.

9219 Umpierre, Luz Maria. Sacrilegio?: peticion hagase con mucho fervor -- 50 ejaculaciones. THIRD WOMAN, Vol. 1, no. 2 (1982), p. 7-8. Spanish.

9220 Umpierre, Luz Maria. Una defensa. BILINGUAL REVIEW, Vol. 10, no. 1 (January, April, 1983), p. 66. Spanish.

9221 Uriarte, Ivan. Introduccion a la poesia revolucionaria de El Salvador. MAIZE, Vol. 6, no. 1-2 (Fall, Winter, 1982, 1983), p. 34-40. Spanish. **DESCR:** *El Salvador; Latin American Literature; Revolutions.

9222 Urrea, Luis Alberto. Living in the usa. MAIZE, Vol. 3, no. 1-2 (Fall, Winter, 1979, 1980), p. 84. English.

9223 Urrea, Luis Alberto. Volcano nights. MAIZE, Vol. 3, no. 1-2 (Fall, Winter, 1979, 1980), p. 80-83. English.

9224 Valdes, Gina. Back to school. MAIZE, Vol. 4, no. 1-2 (Fall, Winter, 1980, 1981), p. 45. English.

9225 Valdes, Gina. Buscando una casa nueva. MAIZE, Vol. 4, no. 1-2 (Fall, Winter, 1980, 1981), p. 46-47. Spanish.

9226 Valdes, Gina. Ko. MAIZE, Vol. 4, no. 1-2 (Fall, Winter, 1980, 1981), p. 48. Spanish.

9227 Valenzuela, Luis E. Caminando. MAIZE, Vol. 6, no. 3-4 (Spring, Summer, 1983), p. 76. Spanish.

9228 Valenzuela, Luis E. Las miradas. MAIZE, Vol. 6, no. 3-4 (Spring, Summer, 1983), p. 75. Spanish.

9229 Valenzuela, Luis E. Los perros. MAIZE, Vol. 6, no. 3-4 (Spring, Summer, 1983), p. 74. Spanish.

9230 Valjalo, David. Bicentenario. CHISMEARTE, (1982), p. 2. Spanish.

9231 Valle, Carmen. Cuando vivimos. THIRD WOMAN, Vol. 1, no. 2 (1982), p. 27. Spanish.

9232 Valle, Carmen. Nursery. THIRD WOMAN, Vol. 1, no. 2 (1982), p. 27. Spanish.

9233 Valle, Victor Manuel. Ciudad de Los Angeles I. CHISMEARTE, (1982), p. 24. Bilingual.

9234 Valle, Victor Manuel. Ciudad de Los Angeles II. CHISMEARTE, (1982), p. 26. Bilingual.

9235 Valle, Victor Manuel. Ciudad de Los Angeles III. CHISMEARTE, (1982), p. 37. Bilingual.

9236 Valle, Victor Manuel. Mode of production. MAIZE, Vol. 2, no. 2 (Winter 1979), p. 52. English.

9237 Valle, Victor Manuel. The work. MAIZE, Vol. 2, no. 2 (Winter 1979), p. 51. English.

9238 Vallin, Violeta. Untitled Poem. COMADRE, no. 1 (Summer 1977), p. 1. English.

9239 Varela, Franklyn P. Electric cowboys, afternoon TV. REVISTA CHICANO-RIQUENA, Vol. 10, no. 3 (Summer 1982), p. 14-15. English.

9240 Varela, Franklyn P. Paulina in the shadows. REVISTA CHICANO-RIQUENA, Vol. 10, no. 3 (Summer 1982), p. 15. English.

9241 Vasquez, Pedro O. Dancing in blue/newday. MAIZE, Vol. 1, no. 1 (Fall 1977), p. 20. English.

9242 Vasquez, Pedro O. Dancing the moon. MAIZE, Vol. 1, no. 1 (Fall 1977), p. 18-19. English.

9243 Vasquez, Ricardo Esquer. No perfectamente romantica. MAIZE, Vol. 3, no. 1-2 (Fall, Winter, 1979, 1980), p. 55-57. Spanish.

9244 Vasquez, Ricardo Esquer. Para rosaura. MAIZE, Vol. 2, no. 1 (Fall 1978), p. 52-53. Spanish.

9245 Vigil, Evangelina. The bridge people. REVISTA CHICANO-RIQUENA, Vol. 11, no. 3-4 (Fall 1983), p. 50-51. English.

9246 Vigil, Evangelina. Dumb broad! REVISTA CHICANO-RIQUENA, Vol. 11, no. 3-4 (Fall 1983), p. 51-53. English.

9247 Vigil, Evangelina. Es todo! REVISTA CHICANO-RIQUENA, Vol. 10, no. 1-2 (Winter, Spring, 1982), p. 142. Bilingual.

9248 Vigil, Evangelina. La loca. MAIZE, Vol. 1, no. 1 (Fall 1977), p. 36-37. Spanish.

9249 Vigil, Evangelina. Mente joven: nothin' like a pensative child, cold north wind flapping against his hair and tender face. REVISTA CHICANO-RIQUENA, Vol. 10, no. 1-2 (Winter, Spring, 1982), p. 145. English.

9250 Vigil, Evangelina. El mercado en san antonio where the tourists trot. MAIZE, Vol. 2, no. 3 (Spring 1979), p. 58-60. Spanish.

9251 Vigil, Evangelina. Para los que piensan con la verga (with due apologies to those who don't). MAIZE, Vol. 1, no. 1 (Fall 1977), p. 35. Bilingual.

9252 Vigil, Evangelina. Pluma asesina. REVISTA CHICANO-RIQUENA, Vol. 10, no. 1-2 (Winter, Spring, 1982), p. 148. Spanish.

Poetry (cont.)

9253 Vigil, Evangelina. Por la calle Zarzamora.
REVISTA CHICANO-RIQUENA, Vol. 10, no. 1-2
(Winter, Spring, 1982), p. 146-147. Calo.

9254 Vigil, Evangelina. Ritual en un instante.
REVISTA CHICANO-RIQUENA, Vol. 10, no. 1-2
(Winter, Spring, 1982), p. 147. Spanish.

9255 Vigil, Evangelina. Ser conforme. REVISTA
CHICANO-RIQUENA, Vol. 10, no. 1-2 (Winter,
Spring, 1982), p. 141. English.

9256 Vigil, Evangelina. Telephone line. REVISTA
CHICANO-RIQUENA, Vol. 11, no. 3-4 (Fall
1983), p. 54-55. English.

9257 Vigil, Evangelina. Was fun running 'round
descalza. REVISTA CHICANO-RIQUENA, Vol. 10,
no. 1-2 (Winter, Spring, 1982), p. 143-144.
Bilingual.

9258 Villanueva, Tino. Haciendo apenas la
recoleccion. REVISTA CHICANO-RIQUENA, Vol.
10, no. 1-2 (Winter, Spring, 1982), p.
149-150. English.

9259 Villareal, Manuel. Que les parece? (una
critica nihilistica). CHISMEARTE, no. 9
(September 1983), p. 29. Spanish.

9260 Volborth, J. Ivaloo. Mad coyote dances.
MAIZE, Vol. 1, no. 4 (Summer 1978), p. 11.
English.

9261 Volborth, J. Ivaloo. Ya-lan. MAIZE, Vol. 1,
no. 4 (Summer 1978), p. 12. English.

9262 Watkins, Vicky. Reflexiones de un mojado.
MAIZE, Vol. 2, no. 1 (Fall 1978), p. 11.
Spanish.

9263 Watkins, Vicky. Salsipuedes. MAIZE, Vol. 2,
no. 1 (Fall 1978), p. 10. Spanish.

9264 Williams, Sherley Anne. The lost nigger
expedition. MAIZE, Vol. 3, no. 3-4 (Spring,
Summer, 1980), p. 45-47. English.

9265 Williams, Sherley Anne. Straight talk from
plain women. MAIZE, Vol. 1, no. 2 (Winter
1977), p. 19. English.

9266 Xelina. Chicharra. MAIZE, Vol. 3, no. 3-4
(Spring, Summer, 1980), p. 57-59. Bilingual.

9267 Xelina. Esterilization. MAIZE, Vol. 1, no. 1
(Fall 1977), p. 44. Spanish.

9268 Xelina. Mendiga. MAIZE, Vol. 1, no. 2
(Winter 1977), p. 16. Bilingual.

9269 Xelina. [Untitled]. MAIZE, Vol. 2, no. 1
(Fall 1978), p. 24-26. Spanish.

9270 Xelina. [Untitled poems]. MAIZE, Vol. 3, no.
1-2 (Fall, Winter, 1979, 1980), p. 49-51.
Bilingual.

9271 Xelina. Urbanization. MAIZE, Vol. 1, no. 1
(Fall 1977), p. 43. English.

9272 Xochicuitcatl. CALMECAC, Vol. 3, (Spring
1982), p. 38. English. **DESCR:** *Musical
Lyrics.

9273 Yanes, Jose. Para no hablarlo nunca con mi
madre. MAIZE, Vol. 3, no. 3-4 (Spring,
Summer, 1980), p. 80-81. Spanish.

9274 Yarbro-Bejarano, Yvonne. Teatropoesia by
Chicanas in the Bay Area: tongues of fire.
REVISTA CHICANO-RIQUENA, Vol. 11, no. 1
(Spring 1983), p. 78-94. English. **DESCR:**
Chicanas; El Teatro Nacional de Aztlan
(TENAZ); Teatro; *TONGUES OF FIRE.

9275 Zapata, Rodger. Cuando la nieve y mis
vecinos me saludan. MAIZE, Vol. 5, no. 1-2
(Fall, Winter, 1981, 1982), p. 52. Spanish.

9276 Zapata, Rodger. Lo que se ha de ver. MAIZE,
Vol. 5, no. 1-2 (Fall, Winter, 1981, 1982),
p. 52. Spanish.

9277 Zimmerman, Enid. An annotated bibliography
of Chicano literature: novels, short
fiction, poetry, and drama, 1970-1980.
BILINGUAL REVIEW, Vol. 9, no. 3 (September,
December, 1982), p. 227-251. English.
DESCR: *Bibliography; Literature; Teatro.

Poets

USE: Authors

Police

9278 Fifth member leaves panel. NUESTRO, Vol. 6,
no. 4 (May 1982), p. 11. English. **DESCR:**
*Lew, Salvador; Little Havana; Miami, FL;
Violence.

9279 Hail to the chief. HISPANIC BUSINESS, Vol.
4, no. 8 (August 1983), p. 10+. English.
DESCR: Criminal Justice System; *Ortega,
Ruben; Phoenix, AZ.

9280 How to resolve police-community conflict.
LATINO, Vol. 54, no. 5 (August, September,
1983), p. 14. English. **DESCR:**
*Police-Community Relations.

9281 Lathrop, Richard A. Out of tragedy. NUESTRO,
Vol. 6, no. 4 (May 1982), p. 19-22+.
English. **DESCR:** *Violence.

9282 Long, William J. and Pohl, Christopher M.
Joint foot patrols succeed in El Paso.
POLICE CHIEF, Vol. 50, no. 4 (April 1983),
p. 49-51. English. **DESCR:** Border Patrol;
Ciudad Juarez, Chihuahua, Mexico; Criminal
Acts; *El Paso, TX; Immigration Regulation
and Control; Undocumented Workers; Youth.

9283 Police and immigration. NUESTRO, Vol. 7, no.
2 (March 1983), p. 7. English. **DESCR:**
*Border Patrol; El Paso, TX; Federal
Government; *Immigration Law; Immigration
Regulation and Control.

9284 Police misconduct [panel discussion at the
LATINOS IN THE LAW symposium, UCLA, 1982].
CHICANO LAW REVIEW, Vol. 6, (1983), p.
63-121. English. **DESCR:** Los Angeles Police
Department; Love, Eulia; Nettles, Ron;
*Police Brutality.

9285 Reporter beaten for story pursuit. NUESTRO,
Vol. 7, no. 1 (January, February, 1983), p.
11-12. English. **DESCR:** *Berio, Yvonne C.;
Journalists; San Juan, Puerto Rico.

9286 Rivas, Mike. Keeping peace in paradise.
NATIONAL HISPANIC JOURNAL, Vol. 1, no. 2
(Winter 1982), p. 13-20. English. **DESCR:**
*Brand, Othal; Casso, Ramiro; Elections;
Police Brutality; *Political Repression; Rio
Grande Valley, TX; THE MEXICAN AMERICAN:
QUEST FOR EQUALITY; Voter Turnout.

9287 Somers, Adele. Improving human relations
between the Hispanic community and law
enforcement. POLICE CHIEF, Vol. 49, no. 3
(March 1982), p. 32-33. English. **DESCR:**
Police-Community Relations; Spanish
Language.

Police (cont.)

9288 [Summary of: race as an employment
qualification to meet police department
operational needs, 54 N.Y.U.L. rev. 413
(1979)]. CHICANO LAW REVIEW, Vol. 5,
(1982), p. 81-82. English. **DESCR**:
Administration of Justice; Employment Tests.

9289 Tenants redo neighborhood. NUESTRO, Vol. 6,
no. 2 (March 1982), p. 14. English. **DESCR**:
*Barrios.

9290 Velez, Larry A. Sonia Berdequez; police
detective. NUESTRO, Vol. 6, no. 1 (January,
February, 1982), p. 20-21. English. **DESCR**:
*Berdeguez, Sonia Estela; Fashion; Latin
Americans.

Police Brutality

9291 Latinos in the law: meeting the challenge [
a symposium]. CHICANO LAW REVIEW, Vol. 6,
(1983), p. 1-121. English. **DESCR**: *Criminal
Justice System; Demography; Legal
Profession; Los Angeles Police Department;
Love, Eulia; Political Representation;
Reapportionment; Settles, Ron.

9292 Police misconduct [panel discussion at the
LATINOS IN THE LAW symposium, UCLA, 1982].
CHICANO LAW REVIEW, Vol. 6, (1983), p.
63-121. English. **DESCR**: Los Angeles Police
Department; Love, Eulia; Nettles, Ron;
Police.

9293 Rivas, Mike. Keeping peace in paradise.
NATIONAL HISPANIC JOURNAL, Vol. 1, no. 2
(Winter 1982), p. 13-20. English. **DESCR**:
*Brand, Othal; Casso, Ramiro; Elections;
Police; *Political Repression; Rio Grande
Valley, TX; THE MEXICAN AMERICAN: QUEST FOR
EQUALITY; Voter Turnout.

Police-Community Relations

9294 How to resolve police-community conflict.
LATINO, Vol. 54, no. 5 (August, September,
1983), p. 14. English. **DESCR**: *Police.

9295 Somers, Adele. Improving human relations
between the Hispanic community and law
enforcement. POLICE CHIEF, Vol. 49, no. 3
(March 1982), p. 32-33. English. **DESCR**:
*Police; Spanish Language.

Policy

9296 Bustamante, Jorge A. The Mexicans are
coming: from ideology to labor relations.
INTERNATIONAL MIGRATION REVIEW, Vol. 17, no.
2 (Summer 1983), p. 323-341. English.
DESCR: Attitude (Psychological);
*Immigration; Immigration Law; Labor Laws
and Legislation; Labor Supply and Market;
Migration; Political Ideology;
*Simpson-Mazzoli Bill; Undocumented Workers.

Policy Formation

9297 Hewlett, Sylvia Ann. Coping with illegal
immigrants. FOREIGN AFFAIRS, Vol. 60, no. 2
(Winter 1981, 1982), p. 358-378. English.
DESCR: Immigrant Labor; Immigration;
Immigration Law; *Immigration Regulation and
Control; Undocumented Workers.

9298 Olivas, Michael A. Federal higher education
policy: the case of Hispanics. EDUCATIONAL
EVALUATION AND POLICY ANALYSIS, Vol. 4, no.
3 (Fall 1982), p. 301-310. English. **DESCR**:
Discrimination in Education; Education
Equalization; Educational Law and

Legislation; Federal Government; *Higher
Education.

9299 Rotberg, Iris C. Some legal and research
considerations in establishing federal
policy in bilingual education. HARVARD
EDUCATIONAL REVIEW, Vol. 52, no. 2 (May
1982), p. 149-168. English. **DESCR**:
*Bilingual Bicultural Education; Educational
Law and Legislation; History; Research
Methodology.

Political Appointments
USE: Appointed Officials

Political Asylum

9300 Cuban-exile community protests deportation
of recent escapee. NUESTRO, Vol. 6, no. 2
(March 1982), p. 32-34. English. **DESCR**:
Cubanos; Immigration and Naturalization
Service (INS); *Rodriguez Hernandez, Andres.

Political Economy

9301 Pedraza Bailey, Silvia. Cubans and Mexicans
in the United States: the functions of
political and economic migration. CUBAN
STUDIES, Vol. 11, no. 2-1 (1981, 1982), p.
70-103. English. **DESCR**: Cubanos; Immigrants;
*Migration; Political Refugees.

9302 Valdez, Abelardo L. From Simon Bolivar to
the Malvinas and beyond. NUESTRO, Vol. 7,
no. 7 (September 1983), p. 38-41. English.
DESCR: *Bolivar, Simon; Latin America;
*Political History and Conditions; South
America.

Political History and Conditions

9303 Breiter, Toni. El Libertador: a profile.
NUESTRO, Vol. 7, no. 7 (September 1983), p.
32-35. English. **DESCR**: Biography; *Bolivar,
Simon; Revolutions; South America.

9304 Cohen, Gaynor. Alliance and conflict among
Mexican-Americans. ETHNIC AND RACIAL
STUDIES, Vol. 5, no. 2 (April 1982), p.
175-195. English. **DESCR**: Identity;
Segregation and Desegregation.

9305 Crisp, James E. Book review of: MEXICANO
RESISTANCE IN THE SOUTHWEST: "THE SACRED
RIGHT OF SELF-PRESERVATION". JOURNAL OF
SOUTHERN HISTORY, Vol. 48, no. 1 (1982), p.
138-139. English. **DESCR**: Book Reviews;
*MEXICANO RESISTANCE IN THE SOUTHWEST: "THE
SACRED RIGHT OF SELF-PRESERVATION";
Rosenbaum, Robert J.; United States-Mexico
Relations.

9306 Cruz, Amaury. El Salvador: realities of a
country at war. NUESTRO, Vol. 6, no. 3
(April 1982), p. 14-17+. English. **DESCR**: *El
Salvador; Poverty; Short Story; Tourism.

9307 Fraser Rothenberg, Irene. Mexican-American
views of U.S. relations with Latin America.
JOURNAL OF ETHNIC STUDIES, Vol. 6, no. 1
(Spring 1978), p. 62-78. English. **DESCR**:
Chicano Movement; Culture; Identity;
International Relations; Latin America;
Lobbying; Mexico; *Nationalism; Politics.

9308 Garcia, Ignacio M. El Salvador: profile of a
nation at war. NUESTRO, Vol. 7, no. 8
(October 1983), p. 26-36. English. **DESCR**:
*El Salvador; Guerrillas; Military; War.

Political History and Conditions (cont.)

9309 Maciel, David R. Nacionalismo cultural y politica liberal en la Republica Restaurada, 1867-1876. AZTLAN, Vol. 14, no. 2 (Fall 1983), p. 267-287. Spanish. **DESCR:** History; *Mexico; *Physical Education; Political Ideology.

9310 Maldonado-Denis, Manuel. El problema de las nacionalidades: la experiencia caribena. Paper presented at the "Dialogo de las Americas" conference. Mexico, D.F. September 9-14, 1982. REVISTA CHICANO-RIQUENA, Vol. 10, no. 4 (Fall 1982), p. 39-45. Spanish. **DESCR:** Capitalism; Carpentier, Alejo; Cuba; El Salvador; Grenada; Guatemala; Imperialism; Marti, Jose; Nicaragua; Puerto Rico; United States.

9311 McDougall, George. The press and Puerto Rico. NUESTRO, Vol. 7, no. 6 (August 1983), p. 21-25. English. **DESCR:** Mass Media; *Puerto Rico.

9312 Morales, Cesareo. El impacto norteamericano en la politica economica de Mexico (1970-1983). CUADERNOS POLITICOS, Vol. 38, (October, December, 1983), p. 81-101. Spanish. **DESCR:** Economic History and Conditions; Mexico; *United States-Mexico Relations.

9313 Munoz, Carlos, Jr. and Barrera, Mario. La Raza Unida Party and the Chicano student movement in California. SOCIAL SCIENCE JOURNAL, Vol. 19, no. 2 (April 1982), p. 101-119. English. **DESCR:** California; *Chicano Movement; *La Raza Unida Party; Political Ideology; Political Parties and Organizations; Student Movements.

9314 Palacios, Gonzalo. Bolivar and contemporary Latin America. NUESTRO, Vol. 7, no. 7 (September 1983), p. 36-37. English. **DESCR:** *Bolivar, Simon; Latin America; Political Ideology; South America.

9315 Pena-Ramos, Alfonso. The Latin American disease: an essay. NUESTRO, Vol. 7, no. 6 (August 1983), p. 42-43. English. **DESCR:** *Latin America; Revolutions; Social History and Conditions.

9316 Rice, Jacqueline. Beyond the cientificos: the educational background of the Porfirian Elite. AZTLAN, Vol. 14, no. 2 (Fall 1983), p. 289-306. English. **DESCR:** History; La Union Liberal; Leadership; *Mexico; Political Parties and Organizations; *Social Classes.

9317 Simon, Jean-Marie. Five days in Nebaj: one perspective. NUESTRO, Vol. 7, no. 1 (January, February, 1983), p. 28-32. English. **DESCR:** *Guatemala; Nebaj, Guatemala.

9318 Valdez, Abelardo L. From Simon Bolivar to the Malvinas and beyond. NUESTRO, Vol. 7, no. 7 (September 1983), p. 38-41. English. **DESCR:** *Bolivar, Simon; Latin America; Political Economy; South America.

Political Ideology

9319 Banas, L. K. Donde estas? Conflicts in the Chicano movement (reprinted CARACOL June 1977). CALMECAC, Vol. 2, (Spring 1981), p. 28-33. English. **DESCR:** *CHICANISMO DEFINED; *Philosophy.

9320 Bustamante, Jorge A. The Mexicans are coming: from ideology to labor relations.

INTERNATIONAL MIGRATION REVIEW, Vol. 17, no. 2 (Summer 1983), p. 323-341. English. **DESCR:** Attitude (Psychological); *Immigration; Immigration Law; Labor Laws and Legislation; Labor Supply and Market; Migration; Policy; *Simpson-Mazzoli Bill; Undocumented Workers.

9321 Davis, James Alston. Does authority generalize? Locus of control perceptions in Anglo-American and Mexican-American adolescents. POLITICAL PSYCHOLOGY, Vol. 4, no. 1 (March 1983), p. 101-120. English. **DESCR:** Comparative Psychology; Family; High School Students; Internal-External Reinforcement Scale; *Locus of Control.

9322 Lamare, James W. Political integration of Mexican American children: a generational analysis. INTERNATIONAL MIGRATION REVIEW, Vol. 16, no. 1 (Spring 1982), p. 169-188. English. **DESCR:** Acculturation; Age Groups; Assimilation; *Children; Immigration; *Political Socialization.

9323 Maciel, David R. Nacionalismo cultural y politica liberal en la Republica Restaurada, 1867-1876. AZTLAN, Vol. 14, no. 2 (Fall 1983), p. 267-287. Spanish. **DESCR:** History; *Mexico; *Physical Education; Political History and Conditions.

9324 Moss, Bernard H. Political values and career aspirations of UCLA law students: the 70's generation. CHICANO LAW REVIEW, Vol. 5, (1982), p. 13-28. English. **DESCR:** *Law Schools; Legal Education; Legal Profession; Student Movements; Students.

9325 Munoz, Carlos, Jr. and Barrera, Mario. La Raza Unida Party and the Chicano student movement in California. SOCIAL SCIENCE JOURNAL, Vol. 19, no. 2 (April 1982), p. 101-119. English. **DESCR:** California; *Chicano Movement; *La Raza Unida Party; Political History and Conditions; Political Parties and Organizations; Student Movements.

9326 Palacios, Gonzalo. Bolivar and contemporary Latin America. NUESTRO, Vol. 7, no. 7 (September 1983), p. 36-37. English. **DESCR:** *Bolivar, Simon; Latin America; Political History and Conditions; South America.

9327 Trevino, Jesus Salvador. Form and technique in Chicano cinema. BILINGUAL REVIEW, Vol. 10, no. 2-3 (May, December, 1983), p. 109-115. English. **DESCR:** *Films.

Political Participation
 USE: Voter Turnout

Political Parties and Organizations

9328 Baca Barragan, Polly; Hamner, Richard; and Guerrero, Lena. [Untitled interview with State Senators (Colorado) Polly Baca-Barragan and Lena Guerrero. NATIONAL HISPANIC JOURNAL, Vol. 1, no. 2 (Winter 1982), p. 8-11. English. **DESCR:** Baca Barragan, Polly; *Carter, Jimmy (President); Chicanas; Democratic Party; Elected Officials; Guerrero, Lena.

9329 Barreto, Julio. Reagan record attacked. LATINO, Vol. 53, no. 5 (September 1982), p. 24. English. **DESCR:** *Reagan Administration.

Political Parties and Organizations (cont.)

9330 Changing Hispanic political loyalties. HISPANIC BUSINESS, Vol. 4, no. 6 (June 1982), p. 23. English. **DESCR:** Los Angeles, CA; Politics; Public Policy; San Antonio, TX; *Surveys.

9331 Conservative Hispanic groups gaining strength attracting suitors. HISPANIC BUSINESS, Vol. 4, no. 2 (February 1982), p. 29. English. **DESCR:** Democratic Party; Politics; Republican Party.

9332 Cruz, Franklin D. Upcoming Republican strategies. HISPANIC BUSINESS, Vol. 4, no. 10 (October 1982), p. 21,30. English. **DESCR:** Republican Party.

9333 Grimond, John. Reconquista begins. ECONOMIST (London), Vol. 283, (April 3, 1982), p. 12-17. English. **DESCR:** *Political Representation; Public Policy; The East Los Angeles Community Union (TELACU); United Neighborhoods Organization (UNO).

9334 Hamner, Richard. Hispanic update: Hispanics and the Republican Party. NATIONAL HISPANIC JOURNAL, Vol. 1, no. 2 (Winter 1982), p. 5. English. **DESCR:** *Republican National Committee; Republican National Hispanic Assembly; Republican Party.

9335 Hispanic caucus announces plans. NUESTRO, Vol. 7, no. 6 (August 1983), p. 12-13. English. **DESCR:** *Congressional Hispanic Caucus; National Hispanic Heritage Week.

9336 Hispanic leader reaction to Governor White: Republicans fail to overcome Democratic one-two punch. NATIONAL HISPANIC JOURNAL, Vol. 1, no. 4 (Spring 1983), p. 8. English. **DESCR:** Clements, Bill; Mexican American Republicans of Texas; *Voter Turnout; White, Mark.

9337 Hispanics wooed by Reagan, Demos. NUESTRO, Vol. 7, no. 8 (October 1983), p. 11-12. English. **DESCR:** Congressional Hispanic Caucus; *National Hispanic Heritage Week; Reagan, Ronald.

9338 Holley, Joe. Page two. TEXAS OBSERVOR, Vol. 75, no. 1 (January 14, 1983), p. 2-3. English. **DESCR:** *Communities Organized for Public Service (COPS); Cultural Organizations; Educational Law and Legislation.

9339 The invisible Puerto Rican vote. HISPANIC BUSINESS, Vol. 5, no. 10 (October 1983), p. 34-36. English. **DESCR:** Elections; Puerto Ricans; *Voter Turnout.

9340 Latino gate to the White House. LATINO, Vol. 54, no. 6 (October 1983), p. 18-19. English. **DESCR:** Politics.

9341 Laws, Bart. Raza unida de Cristal. SOUTHERN EXPOSURE, Vol. 10, no. 2 (March, April, 1982), p. 67-72. English. **DESCR:** Crystal City, TX; Gurule, Dorothy; History; La Raza Unida Party; Mexican American Youth Organization (MAYO); Reyes, Carlos.

9342 Miller, Michael V. Chicano community control in South Texas: problems and prospects. JOURNAL OF ETHNIC STUDIES, Vol. 3, no. 3 (Fall 1975), p. 70-89. English. **DESCR:** Chicano Movement; Crystal City, TX; Gutierrez, Jose Angel; History; La Raza Unida Party; Patron System; Social Classes; Social History and Conditions; *South Texas.

9343 Munoz, Carlos, Jr. and Barrera, Mario. La Raza Unida Party and the Chicano student movement in California. SOCIAL SCIENCE JOURNAL, Vol. 19, no. 2 (April 1982), p. 101-119. English. **DESCR:** California; *Chicano Movement; *La Raza Unida Party; Political History and Conditions; Political Ideology; Student Movements.

9344 New Mexico's gubernatorial race. HISPANIC BUSINESS, Vol. 4, no. 11 (November 1982), p. 27,30. English. **DESCR:** Anaya, Toney; *Biography; Elections; New Mexico.

9345 Politicians you didn't vote for. NUESTRO, Vol. 5, no. 8 (November 1981), p. 18-20. English. **DESCR:** Burgillo, Luis; *Congressional Aides; Latin Americans; *Politics.

9346 Presidential election 1984. NUESTRO, Vol. 7, no. 7 (September 1983), p. 14-19. English. **DESCR:** Anderson, John; Askew, Reubin; Cranston, Alan; Elected Officials; *Elections; Fernandez, Ben; Glenn, John; Hart, Gary; Hispanic Force '84; Hollings, Ernest "Fritz"; Mondale, Walter; Reagan, Ronald.

9347 Rice, Jacqueline. Beyond the cientificos: the educational background of the Porfirian Elite. AZTLAN, Vol. 14, no. 2 (Fall 1983), p. 289-306. English. **DESCR:** History; La Union Liberal; Leadership; *Mexico; Political History and Conditions; *Social Classes.

9348 Rips, Geoffrey. COPS educates. TEXAS OBSERVOR, Vol. 75, no. 4 (February 25, 1983), p. 1-2. English. **DESCR:** *Communities Organized for Public Service (COPS); Cultural Organizations; Educational Law and Legislation.

9349 Rips, Geoffrey. New politics in Texas: COPS comes to Austin. TEXAS OBSERVOR, Vol. 75, no. 1 (January 14, 1983), p. 1+. English. **DESCR:** *Communities Organized for Public Service (COPS); Cultural Organizations; Educational Law and Legislation.

9350 Wells, Miriam J. Political mediation and agricultural cooperation: strawberry farms in California. ECONOMIC DEVELOPMENT AND CULTURAL CHANGE, Vol. 30, no. 2 (January 1982), p. 413-432. English. **DESCR:** *Agricultural Cooperatives; Agricultural Laborers; California; Cooperativa Campesina; Cooperativa Central; Rural Economics.

Political Prisoners

9351 Garcia, Ignacio M. America says, welcome home. NUESTRO, Vol. 6, no. 9 (November 1982), p. 15-19+. English. **DESCR:** *Alvarez, Everett, Jr.; *Veterans; Vietnam; Vietnam War.

9352 Greenfield, Charles. Armando Valladares: twenty-two years of solitude. NUESTRO, Vol. 7, no. 10 (December 1983), p. 14-18+. English. **DESCR:** Cuba; Political Repression; *Valladares, Armando.

9353 Greenfield, Charles. Life imitating art: a profile of Reynaldo Arenas. NUESTRO, Vol. 7, no. 5 (June, July, 1983), p. 40-42. English. **DESCR:** Arenas, Reynaldo; *Authors; *Cuba; *Cubanos; El Morro Prison, Cuba.

Political Prisoners (cont.)

9354 Mimiaga, Hector. Back in the step with
America's Drummers: I feel good again.
NUESTRO, Vol. 6, no. 9 (November 1982), p.
20. English. **DESCR:** *Benavidez, Roy;
Veterans; Vietnam War.

Political Refugees

9355 Camacho de Schmidt, Aurora. Alien smuggling
and the refugee question: the INS and
sojourners from Yalaj. NUESTRO, Vol. 7, no.
5 (June, July, 1983), p. 20. English.
DESCR: *Guatemala; *Immigration Regulation
and Control; Refugees; *Undocumented
Workers.

9356 Chavira, Ricardo. Mexico opens door to
refugees. NUESTRO, Vol. 6, no. 5 (June,
July, 1982), p. 48. English.

9357 Concha, Jaime. Exilio, conciencia: coda
sobre la poesia de Millan. MAIZE, Vol. 5,
no. 1-2 (Fall, Winter, 1981, 1982), p. 7-15.
Spanish. **DESCR:** Chile; Jesuits; Literary
Criticism; Literary History; *Millan,
Gonzalo; Poetry.

9358 Haitian boat people. NUESTRO, Vol. 5, no. 8
(November 1981), p. 10. English. **DESCR:**
*Economic Refugees; *Haiti; World Bank.

9359 Pedraza Bailey, Silvia. Cubans and Mexicans
in the United States: the functions of
political and economic migration. CUBAN
STUDIES, Vol. 11, no. 2-1 (1981, 1982), p.
70-103. English. **DESCR:** Cubanos; Immigrants;
*Migration; Political Economy.

9360 Salvatierra, Richard. Alien smuggling and
the refugee question: U.S. must set a limit
on refugees. NUESTRO, Vol. 7, no. 5 (June,
July, 1983), p. 19. English. **DESCR:**
Federation for American Immigration Reform
(FAIR); *Immigration Regulation and Control;
Refugees; *Undocumented Workers.

Political Representation

9361 "A mi no me afecta" "It doesn't affect me".
CORAZON DE AZTLAN, Vol. 1, no. 2 (March,
April, 1982), p. 4-5. Bilingual. **DESCR:**
*Whittier Blvd., Los Angeles, CA.

9362 Agudelo, C. Wooing the Hispanics. WORLD
PRESS REVIEW, Vol. 30, (November 1983), p.
43. English. **DESCR:** Voter Turnout.

9363 Allende, Luz B. Beyond the Sunday sermon.
APUNTES, Vol. 3, no. 1 (Spring 1983), p.
10-14. English. **DESCR:** *Voter Turnout.

9364 Applebome, Peter. The unkindest cut. TEXAS
MONTHLY, Vol. 11, no. 1 (January 1983), p.
74-80. English. **DESCR:** *Blacks; Corpus
Christi, TX; Voter Turnout.

9365 Barreto, Julio. Amigos o adversarios.
LATINO, Vol. 53, no. 6 (October 1982), p.
13. Spanish.

9366 Barry, Patrick and Zavala, Antonio. Election
'83: Chicago's Latinos awake, but not
united. NUESTRO, Vol. 7, no. 1 (January,
February, 1983), p. 20-23. English. **DESCR:**
*Chicago, IL; *Elections; Voter Turnout.

9367 Cardenas, Leo. The Bonilla years come to an
end. LATINO, Vol. 54, no. 4 (May, June,
1983), p. 8-9+. English. **DESCR:** Biography;
*Bonilla, Tony.

9368 Cardenas, Leo. Five simple words. LATINO,

Vol. 53, no. 7 (November 1982), p. 4.
English.

9369 Equality. LATINO, Vol. 53, no. 6 (October
1982), p. 8-9. English.

9370 Grimond, John. Reconquista begins. ECONOMIST
(London), Vol. 283, (April 3, 1982), p.
12-17. English. **DESCR:** Political Parties and
Organizations; Public Policy; The East Los
Angeles Community Union (TELACU); United
Neighborhoods Organization (UNO).

9371 Hamner, Richard. Hispanics and
redistricting: what you see is not always
what you get. NATIONAL HISPANIC JOURNAL,
Vol. 1, no. 2 (Winter 1982), p. 25-30.
English. **DESCR:** Berlanga, Hugo; Elections;
Hispanic Reapportionment District; National
Association of Latino Elected Officials
(NALEO); Politics; *Reapportionment;
*Roybal, Edward R.; Santillan, Richard.

9372 Hands of unity. LATINO, Vol. 54, no. 3
(April 1983), p. 6+. English.

9373 Latinos in the law: meeting the challenge [
a symposium]. CHICANO LAW REVIEW, Vol. 6,
(1983), p. 1-121. English. **DESCR:** *Criminal
Justice System; Demography; Legal
Profession; Los Angeles Police Department;
Love, Eulia; Police Brutality;
Reapportionment; Settles, Ron.

9374 MacManus, Susan A. and Cassel, Carol A.
Mexican-Americans in city-politics:
participation, representation, and policy
preferences. URBAN INTEREST, Vol. 4, no. 1
(Spring 1982), p. 57-69. English. **DESCR:**
Blacks; Houston, TX; Local Government;
Public Opinion; Public Policy.

9375 Rainbow coalition. LATINO, Vol. 54, no. 6
(October 1983), p. 10. Spanish. **DESCR:**
Bonilla, Tony; *Jackson, Jesse.

9376 Rips, Geoffrey. Mexican Americans jalaron la
palanca, Democrats say ole. TEXAS OBSERVOR,
Vol. 75, (January 1983), p. 6-7. English.
DESCR: Democratic Party; Texas; *Voter
Turnout.

9377 Rodriguez, Roberto. Free and fair elections
are supposed to be what distinguishes a
democracy from a dictatorship. CORAZON DE
AZTLAN, Vol. 1, no. 3 (August, September,
1982), p. 31-34. English. **DESCR:** Voter
Turnout.

9378 Santillan, Richard. The Chicano community
and the redistricting of the Los Angeles
city council, 1971-1973. CHICANO LAW REVIEW,
Vol. 6, (1983), p. 122-145. English.
DESCR: Chicanos for Fair Representation
(CFR), Los Angeles, CA; Los Angeles City
Council; Mexican American Legal Defense and
Educational Fund (MALDEF); Snyder, Art,
Councilman.

9379 Santillan, Richard. [Translating population
numbers into political power]. CHICANO LAW
REVIEW, Vol. 6, (1983), p. 16-21. English.
DESCR: Californios for Fair Representation;
Carrillo v. Whittier Union High School;
LATINOS IN THE LAW [symposium], UCLA, 1982;
MEXICAN AMERICAN LEGAL DEFENSE AND
EDUCATIONAL FUND NEWSLETTER;
Reapportionment; *Voter Turnout.

Political Representation (cont.)

9380 Su voto es su voz. NUESTRO, Vol. 6, no. 7 (September 1982), p. 41. English. DESCR: Congressional Hispanic Caucus; Political System; Politics; *Voter Turnout; *Voting Rights; *Voting Rights Act.

9381 Villarreal, Roberto E. and Kelly, Philip. Mexican Americans as participants in United States-Mexico relations. INTERNATIONAL STUDIES NOTES, Vol. 9, no. 4 (Winter 1982), p. 1-6. English. DESCR: International Relations; Mexico; *United States-Mexico Relations.

9382 Whisler, Kirk. Hispanic candidates: getting serious. CAMINOS, Vol. 3, no. 5 (May 1982), p. 24-25. Bilingual. DESCR: *Elections.

Political Repression

9383 Garcia, Reyes. Politics of flesh: ethnicity and political viability. CACR REVIEW, Vol. 1, no. 1 (September 1982), p. 102-130. English. DESCR: Anaya, Rudolfo A.; Aristotle; Culture; Ethnic Groups; Identity; Locke, John; Nuclear Armament; Philosophy; Urban Communities.

9384 Greenfield, Charles. Armando Valladares: twenty-two years of solitude. NUESTRO, Vol. 7, no. 10 (December 1983), p. 14-18+. English. DESCR: Cuba; *Political Prisoners; *Valladares, Armando.

9385 Peterson, Sarah; Mashek, John W.; and Obledo, Mario. Hispanics set their sights on ballot box. U.S. NEWS & WORLD REPORT, Vol. 95, no. 8 (August 22, 1983), p. 48-49. English. DESCR: Obledo, Mario; *Voter Turnout.

9386 Rivas, Mike. Keeping peace in paradise. NATIONAL HISPANIC JOURNAL, Vol. 1, no. 2 (Winter 1982), p. 13-20. English. DESCR: *Brand, Othal; Casso, Ramiro; Elections; Police; Police Brutality; Rio Grande Valley, TX; THE MEXICAN AMERICAN: QUEST FOR EQUALITY; Voter Turnout.

Political Science

9387 Hispanic caucus offers Washington, fellowships. NUESTRO, Vol. 6, no. 3 (April 1982), p. 62. English. DESCR: *Careers; *Congressional Hispanic Caucus.

9388 McCollough, Dale W. Institutions, governance and confusion in our time. NATIONAL HISPANIC JOURNAL, Vol. 1, no. 4 (Spring 1983), p. 23. English.

Political Socialization

9389 Lamare, James W. Political integration of Mexican American children: a generational analysis. INTERNATIONAL MIGRATION REVIEW, Vol. 16, no. 1 (Spring 1982), p. 169-188. English. DESCR: Acculturation; Age Groups; Assimilation; *Children; Immigration; Political Ideology.

Political System

9390 Su voto es su voz. NUESTRO, Vol. 6, no. 7 (September 1982), p. 41. English. DESCR: Congressional Hispanic Caucus; Political Representation; Politics; *Voter Turnout; *Voting Rights; *Voting Rights Act.

Politicos

USE: Elected Officials

Politics

9391 Anaya, Toney. Una alianza politica hispana. LATINO, Vol. 54, no. 2 (March 1983), p. 14-15. Spanish.

9392 Anaya, Toney. Hispanics need political clout. CAMINOS, Vol. 4, no. 1-2 (January, February, 1983), p. 62-64,76. Bilingual. DESCR: *Voter Turnout.

9393 Arroyo, Antonio M. Stevens. Un hispano para vice-presidente. LATINO, Vol. 53, no. 5 (September 1982), p. 18. Spanish.

9394 Barreto, Julio. Ready for battle; organizations draft legislative agenda. NUESTRO, Vol. 6, no. 3 (April 1982), p. 18-20. English.

9395 Black-Hispanic coalition. LATINO, Vol. 53, no. 2 (March, April, 1982), p. 25. English. DESCR: *Blacks; King, Coretta Scott.

9396 Blanco seeks votes in U.S. NUESTRO, Vol. 6, no. 3 (April 1982), p. 11. English. DESCR: *Blanco, Salvador Jorge.

9397 Bonilla, Tony. 1982 was a memorable year. LATINO, Vol. 53, no. 8 (December 1982), p. 6. English.

9398 California economist considering candidacy. NUESTRO, Vol. 6, no. 5 (June, July, 1982), p. 29. English. DESCR: *Fernandez, Ben.

9399 Changing Hispanic political loyalties. HISPANIC BUSINESS, Vol. 4, no. 6 (June 1982), p. 23. English. DESCR: Los Angeles, CA; *Political Parties and Organizations; Public Policy; San Antonio, TX; *Surveys.

9400 A close look at Mario Obledo. LATINO, Vol. 54, no. 5 (August, September, 1983), p. 10. English. DESCR: Elected Officials; *Obledo, Mario.

9401 Conservative Hispanic groups gaining strength attracting suitors. HISPANIC BUSINESS, Vol. 4, no. 2 (February 1982), p. 29. English. DESCR: Democratic Party; *Political Parties and Organizations; Republican Party.

9402 Education: is it only for the elitist? LATINO, Vol. 53, no. 2 (March, April, 1982), p. 27-28. English. DESCR: *Education.

9403 Five seek league highest office. LATINO, Vol. 54, no. 4 (May, June, 1983), p. 20. English.

9404 Foster, Charles R. Political culture and regional ethnic minorities. JOURNAL OF POLITICS, Vol. 44, no. 2 (May 1982), p. 560-568. English. DESCR: *Ethnic Groups.

9405 Fraser Rothenberg, Irene. Chicanos, the Panama Canal issues and the Reagan campaign: reflections from 1976 and projections for 1980. JOURNAL OF ETHNIC STUDIES, Vol. 7, no. 4 (Winter 1980), p. 37-49. English. DESCR: *International Relations; Lobbying; Nationalism; Newspapers; Panama; *Panama Canal; Reagan, Ronald.

Politics (cont.)

9406 Fraser Rothenberg, Irene. Mexican-American views of U.S. relations with Latin America. JOURNAL OF ETHNIC STUDIES, Vol. 6, no. 1 (Spring 1978), p. 62-78. English. **DESCR:** Chicano Movement; Culture; Identity; International Relations; Latin America; Lobbying; Mexico; *Nationalism; Political History and Conditions.

9407 Garcia, John A. Ethnicity and Chicanos: measurement of ethnic identification, identity and consciousness. HISPANIC JOURNAL OF BEHAVIORAL SCIENCES, Vol. 4, no. 3 (September 1982), p. 295-314. English. **DESCR:** *Identity; *National Chicano Survey of Mexicans.

9408 Gordon, Ronald. A Reagan push. LATINO, Vol. 54, no. 5 (August, September, 1983), p. 20. English.

9409 Gurwitt, Rob. Widespread political efforts open new era for Hispanics. CONGRESSIONAL QUARTERLY WEEKLY REPORT, Vol. 40, (October 23, 1982), p. 2707-2709. English. **DESCR:** Biculturalism; Elected Officials.

9410 Hamner, Richard. Hispanics and redistricting: what you see is not always what you get. NATIONAL HISPANIC JOURNAL, Vol. 1, no. 2 (Winter 1982), p. 25-30. English. **DESCR:** Berlanga, Hugo; Elections; Hispanic Reapportionment District; National Association of Latino Elected Officials (NALEO); Political Representation; *Reapportionment; *Roybal, Edward R.; Santillan, Richard.

9411 Hispanic politics: the power is there. CAMINOS, Vol. 4, no. 3 (March 1983), p. 36-37,51+. Bilingual.

9412 Huerta, John. The future of Latino political power. CAMINOS, Vol. 4, no. 3 (March 1983), p. 44-46,49. English. **DESCR:** Census; *Voter Turnout.

9413 Latino gate to the White House. LATINO, Vol. 54, no. 6 (October 1983), p. 18-19. English. **DESCR:** *Political Parties and Organizations.

9414 League protests appointment to Arizona post. LATINO, Vol. 54, no. 6 (October 1983), p. 21. English. **DESCR:** *Appointed Officials; League of United Latin American Citizens (LULAC).

9415 LULAC 1983 national convention to be in Detroit. LATINO, Vol. 53, no. 8 (December 1982), p. 25. English. **DESCR:** *League of United Latin American Citizens (LULAC).

9416 LULAC board appointments. LATINO, Vol. 54, no. 8 (December 1983), p. 20. English. **DESCR:** *League of United Latin American Citizens (LULAC).

9417 LULAC train is rolling. LATINO, Vol. 53, no. 5 (September 1982), p. 9-11. English. **DESCR:** *League of United Latin American Citizens (LULAC).

9418 Martinez, Chip. Agui vienen los Pena. LATINO, Vol. 54, no. 5 (August, September, 1983), p. 12+. Spanish.

9419 Members to LULAC boards named. LATINO, Vol. 53, no. 8 (December 1982), p. 26. English. **DESCR:** *League of United Latin American Citizens (LULAC).

9420 Mercado, Vicente. El tambor publico. CORAZON DE AZTLAN, Vol. 1, no. 3 (August, September, 1982), p. 38. Spanish.

9421 Mercado, Vicente. El temor publico: la politica puro... CORAZON DE AZTLAN, Vol. 1, no. 2 (March, April, 1982), p. 10-11. Spanish.

9422 Mimiaga, Hector. El rey saluda a America. LATINO, Vol. 53, no. 2 (March, April, 1982), p. 13. English. **DESCR:** *Carlos, Juan, King of Spain.

9423 Montoya, David. Una nacion, divisible. LATINO, Vol. 53, no. 5 (September 1982), p. 14+. Spanish.

9424 Murray, Melissa. Aqui en Tejas: de Zabala youth session set for August: students from throughout state to attend. NATIONAL HISPANIC JOURNAL, Vol. 2, no. 1 (Summer 1983), p. 7. English. **DESCR:** Education; National Hispanic Institute; Students; *Youth.

9425 Murray, Melissa and De Leon, Hector. Texas politics: a frank talk about leadership, Austin, state government and attorney Hector de Leon. NATIONAL HISPANIC JOURNAL, Vol. 1, no. 4 (Spring 1983), p. 10-13. English. **DESCR:** Clements, Bill; De Leon, Hector; Texas; White, Mark.

9426 Lacayo, Carmela G. A response to conservatism: a Democrat's opinion. CAMINOS, Vol. 3, no. 3 (March 1982), p. 42-43,62. Bilingual. **DESCR:** *Democratic Party.

9427 New flavor for Hispanics. LATINO, Vol. 54, no. 5 (August, September, 1983), p. 13. English.

9428 Nieto, Ernesto. Politics: powers that struggled in the Texas Valley. NATIONAL HISPANIC JOURNAL, Vol. 2, no. 1 (Summer 1983), p. 22-23. English. **DESCR:** Elections; McAllen, TX; *Rio Grande Valley, TX; Voter Turnout.

9429 Nuestra gente. LATINO, Vol. 54, no. 8 (December 1983), p. 30. English. **DESCR:** *Biographical Notes; Businesspeople; Carter, Lynda Cordoba; Duran, Sandra; Patino, Lorenzo E.; Rembis, Deborah; Vega, Christopher.

9430 Oaxaca, Fernando. The new Hispanic conservative: a Republican opinion. CAMINOS, Vol. 3, no. 3 (March 1982), p. 40-41,62. Bilingual. **DESCR:** *Republican Party.

9431 Obledo to lecture at University of Madrid. LATINO, Vol. 54, no. 8 (December 1983), p. 21. English. **DESCR:** *Obledo, Mario.

9432 Padilla, Steve. Latinos wield political clout in midterm election. NUESTRO, Vol. 6, no. 9 (November 1982), p. 28-30. English. **DESCR:** De la Garza, Kika; *Elected Officials; Garcia, Robert; Gonzales, Henry B.; Lujan, Manuel, Jr.; Martinez, Matthew G. "Marty", Assemblyman; Ortiz, Solomon; Richardson, William; Roybal, Edward R.; *Torres, Esteban E.

9433 Political charges dismissed against Saldana. LATINO, Vol. 53, no. 8 (December 1982), p. 22. English. **DESCR:** *Saldana, Lupe.

Politics (cont.)

9434 Politicians you didn't vote for. NUESTRO,
Vol. 5, no. 8 (November 1981), p. 18-20.
English. DESCR: Burgillo, Luis;
*Congressional Aides; Latin Americans;
Political Parties and Organizations.

9435 Profile of a public man. NUESTRO, Vol. 7,
no. 2 (March 1983), p. 13-19+. English.
DESCR: Elected Officials; *Gonzalez, Henry
B.; Texas.

9436 Reagan's report card: F. LATINO, Vol. 53,
no. 3 (May 1982), p. 24-25. English. DESCR:
Civil Rights; *Reagan Administration.

9437 The rebirth of MAPA??? CAMINOS, Vol. 3, no.
9 (October 1982), p. 21. English. DESCR:
*Mexican American Political Association
(MAPA); Organizations.

9438 Rivera, Elaine. Fernandez envies Jackson
effort. NUESTRO, Vol. 7, no. 9 (November
1983), p. 13. English. DESCR: Elections;
*Fernandez, Ben; Jackson, Jesse.

9439 Su voto es su voz. NUESTRO, Vol. 6, no. 7
(September 1982), p. 41. English. DESCR:
Congressional Hispanic Caucus; Political
Representation; Political System; *Voter
Turnout; *Voting Rights; *Voting Rights Act.

9440 Turnure, Juan C. Hemisphere bulletin.
AGENDA, Vol. 11, no. 3 (May, June, 1981), p.
56-57. English. DESCR: *Economics; Latin
American Studies; Latin Americans.

9441 Two Hispanics on top ten list. LATINO, Vol.
53, no. 2 (March, April, 1982), p. 14.
English. DESCR: *Bonilla, Ruben; *Cisneros,
Henry, Mayor of San Antonio, TX; U.S. Junior
Chamber of Commerce.

9442 An unwanted favor. LATINO, Vol. 54, no. 6
(October 1983), p. 5. English.

9443 Whisler, Kirk. The California Republican
Hispanic Council: a new force/un nuevo
poder. CAMINOS, Vol. 3, no. 3 (March 1982),
p. 44-46. Bilingual. DESCR: *California
Republican Hispanic Council; Republican
Party.

9444 Whisler, Kirk. Hispanic Democrats. CAMINOS,
Vol. 3, no. 4 (April 1982), p. 37. English.
DESCR: *Democratic Party.

**POLITICS AND LANGUAGE: SPANISH AND ENGLISH IN THE
UNITED STATES**

9445 Macias, Reynaldo Flores. Book review of:
POLITICS AND LANGUAGE: SPANISH AND ENGLISH
IN THE UNITED STATES. NABE JOURNAL, Vol. 7,
no. 1 (Fall 1982), p. 61-66. English.
DESCR: Bilingualism; Book Reviews; Bruckner,
D.J.R.; Cultural Pluralism; Spanish
Language.

POLITICS AND MIGRANT POOR IN MEXICO CITY

9446 Logan, Kathleen. The urban poor in
developing nations. JOURNAL OF URBAN
HISTORY, Vol. 9, no. 1 (November 1982), p.
108-116. English. DESCR: ACCESS TO POWER:
POLITICS AND THE URBAN POOR IN DEVELOPING
NATIONS; *Book Reviews; BORDER BOOM TOWN:
CIUDAD JUAREZ SINCE 1848; Collier, David;
Cornelius, Wayne A.; Eckstein, Susan; Lloyd,
Peter; Martinez, Oscar J.; Nelson, Joan M.;
Perlman, Janice E.; SLUMS OF HOPE? SHANTY
TOWNS OF THE THIRD WORLD; SQUATTERS AND
OLIGARCHS: AUTHORITARIAN RULE AND POLICY
CHANGE IN PERU; THE MYTH OF MARGINALITY:

URBAN POVERTY AND POLITICS IN RIO DE
JANEIRO; THE POVERTY OF REVOLUTION: THE
STATE AND THE URBAN POOR IN MEXICO; Urban
Economics.

**THE POLITICS OF BILINGUAL EDUCATION: A STUDY OF
FOUR SOUTHWEST TEXAS COMMUNITIES**

9447 Dickens, E. Larry. Book review of: THE
POLITICS OF BILINGUAL EDUCATION: A STUDY OF
FOUR SOUTHWEST TEXAS COMMUNITIES. SOUTHWEST
ECONOMY AND SOCIETY, Vol. 1, no. 1 (Spring
1976), p. 47-48. English. DESCR: Bilingual
Bicultural Education; Book Reviews;
Hardgrave, Robert L.; Hinojosa, Santiago.

El Pollo Loco

9448 Business notes. HISPANIC BUSINESS, Vol. 5,
no. 12 (December 1983), p. 35. English.
DESCR: Anheuser-Busch, Inc.; *Business
Enterprises; Denny's Inc.; Des Moines, IA;
Food Industry; Local Government; Martinez,
Vilma Socorro; National Association of
Latino Elected Officials (NALEO); Ochoa,
Juan Pancho.

9449 Ogaz, Armando. The chicken wars. CAMINOS,
Vol. 4, no. 6 (June 1983), p. 10-11.
Bilingual. DESCR: Food Industry; Pioneer
Chicken; *Restaurants.

Pollution

9450 Abrams, Herbert K. Occupational and
environmental health problems along the
U.S.-Mexico Border. SOUTHWEST ECONOMY AND
SOCIETY, Vol. 4, no. 3 (Spring, Summer,
1979), p. 3-20. English. DESCR: Agricultural
Laborers; *Border Region; Housing; Mexican
Border Industrialization Program; Nutrition;
*Public Health; Social History and
Conditions.

9451 Bath, C. Richard. Health and environmental
problems: the role of the border in El
Paso-Ciudad Juarez coordination. JOURNAL OF
INTERAMERICAN STUDIES AND WORLD AFFAIRS,
Vol. 24, no. 3 (August 1982), p. 375-392.
English. DESCR: Border Region; Ciudad
Juarez, Chihuahua, Mexico; *El Paso, TX;
International Boundary and Water Commission;
Nationalism; *Public Health; United
States-Mexico Relations; U.S Border Public
Health Association (AFMES).

9452 Hansen, Niles. Trans boundary environmental
issues in the United States-Mexico
borderlands. SOUTHWESTERN REVIEW OF
MANAGEMENT AND ECONOMICS, Vol. 2, no. 1
(Winter 1982), p. 61-78. English. DESCR: Air
Pollution; Border Region; Water Pollution.

Pompa, Gilbert G.

9453 Nuestra gente. LATINO, Vol. 53, no. 3 (May
1982), p. 26. English. DESCR: Avila, Joaquin
Guadalupe; *Biographical Notes.

9454 President Reagan's appointments. CAMINOS,
Vol. 3, no. 3 (March 1982), p. 48-50.
Bilingual. DESCR: Appointed Officials;
*Federal Government; Flores Buckhart,
Elizabeth; Garcia, Ernest E.; Gonzalez, Luis
A.; Lozano, Diana; Reagan, Ronald; Sanchez,
Nestor D.; Zuniga, Henry.

Ponce, Manuel M.

9455 Lopez, Raymond. Manuel M. Ponce visto por un profesor norteamericano de ascendencia mexicana. HETEROFONIA, Vol. 15, no. 4 (October, December, 1982), p. 30-35. Spanish. **DESCR:** Music.

Ponce, Mary Helen

9456 Ponce, Mary Helen. El jabon de Dona Chonita. NUESTRO, Vol. 7, no. 10 (December 1983), p. 44-45. English. **DESCR:** Autobiography; Prose; *Reminiscences.

Ponce, Phil

9457 Lanier, Alfredo S. The quicksilver world of television news: Phil Ponce's Chicago beat. HISPANIC BUSINESS, Vol. 5, no. 10 (October 1983), p. 18-19+. English. **DESCR:** Journalism; *Television; WBBM-TV, Chicago, IL [television station].

Population

9458 1970s. LATINO, Vol. 53, no. 8 (December 1982), p. 14-15. English.

9459 1983 U.S. population reaches 232.6 million. NUESTRO, Vol. 7, no. 1 (January, February, 1983), p. 47. English. **DESCR:** Census; Population Trends.

9460 American as apple pie and tortillas. AMERICAN DEMOGRAPHICS, Vol. 4, (October 1982), p. 9. English. **DESCR:** *Demography.

9461 Bean, Frank D.; King, Allan G.; and Passel, Jeffrey S. The number of illegal migrants of Mexican origin in the United States: sex ratio-based estimates for 1980. DEMOGRAPHY, Vol. 20, no. 1 (February 1983), p. 99-109. English. **DESCR:** Census; Migration; Statistics; Undocumented Workers.

9462 Cantu, Felipe. Enorme crecimiento. LATINO, Vol. 53, no. 2 (March, April, 1982), p. 19-20. Spanish.

9463 Cantu, Hector. Hispanic numbers rising. NATIONAL HISPANIC JOURNAL, Vol. 1, no. 3 (Summer, Fall, 1982), p. 7. English. **DESCR:** Austin, TX; Census; Demography; *Population Trends.

9464 Garcia, Paco. Tampa: a centennial birthday in 1986. NUESTRO, Vol. 6, no. 10 (December 1982), p. 20-21. English. **DESCR:** Population Trends; *Tampa, FL.

9465 Gottlieb, Karen. Spanish surname as a market of Mexican heritage in Denver, Colorado. AMERICAN JOURNAL OF PHYSICAL ANTHROPOLOGY, Vol. 57, no. 2 (February 1982), p. 194. English. **DESCR:** Demography; *Spanish Surname.

9466 Guernica, Antonio. The Hispanic market: a profile. AGENDA, Vol. 11, no. 3 (May, June, 1981), p. 4-7. English. **DESCR:** *Consumers; Marketing; Mass Media; Population Distribution; Population Trends.

9467 Latino students rapidly increase. NUESTRO, Vol. 6, no. 10 (December 1982), p. 10. English. **DESCR:** *Los Angeles, CA; *Population Distribution; *Population Trends.

9468 Loehr, William. Hispanic phenomenon is not new. LATINO, Vol. 53, no. 4 (June 1982), p. 22+. English. **DESCR:** Biography; *Ferre, Maurice.

9469 Metro market ranking: Spanish-origin population. S & MM [SALES & MARKETING MANAGEMENT], Vol. 13, (July 25, 1983), p. B17. English. **DESCR:** *Consumers; Statistics.

9470 Metro market ranking: Spanish-origin population. S & MM [SALES & MARKETING MANAGEMENT], Vol. 12, no. 2 (July 26, 1982), p. B23. English.

9471 Relethfold, John H., et al. Social class, admixture, and skin color variation in Mexican-Americans and Anglo-Americans living in San Antonio, Texas. AMERICAN JOURNAL OF PHYSICAL ANTHROPOLOGY, Vol. 61, no. 1 (May 1983), p. 97-102. English. **DESCR:** Anglo Americans; San Antonio, TX; *Skin Color.

9472 Research/development: books. HISPANIC BUSINESS, Vol. 4, no. 10 (October 1982), p. 29-30. English.

9473 Russell, Cheryl. The news about Hispanics. AMERICAN DEMOGRAPHICS, Vol. 5, no. 3 (March 1983), p. 14-25. English. **DESCR:** Census; Cubanos; Puerto Ricans.

9474 Segal, Madhav N. and Sosa, Lionel. Marketing to the Hispanic community. CALIFORNIA MANAGEMENT REVIEW, Vol. 26, no. 1 (Fall 1983), p. 120-134. English. **DESCR:** Advertising; *Consumers; Mass Media.

9475 A territorial approach to representation for illegal aliens. MICHIGAN LAW REVIEW, Vol. 80, no. 6 (May 1982), p. 1342-1371. English. **DESCR:** Census; Federation for American Immigration Reform (FAIR); Reapportionment; Reynolds, Steve; *Undocumented Workers; Voting Rights.

9476 Upscale Hispanic consumer demographics in the top 15 SMSAS. HISPANIC BUSINESS, Vol. 4, no. 12 (December 1982), p. 37-38. English. **DESCR:** *Consumers; *Demography; Income.

Population and Family Planning
USE: Family Planning

Population Distribution

9477 Gober, Patricia and Behr, Michelle. Central cities and suburbs as distinct place types: myth or fact? ECONOMIC GEOGRAPHY, Vol. 58, no. 4 (October 1982), p. 371-385. English. **DESCR:** Blacks; Census; Suburban Communities; *Urban Communities.

9478 Government review. NUESTRO, Vol. 7, no. 6 (August 1983), p. 56. English. **DESCR:** Ballet de Puerto Rico; Dance; Education; Employment; *Government Funding Sources; Government Services; Housing; Income; National Fair Housing Law; Urban Development Action Grant (UDAG); Veterans.

9479 Guernica, Antonio. The Hispanic market: a profile. AGENDA, Vol. 11, no. 3 (May, June, 1981), p. 4-7. English. **DESCR:** *Consumers; Marketing; Mass Media; *Population; Population Trends.

9480 Hispanics: will they or won't they? AMERICAN DEMOGRAPHICS, Vol. 5, (October 1983), p. 11. English. **DESCR:** *Population Trends.

9481 Latino students rapidly increase. NUESTRO, Vol. 6, no. 10 (December 1982), p. 10. English. **DESCR:** *Los Angeles, CA; *Population; *Population Trends.

Population Distribution (cont.)

9482 Occupational distribution of Hispanics in California. HISPANIC BUSINESS, Vol. 5, no. 9 (September 1983), p. 33-34. English. **DESCR:** California; Employment; Population Trends.

9483 The Puerto Rican diaspora: the dispersal of a people. NUESTRO, Vol. 6, no. 5 (June, July, 1982), p. 32-41. English. **DESCR:** Espada, Frank; Ethnic Groups; Ethnic Stratification; *Puerto Ricans.

9484 Teschner, Richard V. Hispanics to equal ten percent of population by 2000. HISPANIA, Vol. 66, no. 1 (1983), p. 93. English. **DESCR:** *Population Trends.

Population Genetics

9485 Garber, Ronald A. PGM1 and Ge subtype gene frequencies in a California Hispanic population. AMERICAN JOURNAL OF HUMAN GENETICS, Vol. 35, no. 4 (July 1983), p. 773-776. English. **DESCR:** Genetics; Paternity.

9486 Gottlieb, Karen. Genetic demography of Denver, Colorado: Spanish surname as a market of Mexican ancestry. HUMAN BIOLOGY, Vol. 55, no. 2 (May 1983), p. 227-234. English. **DESCR:** Demography; Denver, CO; Personal Names; Research Methodology; Sociology.

Population Trends

9487 1983 U.S. population reaches 232.6 million. NUESTRO, Vol. 7, no. 1 (January, February, 1983), p. 47. English. **DESCR:** Census; *Population.

9488 Alba, Francisco. La fecundidad entre los Mexicano-Norteamericanos en relacion a los cambiantes patrones reproductivos en Mexico y los Estados Unidos. DEMOGRAFIA Y ECONOMIA, Vol. 16, no. 2 (1982), p. 236-249. Spanish. **DESCR:** Demography; *Fertility; *Mexico; Social Research.

9489 Barberis, Mary. Hispanic America. EDITORIAL RESEARCH REPORTS, no. 7 (30, 1982), p. 551-568. English. **DESCR:** History; Immigration; Marketing.

9490 Cantu, Hector. Hispanic numbers rising. NATIONAL HISPANIC JOURNAL, Vol. 1, no. 3 (Summer, Fall, 1982), p. 7. English. **DESCR:** Austin, TX; Census; Demography; Population.

9491 Ferre, Maurice A. Decade of the Hispanic. ADVERTISING AGE MAGAZINE, Vol. 53, (February 15, 1982), p. II, M14+. English. **DESCR:** Cubanos; Puerto Ricans.

9492 Garcia, Paco. Tampa: a centennial birthday in 1986. NUESTRO, Vol. 6, no. 10 (December 1982), p. 20-21. English. **DESCR:** *Population; *Tampa, FL.

9493 Government review. NUESTRO, Vol. 7, no. 7 (September 1983), p. 55. English. **DESCR:** AIDS Hotline; California; Education; Employment; Food for Survival, New York, NY; Funding Sources; *Government Services; Hewlett Foundation; Laborers; Mathematics, Engineering and Science Achievement (MESA); Public Health; Stanford University, Stanford, CA.

9494 Government review. NUESTRO, Vol. 7, no. 2 (March 1983), p. 42. English. **DESCR:** A WORKING WOMAN'S GUIDE TO HER JOB RIGHTS; Adoption; Business Enterprises; Census; Chicanas; Discrimination in Employment; *Government Services; GUIDE TO FEDERAL MINORITY ENTERPRISE AND RELATED ASSISTANCE PROGRAMS; Study Abroad; U.S. Information Agency (USIA).

9495 Guernica, Antonio. The Hispanic market: a profile. AGENDA, Vol. 11, no. 3 (May, June, 1981), p. 4-7. English. **DESCR:** *Consumers; Marketing; Mass Media; *Population; Population Distribution.

9496 Hayes-Bautista, David E. On comparing studies of different raza populations. AMERICAN JOURNAL OF PUBLIC HEALTH, Vol. 73, no. 3 (March 1983), p. 274-276. English. **DESCR:** *Surveys.

9497 Hispanics: will they or won't they? AMERICAN DEMOGRAPHICS, Vol. 5, (October 1983), p. 11. English. **DESCR:** Population Distribution.

9498 Latino students rapidly increase. NUESTRO, Vol. 6, no. 10 (December 1982), p. 10. English. **DESCR:** *Los Angeles, CA; *Population; *Population Distribution.

9499 Massey, Douglas S. and Schnabel, Kathleen M. Recent trends in Hispanic immigration to the United States. INTERNATIONAL MIGRATION REVIEW, Vol. 17, no. 2 (Summer 1983), p. 212-244. English. **DESCR:** *Immigration; Migration Patterns; Rural Urban Migration; Socioeconomic Factors.

9500 Massey, Douglas S. Research note on residential succession: the Hispanic case. SOCIAL FORCES, Vol. 61, (March 1983), p. 825-833. English. **DESCR:** Barrios; *Residential Segregation; Urban Communities.

9501 Morgan, Thomas B. The Latinization of America. ESQUIRE, Vol. 99, no. 5 (May 1983), p. 47-56. English. **DESCR:** Acculturation; Assimilation; Biculturalism; Bilingualism.

9502 Occupational distribution of Hispanics in California. HISPANIC BUSINESS, Vol. 5, no. 9 (September 1983), p. 33-34. English. **DESCR:** California; Employment; *Population Distribution.

9503 Teschner, Richard V. Hispanics to equal ten percent of population by 2000. HISPANIA, Vol. 66, no. 1 (1983), p. 93. English. **DESCR:** Population Distribution.

9504 Triana, Armando R. Changing demographics, consumer patterns in the Chicago marketplace. HISPANIC BUSINESS, Vol. 5, no. 12 (December 1983), p. 20-21+. English. **DESCR:** *Chicago, IL; Income; *Marketing.

Portales Municipal Schools

9505 Martinez, Paul E. Serna v. Portales: the plight of bilingual education four years later. JOURNAL OF ETHNIC STUDIES, Vol. 7, no. 2 (Summer 1979), p. 109-114. English. **DESCR:** *Bilingual Bicultural Education; Chicano Youth Organization; Civil Rights; *Portales, NM; Serna v. Portales Municipal Schools.

Portales, NM

9506 Martinez, Paul E. Serna v. Portales: the
     plight of bilingual education four years
     later. JOURNAL OF ETHNIC STUDIES, Vol. 7,
     no. 2 (Summer 1979), p. 109-114. English.
     DESCR: *Bilingual Bicultural Education;
     Chicano Youth Organization; Civil Rights;
     Portales Municipal Schools; Serna v.
     Portales Municipal Schools.

Portilla, Marta de la

9507 Feliciano-Foster, Wilma. A comparison of
     three current first-year college-level
     Spanish-for-native-speakers textbooks.
     BILINGUAL REVIEW, Vol. 9, no. 1 (January,
     April, 1982), p. 72-81. English. DESCR:
     *Book Reviews; ESPANOL ESCRITO; Garza-Swan,
     Gloria; *Language Development; Mejias, Hugo
     A.; MEJORA TU ESPANOL; NUESTRO ESPANOL:
     CURSO PARA ESTUDIANTES BILINGUES; Spanish
     Language Textbooks; Teschner, Richard V.;
     Valdes Fallis, Guadalupe; Varela, Beatriz.

Portillo, Irene E.

9508 Fuentes, Diana. Chicana perpectives: Irene
     Portillo. COMADRE, no. 1 (Summer 1977), p.
     42-44. English. DESCR: *Biography; Identity;
     Women's Rights.

Portillo, Rose

9509 Whisler, Kirk. Rose Portillo: a woman on the
     rise. CAMINOS, Vol. 4, no. 4 (April 1983),
     p. 36-39. Bilingual. DESCR: Artists; Films.

Portillo Trambley, Estela

9510 Herrera-Sobek, Maria. La unidad, el hombre y
     el cosmos: reafirmacion del proceso vital en
     Estrella Portillo Trambley. LA PALABRA, Vol.
     4, no. 1-2 (Spring, Fall, 1982, 1983), p.
     127-141. Spanish. DESCR: Authors; *Literary
     Criticism; Literature.

9511 Parr, Carmen Salazar. Surrealism in the work
     of Estela Portillo. MELUS: MULTI-ETHNIC
     LITERATURE OF THE UNITED STATES, Vol. 7, no.
     4 (Winter 1980), p. 85-92. English. DESCR:
     *Literature; Surrealism.

9512 Vowell, Faye Nell and Portillo Trambley,
     Estela. A MELUS interview: Estela
     Portillo-Trambley. MELUS: MULTI-ETHNIC
     LITERATURE OF THE UNITED STATES, Vol. 9, no.
     4 (Winter 1982), p. 59-66. English. DESCR:
     *Literature.

Posada, Jose Guadalupe

9513 Diaz, Katherine A. and Gonzalez, Magdalena.
     Jose Guadalupe Posada: documenting his
     people and his times=informandonos de su
     gente y su epoca. CAMINOS, Vol. 2, no. 6
     (October 1981), p. 18-20. Bilingual. DESCR:
     Artists; Biography; Mexico.

Las Posadas

9514 Lenti, Paul. Mexico's posadas a unique
     experience. NUESTRO, Vol. 6, no. 10
     (December 1982), p. 52-55. English. DESCR:
     *Christmas; Mexico; Tourism.

Positivism

9515 Klor de Alva, Jorge. Gabino Barrera and
     Chicano thought. AZTLAN, Vol. 14, no. 2
     (Fall 1983), p. 343-358. English. DESCR:
     *Barreda, Gabino; Economic History and
     Conditions; History; Mexico; Philosophy.

9516 Leal, Luis. Gabino Barreda y la literatura:
     de la preparatoria al Ateneo. AZTLAN, Vol.
     14, no. 2 (Fall 1983), p. 253-265. Spanish.
     DESCR: Ateneo de la Juventud; *Barreda,
     Gabino; Escuela Nacional Preparatoria;
     History; *Mexican Literature; Philosophy.

9517 Marti, Oscar R. Barrera and moral
     philosophy. AZTLAN, Vol. 14, no. 2 (Fall
     1983), p. 373-403. English. DESCR: *Barreda,
     Gabino; *Ethics; History; Mexico;
     Philosophy.

9518 Marti, Oscar R. Introduction. AZTLAN, Vol.
     14, no. 2 (Fall 1983), p. 209-220. English.
     DESCR: *Barreda, Gabino; *Biography;
     History; Mexico; Philosophy.

9519 Marti, Oscar R., comp. Bibliography. AZTLAN,
     Vol. 14, no. 2 (Fall 1983), p. 405-417.
     English. DESCR: *Barreda, Gabino;
     *Bibliography; History; Mexico; Philosophy.

9520 Raat, W. Dirk. Augusto Comte, Gabino
     Barreda, and positivism in Mexico. AZTLAN,
     Vol. 14, no. 2 (Fall 1983), p. 235-251.
     English. DESCR: *Barreda, Gabino; *Comte,
     Auguste; Education; Educational Theory and
     Practice; History; Mexico; Philosophy.

9521 Rocco, Raymond. Positivism and Mexican
     identity: then and now. AZTLAN, Vol. 14, no.
     2 (Fall 1983), p. 359-371. English. DESCR:
     History; Identity; Mexico; Philosophy.

9522 Skirius, John. Barreda, Vasconcelos, and the
     Mexican educational reforms. AZTLAN, Vol.
     14, no. 2 (Fall 1983), p. 307-341. English.
     DESCR: *Barreda, Gabino; Education;
     *Educational Theory and Practice; History;
     Mexico; *Vasconcelos, Jose.

9523 Zea, Leopoldo. El sentido de la historia en
     Gabino Barreda. AZTLAN, Vol. 14, no. 2 (Fall
     1983), p. 221-233. Spanish. DESCR: *Barreda,
     Gabino; *History; Mexico; Philosophy.

Post Secondary Education
     USE: Higher Education

Posters

9524 Acevedo, Mario (Torero). Big brother speaks
     from the dead [poster]. MAIZE, Vol. 1, no. 2
     (Winter 1978), p. 13. English. DESCR:
     Guevara, Che.

9525 Orozco, Juan Ishi. Celebration of life's
     renewal. CALMECAC, Vol. 3, (Spring 1982),
     p. 41. English.

Poverty

9526 Cruz, Amaury. El Salvador: realities of a
     country at war. NUESTRO, Vol. 6, no. 3
     (April 1982), p. 14-17+. English. DESCR: *El
     Salvador; Political History and Conditions;
     Short Story; Tourism.

9527 Gonzales, Patrisia. Nogales: view from a
     cardboard box. NUESTRO, Vol. 6, no. 9
     (November 1982), p. 21-27. English. DESCR:
     *Mexico; Nogales, Mexico.

9528 Holdenreid, Frank X. Guatemala shantytown.
     NUESTRO, Vol. 7, no. 4 (May 1983), p. 39-41.
     English. DESCR: Ayudantes de los Pobres;
     *Guatemala; Holdenreid, Frank X.; Refugees.

9529 Lopez, Phyllis. Untitled No.2. COMADRE, no.
     2 (Spring 1978), p. 11. English. DESCR:
     *Poetry.

Poverty (cont.)

9530 Migdail, Carl J. Mexico's poverty: driving force for border jumpers. U.S. NEWS & WORLD REPORT, Vol. 94, no. 9 (March 7, 1983), p. 42-44. English. **DESCR:** Economic History and Conditions; Mexico; Migration.

9531 Public housing vital. NUESTRO, Vol. 6, no. 9 (November 1982), p. 9. English. **DESCR:** *Housing.

THE POVERTY OF REVOLUTION: THE STATE AND THE URBAN POOR IN MEXICO

9532 Logan, Kathleen. The urban poor in developing nations. JOURNAL OF URBAN HISTORY, Vol. 9, no. 1 (November 1982), p. 108-116. English. **DESCR:** ACCESS TO POWER: POLITICS AND THE URBAN POOR IN DEVELOPING NATIONS; *Book Reviews; BORDER BOOM TOWN: CIUDAD JUAREZ SINCE 1848; Collier, David; Cornelius, Wayne A.; Eckstein, Susan; Lloyd, Peter; Martinez, Oscar J.; Nelson, Joan M.; Perlman, Janice E.; POLITICS AND MIGRANT POOR IN MEXICO CITY; SLUMS OF HOPE? SHANTY TOWNS OF THE THIRD WORLD; SQUATTERS AND OLIGARCHS: AUTHORITARIAN RULE AND POLICY CHANGE IN PERU; THE MYTH OF MARGINALITY: URBAN POVERTY AND POLITICS IN RIO DE JANEIRO; Urban Economics.

Precolumbian Art

9533 Nicholson, H. B. Treasures of Tenochtitlan. NUESTRO, Vol. 7, no. 10 (December 1983), p. 28-32. English. **DESCR:** Aztecs; *Mexico City.

9534 Ochoa, Victor Orozco. [Untitled photographs]. MAIZE, Vol. 1, no. 3 (Spring 1978), p. 45-47,50+. **DESCR:** *Photography.

9535 A potpourri of pre-Columbian art. NUESTRO, Vol. 7, no. 6 (August 1983), p. 59-60. English. **DESCR:** CERAMIC TOMB SCULPTURE FROM ANCIENT WEST MEXICO; Ceramics; Exhibits; Frederick S. Wright Art Gallery, University of California, Los Angeles; Museum of Cultural History, University of California, Los Angeles; Sculpture.

9536 Quirarte, Jacinto. Book review of: OLMEC: AN EARLY ART STYLE OF PRECOLUMBIAN MEXICO. JOURNAL OF ETHNIC STUDIES, Vol. 1, no. 3 (Fall 1973), p. 92-95. English. **DESCR:** Book Reviews; La Venta, Mexico; *OLMEC: AN EARLY ART STYLE OF PRECOLUMBIAN MEXICO; Precolumbian Society; San Lorenzo, Mexico; Tres Zapotes, Mexico; Wicke, Charles R.

9537 Regional report, antiquities: stolen treasure begins U.S. tour. NUESTRO, Vol. 7, no. 4 (May 1983), p. 12-13. English. **DESCR:** *Criminal Acts; *Peru.

Precolumbian Literature

9538 Carr, Pat and Gingerich, Willard. The vagina dentata motif in Nahuatl and Pueblo mythic narratives: a comparative study. NEW SCHOLAR, Vol. 8, no. 1-2 (Spring, Fall, 1982), p. 85-101. English. **DESCR:** Mythology.

Precolumbian Medicine

9539 Risse, Gunter B. Book review of: CAPITULOS DE HISTORIA MEDICA MEXICANA. BULLETIN OF THE HISTORY OF MEDICINE, Vol. 56, no. 4 (1982), p. 591-592. English. **DESCR:** *CAPITULOS DE HISTORIA MEDICA MEXICANA; Folk Medicine; Medicine; Mexico; Somolinos D'Ardois, German.

Precolumbian Science

9540 Bustamante, Anna Luisa. La ciencia en la tradicion. CALMECAC, Vol. 3, (Spring 1982), p. 11-17. English. **DESCR:** Philosophy.

Precolumbian Society

9541 Brotherston, Gordon. Year 13 reed equals 3113 BC: a clue to Mesoamerican chronology. NEW SCHOLAR, Vol. 8, no. 1-2 (Spring, Fall, 1982), p. 75-84. English. **DESCR:** Codices.

9542 Emboden, William A. The Water Lily and the Maya Scribe: an ethnobotanical interpretation. NEW SCHOLAR, Vol. 8, no. 1-2 (Spring, Fall, 1982), p. 103-127. English. **DESCR:** Narcotics.

9543 Heizer, Robert. Book review of: THE OLMEC WORLD. JOURNAL OF ETHNIC STUDIES, Vol. 15, no. 3 (Fall 1977), p. 124-125. English. **DESCR:** Bernal, Ignacio; Book Reviews; Olmecs; *THE OLMEC WORLD.

9544 Quirarte, Jacinto. Book review of: OLMEC: AN EARLY ART STYLE OF PRECOLUMBIAN MEXICO. JOURNAL OF ETHNIC STUDIES, Vol. 1, no. 3 (Fall 1973), p. 92-95. English. **DESCR:** Book Reviews; La Venta, Mexico; *OLMEC: AN EARLY ART STYLE OF PRECOLUMBIAN MEXICO; Precolumbian Art; San Lorenzo, Mexico; Tres Zapotes, Mexico; Wicke, Charles R.

9545 Vigil, James Diego. Towards a new perspective on understanding the Chicano people: the six C's model of sociocultural change. CAMPO LIBRE, Vol. 1, no. 2 (Summer 1981), p. 141-167. English. **DESCR:** Acculturation; Assimilation; Cultural Characteristics; History; Mexican Nationalism Period; Mexico; Nationalism; Organizations; *Six C's Model (Theoretical Model); Social History and Conditions; Spanish Colonial Period.

Pregnancy

9546 Perez, Robert. Effects of stress, social support and coping style on adjustment to pregnancy among Hispanic women. HISPANIC JOURNAL OF BEHAVIORAL SCIENCES, Vol. 5, no. 2 (June 1983), p. 141-161. English. **DESCR:** *Chicanas; Stress.

Prejudice (Social)

9547 Breiter, Toni. Eddie Olmos and THE BALLAD OF GREGORIO CORTEZ. NUESTRO, Vol. 7, no. 4 (May 1983), p. 14-19. English. **DESCR:** Artists; *BALLAD OF GREGORIO CORTEZ [film]; Corrido; Film Reviews; *Olmos, Edward James.

9548 Candelaria, Nash. The prowler. BILINGUAL REVIEW, Vol. 9, no. 1 (January, April, 1982), p. 66-71. English. **DESCR:** *Racism.

9549 Gonzalez, Alex. Classroom cooperation and ethnic balance: Chicanos and equal status. CACR REVIEW, Vol. 1, no. 1 (September 1982), p. 42-71. English. **DESCR:** Cooperative Education; Curriculum; Intergroup Relations; Segregation and Desegregation.

9550 Latinos and Mrs. Luce. NUESTRO, Vol. 6, no. 8 (October 1982), p. 9. English. **DESCR:** Immigration; *Luce, Claire Boothe.

Prejudices

9551 Lopez, Phyllis. Untitled poem: III. COMADRE, no. 1 (Summer 1977), p. 15-16. English. DESCR: *Poetry.

Prenatal Care

9552 Gaviria, Moises; Stern, Gwen; and Schensul, Stephen L. Sociocultural factors and perinatal health in a Mexican-American community. NATIONAL MEDICAL ASSOCIATION JOURNAL, Vol. 74, no. 10 (October 1982), p. 983-989. English. DESCR: Chicago, IL; Migration Patterns; Public Health; Socioeconomic Factors.

9553 Hunt, Isabelle F., et al. Zinc supplementation during pregnancy: zinc concentration of serum and hair from low-income women of Mexican descent. AMERICAN JOURNAL OF CLINICAL NUTRITION, Vol. 37, no. 4 (April 1983), p. 572-582. English. DESCR: Chicanas; Low Income; Nutrition; Surveys.

Prenatal Influence
USE: Prenatal Care

PREPARED FOR TODAY

9554 Que pasa? NUESTRO, Vol. 7, no. 6 (August 1983), p. 9. English. DESCR: Boy Scouts of America; *Court System; Criminal Justice System; Diabetes; Education; Judicial Review; Petersilia, Joan; RACIAL DISPARITIES IN THE CRIMINAL JUSTICE SYSTEM; Reagan, Ronald.

Presbyterian Church

9555 Arrastia, Cecilio. The Hispanics in the U.S.A.: drama and challenge. CHURCH AND SOCIETY, Vol. 72, no. 4 (March, April, 1982), p. 31-35. English. DESCR: Migration Patterns; Religion.

Preschool Education
USE: Early Childhood Education

President's Commission on Excellence in Education

9556 Garcia, Paco. Voices: Hispanic voices needed in the education debate. NUESTRO, Vol. 7, no. 5 (June, July, 1983), p. 53-54. English. DESCR: Bilingual Bicultural Education; *Discrimination in Education; *Discrimination in Employment; *Education; Federal Government; *Latin Americans; Reagan, Ronald; U.S. Department of Health, Education and Welfare (HEW).

THE PRETEND INDIANS: IMAGES OF NATIVE AMERICANS IN THE MOVIES

9557 Cripps, Thomas. Mexicans, Indians and movies: the need for a history. WIDE ANGLE: A FILM QUARTERLY OF THEORY, CRITICISM, AND PRACTICE, Vol. 5, no. 1 (1982), p. 68-70. English. DESCR: Bataille, Gretchen M.; *Book Reviews; Films; IMAGES OF THE MEXICAN AMERICAN IN FICTION AND FILM; Native Americans; O'Connor, John E.; Pettit, Arthur G.; Silet, Charles L.P.; *Stereotypes; THE HOLLYWOOD INDIAN: STEREOTYPES OF NATIVE AMERICANS IN FILMS.

Preventative Medicine

9558 Effective ways to fight cancer in new publication. LATINO, Vol. 54, no. 8 (December 1983), p. 24. English. DESCR: *Cancer; Public Health.

9559 Hazuda, Helen P. Ethnic differences in health knowledge and behaviors related to the prevention and treatment of coronary heart disease. The San Antonio heart study. AMERICAN JOURNAL OF EPIDEMIOLOGY, Vol. 11, no. 6 (June 1983), p. 717-728. English. DESCR: Anglo Americans; *Coronary Heart Disease; Health Education; San Antonio, TX; Socioeconomic Factors.

9560 Ponce-Adame, Merrihelen. Women and cancer. CORAZON DE AZTLAN, Vol. 1, no. 2 (March, April, 1982), p. 32. English. DESCR: *Cancer; Chicanas; Medical Care.

Prewitt Diaz, Joseph (Jose)

9561 A time for reflection. NUESTRO, Vol. 7, no. 9 (November 1983), p. 42-44. English. DESCR: Anaya, Rudolfo A.; Arias, Beatriz; Bilingual Bicultural Education; Computers; Financial Aid; Folklore; Organizations; Villarreal, Sylvia; *W.K. Kellogg Foundation National Fellowship Program.

Price, Criselda S.

9562 Vazquez, Carol A. Reply to Cuellar and Price. HISPANIC JOURNAL OF BEHAVIORAL SCIENCES, Vol. 4, no. 1 (March 1982), p. 85-88. English. DESCR: *Cuellar, Israel; *Psychological Theory.

Prieto, Carlos

9563 Gente. NUESTRO, Vol. 7, no. 1 (January, February, 1983), p. 63. English. DESCR: Amaya-Espinoza, Isidro; Camargo, Mateo G.; *Latin Americans; Musicians; Radio; Sports; Trevino, Lee.

Primary School Education

9564 Buriel, Raymond, et al. Teacher-student interactions and their relationship to student achievement: a comparison of Mexican-American and Anglo-American children. JOURNAL OF EDUCATIONAL PSYCHOLOGY, Vol. 75, no. 6 (December 1983), p. 889-897. English. DESCR: Academic Achievement; Brophy-Good Dyadic Interaction System; Teacher-pupil Interaction.

9565 Gonzalez, Larry. Serving our students: Larry Gonzalez (interview). CAMINOS, Vol. 4, no. 10 (November 1983), p. 34-36. English. DESCR: Education; *Gonzalez, Larry; Los Angeles Unified School District.

9566 Heathcote, Olivia D. Sex stereotyping in Mexican reading primers. READING TEACHER, Vol. 36, no. 2 (November 1982), p. 158-165. English. DESCR: Comparative Education; Curriculum Materials; Mexico; *Sex Stereotypes.

9567 Johnson, Donna M. Natural language learning by design: a classroom experiment in social interaction and second language acquisition. TESOL QUARTERLY, Vol. 17, no. 1 (March 1983), p. 55-68. English. DESCR: *English as a Second Language; Inter-Ethnolinguistic Peer Tutoring (IEPT); Language Development.

9568 Kugle, Cherry L.; Clements, Richard O.; and Powell, Philip M. Level and stability of self-esteem in relation to academic behavior of second graders. JOURNAL OF PERSONALITY AND SOCIAL PSYCHOLOGY, Vol. 44, no. 1 (January 1983), p. 201-207. English. DESCR: Academic Achievement; *Identity; PIERS-HARRIS CHILDREN'S SELF CONCEPT SCALE.

Primary School Education (cont.)

9569 Oakland, Thomas. Concurrent and predictive validity estimates for the WISC-R IQ's and ELP's by racial-ethnic and SES groups. SCHOOL PSYCHOLOGY REVIEW, Vol. 12, no. 1 (Winter 1983), p. 57-61. English. DESCR: Academic Achievement; Estimated Learning Potential (ELP); *Intelligence Tests; Wechsler Intelligence Scale for Children-Revised (WISC-R).

9570 Obrzut, John E.; Hansen, Robert L.; and Heath, Charles P. The effectiveness of visual information processing training with Hispanic children. JOURNAL OF GENERAL PSYCHOLOGY, Vol. 10, no. 2 (October 1982), p. 165-174. English. DESCR: *Academic Achievement; Bender Gestalt Test; Colorado; Intelligence Tests.

9571 Rodriguez, Imelda and Bethel, Lowell J. Inquiry approach to science and language teaching. JOURNAL OF RESEARCH IN SCIENCE TEACHING, Vol. 20, no. 4 (April 1983), p. 291-296. English. DESCR: Bilingualism; Education; *Educational Tests and Measurements; Language Arts; Learning and Cognition; Science.

9572 Schon, Isabel. Effects of special curricular study of Mexican culture on Anglo and Mexican-American students perceptions of Mexican-Americans. JOURNAL OF EXPERIMENTAL EDUCATION, Vol. 50, no. 4 (Summer 1982), p. 215-218. English. DESCR: Anglo Americans; Perceptions of Mexican Americans Scale (PMAS); *Stereotypes.

9573 Schorr, Burt. Language lab: grade-school project helps Hispanic pupils learn English quickly; but Texas test's avoidance of bilingual approach is source of controversy. WALL STREET JOURNAL, Vol. 202, (November 30, 1983), p. 1. English. DESCR: *English as a Second Language; *Texas.

9574 Strong, Michael. Social styles and the second language acquisition of Spanish-speaking kindergartners. TESOL QUARTERLY, Vol. 17, no. 2 (June 1983), p. 241-258. English. DESCR: *Language Development; Personality.

9575 Walker de Felix, Judith. The language arts approach: planned eclecticism in ESL teaching in the elementary school. BILINGUAL REVIEW, Vol. 10, no. 1 (January, April, 1983), p. 87-89. English. DESCR: *English as a Second Language; *Language Arts Approach (LAA).

Primary School Students

9576 McGhee, Paul E. and Duffy, Nelda S. Children's appreciation of humor victimizing different racial-ethnic groups: racial ethnic differences. JOURNAL OF CROSS-CULTURAL PSYCHOLOGY, Vol. 14, no. 1 (March 1983), p. 29-40. English. DESCR: *Humor; Racism.

9577 Mishra, Shitala P. Validity of WISC-R IQs and factor scores in predicting achievement for Mexican American children. PSYCHOLOGY IN THE SCHOOLS, Vol. 20, no. 4 (October 1983), p. 442-444. English. DESCR: *Academic Achievement; Intelligence Tests; Wechsler Intelligence Scale for Children-Revised (WISC-R).

9578 Scruggs, Thomas E.; Mastropieri, Margo A.; and Argulewicz, Ed N. Stability of performance on the PPVT-R for three ethnic

groups attending a bilingual kindergarten. PSYCHOLOGY IN THE SCHOOLS, Vol. 20, (October 1983), p. 433-435. English. DESCR: *Intelligence Tests; Peabody Picture Vocabulary Test-Revised (PPVT-R).

PRIMEROS ENCUENTROS/FIRST ENCOUNTERS

9579 Mosier, Pat. Book review of: PRIMEROS ENCUENTROS/FIRST ENCOUNTERS. REVISTA CHICANO-RIQUENA, Vol. 10, no. 4 (Fall 1982), p. 69-70. English. DESCR: Book Reviews; Ulibarri, Sabine R.

THE PRINCE

9580 Barrio, Raymond. The bilingual heart and other adventures. BILINGUAL JOURNAL, Vol. 6, no. 2 (Winter 1982), p. 12-15. Bilingual. DESCR: *Early Childhood Education; Ethnic Attitudes; Racism; REVERSING ROLES; THE BILINGUAL HEART.

Print Media

9581 Aguirre, Richard R. Print media at a crossroads. HISPANIC BUSINESS, Vol. 4, no. 5 (May 1982), p. 20-21+. English. DESCR: *Advertising; Magazines; Newspapers.

9582 Bustelo, Manuel A. Una epoca del Foro Nacional Puertorriqueno. LATINO, Vol. 53, no. 2 (March, April, 1982), p. 15. Spanish. DESCR: *Foro Nacional Puertorriqueno; Newspapers.

9583 Chavarria, Jesus. The media scene. HISPANIC BUSINESS, Vol. 4, no. 5 (May 1982), p. 6. English. DESCR: Advertising; Broadcast Media; Caballero Spanish Media, Inc. (CSM); *Mass Media; MIAMI MENSUAL; Radio; Television.

9584 More news for Latinos. LATINO, Vol. 54, no. 6 (October 1983), p. 14. English. DESCR: Magazines.

9585 Stevenson, Robert. Carlos Chavez's United States press coverage. AZTLAN, Vol. 14, no. 1 (Spring 1983), p. 21-33. English. DESCR: *Chavez, Carlos; Ethnomusicology; *Journalism; Musicians.

Prisoners

9586 Devis, Rey. Prisons can't contain freedom. CAMINOS, Vol. 4, no. 11 (December 1983), p. 22-23. English. DESCR: *Flores Magon, Ricardo; Prisons; Yuma Penitentiary.

9587 O`Leary, Tim. David Ruiz brings justice to Texas prisons. NATIONAL HISPANIC JOURNAL, Vol. 1, no. 2 (Winter 1982), p. 21-24. English. DESCR: Clements, Bill; Legal Reform; Prisons; *Ruiz, David; Texas Department of Corrections.

9588 Young Latino goes to prison. NUESTRO, Vol. 6, no. 8 (October 1982), p. 11. English. DESCR: Denver, CO; *Juvenile Delinquency; *Mental Health; Prisons.

Prisoners of War
    USE: Political Prisoners

Prisons

9589 Castro, Agenor L. The case for the bilingual prison. CORRECTIONS TODAY, Vol. 44, no. 4 (August 1982), p. 72-78. English. DESCR: Bilingualism; Social Psychology; Socialization.

Prisons (cont.)

9590 Devis, Rey. Prisons can't contain freedom. CAMINOS, Vol. 4, no. 11 (December 1983), p. 22-23. English. DESCR: *Flores Magon, Ricardo; Prisoners; Yuma Penitentiary.

9591 O`Leary, Tim. David Ruiz brings justice to Texas prisons. NATIONAL HISPANIC JOURNAL, Vol. 1, no. 2 (Winter 1982), p. 21-24. English. DESCR: Clements, Bill; Legal Reform; Prisoners; *Ruiz, David; Texas Department of Corrections.

9592 Young Latino goes to prison. NUESTRO, Vol. 6, no. 8 (October 1982), p. 11. English. DESCR: Denver, CO; *Juvenile Delinquency; *Mental Health; Prisoners.

Private Funding Sources

9593 Allen, Kenneth. Q & A with Kenneth Allen of the President's Task Force on Private Sector initiatives (interview). CAMINOS, Vol. 4, no. 4 (April 1983), p. 49-50,67. Bilingual. DESCR: *Allen, Kenneth.

9594 Caldera, Carmela. Coca-Cola president Bryan Dyson on BRAVISIMO. CAMINOS, Vol. 4, no. 4 (April 1983), p. 44-45,48. Bilingual. DESCR: *BRAVISIMO; Coca-Cola Company; Dyson, Bryan; Television.

9595 Elizalde, Hector. How Anheuser-Busch promotions benefit the Hispanic community. CAMINOS, Vol. 4, no. 4 (April 1983), p. 51-53. Bilingual. DESCR: *Anheuser-Busch, Inc.

9596 Fundraising resources. CAMINOS, Vol. 4, no. 4 (April 1983), p. 58. English. DESCR: *Foundations.

9597 Getting grants. CAMINOS, Vol. 4, no. 4 (April 1983), p. 56-58,67. English.

9598 Ogaz, Antonio and Caldera, Carmela. What do you think of Coca-Cola's sponsorship of Bravisimo? CAMINOS, Vol. 4, no. 4 (April 1983), p. 46-47. English. DESCR: *BRAVISIMO; Coca-Cola Company; Television.

9599 Ogaz, Armando. National menudo cook-off. CAMINOS, Vol. 4, no. 4 (April 1983), p. 60. English. DESCR: *Coors, Adolf.

9600 Pena, Silvia Novo. Open letter to our readers. REVISTA CHICANO-RIQUENA, Vol. 11, no. 2 (Summer 1983), p. 5. English.

9601 Whisler, Kirk. Hispanics and the private sector. CAMINOS, Vol. 3, no. 8 (September 1982), p. 22-23. Bilingual. DESCR: *National Council of La Raza (NCLR); *Organizations.

9602 Yzaguirre, Raul. Hispanics & the private sector: new partnerships. CAMINOS, Vol. 4, no. 4 (April 1983), p. 42-43,66. English.

Private Schools

9603 Dominguez, Simon. A private bilingual summer school in San Jose" an alternative to public education. CAMINOS, Vol. 3, no. 10 (November 1982), p. 44-45. English. DESCR: *Bilingual Bicultural Education.

Production

USE: Industries

Professional Opportunities Program (POP)

9604 Chavez, Rigo. Job counseling, role models mean a lot. HISPANIC BUSINESS, Vol. 4, no. 8 (August 1983), p. 12. English. DESCR: Careers; *Counseling Services (Educational); Cuevas, Hector; Escobedo, Ed; *Stanford University, Stanford, CA.

Professional Organizations

9605 Fostering Hispanic professionalism. HISPANIC BUSINESS, Vol. 5, no. 4 (April 1983), p. 18. English. DESCR: Hispanic Association for Professional Advancement (HAPA); *Organizations.

9606 Quesada-Weiner, Rosemary. Latin Business Association (photoessay). CAMINOS, Vol. 3, no. 2 (February 1982), p. 33. Bilingual. DESCR: Business.

9607 Whisler, Kirk. M.A.B.A. CAMINOS, Vol. 3, no. 5 (May 1982), p. 36-37. English. DESCR: Legal Profession; *Mexican American Bar Association (MABA).

Professional Schools

9608 Webster, David S. Chicano students in American higher education: a review of the literature. CAMPO LIBRE, Vol. 1, no. 2 (Summer 1981), p. 169-192. English. DESCR: Dropouts; Educational Statistics; Enrollment; Graduate Schools; *Higher Education; Literature Reviews.

PROGRAM IMPACT EVALUATIONS: AN INTRODUCTION FOR MANAGERS OF TITLE VII PROJECTS - A DRAFT GUIDEBOOK ESEA TITLE VII

9609 Consalvo, Robert W. Book review of: PROGRAM IMPACT EVALUATIONS: AN INTRODUCTION FOR MANAGERS OF TITLE VII PROJECTS - A DRAFT GUIDEBOOK. BILINGUAL JOURNAL, Vol. 7, no. 2 (Winter 1983), p. 36-37. English. DESCR: Bilingual Bicultural Education; Bissell, Joan; Book Reviews; Educational Administration; ELEMENTARY AND SECONDARY EDUCATION ACT; Evaluation (Educational).

EL PROGRAMA MEXICANO DE MAQUILADORAS: UNA RESPUESTA A LAS NECESIDADES DE LA INDUSTRIA NORTEAMERICANA

9610 Tiano, Susan B. El programa mexicano de maquiladoras: una respuesta a las necesidades de la industria norteamericana. AZTLAN, Vol. 14, no. 1 (Spring 1983), p. 201-208. English. DESCR: Book Reviews; Industrial Workers; Industries; International Labor Activities; Maquiladoras; Woog, Mario Arriola.

Programmed Instruction

9611 Saracho, Olivia N. Effects of a computer-assisted instruction program on basic skills achievement and attitudes toward instruction of Spanish-speaking migrant children. AMERICAN EDUCATIONAL RESEARCH JOURNAL, Vol. 19, no. 2 (Summer 1982), p. 201-219. English. DESCR: Academic Motivation; Audiovisual Instruction; Computers; *Migrant Children; *Migrant Education.

9612 Saracho, Olivia N. Planning computer assisted instruction for Spanish speaking migrant students. JOURNAL OF EDUCATIONAL TECHNOLOGY SYSTEMS, Vol. 10, no. 3 (1981, 1982), p. 257-260. English. DESCR: Academic Achievement; Computers; Migrant Children; *Migrant Education.

Programmed Instruction (cont.)

9613 Walia, Adorna. Book review of: BEGINNING
ENGLISH THROUGH ACTION. BILINGUAL JOURNAL,
Vol. 7, no. 3 (Spring 1983), p. 31-32.
English. **DESCR**: *BEGINNING ENGLISH THROUGH
ACTION (BETA); Book Reviews; English as a
Second Language; Jackson, P.; Language Arts.

Project Literacy, San Francisco, CA

9614 Heaney, Thomas W. "Hanging on" or "gaining
ground": educating marginal adults. NEW
DIRECTIONS FOR CONTINUING EDUCATION, no. 20
(December 1983), p. 53-63. English. **DESCR**:
*Adult Education; Chicago, IL; City
Colleges, Chicago, IL; General Education
Diploma (GED); Gomez, Robert; Instituto del
Progreso Latino; Mission District, San
Francisco, CA; St. Mary's Community
Educational Center; *Universidad Popular,
Chicago, IL.

Project PIE (Parents Involvement in Evaluation)

9615 Cohen, Bernard H. Parent involvement in
program evaluation. BILINGUAL JOURNAL, Vol.
7, no. 2 (Winter 1983), p. 29-34. English.
DESCR: *Bilingual Bicultural Education;
Community School Relationships; Curriculum;
*Evaluation (Educational).

Project WELL (We Enjoy Learning & Leadership)

9616 Community watching. CAMINOS, Vol. 3, no. 5
(May 1982), p. 56-57. Bilingual. **DESCR**:
Adelante Mujer Hispana Conference;
Agricultural Laborers; Beilson, Anthony C.;
Boycotts; Chacon, Peter R.; Chicanas;
*Cultural Organizations; Farm Labor
Organizing Commmittee (FLOC); Financial Aid;
Hollenbeck Junior High School, Los Angeles,
CA; Junior High School Students; National
League of Cities; Optimist Club of Greater
East Los Angeles; Organizations; Torres,
Art.

Property
USE: Real Estate

Proposals

9617 Balasubramonian, Krishna. Not on test scores
alone: the qualitative side to program
evaluation. BILINGUAL JOURNAL, Vol. 7, no. 2
(Winter 1983), p. 17-21,40. English. **DESCR**:
*Bilingual Bicultural Education;
*Curriculum; Educational Tests and
Measurements; ELEMENTARY AND SECONDARY
EDUCATION ACT; Evaluation (Educational).

Prose

9618 Acosta, Armando. Platicame Chicano.
CALMECAC, Vol. 3, (Spring 1982), p. 34.
Bilingual.

9619 Aguirre, Javier. Un corazon sencillo. DE
COLORES, Vol. 6, no. 1-2 (1982), p. 135-136.
English.

9620 Aguirre, Javier. Just another point of view.
DE COLORES, Vol. 6, no. 1-2 (1982), p.
137-139. English.

9621 Alvarez, Julia. El doctor. REVISTA
CHICANO-RIQUENA, Vol. 10, no. 3 (Summer
1982), p. 22-32. English.

9622 Anaya, Rudolfo A. The captain. REVISTA
CHICANO-RIQUENA, Vol. 10, no. 1-2 (Winter,
Spring, 1982), p. 151-160. English.

9623 Anaya, Rudolfo A. The place of the swallows.

9624 Anaya, Rudolfo A. The village which the gods
painted yellow. NUESTRO, Vol. 7, no. 1
(January, February, 1983), p. 48-54.
English. **DESCR**: *Short Story.

9625 Arias, Ron. A house on the island. REVISTA
CHICANO-RIQUENA, Vol. 10, no. 1-2 (Winter,
Spring, 1982), p. 161-166. English.

9626 Arias, Ron. The story machine. REVISTA
CHICANO-RIQUENA, Vol. 10, no. 1-2 (Winter,
Spring, 1982), p. 167-170. English.

9627 Baeza, Joan. A servant of the people.
NUESTRO, Vol. 7, no. 3 (April 1983), p.
41-45. English. **DESCR**: *Short Story.

9628 Berger, Andres. El afilador. REVISTA
CHICANO-RIQUENA, Vol. 10, no. 1-2 (Winter,
Spring, 1982), p. 171-179. Spanish.

9629 Calderon, Hector. To read Chicano narrative:
commentary and metacommentary. MESTER, Vol.
11, no. 2 (1982), p. 3-14. English. **DESCR**:
Anaya, Rudolfo A.; BLESS ME, ULTIMA;
Fiction; Literary Characteristics; *Literary
Criticism; Literature.

9630 Candelaria, Nash. The day the Cisco kid shot
John Wayne. REVISTA CHICANO-RIQUENA, Vol.
11, no. 2 (Summer 1983), p. 52-64. English.

9631 Candelaria, Nash. The retribution. REVISTA
CHICANO-RIQUENA, Vol. 10, no. 1-2 (Winter,
Spring, 1982), p. 180-188. English.

9632 Carrie, Jacques. Suicidal pieces. MAIZE,
Vol. 3, no. 1-2 (Fall, Winter, 1979, 1980),
p. 36-44. English.

9633 Castillo, Rafael C. The Colonel. NUESTRO,
Vol. 7, no. 2 (March 1983), p. 46-48.
English. **DESCR**: *Short Story.

9634 Chavez, Denise. Evening in Paris. REVISTA
CHICANO-RIQUENA, Vol. 11, no. 2 (Summer
1983), p. 65-70. English.

9635 Cota, Claudia Maritza. The scary night.
MAIZE, Vol. 3, no. 1-2 (Fall, Winter, 1979,
1980), p. 34. English.

9636 De la Riva, Osa. She's. MAIZE, Vol. 3, no.
1-2 (Fall, Winter, 1979, 1980), p. 60.
English.

9637 de Leon Hernandez, Victor. Un pecado.
REVISTA CHICANO-RIQUENA, Vol. 10, no. 3
(Summer 1982), p. 39-41. Spanish.

9638 De Vallbona, Rima. Alma-en-pena. REVISTA
CHICANO-RIQUENA, Vol. 11, no. 3-4 (Fall
1983), p. 122-126. Spanish.

9639 De Vallbona, Rima. El nagual de mi amiga
Irene. LA PALABRA, Vol. 4, no. 1-2 (Spring,
Fall, 1982, 1983), p. 151-157. Spanish.
DESCR: Literature; *Short Story.

9640 A decade of Hispanic literature: an
anniversary anthology. REVISTA
CHICANO-RIQUENA, Vol. 10, no. 1-2 (Winter,
Spring, 1982), p. 1-310. Bilingual. **DESCR**:
Essays; *Literature; Poetry.

9641 Engle, Margarita Mondrus. In the rain
forest. NUESTRO, Vol. 7, no. 7 (September
1983), p. 56-60. English. **DESCR**: *Short
Story.

Prose (cont.)

9642 Espinoza, Herbert O. At it ti tac. MAIZE, Vol. 3, no. 1-2 (Fall, Winter, 1979, 1980), p. 58-59. Spanish.

9643 Fernandez, Roberta. Amanda. REVISTA CHICANO-RIQUENA, Vol. 10, no. 1-2 (Winter, Spring, 1982), p. 192-199. Spanish.

9644 Fernandez, Roberta. Zulema. REVISTA CHICANO-RIQUENA, Vol. 11, no. 3-4 (Fall 1983), p. 127-138. Spanish.

9645 Figueredo, D.H. Old Havana. NUESTRO, Vol. 7, no. 3 (April 1983), p. 32-35. English. **DESCR:** *Short Story.

9646 Garzon, Luz Elena. Por que? MAIZE, Vol. 3, no. 3-4 (Spring, Summer, 1980), p. 90-92. Spanish.

9647 Gonzalez Cruz, Luis F. Lazaro volando. REVISTA CHICANO-RIQUENA, Vol. 10, no. 1-2 (Winter, Spring, 1982), p. 200-203. Spanish.

9648 Gonzalez, J. J. The hurricane. NUESTRO, Vol. 7, no. 3 (April 1983), p. 61-64. English. **DESCR:** *Short Story.

9649 Gordils, Yanis. Operacion obras a las manos. REVISTA CHICANO-RIQUENA, Vol. 10, no. 4 (Fall 1982), p. 31-38. Spanish.

9650 Gutierrez-Revuelta, Pedro. Juan perez, teacher de lengua. MAIZE, Vol. 4, no. 3-4 (Spring, Summer, 1981), p. 24-30. Spanish.

9651 Hinojosa-Smith, Rolando R. Don Orfalindo Buitureyra. REVISTA CHICANO-RIQUENA, Vol. 10, no. 1-2 (Winter, Spring, 1982), p. 204-206. Spanish.

9652 Hinojosa-Smith, Rolando R. Un poco de todo. REVISTA CHICANO-RIQUENA, Vol. 10, no. 1-2 (Winter, Spring, 1982), p. 207-210. Spanish.

9653 Hinojosa-Smith, Rolando R. The rites. REVISTA CHICANO-RIQUENA, Vol. 10, no. 1-2 (Winter, Spring, 1982), p. 211-214. English.

9654 Journey on the Inbound 35. CORAZON DE AZTLAN, Vol. 1, no. 3 (August, September, 1982), p. 12-13. English.

9655 Larrosa, Mara. Carta a Zanabria. MAIZE, Vol. 3, no. 3-4 (Spring, Summer, 1980), p. 83-85. Spanish.

9656 Lewis, William. Song of Lia. NUESTRO, Vol. 7, no. 3 (April 1983), p. 46-48. English. **DESCR:** *Short Story.

9657 Lopez-Dzur, Carlos A. Figuraciones de "El Angel". MAIZE, Vol. 5, no. 3-4 (Spring, Summer, 1982), p. 26-27. Bilingual.

9658 Luna, John. Roosevelt High: East Los. MAIZE, Vol. 3, no. 1-2 (Fall, Winter, 1979, 1980), p. 85-92. English.

9659 Martinez, Max. The adventures of the Chicano Kid: a dime novel. REVISTA CHICANO-RIQUENA, Vol. 10, no. 1-2 (Winter, Spring, 1982), p. 215-228. English.

9660 Martinez, Ricardo A. The healing ritual [complete novel]. EL GRITO DEL SOL, Vol. 7, no. 1-2 (1982), p. 1-174. English.

9661 Martinez-Serros, Hugo. Learn! learn! REVISTA CHICANO-RIQUENA, Vol. 10, no. 1-2 (Winter, Spring, 1982), p. 229-237. English.

9662 McEwan-Alvarado, Angela. Naranjas. REVISTA CHICANO-RIQUENA, Vol. 10, no. 1-2 (Winter, Spring, 1982), p. 238-240. Spanish.

9663 McKinney, J.E. Book review of: MOSAICO DE LA VIDA: CHICANO, CUBAN AND PUERTO RICAN PROSE. HISPANIA, Vol. 65, no. 2 (May 1982), p. 321. English. **DESCR:** Book Reviews; Jimenez, Francisco; *MOSAICO DE LA VIDA: CHICANO, CUBAN AND PUERTO RICAN PROSE; Spanish Language; Textbooks.

9664 Mohr, Nicholasa. An awakening... Summer 1956. REVISTA CHICANO-RIQUENA, Vol. 11, no. 3-4 (Fall 1983), p. 107-112. English.

9665 Mora, Pat. Hands. REVISTA CHICANO-RIQUENA, Vol. 10, no. 3 (Summer 1982), p. 33-37. English.

9666 Munoz, Elias Miguel. El sindrome del macho. MAIZE, Vol. 5, no. 1-2 (Fall, Winter, 1981, 1982), p. 39-46. Spanish.

9667 Nava Monreal, David. Mrs. De la Rosa. MAIZE, Vol. 4, no. 1-2 (Fall, Winter, 1980, 1981), p. 78-92. English.

9668 Perez, Hugo Hanriot. El boricua volador. REVISTA CHICANO-RIQUENA, Vol. 10, no. 1-2 (Winter, Spring, 1982), p. 189-191. Spanish.

9669 Ponce, Mary Helen. La despedida. MAIZE, Vol. 6, no. 1-2 (Fall, Winter, 1982, 1983), p. 56. Spanish.

9670 Ponce, Mary Helen. La doctora Barr. REVISTA CHICANO-RIQUENA, Vol. 11, no. 3-4 (Fall 1983), p. 113-115. English.

9671 Ponce, Mary Helen. Las guisas. MAIZE, Vol. 6, no. 1-2 (Fall, Winter, 1982, 1983), p. 54. Bilingual.

9672 Ponce, Mary Helen. El jabon de Dona Chonita. NUESTRO, Vol. 7, no. 10 (December 1983), p. 44-45. English. **DESCR:** Autobiography; *Ponce, Mary Helen; *Reminiscences.

9673 Ponce, Mary Helen. Recuerdo: how I changed the war and won the game. REVISTA CHICANO-RIQUENA, Vol. 11, no. 3-4 (Fall 1983), p. 116. English.

9674 Ponce, Mary Helen. Recuerdo: los piojos. REVISTA CHICANO-RIQUENA, Vol. 11, no. 3-4 (Fall 1983), p. 117-119. English.

9675 Ponce, Mary Helen. Los vatos. MAIZE, Vol. 6, no. 1-2 (Fall, Winter, 1982, 1983), p. 55. Bilingual.

9676 Portillo Trambley, Estela. La jon fontayn. REVISTA CHICANO-RIQUENA, Vol. 10, no. 1-2 (Winter, Spring, 1982), p. 241-250. English.

9677 Ranck, Katherine Quintana. Portrait of Dona Elena [complete novel]. EL GRITO DEL SOL, Vol. 6, no. 3-4 (1981), p. 1-89. English.

9678 Rico, Armando B. Three coffins for Nino Lencho [complete novel]. EL GRITO DEL SOL, Vol. 7, no. 3-4 (1982), p. 1-229. English.

9679 Rivera, Tomas. El Pete Fonseca. REVISTA CHICANO-RIQUENA, Vol. 10, no. 1-2 (Winter, Spring, 1982), p. 251-257. Spanish.

9680 Rubio, Sofia. A matter of faith. NUESTRO, Vol. 7, no. 3 (April 1983), p. 50-55. English. **DESCR:** *Short Story.

Prose (cont.)

9681 Sanchez, Rosaura. Entro y se sento. REVISTA CHICANO-RIQUENA, Vol. 10, no. 1-2 (Winter, Spring, 1982), p. 261-263. Spanish.

9682 Sanchez, Rosaura. Una manana: 1952. REVISTA CHICANO-RIQUENA, Vol. 10, no. 1-2 (Winter, Spring, 1982), p. 258-260. Spanish.

9683 Santana-Bejar, Patricia. In the toolshed. MAIZE, Vol. 4, no. 1-2 (Fall, Winter, 1980, 1981), p. 76-77. English.

9684 Soto, Gary. 1, 2, 3. REVISTA CHICANO-RIQUENA, Vol. 11, no. 2 (Summer 1983), p. 15-24. English.

9685 Soto, Gary; Trejo, Ernesto; and de la Fuente, Patricia. Special focus on Gary Soto. REVISTA CHICANO-RIQUENA, Vol. 11, no. 2 (Summer 1983), p. 7-39. English. **DESCR:** Literary Criticism; *Poetry; *Soto, Gary.

9686 Suarez, Mario. The migrant. REVISTA CHICANO-RIQUENA, Vol. 10, no. 4 (Fall 1982), p. 15-30. English.

9687 Tavera Rivera, Margarita. Sin nombre. MAIZE, Vol. 4, no. 1-2 (Fall, Winter, 1980, 1981), p. 74-75. Spanish.

9688 Trevino, Jesus Salvador. The great pyramid of Aztlan. NUESTRO, Vol. 7, no. 3 (April 1983), p. 36-40. English. **DESCR:** *Short Story.

9689 Trevino, Jesus Salvador. The last night of the mariachi. NUESTRO, Vol. 7, no. 3 (April 1983), p. 23-27. English. **DESCR:** *Short Story.

9690 Valdes, Gina. Te fijaste? MAIZE, Vol. 3, no. 3-4 (Spring, Summer, 1980), p. 86-89. Spanish.

9691 Valdes, Gina. Una vela una luna un sol. MAIZE, Vol. 3, no. 1-2 (Fall, Winter, 1979, 1980), p. 72-73. Spanish.

9692 Valencia, Juan O. Salud Pacheco. LA PALABRA, Vol. 4, no. 1-2 (Spring, Fall, 1982, 1983), p. 159-162. Spanish. **DESCR:** Literature; *Short Story.

9693 de Vallbona, Rima. El monstruo de las cosas. MAIZE, Vol. 5, no. 1-2 (Fall, Winter, 1981, 1982), p. 62-64. Spanish.

9694 Vega, Ed. Back by popular demand. MAIZE, Vol. 3, no. 1-2 (Fall, Winter, 1979, 1980), p. 16-22. English.

9695 Vega, Ed. Felicia Contreras de Manzanet. REVISTA CHICANO-RIQUENA, Vol. 10, no. 1-2 (Winter, Spring, 1982), p. 264-274. English.

9696 Vega, Ed. Fishing. NUESTRO, Vol. 7, no. 3 (April 1983), p. 28-31. English. **DESCR:** *Short Story.

9697 Villanueva, Alma. Her choice. MAIZE, Vol. 4, no. 3-4 (Spring, Summer, 1981), p. 88-92. English.

9698 Viramontes, Helen Maria. The broken web. REVISTA CHICANO-RIQUENA, Vol. 11, no. 3-4 (Fall 1983), p. 99-106. English.

9699 Williams, Christopher. Ramon's run. NUESTRO, Vol. 7, no. 3 (April 1983), p. 56-59. English. **DESCR:** *Short Story.

9700 Wood, Sylvia. Dreams by appointment only.

REVISTA CHICANO-RIQUENA, Vol. 11, no. 3-4 (Fall 1983), p. 82-98. English.

9701 Xochi. Alphabet soup. MAIZE, Vol. 3, no. 1-2 (Fall, Winter, 1979, 1980), p. 74-75. English.

9702 Yuscaran, Guillermo. Rubber sun. NUESTRO, Vol. 7, no. 6 (August 1983), p. 44-46. English. **DESCR:** *Short Story.

Protestant Church

9703 Jaech, Richard E. Latin American undocumented women in the United States. CURRENTS IN THEOLOGY AND MISSION, Vol. 9, no. 4 (August 1982), p. 196-211. English. **DESCR:** Garment Industry; Latin Americans; Socioeconomic Factors; *Undocumented Workers; *Women.

9704 Vigil, James Diego. Human revitalization: the six tasks of victory outreach. DREW GATEWAY, Vol. 52, no. 3 (Spring 1982), p. 49-59. English. **DESCR:** Barrios for Christ Program; Drug Addicts; Drug Programs; Gangs; Identity; Pentecostal Church; Religion; *Victory Outreach; Youth.

Proverbios
USE: Dichos

Proverbs
USE: Dichos

Prueba de Analisis Auditivo (PAA)

9705 Morrison, J. A. and Michael, W.B. Development and validation of an auditory perception test in Spanish for Hispanic children receiving reading instruction in Spanish. EDUCATIONAL AND PSYCHOLOGICAL MEASUREMENT, Vol. 42, (Summer 1982), p. 657-669. English. **DESCR:** Children; Educational Tests and Measurements; *Language Arts; Reading; Spanish Language.

Psychiatry

9706 Arce, A.A. Application of cognitive behavioral techniques in the treatment of Hispanic patients. PSYCHIATRIC QUARTERLY Vol. 54, no. 4 (March 1982), p. 230-236. English. **DESCR:** Attitude (Psychological).

9707 Brink, T. L. Book review of: PSYCHOLOGY MISDIRECTED. HISPANIC JOURNAL OF BEHAVIORAL SCIENCES, Vol. 5, no. 3 (September 1983), p. 363. English. **DESCR:** Book Reviews; *PSYCHOLOGY MISDIRECTED; Sarason, Seymour B.

9708 Escobar, J.I. Post-traumatic stress disorder in Hispanic Vietnam veterans. JOURNAL OF NERVOUS AND MENTAL DISEASE, Vol. 17, no. 10 (October 1983), p. 585-596. English. **DESCR:** Acculturation; Mental Illness; Stress; *Veterans.

9709 Good, Byron J. Reflexivity and countertransference in a psychiatric cultural consultation clinic. CULTURE, MEDICINE & PSYCHIATRY, Vol. 6, no. 3 (September 1982), p. 281-303. English. **DESCR:** Clinical Psychiatry; *Cultural Consultation Clinic.

9710 Maduro, Renaldo J. Working with Latinos and the use of dream analysis. JOURNAL OF THE AMERICAN ACADEMY OF PSYCHOANALYSIS, Vol. 10, no. 4 (October 1982), p. 609-628. English. **DESCR:** Culture; Dream Analysis; *Mental Health.

Psychiatry (cont.)

9711 Vazquez, Carol A. Research on the psychiatric evaluation of the bilingual patient: a methodological critique. HISPANIC JOURNAL OF BEHAVIORAL SCIENCES, Vol. 4, no. 1 (March 1982), p. 75-80. English. **DESCR:** Bilingualism; Mental Health; Research Methodology.

9712 Vernon, Sally W. and Roberts, Robert E. Prevalence of treated and untreated psychiatric disorders in three ethnic groups. SOCIAL SCIENCE AND MEDICINE, Vol. 16, no. 17 (1982), p. 1575-1582. English. **DESCR:** Anglo Americans; Blacks; Comparative Psychology; Mental Illness.

9713 Vernon, Sally W. and Roberts, Robert E. Use of the SADS-RDC in a tri-ethnic community survey. ARCHIVES OF GENERAL PSYCHIATRY, Vol. 39, no. 1 (January 1982), p. 47-52. English. **DESCR:** Ethnic Groups; Mental Health; Psychotherapy; *Schedule for Affective Disorders and Schizophrenia-Research Diagnostic Criteria (SADS-RDC).

Psychological Testing

9714 Adams, Russell L.; Boake, Corwin; and Crain, Charles. Bias in a neuropsychological test classification related to education, age and ethnicity. JOURNAL OF CONSULTING AND CLINICAL PSYCHOLOGY, Vol. 50, no. 1 (February 1982), p. 143-145. English. **DESCR:** Age Groups; Educational Levels; Ethnic Groups; Mentally Handicapped.

9715 Barclay, Lisa K. Using Spanish as the language of instruction with Mexican-American Head Start children: a re-evaluation using meta-analysis. PERCEPTUAL AND MOTOR SKILLS, Vol. 56, no. 2-4 (1983), p. 359-366. English. **DESCR:** Education; Languages; *Spanish Language.

9716 Franco, Juan N. An acculturation scale for Mexican-American children. JOURNAL OF GENERAL PSYCHOLOGY, Vol. 108, (April 1983), p. 175-181. English. **DESCR:** *Acculturation; Children; *Children's Acculturation Scale (CAS).

9717 Gibbs, Jewelle Taylor. Personality patterns of delinquent females: ethnic and sociocultural variations. JOURNAL OF CLINICAL PSYCHOLOGY, Vol. 38, no. 1 (January 1982), p. 198-206. English. **DESCR:** Chicanas; Ethnic Groups; Identity; *Juvenile Delinquency; Personality; Socioeconomic Factors.

9718 Gonzales, Eloy. A cross-cultural comparison of the developmental items of five ethnic groups in the Southwest. JOURNAL OF PERSONALITY ASSESSMENT, Vol. 46, no. 1 (February 1982), p. 26-31. English. **DESCR:** *Comparative Psychology; Draw-A-Person (DAP) [psychological test]; Ethnic Groups; Southwest United States.

9719 Hawley, Peggy and Even, Brenda. Work and sex-role attitudes in relation to education and other characteristics. VOCATIONAL GUIDANCE QUARTERLY, Vol. 31, no. 2 (December 1982), p. 101-108. English. **DESCR:** Careers; Chicanas; Ethnic Groups; *Sex Roles; Working Women.

9720 Hui, C. Harry. Multistrategy approach to cross-cultural research: the case of locus of control. JOURNAL OF CROSS-CULTURAL PSYCHOLOGY, Vol. 14, no. 1 (March 1983), p. 65-83. English. **DESCR:** Comparative Psychology; *Locus of Control; *Military Personnel.

9721 Kagan, Spencer and Knudsen, Kathryn H.M. Relationship of empathy and affective role-taking in young children. JOURNAL OF GENETIC PSYCHOLOGY, Vol. 141, (September 1982), p. 149-150. English. **DESCR:** Anglo Americans; *Attitude (Psychological); Child Study; Socialization.

9722 Knudsen, Kathryn H.M. and Kagan, Spencer. Differential development of empathy and pro-social behavior. JOURNAL OF GENETIC PSYCHOLOGY, Vol. 140, no. 2 (June 1982), p. 249-251. English. **DESCR:** Anglo Americans; *Attitude (Psychological); Child Study; Socialization.

9723 Murray, Anne M. and Mishra, Shitala P. Judgments of item bias in the McCarthy scales of children's abilities. HISPANIC JOURNAL OF BEHAVIORAL SCIENCES, Vol. 5, no. 3 (September 1983), p. 325-336. English. **DESCR:** Culture; *McCarthy Scales for Children's Abilities (MSCA).

9724 O'Donnell, James P., et al. Dimensions of behavior problems in Anglo-American and Mexican-American preschool children: a comparative study. JOURNAL OF CONSULTING AND CLINICAL PSYCHOLOGY, Vol. 50, no. 5 (October 1982), p. 643-651. English. **DESCR:** Anglo Americans; Children; *Comparative Psychology; Cultural Characteristics; Mental Health; Socioeconomic Factors.

9725 Ross-Reynolds, Jane and Reschly, Daniel J. An investigation of item bias on the WISC-R with four sociocultural groups. JOURNAL OF CONSULTING AND CLINICAL PSYCHOLOGY, Vol. 51, no. 1 (February 1983), p. 144-146. English. **DESCR:** Comparative Psychology; Ethnic Groups; *Wechsler Intelligence Scale for Children-Revised (WISC-R).

9726 Sattler, Jerome M. and Gwynne, John. Ethnicity and Bender Visual Motor Gestalt Test performance. JOURNAL OF SCHOOL PSYCHOLOGY, Vol. 20, no. 1 (Spring 1982), p. 69-71. English. **DESCR:** Anglo Americans; *Bender Visual Motor Gestalt Test; System of Multicultural Pluralistic Assessment (SOMPA).

9727 Zamudio, Anthony; Padilla, Amado M.; and Comrey, Andrew L. Personality structure of Mexican Americans using the Comrey Personality Scales. JOURNAL OF PERSONALITY ASSESSMENT, Vol. 47, no. 1 (February 1983), p. 100-106. English. **DESCR:** Colleges and Universities; Comrey Personality Scales (CPS); Minnesota Multiphasic Personality Inventory (MMPI); *Personality; Students.

Psychological Theory

9728 Clements, William M. Way to individuation in Anaya's BLESS ME, ULTIMA. MIDWEST QUARTERLY, Vol. 23, no. 2 (Winter 1982), p. 131-143. English. **DESCR:** Anaya, Rudolfo A.; *BLESS ME, ULTIMA; Literary Criticism.

9729 Cuellar, Israel and Price, Criselda Segovia. Psychiatric evaluation of bilingual patient: a reply to Vazquez. HISPANIC JOURNAL OF BEHAVIORAL SCIENCES, Vol. 4, no. 1 (March 1982), p. 81-83. English. **DESCR:** *Vasquez, Carol.

Psychological Theory (cont.)

9730 Galloway, Linda M. Bilingualism:
     neuropsychological considerations. JOURNAL
     OF RESEARCH AND DEVELOPMENT IN EDUCATION,
     Vol. 15, no. 3 (Spring 1982), p. 12-28.
     English. **DESCR:** *Bilingualism; Language
     Proficiency.

9731 Vazquez, Carol A. Reply to Cuellar and
     Price. HISPANIC JOURNAL OF BEHAVIORAL
     SCIENCES, Vol. 4, no. 1 (March 1982), p.
     85-88. English. **DESCR:** *Cuellar, Israel;
     Price, Criselda S.

Psychology

9732 Brink, T. L. Book review of: AVANCES EN
     PSICOLOGIA CONTEMPORANEA. HISPANIC JOURNAL
     OF BEHAVIORAL SCIENCES, Vol. 5, no. 4
     (December 1983), p. 494-496. English.
     DESCR: *AVANCES EN PSICOLOGIA CONTEMPORANEA;
     Book Reviews; Finley, Gordon E.; Marin,
     Gerardo.

9733 Cortese, Anthony. Moral development in
     Chicano and Anglo children. HISPANIC JOURNAL
     OF BEHAVIORAL SCIENCES, Vol. 4, no. 3
     (September 1982), p. 353-366. English.
     DESCR: Attitude (Psychological); *Ethics;
     Socialization.

9734 Dolgin, Daniel L., et al. Quality of life
     and psychological well-being in a bicultural
     Latino community. HISPANIC JOURNAL OF
     BEHAVIORAL SCIENCES, Vol. 4, no. 4 (December
     1982), p. 433-450. English. **DESCR:**
     Acculturation; *Attitude (Psychological);
     Depression Scale; *Global Acculturation
     Scale; Index of Psychological Adjustment;
     Quality of Life Scale.

9735 Freeman, Frank E.; Gonzalez, Diana; and
     Montgomery, Gary T. Experimenter effects in
     biofeedback training. JOURNAL OF SOCIAL
     PSYCHOLOGY, Vol. 11, no. 1 (February 1983),
     p. 119-123. English. **DESCR:** *Biofeedback;
     *Stress.

9736 Griffith, James. Relationship between
     acculturation and psychological impairment
     in adult Mexican Americans. HISPANIC JOURNAL
     OF BEHAVIORAL SCIENCES, Vol. 5, no. 4
     (December 1983), p. 431-459. English.
     DESCR: *Acculturation.

9737 Lewis, William. Machismo and the will to
     win. NUESTRO, Vol. 7, no. 9 (November 1983),
     p. 32-34. English. **DESCR:** Machismo; *Sports.

9738 Markides, Kyraikos S. Aging, religiosity,
     and adjustment: a longitudinal analysis.
     JOURNAL OF GERONTOLOGY, Vol. 38, no. 5
     (September 1983), p. 621-625. English.
     DESCR: *Ancianos; *Mental Health; Religion.

9739 Markides, Kyraikos S.; Dickson, Harold; and
     Pappas, Christine. Characteristics of
     dropouts in longitudinal research on aging -
     a study of Mexican-Americans and Anglos.
     EXPERIMENTAL AGING RESEARCH, Vol. 8, no. 3-4
     (1982), p. 163-167. English. **DESCR:**
     *Ancianos; Comparative Psychology; *Mental
     Health.

9740 Medina, Antonio S. Adolescent health in
     Alameda county. JOURNAL OF ADOLESCENT HEALTH
     CARE, Vol. 2, no. 3 (March 1982), p.
     175-182. English. **DESCR:** Alameda County, CA;
     *Dentistry; Drug Abuse; Medical Care; Youth.

9741 Murray, James L.; Bruhn, John G.; and Bunce,
     Harvey. Assessment of type A behavior in
     preschoolers. JOURNAL OF HUMAN STRESS, Vol.

9, no. 3 (September 1983), p. 32-39.
English. **DESCR:** Anglo Americans; Blacks;
*Children; Early Childhood Education.

9742 Ruiz, Rene A. and LeVine, Elaine S. Book
     review of: PSYCHOLOGY OF THE MEXICAN CULTURE
     AND PERSONALITY. JOURNAL OF ETHNIC STUDIES,
     Vol. 4, no. 2 (Summer 1976), p. 104-107.
     English. **DESCR:** Book Reviews; *Cultural
     Characteristics; Culture; *Diaz-Guerrero,
     Rogelio; Personality; PSYCHOLOGY OF THE
     MEXICAN CULTURE AND PERSONALITY.

PSYCHOLOGY AND COMMUNITY CHANGE

9743 Hunsaker, Alan. Book review of: PSYCHOLOGY
     AND COMMUNITY CHANGE; SOCIAL AND
     PSYCHOLOGICAL RESEARCH IN COMMUNITY SETTING;
     COMMUNITY PSYCHOLOGY: THEORETICAL AND
     EMPIRICAL APPROACHES. HISPANIC JOURNAL OF
     BEHAVIORAL SCIENCES, Vol. 5, no. 1 (March
     1983), p. 121-124. English. **DESCR:** Book
     Reviews; *COMMUNITY PSYCHOLOGY: THEORETICAL
     AND EMPIRICAL APPROACHES; Gibbs, Margaret
     S.; Heller, Kenneth; Kelly, James G.;
     Lachenmeyer, Juliana Rasic; Monahan, John;
     Munoz, Ricardo F.; Sigal, Janet; Snowden,
     Lonnie R.; *SOCIAL AND PSYCHOLOGICAL
     RESEARCH IN COMMUNITY SETTINGS.

PSYCHOLOGY MISDIRECTED

9744 Brink, T. L. Book review of: PSYCHOLOGY
     MISDIRECTED. HISPANIC JOURNAL OF BEHAVIORAL
     SCIENCES, Vol. 5, no. 3 (September 1983), p.
     363. English. **DESCR:** Book Reviews;
     Psychiatry; Sarason, Seymour B.

PSYCHOLOGY OF THE MEXICAN CULTURE AND PERSONALITY

9745 Ruiz, Rene A. and LeVine, Elaine S. Book
     review of: PSYCHOLOGY OF THE MEXICAN CULTURE
     AND PERSONALITY. JOURNAL OF ETHNIC STUDIES,
     Vol. 4, no. 2 (Summer 1976), p. 104-107.
     English. **DESCR:** Book Reviews; *Cultural
     Characteristics; Culture; *Diaz-Guerrero,
     Rogelio; Personality; Psychology.

Psychotherapy

9746 Cuellar, Israel, et al. Clinical psychiatric
     case presentation; culturally responsive
     diagnostic formulation and treatment in an
     Hispanic female. HISPANIC JOURNAL OF
     BEHAVIORAL SCIENCES, Vol. 5, no. 1 (March
     1983), p. 93-103. English. **DESCR:**
     *ACCULTURATION RATING SCALE FOR MEXICAN
     AMERICANS (ARSMA); Case Study; Chicanas;
     Medical Care.

9747 Delgado, Melvin. Hispanics and
     psychotherapeutic groups. INTERNATIONAL
     JOURNAL OF GROUP PSYCHOTHERAPY, Vol. 33, no.
     4 (October 1983), p. 507-520. English.
     DESCR: Acculturation.

9748 Franklin, Gerald S. and Kaufman, Karen S.
     Group psychotherapy for elderly female
     Hispanic outpatients. HOSPITAL AND COMMUNITY
     PSYCHIATRY, Vol. 33, no. 5 (May 1982), p.
     385-387. English. **DESCR:** Ancianos;
     *Chicanas.

9749 Gomez, Efrain A.; Ruiz, Pedro; and Laval,
     Ramon. Psychotherapy and bilingualism: is
     acculturation important? JOURNAL OF
     OPERATIONAL PSYCHIATRY, Vol. 13, no. 1
     (1982), p. 13-16. English. **DESCR:**
     *Bilingualism.

Psychotherapy (cont.)

9750 Hardy-Fanta, Carol and Montana, Priscila. The Hispanic female adolescent: a group therapy model. INTERNATIONAL JOURNAL OF GROUP PSYCHOTHERAPY, Vol. 32, no. 3 (July 1982), p. 351-366. English. DESCR: Puerto Ricans; *Women; Youth.

9751 Lawson, Harry H.; Kahn, Marrin W.; and Heiman, Elliott M. Psycho-pathology, treatment outcome and attitude toward mental illness in Mexican-American and European patients. INTERNATIONAL JOURNAL OF SOCIAL PSYCHIATRY, Vol. 28, no. 1 (Spring 1982), p. 20-26. English. DESCR: Anglo Americans; *Mental Illness.

9752 LeVine, Elaine S. and Franco, Juan N. Effects of therapist's gender, ethnicity, and verbal style on client's willingness to seek therapy. JOURNAL OF SOCIAL PSYCHOLOGY, Vol. 12, no. 1 (October 1983), p. 51-57. English. DESCR: *Counseling Services (Educational); Jourard's (3) Self-Disclosure Questionnaire; Mental Health; Social Services.

9753 Satow, Robert. A severe case of penis envy: the convergence of cultural and individual intra-psychic factors. JOURNAL OF THE AMERICAN ACADEMY OF PSYCHOANALYSIS, Vol. 11, no. 4 (October 1983), p. 547-556. English. DESCR: Freud, Sigmund; Puerto Ricans; Women.

9754 Vernon, Sally W. and Roberts, Robert E. Use of the SADS-RDC in a tri-ethnic community survey. ARCHIVES OF GENERAL PSYCHIATRY, Vol. 39, no. 1 (January 1982), p. 47-52. English. DESCR: Ethnic Groups; Mental Health; Psychiatry; *Schedule for Affective Disorders and Schizophrenia-Research Diagnostic Criteria (SADS-RDC).

9755 Yamamoto, Joe and Acosta, Frank X. Treatments of Asian Americans and Hispanic Americans: similarities and differences. JOURNAL OF THE AMERICAN ACADEMY OF PSYCHOANALYSIS, Vol. 10, no. 4 (October 1982), p. 585-607. English. DESCR: Asian Americans; Comparative Psychology; Los Angeles, CA; *Mental Health; Socioeconomic Factors.

Public Education
USE: Education

Public Employees
USE: Government Employees

Public Health

9756 Abrams, Herbert K. Occupational and environmental health problems along the U.S.-Mexico Border. SOUTHWEST ECONOMY AND SOCIETY, Vol. 4, no. 3 (Spring, Summer, 1979), p. 3-20. English. DESCR: Agricultural Laborers; *Border Region; Housing; Mexican Border Industrialization Program; Nutrition; *Pollution; Social History and Conditions.

9757 Aging research planned. NUESTRO, Vol. 7, no. 8 (October 1983), p. 9. English. DESCR: *Ancianos; Stanford University Medical Center.

9758 Amigos. LATINO, Vol. 53, no. 7 (November 1982), p. 9-10. English. DESCR: *Amigos de las Americas; Cultural Organizations.

9759 Bailey, Lynn B., et al. Folacin and iron status and hematological finding in Blacks and Spanish-American adolescents from urban low-income households. AMERICAN JOURNAL OF CLINICAL NUTRITION, Vol. 35, no. 5 (May 1982), p. 1023-1032. English. DESCR: Blacks; Low Income; Surveys; *Youth.

9760 Bath, C. Richard. Health and environmental problems: the role of the border in El Paso-Ciudad Juarez coordination. JOURNAL OF INTERAMERICAN STUDIES AND WORLD AFFAIRS, Vol. 24, no. 3 (August 1982), p. 375-392. English. DESCR: Border Region; Ciudad Juarez, Chihuahua, Mexico; *El Paso, TX; International Boundary and Water Commission; Nationalism; Pollution; United States-Mexico Relations; U.S Border Public Health Association (AFMES).

9761 Bose, Aruna; Vashistha, Krishan; and O'Loughlin, Bernard J. Azarcon por empacho - another cause of lead toxicity. PEDIATRICS, Vol. 72, no. 1 (July 1983), p. 106-108. English. DESCR: Children; Folk Medicine; *Lead Poisoning.

9762 Cancer protection project. LATINO, Vol. 54, no. 5 (August, September, 1983), p. 14. English. DESCR: Cancer.

9763 Coping with stress. LATINO, Vol. 53, no. 4 (June 1982), p. 27. English. DESCR: Stress.

9764 Cox, Rebecca A., et al. HLA phenotypes in Mexican-Americans with tuberculosis. AMERICAN REVIEW OF RESPIRATORY DISEASE, Vol. 126, no. 4 (October 1982), p. 653-655. English. DESCR: *Medical Research; Medicine; *Tuberculosis.

9765 Dienhart, Paul. Minnesota support groups help Latinos through medical school. NUESTRO, Vol. 6, no. 6 (August 1982), p. 39-40. English. DESCR: Health Education; Latin Americans; Medical Education; Medical Students; Minnesota; *University of Minnesota.

9766 Dodge, Russell. A comparison of the respiratory health of Mexican-American and non-Mexican American white children. CHEST, Vol. 84, no. 5 (November 1983), p. 587-592. English. DESCR: Anglo Americans; Children.

9767 Effective ways to fight cancer in new publication. LATINO, Vol. 54, no. 8 (December 1983), p. 24. English. DESCR: *Cancer; *Preventative Medicine.

9768 Garcia, Ignacio M. Miracles at Kino Hospital. NUESTRO, Vol. 7, no. 6 (August 1983), p. 11-12. English. DESCR: *Gonzalez, Arthur; Hospitals and the Community; *Kino Community Hospital, Tucson, AZ; Medical Care.

9769 Gaviria, Moises; Stern, Gwen; and Schensul, Stephen L. Sociocultural factors and perinatal health in a Mexican-American community. NATIONAL MEDICAL ASSOCIATION JOURNAL, Vol. 74, no. 10 (October 1982), p. 983-989. English. DESCR: Chicago, IL; Migration Patterns; *Prenatal Care; Socioeconomic Factors.

9770 Giachello, Aida L., et al. Uses of the 1980 census for Hispanic health services research. AMERICAN JOURNAL OF PUBLIC HEALTH, Vol. 73, no. 3 (March 1983), p. 266-274. English. DESCR: Census; Research Methodology; *Surveys.

Public Health (cont.)

9771 Gombeski, William R., Jr., et al. Communicating health information to urban Mexican-Americans: sources of health information. HEALTH EDUCATION QUARTERLY, Vol. 9, no. 4 (Winter 1982), p. 293-309. English. **DESCR:** Doctor Patient Relations; Health Education; Mass Media; Surveys.

9772 Government review. NUESTRO, Vol. 7, no. 7 (September 1983), p. 55. English. **DESCR:** AIDS Hotline; California; Education; Employment; Food for Survival, New York, NY; Funding Sources; *Government Services; Hewlett Foundation; Laborers; Mathematics, Engineering and Science Achievement (MESA); Population Trends; Stanford University, Stanford, CA.

9773 Guendelman, Sylvia. Developing responsiveness to health needs of Hispanic children and families. SOCIAL WORK IN HEALTH CARE, Vol. 8, no. 4 (Summer 1983), p. 1-15. English. **DESCR:** Children; Family; *Social Psychology.

9774 Health fairs set for 10 cities. LATINO, Vol. 54, no. 2 (March 1983), p. 20. English.

9775 Hernandez Arnazzi, H. To your health. LATINA, Vol. 1, no. 1 (1982), p. 8. English.

9776 HHR proposes safety plan for care homes. NUESTRO, Vol. 6, no. 4 (May 1982), p. 57-58. English. **DESCR:** *Ancianos.

9777 Hispanics responding well to health survey. NUESTRO, Vol. 7, no. 1 (January, February, 1983), p. 47. English. **DESCR:** *Hispanic Health and Nutrition Examination Survey (HHANES); National Center for Health Statistics.

9778 Holck, Susan E. Lung cancer mortality and smoking habits: Mexican-American women. AMERICAN JOURNAL OF PUBLIC HEALTH, Vol. 72, no. 1 (January 1982), p. 38-42. English. **DESCR:** Anglo Americans; *Cancer; Chicanas.

9779 Latin health study. NUESTRO, Vol. 5, no. 8 (November 1981), p. 12. English. **DESCR:** U.S. Department of Health and Human Services.

9780 Lewis, Rose. Poisons: handle with care. LATINA, Vol. 1, no. 2 (February, March, 1983), p. 77-78. English.

9781 LULAC-Red Cross agreement. LATINO, Vol. 53, no. 8 (December 1982), p. 25. English. **DESCR:** *League of United Latin American Citizens (LULAC).

9782 Major health survey of Latinos undertaken. NUESTRO, Vol. 6, no. 7 (September 1982), p. 56. English. **DESCR:** *Hispanic Health and Nutrition Examination Survey (HHANES).

9783 Marin, Barbara Van Oss, et al. Utilization of traditional and non-traditional sources of health care among Hispanics. HISPANIC JOURNAL OF BEHAVIORAL SCIENCES, Vol. 5, no. 1 (March 1983), p. 65-80. English. **DESCR:** *Medical Care.

9784 Mendez, Jose A. and Esquer, Cecilia D. The impact of undocumented aliens on health and public health care in Arizona. ARIZONA BUSINESS, Vol. 30, no. 3 (1983), p. 3-7. English. **DESCR:** Arizona; *Arizona Health Care Cost Containment System (AHCCCS); Government Funding Sources; Public Policy; Undocumented Workers.

9785 Nalven, Joseph. Health research on undocumented Mexicans. SOCIAL SCIENCE JOURNAL, Vol. 19, no. 2 (April 1982), p. 73-88. English. **DESCR:** Immigrants; Immigration Law; Medical Care; *Undocumented Workers.

9786 Nalven, Joseph. Who benefits from knowledge about the health of undocumented Mexicans? POLICY STUDIES JOURNAL, Vol. 10, no. 3 (March 1982), p. 556-580. English. **DESCR:** *Undocumented Workers.

9787 New nutritional research center to study aging. NUESTRO, Vol. 6, no. 4 (May 1982), p. 57. English. **DESCR:** *Ancianos; Health Education.

9788 O'Brien, Mary Elizabeth. Pragmatic survivalism: behavior patterns affecting low-level wellness among minority group members. ANS: ADVANCES IN NURSING SCIENCE, Vol. 4, no. 3 (April 1982), p. 13-26. English. **DESCR:** Curanderismo; Ethnic Attitudes; Immigrants; *Medical Care; *Nursing.

9789 Ponce-Adame, Merrihelen. Latinas and breast cancer. NUESTRO, Vol. 6, no. 8 (October 1982), p. 30-31. English. **DESCR:** Cancer; Chicanas.

9790 Roberts, Robert E.; Attkisson, C. Clifford; and Stegner, Bruce L. A client satisfaction scale suitable for use with Hispanics? HISPANIC JOURNAL OF BEHAVIORAL SCIENCES, Vol. 5, no. 4 (December 1983), p. 461-476. English. **DESCR:** *Community Mental Health.

9791 Rodriguez, Josie. Mexican-Americans: factors influencing health practices. JOURNAL OF SCHOOL HEALTH, Vol. 53, no. 2 (Fall 1983), p. 136-139. English. **DESCR:** Curanderismo; Medical Care.

9792 Roeder, Beatrice A. Health care beliefs and practices among the Mexican Americans. AZTLAN, Vol. 13, no. 1-2 (Spring, Fall, 1982), p. 223-256. English. **DESCR:** Folk Medicine; *Literature Reviews; Medical Care.

9793 Samet, Jonathan M., et al. Respiratory disease in a New Mexico population sample of Hispanic and non-Hispanic whites. AMERICAN REVIEW OF RESPIRATORY DISEASE, Vol. 125, no. 2 (February 1982), p. 152-157. English. **DESCR:** Bernalillo County, NM; *Medical Research; Medicine.

9794 Stern, Michael P., et al. Does obesity explain excess prevalence of diabetes among Mexican Americans? Results of the San Antonio Heart Study. DIABETOLOGIA, Vol. 24, no. 4 (April 1983), p. 272-277. English. **DESCR:** *Diabetes; Medical Research; Medicine; Obesity; *San Antonio Heart Study.

9795 Su salud. LATINO, Vol. 53, no. 4 (June 1982), p. 19. Spanish.

9796 Tejani, Amir et al. Lupus nephritis in Black and Hispanic children. AMERICAN JOURNAL OF DISEASES OF CHILDREN, Vol. 137, no. 5 (May 1983), p. 481-483. English. **DESCR:** *Children; Medical Care; *Medical Research.

9797 Trevino, Fernando M. Vital and health statistics for the United States Hispanic population. AMERICAN JOURNAL OF PUBLIC HEALTH, Vol. 72, no. 9 (September 1982), p. 979-982. English. **DESCR:** *Vital Statistics.

Public Health (cont.)

9798 Trotter, Robert T. Contrasting models of the healer's role: south Texas case examples. HISPANIC JOURNAL OF BEHAVIORAL SCIENCES, Vol. 4, no. 3 (September 1982), p. 315-327. English. DESCR: Cultural Characteristics; *Curanderismo; Medical Care.

9799 Wise, Robert P. The persistence of poor health in Guatemala: a preventive medical perspective. JOURNAL OF LATIN COMMUNITY HEALTH, Vol. 1, no. 1 (Fall 1982), p. 71-79. English. DESCR: *Guatemala.

Public Health Legislation

9800 Chavez, Leo R. Undocumented immigrants and access to health services: a game of pass the buck. MIGRATION TODAY, Vol. 11, no. 1 (1983), p. 14-19. English. DESCR: California; *Immigrants; Medical Care; Migrant Health Services; Simpson-Mazzoli Bill; Social Services; Undocumented Workers.

Public Hygiene
USE: Public Health

Public Law 78

9801 Turansick, Michael F. A critique of proposed amendments to the immigration and nationality act. FORDHAM INTERNATIONAL LAW FORUM, Vol. 5, no. 1 (Winter 1981, 1982), p. 213-238. English. DESCR: Border Patrol; Braceros; *Immigration and Nationality Act (INA); Immigration Regulation and Control; Undocumented Workers.

Public Libraries

9802 Cabello-Argandona, Roberto; Crary, Eleanor R.; and Pisano, Vivian M. Subject access for Hispanic library users. LIBRARY JOURNAL, Vol. 107, no. 14 (August 1982), p. 1383-1385. English. DESCR: Catalogues; *HISPANEX (Oakland, CA); Library Services.

9803 Josel, Nathan A. Public library material selection in a bilingual community. CATHOLIC LIBRARY WORLD, Vol. 54, no. 3 (October 1982), p. 113-115. English. DESCR: Bilingualism; El Paso, TX; Library Collections; Spanish Language.

9804 Naismith, Rachael. Field work: outreach to migrants. RQ - REFERENCE AND ADULT SERVICES DIVISION, Vol. 22, no. 1 (Fall 1982), p. 33-35. English. DESCR: Cumberland County Library, NJ; Fresno County Public Library, CA; *Library Services; *Migrant Labor.

9805 Naismith, Rachael. Moveable library: serving migrant farm workers. WILSON LIBRARY BULLETIN, Vol. 57, no. 7 (March 1983), p. 571-575. English. DESCR: *Dodge County Library System, WI; *Fresno County Public Library, CA; Library Services; Migrant Labor.

Public Opinion

9806 MacManus, Susan A. and Cassel, Carol A. Mexican-Americans in city-politics: participation, representation, and policy preferences. URBAN INTEREST, Vol. 4, no. 1 (Spring 1982), p. 57-69. English. DESCR: Blacks; Houston, TX; Local Government; *Political Representation; Public Policy.

9807 Peterson, Robert A. and Kozmetsky, George. Public opinion regarding illegal aliens in Texas. TEXAS BUSINESS REVIEW, Vol. 56, no. 3 (May, June, 1982), p. 118-121. English. DESCR: Surveys; Texas; *Undocumented Workers.

Public Policy

9808 Changing Hispanic political loyalties. HISPANIC BUSINESS, Vol. 4, no. 6 (June 1982), p. 23. English. DESCR: Los Angeles, CA; *Political Parties and Organizations; Politics; San Antonio, TX; *Surveys.

9809 Grimond, John. Reconquista begins. ECONOMIST (London), Vol. 283, (April 3, 1982), p. 12-17. English. DESCR: Political Parties and Organizations; *Political Representation; The East Los Angeles Community Union (TELACU); United Neighborhoods Organization (UNO).

9810 Kjolseth, Rolf. Cultural politics of bilingualism. SOCIETY, Vol. 20, no. 4 (May, June, 1983), p. 40-48. English. DESCR: *Bilingualism; Cultural Pluralism.

9811 MacManus, Susan A. and Cassel, Carol A. Mexican-Americans in city-politics: participation, representation, and policy preferences. URBAN INTEREST, Vol. 4, no. 1 (Spring 1982), p. 57-69. English. DESCR: Blacks; Houston, TX; Local Government; *Political Representation; Public Opinion.

9812 Mendez, Jose A. and Esquer, Cecilia D. The impact of undocumented aliens on health and public health care in Arizona. ARIZONA BUSINESS, Vol. 30, no. 3 (1983), p. 3-7. English. DESCR: Arizona; *Arizona Health Care Cost Containment System (AHCCCS); Government Funding Sources; *Public Health; Undocumented Workers.

9813 Research/development: books. HISPANIC BUSINESS, Vol. 4, no. 2 (February 1982), p. 28. English. DESCR: Book Reviews; Business; Business Enterprises; *FINANCING YOUR BUSINESS; *Loffel, Egon W.; *National Hispanic Center for Advanced Studies and Policy Analysis (NHCAS); *THE STATE OF HISPANIC AMERICA.

Public Relations

9814 Communications/marketing. HISPANIC BUSINESS, Vol. 5, no. 1 (January 1983), p. 23. English. DESCR: Banking Industry; Broadcast Media; Caballero Spanish Media, Inc. (CSM); Fleishman-Hillard, Inc.; *Marketing; Miami, FL; Nogales, Luis G.

9815 Garcia, Art R. Art Garcia's capital gains: staying on top of the public relations games. HISPANIC BUSINESS, Vol. 5, no. 5 (May 1983), p. 12. English. DESCR: *Consultants.

9816 High energy community relations: Con Edison's Carlota M. Maduro. HISPANIC BUSINESS, Vol. 4, no. 2 (February 1982), p. 14. English. DESCR: Biography; Community Services; Consolidated Edison Company of New York, Inc.; *Maduro, Carlota M.

Public Restoration

9817 Snethcamp, P. E. Reflections of the past - public restoration and interpretation of Hispanic sites. AMERICAN JOURNAL OF ARCHAEOLOGY, Vol. 86, no. 2 (April 1982), p. 286. English. DESCR: Architecture.

Public Television

9818 THE BALLAD OF GREGORIO CORTEZ. NUESTRO, Vol.
6, no. 4 (May 1982), p. 63. English. **DESCR:**
*BALLAD OF GREGORIO CORTEZ [film]; Cortez,
Gregorio; Television.

9819 Three PBS reporters seek teenage audience.
NUESTRO, Vol. 6, no. 3 (April 1982), p. 37.
English.

9820 Trevino, Jesus Salvador. Latinos & public
broadcasting: the 2% factor. CAMINOS, Vol.
4, no. 3 (March 1983), p. 25-27,50.
Bilingual. **DESCR:** Television.

9821 Yes, Inc. CAMINOS, Vol. 4, no. 9 (October
1983), p. 22,54-55. Bilingual.

Public Welfare
USE: Welfare

Publications
USE: Books

Publicidad Siboney

9822 Communications/marketing. HISPANIC BUSINESS,
Vol. 4, no. 3 (March 1982), p. 15. English.
DESCR: California; Herrera, Maria Elena;
*Marketing; Philip Morris, Inc.; Siboney
Advertising, Inc.; SRI International.

9823 Communications/marketing. HISPANIC BUSINESS,
Vol. 4, no. 4 (April 1982), p. 15. English.
DESCR: Advertising Agencies; Consumers;
Juarez and Associates, Inc.; Las Americas,
Inc.; *Marketing; Norman, Craig & Kummel
Organization; Siboney Advertising, Inc.

Publicize
USE: Advertising

Publishing Industry

9824 Churchhill, Ward. Implications of publishing
ROOTS OF RESISTANCE. JOURNAL OF ETHNIC
STUDIES, Vol. 9, no. 3 (Fall 1981), p.
83-89. English. **DESCR:** Book Reviews;
Colonialism; Dunbar Ortiz, Roxanne; Land
Tenure; Native Americans; New Mexico; *ROOTS
OF RESISTANCE: LAND TENURE IN NEW MEXICO,
1680-1980; Social History and Conditions.

9825 Communications/marketing. HISPANIC BUSINESS,
Vol. 4, no. 2 (February 1982), p. 15.
English. **DESCR:** Cable Television;
Congressional Hispanic Caucus; El Teatro
Campesino; GalaVision; Labor Unions;
*Marketing; Philip Morris, Inc.; Spanish
International Network (SIN).

9826 Mexican centers advance U.S. ties. NUESTRO,
Vol. 7, no. 1 (January, February, 1983), p.
10-11. English. **DESCR:** Art Galleries; *El
Centro Mexicano del Libro; Los Angeles, CA;
Mexico; Museums; New York, NY.

9827 New calendar salutes Latino military men.
NUESTRO, Vol. 6, no. 4 (May 1982), p. 47.
English. **DESCR:** De Galvez, Bernardo;
*Farragut, David G.

9828 Schon, Isabel. Books in Spanish and
bilingual books for young readers: some
good, some bad. SCHOOL LIBRARY JOURNAL, Vol.
29, (March 1983), p. 87-91. English.
DESCR: *Children's Literature.

9829 See, Lisa. Chicano writers: looking for a
breakout. PUBLISHER'S WEEKLY, Vol. 224,
(September 30, 1983), p. 94. English.
DESCR: *Authors; Literature.

9830 Southern Bell faces directory competition.
NUESTRO, Vol. 6, no. 8 (October 1982), p.
47. English. **DESCR:** *MIAMI EN SUS MANOS;
SPANISH YELLOW PAGES.

Pueblo
USE: Barrios

Pueblo, CO

9831 AM-COR Architects & Engineers, Inc. aligns
growth. HISPANIC BUSINESS, Vol. 4, no. 7
(July 1982), p. 12-13. English. **DESCR:**
Business Enterprises; *Engineering;
Engineering as a Profession.

Pueblo Indians

9832 Dunbar Ortiz, Roxanne. The roots of
resistance: Pueblo land tenure and Spanish
colonization. JOURNAL OF ETHNIC STUDIES,
Vol. 5, no. 4 (Winter 1977), p. 33-53.
English. **DESCR:** *Land Tenure; Native
Americans; New Mexico; Social History and
Conditions.

Puente, Tito

9833 Diaz, Katherine A. El rey del timbal Tito
Puente (interview). CAMINOS, Vol. 4, no. 10
(November 1983), p. 14-16. English. **DESCR:**
*Jazz.

Puerto Rican Day Parade

9834 Puerto Rican observance. NUESTRO, Vol. 6,
no. 6 (August 1982), p. 11. English. **DESCR:**
*Puerto Ricans.

Puerto Rican Education

9835 Improving the schools. NUESTRO, Vol. 6, no.
3 (April 1982), p. 9. English. **DESCR:**
*Bilingual Bicultural Education; Education;
Puerto Ricans.

9836 Olivas, Michael A. Indian, Chicano and
Puerto Rican colleges: status and issues.
BILINGUAL REVIEW, Vol. 9, no. 1 (January,
March, 1982), p. 36-58. English. **DESCR:**
*Colleges and Universities; Education;
Native Americans; Treaties.

9837 Seilhamer, E. Stella and Prewitt-Diaz,
Joseph O. The return and circulatory migrant
student: a perception of teachers, schools
and self. MIGRATION TODAY, Vol. 11, no. 1
(1983), p. 21-23. English. **DESCR:** Cultural
Characteristics; Identity; Migration
Patterns; Puerto Ricans.

Puerto Rican Hawaiians

9838 Espada, Frank. Who am I?: Puerto Rican
Hawaiians ask. NUESTRO, Vol. 6, no. 8
(October 1982), p. 32-33. English. **DESCR:**
Ethnic Groups; Identity; *Puerto Ricans.

Puerto Rican Independence Party

9839 Barrios-Martinez, Ruben. Should Puerto Rico
become a state?: against statehood. NUESTRO,
Vol. 7, no. 5 (June, July, 1983), p. 37-39.
English. **DESCR:** *Colonialism; *International
Relations; *Puerto Rico; Racism; United
States.

Puerto Rican Literature

9840 Algarin, Miguel. Nuyorican literature.
MELUS: MULTI-ETHNIC LITERATURE OF THE UNITED
STATES, Vol. 8, no. 2 (Summer 1981), p.
89-92. English.

Puerto Rican Literature (cont.)

9841 Barradas, Efrain. "Todo lo que digo es cierto...": en memoria de Victor Fernandez Fragoso (1944-1982). REVISTA CHICANO-RIQUENA, Vol. 10, no. 3 (Summer 1982), p. 43-46. Spanish. **DESCR:** Authors; *Biography; Essays; *Fernandez Fragoso, Victor; New York, NY.

9842 Binder, Wolfgang and Thomas, Piri. An interview with Piri Thomas. MINORITY VOICES, Vol. 4, no. 1 (Spring 1980), p. 63-78. English. **DESCR:** DOWN THESE MEAN STREETS; *Thomas, Piri.

9843 Binder, Wolfgang. Book review of: INVENTING A WORD: AN ANTHOLOGY OF TWENTIETH CENTURY PUERTO RICAN POETRY. MELUS: MULTI-ETHNIC LITERATURE OF THE UNITED STATES, Vol. 8, no. 1 (Spring 1981), p. 77-79. English. **DESCR:** INVENTING A WORD, AN ANTHOLOGY OF TWENTIETH CENTURY PUERTO RICAN POETRY; *Marzan, Julio.

9844 Daydi-Tolson, Santiago. The right to belong: a critic's view of Puerto Rican poetry in the United States. BILINGUAL REVIEW, Vol. 10, no. 1 (January, April, 1983), p. 81-86. English. **DESCR:** Barradas, Efrain; Book Reviews; *HEREJES Y MITIFICADORES: MUESTRA DE POESIA PUERTORRIQUENA EN LOS ESTADOS UNIDOS.

9845 Fernandez Olmos, Margarite. From the metropolis: Puerto Rican women poets and the immigration experience. THIRD WOMAN, Vol. 1, no. 2 (1982), p. 40-51. English. **DESCR:** Essays; *Women.

9846 Griffin, Julia Ortiz. Two artists in search of a country: Rafael Rios Rey and Francisco Arrivi. MINORITY VOICES, Vol. 5, no. 1-2 (Spring, Fall, 1981), p. 53-58. English. **DESCR:** *Arrivi, Francisco; Artists; Puerto Ricans; *Rios Rey, Rafael; Teatro.

9847 Laguardia, Gari. The canon and the air-conditioner: modern Puerto Rican poetry. BILINGUAL REVIEW, Vol. 9, no. 2 (May, August, 1982), p. 178-181. English. **DESCR:** Book Reviews; *INVENTING A WORD, AN ANTHOLOGY OF TWENTIETH CENTURY PUERTO RICAN POETRY; Marzan, Julio; Poetry.

9848 Nieto, Sonia. Children's literature on Puerto Rican themes -- the messages of fiction; non-fiction. INTERRACIAL BOOKS FOR CHILDREN, Vol. 14, no. 1-2 (1983), p. 6-12. English. **DESCR:** *Children's Literature; Puerto Ricans.

9849 Rivero, Eliana S. Book review of: HEREJES Y MITIFICADORES: MUESTRA DE POESIA PUERTORRIQUENA EN LOS ESTADOS UNIDOS. THIRD WOMAN, Vol. 1, no. 2 (1982), p. 91-93. Spanish. **DESCR:** Barradas, Efrain; Book Reviews; *HEREJES Y MITIFICADORES: MUESTRA DE POESIA PUERTORRIQUENA EN LOS ESTADOS UNIDOS; Rodriguez, Rafael.

9850 Turner, Faythe. Book review of: THE NUYORICAN EXPERIENCE: LITERATURE OF THE PUERTO RICAN MINORITY. MELUS: MULTI-ETHNIC LITERATURE OF THE UNITED STATES, Vol. 10, no. 2 (Summer 1983), p. 85-88. English. **DESCR:** *Mohr, Eugene V.; THE NUYORICAN EXPERIENCE: LITERATURE OF THE PUERTO RICAN MINORITY.

9851 Umpierre, Luz Maria. Un manifiesto literario: PAPELES DE PANDERA DE ROSARIO FERRE. BILINGUAL REVIEW, Vol. 9, no. 2 (May, August, 1982), p. 120126. Spanish. **DESCR:** Book Reviews; Ferre, Rosario; *PAPELES DE PANDORA; Poetry.

Puerto Rican Music

9852 Andersen, Kurt. A Puerto Rican pop music machine. TIME, Vol. 121, no. 26 (June 27, 1983), p. 46. English. **DESCR:** *Menudo [musical group]; Musicians.

9853 Latino of the Year 1983: Menudo. LATINO, Vol. 54, no. 8 (December 1983), p. 8-11. English. **DESCR:** *Menudo [musical group]; *Musicians.

9854 Mejias-Rentas, Antonio. Una dosis puertorriquena de Menudo. LATINO, Vol. 54, no. 8 (December 1983), p. 12. Spanish. **DESCR:** *Menudo [musical group]; *Musicians.

9855 Mejias-Rentas, Antonio. A Puerto Rican dose of Menudo. NUESTRO, Vol. 7, no. 7 (September 1983), p. 49. English. **DESCR:** *Menudo [musical group]; Musicians.

9856 Menudo: dishing it up in Los Angeles. CAMINOS, Vol. 4, no. 8 (September 1983), p. 46. Bilingual. **DESCR:** Artists; *Menudo [musical group]; Music; Musicians.

Puerto Rican Studies

9857 Vivo, Paquita. Book review of: PUERTO RICO: A POLITICAL AND CULTURAL HISTORY. NUESTRO, Vol. 7, no. 5 (June, July, 1983), p. 63. English. **DESCR:** Book Reviews; Carrion, Arturo Morales; History; Puerto Rico; *PUERTO RICO: A POLITICAL AND CULTURAL HISTORY; United States History.

Puerto Ricans

9858 Barreto, Julio. A new force in the barrio. NUESTRO, Vol. 7, no. 4 (May 1983), p. 43-45. English. **DESCR:** Caballero-Perez, Diana; *Community Development; *Cultural Organizations; National Congress for Puerto Rican Rights (NCPRR).

9859 Borjas, George J. Earnings of male Hispanic immigrants in the United States. INDUSTRIAL AND LABOR RELATIONS REVIEW, Vol. 35, no. 3 (April 1982), p. 343-353. English. **DESCR:** Cubanos; Ethnic Groups; *Immigrants; *Income; Social Mobility.

9860 Borjas, George J. The labor supply of male Hispanic immigrants in the United States. INTERNATIONAL MIGRATION REVIEW, Vol. 17, no. 4 (Winter 1983), p. 653-671. English. **DESCR:** Assimilation; Immigration; Labor Supply and Market; *Native Americans.

9861 Bray, Howard. The new wave of Puerto Rican immigrants. NEW YORK TIMES MAGAZINE, (July 3, 1983), p. 22. English. **DESCR:** Acculturation; Immigration.

9862 De Barbosa, Liliam Coya. "Mastering learning" como metodo psicoeducativo para ninos con problemas especificos de aprendizaje. HISPANIC JOURNAL OF BEHAVIORAL SCIENCES, Vol. 4, no. 4 (December 1982), p. 503-510. Spanish. **DESCR:** Children; Learning and Cognition; *Mastery Learning; *Reading.

9863 Delgado, Melvin. Ethnic and cultural variations in the care of the aged. Hispanic elderly and natural support systems: a special focus on Puerto Ricans. JOURNAL OF GERIATRIC PSYCHIATRY, Vol. 15, no. 2 (1982), p. 239-251. English. **DESCR:** *Ancianos; Cultural Organizations; Curanderas; Family; Natural Support Systems; Religion; Santeros.

Puerto Ricans (cont.)

9864 Diaz, Tom. Turning numbers into clout. NUESTRO, Vol. 7, no. 10 (December 1983), p. 34-35. English. **DESCR:** National Puerto Rican Coalition; *National Puerto Rican/Hispanic Voter Participation Project; *Voter Turnout.

9865 Dvorak, Trisha and Kirschner, Carl. Mary likes fishes: reverse psychological phenomena in New York Puerto Rican Spanish. BILINGUAL REVIEW, Vol. 9, no. 1 (January, April, 1982), p. 59-65. English. **DESCR:** New York; *Spanish Language; *Syntax.

9866 Espada, Frank. Who am I?: Puerto Rican Hawaiians ask. NUESTRO, Vol. 6, no. 8 (October 1982), p. 32-33. English. **DESCR:** Ethnic Groups; Identity; *Puerto Rican Hawaiians.

9867 Ferre honored at concert. NUESTRO, Vol. 6, no. 4 (May 1982), p. 12-13. English. **DESCR:** *Ferre, Don Luis A.

9868 Ferre, Maurice A. Decade of the Hispanic. ADVERTISING AGE MAGAZINE, Vol. 53, (February 15, 1982), p. II, M14+. English. **DESCR:** Cubanos; *Population Trends.

9869 Glick, R. Dealing, demoralization and addiction: heroin in the Chicago Puerto Rican community. JOURNAL OF PSYCHOACTIVE DRUGS, Vol. 15, no. 4 (October, December, 1983), p. 281-292. English. **DESCR:** Chicago, IL; Culture; *Drug Abuse.

9870 Gonzales, Juan. Puerto Rico to Philadelphia: a cure connection. NUESTRO, Vol. 7, no. 5 (June, July, 1983), p. 21-24. English. **DESCR:** *Handicapped; Hospitals and the Community; Medical Care; Shriner's Hospital for Crippled Children, Philadelphia, PA.

9871 Gonzalez, Juan. Arson wave threatens Puerto Ricans in inner cities. NUESTRO, Vol. 6, no. 7 (September 1982), p. 27-28. English. **DESCR:** *Criminal Acts; Firefighters; Hoboken, NJ.

9872 Griffin, Julia Ortiz. Two artists in search of a country: Rafael Rios Rey and Francisco Arrivi. MINORITY VOICES, Vol. 5, no. 1-2 (Spring, Fall, 1981), p. 53-58. English. **DESCR:** *Arrivi, Francisco; Artists; Puerto Rican Literature; *Rios Rey, Rafael; Teatro.

9873 Grijalva, Joshua. The story of Hispanic Southern Baptists. BAPTIST HISTORY AND HERITAGE, Vol. 18, no. 3 (July 1983), p. 40-47. English. **DESCR:** *Baptists; History; Religion; *Southern Baptists.

9874 Gurak, Douglas T. and Fitzpatrick, Joseph P. Intermarriage among Hispanic ethnic groups in New York City. AMERICAN JOURNAL OF SOCIOLOGY, Vol. 87, no. 4 (January 1982), p. 921-934. English. **DESCR:** *Intermarriage; New York, NY.

9875 Hardy-Fanta, Carol and Montana, Priscila. The Hispanic female adolescent: a group therapy model. INTERNATIONAL JOURNAL OF GROUP PSYCHOTHERAPY, Vol. 32, no. 3 (July 1982), p. 351-366. English. **DESCR:** Psychotherapy; *Women; Youth.

9876 Improving the schools. NUESTRO, Vol. 6, no. 3 (April 1982), p. 9. English. **DESCR:** *Bilingual Bicultural Education; Education; Puerto Rican Education.

9877 The invisible Puerto Rican vote. HISPANIC BUSINESS, Vol. 5, no. 10 (October 1983), p. 34-36. English. **DESCR:** Elections; Political Parties and Organizations; *Voter Turnout.

9878 Jones, B.E. Manic-depressive illness among poor urban Hispanics. AMERICAN JOURNAL OF PSYCHIATRY, Vol. 14, no. 9 (September 1983), p. 1208-1210. English. **DESCR:** Bronx, NY; *Mental Health.

9879 Lattin, Vernon E. Book review of: THE DOCILE PUERTO RICAN. MINORITY VOICES, Vol. 2, no. 1 (Spring 1978), p. 62-63. English. **DESCR:** Book Reviews; Marques, Rene; *THE DOCILE PUERTO RICAN.

9880 Mejias-Rentas, Antonio. Reflections on fathers: my three fathers. NUESTRO, Vol. 7, no. 5 (June, July, 1983), p. 61-62. English. **DESCR:** *Family; Marin, Luis Munoz; Partido Popular Democratico (PPD); *Puerto Rico.

9881 Melendez, Carmelo. Mother's Day reflections: "I will get to him". NUESTRO, Vol. 7, no. 4 (May 1983), p. 47. English. **DESCR:** *Family; *Parent and Child Relationships.

9882 Mukherjee, Sukdeb. Misdiagnosis of schizophrenia in bipolar patients: a multiethnic comparison. AMERICAN JOURNAL OF PSYCHIATRY, Vol. 14, no. 12 (December 1983), p. 1571-1574. English. **DESCR:** *Mental Health; NEW YORK.

9883 Naismith, Rachael. Outreach services to Hispanics. ILLINOIS LIBRARIES, Vol. 64, no. 7 (September 1982), p. 962-966. English. **DESCR:** Arrondo, Ondina; Cubanos; La Raza Hispanica, Miami, FL; Latin American Library/Biblioteca Latinoamericana, Oakland, CA; *Library Services; Lopez, Lillian; Ruiz, Deborah; South Bronx Project, New York Public Library; Verges, Bruni.

9884 Nieto, Sonia. Children's literature on Puerto Rican themes -- the messages of fiction; non-fiction. INTERRACIAL BOOKS FOR CHILDREN, Vol. 14, no. 1-2 (1983), p. 6-12. English. **DESCR:** *Children's Literature; Puerto Rican Literature.

9885 Ortiz, Carlos V. Growing old alone. NUESTRO, Vol. 7, no. 4 (May 1983), p. 36-38. English. **DESCR:** *Ancianos; Drinane, Suleika Cabrera; Instituto Puertorriqueno/Hispano Para Personas Mayores; Padilla de Armas, Encarnacion.

9886 The Puerto Rican diaspora: the dispersal of a people. NUESTRO, Vol. 6, no. 5 (June, July, 1982), p. 32-41. English. **DESCR:** Espada, Frank; Ethnic Groups; Ethnic Stratification; Population Distribution.

9887 Puerto Rican observance. NUESTRO, Vol. 6, no. 6 (August 1982), p. 11. English. **DESCR:** *Puerto Rican Day Parade.

9888 Resign, Peter Grace. NUESTRO, Vol. 6, no. 5 (June, July, 1982), p. 9. English. **DESCR:** Barcelo, Carlos Romero; *Grace, J. Peter.

9889 Rios, Lydia E. Determinants of asthma among Puerto Ricans. JOURNAL OF LATIN COMMUNITY HEALTH, Vol. 1, no. 1 (Fall 1982), p. 25-40. English. **DESCR:** *Asthma.

9890 Rizzuto, Anna-Maria. Ethnic and cultural variations in the care of the aged. Discussion: Hispanic elderly and natural support systems: a special focus on Puerto Ricans. JOURNAL OF GERIATRIC PSYCHIATRY, Vol. 15, no. 2 (1982), p. 253-255. English. **DESCR:** *Ancianos; Natural Support Systems.

Puerto Ricans (cont.)

9891 Russell, Cheryl. The news about Hispanics. AMERICAN DEMOGRAPHICS, Vol. 5, no. 3 (March 1983), p. 14-25. English. **DESCR:** Census; Cubanos; *Population.

9892 Satow, Robert. A severe case of penis envy: the convergence of cultural and individual intra-psychic factors. JOURNAL OF THE AMERICAN ACADEMY OF PSYCHOANALYSIS, Vol. 11, no. 4 (October 1983), p. 547-556. English. **DESCR:** Freud, Sigmund; *Psychotherapy; Women.

9893 Seda-Bonilla, Eduardo. On the vicissitudes of being "Puerto Rican": an exploration of Pedro Juan Soto's "Hot land, cold season". MELUS: MULTI-ETHNIC LITERATURE OF THE UNITED STATES, Vol. 6, no. 3 (Fall 1979), p. 27-40. English. **DESCR:** *HOT LAND, COLD SEASON; Soto, Pedro Juan.

9894 Seilhamer, E. Stella and Prewitt-Diaz, Joseph O. The return and circulatory migrant student: a perception of teachers, schools and self. MIGRATION TODAY, Vol. 11, no. 1 (1983), p. 21-23. English. **DESCR:** Cultural Characteristics; Identity; Migration Patterns; *Puerto Rican Education.

9895 Soto, Elaine and Shaver, Phillip. Sex-role traditionalism assertiveness, and symptoms of Puerto Rican women living in the United States. HISPANIC JOURNAL OF BEHAVIORAL SCIENCES, Vol. 4, no. 1 (March 1982), p. 1-19. English. **DESCR:** Sex Roles; *Women.

9896 Tienda, Marta and Angel, Ronald. Headship and household composition among blacks, Hispanics and other whites. SOCIAL FORCES, Vol. 61, no. 2 (December 1982), p. 508-531. English. **DESCR:** Anglo Americans; Blacks; Cultural Characteristics; Extended Family; *Family; Single Parents.

9897 Trilla, Francisco. The plight of the elderly Puerto Rican. JOURNAL OF LATIN COMMUNITY HEALTH, Vol. 1, no. 1 (Fall 1982), p. 89-91. English. **DESCR:** *Ancianos.

9898 Wurzman, Ilyana. Cultural values of Puerto Rican opiate addicts: an exploratory study. AMERICAN JOURNAL OF DRUG AND ALCOHOL ABUSE, Vol. 9, no. 2 (1982, 1983), p. 141-153. English. **DESCR:** Acculturation; Anglo Americans; Blacks; *Drug Abuse; Drug Addicts; Family; Loevinger's Sentence Completion Test; Machismo; New York, NY; Opium; Values.

Puerto Rico

9899 Barrios-Martinez, Ruben. Should Puerto Rico become a state?: against statehood. NUESTRO, Vol. 7, no. 5 (June, July, 1983), p. 37-39. English. **DESCR:** *Colonialism; *International Relations; Puerto Rican Independence Party; Racism; United States.

9900 Business notes. HISPANIC BUSINESS, Vol. 5, no. 11 (November 1983), p. 27. English. **DESCR:** *Business Enterprises; Garment Industry; High Tech '84; Personnel Management; Taxation; U.S. Department of Housing and Urban Development (HUD).

9901 Carrion, Arturo Morales. Puerto Rico: the coming of the Americans. NUESTRO, Vol. 7, no. 5 (June, July, 1983), p. 25-30. English. **DESCR:** Cuba; *International Relations; Spain; *United States History; *War.

9902 Foreign trade. HISPANIC BUSINESS, Vol. 5, no. 4 (April 1983), p. 22. English. **DESCR:** Banking Industry; Brazil; *Electronics Industry; Export Trade; *Foreign Trade; Ibero-American Chamber of Commerce; Miami, FL; Minority Bank Development Program (MBDP); Minority Export Development Consultants Program (MEDC); Peace Corps.

9903 Foreign trade. HISPANIC BUSINESS, Vol. 5, no. 10 (October 1983), p. 29. English. **DESCR:** Agency for International Development (AID); Caribbean Region; Economic History and Conditions; *Foreign Trade; HOW TO EXPORT: A MARKETING MANUAL; Mexico; U.S. Trade Center (Mexico City).

9904 Foreign trade. HISPANIC BUSINESS, Vol. 5, no. 11 (November 1983), p. 31. English. **DESCR:** California; *Foreign Trade; HOW TO EXPORT: A MARKETING MANUAL; Marketing; Miami, FL; Miami Free Zone.

9905 Gonzales, Juan. Town without fear. NUESTRO, Vol. 6, no. 10 (December 1982), p. 15-17. English. **DESCR:** Homeless Persons; *Housing.

9906 Maldonado-Denis, Manuel. El problema de las nacionalidades: la experiencia caribena. Paper presented at the "Dialogo de las Americas" conference. Mexico, D.F. September 9-14, 1982. REVISTA CHICANO-RIQUENA, Vol. 10, no. 4 (Fall 1982), p. 39-45. Spanish. **DESCR:** Capitalism; Carpentier, Alejo; Cuba; El Salvador; Grenada; Guatemala; Imperialism; Marti, Jose; Nicaragua; *Political History and Conditions; United States.

9907 McDougall, George. The press and Puerto Rico. NUESTRO, Vol. 7, no. 6 (August 1983), p. 21-25. English. **DESCR:** Mass Media; Political History and Conditions.

9908 Mejias-Rentas, Antonio. Reflections on fathers: my three fathers. NUESTRO, Vol. 7, no. 5 (June, July, 1983), p. 61-62. English. **DESCR:** *Family; Marin, Luis Munoz; Partido Popular Democratico (PPD); *Puerto Ricans.

9909 Melendez, Carmelo. Chasing a Puerto Rican Christmas. NUESTRO, Vol. 5, no. 8 (November 1981), p. 33. English. **DESCR:** *Christmas; *Family.

9910 Migration: a problem. NUESTRO, Vol. 6, no. 10 (December 1982), p. 8. English. **DESCR:** *Migration.

9911 Panitz, Daniel R., et al. The role of machismo and the Hispanic family in the etiology and treatment of alcoholism in the Hispanic American males. AMERICAN JOURNAL OF FAMILY THERAPY, Vol. 11, no. 1 (Spring 1983), p. 31-44. English. **DESCR:** *Alcoholism; Children; Family; *Machismo; Socioeconomic Factors.

9912 Puerto Rico: images from the past. NUESTRO, Vol. 7, no. 9 (November 1983), p. 48-53. English. **DESCR:** CONTRASTES [exhibit]; *Delano, Jack; Hostos Community College, New York, NY; *Photography.

9913 Romero-Barcelo, Carlos. Should Puerto Rico become a state?: for statehood. NUESTRO, Vol. 7, no. 5 (June, July, 1983), p. 34-37. English. **DESCR:** *Colonialism; *International Relations; Munoz Marin, Luis; United States.

Puerto Rico (cont.)

9914 Vivo, Paquita. Book review of: PUERTO RICO: A POLITICAL AND CULTURAL HISTORY. NUESTRO, Vol. 7, no. 5 (June, July, 1983), p. 63. English. DESCR: Book Reviews; Carrion, Arturo Morales; History; Puerto Rican Studies; *PUERTO RICO: A POLITICAL AND CULTURAL HISTORY; United States History.

PUERTO RICO: A POLITICAL AND CULTURAL HISTORY

9915 Vivo, Paquita. Book review of: PUERTO RICO: A POLITICAL AND CULTURAL HISTORY. NUESTRO, Vol. 7, no. 5 (June, July, 1983), p. 63. English. DESCR: Book Reviews; Carrion, Arturo Morales; History; Puerto Rican Studies; Puerto Rico; United States History.

Puig, Manuel

9916 Alurista. BOQUITAS PINTADAS, produccion folletinesca bajo el militarismo. MAIZE, Vol. 4, no. 1-2 (Fall, Winter, 1980, 1981), p. 21-26. Spanish. DESCR: *BOQUITAS PINTADAS; Literary Criticism.

Purim, Flora

9917 Gonzalez, Johnny. Flora and Airto; making music happen. CAMINOS, Vol. 3, no. 8 (September 1982), p. 10-13,50. Bilingual. DESCR: Artists; Moreira, Airto; *Musicians.

PURO ROLLO

9918 Garcia, Ignacio M. Book review of: PURO ROLLO. NUESTRO, Vol. 6, no. 10 (December 1982), p. 60. English. DESCR: Barrios, Gregg; Book Reviews.

Puruaran, Michoacan, Mexico

9919 Slade, Santiago. From Michoacan to Southern California: the story of an undocumented Mexican. SOUTHWEST ECONOMY AND SOCIETY, Vol. 3, no. 1 (Fall 1977), p. 5-18. English. DESCR: Biography; *Oral History; *Undocumented Workers.

Quality of Life Scale

9920 Dolgin, Daniel L., et al. Quality of life and psychological well-being in a bicultural Latino community. HISPANIC JOURNAL OF BEHAVIORAL SCIENCES, Vol. 4, no. 4 (December 1982), p. 433-450. English. DESCR: Acculturation; *Attitude (Psychological); Depression Scale; *Global Acculturation Scale; Index of Psychological Adjustment; Psychology.

Quesada, Leticia

9921 Diaz, Katherine A. "And this year's winners are...". CAMINOS, Vol. 4, no. 1-2 (January, February, 1983), p. 39-54,74+. English. DESCR: *Awards; Castro, Tony; Elizalde, Hector; Flores, Tom; Martinez, Esperanza; Mendizabal, Maritza; Molina, Gloria; Moya, Connie; Placentia, Joe; Rios, David N.; Ybarra, Lea; Zapata, Carmen.

THE QUESTION OF SEX DIFFERENCES: BIOLOGICAL, CULTURAL, AND PSYCHOLOGICAL ISSUES

9922 Coolson, Freda L. Book review of: THE QUESTION OF SEX DIFFERENCES: BIOLOGICAL, CULTURAL AND PSYCHOLOGICAL ISSUES. HISPANIC JOURNAL OF BEHAVIORAL SCIENCES, Vol. 4, no. 3 (September 1982), p. 391-393. English. DESCR: Book Reviews; Hoyenga, Katherine Blick; Hoyenga, Kermit T.

Quezada, Felipe L.

9923 Gomez, Dalia. Needed: Latino CPA's. NUESTRO, Vol. 6, no. 1 (January, February, 1982), p. 25-28. English. DESCR: *Accounting; Careers; Frank, Eleanor Marie; Karpel, Miguel; Rodriguez, Julio H.; Umpierre, Raphael; Zuzueta, Joseph.

Quezada, Sylvia

9924 People. HISPANIC BUSINESS, Vol. 5, no. 5 (May 1983), p. 8. English. DESCR: Biographical Notes; *Businesspeople; Duron, Armando; Espinoza, Peter; Flores, Juan; Martinez, Vilma Socorro; Molina, Gloria; Moreno, Samuel; Pantin, Leslie, Sr.; Quinones, Sergio.

Quinn, Anthony

9925 A Hispanic turned Greek. LATINO, Vol. 54, no. 4 (May, June, 1983), p. 14. English. DESCR: Artists.

9926 Reyes, Luis. East L.A.'s very own Anthony Quinn. CAMINOS, Vol. 4, no. 7 (July, August, 1983), p. 24-27. Bilingual. DESCR: Artists; Films.

Quinones, Sergio

9927 People. HISPANIC BUSINESS, Vol. 5, no. 5 (May 1983), p. 8. English. DESCR: Biographical Notes; *Businesspeople; Duron, Armando; Espinoza, Peter; Flores, Juan; Martinez, Vilma Socorro; Molina, Gloria; Moreno, Samuel; Pantin, Leslie, Sr.; Quezada, Sylvia.

Quintanilla, Guadalupe

9928 Nuestra gente. LATINO, Vol. 53, no. 6 (October 1982), p. 22. English. DESCR: Alfaro-Garcia, Rafael Antonio; *Biographical Notes; Salazar, Veronica.

9929 People. HISPANIC BUSINESS, Vol. 4, no. 8 (August 1983), p. 7. English. DESCR: Aguilar, Richard; *Businesspeople; Cordero-Badillo, Atilano; del Olmo, Frank; Infante, E. Anthony; Levitan, Aida T.; Nunez, Luis; Rivera, Victor M.

9930 Reagan's new appointee to Civil Rights Commission. NUESTRO, Vol. 6, no. 5 (June, July, 1982), p. 29-30. English. DESCR: Appointed Officials; U.S. Commission on Civil Rights.

Quintero, Jose

9931 Gonzalez, Magdalena. Recognizing Hispanic achievements in entertainment - U.S. and Mexico. CAMINOS, Vol. 3, no. 7 (July, August, 1982), p. 18-24. Bilingual. DESCR: Allende, Fernando; Artists; Awards; Bonilla Giannini, Roxanna; Eynoso, David; Felix, Maria; Films; Gallego, Gina; *Golden Eagle Awards; Hoyos, Rodolfo; Lamas, Lorenzo; Lopez, Conchita; Lopez, Lisa; Montalban, Ricardo; Nosotros [film production company]; Rowe, Arthur; Television; Torres, Liz.

Raat, W. Dirk

9932 Cardoso, Lawrence Anthony. Book review of: REVOLTOSOS: MEXICO'S REBELS IN THE UNITED STATES 1903-1923. JOURNAL OF THE WEST, Vol. 22, no. 1 (1983), p. 90. English. DESCR: Book Reviews; History; Immigration; Mexico; *REVOLTOSOS: MEXICO'S REBELS IN THE UNITED STATES, 1903-1923.

9933 Griswold del Castillo, Richard. Book review of: REVOLTOSOS: MEXICO'S REBELS IN THE UNITED STATES 1903-1923. JOURNAL OF SAN DIEGO HISTORY, Vol. 28, no. 2 (Spring 1982), p. 143-144. English. DESCR: Book Reviews; *REVOLTOSOS: MEXICO'S REBELS IN THE UNITED STATES, 1903-1923.

9934 Martinez, Oscar J. Book review of: REVOLTOSOS: MEXICO'S REBELS IN THE UNITED STATES 1903-1923. ARIZONA AND THE WEST, Vol. 24, no. 1 (Spring 1982), p. 69-70. English. DESCR: Book Reviews; Mexico; *REVOLTOSOS: MEXICO'S REBELS IN THE UNITED STATES, 1903-1923; United States History.

Race Awareness
USE: Identity

Race Identity
USE: Identity

Race Relations
USE: Intergroup Relations

RACIAL DISPARITIES IN THE CRIMINAL JUSTICE SYSTEM

9935 Que pasa? NUESTRO, Vol. 7, no. 6 (August 1983), p. 9. English. DESCR: Boy Scouts of America; *Court System; Criminal Justice System; Diabetes; Education; Judicial Review; Petersilia, Joan; PREPARED FOR TODAY; Reagan, Ronald.

"Racial intelligence testing and the Mexican people"

9936 Cortese, Anthony J.; Santillan, Richard; and Mercado, Olivia. Chicano psychological assessment: a critique of "Racial intelligence and the Mexican people" [sic]. EXPLORATIONS IN ETHNIC STUDIES, Vol. 5, no. 2 (July 1982), p. 50-51. English. DESCR: *Gonzalez, Gilbert G.; *Intelligence Tests.

9937 Santillan, Richard. Critique. EXPLORATIONS IN ETHNIC STUDIES, Vol. 5, no. 2 (July 1982), p. 54-55. English. DESCR: *Gonzalez, Gilbert G.; *Intelligence Tests.

Racism

9938 Aragon, Ellen Weis. The factory raid: an unconstitutional act. SOUTHERN CALIFORNIA LAW REVIEW, Vol. 56, no. 2 (January 1983), p. 605-645. English. DESCR: Blackie's House of Beef v. Castillo; Deportation; Immigration and Naturalization Service (INS); International Ladies Garment Workers Union (ILGWU) v. Sureck; Search and Seizure; *Undocumented Workers.

9939 Barrio, Raymond. The bilingual heart and other adventures. BILINGUAL JOURNAL, Vol. 6, no. 2 (Winter 1982), p. 12-15. Bilingual. DESCR: *Early Childhood Education; Ethnic Attitudes; REVERSING ROLES; THE BILINGUAL HEART; THE PRINCE.

9940 Barrios-Martinez, Ruben. Should Puerto Rico become a state?: against statehood. NUESTRO, Vol. 7, no. 5 (June, July, 1983), p. 37-39. English. DESCR: *Colonialism; *International

Relations; Puerto Rican Independence Party; *Puerto Rico; United States.

9941 Bobby Knight must go. NUESTRO, Vol. 7, no. 1 (January, February, 1983), p. 9. English. DESCR: *Knight, Bobby; Olympic Committee (U.S.); Sports.

9942 Brasch, Walter M. Hanigan case: hung up on racism? SOUTH ATLANTIC QUARTERLY, Vol. 81, no. 4 (Fall 1982), p. 429-435. English. DESCR: Administration of Justice; Arizona; Criminal Justice System; Garcia-Loya, Manuel; *Hanigan, Patrick; Hanigan, Tom; Herrera-Mata, Bernabe; *Laws; Ruelas-Zavala, Eleazar; Undocumented Workers.

9943 Bronfenbrenner, Martin. Hyphenated Americans-economic aspects. LAW AND CONTEMPORARY PROBLEMS, Vol. 45, no. 2 (Spring 1982), p. 9-27. English. DESCR: *Chiswick, Barry R.; *Economics; *Immigrants; Smith, James P.; Welch, Finis R.

9944 Burciaga, Jose Antonio. Me, E.T. and other alien beings. NUESTRO, Vol. 7, no. 2 (March 1983), p. 41. English. DESCR: *Identity.

9945 Candelaria, Nash. The prowler. BILINGUAL REVIEW, Vol. 9, no. 1 (January, April, 1982), p. 66-71. English. DESCR: Prejudice (Social).

9946 Cockcroft, James D. Mexican migration, crisis, and the internationalization of labor struggle. CONTEMPORARY MARXISM, Vol. 5, (Summer 1982), p. 48-61. English. DESCR: International Economic Relations; International Labor Activities; Labor Unions; Legislation; *Undocumented Workers.

9947 Diaz, Tom. "Wetbacks" and other fellow Americans. NUESTRO, Vol. 7, no. 8 (October 1983), p. 63. English. DESCR: Ethnic Attitudes; *Hollings, Ernest "Fritz".

9948 Flaherty, Francis J. The struggle continues: protecting the rights of Hispanics in the U.S. NATIONAL LAW JOURNAL, Vol. 5, (March 14, 1983), p. 1. English. DESCR: Affirmative Action; *Avila, Joaquin Guadalupe; Civil Rights; Hispanic Amendments; *Legal Representation; Mexican American Legal Defense and Educational Fund (MALDEF); Voting Rights.

9949 Fram, Steven J. Restricting inquiry into racial attitudes during the Voir Dire. AMERICAN CRIMINAL REVIEW, Vol. 19, no. 4 (Spring 1982), p. 719-750. English. DESCR: Aldridge v. U.S.; Ham v. South Carolina; Juries; Ristaino v. Ross; Rosales v. U.S.; Rosales-Lopez, Humberto.

9950 Gonzalez, Josue M. The pentagon and genetic inferiority. NUESTRO, Vol. 6, no. 3 (April 1982), p. 44. English. DESCR: *Ethnic Groups; *Government.

9951 Klan resurgence. NUESTRO, Vol. 5, no. 8 (November 1981), p. 11. English. DESCR: *American Friends Service Committee; Ku Klux Klan.

9952 LULAC files complaint against TV networks. NUESTRO, Vol. 6, no. 8 (October 1982), p. 48. English. DESCR: Bonilla, Tony; Employment; Equal Employment Opportunity Commission (EEOC); *League of United Latin American Citizens (LULAC); Television.

Racism (cont.)

9953 Martinez, Arthur D. Mexican-Americans: Qua the assistant-Americans. SOUTHWEST ECONOMY AND SOCIETY, Vol. 2, no. 2 (Winter 1977), p. 34-36. English. DESCR: *Employment; Management; *Self-Determination.

9954 Martinez, Elizabeth. The "Kiko" Martinez case: a sign of our times. CRIME AND SOCIAL JUSTICE, Vol. 17, (Summer 1982), p. 92-95. English. DESCR: Administration of Justice; Martinez Defense Committee; Martinez, Francisco; Miller, Robert.

9955 Matute-Bianchi, Maria Eugenia. A Chicana in academe. WOMEN'S STUDIES QUARTERLY, Vol. 10, no. 1 (Spring 1982), p. 14-17. English. DESCR: *Chicanas; *Higher Education; Matute-Bianchi, Maria Eugenia; Sex Roles; Sexism.

9956 McGhee, Paul E. and Duffy, Nelda S. Children's appreciation of humor victimizing different racial-ethnic groups: racial ethnic differences. JOURNAL OF CROSS-CULTURAL PSYCHOLOGY, Vol. 14, no. 1 (March 1983), p. 29-40. English. DESCR: *Humor; Primary School Students.

9957 Padilla, Steve. A Latino voice on the Parole Commission. NUESTRO, Vol. 7, no. 7 (September 1983), p. 42-43. English. DESCR: *Chicanas; Discrimination in Employment; *Kaslow, Audrey; U.S. Parole Commission.

9958 Park inequity pursued. NUESTRO, Vol. 7, no. 1 (January, February, 1983), p. 9. English. DESCR: *Chicago Park District; Local Government.

9959 Que pasa? NUESTRO, Vol. 7, no. 7 (September 1983), p. 9. English. DESCR: Alcoholism; Anti-Defamation League of B'nai B'rith; *Drug Abuse; Drug Programs; Employment; Kiwanis International; Miller Brewing Company; Sports.

9960 Racial problems at Denver school. NUESTRO, Vol. 6, no. 9 (November 1982), p. 11-12. English. DESCR: *Denver, CO.

9961 "Racist and demeaning". NUESTRO, Vol. 7, no. 2 (March 1983), p. 7. English. DESCR: Agricultural Laborers; Book Reviews; Granada, Pilar; Hagopian, Tom; *SPANISH FOR THE CALIFORNIA FARMERS.

9962 Raymond, Richard and Sesnowitz, Michael. Labor market discrimination against Mexican American college graduates. SOUTHERN ECONOMIC JOURNAL, Vol. 49, no. 4 (April 1983), p. 1122-1136. English. DESCR: College Graduates; *Employment; Income.

9963 Research/development: books. HISPANIC BUSINESS, Vol. 4, no. 1 (January 1982), p. 27. English. DESCR: *Book Reviews; *Discrimination in Employment; *Fernandez, John P.; *RACISM AND SEXISM IN CORPORATE LIFE; Sexism.

9964 Rivera, Roberto. Selected topics on Latino access to Illinois colleges and universities. INTEGRATED EDUCATION, Vol. 20, no. 3-5 (May, October, 1982), p. 101-105. English. DESCR: Colleges and Universities; Discrimination in Education; *Higher Education; Illinois.

9965 Stehno, S. M. Differential treatment of minority children in service systems. SOCIAL WORK, Vol. 27, (January 1982), p. 39-45. English. DESCR: *Ethnic Groups; Social Services; Youth.

9966 Straight, Susan. The homeboys. NUESTRO, Vol. 6, no. 6 (August 1982), p. 17-19. English. DESCR: Barrios; Frias, Gustavo; *Short Story.

9967 [Summary of: Freeman, Legitimizing racial discrimination through anti-discrimination law: a critical review of Supreme Court doctrine, 62 Minn. L. Rev. 1049 (1978)]. CHICANO LAW REVIEW, Vol. 5, (1982), p. 78-79. English. DESCR: Administration of Justice.

9968 Surace, Samuel J. Achievement, discrimination, and Mexican-Americans. COMPARATIVE STUDIES IN SOCIETY AND HISTORY, Vol. 24, no. 2 (1982), p. 315-339. English. DESCR: Academic Achievement; Stereotypes.

9969 Torres, Lorenzo. Short history of Chicano workers. SOUTHWEST ECONOMY AND SOCIETY, Vol. 3, no. 2 (Winter 1977, 1978), p. 4-17. English. DESCR: *Labor Unions; Marxism; *Mine, Mill and Smelter Workers Union; Mining Industry.

RACISM AND SEXISM IN CORPORATE LIFE

9970 Research/development: books. HISPANIC BUSINESS, Vol. 4, no. 1 (January 1982), p. 27. English. DESCR: *Book Reviews; *Discrimination in Employment; *Fernandez, John P.; Racism; Sexism.

Radio

9971 10 member commission to oversee radio Marti. NUESTRO, Vol. 6, no. 2 (March 1982), p. 38. English. DESCR: *Radio Marti.

9972 Anti-Castro effort. NUESTRO, Vol. 6, no. 7 (September 1982), p. 9. English. DESCR: *Cuba; Radio Marti.

9973 Baciu, Joyce A. KBBF in Santa Rosa. CAMINOS, Vol. 3, no. 5 (May 1982), p. 48. Bilingual. DESCR: *Radio Station KBBF, Santa Rosa, CA; Santa Rosa, CA.

9974 Baciu, Joyce A. KUBO-FM 90.9; the nation's fourth bilingual radio station. CAMINOS, Vol. 3, no. 5 (May 1982), p. 44-45,59. Bilingual. DESCR: *KUBO, Salinas, CA [radio station]; Salinas, CA.

9975 Balkan, D. Carlos. Mr. Caballero's Spanish radio network. HISPANIC BUSINESS, Vol. 4, no. 5 (May 1982), p. 18-19,26. English. DESCR: Advertising; Broadcast Media; *Caballero Spanish Media, Inc. (CSM).

9976 Chavarria, Jesus. The media scene. HISPANIC BUSINESS, Vol. 4, no. 5 (May 1982), p. 6. English. DESCR: Advertising; Broadcast Media; Caballero Spanish Media, Inc. (CSM); *Mass Media; MIAMI MENSUAL; Print Media; Television.

9977 Communications and announcements: raices y ritmos/roots and rythms: our heritage of Latin American music. LATIN AMERICAN MUSIC REVIEW, Vol. 3, no. 1 (Spring, Summer, 1982), p. 139-145. English. DESCR: Music; *RAICES Y RITMOS/ROOTS AND RHYTHMS.

Radio (cont.)

9978 Communications/marketing. HISPANIC BUSINESS, Vol. 4, no. 8 (August 1983), p. 22+. English. **DESCR:** Arredondo, Price; Baseball; De la O, Val; Films; Marketing; *Mass Media; San Antonio CineFestival, TX; Television; Val De La O Show; Valenzuela, Fernando; Wright & Arredondo Associates; Wright, Oscar.

9979 Community watching: para la comunidad. CAMINOS, Vol. 3, no. 1 (January 1982), p. 43-44. Bilingual. **DESCR:** Congreso Nacional Para Pueblos Unidos (CPU); *Financial Aid; *Food Programs; *Journalists; National Association for Chicano Studies (NACS); Summer Program for Minority Journalists; Zozaya, Julia S.

9980 Diaz, Katherine A. Commercial radio and Hispanic community. CAMINOS, Vol. 3, no. 5 (May 1982), p. 40-41. Bilingual. **DESCR:** *Castro, Thomas.

9981 Diaz, Katherine A. The Dodger's Spanish voice: Jaime Jarrin. CAMINOS, Vol. 3, no. 5 (May 1982), p. 50-51. English. **DESCR:** *Jarrin, Jaime; Sports.

9982 Fantin, Joyce. Some Hispanic stations trying bilingual approach. BILLBOARD, Vol. 94, (November 13, 1982), p. 164. English. **DESCR:** Broadcast Media; Mass Media.

9983 Gente. NUESTRO, Vol. 7, no. 1 (January, February, 1983), p. 63. English. **DESCR:** Amaya-Espinoza, Isidro; Camargo, Mateo G.; *Latin Americans; Musicians; Prieto, Carlos; Sports; Trevino, Lee.

9984 Hispanic owned stations. HISPANIC BUSINESS, Vol. 4, no. 5 (May 1982), p. 28. English. **DESCR:** *Broadcast Media; Radio Stations; Television; Television Stations.

9985 House panel limits Radio Marti effort. NUESTRO, Vol. 6, no. 4 (May 1982), p. 57. English. **DESCR:** Cubanos; *Radio Marti.

9986 "Jekyll, Hyde" radio station. NUESTRO, Vol. 6, no. 2 (March 1982), p. 13-14. English. **DESCR:** *Radio Station KXEW, Tucson, AZ; Tucson, AZ.

9987 Media/marketing. HISPANIC BUSINESS, Vol. 5, no. 11 (November 1983), p. 30. English. **DESCR:** Caballero Spanish Media, Inc. (CSM); California Chicano News Media Association (CCNMA); Employment Training; Federal Communications Commission (FCC); HISPANEX (Oakland, CA); *Mass Media; Michell, Pat; Radio Station KALI, Los Angeles, CA.

9988 Media/marketing. HISPANIC BUSINESS, Vol. 5, no. 12 (December 1983), p. 38. English. **DESCR:** Albertini, Luis Diaz; Computers; League of United Latin American Citizens (LULAC); Lotus-Albertini Hispanic Reps; Marketing; *Mass Media; Nuestras Noticias; Reading; Television; Tortosa, Cristobal.

9989 Radio station is near reality. LATINO, Vol. 53, no. 1 (January, February, 1982), p. 17. English.

9990 Ramirez, Sylvia E. Bilingual radio: reaching new horizons. CAMINOS, Vol. 3, no. 5 (May 1982), p. 38-39. Bilingual. **DESCR:** *Lopez, Antonio; Ramos, Juan; WCBR (Western Community Bilingual Radio) [radio station].

9991 Reflections of "La Raza". LATINO, Vol. 53, no. 5 (September 1982), p. 4. English.

9992 Research and ownership among Hispanic concerns. BROADCASTING, Vol. 102, no. 15 (April 12, 1982), p. 66. English. **DESCR:** Federal Communications Commission (FCC); Rivera, Henry.

9993 Rivera, Henry M. Hispanics need to effectively translate potential into political and economic clout. TELEVISION/RADIO AGE, Vol. 31, no. 4 (September 12, 1983), p. 117-118. English. **DESCR:** Equal Employment Opportunity Commission (EEOC); Federal Communications Commission (FCC); *Minority Telecommunications Ownership Act of 1983 (HR 2331).

9994 Silva, Vicente. Community supported radio bilingue: FM 91. CAMINOS, Vol. 3, no. 5 (May 1982), p. 46-48. Bilingual. **DESCR:** Fresno, CA; *KSJV, Fresno, CA [radio station].

9995 Skriloff, Lisa. Music, news dominate Spanish-language radio programming. HISPANIC BUSINESS, Vol. 5, no. 12 (December 1983), p. 34. English. **DESCR:** Advertising; Los Angeles, CA; Marketing; Miami, FL; San Antonio, TX.

9996 Spanish language radio: a directory. CAMINOS, Vol. 3, no. 5 (May 1982), p. 52-53. English.

9997 Spanish lesson. TELEVISION/RADIO AGE, Vol. 30, no. 22 (June 6, 1983), p. 18. English. **DESCR:** Advertising; Differential Survey Treatment.

9998 Villegas, Jim. Enfoque nacional: created from a need for information. CAMINOS, Vol. 3, no. 5 (May 1982), p. 42-43. Bilingual. **DESCR:** *ENFOQUE NACIONAL [radio program].

9999 Volsky, George. Miami's radio S-U-A-A-V-E. HISPANIC BUSINESS, Vol. 4, no. 12 (December 1982), p. 22,35. English. **DESCR:** Advertising; Broadcast Media; Language Usage; Marketing; Miami, FL; Radio Station SUAVE, Miami, FL; *Radio Stations; Spanish Language.

10000 Washington has new Spanish radio station. NUESTRO, Vol. 6, no. 1 (January, February, 1982), p. 50. English. **DESCR:** *Radio Station WMDO, Washington, D.C.

Radio Marti

10001 10 member commission to oversee radio Marti. NUESTRO, Vol. 6, no. 2 (March 1982), p. 38. English. **DESCR:** Radio.

10002 Anti-Castro effort. NUESTRO, Vol. 6, no. 7 (September 1982), p. 9. English. **DESCR:** *Cuba; *Radio.

10003 House panel limits Radio Marti effort. NUESTRO, Vol. 6, no. 4 (May 1982), p. 57. English. **DESCR:** Cubanos; Radio.

Radio Station KALI, Los Angeles, CA

10004 Media/marketing. HISPANIC BUSINESS, Vol. 5, no. 11 (November 1983), p. 30. English. **DESCR:** Caballero Spanish Media, Inc. (CSM); California Chicano News Media Association (CCNMA); Employment Training; Federal Communications Commission (FCC); HISPANEX (Oakland, CA); *Mass Media; Michell, Pat; Radio.

Radio Station KBBF, Santa Rosa, CA

10005 Baciu, Joyce A. KBBF in Santa Rosa. CAMINOS, Vol. 3, no. 5 (May 1982), p. 48. Bilingual. DESCR: Radio; Santa Rosa, CA.

Radio Station KXEW, Tucson, AZ

10006 "Jekyll, Hyde" radio station. NUESTRO, Vol. 6, no. 2 (March 1982), p. 13-14. English. DESCR: Radio; Tucson, AZ.

Radio Station SUAVE, Miami, FL

10007 Volsky, George. Miami's radio S-U-A-A-A-V-E. HISPANIC BUSINESS, Vol. 4, no. 12 (December 1982), p. 22,35. English. DESCR: Advertising; Broadcast Media; Language Usage; Marketing; Miami, FL; *Radio; *Radio Stations; Spanish Language.

Radio Station WMDO, Washington, D.C.

10008 Washington has new Spanish radio station. NUESTRO, Vol. 6, no. 1 (January, February, 1982), p. 50. English. DESCR: Radio.

Radio Stations

10009 Hispanic owned stations. HISPANIC BUSINESS, Vol. 4, no. 5 (May 1982), p. 28. English. DESCR: *Broadcast Media; Radio; Television; Television Stations.

10010 Volsky, George. Miami's radio S-U-A-A-A-V-E. HISPANIC BUSINESS, Vol. 4, no. 12 (December 1982), p. 22,35. English. DESCR: Advertising; Broadcast Media; Language Usage; Marketing; Miami, FL; *Radio; Radio Station SUAVE, Miami, FL; Spanish Language.

Ragan, Pauline K.

10011 Burke, Leslie K. Book review of: WORK AND RETIREMENT: POLICY ISSUES. HISPANIC JOURNAL OF BEHAVIORAL SCIENCES, Vol. 4, no. 1 (March 1982), p. 112-114. English. DESCR: Book Reviews; *WORK AND RETIREMENT: POLICY ISSUES.

RAICES DE SANGRE [film]

10012 Morales, Alejandro. Expanding the meaning of Chicano cinema: YO SOY CHICANO, RAICES DE SANGRE, SEGUIN. BILINGUAL REVIEW, Vol. 10, no. 2-3 (May, December, 1983), p. 121-137. English. DESCR: Film Reviews; *Films; SEGUIN [movie]; YO SOY CHICANO [film].

10013 Morales, Sylvia. Chicano-produced celluloid mujeres. BILINGUAL REVIEW, Vol. 10, no. 2-3 (May, December, 1983), p. 89-93. English. DESCR: BALLAD OF GREGORIO CORTEZ [film]; *Chicanas; Film Reviews; *Films; SEGUIN [movie]; *Stereotypes; ZOOT SUIT [film].

10014 Ochoa Thompson, Guadalupe. RAICES DE SANGRE: roots of lineage, sources of life. BILINGUAL REVIEW, Vol. 10, no. 2-3 (May, December, 1983), p. 138-141. English. DESCR: Film Reviews; Trevino, Jesus Salvador.

RAICES (New York, NY)

10015 Valiente-Barksdale, Clara. Recruiting Hispanic families. CHILDREN TODAY, Vol. 12, no. 2 (March, April, 1983), p. 26-28. English. DESCR: *Adoption; New York Council on Adoptable Children (COAC); New York, NY.

RAICES Y RITMOS/ROOTS AND RHYTHMS

10016 Communications and announcements: raices y ritmos/roots and rythms: our heritage of Latin American music. LATIN AMERICAN MUSIC REVIEW, Vol. 3, no. 1 (Spring, Summer, 1982), p. 139-145. English. DESCR: Music; Radio.

Railroads

10017 Weiss, Lawrence D. Industrial reserve armies of the southwest: Navajo and Mexican. SOUTHWEST ECONOMY AND SOCIETY, Vol. 3, no. 1 (Fall 1977), p. 19-29. English. DESCR: Capitalism; History; *Labor Supply and Market; Native Americans; Navaho Indians; *Southwest United States.

Ramirez, Linda

10018 Garcia, Ignacio M. Linda Ramirez: labor leader. NUESTRO, Vol. 6, no. 5 (June, July, 1982), p. 26-28. English. DESCR: *Labor; Labor Unions; Latin Americans; Leadership; San Antonio, TX.

Ramirez, Ricardo (Bishop of Las Cruces, NM)

10019 Day, Mark R. and Ramirez, Ricardo (Bishop of Las Cruces, NM),. Bishop: why have we had to wait so long for Hispanic leaders. NATIONAL CATHOLIC REPORTER, Vol. 19, (December 24, 1982), p. 6-7. English. DESCR: Catholic Church; *Clergy; Leadership.

10020 Ramirez named bishop of Las Cruces diocese. NUESTRO, Vol. 6, no. 8 (October 1982), p. 43. English. DESCR: Catholic Church; *Religion.

Ramirez, Steve

10021 People. HISPANIC BUSINESS, Vol. 4, no. 10 (October 1982), p. 7. English. DESCR: Aguilar, Gloria; Biographical Notes; *Businesspeople; Caldera, Manuel R.; Lopez, Victor M.

Ramos Jimenez, Ynocencio

10022 Calderon, Roberto R. Corridos of Ynocencio Ramos Jimenez. CAMINOS, Vol. 4, no. 10 (November 1983), p. 26-27,48+. Bilingual. DESCR: Corrido.

Ramos, Juan

10023 Ramirez, Sylvia E. Bilingual radio: reaching new horizons. CAMINOS, Vol. 3, no. 5 (May 1982), p. 38-39. Bilingual. DESCR: *Lopez, Antonio; *Radio; WCBR (Western Community Bilingual Radio) [radio station].

Ramos, Samuel

10024 Cantu, Roberto. Nota preliminar: de Samuel Ramos a Emilio Uranga. CAMPO LIBRE, Vol. 1, no. 2 (Summer 1981), p. 239-272. Spanish. DESCR: Cultural Characteristics; Identity; Mexico; Philosophy; *Uranga, Emilio.

10025 Uranga, Emilio. Notas para un estudio del mexicano. CAMPO LIBRE, Vol. 1, no. 2 (Summer 1981), p. 283-295. Spanish. DESCR: Cultural Characteristics; Gaos, Jose; Identity; Mexico; Philosophy.

Random Digit Dialling (RDD)

10026 Parra, Fernando and So, Alvin Yiu-cheong. Changing perceptions of mental illness in a Mexican-American community. JOURNAL OF SOCIAL PSYCHOLOGY, Vol. 29, (Summer 1983), p. 95-100. English. DESCR: Anglo Americans; Assimilation; *Los Angeles, CA; *Mental Health.

Rape

10027 Carmen, Andrea. Rape. LATINA, Vol. 1, no. 3
(1983), p. 34-36. English.

10028 Garza-Livingston, M'Liss and Villa de Romo,
Velma. An interview with Velma Villa de
Romo: bilingual liaison for the Santa
Barbara Rape Crisis Center. COMADRE, no. 3
(Fall 1978), p. 15-16. English. **DESCR:**
*Santa Barbara Rape Crisis Center; Villa de
Romo, Velma.

10029 Villa Romo, Velma. Rape in the barrio.
COMADRE, no. 3 (Fall 1978), p. 19-29.
English. **DESCR:** *Chicanas; Identity; Santa
Barbara Rape Crisis Center; Social History
and Conditions.

Ravard, Rafael Alonzo

10030 Gente. NUESTRO, Vol. 7, no. 7 (September
1983), p. 61. English. **DESCR:** Americas
Award; Chavez, Raul; *Chicanas; Diaz-Cobo,
Christine; Mexico; Ortega, Katherine D.;
Performing Arts; Planas, Vilma; Venezuela.

10031 People. HISPANIC BUSINESS, Vol. 5, no. 9
(September 1983), p. 10. English. **DESCR:**
*Businesspeople; Chavez, Chris; Diez de
Onate, Jorge; Franco Garcia, Freddie;
Garcia, Hector P.; Lozano, Leticia Eugenia;
Rodriguez, Alberto Duque; Sanchez, Philip
V.; Villalpando, Catalina.

La Raza Hispanica, Miami, FL

10032 Naismith, Rachael. Outreach services to
Hispanics. ILLINOIS LIBRARIES, Vol. 64, no.
7 (September 1982), p. 962-966. English.
DESCR: Arrondo, Ondina; Cubanos; Latin
American Library/Biblioteca Latinoamericana,
Oakland, CA; *Library Services; Lopez,
Lillian; Puerto Ricans; Ruiz, Deborah; South
Bronx Project, New York Public Library;
Verges, Bruni.

La Raza Unida Party

10033 Laws, Bart. Raza unida de Cristal. SOUTHERN
EXPOSURE, Vol. 10, no. 2 (March, April,
1982), p. 67-72. English. **DESCR:** Crystal
City, TX; Gurule, Dorothy; History; Mexican
American Youth Organization (MAYO);
*Political Parties and Organizations; Reyes,
Carlos.

10034 Miller, Michael V. Chicano community control
in South Texas: problems and prospects.
JOURNAL OF ETHNIC STUDIES, Vol. 3, no. 3
(Fall 1975), p. 70-89. English. **DESCR:**
Chicano Movement; Crystal City, TX;
Gutierrez, Jose Angel; History; Patron
System; *Political Parties and
Organizations; Social Classes; Social
History and Conditions; *South Texas.

10035 Munoz, Carlos, Jr. and Barrera, Mario. La
Raza Unida Party and the Chicano student
movement in California. SOCIAL SCIENCE
JOURNAL, Vol. 19, no. 2 (April 1982), p.
101-119. English. **DESCR:** California;
*Chicano Movement; Political History and
Conditions; Political Ideology; Political
Parties and Organizations; Student
Movements.

REACHING THE HISPANIC MARKET EFFECTIVELY

10036 Research/development: books. HISPANIC
BUSINESS, Vol. 4, no. 12 (December 1982), p.
36. English. **DESCR:** Book Reviews; Consumers;
Guernica, A.; Kasperuk, I.; Marketing.

Reading

10037 Argulewicz, Ed N. and Sanchez, David T.
Considerations in the assessment of reading
difficulties in bilingual children. SCHOOL
PSYCHOLOGY REVIEW, Vol. 11, no. 3 (Summer
1982), p. 281-289. English. **DESCR:**
Bilingualism; Children; *Language
Assessment; Sociolinguistics.

10038 Chall, Jeanne. Rich and sharp memories of
reading. CHANGE, Vol. 14, no. 7 (October
1982), p. 36-40. English. **DESCR:**
Assimilation; Book Reviews; *HUNGER OF
MEMORY: THE EDUCATION OF RICHARD RODRIGUEZ;
Language Arts; Rodriguez, Richard;
Socioeconomic Factors.

10039 De Barbosa, Liliam Coya. "Mastering
learning" como metodo psicoeducativo para
ninos con problemas especificos de
aprendizaje. HISPANIC JOURNAL OF BEHAVIORAL
SCIENCES, Vol. 4, no. 4 (December 1982), p.
503-510. Spanish. **DESCR:** Children; Learning
and Cognition; *Mastery Learning; Puerto
Ricans.

10040 Lado, Robert. Aula/the classroom:
developmental reading in two languages. NABE
JOURNAL, Vol. 6, no. 2-3 (Winter, Spring,
1981, 1982), p. 99-110. English. **DESCR:**
Bilingual Bicultural Education;
Bilingualism; Language Arts; Language
Development; Learning and Cognition; Spanish
Education Development (SED) Center Bilingual
Reading Project; Spanish Language.

10041 Lalas, Joselito W. The influence of prior
experience in ESL reading. BILINGUAL
JOURNAL, Vol. 6, no. 1 (Fall 1982), p.
10-12. English. **DESCR:** Bilingual Bicultural
Education; English as a Second Language;
Learning and Cognition.

10042 Media/marketing. HISPANIC BUSINESS, Vol. 5,
no. 12 (December 1983), p. 38. English.
DESCR: Albertini, Luis Diaz; Computers;
League of United Latin American Citizens
(LULAC); Lotus-Albertini Hispanic Reps;
Marketing; *Mass Media; Nuestras Noticias;
Radio; Television; Tortosa, Cristobal.

10043 Morrison, J. A. and Michael, W.B.
Development and validation of an auditory
perception test in Spanish for Hispanic
children receiving reading instruction in
Spanish. EDUCATIONAL AND PSYCHOLOGICAL
MEASUREMENT, Vol. 42, (Summer 1982), p.
657-669. English. **DESCR:** Children;
Educational Tests and Measurements;
*Language Arts; Prueba de Analisis Auditivo
(PAA); Spanish Language.

10044 Oakland, Thomas. Joint use of adaptive
behavior and IQ to predict achievement.
JOURNAL OF CONSULTING AND CLINICAL
PSYCHOLOGY, Vol. 51, no. 2 (April 1983), p.
298-301. English. **DESCR:** *Academic
Achievement; Education; Intelligence Tests;
Mathematics.

10045 Peterson, Marilyn L. Mexican-American
children: what do they prefer to read?
READING WORLD, Vol. 22, no. 2 (December
1982), p. 129-131. English. **DESCR:** Child
Study.

Reading (cont.)

10046 Plake, Barbara S., et al. Relationship of ethnic group membership to the measurement and meaning of attitudes towards reading: implications for validity of test score interpretations. EDUCATIONAL AND PSYCHOLOGICAL MEASUREMENT, Vol. 42, no. 4 (Winter 1982), p. 1259-1267. English. DESCR: Anglo Americans; Attitude (Psychological); Educational Tests and Measurements; Estes Reading Attitude Scale; Ethnic Groups; Students.

10047 Schon, Isabel; Hopkins, Kenneth D.; and Davis, W. Alan. Effects of books in Spanish and free reading time on Hispanic students' reading abilities and attitudes. NABE JOURNAL, Vol. 7, no. 1 (Fall 1982), p. 13-20. English. DESCR: Bilingual Bicultural Education; *Language Arts; Language Proficiency; Spanish Language.

Reagan Administration

10048 Barreto, Julio. Reagan record attacked. LATINO, Vol. 53, no. 5 (September 1982), p. 24. English. DESCR: *Political Parties and Organizations.

10049 Mexico y Estados Unidos ante la tercera Confemar: resultados e implicaciones. INFORME: RELACIONES MEXICO-ESTADOS UNIDOS, Vol. 1, no. 3 (July, December, 1982), p. 215-226. Spanish. DESCR: CONFEMAR; *Maritime Law; Multinational Corporations; United States-Mexico Relations.

10050 Reaganomics. LATINO, Vol. 53, no. 7 (November 1982), p. 18-20. English. DESCR: *Economics.

10051 Reagan's report card: F. LATINO, Vol. 53, no. 3 (May 1982), p. 24-25. English. DESCR: Civil Rights; *Politics.

Reagan, Ronald

10052 Babbitt, Bruce. Reagan approach to aliens simply wishful thinking. NATIONAL HISPANIC JOURNAL, Vol. 1, no. 2 (Winter 1982), p. 6-7. English. DESCR: Border Region; Braceros; Immigration Regulation and Control; Select Commission on Immigration and Refugee Policy; *Undocumented Workers; United States-Mexico Relations.

10053 Castillo, Leonel J. A response to the Reagan plan: respuesta al plan Reagan. CAMINOS, Vol. 3, no. 1 (January 1982), p. 13-15. Bilingual. DESCR: *Immigration Regulation and Control.

10054 Fraser Rothenberg, Irene. Chicanos, the Panama Canal issues and the Reagan campaign: reflections from 1976 and projections for 1980. JOURNAL OF ETHNIC STUDIES, Vol. 7, no. 4 (Winter 1980), p. 37-49. English. DESCR: *International Relations; Lobbying; Nationalism; Newspapers; Panama; *Panama Canal; Politics.

10055 El futuro de la cuenca del Caribe segun la administracion Reagan. INFORME: RELACIONES MEXICO-ESTADOS UNIDOS, Vol. 1, no. 2 (July, December, 1982), p. 10-56. Spanish. DESCR: *Iniciativa Para la Cuenca del Caribe (ICC); *United States-Latin American Relations.

10056 Garcia, Paco. Voices: Hispanic voices needed in the education debate. NUESTRO, Vol. 7, no. 5 (June, July, 1983), p. 53-54. English. DESCR: Bilingual Bicultural Education; *Discrimination in Education;

*Discrimination in Employment; *Education; Federal Government; *Latin Americans; President's Commission on Excellence in Education; U.S. Department of Health, Education and Welfare (HEW).

10057 Hispanics wooed by Reagan, Demos. NUESTRO, Vol. 7, no. 8 (October 1983), p. 11-12. English. DESCR: Congressional Hispanic Caucus; *National Hispanic Heritage Week; *Political Parties and Organizations.

10058 King, John S. California Farm Bureau Federation: addressing the issue/conduciendo el topico. CAMINOS, Vol. 3, no. 1 (January 1982), p. 16-17. Bilingual. DESCR: *California Farm Bureau Federation; *Immigration Regulation and Control.

10059 Lowther, William. Reagan hunts for the Hispanic vote. MACLEANS, Vol. 96, no. 34 (August 22, 1983), p. 21-22. English. DESCR: Elections; League of United Latin American Citizens (LULAC); *Voter Turnout.

10060 People. HISPANIC BUSINESS, Vol. 5, no. 10 (October 1983), p. 10. English. DESCR: Anaya, Toney; Arriola, Elvia Rosales; Babbitt, Bruce; Burgos, Tony; Bush, George; *Businesspeople; Cisneros, Henry, Mayor of San Antonio, TX; Cruz, Jose; Kennedy, Edward M.; Montano, Gilbert; White, Mark.

10061 President Reagan's appointments. CAMINOS, Vol. 3, no. 3 (March 1982), p. 48-50. Bilingual. DESCR: Appointed Officials; *Federal Government; Flores Buckhart, Elizabeth; Garcia, Ernest E.; Gonzalez, Luis A.; Lozano, Diana; Pompa, Gilbert G.; Sanchez, Nestor D.; Zuniga, Henry.

10062 Presidential election 1984. NUESTRO, Vol. 7, no. 7 (September 1983), p. 14-19. English. DESCR: Anderson, John; Askew, Reubin; Cranston, Alan; Elected Officials; *Elections; Fernandez, Ben; Glenn, John; Hart, Gary; Hispanic Force '84; Hollings, Ernest "Fritz"; Mondale, Walter; Political Parties and Organizations.

10063 Q & A: in the Hispanic community who are the winners and losers of Reaganomics? CAMINOS, Vol. 3, no. 3 (March 1982), p. 47. Bilingual. DESCR: Casado, Lucy; Echeveste, John; *Federal Government; Flores, Bob; Leon, Virginia; Mendoza, John; Sanchez-Alvarez, Gloria; Vidal de Neri, Julieta.

10064 Que pasa? NUESTRO, Vol. 7, no. 6 (August 1983), p. 9. English. DESCR: Boy Scouts of America; *Court System; Criminal Justice System; Diabetes; Education; Judicial Review; Petersilia, Joan; PREPARED FOR TODAY; RACIAL DISPARITIES IN THE CRIMINAL JUSTICE SYSTEM.

10065 Quevedo. The Reagan administration and affirmative action. CAMINOS, Vol. 4, no. 9 (October 1983), p. 24-26. English. DESCR: *Affirmative Action.

10066 Quinlivan, Robert. CRC's Herman Baca on the issue. CAMINOS, Vol. 3, no. 1 (January 1982), p. 18-20. Bilingual. DESCR: *Baca, Herman; *Committee on Chicano Rights; *Immigration Regulation and Control.

Reagan, Ronald (cont.)

10067 Regional report, Latin America: marchers oppose Reagan polices. NUESTRO, Vol. 7, no. 4 (May 1983), p. 11. English. **DESCR:** Central America; Demonstrations; International Relations; *Latin America; Stanford University, Stanford, CA.

10068 Romero, Tina. The undocumented worker: how will the United States deal with him? NATIONAL HISPANIC JOURNAL, Vol. 1, no. 3 (Summer, Fall, 1982), p. 13-15. English. **DESCR:** Immigration Law; Immigration Regulation and Control; *Undocumented Workers.

10069 A summary of the Reagan administration's proposed immigration policies/compendio de la propuesta politica de inmigracion de la administracion Reagan. CAMINOS, Vol. 3, no. 1 (January 1982), p. 11-12. Bilingual. **DESCR:** *Immigration Regulation and Control.

10070 Zapanta, Albert C. President Reagan and the Hispanic community/El presidente Reagan y la comunidad Hispanica. CAMINOS, Vol. 3, no. 3 (March 1982), p. 38-39. Bilingual. **DESCR:** Federal Government.

Real Estate

10071 Goodman, Gerson. LRF takes on Battery Park City. HISPANIC BUSINESS, Vol. 4, no. 10 (October 1982), p. 16-17,24. English. **DESCR:** Business Enterprises; Construction Industry; *LRF Developers, Inc.; NEW YORK.

10072 Mecht, Richard L. U.S. real estate owners in Mexico face huge losses. CAMINOS, Vol. 3, no. 11 (December 1982), p. 27,52. Bilingual. **DESCR:** Mexico.

10073 Mexican condo buyer in Texas-sized trouble. SOUTHERN EXPOSURE, Vol. 11, no. 1 (January 1983), p. 8-9. English. **DESCR:** Condominiums; Mexico; Peso Devaluation.

Real Property
USE: Real Estate

Reapportionment

10074 Community watching: para la comunidad. CAMINOS, Vol. 2, no. 6 (October 1981), p. 40-41+. English. **DESCR:** *Cultural Organizations; Hispanic Women in Higher Education (HWHE); La Plaza Senior Citizens, Los Angeles, CA; Mexican American Political Association (MAPA).

10075 Hamner, Richard. Hispanics and redistricting: what you see is not always what you get. NATIONAL HISPANIC JOURNAL, Vol. 1, no. 2 (Winter 1982), p. 25-30. English. **DESCR:** Berlanga, Hugo; Elections; Hispanic Reapportionment District; National Association of Latino Elected Officials (NALEO); Political Representation; Politics; *Roybal, Edward R.; Santillan, Richard.

10076 Jurado, Rebecca. Abstract: Dodge and McCauley, REAPPORTIONMENT: A SURVEY OF THE PRACTICALITY OF VOTING EQUALITY, 43 U. PITT. L. Rev. 527 (1982). CHICANO LAW REVIEW, Vol. 6, (1983), p. 156-157. English.

10077 Latinos in the law: meeting the challenge [a symposium]. CHICANO LAW REVIEW, Vol. 6, (1983), p. 1-121. English. **DESCR:** *Criminal Justice System; Demography; Legal Profession; Los Angeles Police Department; Love, Eulia; Police Brutality; Political Representation; Settles, Ron.

10078 Reapportionment [panel discussion at the LATINOS IN THE LAW symposium, UCLA, 1982]. CHICANO LAW REVIEW, Vol. 6, (1983), p. 34-62. English. **DESCR:** California; Californios for Fair Representation; Common Cause.

10079 Santillan, Richard. [Translating population numbers into political power]. CHICANO LAW REVIEW, Vol. 6, (1983), p. 16-21. English. **DESCR:** Californios for Fair Representation; Carrillo v. Whittier Union High School; LATINOS IN THE LAW [symposium], UCLA, 1982; MEXICAN AMERICAN LEGAL DEFENSE AND EDUCATIONAL FUND NEWSLETTER; Political Representation; *Voter Turnout.

10080 A territorial approach to representation for illegal aliens. MICHIGAN LAW REVIEW, Vol. 80, no. 6 (May 1982), p. 1342-1371. English. **DESCR:** Census; Federation for American Immigration Reform (FAIR); Population; Reynolds, Steve; *Undocumented Workers; Voting Rights.

Rechy, John

10081 Bruce Novoa, Juan. In search of the honest outlaw: John Rechy. MINORITY VOICES, Vol. 3, no. 1 (Fall 1979), p. 37-45. English. **DESCR:** Literature.

10082 Tatum, Charles. The sexual underworld of John Rechy. MINORITY VOICES, Vol. 3, no. 1 (Fall 1979), p. 47-52. English. **DESCR:** CITY OF NIGHT; Literature.

10083 Zamora, Carlos. Odysseus in John Rechy's CITY OF NIGHT: the epistemological journey. MINORITY VOICES, Vol. 3, no. 1 (Fall 1979), p. 53-62. English. **DESCR:** *CITY OF NIGHT; Literature.

Recipes

10084 Burritos to Lebanon. LATINA, Vol. 1, no. 2 (February, March, 1983), p. 19. English. **DESCR:** *Cal International; Maria's Burritos.

10085 Crunchy and tasty for brunch or party, bunuelos y atole. LATINA, Vol. 1, no. 2 (February, March, 1983), p. 65. English.

10086 De Leon, Estrella. Stuffed plantains "bolas de platano". LATINA, Vol. 1, no. 3 (1983), p. 32-33. English.

10087 Family favorites. NUESTRO, Vol. 7, no. 10 (December 1983), p. 36-38. English. **DESCR:** Bermudez, Maria Teresa; Book Reviews; *MEXICAN FAMILY FAVORITES COOKBOOK.

10088 Gifts from your kitchen. NUESTRO, Vol. 5, no. 8 (November 1981), p. 53. English.

10089 Gupta, Udayan. Hispanic foods in New York: the race for number two. HISPANIC BUSINESS, Vol. 5, no. 8 (August 1983), p. 18-19+. English. **DESCR:** Condal Distributor, Inc.; Consumers; *Food Industry; Goya Foods; Iberia Foods Corp.; La Cena Fine Foods, Ltd.

10090 Gutierrez, Bonifacia. Una tamalada: a family tradition in the works. LATINA, Vol. 1, no. 2 (February, March, 1983), p. 59-61. English.

Recipes (cont.)

10091 How to stuff a wild chile part II. CAMINOS,
Vol. 3, no. 1 (January 1982), p. 31-32.
English. **DESCR:** Albert, Margo; Chacon, Peter
R.; *Icaya, Rick; Lacayo, Frank L. "Hank";
*Rodriguez, Edmundo; Rodriguez, Edmundo M.;
*Vasquez, Victor.

10092 How to stuff a wild chile part III. CAMINOS,
Vol. 4, no. 6 (June 1983), p. 20-21.
English.

10093 Kopp, April. Chile, spice of the southwest.
NUESTRO, Vol. 6, no. 10 (December 1982), p.
22-25+. English. **DESCR:** *Chile (Food).

10094 Marilyn Monteruego's flan. LATINA, Vol. 1,
no. 1 (1982), p. 23. English.

10095 Martinez, Anita. Tortilla demonstration.
LATINA, Vol. 1, no. 3 (1983), p. 30-31.
English.

10096 Reading to whet your appetite [book
reviews]. CAMINOS, Vol. 4, no. 6 (June
1983), p. 19,66. English. **DESCR:** Barraza
Sanchez, Irene; Book Reviews; *COMIDA
SABROSA; Sanchez Yund, Gloria.

10097 Rivera, Jean. Codfish fritters "bacalao
fritos". LATINA, Vol. 1, no. 3 (1983), p.
32-33. English.

10098 Salazar, Pamela Eoff. Selling $25 million of
Jimenez Food Products. HISPANIC BUSINESS,
Vol. 4, no. 6 (June 1982), p. 20-21,24.
English. **DESCR:** Business Enterprises; Food
Industry; *Jimenez Food Products, Inc.

10099 Shiell, Pancho. The food world's CIA.
NUESTRO, Vol. 7, no. 2 (March 1983), p.
28-32. English. **DESCR:** *Culinary Institute
of America, Hyde Park, NY; Employment
Training; Figueroa, Roberto.

10100 Soto, Manuela. Calientitas y recien hechas!
Tortillas de harina. LATINA, Vol. 1, no. 3
(1983), p. 30. English.

10101 Villegas-Romero, Rosa. Rose
Villegas-Romero's menudo for a Sunday
brunch. LATINA, Vol. 1, no. 1 (1982), p.
24-25. English.

10102 Volsky, George. Miami's premier
Latin-America cafeteria. HISPANIC BUSINESS,
Vol. 5, no. 8 (August 1983), p. 16. English.
DESCR: *Restaurants.

10103 Weber, Robert and Balkan, D. Carlos.
Hispanic foods in Southern California:
anatomy of a market in flux. HISPANIC
BUSINESS, Vol. 5, no. 8 (August 1983), p.
24-25+. English. **DESCR:** *Food Industry.

Recording Industry

10104 Agudelo, Carlos. What about Latin music?
BILLBOARD, Vol. 94, (November 20, 1982), p.
10. English. **DESCR:** *Awards; *Grammy Awards;
Music; National Academy of Recording Arts
and Sciences; Performing Arts.

10105 Fantin, Joyce and Fernandez, Diana.
Undocumented aliens ease concern over
younger generation's cultural drift.
BILLBOARD, Vol. 94, (September 11, 1982),
p. T20+. English. **DESCR:** *Music;
Undocumented Workers.

10106 Fernandez, Enrique. NARAS takes a welcome
step. BILLBOARD, Vol. 95, (June 18, 1983),
p. 59. English. **DESCR:** Awards; Entertainers;
Grammy Awards; Music; *National Academy of
Recording Arts and Sciences; Performing
Arts.

10107 Fernandez, Enrique. Youth acts dominating
markets: labels woo kids with
Spanish-language rock product. BILLBOARD,
Vol. 95, (March 12, 1983), p. 58. English.
DESCR: *Entertainers; Music; Youth.

10108 Record marketing effort aimed at Latino
buyer. NUESTRO, Vol. 6, no. 2 (March 1982),
p. 48. English. **DESCR:** *Marketing; Music.

Recreation

10109 Barrera, Jose J. Jesus "Chuy" Negrete: the
Chicano vote. NUESTRO, Vol. 5, no. 8
(November 1981), p. 40-41. English. **DESCR:**
Chicanismo; *Negrete, Jesus "Chuy".

10110 Cantu, Hector. Softball Texas style.
NATIONAL HISPANIC JOURNAL, Vol. 1, no. 3
(Summer, Fall, 1982), p. 9-11. English.
DESCR: El Paso Jesters; Mexico City All
Stars; Pan American Softball League;
*Softball; Sports.

10111 Entertaiment reviews. CAMINOS, Vol. 3, no. 8
(September 1982), p. 21. English. **DESCR:**
Adams, Bob; Alpert, Herb; Books; Calvert,
Robert; Jimenez, Santiago; Lopez, Lisa;
Music; Myles, Carol; Paredes, Americo;
Pettus, Theodore T.; Television.

10112 Entertainment = diversion. CAMINOS, Vol. 3,
no. 2 (February 1982), p. 40-41. English.
DESCR: Awards; CHECKING IT OUT; Club Hogar
Latino; Dance; Films; Flamenco; Marley, Bob;
Montalban, Ricardo; ON GOLDEN POND;
Television.

10113 Entertainment = diversion. CAMINOS, Vol. 3,
no. 3 (March 1982), p. 55-56. Bilingual.
DESCR: Aztlan Writing Contest; CORAZON DE
AZTLAN; Films; Literary Contests; MISSING
[film]; THE BORDER [film]; Young, Robert.

10114 Entertainment = diversion. CAMINOS, Vol. 3,
no. 4 (April 1982), p. 41. Bilingual.
DESCR: AZTLAN [journal];
Committee in Solidarity with the People of
El Salvador (CISPES); Cultural
Organizations; Directories; DIRECTORY OF
MINORITY ARTS ORGANIZATIONS; El Salvador;
*National Endowment for the Arts; NOTICIERO;
Organizations; Periodicals; Television.

10115 Golden Eagle Awards 1983. CAMINOS, Vol. 4,
no. 8 (September 1983), p. 42-43. English.
DESCR: *Awards; Nosotros [film production
company]; Sesma, Chico.

10116 Greenfield, Charles. Spanish prince of song.
NUESTRO, Vol. 6, no. 5 (June, July, 1982),
p. 18-21. English. **DESCR:** Entertainers;
*Iglesias, Julio.

10117 McManis, Linda. Flying Hispanics: a constant
gamble with death. LATINO, Vol. 54, no. 6
(October 1983), p. 12-13. English. **DESCR:**
*Circus.

10118 New city park for Miamians. NUESTRO, Vol. 6,
no. 9 (November 1982), p. 13. English.
DESCR: Marti, Jose; *Miami, FL.

10119 The world cup: soccer's superbowl. NUESTRO,
Vol. 6, no. 1 (January, February, 1982), p.
43-44. English. **DESCR:** Soccer; Sports; *The
World Cup of Soccer.

Recruitment

10120 Atkinson, Donald R. Ethnic minority
representation in counselor education.
COUNSELOR EDUCATION AND SUPERVISION, Vol.
23, no. 1 (September 1983), p. 7-19.
English. DESCR: Affirmative Action;
Counseling Services (Educational);
*Counselors.

10121 Cantu, Hector. Hispanic students wanted.
NATIONAL HISPANIC JOURNAL, Vol. 1, no. 3
(Summer, Fall, 1982), p. 8. English. DESCR:
*Enrollment; Higher Education; Students;
*University of Texas at Austin.

10122 Fisher, Edith Maureen. Minority
librarianship research: a state-of-the-art
review. LIBRARY AND INFORMATION SCIENCE
RESEARCH, Vol. 5, no. 1 (Spring 1983), p.
5-65. English. DESCR: *Librarians; Library
and Information Studies.

10123 Lourenzo, Susan V. Early outreach: career
awareness for health professions. JOURNAL OF
MEDICAL EDUCATION, Vol. 58, no. 1 (January
1983), p. 39-44. English. DESCR: Affirmative
Action; Careers; College Preparation;
*Medical Education.

10124 Tips for making the right moves in today's
job markets. HISPANIC BUSINESS, Vol. 4, no.
6 (June 1982), p. 26. English. DESCR:
*Employment.

Reference Books
USE: Reference Works

Reference Works

10125 Abu Bakr, Virginia. Book review of:
MENTAL-HEALTH RESEARCH: A REFERENCE GUIDE.
SOCIAL CASEWORK: JOURNAL OF CONTEMPORARY
SOCIAL WORK, Vol. 63, no. 7 (September
1982), p. 443-444. English. DESCR: Book
Reviews; Cota-Robles Newton, Frank;
*HISPANIC MENTAL HEALTH RESEARCH: A
REFERENCE GUIDE; Mental Health.

10126 Chavaria, Elvira. Book review of: THE
MEXICAN AMERICAN: A CRITICAL GUIDE TO
RESEARCH AIDS. AZTLAN, Vol. 14, no. 1
(Spring 1983), p. 192-195. English. DESCR:
Bibliography; Book Reviews; Robinson,
Barbara J.; Robinson, J. Cordell; *THE
MEXICAN AMERICAN: A CRITICAL GUIDE TO
RESEARCH AIDS.

10127 de Cuenca, Pilar and Alvarez, Rudolph, Ines.
Library holdings of the Office of Bilingual
Education, city of New York: a selected
bibliography. BILINGUAL REVIEW, Vol. 9, no.
2 (May, August, 1982), p. 127-152. English.
DESCR: Bibliography; *Bilingual Bicultural
Education; *Office of Bilingual Education
Library, New York, NY.

10128 Jones, Errol D. Book review of: DICTIONARY
OF MEXICAN-AMERICAN HISTORY. WESTERN
HISTORICAL QUARTERLY, Vol. 14, no. 3 (1983),
p. 339-340. English. DESCR: Book Reviews;
*DICTIONARY OF MEXICAN AMERICAN HISTORY;
History; Meier, Matt S.; Rivera, Feliciano.

10129 Marquez, Maria Teresa. Book review of: A
SELECTED AND ANNOTATED BIBLIOGRAPHY OF
CHICANO STUDIES. AZTLAN, Vol. 14, no. 1
(Spring 1983), p. 191-192. English. DESCR:
*A SELECTED AND ANNOTATED BIBLIOGRAPHY OF
CHICANO STUDIES; Bibliography; Book Reviews;
Tatum, Charles.

Refranes
USE: Dichos

Refugees

10130 Camacho de Schmidt, Aurora. Alien smuggling
and the refugee question: the INS and
sojourners from Yalaj. NUESTRO, Vol. 7, no.
5 (June, July, 1983), p. 20. English.
DESCR: *Guatemala; *Immigration Regulation
and Control; *Political Refugees;
*Undocumented Workers.

10131 Equity for camp victims. NUESTRO, Vol. 6,
no. 1 (January, February, 1982), p. 10-11.
English. DESCR: Haiti; Immigration and
Naturalization Service (INS); *Immigration
Law.

10132 Estevez, Guillermo. Resettling the Cuban
refugees in New Jersey. MIGRATION TODAY,
Vol. 11, no. 4-5 (1983), p. 28-33. English.
DESCR: Caribbean Relief Program; *Cubanos;
Immigration; International Rescue Committee;
*New Jersey.

10133 Holdenreid, Frank X. Guatemala shantytown.
NUESTRO, Vol. 7, no. 4 (May 1983), p. 39-41.
English. DESCR: Ayudantes de los Pobres;
*Guatemala; Holdenreid, Frank X.; *Poverty.

10134 Salvatierra, Richard. Alien smuggling and
the refugee question: U.S. must set a limit
on refugees. NUESTRO, Vol. 7, no. 5 (June,
July, 1983), p. 19. English. DESCR:
Federation for American Immigration Reform
(FAIR); *Immigration Regulation and Control;
*Political Refugees; *Undocumented Workers.

10135 Schey, Peter A. Supply side immigration
theory: analysis of the Simpson-Mazzoli
Bill. LA RAZA LAW JOURNAL, Vol. 1, no. 1
(June 1983), p. 53-71. English. DESCR:
Amnesty; Immigration; Mazzoli, Romano L.;
Migration Patterns; Simpson, Alan K.;
*Simpson-Mazzoli Bill; Temporary Worker
Program.

10136 Trevino, Jesus and Ruiz, Jose Luis.
Guatemalan refugees - the tip of the
iceberg. CAMINOS, Vol. 4, no. 5 (May 1983),
p. 13-15,48. English. DESCR: Guatemala;
International Relations; Mexico; MEXICO: THE
FUTURE.

Regional Planning
USE: Urban Planning

Reidel, Johannes

10137 Prof pushes for recognition of Chicano's
music. VARIETY, Vol. 306, (March 10, 1982),
p. 184. English. DESCR: Corrido; *Folk
Songs.

Reisler, Mark

10138 Garcia, Mario T. On Mexican immigration, the
United States, and Chicano history. JOURNAL
OF ETHNIC STUDIES, Vol. 7, no. 1 (Spring
1979), p. 80-88. English. DESCR: Book
Reviews; *BY THE SWEAT OF THEIR BROW:
MEXICAN IMMIGRANT LABOR IN THE UNITED
STATES, 1900-1940; History; Immigrant Labor;
Immigration; Immigration Law; Mexico;
Research Methodology; Southwest United
States.

Religion

10139 Alarcon, Justo S. Hacia la nada ... o la religion en POCHO. MINORITY VOICES, Vol. 1, no. 2 (Fall 1977), p. 17-26. English. DESCR: Literature; *POCHO; Villarreal, Jose Antonio.

10140 Alvarez, Amando. Juana de Arco. LATINO, Vol. 54, no. 7 (November 1983), p. 21-22. English. DESCR: Biography; *De Arco, Juana.

10141 Anderson, Arthur J.O. Aztec hymns of life and love. NEW SCHOLAR, Vol. 8, no. 1-2 (Spring, Fall, 1982), p. 1-72. English. DESCR: *Aztecs.

10142 Arrastia, Cecilio. The Hispanics in the U.S.A.: drama and challenge. CHURCH AND SOCIETY, Vol. 72, no. 4 (March, April, 1982), p. 31-35. English. DESCR: Migration Patterns; *Presbyterian Church.

10143 Carrasco, David. A perspective for a study of religious dimensions in Chicano experience: BLESS ME, ULTIMA as a religious text. AZTLAN, Vol. 13, no. 1-2 (Spring, Fall, 1982), p. 195-221. English. DESCR: Anaya, Rudolfo A.; *BLESS ME, ULTIMA; Literary Criticism; Literature.

10144 Clark, Walter J. Hispanics: the harvest field at home. CHRISTIANITY TODAY, Vol. 26, (November 12, 1982), p. 102. English. DESCR: Religious Education.

10145 Cortez, Hector. The undocumented alien and the law. CHRISTIAN CENTURY, Vol. 100, (July 6, 1983), p. 650-652. English. DESCR: Immigration Regulation and Control; *Undocumented Workers.

10146 Costas, Orlando E. The Hispanics next door. CHRISTIAN CENTURY, Vol. 99, no. 26 (August 18, 1982), p. 851-856. English. DESCR: Cultural Pluralism; Latin Americans; *Liberation Theology.

10147 Day, Mark R. Hispanics 'want more bishops, input in church'. NATIONAL CATHOLIC REPORTER, Vol. 18, (March 12, 1982), p. 1. English. DESCR: *Catholic Church; Clergy; Cursillo Movement; Monterey, CA.

10148 Delgado, Melvin. Ethnic and cultural variations in the care of the aged. Hispanic elderly and natural support systems: a special focus on Puerto Ricans. JOURNAL OF GERIATRIC PSYCHIATRY, Vol. 15, no. 2 (1982), p. 239-251. English. DESCR: *Ancianos; Cultural Organizations; Curanderas; Family; Natural Support Systems; Puerto Ricans; Santeros.

10149 Delgado, Melvin. Hispanic natural support systems: implications for mental health services. JOURNAL OF PSYCHOSOCIAL NURSING AND MENTAL HEALTH SERVICES, Vol. 21, no. 4 (April 1983), p. 19-24. English. DESCR: Curanderas; Family; *Mental Health; Support Groups.

10150 Erdman, Daniel. Liberation and identity: Indo-Hispano youth. RELIGIOUS EDUCATION, Vol. 78, no. 1 (Winter 1983), p. 76-89. English. DESCR: Identity; *Liberation Theology.

10151 Estrada, Antonio; Rabou, Jerome; and Watts, Ronald K. Alcohol use among Hispanic adolescents; a preliminary report. HISPANIC JOURNAL OF BEHAVIORAL SCIENCES, Vol. 4, no. 3 (September 1982), p. 339-351. English. DESCR: *Alcoholism; Youth.

10152 Garcia, Ignacio M. Latino-ization of the Mormon church. NUESTRO, Vol. 7, no. 2 (March 1983), p. 20-24+. English. DESCR: *Church of Jesus Christ of Latter-Day Saints (Mormons); Molina, Alberto.

10153 Gibeau, Dawn. Mexican-American Center forges new vision. NATIONAL CATHOLIC REPORTER, Vol. 18, (July 30, 1982), p. 5+. English. DESCR: Catholic Church; Elizondo, Virgilio; *Mexican American Cultural Center, San Antonio, TX.

10154 Gil, Carlos B. Withstanding time: the miracle of the Virgin of Guadalupe. NUESTRO, Vol. 7, no. 10 (December 1983), p. 46-47. English. DESCR: Catholic Church; *Guadalupanismo; Mexico City; *Virgin of Guadalupe.

10155 Gomez, Roberto L. Pastoral care and counseling in a Mexican American setting. APUNTES, Vol. 2, no. 2 (Summer 1982), p. 31-39. English. DESCR: *Clergy; *Counseling (Religious); Cultural Characteristics.

10156 Gonzalez, Juan. Caribbean voodoo: a Catholic response, a private encounter. NUESTRO, Vol. 7, no. 1 (January, February, 1983), p. 37. English. DESCR: Catholic Church; Gods and Dieties.

10157 Grijalva, Joshua. The story of Hispanic Southern Baptists. BAPTIST HISTORY AND HERITAGE, Vol. 18, no. 3 (July 1983), p. 40-47. English. DESCR: *Baptists; History; Puerto Ricans; *Southern Baptists.

10158 Hispanics keep the faith, but better parish work is needed. MIGRATION TODAY, Vol. 10, no. 5 (1982), p. 35. English. DESCR: Assimilation; Catholic Church; Cultural Customs.

10159 Inter faith unity. LATINA, Vol. 1, no. 2 (February, March, 1983), p. 19. English. DESCR: *National Council of Churches.

10160 Lopez, Hugo L. Toward a theology of migration. APUNTES, Vol. 2, no. 3 (Fall 1982), p. 68-71. English. DESCR: *Immigrants; *Liberation Theology.

10161 Markides, Kyraikos S. Aging, religiosity, and adjustment: a longitudinal analysis. JOURNAL OF GERONTOLOGY, Vol. 38, no. 5 (September 1983), p. 621-625. English. DESCR: *Ancianos; *Mental Health; Psychology.

10162 Mercado, Olivia; Corrales, Ramona; and Segovia, Sara. Las hermanas. COMADRE, no. 2 (Spring 1978), p. 34-41. English. DESCR: Chicanas; *Clergy.

10163 Mexican migration to the United States: challenge to Christian witness and national policy. CHURCH AND SOCIETY, Vol. 72, no. 5 (May, June, 1982), p. 29-46. English. DESCR: Economic History and Conditions; Immigration Regulation and Control; *Undocumented Workers; United States-Mexico Relations.

10164 Morales, Cecilio J. The bishops' pastoral on Hispanic ministry. AMERICA [America Press, New York, NY], Vol. 149, (June, July, 1983), p. 7-9. English. DESCR: *Catholic Church; Clergy.

Religion (cont.)

10165 Morales, Cecilio J. Challenges in Catholicism. NUESTRO, Vol. 6, no. 3 (April 1982), p. 26-27+. English. **DESCR**: Catholic Church.

10166 Ramirez named bishop of Las Cruces diocese. NUESTRO, Vol. 6, no. 8 (October 1982), p. 43. English. **DESCR**: Catholic Church; *Ramirez, Ricardo (Bishop of Las Cruces, NM).

10167 Ramirez, Ricardo. Reflections on the Hispanicization of the liturgy. WORSHIP, Vol. 57, no. 1 (January 1983), p. 26-34. English. **DESCR**: Catholic Church; Clergy; *Liturgy; Third General Conference of the Latin American Episcopate.

10168 Rivas, Yolanda E. Confrontacion y reconciliacion. APUNTES, Vol. 2, no. 2 (Summer 1982), p. 40-47. Spanish. **DESCR**: *Identity.

10169 Rosenhouse-Persson, Sandra and Sabagh, Georges. Attitudes toward abortion among Catholic Mexican-American women: the effects of religiosity and education. DEMOGRAPHY, Vol. 20, no. 1 (February 1983), p. 87-98. English. **DESCR**: Abortion; Attitude (Psychological); *Catholic Church; Education.

10170 Solis, Arnaldo. Traditional Chicano centering. CALMECAC, Vol. 3, (Spring 1982), p. 18-19. English.

10171 Stacy, Gerald F. From stranger to neighbor. CHURCH AND SOCIETY, Vol. 72, no. 5 (May, June, 1982), p. 1-71. English. **DESCR**: Economic History and Conditions; *Migration; Undocumented Workers.

10172 Turner, Kay F. Mexican American home altars: towards their interpretation. AZTLAN, Vol. 13, no. 1-2 (Spring, Fall, 1982), p. 309-326. English. **DESCR**: *Home Altars; Icons.

10173 Vigil, James Diego. Human revitalization: the six tasks of victory outreach. DREW GATEWAY, Vol. 52, no. 3 (Spring 1982), p. 49-59. English. **DESCR**: Barrios for Christ Program; Drug Addicts; Drug Programs; Gangs; Identity; Pentecostal Church; Protestant Church; *Victory Outreach; Youth.

10174 Weber, Kenneth R. Book review of: MY PENITENTE LAND: REFLECTIONS ON SPANISH NEW MEXICO. JOURNAL OF ETHNIC STUDIES, Vol. 3, no. 2 (Summer 1975), p. 119-121. English. **DESCR**: Book Reviews; Chavez, Fray Angelico; *Hermanos Penitentes; MY PENITENTE LAND: REFLECTIONS ON SPANISH NEW MEXICO; *New Mexico.

10175 Zabaleta, Antonio N. The medieval antecedents of border pseudo-religious folk beliefs. BORDERLANDS JOURNAL, Vol. 5, no. 2 (Spring 1982), p. 185-200. English. **DESCR**: Curanderismo.

Religious Art

10176 Lenti, Paul. Accent: the Mexican retablo - a highly collectable folk art. NUESTRO, Vol. 7, no. 4 (May 1983), p. 63-64. English. **DESCR**: *Art History; *Folk Art; *Mexico.

Religious Education

10177 Clark, Walter J. Hispanics: the harvest field at home. CHRISTIANITY TODAY, Vol. 26, (November 12, 1982), p. 102. English. **DESCR**: *Religion.

10178 Deck, Allan Figueroa and Nunez, J. A. Religious enthusiasm and Hispanic youths. AMERICA [America Press, New York, NY], Vol. 147, (October 23, 1982), p. 232-234. English. **DESCR**: *Catholic Church.

10179 Doyle, Janet. Escoja educacion catolica! MOMENTUM, Vol. 14, no. 1 (February 1983), p. 37-38. English. **DESCR**: Catholic Church; *Enrollment; Toledo, OH.

10180 Elford, George. Catholic schools and bilingual education. MOMENTUM, Vol. 14, no. 1 (February 1983), p. 35-37. English. **DESCR**: *Bilingual Bicultural Education; Catholic Church.

Rembis, Deborah

10181 Nuestra gente. LATINO, Vol. 54, no. 8 (December 1983), p. 30. English. **DESCR**: *Biographical Notes; Businesspeople; Carter, Lynda Cordoba; Duran, Sandra; Patino, Lorenzo E.; Politics; Vega, Christopher.

Remedial Teaching
USE: Compensatory Education

Reminiscences

10182 Martinez, Elisa A. Sharing her tiny pieces of the past. NUESTRO, Vol. 7, no. 7 (September 1983), p. 51-52. English. **DESCR**: Autobiography; Chicanas; *Extended Family.

10183 Ponce, Mary Helen. El jabon de Dona Chonita. NUESTRO, Vol. 7, no. 10 (December 1983), p. 44-45. English. **DESCR**: Autobiography; *Ponce, Mary Helen; Prose.

Repatriation
USE: Deportation

Reports and Reporting
USE: Journalism

Republican National Committee

10184 Hamner, Richard. Hispanic update: Hispanics and the Republican Party. NATIONAL HISPANIC JOURNAL, Vol. 1, no. 2 (Winter 1982), p. 5. English. **DESCR**: Political Parties and Organizations; Republican National Hispanic Assembly; Republican Party.

Republican National Hispanic Assembly

10185 Hamner, Richard. Hispanic update: Hispanics and the Republican Party. NATIONAL HISPANIC JOURNAL, Vol. 1, no. 2 (Winter 1982), p. 5. English. **DESCR**: Political Parties and Organizations; *Republican National Committee; Republican Party.

Republican Party

10186 Conservative Hispanic groups gaining strength attracting suitors. HISPANIC BUSINESS, Vol. 4, no. 2 (February 1982), p. 29. English. **DESCR**: Democratic Party; *Political Parties and Organizations; Politics.

10187 Cruz, Franklin D. Upcoming Republican strategies. HISPANIC BUSINESS, Vol. 4, no. 10 (October 1982), p. 21,30. English. **DESCR**: *Political Parties and Organizations.

Republican Party (cont.)

10188 Hamner, Richard. Hispanic update: Hispanics and the Republican Party. NATIONAL HISPANIC JOURNAL, Vol. 1, no. 2 (Winter 1982), p. 5. English. DESCR: Political Parties and Organizations; *Republican National Committee; Republican National Hispanic Assembly.

10189 Kirschten, Dick. The Hispanic vote: parties can't gamble that the sleeping giant won't awaken. NATIONAL JOURNAL, Vol. 15, no. 47 (November 19, 1983), p. 2410-2411. English. DESCR: Democratic Party; *Hispanic Caucus; Southwest Voter Registration Education Project (SVRP); *Voter Turnout.

10190 Oaxaca, Fernando. The new Hispanic conservative: a Republican opinion. CAMINOS, Vol. 3, no. 3 (March 1982), p. 40-41,62. Bilingual. DESCR: Politics.

10191 Whisler, Kirk. The California Republican Hispanic Council: a new force/un nuevo poder. CAMINOS, Vol. 3, no. 3 (March 1982), p. 44-46. Bilingual. DESCR: *California Republican Hispanic Council; Politics.

Research Methodology

10192 Alba, Richard D. A comment on Schoen and Cohen. AMERICAN JOURNAL OF SOCIOLOGY, Vol. 87, no. 4 (January 1982), p. 935-939. English. DESCR: Cohen, Lawrence E.; ETHNIC ENDOGAMY AMONG MEXICAN AMERICAN GROOMS; Intermarriage; Schoen, Robert.

10193 Arce, Carlos H. Language shift among Chicanos: strategies for measuring and assessing direction and rate. SOCIAL SCIENCE JOURNAL, Vol. 19, no. 2 (April 1982), p. 121-132. English. DESCR: Bilingualism; Language Development; *Spanish Language.

10194 Baca Zinn, Maxine. Chicano family research: conceptual distortions and alternative directions. JOURNAL OF ETHNIC STUDIES, Vol. 7, no. 3 (Fall 1979), p. 59-71. English. DESCR: Cultural Characteristics; Culture; *Family; Social Research; Stereotypes.

10195 Chavez, Mauro. Carranza's CHICANISMO: PHILOSOPHICAL FRAGMENTS. JOURNAL OF ETHNIC STUDIES, Vol. 7, no. 3 (Fall 1979), p. 95-100. English. DESCR: Book Reviews; Carranza, Elihu; *Chicanismo; *CHICANISMO: PHILOSOPHICAL FRAGMENTS; Philosophy.

10196 Consalvo, Robert W. and Orlandi, Lisanio R. Principles and practices of data collection and management. BILINGUAL JOURNAL, Vol. 7, no. 2 (Winter 1983), p. 13-16. English. DESCR: *Bilingual Bicultural Education; Educational Statistics; *Evaluation (Educational).

10197 Cornelius, Wayne A. Interviewing undocumented immigrants: methodological reflections based on fieldwork in Mexico and the U.S. INTERNATIONAL MIGRATION REVIEW, Vol. 16, no. 2 (Summer 1982), p. 378-411. English. DESCR: Immigrant Labor; Immigrants; Migrant Labor; *Undocumented Workers.

10198 Dowdall, George W. and Flood, Lawrence G. Correlates and consequences of socioeconomic differences among Chicanos, Blacks and Anglos in the Southwest: a study of metropolitan structure. SOCIAL SCIENCE JOURNAL, Vol. 19, no. 2 (April 1982), p. 25-36. English. DESCR: Anglo Americans; Blacks; *Ethnic Groups; Residential Segregation; Socioeconomic Factors; Southwest United States.

10199 Garcia, Mario T. On Mexican immigration, the United States, and Chicano history. JOURNAL OF ETHNIC STUDIES, Vol. 7, no. 1 (Spring 1979), p. 80-88. English. DESCR: Book Reviews; *BY THE SWEAT OF THEIR BROW: MEXICAN IMMIGRANT LABOR IN THE UNITED STATES, 1900-1940; History; Immigrant Labor; Immigration; Immigration Law; Mexico; Reisler, Mark; Southwest United States.

10200 Giachello, Aida L., et al. Uses of the 1980 census for Hispanic health services research. AMERICAN JOURNAL OF PUBLIC HEALTH, Vol. 73, no. 3 (March 1983), p. 266-274. English. DESCR: Census; Public Health; *Surveys.

10201 Gottlieb, Karen. Genetic demography of Denver, Colorado: Spanish surname as a market of Mexican ancestry. HUMAN BIOLOGY, Vol. 55, no. 2 (May 1983), p. 227-234. English. DESCR: Demography; Denver, CO; Personal Names; *Population Genetics; Sociology.

10202 Growth of U.S. Hispanic income: 1950-1982. HISPANIC BUSINESS, Vol. 5, no. 12 (December 1983), p. 46. English. DESCR: Economics; *Income.

10203 Hoffman, Abraham. Chicano history: problems and potentialities. JOURNAL OF ETHNIC STUDIES, Vol. 1, no. 1 (Spring 1973), p. 6-12. English. DESCR: *History.

10204 The impact of undocumented migration on the U.S. labor market. HOUSTON JOURNAL OF INTERNATIONAL LAW, Vol. 5, no. 2 (Spring 1983), p. 287-321. English. DESCR: Economic History and Conditions; Employment; Immigrant Labor; Immigration and Nationality Act (INA); Immigration Law; Labor Supply and Market; Simpson-Mazzoli Bill; *Undocumented Workers.

10205 Phillips, Susan D., et al. Career development of special populations: a framework for research. JOURNAL OF VOCATIONAL BEHAVIOR, Vol. 22, no. 1 (February 1983), p. 12-29. English. DESCR: Careers; College Graduates; Vocational Education.

10206 Ramos, Reyes. Discovering the production of Mexican American family structure. DE COLORES, Vol. 6, no. 1-2 (1982), p. 120-134. English. DESCR: *Ethnomethodology; *Family.

10207 Role model for aspiring researchers. NUESTRO, Vol. 6, no. 4 (May 1982), p. 34-36. English. DESCR: Gonzales, Ciriaco Q.; *Short Story.

10208 Rotberg, Iris C. Some legal and research considerations in establishing federal policy in bilingual education. HARVARD EDUCATIONAL REVIEW, Vol. 52, no. 2 (May 1982), p. 149-168. English. DESCR: *Bilingual Bicultural Education; Educational Law and Legislation; History; Policy Formation.

10209 Schoen, Robert and Cohen, Lawrence E. Theory and method in the study of ethnic endogamy among Mexican-American grooms - reply. AMERICAN JOURNAL OF SOCIOLOGY, Vol. 87, no. 4 (January 1982), p. 939-942. English. DESCR: Assimilation; ETHNIC ENDOGAMY: THE CASE OF THE MEXICAN-AMERICANS; Intermarriage; Mittelback, Frank G.; Moore, Joan W.

Research Methodology (cont.)

10210 Valdez, Diana. Mexican American family research: a critical review and conceptual framework. DE COLORES, Vol. 6, no. 1-2 (1982), p. 48-63. English. DESCR: *Family.

10211 Vazquez, Carol A. Research on the psychiatric evaluation of the bilingual patient: a methodological critique. HISPANIC JOURNAL OF BEHAVIORAL SCIENCES, Vol. 4, no. 1 (March 1982), p. 75-80. English. DESCR: Bilingualism; Mental Health; *Psychiatry.

10212 Willig, Ann C. The effectiveness of bilingual education: review of a report. NABE JOURNAL, Vol. 6, no. 2-3 (Winter, Spring, 1981, 1982), p. 1-19. English. DESCR: *Bilingual Bicultural Education; Educational Statistics.

Reserve Officer Training Corps (ROTC)

10213 Captor, Rich. College and the Navy. CAMINOS, Vol. 4, no. 1-2 (January, February, 1983), p. 26-27. Bilingual. DESCR: *Careers; *Military; U.S. Navy.

Residential Segregation

10214 Dowdall, George W. and Flood, Lawrence G. Correlates and consequences of socioeconomic differences among Chicanos, Blacks and Anglos in the Southwest: a study of metropolitan structure. SOCIAL SCIENCE JOURNAL, Vol. 19, no. 2 (April 1982), p. 25-36. English. DESCR: Anglo Americans; Blacks; *Ethnic Groups; *Research Methodology; Socioeconomic Factors; Southwest United States.

10215 Krivo, Lauren J. Housing price inequalities: a comparison of Anglos, Blacks, and Spanish-origin populations. URBAN AFFAIRS QUARTERLY, Vol. 17, no. 4 (1982), p. 445-462. English. DESCR: Housing; *Urban Housing.

10216 Massey, Douglas S. Research note on residential succession: the Hispanic case. SOCIAL FORCES, Vol. 61, (March 1983), p. 825-833. English. DESCR: Barrios; Population Trends; Urban Communities.

Restaurants

10217 Diaz, Katherine A. El Adobe Cafe: a recipe for success. CAMINOS, Vol. 3, no. 1 (January 1982), p. 33-34. Bilingual. DESCR: *Casado, Frank.

10218 It's not all rice & beans, part III (restaurant reviews). CAMINOS, Vol. 4, no. 6 (June 1983), p. 15-18. Bilingual. DESCR: Cache Restaurant; El Cochinito Yucateco Restaurant; El Tepeyac Restaurant; La Parrilla Restaurant.

10219 It's not all rice and beans (2nd annual Mexican restaurant guide), part II. CAMINOS, Vol. 3, no. 1 (January 1982), p. 26-30. Bilingual.

10220 Langley, Roger. Roger Langley's Hispanic beat. HISPANIC BUSINESS, Vol. 4, no. 1 (January 1982), p. 22. English. DESCR: *Food Industry.

10221 Ogaz, Armando. The chicken wars. CAMINOS, Vol. 4, no. 6 (June 1983), p. 10-11. Bilingual. DESCR: El Pollo Loco; Food Industry; Pioneer Chicken.

10222 San Antonio restaurant survives urban project. NUESTRO, Vol. 6, no. 5 (June, July, 1982), p. 44. English. DESCR: San Antonio, TX; *Urban Planning.

10223 Volsky, George. Miami's premier Latin-America cafeteria. HISPANIC BUSINESS, Vol. 5, no. 8 (August 1983), p. 16. English. DESCR: Recipes.

RESTLESS SERPENTS

10224 Sanchez, Marta. Inter-sexual and intertextual codes in the poetry of Bernice Zamora. MELUS: MULTI-ETHNIC LITERATURE OF THE UNITED STATES, Vol. 7, no. 3 (Fall 1980), p. 55-68. English. DESCR: *Literature; *Zamora, Bernice.

Resumes

10225 Baciu, Joyce A. How to prepare a resume. CAMINOS, Vol. 3, no. 3 (March 1982), p. 31. English.

10226 Baciu, Joyce A. How to prepare a resume/como redactar un resumen. CAMINOS, Vol. 4, no. 1-2 (January, February, 1983), p. 28. Bilingual. DESCR: Employment.

REVERSING ROLES

10227 Barrio, Raymond. The bilingual heart and other adventures. BILINGUAL JOURNAL, Vol. 6, no. 2 (Winter 1982), p. 12-15. Bilingual. DESCR: *Early Childhood Education; Ethnic Attitudes; Racism; THE BILINGUAL HEART; THE PRINCE.

REVISTA CHICANO-RIQUENA

10228 Kanellos, Nicolas. REVISTA CHICANO-RIQUENA/Arte Publico Press. CAMINOS, Vol. 4, no. 6 (June 1983), p. 52-53,67. English. DESCR: Journals; Periodicals.

THE REVOLT OF THE COCKROACH PEOPLE

10229 Alurista. El caso, la novela y la historia en la obra de Acosta: THE REVOLT OF THE COCKROACH PEOPLE. MAIZE, Vol. 2, no. 3 (Spring 1979), p. 6-13. Spanish. DESCR: Acosta, Oscar Zeta; Literary Criticism.

REVOLTOSOS: MEXICO'S REBELS IN THE UNITED STATES, 1903-1923

10230 Cardoso, Lawrence Anthony. Book review of: REVOLTOSOS: MEXICO'S REBELS IN THE UNITED STATES 1903-1923. JOURNAL OF THE WEST, Vol. 22, no. 1 (1983), p. 90. English. DESCR: Book Reviews; History; Immigration; Mexico; Raat, W. Dirk.

10231 Griswold del Castillo, Richard. Book review of: REVOLTOSOS: MEXICO'S REBELS IN THE UNITED STATES 1903-1923. JOURNAL OF SAN DIEGO HISTORY, Vol. 28, no. 2 (Spring 1982), p. 143-144. English. DESCR: Book Reviews; Raat, W. Dirk.

10232 Martinez, Oscar J. Book review of: REVOLTOSOS: MEXICO'S REBELS IN THE UNITED STATES 1903-1923. ARIZONA AND THE WEST, Vol. 24, no. 1 (Spring 1982), p. 69-70. English. DESCR: Book Reviews; Mexico; Raat, W. Dirk; United States History.

Revolutions

10233 Aldaraca, Bridget. The poetry of Gioconda Belli. MAIZE, Vol. 5, no. 3-4 (Spring, Summer, 1982), p. 18-21. English. DESCR: Belli, Gioconda; Literary Criticism; *Nicaragua; *Poetry.

10234 Baker, Edward, trans. and Dalton, Roque. The poetry of Roque Dalton: We all, Typist, Latinoamerica, Love poem, O.A.S. MAIZE, Vol. 5, no. 3-4 (Spring, Summer, 1982), p. 37-46. English. DESCR: *El Salvador; *Poetry.

10235 Banberger, Ellen. Poesia nicaraguense. MAIZE, Vol. 5, no. 3-4 (Spring, Summer, 1982), p. 64-77. Spanish. DESCR: Belli, Gioconda; Cardenal, Ernesto; Carrillo, Ernesto; Coronel Urtecho, Jose; Gadea, Gerardo; Gomez, Manuel; Murillo, Rosario; *Nicaragua; Ojeda, Mirna; *Poetry; Rugama, Leonel.

10236 Breiter, Toni. El Libertador: a profile. NUESTRO, Vol. 7, no. 7 (September 1983), p. 32-35. English. DESCR: Biography; *Bolivar, Simon; Political History and Conditions; South America.

10237 Pena-Ramos, Alfonso. The Latin American disease: an essay. NUESTRO, Vol. 7, no. 6 (August 1983), p. 42-43. English. DESCR: *Latin America; *Political History and Conditions; Social History and Conditions.

10238 Uriarte, Ivan. Introduccion a la poesia revolucionaria de El Salvador. MAIZE, Vol. 6, no. 1-2 (Fall, Winter, 1982, 1983), p. 34-40. Spanish. DESCR: *El Salvador; Latin American Literature; *Poetry.

Reyes, Carlos

10239 Laws, Bart. Raza unida de Cristal. SOUTHERN EXPOSURE, Vol. 10, no. 2 (March, April, 1982), p. 67-72. English. DESCR: Crystal City, TX; Gurule, Dorothy; History; La Raza Unida Party; Mexican American Youth Organization (MAYO); *Political Parties and Organizations.

Reyes, Gil

10240 Commercial art as a career. CAMINOS, Vol. 4, no. 9 (October 1983), p. 32-35. English. DESCR: Artists; *Careers; Chavez Lichwardt, Leticia; Gomez, Dario; Guerrero, Ernest R.; Melendez, Bill; Santistevan, August.

Reyes, Luis

10241 Los Alvarez. CAMINOS, Vol. 4, no. 4 (April 1983), p. 40-41,66. English. DESCR: Films.

Reyna, Jose

10242 Richardson, Chad and Yanez, Linda. "Equal justice" and Jose Reyna. NUESTRO, Vol. 6, no. 5 (June, July, 1982), p. 17. English. DESCR: Brownsville, TX; *Children; Education; Education Equalization; Immigration Law; *Legislation; Undocumented Workers.

Reynolds, Steve

10243 A territorial approach to representation for illegal aliens. MICHIGAN LAW REVIEW, Vol. 80, no. 6 (May 1982), p. 1342-1371. English. DESCR: Census; Federation for American Immigration Reform (FAIR); Population; Reapportionment; *Undocumented Workers; Voting Rights.

Reynoso, Cruz

10244 Hernandez, Dennis. Group works to ensure Reynoso election. CAMINOS, Vol. 3, no. 9 (October 1982), p. 46. English. DESCR: *Judges.

Rhetoric

10245 Jensen, Richard J. and Hammerback, John C. "No revolutions without poets": the rhetoric of Rodolfo "Corky" Gonzales. WESTERN JOURNAL OF SPEECH COMMUNICATION, Vol. 46, no. 1 (Winter 1982), p. 72-91. English. DESCR: Chicano Movement; *Gonzales, Rodolfo (Corky); Literary Criticism; Poetry.

Ribes Tovar, Federico

10246 Villanueva Collado, Alfredo. Fili-Mele: simbolo y mujer en la poesia de Luis Pales Matos e Ivan Silen. REVISTA CHICANO-RIQUENA, Vol. 10, no. 4 (Fall 1982), p. 47-54. Spanish. DESCR: Chicanas; Literary Criticism; LOS POEMAS DE FILI-MELE; *Pales Matos, Luis; *Silen, Ivan; Symbolism; TUNTUN DE PASA Y GRIFERIA.

Richardson, Bill Lopez

10247 People. HISPANIC BUSINESS, Vol. 5, no. 6 (June 1983), p. 8. English. DESCR: Appointed Officials; *Biographical Notes; Businesspeople; Goizueta, Roberto C.; Guerra, Stella; Huapaya, Sixto Guillermo; Kitano, Pat; Manriquez, Suzanna; Oppenheimer-Nicolau, Siabhan; Ortiz, Solomon; Pachon, Harry P.; Torres, Esteban E.; Torres, Johnny.

Richardson, William

10248 Padilla, Steve. Latinos wield political clout in midterm election. NUESTRO, Vol. 6, no. 9 (November 1982), p. 28-30. English. DESCR: De la Garza, Kika; *Elected Officials; Garcia, Robert; Gonzales, Henry B.; Lujan, Manuel, Jr.; Martinez, Matthew G. "Marty", Assemblyman; Ortiz, Solomon; *Politics; Roybal, Edward R.; *Torres, Esteban E.

Richmond, Frederick W.

10249 Food stamp cheaters. NUESTRO, Vol. 5, no. 8 (November 1981), p. 10. English. DESCR: Food Stamps; Human Resources Administration; *Welfare.

Rico, Jose Hipolito

10250 People. HISPANIC BUSINESS, Vol. 5, no. 11 (November 1983), p. 10. English. DESCR: Aragon, Fermin; *Businesspeople; De Los Reyes, Victor; Di Martino, Rita; Garcia, Ruben; Juarez, Chris; Lopez, Leonard; Nogales, Luis G.; Ozuna, Bob; Tamayo, Roberto; Tapia, Raul R.

Ridge, Martin

10251 Weber, David J. Book review of: THE NEW BILINGUALISM: AN AMERICAN DILEMMA. WESTERN HISTORICAL QUARTERLY, Vol. 14, no. 1 (1983), p. 77-79. English. DESCR: Bilingual Bicultural Education; Bilingualism; Book Reviews; *THE NEW BILINGUALISM: AN AMERICAN DILEMMA.

RIE-RIT

Riesco, Laura

10252 Riesco, Laura. Laura Riesco y el truco de los ojos: entrevista. THIRD WOMAN, Vol. 1, no. 2 (1982), p. 76-82. Spanish. DESCR: Literature; Literature Reviews.

Rio Arriba Valley, New Mexico

10253 Craver, Rebecca McDowell. The impact of intimacy: Mexican-Anglo intermarriage in New Mexico 1821-1846. SOUTHWESTERN STUDIES, no. 66 (1982), p. 1-79. English. DESCR: Acculturation; Assimilation; Chicanas; *Intermarriage; New Mexico.

Rio Grande

10254 Mumme, Stephen P. and Jamail, Milton H. The International Boundary and Water Commission as a conflict management agency in the U.S.-Mexico borderlands. SOCIAL SCIENCE JOURNAL, Vol. 19, no. 1 (January 1982), p. 46-62. English. DESCR: Border Region; Conflict Resolution; *International Boundary and Water Commission; United States-Mexico Relations; *Water.

Rio Grande Valley, TX

10255 Flores, David. 30's gridder recalls pain of prejudice. NUESTRO, Vol. 6, no. 8 (October 1982), p. 25-26. English. DESCR: *Lerma, Everardo Carlos; Sports; Texas.

10256 Mena, Jesus. Violence in the Rio Grande Valley. NUESTRO, Vol. 7, no. 1 (January, February, 1983), p. 41-42. English. DESCR: *Bandidos; Border Region; History; Social History and Conditions.

10257 Nieto, Ernesto. Politics: powers that struggled in the Texas Valley. NATIONAL HISPANIC JOURNAL, Vol. 2, no. 1 (Summer 1983), p. 22-23. English. DESCR: Elections; McAllen, TX; *Politics; Voter Turnout.

10258 Peso devaluation hurts Rio Grande economy. NUESTRO, Vol. 6, no. 3 (April 1982), p. 46. English. DESCR: *Currency.

10259 Rivas, Mike. Keeping peace in paradise. NATIONAL HISPANIC JOURNAL, Vol. 1, no. 2 (Winter 1982), p. 13-20. English. DESCR: *Brand, Othal; Casso, Ramiro; Elections; Police; Police Brutality; *Political Repression; THE MEXICAN AMERICAN: QUEST FOR EQUALITY; Voter Turnout.

Rioja, Pilar

10260 Pilar Rioja and the magic of duende. NUESTRO, Vol. 7, no. 6 (August 1983), p. 47-48. English. DESCR: *Dance; Performing Arts.

Rios, Al

10261 U.S. workers tutor students. NUESTRO, Vol. 6, no. 4 (May 1982), p. 13. English. DESCR: Children; *Education.

Rios, Alberto

10262 Saldivar, Jose David. Book review of: WHISPERING TO FOOL THE WIND. REVISTA CHICANO-RIQUENA, Vol. 11, no. 2 (Summer 1983), p. 72-74. English. DESCR: Book Reviews; *WHISPERING TO FOOL THE WIND.

Rios, Conrad R.

10263 The compleat Hispanic marketing guide. HISPANIC BUSINESS, Vol. 4, no. 1 (January 1982), p. 10. English. DESCR: *Consumers; *Marketing.

Rios, David N.

10264 Diaz, Katherine A. "And this year's winners are...". CAMINOS, Vol. 4, no. 1-2 (January, February, 1983), p. 39-54,74+. English. DESCR: *Awards; Castro, Tony; Elizalde, Hector; Flores, Tom; Martinez, Esperanza; Mendizabal, Maritza; Molina, Gloria; Moya, Connie; Placentia, Joe; Quesada, Leticia; Ybarra, Lea; Zapata, Carmen.

Rios, Isabella

10265 Lomeli, Francisco A. Isabella Rios and the Chicano psychic novel. MINORITY VOICES, Vol. 4, no. 1 (Spring 1980), p. 49-61. English. DESCR: Literature; Lopez, Diana; Novel; VICTUUM.

Rios, John F.

10266 People. HISPANIC BUSINESS, Vol. 4, no. 11 (November 1982), p. 7. English. DESCR: Biographical Notes; *Businesspeople; Diaz, Jose; Garcia-Pedrosa, Jose R.; Garza, Jose; Herrera, Heriberto; Mercado, Anthony; Solano, Faustina V.; Solis, Frank.

Rios Rey, Rafael

10267 Griffin, Julia Ortiz. Two artists in search of a country: Rafael Rios Rey and Francisco Arrivi. MINORITY VOICES, Vol. 5, no. 1-2 (Spring, Fall, 1981), p. 53-58. English. DESCR: *Arrivi, Francisco; Artists; Puerto Rican Literature; Puerto Ricans; Teatro.

Rios-Bustamante, Antonio

10268 Meier, Matt S. Book review of: MEXICAN IMMIGRANT WORKERS IN THE UNITED STATES and OPERATION WETBACK: THE MASS DEPORTATION OF MEXICAN UNDOCUMENTED WORKERS IN 1954. PACIFIC HISTORICAL REVIEW, Vol. 52, no. 1 (February 1983), p. 126-128. English. DESCR: Book Reviews; Garcia, Juan Ramon; *MEXICAN IMMIGRANT WORKERS IN THE U.S.; *Operation Wetback.

Riots

10269 Colorado confrontation. NUESTRO, Vol. 6, no. 6 (August 1982), p. 9. English. DESCR: *Colorado; *Violence.

10270 Lopez, Enrique Hank. Overkill at the silver dollar. CHISMEARTE, (1982), p. 6-8. English. DESCR: *Chicano Movement.

10271 Rodriguez, Luis. La veintinueve. CHISMEARTE, (1982), p. 9-10. English. DESCR: *Chicano Movement.

Ristaino v. Ross

10272 Fram, Steven J. Restricting inquiry into racial attitudes during the Voir Dire. AMERICAN CRIMINAL REVIEW, Vol. 19, no. 4 (Spring 1982), p. 719-750. English. DESCR: Aldridge v. U.S.; Ham v. South Carolina; Juries; *Racism; Rosales v. U.S.; Rosales-Lopez, Humberto.

RITES AND WITNESSES

10273 Garcia, Ed. Quien es Rolando Hinojosa? TEXAS OBSERVER, Vol. 75, no. 5 (March 11,), p. 26-29. English. DESCR: Biography; Book Reviews; *Hinojosa-Smith, Rolando R.; THE VALLEY.

Rivera, Diana

10274 Aparicio, Frances R. Figure in dream. THIRD WOMAN, Vol. 1, no. 2 (1982), p. 83-86. English. DESCR: Art.

Rivera, Diego

10275 Herrera, Hayden. The elephant and the dove. NUESTRO, Vol. 7, no. 8 (October 1983), p. 40-43. English. DESCR: Art; Artists; Biography; *Kahlo, Frida; Paintings.

10276 Rose, Barbara. Frida Kahlo: the Chicana as art heroine. VOGUE, Vol. 173, (April 1983), p. 152-154. English. DESCR: Art; Artists; Biography; *Kahlo, Frida; Mexico.

Rivera, Feliciano

10277 Barber, Gary. Book review of: DICTIONARY OF MEXICAN-AMERICAN HISTORY. REFERENCE SERVICES REVIEW, Vol. 10, no. 3 (October 1982), p. 41. English. DESCR: Book Reviews; Dictionaries; *DICTIONARY OF MEXICAN AMERICAN HISTORY; Meier, Matt S.

10278 Book review of: DICTIONARY OF MEXICAN-AMERICAN HISTORY. LIBRARY JOURNAL, Vol. 108, no. 10 (May 15, 1983), p. 965. English. DESCR: Book Reviews; *DICTIONARY OF MEXICAN AMERICAN HISTORY; Meier, Matt S.

10279 Camarillo, Alberto M. Book review of: DICTIONARY OF MEXICAN-AMERICAN HISTORY. JOURNAL OF AMERICAN HISTORY, Vol. 69, no. 4 (March 1983), p. 953-954. English. DESCR: Book Reviews; *DICTIONARY OF MEXICAN AMERICAN HISTORY; Meier, Matt S.

10280 De Leon, Arnoldo. Book review of: DICTIONARY OF MEXICAN-AMERICAN HISTORY. NEW MEXICO HISTORICAL REVIEW, Vol. 58, no. 1 (January 1983), p. 101-102. English. DESCR: Book Reviews; *DICTIONARY OF MEXICAN AMERICAN HISTORY; Meier, Matt S.

10281 Griswold del Castillo, Richard. Book review of: DICTIONARY OF MEXICAN-AMERICAN HISTORY. SOUTHWESTERN HISTORICAL QUARTERLY, Vol. 86, no. 4 (April 1983), p. 579-580. English. DESCR: Book Reviews; *DICTIONARY OF MEXICAN AMERICAN HISTORY; Meier, Matt S.

10282 Jones, Errol D. Book review of: DICTIONARY OF MEXICAN-AMERICAN HISTORY. WESTERN HISTORICAL QUARTERLY, Vol. 14, no. 3 (1983), p. 339-340. English. DESCR: Book Reviews; *DICTIONARY OF MEXICAN AMERICAN HISTORY; History; Meier, Matt S.; Reference Works.

10283 Laska, Vera. Book review of: DICTIONARY OF MEXICAN-AMERICAN HISTORY. INTERNATIONAL SOCIAL SCIENCE, Vol. 57, no. 3 (Summer 1982), p. 184. English. DESCR: Book Reviews; Dictionaries; *DICTIONARY OF MEXICAN AMERICAN HISTORY; History; Meier, Matt S.

10284 Martinez, Julio A. Book review of: DICTIONARY OF MEXICAN-AMERICAN HISTORY. RQ - REFERENCE AND ADULT SERVICES DIVISION, Vol. 21, no. 3 (Spring 1982), p. 297-298. English. DESCR: Book Reviews; Dictionaries; *DICTIONARY OF MEXICAN AMERICAN HISTORY; History; Meier, Matt S.

Rivera, Geraldo

10285 Baciu, Joyce A. The winners - Los ganadores. CAMINOS, Vol. 3, no. 2 (February 1982), p. 14-20,45. Bilingual. DESCR: *Awards; Caldera, Manuel; Gomez, Ignacio; Huerta, Dolores; Lizarraga, David C.; Obledo, Mario; Olmos, Edward James; Rivera, Tomas.

Rivera, Henry

10286 Gutierrez, Felix. Henry Rivera: our Hispanic on the FCC. CAMINOS, Vol. 4, no. 3 (March 1983), p. 22-24,50. Bilingual. DESCR: Federal Communications Commission (FCC); Mass Media; Television.

10287 Lewels, Francisco J. Un mensaje. LATINO, Vol. 53, no. 7 (November 1982), p. 17. Spanish. DESCR: *Mass Media.

10288 Research and ownership among Hispanic concerns. BROADCASTING, Vol. 102, no. 15 (April 12, 1982), p. 66. English. DESCR: Federal Communications Commission (FCC); *Radio.

Rivera, Joseph, Jr.

10289 People. HISPANIC BUSINESS, Vol. 5, no. 3 (March 1983), p. 9. English. DESCR: Anaya, Toney; Anguiano, Lupe; Appointed Officials; Avila, Joaquin Guadalupe; Awards; *Biographical Notes; de la Fuente, Emilio; del Olmo, Frank; Godoy, Gustavo; Long, Dennis P.; Martinez, Elias (Lee).

Rivera, Julio

10290 Pacific direct mail services. CAMINOS, Vol. 3, no. 2 (February 1982), p. 30-32. Bilingual. DESCR: *Business; Businesspeople; *Pacific Direct Mail Service, Inc., Los Angeles, CA.

Rivera, Lourdes

10291 Math-based careers. HISPANIC BUSINESS, Vol. 5, no. 9 (September 1983), p. 28. English. DESCR: Andrew W. Mellon Foundation; *Careers; Employment; Engineering as a Profession; Financial Aid; Garcia, Mary; Higher Education; National Council for Minorities in Engineering (NACME); National Medical Fellowships (NMF).

Rivera, Tomas

10292 Baciu, Joyce A. The winners - Los ganadores. CAMINOS, Vol. 3, no. 2 (February 1982), p. 14-20,45. Bilingual. DESCR: *Awards; Caldera, Manuel; Gomez, Ignacio; Huerta, Dolores; Lizarraga, David C.; Obledo, Mario; Olmos, Edward James; Rivera, Geraldo.

10293 Diaz, Katherine A. Chancellor Tomas Rivera on today's graduates. CAMINOS, Vol. 3, no. 3 (March 1982), p. 11-13. English. DESCR: *Higher Education.

10294 Lattin, Vernon E. Novelistic structure and myth in ...Y NO SE LO TRAGO LA TIERRA. BILINGUAL REVIEW, Vol. 9, no. 3 (September, December, 1982), p. 220-226. English. DESCR: Literature; Novel; United Mexican Americans, South Bend, IN; *Y NO SE LO TRAGO LA TIERRA/AND THE EARTH DID NOT PART.

10295 Vallejos, Thomas. Ritual process and the family in the Chicano novel. MELUS: MULTI-ETHNIC LITERATURE OF THE UNITED STATES, Vol. 10, no. 4 (Winter 1983, 1984), p. 5-16. English. DESCR: Anaya, Rudolfo A.; BLESS ME, ULTIMA; Family; *Literary Criticism; Novel; Parent and Child Relationships; POCHO; Villarreal, Jose Antonio; Y NO SE LO TRAGO LA TIERRA/AND THE EARTH DID NOT PART.

Rivera, Victor M.

10296 People. HISPANIC BUSINESS, Vol. 4, no. 8
(August 1983), p. 7. English. **DESCR:**
Aguilar, Richard; *Businesspeople;
Cordero-Badillo, Atilano; del Olmo, Frank;
Infante, E. Anthony; Levitan, Aida T.;
Nunez, Luis; Quintanilla, Guadalupe.

Rivero, Horacio

10297 Weinberger, Caspar W. A heritage of valor -
Hispanics in America's defense: remarks... at
the recent unveiling of paintings of
Hispanic heroes at the Pentagon. NUESTRO,
Vol. 7, no. 9 (November 1983), p. 18.
English. **DESCR:** Del Valle, Pedro A.;
Gabaldon, Guy; Lopez, Jose; *Military
Service; Paintings.

Riverside, CA

10298 Riverside's Hispanic Chamber of Commerce.
CAMINOS, Vol. 3, no. 8 (September 1982), p.
46. English. **DESCR:** *Business;
*Organizations.

10299 Whisler, Kirk. Menudo cook-off and much more
(photoessay). CAMINOS, Vol. 3, no. 8
(September 1982), p. 49. English. **DESCR:**
*Cultural Organizations.

Roa Bastos, Augustos

10300 Espinoza, Roberto. Sintesis vs. analysis: un
problema de historicidad en las novelas de
las dictaduras. MAIZE, Vol. 6, no. 1-2
(Fall, Winter, 1982, 1983), p. 7-27.
Spanish. **DESCR:** Carpentier, Alejo;
Dictatorships; Garcia Marquez, Gabriel;
Latin American Literature; *Literary
Criticism; Novel; Valle Inclan, Ramon;
White, Lucas Edward.

THE ROAD TO TAMAZUNCHALE

10301 Arias, Ron. El senor del chivo. JOURNAL OF
ETHNIC STUDIES, Vol. 3, no. 4 (Winter 1976),
p. 58-60. English. **DESCR:** Authors; *Fiction.

10302 Lattin, Vernon E. La meta critica Chicana.
REVISTA CHICANO-RIQUENA, Vol. 10, no. 3
(Summer 1982), p. 53-62. English. **DESCR:**
*Arias, Ron; Death (Concept); Literary
Criticism.

Robb, John Donald

10303 Gifford, Douglas. Book review of: HISPANIC
FOLK MUSIC OF NEW MEXICO AND THE SOUTHWEST:
A SELF-PORTRAIT OF A PEOPLE. BULLETIN OF
HISPANIC STUDIES, Vol. 59, no. 2 (April
1982), p. 162-163. English. **DESCR:** Book
Reviews; Folk Songs; *HISPANIC FOLK MUSIC OF
NEW MEXICO AND THE SOUTHWEST: A
SELF-PORTRAIT OF A PEOPLE; New Mexico.

10304 Pena, Manuel H. Book review of: FOLK MUSIC
OF NEW MEXICO AND THE SOUTHWEST: A
SELF-PORTRAIT OF A PEOPLE. AMERICAN MUSIC,
Vol. 1, no. 2 (Summer 1983), p. 102-105.
English. **DESCR:** Book Reviews; *HISPANIC FOLK
MUSIC OF NEW MEXICO AND THE SOUTHWEST: A
SELF-PORTRAIT OF A PEOPLE; Music.

10305 Vincent, J. Book review of: HISPANIC FOLK
MUSIC OF NEW MEXICO AND THE SOUTHWEST: A
SELF-PORTRAIT OF A PEOPLE. ETHNOMUSICOLOGY,
Vol. 26, no. 2 (May 1982), p. 326-327.
English. **DESCR:** Book Reviews;
Ethnomusicology; Folk Songs; *HISPANIC FOLK
MUSIC OF NEW MEXICO AND THE SOUTHWEST: A
SELF-PORTRAIT OF A PEOPLE; New Mexico; *THE
SOUTHWEST: A SELF-PORTRAIT.

10306 West, John O. Book review of: HISPANIC FOLK
MUSIC OF NEW MEXICO AND THE SOUTHWEST: A
SELF-PORTRAIT OF A PEOPLE. JOURNAL OF
AMERICAN FOLKLORE, Vol. 96, (April, May,
1983), p. 239. English. **DESCR:** Book Reviews;
Folk Songs; *HISPANIC FOLK MUSIC OF NEW
MEXICO AND THE SOUTHWEST: A SELF-PORTRAIT OF
A PEOPLE.

10307 Zalazar, Daniel E. Book review of: HISPANIC
FOLK MUSIC OF NEW MEXICO AND THE SOUTHWEST:
A SELF-PORTRAIT OF A PEOPLE. HISPANIC
JOURNAL, Vol. 3, no. 2 (Spring 1982), p.
139-140. Spanish. **DESCR:** Book Reviews;
*HISPANIC FOLK MUSIC OF NEW MEXICO AND THE
SOUTHWEST: A SELF-PORTRAIT OF A PEOPLE.

Robe, Stanley L.

10308 Weigle, Marta. Book review of: HISPANIC
LEGENDS FROM NEW MEXICO: NARRATIVES FROM THE
R.D. JAMESON COLLECTION. JOURNAL OF AMERICAN
FOLKLORE, Vol. 96, , p. 238-239. English.
DESCR: Book Reviews; Cuentos; *HISPANIC
LEGENDS FROM NEW MEXICO: NARRATIVES FROM THE
R.D. JAMESON COLLECTION.

Robinson, Barbara J.

10309 Chavaria, Elvira. Book review of: THE
MEXICAN AMERICAN: A CRITICAL GUIDE TO
RESEARCH AIDS. AZTLAN, Vol. 14, no. 1
(Spring 1983), p. 192-195. English. **DESCR:**
Bibliography; Book Reviews; Reference Works;
Robinson, J. Cordell; *THE MEXICAN AMERICAN:
A CRITICAL GUIDE TO RESEARCH AIDS.

Robinson, David J.

10310 Hornbeck, David. Book review of: STUDIES IN
SPANISH-AMERICAN POPULATION HISTORY.
PROFESSIONAL GEOGRAPHER, Vol. 34, no. 4
(1982), p. 480. English. **DESCR:** Book
Reviews; Demography; Latin America; *STUDIES
IN SPANISH-AMERICAN POPULATION HISTORY.

Robinson, J. Cordell

10311 Bodayla, Stephen D. Book review of: ORIGINS
OF THE MEXICAN WAR: A DOCUMENTARY SOURCE
BOOK. HISTORY - REVIEWS OF NEW BOOKS, Vol.
11, no. 7 (May, June, 1983), p. 149-150.
English. **DESCR:** Book Reviews; McAfee, Ward;
*ORIGINS OF THE MEXICAN WAR: A DOCUMENTARY
SOURCE BOOK.

10312 Chavaria, Elvira. Book review of: THE
MEXICAN AMERICAN: A CRITICAL GUIDE TO
RESEARCH AIDS. AZTLAN, Vol. 14, no. 1
(Spring 1983), p. 192-195. English. **DESCR:**
Bibliography; Book Reviews; Reference Works;
Robinson, Barbara J.; *THE MEXICAN AMERICAN:
A CRITICAL GUIDE TO RESEARCH AIDS.

10313 Graebner, Norman A. Book review of: ORIGINS
OF THE MEXICAN WAR: A DOCUMENTARY SOURCE
BOOK. NEW MEXICO HISTORICAL REVIEW, Vol. 58,
no. 3 (July 1983), p. 291-292. English.
DESCR: Book Reviews; McAfee, Ward; *ORIGINS
OF THE MEXICAN WAR: A DOCUMENTARY SOURCE
BOOK.

Rocard, Marcienne

10314 Cazemajou, Jean. Book review of: LES FILS DU
SOLEIL: LA MINORITE MEXICAINE A TRAVERS LA
LITTERATURE DES ETATS-UNIS. REVUE FRANCAISE
D'ETUDES AMERICAINES. Vol. 83, no. 16 (February
1983), p. 153-155. Other. **DESCR:** *LES
FILS DU SOLEIL: LA MINORITE MEXICAINE A
TRAVERS LA LITTERATURE DES ETATS-UNIS.

Rocard, Marcienne (cont.)

10315 Fabre, Michel. Book review of: LES FILS DU
      SOLEIL: LA MINORITE MEXICAINE A TRAVERS LA
      LITTERATURE DES ETATS-UNIS. MELUS:
      MULTI-ETHNIC LITERATURE OF THE UNITED
      STATES, Vol. 8, no. 1 (Spring 1981), p.
      65-68. English. **DESCR:** Book Reviews; *LES
      FILS DU SOLEIL: LA MINORITE MEXICAINE A
      TRAVERS LA LITTERATURE DES ETATS-UNIS;
      Literature.

Rocha, Peter

10316 Ysla, Elizabeth. King of jelly bean art.
      NUESTRO, Vol. 6, no. 4 (May 1982), p. 50-52.
      English. **DESCR:** Art; Art History.

Rocky Mountain Spotted Fever

10317 Que pasa? NUESTRO, Vol. 7, no. 3 (April
      1983), p. 9. English. **DESCR:** Border Patrol;
      *Cisneros, Henry, Mayor of San Antonio, TX;
      Elections; Immigration Regulation and
      Control; Servas; Tourism.

Rodeo
      USE: Charreada

Rodino, Peter W.

10318 Immigration reform. NUESTRO, Vol. 5, no. 8
      (November 1981), p. 11. English. **DESCR:**
      *Immigration Law.

Rodolfo H. Castro Fellowship

10319 Community watching: para la comunidad.
      CAMINOS, Vol. 3, no. 3 (March 1982), p.
      58-59. Bilingual. **DESCR:** Cultural
      Organizations; *Engineering as a Profession;
      Financial Aid; Harvard University; Latino
      Business Students Association (LBSA);
      Society for Hispanic Professional Engineers
      (SHPE); Student Organizations; University of
      Southern California.

Rodriguez, Adan

10320 Reavis, Dick J. Growing up gringo. TEXAS
      MONTHLY, Vol. 10, no. 8 (August 1982), p.
      110-112+. English. **DESCR:** Biography; Dumas,
      TX; Zinc Mining.

Rodriguez, Alberto Duque

10321 People. HISPANIC BUSINESS, Vol. 5, no. 9
      (September 1983), p. 10. English. **DESCR:**
      *Businesspeople; Chavez, Chris; Diez de
      Onate, Jorge; Franco Garcia, Freddie;
      Garcia, Hector P.; Lozano, Leticia Eugenia;
      Ravard, Rafael Alonzo; Sanchez, Philip V.;
      Villalpando, Catalina.

Rodriguez, Axel

10322 What bilingual education means to the
      nation. NUESTRO, Vol. 7, no. 2 (March 1983),
      p. 52-53. English. **DESCR:** *Bilingual
      Bicultural Education; Education; Millan,
      Aida; Nguyen, Anh Tuan.

Rodriguez, Demetrio P.

10323 Texan honored for court fight. NUESTRO, Vol.
      7, no. 1 (January, February, 1983), p. 12.
      English. **DESCR:** *School Finance; Taxation.

Rodriguez, Edmundo M.

10325 How to stuff a wild chile part II. CAMINOS,
      Vol. 3, no. 1 (January 1982), p. 31-32.
      English. **DESCR:** Albert, Margo; Chacon, Peter
      R.; *Icaya, Rick; Lacayo, Frank L. "Hank";
      *Recipes; *Rodriguez, Edmundo; *Vasquez,
      Victor.

10326 "Our success is to see someone get a job
      with MGM"; Q and A with Edmundo M.
      Rodriguez. CAMINOS, Vol. 3, no. 11 (December
      1982), p. 48-49,54. English. **DESCR:** Cultural
      Organizations; *Plaza de La Raza, Los
      Angeles, CA.

Rodriguez, Elias C.

10327 People. HISPANIC BUSINESS, Vol. 4, no. 5
      (May 1982), p. 8. English. **DESCR:** Appointed
      Officials; Asociacion Internacional de
      Exportadores e Importadores (EXIMA);
      *Biographical Notes; Businesspeople;
      California Chicano News Media Association
      (CCNMA); de la Ossa, Ernest G.; Foreign
      Trade; Obledo, Mario; Rodriguez, Samuel F.;
      United Way; U.S. Hispanic Chamber of
      Commerce.

Rodriguez Hernandez, Andres

10328 Cuban-exile community protests deportation
      of recent escapee. NUESTRO, Vol. 6, no. 2
      (March 1982), p. 32-34. English. **DESCR:**
      Cubanos; Immigration and Naturalization
      Service (INS); Political Asylum.

10329 Our 1982 Latino awards. NUESTRO, Vol. 7, no.
      1 (January, February, 1983), p. 44-46.
      English. **DESCR:** Awards; Escalante, Jaime;
      Gallegos, Gina; Grace, J. Peter; Immigration
      and Naturalization Service (INS); Knight,
      Bobby; Lamas, Fernando; *Latino Awards;
      Luce, Claire Boothe; Moreno, Rita; National
      Press Foundation; Simpson-Mazzoli Bill;
      Smith, Raymond; Valeri, Michele; Voting
      Rights Act.

Rodriguez, Isidoro

10330 Virginian to head U.S.D.A. minority affairs
      office. NUESTRO, Vol. 6, no. 6 (August
      1982), p. 34. English. **DESCR:** Appointed
      Officials.

Rodriguez, Ismael D.

10331 People. HISPANIC BUSINESS, Vol. 5, no. 12
      (December 1983), p. 9. English. **DESCR:**
      *Businesspeople; Cantu, Norma V.; Cruz,
      Jose; Masvidal, Sergio J.; Ortega, Katherine
      D.; Planas, Maria Bordas; Romero, Estella
      E.

Rodriguez, Julio H.

10332 Gomez, Dalia. Needed: Latino CPA's. NUESTRO,
      Vol. 6, no. 1 (January, February, 1982), p.
      25-28. English. **DESCR:** *Accounting; Careers;
      Frank, Eleanor Marie; Karpel, Miguel;
      Quezada, Felipe L.; Umpierre, Raphael;
      Zuzueta, Joseph.

Rodriguez, Leslie J.

10333 People. HISPANIC BUSINESS, Vol. 4, no. 6 (June 1982), p. 8. English. **DESCR:** Aguirre, Pedro; Arellano, Richard; *Biographical Notes; Businesspeople; Cortez, Pete; De la Colina, Rafael; Hernandez, Sam; Nogales, Luis; Roybal, Edward R.

Rodriguez, Manuel Jaramillo

10334 Manuel Jaramillo Rodriguez; master portrait artist. CAMINOS, Vol. 3, no. 9 (October 1982), p. 16-17. English. **DESCR:** *Artists.

Rodriguez, Paul

10335 Padilla, Steve. The comedian. NUESTRO, Vol. 7, no. 2 (March 1983), p. 25-27. English. **DESCR:** Artists; Humor; Performing Arts.

10336 Paul Rodriguez. LATINA, Vol. 1, no. 2 (February, March, 1983), p. 44-45. English. **DESCR:** *Biography.

Rodriguez, Peter

10337 Morris, Gay. The Mexican Museum has a colorful new home. CAMINOS, Vol. 3, no. 7 (July, August, 1982), p. 30-33. Bilingual. **DESCR:** Art; *Mexican Museum, San Francisco, CA; Museums; San Francisco, CA.

Rodriguez, Rafael

10338 Mullen, E.J. Book review of: HEREJES Y MITIFICADORES: MUESTRA DE POESIA PUERTORRIQUENA EN LOS ESTADOS UNIDOS. REVISTA CHICANO-RIQUENA, Vol. 10, no. 3 (Summer 1982), p. 68-70. English. **DESCR:** Barradas, Efrain; Book Reviews; *HEREJES Y MITIFICADORES: MUESTRA DE POESIA PUERTORRIQUENA EN LOS ESTADOS UNIDOS; Marin, Carmen Lilianne.

10339 Rivero, Eliana S. Book review of: HEREJES Y MITIFICADORES: MUESTRA DE POESIA PUERTORRIQUENA EN LOS ESTADOS UNIDOS. THIRD WOMAN, Vol. 1, no. 2 (1982), p. 91-93. Spanish. **DESCR:** Barradas, Efrain; Book Reviews; *HEREJES Y MITIFICADORES: MUESTRA DE POESIA PUERTORRIQUENA EN LOS ESTADOS UNIDOS; Puerto Rican Literature.

Rodriguez, Raul

10340 Aguilar, George. Raul Rodriguez, parade artist extraordinaire. NUESTRO, Vol. 6, no. 10 (December 1982), p. 11-14. English. **DESCR:** *Art; *Artists.

Rodriguez, Richard

10341 Ano Nuevo de Kerr, Louise. Book review of: HUNGER OF MEMORY: THE EDUCATION OF RICHARD RODRIGUEZ. COMMONWEAL, Vol. 110, no. 1 (January 14, 1983), p. 26-28. English. **DESCR:** Book Reviews; *HUNGER OF MEMORY: THE EDUCATION OF RICHARD RODRIGUEZ.

10342 Bell, Michael Davitt. Fitting into a tradition of autobiography. CHANGE, Vol. 14, no. 7 (October 1982), p. 36-39. English. **DESCR:** Affirmative Action; Assimilation; Bilingual Bicultural Education; Biography; Book Reviews; *HUNGER OF MEMORY: THE EDUCATION OF RICHARD RODRIGUEZ.

10343 Book review of: HUNGER OF MEMORY: THE EDUCATION OF RICHARD RODRIGUEZ. SAN FRANCISCO REVIEW OF BOOKS, Vol. 7, (Summer 1982), p. 11. English. **DESCR:** Attitude (Psychological); Bilingual Bicultural Education; Book Reviews; *HUNGER OF MEMORY: THE EDUCATION OF RICHARD RODRIGUEZ; Identity.

10344 Chall, Jeanne. Rich and sharp memories of reading. CHANGE, Vol. 14, no. 7 (October 1982), p. 36-40. English. **DESCR:** Assimilation; Book Reviews; *HUNGER OF MEMORY: THE EDUCATION OF RICHARD RODRIGUEZ; Language Arts; Reading; Socioeconomic Factors.

10345 Chavez, Linda. HUNGER OF MEMORY: the metamorphosis of a disadvantaged child. AMERICAN EDUCATOR, Vol. 6, no. 3 (Fall 1982), p. 14-16. English. **DESCR:** Book Reviews; *HUNGER OF MEMORY: THE EDUCATION OF RICHARD RODRIGUEZ.

10346 Cotera, Martha P. Rich-heard rod-ree-guess. LATINA, Vol. 1, no. 1 (1982), p. 27+. English. **DESCR:** Book Reviews; *HUNGER OF MEMORY: THE EDUCATION OF RICHARD RODRIGUEZ.

10347 Fainberg, Louise Vasvari. HUNGER OF MEMORY: review of a review. NABE JOURNAL, Vol. 6, no. 2-3 (Winter, Spring, 1981, 1982), p. 115-116. English. **DESCR:** Book Reviews; *HUNGER OF MEMORY: THE EDUCATION OF RICHARD RODRIGUEZ; Zweig, Paul.

10348 Garcia, Ed. Book review of: HUNGER OF MEMORY: THE EDUCATION OF RICHARD RODRIGUEZ. TEXAS OBSERVOR, Vol. 74, no. 12 (June 18, 1982), p. 23-24. English. **DESCR:** Book Reviews; *HUNGER OF MEMORY: THE EDUCATION OF RICHARD RODRIGUEZ.

10349 HUNGER OF MEMORY: THE EDUCATION OF RICHARD RODRIGUEZ. NUESTRO, Vol. 6, no. 3 (April 1982), p. 52-53. English. **DESCR:** Book Reviews; *HUNGER OF MEMORY: THE EDUCATION OF RICHARD RODRIGUEZ.

10350 Krashen, Stephen D. Bilingual education and the case of Richard Rodriguez. CAMINOS, Vol. 3, no. 10 (November 1982), p. 38-40,54. Bilingual. **DESCR:** *Bilingual Bicultural Education.

10351 Madrid, Arturo. Book review of: HUNGER OF MEMORY: THE EDUCATION OF RICHARD RODRIGUEZ. TEXAS OBSERVOR, Vol. 74, no. 13 (July 9, 1982), p. 14+. English. **DESCR:** Book Reviews; *HUNGER OF MEMORY: THE EDUCATION OF RICHARD RODRIGUEZ.

10352 Olivas, Michael A. Painful to write, painful to read. CHANGE, Vol. 14, no. 7 (October 1982), p. 37-42. English. **DESCR:** Biography; Book Reviews; *HUNGER OF MEMORY: THE EDUCATION OF RICHARD RODRIGUEZ.

10353 Olson, James S. Book review of: HUNGER OF MEMORY: THE EDUCATION OF RICHARD RODRIGUEZ. JOURNAL OF THE WEST, Vol. 22, no. 1 (1983), p. 80-81. English. **DESCR:** Bilingual Bicultural Education; Book Reviews; *HUNGER OF MEMORY: THE EDUCATION OF RICHARD RODRIGUEZ; Identity.

10354 Porter, Horace A. Book review of: HUNGER OF MEMORY: THE EDUCATION OF RICHARD RODRIGUEZ. AMERICAN SCHOLAR, Vol. 52, no. 2 (Spring 1983), p. 278-285. English. **DESCR:** Book Reviews; *HUNGER OF MEMORY: THE EDUCATION OF RICHARD RODRIGUEZ.

Rodriguez, Richard (cont.)

10355 Riley, Michael N. Book review of: HUNGER OF MEMORY: THE EDUCATION OF RICHARD RODRIGUEZ. NATIONAL ASSOCIATION OF SECONDARY SCHOOL PRINCIPALS: BULLETIN, Vol. 66, no. 45 (December 1982), p. 112-113. English. **DESCR:** *Book Reviews; HUNGER OF MEMORY: THE EDUCATION OF RICHARD RODRIGUEZ.

10356 Rodriguez, Richard. A minority scholar speaks out. AMERICAN EDUCATION, Vol. 18, no. 9 (November 1982), p. 2-5. English. **DESCR:** Affirmative Action; Authors; Bilingual Bicultural Education; *Biography; HUNGER OF MEMORY: THE EDUCATION OF RICHARD RODRIGUEZ.

10357 Rodriguez, Richard, et al. Education of Richard Rodriguez [excerpts from "HUNGER OF MEMORY", including discussion]. CHANGE, Vol. 14, no. 7 (October 1982), p. 32-42+. English. **DESCR:** Affirmative Action; Assimilation; Bilingual Bicultural Education; Biography; *HUNGER OF MEMORY: THE EDUCATION OF RICHARD RODRIGUEZ.

10358 Smith, Bruce M. Book review of: HUNGER OF MEMORY: THE EDUCATION OF RICHARD RODRIGUEZ. PHI DELTA KAPPAN, Vol. 64, no. 4 (December 1982), p. 289-290. English. **DESCR:** Book Reviews; *HUNGER OF MEMORY: THE EDUCATION OF RICHARD RODRIGUEZ.

10359 Willie, Charles V. First learning unchallenged and untested. CHANGE, Vol. 14, no. 7 (October 1982), p. 37-41. English. **DESCR:** Affirmative Action; Bilingual Bicultural Education; Biography; Book Reviews; Education; *HUNGER OF MEMORY: THE EDUCATION OF RICHARD RODRIGUEZ.

Rodriguez, Rita

10360 People. HISPANIC BUSINESS, Vol. 5, no. 1 (January 1983), p. 7. English. **DESCR:** Appointed Officials; *Biographical Notes; *Businesspeople; Elizalde, Hector; Mackey y Salazar, C.; Madrid, Carlos; Montoya, Velma; Nunez, Carlos; Perea, Stanley; Valdes, Martha.

Rodriguez, Samuel F.

10361 People. HISPANIC BUSINESS, Vol. 4, no. 5 (May 1982), p. 8. English. **DESCR:** Appointed Officials; Asociacion Internacional de Exportadores e Importadores (EXIMA); *Biographical Notes; Businesspeople; California Chicano News Media Association (CCNMA); de la Ossa, Ernest G.; Foreign Trade; Obledo, Mario; Rodriguez, Elias C.; United Way; U.S. Hispanic Chamber of Commerce.

Rodriguez-Brown, Flora V.

10362 Walia, Adorna. Book review of: DO'S AND DONT'S OF BILINGUAL PROGRAM EVALUATION. BILINGUAL JOURNAL, Vol. 7, no. 2 (Winter 1983), p. 38. English. **DESCR:** Bilingual Bicultural Education; Book Reviews; Curriculum; *DO'S AND DONT'S OF BILINGUAL PROGRAM EVALUATION; Evaluation (Educational).

Rodriguez-Fernandez v. Wilkinson

10363 Hopson, Susan B. Immigration: indefinite detention of excluded aliens held illegal. TEXAS INTERNATIONAL LAW JOURNAL, Vol. 17, (Winter 1982), p. 101-110. English. **DESCR:** Civil Rights; Deportation; *Detention of Persons; Immigration; International Law; Shaughnessy v. Mezei; *Undocumented Workers.

10364 Parr, Julie A. Immigration law and the excluded alien: potential for human rights violations. UNIVERSITY OF CALIFORNIA DAVIS LAW REVIEW, Vol. 15, no. 3 (Spring 1982), p. 723-740. English. **DESCR:** *Civil Rights; Deportation; *Detention of Persons; Internal Security Act of 1950; *Undocumented Workers.

Roe v. Wade

10365 [Summary of: Simpson, abortion, poverty, and equal protection of the law, 13 Ga. L. rev. 505 (1979)]. CHICANO LAW REVIEW, Vol. 5, (1982), p. 82-83. English. **DESCR:** Abortion; *Administration of Justice; Maher v. Roe.

Rogg, Eleanor Meyer

10366 Ward, Carmen Carole. Book review of: THE ASSIMILATION OF CUBAN EXILES: THE ROLE OF COMMUNITY AND CLASS. JOURNAL OF ETHNIC STUDIES, Vol. 3, no. 2 (Summer 1975), p. 116-119. English. **DESCR:** Assimilation; Book Reviews; *Cubanos; Miami, FL; Social Classes; Social History and Conditions; THE ASSIMILATION OF CUBAN EXILES: THE ROLE OF COMMUNITY AND CLASS; West New York, NJ.

Romagosa, Guillermo

10367 Common Spanish book provided by Romagosa. NUESTRO, Vol. 6, no. 5 (June, July, 1982), p. 30. English. **DESCR:** Language Patterns; Language Usage; Languages.

Romero, Carlos J.

10368 People. HISPANIC BUSINESS, Vol. 4, no. 9 (September 1982), p. 7. English. **DESCR:** Advertising Agencies; Appointed Officials; Awards; *Biographical Notes; Diaz-Albertini, Luis; Dimartino, Rita; Garza, Jesus; Hispanic Women in Higher Education (HWHE); League of United Latin American Citizens (LULAC); Ortega, Ray; Ortiz, George; Sepulveda, Luis.

Romero, Cesar

10369 Gonzalez, Magdalena. Ole II; BFA honors the 40's. CAMINOS, Vol. 3, no. 7 (July, August, 1982), p. 28-29. Bilingual. **DESCR:** Artists; Awards; *Bilingual Foundation of the Arts; Montalban, Ricardo.

Romero, Estella E.

10370 People. HISPANIC BUSINESS, Vol. 5, no. 12 (December 1983), p. 9. English. **DESCR:** *Businesspeople; Cantu, Norma V.; Cruz, Jose; Masvidal, Sergio J.; Ortega, Katherine D.; Planas, Maria Bordas; Rodriguez, Ismael D.

Romero, Gustavo

10371 Rising star in the music world. NUESTRO, Vol. 6, no. 1 (January, February, 1982), p. 64. English. **DESCR:** Children; Music.

Romero, Orlando

10372 Guerrero, Yolanda E. La funcion del mito: NAMBE-YEAR ONE. MAIZE, Vol. 4, no. 3-4 (Spring, Summer, 1981), p. 51-59. Spanish. **DESCR:** Literary Criticism; Mythology; *NAMBE: YEAR ONE.

Romo, Ricardo

10373 Book review of: EAST LOS ANGELES. LIBRARY
JOURNAL, Vol. 107, no. 22 (December 15,
1982), p. 2349. English. **DESCR:** Book
Reviews; *EAST LOS ANGELES: HISTORY OF A
BARRIO.

10374 Over a million barrio. LATINO, Vol. 54, no.
4 (May, June, 1983), p. 28. English. **DESCR:**
Book Reviews; *EAST LOS ANGELES: HISTORY OF
A BARRIO.

Romo, Vicente

10375 Deportes. CAMINOS, Vol. 3, no. 7 (July,
August, 1982), p. 46. Spanish. **DESCR:**
*Baseball; Guerrero, Pedro; Los Angeles
Dodgers.

**ROOTS OF RESISTANCE: LAND TENURE IN NEW MEXICO,
1680-1980**

10376 Churchhill, Ward. Implications of publishing
ROOTS OF RESISTANCE. JOURNAL OF ETHNIC
STUDIES, Vol. 9, no. 3 (Fall 1981), p.
83-89. English. **DESCR:** Book Reviews;
Colonialism; Dunbar Ortiz, Roxanne; Land
Tenure; Native Americans; New Mexico;
Publishing Industry; Social History and
Conditions.

10377 Gates, Paul W. Book review of: ROOTS OF
RESISTANCE: LAND TENURE IN NEW MEXICO,
1680-1980. WESTERN HISTORICAL QUARTERLY,
Vol. 13, no. 1 (January 1982), p. 76-77.
English. **DESCR:** Book Reviews; Ortiz, Roxanne
Dunbar.

10378 Murphy, Lawrence R. Book review of: ROOTS OF
RESISTANCE: LAND TENURE IN NEW MEXICO,
1680-1980. NEW MEXICO HISTORICAL REVIEW,
Vol. 57, no. 1 (January 1982), p. 89-90.
English. **DESCR:** Book Reviews; New Mexico;
Ortiz, Roxanne Dunbar.

10379 Westphall, Victor. Book review of: ROOTS OF
RESISTANCE: LAND TENURE IN NEW MEXICO,
1680-1980. ARIZONA AND THE WEST, Vol. 24,
no. 2 (Summer 1982), p. 192-193. English.
DESCR: Book Reviews; Land Tenure; Ortiz,
Roxanne Dunbar.

Rosales v. U.S.

10380 Fram, Steven J. Restricting inquiry into
racial attitudes during the Voir Dire.
AMERICAN CRIMINAL REVIEW, Vol. 19, no. 4
(Spring 1982), p. 719-750. English. **DESCR:**
Aldridge v. U.S.; Ham v. South Carolina;
Juries; *Racism; Ristaino v. Ross;
Rosales-Lopez, Humberto.

Rosales-Lopez, Humberto

10381 Fram, Steven J. Restricting inquiry into
racial attitudes during the Voir Dire.
AMERICAN CRIMINAL REVIEW, Vol. 19, no. 4
(Spring 1982), p. 719-750. English. **DESCR:**
Aldridge v. U.S.; Ham v. South Carolina;
Juries; *Racism; Ristaino v. Ross; Rosales
v. U.S.

Rosen, Philip

10382 Fernandez, Celestino. The neglected
dimension: ethnicity in American life.
AZTLAN, Vol. 14, no. 1 (Spring 1983), p.
199-201. English. **DESCR:** Book Reviews;
Ethnic Groups; Identity; *THE NEGLECTED
DIMENSION: ETHNICITY IN AMERICAN LIFE.

Rosenbaum, Robert J.

10383 Camarillo, Alberto M. Book review of:
MEXICANO RESISTANCE IN THE SOUTHWEST: "THE
SACRED RIGHT OF SELF-PRESERVATION". WESTERN
HISTORICAL QUARTERLY, Vol. 14, no. 1 (1983),
p. 79-80. English. **DESCR:** Book Reviews;
History; *MEXICANO RESISTANCE IN THE
SOUTHWEST: "THE SACRED RIGHT OF
SELF-PRESERVATION"; New Mexico.

10384 Crisp, James E. Book review of: MEXICANO
RESISTANCE IN THE SOUTHWEST: "THE SACRED
RIGHT OF SELF-PRESERVATION". JOURNAL OF
SOUTHERN HISTORY, Vol. 48, no. 1 (1982), p.
138-139. English. **DESCR:** Book Reviews;
*MEXICANO RESISTANCE IN THE SOUTHWEST: "THE
SACRED RIGHT OF SELF-PRESERVATION";
Political History and Conditions; United
States-Mexico Relations.

10385 Garcia, Juan R. Book review of: MEXICANO
RESISTANCE IN THE SOUTHWEST: "THE SACRED
RIGHT OF SELF-PRESERVATION". ARIZONA AND THE
WEST, Vol. 24, no. 1 (Spring 1982), p.
81-82. English. **DESCR:** Book Reviews;
*MEXICANO RESISTANCE IN THE SOUTHWEST: "THE
SACRED RIGHT OF SELF-PRESERVATION"; New
Mexico; Social History and Conditions.

10386 Garcia, Mario T. Book review of: MEXICANO
RESISTANCE IN THE SOUTHWEST: "THE SACRED
RIGHT OF SELF-PRESERVATION". PACIFIC
HISTORICAL REVIEW, Vol. 51, no. 3 (August
1982), p. 331-332. English. **DESCR:** Book
Reviews; *MEXICANO RESISTANCE IN THE
SOUTHWEST: "THE SACRED RIGHT OF
SELF-PRESERVATION".

10387 Hoffman, Abraham. Book review of: MEXICANO
RESISTANCE IN THE SOUTHWEST: "THE SACRED
RIGHT OF SELF-PRESERVATION". JOURNAL OF
AMERICAN HISTORY, Vol. 68, no. 4 (March
1982), p. 911. English. **DESCR:** Book Reviews;
*MEXICANO RESISTANCE IN THE SOUTHWEST: "THE
SACRED RIGHT OF SELF-PRESERVATION".

10388 Schmidt, Dorothy. Book review of: MEXICANO
RESISTANCE IN THE SOUTHWEST: "THE SACRED
RIGHT OF SELF-PRESERVATION". WESTERN
AMERICAN LITERATURE, Vol. 17, no. 1 (Spring
1982), p. 75-76. English. **DESCR:** Bandidos;
Book Reviews; Insurrections; *MEXICANO
RESISTANCE IN THE SOUTHWEST: "THE SACRED
RIGHT OF SELF-PRESERVATION".

10389 Vigil, Ralph H. Book review of: MEXICANO
RESISTANCE IN THE SOUTHWEST: "THE SACRED
RIGHT OF SELF-PRESERVATION". NEW MEXICO
HISTORICAL REVIEW, Vol. 58, no. 1 (January
1983), p. 104-105. English. **DESCR:** Book
Reviews; *MEXICANO RESISTANCE IN THE
SOUTHWEST: "THE SACRED RIGHT OF
SELF-PRESERVATION".

10390 Weber, David J. Book review of: MEXICANO
RESISTANCE IN THE SOUTHWEST: "THE SACRED
RIGHT OF SELF-PRESERVATION". AMERICAN
HISTORICAL REVIEW, Vol. 87, no. 1 (February
1982), p. 272-273. English. **DESCR:** Book
Reviews; Insurrections; *MEXICANO RESISTANCE
IN THE SOUTHWEST: "THE SACRED RIGHT OF
SELF-PRESERVATION"; Southwest United States.

ROSIE: THE INVESTIGATION OF A WRONGFUL DEATH

10391 Torres, Sylvia. Book review of: ROSIE: THE INVESTIGATION OF A WRONGFUL DEATH. HISPANIC JOURNAL OF BEHAVIORAL SCIENCES, Vol. 4, no. 2 (June 1982), p. 279-280. English. DESCR: Book Reviews; Frankfort, Ellen; Kissling, Frances.

Ross, Stanley R.

10392 Moore, Richard J. Book review of: "TEMPORARY" ALIEN WORKERS IN THE UNITED STATES: DESIGNING POLICY FROM FACT AND OPINION. INTERNATIONAL MIGRATION REVIEW, Vol. 16, no. 4 (Winter 1982), p. 909-910. English. DESCR: Book Reviews; Braceros; *"TEMPORARY" ALIEN WORKERS IN THE UNITED STATES: DESIGNING POLICY FROM FACT AND OPINION; Undocumented Workers; Weintraub, Sidney.

10393 Moore, Richard J. Book review of: "TEMPORARY" ALIEN WORKERS IN THE UNITED STATES: DESIGNING POLICY FROM FACT AND OPINION. INTERNATIONAL MIGRATION REVIEW, Vol. 16, no. 4 (Winter 1982), p. 909-910. English. DESCR: Book Reviews; Immigration Law; Literature Reviews; *"TEMPORARY" ALIEN WORKERS IN THE UNITED STATES: DESIGNING POLICY FROM FACT AND OPINION; Undocumented Workers; Weintraub, Sidney.

Roubin, Angel

10394 1982 business persons announced by chamber. NUESTRO, Vol. 6, no. 5 (June, July, 1982), p. 44. English. DESCR: Latin Americans; *Vasquez, Victor.

10395 People. HISPANIC BUSINESS, Vol. 5, no. 2 (February 1983), p. 7. English. DESCR: Alvarez, Everett, Jr.; Appointed Officials; *Biographical Notes; Businesspeople; Guzman-Randle, Irene; Vasquez, Victor; Villareal, Luis Maria.

Rowe, Arthur

10396 Gonzalez, Magdalena. Recognizing Hispanic achievements in entertainment - U.S. and Mexico. CAMINOS, Vol. 3, no. 7 (July, August, 1982), p. 18-24. Bilingual. DESCR: Allende, Fernando; Artists; Awards; Bonilla Giannini, Roxanna; Eynoso, David; Felix, Maria; Films; Gallego, Gina; *Golden Eagle Awards; Hoyos, Rodolfo; Lamas, Lorenzo; Lopez, Conchita; Lopez, Lisa; Montalban, Ricardo; Nosotros [film production company]; Quintero, Jose; Television; Torres, Liz.

Roy, Joaquin

10397 Walia, Adorna. Book review of: EL GOBIERNO Y LOS PRESIDENTES DE LOS ESTADOS UNIDOS DE AMERICA. BILINGUAL JOURNAL, Vol. 6, no. 3 (Spring 1982), p. 22. English. DESCR: Book Reviews; Constitution of the United States; *EL GOBIERNO Y LOS PRESIDENTES DE LOS ESTADOS UNIDOS DE AMERICA; *Government; United States; *United States History.

Roybal, Edward R.

10398 Diaz, Katherine A. Congressman Edward Roybal: Los Angeles before the 1960's (interview). CAMINOS, Vol. 4, no. 7 (July, August, 1983), p. 15-17,38. Bilingual. DESCR: History; Los Angeles, CA.

10399 Hamner, Richard. Hispanics and redistricting: what you see is not always what you get. NATIONAL HISPANIC JOURNAL, Vol. 1, no. 2 (Winter 1982), p. 25-30.

English. DESCR: Berlanga, Hugo; Elections; Hispanic Reapportionment District; National Association of Latino Elected Officials (NALEO); Political Representation; Politics; *Reapportionment; Santillan, Richard.

10400 Padilla, Steve. Latinos wield political clout in midterm election. NUESTRO, Vol. 6, no. 9 (November 1982), p. 28-30. English. DESCR: De la Garza, Kika; *Elected Officials; Garcia, Robert; Gonzales, Henry B.; Lujan, Manuel, Jr.; Martinez, Matthew G. "Marty", Assemblyman; Ortiz, Solomon; *Politics; Richardson, William; *Torres, Esteban E.

10401 People. HISPANIC BUSINESS, Vol. 4, no. 6 (June 1982), p. 8. English. DESCR: Aguirre, Pedro; Arellano, Richard; *Biographical Notes; Businesspeople; Cortez, Pete; De la Colina, Rafael; Hernandez, Sam; Nogales, Luis; Rodriguez, Leslie J..

10402 People. HISPANIC BUSINESS, Vol. 4, no. 12 (December 1982), p. 10. English. DESCR: *Biographical Notes; *Businesspeople; Garcia, Frances; Gort, Wilfredo; Ojeda, Armando; Olind, Rebecca Nieto; Philip Morris, Inc.

Ruben Salazar Bicentennial Building

10403 Wittenauer, Cheryl. The economics of culture: L.A.'s most successful Plaza de la Raza. HISPANIC BUSINESS, Vol. 5, no. 1 (January 1983), p. 12-13+. English. DESCR: *Cultural Organizations; Funding Sources; Plaza de La Raza, Los Angeles, CA.

Ruelas-Zavala, Eleazar

10404 Brasch, Walter M. Hanigan case: hung up on racism? SOUTH ATLANTIC QUARTERLY, Vol. 81, no. 4 (Fall 1982), p. 429-435. English. DESCR: Administration of Justice; Arizona; Criminal Justice System; Garcia-Loya, Manuel; *Hanigan, Patrick; Hanigan, Tom; Herrera-Mata, Bernabe; *Laws; Racism; Undocumented Workers.

Rugama, Leonel

10405 Banberger, Ellen. Poesia nicaraguense. MAIZE, Vol. 5, no. 3-4 (Spring, Summer, 1982), p. 64-77. Spanish. DESCR: Belli, Gioconda; Cardenal, Ernesto; Carrillo, Ernesto; Coronel Urtecho, Jose; Gadea, Gerardo; Gomez, Manuel; Murillo, Rosario; *Nicaragua; Ojeda, Mirna; *Poetry; Revolutions.

Ruiz, David

10406 O'Leary, Tim. David Ruiz brings justice to Texas prisons. NATIONAL HISPANIC JOURNAL, Vol. 1, no. 2 (Winter 1982), p. 21-24. English. DESCR: Clements, Bill; Legal Reform; Prisoners; Prisons; Texas Department of Corrections.

Ruiz, Deborah

10407 Naismith, Rachael. Outreach services to Hispanics. ILLINOIS LIBRARIES, Vol. 64, no. 7 (September 1982), p. 962-966. English. DESCR: Arrondo, Ondina; Cubanos; La Raza Hispanica, Miami, FL; Latin American Library/Biblioteca Latinoamericana, Oakland, CA; *Library Services; Lopez, Lillian; Puerto Ricans; South Bronx Project, New York Public Library; Verges, Bruni.

Ruiz Food Products, Inc., Tulare, CA

10408 Business update: West Coast food firm given special honors. NUESTRO, Vol. 7, no. 4 (May 1983), p. 42. English. DESCR: Business Enterprises; Food Industry.

Ruiz, Frederick R.

10409 People. HISPANIC BUSINESS, Vol. 5, no. 8 (August 1983), p. 10. English. DESCR: *Biographical Notes; Businesspeople; Calderon, Charles M.; Esteverena, Rolando C.; General Coffee Corporation; Hispanic Bankers Association (HBA); Martinez, Olivia T.; Pallares, Mariano; Ruiz, Louis F.; Sanchez, Joseph J.

Ruiz, Jose Luis

10410 Whisler, Kirk. Jose Luis Ruiz on sound festival. CAMINOS, Vol. 3, no. 8 (September 1982), p. 6-8. Bilingual. DESCR: Artists; Films; Television.

Ruiz, Louis F.

10411 People. HISPANIC BUSINESS, Vol. 5, no. 8 (August 1983), p. 10. English. DESCR: *Biographical Notes; Businesspeople; Calderon, Charles M.; Esteverena, Rolando C.; General Coffee Corporation; Hispanic Bankers Association (HBA); Martinez, Olivia T.; Pallares, Mariano; Ruiz, Frederick R.; Sanchez, Joseph J.

Ruiz, Pablo

10412 School principal recognized for leadership efforts. NUESTRO, Vol. 6, no. 5 (June, July, 1982), p. 30. English. DESCR: Bilingual Bicultural Education; Leadership; Michigan.

Ruiz, Ramon Eduardo

10413 Knight, Alan. Book review of: THE GREAT REBELLION: MEXICO 1905-1924 and DESERT IMMIGRANTS: THE MEXICANS OF EL PASO 1880-1920. HISTORY: THE JOURNAL OF THE HISTORICAL ASSOCIATION [London], Vol. 67, (October 1982), p. 450-451. English. DESCR: Book Reviews; *DESERT IMMIGRANTS: THE MEXICANS OF EL PASO 1880-1920; Garcia, Mario T.; *THE GREAT REBELLION: MEXICO 1905-1924.

Ruiz, Rene A.

10414 [In memorium: Rene A. Ruiz 1929-1982]. HISPANIC JOURNAL OF BEHAVIORAL SCIENCES, Vol. 5, no. 2 (June 1983), p. 137-140. English. DESCR: *Biography.

Rulfo, Juan

10415 Cantu, Roberto. El relato como articulacion infinitiva: MACARIO y el arte de Juan Rulfo. LA PALABRA, Vol. 4, no. 1-2 (Spring, Fall, 1982, 1983), p. 107-126. Spanish. DESCR: Authors; Literary Characteristics; Literary Criticism; *MACARIO; Mexican Literature.

10416 Menton, Seymour. EL LLANO EN LLAMAS: anti-epopeya de la revolucion. LA PALABRA, Vol. 4, no. 1-2 (Spring, Fall, 1982, 1983), p. 93-96. Spanish. DESCR: *EL LLANO EN LLAMAS; Literary Criticism; Literature.

Rural Economics

10417 Mabry, Donald J. Book review of: ACROSS THE BORDER: RURAL DEVELOPMENT IN MEXICO AND RECENT MIGRATION TO THE UNITED STATES. INTERNATIONAL MIGRATION REVIEW, Vol. 17, no. 2 (Summer 1983), p. 351. English. DESCR:

*ACROSS THE BORDER: RURAL DEVELOPMENT IN MEXICO AND RECENT MIGRATION; Book Reviews; Cross, Harry E.; Migration; Migration Patterns; Sandos, James.

10418 Morrison, Thomas K. The relationship of U.S. aid, trade and investment to migration pressures in major sending countries. INTERNATIONAL MIGRATION REVIEW, Vol. 16, no. 1 (Spring 1982), p. 4-26. English. DESCR: Border Region; International Economic Relations; Investments; Mexican Border Industrialization Program; *Migration Patterns; PIDER Project; Rural Urban Migration; Undocumented Workers; United States-Mexico Relations.

10419 Wells, Miriam J. Political mediation and agricultural cooperation: strawberry farms in California. ECONOMIC DEVELOPMENT AND CULTURAL CHANGE, Vol. 30, no. 2 (January 1982), p. 413-432. English. DESCR: *Agricultural Cooperatives; Agricultural Laborers; California; Cooperativa Campesina; Cooperativa Central; Political Parties and Organizations.

Rural Population

10420 Cockerham, William C. and Alster, Joan M. A comparison of marijuana use among Mexican-American and Anglo rural youth utilizing a matched-set analysis. INTERNATIONAL JOURNAL OF THE ADDICTIONS, Vol. 18, no. 6 (August 1983), p. 759-767. English. DESCR: Anglo Americans; Drug Abuse; *Marijuana; Youth.

10421 Davis, Sally M. and Harris, Mary B. Sexual knowledge, sexual interests, and sources of sexual information of rural and urban adolescents from three cultures. ADOLESCENCE, Vol. 17, no. 66 (Summer 1982), p. 471-492. English. DESCR: Birth Control; Cultural Characteristics; Identity; *Sex Education; Sex Roles; *Sexual Behavior; Urban Communities; Youth.

10422 Reid, Richard A.; Bartlett, Edward E.; and Kozoll, Richard. Checkerboard area health system: delivering comprehensive care in a remote region of New Mexico. HUMAN ORGANIZATION, Vol. 41, no. 2 (Summer 1982), p. 147-155. English. DESCR: *Medical Care; New Mexico.

Rural Urban Migration

10423 Massey, Douglas S. and Schnabel, Kathleen M. Recent trends in Hispanic immigration to the United States. INTERNATIONAL MIGRATION REVIEW, Vol. 17, no. 2 (Summer 1983), p. 212-244. English. DESCR: *Immigration; Migration Patterns; Population Trends; Socioeconomic Factors.

10424 Morrison, Thomas K. The relationship of U.S. aid, trade and investment to migration pressures in major sending countries. INTERNATIONAL MIGRATION REVIEW, Vol. 16, no. 1 (Spring 1982), p. 4-26. English. DESCR: Border Region; International Economic Relations; Investments; Mexican Border Industrialization Program; *Migration Patterns; PIDER Project; Rural Economics; Undocumented Workers; United States-Mexico Relations.

Russell, Philip

10425 Jamail, Milton H. Book review of: MEXICO IN
TRANSITION. SOUTHWEST ECONOMY AND SOCIETY,
Vol. 4, no. 2 (Winter 1978, 1979), p. 47-49.
English. **DESCR:** Book Reviews; History;
Mexico; *MEXICO IN TRANSITION.

**RX: DISCOVERY AND NURTURANCE OF GIFTEDNESS IN THE
CULTURALLY DIFFERENT**

10426 Tabet, Nita. Book review of: RX: DISCOVERY
AND NURTURANCE OF GIFTEDNESS IN THE
CULTURALLY DIFFERENT. HISPANIC JOURNAL OF
BEHAVIORAL SCIENCES, Vol. 4, no. 4 (December
1982), p. 526-527. English. **DESCR:** Book
Reviews; Torrance, E. Paul.

Saavedra, Denise

10427 Gonzalez, Alicia. Women for success.
CAMINOS, Vol. 3, no. 6 (June 1982), p.
42-43. Bilingual. **DESCR:** *Chicanas;
*Hispanic Women's Council; Moreno, Rita;
Organizations; Terrazas, Carmen.

Sacramento, CA

10428 Castro, Mike. Alien smuggling and the
refugee question: caught between the border
patrol and the river. NUESTRO, Vol. 7, no. 5
(June, July, 1983), p. 18. English. **DESCR:**
*Border Patrol; California Rural Legal
Assistance (CRLA); *Immigration Regulation
and Control; *Undocumented Workers.

10429 Flores, Bettina and Flores, Alfredo. Benny
Barrios, Sacramento's living landmark.
NUESTRO, Vol. 6, no. 9 (November 1982), p.
57-58. English. **DESCR:** *Art; Artists;
Barrios, Benny.

10430 Sacramento youth wins leadership
scholarship. NUESTRO, Vol. 6, no. 8 (October
1982), p. 43. English. **DESCR:** *Boy Scouts of
America.

Salamon, Lester M.

10431 Book review of: THE FEDERAL BUDGET AND THE
NON-PROFIT SECTOR. CAMINOS, Vol. 4, no. 4
(April 1983), p. 59. English. **DESCR:**
Abramson, Anal J.; Book Reviews; Federal
Aid; *FEDERAL BUDGET AND THE NON-PROFIT
SECTOR; Non-profit Groups.

Salazar, Alberto

10432 Salazar came, ran, conquered in Miami.
NUESTRO, Vol. 6, no. 2 (March 1982), p. 45.
English. **DESCR:** Sports.

10433 Salazar wins New York race. NUESTRO, Vol. 6,
no. 8 (October 1982), p. 13. English.
DESCR: Athletes; New York City Marathon;
Sports.

Salazar, Ruben

10434 Ericksen, Charles. Holdenreid and Salazar:
unanswered questions. NUESTRO, Vol. 7, no. 4
(May 1983), p. 40-41. English. **DESCR:**
Assassination; Criminal Acts; Guatemala;
*Holdenreid, Frank X.; *Violence.

10435 New Salazar building. NUESTRO, Vol. 6, no. 7
(September 1982), p. 9. English. **DESCR:**
*Art; Culture; Education; Latin Americans;
Los Angeles, CA; *Plaza de La Raza, Los
Angeles, CA.

10436 Ruben Salazar: a most uncommon man. NUESTRO,
Vol. 6, no. 4 (May 1982), p. 44-45. English.
DESCR: *Poetry.

Salazar, Veronica

10437 Historia de exitos. LATINO, Vol. 53, no. 3
(May 1982), p. 9. English. **DESCR:** Authors.

10438 Nuestra gente. LATINO, Vol. 53, no. 6
(October 1982), p. 22. English. **DESCR:**
Alfaro-Garcia, Rafael Antonio; *Biographical
Notes; Quintanilla, Guadalupe.

Saldana, Lupe

10439 Political charges dismissed against Saldana.
LATINO, Vol. 53, no. 8 (December 1982), p.
22. English. **DESCR:** Politics.

Saldana, Teresa

10440 Gente. NUESTRO, Vol. 7, no. 2 (March 1983),
p. 51. English. **DESCR:** Artists; Betancourt,
Jose L.; *Chicanas; Crime Victims Fund;
Federal Government; Juarez, Joe; Military
Service; Vargas, Alberto; Victims for
Victims.

Salinas, CA

10441 Baciu, Joyce A. KUBO-FM 90.9; the nation's
fourth bilingual radio station. CAMINOS,
Vol. 3, no. 5 (May 1982), p. 44-45,59.
Bilingual. **DESCR:** *KUBO, Salinas, CA [radio
station]; Radio.

Salinas, Luis Omar

10442 Soto, Gary. Luis Omar Salinas: Chicano poet.
MELUS: MULTI-ETHNIC LITERATURE OF THE UNITED
STATES, Vol. 9, no. 2 (Summer 1982), p.
47-82. English. **DESCR:** Authors; Poetry.

Salinas, Raul

10443 Gente; FBI head, two agents praised by Texas
house. NUESTRO, Vol. 7, no. 4 (May 1983), p.
52. English. **DESCR:** Careers; *Federal Bureau
of Investigation (FBI); *Texas.

Salinas, Vicente

10444 People on the move. CAMINOS, Vol. 2, no. 6
(October 1981), p. 7. English. **DESCR:**
Alvarado, Angel S.; Arreola, Rafael;
*Biographical Notes; Diaz, Elisa; Diaz,
Elvira A.; Garcia, Jose Joel; Garza,
Florentino; Icaza, Ricardo F.; Lacayo,
Henry; Martinez, Lydia R.; Munoz, Victor M.;
Sanchez, Manuel; Zuniga, Henry.

Salsa

10445 Fernandez, Enrique. Cannes and CROSSOVER
DREAMS, '83. FILM COMMENT, Vol. 19, no. 4-7
(August 1983), p. 2-7. English. **DESCR:** Arce,
Manuel; Blades, Ruben; Cannes Film Festival;
*CROSSOVER DREAMS; Film Reviews; Films.

10446 Fernandez, Enrique. Notas: these ladies are
not waiting. BILLBOARD, Vol. 94, (November
13, 1982), p. 62. English. **DESCR:** Artists;
*Chicanas; Performing Arts; Singers.

10447 UC Latino: salsa music comes to UCLA.
CAMINOS, Vol. 4, no. 5 (May 1983), p. 46,48.
English. **DESCR:** Musicians; *UC Latino;
University of California, Los Angeles
(UCLA).

10448 Ucalatino: salsa music comes to UCLA.
NUESTRO, Vol. 6, no. 9 (November 1982), p.
59-60. English. **DESCR:** *Music; UCALATINO
[musical group]; University of California,
Los Angeles (UCLA).

SALT OF THE EARTH

10449 McCracken, Ellen. Book review of: SALT OF THE EARTH. JOURNAL OF ETHNIC STUDIES, Vol. 8, no. 1 (Spring 1980), p. 116-120. English. **DESCR:** Book Reviews; Chicanas; Films; Hanover, NM; International Union of Mine, Mill and Smelter Workers; Silverton Rosenfelt, Deborah; Strikes and Lockouts; Women Men Relations; Women's Rights.

Salvadorans

10450 Martinez, Danny. Mother's Day reflections: master gardener. NUESTRO, Vol. 7, no. 4 (May 1983), p. 48. English. **DESCR:** *Family; *Parent and Child Relationships.

Samora, Julian

10451 Achor, Shirley. Book review of: GUNPOWDER JUSTICE: A REASSESSMENT OF THE TEXAS RANGERS. INTERNATIONAL MIGRATION REVIEW, Vol. 16, no. 2 (Summer 1982), p. 491-492. English. **DESCR:** Bernal, Joseph; Book Reviews; *GUNPOWDER JUSTICE: A REASSESSMENT OF THE TEXAS RANGERS; Pena, Alberto; Texas Rangers.

10452 Achor, Shirley. Book review of: GUNPOWDER JUSTICE: A REASSESSMENT OF THE TEXAS RANGERS. INTERNATIONAL MIGRATION REVIEW, Vol. 16, no. 2 (Summer 1982), p. 491-492. English. **DESCR:** Bernal, Joseph; Book Reviews; *GUNPOWDER JUSTICE: A REASSESSMENT OF THE TEXAS RANGERS; History; Pena, Alberto; Texas Rangers.

10453 Garcia, Mario T. Book review of: LOS MOJADOS: THE WETBACK STORY. JOURNAL OF ETHNIC STUDIES, Vol. 1, no. 1 (Spring 1973), p. 66-68. English. **DESCR:** Book Reviews; Immigrant Labor; *LOS MOJADOS: THE WETBACK STORY; Mexico; Southwest United States; Undocumented Workers; United States.

10454 Trujillo, Larry. Book review of: GUNPOWDER JUSTICE: A REASSESSMENT OF THE TEXAS RANGERS [reprinted from CRIME AND SOCIAL JUSTICE, 61 (Summer 1980)]. CHICANO LAW REVIEW, Vol. 6, (1983), p. 148-155. English. **DESCR:** Book Reviews; *GUNPOWDER JUSTICE: A REASSESSMENT OF THE TEXAS RANGERS; *Texas Rangers.

San Antonio CineFestival, TX

10455 Broyles, Yolanda Julia. Chicano film festivals: an examination. BILINGUAL REVIEW, Vol. 10, no. 2-3 (May, December, 1983), p. 116-120. English. **DESCR:** Chicano Film Exhibition and Festival, Detroit, Michigan, April 5-9, 1982; *Film Festivals.

10456 Communications/marketing. HISPANIC BUSINESS, Vol. 4, no. 8 (August 1983), p. 22+. English. **DESCR:** Arredondo, Price; Baseball; De la O, Val; Films; Marketing; *Mass Media; Radio; Television; Val De La O Show; Valenzuela, Fernando; Wright & Arredondo Associates; Wright, Oscar.

San Antonio Heart Study

10457 Stern, Michael P., et al. Does obesity explain excess prevalence of diabetes among Mexican Americans? Results of the San Antonio Heart Study. DIABETOLOGIA, Vol. 24, no. 4 (April 1983), p. 272-277. English. **DESCR:** *Diabetes; Medical Research; Medicine; Obesity; Public Health.

San Antonio Police Department

10458 Morton, Carlos. People: back on top with Bernardo Eureste. NATIONAL HISPANIC JOURNAL, Vol. 2, no. 1 (Summer 1983), p. 20-21. English. **DESCR:** Cisneros, Henry, Mayor of San Antonio, TX; Elected Officials; Elections; *Eureste, Bernardo; San Antonio, TX; Valdez, Jesse.

San Antonio School District v. Rodriguez

10459 Heberton Craig N. To educate and not to educate: the plight of undocumented alien children in Texas. WASHINGTON UNIVERSITY LAW QUARTERLY, Vol. 60, no. 1 (Spring 1982), p. 119-159. English. **DESCR:** *Children; Doe v. Plyer [Tyler Independent School District, Texas]; Education; *Undocumented Workers.

10460 Supreme Court recognizes special importance of education. MENTAL DISABILITY LAW REPORTER, Vol. 6, (July, August, 1982), p. 227-229. English. **DESCR:** Doe v. Plyer [Tyler Independent School District, Texas]; *Education; THE PLUM PLUM PICKERS; Undocumented Workers.

San Antonio, TX

10461 Changing Hispanic political loyalties. HISPANIC BUSINESS, Vol. 4, no. 6 (June 1982), p. 23. English. **DESCR:** Los Angeles, CA; *Political Parties and Organizations; Politics; Public Policy; *Surveys.

10462 Cine-festival. CAMINOS, Vol. 4, no. 9 (October 1983), p. 58. English. **DESCR:** Art; *Fiestas; *Films.

10463 City officials decide mural must be removed. NUESTRO, Vol. 6, no. 7 (September 1982), p. 51. English. **DESCR:** *Art; *Hidalgo y Costilla, Miguel; *Mural Art.

10464 Garcia, Ignacio M. Linda Ramirez: labor leader. NUESTRO, Vol. 6, no. 5 (June, July, 1982), p. 26-28. English. **DESCR:** *Labor; Labor Unions; Latin Americans; Leadership; Ramirez, Linda.

10465 Grocery chains fight for San Antonio market. NUESTRO, Vol. 7, no. 2 (March 1983), p. 54. English. **DESCR:** *Food Industry; Marketing.

10466 Hazuda, Helen P. Ethnic differences in health knowledge and behaviors related to the prevention and treatment of coronary heart disease. The San Antonio heart study. AMERICAN JOURNAL OF EPIDEMIOLOGY, Vol. 11, no. 6 (June 1983), p. 717-728. English. **DESCR:** Anglo Americans; *Coronary Heart Disease; Health Education; Preventative Medicine; Socioeconomic Factors.

10467 Kanellos, Nicolas. Two centuries of Hispanic theatre in the Southwest. REVISTA CHICANO-RIQUENA, Vol. 11, no. 1 (Spring 1983), p. 17-39. English. **DESCR:** California; History; Los Angeles, CA; Photography; Southwest United States; *Teatro; Texas.

10468 Math-based careers. HISPANIC BUSINESS, Vol. 5, no. 12 (December 1983), p. 40. English. **DESCR:** *Careers; Council on Legal Education Opportunities (CLEO); Education; Employment Training; Graduate Schools; High Technology High School, San Antonio, TX; Legal Education; Mexican American Legal Defense and Educational Fund (MALDEF); Science as a Profession.

San Antonio, TX (cont.)

10469 Morton, Carlos. People: back on top with
      Bernardo Eureste. NATIONAL HISPANIC JOURNAL,
      Vol. 2, no. 1 (Summer 1983), p. 20-21.
      English. **DESCR:** Cisneros, Henry, Mayor of
      San Antonio, TX; Elected Officials;
      Elections; *Eureste, Bernardo; San Antonio
      Police Department; Valdez, Jesse.

10470 Nowhere else but San Antonio. LATINO, Vol.
      53, no. 4 (June 1982), p. 11-12. English.
      DESCR: Urban Communities.

10471 Old and new in San Antonio. ECONOMIST
      (London), Vol. 288, (August 13, 1983), p.
      26. English. **DESCR:** *Cisneros, Henry, Mayor
      of San Antonio, TX; Voter Turnout.

10472 Perales, Alonso M. Effects of
      teacher-oriented and student-oriented
      strategies on self-concept, English language
      development, and social studies achievement
      of 5th grade Mexican-American students
      [research notes]. TESOL QUARTERLY, Vol. 16,
      no. 1 (March 1982), p. 99-100. English.
      DESCR: Attitude (Psychological); Identity;
      *Teacher Attitudes; Teacher-pupil
      Interaction.

10473 Relethfold, John H., et al. Social class,
      admixture, and skin color variation in
      Mexican-Americans and Anglo-Americans living
      in San Antonio, Texas. AMERICAN JOURNAL OF
      PHYSICAL ANTHROPOLOGY, Vol. 61, no. 1 (May
      1983), p. 97-102. English. **DESCR:** Anglo
      Americans; Population; *Skin Color.

10474 Rosales, John. Holy Cross High: a Texas
      success story. NUESTRO, Vol. 6, no. 9
      (November 1982), p. 41-42. English. **DESCR:**
      Carr, Vikki; *Education; Holy Cross High
      School, San Antonio, TX.

10475 San Antonio: an all American city. CAMINOS,
      Vol. 4, no. 8 (September 1983), p. 35.
      English. **DESCR:** *Artists; Cerda, Daniel;
      Congressional Arts Caucus; Gonzalez, Henry
      B.

10476 San Antonio restaurant survives urban
      project. NUESTRO, Vol. 6, no. 5 (June, July,
      1982), p. 44. English. **DESCR:** Restaurants;
      *Urban Planning.

10477 Skriloff, Lisa. Music, news dominate
      Spanish-language radio programming. HISPANIC
      BUSINESS, Vol. 5, no. 12 (December 1983), p.
      34. English. **DESCR:** Advertising; Los
      Angeles, CA; Marketing; Miami, FL; *Radio.

10478 Southwest may lose theater. NUESTRO, Vol. 6,
      no. 7 (September 1982), p. 11. English.
      DESCR: *Alameda Theater, San Antonio, TX;
      Films; Spanish Language.

10479 Stern, Michael P. Knowledge, attitudes, and
      behavior related to obesity and dieting in
      Mexican-Americans and Anglos: the San
      Antonio heart study. AMERICAN JOURNAL OF
      EPIDEMIOLOGY, Vol. 115, no. 6 (June 1982),
      p. 917-928. English. **DESCR:** Anglo Americans;
      Attitude (Psychological); *Food Practices;
      Obesity; Weight Control.

10480 Wittenauer, Cheryl. The mayor markets San
      Antonio. HISPANIC BUSINESS, Vol. 5, no. 7
      (July 1983), p. 12-13+. English. **DESCR:**
      Cisneros, Henry, Mayor of San Antonio, TX;
      *Economic Development; *Marketing.

San Bernardino, CA

10481 Whisler, Kirk. It can work. CAMINOS, Vol. 3,

no. 6 (June 1982), p. 46. Bilingual. **DESCR:**
*Car Clubs; Low Riders.

San Diego, CA

10482 Chavira, Ricardo. Refugees from poverty: a
      San Diego perspective. NUESTRO, Vol. 7, no.
      4 (May 1983), p. 24-25. English. **DESCR:**
      Border Patrol; *Immigration Regulation and
      Control; *Undocumented Workers.

10483 Ezell, P. Research on Spanish colonial sites
      in San Diego. AMERICAN JOURNAL OF
      ARCHAEOLOGY, Vol. 86, no. 2 (April 1982), p.
      263. English. **DESCR:** *Anthropology; Fort
      Guijanos; San Diego Mission.

10484 Farmer, Mary. Bilingual integration in San
      Diego. HISPANIA, Vol. 65, no. 3 (September
      1982), p. 427-429. English. **DESCR:**
      *Bilingual Bicultural Education.

10485 Foster, Douglas. The desperate migrants of
      Devil's Canyon. THE PROGRESSIVE, Vol. 46,
      no. 11 (November 1982), p. 44-49. English.
      DESCR: *Agricultural Laborers; California;
      *Devil's Canyon, Deer Canyon, CA; Growers;
      Labor Camps; Undocumented Workers.

10486 Pendleton, Jennifer. Battle for the buck is
      the tale of two cities: marketers in San
      Diego and Tijuana square off. ADVERTISING
      AGE MAGAZINE, Vol. 53, (February 15, 1982),
      p. II, M42-43. English. **DESCR:** Advertising;
      Border Region; Business; *Market Research;
      Tijuana, Mexico.

10487 Quinlivan, Robert and Castaneda, Jaime.
      Black & white ball. CAMINOS, Vol. 4, no. 1-2
      (January, February, 1983), p. 68-69.
      Bilingual. **DESCR:** *Alba '80 Society;
      Organizations.

10488 Quinlivan, Robert. The Mexican and American
      Foundation. CAMINOS, Vol. 3, no. 4 (April
      1982), p. 24-25. Bilingual. **DESCR:**
      Castaneda, Jaime; *Organizations; United
      States-Mexico Relations.

10489 Quinlivan, Robert. The need for Hispanic
      senior housing. CAMINOS, Vol. 3, no. 7
      (July, August, 1982), p. 42-43. Bilingual.
      DESCR: *Ancianos; Colonial Barrio Seniors;
      *Housing; Villa Merced Housing Project.

San Diego Chicano Federation, Inc.
      USE: Chicano Federation of San Diego Co.,
      Inc.

San Diego Mission

10490 Ezell, P. Research on Spanish colonial sites
      in San Diego. AMERICAN JOURNAL OF
      ARCHAEOLOGY, Vol. 86, no. 2 (April 1982), p.
      263. English. **DESCR:** *Anthropology; Fort
      Guijanos; San Diego, CA.

San Francisco Bay

10491 Forbes, Jack D. Hispanic-Mexican pioneers of
      the San Francisco Bay region: an analysis of
      racial origins. AZTLAN, Vol. 14, no. 1
      (Spring 1983), p. 175-189. English. **DESCR:**
      Ethnic Groups; Identity; *Pioneers.

San Francisco, CA

10492 Morris, Gay. The Mexican Museum has a
      colorful new home. CAMINOS, Vol. 3, no. 7
      (July, August, 1982), p. 30-33. Bilingual.
      DESCR: Art; *Mexican Museum, San Francisco,
      CA; Museums; Rodriguez, Peter.

San Francisco, CA (cont.)

10493 New mecca for comedians. NUESTRO, Vol. 6, no. 5 (June, July, 1982), p. 12. English. DESCR: *Humor; Simon, Jose.

10494 Ramirez, Belinda. In solidarity with El Salvador. CAMINOS, Vol. 3, no. 5 (May 1982), p. 9. English. DESCR: Benavidez, Virginia; *Committee in Solidarity with the People of El Salvador (CISPES); Organizations.

San Joaquin Valley

10495 Saragoza, Alex M. Mexican children in the U.S.: the Central San Joaquin Valley. DE COLORES, Vol. 6, no. 1-2 (1982), p. 64-74. English. DESCR: Acculturation; *Children; Family; Identity; Parent and Child Relationships.

San Juan Pueblo, NM

10496 Sagel, Jaime. Patriarch of San Juan Pueblo. NUESTRO, Vol. 6, no. 8 (October 1982), p. 52-53. English. DESCR: *Biography; Montoya, Liberato.

San Juan, Puerto Rico

10497 Reporter beaten for story pursuit. NUESTRO, Vol. 7, no. 1 (January, February, 1983), p. 11-12. English. DESCR: *Berio, Yvonne C.; Journalists; Police.

San Lorenzo, Mexico

10498 Quirarte, Jacinto. Book review of: OLMEC: AN EARLY ART STYLE OF PRECOLUMBIAN MEXICO. JOURNAL OF ETHNIC STUDIES, Vol. 1, no. 3 (Fall 1973), p. 92-95. English. DESCR: Book Reviews; La Venta, Mexico; *OLMEC: AN EARLY ART STYLE OF PRECOLUMBIAN MEXICO; Precolumbian Art; Precolumbian Society; Tres Zapotes, Mexico; Wicke, Charles R.

San Miguel de Allende, Mexico

10499 Geary, Richard. The faces of San Miguel: a photo essay. NUESTRO, Vol. 7, no. 4 (May 1983), p. 31-34. English. DESCR: Mexico; *Photography.

Sanchez, Antonia

10500 Walia, Adorna. Book review of: COUNSELING THE BILINGUAL STUDENT. BILINGUAL JOURNAL, Vol. 7, no. 4 (Summer 1983), p. 27-28. English. DESCR: Bilingual Bicultural Education; Book Reviews; Counseling Services (Educational); *COUNSELING THE BILINGUAL STUDENT; Searchlight Series.

Sanchez, George I.

10501 Schlossman, Steven. Self-evident remedy? George I. Sanchez, segregation, and enduring dilemmas in bilingual education. TEACHERS COLLEGE RECORD, Vol. 84, no. 4 (Summer 1983), p. 871-907. English. DESCR: *Bilingual Bicultural Education; Biography; Delgado v. Bastrop Independent School District of Bastrop Co., TX (1948); FORGOTTEN PEOPLE; History.

Sanchez, Joseph J.

10502 People. HISPANIC BUSINESS, Vol. 5, no. 8 (August 1983), p. 10. English. DESCR: *Biographical Notes; Businesspeople; Calderon, Charles M.; Esteverena, Rolando C.; General Coffee Corporation; Hispanic Bankers Association (HBA); Martinez, Olivia T.; Pallares, Mariano; Ruiz, Frederick R.;

Ruiz, Louis F.

Sanchez, Manuel

10503 Manuel Sanchez: the joy of big business. CAMINOS, Vol. 3, no. 2 (February 1982), p. 34-36. Bilingual. DESCR: Blue Cross of Southern California; Businesspeople.

10504 People on the move. CAMINOS, Vol. 2, no. 6 (October 1981), p. 7. English. DESCR: Alvarado, Angel S.; Arreola, Rafael; *Biographical Notes; Diaz, Elisa; Diaz, Elvira A.; Garcia, Jose Joel; Garza, Florentino; Icaza, Ricardo F.; Lacayo, Henry; Martinez, Lydia R.; Munoz, Victor M.; Salinas, Vicente; Zuniga, Henry.

Sanchez, Nestor D.

10505 President Reagan's appointments. CAMINOS, Vol. 3, no. 3 (March 1982), p. 48-50. Bilingual. DESCR: Appointed Officials; *Federal Government; Flores Buckhart, Elizabeth; Garcia, Ernest E.; Gonzalez, Luis A.; Lozano, Diana; Pompa, Gilbert G.; Reagan, Ronald; Zuniga, Henry.

Sanchez, Philip V.

10506 Caldera, Carmela. Two views on Central America (interview). CAMINOS, Vol. 4, no. 8 (September 1983), p. 12-16,50. Bilingual. DESCR: *Central America; *International Relations; Torres, Esteban E.

10507 People. HISPANIC BUSINESS, Vol. 5, no. 9 (September 1983), p. 10. English. DESCR: *Businesspeople; Chavez, Chris; Diez de Onate, Jorge; Franco Garcia, Freddie; Garcia, Hector P.; Lozano, Leticia Eugenia; Ravard, Rafael Alonzo; Rodriguez, Alberto Duque; Villalpando, Catalina.

Sanchez, Ricardo

10508 Ortego y Gasca, Felipe de. An appreciation of "Hechizospells" by Ricardo Sanchez. MELUS: MULTI-ETHNIC LITERATURE OF THE UNITED STATES, Vol. 7, no. 2 (Summer 1980), p. 73-77. English. DESCR: HECHIZOSPELLS; *Literature.

Sanchez, Rosaura

10509 Chavez, Mauro. Book review of: ESSAYS ON LA MUJER. JOURNAL OF ETHNIC STUDIES, Vol. 8, no. 2 (Summer 1980), p. 117-120. English. DESCR: Book Reviews; *Chicanas; Cruz, Rosa Martinez; Economic History and Conditions; *ESSAYS ON LA MUJER; Social History and Conditions; Socioeconomic Factors; Women's Rights.

Sanchez, Saul

10510 Avendano, Fausto. Book review of: HAY PLESHA LICHANS TO DI FLAC. LA PALABRA, Vol. 4, no. 1-2 (Spring, Fall, 1982, 1983), p. 165-167. Spanish. DESCR: Book Reviews; *HAY PLESHA LICHANS TU DI FLAC; Literature.

10511 Portales, Marco A. Anglo villains and Chicano writers. JOURNAL OF ETHNIC STUDIES, Vol. 9, no. 3 (Fall 1981), p. 78-82. English. DESCR: Book Reviews; *HAY PLESHA LICHANS TU DI FLAC; Literature; Stereotypes.

Sanchez, Tony, Jr.

10512 Deibel, Richard and Sanchez, Tony, Jr. Business on the border: attracting venture capital. HISPANIC BUSINESS, Vol. 5, no. 9 (September 1983), p. 20-21+. English. **DESCR:** Border Industries; Border Region; Finance; Texas.

Sanchez Yund, Gloria

10513 Reading to whet your appetite [book reviews]. CAMINOS, Vol. 4, no. 6 (June 1983), p. 19,66. English. **DESCR:** Barraza Sanchez, Irene; Book Reviews; *COMIDA SABROSA; Recipes.

Sanchez-Alvarez, Gloria

10514 Q & A: in the Hispanic community who are the winners and losers of Reaganomics? CAMINOS, Vol. 3, no. 3 (March 1982), p. 47. Bilingual. **DESCR:** Casado, Lucy; Echeveste, John; *Federal Government; Flores, Bob; Leon, Virginia; Mendoza, John; *Reagan, Ronald; Vidal de Neri, Julieta.

Sandos, James

10515 Cardoso, Lawrence Anthony. Book review of: ACROSS THE BORDER: RURAL DEVELOPMENT IN MEXICO AND RECENT MIGRATION TO THE UNITED STATES. AMERICAN HISTORICAL REVIEW, Vol. 88, no. 1 (February 1983), p. 226-227. English. **DESCR:** *ACROSS THE BORDER: RURAL DEVELOPMENT IN MEXICO AND RECENT MIGRATION; Book Reviews; Cross, Harry E.

10516 Cardoso, Lawrence Anthony. Book review of: ACROSS THE BORDER: RURAL DEVELOPMENT IN MEXICO AND RECENT MIGRATION TO THE UNITED STATES. AMERICAN HISTORICAL REVIEW, Vol. 88, (February 1983), p. 226. English. **DESCR:** *ACROSS THE BORDER: RURAL DEVELOPMENT IN MEXICO AND RECENT MIGRATION; Book Reviews; Cross, Harry E.; Immigration.

10517 Mabry, Donald J. Book review of: ACROSS THE BORDER: RURAL DEVELOPMENT IN MEXICO AND RECENT MIGRATION TO THE UNITED STATES. INTERNATIONAL MIGRATION REVIEW, Vol. 17, no. 2 (Summer 1983), p. 351. English. **DESCR:** *ACROSS THE BORDER: RURAL DEVELOPMENT IN MEXICO AND RECENT MIGRATION; Book Reviews; Cross, Harry E.; Migration; Migration Patterns; Rural Economics.

Sandoval, Jose

10518 Martinez, Rick. Migrant worker to M.D. NUESTRO, Vol. 6, no. 1 (January, February, 1982), p. 16-17. English. **DESCR:** Medical Students.

Sandoval, Ruben

10519 Cardenas, Leo. Ruben Sandoval's quiet work. LATINO, Vol. 53, no. 4 (June 1982), p. 4. English. **DESCR:** Legal Aid.

Santa Barbara, CA

10520 Keefe, Susan Emily. Help-seeking behavior among foreign-born and native-born Mexican-Americans. SOCIAL SCIENCE AND MEDICINE, Vol. 16, no. 16 (1982), p. 1467-1472. English. **DESCR:** Acculturation; Immigrants; *Mental Health Programs.

Santa Barbara Rape Crisis Center

10521 Garza-Livingston, M'Liss and Villa de Romo, Velma. An interview with Velma Villa de Romo: bilingual liaison for the Santa Barbara Rape Crisis Center. COMADRE, no. 3 (Fall 1978), p. 15-16. English. **DESCR:** Rape; Villa de Romo, Velma.

10522 Villa Romo, Velma. El centro de violacion de Santa Barbara. COMADRE, no. 3 (Fall 1978), p. 28. Spanish.

10523 Villa Romo, Velma. Rape in the barrio. COMADRE, no. 3 (Fall 1978), p. 19-29. English. **DESCR:** *Chicanas; Identity; Rape; Social History and Conditions.

Santa Clara County, CA

10524 Walia, Adorna. Book review of: THE PLUM PLUM PICKERS. BILINGUAL JOURNAL, Vol. 6, no. 1 (Fall 1982), p. 30-31. English. **DESCR:** Agricultural Laborers; Barrio, Raymond; Book Reviews; California; *Migrant Labor; *THE PLUM PLUM PICKERS.

Santa Clara Valley, CA

10525 Arnold, Frank. A history of struggle: organizing cannery workers in the Santa Clara Valley. SOUTHWEST ECONOMY AND SOCIETY, Vol. 2, no. 1 (October, November, 1976), p. 26-38. English. **DESCR:** Agribusiness; American Labor Union (Santa Clara County, CA); Cannery and Agricultural Worker's Industrial Union; *Cannery Workers; Comite de Trabajadores de Canerias, San Jose, CA; History; Labor Unions; United Cannery Agricultural Packing and Allied Workers of America (UCAPAWA).

Santa Rosa, CA

10526 Baciu, Joyce A. KBBF in Santa Rosa. CAMINOS, Vol. 3, no. 5 (May 1982), p. 48. Bilingual. **DESCR:** Radio; *Radio Station KBBF, Santa Rosa, CA.

Santana, Carlos

10527 Santana's guitar work still sharp and crisp. NUESTRO, Vol. 6, no. 9 (November 1982), p. 60. English. **DESCR:** Guitar Music; Guitarists; Music.

Santeros

10528 Delgado, Melvin. Ethnic and cultural variations in the care of the aged. Hispanic elderly and natural support systems: a special focus on Puerto Ricans. JOURNAL OF GERIATRIC PSYCHIATRY, Vol. 15, no. 2 (1982), p. 239-251. English. **DESCR:** *Ancianos; Cultural Organizations; Curanderas; Family; Natural Support Systems; Puerto Ricans; Religion.

Santiago, Danny
USE: James, Dan

Santillan Munoz, Hector

10529 Ogaz, Armando. "It has been very confusing" Q and A with Hector Santillan. CAMINOS, Vol. 3, no. 11 (December 1982), p. 30-31. Bilingual. **DESCR:** *Currency; *Tijuana, Mexico; *Tourism.

Santillan, Richard

10530 Hamner, Richard. Hispanics and redistricting: what you see is not always what you get. NATIONAL HISPANIC JOURNAL, Vol. 1, no. 2 (Winter 1982), p. 25-30. English. DESCR: Berlanga, Hugo; Elections; Hispanic Reapportionment District; National Association of Latino Elected Officials (NALEO); Political Representation; Politics; *Reapportionment; *Roybal, Edward R.

Santistevan, August

10531 Commercial art as a career. CAMINOS, Vol. 4, no. 9 (October 1983), p. 32-35. English. DESCR: Artists; *Careers; Chavez Lichwardt, Leticia; Gomez, Dario; Guerrero, Ernest R.; Melendez, Bill; Reyes, Gil.

Santos-Killins, Consuelo

10532 Soto, Rose Marie. Consuelo Santos-Killins: a leader in the arts. CAMINOS, Vol. 4, no. 6 (June 1983), p. 56-57,67. Bilingual. DESCR: Art; California Arts Council (C.A.C.); Cultural Organizations.

Sarason, Seymour B.

10533 Brink, T. L. Book review of: PSYCHOLOGY MISDIRECTED. HISPANIC JOURNAL OF BEHAVIORAL SCIENCES, Vol. 5, no. 3 (September 1983), p. 363. English. DESCR: Book Reviews; Psychiatry; *PSYCHOLOGY MISDIRECTED.

Satelco, Inc.

10534 Weber, Robert. Rising star: Satelco. HISPANIC BUSINESS, Vol. 5, no. 9 (September 1983), p. 14. English. DESCR: Business Enterprises; Lagueruela, Andy; Telecommunications; Veve, Rafael.

Satire
USE: Caricature

Saura, Carlos

10535 BLOOD WEDDING. NUESTRO, Vol. 5, no. 8 (November 1981), p. 50. English. DESCR: *Film Reviews; Gades, Antonio; Lorca, Federico Garcia.

Schedule for Affective Disorders and Schizophrenia-Research Diagnostic Criteria (SADS-RDC)

10536 Vernon, Sally W. and Roberts, Robert E. Use of the SADS-RDC in a tri-ethnic community survey. ARCHIVES OF GENERAL PSYCHIATRY, Vol. 39, no. 1 (January 1982), p. 47-52. English. DESCR: Ethnic Groups; Mental Health; Psychiatry; Psychotherapy.

Schement, Jorge Reina

10537 Breiter, Toni. An interview with some experts. AGENDA, Vol. 11, no. 3 (May, June, 1981), p. 48-52. English. DESCR: Guernica, Antonio; Gutierrez, Felix; *Mass Media; Morales, Rosa; Valenzuela, Nicholas.

Schmidhuber de la Mora, Guillermo

10538 Whisler, Kirk. Q & A with Guillermo Schmirdhuber de la Mora, Centro Cultural FONOPAS director: "We try to balance education and culture with entertainment". CAMINOS, Vol. 3, no. 11 (December 1982), p. 19,23. Bilingual. DESCR: *Baja California, Mexico; *Centro Cultural Fondo Nacional para Actividades Sociales (FONOPAS); *Tourism.

Schoen, Robert

10539 Alba, Richard D. A comment on Schoen and Cohen. AMERICAN JOURNAL OF SOCIOLOGY, Vol. 87, no. 4 (January 1982), p. 935-939. English. DESCR: Cohen, Lawrence E.; ETHNIC ENDOGAMY AMONG MEXICAN AMERICAN GROOMS; Intermarriage; *Research Methodology.

Scholarship
USE: Financial Aid

School Finance

10540 Olivas, Michael A. Research and theory on Hispanic education: students, finance, and governance. AZTLAN, Vol. 14, no. 1 (Spring 1983), p. 111-146. English. DESCR: Educational Administration; *Educational Theory and Practice; Students.

10541 Texan honored for court fight. NUESTRO, Vol. 7, no. 1 (January, February, 1983), p. 12. English. DESCR: *Rodriguez, Demetrio P.; Taxation.

10542 Torres, Arnold. Capitol links. LATINO, Vol. 54, no. 4 (May, June, 1983), p. 23. English.

School Integration
USE: Busing

Schooling
USE: Education

Schoonover, Thomas David

10543 Monjaras-Ruiz, Jesus. Book review of: DOLLARS OVER DOMINION: THE TRIUMPH OF LIBERALISM IN MEXICAN-UNITED STATES RELATIONS, 1861-1867. HISTORIA MEXICANA, Vol. 31, no. 4 (April, June, 1982), p. 642-646. Spanish. DESCR: Book Reviews; *DOLLARS OVER DOMINION: THE TRIUMPH OF LIBERALISM IN MEXICAN-UNITED STATES RELATIONS, 1861-1867.

Schuckit, Marc A.

10544 Hunsaker, Alan. Book review of: ANGEL DUST: AN ETHNOGRAPHIC STUDY OF PCP USERS; HEROIN USE IN THE BARRIO; DRUG AND ALCOHOL ABUSE: A CLINICAL GUIDE TO DIAGNOSIS AND TREATMENT. HISPANIC JOURNAL OF BEHAVIORAL SCIENCES, Vol. 4, no. 1 (March 1982), p. 118-121. English. DESCR: Agar, Michael; *ANGEL DUST: AN ETHNOGRAPHIC STUDY OF PCP USERS; Bescher, George; Book Reviews; Bullington, Bruce; *DRUG AND ALCOHOL ABUSE: A CLINICAL GUIDE TO DIAGNOSIS AND TREATMENT; Feldman, Harvey W.; *HEROIN USE IN THE BARRIO.

Science

10545 Griego, Richard J. Crisis in science education: from Sputnik to Pac-man. CAMINOS, Vol. 4, no. 6 (June 1983), p. 47-49,67. English. DESCR: *Education.

10546 Klein, Carol A. Children's concepts of the earth and the sun: a cross cultural study. SCIENCE EDUCATION, Vol. 66, no. 1 (January 1982), p. 95-107. English. DESCR: Anglo Americans; Children; Cultural Pluralism; Education.

Science (cont.)

10547 Research/development: books. HISPANIC BUSINESS, Vol. 5, no. 4 (April 1983), p. 28. English. DESCR: Biographical Notes; *Book Reviews; *"DO IT MY WAY OR YOU'RE FIRED!": EMPLOYEE RIGHTS AND THE CHANGING ROLE OF MANAGEMENT PREROGATIVES; Ewing, David W.; Garcia, Carlos; Garcia, Edward; Industrial Relations; *SCIENCE OF THE SPANISH SPEAKING PEOPLE.

10548 Rodriguez, Imelda and Bethel, Lowell J. Inquiry approach to science and language teaching. JOURNAL OF RESEARCH IN SCIENCE TEACHING, Vol. 20, no. 4 (April 1983), p. 291-296. English. DESCR: Bilingualism; Education; *Educational Tests and Measurements; Language Arts; Learning and Cognition; Primary School Education.

Science as a Profession

10549 Math-based careers. HISPANIC BUSINESS, Vol. 5, no. 10 (October 1983), p. 28. English. DESCR: *Careers; Carnation Company; Chicanas; Education; Engineering as a Profession; Hispanic Policy Development Project; Minority Engineering Education Center, University of California, Los Angeles; University of California, Los Angeles (UCLA).

10550 Math-based careers. HISPANIC BUSINESS, Vol. 5, no. 12 (December 1983), p. 40. English. DESCR: *Careers; Council on Legal Education Opportunities (CLEO); Education; Employment Training; Graduate Schools; High Technology High School, San Antonio, TX; Legal Education; Mexican American Legal Defense and Educational Fund (MALDEF); San Antonio, TX.

10551 Mendoza, Samuel M. Careers for Chicanos: computers, engineering, science/computadoras, ingenieria, ciencia. CAMINOS, Vol. 3, no. 3 (March 1982), p. 14-16. Bilingual. DESCR: *Careers; Computers; Engineering as a Profession.

10552 Vara, Richard. Reaching for the stars: Franklin Chang-Diaz, astronaut and future scientist in space. HISPANIC BUSINESS, Vol. 5, no. 11 (November 1983), p. 18-19+. English. DESCR: Astronauts; *Chang-Diaz, Franklin; National Aeronautics and Space Administration (NASA).

SCIENCE OF THE SPANISH SPEAKING PEOPLE

10553 Research/development: books. HISPANIC BUSINESS, Vol. 5, no. 4 (April 1983), p. 28. English. DESCR: Biographical Notes; *Book Reviews; *"DO IT MY WAY OR YOU'RE FIRED!": EMPLOYEE RIGHTS AND THE CHANGING ROLE OF MANAGEMENT PREROGATIVES; Ewing, David W.; Garcia, Carlos; Garcia, Edward; Industrial Relations; Science.

Scott Paper Company

10554 Think Spanish! MARKETING AND MEDIA DECISIONS, Vol. 17, (October 1982), p. 66-69. English. DESCR: Advertising; Biography; Conill Advertising Associates, New York, NY; Conill, Alicia; Conill, Rafael; *Marketing; Spanish Language.

Screen Actors Guild

10555 Levario, Raquel. Asner tells it like it is. LATINA, Vol. 1, no. 2 (February, March, 1983), p. 14. English. DESCR: *Artists.

Sculptors
USE: Artists

Sculpture

10556 Lewis, William. Tres Plumas and his pantheon of archetypal deities. NUESTRO, Vol. 7, no. 2 (March 1983), p. 38-40. English. DESCR: *Aguilar, Humberto; Artists; Tres Plumas.

10557 A potpourri of pre-Columbian art. NUESTRO, Vol. 7, no. 6 (August 1983), p. 59-60. English. DESCR: CERAMIC TOMB SCULPTURE FROM ANCIENT WEST MEXICO; Ceramics; Exhibits; Frederick S. Wright Art Gallery, University of California, Los Angeles; Museum of Cultural History, University of California, Los Angeles; *Precolumbian Art.

10558 Sculpture results in controversy. NUESTRO, Vol. 7, no. 2 (March 1983), p. 9. English. DESCR: Albuquerque Arts Board; *Jimenez, Luis.

Seaga, Edward

10559 Newsfront. HISPANIC BUSINESS, Vol. 4, no. 3 (March 1982), p. 9. English. DESCR: Appointed Officials; *Biographical Notes; Businesspeople; Chicano Film Exhibition and Festival, Detroit, Michigan, April 5-9, 1982; Garcia, Gloria; League of United Latin American Citizens (LULAC); Martinez, Vilma Socorro; National Association for Bilingual Education; Suarez, Carlos R.

Search and Seizure

10560 Appleson, Gail. Court to review INS stop-and-quiz policy. AMERICAN BAR ASSOCIATION JOURNAL, Vol. 68, (July 1982), p. 791-792. English. DESCR: Constitutional Amendments - Fourth; Immigration and Naturalization Service (INS); Immigration Regulation and Control; *Undocumented Workers.

10561 Aragon, Ellen Weis. The factory raid: an unconstitutional act. SOUTHERN CALIFORNIA LAW REVIEW, Vol. 56, no. 2 (January 1983), p. 605-645. English. DESCR: Blackie's House of Beef v. Castillo; Deportation; Immigration and Naturalization Service (INS); International Ladies Garment Workers Union (ILGWU) v. Sureck; Racism; *Undocumented Workers.

10562 INS sweep searches of work areas must meet fourth amendment standards. CRIMINAL LAW REPORTER, Vol. 31, no. 18 (August 11, 1982), p. 2366-2367. English. DESCR: Constitutional Amendments - Fourth; Immigration and Naturalization Service (INS); Immigration Regulation and Control; International Ladies Garment Workers Union (ILGWU); Undocumented Workers.

Searchlight Series

10563 Walia, Adorna. Book review of: COUNSELING THE BILINGUAL STUDENT. BILINGUAL JOURNAL, Vol. 7, no. 4 (Summer 1983), p. 27-28. English. DESCR: Bilingual Bicultural Education; Book Reviews; Counseling Services (Educational); *COUNSELING THE BILINGUAL STUDENT; Sanchez, Antonia.

Seasonal Labor
USE: Migrant Labor

Seattle, WA

10564 Aguilar, Ricardo D. Chicano poetry and new places. JOURNAL OF ETHNIC STUDIES, Vol. 5, no. 1 (Spring 1977), p. 59-61. English. DESCR: *Literature; Poetry.

THE SECOND RING OF POWER

10565 Nieto, Eva Margarita. El problema de la juventud eterna en tres hechiceras en THE SECOND RING OF POWER, LA MULATA DE CORDOBA y AURA. LA PALABRA, Vol. 4, no. 1-2 (Spring, Fall, 1982, 1983), p. 81-91. Spanish. DESCR: AURA; Castaneda, Carlos; Fuentes, Carlos; Gonzalez Obregon, Luis; LA MULATA DE CORDOBA; *Literary Criticism; Literature; Literature Reviews.

Secondary School Education

10566 Breiter, Toni. Hispanic policy development project. CAMINOS, Vol. 4, no. 10 (November 1983), p. 42-43,54. Bilingual. DESCR: *Hispanic Policy Development Project; *National Commission on Secondary Schooling for Hispanics.

10567 Burciaga, Cecilia Preciado. High school dropouts: remedies. CAMINOS, Vol. 4, no. 10 (November 1983), p. 38-40,54. Bilingual. DESCR: *Dropouts.

10568 Hispanic student study undertaken. NUESTRO, Vol. 7, no. 10 (December 1983), p. 11-12. English. DESCR: Academic Achievement; Dropouts; Educational Statistics; Enrollment; Hispanic Policy Development Project; *National Commission on Secondary Schooling for Hispanics.

10569 Ramirez, Albert and Soriano, Fernando. Social power in educational systems: its effect on Chicanos' attitudes toward the school experience. JOURNAL OF SOCIAL PSYCHOLOGY, Vol. 118, no. 1 (October 1982), p. 113-119. English. DESCR: Educational Tests and Measurements; Identity; *Social Psychology.

10570 Venerable, W. R. Student and parent attitudes toward college at five Hispanic learning centers in Illinois. JOURNAL OF THE NATIONAL ASSOC. OF COLLEGE ADMISSIONS COUNSELORS, Vol. 26, (April 1982), p. 19-23. English. DESCR: Casa Aztlan; Chicago, IL; *Higher Education; Illinois Migrant Council; Lakeview Learning Center, Chicago, IL.

10571 Vigil, James Diego. Chicano high schoolers: educational performance and acculturation. EDUCATIONAL FORUM, Vol. 47, no. 1 (Fall 1982), p. 58-73. English. DESCR: *Academic Achievement; *Acculturation; Identity; Socioeconomic Factors.

Segall, Marshall H.

10572 Beaupre, Shirley. Book review of: CROSS CULTURAL PSYCHOLOGY: HUMAN BEHAVIOR IN GLOBAL PERSPECTIVE. HISPANIC JOURNAL OF BEHAVIORAL SCIENCES, Vol. 4, no. 1 (March 1982), p. 134-137. English. DESCR: Book Reviews; *CROSS CULTURAL PSYCHOLOGY: HUMAN BEHAVIOR IN GLOBAL PERSPECTIVE.

Segovia, Andres

10573 Segovia: un retrato musical. LATINO, Vol. 54, no. 3 (April 1983), p. 10. Spanish. DESCR: Musicians.

Segregation and Desegregation

10574 Cohen, Gaynor. Alliance and conflict among Mexican-Americans. ETHNIC AND RACIAL STUDIES, Vol. 5, no. 2 (April 1982), p. 175-195. English. DESCR: Identity; *Political History and Conditions.

10575 Gonzalez, Alex. Classroom cooperation and ethnic balance: Chicanos and equal status. CACR REVIEW, Vol. 1, no. 1 (September 1982), p. 42-71. English. DESCR: Cooperative Education; Curriculum; Intergroup Relations; *Prejudice (Social).

10576 Hwang, Sean-Shong and Murdock, Steve H. Residential segregation in Texas in 1980. SOCIAL SCIENCE QUARTERLY, Vol. 63, (December 1982), p. 737-748. English. DESCR: Housing; Texas.

10577 Iadicola, Peter and Moore, Helen A. The desegregated school and status relations among Anglo and Hispanic students: the dilemma of school desegregation. AZTLAN, Vol. 14, no. 1 (Spring 1983), p. 147-173. English. DESCR: Comparative Education; Educational Theory and Practice; Students.

10578 Perez, Robert; Padilla, Amado M.; and Ramirez, Alex. Expectations toward school busing by Mexican American youth. AMERICAN JOURNAL OF COMMUNITY PSYCHOLOGY, Vol. 10, no. 2 (April 1982), p. 133-148. English. DESCR: Attitude (Psychological); *Busing; East Los Angeles, CA; Identity; Students; Youth.

10579 San Miguel, Guadalupe. Mexican American organizations and the changing politics of school desegration in Texas, 1945 to 1980. SOCIAL SCIENCE QUARTERLY, Vol. 63, (December 1982), p. 701-715. English. DESCR: American G.I. Forum; League of United Latin American Citizens (LULAC); Mexican American Legal Defense and Educational Fund (MALDEF); Organizations; Texas.

10580 Weinberg, Meyer. Bibliography of desegration: Los Angeles. INTEGRATED EDUCATION, Vol. 20, no. 1- (January, April, 1982), p. 32-33. English. DESCR: Bibliography; Los Angeles, CA.

SEGUIN [movie]

10581 Entertainment = diversion. CAMINOS, Vol. 3, no. 1 (January 1982), p. 41-42. Bilingual. DESCR: ANO NUEVO [film]; Broadcast Media; *CERVANTES [film]; *Films; *Times Mirror Company.

10582 Fregoso, Linda. Sequin: the same side of the Alamo. BILINGUAL REVIEW, Vol. 10, no. 2-3 (May, December, 1983), p. 146-152. English. DESCR: Film Reviews; Trevino, Jesus Salvador.

10583 Levine, Paul G. Remember the Alamo? AMERICAN FILM, Vol. 7, no. 4 (January, February, 1982), p. 47-49. English. DESCR: Film Reviews; Films; LA HISTORIA [film series]; Trevino, Jesus Salvador.

10584 Morales, Alejandro. Expanding the meaning of Chicano cinema: YO SOY CHICANO, RAICES DE SANGRE, SEGUIN. BILINGUAL REVIEW, Vol. 10, no. 2-3 (May, December, 1983), p. 121-137. English. DESCR: Film Reviews; *Films; RAICES DE SANGRE [film]; YO SOY CHICANO [film].

SEGUIN [movie] (cont.)

10585 Morales, Sylvia. Chicano-produced celluloid
      mujeres. BILINGUAL REVIEW, Vol. 10, no. 2-3
      (May, December, 1983), p. 89-93. English.
      DESCR: BALLAD OF GREGORIO CORTEZ [film];
      *Chicanas; Film Reviews; *Films; RAICES DE
      SANGRE [film]; *Stereotypes; ZOOT SUIT
      [film].

10586 A very special gift. LATINO, Vol. 53, no. 5
      (September 1982), p. 7-8+. English. **DESCR:**
      Films; *Martinez, A.

**Select Commission on Immigration and Refugee
Policy**

10587 Babbitt, Bruce. Reagan approach to aliens
      simply wishful thinking. NATIONAL HISPANIC
      JOURNAL, Vol. 1, no. 2 (Winter 1982), p.
      6-7. English. **DESCR:** Border Region;
      Braceros; Immigration Regulation and
      Control; *Reagan, Ronald; *Undocumented
      Workers; United States-Mexico Relations.

10588 Corwin, Arthur F. The numbers game:
      estimates of illegal aliens in the United
      States, 1970-1981. LAW AND CONTEMPORARY
      PROBLEMS, Vol. 45, no. 2 (Spring 1982), p.
      223-297. English. **DESCR:** Bustamante, Jorge
      A.; Centro Nacional de Informacion y
      Estadistica del Trabajo (CENINET);
      Demography; Federation for American
      Immigration Reform (FAIR); Mexican American
      Legal Defense and Educational Fund (MALDEF);
      Simpson-Mazzoli Bill; *Statistics;
      *Undocumented Workers.

10589 Martin, Philip L. Select Commission suggests
      changes in immigration policy: a review
      essay. MONTHLY LABOR REVIEW, Vol. 105, no. 2
      (February 1982), p. 31-37. English. **DESCR:**
      Immigration; *Immigration Regulation and
      Control; Undocumented Workers.

**A SELECTED AND ANNOTATED BIBLIOGRAPHY OF CHICANO
STUDIES**

10590 Marquez, Maria Teresa. Book review of: A
      SELECTED AND ANNOTATED BIBLIOGRAPHY OF
      CHICANO STUDIES. AZTLAN, Vol. 14, no. 1
      (Spring 1983), p. 191-192. English. **DESCR:**
      Bibliography; Book Reviews; Reference Works;
      Tatum, Charles.

Selective Service
      USE: Military Service

Self Concept
      USE: Identity

Self Perception
      USE: Identity

**THE SELF-CONCEPT (REV. ED) VOLUME 2: THEORY AND
RESEARCH ON SELECTED TOPICS**

10591 Nelson, Ann. Book review of: THE
      SELF-CONCEPT (Rev. ed.). Volume 2: THEORY
      AND RESEARCH ON SELECTED TOPICS. HISPANIC
      JOURNAL OF BEHAVIORAL SCIENCES, Vol. 4, no.
      3 (September 1982), p. 396-397. English.
      DESCR: Book Reviews; Wylie, Ruth C.

Self-Concept Self Report Scale

10592 Fu, Victoria R.; Hinkle, Dennis E.; and
      Korslund, Mary K. A development study of
      ethnic self-concept among pre-adolescent
      girls. JOURNAL OF GENETIC PSYCHOLOGY, Vol.
      14, (March 1983), p. 67-73. English.
      DESCR: Chicanas; Comparative Psychology;
      *Identity; Junior High School Students.

Self-Determination

10593 Martinez, Arthur D. Mexican-Americans: Qua
      the assistant-Americans. SOUTHWEST ECONOMY
      AND SOCIETY, Vol. 2, no. 2 (Winter 1977), p.
      34-36. English. **DESCR:** *Employment;
      Management; Racism.

Self-Help Graphics, Los Angeles, CA

10594 Miccaihuitl. CALMECAC, Vol. 1, (Summer
      1980), p. 34-37. Bilingual. **DESCR:** *Cultural
      Customs; *Dia de los Muertos.

Self-Help Groups

10595 Fernandez, John P. Facing the hard realities
      of corporate advancement. HISPANIC BUSINESS,
      Vol. 4, no. 4 (April 1982), p. 18-19,25.
      English. **DESCR:** *Affirmative Action;
      Businesspeople; *Discrimination in
      Employment; Mentors.

10596 Professional network. HISPANIC BUSINESS,
      Vol. 4, no. 9 (September 1982), p. 18,26+.
      English. **DESCR:** California; Castillo,
      Sylvia; Higher Education; Hispanic Women in
      Higher Education (HWHE); Mentors.

SELF-PORTRAIT WITH PORTRAIT OF DR. FARILL

10597 Herrera, Hayden. Making an art of pain.
      PSYCHOLOGY TODAY, Vol. 17, no. 3 (March
      1983), p. 86. English. **DESCR:** Biography;
      HENRY FORD HOSPITAL; *Kahlo, Frida;
      Paintings; THE BROKEN COLUMN; THE LITTLE
      DEER; TREE OF HOPE; WITHOUT HOPE.

Self-Referents

10598 Davila, Luis. Meditaciones. REVISTA
      CHICANO-RIQUENA, Vol. 10, no. 1-2 (Winter,
      Spring, 1982), p. 275-278. Spanish. **DESCR:**
      Bilingualism; Cultural Customs; *Essays;
      Folklore.

10599 Garcia, Richard A. Chicano intellectual
      history: myth and realities. REVISTA
      CHICANO-RIQUENA, Vol. 10, no. 1-2 (Winter,
      Spring, 1982), p. 285-289. English. **DESCR:**
      Chicano Movement; *Essays; History;
      Stereotypes.

10600 Rodriguez, Roberto. Who declared war on the
      word Chicano? CORAZON DE AZTLAN, Vol. 1, no.
      2 (March, April, 1982), p. 17-20. English.
      DESCR: *Chicano Movement.

10601 Sandoval, David A. What do I call them: the
      Chicano experience. CACR REVIEW, Vol. 1, no.
      1 (September 1982), p. 3-25. English.
      DESCR: Colonialism; Identity; Intergroup
      Relations.

Semantics

10602 Kirschner, Carl. Spanish and English
      inchoatives and the Spanish-English
      bilingual: got anything to se? BILINGUAL
      REVIEW, Vol. 9, no. 3 (September, December,
      1982), p. 213-219. English. **DESCR:** *Grammar;
      Slang; Syntax.

10603 Walsh, Catherine E. The phenomenon of
      educated/educado: an example for a
      tripartite system of semantic memory.
      BILINGUAL REVIEW, Vol. 10, no. 1 (January,
      April, 1983), p. 33-40. English. **DESCR:**
      *Bilingualism; Language Development.

Senorita Black Velvet Latina
      USE: Miss Black Velvet Latina

Sephardic Jews
    USE: Jews

September 16
    USE: Dieciseis de Septiembre

Septien, Rafael

10604 Nuestra gente. LATINO, Vol. 53, no. 2
      (March, April, 1982), p. 30. English.
      DESCR: Asip, Patricia V.; *Biographical
      Notes; Ceballos, Sonia Ceban; Gonzales,
      Modesto.

Sepulveda, Bernardo

10605 El nuevo embajador de Mexico en Washington.
      El inicio de un nuevo estilo? INFORME:
      RELACIONES MEXICO-ESTADOS UNIDOS, Vol. 1,
      no. 2 (July, December, 1982), p. 109-111.
      Spanish. **DESCR:** *United States-Mexico
      Relations.

Sepulveda, Luis

10606 People. HISPANIC BUSINESS, Vol. 4, no. 9
      (September 1982), p. 7. English. **DESCR:**
      Advertising Agencies; Appointed Officials;
      Awards; *Biographical Notes; Diaz-Albertini,
      Luis; Dimartino, Rita; Garza, Jesus;
      Hispanic Women in Higher Education (HWHE);
      League of United Latin American Citizens
      (LULAC); Ortega, Ray; Ortiz, George; Romero,
      Carlos J.

SER

10607 1983 SER theme: a new reality. LATINO, Vol.
      54, no. 3 (April 1983), p. 8. English.
      DESCR: *Cultural Organizations.

10608 Full employment is theme of SER annual
      conference. LATINO, Vol. 53, no. 2 (March,
      April, 1982), p. 20. English. **DESCR:**
      *Employment.

10609 Government review. NUESTRO, Vol. 7, no. 10
      (December 1983), p. 48. English. **DESCR:**
      Banking Industry; Child Care Centers; Chile;
      Clinics (Medical); Credit Unions;
      Employment; Employment Training; *Government
      Services; Medical Care; National Credit
      Union Administration; National Oceanic and
      Atmospheric Administration; U.S. Department
      of Health and Human Services; U.S.
      Department of Labor.

10610 New corporate structure approved for
      national SER. LATINO, Vol. 53, no. 6
      (October 1982), p. 16. English. **DESCR:**
      Organizations.

Serin, Enrique

10611 Laguna, Jaime. Enrique Serin: Mexico's
      violin ambassador. CAMINOS, Vol. 4, no. 10
      (November 1983), p. 17-19. Bilingual.
      DESCR: Classical Music; Music.

Serna, Pepe

10612 Madrid, Joe. The multi-faceted Pepe Serna
      (interview). CAMINOS, Vol. 4, no. 4 (April
      1983), p. 32-35,66. Bilingual. **DESCR:**
      Artists; Films.

Serna v. Portales Municipal Schools

10613 Martinez, Paul E. Serna v. Portales: the
      plight of bilingual education four years
      later. JOURNAL OF ETHNIC STUDIES, Vol. 7,
      no. 2 (Summer 1979), p. 109-114. English.
      DESCR: *Bilingual Bicultural Education;
      Chicano Youth Organization; Civil Rights;

Portales Municipal Schools; *Portales, NM.

Servas

10614 Que pasa? NUESTRO, Vol. 7, no. 3 (April
      1983), p. 9. English. **DESCR:** Border Patrol;
      *Cisneros, Henry, Mayor of San Antonio, TX;
      Elections; Immigration Regulation and
      Control; Rocky Mountain Spotted Fever;
      Tourism.

SESAME STREET

10615 Neuman, Susan B. and Pits, Elaine F. A
      review of current North American television
      programs for bilingual children. READING
      TEACHER, Vol. 37, no. 3 (December 1983), p.
      254-260. English. **DESCR:** *Bilingual
      Bicultural Education; Mass Media; Spanish
      Language; THE ELECTRIC COMPANY; VILLA
      ALEGRE.

Sesma, Chico

10616 Golden Eagle Awards 1983. CAMINOS, Vol. 4,
      no. 8 (September 1983), p. 42-43. English.
      DESCR: *Awards; Nosotros [film production
      company]; Recreation.

Settles, Ron

10617 Latinos in the law: meeting the challenge [
      a symposium]. CHICANO LAW REVIEW, Vol. 6,
      (1983), p. 1-121. English. **DESCR:** *Criminal
      Justice System; Demography; Legal
      Profession; Los Angeles Police Department;
      Love, Eulia; Police Brutality; Political
      Representation; Reapportionment.

Sex Discrimination
    USE: Sexism

Sex Education

10618 Davis, Sally M. and Harris, Mary B. Sexual
      knowledge, sexual interests, and sources of
      sexual information of rural and urban
      adolescents from three cultures.
      ADOLESCENCE, Vol. 17, no. 66 (Summer 1982),
      p. 471-492. English. **DESCR:** Birth Control;
      Cultural Characteristics; Identity; Rural
      Population; Sex Roles; *Sexual Behavior;
      Urban Communities; Youth.

Sex Roles

10619 Adams, Phylliss J. and Anderson, Peggy L.
      Comparison of teachers' and Mexican-American
      children's perceptions of the children's
      competence. READING TEACHER, Vol. 36, no. 1
      (October 1982), p. 8-13. English. **DESCR:**
      Attitude (Psychological); Children;
      Colorado; Cultural Characteristics; Learning
      and Cognition; *Teacher Attitudes.

10620 Andrade, Sally J. Social science stereotypes
      of the Mexican American woman: policy
      implications for research. HISPANIC JOURNAL
      OF BEHAVIORAL SCIENCES, Vol. 4, no. 2 (June
      1982), p. 223-244. English. **DESCR:**
      *Chicanas; Stereotypes.

10621 Ayers-Nackamkin, Beverly, et al. Sex and
      ethnic differences in the use of power.
      JOURNAL OF APPLIED PSYCHOLOGY, Vol. 67, no.
      4 (August 1982), p. 464-471. English.
      DESCR: Anglo Americans; Ethnic Groups;
      Management; *Personnel Management; Social
      Psychology.

Sex Roles (cont.)

10622 Baca Zinn, Maxine. Chicano men and masculinity. JOURNAL OF ETHNIC STUDIES, Vol. 10, no. 2 (Summer 1982), p. 29-44. English. **DESCR:** Cultural Characteristics; Ethnic Stratification; *Machismo; Sex Stereotypes; Socioeconomic Factors; Women Men Relations.

10623 Borland, Dolores C. A cohort analysis approach to the empty nest syndrome among three ethnic groups of women: a theoretical position. JOURNAL OF MARRIAGE AND THE FAMILY, Vol. 44, no. 1 (February 1982), p. 117-129. English. **DESCR:** Social Psychology.

10624 Borrego, Richard L.; Chavez, Ernest L.; and Titley, Robert W. Effect of counselor technique on Mexican-American and Anglo-American self-disclosure and counselor perception. JOURNAL OF COUNSELING PSYCHOLOGY, Vol. 29, no. 5 (September 1982), p. 538-541. English. **DESCR:** Anglo Americans; *Counseling (Psychological); Cultural Characteristics; Identity; Personality.

10625 Davis, Sally M. and Harris, Mary B. Sexual knowledge, sexual interests, and sources of sexual information of rural and urban adolescents from three cultures. ADOLESCENCE, Vol. 17, no. 66 (Summer 1982), p. 471-492. English. **DESCR:** Birth Control; Cultural Characteristics; Identity; Rural Population; *Sex Education; *Sexual Behavior; Urban Communities; Youth.

10626 Delgado, Abelardo "Lalo". An open letter to Carolina... or relations between men and women. REVISTA CHICANO-RIQUENA, Vol. 10, no. 1-2 (Winter, Spring, 1982), p. 279-284. English. **DESCR:** Chicanas; *Essays; Machismo; Sex Stereotypes.

10627 Flores, Henry. Some different thoughts concerning "machismo". COMADRE, no. 3 (Fall 1978), p. 7-9. English. **DESCR:** Chicanas; *Machismo; Mythology.

10628 Gonzalez, Alex. Sex role of the traditional Mexican family: a comparison of Chicano and Anglo students' attitudes. JOURNAL OF CROSS-CULTURAL PSYCHOLOGY, Vol. 13, no. 3 (September 1982), p. 330-339. English. **DESCR:** Anglo Americans; *Family; Hembrismo; Machismo.

10629 Greenberg, Julie L. Dating and the elderly. NUESTRO, Vol. 6, no. 5 (June, July, 1982), p. 43. English. **DESCR:** *Ancianos.

10630 Hawley, Peggy and Even, Brenda. Work and sex-role attitudes in relation to education and other characteristics. VOCATIONAL GUIDANCE QUARTERLY, Vol. 31, no. 2 (December 1982), p. 101-108. English. **DESCR:** Careers; Chicanas; Ethnic Groups; Psychological Testing; Working Women.

10631 Herrera-Sobek, Maria. The acculturation process of the Chicana in the corrido. DE COLORES, Vol. 6, no. 1-2 (1982), p. 7-16. English. **DESCR:** Acculturation; *Chicanas; Corrido.

10632 Kranau, Edgar J.; Green, Vicki; and Valencia-Weber, Gloria. Acculturation and the Hispanic woman: attitudes toward women, sex-role attribution, sex-role behavior, and demographics. HISPANIC JOURNAL OF BEHAVIORAL SCIENCES, Vol. 4, no. 1 (March 1982), p. 21-40. English. **DESCR:** Acculturation; *Chicanas; Demography.

10633 Matute-Bianchi, Maria Eugenia. A Chicana in

academe. WOMEN'S STUDIES QUARTERLY, Vol. 10, no. 1 (Spring 1982), p. 14-17. English. **DESCR:** *Chicanas; *Higher Education; Matute-Bianchi, Maria Eugenia; Racism; Sexism.

10634 Mercado, Olivia. Chicanas: myths and roles. COMADRE, no. 1 (Summer 1977), p. 26-32. English. **DESCR:** *Chicanas; Gallo, Juana; Huerta, Dolores; *Identity; Leadership; Women's Rights.

10635 Mirande, Alfredo. The Chicano family and sex roles: an overview and introduction. DE COLORES, Vol. 6, no. 1-2 (1982), p. 1-6. English. **DESCR:** *Family.

10636 Mirande, Alfredo. Machismo: rucas, chingasos, y chingaderas. DE COLORES, Vol. 6, no. 1-2 (1982), p. 17-31. English. **DESCR:** *Machismo.

10637 Soto, Elaine and Shaver, Phillip. Sex-role traditionalism assertiveness, and symptoms of Puerto Rican women living in the United States. HISPANIC JOURNAL OF BEHAVIORAL SCIENCES, Vol. 4, no. 1 (March 1982), p. 1-19. English. **DESCR:** Puerto Ricans; *Women.

10638 Steigelfest, Annette. Ethnicity and sex role socialization. BILINGUAL JOURNAL, Vol. 6, no. 3 (Spring 1982), p. 11-15,24. English. **DESCR:** Ethnic Attitudes; Halacha Institute; *Identity; Orthodox Jews; Sex Stereotypes; Socialization.

10639 Trotter, Robert T. Ethnic and sexual patterns of alcohol use: Anglo and Mexican American college students. ADOLESCENCE, Vol. 17, no. 66 (Summer 1982), p. 305-325. English. **DESCR:** *Alcoholism; Anglo Americans; Chicanas; Cultural Characteristics; Ethnic Groups; Youth.

10640 Vasquez, Melba J. T. Confronting barriers to the participation of Mexican American women in higher education. HISPANIC JOURNAL OF BEHAVIORAL SCIENCES, Vol. 4, no. 2 (June 1982), p. 147-165. English. **DESCR:** Academic Motivation; *Chicanas; Higher Education; Socioeconomic Factors.

10641 Whiteford, Linda. Migrants no longer: changing family structure of Mexican Americans in South Texas. DE COLORES, Vol. 6, no. 1-2 (1982), p. 99-108. English. **DESCR:** Chicanas; *Family; *South Texas.

10642 Ybarra, Lea. Marital decision-making and the role of machismo in the Chicano family. DE COLORES, Vol. 6, no. 1-2 (1982), p. 32-47. English. **DESCR:** Family; *Machismo; Marriage.

10643 Zeff, Shirley B. A cross-cultural study of Mexican American, Black American and white American women of a large urban university. HISPANIC JOURNAL OF BEHAVIORAL SCIENCES, Vol. 4, no. 2 (June 1982), p. 245-261. English. **DESCR:** Anglo Americans; Blacks; *Chicanas; Higher Education.

Sex Stereotypes

10644 Baca Zinn, Maxine. Chicano men and masculinity. JOURNAL OF ETHNIC STUDIES, Vol. 10, no. 2 (Summer 1982), p. 29-44. English. **DESCR:** Cultural Characteristics; Ethnic Stratification; *Machismo; Sex Roles; Socioeconomic Factors; Women Men Relations.

Sex Stereotypes (cont.)

10645 Delgado, Abelardo "Lalo". An open letter to Carolina... or relations between men and women. REVISTA CHICANO-RIQUENA, Vol. 10, no. 1-2 (Winter, Spring, 1982), p. 279-284. English. DESCR: Chicanas; *Essays; Machismo; Sex Roles.

10646 Heathcote, Olivia D. Sex stereotyping in Mexican reading primers. READING TEACHER, Vol. 36, no. 2 (November 1982), p. 158-165. English. DESCR: Comparative Education; Curriculum Materials; Mexico; Primary School Education.

10647 Steigelfest, Annette. Ethnicity and sex role socialization. BILINGUAL JOURNAL, Vol. 6, no. 3 (Spring 1982), p. 11-15,24. English. DESCR: Ethnic Attitudes; Halacha Institute; *Identity; Orthodox Jews; *Sex Roles; Socialization.

10648 Walia, Adorna. Book review of: WOMEN AND MEN SPEAKING: FRAMEWORK FOR ANALYSIS. BILINGUAL JOURNAL, Vol. 6, no. 3 (Spring 1982), p. 20-22. English. DESCR: Book Reviews; Kramarae, Cheris; Language Usage; Sexism; Sociolinguistics; *WOMEN AND MEN SPEAKING: FRAMEWORK FOR ANALYSIS.

Sexism

10649 Hartman, Harriet. Book review of: MEXICAN WOMEN IN THE UNITED STATES: STRUGGLES PAST AND PRESENT. INTERNATIONAL MIGRATION REVIEW, Vol. 16, no. 1 (Spring 1982), p. 228-229. English. DESCR: Book Reviews; Chicanas; Del Castillo, Adelaida R.; *MEXICAN WOMEN IN THE UNITED STATES: STRUGGLES PAST AND PRESENT; Mora, Magdalena.

10650 Lopez, Marcos. And justice for all. LATINA, Vol. 1, no. 1 (1982), p. 7+. English.

10651 Matute-Bianchi, Maria Eugenia. A Chicana in academe. WOMEN'S STUDIES QUARTERLY, Vol. 10, no. 1 (Spring 1982), p. 14-17. English. DESCR: *Chicanas; *Higher Education; Matute-Bianchi, Maria Eugenia; Racism; Sex Roles.

10652 Research/development: books. HISPANIC BUSINESS, Vol. 4, no. 1 (January 1982), p. 27. English. DESCR: *Book Reviews; *Discrimination in Employment; *Fernandez, John P.; Racism; *RACISM AND SEXISM IN CORPORATE LIFE.

10653 Tienda, Marta. Sex, ethnicity and Chicano status attainment. INTERNATIONAL MIGRATION REVIEW, Vol. 16, no. 2 (Summer 1982), p. 435-473. English. DESCR: Academic Achievement; Chicanas; Discrimination in Education; Discrimination in Employment; Identity; Income; Language Proficiency; *Social Classes; Social Mobility.

10654 Walia, Adorna. Book review of: WOMEN AND MEN SPEAKING: FRAMEWORK FOR ANALYSIS. BILINGUAL JOURNAL, Vol. 6, no. 3 (Spring 1982), p. 20-22. English. DESCR: Book Reviews; Kramarae, Cheris; Language Usage; Sex Stereotypes; Sociolinguistics; *WOMEN AND MEN SPEAKING: FRAMEWORK FOR ANALYSIS.

Sexual Behavior

10655 Davis, Sally M. and Harris, Mary B. Sexual knowledge, sexual interests, and sources of sexual information of rural and urban adolescents from three cultures. ADOLESCENCE, Vol. 17, no. 66 (Summer 1982), p. 471-492. English. DESCR: Birth Control;

Cultural Characteristics; Identity; Rural Population; *Sex Education; Sex Roles; Urban Communities; Youth.

Sexual Harrassment
USE: Sexism

Shafer, Robert Jones

10656 Schmitt, Karl M. Book review of: HISPANIC FOLK MUSIC OF NEW MEXICO AND THE SOUTHWEST: A SELF-PORTRAIT OF A PEOPLE. HISPANIC AMERICAN HISTORICAL REVIEW, Vol. 63, no. 1 (1983), p. 209-210. English. DESCR: Book Reviews; Mabry, Donald; *NEIGHBORS, MEXICO AND THE UNITED STATES: WETBACKS AND OIL; United States-Mexico Relations.

Shaughnessy v. Mezei

10657 Hopson, Susan B. Immigration: indefinite detention of excluded aliens held illegal. TEXAS INTERNATIONAL LAW JOURNAL, Vol. 17, (Winter 1982), p. 101-110. English. DESCR: Civil Rights; Deportation; *Detention of Persons; Immigration; International Law; Rodriguez-Fernandez v. Wilkinson; *Undocumented Workers.

Sheehy, Daniel E.

10658 Loza, Steven J. The Son Jarocho: the history, style and repertory of a changing Mexican musical tradition. AZTLAN, Vol. 13, no. 1-2 (Spring, Fall, 1982), p. 327-334. English. DESCR: Dance; Folk Songs; Music; *Son Jarocho; Veracruz, Mexico.

Short Story

10659 Acosta, Daniel. Homeboy. CHISMEARTE, (1982), p. 60-61. English.

10660 Acuna, Mike. Man witnesses his own execution. CORAZON DE AZTLAN, Vol. 1, no. 3 (August, September, 1982), p. 26-28. English.

10661 Alurista. Mojologue. MAIZE, Vol. 2, no. 1 (Fall 1978), p. 36-39. Calo.

10662 Alvarez, Jorge. The sacred spot. CHISMEARTE, (1982), p. 23. English.

10663 Anaya, Rudolfo A. The place of the swallows. NUESTRO, Vol. 7, no. 3 (April 1983), p. 18-19. English. DESCR: Prose.

10664 Anaya, Rudolfo A. The village which the gods painted yellow. NUESTRO, Vol. 7, no. 1 (January, February, 1983), p. 48-54. English. DESCR: Prose.

10665 Aranda, Maria. Agueco awakens. CALMECAC, Vol. 3, (Spring 1982), p. 21-23. English.

10666 Baeza, Joan. A servant of the people. NUESTRO, Vol. 7, no. 3 (April 1983), p. 41-45. English. DESCR: Prose.

10667 Bartlett, Paul Alexander. Against the wall. NUESTRO, Vol. 6, no. 5 (June, July, 1982), p. 49-52. English.

10668 Burciaga, Jose Antonio. Care package. NUESTRO, Vol. 6, no. 3 (April 1982), p. 35-36. English.

10669 Burk, Ronnie. La merced. MAIZE, Vol. 6, no. 3-4 (Spring, Summer, 1982), p. 48-50. English.

Short Story (cont.)

10670 Burns, Robert C. The miracle teachers: portraits of women who challenged themselves and at the same time challenged a system which had relegated them to nonprofessional... NUESTRO, Vol. 6, no. 6 (August 1982), p. 13-16. English. **DESCR:** Bilingual Bicultural Education; *Teaching Profession.

10671 Caldwell, Christy. The power. MAIZE, Vol. 6, no. 3-4 (Spring, Summer, 1983), p. 103-106. English.

10672 Canchola, E. M. School daze: reflections on what school days were like for some Latinos in the 1940's. NUESTRO, Vol. 6, no. 4 (May 1982), p. 30-33. English. **DESCR:** *Education.

10673 Carrasco, Ricardo. Eagle. CORAZON DE AZTLAN, Vol. 1, no. 1 (January, February, 1982), p. 44. English.

10674 Castillo, Ana. A Christmas carol '76. MAIZE, Vol. 1, no. 2 (Winter 1977), p. 34-35. English.

10675 Castillo, Rafael C. The Colonel. NUESTRO, Vol. 7, no. 2 (March 1983), p. 46-48. English. **DESCR:** Prose.

10676 Castro, Tony. Red light district. LATINA, Vol. 1, no. 1 (1982), p. 35. English.

10677 Chavez, Denise. Evening in Paris. NUESTRO, Vol. 5, no. 8 (November 1981), p. 29-31. English.

10678 Chavez, Denise. Willow game. NUESTRO, Vol. 6, no. 1 (January, February, 1982), p. 35-38. English.

10679 Cruz, Amaury. El Salvador: realities of a country at war. NUESTRO, Vol. 6, no. 3 (April 1982), p. 14-17+. English. **DESCR:** *El Salvador; Political History and Conditions; Poverty; Tourism.

10680 De Vallbona, Rima. El nagual de mi amiga Irene. LA PALABRA, Vol. 4, no. 1-2 (Spring, Fall, 1982, 1983), p. 151-157. Spanish. **DESCR:** Literature; Prose.

10681 Duarte, Marialupe. Las norias. MAIZE, Vol. 2, no. 4 (Summer 1979), p. 25-27. Spanish.

10682 Elizondo, Sergio D. Quien le manda. MAIZE, Vol. 2, no. 1 (Fall 1978), p. 12-16. Spanish.

10683 Engle, Margarita Mondrus. In the rain forest. NUESTRO, Vol. 7, no. 7 (September 1983), p. 56-60. English. **DESCR:** Prose.

10684 Espinosa, Monica. Habra? MAIZE, Vol. 1, no. 3 (Spring 1977), p. 18-22. Spanish.

10685 Espinoza, Ana Luisa. Los ninos: la cosecha del futuro. CALMECAC, Vol. 2, (Spring 1981), p. 20-25. English. **DESCR:** Children.

10686 Espinoza, Danny J. Beware of subways. MAIZE, Vol. 2, no. 4 (Summer 1979), p. 30. English.

10687 Espinoza, Danny J. Conversations. MAIZE, Vol. 6, no. 1-2 (Fall, Winter, 1982, 1983), p. 75-79. English.

10688 Espinoza, Herbert O. Alas de carton. MAIZE, Vol. 1, no. 2 (Winter 1977), p. 7-11. Spanish.

10689 Espinoza, Herbert O. Carrousel. MAIZE, Vol.

1, no. 4 (Summer 1978), p. 34-38. Spanish.

10690 Espinoza, Herbert O. La otra novia. MAIZE, Vol. 5, no. 1-2 (Fall, Winter, 1981, 1982), p. 56-60. Spanish.

10691 Espinoza, Herbert O. Viendo morir a teresa. MAIZE, Vol. 2, no. 1 (Fall 1978), p. 54-56. Spanish.

10692 Esquivel, Grace. The East L.A. mysterious lady. CORAZON DE AZTLAN, Vol. 1, no. 2 (March, April, 1982), p. 33. English.

10693 Fernandez, Peter. The incredible F.P. hopper of varrio nuevo. CHISMEARTE, (1982), p. 11-12. English. **DESCR:** *Chicano Movement.

10694 Figueredo, D.H. Old Havana. NUESTRO, Vol. 7, no. 3 (April 1983), p. 32-35. English. **DESCR:** Prose.

10695 Flores, Lauro. A la mitad. MAIZE, Vol. 1, no. 1 (Fall 1977), p. 38-42. Spanish.

10696 Gamboa, Harry, Jr. Ins and outs. CORAZON DE AZTLAN, Vol. 1, no. 2 (March, April, 1982), p. 21-23. English.

10697 Gamboa, Harry, Jr. No grey matter. CORAZON DE AZTLAN, Vol. 1, no. 1 (January, February, 1982), p. 17-18. English.

10698 Gamboa, Harry, Jr. A rival departure. CHISMEARTE, (1982), p. 52-54. English.

10699 Garcia-Camarillo, Mia. Corn dream, january 19, 1978. MAIZE, Vol. 2, no. 1 (Fall 1978), p. 7-8. English.

10700 Garzon, Luz Elena. The beepers. MAIZE, Vol. 1, no. 3 (Spring 1978), p. 39-41. Bilingual.

10701 Gilb, Dagoberto. El fierro. NUESTRO, Vol. 6, no. 10 (December 1982), p. 33-35. English.

10702 Gonzalez, David J. La lucha. MAIZE, Vol. 2, no. 4 (Summer 1979), p. 51-58. English.

10703 Gonzalez, David J. Protesta en los angeles. MAIZE, Vol. 2, no. 2 (Winter 1979), p. 53-56. English.

10704 Gonzalez, J. J. The hurricane. NUESTRO, Vol. 7, no. 3 (April 1983), p. 61-64. English. **DESCR:** Prose.

10705 Govea, Jose. The drunken sermon. CORAZON DE AZTLAN, Vol. 1, no. 3 (August, September, 1982), p. 14-17. English.

10706 Guerra-Cunningham, Lucia. La estafa de Eros. MAIZE, Vol. 6, no. 3-4 (Spring, Summer, 1983), p. 64-73. Spanish.

10707 Haslam, Gerald. Earthquake summer. BILINGUAL REVIEW, Vol. 10, no. 1 (January, April, 1983), p. 60-65. English.

10708 Hernandez, Jesus. Death at Victory Park: silence mars investigation. LATINA, Vol. 1, no. 2 (February, March, 1983), p. 26-29. English.

10709 Hinojosa-Smith, Rolando R. Con el pie en el estribo. MAIZE, Vol. 1, no. 1 (Fall 1977), p. 51-54. Spanish.

10710 Infante, Martha. Their little scheme. CORAZON DE AZTLAN, Vol. 1, no. 1 (January, February, 1982), p. 15. English.

Short Story (cont.)

10711 Lewis, William. The milk of human kindness. NUESTRO, Vol. 6, no. 8 (October 1982), p. 39-41. English.

10712 Lewis, William. Song of Lia. NUESTRO, Vol. 6, no. 4 (May 1982), p. 38-41. English.

10713 Lewis, William. Song of Lia. NUESTRO, Vol. 7, no. 3 (April 1983), p. 46-48. English. **DESCR:** Prose.

10714 Lizarraga Duerfeldt, Martha. The most blessed profession. MAIZE, Vol. 1, no. 1 (Fall 1977), p. 10-17. English.

10715 Lizarraga, Sylvia S. Don? MAIZE, Vol. 1, no. 2 (Winter 1977), p. 20-22. Spanish.

10716 Lomeli, Marta. Si yo. COMADRE, no. 2 (Spring 1978), p. 26-30. Bilingual.

10717 Lopez, Daniel M. The founding of NUESTRO. NUESTRO, Vol. 6, no. 3 (April 1982), p. 41-43. English. **DESCR:** Magazines.

10718 Lopez, Felice. Word woman. NUESTRO, Vol. 7, no. 9 (November 1983), p. 56-59. English. **DESCR:** Fiction.

10719 Mendoza, Phillip. To remember me. CORAZON DE AZTLAN, Vol. 1, no. 3 (August, September, 1982), p. 24-25. English.

10720 Mercado, Vicente. El temor publico. CORAZON DE AZTLAN, Vol. 1, no. 1 (January, February, 1982), p. 36-37. Spanish.

10721 Monleon, Jose. Donde estan las llaves...? MAIZE, Vol. 2, no. 1 (Fall 1978), p. 44-45. Spanish.

10722 Moreno, Robert. Foolish pride. NUESTRO, Vol. 6, no. 9 (November 1982), p. 45-46+. English.

10723 Moyano, Daniel and Francis, H.E., trans. My uncle smiled one Christmas. MAIZE, Vol. 6, no. 3-4 (Spring, Summer, 1983), p. 21-23. English.

10724 Navarro, J.L. Baby hulk. CHISMEARTE, (1982), p. 44-51. English.

10725 Navarro, J.L. Miguel. CORAZON DE AZTLAN, Vol. 1, no. 2 (March, April, 1982), p. 45. English.

10726 Norte, Marisela. Each street/each story. CHISMEARTE, (1982), p. 57. Bilingual.

10727 Obejas, Achy. Argentina: back to Europe where it belongs. NUESTRO, Vol. 6, no. 8 (October 1982), p. 51. English. **DESCR:** *Argentina; Geography.

10728 Padilla, Steve. Granny's bunuelos and other secrets. NUESTRO, Vol. 6, no. 10 (December 1982), p. 45. English. **DESCR:** *Christmas.

10729 Padilla, Steve. Otters don't live in the barrio. NUESTRO, Vol. 6, no. 3 (April 1982), p. 33. English.

10730 Pavoncordero, Jose. The pride I have of being Mexican. CORAZON DE AZTLAN, Vol. 1, no. 3 (August, September, 1982), p. 37. English.

10731 Perez, Hector. Los yonqueros. MAIZE, Vol. 2, no. 3 (Spring 1979), p. 40-43. Spanish.

10732 Ponce, Mary Helen. How I changed the war and

won the game. CORAZON DE AZTLAN, Vol. 1, no. 1 (January, February, 1982), p. 38. English.

10733 Ponce, Mary Helen. El pedo. CHISMEARTE, (1982), p. 17. English.

10734 Ponce, Mary Helen. Los piojos. CHISMEARTE, (1982), p. 16. English.

10735 Quinonez, Naomi. Auroa: reflections. LATINA, Vol. 1, no. 3 (1983), p. 58. English.

10736 Ramirez, Alma Beatrice. Life in a Crackerjack box. MAIZE, Vol. 6, no. 1-2 (Fall, Winter, 1982, 1983), p. 72-74. English.

10737 Ramirez, Alma Beatrice. Pictures and poems. MAIZE, Vol. 5, no. 3-4 (Spring, Summer, 1982), p. 33-34. English.

10738 Ramirez, Henry J. Vatos from the Pentagon. CORAZON DE AZTLAN, Vol. 1, no. 2 (March, April, 1982), p. 41-44. English.

10739 Repetto, Hugo. Nomada, a; lautremont. MAIZE, Vol. 2, no. 4 (Summer 1979), p. 43. Spanish.

10740 Repetto, Hugo. Van! MAIZE, Vol. 2, no. 2 (Winter 1979), p. 21. Spanish.

10741 Rodriguez, Luis. Pobreza. CHISMEARTE, (1982), p. 19. English.

10742 Rodriguez, Luis. The tunnel. CORAZON DE AZTLAN, Vol. 1, no. 1 (January, February, 1982), p. 39. English.

10743 Rodriguez, Luis Javier. A look at the immigration laws. CHISMEARTE, no. 9 (September 1983), p. 24-26. English.

10744 Rodriguez, Roberto. Mazehual: a total war of extermination. CORAZON DE AZTLAN, Vol. 1, no. 3 (August, September, 1982), p. 18-21. English.

10745 Rojas, Mary. Mascutis. MAIZE, Vol. 6, no. 3-4 (Spring, Summer, 1983), p. 55-57. Bilingual.

10746 Role model for aspiring researchers. NUESTRO, Vol. 6, no. 4 (May 1982), p. 34-36. English. **DESCR:** Gonzales, Ciriaco Q.; *Research Methodology.

10747 Romero, Norberto Luis and Francis, H.E., trans. Mirrors. MAIZE, Vol. 6, no. 3-4 (Spring, Summer, 1983), p. 90-95. English.

10748 Rosel, Fernando. Changes. CHISMEARTE, (1982), p. 58-59. English.

10749 Rubio, Sofia. A matter of faith. NUESTRO, Vol. 7, no. 3 (April 1983), p. 50-55. English. **DESCR:** Prose.

10750 Sagel, Jaime. Another Rio Arriba murder. BILINGUAL REVIEW, Vol. 10, no. 1 (January, April, 1983), p. 52-59. English.

10751 Salicrup, Nemesio Caban. Saltan and the hurricane. NUESTRO, Vol. 6, no. 7 (September 1982), p. 36-38. English.

10752 Salvatierra, Richard. Christmas mass at the Vatican: a burning memory. NUESTRO, Vol. 6, no. 10 (December 1982), p. 38-40. English. **DESCR:** Catholic Church.

Short Story (cont.)

10753 Sanchez, Ricardo. El lencho y los chenchos. NATIONAL HISPANIC JOURNAL, Vol. 1, no. 3 (Summer, Fall, 1982), p. 20. Calo. **DESCR:** Border Region; *Ciudad Juarez, Chihuahua, Mexico; El Paso, TX.

10754 Sanchez, Rosaura. El traje nuevo. MAIZE, Vol. 1, no. 1 (Fall 1977), p. 21-24. Spanish.

10755 Sanchez, Saul. Esperanza + turo. MAIZE, Vol. 1, no. 3 (Spring 1978), p. 8-13. Spanish.

10756 Santiago, Esmerelda. Madre de madre. NUESTRO, Vol. 6, no. 1 (January, February, 1982), p. 59. English. **DESCR:** Family.

10757 Shanti. Tres imagenes para rosaura. MAIZE, Vol. 1, no. 4 (Summer 1978), p. 16-19. Spanish.

10758 Shiell, Pancho. My vacation. NUESTRO, Vol. 6, no. 9 (November 1982), p. 52-54. English.

10759 Sifuentes, Frank. Babe and the Cadillac. CORAZON DE AZTLAN, Vol. 1, no. 3 (August, September, 1982), p. 39-41. English.

10760 Sifuentes, Frank. Mi padrino Apolino. CORAZON DE AZTLAN, Vol. 1, no. 1 (January, February, 1982), p. 41-43. English.

10761 Sifuentes, Frank. Tio tacos are people too. CHISMEARTE, (1982), p. 14. English. **DESCR:** *Identity.

10762 Soto, Gary. The savings account. NUESTRO, Vol. 6, no. 6 (August 1982), p. 48-50. English.

10763 Soy Quilaztli... y que? cuento azteca. CALMECAC, Vol. 2, (Spring 1981), p. 45-47. English.

10764 Straight, Susan. The homeboys. NUESTRO, Vol. 6, no. 6 (August 1982), p. 17-19. English. **DESCR:** Barrios; Frias, Gustavo; Racism.

10765 Tapia, Irma. La Llorona. CORAZON DE AZTLAN, Vol. 1, no. 1 (January, February, 1982), p. 10. English.

10766 Trevino, Jesus Salvador. The great pyramid of Aztlan. NUESTRO, Vol. 7, no. 3 (April 1983), p. 36-40. English. **DESCR:** Prose.

10767 Trevino, Jesus Salvador. The last night of the mariachi. NUESTRO, Vol. 7, no. 3 (April 1983), p. 23-27. English. **DESCR:** Prose.

10768 Valdes, Gina. El gallinero. MAIZE, Vol. 2, no. 2 (Winter 1979), p. 43-47. Spanish.

10769 Valencia, Juan O. Salud Pacheco. LA PALABRA, Vol. 4, no. 1-2 (Spring, Fall, 1982, 1983), p. 159-162. Spanish. **DESCR:** Literature; Prose.

10770 Valenzuela, Luisa. Mercado de pulgas. MAIZE, Vol. 6, no. 3-4 (Spring, Summer, 1983), p. 31-33. Spanish.

10771 Vega, Ed. Fishing. NUESTRO, Vol. 7, no. 3 (April 1983), p. 28-31. English. **DESCR:** Prose.

10772 Vigil, Maurilio E. Recollections of New Mexico Christmas. NUESTRO, Vol. 6, no. 10 (December 1982), p. 41-44. English. **DESCR:** *Christmas; New Mexico.

10773 Viramontes, Helen Maria. The moths.

10774 Viramontes, Helen Maria. Snapshots. MAIZE, Vol. 6, no. 1-2 (Fall, Winter, 1982, 1983), p. 64-71. English.

10775 Wilkins, Terry Meyette. Rainbow warrior. CHISMEARTE, no. 9 (September 1983), p. 14-16. English.

10776 Williams, Christopher. Ramon's run. NUESTRO, Vol. 7, no. 3 (April 1983), p. 56-59. English. **DESCR:** Prose.

10777 Xelina. Green card falsa. MAIZE, Vol. 5, no. 1-2 (Fall, Winter, 1981, 1982), p. 47. Spanish.

10778 Yuscaran, Guillermo. Rubber sun. NUESTRO, Vol. 7, no. 6 (August 1983), p. 44-46. English. **DESCR:** Prose.

Showalter, Dennis K.

10779 Bloodworth, William A., Jr. Book review of: IMAGES OF THE MEXICAN-AMERICAN IN FICTION AND FILM. WESTERN AMERICAN LITERATURE, Vol. 16, no. 4 (Winter 1982), p. 323-325. English. **DESCR:** Book Reviews; Chicanos in American Literature; Films; *IMAGES OF THE MEXICAN AMERICAN IN FICTION AND FILM; Pettit, Arthur G.; Stereotypes.

Shriner's Hospital for Crippled Children, Philadelphia, PA

10780 Gonzales, Juan. Puerto Rico to Philadelphia: a cure connection. NUESTRO, Vol. 7, no. 5 (June, July, 1983), p. 21-24. English. **DESCR:** *Handicapped; Hospitals and the Community; Medical Care; Puerto Ricans.

Siberio, Julio

10781 People. HISPANIC BUSINESS, Vol. 5, no. 4 (April 1983), p. 9. English. **DESCR:** Alvarado, Linda M.; *Biographical Notes; Businesspeople; Castillo, Irenemaree; Castillo, Sylvia; Del Junco, Tirso; Gutierrez, Jose Roberto; Juarez, Joe; Mata, Bill; Miyares, Marcelino; Montanez Davis, Grace; Montoya, Velma; Pineda, Pat; Thompson, Edith Lopez.

Siboney Advertising, Inc.

10782 Communications/marketing. HISPANIC BUSINESS, Vol. 4, no. 3 (March 1982), p. 15. English. **DESCR:** California; Herrera, Maria Elena; *Marketing; Philip Morris, Inc.; Publicidad Siboney; SRI International.

10783 Communications/marketing. HISPANIC BUSINESS, Vol. 4, no. 4 (April 1982), p. 15. English. **DESCR:** Advertising Agencies; Consumers; Juarez and Associates, Inc.; Las Americas, Inc.; *Marketing; Norman, Craig & Kummel Organization; Publicidad Siboney.

Sigal, Janet

10784 Hunsaker, Alan. Book review of: PSYCHOLOGY
AND COMMUNITY CHANGE; SOCIAL AND
PSYCHOLOGICAL RESEARCH IN COMMUNITY SETTING;
COMMUNITY PSYCHOLOGY: THEORETICAL AND
EMPIRICAL APPROACHES. HISPANIC JOURNAL OF
BEHAVIORAL SCIENCES, Vol. 5, no. 1 (March
1983), p. 121-124. English. **DESCR:** Book
Reviews; *COMMUNITY PSYCHOLOGY: THEORETICAL
AND EMPIRICAL APPROACHES; Gibbs, Margaret
S.; Heller, Kenneth; Kelly, James G.;
Lachenmeyer, Juliana Rasic; Monahan, John;
Munoz, Ricardo F.; *PSYCHOLOGY AND COMMUNITY
CHANGE; Snowden, Lonnie R.; *SOCIAL AND
PSYCHOLOGICAL RESEARCH IN COMMUNITY
SETTINGS.

Silen, Ivan

10785 Villanueva Collado, Alfredo. Fili-Mele:
simbolo y mujer en la poesia de Luis Pales
Matos e Ivan Silen. REVISTA CHICANO-RIQUENA,
Vol. 10, no. 4 (Fall 1982), p. 47-54.
Spanish. **DESCR:** Chicanas; Literary
Criticism; LOS POEMAS DE FILI-MELE; *Pales
Matos, Luis; Ribes Tovar, Federico;
Symbolism; TUNTUN DE PASA Y GRIFERIA.

THE SILENCE OF THE LLANO

10786 Candelaria, Cordelia. Book review of: THE
SILENCE OF THE LLANO. MELUS: MULTI-ETHNIC
LITERATURE OF THE UNITED STATES, Vol. 10,
no. 2 (Summer 1983), p. 79-82. English.
DESCR: *Anaya, Rudolfo A.; *Literature.

10787 Candelaria, Cordelia. Problems and promise
in Anaya's llano: THE SILENCE OF THE LLANO,
Rudolfo A. Anaya. AMERICAN BOOK REVIEW, Vol.
5, no. 6 (September, October, 1983), p.
18-19. English. **DESCR:** Anaya, Rudolfo A.;
Book Reviews.

10788 Martinez, Douglas R. Book review of: THE
SILENCE OF THE LLANO. NUESTRO, Vol. 7, no. 1
(January, February, 1983), p. 55. English.
DESCR: Anaya, Rudolfo A.; Book Reviews.

10789 Martinez, Douglas R. Sharing the silence.
LATINO, Vol. 54, no. 4 (May, June, 1983), p.
28. English. **DESCR:** Anaya, Rudolfo A.; Book
Reviews.

Silet, Charles L.P.

10790 Cripps, Thomas. Mexicans, Indians and
movies: the need for a history. WIDE ANGLE:
A FILM QUARTERLY OF THEORY, CRITICISM, AND
PRACTICE, Vol. 5, no. 1 (1982), p. 68-70.
English. **DESCR:** Bataille, Gretchen M.; *Book
Reviews; Films; IMAGES OF THE MEXICAN
AMERICAN IN FICTION AND FILM; Native
Americans; O'Connor, John E.; Pettit, Arthur
G.; *Stereotypes; THE HOLLYWOOD INDIAN:
STEREOTYPES OF NATIVE AMERICANS IN FILMS;
THE PRETEND INDIANS: IMAGES OF NATIVE
AMERICANS IN THE MOVIES.

Silva Letters

10791 Schmeltzer, Mike. Mexicans asked to report.
MIGRATION TODAY, Vol. 10, no. 1 (1982), p.
29. English. **DESCR:** Immigration;
*Immigration Regulation and Control; Silva,
Refugio; Visa.

Silva, Refugio

10792 Immigration questions. NUESTRO, Vol. 6, no.
2 (March 1982), p. 10-11. English. **DESCR:**
*Immigrant Labor; Immigration Law.

10793 Schmeltzer, Mike. Mexicans asked to report.
MIGRATION TODAY, Vol. 10, no. 1 (1982), p.
29. English. **DESCR:** Immigration;
*Immigration Regulation and Control; Silva
Letters; Visa.

Silverton Rosenfelt, Deborah

10794 McCracken, Ellen. Book review of: SALT OF
THE EARTH. JOURNAL OF ETHNIC STUDIES, Vol.
8, no. 1 (Spring 1980), p. 116-120. English.
DESCR: Book Reviews; Chicanas; Films;
Hanover, NM; International Union of Mine,
Mill and Smelter Workers; *SALT OF THE
EARTH; Strikes and Lockouts; Women Men
Relations; Women's Rights.

Simic, Andrei

10795 Burke, Leslie K. Book review of: LIFE'S
CAREER-AGING: CULTURAL VARIATIONS ON GROWING
OLD. HISPANIC JOURNAL OF BEHAVIORAL
SCIENCES, Vol. 4, no. 1 (March 1982), p.
103-107. English. **DESCR:** Academic
Achievement; *LIFE'S CAREER--AGING: CULTURAL
VARIATIONS ON GROWING OLD; Myerhoff, Barbara
G.

Simon, Jose

10796 New mecca for comedians. NUESTRO, Vol. 6,
no. 5 (June, July, 1982), p. 12. English.
DESCR: *Humor; *San Francisco, CA.

Simpson, Alan K.

10797 Hing, Bill Ong. Racial disparity: the
unaddressed issues of the Simpson-Mazzoli
Bill. LA RAZA LAW JOURNAL, Vol. 1, no. 1
(June 1983), p. 21-52. English. **DESCR:**
Amnesty; Asian Americans; Ethnic Attitudes;
Family; Immigration; Immigration and
Naturalization Service (INS); Latin
Americans; Mazzoli, Romano L.; Mexican
American Legal Defense and Educational Fund
(MALDEF); *Simpson-Mazzoli Bill; Temporary
Worker Program; U.S. Congresssional
Subcommittee on Immigration, Refugees and
International Law.

10798 Liebowitz, Arnold. Immigration challenge and
the congressional response. LA RAZA LAW
JOURNAL, Vol. 1, no. 1 (June 1983), p. 1-20.
English. **DESCR:** Amnesty; Immigration;
Immigration and Nationality Act (INA);
Mazzoli, Romano L.; *Simpson-Mazzoli Bill;
Temporary Worker Program; Undocumented
Workers; U.S. Congresssional Subcommittee on
Immigration, Refugees and International Law.

10799 Schey, Peter A. Supply side immigration
theory: analysis of the Simpson-Mazzoli
Bill. LA RAZA LAW JOURNAL, Vol. 1, no. 1
(June 1983), p. 53-71. English. **DESCR:**
Amnesty; Immigration; Mazzoli, Romano L.;
Migration Patterns; Refugees;
*Simpson-Mazzoli Bill; Temporary Worker
Program.

10800 Watson, Roy J., Jr. The Simpson-Mazzoli
bill: an analysis of selected policies. SAN
DIEGO LAW REVIEW, Vol. 20, no. 1 (December
1982), p. 97-116. English. **DESCR:**
Employment; Immigration Regulation and
Control; Labor Certification; Mazzoli,
Romano L.; *Simpson-Mazzoli Bill;
*Undocumented Workers.

Simpson, Alan K. (cont.)

10801 Wong, Linda. Simpson-Mazzoli Bill in the
Ninety-eighth Congress. LA RAZA LAW JOURNAL,
Vol. 1, no. 1 (June 1983), p. 72-75.
English. **DESCR:** Immigration and
Naturalization Service (INS); Immigration
Law; Mazzoli, Romano L.; *Simpson-Mazzoli
Bill.

Simpson-Mazzoli Bill

10802 Baruch, Jeremiah (pseud.). Half-open door.
COMMONWEAL, Vol. 110, no. 13 (July 15,
1983), p. 389-390. English. **DESCR:**
Immigration; *Immigration Law.

10803 Bethell, Tom. Immigration and the economy.
NATIONAL REVIEW, Vol. 35, no. 13 (July 8,
1983), p. 802. English. **DESCR:** *Immigration;
Immigration Law.

10804 Bridling at a U.S. immigration bill.
BUSINESS WEEK, (February 28, 1983), p.
43-44. English. **DESCR:** *Immigration Law;
Immigration Regulation and Control;
Undocumented Workers.

10805 Bustamante, Jorge A. The Mexicans are
coming: from ideology to labor relations.
INTERNATIONAL MIGRATION REVIEW, Vol. 17, no.
2 (Summer 1983), p. 323-341. English.
DESCR: Attitude (Psychological);
*Immigration; Immigration Law; Labor Laws
and Legislation; Labor Supply and Market;
Migration; Policy; Political Ideology;
Undocumented Workers.

10806 Can America get control of its border?
ECONOMIST (London), Vol. 286, (February 26,
1983), p. 43-44. English. **DESCR:**
*Immigration; Immigration Regulation and
Control; Undocumented Workers.

10807 Chavez, Cesar E. Relentless struggle for
farm workers' rights. NUESTRO, Vol. 7, no. 9
(November 1983), p. 55. English. **DESCR:**
*Agricultural Laborers; California;
Immigrant Labor.

10808 Chavez, Leo R. Hispanics and immigration
reform. NUESTRO, Vol. 7, no. 8 (October
1983), p. 23-24. English. **DESCR:** Immigration
Law; *Immigration Regulation and Control;
Undocumented Workers.

10809 Chavez, Leo R. Undocumented immigrants and
access to health services: a game of pass
the buck. MIGRATION TODAY, Vol. 11, no. 1
(1983), p. 14-19. English. **DESCR:**
California; *Immigrants; Medical Care;
Migrant Health Services; Public Health
Legislation; Social Services; Undocumented
Workers.

10810 Cohodas, Nadine. Senate passes legislation
to curb illegal immigration. CONGRESSIONAL
QUARTERLY WEEKLY REPORT, Vol. 40, (August
21, 1982), p. 2053-2055. English. **DESCR:**
Immigration Law; *Undocumented Workers.

10811 Congressional hearings proceed on
immigration. NUESTRO, Vol. 6, no. 3 (April
1982), p. 62. English. **DESCR:** Immigration.

10812 Corwin, Arthur F. The numbers game:
estimates of illegal aliens in the United
States, 1970-1981. LAW AND CONTEMPORARY
PROBLEMS, Vol. 45, no. 2 (Spring 1982), p.
223-297. English. **DESCR:** Bustamante, Jorge
A.; Centro Nacional de Informacion y
Estadistica del Trabajo (CENINET);
Demography; Federation for American
Immigration Reform (FAIR); Mexican American

Legal Defense and Educational Fund (MALDEF);
*Select Commission on Immigration and
Refugee Policy; *Statistics; *Undocumented
Workers.

10813 Employers may pay if they hire illegals.
BUSINESS WEEK, (June 21, 1982), p. 38.
English. **DESCR:** *Immigration Law;
Immigration Regulation and Control;
Undocumented Workers.

10814 Evolucion del proyecto Simpson-Mazzoli.
INFORME: RELACIONES MEXICO-ESTADOS UNIDOS,
Vol. 1, no. 3 (July, December, 1982), p.
209-214. Spanish. **DESCR:** *Immigration Law.

10815 Hing, Bill Ong. Racial disparity: the
unaddressed issues of the Simpson-Mazzoli
Bill. LA RAZA LAW JOURNAL, Vol. 1, no. 1
(June 1983), p. 21-52. English. **DESCR:**
Amnesty; Asian Americans; Ethnic Attitudes;
Family; Immigration; Immigration and
Naturalization Service (INS); Latin
Americans; Mazzoli, Romano L.; Mexican
American Legal Defense and Educational Fund
(MALDEF); Simpson, Alan K.; Temporary Worker
Program; U.S. Congresssional Subcommittee on
Immigration, Refugees and International Law.

10816 Immigration and nationality symposium. SAN
DIEGO LAW REVIEW, Vol. 20, no. 1 (December
1982, 1983), p. 1-231. English. **DESCR:**
Akbarian v. INS; Deportation; Employment;
Immigration and Nationality Act (INA);
*Immigration Regulation and Control; Miranda
v. INS; Undocumented Workers.

10817 Immigration pols. NATION, Vol. 237, no. 10
(October 15, 1983), p. 324. English. **DESCR:**
*Immigration Law.

10818 The impact of undocumented migration on the
U.S. labor market. HOUSTON JOURNAL OF
INTERNATIONAL LAW, Vol. 5, no. 2 (Spring
1983), p. 287-321. English. **DESCR:** Economic
History and Conditions; Employment;
Immigrant Labor; Immigration and Nationality
Act (INA); Immigration Law; Labor Supply and
Market; Research Methodology; *Undocumented
Workers.

10819 Keep, Paul M. Overhauling the immigration
code: this year, Congress may finally act.
NATIONAL JOURNAL, Vol. 15, no. 12 (March 19,
1983), p. 616-619. English. **DESCR:** American
Civil Liberties Union; Federation for
American Immigration Reform (FAIR);
Immigration; *Immigration Law; Mexican
American Legal Defense and Educational Fund
(MALDEF).

10820 Liebowitz, Arnold. Immigration challenge and
the congressional response. LA RAZA LAW
JOURNAL, Vol. 1, no. 1 (June 1983), p. 1-20.
English. **DESCR:** Amnesty; Immigration;
Immigration and Nationality Act (INA);
Mazzoli, Romano L.; *Simpson, Alan K.;
Temporary Worker Program; Undocumented
Workers; U.S. Congresssional Subcommittee on
Immigration, Refugees and International Law.

10821 MALDEF critical of FAIR study. NUESTRO, Vol.
7, no. 7 (September 1983), p. 12-13.
English. **DESCR:** Federation for American
Immigration Reform (FAIR); *Immigration
Regulation and Control; *Mexican American
Legal Defense and Educational Fund (MALDEF).

10822 Morganthau, Tom and Camper, Diane. An
amnesty for illegal aliens? NEWSWEEK, Vol.
101, no. 22 (May 30, 1983), p. 41. English.
DESCR: Immigration Law.

Simpson-Mazzoli Bill (cont.)

10823 N.A.L.E.O.'s "Fiesta '83". CAMINOS, Vol. 4, no. 10 (November 1983), p. 28-29. English. **DESCR:** Baca Barragan, Polly; Bilingual Bicultural Education; Central America; Fiesta '83; Garcia, Robert; Immigration; International Relations; Mendez, Olga; *National Association of Latino Elected Officials (NALEO); United States-Mexico Relations.

10824 O'Neill shifts his course on immigration (NEW YORK TIMES 12-4-83). MIGRATION TODAY, Vol. 11, no. 4-5 (1983), p. 52. English. **DESCR:** *Immigration Law; *O'Neill, Thomas P.

10825 Our 1982 Latino awards. NUESTRO, Vol. 7, no. 1 (January, February, 1983), p. 44-46. English. **DESCR:** Awards; Escalante, Jaime; Gallegos, Gina; Grace, J. Peter; Immigration and Naturalization Service (INS); Knight, Bobby; Lamas, Fernando; *Latino Awards; Luce, Claire Boothe; Moreno, Rita; National Press Foundation; Rodriguez Hernandez, Andres; Smith, Raymond; Valeri, Michele; Voting Rights Act.

10826 Plaza, Eva. Interest group politics and U.S. immigration policy towards Mexico. LA RAZA LAW JOURNAL, Vol. 1, no. 1 (June 1983), p. 76-100. English. **DESCR:** Immigration; Immigration Law; Immigration Regulation and Control; *Interest Groups; Mexico; United States-Mexico Relations.

10827 Praise for the speaker. NUESTRO, Vol. 7, no. 8 (October 1983), p. 9. English. **DESCR:** Immigration Law; Mexican American Legal Defense and Educational Fund (MALDEF).

10828 El proyecto Simpson-Mazzoli para el control de la inmigracion de los trabajadores mexicanos a Estados Unidos. INFORME: RELACIONES MEXICO-ESTADOS UNIDOS, Vol. 1, no. 2 (July, December, 1982), p. 75-87. Spanish. **DESCR:** *Immigration Law.

10829 Reza, H. G. Immigration: restriction or reform? CALIFORNIA LAWYER, Vol. 2, no. 11 (December 1982), p. 32-35. English. **DESCR:** *Immigration Law; Immigration Regulation and Control; Undocumented Workers.

10830 Rips, Geoffrey. Supply-side immigration reform. NATION, Vol. 237, no. 10 (October 8, 1983), p. 289,303+. English. **DESCR:** *Immigration Law; Undocumented Workers.

10831 Schey, Peter A. The Reagan and Simpson/Mazzoli immigration proposals: supply side immigration policy. MIGRATION TODAY, Vol. 11, no. 2-3 (1983), p. 35-38. English. **DESCR:** *Immigration Law.

10832 Schey, Peter A. Supply side immigration theory: analysis of the Simpson-Mazzoli Bill. LA RAZA LAW JOURNAL, Vol. 1, no. 1 (June 1983), p. 53-71. English. **DESCR:** Amnesty; Immigration; Mazzoli, Romano L.; Migration Patterns; Refugees; Simpson, Alan K.; Temporary Worker Program.

10833 Senate passes immigration reform bill. CONGRESSIONAL QUARTERLY WEEKLY REPORT, Vol. 41, (May 21, 1983), p. 1006-1007. English. **DESCR:** Immigration; Immigration Law.

10834 Shapiro, Walter, et al. Immigration: failure of will. NEWSWEEK, Vol. 102, no. 16 (October 17, 1983), p. 32. English. **DESCR:** Immigration; *Immigration Law.

10835 Side-by-side comparison of House and Senate bills. MIGRATION TODAY, Vol. 11, no. 2-3 (1983), p. 7. English. **DESCR:** *Immigration Law.

10836 Simpson, Alan K. Immigration reform and control. LABOR LAW JOURNAL, Vol. 34, no. 4 (April 1983), p. 195-200. English. **DESCR:** *Immigration Law.

10837 Stone, Marvin. The illegals: one more try. U.S. NEWS & WORLD REPORT, Vol. 94, no. 15 (April 18, 1983), p. 94. English. **DESCR:** Editorials; Immigration Law; *Immigration Regulation and Control.

10838 Tattered borders. NEW REPUBLIC, Vol. 189, no. 2 (July 11, 1983), p. 9-11. English. **DESCR:** Cubanos; *Immigration; Undocumented Workers.

10839 Taylor, Robert E. New fight on illegal aliens planned amid signs opposition is softening. WALL STREET JOURNAL, Vol. 19, no. 43 (March 10, 1982), p. 33. English. **DESCR:** Immigration Law.

10840 Thomas, Evan. Playing politics with immigration. TIME, Vol. 122, no. 17 (October 17, 1983), p. 19. English. **DESCR:** Immigration Law; *Immigration Regulation and Control.

10841 Through the revolution door: undocumented workers and the U.S. economy. DOLLARS AND SENSE, Vol. 83, (January 1983), p. 8-9+. English. **DESCR:** History; *Immigration Law.

10842 Torres, Arnold. Special report on the Simpson-Mazzoli Bill. LATINO, Vol. 53, no. 8 (December 1982), p. 16-18. English. **DESCR:** *Immigration Law.

10843 Watson, Roy J., Jr. The Simpson-Mazzoli bill: an analysis of selected policies. SAN DIEGO LAW REVIEW, Vol. 20, no. 1 (December 1982), p. 97-116. English. **DESCR:** Employment; Immigration Regulation and Control; Labor Certification; Mazzoli, Romano L.; Simpson, Alan K.; *Undocumented Workers.

10844 Wong, Linda. Simpson-Mazzoli Bill in the Ninety-eighth Congress. LA RAZA LAW JOURNAL, Vol. 1, no. 1 (June 1983), p. 72-75. English. **DESCR:** Immigration and Naturalization Service (INS); Immigration Law; Mazzoli, Romano L.; Simpson, Alan K.

Singers

10845 Diaz, Katherine A. Jose Feliciano. CAMINOS, Vol. 3, no. 8 (September 1982), p. 14-16. Bilingual. **DESCR:** Artists; *Feliciano, Jose; Musicians.

10846 Fernandez, Enrique. Notas: these ladies are not waiting. BILLBOARD, Vol. 94, (November 13, 1982), p. 62. English. **DESCR:** Artists; *Chicanas; Performing Arts; Salsa.

10847 The Julio-ization of America. LATINO, Vol. 54, no. 4 (May, June, 1983), p. 24-25. English. **DESCR:** Artists; *Iglesias, Julio.

10848 Madrid, Joe. Q & A with Joan Baez. CAMINOS, Vol. 3, no. 11 (December 1982), p. 44-45. English. **DESCR:** *Artists; Baez, Joan; Human Rights.

10849 Madrid, Joe. Warrior of the sun. CAMINOS, Vol. 3, no. 11 (December 1982), p. 42-43. English. **DESCR:** *Artists; *Baez, Joan.

Singers (cont.)

10850 Ogaz, Armando. South of the other border. CAMINOS, Vol. 3, no. 6 (June 1982), p. 26-28,36+. Bilingual. **DESCR:** *Artists; Del Rio, Yolanda; Emmanuel; Nunez, Estella.

10851 Quinlivan, Robert. Tony Orlando in concert. CAMINOS, Vol. 3, no. 9 (October 1982), p. 25. English. **DESCR:** Artists; *Orlando, Tony.

Single Parents

10852 Nieto, Daniel S. Hispanic fathers: the growing phenomenon of single fathers keeping their children. NATIONAL HISPANIC JOURNAL, Vol. 1, no. 4 (Spring 1983), p. 15-19. English. **DESCR:** Divorce; Family; Parent and Child Relationships.

10853 Tienda, Marta and Angel, Ronald. Headship and household composition among blacks, Hispanics and other whites. SOCIAL FORCES, Vol. 61, no. 2 (December 1982), p. 508-531. English. **DESCR:** Anglo Americans; Blacks; Cultural Characteristics; Extended Family; *Family; Puerto Ricans.

Six C's Model (Theoretical Model)

10854 Vigil, James Diego. Towards a new perspective on understanding the Chicano people: the six C's model of sociocultural change. CAMPO LIBRE, Vol. 1, no. 2 (Summer 1981), p. 141-167. English. **DESCR:** Acculturation; Assimilation; Cultural Characteristics; History; Mexican Nationalism Period; Mexico; Nationalism; Organizations; Precolumbian Society; Social History and Conditions; Spanish Colonial Period.

Sixteen Personality Factor Questionnaire

10855 De Blassie, Richard R. and Franco, Juan N. The differences between personality inventory scores and self-rating in a sample of Hispanic subjects. JOURNAL OF NON-WHITE CONCERNS IN PERSONNEL AND GUIDANCE, Vol. 11, no. 2 (January 1983), p. 43-46. English. **DESCR:** Chicanas; Hispanic Education [program]; New Mexico State University; *Personality.

Skeet-shooting

10856 Ferrarone, Aida. Olympic skeet-shooter. LATINA, Vol. 1, no. 3 (1983), p. 15. English. **DESCR:** Biography; Olympics; *Ortiz-Sherman, Nuria; Sports.

Skin Color

10857 Relethfold, John H., et al. Social class, admixture, and skin color variation in Mexican-Americans and Anglo-Americans living in San Antonio, Texas. AMERICAN JOURNAL OF PHYSICAL ANTHROPOLOGY, Vol. 61, no. 1 (May 1983), p. 97-102. English. **DESCR:** Anglo Americans; Population; San Antonio, TX.

Slang

10858 Freeman, Marion. La onda and other youthful Mexican expressions. HISPANIA, Vol. 66, (May 1983), p. 260-261. English. **DESCR:** Language Patterns.

10859 Kirschner, Carl. Spanish and English inchoatives and the Spanish-English bilingual: got anything to se? BILINGUAL REVIEW, Vol. 9, no. 3 (September, December, 1982), p. 213-219. English. **DESCR:** *Grammar; *Semantics; Syntax.

SLAVE TRADE TODAY: AMERICAN EXPLOITATION OF ILLEGAL ALIENS

10860 Cardoso, Lawrence Anthony. "Wetbacks" and "slaves": recent additions to the literature. JOURNAL OF AMERICAN ETHNIC HISTORY, Vol. 1, no. 2 (Spring 1982), p. 68-71. English. **DESCR:** Book Reviews; Garcia, Juan Ramon; Lewis, Sasha G.; *OPERATION WETBACK: THE MASS DEPORTATION OF MEXICAN UNDOCUMENTED WORKERS IN 1954; Undocumented Workers.

SLUMS OF HOPE? SHANTY TOWNS OF THE THIRD WORLD

10861 Logan, Kathleen. The urban poor in developing nations. JOURNAL OF URBAN HISTORY, Vol. 9, no. 1 (November 1982), p. 108-116. English. **DESCR:** ACCESS TO POWER: POLITICS AND THE URBAN POOR IN DEVELOPING NATIONS; *Book Reviews; BORDER BOOM TOWN: CIUDAD JUAREZ SINCE 1848; Collier, David; Cornelius, Wayne A.; Eckstein, Susan; Lloyd, Peter; Martinez, Oscar J.; Nelson, Joan M.; Perlman, Janice E.; POLITICS AND MIGRANT POOR IN MEXICO CITY; SQUATTERS AND OLIGARCHS: AUTHORITARIAN RULE AND POLICY CHANGE IN PERU; THE MYTH OF MARGINALITY: URBAN POVERTY AND POLITICS IN RIO DE JANEIRO; THE POVERTY OF REVOLUTION: THE STATE AND THE URBAN POOR IN MEXICO; Urban Economics.

Small Business

10862 A career line. HISPANIC BUSINESS, Vol. 4, no. 11 (November 1982), p. 14-15. English. **DESCR:** *Gallegos, Amanda M.; U.S. Small Business Administration.

10863 Dominguez, Richard M. Capital formulation for small businesses. HISPANIC BUSINESS, Vol. 4, no. 9 (September 1982), p. 8. English. **DESCR:** Banking Industry; California; *Finance.

10864 Foreign trade. HISPANIC BUSINESS, Vol. 5, no. 2 (February 1983), p. 25. English. **DESCR:** *Currency; Mexico; U.S. Small Business Administration; U.S. Trade Center (Mexico City).

10865 SBA update. HISPANIC BUSINESS, Vol. 4, no. 11 (November 1982), p. 22. English. **DESCR:** Small Business Administration 8(a) Program; U.S. Small Business Administration.

10866 SBA update. HISPANIC BUSINESS, Vol. 5, no. 2 (February 1983), p. 14. English. **DESCR:** U.S. Small Business Administration.

10867 SBA update. HISPANIC BUSINESS, Vol. 5, no. 3 (March 1983), p. 18. English. **DESCR:** High Technology Industries; Minority Business Development Agency (MBDA); Small Business Innovation Research Act; Technology.

10868 Triana, Armando R. and Balkan, D. Carlos. Four little-known facts about Hispanic business firms. HISPANIC BUSINESS, Vol. 5, no. 6 (June 1983), p. 10-11. English. **DESCR:** *Business Enterprises.

10869 Washington carousel. HISPANIC BUSINESS, Vol. 4, no. 7 (July 1982), p. 24. English. **DESCR:** *Legislation.

Small Business Administration 8(a) Program

10870 Balkan, D. Carlos. AMEX Systems Inc. at transition point. HISPANIC BUSINESS, Vol. 4, no. 6 (June 1982), p. 18-19,24. English. DESCR: AMEX Systems, Inc.; Business Enterprises; Caldera, Manuel R.; *Corporations; High Technology Industries; U.S. Small Business Administration.

10871 Foster, Richard. Two Alvarados make one sucessful construction firm. HISPANIC BUSINESS, Vol. 4, no. 10 (October 1982), p. 10-11,26. English. DESCR: Alvarado, Bob; Alvarado, Linda M.; *Business Enterprises; Construction Industry; U.S. Small Business Administration.

10872 News at the SBA. HISPANIC BUSINESS, Vol. 4, no. 3 (March 1982), p. 14. English. DESCR: *Business; Business Enterprises; Cardenas, Maria Elena; U.S. Small Business Administration.

10873 SBA update. HISPANIC BUSINESS, Vol. 4, no. 11 (November 1982), p. 22. English. DESCR: *Small Business; U.S. Small Business Administration.

Small Business Innovation Research Act

10874 SBA update. HISPANIC BUSINESS, Vol. 5, no. 3 (March 1983), p. 18. English. DESCR: High Technology Industries; Minority Business Development Agency (MBDA); *Small Business; Technology.

Smith, Anthony D.

10875 Esman, Milton J. Book review of: THE ETHNIC REVIVAL IN THE MODERN WORLD. ETHNIC AND RACIAL STUDIES, Vol. 5, no. 3 (1982), p. 378-379. English. DESCR: Book Reviews; Ethnic Groups; *ETHNIC REVIVAL IN THE MODERN WORLD.

Smith, James P.

10876 Bronfenbrenner, Martin. Hyphenated Americans-economic aspects. LAW AND CONTEMPORARY PROBLEMS, Vol. 45, no. 2 (Spring 1982), p. 9-27. English. DESCR: *Chiswick, Barry R.; *Economics; *Immigrants; Racism; Welch, Finis R.

Smith, Michael M.

10877 Shepperson, Wilbur S. Book review of: THE MEXICANS IN OKLAHOMA. NEW MEXICO HISTORICAL REVIEW, Vol. 57, no. 3 (July 1982), p. 304-305. English. DESCR: Book Reviews; Immigration; Oklahoma; *THE MEXICANS IN OKLAHOMA.

Smith, Raymond

10878 Our 1982 Latino awards. NUESTRO, Vol. 7, no. 1 (January, February, 1983), p. 44-46. English. DESCR: Awards; Escalante, Jaime; Gallegos, Gina; Grace, J. Peter; Immigration and Naturalization Service (INS); Knight, Bobby; Lamas, Fernando; *Latino Awards; Luce, Claire Boothe; Moreno, Rita; National Press Foundation; Rodriguez Hernandez, Andres; Simpson-Mazzoli Bill; Valeri, Michele; Voting Rights Act.

Smuggling

10879 Chaze, William L. Invasion from Mexico: it just keeps growing. U.S. NEWS & WORLD REPORT, Vol. 94, no. 9 (March 7, 1983), p. 37-41. English. DESCR: Border Region; *Immigration Regulation and Control;

*Undocumented Workers.

10880 Chaze, William L. Smuggling aliens into U.S.: booming business. U.S. NEWS & WORLD REPORT, Vol. 93, no. 11 (September 13, 1982), p. 57-58. English. DESCR: Undocumented Workers.

Snowden, Lonnie R.

10881 Hunsaker, Alan. Book review of: PSYCHOLOGY AND COMMUNITY CHANGE; SOCIAL AND PSYCHOLOGICAL RESEARCH IN COMMUNITY SETTING; COMMUNITY PSYCHOLOGY: THEORETICAL AND EMPIRICAL APPROACHES. HISPANIC JOURNAL OF BEHAVIORAL SCIENCES, Vol. 5, no. 1 (March 1983), p. 121-124. English. DESCR: Book Reviews; *COMMUNITY PSYCHOLOGY: THEORETICAL AND EMPIRICAL APPROACHES; Gibbs, Margaret S.; Heller, Kenneth; Kelly, James G.; Lachenmeyer, Juliana Rasic; Monahan, John; Munoz, Ricardo F.; *PSYCHOLOGY AND COMMUNITY CHANGE; Sigal, Janet; *SOCIAL AND PSYCHOLOGICAL RESEARCH IN COMMUNITY SETTINGS.

Snyder, Art, Councilman

10882 Santillan, Richard. The Chicano community and the redistricting of the Los Angeles city council, 1971-1973. CHICANO LAW REVIEW, Vol. 6, (1983), p. 122-145. English. DESCR: Chicanos for Fair Representation (CFR), Los Angeles, CA; Los Angeles City Council; Mexican American Legal Defense and Educational Fund (MALDEF); *Political Representation.

Soccer

10883 Galarza, Carlos V. Deportes en Mexico. CAMINOS, Vol. 3, no. 6 (June 1982), p. 29,40. Bilingual. DESCR: Mexico; *Sports.

10884 The world cup: soccer's superbowl. NUESTRO, Vol. 6, no. 1 (January, February, 1982), p. 43-44. English. DESCR: Recreation; Sports; *The World Cup of Soccer.

SOCIAL AND PSYCHOLOGICAL RESEARCH IN COMMUNITY SETTINGS

10885 Hunsaker, Alan. Book review of: PSYCHOLOGY AND COMMUNITY CHANGE; SOCIAL AND PSYCHOLOGICAL RESEARCH IN COMMUNITY SETTING; COMMUNITY PSYCHOLOGY: THEORETICAL AND EMPIRICAL APPROACHES. HISPANIC JOURNAL OF BEHAVIORAL SCIENCES, Vol. 5, no. 1 (March 1983), p. 121-124. English. DESCR: Book Reviews; *COMMUNITY PSYCHOLOGY: THEORETICAL AND EMPIRICAL APPROACHES; Gibbs, Margaret S.; Heller, Kenneth; Kelly, James G.; Lachenmeyer, Juliana Rasic; Monahan, John; Munoz, Ricardo F.; *PSYCHOLOGY AND COMMUNITY CHANGE; Sigal, Janet; Snowden, Lonnie R.

Social Bandits
    USE: Bandidos

Social Behavior Scale

10886 Knight, George P. and Kagan, Spencer. Sibling, birth order, and cooperative-competitive social behavior: a comparison of Anglo-American and Mexican-American children. JOURNAL OF CROSS-CULTURAL PSYCHOLOGY, Vol. 13, no. 2 (June 1982), p. 239-249. English. DESCR: Anglo Americans; Children; *Competition; Socialization.

Social Classes

10887 Chesney, Alan P., et al. Barriers to medical care of Mexican-Americans: the role of social class, acculturation, and social isolation. MEDICAL CARE, Vol. 20, no. 9 (1982), p. 883-891. English. DESCR: Acculturation; *Medical Care; Surveys.

10888 Johnson, Dale L. and Breckenridge, James N. The Houston Parent-Child Development Center and the primary prevention of behavior problems in young children. AMERICAN JOURNAL OF COMMUNITY PSYCHOLOGY, Vol. 10, no. 3 (June 1982), p. 305-316. English. DESCR: *Child Rearing; Children; Early Childhood Education; *Houston Parent-Child Development Center(PCDC); Parent and Child Relationships.

10889 Miller, Michael V. Chicano community control in South Texas: problems and prospects. JOURNAL OF ETHNIC STUDIES, Vol. 3, no. 3 (Fall 1975), p. 70-89. English. DESCR: Chicano Movement; Crystal City, TX; Gutierrez, Jose Angel; History; La Raza Unida Party; Patron System; *Political Parties and Organizations; Social History and Conditions; *South Texas.

10890 Reichert, Joshua. Town divided: economic stratification and social relations in a Mexican migrant community. SOCIAL PROBLEMS, Vol. 29, no. 4 (April 1982), p. 411-423. English. DESCR: Mexico; *Migration.

10891 Rice, Jacqueline. Beyond the cientificos: the educational background of the Porfirian Elite. AZTLAN, Vol. 14, no. 2 (Fall 1983), p. 289-306. English. DESCR: History; La Union Liberal; Leadership; *Mexico; Political History and Conditions; Political Parties and Organizations.

10892 Rivera, Julius and Goodman, Paul Wershub. Clandestine labor circulation: a case on the U.S.-Mexico border. MIGRATION TODAY, Vol. 10, no. 1 (1982), p. 21-26. English. DESCR: Border Patrol; Border Region; Ciudad Juarez, Chihuahua, Mexico; El Paso, TX; Immigration Regulation and Control; Migration Patterns; Social Mobility; Socioeconomic Factors; *Undocumented Workers.

10893 Tienda, Marta. Sex, ethnicity and Chicano status attainment. INTERNATIONAL MIGRATION REVIEW, Vol. 16, no. 2 (Summer 1982), p. 435-473. English. DESCR: Academic Achievement; Chicanas; Discrimination in Education; Discrimination in Employment; Identity; Income; Language Proficiency; Sexism; Social Mobility.

10894 Ward, Carmen Carole. Book review of: THE ASSIMILATION OF CUBAN EXILES: THE ROLE OF COMMUNITY AND CLASS. JOURNAL OF ETHNIC STUDIES, Vol. 3, no. 2 (Summer 1975), p. 116-119. English. DESCR: Assimilation; Book Reviews; *Cubanos; Miami, FL; *Rogg, Eleanor Meyer; Social History and Conditions; THE ASSIMILATION OF CUBAN EXILES: THE ROLE OF COMMUNITY AND CLASS; West New York, NJ.

Social History and Conditions

10895 Abrams, Herbert K. Occupational and environmental health problems along the U.S.-Mexico Border. SOUTHWEST ECONOMY AND SOCIETY, Vol. 4, no. 3 (Spring, Summer, 1979), p. 3-20. English. DESCR: Agricultural Laborers; *Border Region; Housing; Mexican Border Industrialization Program; Nutrition; *Pollution; *Public Health.

10896 Ano Nuevo de Kerr, Louise. Chicano settlements in Chicago: a brief history. JOURNAL OF ETHNIC STUDIES, Vol. 2, no. 4 (Winter 1975), p. 22-32. English. DESCR: Back of the Yards, Chicago, IL; *Chicago, IL; Near West Side, Chicago, IL; Pilsen, IL; South Chicago, Chicago, IL; *Urban Communities.

10897 Baca-Ramirez, Reynaldo and Bryan, Dexter Edward. The undocumented Mexican worker: a social problem? JOURNAL OF ETHNIC STUDIES, Vol. 8, no. 1 (Spring 1980), p. 55-69. English. DESCR: Government Services; Immigrant Labor; Immigration; Immigration Regulation and Control; Mexico; Social Services; *Undocumented Workers.

10898 Campbell, Jack K. Senator Yarborough and the Texan RWY brand on bilingual education and federal aid. EDUCATIONAL STUDIES, Vol. 12, no. 4 (Winter 1981, 1982), p. 403-415. English. DESCR: *Bilingual Bicultural Education; Educational Law and Legislation; History; Texas; Yarborough, Ralph Webster.

10899 Cardoso, Lawrence Anthony. Book review of: LOS MEXICANOS QUE DEVOLVIO LA CRISIS, 1929-1932. JOURNAL OF ETHNIC STUDIES, Vol. 5, no. 1 (Spring 1977), p. 120-122. Spanish. DESCR: Book Reviews; Carreras de Velasco, Mercedes; Deportation; Immigrant Labor; Immigration; Immigration Regulation and Control; *LOS MEXICANOS QUE DEVOLVIO LA CRISIS 1929-1932; Mexico.

10900 Cardoso, Lawrence Anthony. Book review of: UNWANTED MEXICAN AMERICANS IN THE GREAT DEPRESSION: REPATRIATION PRESSURES, 1929-1939. JOURNAL OF ETHNIC STUDIES, Vol. 5, no. 1 (Spring 1977), p. 120-122. English. DESCR: Book Reviews; Deportation; Hoffman, Abraham; Immigrant Labor; Immigration; Immigration Regulation and Control; Mexico; *UNWANTED MEXICAN AMERICANS IN THE GREAT DEPRESSION.

10901 Carlos, Jess. The Filipinos: our forgotten cultural cousins. NUESTRO, Vol. 7, no. 8 (October 1983), p. 19-21. English. DESCR: Catholic Church; Cultural Characteristics; *Philippines.

10902 Chase, Marilyn. Mired minority: Latins rise in numbers in U.S. but don't win influence or affluence. WALL STREET JOURNAL, Vol. 19, no. 43 (June 9, 1982), p. 1+. English. DESCR: Assimilation; Education; Employment.

10903 Chavez, Mauro. Book review of: ESSAYS ON LA MUJER. JOURNAL OF ETHNIC STUDIES, Vol. 8, no. 2 (Summer 1980), p. 117-120. English. DESCR: Book Reviews; *Chicanas; Cruz, Rosa Martinez; Economic History and Conditions; *ESSAYS ON LA MUJER; Sanchez, Rosaura; Socioeconomic Factors; Women's Rights.

10904 Churchhill, Ward. Implications of publishing ROOTS OF RESISTANCE. JOURNAL OF ETHNIC STUDIES, Vol. 9, no. 3 (Fall 1981), p. 83-89. English. DESCR: Book Reviews; Colonialism; Dunbar Ortiz, Roxanne; Land Tenure; Native Americans; New Mexico; Publishing Industry; *ROOTS OF RESISTANCE: LAND TENURE IN NEW MEXICO, 1680-1980.

10905 Dunbar Ortiz, Roxanne. The roots of resistance: Pueblo land tenure and Spanish colonization. JOURNAL OF ETHNIC STUDIES, Vol. 5, no. 4 (Winter 1977), p. 33-53. English. DESCR: *Land Tenure; Native Americans; New Mexico; Pueblo Indians.

Social History and Conditions (cont.)

10906 Garcia, Juan R. Book review of: MEXICANO RESISTANCE IN THE SOUTHWEST: "THE SACRED RIGHT OF SELF-PRESERVATION". ARIZONA AND THE WEST, Vol. 24, no. 1 (Spring 1982), p. 81-82. English. DESCR: Book Reviews; *MEXICANO RESISTANCE IN THE SOUTHWEST: "THE SACRED RIGHT OF SELF-PRESERVATION"; New Mexico; Rosenbaum, Robert J.

10907 Garcia, Juan R. Midwest Mexicanos in the 1920's: issues, questions, and directions. SOCIAL SCIENCE JOURNAL, Vol. 19, no. 2 (April 1982), p. 89-99. English. DESCR: Identity; Midwestern States; Social Research.

10908 Gil, Carlos B. Miguel Antonio Otero, first Chicano governor. JOURNAL OF ETHNIC STUDIES, Vol. 4, no. 3 (Fall 1976), p. 95-102. English. DESCR: Book Reviews; *Elected Officials; *New Mexico; OTERO: AN AUTOBIOGRAPHICAL TRILOGY; Otero, Miguel A.; United States History.

10909 Goldman, Shifra. Mexican muralism: its social-educative roles in Latin America and the United States. AZTLAN, Vol. 13, no. 1-2 (Spring, Fall, 1982), p. 111-133. Spanish. DESCR: Art; Latin America; *Mexico; *Mural Art.

10910 Griswold del Castillo, Richard. La familia Chicana: social change in the Chicano family of Los Angeles, 1850-1880. JOURNAL OF ETHNIC STUDIES, Vol. 3, no. 1 (Spring 1975), p. 41-58. English. DESCR: *Family; Industrialization; *Los Angeles, CA.

10911 Kanellos, Nicolas. The flourishing of Hispanic theater in the Southwest, 1920-30s. LATIN AMERICAN THEATRE REVIEW, Vol. 16, no. 1 (1982), p. 29-40. English. DESCR: Folk Drama; History; *Teatro.

10912 Life in a Mexican-American barrio: gangs alongside middle-class striving. WALL STREET JOURNAL, Vol. 199, no. 43 (June 9, 1982), p. 26. English. DESCR: East Los Angeles, CA; Frias, Gustavo; *Gangs.

10913 Lotchin, Roger W. New Chicano history: an urban history perspective. HISTORY TEACHER, Vol. 16, no. 2 (February 1983), p. 229-247. English. DESCR: Camarillo, Alberto; CHICANOS IN A CHANGING SOCIETY; DESERT IMMIGRANTS: THE MEXICANS OF EL PASO 1880-1920; Garcia, Mario T.; Griswold del Castillo, Ricardo; *Historiography; History; THE LOS ANGELES BARRIO 1850-1890: A SOCIAL HISTORY; Urban Communities.

10914 Mena, Jesus. Violence in the Rio Grande Valley. NUESTRO, Vol. 7, no. 1 (January, February, 1983), p. 41-42. English. DESCR: *Bandidos; Border Region; History; *Rio Grande Valley, TX.

10915 Miller, Darlis A. Cross-cultural marriages in the Southwest: the New Mexico experience, 1846-1900. NEW MEXICO HISTORICAL REVIEW, Vol. 57, no. 4 (October 1982), p. 335-359. English. DESCR: Assimilation; Chicanas; Ethnic Attitudes; *Intermarriage; New Mexico.

10916 Miller, Michael V. Book review of: CHICANOS AND RURAL POVERTY. JOURNAL OF ETHNIC STUDIES, Vol. 5, no. 3 (Fall 1977), p. 116-117. English. DESCR: Agricultural Laborers; Book Reviews; Briggs, Vernon M.; *CHICANOS AND RURAL POVERTY; Immigration Law; Southwest United States.

10917 Miller, Michael V. Chicano community control in South Texas: problems and prospects. JOURNAL OF ETHNIC STUDIES, Vol. 3, no. 3 (Fall 1975), p. 70-89. English. DESCR: Chicano Movement; Crystal City, TX; Gutierrez, Jose Angel; History; La Raza Unida Party; Patron System; *Political Parties and Organizations; Social Classes; *South Texas.

10918 Myres, Sandra Lynn. Mexican Americans and westering Anglos: a feminine perspective. NEW MEXICO HISTORICAL REVIEW, Vol. 57, no. 4 (October 1982), p. 317-333. English. DESCR: Anglo Americans; Chicanas; *Ethnic Attitudes; Southwest United States; Stereotypes.

10919 Pena-Ramos, Alfonso. The Latin American disease: an essay. NUESTRO, Vol. 7, no. 6 (August 1983), p. 42-43. English. DESCR: *Latin America; *Political History and Conditions; Revolutions.

10920 Phillips, Melody. The Chicana: her attitudes towards the woman's liberation movement. COMADRE, no. 2 (Spring 1978), p. 42-50. English. DESCR: Carr, Vikki; *Chicanas; FAMOUS MEXICAN-AMERICANS; Newton, Clark; Women's Rights.

10921 Reisler, Mark. Book review of: CHICANOS IN A CHANGING SOCIETY: FROM MEXICAN PUEBLOS TO AMERICAN BARRIOS IN SANTA BARBARA AND SOUTHERN CALIFORNIA, 1848-1930. NEW MEXICO HISTORICAL REVIEW, Vol. 57, no. 2 (April 1982), p. 200-201. English. DESCR: Book Reviews; Camarillo, Alberto; *CHICANOS IN A CHANGING SOCIETY.

10922 Richmond, Douglas W. Mexican immigration and border strategy during the revolution, 1910-1920. NEW MEXICO HISTORICAL REVIEW, Vol. 57, no. 3 (July 1982), p. 269-288. English. DESCR: *Border Region; Carranza, Venustiano; History; Immigration; Mexican Revolution - 1910-1920; Mexico; United States-Mexico Relations.

10923 Simon, Daniel T. Mexican repatriation in East Chicago, Indiana. JOURNAL OF ETHNIC STUDIES, Vol. 2, no. 2 (Summer 1974), p. 11-23. English. DESCR: *Deportation; *East Chicago, IN; History; Immigrant Labor; Immigration; Immigration Regulation and Control; Inland Steel Company; Mexico.

10924 Timmons, Wilbert H. American El Paso: the formative years, 1848-1854. SOUTHWESTERN HISTORICAL QUARTERLY, Vol. 87, no. 1 (July 1983), p. 1-36. English. DESCR: Border Region; *El Paso, TX; Guadalupe Hidalgo, Treaty of 1848; History.

10925 Vigil, James Diego. Towards a new perspective on understanding the Chicano people: the six C's model of sociocultural change. CAMPO LIBRE, Vol. 1, no. 2 (Summer 1981), p. 141-167. English. DESCR: Acculturation; Assimilation; Cultural Characteristics; History; Mexican Nationalism Period; Mexico; Nationalism; Organizations; Precolumbian Society; *Six C's Model (Theoretical Model); Spanish Colonial Period.

10926 Villa Romo, Velma. Rape in the barrio. COMADRE, no. 3 (Fall 1978), p. 19-29. English. DESCR: *Chicanas; Identity; Rape; Santa Barbara Rape Crisis Center.

Social History and Conditions (cont.)

10927 Ward, Carmen Carole. Book review of: THE ASSIMILATION OF CUBAN EXILES: THE ROLE OF COMMUNITY AND CLASS. JOURNAL OF ETHNIC STUDIES, Vol. 3, no. 2 (Summer 1975), p. 116-119. English. DESCR: Assimilation; Book Reviews; *Cubanos; Miami, FL; *Rogg, Eleanor Meyer; Social Classes; THE ASSIMILATION OF CUBAN EXILES: THE ROLE OF COMMUNITY AND CLASS; West New York, NJ.

10928 Weber, David J. and Lotchin, Roger W. The new Chicano history: two perspectives. HISTORY TEACHER, Vol. 16, no. 2 (February 1983), p. 219-247. English. DESCR: Camarillo, Alberto; *CHICANOS IN A CHANGING SOCIETY; DESERT IMMIGRANTS: THE MEXICANS OF EL PASO 1880-1920; Garcia, Mario T.; Griswold del Castillo, Ricardo; *Historiography; History; *THE LOS ANGELES BARRIO 1850-1890: A SOCIAL HISTORY; *Urban Communities.

10929 Weber, David J. The new Chicano urban history. HISTORY TEACHER, Vol. 16, no. 2 (February 1983), p. 223-229. English. DESCR: Camarillo, Alberto; *CHICANOS IN A CHANGING SOCIETY; DESERT IMMIGRANTS: THE MEXICANS OF EL PASO 1880-1920; Garcia, Mario T.; Griswold del Castillo, Ricardo; *Historiography; History; *THE LOS ANGELES BARRIO 1850-1890: A SOCIAL HISTORY; Urban Communities.

Social Mobility

10930 Borjas, George J. Earnings of male Hispanic immigrants in the United States. INDUSTRIAL AND LABOR RELATIONS REVIEW, Vol. 35, no. 3 (April 1982), p. 343-353. English. DESCR: Cubanos; Ethnic Groups; *Immigrants; *Income; Puerto Ricans.

10931 Gould, Sam. Correlates of career progression among Mexican-American college graduates. JOURNAL OF VOCATIONAL BEHAVIOR, Vol. 20, no. 1 (February 1982), p. 93-110. English. DESCR: *Careers; *College Graduates; Colleges and Universities; Cultural Characteristics.

10932 Murguia, Edward and Cazares, Ralph B. Intermarriage of Mexican Americans. MARRIAGE & FAMILY REVIEW, Vol. 5, no. 1 (Spring 1982), p. 91-100. English. DESCR: Acculturation; Anglo Americans; *Intermarriage.

10933 Rivera, Julius and Goodman, Paul Wershub. Clandestine labor circulation: a case on the U.S.-Mexico border. MIGRATION TODAY, Vol. 10, no. 1 (1982), p. 21-26. English. DESCR: Border Patrol; Border Region; Ciudad Juarez, Chihuahua, Mexico; El Paso, TX; Immigration Regulation and Control; Migration Patterns; Social Classes; Socioeconomic Factors; *Undocumented Workers.

10934 Snipp, C. Matthew and Tienda, Marta. New perspectives of Chicano intergenerational occupational mobility. SOCIAL SCIENCE JOURNAL, Vol. 19, no. 2 (April 1982), p. 37-49. English. DESCR: Age Groups; Careers; *Employment.

10935 Tienda, Marta. Sex, ethnicity and Chicano status attainment. INTERNATIONAL MIGRATION REVIEW, Vol. 16, no. 2 (Summer 1982), p. 435-473. English. DESCR: Academic Achievement; Chicanas; Discrimination in Education; Discrimination in Employment; Identity; Income; Language Proficiency; Sexism; *Social Classes.

Social Organizations

USE: Cultural Organizations

Social Orientation

10936 Kagan, Spencer and Zahn, G. Lawrence. Cultural differences in individualism? Just artifact. HISPANIC JOURNAL OF BEHAVIORAL SCIENCES, Vol. 5, no. 2 (June 1983), p. 219-232. English. DESCR: Anglo Americans; Blacks; Children; Competition; *Culture.

Social Psychology

10937 Ayers-Nackamkin, Beverly, et al. Sex and ethnic differences in the use of power. JOURNAL OF APPLIED PSYCHOLOGY, Vol. 67, no. 4 (August 1982), p. 464-471. English. DESCR: Anglo Americans; Ethnic Groups; Management; *Personnel Management; Sex Roles.

10938 Bernal, Guillermo and Flores-Ortiz, Yvette. Latino families in therapy: engagement and evaluation. JOURNAL OF MARITAL AND FAMILY THERAPY, Vol. 8, no. 3 (July 1982), p. 357-365. English. DESCR: *Family; Mental Health.

10939 Borland, Dolores C. A cohort analysis approach to the empty nest syndrome among three ethnic groups of women: a theoretical position. JOURNAL OF MARRIAGE AND THE FAMILY, Vol. 44, no. 1 (February 1982), p. 117-129. English. DESCR: *Sex Roles.

10940 Castro, Agenor L. The case for the bilingual prison. CORRECTIONS TODAY, Vol. 44, no. 4 (August 1982), p. 72-78. English. DESCR: Bilingualism; *Prisons; Socialization.

10941 Garza, Raymond T., et al. Biculturalism, locus of control and leader behavior in ethnically mixed small groups. JOURNAL OF APPLIED SOCIAL PSYCHOLOGY, Vol. 12, no. 3 (May, June, 1982), p. 237-253. English. DESCR: Attitude (Psychological); *Biculturalism; Culture; Interpersonal Relations; Leadership; *Locus of Control.

10942 Guendelman, Sylvia. Developing responsiveness to health needs of Hispanic children and families. SOCIAL WORK IN HEALTH CARE, Vol. 8, no. 4 (Summer 1983), p. 1-15. English. DESCR: Children; Family; Public Health.

10943 Korte, Alvin O. Social interaction and morale of Spanish-speaking rural and urban elderly. JOURNAL OF GERONTOLOGICAL SOCIAL WORK, Vol. 4, no. 3- (Spring, Summer, 1982), p. 57-66. English. DESCR: *Ancianos; New Mexico.

10944 Mirowsky, John and Ross, Catherine E. Paranoia and the structure of powerlessness. AMERICAN SOCIOLOGICAL REVIEW, Vol. 48, no. 2 (April 1983), p. 228-239. English. DESCR: Ciudad Juarez, Chihuahua, Mexico; *El Paso, TX.

10945 Perry, Ronald W. Crisis communications: ethnic differentials in interpreting and acting on disaster warnings. SOCIAL BEHAVIOR AND PERSONALITY, Vol. 10, no. 1 (1982), p. 97-104. English. DESCR: Cultural Characteristics; *Disasters.

Social Psychology (cont.)

10946 Ramirez, Albert and Soriano, Fernando. Social power in educational systems: its effect on Chicanos' attitudes toward the school experience. JOURNAL OF SOCIAL PSYCHOLOGY, Vol. 118, no. 1 (October 1982), p. 113-119. English. DESCR: Educational Tests and Measurements; Identity; Secondary School Education.

10947 Wheaton, Blair. A comparison of the moderating effects of personal coping resources in the impact of exposure to stress in two groups. JOURNAL OF COMMUNITY PSYCHOLOGY, Vol. 10, no. 4 (October 1982), p. 293-311. English. DESCR: Anglo Americans; Comparative Psychology; Cultural Characteristics; Mental Health; *Stress.

Social Research

10948 Alba, Francisco. La fecundidad entre los Mexicano-Norteamericanos en relacion a los cambiantes patrones reproductivos en Mexico y los Estados Unidos. DEMOGRAFIA Y ECONOMIA, Vol. 16, no. 2 (1982), p. 236-249. Spanish. DESCR: Demography; *Fertility; *Mexico; Population Trends.

10949 Baca Zinn, Maxine. Chicano family research: conceptual distortions and alternative directions. JOURNAL OF ETHNIC STUDIES, Vol. 7, no. 3 (Fall 1979), p. 59-71. English. DESCR: Cultural Characteristics; Culture; *Family; Research Methodology; Stereotypes.

10950 Baca Zinn, Maxine, ed. Social research on Chicanos: its development and directions: symposium. SOCIAL SCIENCE JOURNAL, Vol. 19, no. 2 (April 1982), p. 1-132. English. DESCR: Social Science.

10951 Garcia, Juan R. Midwest Mexicanos in the 1920's: issues, questions, and directions. SOCIAL SCIENCE JOURNAL, Vol. 19, no. 2 (April 1982), p. 89-99. English. DESCR: Identity; Midwestern States; *Social History and Conditions.

10952 Perez, Lisandro. Comment: Cubans and Mexicans in the United States. CUBAN STUDIES, Vol. 11, no. 2-1 (1981, 1982), p. 99-103. English. DESCR: Cubanos; *Migration.

Social Science

10953 Baca Zinn, Maxine. Book review of: LA CHICANA: THE MEXICAN AMERICAN WOMAN. SIGNS: JOURNAL OF WOMEN IN CULTURE AND SOCIETY, Vol. 8, no. 2 (Winter 1982), p. 259-272. English. DESCR: Book Reviews; Chicanas; Enriquez, Evangelina; *LA CHICANA: THE MEXICAN AMERICAN WOMAN; Literature Reviews; Mirande, Alfredo.

10954 Baca Zinn, Maxine. Book review of: MEXICAN WOMEN IN THE UNITED STATES: STRUGGLES PAST AND PRESENT. SIGNS: JOURNAL OF WOMEN IN CULTURE AND SOCIETY, Vol. 8, no. 2 (Winter 1982), p. 259-272. English. DESCR: Book Reviews; Chicanas; Del Castillo, Adelaida R.; Literature Reviews; *MEXICAN WOMEN IN THE UNITED STATES: STRUGGLES PAST AND PRESENT; Mora, Magdalena.

10955 Baca Zinn, Maxine. Book review of: TWICE A MINORITY; MEXICAN-AMERICAN WOMEN. SIGNS: JOURNAL OF WOMEN IN CULTURE AND SOCIETY, Vol. 8, no. 2 (Winter 1982), p. 259-272. English. DESCR: Book Reviews; Chicanas; Literature Reviews; Melville, Margarita B.; *TWICE A MINORITY: MEXICAN-AMERICAN WOMEN.

10956 Baca Zinn, Maxine. Mexican American women in the social sciences. SIGNS: JOURNAL OF WOMEN IN CULTURE AND SOCIETY, Vol. 8, no. 2 (Winter 1982), p. 259-272. English. DESCR: *Chicanas; *Literature Reviews.

10957 Baca Zinn, Maxine, ed. Social research on Chicanos: its development and directions: symposium. SOCIAL SCIENCE JOURNAL, Vol. 19, no. 2 (April 1982), p. 1-132. English. DESCR: *Social Research.

Social Science Research
USE: Social Research

Social Security Administration

10958 Achievements of social security worker noted. NUESTRO, Vol. 6, no. 10 (December 1982), p. 31. English. DESCR: *Handicapped.

Social Services

10959 Baca-Ramirez, Reynaldo and Bryan, Dexter Edward. The undocumented Mexican worker: a social problem? JOURNAL OF ETHNIC STUDIES, Vol. 8, no. 1 (Spring 1980), p. 55-69. English. DESCR: Government Services; Immigrant Labor; Immigration; Immigration Regulation and Control; Mexico; Social History and Conditions; *Undocumented Workers.

10960 Carlos, Manuel L. Chicano households, the structure of parental information networks, and family use of child-related social services. BORDERLANDS JOURNAL, Vol. 6, no. 1 (Fall 1982), p. 49-68. English. DESCR: Family.

10961 Chavez, Leo R. Undocumented immigrants and access to health services: a game of pass the buck. MIGRATION TODAY, Vol. 11, no. 1 (1983), p. 14-19. English. DESCR: California; *Immigrants; Medical Care; Migrant Health Services; Public Health Legislation; Simpson-Mazzoli Bill; Undocumented Workers.

10962 Lasater, Tonia Tash and Montalvo, Frank F. Understanding Mexican American culture: a training program. CHILDREN TODAY, Vol. 11, no. 3 (May, June, 1982), p. 23-25+. English. DESCR: Cultural Characteristics; *Cultural Customs; Employment Training; Mexican American Culture Simulator.

10963 LeVine, Elaine S. and Franco, Juan N. Effects of therapist's gender, ethnicity, and verbal style on client's willingness to seek therapy. JOURNAL OF SOCIAL PSYCHOLOGY, Vol. 12, no. 1 (October 1983), p. 51-57. English. DESCR: *Counseling Services (Educational); Jourard's (3) Self-Disclosure Questionnaire; Mental Health; Psychotherapy.

10964 The new federalism. NUESTRO, Vol. 6, no. 2 (March 1982), p. 10. English. DESCR: *Federal Aid; *Government; *Government Services.

10965 Salcido, Ramon M. The undocumented alien family. DE COLORES, Vol. 6, no. 1-2 (1982), p. 109-119. English. DESCR: East Los Angeles, CA; Family; Green Carders; *Undocumented Workers.

10966 Stehno, S. M. Differential treatment of minority children in service systems. SOCIAL WORK, Vol. 27, (January 1982), p. 39-45. English. DESCR: *Ethnic Groups; Racism; Youth.

Social Services (cont.)

10967 Watkins, Ted R. and Gonzalez, Richard. Outreach to Mexican-Americans. SOCIAL WORK, Vol. 27, no. 1 (January 1982), p. 68-73. English. **DESCR**: *Counseling Services (Educational); Cultural Organizations.

10968 Watts, Thomas D. Social policy and the aged: transcultural perspectives. HUMAN SERVICES IN THE RURAL ENVIRONMENT, Vol. 7, no. 1 (Winter 1982), p. 32-34. English. **DESCR**: *Ancianos.

10969 Whittaker, Michael. New career opportunity in social services agencies. NUESTRO, Vol. 6, no. 3 (April 1982), p. 28-30. English. **DESCR**: Pan American University, Edinburg, TX.

Social Stratification
USE: Social Classes

Social Studies
USE: Social Science

Social Theory

10970 Morrissey, Marietta. Ethnic stratification and the study of Chicanos. JOURNAL OF ETHNIC STUDIES, Vol. 10, no. 4 (Winter 1983), p. 71-99. English. **DESCR**: Assimilation; *Ethnic Stratification; Internal Colonial Model (Theoretical); Marxism; Paradigm (Theoretical).

Social Work

10971 Delgado, Melvin and Humm-Delgado, Denise. Natural support systems: source of strength in Hispanic communities. SOCIAL WORK, Vol. 27, no. 1 (January 1982), p. 83-89. English. **DESCR**: Cultural Characteristics; Cultural Organizations.

10972 Lum, Doman. Toward a framework for social work practice with minorities. SOCIAL WORK, Vol. 27, no. 3 (May 1982), p. 244-249. English. **DESCR**: Ethnic Groups.

10973 Montalvo, Frank F.; Lasater, Tonia Tash; and Valdez, Nancy Garza. Training child welfare workers for cultural awareness: the culture simulator technique. CHILD WELFARE, Vol. 61, no. 6 (June 1982), p. 341-352. English. **DESCR**: *Child Study; Cultural Pluralism.

Socialization

10974 Castro, Agenor L. The case for the bilingual prison. CORRECTIONS TODAY, Vol. 44, no. 4 (August 1982), p. 72-78. English. **DESCR**: Bilingualism; *Prisons; Social Psychology.

10975 Cortese, Anthony. Moral development in Chicano and Anglo children. HISPANIC JOURNAL OF BEHAVIORAL SCIENCES, Vol. 4, no. 3 (September 1982), p. 353-366. English. **DESCR**: Attitude (Psychological); *Ethics; *Psychology.

10976 Henderson, Ronald W. and Brody, Gene H. Effects of ethnicity and child's age on maternal judgments of children's transgressions against persons and property. JOURNAL OF GENETIC PSYCHOLOGY, Vol. 140, no. 2 (June 1982), p. 253-263. English. **DESCR**: Anglo Americans; Arizona; Behavior Modification; *Child Rearing; Cultural Characteristics; Native Americans; Tucson, AZ.

10977 Hernandez, Leodoro. The socialization of a Chicano family. DE COLORES, Vol. 6, no. 1-2 (1982), p. 75-84. English. **DESCR**: Acculturation; Family.

10978 Hunsaker, Alan. A prompt/reward technique to elicit socially acceptable behavior with Chicano gang delinquents. HISPANIC JOURNAL OF BEHAVIORAL SCIENCES, Vol. 5, no. 1 (March 1983), p. 105-113. English. **DESCR**: Behavior Modification; *Gangs; Juvenile Delinquency.

10979 Kagan, Spencer and Knudsen, Kathryn H.M. Relationship of empathy and affective role-taking in young children. JOURNAL OF GENETIC PSYCHOLOGY, Vol. 141, (September 1982), p. 149-150. English. **DESCR**: Anglo Americans; *Attitude (Psychological); Child Study; Psychological Testing.

10980 Knight, George P.; Kagan, Spencer; and Buriel, Raymond. Perceived parental practices and prosocial development. JOURNAL OF GENETIC PSYCHOLOGY, Vol. 141, (September 1982), p. 57-65. English. **DESCR**: Anglo Americans; Cultural Characteristics; *Parent and Child Relationships; Socioeconomic Factors.

10981 Knight, George P. and Kagan, Spencer. Sibling, birth order, and cooperative-competitive social behavior: a comparison of Anglo-American and Mexican-American children. JOURNAL OF CROSS-CULTURAL PSYCHOLOGY, Vol. 13, no. 2 (June 1982), p. 239-249. English. **DESCR**: Anglo Americans; Children; *Competition; Social Behavior Scale.

10982 Knight, George P., et al. Cooperative-competitive social orientation and school achievement among Anglo-American and Mexican-American children. CONTEMPORARY EDUCATIONAL PSYCHOLOGY, Vol. 7, no. 2 (April 1982), p. 97-106. English. **DESCR**: *Academic Achievement; Anglo Americans; Cultural Characteristics; Students.

10983 Knudsen, Kathryn H.M. and Kagan, Spencer. Differential development of empathy and pro-social behavior. JOURNAL OF GENETIC PSYCHOLOGY, Vol. 140, no. 2 (June 1982), p. 249-251. English. **DESCR**: Anglo Americans; *Attitude (Psychological); Child Study; Psychological Testing.

10984 Maestas, Leo C. Academic performance across cultures: an examination of the effect of value similarity. EDUCATIONAL RESEARCH QUARTERLY, Vol. 7, no. 4 (Winter 1983), p. 24-34. English. **DESCR**: *Academic Achievement; Cultural Customs; Ethnic Groups; Teacher-pupil Interaction.

10985 McMillen, Jay B. The social organization of leisure among Mexican-Americans. JOURNAL OF LEISURE RESEARCH, Vol. 15, no. 2 (1983), p. 164-173. English. **DESCR**: Cultural Characteristics; Leisure.

10986 Steigelfest, Annette. Ethnicity and sex role socialization. BILINGUAL JOURNAL, Vol. 6, no. 3 (Spring 1982), p. 11-15,24. English. **DESCR**: Ethnic Attitudes; Halacha Institute; *Identity; Orthodox Jews; *Sex Roles; Sex Stereotypes.

Society for Hispanic Professional Engineers (SHPE)

10987 Community watching: para la comunidad.
CAMINOS, Vol. 3, no. 3 (March 1982), p.
58-59. Bilingual. DESCR: Cultural
Organizations; *Engineering as a Profession;
Financial Aid; Harvard University; Latino
Business Students Association (LBSA);
Rodolfo H. Castro Fellowship; Student
Organizations; University of Southern
California.

10988 Math-based careers. HISPANIC BUSINESS, Vol.
4, no. 5 (May 1982), p. 22. English. DESCR:
Careers; Education; Engineering as a
Profession; *Financial Aid; National Action
Council for Minorities in Engineering
(NACME).

Socioeconomic Factors

10989 Andreasen, Alan R. Disadvantaged Hispanic
consumers: a research perspective and
agenda. JOURNAL OF CONSUMER AFFAIRS, Vol.
16, no. 1 (Summer 1982), p. 46-61. English.
DESCR: *Consumers; Marketing.

10990 Baca Zinn, Maxine. Chicano men and
masculinity. JOURNAL OF ETHNIC STUDIES, Vol.
10, no. 2 (Summer 1982), p. 29-44. English.
DESCR: Cultural Characteristics; Ethnic
Stratification; *Machismo; Sex Roles; Sex
Stereotypes; Women Men Relations.

10991 Burns, Maureen. Current status of Hispanic
technical professionals: how can we improve
recruitment and retention. INTEGRATED
EDUCATION, Vol. 20, (January, April, 1982),
p. 49-55. English. DESCR: Academic
Achievement; Academic Motivation; Counseling
Services (Educational); *Technical
Education.

10992 Carrison, Muriel Paskin. Bilingual-no!
PRINCIPAL, Vol. 62, no. 3 (January 1983), p.
9. English. DESCR: *Bilingual Bicultural
Education; Cultural Characteristics;
Education Equalization.

10993 Chaikin, Sol C. and Comstock, Phil. Toward a
rational immigration policy. JOURNAL OF THE
INSTITUTE FOR SOCIOECONOMIC STUDIES, Vol. 7,
no. 1 (Spring 1982), p. 48-61. English.
DESCR: Immigration Law; Immigration
Regulation and Control; *Undocumented
Workers.

10994 Chall, Jeanne. Rich and sharp memories of
reading. CHANGE, Vol. 14, no. 7 (October
1982), p. 36-40. English. DESCR:
Assimilation; Book Reviews; *HUNGER OF
MEMORY: THE EDUCATION OF RICHARD RODRIGUEZ;
Language Arts; Reading; Rodriguez, Richard.

10995 Chavez, Mauro. Book review of: ESSAYS ON LA
MUJER. JOURNAL OF ETHNIC STUDIES, Vol. 8,
no. 2 (Summer 1980), p. 117-120. English.
DESCR: Book Reviews; *Chicanas; Cruz, Rosa
Martinez; Economic History and Conditions;
*ESSAYS ON LA MUJER; Sanchez, Rosaura;
Social History and Conditions; Women's
Rights.

10996 Dowdall, George W. and Flood, Lawrence G.
Correlates and consequences of socioeconomic
differences among Chicanos, Blacks and
Anglos in the Southwest: a study of
metropolitan structure. SOCIAL SCIENCE
JOURNAL, Vol. 19, no. 2 (April 1982), p.
25-36. English. DESCR: Anglo Americans;
Blacks; *Ethnic Groups; *Research
Methodology; Residential Segregation;
Southwest United States.

10997 Eberstein, Isaac W. and Pol, Louis G.
Mexican-American ethnicity, socioeconomic
status, and infant mortality: a county level
analysis. SOCIAL SCIENCE JOURNAL, Vol. 19,
no. 2 (April 1982), p. 61-71. English.
DESCR: Identity; *Infant Mortality;
Southwest United States.

10998 Frazier, Donald J. and De Blassie, Richard
R. Comparison of self-concept in Mexican
American and non-Mexican American late
adolescents. ADOLESCENCE, Vol. 17, no. 66
(Summer 1982), p. 327-334. English. DESCR:
Academic Achievement; *Identity; Students;
Youth.

10999 Gaviria, Moises; Stern, Gwen; and Schensul,
Stephen L. Sociocultural factors and
perinatal health in a Mexican-American
community. NATIONAL MEDICAL ASSOCIATION
JOURNAL, Vol. 74, no. 10 (October 1982), p.
983-989. English. DESCR: Chicago, IL;
Migration Patterns; *Prenatal Care; Public
Health.

11000 Gibbs, Jewelle Taylor. Personality patterns
of delinquent females: ethnic and
sociocultural variations. JOURNAL OF
CLINICAL PSYCHOLOGY, Vol. 38, no. 1 (January
1982), p. 198-206. English. DESCR: Chicanas;
Ethnic Groups; Identity; *Juvenile
Delinquency; Personality; Psychological
Testing.

11001 Hazuda, Helen P. Ethnic differences in
health knowledge and behaviors related to
the prevention and treatment of coronary
heart disease. The San Antonio heart study.
AMERICAN JOURNAL OF EPIDEMIOLOGY, Vol. 11,
no. 6 (June 1983), p. 717-728. English.
DESCR: Anglo Americans; *Coronary Heart
Disease; Health Education; Preventative
Medicine; San Antonio, TX.

11002 Jaech, Richard E. Latin American
undocumented women in the United States.
CURRENTS IN THEOLOGY AND MISSION, Vol. 9,
no. 4 (August 1982), p. 196-211. English.
DESCR: Garment Industry; Latin Americans;
Protestant Church; *Undocumented Workers;
*Women.

11003 Jimenez, Ricardo. Understanding the culture
and learning styles of Hispanic students.
MOMENTUM, Vol. 14, no. 1 (February 1983), p.
15-18. English. DESCR: *Cultural
Characteristics; Learning and Cognition.

11004 Knight, George P.; Kagan, Spencer; and
Buriel, Raymond. Perceived parental
practices and prosocial development. JOURNAL
OF GENETIC PSYCHOLOGY, Vol. 141, (September
1982), p. 57-65. English. DESCR: Anglo
Americans; Cultural Characteristics; *Parent
and Child Relationships; *Socialization.

11005 Low, Benson P. and Clement, Paul W.
Relationships of race and socioeconomic
status to classroom behavior, academic
achievement, and referral for special
education. JOURNAL OF SCHOOL PSYCHOLOGY,
Vol. 20, no. 2 (Summer 1982), p. 103-112.
English. DESCR: *Academic Achievement; Anglo
Americans; Blacks; Identity.

11006 Lujan, Sylvia and Zapata, Jesse T.
Personality differences among
Mexican-American college freshmen. JOURNAL
OF COLLEGE STUDENT PERSONNEL, Vol. 24, no. 2
(March 1983), p. 105-111. English. DESCR:
Colleges and Universities; *Personality;
*Students.

Socioeconomic Factors (cont.)

11007 Massey, Douglas S. and Schnabel, Kathleen M. Background and characteristics of undocumented Hispanic migrants to the United States: a review of recent research. MIGRATION TODAY, Vol. 11, no. 1 (1983), p. 6-13. English. DESCR: Immigrants; Migration; Migration Patterns; *Undocumented Workers.

11008 Massey, Douglas S. and Schnabel, Kathleen M. Recent trends in Hispanic immigration to the United States. INTERNATIONAL MIGRATION REVIEW, Vol. 17, no. 2 (Summer 1983), p. 212-244. English. DESCR: *Immigration; Migration Patterns; Population Trends; Rural Urban Migration.

11009 Meredith, Howard V. Compilation and comparison of averages for standing height at late childhood ages on United States boys of several ethnic groups studied between 1875 and 1980. AMERICAN JOURNAL OF PHYSICAL ANTHROPOLOGY, Vol. 61, no. 1 (May 1983), p. 111-124. English. DESCR: *Anthropometry; Ethnic Groups.

11010 Newman, Allen R. The impacts of emigration on the Mexican economy. MIGRATION TODAY, Vol. 10, no. 2 (1982), p. 17-21. English. DESCR: Economic History and Conditions; Employment; *Mexican Economy; *Migration; Undocumented Workers.

11011 O'Donnell, James P., et al. Dimensions of behavior problems in Anglo-American and Mexican-American preschool children: a comparative study. JOURNAL OF CONSULTING AND CLINICAL PSYCHOLOGY, Vol. 50, no. 5 (October 1982), p. 643-651. English. DESCR: Anglo Americans; Children; *Comparative Psychology; Cultural Characteristics; Mental Health; Psychological Testing.

11012 Panitz, Daniel R., et al. The role of machismo and the Hispanic family in the etiology and treatment of alcoholism in the Hispanic American males. AMERICAN JOURNAL OF FAMILY THERAPY, Vol. 11, no. 1 (Spring 1983), p. 31-44. English. DESCR: *Alcoholism; Children; Family; *Machismo; Puerto Rico.

11013 Rivera, Julius and Goodman, Paul Wershub. Clandestine labor circulation: a case on the U.S.-Mexico border. MIGRATION TODAY, Vol. 10, no. 1 (1982), p. 21-26. English. DESCR: Border Patrol; Border Region; Ciudad Juarez, Chihuahua, Mexico; El Paso, TX; Immigration Regulation and Control; Migration Patterns; Social Classes; Social Mobility; *Undocumented Workers.

11014 Valencia, Richard R. Stability of the McCarthy scales of children's abilities over a one-year period for Mexican-American children. PSYCHOLOGY IN THE SCHOOLS, Vol. 20, no. 1 (January 1983), p. 29-34. English. DESCR: Child Study; Cultural Characteristics; *Intelligence Tests; McCarthy Scales for Children's Abilities (MSCA).

11015 Vasquez, Melba J. T. Confronting barriers to the participation of Mexican American women in higher education. HISPANIC JOURNAL OF BEHAVIORAL SCIENCES, Vol. 4, no. 2 (June 1982), p. 147-165. English. DESCR: Academic Motivation; *Chicanas; Higher Education; Sex Roles.

11016 Vigil, James Diego. Chicano high schoolers: educational performance and acculturation. EDUCATIONAL FORUM, Vol. 47, no. 1 (Fall 1982), p. 58-73. English. DESCR: *Academic Achievement; *Acculturation; Identity; Secondary School Education.

11017 Yamamoto, Joe and Acosta, Frank X. Treatments of Asian Americans and Hispanic Americans: similarities and differences. JOURNAL OF THE AMERICAN ACADEMY OF PSYCHOANALYSIS, Vol. 10, no. 4 (October 1982), p. 585-607. English. DESCR: Asian Americans; Comparative Psychology; Los Angeles, CA; *Mental Health; Psychotherapy.

11018 Zavaleta, Anthony N. and Malina, Robert M. Growth and body composition of Mexican-American boys 9 through 14 years of age. AMERICAN JOURNAL OF PHYSICAL ANTHROPOLOGY, Vol. 57, no. 3 (March 1982), p. 261-271. English. DESCR: Age Groups; Anglo Americans; *Anthropometry; Children.

Sociolinguistics

11019 Argulewicz, Ed N. and Sanchez, David T. Considerations in the assessment of reading difficulties in bilingual children. SCHOOL PSYCHOLOGY REVIEW, Vol. 11, no. 3 (Summer 1982), p. 281-289. English. DESCR: Bilingualism; Children; *Language Assessment; Reading.

11020 Carrillo, Federico M. How should Spanish speakers be taught Spanish in the schools? BILINGUAL JOURNAL, Vol. 7, no. 4 (Summer 1983), p. 18-22. English. DESCR: *Bilingual Bicultural Education; *Language Arts; Spanish Language.

11021 Elsenberg, Ann R. Book review of: LATINO LANGUAGE AND COMMUNICATIVE BEHAVIOR. HISPANIC JOURNAL OF BEHAVIORAL SCIENCES, Vol. 5, no. 3 (September 1983), p. 347-349. English. DESCR: Book Reviews; Duran, Richard P.; Languages; *LATINO LANGUAGE AND COMMUNICATIVE BEHAVIOR.

11022 Fishman, Joshua A. Sociolinguistic foundations of bilingual education. BILINGUAL REVIEW, Vol. 9, no. 1 (January, April, 1982), p. 1-35. English. DESCR: *Bilingual Bicultural Education.

11023 Gumperz, John J. Interethnic discourse. SOCIETY, Vol. 20, no. 4 (May, June, 1983), p. 64-69. English. DESCR: Language Usage.

11024 McDowell, John H. Sociolinguistic contours in the verbal art of Chicano children. AZTLAN, Vol. 13, no. 1-2 (Spring, Fall, 1982), p. 166-193. English. DESCR: Bilingualism; Children; Linguistics.

11025 Politzer, Robert L.; Shohamy, Elana; and McGroarty, Mary. Validation of linguistic and communicative oral language tests for Spanish-English bilingual programs. BILINGUAL REVIEW, Vol. 10, no. 1 (January, April, 1983), p. 3-20. English. DESCR: Bahia Oral Language Test (BOLT); Bay Area, CA; *Bilingual Bicultural Education; Bilingual Programs; *Language Assessment; Linguistics.

11026 Valdes, Guadalupe. Language attitudes and their reflection in Chicano theatre: an exploratory study. NEW SCHOLAR, Vol. 8, no. 1-2 (Spring, Fall, 1982), p. 181-200. English. DESCR: *Teatro.

Sociolinguistics (cont.)

11027 Walia, Adorna. Book review of: WOMEN AND MEN SPEAKING: FRAMEWORK FOR ANALYSIS. BILINGUAL JOURNAL, Vol. 6, no. 3 (Spring 1982), p. 20-22. English. DESCR: Book Reviews; Kramarae, Cheris; Language Usage; Sex Stereotypes; Sexism; *WOMEN AND MEN SPEAKING: FRAMEWORK FOR ANALYSIS.

SOCIOLOGICAL THEORY IN EMERGENT CHICANO PERSPECTIVES

11028 Mirande, Alfredo. Sociology of Chicanos or Chicano sociology: a critical assessment of emergent paradigms. PACIFIC SOCIOLOGICAL REVIEW, Vol. 25, no. 4 (October 1982), p. 495-508. English. DESCR: Baca Zinn, Maxine; Internal Colonial Model (Theoretical); *Paradigm (Theoretical); *Sociology.

Sociology

11029 Gottlieb, Karen. Genetic demography of Denver, Colorado: Spanish surname as a market of Mexican ancestry. HUMAN BIOLOGY, Vol. 55, no. 2 (May 1983), p. 227-234. English. DESCR: Demography; Denver, CO; Personal Names; *Population Genetics; Research Methodology.

11030 Mirande, Alfredo. Sociology of Chicanos or Chicano sociology: a critical assessment of emergent paradigms. PACIFIC SOCIOLOGICAL REVIEW, Vol. 25, no. 4 (October 1982), p. 495-508. English. DESCR: Baca Zinn, Maxine; Internal Colonial Model (Theoretical); *Paradigm (Theoretical); SOCIOLOGICAL THEORY IN EMERGENT CHICANO PERSPECTIVES.

11031 Shellenberger, Sylvia. Assessment of Puerto Rican children: a cross-culture study with the Spanish McCarthy scales of children's abilities. BILINGUAL REVIEW, Vol. 9, no. 2 (May, August, 1982), p. 109-119. English. DESCR: *Intelligence Tests; Spanish Language.

Softball

11032 Cantu, Hector. Softball Texas style. NATIONAL HISPANIC JOURNAL, Vol. 1, no. 3 (Summer, Fall, 1982), p. 9-11. English. DESCR: El Paso Jesters; Mexico City All Stars; Pan American Softball League; Recreation; Sports.

EL SOL DE HOUSTON (TX)

11033 Cantu, Hector. Aqui en Tejas: Hispanic newspapers: city, community papers taking a business approach to the news. NATIONAL HISPANIC JOURNAL, Vol. 2, no. 1 (Summer 1983), p. 9. English. DESCR: AUSTIN LIGHT (TX); EL EDITOR (Lubbock, TX); Journalism; *Newspapers; THE TEXICAN (Dallas, TX).

EL SOL Y LOS DE ABAJO

11034 Orozco, Febe Portillo. A bibliography of Hispanic literature. ENGLISH JOURNAL, Vol. 71, no. 7 (November 1982), p. 58-62. English. DESCR: BARRIO BOY; *Bibliography; BLESS ME, ULTIMA; CHICANO; GRITO DEL SOL; HEART OF AZTLAN; *Literature; POCHO; WE ARE CHICANOS.

Solano, Faustina V.

11035 People. HISPANIC BUSINESS, Vol. 4, no. 11 (November 1982), p. 7. English. DESCR: Biographical Notes; *Businesspeople; Diaz, Jose; Garcia-Pedrosa, Jose R.; Garza, Jose; Herrera, Heriberto; Mercado, Anthony; Rios, John F.; Solis, Frank.

Solis, Frank

11036 People. HISPANIC BUSINESS, Vol. 4, no. 11 (November 1982), p. 7. English. DESCR: Biographical Notes; *Businesspeople; Diaz, Jose; Garcia-Pedrosa, Jose R.; Garza, Jose; Herrera, Heriberto; Mercado, Anthony; Rios, John F.; Solano, Faustina V.

Sommers, Joseph

11037 Elizondo, Sergio D. Book review of: LITERATURA CHICANA: TEXTO Y CONTEXTO. JOURNAL OF ETHNIC STUDIES, Vol. 1, no. 1 (Spring 1973), p. 68-70. Bilingual. DESCR: Book Reviews; Castaneda Shular, Antonia; Literary Criticism; Literary History; Literary Influence; *LITERATURA CHICANA: TEXTO Y CONTEXTO; Literature; Teatro; Ybarra-Frausto, Tomas.

Somolinos D'Ardois, German

11038 Risse, Gunter B. Book review of: CAPITULOS DE HISTORIA MEDICA MEXICANA. BULLETIN OF THE HISTORY OF MEDICINE, Vol. 56, no. 4 (1982), p. 591-592. English. DESCR: *CAPITULOS DE HISTORIA MEDICA MEXICANA; Folk Medicine; Medicine; Mexico; Precolumbian Medicine.

Son Jarocho

11039 Loza, Steven J. Origins, form, and development of the Son Jarocho: Veracruz, Mexico. AZTLAN, Vol. 13, no. 1-2 (Spring, Fall, 1982), p. 257-274. English. DESCR: Dance; Folk Songs; Music; Veracruz, Mexico.

11040 Loza, Steven J. The Son Jarocho: the history, style and repertory of a changing Mexican musical tradition. AZTLAN, Vol. 13, no. 1-2 (Spring, Fall, 1982), p. 327-334. English. DESCR: Dance; Folk Songs; Music; Sheehy, Daniel E.; Veracruz, Mexico.

"Song for the pockets"

11041 de la Fuente, Patricia. Ambiguity in the poetry of Gary Soto. REVISTA CHICANO-RIQUENA, Vol. 11, no. 2 (Summer 1983), p. 34-39. English. DESCR: "Avocado Lake"; "Blanco"; "Braley Street"; "Field"; *Literary Criticism; Poetry; *Soto, Gary; TALE OF SUNLIGHT; "Telephoning God"; THE ELEMENTS OF SAN JOAQUIN; "Wind".

Soriano, Esteban

11042 Math-based careers. HISPANIC BUSINESS, Vol. 5, no. 11 (November 1983), p. 32. English. DESCR: *Careers; Education; Employment Training; INROADS; Mathematics, Engineering and Science Achievement (MESA); Mexican American Legal Defense and Educational Fund (MALDEF).

Sosa de Garcia, Manuel

11043 Communications/marketing. HISPANIC BUSINESS, Vol. 4, no. 7 (July 1982), p. 16. English. DESCR: Awards; *Biographical Notes; Buena Vista Cablevision, Inc.; Demy, Caroline; *Marketing.

Sotelo, Isela

11044 Isela Sotelo. LATINA, Vol. 1, no. 1 (1982), p. 15. English. DESCR: *Biography.

Sotelo, Priscilla Elvira

11045 Baltodano, J. C. Success. CAMINOS, Vol. 4, no. 6 (June 1983), p. 32,34+. English. **DESCR**: Colleges and Universities; Gallegos, Genevie; Gutierrez, Jorge; *Students; Torres, Juan; University of California, Berkeley.

Soto, Gary

11046 de la Fuente, Patricia. Ambiguity in the poetry of Gary Soto. REVISTA CHICANO-RIQUENA, Vol. 11, no. 2 (Summer 1983), p. 34-39. English. **DESCR**: "Avocado Lake"; "Blanco"; "Braley Street"; "Field"; *Literary Criticism; Poetry; "Song for the pockets"; TALE OF SUNLIGHT; "Telephoning God"; THE ELEMENTS OF SAN JOAQUIN; "Wind".

11047 Paredes, Raymund A. Book review of: THE ELEMENTS OF SAN JOAQUIN. MINORITY VOICES, Vol. 1, no. 2 (Fall 1977), p. 106-108. English. **DESCR**: Book Reviews; Poetry; *THE ELEMENTS OF SAN JOAQUIN.

11048 Paredes, Raymund A. Book review of: THE TALE OF SUNLIGHT. MINORITY VOICES, Vol. 2, no. 2 (Fall 1978), p. 67-68. English. **DESCR**: Book Reviews; Poetry; *TALE OF SUNLIGHT.

11049 Soto, Gary; Trejo, Ernesto; and de la Fuente, Patricia. Special focus on Gary Soto. REVISTA CHICANO-RIQUENA, Vol. 11, no. 2 (Summer 1983), p. 7-39. English. **DESCR**: Literary Criticism; *Poetry; Prose.

11050 Trejo, Ernesto and Soto, Gary. An interview with Gary Soto. REVISTA CHICANO-RIQUENA, Vol. 11, no. 2 (Summer 1983), p. 25-33. English. **DESCR**: Authors.

Soto, John

11051 Balkan, D. Carlos and Cruz, Franklin D. Space-Craft's strategy for re-industrialization. HISPANIC BUSINESS, Vol. 4, no. 11 (November 1982), p. 16-17,26. English. **DESCR**: Business Enterprises; Connecticut; *High Technology Industries; Space-Craft Manufacturing, Inc.

11052 Padilla, Steve. Choosing a career. NUESTRO, Vol. 7, no. 1 (January, February, 1983), p. 13-19+. English. **DESCR**: Alvarado, Raul, Jr.; *Careers; Computers; Diaz, William; Engineering as a Profession; Esparza, Alma; Flores, Francisco; Garcia, Linda; Medical Care; Yanez, Ricardo.

Soto, Pedro Juan

11053 Seda-Bonilla, Eduardo. On the vicissitudes of being "Puerto Rican": an exploration of Pedro Juan Soto's "Hot land, cold season". MELUS: MULTI-ETHNIC LITERATURE OF THE UNITED STATES, Vol. 6, no. 3 (Fall 1979), p. 27-40. English. **DESCR**: *HOT LAND, COLD SEASON; Puerto Ricans.

South America

11054 Breiter, Toni. El Libertador: a profile. NUESTRO, Vol. 7, no. 7 (September 1983), p. 32-35. English. **DESCR**: Biography; *Bolivar, Simon; Political History and Conditions; Revolutions.

11055 Palacios, Gonzalo. Bolivar and contemporary Latin America. NUESTRO, Vol. 7, no. 7 (September 1983), p. 36-37. English. **DESCR**: *Bolivar, Simon; Latin America; Political History and Conditions; Political Ideology.

11056 Valdez, Abelardo L. From Simon Bolivar to the Malvinas and beyond. NUESTRO, Vol. 7, no. 7 (September 1983), p. 38-41. English. **DESCR**: *Bolivar, Simon; Latin America; Political Economy; *Political History and Conditions.

South Bronx Project, New York Public Library

11057 Naismith, Rachael. Outreach services to Hispanics. ILLINOIS LIBRARIES, Vol. 64, no. 7 (September 1982), p. 962-966. English. **DESCR**: Arrondo, Ondina; Cubanos; La Raza Hispanica, Miami, FL; Latin American Library/Biblioteca Latinoamericana, Oakland, CA; *Library Services; Lopez, Lillian; Puerto Ricans; Ruiz, Deborah; Verges, Bruni.

South Chicago, Chicago, IL

11058 Ano Nuevo de Kerr, Louise. Chicano settlements in Chicago: a brief history. JOURNAL OF ETHNIC STUDIES, Vol. 2, no. 4 (Winter 1975), p. 22-32. English. **DESCR**: Back of the Yards, Chicago, IL; *Chicago, IL; Near West Side, Chicago, IL; Pilsen, IL; Social History and Conditions; *Urban Communities.

South Texas

11059 Miller, Michael V. Chicano community control in South Texas: problems and prospects. JOURNAL OF ETHNIC STUDIES, Vol. 3, no. 3 (Fall 1975), p. 70-89. English. **DESCR**: Chicano Movement; Crystal City, TX; Gutierrez, Jose Angel; History; La Raza Unida Party; Patron System; *Political Parties and Organizations; Social Classes; Social History and Conditions.

11060 Whiteford, Linda. Migrants no longer: changing family structure of Mexican Americans in South Texas. DE COLORES, Vol. 6, no. 1-2 (1982), p. 99-108. English. **DESCR**: Chicanas; *Family; Sex Roles.

Southern Baptists

11061 Grijalva, Joshua. The story of Hispanic Southern Baptists. BAPTIST HISTORY AND HERITAGE, Vol. 18, no. 3 (July 1983), p. 40-47. English. **DESCR**: *Baptists; History; Puerto Ricans; Religion.

Southern California

11062 Casey, G.M. Marketing to Mexican-Americans: just a bit of insight. ADVERTISING AGE MAGAZINE, Vol. 53, no. 11 (March 15, 1982), p. II, M34-35. English. **DESCR**: Food Industry; *Market Research.

THE SOUTHWEST: A SELF-PORTRAIT

11063 Vincent, J. Book review of: HISPANIC FOLK MUSIC OF NEW MEXICO AND THE SOUTHWEST: A SELF-PORTRAIT OF A PEOPLE. ETHNOMUSICOLOGY, Vol. 26, no. 2 (May 1982), p. 326-327. English. **DESCR**: Book Reviews; Ethnomusicology; Folk Songs; *HISPANIC FOLK MUSIC OF NEW MEXICO AND THE SOUTHWEST: A SELF-PORTRAIT OF A PEOPLE; New Mexico; Robb, John Donald.

Southwest United States

11064 Chavez, John A. Aztlan, Cibola, and frontier New Spain. CAMPO LIBRE, Vol. 1, no. 2 (Summer 1981), p. 193-211. English. DESCR: *Aztlan; *Explorations; Folklore; History; Mestizaje; Mexico; Missions; Native Americans.

11065 Dowdall, George W. and Flood, Lawrence G. Correlates and consequences of socioeconomic differences among Chicanos, Blacks and Anglos in the Southwest: a study of metropolitan structure. SOCIAL SCIENCE JOURNAL, Vol. 19, no. 2 (April 1982), p. 25-36. English. DESCR: Anglo Americans; Blacks; *Ethnic Groups; *Research Methodology; Residential Segregation; Socioeconomic Factors.

11066 Eberstein, Isaac W. and Pol, Louis G. Mexican-American ethnicity, socioeconomic status, and infant mortality: a county level analysis. SOCIAL SCIENCE JOURNAL, Vol. 19, no. 2 (April 1982), p. 61-71. English. DESCR: Identity; *Infant Mortality; Socioeconomic Factors.

11067 Garcia, Mario T. Book review of: LOS MOJADOS: THE WETBACK STORY. JOURNAL OF ETHNIC STUDIES, Vol. 1, no. 1 (Spring 1973), p. 66-68. English. DESCR: Book Reviews; Immigrant Labor; *LOS MOJADOS: THE WETBACK STORY; Mexico; Samora, Julian; Undocumented Workers; United States.

11068 Garcia, Mario T. On Mexican immigration, the United States, and Chicano history. JOURNAL OF ETHNIC STUDIES, Vol. 7, no. 1 (Spring 1979), p. 80-88. English. DESCR: Book Reviews; *BY THE SWEAT OF THEIR BROW: MEXICAN IMMIGRANT LABOR IN THE UNITED STATES, 1900-1940; History; Immigrant Labor; Immigration; Immigration Law; Mexico; Reisler, Mark; Research Methodology.

11069 Garcia, Wilfred F. Book review of: NUESTRO ESPANOL: CURSO PARA ESTUDIANTES BILINGUES, BILINGUAL NATIVE SPANISH SPEAKERS FROM THE SOUTHWESTERN UNITED STATES. HISPANIA, Vol. 65, no. 2 (May 1982), p. 320-321. English. DESCR: Book Reviews; Garza-Swan, Gloria; Mejias, Hugo A.; *NUESTRO ESPANOL: CURSO PARA ESTUDIANTES BILINGUES; Spanish Language; Textbooks.

11070 Gonzales, Eloy. A cross-cultural comparison of the developmental items of five ethnic groups in the Southwest. JOURNAL OF PERSONALITY ASSESSMENT, Vol. 46, no. 1 (February 1982), p. 26-31. English. DESCR: *Comparative Psychology; Draw-A-Person (DAP) [psychological test]; Ethnic Groups; Psychological Testing.

11071 Howell, Frances Baseden. Split labor market: Mexican farm workers in the Southwest. SOCIOLOGICAL INQUIRY, Vol. 52, no. 2 (Spring 1982), p. 132-140. English. DESCR: Agricultural Labor Unions; Arizona Farm Workers (AFW); *Labor Supply and Market; Undocumented Workers; United Farmworkers of America (UFW).

11072 John, Elizabeth A.H. Book review of: THE MEXICAN FRONTIER, 1821-1846: THE AMERICAN SOUTHWEST UNDER MEXICO. NEW MEXICO HISTORICAL REVIEW, Vol. 57, no. 3 (July 1982), p. 289-293. English. DESCR: Book Reviews; Border Region; *THE MEXICAN FRONTIER, 1821-1846: THE AMERICAN SOUTHWEST UNDER MEXICO; Weber, David J.

11073 Jones, Oakah L. Book review of: THE MEXICAN FRONTIER, 1821-1846: THE AMERICAN SOUTHWEST UNDER MEXICO. ARIZONA AND THE WEST, Vol. 25, no. 2 (1983), p. 168-169. English. DESCR: Book Reviews; History; Mexico; *THE MEXICAN FRONTIER, 1821-1846: THE AMERICAN SOUTHWEST UNDER MEXICO; Weber, David J.

11074 Kanellos, Nicolas. Two centuries of Hispanic theatre in the Southwest. REVISTA CHICANO-RIQUENA, Vol. 11, no. 1 (Spring 1983), p. 17-39. English. DESCR: California; History; Los Angeles, CA; Photography; San Antonio, TX; *Teatro; Texas.

11075 Meyer, Michael C. Book review of: THE MEXICAN FRONTIER, 1821-1846: THE AMERICAN SOUTHWEST UNDER MEXICO. WESTERN HISTORICAL QUARTERLY, Vol. 14, no. 3 (1983), p. 337-338. English. DESCR: Book Reviews; History; Mexico; *THE MEXICAN FRONTIER, 1821-1846: THE AMERICAN SOUTHWEST UNDER MEXICO; Weber, David J.

11076 Miller, Michael V. Book review of: CHICANOS AND RURAL POVERTY. JOURNAL OF ETHNIC STUDIES, Vol. 5, no. 3 (Fall 1977), p. 116-117. English. DESCR: Agricultural Laborers; Book Reviews; Briggs, Vernon M.; *CHICANOS AND RURAL POVERTY; Immigration Law; Social History and Conditions.

11077 Myres, Sandra Lynn. Mexican Americans and westering Anglos: a feminine perspective. NEW MEXICO HISTORICAL REVIEW, Vol. 57, no. 4 (October 1982), p. 317-333. English. DESCR: Anglo Americans; Chicanas; *Ethnic Attitudes; Social History and Conditions; Stereotypes.

11078 Southwest exhibit traces history. NUESTRO, Vol. 6, no. 8 (October 1982), p. 11-12. English. DESCR: *Teatro.

11079 Weber, David J. Book review of: MEXICANO RESISTANCE IN THE SOUTHWEST: "THE SACRED RIGHT OF SELF-PRESERVATION". AMERICAN HISTORICAL REVIEW, Vol. 87, no. 1 (February 1982), p. 272-273. English. DESCR: Book Reviews; Insurrections; *MEXICANO RESISTANCE IN THE SOUTHWEST: "THE SACRED RIGHT OF SELF-PRESERVATION"; Rosenbaum, Robert J.

11080 Weiss, Lawrence D. Industrial reserve armies of the southwest: Navajo and Mexican. SOUTHWEST ECONOMY AND SOCIETY, Vol. 3, no. 1 (Fall 1977), p. 19-29. English. DESCR: Capitalism; History; *Labor Supply and Market; Native Americans; Navaho Indians; Railroads.

Southwest Voter Registration Education Project (SVRP)

11081 Hispanic voting trends. HISPANIC BUSINESS, Vol. 4, no. 8 (August 1983), p. 28-29. English. DESCR: Bilingual Ballots; Bilingualism; *Elections; Mexican American Legal Defense and Educational Fund (MALDEF); Texas; Voter Turnout.

11082 Kirschten, Dick. The Hispanic vote: parties can't gamble that the sleeping giant won't awaken. NATIONAL JOURNAL, Vol. 15, no. 47 (November 19, 1983), p. 2410-2411. English. DESCR: Democratic Party; *Hispanic Caucus; Republican Party; *Voter Turnout.

Sowell, Thomas

11083 Goldberg, Victor. Ethnic groups in the United States. REVIEWS IN ANTHROPOLOGY, Vol. 9, no. 4 (Fall 1982), p. 375-382. English. **DESCR:** Achor, Shirley; Book Reviews; ETHNIC AMERICA, A HISTORY; MEXICAN AMERICANS IN A DALLAS BARRIO; *THE CHICANOS; Trejo, Arnulfo D.

11084 Van den Berghe, Pierre L. Book review of: ETHNIC AMERICA, A HISTORY. INTERNATIONAL MIGRATION REVIEW, Vol. 16, no. 4 (Winter 1982), p. 900-902. English. **DESCR:** Book Reviews; *ETHNIC AMERICA, A HISTORY; Ethnic Groups; History; Migration.

THE SPACE OF CHICANO LITERATURE

11085 Lizarraga, Sylvia S. Observaciones acerca de la critica literaria Chicana. REVISTA CHICANO-RIQUENA, Vol. 10, no. 4 (Fall 1982), p. 55-64. Spanish. **DESCR:** *Bruce Novoa, Juan; CITY OF NIGHT; El Teatro Campesino; *Literary Criticism; Literature; POCHO.

Space Shuttle

11086 Valenzuela-Crocker, Elvira. Chang-Diaz has space shuttle role. NUESTRO, Vol. 7, no. 9 (November 1983), p. 11-12. English. **DESCR:** *Astronauts; *Chang-Diaz, Franklin; National Aeronautics and Space Administration (NASA).

Space-Craft Manufacturing, Inc.

11087 Balkan, D. Carlos and Cruz, Franklin D. Space-Craft's strategy for re-industrialization. HISPANIC BUSINESS, Vol. 4, no. 11 (November 1982), p. 16-17,26. English. **DESCR:** Business Enterprises; Connecticut; *High Technology Industries; Soto, John.

Spain

11088 Carrion, Arturo Morales. Puerto Rico: the coming of the Americans. NUESTRO, Vol. 7, no. 5 (June, July, 1983), p. 25-30. English. **DESCR:** Cuba; *International Relations; *Puerto Rico; *United States History; *War.

11089 EFE announces opening of Miami News Bureau. NUESTRO, Vol. 6, no. 6 (August 1982), p. 52. English. **DESCR:** Miami, FL; *News Agencies; Spanish Language.

11090 Schon, Isabel. Recent outstanding books for young readers from Spanish speaking countries. READING TEACHER, Vol. 36, no. 2 (November 1982), p. 206-209. English. **DESCR:** Argentina; *Children's Literature; Literature Reviews; Spanish Language; Venezuela.

11091 Schon, Isabel. Spanish books for children. BOOKLIST, Vol. 78, no. 20 (June 15, 1982), p. 1373-1374. English. **DESCR:** Argentina; *Bibliography; *Children's Literature; Mexico; Spanish Language; Venezuela.

11092 Schon, Isabel. Spanish books for children. BOOKLIST, Vol. 79, (February 15, 1983), p. 783-784. English. **DESCR:** *Bibliography; *Children's Literature; Mexico; Spanish Language; Venezuela.

Spanish Advertising and Marketing Services (S.A.M.S.)

11093 Balkan, D. Carlos. The advent of Uniworld/Hispanic: an interview. HISPANIC BUSINESS, Vol. 5, no. 3 (March 1983), p. 10-11+. English. **DESCR:** *Advertising Agencies; Blacks; Consumers; Diaz-Albertini, Luis; Lewis, Byron; *Marketing; Uniworld Group, Inc.; UniWorld Hispanic.

11094 Communications/marketing. HISPANIC BUSINESS, Vol. 5, no. 3 (March 1983), p. 21. English. **DESCR:** *Advertising; Awards; Consumers; El Cervantes Media Awards; Marketing.

SPANISH AND ENGLISH OF U.S. HISPANOS: A CRITICAL, ANNOTATED, LINGUISTIC BIBLIOGRAPHY

11095 Woods, Richard D. Book review of: SPANISH AND ENGLISH OF UNITED STATES HISPANOS: A CRITICAL, ANNOTATED, LINGUISTIC BIBLIOGRAPHY. JOURNAL OF ETHNIC STUDIES, Vol. 4, no. 3 (Fall 1976), p. 116. English. **DESCR:** Accentedness; Bibliography; Bills, Garland D.; Book Reviews; Craddock, Jerry R.; Language Patterns; Spanish Language; Teschner, Richard V.

SPANISH AND MEXICAN LAND GRANTS IN NEW MEXICO AND COLORADO

11096 Salmon, Roberto Mario. Book review of: SPANISH AND MEXICAN LAND GRANTS IN NEW MEXICO AND COLORADO. JOURNAL OF ETHNIC STUDIES, Vol. 9, no. 3 (Fall 1981), p. 120-121. English. **DESCR:** Book Reviews; Colorado; *Land Grants; New Mexico; Van Ness, Christine M.; Van Ness, John R.

Spanish Colonial Period

11097 Vigil, James Diego. Towards a new perspective on understanding the Chicano people: the six C's model of sociocultural change. CAMPO LIBRE, Vol. 1, no. 2 (Summer 1981), p. 141-167. English. **DESCR:** Acculturation; Assimilation; Cultural Characteristics; History; Mexican Nationalism Period; Mexico; Nationalism; Organizations; Precolumbian Society; *Six C's Model (Theoretical Model); Social History and Conditions.

Spanish Education Development (SED) Center Bilingual Reading Project

11098 Lado, Robert. Aula/the classroom: developmental reading in two languages. NABE JOURNAL, Vol. 6, no. 2-3 (Winter, Spring, 1981, 1982), p. 99-110. English. **DESCR:** Bilingual Bicultural Education; Bilingualism; Language Arts; Language Development; Learning and Cognition; *Reading; Spanish Language.

SPANISH FOR THE CALIFORNIA FARMERS

11099 "Racist and demeaning". NUESTRO, Vol. 7, no. 2 (March 1983), p. 7. English. **DESCR:** Agricultural Laborers; Book Reviews; Granada, Pilar; Hagopian, Tom; Racism.

Spanish Influence

11100 Martinez, Douglas R. Down on the farm with the Cisco Kid. NUESTRO, Vol. 7, no. 2 (March 1983), p. 49. English. **DESCR:** *Agriculture; Agriculture Day USDA; Cisco Kid.

11101 Mathes, W. Michael. Sources in Mexico for the history of Spanish California. CALIFORNIA HISTORY, Vol. 61, no. 3 (1982), p. 223-226. English. **DESCR:** *California; *Historiography; Mexico.

Spanish Influence (cont.)

11102 Myres, Sandra Lynn. The cowboy's Hispanic heritage. NUESTRO, Vol. 7, no. 7 (September 1983), p. 44-48. English. **DESCR:** United States History; *Vaqueros.

Spanish International Network (SIN)

11103 Bagamery, Anne. SIN, the original. FORBES, Vol. 13, no. 11 (November 22, 1982), p. 96-97. English. **DESCR:** Anselmo, Rene; Broadcast Media; Spanish Language; Television.

11104 Chavarria, Jesus. How long will it last? HISPANIC BUSINESS, Vol. 4, no. 1 (January 1982), p. 6. English. **DESCR:** Anselmo, Rene; Businesspeople; Lasa, Luis; *Marketing.

11105 Chavez, Lydia. The fourth network's chief executive. HISPANIC BUSINESS, Vol. 4, no. 1 (January 1982), p. 16-18. English. **DESCR:** Advertising; Anselmo, Rene; *Biography; Cable Television; Marketing.

11106 Communications/marketing. HISPANIC BUSINESS, Vol. 4, no. 2 (February 1982), p. 15. English. **DESCR:** Cable Television; Congressional Hispanic Caucus; El Teatro Campesino; GalaVision; Labor Unions; *Marketing; Philip Morris, Inc.; Publishing Industry.

11107 McGuire, Jack. Hispanic TV network thrives: this SIN is legit. ADVERTISING AGE MAGAZINE, Vol. 53, (February 15, 1982), p. II, M34-35. English. **DESCR:** Broadcast Media; Spanish Language; Television.

11108 SIN seeks FCC review of Hughes performance. NUESTRO, Vol. 6, no. 1 (January, February, 1982), p. 50. English. **DESCR:** Laws; Television.

Spanish Language

11109 Alvarez, Amando. How the Spanish language is changing. LATINO, Vol. 54, no. 6 (October 1983), p. 11. English.

11110 Alvarez, Amando. El ingles en el espanol. LATINO, Vol. 54, no. 6 (October 1983), p. 15. Spanish.

11111 Alvarez, Amando. La lengua espanol. LATINO, Vol. 53, no. 6 (October 1982), p. 11+. Spanish.

11112 Aparicio, Frances R. Teaching Spanish to the native speaker at the college level. HISPANIA, Vol. 66, (May 1983), p. 232-239. English. **DESCR:** *Bilingual Bicultural Education.

11113 Arce, Carlos H. Language shift among Chicanos: strategies for measuring and assessing direction and rate. SOCIAL SCIENCE JOURNAL, Vol. 19, no. 2 (April 1982), p. 121-132. English. **DESCR:** Bilingualism; Language Development; Research Methodology.

11114 Armengol, Armando; Manley, Joan H.; and Teschner, Richard V. The international bilingual city: how a university meets the challenge. FOREIGN LANGUAGE ANNALS, Vol. 15, no. 4 (September 1982), p. 289-295. English. **DESCR:** Biculturalism; Bilingualism; Border Region; Ciudad Juarez, Chihuahua, Mexico; El Paso, TX; *Language Development; University of Texas at El Paso.

11115 Arora, Shirley L. Proverbs in Mexican American tradition. AZTLAN, Vol. 13, no. 1-2

(Spring, Fall, 1982), p. 43-69. English. **DESCR:** *Dichos; Identity; Surveys.

11116 Bagamery, Anne. SIN, the original. FORBES, Vol. 13, no. 11 (November 22, 1982), p. 96-97. English. **DESCR:** Anselmo, Rene; Broadcast Media; *Spanish International Network (SIN); Television.

11117 Barclay, Lisa K. Using Spanish as the language of instruction with Mexican-American Head Start children: a re-evaluation using meta-analysis. PERCEPTUAL AND MOTOR SKILLS, Vol. 56, no. 2-4 (1983), p. 359-366. English. **DESCR:** Education; Languages; Psychological Testing.

11118 Beyer, Sandra S. and Kluck, Frederick J. French via Spanish: a positive approach to language learning for minority students. FOREIGN LANGUAGE ANNALS, Vol. 15, no. 2 (April 1982), p. 123-126. English. **DESCR:** Educational Innovations; *French Language; Language Development; University of Texas at El Paso.

11119 Blake, Robert. Mood selection among Spanish-speaking children, ages 4 to 12. BILINGUAL REVIEW, Vol. 10, no. 1 (January, April, 1983), p. 21-32. English. **DESCR:** Children; Grammar; *Language Development; Language Usage.

11120 Carrillo, Federico M. How should Spanish speakers be taught Spanish in the schools? BILINGUAL JOURNAL, Vol. 7, no. 4 (Summer 1983), p. 18-22. English. **DESCR:** *Bilingual Bicultural Education; *Language Arts; Sociolinguistics.

11121 Chavez, Ernest L. Analysis of a Spanish translation of the Peabody Picture Vocabulary Test. PERCEPTUAL AND MOTOR SKILLS, Vol. 54, no. 3 (June 1982), p. 1335-1338. English. **DESCR:** Bilingualism; Educational Tests and Measurements; *Peabody Picture Vocabulary Test (PPVT).

11122 Communications/marketing. HISPANIC BUSINESS, Vol. 5, no. 4 (April 1983), p. 23. English. **DESCR:** Faultless Starch/Bon Ami Company; Garcia, Marti; *Marketing; Mejias, Hugo A.; Pan American University, Edinburg, TX.

11123 DeOrtega, Manuel R. In the stomach of the shark: echoes of a culture in captivity. SOUTHWEST ECONOMY AND SOCIETY, Vol. 6, no. 1 (Fall 1982), p. 35-48. Bilingual. **DESCR:** *Assimilation; Culture; Poetry.

11124 Dvorak, Trisha and Kirschner, Carl. Mary likes fishes: reverse psychological phenomena in New York Puerto Rican Spanish. BILINGUAL REVIEW, Vol. 9, no. 1 (January, April, 1982), p. 59-65. English. **DESCR:** New York; Puerto Ricans; *Syntax.

11125 Dyer, Nancy Joe. Book review of: TEACHING SPANISH TO THE HISPANIC BILINGUAL: ISSUES, AIMS AND METHODS. HISPANIA, Vol. 65, no. 3 (September 1982), p. 474-475. English. **DESCR:** Book Reviews; Garcia-Moya, Rodolfo; Lozano, Anthony G.; *TEACHING SPANISH TO THE HISPANIC BILINGUAL: ISSUES, AIMS AND METHODS; Valdez, Guadalupe.

11126 EFE announces opening of Miami News Bureau. NUESTRO, Vol. 6, no. 6 (August 1982), p. 52. English. **DESCR:** Miami, FL; *News Agencies; Spain.

Spanish Language (cont.)

11127 Estrada, Leobardo F. [Demographic
characteristics of Latinos]. CHICANO LAW
REVIEW, Vol. 6, (1983), p. 9-16. English.
DESCR: *Demography; Internal Migration;
LATINOS IN THE LAW [symposium], UCLA, 1982;
Los Angeles County, CA; Migration; Migration
Patterns.

11128 Fallows, James. Language. ATLANTIC, Vol.
252, (November 1983), p. 62+. English.
DESCR: Language Development; *Languages.

11129 Flori, Monica. The Hispanic community as a
resource for a practical Spanish program.
FOREIGN LANGUAGE ANNALS, Vol. 15, no. 3 (May
1982), p. 213-215. English. **DESCR:** Community
School Relationships; Curriculum;
Educational Innovations; Language
Development; Lewis and Clark College,
Portland, OR.

11130 Friedman, Mary Lusky. Notes on the grading
of advanced placement Spanish language
examination. HISPANIA, Vol. 66, (May 1983),
p. 239-241. English. **DESCR:** Educational
Tests and Measurements.

11131 Garcia, Wilfred F. Book review of: NUESTRO
ESPANOL: CURSO PARA ESTUDIANTES BILINGUES,
BILINGUAL NATIVE SPANISH SPEAKERS FROM THE
SOUTHWESTERN UNITED STATES. HISPANIA, Vol.
65, no. 2 (May 1982), p. 320-321. English.
DESCR: Book Reviews; Garza-Swan, Gloria;
Mejias, Hugo A.; *NUESTRO ESPANOL: CURSO
PARA ESTUDIANTES BILINGUES; Southwest United
States; Textbooks.

11132 Goldin, Mark G. Book review of: TEACHING
SPANISH TO THE HISPANIC BILINGUAL: ISSUES,
AIMS AND METHODS. NABE JOURNAL, Vol. 7, no.
1 (Fall 1982), p. 53-56. English. **DESCR:**
Bilingualism; Book Reviews; Garcia-Moya,
Rodolfo; Language Proficiency; Language
Usage; Lozano, Anthony G.; *TEACHING SPANISH
TO THE HISPANIC BILINGUAL: ISSUES, AIMS AND
METHODS; Valdez, Guadalupe.

11133 Gonzalez, Gustavo. Expressing time through
verb tenses and temporal expressions in
Spanish: age 2.0-4.6. NABE JOURNAL, Vol. 7,
no. 2 (Winter 1983), p. 69-82. English.
DESCR: *Bilingual Bicultural Education;
*Language Development; *Language Usage.

11134 Gutierrez, John R. Book review of: TEACHING
SPANISH TO THE HISPANIC BILINGUAL: ISSUES,
AIMS AND METHODS. MODERN LANGUAGE JOURNAL,
Vol. 66, no. 2 (Summer 1982), p. 234.
English. **DESCR:** Bilingualism; Book Reviews;
Garcia-Moya, Rodolfo; Lozano, Anthony G.;
*TEACHING SPANISH TO THE HISPANIC BILINGUAL:
ISSUES, AIMS AND METHODS; Valdez, Guadalupe.

11135 Hernandez, Rudy. English, yes! Spanish, si!
Spanglish, no! NUESTRO, Vol. 7, no. 8
(October 1983), p. 53. English. **DESCR:**
English Language; Language Proficiency;
*Language Usage.

11136 Hudelson, Sarah. An introductory examination
of children's invented spelling in Spanish.
NABE JOURNAL, Vol. 6, no. 2-3 (Winter,
Spring, 1981, 1982), p. 53-67. English.
DESCR: Bilingual Bicultural Education;
Children; *Language Arts; Learning and
Cognition.

11137 Jensen, Joan M. Women teachers, class and
ethnicity: New Mexico 1900-1950. SOUTHWEST
ECONOMY AND SOCIETY, Vol. 4, no. 2 (Winter
1978, 1979), p. 3-13. English. **DESCR:**
Alternative Education; *Chicanas; Cultural
Pluralism; History; *New Mexico; Teaching
Profession.

11138 Johnson, Greg. Administracion en un medio
ambiente hispanico. INDUSTRY WEEK, Vol. 212,
no. 2 (January 25, 1982), p. 30-34. English.
DESCR: Industries; *Labor Supply and Market;
Undocumented Workers.

11139 Josel, Nathan A. Public library material
selection in a bilingual community. CATHOLIC
LIBRARY WORLD, Vol. 54, no. 3 (October
1982), p. 113-115. English. **DESCR:**
Bilingualism; El Paso, TX; Library
Collections; *Public Libraries.

11140 Karno, M. Development of the
Spanish-language version of the National
Institute of Mental Health Diagnostic
Interview Schedule. ARCHIVES OF GENERAL
PSYCHIATRY, Vol. 40, no. 11 (November 1983),
p. 1183-1188. English. **DESCR:** Culture;
Languages; Mental Health; *National
Institute of Mental Health Diagnostic
Interview Schedule.

11141 Kramer, Virginia Reyes and Schell, Leo M.
English auditory discrimination skills of
Spanish-speaking children. ALBERTA JOURNAL
OF EDUCATIONAL RESEARCH, Vol. 28, no. 1
(March 1982), p. 1-8. English. **DESCR:**
Accentedness; Bilingualism; English
Language; *Language Development.

11142 Lado, Robert. Aula/the classroom:
developmental reading in two languages. NABE
JOURNAL, Vol. 6, no. 2-3 (Winter, Spring,
1981, 1982), p. 99-110. English. **DESCR:**
Bilingual Bicultural Education;
Bilingualism; Language Arts; Language
Development; Learning and Cognition;
*Reading; Spanish Education Development
(SED) Center Bilingual Reading Project.

11143 Macias, Reynaldo Flores. Book review of:
POLITICS AND LANGUAGE: SPANISH AND ENGLISH
IN THE UNITED STATES. NABE JOURNAL, Vol. 7,
no. 1 (Fall 1982), p. 61-66. English.
DESCR: Bilingualism; Book Reviews; Bruckner,
D.J.R.; Cultural Pluralism; *POLITICS AND
LANGUAGE: SPANISH AND ENGLISH IN THE UNITED
STATES.

11144 McGuire, Jack. Hispanic TV network thrives:
this SIN is legit. ADVERTISING AGE MAGAZINE,
Vol. 53, (February 15, 1982), p. II,
M34-35. English. **DESCR:** Broadcast Media;
*Spanish International Network (SIN);
Television.

11145 McKinney, J.E. Book review of: MOSAICO DE LA
VIDA: CHICANO, CUBAN AND PUERTO RICAN PROSE.
HISPANIA, Vol. 65, no. 2 (May 1982), p. 321.
English. **DESCR:** Book Reviews; Jimenez,
Francisco; *MOSAICO DE LA VIDA: CHICANO,
CUBAN AND PUERTO RICAN PROSE; Prose;
Textbooks.

11146 McKone, Jerry. Texas Spanish: not standard:
but not bad. NATIONAL HISPANIC JOURNAL, Vol.
1, no. 4 (Spring 1983), p. 20-21. English.
DESCR: Education; Folk Medicine; Mejias,
Hugo A.

Spanish Language (cont.)

11147 Morrison, J. A. and Michael, W.B. Development and validation of an auditory perception test in Spanish for Hispanic children receiving reading instruction in Spanish. EDUCATIONAL AND PSYCHOLOGICAL MEASUREMENT, Vol. 42, (Summer 1982), p. 657-669. English. **DESCR:** Children; Educational Tests and Measurements; *Language Arts; Prueba de Analisis Auditivo (PAA); Reading.

11148 Neuman, Susan B. and Pits, Elaine F. A review of current North American television programs for bilingual children. READING TEACHER, Vol. 37, no. 3 (December 1983), p. 254-260. English. **DESCR:** *Bilingual Bicultural Education; Mass Media; SESAME STREET; THE ELECTRIC COMPANY; VILLA ALEGRE.

11149 Ramirez, Arnulfo G.; Milk, Robert H.; and Sapiens, Alexander. Intragroup differences and attitudes toward varieties of Spanish among bilingual pupils from California and Texas. HISPANIC JOURNAL OF BEHAVIORAL SCIENCES, Vol. 5, no. 4 (December 1983), p. 417-429. English. **DESCR:** *Bilingualism.

11150 Savage, David G. Is the market going English? HISPANIC BUSINESS, Vol. 4, no. 12 (December 1982), p. 20-21. English. **DESCR:** English Language; Language Proficiency; *Language Usage.

11151 Schement, Jorge Reina. U.S. communication policy: catching up with Spanish language broadcasting. AGENDA, Vol. 11, no. 3 (May, June, 1981), p. 41-44. English. **DESCR:** *Television.

11152 Schon, Isabel; Hopkins, Kenneth D.; and Davis, W. Alan. Effects of books in Spanish and free reading time on Hispanic students' reading abilities and attitudes. NABE JOURNAL, Vol. 7, no. 1 (Fall 1982), p. 13-20. English. **DESCR:** Bilingual Bicultural Education; *Language Arts; Language Proficiency; *Reading.

11153 Schon, Isabel. Recent outstanding books for young readers from Spanish speaking countries. READING TEACHER, Vol. 36, no. 2 (November 1982), p. 206-209. English. **DESCR:** Argentina; *Children's Literature; Literature Reviews; Spain; Venezuela.

11154 Schon, Isabel. Spanish books for children. BOOKLIST, Vol. 78, no. 20 (June 15, 1982), p. 1373-1374. English. **DESCR:** Argentina; *Bibliography; *Children's Literature; Mexico; Spain; Venezuela.

11155 Schon, Isabel. Spanish books for children. BOOKLIST, Vol. 79, (February 15, 1983), p. 783-784. English. **DESCR:** *Bibliography; *Children's Literature; Mexico; Spain; Venezuela.

11156 Shellenberger, Sylvia. Assessment of Puerto Rican children: a cross-culture study with the Spanish McCarthy scales of children's abilities. BILINGUAL REVIEW, Vol. 9, no. 2 (May, August, 1982), p. 109-119. English. **DESCR:** *Intelligence Tests; Sociology.

11157 Sohn, Jeanne and Davidson, Russ. Out of the morass: acquiring Spanish language materials from Latin America. LIBRARY JOURNAL, Vol. 10, no. 13 (July 1982), p. 1290-1293. English. **DESCR:** Latin American Literature; *Library Collections; Library Services.

11158 Somers, Adele. Improving human relations

between the Hispanic community and law enforcement. POLICE CHIEF, Vol. 49, no. 3 (March 1982), p. 32-33. English. **DESCR:** *Police; Police-Community Relations.

11159 Southwest may lose theater. NUESTRO, Vol. 6, no. 7 (September 1982), p. 11. English. **DESCR:** *Alameda Theater, San Antonio, TX; Films; San Antonio, TX.

11160 Spanish farm primer. LATINO, Vol. 53, no. 4 (June 1982), p. 24. English.

11161 Staczek, John J. Code-switching in Miami Spanish: the domain of health care services. BILINGUAL REVIEW, Vol. 10, no. 1 (January, April, 1983), p. 41-46. English. **DESCR:** *Bilingualism; *Language Interference; Medical Care; Miami, FL.

11162 Think Spanish! MARKETING AND MEDIA DECISIONS, Vol. 17, (October 1982), p. 66-69. English. **DESCR:** Advertising; Biography; Conill Advertising Associates, New York, NY; Conill, Alicia; Conill, Rafael; *Marketing; Scott Paper Company.

11163 Tio Pepe habla espanol. CAMINOS, Vol. 4, no. 10 (November 1983), p. 31. English. **DESCR:** Education; *Suarez Weiss, Patricia.

11164 Volsky, George. Miami's radio S-U-A-A-V-E. HISPANIC BUSINESS, Vol. 4, no. 12 (December 1982), p. 22,35. English. **DESCR:** Advertising; Broadcast Media; Language Usage; Marketing; Miami, FL; *Radio; Radio Station SUAVE, Miami, FL; *Radio Stations.

11165 Wittenauer, Cheryl. Dallas Hispanic media. HISPANIC BUSINESS, Vol. 5, no. 2 (February 1983), p. 12-13+. English. **DESCR:** Broadcast Media; *Consumers; Dallas, TX; English Language; Marketing; Mass Media; Newspapers.

11166 Woods, Richard D. Book review of: SPANISH AND ENGLISH OF UNITED STATES HISPANOS: A CRITICAL, ANNOTATED, LINGUISTIC BIBLIOGRAPHY. JOURNAL OF ETHNIC STUDIES, Vol. 4, no. 3 (Fall 1976), p. 116. English. **DESCR:** Accentedness; Bibliography; Bills, Garland D.; Book Reviews; Craddock, Jerry R.; Language Patterns; *SPANISH AND ENGLISH OF U.S. HISPANOS: A CRITICAL, ANNOTATED, LINGUISTIC BIBLIOGRAPHY; Teschner, Richard V.

11167 Woods, Richard D. Sources of identification of Spanish names. JOURNAL OF ETHNIC STUDIES, Vol. 4, no. 2 (Summer 1976), p. 92-94. English. **DESCR:** Names, Spanish; *Personal Names.

11168 Zotti, Ed. An idea whose time has not quite arrived: Spanish sections in newspapers still struggling. ADVERTISING AGE MAGAZINE, Vol. 53, (February 15, 1982), p. II, M29+. English. **DESCR:** Market Research; *Newspapers.

Spanish Language Textbooks

11169 Feliciano-Foster, Wilma. A comparison of three current first-year college-level Spanish-for-native-speakers textbooks. BILINGUAL REVIEW, Vol. 9, no. 1 (January, April, 1982), p. 72-81. English. **DESCR:** *Book Reviews; ESPANOL ESCRITO; Garza-Swan, Gloria; *Language Development; Mejias, Hugo A.; MEJORA TU ESPANOL; NUESTRO ESPANOL: CURSO PARA ESTUDIANTES BILINGUES; Portilla, Marta de la; Teschner, Richard V.; Valdes Fallis, Guadalupe; Varela, Beatriz.

Spanish Satellite Network (SSN)

11170 Communications/marketing. HISPANIC BUSINESS, Vol. 5, no. 7 (July 1983), p. 24. English. DESCR: AltaVision, Inc. (Denver, CO); Boycotts; Cable Television; Marketing; Operation PUSH; *Television.

Spanish Surname

11171 Gottlieb, Karen. Spanish surname as a market of Mexican heritage in Denver, Colorado. AMERICAN JOURNAL OF PHYSICAL ANTHROPOLOGY, Vol. 57, no. 2 (February 1982), p. 194. English. DESCR: Demography; Population.

SPANISH YELLOW PAGES

11172 Southern Bell faces directory competition. NUESTRO, Vol. 6, no. 8 (October 1982), p. 47. English. DESCR: *MIAMI EN SUS MANOS; Publishing Industry.

Special Education

11173 Ambert, Alba N. The identification of LEP children with special needs. BILINGUAL JOURNAL, Vol. 6, no. 1 (Fall 1982), p. 17-22. English. DESCR: Cultural Characteristics; Handicapped; Language Interference; Limited-English Proficient (LEP).

11174 Argulewicz, Ed N. and Sanchez, David T. Special education evaluation process as a moderator of false positives. EXCEPTIONAL CHILDREN, Vol. 49, no. 5 (1983), p. 452-454. English. DESCR: Anglo Americans; Blacks.

Speech Patterns
USE: Accentedness

Spillis Candela & Partners

11175 Volsky, George. Hilario Candela: designing for Florida's future. HISPANIC BUSINESS, Vol. 5, no. 11 (November 1983), p. 20-22. English. DESCR: Architecture; *Candela, Hilario; Miami, FL; Urban Development.

Spiro, Herbert T.

11176 Research/development: books. HISPANIC BUSINESS, Vol. 4, no. 7 (July 1982), p. 27. English. DESCR: *Book Reviews; De Leon, Arnoldo; Finance; History; Texas; THE TEJANO COMMUNITY, 1836-1900.

Sports

11177 Alvarez, Amando. Tall and mighty proud. LATINO, Vol. 53, no. 6 (October 1982), p. 18+. English. DESCR: *Flores, Tom.

11178 Bobby Knight must go. NUESTRO, Vol. 7, no. 1 (January, February, 1983), p. 9. English. DESCR: *Knight, Bobby; Olympic Committee (U.S.); Racism.

11179 Caldera, Carmela. Dan Cruz: making the Olympics happen for the community. CAMINOS, Vol. 4, no. 4 (April 1983), p. 10-13,64. Bilingual. DESCR: *Cruz, Dan; *Los Angeles Olympic Organizing Committee; Olympics.

11180 Caldera, Carmela. You and the 1984 Olympics. CAMINOS, Vol. 4, no. 4 (April 1983), p. 7-9,64. Bilingual. DESCR: *Olympics.

11181 Cantu, Hector. Softball Texas style. NATIONAL HISPANIC JOURNAL, Vol. 1, no. 3 (Summer, Fall, 1982), p. 9-11. English. DESCR: El Paso Jesters; Mexico City All Stars; Pan American Softball League; Recreation; *Softball.

11182 Cardenas, Leo. Family unit. LATINO, Vol. 53, no. 6 (October 1982), p. 14-15. English. DESCR: *Lopez, Nancy.

11183 Corrida clasica Aztlan internacional de 10 km. en Noviembre. LATINO, Vol. 54, no. 6 (October 1983), p. 9. Spanish.

11184 Diaz, Katherine A. The Dodger's Spanish voice: Jaime Jarrin. CAMINOS, Vol. 3, no. 5 (May 1982), p. 50-51. English. DESCR: *Jarrin, Jaime; Radio.

11185 Ferrarone, Aida. Olympic skeet-shooter. LATINA, Vol. 1, no. 3 (1983), p. 15. English. DESCR: Biography; Olympics; *Ortiz-Sherman, Nuria; Skeet-shooting.

11186 Flores, David. 30's gridder recalls pain of prejudice. NUESTRO, Vol. 6, no. 8 (October 1982), p. 25-26. English. DESCR: *Lerma, Everardo Carlos; Rio Grande Valley, TX; Texas.

11187 Galarza, Carlos V. Deportes en Mexico. CAMINOS, Vol. 3, no. 6 (June 1982), p. 29,40. Bilingual. DESCR: Mexico; Soccer.

11188 Garcia, Ignacio M. Realizing the dream. NUESTRO, Vol. 6, no. 8 (October 1982), p. 27-29. English. DESCR: *Lerma, Everardo Carlos.

11189 Gente. NUESTRO, Vol. 7, no. 1 (January, February, 1983), p. 63. English. DESCR: Amaya-Espinoza, Isidro; Camargo, Mateo G.; *Latin Americans; Musicians; Prieto, Carlos; Radio; Trevino, Lee.

11190 Heuer, Robert J. Baseball expansion: why not Latin America? NUESTRO, Vol. 7, no. 10 (December 1983), p. 41. English. DESCR: *Baseball; *Latin America.

11191 Lewis, William. Machismo and the will to win. NUESTRO, Vol. 7, no. 9 (November 1983), p. 32-34. English. DESCR: Machismo; Psychology.

11192 Ortiz, Carlos V. The Hall at last. NUESTRO, Vol. 7, no. 1 (January, February, 1983), p. 33-35. English. DESCR: *Baseball; Baseball Hall of Fame; *Marichal, Juan.

11193 Ortiz, Carlos V. NUESTRO's 1981 all-star baseball team. NUESTRO, Vol. 6, no. 2 (March 1982), p. 55-58. English. DESCR: Lopez, Aurelia; Martinez, Felix.

11194 Ortiz, Carlos V. NUESTRO'S sixth annual all-star baseball team. NUESTRO, Vol. 7, no. 2 (March 1983), p. 33-37. English. DESCR: Andujar, Joaquin; Barojas, Salome; *Baseball; Castillo, Manny; Concepcion, Dave; Cruz, Jose; Garcia, Damaso; Guerrero, Pedro; Hernandez, Keith; Lezcano, Sixto; Martinez, Tippy; Pena, Tony; Piniella, Lou; Valenzuela, Fernando.

11195 Que pasa? NUESTRO, Vol. 7, no. 7 (September 1983), p. 9. English. DESCR: Alcoholism; Anti-Defamation League of B'nai B'rith; *Drug Abuse; Drug Programs; Employment; Kiwanis International; Miller Brewing Company; Racism.

Sports (cont.)

11196 Rios-Bustamante, Antonio and Estrada, William. The Latino Olympians: Latin American participation in the Olympic Games 1896-1980. CAMINOS, Vol. 4, no. 4 (April 1983), p. 14-18,20+. Bilingual. **DESCR:** *Olympics.

11197 Rios-Bustamante, Antonio. The Latino Olympians project and what it means to you. CAMINOS, Vol. 4, no. 4 (April 1983), p. 19. Bilingual. **DESCR:** *Latino Olympians Project; Mass Media; Olympics.

11198 Rios-Bustamante, Antonio. The Pan American games 1951-1983. CAMINOS, Vol. 4, no. 8 (September 1983), p. 31-33,51+. Bilingual. **DESCR:** History; Latin America; *Pan American Games.

11199 Salazar came, ran, conquered in Miami. NUESTRO, Vol. 6, no. 2 (March 1982), p. 45. English. **DESCR:** *Salazar, Alberto.

11200 Salazar wins New York race. NUESTRO, Vol. 6, no. 8 (October 1982), p. 13. English. **DESCR:** Athletes; New York City Marathon; *Salazar, Alberto.

11201 Three Latinos in training. NUESTRO, Vol. 6, no. 5 (June, July, 1982), p. 10-11. English. **DESCR:** Latin Americans.

11202 The world cup: soccer's superbowl. NUESTRO, Vol. 6, no. 1 (January, February, 1982), p. 43-44. English. **DESCR:** Recreation; Soccer; *The World Cup of Soccer.

SQUATTERS AND OLIGARCHS: AUTHORITARIAN RULE AND POLICY CHANGE IN PERU

11203 Logan, Kathleen. The urban poor in developing nations. JOURNAL OF URBAN HISTORY, Vol. 9, no. 1 (November 1982), p. 108-116. English. **DESCR:** ACCESS TO POWER: POLITICS AND THE URBAN POOR IN DEVELOPING NATIONS; *Book Reviews; BORDER BOOM TOWN: CIUDAD JUAREZ SINCE 1848; Collier, David; Cornelius, Wayne A.; Eckstein, Susan; Lloyd, Peter; Martinez, Oscar J.; Nelson, Joan M.; Perlman, Janice E.; POLITICS AND MIGRANT POOR IN MEXICO CITY; SLUMS OF HOPE? SHANTY TOWNS OF THE THIRD WORLD; THE MYTH OF MARGINALITY: URBAN POVERTY AND POLITICS IN RIO DE JANEIRO; THE POVERTY OF REVOLUTION: THE STATE AND THE URBAN POOR IN MEXICO; Urban Economics.

SRI International

11204 Communications/marketing. HISPANIC BUSINESS, Vol. 4, no. 3 (March 1982), p. 15. English. **DESCR:** California; Herrera, Maria Elena; *Marketing; Philip Morris, Inc.; Publicidad Siboney; Siboney Advertising, Inc.

St. Mary's Community Educational Center

11205 Heaney, Thomas W. "Hanging on" or "gaining ground": educating marginal adults. NEW DIRECTIONS FOR CONTINUING EDUCATION, no. 20 (December 1983), p. 53-63. English. **DESCR:** *Adult Education; Chicago, IL; City Colleges, Chicago, IL; General Education Diploma (GED); Gomez, Robert; Instituto del Progreso Latino; Mission District, San Francisco, CA; Project Literacy, San Francisco, CA; *Universidad Popular, Chicago, IL.

Standard of Living

USE: Economic History and Conditions

Standard Oil Corp.

11206 Lanier, Alfredo S. Making it seem easy, from intern to account executive. HISPANIC BUSINESS, Vol. 4, no. 8 (August 1983), p. 16-17+. English. **DESCR:** *Accountants; Careers; Chicanas; Employment Training; *Fernandez, Margarita; INROADS.

Stanford Achievement Test

11207 Llabre, Maria M. and Cuevas, Gilberto. Effects of test language and mathematical skills assessed on the scores of bilingual Hispanic students. JOURNAL FOR RESEARCH IN MATHEMATICS EDUCATION, Vol. 14, no. 4 (November 1983), p. 318-324. English. **DESCR:** Comprehensive Test of Basic Skills (CTBS); Dade County, FL; *Educational Tests and Measurements; Mathematics.

Stanford University, Stanford, CA

11208 Chavez, Rigo. Job counseling, role models mean a lot. HISPANIC BUSINESS, Vol. 4, no. 8 (August 1983), p. 12. English. **DESCR:** Careers; *Counseling Services (Educational); Cuevas, Hector; Escobedo, Ed; Professional Opportunities Program (POP).

11209 Government review. NUESTRO, Vol. 7, no. 7 (September 1983), p. 55. English. **DESCR:** AIDS Hotline; California; Education; Employment; Food for Survival, New York, NY; Funding Sources; *Government Services; Hewlett Foundation; Laborers; Mathematics, Engineering and Science Achievement (MESA); Population Trends; Public Health.

11210 A new global approach. NUESTRO, Vol. 7, no. 10 (December 1983), p. 9. English. **DESCR:** *Bay Area Global Education Program (BAGEP); Curriculum; Education; Educational Innovations.

11211 Regional report, Latin America: marchers oppose Reagan polices. NUESTRO, Vol. 7, no. 4 (May 1983), p. 11. English. **DESCR:** Central America; Demonstrations; International Relations; *Latin America; *Reagan, Ronald.

Stanford University Medical Center

11212 Aging research planned. NUESTRO, Vol. 7, no. 8 (October 1983), p. 9. English. **DESCR:** *Ancianos; *Public Health.

11213 Training, fellowships. NUESTRO, Vol. 7, no. 1 (January, February, 1983), p. 9. English. **DESCR:** *Community Outreach Project; Employment Training; Financial Aid; Medical Personnel.

Stanislaus County, CA

11214 Luevano, Richard L. Attitudes of elderly Mexican Americans towards nursing homes in Stanislaus county. CAMPO LIBRE, Vol. 1, no. 2 (Summer 1981), p. 213-228. English. **DESCR:** *Ancianos; Attitude (Psychological); Cultural Characteristics; Medical Care; *Nursing Homes; Surveys.

Star-Adair Insulation, Inc.

11215 Chavarria, Jesus. Varieties of energy. HISPANIC BUSINESS, Vol. 4, no. 2 (February 1982), p. 6. English. **DESCR:** Business Enterprises; *Cataract Engineering and Construction, Inc.; Energy Industries.

Star-Adair Insulation, Inc. (cont.)

11216 Garcia, Art R. Star Adair Insulation Inc. spurts to new growth. HISPANIC BUSINESS, Vol. 4, no. 2 (February 1982), p. 18-19+. English. DESCR: Biography; Business Enterprises; Businesspeople; *Cisneros, Ignacio; Minority Enterprise Small Business Investment Corporation (MESBIC).

Starr County, TX

11217 Hanis, Craig L., et al. Diabetes among Mexican Americans in Starr County, Texas. AMERICAN JOURNAL OF EPIDEMIOLOGY, Vol. 118, no. 5 (November 1983), p. 659-672. English. DESCR: *Diabetes.

State Government

11218 Marquez, Roberto. Experiencing state government. NATIONAL HISPANIC JOURNAL, Vol. 1, no. 3 (Summer, Fall, 1982), p. 16-18. English. DESCR: Lorenzo de Zavala Mock Legislative Session; *National Hispanic Institute.

11219 Tom Bradley. CAMINOS, Vol. 3, no. 4 (April 1982), p. 21-23. Bilingual. DESCR: *Bradley, Tom; Obledo, Mario.

11220 Whisler, Kirk. Mario Obledo. CAMINOS, Vol. 3, no. 4 (April 1982), p. 18-20. Bilingual. DESCR: *Obledo, Mario.

THE STATE OF HISPANIC AMERICA

11221 Research/development: books. HISPANIC BUSINESS, Vol. 4, no. 2 (February 1982), p. 28. English. DESCR: Book Reviews; Business; Business Enterprises; *FINANCING YOUR BUSINESS; *Loffel, Egon W.; *National Hispanic Center for Advanced Studies and Policy Analysis (NHCAS); Public Policy.

Statesmanship

11222 Kennedy, Edward M. Twentieth anniversary tribute to President John F. Kennedy. NUESTRO, Vol. 7, no. 9 (November 1983), p. 9. English. DESCR: *Kennedy, John Fitzgerald.

Statistics

11223 Bean, Frank D.; King, Allan G.; and Passel, Jeffrey S. The number of illegal migrants of Mexican origin in the United States: sex ratio-based estimates for 1980. DEMOGRAPHY, Vol. 20, no. 1 (February 1983), p. 99-109. English. DESCR: Census; Migration; *Population; Undocumented Workers.

11224 Corwin, Arthur F. The numbers game: estimates of illegal aliens in the United States, 1970-1981. LAW AND CONTEMPORARY PROBLEMS, Vol. 45, no. 2 (Spring 1982), p. 223-297. English. DESCR: Bustamante, Jorge A.; Centro Nacional de Informacion y Estadistica del Trabajo (CENINET); Demography; Federation for American Immigration Reform (FAIR); Mexican American Legal Defense and Educational Fund (MALDEF); *Select Commission on Immigration and Refugee Policy; Simpson-Mazzoli Bill; *Undocumented Workers.

11225 From the SBA. CAMINOS, Vol. 3, no. 2 (February 1982), p. 42. English. DESCR: *Business; *U.S. Small Business Administration.

11226 Garcia, Philip and Maldonado, Lionel A. America's Mexicans: a plea for specificity.

SOCIAL SCIENCE JOURNAL, Vol. 19, no. 2 (April 1982), p. 9-24. English. DESCR: Census; *Demography; Ethnic Groups.

11227 Hedderson, John and Daudistel, Howard C. Infant mortality of the Spanish surname population. SOCIAL SCIENCE JOURNAL, Vol. 19, no. 4 (October 1982), p. 67-78. English. DESCR: Demography; El Paso County, TX; *Infant Mortality; Medical Care; Vital Statistics.

11228 Mamer, John W. and Martin, Philip. Hired workers on California farms. CALIFORNIA AGRICULTURE, Vol. 36, no. 9-10 (September, October, 1982), p. 21-23. English. DESCR: *Agricultural Laborers; *California; *Labor Supply and Market; Undocumented Workers.

11229 Manpower Inc. Hispanics in the labor force: data. CAMINOS, Vol. 3, no. 3 (March 1982), p. 23-25. English. DESCR: *Labor Supply and Market.

11230 Metro market ranking: Spanish-origin population. S & MM [SALES & MARKETING MANAGEMENT], Vol. 13, (July 25, 1983), p. B17. English. DESCR: *Consumers; Population.

11231 Mexican American Legal Defense and Education Fund (MALDEF). Chicana rights: a major MALDEF issue (reprinted from MALDEF Newsletter, Fall 1977). COMADRE, no. 2 (Spring 1978), p. 31-33. English. DESCR: Chicana Rights Project; Chicanas; *Mexican American Legal Defense and Educational Fund (MALDEF); Vasquez, Patricia; *Women's Rights.

11232 Mexican American Legal Defense and Education Fund (MALDEF). Chicana rights: a major MALDEF issue (reprinted from MALDEF Newsletter, Fall 1977). COMADRE, no. 3 (Fall 1978), p. 31-35. English. DESCR: Chicana Rights Project; Chicanas; *Mexican American Legal Defense and Educational Fund (MALDEF); Vasquez, Patricia; *Women's Rights.

11233 Nickel, Kenneth N. Bilingual education in the eighties. PHI DELTA KAPPAN, Vol. 63, (May 1982), p. 638. English. DESCR: *Bilingual Bicultural Education.

11234 A statistical profile of California public schools. CAMINOS, Vol. 3, no. 10 (November 1982), p. 46-47. English. DESCR: *California; *Education.

Statue of Liberty

11235 Statue of Liberty has 95th birthday. NUESTRO, Vol. 5, no. 8 (November 1981), p. 12. English.

Steinbeck, John

11236 Ortego y Gasca, Philip D. Fables of identity: stereotype and caricature of Chicanos in Steinbeck's TORTILLA FLAT. JOURNAL OF ETHNIC STUDIES, Vol. 1, no. 1 (Spring 1973), p. 39-43. English. DESCR: Caricature; Chicanos in American Literature; Literature; *Stereotypes; TORTILLA FLAT.

Steiner, Barry R.

11237 Research/development: books. HISPANIC BUSINESS, Vol. 4, no. 4 (April 1982), p. 28. English. DESCR: *Book Reviews; Engineering; Financial Aid; FINANCIAL AID FOR MINORITIES IN ENGINEERING; Kennedy, David W.; PERFECTLY LEGAL - 275 FOOLPROOF METHODS FOR PAYING LESS TAXES; Swann, Ruth N.; Taxation.

Stereotypes

11238 Andrade, Sally J. Social science stereotypes of the Mexican American woman: policy implications for research. HISPANIC JOURNAL OF BEHAVIORAL SCIENCES, Vol. 4, no. 2 (June 1982), p. 223-244. English. DESCR: *Chicanas; Sex Roles.

11239 Armas, Jose. ANTONIO AND THE MAYOR: a cultural review of the film. JOURNAL OF ETHNIC STUDIES, Vol. 3, no. 3 (Fall 1975), p. 98-101. English. DESCR: *ANTONIO AND THE MAYOR; Broadcast Media; Columbia Broadcasting Studios (CBS); Cultural Characteristics; Film Reviews; Films; Mass Media.

11240 Baca Zinn, Maxine. Chicano family research: conceptual distortions and alternative directions. JOURNAL OF ETHNIC STUDIES, Vol. 7, no. 3 (Fall 1979), p. 59-71. English. DESCR: Cultural Characteristics; Culture; *Family; Research Methodology; Social Research.

11241 Bloodworth, William A., Jr. Book review of: IMAGES OF THE MEXICAN-AMERICAN IN FICTION AND FILM. WESTERN AMERICAN LITERATURE, Vol. 16, no. 4 (Winter 1982), p. 323-325. English. DESCR: Book Reviews; Chicanos in American Literature; Films; *IMAGES OF THE MEXICAN AMERICAN IN FICTION AND FILM; Pettit, Arthur G.; Showalter, Dennis E.

11242 Candelaria, Cordelia. Social equity in film criticism. BILINGUAL REVIEW, Vol. 10, no. 2-3 (May, December, 1983), p. 64-70. English. DESCR: Chicanas; *Film Criticism.

11243 Cortes, Carlos E. Chicanas in film: history of an image. BILINGUAL REVIEW, Vol. 10, no. 2-3 (May, December, 1983), p. 94-108. English. DESCR: *Chicanas; Film Criticism; *Films.

11244 Cripps, Thomas. Mexicans, Indians and movies: the need for a history. WIDE ANGLE: A FILM QUARTERLY OF THEORY, CRITICISM, AND PRACTICE, Vol. 5, no. 1 (1982), p. 68-70. English. DESCR: Bataille, Gretchen M.; *Book Reviews; Films; IMAGES OF THE MEXICAN AMERICAN IN FICTION AND FILM; Native Americans; O'Connor, John E.; Pettit, Arthur G.; Silet, Charles L.P.; THE HOLLYWOOD INDIAN: STEREOTYPES OF NATIVE AMERICANS IN FILMS; THE PRETEND INDIANS: IMAGES OF NATIVE AMERICANS IN THE MOVIES.

11245 Dujoune, Marta. The image of Latin America in children's literature of developed countries. BOOKBIRD, Vol. 20, no. 1-2 (1982), p. 5-10. English. DESCR: *Children's Literature.

11246 Exum, Herbert A. The most invisible minority: the culturally diverse elderly. SCHOOL COUNSELOR, Vol. 30, no. 1 (September 1982), p. 15-24. English. DESCR: *Ancianos; Asian Americans; Blacks; Counseling (Psychological); Cultural Customs; Ethnic Groups; Family; Native Americans.

11247 Garcia, Ignacio M. Regional report, television: "Condo" canceled. NUESTRO, Vol. 7, no. 5 (June, July, 1983), p. 13. English. DESCR: Avalos, Luis; Carmen, Julie; CONDO [televison series]; Latin Americans; *Television.

11248 Garcia, Richard A. Chicano intellectual history: myth and realities. REVISTA CHICANO-RIQUENA, Vol. 10, no. 1-2 (Winter, Spring, 1982), p. 285-289. English. DESCR:

Chicano Movement; *Essays; History; Self-Referents.

11249 Jaramillo, Patricio T.; Zapata, Jesse T.; and McPherson, Robert. Concerns of college bound Mexican-American students. SCHOOL COUNSELOR, Vol. 29, no. 5 (May 1982), p. 375-380. English. DESCR: *Attitude (Psychological); College Preparation; Counseling Services (Educational); Identity; Students.

11250 Kanellos, Nicolas. Devorados pero no digeridos. Paper presented at the "Dialogo de las Americas" conference. Mexico, D.F. September 9-13, 1982. REVISTA CHICANO-RIQUENA, Vol. 10, no. 4 (Fall 1982), p. 5-6. Spanish. DESCR: *Biculturalism; Ethnic Groups.

11251 Keller, Gary. The image of the Chicano in Mexican, Chicano, and Chicano cinema: an overview. BILINGUAL REVIEW, Vol. 10, no. 2-3 (May, December, 1983), p. 13-58. English. DESCR: Film Reviews; *Films.

11252 Langum, D.J. From condemnation to praise: shifting perspectives on Hispanic California. CALIFORNIA HISTORY, Vol. 61, no. 4 (1983), p. 282-291. English. DESCR: *California; *Cultural Characteristics; Ethnic Attitudes.

11253 Levario, Raquel. Our children are watching. LATINA, Vol. 1, no. 1 (1982), p. 30. English. DESCR: *Chicanas; Television.

11254 Marquez, Antonio. A discordant image: the Mexican in American literature. MINORITY VOICES, Vol. 5, no. 1-2 (Spring, Fall, 1981), p. 41-51. English. DESCR: *Literature.

11255 Morales, Sylvia. Chicano-produced celluloid mujeres. BILINGUAL REVIEW, Vol. 10, no. 2-3 (May, December, 1983), p. 89-93. English. DESCR: BALLAD OF GREGORIO CORTEZ [film]; *Chicanas; Film Reviews; *Films; RAICES DE SANGRE [film]; SEGUIN [movie]; ZOOT SUIT [film].

11256 Myres, Sandra Lynn. Mexican Americans and westering Anglos: a feminine perspective. NEW MEXICO HISTORICAL REVIEW, Vol. 57, no. 4 (October 1982), p. 317-333. English. DESCR: Anglo Americans; Chicanas; *Ethnic Attitudes; Social History and Conditions; Southwest United States.

11257 Nevarez, Armando. We're with you, Norman Lear, but watching you closely. NUESTRO, Vol. 7, no. 8 (October 1983), p. 47. English. DESCR: Embassy Communications; *Lear, Norman; *Television.

11258 Olguin, Hank S. Images: minorities in the media. LATINA, Vol. 1, no. 2 (February, March, 1983), p. 21. English. DESCR: *Human Relations Commission, Los Angeles, CA; *Mass Media; Media Artists Against Discrimination (MAAD).

11259 Ortego y Gasca, Felipe de. Fables of identity: stereotype and caricature of Chicanos in Steinbeck's TORTILLA FLAT. JOURNAL OF ETHNIC STUDIES, Vol. 1, no. 1 (Spring 1973), p. 39-43. English. DESCR: Caricature; Chicanos in American Literature; Literature; Steinbeck, John; TORTILLA FLAT.

Stereotypes (cont.)

11260 Portales, Marco A. Anglo villains and
      Chicano writers. JOURNAL OF ETHNIC STUDIES,
      Vol. 9, no. 3 (Fall 1981), p. 78-82.
      English. DESCR: Book Reviews; *HAY PLESHA
      LICHANS TU DI FLAC; Literature; Sanchez,
      Saul.

11261 Reisberg, Barry and Vasquez, Richard.
      Stereotypes of Mexican descent persons:
      attitudes of three generations of Mexican
      American and Anglo-American adolescents.
      JOURNAL OF CROSS-CULTURAL PSYCHOLOGY, Vol.
      13, no. 1 (March 1982), p. 59-70. English.
      DESCR: Age Groups; Anglo Americans.

11262 Reyes, Luis. The Hispanic image on network
      television: past & present. CAMINOS, Vol. 4,
      no. 3 (March 1983), p. 10-16. Bilingual.
      DESCR: *Television.

11263 Schon, Isabel. Effects of special curricular
      study of Mexican culture on Anglo and
      Mexican-American students perceptions of
      Mexican-Americans. JOURNAL OF EXPERIMENTAL
      EDUCATION, Vol. 50, no. 4 (Summer 1982), p.
      215-218. English. DESCR: Anglo Americans;
      Perceptions of Mexican Americans Scale
      (PMAS); Primary School Education.

11264 Surace, Samuel J. Achievement,
      discrimination, and Mexican-Americans.
      COMPARATIVE STUDIES IN SOCIETY AND HISTORY,
      Vol. 24, no. 2 (1982), p. 315-339. English.
      DESCR: Academic Achievement; *Racism.

11265 Sutton, Susan Buck and Brunner, Tracy. Life
      on the road: Midwestern migrant farmworker
      survival skills. MIGRATION TODAY, Vol. 11,
      no. 1 (1983), p. 24-31. English. DESCR:
      Agribusiness; Agricultural Laborers;
      Economic History and Conditions; Indiana;
      Migrant Children; Migrant Education;
      *Migrant Labor.

11266 Torres, Luis. The Chicano image in film.
      CAMINOS, Vol. 3, no. 10 (November 1982), p.
      8-11,51. Bilingual. DESCR: *Films.

11267 Triandis, H.C., et al. Stereotyping among
      Hispanics and Anglos: the uniformity,
      intensity, direction and quality of auto-
      and heterosterotypes. JOURNAL OF
      CROSS-CULTURAL PSYCHOLOGY, Vol. 13, no. 4
      (December 1982), p. 409-426. English.
      DESCR: Anglo Americans; Blacks.

11268 Wagoner, Shirley A. Mexican-Americans in
      children's literature since 1970. READING
      TEACHER, Vol. 36, no. 3 (December 1982), p.
      274-279. English. DESCR: *Children's
      Literature; Literature Reviews.

11269 West, Dennis. Book review of: IMAGES OF THE
      MEXICAN-AMERICAN IN FICTION AND FILM.
      CINEASTE, Vol. 12, no. 1 (1982), p. 41.
      English. DESCR: Book Reviews; Chicanos in
      American Literature; Films; *IMAGES OF THE
      MEXICAN AMERICAN IN FICTION AND FILM;
      Pettit, Arthur G.

11270 Williams, Linda. Type and stereotype:
      Chicano images in film. BILINGUAL REVIEW,
      Vol. 10, no. 2-3 (May, December, 1983), p.
      59-63. English. DESCR: *Films.

Stiehl-Rios, Edward

11271 Ponti, Gino. Courage all the way. NUESTRO,
      Vol. 6, no. 4 (May 1982), p. 14-15+.
      English. DESCR: Veterans.

Stoddard, Ellwyn R.

11272 Book review of: BORDERLANDS SOURCEBOOK.
      LIBRARY JOURNAL, Vol. 108, no. 4 (February
      15, 1983), p. 385. English. DESCR: Book
      Reviews; *BORDERLANDS SOURCEBOOK.

Strachwitz, Chris

11273 Herrera-Sobek, Maria. Film review of: DEL
      MERO CORAZON (STRAIGHT FROM THE HEART).
      JOURNAL OF AMERICAN FOLKLORE, Vol. 95,
      (March 1982), p. 123. English. DESCR: Blank,
      Les; *DEL MERO CORAZON; Film Reviews;
      Gosling, Maureen; Hernandez, Guillermo;
      Norteno.

Street Theater
      USE: Teatro

Strenio, Andrew J., Jr.

11274 Tucker, Sally. Book review of: THE TESTING
      TRAP. HISPANIC JOURNAL OF BEHAVIORAL
      SCIENCES, Vol. 5, no. 2 (June 1983), p.
      241-244. English. DESCR: Book Reviews; *THE
      TESTING TRAP.

Stress

11275 Coping with stress. LATINO, Vol. 53, no. 4
      (June 1982), p. 27. English. DESCR: *Public
      Health.

11276 Escobar, J.I. Post-traumatic stress disorder
      in Hispanic Vietnam veterans. JOURNAL OF
      NERVOUS AND MENTAL DISEASE, Vol. 17, no. 10
      (October 1983), p. 585-596. English. DESCR:
      Acculturation; Mental Illness; Psychiatry;
      *Veterans.

11277 Freeman, Frank E.; Gonzalez, Diana; and
      Montgomery, Gary T. Experimenter effects in
      biofeedback training. JOURNAL OF SOCIAL
      PSYCHOLOGY, Vol. 11, no. 1 (February 1983),
      p. 119-123. English. DESCR: *Biofeedback;
      Psychology.

11278 Perez, Robert. Effects of stress, social
      support and coping style on adjustment to
      pregnancy among Hispanic women. HISPANIC
      JOURNAL OF BEHAVIORAL SCIENCES, Vol. 5, no.
      2 (June 1983), p. 141-161. English. DESCR:
      *Chicanas; *Pregnancy.

11279 Warheit, George. Interpersonal coping
      networks and mental health problems among
      four race-ethnic groups. JOURNAL OF
      COMMUNITY PSYCHOLOGY, Vol. 10, no. 4
      (October 1982), p. 312-324. English. DESCR:
      Comparative Psychology; Family; Mental
      Health; *Support Groups.

11280 Wheaton, Blair. A comparison of the
      moderating effects of personal coping
      resources in the impact of exposure to
      stress in two groups. JOURNAL OF COMMUNITY
      PSYCHOLOGY, Vol. 10, no. 4 (October 1982),
      p. 293-311. English. DESCR: Anglo Americans;
      Comparative Psychology; Cultural
      Characteristics; Mental Health; Social
      Psychology.

STRESSFUL LIFE EVENTS: THEIR NATURE AND EFFECTS

11281 Hunsaker, Alan. Book review of: STRESSFUL
      LIFE EVENTS: THEIR NATURE AND EFFECTS.
      HISPANIC JOURNAL OF BEHAVIORAL SCIENCES,
      Vol. 5, no. 1 (March 1983), p. 130-132.
      English. DESCR: Book Reviews; Dohrenwend,
      Barbara Snell; Dohrenwend, Bruce P.

Strikes and Lockouts

11282 Barry, Tom. On strike! Undocumented workers in Arizona. SOUTHWEST ECONOMY AND SOCIETY, Vol. 3, no. 3 (Spring 1978), p. 52-60. English. **DESCR:** Agribusiness; Agricultural Laborers; Arizona; *Goldmar Citrus Ranch, Phoenix, AZ; Labor Organizing; *Maricopa County Organizing Project (MCOP); Phoenix, AZ; Undocumented Workers.

11283 Byrkit, James W. Walter Douglas and labor struggles in early 20th century Arizona. SOUTHWEST ECONOMY AND SOCIETY, Vol. 1, no. 1 (Spring 1976), p. 14-27. English. **DESCR:** Arizona; *Biography; Bisbee, AZ; Clifton Morenci Strike, June 1903; Copper Queen Mining Co., Bisbee, AZ; *Douglas, Walter; International Workers of the World (IWW); Labor Unions; Mining Industry.

11284 Casillas, Mike. The Cananea strike of 1906. SOUTHWEST ECONOMY AND SOCIETY, Vol. 3, no. 2 (Winter 1977, 1978), p. 18-32. English. **DESCR:** Arizona; *Cananea Mining Strike of 1906; Cananea, Sonora, Mexico; History; Mining Industry; Partido Liberal Mexicano (PLM).

11285 McCracken, Ellen. Book review of: SALT OF THE EARTH. JOURNAL OF ETHNIC STUDIES, Vol. 8, no. 1 (Spring 1980), p. 116-120. English. **DESCR:** Book Reviews; Chicanas; Films; Hanover, NM; International Union of Mine, Mill and Smelter Workers; *SALT OF THE EARTH; Silverton Rosenfelt, Deborah; Women Men Relations; Women's Rights.

11286 Rubenstein, Harry R. The great Gallup Coal strike of 1933. SOUTHWEST ECONOMY AND SOCIETY, Vol. 3, no. 2 (Winter 1977, 1978), p. 34-53. English. **DESCR:** *Gallup Coal Strike of 1933; Labor Unions; Mining Industry; National Miner's Union (NMU); New Mexico; United Mineworkers of America (UMWA).

Student Advocates for Bilingual Education (SABE)

11287 Community watching: para la comunidad. CAMINOS, Vol. 2, no. 7 (December 1981), p. 42-43. Bilingual. **DESCR:** Bilingual Education; Mexican American Correctional Association (MACE); *Organizations.

Student Ambassador Recruitment Program, California State University, Stanislaus

11288 Hernandez, Leodoro and Luevano, Richard L. A program for the recruitment of Chicanos into higher education. COLLEGE STUDENT JOURNAL, Vol. 17, no. 2 (Summer 1983), p. 166-171. English. **DESCR:** California; California State University, Stanislaus; *Enrollment; Higher Education.

Student Movements

11289 Moss, Bernard H. Political values and career aspirations of UCLA law students: the 70's generation. CHICANO LAW REVIEW, Vol. 5, (1982), p. 13-28. English. **DESCR:** *Law Schools; Legal Education; Legal Profession; Political Ideology; Students.

11290 Munoz, Carlos, Jr. and Barrera, Mario. La Raza Unida Party and the Chicano student movement in California. SOCIAL SCIENCE JOURNAL, Vol. 19, no. 2 (April 1982), p. 101-119. English. **DESCR:** California; *Chicano Movement; *La Raza Unida Party; Political History and Conditions; Political Ideology; Political Parties and Organizations.

Student Organizations

11291 Community watching: para la comunidad. CAMINOS, Vol. 3, no. 3 (March 1982), p. 58-59. Bilingual. **DESCR:** Cultural Organizations; *Engineering as a Profession; Financial Aid; Harvard University; Latino Business Students Association (LBSA); Rodolfo H. Castro Fellowship; Society for Hispanic Professional Engineers (SHPE); University of Southern California.

11292 Flores, Rogelio. The struggle for minority admissions: the UCLA experience. CHICANO LAW REVIEW, Vol. 5, (1982), p. 1-12. English. **DESCR:** Bakke v. Regents of University of California; *Law Schools; Legal Education; Legal Profession; Students; UCLA Law School.

11293 Wittenauer, Cheryl. Harvard's Latino Association. HISPANIC BUSINESS, Vol. 5, no. 4 (April 1983), p. 12-13+. English. **DESCR:** Business Schools and Colleges; *Harvard Business School's Latino Association; Harvard University.

Student Teachers
USE: Teacher Training

Students

11294 Amador, Richard S. Raising our expectations of Hispanic students. CAMINOS, Vol. 4, no. 10 (November 1983), p. 30. English. **DESCR:** *Education.

11295 Baca, Judith F. Class II: young and energetic leaders. LATINO, Vol. 54, no. 2 (March 1983), p. 29-30. English. **DESCR:** *Financial Aid.

11296 Baltodano, J. C. Success. CAMINOS, Vol. 4, no. 6 (June 1983), p. 32,34+. English. **DESCR:** Colleges and Universities; Gallegos, Genevie; Gutierrez, Jorge; Sotelo, Priscilla Elvira; Torres, Juan; University of California, Berkeley.

11297 Cantu, Hector. Hispanic students wanted. NATIONAL HISPANIC JOURNAL, Vol. 1, no. 3 (Summer, Fall, 1982), p. 8. English. **DESCR:** *Enrollment; Higher Education; Recruitment; *University of Texas at Austin.

11298 de los Santos, Alfredo G. Jr.; Montemayor, Joaquin; and Solis, Enrique, Jr. Chicano students in institutions of higher education: access, attrition, and achievement. AZTLAN, Vol. 14, no. 1 (Spring 1983), p. 79-110. English. **DESCR:** Academic Achievement; Educational Statistics; Enrollment; *Higher Education.

11299 Father, son attend UCLA school of law. NUESTRO, Vol. 5, no. 8 (November 1981), p. 42. English. **DESCR:** *Family; UCLA Law School.

11300 Flores, Rogelio. The struggle for minority admissions: the UCLA experience. CHICANO LAW REVIEW, Vol. 5, (1982), p. 1-12. English. **DESCR:** Bakke v. Regents of University of California; *Law Schools; Legal Education; Legal Profession; Student Organizations; UCLA Law School.

Students (cont.)

11301 Frazier, Donald J. and De Blassie, Richard R. Comparison of self-concept in Mexican American and non-Mexican American late adolescents. ADOLESCENCE, Vol. 17, no. 66 (Summer 1982), p. 327-334. English. DESCR: Academic Achievement; *Identity; Socioeconomic Factors; Youth.

11302 Haft, Jonathan D. Assuring equal educational opportunity for language-minority students: bilingual education and the Equal Educational Opportunity Act of 1974. COLUMBIA JOURNAL OF LAW AND SOCIAL PROBLEMS, Vol. 18, no. 2 (1983), p. 209-293. English. DESCR: *Bilingual Bicultural Education; Civil Rights; Educational Law and Legislation; English as a Second Language; *Equal Educational Opportunity Act of 1974 (EEOA); Laws.

11303 Haro, Carlos Manuel. Chicanos and higher education: a review of selected literature. AZTLAN, Vol. 14, no. 1 (Spring 1983), p. 35-77. English. DESCR: California; Education; *Higher Education; Literature Reviews.

11304 Iadicola, Peter and Moore, Helen A. The desegregated school and status relations among Anglo and Hispanic students: the dilemma of school desegregation. AZTLAN, Vol. 14, no. 1 (Spring 1983), p. 147-173. English. DESCR: Comparative Education; Educational Theory and Practice; *Segregation and Desegregation.

11305 Jaramillo, Patricio T.; Zapata, Jesse T.; and McPherson, Robert. Concerns of college bound Mexican-American students. SCHOOL COUNSELOR, Vol. 29, no. 5 (May 1982), p. 375-380. English. DESCR: *Attitude (Psychological); College Preparation; Counseling Services (Educational); Identity; Stereotypes.

11306 Knight, George P., et al. Cooperative-competitive social orientation and school achievement among Anglo-American and Mexican-American children. CONTEMPORARY EDUCATIONAL PSYCHOLOGY, Vol. 7, no. 2 (April 1982), p. 97-106. English. DESCR: *Academic Achievement; Anglo Americans; Cultural Characteristics; Socialization.

11307 A Latino summer. LATINO, Vol. 54, no. 5 (August, September, 1983), p. 13. English.

11308 Lujan, Sylvia and Zapata, Jesse T. Personality differences among Mexican-American college freshmen. JOURNAL OF COLLEGE STUDENT PERSONNEL, Vol. 24, no. 2 (March 1983), p. 105-111. English. DESCR: Colleges and Universities; *Personality; Socioeconomic Factors.

11309 Magallan, Rafael J. Resume/overview: insights into the needs of a new source of students. CASE CURRENTS, Vol. 9, no. 4 (April 1983), p. 8-10. English. DESCR: *Higher Education.

11310 Moss, Bernard H. Political values and career aspirations of UCLA law students: the 70's generation. CHICANO LAW REVIEW, Vol. 5, (1982), p. 13-28. English. DESCR: *Law Schools; Legal Education; Legal Profession; Political Ideology; Student Movements.

11311 Murray, Melissa. Aqui en Tejas: de Zabala youth session set for August: students from throughout state to attend. NATIONAL HISPANIC JOURNAL, Vol. 2, no. 1 (Summer 1983), p. 7. English. DESCR: Education; National Hispanic Institute; Politics; *Youth.

11312 Olivas, Michael A. Research and theory on Hispanic education: students, finance, and governance. AZTLAN, Vol. 14, no. 1 (Spring 1983), p. 111-146. English. DESCR: Educational Administration; *Educational Theory and Practice; School Finance.

11313 Padilla, Eligio R.; Olmedo, Esteban L.; and Loya, Fred. Acculturation and the MMPI performance of Chicano and Anglo college students. HISPANIC JOURNAL OF BEHAVIORAL SCIENCES, Vol. 4, no. 4 (December 1982), p. 451-466. English. DESCR: *Acculturation; *Minnesota Multiphasic Personality Inventory (MMPI).

11314 The path to college. LATINO, Vol. 54, no. 2 (March 1983), p. 8-11+. English. DESCR: Financial Aid; Higher Education.

11315 Perez, Robert; Padilla, Amado M.; and Ramirez, Alex. Expectations toward school busing by Mexican American youth. AMERICAN JOURNAL OF COMMUNITY PSYCHOLOGY, Vol. 10, no. 2 (April 1982), p. 133-148. English. DESCR: Attitude (Psychological); *Busing; East Los Angeles, CA; Identity; Segregation and Desegregation; Youth.

11316 Plake, Barbara S., et al. Relationship of ethnic group membership to the measurement and meaning of attitudes towards reading: implications for validity of test score interpretations. EDUCATIONAL AND PSYCHOLOGICAL MEASUREMENT, Vol. 42, no. 4 (Winter 1982), p. 1259-1267. English. DESCR: Anglo Americans; Attitude (Psychological); Educational Tests and Measurements; Estes Reading Attitude Scale; Ethnic Groups; *Reading.

11317 Students view career option. NUESTRO, Vol. 6, no. 6 (August 1982), p. 12. English. DESCR: *Business; Careers; Phoenix, AZ.

11318 UCLA effort aids students. NUESTRO, Vol. 6, no. 5 (June, July, 1982), p. 11. English. DESCR: *Intergroup Relations; *University of California, Los Angeles (UCLA).

11319 Zamudio, Anthony; Padilla, Amado M.; and Comrey, Andrew L. Personality structure of Mexican Americans using the Comrey Personality Scales. JOURNAL OF PERSONALITY ASSESSMENT, Vol. 47, no. 1 (February 1983), p. 100-106. English. DESCR: Colleges and Universities; Comrey Personality Scales (CPS); Minnesota Multiphasic Personality Inventory (MMPI); *Personality; Psychological Testing.

STUDIES IN SPANISH-AMERICAN POPULATION HISTORY

11320 Hornbeck, David. Book review of: STUDIES IN SPANISH-AMERICAN POPULATION HISTORY. PROFESSIONAL GEOGRAPHER, Vol. 34, no. 4 (1982), p. 480. English. DESCR: Book Reviews; Demography; Latin America; Robinson, David J.

Study Abroad

11321 Government review. NUESTRO, Vol. 7, no. 2
(March 1983), p. 42. English. DESCR: A
WORKING WOMAN'S GUIDE TO HER JOB RIGHTS;
Adoption; Business Enterprises; Census;
Chicanas; Discrimination in Employment;
*Government Services; GUIDE TO FEDERAL
MINORITY ENTERPRISE AND RELATED ASSISTANCE
PROGRAMS; Population Trends; U.S.
Information Agency (USIA).

Style and Composition

11322 Gonzalez, Roseann Duenas. Teaching Mexican
American students to write: capitalizing on
the culture. ENGLISH JOURNAL, Vol. 71, no. 7
(November 1982), p. 20-24. English. DESCR:
Cultural Characteristics; Education;
Educational Innovations; *Language Arts.

Suarez, Carlos R.

11323 Newsfront. HISPANIC BUSINESS, Vol. 4, no. 3
(March 1982), p. 9. English. DESCR:
Appointed Officials; *Biographical Notes;
Businesspeople; Chicano Film Exhibition and
Festival, Detroit, Michigan, April 5-9,
1982; Garcia, Gloria; League of United Latin
American Citizens (LULAC); Martinez, Vilma
Socorro; National Association for Bilingual
Education; Seaga, Edward.

Suarez Weiss, Patricia

11324 Tio Pepe habla espanol. CAMINOS, Vol. 4, no.
10 (November 1983), p. 31. English. DESCR:
Education; *Spanish Language.

Suarez, Xavier

11325 Hines, Bea L. and Fabricio, Roberto. Voices.
NUESTRO, Vol. 7, no. 10 (December 1983), p.
57-58. English. DESCR: Blacks; Cubanos;
*Elections; Ferre, Maurice; *Miami, FL.

Suburban Communities

11326 Gober, Patricia and Behr, Michelle. Central
cities and suburbs as distinct place types:
myth or fact? ECONOMIC GEOGRAPHY, Vol. 58,
no. 4 (October 1982), p. 371-385. English.
DESCR: Blacks; Census; Population
Distribution; *Urban Communities.

Success

11327 Gupta, Udayan. Netting success: Apoca's
approach. HISPANIC BUSINESS, Vol. 5, no. 7
(July 1983), p. 20-21+. English. DESCR:
Abrilz, Santos T. (Sandy); Business
Enterprises; Businesspeople;
*Telecommunications.

11328 Wittenauer, Cheryl. Stanford students set it
straight. HISPANIC BUSINESS, Vol. 5, no. 7
(July 1983), p. 15. English. DESCR:
*Leadership.

Sue, Derald Wing

11329 Borland, James J. Book review of: COUNSELING
THE CULTURALLY DIFFERENT. INTERNATIONAL
MIGRATION REVIEW, Vol. 16, no. 4 (Winter
1982), p. 910-911. English. DESCR: Book
Reviews; Counseling (Psychological);
*COUNSELING THE CULTURALLY DIFFERENT.

Suffrage
USE: Voting Rights

Sugarman v. Dougall

11330 Richard, John E. Public employment rights of

aliens. BAYLOR LAW REVIEW, Vol. 34, no. 3
(Summer 1982), p. 371-385. English. DESCR:
Cabell v. Chavez-Salido; Employment;
*Naturalization.

Summa Medical Corporation

11331 Weber, Robert. Summa's Tumortec/hCG.
HISPANIC BUSINESS, Vol. 5, no. 7 (July
1983), p. 18-19+. English. DESCR: *Business
Enterprises; Businesspeople; *Medical
Research.

Summer Program for Minority Journalists

11332 Community watching: para la comunidad.
CAMINOS, Vol. 3, no. 1 (January 1982), p.
43-44. Bilingual. DESCR: Congreso Nacional
Para Pueblos Unidos (CPU); *Financial Aid;
*Food Programs; *Journalists; National
Association for Chicano Studies (NACS);
*Radio; Zozaya, Julia S.

Sun Harvest, Inc.

11333 Produce firm to close doors. NUESTRO, Vol.
7, no. 6 (August 1983), p. 12. English.
DESCR: *Agribusiness; Agricultural Labor
Unions; Business Enterprises; United
Farmworkers of America (UFW).

EL SUPER

11334 West, Dennis. Film review of: EL SUPER.
MINORITY VOICES, Vol. 4, no. 2 (Fall 1980),
p. 85-87. English. DESCR: Cubanos; Film
Reviews; Ichaso, Leon; Jimenez-Leal,
Orlando.

Support Groups

11335 Delgado, Melvin. Hispanic natural support
systems: implications for mental health
services. JOURNAL OF PSYCHOSOCIAL NURSING
AND MENTAL HEALTH SERVICES, Vol. 21, no. 4
(April 1983), p. 19-24. English. DESCR:
Curanderas; Family; *Mental Health;
Religion.

11336 Warheit, George. Interpersonal coping
networks and mental health problems among
four race-ethnic groups. JOURNAL OF
COMMUNITY PSYCHOLOGY, Vol. 10, no. 4
(October 1982), p. 312-324. English. DESCR:
Comparative Psychology; Family; Mental
Health; Stress.

Sure-Tan

11337 Bracamonte, Jose A. The national labor
relations act and undaunted workers: the
alienation of American labor. SAN DIEGO LAW
REVIEW, Vol. 21, no. 1 (December 1983), p.
29-86. English. DESCR: Immigration Law;
Labor Unions; National Labor Relations Act
(NLRA); *Undocumented Workers.

Surrealism

11338 Parr, Carmen Salazar. Surrealism in the work
of Estela Portillo. MELUS: MULTI-ETHNIC
LITERATURE OF THE UNITED STATES, Vol. 7, no.
4 (Winter 1980), p. 85-92. English. DESCR:
*Literature; *Portillo Trambley, Estela.

SURVEY OF PROMOTIONAL PRACTICES

11339 Communications/marketing. HISPANIC BUSINESS,
Vol. 5, no. 9 (September 1983), p. 26.
English. DESCR: Aguirre, Horacio; Business
Enterprises; Consumers; DIARIO DE LAS
AMERICAS; La Ventana; *Marketing; Miller
Brewing Company.

Survey Research

11340 Camayd-Freixas, Yohel. A critical assessment of a computer program designed to identify Hispanic surnames in archival data. JOURNAL OF LATIN COMMUNITY HEALTH, Vol. 1, no. 1 (Fall 1982), p. 41-54. English. DESCR: *Generally Useful Ethnic Search System (GUESS).

Surveys

11341 100 influentials survey findings. HISPANIC BUSINESS, Vol. 5, no. 5 (May 1983), p. 36+. English. DESCR: Leadership.

11342 Ailinger, Rita L. Hypertension knowledge in a Hispanic community. NURSING RESEARCH, Vol. 31, no. 4 (July, August, 1982), p. 207-210. English. DESCR: *Hypertension; Medical Care.

11343 Arora, Shirley L. Proverbs in Mexican American tradition. AZTLAN, Vol. 13, no. 1-2 (Spring, Fall, 1982), p. 43-69. English. DESCR: *Dichos; Identity; Spanish Language.

11344 Bailey, Lynn B., et al. Folacin and iron status and hematological finding in Blacks and Spanish-American adolescents from urban low-income households. AMERICAN JOURNAL OF CLINICAL NUTRITION, Vol. 35, no. 5 (May 1982), p. 1023-1032. English. DESCR: Blacks; Low Income; Public Health; *Youth.

11345 Balkan, D. Carlos. 100 influentials and their critical issues for the eighties. HISPANIC BUSINESS, Vol. 5, no. 5 (May 1983), p. 14-22. English. DESCR: Leadership.

11346 Changing Hispanic political loyalties. HISPANIC BUSINESS, Vol. 4, no. 6 (June 1982), p. 23. English. DESCR: Los Angeles, CA; *Political Parties and Organizations; Politics; Public Policy; San Antonio, TX.

11347 Chesney, Alan P., et al. Barriers to medical care of Mexican-Americans: the role of social class, acculturation, and social isolation. MEDICAL CARE, Vol. 20, no. 9 (1982), p. 883-891. English. DESCR: Acculturation; *Medical Care; Social Classes.

11348 Dear reader. LATINA, Vol. 1, no. 3 (1983), p. 76-78. English. DESCR: *Marketing.

11349 Giachello, Aida L., et al. Uses of the 1980 census for Hispanic health services research. AMERICAN JOURNAL OF PUBLIC HEALTH, Vol. 73, no. 3 (March 1983), p. 266-274. English. DESCR: Census; Public Health; Research Methodology.

11350 Gombeski, William R., Jr., et al. Communicating health information to urban Mexican-Americans: sources of health information. HEALTH EDUCATION QUARTERLY, Vol. 9, no. 4 (Winter 1982), p. 293-309. English. DESCR: Doctor Patient Relations; Health Education; Mass Media; *Public Health.

11351 Hayes-Bautista, David E. On comparing studies of different raza populations. AMERICAN JOURNAL OF PUBLIC HEALTH, Vol. 73, no. 3 (March 1983), p. 274-276. English. DESCR: Population Trends.

11352 Howard, David. For "illegals" migration goes both ways. R & D MEXICO, Vol. 2, no. 3-4 (December, January, 1981, 1982), p. 14-17. English. DESCR: Immigration; Migration; Migration Patterns; NATIONAL SURVEY ON EMIGRATION TO THE NORTHERN BORDER AND THE UNITED STATES; *Undocumented Workers.

11353 Hunt, Isabelle F., et al. Zinc supplementation during pregnancy: zinc concentration of serum and hair from low-income women of Mexican descent. AMERICAN JOURNAL OF CLINICAL NUTRITION, Vol. 37, no. 4 (April 1983), p. 572-582. English. DESCR: Chicanas; Low Income; Nutrition; *Prenatal Care.

11354 Kerr, G. R. Supermarket sales high-sugar products in predominantly Black, Hispanic and white census tracts of Houston, Texas. AMERICAN JOURNAL OF CLINICAL NUTRITION, Vol. 37, no. 4 (April 1983), p. 622-631. English. DESCR: Anglo Americans; Blacks; Food Practices; *Nutrition.

11355 Luevano, Richard L. Attitudes of elderly Mexican Americans towards nursing homes in Stanislaus county. CAMPO LIBRE, Vol. 1, no. 2 (Summer 1981), p. 213-228. English. DESCR: *Ancianos; Attitude (Psychological); Cultural Characteristics; Medical Care; *Nursing Homes; Stanislaus County, CA.

11356 LULAC survey approved. LATINO, Vol. 53, no. 8 (December 1982), p. 26. English. DESCR: *League of United Latin American Citizens (LULAC).

11357 The Mexican-American electorate. HISPANIC BUSINESS, Vol. 5, no. 8 (August 1983), p. 34-36. English. DESCR: *Mass Media.

11358 Peterson, Robert A. and Kozmetsky, George. Public opinion regarding illegal aliens in Texas. TEXAS BUSINESS REVIEW, Vol. 56, no. 3 (May, June, 1982), p. 118-121. English. DESCR: Public Opinion; Texas; *Undocumented Workers.

Susto

11359 Richardson, Lynette. Caring through understanding, part II: folk medicine in the Hispanic population. IMPRINT, Vol. 29, no. 2 (April 1982), p. 21, 72-77. English. DESCR: Brujo; Caida de Mollera; Curanderas; Empacho; *Folk Medicine; Mal de Ojo; Mal Puesto.

11360 Trotter, Robert T. Susto: the context of community morbidity patterns. ETHNOLOGY, Vol. 21, no. 3 (July 1982), p. 215-226. English. DESCR: Folk Medicine; Medical Anthropology.

Swann, Ruth N.

11361 Research/development: books. HISPANIC BUSINESS, Vol. 4, no. 4 (April 1982), p. 28. English. DESCR: *Book Reviews; Engineering; Financial Aid; FINANCIAL AID FOR MINORITIES IN ENGINEERING; Kennedy, David W.; PERFECTLY LEGAL - 275 FOOLPROOF METHODS FOR PAYING LESS TAXES; Steiner, Barry R.; Taxation.

Symbolism

11362 Gonzalez, Cesar A. LA FAMILIA de Joaquin Chinas. DE COLORES, Vol. 6, no. 1-2 (1982), p. 146-149. English. DESCR: Artists; Chicano Movement; Chinas, Joaquin; *LA FAMILIA [poster].

Symbolism (cont.)

11363 Villanueva Collado, Alfredo. Fili-Mele: simbolo y mujer en la poesia de Luis Pales Matos e Ivan Silen. REVISTA CHICANO-RIQUENA, Vol. 10, no. 4 (Fall 1982), p. 47-54. Spanish. DESCR: Chicanas; Literary Criticism; LOS POEMAS DE FILI-MELE; *Pales Matos, Luis; Ribes Tovar, Federico; *Silen, Ivan; TUNTUN DE PASA Y GRIFERIA.

Syntax

11364 Dvorak, Trisha and Kirschner, Carl. Mary likes fishes: reverse psychological phenomena in New York Puerto Rican Spanish. BILINGUAL REVIEW, Vol. 9, no. 1 (January, April, 1982), p. 59-65. English. DESCR: New York; Puerto Ricans; *Spanish Language.

11365 Kirschner, Carl. Spanish and English inchoatives and the Spanish-English bilingual: got anything to se? BILINGUAL REVIEW, Vol. 9, no. 3 (September, December, 1982), p. 213-219. English. DESCR: *Grammar; *Semantics; Slang.

System of Multicultural Pluralistic Assessment (SOMPA)

11366 Sattler, Jerome M. and Gwynne, John. Ethnicity and Bender Visual Motor Gestalt Test performance. JOURNAL OF SCHOOL PSYCHOLOGY, Vol. 20, no. 1 (Spring 1982), p. 69-71. English. DESCR: Anglo Americans; *Bender Visual Motor Gestalt Test; Psychological Testing.

11367 Scott, Leigh S., et al. Adaptive behavior inventory for children: the need for local norms. JOURNAL OF SCHOOL PSYCHOLOGY, Vol. 20, no. 1 (Spring 1982), p. 39-44. English. DESCR: *Adaptive Behavior Inventory for Children (ABIC); Anglo Americans; Blacks; Corpus Christi Independent School District; Corpus Christi, TX; Placement.

Tafoya, Tony

11368 Nuestra gente. LATINO, Vol. 53, no. 4 (June 1982), p. 30. English. DESCR: Batine, Rafael; *Biographical Notes; Gimeno, Emil.

TALE OF SUNLIGHT

11369 de la Fuente, Patricia. Ambiguity in the poetry of Gary Soto. REVISTA CHICANO-RIQUENA, Vol. 11, no. 2 (Summer 1983), p. 34-39. English. DESCR: "Avocado Lake"; "Blanco"; "Braley Street"; "Field"; *Literary Criticism; Poetry; "Song for the pockets"; *Soto, Gary; "Telephoning God"; THE ELEMENTS OF SAN JOAQUIN; "Wind".

11370 Paredes, Raymund A. Book review of: THE TALE OF SUNLIGHT. MINORITY VOICES, Vol. 2, no. 2 (Fall 1978), p. 67-68. English. DESCR: Book Reviews; Poetry; Soto, Gary.

TALLER DE IMAGENES

11371 Katra, William H. 'Taller de imagenes': a poetic cosmovision. MINORITY VOICES, Vol. 4, no. 2 (Fall 1980), p. 75-84. English. DESCR: Mendez M., Miguel; Poetry.

Tamayo, Roberto

11372 People. HISPANIC BUSINESS, Vol. 5, no. 11 (November 1983), p. 10. English. DESCR: Aragon, Fermin; *Businesspeople; De Los Reyes, Victor; Di Martino, Rita; Garcia, Ruben; Juarez, Chris; Lopez, Leonard; Nogales, Luis G.; Ozuna, Bob; Rico, Jose Hipolito; Tapia, Raul R.

Tamayo, Rufino

11373 Entertainment = diversion. CAMINOS, Vol. 3, no. 5 (May 1982), p. 54. Bilingual. DESCR: Artists; Buena Vista Cablevision, Inc.; Cinco de Mayo; *Holidays; Knott's Berry Farm, Buena Park, CA; Television.

11374 Gomez, Imelda. Tamayo interview. CAMINOS, Vol. 3, no. 9 (October 1982), p. 7,44. Bilingual. DESCR: *Artists.

11375 Rodriguez, Antonio. Tamayo: artist of great synthesis. CAMINOS, Vol. 3, no. 9 (October 1982), p. 6,8-9,44. English. DESCR: *Artists.

Tampa, FL

11376 Fletcher and Valenti: Tampa's growing arquitectural firm. HISPANIC BUSINESS, Vol. 4, no. 10 (October 1982), p. 15,26. English. DESCR: *Architecture; Business Enterprises; Fletcher & Valenti Architects/Planners, Inc.; Valenti, Frank S.

11377 Garcia, Paco. Tampa: a centennial birthday in 1986. NUESTRO, Vol. 6, no. 10 (December 1982), p. 20-21. English. DESCR: *Population; Population Trends.

Tape & Label Converters (TLC)

11378 Roberto Varela and TLC. CAMINOS, Vol. 3, no. 2 (February 1982), p. 27-29. Bilingual. DESCR: Business; *Businesspeople; *Varela, Robert.

Tapia, Raul R.

11379 People. HISPANIC BUSINESS, Vol. 5, no. 11 (November 1983), p. 10. English. DESCR: Aragon, Fermin; *Businesspeople; De Los Reyes, Victor; Di Martino, Rita; Garcia, Ruben; Juarez, Chris; Lopez, Leonard; Nogales, Luis G.; Ozuna, Bob; Rico, Jose Hipolito; Tamayo, Roberto.

Taracido, Manuel E.

11380 Sargeant, Georgia. Young turks set new standards. HISPANIC BUSINESS, Vol. 5, no. 11 (November 1983), p. 8-9. English. DESCR: Alvarez, Julio E.; *Architecture; Business Enterprises; Management; Marketing; Miami, FL; Wolfberg, David A.; *Wolfberg/Alvarez/Taracido (WAT).

TAT

11381 Constantino, Guiseppe and Malgady, Robert G. Verbal fluency of Hispanic, Black and white children on TAT and TEMAS, a new thematic apperception test. HISPANIC JOURNAL OF BEHAVIORAL SCIENCES, Vol. 5, no. 2 (June 1983), p. 199-206. English. DESCR: Children; Ethnic Groups; *Language Proficiency; TEMAS.

Tatum, Charles

11382 Marquez, Maria Teresa. Book review of: A SELECTED AND ANNOTATED BIBLIOGRAPHY OF CHICANO STUDIES. AZTLAN, Vol. 14, no. 1 (Spring 1983), p. 191-192. English. DESCR: *A SELECTED AND ANNOTATED BIBLIOGRAPHY OF CHICANO STUDIES; Bibliography; Book Reviews; Reference Works.

Tatum, Charles (cont.)

11383 Olszewski, Lawrence. Book review of: CHICANO LITERATURE: A CRITICAL HISTORY. LIBRARY JOURNAL, Vol. 108, no. 2 (January 15, 1983), p. 132. English. **DESCR:** Book Reviews; *CHICANO LITERATURE: A CRITICAL HISTORY; History; Poetry.

Taxation

11384 Business notes. HISPANIC BUSINESS, Vol. 5, no. 10 (October 1983), p. 13. English. **DESCR:** *Business Administration; Business Enterprises; Claudio, Irma; Investments; Los Angeles Board of Public Works; Oakland, CA; Tri-Oakland Development Corporation; Wisconsin Minority Business Forum '83.

11385 Business notes. HISPANIC BUSINESS, Vol. 5, no. 11 (November 1983), p. 27. English. **DESCR:** *Business Enterprises; Garment Industry; High Tech '84; Personnel Management; Puerto Rico; U.S. Department of Housing and Urban Development (HUD).

11386 Research/development: books. HISPANIC BUSINESS, Vol. 4, no. 4 (April 1982), p. 28. English. **DESCR:** *Book Reviews; Engineering; Financial Aid; FINANCIAL AID FOR MINORITIES IN ENGINEERING; Kennedy, David W.; PERFECTLY LEGAL - 275 FOOLPROOF METHODS FOR PAYING LESS TAXES; Steiner, Barry R.; Swann, Ruth N.

11387 Texan honored for court fight. NUESTRO, Vol. 7, no. 1 (January, February, 1983), p. 12. English. **DESCR:** *Rodriguez, Demetrio P.; *School Finance.

11388 Woman chosen by Brown to head tax agency. NUESTRO, Vol. 6, no. 4 (May 1982), p. 27. English. **DESCR:** Appointed Officials; *Becerra, Gloria V.

Teacher Attitudes

11389 Adams, Phylliss J. and Anderson, Peggy L. Comparison of teachers' and Mexican-American children's perceptions of the children's competence. READING TEACHER, Vol. 36, no. 1 (October 1982), p. 8-13. English. **DESCR:** Attitude (Psychological); Children; Colorado; Cultural Characteristics; Learning and Cognition; Sex Roles.

11390 Anderson, Alfred. Training teachers for the bicultural part of bilingual-bicultural education. INTEGRATED EDUCATION, Vol. 20, no. 1-2 (January, April, 1982), p. 73-75. English. **DESCR:** Biculturalism; *Bilingual Bicultural Education; *Teacher Training.

11391 Buriel, Raymond, et al. Mexican- and Anglo-American children's locus of control and achievement in relation to teachers attitudes. JOURNAL OF GENETIC PSYCHOLOGY, Vol. 140, no. 1 (March 1982), p. 131-143. English. **DESCR:** *Academic Achievement; Anglo Americans; Children; Comparative Education.

11392 Elliott, Stephen N. and Argulewicz, Ed N. The influence of student ethnicity on teachers' behavior ratings of normal and learning disabled children. HISPANIC JOURNAL OF BEHAVIORAL SCIENCES, Vol. 5, no. 3 (September 1983), p. 337-345. English. **DESCR:** *Devereux Elementary School Behavior Rating Scale (DESBRS); *Ethnic Attitudes.

11393 Miller, Robert. Reading instruction and primary school education - Mexican teachers' viewpoints. READING TEACHER, Vol. 35, no. 8 (May 1982), p. 890-894. English. **DESCR:**

*Curriculum; Early Childhood Education; Educational Theory and Practice; Mexico.

11394 Perales, Alonso M. Effects of teacher-oriented and student-oriented strategies on self-concept, English language development, and social studies achievement of 5th grade Mexican-American students [research notes]. TESOL QUARTERLY, Vol. 16, no. 1 (March 1982), p. 99-100. English. **DESCR:** Attitude (Psychological); Identity; San Antonio, TX; Teacher-pupil Interaction.

11395 Tikunoff, William J. and Vazquez-Faria, Jose A. Successful instruction for bilingual schooling. PEABODY JOURNAL OF EDUCATION, Vol. 59, no. 4 (July 1982), p. 234-271. English. **DESCR:** *Bilingual Bicultural Education; Curriculum; Educational Theory and Practice.

Teacher Training

11396 Anderson, Alfred. Training teachers for the bicultural part of bilingual-bicultural education. INTEGRATED EDUCATION, Vol. 20, no. 1-2 (January, April, 1982), p. 73-75. English. **DESCR:** Biculturalism; *Bilingual Bicultural Education; Teacher Attitudes.

11397 Baldonado, Lisa. A university program to meet Chicago's bilingual needs. BILINGUAL JOURNAL, Vol. 7, no. 4 (Summer 1983), p. 15-17,28. English. **DESCR:** *Bilingual Bicultural Education; Chicago, IL; Curriculum; Urban Education.

11398 Mahan, James M. and Miller, Shawn M. Concerns of Anglo secondary student teachers in Hispanic communities: a pilot study. ILLINOIS SCHOOL RESEARCH AND DEVELOPMENT, Vol. 19, no. 2 (Winter 1983), p. 28-34. English. **DESCR:** Comparative Education; *Frequent Concerns of Student Teachers Survey.

11399 Riley, Mary Tom and Taylor, Vincent. Threading the needle: IEP's for teachers? EDUCATIONAL RESEARCH QUARTERLY, Vol. 7, no. 1 (Spring 1982), p. 2-6. English. **DESCR:** Child Development Associate (CDA) Program; Ethnic Groups.

11400 Rugsaken, Kris T. Qualifications for the bilingual vocational teacher. BILINGUAL JOURNAL, Vol. 6, no. 4 (Summer 1982), p. 22-25. English. **DESCR:** Adult Education; *Bilingual Bicultural Education; *Vocational Education; Vocational Education Act of 1963.

11401 Saracho, Olivia N. Essential requirements for teachers in early childhood bilingual/bicultural programs. CHILDHOOD EDUCATION, Vol. 60, no. 2 (November, December, 1983), p. 96-101. English. **DESCR:** Bilingual Bicultural Education.

Teacher-pupil Interaction

11402 Bradley, Curtis H. and Friedenberg, Joan E. Tips for the English speaking multicultural vocational teacher. BILINGUAL JOURNAL, Vol. 6, no. 1 (Fall 1982), p. 6-9. English. **DESCR:** *Cultural Pluralism; Educational Innovations; Limited-English Proficient (LEP); *Vocational Education.

Teacher-pupil Interaction (cont.)

11403 Buriel, Raymond, et al. Teacher-student interactions and their relationship to student achievement: a comparison of Mexican-American and Anglo-American children. JOURNAL OF EDUCATIONAL PSYCHOLOGY, Vol. 75, no. 6 (December 1983), p. 889-897. English. DESCR: Academic Achievement; Brophy-Good Dyadic Interaction System; *Primary School Education.

11404 Burns, Allan F. Politics, pedagogy, and culture in bilingual classrooms: a case study. NABE JOURNAL, Vol. 6, no. 2-3 (Winter, Spring, 1981, 1982), p. 35-51. English. DESCR: Biculturalism; *Bilingual Bicultural Education; Bilingualism; Cultural Characteristics.

11405 Chesterfield, Ray, et al. The influence of teachers and peers on second language acquisition in bilingual preschool programs. TESOL QUARTERLY, Vol. 17, no. 3 (September 1983), p. 401-419. English. DESCR: Bilingual Bicultural Education; Early Childhood Education; *English as a Second Language; Language Development.

11406 De Anda, Diane. A study of the interaction of Hispanic junior high school students and their teachers. HISPANIC JOURNAL OF BEHAVIORAL SCIENCES, Vol. 4, no. 1 (March 1982), p. 57-74. English. DESCR: *Chicanas; Dropouts.

11407 Maestas, Leo C. Academic performance across cultures: an examination of the effect of value similarity. EDUCATIONAL RESEARCH QUARTERLY, Vol. 7, no. 4 (Winter 1983), p. 24-34. English. DESCR: *Academic Achievement; Cultural Customs; Ethnic Groups; Socialization.

11408 Perales, Alonso M. Effects of teacher-oriented and student-oriented strategies on self-concept, English language development, and social studies achievement of 5th grade Mexican-American students [research notes]. TESOL QUARTERLY, Vol. 16, no. 1 (March 1982), p. 99-100. English. DESCR: Attitude (Psychological); Identity; San Antonio, TX; *Teacher Attitudes.

Teaching
USE: Education

Teaching Profession

11409 Bilingual effort offers few jobs. NUESTRO, Vol. 7, no. 6 (August 1983), p. 13. English. DESCR: *Bilingual Bicultural Education; California; Education.

11410 Burns, Robert C. The miracle teachers: portraits of women who challenged themselves and at the same time challenged a system which had relegated them to nonprofessional... NUESTRO, Vol. 6, no. 6 (August 1982), p. 13-16. English. DESCR: Bilingual Bicultural Education; Short Story.

11411 Cuban exile chosen teacher of the year. NUESTRO, Vol. 6, no. 3 (April 1982), p. 37. English. DESCR: Cubanos.

11412 Dejnozka, Edward L. and Smiley, Lydia R. Selective admissions criteria in graduate teacher education programs. JOURNAL OF TEACHER EDUCATION, Vol. 34, no. 1 (January, February, 1983), p. 24-27. English. DESCR: *Educational Tests and Measurements; Graduate Schools.

11413 Forster, Merlin H. Luis Leal. LA PALABRA, Vol. 4, no. 1-2 (Spring, Fall, 1982, 1983), p. 19-20. Spanish. DESCR: Authors; *Biography; Higher Education; Latin American Literature; *Leal, Luis.

11414 Fuentes, Diana. Chicana perpectives: Ester Reyes Aguilar. COMADRE, no. 1 (Summer 1977), p. 45-48. English. DESCR: Affirmative Action; *Aguilar, Ester Reyes; Ballet Folklorico; *Biography.

11415 Jensen, Joan M. Women teachers, class and ethnicity: New Mexico 1900-1950. SOUTHWEST ECONOMY AND SOCIETY, Vol. 4, no. 2 (Winter 1978, 1979), p. 3-13. English. DESCR: Alternative Education; *Chicanas; Cultural Pluralism; History; *New Mexico; Spanish Language.

11416 Lamento por la jubilacion de un insigne hispanista y viejo amigo (una carta anonima). LA PALABRA, Vol. 4, no. 1-2 (Spring, Fall, 1982, 1983), p. 21-24. Spanish. DESCR: Authors; *Biography; Higher Education; Latin American Literature; *Leal, Luis.

11417 Michel, Jose R. For the new breed of bilingual teachers: what the future holds. CAMINOS, Vol. 2, no. 7 (December 1981), p. [29]. English. DESCR: Bilingual Bicultural Education.

11418 Ortiz, Flora Ida. The distribution of Mexican American women in school organizations. HISPANIC JOURNAL OF BEHAVIORAL SCIENCES, Vol. 4, no. 2 (June 1982), p. 181-198. English. DESCR: *Chicanas; Educational Administration; Educational Organizations.

11419 Plata, Maximino and Jones, Priscilla. Bilingual vocational education for handicapped students. EXCEPTIONAL CHILDREN, Vol. 48, no. 4 (April 1982), p. 538-540. English. DESCR: *Bilingual Bicultural Education; *Handicapped; Limited- or Non-English Speaking Handicapped Students (LONESHS); Vocational Education.

11420 Villarreal, Maria; Tirado, Miguel David; and Lopez, Ronald W. Abelardo Villarreal: a teacher's teacher. CAMINOS, no. 12 (1981), p. 30, 46. Bilingual. DESCR: Biography; *Villarreal, Abelardo.

TEACHING SPANISH TO THE HISPANIC BILINGUAL: ISSUES, AIMS AND METHODS

11421 Dyer, Nancy Joe. Book review of: TEACHING SPANISH TO THE HISPANIC BILINGUAL: ISSUES, AIMS AND METHODS. HISPANIA, Vol. 65, no. 3 (September 1982), p. 474-475. English. DESCR: Book Reviews; Garcia-Moya, Rodolfo; Lozano, Anthony G.; Spanish Language; Valdez, Guadalupe.

11422 Goldin, Mark G. Book review of: TEACHING SPANISH TO THE HISPANIC BILINGUAL: ISSUES, AIMS AND METHODS. NABE JOURNAL, Vol. 7, no. 1 (Fall 1982), p. 53-56. English. DESCR: Bilingualism; Book Reviews; Garcia-Moya, Rodolfo; Language Proficiency; Language Usage; Lozano, Anthony G.; Spanish Language; Valdez, Guadalupe.

TEACHING SPANISH TO THE HISPANIC BILINGUAL: ISSUES, AIMS AND METHODS (cont.)

11423 Gutierrez, John R. Book review of: TEACHING SPANISH TO THE HISPANIC BILINGUAL: ISSUES, AIMS AND METHODS. MODERN LANGUAGE JOURNAL, Vol. 66, no. 2 (Summer 1982), p. 234. English. **DESCR:** Bilingualism; Book Reviews; Garcia-Moya, Rodolfo; Lozano, Anthony G.; Spanish Language; Valdez, Guadalupe.

Teatro

11424 Arias, Ron. Book review of: CONTEMPORARY CHICANO THEATRE. JOURNAL OF ETHNIC STUDIES, Vol. 5, no. 1 (Spring 1977), p. 122-123. English. **DESCR:** Book Reviews; *CONTEMPORARY CHICANO THEATRE; Garza, Roberto.

11425 Asco 83. CAMINOS, Vol. 4, no. 9 (October 1983), p. 36. English. **DESCR:** *Artists.

11426 Astol, Leonardo, et al. El Raja. REVISTA CHICANO-RIQUENA, Vol. 11, no. 1 (Spring 1983), p. 9-11. Spanish.

11427 Barrientos, L. S. The manana show - starring johnny calzon. MAIZE, Vol. 2, no. 3 (Spring 1979), p. 22-31. English.

11428 Book review of: CHICANO THEATER: THEMES AND FORMS. CHOICE, Vol. 20, no. 2 (October 1982), p. 280. English. **DESCR:** Book Reviews; *CHICANO THEATER: THEMES AND FORMS; History; Huerta, Jorge A.

11429 Brown, Edward G. The Teatro Campesino's Vietnam trilogy. MINORITY VOICES, Vol. 4, no. 1 (Spring 1980), p. 29-38. English. **DESCR:** *El Teatro Campesino; Veterans; Vietnam War.

11430 Bruce Novoa, Juan. Round table on Chicano literature. JOURNAL OF ETHNIC STUDIES, Vol. 3, no. 1 (Spring 1975), p. 99-103. English. **DESCR:** *Bruce Novoa, Juan; *Literature; Montejano, David; Morton, Carlos; Ortego y Gasca, Felipe de.

11431 Caldera, Carmela and Martinez, Alma. Alma Martinez: "I'm keeping my fingers crossed" (interview). CAMINOS, Vol. 4, no. 11 (December 1983), p. 32-35. English. **DESCR:** Artists; Films; *Martinez, Alma.

11432 Carmen Zapata and the B.F.A. CAMINOS, Vol. 3, no. 4 (April 1982), p. 38-40. Bilingual. **DESCR:** Artists; Bilingual Foundation of the Arts; *Zapata, Carmen.

11433 Elizondo, Sergio D. Book review of: LITERATURA CHICANA: TEXTO Y CONTEXTO. JOURNAL OF ETHNIC STUDIES, Vol. 1, no. 1 (Spring 1973), p. 68-70. Bilingual. **DESCR:** Book Reviews; Castaneda Shular, Antonia; Literary Criticism; Literary History; Literary Influence; *LITERATURA CHICANA: TEXTO Y CONTEXTO; Literature; Sommers, Joseph; Ybarra-Frausto, Tomas.

11434 Garcia Astol, Leonardo. Monologo. REVISTA CHICANO-RIQUENA, Vol. 11, no. 1 (Spring 1983), p. 8. Spanish.

11435 Garcia Astol, Leonardo. La viajera mundial. REVISTA CHICANO-RIQUENA, Vol. 11, no. 1 (Spring 1983), p. 12-14. Spanish.

11436 Garcia, La Carpa. El fotografo. REVISTA CHICANO-RIQUENA, Vol. 11, no. 1 (Spring 1983), p. 15-16. Spanish.

11437 Greenfield, Charles. Cuban theater in exile: Miami's little Broadway. NUESTRO, Vol. 6, no. 9 (November 1982), p. 36-38. English. **DESCR:** Cubanos; Little Havana; *Miami, FL.

11438 Griffin, Julia Ortiz. Two artists in search of a country: Rafael Rios Rey and Francisco Arrivi. MINORITY VOICES, Vol. 5, no. 1-2 (Spring, Fall, 1981), p. 53-58. English. **DESCR:** *Arrivi, Francisco; Artists; Puerto Rican Literature; Puerto Ricans; *Rios Rey, Rafael.

11439 Guerra, Victor and Duarte, Rodrigo. An interview with Rodrigo Duarte of Teatro de la Esperanza, August 13, 1982/New York City. REVISTA CHICANO-RIQUENA, Vol. 11, no. 1 (Spring 1983), p. 112-120. English. **DESCR:** Duarte, Rodrigo; *El Teatro de la Esperanza.

11440 Huerta, Jorge A. Book review of: CHICANO THEATER: THEMES AND FORMS. NUESTRO, Vol. 6, no. 8 (October 1982), p. 45. English. **DESCR:** *Book Reviews.

11441 Huerta, Jorge A. The influences of Latin American theatre on teatro Chicano. REVISTA CHICANO-RIQUENA, Vol. 11, no. 1 (Spring 1983), p. 68-77. English. **DESCR:** *El Teatro Campesino; Latin America; Valdez, Luis.

11442 Kanellos, Nicolas. The flourishing of Hispanic theater in the Southwest, 1920-30s. LATIN AMERICAN THEATRE REVIEW, Vol. 16, no. 1 (1982), p. 29-40. English. **DESCR:** Folk Drama; History; Social History and Conditions.

11443 Kanellos, Nicolas. Two centuries of Hispanic theatre in the Southwest. REVISTA CHICANO-RIQUENA, Vol. 11, no. 1 (Spring 1983), p. 17-39. English. **DESCR:** California; History; Los Angeles, CA; Photography; San Antonio, TX; Southwest United States; Texas.

11444 Kanellos, Nicolas, ed. Mexican American theatre: then and now. REVISTA CHICANO-RIQUENA, Vol. 11, no. 1 (Spring 1983), p. 1-120. Bilingual.

11445 Lira, Pedro Antonio. El Onceno Festival Chicano-Latino de Teatro. CONJUNTO, no. 51 (January, March, 1982), p. 113-117. Spanish. **DESCR:** *Eleventh International Chicano Latino Teatro Festival, Mission Cultural Center, San Francisco, CA.

11446 Lomeli, Marta. Si yo. MAIZE, Vol. 1, no. 2 (Winter 1977), p. 40-48. English.

11447 Lopez, Yvette. Victoria Espinoza and the development of theater in Puerto Rico. THIRD WOMAN, Vol. 1, no. 2 (1982), p. 56-64. English. **DESCR:** *Espinosa, Victoria.

11448 Miguelez, Armando. El teatro Carmen (1915-1923): centro del arte escenico hispano en Tucson. REVISTA CHICANO-RIQUENA, Vol. 11, no. 1 (Spring 1983), p. 52-67. Spanish. **DESCR:** *Teatro Carmen; Tucson, AZ.

11449 Miller, John C. Book review of: NUEVOS PASOS: CHICANO AND PUERTO RICAN DRAMA. MELUS: MULTI-ETHNIC LITERATURE OF THE UNITED STATES, Vol. 6, no. 3 (Fall 1979), p. 99-100. English. **DESCR:** Book Reviews; Huerta, Jorge A.; *Kanellos, Nicolas; NUEVOS PASOS: CHICANO AND PUERTO RICAN DRAMA (thematic issue of REVISTA CHICANO-RIQUENA).

11450 Morton, Carlos and Valdez, Luis. An interview with Luis Valdez. LATIN AMERICAN THEATRE REVIEW, Vol. 15, no. 2 (Spring 1982), p. 73-76. English. **DESCR:** Agricultural Laborers; *Valdez, Luis.

Teatro (cont.)

11451 Navarro, J.L. Homecoming: a play in one act
in the tradition of the mildly absurd &
surreal. BILINGUAL REVIEW, Vol. 9, no. 3
(September, December, 1982), p. 252-271.
English.

11452 Nontraditional street group. NUESTRO, Vol.
6, no. 6 (August 1982), p. 12. English.
DESCR: Artists; *New Mexico; *Teatro
Claridad, South Valley, NM.

11453 Orona-Cordova, Roberta and Valdez, Luis.
ZOOT SUIT and the Pachuco phenomenon: an
interview with Luis Valdez. REVISTA
CHICANO-RIQUENA, Vol. 11, no. 1 (Spring
1983), p. 95-111. English. **DESCR:** Pachucos;
Valdez, Luis; *ZOOT SUIT [play].

11454 Ortiz Griffin, Julia. The Puerto Rican woman
in Rene Marques' drama. REVISTA
CHICANO-RIQUENA, Vol. 11, no. 3-4 (Fall
1983), p. 169-176. English. **DESCR:** Literary
Criticism; *Marques, Rene; Women.

11455 Padilla-Sanchez, Beverly. T.E.N.A.Z.: Teatro
Chicano/Teatro Latino. CAMINOS, Vol. 2, no.
7 (December 1981), p. 34-35. Bilingual.
DESCR: *Eleventh International Chicano
Latino Teatro Festival, Mission Cultural
Center, San Francisco, CA; Huerta, Jorge A.

11456 Prida, Dolores. Playwrights Laboratory: in
search of a creative formula. NUESTRO, Vol.
7, no. 10 (December 1983), p. 43. English.
DESCR: Authors; Education; *Hispanic
Playwrights-in-Residence Laboratory; INTAR.

11457 Southwest exhibit traces history. NUESTRO,
Vol. 6, no. 8 (October 1982), p. 11-12.
English. **DESCR:** *Southwest United States.

11458 Umpierre, Luz Maria. Introduccion al teatro
de Myrna Casas. THIRD WOMAN, Vol. 1, no. 2
(1982), p. 52-58. Spanish. **DESCR:** *Casas,
Myrna.

11459 Valdes, Guadalupe. Language attitudes and
their reflection in Chicano theatre: an
exploratory study. NEW SCHOLAR, Vol. 8, no.
1-2 (Spring, Fall, 1982), p. 181-200.
English. **DESCR:** Sociolinguistics.

11460 Walia, Adorna. Book review of: THE BILINGUAL
PLAY: PINOCCHIO. BILINGUAL JOURNAL, Vol. 7,
no. 3 (Spring 1983), p. 31. English. **DESCR:**
Bilingual Bicultural Education; Book
Reviews; Pastore Passaro, Maria C.; *THE
BILINGUAL PLAY: PINOCCHIO.

11461 Whisler, Kirk. Exito - an East coast play
for the whole nation. CAMINOS, Vol. 4, no. 6
(June 1983), p. 58,67. Bilingual. **DESCR:**
*EXITO; Gala Hispanic Theatre.

11462 Yarbro-Bejarano, Yvonne. Teatropoesia by
Chicanas in the Bay Area: tongues of fire.
REVISTA CHICANO-RIQUENA, Vol. 11, no. 1
(Spring 1983), p. 78-94. English. **DESCR:**
Chicanas; El Teatro Nacional de Aztlan
(TENAZ); Poetry; *TONGUES OF FIRE.

11463 Ybarra-Frausto, Tomas. La Chata Noloesca:
figura del donaire. REVISTA CHICANO-RIQUENA,
Vol. 11, no. 1 (Spring 1983), p. 41-51.
English. **DESCR:** Biography; *La Chata
Noloesca.

11464 Zimmerman, Enid. An annotated bibliography
of Chicano literature: novels, short
fiction, poetry, and drama, 1970-1980.
BILINGUAL REVIEW, Vol. 9, no. 3 (September,
December, 1982), p. 227-251. English.

DESCR: *Bibliography; Literature; Poetry.

El Teatro Campesino

11465 Brown, Edward G. The Teatro Campesino's
Vietnam trilogy. MINORITY VOICES, Vol. 4,
no. 1 (Spring 1980), p. 29-38. English.
DESCR: Teatro; Veterans; Vietnam War.

11466 Burciaga, Jose Antonio. Theatre: CORRIDOS -
sad and happy masks. NUESTRO, Vol. 7, no. 4
(May 1983), p. 53. English. **DESCR:** Corrido;
*CORRIDOS [play]; Valdez, Luis.

11467 Communications/marketing. HISPANIC BUSINESS,
Vol. 4, no. 2 (February 1982), p. 15.
English. **DESCR:** Cable Television;
Congressional Hispanic Caucus; GalaVision;
Labor Unions; *Marketing; Philip Morris,
Inc.; Publishing Industry; Spanish
International Network (SIN).

11468 Huerta, Jorge A. The influences of Latin
American theatre on teatro Chicano. REVISTA
CHICANO-RIQUENA, Vol. 11, no. 1 (Spring
1983), p. 68-77. English. **DESCR:** Latin
America; Teatro; Valdez, Luis.

11469 Lizarraga, Sylvia S. Observaciones acerca de
la critica literaria Chicana. REVISTA
CHICANO-RIQUENA, Vol. 10, no. 4 (Fall 1982),
p. 55-64. Spanish. **DESCR:** *Bruce Novoa,
Juan; CITY OF NIGHT; *Literary Criticism;
Literature; POCHO; THE SPACE OF CHICANO
LITERATURE.

Teatro Carmen

11470 Miguelez, Armando. El teatro Carmen
(1915-1923): centro del arte escenico
hispano en Tucson. REVISTA CHICANO-RIQUENA,
Vol. 11, no. 1 (Spring 1983), p. 52-67.
Spanish. **DESCR:** Teatro; Tucson, AZ.

Teatro Claridad, South Valley, NM

11471 Nontraditional street group. NUESTRO, Vol.
6, no. 6 (August 1982), p. 12. English.
DESCR: Artists; *New Mexico; *Teatro.

El Teatro de la Esperanza

11472 Guerra, Victor and Duarte, Rodrigo. An
interview with Rodrigo Duarte of Teatro de
la Esperanza, August 13, 1982/New York City.
REVISTA CHICANO-RIQUENA, Vol. 11, no. 1
(Spring 1983), p. 112-120. English. **DESCR:**
Duarte, Rodrigo; Teatro.

Technical Education

11473 Burns, Maureen. Current status of Hispanic
technical professionals: how can we improve
recruitment and retention. INTEGRATED
EDUCATION, Vol. 20, (January, April, 1982),
p. 49-55. English. **DESCR:** Academic
Achievement; Academic Motivation; Counseling
Services (Educational); Socioeconomic
Factors.

Technology

11474 Garcia, Ray J. The technological challenge:
Hispanics as participants or observers.
HISPANIC BUSINESS, Vol. 4, no. 7 (July
1982), p. 20-21,26. English. **DESCR:**
*Careers; Education; *Engineering as a
Profession.

Technology (cont.)

11475 SBA update. HISPANIC BUSINESS, Vol. 5, no. 3 (March 1983), p. 18. English. DESCR: High Technology Industries; Minority Business Development Agency (MBDA); *Small Business; Small Business Innovation Research Act.

THE TEJANO COMMUNITY, 1836-1900

11476 Acuna, Rodolfo. Book review of: THE TEJANO COMMUNITY 1836-1900. WESTERN HISTORICAL QUARTERLY, Vol. 14, no. 2, p. 207-208. English. DESCR: Book Reviews; De Leon, Arnoldo; Texas.

11477 Crisp, James E. Book review of: THE TEJANO COMMUNITY 1836-1900. JOURNAL OF ECONOMIC HISTORY, Vol. 42, no. 4 (December 1982), p. 951-953. English. DESCR: Book Reviews; De Leon, Arnoldo; Texas.

11478 Research/development: books. HISPANIC BUSINESS, Vol. 4, no. 7 (July 1982), p. 27. English. DESCR: *Book Reviews; De Leon, Arnoldo; Finance; History; Spiro, Herbert T.; Texas.

Tejano Music Awards

11479 Top talent at Tejano awards. BILLBOARD, Vol. 95, (January 29, 1983), p. 65. English. DESCR: Awards; Entertainers; Music; Performing Arts; Texas.

Tejeda-Mata v. INS

11480 Helbush, Terry. INS violations of its own regulations: relief for the aliens. GOLDEN GATE UNIVERSITY LAW REVIEW, Vol. 12, (Spring 1982), p. 217-225. English. DESCR: Deportation; *Immigration Law; Undocumented Workers; U.S. v. Calderon-Medina.

Telecommunications

11481 Gupta, Udayan. Netting success: Apoca's approach. HISPANIC BUSINESS, Vol. 5, no. 7 (July 1983), p. 20-21+. English. DESCR: Abrilz, Santos T. (Sandy); Business Enterprises; Businesspeople; Success.

11482 Valenzuela, Nicholas. Ensuring future Hispanic participation in telecommunications. AGENDA, Vol. 11, no. 3 (May, June, 1981), p. 24-27. English. DESCR: Mass Media; Television.

11483 Weber, Robert. Rising star: Satelco. HISPANIC BUSINESS, Vol. 5, no. 9 (September 1983), p. 14. English. DESCR: Business Enterprises; Lagueruela, Andy; *Satelco, Inc.; Veve, Rafael.

"Telephoning God"

11484 de la Fuente, Patricia. Ambiguity in the poetry of Gary Soto. REVISTA CHICANO-RIQUENA, Vol. 11, no. 2 (Summer 1983), p. 34-39. English. DESCR: "Avocado Lake"; "Blanco"; "Braley Street"; "Field"; *Literary Criticism; Poetry; "Song for the pockets"; *Soto, Gary; TALE OF SUNLIGHT; THE ELEMENTS OF SAN JOAQUIN; "Wind".

Tele-Signal Corporation

11485 New York's tele-signal corporation. HISPANIC BUSINESS, Vol. 4, no. 11 (November 1982), p. 20. English. DESCR: Business Enterprises; *High Technology Industries; NEW YORK; Toracida, Esteben.

Television

11486 Alvarez, Amando. Bravisimo. LATINO, Vol. 54, no. 1 (January, February, 1983), p. 10. English.

11487 Bagamery, Anne. SIN, the original. FORBES, Vol. 13, no. 11 (November 22, 1982), p. 96-97. English. DESCR: Anselmo, Rene; Broadcast Media; *Spanish International Network (SIN); Spanish Language.

11488 THE BALLAD OF GREGORIO CORTEZ. NUESTRO, Vol. 6, no. 4 (May 1982), p. 63. English. DESCR: *BALLAD OF GREGORIO CORTEZ [film]; Cortez, Gregorio; Public Television.

11489 Bunnell, Robert. Bravisimo! NUESTRO, Vol. 7, no. 9 (November 1983), p. 21-25. English. DESCR: Anacani; Coca-Cola Company; Miller Brewing Company; Palomino, Carlos; Pena, Samm; Performing Arts.

11490 Caldera, Carmela. Coca-Cola president Bryan Dyson on BRAVISIMO. CAMINOS, Vol. 4, no. 4 (April 1983), p. 44-45,48. Bilingual. DESCR: *BRAVISIMO; Coca-Cola Company; Dyson, Bryan; Private Funding Sources.

11491 Caldera, Carmela. Luis Avalos - he has it all - talent, wit, and a TV show of his own (interview). CAMINOS, Vol. 4, no. 5 (May 1983), p. 36-38. English. DESCR: Artists; *Avalos, Luis.

11492 Cantu, Hector. Aqui en Austin: this is Olga Campos reporting. NATIONAL HISPANIC JOURNAL, Vol. 1, no. 3 (Summer, Fall, 1982), p. 7. English. DESCR: Campos, Olga; Careers; *KTBC-TV, Austin, TX [television station]; Mass Media.

11493 Chavarria, Jesus. The media scene. HISPANIC BUSINESS, Vol. 4, no. 5 (May 1982), p. 6. English. DESCR: Advertising; Broadcast Media; Caballero Spanish Media, Inc. (CSM); *Mass Media; MIAMI MENSUAL; Print Media; Radio.

11494 Communications/marketing. HISPANIC BUSINESS, Vol. 4, no. 5 (May 1982), p. 15. English. DESCR: Anheuser-Busch, Inc.; Farres, Osvaldo; Girl Scouts of the United States of America; *Marketing; Organizations; Vocational Education; Voter Turnout.

11495 Communications/marketing. HISPANIC BUSINESS, Vol. 4, no. 11 (November 1982), p. 18. English. DESCR: California Chicano News Media Association (CCNMA); Diaz-Albertini, Luis; Domecq Importers, Inc.; *Marketing; National Hispanic Media Conference, San Diego, CA, December 2-5, 1982; Pacific Telephone.

11496 Communications/marketing. HISPANIC BUSINESS, Vol. 5, no. 5 (May 1983), p. 24. English. DESCR: Anheuser-Busch, Inc.; Arbitron; Awards; California Chicano News Media Association (CCNMA); Coca-Cola Company; Elizalde, Hector; *Marketing.

11497 Communications/marketing. HISPANIC BUSINESS, Vol. 5, no. 7 (July 1983), p. 24. English. DESCR: AltaVision, Inc. (Denver, CO); Boycotts; Cable Television; Marketing; Operation PUSH; Spanish Satellite Network (SSN).

Television (cont.)

11498 Communications/marketing. HISPANIC BUSINESS, Vol. 4, no. 8 (August 1983), p. 22+. English. **DESCR:** Arredondo, Price; Baseball; De la O, Val; Films; Marketing; *Mass Media; Radio; San Antonio CineFestival, TX; Val De La O Show; Valenzuela, Fernando; Wright & Arredondo Associates; Wright, Oscar.

11499 Diaz, Katherine A. The model of reflection: Rita Moreno. CAMINOS, Vol. 4, no. 3 (March 1983), p. 18-21. Bilingual. **DESCR:** Artists; *Moreno, Rita.

11500 Endicott, Craig. Chicago Hispanics to get new channel. ADVERTISING AGE MAGAZINE, Vol. 53, (February 15, 1982), p. II, M36-37. English. **DESCR:** Chicago, IL; *HATCO/60 [television station], Chicago IL.

11501 Entertaiment reviews. CAMINOS, Vol. 3, no. 8 (September 1982), p. 21. English. **DESCR:** Adams, Bob; Alpert, Herb; Books; Calvert, Robert; Jimenez, Santiago; Lopez, Lisa; Music; Myles, Carol; Paredes, Americo; Pettus, Theodore T.; *Recreation.

11502 Entertainment = diversion. CAMINOS, Vol. 3, no. 2 (February 1982), p. 40-41. English. **DESCR:** Awards; CHECKING IT OUT; Club Hogar Latino; Dance; Films; Flamenco; Marley, Bob; Montalban, Ricardo; ON GOLDEN POND; *Recreation.

11503 Entertainment = diversion. CAMINOS, Vol. 3, no. 4 (April 1982), p. 41. Bilingual. **DESCR:** AZTLAN [journal]; Committee in Solidarity with the People of El Salvador (CISPES); Cultural Organizations; Directories; DIRECTORY OF MINORITY ARTS ORGANIZATIONS; El Salvador; *National Endowment for the Arts; NOTICIERO; Organizations; Periodicals; *Recreation.

11504 Entertainment = diversion. CAMINOS, Vol. 3, no. 5 (May 1982), p. 54. Bilingual. **DESCR:** Artists; Buena Vista Cablevision, Inc.; Cinco de Mayo; *Holidays; Knott's Berry Farm, Buena Park, CA; Tamayo, Rufino.

11505 Figueroa, John. Pueden los Hispanos costearse la television por cable? LATINO, Vol. 53, no. 7 (November 1982), p. 15. Spanish. **DESCR:** *Cable Television.

11506 Five-part series on youth jobs. NUESTRO, Vol. 7, no. 7 (September 1983), p. 13. English. **DESCR:** *Employment Training; KCET-TV, Los Angeles, CA [television station]; *Y.E.S. INC.; Youth.

11507 Garcia, Ignacio M. Regional report, television: "Condo" canceled. NUESTRO, Vol. 7, no. 5 (June, July, 1983), p. 13. English. **DESCR:** Avalos, Luis; Carmen, Julie; CONDO [televison series]; Latin Americans; Stereotypes.

11508 Gonzalez, Magdalena. Recognizing Hispanic achievements in entertainment - U.S. and Mexico. CAMINOS, Vol. 3, no. 7 (July, August, 1982), p. 18-24. Bilingual. **DESCR:** Allende, Fernando; Artists; Awards; Bonilla Giannini, Roxanna; Eynoso, David; Felix, Maria; Films; Gallego, Gina; *Golden Eagle Awards; Hoyos, Rodolfo; Lamas, Lorenzo; Lopez, Conchita; Lopez, Lisa; Montalban, Ricardo; Nosotros [film production company]; Quintero, Jose; Rowe, Arthur; Torres, Liz.

11509 Greenberg, Bradley S. and Heeter, Carrie. Mass media orientations among Hispanic youth. HISPANIC JOURNAL OF BEHAVIORAL SCIENCES, Vol. 5, no. 3 (September 1983), p. 305-323. English. **DESCR:** Broadcast Media; *Mass Media.

11510 Gupta, Udayan. New York's WNJU Channel 47: Spanish TV's hottest item. HISPANIC BUSINESS, Vol. 5, no. 3 (March 1983), p. 16-17+. English. **DESCR:** *Advertising; Broadcast Media; Consumers; Marketing; WNJU-TV, Newark, NJ [television station].

11511 Gutierrez, Felix. Henry Rivera: our Hispanic on the FCC. CAMINOS, Vol. 4, no. 3 (March 1983), p. 22-24,50. Bilingual. **DESCR:** Federal Communications Commission (FCC); Mass Media; *Rivera, Henry.

11512 The Hispanic business directory of the 400 largest corporations. HISPANIC BUSINESS, Vol. 4, no. 6 (June 1982), p. 11-16. English. **DESCR:** Business Enterprises; *Corporations.

11513 Hispanic owned stations. HISPANIC BUSINESS, Vol. 4, no. 5 (May 1982), p. 28. English. **DESCR:** *Broadcast Media; Radio; Radio Stations; Television Stations.

11514 Hispanic television. AMERICAN DEMOGRAPHICS, Vol. 4, no. 6 (June 1982), p. 11. English. **DESCR:** Marketing.

11515 Holston, Mark. The Walter Cronkite of Mexico. NUESTRO, Vol. 7, no. 5 (June, July, 1983), p. 58-59. English. **DESCR:** Cronkite, Walter; Journalists; *Zabludovsky, Jacobo.

11516 Hospital produces television series for Spanish-speaking viewers. HOSPITALS, Vol. 56, no. 8 (April 16, 1982), p. 36. English. **DESCR:** *Hospitals and the Community.

11517 Hulin-Salkin, Belinda. Films need mass appeal. ADVERTISING AGE MAGAZINE, Vol. 53, (February 15, 1982), p. II, M10. English. **DESCR:** Broadcast Media; Films; *Market Research.

11518 KMEX-TV dominates the Hispanic market. HISPANIC BUSINESS, Vol. 5, no. 12 (December 1983), p. 16-17. English. **DESCR:** Advertising; *KMEX, Los Angeles, CA [television station]; Los Angeles, CA; Marketing.

11519 Langley, Roger. Roger Langley's Hispanic beat. HISPANIC BUSINESS, Vol. 4, no. 5 (May 1982), p. 24. English. **DESCR:** Broadcast Media.

11520 Lanier, Alfredo S. The quicksilver world of television news: Phil Ponce's Chicago beat. HISPANIC BUSINESS, Vol. 5, no. 10 (October 1983), p. 18-19+. English. **DESCR:** Journalism; *Ponce, Phil; WBBM-TV, Chicago, IL [television station].

11521 Levario, Raquel. Our children are watching. LATINA, Vol. 1, no. 1 (1982), p. 30. English. **DESCR:** *Chicanas; Stereotypes.

11522 LULAC files complaint against TV networks. NUESTRO, Vol. 6, no. 8 (October 1982), p. 48. English. **DESCR:** Bonilla, Tony; Employment; Equal Employment Opportunity Commission (EEOC); *League of United Latin American Citizens (LULAC); Racism.

Television (cont.)

11523 McGuire, Jack. Hispanic TV network thrives: this SIN is legit. ADVERTISING AGE MAGAZINE, Vol. 53, (February 15, 1982), p. II, M34-35. English. **DESCR:** Broadcast Media; *Spanish International Network (SIN); Spanish Language.

11524 Media/marketing. HISPANIC BUSINESS, Vol. 5, no. 12 (December 1983), p. 38. English. **DESCR:** Albertini, Luis Diaz; Computers; League of United Latin American Citizens (LULAC); Lotus-Albertini Hispanic Reps; Marketing; *Mass Media; Nuestras Noticias; Radio; Reading; Tortosa, Cristobal.

11525 Miller Brewing is airing bilingual commercial. NUESTRO, Vol. 7, no. 9 (November 1983), p. 36. English. **DESCR:** Advertising; Bilingualism; *Miller Brewing Company.

11526 Nevarez, Armando. We're with you, Norman Lear, but watching you closely. NUESTRO, Vol. 7, no. 8 (October 1983), p. 47. English. **DESCR:** Embassy Communications; *Lear, Norman; Stereotypes.

11527 Obledo, Mario. Where are the Latinos? LATINO, Vol. 54, no. 7 (November 1983), p. 4. English. **DESCR:** *Broadcast Media.

11528 Ogaz, Antonio and Caldera, Carmela. What do you think of Coca-Cola's sponsorship of Bravisimo? CAMINOS, Vol. 4, no. 4 (April 1983), p. 46-47. English. **DESCR:** *BRAVISIMO; Coca-Cola Company; Private Funding Sources.

11529 Ole carnival! CAMINOS, Vol. 4, no. 7 (July, August, 1983), p. 32-33. English. **DESCR:** *Bilingual Foundation of the Arts.

11530 Pay TV or free broadcast. LATINO, Vol. 54, no. 1 (January, February, 1983), p. 6. English.

11531 Prime time brown out. LATINO, Vol. 54, no. 8 (December 1983), p. 16-17. English. **DESCR:** Broadcast Media.

11532 Reyes, Luis. Henry Darrow: the man behind the actor. CAMINOS, Vol. 4, no. 6 (June 1983), p. 23-25,66. Bilingual. **DESCR:** Artists; *Darrow, Henry; Films.

11533 Reyes, Luis. The Hispanic image on network television: past & present. CAMINOS, Vol. 4, no. 3 (March 1983), p. 10-16. Bilingual. **DESCR:** Stereotypes.

11534 Ruiz, Jose Luis. Hispanics on TV: who is calling the shots. CAMINOS, Vol. 4, no. 3 (March 1983), p. 7-9. Bilingual.

11535 Schement, Jorge Reina. U.S. communication policy: catching up with Spanish language broadcasting. AGENDA, Vol. 11, no. 3 (May, June, 1981), p. 41-44. English. **DESCR:** Spanish Language.

11536 Siccardi, Maria C. Cable T.V.: new opportunities for Hispanic communities. AGENDA, Vol. 11, no. 3 (May, June, 1981), p. 20-22. English. **DESCR:** *Cable Television.

11537 SIN seeks FCC review of Hughes performance. NUESTRO, Vol. 6, no. 1 (January, February, 1982), p. 50. English. **DESCR:** Laws; *Spanish International Network (SIN).

11538 Sutherland, Sam. TV series eyes crossover: BRAVISIMO sets its sights on mainstream audience. BILLBOARD, Vol. 95, (July 30, 1983), p. 50. English. **DESCR:** *BRAVISIMO;

Broadcast Media; Mass Media.

11539 Television: Hispanics: unexplored territory. LATINO, Vol. 53, no. 2 (March, April, 1982), p. 21+. English. **DESCR:** NBC [television network].

11540 Too much TV and violence in cartoons. LATINA, Vol. 1, no. 2 (February, March, 1983), p. 74. English. **DESCR:** National Coalition on Violence; *Violence.

11541 A torch of diversity. LATINO, Vol. 54, no. 8 (December 1983), p. 15. English. **DESCR:** *Mass Media.

11542 Trevino, Jesus Salvador. Latinos & public broadcasting: the 2% factor. CAMINOS, Vol. 4, no. 3 (March 1983), p. 25-27,50. Bilingual. **DESCR:** *Public Television.

11543 Valenzuela, Nicholas. Ensuring future Hispanic participation in telecommunications. AGENDA, Vol. 11, no. 3 (May, June, 1981), p. 24-27. English. **DESCR:** Mass Media; *Telecommunications.

11544 Whisler, Kirk. Jose Luis Ruiz on sound festival. CAMINOS, Vol. 3, no. 8 (September 1982), p. 6-8. Bilingual. **DESCR:** Artists; Films; *Ruiz, Jose Luis.

11545 Whisler, Kirk. Nosotros on film in Hollywood and Latin America. CAMINOS, Vol. 3, no. 7 (July, August, 1982), p. 15-17. Bilingual. **DESCR:** Artists; Cardinale, Marcela; Espinoza, Jimmy; Films; Gomez, Mike; *Nosotros [film production company]; Ortiz, Yolanda; Velasco, Jerry.

11546 Wittenauer, Cheryl. Rating Hispanic media. HISPANIC BUSINESS, Vol. 5, no. 3 (March 1983), p. 14-15. English. **DESCR:** A.C. Nielsen Company; Advertising; Arbitron; *Broadcast Media.

Television Stations SEE ALSO: Specific call letters of television stations, e.g., KMEX.
11547 Hispanic owned stations. HISPANIC BUSINESS, Vol. 4, no. 5 (May 1982), p. 28. English. **DESCR:** *Broadcast Media; Radio; Radio Stations; Television.

TEMAS

11548 Constantino, Guiseppe and Malgady, Robert G. Verbal fluency of Hispanic, Black and white children on TAT and TEMAS, a new thematic apperception test. HISPANIC JOURNAL OF BEHAVIORAL SCIENCES, Vol. 5, no. 2 (June 1983), p. 199-206. English. **DESCR:** Children; Ethnic Groups; *Language Proficiency; TAT.

"TEMPORARY" ALIEN WORKERS IN THE UNITED STATES: DESIGNING POLICY FROM FACT AND OPINION

11549 Moore, Richard J. Book review of: "TEMPORARY" ALIEN WORKERS IN THE UNITED STATES: DESIGNING POLICY FROM FACT AND OPINION. INTERNATIONAL MIGRATION REVIEW, Vol. 16, no. 4 (Winter 1982), p. 909-910. English. **DESCR:** Book Reviews; Braceros; Ross, Stanley R.; Undocumented Workers; Weintraub, Sidney.

11550 Moore, Richard J. Book review of: "TEMPORARY" ALIEN WORKERS IN THE UNITED STATES: DESIGNING POLICY FROM FACT AND OPINION. INTERNATIONAL MIGRATION REVIEW, Vol. 16, no. 4 (Winter 1982), p. 909-910. English. **DESCR:** Book Reviews; Immigration Law; Literature Reviews; Ross, Stanley R.; Undocumented Workers; Weintraub, Sidney.

Temporary Worker Program

11551 Hing, Bill Ong. Racial disparity: the unaddressed issues of the Simpson-Mazzoli Bill. LA RAZA LAW JOURNAL, Vol. 1, no. 1 (June 1983), p. 21-52. English. DESCR: Amnesty; Asian Americans; Ethnic Attitudes; Family; Immigration; Immigration and Naturalization Service (INS); Latin Americans; Mazzoli, Romano L.; Mexican American Legal Defense and Educational Fund (MALDEF); Simpson, Alan K.; *Simpson-Mazzoli Bill; U.S. Congresssional Subcommittee on Immigration, Refugees and International Law.

11552 Liebowitz, Arnold. Immigration challenge and the congressional response. LA RAZA LAW JOURNAL, Vol. 1, no. 1 (June 1983), p. 1-20. English. DESCR: Amnesty; Immigration; Immigration and Nationality Act (INA); Mazzoli, Romano L.; *Simpson, Alan K.; *Simpson-Mazzoli Bill; Undocumented Workers; U.S. Congresssional Subcommittee on Immigration, Refugees and International Law.

11553 Schey, Peter A. Supply side immigration theory: analysis of the Simpson-Mazzoli Bill. LA RAZA LAW JOURNAL, Vol. 1, no. 1 (June 1983), p. 53-71. English. DESCR: Amnesty; Immigration; Mazzoli, Romano L.; Migration Patterns; Refugees; Simpson, Alan K.; *Simpson-Mazzoli Bill.

Tenayuca, Emma

11554 Monroy, Douglas. Anarquismo y comunismo: Mexican radicalism and the Communist Party in Los Angeles during the 1930's. LABOR HISTORY, Vol. 24, no. 1 (Winter 1983), p. 34-59. English. DESCR: Cannery and Agricultural Worker's Industrial Union; *Communist Party; Confederacion de Uniones de Obreros Mexicanos (CUOM); History; International Ladies Garment Workers Union (ILGWU); Labor; Labor Organizing; *Los Angeles, CA; Worker's Alliance (WA), Los Angeles, CA.

"Tenochtitlan's glory"

11555 Ruiz, Rene A. [Article review of: "The Aztecs"; "Tenochtitlan's glory"; "The Great Temple"]. HISPANIC JOURNAL OF BEHAVIORAL SCIENCES, Vol. 4, no. 3 (September 1982), p. 394-395. English. DESCR: Book Reviews; NATIONAL GEOGRAPHIC [magazine]; *"The Aztecs"; *"The Great Temple".

El Tepeyac Restaurant

11556 It's not all rice & beans, part III (restaurant reviews). CAMINOS, Vol. 4, no. 6 (June 1983), p. 15-18. Bilingual. DESCR: Cache Restaurant; El Cochinito Yucateco Restaurant; La Parrilla Restaurant; *Restaurants.

Term Papers
USE: Style and Composition

Terrazas, Carmen

11557 Gonzalez, Alicia. Women for success. CAMINOS, Vol. 3, no. 6 (June 1982), p. 42-43. Bilingual. DESCR: *Chicanas; *Hispanic Women's Council; Moreno, Rita; Organizations; Saavedra, Denise.

Terrazas, Francisco Barrio

11558 Burciaga, Jose Antonio. Mosca en la leche. LATINO, Vol. 54, no. 5 (August, September, 1983), p. 15. Spanish. DESCR: Elected Officials.

Teschner, Richard V.

11559 Feliciano-Foster, Wilma. A comparison of three current first-year college-level Spanish-for-native-speakers textbooks. BILINGUAL REVIEW, Vol. 9, no. 1 (January, April, 1982), p. 72-81. English. DESCR: *Book Reviews; ESPANOL ESCRITO; Garza-Swan, Gloria; *Language Development; Mejias, Hugo A.; MEJORA TU ESPANOL; NUESTRO ESPANOL: CURSO PARA ESTUDIANTES BILINGUES; Portilla, Marta de la; Spanish Language Textbooks; Valdes Fallis, Guadalupe; Varela, Beatriz.

11560 Woods, Richard D. Book review of: SPANISH AND ENGLISH OF UNITED STATES HISPANOS: A CRITICAL, ANNOTATED, LINGUISTIC BIBLIOGRAPHY. JOURNAL OF ETHNIC STUDIES, Vol. 4, no. 3 (Fall 1976), p. 116. English. DESCR: Accentedness; Bibliography; Bills, Garland D.; Book Reviews; Craddock, Jerry R.; Language Patterns; *SPANISH AND ENGLISH OF U.S. HISPANOS: A CRITICAL, ANNOTATED, LINGUISTIC BIBLIOGRAPHY; Spanish Language.

Test of Social Problem Solving

11561 Rueda, Robert. Interpersonal tactics and communicative strategies of Anglo-American and Mexican American mildly mentally retarded and nonretarded students. APPLIED RESEARCH IN MENTAL RETARDATION, Vol. 4, no. 2 (1983), p. 153-161. English. DESCR: Anglo Americans; Children; Intelligence Tests; *Mentally Handicapped.

THE TESTING TRAP

11562 Tucker, Sally. Book review of: THE TESTING TRAP. HISPANIC JOURNAL OF BEHAVIORAL SCIENCES, Vol. 5, no. 2 (June 1983), p. 241-244. English. DESCR: Book Reviews; Strenio, Andrew J., Jr.

Tewa Basin, NM

11563 Weber, Kenneth R. Book review of: HISPANIC VILLAGES OF NORTHERN NEW MEXICO. SOUTHWEST ECONOMY AND SOCIETY, Vol. 1, no. 1 (Spring 1976), p. 48. English. DESCR: Book Reviews; Economic History and Conditions; Great Depression, 1929-1933; *HISPANIC VILLAGES OF NORTHERN NEW MEXICO; New Mexico; Weigle, Marta.

Texas

11564 Acuna, Rodolfo. Book review of: THE TEJANO COMMUNITY 1836-1900. WESTERN HISTORICAL QUARTERLY, Vol. 14, no. 2, p. 207-208. English. DESCR: Book Reviews; De Leon, Arnoldo; *THE TEJANO COMMUNITY, 1836-1900.

11565 Appeals court overturns Texas bilingual order. PHI DELTA KAPPAN, Vol. 64, no. 1 (September 1982), p. 75. English. DESCR: Bilingual Bicultural Education; *Educational Law and Legislation.

11566 Aptekar, Lewis. Mexican-American high school students' perception of school. ADOLESCENCE, Vol. 18, no. 70 (Summer 1983), p. 345-357. English. DESCR: Anthony, TX; *Attitude (Psychological); Canutillo, TX; High School Students.

Texas (cont.)

11567 Bradshaw, Benjamin S. and Frisbie, W. Parker. Potential labor force supply and replacement in Mexico and the states of the Mexican cession and Texas: 1980-2000. INTERNATIONAL MIGRATION REVIEW, Vol. 17, no. 3 (Fall 1983), p. 394-409. English. **DESCR:** Immigration; *Labor Supply and Market; *Mexico.

11568 Campbell, Jack K. Senator Yarborough and the Texan RWY brand on bilingual education and federal aid. EDUCATIONAL STUDIES, Vol. 12, no. 4 (Winter 1981, 1982), p. 403-415. English. **DESCR:** *Bilingual Bicultural Education; Educational Law and Legislation; History; Social History and Conditions; Yarborough, Ralph Webster.

11569 Crisp, James E. Book review of: THE TEJANO COMMUNITY 1836-1900. JOURNAL OF ECONOMIC HISTORY, Vol. 42, no. 4 (December 1982), p. 951-953. English. **DESCR:** Book Reviews; De Leon, Arnoldo; *THE TEJANO COMMUNITY, 1836-1900.

11570 De Leon, Arnoldo. Book review of: ON THE BORDER: PORTRAITS OF AMERICA'S SOUTHWESTERN FRONTIER. SOUTHWESTERN HISTORICAL QUARTERLY, Vol. 86, no. 2 (1982), p. 367-368. English. **DESCR:** Book Reviews; History; Mexico; Miller, Tom; *ON THE BORDER: PORTRAITS OF AMERICA'S SOUTHWESTERN FRONTIER.

11571 De Leon, Arnoldo and Stewart, Kenneth L. Lost dream and found fortunes: Mexican and Anglo immigrants in South Texas,1850 -1900. WESTERN HISTORICAL QUARTERLY, Vol. 14, no. 3 (1983), p. 291-310. English. **DESCR:** History; Migrant Labor; *Migration.

11572 Deep in the heart of Texas. LATINO, Vol. 53, no. 4 (June 1982), p. 8. English. **DESCR:** *Holidays.

11573 Deibel, Richard and Sanchez, Tony, Jr. Business on the border: attracting venture capital. HISPANIC BUSINESS, Vol. 5, no. 9 (September 1983), p. 20-21+. English. **DESCR:** Border Industries; Border Region; Finance; *Sanchez, Tony, Jr.

11574 Flores, David. 30's gridder recalls pain of prejudice. NUESTRO, Vol. 6, no. 8 (October 1982), p. 25-26. English. **DESCR:** *Lerma, Everardo Carlos; Rio Grande Valley, TX; Sports.

11575 Gente; FBI head, two agents praised by Texas house. NUESTRO, Vol. 7, no. 4 (May 1983), p. 52. English. **DESCR:** Careers; *Federal Bureau of Investigation (FBI); Salinas, Raul.

11576 Hansen, Niles. Location preference and opportunity cost: a South Texas perspective. SOCIAL SCIENCE QUARTERLY, Vol. 63, (September 1982), p. 506-516. English. **DESCR:** *Economic History and Conditions; Employment.

11577 Hispanic voting trends. HISPANIC BUSINESS, Vol. 4, no. 8 (August 1983), p. 28-29. English. **DESCR:** Bilingual Ballots; Bilingualism; California; *Elections; Mexican American Legal Defense and Educational Fund (MALDEF); Southwest Voter Registration Education Project (SVRP); Voter Turnout.

11578 Hwang, Sean-Shong and Murdock, Steve H. Residential segregation in Texas in 1980. SOCIAL SCIENCE QUARTERLY, Vol. 63, (December 1982), p. 737-748. English. **DESCR:** Housing; *Segregation and Desegregation.

11579 Kanellos, Nicolas. Two centuries of Hispanic theatre in the Southwest. REVISTA CHICANO-RIQUENA, Vol. 11, no. 1 (Spring 1983), p. 17-39. English. **DESCR:** California; History; Los Angeles, CA; Photography; San Antonio, TX; Southwest United States; *Teatro.

11580 Leigh, Monroe. United States Constitution - equal protection deprivation of education in illegal alien school-children not justified by substantial state goal. AMERICAN JOURNAL OF INTERNATIONAL LAW, Vol. 77, no. 1 (January 1983), p. 151-153. English. **DESCR:** *Children; Discrimination in Education; Doe v. Plyer [Tyler Independent School District, Texas]; *Education; *Undocumented Workers.

11581 Limon, Jose. History, Chicano joking, and the varieties of higher-education: tradition and performance as critical symbolic action. JOURNAL OF THE FOLKLORE INSTITUTE, Vol. 19, no. 2-3 (1982), p. 146-166. English. **DESCR:** *Chistes; Folklore; Higher Education; Humor; Interpersonal Relations; University of Texas at Austin.

11582 McCarthy, Martha. Legal forum. The right to an education: illegal aliens. JOURNAL OF EDUCATIONAL EQUITY AND LEADERSHIP, Vol. 2, no. 4 (Summer 1982), p. 282-287. English. **DESCR:** Administration of Justice; Doe v. Plyer [Tyler Independent School District, Texas]; Education; *Educational Law and Legislation; Migrant Children; *Migrant Education; Undocumented Workers.

11583 Miller, Lawrence W. A note on cultural assimilation in south Texas. BORDERLANDS JOURNAL, Vol. 6, no. 1 (Fall 1982), p. 93-98. English. **DESCR:** *Assimilation.

11584 Murray, Melissa and De Leon, Hector. Texas politics: a frank talk about leadership, Austin, state government and attorney Hector de Leon. NATIONAL HISPANIC JOURNAL, Vol. 1, no. 4 (Spring 1983), p. 10-13. English. **DESCR:** Clements, Bill; De Leon, Hector; *Politics; White, Mark.

11585 Paull, Gene J. and Zavaleta, Anthony N. Archaeology and ethnohistory of the Boscaje de Palmas. BORDERLANDS JOURNAL, Vol. 6, no. 2 (Spring 1983), p. 111-150. English. **DESCR:** *Anthropology.

11586 Peterson, Robert A. and Kozmetsky, George. Public opinion regarding illegal aliens in Texas. TEXAS BUSINESS REVIEW, Vol. 56, no. 3 (May, June, 1982), p. 118-121. English. **DESCR:** Public Opinion; Surveys; *Undocumented Workers.

11587 Powell-Griner, Eve and Streck, Dan. A closer examination of neonatal mortality rates among the Texas Spanish surname population. AMERICAN JOURNAL OF PUBLIC HEALTH, Vol. 72, no. 9 (September 1982), p. 993-999. English. **DESCR:** *Infant Mortality.

11588 Profile of a public man. NUESTRO, Vol. 7, no. 2 (March 1983), p. 13-19+. English. **DESCR:** Elected Officials; *Gonzalez, Henry B.; Politics.

11589 Research/development: books. HISPANIC BUSINESS, Vol. 4, no. 7 (July 1982), p. 27. English. **DESCR:** *Book Reviews; De Leon, Arnoldo; Finance; History; Spiro, Herbert T.; THE TEJANO COMMUNITY, 1836-1900.

Texas (cont.)

11590 Reyna, Jose R. Musica tejana. CAMINOS, Vol. 4, no. 10 (November 1983), p. 25,48. English. DESCR: *Music.

11591 Reyna, Jose R. Notes on Tejano music. AZTLAN, Vol. 13, no. 1-2 (Spring, Fall, 1982), p. 81-94. English. DESCR: Conjunto; Ethnomusicology; *Music.

11592 Rips, Geoffrey. Mexican Americans jalaron la palanca, Democrats say ole. TEXAS OBSERVOR, Vol. 75, (January 1983), p. 6-7. English. DESCR: Democratic Party; Political Representation; *Voter Turnout.

11593 Rosales, Francisco Arturo. Book review of: DESERT IMMIGRANTS: THE MEXICANS OF EL PASO 1880-1920. ARIZONA AND THE WEST, Vol. 24, no. 1 (Spring 1982), p. 79-80. English. DESCR: Book Reviews; *DESERT IMMIGRANTS: THE MEXICANS OF EL PASO 1880-1920; Garcia, Mario T.; Immigrants.

11594 San Miguel, Guadalupe. In the background: conflict and controversy in the evolution of bilingual legislation in Texas, 1965-73. NABE JOURNAL, Vol. 7, no. 3 (Spring 1983), p. 23-40. English. DESCR: *Bilingual Bicultural Education; *Educational Law and Legislation; Educational Theory and Practice.

11595 San Miguel, Guadalupe. Mexican American organizations and the changing politics of school desegration in Texas, 1945 to 1980. SOCIAL SCIENCE QUARTERLY, Vol. 63, (December 1982), p. 701-715. English. DESCR: American G.I. Forum; League of United Latin American Citizens (LULAC); Mexican American Legal Defense and Educational Fund (MALDEF); Organizations; *Segregation and Desegregation.

11596 School house door must be open to children of illegal aliens. CHILDREN'S LEGAL RIGHTS JOURNAL, Vol. 3, (June 1982), p. 19-21. English. DESCR: Constitutional Amendments - Fourteenth; Doe v. Plyer [Tyler Independent School District, Texas]; *Education; Undocumented Workers.

11597 Schorr, Burt. Language lab: grade-school project helps Hispanic pupils learn English quickly; but Texas test's avoidance of bilingual approach is source of controversy. WALL STREET JOURNAL, Vol. 202, (November 30, 1983), p. 1. English. DESCR: *English as a Second Language; Primary School Education.

11598 Sun Belt dominates in top housing markets. NUESTRO, Vol. 7, no. 1 (January, February, 1983), p. 36. English. DESCR: Arizona; *Housing.

11599 Texas voting report. NUESTRO, Vol. 6, no. 4 (May 1982), p. 8-9. English. DESCR: *Voter Turnout.

11600 Top talent at Tejano awards. BILLBOARD, Vol. 95, (January 29, 1983), p. 65. English. DESCR: Awards; Entertainers; Music; Performing Arts; *Tejano Music Awards.

11601 Zuniga, Jo Ann and Bonilla, Tony. Talking Texas: turning the tables with LULAC. HISPANIC BUSINESS, Vol. 5, no. 9 (September 1983), p. 18-19+. English. DESCR: *Bonilla, Tony; Business Enterprises; Consumers; Economic History and Conditions; League of United Latin American Citizens (LULAC); Marketing.

Texas Association of Chicanos in Higher Education (TACHE)

11602 Valverde, Leonard. Hispanic academics organized for the greater good. CAMINOS, Vol. 4, no. 6 (June 1983), p. 50-51. Bilingual. DESCR: Colleges and Universities; Higher Education; Organizations.

Texas Department of Corrections

11603 O`Leary, Tim. David Ruiz brings justice to Texas prisons. NATIONAL HISPANIC JOURNAL, Vol. 1, no. 2 (Winter 1982), p. 21-24. English. DESCR: Clements, Bill; Legal Reform; Prisoners; Prisons; *Ruiz, David.

Texas Panhandle

11604 Garcia, Ruperto. No help yet for farmworkers in Panhandle. TEXAS OBSERVOR, Vol. 74, no. 16 (September 3, 1982), p. 6-7. English. DESCR: *Agricultural Laborers; Crops; Disasters; Economic History and Conditions.

Texas Public Schools

11605 Schey, Peter A. Unnamed witness number 1: now attending the Texas public schools. MIGRATION TODAY, Vol. 10, no. 5 (1982), p. 22-27. English. DESCR: Constitutional Amendments - Fourteenth; Education; Education Equalization; Educational Law and Legislation; Equal Protection Clause; Migrant Children; *Undocumented Children; U.S. Supreme Court Case.

Texas Rangers

11606 Achor, Shirley. Book review of: GUNPOWDER JUSTICE: A REASSESSMENT OF THE TEXAS RANGERS. INTERNATIONAL MIGRATION REVIEW, Vol. 16, no. 2 (Summer 1982), p. 491-492. English. DESCR: Bernal, Joseph; Book Reviews; *GUNPOWDER JUSTICE: A REASSESSMENT OF THE TEXAS RANGERS; Pena, Alberto; Samora, Julian.

11607 Achor, Shirley. Book review of: GUNPOWDER JUSTICE: A REASSESSMENT OF THE TEXAS RANGERS. INTERNATIONAL MIGRATION REVIEW, Vol. 16, no. 2 (Summer 1982), p. 491-492. English. DESCR: Bernal, Joseph; Book Reviews; *GUNPOWDER JUSTICE: A REASSESSMENT OF THE TEXAS RANGERS; History; Pena, Alberto; Samora, Julian.

11608 Trujillo, Larry. Book review of: GUNPOWDER JUSTICE: A REASSESSMENT OF THE TEXAS RANGERS [reprinted from CRIME AND SOCIAL JUSTICE, 61 (Summer 1980)]. CHICANO LAW REVIEW, Vol. 6, (1983), p. 148-155. English. DESCR: Book Reviews; *GUNPOWDER JUSTICE: A REASSESSMENT OF THE TEXAS RANGERS; Samora, Julian.

Texas v. Certain Undocumented Alien Children

11609 Witt, Elder. Court rules illegal aliens entitled to public schooling. CONGRESSIONAL QUARTERLY WEEKLY REPORT, Vol. 40, (June 19, 1982), p. 1479-1480. English. DESCR: Doe v. Plyer [Tyler Independent School District, Texas]; Education; Immigration; Undocumented Children; *Undocumented Workers.

THE TEXICAN (Dallas, TX)

11610 Cantu, Hector. Aqui en Tejas: Hispanic newspapers: city, community papers taking a business approach to the news. NATIONAL HISPANIC JOURNAL, Vol. 2, no. 1 (Summer 1983), p. 9. English. DESCR: AUSTIN LIGHT (TX); EL EDITOR (Lubbock, TX); EL SOL DE HOUSTON (TX); Journalism; *Newspapers.

Textbooks

11611 Englebrecht, Guillermina. And now Domingo... in school in the United States. CHILDHOOD EDUCATION, Vol. 60, no. 2 (November, December, 1983), p. 90-95. English. DESCR: Curriculum; Education; Mexico; *Undocumented Children.

11612 Flemming, Donald N. Book review of: EXPLORACIONES CHICANO-RIQUENAS. MODERN LANGUAGE JOURNAL, Vol. 66, no. 2 (Summer 1982), p. 233-234. English. DESCR: Book Reviews; Burgos-Sasscer. Ruth; *EXPLORACIONES CHICANO-RIQUENAS; Williams, Shirley.

11613 Garcia, Wilfred F. Book review of: NUESTRO ESPANOL: CURSO PARA ESTUDIANTES BILINGUES, BILINGUAL NATIVE SPANISH SPEAKERS FROM THE SOUTHWESTERN UNITED STATES. HISPANIA, Vol. 65, no. 2 (May 1982), p. 320-321. English. DESCR: Book Reviews; Garza-Swan, Gloria; Mejias, Hugo A.; *NUESTRO ESPANOL: CURSO PARA ESTUDIANTES BILINGUES; Southwest United States; Spanish Language.

11614 McKinney, J.E. Book review of: MOSAICO DE LA VIDA: CHICANO, CUBAN AND PUERTO RICAN PROSE. HISPANIA, Vol. 65, no. 2 (May 1982), p. 321. English. DESCR: Book Reviews; Jimenez, Francisco; *MOSAICO DE LA VIDA: CHICANO, CUBAN AND PUERTO RICAN PROSE; Prose; Spanish Language.

11615 Somoza, Oscar U. Book review of: EXPLORACIONES CHICANO-RIQUENAS. HISPANIA, Vol. 65, no. 4 (December 1982), p. 668-669. Spanish. DESCR: Book Reviews; Burgos-Sasscer. Ruth; *EXPLORACIONES CHICANO-RIQUENAS; Williams, Shirley.

The East Los Angeles Community Union (TELACU)

11616 Grimond, John. Reconquista begins. ECONOMIST (London), Vol. 283, (April 3, 1982), p. 12-17. English. DESCR: Political Parties and Organizations; *Political Representation; Public Policy; United Neighborhoods Organization (UNO).

11617 Newsfront. HISPANIC BUSINESS, Vol. 4, no. 1 (January 1982), p. 7. English. DESCR: *Biographical Notes; Businesspeople; Community Development; Jimenez, Richard D.; Macias, Miguel (Mike); Oaxaca, Jaime; Viramontes, Carlos.

"The Great Temple"

11618 Ruiz, Rene A. [Article review of: "The Aztecs"; "Tenochtitlan's glory"; "The Great Temple"]. HISPANIC JOURNAL OF BEHAVIORAL SCIENCES, Vol. 4, no. 3 (September 1982), p. 394-395. English. DESCR: Book Reviews; NATIONAL GEOGRAPHIC [magazine]; *"Tenochtitlan's glory"; *"The Aztecs".

Theater

USE: Teatro

THEY CALLED THEM GREASERS: ANGLO ATTITUDES TOWARD MEXICANS IN TEXAS, 1821-1900

11619 Alvarez, Amando. A clash of cultures. LATINO, Vol. 54, no. 8 (December 1983), p. 18+. English. DESCR: Book Reviews; De Leon, Arnoldo.

THINGS ARE TOUGH ALL OVER

11620 Gutierrez, Chela. Flicks in review. LATINA, Vol. 1, no. 1 (1982), p. 46+. English. DESCR: *AN OFFICER AND A GENTLEMAN; Film Reviews.

Third General Conference of the Latin American Episcopate

11621 Ramirez, Ricardo. Reflections on the Hispanicization of the liturgy. WORSHIP, Vol. 57, no. 1 (January 1983), p. 26-34. English. DESCR: Catholic Church; Clergy; *Liturgy; Religion.

THIRD WOMAN: MINORITY WOMEN WRITERS OF THE UNITED STATES

11622 Hill, Patricia Liggins. Book review of: THE THIRD WOMAN: MINORITY WRITERS OF THE UNITED STATES. MELUS: MULTI-ETHNIC LITERATURE OF THE UNITED STATES, Vol. 7, no. 3 (Fall 1980), p. 87-89. English. DESCR: Book Reviews; *Fisher, Dexter; *Third World Literature (U.S.)

Third World Literature (U.S.)

11623 Hill, Patricia Liggins. Book review of: THE THIRD WOMAN: MINORITY WRITERS OF THE UNITED STATES. MELUS: MULTI-ETHNIC LITERATURE OF THE UNITED STATES, Vol. 7, no. 3 (Fall 1980), p. 87-89. English. DESCR: Book Reviews; *Fisher, Dexter; THIRD WOMAN: MINORITY WOMEN WRITERS OF THE UNITED STATES.

Thomas, Piri

11624 Binder, Wolfgang and Thomas, Piri. An interview with Piri Thomas. MINORITY VOICES, Vol. 4, no. 1 (Spring 1980), p. 63-78. English. DESCR: DOWN THESE MEAN STREETS; Puerto Rican Literature.

Thompson, Edith Lopez

11625 People. HISPANIC BUSINESS, Vol. 5, no. 4 (April 1983), p. 9. English. DESCR: Alvarado, Linda M.; *Biographical Notes; Businesspeople; Castillo, Irenemaree; Castillo, Sylvia; Del Junco, Tirso; Gutierrez, Jose Roberto; Juarez, Joe; Mata, Bill; Miyares, Marcelino; Montanez Davis, Grace; Montoya, Velma; Pineda, Pat; Siberio, Julio.

Tierra [musical group]

11626 Hernandez, Al Carlos. BAD CITY BOYS: Tierra. NUESTRO, Vol. 6, no. 8 (October 1982), p. 46. English. DESCR: Music; Musicians.

11627 Mismanagement hampers TOGETHER AGAIN album. NUESTRO, Vol. 6, no. 3 (April 1982), p. 54. English. DESCR: *Music.

11628 Tierra. LATINO, Vol. 54, no. 1 (January, February, 1983), p. 8. English. DESCR: Music; Musicians.

Tijerina, Pete

11629 Beyette, Beverly. A time of transition for MALDEF. CALIFORNIA LAWYER, Vol. 2, no. 5 (May 1982), p. 28-32. English. DESCR: *Legal Representation; Martinez, Vilma Socorro; Mexican American Legal Defense and Educational Fund (MALDEF).

Tijuana, Baja California, Mexico

11630 Chavira, Ricardo. "New" Tijuana defies the stereotypes. NUESTRO, Vol. 6, no. 4 (May 1982), p. 17-18. English. DESCR: *Urban Renewal.

11631 Esparza, Antonio. The new spectacular Tijuana cultural center. CAMINOS, Vol. 3, no. 11 (December 1982), p. 18,20,22. English. DESCR: *Centro Cultural Fondo Nacional para Actividades Sociales (FONOPAS); *Tourism.

11632 Historic Baja captured on film. CAMINOS, Vol. 3, no. 11 (December 1982), p. 21. English. DESCR: *Baja California, Mexico; *Centro Cultural Fondo Nacional para Actividades Sociales (FONOPAS); Photography; *Tourism.

11633 Ogaz, Armando. "It has been very confusing" Q and A with Hector Santillan. CAMINOS, Vol. 3, no. 11 (December 1982), p. 30-31. Bilingual. DESCR: *Currency; *Santillan Munoz, Hector; *Tourism.

11634 Pendleton, Jennifer. Battle for the buck is the tale of two cities: marketers in San Diego and Tijuana square off. ADVERTISING AGE MAGAZINE, Vol. 53, (February 15, 1982), p. II, M42-43. English. DESCR: Advertising; Border Region; Business; *Market Research; San Diego, CA.

Times Mirror Company

11635 Entertainment = diversion. CAMINOS, Vol. 3, no. 1 (January 1982), p. 41-42. Bilingual. DESCR: ANO NUEVO [film]; Broadcast Media; *CERVANTES [film]; *Films; *SEGUIN [movie].

TIRANO BANDERAS

11636 Espinoza, Herbert O. Lope de Aguirre y santos banderas, la manipulacion del mito. MAIZE, Vol. 4, no. 3-4 (Spring, Summer, 1981), p. 32-43. Spanish. DESCR: De Valle-Inclan, Ramon; Literary Criticism; Mythology.

Tixier y Vigil, Yvonne

11637 Ybarra, Lea. Book review of: LAS MUJERES: CONVERSATIONS FROM A HISPANIC COMMUNITY [reprinted from LA RED/THE NET 5 (Sept. 1982)]. CHICANO LAW REVIEW, Vol. 6, (1983), p. 146-147. English. DESCR: Book Reviews; Chicanas; Elsasser, Nan; *LAS MUJERES: CONVERSATIONS FROM A HISPANIC COMMUNITY; MacKenzie, Kyle; Oral History.

TODAY'S IMMIGRANTS, THEIR STORIES

11638 Reimers, David M. Book review of: TODAY'S IMMIGRANTS, THEIR STORIES. INTERNATIONAL MIGRATION REVIEW, Vol. 16, no. 4 (Winter 1982), p. 900. English. DESCR: Book Reviews; Caroli, Betty; Immigrants; Kessner, Thomas; Oral History.

Toledo, OH

11639 Doyle, Janet. Escoja educacion catolica! MOMENTUM, Vol. 14, no. 1 (February 1983), p. 37-38. English. DESCR: Catholic Church; *Enrollment; *Religious Education.

Tonatiuh-Quinto Sol Award for Literature, 1977-78

11640 Community watching: para la comunidad. CAMINOS, Vol. 3, no. 2 (February 1982), p. 43-44. Bilingual. DESCR: Casa Blanca Youth Project; Colegio Cesar Chavez, Mt. Angel, OR; Colleges and Universities; *Cultural Organizations; Financial Aid; LULAC National Education Service Centers (LNESC); University of California, Riverside.

TONGUES OF FIRE

11641 Yarbro-Bejarano, Yvonne. Teatropoesia by Chicanas in the Bay Area: tongues of fire. REVISTA CHICANO-RIQUENA, Vol. 11, no. 1 (Spring 1983), p. 78-94. English. DESCR: Chicanas; El Teatro Nacional de Aztlan (TENAZ); Poetry; Teatro.

Toracida, Esteben

11642 New York's tele-signal corporation. HISPANIC BUSINESS, Vol. 4, no. 11 (November 1982), p. 20. English. DESCR: Business Enterprises; *High Technology Industries; NEW YORK; *Tele-Signal Corporation.

Torrance, E. Paul

11643 Tabet, Nita. Book review of: RX: DISCOVERY AND NURTURANCE OF GIFTEDNESS IN THE CULTURALLY DIFFERENT. HISPANIC JOURNAL OF BEHAVIORAL SCIENCES, Vol. 4, no. 4 (December 1982), p. 526-527. English. DESCR: Book Reviews; *RX: DISCOVERY AND NURTURANCE OF GIFTEDNESS IN THE CULTURALLY DIFFERENT.

Torres, Art

11644 Community watching. CAMINOS, Vol. 3, no. 5 (May 1982), p. 56-57. Bilingual. DESCR: Adelante Mujer Hispana Conference; Agricultural Laborers; Beilson, Anthony C.; Boycotts; Chacon, Peter R.; Chicanas; *Cultural Organizations; Farm Labor Organizing Commmittee (FLOC); Financial Aid; Hollenbeck Junior High School, Los Angeles, CA; Junior High School Students; National League of Cities; Optimist Club of Greater East Los Angeles; Organizations; Project WELL (We Enjoy Learning & Leadership).

Torres Chabert, Hugo

11645 "Tourism was benefited by the devaluation." Q and A with Hugo Torres Chabert. CAMINOS, Vol. 3, no. 11 (December 1982), p. 32-33,52+. Bilingual. DESCR: *Baja California, Mexico; *Currency; *Tourism.

Torres, Daniel

11646 Ponce, Mary Helen. Recuerdo: the funeral of Daniel Torres, winner of the Medal of Honor. CHISMEARTE, no. 9 (September 1983), p. 35-37. English. DESCR: Medal of Honor; Military Service.

Torres, Esteban E.

11647 Caldera, Carmela. Two views on Central America (interview). CAMINOS, Vol. 4, no. 8 (September 1983), p. 12-16,50. Bilingual. DESCR: *Central America; *International Relations; Sanchez, Philip V.

Torres, Esteban E. (cont.)

11648 Padilla, Steve. Latinos wield political clout in midterm election. NUESTRO, Vol. 6, no. 9 (November 1982), p. 28-30. English. DESCR: De la Garza, Kika; *Elected Officials; Garcia, Robert; Gonzales, Henry B.; Lujan, Manuel, Jr.; Martinez, Matthew G. "Marty", Assemblyman; Ortiz, Solomon; *Politics; Richardson, William; Roybal, Edward R.

11649 People. HISPANIC BUSINESS, Vol. 5, no. 6 (June 1983), p. 8. English. DESCR: Appointed Officials; *Biographical Notes; Businesspeople; Goizueta, Roberto C.; Guerra, Stella; Huapaya, Sixto Guillermo; Kitano, Pat; Manriquez, Suzanna; Oppenheimer-Nicolau, Siabhan; Ortiz, Solomon; Pachon, Harry P.; Richardson, Bill Lopez; Torres, Johnny.

Torres, Jaime

11650 White House honors three minority firms. NUESTRO, Vol. 7, no. 8 (October 1983), p. 51. English. DESCR: *Business Enterprises; Businesspeople; Carson, Norris L.; H & H Meat Products, Mercedes, TX; Hinojosa, Liborio; J.T. Construction Co., El Paso, TX; National Minority Enterprise Development Week; N.L. Carson Construction, Inc., Carthage, MS.

Torres, Johnny

11651 People. HISPANIC BUSINESS, Vol. 5, no. 6 (June 1983), p. 8. English. DESCR: Appointed Officials; *Biographical Notes; Businesspeople; Goizueta, Roberto C.; Guerra, Stella; Huapaya, Sixto Guillermo; Kitano, Pat; Manriquez, Suzanna; Oppenheimer-Nicolau, Siabhan; Ortiz, Solomon; Pachon, Harry P.; Richardson, Bill Lopez; Torres, Esteban E.

Torres, Juan

11652 Baltodano, J. C. Success. CAMINOS, Vol. 4, no. 6 (June 1983), p. 32,34+. English. DESCR: Colleges and Universities; Gallegos, Genevie; Gutierrez, Jorge; Sotelo, Priscilla Elvira; *Students; University of California, Berkeley.

Torres, Liz

11653 Gonzalez, Magdalena. Recognizing Hispanic achievements in entertainment - U.S. and Mexico. CAMINOS, Vol. 3, no. 7 (July, August, 1982), p. 18-24. Bilingual. DESCR: Allende, Fernando; Artists; Awards; Bonilla Giannini, Roxanna; Eynoso, David; Felix, Maria; Films; Gallego, Gina; *Golden Eagle Awards; Hoyos, Rodolfo; Lamas, Lorenzo; Lopez, Conchita; Lopez, Lisa; Montalban, Ricardo; Nosotros [film production company]; Quintero, Jose; Rowe, Arthur; Television.

Torres, Luis

11654 Gutierrez, Felix. Breaking through the media employment wall. AGENDA, Vol. 11, no. 3 (May, June, 1981), p. 13-19. English. DESCR: *Employment; Journalism; Mass Media.

Torrez, Juan

11655 Holley, Joe. Farmworker wins the right to sue. TEXAS OBSERVOR, Vol. 74, no. 13 (July 9, 1982), p. 15. English. DESCR: *Agricultural Laborers; Donna Fruit Company; Laws; Legal Representation; Occupational Hazards.

TORTILLA FLAT

11656 Ortego y Gasca, Felipe de. Fables of identity: stereotype and caricature of Chicanos in Steinbeck's TORTILLA FLAT. JOURNAL OF ETHNIC STUDIES, Vol. 1, no. 1 (Spring 1973), p. 39-43. English. DESCR: Caricature; Chicanos in American Literature; Literature; Steinbeck, John; *Stereotypes.

TORTILLITAS PARA MAMA

11657 Villarreal, Diana Judith. For Spanish children. HORN BOOK MAGAZINE, Vol. 58, (June 1982), p. 312-313. English. DESCR: Book Reviews; Griego, Margo C.; *PARA LOS NINOS, vols. 1&2; Pena, Graciela.

Tortosa, Cristobal

11658 Media/marketing. HISPANIC BUSINESS, Vol. 5, no. 12 (December 1983), p. 38. English. DESCR: Albertini, Luis Diaz; Computers; League of United Latin American Citizens (LULAC); Lotus-Albertini Hispanic Reps; Marketing; *Mass Media; Nuestras Noticias; Radio; Reading; Television.

TORTUGA

11659 Candelaria, Cordelia. Book review of: TORTUGA. LA PALABRA, Vol. 4, no. 1-2 (Spring, Fall, 1982, 1983), p. 167-169. Spanish. DESCR: Anaya, Rudolfo A.; Book Reviews; Literature.

11660 Elias, Edward. TORTUGA: a novel of archetypal structure. BILINGUAL REVIEW, Vol. 9, no. 1 (January, April, 1982), p. 82-87. English. DESCR: Anaya, Rudolfo A.; Book Reviews.

Tourism

11661 Casanova, Steve. Oaxaca and the ancient ruins of Monte Alban and Mitla. NUESTRO, Vol. 6, no. 9 (November 1982), p. 62-64. English. DESCR: Mexico; *Oaxaca, Mexico.

11662 Cruz, Amaury. El Salvador: realities of a country at war. NUESTRO, Vol. 6, no. 3 (April 1982), p. 14-17+. English. DESCR: *El Salvador; Political History and Conditions; Poverty; Short Story.

11663 Esparza, Antonio. The new spectacular Tijuana cultural center. CAMINOS, Vol. 3, no. 11 (December 1982), p. 18,20,22. English. DESCR: *Centro Cultural Fondo Nacional para Actividades Sociales (FONOPAS); Tijuana, Mexico.

11664 Historic Baja captured on film. CAMINOS, Vol. 3, no. 11 (December 1982), p. 21. English. DESCR: *Baja California, Mexico; *Centro Cultural Fondo Nacional para Actividades Sociales (FONOPAS); Photography; *Tijuana, Mexico.

11665 Lenti, Paul. Mexico's posadas a unique experience. NUESTRO, Vol. 6, no. 10 (December 1982), p. 52-55. English. DESCR: *Christmas; Las Posadas; Mexico.

11666 Miller, Shirley and Miller, Tom. Cabo San Lucas - revisited; border updates. CAMINOS, Vol. 3, no. 1 (January 1982), p. 8-9. Bilingual. DESCR: *Baja California, Mexico; Border Region.

Tourism (cont.)

11667 Ogaz, Armando. "It has been very confusing" Q and A with Hector Santillan. CAMINOS, Vol. 3, no. 11 (December 1982), p. 30-31. Bilingual. **DESCR:** *Currency; *Santillan Munoz, Hector; *Tijuana, Mexico.

11668 Olvera Street - a Mexican mercado in the heart of Los Angeles. CAMINOS, Vol. 4, no. 5 (May 1983), p. 26-35,51+. Bilingual. **DESCR:** Los Angeles, CA; *Olvera Street, Los Angeles, CA.

11669 Que pasa? NUESTRO, Vol. 7, no. 3 (April 1983), p. 9. English. **DESCR:** Border Patrol; *Cisneros, Henry, Mayor of San Antonio, TX; Elections; Immigration Regulation and Control; Rocky Mountain Spotted Fever; Servas.

11670 Some useful advise [sic] on currency regulations in Mexico. CAMINOS, Vol. 3, no. 11 (December 1982), p. 28. English. **DESCR:** *Currency; *Mexico.

11671 "Tourism was benefited by the devaluation." Q and A with Hugo Torres Chabert. CAMINOS, Vol. 3, no. 11 (December 1982), p. 32-33,52+. Bilingual. **DESCR:** *Baja California, Mexico; *Currency; *Torres Chabert, Hugo.

11672 Whisler, Kirk. Q & A with Guillermo Schmirdhuber de la Mora, Centro Cultural FONOPAS director: "We try to balance education and culture with entertainment". CAMINOS, Vol. 3, no. 11 (December 1982), p. 19,23. Bilingual. **DESCR:** *Baja California, Mexico; *Centro Cultural Fondo Nacional para Actividades Sociales (FONOPAS); *Schmidhuber de la Mora, Guillermo.

TOWARD ECONOMIC DEVELOPMENT OF THE CHICANO BARRIO

11673 Castillo, Pedro. Letter to the editor. SOUTHWEST ECONOMY AND SOCIETY, Vol. 3, no. 1 (Fall 1977), p. 55-56. English. **DESCR:** Economic History and Conditions; Internal Colonial Model (Theoretical); *Manta, Ben.

EL TRABAJO Y LOS TRABAJADORES EN LA HISTORIA DE MEXICO = LABOR AND LABORERS THROUGH MEXICAN HISTORY

11674 Taylor, William B. Book review of: LABOR AND LABORERS THROUGH MEXICAN HISTORY. NEW MEXICO HISTORICAL REVIEW, Vol. 57, no. 1 (January 1982), p. 91-92. English. **DESCR:** Book Reviews; Frost, Elsa Cecilia; Laborers; Mexico.

Tracking (Educational)

11675 Gonzalez, Gilbert G. Educational reform and the Mexican community in Los Angeles. SOUTHWEST ECONOMY AND SOCIETY, Vol. 3, no. 3 (Spring 1978), p. 24-51. English. **DESCR:** Counseling Services (Educational); Curriculum; *Education; Enrollment; *History; Intelligence Tests; Los Angeles, CA; *Los Angeles City School District; Vocational Education.

Training Programs
        USE: Employment Training

Trambley, Estela Portillo
        USE: Portillo Trambley, Estela

Transamerica Occidental Life

11676 Haggerty, Alfred G. Occidental goes after Hispanic market. NATIONAL UNDERWRITER LIFE AND HEALTH INSURANCE EDITION, Vol. 86, no. 1 (January 2, 1982), p. 22. English. **DESCR:** Cubanos; *Insurance; Market Research.

Transitional Labor

11677 Morales, Rebecca. Transitional labor: undocumented workers in the Los Angeles automobile industry. INTERNATIONAL MIGRATION REVIEW, Vol. 17, no. 4 (Winter 1983), p. 570-596. English. **DESCR:** Automobile Industry; Los Angeles, CA; *Undocumented Workers.

Translations

11678 Acosta, Frank X. and Cristo, Martha H. Bilingual-Bicultural interpreters as psychotherapeutic bridges: a program note. JOURNAL OF COMMUNITY PSYCHOLOGY, Vol. 10, no. 1 (January 1982), p. 54-56. English. **DESCR:** Biculturalism; Bilingualism; Community Mental Health; Doctor Patient Relations; East Los Angeles, CA; *Mental Health Personnel; Mental Health Programs.

Transportation

11679 Applebome, Peter. The Laredo express. TEXAS MONTHLY, Vol. 10, no. 4 (April 1982), p. 100-106. English. **DESCR:** Garza Travel Bureau, San Antonio, TX.

Treaties

11680 Burciaga, Jose Antonio. The Mexican archipelago. NUESTRO, Vol. 6, no. 6 (August 1982), p. 47. English. **DESCR:** *Mexico.

11681 Hernandez, Philip A. The Treaty of Guadalupe Hidalgo: a matter of precision. CACR REVIEW, Vol. 1, no. 1 (September 1982), p. 26-41. English. **DESCR:** *Guadalupe Hidalgo, Treaty of 1848; United States History.

11682 Olivas, Michael A. Indian, Chicano and Puerto Rican colleges: status and issues. BILINGUAL REVIEW, Vol. 9, no. 1 (January, March, 1982), p. 36-58. English. **DESCR:** *Colleges and Universities; Education; Native Americans; Puerto Rican Education.

TREE OF HOPE

11683 Herrera, Hayden. Making an art of pain. PSYCHOLOGY TODAY, Vol. 17, no. 3 (March 1983), p. 86. English. **DESCR:** Biography; HENRY FORD HOSPITAL; *Kahlo, Frida; Paintings; SELF-PORTRAIT WITH PORTRAIT OF DR. FARILL; THE BROKEN COLUMN; THE LITTLE DEER; WITHOUT HOPE.

Trejo, Arnulfo D.

11684 Goldberg, Victor. Ethnic groups in the United States. REVIEWS IN ANTHROPOLOGY, Vol. 9, no. 4 (Fall 1982), p. 375-382. English. **DESCR:** Achor, Shirley; Book Reviews; ETHNIC AMERICA, A HISTORY; MEXICAN AMERICANS IN A DALLAS BARRIO; Sowell, Thomas; *THE CHICANOS.

Tres Plumas

11685 Lewis, William. Tres Plumas and his pantheon of archetypal deities. NUESTRO, Vol. 7, no. 2 (March 1983), p. 38-40. English. **DESCR:** *Aguilar, Humberto; Artists; Sculpture.

Tres Zapotes, Mexico

11686 Quirarte, Jacinto. Book review of: OLMEC: AN EARLY ART STYLE OF PRECOLUMBIAN MEXICO. JOURNAL OF ETHNIC STUDIES, Vol. 1, no. 3 (Fall 1973), p. 92-95. English. DESCR: Book Reviews; La Venta, Mexico; *OLMEC: AN EARLY ART STYLE OF PRECOLUMBIAN MEXICO; Precolumbian Art; Precolumbian Society; San Lorenzo, Mexico; Wicke, Charles R.

Trevino, Jesus Salvador

11687 Fregoso, Linda. Sequin: the same side of the Alamo. BILINGUAL REVIEW, Vol. 10, no. 2-3 (May, December, 1983), p. 146-152. English. DESCR: Film Reviews; *SEGUIN [movie].

11688 Levine, Paul G. Remember the Alamo? AMERICAN FILM, Vol. 7, no. 4 (January, February, 1982), p. 47-49. English. DESCR: Film Reviews; Films; LA HISTORIA [film series]; *SEGUIN [movie].

11689 Ochoa Thompson, Guadalupe. RAICES DE SANGRE: roots of lineage, sources of life. BILINGUAL REVIEW, Vol. 10, no. 2-3 (May, December, 1983), p. 138-141. English. DESCR: Film Reviews; *RAICES DE SANGRE [film].

Trevino, Lee

11690 Gente. NUESTRO, Vol. 7, no. 1 (January, February, 1983), p. 63. English. DESCR: Amaya-Espinoza, Isidro; Camargo, Mateo G.; *Latin Americans; Musicians; Prieto, Carlos; Radio; Sports.

Trimble, Joseph E.

11691 Franco, Juan N. Book review of: COUNSELING ACROSS CULTURES. HISPANIC JOURNAL OF BEHAVIORAL SCIENCES, Vol. 5, no. 2 (June), p. 233-237. English. DESCR: Book Reviews; *COUNSELING ACROSS CULTURES; Draguns, Juris G.; Lonner, Walter J.; Pedersen, Paul P.

Tri-Oakland Development Corporation

11692 Business notes. HISPANIC BUSINESS, Vol. 5, no. 10 (October 1983), p. 13. English. DESCR: *Business Administration; Business Enterprises; Claudio, Irma; Investments; Los Angeles Board of Public Works; Oakland, CA; Taxation; Wisconsin Minority Business Forum '83.

Trotter, Robert

11693 Folk remedy dangerous. NUESTRO, Vol. 7, no. 2 (March 1983), p. 7. English. DESCR: Federal Drug Administration (FDA); *Folk Medicine; Medicine.

Trueba, Henry T.

11694 Walia, Adorna. Book review of: CULTURE AND THE BILINGUAL CLASSROOM: STUDIES IN CLASSROOM ETHNOGRAPHY. BILINGUAL JOURNAL, Vol. 6, no. 4 (Summer 1982), p. 30-31. English. DESCR: Au, Kathryn Hu-Pei; Biculturalism; *Bilingual Bicultural Education; Book Reviews; Cultural Pluralism; *CULTURE AND THE BILINGUAL CLASSROOM: STUDIES IN CLASSROOM ETHNOLOGY; Guthrie, Grace Pung.

Trujillo, Robert

11695 Martinez, Julio A. Book review of: A DECADE OF CHICANO LITERATURE (1970-1979)-CRITICAL ESSAYS AND BIBLIOGRAPHY. RQ - REFERENCE AND ADULT SERVICES DIVISION, Vol. 22, no. 1 (Fall 1982), p. 90. English. DESCR: *A DECADE OF CHICANO LITERATURE (1970-1979): CRITICAL ESSAYS AND BIBLIOGRAPHY; Bibliography; Book Reviews; Gonzalez, Raquel Quiroz; Literary Criticism; Literatura Chicanesca; Literature.

TRW Defense Systems Group

11696 Whisler, Kirk. Martha Cornejo Rottenberg: on opportunities & advancement. CAMINOS, Vol. 4, no. 1-2 (January, February, 1983), p. 17-18,71+. English. DESCR: Careers; *Cornejo Rottenberg, Martha; Electronics Industry; Mining Industry.

Tuberculosis

11697 Cox, Rebecca A., et al. HLA phenotypes in Mexican-Americans with tuberculosis. AMERICAN REVIEW OF RESPIRATORY DISEASE, Vol. 126, no. 4 (October 1982), p. 653-655. English. DESCR: *Medical Research; Medicine; Public Health.

Tucson, AZ

11698 Conflict occurs over city statue. NUESTRO, Vol. 6, no. 9 (November 1982), p. 11. English. DESCR: History; Mexico; *Villa, Pancho.

11699 Gannett's Gerald Garcia goes to Tucson. HISPANIC BUSINESS, Vol. 4, no. 5 (May 1982), p. 13. English. DESCR: *Biography; Gannett Co., Inc.; Garcia, Gerald; Newspapers.

11700 Gonzales, Patrisia. The two cities of Tucson. NUESTRO, Vol. 7, no. 4 (May 1983), p. 20-23. English. DESCR: Accion 80s; Cultural Organizations; *Discrimination in Education; *Discrimination in Employment; Garcia, Gerald; Lopez-Grant, Lillian; Valdez, Joel.

11701 Henderson, Ronald W. and Brody, Gene H. Effects of ethnicity and child's age on maternal judgments of children's transgressions against persons and property. JOURNAL OF GENETIC PSYCHOLOGY, Vol. 140, no. 2 (June 1982), p. 253-263. English. DESCR: Anglo Americans; Arizona; Behavior Modification; *Child Rearing; Cultural Characteristics; Native Americans; *Socialization.

11702 "Jekyll, Hyde" radio station. NUESTRO, Vol. 6, no. 2 (March 1982), p. 13-14. English. DESCR: Radio; *Radio Station KXEW, Tucson, AZ.

11703 Karam, Bruce G. The murals of Tucson. NUESTRO, Vol. 5, no. 8 (November 1981), p. 58-61. English. DESCR: *Art; Mural Art.

11704 Miguelez, Armando. El teatro Carmen (1915-1923): centro del arte escenico hispano en Tucson. REVISTA CHICANO-RIQUENA, Vol. 11, no. 1 (Spring 1983), p. 52-67. Spanish. DESCR: Teatro; *Teatro Carmen.

11705 Vigil, Maria. Regional report, health: Tucson students study herbal arts. NUESTRO, Vol. 7, no. 5 (June, July, 1983), p. 12-13. English. DESCR: *Folk Medicine; Herbal Medicine.

Tucson International Airport

11706 Airport charge causes conflict. NUESTRO, Vol. 7, no. 7 (September 1983), p. 12. English. DESCR: Bilingualism; Language Proficiency.

TUNTUN DE PASA Y GRIFERIA

11707 Villanueva Collado, Alfredo. Fili-Mele:
simbolo y mujer en la poesia de Luis Pales
Matos e Ivan Silen. REVISTA CHICANO-RIQUENA,
Vol. 10, no. 4 (Fall 1982), p. 47-54.
Spanish. DESCR: Chicanas; Literary
Criticism; LOS POEMAS DE FILI-MELE; *Pales
Matos, Luis; Ribes Tovar, Federico; *Silen,
Ivan; Symbolism.

Turincio, Giovanne

11708 Texas teenager wins scholarship. NUESTRO,
Vol. 7, no. 10 (December 1983), p. 13.
English. DESCR: *Financial Aid; Girl Scouts
of the United States of America; Leadership.

Turner, Paul R.

11709 Enright, Scott. Book review of: BILINGUALISM
IN THE SOUTHWEST. EDUCATIONAL STUDIES, Vol.
13, no. 3-4 (Fall, Winter, 1982), p.
494-498. English. DESCR: *BILINGUALISM IN
THE SOUTHWEST; Book Reviews.

Tutorow, Norman E.

11710 Bauer, Karl Jack. Book review of: THE
MEXICAN-AMERICAN WAR: AN ANNOTATED
BIBLIOGRAPHY. JOURNAL OF THE WEST, Vol. 21,
no. 3 (April 1982), p. 73. English. DESCR:
Book Reviews; Mexican American War; *THE
MEXICAN-AMERICAN WAR: AN ANNOTATED
BIBLIOGRAPHY; United States-Mexico
Relations.

11711 Mathes, W. Michael. Book review of: THE
MEXICAN-AMERICAN WAR: AN ANNOTATED
BIBLIOGRAPHY. CALIFORNIA HISTORY, Vol. 60,
no. 4 (Winter 1981, 1982), p. 379-380.
English. DESCR: Book Reviews; *THE
MEXICAN-AMERICAN WAR: AN ANNOTATED
BIBLIOGRAPHY; United States-Mexico War.

11712 Nasatir, A. P. Book review of: THE
MEXICAN-AMERICAN WAR: AN ANNOTATED
BIBLIOGRAPHY. JOURNAL OF SAN DIEGO HISTORY,
Vol. 28, no. 3 (Summer 1982), p. 210-211.
English. DESCR: Book Reviews; Mexican
American War; *THE MEXICAN-AMERICAN WAR: AN
ANNOTATED BIBLIOGRAPHY; United States-Mexico
Relations.

11713 Robinson, Barbara J. Book review of: THE
MEXICAN-AMERICAN WAR: AN ANNOTATED
BIBLIOGRAPHY. REVISTA INTERAMERICANA DE
BIBLIOGRAFIA, Vol. 32, no. 2 (1982), p.
222-223. English. DESCR: Bibliography; Book
Reviews; *THE MEXICAN-AMERICAN WAR: AN
ANNOTATED BIBLIOGRAPHY; War.

TWICE A MINORITY: MEXICAN-AMERICAN WOMEN

11714 Baca Zinn, Maxine. Book review of: TWICE A
MINORITY; MEXICAN-AMERICAN WOMEN. SIGNS:
JOURNAL OF WOMEN IN CULTURE AND SOCIETY,
Vol. 8, no. 2 (Winter 1982), p. 259-272.
English. DESCR: Book Reviews; Chicanas;
Literature Reviews; Melville, Margarita B.;
Social Science.

11715 Fernandez, Maria Patricia. Book review of:
TWICE A MINORITY; MEXICAN-AMERICAN WOMEN.
CONTEMPORARY SOCIOLOGY: A JOURNAL OF
REVIEWS, Vol. 11, no. 3 (May 1982), p.
342-343. English. DESCR: Book Reviews;
Melville, Margarita B.

Tyler Independent School District, Texas

11716 Gallagher, Michael P. Constitutional law -
equal protection: a Texas statute which

withholds state funds for the education of
illegal alien children ... VILLANOVA LAW
REVIEW, Vol. 28, no. 1 (November 1982), p.
198-224. English. DESCR: Constitutional
Amendments - Fourteenth; Doe v. Plyer [Tyler
Independent School District, Texas];
Education; *Undocumented Workers.

UC Latino

11717 UC Latino: salsa music comes to UCLA.
CAMINOS, Vol. 4, no. 5 (May 1983), p. 46,48.
English. DESCR: Musicians; Salsa; University
of California, Los Angeles (UCLA).

UCALATINO [musical group]

11718 Ucalatino: salsa music comes to UCLA.
NUESTRO, Vol. 6, no. 9 (November 1982), p.
59-60. English. DESCR: *Music; Salsa;
University of California, Los Angeles
(UCLA).

UCLA Law School

11719 Father, son attend UCLA school of law.
NUESTRO, Vol. 5, no. 8 (November 1981), p.
42. English. DESCR: *Family; Students.

11720 Flores, Rogelio. The struggle for minority
admissions: the UCLA experience. CHICANO LAW
REVIEW, Vol. 5, (1982), p. 1-12. English.
DESCR: Bakke v. Regents of University of
California; *Law Schools; Legal Education;
Legal Profession; Student Organizations;
Students.

Ulibarri, Sabine R.

11721 Irizarry, Estelle. La abuelita in
literature. NUESTRO, Vol. 7, no. 7
(September 1983), p. 50. English. DESCR:
Alonso, Luis Ricardo; *Ancianos; Chicanas;
Cotto-Thorner, Guillermo; Family; Valero,
Robert.

11722 Mosier, Pat. Book review of: PRIMEROS
ENCUENTROS/FIRST ENCOUNTERS. REVISTA
CHICANO-RIQUENA, Vol. 10, no. 4 (Fall 1982),
p. 69-70. English. DESCR: Book Reviews;
*PRIMEROS ENCUENTROS/FIRST ENCOUNTERS.

Umpierre, Maria

11723 Barradas, Efrain. Book review of: EN EL PAIS
DE LAS MARAVILLAS (KEMPIS PUERTORRIQUENO).
REVISTA CHICANO-RIQUENA, Vol. 10, no. 4
(Fall 1982), p. 67-68. Spanish. DESCR: *Book
Reviews; *EN EL PAIS DE LAS MARAVILLAS
(KEMPIS PUERTORRIQUENO).

Umpierre, Raphael

11724 Gomez, Dalia. Needed: Latino CPA's. NUESTRO,
Vol. 6, no. 1 (January, February, 1982), p.
25-28. English. DESCR: *Accounting; Careers;
Frank, Eleanor Marie; Karpel, Miguel;
Quezada, Felipe L.; Rodriguez, Julio H.;
Zuzueta, Joseph.

Undocumented Children

11725 Arroyo, Sara G. and Tucker, M. Belinda.
Black residential mobility: trends and
characteristics. JOURNAL OF SOCIAL ISSUES,
Vol. 38, no. 3 (1982), p. 51-74. English.
DESCR: *Housing; Los Angeles, CA; Watts, CA.

11726 Englebrecht, Guillermina. And now Domingo...
in school in the United States. CHILDHOOD
EDUCATION, Vol. 60, no. 2 (November,
December, 1983), p. 90-95. English. DESCR:
Curriculum; Education; Mexico; Textbooks.

Undocumented Children (cont.)

11727 Schey, Peter A. Unnamed witness number 1: now attending the Texas public schools. MIGRATION TODAY, Vol. 10, no. 5 (1982), p. 22-27. English. **DESCR**: Constitutional Amendments - Fourteenth; Education; Education Equalization; Educational Law and Legislation; Equal Protection Clause; Migrant Children; Texas Public Schools; U.S. Supreme Court Case.

11728 Vasquez, Ivan. Analysis of June 15, 1982 opinion issued by the U.S. Supreme Court in the case of Texas undocumented children. MIGRATION TODAY, Vol. 10, no. 3-4 (1982), p. 49-51. English. **DESCR**: Constitutional Amendments - Fourteenth; Education; *Education Equalization; Educational Law and Legislation; Equal Protection Clause; Migrant Children; U.S. Supreme Court Case.

11729 Witt, Elder. Court rules illegal aliens entitled to public schooling. CONGRESSIONAL QUARTERLY WEEKLY REPORT, Vol. 40, (June 19, 1982), p. 1479-1480. English. **DESCR**: Doe v. Plyer [Tyler Independent School District, Texas]; Education; Immigration; Texas v. Certain Undocumented Alien Children; *Undocumented Workers.

*Undocumented migration from Mexico: some geographical questions"

11730 Austin, Robert F. Comment on "Undocumented migration from Mexico: some geographical questions". ANNALS OF THE ASSOCIATION OF AMERICAN GEOGRAPHERS, Vol. 72, no. 4 (December 1982), p. 559-560. English. **DESCR**: Jones, Richard C.; Migration Patterns.

11731 Jones, Richard C. Reply to Robert Austin's "Comment on 'Undocumented migration from Mexico: some geographical questions'." ANNALS OF THE ASSOCIATION OF AMERICAN GEOGRAPHERS, Vol. 72, no. 4 (December 1982), p. 561-562. English. **DESCR**: Austin, Robert F.; Migration Patterns.

Undocumented Workers

11732 Alvarez, Alejandro. Economic crisis and migration: comments on James Cockcroft's article. CONTEMPORARY MARXISM, Vol. 5, (Summer 1982), p. 62-66. English. **DESCR**: Cockroft, James; International Economic Relations; Laboring Classes; Legislation; MEXICAN MIGRATION, CRISIS, AND THE INTERNATIONALIZATION OF LABOR STRUGGLES.

11733 Alvarez, Amando. From Texas to Idaho. LATINO, Vol. 53, no. 4 (June 1982), p. 26. English. **DESCR**: Migrant Children.

11734 Appleson, Gail. Court to review INS stop-and-quiz policy. AMERICAN BAR ASSOCIATION JOURNAL, Vol. 68, (July 1982), p. 791-792. English. **DESCR**: Constitutional Amendments - Fourth; Immigration and Naturalization Service (INS); Immigration Regulation and Control; Search and Seizure.

11735 Aragon, Ellen Weis. The factory raid: an unconstitutional act. SOUTHERN CALIFORNIA LAW REVIEW, Vol. 56, no. 2 (January 1983), p. 605-645. English. **DESCR**: Blackie's House of Beef v. Castillo; Deportation; Immigration and Naturalization Service (INS); International Ladies Garment Workers Union (ILGWU) v. Sureck; Racism; Search and Seizure.

11736 Arias, Ron. The rooster that called me home.

NATION, Vol. 236, no. 24 (June 18, 1983), p. 758-761. English. **DESCR**: Arias, Ron; Essays.

11737 Ashman, Allan. What's new in the law: immigration ... detained aliens. AMERICAN BAR ASSOCIATION JOURNAL, Vol. 68, (June 1982), p. 745. English. **DESCR**: Arias v. Rogers; Deportation; Immigration Law.

11738 Babbitt, Bruce. Reagan approach to aliens simply wishful thinking. NATIONAL HISPANIC JOURNAL, Vol. 1, no. 2 (Winter 1982), p. 6-7. English. **DESCR**: Border Region; Braceros; Immigration Regulation and Control; *Reagan, Ronald; Select Commission on Immigration and Refugee Policy; United States-Mexico Relations.

11739 Baca, Reynaldo and Bryan, Dexter Edward. The "Assimilation" of unauthorized Mexican workers: another social science fiction? HISPANIC JOURNAL OF BEHAVIORAL SCIENCES, Vol. 5, no. 1 (March 1983), p. 1-20. English. **DESCR**: Assimilation; *Binationalism; Immigrants.

11740 Baca-Ramirez, Reynaldo and Bryan, Dexter Edward. The undocumented Mexican worker: a social problem? JOURNAL OF ETHNIC STUDIES, Vol. 8, no. 1 (Spring 1980), p. 55-69. English. **DESCR**: Government Services; Immigrant Labor; Immigration; Immigration Regulation and Control; Mexico; Social History and Conditions; Social Services.

11741 Barber, Bob. UFW and the class struggle. SOUTHWEST ECONOMY AND SOCIETY, Vol. 1, no. 1 (Spring 1976), p. 28-35. English. **DESCR**: California; *Labor Unions; *United Farmworkers of America (UFW).

11742 Barry, Tom. On strike! Undocumented workers in Arizona. SOUTHWEST ECONOMY AND SOCIETY, Vol. 3, no. 3 (Spring 1978), p. 52-60. English. **DESCR**: Agribusiness; Agricultural Laborers; Arizona; *Goldmar Citrus Ranch, Phoenix, AZ; Labor Organizing; *Maricopa County Organizing Project (MCOP); Phoenix, AZ; *Strikes and Lockouts.

11743 Bean, Frank D.; King, Allan G.; and Passel, Jeffrey S. The number of illegal migrants of Mexican origin in the United States: sex ratio-based estimates for 1980. DEMOGRAPHY, Vol. 20, no. 1 (February 1983), p. 99-109. English. **DESCR**: Census; Migration; *Population; Statistics.

11744 Boiston, Bernard G. The Simpson-Mazzoli bill: the first major immigration bill in thirty years. OHIO STATE BAR ASSOCIATION REPORT, Vol. 55, no. 39 (October 11, 1982), p. 1738-1743. English. **DESCR**: Employment; Immigration; Visa.

11745 Bracamonte, Jose A. The national labor relations act and undaunted workers: the alienation of American labor. SAN DIEGO LAW REVIEW, Vol. 21, no. 1 (December 1983), p. 29-86. English. **DESCR**: Immigration Law; Labor Unions; National Labor Relations Act (NLRA); Sure-Tan.

11746 Brasch, Walter M. Hanigan case: hung up on racism? SOUTH ATLANTIC QUARTERLY, Vol. 81, no. 4 (Fall 1982), p. 429-435. English. **DESCR**: Administration of Justice; Arizona; Criminal Justice System; Garcia-Loya, Manuel; *Hanigan, Patrick; Hanigan, Tom; Herrera-Mata, Bernabe; *Laws; Racism; Ruelas-Zavala, Eleazar.

Undocumented Workers (cont.)

11747 Bridling at a U.S. immigration bill. BUSINESS WEEK, (February 28, 1983), p. 43-44. English. **DESCR:** *Immigration Law; Immigration Regulation and Control; *Simpson-Mazzoli Bill.

11748 Brooks, Douglas Montgomery. Aliens - civil rights - illegal aliens are inhabitants within meaning of U.S.C 242. SUFFOLK TRANSNATIONAL LAW JOURNAL, Vol. 6, no. 1 (Spring 1982), p. 117-131. English. **DESCR:** Border Patrol; Constitutional Amendments - Fourteenth; Immigration Regulation and Control; U.S. v. Otherson.

11749 Buffenstein, Darryl F. The proposed immigration reform and control act of 1982: a new epoch in immigration law and a new headache for employers. EMPLOYEE RELATIONS LAW JOURNAL, Vol. 8, no. 3 (Winter 1983), p. 450-462. English. **DESCR:** Employment; Immigration Law; *Immigration Regulation and Control; Labor Certification.

11750 Bustamante, Jorge A. The Mexicans are coming: from ideology to labor relations. INTERNATIONAL MIGRATION REVIEW, Vol. 17, no. 2 (Summer 1983), p. 323-341. English. **DESCR:** Attitude (Psychological); *Immigration; Immigration Law; Labor Laws and Legislation; Labor Supply and Market; Migration; Policy; Political Ideology; *Simpson-Mazzoli Bill.

11751 Bustamante, Jorge A. Relief from illegals? Perhaps in 50 years. U.S. NEWS & WORLD REPORT, Vol. 94, no. 9 (March 7, 1983), p. 44. English. **DESCR:** Bustamante, Jorge A.; *Migration.

11752 Camacho de Schmidt, Aurora. Alien smuggling and the refugee question: the INS and sojourners from Yalaj. NUESTRO, Vol. 7, no. 5 (June, July, 1983), p. 20. English. **DESCR:** *Guatemala; *Immigration Regulation and Control; *Political Refugees; Refugees.

11753 Can America get control of its border? ECONOMIST (London), Vol. 286, (February 26, 1983), p. 43-44. English. **DESCR:** *Immigration; Immigration Regulation and Control; Simpson-Mazzoli Bill.

11754 Cardoso, Lawrence Anthony. "Wetbacks" and "slaves": recent additions to the literature. JOURNAL OF AMERICAN ETHNIC HISTORY, Vol. 1, no. 2 (Spring 1982), p. 68-71. English. **DESCR:** Book Reviews; Garcia, Juan Ramon; Lewis, Sasha G.; *OPERATION WETBACK: THE MASS DEPORTATION OF MEXICAN UNDOCUMENTED WORKERS IN 1954; *SLAVE TRADE TODAY: AMERICAN EXPLOITATION OF ILLEGAL ALIENS.

11755 Castagnera-Cain, Jim. Garreau's nine nations offer immigration insights. TEXAS OBSERVER, Vol. 74, (October 15, 1982), p. 12+. English. **DESCR:** Garreau, Joel; Immigration Law; Immigration Regulation and Control; *THE NINE NATIONS OF NORTH AMERICA.

11756 Castro, Mike. Alien smuggling and the refugee question: caught between the border patrol and the river. NUESTRO, Vol. 7, no. 5 (June, July, 1983), p. 18. English. **DESCR:** *Border Patrol; California Rural Legal Assistance (CRLA); *Immigration Regulation and Control; *Sacramento, CA.

11757 Chaikin, Sol C. and Comstock, Phil. Toward a rational immigration policy. JOURNAL OF THE INSTITUTE FOR SOCIOECONOMIC STUDIES, Vol. 7, no. 1 (Spring 1982), p. 48-61. English. **DESCR:** Immigration Law; Immigration Regulation and Control; Socioeconomic Factors.

11758 Chavez, Leo R. Hispanics and immigration reform. NUESTRO, Vol. 7, no. 8 (October 1983), p. 23-24. English. **DESCR:** Immigration Law; *Immigration Regulation and Control; *Simpson-Mazzoli Bill.

11759 Chavez, Leo R. Undocumented immigrants and access to health services: a game of pass the buck. MIGRATION TODAY, Vol. 11, no. 1 (1983), p. 14-19. English. **DESCR:** California; *Immigrants; Medical Care; Migrant Health Services; Public Health Legislation; Simpson-Mazzoli Bill; Social Services.

11760 Chavira, Ricardo. Refugees from poverty: a San Diego perspective. NUESTRO, Vol. 7, no. 4 (May 1983), p. 24-25. English. **DESCR:** Border Patrol; *Immigration Regulation and Control; *San Diego, CA.

11761 Chaze, William L. Invasion from Mexico: it just keeps growing. U.S. NEWS & WORLD REPORT, Vol. 94, no. 9 (March 7, 1983), p. 37-41. English. **DESCR:** Border Region; *Immigration Regulation and Control; Smuggling.

11762 Chaze, William L. Smuggling aliens into U.S.: booming business. U.S. NEWS & WORLD REPORT, Vol. 93, no. 11 (September 13, 1982), p. 57-58. English. **DESCR:** *Smuggling.

11763 Cockcroft, James D. Mexican migration, crisis, and the internationalization of labor struggle. CONTEMPORARY MARXISM, Vol. 5, (Summer 1982), p. 48-61. English. **DESCR:** International Economic Relations; International Labor Activities; Labor Unions; Legislation; Racism.

11764 Cohodas, Nadine. Senate passes legislation to curb illegal immigration. CONGRESSIONAL QUARTERLY WEEKLY REPORT, Vol. 40, (August 21, 1982), p. 2053-2055. English. **DESCR:** Immigration Law; Simpson-Mazzoli Bill.

11765 Cornelius, Wayne A. Interviewing undocumented immigrants: methodological reflections based on fieldwork in Mexico and the U.S. INTERNATIONAL MIGRATION REVIEW, Vol. 16, no. 2 (Summer 1982), p. 378-411. English. **DESCR:** Immigrant Labor; Immigrants; Migrant Labor; Research Methodology.

11766 Cortez, Hector. The undocumented alien and the law. CHRISTIAN CENTURY, Vol. 100, (July 6, 1983), p. 650-652. English. **DESCR:** Immigration Regulation and Control; Religion.

11767 Corwin, Arthur F. The numbers game: estimates of illegal aliens in the United States, 1970-1981. LAW AND CONTEMPORARY PROBLEMS, Vol. 45, no. 2 (Spring 1982), p. 223-297. English. **DESCR:** Bustamante, Jorge A.; Centro Nacional de Informacion y Estadistica del Trabajo (CENINET); Demography; Federation for American Immigration Reform (FAIR); Mexican American Legal Defense and Educational Fund (MALDEF); *Select Commission on Immigration and Refugee Policy; Simpson-Mazzoli Bill; *Statistics.

Undocumented Workers (cont.)

11768 Day, Mark R. Hopes of jobs lure Mexicans.
NATIONAL CATHOLIC REPORTER, Vol. 19,
(October 29, 1982), p. 3. English. DESCR:
Border Region; U.S. Border Patrol.

11769 Day, Mark R. Immigrants ... and Mexican
citizens. NATIONAL CATHOLIC REPORTER, Vol.
18, (February 5, 1982), p. 3. English.
DESCR: Catholic Church; *Immigrants;
Immigration and Naturalization Service
(INS).

11770 Day, Mark R. 'Traffic darn heavy' to U.S.
NATIONAL CATHOLIC REPORTER, Vol. 19,
(October 29, 1982), p. 3. English. DESCR:
Border Patrol; Immigration Regulation and
Control.

11771 Developments in migrant workers programs:
1981. CLEARINGHOUSE REVIEW, Vol. 15,
(January 1982), p. 797-805. English. DESCR:
Fair Labor Standards Act (FLSA); Farm Labor
Contractor Registration Act (FLCRA); Migrant
Education; Migrant Housing; *Migrant Labor;
Migrant Legal Action Program (MLAP);
Occupational Safety and Health
Administration; Pesticides; Wagner-Peyser
Act.

11772 Diez-Canedo, Juan. Undocumented migration to
the United States: a new perspective.
SOUTHWESTERN REVIEW OF MANAGEMENT AND
ECONOMICS, Vol. 2, no. 1 (Winter 1982), p.
1-59. English. DESCR: *Immigration.

11773 Employers may pay if they hire illegals.
BUSINESS WEEK, (June 21, 1982), p. 38.
English. DESCR: *Immigration Law;
Immigration Regulation and Control;
*Simpson-Mazzoli Bill.

11774 Equal protection: right of illegal alien
children to state provided education.
HARVARD LAW REVIEW, Vol. 96, no. 1 (November
1982), p. 130-140. English. DESCR:
*Children; Civil Rights; Discrimination in
Education; Doe v. Plyer [Tyler Independent
School District, Texas]; *Education.

11775 Fantin, Joyce and Fernandez, Diana.
Undocumented aliens ease concern over
younger generation's cultural drift.
BILLBOARD, Vol. 94, (September 11, 1982),
p. T20+. English. DESCR: *Music; Recording
Industry.

11776 Farmworkers win Arkansas contract. SOUTHERN
EXPOSURE, Vol. 10, no. 5 (September,
October, 1982), p. 4. English. DESCR:
Agricultural Laborers; Arkansas; *Arkansas
Farmworker Civil Rights Organizing Project
(AFCROP); Labor Disputes.

11777 Foster, Douglas. The desperate migrants of
Devil's Canyon. THE PROGRESSIVE, Vol. 46,
no. 11 (November 1982), p. 44-49. English.
DESCR: *Agricultural Laborers; California;
*Devil's Canyon, Deer Canyon, CA; Growers;
Labor Camps; San Diego, CA.

11778 Furin, Gary C. Immigration law: alien
employment certification. INTERNATIONAL
LAWYER, Vol. 16, no. 1 (Winter 1982), p.
111-119. English. DESCR: Employment;
Immigration and Nationality Act (INA);
*Labor Certification.

11779 Gallagher, Michael P. Constitutional law -
equal protection: a Texas statute which
withholds state funds for the education of
illegal alien children ... VILLANOVA LAW
REVIEW, Vol. 28, no. 1 (November 1982), p.

198-224. English. DESCR: Constitutional
Amendments - Fourteenth; Doe v. Plyer [Tyler
Independent School District, Texas];
Education; Tyler Independent School
District, Texas.

11780 Garcia, Mario T. Book review of: LOS
MOJADOS: THE WETBACK STORY. JOURNAL OF
ETHNIC STUDIES, Vol. 1, no. 1 (Spring 1973),
p. 66-68. English. DESCR: Book Reviews;
Immigrant Labor; *LOS MOJADOS: THE WETBACK
STORY; Mexico; Samora, Julian; Southwest
United States; United States.

11781 Heberton Craig N. To educate and not to
educate: the plight of undocumented alien
children in Texas. WASHINGTON UNIVERSITY LAW
QUARTERLY, Vol. 60, no. 1 (Spring 1982), p.
119-159. English. DESCR: *Children; Doe v.
Plyer [Tyler Independent School District,
Texas]; Education; San Antonio School
District v. Rodriguez.

11782 Helbush, Terry. INS violations of its own
regulations: relief for the aliens. GOLDEN
GATE UNIVERSITY LAW REVIEW, Vol. 12,
(Spring 1982), p. 217-225. English. DESCR:
Deportation; *Immigration Law; Tejeda-Mata
v. INS; U.S. v. Calderon-Medina.

11783 Hewlett, Sylvia Ann. Coping with illegal
immigrants. FOREIGN AFFAIRS, Vol. 60, no. 2
(Winter 1981, 1982), p. 358-378. English.
DESCR: Immigrant Labor; Immigration;
Immigration Law; *Immigration Regulation and
Control; Policy Formation.

11784 Hopson, Susan B. Immigration: indefinite
detention of excluded aliens held illegal.
TEXAS INTERNATIONAL LAW JOURNAL, Vol. 17,
(Winter 1982), p. 101-110. English. DESCR:
Civil Rights; Deportation; *Detention of
Persons; Immigration; International Law;
Rodriguez-Fernandez v. Wilkinson;
Shaughnessy v. Mezei.

11785 Howard, David. For "illegals" migration goes
both ways. R & D MEXICO, Vol. 2, no. 3-4
(December, January, 1981, 1982), p. 14-17.
English. DESCR: Immigration; Migration;
Migration Patterns; NATIONAL SURVEY ON
EMIGRATION TO THE NORTHERN BORDER AND THE
UNITED STATES; Surveys.

11786 Howell, Frances Baseden. Split labor market:
Mexican farm workers in the Southwest.
SOCIOLOGICAL INQUIRY, Vol. 52, no. 2 (Spring
1982), p. 132-140. English. DESCR:
Agricultural Labor Unions; Arizona Farm
Workers (AFW); *Labor Supply and Market;
Southwest United States; United Farmworkers
of America (UFW).

11787 Hull, Elizabeth. Los indocumentados:
practices, recommendations, and proposals.
POLICY STUDIES JOURNAL, Vol. 10, no. 4 (June
1982), p. 638-651. English.

11788 Illegal aliens vital to economy, mayor says.
NUESTRO, Vol. 7, no. 2 (March 1983), p. 54.
English. DESCR: Border Region; Cisneros,
Henry, Mayor of San Antonio, TX; Economics.

11789 Immigration and nationality symposium. SAN
DIEGO LAW REVIEW, Vol. 20, no. 1 (December
1982, 1983), p. 1-231. English. DESCR:
Akbarian v. INS; Deportation; Employment;
Immigration and Nationality Act (INA);
*Immigration Regulation and Control; Miranda
v. INS; Simpson-Mazzoli Bill.

Undocumented Workers (cont.)

11790 Immigration, jobs. NUESTRO, Vol. 6, no. 4 (May 1982), p. 8. English. **DESCR:** *Immigration; *Immigration and Naturalization Service (INS); Immigration Law.

11791 The impact of undocumented migration on the U.S. labor market. HOUSTON JOURNAL OF INTERNATIONAL LAW, Vol. 5, no. 2 (Spring 1983), p. 287-321. English. **DESCR:** Economic History and Conditions; Employment; Immigrant Labor; Immigration and Nationality Act (INA); Immigration Law; Labor Supply and Market; Research Methodology; Simpson-Mazzoli Bill.

11792 INS raids challenged. NUESTRO, Vol. 6, no. 6 (August 1982), p. 9. English. **DESCR:** *Immigration and Naturalization Service (INS); Immigration Regulation and Control.

11793 INS sweep searches of work areas must meet fourth amendment standards. CRIMINAL LAW REPORTER, Vol. 31, no. 18 (August 11, 1982), p. 2366-2367. English. **DESCR:** Constitutional Amendments - Fourth; Immigration and Naturalization Service (INS); Immigration Regulation and Control; International Ladies Garment Workers Union (ILGWU); *Search and Seizure.

11794 Jaech, Richard E. Latin American undocumented women in the United States. CURRENTS IN THEOLOGY AND MISSION, Vol. 9, no. 4 (August 1982), p. 196-211. English. **DESCR:** Garment Industry; Latin Americans; Protestant Church; Socioeconomic Factors; *Women.

11795 Joe, Harry J. Judicial recommendation against deportation. TEXAS BAR JOURNAL, Vol. 45, no. 6 (June 1982), p. 712-716. English. **DESCR:** *Deportation; Legal Aid.

11796 Johnson, Greg. Administracion en un medio ambiente hispanico. INDUSTRY WEEK, Vol. 212, no. 2 (January 25, 1982), p. 30-34. English. **DESCR:** Industries; *Labor Supply and Market; Spanish Language.

11797 Jones, Richard C. Undocumented migration from Mexico: some geographical questions. ANNALS OF THE ASSOCIATION OF AMERICAN GEOGRAPHERS, Vol. 72, no. 1 (March 1982), p. 77-87. English. **DESCR:** Geography; Immigration; Mexico; *Migration Patterns.

11798 Jones, Robert C. Channelization of undocumented Mexican migrants to the U.S. ECONOMIC GEOGRAPHY, Vol. 58, (April 1982), p. 156-176. English. **DESCR:** Immigration.

11799 Kelly, Philip. Book review of: OPERATION WETBACK: THE MASS DEPORTATION OF MEXICAN UNDOCUMENTED WORKERS IN 1954. SOCIAL SCIENCE JOURNAL, Vol. 19, no. 2 (April 1982), p. 133-134. English. **DESCR:** Book Reviews; Garcia, Juan Ramon; *OPERATION WETBACK: THE MASS DEPORTATION OF MEXICAN UNDOCUMENTED WORKERS IN 1954.

11800 Leigh, Monroe. United States Constitution - equal protection deprivation of education in illegal alien school-children not justified by substantial state goal. AMERICAN JOURNAL OF INTERNATIONAL LAW, Vol. 77, no. 1 (January 1983), p. 151-153. English. **DESCR:** *Children; Discrimination in Education; Doe v. Plyer [Tyler Independent School District, Texas]; *Education; Texas.

11801 Liebowitz, Arnold. Immigration challenge and the congressional response. LA RAZA LAW JOURNAL, Vol. 1, no. 1 (June 1983), p. 1-20. English. **DESCR:** Amnesty; Immigration; Immigration and Nationality Act (INA); Mazzoli, Romano L.; *Simpson, Alan K.; *Simpson-Mazzoli Bill; Temporary Worker Program; U.S. Congresssional Subcommittee on Immigration, Refugees and International Law.

11802 Long, William J. and Pohl, Christopher M. Joint foot patrols succeed in El Paso. POLICE CHIEF, Vol. 50, no. 4 (April 1983), p. 49-51. English. **DESCR:** Border Patrol; Ciudad Juarez, Chihuahua, Mexico; Criminal Acts; *El Paso, TX; Immigration Regulation and Control; *Police; Youth.

11803 Lopez, Phyllis. Migrant life. COMADRE, no. 3 (Fall 1978), p. 4. English. **DESCR:** *Poetry.

11804 Lopez, Phyllis. The unwanted emigrants. COMADRE, no. 3 (Fall 1978), p. 3. Bilingual. **DESCR:** *Poetry.

11805 Lopez, Victor Manuel. Equal protection for undocumented aliens. CHICANO LAW REVIEW, Vol. 5, (1982), p. 29-54. English. **DESCR:** Civil Rights; Discrimination in Education; Legal Reform; Medical Care Laws and Legislation.

11806 Maciel, David R. Visions of the other Mexico: Chicanos and undocumented workers in Mexican cinema, 1954-1982. BILINGUAL REVIEW, Vol. 10, no. 2-3 (May, December, 1983), p. 71-88. English. **DESCR:** Film Reviews; *Films; Mexican Cinema; *Mexico.

11807 Mamer, John W. and Martin, Philip. Hired workers on California farms. CALIFORNIA AGRICULTURE, Vol. 36, no. 9-10 (September, October, 1982), p. 21-23. English. **DESCR:** *Agricultural Laborers; *California; *Labor Supply and Market; Statistics.

11808 Martin, Philip and Mines, Richard. Foreign workers in selected California crops. CALIFORNIA AGRICULTURE, Vol. 37, no. 3-4 (March, April, 1983), p. 6-8. English. **DESCR:** Agricultural Laborers; California.

11809 Martin, Philip L. Select Commission suggests changes in immigration policy: a review essay. MONTHLY LABOR REVIEW, Vol. 105, no. 2 (February 1982), p. 31-37. English. **DESCR:** Immigration; *Immigration Regulation and Control; Select Commission on Immigration and Refugee Policy.

11810 Martinez, Oscar J. Book review of: OPERATION WETBACK: THE MASS DEPORTATION OF MEXICAN UNDOCUMENTED WORKERS IN 1954. NEW MEXICO HISTORICAL REVIEW, Vol. 57, no. 2 (April 1982), p. 201-202. English. **DESCR:** Book Reviews; Garcia, Juan Ramon; *OPERATION WETBACK: THE MASS DEPORTATION OF MEXICAN UNDOCUMENTED WORKERS IN 1954.

11811 Massey, Douglas S. and Schnabel, Kathleen M. Background and characteristics of undocumented Hispanic migrants to the United States: a review of recent research. MIGRATION TODAY, Vol. 11, no. 1 (1983), p. 6-13. English. **DESCR:** Immigrants; Migration; Migration Patterns; Socioeconomic Factors.

Undocumented Workers (cont.)

11812 McCarthy, Martha. Legal forum. The right to an education: illegal aliens. JOURNAL OF EDUCATIONAL EQUITY AND LEADERSHIP, Vol. 2, no. 4 (Summer 1982), p. 282-287. English. **DESCR:** Administration of Justice; Doe v. Plyer [Tyler Independent School District, Texas]; Education; *Educational Law and Legislation; Migrant Children; *Migrant Education; Texas.

11813 Mena, Jesus. Refugees from poverty: a Brownsville perspective. NUESTRO, Vol. 7, no. 4 (May 1983), p. 26. English. **DESCR:** Border Patrol; Brownsville, TX; *Immigration Regulation and Control.

11814 Mendez Gonzalez, Rosalinda. Mexican women and families: rural-to-urban and international migration. SOUTHWEST ECONOMY AND SOCIETY, Vol. 4, no. 2 (Winter 1978, 1979), p. 14-27. English. **DESCR:** Chicanas; Employment; *Family; Garment Industry; Immigration; International Ladies Garment Workers Union (ILGWU); Labor Organizing; Los Angeles, CA.

11815 Mendez, Jose A. and Esquer, Cecilia D. The impact of undocumented aliens on health and public health care in Arizona. ARIZONA BUSINESS, Vol. 30, no. 3 (1983), p. 3-7. English. **DESCR:** Arizona; *Arizona Health Care Cost Containment System (AHCCCS); Government Funding Sources; *Public Health; Public Policy.

11816 Mexican migration to the United States: challenge to Christian witness and national policy. CHURCH AND SOCIETY, Vol. 72, no. 5 (May, June, 1982), p. 29-46. English. **DESCR:** Economic History and Conditions; Immigration Regulation and Control; Religion; United States-Mexico Relations.

11817 Moore, Richard J. Book review of: "TEMPORARY" ALIEN WORKERS IN THE UNITED STATES: DESIGNING POLICY FROM FACT AND OPINION. INTERNATIONAL MIGRATION REVIEW, Vol. 16, no. 4 (Winter 1982), p. 909-910. English. **DESCR:** Book Reviews; Braceros; Ross, Stanley R.; *"TEMPORARY" ALIEN WORKERS IN THE UNITED STATES: DESIGNING POLICY FROM FACT AND OPINION; Weintraub, Sidney.

11818 Moore, Richard J. Book review of: "TEMPORARY" ALIEN WORKERS IN THE UNITED STATES: DESIGNING POLICY FROM FACT AND OPINION. INTERNATIONAL MIGRATION REVIEW, Vol. 16, no. 4 (Winter 1982), p. 909-910. English. **DESCR:** Book Reviews; Immigration Law; Literature Reviews; Ross, Stanley R.; *"TEMPORARY" ALIEN WORKERS IN THE UNITED STATES: DESIGNING POLICY FROM FACT AND OPINION; Weintraub, Sidney.

11819 Morales, Rebecca. Transitional labor: undocumented workers in the Los Angeles automobile industry. INTERNATIONAL MIGRATION REVIEW, Vol. 17, no. 4 (Winter 1983), p. 570-596. English. **DESCR:** Automobile Industry; Los Angeles, CA; Transitional Labor.

11820 Morales, Rebecca. Unions and undocumented workers. SOUTHWEST ECONOMY AND SOCIETY, Vol. 6, no. 1 (Fall 1982), p. 3-11. English. **DESCR:** Employment; Immigration and Naturalization Service (INS); Labor Unions; *Operation Jobs.

11821 Morrison, Thomas K. The relationship of U.S. aid, trade and investment to migration pressures in major sending countries. INTERNATIONAL MIGRATION REVIEW, Vol. 16, no. 1 (Spring 1982), p. 4-26. English. **DESCR:** Border Region; International Economic Relations; Investments; Mexican Border Industrialization Program; *Migration Patterns; PIDER Project; Rural Economics; Rural Urban Migration; United States-Mexico Relations.

11822 Movement of illegal alien laborers into United States is Hobbs act "Commerce". CRIMINAL LAW REPORTER, Vol. 31, no. 19 (August 18, 1982), p. 2394. English. **DESCR:** Business; Hobbs Act; U.S. v. Hanigan.

11823 Nalven, Joseph. Health research on undocumented Mexicans. SOCIAL SCIENCE JOURNAL, Vol. 19, no. 2 (April 1982), p. 73-88. English. **DESCR:** Immigrants; Immigration Law; Medical Care; *Public Health.

11824 Nalven, Joseph. Resolving the undocumented worker problem. NEW SCHOLAR, Vol. 8, no. 1-2 (Spring, Fall, 1982), p. 473-481. English. **DESCR:** Book Reviews; *MEXICAN WORKERS IN THE UNITED STATES; *MIGRANT WORKERS IN WESTERN EUROPE AND THE UNITED STATES.

11825 Nalven, Joseph. Who benefits from knowledge about the health of undocumented Mexicans? POLICY STUDIES JOURNAL, Vol. 10, no. 3 (March 1982), p. 556-580. English. **DESCR:** Public Health.

11826 Negrete, Louis R. Labor unions and undocumented workers. BORDERLANDS JOURNAL, Vol. 6, no. 1 (Fall 1982), p. 1-10. English. **DESCR:** Labor Unions.

11827 Newman, Allen R. The impacts of emigration on the Mexican economy. MIGRATION TODAY, Vol. 10, no. 2 (1982), p. 17-21. English. **DESCR:** Economic History and Conditions; Employment; *Mexican Economy; *Migration; Socioeconomic Factors.

11828 No hay ilegales - There are no illegal aliens. CORAZON DE AZTLAN, Vol. 1, no. 3 (August, September, 1982), p. 4-5. Bilingual.

11829 North, David S. Book review of: ILLEGAL ALIENS IN THE WESTERN HEMISPHERE: POLITICAL AND ECONOMIC FACTORS. INTERNATIONAL MIGRATION REVIEW, Vol. 16, no. 3 (Fall 1982), p. 682-683. English. **DESCR:** Book Reviews; *ILLEGAL ALIENS IN THE WESTERN HEMISPHERE: POLITICAL AND ECONOMIC FACTORS; Johnson, Kenneth F.; Williams, Miles W.

11830 Olson, James S. Book review of: OPERATION WETBACK: THE MASS DEPORTATION OF MEXICAN UNDOCUMENTED WORKERS IN 1954. JOURNAL OF THE WEST, Vol. 22, no. 1 (1983), p. 80-81. English. **DESCR:** Agricultural Laborers; Book Reviews; Braceros; Garcia, Juan Ramon; *OPERATION WETBACK: THE MASS DEPORTATION OF MEXICAN UNDOCUMENTED WORKERS IN 1954.

11831 Opportunity knocks ... but it needn't be equal. CHILDREN'S LEGAL RIGHTS JOURNAL, Vol. 4, no. 1 (August 1982), p. 14-17. English. **DESCR:** Board of Education of Hudson Central School District v. Rowley Individualized Educational Program (IEP); Doe v. Plyer [Tyler Independent School District, Texas]; Handicapped.

Undocumented Workers (cont.)

11832 Osifchok, Diane I. The utilization of immediate scrutiny in establishing the right to education for undocumented alien children. PEPPERDINE LAW REVIEW, Vol. 10, no. 1 (December 1982), p. 139-165. English. DESCR: Civil Rights; Doe v. Plyer [Tyler Independent School District, Texas]; Education.

11833 Packard, Mark. Equal protection clause requires a free public education for illegal alien children. TEXAS TECH LAW REVIEW, Vol. 14, (May 1983), p. 531-547. English. DESCR: Constitutional Amendments - Fourteenth; Doe v. Plyer [Tyler Independent School District, Texas]; Education.

11834 Padilla, Steve. Alien smuggling and the refugee question: undercover agent for the border patrol. NUESTRO, Vol. 7, no. 5 (June, July, 1983), p. 15-17. English. DESCR: Acosta, Hipolito; *Border Patrol; *Immigration Regulation and Control.

11835 Parr, Julie A. Immigration law and the excluded alien: potential for human rights violations. UNIVERSITY OF CALIFORNIA DAVIS LAW REVIEW, Vol. 15, no. 3 (Spring 1982), p. 723-740. English. DESCR: *Civil Rights; Deportation; *Detention of Persons; Internal Security Act of 1950; Rodriguez-Fernandez v. Wilkinson.

11836 Peterson, Robert A. and Kozmetsky, George. Public opinion regarding illegal aliens in Texas. TEXAS BUSINESS REVIEW, Vol. 56, no. 3 (May, June, 1982), p. 118-121. English. DESCR: Public Opinion; Surveys; Texas.

11837 Quinn, Michael Sean. Educating alien kids. TEXAS OBSERVOR, Vol. 74, no. 18 (September 17, 1982), p. 5-6. English. DESCR: Children; *Doe v. Plyer [Tyler Independent School District, Texas]; Education.

11838 Reaves, Gayle. Supreme Court rules for alien children. NUESTRO, Vol. 6, no. 5 (June, July, 1982), p. 14-16. English. DESCR: *Children; Education; Education Equalization; Immigration Law; *Legislation; U.S. Supreme Court.

11839 Reza, H. G. Immigration: restriction or reform? CALIFORNIA LAWYER, Vol. 2, no. 11 (December 1982), p. 32-35. English. DESCR: *Immigration Law; Immigration Regulation and Control; Simpson-Mazzoli Bill.

11840 Richardson, Chad and Feagin, Joe. After crossing Rio Bravo. TEXAS OBSERVOR, Vol. 74, no. 12 (June 18, 1982), p. 1, 4-7. English. DESCR: Immigration and Naturalization Service (INS); *Immigration Regulation and Control.

11841 Richardson, Chad and Yanez, Linda. "Equal justice" and Jose Reyna. NUESTRO, Vol. 6, no. 5 (June, July, 1982), p. 17. English. DESCR: Brownsville, TX; *Children; Education; Education Equalization; Immigration Law; *Legislation; Reyna, Jose.

11842 Rios, Madeline. Operation Jobs: one year later. CAMINOS, Vol. 4, no. 11 (December 1983), p. 28-30. Bilingual. DESCR: Immigration Regulation and Control; *Operation Jobs.

11843 Rips, Geoffrey. Supply-side immigration reform. NATION, Vol. 237, no. 10 (October 8, 1983), p. 289,303+. English. DESCR: *Immigration Law; Simpson-Mazzoli Bill.

11844 Rivera, Julius and Goodman, Paul Wershub. Clandestine labor circulation: a case on the U.S.-Mexico border. MIGRATION TODAY, Vol. 10, no. 1 (1982), p. 21-26. English. DESCR: Border Patrol; Border Region; Ciudad Juarez, Chihuahua, Mexico; El Paso, TX; Immigration Regulation and Control; Migration Patterns; Social Classes; Social Mobility; Socioeconomic Factors.

11845 Rogg, Eleanor Meyer. Film review of: ANO NUEVO. MIGRATION TODAY, Vol. 10, no. 5 (1982), p. 36. English. DESCR: *ANO NUEVO [film]; Darling, Todd; Film Reviews; Films.

11846 Romero, Tina. The undocumented worker: how will the United States deal with him? NATIONAL HISPANIC JOURNAL, Vol. 1, no. 3 (Summer, Fall, 1982), p. 13-15. English. DESCR: Immigration Law; Immigration Regulation and Control; Reagan, Ronald.

11847 Salcido, Ramon M. The undocumented alien family. DE COLORES, Vol. 6, no. 1-2 (1982), p. 109-119. English. DESCR: East Los Angeles, CA; Family; Green Carders; Social Services.

11848 Salgado, J. F. Alien smugglers: an escalating war. NUESTRO, Vol. 7, no. 1 (January, February, 1983), p. 39. English. DESCR: Border Patrol; Immigration and Naturalization Service (INS); Immigration Regulation and Control.

11849 Salvadorans left in truck to die. NUESTRO, Vol. 6, no. 8 (October 1982), p. 12. English. DESCR: Death (Concept); Deportation; *Edinburg, TX.

11850 Salvatierra, Richard. Alien smuggling and the refugee question: U.S. must set a limit on refugees. NUESTRO, Vol. 7, no. 5 (June, July, 1983), p. 19. English. DESCR: Federation for American Immigration Reform (FAIR); *Immigration Regulation and Control; *Political Refugees; Refugees.

11851 Schmitt, Richard B. Desperate journey: hard times at home cause more Mexicans to enter U.S. illegally. WALL STREET JOURNAL, Vol. 200, (November 17, 1982), p. 1, 20+. English.

11852 School house door must be open to children of illegal aliens. CHILDREN'S LEGAL RIGHTS JOURNAL, Vol. 3, (June 1982), p. 19-21. English. DESCR: Constitutional Amendments - Fourteenth; Doe v. Plyer [Tyler Independent School District, Texas]; *Education; Texas.

11853 Slade, Santiago. From Michoacan to Southern California: the story of an undocumented Mexican. SOUTHWEST ECONOMY AND SOCIETY, Vol. 3, no. 1 (Fall 1977), p. 5-18. English. DESCR: Biography; *Oral History; *Puruaran, Michoacan, Mexico.

11854 Smith, William French. A look at the immigration laws. TEXAS BAR JOURNAL, Vol. 45, no. 2 (February 1982), p. 224-225. English. DESCR: *Immigration Law.

11855 Stacy, Gerald F. From stranger to neighbor. CHURCH AND SOCIETY, Vol. 72, no. 5 (May, June, 1982), p. 1-71. English. DESCR: Economic History and Conditions; *Migration; Religion.

Undocumented Workers (cont.)

11856 [Summary of: Hollander, defending the criminal alien in New Mexico: tactics and strategy to avoid deportation, 9 N.M.L. rev. 45 (1979)]. CHICANO LAW REVIEW, Vol. 5, (1982), p. 79-80. English. **DESCR:** Criminal Acts; Deportation; *Legal Representation.

11857 [Summary of: Note, medical benefits awarded to an alien: Perez v. health and social services, 9 N.M.L. rev. 89 (1979)]. CHICANO LAW REVIEW, Vol. 5, (1982), p. 80-81. English. **DESCR:** Medical Care; *Medical Care Laws and Legislation; Perez v. Health and Social Services.

11858 Supreme Court recognizes special importance of education. MENTAL DISABILITY LAW REPORTER, Vol. 6, (July, August, 1982), p. 227-229. English. **DESCR:** Doe v. Plyer [Tyler Independent School District, Texas]; *Education; San Antonio School District v. Rodriguez; THE PLUM PLUM PICKERS.

11859 Tattered borders. NEW REPUBLIC, Vol. 189, no. 2 (July 11, 1983), p. 9-11. English. **DESCR:** Cubanos; *Immigration; *Simpson-Mazzoli Bill.

11860 A territorial approach to representation for illegal aliens. MICHIGAN LAW REVIEW, Vol. 80, no. 6 (May 1982), p. 1342-1371. English. **DESCR:** Census; Federation for American Immigration Reform (FAIR); Population; Reapportionment; Reynolds, Steve; Voting Rights.

11861 Turansick, Michael F. A critique of proposed amendments to the immigration and nationality act. FORDHAM INTERNATIONAL LAW FORUM, Vol. 5, no. 1 (Winter 1981, 1982), p. 213-238. English. **DESCR:** Border Patrol; Braceros; *Immigration and Nationality Act (INA); Immigration Regulation and Control; Public Law 78.

11862 Watson, Roy J., Jr. The Simpson-Mazzoli bill: an analysis of selected policies. SAN DIEGO LAW REVIEW, Vol. 20, no. 1 (December 1982), p. 97-116. English. **DESCR:** Employment; Immigration Regulation and Control; Labor Certification; Mazzoli, Romano L.; Simpson, Alan K.; *Simpson-Mazzoli Bill.

11863 Weintraub, Sidney and Ross, Stanley R. Poor United States, so close to Mexico. ACROSS THE BOARD, Vol. 19, no. 3 (March 1982), p. 54-61. English. **DESCR:** Braceros; Immigrants; *Immigration.

11864 Witt, Elder. Court rules illegal aliens entitled to public schooling. CONGRESSIONAL QUARTERLY WEEKLY REPORT, Vol. 40, (June 19, 1982), p. 1479-1480. English. **DESCR:** Doe v. Plyer [Tyler Independent School District, Texas]; Education; Immigration; Texas v. Certain Undocumented Alien Children; Undocumented Children.

11865 Wolin, Merle Linda. Dirty work: Americans turn down many jobs vacated by ouster of aliens. WALL STREET JOURNAL, Vol. 200, (December 6, 1982), p. 1. English. **DESCR:** Immigrant Labor; Labor.

11866 Young, Rowland L. Exclusion hearing enough for illegal alien smuggler. AMERICAN BAR ASSOCIATION JOURNAL, Vol. 69, (March 1983), p. 352. English. **DESCR:** Chicana Welfare Rights Organization; Landon v. Plasencia; Laws.

11867 Young, Rowland L. Schools ... illegal aliens ... AMERICAN BAR ASSOCIATION JOURNAL, Vol. 68, (September 1982), p. 1156-1157. English. **DESCR:** Constitutional Amendments - Fourteenth; *Education.

11868 Young, Rowland L. Witnesses ... deportation. AMERICAN BAR ASSOCIATION JOURNAL, Vol. 68, (November 1982), p. 1493. English. **DESCR:** *Deportation; Jury Trials; U.S. v. Valenzuela-Bernal.

Unemployment
USE: Employment

Unemployment Insurance
USE: Employment

Unification Church

11869 Uehling, Mark D. Rivalry in New York: a profile of two newspapers. NUESTRO, Vol. 7, no. 7 (September 1983), p. 20-21. English. **DESCR:** Bustelo, Manuel A.; DIARIO LA PRENSA [newspaper], New York, NY; Espinal, Antonio; Gannett Co., Inc.; Journalism; New York, NY; *Newspapers; NOTICIAS DEL MUNDO; Patino, Luis.

Union City, NJ

11870 Cubans enjoy New Jersey town. NUESTRO, Vol. 7, no. 3 (April 1983), p. 10-11. English. **DESCR:** Cubanos; New Jersey.

La Union Liberal

11871 Rice, Jacqueline. Beyond the cientificos: the educational background of the Porfirian Elite. AZTLAN, Vol. 14, no. 2 (Fall 1983), p. 289-306. English. **DESCR:** History; Leadership; *Mexico; Political History and Conditions; Political Parties and Organizations; *Social Classes.

United Cannery Agricultural Packing and Allied Workers of America (UCAPAWA)

11872 Arnold, Frank. A history of struggle: organizing cannery workers in the Santa Clara Valley. SOUTHWEST ECONOMY AND SOCIETY, Vol. 2, no. 1 (October, November, 1976), p. 26-38. English. **DESCR:** Agribusiness; American Labor Union (Santa Clara County, CA); Cannery and Agricultural Worker's Industrial Union; *Cannery Workers; Comite de Trabajadores de Canerias, San Jose, CA; History; Labor Unions; *Santa Clara Valley, CA.

United Farmworkers of America (UFW)

11873 Barber, Bob. UFW and the class struggle. SOUTHWEST ECONOMY AND SOCIETY, Vol. 1, no. 1 (Spring 1976), p. 28-35. English. **DESCR:** California; *Labor Unions; Undocumented Workers.

11874 California farmworkers: back to the barricades? BUSINESS WEEK, no. 28 (September 26, 1983), p. 86+. English. **DESCR:** *Agricultural Labor Relations Board (ALRB); Agricultural Labor Unions; *Agricultural Laborers; California.

11875 Chavez pinpoints Texas for bargaining efforts. NUESTRO, Vol. 6, no. 8 (October 1982), p. 47-48. English. **DESCR:** Agricultural Labor Unions; Agricultural Laborers; Collective Bargaining.

United Farmworkers of America (UFW) (cont.)

11876 Chavez' union decentralizes. NUESTRO, Vol. 6, no. 7 (September 1982), p. 11-12. English. DESCR: Agricultural Laborers; Chavez, Cesar E.; Farmer Organizations.

11877 Howell, Frances Baseden. Split labor market: Mexican farm workers in the Southwest. SOCIOLOGICAL INQUIRY, Vol. 52, no. 2 (Spring 1982), p. 132-140. English. DESCR: Agricultural Labor Unions; Arizona Farm Workers (AFW); *Labor Supply and Market; Southwest United States; Undocumented Workers.

11878 Kivisto, Peter. Book review of: FARM WORKERS, AGRIBUSINESS, AND THE STATE. INTERNATIONAL MIGRATION REVIEW, Vol. 17, no. 4 (Winter 1983), p. 724-726. English. DESCR: Agribusiness; Agricultural Laborers; Book Reviews; *FARMWORKERS, AGRIBUSINESS, AND THE STATE; Majka, Linda C.; Majka, Theo J.

11879 Produce firm to close doors. NUESTRO, Vol. 7, no. 6 (August 1983), p. 12. English. DESCR: *Agribusiness; Agricultural Labor Unions; Business Enterprises; *Sun Harvest, Inc.

11880 Rodriguez, Vicente and Costello, Guy. United farm workers. SOUTHERN EXPOSURE, Vol. 10, no. 4 (July, August, 1982), p. 14-15. English. DESCR: Agricultural Labor Relations Board (ALRB); Agricultural Laborers.

United Food and Commercial Workers

11881 Rick Icaza on career opportunities in unions. CAMINOS, Vol. 3, no. 8 (September 1982), p. 44-45. Bilingual. DESCR: *Affirmative Action; Chicano Youth Leadership Conference; Labor Unions.

United Mexican Americans, South Bend, IN

11882 Lattin, Vernon E. Novelistic structure and myth in ...Y NO SE LO TRAGO LA TIERRA. BILINGUAL REVIEW, Vol. 9, no. 3 (September, December, 1982), p. 220-226. English. DESCR: Literature; Novel; Rivera, Tomas; *Y NO SE LO TRAGO LA TIERRA/AND THE EARTH DID NOT PART.

United Mineworkers of America (UMWA)

11883 Rubenstein, Harry R. The great Gallup Coal strike of 1933. SOUTHWEST ECONOMY AND SOCIETY, Vol. 3, no. 2 (Winter 1977, 1978), p. 34-53. English. DESCR: *Gallup Coal Strike of 1933; Labor Unions; Mining Industry; National Miner's Union (NMU); New Mexico; *Strikes and Lockouts.

United Nations

11884 Lamm, Richard D. Why the U.S. closed its borders. FUTURIST, Vol. 16, no. 6 (December 1982), p. 4-8. English. DESCR: *Immigration.

United Neighborhoods Organization (UNO)

11885 Grimond, John. Reconquista begins. ECONOMIST (London), Vol. 283, (April 3, 1982), p. 12-17. English. DESCR: Political Parties and Organizations; *Political Representation; Public Policy; The East Los Angeles Community Union (TELACU).

11886 Grimond, John. The reconquista begins. LOS ANGELES, Vol. 27, (May 1982), p. 190-195. English. DESCR: Demography; *Los Angeles, CA.

United States

11887 Barrios-Martinez, Ruben. Should Puerto Rico become a state?: against statehood. NUESTRO, Vol. 7, no. 5 (June, July, 1983), p. 37-39. English. DESCR: *Colonialism; *International Relations; Puerto Rican Independence Party; *Puerto Rico; Racism.

11888 Diaz, Katherine A. Henry G. Cisneros on Central American commission (interview). CAMINOS, Vol. 4, no. 8 (September 1983), p. 10,48. English. DESCR: Central America; *Cisneros, Henry, Mayor of San Antonio, TX; International Relations; National Bipartisan Commission on Central America.

11889 Garcia, Mario T. Book review of: LOS MOJADOS: THE WETBACK STORY. JOURNAL OF ETHNIC STUDIES, Vol. 1, no. 1 (Spring 1973), p. 66-68. English. DESCR: Book Reviews; Immigrant Labor; *LOS MOJADOS: THE WETBACK STORY; Mexico; Samora, Julian; Southwest United States; Undocumented Workers.

11890 Gonzalez, Raymond J. U.S. support of military in Latin America. CAMINOS, Vol. 4, no. 8 (September 1983), p. 18-19,50. Bilingual. DESCR: *International Relations; *Latin America.

11891 Maldonado-Denis, Manuel. El problema de las nacionalidades: la experiencia caribena. Paper presented at the "Dialogo de las Americas" conference. Mexico, D.F. September 9-14, 1982. REVISTA CHICANO-RIQUENA, Vol. 10, no. 4 (Fall 1982), p. 39-45. Spanish. DESCR: Capitalism; Carpentier, Alejo; Cuba; El Salvador; Grenada; Guatemala; Imperialism; Marti, Jose; Nicaragua; *Political History and Conditions; Puerto Rico.

11892 Reagan, Ronald. "There is a war in Central America" (speech). CAMINOS, Vol. 4, no. 8 (September 1983), p. 9. English. DESCR: Central America; *International Relations.

11893 Romero-Barcelo, Carlos. Should Puerto Rico become a state?: for statehood. NUESTRO, Vol. 7, no. 5 (June, July, 1983), p. 34-37. English. DESCR: *Colonialism; *International Relations; Munoz Marin, Luis; *Puerto Rico.

11894 Serafino, Nina M. U.S.-Latinoamerican relations: 1960 to the present. CAMINOS, Vol. 4, no. 8 (September 1983), p. 6-8,48. Bilingual. DESCR: History; *International Relations; Latin America; United States-Mexico Relations.

11895 Walia, Adorna. Book review of: EL GOBIERNO Y LOS PRESIDENTES DE LOS ESTADOS UNIDOS DE AMERICA. BILINGUAL JOURNAL, Vol. 6, no. 3 (Spring 1982), p. 22. English. DESCR: Book Reviews; Constitution of the United States; *EL GOBIERNO Y LOS PRESIDENTES DE LOS ESTADOS UNIDOS DE AMERICA; *Government; Roy, Joaquin; *United States History.

United States History

11896 Bell, Samuel E. and Smallwood, James M. Zona libre: trade and diplomacy on the Mexican border, 1858-1905. ARIZONA AND THE WEST, Vol. 24, no. 2 (Summer 1982), p. 119-152. English. DESCR: Border Region; *Foreign Trade; International Relations; Mexico.

United States History (cont.)

11897 Carrion, Arturo Morales. Puerto Rico: the coming of the Americans. NUESTRO, Vol. 7, no. 5 (June, July, 1983), p. 25-30. English. DESCR: Cuba; *International Relations; *Puerto Rico; Spain; *War.

11898 Gil, Carlos B. Miguel Antonio Otero, first Chicano governor. JOURNAL OF ETHNIC STUDIES, Vol. 4, no. 3 (Fall 1976), p. 95-102. English. DESCR: Book Reviews; *Elected Officials; *New Mexico; OTERO: AN AUTOBIOGRAPHICAL TRILOGY; Otero, Miguel A.; Social History and Conditions.

11899 Hernandez, Philip A. The Treaty of Guadalupe Hidalgo: a matter of precision. CACR REVIEW, Vol. 1, no. 1 (September 1982), p. 26-41. English. DESCR: *Guadalupe Hidalgo, Treaty of 1848; Treaties.

11900 Martinez, Oscar J. Book review of: REVOLTOSOS: MEXICO'S REBELS IN THE UNITED STATES 1903-1923. ARIZONA AND THE WEST, Vol. 24, no. 1 (Spring 1982), p. 69-70. English. DESCR: Book Reviews; Mexico; Raat, W. Dirk; *REVOLTOSOS: MEXICO'S REBELS IN THE UNITED STATES, 1903-1923.

11901 Myres, Sandra Lynn. The cowboy's Hispanic heritage. NUESTRO, Vol. 7, no. 7 (September 1983), p. 44-48. English. DESCR: Spanish Influence; *Vaqueros.

11902 Vivo, Paquita. Book review of: PUERTO RICO: A POLITICAL AND CULTURAL HISTORY. NUESTRO, Vol. 7, no. 5 (June, July, 1983), p. 63. English. DESCR: Book Reviews; Carrion, Arturo Morales; History; Puerto Rican Studies; Puerto Rico; *PUERTO RICO: A POLITICAL AND CULTURAL HISTORY.

11903 Walia, Adorna. Book review of: EL GOBIERNO Y LOS PRESIDENTES DE LOS ESTADOS UNIDOS DE AMERICA. BILINGUAL JOURNAL, Vol. 6, no. 3 (Spring 1982), p. 22. English. DESCR: Book Reviews; Constitution of the United States; *EL GOBIERNO Y LOS PRESIDENTES DE LOS ESTADOS UNIDOS DE AMERICA; *Government; Roy, Joaquin; United States.

United States-Latin American Relations

11904 El futuro de la cuenca del Caribe segun la administracion Reagan. INFORME: RELACIONES MEXICO-ESTADOS UNIDOS, Vol. 1, no. 2 (July, December, 1982), p. 10-56. Spanish. DESCR: *Iniciativa Para la Cuenca del Caribe (ICC); Reagan, Ronald.

United States-Mexico War

11905 Mathes, W. Michael. Book review of: THE MEXICAN-AMERICAN WAR: AN ANNOTATED BIBLIOGRAPHY. CALIFORNIA HISTORY, Vol. 60, no. 4 (Winter 1981, 1982), p. 379-380. English. DESCR: Book Reviews; *THE MEXICAN-AMERICAN WAR: AN ANNOTATED BIBLIOGRAPHY; Tutorow, Norman E.

United States-Mexico Governors' Conference

11906 Juarez, Richard. Third international conference of the U.S.- Mexico border governors. CAMINOS, Vol. 3, no. 11 (December 1982), p. 35-36. English. DESCR: *Border Region; *United States-Mexico Relations.

United States-Mexico Relations

11907 Babbitt, Bruce. Reagan approach to aliens simply wishful thinking. NATIONAL HISPANIC JOURNAL, Vol. 1, no. 2 (Winter 1982), p. 6-7. English. DESCR: Border Region; Braceros; Immigration Regulation and Control; *Reagan, Ronald; Select Commission on Immigration and Refugee Policy; *Undocumented Workers.

11908 Bath, C. Richard. Health and environmental problems: the role of the border in El Paso-Ciudad Juarez coordination. JOURNAL OF INTERAMERICAN STUDIES AND WORLD AFFAIRS, Vol. 24, no. 3 (August 1982), p. 375-392. English. DESCR: Border Region; Ciudad Juarez, Chihuahua, Mexico; *El Paso, TX; International Boundary and Water Commission; Nationalism; Pollution; *Public Health; U.S Border Public Health Association (AFMES).

11909 Bauer, Karl Jack. Book review of: THE MEXICAN-AMERICAN WAR: AN ANNOTATED BIBLIOGRAPHY. JOURNAL OF THE WEST, Vol. 21, no. 3 (April 1982), p. 73. English. DESCR: Book Reviews; Mexican American War; *THE MEXICAN-AMERICAN WAR: AN ANNOTATED BIBLIOGRAPHY; Tutorow, Norman E.

11910 Cantu, Hector. Border business report: the Rio Grande Valley's economy and Mexico's lingering peso devaluation effects. NATIONAL HISPANIC JOURNAL, Vol. 2, no. 1 (Summer 1983), p. 10-13. English. DESCR: Aguirre, Lionel; Border Region; Cano, Eddie; Coors Distributing Company, McAllen, TX; Cruz, Conrado; Cuevas, Betty; *Currency; Economic Development; Laredo, TX, Chamber of Commerce; Mexican American Chamber of Commerce, Austin, TX.

11911 Crisp, James E. Book review of: MEXICANO RESISTANCE IN THE SOUTHWEST: "THE SACRED RIGHT OF SELF-PRESERVATION". JOURNAL OF SOUTHERN HISTORY, Vol. 48, no. 1 (1982), p. 138-139. English. DESCR: Book Reviews; *MEXICANO RESISTANCE IN THE SOUTHWEST: "THE SACRED RIGHT OF SELF-PRESERVATION"; Political History and Conditions; Rosenbaum, Robert J.

11912 Cronologia de las relaciones Mexico-Estados Unidos (julio-noviembre de 1982). INFORME: RELACIONES MEXICO-ESTADOS UNIDOS, Vol. 1, no. 3 (July, December, 1982), p. 313-332. Spanish.

11913 Cronologia de las relaciones Mexico-Estados Unidos (octubre de 1981-junio de 1982). INFORME: RELACIONES MEXICO-ESTADOS UNIDOS, Vol. 1, no. 2 (July, December, 1982), p. 213-223. Spanish.

11914 Deukmejian, George. Welcoming the Commission of the Californias. CAMINOS, Vol. 4, no. 11 (December 1983), p. 19. English. DESCR: Border Region; California; *Commission of the Californias.

11915 Dr. Julian Nava on Mexico. CAMINOS, Vol. 3, no. 6 (June 1982), p. 7-8. Bilingual. DESCR: Mexico; Nava, Julian.

11916 Edmunds, Stahrl W. California-Mexico trade relations. CAMINOS, Vol. 4, no. 11 (December 1983), p. 20-21,38. Bilingual. DESCR: Border Region; Business; *California.

11917 Fichas biograficas de los funcionarios norteamericanos responsables de la politica de Estados Unidos hacia Mexico, Centroamerica y el Caribe. INFORME: RELACIONES MEXICO-ESTADOS UNIDOS, Vol. 1, no. 2 (July, December, 1982), p. 224-232. Spanish.

United States-Mexico Relations (cont.)

11918 Ford, Charles A. and Violante Morlock, Alejandro A. Policy concerns over the impact of trade-related performance requirements and investment incentives on the international economy: Mexican automotive policy and U.S.-Mexican relations. INTER-AMERICAN ECONOMIC AFFAIRS, Vol. 36, no. 2 (Fall 1982), p. 3-42. English. **DESCR:** Automobile Industry; Economic History and Conditions; *Mexico.

11919 Gavin, John. A productive year. CAMINOS, Vol. 3, no. 6 (June 1982), p. 6-17,36. English. **DESCR:** Mexico.

11920 Hamner, Richard. Hispanic update: border governors tackle U.S.-Mexico relations: much ado: but nothing on immigration. NATIONAL HISPANIC JOURNAL, Vol. 1, no. 2 (Winter 1982), p. 4-5. English. **DESCR:** Babbitt, Bruce; Border Region; Brown, Edmund G., Jr., Governor of California; *Clements, Bill; Immigration; Immigration Regulation and Control; Moreno, Paul.

11921 Juarez, Richard. Third international conference of the U.S.- Mexico border governors. CAMINOS, Vol. 3, no. 11 (December 1982), p. 35-36. English. **DESCR:** *Border Region; United States-Mexico Governors' Conference.

11922 Mexican border crossing survey. CAMINOS, Vol. 3, no. 11 (December 1982), p. 40-41. English. **DESCR:** *Border Region.

11923 Mexican migration to the United States: challenge to Christian witness and national policy. CHURCH AND SOCIETY, Vol. 72, no. 5 (May, June, 1982), p. 29-46. English. **DESCR:** Economic History and Conditions; Immigration Regulation and Control; Religion; *Undocumented Workers.

11924 Mexico y Estados Unidos ante la tercera Confemar: resultados e implicaciones. INFORME: RELACIONES MEXICO-ESTADOS UNIDOS, Vol. 1, no. 3 (July, December, 1982), p. 215-226. Spanish. **DESCR:** CONFEMAR; *Maritime Law; Multinational Corporations; Reagan Administration.

11925 Meyer, Lorenzo. Mexico frente a los Estados Unidos, 1971-1980. DIALOGOS, Vol. 18, (January, February, 1982), p. 3-12. Spanish. **DESCR:** Economic History and Conditions; *Mexico.

11926 Moody, George F. Mexicans and Americans should be the best of friends. CAMINOS, Vol. 3, no. 11 (December 1982), p. 37. Bilingual. **DESCR:** *Border Region.

11927 Morales, Cesareo. El impacto norteamericano en la politica economica de Mexico (1970-1983). CUADERNOS POLITICOS, Vol. 38, (October, December, 1983), p. 81-101. Spanish. **DESCR:** Economic History and Conditions; Mexico; Political History and Conditions.

11928 Morrison, Thomas K. The relationship of U.S. aid, trade and investment to migration pressures in major sending countries. INTERNATIONAL MIGRATION REVIEW, Vol. 16, no. 1 (Spring 1982), p. 4-26. English. **DESCR:** Border Region; International Economic Relations; Investments; Mexican Border Industrialization Program; *Migration Patterns; PIDER Project; Rural Economics; Rural Urban Migration; Undocumented Workers.

11929 Mumme, Stephen P. and Jamail, Milton H. The International Boundary and Water Commission as a conflict management agency in the U.S.-Mexico borderlands. SOCIAL SCIENCE JOURNAL, Vol. 19, no. 1 (January 1982), p. 46-62. English. **DESCR:** Border Region; Conflict Resolution; *International Boundary and Water Commission; Rio Grande; *Water.

11930 N.A.L.E.O.'s "Fiesta '83". CAMINOS, Vol. 4, no. 10 (November 1983), p. 28-29. English. **DESCR:** Baca Barragan, Polly; Bilingual Bicultural Education; Central America; Fiesta '83; Garcia, Robert; Immigration; International Relations; Mendez, Olga; *National Association of Latino Elected Officials (NALEO); Simpson-Mazzoli Bill.

11931 Nasatir, A. P. Book review of: THE MEXICAN-AMERICAN WAR: AN ANNOTATED BIBLIOGRAPHY. JOURNAL OF SAN DIEGO HISTORY, Vol. 28, no. 3 (Summer 1982), p. 210-211. English. **DESCR:** Book Reviews; Mexican American War; *THE MEXICAN-AMERICAN WAR: AN ANNOTATED BIBLIOGRAPHY; Tutorow, Norman E.

11932 El nuevo embajador de Mexico en Washington. El inicio de un nuevo estilo? INFORME: RELACIONES MEXICO-ESTADOS UNIDOS, Vol. 1, no. 2 (July, December, 1982), p. 109-111. Spanish. **DESCR:** *Sepulveda, Bernardo.

11933 Plaza, Eva. Interest group politics and U.S. immigration policy towards Mexico. LA RAZA LAW JOURNAL, Vol. 1, no. 1 (June 1983), p. 76-100. English. **DESCR:** Immigration; Immigration Law; Immigration Regulation and Control; *Interest Groups; Mexico; *Simpson-Mazzoli Bill.

11934 Que pasa?: Mexican border caucus. NUESTRO, Vol. 7, no. 5 (June, July, 1983), p. 9. English. **DESCR:** Border Region; Congressional Border Caucus.

11935 Quinlivan, Robert. The Mexican and American Foundation. CAMINOS, Vol. 3, no. 4 (April 1982), p. 24-25. Bilingual. **DESCR:** Castaneda, Jaime; *Organizations; San Diego, CA.

11936 Research/development: books. HISPANIC BUSINESS, Vol. 4, no. 11 (November 1982), p. 28. English. **DESCR:** Book Reviews; Border Industries; Border Region; *ESTUDIOS FRONTERIZOS: PONENCIAS Y COMENTARIOS; Jamail, Milton H.; *THE UNITED STATES-MEXICO BORDER: A GUIDE TO INSTITUTIONS, ORGANIZATIONS AND SCHOLARS.

11937 Richmond, Douglas W. Mexican immigration and border strategy during the revolution, 1910-1920. NEW MEXICO HISTORICAL REVIEW, Vol. 57, no. 3 (July 1982), p. 269-288. English. **DESCR:** *Border Region; Carranza, Venustiano; History; Immigration; Mexican Revolution - 1910-1920; Mexico; Social History and Conditions.

11938 Sanchez-Devanny, Jorge. Inseparable United States Mexico business relations. CAMINOS, Vol. 3, no. 6 (June 1982), p. 12-14. English. **DESCR:** Foreign Trade; Mexico.

11939 Schmitt, Karl M. Book review of: HISPANIC FOLK MUSIC OF NEW MEXICO AND THE SOUTHWEST: A SELF-PORTRAIT OF A PEOPLE. HISPANIC AMERICAN HISTORICAL REVIEW, Vol. 63, no. 1 (1983), p. 209-210. English. **DESCR:** Book Reviews; Mabry, Donald; *NEIGHBORS, MEXICO AND THE UNITED STATES: WETBACKS AND OIL; Shafer, Robert Jones.

United States-Mexico Relations (cont.)

11940 Seis meses despues, algunas lecciones que aprender: Mexico y Estados Unidos ante Cancun. INFORME: RELACIONES MEXICO-ESTADOS UNIDOS, Vol. 1, no. 2 (July, December, 1982), p. 58-74. Spanish.

11941 Sepulveda, Bernardo. Nueva evolucion. LATINO, Vol. 53, no. 8 (December 1982), p. 10-12. Spanish.

11942 Serafino, Nina M. U.S.-Latinoamerican relations: 1960 to the present. CAMINOS, Vol. 4, no. 8 (September 1983), p. 6-8,48. Bilingual. DESCR: History; *International Relations; Latin America; United States.

11943 Starr, Mark; McGuire, Stryker; and Contreras, Joe. The border: a world apart. NEWSWEEK, Vol. 10, (April 11, 1983), p. 36-40. English. DESCR: *Border Region; Immigration.

11944 Las tendencias de la relacion economica Mexico-Estados Unidos. INFORME: RELACIONES MEXICO-ESTADOS UNIDOS, Vol. 1, no. 2 (July, December, 1982), p. 88-108. Spanish. DESCR: *International Economic Relations.

11945 UC MEXUS consortium established. CAMINOS, Vol. 3, no. 6 (June 1982), p. 38. English. DESCR: Border Region; University of California; *University of California Consortium on Mexico and the United States (UC MEXUS).

11946 U.S. Mexico border region economic report. CAMINOS, Vol. 3, no. 11 (December 1982), p. 38-39. English. DESCR: *Border Region; *Economic Development.

11947 US-Mexican trade relations. HISPANIC BUSINESS, Vol. 4, no. 9 (September 1982), p. 23. English. DESCR: California; Export Trade; *Foreign Trade; Mexico.

11948 Vidal, Jose. Oil pluses - economic woes. CAMINOS, Vol. 3, no. 6 (June 1982), p. 18-19. Bilingual. DESCR: Economic Development; Mexico; Petroleum Industry.

11949 Villarreal, Roberto E. and Kelly, Philip. Mexican Americans as participants in United States-Mexico relations. INTERNATIONAL STUDIES NOTES, Vol. 9, no. 4 (Winter 1982), p. 1-6. English. DESCR: International Relations; Mexico; Political Representation.

THE UNITED STATES-MEXICO BORDER: A GUIDE TO INSTITUTIONS, ORGANIZATIONS AND SCHOLARS

11950 Research/development: books. HISPANIC BUSINESS, Vol. 4, no. 11 (November 1982), p. 28. English. DESCR: Book Reviews; Border Industries; Border Region; *ESTUDIOS FRONTERIZOS: PONENCIAS Y COMENTARIOS; Jamail, Milton H.; United States-Mexico Relations.

United Way

11951 People. HISPANIC BUSINESS, Vol. 4, no. 5 (May 1982), p. 8. English. DESCR: Appointed Officials; Asociacion Internacional de Exportadores e Importadores (EXIMA); *Biographical Notes; Businesspeople; California Chicano News Media Association (CCNMA); de la Ossa, Ernest G.; Foreign Trade; Obledo, Mario; Rodriguez, Elias C.; Rodriguez, Samuel F.; U.S. Hispanic Chamber of Commerce.

Universidad Popular, Chicago, IL

11952 Heaney, Thomas W. "Hanging on" or "gaining ground": educating marginal adults. NEW DIRECTIONS FOR CONTINUING EDUCATION, no. 20 (December 1983), p. 53-63. English. DESCR: *Adult Education; Chicago, IL; City Colleges, Chicago, IL; General Education Diploma (GED); Gomez, Robert; Instituto del Progreso Latino; Mission District, San Francisco, CA; Project Literacy, San Francisco, CA; St. Mary's Community Educational Center.

Universities

USE: Colleges and Universities

University of California

11953 UC MEXUS consortium established. CAMINOS, Vol. 3, no. 6 (June 1982), p. 38. English. DESCR: Border Region; United States-Mexico Relations; *University of California Consortium on Mexico and the United States (UC MEXUS).

University of California, Berkeley

11954 Baltodano, J. C. Success. CAMINOS, Vol. 4, no. 6 (June 1983), p. 32,34+. English. DESCR: Colleges and Universities; Gallegos, Genevie; Gutierrez, Jorge; Sotelo, Priscilla Elvira; *Students; Torres, Juan.

University of California, Riverside

11955 Community watching: para la comunidad. CAMINOS, Vol. 3, no. 2 (February 1982), p. 43-44. Bilingual. DESCR: Casa Blanca Youth Project; Colegio Cesar Chavez, Mt. Angel, OR; Colleges and Universities; *Cultural Organizations; Financial Aid; LULAC National Education Service Centers (LNESC); Tonatiuh-Quinto Sol Award for Literature, 1977-78.

University of California, Santa Barbara

11956 Math-based careers. HISPANIC BUSINESS, Vol. 5, no. 5 (May 1983), p. 26. English. DESCR: *Careers; Engineering as a Profession; Financial Aid; Income; Labor Supply and Market; Mexican American Engineering Society (MAES) National Symposium (5th), Fullerton, CA, April 13-15, 1980.

University of California, Los Angeles (UCLA)

11957 Hughes invests in the future. HISPANIC BUSINESS, Vol. 4, no. 11 (November 1982), p. 8-9,26. English. DESCR: Careers; *Educational Opportunities; *Engineering as a Profession; Minority Introduction to Engineering (MITE).

11958 Math-based careers. HISPANIC BUSINESS, Vol. 5, no. 10 (October 1983), p. 28. English. DESCR: *Careers; Carnation Company; Chicanas; Education; Engineering as a Profession; Hispanic Policy Development Project; Minority Engineering Education Center, University of California, Los Angeles; Science as a Profession.

11959 Minority students given assistance. NUESTRO, Vol. 7, no. 2 (March 1983), p. 10. English. DESCR: Education; Engineering as a Profession; *Minority Engineering Education Center, University of California, Los Angeles.

University of California, Los Angeles (UCLA)
(cont.)

11960 UC Latino: salsa music comes to UCLA.
CAMINOS, Vol. 4, no. 5 (May 1983), p. 46,48.
English. DESCR: Musicians; Salsa; *UC
Latino.

11961 Ucalatino: salsa music comes to UCLA.
NUESTRO, Vol. 6, no. 9 (November 1982), p.
59-60. English. DESCR: *Music; Salsa;
UCALATINO [musical group].

11962 UCLA effort aids students. NUESTRO, Vol. 6,
no. 5 (June, July, 1982), p. 11. English.
DESCR: *Intergroup Relations; Students.

University of California Consortium on Mexico and the United States (UC MEXUS)

11963 UC MEXUS consortium established. CAMINOS,
Vol. 3, no. 6 (June 1982), p. 38. English.
DESCR: Border Region; United States-Mexico
Relations; University of California.

University of Illinois at Urbana

11964 Anderson, John W. The effects of culture and
social class on client preference for
counseling methods. JOURNAL OF NON-WHITE
CONCERNS IN PERSONNEL AND GUIDANCE, Vol. 11,
no. 3 (April 1983), p. 84-88. English.
DESCR: Anglo Americans; Blacks; Counseling
Effectiveness Scale; *Counseling
(Psychological); *Educational Opportunity
Program (EOP); Locus of Control.

University of Minnesota

11965 Dienhart, Paul. Minnesota support groups
help Latinos through medical school.
NUESTRO, Vol. 6, no. 6 (August 1982), p.
39-40. English. DESCR: Health Education;
Latin Americans; Medical Education; Medical
Students; Minnesota; Public Health.

University of Missouri-Kansas City School of Medicine

11966 Calkins, E. Virginia; Willoughby, T. Lee;
and Arnold, Louise M. Predictors of
performance of minority students in the
first two years of a BA/MD program. NATIONAL
MEDICAL ASSOCIATION JOURNAL, Vol. 74, no. 7
(July 1982), p. 625-632. English. DESCR:
Academic Achievement; Academic Motivation;
Affirmative Action Programs; *Medical
Education.

University of Southern California

11967 Community watching: para la comunidad.
CAMINOS, Vol. 3, no. 3 (March 1982), p.
58-59. Bilingual. DESCR: Cultural
Organizations; *Engineering as a Profession;
Financial Aid; Harvard University; Latino
Business Students Association (LBSA);
Rodolfo H. Castro Fellowship; Society for
Hispanic Professional Engineers (SHPE);
Student Organizations.

11968 Cuenca, Ramon Araluce. USC forms institute
for Hispanic media & culture. CAMINOS, Vol.
4, no. 3 (March 1983), p. 32. English.
DESCR: *Institute for Hispanic Media and
Culture; Mass Media.

11969 The future beckons, USC's LBSA responds.
HISPANIC BUSINESS, Vol. 4, no. 4 (April
1982), p. 12, 25. English. DESCR: Business;
Business Education; Business Schools and
Colleges; Educational Opportunities; *Latino
Business Students Association (LBSA).

University of Texas at El Paso

11970 Armengol, Armando; Manley, Joan H.; and
Teschner, Richard V. The international
bilingual city: how a university meets the
challenge. FOREIGN LANGUAGE ANNALS, Vol. 15,
no. 4 (September 1982), p. 289-295. English.
DESCR: Biculturalism; Bilingualism; Border
Region; Ciudad Juarez, Chihuahua, Mexico; El
Paso, TX; *Language Development; Spanish
Language.

11971 Beyer, Sandra S. and Kluck, Frederick J.
French via Spanish: a positive approach to
language learning for minority students.
FOREIGN LANGUAGE ANNALS, Vol. 15, no. 2
(April 1982), p. 123-126. English. DESCR:
Educational Innovations; *French Language;
Language Development; Spanish Language.

University of Texas at Austin

11972 Cantu, Hector. Hispanic students wanted.
NATIONAL HISPANIC JOURNAL, Vol. 1, no. 3
(Summer, Fall, 1982), p. 8. English. DESCR:
*Enrollment; Higher Education; Recruitment;
Students.

11973 Limon, Jose. History, Chicano joking, and
the varieties of higher-education: tradition
and performance as critical symbolic action.
JOURNAL OF THE FOLKLORE INSTITUTE, Vol. 19,
no. 2-3 (1982), p. 146-166. English. DESCR:
*Chistes; Folklore; Higher Education; Humor;
Interpersonal Relations; Texas.

11974 LULAC: 53 years of continued achievement
(photoessay). CAMINOS, Vol. 4, no. 5 (May
1983), p. 40-41. English. DESCR: Benson
Latin American Collection; *League of United
Latin American Citizens (LULAC);
Organizations.

Uniworld Group, Inc.

11975 Balkan, D. Carlos. The advent of
Uniworld/Hispanic: an interview. HISPANIC
BUSINESS, Vol. 5, no. 3 (March 1983), p.
10-11+. English. DESCR: *Advertising
Agencies; Blacks; Consumers; Diaz-Albertini,
Luis; Lewis, Byron; *Marketing; Spanish
Advertising and Marketing Services
(S.A.M.S.); UniWorld Hispanic.

UniWorld Hispanic

11976 Balkan, D. Carlos. The advent of
Uniworld/Hispanic: an interview. HISPANIC
BUSINESS, Vol. 5, no. 3 (March 1983), p.
10-11+. English. DESCR: *Advertising
Agencies; Blacks; Consumers; Diaz-Albertini,
Luis; Lewis, Byron; *Marketing; Spanish
Advertising and Marketing Services
(S.A.M.S.); Uniworld Group, Inc.

11977 Communications/marketing. HISPANIC BUSINESS,
Vol. 4, no. 12 (December 1982), p. 11.
English. DESCR: Advertising; Advertising
Agencies; Diaz-Albertini, Luis; *Marketing.

UNO [magazine], Fremont, CA

11978 New tabloid magazines developed in Bay Area.
NUESTRO, Vol. 6, no. 2 (March 1982), p. 48.
English. DESCR: ESENCIA [magazine];
*Magazines.

THE UNWANTED

11979 Munoz, Carlos, Jr. The unwanted. BILINGUAL REVIEW, Vol. 10, no. 2-3 (May, December, 1983), p. 187-188. English. DESCR: Film Reviews.

UNWANTED MEXICAN AMERICANS IN THE GREAT DEPRESSION

11980 Cardoso, Lawrence Anthony. Book review of: UNWANTED MEXICAN AMERICANS IN THE GREAT DEPRESSION: REPATRIATION PRESSURES, 1929-1939. JOURNAL OF ETHNIC STUDIES, Vol. 5, no. 1 (Spring 1977), p. 120-122. English. DESCR: Book Reviews; Deportation; Hoffman, Abraham; Immigrant Labor; Immigration; Immigration Regulation and Control; Mexico; Social History and Conditions.

Upper Class
USE: Social Classes

Uranga, Emilio

11981 Cantu, Roberto. Nota preliminar: de Samuel Ramos a Emilio Uranga. CAMPO LIBRE, Vol. 1, no. 2 (Summer 1981), p. 239-272. Spanish. DESCR: Cultural Characteristics; Identity; Mexico; Philosophy; *Ramos, Samuel.

11982 Ramos, Manuel. En torno a las ideas sobre EL MEXICANO. CAMPO LIBRE, Vol. 1, no. 2 (Summer 1981), p. 273-282. Spanish. DESCR: Cultural Characteristics; *EL MEXICANO; Identity; Mexico; Philosophy.

Urban Communities

11983 Ano Nuevo de Kerr, Louise. Chicano settlements in Chicago: a brief history. JOURNAL OF ETHNIC STUDIES, Vol. 2, no. 4 (Winter 1975), p. 22-32. English. DESCR: Back of the Yards, Chicago, IL; *Chicago, IL; Near West Side, Chicago, IL; Pilsen, IL; Social History and Conditions; South Chicago, Chicago, IL.

11984 Baca Zinn, Maxine. Urban kinship and Midwest Chicano families: evidence in support of revision. DE COLORES, Vol. 6, no. 1-2 (1982), p. 85-98. English. DESCR: Compadrazgo; *Extended Family; Family; *Midwestern States.

11985 Chavarria, Jesus. The world according to Miami. HISPANIC BUSINESS, Vol. 4, no. 3 (March 1982), p. 6. English. DESCR: *Business; Carnaval Miami 82; Cubanos; Miami, FL.

11986 Davis, Sally M. and Harris, Mary B. Sexual knowledge, sexual interests, and sources of sexual information of rural and urban adolescents from three cultures. ADOLESCENCE, Vol. 17, no. 66 (Summer 1982), p. 471-492. English. DESCR: Birth Control; Cultural Characteristics; Identity; Rural Population; *Sex Education; Sex Roles; *Sexual Behavior; Youth.

11987 Election change sought by Garcia. NUESTRO, Vol. 6, no. 10 (December 1982), p. 9-10. English. DESCR: *Corpus Christi, TX; Garcia, Hector; Government.

11988 Ferre, Maurice A. Marketplace of the Americas. HISPANIC BUSINESS, Vol. 4, no. 3 (March 1982), p. 8. English. DESCR: Business; Miami, FL.

11989 Garcia, Reyes. Politics of flesh: ethnicity and political viability. CACR REVIEW, Vol. 1, no. 1 (September 1982), p. 102-130. English. DESCR: Anaya, Rudolfo A.; Aristotle; Culture; Ethnic Groups; Identity; Locke, John; Nuclear Armament; Philosophy; *Political Repression.

11990 Gober, Patricia and Behr, Michelle. Central cities and suburbs as distinct place types: myth or fact? ECONOMIC GEOGRAPHY, Vol. 58, no. 4 (October 1982), p. 371-385. English. DESCR: Blacks; Census; Population Distribution; Suburban Communities.

11991 Hines, Thomas S. Housing, baseball, and creeping socialism: the battle of Chavez Ravine, Los Angeles, 1949-1959. JOURNAL OF URBAN HISTORY, Vol. 8, no. 2 (1982), p. 123-143. English. DESCR: Barrios; *Chavez Ravine, Los Angeles, CA; Los Angeles, CA; Urban Renewal.

11992 Lanier, Alfredo S. Continental's Fidel Lopez takes an encompassing view. HISPANIC BUSINESS, Vol. 4, no. 4 (April 1982), p. 16-17,24. English. DESCR: Biography; Chicago, IL; *Lopez, Fidel; Urban Development.

11993 Lotchin, Roger W. New Chicano history: an urban history perspective. HISTORY TEACHER, Vol. 16, no. 2 (February 1983), p. 229-247. English. DESCR: Camarillo, Alberto; CHICANOS IN A CHANGING SOCIETY; DESERT IMMIGRANTS: THE MEXICANS OF EL PASO 1880-1920; Garcia, Mario T.; Griswold del Castillo, Ricardo; *Historiography; History; Social History and Conditions; THE LOS ANGELES BARRIO 1850-1890: A SOCIAL HISTORY.

11994 Massey, Douglas S. Research note on residential succession: the Hispanic case. SOCIAL FORCES, Vol. 61, (March 1983), p. 825-833. English. DESCR: Barrios; Population Trends; *Residential Segregation.

11995 Mata, Alberto G. Book review of: MEXICAN AMERICANS IN A DALLAS BARRIO. AZTLAN, Vol. 14, no. 1 (Spring 1983), p. 196-198. English. DESCR: Achor, Shirley; Barrios; Book Reviews; Dallas, TX; *MEXICAN AMERICANS IN A DALLAS BARRIO.

11996 Nowhere else but San Antonio. LATINO, Vol. 53, no. 4 (June 1982), p. 11-12. English. DESCR: *San Antonio, TX.

11997 Weber, David J. and Lotchin, Roger W. The new Chicano history: two perspectives. HISTORY TEACHER, Vol. 16, no. 2 (February 1983), p. 219-247. English. DESCR: Camarillo, Alberto; *CHICANOS IN A CHANGING SOCIETY; DESERT IMMIGRANTS: THE MEXICANS OF EL PASO 1880-1920; Garcia, Mario T.; Griswold del Castillo, Ricardo; *Historiography; History; Social History and Conditions; *THE LOS ANGELES BARRIO 1850-1890: A SOCIAL HISTORY.

11998 Weber, David J. The new Chicano urban history. HISTORY TEACHER, Vol. 16, no. 2 (February 1983), p. 223-229. English. DESCR: Camarillo, Alberto; *CHICANOS IN A CHANGING SOCIETY; DESERT IMMIGRANTS: THE MEXICANS OF EL PASO 1880-1920; Garcia, Mario T.; Griswold del Castillo, Ricardo; *Historiography; History; Social History and Conditions; *THE LOS ANGELES BARRIO 1850-1890: A SOCIAL HISTORY.

11999 Whitefield, Mimi. Miami, Caribbean megalopolis. HISPANIC BUSINESS, Vol. 4, no. 3 (March 1982), p. 18-19+. English. DESCR: Business; Dade County, FL; Foreign Trade; Miami, FL.

Urban Communities (cont.)

12000 Zavala, Antonio. The end of another summer.
      NUESTRO, Vol. 7, no. 8 (October 1983), p.
      64. English. **DESCR:** *Chicago, IL.

Urban Development

12001 Lanier, Alfredo S. Continental's Fidel Lopez
      takes an encompassing view. HISPANIC
      BUSINESS, Vol. 4, no. 4 (April 1982), p.
      16-17,24. English. **DESCR:** Biography;
      Chicago, IL; *Lopez, Fidel; Urban
      Communities.

12002 Thomas Fuentes: community builder. HISPANIC
      BUSINESS, Vol. 5, no. 11 (November 1983), p.
      16-17. English. **DESCR:** Engineering as a
      Profession; *Fuentes, Thomas; Local
      Government; Orange County, CA.

12003 Volsky, George. Hilario Candela: designing
      for Florida's future. HISPANIC BUSINESS,
      Vol. 5, no. 11 (November 1983), p. 20-22.
      English. **DESCR:** Architecture; *Candela,
      Hilario; Miami, FL; Spillis Candela &
      Partners.

Urban Development Action Grant (UDAG)

12004 Government review. NUESTRO, Vol. 7, no. 6
      (August 1983), p. 56. English. **DESCR:** Ballet
      de Puerto Rico; Dance; Education;
      Employment; *Government Funding Sources;
      Government Services; Housing; Income;
      National Fair Housing Law; Population
      Distribution; Veterans.

Urban Economics

12005 Logan, Kathleen. The urban poor in
      developing nations. JOURNAL OF URBAN
      HISTORY, Vol. 9, no. 1 (November 1982), p.
      108-116. English. **DESCR:** ACCESS TO POWER:
      POLITICS AND THE URBAN POOR IN DEVELOPING
      NATIONS; *Book Reviews; BORDER BOOM TOWN:
      CIUDAD JUAREZ SINCE 1848; Collier, David;
      Cornelius, Wayne A.; Eckstein, Susan; Lloyd,
      Peter; Martinez, Oscar J.; Nelson, Joan M.;
      Perlman, Janice E.; POLITICS AND MIGRANT
      POOR IN MEXICO CITY; SLUMS OF HOPE? SHANTY
      TOWNS OF THE THIRD WORLD; SQUATTERS AND
      OLIGARCHS: AUTHORITARIAN RULE AND POLICY
      CHANGE IN PERU; THE MYTH OF MARGINALITY:
      URBAN POVERTY AND POLITICS IN RIO DE
      JANEIRO; THE POVERTY OF REVOLUTION: THE
      STATE AND THE URBAN POOR IN MEXICO.

Urban Education

12006 Baldonado, Lisa. A university program to
      meet Chicago's bilingual needs. BILINGUAL
      JOURNAL, Vol. 7, no. 4 (Summer 1983), p.
      15-17,28. English. **DESCR:** *Bilingual
      Bicultural Education; Chicago, IL;
      Curriculum; *Teacher Training.

Urban Housing

12007 Krivo, Lauren J. Housing price inequalities:
      a comparison of Anglos, Blacks, and
      Spanish-origin populations. URBAN AFFAIRS
      QUARTERLY, Vol. 17, no. 4 (1982), p.
      445-462. English. **DESCR:** Housing;
      Residential Segregation.

Urban Planning

12008 San Antonio restaurant survives urban
      project. NUESTRO, Vol. 6, no. 5 (June, July,
      1982), p. 44. English. **DESCR:** Restaurants;
      San Antonio, TX.

Urban Poverty
      USE: Urban Economics

Urban Relocation
      USE: Urban Renewal

Urban Renewal

12009 Chavira, Ricardo. "New" Tijuana defies the
      stereotypes. NUESTRO, Vol. 6, no. 4 (May
      1982), p. 17-18. English. **DESCR:** *Tijuana,
      Mexico.

12010 Hines, Thomas S. Housing, baseball, and
      creeping socialism: the battle of Chavez
      Ravine, Los Angeles, 1949-1959. JOURNAL OF
      URBAN HISTORY, Vol. 8, no. 2 (1982), p.
      123-143. English. **DESCR:** Barrios; *Chavez
      Ravine, Los Angeles, CA; Los Angeles, CA;
      Urban Communities.

Urbanization
      USE: Urban Communities

U.S. Border Patrol

12011 Day, Mark R. Hopes of jobs lure Mexicans.
      NATIONAL CATHOLIC REPORTER, Vol. 19,
      (October 29, 1982), p. 3. English. **DESCR:**
      Border Region; *Undocumented Workers.

U.S Border Public Health Association (AFMES)

12012 Bath, C. Richard. Health and environmental
      problems: the role of the border in El
      Paso-Ciudad Juarez coordination. JOURNAL OF
      INTERAMERICAN STUDIES AND WORLD AFFAIRS,
      Vol. 24, no. 3 (August 1982), p. 375-392.
      English. **DESCR:** Border Region; Ciudad
      Juarez, Chihuahua, Mexico; *El Paso, TX;
      International Boundary and Water Commission;
      Nationalism; Pollution; *Public Health;
      United States-Mexico Relations.

U.S. Chamber of Commerce

12013 Latinos from 21 states attend chamber
      confab. NUESTRO, Vol. 6, no. 6 (August
      1982), p. 51. English. **DESCR:** Conventions;
      Latin Americans.

U.S. Commission on Civil Rights

12014 Civil Rights Commission. LATINO, Vol. 54,
      no. 8 (December 1983), p. 21. English.
      DESCR: Civil Rights.

12015 Reagan's new appointee to Civil Rights
      Commission. NUESTRO, Vol. 6, no. 5 (June,
      July, 1982), p. 29-30. English. **DESCR:**
      Appointed Officials; *Quintanilla,
      Guadalupe.

12016 Valenzuela-Crocker, Elvira. Confrontation
      over the Civil Rights Commission. NUESTRO,
      Vol. 7, no. 10 (December 1983), p. 21-27.
      English. **DESCR:** Administration of Justice;
      Affirmative Action; *Civil Rights; Education
      Equalization; Employment; Voting Rights.

U.S. Commission on Farmworkers

12017 Migrant farm workers. NUESTRO, Vol. 5, no. 8
      (November 1981), p. 10-11. English. **DESCR:**
      *Chisholm, Shirley; *Migrant Labor.

U.S. Congress

12018 Candidates for congressional seats. CAMINOS,
      Vol. 3, no. 5 (May 1982), p. 26-34. English.
      DESCR: *Elected Officials.

U.S. Congresssional Subcommittee on Immigration, Refugees and International Law

12019 Hing, Bill Ong. Racial disparity: the unaddressed issues of the Simpson-Mazzoli Bill. LA RAZA LAW JOURNAL, Vol. 1, no. 1 (June 1983), p. 21-52. English. DESCR: Amnesty; Asian Americans; Ethnic Attitudes; Family; Immigration; Immigration and Naturalization Service (INS); Latin Americans; Mazzoli, Romano L.; Mexican American Legal Defense and Educational Fund (MALDEF); Simpson, Alan K.; *Simpson-Mazzoli Bill; Temporary Worker Program.

12020 Liebowitz, Arnold. Immigration challenge and the congressional response. LA RAZA LAW JOURNAL, Vol. 1, no. 1 (June 1983), p. 1-20. English. DESCR: Amnesty; Immigration; Immigration and Nationality Act (INA); Mazzoli, Romano L.; *Simpson, Alan K.; *Simpson-Mazzoli Bill; Temporary Worker Program; Undocumented Workers.

U.S. Constitution
USE: Constitution of the United States

U.S. Customs

12021 Carreras, Peter Nares. Strong concern over searches. NUESTRO, Vol. 7, no. 10 (December 1983), p. 12-13. English. DESCR: Colombia; *Drug Laws; Drug Traffic.

U.S. Department of Defense (DOD)

12022 NALEO audits the Feds. HISPANIC BUSINESS, Vol. 5, no. 10 (October 1983), p. 16. English. DESCR: Business Enterprises; Federal Government; *Government Contracts; Minority Business Development Agency (MBDA); *National Association of Latino Elected Officials (NALEO); U.S. Department of Health and Human Services.

U.S. Department of Health and Human Services

12023 Government review. NUESTRO, Vol. 7, no. 10 (December 1983), p. 48. English. DESCR: Banking Industry; Child Care Centers; Chile; Clinics (Medical); Credit Unions; Employment; Employment Training; *Government Services; Medical Care; National Credit Union Administration; National Oceanic and Atmospheric Administration; SER; U.S. Department of Labor.

12024 Latin health study. NUESTRO, Vol. 5, no. 8 (November 1981), p. 12. English. DESCR: *Public Health.

12025 NALEO audits the Feds. HISPANIC BUSINESS, Vol. 5, no. 10 (October 1983), p. 16. English. DESCR: Business Enterprises; Federal Government; *Government Contracts; Minority Business Development Agency (MBDA); *National Association of Latino Elected Officials (NALEO); U.S. Department of Defense (DOD).

U.S. Department of Health, Education and Welfare (HEW)

12026 Garcia, Paco. Voices: Hispanic voices needed in the education debate. NUESTRO, Vol. 7, no. 5 (June, July, 1983), p. 53-54. English. DESCR: Bilingual Bicultural Education; *Discrimination in Education; *Discrimination in Employment; *Education; Federal Government; *Latin Americans; President's Commission on Excellence in Education; Reagan, Ronald.

U.S. Department of Housing and Urban Development (HUD)

12027 Business notes. HISPANIC BUSINESS, Vol. 5, no. 11 (November 1983), p. 27. English. DESCR: *Business Enterprises; Garment Industry; High Tech '84; Personnel Management; Puerto Rico; Taxation.

U.S. Department of Labor

12028 Government review. NUESTRO, Vol. 7, no. 10 (December 1983), p. 48. English. DESCR: Banking Industry; Child Care Centers; Chile; Clinics (Medical); Credit Unions; Employment; Employment Training; *Government Services; Medical Care; National Credit Union Administration; National Oceanic and Atmospheric Administration; SER; U.S. Department of Health and Human Services.

U.S. Hispanic Chamber of Commerce

12029 Chavarria, Jesus. Chambers meet, Minnesota shines. HISPANIC BUSINESS, Vol. 4, no. 10 (October 1982), p. 6. English. DESCR: Businesspeople; *Chamber of Commerce.

12030 People. HISPANIC BUSINESS, Vol. 4, no. 5 (May 1982), p. 8. English. DESCR: Appointed Officials; Asociacion Internacional de Exportadores e Importadores (EXIMA); *Biographical Notes; Businesspeople; California Chicano News Media Association (CCNMA); de la Ossa, Ernest G.; Foreign Trade; Obledo, Mario; Rodriguez, Elias C.; Rodriguez, Samuel F.; United Way.

12031 Rinco, Marcos. U.S. Hispanic Chamber's national convention. CAMINOS, Vol. 3, no. 10 (November 1982), p. 30-31. English. DESCR: Business.

12032 Southwest regional conference of Hispanic Chamber of Commerce. CAMINOS, Vol. 4, no. 9 (October 1983), p. 60. English. DESCR: Business; Clergy.

U.S. Information Agency (USIA)

12033 Government review. NUESTRO, Vol. 7, no. 2 (March 1983), p. 42. English. DESCR: A WORKING WOMAN'S GUIDE TO HER JOB RIGHTS; Adoption; Business Enterprises; Census; Chicanas; Discrimination in Employment; *Government Services; GUIDE TO FEDERAL MINORITY ENTERPRISE AND RELATED ASSISTANCE PROGRAMS; Population Trends; Study Abroad.

U.S. Junior Chamber of Commerce

12034 Two Hispanics on top ten list. LATINO, Vol. 53, no. 2 (March, April, 1982), p. 14. English. DESCR: *Bonilla, Ruben; *Cisneros, Henry, Mayor of San Antonio, TX; Politics.

U.S. Navy

12035 Bunnell, Robert. A conversation with Commodore Diego Hernandez. NUESTRO, Vol. 7, no. 8 (October 1983), p. 15-17. English. DESCR: Caribbean Region; *Hernandez, Diego; Military Service.

12036 Captor, Rich. College and the Navy. CAMINOS, Vol. 4, no. 1-2 (January, February, 1983), p. 26-27. Bilingual. DESCR: *Careers; *Military; Reserve Officer Training Corps (ROTC).

U.S. Parole Commission

12037 Padilla, Steve. A Latino voice on the Parole Commission. NUESTRO, Vol. 7, no. 7 (September 1983), p. 42-43. English. **DESCR:** *Chicanas; Discrimination in Employment; *Kaslow, Audrey; Racism.

U.S. Postal Service

12038 "With pride and courage". NUESTRO, Vol. 7, no. 8 (October 1983), p. 9. English. **DESCR:** Military Service; *Veterans.

U.S. Small Business Administration

12039 Acosta, Maria D. Hispanic business in the 80's/el negocio Hispanico en los ochentas. CAMINOS, Vol. 3, no. 2 (February 1982), p. 24-26. Bilingual. **DESCR:** *Business.

12040 Balkan, D. Carlos. AMEX Systems Inc. at transition point. HISPANIC BUSINESS, Vol. 4, no. 6 (June 1982), p. 18-19,24. English. **DESCR:** AMEX Systems, Inc.; Business Enterprises; Caldera, Manuel R.; *Corporations; High Technology Industries; Small Business Administration 8(a) Program.

12041 A career line. HISPANIC BUSINESS, Vol. 4, no. 11 (November 1982), p. 14-15. English. **DESCR:** *Gallegos, Amanda M.; Small Business.

12042 Chamber, construction group given SBA aid. NUESTRO, Vol. 6, no. 7 (September 1982), p. 51. English. **DESCR:** *Business; *Businesspeople.

12043 Foreign trade. HISPANIC BUSINESS, Vol. 5, no. 2 (February 1983), p. 25. English. **DESCR:** *Currency; Mexico; Small Business; U.S. Trade Center (Mexico City).

12044 Foster, Richard. Two Alvarados make one sucessful construction firm. HISPANIC BUSINESS, Vol. 4, no. 10 (October 1982), p. 10-11,26. English. **DESCR:** Alvarado, Bob; Alvarado, Linda M.; *Business Enterprises; Construction Industry; Small Business Administration 8(a) Program.

12045 From the SBA. CAMINOS, Vol. 3, no. 2 (February 1982), p. 42. English. **DESCR:** *Business; *Statistics.

12046 Houstonite builds successful business: home-started business exceeds millions in foreign trade sales. NATIONAL HISPANIC JOURNAL, Vol. 1, no. 4 (Spring 1983), p. 7. English. **DESCR:** Business; *Business Enterprises; Businesspeople; Cavazos, Roy; Minority Business Development Agency (MBDA); *National Economic Development Association (NEDA).

12047 News at SBA: Cardenas removed as SBA chief. HISPANIC BUSINESS, Vol. 4, no. 4 (April 1982), p. 11. English. **DESCR:** Appointed Officials; *Cardenas, Michael.

12048 News at the SBA. HISPANIC BUSINESS, Vol. 4, no. 2 (February 1982), p. 22. English. **DESCR:** *Biographical Notes; Cardenas, Michael; Castillo, Irenemaree; Lopez, Reynaldo H.

12049 News at the SBA. HISPANIC BUSINESS, Vol. 4, no. 3 (March 1982), p. 14. English. **DESCR:** *Business; Business Enterprises; Cardenas, Maria Elena; Small Business Administration 8(a) Program.

12050 Peso pack announced for border businesses. NUESTRO, Vol. 6, no. 7 (September 1982), p.

52. English. **DESCR:** *Economic History and Conditions; *Economic Policy; *Economics.

12051 SBA reports on help to minority businesses. NUESTRO, Vol. 6, no. 4 (May 1982), p. 48. English. **DESCR:** *Businesspeople; Ethnic Groups.

12052 SBA update. HISPANIC BUSINESS, Vol. 4, no. 11 (November 1982), p. 22. English. **DESCR:** *Small Business; Small Business Administration 8(a) Program.

12053 SBA update. HISPANIC BUSINESS, Vol. 5, no. 2 (February 1983), p. 14. English. **DESCR:** *Small Business.

12054 Stockton woman named regional head of SBA. NUESTRO, Vol. 6, no. 1 (January, February, 1982), p. 47. English. **DESCR:** *Castillo, Irenemaree.

12055 Top ranking Latino resigns from SBA. NUESTRO, Vol. 6, no. 2 (March 1982), p. 45. English. **DESCR:** *Cardenas, Michael; Government.

12056 Women entrepreneurs offered SBA assistance. NUESTRO, Vol. 7, no. 1 (January, February, 1983), p. 47. English. **DESCR:** *Business Enterprises; Businesspeople; *Chicanas.

U.S. Supreme Court

12057 Reaves, Gayle. Supreme Court rules for alien children. NUESTRO, Vol. 6, no. 5 (June, July, 1982), p. 14-16. English. **DESCR:** *Children; Education; Education Equalization; Immigration Law; *Legislation; Undocumented Workers.

U.S. Supreme Court Case

12058 Schey, Peter A. Unnamed witness number 1: now attending the Texas public schools. MIGRATION TODAY, Vol. 10, no. 5 (1982), p. 22-27. English. **DESCR:** Constitutional Amendments - Fourteenth; Education; Education Equalization; Educational Law and Legislation; Equal Protection Clause; Migrant Children; Texas Public Schools; *Undocumented Children.

12059 Vasquez, Ivan. Analysis of June 15, 1982 opinion issued by the U.S. Supreme Court in the case of Texas undocumented children. MIGRATION TODAY, Vol. 10, no. 3-4 (1982), p. 49-51. English. **DESCR:** Constitutional Amendments - Fourteenth; Education; *Education Equalization; Educational Law and Legislation; Equal Protection Clause; Migrant Children; *Undocumented Children.

U.S. Trade Center (Mexico City)

12060 Foreign trade. HISPANIC BUSINESS, Vol. 5, no. 2 (February 1983), p. 25. English. **DESCR:** *Currency; Mexico; Small Business; U.S. Small Business Administration.

12061 Foreign trade. HISPANIC BUSINESS, Vol. 5, no. 10 (October 1983), p. 29. English. **DESCR:** Agency for International Development (AID); Caribbean Region; Economic History and Conditions; *Foreign Trade; HOW TO EXPORT: A MARKETING MANUAL; Mexico; Puerto Rico.

U.S. v. Calderon-Medina

12062 Helbush, Terry. INS violations of its own regulations: relief for the aliens. GOLDEN GATE UNIVERSITY LAW REVIEW, Vol. 12, (Spring 1982), p. 217-225. English. **DESCR:** Deportation; *Immigration Law; Tejeda-Mata v. INS; Undocumented Workers.

U.S. v. Contreras

12063 Miranda warnings were adequate despite deviations from strict form. CRIMINAL LAW REPORTER, Vol. 30, no. 22 (October 3, 1982), p. 2427-2428. English. **DESCR:** California v. Prysock; Drug Traffic; *Legal Aid.

U.S. v. Hanigan

12064 Movement of illegal alien laborers into United States is Hobbs act "Commerce". CRIMINAL LAW REPORTER, Vol. 31, no. 19 (August 18, 1982), p. 2394. English. **DESCR:** Business; Hobbs Act; *Undocumented Workers.

U.S. v. Otherson

12065 Brooks, Douglas Montgomery. Aliens - civil rights - illegal aliens are inhabitants within meaning of U.S.C 242. SUFFOLK TRANSNATIONAL LAW JOURNAL, Vol. 6, no. 1 (Spring 1982), p. 117-131. English. **DESCR:** Border Patrol; Constitutional Amendments - Fourteenth; Immigration Regulation and Control; *Undocumented Workers.

U.S. v. Valenzuela-Bernal

12066 Young, Rowland L. Witnesses ... deportation. AMERICAN BAR ASSOCIATION JOURNAL, Vol. 68, (November 1982), p. 1493. English. **DESCR:** *Deportation; Jury Trials; Undocumented Workers.

U.S.A. Bicentennial

12067 201 [special issue of CHISMEARTE]. CHISMEARTE, (1982), p. 6-66. Bilingual. **DESCR:** *Los Angeles Bicentennial; *Los Angeles, CA.

U.S.-Mexico Joint Commission on Commerce and Trade

12068 Mexican business update. HISPANIC BUSINESS, Vol. 4, no. 1 (January 1982), p. 24. English. **DESCR:** Business; Export Trade; *Foreign Trade; Mexico.

Val De La O Show

12069 Communications/marketing. HISPANIC BUSINESS, Vol. 4, no. 8 (August 1983), p. 22+. English. **DESCR:** Arredondo, Price; Baseball; De la O, Val; Films; Marketing; *Mass Media; Radio; San Antonio CineFestival, TX; Television; Valenzuela, Fernando; Wright & Arredondo Associates; Wright, Oscar.

Valdes Fallis, Guadalupe

12070 Feliciano-Foster, Wilma. A comparison of three current first-year college-level Spanish-for-native-speakers textbooks. BILINGUAL REVIEW, Vol. 9, no. 1 (January, April, 1982), p. 72-81. English. **DESCR:** *Book Reviews; ESPANOL ESCRITO; Garza-Swan, Gloria; *Language Development; Mejias, Hugo A.; MEJORA TU ESPANOL; NUESTRO ESPANOL: CURSO PARA ESTUDIANTES BILINGUES; Portilla, Marta de la; Spanish Language Textbooks; Teschner, Richard V.; Varela, Beatriz.

Valdes, Martha

12071 People. HISPANIC BUSINESS, Vol. 5, no. 1 (January 1983), p. 7. English. **DESCR:** Appointed Officials; *Biographical Notes; *Businesspeople; Elizalde, Hector; Mackey y Salazar, C.; Madrid, Carlos; Montoya, Velma; Nunez, Carlos; Perea, Stanley; Rodriguez, Rita.

Valdes y Tapia, Daniel T.

12072 LA LUZ MAGAZINE founder victim of cancer. LATINO, Vol. 53, no. 4 (June 1982), p. 8. English. **DESCR:** Biography.

Valdes-Fauli, Gonzalo

12073 Volsky, George. Four careers in Miami. HISPANIC BUSINESS, Vol. 5, no. 4 (April 1983), p. 10-11+. English. **DESCR:** Balestra, Victor C.; *Banking Industry; Biographical Notes; *Businesspeople; Harvard Business School's Latino Association; Huston, Maria Padilla; Masvidal, Sergio J.; Miami, FL.

Valdez, Abelardo L.

12074 People. HISPANIC BUSINESS, Vol. 5, no. 7 (July 1983), p. 8. English. **DESCR:** Alvarado, Anthony J.; Appointed Officials; *Biographical Notes; Businesspeople; Candela, Hilario; Garcia, Marlene; Gonzalez, Julio; Martinez, Tony; Pla, George.

Valdez, Daniel

12075 Alvarez, Amando. Daniel Valdez: su vida y su carrera. LATINO, Vol. 53, no. 2 (March, April, 1982), p. 16-17. Spanish. **DESCR:** Films; ZOOT SUIT [film].

12076 Diaz, Katherine A. The many faceted talents of Danny Valdez=Los muchos y variados talentos de Danny Valdez. CAMINOS, Vol. 2, no. 6 (October 1981), p. [34]-36. Bilingual. **DESCR:** Biography; Entertainers.

12077 Lopez, Rafael and Miller, Robert. Daniel Valley and the American Zoot Band (band review). CAMINOS, Vol. 4, no. 5 (May 1983), p. 42-43,52. English. **DESCR:** Artists; Films; ZOOT SUIT [film].

Valdez, Guadalupe

12078 Dyer, Nancy Joe. Book review of: TEACHING SPANISH TO THE HISPANIC BILINGUAL: ISSUES, AIMS AND METHODS. HISPANIA, Vol. 65, no. 3 (September 1982), p. 474-475. English. **DESCR:** Book Reviews; Garcia-Moya, Rodolfo; Lozano, Anthony G.; Spanish Language; *TEACHING SPANISH TO THE HISPANIC BILINGUAL: ISSUES, AIMS AND METHODS.

12079 Goldin, Mark G. Book review of: TEACHING SPANISH TO THE HISPANIC BILINGUAL: ISSUES, AIMS AND METHODS. NABE JOURNAL, Vol. 7, no. 1 (Fall 1982), p. 53-56. English. **DESCR:** Bilingualism; Book Reviews; Garcia-Moya, Rodolfo; Language Proficiency; Language Usage; Lozano, Anthony G.; Spanish Language; *TEACHING SPANISH TO THE HISPANIC BILINGUAL: ISSUES, AIMS AND METHODS.

Valdez, Guadalupe (cont.)

12080 Gutierrez, John R. Book review of: TEACHING
      SPANISH TO THE HISPANIC BILINGUAL: ISSUES,
      AIMS AND METHODS. MODERN LANGUAGE JOURNAL,
      Vol. 66, no. 2 (Summer 1982), p. 234.
      English. **DESCR**: Bilingualism; Book Reviews;
      Garcia-Moya, Rodolfo; Lozano, Anthony G.;
      Spanish Language; *TEACHING SPANISH TO THE
      HISPANIC BILINGUAL: ISSUES, AIMS AND
      METHODS.

Valdez, Jesse

12081 Morton, Carlos. People: back on top with
      Bernardo Eureste. NATIONAL HISPANIC JOURNAL,
      Vol. 2, no. 1 (Summer 1983), p. 20-21.
      English. **DESCR**: Cisneros, Henry, Mayor of
      San Antonio, TX; Elected Officials;
      Elections; *Eureste, Bernardo; San Antonio
      Police Department; San Antonio, TX.

Valdez, Joel

12082 Gonzales, Patrisia. The two cities of
      Tucson. NUESTRO, Vol. 7, no. 4 (May 1983),
      p. 20-23. English. **DESCR**: Accion 80s;
      Cultural Organizations; *Discrimination in
      Education; *Discrimination in Employment;
      Garcia, Gerald; Lopez-Grant, Lillian;
      *Tucson, AZ.

Valdez, Luis

12083 Barrios, Gregg. Zoot Suit: the man, the
      myth, still lives. BILINGUAL REVIEW, Vol.
      10, no. 2-3 (May, December, 1983), p.
      159-164. English. **DESCR**: Film Reviews; *ZOOT
      SUIT [film].

12084 Burciaga, Jose Antonio. Theatre: CORRIDOS -
      sad and happy masks. NUESTRO, Vol. 7, no. 4
      (May 1983), p. 53. English. **DESCR**: Corrido;
      *CORRIDOS [play]; El Teatro Campesino.

12085 Grelier, Robert. Film review of: CHICANOS
      STORY. REVUE DU CINEMA - IMAGE ET SON -
      ECRAN, (May 1983), p. 30. Other. **DESCR**:
      Film Reviews; ZOOT SUIT [film].

12086 Hinojosa-Smith, Rolando R. I AM JOAQUIN:
      relationships between the text and the film.
      BILINGUAL REVIEW, Vol. 10, no. 2-3 (May,
      December, 1983), p. 142-145. English.
      DESCR: Film Reviews; Gonzales, Rodolfo
      (Corky); I AM JOAQUIN [book]; *I AM JOAQUIN
      [film].

12087 Huerta, Jorge A. The influences of Latin
      American theatre on teatro Chicano. REVISTA
      CHICANO-RIQUENA, Vol. 11, no. 1 (Spring
      1983), p. 68-77. English. **DESCR**: *El Teatro
      Campesino; Latin America; Teatro.

12088 Morton, Carlos and Valdez, Luis. An
      interview with Luis Valdez. LATIN AMERICAN
      THEATRE REVIEW, Vol. 15, no. 2 (Spring
      1982), p. 73-76. English. **DESCR**:
      Agricultural Laborers; *Teatro.

12089 Orona-Cordova, Roberta and Valdez, Luis.
      ZOOT SUIT and the Pachuco phenomenon: an
      interview with Luis Valdez. REVISTA
      CHICANO-RIQUENA, Vol. 11, no. 1 (Spring
      1983), p. 95-111. English. **DESCR**: Pachucos;
      Teatro; *ZOOT SUIT [play].

12090 Ostria, Vincent. Film review of: CHICANOS
      STORY. CAHIERS DU CINEMA, Vol. 36, (June,
      July, 1983), p. 90. Other. **DESCR**: Film
      Reviews; *ZOOT SUIT [film].

Valencia, Gloria

12091 Gloria Valencia: woman on the move. LATINA,
      Vol. 1, no. 3 (1983), p. 50-51. English.
      DESCR: Biography; Valencia, Tony.

Valencia, Tony

12092 Gloria Valencia: woman on the move. LATINA,
      Vol. 1, no. 3 (1983), p. 50-51. English.
      DESCR: Biography; *Valencia, Gloria.

Valenti, Frank S.

12093 Fletcher and Valenti: Tampa's growing
      arquitectural firm. HISPANIC BUSINESS, Vol.
      4, no. 10 (October 1982), p. 15,26. English.
      DESCR: *Architecture; Business Enterprises;
      Fletcher & Valenti Architects/Planners,
      Inc.; Tampa, FL.

12094 People. HISPANIC BUSINESS, Vol. 4, no. 7
      (July 1982), p. 7. English. **DESCR**: Aguilar,
      Richard; *Biographical Notes;
      Businesspeople; Coronado, Julius; Enriquez,
      Rene; Garza, Jose S.; Guerra-Martinez,
      Celina; Medrano, Adan; Mota, Manny.

Valentino

12095 Diaz, Barbara M. The great Valentino.
      CAMINOS, Vol. 3, no. 9 (October 1982), p.
      22-23,44. Bilingual. **DESCR**: Artists.

Valenzuela, Fernando

12096 CAMINO'S 1981 Chicano of the year: Fernando
      Valenzuela. CAMINOS, Vol. 3, no. 2 (February
      1982), p. 10-13. Bilingual. **DESCR**: Awards;
      *CAMINOS' Chicano of the Year Award.

12097 Communications/marketing. HISPANIC BUSINESS,
      Vol. 4, no. 8 (August 1983), p. 22+.
      English. **DESCR**: Arredondo, Price; Baseball;
      De la O, Val; Films; Marketing; *Mass Media;
      Radio; San Antonio CineFestival, TX;
      Television; Val De La O Show; Wright &
      Arredondo Associates; Wright, Oscar.

12098 Ortiz, Carlos V. NUESTRO'S sixth annual
      all-star baseball team. NUESTRO, Vol. 7, no.
      2 (March 1983), p. 33-37. English. **DESCR**:
      Andujar, Joaquin; Barojas, Salome;
      *Baseball; Castillo, Manny; Concepcion,
      Dave; Cruz, Jose; Garcia, Damaso; Guerrero,
      Pedro; Hernandez, Keith; Lezcano, Sixto;
      Martinez, Tippy; Pena, Tony; Piniella, Lou;
      Sports.

12099 Sports updates. CAMINOS, Vol. 3, no. 4
      (April 1982), p. 42. English. **DESCR**:
      *Baseball; Maldonado, Candy; Orta, Jorge;
      Pena, Alejandro.

Valenzuela, Nicholas

12100 Breiter, Toni. An interview with some
      experts. AGENDA, Vol. 11, no. 3 (May, June,
      1981), p. 48-52. English. **DESCR**: Guernica,
      Antonio; Gutierrez, Felix; *Mass Media;
      Morales, Rosa; Schement, Jorge Reina.

Valeri, Michele

12101 Mi casa es su casa. NUESTRO, Vol. 6, no. 4
      (May 1982), p. 64. English. **DESCR**: *Music.

Valeri, Michele (cont.)

12102 Our 1982 Latino awards. NUESTRO, Vol. 7, no.
1 (January, February, 1983), p. 44-46.
English. **DESCR:** Awards; Escalante, Jaime;
Gallegos, Gina; Grace, J. Peter; Immigration
and Naturalization Service (INS); Knight,
Bobby; Lamas, Fernando; *Latino Awards;
Luce, Claire Boothe; Moreno, Rita; National
Press Foundation; Rodriguez Hernandez,
Andres; Simpson-Mazzoli Bill; Smith,
Raymond; Voting Rights Act.

Valero, Robert

12103 Irizarry, Estelle. La abuelita in
literature. NUESTRO, Vol. 7, no. 7
(September 1983), p. 50. English. **DESCR:**
Alonso, Luis Ricardo; *Ancianos; Chicanas;
Cotto-Thorner, Guillermo; Family; Ulibarri,
Sabine R.

Valladares, Armando

12104 Greenfield, Charles. Armando Valladares:
twenty-two years of solitude. NUESTRO, Vol.
7, no. 10 (December 1983), p. 14-18+.
English. **DESCR:** Cuba; *Political Prisoners;
Political Repression.

Valle Inclan, Ramon

12105 Espinoza, Roberto. Sintesis vs. analysis: un
problema de historicidad en las novelas de
las dictaduras. MAIZE, Vol. 6, no. 1-2
(Fall, Winter, 1982, 1983), p. 7-27.
Spanish. **DESCR:** Carpentier, Alejo;
Dictatorships; Garcia Marquez, Gabriel;
Latin American Literature; *Literary
Criticism; Novel; Roa Bastos, Augustos;
White, Lucas Edward.

THE VALLEY

12106 Garcia, Ed. Quien es Rolando Hinojosa? TEXAS
OBSERVOR, Vol. 75, no. 5 (March 11,), p.
26-29. English. **DESCR:** Biography; Book
Reviews; *Hinojosa-Smith, Rolando R.; *RITES
AND WITNESSES.

Values

12107 Cortese, Anthony J., ed. A comparative
analysis of ethnicity and moral judgment.
CACR REVIEW, Vol. 1, no. 1 (September 1982),
p. 72-101. English. **DESCR:** Anglo Americans;
Blacks; Cultural Characteristics; Identity.

12108 Solis, Arnaldo. Chicano mental health.
CALMECAC, Vol. 1, (Summer 1980), p. 49-56.
Bilingual. **DESCR:** Aztecs; *Mental Health.

12109 Solis, Arnaldo. Chicano values: living in
balance. CALMECAC, Vol. 3, (Spring 1982),
p. 30-32. English.

12110 Tello, Jerry. Relationship entre nuestra
gente II. CALMECAC, Vol. 1, (Summer 1980),
p. 12-15. Bilingual. **DESCR:** *Interpersonal
Relations.

12111 Wurzman, Ilyana. Cultural values of Puerto
Rican opiate addicts: an exploratory study.
AMERICAN JOURNAL OF DRUG AND ALCOHOL ABUSE,
Vol. 9, no. 2 (1982, 1983), p. 141-153.
English. **DESCR:** Acculturation; Anglo
Americans; Blacks; *Drug Abuse; Drug
Addicts; Family; Loevinger's Sentence
Completion Test; Machismo; New York, NY;
Opium; Puerto Ricans.

Van Ness, Christine M.

12112 Salmon, Roberto Mario. Book review of:

SPANISH AND MEXICAN LAND GRANTS IN NEW
MEXICO AND COLORADO. JOURNAL OF ETHNIC
STUDIES, Vol. 9, no. 3 (Fall 1981), p.
120-121. English. **DESCR:** Book Reviews;
Colorado; *Land Grants; New Mexico; *SPANISH
AND MEXICAN LAND GRANTS IN NEW MEXICO AND
COLORADO; Van Ness, John R.

Van Ness, John R.

12113 Carlson, Alvar W. Book review of: CANONES:
VALUES, CRISIS, AND SURVIVAL IN A NORTHERN
NEW MEXICO VILLAGE. NEW MEXICO HISTORICAL
REVIEW, Vol. 58, no. 3 (July 1983), p. 294.
English. **DESCR:** Book Reviews; *CANONES:
VALUES, CRISIS AND SURVIVAL IN A NORTHERN
NEW MEXICO VILLAGE; Kutsche, Paul.

12114 Salmon, Roberto Mario. Book review of:
SPANISH AND MEXICAN LAND GRANTS IN NEW
MEXICO AND COLORADO. JOURNAL OF ETHNIC
STUDIES, Vol. 9, no. 3 (Fall 1981), p.
120-121. English. **DESCR:** Book Reviews;
Colorado; *Land Grants; New Mexico; *SPANISH
AND MEXICAN LAND GRANTS IN NEW MEXICO AND
COLORADO; Van Ness, Christine M.

12115 Weber, Kenneth R. Book review of: CANONES:
VALUES, CRISIS, AND SURVIVAL IN A NORTHERN
NEW MEXICO VILLAGE. JOURNAL OF ETHNIC
STUDIES, Vol. 11, no. 2 (Summer 1983), p.
119-123. English. **DESCR:** Book Reviews;
Canones, NM; *CANONES: VALUES, CRISIS AND
SURVIVAL IN A NORTHERN NEW MEXICO VILLAGE;
Ethnology; History; Kutsche, Paul; New
Mexico; Northern New Mexico.

Vanderwood, Paul J.

12116 Powell, T. G. Book review of: DISORDER AND
PROGRESS: BANDITS, POLICE, AND MEXICAN
DEVELOPMENT. AMERICAS, Vol. 38, no. 4
(1982), p. 540-541. English. **DESCR:** Book
Reviews; *DISORDER AND PROGRESS: BANDITS,
POLICE AND MEXICAN DEVELOPMENT.

12117 Ruiz, Ramon Eduardo. Book review of:
DISORDER AND PROGRESS: BANDITS, POLICE, AND
MEXICAN DEVELOPMENT. ARIZONA AND THE WEST,
Vol. 24, no. 1 (Spring 1982), p. 75-76.
English. **DESCR:** Bandidos; Book Reviews;
Diaz, Porfirio; *DISORDER AND PROGRESS:
BANDITS, POLICE AND MEXICAN DEVELOPMENT.

Vaqueros

12118 Myres, Sandra Lynn. The cowboy's Hispanic
heritage. NUESTRO, Vol. 7, no. 7 (September
1983), p. 44-48. English. **DESCR:** Spanish
Influence; United States History.

Varela, Beatriz

12119 Feliciano-Foster, Wilma. A comparison of
three current first-year college-level
Spanish-for-native-speakers textbooks.
BILINGUAL REVIEW, Vol. 9, no. 1 (January,
April, 1982), p. 72-81. English. **DESCR:**
*Book Reviews; ESPANOL ESCRITO; Garza-Swan,
Gloria; *Language Development; Mejias, Hugo
A.; MEJORA TU ESPANOL; NUESTRO ESPANOL:
CURSO PARA ESTUDIANTES BILINGUES; Portilla,
Marta de la; Spanish Language Textbooks;
Teschner, Richard V.; Valdes Fallis,
Guadalupe.

Varela, Gilbert

12120 Bachelor of the month. LATINA, Vol. 1, no. 1
(1982), p. 13. English. **DESCR:** *Biography.

Varela, Robert

12121 Roberto Varela and TLC. CAMINOS, Vol. 3, no. 2 (February 1982), p. 27-29. Bilingual. **DESCR:** Business; *Businesspeople; Tape & Label Converters (TLC).

Vargas, Alberto

12122 Gente. NUESTRO, Vol. 7, no. 2 (March 1983), p. 51. English. **DESCR:** Artists; Betancourt, Jose L.; *Chicanas; Crime Victims Fund; Federal Government; Juarez, Joe; Military Service; Saldana, Teresa; Victims for Victims.

Vargas, Raul

12123 Taylor, Karla and Vargas, Raul. Entrevista/interview: Q: How to raise money for your Hispanic students? A: Involve your alumni and their corporate contacts. CASE CURRENTS, Vol. 9, no. 4 (April 1983), p. 18-21. English. **DESCR:** College Graduates; Funding Sources; Higher Education; *Office for Mexican American Programs, University of Southern California.

Vasconcelos, Jose

12124 Skirius, John. Barreda, Vasconcelos, and the Mexican educational reforms. AZTLAN, Vol. 14, no. 2 (Fall 1983), p. 307-341. English. **DESCR:** *Barreda, Gabino; Education; *Educational Theory and Practice; History; Mexico; Positivism.

Vasquez, Carol

12125 Cuellar, Israel and Price, Criselda Segovia. Psychiatric evaluation of bilingual patient: a reply to Vazquez. HISPANIC JOURNAL OF BEHAVIORAL SCIENCES, Vol. 4, no. 1 (March 1982), p. 81-83. English. **DESCR:** *Psychological Theory.

Vasquez, Hector G.

12126 Study details minority access to legal education. NEW JERSEY LAW JOURNAL, Vol. 112, no. 1 (July 7, 1983), p. 28. English. **DESCR:** Brown, Susan E.; *Ethnic Groups; *Legal Education; Mexican American Legal Defense and Educational Fund (MALDEF); PLURALISM IN THE LEGAL PROFESSION: MODELS FOR MINORITY ACCESS.

Vasquez, Patricia

12127 Mexican American Legal Defense and Education Fund (MALDEF). Chicana rights: a major MALDEF issue (reprinted from MALDEF Newsletter, Fall 1977). COMADRE, no. 2 (Spring 1978), p. 31-33. English. **DESCR:** Chicana Rights Project; Chicanas; *Mexican American Legal Defense and Educational Fund (MALDEF); Statistics; *Women's Rights.

12128 Mexican American Legal Defense and Education Fund (MALDEF). Chicana rights: a major MALDEF issue (reprinted from MALDEF Newsletter, Fall 1977). COMADRE, no. 3 (Fall 1978), p. 31-35. English. **DESCR:** Chicana Rights Project; Chicanas; *Mexican American Legal Defense and Educational Fund (MALDEF); Statistics; *Women's Rights.

Vasquez, Victor

12129 1982 business persons announced by chamber. NUESTRO, Vol. 6, no. 5 (June, July, 1982), p. 44. English. **DESCR:** Latin Americans; *Roubin, Angel.

12130 How to stuff a wild chile part II. CAMINOS, Vol. 3, no. 1 (January 1982), p. 31-32. English. **DESCR:** Albert, Margo; Chacon, Peter R.; *Icaya, Rick; Lacayo, Frank L. "Hank"; *Recipes; *Rodriguez, Edmundo; Rodriguez, Edmundo M.

12131 People. HISPANIC BUSINESS, Vol. 5, no. 2 (February 1983), p. 7. English. **DESCR:** Alvarez, Everett, Jr.; Appointed Officials; *Biographical Notes; Businesspeople; Guzman-Randle, Irene; Roubin, Angel; Villareal, Luis Maria.

Vazquez-Castro, Javier

12132 Gonzalez, Maria R. Book review of: ACERCA DE LITERATURA (Dialogo con tres autores chicanos). LA PALABRA, Vol. 4, no. 1-2 (Spring, Fall, 1982, 1983), p. 170-171. Spanish. **DESCR:** *ACERCA DE LITERATURA; Book Reviews; Literature.

Vega, Christopher

12133 Nuestra gente. LATINO, Vol. 54, no. 8 (December 1983), p. 30. English. **DESCR:** *Biographical Notes; Businesspeople; Carter, Lynda Cordoba; Duran, Sandra; Patino, Lorenzo E.; Politics; Rembis, Deborah.

Vela, Roque

12134 Vietnam war hero treated unjustly. NUESTRO, Vol. 5, no. 8 (November 1981), p. 43. English. **DESCR:** *Veterans; *Vietnam War.

Velasco, Eugenio

12135 Perales, Velasco win special Durfee award. NUESTRO, Vol. 6, no. 8 (October 1982), p. 43. English. **DESCR:** *Durfee Award; *Perales, Cesar A.

Velasco, Jerry

12136 Whisler, Kirk. Nosotros on film in Hollywood and Latin America. CAMINOS, Vol. 3, no. 7 (July, August, 1982), p. 15-17. Bilingual. **DESCR:** Artists; Cardinale, Marcela; Espinoza, Jimmy; Films; Gomez, Mike; *Nosotros [film production company]; Ortiz, Yolanda; Television.

Velasquez, Baldemar

12137 Latinos evident in 1983 march. NUESTRO, Vol. 7, no. 7 (September 1983), p. 11-12. English. **DESCR:** Bonilla, Tony; Cuban-American Coordinating Committee; *Demonstrations; IMAGE, Washington, DC; Jackson, Jesse; League of United Latin American Citizens (LULAC); National Congress for Puerto Rican Rights (NCPRR); National Council of La Raza (NCLR); Zamora, Reuben.

Velez, Tom

12138 Tom Velez: a man in control of his future. CAMINOS, Vol. 4, no. 1-2 (January, February, 1983), p. 9-10+. English. **DESCR:** Careers; Computer Technology Associates (CTA); Computers.

Venezuela

12139 Gente. NUESTRO, Vol. 7, no. 7 (September 1983), p. 61. English. **DESCR:** Americas Award; Chavez, Raul; *Chicanas; Diaz-Cobo, Christine; Mexico; Ortega, Katherine D.; Performing Arts; Planas, Vilma; Ravard, Rafael Alonzo.

Venezuela (cont.)

12140 PA trained for Venezuela. NUESTRO, Vol. 6, no. 6 (August 1982), p. 10. English. **DESCR**: *Estassi, Pilar; Medical Care.

12141 Schon, Isabel. Recent outstanding books for young readers from Spanish speaking countries. READING TEACHER, Vol. 36, no. 2 (November 1982), p. 206-209. English. **DESCR**: Argentina; *Children's Literature; Literature Reviews; Spain; Spanish Language.

12142 Schon, Isabel. Spanish books for children. BOOKLIST, Vol. 78, no. 20 (June 15, 1982), p. 1373-1374. English. **DESCR**: Argentina; *Bibliography; *Children's Literature; Mexico; Spain; Spanish Language.

12143 Schon, Isabel. Spanish books for children. BOOKLIST, Vol. 79, (February 15, 1983), p. 783-784. English. **DESCR**: *Bibliography; *Children's Literature; Mexico; Spain; Spanish Language.

La Ventana

12144 Communications/marketing. HISPANIC BUSINESS, Vol. 5, no. 9 (September 1983), p. 26. English. **DESCR**: Aguirre, Horacio; Business Enterprises; Consumers; DIARIO DE LAS AMERICAS; *Marketing; Miller Brewing Company; SURVEY OF PROMOTIONAL PRACTICES.

Ventriglia, Linda

12145 Walia, Adorna. Book review of: CONVERSATIONS OF MIGUEL AND MARIA: HOW CHILDREN LEARN ENGLISH AS A SECOND LANGUAGE; IMPLICATIONS FOR CLASSROOM TEACHING. BILINGUAL JOURNAL, Vol. 6, no. 1 (Fall 1982), p. 28-29. English. **DESCR**: Bilingual Bicultural Education; Book Reviews; *CONVERSATIONS OF MIGUEL AND MARIA: HOW CHILDREN LEARN ENGLISH AS A SECOND LANGUAGE; IMPLICATIONS FOR CLASSROOM TEACHING; English as a Second Language.

Veracruz, Mexico

12146 Loza, Steven J. Origins, form, and development of the Son Jarocho: Veracruz, Mexico. AZTLAN, Vol. 13, no. 1-2 (Spring, Fall, 1982), p. 257-274. English. **DESCR**: Dance; Folk Songs; Music; *Son Jarocho.

12147 Loza, Steven J. The Son Jarocho: the history, style and repertory of a changing Mexican musical tradition. AZTLAN, Vol. 13, no. 1-2 (Spring, Fall, 1982), p. 327-334. English. **DESCR**: Dance; Folk Songs; Music; Sheehy, Daniel E.; *Son Jarocho.

UN VERANO

12148 Ayala, Ernesto. My machine. NUESTRO, Vol. 6, no. 7 (September 1982), p. 31. English. **DESCR**: Ayala, Ernesto; *Poetry.

12149 Montoya, Deborah. Creativity. NUESTRO, Vol. 6, no. 7 (September 1982), p. 31. English. **DESCR**: *Poetry.

LA VERDAD SIN VOZ

12150 Gonzales-Berry, Erlinda. Doctor, writer, warrior chief. BILINGUAL REVIEW, Vol. 9, no. 3 (September, December, 1982), p. 276-279. English. **DESCR**: *Morales, Alejandro.

12151 Monleon, Jose. Dos novelas de Alejandro Morales. MAIZE, Vol. 4, no. 1-2 (Fall, Winter, 1980, 1981), p. 6-8. Spanish. **DESCR**: *CARAS VIEJAS Y VINO NUEVO; Literary Criticism; Morales, Alejandro.

Verges, Bruni

12152 Naismith, Rachael. Outreach services to Hispanics. ILLINOIS LIBRARIES, Vol. 64, no. 7 (September 1982), p. 962-966. English. **DESCR**: Arrondo, Ondina; Cubanos; La Raza Hispanica, Miami, FL; Latin American Library/Biblioteca Latinoamericana, Oakland, CA; *Library Services; Lopez, Lillian; Puerto Ricans; Ruiz, Deborah; South Bronx Project, New York Public Library.

Veterans

12153 Brown, Edward G. The Teatro Campesino's Vietnam trilogy. MINORITY VOICES, Vol. 4, no. 1 (Spring 1980), p. 29-38. English. **DESCR**: *El Teatro Campesino; Teatro; Vietnam War.

12154 Escobar, J.I. Post-traumatic stress disorder in Hispanic Vietnam veterans. JOURNAL OF NERVOUS AND MENTAL DISEASE, Vol. 17, no. 10 (October 1983), p. 585-596. English. **DESCR**: Acculturation; Mental Illness; Psychiatry; Stress.

12155 Garcia, Ignacio M. America says, welcome home. NUESTRO, Vol. 6, no. 9 (November 1982), p. 15-19+. English. **DESCR**: *Alvarez, Everett, Jr.; Political Prisoners; Vietnam; Vietnam War.

12156 Government review. NUESTRO, Vol. 7, no. 8 (October 1983), p. 54. English. **DESCR**: Alcoholism; Employment; *Government Services; National Endowment for the Arts; Plaza de La Raza, Los Angeles, CA; Working Women; Youth.

12157 Government review. NUESTRO, Vol. 7, no. 6 (August 1983), p. 56. English. **DESCR**: Ballet de Puerto Rico; Dance; Education; Employment; *Government Funding Sources; Government Services; Housing; Income; National Fair Housing Law; Population Distribution; Urban Development Action Grant (UDAG).

12158 Mimiaga, Hector. Back in the step with America's Drummers: I feel good again. NUESTRO, Vol. 6, no. 9 (November 1982), p. 20. English. **DESCR**: *Benavidez, Roy; Political Prisoners; Vietnam War.

12159 Ponti, Gino. Courage all the way. NUESTRO, Vol. 6, no. 4 (May 1982), p. 14-15+. English. **DESCR**: *Stiehl-Rios, Edward.

12160 Vietnam war hero treated unjustly. NUESTRO, Vol. 5, no. 8 (November 1981), p. 43. English. **DESCR**: Vela, Roque; *Vietnam War.

12161 "With pride and courage". NUESTRO, Vol. 7, no. 8 (October 1983), p. 9. English. **DESCR**: Military Service; *U.S. Postal Service.

Veteran's Administration

12162 Hann, Donna; Ferree, W. P.; and Flores, Larry. Affirmative action means progress: 2 corporations and one federal agency look at affirmative action. CAMINOS, Vol. 3, no. 8 (September 1982), p. 39-42. English. **DESCR**: *Affirmative Action; General Telephone Company; Imperial Savings.

12163 NATIVE ALIENS (videotape). CAMINOS, Vol. 3, no. 8 (September 1982), p. 43. English. **DESCR**: Hispanic Employment Program (HEP); *Manpower Programs.

Veve, Rafael

12164 Weber, Robert. Rising star: Satelco. HISPANIC BUSINESS, Vol. 5, no. 9 (September 1983), p. 14. English. **DESCR:** Business Enterprises; Lagueruela, Andy; *Satelco, Inc.; Telecommunications.

Victims for Victims

12165 Gente. NUESTRO, Vol. 7, no. 2 (March 1983), p. 51. English. **DESCR:** Artists; Betancourt, Jose L.; *Chicanas; Crime Victims Fund; Federal Government; Juarez, Joe; Military Service; Saldana, Teresa; Vargas, Alberto.

Victory Outreach

12166 Vigil, James Diego. Human revitalization: the six tasks of victory outreach. DREW GATEWAY, Vol. 52, no. 3 (Spring 1982), p. 49-59. English. **DESCR:** Barrios for Christ Program; Drug Addicts; Drug Programs; Gangs; Identity; Pentecostal Church; Protestant Church; Religion; Youth.

VICTUUM

12167 Lomeli, Francisco A. Isabella Rios and the Chicano psychic novel. MINORITY VOICES, Vol. 4, no. 1 (Spring 1980), p. 49-61. English. **DESCR:** Literature; Lopez, Diana; Novel; *Rios, Isabella.

Vidal de Neri, Julieta

12168 Q & A: in the Hispanic community who are the winners and losers of Reaganomics? CAMINOS, Vol. 3, no. 3 (March 1982), p. 47. Bilingual. **DESCR:** Casado, Lucy; Echeveste, John; *Federal Government; Flores, Bob; Leon, Virginia; Mendoza, John; *Reagan, Ronald; Sanchez-Alvarez, Gloria.

Vietnam

12169 Garcia, Ignacio M. America says, welcome home. NUESTRO, Vol. 6, no. 9 (November 1982), p. 15-19+. English. **DESCR:** *Alvarez, Everett, Jr.; Political Prisoners; *Veterans; Vietnam War.

Vietnam War

12170 Brown, Edward G. The Teatro Campesino's Vietnam trilogy. MINORITY VOICES, Vol. 4, no. 1 (Spring 1980), p. 29-38. English. **DESCR:** *El Teatro Campesino; Teatro; Veterans.

12171 Garcia, Ignacio M. America says, welcome home. NUESTRO, Vol. 6, no. 9 (November 1982), p. 15-19+. English. **DESCR:** *Alvarez, Everett, Jr.; Political Prisoners; *Veterans; Vietnam.

12172 Mimiaga, Hector. Back in the step with America's Drummers: I feel good again. NUESTRO, Vol. 6, no. 9 (November 1982), p. 20. English. **DESCR:** *Benavidez, Roy; Political Prisoners; Veterans.

12173 The Vietnam void. LATINO, Vol. 54, no. 1 (January, February, 1983), p. 22. English. **DESCR:** *War.

12174 Vietnam war hero treated unjustly. NUESTRO, Vol. 5, no. 8 (November 1981), p. 43. English. **DESCR:** Vela, Roque; *Veterans.

VIEWS ACROSS THE BORDER: THE UNITED STATES AND MEXICO

12175 Garcia, Mario T. History, culture, and society of the borderlands. NEW SCHOLAR, Vol. 8, no. 1-2 (Spring, Fall, 1982), p. 467-472. English. **DESCR:** Book Reviews; Border Studies.

VILLA ALEGRE

12176 Neuman, Susan B. and Pits, Elaine F. A review of current North American television programs for bilingual children. READING TEACHER, Vol. 37, no. 3 (December 1983), p. 254-260. English. **DESCR:** *Bilingual Bicultural Education; Mass Media; SESAME STREET; Spanish Language; THE ELECTRIC COMPANY.

Villa de Romo, Velma

12177 Garza-Livingston, M'Liss and Villa de Romo, Velma. An interview with Velma Villa de Romo: bilingual liaison for the Santa Barbara Rape Crisis Center. COMADRE, no. 3 (Fall 1978), p. 15-16. English. **DESCR:** Rape; *Santa Barbara Rape Crisis Center.

Villa, Eduardo

12178 A salute to the arts. NUESTRO, Vol. 6, no. 7 (September 1982), p. 44-45. English. **DESCR:** *Art; Artists; Congressional Hispanic Caucus; National Hispanic Heritage Week.

Villa, Esteban

12179 Villa, Esteban. Chicano wisdom. CALMECAC, Vol. 2, (Spring 1981), p. 16-17. English. **DESCR:** *Biography.

Villa Merced Housing Project

12180 Quinlivan, Robert. The need for Hispanic senior housing. CAMINOS, Vol. 3, no. 7 (July, August, 1982), p. 42-43. Bilingual. **DESCR:** *Ancianos; Colonial Barrio Seniors; *Housing; San Diego, CA.

Villa, Pancho

12181 Conflict occurs over city statue. NUESTRO, Vol. 6, no. 9 (November 1982), p. 11. English. **DESCR:** History; Mexico; *Tucson, AZ.

Villalpando, Catalina

12182 People. HISPANIC BUSINESS, Vol. 5, no. 9 (September 1983), p. 10. English. **DESCR:** *Businesspeople; Chavez, Chris; Diez de Onate, Jorge; Franco Garcia, Freddie; Garcia, Hector P.; Lozano, Leticia Eugenia; Ravard, Rafael Alonzo; Rodriguez, Alberto Duque; Sanchez, Philip V.

Villanueva, Tino

12183 Alves Pereira, Teresinka. Book review of: CHICANOS: ANTOLOGIA HISTORICA Y LITERARIA. ROCKY MOUNTAIN REVIEW OF LANGUAGE AND LITERATURE, Vol. 36, no. 4 (1982), p. 301-302. Spanish. **DESCR:** Book Reviews; *CHICANOS: ANTOLOGIA HISTORICA Y LITERARIA.

12184 de Armas, Isabel. Chicano, un vocablo colonizador. CUADERNOS HISPANOAMERICANOS, Vol. 394, (April 1983), p. 193-201. Spanish. **DESCR:** Agricultural Laborers; Book Reviews; Calvo Buezas, Tomas; *CHICANOS: ANTOLOGIA HISTORICA Y LITERARIA; Identity; *LOS MAS POBRES EN EL PAIS MAS RICO.

Villanueva, Tino (cont.)

12185 Soens. Adolph L. Book review of: CHICANOS: ANTOLOGIA HISTORICA Y LITERARIA. MINORITY VOICES, Vol. 5, no. 1-2 (Spring, Fall, 1981), p. 69-71. English. **DESCR:** Book Reviews; *CHICANOS: ANTOLOGIA HISTORICA Y LITERARIA; Literature.

Villareal, Luis Maria

12186 People. HISPANIC BUSINESS, Vol. 5, no. 2 (February 1983), p. 7. English. **DESCR:** Alvarez, Everett, Jr.; Appointed Officials; *Biographical Notes; Businesspeople; Guzman-Randle, Irene; Roubin, Angel; Vasquez, Victor.

Villarreal, Abelardo

12187 Villarreal, Maria; Tirado, Miguel David; and Lopez, Ronald W. Abelardo Villarreal: a teacher's teacher. CAMINOS, no. 12 (1981), p. 30, 46. Bilingual. **DESCR:** Biography; Teaching Profession.

Villarreal, Jose Antonio

12188 Alarcon, Justo S. Hacia la nada ... o la religion en POCHO. MINORITY VOICES, Vol. 1, no. 2 (Fall 1977), p. 17-26. English. **DESCR:** Literature; *POCHO; Religion.

12189 Leudtke, Luther S. POCHO and the American dream. MINORITY VOICES, Vol. 1, no. 2 (Fall 1977), p. 1-16. English. **DESCR:** Literature; *POCHO.

12190 Vallejos, Thomas. Ritual process and the family in the Chicano novel. MELUS: MULTI-ETHNIC LITERATURE OF THE UNITED STATES, Vol. 10, no. 4 (Winter 1983, 1984), p. 5-16. English. **DESCR:** Anaya, Rudolfo A.; BLESS ME, ULTIMA; Family; *Literary Criticism; Novel; Parent and Child Relationships; POCHO; Rivera, Tomas; Y NO SE LO TRAGO LA TIERRA/AND THE EARTH DID NOT PART.

Villarreal, Sylvia

12191 A time for reflection. NUESTRO, Vol. 7, no. 9 (November 1983), p. 42-44. English. **DESCR:** Anaya, Rudolfo A.; Arias, Beatriz; Bilingual Bicultural Education; Computers; Financial Aid; Folklore; Organizations; Prewitt Diaz, Joseph (Jose); *W.K. Kellogg Foundation National Fellowship Program.

Violence

12192 Colorado confrontation. NUESTRO, Vol. 6, no. 6 (August 1982), p. 9. English. **DESCR:** *Colorado; Riots.

12193 Ericksen, Charles. Holdenreid and Salazar: unanswered questions. NUESTRO, Vol. 7, no. 4 (May 1983), p. 40-41. English. **DESCR:** Assassination; Criminal Acts; Guatemala; *Holdenreid, Frank X.; *Salazar, Ruben.

12194 Fifth member leaves panel. NUESTRO, Vol. 6, no. 4 (May 1982), p. 11. English. **DESCR:** *Lew, Salvador; Little Havana; Miami, FL; Police.

12195 Lathrop, Richard A. Out of tragedy. NUESTRO, Vol. 6, no. 4 (May 1982), p. 19-22+. English. **DESCR:** *Police.

12196 McCurdy, Jack. L.A. violence linked to Chicano-studies dispute. CHRONICLE OF HIGHER EDUCATION, Vol. 24, no. 14 (June 2, 1982), p. 8. English. **DESCR:** California State

University, Los Angeles; *Chicano Studies; Corona, Bert; Faculty.

12197 Too much TV and violence in cartoons. LATINA, Vol. 1, no. 2 (February, March, 1983), p. 74. English. **DESCR:** National Coalition on Violence; *Television.

Viramontes, Carlos

12198 Newsfront. HISPANIC BUSINESS, Vol. 4, no. 1 (January 1982), p. 7. English. **DESCR:** *Biographical Notes; Businesspeople; Community Development; Jimenez, Richard D.; Macias, Miguel (Mike); Oaxaca, Jaime; The East Los Angeles Community Union (TELACU).

Viramontes, Helen

12199 Alurista and Monleon, Jose. Mesa redonda. MAIZE, Vol. 4, no. 3-4 (Spring, Summer, 1981), p. 6-23. English. **DESCR:** Alurista; Anaya, Rudolfo A.; Herrera Sobek, Maria; Identity; Literature; Morales, Alejandro; *Mythology.

Virgin of Guadalupe

12200 Gil, Carlos B. Withstanding time: the miracle of the Virgin of Guadalupe. NUESTRO, Vol. 7, no. 10 (December 1983), p. 46-47. English. **DESCR:** Catholic Church; *Guadalupanismo; Mexico City; Religion.

12201 Lopez, Yolanda M. [Untitled montage from the SERIE GUADALUPE]. MAIZE, Vol. 1, no. 4 (Summer 1978), p. Ft cover. English. **DESCR:** *Montage.

12202 Lopez, Yolanda M. [Untitled montage from the SERIE GUADALUPE]. MAIZE, Vol. 1, no. 4 (Summer 1978), p. 55-59. English. **DESCR:** *Montage.

Visa

12203 Boiston, Bernard G. The Simpson-Mazzoli bill: the first major immigration bill in thirty years. OHIO STATE BAR ASSOCIATION REPORT, Vol. 55, no. 39 (October 11, 1982), p. 1738-1743. English. **DESCR:** Employment; Immigration; *Undocumented Workers.

12204 Roma, Thomas E., Jr. Not my father's son: obtaining preferred immigration status through paternal affiliation. JOURNAL OF FAMILY LAW, Vol. 20, no. 2 (January 1982), p. 323-335. English. **DESCR:** Board of Immigration Appeals (BIA); Immigration; Immigration and Nationality Act (INA).

12205 Schmeltzer, Mike. Mexicans asked to report. MIGRATION TODAY, Vol. 10, no. 1 (1982), p. 29. English. **DESCR:** Immigration; *Immigration Regulation and Control; Silva Letters; Silva, Refugio.

Vital Statistics

12206 Hedderson, John and Daudistel, Howard C. Infant mortality of the Spanish surname population. SOCIAL SCIENCE JOURNAL, Vol. 19, no. 4 (October 1982), p. 67-78. English. **DESCR:** Demography; El Paso County, TX; *Infant Mortality; Medical Care; Statistics.

12207 Trevino, Fernando M. Vital and health statistics for the United States Hispanic population. AMERICAN JOURNAL OF PUBLIC HEALTH, Vol. 72, no. 9 (September 1982), p. 979-982. English. **DESCR:** Public Health.

Vocational Aspirations

USE: Vocational Education

Vocational Education

12208 Bradley, Curtis H. and Friedenberg, Joan E. Tips for the English speaking multicultural vocational teacher. BILINGUAL JOURNAL, Vol. 6, no. 1 (Fall 1982), p. 6-9. English. DESCR: *Cultural Pluralism; Educational Innovations; Limited-English Proficient (LEP); Teacher-pupil Interaction.

12209 Buckholtz, Marjorie Weidenfeld. Technical training in two languages helps Houston stay cool. AMERICAN EDUCATION, Vol. 18, no. 3 (April 1982), p. 11-14. English. DESCR: *Employment Training; Houston Community College; Language Arts; Language Proficiency.

12210 Chavez, Ruth and Ramirez, Albert. Employment aspirations, expectations, and attitudes among employed and unemployed Chicanos. JOURNAL OF SOCIAL PSYCHOLOGY, Vol. 11, no. 1 (February 1983), p. 143-144. English. DESCR: Attitude (Psychological); *Employment.

12211 Communications/marketing. HISPANIC BUSINESS, Vol. 4, no. 5 (May 1982), p. 15. English. DESCR: Anheuser-Busch, Inc.; Farres, Osvaldo; Girl Scouts of the United States of America; *Marketing; Organizations; Television; Voter Turnout.

12212 Gonzalez, Gilbert G. Educational reform and the Mexican community in Los Angeles. SOUTHWEST ECONOMY AND SOCIETY, Vol. 3, no. 3 (Spring 1978), p. 24-51. English. DESCR: Counseling Services (Educational); Curriculum; *Education; Enrollment; *History; Intelligence Tests; Los Angeles, CA; *Los Angeles City School District; Tracking (Educational).

12213 Phillips, Susan D., et al. Career development of special populations: a framework for research. JOURNAL OF VOCATIONAL BEHAVIOR, Vol. 22, no. 1 (February 1983), p. 12-29. English. DESCR: Careers; College Graduates; *Research Methodology.

12214 Plata, Maximino and Jones, Priscilla. Bilingual vocational education for handicapped students. EXCEPTIONAL CHILDREN, Vol. 48, no. 4 (April 1982), p. 538-540. English. DESCR: *Bilingual Bicultural Education; *Handicapped; Limited- or Non-English Speaking Handicapped Students (LONESHS); Teaching Profession.

12215 Rugsaken, Kris T. Qualifications for the bilingual vocational teacher. BILINGUAL JOURNAL, Vol. 6, no. 4 (Summer 1982), p. 22-25. English. DESCR: Adult Education; *Bilingual Bicultural Education; Teacher Training; Vocational Education Act of 1963.

Vocational Education Act of 1963

12216 Rugsaken, Kris T. Qualifications for the bilingual vocational teacher. BILINGUAL JOURNAL, Vol. 6, no. 4 (Summer 1982), p. 22-25. English. DESCR: Adult Education; *Bilingual Bicultural Education; Teacher Training; *Vocational Education.

Vocational Guidance

12217 Mestre, Jose P. and Robinson, Holly. Academic, socio-economic, and motivational characteristics of Hispanic college students enrolled in technical programs. VOCATIONAL GUIDANCE QUARTERLY, Vol. 31, no. 3 (March 1983), p. 187-194. English. DESCR: *College and University Students; Counseling Services (Educational); Enrollment.

LAS VOCES DE LOS CAMPESINOS

12218 McNeil, W. K. Record Review: LAS VOCES DE LOS CAMPESINOS. JOURNAL OF AMERICAN FOLKLORE, Vol. 96, (1983), p. 370. English. DESCR: Agricultural Laborers; Corrido; Music Review; Musical Lyrics.

VOLVER A EMPEZAR

12219 Gutierrez, Silvio. Cinema. LATINA, Vol. 1, no. 3 (1983), p. 18-19+. English. DESCR: Film Reviews; *LIANNA.

Voter Turnout

12220 Agudelo, C. Wooing the Hispanics. WORLD PRESS REVIEW, Vol. 30, (November 1983), p. 43. English. DESCR: *Political Representation.

12221 Allende, Luz B. Beyond the Sunday sermon. APUNTES, Vol. 3, no. 1 (Spring 1983), p. 10-14. English. DESCR: *Political Representation.

12222 Alter, Jonathan. Hispanic power at the polls. NEWSWEEK, Vol. 102, no. 1 (July 4, 1983), p. 23-24. English.

12223 Anaya, Toney. Hispanics need political clout. CAMINOS, Vol. 4, no. 1-2 (January, February, 1983), p. 62-64,76. Bilingual. DESCR: Politics.

12224 Applebome, Peter. The unkindest cut. TEXAS MONTHLY, Vol. 11, no. 1 (January 1983), p. 74-80. English. DESCR: *Blacks; Corpus Christi, TX; Political Representation.

12225 Barry, Patrick and Zavala, Antonio. Election '83: Chicago's Latinos awake, but not united. NUESTRO, Vol. 7, no. 1 (January, February, 1983), p. 20-23. English. DESCR: *Chicago, IL; *Elections; Political Representation.

12226 Chavarria, Jesus. How are we doing? HISPANIC BUSINESS, Vol. 4, no. 8 (August 1983), p. 6. English. DESCR: Economics; Elected Officials; *Finance.

12227 Chicago's mayoralty race. HISPANIC BUSINESS, Vol. 5, no. 7 (July 1983), p. 27-28. English. DESCR: Chicago, IL; Elections; Local Government.

12228 Communications/marketing. HISPANIC BUSINESS, Vol. 4, no. 5 (May 1982), p. 15. English. DESCR: Anheuser-Busch, Inc.; Farres, Osvaldo; Girl Scouts of the United States of America; *Marketing; Organizations; Television; Vocational Education.

12229 de Avila, Edward A. [Combining political strategies for effective representation]. CHICANO LAW REVIEW, Vol. 6, (1983), p. 24-29. English. DESCR: LATINOS IN THE LAW [symposium], UCLA, 1982.

12230 Diaz, Tom. Turning numbers into clout. NUESTRO, Vol. 7, no. 10 (December 1983), p. 34-35. English. DESCR: National Puerto Rican Coalition; *National Puerto Rican/Hispanic Voter Participation Project; Puerto Ricans.

Voter Turnout (cont.)

12231 Election '82: the Hispanic vote. CAMINOS,
Vol. 4, no. 1-2 (January, February, 1983),
p. 65,75. English. **DESCR:** *Elections.

12232 Garcia, Miguel. Are you registered to vote?
CAMINOS, Vol. 3, no. 4 (April 1982), p.
33-34. English. **DESCR:** Congress for United
Communities (CPU); Mexican American Latino
Voter Registration Alliance (MALVRA).

12233 Hispanic leader reaction to Governor White:
Republicans fail to overcome Democratic
one-two punch. NATIONAL HISPANIC JOURNAL,
Vol. 1, no. 4 (Spring 1983), p. 8. English.
DESCR: Clements, Bill; Mexican American
Republicans of Texas; Political Parties and
Organizations; White, Mark.

12234 Hispanic power arrives at the ballot box.
BUSINESS WEEK, no. 27 (July 4, 1983), p. 32.
English. **DESCR:** Denver, CO; *Pena, Federico.

12235 Hispanic voting trends. HISPANIC BUSINESS,
Vol. 4, no. 8 (August 1983), p. 28-29.
English. **DESCR:** Bilingual Ballots;
Bilingualism; California; *Elections;
Mexican American Legal Defense and
Educational Fund (MALDEF); Southwest Voter
Registration Education Project (SVRP);
Texas.

12236 Huerta, John. The future of Latino political
power. CAMINOS, Vol. 4, no. 3 (March 1983),
p. 44-46,49. English. **DESCR:** Census;
*Politics.

12237 The invisible Puerto Rican vote. HISPANIC
BUSINESS, Vol. 5, no. 10 (October 1983), p.
34-36. English. **DESCR:** Elections; Political
Parties and Organizations; Puerto Ricans.

12238 Is a computer following you? LATINO, Vol.
54, no. 4 (May, June, 1983), p. 26. English.

12239 Kirschten, Dick. The Hispanic vote: parties
can't gamble that the sleeping giant won't
awaken. NATIONAL JOURNAL, Vol. 15, no. 47
(November 19, 1983), p. 2410-2411. English.
DESCR: Democratic Party; *Hispanic Caucus;
Republican Party; Southwest Voter
Registration Education Project (SVRP).

12240 Lowther, William. Reagan hunts for the
Hispanic vote. MACLEANS, Vol. 96, no. 34
(August 22, 1983), p. 21-22. English.
DESCR: Elections; League of United Latin
American Citizens (LULAC); Reagan, Ronald.

12241 LULAC reports new stance. NUESTRO, Vol. 6,
no. 3 (April 1982), p. 13. English. **DESCR:**
*League of United Latin American Citizens
(LULAC).

12242 Martinez, Chip. Federico Pena: Denver's
first Hispanic mayor. NUESTRO, Vol. 7, no. 6
(August 1983), p. 14-20. English. **DESCR:**
Denver, CO; Elections; Local Government;
*Pena, Federico.

12243 Mexican-American voting trends. HISPANIC
BUSINESS, Vol. 5, no. 3 (March 1983), p.
29-30. English.

12244 Mile high Pena fever. LATINO, Vol. 54, no. 4
(May, June, 1983), p. 4. English. **DESCR:**
Elected Officials; *Pena, Federico.

12245 Navarro, Armando. Latino power in the 80's:
ilusion o realidad? CAMINOS, Vol. 3, no. 5
(May 1982), p. 20-22. Bilingual.

12246 Nieto, Ernesto. Politics: powers that

struggled in the Texas Valley. NATIONAL
HISPANIC JOURNAL, Vol. 2, no. 1 (Summer
1983), p. 22-23. English. **DESCR:** Elections;
McAllen, TX; *Politics; *Rio Grande Valley,
TX.

12247 Obledo, Mario. Challenging nuestro orgullo.
LATINO, Vol. 54, no. 5 (August, September,
1983), p. 6. English.

12248 Old and new in San Antonio. ECONOMIST
(London), Vol. 288, (August 13, 1983), p.
26. English. **DESCR:** *Cisneros, Henry, Mayor
of San Antonio, TX; San Antonio, TX.

12249 Padilla, Steve. In search of Hispanic
voters. NUESTRO, Vol. 7, no. 6 (August
1983), p. 20. English. **DESCR:** Elections;
National Hispanic Voter Registration
Campaign.

12250 Peterson, Sarah; Mashek, John W.; and
Obledo, Mario. Hispanics set their sights on
ballot box. U.S. NEWS & WORLD REPORT, Vol.
95, no. 8 (August 22, 1983), p. 48-49.
English. **DESCR:** Obledo, Mario; Political
Repression.

12251 Rips, Geoffrey. Mexican Americans jalaron la
palanca, Democrats say ole. TEXAS OBSERVOR,
Vol. 75, (January 1983), p. 6-7. English.
DESCR: Democratic Party; Political
Representation; Texas.

12252 Rivas, Mike. Keeping peace in paradise.
NATIONAL HISPANIC JOURNAL, Vol. 1, no. 2
(Winter 1982), p. 13-20. English. **DESCR:**
*Brand, Othal; Casso, Ramiro; Elections;
Police; Police Brutality; *Political
Repression; Rio Grande Valley, TX; THE
MEXICAN AMERICAN: QUEST FOR EQUALITY.

12253 Rodriguez, Roberto. Free and fair elections
are supposed to be what distinguishes a
democracy from a dictatorship. CORAZON DE
AZTLAN, Vol. 1, no. 3 (August, September,
1982), p. 31-34. English. **DESCR:** *Political
Representation.

12254 Santillan, Richard. [Translating population
numbers into political power]. CHICANO LAW
REVIEW, Vol. 6, (1983), p. 16-21. English.
DESCR: Californios for Fair Representation;
Carrillo v. Whittier Union High School;
LATINOS IN THE LAW [symposium], UCLA, 1982;
MEXICAN AMERICAN LEGAL DEFENSE AND
EDUCATIONAL FUND NEWSLETTER; Political
Representation; Reapportionment.

12255 Su voto es su voz. NUESTRO, Vol. 6, no. 7
(September 1982), p. 41. English. **DESCR:**
Congressional Hispanic Caucus; Political
Representation; Political System; Politics;
*Voting Rights; *Voting Rights Act.

12256 Su voto es su voz. LATINO, Vol. 53, no. 7
(November 1982), p. 6-8. English.

12257 Texas voting report. NUESTRO, Vol. 6, no. 4
(May 1982), p. 8-9. English. **DESCR:** *Texas.

12258 Valadez, Esther. [The role of the Latina].
CHICANO LAW REVIEW, Vol. 6, (1983), p.
21-24. English. **DESCR:** *Chicanas; LATINOS IN
THE LAW [symposium], UCLA, 1982.

12259 Velasquez, William C. The Hispanic vote: a
profile. CAMINOS, Vol. 3, no. 4 (April
1982), p. 28-30. Bilingual.

12260 Velasquez, William C. Vote vote vote.
CAMINOS, Vol. 3, no. 4 (April 1982), p. 26.
Bilingual.

Voter Turnout (cont.)

12261 Viva Obledo. LATINO, Vol. 54, no. 5 (August, September, 1983), p. 8-9. English. **DESCR:** *Obledo, Mario.

12262 Why politicians cry 'Viva Hispanics'. U.S. NEWS & WORLD REPORT, Vol. 95, no. 13 (September 26, 1983), p. 15. English.

Voting Rights

12263 Burciaga, Jose Antonio. Wii dii piipo. LATINO, Vol. 53, no. 5 (September 1982), p. 15. Spanish.

12264 Flaherty, Francis J. The struggle continues: protecting the rights of Hispanics in the U.S. NATIONAL LAW JOURNAL, Vol. 5, (March 14, 1983), p. 1. English. **DESCR:** Affirmative Action; *Avila, Joaquin Guadalupe; Civil Rights; Hispanic Amendments; *Legal Representation; Mexican American Legal Defense and Educational Fund (MALDEF); Racism.

12265 An Indian treaty. NUESTRO, Vol. 6, no. 5 (June, July, 1982), p. 9. English. **DESCR:** Jackson, Jesse; *Voting Rights Act.

12266 Molina, Lilia. Voting Rights Act. CAMINOS, Vol. 3, no. 4 (April 1982), p. 31-32. Bilingual. **DESCR:** *Voting Rights Act.

12267 New bilingual effort. NUESTRO, Vol. 6, no. 1 (January, February, 1982), p. 10. English. **DESCR:** *Bilingualism.

12268 Padilla, Steve. A pipe dream. LATINO, Vol. 54, no. 6 (October 1983), p. 20. English.

12269 Rendon, Josefina Muniz. How to get Hispanics elected to office. LATINO, Vol. 54, no. 5 (August, September, 1983), p. 26-27. English.

12270 Su voto es su voz. NUESTRO, Vol. 6, no. 7 (September 1982), p. 41. English. **DESCR:** Congressional Hispanic Caucus; Political Representation; Political System; Politics; *Voter Turnout; *Voting Rights Act.

12271 A territorial approach to representation for illegal aliens. MICHIGAN LAW REVIEW, Vol. 80, no. 6 (May 1982), p. 1342-1371. English. **DESCR:** Census; Federation for American Immigration Reform (FAIR); Population; Reapportionment; Reynolds, Steve; *Undocumented Workers.

12272 Valenzuela-Crocker, Elvira. Confrontation over the Civil Rights Commission. NUESTRO, Vol. 7, no. 10 (December 1983), p. 21-27. English. **DESCR:** Administration of Justice; Affirmative Action; *Civil Rights; Education Equalization; Employment; *U.S. Commission on Civil Rights.

Voting Rights Act

12273 An Indian treaty. NUESTRO, Vol. 6, no. 5 (June, July, 1982), p. 9. English. **DESCR:** Jackson, Jesse; *Voting Rights.

12274 Molina, Lilia. Voting Rights Act. CAMINOS, Vol. 3, no. 4 (April 1982), p. 31-32. Bilingual. **DESCR:** *Voting Rights.

12275 Our 1982 Latino awards. NUESTRO, Vol. 7, no. 1 (January, February, 1983), p. 44-46. English. **DESCR:** Awards; Escalante, Jaime; Gallegos, Gina; Grace, J. Peter; Immigration and Naturalization Service (INS); Knight, Bobby; Lamas, Fernando; *Latino Awards;

Luce, Claire Boothe; Moreno, Rita; National Press Foundation; Rodriguez Hernandez, Andres; Simpson-Mazzoli Bill; Smith, Raymond; Valeri, Michele.

12276 Su voto es su voz. NUESTRO, Vol. 6, no. 7 (September 1982), p. 41. English. **DESCR:** Congressional Hispanic Caucus; Political Representation; Political System; Politics; *Voter Turnout; *Voting Rights.

Wages

USE: Income

Wagner-Peyser Act

12277 Developments in migrant workers programs: 1981. CLEARINGHOUSE REVIEW, Vol. 15, (January 1982), p. 797-805. English. **DESCR:** Fair Labor Standards Act (FLSA); Farm Labor Contractor Registration Act (FLCRA); Migrant Education; Migrant Housing; *Migrant Labor; Migrant Legal Action Program (MLAP); Occupational Safety and Health Administration; Pesticides; Undocumented Workers.

Wall, Evern R.

12278 Positioning growth at El Paso Electric Co. HISPANIC BUSINESS, Vol. 4, no. 2 (February 1982), p. 10+. English. **DESCR:** El Paso Electric Company; El Paso, TX; Employment; *Energy Industries; *Labor Supply and Market.

WALL STREET JOURNAL

12279 Miguel de la Madrid en la prensa norteamericana. INFORME: RELACIONES MEXICO-ESTADOS UNIDOS, Vol. 1, no. 2 (July, December, 1982), p. 176-183. Spanish. **DESCR:** *De la Madrid, Miguel; *Journalism; Lopez Portillo, Jose; LOS ANGELES TIMES; NEW YORK TIMES; Newspapers; WASHINGTON POST.

War

12280 Altman, Barbara. El Salvador. LATINO, Vol. 54, no. 4 (May, June, 1983), p. 10-11. English. **DESCR:** *El Salvador; Latin Americans.

12281 Burciaga, Jose Antonio. 20 nuclear years later: still holding my breath. NUESTRO, Vol. 6, no. 8 (October 1982), p. 35. English. **DESCR:** Cuba; *Cuban Missile Crisis, October 1962; Nuclear Armament.

12282 Carrion, Arturo Morales. Puerto Rico: the coming of the Americans. NUESTRO, Vol. 7, no. 5 (June, July, 1983), p. 25-30. English. **DESCR:** Cuba; *International Relations; *Puerto Rico; Spain; *United States History.

12283 Garcia, Ignacio M. El Salvador: profile of a nation at war. NUESTRO, Vol. 7, no. 8 (October 1983), p. 26-36. English. **DESCR:** *El Salvador; Guerrillas; Military; Political History and Conditions.

12284 Robinson, Barbara J. Book review of: THE MEXICAN-AMERICAN WAR: AN ANNOTATED BIBLIOGRAPHY. REVISTA INTERAMERICANA DE BIBLIOGRAFIA, Vol. 32, no. 2 (1982), p. 222-223. English. **DESCR:** Bibliography; Book Reviews; *THE MEXICAN-AMERICAN WAR: AN ANNOTATED BIBLIOGRAPHY; Tutorow, Norman E.

12285 The Vietnam void. LATINO, Vol. 54, no. 1 (January, February, 1983), p. 22. English. **DESCR:** *Vietnam War.

War on Drugs

12286 Ballard, Lee. Tom Marquez and the EDS mode. HISPANIC BUSINESS, Vol. 5, no. 2 (February 1983), p. 10-11+. English. **DESCR**: *Biography; Businesspeople; Electronic Data Systems (EDS); Marquez, Tom; Perot, Ross.

Washington, DC

12287 70.000 enjoy cultural confab. NUESTRO, Vol. 6, no. 7 (September 1982), p. 12. English. **DESCR**: *Fiesta en Washington; Fiestas.

12288 Dorn, Georgette Magassy. Hispanic collections of the Library of Congress. NUESTRO, Vol. 6, no. 6 (August 1982), p. 35-38. English. **DESCR**: *Hispanic Reading Room, Library of Congress; Libraries; Library Collections; Library of Congress.

12289 Rosales, John. Life at the "Chicano Hilton". NUESTRO, Vol. 6, no. 4 (May 1982), p. 23-26. English. **DESCR**: *Housing.

WASHINGTON POST

12290 Miguel de la Madrid en la prensa norteamericana. INFORME: RELACIONES MEXICO-ESTADOS UNIDOS, Vol. 1, no. 2 (July, December, 1982), p. 176-183. Spanish. **DESCR**: *De la Madrid, Miguel; *Journalism; Lopez Portillo, Jose; LOS ANGELES TIMES; NEW YORK TIMES; Newspapers; WALL STREET JOURNAL.

Water

12291 Mumme, Stephen P. and Jamail, Milton H. The International Boundary and Water Commission as a conflict management agency in the U.S.-Mexico borderlands. SOCIAL SCIENCE JOURNAL, Vol. 19, no. 1 (January 1982), p. 46-62. English. **DESCR**: Border Region; Conflict Resolution; *International Boundary and Water Commission; Rio Grande; United States-Mexico Relations.

12292 Utton, Albert E. The present status of water issues in the United States-Mexico border region. SOUTHWESTERN REVIEW OF MANAGEMENT AND ECONOMICS, Vol. 2, no. 1 (Winter 1982), p. 79-81. English. **DESCR**: *Border Region.

Water Pollution

12293 Hansen, Niles. Trans boundary environmental issues in the United States-Mexico borderlands. SOUTHWESTERN REVIEW OF MANAGEMENT AND ECONOMICS, Vol. 2, no. 1 (Winter 1982), p. 61-78. English. **DESCR**: Air Pollution; Border Region; *Pollution.

Watts, CA

12294 Arroyo, Sara G. and Tucker, M. Belinda. Black residential mobility: trends and characteristics. JOURNAL OF SOCIAL ISSUES, Vol. 38, no. 3 (1982), p. 51-74. English. **DESCR**: *Housing; Los Angeles, CA; Undocumented Children.

WBBM-TV, Chicago, IL [television station]

12295 Lanier, Alfredo S. The quicksilver world of television news: Phil Ponce's Chicago beat. HISPANIC BUSINESS, Vol. 5, no. 10 (October 1983), p. 18-19+. English. **DESCR**: Journalism; *Ponce, Phil; *Television.

WCBR (Western Community Bilingual Radio) [radio station]

12296 Ramirez, Sylvia E. Bilingual radio: reaching new horizons. CAMINOS, Vol. 3, no. 5 (May 1982), p. 38-39. Bilingual. **DESCR**: *Lopez, Antonio; *Radio; Ramos, Juan.

WE ARE CHICANOS

12297 Orozco, Febe Portillo. A bibliography of Hispanic literature. ENGLISH JOURNAL, Vol. 71, no. 7 (November 1982), p. 58-62. English. **DESCR**: BARRIO BOY; *Bibliography; BLESS ME, ULTIMA; CHICANO; EL SOL Y LOS DE ABAJO; GRITO DEL SOL; HEART OF AZTLAN; *Literature; POCHO.

Weber, David J.

12298 Acuna, Rodolfo. Book review of: THE MEXICAN FRONTIER 1821-1846: THE AMERICAN SOUTHWEST UNDER MEXICO. AMERICAN HISTORICAL REVIEW, Vol. 88, no. 2 (April 1983), p. 504-505. English. **DESCR**: Book Reviews; *THE MEXICAN FRONTIER, 1821-1846: THE AMERICAN SOUTHWEST UNDER MEXICO.

12299 Book review of: THE MEXICAN FRONTIER, 1821-1846: THE AMERICAN SOUTHWEST UNDER MEXICO. CHOICE, Vol. 20, no. 3 (November 1982), p. 494. English. **DESCR**: Book Reviews; *THE MEXICAN FRONTIER, 1821-1846: THE AMERICAN SOUTHWEST UNDER MEXICO.

12300 Brack, Gene M. Book review of: THE MEXICAN FRONTIER, 1821-1846: THE AMERICAN SOUTHWEST UNDER MEXICO. HISPANIC AMERICAN HISTORICAL REVIEW, Vol. 63, no. 2 (1983), p. 396-397. English. **DESCR**: Book Reviews; *THE MEXICAN FRONTIER, 1821-1846: THE AMERICAN SOUTHWEST UNDER MEXICO.

12301 Cummins, Light Townsend. Book review of: THE MEXICAN FRONTIER 1821-1846: THE AMERICAN SOUTHWEST UNDER MEXICO. JOURNAL OF SOUTHERN HISTORY, Vol. 49, no. 3 (August 1983), p. 453-455. English. **DESCR**: Book Reviews; *THE MEXICAN FRONTIER, 1821-1846: THE AMERICAN SOUTHWEST UNDER MEXICO.

12302 Henson, Margaret S. Book review of: THE MEXICAN FRONTIER 1821-1846: THE AMERICAN SOUTHWEST UNDER MEXICO. SOUTHWESTERN HISTORICAL QUARTERLY, Vol. 86, no. 3 (1983), p. 441-443. English. **DESCR**: Book Reviews; *THE MEXICAN FRONTIER, 1821-1846: THE AMERICAN SOUTHWEST UNDER MEXICO.

12303 John, Elizabeth A.H. Book review of: THE MEXICAN FRONTIER, 1821-1846: THE AMERICAN SOUTHWEST UNDER MEXICO. NEW MEXICO HISTORICAL REVIEW, Vol. 57, no. 3 (July 1982), p. 289-293. English. **DESCR**: Book Reviews; Border Region; Southwest United States; *THE MEXICAN FRONTIER, 1821-1846: THE AMERICAN SOUTHWEST UNDER MEXICO.

12304 Jones, Oakah L. Book review of: THE MEXICAN FRONTIER, 1821-1846: THE AMERICAN SOUTHWEST UNDER MEXICO. ARIZONA AND THE WEST, Vol. 25, no. 2 (1983), p. 168-169. English. **DESCR**: Book Reviews; History; Mexico; Southwest United States; *THE MEXICAN FRONTIER, 1821-1846: THE AMERICAN SOUTHWEST UNDER MEXICO.

12305 Meyer, Michael C. Book review of: THE MEXICAN FRONTIER, 1821-1846: THE AMERICAN SOUTHWEST UNDER MEXICO. WESTERN HISTORICAL QUARTERLY, Vol. 14, no. 3 (1983), p. 337-338. English. **DESCR**: Book Reviews; History; Mexico; Southwest United States; *THE MEXICAN FRONTIER, 1821-1846: THE AMERICAN SOUTHWEST UNDER MEXICO.

Wechsler Intelligence Scale for Children-Revised (WISC-R)

12306 Mishra, Shitala P. Validity of WISC-R IQs and factor scores in predicting achievement for Mexican American children. PSYCHOLOGY IN THE SCHOOLS, Vol. 20, no. 4 (October 1983), p. 442-444. English. DESCR: *Academic Achievement; Intelligence Tests; Primary School Students.

12307 Oakland, Thomas. Concurrent and predictive validity estimates for the WISC-R IQ's and ELP's by racial-ethnic and SES groups. SCHOOL PSYCHOLOGY REVIEW, Vol. 12, no. 1 (Winter 1983), p. 57-61. English. DESCR: Academic Achievement; Estimated Learning Potential (ELP); *Intelligence Tests; Primary School Education.

12308 Ross-Reynolds, Jane and Reschly, Daniel J. An investigation of item bias on the WISC-R with four sociocultural groups. JOURNAL OF CONSULTING AND CLINICAL PSYCHOLOGY, Vol. 51, no. 1 (February 1983), p. 144-146. English. DESCR: Comparative Psychology; Ethnic Groups; Psychological Testing.

12309 Sandoval, Jonathan; Zimmerman, Irla L.; and Woo-Sam, James M. Cultural difference on WISC-R verbal items. JOURNAL OF SCHOOL PSYCHOLOGY, Vol. 21, no. 1 (Spring 1983), p. 49-55. English. DESCR: Educational Tests and Measurements; *Intelligence Tests.

12310 Sandoval, Joseph. WISC-R factoral validity for minority groups and Spearman's hypothesis. JOURNAL OF SCHOOL PSYCHOLOGY, Vol. 20, (Fall 1982), p. 198-204. English. DESCR: Educational Tests and Measurements; *Intelligence Tests.

Weddings

12311 Barry, Patrick. Saturdays are wedding cakes. NUESTRO, Vol. 6, no. 9 (November 1982), p. 31-33. English. DESCR: *Businesspeople; Chicago, IL; Fasco, Luis.

Weight Control

12312 Stern, Michael P. Knowledge, attitudes, and behavior related to obesity and dieting in Mexican-Americans and Anglos: the San Antonio heart study. AMERICAN JOURNAL OF EPIDEMIOLOGY, Vol. 115, no. 6 (June 1982), p. 917-928. English. DESCR: Anglo Americans; Attitude (Psychological); *Food Practices; Obesity; San Antonio, TX.

Weigle, Marta

12313 Weber, Kenneth R. Book review of: HISPANIC VILLAGES OF NORTHERN NEW MEXICO. SOUTHWEST ECONOMY AND SOCIETY, Vol. 1, no. 1 (Spring 1976), p. 48. English. DESCR: Book Reviews; Economic History and Conditions; Great Depression, 1929-1933; *HISPANIC VILLAGES OF NORTHERN NEW MEXICO; New Mexico; Tewa Basin, NM.

Weintraub, Sidney

12314 Moore, Richard J. Book review of: "TEMPORARY" ALIEN WORKERS IN THE UNITED STATES: DESIGNING POLICY FROM FACT AND OPINION. INTERNATIONAL MIGRATION REVIEW, Vol. 16, no. 4 (Winter 1982), p. 909-910. English. DESCR: Book Reviews; Braceros; Ross, Stanley R.; *"TEMPORARY" ALIEN WORKERS IN THE UNITED STATES: DESIGNING POLICY FROM FACT AND OPINION; Undocumented Workers.

12315 Moore, Richard J. Book review of:

"TEMPORARY" ALIEN WORKERS IN THE UNITED STATES: DESIGNING POLICY FROM FACT AND OPINION. INTERNATIONAL MIGRATION REVIEW, Vol. 16, no. 4 (Winter 1982), p. 909-910. English. DESCR: Book Reviews; Immigration Law; Literature Reviews; Ross, Stanley R.; *"TEMPORARY" ALIEN WORKERS IN THE UNITED STATES: DESIGNING POLICY FROM FACT AND OPINION; Undocumented Workers.

Welch, Finis R.

12316 Bronfenbrenner, Martin. Hyphenated Americans-economic aspects. LAW AND CONTEMPORARY PROBLEMS, Vol. 45, no. 2 (Spring 1982), p. 9-27. English. DESCR: *Chiswick, Barry R.; *Economics; *Immigrants; Racism; Smith, James P.

Welfare

12317 Food stamp cheaters. NUESTRO, Vol. 5, no. 8 (November 1981), p. 10. English. DESCR: Food Stamps; Human Resources Administration; *Richmond, Frederick W.

12318 Ramos, Alfonso Pena. Voices: Gandhi: the Mahatma's message to Hispanics. NUESTRO, Vol. 7, no. 4 (May 1983), p. 59-60. English. DESCR: *Ethnic Groups; Gandhi, Mahatma; *Identity; *Philosophy.

West New York, NJ

12319 Ward, Carmen Carole. Book review of: THE ASSIMILATION OF CUBAN EXILES: THE ROLE OF COMMUNITY AND CLASS. JOURNAL OF ETHNIC STUDIES, Vol. 3, no. 2 (Summer 1975), p. 116-119. English. DESCR: Assimilation; Book Reviews; *Cubanos; Miami, FL; *Rogg, Eleanor Meyer; Social Classes; Social History and Conditions; THE ASSIMILATION OF CUBAN EXILES: THE ROLE OF COMMUNITY AND CLASS.

Western Union Corporation

12320 Communications/marketing. HISPANIC BUSINESS, Vol. 4, no. 9 (September 1982), p. 22. English. DESCR: Awards; Coca-Cola Company; Domecq Importers, Inc.; *Marketing.

Westfried, Alex Huxley

12321 Brue de Lorenzo, Kathryn. Book review of: ETHNIC LEADERSHIP IN A NEW ENGLAND COMMUNITY: THREE PUERTO RICAN FAMILIES. HISPANIC JOURNAL OF BEHAVIORAL SCIENCES, Vol. 5, no. 2 (June 1983), p. 245-247. English. DESCR: Book Reviews; *ETHNIC LEADERSHIP IN A NEW ENGLAND COMMUNITY: THREE PUERTO RICAN FAMILIES.

WHISPERING TO FOOL THE WIND

12322 Saldivar, Jose David. Book review of: WHISPERING TO FOOL THE WIND. REVISTA CHICANO-RIQUENA, Vol. 11, no. 2 (Summer 1983), p. 72-74. English. DESCR: Book Reviews; Rios, Alberto.

White, Lucas Edward

12323 Espinoza, Roberto. Sintesis vs. analysis: un problema de historicidad en las novelas de las dictaduras. MAIZE, Vol. 6, no. 1-2 (Fall, Winter, 1982, 1983), p. 7-27. Spanish. DESCR: Carpentier, Alejo; Dictatorships; Garcia Marquez, Gabriel; Latin American Literature; *Literary Criticism; Novel; Roa Bastos, Augustos; Valle Inclan, Ramon.

White, Mark

12324 Hispanic leader reaction to Governor White: Republicans fail to overcome Democratic one-two punch. NATIONAL HISPANIC JOURNAL, Vol. 1, no. 4 (Spring 1983), p. 8. English. DESCR: Clements, Bill; Mexican American Republicans of Texas; Political Parties and Organizations; *Voter Turnout.

12325 Murray, Melissa and De Leon, Hector. Texas politics: a frank talk about leadership, Austin, state government and attorney Hector de Leon. NATIONAL HISPANIC JOURNAL, Vol. 1, no. 4 (Spring 1983), p. 10-13. English. DESCR: Clements, Bill; De Leon, Hector; *Politics; Texas.

12326 People. HISPANIC BUSINESS, Vol. 5, no. 10 (October 1983), p. 10. English. DESCR: Anaya, Toney; Arriola, Elvia Rosales; Babbitt, Bruce; Burgos, Tony; Bush, George; *Businesspeople; Cisneros, Henry, Mayor of San Antonio, TX; Cruz, Jose; Kennedy, Edward M.; Montano, Gilbert; Reagan, Ronald.

Whittier Blvd., Los Angeles, CA

12327 "A mi no me afecta" "It doesn't affect me". CORAZON DE AZTLAN, Vol. 1, no. 2 (March, April, 1982), p. 4-5. Bilingual. DESCR: Political Representation.

Wicke, Charles R.

12328 Quirarte, Jacinto. Book review of: OLMEC: AN EARLY ART STYLE OF PRECOLUMBIAN MEXICO. JOURNAL OF ETHNIC STUDIES, Vol. 1, no. 3 (Fall 1973), p. 92-95. English. DESCR: Book Reviews; La Venta, Mexico; *OLMEC: AN EARLY ART STYLE OF PRECOLUMBIAN MEXICO; Precolumbian Art; Precolumbian Society; San Lorenzo, Mexico; Tres Zapotes, Mexico.

Williams, Miles W.

12329 North, David S. Book review of: ILLEGAL ALIENS IN THE WESTERN HEMISPHERE: POLITICAL AND ECONOMIC FACTORS. INTERNATIONAL MIGRATION REVIEW, Vol. 16, no. 3 (Fall 1982), p. 682-683. English. DESCR: Book Reviews; *ILLEGAL ALIENS IN THE WESTERN HEMISPHERE: POLITICAL AND ECONOMIC FACTORS; Johnson, Kenneth F.; Undocumented Workers.

Williams, Shirley

12330 Flemming, Donald N. Book review of: EXPLORACIONES CHICANO-RIQUENAS. MODERN LANGUAGE JOURNAL, Vol. 66, no. 2 (Summer 1982), p. 233-234. English. DESCR: Book Reviews; Burgos-Sasscer. Ruth; *EXPLORACIONES CHICANO-RIQUENAS; Textbooks.

12331 Somoza, Oscar U. Book review of: EXPLORACIONES CHICANO-RIQUENAS. HISPANIA, Vol. 65, no. 4 (December 1982), p. 668-669. Spanish. DESCR: Book Reviews; Burgos-Sasscer. Ruth; *EXPLORACIONES CHICANO-RIQUENAS; Textbooks.

Wille , Herm M.

12332 Newsfront. HISPANIC BUSINESS, Vol. 4, no. 4 (April 1982), p. 8, 24. English. DESCR: *Biographical Notes; Burgos, Elizabeth; *Businesspeople; Flores, Arturo; Garcia, Carlos E.; Garcia, Edward T.; Guzman, Ralph C.; Hernandez, Richard; National Coalition of Hispanic Mental Health and Human Services Organizations (COSSMHO); Parra, Oscar C.

Wilmot, Luis G.

12333 Only two remain. LATINO, Vol. 54, no. 1 (January, February, 1983), p. 4. English. DESCR: League of United Latin American Citizens (LULAC).

"Wind"

12334 de la Fuente, Patricia. Ambiguity in the poetry of Gary Soto. REVISTA CHICANO-RIQUENA, Vol. 11, no. 2 (Summer 1983), p. 34-39. English. DESCR: "Avocado Lake"; "Blanco"; "Braley Street"; "Field"; *Literary Criticism; Poetry; "Song for the pockets"; *Soto, Gary; TALE OF SUNLIGHT; "Telephoning God"; THE ELEMENTS OF SAN JOAQUIN.

Wisconsin Minority Business Forum '83

12335 Business notes. HISPANIC BUSINESS, Vol. 5, no. 10 (October 1983), p. 13. English. DESCR: *Business Administration; Business Enterprises; Claudio, Irma; Investments; Los Angeles Board of Public Works; Oakland, CA; Taxation; Tri-Oakland Development Corporation.

WITH HIS PISTOL IN HIS HAND

12336 Sorell, Victor A. Ethnomusicology, folklore, and history in the filmmaker's art: THE BALLAD OF GREGORIO CORTEZ. BILINGUAL REVIEW, Vol. 10, no. 2-3 (1983), p. 153-158. English. DESCR: *BALLAD OF GREGORIO CORTEZ [film]; Film Reviews; Paredes, Americo.

WITHOUT HOPE

12337 Herrera, Hayden. Making an art of pain. PSYCHOLOGY TODAY, Vol. 17, no. 3 (March 1983), p. 86. English. DESCR: Biography; HENRY FORD HOSPITAL; *Kahlo, Frida; Paintings; SELF-PORTRAIT WITH PORTRAIT OF DR. FARILL; THE BROKEN COLUMN; THE LITTLE DEER; TREE OF HOPE.

W.K. Kellogg Foundation

12338 Academic furlough for the working professional. HISPANIC BUSINESS, Vol. 4, no. 8 (August 1983), p. 15. English. DESCR: Arias, Beatriz; Financial Aid; Funding Sources; Kellogg, W.K.

W.K. Kellogg Foundation National Fellowship Program

12339 A time for reflection. NUESTRO, Vol. 7, no. 9 (November 1983), p. 42-44. English. DESCR: Anaya, Rudolfo A.; Arias, Beatriz; Bilingual Bicultural Education; Computers; Financial Aid; Folklore; Organizations; Prewitt Diaz, Joseph (Jose); Villarreal, Sylvia.

WNJU-TV, Newark, NJ [television station]

12340 Gupta, Udayan. New York's WNJU Channel 47: Spanish TV's hottest item. HISPANIC BUSINESS, Vol. 5, no. 3 (March 1983), p. 16-17+. English. DESCR: *Advertising; Broadcast Media; Consumers; Marketing; Television.

Wolfberg, David A.

12341 Sargeant, Georgia. Young turks set new
      standards. HISPANIC BUSINESS, Vol. 5, no. 11
      (November 1983), p. 8-9. English. **DESCR:**
      Alvarez, Julio E.; *Architecture; Business
      Enterprises; Management; Marketing; Miami,
      FL; Taracido, Manuel E.;
      *Wolfberg/Alvarez/Taracido (WAT).

Wolfberg/Alvarez/Taracido (WAT)

12342 Sargeant, Georgia. Young turks set new
      standards. HISPANIC BUSINESS, Vol. 5, no. 11
      (November 1983), p. 8-9. English. **DESCR:**
      Alvarez, Julio E.; *Architecture; Business
      Enterprises; Management; Marketing; Miami,
      FL; Taracido, Manuel E.; Wolfberg, David A.

**A WOMAN OF GENIUS: THE INTELLECTUAL AUTOBIOGRAPHY
OF SOR JUANA INES DE LA CRUZ**

12343 Sabat-Rivers, Georgina. Book review of: A
      WOMAN OF GENIUS: THE INTELLECTUAL
      AUTOBIOGRAPHY OF SOR JUANA INES DE LA CRUZ.
      NUESTRO, Vol. 7, no. 6 (August 1983), p.
      62-64. English. **DESCR:** Autobiography; Book
      Reviews; Juana Ines de la Cruz, Sor; Peden,
      Margaret Sayers.

Women Here are entered works about non-Chicanas.
      For Mexican-American women USE Chicanas

12344 Fernandez Olmos, Margarite. From the
      metropolis: Puerto Rican women poets and the
      immigration experience. THIRD WOMAN, Vol. 1,
      no. 2 (1982), p. 40-51. English. **DESCR:**
      Essays; *Puerto Rican Literature.

12345 Hardy-Fanta, Carol and Montana, Priscila.
      The Hispanic female adolescent: a group
      therapy model. INTERNATIONAL JOURNAL OF
      GROUP PSYCHOTHERAPY, Vol. 32, no. 3 (July
      1982), p. 351-366. English. **DESCR:**
      Psychotherapy; Puerto Ricans; Youth.

12346 Jaech, Richard E. Latin American
      undocumented women in the United States.
      CURRENTS IN THEOLOGY AND MISSION, Vol. 9,
      no. 4 (August 1982), p. 196-211. English.
      DESCR: Garment Industry; Latin Americans;
      Protestant Church; Socioeconomic Factors;
      *Undocumented Workers.

12347 Ortiz Griffin, Julia. The Puerto Rican woman
      in Rene Marques' drama. REVISTA
      CHICANO-RIQUENA, Vol. 11, no. 3-4 (Fall
      1983), p. 169-176. English. **DESCR:** Literary
      Criticism; *Marques, Rene; Teatro.

12348 Satow, Robert. A severe case of penis envy:
      the convergence of cultural and individual
      intra-psychic factors. JOURNAL OF THE
      AMERICAN ACADEMY OF PSYCHOANALYSIS, Vol. 11,
      no. 4 (October 1983), p. 547-556. English.
      DESCR: Freud, Sigmund; *Psychotherapy;
      Puerto Ricans.

12349 Soto, Elaine and Shaver, Phillip. Sex-role
      traditionalism assertiveness, and symptoms
      of Puerto Rican women living in the United
      States. HISPANIC JOURNAL OF BEHAVIORAL
      SCIENCES, Vol. 4, no. 1 (March 1982), p.
      1-19. English. **DESCR:** Puerto Ricans; Sex
      Roles.

WOMEN AND MEN SPEAKING: FRAMEWORK FOR ANALYSIS

12350 Walia, Adorna. Book review of: WOMEN AND MEN
      SPEAKING: FRAMEWORK FOR ANALYSIS. BILINGUAL
      JOURNAL, Vol. 6, no. 3 (Spring 1982), p.
      20-22. English. **DESCR:** Book Reviews;
      Kramarae, Cheris; Language Usage; Sex
      Stereotypes; Sexism; Sociolinguistics.

Women for Success Awards

12351 Diaz, Barbara M. Continuing the success: the
      Hispanic Women's Council. CAMINOS, Vol. 4,
      no. 6 (June 1983), p. 62. English. **DESCR:**
      Awards; Chicanas; *Hispanic Women's Council;
      Organizations.

Women Men Relations

12352 Baca Zinn, Maxine. Chicano men and
      masculinity. JOURNAL OF ETHNIC STUDIES, Vol.
      10, no. 2 (Summer 1982), p. 29-44. English.
      DESCR: Cultural Characteristics; Ethnic
      Stratification; *Machismo; Sex Roles; Sex
      Stereotypes; Socioeconomic Factors.

12353 Benardo, Margot L. and Anthony, Darius.
      Hispanic women and their men. LATINA, Vol.
      1, no. 3 (1983), p. 24-29. English. **DESCR:**
      Chicanas; Photography.

12354 Cotera, Martha P. ERA: the Latina challenge.
      NUESTRO, Vol. 5, no. 8 (November 1981), p.
      47-48. English. **DESCR:** *Equal Rights
      Amendment (ERA); Women's Rights.

12355 Fostering the advancement of Latinas.
      NUESTRO, Vol. 6, no. 10 (December 1982), p.
      48-49. English. **DESCR:** *Chicanas; *Mexican
      American Women's National Association
      (MANA).

12356 McCracken, Ellen. Book review of: SALT OF
      THE EARTH. JOURNAL OF ETHNIC STUDIES, Vol.
      8, no. 1 (Spring 1980), p. 116-120. English.
      DESCR: Book Reviews; Chicanas; Films;
      Hanover, NM; International Union of Mine,
      Mill and Smelter Workers; *SALT OF THE
      EARTH; Silverton Rosenfelt, Deborah; Strikes
      and Lockouts; Women's Rights.

Women's Rights

12357 Chavez, Mauro. Book review of: ESSAYS ON LA
      MUJER. JOURNAL OF ETHNIC STUDIES, Vol. 8,
      no. 2 (Summer 1980), p. 117-120. English.
      DESCR: Book Reviews; *Chicanas; Cruz, Rosa
      Martinez; Economic History and Conditions;
      *ESSAYS ON LA MUJER; Sanchez, Rosaura;
      Social History and Conditions; Socioeconomic
      Factors.

12358 Cotera, Martha P. ERA: the Latina challenge.
      NUESTRO, Vol. 5, no. 8 (November 1981), p.
      47-48. English. **DESCR:** *Equal Rights
      Amendment (ERA); *Women Men Relations.

12359 Engle, Margarita Mondrus. Mother's Day
      reflections: a "traditional" Latina.
      NUESTRO, Vol. 7, no. 4 (May 1983), p. 46.
      Portuguese. **DESCR:** *Cubanos; *Family.

12360 Fuentes, Diana. Chicana perpectives: Irene
      Portillo. COMADRE, no. 1 (Summer 1977), p.
      42-44. English. **DESCR:** *Biography; Identity;
      *Portillo, Irene E.

12361 McCracken, Ellen. Book review of: SALT OF
      THE EARTH. JOURNAL OF ETHNIC STUDIES, Vol.
      8, no. 1 (Spring 1980), p. 116-120. English.
      DESCR: Book Reviews; Chicanas; Films;
      Hanover, NM; International Union of Mine,
      Mill and Smelter Workers; *SALT OF THE
      EARTH; Silverton Rosenfelt, Deborah; Strikes
      and Lockouts; Women Men Relations.

12362 Mercado, Olivia. Chicanas: myths and roles.
      COMADRE, no. 1 (Summer 1977), p. 26-32.
      English. **DESCR:** *Chicanas; Gallo, Juana;
      Huerta, Dolores; *Identity; Leadership; Sex
      Roles.

Women's Rights (cont.)

12363 Mexican American Legal Defense and Education Fund (MALDEF). Chicana rights: a major MALDEF issue (reprinted from MALDEF Newsletter, Fall 1977). COMADRE, no. 2 (Spring 1978), p. 31-33. English. DESCR: Chicana Rights Project; Chicanas; *Mexican American Legal Defense and Educational Fund (MALDEF); Statistics; Vasquez, Patricia.

12364 Mexican American Legal Defense and Education Fund (MALDEF). Chicana rights: a major MALDEF issue (reprinted from MALDEF Newsletter, Fall 1977). COMADRE, no. 3 (Fall 1978), p. 31-35. English. DESCR: Chicana Rights Project; Chicanas; *Mexican American Legal Defense and Educational Fund (MALDEF); Statistics; Vasquez, Patricia.

12365 Phillips, Melody. The Chicana: her attitudes towards the woman's liberation movement. COMADRE, no. 2 (Spring 1978), p. 42-50. English. DESCR: Carr, Vikki; *Chicanas; FAMOUS MEXICAN-AMERICANS; Newton, Clark; Social History and Conditions.

Woog, Mario Arriola

12366 Tiano, Susan B. El programa mexicano de maquiladoras: una respuesta a las necesidades de la industria norteamericana. AZTLAN, Vol. 14, no. 1 (Spring 1983), p. 201-208. English. DESCR: Book Reviews; *EL PROGRAMA MEXICANO DE MAQUILADORAS: UNA RESPUESTA A LAS NECESIDADES DE LA INDUSTRIA NORTEAMERICANA; Industrial Workers; Industries; International Labor Activities; Maquiladoras.

WORK AND RETIREMENT: POLICY ISSUES

12367 Burke, Leslie K. Book review of: WORK AND RETIREMENT: POLICY ISSUES. HISPANIC JOURNAL OF BEHAVIORAL SCIENCES, Vol. 4, no. 1 (March 1982), p. 112-114. English. DESCR: Book Reviews; Ragan, Pauline K.

WORKBOOK ON PROGRAM EVALUATION

12368 Orlandi, Lisanio R. Book review of: WORKBOOK ON PROGRAM EVALUATION. BILINGUAL JOURNAL, Vol. 7, no. 2 (Winter 1983), p. 35-36. English. DESCR: Babcock, R.; Bilingual Bicultural Education; Book Reviews; Evaluation (Educational); Plakos, J.; Plakos, M.

Workers

USE: Laborers

Worker's Alliance (WA), Los Angeles, CA

12369 Monroy, Douglas. Anarquismo y comunismo: Mexican radicalism and the Communist Party in Los Angeles during the 1930's. LABOR HISTORY, Vol. 24, no. 1 (Winter 1983), p. 34-59. English. DESCR: Cannery and Agricultural Worker's Industrial Union; *Communist Party; Confederacion de Uniones de Obreros Mexicanos (CUOM); History; International Ladies Garment Workers Union (ILGWU); Labor; Labor Organizing; *Los Angeles, CA; Tenayuca, Emma.

WORKING CLASS EMIGRES FROM CUBA

12370 Brink, T. L. Book review of: WORKING-CLASS EMIGRES FROM CUBA. HISPANIC JOURNAL OF BEHAVIORAL SCIENCES, Vol. 5, no. 3 (September 1983), p. 363-365. English. DESCR: Book Reviews; Cubanos; Fox, Geoffrey E.; Laborers.

Working Force

USE: Laborers

A WORKING WOMAN'S GUIDE TO HER JOB RIGHTS

12371 Government review. NUESTRO, Vol. 7, no. 2 (March 1983), p. 42. English. DESCR: Adoption; Business Enterprises; Census; Chicanas; Discrimination in Employment; *Government Services; GUIDE TO FEDERAL MINORITY ENTERPRISE AND RELATED ASSISTANCE PROGRAMS; Population Trends; Study Abroad; U.S. Information Agency (USIA).

Working Women

12372 Cooney, Rosemary Santana and Ortiz, Vilma. Nativity, national origin, and Hispanic female participation in the labor force. SOCIAL SCIENCE QUARTERLY, Vol. 64, (September 1983), p. 510-523. English. DESCR: *Chicanas.

12373 Government review. NUESTRO, Vol. 7, no. 8 (October 1983), p. 54. English. DESCR: Alcoholism; Employment; *Government Services; National Endowment for the Arts; Plaza de La Raza, Los Angeles, CA; Veterans; Youth.

12374 Hawley, Peggy and Even, Brenda. Work and sex-role attitudes in relation to education and other characteristics. VOCATIONAL GUIDANCE QUARTERLY, Vol. 31, no. 2 (December 1982), p. 101-108. English. DESCR: Careers; Chicanas; Ethnic Groups; Psychological Testing; *Sex Roles.

12375 Montenegro, Marilyn. Latinas in the work force. LATINA, Vol. 1, no. 1 (1982), p. 16. English. DESCR: Chicanas.

12376 Padilla, Steve. Adelina Pena Callahan: restaurateur. NUESTRO, Vol. 7, no. 4 (May 1983), p. 26-29. English. DESCR: Businesspeople; *Callahan, Adelina Pena; *Careers; Food Industry; La Fonda Restaurant.

12377 Tips for making the right moves in today's job markets. HISPANIC BUSINESS, Vol. 5, no. 5 (May 1983), p. 30. English. DESCR: Advertising; *Careers; Employment; Hispanic Access to Services (HAS), Denver, CO.

12378 Women & economic progress. HISPANIC BUSINESS, Vol. 4, no. 1 (January 1982), p. 28. English. DESCR: *National Commission on Working Women (NCWW).

12379 Ybarra, Lea. When wives work: the impact on the Chicano family. JOURNAL OF MARRIAGE AND THE FAMILY, Vol. 44, (February 1982), p. 169-178. English. DESCR: Family.

World Bank

12380 Haitian boat people. NUESTRO, Vol. 5, no. 8 (November 1981), p. 10. English. DESCR: *Economic Refugees; *Haiti; Political Refugees.

The World Cup of Soccer

12381 The world cup: soccer's superbowl. NUESTRO, Vol. 6, no. 1 (January, February, 1982), p. 43-44. English. DESCR: Recreation; Soccer; Sports.

World War II

12382 Gamboa, Erasmo. Mexican labor in the Pacific Northwest, 1943-1947: a photographic essay. PACIFIC NORTHWEST QUARTERLY, Vol. 73, no. 4 (October 1982), p. 175-181. English. DESCR: *Agricultural Laborers; International Labor Activities; Labor Camps; Labor Supply and Market; Northwestern United States.

12383 Hewitt, William L. Mexican workers in Wyoming during World War II: necessity, discrimination and protest. ANNALS OF WYOMING, Vol. 54, no. 2 (1982), p. 20-33. English. DESCR: *Agricultural Laborers; Braceros; Migrant Labor; Wyoming.

Wright & Arredondo Associates

12384 Communications/marketing. HISPANIC BUSINESS, Vol. 4, no. 8 (August 1983), p. 22+. English. DESCR: Arredondo, Price; Baseball; De la O, Val; Films; Marketing; *Mass Media; Radio; San Antonio CineFestival, TX; Television; Val De La O Show; Valenzuela, Fernando; Wright, Oscar.

Wright, Oscar

12385 Communications/marketing. HISPANIC BUSINESS, Vol. 4, no. 8 (August 1983), p. 22+. English. DESCR: Arredondo, Price; Baseball; De la O, Val; Films; Marketing; *Mass Media; Radio; San Antonio CineFestival, TX; Television; Val De La O Show; Valenzuela, Fernando; Wright & Arredondo Associates.

Writers

USE: Authors

Wylie, Ruth C.

12386 Nelson, Ann. Book review of: THE SELF-CONCEPT (Rev. ed.). Volume 2: THEORY AND RESEARCH ON SELECTED TOPICS. HISPANIC JOURNAL OF BEHAVIORAL SCIENCES, Vol. 4, no. 3 (September 1982), p. 396-397. English. DESCR: Book Reviews; *THE SELF-CONCEPT (REV. ED) VOLUME 2: THEORY AND RESEARCH ON SELECTED TOPICS.

Wyoming

12387 Hewitt, William L. Mexican workers in Wyoming during World War II: necessity, discrimination and protest. ANNALS OF WYOMING, Vol. 54, no. 2 (1982), p. 20-33. English. DESCR: *Agricultural Laborers; Braceros; Migrant Labor; World War II.

Y NO SE LO TRAGO LA TIERRA/AND THE EARTH DID NOT PART

12388 Lattin, Vernon E. Ethnicity and identity in the contemporary Chicano novel. MINORITY VOICES, Vol. 2, no. 2 (Fall 1978), p. 37-44. English. DESCR: BLESS ME, ULTIMA; Identity; Literary Criticism; Literature; MEMORIES OF THE ALHAMBRA; *Novel; POCHO; THE AUTOBIOGRAPHY OF A BROWN BUFFALO.

12389 Lattin, Vernon E. Novelistic structure and myth in ...Y NO SE LO TRAGO LA TIERRA. BILINGUAL REVIEW, Vol. 9, no. 3 (September, December, 1982), p. 220-226. English. DESCR: Literature; Novel; Rivera, Tomas; United Mexican Americans, South Bend, IN.

12390 Vallejos, Thomas. Ritual process and the family in the Chicano novel. MELUS: MULTI-ETHNIC LITERATURE OF THE UNITED STATES, Vol. 10, no. 4 (Winter 1983, 1984), p. 5-16. English. DESCR: Anaya, Rudolfo A.; BLESS ME, ULTIMA; Family; *Literary

Criticism; Novel; Parent and Child Relationships; POCHO; Rivera, Tomas; Villarreal, Jose Antonio.

Yakima, WA

12391 Oliver, Gordon. Worker abuses claimed. NATIONAL CATHOLIC REPORTER, Vol. 19, (October 29, 1982), p. 7. English. DESCR: Agricultural Laborers; Border Patrol; *Citizens United for Farmworkers, Yakima WA; Immigration and Naturalization Service (INS); *Immigration Regulation and Control.

Yanez, Ricardo

12392 Padilla, Steve. Choosing a career. NUESTRO, Vol. 7, no. 1 (January, February, 1983), p. 13-19+. English. DESCR: Alvarado, Raul, Jr.; *Careers; Computers; Diaz, William; Engineering as a Profession; Esparza, Alma; Flores, Francisco; Garcia, Linda; Medical Care; Soto, John.

Yarborough, Ralph Webster

12393 Campbell, Jack K. Senator Yarborough and the Texan RWY brand on bilingual education and federal aid. EDUCATIONAL STUDIES, Vol. 12, no. 4 (Winter 1981, 1982), p. 403-415. English. DESCR: *Bilingual Bicultural Education; Educational Law and Legislation; History; Social History and Conditions; Texas.

Ybarra, Lea

12394 Diaz, Katherine A. "And this year's winners are...". CAMINOS, Vol. 4, no. 1-2 (January, February, 1983), p. 39-54,74+. English. DESCR: *Awards; Castro, Tony; Elizalde, Hector; Flores, Tom; Martinez, Esperanza; Mendizabal, Maritza; Molina, Gloria; Moya, Connie; Placentia, Joe; Quesada, Leticia; Rios, David N.; Zapata, Carmen.

Ybarra-Frausto, Tomas

12395 Elizondo, Sergio D. Book review of: LITERATURA CHICANA: TEXTO Y CONTEXTO. JOURNAL OF ETHNIC STUDIES, Vol. 1, no. 1 (Spring 1973), p. 68-70. Bilingual. DESCR: Book Reviews; Castaneda Shular, Antonia; Literary Criticism; Literary History; Literary Influence; *LITERATURA CHICANA: TEXTO Y CONTEXTO; Literature; Sommers, Joseph; Teatro.

Y.E.S. INC.

12396 Five-part series on youth jobs. NUESTRO, Vol. 7, no. 7 (September 1983), p. 13. English. DESCR: *Employment Training; KCET-TV, Los Angeles, CA [television station]; Television; Youth.

YMCA

12397 YMCA. LATINA, Vol. 1, no. 3 (1983), p. 44-45+. English. DESCR: Early Childhood Education.

YO SOY CHICANO [film]

12398 Morales, Alejandro. Expanding the meaning of Chicano cinema: YO SOY CHICANO, RAICES DE SANGRE, SEGUIN. BILINGUAL REVIEW, Vol. 10, no. 2-3 (May, December, 1983), p. 121-137. English. DESCR: Film Reviews; *Films; RAICES DE SANGRE [film]; SEGUIN [movie].

Young, Robert

12399 Entertainment = diversion. CAMINOS, Vol. 3, no. 3 (March 1982), p. 55-56. Bilingual. **DESCR:** Aztlan Writing Contest; CORAZON DE AZTLAN; Films; Literary Contests; MISSING [film]; *Recreation; THE BORDER [film].

12400 Olmos, Edward James. Edward James Olmos and Robert Young with 21 reasons why you should see THE BALLAD OF GREGORIO CORTEZ. CAMINOS, Vol. 3, no. 8 (September 1982), p. 26-27, 50. Bilingual. **DESCR:** *BALLAD OF GREGORIO CORTEZ [film]; Film Reviews; Olmos, Edward James.

Youth

12401 Bailey, Lynn B., et al. Folacin and iron status and hematological finding in Blacks and Spanish-American adolescents from urban low-income households. AMERICAN JOURNAL OF CLINICAL NUTRITION, Vol. 35, no. 5 (May 1982), p. 1023-1032. English. **DESCR:** Blacks; Low Income; Public Health; Surveys.

12402 Capital events honor achievers. NUESTRO, Vol. 6, no. 9 (November 1982), p. 12. English. **DESCR:** *National Coalition of Hispanic Mental Health and Human Services Organizations (COSSMHO).

12403 Cockerham, William C. and Alster, Joan M. A comparison of marijuana use among Mexican-American and Anglo rural youth utilizing a matched-set analysis. INTERNATIONAL JOURNAL OF THE ADDICTIONS, Vol. 18, no. 6 (August 1983), p. 759-767. English. **DESCR:** Anglo Americans; Drug Abuse; *Marijuana; Rural Population.

12404 Creswell, John L. and Exezidis, Roxane H. Research brief: sex and ethnic differences in mathematics achievement of Black and Mexican-American adolescents. TEXAS TECH JOURNAL OF EDUCATION, Vol. 9, no. 3 (Fall 1982), p. 219-222. English. **DESCR:** Blacks; Chicanas; Gender; *Mathematics.

12405 Creswell, John L. Sex-related differences in the problem-solving abilities of rural Black, Anglo, and Chicano adolescents. TEXAS TECH JOURNAL OF EDUCATION, Vol. 10, no. 1 (Winter 1983), p. 29-33. English. **DESCR:** Aiken and Preger Revised Math Attitude Scale; Anglo Americans; Blacks; California Achievement Test; Chicanas; Gender; Mathematics; National Assessment of Educational Progress; *National Council of Teachers of Mathematics (NCTM).

12406 Davis, Sally M. and Harris, Mary B. Sexual knowledge, sexual interests, and sources of sexual information of rural and urban adolescents from three cultures. ADOLESCENCE, Vol. 17, no. 66 (Summer 1982), p. 471-492. English. **DESCR:** Birth Control; Cultural Characteristics; Identity; Rural Population; *Sex Education; Sex Roles; *Sexual Behavior; Urban Communities.

12407 Dean, Raymond S. Intelligence-achievement discrepancies in diagnosing pediatric learning disabilities. CLINICAL NEUROPSYCHOLOGY, Vol. 4, no. 2 (1982), p. 58-62. English. **DESCR:** Anglo Americans; *Handicapped; Intelligence Tests; Peabody Individual Achievement Test (PIAT); ZOOT SUIT [film].

12408 Estrada, Antonio; Rabou, Jerome; and Watts, Ronald K. Alcohol use among Hispanic adolescents; a preliminary report. HISPANIC JOURNAL OF BEHAVIORAL SCIENCES, Vol. 4, no. 3 (September 1982), p. 339-351. English. **DESCR:** *Alcoholism; Religion.

12409 Fernandez, Enrique. Youth acts dominating markets: labels woo kids with Spanish-language rock product. BILLBOARD, Vol. 95, (March 12, 1983), p. 58. English. **DESCR:** *Entertainers; Music; Recording Industry.

12410 Five-part series on youth jobs. NUESTRO, Vol. 7, no. 7 (September 1983), p. 13. English. **DESCR:** *Employment Training; KCET-TV, Los Angeles, CA [television station]; Television; *Y.E.S. INC.

12411 Frazier, Donald J. and De Blassie, Richard R. Comparison of self-concept in Mexican American and non-Mexican American late adolescents. ADOLESCENCE, Vol. 17, no. 66 (Summer 1982), p. 327-334. English. **DESCR:** Academic Achievement; *Identity; Socioeconomic Factors; Students.

12412 Government review. NUESTRO, Vol. 7, no. 8 (October 1983), p. 54. English. **DESCR:** Alcoholism; Employment; *Government Services; National Endowment for the Arts; Plaza de La Raza, Los Angeles, CA; Veterans; Working Women.

12413 Hardy-Fanta, Carol and Montana, Priscila. The Hispanic female adolescent: a group therapy model. INTERNATIONAL JOURNAL OF GROUP PSYCHOTHERAPY, Vol. 32, no. 3 (July 1982), p. 351-366. English. **DESCR:** Psychotherapy; Puerto Ricans; *Women.

12414 Kincaid, Jill. LULAC opposes youth subminimum wage proposal. LATINO, Vol. 54, no. 4 (May, June, 1983), p. 27. English. **DESCR:** *Income; *League of United Latin American Citizens (LULAC).

12415 Lindemann, Constance and Scott, Wilbur. The fertility related behavior of Mexican American adolescents. JOURNAL OF EARLY ADOLESCENCE, Vol. 2, no. 1 (Spring 1982), p. 31-38. English. **DESCR:** *Fertility; Migration Patterns.

12416 Long, William J. and Pohl, Christopher M. Joint foot patrols succeed in El Paso. POLICE CHIEF, Vol. 50, no. 4 (April 1983), p. 49-51. English. **DESCR:** Border Patrol; Ciudad Juarez, Chihuahua, Mexico; Criminal Acts; *El Paso, TX; Immigration Regulation and Control; *Police; Undocumented Workers.

12417 Mayers, Raymond Sanchez. The school and labor-force status of Hispanic youth: implications for social policy. CHILDREN AND YOUTH SERVICES REVIEW, Vol. 4. no. 1- (1982), p. 175-192. English. **DESCR:** Education; Laborers.

12418 Medina, Antonio S. Adolescent health in Alameda county. JOURNAL OF ADOLESCENT HEALTH CARE, Vol. 2, no. 3 (March 1982), p. 175-182. English. **DESCR:** Alameda County, CA; *Dentistry; Drug Abuse; Medical Care; Psychology.

12419 Mena, Kristena. Tomorrow's leaders (photoessays). CAMINOS, Vol. 3, no. 8 (September 1982), p. 48. English. **DESCR:** *Association of Mexican American Educators, Inc. (AMAE); Chicano Youth Leadership Conference.

Youth (cont.)

12420 Murray, Melissa. Aqui en Tejas: de Zabala youth session set for August: students from throughout state to attend. NATIONAL HISPANIC JOURNAL, Vol. 2, no. 1 (Summer 1983), p. 7. English. **DESCR:** Education; National Hispanic Institute; Politics; Students.

12421 Perez, Robert; Padilla, Amado M.; and Ramirez, Alex. Expectations toward school busing by Mexican American youth. AMERICAN JOURNAL OF COMMUNITY PSYCHOLOGY, Vol. 10, no. 2 (April 1982), p. 133-148. English. **DESCR:** Attitude (Psychological); *Busing; East Los Angeles, CA; Identity; Segregation and Desegregation; Students.

12422 Stehno, S. M. Differential treatment of minority children in service systems. SOCIAL WORK, Vol. 27, (January 1982), p. 39-45. English. **DESCR:** *Ethnic Groups; Racism; Social Services.

12423 Trotter, Robert T. Ethnic and sexual patterns of alcohol use: Anglo and Mexican American college students. ADOLESCENCE, Vol. 17, no. 66 (Summer 1982), p. 305-325. English. **DESCR:** *Alcoholism; Anglo Americans; Chicanas; Cultural Characteristics; Ethnic Groups; Sex Roles.

12424 Vigil, James Diego. Human revitalization: the six tasks of victory outreach. DREW GATEWAY, Vol. 52, no. 3 (Spring 1982), p. 49-59. English. **DESCR:** Barrios for Christ Program; Drug Addicts; Drug Programs; Gangs; Identity; Pentecostal Church; Protestant Church; Religion; *Victory Outreach.

Youth Offenders
USE: Juvenile Delinquency

YUCATAN BEFORE AND AFTER THE CONQUEST

12425 Hartzler, Kaye. Book review of: YUCATAN BEFORE AND AFTER THE CONQUEST. HISPANIC JOURNAL OF BEHAVIORAL SCIENCES, Vol. 4, no. 3 (September 1982), p. 381-383. English. **DESCR:** Book Reviews; De Landa, Friar Diego; Gates, William.

Yuma Penitentiary

12426 Devis, Rey. Prisons can't contain freedom. CAMINOS, Vol. 4, no. 11 (December 1983), p. 22-23. English. **DESCR:** *Flores Magon, Ricardo; Prisoners; Prisons.

Yzaguirre, Raul

12427 Latinas on the march, NUESTRO survey reveals: organizations assess achievements during 1981. NUESTRO, Vol. 6, no. 2 (March 1982), p. 16-28+. English. **DESCR:** Forum of National Hispanic Organizations; Hispanic Health Council; Latin Americans; League of United Latin American Citizens (LULAC); National Coalition of Hispanic Mental Health and Human Services Organizations (COSSMHO); National Council of La Raza (NCLR); National Hispanic Bar Association; *National Image, Inc.; National Puerto Rican Forum, Inc.; *Organizations.

Zabludovsky, Jacobo

12428 Holston, Mark. The Walter Cronkite of Mexico. NUESTRO, Vol. 7, no. 5 (June, July, 1983), p. 58-59. English. **DESCR:** Cronkite, Walter; Journalists; *Television.

Zamora, Bernice

12429 Candelaria, Cordelia. Another reading of three poems by Zamora. MELUS: MULTI-ETHNIC LITERATURE OF THE UNITED STATES, Vol. 7, no. 4 (Winter 1980), p. 102-104. English. **DESCR:** *Literature.

12430 Sanchez, Marta. Inter-sexual and intertextual codes in the poetry of Bernice Zamora. MELUS: MULTI-ETHNIC LITERATURE OF THE UNITED STATES, Vol. 7, no. 3 (Fall 1980), p. 55-68. English. **DESCR:** *Literature; RESTLESS SERPENTS.

Zamora, Reuben

12431 Latinos evident in 1983 march. NUESTRO, Vol. 7, no. 7 (September 1983), p. 11-12. English. **DESCR:** Bonilla, Tony; Cuban-American Coordinating Committee; *Demonstrations; IMAGE, Washington, DC; Jackson, Jesse; League of United Latin American Citizens (LULAC); National Congress for Puerto Rican Rights (NCPRR); National Council of La Raza (NCLR); Velasquez, Baldemar.

Zapata, Carmen

12432 Carmen Zapata and the B.F.A. CAMINOS, Vol. 3, no. 4 (April 1982), p. 38-40. Bilingual. **DESCR:** Artists; Bilingual Foundation of the Arts; Teatro.

12433 Diaz, Katherine A. "And this year's winners are...". CAMINOS, Vol. 4, no. 1-2 (January, February, 1983), p. 39-54,74+. English. **DESCR:** *Awards; Castro, Tony; Elizalde, Hector; Flores, Tom; Martinez, Esperanza; Mendizabal, Maritza; Molina, Gloria; Moya, Connie; Placentia, Joe; Quesada, Leticia; Rios, David N.; Ybarra, Lea.

Zavala, Iris M.

12434 Umpierre, Luz Maria. Book review of: KILIAGONIA. THIRD WOMAN, Vol. 1, no. 2 (1982), p. 87-90. Spanish. **DESCR:** Book Reviews; *KILIAGONIA.

Zeta Acosta, Oscar
USE: Acosta, Oscar Zeta

Zinc Mining

12435 Reavis, Dick J. Growing up gringo. TEXAS MONTHLY, Vol. 10, no. 8 (August 1982), p. 110-112+. English. **DESCR:** Biography; Dumas, TX; *Rodriguez, Adan.

Zooarchaeology

12436 Langenwalter, P. E. Problems in California Hispanic ethno-zoology [meeting abstract]. AMERICAN JOURNAL OF ARCHAEOLOGY, Vol. 86, no. 2 (April 1982), p. 274. English.

ZOOT SUIT [film]

12437 Alvarez, Amando. Daniel Valdez: su vida y su carrera. LATINO, Vol. 53, no. 2 (March, April, 1982), p. 16-17. Spanish. **DESCR:** Films; *Valdez, Daniel.

12438 Barrios, Gregg. Zoot Suit: the man, the myth, still lives. BILINGUAL REVIEW, Vol. 10, no. 2-3 (May, December, 1983), p. 159-164. English. **DESCR:** Film Reviews; Valdez, Luis.

ZOOT SUIT [film] (cont.)

12439 Dean, Raymond S. Intelligence-achievement discrepancies in diagnosing pediatric learning disabilities. CLINICAL NEUROPSYCHOLOGY, Vol. 4, no. 2 (1982), p. 58-62. English. DESCR: Anglo Americans; *Handicapped; Intelligence Tests; Peabody Individual Achievement Test (PIAT); Youth.

12440 Grelier, Robert. Film review of: CHICANOS STORY. REVUE DU CINEMA - IMAGE ET SON - ECRAN, (May 1983), p. 30. Other. DESCR: Film Reviews; *Valdez, Luis.

12441 Lopez, Rafael and Miller, Robert. Daniel Valley and the American Zoot Band (band review). CAMINOS, Vol. 4, no. 5 (May 1983), p. 42-43,52. English. DESCR: Artists; Films; *Valdez, Daniel.

12442 Morales, Sylvia. Chicano-produced celluloid mujeres. BILINGUAL REVIEW, Vol. 10, no. 2-3 (May, December, 1983), p. 89-93. English. DESCR: BALLAD OF GREGORIO CORTEZ [film]; *Chicanas; Film Reviews; *Films; RAICES DE SANGRE [film]; SEGUIN [movie]; *Stereotypes.

12443 Ostria, Vincent. Film review of: CHICANOS STORY. CAHIERS DU CINEMA, Vol. 36, (June, July, 1983), p. 90. Other. DESCR: Film Reviews; Valdez, Luis.

12444 Quesada-Weiner, Rosemary and Diaz, Katherine A. ZOOT SUIT. CAMINOS, Vol. 2, no. 7 (December 1981), p. 38-39. English. DESCR: Film Reviews.

12445 Ramirez Berg, Charles. ZOOT SUIT. BILINGUAL REVIEW, Vol. 10, no. 2-3 (May, December, 1983), p. 189-190. English. DESCR: Film Reviews.

12446 ZOOT SUIT. NUESTRO, Vol. 6, no. 2 (March 1982), p. 46-47. English. DESCR: Films.

ZOOT SUIT [play]

12447 Orona-Cordova, Roberta and Valdez, Luis. ZOOT SUIT and the Pachuco phenomenon: an interview with Luis Valdez. REVISTA CHICANO-RIQUENA, Vol. 11, no. 1 (Spring 1983), p. 95-111. English. DESCR: Pachucos; Teatro; Valdez, Luis.

Zoot Suiter
USE: Pachucos

Zozaya, Julia S.

12448 Community watching: para la comunidad. CAMINOS, Vol. 3, no. 1 (January 1982), p. 43-44. Bilingual. DESCR: Congreso Nacional Para Pueblos Unidos (CPU); *Financial Aid; *Food Programs; *Journalists; National Association for Chicano Studies (NACS); *Radio; Summer Program for Minority Journalists.

Zubi Inc., Miami, FL

12449 Communications/marketing. HISPANIC BUSINESS, Vol. 5, no. 6 (June 1983), p. 16. English. DESCR: *Advertising Agencies; *Broadcast Media; Castillo & Castillo Public Relations and Advertising; Castillo, Cid; Castillo, Patricia; Latino Consortium, Los Angeles, CA; Montemayor, Carlos R.; Montemayor y Asociados, Inc.

Zuniga, Francisco

12450 Diaz, Katherine A. Francisco Zuniga; el pueblo Mexicano su inspiracion. CAMINOS, Vol. 4, no. 1-2 (January, February, 1983), p. 34-38. Bilingual. DESCR: Artists; Mexico.

Zuniga, Henry

12451 People on the move. CAMINOS, Vol. 2, no. 6 (October 1981), p. 7. English. DESCR: Alvarado, Angel S.; Arreola, Rafael; *Biographical Notes; Diaz, Elisa; Diaz, Elvira A.; Garcia, Jose Joel; Garza, Florentino; Icaza, Ricardo F.; Lacayo, Henry; Martinez, Lydia R.; Munoz, Victor M.; Salinas, Vicente; Sanchez, Manuel.

12452 President Reagan's appointments. CAMINOS, Vol. 3, no. 3 (March 1982), p. 48-50. Bilingual. DESCR: Appointed Officials; *Federal Government; Flores Buckhart, Elizabeth; Garcia, Ernest E.; Gonzalez, Luis A.; Lozano, Diana; Pompa, Gilbert G.; Reagan, Ronald; Sanchez, Nestor D.

Zuzueta, Joseph

12453 Gomez, Dalia. Needed: Latino CPA's. NUESTRO, Vol. 6, no. 1 (January, February, 1982), p. 25-28. English. DESCR: *Accounting; Careers; Frank, Eleanor Marie; Karpel, Miguel; Quezada, Felipe L.; Rodriguez, Julio H.; Umpierre, Raphael.

Zweig, Paul

12454 Fainberg, Louise Vasvari. HUNGER OF MEMORY: review of a review. NABE JOURNAL, Vol. 6, no. 2-3 (Winter, Spring, 1981, 1982), p. 115-116. English. DESCR: Book Reviews; *HUNGER OF MEMORY: THE EDUCATION OF RICHARD RODRIGUEZ; Rodriguez, Richard.

AUTHOR INDEX

Abelardo
USE: Delgado, Abelardo "Lalo"

Abrams, Herbert K.
Occupational and environmental health problems along the U.S.-Mexico Border, 211.

Abu Bakr, Virginia
Book review of: HISPANIC MENTAL HEALTH RESEARCH: A REFERENCE GUIDE, 1371.

Acevedo, Guillermo
Portfolio-arte, 3629.

Acevedo, Mario (Torero)
Big brother speaks from the dead [poster], 5107.
[La race (drawing)], 3630.
Trapezoid man [painting], 8245.
[Untitled painting], 8246.

Achor, Shirley
Book review of: GUNPOWDER JUSTICE: A REASSESSMENT OF THE TEXAS RANGERS, 946.
Book review of: GUNPOWDER JUSTICE: A REASSESSMENT OF THE TEXAS RANGERS, 947.

Acosta, Armando
Platicame Chicano, 9618.

Acosta, Daniel
Homeboy, 10659.

Acosta, Frank X.
Bilingual-Bicultural interpreters as psychotherapeutic bridges: a program note, 978.
Treatments of Asian Americans and Hispanic Americans: similarities and differences, 643.

Acosta, Maria D.
Hispanic business in the 80's/el negocio Hispanico en los ochentas, 1888.

Acuna, Carlos
Alcon Moco's ballet (a border question), 8489.

Acuna, Mike
Man witnesses his own execution, 10660.

Acuna, Rodolfo
Book review of: THE MEXICAN FRONTIER 1821-1846: THE AMERICAN SOUTHWEST UNDER MEXICO, 1374.
Book review of: THE TEJANO COMMUNITY 1836-1900, 1375.
La generacion de '68: unfulfilled dreams, 2587.

Adams, Alice
To see you again, 1376.

Adams, Phylliss J.
Comparison of teachers' and Mexican-American children's perceptions of the children's competence, 685.

Adams, Russell L.
Bias in a neuropsychological test classification related to education, age and ethnicity, 190.

Adkins, Lynn
New strategies to sell Hispanics, 118.

Adnan, Etel
Pablo Neruda is a banana tree, 8490.

Adrienne, K.
Memories of you, 8491.

Agosin, Marjorie
Book review of: ENTRE LA VIGILIA Y EL SUENO, 1377.
Donde estan?, 8492.
Elucubraciones y antielucubraciones: critica feminista desde perspectivas poeticas, 2444.
Estados Unidos, 8493.
La mesa de billar en New Bedford, Mass., 8494.

Agudelo, C.
Wooing the Hispanics, 9362.

Agudelo, Carlos
What about Latin music?, 767.

Aguila, Pancho
Before the aquarians, 8495.
Existential, 8496.
The ex-marine, 8497.
Folsom, 8498.
Marilyn, 8499.
The nuts and bolts, 8500.

Aguilar, George
Raul Rodriguez, parade artist extraordinaire, 528

Aguilar, Nacho
Cultural awareness and sensitivity in mental health with Chicanos, 7186.

Aguilar, Ricardo D.
Aeroplanos de papel, 8501.
Al regreso, 8502.
Cancion de viaje, 8503.
Chicano poetry and new places, 6597.
Definicion de la vida -o- agarrala que se escapa, 8505.
Gabi, 8506.
Hacia donde?, 8507.
Marinero, 8508.
Pica pica pica perico pica pica pica la rama, 8509.

Aguirre, Javier
Un corazon sencillo, 9619.
Just another point of view, 9620.
Las lagrimas se secan, 8510.
Oda para la jefita, 8511.
Pa' mi asi fue, 8512.

Aguirre, Richard R.
Print media at a crossroads, 119.

Ailinger, Rita L.
Hypertension knowledge in a Hispanic community, 5499.

Akbar, Karim
Death, 8513.
I am tired, 8514.
People, 8515.

Alarcon, Justo S.
Book review of: CHULIFEAS FRONTERAS, 1442.
Hacia la nada ... o la religion en POCHO, 6598.
La meta critica Chicana, 4260.
Resena de EL DIABLO EN TEXAS, 1378.

Alatorre, Alva Sylvia
Book review of: LIFE WITH TWO LANGUAGES: AN INTRODUCTION TO BILINGUALISM, 1136.

Alba, Francisco
La fecundidad entre los Mexicano-Norteamericanos en relacion a los cambiantes patrones reproductivos en Mexico y los Estados Unidos, 3451.

Alba, Richard D.
A comment on Schoen and Cohen, 2811.

Alcaraz, Edward
Tecate soldiers, 8516.

Aldaraca, Bridget
The poetry of Gioconda Belli, 929.

Aldridge, Henry B.
Angel and big Joe, 374.

Alegria, Claribel
Requiem, 8518.

Alejandro, Brenda
La paraplejica se vistio de largo, 8519.

Alejandro, Marcial
Un canto, 8655.

Algarin, Miguel
Albuquerque, 8520.
El jibarito moderno, 8521.
Nuyorican literature, 9840.
Paris, 8522.
Paterson, 8523.
Taos Pueblo Indians: 700 strong according to Bobby's last census, 8524.

Allen, Kenneth
Q & A with Kenneth Allen of the President's Task Force on Private Sector initiatives (interview), 286.

Allen, Virginia
Book review of: A CHICANO CHRISTMAS STORY, 1380.

Allende, Luz B.
Beyond the Sunday sermon, 9363.

Almanza, Antonio
A......lone, 8525.
Charade, 8526.
The panhandle, 8527.

Almaraz, Felix D., Jr.
Book review of: MEXICAN EMIGRATION TO THE UNITED STATES, 1897-1931: SOCIO-ECONOMIC PATTERNS, 1381.

Arce, A.A.
    Application of cognitive behavioral techniques
        in the treatment of Hispanic patients, 687.
Arce, Carlos H.
    Language shift among Chicanos: strategies for
        measuring and assessing direction and rate,
        1138.
Arguelles, Ivan
    The conquest of Mexico, 8554.
    "The Cuban decision", 8555.
    Echoes of life, 8556.
    Maquina de coser, 8557.
    Modern Mexico, 8558.
    Mr. Gonzalez makes a speech, 8559.
    El Quijote de la maquina de coser, 8560.
    Republica Mexicana, 8561.
    La vida no es un sueno, 8562.
Argulewicz, Ed N.
    Comparison of behavioral ratings of
        Anglo-American and Mexican-American gifted
        children, 377.
    Considerations in the assessment of reading
        difficulties in bilingual children, 1139.
    The influence of student ethnicity on
        teachers' behavior ratings of normal and
        learning disabled children, 3516.
    Special education evaluation process as a
        moderator of false positives, 378.
    Stability of performance on the PPVT-R for
        three ethnic groups attending a bilingual
        kindergarten, 5911.
Arias, Ron
    Book review of: CONTEMPORARY CHICANO THEATRE,
        1387.
    A house on the island, 9625.
    Interview with Ron Arias, 499.
    Los que emigran desde Costa Rica hacia el
        norte, 3065.
    The road to Tamazunchale (excerpt from novel),
        8056.
    The rooster that called me home, 498.
    El senor del chivo, 715.
    The story machine, 9626.
Armas, Jose
    ANTONIO AND THE MAYOR: a cultural review of
        the film, 453.
Armengol, Armando
    The international bilingual city: how a
        university meets the challenge, 980.
Arnold, Bill R.
    Attitudinal research and Hispanic handicapped:
        a review of selected needs, 688.
Arnold, Frank
    A history of struggle: organizing cannery
        workers in the Santa Clara Valley, 199.
Arnold, Louise M.
    Predictors of performance of minority students
        in the first two years of a BA/MD program,
        13.
Arora, Shirley L.
    A critical bibliography of Mexican American
        proverbs, 954.
    Proverbs in Mexican American tradition, 3543.
Arrastia, Cecilio
    The Hispanics in the U.S.A.: drama and
        challenge, 7551.
Arroyo, Antonio M. Stevens
    Un hispano para vice-presidente, 9393.
Arroyo, Sara G.
    Black residential mobility: trends and
        characteristics, 5433.
Ashman, Allan
    What's new in the law: immigration ...
        detained aliens, 501.
Askin, Steve
    Boston church encourages labor talks, 1792.
Astol, Leonardo, et al.
    El Raja, 11426.
Atkinson, Donald R.
    Ethnic minority representation in counselor
        education, 160.
    Mexican-American cultural commitment,
        preference for counselor ethnicity, and
        willingness to use counseling, 3082.

Attkisson, C. Clifford
    A client satisfaction scale suitable for use
        with Hispanics?, 2871.
Austin, Robert F.
    Comment on "Undocumented migration from
        Mexico: some geographical questions", 6026.
Avendano, Fausto
    Book review of: HAY PLESHA LICHANS TO DI FLAC,
        1388.
Avila, Carmen
    Assessing the casa study, 2858.
Avila, Joaquin G.
    The computer revolution: only for the few?,
        2905.
    Remembering Matt Garcia, 1223.
Ayala, Ernesto
    My machine, 798.
Ayers-Nackamkin, Beverly, et al.
    Sex and ethnic differences in the use of
        power, 379.
Aztlan, Perico
    The sewer society, 8564.
Babbitt, Bruce
    Reagan approach to aliens simply wishful
        thinking, 1750.
Baca Barragan, Polly
    [Untitled interview with State Senators
        (Colorado) Polly Baca-Barragan and Lena
        Guerrero, 815.
Baca, Jimmy Santiago
    For a Chicano brother of mine, 8565.
    Sun calendar, 8566.
    They're used to putting things in the ground,
        8567.
    We knew it, 8568.
    The word love, 8569.
Baca, Judith F.
    Class II: young and energetic leaders, 4681.
    Secretary of Education Terrell Bell speaks
        out, 927.
Baca, Reynaldo
    The "Assimilation" of unauthorized Mexican
        workers: another social science fiction?,
        651.
Baca Zinn, Maxine
    Book review of: LA CHICANA: THE MEXICAN
        AMERICAN WOMAN, 1389.
    Book review of: MEXICAN WOMEN IN THE UNITED
        STATES: STRUGGLES PAST AND PRESENT, 1390.
    Book review of: TWICE A MINORITY;
        MEXICAN-AMERICAN WOMEN, 1391.
    Chicano family research: conceptual
        distortions and alternative directions,
        3206.
    Chicano men and masculinity, 3207.
    Mexican American women in the social sciences,
        2451.
    Urban kinship and Midwest Chicano families:
        evidence in support of revision, 2880.
Baca Zinn, Maxine, ed.
    Social research on Chicanos: its development
        and directions: symposium, 10950.
Baca-Ramirez, Reynaldo
    The undocumented Mexican worker: a social
        problem?, 5024.
Baciu, Joyce A.
    How to handle a job interview, 6022.
    How to handle a job interview/como prepararse
        para una entrevista, 6023.
    How to prepare a resume, 10225.
    How to prepare a resume/como redactar un
        resumen, 4082.
    KBBF in Santa Rosa, 9973.
    KUBO-FM 90.9; the nation's fourth bilingual
        radio station, 6115.
    The winners - Los ganadores, 768.
Baeza, Joan
    A servant of the people, 9627.
Bagamery, Anne
    SIN, the original, 441.
Bailey, Lynn B., et al.
    Folacin and iron status and hematological
        finding in Blacks and Spanish-American
        adolescents from urban low-income

households, 1310.

Baker, Catherine A.
Bilingual education: que pasa?, 995.

Baker, Edward, trans.
The poetry of Roque Dalton: We all, Typist,
Latinoamerica, Love poem, O.A.S., 4000.

Balakian, Anna
Book review of: THE PERPETUAL PRESENT: THE
POETRY AND PROSE OF OCTAVIO PAZ, 1392.

Balasubramonian, Krishna
Not on test scores alone: the qualitative side
to program evaluation, 996.

Baldonado, Lisa
A university program to meet Chicago's
bilingual needs, 997.

Baldwin, Deirdra
The empty room, 8571.
Stopping by the sauna, 8572.

Balkan, D. Carlos
100 influentials and their critical issues for
the eighties, 6377.
The advent of Uniworld/Hispanic: an interview,
151.
AMEX Systems Inc. at transition point, 319.
Being a start-up manager at San Onofre II &
III, 2071.
The crisis in Hispanic marketing, 121.
Four little-known facts about Hispanic
business firms, 1979.
The Hispanic business top 400 in sales, 1940.
Hispanic foods in Southern California: anatomy
of a market in flux, 4779.
The Hispanic market: leading indicators, 122.
Mr. Caballero's Spanish radio network, 123.
The nation's largest little bank: Laredo's
International Bank of Commerce, 858.
The nuclear powered Mr. Carlos Pimentel, 1225.
Packaging the Dallas Hispanic consumer, 2993.
Space-Craft's strategy for
re-industrialization, 1943.
The subtleties of corporate boardsmanship,
3030.

Ballard, Lee
Tom Marquez and the EDS mode, 1226.

Baltodano, J. C.
Success, 2823.

Banas, L. K.
Donde estas? Conflicts in the Chicano movement
(reprinted CARACOL June 1977), 2573.

Banberger, Ellen
Poesia nicaraguense, 930.

Barajas, Salvador
A mi amor [painting], 8247.
Primavera [painting], 8248.

Barber, Bob
UFW and the class struggle, 2073.

Barber, Gary
Book review of: DICTIONARY OF MEXICAN-AMERICAN
HISTORY, 1393.

Barberis, Mary
Hispanic America, 5321.

Barclay, Lisa K.
Using Spanish as the language of instruction
with Mexican-American Head Start children: a
re-evaluation using meta-analysis, 3797.

Barradas, Efrain
Book review of: EN EL PAIS DE LAS MARAVILLAS
(KEMPIS PUERTORRIQUENO), 1394.
Conciencia femenina, conciencia social: la voz
poetica de Sandra Maria Esteves, 4275.
NOO JORK, 1395.
"Todo lo que digo es cierto...": en memoria de
Victor Fernandez Fragoso (1944-1982), 716.

Barrera, Jose J.
Jesus "Chuy" Negrete: the Chicano vote, 2569.

Barrera, Mario
La Raza Unida Party and the Chicano student
movement in California, 2098.

Barreto, Julio
Amigos o adversarios, 9365.
Cecilio's dream, 4407.
Gathering of the Ojedas, 710.
A new force in the barrio, 2052.
Ready for battle; organizations draft

legislative agenda, 9394.
Reagan record attacked, 9329.
Seven women honored, 2452.
Where the jobs are: tips from Latinos in key
occupations, 1890.

Barrientos, L. S.
The manana show - starring johnny calzon,
11427.

Barrio, Raymond
The bilingual heart and other adventures,
1129.
Un breviario mexicano, 8574.
Dando gracias al Rey Ocho Ciervos, 4383.
Resurrection 1999, 4001.

Barrios, Gregg
Advertisement for Chicano unity, 8575.
Alambrista! a modern odyssey, 260.
A cinema of failure, a cinema of hunger: the
films of Efrain Gutierrez, 4574.
Del mero corazon, 8576.
I am an American too, 8577.
The Latino genre in American film 1980-81,
4613.
Our Lady of the Angels has no papers, 822.
Zoot Suit: the man, the myth, still lives,
4575.

Barrios-Martinez, Ruben
Should Puerto Rico become a state?: against
statehood, 2841.

Barry, Joseph E.
Politics, bilingual education, and the
curriculum, 998.

Barry, Patrick
Alternative high school provides dropouts a
second chance, 3673.
Election '83: Chicago's Latinos awake, but not
united, 2417.
Progress at La Paz: a chance for the retarded,
2418.
Saturdays are wedding cakes, 1993.
Trouble in the bush: neighborhood house fights
back, 2420.

Barry, Tom
On strike! Undocumented workers in Arizona.,
200.

Bartlett, Edward E.
Checkerboard area health system: delivering
comprehensive care in a remote region of New
Mexico, 7118.

Bartlett, Paul Alexander
Against the wall, 10667.

Baruch, Jeremiah (pseud.)
Half-open door, 5641.

Bath, C. Richard
Health and environmental problems: the role of
the border in El Paso-Ciudad Juarez
coordination, 1751.

Bauer, Karl Jack
Book review of: THE MEXICAN-AMERICAN WAR: AN
ANNOTATED BIBLIOGRAPHY, 1396.

Baxter, Carolyn
E. 100th st. (8th grade), 8579.
Street, 8580.

Bean, Frank D.
Book review of: MEXICAN EMIGRATION TO THE
UNITED STATES, 1897-1931: SOCIO-ECONOMIC
PATTERNS, 1397.
Generation, female education and Mexican
American fertility, 2453.
The number of illegal migrants of Mexican
origin in the United States: sex ratio-based
estimates for 1980, 2348.

Beard, Timothy
Ernesto Galarza: early organizing efforts and
the community, 4858.

Beaupre, Shirley
Book review of: CROSS CULTURAL PSYCHOLOGY:
HUMAN BEHAVIOR IN GLOBAL PERSPECTIVE, 1398.

Beaver, Frank E.
CHULAS FRONTERAS, 1339.
DEL MERO CORAZON, 3437.

Bedard, Evelyn M.
Book review of: HISPANIC MENTAL HEALTH
RESEARCH: A REFERENCE GUIDE, 955.

Behr, Michelle
    Central cities and suburbs as distinct place
        types: myth or fact?, 1320.
Bejar, Rebecca
    Mejor en grupo, 3304.
Bejarano, Guillermo
    USE: Bejarano, William
Bejarano, William
    Murals of Los Angeles, 7712.
Bell, Michael Davitt
    Fitting into a tradition of autobiography,
        161.
Bell, Samuel E.
    Zona libre: trade and diplomacy on the Mexican
        border, 1858-1905, 1752.
Bellenger, Danny N.
    Understanding the Hispanic market, 2976.
Belli, Gioconda
    Dynamite dresses: vestidos de dinamita, 8025.
Bell-Villada, G. H.
    Book review of: CHICANO AUTHORS, INQUIRY BY
        INTERVIEW v. 228, 1401.
Belton, Robert T.
    Book review of: CANNIBALS AND KINGS: THE
        ORIGINS OF CULTURE and THE MAN-EATING MYTH:
        ANTHROPOLOGY AND ANTHROPOPHAGY, 491.
Benardo, Margot L.
    Hispanic women and their men, 2454.
Benavidez, Max
    Los Angeles, 8582.
    Los Angeles, 8583.
    Nada, 8584.
Benson, Nancy C.
    The art of colcha-stitch embroidery: an
        Hispanic heritage, 559.
Benton, Patricia Moran
    Mother's Day reflections: keepers of the
        faith, 2455.
Berg, Charles
    Book review of: CHRONIQUE OF A DEATH FORETOLD,
        1403.
Bergaila, Christine
    Book review of: CHICANOS: THE STORY OF THE
        MEXICAN AMERICANS, 1561.
Berger, Andres
    El afilador, 9628.
Bernal, Guillermo
    Latino families in therapy: engagement and
        evaluation, 4410.
Bernal, Juan Manuel
    [Cheech and Chong together], 8585.
    Happy happy, 8026.
    [It took ten powerful trucks to haul], 8587.
    Mientras, 8027.
    Monologo congruente, 8589.
    Oda a garcia lorca, 8590.
    [Quiero jugar bebeleche y la cebolla], 8591.
    La vida fascinante de un individuo trivial,
        8592.
Berssenbrugge, Mei Mei
    The beautiful moth, 8593.
Betancourt, Mary
    La educacion de Jesus, 8594.
Bethel, Lowell J.
    Inquiry approach to science and language
        teaching, 1175.
Bethell, Tom
    Immigration and the economy, 5642.
Beveridge, John
    Bi-lingual programs: some doubts and comments,
        1000.
Beveridge, Kriss
    Chubasco, 8595.
    La isla de nadie, 8596.
Beverley, John
    The revolution betrayed: a note on Mariano
        Azuela's estridentista trilogy, 811.
Beyer, Sandra S.
    French via Spanish: a positive approach to
        language learning for minority students,
        3899

Beyette, Beverly
    A time of transition for MALDEF, 6474.
Binder, Wolfgang
    An interview with Piri Thomas, 3626.
    Book review of: INVENTING A WORD: AN ANTHOLOGY
        OF TWENTIETH CENTURY PUERTO RICAN POETRY,
        5982.
Bisconte, Sarah R.
    [Untitled poems], 8597.
Black, Bill
    Housing for farm laborers: a California
        solution, 213.
Blake, Robert
    Mood selection among Spanish-speaking
        children, ages 4 to 12, 2652.
Blanche, Ella
    Ghost people, 8598.
    I have seen her, 8599.
Blea, Irene I.
    Book review of: BUT TIME AND CHANCE, 1404.
Bletzer, Keith V.
    A follow-up note on census techniques for
        enumerating the Hispanic population, 2349.
Blomstedt, Robert
    Applying existential thought to bilingual
        education, 1003.
Bloodworth, William A., Jr.
    Book review of: IMAGES OF THE MEXICAN-AMERICAN
        IN FICTION AND FILM, 1405.
Boake, Corwin
    Bias in a neuropsychological test
        classification related to education, age and
        ethnicity, 190.
Bodayla, Stephen D.
    Book review of: ORIGINS OF THE MEXICAN WAR: A
        DOCUMENTARY SOURCE BOOK, 1406.
Bogrand, Ricardo
    Dentro de un pozo, 8600.
Boiston, Bernard G.
    The Simpson-Mazzoli bill: the first major
        immigration bill in thirty years, 4084.
Bolano, Roberto
    Bienvenida, 8601.
    Estos patios parecen playas, 8602.
    Rojo/burbujeante, 8603.
Bolivar, Maria Dolores
    Al hombre, 8604.
Bonham, G.W.
    Moral imperative, 4085.
Bonilla, Ruben
    Soliciten aqui dentro el presidente continua
        su busqueda, 4615.
Bonilla, Tony
    1982 was a memorable year, 9397.
    A decade of success, 2653.
    Hispanics in the media, 7010.
    It's time for us to watch the media, 7011.
    Law services for the poor, 6449.
    Life in these United States, 7012.
    Local government is no answer, 6703.
    New doors of opportunity, 3769.
    Talking Texas: turning the tables with LULAC,
        1370.
    There is trouble in our schools, 3800.
    Toward a land of opportunity, 5323.
    'We gave it our best shot', 1362.
Borjas, George J.
    Earnings of male Hispanic immigrants in the
        United States, 3157.
    The labor supply of male Hispanic immigrants
        in the United States, 653.
    The substitutability of Black, Hispanic and
        white labor, 5854.
Borland, Dolores C.
    A cohort analysis approach to the empty nest
        syndrome among three ethnic groups of women:
        a theoretical position, 10623.
Borland, James J.
    Book review of: COUNSELING THE CULTURALLY
        DIFFERENT, 1424.
Borman, Adele T.
    "Who do you think you are, anyway?, 2193.
Borrego, Richard L.

Effect of counselor technique on
Mexican-American and Anglo-American
self-disclosure and counselor perception,
380.

Bose, Aruna
Azarcon por empacho - another cause of lead
toxicity, 2654.

Bracamonte, Jose A.
The national labor relations act and undaunted
workers: the alienation of American labor,
5730.

Brack, Gene M.
Book review of: THE MEXICAN FRONTIER,
1821-1846: THE AMERICAN SOUTHWEST UNDER
MEXICO, 1425.

Bradley, Curtis H.
Tips for the English speaking multicultural
vocational teacher, 3287.

Bradshaw, Benjamin S.
Potential labor force supply and replacement
in Mexico and the states of the Mexican
cession and Texas: 1980-2000, 5645.

Brasch, Walter M.
Hanigan case: hung up on racism?, 103.

Bray, Howard
The new wave of Puerto Rican immigrants, 58.

Breckenridge, James N.
The Houston Parent-Child Development Center
and the primary prevention of behavior
problems in young children, 2636.

Breiter, Toni
Eddie Olmos and THE BALLAD OF GREGORIO CORTEZ,
565.
First to fall: "God just chose him to be a
Marine", 1230.
Hispanic policy development project, 5294.
An interview with some experts, 5099.
El Libertador: a profile, 1231.
La raza, 4254.

Brigham, Jack
Tribute to Cesar Chavez, 2401.

Brink, T. L.
Book review of: AVANCES EN PSICOLOGIA
CONTEMPORANEA, 760.
Book review of: PSYCHOLOGY MISDIRECTED, 1427.
Book review of: WORKING-CLASS EMIGRES FROM
CUBA, 1428.

Brinson-Pineda, Barbara
Fire, 8605.
Maria la O, 8606.

Britt, Anita
Book review of: THE LOS ANGELES BARRIO
1850-1890: A SOCIAL HISTORY, 1429.

Brody, Gene H.
Effects of ethnicity and child's age on
maternal judgments of children's
transgressions against persons and property,
392.

Bronfenbrenner, Martin
Hyphenated Americans-economic aspects, 2723.

Brooks, C. K.
Verbal giftedness in the minority student: a
NEWT questions a SOT, 3288.

Brooks, Douglas Montgomery
Aliens - civil rights - illegal aliens are
inhabitants within meaning of U.S.C 242,
1732.

Brotherston, Gordon
Year 13 reed equals 31113 BC: a clue to
Mesoamerican chronology, 2807.

Brown, Edward G.
The Teatro Campesino's Vietnam trilogy, 11429.

Brown, Susan E.
Melendez v. Burciaga: revealing the state of
the art in bar examinations, 6105.

Broyles, Yolanda Julia
Chicano film festivals: an examination, 2581.

Bruce Novoa, Juan
Artistic perceptions of Mexico City, 531.
La critica chicana de Luis Leal, 717.
Fear and loathing on the buffalo trail, 92.
In search of the honest outlaw: John Rechy,
6604.
Interview with Ron Arias, 499.

Round table on Chicano literature, 1867.

Brue de Lorenzo, Kathryn
Book review of: ETHNIC LEADERSHIP IN A NEW
ENGLAND COMMUNITY: THREE PUERTO RICAN
FAMILIES, 1430.

Bruhn, John G.
Assessment of type A behavior in preschoolers,
408.

Brunner, Tracy
Life on the road: Midwestern migrant
farmworker survival skills, 203.

Brusco, Bernadette A.
Hispanic marketing: new applications for old
methodologies, 2977.

Bryan, Dexter Edward
The "Assimilation" of unauthorized Mexican
workers: another social science fiction?,
651.
The undocumented Mexican worker: a social
problem?, 5024.

Bubriski, Kevin
THE BALLAD OF GREGORIO CORTEZ (photoessay),
840.

Buckholtz, Marjorie Weidenfeld
Technical training in two languages helps
Houston stay cool, 4145.

Buckley, William F.
Doing the impossible, 942.

Buffenstein, Darryl F.
The proposed immigration reform and control
act of 1982: a new epoch in immigration law
and a new headache for employers, 4086.

Buitron, Robert C.
Loteria: las manos, 8428.
[Untitled], 8429.

Bunce, Harvey
Assessment of type A behavior in preschoolers,
408.

Bunker, Stephen G.
Book review of: THE CHANGING DEMOGRAPHY OF
SPANISH-AMERICANS, 1431.

Bunnell, Robert
Bravisimo!, 326.
A conversation with Commodore Diego Hernandez,
2251.

Bunuel, Janie
The need for goal setting, 2194.

Burciaga, Cecilia Preciado
Cap and gown vs. cap and apron, 3674.
High school dropouts: remedies, 3675.

Burciaga, Jose Antonio
20 nuclear years later: still holding my
breath, 3144.
Care package, 10668.
Death of el senor Peso, 3744.
La dieta del ano, 8082.
Ghost riders, 8607.
Hannukkah, navidad and christmas, 2724.
Me, E.T. and other alien beings, 5517.
The Mexican archipelago, 7356.
Mosca en la leche, 4010.
Theatre: CORRIDOS - sad and happy masks, 3042.
Wii dii piipo, 12263.

Buriel, Raymond
Perceived parental practices and prosocial
development, 401.
The relationship of traditional Mexican
American culture to adjustment and
delinquency among three generations of
Mexican American male adolescents, 3305.

Buriel, Raymond, et al.
Mexican- and Anglo-American children's locus
of control and achievement in relation to
teachers attitudes, 9.
Teacher-student interactions and their
relationship to student achievement: a
comparison of Mexican-American and
Anglo-American children, 10.

Burk, Ronnie
Cihuacoatl, 8608.
In the park, 8609.
La merced, 10669.
Ogre woman's song, 8610.

Burke, Leslie K.

The day the Cisco kid shot John Wayne, 9630.
The prowler, 9548.
The retribution, 9631.
Cannstatt, Christian
On sancta maria-ave euroshima, 8631.
Cantu, Felipe
Enorme crecemiento, 9462.
Cantu, Hector
Aqui en Austin: this is Olga Campos reporting,
2144.
Aqui en Tejas: Hispanic newspapers: city,
community papers taking a business approach
to the news, 708.
Aqui en Texas: ex-boxer finds success in
restaurant: Matt's of Austin one of Texas's
most successful restaurants, 1951.
Border business report: the Rio Grande
Valley's economy and Mexico's lingering peso
devaluation effects, 254.
Hispanic numbers rising, 711.
Hispanic students wanted, 4219.
The island, 1952.
Softball Texas style, 3984.
Cantu, Roberto
Nota preliminar: de Samuel Ramos a Emilio
Uranga, 3210.
El relato como articulacion infinitiva:
MACARIO y el arte de Juan Rulfo, 719.
Captor, Rich
College and the Navy, 2196.
Cardenas de Dwyer, Carlota
Cultural nationalism and Chicano literature in
the eighties, 6611.
Cardenas, Leo
The Bonilla years come to an end, 1234.
The day E.T. met T.B. and A.T., 5467.
Editor's view: invisible in advertising world,
125.
Family unit, 6736.
How Hispanics are really influencing the
networks, 7017.
Ruben Sandoval's quiet work, 6450.

Five simple words, 9368.
Cardenas, Lupe
Book review of: CHULIFEAS FRONTERAS, 1442.
Cardona-Hine, Alvaro
The croupiers, 8632.
Cardoso, Lawrence Anthony
Book review of: ACROSS THE BORDER: RURAL
DEVELOPMENT IN MEXICO AND RECENT MIGRATION
TO THE UNITED STATES, 93.
Book review of: ACROSS THE BORDER: RURAL
DEVELOPMENT IN MEXICO AND RECENT MIGRATION
TO THE UNITED STATES, 94.
Book review of: DESERT IMMIGRANTS: THE
MEXICANS OF EL PASO 1880-1920, 1445.
Book review of: LOS MEXICANOS QUE DEVOLVIO LA
CRISIS, 1929-1932, 1446.
Book review of: REVOLTOSOS: MEXICO'S REBELS IN
THE UNITED STATES 1903-1923, 1447.
Book review of: UNWANTED MEXICAN AMERICANS IN
THE GREAT DEPRESSION: REPATRIATION
PRESSURES, 1929-1939, 1448.
"Wetbacks" and "slaves": recent additions to
the literature, 1449.
Carlos, Jess
The Filipinos: our forgotten cultural cousins,
2320.
Carlos, Manuel L.
Chicano households, the structure of parental
information networks, and family use of
child-related social services, 4412.
Carlson, Alvar W.
Book review of: CANONES: VALUES, CRISIS, AND
SURVIVAL IN A NORTHERN NEW MEXICO VILLAGE,
1450.
Carmen, Andrea
Rape, 10027.
Carr, Pat
The vagina dentata motif in Nahuatl and Pueblo
mythic narratives: a comparative study,
7817.
Carrasco, David

A perspective for a study of religious
dimensions in Chicano experience: BLESS ME,
ULTIMA as a religious text, 334.
Carrasco, Ricardo
Eagle, 10673.
Carreon, Ernesto
[Untitled drawing], 5047.
Carreras, Peter Nares
Strong concern over searches, 2838.
Carrie, Jacques
Suicidal pieces, 9632.
Carrillo, Federico M.
How should Spanish speakers be taught Spanish
in the schools?, 1011.
Carrion, Arturo Morales
Puerto Rico: the coming of the Americans,
3145.
Carrison, Muriel Paskin
Bilingual-no!, 1012.
Casanova, Steve
Oaxaca and the ancient ruins of Monte Alban
and Mitla, 7361.
Casey, G.M.
Marketing to Mexican-Americans: just a bit of
insight, 4767.
Casillas, Mike
The Cananea strike of 1906, 507.
Cassel, Carol A.
Mexican-Americans in city-politics:
participation, representation, and policy
preferences, 1326.
Castagnera-Cain, Jim
Garreau's nine nations offer immigation
insights, 4936.
Castaneda, Jaime
Black & white ball, 264.
Castillo, Ana
1975, 8633.
The antihero, 8634.
Cartas, 8635.
A Christmas carol '76, 10674.
Encuentros #1, 8636.
I don't want to know, 8637.
Napa, California, 8638.
Not just because my husband said, 8639.
Castillo, Leonel J.
A response to the Reagan plan: respuesta al
plan Reagan, 5795.
Castillo, Pedro
Letter to the editor, 3745.
Castillo, Rafael C.
The Colonel, 9633.
Castro, Agenor L.
The case for the bilingual prison, 1143.
Castro, Mike
Alien smuggling and the refugee question:
caught between the border patrol and the
river, 1733.
OAS investigates California deaths, 1734.
Castro, Rafaela
Mexican women's sexual jokes, 2457.
Castro, Tony
I still love you, 8640.
Red light district, 10676.
Catala, Rafael
Danzon Peruano, 8641.
Cavazos, David S.
Chile bruja, 8642.
Caviness, Denise
The battered woman, 8643.
The battering, 8644.
Cayer, Shirley
Chicago's new Hispanic health alliance, 274.
Cazares, Allen E.
Adventures in careers: los desafios del
periodismo y la profesion legal, 6463.
Cazares, Ralph B.
Intermarriage of Mexican Americans, 78.
Cazemajou, Jean
Book review of: LES FILS DU SOLEIL: LA
MINORITE MEXICAINE A TRAVERS LA LITTERATURE
DES ETATS-UNIS, 1451.
Cea, Jose Roberto
El potrero, 8645.

Crisp, James E.
    Book review of: MEXICANO RESISTANCE IN THE
        SOUTHWEST: "THE SACRED RIGHT OF
        SELF-PRESERVATION", 1468.
    Book review of: THE TEJANO COMMUNITY
        1836-1900, 1469.
Cristo, Martha H.
    Bilingual-Bicultural interpreters as
        psychotherapeutic bridges: a program note,
        978.
Crocker, Elvira Valenzuela
    USE: Valenzuela-Crocker, Elvira
Cross, Harry E.
    National development and international labour
        migration: Mexico 1940-1965, 1812.
Cruz, Amaury
    Book review of: AZTEC, 1543.
    El Salvador: realities of a country at war,
        4002.
Cruz, Franklin D.
    Space-Craft's strategy for
        re-industrialization, 1943.
    Upcoming Republican strategies, 9332.
Cuellar, Israel
    Psychiatric evaluation of bilingual patient: a
        reply to Vazquez, 9729.
Cuellar, Israel, et al.
    Clinical psychiatric case presentation;
        culturally responsive diagnostic formulation
        and treatment in an Hispanic female, 84.
Cuello, J.
    Book review of: IN DEFENSE OF LA RAZA: THE LOS
        ANGELES MEXICAN CONSULATE AND THE MEXICAN
        COMMUNITY, 833.
Cuenca, Ramon Araluce
    USC forms institute for Hispanic media &
        culture, 5888.
Cuervo, Jose S.
    Los estragos del progreso, 8681.
Cuevas, Gilberto
    Effects of test language and mathematical
        skills assessed on the scores of bilingual
        Hispanic students, 2903.
Cummins, Light Townsend
    Book review of: THE MEXICAN FRONTIER
        1821-1846: THE AMERICAN SOUTHWEST UNDER
        MEXICO, 1471.
Cunningham, John W.
    Library services for the Spanish speaking,
        1028.
Curiel, Marco Antonio
    Black Greg, 8682.
    Carlitos, 8683.
    Fears, 8684.
    Para vicente, 8685.
Dalton, Roque
    Poema de amor, 4003.
    The poetry of Roque Dalton: We all, Typist,
        Latinoamerica, Love poem, O.A.S., 4000.
Daudistel, Howard C.
    Infant mortality of the Spanish surname
        population, 3462.
Davidson, Russ
    Out of the morass: acquiring Spanish language
        materials from Latin America, 6321.
Davila, Luis
    Meditaciones, 1145.
Davila, Martin
    Cuando hay nieve, 8687.
Davis, James Alston
    Does authority generalize? Locus of control
        perceptions in Anglo-American and
        Mexican-American adolescents, 2888.
Davis, Lisa
    La mujer hispana, 2468.
    Workers or owners, 1902.
Davis, Sally M.
    Sexual knowledge, sexual interests, and
        sources of sexual information of rural and
        urban adolescents from three cultures, 1302.
Davis, Susan M.
    A sparkling alternative to the cocktail party,
        270.

Davis, W. Alan
    Effects of books in Spanish and free reading
        time on Hispanic students' reading abilities
        and attitudes, 1094.
Day, Mark R.
    Bishop: why have we had to wait so long for
        Hispanic leaders, 2321.
    Border group feeds, clothes dispossessed,
        1756.
    Hispanics 'want more bishops, input in
        church', 2323.
    Hopes of jobs lure Mexicans, 1757.
    Immigrants ... and Mexican citizens, 2324.
    'Traffic darn heavy' to U.S., 1736.
Daydi-Tolson, Santiago
    The right to belong: a critic's view of Puerto
        Rican poetry in the United States, 879.
De Anda, Diane
    A study of the interaction of Hispanic junior
        high school students and their teachers,
        2469.
de Armas, Isabel
    Chicano, un vocablo colonizador, 219.
de Avila, Edward A.
    [Combining political strategies for effective
        representation], 6359.
De Barbosa, Liliam Coya
    "Mastering learning" como metodo
        psicoeducativo para ninos con problemas
        especificos de aprendizaje, 2660.
De Blassie, Richard R.
    Comparison of self-concept in Mexican American
        and non-Mexican American late adolescents,
        16.
    The differences between personality inventory
        scores and self-rating in a sample of
        Hispanic subjects, 2470.
    Ethnic designation, identification, and
        preference as they relate to Chicano
        children, 2694.
de Cuenca, Pilar
    Library holdings of the Office of Bilingual
        Education, city of New York: a selected
        bibliography, 957.
De George, George P.
    The guest editor speaks, 1030.
    Selecting tests for bilingual program
        evaluation, 1031.
De Hoyos, Angela
    The final laugh, 8688.
    How to eat crow on a cold Sunday morning,
        8689.
    Un llanto en seco, 8690.
    The missing ingredient, 8691.
    San antonio rose era xicana, 8692.
    Ten dry summers ago, 8693.
de Janvry, Alain
    Migration to the United States and Mexican
        rural developments: a case study, 7544.
De la Carcela, Victor
    An analysis of culturalism in Latino mental
        health: folk medicine as a case in point,
        3307.
de la Fuente, Patricia
    Ambiguity in the poetry of Gary Soto, 765.
    Special focus on Gary Soto, 6581.
De la Garza, Rodolfo O.
    Chicano-Mexican relations: a framework for
        research., 3773.
de la Isla, Jose
    Math-based careers, 2204.
De la Riva, Osa
    She's, 9636.
De la Rosa, Carlos
    Esai Morales: a new and exciting Latino talent
        on the rise, 821.
De Leon, Arnoldo
    Book review of: DICTIONARY OF MEXICAN-AMERICAN
        HISTORY, 1474.
    Book review of: IN DEFENSE OF LA RAZA: THE LOS
        ANGELES MEXICAN CONSULATE AND THE MEXICAN
        COMMUNITY, 834.
    Book review of: ON THE BORDER: PORTRAITS OF
        AMERICA'S SOUTHWESTERN FRONTIER, 1476.

Lost dream and found fortunes: Mexican and Anglo immigrants in South Texas,1850 -1900, 5336.

De Leon, David
Book review of: BITTER HARVEST: A HISTORY OF CALIFORNIA FARMWORKERS 1870-1941, 220.

De Leon, Estrella
Stuffed plantains "bolas de platano", 10086.

De Leon, Hector
Texas politics: a frank talk about leadership, Austin, state government and attorney Hector de Leon, 2781.

de Leon Hernandez, Victor
Un pecado, 9637.
Recuerdos de Manolo, 8695.

De los Angeles Ruano, Isabel
El cadaver, 8696.
No son muchos, 8697.

de los Santos, Alfredo G. Jr.
Chicano students in institutions of higher education: access, attrition, and achievement, 14.

de Olmedo, Jose Joaquin
The victory at Junin: song to Bolivar, 1356.

De Snyder, Nelly Salgado
USE: Salgado de Snyder, Nelly

De Soto, Rosana
Rosana de Soto: breaking the mold (interview), 568.

de Vallbona, Rima
El monstruo de las cosas, 9693.

Alma-en-pena, 9638.
El nagual de mi amiga Irene, 6614.

Dean, Raymond S.
Intelligence-achievement discrepancies in diagnosing pediatric learning disabilities, 386.

Deck, Allan Figueroa
Religious enthusiasm and Hispanic youths, 2325.

Decormier-Shekerjian, Regina
Her hands, 8700.
Pigeons limping in Venice...special to the New York Times, 8701.

Deibel, Richard
Business along la frontera, 1758.
Business on the border: attracting venture capital, 1730.
The nation's largest little bank: Laredo's International Bank of Commerce, 858.

Dejnozka, Edward L.
Selective admissions criteria in graduate teacher education programs, 3952.

del Castillo, Amelia
Cara al viento, 8706.
Mi poesia y yo, 8707.

Del Olmo, Frank
Latinos: they were a people living between two worlds (reprinted LOS ANGELES TIMES August 14, 1983), 6760.

Delgado, Abelardo "Lalo"
From Garden City to Hays, 8708.
The last wow, 8709.
An open letter to Carolina... or relations between men and women, 2471.

Delgado, Alberto
Los mexicanos, 8710.

Delgado, Melvin
Book review of: BASIC PROBLEMS OF ETHNOPSYCHIATRY, 911.
Ethnic and cultural variations in the care of the aged. Hispanic elderly and natural support systems: a special focus on Puerto Ricans, 350.
Hispanic natural support systems: implications for mental health services, 3328.
Hispanics and psychotherapeutic groups, 63.
Natural support systems: source of strength in Hispanic communities, 3217.

DeMauro, Gerald E.
Models and assumptions for bilingual education evaluation, 1032.

DeOrtega, Manuel R.

In the stomach of the shark: echoes of a culture in captivity, 657.

Desleal, Alvaro Menen
Oracion que ayuda a bien condenarse a un tirano, 8712.

Deukmejian, George
Welcoming the Commission of the Californias, 1760.

Devis, Rey
Prisons can't contain freedom, 4725.

Diaz, Barbara M.
Continuing the success: the Hispanic Women's Council, 782.
The great Valentino, 574.

Diaz, David
Cosmopolitan Angel Dust, 8713.

Diaz, Elisa G.
Bilingualism - a reality in these United States, 1146.

Diaz, Katherine A.
El Adobe Cafe: a recipe for success, 2290.
"And this year's winners are...", 783.
Chancellor Tomas Rivera on today's graduates, 5225.
Commercial radio and Hispanic community, 2312.
Congressman Edward Roybal: Los Angeles before the 1960's (interview), 5337.
The Dodger's Spanish voice: Jaime Jarrin, 6002.
Enrique Martinez: why I became a U.S. citizen, 6983.
Francisco Zuniga; el pueblo Mexicano su inspiracion, 575.
Henry Cisneros: our hope for today & tomorrow, 2741.
Henry G. Cisneros on Central American commission (interview), 2368.
Jose Feliciano, 576.
Jose Guadalupe Posada: documenting his people and his times=informandonos de su gente y su epoca, 577.
The many faceted talents of Danny Valdez=Los muchos y variados talentos de Danny Valdez, 1238.
Mike Gomez; pursuing his dream, 578.
The model of reflection: Rita Moreno, 579.
The people who make films happen, 4627.
El rey del timbal Tito Puente (interview), 6003.
ZOOT SUIT, 4601.

Diaz, Tom
Turning numbers into clout, 7912.
"Wetbacks" and other fellow Americans, 4284.

Diaz-Diocaretz, Myriam
Mujer de la tierra, 8714.
Musa amordazada, 8715.

Dickens, E. Larry
Book review of: THE POLITICS OF BILINGUAL EDUCATION: A STUDY OF FOUR SOUTHWEST TEXAS COMMUNITIES, 1033.

Dicker, Lois
Occupational health hazards faced by Hispanic workers: an exploratory discussion, 8102.

Dicker, Marvin
Occupational health hazards faced by Hispanic workers: an exploratory discussion, 8102.

Dickey, Dan W.
La musica nortena: a photographic essay, 6006.

Dickson, Harold
Characteristics of dropouts in longitudinal research on aging - a study of Mexican-Americans and Anglos, 360.

Dienhart, Paul
Minnesota support groups help Latinos through medical school, 5162.

Diez-Canedo, Juan
Undocumented migration to the United States: a new perspective, 5656.

Dochniak, Jim
Pro-life)maybe(/el salvador, 8716.

Dodge, Russell
A comparison of the respiratory health of Mexican-American and non-Mexican American white children, 387.

Power, 8729.
Tato hates the New York Yankees, 8730.

Esparza, Antonio
The new spectacular Tijuana cultural center, 2374.

Espinosa, Luis P.
Erendira, 8731.

Espinosa, Monica
Habra?, 10684.

Espinoza, Ana Luisa
Approaching our familias con corazon, 4404.
La Chicana cosmica, 2475.
Los ninos: la cosecha del futuro, 2665.
Los tatas, 4419.
Untitled Poem, 8732.

Espinoza, Danny J.
Beware of subways, 10686.
Conversations, 10687.
Life is, 8733.
Video games video games, 8734.

Espinoza, Herbert O.
Alas de carton, 10688.
At it ti tac, 9642.
Carrousel, 10689.
Examen final de literatura, 8735.
Lope de Aguirre y santos banderas, la manipulacion del mito, 3425.
La otra novia, 10690.
Viendo morir a teresa, 10691.

Espinoza, Roberto
Sintesis vs. analysis: un problema de historicidad en las novelas de las dictaduras, 2271.

Esquer, Cecilia D.
The impact of undocumented aliens on health and public health care in Arizona, 511.

Esquivel, Grace
The East L.A. mysterious lady, 10692.

Esteves, Sandra Maria
Amor negro, 8736.
A celebration of home birth, 8737.
For Noel Rico, 8738.
A Julia y a mi, 8739.
Portraits for Shamsul Alam, 8740.
Transference, 8741.
[Untitled poem], 8742.
[Untitled poem], 8743.

Estevez, Guillermo
Resettling the Cuban refugees in New Jersey, 2255.

Estrada, Antonio
Alcohol use among Hispanic adolescents; a preliminary report, 275.

Estrada, Leobardo F.
[Demographic characteristics of Latinos], 3457.
Significance of the 1980 census to Latinos, 2354.

Estrada, William
The Latino Olympians: Latin American participation in the Olympic Games 1896-1980, 8138.

Even, Brenda
Work and sex-role attitudes in relation to education and other characteristics, 2209.

Exezidis, Roxane H.
Research brief: sex and ethnic differences in mathematics achievement of Black and Mexican-American adolescents, 1314.

Exum, Herbert A.
The most invisible minority: the culturally diverse elderly, 351.

Ezell, P.
Research on Spanish colonial sites in San Diego, 446.

Fabre, Michel
Book review of: LES FILS DU SOLEIL: LA MINORITE MEXICAINE A TRAVERS LA LITTERATURE DES ETATS-UNIS, 1489.

Fabricio, Roberto
Voices, 1321.

Fainberg, Louise Vasvari
HUNGER OF MEMORY: review of a review, 1490.

Fallows, James

Language, 6231.

Fantin, Joyce
Some Hispanic stations trying bilingual approach, 1840.
Undocumented aliens ease concern over younger generation's cultural drift, 7745.

Farias, Eddie Jaime
Aztlan begins with the heart and the mind, 808.

Farmer, Mary
Bilingual integration in San Diego, 1038.

Feagin, Joe
After crossing Rio Bravo, 5723.

Feliciano, Jose
Escenas de amor: Jose Feliciano, 7746.

Feliciano-Foster, Wilma
A comparison of three current first-year college-level Spanish-for-native-speakers textbooks, 1492.

Fernandez, Angel Jose
Balada (en tono menor) para el culpable, 8744.

Fernandez, Celestino
Chicano-Anglo intermarriage in Arizona, 1960-1980: an exploratory study of eight counties, 508.
The neglected dimension: ethnicity in American life, 1493.

Fernandez, Diana
Undocumented aliens ease concern over younger generation's cultural drift, 7745.

Fernandez, Enrique
Cannes and CROSSOVER DREAMS, '83, 481.
Latin drop: retail sales decrease attributed to sweeps by Dept. of Immigration raids, 3484.
NARAS takes a welcome step, 785.
Notas: these ladies are not waiting, 582.
Youth acts dominating markets: labels woo kids with Spanish-language rock product, 4231.

Fernandez, John P.
Facing the hard realities of corporate advancement, 164.

Fernandez, Jose B.
Book review of: HISPANICS IN THE UNITED STATES: AN ANTHOLOGY OF CREATIVE LITERATURE, 1494.
Book review of: LA LLEGADA, 1495.

Fernandez, Maria Patricia
Book review of: TWICE A MINORITY; MEXICAN-AMERICAN WOMEN, 1496.

Fernandez Olmos, Margarite
From the metropolis: Puerto Rican women poets and the immigration experience, 4266.

Fernandez, Peter
The incredible F.P. hopper of varrio nuevo, 2588.

Fernandez, Roberta
Amanda, 9643.
Zulema, 9644.

Ferrarone, Aida
The aquarium conspiracy: personal and social transformation in the 80's: a review, 476.
Chasqui: a children's story, 2707.
Olympic skeet-shooter, 1240.

Ferre, Maurice A.
Decade of the Hispanic, 3166.
Marketplace of the Americas, 1904.

Ferree, W. P.
Affirmative action means progress: 2 corporations and one federal agency look at affirmative action, 168.

Ferullo, R. J.
Objectivity in the assessment of pre-school hearing impaired bilingual-Hispanic children, 1148.

Figueredo, D.H.
Old Havana, 9645.

Figueroa, John
Pueden los Hispanos costearse la television por cable?, 2058.

Fillmore, Lili Wong
Language minority students and school participation: what kind of English is needed?, 1039.

Fischman, Gladys, et al.
    Day treatment programs for the Spanish
        speaking: a response to underutilization,
        5425.
Fisher, Edith Maureen
    Minority librarianship research: a
        state-of-the-art review, 6504.
Fishman, Joshua A.
    Sociolinguistic foundations of bilingual
        education, 1040.
Fitzpatrick, Joseph P.
    Intermarriage among Hispanic ethnic groups in
        New York City, 5925.
La Flaca
    USE: Bustamante, Anna Luisa
Flaherty, Francis J.
    The struggle continues: protecting the rights
        of Hispanics in the U.S., 165.
Flaskerud, Jacquelyn H.
    Community mental health nursing: its unique
        role in the delivery of services to ethnic
        minorities, 641.
Fleming, Marilyn B.
    Problems experienced by Anglo, Hispanic and
        Navajo Indian women college students, 2477.
Flemming, Donald N.
    Book review of: EXPLORACIONES
        CHICANO-RIQUENAS, 1498.
Flood, Lawrence G.
    Correlates and consequences of socioeconomic
        differences among Chicanos, Blacks and
        Anglos in the Southwest: a study of
        metropolitan structure, 388.
Flores, Alfredo
    Benny Barrios, Sacramento's living landmark,
        534.
Flores, Bettina
    Benny Barrios, Sacramento's living landmark,
        534.
Flores, David
    30's gridder recalls pain of prejudice, 6490.
Flores de Apodaca, Roberto
    Quick socio-emotional screening of
        Mexican-American and other ethnic head start
        children, 322.
Flores, Fernando
    Flores on fashion, 4480.
Flores, Henry
    Some different thoughts concerning "machismo",
        2478.
Flores, Jose
    Bilingual success: a second language program
        that is making everyone happy (and smarter),
        1068.
    Las manos (para 'pa Agapito), 8747.
    Sabado, 8748.
Flores, Larry
    Affirmative action means progress: 2
        corporations and one federal agency look at
        affirmative action, 168.
Flores, Lauro
    A la mitad, 10695.
Flores, Rogelio
    The struggle for minority admissions: the UCLA
        experience, 831.
Flores-Ortiz, Yvette
    Latino families in therapy: engagement and
        evaluation, 4410.
Flori, Monica
    The Hispanic community as a resource for a
        practical Spanish program, 2875.
Forbes, Jack D.
    Hispanic-Mexican pioneers of the San Francisco
        Bay region: an analysis of racial origins,
        4312.
Ford, Charles A.
    Policy concerns over the impact of
        trade-related performance requirements and
        investment incentives on the international
        economy: Mexican automotive policy and
        U.S.-Mexican relations, 753.
Ford, Martin Z.
    Locus of control: a cross-cultural comparison,
        4488.

Forster, Merlin H.
    Luis Leal, 721.
Foster, Charles R.
    Defusing the issues in bilingualism and
        bilingual education, 1041.
    Political culture and regional ethnic
        minorities, 4313.
Foster, Douglas
    The desperate migrants of Devil's Canyon, 222.
Foster, Richard
    Two Alvarados make one sucessful construction
        firm, 299.
Fox, Martin
    Grand Jury selection upheld against test by
        Hispanics, 1858.
Fox-Chandonnet, Ann
    Masks, 8749.
Fradd, Sandra
    Cubans to Cuban Americans: assimilation in the
        United States, 658.
Fram, Steven J.
    Restricting inquiry into racial attitudes
        during the Voir Dire, 280.
France, Pauline
    Working with young bilingual children, 1150.
Francis, H.E., trans.
    Mirrors, 10747.
    My uncle smiled one Christmas, 10723.
Francis, Reynold S.
    Cost efficency, 8750.
Franco, Juan N.
    An acculturation scale for Mexican-American
        children, 66.
    Book review of: COUNSELING ACROSS CULTURES,
        1499.
    A developmental analysis of self concept in
        Mexican American and Anglo school children,
        67.
    The differences between personality inventory
        scores and self-rating in a sample of
        Hispanic subjects, 2470.
    Effects of therapist's gender, ethnicity, and
        verbal style on client's willingness to seek
        therapy, 3091.
Franklin, Gerald S.
    Group psychotherapy for elderly female
        Hispanic outpatients, 353.
Fraser Rothenberg, Irene
    Chicanos, the Panama Canal issues and the
        Reagan campaign: reflections from 1976 and
        projections for 1980, 5963.
    Mexican-American views of U.S. relations with
        Latin America, 2589.
Frazier, Donald J.
    Comparison of self-concept in Mexican American
        and non-Mexican American late adolescents,
        16.
Freed, Ray
    Josephina, 8751.
Freeman, Frank E.
    Experimenter effects in biofeedback training,
        1189.
Freeman, Marion
    La onda and other youthful Mexican
        expressions, 6248.
Fregoso, Linda
    Sequin: the same side of the Alamo, 4583.
Frerichs, Ralph R.
    Race, ethnicity, and depression: a
        confirmatory analysis, 2887.
Friedenberg, Joan E.
    Tips for the English speaking multicultural
        vocational teacher, 3287.
Friedman, Florence
    Living and working in a lighthouse, 6017.
Friedman, Mary Lusky
    Notes on the grading of advanced placement
        Spanish language examination, 3955.
Frisbie, W. Parker
    Potential labor force supply and replacement
        in Mexico and the states of the Mexican
        cession and Texas: 1980-2000, 5645.
Fu, Victoria R.
    A development study of ethnic self-concept

Greenberg, Julie L.
    Dating and the elderly, 354.
Greenblatt, Milton
    Hispanic mental health and use of mental
        health services: a critical review of the
        literature, 6677.
Greenfield, Charles
    Armando Valladares: twenty-two years of
        solitude, 3148.
    Cuban theater in exile: Miami's little
        Broadway, 3171.
    Cuba's matriarch of letters: Lydia Cabrera,
        723.
    Life imitating art: a profile of Reynaldo
        Arenas, 489.
    Q & A with Lydia Cabrera, 725.
    Spanish prince of song, 4232.
    Writing in exile, 726.
Greenleaf, Cynthia
    Legacy, 8796.
Grelier, Robert
    Film review of: CHICANOS STORY, 4585.
Griego, Richard J.
    Crisis in science education: from Sputnik to
        Pac-man, 3822.
Griffin, Julia Ortiz
    Two artists in search of a country: Rafael
        Rios Rey and Francisco Arrivi, 524.
Griffith, James
    Re-examination of Mexican American service
        utilization and mental health need, 4396.
    Relationship between acculturation and
        psychological impairment in adult Mexican
        Americans, 69.
Grijalva, Joshua
    The story of Hispanic Southern Baptists, 875.
Grimond, John
    Reconquista begins, 9333.
    The reconquista begins, 3461.
Griswold del Castillo, Richard
    Book review of: DICTIONARY OF MEXICAN-AMERICAN
        HISTORY, 1521.
    Book review of: IMAGES OF THE MEXICAN-AMERICAN
        IN FICTION AND FILM, 1522.
    Book review of: REVOLTOSOS: MEXICO'S REBELS IN
        THE UNITED STATES 1903-1923, 1523.
    Book review of: THE CHICANOS OF EL PASO: AN
        ASSESSMENT OF PROGRESS, 1524.
    La familia Chicana: social change in the
        Chicano family of Los Angeles, 1850-1880,
        4424.
Guckert, John C.
    Multiculturalism: a democratic approach to
        education, 3292.
Guendelman, Sylvia
    Developing responsiveness to health needs of
        Hispanic children and families, 2670.
Guernica, Antonio
    Consumer Hispanic: a dual identity, 135.
    The Hispanic market: a profile, 2990.
    El mercado hispano, 1907.
Guerra, Vicente
    Hermandad iberoamericana, 8797.
Guerra, Victor
    An interview with Rodrigo Duarte of Teatro de
        la Esperanza, August 13, 1982/New York City,
        3695.
Guerra-Cunningham, Lucia
    La estafa de Eros, 10706.
Guerra-Garza, Victor
    Ecos del barrio, 8798.
Guerrero, Lena
    [Untitled interview with State Senators
        (Colorado) Polly Baca-Barragan and Lena
        Guerrero, 815.
Guerrero, Yolanda E.
    La funcion del mito: NAMBE-YEAR ONE, 6560.
Guillen, Pablo
    Que puedo darte..., 8799.
    Volver a empezar, 8800.
    Voy a denunciar al silencio, 8801.
Gumperz, John J.
    Hispanic Catholics, 2331.

Interethnic discourse, 6271.
Gupta, Udayan
    Hispanic foods in New York: the race for
        number two, 2345.
    Netting success: Apoca's approach, 7.
    New York's WNJU Channel 47: Spanish TV's
        hottest item, 136.
Gurak, Douglas T.
    Intermarriage among Hispanic ethnic groups in
        New York City, 5925.
Gurwitt, Rob
    Widespread political efforts open new era for
        Hispanics, 983.
Gutierrez, Adolfo
    El cinco, 8802.
Gutierrez, Bonifacia
    Una tamalada: a family tradition in the works,
        10090.
Gutierrez, Chela
    Flicks in review, 4586.
Gutierrez, Felix
    Breaking through the media employment wall,
        4102.
    Henry Rivera: our Hispanic on the FCC, 4500.
Gutierrez, John R.
    Book review of: TEACHING SPANISH TO THE
        HISPANIC BILINGUAL: ISSUES, AIMS AND
        METHODS, 1158.
Gutierrez, Mary Grace
    Ethno-medical beliefs and practices of
        Mexican-Americans, 3331.
Gutierrez, Silvio
    Cinema, 4587.
    Fernando Favela: street wise and sexy, 1254.
Gutierrez-Revuelta, Pedro
    A marilyn con unas violetas, 8803.
    Democracia a blas de otero, 8804.
    Juan perez, teacher de lengua, 9650.
    No draft, no war, U.S. out of El Salvador,
        8805.
    Oda a san diego, 8806.
    Oda a walt disney (pacto con china), 8807.
    Take 5, 8808.
    Una dos y tres, 8809.
    U.s.a., 8810.
Gwynne, John
    Ethnicity and Bender Visual Motor Gestalt Test
        performance, 417.
Haft, Jonathan D.
    Assuring equal educational opportunity for
        language-minority students: bilingual
        education and the Equal Educational
        Opportunity Act of 1974, 1047.
Haggerty, Alfred G.
    Occidental goes after Hispanic market, 3176.
Hall, Robert
    Comparison of behavioral ratings of
        Anglo-American and Mexican-American gifted
        children, 377.
Hammerback, John C.
    "No revolutions without poets": the rhetoric
        of Rodolfo "Corky" Gonzales, 2592.
Hamner, Richard
    Hispanic update: border governors tackle
        U.S.-Mexico relations: much ado: but
        nothing on immigration, 812.
    Hispanic update: changing of the LULAC
        guard--almost, 1360.
    Hispanic update: Hispanics and the Republican
        Party, 9334.
    Hispanics and redistricting: what you see is
        not always what you get, 941.
    [Untitled interview with State Senators
        (Colorado) Polly Baca-Barragan and Lena
        Guerrero, 815.
Haner, Lisa G.
    The new wave: strangers in our land, 659.
Hanis, Craig L., et al.
    Diabetes among Mexican Americans in Starr
        County, Texas, 3522.
Hann, Donna
    Affirmative action means progress: 2
        corporations and one federal agency look at
        affirmative action, 168.

Hill, Patricia Liggins
    Book review of: THE THIRD WOMAN: MINORITY
        WRITERS OF THE UNITED STATES, 1531.
Hines, Bea L.
    Voices, 1321.
Hines, Thomas S.
    Housing, baseball, and creeping socialism: the
        battle of Chavez Ravine, Los Angeles,
        1949-1959, 896.
Hinestrosa, Dukardo
    Canto sin estrellas, 8831.
Hing, Bill Ong
    Racial disparity: the unaddressed issues of
        the Simpson-Mazzoli Bill, 323.
Hinkle, Dennis E.
    A development study of ethnic self-concept
        among pre-adolescent girls, 2481.
Hinojosa-Smith, Rolando R.
    Con el pie en el estribo, 10709.
    Don Orfalindo Buitureyra, 9651.
    I AM JOAQUIN: relationships between the text
        and the film, 4589.
    Luis (el amigo) Leal, 728.
    Un poco de todo, 9652.
    Reflections on fathers: out of many lives:
        one, 4428.
    Retaguardia en no noviembre which means: the
        219th isn't doing well at all, 8832.
    The rites, 9653.
    Rolando Hinojosa: entrevista, 734.
Hitchens, Theresa
    Astronomy, 8833.
    Harvest, 8834.
    In black and white, 8835.
    Tristan, 8836.
    Winter feeding (to little sis), 8837.
Hoffer, Bates L.
    Sociology by value systems: explication and
        some implications of two studies on the
        folklore of Hispanics in the United States,
        937.
Hoffman, Abraham
    Book review of: MEXICANO RESISTANCE IN THE
        SOUTHWEST: "THE SACRED RIGHT OF
        SELF-PRESERVATION", 1532.
    Book review of: MEXICANO RESISTANCE IN THE
        SOUTHWEST: "THE SACRED RIGHT OF
        SELF-PRESERVATION", 1533.
    Chicano history: problems and potentialities,
        5345.
Holck, Susan E.
    Lung cancer mortality and smoking habits:
        Mexican-American women, 393.
Holck, Susan E., et al.
    Need for family planning services among Anglo
        and Hispanic women in the United States
        counties bordering Mexico, 394.
Holdenreid, Frank X.
    Guatemala shantytown, 799.
Holley, Joe
    Farmworker wins the right to sue, 226.
    Page two, 2861.
Holmberg, Joan J.
    The assimilation of Cubans in the United
        States, 665.
    Book review of: THE CHANGING DEMOGRAPHY OF
        SPANISH-AMERICANS, 1534.
Holscher, Louis M.
    Chicano-Anglo intermarriage in Arizona,
        1960-1980: an exploratory study of eight
        counties, 508.
    Tiene arte valor afuera del barrio: the murals
        of East Los Angeles and Boyle Heights, 539.
Holston, Mark
    The Walter Cronkite of Mexico, 3124.
Holzman, Michael
    Tar, 8838.
Honomichl, Jack
    How to research U.S. Hispanic market, 6891.
    Never lose sight of Hispanic pride, 139.
Hopkins, Kenneth D.
    Effects of books in Spanish and free reading
        time on Hispanic students' reading abilities
        and attitudes, 1094.

Hopson, Susan B.
    Immigration: indefinite detention of excluded
        aliens held illegal, 2766.
Hornbeck, David
    Book review of: STUDIES IN SPANISH-AMERICAN
        POPULATION HISTORY, 1535.
Hough, Richard
    The Los Angeles Epidemiologic Catchment Area
        research program and the epidemiology of
        psychiatric disorders among Mexican
        Americans, 72.
Howard, David
    For "illegals" migration goes both ways, 5670.
Howell, Frances Baseden
    Split labor market: Mexican farm workers in
        the Southwest, 209.
HRV
    Time and time again, 8839.
Hsi, Bartholomew P.
    Ventilatory functions of normal children and
        young adults: Mexican-American, white and
        black. III. Sitting height as a predictor,
        395.
Hsu, Katherine H.
    Ventilatory functions of normal children and
        young adults: Mexican-American, white and
        black. III. Sitting height as a predictor,
        395.
Hudelson, Sarah
    An introductory examination of children's
        invented spelling in Spanish, 1048.
Huerta, Grace C.
    Mother's day reflections: a woman of means,
        2500.
Huerta, John
    The future of Latino political power, 2362.
Huerta, Jorge A.
    Book review of: CHICANO THEATER: THEMES AND
        FORMS, 1536.
    The influences of Latin American theatre on
        teatro Chicano, 6301.
Hui, C. Harry
    Analysis of the modernity scale: an item
        response theory approach, 2891.
    Multistrategy approach to cross-cultural
        research: the case of locus of control,
        2892.
Hulin-Salkin, Belinda
    Films need mass appeal, 1844.
Hull, Elizabeth
    Los indocumentados: practices,
        recommendations, and proposals, 11787.
Humm-Delgado, Denise
    Natural support systems: source of strength in
        Hispanic communities, 3217.
Hunsaker, Alan
    Book review of: ALMA ABIERTA: PINTO POETRY,
        MAYO DE CRC, 289.
    Book review of: ANGEL DUST: AN ETHNOGRAPHIC
        STUDY OF PCP USERS; HEROIN USE IN THE
        BARRIO; DRUG AND ALCOHOL ABUSE: A CLINICAL
        GUIDE TO DIAGNOSIS AND TREATMENT, 189.
    Book review of: PSYCHOLOGY AND COMMUNITY
        CHANGE; SOCIAL AND PSYCHOLOGICAL RESEARCH IN
        COMMUNITY SETTING; COMMUNITY PSYCHOLOGY:
        THEORETICAL AND EMPIRICAL APPROACHES, 1540.
    Book review of: STRESSFUL LIFE EVENTS: THEIR
        NATURE AND EFFECTS, 1541.
    A prompt/reward technique to elicit socially
        acceptable behavior with Chicano gang
        delinquents, 924.
Hunt, Isabelle F., et al.
    Zinc supplementation during pregnancy: zinc
        concentration of serum and hair from
        low-income women of Mexican descent, 2501.
Hwang, Sean-Shong
    Residential segregation in Texas in 1980,
        5438.
Iadicola, Peter
    The desegregated school and status relations
        among Anglo and Hispanic students: the
        dilemma of school desegregation, 2883.
    Schooling and symbolic violence: the effect of
        power differences and curriculum factors on

Hispanic students' attitudes toward their
own ethnicity, 5545.
Ibargoyen Islas, Saul
Soledad propia, 8840.
Inclan, Jaime
Structural family therapy training in family
medicine, 4459.
Infante, Martha
Their little scheme, 10710.
Irizarry, Estelle
La abuelita in literature, 291.
Frijoles boiling musically, 4781.
Islas, Maya
He dudado, 8841.
Palabras del ave, 8842.
Islas, Saul
Otra vez octubre, 8843.
Jacobs, Teresa
Ara, 8844.
Ceremonies, 8845.
Metamorfose, 8846.
Jaech, Richard E.
Latin American undocumented women in the
United States, 4934.
Jamail, Milton H.
Book review of: MEXICO IN TRANSITION, 1542.
The International Boundary and Water
Commission as a conflict management agency
in the U.S.-Mexico borderlands, 1774.
Jaramillo, Patricio T.
Concerns of college bound Mexican-American
students, 695.
Jenkins, Daniel E.
Ventilatory functions of normal children and
young adults: Mexican-American, white and
black. III. Sitting height as a predictor,
395.
Jenoveva
La Chicana: principle of life, survival and
endurance, 2504.
Jensen, Carol
Cleofas M. Jaramillo on marriage in
territorial Northern New Mexico, 6001.
Jensen, Gary F.
Ethnic status and adolescent self-evaluations:
an extension of research on minority
self-esteem, 510.
Jensen, Joan M.
Canning comes to New Mexico: women and the
agricultural extension service, 1914-1919,
2161.
Women teachers, class and ethnicity: New
Mexico 1900-1950, 294.
Jensen, Richard J.
"No revolutions without poets": the rhetoric
of Rodolfo "Corky" Gonzales, 2592.
Jimenez, Carlos M.
Crisis in Chicano schools, 3826.
Jimenez, Ricardo
Understanding the culture and learning styles
of Hispanic students, 3225.
Joe, Harry J.
Judicial recommendation against deportation,
3488.
John, Elizabeth A.H.
Book review of: THE MEXICAN FRONTIER,
1821-1846: THE AMERICAN SOUTHWEST UNDER
MEXICO, 1544.
Johnson, Dale L.
The Houston Parent-Child Development Center
and the primary prevention of behavior
problems in young children, 2636.
Johnson, Donna M.
Natural language learning by design: a
classroom experiment in social interaction
and second language acquisition, 4197.
Johnson, Greg
Administracion en un medio ambiente hispanico,
5877.
Jones, B.E.
Manic-depressive illness among poor urban
Hispanics, 1857.
Jones, Errol D.
Book review of: DICTIONARY OF MEXICAN-AMERICAN

HISTORY, 1545.
Jones, Oakah L.
Book review of: THE MEXICAN FRONTIER,
1821-1846: THE AMERICAN SOUTHWEST UNDER
MEXICO, 1546.
Jones, Priscilla
Bilingual vocational education for handicapped
students, 1080.
Jones, Richard C.
Reply to Robert Austin's "Comment on
undocumented migration from Mexico: some
geographical questions", 709.
Undocumented migration from Mexico: some
geographical questions, 4957.
Jones, Robert C.
Channelization of undocumented Mexican
migrants to the U.S., 5675.
Josber
A la siega, 8848.
Ansias, 8849.
Josel, Nathan A.
Public library material selection in a
bilingual community, 1161.
Juarez, Richard
Third international conference of the U.S.-
Mexico border governors, 1767.
Jurado, Rebecca
Abstract: Dodge and McCauley, REAPPORTIONMENT:
A SURVEY OF THE PRACTICALITY OF VOTING
EQUALITY, 43 U. PITT. L. Rev. 527 (1982),
10076.
Justiz, Manuel J.
Six community colleges share resources to meet
the needs of Mexican-American students
linking together to solve a common need,
2827.
Kagan, Spencer
Cultural differences in individualism? Just
artifact, 396.
Culture and the development of conflict
resolution style, 397.
Differential development of empathy and
pro-social behavior, 404.
Perceived parental practices and prosocial
development, 401.
Relationship of empathy and affective
role-taking in young children, 398.
Sibling, birth order, and
cooperative-competitive social behavior: a
comparison of Anglo-American and
Mexican-American children, 402.
Kahn, Marrin W.
Psycho-pathology, treatment outcome and
attitude toward mental illness in
Mexican-American and European patients, 405.
Kanellos, Nicolas
Devorados pero no digeridos. Paper presented
at the "Dialogo de las Americas" conference.
Mexico, D.F. September 9-13, 1982, 984.
The flourishing of Hispanic theater in the
Southwest, 1920-30s, 4731.
REVISTA CHICANO-RIQUENA/Arte Publico Press,
6049.
Two centuries of Hispanic theatre in the
Southwest, 2092.
Kanellos, Nicolas, ed.
Mexican American theatre: then and now, 11444.
Kappel, Mark
A new career direction for Hilda Morales,
3384.
Karam, Bruce G.
The murals of Tucson, 540.
Karanikas, Marianthe
A boa from Brazil, 8850.
Tu companera Guachita, 8851.
Karno, M.
Development of the Spanish-language version of
the National Institute of Mental Health
Diagnostic Interview Schedule, 3318.
Katra, William H.
'Taller de imagenes': a poetic cosmovision,
7181.
Kaufman, Karen S.
Group psychotherapy for elderly female

Hispanic outpatients, 353.

Keefe, Susan Emily
Help-seeking behavior among foreign-born and
native-born Mexican-Americans, 73.

Keep, Paul M.
Overhauling the immigration code: this year,
Congress may finally act, 308.

Keller, Gary
Ballad of an unsung hero, 836.
The image of the Chicano in Mexican, Chicano,
and Chicano cinema: an overview, 4591.

Keller, Gary D., ed.
Chicano cinema research, reviews, and
resources, 4640.

Kelly, Philip
Book review of: OPERATION WETBACK: THE MASS
DEPORTATION OF MEXICAN UNDOCUMENTED WORKERS
IN 1954, 1547.
Mexican Americans as participants in United
States-Mexico relations, 5972.

Kennedy, Edward M.
Twentieth anniversary tribute to President
John F. Kennedy, 6094.

Keogh, Barbara K.
Testwiseness as a factor in readiness test
performance of young Mexican-American
children, 15.

Kerns, Chloe Jane
Now, I just dance, 8853.
Shock treatment, 8854.
Untitled #73, 8855.

Kerr, G. R.
Supermarket sales high-sugar products in
predominantly Black, Hispanic and white
census tracts of Houston, Texas, 399.

Kincaid, Jill
LULAC opposes youth subminimum wage proposal,
5862.
You can help 3.6 million children, 1050.

King, Allan G.
The number of illegal migrants of Mexican
origin in the United States: sex ratio-based
estimates for 1980, 2348.

King, John S.
California Farm Bureau Federation: addressing
the issue/conduciendo el topico, 2119.

King, Karen
Hope comes to Apopka: on working alongside the
poor, 454.

Kirschner, Carl
Mary likes fishes: reverse psychological
phenomena in New York Puerto Rican Spanish,
7994.
Spanish and English inchoatives and the
Spanish-English bilingual: got anything to
se?, 5042.

Kirschten, Dick
The Hispanic vote: parties can't gamble that
the sleeping giant won't awaken, 3447.

Kivisto, Peter
Book review of: FARM WORKERS, AGRIBUSINESS,
AND THE STATE, 201.

Kjolseth, Rolf
Cultural politics of bilingualism, 1162.

Klein, Carol A.
Children's concepts of the earth and the sun:
a cross cultural study, 400.

Klor de Alva, Jorge
Book review of: PELON DROPS OUT, 1549.
Gabino Barrera and Chicano thought, 884.

Kluck, Frederick J.
French via Spanish: a positive approach to
language learning for minority students,
3899.

Knight, Alan
Book review of: THE GREAT REBELLION: MEXICO
1905-1924 and DESERT IMMIGRANTS: THE
MEXICANS OF EL PASO 1880-1920, 1550.

Knight, George P.
Culture and the development of conflict
resolution style, 397.
Perceived parental practices and prosocial
development, 401.
Sibling, birth order, and

cooperative-competitive social behavior: a
comparison of Anglo-American and
Mexican-American children, 402.

Knight, George P., et al.
Cooperative-competitive social orientation and
school achievement among Anglo-American and
Mexican-American children, 19.

Knudsen, Kathryn H.M.
Differential development of empathy and
pro-social behavior, 404.
Relationship of empathy and affective
role-taking in young children, 398.

Kopp, April
Chile, spice of the southwest, 2718.

Korslund, Mary K.
A development study of ethnic self-concept
among pre-adolescent girls, 2481.

Korte, Alvin O.
Social interaction and morale of
Spanish-speaking rural and urban elderly,
357.

Kozmetsky, George
Public opinion regarding illegal aliens in
Texas, 9807.

Kozoll, Richard
Checkerboard area health system: delivering
comprehensive care in a remote region of New
Mexico, 7118.

Kramer, Virginia Reyes
English auditory discrimination skills of
Spanish-speaking children, 49.

Kranau, Edgar J.
Acculturation and the Hispanic woman:
attitudes toward women, sex-role
attribution, sex-role behavior, and
demographics, 74.

Krashen, Stephen D.
Bilingual education and the case of Richard
Rodriguez, 1051.

Krivo, Lauren J.
Housing price inequalities: a comparison of
Anglos, Blacks, and Spanish-origin
populations, 5439.

Kugle, Cherry L.
Level and stability of self-esteem in relation
to academic behavior of second graders, 20.

La Fond, Vita
Calexico, where windows, 8856.

Lacayo, Carmela G.
A response to conservatism: a Democrat's
opinion, 3448.

Lado, Robert
Aula/the classroom: developmental reading in
two languages, 1052.

Laguardia, Gari
The canon and the air-conditioner: modern
Puerto Rican poetry, 1551.

Laguna, Jaime
Enrique Serin: Mexico's violin ambassador,
2777.

Lalas, Joselito W.
The influence of prior experience in ESL
reading, 1053.

Lamare, James W.
Political integration of Mexican American
children: a generational analysis, 75.

Lamm, Richard D.
Why the U.S. closed its borders, 5678.

Lampe, Philip E.
Female Mexican Americans: minority within a
minority, 2508.

Langenwalter, P. E.
Problems in California Hispanic ethno-zoology
[meeting abstract], 12436.

Langley, Roger
Roger Langley's Hispanic beat, 4772.
Roger Langley's Hispanic beat, 457.
Roger Langley's Hispanic beat, 5019.
Roger Langley's Hispanic beat, 1846.
Roger Langley's Hispanic beat, 7393.

Langum, D.J.
From condemnation to praise: shifting
perspectives on Hispanic California, 2093.

Lanier, Alfredo S.

Continental's Fidel Lopez takes an
encompassing view, 1263.
Making it seem easy, from intern to account
executive, 54.
The quicksilver world of television news: Phil
Ponce's Chicago beat, 6034.

Laosa, Luis M.
School occupation, culture, and family: the
impact of parental schooling on the
parent-child relationship, 21.

Laraque, Paul
El reino del hombre, 8858.

Larrosa, Mara
Carta a Zanabria, 9655.
Espaldas negras, 8859.

Lasater, Tonia Tash
Training child welfare workers for cultural
awareness: the culture simulator technique,
2647.
Understanding Mexican American culture: a
training program, 3229.

Laska, Vera
Book review of: DICTIONARY OF MEXICAN-AMERICAN
HISTORY, 1552.

Lathrop, Richard A.
Out of tragedy, 9281.

Lattin, Vernon E.
Book review of: THE DOCILE PUERTO RICAN, 1553.
Ethnicity and identity in the contemporary
Chicano novel, 751.
La meta critica Chicana, 500.
Novelistic structure and myth in ...Y NO SE LO
TRAGO LA TIERRA, 6625.

Laval, Ramon
Psychotherapy and bilingualism: is
acculturation important?, 1156.

Laviera, Tato
Angelito's eulogy in anger, 8860.
The song of an oppressor, 8861.
Standards, 8862.
Tito Madera Smith, 8863.

Laws, Bart
Raza unida de Cristal, 3139.

Lawson, Harry H.
Psycho-pathology, treatment outcome and
attitude toward mental illness in
Mexican-American and European patients, 405.

Lazarus, Philip J.
Cross-cultural child-rearing practices:
implications for school psychologists, 2634.

Leal, Luis
Aves zancudas, 8864.
Caracol, 8865.
Con Borges en el sueno, 8866.
Coyolxauhqui, 8867.
El Dios viejo, 8868.
Fabula de la luna y el astro, 8869.
Gabino Barreda y la literatura: de la
preparatoria al Ateneo, 682.
Magueyes, 8870.
La noche triste, 8871.
La noria del tiempo, 8872.
Pavo irreal, 8873.
El retorno, 8874.
El sarape de la existencia, 8875.
Tlapala, 8876.
Los voladores: from ritual to game, 3385.
Xibalba, 8877.

LeCompte, Mary Lou
The first American rodeo never happened, 2396.

Leigh, Monroe
United States Constitution - equal protection
deprivation of education in illegal alien
school-children not justified by substantial
state goal, 2679.

Lenti, Paul
Accent: the Mexican retablo - a highly
collectable folk art, 556.
Frida Kahlo, 597.
Mexico's posadas a unique experience, 2725.
Special honor goes to Montalban, 598.

Leudtke, Luther S.
POCHO and the American dream, 6626.

Levario, Raquel

Asner tells it like it is, 599.
LULAC takes a stand against mainstream media,
4239.
Our children are watching, 2510.

Levin, Betsy
An analysis of the federal attempt to regulate
bilingual education: protecting civil rights
or controlling curriculum?, 188.

LeVine, Elaine S.
Book review of: PSYCHOLOGY OF THE MEXICAN
CULTURE AND PERSONALITY, 1644.
Effects of therapist's gender, ethnicity, and
verbal style on client's willingness to seek
therapy, 3091.

Levine, Paul G.
Remember the Alamo?, 4592.

Levoy, Claire
Melendez v. Burciaga: revealing the state of
the art in bar examinations, 6105.

Lewels, Francisco J.
Un mensaje, 7034.

Lewis, Marvin A.
Book review of: THE IDENTIFICATION AND
ANALYSIS OF CHICANO LITERATURE, 1554.

Lewis, Rose
Poisons: handle with care, 9780.

Lewis, William
Machismo and the will to win, 6831.
The milk of human kindness, 10711.
Song of Lia, 10712.
Song of Lia, 9656.
Tres Plumas and his pantheon of archetypal
deities, 249.

Leyna, Mariano
El miedo de la muerte, 8879.

Lezcano, Manuel
Read this when I die (again) please, 8880.

Liberty, Paul G.
Director's notebook, 1055.
Director's notebook, 1056.
Director's notebook, 1057.
Director's notebook, 1058.

Liberty, Paul G., et al.
[Evaluation in bilingual education], 1059.

Liebowitz, Arnold
Immigration challenge and the congressional
response, 324.

Limon, Jose
History, Chicano joking, and the varieties of
higher-education: tradition and performance
as critical symbolic action, 2722.

Limon, Margarita
Las flores, 8881.

Limon, Mercedes
Esperame en la historia Che Guevara, 8882.
Mentira, 8883.

Lindemann, Constance
The fertility related behavior of Mexican
American adolescents, 4546.

Lindsey, Alfred J.
Ethnic pluralism: a misguided approach to
schooling, 662.

Lippard, Lucy R.
Book review of: FRIDA: A BIOGRAPHY OF FRIDA
KAHLO, 1555.

Lipski, John M.
Spanish-English language switching in speech
and literature: theories and models, 50.

Lipton, Jack P.
Racism in the jury box: the Hispanic
defendant, 3098.
Theoretical perspectives on Chicano
personality development, 3312.

Lira, Pedro Antonio
El Onceno Festival Chicano-Latino de Teatro,
4069.

Lizarraga Duerfeldt, Martha
The most blessed profession, 10714.

Lizarraga, Sylvia S.
Don?, 10715.
Observaciones acerca de la critica literaria
Chicana, 1868.

Llabre, Maria M.
Effects of test language and mathematical

undocumented workers in Mexican cinema,
1954-1982, 4593.
MacManus, Susan A.
Mexican-Americans in city-politics:
participation, representation, and policy
preferences, 1326.
Madrid, A.
The problematics of the Chicano experience and
its literature, 6566.
Madrid, Arturo
Book review of: HUNGER OF MEMORY: THE
EDUCATION OF RICHARD RODRIGUEZ, 1563.
The mis-education of rich-heard
road-ree-guess, 663.
Madrid, Joe
The brat; looking for the best, 1818.
Los Illegals, 5592.
The multi-faceted Pepe Serna (interview), 604.
NALEO - honoring the Hispanic Medal of Honor
winners, 7093.
Q & A with Joan Baez, 605.
Warrior of the sun, 606.
Maduro, Renaldo J.
Working with Latinos and the use of dream
analysis, 3319.
Maestas, Leo C.
Academic performance across cultures: an
examination of the effect of value
similarity, 23.
Maestas, R. W.
Bilingualism in business education, 1167.
Magallan, Rafael J.
Resume/overview: insights into the needs of a
new source of students, 5236.
Magorian, James
Blizzard, 8919.
Small town, 8920.
Mahan, James M.
Concerns of Anglo secondary student teachers
in Hispanic communities: a pilot study,
2884.
Maiz, Magdalena
Book review of: OCCUPIED AMERICA, 99.
MALDEF
USE: Mexican American Legal Defense and
Education Fund (MALDEF)
Maldonado, Lionel A.
America's Mexicans: a plea for specificity,
2355.
Maldonado-Denis, Manuel
El problema de las nacionalidades: la
experiencia caribena. Paper presented at
the "Dialogo de las Americas" conference.
Mexico, D.F. September 9-14, 1982, 2172.
Malgady, Robert G.
Verbal fluency of Hispanic, Black and white
children on TAT and TEMAS, a new thematic
apperception test, 2659.
Malina, Robert M.
Growth and body composition of
Mexican-American boys 9 through 14 years of
age, 194.
Mamer, John W.
Hired workers on California farms, 229.
Manazar
USE: Gamboa, Manuel "Manazar"
Manley, Joan H.
The international bilingual city: how a
university meets the challenge, 980.
Manning, Roberta
Book review of: CHICANO INTERMARRIAGE: A
THEORETICAL AND EMPIRICAL STUDY, 1566.
Manpower Inc.
Hispanics in the labor force: data, 6160.
Mansilla, Juan
Alabanza a pinochet, 8921.
Manta, Ben
Toward economic development of the Chicano
barrio: alternative strategies and their
implications [reprint of DE COLORES
article], 2173.
Mariaurelia
Explanation, 8922.
Mallory Docks, Key West, 8923.

Marin, Barbara Van Oss, et al.
Utilization of traditional and non-traditional
sources of health care among Hispanics,
7109.
Markides, Kyraikos S.
Aging, religiosity, and adjustment: a
longitudinal analysis, 359.
Characteristics of dropouts in longitudinal
research on aging - a study of
Mexican-Americans and Anglos, 360.
Markiewicz, Dana
Book review of: MEXICAN CINEMA: REFLECTIONS OF
SOCIETY, 1896-1980, 1567.
Marquez, Alberto
Bomba de gasolina, 8924.
Madre, 8925.
Marquez, Antonio
The American dream in the Chicano novel, 6567.
A discordant image: the Mexican in American
literature, 6633.
Marquez, Maria Teresa
Book review of: A SELECTED AND ANNOTATED
BIBLIOGRAPHY OF CHICANO STUDIES, 962.
Marquez, Roberto
Experiencing state government, 6744.
Marshall, Peter
[Untitled photograph], 8437.
Marta
[Untitled graphic], 5055.
Marti, Oscar R.
Barrera and moral philosophy, 886.
Introduction, 887.
Marti, Oscar R., comp.
Bibliography, 888.
Martin, Philip
Foreign workers in selected California crops,
230.
Hired workers on California farms, 229.
Martin, Philip L.
Select Commission suggests changes in
immigration policy: a review essay, 5681.
Martinez, Alma
Alma Martinez: "I'm keeping my fingers
crossed" (interview), 566.
Martinez, Anita
Tortilla demonstration, 10095.
Martinez, Arthur D.
Mexican-Americans: Qua the
assistant-Americans, 4114.
Martinez, Chip
Agui vienen los Pena, 9418.
Federico Pena: Denver's first Hispanic mayor,
3476.
Martinez, D. G.
[Untitled drawing], 3637.
Martinez, Danny
Mother's Day reflections: master gardener,
4431.
Martinez, Douglas R.
American spelling bee: enchilada, llano,
amigo, maraca, 316.
Book review of: THE SILENCE OF THE LLANO, 338.
Down on the farm with the Cisco Kid, 245.
Sharing the silence, 339.
Martinez, Elisa A.
Sharing her tiny pieces of the past, 748.
Sharing her tiny pieces of the past, 4432.
Martinez, Elizabeth
The "Kiko" Martinez case: a sign of our times,
104.
Martinez, Iris Zavala
An analysis of culturalism in Latino mental
health: folk medicine as a case in point,
3307.
Martinez, Julio A.
Book review of: A BIBLIOGRAPHY OF CRITICISM OF
CONTEMPORARY CHICANO LITERATURE, 964.
Book review of: A DECADE OF CHICANO LITERATURE
(1970-1979)-CRITICAL ESSAYS AND
BIBLIOGRAPHY, 965.
Book review of: DICTIONARY OF MEXICAN-AMERICAN
HISTORY, 1573.
Martinez, Mardell
La banda, 8926.

Come again, 8927.

Por mi padre, 8928.

Martinez, Maria

The kiss of the butterfly, 8929.

Sterling silver roses, 8930.

Martinez, Marie

CORRIDO run clipped by national film
distributors, 841.

Luis Avalos: what a man, and what a talent,
759.

Lynda Cordoba Carter, 1273.

A morenita and a rubia visit Rodeo Drive for a
sleek make-over, 3063.

Martinez, Max

The adventures of the Chicano Kid: a dime
novel, 9659.

Martinez, Olivia

Bilingual education today, 1060.

Martinez, Ollin

Visitas e imagenes mexicanas; reflections of a
photographer (photoessay), 7405.

Martinez, Oscar J.

Book review of: DESERT IMMIGRANTS: THE
MEXICANS OF EL PASO 1880-1920, 1574.

Book review of: OPERATION WETBACK: THE MASS
DEPORTATION OF MEXICAN UNDOCUMENTED WORKERS
IN 1954, 1575.

Book review of: REVOLTOSOS: MEXICO'S REBELS IN
THE UNITED STATES 1903-1923, 1576.

Martinez, Paul E.

Serna v. Portales: the plight of bilingual
education four years later, 1061.

Martinez, Ramon E.

The jockey, 8931.

Martinez, Renato

Cancion de cuna para una nina que no comio
pan, 8932.

Martinez, Ricardo A.

The healing ritual [complete novel], 9660.

Martinez, Rick

Migrant worker to M.D., 7149.

Martinez, Vilma

Working with de la Madrid, 3410.

Martinez-Romero, Sergio

Culture and the development of conflict
resolution style, 397.

Martinez-Serros, Hugo

Learn! learn!, 9661.

Mascarenas, Etta Delgado

Corrido de las comadres: (sung to the music of
a traditional Mexican corrido), 3047.

Mascarenas, Stella

[Untitled drawings], 3638.

Mashek, John W.

Hispanics set their sights on ballot box,
8096.

Massey, Douglas S.

Background and characteristics of undocumented
Hispanic migrants to the United States: a
review of recent research, 5629.

Recent trends in Hispanic immigration to the
United States, 5683.

Research note on residential succession: the
Hispanic case, 897.

Mastropieri, Margo A.

Stability of performance on the PPVT-R for
three ethnic groups attending a bilingual
kindergarten, 5911.

Masvidal, Raul

An interview with Raul Masvidal, 872.

Mata, Alberto G.

Book review of: MEXICAN AMERICANS IN A DALLAS
BARRIO, 88.

Mathes, W. Michael

Book review of: JOAQUIN MURRIETA AND HIS HORSE
GANGS, 1578.

Book review of: THE MEXICAN-AMERICAN WAR: AN
ANNOTATED BIBLIOGRAPHY, 1579.

Sources in Mexico for the history of Spanish
California, 2097.

Matute-Bianchi, Maria Eugenia

A Chicana in academe, 2515.

Mayers, Raymond Sanchez

The school and labor-force status of Hispanic

youth: implications for social policy, 3840.

Mazzone, Ernest

Newsmakers forum (interviews with Gloria
Zamora and Ernest Mazzone), 1116.

McCaffrey, Mark

Laura Allende, 8934.

McCarthy, Martha

Legal forum. The right to an education:
illegal aliens, 105.

McCloud, George E.

Film review of: CONSUELO: QUIENES SOMOS?,
2967.

McCollough, Dale W.

Institutions, governance and confusion in our
time, 9388.

McConnell, Beverly B.

Evaluating bilingual education using a time
series design, 1062.

McCracken, Ellen

Book review of: IDENTIFICATION AND ANALYSIS OF
CHICANO LITERATURE, 1580.

Book review of: SALT OF THE EARTH, 1581.

McCurdy, Jack

Chicanos mark their gains in colleges, call
for more, 24.

L.A. violence linked to Chicano-studies
dispute, 2125.

McDougall, George

The press and Puerto Rico, 7035.

McDowell, John H.

Sociolinguistic contours in the verbal art of
Chicano children, 1168.

McEwan-Alvarado, Angela

Naranjas, 9662.

McFadden, Bernard J.

Bilingual education and the law, 106.

McGhee, Paul E.

Children's appreciation of humor victimizing
different racial-ethnic groups: racial
ethnic differences, 5470.

McGroarty, Mary

English language test, school language use,
and achievement in Spanish-speaking high
school students, 25.

Validation of linguistic and communicative
oral language tests for Spanish-English
bilingual programs, 825.

McGuire, Jack

Hispanic TV network thrives: this SIN is
legit, 1847.

McGuire, Stryker

The border: a world apart, 1781.

McKinney, J.E.

Book review of: MOSAICO DE LA VIDA: CHICANO,
CUBAN AND PUERTO RICAN PROSE, 1582.

McKone, Jerry

Texas Spanish: not standard: but not bad,
3842.

McManis, Linda

Fashion is international, 4483.

First impressions, 608.

Flying Hispanics: a constant gamble with
death, 2738.

McMillen, Jay B.

The social organization of leisure among
Mexican-Americans, 3231.

McNeil, W.K.

Record Review: LAS VOCES DE LOS CAMPESINOS,
231.

McPherson, Robert

Concerns of college bound Mexican-American
students, 695.

Mead, R.H.

Latin American accents in new music, 2398.

Mecht, Richard L.

U.S. real estate owners in Mexico face huge
losses, 7409.

Medina, Antonio S.

Adolescent health in Alameda county, 261.

Medina, Jose M.

Angela before an earthquake, 8935.

Holy week, 8936.

Pool of bad luck, 8937.

Medina, Ruben

Acuarela, 8938.
Angels of the city, 8939.
Clasificados, 8940.
Desaparecido, 8941.
Fotografias, 8942.
Has vuelto a casa como un silencio: rimbaud, 8943.
Los muchachos de matagalpa, 8944.
Para un album, 8945.
Post card, 8946.
Rolando Hinojosa: entrevista, 734.
Medina-Nguyen, Suzanne
Age, 8947.
One, two, three, 8948.
Reality, 8949.
Medinnus, Gene R.
Locus of control: a cross-cultural comparison, 4488.
Meier, Matt S.
Book review of: MEXICAN IMMIGRANT WORKERS IN THE UNITED STATES and OPERATION WETBACK: THE MASS DEPORTATION OF MEXICAN UNDOCUMENTED WORKERS IN 1954, 1583.
Mejias-Rentas, Antonio
Cantinflas give D.C. tribute, 609.
Una dosis puertorriquena de Menudo, 7240.
"I love Latinos because they love to smile", 4289.
A Puerto Rican dose of Menudo, 7241.
Reflections on fathers: my three fathers, 4433.
Melendez, Carmelo
Chasing a Puerto Rican Christmas, 2726.
Mother's Day reflections: "I will get to him", 4435.
Melendez, Jesus Papoleto
Antonia, 8950.
Story from a mountain, 8951.
Who i am/who i touch, 8952.
Melendez, Melinda
Bilingual education interest groups: their past and their future=Grupos interesados en educacion bilingue: su pasado y su futuro [sic], 1064.
Melendez, Theresa
Coyote: towards a definition of a concept, 3104.
Mena, Jesus
Refugees from poverty: a Brownsville perspective, 1739.
Testimonio de Bert Corona: struggle is the ultimate teacher, 3025.
Violence in the Rio Grande Valley, 852.
Mena, Kristena
Tomorrow's leaders (photoessays), 678.
Mendez, Cuauhtemoc
Cancion cansada, 8953.
Mendez, Gloria I.
Bilingual children's adaptation after a transitional bilingual education, 26.
Mendez Gonzalez, Rosalinda
Mexican women and families: rural-to-urban and international migration, 2518.
Mendez, Jose A.
The impact of undocumented aliens on health and public health care in Arizona, 511.
Mendez, Luis
La muerte que adelanto, 8954.
Mendoza, Amelia
Son paginas, 8955.
Mendoza, Pablo
Dreams, 8956.
Mendoza, Phillip
To remember me, 10719.
Mendoza, Rafael
Secreto profesional, 8957.
Mendoza, Ruben G.
The lowrider happening: hydraulics and the hopping competition, 2176.
Mendoza, Samuel M.
Careers for Chicanos: computers, engineering, science/computadoras, ingenieria, ciencia, 2229.
Menton, Seymour

EL LLANO EN LLAMAS: anti-epopeya de la revolucion, 6570.
Mercado, Anthony
Do Hispanics use coupons?, 141.
Mercado, Olivia
Chicanas: myths and roles, 2519.
Chicano psychological assessment: a critique of "Racial intelligence and the Mexican people" [sic], 4989.
Las hermanas, 2520.
Mercado, Olivia, ed.
Chicana journals, 2484.
New book on the Chicana, 2432.
Mercado, Vicente
El tambor publico, 9420.
El temor publico, 10720.
El temor publico: la politica puro..., 9421.
Meredith, Howard V.
Compilation and comparison of averages for standing height at late childhood ages on United States boys of several ethnic groups studied between 1875 and 1980, 450.
Merino, Barbara J.
Language development in normal and language handicapped Spanish-speaking children, 6239.
Mestre, Jose P.
Academic, socio-economic, and motivational characteristics of Hispanic college students enrolled in technical programs, 2814.
Mestre, Mercedes
Paving the path, 1934.
Mexican American Legal Defense and Education Fund (MALDEF)
Chicana rights: a major MALDEF issue (reprinted from MALDEF Newsletter, Fall 1977), 2434.
Chicana rights: a major MALDEF issue (reprinted from MALDEF Newsletter, Fall 1977), 2435.
MALDEF on the Reagan plan, 3396.
Meyer, Lorenzo
Mexico frente a los Estados Unidos, 1971-1980, 3757.
Meyer, Michael C.
Book review of: THE MEXICAN FRONTIER, 1821-1846: THE AMERICAN SOUTHWEST UNDER MEXICO, 1584.
Meyer Rogg, Eleanor
The assimilation of Cubans in the United States, 665.
Michael, W.B.
Development and validation of an auditory perception test in Spanish for Hispanic children receiving reading instruction in Spanish, 2682.
Michel, Jose R.
For the new breed of bilingual teachers: what the future holds, 1066.
Migdail, Carl J.
Mexico's poverty: driving force for border jumpers, 3758.
Miguelez, Armando
El teatro Carmen (1915-1923): centro del arte escenico hispano en Tucson, 11448.
Milk, Robert H.
Intragroup differences and attitudes toward varieties of Spanish among bilingual pupils from California and Texas, 1174.
Millar, Pat
Ce Acatl, 8958.
Miller, Darlis A.
Book review of: THE IMPACT OF INTIMACY: MEXICAN-ANGLO INTERMARRIAGE IN NEW MEXICO, 1821-1846, 1585.
Cross-cultural marriages in the Southwest: the New Mexico experience, 1846-1900, 666.
Miller, John C.
Book review of: NUEVOS PASOS: CHICANO AND PUERTO RICAN DRAMA, 1586.
Miller, Lawrence W.
A note on cultural assimilation in south Texas, 667.
Miller, Michael V.
Book review of: CHICANOS AND RURAL POVERTY, 233

Chicano community control in South Texas: problems and prospects, 2595.

Miller, Robert
Bilingual education in Mexico, 1588.
Daniel Valley and the American Zoot Band (band review), 601.
The Mexican approach to developing bilingual materials and teaching literacy to bilingual students, 1067.
Reading instruction and primary school education - Mexican teachers' viewpoints, 3360.

Miller, Shawn M.
Concerns of Anglo secondary student teachers in Hispanic communities: a pilot study, 2884.

Miller, Shirley
Cabo San Lucas - revisited; border updates, 828.

Miller, Tom
Cabo San Lucas - revisited; border updates, 828.

Mimiaga, Hector
Back in the step with America's Drummers: I feel good again, 933.
Greatest ambition, 1274.
El rey saluda a America, 2263.
Una semana de lujo, 5412.

Mines, Richard
Foreign workers in selected California crops, 230.
Migration to the United States and Mexican rural developments: a case study, 7544.

Mirande, Alfredo
The Chicano family and sex roles: an overview and introduction, 4437.
Machismo: rucas, chingasos, y chingaderas, 6832.
Sociology of Chicanos or Chicano sociology: a critical assessment of emergent paradigms, 818.

Mirowsky, John
Paranoia and the structure of powerlessness, 2759.
Social class, Mexican culture, and fatalism: their effects on psychological distress, 3322.

Mishra, Shitala P.
Judgments of item bias in the McCarthy scales of children's abilities, 3320.
Validity of WISC-R IQs and factor scores in predicting achievement for Mexican American children, 27.

Mohr, Nicholasa
An awakening... Summer 1956, 9664.

Molina, Lilia
Voting Rights Act, 12266.

Molina, Raymond
Como mantener la tecnologia moderna?, 1913.

Molina, Robert A.
The Mexican food industry, 4773.

Molina-Pick, Gracia
The emergence of Chicano leadership: 1930-1950, 2596.

Moll, Luis C.
A naturalistic approach for evaluation, 1019.

Monjaras-Ruiz, Jesus
Book review of: DOLLARS OVER DOMINION: THE TRIUMPH OF LIBERALISM IN MEXICAN-UNITED STATES RELATIONS, 1861-1867, 1589.

Monleon, Jose
Democracia a blas de otero, 8804.
Donde estan las llaves...?, 10721.
Dos novelas de Alejandro Morales, 2178.
Entrevista con Alejandro Morales, 6638.
Este hombre, 8959.
Historia de una contradiccion, 2735.
Mesa redonda, 296.
Oda a san diego, 8806.
Oda a walt disney (pacto con china), 8807.
Take 5, 8808.
U.s.a., 8810.

Monroy, Douglas
Anarquismo y comunismo: Mexican radicalism and the Communist Party in Los Angeles during the 1930's, 2159.

Monsivais, Carlos
No te muevas, paisaje (sobre el cincuentenario del cine sonoro en Mexico), 1880.

Montalvo, Frank F.
Training child welfare workers for cultural awareness: the culture simulator technique, 2647.
Understanding Mexican American culture: a training program, 3229.

Montana, Priscila
The Hispanic female adolescent: a group therapy model, 9750.

Montane, Bruno
Cronica de los anos azules: mareas de metal n.4, 8960.
Cronica de los anos azules: mareas de metal n.2, 8961.
Exilio, 8962.

Montanez, Mary Ann
Old Lady -- New Woman: (a poem -- cycle), 8963.

Montecino A., Sonia
Tres poemas y una impresion etnografica, 8964.

Montemayor, Joaquin
Chicano students in institutions of higher education: access, attrition, and achievement, 14.

Montenegro, Marilyn
Latinas in the work force, 2524.

Montenegro, Raquel
Ausencia, 8965.

Montes, Ana
Adelita, 8966.
Bus stop macho, 8967.

Montez, Philip
How to spot a Chicano from New Texicaloradizona, 5471.

Montgomery, Gary T.
Experimenter effects in biofeedback training, 1189.

Montoya, David
Una nacion, divisible, 9423.

Montoya, Deborah
Creativity, 8968.

Montoya, Delilah Merriman
[Untitled photograph], 8439.
[Untitled photograph], 8440.

Montoya, Emmanuel
Reagan's carcajada/ Reagan's sarcastic laugh: detail..., 7725.

Montoya, Jose E.
Chuco series [drawings], 3639.
El corrido de mi jefe, 8969.
Eslipping and esliding, 8970.
It's my turn to kick the can, 8971.
[Untitled drawing], 3640.
[Untitled drawings], 3641.
[Untitled drawings], 3642.
[Untitled drawings], 3643.
[Untitled drawings from the CHUCO SERIES], 3644.

Moody, George F.
Mexicans and Americans should be the best of friends, 1772.

Moore, Helen A.
The desegregated school and status relations among Anglo and Hispanic students: the dilemma of school desegregation, 2883.
Hispanic women: schooling for conformity in public education, 28.

Moore, Richard J.
Book review of: "TEMPORARY" ALIEN WORKERS IN THE UNITED STATES: DESIGNING POLICY FROM FACT AND OPINION, 1590.
Book review of: "TEMPORARY" ALIEN WORKERS IN THE UNITED STATES: DESIGNING POLICY FROM FACT AND OPINION, 1591.

Mora, Pat
Bailando, 8972.
Chuparrosa: humingbird, 8973.
Cool love, 8974.

Parr, Julie A.
Immigration law and the excluded alien:
potential for human rights violations, 2772.
Parra, Fernando
Changing perceptions of mental illness in a
Mexican-American community, 411.
Passel, Jeffrey S.
The number of illegal migrants of Mexican
origin in the United States: sex ratio-based
estimates for 1980, 2348.
Paul, Jan S.
The changing work week, 4125.
Paull, Gene J.
Archaeology and ethnohistory of the Boscaje de
Palmas, 448.
Pau-Llosa, Ricardo
The sugar mill, 9021.
Pavoncordero, Jose
The pride I have of being Mexican, 10730.
Pazos, Antonio
[Untitled graphics], 5058.
Pearlman, Steven Ray
Mariachi music in Los Angeles, 3723.
Pedraza Bailey, Silvia
Cubans and Mexicans in the United States: the
functions of political and economic
migration, 3183.
Pena, Devon G.
Migra three points blue, 9022.
Untitled, 9023.
Pena, Gerardo
Sidro, 5059.
Pena, Manuel H.
Book review of: FOLK MUSIC OF NEW MEXICO AND
THE SOUTHWEST: A SELF-PORTRAIT OF A PEOPLE,
1609.
Folksong and social change: two corridos as
interpretive sources, 3050.
Pena, Silvia Novo
Open letter to our readers, 9600.
Sonata nuevomejicana, 9024.
Pena-Ramos, Alfonso
The Latin American disease: an essay, 6305.
Pendleton, Jennifer
Battle for the buck is the tale of two cities:
marketers in San Diego and Tijuana square
off, 143.
Penichet, Carlos
Carlos Penichet on the market for bilingual
materials, 1079.
Perales, Alonso M.
Effects of teacher-oriented and
student-oriented strategies on self-concept,
English language development, and social
studies achievement of 5th grade
Mexican-American students [research notes],
699.
Perales, Leon
Rockwell International's highest ranking
Hispanic, 1280.
Pereira, Teresinka
USE: Alves Pereira, Teresinka
Perez, Ana M.
Issues in Hispanic foster care: the Boston
experience, 1793.
Perez Firmat, Gustavo
Carolina Cuban, 9026.
Home, 9027.
Perez, Hector
Los yonqueros, 10731.
Perez, Hugo Hanriot
El boricua volador, 9668.
Perez, Juan
Chile, poema en cuatro augustias y un iris
aura, 2717.
Perez, Lisandro
Comment: Cubans and Mexicans in the United
States, 3184.
Perez, Ray
A naturalistic approach for evaluation, 1019.
Perez, Robert
Effects of stress, social support and coping
style on adjustment to pregnancy among
Hispanic women, 2534.

Expectations toward school busing by Mexican
American youth, 700.
Perry, Charles E.
Book review of: DEVELOPING LIBRARY AND
INFORMATION SERVICES FOR AMERICANS OF
HISPANIC ORIGIN, 41.
Perry, Ronald W.
Crisis communications: ethnic differentials in
interpreting and acting on disaster
warnings, 3233.
Peterson, Marilyn L.
Mexican-American children: what do they prefer
to read?, 2648.
Peterson, Robert A.
Public opinion regarding illegal aliens in
Texas, 9807.
Peterson, Sarah
Hispanics set their sights on ballot box,
8096.
Phillips, Melody
The Chicana: her attitudes towards the woman's
liberation movement, 2273.
Phillips, Susan D., et al.
Career development of special populations: a
framework for research, 2232.
Piersel, Wayne C., et al.
Bias in content validity on the Boehm test of
basic concepts for white and
Mexican-American children, 412.
Pilar
Ask pilar, 3081.
Pinero, Miguel
A Lower East Side poem, 9029.
New York City hard times blues, 9030.
Requiem for the men's shelter, 9031.
Pisano, Vivian M.
Subject access for Hispanic library users,
2315.
Pits, Elaine F.
A review of current North American television
programs for bilingual children, 1072.
Plake, Barbara S., et al.
Relationship of ethnic group membership to the
measurement and meaning of attitudes towards
reading: implications for validity of test
score interpretations, 413.
Plata, Maximino
Bilingual vocational education for handicapped
students, 1080.
Plaza, Eva
Interest group politics and U.S. immigration
policy towards Mexico, 5687.
Pohl, Christopher M.
Joint foot patrols succeed in El Paso, 1738.
Pol, Louis G.
Mexican-American ethnicity, socioeconomic
status, and infant mortality: a county level
analysis, 5525.
Politzer, Robert L.
Validation of linguistic and communicative
oral language tests for Spanish-English
bilingual programs, 825.
Polkinhorn, Harry
[Untitled], 8443.
[Untitled], 5060.
[Untitled graphics], 5061.
Poma, Pedro A.
Hispanic cultural influences on medical
practices, 3234.
Ponce, Mary Helen
La despedida, 9669.
La doctora Barr, 9670.
Las guisas, 9671.
How I changed the war and won the game, 10732.
El jabon de Dona Chonita, 749.
Juan Gomez-Quinones: escolar y poeta, 735.
El pedo, 10733.
Los piojos, 10734.
Recuerdo: how I changed the war and won the
game, 9673.
Recuerdo: los piojos, 9674.
Recuerdo: the funeral of Daniel Torres, winner
of the Medal of Honor, 7094.
Los vatos, 9675.

Ponce, Miguel
    [Untitled photographs], 8444.
Ponce-Adame, Merrihelen
    Latinas and breast cancer, 2152.
    Women and cancer, 2153.
Ponti, Gino
    Courage all the way, 11271.
Popp, Gary E.
    Fears of success and women employees, 2538.
Portales, Marco A.
    Anglo villains and Chicano writers, 1611.
Porter, Horace A.
    Book review of: HUNGER OF MEMORY: THE
        EDUCATION OF RICHARD RODRIGUEZ, 1612.
Portillo Trambley, Estela
    La jon fontayn, 9676.
    A MELUS interview: Estela Portillo-Trambley,
        6662.
Powell, Philip M.
    Level and stability of self-esteem in relation
        to academic behavior of second graders, 20.
Powell, T. G.
    Book review of: DISORDER AND PROGRESS:
        BANDITS, POLICE, AND MEXICAN DEVELOPMENT,
        1613.
Powell-Griner, Eve
    A closer examination of neonatal mortality
        rates among the Texas Spanish surname
        population, 5881.
Powers, Stephen
    Correlates of self-esteem of Mexican American
        adolescents, 33.
Prewitt-Diaz, Joseph O.
    The return and circulatory migrant student: a
        perception of teachers, schools and self,
        3238.
Price, Criselda Segovia
    Psychiatric evaluation of bilingual patient: a
        reply to Vazquez, 9729.
Prichard, Sue
    Book review of: HISTORY AS NEUROSIS:
        PATERNALISM AND MACHISMO IN SPANISH AMERICA,
        1614.
Prida, Dolores
    Latin American women writers meet in New
        England, 736.
    Playwrights Laboratory: in search of a
        creative formula, 737.
Pursifull, Carmen M.
    Going for the land of the living, 9034.
    Papa, 9035.
    The poltergeist, 9036.
Quammen, David
    Book review of: FAMOUS ALL OVER TOWN, 1615.
Quesada-Weiner, Rosemary
    Blowing out the candles on 200 years=Apagando
        las velas de los 200 anos de L.A., 6752.
    CAMINOS second annual Chicano of the year
        awards, 795.
    Chicana Service Action Center, 2436.
    EL ARCA, 3725.
    Latin Business Association (photoessay), 1920.
    MALDEF (photoessay), 7279.
    NALEO's Fiesta '81, 7844.
    Relampago del Cielo, 3389.
    Soy Chicana, 2541.
    The third annual Hispanic of the Year Awards:
        it was an event not to be missed
        (photoessay), 796.
    ZOOT SUIT, 4601.
Quevedo
    The Reagan administration and affirmative
        action, 173.
Quijada
    What the corporate world wants and expects,
        1921.
Quinlivan, Robert
    Another milestone for the Chicano federation,
        2580.
    Black & white ball, 264.
    CRC's Herman Baca on the issue, 817.
    An evening with the stars '82, 4847.
    The Mexican and American Foundation, 2297.
    The need for Hispanic senior housing, 363.

The photographs of Agustin V. Casasola; un
    epilogo de la revolucion Mexicana de 1910,
    2293.
Tony Orlando in concert, 617.
Quinn, Michael Sean
    Educating alien kids, 2689.
Quinonez, Naomi
    Auroa: reflections, 10735.
    Central Califas, 9037.
    Educators, 9038.
    L.A.: a face only a mother could love, 9039.
    El Salvador, 9040.
Quintana Pigno, Antonia
    Isleta, 9041.
Quintana, Vicente
    Mourn not, 9042.
Quirarte, Jacinto
    Book review of: OLMEC: AN EARLY ART STYLE OF
        PRECOLUMBIAN MEXICO, 1616.
Raat, W. Dirk
    Augusto Comte, Gabino Barreda, and positivism
        in Mexico, 889.
Rabou, Jerome
    Alcohol use among Hispanic adolescents; a
        preliminary report, 275.
Ramirez, Albert
    Employment aspirations, expectations, and
        attitudes among employed and unemployed
        Chicanos, 691.
    Social power in educational systems: its
        effect on Chicanos' attitudes toward the
        school experience, 3960.
Ramirez, Alex
    Expectations toward school busing by Mexican
        American youth, 700.
Ramirez, Alma Beatrice
    Life in a Crackerjack box, 10736.
    Pictures and poems, 10737.
Ramirez, Arnulfo G.
    Intragroup differences and attitudes toward
        varieties of Spanish among bilingual pupils
        from California and Texas, 1174.
Ramirez, Arthur
    Book review of: OLD FACES AND NEW WINE, 1618.
Ramirez, Belinda
    In solidarity with El Salvador, 934.
Ramirez Berg, Charles
    ZOOT SUIT, 4602.
Ramirez Garcia, Raul
    A las botas que me dio mi apa, 9043.
    Mi fella epoca, 9044.
    El tiempo es un suicida que nos arrastra,
        9045.
Ramirez, Henry J.
    Vatos from the Pentagon, 10738.
Ramirez, Nora E.
    Book review of: OPERATION WETBACK: THE MASS
        DEPORTATION OF MEXICAN UNDOCUMENTED WORKERS
        IN 1954, 1619.
Ramirez, Ricardo
    Reflections on the Hispanicization of the
        liturgy, 2337.
Ramirez, Ricardo (Bishop of Las Cruces, NM),
    Bishop: why have we had to wait so long for
        Hispanic leaders, 2321.
Ramirez, Sylvia E.
    Bilingual radio: reaching new horizons, 6723.
Ramos, Alfonso Pena
    Voices: Gandhi: the Mahatma's message to
        Hispanics, 4331.
Ramos, Manuel
    En torno a las ideas sobre EL MEXICANO, 3235.
Ramos, Reyes
    Discovering the production of Mexican American
        family structure, 4349.
Ranck, Katherine Quintana
    Portrait of Dona Elena [complete novel], 9677.
Rangel, Irma "La Cui Cui"
    The children are the healing, 7783.
    L.A.'s dust, 7784.
    Lullaby for baby, 7785.
    A tender gift, 9048.
Rangel, Jesus
    Hispanic print media: alive and growing, 7043.

New politics in Texas: COPS comes to Austin, 2863.
Supply-side immigration reform, 5767.

Risse, Gunter B.
Book review of: CAPITULOS DE HISTORIA MEDICA MEXICANA, 2175.

Rivas, Mike
Keeping peace in paradise, 1817.

Rivas, Yolanda E.
Confrontacion y reconciliacion, 5568.

Rivera, Diana
ChildEternal, 9068.
Woman with black kerchief, 3652.

Rivera, Elaine
Fernandez envies Jackson effort, 4054.

Rivera, Henry M.
Hispanics need to effectively translate potential into political and economic clout, 4241.

Rivera, Jean
Codfish fritters "bacalao fritos", 10097.

Rivera, Julius
Book review of: VARIETIES OF AMERICA, 1634.
Clandestine labor circulation: a case on the U.S.-Mexico border, 1745.

Rivera, Marina
Bees, birds, moths, chickens, 9069.
Esteban, 9070.
Pan, 9071.
Villa, 9072.
Why, 9073.

Rivera, Mario A.
Book review of: CUBAN AMERICANS: MASTERS OF SURVIVAL, 1635.

Rivera, Roberto
Selected topics on Latino access to Illinois colleges and universities, 2831.

Rivera, Tomas
The importance of college, 2832.
El Pete Fonseca, 9679.

Rivera, Victor M.
Goal for the 1980s for minority-owned businesses is expansion, 1924.
Trends in minority business enterprise, 1976.

Rivera-Cano, Andrea
Parenting: four families' stories, 2637.

Rivero, Eliana S.
Book review of: HEREJES Y MITIFICADORES: MUESTRA DE POESIA PUERTORRIQUENA EN LOS ESTADOS UNIDOS, 881.
En el lugar que corresponde, 9074.
Gloria, 9075.
Salutacion: Ave, 9076.

Riveros, Enrique
Carta a un poeta, 9077.
Despues del golpe, 9078.
La esperanza vuelve desde el horizonte, 9079.
Mientras tanto, 9080.
Paisaje, 9081.

Rivers, J.W.
Guerrillas, 9082.
MSFW: migrant seasonal farm worker, 9083.
The municipal president of tequistalpa to general felix diaz, 9084.
Pascual orozco, 9085.

Rizzuto, Anna-Maria
Ethnic and cultural variations in the care of the aged. Discussion: Hispanic elderly and natural support systems: a special focus on Puerto Ricans, 365.

Roberts, Catharine Ramsay
Marriage, work and depressive symptoms among Mexican Americans, 2545.

Roberts, Robert E.
A client satisfaction scale suitable for use with Hispanics?, 2871.
Marriage, work and depressive symptoms among Mexican Americans, 2545.
Prevalence of treated and untreated psychiatric disorders in three ethnic groups, 425.
Use of the SADS-RDC in a tri-ethnic community survey, 4340.

Robertson, Sandra

Para que me mueras, 9086.

Robertson-Kozan, Concha
Hispanics in the U.S.: implications for library service, 1036.

Robey, Bryant
Speaking of Hispanics, 6240.

Robinson, Barbara J.
Book review of: THE MEXICAN-AMERICAN WAR: AN ANNOTATED BIBLIOGRAPHY, 968.

Robinson, Holly
Academic, socio-economic, and motivational characteristics of Hispanic college students enrolled in technical programs, 2814.

Robles, Mireya
Trilogia en punto final, 9087.

Rocco, Raymond
Positivism and Mexican identity: then and now, 5381.

Rocha, Julie
Ano de la mujer-Tenochtitlan [photograph], 8447.

Rocha, Thomas
Drink into the early dawn: on the death of an uncle, 9088.
Reflejos, 9089.
Torment, 9090.

Rochat, Roger W.
Differentials in the planning status of the most recent live birth to Mexican Americans and Anglos, 426.

Rochester, R. C.
Book review of: IMPACT OF RACISM ON WHITE AMERICANS, 1638.

Rodriguez, Alfonso
Ideologia, 9091.

Rodriguez, Andres
Ethnic designation, identification, and preference as they relate to Chicano children, 2694.
Hunters tell at midnight, 9092.
Irises, 9093.
The island, 9094.

Rodriguez, Antonio
Tamayo: artist of great synthesis, 622.

Rodriguez del Pino, Salvador
Implorasion a mi lengua, 9095.
La intimidad poetica de Luis Leal, 739.

Rodriguez, Eddie
Computer sciences: a special challenge, 2910.

Rodriguez, Imelda
Inquiry approach to science and language teaching, 1175.

Rodriguez, Joe
Chicano poetry: mestizaje and the use of irony, 5571.

Rodriguez, Josie
Mexican-Americans: factors influencing health practices, 3333.

Rodriguez, Luis
Pobreza, 10741.
Soldados, 9098.
The tunnel, 10742.
La veintinueve, 2599.
Vengan, 9099.

Rodriguez, Luis Javier
A look at the immigration laws, 10743.
Profile of Luis Carlos Bernal, 948.

Rodriguez, Patricia
Goddess Tlazolteotl, 7727.

Rodriguez, Raquel
Children of the earth, 240.
Cry to the wind, 9101.
My mother will no longer cry, 9102.
This woman, 9103.
Tomorrow, 9104.
Yo soy mujer, 9105.

Rodriguez, Richard
A minority scholar speaks out, 176.
The mis-education of rich-heard road-ree-guess, 663.

Rodriguez, Richard, et al.
Education of Richard Rodriguez [excerpts from "HUNGER OF MEMORY", including discussion], 177.

Rodriguez, Roberto
    Book review of: BARRIO WARRIORS HOMEBOYS OF
        PEACE, 894.
    Cal Worthington politics and 1982, 4028.
    Free and fair elections are supposed to be
        what distinguishes a democracy from a
        dictatorship, 9377.
    "Guest worker program", 1806.
    The Maya: from oppression to resistence, 7078.
    Mazehual: a total war of extermination, 10744.
    Who declared war on the word Chicano?, 2600.
Rodriguez, Roy
    Los inocentes: considering the special need of
        the Mexican American child, 1042.
Rodriguez, Vicente
    United farm workers, 206.
Roeder, Beatrice A.
    Health care beliefs and practices among the
        Mexican Americans, 4740.
Rogg, Eleanor Meyer
    Film review of: ANO NUEVO, 440.
Roitman, Daniel
    [Untitled], 8449.
Rojas, Mary
    Mascutis, 10745.
Roma, Thomas E., Jr.
    Not my father's son: obtaining preferred
        immigration status through paternal
        affiliation, 1352.
Roman, James
    Haiku, 9106.
Romano, Branko E.
    Chicken toons, 2262.
Romano, James V.
    Spanish scene, 9107.
Romero, Karen
    A sense of inner beauty, 4485.
Romero, Leo
    The dark side of the moon, 9108.
    Earth, Texas, 9109.
    Fear of the moon, 9110.
    I came to earth, 9111.
    The moon is lost, 9112.
    Moonstruck, 9113.
    The night is overwhelmed, 9114.
    The ocean is not red, 9115.
Romero, Norberto Luis
    Mirrors, 10747.
Romero, Pedro Sababu
    Pete Escovedo: a study in versatility, 623.
Romero, Tina
    The undocumented worker: how will the United
        States deal with him?, 5768.
Romero-Barcelo, Carlos
    Should Puerto Rico become a state?: for
        statehood, 2843.
Romo, Ricardo
    Book review of: MEXICAN EMIGRATION TO THE
        UNITED STATES, 1897-1931: SOCIO-ECONOMIC
        PATTERNS, 1640.
    Unfinished story: Chicanos in the West, 2607.
Rosales, Francisco Arturo
    Book review of: DESERT IMMIGRANTS: THE
        MEXICANS OF EL PASO 1880-1920, 1641.
Rosales, John
    Holy Cross High: a Texas success story, 2274.
    Life at the "Chicano Hilton", 5444.
    El perro favorito, 7045.
Rose, Barbara
    Frida Kahlo: the Chicana as art heroine, 546.
Rosel, Fernando
    Changes, 10748.
Rosenhouse-Persson, Sandra
    Attitudes toward abortion among Catholic
        Mexican-American women: the effects of
        religiosity and education, 4.
Ross, Catherine E.
    Paranoia and the structure of powerlessness,
        2759.
    Social class, Mexican culture, and fatalism:
        their effects on psychological distress,
        3322.
Ross, Stanley R.
    Poor United States, so close to Mexico, 1814.

Rossier, Robert E.
    Bilingual education: training for the ghetto,
        1086.
Ross-Reynolds, Jane
    An investigation of item bias on the WISC-R
        with four sociocultural groups, 2895.
Rotberg, Iris C.
    Some legal and research considerations in
        establishing federal policy in bilingual
        education, 1087.
Rout, Lawrence
    For most Mexicans, legal entry to U.S. is
        impossible dream, 5724.
Royal Chicano Air Force (RCAF)
    Untitled, 7728.
Rubenstein, Harry R.
    The great Gallup Coal strike of 1933, 4867.
Rubio, Sofia
    A matter of faith, 9680.
Rueda, Robert
    Interpersonal tactics and communicative
        strategies of Anglo-American and Mexican
        American mildly mentally retarded and
        nonretarded students, 416.
Rugsaken, Kris T.
    Qualifications for the bilingual vocational
        teacher, 116.
    Toward a true bilingual education: when
        federal funding ends, 1089.
Ruiz, Jose Luis
    Guatemalan refugees - the tip of the iceberg,
        5096.
    Hispanics on TV: who is calling the shots,
        11534.
Ruiz, Pedro
    Psychotherapy and bilingualism: is
        acculturation important?, 1156.
Ruiz, Ramon Eduardo
    Book review of: DISORDER AND PROGRESS:
        BANDITS, POLICE, AND MEXICAN DEVELOPMENT,
        854.
Ruiz, Rene A.
    [Article review of: "The Aztecs";
        "Tenochtitlan's glory"; "The Great Temple"],
        800.
    Book review of: PSYCHOLOGY OF THE MEXICAN
        CULTURE AND PERSONALITY, 1644.
Ruiz, Reynaldo
    BORDERLANDS, 1789.
    CINCO VIDAS, 2737.
Ruskin, Ellen Maria
    Book review of: THE BILINGUAL BRAIN:
        NEURO-PSYCHOLOGICAL AND NEUROLINGUISTIC
        ASPECTS OF BILINGUALISM, 266.
Russell, Cheryl
    The news about Hispanics, 2363.
Sabagh, Georges
    Attitudes toward abortion among Catholic
        Mexican-American women: the effects of
        religiosity and education, 4.
Sabat-Rivers, Georgina
    Book review of: A WOMAN OF GENIUS: THE
        INTELLECTUAL AUTOBIOGRAPHY OF SOR JUANA INES
        DE LA CRUZ, 750.
Sabino, Osvaldo R.
    La magia y el mito, 9117.
    Ronda infantil, 9118.
Sagarin, Edward
    Book review of: LIFE WITH TWO LANGUAGES: AN
        INTRODUCTION TO BILINGUALISM, 1647.
Sagel, Jaime
    Abuela, 9119.
    Another Rio Arriba murder, 10750.
    Frigid, 9120.
    Low rider, 9121.
    Patriarch of San Juan Pueblo, 1288.
Salazar, Alejandro
    Indio, 9122.
Salazar, Pamela Eoff
    Selling $25 million of Jimenez Food Products,
        1977.
Salcido, Ramon M.
    The undocumented alien family, 3726.
Saldivar, Jose David

Book review of: CHICANO POETRY: A RESPONSE TO
    CHAOS, 1648.
Book review of: WHISPERING TO FOOL THE WIND,
    1649.
Saldivar, Ramon
    Chicano literature and ideology: prospectus
        for the 80's: part II: the present, 6651.
    A dialectic of difference: towards a theory of
        the Chicano novel, 6652.
Salgado de Snyder, Nelly
    Book review of: LA CHICANA: THE MEXICAN
        AMERICAN WOMAN, 1650.

    Cultural and ethnic maintenance of
        interethnically married Mexican-Americans,
        62.
Salgado, J. F.
    Alien smugglers: an escalating war, 1746.
Salicrup, Nemesio Caban
    Saltan and the hurricane, 10751.
Salinas Jaramillo, Miguel A.
    Canto al hombre nuevo, 9124.
Salinas, Omar
    As I look to the literate, 9125.
    I am America, 9126.
    My father is a simple man, 9127.
    When this life no longer smells of roses,
        9128.
Salmon, Roberto Mario
    Book review of: SPANISH AND MEXICAN LAND
        GRANTS IN NEW MEXICO AND COLORADO, 1651.
    Comment: is this our decade in the sun?, 5572.
Salvatierra, Richard
    Alien smuggling and the refugee question: U.S.
        must set a limit on refugees, 4520.
    Christmas mass at the Vatican: a burning
        memory, 2339.
    Debtors' row expands in Latin America, 867.
    Tiempos dificiles, 3412.
Samet, Jonathan M., et al.
    Respiratory disease in a New Mexico population
        sample of Hispanic and non-Hispanic whites,
        949.
San Miguel, Guadalupe
    In the background: conflict and controversy in
        the evolution of bilingual legislation in
        Texas, 1965-73, 1090.
    Mexican American organizations and the
        changing politics of school desegration in
        Texas, 1945 to 1980, 313.
Sanchez, Arthur R.
    Mexican-American cultural commitment,
        preference for counselor ethnicity, and
        willingness to use counseling, 3082.
Sanchez, David T.
    Considerations in the assessment of reading
        difficulties in bilingual children, 1139.
    Special education evaluation process as a
        moderator of false positives, 378.
Sanchez, Marta
    Inter-sexual and intertextual codes in the
        poetry of Bernice Zamora, 6653.
Sanchez, Ricardo
    Canto towards Ateneo, 741.
    Coronado, 9130.
    Entequila, 9131.
    El lencho y los chenchos, 1780.
    Letter to my ex-Texas sanity, 9132.
Sanchez, Rita
    [Untitled drawing], 3653.
    [Untitled painting], 8246.
Sanchez, Rosaura
    Entro y se sento, 9681.
    Una manana: 1952, 9682.
    El traje nuevo, 10754.
Sanchez, Saul
    Esperanza + turo, 10755.
    La incipiente narrativa chicana: un espejo de
        telaranas, 5574.
Sanchez, Teresa S.
    Banking: a diversified industry, 868.
Sanchez, Tony, Jr.
    Business on the border: attracting venture
        capital, 1730.

Sanchez, Virginia V.
    Correlates of self-esteem of Mexican American
        adolescents, 33.
Sanchez-Devanny, Jorge
    Inseparable United States Mexico business
        relations, 4797.
Sandos, James A.
    National development and international labour
        migration: Mexico 1940-1965, 1812.
Sandoval, Alicia
    Images and the media, 7047.
Sandoval, David A.
    What do I call them: the Chicano experience,
        2844.
Sandoval, Jonathan
    Cultural difference on WISC-R verbal items,
        3962.
Sandoval, Joseph
    WISC-R factoral validity for minority groups
        and Spearman's hypothesis, 3963.
Sandoval, Moises
    Why LULAC was founded, 6428.
Sandoval-Martinez, Steven
    Findings from the Head Start bilingual
        curriculum development and evaluation
        effort, 1091.
Santana-Bejar, Patricia
    In the toolshed, 9683.
Santiago Baca, Jimmy
    Dark innocence, 9133.
    Mr. Valdez, 9134.
    On this side of the mountain, 9135.
    Spring burning, 9136.
Santiago, Esmerelda
    Madre de madre, 4442.
    Paseo, 9137.
    Recordando un verano, 9138.
    Wintercool, 9139.
Santiago, Mario
    Imaginense, 9140.
Santillan, Richard
    The Chicano community and the redistricting of
        the Los Angeles city council, 1971-1973,
        2617.
    Chicano psychological assessment: a critique
        of "Racial intelligence and the Mexican
        people" [sic], 4989.
    Critique, 4990.
    [Translating population numbers into political
        power], 2129.
Santos, Richard
    Earning among Spanish-origin males in the
        Midwest, 4134.
Sapia, Yvonne
    Another poem about breasts, 9141.
    Del medio del sueno, 9142.
    The figure at the door, 9143.
    Inside the room of ruined light, 9144.
    The landlord's dream of hell, 9145.
    The posture of the dance, 9146.
    The second person, 9147.
    Southern boulevard, 9148.
Sapiens, Alexander
    Intragroup differences and attitudes toward
        varieties of Spanish among bilingual pupils
        from California and Texas, 1174.
Saracho, Olivia N.
    Cultural differences in the cognitive style of
        Mexican American students, 2809.
    Effects of a computer-assisted instruction
        program on basic skills achievement and
        attitudes toward instruction of
        Spanish-speaking migrant children, 44.
    Essential requirements for teachers in early
        childhood bilingual/bicultural programs,
        1092.
    Planning computer assisted instruction for
        Spanish speaking migrant students, 34.
Saragoza, Alex M.
    The florescence of Chicano historical
        scholarship, 1652.
    Mexican children in the U.S.: the Central San
        Joaquin Valley, 80.
Sargeant, Georgia

The food world's CIA, 3201.
My vacation, 10758.
Sebastian Castro Vallejo: artist on stage and
  on canvas, 548.
Shirley, Paula
  Book review of: MEMORIES OF THE ALHAMBRA,
    1658.
Shohamy, Elana
  Validation of linguistic and communicative
    oral language tests for Spanish-English
    bilingual programs, 825.
Siccardi, Maria C.
  Cable T.V.: new opportunities for Hispanic
    communities, 2059.
Sierra, Christine Marie
  Book review of: ASSIMILATION, COLONIALISM, AND
    THE MEXICAN AMERICAN PEOPLE, 676.
Sierra, Jerry A.
  Faces [photographs], 3188.
Sifuentes, Frank
  Babe and the Cadillac, 10759.
  Mi padrino Apolino, 10760.
  Notes from a 9 to 5 Hispanic, 5579.
  Tio tacos are people too, 5580.
Sifuentes, Roberto
  Aproximaciones al "Corrido de los Hermanos
    Hernandez ejecutados en la camara de gas de
    la penitenciaria de Florence, Arizona el dia
    6 de julio de 1934", 290.
Silber, Joan
  Book review of: FRIDA: A BIOGRAPHY OF FRIDA
    KAHLO, 1660.
Silva, Vicente
  Community supported radio bilingue: FM 91,
    4821.
Silver, Chitra
  At a pipe factory in Fontana, 9158.
Simon, Daniel T.
  Mexican repatriation in East Chicago, Indiana,
    3491.
Simon, Jean-Marie
  Five days in Nebaj: one perspective, 5094.
Simpson, Alan K.
  Immigration reform and control, 5773.
Skirius, John
  Barreda, Vasconcelos, and the Mexican
    educational reforms, 890.
Skriloff, Lisa
  Music, news dominate Spanish-language radio
    programming, 145.
Slade, Santiago
  From Michoacan to Southern California: the
    story of an undocumented Mexican, 1292.
Smallwood, James M.
  Zona libre: trade and diplomacy on the Mexican
    border, 1858-1905, 1752.
Smiley, Lydia R.
  Selective admissions criteria in graduate
    teacher education programs, 3952.
Smith, Bruce M.
  Book review of: HUNGER OF MEMORY: THE
    EDUCATION OF RICHARD RODRIGUEZ, 1661.
Smith, Dana M.
  [Untitled photographs], 8452.
Smith, Jack C.
  Differentials in the planning status of the
    most recent live birth to Mexican Americans
    and Anglos, 426.
  Trends in the incidence of breastfeeding for
    Hispanics of Mexican origin and Anglos on
    the US-Mexican border, 420.
Smith, Sherman W.
  Book review of: FAMOUS ALL OVER TOWN, 1662.
Smith, William French
  A look at the immigration laws, 5774.
Snethcamp, P. E.
  Reflections of the past - public restoration
    and interpretation of Hispanic sites, 484.
Snipp, C. Matthew
  New perspectives of Chicano intergenerational
    occupational mobility, 193.
So, Alvin Yiu-cheong
  Changing perceptions of mental illness in a
    Mexican-American community, 411.

Soens. Adolph L.
  Book review of: CHICANOS: ANTOLOGIA HISTORICA
    Y LITERARIA, 1663.
Sohn, Jeanne
  Out of the morass: acquiring Spanish language
    materials from Latin America, 6321.
Solis, A.
  A Chicano Tloque Nahuaque in the 20th century,
    2572.
Solis, Arnaldo
  The birth of the Ranfla, 756.
  Calmecac, 8420.
  La Chicana: principle of life, survival and
    endurance, 2504.
  Chicano mental health, 805.
  Chicano values: living in balance, 12109.
  El oro del barrio: maestro Montoya, 629.
  Prevention in Chicano mental health, 7211.
  Raices of the Chicano spirit, 806.
  Theory of biculturality, 987.
  Theory of biculturality, 851.
  Traditional Chicano centering, 10170.
Solis, Enrique, Jr.
  Chicano students in institutions of higher
    education: access, attrition, and
    achievement, 14.
Somers, Adele
  Improving human relations between the Hispanic
    community and law enforcement, 9287.
Somoza, Oscar U.
  Book review of: CHICANO AUTHORS: INQUIRY BY
    INTERVIEW, 1664.
  Book review of: EXPLORACIONES
    CHICANO-RIQUENAS, 1665.
Sorell, Victor A.
  Ethnomusicology, folklore, and history in the
    filmmaker's art: THE BALLAD OF GREGORIO
    CORTEZ, 845.
Soriano, Fernando
  Social power in educational systems: its
    effect on Chicanos' attitudes toward the
    school experience, 3960.
Sosa, Lionel
  Marketing to the Hispanic community, 144.
Soto, Elaine
  Sex-role traditionalism assertiveness, and
    symptoms of Puerto Rican women living in the
    United States, 9895.
Soto, Gary
  1, 2, 3, 9684.
  Black hair, 9159.
  Brown like us, 9160.
  Eating, 9161.
  A few coins, 9162.
  Girls among waves, 1967, 9163.
  Hard times, 9164.
  In the madness of love, 9165.
  An interview with Gary Soto, 745.
  Joey the midget, 9166.
  Litany after a mexican prayer of the poor,
    9167.
  Luis Omar Salinas: Chicano poet, 743.
  Mexicans begin jogging, 9169.
  Mission tire factory, 1969, 9170.
  Nada, 9171.
  The ring, 9172.
  Ritual, 9173.
  The savings account, 10762.
  Special focus on Gary Soto, 6581.
  Uncle: 1957: after being rejected by the
    Marines, 9175.
  Who are you?, 9176.
Soto, Grace
  Editorial, 2549.
Soto, Manuela
  Calientitas y recien hechas! Tortillas de
    harina, 10100.
Soto, Rose Marie
  Consuelo Santos-Killins: a leader in the arts,
    549.
Soto, Shirlene Ann
  The emerging Chicana: a review of the
    journals, 2550.
Speight, Tamara D.

Current legislation of significance to the English as a second language and bilingual education communities, 3927.

Spiridakis, John N.
Three diagnostics tools for use with the bilingual child, 1096.

Stacy, Gerald F.
From stranger to neighbor, 3762.

Staczek, John J.
Code-switching in Miami Spanish: the domain of health care services, 1178.

Starr, Mark
The border: a world apart, 1781.

Stegner, Bruce L.
A client satisfaction scale suitable for use with Hispanics?, 2871.

Stehno, S. M.
Differential treatment of minority children in service systems, 4336.

Steigelfest, Annette
Ethnicity and sex role socialization, 4293.

Stephens, Doris T.
Book review of: IMAGES OF THE MEXICAN-AMERICAN IN FICTION AND FILM, 1666.

Stern, Gwen
Sociocultural factors and perinatal health in a Mexican-American community, 2424.

Stern, Michael P.
Knowledge, attitudes, and behavior related to obesity and dieting in Mexican-Americans and Anglos: the San Antonio heart study, 421.

Stern, Michael P., et al.
Does obesity explain excess prevalence of diabetes among Mexican Americans? Results of the San Antonio Heart Study, 3524.

Stevenson, Robert
Carlos Chavez's United States press coverage, 2399.
Relaciones de Carlos Chavez en Los Angeles, 2400.

Stewart, Kenneth L.
Lost dream and found fortunes: Mexican and Anglo immigrants in South Texas,1850 -1900, 5336.

Stoddard, Ellwyn R.
Multidisciplinary research funding: a "Catch 22" enigma, 1788.

Stoller, Marianne L.
Book review of: LA CHICANA: THE MEXICAN AMERICAN WOMAN, 1667.

Stone, Marvin
The illegals: one more try, 3791.

Storr, Robert
Book review of: FRIDA: A BIOGRAPHY OF FRIDA KAHLO, 630.

Straight, Susan
The homeboys, 899.

Streck, Dan
A closer examination of neonatal mortality rates among the Texas Spanish surname population, 5881.

Strong, Michael
Social styles and the second language acquisition of Spanish-speaking kindergartners, 6241.

Stroud, Ruth
New products target Hispanics, men, 2998.

Stumphauzer, J.S.
Training Mexican American mental health personnel in behavior therapy, 925.

Suarez, Elena
Encuentro de dos expatriados, 9177.
Marginacion, 9178.

Suarez, Mario
The migrant, 9686.

Sullivan, Jim
The Puerto Rican powerhouse: Goya, 4777.

Sunseri, Alvin R.
Book review of: DESERT IMMIGRANTS: THE MEXICANS OF EL PASO 1880-1920, 1669.

Surace, Samuel J.
Achievement, discrimination, and Mexican-Americans, 35.

Suro, Xiomara

Do you remember my love, 9179.
The horizon, 9180.
Loneliness, 9181.

Sussman, Leon N.
Paternity blood tests, 1348.

Sutherland, Sam
TV series eyes crossover: BRAVISIMO sets its sights on mainstream audience, 1821.

Sutton, Susan Buck
Life on the road: Midwestern migrant farmworker survival skills, 203.

Swicegood, Gray
Generation, female education and Mexican American fertility, 2453.

Swink, Sue
Book review of: LA CHICANA: THE MEXICAN AMERICAN WOMAN, 1670.

Szapocznik, Jose, et al.
Ethnic and cultural variations in the care of the aged. New directions in the treatment of represion in the elderly: a life enhancement counseling approach, 367.
Life enhancement counseling and the treatment of the depressed Cuban American elders, 368.

Tabet, Nita
Book review of: RX: DISCOVERY AND NURTURANCE OF GIFTEDNESS IN THE CULTURALLY DIFFERENT, 1671.

Tack-Robinson, Susan
Locus of control: a cross-cultural comparison, 4488.

Tafolla, Carmen
Caminitos, 9182.
Casa, 9183.
MotherMother, 9184.
Soulpain, 9185.
Woman-hole, 9186.

Tammaro, Thom
Book review of: CHICANO POETRY: A RESPONSE TO CHAOS, 1672.

Tapia, Irma
La Llorona, 10765.

Tatum, Charles
Book review of: CHICANO AUTHORS: INQUIRY BY INTERVIEW, 744.
The sexual underworld of John Rechy, 2754.

Tavera Rivera, Margarita
Sin nombre, 9687.

Tawese
Tia Ester, 9187.

Taylor, Karla
Accion/action: a coast-to-coast sampling of innovative Hispanic programs, 3907.
Entrevista/interview: Q: How to raise money for your Hispanic students? A: Involve your alumni and their corporate contacts, 2820.

Taylor, Robert E.
New fight on illegal aliens planned amid signs opposition is softening, 5777.

Taylor, Vincent
Threading the needle: IEP's for teachers?, 2633.

Taylor, William B.
Book review of: LABOR AND LABORERS THROUGH MEXICAN HISTORY, 1674.

Tejani, Amir et al.
Lupus nephritis in Black and Hispanic children, 2699.

Tejeda, Juan
Aztlan 1976, 9188.

Tello, Jerry
De donde eres? que te importa, 9189.
Platicando (relationships III), 4444.
Relationship entre nuestra gente, 4445.
Relationship entre nuestra gente II, 5981.
[Untitled drawing], 3655.

Terronez, Irene R.
[Untitled painting], 8264.
[Untitled paintings], 8265.

Teschner, Richard V.
Hispanics to equal ten percent of population by 2000, 9484.
The international bilingual city: how a university meets the challenge, 980.

Teyna, Tadeo
    Applying existential thought to bilingual
        education, 1003.
Thomas, Evan
    Playing politics with immigration, 5778.
Thomas, Jackie
    Applying existential thought to bilingual
        education, 1003.
Thomas, Piri
    An interview with Piri Thomas, 3626.
Thomas, William
    Affirmative action under fire, 178.
Thompson, Laurie
    Active verbs, 9190.
    Amen, 9191.
    Far away, 9192.
    Manzanas amargas, 9193.
    To the quetzal, 9194.
Tiano, Susan B.
    El programa mexicano de maquiladoras: una
        respuesta a las necesidades de la industria
        norteamericana, 1675.
Tienda, Marta
    Determinants of extended household structure:
        cultural pattern or economical need?, 4393.
    Headship and household composition among
        blacks, Hispanics and other whites, 422.
    Market characteristics and Hispanic earnings:
        a comparison of natives and immigrants,
        5867.
    New perspectives of Chicano intergenerational
        occupational mobility, 193.
    Sex, ethnicity and Chicano status attainment,
        36.
Tikunoff, William J.
    Successful instruction for bilingual
        schooling, 1099.
Timm, Lenora A.
    Does code switching take time?: a comparison
        of results in experimental and natural
        setting, with some implications for
        bilingual language processing, 1179.
Timmons, Wilbert H.
    American El Paso: the formative years,
        1848-1854, 1782.
Tirado, Evie
    In the damp sienna hills, 9195.
    Today, 9196.
Tirado, Miguel David
    Abelardo Villarreal: a teacher's teacher,
        1297.
Titley, Robert W.
    Effect of counselor technique on
        Mexican-American and Anglo-American
        self-disclosure and counselor perception,
        380.
Tizoc
    Arte, 3656.
    Breaking the needle [drawing], 3657.
    [Levantate campesino! (drawing)], 3658.
    [Untitled graphics], 5062.
Tizocurista
    Papa sun, 9197.
    [Untitled pen line drawings], 5063.
    [Untitled pen line drawings], 5064.
Tomasi, Lydio F.
    Of diversity and strength [editorial], 3240.
Tomayo, Maria
    Book review of: CUNDE AMORES, 1676.
Tony Blue Crow de Sacra
    USE: Cervantez, Tony "Blue Crow"
Tony de Sacra
    USE: Cervantez, Tony "Blue Crow"
Torbert, Eugene C.
    Book review of: NUEVOS HORIZONTES: CHICANO,
        PUERTO-RICAN AND CUBAN SHORT STORIES, 1677.
Torero
    USE: Acevedo, Mario (Torero)
Torrens, James
    The American way, 9198.
    Shine on, la rubia, 9199.
Torres, Arnold
    Capitol links, 10542.
    Immigration bill defeated, 5780.

    Looking out for America's children, 2700.
    Special report on the Simpson-Mazzoli Bill,
        5781.
Torres, Lorenzo
    Short history of Chicano workers, 6178.
Torres, Luis
    The Chicano image in film, 4657.
    Distortions in celluloid: Hispanics and film,
        4658.
Torres, Sylvia
    Book review of: ROSIE: THE INVESTIGATION OF A
        WRONGFUL DEATH, 1678.
Tovar, Irene
    Affirmative action in California, 179.
Trejo, Ernesto
    An interview with Gary Soto, 745.
    Special focus on Gary Soto, 6581.
Tremblay, Gail
    Night gives old woman the word, 9200.
    Remembering the way ... old woman's fire,
        5065.
    Young man's fire, 5066.
Trevino, Fernando M.
    Vital and health statistics for the United
        States Hispanic population, 9797.
Trevino, Gloria L.
    Recuerdos, 9201.
Trevino, Jesus
    Guatemalan refugees - the tip of the iceberg,
        5096.
Trevino, Jesus Salvador
    Chicano cinema, 4659.
    Chicano films and beyond, 4660.
    Form and technique in Chicano cinema, 4661.
    The great pyramid of Aztlan, 9688.
    The last night of the mariachi, 9689.
    Latinos & public broadcasting: the 2% factor,
        9820.
Treviso, Ruben
    EL CORRIDO DE GREGORIO CORTEZ, 846.
    Latino journalists make their move, 2114.
    National IMAGE, 7901.
    Strength through dollars, 7569.
Triana, Armando R.
    Changing demographics, consumer patterns in
        the Chicago marketplace, 2428.
    Four little-known facts about Hispanic
        business firms, 1979.
    The trendy Hispanic market, 2999.
Triandis, H.C., et al.
    Stereotyping among Hispanics and Anglos: the
        uniformity, intensity, direction and quality
        of auto- and heterosterotypes, 423.
Trilla, Francisco
    The plight of the elderly Puerto Rican, 369.
Troike, Rudolph C.
    Bilingual-si!, 37.
Trotter, Robert T.
    Contrasting models of the healer's role: south
        Texas case examples, 3241.
    Ethnic and sexual patterns of alcohol use:
        Anglo and Mexican American college students,
        279.
    Susto: the context of community morbidity
        patterns, 4741.
Trujillo, Larry
    Book review of: GUNPOWDER JUSTICE: A
        REASSESSMENT OF THE TEXAS RANGERS [reprinted
        from CRIME AND SOCIAL JUSTICE, 61 (Summer
        1980)], 1679.
Trujillo, Leo G.
    Don't forget corporate business as a career,
        1930.
Trujillo Munoz, Gabriel
    Alien, 9202.
    Anos luz, 9203.
Trujillo, Paul
    Before and after noon, 9204.
    Damage, 9205.
    Letters, 9206.
    Motion, 9207.
    Prayer for evening, 9208.
    Winter, 9209.
Tucker, M. Belinda

Vargas, Raul
    Entrevista/interview: Q: How to raise money
        for your Hispanic students? A: Involve your
        alumni and their corporate contacts, 2820.
Varnez, Ginger
    Film review of: THE BALLAD OF GREGORIO CORTEZ,
        847.
Vashistha, Krishan
    Azarcon por empacho - another cause of lead
        toxicity, 2654.
Vasquez, Ivan
    Analysis of June 15, 1982 opinion issued by
        the U.S. Supreme Court in the case of Texas
        undocumented children, 2959.
Vasquez, Melba J. T.
    Confronting barriers to the participation of
        Mexican American women in higher education,
        45.
Vasquez, Pedro O.
    Dancing in blue/newday, 9241.
    Dancing the moon, 9242.
Vasquez, Ricardo Esquer
    No perfectamente romantica, 9243.
    Para rosaura, 9244.
Vasquez, Richard
    The relationship of traditional Mexican
        American culture to adjustment and
        delinquency among three generations of
        Mexican American male adolescents, 3305.
    Stereotypes of Mexican descent persons:
        attitudes of three generations of Mexican
        American and Anglo-American adolescents,
        192.
Vazquez, Carol A.
    Reply to Cuellar and Price, 3196.
    Research on the psychiatric evaluation of the
        bilingual patient: a methodological
        critique, 1181.
Vazquez-Faria, Jose A.
    Successful instruction for bilingual
        schooling, 1099.
Vega, Ed
    Back by popular demand, 9694.
    Book review of: OUR HOUSE IN THE LAST WORLD,
        1686.
    Felicia Contreras de Manzanet, 9695.
    Fishing, 9696.
Velasquez, William C.
    The Hispanic vote: a profile, 12259.
    Vote vote vote, 12260.
Velez, Larry A.
    Sonia Berdequez; police detective, 939.
Velez-I., Carlos G.
    Social diversity, commercialization, and
        organizational complexity of urban Mexican
        Chicano rotating credit associations-
        theorical and empirical issues of
        adaptation, 3108.
Venerable, W. R.
    Student and parent attitudes toward college at
        five Hispanic learning centers in Illinois,
        2288.
Venier, M.E.
    Literatura chicana, 1687.
Vernon, Sally W.
    Prevalence of treated and untreated
        psychiatric disorders in three ethnic
        groups, 425.
    Use of the SADS-RDC in a tri-ethnic community
        survey, 4340.
Viamonte, Norberto
    Media and politics, 7054.
Vidal
    The next president of Mexico: Miguel de la
        Madrid, 3413.
Vidal, Jose
    CAMINO'S census effectiveness poll, 2365.
    Cantinflas: Mario Moreno, 632.
    Lopez Portillo's accomplishments, 4030.
    Mexican film - a short history, 633.
    Oil pluses - economic woes, 3741.
Vierra, Andrea
    Book review of: BEYOND THE NUCLEAR FAMILY
        MODEL: CROSS CULTURAL PERSPECTIVES, 953.

Vigil, Evangelina
    The bridge people, 9245.
    Dumb broad!, 9246.
    Es todo!, 9247.
    La loca, 9248.
    Mente joven: nothin' like a pensative child,
        cold north wind flapping against his hair
        and tender face, 9249.
    El mercado en san antonio where the tourists
        trot, 9250.
    Para los que piensan con la verga (with due
        apologies to those who don't), 9251.
    Pluma asesina, 9252.
    Por la calle Zarzamora, 9253.
    Ritual en un instante, 9254.
    Ser conforme, 9255.
    Telephone line, 9256.
    Was fun running 'round descalza, 9257.
Vigil, Evangelina, ed.
    Woman of her word: Hispanic women write, 746.
Vigil, James Diego
    Chicano high schoolers: educational
        performance and acculturation, 39.
    Human revitalization: the six tasks of victory
        outreach, 902.
    Towards a new perspective on understanding the
        Chicano people: the six C's model of
        sociocultural change, 82.
Vigil, Maria
    Regional report, health: Tucson students study
        herbal arts, 4742.
Vigil, Maurilio E.
    Recollections of New Mexico Christmas, 2729.
Vigil, Ralph H.
    Book review of: DESERT IMMIGRANTS: THE
        MEXICANS OF EL PASO 1880-1920, 1689.
    Book review of: MEXICANO RESISTANCE IN THE
        SOUTHWEST: "THE SACRED RIGHT OF
        SELF-PRESERVATION", 1690.
Villa de Romo, Velma
    An interview with Velma Villa de Romo:
        bilingual liaison for the Santa Barbara Rape
        Crisis Center, 10028.
Villa, Esteban
    Chicano wisdom, 1296.
    Coacihuatl - serpent woman, 3662.
    La Colonia, 3663.
    La jennie de sacra, 3664.
    RCAF c/s, 3665.
    Reflection = action c/s, 3666.
    [Untitled art work], 550.
    [Untitled drawings], 3667.
    [Untitled drawings], 3668.
    [Untitled drawings], 3669.
    [Untitled drawings], 3670.
Villa Romo, Velma
    El centro de violacion de Santa Barbara,
        10522.
    Rape in the barrio, 2558.
Villalvazo Briggs, June
    Is affirmative action working?, 181.
Villanueva, Alma
    Her choice, 9697.
Villanueva Collado, Alfredo
    Fili-Mele: simbolo y mujer en la poesia de
        Luis Pales Matos e Ivan Silen, 2559.
Villanueva, Tino
    Haciendo apenas la recoleccion, 9258.
Villareal, Manuel
    Que les parece? (una critica nihilistica),
        9259.
Villarreal, Diana Judith
    For Spanish children, 1691.
Villarreal, Jose Antonio
    Jose Antonio Villarreal: entrevista, 713.
Villarreal, Maria
    Abelardo Villarreal: a teacher's teacher,
        1297.
Villarreal, Roberto E.
    Mexican Americans as participants in United
        States-Mexico relations, 5972.
Villegas, Jim
    Enfoque nacional: created from a need for
        information, 4164.

Villegas-Romero, Rosa
    Rose Villegas-Romero's menudo for a Sunday
        brunch, 10101.
Vincent, J.
    Book review of: HISPANIC FOLK MUSIC OF NEW
        MEXICO AND THE SOUTHWEST: A SELF-PORTRAIT OF
        A PEOPLE, 1692.
Violante Morlock, Alejandro A.
    Policy concerns over the impact of
        trade-related performance requirements and
        investment incentives on the international
        economy: Mexican automotive policy and
        U.S.-Mexican relations, 753.
Viramontes, Helen Maria
    The broken web, 9698.
    The moths, 10773.
    Snapshots, 10774.
Vivo, Paquita
    Book review of: PUERTO RICO: A POLITICAL AND
        CULTURAL HISTORY, 1693.
Volborth, J. Ivaloo
    Mad coyote dances, 9260.
    Ya-lan, 9261.
Volsky, George
    The American club, 309.
    Four careers in Miami, 835.
    Hilario Candela: designing for Florida's
        future, 485.
    An interview with Raul Masvidal, 872.
    Miami's premier Latin-America cafeteria,
        10102.
    Miami's radio S-U-A-A-V-E, 149.
Vowell, Faye Nell
    A MELUS interview: Estela Portillo-Trambley,
        6662.
Wagatsuma, Yuria
    Book review of: EARLY CHILDHOOD BILINGUALISM:
        WITH SPECIAL REFERENCE TO THE
        MEXICAN-AMERICAN CHILD, 1182.
Wagoner, Shirley A.
    Mexican-Americans in children's literature
        since 1970, 2713.
Walden, Daniel
    Parallels between Chicano and Jewish-American
        writing, 6005.
Walia, Adorna
    Book review of: BEGINNING ENGLISH THROUGH
        ACTION, 922.
    Book review of: BILINGUAL EDUCATION TEACHER
        HANDBOOK: LANGUAGE ISSUES IN MULTICULTURAL
        SETTINGS. vol. II, 1103.
    Book review of: CONVERSATIONS OF MIGUEL AND
        MARIA: HOW CHILDREN LEARN ENGLISH AS A
        SECOND LANGUAGE; IMPLICATIONS FOR CLASSROOM
        TEACHING, 1104.
    Book review of: COUNSELING THE BILINGUAL
        STUDENT, 1105.
    Book review of: CULTURE AND THE BILINGUAL
        CLASSROOM: STUDIES IN CLASSROOM ETHNOGRAPHY,
        705.
    Book review of: DATA FORMS FOR EVALUATING
        BILINGUAL EDUCATION PROGRAM, 1107.
    Book review of: DO'S AND DONT'S OF BILINGUAL
        PROGRAM EVALUATION, 1108.
    Book review of: EL GOBIERNO Y LOS PRESIDENTES
        DE LOS ESTADOS UNIDOS DE AMERICA, 1702.
    Book review of: THE BILINGUAL PLAY: PINOCCHIO,
        1109.
    Book review of: THE PLUM PLUM PICKERS, 243.
    Book review of: WOMEN AND MEN SPEAKING:
        FRAMEWORK FOR ANALYSIS, 1705.
Walker de Felix, Judith
    The language arts approach: planned
        eclecticism in ESL teaching in the
        elementary school, 4206.
Walsh, Catherine E.
    The phenomenon of educated/educado: an example
        for a tripartite system of semantic memory,
        1183.
Ward, Carmen Carole
    Book review of: THE ASSIMILATION OF CUBAN
        EXILES: THE ROLE OF COMMUNITY AND CLASS,
        674.
Warheit, George

Interpersonal coping networks and mental
    health problems among four race-ethnic
    groups, 2897.
Warren, Charles W.
    Differentials in the planning status of the
        most recent live birth to Mexican Americans
        and Anglos, 426.
Watkins, Ted R.
    Outreach to Mexican-Americans, 3094.
Watkins, Vicky
    Reflexiones de un mojado, 9262.
    Salsipuedes, 9263.
Watson, Roy J., Jr.
    The Simpson-Mazzoli bill: an analysis of
        selected policies, 4143.
Watts, Ronald K.
    Alcohol use among Hispanic adolescents; a
        preliminary report, 275.
Watts, Thomas D.
    Social policy and the aged: transcultural
        perspectives, 370.
Weber, David J.
    Book review of: MEXICANO RESISTANCE IN THE
        SOUTHWEST: "THE SACRED RIGHT OF
        SELF-PRESERVATION", 1707.
    Book review of: THE NEW BILINGUALISM: AN
        AMERICAN DILEMMA, 1110.
    The new Chicano history: two perspectives,
        2138.
    The new Chicano urban history, 2139.
Weber, Devra
    Oral sources and the history of Mexican
        workers in the United States, 8166.
Weber, Kenneth R.
    Book review of: CANONES: VALUES, CRISIS, AND
        SURVIVAL IN A NORTHERN NEW MEXICO VILLAGE,
        1709.
    Book review of: HISPANIC VILLAGES OF NORTHERN
        NEW MEXICO, 1710.
    Book review of: MY PENITENTE LAND: REFLECTIONS
        ON SPANISH NEW MEXICO, 1711.
Weber, Robert
    Hispanic foods in Southern California: anatomy
        of a market in flux, 4779.
    Rising star: Satelco, 1982.
    The special talent of digitron's Nestor
        Fernandez, 1983.
    Summa's Tumortec/hCG, 1984.
    Turbo-charged MST, Inc, 269.
Webster, David S.
    Chicano students in American higher education:
        a review of the literature, 3679.
Weigle, Marta
    Book review of: HISPANIC LEGENDS FROM NEW
        MEXICO: NARRATIVES FROM THE R.D. JAMESON
        COLLECTION, 1712.
Weinberg, Meyer
    Bibliography of desegration: Los Angeles, 972.
    Special higher education bibliography, 973.
Weinberger, Caspar W.
    A heritage of valor - Hispanics in America's
        defense: remarks... at the recent unveiling
        of paintings of Hispanic heroes at the
        Pentagon, 3442.
Weiner, Richard E.
    Teaching the immigrant's child: a model plan
        for court-ordered bilingual education, 1111.
Weintraub, Sidney
    Poor United States, so close to Mexico, 1814.
Weiss, Lawrence D.
    Industrial reserve armies of the southwest:
        Navajo and Mexican, 2174.
Weiss, Richard
    Book review of: LEGISLATIVE HISTORY OF
        AMERICAN IMMIGRATION POLICY, 1798-1965,
        1713.
Wells, Miriam J.
    Political mediation and agricultural
        cooperation: strawberry farms in California,
        204.
West, Dennis
    Book review of: IMAGES OF THE MEXICAN-AMERICAN
        IN FICTION AND FILM, 1714.
    Film review of: EL SUPER, 3195.

machismo in the Chicano family, 4453.
When wives work: the impact on the Chicano
family, 4454.

Ybarra-Frausto, Tomas
La Chata Noloesca: figura del donaire, 1301.

Young, Rowland L.
Exclusion hearing enough for illegal alien
smuggler, 2442.
Schools ... illegal aliens ..., 2960.
Witnesses ... deportation, 3493.

Yovovich, B.G.
Cultural pride galvanizes heritages, 675.

Ysla, Elizabeth
King of jelly bean art, 551.

Yuscaran, Guillermo
Rubber sun, 9702.

Yvon, Bernard R.
Effects of the language of a diagnostic test
on math scores, 1115.

Yzaguirre, Raul
Hispanics & the private sector: new
partnerships, 9602.

Zabaleta, Antonio N.
The medieval antecedents of border
pseudo-religious folk beliefs, 3335.

Zahn, G. Lawrence
Cultural differences in individualism? Just
artifact, 396.

Zaks, Vivian Calderon
Book review of: ETHNIC FAMILIES IN AMERICA:
PATTERNS AND VARIATIONS, 1723.

Zalazar, Daniel E.
Book review of: HISPANIC FOLK MUSIC OF NEW
MEXICO AND THE SOUTHWEST: A SELF-PORTRAIT OF
A PEOPLE, 1724.

Zamora, Carlos
Book review of: MOSAICO DE LA VIDA: CHICANO,
CUBAN AND PUERTO RICAN PROSE, 1725.
Odysseus in John Rechy's CITY OF NIGHT: the
epistemological journey, 2755.

Zamora, Gloria L.
Newsmakers forum (interviews with Gloria
Zamora and Ernest Mazzone), 1116.
Zamora speaks on bilingual education, 1117.

Zamudio, Anthony
Personality structure of Mexican Americans
using the Comrey Personality Scales, 2835.

Zapanta, Albert C.
President Reagan and the Hispanic community/El
presidente Reagan y la comunidad Hispanica,
4515.

Zapata, Jesse T.
Concerns of college bound Mexican-American
students, 695.
Personality differences among Mexican-American
college freshmen, 2828.

Zapata, Rodger
Cuando la nieve y mis vecinos me saludan,
9275.
Lo que se ha de ver, 9276.

Zavala, Antonio
Election '83: Chicago's Latinos awake, but not
united, 2417.
The end of another summer, 2430.

Zavala, Iris M.
Ideologias y autobiografias: perspectivas
femeninas, 2565.

Zavaleta, Anthony N.
Archaeology and ethnohistory of the Boscaje de
Palmas, 448.
Growth and body composition of
Mexican-American boys 9 through 14 years of
age, 194.

Zea, Leopoldo
El sentido de la historia en Gabino Barreda,
891.

Zeff, Shirley B.
A cross-cultural study of Mexican American,
Black American and white American women of a
large urban university, 431.

Zeidler, Adina S.
Histocompatibility antigens and immunoglobulin
G insulin antibodies in Mexican-American
insulin-dependent diabetic patients, 3525.

Pancreatic islet cell and thyroid antibodies,
and islet cell function in diabetic patients
of Mexico-American origin, 3526.

Zepeda, Marlene
Selected maternal-infant care practices of
Spanish-speaking women, 2638.

Zimmerman, Enid
An annotated bibliography of Chicano
literature: novels, short fiction, poetry,
and drama, 1970-1980, 975.

Zimmerman, Irla L.
Cultural difference on WISC-R verbal items,
3962.

Zotti, Ed
An idea whose time has not quite arrived:
Spanish sections in newspapers still
struggling, 6896.

Zuniga, Jo Ann
Talking Texas: turning the tables with LULAC,
1370.

TITLE INDEX

--   --

Alternative high school provides dropouts a second
         chance, 3673.
Los Alvarez, 4610.
Amanda, 9643.
Ambiguity in the poetry of Gary Soto, 765.
AM-COR Architects & Engineers, Inc. aligns growth,
         1938.
Amen, 9191.
America linda, 8650.
America needs to invest in the right kind of
         education, 310.
America says, welcome home, 303.
American as apple pie and tortillas, 3452.
The American club, 309.
The American dream in the Chicano novel, 6567.
American El Paso: the formative years, 1848-1854,
         1782.
American spelling bee: enchilada, llano, amigo,
         maraca, 316.
The American way, 9198.
Americanization and the Mexican immigrant,
         1880-1930, 68.
America's Mexicans: a plea for specificity, 2355.
America's most important investment, 3793.
AMEX Systems Inc. at transition point, 319.
Amigos, 321.
Amigos o adversarios, 9365.
An amnesty for illegal aliens?, 5757.
Amor negro, 8736.
An idea whose time has not quite arrived: Spanish
         sections in newspapers still struggling,
         6896.
An interview with Piri Thomas, 3626.
An investigation of item bias on the WISC-R with
         four sociocultural groups, 2895.
Ana Alicia, 284.
Analysis of a Spanish translation of the Peabody
         Picture Vocabulary Test, 1144.
An analysis of culturalism in Latino mental
         health: folk medicine as a case in point,
         3307.
Analysis of June 15, 1982 opinion issued by the
         U.S. Supreme Court in the case of Texas
         undocumented children, 2959.
An analysis of the federal attempt to regulate
         bilingual education: protecting civil rights
         or controlling curriculum?, 188.
Analysis of the modernity scale: an item response
         theory approach, 2891.
Anarquismo y comunismo: Mexican radicalism and the
         Communist Party in Los Angeles during the
         1930's, 2159.
And, 8782.
And justice for all, 10650.
And now Domingo... in school in the United States,
         3353.
"And this year's winners are...", 783.
And thus and thus, 8678.
Ando sangrando! (I am bleeding), a study of
         Mexican American - Police conflict and an
         analysis of the East Los Angeles 1970 riots,
         8553.
Angel and big Joe, 374.
Angela before an earthquake, 8935.
Angelito's eulogy in anger, 8860.
Angels of the city, 8939.
Anglo villains and Chicano writers, 1611.
An anniversary is observed, 914.
Annotated bibliography of selected materials on la
         mujer y la chicana, 959, 960.
An annotated bibliography of Chicano literature:
         novels, short fiction, poetry, and drama,
         1970-1980, 975.
Ano de la mujer-Tenochtitlan [photograph], 8447.
Anos luz, 9203.
Another graphic award for Francisco Masseria, 529.
Another milestone for the Chicano federation,
         2580.
Another poem about breasts, 9141.
Another reading of three poems by Zamora, 6608.
Another Rio Arriba murder, 10750.
Ansias, 8849.
La ansiedad de la influencia en Sandra Maria
         Esteves y Marjorie Agosin, 1.

Anti-Castro effort, 3143.
The antihero, 8634.
Antonia, 8950.
ANTONIO AND THE MAYOR: a cultural review of the
         film, 453.
Appeals court overturns Texas bilingual order,
         994.
Applicants to U.S. medical schools, 1977-78 to
         1981-82, 3946.
Application of cognitive behavioral techniques in
         the treatment of Hispanic patients, 687.
Applying existential thought to bilingual
         education, 1003.
An appreciation of "Hechizospells" by Ricardo
         Sanchez, 5167.
Approaching our familias con corazon, 4404.
Aproximaciones al "Corrido de los Hermanos
         Hernandez ejecutados en la camara de gas de
         la penitenciaria de Florence, Arizona el dia
         6 de julio de 1934", 290.
The aquarium conspiracy: personal and social
         transformation in the 80's: a review, 476.
Aqui en Austin: this is Olga Campos reporting,
         2144.
Aqui en Tejas: de Zabala youth session set for
         August: students from throughout state to
         attend, 3847.
Aqui en Tejas: Hispanic newspapers: city,
         community papers taking a business approach
         to the news, 708.
Aqui en Tejas: staying on that long road to
         success: mentors, how to find a helping hand
         to assist you achieve educational goals,
         2192.
Aqui en Texas: ex-boxer finds success in
         restaurant: Matt's of Austin one of Texas's
         most successful restaurants, 1951.
Ara, 8844.
Archaeology and ethnohistory of the Boscaje de
         Palmas, 448.
Arco iris, 487.
"Are there U.S. Hispanic writers?", 720.
Are you a good job hunter? Test yourself, 4081.
Are you registered to vote?, 2928.
Argentina: back to Europe where it belongs, 493.
Arizona conference, 159.
Armando Valladares: twenty-two years of solitude,
         3148.
Arson wave threatens Puerto Ricans in inner
         cities, 3113.
Art currents from Mexico, 571.
Art Garcia's capital gains: keeping down legal
         fees, 6476.
Art Garcia's capital gains: the consultant's
         consultant, 2968.
Art Garcia's capital gains: staying on top of the
         public relations games, 2969.
The art of colcha-stitch embroidery: an Hispanic
         heritage, 559.
Arte, 3656.
[Article review of: "The Aztecs"; "Tenochtitlan's
         glory"; "The Great Temple"], 800.
The artist in bourgeois society, as seen in
         Carpentier's LA CONSAGRACION DE LA
         PRIMAVERA, 569.
Artistic perceptions of Mexico City, 531.
Arturo Burro, 8657.
As I look to the literate, 9125.
Asco 83, 563.
Ask pilar, 3081.
Asner tells it like it is, 599.
Assault and battery, 9061.
Assembling 100 influentials, 6378.
Assessing the casa study, 2858.
Assessment of Puerto Rican children: a
         cross-culture study with the Spanish
         McCarthy scales of children's abilities,
         5912.
Assessment of type A behavior in preschoolers,
         408.
The assimilation of Cubans in the United States,
         665.
The "Assimilation" of unauthorized Mexican
         workers: another social science fiction?, 651

Book review of: FRIDA: A BIOGRAPHY OF FRIDA KAHLO,
564, 627, 630, 1233, 1555, 1660.
Book review of: GUNPOWDER JUSTICE: A REASSESSMENT
OF THE TEXAS RANGERS, 946, 947.
Book review of: GUNPOWDER JUSTICE: A REASSESSMENT
OF THE TEXAS RANGERS [reprinted from CRIME
AND SOCIAL JUSTICE, 61 (Summer 1980)], 1679.
Book review of: HAY PLESHA LICHANS TO DI FLAC,
1388.
Book review of: HEREJES Y MITIFICADORES: MUESTRA
DE POESIA PUERTORRIQUENA EN LOS ESTADOS
UNIDOS, 880, 881.
Book review of: HISPANIC MENTAL HEALTH RESEARCH: A
REFERENCE GUIDE, 955, 1371.
Book review of: HISPANIC FOLK MUSIC OF NEW MEXICO
AND THE SOUTHWEST: A SELF-PORTRAIT OF A
PEOPLE, 1513, 1655, 1692, 1715, 1724.
Book review of: HISPANIC LEGENDS FROM NEW MEXICO:
NARRATIVES FROM THE R.D. JAMESON COLLECTION,
1712.
Book review of: HISPANIC VILLAGES OF NORTHERN NEW
MEXICO, 1710.
Book review of: HISPANICS IN THE UNITED STATES: AN
ANTHOLOGY OF CREATIVE LITERATURE, 1494.
Book review of: HISTORY AS NEUROSIS: PATERNALISM
AND MACHISMO IN SPANISH AMERICA, 1614.
Book review of: HUNGER OF MEMORY: THE EDUCATION OF
RICHARD RODRIGUEZ, 689, 1075, 1386, 1501,
1563, 1612, 1633, 1661.
Book review of: IDENTIFICATION AND ANALYSIS OF
CHICANO LITERATURE, 1580.
Book review of: ILLEGAL ALIENS IN THE WESTERN
HEMISPHERE: POLITICAL AND ECONOMIC FACTORS,
1598.
Book review of: IMAGES OF THE MEXICAN-AMERICAN IN
FICTION AND FILM, 1405, 1417, 1522, 1666,
1714.
Book review of: IMPACT OF RACISM ON WHITE
AMERICANS, 1638.
Book review of: IN DEFENSE OF LA RAZA: THE LOS
ANGELES MEXICAN CONSULATE AND THE MEXICAN
COMMUNITY, 832, 833, 834.
Book review of: INTELLIGENCE AND RACE. THE
ORIGINS AND DIMENSIONS OF THE IQ
CONTROVERSY, 1717.
Book review of: INVENTING A WORD: AN ANTHOLOGY OF
TWENTIETH CENTURY PUERTO RICAN POETRY, 5982.
Book review of: JOAQUIN MURRIETA AND HIS HORSE
GANGS, 1578.
Book review of: KILIAGONIA, 1682.
Book review of: LA CARRETA MADE A U-TURN, 2280.
Book review of: LA CHICANA: THE MEXICAN AMERICAN
WOMAN, 1389, 1606, 1650, 1667, 1670.
Book review of: LA CLASE OBRERA EN LA HISTORIA DE
MEXICO: AL NORTE DEL RIO BRAVO (PASADO
INMEDIATO, 1930-1981), 1505.
Book review of: LA LLEGADA, 1495.
Book review of: LABOR AND LABORERS THROUGH MEXICAN
HISTORY, 1674.
Book review of: LAS MUJERES: CONVERSATIONS FROM A
HISPANIC COMMUNITY [reprinted from LA
RED/THE NET 5 (Sept. 1982)], 1722.
Book review of: LATINO LANGUAGE AND COMMUNICATIVE
BEHAVIOR, 1484.
Book review of: LEGISLATIVE HISTORY OF AMERICAN
IMMIGRATION POLICY, 1798-1965, 1713.
Book review of: LES FILS DU SOLEIL: LA MINORITE
MEXICAINE A TRAVERS LA LITTERATURE DES
ETATS-UNIS, 1451, 1489.
Book review of: LIFE WITH TWO LANGUAGES: AN
INTRODUCTION TO BILINGUALISM, 1136, 1647.
Book review of: LIFE'S CAREER-AGING: CULTURAL
VARIATIONS ON GROWING OLD, 11.
Book review of: LITERATURA CHICANA: TEXTO Y
CONTEXTO, 1483.
Book review of: LOS ANGELES BARRIO 1850-1890: A
SOCIAL HISTORY, 895.
Book review of: LOS MEXICANOS QUE DEVOLVIO LA
CRISIS, 1929-1932, 1446.
Book review of: LOS MOJADOS: THE WETBACK STORY,
1507.
Book review of: MEGATRENDS, 1419.
Book review of: MEMORIES OF THE ALHAMBRA, 1658.

Book review of: MEXICAN WOMEN IN THE UNITED
STATES: STRUGGLES PAST AND PRESENT, 1526.
Book review of: MEXICAN EMIGRATION TO THE UNITED
STATES, 1897-1931: SOCIO-ECONOMIC PATTERNS,
1381, 1397, 1640.
Book review of: MEXICANO RESISTANCE IN THE
SOUTHWEST: "THE SACRED RIGHT OF
SELF-PRESERVATION", 855, 1438, 1468, 1504,
1508, 1532, 1533, 1690, 1707.
Book review of: MEXICAN IMMIGRANT WORKERS IN THE
UNITED STATES and OPERATION WETBACK: THE
MASS DEPORTATION OF MEXICAN UNDOCUMENTED
WORKERS IN 1954, 1583.
Book review of: MEXICAN WOMEN IN THE UNITED
STATES: STRUGGLES PAST AND PRESENT, 1390.
Book review of: MEXICO IN TRANSITION, 1542.
Book review of: MEXICAN CINEMA: REFLECTIONS OF
SOCIETY, 1896-1980, 1420, 1567.
Book review of: MEXICAN AMERICANS IN A DALLAS
BARRIO, 86, 88.
Book review of: MOSAICO DE LA VIDA: CHICANO, CUBAN
AND PUERTO RICAN PROSE, 1582, 1725.
Book review of: MY PENITENTE LAND: REFLECTIONS ON
SPANISH NEW MEXICO, 1557, 1558, 1711.
Book review of: NUESTRO ESPANOL: CURSO PARA
ESTUDIANTES BILINGUES, BILINGUAL NATIVE
SPANISH SPEAKERS FROM THE SOUTHWESTERN
UNITED STATES, 1511.
Book review of: NUEVOS PASOS: CHICANO AND PUERTO
RICAN DRAMA, 1586.
Book review of: NUEVOS HORIZONTES: CHICANO,
PUERTO-RICAN AND CUBAN SHORT STORIES, 1677.
Book review of: OCCUPIED AMERICA, 99.
Book review of: OLD FACES AND NEW WINE, 1618.
Book review of: OLMEC: AN EARLY ART STYLE OF
PRECOLUMBIAN MEXICO, 1616.
Book review of: ON THE BORDER: PORTRAITS OF
AMERICA'S SOUTHWESTERN FRONTIER, 1476, 1654.
Book review of: OPERATION WETBACK: THE MASS
DEPORTATION OF MEXICAN UNDOCUMENTED WORKERS
IN 1954, 238, 1547, 1575, 1619.
Book review of: ORIGINS OF THE MEXICAN WAR: A
DOCUMENTARY SOURCE BOOK, 1406, 1520.
Book review of: OUR HOUSE IN THE LAST WORLD, 1686.
Book review of: OVER THE CHIHUAHUA AND SANTA FE
TRAILS, 1847-1848: GEORGE RUTLEDGE GIBSON'S
JOURNAL, 1421.
Book review of: PARENTING IN A MULTI-CULTURAL
SOCIETY, 1459.
Book review of: PELON DROPS OUT, 1549.
Book review of: POLITICS AND LANGUAGE: SPANISH AND
ENGLISH IN THE UNITED STATES, 1166.
Book review of: PRIMEROS ENCUENTROS/FIRST
ENCOUNTERS, 1592.
Book review of: PROGRAM IMPACT EVALUATIONS: AN
INTRODUCTION FOR MANAGERS OF TITLE VII
PROJECTS - A DRAFT GUIDEBOOK, 1024.
Book review of: PSYCHOLOGY AND COMMUNITY CHANGE;
SOCIAL AND PSYCHOLOGICAL RESEARCH IN
COMMUNITY SETTING; COMMUNITY PSYCHOLOGY:
THEORETICAL AND EMPIRICAL APPROACHES, 1540.
Book review of: PSYCHOLOGY OF THE MEXICAN CULTURE
AND PERSONALITY, 1644.
Book review of: PSYCHOLOGY MISDIRECTED, 1427.
Book review of: PUERTO RICO: A POLITICAL AND
CULTURAL HISTORY, 1693.
Book review of: PURO ROLLO, 903.
Book review of: REVOLTOSOS: MEXICO'S REBELS IN THE
UNITED STATES 1903-1923, 1447, 1523, 1576.
Book review of: ROOTS OF RESISTANCE: LAND TENURE
IN NEW MEXICO, 1680-1980, 1512, 1594, 1716.
Book review of: ROSIE: THE INVESTIGATION OF A
WRONGFUL DEATH, 1678.
Book review of: RX: DISCOVERY AND NURTURANCE OF
GIFTEDNESS IN THE CULTURALLY DIFFERENT,
1671.
Book review of: SALT OF THE EARTH, 1581.
Book review of: SPANISH AND ENGLISH OF UNITED
STATES HISPANOS: A CRITICAL, ANNOTATED,
LINGUISTIC BIBLIOGRAPHY, 51.
Book review of: SPANISH AND MEXICAN LAND GRANTS IN
NEW MEXICO AND COLORADO, 1651.
Book review of: STRESSFUL LIFE EVENTS: THEIR
NATURE AND EFFECTS, 1541.

Book review of: STUDIES IN SPANISH-AMERICAN
    POPULATION HISTORY, 1535.
Book review of: TEACHING SPANISH TO THE HISPANIC
    BILINGUAL: ISSUES, AIMS AND METHODS, 1155,
    1158, 1480.
Book review of: "TEMPORARY" ALIEN WORKERS IN THE
    UNITED STATES: DESIGNING POLICY FROM FACT
    AND OPINION, 1590, 1591.
Book review of: THE ASSIMILATION OF CUBAN EXILES:
    THE ROLE OF COMMUNITY AND CLASS, 674.
Book review of: THE BILINGUAL PLAY: PINOCCHIO,
    1109.
Book review of: THE BILINGUAL BRAIN:
    NEURO-PSYCHOLOGICAL AND NEUROLINGUISTIC
    ASPECTS OF BILINGUALISM, 266.
Book review of: THE CHICANOS OF EL PASO: AN
    ASSESSMENT OF PROGRESS, 1524.
Book review of: THE CHANGING DEMOGRAPHY OF
    SPANISH-AMERICANS, 1431, 1534.
Book review of: THE DOCILE PUERTO RICAN, 1553.
Book review of: THE ETHNIC REVIVAL IN THE MODERN
    WORLD., 1488.
Book review of: THE ELEMENTS OF SAN JOAQUIN, 1607.
Book review of: THE FEDERAL BUDGET AND THE
    NON-PROFIT SECTOR, 6.
Book review of: THE GREAT REBELLION: MEXICO
    1905-1924 and DESERT IMMIGRANTS: THE
    MEXICANS OF EL PASO 1880-1920, 1550.
Book review of: THE IMPACT OF INTIMACY:
    MEXICAN-ANGLO INTERMARRIAGE IN NEW MEXICO,
    1821-1846, 1585.
Book review of: THE INTELLIGENCE CONTROVERSY,
    1530.
Book review of: THE IDENTIFICATION AND ANALYSIS OF
    CHICANO LITERATURE, 1554.
Book review of: THE KENNEDY CORRIDOS: A STUDY OF
    THE BALLADS OF A MEXICAN AMERICAN HERO,
    1562.
Book review of: THE LATER YEARS: SOCIAL
    APPLICATIONS OF GERONTOLOGY, 1435.
Book review of: THE LOS ANGELES BARRIO 1850-1890:
    A SOCIAL HISTORY, 1429.
Book review of: THE MEXICAN-AMERICAN WAR: AN
    ANNOTATED BIBLIOGRAPHY, 968, 1396, 1596.
Book review of: THE MEXICAN FRONTIER, 1821-1846:
    THE AMERICAN SOUTHWEST UNDER MEXICO, 1423,
    1425, 1544, 1546, 1584.
Book review of: THE MEXICANS IN OKLAHOMA, 1657.
Book review of: THE MEXICAN-AMERICAN WAR: AN
    ANNOTATED BIBLIOGRAPHY, 1579.
Book review of: THE MEXICAN FRONTIER 1821-1846:
    THE AMERICAN SOUTHWEST UNDER MEXICO, 1374,
    1471, 1529.
Book review of: THE MEXICAN AMERICAN: A CRITICAL
    GUIDE TO RESEARCH AIDS, 956.
Book review of: THE NEW BILINGUALISM: AN AMERICAN
    DILEMMA, 1110.
Book review of: THE NUYORICAN EXPERIENCE:
    LITERATURE OF THE PUERTO RICAN MINORITY,
    7640.
Book review of: THE OLMEC WORLD, 945.
Book review of: THE PLUM PLUM PICKERS, 243.
Book review of: THE PERPETUAL PRESENT: THE POETRY
    AND PROSE OF OCTAVIO PAZ, 1392.
Book review of: THE POLITICS OF BILINGUAL
    EDUCATION: A STUDY OF FOUR SOUTHWEST TEXAS
    COMMUNITIES, 1033.
Book review of: THE QUESTION OF SEX DIFFERENCES:
    BIOLOGICAL, CULTURAL AND PSYCHOLOGICAL
    ISSUES, 1461.
Book review of: THE SELF-CONCEPT (Rev. ed.).
    Volume 2: THEORY AND RESEARCH ON SELECTED
    TOPICS, 1597.
Book review of: THE SILENCE OF THE LLANO, 331,
    338.
Book review of: THE TEJANO COMMUNITY 1836-1900,
    1375, 1469.
Book review of: THE TESTING TRAP, 1680.
Book review of: THE TALE OF SUNLIGHT, 1608.
Book review of: THE THIRD WOMAN: MINORITY WRITERS
    OF THE UNITED STATES, 1531.
Book review of: TODAY'S IMMIGRANTS, THEIR STORIES,
    1622.
Book review of: TORTUGA, 332.

Book review of: TWICE A MINORITY; MEXICAN-AMERICAN
    WOMEN, 1391, 1496.
Book review of: UNWANTED MEXICAN AMERICANS IN THE
    GREAT DEPRESSION: REPATRIATION PRESSURES,
    1929-1939, 1448.
Book review of: VARIETIES OF AMERICA, 1634.
Book review of: WHISPERING TO FOOL THE WIND, 1649.
Book review of: WOMEN AND MEN SPEAKING: FRAMEWORK
    FOR ANALYSIS, 1705.
Book review of: WORK AND RETIREMENT: POLICY
    ISSUES, 1436.
Book review of: WORKBOOK ON PROGRAM EVALUATION,
    814.
Book review of: WORKING-CLASS EMIGRES FROM CUBA,
    1428.
Book review of: YUCATAN BEFORE AND AFTER THE
    CONQUEST, 1527.
Books in Spanish and bilingual books for young
    readers: some good, some bad, 2709.
Booming Latino business, 1891.
Boost for Hispanic business, 1892.
BOQUITAS PINTADAS, produccion folletinesca bajo el
    militarismo, 1727.
The border: a world apart, 1781.
Border business report: the Rio Grande Valley's
    economy and Mexico's lingering peso
    devaluation effects, 254.
Border group feeds, clothes dispossessed, 1756.
BORDERLANDS, 1789.
El boricua volador, 9668.
Un borracho cargado a tu cuenta bancaria, 8980.
Boston church encourages labor talks, 1792.
Boycott threat leads to negociation table, 162.
The brat; looking for the best, 1818.
Bravisimo!, 326.
Bravisimo, 11486.
Breaking the needle [drawing], 3657.
Breaking through the media employment wall, 4102.
Breast examination, 2148.
Un breviario mexicano, 8574.
The bridge people, 9245.
Bridling at a U.S. immigration bill, 5731.
Broadcasting role model, 1848.
Brocksbank, Bonilla are winners of LNESC award,
    1363.
The broken web, 9698.
The Bronx, 1979, 9053.
Brown like us, 9160.
Burritos to Lebanon, 2065.
Bus stop macho, 8967.
Buscando una casa nueva, 9225.
Business along la frontera, 1758.
Business notes, 433, 1932, 1945.
Business on the border: attracting venture
    capital, 1730.
Business savvy and Capricorn spirit: How do you
    spell entrepreneurship?, 527.
Business update: Ibero-American chamber has gala,
    makes awards, 769.
Business update: phone company issues Spanish
    yellow pages, 124.
Business update: West Coast food firm given
    special honors, 1948.
Business/negocios, 492.
Buttonwillow, 8756.
Cabezeando, 8533.
Cable T.V.: new opportunities for Hispanic
    communities, 2059.
Cabo San Lucas - revisited; border updates, 828.
Cactus prisoner, 5051.
El cadaver, 8696.
Cadiz de lien tan, 8623.
Cal Worthington politics and 1982, 4028.
Calexico, where windows, 8856.
Calientitas y recien hechas! Tortillas de harina,
    10100.
California economist considering candidacy, 4528.
California Farm Bureau Federation: addressing the
    issue/conduciendo el topico, 2119.
California farmworkers: back to the barricades?,
    205.
The California GI Forum 1982 convention, 312.
The California National Guard, 2120.
The California Republican Hispanic Council: a new

The Chicano community and the redistricting of the
Los Angeles city council, 1971-1973, 2617.
Chicano community control in South Texas: problems
and prospects, 2595.
The Chicano family and sex roles: an overview and
introduction, 4437.
Chicano family research: conceptual distortions
and alternative directions, 3206.
Chicano film festivals: an examination, 2581.
Chicano films and beyond, 4660.
Chicano high schoolers: educational performance
and acculturation, 39.
Chicano history: problems and potentialities,
5345.
Chicano households, the structure of parental
information networks, and family use of
child-related social services, 4412.
The Chicano image in film, 4657.
Chicano intellectual history: myth and realities,
2590.
Chicano literature and ideology: prospectus for
the 80's: part II: the present, 6651.
Chicano men and masculinity, 3207.
Chicano mental health, 805.
Chicano music: from country and rock to soul and
Mexican rancheras, 3395.
Chicano nights [painting], 8250.
Chicano poetry and new places, 6597.
Chicano poetry: mestizaje and the use of irony,
5571.
Chicano psychological assessment: a critique of
"Racial intelligence and the Mexican people"
[sic], 4989.
Chicano settlements in Chicago: a brief history,
820.
Chicano students in institutions of higher
education: access, attrition, and
achievement, 14.
Chicano students in American higher education: a
review of the literature, 3679.
A Chicano Tloque Nahuaque in the 20th century,
2572.
Chicano, un vocablo colonizador, 219.
Chicano values: living in balance, 12109.
Chicano wisdom, 1296.
Chicano writers: looking for a breakout, 742.
Chicano-Anglo intermarriage in Arizona, 1960-1980:
an exploratory study of eight counties, 508.
Chicano-Mexican relations: a framework for
research., 3773.
Chicano-produced celluloid mujeres, 842.
Chicanos and higher education: a review of
selected literature, 2088.
Chicanos mark their gains in colleges, call for
more, 24.
Chicanos, the Panama Canal issues and the Reagan
campaign: reflections from 1976 and
projections for 1980, 5963.
Chicharra, 9266.
Chicken toons, 2262.
The chicken wars, 4774.
La chiclera [drawing], 3660.
ChildEternal, 9068.
The children are the healing, 7783.
Children of Guatemala: a pictoral essay, 2669.
Children of the earth, 240.
Children of the sun [painting], 8255.
Children's appreciation of humor victimizing
different racial-ethnic groups: racial
ethnic differences, 5470.
Children's concepts of the earth and the sun: a
cross cultural study, 400.
Children's literature on Puerto Rican themes --
the messages of fiction; non-fiction, 2708.
Chile bruja, 8642.
Chile, poema en cuatro augustias y un iris aura,
2717.
Chile, spice of the southwest, 2718.
Chingaderas in mental health funding, 4849.
Chivo, 8759.
Choosing a career, 302.
A Christmas carol '76, 10674.
Christmas mass at the Vatican: a burning memory,
2339.

Chubasco, 8595.
Chuck, 8535.
Chuco series [drawings], 3639.
CHULAS FRONTERAS, 1339.
Chuparrosa: humingbird, 8973.
La ciencia en la tradicion, 8407.
Cihuacoatl, 8608.
El cinco, 8802.
El Cinco de Mayo, 5406.
CINCO VIDAS, 2737.
Cine-festival, 532.
Cinema, 4587.
A cinema of failure, a cinema of hunger: the films
of Efrain Gutierrez, 4574.
City officials decide mural must be removed, 533.
Ciudad de Los Angeles I, 9233.
Ciudad de Los Angeles II, 9234.
Ciudad de Los Angeles III, 9235.
Civil Rights Commission, 2762.
Clandestine labor circulation: a case on the
U.S.-Mexico border, 1745.
Clarence and angel, 2191.
A clash of cultures, 1382.
Clasificados, 8940.
Class II: young and energetic leaders, 4681.
Classroom cooperation and ethnic balance: Chicanos
and equal status, 3012.
Cleofas M. Jaramillo on marriage in territorial
Northern New Mexico, 6001.
A client satisfaction scale suitable for use with
Hispanics?, 2871.
Clinical psychiatric case presentation; culturally
responsive diagnostic formulation and
treatment in an Hispanic female, 84.
A close look at Mario Obledo, 4014.
A closer examination of neonatal mortality rates
among the Texas Spanish surname population,
5881.
Coacihuatl - serpent woman, 3662.
Coca-Cola president Bryan Dyson on BRAVISIMO,
1819.
Coca-Cola USA Today outlines Latino agenda, 1900.
Code-switching in Miami Spanish: the domain of
health care services, 1178.
Codfish fritters "bacalao fritos", 10097.
A cohort analysis approach to the empty nest
syndrome among three ethnic groups of women:
a theoretical position, 10623.
College and the Navy, 2196.
The Colonel, 9633.
La Colonia, 3663.
Colorado confrontation, 2846.
Colores de un hombre fuerte, 8823.
Combing my hair, 8912.
[Combining political strategies for effective
representation], 6359.
Come again, 8927.
The comedian, 615.
Comment: Cubans and Mexicans in the United States,
3184.
Comment: is this our decade in the sun?, 5572.
A comment on Schoen and Cohen, 2811.
Comment on "Undocumented migration from Mexico:
some geographical questions", 6026.
Commerce department releases census data, 2352.
Commercial art as a career, 572.
Commercial radio and Hispanic community, 2312.
Committed to keep the culture alive, 648.
Common Spanish book provided by Romagosa, 6247.
Communicating health information to urban
Mexican-Americans: sources of health
information, 3602.
Communications and announcements: raices y
ritmos/roots and rythms: our heritage of
Latin American music, 7742.
Communications/marketing, 129, 130, 131, 152, 154,
155, 252, 293, 435, 436, 521, 777, 778, 779,
857, 917, 1834, 2056, 2079, 2112, 4490.
Community development, 2866.
Community mental health nursing: its unique role
in the delivery of services to ethnic
minorities, 641.
Community supported radio bilingue: FM 91, 4821.
Community watching, 102.

A cross-cultural comparison of the developmental
    items of five ethnic groups in the
    Southwest, 2890.
Cross-cultural marriages in the Southwest: the New
    Mexico experience, 1846-1900, 666.
A cross-cultural study of Mexican American, Black
    American and white American women of a large
    urban university, 431.
The croupiers, 8632.
Crunchy and tasty for brunch or party, bunuelos y
    atole, 10085.
Cry to the wind, 9101.
Cuando hay nieve, 8687.
Cuando la nieve y mis vecinos me saludan, 9275.
Cuando vivimos, 9231.
"The Cuban decision", 8555.
Cuban exile chosen teacher of the year, 3161.
Cuban theater in exile: Miami's little Broadway,
    3171.
Cuban-exile community protests deportation of
    recent escapee, 3162.
Cubans and Mexicans in the United States: the
    functions of political and economic
    migration, 3183.
Cubans enjoy New Jersey town, 3163.
Cubans to Cuban Americans: assimilation in the
    United States, 658.
Cuba's matriarch of letters: Lydia Cabrera, 723.
Cuento sin hadas, 9215.
Cultural and ethnic maintenance of interethnically
    married Mexican-Americans, 62.
Cultural awareness and sensitivity in mental
    health with Chicanos, 7186.
Cultural difference on WISC-R verbal items, 3962.
Cultural differences in individualism? Just
    artifact, 396.
Cultural differences in the cognitive style of
    Mexican American students, 2809.
Cultural nationalism and Xicano literature during
    the decade of 1965-1975, 6599.
Cultural nationalism and Chicano literature in the
    eighties, 6611.
Cultural politics of bilingualism, 1162.
Cultural pride galvanizes heritages, 675.
Cultural values of Puerto Rican opiate addicts: an
    exploratory study, 83.
Culture and the development of conflict resolution
    style, 397.
The culture is alive at the schools of East Los
    Angeles, 3381.
Current legislation of significance to the English
    as a second language and bilingual education
    communities, 3927.
Current status of Hispanic technical
    professionals: how can we improve
    recruitment and retention, 12.
Dallas, 2978.
The Dallas bilingual yellow pages, 2984.
Dallas Hispanic media, 1853.
Damage, 9205.
Dan Cruz: making the Olympics happen for the
    community, 3132.
Dancing in blue/newday, 9241.
Dancing the moon, 9242.
Dando gracias al Rey Ocho Ciervos, 4383.
Dando una mano, 1268.
Daniel Valdez: su vida y su carrera, 4611.
Daniel Valley and the American Zoot Band (band
    review), 601.
Danzon Peruano, 8641.
Dark innocence, 9133.
The dark side of the moon, 9108.
Data sources for information on Hispanics, 2353.
Dating and the elderly, 354.
David Ruiz brings justice to Texas prisons, 2782.
The day E.T. met T.B. and A.T., 5467.
The day the Cisco kid shot John Wayne, 9630.
Day treatment programs for the Spanish speaking: a
    response to underutilization, 5425.
De donde eres? que te importa, 9189.
De la vina, 8892.
Dealing, demoralization and addiction: heroin in
    the Chicago Puerto Rican community, 2425.
Dear reader, 6350, 6930.

Dear Santa, we want to see more Hispanics on
    television, movies, radio, magazines, and
    newspapers, Teresa and Carlos, 7024.
Death, 8513.
Death at Victory Park: silence mars investigation,
    10708.
Death of a homeboy, 7714.
Death of el senor Peso, 3744.
Death of mi abuelito, 9152.
Debtors' row expands in Latin America, 867.
A decade of Hispanic literature: an anniversary
    anthology, 4264.
A decade of success, 2653.
Decade of the Hispanic, 3166.
Decadecima, 9007.
Decia grandpa, 9051.
Dedicacion, 8702, 8703, 8704, 8705.
Deep in the heart of Texas, 5409.
Una defensa, 9220.
Definicion de la vida -o- agarrala que se escapa,
    8505.
Defusing the issues in bilingualism and bilingual
    education, 1041.
Del medio del sueno, 9142.
Del mero corazon, 8576.
DEL MERO CORAZON, 3437.
Democracia a blas de otero, 8804.
[Demographic characteristics of Latinos], 3457.
Demographic profile of Hispanics in the
    Dallas/Fort Worth SMSA, 2985.
Dentro de un pozo, 8600.
Denuncia, 8676.
Deportes, 905.
Deportes en Mexico, 7377.
Desaparecido, 8941.
Desde Anchorage hasta San Juan, 1837.
The desegregated school and status relations among
    Anglo and Hispanic students: the dilemma of
    school desegregation, 2883.
Desempleo, 8775.
La despedida, 9669.
Desperate journey: hard times at home cause more
    Mexicans to enter U.S. illegally, 11851.
The desperate migrants of Devil's Canyon, 222.
Despues del golpe, 9078.
Despues del sueno, 8664.
Determinants of asthma among Puerto Ricans, 679.
Determinants of extended household structure:
    cultural pattern or economical need?, 4393.
Detroit's great mural battle, 3513.
Developing responsiveness to health needs of
    Hispanic children and families, 2670.
Development and validation of an auditory
    perception test in Spanish for Hispanic
    children receiving reading instruction in
    Spanish, 2682.
Development of the Spanish-language version of the
    National Institute of Mental Health
    Diagnostic Interview Schedule, 3318.
A development study of ethnic self-concept among
    pre-adolescent girls, 2481.
A developmental analysis of self concept in
    Mexican American and Anglo school children,
    67.
Developments in migrant workers programs: 1981,
    4402.
Devorados pero no digeridos. Paper presented at
    the "Dialogo de las Americas" conference.
    Mexico, D.F. September 9-13, 1982, 984.
El dia de los enamorados, 5410.
Diabetes among Mexican Americans in Starr County,
    Texas, 3522.
A dialectic of difference: towards a theory of the
    Chicano novel, 6652.
Did you know, 285.
La dieta del ano, 8082.
The differences between personality inventory
    scores and self-rating in a sample of
    Hispanic subjects, 2470.
Differential development of empathy and pro-social
    behavior, 404.
Differential treatment of minority children in
    service systems, 4336.
Differentials in the planning status of the most

The executive market, 4096.
Executives challenge first impressions, 883.
Executives expect little affirmative action
      change, 163.
Exilio, 8777, 8962.
Exilio, conciencia: coda sobre la poesia de
      Millan, 2715.
Existential, 8496.
Exito - an East coast play for the whole nation,
      4379.
The ex-marine, 8497.
Expanding the meaning of Chicano cinema: YO SOY
      CHICANO, RAICES DE SANGRE, SEGUIN, 4595.
Expectations toward school busing by Mexican
      American youth, 700.
Expected but shocking, 4093.
Experiencing state government, 6744.
Experimenter effects in biofeedback training,
      1189.
Explanation, 8922.
Expressing time through verb tenses and temporal
      expressions in Spanish: age 2.0-4.6, 1046.
Eye don't, eye do's, 3061.
Fables of identity: stereotype and caricature of
      Chicanos in Steinbeck's TORTILLA FLAT, 2261.
Fabula de la luna y el astro, 8869.
The faces of San Miguel: a photo essay, 7381.
Faces [photographs], 3188.
Facing the hard realities of corporate
      advancement, 164.
The factory raid: an unconstitutional act, 1306.
La familia Chicana: social change in the Chicano
      family of Los Angeles, 1850-1880, 4424.
LA FAMILIA de Joaquin Chinas, 586.
La familia [special issue of DE COLORES], 4421.
Family displays special courage, 6693.
Family favorites, 944.
Family unit, 6736.
Fandangos and bailes: dancing and dance events in
      early California, 3390.
Far away, 9192.
Farmworker wins the right to sue, 226.
Farmworkers win Arkansas contract, 221.
Fashion is international, 4483.
Father, son attend UCLA school of law, 4422.
Fear and loathing on the buffalo trail, 92.
Fear of the moon, 9110.
Fears, 8684.
Fears of success and women employees, 2538.
Febrero, 8820.
La fecundidad entre los Mexicano-Norteamericanos
      en relacion a los cambiantes patrones
      reproductivos en Mexico y los Estados
      Unidos, 3451.
Federal higher education policy: the case of
      Hispanics, 3583.
Federico Pena: Denver's first Hispanic mayor,
      3476.
Felicia Contreras de Manzanet, 9695.
Female Mexican Americans: minority within a
      minority, 2508.
Fernandez envies Jackson effort, 4054.
Fernando Allende, 287.
Fernando Favela: street wise and sexy, 1254.
Ferre honored at concert, 4539.
The fertility related behavior of Mexican American
      adolescents, 4546.
Festival a puertas abiertas, 8616.
Festival international Cervantino, 4547.
A few coins, 9162.
Fichas biograficas de los funcionarios
      norteamericanos responsables de la politica
      de Estados Unidos hacia Mexico,
      Centroamerica y el Caribe, 11917.
Field work: outreach to migrants, 3325.
El fierro, 10701.
Fiesta de los colores de sacra: fiesta de colores,
      8745.
Fifth member leaves panel, 6494.
Figuraciones de "El Angel", 9657.
The figure at the door, 9143.
Figure in dream, 530.
Fili-Mele: simbolo y mujer en la poesia de Luis
      Pales Matos e Ivan Silen, 2559.

The Filipinos: our forgotten cultural cousins,
      2320.
Film distributors, 4632.
Film portrayals of La Mujer Hispana, 2462.
Film review of: ANO NUEVO, 440.
Film review of: CHICANOS STORY, 4585, 4600.
Film review of: CONSUELO: QUIENES SOMOS?, 2967.
Film review of: DEL MERO CORAZON (STRAIGHT FROM
      THE HEART), 1340.
Film review of: EL SUPER, 3195.
Film review of: THE BALLAD OF GREGORIO CORTEZ,
      847.
Films need mass appeal, 1844.
The final laugh, 8688.
Findings from the Head Start bilingual curriculum
      development and evaluation effort, 1091.
Fire, 8605.
The firing squad is singing in Chile, 8728.
Firm honors Latino workers, 90.
The first American rodeo never happened, 2396.
First Cuban since 1890 in Florida legislature,
      3167.
First impressions, 608.
First learning unchallenged and untested, 183.
The first place, 9060.
First race for scouts occurs in East L.A., 4842.
First to fall: "God just chose him to be a
      Marine", 1230.
Fishing, 9696.
Fitting into a tradition of autobiography, 161.
Five days in Nebaj: one perspective, 5094.
Five seek league highest office, 9403.
Five simple words, 9368.
Five-part series on youth jobs, 4147.
Fletcher and Valenti: Tampa's growing
      arquitectural firm, 482.
Flicks in review, 4586.
FLOC, Campbell labels, 1802.
Flora and Airto; making music happen, 587.
Las flores, 8881.
Flores de Aztlan, 8746.
Flores on fashion, 4480.
The florescence of Chicano historical scholarship,
      1652.
The flourishing of Hispanic theater in the
      Southwest, 1920-30s, 4731.
Floyd Aragon: filling voids with his
      entrepreneurship, 478.
Flying Hispanics: a constant gamble with death,
      2738.
Folacin and iron status and hematological finding
      in Blacks and Spanish-American adolescents
      from urban low-income households, 1310.
Folk remedy dangerous, 4504.
Folklore, lo mexicano, and proverbs, 3544.
Folksong and social change: two corridos as
      interpretive sources, 3050.
A follow-up note on census techniques for
      enumerating the Hispanic population, 2349.
Folsom, 8498.
Food stamp cheaters, 4785.
Food stamp recovery, 3038.
The food world's CIA, 3201.
Foolish pride, 10722.
For a Chicano brother of mine, 8565.
For children - Centros de Ninos, 2377.
For "illegals" migration goes both ways, 5670.
For most Mexicans, legal entry to U.S. is
      impossible dream, 5724.
For Noel Rico, 8738.
For Spanish children, 1691.
For the Apache infants in the mountains of
      Arizona, 2680.
For the new breed of bilingual teachers: what the
      future holds, 1066.
Foreign trade, 195, 860, 2085, 2252, 2253, 3339.
Foreign trade: outlook for the Caribbean Basin
      Initiative, 2250.
Foreign workers in selected California crops, 230.
Forging technologies, 5215.
Form and technique in Chicano cinema, 4661.
Forum to address concerns of elderly, 352.
Fostering Hispanic professionalism, 5269.
Fostering the advancement of Latinas, 2479.

Fotografias, 8942.
El fotografo, 11436.
The founding of NUESTRO, 6847.
Four careers in Miami, 835.
Four little-known facts about Hispanic business
    firms, 1979.
The fourth network's chief executive, 128.
Francisco Zuniga; el pueblo Mexicano su
    inspiracion, 575.
Fred Maes builds a multi-level system, 1242.
Free and fair elections are supposed to be what
    distinguishes a democracy from a
    dictatorship, 9377.
French via Spanish: a positive approach to
    language learning for minority students,
    3899.
Fresh mint garden, 8629.
Frida Kahlo, 597.
Frida Kahlo: the Chicana as art heroine, 546.
Frigid, 9120.
Frijoles boiling musically, 4781.
From condemnation to praise: shifting perspectives
    on Hispanic California, 2093.
From Garden City to Hays, 8708.
From Michoacan to Southern California: the story
    of an undocumented Mexican, 1292.
From Simon Bolivar to the Malvinas and beyond,
    1358.
From stranger to neighbor, 3762.
From Texas to Idaho, 7499.
From the daughter of the deceased, 5542.
From the metropolis: Puerto Rican women poets and
    the immigration experience, 4266.
From the SBA, 1905.
Full employment is theme of SER annual conference,
    4094.
La funcion del mito: NAMBE-YEAR ONE, 6560.
Fundraising resources, 4809.
The future beckons, USC's LBSA responds, 1906.
The future of Latino political power, 2362.
The future of minority engineering, 4175.
Future scenarios for Hispanics in higher
    education, 5235.
El futuro de la cuenca del Caribe segun la
    administracion Reagan, 5884.
Gabi, 8506.
Gabino Barreda y la literatura: de la preparatoria
    al Ateneo, 682.
Gabino Barrera and Chicano thought, 884.
El gallinero, 10768.
Game theory in Chicana poetry, 2543.
Games helps study effort, 4868.
Gannett's Gerald Garcia goes to Tucson, 1246.
Garreau's nine nations offer immigration insights,
    4936.
Gathering of the Ojedas, 710.
Gautum, 8814.
La generacion de '68: unfulfilled dreams, 2587.
Generation, female education and Mexican American
    fertility, 2453.
Genetic demography of Denver, Colorado: Spanish
    surname as a market of Mexican ancestry,
    3459.
Gente, 307, 317, 584.
Gente; FBI head, two agents praised by Texas
    house, 2206.
Gente: Miguel Aleman, former president, Mexico,
    dies, 281.
Getting grants, 9597.
Ghost people, 8598.
Ghost riders, 8607.
Gifts from your kitchen, 10088.
Gilbert L. Hernandez, 5181.
Girls among waves, 1967, 9163.
Girls explore new job fields, 2490.
Gloria, 9075.
Gloria Molina spells winner, 2491.
Gloria Valencia: woman on the move, 1250.
Goal for the 1980s for minority-owned businesses
    is expansion, 1924.
Goddess Tlazolteotl, 7727.
Going for the land of the living, 9034.
Gold coins of Mexico, 861.
Golden Eagle Awards 1983, 786.

Government has a role to promote access to
    education, 3816.
Government maze, 5011.
Government review, 112, 256, 276, 848, 862.
Gozando de la vida, 1251.
Grand Jury selection upheld against test by
    Hispanics, 1858.
Grandmother's ghetto, 8795.
Grandparental-grandchild interaction in a Mexican
    American group, 366.
Granny's bunuelos and other secrets, 2727.
The great Gallup Coal strike of 1933, 4867.
The great Mexican legends in music, 7399.
The great pyramid of Aztlan, 9688.
The great Valentino, 574.
The great wall of Los Angeles, 6765.
Greatest ambition, 1274.
El Greco of Toledo: his life and his art, 537.
Green card falsa, 10777.
El Grito de Dolores, 5407.
El grito de las madres dolorosas, 2949.
Gritos, 8783.
Grocery chains fight for San Antonio market, 4769.
Group psychotherapy for elderly female Hispanic
    outpatients, 353.
Group works to ensure Reynoso election, 6058.
Growing, 8770.
Growing old alone, 362.
Growing up gringo, 1282.
Growth and body composition of Mexican-American
    boys 9 through 14 years of age, 194.
Growth of U.S. Hispanic income: 1950-1982, 3777.
Guatemala shantytown, 799.
Guatemalan refugees - the tip of the iceberg,
    5096.
Guernica 1980, 8986.
Guerrillas, 9082.
The guest editor speaks, 1030.
"Guest worker program", 1806.
Las guisas, 9671.
Gum disease: a problem of epidemic proportions,
    3472.
Gus Garcia Foundation, 2070.
Gutierrez, first Latino recipient, 4682.
Habana! comes to Manhattan, 5127.
Habra?, 10684.
Hace un chingo de anos ... [drawing], 2260.
Hacia donde?, 8507.
Hacia la nada ... o la religion en POCHO, 6598.
Haciendo apenas la recoleccion, 9258.
Haiku, 9106.
Hail to the chief, 3120.
Haitian boat people, 3768.
Half-open door, 5641.
The Hall at last, 907.
Hands, 9665.
Hands of unity, 9372.
"Hanging on" or "gaining ground": educating
    marginal adults, 115.
Hanigan case: hung up on racism?, 103.
Hannukkah, navidad and christmas, 2724.
Happy happy, 8026.
Hard times, 9164.
Harvard's Latino Association, 1989.
Harvest, 8834.
Has vuelto a casa como un silencio: rimbaud, 8943.
Hasta siempre companero revueltas!, 8778.
He dudado, 8841.
He sabido, Carnala, 8724.
Headship and household composition among blacks,
    Hispanics and other whites, 422.
The healing ritual [complete novel], 9660.
Health and environmental problems: the role of the
    border in El Paso-Ciudad Juarez
    coordination, 1751.
Health care beliefs and practices among the
    Mexican Americans, 4740.
Health fairs set for 10 cities, 9774.
Health research on undocumented Mexicans, 5631.
Healthy prospects for bilingual
    education=Prospectos fructiferos para la
    educacion bilingue, 1013.
Help-seeking behavior among foreign-born and
    native-born Mexican-Americans, 73.

Hemisphere bulletin, 3786.
Henry Cisneros: our hope for today & tomorrow, 2741.
Henry Darrow: the man behind the actor, 620.
Henry G. Cisneros on Central American commission (interview), 2368.
Henry Rivera: our Hispanic on the FCC, 4500.
Her choice, 9697.
Her hands, 8700.
Heritage, 8646.
A heritage of valor - Hispanics in America's defense: remarks... at the recent unveiling of paintings of Hispanic heroes at the Pentagon, 3442.
Herlinda Maxima Gonzales, 1247.
Las hermanas, 2520.
Hermandad iberoamericana, 8797.
Heublein's Miss Black Velvet II, 137.
HHR proposes safety plan for care homes, 355.
The hidden threat of underemployment, 3807.
High energy community relations: Con Edison's Carlota M. Maduro, 1257.
High school dropouts: remedies, 3675.
El hijo del pueblo: Jose Alfredo Jimenez and the Mexican cancion ranchera, 1252.
Los hijos de Quetzalcoatl, 8830.
Hilario Candela: designing for Florida's future, 485.
Hired workers on California farms, 229.
Hiring N.J. fire fighters, 169.
Hispanic academics organized for the greater good, 2834.
Hispanic America, 5321.
The Hispanic business directory of the 400 largest corporations, 1967.
Hispanic business in the 80's/el negocio Hispanico en los ochentas, 1888.
The Hispanic business top 400 in sales, 1940.
Hispanic candidates: getting serious, 4056.
Hispanic Catholics, 2331.
Hispanic caucus announces plans, 2934.
Hispanic caucus offers Washington, fellowships, 2210.
Hispanic coalition formed on economy, 3399.
Hispanic collections of the Library of Congress, 5297.
The Hispanic community as a resource for a practical Spanish program, 2875.
Hispanic cultural influences on medical practices, 3234.
Hispanic Democrats, 3450.
The Hispanic educational dilemma: a strategy for change, 29.
Hispanic employment reviews, 4104.
Hispanic engineers, 4166.
Hispanic fathers: the growing phenomenon of single fathers keeping their children, 3598.
The Hispanic female adolescent: a group therapy model, 9750.
Hispanic food producers: the top ten, 4768.
Hispanic foods in New York: the race for number two, 2345.
Hispanic foods in Southern California: anatomy of a market in flux, 4779.
Hispanic heritage month celebrated by Newark public, 3252.
The Hispanic image on network television: past & present, 11262.
Hispanic income still lower, 4105.
Hispanic journalists assemble in California, 3069.
Hispanic leader reaction to Governor White: Republicans fail to overcome Democratic one-two punch, 2780.
The Hispanic market: a profile, 2990.
The Hispanic market: a reality of the 1980s, 1908.
The Hispanic market: leading indicators, 122.
Hispanic marketing: new applications for old methodologies, 2977.
Hispanic mental health and use of mental health services: a critical review of the literature, 6677.
Hispanic mental health and the Omnibus Budget Reconciliation Act of 1981 (editorial board special report), 4839.

The Hispanic movie market, 4654.
Hispanic natural support systems: implications for mental health services, 3328.
Hispanic numbers rising, 711.
Hispanic owned banks, 863.
Hispanic owned stations, 1843.
Hispanic phenomenon is not new, 1265.
Hispanic policy development project, 5294.
Hispanic politics: the power is there, 9411.
Hispanic power arrives at the ballot box, 3475.
Hispanic power at the polls, 12222.
Hispanic print media: alive and growing, 7043.
Hispanic representation in California's cities: progress???, 2108.
Hispanic solidarity, 6124.
Hispanic student study undertaken, 18.
Hispanic students wanted, 4219.
Hispanic television, 6944.
A Hispanic turned Greek, 594.
Hispanic TV network thrives: this SIN is legit, 1847.
Hispanic update: border governors tackle U.S.-Mexico relations: much ado: but nothing on immigration, 812.
Hispanic update: changing of the LULAC guard--almost, 1360.
Hispanic update: Hispanics and the Republican Party, 9334.
Hispanic victories; seats gained, 2090.
An Hispanic view of the 1983 Academy Awards, 47.
The Hispanic vote: a profile, 12259.
The Hispanic vote: parties can't gamble that the sleeping giant won't awaken, 3447.
Hispanic voting trends, 990.
Hispanic wages and employment slow to rise, 2498.
Hispanic women and their men, 2454.
Hispanic women: schooling for conformity in public education, 28.
Hispanic-Mexican pioneers of the San Francisco Bay region: an analysis of racial origins, 4312.
Hispanic-owned bank far exceeds expectations, 864.
Hispanics & the private sector: new partnerships, 9602.
Hispanics and immigration reform, 5737.
Hispanics and psychotherapeutic groups, 63.
Hispanics and redistricting: what you see is not always what you get, 941.
Hispanics and the census, 2361.
Hispanics and the private sector, 7872.
Hispanics are moving toward the front pew, 2335.
Hispanics: don't they know there's a recession on?, 5861.
Hispanics in Communications, Inc., 138.
Hispanics in federal agencies, 170.
Hispanics in the labor force: data, 6160.
Hispanics in the media, 7010.
Hispanics in the U.S.: implications for library service, 1036.
Hispanics keep the faith, but better parish work is needed, 660.
Hispanics need political clout, 9392.
Hispanics need to effectively translate potential into political and economic clout, 4241.
The Hispanics next door, 3291.
Hispanics on TV: who is calling the shots, 11534.
Hispanics receive appointments, 455.
Hispanics responding well to health survey, 5284.
Hispanics set their sights on ballot box, 8096.
Hispanics still ignored, 7025.
Hispanics: the harvest field at home, 10144.
Hispanics to equal ten percent of population by 2000, 9484.
Hispanics 'want more bishops, input in church', 2323.
Hispanics: will they or won't they?, 9480.
Hispanics win Nobel Prizes, 729.
Hispanics wooed by Reagan, Demos, 2938.
Hispanidad parades: New York and world, 4564.
Un hispano para vice-presidente, 9393.
Histocompatibility antigens and immunoglobulin G insulin antibodies in Mexican-American insulin-dependent diabetic patients, 3525.
Historia de exitos, 730.
Historia de una contradiccion, 2735.

Improving human relations between the Hispanic
    community and law enforcement, 9287.
Improving the schools, 1049.
In black and white, 8835.
In ixtli, in yollotl - rostro y corazon, 8613.
[In memorium: Rene A. Ruiz 1929-1982], 1259.
In search of Hispanic voters, 4050.
In search of the honest outlaw: John Rechy, 6604.
In solidarity with El Salvador, 934.
In the background: conflict and controversy in the
    evolution of bilingual legislation in Texas,
    1965-73, 1090.
In the damp sienna hills, 9195.
In the madness of love, 9165.
In the park, 8609.
In the rain forest, 9641.
In the stomach of the shark: echoes of a culture
    in captivity, 657.
In the toolshed, 9683.
La incipiente narrativa chicana: un espejo de
    telaranas, 5574.
Increasingly educated work force, 5231.
The incredible F.P. hopper of varrio nuevo, 2588.
An indian, 5053.
Indian, Chicano and Puerto Rican colleges: status
    and issues, 2830.
An Indian treaty, 5987.
Indio, 9122.
Los indocumentados: practices, recommendations,
    and proposals, 11787.
Industrial reserve armies of the southwest: Navajo
    and Mexican, 2174.
Infant mortality of the Spanish surname
    population, 3462.
Infantes, 5057.
The influence of prior experience in ESL reading,
    1053.
The influence of student ethnicity on teachers'
    behavior ratings of normal and learning
    disabled children, 3516.
The influence of teachers and peers on second
    language acquisition in bilingual preschool
    programs, 1018.
The influences of Latin American theatre on teatro
    Chicano, 6301.
El ingles en el espanol, 11110.
Inlak'ech, 8996.
Los inocentes: considering the special need of the
    Mexican American child, 1042.
Inquiry approach to science and language teaching,
    1175.
Ins and outs, 10696.
INS raids challenged, 5718.
INS sweep searches of work areas must meet fourth
    amendment standards, 2962.
INS violations of its own regulations: relief for
    the aliens, 3485.
Inseparable United States Mexico business
    relations, 4797.
Inside the room of ruined light, 9144.
Institutions, governance and confusion in our
    time, 9388.
Intellectual assessment of Hispanic children, 382.
Intelligence-achievement discrepancies in
    diagnosing pediatric learning disabilities,
    386.
Inter faith unity, 7867.
The Inter-American Development Bank at work
    (photoessay), 865.
Interest group politics and U.S. immigration
    policy towards Mexico, 5687.
Interethnic discourse, 6271.
Intermarriage among Hispanic ethnic groups in New
    York City, 5925.
Intermarriage of Mexican Americans, 78.
The international bilingual city: how a university
    meets the challenge, 980.
The International Boundary and Water Commission as
    a conflict management agency in the
    U.S.-Mexico borderlands, 1774.
Interpersonal coping networks and mental health
    problems among four race-ethnic groups,
    2897.
Interpersonal tactics and communicative strategies

of Anglo-American and Mexican American
    mildly mentally retarded and nonretarded
    students, 416.
Inter-sexual and intertextual codes in the poetry
    of Bernice Zamora, 6653.
An interview with Gary Soto, 745.
An interview with Luis Valdez, 234.
An interview with Raul Masvidal, 872.
An interview with Rodrigo Duarte of Teatro de la
    Esperanza, August 13, 1982/New York City,
    3695.
Interview with Ron Arias, 499.
An interview with some experts, 5099.
An interview with Velma Villa de Romo: bilingual
    liaison for the Santa Barbara Rape Crisis
    Center, 10028.
Interviewing undocumented immigrants:
    methodological reflections based on
    fieldwork in Mexico and the U.S, 5607.
La intimidad poetica de Luis Leal, 739.
Intragroup differences and attitudes toward
    varieties of Spanish among bilingual pupils
    from California and Texas, 1174.
Introduccion a la poesia revolucionaria de El
    Salvador, 4007.
Introduccion al teatro de Myrna Casas, 2292.
Introduction, 887, 2502.
An introductory examination of children's invented
    spelling in Spanish, 1048.
Invasion from Mexico: it just keeps growing, 1755.
The invisible American, 1845.
The invisible Puerto Rican vote, 4044.
Irises, 9093.
Is a computer following you?, 12238.
Is affirmative action working?, 181.
Is the answer right at home?, 2767.
Is the market going English?, 4211.
Isabella Rios and the Chicano psychic novel, 6631.
Isela Sotelo, 1260.
La isla de nadie, 8596.
The island, 1952, 9094.
Isleta, 9041.
The issue of language proficiency, 263.
Issues in Hispanic foster care: the Boston
    experience, 1793.
Issues in the delivery of mental health services
    to Cuban entrants, 3153.
It can work, 2177.
"It has been very confusing" Q and A with Hector
    Santillan, 3340.
It is only the flowers, 9057.
[It took ten powerful trucks to haul], 8587.
It's called mainstreaming, 1021.
It's in the cut, 3062.
It's my turn to kick the can, 8971.
It's not all rice & beans, part III (restaurant
    reviews), 2062.
It's not all rice and beans (2nd annual Mexican
    restaurant guide), part II, 10219.
It's time for us to watch the media, 7011.
El jabon de Dona Chonita, 749.
Jan D'Esopo: a talented artist, 595.
El jazz del vagabundo, 8617.
Jc's mono jog at camp slingshot, 8542.
"Jekyll, Hyde" radio station, 9986.
La jennie de sacra, 3664.
Jesus "Chuy" Negrete: the Chicano vote, 2569.
El jibarito moderno, 8521.
Jim Blancarte, "an ace in the deck", 1261.
Job counseling, role models mean a lot, 2202.
Job hunting & bolts, 2212.
Jobs for peace initiative, 4110.
The jockey, 8931.
Joey the midget, 9166.
Joint foot patrols succeed in El Paso, 1738.
Joint use of adaptive behavior and IQ to predict
    achievement, 31.
La jon fontayn, 9676.
Jose, 8785.
Jose Antonio Villarreal: entrevista, 713.
Jose Feliciano, 576.
Jose Guadalupe Posada: documenting his people and
    his times=informandonos de su gente y su
    epoca, 577.

----

bibliography, 957.

Library services for the Spanish speaking, 1028.

Life at the "Chicano Hilton", 5444.

Life enhancement counseling and the treatment of
     the depressed Cuban American elders, 368.

Life imitating art: a profile of Reynaldo Arenas,
     489.

Life in a Crackerjack box, 10736.

Life in a Mexican-American barrio: gangs alongside
     middle-class striving, 3722.

Life in these United States, 7012.

Life is, 8733.

Life on the road: Midwestern migrant farmworker
     survival skills, 203.

Limbo, 8670.

Linda Ramirez: labor leader, 6123.

Linguistic confusion, 7523.

Litany after a mexican prayer of the poor, 9167.

Literatura chicana, 1687.

The little bighorn, montana, 1980, 8811.

The Little Havana development authority, 2267.

Living and working in a lighthouse, 6017.

Living in the usa, 9222.

Living traditions of the days of the dead, 3255.

EL LLANO EN LLAMAS: anti-epopeya de la revolucion,
     6570.

Un llanto en seco, 8690.

La Llorona, 9153, 10765.

LNESC tenth anniversary banquet set for March 24,
     3274.

Loaned lawns, 9212.

La loca, 9248.

La loca de la raza cosmica, 5520.

Local government is no answer, 6703.

Location preference and opportunity cost: a South
     Texas perspective, 3752.

Locus of control: a cross-cultural comparison,
     4488.

Loneliness, 9181.

Long journey home, 8767.

A look at the immigration laws, 5774, 10743.

Looking backwards down, 9063.

Looking out for America's children, 2700.

Lope de Aguirre y santos banderas, la manipulacion
     del mito, 3425.

Lopez Portillo's accomplishments, 4030.

Lorenzo Lamas, 602.

Los Angeles, 8582, 8583.

The Los Angeles Epidemiologic Catchment Area
     research program and the epidemiology of
     psychiatric disorders among Mexican
     Americans, 72.

Los que emigran desde Costa Rica hacia el norte,
     3065.

Losing control of the borders, 1737.

Lost dream and found fortunes: Mexican and Anglo
     immigrants in South Texas,1850 -1900, 5336.

The lost nigger expedition, 9264.

Loteria: las manos, 8428.

Love poem # 1, 8659.

Low rider, 9121.

Low riding to positive mental health, 6802.

The Lower East Side: after having witnessed a man
     beating up a woman underneath a balcony
     overlooking Avenue C, 9059.

A Lower East Side poem, 9029.

The lowrider happening: hydraulics and the hopping
     competition, 2176.

LRF takes on Battery Park City, 1964.

Lt. Governor Mike Curb, 3336.

La lucha, 10702.

La lucha por la independencia, 1269.

Luis Avalos - he has it all - talent, wit, and a
     TV show of his own (interview), 567.

Luis Avalos: what a man, and what a talent, 759.

Luis (el amigo) Leal, 728.

Luis Leal, 721.

Luis Mayorga, 588.

Luis Omar Salinas: Chicano poet, 743.

Luisa/louise (mothersong), 9155.

LULAC 1983 national convention to be in Detroit,
     6407.

LULAC: 53 years of continued achievement
     (photoessay), 938.

LULAC '83: 54th annual LULAC national convention
     agenda, 6409.

LULAC board appointments, 6410.

LULAC board's Washington meeting set October 6-8,
     6411.

LULAC files complaint against TV networks, 1367.

LULAC foundation moves to Washington D.C., 6413.

LULAC is building $2.6 million housing project in
     Corpus Christi, 3039.

LULAC national scholarship fund, 3508.

LULAC opposes youth subminimum wage proposal,
     5862.

LULAC reports new stance, 6416.

LULAC survey approved, 6417.

LULAC takes a stand against mainstream media,
     4239.

LULAC train is rolling, 6418.

The LULAC/PUSH dialog, 1368.

LULAC-Red Cross agreement, 6420.

Lullaby for baby, 7785.

Lung cancer mortality and smoking habits:
     Mexican-American women, 393.

Lupus nephritis in Black and Hispanic children,
     2699.

Luring the Hispanic dollar: retailers boost ethnic
     image, 134.

LA LUZ MAGAZINE founder victim of cancer, 1270.

Lynda Cordoba Carter, 1273.

M.A.B.A., 6470.

Machismo and the will to win, 6831.

Machismo: rucas, chingasos, y chingaderas, 6832.

Mad coyote dances, 9260.

Madre, 8925.

Madre de madre, 4442.

Madre tierra press, 603.

Las madres de la Plaza de Mayo en Buenos Aires,
     8998.

Madrugada, 8651.

MAGA annual scholarship awards banquet, 790.

The Maga Saga, 3003.

La magia y el mito, 9117.

Magueyes, 8870.

Mainstream Hispanic, 664.

Major health survey of Latinos undertaken, 5285.

Making a dent in the corporate hierarchy, 3750.

Making an art of pain, 1256.

Making it seem easy, from intern to account
     executive, 54.

Mal vino el tango, 96, 97.

MALDEF critical of FAIR study, 4519.

MALDEF on the Reagan plan, 3396.

MALDEF (photoessay), 7279.

MALDEF's goal: a fair opportunity for Hispanics to
     compete, 3833.

MALDEF's strategies for leadership, 6389.

Mallory Docks, Key West, 8923.

Man witnesses his own execution, 10660.

Una manana: 1952, 9682.

The manana show - starring johnny calzon, 11427.

Manic-depressive illness among poor urban
     Hispanics, 1857.

Un manifiesto literario: PAPELES DE PANDERA DE
     ROSARIO FERRE, 1683.

Las manos (para 'pa Agapito), 8747.

Mantillas, 8824.

Manuel Bustelo heads youth effort, 2043.

Manuel Jaramillo Rodriguez; master portrait
     artist, 607.

Manuel M. Ponce visto por un profesor
     norteamericano de ascendencia mexicana,
     7755.

Manuel Sanchez: the joy of big business, 1350.

The many faceted talents of Danny Valdez=Los
     muchos y variados talentos de Danny Valdez,
     1238.

Manzanas amargas, 9193.

Maquina de coser, 8557.

Marginacion, 9178.

Maria la 0, 8606.

Mariachi music in Los Angeles, 3723.

Marilyn, 8499.

Marilyn Monteruego's flan, 10094.

Marinero, 8508.

Mario Obledo, 8099.

Mariposas, 8910.

Marital decision-making and the role of machismo in the Chicano family, 4453.

Market characteristics and Hispanic earnings: a comparison of natives and immigrants, 5867.

Marketing to Mexican-Americans: just a bit of insight, 4767.

Marketing to the Hispanic community, 144.

Marketplace of the Americas, 1904.

Marriage, work and depressive symptoms among Mexican Americans, 2545.

Martha Cornejo Rottenberg: on opportunities & advancement, 2248.

Mary likes fishes: reverse psychological phenomena in New York Puerto Rican Spanish, 7994.

Mascutis, 10745.

Masks, 8749.

Mass media orientations among Hispanic youth, 1841.

"Mastering learning" como metodo psicoeducativo para ninos con problemas especificos de aprendizaje, 2660.

Math-based careers, 372, 1827, 2204, 2215, 2216, 2217, 2218, 2219, 2220, 2221, 2222, 2223, 2225, 2226, 2227.

A matter of faith, 9680.

The Maya: from oppression to resistence, 7078.

The mayor markets San Antonio, 2749.

Mazehual: a total war of extermination, 10744.

Me, E.T. and other alien beings, 5517.

Me imagino una lucha llena de amor, 8621.

Media and politics, 7054.

The media scene, 127.

Media/marketing, 267, 2051.

Median administrative salaries in 1981-82 for men and women and minority-group members, 111.

Medianoche [graphic], 5052.

The medieval antecedents of border pseudo-religious folk beliefs, 3335.

Meditaciones, 1145.

Mejico [drawing], 3635.

Mejor en grupo, 3304.

Melendez v. Burciaga: revealing the state of the art in bar examinations, 6105.

A MELUS interview: Estela Portillo-Trambley, 6662.

Members of the caucus, 2940.

Members to LULAC boards named, 6422.

Memories of you, 8491.

Mendiga, 9268.

Un mensaje, 7034.

Mente joven: nothin' like a pensative child, cold north wind flapping against his hair and tender face, 9249.

Mentira, 8883.

Menudo cook-off and much more (photoessay), 3284.

Menudo: dishing it up in Los Angeles, 610.

Mercado de pulgas, 10770.

El mercado en san antonio where the tourists trot, 9250.

El mercado hispano, 1907.

La merced, 10669.

La mesa de billar en New Bedford, Mass., 8494.

Mesa redonda, 296.

Message to Rudy Acuna...stop... the Spanish boys have returned...stop... business as usual...stop,spot, 7724.

La meta critica Chicana, 500, 4260.

Metamorfose, 8846.

Metro market ranking: Spanish-origin population, 2995, 9470.

Mexican American authors and the American dream, 6645.

Mexican American family research: a critical review and conceptual framework, 4447.

Mexican American home altars: towards their interpretation, 5421.

Mexican American organizations and the changing politics of school desegregation in Texas, 1945 to 1980, 313.

Mexican American theatre: then and now, 11444.

Mexican American women in the social sciences, 2451.

Mexican Americans and westering Anglos: a feminine perspective, 409.

Mexican Americans as participants in United States-Mexico relations, 5972.

Mexican Americans jalaron la palanca, Democrats say ole, 3449.

The Mexican and American Foundation, 2297, 3275.

Mexican- and Anglo-American children's locus of control and achievement in relation to teachers attitudes, 9.

The Mexican approach to developing bilingual materials and teaching literacy to bilingual students, 1067.

The Mexican archipelago, 7356.

Mexican border crossing survey, 1769.

Mexican border sounds travel the folk circuit, 1770.

Mexican business update, 1911.

Mexican centers advance U.S. ties, 552.

Mexican children in the U.S.: the Central San Joaquin Valley, 80.

Mexican condo buyer in Texas-sized trouble, 2921.

Mexican film - a short history, 633.

The Mexican food industry, 4773.

Mexican immigration and border strategy during the revolution, 1910-1920, 1778.

Mexican labor in the Pacific Northwest, 1943-1947: a photographic essay, 223.

Mexican market hints, 4795.

Mexican migration, crisis, and the internationalization of labor struggle, 5944.

Mexican migration to the United States: challenge to Christian witness and national policy, 3756.

Mexican muralism: its social-educative roles in Latin America and the United States, 535.

The Mexican Museum has a colorful new home, 541.

Mexican repatriation in East Chicago, Indiana, 3491.

Mexican woman seriously injured, 1740.

Mexican women and families: rural-to-urban and international migration, 2518.

Mexican women's sexual jokes, 2457.

Mexican workers in Wyoming during World War II: necessity, discrimination and protest, 225.

Mexican-American Center forges new vision, 2328.

Mexican-American children: what do they prefer to read?, 2648.

Mexican-American cultural commitment, preference for counselor ethnicity, and willingness to use counseling, 3082.

The Mexican-American electorate, 7038.

Mexican-American ethnicity, socioeconomic status, and infant mortality: a county level analysis, 5525.

Mexican-American high school students' perception of school, 444.

Mexican-American views of U.S. relations with Latin America, 2589.

Mexican-American voting trends, 12243.

Mexican-Americans: factors influencing health practices, 3333.

Mexican-Americans in children's literature since 1970, 2713.

Mexican-Americans in city-politics: participation, representation, and policy preferences, 1326.

Mexican-Americans: Qua the assistant-Americans, 4114.

Los mexicanos, 8710.

Mexicans and Americans should be the best of friends, 1772.

The Mexicans are coming: from ideology to labor relations, 690.

Mexicans asked to report, 5693.

Mexicans begin jogging, 9169.

Mexicans, Indians and movies: the need for a history, 912.

Mexico & its economy - some keen insights, 3739.

Mexico en crisis: la incomprendida prensa norteamericana, 2.

Mexico frente a los Estados Unidos, 1971-1980, 3757.

Mexico opens door to refugees, 9356.

Mexico y Estados Unidos ante la tercera Confemar:

Hispanic students' attitudes toward their own ethnicity, 5545.

Schools ... illegal aliens ..., 2960.

Scratching six, plucking one, 8546.

Sculpture results in controversy, 268.

Sebastian Castro Vallejo: artist on stage and on canvas, 548.

Second Latino assumes new duties at EEOC, 472.

The second person, 9147.

Secretary of Education Terrell Bell speaks out, 927.

Secreto profesional, 8957.

Segovia: un retrato musical, 7806.

Seis meses despues, algunas lecciones que aprender: Mexico y Estados Unidos ante Cancun, 11940.

Select Commission suggests changes in immigration policy: a review essay, 5681.

Selected maternal-infant care practices of Spanish-speaking women, 2638.

Selected topics on Latino access to Illinois colleges and universities, 2831.

Selecting tests for bilingual program evaluation, 1031.

Selective admissions criteria in graduate teacher education programs, 3952.

Self-evident remedy? George I. Sanchez, segregation, and enduring dilemmas in bilingual education, 1093.

Selling $25 million of Jimenez Food Products, 1977.

Una semana de lujo, 5412.

Senate passes immigration reform bill, 5694.

Senate passes legislation to curb illegal immigration, 5738.

Senator Yarborough and the Texan RWY brand on bilingual education and federal aid, 1010.

El senor del chivo, 715.

Senor Pascua, 8615.

A sense of inner beauty, 4485.

El sentido de la historia en Gabino Barreda, 891.

Sentimientos sin nombre, 5551.

Sequin: the same side of the Alamo, 4583.

Ser conforme, 9255.

Serna v. Portales: the plight of bilingual education four years later, 1061.

A servant of the people, 9627.

Serving our students: Larry Gonzalez (interview), 3818.

Seven page note to a choctaw indian girl at a claiborne county school in mississippi, 8813.

Seven women honored, 2452.

A severe case of penis envy: the convergence of cultural and individual intra-psychic factors, 4824.

The sewer society, 8564.

Sex and ethnic differences in the use of power, 379.

Sex, ethnicity and Chicano status attainment, 36.

Sex role of the traditional Mexican family: a comparison of Chicano and Anglo students' attitudes, 390.

Sex stereotyping in Mexican reading primers, 2882.

Sex-related differences in the problem-solving abilities of rural Black, Anglo, and Chicano adolescents, 257.

Sex-role traditionalism assertiveness, and symptoms of Puerto Rican women living in the United States, 9895.

Sexual knowledge, sexual interests, and sources of sexual information of rural and urban adolescents from three cultures, 1302.

The sexual underworld of John Rechy, 2754.

The shaping of a career, 684.

Sharing her tiny pieces of the past, 748, 4432.

Sharing the silence, 339.

Sharing with a spiritual sister, 2461.

Shells, 8648.

A sheriff's X-mas, 932.

She's, 9636.

Shine on, la rubia, 9199.

Shock treatment, 8854.

Short history of Chicano workers, 6178.

Should Puerto Rico become a state?: for statehood, 2843.

Should Puerto Rico become a state?: against statehood, 2841.

A showcase of fiction: NUESTRO's sixth anniversary edition, 4554.

Si no fuera por la gente: podriamos servir el publico, 5025.

Si yo, 10716, 11446.

Sibling, birth order, and cooperative-competitive social behavior: a comparison of Anglo-American and Mexican-American children, 402.

Side-by-side comparison of House and Senate bills, 5772.

Sidro, 5059.

Sierra Foothills, 9157.

Siers robo, 8547.

Significance of the 1980 census to Latinos, 2354.

Signs your wife is going crazy, 8672.

Simon Bolivar, 1354.

The Simpson-Mazzoli bill: the first major immigration bill in thirty years, 4084.

The Simpson-Mazzoli bill: an analysis of selected policies, 4143.

Simpson-Mazzoli Bill in the Ninety-eighth Congress, 5726.

Sin nombre, 9687.

Sin que nadie la vea..., 8780.

Sin raices hay flor?, 8630.

SIN seeks FCC review of Hughes performance, 6373.

SIN, the original, 441.

El sindrome del macho, 9666.

Singing of life en el Valle de Califas, 3654.

Sintesis vs. analysis: un problema de historicidad en las novelas de las dictaduras, 2271.

The siren rang, 8528.

Six community colleges share resources to meet the needs of Mexican-American students linking together to solve a common need, 2827.

Small town, 8920.

Smuggling aliens into U.S.: booming business, 10880.

Snapshots, 10774.

The so-and-so's, 8662.

Social class, admixture, and skin color variation in Mexican-Americans and Anglo-Americans living in San Antonio, Texas, 415.

Social class, Mexican culture, and fatalism: their effects on psychological distress, 3322.

Social diversity, commercialization, and organizational complexity of urban Mexican Chicano rotating credit associations-theorical and empirical issues of adaptation, 3108.

Social equity in film criticism, 2456.

Social interaction and morale of Spanish-speaking rural and urban elderly, 357.

The social organization of leisure among Mexican-Americans, 3231.

Social policy and the aged: transcultural perspectives, 370.

Social power in educational systems: its effect on Chicanos' attitudes toward the school experience, 3960.

Social research on Chicanos: its development and directions: symposium, 10950.

Social science stereotypes of the Mexican American woman: policy implications for research, 2446.

Social styles and the second language acquisition of Spanish-speaking kindergartners, 6241.

Social workers?, 8898.

The socialization of a Chicano family, 70.

Sociocultural and educational correlates of success-failure attributions and evaluation anxiety in the school setting for Black, Hispanic, and Anglo children, 40.

Sociocultural factors and perinatal health in a Mexican-American community, 2424.

Sociolinguistic contours in the verbal art of Chicano children, 1168.

Sociolinguistic foundations of bilingual education, 1040.

Sociology by value systems: explication and some implications of two studies on the folklore of Hispanics in the United States, 937.

Sociology of Chicanos or Chicano sociology: a critical assessment of emergent paradigms, 818.

Softball Texas style, 3984.

Sola, 8977.

Soldados, 9098.

La soledad de la America Latina, 6296.

Soledad propia, 8840.

Soliciten aqui dentro el presidente continua su busqueda, 4615.

The solitude of Latin America, 722.

Solon opposes military support for Guatemala, 4925.

Some different thoughts concerning "machismo", 2478.

Some Hispanic stations trying bilingual approach, 1840.

Some legal and research considerations in establishing federal policy in bilingual education, 1087.

Some useful advise [sic] on currency regulations in Mexico, 3342.

Somewhere, 4267.

The Son Jarocho: the history, style and repertory of a changing Mexican musical tradition, 3387.

Son paginas, 8955.

Sonata nuevomejicana, 9024.

Soneto, 9001.

The song of an oppressor, 8861.

Song of Lia, 9656, 10712.

A song to women, 8619.

Sonia Berdequez; police detective, 939.

Soulpain, 9185.

Sound impact, 7774.

Sources in Mexico for the history of Spanish California, 2097.

Sources of identification of Spanish names, 7823.

South of the other border, 614.

Southern Bell faces directory competition, 7465.

Southern boulevard, 9148.

Southern California's HBA, 870.

Southwest exhibit traces history, 11078.

Southwest may lose theater, 262.

Southwest regional conference of Hispanic Chamber of Commerce, 1927.

Soy Chicana, 2541.

Soy Quilaztli... y que? cuento azteca, 10763.

Space-Craft's strategy for re-industrialization, 1943.

Spanish and English inchoatives and the Spanish-English bilingual: got anything to se?, 5042.

Spanish books for children, 495, 970.

Spanish farm primer, 11160.

Spanish language radio: a directory, 9996.

Spanish lesson, 146.

Spanish prince of song, 4232.

Spanish scene, 9107.

Spanish surname as a market of Mexican heritage in Denver, Colorado, 3460.

Spanish-English language switching in speech and literature: theories and models, 50.

The Spanish-speaking migrant child, 1077.

A sparkling alternative to the cocktail party, 270.

Speaking of Hispanics, 6240.

A special dress for a special person, 2551.

Special education evaluation process as a moderator of false positives, 378.

Special focus on Gary Soto, 6581.

Special higher education bibliography, 973.

Special honor goes to Montalban, 598.

Special report on the Simpson-Mazzoli Bill, 5781.

The special talent of digitron's Nestor Fernandez, 1983.

Split labor market: Mexican farm workers in the Southwest, 209.

Sports updates, 909.

Spring burning, 9136.

Stability of performance on the PPVT-R for three

ethnic groups attending a bilingual kindergarten, 5911.

Stability of the McCarthy scales of children's abilities over a one-year period for Mexican-American children, 2649.

Standards, 8862.

Stanford students set it straight, 6390.

Star Adair Insulation Inc. spurts to new growth, 1248.

State considers English bill, 1097.

State of the art, 4168.

State Senator John Garamendi, 4035.

A statistical profile of California public schools, 2104.

Statue of Liberty has 95th birthday, 11235.

The status of bilingual education in California, 1083.

Stereotypes of Mexican descent persons: attitudes of three generations of Mexican American and Anglo-American adolescents, 192.

Stereotyping among Hispanics and Anglos: the uniformity, intensity, direction and quality of auto- and heterosterotypes, 423.

Sterling silver roses, 8930.

Stockton woman named regional head of SBA, 2304.

Stone men, 8663.

Stopping by the sauna, 8572.

Story from a mountain, 8951.

The story machine, 9626.

The story of Hispanic Southern Baptists, 875.

Straight talk from plain women, 9265.

Street, 8580.

Strength through dollars, 7569.

Strong concern over searches, 2838.

Structural family therapy training in family medicine, 4459.

The struggle continues: protecting the rights of Hispanics in the U.S., 165.

The struggle for minority admissions: the UCLA experience, 831.

Student and parent attitudes toward college at five Hispanic learning centers in Illinois, 2288.

Student at New Jersey school saves classmate, 2698.

Students view career option, 1928.

Study details minority access to legal education, 1862.

A study of the interaction of Hispanic junior high school students and their teachers, 2469.

Stuffed plantains "bolas de platano", 10086.

Su calle, 8991.

Su salud, 9795.

Su voto es su voz, 2942, 12256.

Subject access for Hispanic library users, 2315.

The substitutability of Black, Hispanic and white labor, 5854.

Subtle as growth, the process has begun, 8673.

The subtleties of corporate boardsmanship, 3030.

Success, 2823.

Successful instruction for bilingual schooling, 1099.

Suenos de plomo, 8791.

The sugar mill, 9021.

Sugarcane, 8990.

Suggested reading, 971.

Suicidal pieces, 9632.

A suite of locals, 8752.

[Summary of: Freeman, Legitimizing racial discrimination through anti-discrimination law: a critical review of Supreme Court doctrine, 62 Minn. L. Rev. 1049 (1978)], 107.

[Summary of: Hollander, defending the criminal alien in New Mexico: tactics and strategy to avoid deportation, 9 N.M.L. rev. 45 (1979)], 3118.

[Summary of: Note, medical benefits awarded to an alien: Perez v. health and social services, 9 N.M.L. rev. 89 (1979)], 7122.

[Summary of: race as an employment qualification to meet police department operational needs, 54 N.Y.U.L. rev. 413 (1979)], 108.

Summary of selected bilingual legislation, 1098.

A DIRECTORY OF CHICANO PERIODICALS

The following list reflects the holdings of the Chicano Studies Library at the University of California, Berkeley. Uncertainty about the status of a given periodical is indicated by the use of an asterisk (*) followed by the date of the last issue received. In all cases the institutional subscription rate is provided. Prices are current as of July 1986.

JOURNALS

Aztlán
Chicano Studies Research Center
Publications Unit
UCLA
Los Angeles, CA 90024
$20.00/year

Bilingual Journal
EDAC/Lesley College
49 Washington Avenue
Cambridge, MA 02140
$7.50/year

Bilingual Review
Box M, Campus Post Office
SUNY, Binghamton
Binghamton, NY 13901
$18.00/year

Chicano Law Review
UCLA School of Law
405 Hilgard Avenue
Los Angeles, CA 90024
$10.00/volume

Crítica: A Journal of Critical Essays
Chicano Studies, C-009
University of California, San Diego
La Jolla, CA 92093
$10.00/volume (two issues)

Grito del Sol
TQS Publications
P.O. Box 9275
Berkeley, CA 94709
$42.00/two years

Hispanic Journal of Behavioral Sciences
Spanish Speaking Mental Health Center
A352 Franz Hall
UCLA
Los Angeles, CA 90024
$18.00/year

Huehuetitlan
M & A Editions
Rt. 5 Box 332
San Antonio, TX 78211
donations accepted

Imagine: International Chicano Poetry Journal
645 Beacon Street
Suite 7
Boston, MA 02215
$18.00/two years

International Migration Review
209 Flagg Place
Staten Island, New York 10304
$37.50/year

Journal of Ethnic Studies
Western Washington University
Bellingham, WA 98225
$12.00/year

Llueve Tlaloc
Bilingual & International Studies
Pima Community College
200 N. Stone Avenue
Tucson, AZ 85702
free

**MELUS: The Society for the Study of
Multi-ethnic Literature of the U.S.A.**
    Office of the Dean
    School of Human Sciences & Humanities
    University of Houston, Clear Lake
    Houston, TX 77058
    $25.00/year

Mexican Studies/Estudios Mexicanos
    University of California Press
    2120 Berkeley Way
    Berkeley, CA 94720
    $27.00/two years

NABE Journal
    National Association for Bilingual Education
    1201 16th Street N.W.
    Room 407
    Washington, DC 20036
    $100.00/year
    Price includes subscription to NABE News

National Hispanic Journal
    P.O. Box 1812
    Austin, TX 78767
    $9.00/year

La Raza Law Journal
    Boalt Hall School of Law, Room 37
    University of California, Berkeley
    Berkeley, CA 94720
    *Spring 1983

Revista Chicano-Riqueña
    University of Houston
    Houston, TX 77004
    $15.00/year

    Subsequently will be titled
    The Americas Review: The Review of
    Hispanic Literature and Art of the USA

Revista Mujeres
    Merrill College
    University of California, Santa Cruz
    Santa Cruz, CA 95064
    donations accepted

Saguaro
    Mexican American Studies Research Center
    University of Arizona
    Tucson, AZ 85721
    $8.00/year

Southwest Economy and Society
    P.O. Box 4482
    Albuquerque, NM 87106
    $18.00/year

Third Woman
    Chicano-Riqueña Studies
    Ballantine Hall 849
    Indiana University
    Bloomington, IN 47405
    $12.00/year

MAGAZINES

Caminos
    P.O. Box 54307
    Los Angeles, CA 90054
    *February 1986

La Comunidad
    La Opinion
    P.O. Box 15093
    Los Angeles, CA 90015
    $40.00/year
    Price reflects subscription to
    Sunday edition of La Opinion newspaper.
    La Comunidad is a Sunday supplement.

Fem
    Av. Universidad No. 1855, 4 piso
    Col. Oxtopulco Universidad
    Mexico 04310 D.F., Mexico
    $30.00/year

Hispanic Business
    360 S. Hope Ave., Ste. 100C
    Santa Barbara, CA 93105
    $18.00/year

Hispanic Engineer
    280 South Sadler Avenue
    Los Angeles, CA 90022
    $15.00/year

Hispanic Review of Business (HRB)
    P.O. Box 40874
    Washington, DC 20016
    $26.00/year
    Formerly appeared in Nuestro Magazine

Latina!
2801 B Ocean Park Blvd., Suite 145
Santa Monica, CA 90405
$19.00/year

Latino
125 South Kalamath
Denver, CO 80223

El Malcriado (Food and Justice)
United Farm Workers of America
AFL-CIO
Keene, CA 93531
$5.00/year

Nuestro: The Magazine for Latinos
Box 40874
Washington, DC 20016
$20.00/year

La Raza Habla
Chicano Affairs Office
Box 4188
New Mexico State University
Las Cruces, NM 88003
free

La Voz
P.O. Box 19206 - Diamond Lake Station
Minneapolis, Minnesota 55419
$6.00/year

NEWSLETTERS

Adelante!
Centro de Servicios Para Mexicanos
1109 Seward
Topeka, Kansas 66616
free

Arriba
Committee for Hispanic Arts & Research
P.O. Box 12865
Austin, TX 78711
free

Avance
504 "C" Street, NE
Washington, DC 20002
free

Previously titled Congressional
Hispanic Caucus

Bibliotecas Para La Gente Newsletter
c/o Mission Branch Library
3359 24th Street
San Francisco, CA 94110
$25.00/year

**California Chicano News Media
Association Newsletter**
School of Journalism
University of Southern California
Los Angeles, CA 90089-1695
$10.00/year

Los Camaradas
Raza Recruitment Center
500 Eshleman Hall
University of California, Berkeley
Berkeley, CA 94720
free

**Center for Inter-American and Border
Studies Newsletter**
University of Texas at El Paso
El Paso, TX 79968-0605
free

Chicanos: A Checklist of Current Material
Library
University of California, Santa Barbara
Santa Barbara, CA 93106
free

Cine Acción News
3181-A Mission Street
San Francisco, CA 94110
$20.00/yearly membership to Cine Acción

Cuento Books and Review
P.O. Box H
Las Cruces, NM 88004
$10.00/year

Encuentro: EOP Newsletter
EOP
Bldg. 406, Room 129
Santa Barbara, CA 93106
free

El Faro
National Association of Hispanic Nurses
4359 Stockdale
San Antonio, TX 78233
$25.00/yearly membership

Forum: National Clearinghouse for Bilingual Education
1555 Wilson Blvd., Suite 605
Rosslyn, VA 22209
free

Frente a Frente
Spanish Speaking Catholic Commission
Holy Cross Annex
P.O. Box 703
Notre Dame, IN 46556
free

Health Advocate
National Health Law Program
2639 South La Cienega Blvd.
Los Angeles, CA 90034
$15.00/year

Previously published as Health Law Newsletter

Hispanic Hotline
P.O. Box 163510
Sacramento, CA 95816
$12.00/year or $1.00/issue
All subscriptions must be
renewed in June

Hispanic Legislative Alert
Senator David Roberti
State Capitol, Room 205
Sacramento, CA 95814
free

Hispanic Link Weekly Report
1420 "N" Street, N.W.
Washington, DC 20016
$96.00/year

Hispanic Media Notes
1420 N Street NW
Washington, DC 20005
$15.00/year

El Kaite
1828 Sunset Blvd.
Los Angeles, CA 90026
*Sept/Oct 1984

Latino Consortium
4401 Sunset Blvd
Los Angeles, Ca 90027
*Winter/Spring 1985

Latinograma: El Pulso Latino
Moraga and Associates
3752 Moore Street
Los Angeles, CA 90066
$55.00/two years

Lector
Hispanex
P.O. Box 4273
Berkeley, Ca 94704
*Vol. 3, no. 6 (no date)

Legislative Bulletin--Boletin Legislativo
National Association for Hispanic Elderly
2727 West Sixth Street, Suite 270
Los Angeles, CA 90057
$20.00/year

La Letra
Chicano Studies Program
3404 Dwinelle Hall
University of California, Berkeley
Berkeley, CA 94720
free

MALDEF Newsletter
Mexican-American Legal Defense and
Education Fund
145 Ninth Street
San Francisco, CA 94103
free

El Mirlo
Chicano Resource Center
University of California, Los Angeles
405 Hilgard Avenue
Los Angeles, Ca 90024
*Winter 1984
Continued by Noticias de Aztlan

NFWM Newsletter
National Farm Workers Ministry
111-A Fairmount Avenue
Oakland, CA 94611
free

NABE News
National Association for Bilingual Education
1201 16th Street N.W.
Room 407
Washington, DC 20036
$100.00/year
Price includes subscription to NABE Journal

NALEO: National Report
National Association of Latino Elected
and Appointed Officials
504 C Street, N.E.
Washington, DC 20002
$25.00/year
formerly NALEO: Washington Report

Newsletter: Chicano Studies Library
Chicano Studies Library Publications Unit
3404 Dwinelle Hall
University of California, Berkeley
Berkeley, CA 94720
free

Newsletter: Mexican American Commission, Nebraska
P.O. Box 94965
Lincoln, Nebraska 68509-4965
free

News: Washington State Migrant Education
P.O. Box 719
Sunnyside, WA 98944
free

Noticias de Aztlán
Chicano Resource Center
UCLA
405 Hilgard
Los Angeles, CA 90024
$12.00/year
formerly El Mirlo

Noticias de B.A.S.S.T.A.
Bay Area Spanish Speaking Therapists Association
P.O. Box 40598
San Francisco, CA 94140
$6.00/year

Noticias de la Semana: A News Summary for Hispanics
U.S. Department of labor
Office of Information
Publications and Reports
Washington,, DC 20210
free

Noticiera de MALCS
Mujeres Activas en Letras y
Cambio Social
Chicano Studies
University of California, Davis
Davis, CA 95616
$100/institutional membership

Nuestro Bienestar
Chicano Health Policy Development, Inc.
2300 W. Commerce Ste. 304
San Antonio, TX 78207
*May/June 1984

Oregon Migrant Education News
700 Church Street S.E.
Administration Bldg., 2nd Floor
Salem, OR 97301
free

Raza Alumni Club, U.C. Berkeley
P.O. Box 187
Berkeley, CA 94704
free

La Red/The Net
National Chicano Council of
Higher Education
710 College Avenue
Claremont, CA 91711
$50.00/year

Reforma Newsletter
National Association of Spanish
Speaking Librarians in the U.S.
c/o Susana Luevano
Rancho Santiago College Library
17th Street at Bristol
Santa Ana, CA 92706
$12.00/year

Also publishes: The Amoxcalli
Newsletter; Reforma: Arizona Chapter
Newsletter

Research Bulletin: Hispanic Research Center
  Hispanic Research Center
  Fordham University
  Bronx, NY 10458
  free

Research Bulletin: Spanish Speaking Mental Health Research Center
  Spanish Speaking Mental Health Research Center
  University of California
  Los Angeles, CA 90024
  free

SACNAS News
  Society for Advancement of Chicanos and
  Native Americans in Science
  P.O. Box 30040
  Bethesda, MD 20814
  $5.00/year

Society of Hispanic Professional Engineers National Newsletter
  Society of Hispanic Professional Engineers
  P.O. Box 48
  Los Angeles, CA 90053
  *June/July 1982

U.C. MEXUS News
  2121E Watkins Hall
  University of California
  Riverside, CA 92521
  free

Visión
  Mexican American Cultural Center
  San Antonio, TX 78228
  free

Voz del Llano
  Kansas Advisory Committee on
  Mexican American Affairs
  512 W. 6th Street
  Topeka, KS 66603
  free

La Voz Latina
  Labor Council for Latin American Advancement
  815 Sixteenth St. NW, Suite 707
  AFL-CIO Building
  Washington, DC 20006
  free

NEWSPAPERS

Austin Light
  100 N. Interregional Suite 3500 M
  Austin, TX 78701
  $12.50/year

El Bautista Mexicano
  511 N. Akard
  Dallas, TX 75201-3355
  $3.00/year

Cambio
  138 Monte Cresta Ave., No. 203
  Oakland, CA 94611
  $12.00/year

El Editor
  Amigo Publications
  P.O. Box 11250
  Lubbock, TX 79408
  $35.00/year

Eastside Sun
  Eastern Group Publications
  P.O. Box 33803
  Los Angeles, CA 90033
  $29.50/year

El Hispano
  P.O. Box 989
  Albuquerque, NM 87103
  $7.00/year

Horizontes
  P.O. Box 14,432
  San Francisco, Ca 94114
  $20.00/year

Justicia
  International Ladies' Garment Workers
  1710 Broadway
  New York, NY 10019
  $2.00/year

Latin Times
  Figueroa Printers
  3805 Main Street
  East Chicago, Indiana 46312
  *Dec. 1984

Mexicalo
931 Niles Street
Bakersfield, CA 93305
$24.00/year

El Mundo: Seminario Latino del Norte de California
Alameda Publishing Corporation
The Post Newspaper Group
P.O. Box 1350
Oakland, CA 94604-1350
$25.00/year

La Nación
Chavez Publishing Company
2735 N. Teepee Dr. Suite C
Stockton, CA 95205
$12.00/year
$14.00/year (out of state)

El Observador
P.O. Box 1990
San Jose, CA 95109
$10.00/year

El Paseño
c/o Salazar Public Relations
503 Prospect
El Paso, TX 79902
$20.00/year

La Prensa
1950 Fifth Avenue
San Diego, CA 92101
*Sept 1984

La República
Chavez Publishing Co.
415 N. Abby Street
Fresno, CA 93721
$14.00/year
$16.00/year (out of state)

Semanario Azteca
P.O. Box 207
Santa Ana, CA 92702
$30.00/year

El Sembrador: La Voz del Pueblo Mexicano
P.O. Box 13
San Fernando, CA 91341
$5.00/year

El Sol
Houston Sun
El Sol Publishing Corporation
2434 Navigation
Houston, TX 77003
*November 28, 1984

El Tecolote
3240 21st Street
San Francisco, CA 94110
$20.00/year

La Voz
685 W. Mission Blvd.
Pomona, CA 91766
$15.00/year

STUDENT NEWSPAPERS

La Carta Informativa
La Casa Cultural Latina
University of Illinois
510 E. Chalmers Street
Champaign, IL 61820
free

La Gente de Aztlán
MEChA
A.S.U.C.L.A. Communications Board
308 Westwood Plaza
Los Angeles, Ca 90024
free

El Popo
MEChA
c/o Chicano Studies Dept.
California State University
Northridge, CA 91324
free

Voz Fronteriza
B-203 Student Organizations
University of California, San Diego
La Jolla, CA 92093
free